Annotated Guide to Insolvency Legislation and Practice

While every care has been taken to ensure the accuracy of this work, no responsibility for loss or damage occasioned to any person acting or refraining from action as a result of any statement in it can be accepted by the authors, editors or publishers.

Annotated Guide to Insolvency Legislation and Practice

Hugo Groves
Enterprise Chambers, Leeds

Peter Arden
Enterprise Chambers, Leeds

Tim Calland
Enterprise Chambers, Leeds

Olivier Kalfon
Enterprise Chambers, Leeds

LexisNexis®
Butterworths

Members of the LexisNexis Group worldwide

United Kingdom	LexisNexis Butterworths, a Division of Reed Elsevier (UK) Ltd, Halsbury House, 35 Chancery Lane, LONDON, WC2A 1EL, and RSH, 1–3 Baxter's Place, Leith Walk EDINBURGH EH1 3AF
Argentina	LexisNexis Argentina, BUENOS AIRES
Australia	LexisNexis Butterworths, CHATSWOOD, New South Wales
Austria	LexisNexis Verlag ARD Orac GmbH & Co KG, VIENNA
Canada	LexisNexis Butterworths, MARKHAM, Ontario
Chile	LexisNexis Chile Ltda, SANTIAGO DE CHILE
Czech Republic	Nakladatelství Orac sro, PRAGUE
France	LexisNexis SA, PARIS
Germany	LexisNexis Deutschland GmbH, FRANKFURT and MUNSTER
Hong Kong	LexisNexis Butterworths, HONG KONG
Hungary	HVG-Orac, BUDAPEST
India	LexisNexis Butterworths, NEW DELHI
Italy	Giuffrè Editore, MILAN
Malaysia	Malayan Law Journal Sdn Bhd, KUALA LUMPUR
New Zealand	LexisNexis Butterworths, WELLINGTON
Poland	Wydawnictwo Prawnicze LexisNexis, WARSAW
Singapore	LexisNexis Butterworths, SINGAPORE
South Africa	LexisNexis Butterworths, DURBAN
Switzerland	Stämpfli Verlag AG, BERNE
USA	LexisNexis, DAYTON, Ohio

First published in 2006

© Reed Elsevier (UK) Ltd 2006

Published by LexisNexis Butterworths

A CIP Catalogue record for this book is available from the British Library.

ISBN for this volume

ISBN 10: 0 4069 5065 2	0 4069 5065 2
ISBN 13: 978 0 4069 5065 9	978 0 4069 5065 9

Typeset by Letterpart Limited, Reigate, Surrey

Printed and bound in Great Britain by William Clowes Ltd, Beccles, Suffolk

Visit LexisNexis Butterworths at www.lexisnexis.co.uk

Foreword

When he wrote the foreword to the 30th edition of Snell's Equity Lord Millett observed that equity was on the march again. A modification of the metaphor is required for insolvency law. Ever since it was first discovered to be a discrete area of practice some 30 years or so ago, it has proceeded at more of a brisk trot, occasionally breaking into something faster. This makes life very difficult for the practitioner, who has to keep up. The subject is essentially statute-based, and the legislators do not so much keep moving the goalposts as introducing additional ones when you are not looking. Inevitably, not only does a large and growing body of statutory law have to be dealt with, but an eye needs to be kept on the ever burgeoning case law which (we like to think) helps towards a sensible development and understanding of the law. The most useful practitioner's *vade mecum* will cater for that.

That is why this book is indispensable. It contains all the essential legislation, and does not confine itself to the obvious. Thus in addition to the Insolvency Act 1986 and its younger relations, one finds such things as section 39 of the Matrimonial Causes Act 1973, the Third Parties Rights Against Insurers Act 1930, the Proceeds of Crime Act 2002 and various environmental provisions which are capable of impacting on the life of an insolvency practitioner. The pace with which new laws are introduced means that it has not been possible to annotate absolutely everything (thus the UNCITRAL Model Law and Rules have been included but not annotated), but most of the material has thorough notes, as is required of the most useful practitioner's handbook.

It is a commonplace in forewords like this to observe that the book in question should be kept at the elbow of all serious practitioners in the area, but I can't think of a better figure of speech, and the sentiment is particularly true in relation to this book. It was a privilege to have been in chambers with the authors and editors of this book, and I only wish they had managed to produce it while I was still in practice with them. It would have made my life much easier.

The Honourable Mr Justice Mann

Preface

The aim of this work by the Enterprise Chambers Insolvency Group is to provide a practical and informative commentary on the insolvency legislation and related material that is commonly encountered in practice by insolvency lawyers and insolvency practitioners. The work is divided into four Parts. The first Part contains material that is consulted most frequently by practitioners. The second Part consists of a variety of statutes which from time to time may be of relevance in an insolvency context. The third Part contains annotated statutory instruments and the UNCITRAL Model Law on Cross Border Insolvency which itself will be annotated in a future edition. The fourth Part contains Practice Directions.

The Enterprise Chambers Insolvency Group wish to thank the Honourable Mr Justice Mann for kindly providing the Foreword and also Cara Annett, Peter Wood and all the staff at the publishers Lexis Nexis Butterworths for their patience and assistance throughout.

The aim has been to ensure that the Enterprise Chambers Annotated Guide to Insolvency Legislation is up to date to 1 October 2006.

Enterprise Chambers Insolvency Group

1 October 2006

List of authors and contributors

General Editor

Hugo Groves

Editors

Peter Arden QC

Tim Calland

Rebecca Page

Olivier Kalfon

Contributors

Bernard Weatherill QC

Michael James

Linden Ife

Geoffrey Zelin

James Barker

James Pickering

Hugh Jory

Bridget Williamson

Sarah Richardson

Edward Francis

Shanti Mauger

Shaiba Ilyas

Niall McCulloch

Claire Jackson

Jeremy Child

Matthew West

Kavan Gunaratna

Cristin Toman

Contents

Part Four

Index

Table of Cases

B

C

D

F

G

H

J

K

L

M

N

O

P

Q

R

1

S

T

U

V

W

X

Y

Z

Table of Statutes

Paragraph references printed in **bold** type indicate where the Statute is set out in part or in full.

Table of Statutory Instruments

Paragraph references printed in **bold** type indicate where the Statutory Instrument is set out in part or in full.

E

J

L

Table of European and International Legislation

Paragraph references printed in **bold** type indicate where the Legislation is set out in part or in full.

Primary Legislation

Conventions, Treaties and Commissions

Secondary Legislation

Regulations

C

Part One

Insolvency Act 1986

The First Group of Parts
Company Insolvency; Companies Winding Up

Part I
Company Voluntary Arrangements

Arrangement of Sections

The First Group of Parts
Company Insolvency; Companies Winding Up

Part I
Company Voluntary Arrangements

The proposal

Part II
Administration

Part III
Receivership

Chapter I
Receivers and Managers (England and Wales)

Preliminary and general provisions

Chapter II
Voluntary Winding Up (Introductory and General)

Resolutions for, and commencement of, voluntary winding up

Consequences of resolution to wind up

Declaration of solvency

Chapter III
Members' Voluntary Winding Up

Chapter IV
Creditors' Voluntary Winding Up

Chapter V
Provisions Applying to Both Kinds of Voluntary Winding Up

7

Part VI
Miscellaneous Provisions Applying to Companies
Which Are Insolvent Or in Liquidation

Office-holders

Management by administrators, liquidators, etc

Adjustment of prior transactions (administration and liquidation)

Part VII
Interpretation for First Group of Parts

The Second Group of Parts
Insolvency of Individuals; Bankruptcy

Part VIII
Individual Voluntary Arrangements

Moratorium for insolvent debtor

Procedure where no interim order made

Chapter V
Effect of Bankruptcy On Certain Rights, Transactions, etc

Rights under trusts of land

Rights of occupation

Adjustment of prior transactions, etc

Chapter VI
Bankruptcy Offences

Preliminary

Wrongdoing by the bankrupt before and after bankruptcy

> Part III—Transitional effect of Part XVI
> Part IV—Insolvency practitioners
> Part V—General transitional provisions and savings

Introductory

Company voluntary arrangements were an innovation of the Insolvency Act 1986. The Review Committee on Insolvency on Law and Practice (the Cork Committee) had identified as a weakness of the existing insolvency legislation that a company was not able to enter into a binding arrangement with its creditors for the composition of its indebtedness by a straightforward and inexpensive procedure. CVAs were intended to fill the gap, providing (by contrast with schemes of arrangement under CA 1985 s 425) a simpler mechanism in which court-involvement was limited.

A 'company' is defined by reference to the Companies Act definition (IA 1986 s 251, CA 1985 s 735) and by using IA 1986 s 426 foreign companies may adopt the company voluntary arrangement provisions too: *Re Television Trade Rentals Ltd* [2002] BCC 807. Although the EC Regulation on Insolvency Proceedings 2000 extended the definition of 'company' to unregistered companies for the purposes of the above provisions *Re Salvage Association* [2004] 1 WLR 174; [2003] BPIR 1181 the voluntary arrangement (and administration) provisions were amended by the Insolvency Act 1986 (Amendment) Regulations 2005, SI 2005/879. The effect was to amend the definition of 'company' in IA 1986 s 1(4) (*voluntary arrangements*) and Sch B1 para 111 (*administrations*) to reverse *Re Salvage Association* so that companies such as those incorporated by charter and other bodies falling outside the definition in s 1(4) cannot now enter into a voluntary arrangement. The definition of company in gist now covers only: (a) registered companies under Companies Act; (b) companies incorporated in European Economic Association states other than the UK (this would include Danish companies); and (c) companies registered outside the European Union but with a centre of main interest in an European Union member state (other than Denmark), for instance as in *Re Brac Rent-a-Car International Inc* [2004] BCC 248, *Re Sendo Ltd* [2006] 1 BCLC 395.

The CVA provides a free-standing insolvency procedure under which a troubled company can typically:

- seek to survive and to trade out of its difficulties under the continued control of its directors, either agreeing to pay its creditors a dividend in settlement of its existing debts, or at least obtaining a period of moratorium from enforcement of those debts (a 'trading out' CVA); and/or
- achieve a better (and cheaper) realisation of its business or assets than it could in a liquidation for the benefit of its creditors (an 'asset-based' CVA).

Under a typical trading out CVA, a company agrees to make regular (typically monthly) contributions over a defined period from its trading income to a supervisor (or, or possibly topped up by, injections of funds from third parties), who will hold such monies for the benefit of the creditors bound by the arrangement, and will divide up the fund on completion of the arrangement and after deduction of his expenses pari passu amongst those creditors. Under an asset based CVA, a company may transfer its business, or part of its business, or specific property or assets to a supervisor to be realised to provide a fund for division amongst creditors. In either case, while the company complies with its obligations under the arrangement, the creditors bound by the arrangement can only look to that fund for payment of a dividend in satisfaction of their debt, and cannot enforce the original debt against the company. However proceedings can still be continued against the company in a voluntary arrangement unless expressly or implicitly prohibited by the terms of the arrangement *Alman v Approach Housing Ltd* [2001] BPIR 203; further a secured creditor is not prevented from enforcing its security by an express clause preventing creditors from taking proceedings to enforce the personal liability of a debtor to his creditors *Joseph Manuel Rey v FNCB Ltd* [2006] EWHC 1386 (Ch).

Once approved by a majority of creditors (in excess of 75% in value of the creditors attending in person or by proxy at a creditors' meeting), the arrangement is binding on the company's creditors, whether or not such creditors have voted in its favour and (now, as a consequence of the amendments to IA 1986 s 5 made by the IA 2000) whether or not they had notice of the creditors' meeting. In this way, the procedure enables a company to trade out of its difficulties free from the threat of enforcement action or, as the case may be, provides the conditions in which the company's business or assets can be sold in an orderly way as best preserves their going-concern value.

The CVA procedure as introduced, however, differed from the voluntary arrangement procedure for individual debtors under IA 1986 s 252 to 263 in that it made no provision for any interim moratorium protecting the company from enforcement action (which could trigger the collapse of the company) by a dissenting creditor who had caught wind of the company's difficulties in the period while the proposals were being prepared but before the arrangement was approved. To obtain such protection, it was necessary to pursue the much more expensive and cumbersome route of obtaining an administration order under the provisions of IA 1986 ss 8 to 27 which were then in force. At least partly due to the above, take-up of the CVA procedure proved disappointing. In 1990 only 58 CVAs were registered with the Registrar of Companies (and many of those were only put in place as an exit from administrations) and while this later rose to an average of about 500 per year it still fell far short of the take up of IVAs.

As a result, the IA 2000 introduced a new optional CVA procedure which is available to small companies (as defined by s 247 CA 1985) which meet the eligibility criteria. This provides for an automatic moratorium (without the need for any court order) for an initial period of 28 days (and extendable for a further two months with creditors' consent) with effect from the date the directors of the company file notice with the court during which the company is protected from most forms of enforcement action. It also provides a much more tightly regulated procedure for the approval and implementation of CVAs which have the benefit of the moratorium. The detailed provisions relating to the new CVA procedure are contained in the new s 1A and schedule A1 to IA 1986 together with the new IR 1986 r 1.35 to 1.54.

The old CVA procedure, however, remains in operation as the only procedure available for companies which do not meet the eligibility criteria for the new procedure (as well being an option for those companies which do meet them). This procedure is set out in 1A 1986 s 2–7 below and in IR 1986 r 1.2 to 1.29.

The First Group of Parts
Company Insolvency; Companies Winding Up

Part 1
Company Voluntary Arrangements

The proposal

1.1

1 Those who may propose an arrangement

(1) The directors of a company (other than one which is in administration or being wound up) may make a proposal under this Part to the company and to its creditors for a composition in satisfaction of its debts or a scheme of arrangement of its affairs (from here on referred to, in either case, as a 'voluntary arrangement').

(2) A proposal under this Part is one which provides for some person ('the nominee') to act in relation to the voluntary arrangement either as

trustee or otherwise for the purpose of supervising its implementation; and the nominee must be a person who is qualified to act as an insolvency practitioner [or authorised to act as nominee, in relation to the voluntary arrangement].

(3) Such a proposal may also be made—
    (a) where the company is in administration by the administrator, and
    (b) where the company is being wound up, by the liquidator.

(4) In this Part 'company' means –
    (a) a company within the meaning of section 735(1) of the Companies Act 1985,
    (b) a company incorporated in an EEA State other than the United Kingdom; or
    (c) a company not incorporated in an EEA State but having its centre of main interests in a member State other than Denmark.

(5) In subsection (4), in relation to a company, 'centre of main interests' has the same meaning as in the EC Regulation and, in the absence of proof to the contrary, is presumed to be the place of its registered office (within the meaning of that Regulation).

(6) If a company incorporated outside the United Kingdom has a principal place of business in Northern Ireland, no proposal under this Part shall be made in relation to it unless it also has a principal place of business in England and Wales or Scotland (or both in England and Wales or Scotland)

Who may propose a CVA?

A CVA proposal may be submitted for consideration and approval by the company's members and creditors:-

(a) by the directors of the company, at any time prior to the company going into administration or liquidation;

(b) if the company is in administration, by its administrator; and

(c) if the company has gone into liquidation, by its liquidator.

Note that IA 1986 only gives authority to submit a CVA proposal to the directors of the company acting together, rather than to the company itself, its members or any individual director. In the absence of unanimity, however, it is likely that the directors can act by majority vote.

Consideration was given to the obligations of a liquidator or administrator proposing a CVA in *Sisu Capital Fund Ltd v Tucker* [2005] EWHC 2170 (Ch), [2006] BPIR 154. The office holder should:

• try to structure a proposal that had a reasonable prospect of achieving the necessary majorities without being unfairly prejudicial to any creditor, and

• seek to achieve sufficient consensus among the majority of creditors

In doing so the office holder would be acting as a broker and to some extent mediator between different creditors or groups of creditors and there would be a number of approaches he could adopt. There would be a range of reasonable proposals that could be made. Accordingly the office holder should

• only put forward a proposal that fell within that reasonable range

• only put forward a proposal that he considered had a reasonable prospect of achieving sufficient support for it to be adopted.

By the same token, he should not

• put forward a proposal that he did not consider had a reasonable prospect of being adopted (e g if he knows that a sufficient minority is adamantly opposed to it)

• put forward a proposal that fell outside the reasonable range

• put forward a proposal that he considered unfairly prejudicial to any creditor.

The statutory definition of a CVA

Section 1(1) describes a CVA as 'a composition in satisfaction of [the company's] debts' or 'a scheme of arrangement of its affairs'. A 'composition' was described by Rimer J in *Re Bradley Hole* [1995] 1 WLR 1097 (at 1118H) as an arrangement between a debtor and his or her creditors under which 'each creditor compromises or releases his rights against the debtor in respect of his pre-existing debt and receives in exchange and in full satisfaction whatever payment terms are being offered by the debtor'. A 'scheme of arrangement' was explained by Lightman J in *March Estates plc v Gunmark Ltd* [1996] 2 BCLC 1 as involving something less than the release or discharge of creditors' debts, such as a mere moratorium on payment during the term of the arrangement.

In *IRC v Adams* [2001] 1 BCLC 222 the Court of Appeal had to consider whether a purported voluntary arrangement which had been approved in fact fell within the statutory regime as either a composition or voluntary arrangement. The proposal provided for a moratorium on creditors' claims for the three year duration of the arrangement but made no provision for payment to either preferential or unsecured creditors. The court held that the proposal was not a composition because those creditors were not receiving payment of any lesser sum in consideration for their forbearing to sue upon or the release of their debts. However the proposal did constitute a scheme of arrangement because (i) the scheme involved a moratorium and (ii) the scheme did not prevent creditors who received no payment from subsequently asserting their contractual rights after the moratorium ended. As a result, the scheme had the requisite element of give and take as between creditors to qualify as a scheme of arrangement. The Court of Appeal therefore upheld the first instance decision ([1999] 2 BCLC 730) on somewhat narrower grounds. In *Commissioners of Inland Revenue v Bland* [2003] BPIR 1274, however, a proposal which offered nothing to creditors was unsurprisingly held not to be a composition and treated as a nullity.

Creditors

Neither IA 1986 nor IR 1986 expressly define who qualifies as a creditor for the purposes of a CVA or what qualifies as a debt which may potentially be caught within a CVA. See by contrast:

• IR 1986 r 12.3 which defines what debts are provable in administration, winding up and bankruptcy

• IA 1986 s 383(2) which defines 'debt' and 'liability' for the purpose of the provisions of IA 1986 relating to personal insolvency as including 'debts or liabilities which are present or future, certain or contingent, or in respect of an amount which is fixed or liquidated or is capable of being ascertained by fixed rules or as a matter of opinion.'

• IR 1986 r 13.12(3) which defines 'debt' and 'liability' in similar terms for the purpose of the winding up provisions of IA 1986 and IR 1986.

However, in the context of creditors' voting rights at the meeting convened to consider the CVA proposal, IR 1986 r 1.17(3) expressly provides that a creditor may vote in respect of an unliquidated or unascertained claim at a value of £1 unless the chairman agrees to place a higher value on it. This points to 'debt' and 'creditor' having a similarly wide meaning for the purposes of a CVA as it has elsewhere.

As a matter of principle, the class of creditors capable of being bound by a CVA ought to be defined in as wide terms as possible, since the purpose of the CVA provisions is to encourage arrangements with creditors which avoid liquidation and facilitate the rehabilitation of companies. That is the approach which was adopted for schemes of arrangement under CA 1985 s 425: see *Re Midland Coal, Coke and Iron Co* [1895] 1 Ch 267. This case was followed in *Re Cancol Ltd* [1996] 1 BCLC 100 where Knox J held that the term 'creditor' included those entitled to future payments under an existing agreement and that as a result a CVA was not as a matter of law confined to debts which were presently payable but could, depending on its terms, bind persons entitled to future or contingent debts – in that case the company's landlord in respect of post-arrangement rent. The issue has now been dealt with in detail by David Richards J in *Re T&N Ltd* [2005] EWHC 2870 (Ch), [2006] BPIR 532. In that case, the issues were (a) whether future tort claimants (where the tortious act – exposure to asbestos – had occurred, but no material damage had been suffered and no cause of action had accrued and (b) whether future tort claimants could prove in a liquidation. It was held that they were contingent creditors and creditors for the purposes of schemes of arrangement and CVAs. It was held, further, that although future tort claimants were creditors for the purposes of IR 1986 r 12.3, they were not entitled to prove because of the provisions of IR 1986 r 13.12(2) (a position that has now been changed by amendment to rule 13.12). Contrast, however, *R (on the application of Steele) v Birmingham City Council* [2005] EWCA Civ 1824, [2005] BPIR 532, where Arden LJ adopted a different approach to the meaning of contingent creditor for the purposes of IR 1986 r 12.3 and IA s 382. It is arguable that her approach is itself inconsistent with the decision of the House of Lords in *Secretary of State for Trade and Industry v Frid* [2004] 2 AC 506, a case which David Richards J relied on. Further, Arden LJ made it clear that her approach was confined to the meaning of the term contingent creditor for the purposes of proof and locus to petition for a winding up order. It does not undermine, therefore, David Richards J's approach so far as schemes of arrangement and CVAs are concerned. Sir Martin Nourse's judgment in *Steele* is consistent with that of David Richards J. The third member of the Court of Appeal, May LJ, simply gave a short judgment agreeing with the other two. In *Re T&N Ltd* [2006] EWHC 1447 (Ch), [2006] 1 WLR 1728, David Richards J. affirmed his earlier decision. For the purposes of other statutory provisions, however, the meaning of the term contingent creditor may be regarded as unsettled.

The Nominee

As originally enacted, IA 1986 required the nominee to be a qualified insolvency practitioner. Sections 390 to 398 IA 1986 set out the relevant provisions relating to such qualification. IA 2000 extends the class of person who may act as nominee (or supervisor) of a CVA to include other 'authorised persons' as defined by s 389A of IA 1986 (i e members of a body recognised by the Secretary of State for the purpose of acting in relation to voluntary arrangements). As part of the promotion of the 'business rescue' culture, and in particular in regard to small companies proposing to use the new CVA moratorium procedure, the aim is to open up the market to business rescue specialists though so far this has not occurred. For commentary on the function and obligations of the nominee, see the notes to IA 1986 s 2 below.

S 1(2)

This provision refers to the nominee acting in relation to the voluntary arrangement either as trustee or otherwise for the purpose of supervising its implementation. In many cases, where the CVA provides for the supervisor of the arrangement to collect in or hold funds – whether from asset realisations or monthly contributions made by the company – the supervisor will hold such funds as trustee for the benefit of creditors entitled to distributions under the CVA: see *Re Leisure Study Group Ltd* [1994] 2 BCLC 65 and the commentary to IA 1986 s 7 below.

S 1(4)

This provision was introduced by Insolvency Act 1986 (Amendment) Regulations 2005 (SI 2005 No 879). The effect of the amendment is to reverse *Re Salvage Association [2003] EWHC 1028 (Ch), [2004] 1 WLR 174*, [2003] BCC 504 so that companies such as those incorporated by charter and other bodies falling outside the definition in this provision cannot now enter a voluntary arrangement (or administration) unless there is a specific statutory power to do so); see notes to IA 1986 Sch B1 para 111(1A).

———

1.2

1A Moratorium

(1) Where the directors of an eligible company intend to make a proposal for a voluntary arrangement, they may take steps to obtain a moratorium for the company.

(2) The provisions of Schedule A1 to this Act have effect with respect to—
- (a) companies eligible for a moratorium under this section,
- (b) the procedure for obtaining such a moratorium,
- (c) the effects of such a moratorium, and
- (d) the procedure applicable (in place of sections 2 to 6 and 7) in relation to the approval and implementation of a voluntary arrangement where such a moratorium is or has been in force.

Notes

S 1A(2)

Section 1A introduces the new CVA procedure for eligible companies which wish to take the benefit of a 28 day moratorium while the company puts together its CVA proposals for consideration by its creditors. The detailed code which applies to the new procedure (in place of the provisions of IA 1986 s 2 to 7 below) is contained in the new Schedule A1. This includes provisions:-
- (a) as to the companies eligible for a moratorium: see paragraphs 2 to 5 of the Schedule;
- (b) as to the procedure for obtaining the moratorium: see paragraphs 6 to 11;
- (c) as to the effect of the moratorium: see paragraphs 12 to 23;
- (d) as to the function and duties of the nominee during the moratorium: see paragraphs 24 to 28;
- (e) as to the consideration and implementation of the CVA: see paragraphs 29 to 40;
- (f) on miscellaneous matters including challenges to decisions made by directors during the moratorium and new moratorium offences which apply to officers of the company: see paragraphs 31 to 44.

The provisions of Schedule A1 are further supplemented by the new IR 1986 r 1.35 to 1.54.

1.3

2 Procedure where nominee is not the liquidator or administrator

(1) This section applies where the nominee under section 1 is not the liquidator or administrator of the company [and the directors do not propose to take steps to obtain a moratorium under section 1A for the company].

(2) The nominee shall, within 28 days (or such longer period as the court may allow) after he is given notice of the proposal for a voluntary arrangement, submit a report to the court stating—
- (a) whether, in his opinion, the proposed voluntary arrangement has a reasonable prospect of being approved and implemented,
- (aa) whether, in his opinion, meetings of the company and of its creditors should be summoned to consider the proposal, and

(b)   if in his opinion such meetings should be summoned, the date on which, and time and place at which, he proposes the meetings should be held.

(3) For the purposes of enabling the nominee to prepare his report, the person intending to make the proposal shall submit to the nominee—

(a)   a document setting out the terms of the proposed voluntary arrangement, and

(b)   a statement of the company's affairs containing—

(i)   such particulars of its creditors and of its debts and other liabilities and of its assets as may be prescribed, and

(ii)   such other information as may be prescribed.

(4) The court may—

(a)   on an application made by the person intending to make the proposal, in a case where the nominee has failed to submit the report required by this section or has died, or

(b)   on an application made by that person or the nominee, in a case where it is impracticable or inappropriate for the nominee to continue to act as such,

direct that the nominee be replaced as such by another person qualified to act as an insolvency practitioner, or authorised to act as nominee, in relation to the voluntary arrangement.

Notes

S 2

This section and IR 1986 r 1.2 to 1.9 (in the case of a proposal by the directors) or IR 1986 r 1.12 (in the case of a proposal by an administrator or liquidator) lay down a detailed procedure under which the nominee is required to scrutinise the proposal and report to the court before any steps can be taken to implement the proposal.

The above provisions, however, only apply where:

- the nominee is not the liquidator or administrator of the company, and
- the directors do not propose to take steps to obtain a moratorium for the company.

The stipulated procedure is as follows:

- The directors (or responsible insolvency practitioner, as the case may be) prepare a CVA proposal in accordance with IR 1986 r 1.3, having identified a person qualified and willing to act as nominee in relation to the proposal.
- The directors give notice of the proposal to the nominee accompanied by a copy of the proposal (IR 1986 r 1.4). Within 7 days, they then provide the nominee with a statement of the company's affairs prepared in accordance with IR 1986 r 1.5. In practice, these documents will often by prepared by the nominee him or herself (see further below).
- The nominee has an initial 28 days (which may be extended by the court) from receipt of the notice to prepare a report to the court. In preparing that report, the nominee may require the directors to provide further information of the matters set out in IR 1986 r 1.6.
- In reporting to the court the nominee must consider both whether the proposal has reasonable prospects of being approved and implemented and whether meetings should be summoned. If both questions can be concluded positively, the nominee should so report to the court (annexing his or her comments on the proposal) and fix a time, date and place for the meetings (IA 1986 s 2(2) and IR 1986 r 1.7(2)). If the nominee concludes that the proposal should not proceed further, he or she should report to the court the reasons for reaching a negative conclusion (IR 1986 r 1.7(2).

The stipulated procedure is premised on the assumption that it is the company directors themselves who have prepared the proposal and who then pass the proposal for consideration by an intended nominee. What happens in practice is usually rather different. The intended nominee will usually have been retained by the company from a much earlier stage to analyse the company's position, advise on appropriate insolvency procedures and (if considered appropriate) to formulate the CVA proposal. Accordingly, the nominee will very often already have considered both the viability of the proposal and its chances of being approved before proceeding him or herself to draft the proposal.

It should further be noted that the court generally plays a purely administrative role in the process. It receives the report and must make it available for inspection by any director, member or creditor of the company: IR 1986 r 1.7(3). There will, however, usually be no judicial involvement in the decision whether or not to convene a meeting: see further the commentary to s 3(1).

Obligations of Nominee

Although IA 1986 imposes no statutory duties of investigation, the nominee is an officer of the court. Accordingly, when preparing the report under section 2(2) the nominee must (within the time and financial constraints under which it is necessary to operate) satisfy him or herself that the proposal can properly be taken forward and is based on reliable information as to the company's financial position. The nominee should not accept without query the information which is supplied by the company's officers. For its part, the company through its officers must act with complete candour in supplying full and accurate information to the nominee.

In *Re a Debtor (No 140 IO of 1995)* [1996] 2 BCLC 429 (also reported under *Greystoke v Hamilton-Smith* [1997] BPIR 24) Lindsay J stated (in the context of an IVA) that before concluding whether or not a meeting should be summoned to consider a proposed voluntary arrangement, the nominee should, at least in circumstances where the fullness or candour of the debtor's information has properly come into question, take such steps as are in all the circumstances reasonable to satisfy him or herself on three counts:

- that the debtor's true position as to assets and liabilities did not appear to him or her in any material respect to be different substantially from those to be represented to the creditors;
- that it appeared to him or her that the debtor's proposals as put to the creditors' meeting had a real prospect of being implemented making due allowance for the fact the proposal could be modified at the meeting in response to any concerns (now an express requirement of the report under s 2(2)(a)); and
- that he or she had information that provided a basis for forming the opinion that there was no already manifest yet unavoidable prospective unfairness in relation to any class of creditor.

Where the nominee cannot be satisfied of any of the above conditions, he or she should not unequivocally report that a meeting of creditors should be summoned; in such circumstances the nominee should either not recommend the summoning of the meeting or should make such a recommendation but qualify the report accordingly.

See also:

- The Association of Business Recovery Professionals guidance notes contained in its *Statement of Insolvency Practice 3* section 6 (issued in November 1997 and amended in June 2002). This adopts the principles stated by Lindsay J in *Greystoke* and also sets out the information which the nominee should as good practice include within his report to the court.
- The DTI's Insolvency Service guidance notes (the *Dear IP* letters) Millennium edition, chapter 24 Voluntary Arrangements, section 1. This guidance (which relates specifically to IVAs) sets out the matters which nominees should consider in exercising their professional judgment as to whether a proposal should go forward.
- Guidance Leaflet CWL5 produced by the Voluntary Arrangement Service (VAS) and available from HM Revenue & Customs website www.inlandrevenue.gov.uk/leaflets. The VAS (based at Durrington Bridge House, Barrington Road, Worthing, West Sussex

BN12 4SE) is a single unit which was set up jointly by the Inland Revenue and Customs & Excise to handle voluntary arrangements. Since the two Crown debtors will very frequently be substantial creditors in any arrangement, the VAS (on their behalf) plays a crucial role in the approval of any proposal. The leaflet sets out its approach to proposals, including its expectations of the nominee in reporting on the financial position of the company and the prospects of the proposal being implemented.

Liability of Nominee

It is important to distinguish between, on the one hand, the private role played by an insolvency practitioner in advising an insolvent company or individual as to the available insolvency procedures and the nature and form of a proposal for a voluntary arrangement and, on the other hand, the public role undertaken by the insolvency practitioner in undertaking his functions as nominee under Part 1 IA 1986 as an officer of the court. In the former capacity, the insolvency practitioner may owe contractual and tortious duties of care to his client: see for example *Pitt v Mond* [2001] BPIR 624. In the latter capacity, the circumstances in which an insolvency practitioner might owe a duty of care either to the debtor company or individual or to creditors affected by the proposal are much more limited:

- The general principles governing private law liability for breach of statutory obligations are set out by Lord Browne-Wilkinson in *X v Bedfordshire county council* [1995] 2 AC 633. Where a statute provides its own means of enforcing the duty (or provides a remedy for its breach) this will normally indicate that the duty is intended to be enforceable by those means rather than by private right of action. Further, no common law duty of care will generally be imposed which either is inconsistent with a statutory duty or would enable a claimant by private right of action to circumvent the statutory means of enforcement.

- IA 1986 s 6 provides a statutory remedy (by way of revocation of any approval) available to creditors in circumstances where a CVA has been approved which unfairly prejudices the interests of a creditor, member or contributory of a company, or where there was a material irregularity at or in relation to either of the meetings at which the proposal was approved (and see also the remedy under IR 1986 r 1.17 in respect of decisions on voting entitlement at meetings). Accordingly, no private law claim lies against the nominee in relation to matters falling within the scope of that section: *King v Anthony* [1998] 2 BCLC 517, CA; *Prosser v Castle Sanderson* [2002] EWCA Civ 1140, [2003] BCC 440.

- Likewise IA 1986 s 7 provides a statutory remedy (subjecting the supervisor to the overriding supervisory role of the court) available to creditors and anyone else dissatisfied with any act, omission or decision of the supervisor subsequent to approval of the arrangement, inconsistent with the existence of any private law right of action in favour of individual creditors: *King v Anthony* [1998] 2 BCLC 517, CA.

- Accordingly, a private law claim only conceivably arises in respect of acts or omissions of the nominee in the performance of his statutory functions causing loss to one or more creditors which cannot be remedied by a challenge to the approval under s 6. It remains to be decided whether or not such a claim could be brought where the nominee has approved a proposal in his or her report to the court having failed to exercise any proper scrutiny or investigation of a debtor's proposal or statement of affairs where no reasonable nominee exercising such scrutiny could have made a positive report to the court.

Note, however, the nominee's potential liability in costs where a creditor is forced to seek relief under one of the statutory remedies as a result of the nominee's breach of duty: see *Re a Debtor (No 222 of 1990) ex p Bank of Ireland (No 2)* [1993] BCLC 233; *Smurthwaite v Simpson-Smith*, 25 July 2006, LTL 25/07/06, CA.

S 2(4) Replacement of nominee

The filing by the nominee of his report is a prerequisite to the summoning of meetings to consider the proposal. If, for any reason, the nominee fails to file his report timeously, the directors (or, as the case may be, the liquidator/administrator) may apply to the court for a direction replacing the nominee. In such circumstances, however, there is no obvious reason why the directors should not, for the sake of speed, simply start the process afresh with a replacement nominee without the need for the involvement of the court. As amended by IA 2000, s 2(4) now also makes provision for the nominee to be replaced on his own application or on the application of the proposer of the CVA where it is 'impracticable or inappropriate' for the nominee to continue to act as such.

1.4

3 Summoning of meetings

(1) Where the nominee under section 1 is not the liquidator or administrator, and it has been reported to the court that such meetings as are mentioned in section 2(2) should be summoned, the person making the report shall (unless the court otherwise directs) summon those meetings for the time, date and place proposed in the report.

(2) Where the nominee is the liquidator or administrator, he shall summon meetings of the company and of its creditors to consider the proposal for such a time, date and place as he thinks fit.

(3) The persons to be summoned to a creditors' meeting under this section are every creditor of the company of whose claim and address the person summoning the meeting is aware.

Notes

S 3(1) Summoning of meetings where the nominee is not the liquidator or administrator of the company

Once the nominee has filed his report with the court stating that meetings of the company's members and creditors should be summoned to consider the proposal, he is then required to summon such meetings. Note that the nominee cannot summon any such meeting without having first reported to the court that one should be summoned; any meeting summoned in such circumstances (as well as any CVA approved by such meeting) would be a nullity: *Fletcher v Vooght* [2000] BPIR 435.

Section 3(1) provides for the meeting to be summoned unless the court otherwise directs. In the ordinary case, the court will not have cause to consider the report in any judicial capacity at all at this stage. Neither IA 1986 nor IR 1986 set out the circumstances in which a court might direct that a meeting should not be held despite the positive report of the nominee, nor the classes of person who have *locus standi* to apply to the court for such a direction. Some assistance may perhaps be derived from IR 1986 r 5.7(4) which in relation to an IVA gives only the debtor, the official receiver, the trustee and any petitioning creditor entitlement to receive notice of and attend a hearing to consider the nominee's report.

In considering whether or not to make a direction that no meeting should be summoned, the court will primarily be guided by the nominee's report itself. The following, however, may be grounds which the court may take into account, at least if it can be demonstrated that the nominee had wrongly failed to take such matters into account in his report:
- The proposal fails to comply with IA 1986 or IR 1986 in some crucial respect.
- The proposal in its current or any modified form has no reasonable prospects of being approved at any creditors' meeting by reason of the opposition of a creditor or creditors holding at least 25% of eligible votes: see *Re a Debtor (No 83 of 1988)* [1990] 1 WLR 708 (a decision under IA 1986 s 257(1)).

- Where the company through its officers has demonstrably failed to be open and honest and provide all material information relevant to the proposal: *In re a Debtor (No 2389 of 1989)* [1991] Ch 326.
- Where the proposal is demonstrably not serious or viable: *Cooper v Fearnley* [1997] BPIR 20; *Hook v Jewson Ltd* [1997] 1 BCLC 664 (both cases relate to refusals to make interim orders under s 255(1) so are not directly analogous).

For the rules relating to the summoning of the members' and creditors meetings, see IR 1986 r 1.9 and r 1.12(7); see also the notes to s 5(2) below.

S 3(2) Summoning of meetings where the nominee is liquidator or administrator of the company

In this case, there is no prior requirement on the nominee to report to the court, and no power for the court to direct that the meetings should not be held where the nominee has decided to summon them. For the relevant rules, see IR 1986 r 1.11; see also the notes to s 5(2) below.

Consideration and implementation of proposal

1.5

4 Decisions of meetings

(1) The meetings summoned under section 3 shall decide whether to approve the proposed voluntary arrangement (with or without modifications).

(2) The modifications may include one conferring the functions proposed to be conferred on the nominee on another person qualified to act as an insolvency practitioner [or authorised to act as nominee, in relation to the voluntary arrangement].

But they shall not include any modification by virtue of which the proposal ceases to be a proposal such as is mentioned in section 1.

(3) A meeting so summoned shall not approve any proposal or modification which affects the right of a secured creditor of the company to enforce his security, except with the concurrence of the creditor concerned.

(4) Subject as follows, a meeting so summoned shall not approve any proposal or modification under which—

    (a)   any preferential debt of the company is to be paid otherwise than in priority to such of its debts as are not preferential debts, or

    (b)   a preferential creditor of the company is to be paid an amount in respect of a preferential debt that bears to that debt a smaller proportion than is borne to another preferential debt by the amount that is to be paid in respect of that other debt.

However, the meeting may approve such a proposal or modification with the concurrence of the preferential creditor concerned.

(5) Subject as above, each of the meetings shall be conducted in accordance with the rules.

(6) After the conclusion of either meeting in accordance with the rules, the chairman of the meeting shall report the result of the meeting to the

court, and, immediately after reporting to the court, shall give notice of the result of the meeting to such persons as may be prescribed.

(7) References in this section to preferential debts and preferential creditors are to be read in accordance with section 386 in Part XII of this Act.

Notes

S 4

The creditors' meeting, and now to a rather lesser degree (as set out in IA 1986 s 4A below) the meeting of the members of the company, summoned in each case to consider the CVA proposal, form the essential keystone of the CVA procedure. When approved by the requisite majorities at the meetings, the CVA becomes binding under IA 1986 s 5(2). Where, however, the meetings are not convened in accordance with the statutory scheme, any proposal approved at the same may not take effect at all as a binding arrangement: see *Fletcher v Vooght* [2000] BPIR 435. The full implications of this decision in cases where the statutory scheme has not been followed to the letter are yet to be fully worked out by the court: see for example the decision in *Re N (a debtor)* [2002] BPIR 1024. For the rules relating to the conduct of the meetings of members and creditors, see IR 1986 r 1.13 to 1.21.

S 4(2) Modifications to the proposal

(i) **Prior to the meetings**

As provided by IR 1986 r 1.3(3) a proposal can be modified by the directors with the written agreement of the nominee at any time up to the date when the nominee files his report with the court. Through consultation by the nominee in the course of formulating or considering proposals under his reporting obligations, substantial creditors (including in particular the Crown creditors acting through the Voluntary Arrangement Service: see commentary to s 2 above) may seek the directors' agreement to modifications by this method at an early stage.

(ii) **At the meetings**

Alternatively, the proposal may be (and frequently is) modified at the creditors' meeting itself at the behest of one or more creditors and subject to the vote of the requisite majority. Any such modification formerly also required the approval of the company through the votes of its members at the company meeting (and compare IA 1986 s 258(2) under which any modification to an IVA proposal requires the consent of the debtor) but now may take effect even without the approval of the company meeting unless otherwise ordered by the court (IA 1986 s 4A).

No modification may be made by which the proposal ceases to be a composition or a scheme of arrangement within IA 1986 s 1 (see further the commentary to that section) or which affects the rights of secured and preferential creditors without their consent (see the commentary below).

There is at present no judicial guidance on the use or validity of proxy votes in a case where a proposal has been altered substantially by modifications proposed at the creditors' meeting but unseen by the proxy voter. Where proposed modifications make substantial alterations, the safest course will be for the chairman to adjourn the creditors' meeting in accordance with the procedure in IR 1986 r 1.21 to enable proxy voters to consider the proposed modifications before proceeding further; see in a different context *Cadbury Schweppes plc v Somji* [2001] 1 WLR 615 para 25.

(iii) **Subsequent to the meetings**

There is no statutory power to modify a proposal once the meetings at which the proposal is considered have been concluded (regardless of whether the meetings have approved or rejected the proposal). Accordingly:

- In *Re Symes* [1995] 2 BCLC 651 (an IVA case) it was held that after creditors had rejected the original proposal at their meeting the court had no jurisdiction to call a second meeting at which modified proposals might be considered. It therefore followed that a meeting which was erroneously called for the above purpose at which the modified proposals were approved was invalid and the purported approval of no effect.
- In *Re Alpa Lighting Ltd* [1997] BPIR 341, CA it was held that where during the course of a CVA it became apparent that the company was unable to maintain the monthly contributions it had agreed to pay under its terms, the court had no power on an application by the supervisor for directions under IA 1986 s 7(4) to vary the terms of the CVA.

A variation, however, may be effected in one or more of the following ways:

- In the case of non-moratorium CVAs (for which there is no time bar precluding a company from proposing or entering into a second CVA following the rejection or failure of the first), there is no reason why, in order to effect a modification, an entirely new CVA should not be proposed to supersede the existing CVA which may then be considered and voted upon by creditors and members at their respective statutory meetings.
- An arrangement may be modified (as a matter of contract) by the unanimous consent of all creditors affected by the modifications: *Raja v Rubin* [2000] Ch 274, CA.
- Where the arrangement itself contains a variation clause, such clause is not *ipso facto* repugnant to the arrangement. Accordingly, an arrangement may be validly varied in accordance with its terms provided that such variation does not affect the rights of secured and preferential creditors or take the scheme outside IA 1986 s 1: *Re Broome (a debtor)* [1999] 1 BCLC 356. See also *Re Cape Plc* [2006] EWHC 1316 (Ch), a case concerning a scheme of arrangement under CA 1985 s 425 where a long term arrangement (in that case the arrangement was expected to last 50 to 60 years) required flexibility. Given the exceptional circumstances the court sanctioned a scheme which involved ancillary documents that permitted variations in the event of future changes in the law.

S 4(3), (4) Limitations on approval

(i) Secured creditors

No CVA can affect the right of a secured creditor to enforce his security except where the secured creditor consents. This accords with the general scheme of Part I which is to leave secured creditors outside the arrangement and free to enforce their security as they see fit.

Secured creditors include a judgment creditor on whose behalf goods have been seized under a writ of *fi.fa.*: *Peck v Craighead* [1995] 1 BCLC 337; and a creditor with an interim charging order: *Calor Gas v Piercy* [1994] 2 BCLC 321. It seems, however, that a landlord's right of re-entry on non-payment of rent does not constitute security within the meaning of IA 1986: *Re Park Air Services* [2000] 2 AC 172 (decided under IA 1986 s 248 but likely to be followed in interpreting the meaning of security elsewhere under IA 1986); *Razzaq v Pala* [1997] 1 WLR 1336; cf *March Estates v Gunmark* [1996] 2 BCLC 1.

Khan v Permayer [2001] BPIR 95, CA provides a salutary example of a case where the rights of a secured creditor were affected by the terms of the arrangement on their true construction and where the secured creditor (inadvertently) concurred by voting in favour of the arrangement. The arrangement treated P, who was in fact a secured creditor, as having only an unsecured claim in respect of which a dividend was payable in common with other unsecured claims, and in contrast to the treatment of secured creditors. P voted in favour of the arrangement (which was approved by a requisite majority) and subsequently received a dividend in respect of his claim on the successful conclusion of the arrangement. He was held to have lost his right to recover the full amount of his secured debt under the terms of the arrangement, and to have concurred in this by voting in favour of the arrangement and by his subsequent conduct in accepting the dividend.

Where the value of a secured creditor's claim exceeds the value of his security, it is entitled to participate in the arrangement and receive a dividend in respect of its estimated unsecured balance. In the absence of an express term in the arrangement to that effect or a subsequent express waiver of its rights, a secured creditor who receives a dividend in respect of its estimated unsecured balance will not be prohibited when the value of the security subsequently rises from applying the proceeds of sale of its security in discharge of the full amount of the debt including that part which was thought to be unsecured and in respect of which a dividend was paid: *Whitehead v Household Mortgage Corporation plc* [2002] EWCA [2003] 1 WLR 1173; [2003] 1 All ER 319.

See further the commentary to IR 1986 r 1.19(3) on the voting rights of secured creditors in respect of any unsecured shortfall

(ii) **Preferential creditors**

Similarly, a CVA cannot affect the priority rights of preferential creditors, or their rights of equal treatment between themselves. Note that the preferential status of Crown creditors is abolished under s 251 EA 2002, leaving employee's remuneration, occupational pension scheme contributions and ECSC levies (all as defined and limited by IA 1986 Sch 6) as the only remaining preferential debts.

The section is aimed at preserving the priority of preferential creditors on distribution of the company's assets. S 4(4)(a) does not prevent the payment of non preferential creditors in full by a third party leaving preferential creditors to receive a dividend, and such an arrangement is not unfairly prejudicial to the preferential creditors within either s 6 or Sch A1 para 38 where they might otherwise receive nothing on a winding up. Thus in *Inland Revenue Commissioners v Wimbledon Football Club Ltd* [2004] EWCA Civ 655, [2004] BPIR 700 the Court of Appeal refused to interfere where a sale of the business (a) required the buyer to discharge the debts of all 'football creditors' in full and (b) was conditional on the approval of a CVA under which the preferential creditors would receive 30 pence in the pound. The football creditors were not being paid out of cash realised on the sale of the company's assets (ie at the company's cost) but out of the purchaser's 'free money.'

S 4(6) Reporting requirements

See IR 1986 r 1.24 for supplemental rules on the filing by the chairman of his report with the court and (where approved) with the Registrar of Companies and the giving of notice of the result of the meetings to creditors.

1.6

4A Approval of arrangement

(1) This section applies to a decision, under section 4, with respect to the approval of a proposed voluntary arrangement.

(2) The decision has effect if, in accordance with the rules—

  (a) it has been taken by both meetings summoned under section 3, or

  (b) (subject to any order made under subsection (4)) it has been taken by the creditors' meeting summoned under that section.

(3) If the decision taken by the creditors' meeting differs from that taken by the company meeting, a member of the company may apply to the court.

(4) An application under subsection (3) shall not be made after the end of the period of 28 days beginning with—

  (a) the day on which the decision was taken by the creditors' meeting, or

  (b) where the decision of the company meeting was taken on a later day, that day.

(5) Where a member of a regulated company, within the meaning given by paragraph 44 of Schedule A1, applies to the court under subsection (3), the Financial Services Authority is entitled to be heard on the application.

(6) On an application under subsection (3), the court may—
  (a) order the decision of the company meeting to have effect instead of the decision of the creditors' meeting, or
  (b) make such other order as it thinks fit.

Notes

S 4A

Under IA 1986 as originally enacted, a CVA required the approval both of the creditors' meeting and of the company meeting by their requisite majorities. As amended by IA 2000, a CVA may now be approved:

(a) by the creditors' meeting alone, where the company meeting has failed to approve it, unless the court otherwise orders on an application by a member; or

(b) where the company meeting has voted with the requisite majority in favour, but the creditors' meeting has not, by order of the court made on the application of a member.

Under scenario (a), the presumption is that once approved by the creditors' meeting, the CVA takes effect unless a member applies to the court for an order that the decision of the company meeting (voting down the proposal) should take effect in place of the decision of the creditors' meeting. The section does not provide any guidance as to the circumstances in which the court should exercise its discretion in favour of the members. Presumably, however, the court may take into account:

- the percentage share of members respectively in favour and against the proposal;
- how the CVA will prejudicially affect the dissenting members in their capacity as members;
- any material misstatements or omissions within the proposal or statement of affairs not identified by the nominee; and any other failures on the part of the directors or nominee to disclose material information to the creditors which may have affected the creditors' decision;
- any material irregularities in the conduct of the creditors' meeting.

Under scenario (b), the presumption is, again, that the decision of the creditors' meeting (voting down the proposal) takes precedence. Where the members have voted in favour, the court has power to intervene either by ordering that the decision of the company meeting takes effect instead of that of the creditors' meeting, or by making other some order. The court might, for example, make an order setting aside the decision of the first meeting and ordering a fresh meeting to take place. It is submitted that the court would make an order imposing a CVA on creditors despite their rejection of the proposal only in exceptional circumstances.

Under either scenario, a member has only 28 days from the decision of the creditors' meeting or the company meeting (whichever is the later) in which to make his application. The court has no power to extend the time for bringing such application: see by analogy *Bournemouth & Boscombe Athletic Football Club Co Ltd* [1998] BPIR 183.

1.7

5 Effect of approval

(1) This section applies where a decision approving a voluntary arrangement has effect under section 4A.

(2) The voluntary arrangement—

   (a)   takes effect as if made by the company at the creditors' meeting, and

   (b)   binds every person who in accordance with the rules—

       (i)   was entitled to vote at that meeting (whether or not he was present or represented at it), or

      (ii) would have been so entitled if he had had notice of it,

   as if he were a party to the voluntary arrangement.

(2A) If—

   (a)   when the arrangement ceases to have effect any amount payable under the arrangement to a person bound by virtue of subsection (2)(b)(ii) has not been paid, and

   (b)   the arrangement did not come to an end prematurely,

the company shall at that time become liable to pay to that person the amount payable under the arrangement.]

(3) Subject as follows, if the company is being wound up or is in administration, the court may do one or both of the following, namely—

   (a)   by order stay or sist all proceedings in the winding up or provide for the appointment of the administrator to cease to have effect;

   (b)   give such directions with respect to the conduct of the winding up or the administration as it thinks appropriate for facilitating the implementation of the voluntary arrangement.

(4) The court shall not make an order under subsection (3)(a)—

   (a)   at any time before the end of the period of 28 days beginning with the first day on which each of the reports required by section 4(6) has been made to the court, or

   (b)   at any time when an application under the next section or an appeal in respect of such an application is pending, or at any time in the period within which such an appeal may be brought.

   (5)   Where the company is in energy administration, the court shall not make an order or give a direction under subsection (3) unless –

   (a) the court has given the Secretary of State or the Gas and Electricity Markets Authority a reasonable opportunity of making representations to it about the proposed order or direction; and

   (b) the order or direction is consistent with the objective of the energy administration

(6) In subsection (5) 'in energy administration' and 'objective of the energy administration' are to be construed in accordance with Schedule B1 to this Act, as applied by Part 1 of Schedule 20 to the Energy Act 2004.

Notes

S 5

Once approved in the manner provided under section 4A, the CVA is binding on all creditors falling within its ambit (as explained below) whether or not such creditors voted in its favour. As explained by the Court of Appeal in *Johnson v Davies* [1999] Ch 117 at 131–2, this section (and in particular subsection 2(b)) does not purport to impose the CVA directly on a dissenting creditor. Rather the creditor is bound by the arrangement as a result of a statutory hypothesis which requires that creditor to be treated as if he or she had consented.

Although this distinction appears at first sight a mere technicality, it has crucial consequences as to the effect of a voluntary arrangement on third parties liable to a creditor in respect of the same debt as the debtor company/individual entering into the arrangement. It was previously considered that a voluntary arrangement could not, as a matter of law, operate to release third parties liable in respect of the same debt as the debtor because a voluntary arrangement was not a consensual agreement between the debtor and his creditor but rather a 'statutory binding' on his creditor which could not and should not by a side wind affect that creditor's rights in respect of that debt against any other party: see Jacob J in *R A Securities Ltd v Mercantile Credit Co Ltd* [1994] 3 All ER 581; [1994] 2 BCLC 721. That analysis, however, is incorrect if the creditor is to be treated as if he had consented to the arrangement. As stated in *Johnson v Davies*, it is rather purely a question of construction of the arrangement as to whether or not it operates to discharge third parties liable in respect of the same debt as the debtor. The relevant question of construction is whether the arrangement operates as an absolute and unconditional release of the debt in question without any reservation by the creditor of his or her rights against others liable in respect of the same debt.

S 5(2)(b) Creditors bound by the arrangement

Under IA 1986 s 5(2)(b) as originally enacted, the arrangement bound only those creditors who had notice in accordance with the rules of the creditors' meeting convened to consider the proposal and who were entitled to vote at that meeting. Creditors who were overlooked were not bound by the arrangement and could not participate in it. Nor did such a creditor have standing to apply to set aside the arrangement. He was left either to come to some separate arrangement with the company or to force the issue by presenting a winding up petition of his own. Even then, however, potential injustice resulted; a winding up order made on such a petition did not operate to bring to an end the voluntary arrangement or the trusts on which the assets of the arrangement were held. The result, as recognised in a bankruptcy context in *Re Bradley-Hole (a bankrupt)* [1995] 1 WLR 1097, was that such creditor could find that there were no free assets in the winding up available for distribution, all such assets being held by the supervisor of the arrangement for the benefit of those creditors participating in the voluntary arrangement. On the treatment of creditors outside the CVA see *Re Oakley Smith v Greenberg* [2002] EWCA Civ 1217, [2005] 2 BCLC 74.

The present s 5(2)(b) was introduced by amendment effected by IA 2000. Under the new provision, a creditor is bound notwithstanding that he was not given notice of the proposal or the meeting at which the proposal was to be considered by creditors. Any injustice which may result from the failure to give him notice is addressed in two ways. First, the scope of persons entitled to challenge the CVA has been expanded to include a creditor who would have been entitled to vote at the meeting had they had notice of it: see IA s 6(2)(aa). That creditor's period for challenge is extended so that it runs from the day on which that person became aware that the meeting had taken place: IA s 6(3)(b). Secondly, under IA s 5(2)(A), where the CVA has come to an end (but not prematurely) and that creditor has not received the sums due to it under the CVA, the company becomes liable to pay that sum.

The question whether a creditor had received proper notice of the meeting was previously crucial to the question whether he was bound, and will continue to be of some importance to his right of challenge to an approval. The court has generally taken a strict approach on due notice being given in accordance with the rules:

- Under IR 1986 r 1.9(2) notice of the meeting must be sent to creditors not less than 14 days before the date of the meeting. In *Mytre Investments v Reynolds (No 2)* [1996] BPIR 464 (an IVA case but decided on identically worded provisions) it was held that the requirement for 14 days notice of the meeting was for 14 clear days notice of the first meeting of creditors (as distinct from any reconvened meeting following its adjournment). This requirement had to be strictly complied with and, where it was not, the creditor was not bound (under the former provisions of the IA 1986).

- Solicitors do not have implied authority to accept service of notices of meetings on behalf of their clients: *Re Munro and Rowe* [1981] 1 WLR 1358 at 1361; affirmed in *Mytre Investments v Reynolds (No 2)* [1996] BPIR 464.
- For a notice to have been given, and for a creditor to have had that notice, it is necessary that the creditor should actually have received that notice: *Re a Debtor (No 64 of 1992)* [1994] 1 WLR 264; *Skipton Building Society v Collins* [1998] BPIR 267.
- IR Parts 12 and 13 contain a number of rules relating to the giving of notice and the service of documents.
- By IR 1986 r 13.3(3), personal service is always permissible. By IR 1986 r 13.3(1) and (2), a notice may be given by post, and any form of post may be used, unless a particular rule requires otherwise. Further, if a person to whom a notice has to be given has indicated that a solicitor is authorised to accept service, notice may be given to that solicitor: IR 13.4. By IR 12.4(3), the sending or giving of a notice by post may be proved by a certificate to the effect that the notice was posted.
- In addition to these essentially permissive provisions which do not preclude the giving of notice in any other way (provided always that the fundamental condition of actual receipt within the requisite period is satisfied), there are two further sets of provisions – all mandatory and all concerned with the service of documents – which have been held to apply. These are the provisions of IR 1986 r 12.10 and 12.11.
- IR 1986 r 12.11 applies the provisions of Part 6 of the Civil Procedure Rules to the service of documents and giving of notice in insolvency proceedings, subject to IR 1986 r 12.10 and 12.12. Rule 12.10 provides that documents served by post are treated, in the case of first class post as being served on the second business day after posting, and in the case of second class post on the fourth business day after posting unless, in either case, the contrary is shown.
- In a series of voluntary arrangement cases, it has been held that the giving of a notice of a section 3 meeting must be in accordance with these provisions: *Re a Debtor (No 64 of 1992)* [1994] 1 WLR 264; *Beverley Group plc v McClue* [1995] 2 BCLC 405; *Skipton Building Society v Collins* [1998] BPIR 267.
- In *Re a Debtor (No 64 of 1992)* [1994] 1 WLR 264 the court rejected the suggestion that a building society creditor who had not actually received notice of a meeting which had been sent by post wrongly addressed to the society at a branch office rather than its registered or principal office should be treated as having constructive notice of the meeting.
- In *Skipton Building Society v Collins* [1998] BPIR 267 (again an IVA case) it was held that the requirement in r 5.17(2)-the equivalent to r 1.9(2)-that the notice be sent not less than 14 days before the meeting comprehended not merely the act of posting but the entire process of sending a document including delivery. Accordingly, it was for the debtor to establish that the notice had been posted so that it was to be treated under r 12.10 as having been delivered not less than 14 days before the meeting. Importantly, however, even if this were to be established it still remained open for the creditor to rebut the presumption of delivery by showing that notice had not in fact been received in accordance with the statutory presumption or at all.
- The above case, however, can be contrasted with *Beverley Group plc v McClue* [1995] 2 BCLC 407 where it was held that a creditor did have the requisite notice of the meeting where (i) the notice was sent addressed to him at his last known address in accordance with the rules not less than 14 days before the meeting even though that notice had not in fact been received by the creditor, but (ii) where the creditor was actually aware of the notice (from a third party) before the meeting took place.
- In *Re T&N Limited* [2006] EWHC 842 (Ch), [2006] All ER (D) 292 (Apr), [2006] BPIR 632, David Richards J accepted that IR 1986 r 12.10 to 12.11 applied to the giving of notices of section 3 meetings, following the authorities referred to above. However, he held that IR 1986 r 12.12, which deals with service out of the jurisdiction, did not, so that it was not necessary for the court to give leave for the giving of notice to overseas creditors.

S 5(2A)

An omitted creditor who finds him or herself bound to the arrangement by virtue of the new s 5(2)(b) will be entitled to receive the same dividend or other payments as are due to other creditors. While the arrangement remains in effect (or while any trusts created under the same by which the supervisor holds funds for the benefit of the CVA creditors remain in being), it is suggested that the omitted creditor should apply to the supervisor, who should meet the claim from available funds *pari passu* with other creditors.

Section 5(2A) contemplates the case where the arrangement has been successfully concluded but an omitted creditor has not received a dividend in common with other creditors (presumably because the creditor did not become aware of the CVA or appreciate that he or she was bound by the same). In such a case, the company is liable to meet the claim to the dividend or payment to which the omitted creditor was entitled under the arrangement.

'The amount payable under the arrangement' is, it is suggested, the amount of the dividend or payment which the creditor would actually have received as another creditor in common with that actually received by other creditors – rather than (if different) the amount of the dividend originally contemplated in the proposal.

Subsection 2A only applies where the arrangement did not 'come to an end prematurely'. The meaning of this phrase is set out in the new IA 1986 s 7B. An arrangement will have ended prematurely where, when it ceases to have effect, 'it has not been fully implemented in respect of all persons bound by the arrangement'. IA 1986 is silent as to the position of the omitted creditor in such circumstances. It is suggested, however, as follows:

- Where the supervisor holds funds on trust for the benefit of the CVA creditors (the trust having survived the premature termination of the arrangement) the omitted creditor should have the same entitlement to a share of such funds as other CVA creditors.
- Where, however, before receiving notice of the omitted creditor's claim, the supervisor has already distributed the funds held on trust to the other CVA creditors, the omitted creditor may find him or herself with little or no recourse.

1.8

6 Challenge of decisions

(1) Subject to this section, an application to the court may be made, by any of the persons specified below, on one or both of the following grounds, namely—

    (a) that a voluntary arrangement [which has effect under section 4A unfairly prejudices the interests of a creditor, member or contributory of the company;

    (b) that there has been some material irregularity at or in relation to either of the meetings.

(2) The persons who may apply under this section are—

    (a) a person entitled, in accordance with the rules, to vote at either of the meetings;

    (aa) a person who would have been entitled, in accordance with the rules, to vote at the creditors' meeting if he had had notice of it;

    (b) the nominee or any person who has replaced him under section 2(4) or 4(2); and

    (c) if the company is being wound up or is in administration, the liquidator or administrator.

(2A) Subject to this section, where a voluntary arrangement in relation to a company in energy administration is approved at the meeting summoned under section 3, an application to the court may be made-

(a)   by the Secretary of State, or
(b)   with the consent of the Secretary of State, by the Gas and Electricity Markets Authority,
(c)   on the ground that the voluntary arrangement is not consistent with the achievement of the objective of the energy administration

(3) An application under this section shall not be made
(a)   after the end of the period of 28 days beginning with the first day on which each of the reports required by section 4(6) has been made to the court or
(b)   in the case of a person who was not given notice of the creditors' meeting, after the end of the period of 28 days beginning with the day on which he became aware that the meeting had taken place,
but (subject to that) an application made by a person within subsection (2)(aa) on the ground that the voluntary arrangement prejudices his interests may be made after the arrangement has ceased to have effect, unless it came to an end prematurely.

(4) Where on such an application the court is satisfied as to either of the grounds mentioned in subsection (1) or, in the case of an application under subsection (2A), as to the ground mentioned in that subsection, it may do one or both of the following, namely—
(a)   revoke or suspend any decision approving the voluntary arrangement which has effect under section 4A or, in a case falling within subsection (1)(b), any decision taken by the meeting in question which has effect under that section;
(b)   give a direction to any person for the summoning of further meetings to consider any revised proposal the person who made the original proposal may make or, in a case falling within subsection (1)(b), a further company or (as the case may be) creditors' meeting to reconsider the original proposal.

(5) Where at any time after giving a direction under subsection (4)(b) for the summoning of meetings to consider a revised proposal the court is satisfied that the person who made the original proposal does not intend to submit a revised proposal, the court shall revoke the direction and revoke or suspend any decision approving the voluntary arrangement which has effect under section 4A.

(6) In a case where the court, on an application under this section with respect to any meeting—
(a)   gives a direction under subsection (4)(b), or
(b)   revokes or suspends an approval under subsection (4)(a) or (5),
the court may give such supplemental directions as it thinks fit and, in particular, directions with respect to things done [under the voluntary arrangement since it took effect].

(7) Except in pursuance of the preceding provisions of this section, [a decision taken] at a meeting summoned under section 3 is not invalidated by any irregularity at or in relation to the meeting.

> (8) In this section 'in energy administration' and 'objective of the energy administration' are to be construed in accordance with Schedule B1 to this Act, as applied by Part 1 of Schedule 20 to the Energy Act 2004.

Notes

S 6

Once approved, a CVA may be challenged under s 6 on grounds either (a) of unfair prejudice (as discussed below) or (b) of material irregularity at or in relation to the meeting at which it was approved. Where a meeting has rejected a proposal that decision may also be challenged on the material irregularity ground.

Apart from the parallel process for appealing decisions of the chairman relating to voting rights under IR 1986 r 1.17 and the new provisions of s 4A, the above section provides the only means of challenging creditors' approval of a CVA. Indeed, s 6(7) expressly provides that an approval given at a meeting summoned under s 3 is not invalidated by an irregularity at or in relation to the meeting otherwise than by a challenge under s 6. The above, however, can be contrasted with the position where a meeting purportedly held to consider a CVA proposal (together with any approval purportedly given) is a nullity due to a failure to follow the procedure set out in s 3: *Fletcher v Vooght* [2000] BPIR 435.

With the exception of creditors who find themselves bound to a CVA of which they did not receive notice, s 6 provides a short 28 day window after the filing by the chairman of his report of the meeting within which any challenge must be made. The aim, where a CVA has been approved, is that the CVA may thereafter proceed without fear of subsequent challenge.

Note that there are no provisions analogous to IA 1986 s 276(1)(b) as apply to IVAs entitling a creditor bound by a CVA to present a winding up petition on the grounds that the CVA was procured by false or misleading information (or omissions) contained in the proposal, statement of affairs or other document or otherwise made available by the debtor to his creditors at or in connection with the creditors meeting. Accordingly, s 6(1)(b) 'material irregularity' provides the only established means of challenge to a CVA so procured. See, however, the discussion relating to the debtor's duty of good faith to his creditors in *Cadbury Schweppes plc v Somji* [2001]1 WLR 615, [2000] BPIR 951.

Grounds of Challenge

S 6(1)(a) Unfair prejudice

A challenge under (a) can only be made in respect of prejudice to a creditor or member/contributory brought about by unfairness stemming from the actual terms of the scheme itself: *Re a Debtor (No 259 of 1990)* [1992] 1 WLR 226, *Sisu Capital Trust Ltd v Tucker* [2005] EWHC 2170 (Ch), [2006] BCC 463, [2006] BPIR 154. It is not apt to cover complaints that the arrangement should not have been approved at all but was procured by misrepresentations or material non-disclosure within the proposal or the statement of affairs, or by the votes of sham creditors, which rather constitute material irregularities at or in connection with the meetings of creditors or the company falling within ground (b): *Re a Debtor (No 87 of 1993) (No 2)* [1996] 1 BCLC 63.

A voluntary arrangement is by its nature prejudicial to creditors where it prevents full recovery of a debt; if no prejudice is shown the application will be dismissed: *Swindon Town Properties Ltd v Swindon Town Football Co Ltd* [2003] BPIR 253. There may be a range of possible compromises and the court will not investigate whether the arrangement represents the best deal that could have been obtained for creditors or a particular creditor or group of creditors: *Sisu Capital Fund Ltd v Tucker* [2005] EWHC 2170 (Ch), [2006] BCC 463, [2006] BPIR 154, although an arrangement may be unfairly prejudicial if it is one that falls outside the range of reasonableness: *Re T&N Ltd* [2004] EWHC 2361 (Ch), [2005] 2 BCLC 488. It is therefore not sufficient that a creditor has a reasonable objection: *Re British Aviation Insurance Company Ltd* [2005] EWHC 1621, [2006] BCC 14.

The concept of unfair prejudice denotes differential treatment between one or more creditors and others falling within the same class for which there is no reasonable objective justification. This may arise in the following types of circumstances:

* where one or more creditors are to receive a lower dividend than other creditors within the same class;
* where, although all creditors receive equal treatment within the arrangement, a particular creditor is prevented by the operation of the arrangement from pursuing his or her rights in respect of the debt against third parties: see for example *Sea Voyager Maritime Inc v Bielecki* [1999] 1 All ER 628 where a creditor succeeded in a challenge to an IVA under IA 1986 s 262(1)(a) on the basis that the arrangement prevented him from obtaining judgment against the debtor which was a prerequisite to exercising his rights under the Third Parties (Rights against Insurers) Act 1930;
* similarly, where a creditor loses his or her right of recourse against co-debtors or sureties liable in respect of the same debt because the arrangement on its true construction operates as a release of the debt: *Johnson v Davies* [1999] Ch 117 per Chadwick LJ at 138G;
* where some creditors receive collateral benefits arising as a result of the operation of the scheme not available to other creditors: *Re a Debtor (No 101 of 1999) (No 2)* [2001] BPIR 996; but cf *Cadbury Schweppes plc v Somji* [2001] 1 WLR 615 where undisclosed collateral payments made to two creditors in order to procure their approval to the scheme was held not to constitute unfair prejudice arising from the terms of the scheme itself.

The court must consider all the circumstances of the case in deciding whether the interests of a creditor have been unfairly prejudiced, and not base its decision on the mere fact of differential treatment itself: see Ferris J in *Re a Debtor (No 101 of 1999)* [2001] BCLC 54 at 63. In particular:

(1) There may be reasonable objective justification for differential treatment between creditors falling with the same class. So, for instance:
* It may be justifiable for specific essential suppliers to be paid in full to maintain supply in order to enable the debtor company/individual to continue trading (from the fruits of which monthly contributions are to be made to provide for a dividend for creditors).
* Similarly, where equipment hired under lease contracts is required for the continued operation of the debtor's business, it may be justifiable to provide for payment of future rent on such contracts in full where the landlord of the debtor's premises which are no longer required receives only a dividend in respect of his claim for future rent: *Re Cancol Ltd* [1996] 1 All ER 37.

(2) It may be relevant to compare the position of creditors under the arrangement with that under winding-up/bankruptcy, although this cannot be the determinative test: see *Re a Debtor (No 101 of 1999)* [2001] BCLC 54.

The unfair prejudice must be caused by the arrangement itself, and not by the way in which it came to be promulgated and approved: *Sisu Capital Fund Ltd v Tucker* [2006] BCC 463, [2006] BPIR 154 (although that may amount to a material irregularity within subsection (1)(b)). The section is concerned with prejudice caused by the distribution of the company's assets under the arrangement. Thus an arrangement whereby one class of creditors is to be paid in full by a third party leaving other creditors to receive a dividend is not unfairly prejudicial within either s 6 or Sch A1 para 38 where the other creditors might otherwise receive nothing on a winding up. Thus in *Inland Revenue Commissioners v Wimbledon Football Club Ltd* [2004] EWCA Civ 655, [2004] BCC 638 the Court of Appeal refused to interfere where a sale of the business (a) required the buyer to discharge the debts of all 'football creditors' in full and (b) was conditional on the approval of a CVA under which the preferential creditors would receive 30p in the pound. The football creditors were not being paid out of cash realised on the sale of the company's assets (i e at the company's cost) but out of the purchaser's 'free money.' See also *Inland Revenue Commissioners v Exeter City AFC Ltd* [2004] BCC 519.

Furthermore, in determining whether a creditor is unfairly prejudiced by the terms of an arrangement, the court is concerned not with theoretical inequities, but with commercial reality.

Where under the terms of an IVA a bank was prevented from pursuing its debt against a co-debtor, the debtor's wife, there was no unfair prejudice where on the debtor's unchallenged evidence his wife had no assets and no income against which the bank would have been able to enforce its claim: *Re a debtor (No 574 of 1995)* [1998] 2 BCLC 124 at p. 130j – 131a. For the same reason the fact that a proposal is put forward by an administrator or liquidator, and the office holder is in a position of conflict of interest (even a serious conflict) and in breach of his obligations of professional conduct, will not by itself make the arrangement unfairly prejudicial, although the conflict and professional misconduct will not be irrelevant factors. The office holder must do his best to out forward a proposal that will have some prospect of being accepted by the requisite majority, provided that he may not put forward a proposal that he considers to be unfairly prejudicial any of the creditors: *Sisu Capital Trust Ltd v Tucker*), [2006] BCC 463 ,[2006] BPIR 154.

S 6(1)(b) Material Irregularity

A challenge may be brought on the grounds of material irregularities at or in relation to either of the meetings in the following circumstances:

- Were the proposal or statement of affairs or other documents provided for consideration at the meetings contain false or misleading information or material omissions: *Re a debtor (No 87 of 1993) (No 2)* [1996] 1 BCLC 63; *Re Bradburn v Kaye* [2006] BPIR 605.
- Failure to give proper notice of the meeting to one or more creditors or to provide all the documentation prescribed under the rules.
- A wrong decision on the voting entitlement of one or more creditors or as to whether a creditor's vote should count under IR 1986 r 1.19(3) or (4) (where the ground of challenge under IA 1986 s 6(1)(b) runs in parallel with the right of appeal under IR 1986 r 1.17A(3).
- A refusal by a chairman to admit a valid proxy for voting: *Roberts v Pinnacle Entertainment Ltd* [2003] EWHC 2394, [2004] BPIR 208; or the improper use of a proxy vote by the chairman: see for example *Re Cardona* [1997] BPIR 604.
- Where further information has come to light at or before the meeting which is germane to the commercial merits of the proposal and/or may affect the decision of creditors who have already cast their votes by proxy in ignorance of such information, but where the chairman has not given such creditors the opportunity to reconsider their proxy in the light of such further information: *Cadbury Schweppes plv v Somji* [2001] 1 WLR 615, para 25. Where, however, the further information would have not made a material difference to the creditors' decision a challenge based on material irregularity would ordinarily fail: *Re Trident Fashions plc (No 2)* [2004] EWHC 293 (Ch), [2004] 2 BCLC 35.

Where the objection taken relates to the information available to the creditors, the test to be applied is whether, had the truth been told, the creditors would have voted differently. It is not enough that the meeting would have been adjourned to allow them to reconsider their position in the light of the truth: *Sisu Capital Fund Ltd v Tucker* [2006] BCC 463, [2006] BPIR 154, following *Cadbury Schweppes plc v Somji* and *Re Trident Fashions plc (No 2)*.

Following the amendment to IA 1986 s 5(2)(b) effected by IA 2000 (making an arrangement binding not just on creditors who had notice of the meeting but also those omitted creditors who were entitled to but did not receive notice of the meeting), IA 1986 s 6(1)(b) provides a crucial means of challenge to an approved arrangement by an omitted creditor; see further the commentary to that sub-section.

For a challenge to succeed in any case, however, the irregularity must be material in that it would or might have affected the outcome of the meeting. Where the irregularity consists of significant misrepresentations or non-disclosure, it may not be difficult to satisfy a court that this may have affected the outcome of the meeting and that it would be appropriate to set aside the existing approval and reconvene a further meeting to consider the proposal afresh. Where, however, the irregularity comprises a failure to notify one or more creditors whose votes would not directly have affected the outcome of the meeting, it may be more difficult to establish materiality even allowing for the fact that other creditors' voting intentions may not have been fixed in advance of the meeting. Nevertheless the right to attend and speak (and possibly persuade others) at a meeting is an important one.

S 6(2) Persons entitled to challenge

The persons entitled to challenge the CVA itself or a decision approving or rejecting it are for the large part self-explanatory. It is submitted, however, that anyone mounting a challenge must have a proper interest in so doing. So, for instance, a creditor who makes a challenge on grounds of unfair prejudice must do so on the grounds that he or she rather than some other creditor is unfairly prejudiced by the CVA. In that regard, it is not clear what interest a nominee (under IA 1986 s 6(2)(b)) might properly have in seeking to mount a challenge under s 6(1)(a).

S 6(3)(a) Time for challenge

The court has no power to extend the time for bringing an application beyond the 28 day time limit provided. IR 1986 r.12.9 does not assist because the limitation period is one imposed by statute rather than under the rules: *Bournemouth & Boscombe Athletic Football Club Co Ltd* [1998] BPIR 183. The above is to be contrasted with appeals to the decisions of chairman on voting entitlement etc. under IR 1986 r 1.17A(3) to which r 12.9 does apply; see also the commentary to IR 1986 r 1.17A(6). Note that the position is not the same for IVAs, although the courts have adopted a strict approach to applications under IA 1986 s 376 for extensions of time: see *Re Timothy* [2006] BPIR 329.

S 6(3)(b) Time for challenge; omitted creditors

An omitted creditor has 28 days from the date he becomes aware that the meeting took place to mount his challenge. This wording does not sit easily in the case of an omitted creditor who first learns (i) of the existence of the arrangement and (ii) that he is bound by it, some months or years after it has been approved. The 28 day period ought in such circumstances run from the date when the creditor learns one or both of the above facts, rather than when he becomes 'aware' of the meeting – which is surely not in itself the material fact and may indeed not be something which the creditor actually becomes aware of at all. A purposive construction of this provision (equating 'awareness' of the meeting with knowledge of the existence of the arrangement) might avoid these difficulties. It is also unclear why an omitted creditor should necessarily be barred from challenge where an arrangement has ended 'prematurely' (for the meaning of which see IA 1986 s 7B). The premature termination of a CVA does not necessarily revoke or determine any trust created by the CVA under which CVA assets may be held for the sole benefit of CVA creditors. Where such a trust survives, this may not be of benefit but may be prejudicial to an omitted creditor.

S 6(4) Powers of the court

Where an approved arrangement is successfully challenged on either ground (a) or (b), the court may revoke or suspend any decision approving the arrangement. It may also give directions for the summoning of further meetings at which a revised proposal may be considered. However:

- The court may, before giving such directions, require any revised proposals to be put before it to determine whether such proposal is free from objection: see *Re a Debtor (No 101 of 1999)* [2001] BCLC 54 (order made on successful challenge to first proposal), and *Re a Debtor (No 101 of 1999) (No 2)* [2001] BPIR 996 (order refusing to convene second meeting to consider revised proposal which introduced new objectionable elements).
- The court may refuse to convene any further meeting where it is clear that any revised proposal has no reasonable prospects of being approved: *Re a Debtor (No 83 of 1988)* [1990] 1 WLR 708; *Re a Debtor (No 222 of 1990)* [1992] BCLC 137.
- Where an approval has been revoked as a result of material irregularities, in determining whether to order a further meeting the court may take into account the seriousness of the irregularities. Further, where the conduct of the nominee/chairman is called into question in failing to correct such irregularities, the court may make any direction for a new meeting conditional upon such nominee being replaced: *IRC v Duce* [1999] BPIR 189.

Where the decision of a meeting rejecting a proposal is successfully challenged on the ground of material irregularity, the court may direct a further meeting to be held to reconsider the proposal. It has, however, no power to order that an arrangement stand approved – even if, but for the material irregularity, the arrangement would have been approved at the original meeting.

S 6(6) Consequential directions

This subsection makes provision for orders validating acts done by a supervisor (or others) under and with the authority of an arrangement where that arrangement (and the authority) is subsequently revoked by an order under IA 1986 s 6(4) or (5). Where a proposed direction affects the rights of third parties, such third parties may need to be joined before the direction is made.

Procedural matters and costs

It is generally unnecessary and inappropriate to join either the nominee or other creditors as respondents to a challenge based on unfair prejudice: *Re Naeem* [1990] 1 WLR 48. The nominee acts simply as agent of the debtor in drafting and putting the proposal before creditors. By contrast, on an application based on material irregularity, it will be appropriate to join the nominee where his own conduct is in issue, and it will be necessary to do so where an order for costs is sought against him. Further, in determining whether an irregularity was material and whether a further meeting should be summoned, the views and attitude of other creditors will also be relevant. In the absence of any specific requirement that such creditors be notified of the application, however, the court itself will have to act, so far as possible, as a watchdog for their interests: see *IRC v Duce* [1999] BPIR 189 at 200G.

Applications under s 6 may raise serious questions relating to the truth or accuracy of information supplied in the proposal or statement of affairs or on the failure to disclose material facts. In such cases, where allegations of misrepresentation or non-disclosure are challenged, the court may be unable to determine the matter on the basis of competing affidavit evidence without cross-examination: see for example *Re a Debtor (No 574 of 1995)* [1998] 2 BCLC 124. Orders for disclosure and further information may also be made where appropriate. See also *Re Primlaks (UK) Ltd (No 2)* [1990] BCLC 234.

A nominee will not generally be liable for the costs of a successful application under ground (a); in preparing a proposal for consideration the nominee acts as agent of the directors. In cases of material irregularity under ground (b), however, a nominee may be personally liable in costs where, exceptionally, the nominee in performing his or her duties has fallen so far below the proper standard of duty required of the profession as to justify such an order: *Re a Debtor (No 222 of 1990) (No 2)* [1993] BCLC 233, *Smurthwaite v Simpson-Smith*, 25 July 2006, LTL 25/07/06 CA. In *Harmony Carpets v Chaffin-Laird* [2000] BPIR 61 the court made it clear that for the nominee to be liable for the costs of a challenge in such circumstances it must also be shown that the costs claimed were caused by the nominee's misconduct.

1.9

6A False representations, etc

(1) If, for the purpose of obtaining the approval of the members or creditors of a company to a proposal for a voluntary arrangement, a person who is an officer of the company—

    (a)   makes any false representation, or

    (b)   fraudulently does, or omits to do, anything,

he commits an offence.

(2) Subsection (1) applies even if the proposal is not approved.

(3) For purposes of this section 'officer' includes a shadow director.

(4) A person guilty of an offence under this section is liable to imprisonment or a fine, or both.

―――――

Notes

S 6A

This provision was added by IA 2000. It enacts by primary legislation an offence which was formerly contained in IR 1986 r 1.30. As now enacted, the offence applies whether or not the voluntary arrangement proposal is in fact approved. The penalties for the offence are to be found in IA 1986, Schedule 10.

―――――

1.10

7 Implementation of proposal

(1) This section applies where a voluntary arrangement has effect under section 4A.

(2) The person who is for the time being carrying out in relation to the voluntary arrangement the functions conferred―
   (a) on the nominee by virtue of the approval given at one or both of the meetings summoned under section 3
   (b) by virtue of section 2(4) or 4(2) on a person other than the nominee,
shall be known as the supervisor of the voluntary arrangement.

(3) If any of the company's creditors or any other person is dissatisfied by any act, omission or decision of the supervisor, he may apply to the court; and on the application the court may―
   (a) confirm, reverse or modify any act or decision of the supervisor,
   (b) give him directions, or
   (c) make such other order as it thinks fit.

(4) The supervisor―
   (a) may apply to the court for directions in relation to any particular matter arising under the voluntary arrangement, and
   (b) is included among the persons who may apply to the court for the winding up of the company or for an administration order to be made in relation to it.

(5) The court may, whenever―
   (a) it is expedient to appoint a person to carry out the functions of the supervisor, and
   (b) it is inexpedient, difficult or impracticable for an appointment to be made without the assistance of the court,
make an order appointing a person who is qualified to act as an insolvency practitioner or authorised to act as supervisor, in relation to the voluntary arrangement, either in substitution for the existing supervisor or to fill a vacancy.

> (6) The power conferred by subsection (5) is exercisable so as to increase the number of persons exercising the functions of supervisor or, where there is more than one person exercising those functions, so as to replace one or more of those persons.

Notes

S 7

Following the approval of the voluntary arrangement, its implementation is largely governed by the terms of the arrangement itself. The person on whom responsibility has been placed for carrying out the functions conferred by the arrangement is known as the supervisor. Usually, this will be the same person as the nominee but the creditors' meeting may instead appoint one or more other person in place of or in addition to the nominee to carry out such functions.

The supervisor's functions and activities will be determined by the terms of the arrangement. The supervisor will have only such powers as are vested in him or her by the arrangement whether under its express terms or under such implied terms as may be necessary in order to give the arrangement business efficacy. Neither IA 1986 nor IR 1986 confer any additional powers on the supervisor and neither does the court have power to vary the arrangement to confer additional powers to assist in the operation of the arrangement. See, however, the commentary to IA s 4 above on the means by which an arrangement may be varied during its operation either by the unanimity of creditors or pursuant to a power of variation contained within the arrangement itself.

In carrying out his or her tasks under an approved arrangement, the supervisor will be subject to the control of the court which has power at the request of any person dissatisfied with any act, omission or decision of the supervisor to give directions to the supervisor (under IA 1986 s 7(3)) or even to replace the supervisor (under IA 1986 s 7(5)). See the commentary below for the principles which apply to the operation of these provisions. It has been held that these provisions comprise a self-contained statutory scheme under which the court may enforce the duties owed by a supervisor and adjudicate any complaint; accordingly, no private right of action lies against a supervisor for breach of any statutory duty or duty of care in undertaking his functions: *King v Anthony* [1998] 2 BCLC 517, and see commentary to IA 1986, s 2 above.

Where the arrangement provides for the supervisor to hold assets or their proceeds or funds received by way of voluntary contributions or otherwise for distribution to creditors under the CVA, this will generally constitute the supervisor a trustee to hold such assets or funds to be applied in accordance with the terms of the arrangement. This will be so whether or not the arrangement expressly creates a trust: see *In Re Leisure Study Group Ltd* [1994] 2 BCLC 65, approved by the Court of Appeal in *In re N T Gallagher & Son Ltd* [2002] 1 WLR 2380 at para 26–30; see also *Welburn v Dibb Lupton Broomhead* [2002] EWCA Civ 1601, [2003] BPIR 768.

S 7(3) Power of the court to give directions to supervisor

Persons who may apply

Any person 'dissatisfied' with an act, omission, or decision of the supervisor may apply to the court for directions under s 7(3). IA 1986 does not define the term 'dissatisfied' but it probably extends to any person (i) directly affected by the acts, omissions or decision of the supervisor in undertaking his functions under the arrangement, and (ii) who has no other right of action (for example pursuant to a contract). See:

- Re Cook [1999] BPIR 881 – a decision under IA 1986, s 303 on the right of a person dissatisfied with the act of a trustee in bankruptcy to apply to court. It was held that the term 'dissatisfied' should be given as wide a meaning as the term 'aggrieved' used elsewhere in the insolvency legislation, so as not to include '*a mere busybody who is interfering with things which do not concern him*', but to include '*a person who has a genuine grievance because an order has been made which prejudicially affects his interests*' (citing *A-G of The Gambia v N'Jie* [1961] AC 617).

- *Mahomed v Morris* [2000] 2 BCLC 536 – a decision under IA 1986 s 168(5) on the right of a person 'aggrieved' with the act etc of a liquidator in a compulsory winding up to apply to the court – where the Court of Appeal applied the formula set out above ie person (i) directly affected by decision (ii) with no other right of action.

Powers of court to intervene

The court has been slow to interfere with the commercial acts or decisions of office-holders (typically decisions on the disposal of assets) in the day to day administration of estates under IA 1986 or previous insolvency legislation (whether liquidators, trustees in bankruptcy or otherwise). The test applied has been one of fraud, bad faith or perversity on the part of the office-holder: see for example *Re Hans Place Ltd* [1993] BCLC 768; *Re Edennote Ltd* [1996] 2 BCLC 389; *Hamilton v Official Receiver* [1998] BPIR 602 and *Mahomed v Morris (above)*. Contrast decisions such as those on the true construction of the arrangement or scope of powers conferred under it and the admission, or valuation of a creditor's proof for dividend purposes where the court will intervene on being satisfied that the supervisor is wrong.

S 7(4)(a) Application by supervisor for directions

The supervisor may apply for directions in relation to any particular matter arising under the voluntary arrangement. However:

- This subsection does not confer jurisdiction on the court to sanction a variation to the terms of the arrangement: *Re Alpa Lighting Ltd* [1997] BPIR 341, distinguishing *Re FMS Financial Management Services Ltd* (1988) 5 BCC 191.
- The provision should not generally be used for the purpose of obtaining directions on commercial decisions/administrative matters which are properly matters for the discretion of the supervisor: see *Re T & D Industries* [2000] 1 WLR 646 (an administration case); see also the note to ss (3) above.

In determining questions of construction of a voluntary arrangement, the observations of Blackburne J in *Re Brelec Installations Ltd* [2000] 2 BCLC 576 at 585–6 should be borne in mind. An arrangement is usually put together in some haste. Modifications to it are frequently made at the creditors' meeting with little time to reflect on how they relate to the other terms of the proposal, often resulting in clumsily worded terms. The arrangement ought therefore to be construed in a practical fashion. There is otherwise a risk that careless drafting coupled with a too literal approach to its construction will serve to frustrate rather than to achieve the purpose of the arrangement.

A common question put before the court for directions under IA 1986 s 7(4) (and the subject of a number of first instance decisions) is the effect of any subsequent liquidation (whether voluntary or compulsory) on the voluntary arrangement and on any trust created thereby under which assets are held. The Court of Appeal has now sought to clarify the law in *Re N T Gallagher Ltd* [2002] 1 WLR 2380 in the following propositions:

(1)   Where a CVA or IVA provides for moneys or other assets to be paid to or transferred or held for the benefit of CVA or IVA creditors, this will create a trust of those moneys or assets for those creditors.

(2)   The effect of the liquidation of the company or bankruptcy of the debtor on a trust created by the CVA or IVA will depend on the provisions of the CVA or IVA relating thereto.

(3)   If the CVA or IVA provides what is to happen on liquidation or bankruptcy (or a failure of the CVA or IVA), effect must be given thereto; see also *Re Brelec Installations Ltd* [2000] 2 BCLC 576 at 579.

(4)   If the CVA or IVA does not so provide, the trust will continue notwithstanding the liquidation, bankruptcy or failure and must take effect according to its terms.

(5)   The CVA or IVA creditors can prove in the liquidation or bankruptcy for so much of their debt as remains after payment of what has been or will be recovered under the trust.

S 7(4)(b) Power of supervisor to present petition for the winding up of company

The supervisor of a CVA has power to present a petition for the winding up of the company in the same way as the supervisor of an IVA has power to present a petition for the bankruptcy of the debtor under IA 1986 s 264(1)(c). However, whereas in the latter case the grounds for such a petition are specifically provided for in IA 1986 s 276(1) (failure to comply with obligations under arrangement; provision to creditors of false or misleading information; failure to co-operate with supervisor), there are no such grounds provided in respect of a petition under IA 1986 s 7(4).

It is usual for an arrangement to provide for a supervisor to present a petition in the event of the 'failure' of the arrangement. What constitutes a 'failure' of the arrangement, whether such failure operates automatically to terminate the arrangement or simply provides the threshold conditions under which the supervisor may decide to bring the arrangement to an end (typically by serving a certificate of non-compliance) and (likewise) whether the supervisor may or must in such circumstances present a petition, are all matters which ultimately depend on the construction of the arrangement itself: see *Re Brelec Installations Ltd* (above). However:

- In *Re Brelec Installations Ltd* the court leaned against a construction of the terms which would result in any default on the part of the company in complying with the terms of a trading out CVA bringing the arrangement to an end automatically, no matter how trivial the default and regardless of whether or not the default has or can be remedied, rather than just a permissive threshold requirement entitling the supervisor to bring it to an end.
- By contrast, in *Re Maple Environmental Services Ltd* [2000] BCC 93 it was held that (i) a trading out CVA had failed in circumstances where the company continued to make contributions under the arrangement only at the expense of post CVA creditors, and (ii) the question whether or not the arrangement had failed in such circumstances was not a matter for the discretion of the supervisor; he had been obliged to present a petition. See also the obiter comments of Peter Gibson LJ in *Re N T Gallagher* (cited above) at paragraph 20.

A winding-up petition presented by a supervisor under IA 1986 s 7(4) is treated under IR 1986 r 4.7(9) as if it were a petition filed by a company's contributories and the procedure laid down in IR Part 4 Chapter 4 applies accordingly.

S 7(5) Power to remove supervisor, or to add a further supervisor

An application to remove a supervisor may be made as a single application:
- by the supervisor him or herself (where the supervisor wishes to resign),
- by a disgruntled creditor or (presumably) member or other person interested in the arrangement,

where in either case there is no provision within the arrangement itself for the resignation or removal (as the case may be) of the supervisor and for the appointment of a replacement.

Where it is sought to remove a supervisor for cause, the same principles should apply as those which govern removal of office-holders under other provisions of IA 1986. For a summary of those principles, and the authorities, see *Sisu Capital Fund Ltd v Tucker* [2006] BCC 463, [2006] BPIR 154.

An application to remove a supervisor from one or more offices may also be made as part of a block application for his or her removal from all the appointments held by him or her; see Practice Direction Insolvency Proceedings para 1.6, Vol 2, Civil Procedure, Section 3E. Such block applications may be brought in appropriate cases not only by a resigning supervisor but also:
- in circumstances where the supervisor has left the firm which is handling the day to day administration of the various offices held by him or her, by another member of the same firm who is the intended replacement: *Re A & C Supplies Ltd* [1998] BPIR 303.
- by the professional body responsible for the licensing of insolvency practitioners (or, now, other recognised body) in circumstances where the supervisor has been disqualified from acting: *Re Stella Metals Ltd* [1997] BPIR 293.

1.11

7A Prosecution of delinquent officers of company

(1) This section applies where a moratorium under section 1A has been obtained for a company or the approval of a voluntary arrangement in relation to a company has taken effect under section 4A or paragraph 36 of Schedule A1.

(2) If it appears to the nominee or supervisor that any past or present officer of the company has been guilty of any offence in connection with the moratorium or, as the case may be, voluntary arrangement for which he is criminally liable, the nominee or supervisor shall forthwith-

    (a)   report the matter to the appropriate authority, and

    (b)   provide the appropriate authority with such information and give the authority such access to and facilities for inspecting and taking copies of documents (being information or documents in the possession or under the control of the nominee or supervisor and relating to the matter in question) as the authority requires.

In this subsection, 'the appropriate authority' means-

    (i)   in the case of a company registered in England and Wales, the Secretary of State, and

    (ii)   in the case of a company registered in Scotland, the Lord Advocate.

(3) Where a report is made to the Secretary of State under subsection (2), he may, for the purpose of investigating the matter reported to him and such other matters relating to the affairs of the company as appear to him to require investigation, exercise any of the powers which are exercisable by inspectors appointed under section 431 or 432 of the Companies Act to investigate a company's affairs.

(4) For the purpose of such an investigation any obligation imposed on a person by any provision of the Companies Act to produce documents or give information to, or otherwise to assist, inspectors so appointed is to be regarded as an obligation similarly to assist the Secretary of State in his investigation.

(5) An answer given by a person to a question put to him in exercise of the powers conferred by subsection (3) may be used in evidence against him.

(6) However, in criminal proceedings in which that person is charged with an offence to which this subsection applies-

    (a) no evidence relating to the answer may be adduced, and

    (b) no question relating to it may be asked,

by or on behalf of the prosecution, unless evidence relating to it is adduced, or a question relating to it is asked, in the proceedings by or on behalf of that person.

(7) Subsection (6) applies to any offence other than

    (a)   an offence under section 2 or 5 of the Perjury Act 1911 (false statements made on oath otherwise than in judicial proceedings or made otherwise than on oath), or

    (b)   an offence under section 44(1) or (2) of the Criminal Law (Consolidation) (Scotland) Act 1995 (false statements made on oath or otherwise than on oath).

(8) Where a prosecuting authority institutes criminal proceedings following any report under subsection (2), the nominee or supervisor, and every officer and agent of the company past and present (other than the defendant or defender), shall give the authority all assistance in connection with the prosecution which he is reasonably able to give.

For this purpose-

'agent' includes any banker or solicitor of the company and any person employed by the company as auditor, whether that person is or is not an officer of the company,

'prosecuting authority' means the Director of Public Prosecutions, the Lord Advocate or the Secretary of State.

(9) The court may, on the application of the prosecuting authority, direct any person referred to in subsection (8) to comply with that subsection if he has failed to do so.

1.12

7B Arrangements coming to an end prematurely.

For the purposes of this Part, a voluntary arrangement the approval of which has taken effect under section 4A or paragraph 36 of Schedule A1 comes to an end prematurely if, when it ceases to have effect, it has not been fully implemented in respect of all persons bound by the arrangement by virtue of section 5(2)(b)(i) or, as the case may be, paragraph 37(2)(b)(i) of Schedule A1.

Notes

IA 1986, sections 5(2A)(b) and 6(3) refer to the concept of a CVA coming to an end prematurely. This provision sets out the relevant definition of this term. See further the commentary to section 5(2A)(b) above.

[Part II Administration]

1.13

8 Administration

[Schedule B1 to this Act (which makes provision about the administration of companies) shall have effect.]

Notes

S 8

This section introduces the substantive provisions of the new administration regime which are to be found in Sch B1. As well as containing provisions dealing with the new administration regime, Sch B1 also contains provisions which applied to 'old' administrations but which were formerly to be found in other Parts of IA 1986.

The old Part 2 of IR 1986 continues to apply to all administrations which either were or continue to be subject to the old Part II of IA 1986: art 5(3) of the Insolvency (Amendment) Rules 2003, SI 2003/1730. The old Part II of IA 1986 (ss 8–27) appear below.

Part II (the new IA 1986 s 8 and IA 1986 Sch B1) and the new Part 2 IR 1986 were brought into effect with effect from 15 September 2003 by the Enterprise Act 2002 (Commencement No 4 and Transitional Provisions and Savings) Order 2003, SI 2003/2093 and the Insolvency (Amendment) Rules 2003, SI 2003/1730.

From 15 September 2003, the existing provisions of Part II of the 1986 Act ceased to have effect save as follows:
- Where the petition for the administration order was presented before 15 September 2003: art 3(2) of the Enterprise Act 2002 (Commencement No 4 and Transitional Provisions and Savings) Order 2003, SI 2003/2093. Thus, all pre-existing administrations, plus any administration commenced by an order made on or after 15 September 2003 but pursuant to a petition presented before that date, continue to be governed by the old provisions.
- Undertakings carrying on business of the type identified in **s** 249 EA 2002 are excluded from the provisions of the new Part II. Those undertakings are:
    - Water and sewage undertakers within Chapter 1 of Part II of the Water Industry Act 1991;
    - Protected railway companies within section 59 of the Railways Act 1993 as extended;
    - Air traffic service companies within section 26 of the Transport Act 2000,
    - Public private partnerships within section 210 of the Greater London Authority Act 1999; and
    - Building societies within section 119 of the Building Societies Act 1986.

In these cases, the exclusionary provisions of s 249(2) EA 2002 may be modified by order of the Treasury (building societies) or the Secretary of State (all other cases); at present, no such orders have been made.

By art 3 Enterprise Act 2002 (Commencement No 4 and Transitional Provisions and Savings) Order 2003, SI 2003/2093, the provisions of the old Part II continued to apply to administrations in relation to the following undertakings:
- Insolvent partnerships.
- Limited liability partnerships.
- Insurers within the Financial Services and Markets Act 2000 (Administration Orders relating to Insurers) Order 2002.

However from 1 July 2005 the Insolvent Partnerships (Amendment) Order 2005 (SI 2005/1516) extended the new administration regime (with certain modifications) to partnerships including importantly the ability to make an out of court appointment of an administrator to an insolvent partnership; further amendments effective from 6 April 2006 were made to the insolvent partnership regime under the Insolvent Partnerships (Amendment) Order 2006 (SI 2006/622). The Insolvency Service website is a useful source for checking for checking the chronology of those recent changes (www.insolvency.gov.uk). As from 1 October 2005 the new administration regime was also extended to limited liability partnerships under the Limited Liability Partnerships (Amendment) Regulations 2005 (SI 2005/1989).

'Company'

The definition of company' is in IA 1986 Sch B1 para 111A. It should be noted that s 254 EA 2002 gives the Secretary of State the power by order to provide for the application of provisions of IA 1986 to foreign companies but unfortunately no such order has yet been made. There has been considerable confusion whether the term 'company' in IA 1986 was capable of extending to foreign corporations: see *Re Dallhold Estates (UK) Ltd* [1992] BCC 394. The position was made a little clearer as result of the EC Regulation on Insolvency Proceedings 2000 art 3. This extended the definition of 'company' so that certain unregistered companies could fall within the company voluntary arrangement/administration provisions *Re*

Salvage Association [2003] BCC 504. However Insolvency Act 1986 (Amendment) Regulations 2005 (SI 2005/879) para 2 amended the definition of 'company' in IA 1986 s 1(4) and Sch B1 para 111 to reverse *Re Salvage Association* [2003] EWHC 1028 (Ch), [2003] BCC 504 so that companies such as those incorporated by charter and other bodies falling outside the definition in this provision cannot now to do so or voluntary arrangement unless there is a specific statutory power to do so. The definition of company in summary covers: (a) registered companies under Companies Act; (b) companies incorporated in European Economic Association states other than the UK (this would include Danish companies); and (c) companies registered outside the European Union but with a centre of main interest in an European Union member state (other than Denmark), for example *Re Brac Rent-a-Car International Inc* [2004] BCC 248.

It should further be noted that s 255 EA 2002 gives the Treasury, with the concurrence of the Secretary of State, the power by order to provide for the application of the provisions relating to company arrangements and administration to the following:

- Societies registered under the Industrial and Provident Societies Act 1965.
- Societies registered under the Friendly Societies Act 1974, societies within the Friendly Societies Act 1992 and unregistered Friendly Societies.

The former Part II relating to administrations prior to its substitution by the Enterprise Act 2002 read as follows:

'Part II
Administration Orders

Making etc of administration order

1.14

8 Power of court to make order

(1) *Subject to this section, if the court—*

    (a)   *is satisfied that a company is or is likely to become unable to pay its debts (within the meaning given to that expression by section 123 of this Act), and*

    (b)   *considers that the making of an order under this section would be likely to achieve one or more of the purposes mentioned below,*

the court may make an administration order in relation to the company.

[(1A) For the purposes of a petition presented by the Financial Services Authority alone or together with any other party, an authorised deposit taker who defaults in an obligation to pay any sum due and payable in respect of a relevant deposit is deemed to be unable to pay its debts as mentioned in subsection (1).

(1B) In subsection (1A)—

    (a)   *'authorised deposit taker' means a person who has permission under Part 4 of the Financial Services and Markets Act 2000 to accept deposits, but excludes a person who has such permission only for the purpose of carrying on another regulated activity in accordance with that permission; and*

    (b)   *'relevant deposit' must be read with—*

        (i)   *section 22 of the Financial Services and Markets Act 2000,*

        (ii)   *any relevant order under that section, and*

        (iii)   *Schedule 2 to that Act,*

but any restriction on the meaning of deposit which arises from the identity of the person making it is to be disregarded.]

(2) *An administration order is an order directing that, during the period for which the order is in force, the affairs, business and property of the company shall be managed by a person ('the administrator') appointed for the purpose by the court.*

(3) *The purposes for whose achievement an administration order may be made are—*

(a) *the survival of the company, and the whole or any part of its undertaking, as a going concern;*

(b) *the approval of a voluntary arrangement under Part I;*

(c) *the sanctioning under section 425 of the Companies Act of a compromise or arrangement between the company and any such persons as are mentioned in that section; and*

(d) *a more advantageous realisation of the company's assets than would be effected on a winding up;*

and the order shall specify the purpose or purposes for which it is made.

[(4) An administration order shall not be made in relation to a company after it has gone into liquidation.

(5) *An administration order shall not be made against a company if—*

[(a) *it effects or carries out contracts of insurance, but is not—*

(i) *exempt from the general prohibition, within the meaning of section 19 of the Financial Services and Markets Act 2000, in relation to effecting or carrying out contracts of insurance, or*

(ii) *an authorised deposit taker within the meaning given by subsection (IB), and effecting or carrying out contracts of insurance in the course of a banking business;]*

(b) *it continues to have a liability in respect of a deposit which was held by it in accordance with the Banking Act 1979 or the Banking Act 1987[, but is not an authorised deposit taker, within the meaning given by subsection (1B)].*

(6) *Subsection (5)(a) must be read with—*

(a) *section 22 of the Financial Services and Markets Act 2000;*

(b) *any relevant order under that section; and*

(c) *Schedule 2 to that Act.]*

[(7) In this Part a reference to a company includes a reference to a company in relation to which an administration order may be made by virtue of Article 3 of the EC Regulation.]

1.15

9 Application for order

(1) *An application to the court for an administration order shall be by petition presented either by the company or the directors, or by a creditor or creditors (including any contingent or prospective creditor or creditors), [or by [a justices' chief executive] in the exercise of the power conferred by section 87A of the Magistrates' Courts Act 1980 (enforcement of fines imposed on companies)] or by all or any of those parties, together or separately.*

(2) *Where a petition is presented to the court—*

(a) notice of the petition shall be given forthwith to any person who has appointed, or is or may be entitled to appoint, an administrative receiver of the company, and to such other persons as may be prescribed, and

(b) the petition shall not be withdrawn except with the leave of the court.

(3) Where the court is satisfied that there is an administrative receiver of the company, the court shall dismiss the petition unless it is also satisfied either—

(a) that the person by whom or on whose behalf the receiver was appointed has consented to the making of the order, or

(b) that, if an administration order were made, any security by virtue of which the receiver was appointed would—

[(i) be void against the administrator to any extent by virtue of the provisions of Part XII of the Companies Act 1985 (registration of company changes),]

[(ii)] be liable to be released or discharged under sections 238 to 240 in Part VI (transactions at an undervalue and preferences),

[(iii)] be avoided under section 245 in that Part (avoidance of floating charges), or

[(iv)] be challengeable under section 242 (gratuitous alienations) or 243 (unfair preferences) in that Part, or under any rule of law in Scotland.

(4) Subject to subsection (3), on hearing a petition the court may dismiss it, or adjourn the hearing conditionally or unconditionally, or make an interim order or any other order that it thinks fit.

(5) Without prejudice to the generality of subsection (4), an interim order under that subsection may restrict the exercise of any powers of the directors or of the company (whether by reference to the consent of the court or of a person qualified to act as an insolvency practitioner in relation to the company, or otherwise).

1.16

10 Effect of application

(1) During the period beginning with the presentation of a petition for an administration order and ending with the making of such an order or the dismissal of the petition—

(a) no resolution may be passed or order made for the winding up of the company;

[(aa) no landlord or other person to whom rent is payable may exercise any right of forfeiture by peaceable re-entry in relation to premises let to the company in respect of a failure by the company to comply with any term or condition of its tenancy of such premises, except with the leave of the court and subject to such terms as the court may impose]

(b) no steps may be taken to enforce any security over the company's property, or to repossess goods in the company's possession under any hire-purchase agreement, except with the leave of the court and subject to such terms as the court may impose; and

(c) no other proceedings and no execution or other legal process may be commenced or continued, and no distress may be levied, against the company or its property except with the leave of the court and subject to such terms as aforesaid.

(2) Nothing in subsection (1) requires the leave of the court—

(a)   for the presentation of a petition for the winding up of the company,

(b)   for the appointment of an administrative receiver of the company, or

(c)   for the carrying out by such a receiver (whenever appointed) of any of his functions.

(3) Where—

(a)   a petition for an administration order is presented at a time when there is an administrative receiver of the company, and

(b)   the person by or on whose behalf the receiver was appointed has not consented to the making of the order,

the period mentioned in subsection (1) is deemed not to begin unless and until that person so consents.

(4) References in this section and the next to hire-purchase agreements include conditional sale agreements, chattel leasing agreements and retention of title agreements.

(5) In the application of this section and the next to Scotland, references to execution being commenced or continued include references to diligence being carried out or continued, and references to distress being levied shall be omitted.

1.17

11 Effect of order

(1) On the making of an administration order—

(a)   any petition for the winding up of the company shall be dismissed, and

(b)   any administrative receiver of the company shall vacate office.

(2) Where an administration order has been made, any receiver of part of the company's property shall vacate office on being required to do so by the administrator.

(3) During the period for which an administration order is in force—

(a)   no resolution may be passed or order made for the winding up of the company;

(b)   no administrative receiver of the company may be appointed;

[(ba) no landlord or other person to whom rent is payable may exercise any right of forfeiture by peaceable re-entry in relation to premises let to the company in respect of a failure by the company to comply with any term or condition of its tenancy of such premises, except with the consent of the administrator or the leave of the court and subject (where the court gives leave) to such terms as the court may impose;]

(c)   no other steps may be taken to enforce any security over the company's property, or to repossess goods in the company's possession under any hire-purchase agreement, except with the consent of the administrator or the leave of the court and subject (where the court gives leave) to such terms as the court may impose; and

(d)   no other proceedings and no execution or other legal process may be commenced or continued, and no distress may be levied, against the company or its property except with the consent of the administrator or the leave of the court and subject (where the court gives leave) to such terms as aforesaid.

(4) Where at any time an administrative receiver of the company has vacated office under subsection (1)(b), or a receiver of part of the company's property has vacated office under subsection (2)—

(*a*) *his remuneration and any expenses properly incurred by him, and*

(*b*) *any indemnity to which he is entitled out of the assets of the company,*

shall be charged on and (subject to subsection (3) above) paid out of any property of the company which was in his custody or under his control at that time in priority to any security held by the person by or on whose behalf he was appointed.

(5) Neither an administrative receiver who vacates office under subsection (1)(b) nor a receiver who vacates office under subsection (2) is required on or after so vacating office to take any steps for the purpose of complying with any duty imposed on him by section 40 or 59 of this Act (duty to pay preferential creditors).

1.18

12 Notification of order

(1) Every invoice, order for goods or business letter which, at a time when an administration order is in force in relation to a company, is issued by or on behalf of the company or the administrator, being a document on or in which the company's name appears, shall also contain the administrator's name and a statement that the affairs, business and property of the company are being managed by the administrator.

(2) If default is made in complying with this section, the company and any of the following persons who without reasonable excuse authorises or permits the default, namely, the administrator and any officer of the company, is liable to a fine.

Administrators

1.19

13 Appointment of administrator

(1) The administrator of a company shall be appointed either by the administration order or by an order under the next subsection.

(2) If a vacancy occurs by death, resignation or otherwise in the office of the administrator, the court may by order fill the vacancy.

(3) An application for an order under subsection (2) may be made—

(*a*) *by any continuing administrator of the company; or*

(*b*) *where there is no such administrator, by a creditors' committee established under section 26 below; or*

(*c*) *where there is no such administrator and no such committee, by the company or the directors or by any creditor or creditors of the company.*

1.20

14 General powers

(1) The administrator of a company—

(*a*) *may do all such things as may be necessary for the management of the affairs, business and property of the company, and*

(*b*) *without prejudice to the generality of paragraph (a), has the powers specified in Schedule 1 to this Act;*

and in the application of that Schedule to the administrator of a company the words 'he' and 'him' refer to the administrator.

(2) The administrator also has power—

(a) to remove any director of the company and to appoint any person to be a director of it, whether to fill a vacancy or otherwise, and

(b) to call any meeting of the members or creditors of the company.

(3) The administrator may apply to the court for directions in relation to any particular matter arising in connection with the carrying out of his functions.

(4) Any power conferred on the company or its officers, whether by this Act or the Companies Act or by the memorandum or articles of association, which could be exercised in such a way as to interfere with the exercise by the administrator of his powers is not exercisable except with the consent of the administrator, which may be given either generally or in relation to particular cases.

(5) In exercising his powers the administrator is deemed to act as the company's agent.

(6) A person dealing with the administrator in good faith and for value is not concerned to inquire whether the administrator is acting within his powers.

1.21

15 Power to deal with charged property, etc

(1) The administrator of a company may dispose of or otherwise exercise his powers in relation to any property of the company which is subject to a security to which this subsection applies as if the property were not subject to the security.

(2) Where, on an application by the administrator, the court is satisfied that the disposal (with or without other assets) of—

(a) any property of the company subject to a security to which this subsection applies, or

(b) any goods in the possession of the company under a hire-purchase agreement,

would be likely to promote the purpose or one or more of the purposes specified in the administration order, the court may by order authorise the administrator to dispose of the property as if it were not subject to the security or to dispose of the goods as if all rights of the owner under the hire-purchase agreement were vested in the company.

(3) Subsection (1) applies to any security which, as created, was a floating charge; and subsection (2) applies to any other security.

(4) Where property is disposed of under subsection (1), the holder of the security has the same priority in respect of any property of the company directly or indirectly representing the property disposed of as he would have had in respect of the property subject to the security.

(5) It shall be a condition of an order under subsection (2) that—

(a) the net proceeds of the disposal, and

(b) where those proceeds are less than such amount as may be determined by the court to be the net amount which would be realised on a sale of the property or goods in the open market by a willing vendor, such sums as may be required to make good the deficiency,

shall be applied towards discharging the sums secured by the security or payable under the hire-purchase agreement.

(6) Where a condition imposed in pursuance of subsection (5) relates to two or more securities, that condition requires the net proceeds of the disposal and, where

paragraph (b) of that subsection applies, the sums mentioned in that paragraph to be applied towards discharging the sums secured by those securities in the order of their priorities.

(7) An office copy of an order under subsection (2) shall, within 14 days after the making of the order, be sent by the administrator to the registrar of companies.

(8) If the administrator without reasonable excuse fails to comply with subsection (7), he is liable to a fine and, for continued contravention, to a daily default fine.

(9) References in this section to hire-purchase agreements include conditional sale agreements, chattel leasing agreements and retention of title agreements.

1.22–1.23

16 Operation of s 15 in Scotland

(1) Where property is disposed of under section 15 in its application to Scotland, the administrator shall grant to the disponee an appropriate document of transfer or conveyance of the property, and—

  (a)   that document, or
  (b)   where any recording, intimation or registration of the document is a legal requirement for completion of title to the property, that recording, intimation or registration,

has the effect of disencumbering the property of or, as the case may be, freeing the property from the security.

(2) Where goods in the possession of the company under a hire-purchase agreement, conditional sale agreement, chattel leasing agreement or retention of title agreement are disposed of under section 15 in its application to Scotland, the disposal has the effect of extinguishing, as against the disponee, all rights of the owner of the goods under the agreement.

1.24

17 General duties

(1) The administrator of a company shall, on his appointment, take into his custody or under his control all the property to which the company is or appears to be entitled.

(2) The administrator shall manage the affairs, business and property of the company—

  (a)   at any time before proposals have been approved (with or without modifications) under section 24 below, in accordance with any directions given by the court, and
  (b)   at any time after proposals have been so approved, in accordance with those proposals as from time to time revised, whether by him or a predecessor of his.

(3) The administrator shall summon a meeting of the company's creditors if—

  (a)   he is requested, in accordance with the rules, to do so by one-tenth, in value, of the company's creditors, or
  (b)   he is directed to do so by the court.

1.25

18 Discharge or variation of administration order

(1) The administrator of a company may at any time apply to the court for the administration order to be discharged, or to be varied so as to specify an additional purpose.

(2) The administrator shall make an application under this section if—
   (a) it appears to him that the purpose or each of the purposes specified in the order either has been achieved or is incapable of achievement; or
   (b) he is required to do so by a meeting of the company's creditors summoned for the purpose in accordance with the rules.

(3) On the hearing of an application under this section, the court may by order discharge or vary the administration order and make such consequential provision as it thinks fit, or adjourn the hearing conditionally or unconditionally, or make an interim order or any other order it thinks fit.

(4) Where the administration order is discharged or varied the administrator shall, within 14 days after the making of the order effecting the discharge or variation, send an office copy of that order to the registrar of companies.

(5) If the administrator without reasonable excuse fails to comply with subsection (4), he is liable to a fine and, for continued contravention, to a daily default fine.

1.26

19 Vacation of office

(1) The administrator of a company may at any time be removed from office by order of the court and may, in the prescribed circumstances, resign his office by giving notice of his resignation to the court.

(2) The administrator shall vacate office if—
   (a) he ceases to be qualified to act as an insolvency practitioner in relation to the company, or
   (b) the administration order is discharged.

(3) Where at any time a person ceases to be administrator, the [following] subsections apply.

(4) His remuneration and any expenses properly incurred by him shall be charged on and paid out of any property of the company which is in his custody or under his control at that time in priority to any security to which section 15(1) then applies.

(5) Any sums payable in respect of debts or liabilities incurred, while he was administrator, under contracts entered into ... by him or a predecessor of his in the carrying out of his or the predecessor's functions shall be charged on and paid out of any such property as is mentioned in subsection (4) in priority to any charge arising under that subsection.

[(6) Any sums payable in respect of liabilities incurred, while he was administrator, under contracts of employment adopted by him or a predecessor of his in the carrying out of his or the predecessor's functions shall, to the extent that the liabilities are qualifying liabilities, be charged on and paid out of any such property as is mentioned in subsection (4) and enjoy the same priority as any sums to which subsection (5) applies.]

For this purpose, the administrator is not to be taken to have adopted a contract of employment by reason of anything done or omitted to be done within 14 days after his appointment.

[(7) For the purposes of subsection (6), a liability under a contract of employment is a qualifying liability if—
  (a)   it is a liability to pay a sum by way of wages or salary or contribution to an occupational pension scheme, and
  (b)   it is in respect of services rendered wholly or partly after the adoption of the contract.

(8) There shall be disregarded for the purposes of subsection (6) so much of any qualifying liability as represents payment in respect of services rendered before the adoption of the contract.

(9) For the purposes of subsections (7) and (8)—
  (a)   wages or salary payable in respect of a period of holiday or absence from work through sickness or other good cause are deemed to be wages or (as the case may be) salary in respect of services rendered in that period, and
  (b)   a sum payable in lieu of holiday is deemed to be wages or (as the case may be) salary in respect of services rendered in the period by reference to which the holiday entitlement arose.

(10) In subsection (9)(a), the reference to wages or salary payable in respect of a period of holiday includes any sums which, if they had been paid, would have been treated for the purposes of the enactments relating to social security as earnings in respect of that period.]

1.27

20 Release of administrator

(1) A person who has ceased to be the administrator of a company has his release with effect from the following time, that is to say—
  (a)   in the case of a person who has died, the time at which notice is given to the court in accordance with the rules that he has ceased to hold office;
  (b)   in any other case, such time as the court may determine.

(2) Where a person has his release under this section, he is, with effect from the time specified above, discharged from all liability both in respect of acts or omissions of his in the administration and otherwise in relation to his conduct as administrator.

(3) However, nothing in this section prevents the exercise, in relation to a person who has had his release as above, of the court's powers under section 212 in Chapter X of Part IV (summary remedy against delinquent directors, liquidators, etc).

Ascertainment and investigation of company's affairs

1.28

21 Information to be given by administrator

(1) Where an administration order has been made, the administrator shall—
  (a)   forthwith send to the company and publish in the prescribed manner a notice of the order, and

(b)   *within 28 days after the making of the order, unless the court otherwise directs, send such a notice to all creditors of the company (so far as he is aware of their addresses).*

(2) *Where an administration order has been made, the administrator shall also, within 14 days after the making of the order, send an office copy of the order to the registrar of companies and to such other persons as may be prescribed.*

(3) *If the administrator without reasonable excuse fails to comply with this section, he is liable to a fine and, for continued contravention, to a daily default fine.*

1.29

22 Statement of affairs to be submitted to administrator

(1) *Where an administration order has been made, the administrator shall forthwith require some or all of the persons mentioned below to make out and submit to him a statement in the prescribed form as to the affairs of the company.*

(2) *The statement shall be verified by affidavit by the persons required to submit it and shall show—*
(a)   *particulars of the company's assets, debts and liabilities;*
(b)   *the names and addresses of its creditors;*
(c)   *the securities held by them respectively;*
(d)   *the dates when the securities were respectively given; and*
(e)   *such further or other information as may be prescribed.*

(3) *The persons referred to in subsection (1) are—*
(a)   *those who are or have been officers of the company;*
(b)   *those who have taken part in the company's formation at any time within one year before the date of the administration order;*
(c)   *those who are in the company's employment or have been in its employment within that year, and are in the administrator's opinion capable of giving the information required;*
(d)   *those who are or have been within that year officers of or in the employment of a company which is, or within that year was, an officer of the company.*

In this subsection 'employment' includes employment under a contract for services.

(4) *Where any persons are required under this section to submit a statement of affairs to the administrator, they shall do so (subject to the next subsection) before the end of the period of 21 days beginning with the day after that on which the prescribed notice of the requirement is given to them by the administrator.*

(5) *The administrator, if he thinks fit, may—*
(a)   *at any time release a person from an obligation imposed on him under subsection (1) or (2), or*
(b)   *either when giving notice under subsection (4) or subsequently, extend the period so mentioned;*
and where the administrator has refused to exercise a power conferred by this subsection, the court, if it thinks fit, may exercise it.

(6) *If a person without reasonable excuse fails to comply with any obligation imposed under this section, he is liable to a fine and, for continued contravention, to a daily default fine.*

Administrator's proposals

1.30

23 Statement of proposals

(1) Where an administration order has been made, the administrator shall, within 3 months (or such longer period as the court may allow) after the making of the order—

    (a)   send to the registrar of companies and (so far as he is aware of their addresses) to all creditors a statement of his proposals for achieving the purpose or purposes specified in the order, and

    (b)   lay a copy of the statement before a meeting of the company's creditors summoned for the purpose on not less than 14 days' notice.

(2) The administrator shall also, within 3 months (or such longer period as the court may allow) after the making of the order, either—

    (a)   send a copy of the statement (so far as he is aware of their addresses) to all members of the company, or

    (b)   publish in the prescribed manner a notice stating an address to which members of the company should write for copies of the statement to be sent to them free of charge.

(3) If the administrator without reasonable excuse fails to comply with this section, he is liable to a fine and, for continued contravention, to a daily default fine.

1.31

24 Consideration of proposals by creditors' meeting

(1) A meeting of creditors summoned under section 23 shall decide whether to approve the administrator's proposals.

(2) The meeting may approve the proposals with modifications, but shall not do so unless the administrator consents to each modification.

(3) Subject as above, the meeting shall be conducted in accordance with the rules.

(4) After the conclusion of the meeting in accordance with the rules, the administrator shall report the result of the meeting to the court and shall give notice of that result to the registrar of companies and to such persons as may be prescribed.

(5) If a report is given to the court under subsection (4) that the meeting has declined to approve the administrator's proposals (with or without modifications), the court may by order discharge the administration order and make such consequential provision as it thinks fit, or adjourn the hearing conditionally or unconditionally, or make an interim order or any other order that it thinks fit.

(6) Where the administration order is discharged, the administrator shall, within 14 days after the making of the order effecting the discharge, send an office copy of that order to the registrar of companies.

(7) If the administrator without reasonable excuse fails to comply with subsection (6), he is liable to a fine and, for continued contravention, to a daily default fine.

1.32

25 Approval of substantial revisions

(*1*) *This section applies where—*
  (*a*) *proposals have been approved (with or without modifications) under section 24, and*
  (*b*) *the administrator proposes to make revisions of those proposals which appear to him substantial.*

(*2*) *The administrator shall—*
  (*a*) *send to all creditors of the company (so far as he is aware of their addresses) a statement in the prescribed form of his proposed revisions, and*
  (*b*) *lay a copy of the statement before a meeting of the company's creditors summoned for the purpose on not less than 14 days' notice; and he shall not make the proposed revisions unless they are approved by the meeting.*

(*3*) *The administrator shall also either—*
  (*a*) *send a copy of the statement (so far as he is aware of their addresses) to all members of the company, or*
  (*b*) *publish in the prescribed manner a notice stating an address to which members of the company should write for copies of the statement to be sent to them free of charge.*

(*4*) *The meeting of creditors may approve the proposed revisions with modifications, but shall not do so unless the administrator consents to each modification.*

(*5*) *Subject as above, the meeting shall be conducted in accordance with the rules.*

(*6*) *After the conclusion of the meeting in accordance with the rules, the administrator shall give notice of the result of the meeting to the registrar of companies and to such persons as may be prescribed.*

Miscellaneous

1.33

26 Creditors' committee

(*1*) *Where a meeting of creditors summoned under section 23 has approved the administrator's proposals (with or without modifications), the meeting may, if it thinks fit, establish a committee ('the creditors' committee') to exercise the functions conferred on it by or under this Act.*

(*2*) *If such a committee is established, the committee may, on giving not less than 7 days' notice, require the administrator to attend before it at any reasonable time and furnish it with such information relating to the carrying out of his functions as it may reasonably require.*

1.34

27 Protection of interests of creditors and members

(*1*) *At any time when an administration order is in force, a creditor or member of the company may apply to the court by petition for an order under this section on the ground—*

(a)   that the company's affairs, business and property are being or have been managed by the administrator in a manner which is unfairly prejudicial to the interests of its creditors or members generally, or of some part of its creditors or members (including at least himself), or

(b)   that any actual or proposed act or omission of the administrator is or would be so prejudicial.

(2) On an application for an order under this section the court may, subject as follows, make such order as it thinks fit for giving relief in respect of the matters complained of, or adjourn the hearing conditionally or unconditionally, or make an interim order or any other order that it thinks fit.

(3) An order under this section shall not prejudice or prevent—

(a)   the implementation of a voluntary arrangement approved under … Part I, or any compromise or arrangement sanctioned under section 425 of the Companies Act; or

(b)   where the application for the order was made more than 28 days after the approval of any proposals or revised proposals under section 24 or 25, the implementation of those proposals or revised proposals.

(4) Subject as above, an order under this section may in particular—

(a)   regulate the future management by the administrator of the company's affairs, business and property;

(b)   require the administrator to refrain from doing or continuing an act complained of by the petitioner, or to do an act which the petitioner has complained he has omitted to do;

(c)   require the summoning of a meeting of creditors or members for the purpose of considering such matters as the court may direct;

(d)   discharge the administration order and make such consequential provision as the court thinks fit.

(5) Nothing in section 15 or 16 is to be taken as prejudicing applications to the court under this section.

(6) Where the administration order is discharged, the administrator shall, within 14 days after the making of the order effecting the discharge, send an office copy of that order to the registrar of companies; and if without reasonable excuse he fails to comply with this subsection, he is liable to a fine and, for continued contravention, to a daily default fine.

Part III
Receivership

Chapter I
Receivers and Managers (England and Wales)Preliminary and general provisions

1.35

28 Extent of this Chapter

This Chapter does not apply to receivers appointed under Chapter II of this Part (Scotland).

Notes

S 28

An administrative receiver may no longer be appointed under a qualifying floating charge (defined by IA 1986 Sch B1 para 14(2)) which was created on or after 15 September 2003: IA 1986 s 72A. This is subject to the exceptions for charges created pursuant to the arrangements identified in IA 1986 s 72B to G. In general, a holder of a qualifying floating charge can now appoint an administrator. An administrative receiver may still be appointed under a charge created prior to 15 September 2003 provided that the charge, as created, was a floating charge as provided in IA 1986 s 29(2); alternatively the holder of such a charge may appoint an administrator under IA 1986 Sch B1 para 14.

1.36

29 Definitions

(1) It is hereby declared that, except where the context otherwise requires—
  (a) any reference in the Companies Act or this Act to a receiver or manager of the property of a company, or to a receiver of it, includes a receiver or manager, or (as the case may be) a receiver of part only of that property and a receiver only of the income arising from the property or from part of it; and
  (b) any reference in the Companies Act or this Act to the appointment of a receiver or manager under powers contained in an instrument includes an appointment made under powers which, by virtue of any enactment, are implied in and have effect as if contained in an instrument.

(2) In this Chapter 'administrative receiver' means—
  (a) a receiver or manager of the whole (or substantially the whole) of a company's property appointed by or on behalf of the holders of any debentures of the company secured by a charge which, as created, was a floating charge, or by such a charge and one or more other securities; or

> (b) a person who would be such a receiver or manager but for the appointment of some other person as the receiver of part of the company's property.

Notes

S 29(1)

'Receiver' and 'manager' includes those receivers of only part of the company's property or a receiver of income arising from company property or from part of it.

S 29(2)

This defines, 'administrative receiver'. Administrative receivers were a new kind of receiver introduced by IA 1986. Previously receivers appointed under a debenture had the powers conferred by the Law of Property Act 1925, supplemented by the provisions of the charge under which they were appointed. 'Administrative Receivers' have the powers and duties conferred by Part III and schedule 1 of IA 1986 and Part 3 of IR 1986. Those powers enable the administrative receiver to carry on the company's business with a view to a realisation of assets for the benefit of the debenture holder: *Newhart v Co-op Commercial Bank* [1978] QB 814. IR 1986 r 3.1 to 3.38 apply to administrative receivers only; IR 1986 r 3.39 and 3.40 concerning a receiver's obligations in respect of dealing with the 'prescribed part' under IA 1986 s 176A apply to all receivers except administrative receivers.

The appointment of an administrative receiver does not effect a total termination of directors' authority but the management function of the board is in effect 'suspended,' at least so far as it is concurrent with the powers and functions of the administrative receiver and affects the assets that are the subject of the charge under which the administrative receiver is appointed. The residual power of the board following the appointment of the administrative receiver to use the company's name in litigation (or otherwise act on the company's behalf) is very limited; the directors may act if it is in the company's interest and does not impinge prejudicially on the debenture holders qua debenture holders by threatening or imperiling the assets which are the subject of the charge: *Newhart v Co-op Commercial Bank supra*; and see *Re GE Capital Commercial Finance Ltd v Sutton* [2004] EWCA Civ 315, [2004] 2 BCLC 662 where the directors were able to restrain use of confidential and privileged material by the administrative receiver where the purported waiver was not in the interests of the company and was either outside the powers conferred by the debenture or an improper use of statutory powers. By contrast in *Tudor Grange Holdings Ltd v Citibank NV* [1992] Ch 53 a claim brought by the directors in the company's name against the debenture holder was struck out on the ground that they were starting proceedings which could directly impinge on the property subject to the receiver's powers, in that they held no indemnity to protect the company's assets in the event of a hostile order for costs made against the company. It was pointed out that the receivers could have brought the claim had they thought fit to do so, and that any embarrassment caused by the fact they would have been suing their appointors could have been resolved by seeking directions from the court. In *Sheppard & Cooper V TSB Bank PLC* [1997] 2 BCLC 222 directors exercised their powers to seek a change in the identity of the administrative receivers appointed on the basis that the persons that the bank had appointed had disqualified themselves by contract from acting. In *Sheppard & Cooper v TSB Bank PLC (No 2)* [1996] 2 All ER 654, the directors unsuccessfully sought to challenge the validity of the first receivers' appointment and to bring a claim against them for trespass and conversion. A subsequent application to make the directors liable for the defendants' costs failed.

Under the former administration regime the holder of a floating charge with the power to appoint an administrative receiver could veto an administration. The practice therefore grew of taking a floating charge, even where the assets were also charged by a fixed charge. If all or substantially all of the company's property is charged under a debenture and at least one of those charges under the debenture is a floating charge, then despite the fact that the assets are already charged by a fixed charge a receiver appointed under the debenture will generally be an administrative receiver: *Re Croftbell Ltd* [1990] BCLC 844. However, if an appointment is made only under the fixed charge element of the debenture, the receiver will not be an administrative receiver: *Meadrealm Ltd v Transcontinental Golf Construction* (Vinelott J, 29 November 1991, unreported). For the effect of an administrative receivership on the new administration regime see IA 1986 Sch B1 paras 17, 25, 39.

S 29(2)(a)

A 'debenture' has been described as an instrument acknowledging an indebtedness of its maker to its holder: *Levy v Abercorris Slate and Slab Company* (1887) 37 Ch D 260; see also CA 1985, s 744. An administrative receiver can only be appointed in respect of a 'company', which is generally defined as a company registered under the CA 1985, unless the contrary intention appears (IA 1986 s 251, CA 1985 s 735). In *Re International Bulk Commodities Ltd* [1992] BCLC 1074 it was held that a contrary intention could be derived from the IA 1986 when looked at as a whole and the provisions relating to administrative receivers in particular. It was held that 'company' in IA 1986 s 29(2)(a) includes unregistered companies liable to be wound up under Part V of the IA 1986. However in *Re Devon and Somerset Farmers Ltd* [1994] Ch 57 it was held that s 29(2) did not extend to industrial and provident societies which are the subject of their own legislative scheme.

S 29(2)(b)

This provision determines whether the appointment of a receiver creates an administrative receivership when a receiver has already been appointed by the court or under a fixed charge. An administrative receivership is created if the latter receiver would be an administrative receiver but for the former appointment/s. It does not appear that there can be concurrent administrative receivers appointed.

1.37

30 Disqualification of body corporate from acting as receiver

A body corporate is not qualified for appointment as receiver of the property of a company, and any body corporate which acts as such a receiver is liable to a fine.

1.38

31 Disqualification of undischarged bankrupt

(1) A person commits an offence if he acts as a receiver or manager of the property of a company on behalf of debenture holders while-
  (a)   he is an undischarged bankrupt, or
  (b)   a bankruptcy restrictions order is in force in respect of him.

(2) A person guilty of an offence under subsection (1) shall be liable to imprisonment, a fine or both

(3) This section does not apply to a receiver or manager acting under an appointment made by the court

---

Notes

S 31

This is a new provision inserted by schedule 21 para 21 EA 2002 to deal with the effect of bankruptcy restriction orders (see IA 1986 section 281A and Sch 4A).

1.39

32 Power for court to appoint official receiver

Where application is made to the court to appoint a receiver on behalf of the debenture holders or other creditors of a company which is being wound up by the court, the official receiver may be appointed.

Notes

S 32

This section enables the court to appoint the official receiver as a receiver in the unusual situation where a debenture holder applies to court for the appointment of a receiver.

Receivers and managers appointed out of court

1.40

33 Time for which appointment is effective

(1) The appointment of a person as a receiver or manager of a company's property under powers contained in an instrument—

(a)   is of no effect unless it is accepted by that person before the end of the business day next following that on which the instrument of appointment is received by him or on his behalf, and

(b)   subject to this, is deemed to be made at the time at which the instrument of appointment is so received.

(2) This section applies to the appointment of two or more persons as joint receivers or managers of a company's property under powers contained in an instrument, subject to such modifications as may be prescribed by the rules.

Notes

S 33(1)

Receivers and managers appointed out of court are deemed to be appointed when the letter of appointment is received. However, the appointment is not effective unless he accepts the appointment before the end of the next business day.

S 33(2)

The section also applies to joint receivers subject to modifications prescribed by the rules (see IR 1986 r 3.1).

1.41

34 Liability for invalid appointment

Where the appointment of a person as the receiver or manager of a company's property under powers contained in an instrument is discovered to be invalid (whether by virtue of the invalidity of the instrument or

> otherwise), the court may order the person by whom or on whose behalf
> the appointment was made to indemnify the person appointed against any
> liability which arises solely by reason of the invalidity of the appointment.

Notes

S 34

The court may order that the person who appointed the receiver indemnify the appointee against liability arising solely by reason of the invalidity of that appointment. This section provides protection to a receiver in the event that his appointment is challenged. There are a number of situations in which the appointment of a receiver may be challenged:

(i)   there has been a failure to comply with the registration requirements of CA 1985 s 395;

(ii)   the floating charge under the debenture is invalid under IA 1986 s 245;

(iii)   the fixed charge under the debenture is avoided as a preference under IA 1986 s 239 or possibly as a transaction at an undervalue under IA 1986 s 238, *Re Nurokowksi, Hill v Spread Trustee Company Ltd* [2006] BPIR 789;

(iv)   the sums secured by the debenture have not become due and payable. In most cases the facilities will be repayable 'on demand' and the period between demand and appointment of the administrative receiver need only be as long as would enable the company to implement 'the mechanics of payment,' ie to obtain the money and pay the debt assuming that the company has sufficient funds readily available. The company is not entitled to sufficient time to realise assets or arrange finance: *Sheppard and Cooper Ltd v TSB Bank (No 2)* [1996] 2 All ER 654, following *RA Cripps & Sons Ltd v Wickenden* [1973] 1 WLR 944 and *Bank of Baroda v Panessar* [1987] Ch 335. A demand need not specify the amount due and will be valid even if the amount due is overstated: *Bank of Baroda v Panessar*; On the mechanics of payment test, and the validity of an overstated demand, see also paras 107 to 109 of the judgment of Patten J in *Silven Properties Ltd v Royal Bank of Scotland plc* [2002] EWHC 1976 (Ch), [2004] 1 WLR 997;

(v)   the debt in question was not covered by the security under which the administrative receiver was purportedly appointed. For example in *OBG v Allan* [2001] Lloyds Rep Bank 365, the appointor was the assignee of a charge and sought to appoint administrative receivers on the basis of indebtedness incurred prior to the assignment;

(vi)   the purported appointment is not made under a written instrument.

In *Sheppard & Cooper v TSB Bank PLC* [1997] 2 BCLC 222 a firm of insolvency practitioners had agreed not to become involved in the management of the company. Some years later the company's bankers appointed administrative receivers who were partners in the same firm of insolvency practitioners. It was held that whilst the appointment was not itself invalid, partners and employees of the firm in question were disqualified by contract from acting, so new receivers had to be appointed.

An invalidly appointed administrative receiver may be liable for torts such as trespass and conversion, but in *OBG v Allan* [2005] QB 762 the Court of Appeal held by a majority that the invalidly appointed administrative receivers were not liable for the tort of interference with contractual relations because they lacked the relevant intention to procure an actionable wrong such as a breach of contract by the company. This decision is the subject of a pending appeal to the House of Lords.

1.42

35 Application to court for directions

(1) A receiver or manager of the property of a company appointed under powers contained in an instrument, or the persons by whom or on whose

behalf a receiver or manager has been so appointed, may apply to the court for directions in relation to any particular matter arising in connection with the performance of the functions of the receiver or manager.

(2) On such an application, the court may give such directions, or may make such order declaring the rights of persons before the court or otherwise, as it thinks just.

Notes

S 35(1)

A receiver or debenture holder can apply to the court for directions in relation to any particular matter arising in connection with the performance of his functions. Clearly, the court has a wide discretion under s 35(2) to deal with any matters raised: see for example *Re Therm-a-Stor Ltd* [1996] 2 BCLC 400; *Re Beam Tube Products Ltd* [2006] BCC 615, [2006] EWHC 486 (Ch). Although the jurisdiction to give directions is a useful one, and a means by which disputed issues may be determined, a receiver should only apply for directions in cases of real doubt. The court may refuse to entertain an application where the receiver has funds and the matter can best be dealt with by ordinary litigation: *Re Stetzel Thomson & Co Ltd* (1988) 4 BCC 74. Moreover, the jurisdiction is not to be used for the purposes of seeking directions on matters which are within the commercial judgment of the receiver: see *Re T&D Automotive plc* [2000] 1 BCLC 471.

After *Mirror Group Newspapers v Maxwell* [1998] BCC 324 (also, see the taxing officer's judgment at [1999] BCC 684) and the Statement of Insolvency Practice ('SIP 9'), a receiver (or debenture holder: see *Munns v Perkins* [2002] BPIR 120) can apply for directions under IA 1986 s 35 if he is concerned about the level of remuneration that is intended to be charged. If the receiver does not make this application then his fees may be vulnerable to challenge by a liquidator under IA 1986 s 36 below. The *Practice Statement- the Fixing and Approval of the Remuneration of Appointees* (*2004*) [2004] BPIR 953 does not apply to receivers of companies.

1.43

36 Court's power to fix remuneration

(1) The court may, on an application made by the liquidator of a company, by order fix the amount to be paid by way of remuneration to a person who, under powers contained in an instrument, has been appointed receiver or manager of the company's property.

(2) The court's power under subsection (1), where no previous order has been made with respect thereto under the subsection—

    (a)   extends to fixing the remuneration for any period before the making of the order or the application for it,

    (b)   is exercisable notwithstanding that the receiver or manager has died or ceased to act before the making of the order or the application, and

    (c)   where the receiver or manager has been paid or has retained for his remuneration for any period before the making of the order any amount in excess of that so fixed for that period, extends to requiring him or his personal representatives to account for the excess or such part of it as may be specified in the order.

But the power conferred by paragraph (c) shall not be exercised as respects any period before the making of the application for the order under this section, unless in the court's opinion there are special circumstances making it proper for the power to be exercised.

(3) The court may from time to time on an application made either by the liquidator or by the receiver or manager, vary or amend an order made under subsection (1).

Notes

S 36(1)

A liquidator may apply to court to fix a receiver's fees. The court can therefore prevent an unreasonable amount being charged in a receivership where the debenture holder is comfortably secured. However, the court is unlikely to become involved in fee disputes and interfere unless the remuneration is demonstrably excessive; *Re Potters Oils Ltd (No 2)* [1986] 1 WLR 201. The *Practice Statement – the Fixing and Approval of the Remuneration of Appointees* [2004] BPIR 953 does not apply to receivers of companies.

1.44

37 Liability for contracts, etc

(1) A receiver or manager appointed under powers conferred in an instrument (other than an administrative receiver) is, to the same extent as if he had been appointed by order of the court—
    (a)   personally liable on any contract entered into by him in the performance of his functions (except in so far as the contract otherwise provides) and on any contract of employment adopted by him in the performance of those functions, and
    (b)   entitled in respect of that liability to indemnity out of the assets.

(2) For the purposes of subsection (1)(a), the receiver or manager is not to be taken to have adopted a contract of employment by reason of anything done or omitted to be done within 14 days after his appointment.

(3) Subsection (1) does not limit any right to indemnity which the receiver or manager would have apart from it, nor limit his liability on contracts entered into without authority, nor confer any right to indemnity in respect of that liability.

(4) Where at any time the receiver or manager so appointed vacates office—
    (a)   his remuneration and any expenses properly incurred by him, and
    (b)   any indemnity to which he is entitled out of the assets of the company,

> shall be charged on and paid out of any property of the company which is in his custody or under his control at that time in priority to any charge or other security held by the person by or on whose behalf he was appointed.

Notes

S 37

This provision does not apply to administrative receivers. The position in relation to administrative receivers is dealt with in IA 1986 s 44.

S 37(1)(a)

Where a receiver appointed out of court does not make express provision in a contract to exclude any personal liability, he will be personally liable on the contract. As to existing contracts, the company remains bound by them but the receiver is not personally liable unless he adopts them.

S 37(1)(b)

The receiver is entitled to the statutory indemnity 'out of the assets'; where the receiver's liability may exceed the value of the assets, the receiver can limit his liability to the available assets *Re Ernest Hawkins & Co Ltd* (1915) 31 TLR 247.

S 37(2)

A receiver can adopt contracts of employment and he has 14 days to decide whether to do so. This provision departs from the common law position where employees continued in employment with the company as employer, and the office holder acting as the agent of the company had no personal responsibility in respect of the employment contracts, including the obligation to pay wages: see *Nicoll v Cutts* [1985] BCLC 322. If the receiver does adopt a contract of employment this will bring with it the accrued liabilities which the company previously had to the employee under the contract of employment in question: *Powdrill v Watson, Re Paramount Airways Ltd* [1995] 2 AC 394. The IA 1994 (see notes to IA 1986 s 44) limiting the liability of office holders in respect of the adoption of employment contracts does not apply to non-administrative receivers so the accrued liabilities of the relevant employee are not limited to the 'qualifying liabilities' referred to in IA 1986 s 44(2A).

A receiver may decide not to adopt employment contracts in order to avoid any difficulties arising under the Transfer of Undertakings (Protection of Employment) Regulations 2006 (SI 2006/246):

S 37(3)

See *Litster v Forth Dry Dock and Engineering Co Ltd* [1990] 1 AC 546 (a case on the former TUPE regulations). The old practice of writing to employees undertaking to ensure that the company would pay the present salary if the employee continued working for the company but denying that the receiver was adopting the contract of employment, was firmly rejected in *Powdrill v Watson, Re Paramount Airways Ltd* [1995] 2 AC 394.

S 37(4)

This provision creates a charge to ensure that the receiver's remuneration, costs and expenses and any indemnity are paid, without the requirement to retain assets for payment. However, a receiver will usually avoid paying off a charge holder until he has in fact been paid or secured payment; this will avoid the problems which might be caused by court intervention which may result in preventing further realisations being made pending resolution of a fee dispute. The court is likely to intervene where there is an arguable case that the receiver has already realised sufficient assets to pay both himself and the secured creditors so that his authority to act is effectively at an end: see eg *Rottenberg v Monjack* [1993] BCLC 374 a case on administrative receivers.

Further, a receiver is unlikely to part with assets and rely on the charge created by IA 1986 s 37(4) because such a charge does not appear to be effective as against bona fide purchasers for value without notice. The charge created by this subsection only has priority over other charges held by the receiver's appointor. The provision does not re-order the priorities of other charges, so if any charge was granted by the company in priority to the charge under which the receiver was appointed, then the debts secured by the prior charge take priority and must be paid before the receiver's fees and expenses *Choudri v Palta* [1992] BCC 787.

1.45

38 Receivership accounts to be delivered to registrar

(1) Except in the case of an administrative receiver, every receiver or manager of a company's property who has been appointed under powers contained in an instrument shall deliver to the registrar of companies for registration the requisite accounts of his receipts and payments.

(2) The accounts shall be delivered within one month (or such longer period as the registrar may allow) after the expiration of 12 months from the date of his appointment and of every subsequent period of 6 months, and also within one month after he ceases to act as receiver or manager.

(3) The requisite accounts shall be an abstract in the prescribed form showing—

   (a)   receipts and payments during the relevant period of 12 or 6 months, or

   (b)   where the receiver or manager ceases to act, receipts and payments during the period from the end of the period of 12 or 6 months to which the last preceding abstract related (or, if no preceding abstract has been delivered under this section, from the date of his appointment) up to the date of his so ceasing, and the aggregate amount of receipts and payments during all preceding periods since his appointment.

(4) In this section 'prescribed' means prescribed by regulations made by statutory instrument by the Secretary of State.

(5) A receiver or manager who makes default in complying with this section is liable to a fine and, for continued contravention, to a daily default fine.

Notes

S 38(1), (2)

Receivers and managers except administrative receivers must deliver accounts to the registrar of companies; see IA 1986 s 48 and IR 1986 r 3.32, for the duty of reporting and accounting placed on administrative receivers.

Provisions applicable to every receivership

1.46

39 Notification that receiver or manager appointed

(1) When a receiver or manager of the property of a company has been appointed, every invoice, order for goods or business letter issued by or on behalf of the company or the receiver or manager or the liquidator of the company, being a document on or in which the company's name appears, shall contain a statement that a receiver or manager has been appointed.

(2) If default is made in complying with this section, the company and any of the following persons, who knowingly and wilfully authorises or permits the default, namely, any officer of the company, any liquidator of the company and any receiver or manager, is liable to a fine.

1.47

40 Payment of debts out of assets subject to floating charge

(1) The following applies, in the case of a company, where a receiver is appointed on behalf of the holders of any debentures of the company secured by a charge which, as created, was a floating charge.

(2) If the company is not at the time in course of being wound up, its preferential debts (within the meaning given to that expression by section 386 in Part XII) shall be paid out of the assets coming to the hands of the receiver in priority to any claims for principal or interest in respect of the debentures.

(3) Payments made under this section shall be recouped, as far as may be, out of the assets of the company available for payment of general creditors.

Notes

S 40

The obligation on the receiver to pay the preferential creditors must now be read in the light of IA 1986 s 175A under which a receiver must make a prescribed part of the company's net property available for the satisfaction of unsecured debts; see notes to IA 1986 s 176A and IR 1986 r 3.8, 3.39 to 3.40). Section 40 does not apply to receivers of industrial provident societies registered under the Industrial and Provident Societies Act 1986: *Re Devon & Somerset Farmers Ltd* [1994] Ch 57.

S 40(1)

This provision applies where the receiver is appointed under a debenture secured by a charge 'which, *as created*, was a floating charge' – this wording is of course that used to define a floating charge in IA 1986 s 251. This definition ensures that crystallisation of a charge on or before the appointment of a receiver does not alter the duty to pay preferential creditors under IA 1986 s 40 see *H & K Medway Ltd* [1997] 1 BCLC 545, disapproving *Griffiths v Yorkshire Bank plc* [1994] 1 WLR 1427. The duty to pay the preferential creditors ahead of the floating charge holder is personal to the receiver *IRC v Goldblatt* [1972] Ch 498 and it does not cease upon payment of the floating charge holder *Re Pearl Maintenance Services Ltd* [1995] BCC

657. The operation of this section was considered by the House of Lords in *Buchler v Talbot* [2004] UKHL 9, [2004] 2 AC 298: see the notes to IA 1986 s 175 where the effect of the decision is more fully discussed.

However, the classification of charges has led to difficulty. The question is usually whether a charge described in a debenture as a fixed is in fact a fixed or a floating charge, and the issue has been most hotly contested in relation to charges over book debts. *Re Bullas Trading Ltd* [1994] BCC 36 approved the practice of dividing security over book debts into a fixed charge over uncollected book debts and a floating charge once those debts were collected. *Re Bullas* was distinguished on a number of occasions and the attacks culminated in *Agnew v IRC (Re Brumark Investments Ltd)* [2001] UKPC 28, [2001] 2 AC 710 where the Privy Council considered that *Re Bullas Trading* was wrongly decided.

In *Re Spectrum Plus Ltd* [2005] 2 AC 680, the House of Lords held that the essential characteristic of a floating charge was that the asset subject to the charge was not finally appropriated as a security for the payment of the debt until the occurrence of some future event, and in the meantime the chargor was free to use the charged asset and remove it from the security. Whether a charge was fixed or floating would depend on the construction of the charge and the facts of any particular case. Although the company was subject to restrictions in relation to book debts prior to their collection, once the book debts had been collected and paid into the company's current account, the bank's debenture placed no restriction on the use that the company could make of the balance on the account. Since it was not a blocked account the company could continue to draw on it and the bank was obliged to honour the company's cheques. The charge over the company's book debts therefore had the characteristics of a floating charge. It was further held that it did not matter whether debts were received into an overdrawn account or into an account with a credit balance. Accordingly, the debenture, although expressed to grant the bank a fixed charge, in law granted only a floating charge which would not have priority over the claims of preferential creditors. *Agnew v CIR (Re Brumark Investments Ltd) was approved and Siebe Gorman v Barclays bank Ltd* [1979] 2 Lloyd's Rep 142 was overruled. The analysis in *Re Spectrum Plus Ltd was applied in Re Bean Tube Products Ltd* [2006] EWHC 486 (Ch), [2006] BCC 615.

Although the question is, in theory a mixed question of construction of the charge and fact (the way in which the charge operates in practice), in practice it is unlikely that a charge on book debts would be operated in such a way as to allow the debenture holder sufficient control over the proceeds of the debts once paid into the company's bank account. The current position is therefore that, in general, charges on book debts will be treated as floating charges unless the accounts into which they are paid is genuinely blocked.

S 40(2)

A receiver appointed under a floating charge is under a personal duty to pay preferential creditors: see *IRC v Goldblatt* [1972] Ch 498; *Westminster City Council v Haste* [1950] Ch 442). A failure to pay preferential creditors renders the receiver personally liable: *Re H & K Medway* [1997] 1 BCLC 545; *Woods v Winskill* [1913] 2 Ch 303. The receiver is under a duty to pay the preferential creditors before the charge holder is paid, as the preferential claims rank above the floating charge albeit that on crystallisation the charged assets belong to the charge holder as opposed to the company: *Re BHT (UK) Ltd* [2004] BCC 301. This duty is not abrogated by the company entering liquidation but the receiver is relieved from taking any further steps to comply with IA 1986 s 40 if he vacates office as a result of an administration in the circumstances set out in IA 1986 Sch B1 para 41(3).

S 40(3)

The funds available for unsecured creditors may then be used to recoup the cost of meeting preferential creditors' claims see *Buchler v Talbot* [2004] UKHL 9, [2004] 2 AC 298 and the notes to IA s 175 post.

1.48

41 Enforcement of duty to make returns

(1) If a receiver or manager of a company's property—
 (a) having made default in filing, delivering or making any return, account or other document, or in giving any notice, which a receiver or manager is by law required to file, deliver, make or give, fails to make good the default within 14 days after the service on him of a notice requiring him to do so, or
 (b) having been appointed under powers contained in an instrument, has, after being required at any time by the liquidator of the company to do so, failed to render proper accounts of his receipts and payments and to vouch them and pay over to the liquidator the amount properly payable to him,
the court may, on an application made for the purpose, make an order directing the receiver or manager (as the case may be) to make good the default within such time as may be specified in the order.

(2) In the case of the default mentioned in subsection (1)(a), application to the court may be made by any member or creditor of the company or by the registrar of companies; and in the case of the default mentioned in subsection (1)(b), the application shall be made by the liquidator.

In either case the court's order may provide that all costs of and incidental to the application shall be borne by the receiver or manager, as the case may be.

(3) Nothing in this section prejudices the operation of any enactment imposing penalties on receivers in respect of any such default as is mentioned in subsection (1).

Notes

S 41(2)

This section deals with locus for an application. The court may provide that the receiver bear all costs of the application.

Administrative receivers: general

1.49

42 General powers

(1) The powers conferred on the administrative receiver of a company by the debentures by virtue of which he was appointed are deemed to include (except in so far as they are inconsistent with any of the provisions of those debentures) the powers specified in Schedule 1 to this Act.

(2) In the application of Schedule 1 to the administrative receiver of a company—
 (a) the words 'he' and 'him' refer to the administrative receiver, and

> (b) references to the property of the company are to the property of which he is or, but for the appointment of some other person as the receiver of part of the company's property, would be the receiver or manager.
>
> (3) A person dealing with the administrative receiver in good faith and for value is not concerned to inquire whether the receiver is acting within his powers.

Notes

S 42

An administrative receiver's powers have two sources: contract – the charge and the instrument of appointment – and statute, notably this section and IA 1986 Sch 1. Note that where the administrative receiver exercises his power to sell assets and the sale is to a director of the company or to a company in which he is interested, then the transaction must also be approved by an ordinary resolution of the shareholders under CA 1985 s 320: *Demite Ltd v Protec Health Ltd* [1998] BCC 638. The administrative receiver also benefits from the investigatory powers of IA 1986 s 235 and 236 and a number of particular statutory powers such as IA 1986 s 43 below, and IA 1986, s 233 and 234.

The extent and nature of a receiver's duty of care has been much litigated. The paramount duty of an administrative receiver is to realise the security in question in the best interests of the chargee: see *Downsview Nominees Ltd v First City Corporation Ltd* [1993] AC 295 and *Medforth v Blake* [2000] Ch 86. In doing so he owes duties imposed by equity to the chargee and to those interested in the equity of redemption. The equitable duties leave no scope for a common law duty of care. The receiver's duties require him to act in good faith and to take reasonable care in realising the assets for the benefit of the chargee, but they do not require him to carry on the business previously carried on by the company (although he should consider whether he ought to do so in order to preserve goodwill). However if he does so then he will be under a duty to take care in doing so. His duties do not require him to expend money in maximising the potential realisations, for example by obtaining planning permission for the development of property that is the subject of the charge: *Sylven Properties Ltd v Royal Bank of Scotland PLC* [2003] EWCA Civ 1409, [2004] 1 WLR 997.

The receiver is not permitted to use his powers to obtain and pass on information/ documentation to assist the appointing debenture holder in pursuing a guarantor of the company's debt where this would not serve the company's interests: *GE Capital Commercial Finance Ltd v Sutton* [2004] 2 BCLC 662.

1.50

43 Power to dispose of charged property, etc

(1) Where, on an application by the administrative receiver, the court is satisfied that the disposal (with or without other assets) of any relevant property which is subject to a security would be likely to promote a more advantageous realisation of the company's assets than would otherwise be effected, the court may by order authorise the administrative receiver to dispose of the property as if it were not subject to the security.

(2) Subsection (1) does not apply in the case of any security held by the person by or on whose behalf the administrative receiver was appointed, or of any security to which a security so held has priority.

(3) It shall be a condition of an order under this section that—

(a)   the net proceeds of the disposal, and

(b)   where those proceeds are less than such amount as may be determined by the court to be the net amount which would be realised on a sale of the property in the open market by a willing vendor, such sums as may be required to make good the deficiency,

shall be applied towards discharging the sums secured by the security.

(4) Where a condition imposed in pursuance of subsection (3) relates to two or more securities, that condition shall require the net proceeds of the disposal and, where paragraph (b) of that subsection applies, the sums mentioned in that paragraph to be applied towards discharging the sums secured by those securities in the order of their priorities.

(5) An office copy of an order under this section shall, within 14 days of the making of the order, be sent by the administrative receiver to the registrar of companies.

(6) If the administrative receiver without reasonable excuse fails to comply with subsection (5), he is liable to a fine and, for continued contravention, to a daily default fine.

(7) In this section 'relevant property', in relation to the administrative receiver, means the property of which he is or, but for the appointment of some other person as the receiver of part of the company's property, would be the receiver or manager.

Notes

S 43(1)

An administrative receiver can apply to court to dispose of 'relevant property' (defined in IA 1986 s 43(7)) subject to a prior charge as if it were not subject to that security. The court must be satisfied that the disposal would be likely to result in the more advantageous realisation of the company's assets than would otherwise be effected. That result will be 'likely' where it appears that there is a real prospect of its being achieved. The section does not require the court to be satisfied on a balance of probabilities that a more advantageous realisation is more likely to be achieved than not: see the approach taken in Re Harris Simons Construction Ltd [1989] 1 WLR 368 to the requirement in former IA 1986 s 8 that the court should consider the achievement of one of the purposes in s 8(3) to be 'likely.' This is a useful power to employ in a situation where the administrative receiver wishes to sell the whole of a business and the holder of a prior charge over part of the company's assets or business refuses to consent to the sale: see Re ARV Aviation Ltd (1988) 4 BCC 708 for how the court dealt with a similar provision used by administrators (IA 1986 s 15(2); and see notes to IA 1986 Sch B1 para 71).

S 43(2)

This provision disapplies s 43(1) in respect of any security held by the appointor of the administrative receiver or any security which ranks after such a security.

S 43(3)

The court must impose conditions in the order as set out in IA 1986 s 43(3)(a) and (b).

S 43(4)

Where there are two or more securities, the application of net proceeds or any sum under IA 1986 s 43(3)(b) must be applied towards discharging the securities in order of their priorities.

1.51

44 Agency and liability for contracts

(1) The administrative receiver of a company—
  (a) is deemed to be the company's agent, unless and until the company goes into liquidation;
  (b) is personally liable on any contract entered into by him in the carrying out of his functions (except in so far as the contract otherwise provides) and, [to the extent of any qualifying liability,] on any contract of employment adopted by him in the carrying out of those functions; and
  (c) is entitled in respect of that liability to an indemnity out of the assets of the company.

(2) For the purposes of subsection (1)(b) the administrative receiver is not to be taken to have adopted a contract of employment by reason of anything done or omitted to be done within 14 days after his appointment.

(2A) For the purposes of subsection (1)(b), a liability under a contract of employment is a qualifying liability if—
  (a) it is a liability to pay a sum by way of wages or salary or contribution to an occupational pension scheme,
  (b) it is incurred while the administrative receiver is in office, and
  (c) it is in respect of services rendered wholly or partly after the adoption of the contract.

(2B) Where a sum payable in respect of a liability which is a qualifying liability for the purposes of subsection (1)(b) is payable in respect of services rendered partly before and partly after the adoption of the contract, liability under subsection (1)(b) shall only extend to so much of the sum as is payable in respect of services rendered after the adoption of the contract.

(2C) For the purposes of subsections (2A) and (2B)—
  (a) wages or salary payable in respect of a period of holiday or absence from work through sickness or other good cause are deemed to be wages or (as the case may be) salary in respect of services rendered in that period, and
  (b) a sum payable in lieu of holiday is deemed to be wages or (as the case may be) salary in respect of services rendered in the period by reference to which the holiday entitlement arose.

(2D) In subsection (2C)(a), the reference to wages or salary payable in respect of a period of holiday includes any sums which, if they had been paid, would have been treated for the purposes of the enactments relating to social security as earnings in respect of that period.

(3) This section does not limit any right to indemnity which the administrative receiver would have apart from it, nor limit his liability on

> contracts entered into or adopted without authority, nor confer any right to indemnity in respect of that liability.

Notes

S 44

The words in square brackets in s 44(1) were inserted in relation to contracts of employment adopted on or after 15 March 1994, by the IA 1994.

S 44(1)(a)

The administrative receiver is deemed to be the company's agent unless and until the company goes into liquidation. However, the fact that he is the company's agent does not alter the fact that his function is, first and foremost, to realise the company's assets for the benefit of the debenture holder who appointed him.

The administrative receiver does not incur the company's liability for paying business rates whilst he is in occupation of the company's premises as the company's agent so long as he has not dispossessed the company: *Ratford and Hayward v Northavon RDC* [1987] QB 357; *Brown v City of London Corporation* [1996] 1 WLR 1070. Although the appointment of liquidators puts an end to the receiver's agency, he is nevertheless not liable for rates after such an appointment: *Re Becks Foods Ltd* [2001] 2 BCLC 663.

S 44(1)(b)

Where an administrative receiver does not expressly provide in the contract that he has no personal liability, he is personally liable on the contract (see IA 1986 s 37(1)(a) for non-administrative receivers appointed out of court). Express terms in the debenture (which is a contract between the company and the charge holder alone) providing that the administrative receiver has no personal liability and acts as the company's agent at all times, do not prevent personal liability attaching under IA 1986 s 44(1)(b), *Hill Samuel & Co Ltd v Laing* [1991] BCC 665.

In respect of pre-existing contracts at the date of the receivership the contract continues between the third party and the company and the normal remedies are available to the third party for breach of that contract: see *Freevale v Metrostore Holding Ltd* [1984] Ch 199 (specific performance); *Ash & Newman Ltd v Creative Devices Research Ltd* [1991] BCLC 403 (injunction). However an administrative receiver may cause the company to repudiate existing contracts unless he or the chargee knows that the property the subject of the security is bound by a third party's contractual rights: *Swiss Bank v Lloyd's Bank* [1979] Ch 548. Further the administrative receiver whilst acting as agent for the company does not become personally liable for procuring the breach of contract so long as he is acting in good faith and within the scope of his powers: *Lathia v Dronsfield* [1987] BCLC 321; *Welsh Development Agency v Export Finance [1992] BCLC 148*. The position may be different in respect of a receiver appointed by the court because such a receiver is not an agent: *see Re Botibol* [1947] 1 All ER 26, referred to in *Telemetrix plc v Modern Engineers* [1985] 1 BCC 99, 417.

S 44(1)(c)

An administrative receiver is entitled to a statutory indemnity out of the assets of the company for personal liability and in addition he would usually try to obtain a full contractual indemnity from the charge holder.

S 44(2), (2A)-(2D)

See notes to IA 1986 s 37 above for the background to these provisions and *Powdrill v Watson, Re Paramount Airways Ltd* [1995] 2 AC 394. The IA 1994 was passed after *Powdrill v Watson* introducing subsections (2A) to (2D) which apply only to contracts of employment adopted on or after 15 March 1994. The administrative receiver's personal liability is limited to 'any qualifying liability' under those contracts of employment as defined in (2A) to (2D). Under these provisions the administrative receiver does not assume personal liability for liabilities accruing before his adoption of a contract.

In relation to contracts of employment adopted before 15 March 1994 the former law (see notes to IA 1986 s 37 dealing with non administrative receivers) continues to apply to impose all accrued liabilities under contracts of employment on the receiver as opposed to the 'qualifying liabilities' under this provision.

S 44(3)

This applies the provision in IA 1986 s 37(3) to administrative receivers.

1.52

45 Vacation of office

(1) An administrative receiver of a company may at any time be removed from office by order of the court (but not otherwise) and may resign his office by giving notice of his resignation in the prescribed manner to such persons as may be prescribed.

(2) An administrative receiver shall vacate office if he ceases to be qualified to act as an insolvency practitioner in relation to the company.

(3) Where at any time an administrative receiver vacates office—
   (a)   his remuneration and any expenses properly incurred by him, and
   (b)   any indemnity to which he is entitled out of the assets of the company,
shall be charged on and paid out of any property of the company which is in his custody or under his control at that time in priority to any security held by the person by or on whose behalf he was appointed.

(4) Where an administrative receiver vacates office otherwise than by death, he shall, within 14 days after his vacation of office, send a notice to that effect to the registrar of companies.

(5) If an administrative receiver without reasonable excuse fails to comply with subsection (4), he is liable to a fine and, *for continued contravention, to a daily default fine*.

Notes

S 45(1), (2)

These provisions deal with the vacation of office. The only mechanisms available for removal of an administrative receiver are resignation and a court order. A debenture holder cannot simply remove its appointee, and if it wishes to remove him it must apply to the court. This is an important provision emphasising and reinforcing the special and independent position held by an administrative receiver. The court does not have power to appoint an administrative receiver either by way of replacement or otherwise: *Re A & C Suppliers Ltd* [1998] 1 BCLC 603; appointment of a new administrative receiver is a matter for the charge holder. The IA 1986 does not impose any restriction on who may apply for the removal of an administrative receiver. In *Sheppard & Cooper Ltd v TSB Bank PLC* [1997] 2 BCLC 222 the company applied for an injunction restraining the bank's appointees from acting on the basis that they had disqualified themselves by contract from taking an appointment. No injunction was granted because the administrative receivers undertook to resign once the court had decided that that agreement was enforceable. The bank then appointed new administrative receivers in place of those originally appointed.

Where it is sought to remove an administrative receiver for cause, the same principles should apply as those which govern removal of office-holders under other provisions of IA 1986. For a summary of those principles, and the authorities, see *Sisu Capital Fund Ltd v Tucker* [2006] BCC 463, [2006] BPIR 154. The administrative receiver must resign if he ceases to be qualified as an insolvency practitioner. IR 1986 3.35 requires notification of completion vacation from office for this reason or on completion of the receivership forthwith.

S 45(4)

The administrative receiver should provide notice to the registrar of companies within 14 days of his resignation. See IR 1986 r 3.33 for notice of intention to resign and IR 1986 3.33–3.35 generally. It should be noted that whereas liquidators and administrators apply for release from office, no such obligation exists in administrative receivership.

S 45(5)

The words in italics are prospectively repealed by the CA 1989, s 107, 212, Sch 16, para 3(3), Sch 24, as from a day to be appointed.

Administrative receivers: ascertainment and investigation of company's affairs

1.53

46 Information to be given by administrative receiver

(1) Where an administrative receiver is appointed, he shall—
   (a)   forthwith send to the company and publish in the prescribed manner a notice of his appointment, and
   (b)   within 28 days after his appointment, unless the court otherwise directs, send such a notice to all the creditors of the company (so far as he is aware of their addresses).

(2) This section and the next do not apply in relation to the appointment of an administrative receiver to act—
   (a)   with an existing administrative receiver, or
   (b)   in place of an administrative receiver dying or ceasing to act,
except that, where they apply to an administrative receiver who dies or ceases to act before they have been fully complied with, the references in this section and the next to the administrative receiver include (subject to the next subsection) his successor and any continuing administrative receiver.

(3) If the company is being wound up, this section and the next apply notwithstanding that the administrative receiver and the liquidator are the same person, but with any necessary modifications arising from that fact.

(4) If the administrative receiver without reasonable excuse fails to comply with this section, he is liable to a fine and, for continued contravention, to a daily default fine.

Notes

S 46(1), (4)

These sections deal with the administrative receiver's obligations to give notice to specific parties. The debenture holder is also obliged to file notice of the administrative receiver's appointment within 7 days to the registrar of companies who will enter the appointment in the register of charges: CA 1985, s 405. See also IA 1986 s 39(1) which ensures that documents contain a statement that a receiver or manager has been appointed and IR 1986 r 3.2 which deals with notice and advertisement of appointment.

S 46(2)

Once notice has been provided in accordance with IA 1986 s 46, it need not be provided again, for example, by a successor administrative receiver.

S 46(3)

This section deals with the situation where the administrative receiver and the liquidator are the same person, with IA 1986 s 46 and 47 applying with necessary modifications.

1.54

47 Statement of affairs to be submitted

(1) Where an administrative receiver is appointed, he shall forthwith require some or all of the persons mentioned below to make out and submit to him a statement in the prescribed form as to the affairs of the company.

(2) A statement submitted under this section shall be verified by affidavit by the persons required to submit it and shall show—
    (a)   particulars of the company's assets, debts and liabilities;
    (b)   the names and addresses of its creditors;
    (c)   the securities held by them respectively;
    (d)   the dates when the securities were respectively given; and
    (e)   such further or other information as may be prescribed.

(3) The persons referred to in subsection (1) are—
    (a)   those who are or have been officers of the company;
    (b)   those who have taken part in the company's formation at any time within one year before the date of the appointment of the administrative receiver;
    (c)   those who are in the company's employment, or have been in its employment within that year, and are in the administrative receiver's opinion capable of giving the information required;
    (d)   those who are or have been within that year officers of or in the employment of a company which is, or within that year was, an officer of the company.

In this subsection 'employment' includes employment under a contract for services.

(4) Where any persons are required under this section to submit a statement of affairs to the administrative receiver, they shall do so (subject to the next subsection) before the end of the period of 21 days beginning with the day after that on which the prescribed notice of the requirement is given to them by the administrative receiver.

(5) The administrative receiver, if he thinks fit, may—

    (a)   at any time release a person from an obligation imposed on him under subsection (1) or (2), or

    (b)   either when giving notice under subsection (4) or subsequently, extend the period so mentioned;

and where the administrative receiver has refused to exercise a power conferred by this subsection, the court, if it thinks fit, may exercise it.

(6) If a person without reasonable excuse fails to comply with any obligation imposed under this section, he is liable to a fine and, for continued contravention, to a daily default fine.

Notes

S 47

The administrative receiver must 'forthwith' upon his appointment require some or all of the persons identified in IA 1986 s 47(3)) to submit statements of affairs detailing the matters set out in IA 1986 s 47(2). The statement of affairs must be in the prescribed form and must be provided within 21 days of receipt of the notice requiring the officer or employee as the case may be to provide the statement of affairs. The section does allow a certain amount of flexibility. Under IA 1986 s 47(5) the administrative receiver can, if he thinks fit, extend the 21 day period and can release a person from any obligation under IA 1986 s 47(1) and (2). If the administrative receiver refuses a request for an extension or release, then the person seeking that extension or release can apply to the court under IR 1986 r 3.6(2). See generally IR 1986 r 3.3. to 3.7 and r 7.20 for requirements relating to the statement of affairs and for applications for enforcement in the event of default.

There are sanctions in subsection (6) in the form of fines and daily default fines for failure to comply, and subsection (6) extends to the administrative receiver's own obligation forthwith to require one or more of the persons listed in subsection (3) to provide a statement of affairs.

1.55

48 Report by administrative receiver

(1) Where an administrative receiver is appointed, he shall, within 3 months (or such longer period as the court may allow) after his appointment, send to the registrar of companies, to any trustees for secured creditors of the company and (so far as he is aware of their addresses) to all such creditors a report as to the following matters, namely—

    (a)   the events leading up to his appointment, so far as he is aware of them;

    (b)   the disposal or proposed disposal by him of any property of the company and the carrying on or proposed carrying on by him of any business of the company;

    (c)   the amounts of principal and interest payable to the debenture holders by whom or on whose behalf he was appointed and the amounts payable to preferential creditors; and

(d) the amount (if any) likely to be available for the payment of other creditors.

(2) The administrative receiver shall also, within 3 months (or such longer period as the court may allow) after his appointment, either—
    (a) send a copy of the report (so far as he is aware of their addresses) to all unsecured creditors of the company; or
    (b) publish in the prescribed manner a notice stating an address to which unsecured creditors of the company should write for copies of the report to be sent to them free of charge,
and (in either case), unless the court otherwise directs, lay a copy of the report before a meeting of the company's unsecured creditors summoned for the purpose on not less than 14 days' notice.

(3) The court shall not give a direction under subsection (2) unless—
    (a) the report states the intention of the administrative receiver to apply for the direction, and
    (b) a copy of the report is sent to the persons mentioned in paragraph (a) of that subsection, or a notice is published as mentioned in paragraph (b) of that subsection, not less than 14 days before the hearing of the application.

(4) Where the company has gone or goes into liquidation, the administrative receiver—
    (a) shall, within 7 days after his compliance with subsection (1) or, if later, the nomination or appointment of the liquidator, send a copy of the report to the liquidator, and
    (b) where he does so within the time limited for compliance with subsection (2), is not required to comply with that subsection.

(5) A report under this section shall include a summary of the statement of affairs made out and submitted to the administrative receiver under section 47 and of his comments (if any) upon it.

(6) Nothing in this section is to be taken as requiring any such report to include any information the disclosure of which would seriously prejudice the carrying out by the administrative receiver of his functions.

(7) Section 46(2) applies for the purposes of this section also.

(8) If the administrative receiver without reasonable excuse fails to comply with this section, he is liable to a fine and, for continued contravention, to a default fine.

Notes

S 48(1), (4), (7)

An administrative receiver must within 3 months of his appointment (or such longer period as the court may afford) report to a number of parties. The report must be sent to the registrar of companies, any trustee for secured creditors and all secured creditors. In addition IA 1986 s 48(4) requires that any liquidator of the company be sent a copy of the report, and in certain cases FSMA 2000 s 363 imposes an obligation to report to the FSA. IA 1986 s 48(7) expressly applies IA 1986 s 46(2) so that if a receiver vacates office for whatever reason before compliance with his obligations, those obligations fall on his successor(s).

S 48(2)

The administrative receiver is also obliged to send a copy of the report to unsecured creditors or publish a notice providing an address to which unsecured creditors can write to requesting a copy. He must also call a meeting of unsecured creditors and put a copy of the report before them on that occasion. See IR 1986 r 3.9 to 3.15 for detailed provisions relating to the meeting.

S 48(3)

The court may release the administrative receiver from his obligation to call a meeting of creditors under IA 1986 s 46(2) if (a) the report states that the administrative receiver intends to apply for such a direction and (b) the report is sent or a notice published in accordance with s 48(2) at least 14 days before the hearing.

S 48(5)

The report must set out the matters required in s 48(1), summarise the statement of affairs and contain the administrative receiver's own comments on the statement of affairs. Regard must also be had to the requirements of IR 1986 r 3.8 (as amended following the changes effected by the EA 2002) and to IA 1986 s 176A under which a prescribed part of the assets caught by a floating charge are to be made available to satisfy the claims of unsecured creditors unless either the company's assets are less than the minimum prescribed under IA 1986 s 176A or an application is made under IA 1986 s 176A(5) for exemption on the grounds that the costs of making a distribution to unsecured creditors would be disproportionate. However, IR 1986 r 3.8(5) applies whether or not the assets exceed the prescribed minimum or the administrative receiver intends to make an application. The report must therefore state what the value of the prescribed part would be, even if there will be no distribution to unsecured creditors. The report must also state the grounds of any proposed application under IA 1986 s 176A(5).

S 48(6)

This section excludes the inclusion of information the disclosure of which would seriously prejudice the carrying out by the administrative receiver of his functions. There is no statutory guidance on how this test is to be applied.

1.56

49 Committee of creditors

(1) Where a meeting of creditors is summoned under section 48, the meeting may, if it thinks fit, establish a committee ('the creditors' committee') to exercise the functions conferred on it by or under this Act.

(2) If such a committee is established, the committee may, on giving not less than 7 days' notice, require the administrative receiver to attend before it at any reasonable time and furnish it with such information relating to the carrying out by him of his functions as it may reasonably require.

Notes

S 49

Provision for a creditors' committee in receiverships was introduced by the IA 1986. Further provisions relating to the constitution and proceedings of the committee are contained in IR 1986 r 3.16 to 3.30A.

S 49(2)

The creditors' committee can require the administrative receiver to attend before it on 7 days' notice and provide it with such information 'as it may reasonably require'. The reasonableness qualification is intended to prevent onerous requests being made of the administrative receiver or requests for information protected by IA 1986 s 48(6).

Chapter II
Receivers (Scotland)

1.57

50 Extent of this Chapter

This Chapter extends to Scotland only.

1.58

51 Power to appoint receiver

(1) It is competent under the law of Scotland for the holder of a floating charge over all or any part of the property (including uncalled capital), which may from time to time be comprised in the property and undertaking of an incorporated company (whether a company within the meaning of the Companies Act or not) which the Court of Session has jurisdiction to wind up, to appoint a receiver of such part of the property of the company as is subject to the charge.

(2) It is competent under the law of Scotland for the court, on the application of the holder of such a floating charge, to appoint a receiver of such part of the property of the company as is subject to the charge.

[(2A) Subsections (1) and (2) are subject to section 72A.]

(3) The following are disqualified from being appointed as receiver—
    (a)   a body corporate;
    (b)   an undischarged bankrupt; and
    (c)   a firm according to the law of Scotland.

(4) A body corporate or a firm according to the law of Scotland which acts as a receiver is liable to a fine.

(5) An undischarged bankrupt who so acts is liable to imprisonment or a fine, or both.

(6) In this section, 'receiver' includes joint receivers.

1.59

52 Circumstances justifying appointment

(1) A receiver may be appointed under section 51(1) by the holder of the floating charge on the occurrence of any event which, by the provisions of the instrument creating the charge, entitles the holder of the charge to make that appointment and, in so far as not otherwise provided for by the instrument, on the occurrence of any of the following events, namely—
    (a)   the expiry of a period of 21 days after the making of a demand for payment of the whole or any part of the principal sum secured by the charge, without payment having been made;

(b)   the expiry of a period of 2 months during the whole of which interest due and payable under the charge has been in arrears;

(c)   the making of an order or the passing of a resolution to wind up the company;

(d)   the appointment of a receiver by virtue of any other floating charge created by the company.

(2) A receiver may be appointed by the court under section 51(2) on the occurrence of any event which, by the provisions of the instrument creating the floating charge, entitles the holder of the charge to make that appointment and, in so far as not otherwise provided for by the instrument, on the occurrence of any of the following events, namely—

(a)   where the court, on the application of the holder of the charge, pronounces itself satisfied that the position of the holder of the charge is likely to be prejudiced if no such appointment is made;

(b)   any of the events referred to in paragraphs (a) to (c) of subsection (1).

1.60

53 Mode of appointment by holder of charge

(1) The appointment of a receiver by the holder of the floating charge under section 51(1) shall be by means of [an instrument subscribed in accordance with the Requirements of Writing (Scotland) Act 1995] ('the instrument of appointment'), a copy (certified in the prescribed manner to be a correct copy) whereof shall be delivered by or on behalf of the person making the appointment to the registrar of companies for registration within 7 days of its execution and shall be accompanied by a notice in the prescribed form.

(2) If any person without reasonable excuse makes default in complying with the requirements of subsection (1), he is liable to a fine *and, for continued contravention, to a daily default fine.*

(3) ...

[(4) If the receiver is to be appointed by the holders of a series of secured debentures, the instrument of appointment may be executed on behalf of the holders of the floating charge by any person authorised by resolution of the debenture-holders to execute the instrument.]

(5) On receipt of the certified copy of the instrument of appointment in accordance with subsection (1), the registrar shall, on payment of the prescribed fee, enter the particulars of the appointment in the register of charges.

(6) The appointment of a person as a receiver by an instrument of appointment in accordance with subsection (1)—

(a)   is of no effect unless it is accepted by that person before the end of the business day next following that on which the instrument of appointment is received by him or on his behalf, and

(b)   subject to paragraph (a), is deemed to be made on the day on and at the time at which the instrument of appointment is so received, as evidenced by a written docquet by that person or on his behalf;

and this subsection applies to the appointment of joint receivers subject to such modifications as may be prescribed.

(7) On the appointment of a receiver under this section, the floating charge by virtue of which he was appointed attaches to the property then subject to the charge; and such attachment has effect as if the charge was a fixed security over the property to which it has attached.

1.61

54 Appointment by court

(1) Application for the appointment of a receiver by the court under section 51(2) shall be by petition to the court, which shall be served on the company.

(2) On such an application, the court shall, if it thinks fit, issue an interlocutor making the appointment of the receiver.

(3) A copy (certified by the clerk of the court to be a correct copy) of the court's interlocutor making the appointment shall be delivered by or on behalf of the petitioner to the registrar of companies for registration, accompanied by a notice in the prescribed form, within 7 days of the date of the interlocutor or such longer period as the court may allow.

If any person without reasonable excuse makes default in complying with the requirements of this subsection, he is liable to a fine *and, for continued contravention, to a daily default fine.*

(4) On receipt of the certified copy interlocutor in accordance with subsection (3), the registrar shall, on payment of the prescribed fee, enter the particulars of the appointment in the register of charges.

(5) The receiver is to be regarded as having been appointed on the date of his being appointed by the court.

(6) On the appointment of a receiver under this section, the floating charge by virtue of which he was appointed attaches to the property then subject to the charge; and such attachment has effect as if the charge were a fixed security over the property to which it has attached.

(7) In making rules of court for the purposes of this section, the Court of Session shall have regard to the need for special provision for cases which appear to the court to require to be dealt with as a matter of urgency.

1.62

55 Powers of receiver

(1) Subject to the next subsection, a receiver has in relation to such part of the property of the company as is attached by the floating charge by virtue of which he was appointed, the powers, if any, given to him by the instrument creating that charge.

(2) In addition, the receiver has under this Chapter the powers as respects that property (in so far as these are not inconsistent with any provision contained in that instrument) which are specified in Schedule 2 to this Act.

(3) Subsections (1) and (2) apply—

(a) subject to the rights of any person who has effectually executed diligence on all or any part of the property of the company prior to the appointment of the receiver, and

(b) subject to the rights of any person who holds over all or any part of the property of the company a fixed security or floating charge having priority over, or ranking pari passu with, the floating charge by virtue of which the receiver was appointed.

(4) A person dealing with a receiver in good faith and for value is not concerned to enquire whether the receiver is acting within his powers.

1.63

56 Precedence among receivers

(1) Where there are two or more floating charges subsisting over all or any part of the property of the company, a receiver may be appointed under this Chapter by virtue of each such charge; but a receiver appointed by, or on the application of, the holder of a floating charge having priority of ranking over any other floating charge by virtue of which a receiver has been appointed has the powers given to a receiver by section 55 and Schedule 2 to the exclusion of any other receiver.

(2) Where two or more floating charges rank with one another equally, and two or more receivers have been appointed by virtue of such charges, the receivers so appointed are deemed to have been appointed as joint receivers.

(3) Receivers appointed, or deemed to have been appointed, as joint receivers shall act jointly unless the instrument of appointment or respective instruments of appointment otherwise provide.

(4) Subject to subsection (5) below, the powers of a receiver appointed by, or on the application of, the holder of a floating charge are suspended by, and as from the date of, the appointment of a receiver by, or on the application of, the holder of a floating charge having priority of ranking over that charge to such extent as may be necessary to enable the receiver second mentioned to exercise his powers under section 55 and Schedule 2; and any powers so suspended take effect again when the floating charge having priority of ranking ceases to attach to the property then subject to the charge, whether such cessation is by virtue of section 62(6) or otherwise.

(5) The suspension of the powers of a receiver under subsection (4) does not have the effect of requiring him to release any part of the property (including any letters or documents) of the company from his control until he receives from the receiver superseding him a valid indemnity (subject to the limit of the value of such part of the property of the company as is subject to the charge by virtue of which he was appointed) in respect of any expenses, charges and liabilities he may have incurred in the performance of his functions as receiver.

(6) The suspension of the powers of a receiver under subsection (4) does not cause the floating charge by virtue of which he was appointed to cease to attach to the property to which it attached by virtue of section 53(7) or 54(6).

(7) Nothing in this section prevents the same receiver being appointed by virtue of two or more floating charges.

1.64

57 Agency and liability of receiver for contracts

(1) A receiver is deemed to be the agent of the company in relation to such property of the company as is attached by the floating charge by virtue of which he was appointed.

[(1A) Without prejudice to subsection (1), a receiver is deemed to be the agent of the company in relation to any contract of employment adopted by him in the carrying out of his functions.]

(2) A receiver (including a receiver whose powers are subsequently suspended under section 56) is personally liable on any contract entered into by him in the performance of his functions, except in so far as the contract otherwise provides, and[, to the extent of any qualifying liability,] on any contract of employment adopted by him in the carrying out of those functions.

[(2A) For the purposes of subsection (2), a liability under a contract of employment is a qualifying liability if—
   (a)   it is a liability to pay a sum by way of wages or salary or contribution to an occupational pension scheme,
   (b)   it is incurred while the receiver is in office, and
   (c)   it is in respect of services rendered wholly or partly after the adoption of the contract.

(2B) Where a sum payable in respect of a liability which is a qualifying liability for the purposes of subsection (2) is payable in respect of services rendered partly before and partly after the adoption of the contract, liability under that subsection shall only extend to so much of the sum as is payable in respect of services rendered after the adoption of the contract.

(2C) For the purposes of subsections (2A) and (2B)—
   (a)   wages or salary payable in respect of a period of holiday or absence from work through sickness or other good cause are deemed to be wages or (as the case may be) salary in respect of services rendered in that period, and
   (b)   a sum payable in lieu of holiday is deemed to be wages or (as the case may be) salary in respect of services rendered in the period by reference to which the holiday entitlement arose.

(2D) In subsection (2C)(a), the reference to wages or salary payable in respect of a period of holiday includes any sums which, if they had been paid, would have been treated for the purposes of the enactments relating to social security as earnings in respect of that period.]

(3) A receiver who is personally liable by virtue of subsection (2) is entitled to be indemnified out of the property in respect of which he was appointed.

(4) Any contract entered into by or on behalf of the company prior to the appointment of a receiver continues in force (subject to its terms)

notwithstanding that appointment, but the receiver does not by virtue only of his appointment incur any personal liability on any such contract.

(5) For the purposes of subsection (2), a receiver is not to be taken to have adopted a contract of employment by reason of anything done or omitted to be done within 14 days after his appointment.

(6) This section does not limit any right to indemnity which the receiver would have apart from it, nor limit his liability on contracts entered into or adopted without authority, nor confer any right to indemnity in respect of that liability.

(7) Any contract entered into by a receiver in the performance of his functions continues in force (subject to its terms) although the powers of the receiver are subsequently suspended under section 56.

1.65

58 Remuneration of receiver

(1) The remuneration to be paid to a receiver is to be determined by agreement between the receiver and the holder of the floating charge by virtue of which he was appointed.

(2) Where the remuneration to be paid to the receiver has not been determined under subsection (1), or where it has been so determined but is disputed by any of the persons mentioned in paragraphs (a) to (d) below, it may be fixed instead by the Auditor of the Court of Session on application made to him by—

    (a)   the receiver;
    (b)   the holder of any floating charge or fixed security over all or any part of the property of the company;
    (c)   the company; or
    (d)   the liquidator of the company.

(3) Where the receiver has been paid or has retained for his remuneration for any period before the remuneration has been fixed by the Auditor of the Court of Session under subsection (2) any amount in excess of the remuneration so fixed for that period, the receiver or his personal representatives shall account for the excess.

1.66

59 Priority of debts

(1) Where a receiver is appointed and the company is not at the time of the appointment in course of being wound up, the debts which fall under subsection (2) of this section shall be paid out of any assets coming to the hands of the receiver in priority to any claim for principal or interest by the holder of the floating charge by virtue of which the receiver was appointed.

(2) Debts falling under this subsection are preferential debts (within the meaning given by section 386 in Part XII) which, by the end of a period of 6 months after advertisement by the receiver for claims in the Edinburgh Gazette and in a newspaper circulating in the district where the company carries on business either—

    (i)   have been intimated to him, or

    (ii)   have become known to him.

(3) Any payments made under this section shall be recouped as far as may be out of the assets of the company available for payment of ordinary creditors.

1.67

60 Distribution of moneys

(1) Subject to the next section, and to the rights of any of the following categories of persons (which rights shall, except to the extent otherwise provided in any instrument, have the following order of priority), namely—

    (a)   the holder of any fixed security which is over property subject to the floating charge and which ranks prior to, or pari passu with, the floating charge;

    (b)   all persons who have effectually executed diligence on any part of the property of the company which is subject to the charge by virtue of which the receiver was appointed;

    (c)   creditors in respect of all liabilities, charges and expenses incurred by or on behalf of the receiver;

    (d)   the receiver in respect of his liabilities, expenses and remuneration, and any indemnity to which he is entitled out of the property of the company; and

    (e)   the preferential creditors entitled to payment under section 59,

the receiver shall pay moneys received by him to the holder of the floating charge by virtue of which the receiver was appointed in or towards satisfaction of the debt secured by the floating charge.

(2) Any balance of moneys remaining after the provisions of subsection (1) and section 61 below have been satisfied shall be paid in accordance with their respective rights and interests to the following persons, as the case may require—

    (a)   any other receiver;

    (b)   the holder of a fixed security which is over property subject to the floating charge;

    (c)   the company or its liquidator, as the case may be.

(3) Where any question arises as to the person entitled to a payment under this section, or where a receipt or a discharge of a security cannot be obtained in respect of any such payment, the receiver shall consign the amount of such payment in any joint stock bank of issue in Scotland in name of the Accountant of Court for behoof of the person or persons entitled thereto.

1.68

61 Disposal of interest in property

(1) Where the receiver sells or disposes, or is desirous of selling or disposing, of any property or interest in property of the company which is subject to the floating charge by virtue of which the receiver was appointed and which is—

    (a)   subject to any security or interest of, or burden or encumbrance in favour of, a creditor the ranking of which is prior to, or pari passu with, or postponed to the floating charge, or

(b)   property or an interest in property affected or attached by effectual diligence executed by any person,

and the receiver is unable to obtain the consent of such creditor or, as the case may be, such person to such a sale or disposal, the receiver may apply to the court for authority to sell or dispose of the property or interest in property free of such security, interest, burden, encumbrance or diligence.

(2) Subject to the next subsection, on such an application the court may, if it thinks fit, authorise the sale or disposal of the property or interest in question free of such security, interest, burden, encumbrance or diligence, and such authorisation may be on such terms or conditions as the court thinks fit.

(3) In the case of an application where a fixed security over the property or interest in question which ranks prior to the floating charge has not been met or provided for in full, the court shall not authorise the sale or disposal of the property or interest in question unless it is satisfied that the sale or disposal would be likely to provide a more advantageous realisation of the company's assets than would otherwise be effected.

(4) It shall be a condition of an authorisation to which subsection (3) applies that—
(a)   the net proceeds of the disposal, and
(b)   where those proceeds are less than such amount as may be determined by the court to be the net amount which would be realised on a sale of the property or interest in the open market by a willing seller, such sums as may be required to make good the deficiency,

shall be applied towards discharging the sums secured by the fixed security.

(5) Where a condition imposed in pursuance of subsection (4) relates to two or more such fixed securities, that condition shall require the net proceeds of the disposal and, where paragraph (b) of that subsection applies, the sums mentioned in that paragraph to be applied towards discharging the sums secured by those fixed securities in the order of their priorities.

(6) A copy of an authorisation under subsection (2) certified by the clerk of court shall, within 14 days of the granting of the authorisation, be sent by the receiver to the registrar of companies.

(7) If the receiver without reasonable excuse fails to comply with subsection (6), he is liable to a fine and, for continued contravention, to a daily default fine.

(8) Where any sale or disposal is effected in accordance with the authorisation of the court under subsection (2), the receiver shall grant to the purchaser or disponee an appropriate document of transfer or conveyance of the property or interest in question, and that document has the effect, or, where recording, intimation or registration of that document is a legal requirement for completion of title to the property or interest, then that recording, intimation or registration (as the case may be) has the effect, of—
(a)   disencumbering the property or interest of the security, interest, burden or encumbrance affecting it, and

    (b)   freeing the property or interest from the diligence executed upon it.

(9) Nothing in this section prejudices the right of any creditor of the company to rank for his debt in the winding up of the company.

1.69

62 Cessation of appointment of receiver

(1) A receiver may be removed from office by the court under subsection (3) below and may resign his office by giving notice of his resignation in the prescribed manner to such persons as may be prescribed.

(2) A receiver shall vacate office if he ceases to be qualified to act as an insolvency practitioner in relation to the company.

(3) Subject to the next subsection, a receiver may, on application to the court by the holder of the floating charge by virtue of which he was appointed, be removed by the court on cause shown.

(4) Where at any time a receiver vacates office—
    (a)   his remuneration and any expenses properly incurred by him, and
    (b)   any indemnity to which he is entitled out of the property of the company,
shall be paid out of the property of the company which is subject to the floating charge and shall have priority as provided for in section 60(1).

(5) When a receiver ceases to act as such otherwise than by death he shall, and, when a receiver is removed by the court, the holder of the floating charge by virtue of which he was appointed shall, within 14 days of the cessation or removal (as the case may be) give the registrar of companies notice to that effect, and the registrar shall enter the notice in the register of charges.

If the receiver or the holder of the floating charge (as the case may require) makes default in complying with the requirements of this subsection, he is liable to a fine *and, for continued contravention, to a daily default fine.*

(6) If by the expiry of a period of one month following upon the removal of the receiver or his ceasing to act as such no other receiver has been appointed, the floating charge by virtue of which the receiver was appointed—
    (a)   thereupon ceases to attach to the property then subject to the charge, and
    (b)   again subsists as a floating charge;
and for the purposes of calculating the period of one month under this subsection no account shall be taken of any period during which [the company is in administration,] under Part II of this Act ...

1.70

63 Powers of court

(1) The court on the application of—
    (a)   the holder of a floating charge by virtue of which a receiver was appointed, or

(b)   a receiver appointed under section 51,

may give directions to the receiver in respect of any matter arising in connection with the performance by him of his functions.

(2) Where the appointment of a person as a receiver by the holder of a floating charge is discovered to be invalid (whether by virtue of the invalidity of the instrument or otherwise), the court may order the holder of the floating charge to indemnify the person appointed against any liability which arises solely by reason of the invalidity of the appointment.

1.71

64 Notification that receiver appointed

(1) Where a receiver has been appointed, every invoice, order for goods or business letter issued by or on behalf of the company or the receiver or the liquidator of the company, being a document on or in which the name of the company appears, shall contain a statement that a receiver has been appointed.

(2) If default is made in complying with the requirements of this section, the company and any of the following persons who knowingly and wilfully authorises or permits the default, namely any officer of the company, any liquidator of the company and any receiver, is liable to a fine.

1.72

65 Information to be given by receiver

(1) Where a receiver is appointed, he shall—
  (a)   forthwith send to the company and publish notice of his appointment, and
  (b)   within 28 days after his appointment, unless the court otherwise directs, send such notice to all the creditors of the company (so far as he is aware of their addresses).

(2) This section and the next do not apply in relation to the appointment of a receiver to act—
  (a)   with an existing receiver, or
  (b)   in place of a receiver who has died or ceased to act,
except that, where they apply to a receiver who dies or ceases to act before they have been fully complied with, the references in this section and the next to the receiver include (subject to subsection (3) of this section) his successor and any continuing receiver.

(3) If the company is being wound up, this section and the next apply notwithstanding that the receiver and the liquidator are the same person, but with any necessary modifications arising from that fact.

(4) If a person without reasonable excuse fails to comply with this section, he is liable to a fine and, for continued contravention, to a daily default fine.

1.73

66 Company's statement of affairs

(1) Where a receiver of a company is appointed, the receiver shall forthwith require some or all of the persons mentioned in subsection (3) below to make out and submit to him a statement in the prescribed form as to the affairs of the company.

(2) A statement submitted under this section shall be verified by affidavit by the persons required to submit it and shall show—
- (a)   particulars of the company's assets, debts and liabilities;
- (b)   the names and addresses of its creditors;
- (c)   the securities held by them respectively;
- (d)   the dates when the securities were respectively given; and
- (e)   such further or other information as may be prescribed.

(3) The persons referred to in subsection (1) are—
- (a)   those who are or have been officers of the company;
- (b)   those who have taken part in the company's formation at any time within one year before the date of the appointment of the receiver;
- (c)   those who are in the company's employment or have been in its employment within that year, and are in the receiver's opinion capable of giving the information required;
- (d)   those who are or have been within that year officers of or in the employment of a company which is, or within that year was, an officer of the company.

In this subsection 'employment' includes employment under a contract for services.

(4) Where any persons are required under this section to submit a statement of affairs to the receiver they shall do so (subject to the next subsection) before the end of the period of 21 days beginning with the day after that on which the prescribed notice of the requirement is given to them by the receiver.

(5) The receiver, if he thinks fit, may—
- (a)   at any time release a person from an obligation imposed on him under subsection (1) or (2), or
- (b)   either when giving the notice mentioned in subsection (4) or subsequently extend the period so mentioned,

and where the receiver has refused to exercise a power conferred by this subsection, the court, if it thinks fit, may exercise it.

(6) If a person without reasonable excuse fails to comply with any obligation imposed under this section, he is liable to a fine and, for continued contravention, to a daily default fine.

1.74

67 Report by receiver

(1) Where a receiver is appointed under section 51, he shall within 3 months (or such longer period as the court may allow) after his appointment, send to the registrar of companies, to the holder of the floating charge by virtue of which he was appointed and to any trustees for secured creditors of the company and (so far as he is aware of their addresses) to all such creditors a report as to the following matters, namely—
- (a)   the events leading up to his appointment, so far as he is aware of them;
- (b)   the disposal or proposed disposal by him of any property of the company and the carrying on or proposed carrying on by him of any business of the company;

(c) the amounts of principal and interest payable to the holder of the floating charge by virtue of which he was appointed and the amounts payable to preferential creditors; and

(d) the amount (if any) likely to be available for the payment of other creditors.

(2) The receiver shall also, within 3 months (or such longer period as the court may allow) after his appointment, either—

(a) send a copy of the report (so far as he is aware of their addresses) to all unsecured creditors of the company, or

(b) publish in the prescribed manner a notice stating an address to which unsecured creditors of the company should write for copies of the report to be sent to them free of charge,

and (in either case), unless the court otherwise directs, lay a copy of the report before a meeting of the company's unsecured creditors summoned for the purpose on not less than 14 days' notice.

(3) The court shall not give a direction under subsection (2) unless—

(a) the report states the intention of the receiver to apply for the direction; and

(b) a copy of the report is sent to the persons mentioned in paragraph (a) of that subsection, or a notice is published as mentioned in paragraph (b) of that subsection, not less than 14 days before the hearing of the application.

(4) Where the company has gone or goes into liquidation, the receiver—

(a) shall, within 7 days after his compliance with subsection (1) or, if later, the nomination or appointment of the liquidator, send a copy of the report to the liquidator, and

(b) where he does so within the time limited for compliance with subsection (2), is not required to comply with that subsection.

(5) A report under this section shall include a summary of the statement of affairs made out and submitted under section 66 and of his comments (if any) on it.

(6) Nothing in this section shall be taken as requiring any such report to include any information the disclosure of which would seriously prejudice the carrying out by the receiver of his functions.

(7) Section 65(2) applies for the purposes of this section also.

(8) If a person without reasonable excuse fails to comply with this section, he is liable to a fine and, for continued contravention, to a daily default fine.

(9) In this section 'secured creditor', in relation to a company, means a creditor of the company who holds in respect of his debt a security over property of the company, and 'unsecured creditor' shall be construed accordingly.

1.75

68 Committee of creditors

(1) Where a meeting of creditors is summoned under section 67, the meeting may, if it thinks fit, establish a committee ('the creditors' committee') to exercise the functions conferred on it by or under this Act.

(2) If such a committee is established, the committee may on giving not less than 7 days' notice require the receiver to attend before it at any reasonable time and furnish it with such information relating to the carrying out by him of his functions as it may reasonably require.

1.76

69 Enforcement of receiver's duty to make returns, etc

(1) If any receiver—
    (a)   having made default in filing, delivering or making any return, account or other document, or in giving any notice, which a receiver is by law required to file, deliver, make or give, fails to make good the default within 14 days after the service on him of a notice requiring him to do so; or
    (b)   has, after being required at any time by the liquidator of the company so to do, failed to render proper accounts of his receipts and payments and to vouch the same and to pay over to the liquidator the amount properly payable to him,
the court may, on an application made for the purpose, make an order directing the receiver to make good the default within such time as may be specified in the order.

(2) In the case of any such default as is mentioned in subsection (1)(a), an application for the purposes of this section may be made by any member or creditor of the company or by the registrar of companies; and, in the case of any such default as is mentioned in subsection (1)(b), the application shall be made by the liquidator; and, in either case, the order may provide that all expenses of and incidental to the application shall be borne by the receiver.

(3) Nothing in this section prejudices the operation of any enactments imposing penalties on receivers in respect of any such default as is mentioned in subsection (1).

1.77

70 Interpretation for Chapter II

(1) In this Chapter, unless the contrary intention appears, the following expressions have the following meanings respectively assigned to them—
    'company' means an incorporated company (whether or not a company within the meaning of the Companies Act) which the Court of Session has jurisdiction to wind up;
    'fixed security', in relation to any property of a company, means any security, other than a floating charge or a charge having the nature of a floating charge, which on the winding up of the company in Scotland would be treated as an effective security over that property, and (without prejudice to that generality) includes a security over that property, being a heritable security within the meaning of the Conveyancing and Feudal Reform (Scotland) Act 1970;
    'instrument of appointment' has the meaning given by section 53(1);
    'prescribed' means prescribed by regulations made under this Chapter by the Secretary of State;

'receiver' means a receiver of such part of the property of the company as is subject to the floating charge by virtue of which he has been appointed under section 51;

'register of charges' means the register kept by the registrar of companies for the purposes of Chapter II of Part XII of the Companies Act;

'secured debenture' means a bond, debenture, debenture stock or other security which, either itself or by reference to any other instrument, creates a floating charge over all or any part of the property of the company, but does not include a security which creates no charge other than a fixed security; and

'series of secured debentures' means two or more secured debentures created as a series by the company in such a manner that the holders thereof are entitled pari passu to the benefit of the floating charge.

(2) Where a floating charge, secured debenture or series of secured debentures has been created by the company, then, except where the context otherwise requires, any reference in this Chapter to the holder of the floating charge shall—

    (a)   where the floating charge, secured debenture or series of secured debentures provides for a receiver to be appointed by any person or body, be construed as a reference to that person or body;

    (b)   where, in the case of a series of secured debentures, no such provision has been made therein but—

        (i)   there are trustees acting for the debenture-holders under and in accordance with a trust deed, be construed as a reference to those trustees, and

        (ii)   where no such trustees are acting, be construed as a reference to—

            (aa)   a majority in nominal value of those present or represented by proxy and voting at a meeting of debenture-holders at which the holders of at least one-third in nominal value of the outstanding debentures of the series are present or so represented, or

            (bb)   where no such meeting is held, the holders of at least one-half in nominal value of the outstanding debentures of the series.

(3) Any reference in this Chapter to a floating charge, secured debenture, series of secured debentures or instrument creating a charge includes, except where the context otherwise requires, a reference to that floating charge, debenture, series of debentures or instrument as varied by any instrument.

(4) References in this Chapter to the instrument by which a floating charge was created are, in the case of a floating charge created by words in a bond or other written acknowledgement, references to the bond or, as the case may be, the other written acknowledgement.

1.78

71 Prescription of forms etc; regulations

(1) The notice referred to in section 62(5), and the notice referred to in section 65(1)(a) shall be in such form as may be prescribed.

(2) Any power conferred by this Chapter on the Secretary of State to make regulations is exercisable by statutory instrument; and a statutory instrument made in the exercise of the power so conferred to prescribe a fee is subject to annulment in pursuance of a resolution of either House of Parliament.

Chapter III
Receivers' Powers in Great Britain as a whole

1.79

72 Cross-border operation of receivership provisions

(1) A receiver appointed under the law of either part of Great Britain in respect of the whole or any part of any property or undertaking of a company and in consequence of the company having created a charge which, as created, was a floating charge may exercise his powers in the other part of Great Britain so far as their exercise is not inconsistent with the law applicable there.

(2) In subsection (1) 'receiver' includes a manager and a person who is appointed both receiver and manager.

Notes

S 72

'Either part of Great Britain' This refers to the two jurisdictions or law districts which encompass Great Britain: England and Wales, and Scotland. This provision dates back to 1970, when Scottish law did not give effect to floating charges. It follows that IA 1986 s 72 does not apply to Northern Ireland. However The Administration of Justice Act 1977, section 7 contains a similar provision covering Northern Ireland.

Chapter IV
Prohibition of Appointment of Administrative Receiver

1.80

72A Floating charge holder not to appoint administrative receiver

(1) The holder of a qualifying floating charge in respect of a company's property may not appoint an administrative receiver of the company.

(2) In Scotland, the holder of a qualifying floating charge in respect of a company's property may not appoint or apply to the court for the appointment of a receiver who on appointment would be an administrative receiver of property of the company.

(3) In subsections (1) and (2)—
'holder of a qualifying floating charge in respect of a company's property' has the same meaning as in paragraph 14 of Schedule B1 to this Act, and

'administrative receiver' has the meaning given by section 251.

(4) This section applies—
- (a) to a floating charge created on or after a date appointed by the Secretary of State by order made by statutory instrument, and
- (b) in spite of any provision of an agreement or instrument which purports to empower a person to appoint an administrative receiver (by whatever name).

(5) An order under subsection (4)(a) may—
- (a) make provision which applies generally or only for a specified purpose;
- (b) make different provision for different purposes;
- (c) make transitional provision.

(6) This section is subject to the exceptions specified in sections 72B to 72GA.

Notes

S 72A

This provision was inserted by EA 2002 s 250 to prohibit the holder of a 'qualifying' floating charge (defined in IA 1986 Sch B1 para 14(2)). In respect of floating which was entered into on or after 15 September 2003 from appointing an administrative receiver. The prohibition applies to limited liability partnerships: *Cabvision Ltd v Feetum, Marsden and Smith* [2006] BPIR 379. A 'standard form' bank debenture is very likely to include a qualifying floating charge although it will always be necessary to check the relevant debenture against IA 1986 Sch B1 para 14(2). In respect of floating charges created prior to 15 September 2003 which enable a charge-holder to appoint an administrative receiver (as defined in IA 1986 s 29(2)) such a chargeholder has the choice of appointing an administrative receiver or an administrator.

IA 1986 s 72B to 72GA then set out various exceptions to the general prohibition in IA 1986 s 72A and provide that in certain circumstances an administrative receiver may still be appointed notwithstanding the creation of the floating charge on or after 15 September 2003.

1.81

72B First exception: capital market

(1) S 72A does not prevent the appointment of an administrative receiver in pursuance of an agreement which is or forms part of a capital market arrangement if—
- (a) a party incurs or, when the agreement was entered into was expected to incur, a debt of at least £50 million under the arrangement, and
- (b) the arrangement involves the issue of a capital market investment.

(2) In subsection (1)—
'capital market arrangement' means an arrangement of a kind described in paragraph 1 of Schedule 2A, and
'capital market investment' means an investment of a kind described in paragraph 2 or 3 of that Schedule.

1.82

72C Second exception: public-private partnership

(1) Section 72A does not prevent the appointment of an administrative receiver of a project company of a project which—
  (a)   is a public-private partnership project, and
  (b)   includes step-in rights.

(2) In this section 'public-private partnership project' means a project—
  (a)   the resources for which are provided partly by one or more public bodies and partly by one or more private persons, or
  (b)   which is designed wholly or mainly for the purpose of assisting a public body to discharge a function.

(3) In this section—
'step-in rights' has the meaning given by paragraph 6 of Schedule 2A, and
'project company' has the meaning given by paragraph 7 of that Schedule.

1.83

72D Third exception: utilities

(1) Section 72A does not prevent the appointment of an administrative receiver of a project company of a project which—
  (a)   is a utility project, and
  (b)   includes step-in rights.

(2) In this section—
  (a)   'utility project' means a project designed wholly or mainly for the purpose of a regulated business,
  (b)   'regulated business' means a business of a kind listed in paragraph 10 of Schedule 2A,
  (c)   'step-in rights' has the meaning given by paragraph 6 of that Schedule, and
  (d)   'project company' has the meaning given by paragraph 7 of that Schedule.

1.84

72DA Exception in respect of urban regeneration projects

(1) Section 72A does not prevent the appointment of an administrative receiver of a project company of a project which—
  (a)   is designed wholly or mainly to develop land which at the commencement of the project is wholly or partly in a designated disadvantaged area outside Northern Ireland, and
  (b)   includes step-in rights.

(2) In subsection (1) 'develop' means to carry out
  (a)   building operations,
  (b)   any operation for the removal of substances or waste from land and the levelling of the surface of the land, or
  (c)   engineering operations in connection with the activities mentioned in paragraph (a) or (b).

(3) In this section—

'building' includes any structure or er., and any part of a building as so defined, but does not include plant and machinery comprised in a building,

'building operations' includes—
  (a)   demolition of buildings,
  (b)   filling in of trenches,
  (c)   rebuilding,
  (d)   structural alterations of, or additions to, buildings and
  (e)   other operations normally undertaken by a person carrying on business as a builder,

'designated disadvantaged area' means an area designated as a disadvantaged area under section 92 of the Finance Act 2001,

'engineering operations' includes the formation and laying out of means of access to highways,

'project company' has the meaning given by paragraph 7 of Schedule 2A,

'step-in rights' has the meaning given by paragraph 6 of that Schedule,

'substance' means any natural or artificial substance whether in solid or liquid form or in the form of a gas or vapour, and

'waste' includes any waste materials, spoil, refuse or other matter deposited on land.

1.85

72E Fourth exception: project finance

(1) Section 72A does not prevent the appointment of an administrative receiver of a project company of a project which—
  (a)   is a financed project, and
  (b)   includes step-in rights.

(2) In this section—
  (a)   a project is 'financed' if under an agreement relating to the project a project company incurs, or when the agreement is entered into is expected to incur, a debt of at least £50 million for the purposes of carrying out the project,
  (b)   'project company' has the meaning given by paragraph 7 of Schedule 2A, and
  (c)   'step-in rights' has the meaning given by paragraph 6 of that Schedule.

Notes

S 72E

For a discussion of the phrases '*financed project*' and '*step in rights*' where an administrative receiver was purportedly appointed to a limited liability partnership see *Cabvision Ltd v Feetum, Marsden and Smith* [2006] BCC 340, [2006] BPIR 379).

1.86

72F Fifth exception: financial market

Section 72A does not prevent the appointment of an administrative receiver of a company by virtue of—

(a) a market charge within the meaning of section 173 of the Companies Act 1989 (c 40),

(b) a system-charge within the meaning of the Financial Markets and Insolvency Regulations 1996 (SI 1996/1469),

(c) a collateral security charge within the meaning of the Financial Markets and Insolvency (Settlement Finality) Regulations 1999 (SI 1999/2979).

1.87

72G Sixth exception: registered social landlord

Section 72A does not prevent the appointment of an administrative receiver of a company which is registered as a social landlord under Part I of the Housing Act 1996 (c 52) or under Part 3 of the Housing (Scotland) Act 2001 (asp 10).

1.88

72GA Exception in relation to protected railway companies etc

Section 72A does not prevent the appointment of an administrative receiver of—

(a) a company holding an appointment under Chapter I of Part II of the Water Industry Act 1991,

(b) a protected railway company within the meaning of section 59 of the Railways Act 1993 (including that section as it has effect by virtue of section 19 of the Channel Tunnel Rail Link Act 1996, or

(c) a licence company within the meaning of section 26 of the Transport Act 2000.

1.89

72H Sections 72A to 72G: supplementary

(1) Schedule 2A (which supplements sections 72B to 72G) shall have effect.

(2) The Secretary of State may by order—

(a) insert into this Act provision creating an additional exception to section 72A(1) or (2);

(b) provide for a provision of this Act which creates an exception to section 72A(1) or (2) to cease to have effect;

(c) amend section 72A in consequence of provision made under paragraph (a) or (b);

(d) amend any of subsection 72B to 72G;

(e) amend Schedule 2A.

(3) An order under subsection (2) must be made by statutory instrument.

(4) An order under subsection (2) may make—

(a) provision which applies generally or only for a specified purpose;

(b) different provision for different purposes;

(c) consequential or supplementary provision;

(d) transitional provision.

(5) An order under subsection (2)—

(a) in the case of an order under subsection (2)(e), shall be subject to annulment in pursuance of a resolution of either House of Parliament,

(b) in the case of an order under subsection (2)(d) varying the sum specified in section 72B(1)(a) or 72E(2)(a) (whether or not the order also makes consequential or transitional provision), shall be subject to annulment in pursuance of a resolution of either House of Parliament, and

(c) in the case of any other order under subsection (2)(a) to (d), may not be made unless a draft has been laid before and approved by resolution of each House of Parliament.

Part IV Winding up of companies registered under the Companies Acts

Chapter I
Preliminary

Modes of winding up

1.90

73 Alternative modes of winding up

(1) The winding up of a company, within the meaning given to that expression by section 735 of the Companies Act, may be either voluntary (Chapters II, III, IV and V in this Part) or by the court (Chapter VI).

(2) This Chapter, and Chapters VII to X, relate to winding up generally, except where otherwise stated.

Notes

Introduction

This section identifies the two means by which companies may be wound up:

- Voluntarily, in which case the winding up is governed by Chapters II to V (sections 84 to 116); and
- By the court, in which case the winding up is governed by Chapter VI (sections 117 to 162).

In either case, the winding up is also subject to the provisions applicable to both types of winding up contained in Chapters I and VII to X (sections 73 to 83 and 163 to 246), as well as the provisions of the relevant rules, many of which contain important substantive provisions which might perhaps have been better included in IA 1986 itself.

'Company'

IA 1986 defines 'company', for the purposes of winding up, by reference to the definition contained in CA 1985 s 735.

Part IV is applied with appropriate modifications to various other bodies besides companies as defined above including:

- Friendly societies: Friendly Societies Act 1992, s 21, 22, 23 and Schedule 10;
- Industrial and provident societies: Industrial and Provident Societies Act 1965 s 55; *Re Norse Self Build Association Ltd* (1985) 1 BCC 99, 436;
- Building societies: Building Societies Act 1986 s 90 and Schedule 5;

- Limited liability partnerships: Limited Liability Partnerships Regulations SI 2001/1090, paragraph 5;

Note also that:
- 'Unregistered companies' may be wound up pursuant to the provisions of IA 1986 Part V (sections 220 to 229) which applies the provisions of Part IV as modified;
- An insolvent partnership may be wound up as an unregistered company: Insolvent Partnerships Order 1994, SI 1994/2421;
- Financial Services and Markets Act 2000 s 367 enables the Financial Services Authority to petition to wind up certain types of company;

Voluntary Winding Up

There are two types of voluntary winding up:
- Members' voluntary winding up, which is governed by Chapter III (sections 91 to 96); and
- Creditors' voluntary winding up, which is governed by Chapter IV (sections 97 to 106).

In either case, a voluntary winding up is also subject to the provisions applicable to both types of voluntary winding up contained in Chapter V (sections 107 to 116).

A voluntary winding up of either type commences at the time that the resolution to wind up is passed: IA 1986 s 86.

The feature which distinguishes voluntary winding up from winding up by the court is, in the latter case, the control of the court and the involvement of the official receiver. A voluntary winding up is initiated by the members, or by the members and the creditors, who resolve that the company should be wound up and appoint the liquidator. By contrast, a winding up by the court is initiated by court order and the official receiver is appointed the first (and sometimes the only) liquidator. The liquidator in a winding up by the court proceeds to wind up the company on behalf of the court and performs its functions, or his own functions but on behalf of the court. In a voluntary winding up, the role of the court is more limited and must be invoked by a relevant application.

Members' Voluntary Winding Up

The distinguishing feature of a members' voluntary winding up is that it is, or is supposed to be, a solvent winding up, initiated by the members, for their benefit and to some extent under their control. A winding up is a members winding up if, and only if, the directors swear a statutory declaration of solvency in accordance with the provisions of IA 1986 s 89. If the statutory declaration is not made, the winding up is a creditors' voluntary winding up: IA 1986 s 90.

If, during the course of a members' voluntary winding, the liquidator is of the opinion that the company is in fact insolvent, he must summon a meeting of creditors in accordance with the provisions of IA 1986 s 95 and, as from the day on which that meeting is held, the winding up will be a creditors' voluntary winding up in accordance with the provisions of IA 1986 s 96.

Before IA 1986, there were substantial differences between solvent and insolvent windings up. In particular, there were significant differences between the classes of debts provable in each. Proof in solvent liquidations was governed only by the provisions of the Companies Acts, whereas in insolvent liquidations, proof was governed by the law and practice applicable to bankruptcy. This distinction was capable of leading to absurd results, where a winding up could be considered to be solvent under the bankruptcy regime (which had a more restricted class of provable debts), yet insolvent under the provisions of the Companies Acts (which had a more general class). That led to the form of eternal oscillation between the two regimes addressed by Vinelott J in *Re Berkeley Securities (Property) Ltd* [1980] 1 WLR 1589 and attempted to be squared by Harman J in the second part of his judgment in *Re Islington Metal and Plating Works Ltd* [1984] 1 WLR 14. This particular problem has now gone.

There remains, however, an as yet unresolved problem. Certain claims against companies are not provable, either because they are specifically excluded from proof under IR 1986 r 12.3, or because they did not have a sufficient existence as at the commencement of the winding up. If all provable debts are paid in full, should those claims be paid in advance of any distribution to members, or are those claims simply disregarded in their entirety? Logically, the latter answer, however unpalatable, would appear to be correct. However, in *Re T & N Ltd* [2005] EWHC 2870 (Ch), [2006] BPIR 532, David Richards J. suggested (but without deciding the question) that this was not correct. In his view, the court would restrain the distribution of surplus assets and permit the creditor to bring proceedings against the company and enforce against the surplus assets: see paragraphs 106 to 107 of his judgment. In that way, the creditor with the unprovable debt, whilst postponed to those with provable claims, would nevertheless be paid in priority to members.

Creditors' Voluntary Winding Up

Both types of voluntary liquidations are initiated by resolution of the members (general, special or extraordinary, depending upon which of the circumstances specified in IA 1986 s 84(1) applies). In a members' voluntary winding up, the members appoint the liquidator: IA 1986 s 91(1). By contrast, in a creditors' voluntary winding up, there is both a meeting of the company under IA 1986 s 84 and a meeting of the creditors under IA 1986 s 98. Each meeting may nominate a person to be liquidator, but where different persons are nominated, the creditors' nomination prevails: IA 1986 s 100(1) and (2). Further, the creditors may appoint a liquidation committee under IA 1986 s 101 and there are annual and final meetings of both members and creditors under IA 1986 s 105 and 106 (contrast the members only meetings in members' voluntary windings up under IA 1986 s 93 and 94). Essentially, and in accordance with underlying commercial interests intended to be served by a creditors' voluntary winding up, the creditors have a far greater say in, and control over, the process.

Winding up by the Court

Winding up by the court is initiated by an order of the court made under IA 1986 s 125 in the circumstances set out in IA 1986 s 122.

The winding up commences at the time of the presentation of the petition for winding up, unless (a) there was a pre-existing voluntary winding up (in which case the winding up commences as at the time of the resolution) or (b) the order was made under IA 1986 Schedule B1 paragraph 13(1)(1)(e) on the hearing of an administration application (in which case the winding up commences on the making of the order); see IA 1986 s 129.

Once the winding up order is made, the official receiver and any subsequently appointed liquidator performs his own functions (for example, those specified in IA 1986 s 143 to 146), as well those entrusted to the court but which have been delegated to the liquidator under IA 1986 s 160 (for example, the duty to settle a list of contributories and apply assets under IA 1986 s 148(1)).

1.91

74 Liability as contributories of present and past members

(1) When a company is wound up, every present and past member is liable to contribute to its assets to any amount sufficient for payment of its debts and liabilities, and the expenses of the winding up, and for the adjustment of the rights of the contributories among themselves.

(2) This is subject as follows—

    (a)   a past member is not liable to contribute if he has ceased to be a member for one year or more before the commencement of the winding up;

    (b)   a past member is not liable to contribute in respect of any debt or liability of the company contracted after he ceased to be a member;

(c)   a past member is not liable to contribute, unless it appears to the court that the existing members are unable to satisfy the contributions required to be made by them in pursuance of the Companies Act and this Act;

(d)   in the case of a company limited by shares, no contribution is required from any member exceeding the amount (if any) unpaid on the shares in respect of which he is liable as a present or past member;

(e)   nothing in the Companies Act or this Act invalidates any provision contained in a policy of insurance or other contract whereby the liability of individual members on the policy or contract is restricted, or whereby the funds of the company are alone made liable in respect of the policy or contract;

(f)   a sum due to any member of the company (in his character of a member) by way of dividends, profits or otherwise is not deemed to be a debt of the company, payable to that member in a case of competition between himself and any other creditor not a member of the company, but any such sum may be taken into account for the purpose of the final adjustment of the rights of the contributories among themselves.

(3) In the case of a company limited by guarantee, no contribution is required from any member exceeding the amount undertaken to be contributed by him to the company's assets in the event of its being wound up; but if it is a company with a share capital, every member of it is liable (in addition to the amount so undertaken to be contributed to the assets), to contribute to the extent of any sums unpaid on shares held by him.

Notes

Liability of Past and Present Members to Contribute

IA 1986 s 74(1) provides that every past and present member of a company is liable to contribute to its assets an amount sufficient (a) to pay its debts and liabilities and the expenses of its winding up and (b) for the adjustment of the rights of the contributories among themselves.

The liability to contribute is qualified in the various ways set out in IA 1986 s 74(2). In particular, the liability to contribute is:
*   In the case of a past member, barred if he has ceased to be a member for at least one year prior to the commencement of the winding up: IA 1986 s 74(2)(a);
*   In the case of a past member, limited to debts or liabilities 'contracted' after he ceased to be a member: IA 1986 s 74(2)(b);
*   In the case of a past member, barred unless the existing members are unable to satisfy the contributions required to be made by them: IA 1986 s 74(2)(c);
*   In the case of all members of companies limited by shares, limited to the unpaid amount of any share in respect of which he is liable to contribute: IA 1986 s 74(2)(d).

A person who has been induced to acquire shares by misrepresentation cannot rescind his contract, and thereby avoid his liability to contribute, after the commencement of the winding: *Oakes v Turquand* (1867) LR 2 HL 325. This is so even where the assets are sufficient for the payment in full of creditors and liquidation expenses: *Re Hull & County Bank, Burgess's Case* (1880) 15 Ch D 507. However, where a person appears or has appeared as a member in the register of members the court may delete his or her name retrospectively if it is satisfied that the register should be rectified even if the company has entered liquidation: *Barbor v Middleton* (1988) 4 BCC 681 (Court of Session).

A person whose shares have been forfeited, but who remains liable in respect of pre-forfeiture calls, is not a contributory if the forfeiture took place more than one year before the commencement of winding up: *Ladies' Dress Association v Pulbrook* [1900] 2 QB 376. However, such a person may still be liable as a debtor of the company in respect of the unpaid calls.

Subordination of Members' Claims

Any sum due to a member in his character as member is subordinated to the claims of the company's non member creditors, *'so that all creditors not members of the company must have been satisfied in full, before a present or past member, to whom a sum is owed in his character of a member by way of dividends, profits or otherwise, may receive anything at all in the liquidation. Only after provision has been made for all creditors not members of the company to be satisfied in full is it permissible to take such a sum into account 'for the purpose of the final adjustment of the rights of the contributories among themselves'*: see *Re Compania de Electricidad de la Provincia de Buenos Aires Ltd* [1980] Ch 146 at 170 per Slade J.

As to the meaning of 'in his character of a member'

- See *Soden v British & Commonwealth Holdings Plc* [1998] AC 321 where it was held that a claim by a member against the company for damages for misrepresentations which induced the member to purchase from a third party the relevant shares in the company would not result in sums being payable to the member 'in his character of a member'. Sums due *as a member* means sums due under the 'statutory contract' created by the binding effect of the memorandum and articles of association of a company as set out in CA 1985 s 14(1).
- *Soden* expressly leaves open the question whether damages for misrepresentation relating to the issue of shares at the time of issue of the shares would be treated as sums payable to a member as a member: see the speech of Lord Browne Wilkinson at page 326H.
- Two cases suggest that sums due in respect of such claims would fall within IA 1986 s 74(1)(f): *Re Addlestone Linoleum Co* (1887) 37 Ch D 191 and *Webb Distributors (Aus.) Pty Ltd v State of Victoria* (1993) 11 ACSR 731. What is not clear, as Lord Brown Wilkinson observed, was whether CA 1985 s 111A reverses that position.

'Members' includes past members, so that the claim of a past member claiming to be a creditor in respect of unclaimed dividends will be postponed to the claims of non-member creditors under IA 1986 s 74(2)(f): see *Re Consolidated Goldfields of New Zealand Ltd* [1953] Ch 689, referred to with approval *by Slade J in Compania de Electricidad (above)*.

Adjustment of Contributories' Rights

'Contributories' are defined in IA 1986 s 79. The expression includes every person who is liable to contribute to the assets of the company in the event of it being wound up, including every person alleged to be so liable (until the conclusion of any proceedings for determining whether that person is a contributory: IA 1986 s 79(1)). It excludes, however, any person made liable to contribute to the company's assets by virtue of fraudulent or wrongful trading proceedings under IA 1986 s 213 and 214.

'Contributories' include the holders of fully paid up shares: see *Re Anglesea Colliery Company* (1866) 1 Ch App 597, where it was held that liquidators were justified in making calls on the holders of partly paid shares for the purposes of adjusting rights between the holders of partly paid and fully paid shares. This case was followed in *Re National Savings Bank Association* (1866) 1 Ch App 547, *where it was held that the holder of fully paid shares was a contributory and had locus to present a winding up petition, and in Re Phoenix Oil and Transport Ltd* [1958] Ch 560, where it was held that, although the holders of fully paid shares were contributories, the distribution of surplus assets where all shares were fully paid did not amount to an adjustment of rights and contributories and accordingly settlement of a list of contributories was dispensed with. This last case was approved by Slade J in *Compania de Electricidad* (above) at page 173.

1.92

75 Directors, etc with unlimited liability

(1) In the winding up of a limited company, any director or manager (whether past or present) whose liability is under the Companies Act unlimited is liable, in addition to his liability (if any) to contribute as an ordinary member, to make a further contribution as if he were at the commencement of the winding up a member of an unlimited company.

(2) However—
    (a)   a past director or manager is not liable to make such further contribution if he has ceased to hold office for a year or more before the commencement of the winding up;
    (b)   a past director or manager is not liable to make such further contribution in respect of any debt or liability of the company contracted after he ceased to hold office;
    (c)   subject to the company's articles, a director or manager is not liable to make such further contribution unless the court deems it necessary to require that contribution in order to satisfy the company's debts and liabilities, and the expenses of the winding up.

Notes

S 75

Under CA 1985 s 306 a director or manager of a limited company may have unlimited liability if so provided in the memorandum. However, it is very rare to find directors whose liability is extended in this manner and accordingly in practice this section is of limited application.

1.93

76 Liability of past directors and shareholders

(1) This section applies where a company is being wound up and—
    (a)   it has under Chapter VII of Part V of the Companies Act (redeemable shares; purchase by a company of its own shares) made a payment out of capital in respect of the redemption or purchase of any of its own shares (the payment being referred to below as 'the relevant payment'), and
    (b)   the aggregate amount of the company's assets and the amounts paid by way of contribution to its assets (apart from this section) is not sufficient for payment of its debts and liabilities, and the expenses of the winding up.

(2) If the winding up commenced within one year of the date on which the relevant payment was made, then—

(a)   the person from whom the shares were redeemed or purchased, and

(b)   the directors who signed the statutory declaration made in accordance with section 173(3) of the Companies Act for purposes of the redemption or purchase (except a director who shows that he had reasonable grounds for forming the opinion set out in the declaration),

are, so as to enable that insufficiency to be met, liable to contribute to the following extent to the company's assets.

(3) A person from whom any of the shares were redeemed or purchased is liable to contribute an amount not exceeding so much of the relevant payment as was made by the company in respect of his shares; and the directors are jointly and severally liable with that person to contribute that amount.

(4) A person who has contributed any amount to the assets in pursuance of this section may apply to the court for an order directing any other person jointly and severally liable in respect of that amount to pay him such amount as the court thinks just and equitable.

(5) Sections 74 and 75 do not apply in relation to liability accruing by virtue of this section.

(6) This section is deemed included in Chapter VII of Part V of the Companies Act for the purposes of the Secretary of State's power to make regulations under section 179 of that Act.

Notes

S 76

Under CA 1985 s 173, a payment out of capital by a private company for the redemption or purchase of its shares is lawful only if the provisions of CA 1985 s 173 to 175 are satisfied.

Section 173 provides inter alia as follows:

'173(3) [Statutory declaration by directors] The company's directors must make a statutory declaration specifying the amount of the permissible capital payment for the shares in question and stating that, having made full inquiry into the affairs and prospects of the company, they have formed the opinion–

(a)as regards its initial situation immediately following the date on which the payment out of capital is proposed to be made, that there will be no grounds on which the company could then be found unable to pay its debts, and

(b)as regards its prospects for the year immediately following that date, that, having regard to their intentions with respect to the management of the company's business during that year and to the amount and character of the financial resources which will in their view be available to the company during that year, the company will be able to continue to carry on business as a going concern (and will accordingly be able to pay its debts as they fall due) throughout that year.

173(4) [Directors' opinion in s 173(3)(a)] In forming their opinion for purposes of subsection (3)(a), the directors shall take into account the same liabilities (including prospective and contingent liabilities) as would be relevant under section 122 of the Insolvency Act (winding up by the court) to the question whether a company is unable to pay its debts.'

Where the winding up of a company commences within one year of the date on which a payment from capital was made for these purposes, the person whose shares were redeemed or purchased and the director who made the statutory declaration may be liable as a contributory, pursuant and subject to the conditions of IA 1986 s 76.

Liability under IA 1986 s 76

Potential liability arises where the winding up is insolvent; that is, the assets and any contribution made otherwise than pursuant to IA 1986 s 76 are insufficient for the discharge of the company's debts liabilities and the expenses of the winding up: IA 1986 s 76(1)(b).

The person whose shares were redeemed or purchased is liable in an amount not exceeding the amount of a payment from capital made in respect of his shares: IA 1986 s 76(2)(a) and 76(3).

In addition any director who signed the statutory declaration made for the purposes of the redemption or purchase will be jointly and severally liable with the person whose shares were redeemed or purchased: IA 1986 s 76(2)(b) and 76(3). A director who can show that he had reasonable grounds for forming the opinion set out in the declaration is not liable: IA 1986 s 76(2)(b).

Any person who has actually contributed pursuant to IA 1986 s 76 may apply to court for an order that any other person jointly and severally liable with him should pay to him such amount as the court thinks just and equitable: IA 1986 s 76(4). The court's discretion to order an indemnity or contribution is a wide one and would presumably be directed or influenced by considerations, such as relative blameworthiness, which govern the court's general power to order contribution under the Civil Liability (Contribution) Act 1978.

1.94

77 Limited company formerly unlimited

(1) This section applies in the case of a company being wound up which was at some former time registered as unlimited but has re-registered—
  (a)   as a public company under section 43 of the Companies Act (or the former corresponding provision, section 5 of the Companies Act 1980), or
  (b)   as a limited company under section 51 of the Companies Act (or the former corresponding provision, section 44 of the Companies Act 1967).

(2) Notwithstanding section 74(2)(a) above, a past member of the company who was a member of it at the time of re-registration, if the winding up commences within the period of 3 years beginning with the day on which the company was re-registered, is liable to contribute to the assets of the company in respect of debts and liabilities contracted before that time.

(3) If no persons who were members of the company at that time are existing members of it, a person who at that time was a present or past member is liable to contribute as above notwithstanding that the existing members have satisfied the contributions required to be made by them under the Companies Act and this Act.

This applies subject to section 74(2)(a) above and to subsection (2) of this section, but notwithstanding section 74(2)(c).

(4) Notwithstanding section 74(2)(d) and (3), there is no limit on the amount which a person who, at that time, was a past or present member of the company is liable to contribute as above.

Notes

S 77

This section deals with the liability of members of a company, formerly unlimited, but which re-registers as a public company or limited company under CA 1985.

- If winding up commences less than 3 years after re-registration, a past member who was a member at the time of registration is liable to contribute in respect of outstanding debts and liabilities contracted prior to re-registration: IA 1986 s 77(2).
- If there are no existing members who were also members at the time of re-registration, a person who at the time of re-registration was a present or past member is liable to contribute even though existing members have satisfied the contributions required to be made by them.

1.95–1.96

78 Unlimited company formerly limited

(1) This section applies in the case of a company being wound up which was at some former time registered as limited, but has been re-registered as unlimited under section 49 of the Companies Act (or the former corresponding provision, section 43 of the Companies Act 1967).

(2) A person who, at the time when the application for the company to be re-registered was lodged, was a past member of the company and did not after that again become a member of it is not liable to contribute to the assets of the company more than he would have been liable to contribute had the company not been re-registered.

1.97

79 Meaning of 'contributory'

(1) In this Act and the Companies Act the expression 'contributory' means every person liable to contribute to the assets of a company in the event of its being wound up, and for the purposes of all proceedings for determining, and all proceedings prior to the final determination of, the persons who are to be deemed contributories, includes any person alleged to be a contributory.

(2) The reference in subsection (1) to persons liable to contribute to the assets does not include a person so liable by virtue of a declaration by the court under section 213 (imputed responsibility for company's fraudulent trading) or section 214 (wrongful trading) in Chapter X of this Part.

(3) A reference in a company's articles to a contributory does not (unless the context requires) include a person who is a contributory only by virtue of section 76.

This subsection is deemed included in Chapter VII of Part V of the Companies Act for the purposes of the Secretary of State's power to make regulations under section 179 of that Act.

Notes

S 79

See the notes to IA 1986 s 74 above. In addition an office holder who has been held liable for misfeasance under IA 1986 s 212 is not a contributory: *Re AMF International Ltd* [1996] 1 WLR 77. In that case, a liquidator in a members' voluntary liquidation had distributed assets without providing for payment of rent due under a lease. A misfeasance claim was made against him by a subsequently appointed liquidator under IA 1986 s 212. Despite the wording of that section (which refers to an order that a person liable should contribute to the company's assets), and the limited exclusionary provisions of IA 1986 s 79(2), Ferris J held that the former liquidator was not a contributory.

I.98

80 Nature of contributory's liability

The liability of a contributory creates a debt (in England and Wales in the nature of a specialty) accruing due from him at the time when his or her liability commenced, but payable at the times when calls are made for enforcing the liability.

Notes

S 80

The period of limitation for specialty debts is 12 years under Limitation Act 1980 s 8.

I.99

81 Contributories in case of death of a member

(1) If a contributory dies either before or after he has been placed on the list of contributories, his personal representatives, and the heirs and legatees of heritage of his heritable estate in Scotland, are liable in a due course of administration to contribute to the assets of the company in discharge of his liability and are contributories accordingly

(2) Where the personal representatives are placed on the list of contributories, the heirs or legatees of heritage need not be added, but they may be added as and when the court thinks fit.

(3) If in England and Wales the personal representatives make default in paying any money ordered to be paid by them, proceedings may be taken

for administering the estate of the deceased contributory and for compelling payment out of it of the money due.

Notes

S 81

In this connection, see *Re Bayswater Trading Co Ltd* [1970] 1 WLR 343, where a personal representative of a deceased member was held entitled (a) as a member to petition to restore a dissolved company, and (b) as a contributory to petition for its winding up.

1.100

82 Effect of contributory's bankruptcy

(1) The following applies if a contributory becomes bankrupt, either before or after he has been placed on the list of contributories.

(2) His trustee in bankruptcy represents him for all purposes of the winding up, and is a contributory accordingly.

(3) The trustee may be called on to admit to proof against the bankrupt's estate, or otherwise allow to be paid out of the bankrupt's assets in due course of law, any money due from the bankrupt in respect of his liability to contribute to the company's assets.

(4) There may be proved against the bankrupt's estate the estimated value of his liability to future calls as well as calls already made.

Notes

S 82

The trustee in bankruptcy of the contributory becomes the contributory under this provision for all purposes of the winding up. So, the trustee in bankruptcy is the contributory, and may exercise the rights of a contributory, even in respect of shares which were not beneficially owned by the bankrupt and so did not fall into the bankrupt's estate: *Re Wolverhampton Steel & Iron Co. Ltd* [1977] 1 WLR 860. However, this only applies in the event that the company in question is in liquidation. A trustee in bankruptcy of a member is not a contributory entitled to petition for the winding up of a company: *Re H L Bolton Engineering Co. Ltd* [1956] Ch 577.

1.101

83 Companies registered under Companies Act, Part XXII, Chapter II

(1) The following applies in the event of a company being wound up which has been registered under section 680 of the Companies Act (or previous corresponding provisions in the Companies Act 1948 or earlier Acts).

(2) Every person is a contributory, in respect of the company's debts and liabilities contracted before registration, who is liable—

(a)   to pay, or contribute to the payment of, any debt or liability so contracted, or

(b)   to pay, or contribute to the payment of, any sum for the adjustment of the rights of the members among themselves in respect of any such debt or liability, or

(c)   to pay, or contribute to the amount of, the expenses of winding up the company, so far as relates to the debts or liabilities above-mentioned.

(3) Every contributory is liable to contribute to the assets of the company, in the course of the winding up, all sums due from him in respect of any such liability.

(4) In the event of the death, bankruptcy or insolvency of any contributory, provisions of this Act, with respect to the personal representatives, to the heirs and legatees of heritage of the heritable estate in Scotland of deceased contributories and to the trustees of bankrupt or insolvent contributories respectively, apply.

Notes

S 83

Broadly speaking, CA 1985 s 680 provides for the registration under the CA 1985 of old companies which were already in existence on 2 November 1862 (including companies registered under the Joint Stock Companies Acts) and companies registered under an Act of Parliament after 1862. This provision does not apply until the company is in liquidation; it cannot apply merely because a winding up petition has been presented: *Wightman v Bennett* [2005] BPIR 470.

Chapter II
Voluntary winding up (Introductory and General)

1.102

84 Circumstances in which company may be wound up voluntarily

(1) A company may be wound up voluntarily—
   (a)   when the period (if any) fixed for the duration of the company by the articles expires, or the event (if any) occurs, on the occurrence of which the articles provide that the company is to be dissolved, and the company in general meeting has passed a resolution requiring it to be wound up voluntarily;
   (b)   if the company resolves by special resolution that it be wound up voluntarily;
   (c)   if the company resolves by extraordinary resolution to the effect that it cannot by reason of its liabilities continue its business, and that it is advisable to wind up.

(2) In this Act the expression 'a resolution for voluntary winding up' means a resolution passed under any of the paragraphs of subsection (1).

(2A) Before a company passes a resolution for voluntary winding up it must give written notice of the resolution to the holder of any qualifying floating charge to which section 72A applies.

(2B) Where notice is given under subsection (2A) a resolution for voluntary winding up may be passed only-
  (a)   after the end of the period of five business days beginning with the day on which the notice was given, or
  (b)   if the person to whom the notice was given has consented in writing to the passing of the resolution.

(3) A resolution passed under paragraph (a) of subsection (1), as well as a special resolution under paragraph (b) and an extraordinary resolution under paragraph (c), is subject to section 380 of the Companies Act (copy of resolution to be forwarded to registrar of companies within 15 days).

(4) This section has effect subject to section 43 of the Commonhold and Leasehold Reform Act 2002.

Notes

S 84(1) The Resolution to Wind Up

Voluntary winding up is initiated by the company itself when it resolves by resolution in general meeting to enter into a winding up. IA 1986 s 84(1) identifies the three events, upon the happening of which, the company may resolve that it be wound up voluntarily.

Different types of resolution are required.
- IA 1986 s 84(1)(a) – the expiry of time or occurrence of an event specified in the articles as being one on which the company is to be dissolved – requires an ordinary resolution.
- IA 1986 s 84(1)(b) – resolution that the company be wound up voluntarily – requires a special resolution. A special resolution is one that is passed by a majority of not less than three-fourths of such members as (being entitled to do so) vote in person or, where proxies are allowed, by proxy, at a general meeting of which not less than 21 days notice has been given specifying the intention to propose the resolution as a special resolution: CA 1985 s 378(2). The period may be shortened if is so agreed by a majority in number of the members having the right to attend and vote at such a meeting, being a majority together holding not less than 95% in nominal value of the shares giving that right: CA 1985 s 378(3).
- IA 1986 s 84(1)(c) – resolution that it cannot continue its business by reason of its liabilities and that it is advisable to wind up – requires an extraordinary resolution. This is one passed by the same majority as a special resolution and at a general meeting of which notice specifying the intention to propose the resolution as an extraordinary resolution has been given: CA 1985 s 378(1). The notice period in this case is 14 days: CA 1985 s 369(1)(b)(ii).

Where the relevant formalities have not been properly complied with in relation to the holding of the meeting of the company which purported to pass the relevant resolution, the resolution may be held invalid. In *Re Caratal (New) Mines Ltd* [1902] 2 Ch 498, the chairman wrongly counted a number of proxies and declared the resolution passed. This was challenged, successfully, on a petition for a compulsory winding up order.

Any defect may be cured if the shareholders in fact unanimously consented to the resolution, or subsequently ratified it, under the "Duomatic" principle: see *Re Duomatic Ltd* [1969] 2 Ch 365 and, for a recent example of the application of the principle, *Euro Brokers Holdings Ltd v Monecor (London) Ltd* [2003] EWCA Civ 105, [2003] BCC 573. Alternatively, persons seeking to rely on the invalidity of the resolution may by their behaviour be estopped from denying that the company is in fact in liquidation. In *Re Bailey, Hay & Co Ltd* [1971] 1 WLR 1357, the notice summoning the meeting was short. All shareholders attended and the resolution was passed, with three shareholders deliberately abstaining. The dissentient shareholders subsequently found out that the notice was defective, but refrained from challenging the validity of the resolution for a considerable period of time. They were held to be barred from challenging the validity of the resolution by their acquiescence both at and subsequent to the meeting and, further, by laches.

If the validity of the resolution is challenged, a liquidator would be well advised to seek directions under IA 1986 s 112 as soon as possible. Although the liquidator may have some protection under the provisions of IA 1986 s 232, the ambit of that section is uncertain. Whilst it may protect third parties, and therefore liquidators from claims by third parties, it is less clear that it protects the invalidly appointed liquidator himself.

Once the resolution has been passed the company is in liquidation and it cannot be rescinded by a subsequent resolution: *Ross v P J Herringa Ltd* [1970] NZLR 170. In such circumstances an application could be made to stay the liquidation under IA 1986 s 112 and 147: *Re Stephen Walters & Sons Ltd* [1926] WN 236.

There is nothing to prevent the presentation or progress of a winding up petition against a company in voluntary liquidation although the burden is on the petitioner to show that the continuation of the voluntary liquidation is in some way injurious to the interests of the creditors: see further the commentary to IA 1986 s 125.

S 84(2A), (2B) Notice to Qualifying Floating Chargeholder

The aim of these provisions is to prevent a company entering into a voluntary liquidation without notification to the holder of a qualifying floating charge. Once notified the qualifying floating chargeholder has an opportunity to appoint an administrator out of court: IA 1986 Sch B1 paragraph 14. Note however that no notice need be given to the holder of a qualifying floating charge that was created before 15 September 2003. The requirement to give notice only applies in favour of 'any *qualifying floating charge to which section 72A applies*' and IA 1986 s 72A clearly applies only to floating charges created on or after 15 September 2003.

S 84(4) Commonhold Associations

The Commonhold and Leasehold Reform Act 2002 s 43 provides that a winding up resolution in respect of a commonhold association shall be of no effect unless

- the resolution is preceded by a declaration of solvency (*see* IA 1986 s 89),
- the commonhold association passes a termination-statement resolution before it passes the winding up resolution, and
- each resolution is passed with at least 80% of the members of the association voting in favour.

A 'termination statement' is defined in CLRA 2002 s 47.

> **1.103**
>
> **85 Notice of resolution to wind up**
>
> (1) When a company has passed a resolution for voluntary winding up, it shall, within 14 days after the passing of the resolution, give notice of the resolution by advertisement in the Gazette.
>
> (2) If default is made in complying with this section, the company and every officer of it who is in default is liable to a fine and, for continued contravention, to a daily default fine.
>
>   For the purposes of this subsection the liquidator is deemed an officer of the company.

Notes

S 85(1)

In addition to the publicity required by this section, a liquidator is also required to publish a notice of his appointment within 14 days of that appointment: IA 1986 s 109.

S 85(2)

IA 1986 s 430 and Schedule 10 set out the amount of the fine that can be imposed.

1.104

86 Commencement of winding up

A voluntary winding up is deemed to commence at the time of the passing of the resolution for voluntary winding up.

Notes

S 86

If the meeting is adjourned, and the resolution passed at the adjourned meeting, it is the date on which the resolution is in fact passed that is the date on which the voluntary winding up is deemed to commence. In *Re Norditrack (UK) Ltd* [2000] BCC 441 it was decided that because of the terms of IA 1986 s 86 the court could not approve conditional resolutions for voluntary winding up which remained inchoate until the court made an order discharging an administration order. Arden J held that where an administrator sought the discharge of an administration order on the basis that the company would then enter into voluntary liquidation, the correct course was for the court to make an order for discharge to take effect at the time proposed for the extraordinary general meeting (when the resolution was to be considered), on the basis that the order would lie in the court office until the administrator's solicitor had filed a certificate confirming the passing of the resolution to place the company into voluntary liquidation. In the event that the resolution was not passed an undertaking would have to be given on the discharge application to bring the matter back to court to consider whether the date for discharge should be extended or whether the order made earlier should be discharged or rescinded. The 'Norditrack' exit from administration is no longer relevant for administrations initiated on or after 15 September 2003: IA 1986 Sch B1 paragraphs 65 and 83.

If a voluntary winding up is superseded by a winding up by the court, the date on which the winding up commenced nevertheless remains the date of the resolution: IA 1986 s 129(1). The concept of the commencement of a winding up is of critical importance to all liquidations. On that date, the creditors of the company become subject to the collective enforcement procedure which is the characteristic of a winding up. The creditors' claims are untouched but the collective procedure ensures a pari passu distribution of the company's assets in satisfaction of those claims. The debts crystallise and are valued as at the commencement of the winding up, this being the means by which the principle of a pari passu distribution is achieved: see *Wight v Eckhardt Marine Gmbh* [2003] UKPC 37, [2004] 1 AC 147. For the same reason, it is as at that date that one determines which debts are provable and which are subject to set-off: see *Stein v Blake* [1996] AC 243.

Consequences of resolution to wind up

1.105

87 Effect on business and status of company

(1) In case of a voluntary winding up, the company shall from the commencement of the winding up cease to carry on its business, except so far as may be required for its beneficial winding up.

> (2) However, the corporate state and corporate powers of the company, notwithstanding anything to the contrary in its articles, continue until the company is dissolved.

Notes

S 87

The winding up is deemed to commence at the date of the passing of the resolution that the company be wound up: IA 1986 s 86. In a members' voluntary liquidation, the liquidator will be appointed by the company in general meeting: IA 1986 s 91(1). In a creditors' voluntary liquidation, the company may fail to nominate a liquidator, or the creditors may nominate a different person, in which case it will be the creditors' nominee who becomes liquidator: IA 1986 s 100. There may therefore be a gap between the commencement of the winding up and the appointment of a liquidator. In that event, the directors' clearly retain their powers of management and control, but these are heavily circumscribed, not merely by the provisions of IA 1986 s 87, but also s 114. For a commentary on those restrictions, see the notes to s 114.

After the passing of the resolution the company may not continue its business after the passing of the resolution 'except so far as may be required for its beneficial winding up'. By IA 1986 s 165(3) and Sch 4 paragraph 5, a liquidator is given the power (exercisable without sanction in a voluntary winding up, and with sanction in a winding up by the court) 'to carry on the business of the company so far as may be necessary for its beneficial winding up'. Despite the slight difference in language, the prohibition and the power appear to be two sides of the same coin.

If a voluntary liquidator believes that a sale of a business as a going concern may be achieved, then a continuation of the business pending such sale is justifiable: see *Re Great Eastern Electric Company Ltd* [1941] Ch 241. By contrast, a liquidator may not use his powers to carry on business with a view to achieving a resuscitation of the company: see in *Re Wreck Recovery and Salvage Co* (1880) 15 Ch D 353, where the Court of Appeal refused to sanction the exercise of the power in a winding up by the court, holding that it was not being exercised for a proper purpose. Whilst making clear that everything depended upon the facts of the case, the word 'necessary' was said to mean that the exercise of the power had to be more than beneficial – that is highly expedient or a matter of mercantile necessity.

It is for a person claiming that the continuation of business is not required for the beneficial winding up of the company to prove that the section has been contravened: see *The Hire Purchase Furnishing Company Ltd v Richens* (1880) 20 QBD 387. A contract entered into in breach of this section is not illegal: see *Bateman v Ball* (1887) 56 LJQB 291.

1.106

88 Avoidance of share transfers, etc after winding-up resolution

Any transfer of shares, not being a transfer made to or with the sanction of the liquidator, and any alteration in the status of the company's members, made after the commencement of a voluntary winding up, is void

---

Notes

S 88

The rendering void of transfers of shares made after the commencement of the winding up is intended to prevent a transfer of partly paid shares to a person who may not be able to meet a call: *Rudge v Bowman* (1868) LR 3 QB 689 at 696 per Blackburn J.

Although any transfer is rendered void, the underlying contract is neither void nor illegal: *Chapman v Shepherd* (1867) LR 2 CP 228; *Hirsch v Burns* (1897) 77 LT 377. Thus, in *Biederman v Stone* (1867) LR 2 CP 504, the plaintiff sold, on behalf of the defendant, shares in a company which was in voluntary liquidation. The liquidator had not sanctioned the transfer and the defendant refused to execute a transfer in favour of the buyer. It was held that the seller was bound to execute the transfer, whether or not the sanction of the liquidator was obtained.

In *Re National Bank of Wales* [1896] 2 Ch 851 (Vaughan Williams J) and [1897] 1 Ch 298, CA, it was held as follows:

* Whether sanction should be given depends upon the facts of the case. Where the company is insolvent, sanction should only be given where the liquidator is sure that the transferee will contribute any sums due in respect of his shares. Different considerations might apply where, as in that case, liquidation was with a view to sale and amalgamation.
* A liquidator may sanction a transfer of shares, and register the transfer.
* A liquidator may also amend the list of contributories, recording the transferor as a past member, and the transferee as a present member.

For liability to contribute and adjustment of rights amongst contributories, see further IA 1986 s 74 and the notes thereto. The right to transfer debentures, and to have those debentures registered, is unaffected by this section: *Re Goy & Company Ltd* [1900] 2 Ch 149.

Declaration of solvency

1.107

89 Statutory declaration of solvency

(1) Where it is proposed to wind up a company voluntarily, the directors (or, in the case of a company having more than two directors, the majority of them) may at a directors' meeting make a statutory declaration to the effect that they have made a full inquiry into the company's affairs and that, having done so, they have formed the opinion that the company will be able to pay its debts in full, together with interest at the official rate (as defined in section 251), within such period, not exceeding 12 months from the commencement of the winding up, as may be specified in the declaration.

(2) Such a declaration by the directors has no effect for purposes of this Act unless—

    (a)   it is made within the 5 weeks immediately preceding the date of the passing of the resolution for winding up, or on that date but before the passing of the resolution, and

    (b)   it embodies a statement of the company's assets and liabilities as at the latest practicable date before the making of the declaration.

(3) The declaration shall be delivered to the registrar of companies before the expiration of 15 days immediately following the date on which the resolution for winding up is passed.

(4) A director making a declaration under this section without having reasonable grounds for the opinion that the company will be able to pay its debts in full, together with interest at the official rate, within the period specified is liable to imprisonment or a fine, or both.

(5) If the company is wound up in pursuance of a resolution passed within 5 weeks after the making of the declaration, and its debts (together

with interest at the official rate) are not paid or provided for in full within the period specified, it is to be presumed (unless the contrary is shown) that the director did not have reasonable grounds for his opinion.

(6) If a declaration required by subsection (3) to be delivered to the registrar is not so delivered within the time prescribed by that subsection, the company and every officer in default is liable to a fine and, for continued contravention, to a daily default fine.

Notes

S 89

A voluntary winding up will be a members' voluntary liquidation only if a statutory declaration of solvency is made by the directors under IA 1986 s 89: IA 1986 s 90. That declaration must be made within the period of 5 weeks before the passing of the resolution to wind up: IA 1986 s 89(2)(a).

A statutory declaration under section 89 has a number of features which need to be borne in mind:

- What is required is something that may reasonably be described as a statement of assets and liabilities showing (and justifying the directors' opinion) that the company will be able to pay its debts within a period of not more than 12 months from the commencement of the winding up.
- So far as assets are concerned, the company need not have assets sufficient to discharge its liabilities if third parties (for example, a parent company) have provided some form of non-recourse commitment to meet its liabilities.
- IA 1986 s 89(1) refers simply to 'debts', without defining the term. The converse of the statutory declaration of solvency is to be found in the definition of insolvency in IA 1986 s 123, which makes it clear that 'debts' include a company's future, prospective and contingent liabilities. Section 89 is silent as to the manner in which such liabilities should be dealt with. It has been suggested that, in order to make a statutory declaration under section 89, the directors must form the view that debts which would or might fall due after the 12 month period must be capable of some form of commutation (either as a matter of right, or negotiation); otherwise, the directors cannot declare that the company will be able to pay its debts within the requisite period.
- In the case of a long lease where rent will fall due for payment on dates outside the 12 month period, it is likely that the directors can take into account the fact that a liquidator will assign a valuable lease or disclaim a lease with no value. That appears to have been the course adopted, without adverse comment, in *Re Park Air Services Ltd, Christopher Moran Holdings Ltd v Bairstow* [2000] 2 AC 172.

IA 1986 s 89 imposes stringent and onerous requirement on directors. The penalties for making a false declaration are severe and there is, in certain circumstances, a presumption of guilt: cee section 89(4) and (5); *Re Surplus Properties (Huddersfield) Ltd* [1984] BCLC 89 at 92; *Re Leading Guides International Ltd* [1998] 1 BCLC 620. Errors and omissions which are not such that they present a misleading picture of the company's position will not invalidate the statement: *De Courcy v Clements* [1971] Ch 693; *Re New Millennium Experience Co Ltd* [2004] 1 BCLC 19.

1.108

90 Distinction between 'members" and 'creditors" voluntary winding up

A winding up in the case of which a directors' statutory declaration under section 89 has been made is a 'members' voluntary winding up'; and a winding up in the case of which such a declaration has not been made is a 'creditors' voluntary winding up'.

Notes

S 90

Where a declaration has not been sworn the liquidation proceeds as a creditors' voluntary winding up irrespective of whether the company is in fact solvent. This would appear to enable a company to exit administration into a creditors' voluntary liquidation under IA 1986 Sch B1 para 83 albeit that the company is solvent . Where the declaration has been made, but it subsequently appears that the company is in fact insolvent, the winding up is converted under IA 1986 s 95.

Chapter III
Members' Voluntary Winding Up

1.109

91 Appointment of liquidator

(1) In a members' voluntary winding up, the company in general meeting shall appoint one or more liquidators for the purpose of winding up the company's affairs and distributing its assets.

(2) On the appointment of a liquidator all the powers of the directors cease, except so far as the company in general meeting or the liquidator sanctions their continuance.

Notes

S 91(1) Appointment of liquidator

The appointment of the liquidator by members may be by ordinary resolution (simple majority) and it is normally done at the meeting which resolves to liquidate the company; that practice is so common that no separate notice need be given of the appointment of the liquidator: *Re Trench Tubeless Tyre Co* [1900] 1 Ch 408. See IR 1986 r 4.139 and 4.141 for the appropriate rules on the certification and authentication of the appointment. The company may appoint one or more liquidators, and if it does the resolution must state whether any act required or authorised under any enactment to be done by the liquidator is to be done by all or any one or more of the persons for the time being acting as liquidator: IA 1986 s 231(2).

S 91(2) Effect on directors

The passing of a resolution to wind up does not automatically terminate contracts of employment: *Midland Counties District Bank Ltd v Attwood* [1905] 1 Ch 357; *Reigate v Union Manufacturing Company (Ramsbottom) Ltd* [1981] 1 KB 592. Nor does it appear to terminate the offices of directors, although their powers are limited by the provisions of this subsection and IA 1986 s 114(2) and (3). Although it would be unusual for a liquidator to sanction the continuance of the directors' powers there may be situations where a power under the articles of association can only be exercised by the directors: see *Re Fairbairn Engineering Co* [1893] 3 Ch 450 where it was held that a company in liquidation could in general meeting elect directors and sanction the exercise by them of the power of enforcing calls by sale or forfeiture.

1.110

92 Power to fill vacancy in office of liquidator

(1) If a vacancy occurs by death, resignation or otherwise in the office of liquidator appointed by the company, the company in general meeting may, subject to any arrangement with its creditors, fill the vacancy.

(2) For that purpose a general meeting may be convened by any contributory or, if there were more liquidators than one, by the continuing liquidators.

(3) The meeting shall be held in manner provided by this Act or by the articles, or in such manner as may, on application by any contributory or by the continuing liquidators, be determined by the court.

Notes

S 92(1) Filling vacancies

See the notes to IR 1986 r 4.139 and 4 141 as to the certification and authentication of the appointment; clearly a liquidator cannot be appointed without his consent IR 1986 r 4.100(2) and 4.101(2) and *Re Charles* (1964) SC 1.

S 92(3) Mode of appointment

In the absence of any application by a contributory or by a continuing liquidator (if any) to court, the meeting will be held in accordance with the relevant provisions contained in the company's articles and the CA 1985.

1.111

93 General company meeting at each year's end

(1) Subject to sections 96 and 102, in the event of the winding up continuing for more than one year, the liquidator shall summon a general meeting of the company at the end of the first year from the commencement of the winding up, and of each succeeding year, or at the first convenient date within 3 months from the end of the year or such longer period as the Secretary of State may allow.

(2) The liquidator shall lay before the meeting an account of his acts and dealings, and of the conduct of the winding up, during the preceding year.

(3) If the liquidator fails to comply with this section, he is liable to a fine

---

Notes

S 93

If it is desired to have a general meeting at some other time there is no specific power to requisition a meeting of members as there is in a compulsory liquidation: IA 1986 s 168(2).

However, an application could be made under IA 1986 s 112 for the court to direct the holding of a meeting to ascertain 'the wishes of the creditors or contributories' pursuant to the provisions of IA 1986 s 195.

1.112

94 Final meeting prior to dissolution

(1) As soon as the company's affairs are fully wound up, the liquidator shall make up an account of the winding up, showing how it has been conducted and the company's property has been disposed of, and thereupon shall call a general meeting of the company for the purpose of laying before it the account, and giving an explanation of it.

(2) The meeting shall be called by advertisement in the Gazette, specifying its time, place and object and published at least one month before the meeting.

(3) Within one week after the meeting, the liquidator shall send to the registrar of companies a copy of the account, and shall make a return to him of the holding of the meeting and of its date.

(4) If the copy is not sent or the return is not made in accordance with subsection (3), the liquidator is liable to a fine and, for continued contravention, to a daily default fine.

(5) If a quorum is not present at the meeting, the liquidator shall, in lieu of the return mentioned above, make a return that the meeting was duly summoned and that no quorum was present; and upon such a return being made, the provisions of subsection (3) as to the making of the return are deemed complied with.

(6) If the liquidator fails to call a general meeting of the company as required by subsection (1), he is liable to a fine.

Notes

S 94

The liquidator is to make up his final account of the liquidation 'as soon as the company's affairs are fully wound up'. In order to be fully wound up, not all a company's assets need be realised provided the liquidator has done all he can to achieve that result: see *Re London and Caledonian Marine Insurance Co* (1879) 11 Ch D 140; *Re Wilmott Trading Ltd (No 2)* [2000] BCC 321.

It is sufficient that the account is made up as soon as the affairs are fully wound up so far as the liquidator is aware: see *Re Cornish Manures Ltd* [1967] 1 WLR 807 where the liquidator became aware of a further demand after the final meeting, and sent his account with a note relating to the demand to the Registrar of Companies. It was held that the dissolution of the company was not void. Dissolution of the company normally take place three months after the liquidator sends the Registrar of Companies the final account: IA 1986 s 201.

1.113

95 Effect of company's insolvency

(1) This section applies where the liquidator is of the opinion that the company will be unable to pay its debts in full (together with interest at the official rate) within the period stated in the directors' declaration under section 89.

(2) The liquidator shall—
   (a)   summon a meeting of creditors for a day not later than the twenty-eighth day after the day on which he formed that opinion;
   (b)   send notices of the creditors' meeting to the creditors by post not less than 7 days before the day on which that meeting is to be held;
   (c)   cause notice of the creditors' meeting to be advertised once in the Gazette and once at least in 2 newspapers circulating in the relevant locality (that is to say the locality in which the company's principal place of business in Great Britain was situated during the relevant period); and
   (d)   during the period before the day on which the creditors' meeting is to be held, furnish creditors free of charge with such information concerning the affairs of the company as they may reasonably require;

and the notice of the creditors' meeting shall state the duty imposed by paragraph (d) above.

(3) The liquidator shall also—
   (a)   make out a statement in the prescribed form as to the affairs of the company;
   (b)   lay that statement before the creditors' meeting; and
   (c)   attend and preside at that meeting.

(4) The statement as to the affairs of the company shall be verified by affidavit by the liquidator and shall show—
   (a)   particulars of the company's assets, debts and liabilities;
   (b)   the names and addresses of the company's creditors;
   (c)   the securities held by them respectively;
   (d)   the dates when the securities were respectively given; and
   (e)   such further or other information as may be prescribed.

(5) Where the company's principal place of business in Great Britain was situated in different localities at different times during the relevant period, the duty imposed by subsection (2)(c) applies separately in relation to each of those localities.

(6) Where the company had no place of business in Great Britain during the relevant period, references in subsections (2)(c) and (5) to the company's principal place of business in Great Britain are replaced by references to its registered office.

(7) In this section 'the relevant period' means the period of 6 months immediately preceding the day on which were sent the notices summoning the company meeting at which it was resolved that the company be wound up voluntarily.

> (8) If the liquidator without reasonable excuse fails to comply with this section, he is liable to a fine.

Notes

S 95

A liquidator in a members' voluntary winding up should from time to time consider whether the company is in fact insolvent, particularly before making any distribution to members. A liquidator who distributes to members if the company is in fact insolvent, or without making proper provision for debts and liabilities, may be made liable to unpaid creditors in misfeasance proceedings under IA 1986 s 212: see *AMF International Ltd* [1995] BCC 439, where a former liquidator was ordered to pay on an indemnity basis the costs of an application by an unpaid creditor for orders removing the liquidator and for the admission and payment of its proof, and *Re AMF International Ltd* [1996] BCC 335, which deals with the subsequent misfeasance summons against the former liquidator. The court made it clear in these cases that a liquidator pays a supposed surplus to members at his peril. The cases are also salutary lessons on the failure to take effective (that is, secured) indemnities in these circumstances.

S 95(1), (2) Insolvency and summoning Creditors' Meeting

If a liquidator forms the opinion that the company will be unable to pay its debts in full within the period stated by the directors in their statutory declaration of solvency (IA 1986 s 89(1)), the liquidator then has to summon a meeting of creditors within the prescribed time limit to enable the creditors to convert the members' voluntary liquidation into a creditors' voluntary winding up. The business of the meeting is more particularly described in IR 1986 r 4.53, r 4.52.

S 95(3), (4) The Statement of Affairs

The contents of the statement of affairs are prescribed by IA 1986 s 95(4); the form to be used is Form 4.18: IR 1986, Schedule 4. The requirements are substantially the same as those imposed by IA 1986 s 99, where the directors have to lay a statement of affairs before creditors. However under this section the person who prepares the statement is the liquidator; see also IR 1986 r 4.34ff. The creditors and the contributories must be provided with a copy or summary of the statement of affairs and a report of the meeting of creditors: IR 1986 r 4.49.

1.114

96 Conversion to creditors' voluntary winding up

As from the day on which the creditors' meeting is held under section 95, this Act has effect as if—

    (a)   the directors' declaration under section 89 had not been made; and

    (b)   the creditors' meeting and the company meeting at which it was resolved that the company be wound up voluntarily were the meetings mentioned in section 98 in the next Chapter;

and accordingly the winding up becomes a creditors' voluntary winding up.

Notes

S 96

The members' voluntary liquidation is thus converted into a creditors' voluntary liquidation as from the day on which the creditors' meeting is held. The liquidation then proceeds as if the declaration of solvency had not been made, and as if the meeting of creditors and the meeting of the members which resolved to put the company into members' voluntary liquidation were the meetings required under IA 1986 s 98 to put the company into creditors' voluntary liquidation. Further meetings do not therefore have to be held: IA 1986 s 97(2). The creditors may, if they wish, appoint another insolvency practitioner as liquidator in place of the members' choice of liquidator under IA 1986 section 100, and they may also appoint a liquidation committee: IA 1986 section 101.

Chapter IV
Creditors' Voluntary Winding Up

1.115

97 Application of this Chapter

(1) Subject as follows, this Chapter applies in relation to a creditors' voluntary winding up.

(2) Sections 98 and 99 do not apply where, under section 96 in Chapter III, a members' voluntary winding up has become a creditors' voluntary winding up.

Notes

S 97

Where the directors have not made a declaration of solvency or a members' voluntary winding up is converted under IA 1986 s 96, then the winding up proceeds under IA 1986 Chapter IV as a creditors' voluntary winding up. Article 1(1) of the EC Regulation on Insolvency Proceedings 2000 and applies to 'collective insolvency proceedings' which are listed in Annex A of the Regulation. Annex A includes creditors' voluntary winding up (with confirmation by the court). The procedure for making an application for a order confirming the creditors' voluntary winding up for the purposes of the EC Regulation is set out in IR 1986 r 7.62; and see *Re TXU German Finance BV* [2005] BCC 90. Such confirmation is necessary so as to ensure that the winding up is recognised throughout the EU.

S 97(2)

This provision dispenses with the requirements for a further meeting of creditors under IA 1986 s 98 and the presentation of a statement of affairs by the directors of the company under IA 1986 s 99 where a members' voluntary winding up has become a creditors' voluntary winding up.

1.116

98 Meeting of creditors

(1) The company shall—
    (a)   cause a meeting of its creditors to be summoned for a day not later than the 14th day after the day on which there is to be held the company meeting at which the resolution for voluntary winding up is to be proposed;

    (b)   cause the notices of the creditors' meeting to be sent by post to the creditors not less than 7 days before the day on which that meeting is to be held; and

    (c)   cause notice of the creditors' meeting to be advertised once in the Gazette and once at least in two newspapers circulating in the relevant locality (that is to say the locality in which the company's principal place of business in Great Britain was situated during the relevant period).

(2) The notice of the creditors' meeting shall state either—

    (a)   the name and address of a person qualified to act as an insolvency practitioner in relation to the company who, during the period before the day on which that meeting is to be held, will furnish creditors free of charge with such information concerning the company's affairs as they may reasonably require; or

    (b)   a place in the relevant locality where, on the two business days falling next before the day on which that meeting is to be held, a list of the names and addresses of the company's creditors will be available for inspection free of charge.

(3) Where the company's principal place of business in Great Britain was situated in different localities at different times during the relevant period, the duties imposed by subsections (1)(c) and (2)(b) above apply separately in relation to each of those localities.

(4) Where the company had no place of business in Great Britain during the relevant period, references in subsections (1)(c) and (3) to the company's principal place of business in Great Britain are replaced by references to its registered office.

(5) In this section 'the relevant period' means the period of 6 months immediately preceding the day on which were sent the notices summoning the company meeting at which it was resolved that the company be wound up voluntarily.

(6) If the company without reasonable excuse fails to comply with subsection (1) or (2), it is guilty of an offence and liable to a fine.

Notes

S 98

This section contemplates that a period of time may elapse between the meeting of the company at which the resolution to wind up is passed, and the creditors' meeting at which a statement of affairs will be lodged and the creditors consider whether to nominate a liquidator under IA 1986 s 100 and form a creditors' committee under IA 1986 s 101. During that period, if the company has not nominated a liquidator, the directors remain in charge of the management of the company. If the company has appointed a liquidator, then that person is liquidator even if his nomination is not subsequently confirmed by the creditors: see *Re Centrebind Ltd* [1967] 1 WLR 377, where short notice was served of the company's meeting creating a gap between that meeting and the meeting of creditors. Although the law then required that the creditors' meeting be held on the same day as, or the day following, the company's meeting, it was held that the nomination by the company of a liquidator meant that that person was liquidator of the company. This principle was exploited and gave rise to abuse.

Companies would nominate 'friendly' liquidators who would, in the period between meetings, take steps that were within their powers: for example, the sale of assets to a successor company.

IA 1986 s 98(1) contemplates that there may be a gap between meetings. The purpose of allowing the period of up to 14 days is to enable the directors of the company to prepare the statement of affairs in accordance with IA 1986 s 99(1) and (2) and IR 1986 r 4.34 ff.

To prevent abuse:
- Where no liquidator has been nominated by the company, the powers of the directors in the intervening period are heavily circumscribed by IA 1986 s 114. The directors can do what is necessary in order to comply with IA 1986 s 98 and 99, may dispose of perishable goods and goods of depreciating value, and may take steps to protect the company's assets. Otherwise, they may not exercise their powers without the sanction of the court;
- Where a liquidator has been nominated by the company, his powers are also circumscribed during the intervening period by IA 1986 s 166(1) to (3). During that period, the liquidator may not exercise his powers without the sanction of the court, except that he may take steps to take into his custody or under his control the assets of the company, dispose of perishable and depreciating goods and take steps to protect the company's assets.

For details regarding the contents of the notice required under IA 1986 s 98(2), see IR 1986 r 4.51(2). Where part of a creditor's claim is rejected for voting purposes at the meeting of creditors under s 98 as being for an unliquidated amount the fact that it is later reduced to a judgment does not mean that the chairman of the s 98 meeting was wrong to have treated it as unliquidated at the s 98 meeting *Re Shruth Limited* [2005] BPIR 1455.

1.117

99 Directors to lay statement of affairs before creditors

(1) The directors of the company shall—
    (a) make out a statement in the prescribed form as to the affairs of the company;
    (b) cause that statement to be laid before the creditors' meeting under section 98; and
    (c) appoint one of their number to preside at that meeting;

and it is the duty of the director so appointed to attend the meeting and preside over it.

(2) The statement as to the affairs of the company shall be verified by affidavit by some or all of the directors and shall show—
    (a) particulars of the company's assets, debts and liabilities;
    (b) the names and addresses of the company's creditors;
    (c) the securities held by them respectively;
    (d) the dates when the securities were respectively given; and
    (e) such further or other information as may be prescribed

(3) If—
    (a) the directors without reasonable excuse fail to comply with subsection (1) or (2); or
    (b) any director without reasonable excuse fails to comply with subsection (1), so far as requiring him to attend and preside at the creditors' meeting,

> the directors are or (as the case may be) the director is guilty of an offence
> and liable to a fine.

Notes

S 99

The creditors of the company are to be provided with information as to the financial state of the company in the prescribed form: IR 1986 r 4.34. The statement of affairs must be made up to a date not more than 14 days before the date on which the resolution for winding up is passed by the company: IR 1986 r 4.34(4). At least one director must be present to preside at the meeting. It is the duty of the appointed director to attend the meeting and to preside. In *Re Salcombe Hotel Development Co Ltd* (1989) 5 BCC 807 the court held that under the general law relating to meetings if the person who ought to preside over a certain meeting is absent, those entitled to attend may appoint their own nominee to preside. The court further held that there was no obligation on the liquidators under IA 1986 s 166(5) to apply for directions in a case where there was no need for directions; the language of that subsection was 'permissive and directory rather than mandatory'.

1.118

100 Appointment of liquidator

(1) The creditors and the company at their respective meetings mentioned in section 98 may nominate a person to be liquidator for the purpose of winding up the company's affairs and distributing its assets.

(2) The liquidator shall be the person nominated by the creditors or, where no person has been so nominated, the person (if any) nominated by the company.

(3) In the case of different persons being nominated, any director, member or creditor of the company may, within 7 days after the date on which the nomination was made by the creditors, apply to the court for an order either—

   (a)   directing that the person nominated as liquidator by the company shall be liquidator instead of or jointly with the person nominated by the creditors, or

   (b)   appointing some other person to be liquidator instead of the person nominated by the creditors.

(4) The court shall grant an application under subsection (3) made by the holder of a qualifying floating charge in respect of the company's property (within the meaning of paragraph 14 of Schedule B1) unless the court thinks it right to refuse the application because of the particular circumstances of the case.

Notes

S 100(1)–(3) Appointment of Liquidator

Both the company and the creditors may nominate a liquidator at their respective meetings though the creditors' choice of liquidator prevails over that of the members. See also IR 1986 r 4.101 for the certification of the appointment. A liquidator in a voluntary liquidation is not an officer of the court: *Re T H Knitwear (Wholesale) Ltd* (1988) 4 BCC 102.

S 100(4) Rights of Qualifying Floating Charge Holder

This provision ensures that the holder of a qualifying floating charge (IA 1986 Sch B1 para 14) will have its nominee appointed as liquidator unless the court can be persuaded otherwise '*...because of the particular circumstances of the case*'; see also the notes to Sch B1 para 36, para 17. The burden to prove the *'particular circumstances'* appears to be on the party supporting the company's or the creditors' nominee. The aim is to ensure that a voluntary liquidation cannot be initiated (IA 1986 s 84(2A)) nor progressed without the qualifying floating chargeholder being given an opportunity to secure its nominee as liquidator.

1.119

101 Appointment of liquidation committee

(1) The creditors at the meeting to be held under section 98 or at any subsequent meeting may, if they think fit, appoint a committee ('the liquidation committee') of not more than 5 persons to exercise the functions conferred on it by or under this Act.

(2) If such a committee is appointed, the company may, either at the meeting at which the resolution for voluntary winding up is passed or at any time subsequently in general meeting, appoint such number of persons as they think fit to act as members of the committee, not exceeding 5.

(3) However, the creditors may, if they think fit, resolve that all or any of the persons so appointed by the company ought not to be members of the liquidation committee; and if the creditors so resolve—
   (a) the persons mentioned in the resolution are not then, unless the court otherwise directs, qualified to act as members of the committee; and
   (b) on any application to the court under this provision the court may, if it thinks fit, appoint other persons to act as such members in place of the persons mentioned in the resolution.

(4) In Scotland, the liquidation committee has, in addition to the powers and duties conferred and imposed on it by this Act, such of the powers and duties of commissioners on a bankrupt estate as may be conferred and imposed on liquidation committees by the rules.

Notes

S 101

The liquidation committee is intended to provide creditors with an ability to exercise some control over the administration of the liquidation. The liquidator is under a specific obligation to report to the liquidation committee matters which may concern the creditors though the liquidator is released from that obligation in certain circumstances IR 1986 r 4.155(1), (2). The detailed rules in relation to the liquidation committee appear in IR 1986 r 4.151 ff.

S 101(2)

The members of the liquidation committee are fiduciaries with respect to the company's assets and may not be involved in any transaction involving the company's assets without the leave of the court or of the liquidation committee: see IR 1986 r 4.170, *Re Gallard* (1896) 1 QB 68 and *Re F T Hawkins & Co Ltd* [1952] Ch 881, where the costs of solicitors retained by the committee were disallowed because an employee of those solicitors was a member of the committee.

1.120

102 Creditors' meeting where winding up converted under s 96

Where, in the case of a winding up which was, under section 96 in Chapter III, converted to a creditors' voluntary winding up, a creditors' meeting is held in accordance with section 95, any appointment made or committee established by that meeting is deemed to have been made or established by a meeting held in accordance with section 98 in this Chapter.

Notes

S 102

This section provides for the avoidance of doubt that where a members' voluntary winding up has been converted into a creditors' voluntary winding up, any appointment of a liquidator or establishment of a liquidation committee is deemed to have been made by the first meeting of creditors.

1.121

103 Cesser of directors' powers

On the appointment of a liquidator, all the powers of the directors cease, except so far as the liquidation committee (or, if there is no such committee, the creditors) sanction their continuance.

Notes

S 103

The passing of a resolution to wind up does not cause an automatic cessation of office of the director: see IA 1986 s 114(2) and (3); *Midland Counties District Bank Ltd v Attwood* [1905] 1 Ch 357; *Reigate v Union Manufacturing Company (Ramsbottom) Ltd* [1981] 1 KB 592; *Re Fairbairn Engineering Co* [1893] 3 Ch 450 where it was held that a company in liquidation could in a general meeting elect directors and sanction the exercise by them of the power of enforcing calls by sale or forfeiture. However, the powers of the directors do cease unless sanction under this provision is obtained. It would be unusual for a liquidator to sanction the continuance of the directors' powers but there may be situations where a power under the articles of association can only be exercised by the directors.

1.122

104 Vacancy in office of liquidator

If a vacancy occurs, by death, resignation or otherwise, in the office of a liquidator (other than a liquidator appointed by, or by the direction of, the court) the creditors may fill the vacancy.

Notes

S 104

If the court has made an appointment under IA 1986 s 100(3), or an appointment is sought as part of a block transfer under IA 1986 s 108 (*see notes to* Practice Direction: Insolvency Proceedings para 1.6(2) (*Civil Procedure Vol 2 Section 3E*), an application would have to be made to the court.

1.123

105 Meetings of company and creditors at each year's end

(1) If the winding up continues for more than one year, the liquidator shall summon a general meeting of the company and a meeting of the creditors at the end of the first year from the commencement of the winding up, and of each succeeding year, or at the first convenient date within 3 months from the end of the year or such longer period as the Secretary of State may allow.

(2) The liquidator shall lay before each of the meetings an account of his acts and dealings and of the conduct of the winding up during the preceding year.

(3) If the liquidator fails to comply with this section, he is liable to a fine.

(4) Where under section 96 a members' voluntary winding up has become a creditors' voluntary winding up, and the creditors' meeting under section 95 is held 3 months or less before the end of the first year from the commencement of the winding up, the liquidator is not required by this section to summon a meeting of creditors at the end of that year.

Notes

S 105

If the liquidator refuses to summon the meeting an application could be made under IA 1986 s 112 for a suitable direction. There is similar provision in a members' voluntary liquidation for the holding of a members' meeting only: IA 1986 s 93.

1.124

106 Final meeting prior to dissolution

(1) As soon as the company's affairs are fully wound up, the liquidator shall make up an account of the winding up, showing how it has been

conducted and the company's property has been disposed of, and there-upon shall call a general meeting of the company and a meeting of the creditors for the purpose of laying the account before the meetings and giving an explanation of it.

(2) Each such meeting shall be called by advertisement in the Gazette specifying the time, place and object of the meeting, and published at least one month before it.

(3) Within one week after the date of the meetings (or, if they are not held on the same date, after the date of the later one) the liquidator shall send to the registrar of companies a copy of the account, and shall make a return to him of the holding of the meetings and of their dates.

(4) If the copy is not sent or the return is not made in accordance with subsection (3), the liquidator is liable to a fine and, for continued contravention, to a daily default fine.

(5) However, if a quorum is not present at either such meeting, the liquidator shall, in lieu of the return required by subsection (3), make a return that the meeting was duly summoned and that no quorum was present; and upon such return being made the provisions of that subsection as to the making of the return are, in respect of that meeting, deemed complied with.

(6) If the liquidator fails to call a general meeting of the company or a meeting of the creditors as required by this section, he is liable to a fine.

Notes

S 106

In order to be fully wound up, not all the company's assets need be realised provided the liquidator has done all he can to achieve that result: see *Re London and Caledonian Marine Insurance Co* (1879) 11 Ch D 140; *Re Wilmott Trading Ltd* [2000] BCC 321. The liquidator is to make up his final account of the liquidation 'as soon as the company's affairs are fully wound up'. It is sufficient that the account is made up as soon as the affairs are fully wound up so far as the liquidator is aware: see *Re Cornish Manures Ltd* [1967] 1 WLR 807 where the liquidator became aware of a further demand after the final meeting, and sent his account with a note relating to the demand to the Registrar of Companies. It was held that the dissolution of the company was not void.

For the corresponding provisions in members' voluntary winding up, see IA 1986 s 94.

Chapter V
Provisions Applying to Both Kinds of Voluntary Winding Up

1.125

107 Distribution of company's property

Subject to the provisions of this Act as to preferential payments, the company's property in a voluntary winding up shall on the winding up be applied in satisfaction of the company's liabilities pari passu and, subject

> to that application, shall (unless the articles otherwise provide) be distributed among the members according to their rights and interests in the company.

Notes

Introduction

This section expresses the fundamental principle of an insolvent winding up: namely, that the company's assets are to be collected in, realised and then (after payment of claims afforded priority) applied pari passu in satisfaction of the company's liabilities. This is the essence of the statutory scheme for the collective enforcement of debts. The debts are left unaffected by the winding up, but the rights of the creditors are restricted to collective enforcement in accordance with the provisions of the statutory scheme: see *Wight v Eckhardt Marine Gmbh* [2004] 1 AC 147.

The Statutory Scheme

The statutory scheme has a number of features (see generally *Re HIH Casualty & General Insurance Ltd* [2006] 2 All ER 671 and *(in the Court of Appeal)* [2006] EWCA Civ 732, a case dealing with the power of the court to order the transmission of assets to a liquidator in the place of the principal liquidation, where the winding up in England is ancillary):

- All creditors, wherever situated, as at the commencement of the winding up (other than those specifically excluded by the provisions of, for example, IR 1986 r 12.3) are entitled to prove in the winding up.
- With specific and limited exceptions (for example, the special regime applicable to insurance companies, and the 'cut-through' rights conferred by the Third Party (Rights against Insurers) Act 1930), there is no ring fencing of the company's assets to satisfy the claims of particular creditors.
- Subject to those exceptions, and limited categories of preferential claims, distribution is on a pari passu basis.
- The company's assets are held on terms that they are to be applied in accordance with the statutory scheme: see *Ayerst v C&K (Construction) Ltd* [1976] AC 167; *Mitchell v Carter* [1997] 1 BCLC 673 at 686; *Re Polly Peck International plc (No 2)* [1998] 2 BCLC 185 at 201. However, a creditor does not acquire a proprietary interest in the company's property merely because the company is in liquidation: *Banque Nationelle de Paris plc v Montman* [2000] 1 BCLC 576.
- The scheme confers personal rights on creditors which may in an appropriate case be enforced by that creditor against a liquidator in an action for breach of statutory duty: see *Pulsford v Devenish* [1903] 2 Ch 625; *James Smith & Sons (Norwood) v Goodman* [1936] Ch 216; *IRC v Goldblatt* [1972] Ch 498.

Mandatory Nature of the Statutory Scheme

The statutory scheme is mandatory and cannot be departed from, except to a very limited degree: see *Re Bank of Credit & Commerce International (No 10)* [1997] Ch 213; *Re HIH Casualty & General Insurance Ltd* [2006] 2 All ER 671. On the appeal of the HIH decision the Court of Appeal made clear that the court has a discretion under IA 1986 s 426, to order the transmission of assets to a place (out of the jurisdiction) where a 'principal' liquidation is being conducted, even though the effect of such order might be to interfere with the statutory scheme imposed on those assets by IA 1986: [2006] EWCA Civ 732, [2006] All ER (D) 65 (Jun). Nor may the scheme be varied by contractual arrangement: see *National Westminster Bank Ltd v Halesowen Presswork & Assemblies Ltd* [1972] AC 785; *British Eagle International Air Lines Ltd v Cie Nationale Air France* [1975] 1 WLR 758.

However, a creditor may validly subordinate its rights in a winding up, provided that the agreement does not adversely affect the rights of other third parties on insolvency: see *Re*

Maxwell Communications Corporation plc (No 3) [1993] BCC 369; *North Atlantic Insurance Company Ltd v Nationwide General Insurance Company* [2004] EWCA Civ 423, [2004] 2 All ER (Comm) 351.

The Company's Assets

The statutory scheme applies to the company's assets. It does not apply to those held by the company on trust for third parties: see for example *Barclays Bank Ltd v Quistclose Investments Ltd* [1970] AC 567; *Twinsectra Ltd v Yardley* [2002] 2 AC 164.

The Order of Distribution

The order of payments (not all of which are described in s 107) are:
- Expenses and remuneration are paid out in priority to all other claims: IA 1986 s 115.
- Preferential claims: for these, see IA 1986 s 386 and 387.
- The company's ordinary unsecured creditors whose debts are provable pursuant to IR 1986 r 12.3 and 13.12. See IR 1986 r 4.182A for the rules regarding proof and payment of debts in a members' voluntary winding up. See IR 1986 r 4.73 onwards and IR 1986 r 4.180 for the equivalent rules applicable in a creditors' voluntary winding up.
- Possibly, the company's ordinary unsecured creditors whose debts are not provable for any reason: see *Re T&N Ltd* [2005] EWHC 2870 (Ch), [2006] BPIR 532 at paragraphs 107 and 108, and see the notes to IA 1986 s 73.

Subject to adjustment between their rights, any surplus goes to members.

1.126

108 Appointment or removal of liquidator by the court

(1) If from any cause whatever there is no liquidator acting, the court may appoint a liquidator.

(2) The court may, on cause shown, remove a liquidator and appoint another.

Notes

S 108(2) Removal of Liquidator

This places a burden on the applicant to show cause why the liquidator should be removed. In order to effect the removal of a liquidator the court need only be satisfied that the removal is for the general advantage of those interested in the assets of the company, notwithstanding that no personal misconduct or unfitness could be shown on the part of the liquidator. In such cases it might be appropriate to remove a liquidator even though nothing could be said against him or her either personally or in his or her conduct of the particular liquidation: *Re Keypak Homecare Ltd* (1987) 3 BCC 558, *Sisu Capital Fund Ltd v Tucker* [2006] BPIR 154, para 82ff. Good cause for the removal must be shown and it is not sufficient to establish simply that the liquidator has made a wrong decision: *Re Shruth Ltd* [2005] BPIR 1455. However, it is not necessary to prove a breach of duty: *Re Buildlead Ltd* [2004] BPIR 1139, [2005] BCC 138.

In the event that a liquidator has to cease practising due to ill health, disqualification or retirement, the court has jurisdiction to remove the outgoing liquidator and appoint a new one. In most cases, the liquidator will also be appointed to other offices in various insolvencies, both corporate and personal in various courts throughout the country. The High Court has the power to make a single order removing the office-holder from his various appointments and replacing him or her in each case with one or more insolvency practitioners: *Re Bullard & Taplin Ltd* [1996] BCC 973; *Re a Licence Holder, Abbot* [1997] BCC 666. See also para 1.6(2) Practice

Direction: Insolvency Proceedings, (Civil Procedure Vol 2 Section 3E). In *Darrell v Miller* [2003] EWHC 2811 (Ch), [2004] BPIR 470 the court refused to backdate a transfer order.

In *Supperstone v Auger* [1999] BPIR 152 Park J made an order replacing an insolvency practitioner in multiple appointments (which appointments included offices held in pre–1986 insolvencies). Contained in the report is a very useful table setting out the various statutory sources of jurisdiction for a block order together with explanatory notes.

It is particularly important when making an application to consider the requirements of para 1.6(5) and (6) Practice Direction: Insolvency Proceedings (Civil Procedure Vol 2 Section 3E) as to the provision of relevant schedules and supporting evidence. Para 1.6(3) of the Practice Direction identifies various persons who can make an application. In addition, prior to the Practice Direction containing specific provisions in relation to 'block transfers', applications had been made by others including a former liquidator (*Re A J Adams (Builders) Ltd* [1991] BCC 62) and the responsible licensing body of the incumbent liquidator (*Re Stella Metals Ltd* [1997] BCC 626). The application should be served on the liquidator who is to be removed: *Clements v Udal* [2001] BCC 658.

In *Re Equity Nominees Ltd* [2000] BCC 84 Neuberger J held that in order for the court to determine whether a removal and replacement order should be made, the question that should be asked is whether the convening of the meetings required by the IR 1986 would serve any useful purpose. If the court was satisfied that the convening of the meetings would not serve any useful purpose, then it should adopt a practical and sensible approach of avoiding the expense of the statutory resignation procedure (provided the order was drafted in terms to protect the interests of creditors by imposing a requirement on the applicant to send a letter in relation to each insolvency explaining the effect of the order and informing each creditor of their right to require the applicant to comply with the requirements of IA 1986 r 4.108(3) or r 6.126(2)).

In multiple removal and replacement applications the costs orders that have been made are against the various estates divided in equal proportions between the cases involved. In *Re Equity Nominees Ltd* itself (in circumstances where the office holder wished to retire) the following costs order was made:

'(1)*insofar as the costs are referable to an individual insolvency, as costs and expenses of each individual insolvency;*

(2)*in relation to the remainder of the costs which are not so referable, by apportioning that sum equally as between the various insolvencies as part of the costs and expenses of each insolvency;*

provided that in no circumstances should the costs payable in relation to any individual insolvency or voluntary arrangement exceed ten per cent of the value of the realised assets in that particular insolvency or voluntary arrangement.'

In *Saville v Gerrard* [2004] EWHC 1363, [2004] BPIR 1332, however, where the orders sought were for the benefit of the insolvency practitioner's firm, the court made no order made as to costs. Following appointment by the court the liquidator must file a statement of qualification and consent in court and notify the creditors: IR 1986 r 4.103 and 4.140.

1.127

109 Notice by liquidator of his appointment

(1) The liquidator shall, within 14 days after his appointment, publish in the Gazette and deliver to the registrar of companies for registration a notice of his appointment in the form prescribed by statutory instrument made by the Secretary of State.

(2) If the liquidator fails to comply with this section, he is liable to a fine and, for continued contravention, to a daily default fine.

————

Notes

S 109

The winding up resolution has to be gazetted (IA 1986 s 85) and this provision also requires the appointment of the liquidator to be gazetted. Unless it is gazetted the appointment will not have been 'officially notified' and the effect of CA 1985 s 42(1) may be to prevent the company relying on the appointment having taken place. CA 1985 s 42 provides amongst other things that: '*A company is not entitled to rely against other persons on the happening of any of the following events – (a) ... the appointment of a liquidator in a voluntary winding up of the company ... if the event had not been officially notified at the material time and is not shown by the company to have been known at that time to the person concerned, or if the material time fell on or before the fifteenth day after the date of official notification (or, where the fifteenth day was a non-business day, on or before the next day that was not) and it is shown that the person concerned was unavoidably prevented from knowing of the event at that time.*' CA 1985 s 711(2)(b) provides that 'official notification' means, in relation to the appointment of a liquidator in a voluntary winding up, the notification of it in the Gazette under IA 1986 s 109.'

————

1.128

110 Acceptance of shares, etc, as consideration for sale of company property

(1) This section applies, in the case of a company proposed to be, or being, wound up voluntarily, where the whole or part of the company's business or property is proposed to be transferred or sold
  (a)   to another company ('the transferee company'), whether or not the latter is a company within the meaning of the Companies Act, or
  (b)   to a limited liability partnership (the 'transferee limited liability partnership').

(2) With the requisite sanction, the liquidator of the company being, or proposed to be, wound up ('the transferor company') may receive, in compensation or part compensation for the transfer or [sale—
  (a)   in the case of the transferee company, shares, policies or other like interests in the transferee company for distribution among the members of the transferor company, or
  (b)   in the case of the transferee limited liability partnership, membership in the transferee limited liability partnership for distribution among the members of the transferor company].

(3) The sanction requisite under subsection (2) is—
  (a)   in the case of a members' voluntary winding up, that of a special resolution of the company, conferring either a general authority on the liquidator or an authority in respect of any particular arrangement, and
  (b)   in the case of a creditors' voluntary winding up, that of either the court or the liquidation committee.

(4) Alternatively to subsection (2), the liquidator may (with that sanction) enter into any other arrangement whereby the members of the transferor company may—

    (a)   in the case of the transferee company, in lieu of receiving cash, shares, policies or other like interests (or in addition thereto) participate in the profits of, or receive any other benefit from, the transferee company, or

    (b)   in the case of the transferee limited liability partnership, in lieu of receiving cash or membership (or in addition thereto), participate in some other way in the profits of, or receive any other benefit from, the transferee limited liability partnership.

(5) A sale or arrangement in pursuance of this section is binding on members of the transferor company.

(6) A special resolution is not invalid for purposes of this section by reason that it is passed before or concurrently with a resolution for voluntary winding up or for appointing liquidators; but, if an order is made within a year for winding up the company by the court, the special resolution is not valid unless sanctioned by the court.

This provision is made use of in reconstructions or amalgamations. Provision is made for a dissenting member to require the liquidator to purchase the interest of the dissenting member, section 111.

Notes

S 110

A liquidator may wish to sell the whole or part of the business of the company to another company (described as the transferee company) in return for shares (or the equivalent) in the transferee company. For the position of a dissenting member, see IA 1986 s 111.

1.129

111 Dissent from arrangement under s 110

(1) This section applies in the case of a voluntary winding up where, for the purposes of section 110(2) or (4), there has been passed a special resolution of the transferor company providing the sanction requisite for the liquidator under that section.

(2) If a member of the transferor company who did not vote in favour of the special resolution expresses his dissent from it in writing, addressed to the liquidator and left at the company's registered office within 7 days after the passing of the resolution, he may require the liquidator either to abstain from carrying the resolution into effect or to purchase his interest at a price to be determined by agreement or by arbitration under this section.

(3) If the liquidator elects to purchase the member's interest, the purchase money must be paid before the company is dissolved and be raised by the liquidator in such manner as may be determined by special resolution.

(4) For purposes of an arbitration under this section, the provisions of the Companies Clauses Consolidation Act 1845 or, in the case of a winding up in Scotland, the Companies Clauses Consolidation (Scotland) Act 1845 with respect to the settlement of disputes by arbitration are incorporated with this Act, and—

   (a)   in the construction of those provisions this Act is deemed the special Act and 'the company' means the transferor company, and

   (b)   any appointment by the incorporated provisions directed to be made under the hand of the secretary or any two of the directors may be made in writing by the liquidator (or, if there is more than one liquidator, then any two or more of them).

Notes

S 111

A member who dissents to an arrangement under IA 1986 s 110 has the right to have his or her interest bought out at a price to be determined by agreement or arbitration. The relevant mechanism is set out in IA 1986 s 111.

1.130

112 Reference of questions to court

(1) The liquidator or any contributory or creditor may apply to the court to determine any question arising in the winding up of a company, or to exercise, as respects the enforcing of calls or any other matter, all or any of the powers which the court might exercise if the company were being wound up by the court.

(2) The court, if satisfied that the determination of the question or the required exercise of power will be just and beneficial, may accede wholly or partially to the application on such terms and conditions as it thinks fit, or may make such other order on the application as it thinks just.

(3) A copy of an order made by virtue of this section staying the proceedings in the winding up shall forthwith be forwarded by the company, or otherwise as may be prescribed, to the registrar of companies, who shall enter it in his records relating to the company.

Notes

S 112

The nature of voluntary winding up is that is takes place under the control of either the members or the creditors and does not involve court proceedings. However a dissatisfied creditor who has a genuine concern may petition for compulsory liquidation notwithstanding that the company is already in voluntary liquidation: see notes to IA 1986 s 125.

IA 1986 s 112 enables a liquidator, creditor or contributory to apply to court for directions without taking the compulsory liquidation route: *Re Ricksmith (Manufacturing) Ltd* [1999] 2 BCLC 686. Alternatively, the applicant may seek within the voluntary liquidation the exercise of a power normally only exercisable in a compulsory liquidation: *Re Stephen Walters & Sons Ltd* [1926] WN 236. However, a creditor may not apply for a private examination of a director under this section when IA 1986 s 236 only allows a specified class of persons to apply for private examination; it would be contrary to the whole scheme of IA 1986 to have wider powers available in voluntary liquidation than in compulsory liquidation: *Re James McHale Automobiles Ltd* [1997] BCC 202. An application for pre-action disclosure under this provision could be entertained if it was for a legitimate purpose of the winding up *Commissioners of Inland Revenue v Blueslate Ltd* (Ch D Hart J, 23 September 2003). A secured creditor may bring an application for a declaration as to the true construction of the debenture and for directions: *Re Alfred Priestman & Co* [1936] 2 All ER 1340.

Although the jurisdiction to give directions is a useful one, and a means by which disputed issues may be determined, a liquidator should only apply for directions in cases of real doubt. The court may refuse to entertain an application where the liquidator has funds and the matter can best be dealt with by ordinary litigation: *Re Stetzel Thomson & Co Ltd* (1988) 4 BCC 74. Moreover, the jurisdiction is not to be used for the purposes of seeking directions on matters which are within the commercial judgment of the liquidator: see *Re T&D Industries plc* [2000] 1 BCLC 471.

It is possible for a liquidator to make a single application for directions under IA 1986 s 112 entitled '*In the Matter of [listing names of all the relevant companies]*', rather than make a separate application in respect of each company, provided that the same subject matter of the application is related to all the companies included in the single application: *Re William Pickles plc* [1996] BCC 408; see also *Saville v Gerrard* [2005] BCC 433.

1.131

113 Court's power to control proceedings (Scotland)

If the court, on the application of the liquidator in the winding up of a company registered in Scotland, so directs, no action or proceeding shall be proceeded with or commenced against the company except by leave of the court and subject to such terms as the court may impose.

1.132

114 No liquidator appointed or nominated by company

(1) This section applies where, in the case of a voluntary winding up, no liquidator has been appointed or nominated by the company.

(2) The powers of the directors shall not be exercised, except with the sanction of the court or (in the case of a creditors' voluntary winding up) so far as may be necessary to secure compliance with sections 98 (creditors' meeting) and 99 (statement of affairs), during the period before the appointment or nomination of a liquidator of the company.

(3) Subsection (2) does not apply in relation to the powers of the directors—
  (a) to dispose of perishable goods and other goods the value of which is likely to diminish if they are not immediately disposed of, and
  (b) to do all such other things as may be necessary for the protection of the company's assets.

> (4) If the directors of the company without reasonable excuse fail to comply with this section, they are liable to a fine.

Notes

S 114(1)–(3)

Where no liquidator has been appointed or nominated by the company in a voluntary winding up, the directors' powers are accordingly restricted. Where a transaction is entered into on behalf of the company by directors outside these restricted powers it is invalid, except that it may be possible for a third party to argue that it dealt with the director in good faith and could not reasonably have known about the resolution to place the company into liquidation: *Re a Company (No 006341 of 1992), ex parte B Ltd* [1994] 1 BCLC 225.

1.133

115 Expenses of voluntary winding up

All expenses properly incurred in the winding up, including the remuneration of the liquidator, are payable out of the company's assets in priority to all other claims.

Notes

S 115

This provision does not define what constitutes an 'expense'; the definitive statement of what is regarded as an expense of the liquidation is provided by IR 1986 r 4.218: *Re Toshoku Finance plc* [2002] UKHL 6, [2002] 1 WLR 671. Such expenses rank above any claims by the preferential creditors (for which see IA 1986 s 175), the creditors generally (excepting fixed charge holders) and the members.

The concept of a liquidation expense as set out in IR 1986 r 4.218 has been expanded by equity: *Re Lundy Granite Co* (1871) 6 Ch App 462. For instance, it is clear that costs incurred prior to liquidation may be considered as expenses of the liquidation if they were incurred for the purpose of putting the company into voluntary liquidation: *Re A V Sorge & Co Ltd* (1986) 2 BCC 99 at 306. Where a liquidator takes possession of premises for the purpose of carrying on the company's business this will be an expense of the liquidation: *Re Oak Pitts Colliery Co* (1882) 21 Ch D 322. Where, however, a liquidator took formal possession of leased premises simply to preserve the assets the rent was not a liquidation expense: *Re ABC Coupler and Engineering Co Ltd (No 3)* [1970] 1 WLR 702.

Costs may be charged as expenses against assets which the company holds on trust for another where the liquidator has properly incurred costs in investigating the status of the assets: *Re Berkeley Applegate (Investment Consultants) Ltd (No 2)* (1988) 4 BCC 279 cf *Tom Wise Ltd v Fillimore* [1999] BCC 129. It will not be proper to investigate beneficial ownership where that matter is being determined in other proceedings; in the meantime, however, where the liquidator incurs costs administering the relevant assets he or she should be entitled to the costs of that administration: *Re Local London Residential Ltd* [2004] EWHC 144, [2004] BPIR 599.

The company's assets under IA 1986 s 115 do not include assets subject to a charge which as created was a floating charge notwithstanding that it crystallises prior to the commencement of the liquidation. Therefore liquidation expenses are not payable from assets the subject of a floating charge whether or not it has crystallised prior to or after liquidation: *Buchler v Talbot (Re Leyland Daf Ltd)* [2004] 2 AC 298 (overruling *Re Barleycorn Enterprises Ltd* [1970] Ch

465). See further the commentary to IA 1986 s 175 for further commentary on the effect of *Buchler v Talbot* and the proposed reversal of the same in this respect in Clause 1246 the Companies Bill 2006.

Where the company's assets are insufficient to pay all the expenses, they are paid out in the order of priority listed in IR 1986 r 4.218 unless otherwise directed by the court in a voluntary liquidation (IA 1986 s 112 and 156; *Re Linda Marie Ltd* [1989] BCLC 46) or in a compulsory liquidation (IA 1986 s 156, IR 1986 r 4.220). For example, in *Re Grey Marlin Ltd* [1999] 2 BCLC 658 (which concerned a compulsory liquidation) the court ordered under IA 1986 s 156 that tax liabilities arising during the course of trading in a liquidation were to be paid in priority to all other expenses in the liquidation. Corporation tax which is chargeable on a company's post-liquidation profits, including income which has to be brought into the computation of those profits even though it has not been received and will never be received, is payable as an expense of the winding up, as is council tax: *Kahn & anr v IRC* [2001] BCC 373.

1.134

116 Saving for certain rights

The voluntary winding up of a company does not bar the right of any creditor or contributory to have it wound up by the court; but in the case of an application by a contributory the court must be satisfied that the rights of the contributories will be prejudiced by a voluntary winding up.

Notes

S 116

The burden of proof in persuading the court to grant an order if a voluntary liquidation is in progress is on the petitioner who has to show a special reason why a compulsory liquidation should be ordered: *Re Zirceram Ltd* [2000] BCC 1048. The court is more cautious about ordering a compulsory winding up where a voluntary winding up is already in place given that the class remedy of liquidation is already being enforced: *Re J D Swain Ltd* [1965] 1 WLR 909 (see further the notes to IA 1986 s 125). Where a voluntary liquidation is not yet in progress the creditors supporting such a course of action must give their reasons at the hearing of the winding up petition for their opposition to a compulsory liquidation; however, even where there was a voluntary liquidation in existence at the date when the court was asked to make a winding-up order, the court might in appropriate circumstances properly exercise its discretion in favour of making a compulsory winding-up order notwithstanding the opposition of the majority of creditors: *Re Television Parlour plc* (1988) 4 BCC 95.

Part IV
Winding Up of Companies Registered under the Companies Acts

Chapter VI
Winding Up by the Court

Jurisdiction (England and Wales)

1.135

117 High Court and county court jurisdiction

(1) The High Court has jurisdiction to wind up any company registered in England and Wales.

(2) Where the amount of a company's share capital paid up or credited as paid up does not exceed £120,000, then (subject to this section) the county court of the district in which the company's registered office is situated has concurrent jurisdiction with the High Court to wind up the company.

(3) The money sum for the time being specified in subsection (2) is subject to increase or reduction by order under section 416 in Part XV.

(4) The Lord Chancellor *may by order* [may, with the concurrence of the Lord Chief Justice, by order] in a statutory instrument exclude a county court from having winding-up jurisdiction, and for the purposes of that jurisdiction may attach its district, or any part thereof, to any other county court, and may by statutory instrument revoke or vary any such order.

In exercising the powers of this section, the Lord Chancellor shall provide that a county court is not to have winding-up jurisdiction unless it has for the time being jurisdiction for the purposes of Parts VIII to XI of this Act (individual insolvency).

(5) Every court in England and Wales having winding-up jurisdiction has for the purposes of that jurisdiction all the powers of the High Court; and every prescribed officer of the court shall perform any duties which an officer of the High Court may discharge by order of a judge of that court or otherwise in relation to winding up.

(6) For the purposes of this section, a company's 'registered office' is the place which has longest been its registered office during the 6 months immediately preceding the presentation of the petition for winding up.

(7) This section is subject to Article 3 of the EC Regulation (jurisdiction under EC Regulation)

(8) The Lord Chief Justice may nominate a judicial office holder (as defined in section 109(4) of the Constitutional Reform Act 2005) to exercise his functions under this section

Notes

S 117

Practitioners tend to use the High Court for winding up proceedings although in some cases it would in practice be more convenient to use the County Court. The presentation of a winding up petition in a County Court ought to be recorded on the central database maintained by the Companies Court called 'the Central Registry of Winding up Petitions': para 20.19 of the Chancery Guide, October 2005, Civil Procedure 2006, Vol 2, para 1A-166. Provided the County Court petition is properly recorded, the presentation of another petition against the same company in another court is usually avoided. If different petitioners present petitions, one in the Companies Court and the other in the County Court, then if the former makes a winding up order first the County Court proceedings will be transferred to it and stayed *Re Audio Systems Ltd* [1965] 1 WLR 1096. If a petition is presented in the Companies Court after the petition in the County Court the latter proceedings will be transferred to the Companies Court and an order will be made on both petitions *Re Filby Bros (Provender) Ltd* [1958] 1 WLR 683; in such a case the winding up will backdate to the date of the County Court petition. Whether or not a petition has been presented can be checked personally by attendance at the Companies Court General Office, or by phoning the Companies Court on 0906 754 0043. A party dealing with a company of doubtful solvency would be well advised to use this facility to avoid the problems which might otherwise arise under IA 1986 s 127: see for example *Re Dewrun Limited* [2002] BCC 57 and the notes to IA 1986 s 127.

S 117(1), (2)

A company's registered office is the place which has longest been its registered office during the six months immediately preceding the winding up petition: IA 1986 s 117(6). If an application is made during the course of a voluntary winding up (for instance under the general enabling provision IA 1986 s 112) then the relevant court is that which has jurisdiction to wind up the company. For the definition of 'the court' see IA 1986 s 251 which adopts the definition in CA 1985 s 744. In a directors' disqualification context the appropriate date for determining jurisdiction was held to be the date when proceedings were initiated rather than the date of liquidation: *Re Lichfield Freight Terminal Ltd* [1997] BCC 11.

A company without a share capital cannot be wound up in the County Court: *Re North of England Iron SS Insurance Association* [1900] 1 Ch 481. If the registered office of the company is in central London the petition must be presented in the High Court: *Re Southsea Garage Ltd* (1911) 55 SJ 314. District Registries do not have jurisdiction unless specifically authorised, although IA 1986 s 118 may then be relied upon to validate the proceedings: *Re Pleatfine Ltd* [1983] BCLC 102, (1983) 1 BCC 98, 942. The High Court jurisdiction is exercised by the judges of the Chancery Division nominated by the Lord Chancellor and it is then referred to as 'the Companies Court': *Re Shilena Hosiery Co Ltd* [1979] 2 All ER 6, 9 per Brightman J, *Fabric Sales Ltd v Eratex Ltd* [1984] 1 WLR 863, *Re Tasbian Ltd (No 2)* [1990] BCC 322, 324 per Dillon LJ. Companies Court matters are listed for hearing on any day of the week and a Companies Judge is no longer designated to deal with company matters: Practice Statement: Companies Judge [2000] BCC 256; para 20.8 of the Chancery Guide, October 2005, Civil Procedure 2006, Vol 2, para 1A-160. All judges of the High Court have equal authority and jurisdiction unless otherwise stated: Supreme Court Act 1981 s 4(3), 5(5) and 61(6). Jurisdiction in winding up proceedings is assigned to the Chancery Division: see Supreme Court Act 1981 s 61(1) and Sch 1, *Re Shilena Hosiery Co Ltd* [1980] Ch 219 and the commentary to Applications under the Companies Act 1985, Civil Procedure 2006, Vol 2, para 2G-17).

S 117(4)

The County Courts with winding up jurisdiction are listed in the Civil Courts Order 1983, s 1 1983/713, art 10, Sch 3 as amended. The words in square brackets were inserted by the Constitutional Reform Act 2005 s 15

S 117(5)

Whilst the County Court is exercising its winding up jurisdiction it has the same powers as the High Court; thus if a matter falls solely within the winding up jurisdiction it is not relevant that the claim in question is beyond the normal County Court limit *Re F & E Stanton Ltd* [1928] 1 KB 464. However if a claim is brought by or against a company in liquidation which could have been brought were it not being wound up then the County Court is subject to the normal County Court limit *Re Ilkley Hotel Co* [1893] 1 QB 248.

S 117(7)

If the court is to open 'main' insolvency proceedings in England a winding up petition must state that the proceedings are 'main proceedings' within Art 3 EC Regulation Insolvency Proceedings 2000: see the commentary on the EC Regulation.

1.136

118 Proceedings taken in wrong court

(1) Nothing in section 117 invalidates a proceeding by reason of its being taken in the wrong court.

> (2) The winding up of a company by the court in England and Wales, or any proceedings in the winding up, may be retained in the court in which the proceedings were commenced, although it may not be the court in which they ought to have been commenced.

Notes

S 118(1)

Though the jurisdiction to validate appears wide (*Re Pleatfine Ltd* [1983] BCLC 102, (1983) 1 BCC 98, 942), the court is unlikely to exercise it where proceedings have been intentionally initiated in the wrong court *Re Brightmore, ex p May* (1884) 14 QBD 37.

S 118(2)

Apart from the power to allow the proceedings to continue (*Re Sankey Furniture Ltd* [1995] 2 BCLC 594) a transfer to the correct court may be ordered or the proceedings may be struck out: IR 1986 r 7.12.

1.137

119 Proceedings in county court; case stated for High Court

(1) If any question arises in any winding-up proceedings in a county court which all the parties to the proceedings, or which one of them and the judge of the court, desire to have determined in the first instance in the High Court, the judge shall state the facts in the form of a special case for the opinion of the High Court.

(2) Thereupon the special case and the proceedings (or such of them as may be required) shall be transmitted to the High Court for the purposes of the determination.

Notes

S 119(1)

The power to state a special case for the High Court is rarely used in practice. The more convenient course would be for the County Court Judge to transfer the proceedings to the High Court in their entirety: County Courts Act 1984 s 40(1) and 41(1); IR 1986 r 7.11. A transfer can be ordered before a winding up order is made: *Re Laxon & Co* [1892] 3 Ch 31. The reference to transferring the proceedings means the whole file and not just a part of the proceedings: IR 1986 r 7.11, 7.14 and r 7.30; *Re Kouyououmdjian* [1956] 1 WLR 558; *Re a Debtor (26A of 1975)* [1985] 1 WLR 6.

Jurisdiction (Scotland)

1.138

120 Court of Session and sheriff court jurisdiction

(1) The Court of Session has jurisdiction to wind up any company registered in Scotland.

(2) When the Court of Session is in vacation, the jurisdiction conferred on that court by this section may (subject to the provisions of this Part) be exercised by the judge acting as vacation judge ...

(3) Where the amount of a company's share capital paid up or credited as paid up does not exceed £120,000, the sheriff court of the sheriffdom in which the company's registered office is situated has concurrent jurisdiction with the Court of Session to wind up the company; but—
    (a)   the Court of Session may, if it thinks expedient having regard to the amount of the company's assets to do so—
        (i)   remit to sheriff court any petition presented to the Court of Session for winding up such a company, or
        (ii)   require such a petition presented to a sheriff court to be remitted to the Court of Session; and
    (b)   the Court of Session may require any such petition as abovementioned presented to one sheriff court to be remitted to another sheriff court; and
    (c)   in a winding up in the sheriff court the sheriff may submit a stated case for the opinion of the Court of Session on any question of law arising in that winding up.

(4) For purposes of this section, the expression 'registered office' means the place which has longest been the company's registered office during the 6 months immediately preceding the presentation of the petition for winding up.

(5) The money sum for the time being specified in subsection (3) is subject to increase or reduction by order under section 416 in Part XV.

1.139

121 Power to remit winding up to Lord Ordinary

(1) The Court of Session may, by Act of Sederunt, make provision for the taking of proceedings in a winding up before one of the Lords Ordinary; and, where provision is so made, the Lord Ordinary has, for the purposes of the winding up, all the powers and jurisdiction of the court.

(2) However, the Lord Ordinary may report to the Inner House any matter which may arise in the course of a winding up.

Grounds and effect of winding-up petition

1.140–1.141

122 Circumstances in which company may be wound up by the court

(1) A company may be wound up by the court if—
    (a)   the company has by special resolution resolved that the company be wound up by the court,
    (b)   being a public company which was registered as such on its original incorporation, the company has not been issued with a certificate under section 117 of the Companies Act (public company share capital requirements) and more than a year has expired since it was so registered,

(c) it is an old public company, within the meaning of the Consequential Provisions Act,

(d) the company does not commence its business within a year from its incorporation or suspends its business for a whole year,

(e) [except in the case of a private company limited by shares or by guarantee,] the number of members is reduced below 2,

(f) the company is unable to pay its debts,

(fa) at the time at which a moratorium for the company under section 1A comes to an end, no voluntary arrangement approved under Part I has effect in relation to the company,

(g) the court is of the opinion that it is just and equitable that the company should be wound up.

(2) In Scotland, a company which the Court of Session has jurisdiction to wind up may be wound up by the Court if there is subsisting a floating charge over property comprised in the company's property and undertaking, and the court is satisfied that the security of the creditor entitled to the benefit of the floating charge is in jeopardy.

For this purpose a creditor's security is deemed to be in jeopardy if the Court is satisfied that events have occurred or are about to occur which render it unreasonable in the creditor's interests that the company should retain power to dispose of the property which is subject to the floating charge.

Notes

S 122

Though the IA 1986 does not use the phrase 'compulsory liquidation' it is commonly used in practice to describe a 'winding up by the court'. The circumstances in which a company may be wound up by the court are not exhaustively stated by s 122; for example the official receiver may petition for the winding up of a company in voluntary liquidation under IA 1986 s 124(5) and the Secretary of State for Trade and Industry may petition on public interest grounds under IA 1986 s 124A. Notwithstanding that the appropriate circumstances are established, it remains a matter of discretion whether or not a winding up will be made: *Re Walter L Jacob Ltd* [1993] BCC 512. A petitioner may rely on any one or more of the circumstances stated in IA 1986 s 122 and the standard form petition includes in any event reference to the 'just and equitable' ground in addition to the specific grounds which are relied upon by a petitioner: Form 4.2, IR 1986 r 4.7 and Sch 4.

S 122(1)(a) Special resolution

This is seldom encountered in practice. If the requisite majority of members desire a liquidation, the company is more likely to go into voluntary liquidation, thereby avoiding the fees otherwise payable to the official receiver under Insolvency Regulations 1994 SI 1994/2507. Where a 75% majority cannot be obtained but a compulsory liquidation is thought desirable, the company may by ordinary resolution present a petition relying on the other sub-paragraphs of IA 1986 s 122.

S 122(1)(b), (c) Public companies

The insolvency regime generally does not differentiate between public and private companies. However the failure to obtain a trading certificate under CA 1985 s 117 within one year of incorporation or the failure of an old public company to re-register by 22 March 1982 are specific grounds for a compulsory liquidation of a public company

S 122(1)(d) Non-commencement of business

This is rarely encountered. A cheaper form of securing the dissolution of the company is to invoke the striking off procedure under CA 1985 s 652. Where the ground is relied upon the court will consider the interests of the majority shareholders: *Re Tomlin Patent Horse Shoe Co Ltd* (1866) 55 LT 314; where past delay is satisfactorily explained and it is not improbable that business will commence shortly the court is likely to refuse an order: *Re Metropolitan Rly Warehousing Co Ltd* (1867) 36 LJ CH 827. Where the non-commencement of business within a year of its incorporation is relied upon the court is unlikely to make an order unless it is clear that there is no prospect of the company carrying on business: *Re London and County Coal Co* (1866) LR 3 Eq 355; *Re Langham Skating Rink Co* (1877) 5 Ch D 669. The carrying on of business requires a substantive business activity and not the mere holding of directors' meetings: *Re Capital Fire Insurance Association* (1882) 21 ChD 209; nor simply litigating a claim: *Re Perfectair Holdings Ltd* [1990] BCLC 423.

Suspension of business

Something more than the cesser of trade for seasonal reasons is required *Re Tomlin Patent Horse Shoe Co Ltd* (1866) 55 LT 314 or suspension as a temporary measure *Re Middlesborough Assembly Rooms Co* (1880) 14 Ch D 104. The court will enquire whether the business has been abandoned in its entirety and the reasons why that has occurred (*Re Madrid & Valencia Rly Co, ex p James* (1850) 19 LJ Ch 260).

S 122(1)(e) Reduction in members

Personal liability may be incurred when the statutory minimum number of two members for a public company or an unlimited company is not complied with for a period of 6 months: CA 1985 s 24. This ground enables the remaining member to avoid losing the protection of the company's limited liability status by petitioning for its winding up. From 15 July 1992 a private company limited by shares or guarantee may be constituted with only one member: The Companies (Single Member Private Limited Companies) Regulations 1992, SI 1992/1699.

S 122(1)(f) Company is unable to pay its debts

In practice this is the most commonly relied upon ground of compulsory liquidation. Proof is required that the company is insolvent either on cash flow or a balance sheet basis. IA 1986 s 123 defines the circumstances in which a company is deemed to be insolvent; see the commentary to that section.

S 122(1)(fa) End of Moratorium

A moratorium under IA 2000 s 1A may come to an end in a variety of ways: IA 1986 Sch A1 para 8. But it is not simply the ending of a moratorium which will enable the court to make a winding up order. It must also be the case that no voluntary arrangement approved under IA 1986 Part 1 is in effect in relation to the company at the time of the ending of the moratorium. Presumably a voluntary arrangement has 'effect' in this context when the decision approving the voluntary arrangement has effect under IA 1986 Sch A1 para 36; see also IA 1986 Sch A1 para 37.

S 122(1)(g) Just and equitable

This is the ground on which a solvent company is usually wound up by the court on the petition of a 'contributory', which includes but is not limited to an existing member of the company: IA 1986 s 79. Though a creditor or a prospective/contingent creditor can petition on the just and equitable ground this would be highly unusual: *Re a Company (No 003028 of 1987)* (1987) 3 DCC 575, *Re Millenium Advanced Technology Ltd* [2004] 1 WLR 2177. A contributory petitioning on the just and equitable ground must show that he has a 'tangible interest' in the liquidation; ie that the company is solvent on a balance sheet basis so that there is some return contemplated for contributories. However it is not necessary to prove such an interest in certain circumstances, for example in the case of an insolvent unlimited company: *Re Norwich Yarn Co* (1850) 12 Beav 366; or where the petitioner is denied the necessary financial information to prove solvency: *Re Newman and Howard Ltd* [1962] Ch 257. The jurisdiction to make an order on this ground is wide and its categories are not closed: *Re St Piran Ltd* [1981] 1 WLR 1300 (*failure to comply with directions of the Take Over Panel*); *Re Perfectair Holdings Ltd* (1989) 5 BCC 837 (*prevention of an informal liquidation*). However there are well-recognised situations which give rise to this ground for winding up:

(i)   *Loss of substratum*

This applies where a company cannot pursue all or any of its 'main objects'. It is said that the company's 'substratum' has been lost: *Re German Date Coffee Co* (1882) 20 Ch D 169; *Re Kitson & Co Ltd* [1946] 1 All ER 435. As a matter of principle the members are entitled to liquidate the company: *Re Red Rock Gold Mining Co* (1889) 61 LT 785.

(ii)   *Impossibility*

Where there is no reasonable prospect of the company's main objects being attained the court may be wound up (*Davis & Co Ltd v Brunswick (Australia) Ltd* [1936] 1 All ER 299); the court is not required to find that the attainment of the main objects is absolutely impossible.

(iii)   *Illegality/fraud*

This enables a company to be wound up by the court where it is formed for an illegal or fraudulent purpose. The illegality may arise due to a change in the law: *Princess of Reuss v Bos* (1871) LR 5 HL 176. There must be some element of defrauding potential members or other substantive matters requiring investigation to justify a winding up order: *Re Thomas Edward Brinsmead & Sons Ltd* [1897] 1 Ch 45; *Re West Surrey Tanning Co* (1866) LR 2 Eq 737.

(iv)   *Inability to carry on business*

Where the management of a company cannot function properly or at all (often arising from a refusal of the directors to work together) the court may be prepared to wind up the company because of 'deadlock': *Re Yenidje Tobacco Co Ltd* [1916] 2 Ch 426. It is not necessary that actual deadlock be proved (*Re Davis and Collett Ltd* [1935] Ch 693) but something more than loose allegations of a breakdown in communication amongst the participators is required: *Re W R Willcocks & Co Ltd* [1974] Ch 163. The fact that the deadlock can as a matter of theory be broken will not prevent the making of an order, because the company may be unable to carry on its business even though voting power is not divided equally between the opposing factions: *Re American Pioneer Leather Co* [1918] 1 Ch 556.

(v)   *Quasi partnership*

In the leading case of *Ebrahimi v Westbourne Galleries Ltd* [1973] AC 360, 379, Lord Wilberforce referred to the phrase 'quasi partnership' as being convenient but also one that may cause confusion. It was convenient in the sense of neatly describing a company where one or more of the following factors are present: (a) it is formed or continued on the basis of a personal relationship involving mutual confidence; (b) there is an agreement that all or some of the shareholders will participate in the conduct of the business; (c) there is a restriction on the transfer of shares; see also *Strahan v Wilcock* [2006] BCC 320. In the case of a quasi partnership if a participant is excluded from management participation then it may be just and equitable to wind up the company: *Re A and BC Chewing Gum Ltd* [1975] 1 WLR 529. However, the availability of an alternative and more suitable remedy under CA 1985 s 459 or otherwise may be a good reason for declining to make such an order: *CVC/Opportunity Equity Partners Ltd v Demarco Alemida* [2002] BCC 684 (PC); IA 1986 s 125(2).

(vi)   *Misconduct/oppression*

The thrust of this ground is that the affairs of the company are being managed in a manner which is oppressive to the petitioner: *Loch v John Blackwood Ltd* [1924] AC 783. Before a member considers petitioning on this ground ihe must consider whether there is any alternative relief falling short of a winding up; in particular an unfair prejudice petition under CA 1985 s 459: IA 1986 s 125(2); *Re a Company No. 002567 of 1982* [1983] 1 WLR 927. Where a winding up is desired there is a substantial burden on the petitioner to prove oppression requiring, for example, proof of a series of serious breaches of directors' duties: *Re Bleriot Manufacturing Air Craft Co Ltd* (1916) 32 TLR 253; *Thomson v Drysdale* [1925] SC 311 *and*

Baird v Lees [1924] SC 83) and not merely a one off or trivial breach of duty: *Re Gold Co* (1879) 11 Ch D 701 and *Re Diamond Fuel Co* (1879) 13 Ch D 400).

1.142

123 Definition of inability to pay debts

(1) A company is deemed unable to pay its debts—
  (a) if a creditor (by assignment or otherwise) to whom the company is indebted in a sum exceeding £750 then due has served on the company, by leaving it at the company's registered office, a written demand (in the prescribed form) requiring the company to pay the sum so due and the company has for 3 weeks thereafter neglected to pay the sum or to secure or compound for it to the reasonable satisfaction of the creditor, or
  (b) if, in England and Wales, execution or other process issued on a judgment, decree or order of any court in favour of a creditor of the company is returned unsatisfied in whole or in part, or
  (c) if, in Scotland, the induciae of a charge for payment on an extract decree, or an extract registered bond, or an extract registered protest, have expired without payment being made, or
  (d) if, in Northern Ireland, a certificate of unenforceability has been granted in respect of a judgment against the company, or
  (e) if it is proved to the satisfaction of the court that the company is unable to pay its debts as they fall due.

(2) A company is also deemed unable to pay its debts if it is proved to the satisfaction of the court that the value of the company's assets is less than the amount of its liabilities, taking into account its contingent and prospective liabilities.

(3) The money sum for the time being specified in subsection (1)(a) is subject to increase or reduction by order under section 416 in Part XV.

Notes

S 123

A creditor will have to satisfy the court on the hearing of the petition that the company is insolvent. IA 1986 s 123 defines the circumstances in which a company is 'deemed' to be unable to pay its debts and, once the requirements of the provision are fulfilled, the court may make a winding up order notwithstanding that, as a matter of commercial reality, it is inconceivable that the company is in fact insolvent: *Cornhill Insurance plc v Improvement Services Ltd* [1986] BCLC 26. However the fact that the petitioner proves insolvency in any of the ways set out in IA 1986 s 123 does not mean that a winding up order is automatically granted; it remains a matter within the discretion of the court: *Byblos Bank SAL v Al-Khudhairy* [1987] BCLC 232. 'Debt' is given a very wide definition in IR 1900 r 13.12 and may include contingent and/or unliquidated claims. The court will be careful to ensure that the petition is not being used as a means of bringing illegitimate pressure to bear on the debtor company to pay out on an uncertain liability. But *'it is not the law that only a creditor who feels goodwill towards his debtor is entitled to a winding up order'*: *IOC Australia Pty Ltd v Mobil Oil Australia Ltd* (1975) 2 ACLR 122, 131. The line between abuse of the process and a legitimate petition can be a fine one. To pursue a substantial claim in accordance with the winding up procedure provided and in the normal manner, even though with personal hostility or even venom and from some ulterior motive is not an abuse: *Mann v Goldstein* [1968] 1 WLR 1091, 1095.

It is common for insolvency to be proved merely by relying on the fact that the company owes monies to the creditor and the company has not paid the debt; that will satisfy the court of insolvency under IA 1986 s 123(1)(e) without using the statutory demand procedure: *Re Taylor's Industrial Flooring Ltd* [1990] BCLC 216. The fact that a debt cannot be enforced because of the Limitation Act 1980 does not prevent a creditor relying on a judgment debt as the basis for a petition more than six years after the judgment has become enforceable: *Ridgeway Motors v ALTS Ltd* [2005] BPIR 423. A creditor is not bound to give a company an extended time to pay before petitioning: *Re Home Assurance Association (No 2)* (1871) LR 12 Eq 112. It is very unusual for a contributory to petition to wind up an insolvent company and such a petition is unlikely to be successful without a creditor being joined: *Re London Surbuban Bank* (1871) 6 Ch App 641.

S 123(1)(a)

The statutory demand in a corporate context is but one way of proving insolvency at the hearing of the petition (*cf Re a Debtor (No.544/SD/98)* [2000] 1 BCLC 103 in a bankruptcy context) and it is made by serving a written demand for a sum in excess of £750 in a prescribed form (Form 4.1 IR 1986 Sch 4); the use of a 'homemade' form should be avoided. Before serving a statutory demand reference should be made to IR 1986 r 4.4–4.6.

The figure of £750 was set in 1984 and though there is power to increase the figure by statutory instrument (IA 1986 s 123(3), s 416) this has not been exercised. Service is effected by 'leaving' the statutory demand at the registered office of the company though service may be effective in limited circumstances even though the registered office may have changed: CA 1985 s 287(4). To avoid any debate about whether or not service has occurred it is advisable to use a process server or, if it to be served by post, by way of recorded delivery; if it is served only by ordinary post or fax there may be scope for argument about whether or not it was properly served: *Re a Company* [1985] BCLC 37 (*a demand sent by telex was not a valid statutory demand*); cf *Re a Company (No 008790)* [1991] BCLC 561 (*a demand which was posted was a valid statutory demand though there was an admission that it had been received through registered post*).

The mandatory contents of a statutory demand include specifying the amount of the debt and the consideration for it. The sum claimed must be limited to the amount accrued due at the date of the demand and it must be dated and signed by the creditor or his agent: IR 1986 r 4.4(3), 4.5. The fact that the amount owed is misstated does not invalidate the demand so long as the petitioner is clearly owed more than the statutory demand minimum figure of £750: *Cardiff Preserved Coal and Coke Co v Norton* (1867) 2 Ch App 405; *Re Tweeds Garage Ltd* [1962] Ch 406. This is in line with the statutory demand cases under the bankruptcy regime (IA 1986 s 268; *Re a Debtor* [1992] 1 WLR 507; and see the notes to IR 1986 r 6.5). Where a debt is in a foreign currency the debt should be stated in that currency together with its sterling equivalent: IR 1986 r 4.91(2). The prescribed form of statutory demand (Form 4.1, IR 1986 Sch 4) contains helpful guidance notes to assist in fulfilling these requirements. The fact that there must be stated the amount accrued due at the date of the demand excludes its use insofar as the creditor is contingent or prospective: *Re Bryant Investment Co Ltd* [1974] 1 WLR 826; *Re Humberstone Jersey Ltd* [1977] LS Gaz R 31, notwithstanding that the definition of 'debt' (IR 1986 r 13.12) is wide. A statutory demand served by one creditor can be relied upon by another to prove insolvency: *Re Anglesea Island Coal and Coke Co* (1861) 4 LT 684. Further an assignee in law may serve a statutory demand (IA 1986 s 123(1)(a) – '*if a creditor (by assignment or otherwise) ...*' as may an equitable assignee of the whole of the debt: *Re Steel Wing Co Ltd* [1921] 1 Ch 349, 356 per Lawrence J.

For the statutory demand to be relied upon to prove insolvency the company must 'neglect' to pay the debt for a period of three weeks following service. A company does not 'neglect' to pay a debt if and insofar as the debt is disputed: *Re Brighton Club and Norfolk Hotel Co Ltd* (1865) 35 Beav 204; *Stonegate Securities Ltd v Gregory* [1980] Ch 576. The three week period which must elapse before the statutory demand can be relied upon does not include the day on which the demand is served or any part of a day: *Trow v Ind Coope (West Midlands) Ltd* [1967] 2 QB 899; *Re Lympne Investments Ltd* [1972] 1 WLR 523. The advantage of the statutory demand for the creditor is that it may by itself produce payment of the debt; the disadvantage is that the creditor has to allow the company a three week period in which to carry on business before it can be relied upon to support a petition. Any defence raised to the statutory demand by the company should be seriously considered by the creditor because if the company bona fide disputes the debt (and the petitioner relies on nothing more than non payment of the demand to prove insolvency), the court will not make a winding up order: *Re London and Paris Banking Corpn* (1874) LR 19 Eq 444. In those circumstances the safer course for the creditor would be to issue ordinary proceedings; otherwise, if it later transpires that the debt is genuinely disputed, there may be a costs penalty: *Re a Company (No 007456/98) (ITC Infotech Inc)* [2000] BCC 214. The creditor should also take care where it is likely that the debtor company will assert a cross-claim which equals or exceeds the debt demanded. Here 'cross-claim' means something other than a claim which extinguishes the debt by equitable set-off (as to which see *Hanak v Green* [1958] 2 QB 9). A cross-claim that is completely unrelated to the creditor's debt may still give a ground for striking out a winding up petition: see *Re Bayoil SA* [1999] 1 All ER 374; *Montgomery v Wanda Modes Ltd* [2002] 1 BCLC 289; *Re VP Developments Ltd* [2005] BCC 393; and see further notes to IR 1986 r 4.11 dealing with the restraint of presentation and advertisement of a winding up petition.

Restraining winding up petition

From the company's perspective the service of a statutory demand serves as a warning that a creditor may present a petition and a decision will have to be made whether to pay the undisputed amount and/or apply to restrain the presentation of a petition. The company must respond to the statutory demand as quickly as possible and if a debt is disputed it is imperative to detail the dispute in that response. Though ignoring a statutory demand does not prevent a company fighting a petition or the presentation of a petition based on the demand (*Cannon Screen Entertainment Ltd v Handmade Films (Distributors) Ltd* (1989) 5 BCC 207) an unchallenged statutory demand puts unnecessary pressure on a company *Cornhill Insurance plc v Improvement Services Ltd* [1986] BCLC 26. Where the statutory demand is challenged the company should ask for an undertaking that no petition will be presented based on the demand and if that is refused the company should apply (on short notice if necessary) to restrain the presentation of a petition; see the notes to IR 1986 r 4.11 for a more detailed consideration of applications to restrain presentation or advertisement of the petition.

S 123(1)(b)

In practice this is rarely relied upon as by the time execution is returned unsatisfied the company will be heavily insolvent. In order to prove unsatisfied execution it is necessary that the execution was actually carried out; thus it is not sufficient to evidence that the enforcement officer reports that access to the relevant premises was not possible *Re Flagstaff Silver Mining Co of Utah* (1875) LR 20 Eq 268, *The Debtor v First National Commercial Bank plc* [1994] 2 BCLC 171. A petition relying on unsatisfied execution may still be presented notwithstanding that the judgment giving rise to the execution is under appeal *Re Amalgamated Properties of Rhodesia (1913) Ltd* [1917] 2 Ch 115 or that the company has a cross claim against the judgment creditor *Re Douglas (Griggs) Engineering Ltd* [1963] Ch 19.

S 123(1)(e)

This provision deals with insolvency of a liquid nature whereas IA 1986 s 123(2) is concerned with balance sheet insolvency. Often a creditor is unable to obtain current or management accounts to prove illiquidity, and proof of illiquidity is usually established by proving that the petitioner is owed money by the company and the company has not paid the debt. Although there is no requirement to serve a statutory demand (*Re Taylor's Industrial Flooring Ltd* [1990] BCLC 216), it would be expected that some form of demand/request to pay is made of the company before presenting a petition: *Re a Company (No 001573 of 1983)* [1983] BCLC 492.

Illiquidity therefore concentrates on whether the company can meet current debts from cash and other assets which can be easily realised; if it is unable to do this then it is insolvent within the meaning of this section. In calculating the debts owed by the company the court only takes account of the debts actually then due and demanded; if the company has sufficient liquid assets to meet those debts then it is solvent: *Re Capital Annuities Ltd* [1979] 1 WLR 170, 187 per Slade J. Thus contingent and prospective liabilities are ignored as are current debts payable in the future: *Re European Life Assurance Society* (1869) LR 9 EQ 122. The current debts test contrasts the creditors of the company who are presently entitled to payment with the resources the company has immediately available to meet those demands. It does not take into account the overall financial position of the company; if a creditor cannot prove insolvency on the current debts test then he is thrown back on IA 1986 s 123(2) which deals with balance sheet insolvency.

Other indicia of current debts insolvency include cases where the directors admit the company has no assets upon which a creditor can execute: *Re Flagstaff Silver Mining Co of Utah* (1875) LR 20 Eq 268; *Re Douglas Griggs Engineering Ltd* [1963] Ch 19; where the company's business is under the control of the debenture holders and there will be nothing left after the payment of the charges: *Re Chic Ltd* [1905] 2 Ch 345; or where there are outstanding judgments against the company and creditors are pressing for payment: *Re Tweeds Garage Ltd* [1962] Ch 406). However deemed insolvency of the company in these circumstances can be rebutted if it can be shown that the company can in fact pay its debts: *Re Bradford Tramways Co* (1876) 4 Ch D 18.

S 123(2)

This provision deals with balance sheet insolvency. In the leading case of *Re European Life Assurance Society* (1869) LR 9 EQ 122 the court approached the matter on the basis that it was necessary to take account of all existing liabilities of a company which would include liabilities arising under contracts already entered into prior to the petition although they are not destined to materialise until some point in the future. The court may be satisfied of a company's insolvency if the company's assets are less than its liabilities taking into account its contingent and prospective liabilities *Re European Life Assurance Society* (1869) LR 9 EQ 122 but not contingent assets *Byblos Bank SAL v Al-Khudhairy* [1987] BCLC 232 and *Securum Finance Ltd v Camswell* [1994] BCC 434; uncalled capital is included as an asset *Re National Live Stock Insurance Co* (1858) 26 Beav 153 but it is doubtful whether 'prospective' assets could be included in the assessment of balance sheet solvency. The word 'liabilities' is obviously wider than 'debts' and the reference to 'contingent and prospective' will involve the court in some degree of guesswork perhaps assisted by expert accountancy evidence *Re London and Manchester Industrial Association* (1875) 1 Ch D 466, 472 per Bacon VC. A 'contingent' liability does not include all liabilities which may possibly be incurred by the company in the future, rather it is confined to liabilities which may arise in the future on the fulfilment of a contingency under obligations already binding on it, for example as surety: see also the notes relating to 'contingent or prospective' creditor under IA 1986 s 124 and IR 1986 r 13.12 below.

1.143–1.145

124 Application for winding up

(1) Subject to the provisions of this section, an application to the court for the winding up of a company shall be by petition presented either by the company, or the directors, or by any creditor or creditors (including any contingent or prospective creditor or creditors), contributory or contributories or by a liquidator (within the meaning of Article 2(b) of the EC Regulation) appointed in proceedings by virtue of Article 3(1) of the EC Regulation or a temporary administrator (within the meaning of Article 38 of the EC Regulation) or by a *justices' chief executive* [the designated officer for a magistrates' court] in the exercise of the power

conferred by section 87A of the Magistrates' Courts Act 1980 (enforcement of fines imposed on companies), or by all or any of those parties, together or separately.

(2) Except as mentioned below, a contributory is not entitled to present a winding-up petition unless either—
- (a) the number of members is reduced below 2, or
- (b) the shares in respect of which he is a contributory, or some of them, either were originally allotted to him, or have been held by him, and registered in his name, for at least 6 months during the 18 months before the commencement of the winding up, or have devolved on him through the death of a former holder.

(3) A person who is liable under section 76 to contribute to a company's assets in the event of its being wound up may petition on either of the grounds set out in section 122(1)(f) and (g), and subsection (2) above does not then apply; but unless the person is a contributory otherwise than under section 76, he may not in his character as contributory petition on any other ground.

This subsection is deemed included in Chapter VII of Part V of the Companies Act (redeemable shares; purchase by a company of its own shares) for the purposes of the Secretary of State's power to make regulations under section 179 of that Act.

(3A) A winding-up petition on the ground set out in section 122(1)(fa) may only be presented by one or more creditors

(4) A winding-up petition may be presented by the Secretary of State—
- (a) if the ground of the petition is that in section 122(1)(b) or (c), or
- (b) in a case falling within section 124A below.

(5) Where a company is being wound up voluntarily in England and Wales, a winding-up petition may be presented by the official receiver attached to the court as well as by any other person authorised in that behalf under the other provisions of this section; but the court shall not make a winding-up order on the petition unless it is satisfied that the voluntary winding up cannot be continued with due regard to the interests of the creditors or contributories.

Notes

S 124

The court will not generally make a winding up order unless a petition is presented: see *Re Brooke Marine Ltd* [1988] BCLC 546; although it may decide of its own motion to do so, such jurisdiction will be exercised only rarely: *Lancefield v Lancefield* [2002] BPIR 1108. A petition may be presented by a judgment creditor more than six years from the date the judgment became enforceable: *Ridgeway Motors v ALTS Ltd* [2005] BPIR 423. The effect of presenting a petition can be dramatic and it is not a step to be taken lightly as it initiates a class remedy which operates in favour of all creditors and/or contributories (IA 1986 s 130(4)) and the court has stated that it should not be regarded as a debt collection device: *Re a Company* [1983] BCLC 492. A petition can be presented by all or any of the parties listed in IA 1986 s 124(1) together or separately. A company threatened with the presentation of a petition can seek its restraint by originating application supported by affidavit or witness statement; para 8.1 of the Practice Direction: Insolvency Proceedings, (Civil Procedure 2006 Vol 2 Section 3E) and see notes to IR 1986 r 4.11.

S 124(1)

Though most petitions are presented by a creditor there are other persons who may petition to wind up a company and most of them are detailed in IA 1986 s 124. Petitioners outside IA 1986 s 124 include: (i) the Bank of England which may petition in respect of an authorised or formerly authorised institution under the Banking Act 1987 s 92 on the grounds of either inability to pay debts or that it is just and equitable to wind up the institution: *Re Bank of Credit and Commerce International SA* [1992] BCLC 570; (ii) the Attorney General under the Charities Act 1993 s 63 in relation to a company which is formed for a charitable purpose; (iii) the Financial Services Authority in the case of a variety of bodies which carry on investment business under the Financial Services and Markets Act 2000 s 367; (iv) an administrative receiver under IA 1986 s 42 Sch 1 para 21 and an administrator under Sch B1 para 60, Sch 1 para 21; (v) a supervisor of a company voluntary arrangement IA 1986 s 7(4)(b).

A Law of Property Act receiver is not authorised by statute to present a petition and it would be necessary to look at the instrument of appointment and the terms of the debenture for an express power. Alternatively the court may regard the ability to present a petition as an incidental power to the usual power which enables a receiver to take steps to protect and preserve a company's assets from attack: *Re Emmadart Ltd* [1979] Ch 540, 547–548 per Brightman J. A receiver appointed by the court is not an agent of the debenture holder (*Moss SS Co Ltd v Whinney* [1912] AC 254) and cannot present a petition in the company's name: *Parsons v Sovereign Bank of Canada* [1913] AC 160.

Company

The company may present a petition under the authority of an ordinary resolution provided that a statutory ground can be established: *Smith v Duke of Manchester* (1883) 24 Ch D 611. If an extraordinary resolution can be passed the company would normally go into a voluntary liquidation: IA 1986 s 84(1). There is a separate ground for a petition where the company by special resolution resolves to wind up (IA 1986 s 122(1)(a)) but in practice this is rarely employed. The court is not obliged to make a winding up order merely because an ordinary resolution is passed nor can the passing of an ordinary resolution in itself provide a sufficient reason for winding up on the just and equitable ground: *Re Anglo-Continental Produce Co Ltd* [1939] 1 All ER 99.

Directors

To avoid any difficulties a formal board meeting should be called to pass a resolution to authorise the presentation of a petition. A formal board meeting is usually by way of a physical meeting but the articles of association may enable such a meeting to be held in other ways (for example Companies (Tables A–F) Regulations 1985 SI 805/1985 reg 53 Table A). Once the resolution is passed any director has authority to present the petition on behalf of the board notwithstanding that the resolution was not passed unanimously: *Re Equitcorp International plc* [1989] 1 WLR 1010. If no formal board meeting is held then the individual assent of each director must be obtained before the petition is presented by 'the directors' under IA 1986 s 124: *Re Instrumentation Electrical Services Ltd* [1988] BCLC 550.

Creditor

There is no statutory definition of 'creditor' though there is a wide definition of 'debt' in IR 1986 r 13.12 which has been used to support a wide definition of 'creditor' for the purpose of IA 1986 s 124: *Tottenham Hotspur plc v Edennote plc* [1994] BCC 681. There is no minimum amount which a creditor has to be owed before presenting a petition and the court can make a winding up order in respect of a debt less than £750: *Re World Industrial Bank Ltd* [1909] WN 148, though it would be unusual to see such a petition in practice.

A secured creditor may petition (*Moor v Anglo-Italian Bank* (1879) 10 Ch D 681) notwithstanding that a receiver has been appointed: *Re Borough of Portsmouth (Kingston, Fratton and Southsea) Tramways Co* [1892] 2 Ch 362. Where there is an equitable assignment of a debt the assignee can petition without joining in the assignor: *Re Steel Wing Co Ltd* [1921] 1 Ch

349. If the whole of a debt is assigned the assignor cannot petition unless the assignee is joined as a party to the petition: *Re Pentalta Exploration Co* [1898] WN 55.

A contingent creditor is a *'person towards whom under an existing obligation the company may or will become subject to a present liability on the happening of some future event or at some future date'* *Re William Hockley Ltd* [1962] 2 All ER 111, 113 per Pennycuick J, *Re Austral Group Investments Ltd* [1993] 2 NZLR 692 and *Re Lummus Agricultural Services Ltd* [1999] BCC 953. A typical example would be a guarantor of the company's overdraft though such a person cannot petition as a contingent creditor until the whole of the guaranteed debt is paid off: *Re Fitness Centre (South East) Ltd* (1986) 2 BCC 99, 535. A prospective creditor is a *'creditor in respect of a debt which will certainly become due in the future, either on some date which has already been determined or on some date determinable by reference to future events'*: *Stonegate Securities Ltd v Gregory* [1980] Ch 576, 579 per Buckley LJ, *Re Healing Research Trustee Co Ltd* [1991] BCLC 716.

Such a definition of 'contingent' and 'prospective' enables a judgment creditor to present a petition against a company in respect of the costs awarded despite the costs not having been taxed: *Tottenham Hotspur plc v Edennote* [1995] 1 BCLC 65 and *Re Portedge Ltd* [1997] BCC 23. However a creditor who has obtained a judgment for damages which are not yet assessed must first prove that it is balance sheet insolvent before a winding up order will be made: *Securum Finance Ltd v Camswell* [1994] BCC 434.

However, it should be noted that the definition of 'contingent creditor' for the purposes of locus to present a winding up petition may be narrower than the definition of the same term for the purposes of other provisions of the IA 1986: see the judgment of Arden LJ in *R (on the application of Steele) v Birmingham City Council* [2005] EWCA Civ 1824, [2006] BPIR 856 and BPIR 532, and compare the judgments of David Richards J in *Re T&N Ltd* [2006] All ER (D) 188 (Jun), [2005] EWHC 2870 (Ch) and *Re T&N Ltd* [2006] EWHC 1447 (Ch), [2006] BPIR 532. Arden LJ's approach requires that there be a subsisting legal obligation, consistently with the test adopted by Pennycuick J in *Re William Hockley Ltd* (above). Contrast *Re Sutherland* [1963] AC 235, and the judgment of Pennycuick J in *Re SBA Properties Limited* [1967] 1 WLR 799 in which he (like David Richards J) adopted the wider definition set out by the majority in *Re Sutherland* (above).

Contributory

In practice a contributory's petition is often presented as a result of a dispute amongst shareholders. It may be a 'free standing' petition or else part of an unfair prejudice petition under CA 1986 s 459. A 'contributory' (IA 1986 s 79, 82(2), 74, 76(2) and 124(3)) is not synonymous with a 'member' (CA 1985 s 22); those definitions inevitably produce an overlap but it is the status of membership rather than the liability to contribute which defines who may petition as a contributory: *Re Chesterfield Catering Co Ltd* [1977] Ch 373; *Re National Savings Bank Association* (1866) 1 Ch App 547. For instance there are a number of exceptions which apply to exclude or limit the amount that certain contributories may be called upon to pay (eg IA 1986 s 74(2)) but that in itself does not prevent the contributory petitioning (eg the shares are fully paid: *Re Anglesea Colliery Co* (1866) 1 Ch App 555; membership had ceased many years previously: *Re Consolidated Goldfields of New Zealand Ltd* [1953] Ch 689). Every past and present member is a contributory (IA 1986 s 74(1)) as is a trustee in bankruptcy of a contributory (IA 1986 s 82(2)). The trustee in bankruptcy cannot petition until registered for the requisite period (IA 1986 s 124(2)(b)) as a member: *Re HL Bolton (Engineering) Co Ltd* [1956] Ch 577; and the bankrupt contributory himself cannot petition: *Re Wolverhampton Steel and Iron Co Ltd* [1977] 1 WLR 860. A contributory cannot contract away the right to petition in the articles of association because it would offend statute. *Re Peveril Gold Mines Ltd* [1898] 1 Ch 122, 126 per Lindley MR; and presumably the same reasoning would apply to such a provision in a shareholders' agreement.

Where the status of the petitioner as a contributory is challenged the basic principle is that the register of members is prima facie evidence of the fact that a person is a member (CA 1985 s 61) but it is not only persons presently appearing on the register who qualify as a contributory: *Re a Company (No 003160 of 1986)* [1986] BCLC 391. In some circumstances it may include those who are not members at all (eg a personal representative of deceased shareholder IA 1986 s 81; *Re Bayswater Trading Co Ltd* [1970] 1 WLR 343; *Re JN2 Ltd* [1978] 1 WLR 183). A challenge to the status of a petitioner can be determined in the petition proceedings themselves if the challenge emanates from other shareholders: *Re UOC Corpn, Alipour v Ary* [1997] 1 BCLC 557; however if the challenge is by the company itself then separate proceedings may be necessary (*Re JN2 Ltd* [1978] 1 WLR 183) though this is likely to be regarded as a technicality which may not be followed. No doubt such proceedings could be consolidated if necessary with the petition proceedings or the petition could be stayed pending the outcome of those proceedings.

There are a number of statutory restrictions on the ability of a contributory to petition (see IA 1986 s 124(2)) and also common law restrictions. The main restriction at common law is that a contributory must have a 'tangible interest' in a liquidation. In the case of a holder of fully paid shares this means that there is a surplus available for distribution after payment of creditors; in other words the company is solvent: *Re Rica Gold Washing Co* (1879) 11 Ch D 36, 43 per Jessel MR: *Re S A Hawken Ltd* [1950] 2 All ER 408. In the case of a holder of partly paid shares a tangible interest is clear because a liquidation will prevent the company from incurring further liabilities which the contributory may be called upon to meet; the same principle would apply to a contributory in a guarantee or unlimited company: *Re Chesterfield Catering Co Ltd* [1977] Ch 373.

If the company maintains that there will be no surplus it may apply to strike out the petition though the evidence of insolvency would have to be convincing to succeed: *Re Martin Coulter Enterprises Ltd* (1988) 4 BCC 210 (*strike out refused*). Where a contributory cannot discover whether there will be a surplus or not because of a failure to provide financial information a petition can still be presented: *Re Newman and Howard Ltd* [1962] Ch 257; *Re Wessex Computer Stations Ltd* [1992] BCLC 366; *Re a Company (No 007936)* [1995] BCC 705.

S 124(2)

This provision and the following subsection provide statutory restrictions on the ability of a contributory to petition. The rationale for preventing a contributory from petitioning unless the number of members is reduced below two (in the case of a public or unlimited company; for private companies, see the Companies (Single Member Private Companies) Regulations 1992) is to allow the contributory to curtail liability which he would otherwise attract under CA 1985 s 24. The principle behind the restriction based on the manner in which the shareholding was obtained and/or the period of registration is to prevent a person acquiring a share in a company for the purpose of immediately presenting a petition: *Re a Company* [1894] 2 Ch 349; however the restriction does not apply if the non registration of the petitioner was due to the company's own fault: *Re Patent Steam Engine Co* (1879) 8 Ch D 464. The fact that beneficial ownership may have changed in the course of the relevant period is irrelevant provided that the contributory has remain registered for that period: *Re Wala Wynaad Indian Gold Mining Co* (1882) 21 Ch D 849.

S 124(3)

This extends the definition of contributory to include the shareholders whose shares were redeemed or purchased if the company enters liquidation within one year of making the redemption/purchase payment and the directors who swore the relevant statutory declaration IA 1986 s 76(2). If that is the only basis upon which a person is a contributory then a petition may only be presented on the grounds of inability to pay debts or that it is just and equitable to wind up the company.

S 124(3A)

Presumably this ground is confined to creditors because the company will inevitably be insolvent.

S 124(4)

The Financial Services Authority may also petition in respect of an insurance company that is unable to pay its debts or on just and equitable grounds: Financial Services and Markets Act 2000 s 367.

S 124(5)

Where the official receiver petitions in respect of a company already in voluntary liquidation the burden of proof imposed by this provision may be discharged by showing that the liquidator is grossly incompetent *Re Ryder Installations Ltd* [1966] 1 WLR 524 or that the liquidator's conduct demands investigation *Re Hewitt Brannan (Tools) Ltd* [1991] BCLC 80, *Re Gordon & Breach Science Publishers Ltd* [1995] BCC 261. Petitioners other than the official receiver in respect of a company in voluntary liquidation have to show a special reason why a compulsory liquidation should be ordered *Re Zirceram Ltd* [2000] BCC 1048; see further the notes to IA 1986 s 125 below.

1.146

124A Petition for winding up on grounds of public interest

(1) Where it appears to the Secretary of State from—
    (a) any report made or information obtained under Part XIV of the Companies Act 1985 (company investigations, &c.),
    (b) any report made by inspectors under—
        (i) section 167, 168, 169 or 284 of the Financial Services and Markets Act 2000, or
        (ii) where the company is an open-ended investment company (within the meaning of that Act), regulations made as a result of section 262(2)(k) of that Act;
    (bb) any information or documents obtained under section 165, 171, 172, 173 or 175 of that Act,
    (c) any information obtained under section 2 of the Criminal Justice Act 1987 or section 52 of the Criminal Justice (Scotland) Act 1987 (fraud investigations), or
    (d) any information obtained under section 83 of the Companies Act 1989 (powers exercisable for purpose of assisting overseas regulatory authorities),

that it is expedient in the public interest that a company should be wound up, he may present a petition for it to be wound up if the court thinks it just and equitable for it to be so.

(2) This section does not apply if the company is already being wound up by the court.

Notes

S 124(A)(1)

Although other petitioners may refer to the 'public interest' in a winding up petition, it is only the Secretary of State who may petition on this ground: *Re Millenium Advanced Technology Ltd* [2004] 1 WLR 2177. The purpose of the Secretary of State being able to petition is to ensure that the affairs of the company can be thoroughly investigated through the compulsory winding-up regime where to do so would be in the public interest: *Re Walter L.Jacob & Co Ltd*

(1989) 5 BCC 244; *Re Normandy Marketing Ltd* [1993] BCC 879; *Secretary of State for Trade & Industry v Leyton Housing Trustees Ltd* [2000] 2 BCLC 808; *Re Supporting Link Ltd* [2004] BCC 764. Very often winding up orders are made following findings that the activities of the directors are unacceptable *Re Equity and Provident Ltd* [2002] 2 BCLC 78; *Re ForceSun Ltd*; *Re Tidesdale Ltd* [2002] 2 BCLC 302. Insolvency will not in itself justify a winding up order on public interest grounds: *Re Marann Brooks CSV* [2003] BCC 239. The burden of proof is on the Secretary of State to establish on the balance of probabilities that it is just and equitable to wind up the company; it requires weighty and substantial reasons to be produced *Re Portfolios of Distinction Ltd* [2006] 2 BCLC 261.

In the case of a public interest petition the interests of creditors and contributories weigh lighter in the balance than they would otherwise do on the hearing of the petition: *Re Lubin, Rosen and Associates Ltd* [1975] 1 WLR 122; *Re SHV Senator Hanseatische Vervaltungs Gesellschaft mbh* [1996] 2 BCLC 562. However it is never a foregone conclusion that a winding up order will be made on a public interest petition and orders have been refused in a number of cases: *Re Titan International Inc* [1998] 1 BCLC 102 (*foreign company with no sufficient connection to the jurisdiction*); *Secretary of State for Trade & Industry v Travel Time (UK) Ltd* [2000] BCC 792. It is not necessary that the Secretary of State personally has to form the required view before a petition can be presented; rather this can be delegated to a suitably qualified member of his department: *Re Golden Chemical Products Ltd* [1976] Ch 300.

A petition may be presented by the Secretary of State notwithstanding that the company is already in a members' voluntary liquidation: *Re ForceSun Ltd*, *Re Tidesdale Ltd* [2002] 2 BCLC 302; or creditors' voluntary liquidation: *Re Alpha Club (UK) Ltd* [2002] 2 BCLC 612. The costs of the petition to wind up may be ordered to be paid by the directors of the company: *Re North West Holdings plc* [2002] BCC 441; *Secretary of State for Trade and Industry v Aurum Marketing Ltd* [2002] BCC 31; or other parties, such as its majority shareholder: *Secretary of State for Trade and Industry v Liquid Acquisitions Ltd* [2003] 1BCLC 375. An order dismissing a public interest petition may be made conditional on undertakings being given to the court: *Bell Davies Trading v Secretary of State for Trade and Industry* [2005] 1 BCLC 516.

S 124(A)(2)

Presumably this provision appears for the avoidance of doubt and on the basis that a compulsory liquidation is already under way together with the investigatory duties/powers of the official receiver. A company already in compulsory liquidation cannot be made the subject of a fresh winding up petition.

1.147–1.148

124B Petition for winding up of SE

[(1) Where—
    (a)   an SE whose registered office is in Great Britain is not in compliance with Article 7 of Council Regulation (EC) No 2157/2001 on the Statute for a European company (the 'EC Regulation') (location of head office and registered office), and
    (b)   it appears to the Secretary of State that the SE should be wound up, he may present a petition for it to be wound up if the court thinks it is just and equitable for it to be so.

(2) This section does not apply if the SE is already being wound up by the court.

(3) In this section 'SE' has the same meaning as in the EC Regulation.]

1.149

125 Powers of court on hearing of petition

(1) On hearing a winding-up petition the court may dismiss it, or adjourn the hearing conditionally or unconditionally, or make an interim order, or any other order that it thinks fit; but the court shall not refuse to make a winding-up order on the ground only that the company's assets have been mortgaged to an amount equal to or in excess of those assets, or that the company has no assets.

(2) If the petition is presented by members of the company as contributories on the ground that it is just and equitable that the company should be wound up, the court, if it is of opinion—

(a)   that the petitioners are entitled to relief either by winding up the company or by some other means, and

(b)   that in the absence of any other remedy it would be just and equitable that the company should be wound up,

shall make a winding-up order; but this does not apply if the court is also of the opinion both that some other remedy is available to the petitioners and that they are acting unreasonably in seeking to have the company wound up instead of pursuing that other remedy.

Notes

S 125

The discretion of the court on the hearing of a petition is largely unfettered. It may refuse to make a winding up order even though the grounds in the petition have been made out; or it may refuse to make an order because it is believed that the matter would best be decided in another jurisdiction: *Re Harrods (Buenos Aires) Ltd* [1992] Ch 72; in that case the petition in England was stayed on the basis that the courts in Argentina were best suited to deal with the matter. Though the court is given a wide discretion under IA 1986 s 125, the hearing of the petition cannot be used as an occasion to determine a claim arising independently of the petition such as a claim for damages: *Partizan Ltd v O J Kilkenny & Co Ltd* [1998] 1 BCLC 157. The discretion conferred by IA 1986 s 125 is complemented by the court's inherent jurisdiction to restrain presentation or advertisement of the petition: see the notes to IR 1986 r 4.11 on such restraint applications. In practice where there is a dispute about the basis of a debt in a creditor's petition it is normally the case that the company issues a restraint application and the status of the debt is usually decided by the court at that stage rather than the parties awaiting the hearing of the petition itself.

The court will not decline to make a winding up order solely because the company's assets appear to be subject to a charge or that it appears to have no assets: *Re Crigglestone Coal Co Ltd* [1906] 2 Ch 327. This means that a creditor does not have to show the 'tangible interest' that would have to be shown by a petitioner who proceeds on the just and equitable ground (s 122(1)(g) IA 1986). The court may order a winding up to allow an investigation of the company's affairs, perhaps with a view to a liquidator making claims to recover assets: *Bell Group Finance (Pty) v Bell Group (UK) Holdings Ltd* [1996] 1 BCLC 304.

Creditor's Petition

Hearing

On presentation the petition will be given a return date for hearing in the unopposed winding up list. In the High Court in London these usually take place on alternate Wednesdays before a registrar. Outside London, district judges in the appropriate Chancery District Registry take the place of the Companies Court registrars. This hearing will be the first time that the petition is heard, although the papers will have been checked over by the court staff. Parties should be represented by solicitors or counsel (at present, appropriately robed): *Radford Freeway Classics Ltd* [1994] 1 BCLC 445. However the court has a discretion to allow a director of the company to speak on behalf of the company in exceptional circumstances *Arbuthnot Leasing International Ltd v Havelet Leasing Ltd* [1990] BCLC 802. In practice the court is likely to allow a director to address the court briefly. Persons other than creditors or contributories who are interested in the property of the company do not have a right to be heard on the petition but the court may permit them to appear and make representations: *Re Bradford Navigation Company* (1870) LR 5 Ch App Cas 600. The list usually contains hundreds of petitions, which are heard in quick succession. Copies of the list can usually be obtained in court before the hearing itself. Otherwise, it can be found on the court service website from the afternoon of the day before: *www.hmcourts-service.gov.uk*. If the petition is missed the petitioner should speak to the clerk to ask the court to return to it as soon as possible.

Because the list contains so many cases, there is not time to hear any substantive argument on a petition and nor is there time to ask the court summarily to assess costs. In practice any dispute that cannot be disposed of in a very short time (ie where the petition debt is disputed or is opposed by other creditors) will be adjourned to a contested hearing. The court will give directions as to evidence and the filing of listing certificates to enable it to decide whether the matter should be heard before a judge or a registrar. Either may hear it: see Practice Note on the Hearing of Insolvency Proceedings [2005] BPIR 688.

Provided that the papers are in order, and there is no opposition, the court will always make the 'usual compulsory order'. This is an order that the company be wound up, that the official receiver be appointed as liquidator and that the petitioner's costs be an expense in the liquidation. If the papers are not in order (see notes to IR 1986 r 4.7ff), and it is the first hearing, the court will usually allow the petition to stand over to a later date for the purpose of putting them in order. However, the court's patience is not inexhaustible. For instance it is quite common for petitioners to hold off advertising the petition if there is a prospect of the debt being settled but where the petition is not advertised by the time of its second hearing, it will normally be dismissed: see Practice Direction Insolvency Proceedings para 2.1 Civil Procedure 2006 Vol 2 Section 3E. Where there has been some failure to comply with the proper procedures laid out by the rules, the court does have a jurisdiction to waive the defect (IR 1986 r 7.55) but it will not do so if the defect may cause prejudice. An error of one day in the timing of the advertisement will usually be waived (but generally no more than one day). Errors in the wording of the advert may also be waived if they are inconsequential but defects in the petition itself will usually require amendment.

Adjournment

On the hearing of the petition the court is not readily disposed to granting adjournments to the petitioner because of the effect this may have on the company's business and other creditors are prevented from presenting their own petitions: *Re Boston Timber Fabrications Ltd* [1984] BCLC 328, 333 per Oliver LJ. A short adjournment may be granted on the first hearing of the petition but as a matter of practice it is increasingly difficult to secure longer or repeated adjournments: *Re Piccadilly Property Management Ltd* [2000] BCC 44, where an adjournment to enable company to consider proposals for a voluntary arrangement was refused); in exceptional circumstances the court is prepared to grant a lengthy adjournment: eg *Re Bank of Credit and Commerce International SA* [1992] BCC 83 (adjournment of 4 months). In practice, the court's willingness to grant an adjournment to the debtor company is influenced by the petitioner's attitude. If the petitioner does not oppose the application, the court will usually allow it. An adjournment will usually be sought to allow time for money to be raised to settle the petition debt (notwithstanding that the fact that time to find the money is required indicates strongly that the company actually is insolvent) or to allow the debtor company to prepare CVA proposals. However, the company should be prepared to explain how this time is likely to make a difference. Where a petitioner is consenting to an application for an adjournment, there is a risk that a supporting creditor will seek to be substituted as petitioner: IR 1986 r 4.19.

Appeal

Appeals are dealt with in Practice Direction Insolvency Proceedings para 2.1 Civil Procedure 2006 Vol 2 Section 3E and IR 1986 r 7.47. Where the court on the hearing of the petition decides that a debt is disputed in good faith and on reasonable grounds the Court of Appeal is unlikely to overturn that decision: *London and Global Ltd v Sahara Petroleum* (1998) Times 3 December; *Pentagin Technologies International v Express Company Securities* (1995) Times 7 April.

Defence to a petition

In raising a dispute on the petition (i.e. at the hearing of the contested petition, rather than the first hearing), the company must show that the grounds are substantial and it must support its case up with proper evidence: see e g *Re a Company (No 0012209 of 1991)* [1992] 1 WLR 351. It is not enough simply to assert that the debt is disputed. However, in every case, the court retains a discretion as to how far it allows the question of the bona fides of the dispute to be explored – in some cases it may be easy to decide this on the petition: *Re QBS Pty Ltd* [1967] QDR 218, 225; *Brinds Ltd v Offshore Oil NL* [1986] 2 BCC 98, 916, *Re a Company (No 001259 of 1991)* [1991] BCLC 594. It is not enough that the company honestly but foolishly believes it is not bound to pay: *Re General Exchange Bank Ltd* (1866) 14 LT 582, 583 per Lord Romilly. If the dispute is based on the interpretation of documents which are before the court at the hearing then it may determine the issue at the hearing of the petition: *Re Janeash Ltd* [1990] BCC 250; however the court will not allow the winding up proceedings to be used as a forum for resolving substantial disputes of fact: *Alipour v Ary [1997] 1 WLR 534*. Generally where there is a genuine dispute over the petition debt based on substantial grounds the court will strike out the petition: *Re a Company No 006685 of 1996* [1997] BCC 830; see also the note to IA 1986 s 123 above. If the petition is struck out, indemnity costs may well be ordered against the petitioner: see *Re a Company (2507 of 2003)* [2003] 2 BCLC 346.

A common defence to a petition is that the company has a cross claim against the petitioner; often this matter is raised on a restraint of presentation/advertisement application (see notes IR 1986 r 4.11 and IA 1986 s 123(1)(a)) but it may be left to the hearing of the petition. Where the company has a serious and genuine cross claim which overtops the admitted petition debt the court is very likely to dismiss the petition and leave the petitioner to take claim proceedings: *Re Bayoil SA* [1999] 1 WLR 147, *Marchands Associates LLP v The Thompson Partnership [2004] EWCA Civ 878*; *Re Portman Provincial Cinemas Ltd* [1999] 1 WLR 157; *Europa Investments Ltd v Andrew Downs & Co Ltd* (25th June 1996 unreported, Peter Gibson J); *Montgomery v Wanda Modes Ltd* [2002] 1 BCLC 289; though the court always has a discretion whether to make an order or not: *Re FSA Business Software Ltd* [1990] BCC 465. The older cases tended to differentiate between a counterclaim and a set off; the more modern authorities generally refer to a 'cross claim' to include both. In certain circumstances the Court has taken the view that the cross claim can be dealt with in the liquidation process: *Atlantic & General Investment Trust Ltd v Richbell Information Services Inc* [2000] BCC 111. For a recent discussion of the principles applicable in disputed debt and cross-claim cases, see *Re VP Developments Ltd* [2005] BCC 396; and also see the notes to IR 1986 r 4.11 dealing with restraint of presentation/advertisement applications.

Judgment creditor

Clearly a creditor who has judgment against a company is in a strong position to petition for a winding up: *Re a Company* (1983) 1 BCC 98, 901. The fact that the judgment is under appeal will not prevent a winding up order being made (*Re Amalgamated Properties of Rhodesia (1913) Ltd* [1917] 2 Ch 115) albeit that the court can in its discretion stay the proceedings pending the outcome of the appeal: *Re LHF Wools Ltd* [1970] Ch 27. The court would be unlikely to grant a stay where the other creditors would be prejudiced: *Re R A Foulds Ltd* (1986) 2 BCC 99,269. However where a petition is based on a judgment which has been reversed on appeal the court will not make a winding up order nor adjourn the petition until an appeal against the reversal of the judgment is heard; the petition will be dismissed: *Re Anglo Bavarian Steel Ball Co* [1899] WN 80. A petition will also be dismissed if it is based on the same debt as that of a previously dismissed petition: *Re a Company (No 00928 of 1991), ex p*

City Electrical Factors Ltd [1991] BCLC 514. In *Ridgeway Motors Ltd v ALTS Ltd* [2005] BCC 496, the Court of Appeal considered the impact of the statutory limitation provisions on the right of a judgment creditor to present a winding up petition and it was held that a judgment creditor was not barred from presenting a petition more than six years after the judgment became enforceable, notwithstanding that it could no longer be enforced through the courts in the ordinary way.

Views of other parties

Nothwithstanding that a petitioner has established the company has no defence to the petition the court retains its discretion on the hearing of the petition and the wish of the petitioner may be displaced by the wishes of other creditors *Re Brendaco Ltd* (1986) 2 BCC 99,164. The wishes of the shareholders and/or the company are largely ignored as the company is insolvent *Re Camburn Petroleum Products Ltd* [1980] 1 WLR 86.

Classes of creditor interest

The court is directed to have regard to the interests of creditors under IA 1986 s 195 and it is incumbent on the court to consider the views of both supporting and opposing creditors at the hearing of the petition (*Re Crigglestone Coal Co* [1906] 2 Ch 327) including the views of secured creditors insofar as they are unsecured *Re Leigh Estates (UK) Ltd* [1994] BCC 292). Where creditors appear on the petition the court will be interested in discovering the amount of their claims and whether they are creditors of the same class as the petitioner; though neither of those matters will be decisive *Re Vuma Ltd* [1960] 1 WLR 1283. Insofar as a creditor is secured the court will give little weight to its view (*Re Crigglestone Coal Co Ltd* [1906] 2 Ch 327) and certainly not it if its aim in opposing the petition is to prevent an investigation into its security *Bell Finance (UK) Holdings Ltd* [1966] 1 BCLC 304.The petitioner must produce a list of appearances under IR 1986 r 4.17 detailing the supporting and opposing creditors. It is not necessary for creditors to be represented as often the petitioner and the company can rely on the list of appearances itself and/or letters from creditors

If there is majority opposition to the petition from the same class of creditors as the petitioner the court will be concerned to discover whether the majority are seeking to promote their own personal interests (*Re P & J Macrae Ltd* [1961] 1 All ER 302) and whether they are independent creditors or connected with the directors: *Re Lummus Agricultural Services Ltd* [1999] BCC 953. Less weight will be given to the opposition of connected creditors; there is no statutory definition of 'connected' in this context. Where the majority of the same class oppose the petition for a good reason then the burden may shift back to the petitioner to show that there are special circumstances supporting the making of an order (*Re Krasnapolsky Restaurant and Winter Garden Co* [1892] 3 Ch 174) but in any event the court is not bound to dismiss the petition: *Re Hewitt Brannan (Tools) Co Ltd* [1990] BCC 354.

Examples of good reasons for opposing the petition in the older authorities have included proving that payment to the petitioner is forthcoming: *Re Western of Canada Oil, Lands and Works Co* (1873) LR 17 Eq 1; or a reorganisation of the company is imminent (*Re East Kent Colliery Co* (1914) 30 TLR 659. However a minority creditor will obtain a winding up order notwithstanding majority opposition where it is shown that the company is irretrievably insolvent and has no assets: *Re Vuma Ltd* [1960] 1 WLR 1283; or the opposition is fuelled by personal interests: *Re Ithaca Shipping Co* (1950) 84 Ll L Rep 507. If the majority creditors desire a voluntary liquidation but the company has not yet resolved to wind up then the opposition to the compulsory liquidation should be explained: *Re Television Parlour plc* (1988) 4 BCC 95.

Existing voluntary liquidation

A creditor or contributory can petition to wind up a company which is already in a creditors' or members' voluntary liquidation: IA 1986 s 116; *Re Leading Guides International Ltd* [1998] 1 BCLC 620; *Re Surplus Properties (Huddersfield) Ltd* [1984] BCLC 89. The petition may be based on a debt arising before or after the voluntary liquidation: *Re Greenwood & Co* [1900] 2 QB 306. A contributory cannot obtain a winding up order unless the court is satisfied that the rights of the contributories will be prejudiced by the voluntary winding up IA 1986 s 116. The official receiver has to satisfy the court that the voluntary winding up cannot be continued with due regard to the interests of the creditors or contributories: IA 1986 s 124(5); *Re Hewitt Brannan (Tools) Ltd* [1991] BCLC 80.

On the hearing of the petition the voluntary liquidator should appear and assist the court but it is improper for the liquidator to take a partisan approach and/or 'fight' for his continuance in office: *Re Roselmar Properties Ltd (No 2)* (1986) 2 BCC 99; *Re Medisco Equipment Ltd* [1983] BCLC 305. Where the petition itself is based on the voluntary liquidator being partisan the court may appoint a different liquidator rather than make a winding up order: IA 1986 s 171; *Re Inside Sport Ltd* [2000] 1 BCLC 286 (though in this case a winding up order was actually made; *cf Re A B (Handling) Ltd*, 5th February 1999, LTL 5/2/99). If a winding up order is made, the court may order that the remuneration of the voluntary liquidator and the costs and expenses of liquidation should rank as an expense of the compulsory liquidation in priority to the other expenses: IR 1986 r 4.219; *Re Tony Rowse NMC Ltd* [1996] BCC 196.

The discretion of the court to refuse a winding up order is considerably wider in this situation as the 'class remedy' of liquidation is already being enforced (*Re J D Swain Ltd* [1965] 1 WLR 909) and the burden of proof is on the petitioner to show a special reason why the compulsory liquidation should be ordered: *Re Zirceram Ltd* [2000] BCC 1048; *Re Magnus Consultants Ltd* [1995] 1 BCLC 203. In making its decision the court is much influenced by the views of the majority of the independent creditors: *Re William Thorpe & Son Ltd* (1989) 5 BCC 156; *Re Zirceram Ltd* [2000] BCC 1048. A winding up order will not be made unless there is some likelihood that assets will be recovered in the compulsory liquidation: *Re National Distribution of Electricity Co* [1902] 2 Ch 34. Special reasons persuading the court to order a winding up have included a potential conflict situation for the voluntary liquidator, or the voluntary liquidation was initiated a considerable time after the petition was presented: *Re Zinotty Properties Ltd* [1984] 1 WLR 1249; the voluntary liquidator has been in default: *Re Hewitt Brannan (Tools) Co Ltd* [1990] BCC 354; the voluntary liquidator is not seen to be independent: *Re Palmer Marine Surveys Ltd* [1986] 1 WLR 573; there are matters which require urgent investigation: *Re Lowestoft Traffic Services Ltd* (1986) 2 BCC 98, 945; *Re Leading Guides International Ltd* [1998] 1 BCLC 620 (declaration of solvency described as 'totally incredible'); or support for the voluntary liquidation only comes from connected creditors: *Re Falcon RJ Development Ltd* (1987) 3 BCC 146; *Re MCH Services Ltd* [1987] BCLC 535.

Contributory's Petition

A contributory's petition follows a different course from a creditor's petition as it normally involves a shareholder dispute in a solvent company; in particular the return date on the petition is used as a directions hearing. Reference should be made to IR 1986 r 4.22–4.24 for procedural matters in respect of the presentation and progress of a contributory's petition. Often a prayer for winding up is included as part of the relief claimed in an unfair prejudice petition (CA 1985 s 459) though such a request should not be lightly made. Practice Direction – Applications under the Companies Act 1985, para 9, Civil Procedure Vol 2, Section 2G.

Hearing

The majority of contributory petitions do not make it to trial due to the expense and time involved in fighting shareholder disputes. Where a petition proceeds to a hearing it is clear that a contributory does not possess the prima facie right of an unpaid creditor to a winding up order: *Re Metropolitan Rly Warehousing Co Ltd* (1867) 36 LJ Ch 287. The usual ground for such a petition is the 'just and equitable' ground considered above (IA 1986 s 122(1)(g)) as a contributory generally has no business winding up an insolvent company unless there are special circumstances: *Re Norwich Yarn Co* (1850) 12 Beav 366 (contributory of unlimited company; *Re Chesterfield Catering Co Ltd* [1977] Ch 373 (contributory holding partly paid shares). The fact that the company is already in voluntary liquidation is no bar to the making of an order on the petition of a contributory: *Re Beaujolais Wine Co* (1867) 3 Ch App 15.

As a general principle where the opposition to the petition is simply from other shareholders the court will not lightly interfere with the wishes of the majority (*Re Langham Skating Rink Co* (1877) 5 Ch D 669) though this stance will inevitably be influenced by the ground upon which the petition is presented (see notes to IA 1986 s 122(1)(g) above). Though the court has a wide discretion under IA 1986 s 125(1) it is very likely to make a winding up order if there are suspicious circumstances which require investigation: *Re Varieties Ltd* [1893] 2 Ch 235; or the majority opposing a winding up have been guilty of a fraud on the minority: *Re West Surrey Tanning Co* (1866) LR 2 Eq 737. The court is likely to dismiss or restrain a petition if it is not presented for the purpose of winding up the company's affairs but rather for some ancillary motive: *Charles Forte Investments Ltd v Amanda* [1964] Ch 240.

S 125(2)

The availability of other remedies to a contributory does not bar a contributory's petition unless the contributory is acting unreasonably in not pursuing another remedy. There may be less drastic options than a winding up. Other available 'remedies' might include the sale of shares, a voluntary liquidation or, more commonly, an unfair prejudice petition CA 1985 s 459. The orders that can be made under CA 1985 s 461 are wide ranging including a buy-out order or an order regulating the management of the affairs of the company in the future.

1.150

126 Power to stay or restrain proceedings against company

(1) At any time after the presentation of a winding-up petition, and before a winding-up order has been made, the company, or any creditor or contributory, may—

    (a)   where any action or proceeding against the company is pending in the High Court or Court of Appeal in England and Wales or Northern Ireland, apply to the court in which the action or proceeding is pending for a stay of proceedings therein, and

    (b)   where any other action or proceeding is pending against the company, apply to the court having jurisdiction to wind up the company to restrain further proceedings in the action or proceeding;

and the court to which application is so made may (as the case may be) stay, sist or restrain the proceedings accordingly on such terms as it thinks fit.

(2) In the case of a company registered under section 680 of the Companies Act (pre-1862 companies; companies formed under legislation other than the Companies Acts) or the previous corresponding legislation, where the application to stay, sist or restrain is by a creditor, this section extends to actions and proceedings against any contributory of the company

---

Notes

S 126

It is important to note that the mere presentation of a winding up petition (unlike the making of a winding up order or appointment of a provisional liquidator: IA 1986 s 130(2)) does not automatically stay actions or proceedings against the company. A stay will not be effected prior to the hearing of a winding up petition without an application under IA 1986 s 126. This can be made by the company, and any creditor or contributory, to the relevant court in accordance with IA 1986 s 126(1)(a) by way of interim application. Where the action or proceeding is not proceeding in one of courts set out in IA 1986 s 126(1)(a) then an ordinary application should be made to the court having jurisdiction to wind up the company (see IA 1986 s 117). Where more than one action is proceeding in the same division of the High Court, one order can be made in relation to all of them: *Re People's Garden Co* (1875) 1 ChD 44. In the case of unregistered companies, IA 1986 s 126 applies pursuant to IA 1986, s 221(1).

S 126(1)

'.. action or proceeding..' includes any existing litigation and enforcement procedures including steps to distrain: *R: Roundwood Colliery Co* [1897] 1 Ch 373, *Herbert Berry Associates v IRC* [1977] 1 WLR 1437, *Re Memco Engineering Ltd* [1985] 3 WLR 875); sale by an enforcement officer under an execution put before the presentation of the petition: *Re Perkins Beach Lead Mining Co* (1877) 7 Ch D 371); garnishee proceedings: *Anglo Baltic & Mediterranean Bank v Barber* [1924] 2 KB 410, CA; and criminal proceedings: *R v Dickson* [1991] BCC 719. It applies to actions and proceedings in Scotland: *Re Dynamics Corporation of America* [1973] 1 WLR 63; and whilst in general it does not apply to proceedings in a foreign country (*Re Vocalion (Foreign) Ltd* [1932] 2 Ch 196) it may apply where the claimant is within the jurisdiction: *Re Oriental Inland Steam Co* (1874) 9 Ch App 557); see also the notes to IA 1986 s 130(2) where the phrase 'action or proceeding' is also used. Since the outcome of the petition will be unknown at the stage of an application under IA 1986 s 126 and the petition may not in fact result in liquidation, it is for the applicant to satisfy the court that there is some special reason why the action or proceeding should be restrained: *Venner's Electrical Cooking and Heating Appliances Ltd v Thorpe* [1915] 2 Ch 404, CA. In the case of distress for example, special reasons include fraud or unfair dealing but not the fact that a sale under the distress would realise less for creditors than a sale by the liquidator: *Re Bellaglade Ltd* [1977] 1 All ER 319. An application may be made retrospectively: *Re Linkrealm Ltd* [1998] BCC 478. By way of exception CA 1989, s 161(4) provides that nothing in IA 1986 s 126 shall affect any action taken by an exchange or clearing house for the purpose of its default proceedings.

1.151

127 Avoidance of property dispositions, etc

(1) In a winding up by the court, any disposition of the company's property, and any transfer of shares, or alteration in the status of the company's members, made after the commencement of the winding up is, unless the court otherwise orders, void.

(2) This section has no effect in respect of anything done by an administrator of a company while a winding up petition is suspended under paragraph 40 of Schedule B1.

Notes

S 127

This provision applies to a winding up by the court, and not to a voluntary liquidation unless superseded by a compulsory liquidation: IA 1986 s 129(1). It only applies to dispositions made between the presentation of the petition and the making of the winding-up order. *Re Oriental Bank Corporation, ex p Guilemin* (1884) 28 ChD 634; *Re Wiltshire Iron Co, ex p Pearson* (1868) 3 Ch App 443). The wording of the provision is wide and on the face of it unfettered; the possible range of applicants as persons interested in a validation is extensive: *Re Dewrun Ltd* [2002] BCC 57. Normally parties other than the company and the petitioner will not know whether or not a winding up petition has been presented against the company because of the restrictions on advertising the petition (see notes to IR 1986 r 4.11). Where a party is involved in a disposition of property by a company it is therefore advisable to check whether or not a petition has been presented against the company by using the Companies Court search facility 0906 754 0043.

S 127(1)

The significance of this provision is that the winding up is deemed to have occurred when the petition was presented (IA 1986 s 129(2)) and not when the order was made and it applies to transactions taking place during the interval between presentation of a petition and winding up (other than where there is a moratorium in force pursuant to a CVA (IA 1986 Sch A1 para 12(2)). IA 1986 s 127 aims to ensure the rateable division of the assets amongst creditors and that such assets are not alienated and dissipated in the run up to the making of the order: *Re Wiltshire Iron Co* (1868) 3 Ch App 443, 466. Not only are dispositions of a company's property after the commencement of a winding up void unless the court orders otherwise, but directors who permit disposals without a court order (otherwise than in good faith and for the purpose of carrying on the company's business) are exposed to the risk of misfeasance proceedings: *Re Neath Harbour Smelting and Rolling Works* [1887] WN 87.

Commonly applications are made under IA 1986 s 127 for a validation order in relation to a disposition of a company's property where it might be argued that the assets of the company have been depleted. To be depleted the property being disposed of must be beneficially owned by the company (*Re Branston & Gothard Ltd* [1999] BPIR 466) and the avoidance effect of IA 1986 s 127 does not apply where the beneficial interest has already passed, for example where the proceeds of assets covered by a floating charge are paid over to the charge holder: *Re Margart Pty, Hamilton v Westpac Banking Corp* [1985] BCLC 314. However where property subject to a floating charge is recovered by the liquidator from a third party the charge remains over that property for the benefit of the chargeholder: *Re R S & M Engineering Co Ltd* [2000] BCC 445. Even where the beneficial ownership of an asset has been transferred prior to presentation of a petition, (for example the exchange of contracts for the sale of land), it would be appropriate to seek an order validating the transaction in so far as it may involve a disposition of any property (*Re French's Wine Bar Ltd* (1987) 3 BCC 88) so as to avoid any potential argument, and a prudent purchaser would ordinarily require such an order before completion.

Financial markets

So far as financial markets are concerned, this section does not apply to:
(i)   a market contract, or any disposition of property in pursuance of such a contract, the provision of margin in relation to market contracts and some other connected dispositions (for details see CA 1989 s 164(3)–(5)) save that where the other party to the disposition had notice that a petition had been presented the value of profit/margin is recoverable from him by the office-holder (unless the court directs otherwise).
(ii)   dispositions of property as a result of which it becomes subject to a market charge or a transaction pursuant to which that disposition is made save that where the other party to the disposition had notice that a petition had been presented the value of the profit is recoverable from him by the office-holder (unless the court directs otherwise) CA 1989 s 175(3)–(5).

Application for a validation order

An application for an order to validate a disposition can be made before or after the disposition has taken place: *Re A Levy (Holdings) Ltd* [1964] Ch 19; or after a winding up order has been made. The application can be made by any person with an interest in the liquidation by ordinary application supported by an affidavit or a witness statement: *Re Dewrun Ltd* [2002] BCC 57. The application must be supported by satisfactory evidence; thus validation of the sale of a freehold property was refused where there was no evidence that it had been properly marketed: *Re Rescupine Ltd* [2003] 1 BCLC 661. The application is made to a Judge: Practice Direction: Insolvency Proceedings Civil Procedure 2006 Vol 2 Section 3E para 5.1(2); Practice Note: The Hearing of Insolvency Proceedings [2005] BCC 456. Where made by the company, the petitioning creditor should be joined as respondent and in practice is often asked to agree to abridgement of time under IR 1986 r 12.9. Persons with an interest include the company, a contributory or creditor: *Re Argentum Reductions (UK) Ltd* [1975] 1 WLR 186; including a creditor by subrogation: *Re Tramway Building and Construction Co Ltd* [1988] 2 WLR 640. The right to apply for a validation order has held been held not to be assignable by a liquidator: *Re Ayala Holdings Ltd (No.2)* [1996] 1BCLC 467.

It is advisable to ensure in advance of the hearing of the application that the form of the order requested satisfies the person (usually the bank) on whom it is served. A bank is likely to require the addition of the proviso in the order; *'Providing that (the bank) shall be under no obligation to verify for itself whether any transaction through the company's bank accounts is in the ordinary course of business or that it represents full market value for the relevant transaction'* as approved in *Re a Company (No. 00687 of 1991)* [1991] BCC 210.

Validation application in respect of insolvent company

The basic principle behind IA 1986 s 127 is that the assets of an insolvent company should be distributed pari passu amongst the unsecured creditors and that those creditors should receive equal treatment: *Airfreight Express (UK) Ltd v AFX Engineering* [2005] BPIR 250. The court's discretion whilst unfettered (*Re Steane's (Bournmouth) Ltd* [1950] 1 All ER 21) is exercised according to principles well established since *Re Gray's Inn Construction* [1980] 1 WLR 711, 724 intended to achieve a just and fair result in respect of creditors in general as opposed to the giving of an advantage to any one of them, for example to a director: *Re Webb Electrical Ltd* (1988) 4 BCC 230; or to an individual creditor: *Re Rafidain Bank* [1992] BCC 376; *Airfreight Express (UK) Ltd v AFX Engineering* [2005] BPIR 250).

Where a company is insolvent a disposition may be validated where it brings the benefit of improving or protecting the assets, for example by allowing continuation of trade which would necessarily involve paying salaries, essential suppliers and utilities. An insolvent company should not be supported in unprofitable trading: *Re a Company No.007523 of 1986* (1987) 3 BCC 57; unless it is likely to benefit the general body of creditors: *Re Gray's Inn Construction* [1980] 1 WLR 711, 724; *Re Fairway Graphics Ltd* [1991] BCLC 468, for example the preservation of the value of a going concern which could be sold by a liquidator at a price which would outweigh the loss on trading. Where more fuel oil from an existing supplier was required to allow continued trading, and would not be supplied without payment of the outstanding account that payment was validated: *Denney v John Hudson & Co Ltd* [1992] BCC 503; as were payments made to the bank to reduce an overdraft specifically granted to allow trading to continue: *Re TW Construction Ltd* [1954] 1 All ER 744. Similarly, perishable assets including a claim at risk of being struck out may justify expenditure to enable them to be preserved: *Rothschild v Bell* [2000] QB 33.

Transactions which do not involve a reduction in the company's assets are likely to be validated, for example sales of shares in racehorses (*Re Sugar Properties (Derisley Wood) Ltd* (1987) 3 BCC 88) where it was noted that there can be value in having certainty in the price to be realised; similarly in respect of transfers of land: *Re Tramway Building and Construction Co Ltd* [1988] 2 WLR 640; and completion of an unconditional sale of property entered into before presentation of a petition which was specifically enforceable. Where a contract is conditional or voidable or there is a potential argument that waiver or confirmation or variation of terms may constitute a disposition the prudent purchaser will require a validation order: *Re French's Wine Bar Ltd* (1987) 3 BCC 88. Transactions which are in direct conflict with contractual rights however, would not ordinarily be validated, such as where the disposal of a particular asset requires a creditor to consent: *Rothschild v Bell* [2000] QB 33.

Prospective application

The court is unwilling to usurp the function of a liquidator to decide on disposal of assets *Re Bransfield Engineering Ltd* (1985) 1 BCC 99,409. It is in the nature of a proper prospective application that the disposition needs to be effected before the winding up order is made. The evidence on an application should explain the nature, urgency and benefits of the proposed transaction(s). If the application concerns trading expenses the court expects a list of required payments, the identities of the recipients, and the reasons for each payment being required at that stage. Specific care is needed in relation to intended payments of debts incurred prior to the date of the presentation of the petition, which should be highlighted in the evidence. There should also be credible evidence to demonstrate that looking at the circumstances as a whole continued trading will benefit creditors generally, the burden of proof being on the applicant *Re McGuinness Bros (UK) Ltd* (1987) 3 BCC 571.

Retrospective application

Where a recipient of a company's property knows the company is already subject to a winding up petition this might suggest the taking of an advantage as against creditors in general and the task of persuading the court to make a validation order is more difficult: *Re Civil Service and General Store Ltd* (1887) 57 LJ Ch 119; the recipient could have declined to enter into the transaction until the company obtained a validation order: *Re Gray's Inn Construction* [1980] 1 WLR 711, 718. However, good faith and absence of knowledge of the petition are not in themselves enough to satisfy the court that a transaction should be validated though they will be relevant factors to be considered in exercising the discretion: *Re J Leslie Engineers Co Ltd* [1976] 1 WLR 292, 304. In practice ordinary arm's length transactions taking place before advertisement of a petition where the other party had no notice of it will normally be upheld and are therefore unlikely to be challenged by a liquidator.

Where payment has been made to a single creditor (particularly if it is in respect of the petition debt) it will be particularly hard to justify as meriting validation: *Re Liverpool Civil Service Association* (1874) 9 Ch App 511. The petitioning creditor who is paid off by the company prior to the hearing of the petition remains in jeopardy because another creditor may be substituted subsequently (IR 1986 r 4.19) and a winding up order made. In those circumstances the petitioner would be better advised to ensure that the petition debt is paid off with third party monies. Where a purchaser of a property from a company subject to a winding up petition granted a charge over the property to a bank to assist the financing of the transfer the bank successfully applied for a retrospective validation order after winding up to the extent of its charge; title to the property had remained in the company at all material times which created practical problems in relation to registration of the charge: *Re Dewrun Ltd* [2002] BCC 57.

Validation application in respect of solvent company

The fact that a company can show that it is solvent when applying for a validation order puts the onus on any person opposing it to satisfy the court that an order should not be made: *Re Burton and Deakin Ltd* [1977] 1 WLR 390. Ordinarily the court will readily permit all transactions in the ordinary course of business, since there would be no adverse impact on creditors. An exception to this approach is where a petition has been presented on public interest grounds where there is evidence of irregularities in the conduct of the company by its management: *Re: a Company (No.007130 of 1998)* [2000] 1 BCLC 582.

Banking Transactions

In *Bank of Ireland v Hollicourt (Contractors) Ltd* [2001] Ch 555 the Court of Appeal held that payments made by cheque out of a company's bank account to a third party involve no disposition of the company's property to the bank on the basis that the bank is merely the company's agent in making a disposition to the third party, against whom the disposition is avoided. The same analysis applies to payments out to third parties whether the account is in credit or overdrawn, though payments into an overdrawn account are dispositions to the bank itself to the extent that they diminish any overdrawn balance since commencement of the winding up. It is not the case that validation of payments into a bank account will be ordered where the petition had not yet been advertised and before the recipient knew of the petition: *Re Tain Construction Ltd* [2004] BCC 11. The court in that case was concerned to establish whether the parties were acting in the ordinary course of business and that the principle of pari passu distribution was respected. The court will be keen to ensure that the interests of unsecured creditors are not prejudiced and it is only in exceptional circumstances where it is in the interests of creditors generally that the court would validate a disposition which would see pre-liquidation creditors paid in full whilst others were not. The court will not validate a disposition where there are grounds for believing that it was made in an effort to prefer one creditor over another: *Re Tain Construction Ltd* [2004] BCC 11.

Unfair prejudice petitions – winding up as a remedy under CA 1985 s 459–461

Where a winding up order is sought by a petitioner in an unfair prejudice petition he must state whether or not he consents to a standard form of validation. That enables the court to make the order without a hearing or filing of evidence where such consent is given (Practice Direction – Applications under the Companies Act 1985, Civil Procedure Vol 2, Section 2G). Where consent is refused, the court will attach great weight to the wishes of the directors since the mere presentation of a petition by one shareholder should not be allowed to interfere with the management of the company's business. However where there is serious doubt as to the company's solvency and continuing trading would deplete the company's assets the court will uphold the overriding purpose of IA 1986 s 127, and refuse to validate transactions: *Re a Company (No 007523 of 1986)* [1987] BCLC 200. Where the company is solvent and the disposition is required for reasons which an intelligent and honest man could hold, the court is likely to approve the disposition in the absence of persuasive evidence of injury to the interests of the company: *Re Burton and Deakin Ltd* [1977] 1 WLR 390.

However, ordinarily the company should not spend money on defending the petition, in contrast to the position relating to a trade creditor's winding up petition: *Re Crossmore Electrical and Civil Engineering Ltd* [1989] BCLC 137). A petitioner will usually seek confirmation at the outset that the company's monies are not being put to that use, save in respect of the company's disclosure obligations and the petitioner may obtain injunctive relief in the absence of suitable undertakings: *Corbett v Corbett* [1998] BCC 93. The court has however approved expenditure on litigation relating to a proposed management buy-out even though it was in substance a dispute between shareholders: *Re a Company (No.005685 of 1988) ex p Schwarcz* [1989] BCLC 424.

S 127(2)

Under IA 1986 Sch B1 para 40(1)(b), if a company goes into administration as a result of an appointment by a qualifying floating charge holder the winding up petition is suspended and IA 1986 s 127(2) ensures that any disposition of the company's property whilst it is in such an administration is not prohibited by the avoidance provision of IA 1986 s 127(1). The winding up petition remains suspended until the court makes an order on the petition in the event that the administrator's proposals are not approved (IA 1986 Sch B1 para 55(2)(d)) or the company exits administration and an order is made on the petition. Where an administration order is made by the court, the suspension of the winding up petition does not arise because the winding up petition is dismissed on the making of the order: IA 1986 Sch B1 para 40(1)(a)); in the case of an appointment of an administrator by the company or the directors out of court no such appointment can be made if the winding up petition has not been disposed of, IA 1986 Sch B1 para 25(a).

1.152

128 Avoidance of attachments, etc

(1) Where a company registered in England and Wales is being wound up by the court, any attachment, sequestration, distress or execution put in force against the estate or effects of the company after the commencement of the winding up is void.

(2) This section, so far as relates to any estate or effects of the company situated in England and Wales, applies in the case of a company registered in Scotland as it applies in the case of a company registered in England and Wales.

Notes

S 128

This provision applies in a compulsory liquidation to all attachments, distress and executions initiated after the commencement of the liquidation winding up; IA 1986 s 129 defines the 'commencement of the winding up'. Notwithstanding the use of the word 'void' an application can be made to stay or set aside under IA 1986 s 126(1) or 130(2), or to permit the attachment, distress or execution to proceed: *The Constellation* [1966] 1 WLR 272, *Armourduct Manufacturing Co v General Incandescent Co* [1911] 2 KB 143). For attachments, distress or executions begun but not completed at the commencement of winding up, see IA 1986 s 183–184. Without prejudice to the avoidance provided in IA 1986 s 128, where during the 3 months prior to a winding up order goods or effects of the company have been distrained upon, they are charged for the benefit of the company with the preferential debts to the extent that the company has insufficient assets to pay its preferential debts: IA 1986 s 176(2).

So far as financial markets are concerned nothing in this provision affects any action taken by an exchange or clearing house for the purpose of its default proceedings: CA 1989 s 161(4).

Chapter VI
Winding Up by the Court

Commencement of winding up

1.153

129 Commencement of winding up by the court

(1) If, before the presentation of a petition for the winding up of a company by the court, a resolution has been passed by the company for voluntary winding up, the winding up of the company is deemed to have commenced at the time of the passing of the resolution; and unless the court, on proof of fraud or mistake, directs otherwise, all proceedings taken in the voluntary winding up are deemed to have been validly taken.

(1A) Where the court makes a winding up order by virtue of paragraph 13(1)(e) of Schedule B1, the winding up is deemed to commence on the making of the order.

(2) In any other case, the winding up of a company by the court is deemed to commence at the time of the presentation of the petition for winding up.

Notes

S 129(1)

Where a resolution to wind up is passed before the presentation of a winding up petition the voluntary winding up commences on the date of the resolution; see also IA 1986 s 86.

S 129(1A)

This provision does not apply in respect of a company where an administration petition was presented prior to 15 September 2003; it is highly unlikely that any such petition would still be extant. The new provision is designed to deal with the situation where the court is faced with an administration application and the court decides it would be more appropriate to order a liquidation. The liquidation can then be ordered without the presentation of a winding up petition; see notes to IA 1986 Sch B1 para 13.

S 129(2)

Subject to the situation where a resolution to wind up has been passed prior to a petition for winding up (see IA 1986 s 129(1)) the winding up by the court is deemed to have commenced at the time of presentation of the winding up petition at court if an order is made on the petition. This is important for calculation of time in various circumstances, including when trying to set aside transactions at an undervalue and preferences (see IA 1986 s 238 and 239) and the avoidance of dispositions between the presentation of the petition and the order (IA 1986 s 127).

1.154

130 Consequences of winding-up order

(1) On the making of a winding-up order, a copy of the order must forthwith be forwarded by the company (or otherwise as may be prescribed) to the registrar of companies, who shall enter it in his records relating to the company.

(2) When a winding-up order has been made or a provisional liquidator has been appointed, no action or proceeding shall be proceeded with or commenced against the company or its property, except by leave of the court and subject to such terms as the court may impose.

(3) When an order has been made for winding up a company registered under section 680 of the Companies Act, no action or proceeding shall be commenced or proceeded with against the company or its property or any contributory of the company, in respect of any debt of the company, except by leave of the court, and subject to such terms as the court may impose.

(4) An order for winding up a company operates in favour of all the creditors and of all contributories of the company as if made on the joint petition of a creditor and of a contributory.

Notes

S 130(1)

The court draws up the winding up order and sends 3 sealed copies to the official receiver, who in turn sends a copy to each of the company, the registrar of companies and the London Gazette and then the official receiver advertises the order; see IR 1986 r 4.21

S 130(2)

This provision, which stays actions and proceedings against the company after the making of the winding-up order should be compared to IA 1986 s 126(1) IA 1986, which governs the position between presentation of the petition and the making of the order. For the meaning of 'action and proceeding' see the notes under IA 1986 s 126. The phrase also appears to include criminal proceedings; in *R v Dickson* [1991] BCC 719, 722 the Court of Appeal was *'prepared to assume that leave was required in the present case before criminal proceedings could lawfully be instituted '* against the company in liquidation. The need to obtain permission of the court to bring, or more particularly to continue, proceedings against a company in compulsory liquidation is often overlooked. However, permission can be granted retrospectively, provided there is no prejudice to other creditors: *Re Saunders (a Bankrupt)* [1997] Ch 60; *Re Linkrealm Ltd* [1998] BCC 478.

The provision does not expressly apply to voluntary liquidation but an application may nevertheless be made by way of an application under IA 1986 s 112: *Anglo-Baltic & Mediterranean Bank v Barber & Co* [1924] 2 KB 410. The burden in that event is on the liquidator to satisfy the court that there is a good reason to grant the stay: *Currie v Consolidated Kent Collieries Corpn Ltd* [1906] 1 KB 134. The court will not make an order to stay proceedings where the purpose is to stifle a personal claim against the directors of the company: *Re J Burrows (Leeds) Ltd* [1982] 1 WLR 1177. The automatic stay does apply to the winding up of a foreign company as an unregistered company but it does not apply to a foreign insolvency proceeding; the court does have an inherent power to stay such proceedings but it would require exceptional circumstances: *Mazur Media Ltd v Mazur Media Gmbh* [2004] BPIR 1253.

In deciding whether or not to grant permission to issue or proceed with proceedings against a company in compulsory liquidation the court will be concerned to see that matters which can readily, and perhaps more cheaply, be resolved in the course of the winding up through the proof procedure are so resolved, and not through the medium of separate proceedings: *Re Exchange Securities & Commodities Ltd* [1983] BCLC 186. In particular where the liquidator in a compulsory liquidation opposes the lifting of a stay it is unlikely that the court will sanction the continuation of proceedings: *Bawejem Ltd v MC Fabrications Ltd* [1999] 1 BCLC 174. The court will not be concerned to go into the merits of the claim itself: *Re BCCI (No. 4)* [1994] 1 BCLC 419. However the court will look at all the circumstances and where it is right and fair it will lift the stay. For instance in a case where a claim was being made against the company and also against third parties and common issues arose the court allowed the proceedings involving the company to continue; this was because a trial of the proceedings between the claimant and the third parties was to be heard shortly: *New Cap Reinsurance Corp Ltd v HIH Casualty & General Insurance Ltd* [2002] 2 BCLC 228. Further where the nature of the applicant's claim is that the company is using the applicant's property without payment and/or for no good reason the court is likely to grant leave; in line with that principle a landlord will usually be allowed to re-enter for breach of covenant: *Re Strand Hotel Co* [1868] WN 2; chargeholders may enforce their security: *Re David Lloyd & Co* (1877) 6 Ch D 339; and where rights have passed to the claimant under pre-liquidation contracts the court is likely to allow specific performance rather than relegate the claimant to proof: *Re Coregrange Ltd* [1984] BCLC 453. In *Re Swiss Air Schweizerische Luftverkehr-Aktiengesellschaft* [2003] BCC 361 it was held that it was wrong to grant permission to proceed with a claim in circumstances where the claimant had obtained a freezing order, which was discharged by consent on payment of various sums into a joint bank account; this did not create a charge, and therefore it was wrong to give the claimant permission to continue after the company had been compulsorily wound up.

S 130(3)

Companies registered under CA 1985 s 680 are those old companies in existence prior to 2 November 1862, or registered under Acts of Parliament after that date but before the CA 1985 which have since registered under CA 1985.

_____

Investigation procedures

1.155

131 Company's statement of affairs

(1) Where the court has made a winding-up order or appointed a provisional liquidator, the official receiver may require some or all of the persons mentioned in subsection (3) below to make out and submit to him a statement in the prescribed form as to the affairs of the company.

(2) The statement shall be verified by affidavit by the persons required to submit it and shall show—
(a) particulars of the company's assets, debts and liabilities;
(b) the names and addresses of the company's creditors;
(c) the securities held by them respectively;
(d) the dates when the securities were respectively given; and
(e) such further or other information as may be prescribed or as the official receiver may require.

(3) The persons referred to in subsection (1) are—
(a) those who are or have been officers of the company;
(b) those who have taken part in the formation of the company at any time within one year before the relevant date;
(c) those who are in the company's employment, or have been in its employment within that year, and are in the official receiver's opinion capable of giving the information required;
(d) those who are or have been within that year officers of, or in the employment of, a company which is, or within that year was, an officer of the company.

(4) Where any persons are required under this section to submit a statement of affairs to the official receiver, they shall do so (subject to the next subsection) before the end of the period of 21 days beginning with the day after that on which the prescribed notice of the requirement is given to them by the official receiver.

(5) The official receiver, if he thinks fit, may—
(a) at any time release a person from an obligation imposed on him under subsection (1) or (2) above; or
(b) either when giving the notice mentioned in subsection (4) or subsequently, extend the period so mentioned;
and where the official receiver has refused to exercise a power conferred by this subsection, the court, if it thinks fit, may exercise it.

(6) In this section—
'employment' includes employment under a contract for services; and
'the relevant date' means—
(a) in a case where a provisional liquidator is appointed, the date of his appointment; and
(b) in a case where no such appointment is made, the date of the winding-up order.

(7) If a person without reasonable excuse fails to comply with any obligation imposed under this section, he is liable to a fine and, for continued contravention, to a daily default fine.

> (8) In the application of this section to Scotland references to the official receiver are to the liquidator or, in a case where a provisional liquidator is appointed, the provisional liquidator.

Notes

S 131(1)

Once a winding up order has been made, the investigation of the company's affairs will begin. Unless the company has gone into compulsory liquidation following a CVA or administration, and a liquidator has been appointed under IA 1986 s 140, the official receiver will be the first liquidator of the company: IA 1986 s 136(2). The statement of affairs is usually the starting point, with insolvent liquidations, for the official receiver in the performance of his duties of investigation and IR 1986 r 4.32ff should be read in conjunction with IA 1986 s 131. The official receiver may give certain forms of assistance to the persons required to produce the statement of affairs: IR 1986 r 4.32(5), 4.37.

S 131(2)

The statement of affairs, given on oath or affirmation, is particularly useful, as it is generally available for use in evidence in civil proceedings: IA 1986 s 433(1); *Re Keypak Homecare Ltd* [1990] BCLC 440. However, the statement of affairs is not available for use as evidence in all criminal cases: IA 1986 s 433(2). An affidavit rather than a witness statement must be used: IR 1986 r 7.57(6).

S 131(3)

Under IR 1986 r 4.39 the official receiver can require any of the persons set out in this provision to supply him with the accounts of the company over the previous 3 years.

S 131(4)

The statement of affairs is filed in court and it is open therefore to public inspection (IR 1986 r 7.28) and possibly open to searches by commercial agencies: *Re Austintel Ltd* [1997] BCC 363. If the official receiver thinks that public inspection would be prejudicial to the conduct of the liquidation he may apply for an order for limited disclosure: IR 1986 r 4.35.

S 131(5)

Such release might for instance be given in the case of a clearly solvent company.

S 131(6)

Given that 'employment' includes employment under a contract for services an auditor could for example be asked to provide a statement of affairs.

S 131(7)

In the event of non-compliance with a request to submit a statement of affairs, the court can compel enforcement by virtue of IR 1986 r 7.20. This is the proper course, rather than trying to obtain the information through public examination: *Re Wallace Smith Trust Co Ltd* [1992] BCC 707.

1.156

132 Investigation by official receiver

(1) Where a winding-up order is made by the court in England and Wales, it is the duty of the official receiver to investigate—

(a)   if the company has failed, the causes of the failure; and
(b)   generally, the promotion, formation, business, dealings and affairs of the company,
and to make such report (if any) to the court as he thinks fit.

(2) The report is, in any proceedings, prima facie evidence of the facts stated in it.

Notes

S 132(1)

The official receiver is under a duty to investigate, but has discretion whether to make a report. In the case of solvent liquidations the report will usually be cursory, stating the issued and the paid up share capital and estimating the assets and liabilities only.

1.157

133 Public examination of officers

(1) Where a company is being wound up by the court, the official receiver or, in Scotland, the liquidator may at any time before the dissolution of the company apply to the court for the public examination of any person who—
(a)   is or has been an officer of the company; or
(b)   has acted as liquidator or administrator of the company or as receiver or manager or, in Scotland, receiver of its property; or
(c)   not being a person falling within paragraph (a) or (b), is or has been concerned, or has taken part, in the promotion, formation or management of the company.

(2) Unless the court otherwise orders, the official receiver or, in Scotland, the liquidator shall make an application under subsection (1) if he is requested in accordance with the rules to do so by—
(a)   one-half, in value, of the company's creditors; or
(b)   three-quarters, in value, of the company's contributories.

(3) On an application under subsection (1), the court shall direct that a public examination of the person to whom the application relates shall be held on a day appointed by the court; and that person shall attend on that day and be publicly examined as to the promotion, formation or management of the company or as to the conduct of its business and affairs, or his conduct or dealings in relation to the company.

(4) The following may take part in the public examination of a person under this section and may question that person concerning the matters mentioned in subsection (3), namely—
(a)   the official receiver;
(b)   the liquidator of the company;
(c)   any person who has been appointed as special manager of the company's property or business;
(d)   any creditor of the company who has tendered a proof or, in Scotland, submitted a claim in the winding up;

> (e)   any contributory of the company.

Notes

S 133

In practice this provision is only rarely used. The public examination does remain a useful fallback in situations where rogue company officers refuse to give full information in the statement of affairs or in informal interviews. For the relevant rules see IR 1986 r 4.211–4.217 As to the power of the court to govern procedure of a public examination see *Re Richbell Strategic Holdings Ltd (No 2)* [2001] BCC 409. The public examination procedure has the following advantages:

- The examination is in open court and creditors are allowed to attend *Re Grey's Brewery Co* (1883) 25 Ch D 400, IA 1986 s 133(4).
- There is no privilege against self-incrimination *Bishopsgate Investment Management Ltd (in liquidation) v Maxwell* [1993] Ch 1 although the evidence obtained will not necessarily be available for use in criminal proceedings (see IA 1986 s 433).
- The court does not have the power to refuse to order a public examination if the official receiver applies (IA 1986 s 133(3)), although the subject of the order may apply under IR 1986 r 7.47 to review, vary or rescind the order (*Re Casterbridge Properties Ltd* [2003] EWHC 1731, [2003] BCC 724 and there is a specific power of recission exercisable in the circumstances stated in IR 1986 r 4.211(4).

S 133(1)

Any person falling within the category of persons set out can be the subject of an order for public examination, whether or not a British subject or resident within the jurisdiction: *Re Seagull Manufacturing Co Ltd* [1991] BCC 550. There is jurisdiction to order a public examination in a voluntary winding up, by virtue of IA 186 s 112, and see *Re Campbell Coverings Ltd (No 2)* [1954] Ch 225.

S 133(2)

The official receiver makes the application although he may be requisitioned to do so; see also IR 1986 r 4.213.

S 133(3)

Where the official receiver makes the appropriate application for an order the court will generally make an order as a matter of right unless it was satisfied that there was no useful purpose to be served by a public examination: *Jeeves v Official Receiver* [2003] BCC 912. The court has a wide discretion to grant or refuse an order if it is applied for on the basis of a requisition: IR 1986 r 4.213(5).

1.158

134 Enforcement of s 133

(1) If a person without reasonable excuse fails at any time to attend his public examination under section 133, he is guilty of a contempt of court and liable to be punished accordingly.

(2) In a case where a person without reasonable excuse fails at any time to attend his examination under section 133 or there are reasonable grounds for believing that a person has absconded, or is about to abscond, with a

view to avoiding or delaying his examination under that section, the court may cause a warrant to be issued to a constable or prescribed officer of the court—

(a)   for the arrest of that person; and

(b)   for the seizure of any books, papers, records, money or goods in that person's possession.

(3) In such a case the court may authorise the person arrested under the warrant to be kept in custody, and anything seized under such a warrant to be held, in accordance with the rules, until such time as the court may order.

Notes

S 134(1)

See for warrants IR 1986 r 7.22.

Appointment of liquidator

1.159

135 Appointment and powers of provisional liquidator

(1) Subject to the provisions of this section, the court may, at any time after the presentation of a winding-up petition, appoint a liquidator provisionally.

(2) In England and Wales, the appointment of a provisional liquidator may be made at any time before the making of a winding-up order; and either the official receiver or any other fit person may be appointed.

(3) In Scotland, such an appointment may be made at any time before the first appointment of liquidators.

(4) The provisional liquidator shall carry out such functions as the court may confer on him.

(5) When a liquidator is provisionally appointed by the court, his powers may be limited by the order appointing him.

Notes

S 135

A provisional liquidator may be appointed for a variety of purposes, but most commonly where it appears that there is a risk of dissipation of company assets, the winding up petition is a public interest petition (IA 1986 s 124A), or in the case of insolvent insurance companies for which the administration procedure was not previously available: *Smith v UIC Insurance Co. Ltd* [2001] BCC 11; *Re Latreefers Inc* [2001] BCC 174. Though it is not a step taken lightly the power to appoint is stated in general terms and the modern tendency is not to restrict or confine its possible application: *Re Namco Ltd* [2003] BPIR 1170, *MHMH Ltd v Carwood Baxter Holdings Ltd* [2006] 1 BCLC 279. The effect of appointment is dramatic including the termination of the authority of any agents appointed by the company: *Pacific and General Insurance v Hazell* [1997] BCC 400. The appointment of provisional liquidators is intended to be a short-term measure, to hold the ring until a winding up order is made. It must be shown that a winding up order is likely to be made: *Re Highfield Commodities Ltd* [1985] 1 WLR 149, *Re Treasure Traders Corporation Ltd [2005] EWHC 2774 (Ch)), [2005] All ER (D) 25 (Dec).* However, the exercise of the jurisdiction to appoint provisional liquidators over insurance companies with a view to the approval of a scheme of arrangement, or indeed to enable the company's affairs to be run off (for example, in the case of corporate underwriters at Lloyds) shows that the procedure is capable of being used flexibly and in novel situations. IA 1986 s 135 should be read in conjunction with IR 1986 rr 4.25–4.31, r 4.218(1)(e).

The provisional liquidator is generally intended to be appointed for short period pending the hearing of the petition: *Re ABC Coupler & Engineering Co Ltd (No 3)* [1970] 1 WLR 702, 715. The position of provisional liquidator ceases when a winding up order is made or the petition is dismissed: *Re North Wales Gunpowder Co* [1892] 2 QB 220; but the court must make a formal order for his removal: IA 1986 s 172(2). The application may, in urgent circumstances be made without notice, and generally a cross-undertaking in damages will be required unless the applicant is the Secretary of State: *Re Highfield Commodities Ltd* [1985] 1 WLR 149. Under the usual liberty to apply provision inherent in an order appointing a provisional liquidator, the board retains authority to apply for its discharge on short notice: *Re Union Accident Insurance Co Ltd* [1972] 1 WLR 640. If it transpires that a without notice application was inappropriate the petitioner may be ordered to pay the remuneration and expenses of the provisional liquidator directly: *Re Secure & Provide plc* [1992] BCC 405. The application is made to the Judge, not the Registrar: Practice Note: the Hearing of Insolvency Proceedings para 4 [2005] BCC 456. The appointment of a provisional liquidator effects a stay on actions and proceedings against the company: see notes to IA 1986 s 130(2).

S 135(1)

Prior to the introduction of the new administration regime the court could not appoint a provisional liquidator unless there was a subsisting winding up petition: *Re a Company* [1973] 1 WLR 1566. This probably remains the position despite the width of the orders that the court can make on the hearing of an administration application: IA 1986 Sch B1 para 13; and see notes to IA 1986 Sch B1 para 79(4)(d) and *Lancefield v Lancefield* [2002] BPIR 1108. If a provisional liquidator has already been appointed neither a qualifying floating chargeholder nor the company nor the directors can effect an out of court appointment of an administrator: IA 1986, Sch B1, para 17(a), 25(a).

S 135(2)

If someone other than the official receiver is appointed that person must be a licensed insolvency practitioner: IA 1986 s 230(5), s 388(5).

S 135(4)

Usually the order will confine the exercise of powers to taking possession of the assets; if it is desirable that the business of the company is carried on until the petition is heard the provisional liquidator can apply for the appointment of a special manager: IA 1986 s 177; IR 1986 rr 4.206–210; *Re US Ltd* (1983) 1 BCC 98, 985; *Re Pinstripe Farming Co Ltd* [1996] BCC 913. In an appropriate case the court can order that the provisional liquidator circulate information to creditors: *Equitas Ltd v Jacob* [2005] BPIR 1312.

S 135(5)

Occasionally the powers granted can be wider, for example to include the settling a list of contributories: *Re English Bank of the River Plate* [1892] 1 Ch 391; but they ought not ordinarily to include any distribution of the assets: *Re Hammersmith Town Hall* (1877) 6 Ch D 112.

1.160

136 Functions of official receiver in relation to office of liquidator

(1) The following provisions of this section have effect, subject to section 140 below, on a winding-up order being made by the court in England and Wales.

(2) The official receiver, by virtue of his office, becomes the liquidator of the company and continues in office until another person becomes liquidator under the provisions of this Part.

(3) The official receiver is, by virtue of his office, the liquidator during any vacancy.

(4) At any time when he is the liquidator of the company, the official receiver may summon separate meetings of the company's creditors and contributories for the purpose of choosing a person to be liquidator of the company in place of the official receiver.

(5) It is the duty of the official receiver—
(a) as soon as practicable in the period of 12 weeks beginning with the day on which the winding-up order was made, to decide whether to exercise his power under subsection (4) to summon meetings, and
(b) if in pursuance of paragraph (a) he decides not to exercise that power, to give notice of his decision, before the end of that period, to the court and to the company's creditors and contributories, and
(c) (whether or not he has decided to exercise that power) to exercise his power to summon meetings under subsection (4) if he is at any time requested, in accordance with the rules, to do so by one-quarter, in value, of the company's creditors;

and accordingly, where the duty imposed by paragraph (c) arises before the official receiver has performed a duty imposed by paragraph (a) or (b), he is not required to perform the latter duty.

(6) A notice given under subsection (5)(b) to the company's creditors shall contain an explanation of the creditors' power under subsection (5)(c) to require the official receiver to summon meetings of the company's creditors and contributories.

Notes

S 136(1)

The appointment of the supervisor of a voluntary arrangement or the administrator of a company in administration as the liquidator, (as opposed to the official receiver) is dealt with in IA 1986 s 140.

S 136(2)

The official receiver automatically becomes liquidator on the making of a winding up order; consequently a voluntary liquidator will be replaced by the official receiver as liquidator IR 1986 r 4.136, r 4.14/.

S 136(4)

The procedure in relation to the 'first meetings' is dealt with in IR 1986 r 4.50ff and the business of such meetings is limited IR 1986 r 4.52(1). Where the official receiver wishes another person to be liquidator he may apply at any time to the Secretary of State under IA 1986 s 137(1) for an appointment to be made; this could be prior to the first meetings.

S 136(5)

The official receiver is given a 12 week period beginning with the date of the order to decide whether or not to summon such meetings; if he decides not to then he must notify the creditors and contributories before the end of that period; the creditors may require him to summon the meetings if one quarter in value of the creditors make the request.

1.161

137 Appointment by Secretary of State

(1) In a winding up by the court in England and Wales the official receiver may, at any time when he is the liquidator of the company, apply to the Secretary of State for the appointment of a person as liquidator in his place.

(2) If meetings are held in pursuance of a decision under section 136(5)(a), but no person is chosen to be liquidator as a result of those meetings, it is the duty of the official receiver to decide whether to refer the need for an appointment to the Secretary of State.

(3) On an application under subsection (1), or a reference made in pursuance of a decision under subsection (2), the Secretary of State shall either make an appointment or decline to make one.

(4) Where a liquidator has been appointed by the Secretary of State under subsection (3), the liquidator shall give notice of his appointment to the company's creditors or, if the court so allows, shall advertise his appointment in accordance with the directions of the court.

(5) In that notice or advertisement the liquidator shall—
- (a) state whether he proposes to summon a general meeting of the company's creditors under section 141 below for the purpose of determining (together with any meeting of contributories) whether a liquidation committee should be established under that section, and
- (b) if he does not propose to summon such a meeting, set out the power of the company's creditors under that section to require him to summon one.

Notes

S 137(1)

It may be necessary for the official receiver to secure an appointment of a licensed insolvency practitioner as a matter of urgency due to the specialist nature of the work that may be involved in the liquidation or simply because the official receiver does not have the necessary resources. This provision (and see IR 1986 r 4.104, 4.107) enables the official receiver to apply to the Secretary of State without having to await an appointment at a creditors' meeting.

S 137(3)

If the Secretary of State declines to make an appointment the official receiver continues in office as liquidator IA 1986 s 136(2).

1.162

138 Appointment of liquidator in Scotland

(1) Where a winding-up order is made by the court in Scotland, a liquidator shall be appointed by the court at the time when the order is made.

(2) The liquidator so appointed (here referred to as 'the interim liquidator') continues in office until another person becomes liquidator in his place under this section or the next.

(3) The interim liquidator shall (subject to the next subsection) as soon as practicable in the period of 28 days beginning with the day on which the winding-up order was made or such longer period as the court may allow, summon separate meetings of the company's creditors and contributories for the purpose of choosing a person (who may be the person who is the interim liquidator) to be liquidator of the company in place of the interim liquidator.

(4) If it appears to the interim liquidator, in any case where a company is being wound up on grounds including its inability to pay its debts, that it would be inappropriate to summon under subsection (3) a meeting of the company's contributories, he may summon only a meeting of the company's creditors for the purpose mentioned in that subsection.

(5) If one or more meetings are held in pursuance of this section but no person is appointed or nominated by the meeting or meetings, the interim liquidator shall make a report to the court which shall appoint either the interim liquidator or some other person to be liquidator of the company.

(6) A person who becomes liquidator of the company in place of the interim liquidator shall, unless he is appointed by the court, forthwith notify the court of that fact.

1.163

139 Choice of liquidator at meetings of creditors and contributories

(1) This section applies where a company is being wound up by the court and separate meetings of the company's creditors and contributories are summoned for the purpose of choosing a person to be liquidator of the company.

(2) The creditors and the contributories at their respective meetings may nominate a person to be liquidator.

(3) The liquidator shall be the person nominated by the creditors or, where no person has been so nominated, the person (if any) nominated by the contributories.

(4) In the case of different persons being nominated, any contributory or creditor may, within 7 days after the date on which the nomination was made by the creditors, apply to the court for an order either—
   (a) appointing the person nominated as liquidator by the contributories to be a liquidator instead of, or jointly with, the person nominated by the creditors; or

> (b) appointing some other person to be liquidator instead of the person nominated by the creditors.

Notes

S 139(4)

Where there is a conflict between the wishes of the creditors and those of the contributories, the presumption is in favour of the creditors' choice of liquidator, subject to the right of the contributories to apply to the court to have their choice replace or join with the creditors' choice; and see IR 1986 r 4.100, 4.102.

> **1.163A**
>
> **140 Appointment by the court following administration or voluntary arrangement**
>
> (1) Where a winding-up order is made immediately upon the appointment of an administrator ceasing to have effect the court may appoint as liquidator of the company the person whose appointment as administrator has ceased to have effect.
>
> (2) Where a winding-up order is made at a time when there is a supervisor of a voluntary arrangement approved in relation to the company under Part I, the court may appoint as liquidator of the company the person who is the supervisor at the time when the winding-up order is made.
>
> (3) Where the court makes an appointment under this section, the official receiver does not become the liquidator as otherwise provided by section 136(2), and he has no duty under section 136(5)(a) or (b) in respect of the summoning of creditors' or contributories' meetings.

Notes

S 140(1)

This section provides for continuity on the part of the insolvency practitioner where the company goes into a compulsory liquidation from an administration. Note that the winding up petition should contain a request for the appointment of the relevant practitioner in the prayer. Although it may be convenient and cost efficient for the insolvency practitioner with knowledge of the company's affairs to continue in situ, the creditors may not wish to see the same insolvency practitioner remain in control: *Re Charnley Davies Business Services Ltd* (1987) 3 BCC 408. The court requires the creditors to be notified in advance if an appointment under this section is requested, and a report to be filed at court 2 days before the hearing of the petition: IR 1986 r 4.7(9); see also IR 1986 r 4.49A, 4.102. It is possible to exit an administration into a creditors' voluntary liquidation (IA 1986 Sch B1 para 83) rather than using the compulsory liquidation route; in that event the administrator's proposals must contain provisions informing the creditors of their ability to choose as liquidator someone other than the administrator: IR 1986 r 2.117, 2.33(2)(m), 2.45(2)(g).

Liquidation committees

1.164

141 Liquidation committee (England and Wales)

(1) Where a winding-up order has been made by the court in England and Wales and separate meetings of creditors and contributories have been summoned for the purpose of choosing a person to be liquidator, those meetings may establish a committee ('the liquidation committee') to exercise the functions conferred on it by or under this Act.

(2) The liquidator (not being the official receiver) may at any time, if he thinks fit, summon separate general meetings of the company's creditors and contributories for the purpose of determining whether such a committee should be established and, if it is so determined, of establishing it.

The liquidator (not being the official receiver) shall summon such a meeting if he is requested, in accordance with the rules, to do so by one-tenth, in value, of the company's creditors.

(3) Where meetings are summoned under this section, or for the purpose of choosing a person to be liquidator, and either the meeting of creditors or the meeting of contributories decides that a liquidation committee should be established, but the other meeting does not so decide or decides that a committee should not be established, the committee shall be established in accordance with the rules, unless the court otherwise orders.

(4) The liquidation committee is not to be able or required to carry out its functions at any time when the official receiver is liquidator; but at any such time its functions are vested in the Secretary of State except to the extent that the rules otherwise provide.

(5) Where there is for the time being no liquidation committee, and the liquidator is a person other than the official receiver, the functions of such a committee are vested in the Secretary of State except to the extent that the rules otherwise provide.

Notes

S 141(1)

The function of the liquidation committee is to provide guidance and assistance to the liquidator, and can be most helpful in large and complex liquidations. The liquidator cannot be obliged by the committee to disclose the reports he has made under the CDDA 1986: *Re W and A Glasor Ltd* [1994] BCC 199. There can only be a liquidation committee if a liquidator, other than the official receiver, has been appointed. The relevant rules are in IR 1986 r 4.151–4.178.

S 141(4)

When the official receiver is in office as liquidator, the Secretary of State carries out the functions of the liquidation committee.

1.165

142 Liquidation committee (Scotland)

(1) Where a winding-up order has been made by the court in Scotland and separate meetings of creditors and contributories have been summoned for the purpose of choosing a person to be liquidator or, under section 138(4), only a meeting of creditors has been summoned for that purpose, those meetings or (as the case may be) that meeting may establish a committee ('the liquidation committee') to exercise the functions conferred on it by or under this Act.

(2) The liquidator may at any time, if he thinks fit, summon separate general meetings of the company's creditors and contributories for the purpose of determining whether such a committee should be established and, if it is so determined, of establishing it.

(3) The liquidator, if appointed by the court otherwise than under section 139(4)(a), is required to summon meetings under subsection (2) if he is requested, in accordance with the rules, to do so by one-tenth, in value, of the company's creditors.

(4) Where meetings are summoned under this section, or for the purpose of choosing a person to be liquidator, and either the meeting of creditors or the meeting of contributories decides that a liquidation committee should be established, but the other meeting does not so decide or decides that a committee should not be established, the committee shall be established in accordance with the rules, unless the court otherwise orders.

(5) Where in the case of any winding up there is for the time being no liquidation committee, the functions of such a committee are vested in the court except to the extent that the rules otherwise provide.

(6) In addition to the powers and duties conferred and imposed on it by this Act, a liquidation committee has such of the powers and duties of commissioners in a sequestration as may be conferred and imposed on such committees by the rules.

The liquidator's functions

1.166

143 General functions in winding up by the court

(1) The functions of the liquidator of a company which is being wound up by the court are to secure that the assets of the company are got in, realised and distributed to the company's creditors and, if there is a surplus, to the persons entitled to it.

(2) It is the duty of the liquidator of a company, which is being wound up by the court in England and Wales, if he is not the official receiver—
    (a)   to furnish the official receiver with such information,
    (b)   to produce to the official receiver, and permit inspection by the official receiver of, such books, papers and other records, and
    (c)   to give the official receiver such other assistance,

as the official receiver may reasonably require for the purposes of carrying out his functions in relation to the winding up.

Notes

S 143(1)

A liquidator is an officer of the company: *Re X Co Ltd* [1907] 2 Ch 92; and he is a fiduciary who is under a duty to carry out his statutory duties: *Re P Turner (Wilsden) Ltd* [1987] BCLC 149. A liquidator in a compulsory liquidation is also an officer of the court and he is required to act in a fair and honest manner and to be independent: *Re Condon, ex p James* (1874) 9 Ch App 609. The same principle does not apply directly to a voluntary liquidator: *Customs and Excise Commrs v TH Knitwear Ltd* [1988] BCLC 195 cf *Re John Bateson & Co Ltd* [1985] BCLC 259. There are a number of other provisions dealing with powers, duties and functions of liquidators; for instance IA 1986 s 163, 167, 168, and Sch 4. In an insolvent liquidation the liquidator will distribute assets broadly in the following order of priority: (i) expenses of the winding up (IA 1986 s 156)(ii) preferential debts (IA 1986 s 175 (1))(iii) debts secured by floating charge holders (IA 1986 s 175(2)) (iv) ordinary debts (IA 1986 s 175(2)).

S 143(2)

Aside from the specific duties listed in this provision and elsewhere it is clear that a liquidator has a duty to act in the interests of creditors and contributories generally. Unless a liquidator contractually assumes a direct duty to a creditor (*A & J Fabrications (Batley) Ltd v Grant Thornton* [1999] BCC 807) no fiduciary duty or duty of care is owed to individual creditors *Leon v York-O-Matic* [1966] 1 WLR 1450; *Kyrris v Oldham* [2003] EWCA Civ 1506, [2004] 1 BCLC 305; *Re HIH Casualty & General Insurance Ltd* [2005] EWHC 2125 (Ch), [2006] 2 All ER 671, at para 119. However, a liquidator may be liable to an individual creditor if held to be in breach of a statutory duty owed to that creditor: *Pulsford v Devenish* [1903] 2 Ch 625; *James Smith & Sons (Norwood) Ltd v Goodman* [1936] Ch 216.

At all times a liquidator must act impartially and independently: *Re Lubin, Rosen & Associates Ltd* [1975] 1 WLR 122.

1.167

144 Custody of company's property

(1) When a winding-up order has been made, or where a provisional liquidator has been appointed, the liquidator or the provisional liquidator (as the case may be) shall take into his custody or under his control all the property and things in action to which the company is or appears to be entitled.

(2) In a winding up by the court in Scotland, if and so long as there is no liquidator, all the property of the company is deemed to be in the custody of the court.

Notes

S 144(1)

'Property' has a very wide meaning under IA 1986 s 436.

1.168

145 Vesting of company property in liquidator

(1) When a company is being wound up by the court, the court may on the application of the liquidator by order direct that all or any part of the property of whatsoever description belonging to the company or held by trustees on its behalf shall vest in the liquidator by his official name; and thereupon the property to which the order relates vests accordingly.

(2) The liquidator may, after giving such indemnity (if any) as the court may direct, bring or defend in his official name any action or other legal proceeding which relates to that property or which it is necessary to bring or defend for the purpose of effectually winding up the company and recovering its property.

Notes

S 145(1)

The company remains a separate legal entity in liquidation, and so assets of the company do not vest automatically in the liquidator, unlike the position with a trustee in bankruptcy (see IA 1986 s 306). The liquidator can deal with the assets of the company, and bring and defend proceedings in the name of the company, and so the provisions of this section are rarely used: see IA 1986 Sch 4 for the powers of a liquidator to deal with inter alia the 'property' of the company which is widely defined in IA 1986 s 436.

1.169

146 Duty to summon final meeting

(1) Subject to the next subsection, if it appears to the liquidator of a company which is being wound by the court that the winding up of the company is for practical purposes complete and the liquidator is not the official receiver, the liquidator shall summon a final general meeting of the company's creditors which—
  (a) shall receive the liquidator's report of the winding up, and
  (b) shall determine whether the liquidator should have his release under section 174 in Chapter VII of this Part.

(2) The liquidator may, if he thinks fit, give the notice summoning the final general meeting at the same time as giving notice of any final distribution of the company's property but, if summoned for an earlier date, that meeting shall be adjourned (and, if necessary, further adjourned) until a date on which the liquidator is able to report to the meeting that the winding up of the company is for practical purposes complete.

> (3) In the carrying out of his functions in the winding up it is the duty of the liquidator to retain sufficient sums from the company's property to cover the expenses of summoning and holding the meeting required by this section.

Notes

S 146(1)

For final meetings in voluntary windings up, see IA 1986 s 96 and 104, and the notes to those sections. Where the official receiver is the liquidator, he simply gives notice that the winding up is effectively complete to the Secretary of State: IA 1986 s 174(3). For the procedure in relation to meetings see IR 1986 r 4.125, 4.126. At the meeting the liquidator gives details of the course of the winding up, including a summary of receipts and payments. The liquidator will vacate office as soon as he has given notice to the court and to the registrar of companies that the meeting has been held and of the decisions (if any) of the meeting: IA 1986 s 172(8).

General powers of court

1.170

147 Power to stay or sist winding up

(1) The court may at any time after an order for winding up, on the application either of the liquidator or the official receiver or any creditor or contributory, and on proof to the satisfaction of the court that all proceedings in the winding up ought to be stayed or sisted, make an order staying or sisting the proceedings, either altogether or for a limited time, on such terms and conditions as the court thinks fit.

(2) The court may, before making an order, require the official receiver to furnish to it a report with respect to any facts or matters which are in his opinion relevant to the application.

(3) A copy of every order made under this section shall forthwith be forwarded by the company, or otherwise as may be prescribed, to the registrar of companies, who shall enter it in his records relating to the company.

1.171

Notes

S 147

If a stay of the liquidation is ordered *'altogether'* its effect is to end the liquidation for all practical purposes and the control of the company passes back to the directors; otherwise it can be stayed for a *'limited time'*. A stay of a winding up order may be granted for a variety of reasons, for example on the grounds of forum non conveniens: *Re Harrods (Buenos Aires) Ltd* [1992] Ch 72 *cf Re HIH Casualty & General Insurance Ltd* [2006] EWHC Civ 732, [2006] All ER (D) 65 (Jun), para 57 to 60; or because the company is in fact not insolvent, and wishes to continue to trade, although consideration in that case should be given to a rescission of the winding up order under IR 1986 r 7.47. Prior to perfection of the winding-up order it is possible to rescind the order within 7 days of the making of the order: *Re Virgo Systems Ltd* (1989) 5 BCC 833.

S 147(1)

The respondents to the application would normally include the official receiver and any liquidator where the official receiver is not liquidator; the winding up petitioner should also be joined if he does not consent to a stay being granted. The evidence in support should detail the consent of creditors and the holders of partly paid shares, and confirm that there has been no return of capital and that the company will have sufficient capital to carry on business: *Re Calgary & Edmonton Land Co Ltd* [1975] 1 WLR 355. If the evidence does not prove that all creditors will be protected the court must be satisfied that there is good reason for a stay; for instance substantive error in the proceedings: *Re Intermain Properties Ltd* (1985) 1 BCC 99; or a need to investigate possible claims (*Re Telescriptor Syndicate Ltd* [1903] 2 Ch 174.

The court in exercising its discretion will require a good reason for the stay and must be sure that creditors and contributories are not prejudiced. The burden is on the applicant. The court will not grant a stay merely because there is an appeal against a winding up order: *Re Calgary and Edmonton Land Co Ltd* [1975] 1WLR 355; *Re Lowston Ltd* [1991] BCLC 570. The court may also grant a stay on the application of contributories where all the creditors have been paid: *Re South Barrule Slate Quarry* (1869) LR 8 Eq 688; or otherwise provided for: *Re Baxters Ltd* [1898] WN 60, *Re Stephen Walters & Sons Ltd* [1926] WN 236. Further the court may impose terms in the order, for instance that dissenting shareholders be bought out: *Re South Barrule Slate Quarry* (1869) LR 8 Eq 688; or that dissenters can apply to remove the stay within a stated period: *Re Baxters Ltd* [1898] WN 236. The court will not grant a stay unless the fees and remuneration of the liquidator are paid or otherwise provided for: *Re Calgary and Edmonton Land Co* [1975] 1 WLR 355.

S 147(2)

It is therefore necessary to contact the official receiver before applying for a stay to confirm his position on the matter.

1.172

148 Settlement of list of contributories and application of assets

(1) As soon as may be after making a winding-up order, the court shall settle a list of contributories, with power to rectify the register of members in all cases where rectification is required in pursuance of the Companies Act or this Act, and shall cause the company's assets to be collected, and applied in discharge of its liabilities.

(2) If it appears to the court that it will not be necessary to make calls on or adjust the rights of contributories, the court may dispense with the settlement of a list of contributories.

(3) In settling the list, the court shall distinguish between persons who are contributories in their own right and persons who are contributories as being representatives of or liable for the debts of others.

Notes

S 148(1)

For the definition of 'contributory' see IA 1986 s 79(1) and the notes to that section. Note that preparation of the list is the duty of the court, but this duty is expressly delegated to the liquidator by IA 1986 s 160(1)(b) and IR 1986 r 4.195. In practice two lists are drawn up: the A-list and the B-list: see notes to IA 1986 s 73ff. The A-list consists of those who are members at the date of commencement of winding up. The B list will be those who are liable as contributories because they have ceased to be members within one year of the commencement of winding up, under the provisions of IA 1986 s 74(2). The B-list will only need to be compiled if it appears that the contributories on the A-list will be unable to meet the calls made on them to contribute. The most obvious example of a situation where it would not be necessary to compile a list of contributories is where all the shares are fully paid. In a voluntary liquidation the liquidator may exercise the court's power to settle the list: IA 1986 s 165(4). The rules relating to the settling of the list are contained in IR 1986 r 4.195–201.

1.173

149 Debts due from contributory to company

(1) The court may, at any time after making a winding-up order, make an order on any contributory for the time being on the list of contributories to pay, in manner directed by the order, any money due from him (or from the estate of the person who he represents) to the company, exclusive of any money payable by him or the estate by virtue of any call in pursuance of the Companies Act or this Act.

(2) The court in making such an order may—
    (a)   in the case of an unlimited company, allow to the contributory by way of set-off any money due to him or the estate which he represents from the company on any independent dealing or contract with the company, but not any money due to him as a member of the company in respect of any dividend or profit, and
    (b)   in the case of a limited company, make to any director or manager whose liability is unlimited or to his estate the like allowance.

(3) In the case of any company, whether limited or unlimited, when all the creditors are paid in full (together with interest at the official rate), any money due on any account whatever to a contributory from the company may be allowed to him by way of set-off against any subsequent call.

Notes

S 149(1)

This section provides the liquidator with a summary remedy against contributories for debts owed to the company other than uncalled capital, without having to issue ordinary civil proceedings, and gives the contributory only limited rights of set-off: IA 1986 s 149(2); for the general liabilities of contributories see the notes to IA 1986 s 73ff. The position is however different if the contributory is bankrupt. In that event the bankruptcy set off rule (IA 1986 s 323) applies and there will be a set off of calls against a company's debt irrespective of whether the company debt exceeds the call or the call exceeds the company's debt: *Re Universal Banking Corpn* (1879) 5 Ch App 492, *Re Duckworth* (1867) 2 Ch App 578. The balance will be proved for by the liquidator or the trustee as the case may be. If the contributory is itself a company in liquidation the insolvency set off rules do not apply: *Re Auriferous Properties Ltd (No 2)* [1898] 2 Ch 428. The wording of IA 1986 s 149(1) is wide ('any money due'). *Re Marlborough Club Company* (1868) LR 5 Eq 365 is sometimes cited as authority for the proposition that only sums owed by the contributory in his character as a member can be recovered under this section. However, the case is actually decided on the basis that there was, under CA 1862 s 101 no jurisdiction to add to a settled list of contributories, and that a fully paid up shareholder was not a contributory, which is no longer good law: *Re Phoenix Oil and Transport Company Ltd* [1958] 1 Ch 560.

S 149(2), (3)

The general principle is that a contributory may not set off a debt owed to him by the company against a call made by a liquidator: *Re Overend, Gurney & Co* (1866) 1 Ch App 528; neither may a company debt be set off against an unpaid call made by the directors and falling due before the commencement of the liquidation: *Re Hiram Maxim Lamp Co Ltd* [1903] 1 Ch 70. These provisions contain exceptions to those general principles.

1.174

150 Power to make calls

(1) The court may, at any time after making a winding-up order, and either before or after it has ascertained the sufficiency of the company's assets, make calls on all or any of the contributories for the time being settled on the list of the contributories to the extent of their liability, for payment of any money which the court considers necessary to satisfy the company's debts and liabilities, and the expenses of winding up, and for the adjustment of the rights of the contributories among themselves, and make an order for payment of any calls so made.

(2) In making a call the court may take into consideration the probability that some of the contributories may partly or wholly fail to pay it.

Notes

S 150(1)

The power of the court to make calls is delegated to the liquidator, but subject to the control of the court or liquidation committee by the combined effect of IA 1986 s 160(1)(d), 160(2) and 165(4)(b) (voluntary liquidation), and IR 1986 r 4.202. For the procedure for making calls see IR 1986 r 4.202ff. In a compulsory liquidation the liquidator must obtain leave of court or sanction of the liquidation committee before making a call s 160(2).

S 150(2)

The liquidator need not wait for a court order to make calls and he can make a call after settling the list of contributories without first determining the sufficiency of the company's assets. If there is a surplus it will be returned to the contributories. Though the call is likely to be for the full amount of the unpaid liability the liquidator may call in a lesser sum if he thinks appropriate. The liquidator can enforce a call left unpaid with the applicable interest from prior to liquidation: *Stone v City and County Bank* (1871) 3 Ch D 282; however where the liquidator himself makes the call he cannot require interest to be paid unless a court order is required to enforce the call: *Re Welsh Flannel and Tweed Co* (1875) LR 20 Eq 360.

1.175

151 Payment into bank of money due to company

(1) The court may order any contributory, purchaser or other person from whom money is due to the company to pay the amount due into the

Bank of England (or any branch of it) to the account of the liquidator instead of to the liquidator, and such an order may be enforced in the same manner as if it had directed payment to the liquidator.

(2) All money and securities paid or delivered into the Bank of England (or branch) in the event of a winding up by the court are subject in all respects to the orders of the court.

1.176

152 Order on contributory to be conclusive evidence

(1) An order made by the court on a contributory is conclusive evidence that the money (if any) thereby appearing to be due or ordered to be paid is due, but subject to any right of appeal.

(2) All other pertinent matters stated in the order are to be taken as truly stated as against all persons and in all proceedings except proceedings in Scotland against the heritable estate of a deceased contributory; and in that case the order is only prima facie evidence for the purpose of charging his heritable estate, unless his heirs or legatees of heritage were on the list of contributories at the time of the order being made.

Notes

S 152(1)

This underlines the importance of objecting at an early stage to inclusion on the list of contributories, if appropriate (IR 1986 r 4.199).

1.177

153 Power to exclude creditors not proving in time

The court may fix a time or times within which creditors are to prove their debts or claims or to be excluded from the benefit of any distribution made before those debts are proved.

Notes

S 153

The power of the court is delegated to the liquidator in practice (IA 1986 s 160). If a creditor fails to prove his debt within the time allowed he will not be entitled to upset any dividend paid in that time. However, he will be entitled to receive a dividend if there is another round of payments after he has proved his debt: IR 1986 r 4.182(2).

1.178

154 Adjustment of rights of contributories

The court shall adjust the rights of the contributories among themselves and distribute any surplus among the persons entitled to it.

Notes

S 154

For the procedure in any return of capital see IR 1986 r 4.221–4.222; a similar provision for a voluntary liquidation appears in IA 1986 s 107.

1.179

155 Inspection of books by creditors, etc

(1) The court may, at any time after making a winding-up order, make such order for inspection of the company's books and papers by creditors and contributories as the court thinks just; and any books and papers in the company's possession may be inspected by creditors and contributories accordingly, but not further or otherwise.

(2) Nothing in this section excludes or restricts any statutory rights of a government department or person acting under the authority of a government department.

(3) For the purposes of subsection (2) above, references to a government department shall be construed as including references to any part of the Scottish Administration.

Notes

S 155(1)

This power attaches only to documents in the company's possession, and will generally only be used for purposes connected with the winding up: *Re North Brazilian Sugar Factories Ltd* (1887) 37 Ch D 83, *Re DPR Futures Ltd* [1989] 1 WLR 778. For a definition of 'books and papers' see CA 1985 s 744, which provides that the phrase includes: 'accounts, deeds, writings and documents'.

1.180

156 Payment of expenses of winding up

The court may, in the event of the assets being insufficient to satisfy the liabilities, make an order as to the payment out of the assets of the expenses incurred in the winding up in such order of priority as the court thinks just.

Notes

S 156

The expenses of the liquidation are paid in priority over other debts: IA 1986 s 115. The order of priority of payments of liquidation expenses is stated in IR 1986 r 4.218–4.220 and IA 1986 *s* 156 enables that priority to be ordered differently: *Digital Equipment Co Ltd v Bower* [2004] BCC 509; although the burden is on the applicant to persuade the court to depart from the order set out in IR 1986 r 4.218: *Re Grey Marlin Ltd* [2000] 1 WLR 370. Thus, the court will only rarely order that the liquidator's remuneration be given a higher priority than that specified in r 4.218: *Re Linda Marie Ltd (in liquidation)* (1988) 4 BCC 463. Note that the power provided by this section applies only to expenses properly incurred: *Mond v Hammond Suddards (a firm)* [2000] Ch 40.

Assets which are not beneficially owned by the company are not assets within IA 1986 s 115 nor s 156. However, an order may be made for the liquidator to be paid expenses out of such assets where his skill and labour has preserved and/or added value to those assets; *Re Berkeley Applegate (Investment Consultants) Ltd (No 2)* (1988) 4 BCC 279; *Re Berkeley Applegate (Investment Consultants) Ltd (No 3)* (1989) 5 BCC 803; cf *Tom Wise Ltd v Fillimore* [1999] BCC 129; *Re Local London Residential Ltd* [2004] EWHC 114 (Ch), [2004] 2 BCLC 72.

1.181

157 Attendance at company meetings (Scotland)

In the winding up by the court of a company registered in Scotland, the court has power to require the attendance of any officer of the company at any meeting of creditors or of contributories, or of a liquidation committee, for the purpose of giving information as to the trade, dealings, affairs or property of the company.

1.182

158 Power to arrest absconding contributory

The court, at any time either before or after making a winding-up order, on proof of probable cause for believing that a contributory is about to quit the United Kingdom or otherwise to abscond or to remove or conceal any of his property for the purpose of evading payment of calls, may cause the contributory to be arrested and his books and papers and movable personal property to be seized and him and them to be kept safely until such time as the court may order.

Notes

S 158

There are no specific rules accompanying this section, but see IR 1986 r 7.21ff for the procedure in relation to warrants under other sections (eg IA 1986 s 134(2), 236(5), 364(1), 365(3) and 366(3)).

1.183

159 Powers of court to be cumulative

Powers conferred by this Act and the Companies Act on the court are in addition to, and not in restriction of, any existing powers of instituting proceedings against a contributory or debtor of the company, or the estate of any contributory or debtor, for the recovery of any call or other sums.

1.184

160 Delegation of powers to liquidator (England and Wales)

(1) Provision may be made by rules for enabling or requiring all or any of the powers and duties conferred and imposed on the court in England and Wales by the Companies Act and this Act in respect of the following matters—

  (a) the holding and conducting of meetings to ascertain the wishes of creditors and contributories,

  (b) the settling of lists of contributories and the rectifying of the register of members where required, and the collection and application of the assets,

  (c) the payment, delivery, conveyance, surrender or transfer of money, property, books or papers to the liquidator,

  (d) the making of calls,

  (e) the fixing of a time within which debts and claims must be proved,

to be exercised or performed by the liquidator as an officer of the court, and subject to the court's control.

(2) But the liquidator shall not, without the special leave of the court, rectify the register of members, and shall not make any call without either that special leave or the sanction of the liquidation committee.

Notes

S 160

These powers have been touched on elsewhere, but for ease of reference the rules made under this section are as follows:

•	Creditors/contributories meetings	IR 1986 r 4.54ff
•	Lists of contributories	IR 1986 r 4.195ff
•	Collection of assets	IR 1986 r 4.179
•	Delivery of books/papers	IR 1986 r 4.185
•	Making calls	IR 1986 r 4.202ff
•	Fixing of time for claims	none, but see IR 1986 r 11.2, 11.3

Enforcement of, and appeal from, orders

1.185

161 Orders for calls on contributories (Scotland)

(1) In Scotland, where an order, interlocutor or decree has been made for winding up a company by the court, it is competent to the court, on production by the liquidators of a list certified by them of the names of the contributories liable in payment of any calls, and of the amount due by each contributory, and of the date when that amount became due, to pronounce forthwith a decree against those contributories for payment of the sums so certified to be due, with interest from that date until payment

(at 5 per cent. per annum) in the same way and to the same effect as if they had severally consented to registration for execution, on a charge of 6 days, of a legal obligation to pay those calls and interest.

(2) The decree may be extracted immediately, and no suspension of it is competent, except on caution or consignation, unless with special leave of the court.

1.186

162 Appeals from orders in Scotland

(1) Subject to the provisions of this section and to rules of court, an appeal from any order or decision made or given in the winding up of a company by the court in Scotland under this Act lies in the same manner and subject to the same conditions as an appeal from an order or decision of the court in cases within its ordinary jurisdiction.

(2) In regard to orders or judgments pronounced by the judge acting as vacation judge ... —
  (a) none of the orders specified in Part I of Schedule 3 to this Act are subject to review, reduction, suspension or stay of execution, and
  (b) every other order or judgment (except as mentioned below) may be submitted to review by the Inner House by reclaiming motion enrolled within 14 days from the date of the order or judgment.

(3) However, an order being one of those specified in Part II of that Schedule shall, from the date of the order and notwithstanding that it has been submitted to review as above, be carried out and receive effect until the Inner House have disposed of the matter.

(4) In regard to orders or judgments pronounced in Scotland by a Lord Ordinary before whom proceedings in a winding up are being taken, any such order or judgment may be submitted to review by the Inner House by reclaiming motion enrolled within 14 days from its date; but should it not be so submitted to review during session, the provisions of this section in regard to orders or judgments pronounced by the judge acting as vacation judge apply.

(5) Nothing in this section affects provisions of the Companies Act or this Act in reference to decrees in Scotland for payment of calls in the winding up of companies, whether voluntary or by the court.

Chapter VII
Liquidators

Preliminary

1.187

163 Style and title of liquidators

The liquidator of a company shall be described—
  (a) where a person other than the official receiver is liquidator, by the style of 'the liquidator' of the particular company, or
  (b) where the official receiver is liquidator, by the style of 'the official receiver and liquidator' of the particular company;

> and in neither case shall he be described by an individual name.

Notes

S 163

In applications made by a liquidator under IA 1986 (as opposed to ordinary proceedings where the name of the company in liquidation will generally be used) it is however common for the liquidator to appear as applicant using his or her own name rather than as 'Liquidator of X Limited'. It is also advisable for the liquidator to sign cheques as 'Liquidator of X Limited' rather than in any other style: see further the commentary to IA 1986 Sch 4 para 9.

1.188

164 Corrupt inducement affecting appointment

A person who gives, or agrees or offers to give, to any member or creditor of a company any valuable consideration with a view to securing his own appointment or nomination, or to securing or preventing the appointment or nomination of some person other than himself, as the company's liquidator is liable to a fine.

Notes

S 164

This section also needs to be read together with IR 1986 r 4.150 which gives the court power to disallow any remuneration out of the company's assets where it is satisfied that there has been any improper solicitation of votes or proxies either by or on behalf of the liquidator; such an order of the court will overrule any resolution of the liquidation committee. It is also relevant to consider IR 1986 r 8.6 which should cause a liquidator once appointed to consider carefully before voting as a proxy holder if it might place him/her or an associate in a position to earn remuneration from an insolvent estate; although there is no express restriction it appears that IR 1986 r 8.6 would not apply to a person nominated as a liquidator under an IA 1985 s 84 resolution as the proxy rules would arguably be governed by the CA 1985 rather than the insolvency legislation.

Liquidator's powers and duties

1.189

165 Voluntary winding up

(1) This section has effect where a company is being wound up voluntarily, but subject to section 166 below in the case of a creditors' voluntary winding up.

(2) The liquidator may—

    (a)   in the case of a member's voluntary winding up, with the sanction of an extraordinary resolution of the company, and

    (b)   in the case of a creditors' voluntary winding up, with the sanction of the court or the liquidation committee (or, if there is no such committee, a meeting of the company's creditors), exercise any of the powers specified in Part I of Schedule 4 to this Act (payment of debts, compromise of claims, etc.).

(3) The liquidator may, without sanction, exercise either of the powers specified in Part II of that Schedule (institution and defence of proceedings; carrying on the business of the company) and any of the general powers specified in Part III of that Schedule.

(4) The liquidator may—
   (a) exercise the court's power of settling a list of contributories (which list is prima facie evidence of the liability of the persons named in it to be contributories),
   (b) exercise the court's power of making calls,
   (c) summon general meetings of the company for the purpose of obtaining its sanction by special or extraordinary resolution or for any other purpose he may think fit.

(5) The liquidator shall pay the company's debts and adjust the rights of the contributories among themselves.

(6) Where the liquidator in exercise of the powers conferred on him by this Act disposes of any property of the company to a person who is connected with the company (within the meaning of section 249 in Part VII), he shall, if there is for the time being a liquidation committee, give notice to the committee of that exercise of his powers.

Notes

S 165

This provision applies to both members' and creditors' voluntary winding up. IA 1986 s 166 only applies to creditors' voluntary liquidation and limits the powers of the liquidator in the period between the appointment in general meeting and the IA 1986 s 98 meeting of creditors. Sanction where required ought to be obtained before the exercise of the relevant power. If a court application is required then the court would expect to see evidence in support of the particular exercise of a power; it would be most unusual in modern times to obtain a 'blanket' permission as was given in *Re Rochdale Property & General Finance Co* (1879) 12 Ch D 775. Retrospective sanction may also be obtained in cases where the liquidator has otherwise acted properly: *Re Associated Travel and Leisure Services Ltd* [1978] 1 WLR 547.

IA 1986 Sch 4 divides a liquidator's powers into three groups, which are reflected in the three parts of Sch 4. Part I contains powers exercisable 'with sanction' in all types of winding up. These are powers to pay any class of creditors in full and powers of compromise. The EA 2002 s 253 inserted a new paragraph 3A to Part 1 of Sch 4. Proceedings under IA 1986 s 213 and 214 (fraudulent and wrongful trading), IA 1986 s 238 and 239 and 242 and 243 (transactions at an undervalue, gratuitous alienations and preferences) and s 423 (transactions defrauding creditors) may only be brought with sanction. The requirement to seek sanction for such proceedings (and the corresponding comfort obtained by a liquidator) does not apply to such proceedings commenced prior to 15 September 2003. The Enterprise Act 2002 (Commencement No.4 and Transitional Provisions and Savings) Order 2003. Part II of Sch 4 contains powers that are exercisable with sanction in a winding up by the court or without sanction in a voluntary winding up. These are the powers to bring and defend proceedings and the power to carry on the business of the company so far as may be necessary for the beneficial winding up of the company. Part III of Sch 4 contains a list of general powers relating to the management of the company's affairs, for example, powers of sale, powers to execute deeds and documents in the company's name, power to raise money against the security of the company's assets, power to appoint agents and power to do all such other things as may be necessary for winding up the company's affairs and distributing its assets.

S 165(2)

In a members' voluntary winding up 'with sanction' means with the sanction of an extraordinary resolution of the company which requires a 75% majority. In a creditors' voluntary winding up the sanction is that of the court or liquidation committee if there is one; otherwise the sanction required is that of a meeting of creditors by a majority in value of those entitled to vote IR 1986 r 4.63, 4.67. This is in contrast to a compulsory liquidation where if there is no liquidation committee its functions are vested in the Secretary of State IA 1986 s 141(5).

S 165(4)

The powers referred to in paragraphs (a) and (b) (power to settle a list of contributories and to make calls) are powers that, in a compulsory winding up, would be exercisable by the court in the first instance (IA 1986 s 148 to 150) or delegated to the liquidator under s 160. Paragraph (c) expressly confers power to summon meetings for obtaining sanction or for any other purpose.

S 165(5)

This provision sets out one of the primary statutory duties of a liquidator. The assets of the company must be applied in accordance with the rules of priority found elsewhere in the IA 1986 (see for example IA 1986 s 107, 105, 386 and Sch 6).

S 165(6)

The requirement is to give notice rather than to obtain the sanction of the committee.

1.190

166 Creditors' voluntary winding up

(1) This section applies where, in the case of a creditors' voluntary winding up, a liquidator has been nominated by the company.

(2) The powers conferred on the liquidator by section 165 shall not be exercised, except with the sanction of the court, during the period before the holding of the creditors' meeting under section 98 in Chapter IV.

(3) Subsection (2) does not apply in relation to the power of the liquidator—

    (a)   to take into his custody or under his control all the property to which the company is or appears to be entitled;

    (b)   to dispose of perishable goods and other goods the value of which is likely to diminish if they are not immediately disposed of; and

    (c)   to do all such other things as may be necessary for the protection of the company's assets.

(4) The liquidator shall attend the creditors' meeting held under section 98 and shall report to the meeting on any exercise by him of his powers (whether or not under this section or under section 112 or 165).

(5) If default is made—

    (a)   by the company in complying with subsection (1) or (2) of section 98, or

(b) by the directors in complying with subsection (1) or (2) of section 99,

the liquidator shall, within 7 days of the relevant day, apply to the court for directions as to the manner in which that default is to be remedied.

(6) 'The relevant day' means the day on which the liquidator was nominated by the company or the day on which he first became aware of the default, whichever is the later.

(7) If the liquidator without reasonable excuse fails to comply with this section, he is liable to a fine.

_____

Notes

S 166

A voluntary liquidation is initiated by a members' resolution (IA 1986 s 84) and (unless a members' voluntary liquidation is converted by the liquidator under IA 1986 s 95) a creditors' voluntary liquidation additionally requires a creditors' meeting to be held under IA 1986 s 98. In practice the creditors' meeting follows on immediately after the members' meeting. In *Re Centrebind Ltd* [1967] 1 WLR 377 it was held that under the CA 1948 a liquidator had power to act prior to the creditors' meeting. IA 1986 s 166 was introduced to put a stop to the situation whereby a friendly liquidator appointed by the members might postpone the creditors' meeting and in the meantime exercise some of his powers. Whilst this might be done for proper reasons (as in the *Centrebind* case itself), the rule opened the way to abuse and, for example, allowed a liquidator dispose of the company's assets on favourable terms to the members or their associates to the detriment of creditors. See further the commentary to IA 1986, s 98.

S 166(1)

If a resolution is passed to wind up, the liquidation commences IA 1986 s 86. It may be, however, that a liquidator is not appointed or nominated at the time that the resolution to wind up is passed; in that event under IA 1986 s 114 the directors' powers are not to be exercised during the period before the appointment or nomination (other than to dispose of perishable goods or to protect the company's assets) except with the sanction of the court or so far as may be necessary to secure compliance with IA 1986 s 98, 99.

S 166(2), (3)

Creditors' interests are now protected in the period between the nomination of the liquidator at the members' meeting and the creditors' meeting. The protection is effected by these provisions under which the general rule is that the liquidator may not act until after the creditors' meeting. However, the liquidator is allowed in this period to take control of the company's property or what appears to be its property and do such things as may be necessary for the protection of the company's assets. Further, the liquidator may sell perishable goods or other items whose value is likely to diminish if they are not sold quickly. In a creditors' voluntary winding up the 'nomination' of a liquidator is different from an 'appointment'; if the members at their meeting purport to 'appoint' a liquidator, it is treated as a 'nomination' under IA 1986 s 100.

S 166(4)

The liquidator must attend the creditors' meeting and report on any prior exercise of his or her powers. It is the duty of the board of directors to appoint a director to preside at the creditors' meeting (IA 1986 s 99(1)) although in practice the nominated liquidator usually takes an active role in managing and addressing the meeting.

S 166(5), (6)

There is a responsibility on the company to ensure that a creditor's meeting is properly called and on the directors to make a statement of affairs in the proper form and lay it before the meeting: IA 1986 s 98(1), (2); s 99(1), (2). In the event of default, the liquidator must within 7 days of the later of either his or her nomination by the company or his or her becoming aware of the default apply to the court for directions. In the absence of reasonable excuse, any such failure to comply renders the liquidator liable to a fine. The failure of director to preside as chairman at the creditors' meeting is a default but the meeting is not thereby invalidated and despite the mandatory language of IA 1986 s 166(5) there is no need for the liquidator to apply for directions: *Re Salcombe Hotel Development Co Ltd* (1989) 5 BCC 807.

1.191

167 Winding up by the court

(1) Where a company is being wound up by the court, the liquidator may—

    (a) with the sanction of the court or the liquidation committee, exercise any of the powers specified in Parts I and II of Schedule 4 to this Act (payment of debts; compromise of claims, etc; institution and defence of proceedings; carrying on of the business of the company), and

    (b) with or without that sanction, exercise any of the general powers specified in Part III of that Schedule.

(2) Where the liquidator (not being the official receiver), in exercise of the powers conferred on him by this Act—

    (a) disposes of any property of the company to a person who is connected with the company (within the meaning of section 249 in Part VII), or

    (b) employs a solicitor to assist him in the carrying out of his functions,

he shall, if there is for the time being a liquidation committee, give notice to the committee of that exercise of his powers.

(3) The exercise by the liquidator in a winding up by the court of the powers conferred by this section is subject to the control of the court, and any creditor or contributory may apply to the court with respect to any exercise or proposed exercise of any of those powers.

Notes

S 167

The general powers conferred by this section are additional to other specific powers provided for elsewhere in the IA 1986. Note the distinction between the powers of a liquidator in a compulsory winding up and a voluntary winding up in relation to Part II Sch 4. Any such sanction by the liquidation committee or the court must be specific in its nature and not a general permission IR 1986 r 4.184. In a compulsory winding up the liquidator requires the sanction of the court or the liquidation committee to bring or defend proceedings or to carry on the business of the company. Existing proceedings against the company are stayed (subject to leave of the court) under IA 1986 s 130(2). If there is no liquidation committee its functions are generally vested in the Secretary of State: IA 1986 s 141(5).

S 167(1)

When the sanction of the court is sought, the court exercises its own discretion. Whilst great weight will usually be given to the liquidator's views (*Re Edennote Ltd (No 2)* [1997] 2 BCLC 89; *Re Don Basil Williams* [2003] BPIR 545) creditors and contributories are also entitled to be heard and to have their views taken into account. It is therefore important to ensure that all parties who may be affected are joined in the application for directions. However, the views of a creditor or contributory who, having regard to the claims of creditors having priority, had no real or tangible interest in the assets carry little weight: *Re Barings plc (No 7)* [2002] 1 BCLC 401 and *Re Greenhaven Motors Ltd* [1999] BCC 463. In considering whether to grant sanction, the court will consider what is in the best interests of all those concerned in the winding up: *Re Barings plc (No 7)* (above).

S 167(2)

This subsection does not apply where the liquidator is the official receiver.

S 167(3)

The actions and proposed actions of the liquidator are always subject to the scrutiny of the court on the application of any creditor or contributory. In a voluntary winding up, application may be made under IA 1986 s 112. Where this subsection is used, the court is reviewing the liquidator's exercise or proposed exercise of his or her powers and what is being reviewed is normally an exercise of discretion. As a general rule the court will not interfere unless it is satisfied that the liquidator has acted in bad faith or irrationally in the sense that no reasonable liquidator could properly have acted as he did: *Re Edennote Ltd* [1996] 2 BCLC 389; *Hamilton v Official Receiver* [1998] BPIR 602. This subsection provides that any creditor or contributory may apply (contrast with IA 1986 s 168(5) which provides for applications to be made by any 'aggrieved person'). It appears to be an open question whether a person with no real or tangible interest may apply under this section, or whether, whilst such a person may be entitled to apply, his or her views will carry little weight.

1.192

168 Supplementary powers (England and Wales)

(1) This section applies in the case of a company which is being wound up by the court in England and Wales.

(2) The liquidator may summon general meetings of the creditors or contributories for the purpose of ascertaining their wishes; and it is his duty to summon meetings at such times as the creditors or contributories by resolution (either at the meeting appointing the liquidator or otherwise) may direct, or whenever requested in writing to do so by one-tenth in value of the creditors or contributories (as the case may be).

(3) The liquidator may apply to the court (in the prescribed manner) for directions in relation to any particular matter arising in the winding up.

(4) Subject to the provisions of this Act, the liquidator shall use his own discretion in the management of the assets and their distribution among the creditors.

(5) If any person is aggrieved by an act or decision of the liquidator, that person may apply to the court; and the court may confirm, reverse or modify the act or decision complained of, and make such order in the case as it thinks just.

(5A) Where at any time after a winding-up petition has been presented to the court against any person (including an insolvent partnership or other body which may be wound up under Part V of the Act as an unregistered company), whether by virtue of the provisions of the Insolvent Partnerships Order 1994 or not, the attention of the court is drawn to the fact that the person in question is a member of an insolvent partnership, the court may make an order as to the future conduct of the insolvency proceedings and any such order may apply any provisions of that Order with any necessary modifications.

(5B) Any order or directions under subsection (5A) may be made or given on the application of the official receiver, any responsible insolvency practitioner, the trustee of the partnership or any other interested person and may include provisions as to the administration of the joint estate of the partnership, and in particular how it and the separate estate of any member are to be administered.

(5C) Where the court makes an order for the winding up of an insolvent partnership under –
    (a)   section 72(1)(a) of the Financial Services Act 1986;
    (b)   section 92(1)(a) of the Banking Act 1987; or
    (c)   section 367(3)(a) of the Financial Services and Markets Act 2000,

the court may make an order as to the future conduct of the winding up proceedings and any such order may apply any provisions of the Insolvent Partnerships Order 1994 with any necessary modifications.

Notes

S 168

This section provides for consultation in a winding up by the court between the liquidator and the creditors and contributories. The liquidator may call meetings of his or her own volition and must do so on the requisition of 10% by value of the creditors or contributories as the case may be. IR 1986 r 4.54 to 4.71 make provision for the summoning and conduct of meetings. The court of its own motion may also order the holding of creditors or contributories: IA 1986 s 195.

S 168(2)

Although the liquidator may be requested to hold a meeting the court can direct the liquidator not to comply with the request: *Hamilton v Law Debenture Trustees Ltd* [2001] 2 BCLC 159.

S 168(3), (4)

Although IA 1986 s 168(3) provides for the liquidator to make applications for directions, IA 1986 s 168(4) makes it clear that in general the liquidator is to exercise his or her own discretion. Unnecessary or 'rubber stamping' applications should not be made and the jurisdiction is not to be used for the purposes of seeking directions on matters which are within the commercial judgment of the liquidator: see *Re T&D Industries plc* [2000] 1 BCLC 471. This applies equally to the decision whether or not to call meetings and consult. Consultation and application to the court will be appropriate, for example, where there are competing claims to priorities. It will not be appropriate to consult or seek directions where, for example, the liquidator decides to realise an asset where the asset is charged to the company and the amount realised will be insufficient to discharge the chargor's secured debt. In such a case there is no obligation to consult either the debtor or its surety: *Mahomed v Morris* [2001] BCC 233.

S 168(5)

Although this provision states that any person 'aggrieved' may apply, to qualify the applicant must be affected by the act/decision that is the subject of the application: *Re Edennote Ltd (No 2)* [1997] 2 BCLC 89. Contributories and creditors may apply as may others directly affected by the exercise of a power given specifically to a liquidator (for example, a landlord affected by the decision to disclaim a lease) who would not otherwise have any means of challenging the exercise of the power. A surety asserting a right of subrogation that does not depend on the liquidation is not within the section: *Mahomed v Morris (supra)*. Nor can the section be used to make the liquidator personally liable to pay compensation for his or her actions. The liquidator acts as agent and is not generally personally liable; the liquidator is not a fiduciary for the creditors or contributories: *Mahomed v Morris (supra)*.

As to the court's approach generally, see the notes to IA 1986 s 167(3). Whilst IA 1986 s 168(5) states that the court may make such order as it thinks just, its discretion must be exercised judicially and the court will not ordinarily make orders that contradict the statutory scheme of priority and pari passu distribution: *Re HIH Casualty & General Insurance Ltd* [2006] 2 All ER 671 (David Richards J) and [2006] EWHC Civ 732, CA which contains an extensive analysis of the court's powers to limit the ambit of an English ancillary liquidation and to order the remission of assets to the foreign principal liquidation. This jurisdiction cannot be used to give a creditor or class of creditors a preference to which it would not otherwise be entitled.

1.193

169 Supplementary powers (Scotland)

(1) In the case of a winding up in Scotland, the court may provide by order that the liquidator may, where there is no liquidation committee, exercise any of the following powers, namely—

    (a)   to bring or defend any action or other legal proceeding in the name and on behalf of the company, or

    (b)   to carry on the business of the company so far as may be necessary for its beneficial winding up,

without the sanction or intervention of the court.

(2) In a winding up by the court in Scotland, the liquidator has (subject to the rules) the same powers as a trustee on a bankrupt estate.

1.194

170 Enforcement of liquidator's duty to make returns, etc

(1) If a liquidator who has made any default—

    (a)   in filing, delivering or making any return, account or other document, or

    (b)   in giving any notice which he is by law required to file, deliver, make or give,

fails to make good the default within 14 days after the service on him of a notice requiring him to do so, the court has the following powers.

(2) On an application made by any creditor or contributory of the company, or by the registrar of companies, the court may make an order directing the liquidator to make good the default within such time as may be specified in the order.

(3) The court's order may provide that all costs of and incidental to the application shall be borne by the liquidator.

(4) Nothing in this section prejudices the operation of any enactment imposing penalties on a liquidator in respect of any such default as is mentioned above.

Removal; vacation of office

1.195

171 Removal, etc (voluntary winding up)

(1) This section applies with respect to the removal from office and vacation of office of the liquidator of a company which is being wound up voluntarily.

(2) Subject to the next subsection, the liquidator may be removed from office only by an order of the court or—
  (a) in the case of a members' voluntary winding up, by a general meeting of the company summoned specially for that purpose, or
  (b) in the case of a creditors' voluntary winding up, by a general meeting of the company's creditors summoned specially for that purpose in accordance with the rules.

(3) Where the liquidator was appointed by the court under section 108 in Chapter V, a meeting such as is mentioned in subsection (2) above shall be summoned for the purpose of replacing him only if he thinks fit or the court so directs or the meeting is requested, in accordance with the rules—
  (a) in the case of a members' voluntary winding up, by members representing not less than one-half of the total voting rights of all the members having at the date of the request a right to vote at the meeting, or
  (b) in the case of a creditors' voluntary winding up, by not less than one-half, in value, of the company's creditors.

(4) A liquidator shall vacate office if he ceases to be a person who is qualified to act as an insolvency practitioner in relation to the company.

(5) A liquidator may, in the prescribed circumstances, resign his office by giving notice of his resignation to the registrar of companies.

(6) Where—
  (a) in the case of a members' voluntary winding up, a final meeting of the company has been held under section 94 in Chapter III, or
  (b) in the case of a creditors' voluntary winding up, final meetings of the company and of the creditors have been held under section 106 in Chapter IV,

the liquidator whose report was considered at the meeting or meetings shall vacate office as soon as he has complied with subsection (3) of that section and has given notice to the registrar of companies that the meeting or meetings have been held and of the decisions (if any) of the meeting or meetings.

Notes

S 171

IA 1986 s 108(2), 171 and 172 provide a complete code dealing with the circumstances in which a liquidator can be removed and the means of removing such a liquidator. IA 1986 s 108(2) applies only to a voluntarily winding up and enables the court to remove a liquidator 'on cause shown'. The more complex IA 1986 s 171 also applies only to a voluntary winding up, while IA 1986 s 172 applies only where the company is being wound up by the court.

S 171(2)

In a members' voluntary winding up the liquidator may be removed by a meeting of the company. In a creditor's voluntary liquidation removal of the liquidator is matter for the creditors. In either case the meeting must be called specifically for the purpose of considering a resolution to remove the liquidator. IR 1986 r 4.113 to 4.115 govern meetings called to remove the liquidator. For consideration of the court's power to remove a liquidator see *Sisu Capital Fund Ltd v Tucker* [2006] BPIR 154, para 82ff.

S 171(3)

Where the liquidator was appointed by the court under IA 1986 s 108(1) the meeting may only be held where (i) the meeting is requested by not less than one half of the members (by voting rights) or creditors (by value) as the case may be, or (ii) the liquidator him or herself thinks fit or (iii) the court so directs.

S 171(4)

Qualification and acting as an insolvency practitioner are governed by IA 1986 s 388(1) and 390. If the liquidator ceases to be qualified to act as an insolvency practitioner in relation to the company then the appointment ends automatically.

S 171(5)

The circumstances in which a liquidator may resign are set out in IR 1986 r 4.108(4) and 4.142(3). Under these rules, the liquidator may only resign (i) on grounds of ill health or (ii) where he or she intends to cease practice as an insolvency practitioner or (iii) where a conflict of interest arises, or there is some change in his or her personal circumstances which precludes or makes it impractical for him or her to continue acting. Before resigning the liquidator must (unless the court dispenses with this requirement) convene a meeting of creditors or members according to the type of winding up to receive the resignation and decide whether to accept it. If the meeting declines to accept the liquidator's resignation, the liquidator may apply to the court under IR 1986 r 4.111.

Transfer of office applications are fairly commonplace and para 1.6 Practice Direction: Insolvency Proceedings, (Civil Procedure 2006 Vol 2 Section 3E) deals with the same in detail. The court will dispense with the requirement for meetings where a liquidator has a large number of appointments to give up and it would be inconvenient to call a large number of meetings. Other situations in which a 'block' transfer can be considered include the dissolution of the liquidator's partnership or his or expulsion from his or her firm, or where convening the meeting would serve no useful purpose: see for example *Re Equity Nominees* [1999] 2 BCLC 19 where the court set out guidelines for the terms of the order which were intended to ensure that creditors were not unduly prejudiced by the absence of the meeting, including provision of information and a right to apply, as to which see notes to IA 1986 s 172.

S 171(6)

Specific provision is also made in IA 1986 s 94(5) and 106(5) for the situation where the final meetings are inquorate. In such a case, subject to compliance with those subsections, the requirements relating to the final meeting are deemed complied with. A liquidator who is deemed to have complied should be treated as having had his report considered for the purposes of IA 1986 s 171(6).

1.196

172 Removal, etc (winding up by the court)

(1) This section applies with respect to the removal from office and vacation of office of the liquidator of a company which is being wound up by the court, or of a provisional liquidator.

(2) Subject as follows, the liquidator may be removed from office only by an order of the court or by a general meeting of the company's creditors summoned specially for that purpose in accordance with the rules; and a provisional liquidator may be removed from office only by an order of the court.

(3) Where—
- (a) the official receiver is liquidator otherwise than in succession under section 136(3) to a person who held office as a result of a nomination by a meeting of the company's creditors or contributories, or
- (b) the liquidator was appointed by the court otherwise than under section 139(4)(a) or 140(1), or was appointed by the Secretary of State,

a general meeting of the company's creditors shall be summoned for the purpose of replacing him only if he thinks fit, or the court so directs, or the meeting is requested, in accordance with the rules, by not less that one-quarter, in value, of the creditors.

(4) If appointed by the Secretary of State, the liquidator may be removed from office by a direction of the Secretary of State.

(5) A liquidator or provisional liquidator, not being the official receiver, shall vacate office if he ceases to be a person who is qualified to act as an insolvency practitioner in relation to the company.

(6) A liquidator may, in the prescribed circumstances, resign his office by giving notice of his resignation to the court.

(7) Where an order is made under section 204 (early dissolution in Scotland) for the dissolution of the company, the liquidator shall vacate office when the dissolution of the company takes effect in accordance with that section.

(8) Where a final meeting has been held under section 146 (liquidator's report on completion of winding up), the liquidator whose report was considered at the meeting shall vacate office as soon as he has given notice to the court and the registrar of companies that the meeting has been held and of the decisions (if any) of the meeting.

Notes

S 172(1) and (2)

A provisional liquidator may only be removed by order of the court. After the winding up order is made the liquidator may be removed by a meeting of creditors called specifically for that purpose. To justify a removal of a liquidator by the court it is not necessary to prove misfeasance or negligence, merely there may be a case of misfeasance or negligence. Where a liquidator unsuccessfully resists an order for removal, indemnity costs may be ordered: *Shepheard v Lamey [2001]* BPIR 939. For a detailed review of the authorities relating to remove of office-holders, see *Sisu Capital Fund Ltd v Tucker* [2006] BPIR 154, *para* 82ff; see also the notes to IA 1986 s 108(2) for a fuller discussion of this topic.

S 172(3) and (4)

Where the official receiver is liquidator (other than under IA 1986 s 163(3)) or where the liquidator was appointed by the court (other than under IA 1986 s 139(4) or 140(1)), or by the Secretary of State, a meeting to replace him or her may only be summoned (i) where the liquidator him or her self thinks fit, or (ii) where the court so directs, or (iii) where the meeting is requested by not less than one quarter (by value) of the creditors. Where the liquidator was appointed by the Secretary of State he or she may be removed from office by direction of the Secretary of State.

S 172(6)

As with a voluntary liquidation (for which see (IA 1986, s 171(5)), in a winding up by the court a liquidator may only resign in the prescribed circumstances. Those circumstances are set out in IR 1986 r 4.108(4) and 4.142(3): see further the notes to IA 1986, s 171(5). However, whereas in a voluntary liquidation the relevant notice is given to the registrar of companies, in a winding up by the court, such notice is given to the court.

The rules require the creditors to consider the resignation but the court may dispense with the same if appropriate. For the form of order dealing with the information to be given to the creditors and providing for the creditors to have an opportunity to apply to the court if they object to the new appointment, see further *Re Equity Nominees Ltd* [1999] 2 BCLC 19 and the notes to IA 1986 s 171(5). Where a creditor does so apply, the hearing is not an appeal but is a review or rehearing. It therefore follows that although the new liquidator will have been appointed by the court he or she is not to be treated as having been duly appointed. Accordingly, the question is not whether or not the new liquidator ought to be removed; instead, the judge should ask whether or not on the facts now known the court would still make the order that is the subject of the review applying the same tests that were applicable on the first hearing. Where the court is not so satisfied (for example if it is not satisfied that convening a creditors meeting would serve no useful purpose) then the correct course is to refer the matter to the creditors for a decision.

If the objection is from a minority of creditors the circumstances may be such that the court can determine the issue. Where the objectors are the majority and there is no reasonable basis for objecting to their proposed appointee, then the court can dispense with a meeting and make the new appointment. If the objection is upheld, the first appointment should be discharged with immediate effect, but the order should preserve the discharged liquidator's rights to remuneration and expenses in respect of work done in the period when he or she held office. In the case of a compulsory liquidation there is, strictly speaking, no need to appoint a new liquidator since it would fall to the official receiver to administer the estate: see *HM Customs & Excise v Allen* [2003] BPIR 830.

S 172(8)

Under IR 1986 r 4.138(3) where this subsection applies the liquidator must deliver the company's books and records to the official receiver.

Release of liquidator

1.197

173 Release (voluntary winding up)

(1) This section applies with respect to the release of the liquidator of a company which is being wound up voluntarily.

(2) A person who has ceased to be a liquidator shall have his release with effect from the following time, that is to say—

(a)   in the case of a person who has been removed from office by a general meeting of the company or by a general meeting of the company's creditors that has not resolved against his release or who has died, the time at which notice is given to the registrar of companies in accordance with the rules that that person has ceased to hold office;

(b)   in the case of a person who has been removed from office by a general meeting of the company's creditors that has resolved against his release, or by the court, or who has vacated office under section 171(4) above, such time as the Secretary of State may, on the application of that person, determine;

(c)   in the case of a person who has resigned, such time as may be prescribed;

(d)   in the case of a person who has vacated office under subsection (6)(a) of section 171, the time at which he vacated office;

(e)   in the case of a person who has vacated office under subsection (6)(b) of that section—

    (i)   if the final meeting of the creditors referred to in that subsection has resolved against that person's release, such time as the Secretary of State may, on an application by that person, determine, and

    (ii)   if that meeting has not resolved against that person's release, the time at which he vacated office.

(3) In the application of subsection (2) to the winding up of a company registered in Scotland, the references to a determination by the Secretary of State as to the time from which a person who has ceased to be liquidator shall have his release are to be read as references to such a determination by the Accountant of Court.

(4) Where a liquidator has his release under subsection (2), he is, with effect from the time specified in that subsection, discharged from all liability both in respect of acts or omissions of his in the winding up and otherwise in relation to his conduct as liquidator.

But nothing in this section prevents the exercise, in relation to a person who has had his release under subsection (2), of the court's powers under section 212 of this Act (summary remedy against delinquent directors, liquidators, etc.)

Notes

S 173

This section deals with release within a voluntary liquidation. The relevant rules are found in IR 1986, r 4.111(2), 4.114(2), 4.122, 4.126, 4.144, 4.147 depending on the particular circumstances of the case. The reason why a release is so important for a liquidator is because (as IA 1986 s 173(4) makes clear) it generally operates as a discharge from liability for the liquidator. However proceedings may still be brought against the liquidator for misfeasance under IA 1986 s 212, but the person who wishes to apply must first obtain leave of court: IA 1986 s 212(4).

1.198

174 Release (winding up by the court)

(1) This section applies with respect to the release of the liquidator of a company which is being wound up by the court, or of a provisional liquidator.

(2) Where the official receiver has ceased to be liquidator and a person becomes liquidator in his stead, the official receiver has his release with effect from the following time, that is to say—

(a) in a case where that person was nominated by a general meeting of creditors or contributories, or was appointed by the Secretary of State, the time at which the official receiver gives notice to the court that he has been replaced;

(b) in a case where that person is appointed by the court, such time as the court may determine.

(3) If the official receiver while he is a liquidator gives notice to the Secretary of State that the winding up is for practical purposes complete, he has his release with effect from such time as the Secretary of State may determine.

(4) A person other than the official receiver who has ceased to be a liquidator has his release with effect from the following time, that is to say—

(a) in the case of a person who has been removed from office by a general meeting of creditors that has not resolved against his release or who has died, the time at which notice is given to the court in accordance with the rules that that person has ceased to hold office;

(b) in the case of a person who has been removed from office by a general meeting of creditors that has resolved against his release, or by the court or the Secretary of State, or who has vacated office under section 172(5) or (7), such time as the Secretary of State may, on an application by that person, determine;

(c) in the case of a person who has resigned, such time as may be prescribed;

(d) in the case of a person who has vacated office under section 172(8)—

(i) if the final meeting referred to in that subsection has resolved against that person's release, such time as the Secretary of State may, on an application by that person, determine, and

(ii) if that meeting has not so resolved, the time at which that person vacated office.

(5) A person who has ceased to hold office as a provisional liquidator has his release with effect from such time as the court may, on an application by him, determine.

(6) Where the official receiver or a liquidator or provisional liquidator has his release under this section, he is, with effect from the time specified in the preceding provisions of this section, discharged from all liability both in respect of acts or omissions of his in the winding up and otherwise in relation to his conduct as liquidator or provisional liquidator.

But nothing in this section prevents the exercise, in relation to a person who has had his release under this section, of the court's powers under section 212 (summary remedy against delinquent directors, liquidators, etc.).

(7) In the application of this section to a case where the order for winding up has been made by the court in Scotland, the references to a determination by the Secretary of State as to the time from which a person who has ceased to be liquidator has his release are to such a determination by the Accountant of Court.

Notes

S 174

This section deals with release within a winding up by the court. The relevant rules are found in IR 1986, r 4.121 to 4.125. The release is as important for a liquidator in a compulsory liquidation as it is in a voluntary liquidation: see the notes to IA 1986 s 173 above.

Chapter VIII
Provisions of general application in winding up

Preferential debts

1.198A

175 Preferential debts (general provision)

(1) In a winding up the company's preferential debts (within the meaning given by section 386 in Part XII) shall be paid in priority to all other debts.

(2) Preferential debts—
   (a) rank equally among themselves after the expenses of the winding up and shall be paid in full, unless the assets are insufficient to meet them, in which case they abate in equal proportions; and
   (b) so far as the assets of the company available for payment of general creditors are insufficient to meet them, have priority over the claims of holders of debentures secured by, or holders of, any floating charge created by the company, and shall be paid accordingly out of any property comprised in or subject to that charge.

Notes

S 175(1)

This provision (together with IA 1986 s 107) contains the basic rule that certain debts, (preferential debts) are to be paid in priority to all other debts. The categories of preferential debts are set out in IA 1986 s 386 and Sch 6. Prior to the coming into force of the relevant parts of the EA 2002 on 15 September 2003, the main classes of preferential debts could be broadly described as Crown debts (i.e. debts due to the Inland Revenue and HM Customs and Excise and Class 1, Class 2 and Class 4 National Insurance contributions), contributions to occupational pension schemes and employees' remuneration. In addition, with effect from

1 January 1988 levies in respect of coal and steel production under the ECSC Treaty were also given preferential status under the Insolvency (ESCS Levy Debts) Regulations 1987 (SI 1987/2093). Following the coming into force of the amendments made under the EA 2002, s 251, Crown debts have not enjoyed preferential status in liquidations occurring since 15 September 2003.

The list of preferential debts must be settled as at a 'relevant date' as defined in IA 1986 s 387, which varies according to the type of insolvency process concerned: see, for example, IA 1986 s 40 (receivership), IA 1986 Sch B1, para 65(2) (administration), IA 1986 s 4(3) (company voluntary arrangements), IA 1986 s 258(5) (individual voluntary arrangements) and IA 1986 s 328 (bankruptcy). As between themselves preferential debts rank pari passu and abate rateably if the assets available are insufficient. The available assets do not include assets caught by fixed charge assets (IA 1986 s 175(2)(b)). The general rules are also modified in relation to certain financial market transactions by the Financial Markets and Insolvency (Settlement Finality) Regulations 1999 (SI 1999/2979). Where those regulations apply, if collateral security has been provided then claims under that security must be paid ahead of all other claims including the costs and expenses of the winding up unless the terms on which the security was provided expressly provide otherwise.

S 175(2)(a)

The costs of applications by a liquidator under IA 1986 s 213 (fraudulent trading), IA 1986 s 214 (wrongful trading), IA 1986 s 238 and 242 (transactions at undervalues), IA 1986 s 239 and 243 (preferences) and IA 1986 s 423 (transactions defrauding creditors) were held not to be 'expenses of the winding up': see *Re MC Bacon Ltd (No 2)* [1991] Ch 127; *Re RS & M Engineering Co Ltd* [2000] BCC 445 and *Re Floor Fourteen* [2000] BCC 416. This is no longer the position, however, due to the new IR 1986 r 4.218 (1)(a)(i), which was introduced to reverse the effect of *Floor Fourteen*. Further, pursuant to IA 1986 s 165, 167 and Sch 4 a liquidator must obtain sanction to take proceedings under IA 1986 s 213, 214, 238, 239, 242, 243 and 423.

S 175(2)(b)

For the purposes of IA 1986 a charge is a floating charge if it was such a charge at the time of its creation (see IA 1986 s 251), so debts caught by a floating charge which crystallised before the 'relevant date' (as defined in IA 1986 s 387) will, where necessary, still be available for payment of preferential debts. IA 1986 s 175(2)(b) makes assets that are the subject of a floating charge available for payment of preferential debts, but only so far as the other assets of the company are insufficient to pay them. The operation of IA 1986 s 175 was considered by the House of Lords in *Buchler v Talbot* [2004] 2 AC 298, *(Re Leyland Daf)* where it was made clear that, whilst the section made a significant incursion into the proprietary rights of floating charge holders, that derogation was limited to the payment of preferential debts and did not extend to payment of other costs and expenses of the liquidation ahead of the rights of the charge holder. *Re Barleycorn Enterprises* [1970] Ch 465 was overruled. Nor does IA 1986 s 115 or any other statutory provision allow a liquidator to claim the costs and expenses of the winding up out of assets caught by a floating charge, because the proprietary rights of the charge holder mean that the assets in question are not 'the company's assets' for the purposes of that section: *Buchler v Talbot* [2004] 2 AC 298.

Where part of the company's assets are caught by a floating charge then the sums realised on the disposal of those assets form a separate fund to which recourse may only be had for the costs of preserving and realising those assets and the liquidator cannot look to the floating charge assets for their fees and the other expenses of the liquidation. In effect there are two separate funds being: (i) the proceeds of the assets subject to the floating charge which belong to the chargeholder ('the Floating Charge Fund'); and (ii) other free assets which belong to the company and can be dealt with by the liquidator ('the Free Asset Fund').

Each one of those funds bears its own costs and expenses with its own order of priority of payments, which are set out by Lord Millett in *Buchler v Talbot* [2004] 2 AC 298 para 88 as follows:

The Floating Charge Fund:
(a) costs of preserving and realising assets;
(b) remuneration and expenses of receivership;
(c) preferential debts in receivership;
(d) principal and interest owed to chargeholder; and
(e) surplus (if any) to the company/liquidator.

The Free Asset Fund:
(a) costs of preserving and realising assets;
(b) remuneration and expenses of liquidation;
(c) preferential debts in liquidation;
(d) the chargeholder to the extent that preferential debts have been paid out of floating charge assets; and
(e) surplus (if any) to the unsecured creditors.

However, these priorities are now affected by IA 1986 s 176A which subject to certain exceptions would require the unsecured creditors to be paid the *'prescribed part'* before any payment was made to the floating charge holder.

Note that the position is different in an administration given the express provisions of Sch B1 para 99(3); an administrator may charge his remuneration and expenses on the floating charge assets. It is presently proposed (under clause 1246 Companies Bill 2006 inserting new IA 1986 s 176ZA) that the costs and expenses of the liquidation may be paid out of floating charge property to bring the position into line with administrations.

1.199

176 Preferential charge on goods distrained

(1) This section applies where a company is being wound up by the court in England and Wales, and is without prejudice to section 128 (avoidance of attachments, etc).

(2) Where any person (whether or not a landlord or person entitled to rent) has distrained upon the goods or effects of the company in the period of 3 months ending with the date of the winding-up order, those goods or effects, or the proceeds of their sale, shall be charged for the benefit of the company with the preferential debts of the company to the extent that the company's property is for the time being insufficient for meeting them.

(3) Where by virtue of a charge under subsection (2) any person surrenders any goods or effects to a company or makes a payment to a company, that person ranks, in respect of the amount of the proceeds of sale of those goods or effects by the liquidator or (as the case may be) the amount of the payment, as a preferential creditor of the company, except as against so much of the company's property as is available for the payment of preferential creditors by virtue of the surrender or payment.

Notes

S 176

This provision only applies where the company is being wound up by the court and is without prejudice to IA 1986 s 128, which provides that any attachment, sequestration, distress or execution put in force against the company's assets after the presentation of the petition is void. IA 1986 s 176(2), (3) only apply where a creditor has levied distress (whether the creditor is a landlord distraining for rent or some other creditor exercising some statutory right) and does not apply to other forms of execution or attachment or sequestration: *Re Herbert Berry Associates Ltd* [1977] 1 WLR 1437. Whereas IA 1986 s 128 deals with the effect of the presentation of the petition, IA 1986 s 176 is concerned with distress, execution etc levied within the three months ending with the making of the winding up order. There will therefore be an overlap in the periods covered by the two sections. Once a petition is presented, IA 1986 s 128 will prevail and any distress after that date will be void.

S 176(2)

The general effect of this provision is that where any person has levied distress against any assets of the company within a period of 3 months ending with the date of the winding up order, then those assets or the proceeds of their sale are charged with payment of the preferential debts, but only to the extent that the company's other assets are insufficient to meet them. The treatment of the assets against which distress has been levied is therefore similar to that applicable to floating charge assets under IA 1986 s 175(2)(b). Where a distress occurred after the presentation of the petition it is void by virtue of IA 1986 s 128 and IA 1986 s 176(2) does not apply.

S 176(3)

Where a person surrenders goods or effects or makes a payment to the company under IA 1986 s 176(2) then that person ranks as a preferential creditor to the extent of the proceeds of sale of the goods or the amount of the payment and will rank pari passu with the other preferential creditors; accordingly, the charge imposed under IA 1986 s 175(2) is as much for his benefit as for that of the other preferential creditors: *Re Memco Engineering Ltd* [1986] Ch 86.

Property subject to floating charge

1.200

176A Share of assets for unsecured creditors

(1) This section applies where a floating charge relates to property of a company—
- (a) which has gone into liquidation,
- (b) which is in administration,
- (c) of which there is a provisional liquidator, or
- (d) of which there is a receiver.

(2) The liquidator, administrator or receiver—
- (a) shall make a prescribed part of the company's net property available for the satisfaction of unsecured debts, and
- (b) shall not distribute that part to the proprietor of a floating charge except in so far as it exceeds the amount required for the satisfaction of unsecured debts.

(3) Subsection (2) shall not apply to a company if—
- (a) the company's net property is less than the prescribed minimum, and
- (b) the liquidator, administrator or receiver thinks that the cost of making a distribution to unsecured creditors would be disproportionate to the benefits.

(4) Subsection (2) shall also not apply to a company if or in so far as it is disapplied by—

> (a) a voluntary arrangement in respect of the company, or
> (b) a compromise or arrangement agreed under section 425 of the Companies Act (compromise with creditors and members).
>
> (5) Subsection (2) shall also not apply to a company if—
> (a) the liquidator, administrator or receiver applies to the court for an order under this subsection on the ground that the cost of making a distribution to unsecured creditors would be disproportionate to the benefits, and
> (b) the court orders that subsection (2) shall not apply.
>
> (6) In subsections (2) and (3) a company's net property is the amount of its property which would, but for this section, be available for satisfaction of claims of holders of debentures secured by, or holders of, any floating charge created by the company.
>
> (7) An order under subsection (2) prescribing part of a company's net property may, in particular, provide for its calculation—
> (a) as a percentage of the company's net property, or
> (b) as an aggregate of different percentages of different parts of the company's net property.
>
> (8) An order under this section—
> (a) must be made by statutory instrument, and
> (b) shall be subject to annulment pursuant to a resolution of either House of Parliament.
>
> (9) In this section—
> 'floating charge' means a charge which is a floating charge on its creation and which is created after the first order under subsection (2)(a) comes into force, and
> 'prescribed' means prescribed by order by the Secretary of State.
>
> (10) An order under this section may include transitional or incidental provision.

Notes

S 176A

This provision was inserted by the Enterprise Act 2002 and came into force on 15 September 2003: Insolvency Act 1986 (Prescribed Part) Order 2003 (SI 2003/2097). It only apples to charges which were floating charges on their creation and which were created on or after 15 September 2003: IA 1986 s 176A(9). Therefore, a pre-15 September 2003 floating charge will not be subject to the prescribed part regime. Further, where the relevant insolvency procedure has been commenced on or after 15 September 2003 the preferential status of the Crown is abolished.

IA 1986 s 176A reflects a general policy to provide something for unsecured creditors at the expense of the floating chargeholder. Where a company goes into a relevant insolvency procedure, then, if its assets exceed a prescribed minimum, a prescribed part of the assets secured under a floating charge must be made available for distribution among unsecured creditors and no part of that fund may be paid to the charge holder unless it exceeds the amount needed to pay the unsecured debts. If the assets are less than the prescribed minimum and the administrator liquidator or receiver thinks that the cost of making a distribution to the unsecured creditors would be disproportionate, then the section does not apply; and even where the assets exceed the prescribed minimum, the liquidator, receiver or administrator may apply to the court for an order that the section shall not apply on the ground that the cost of making a distribution to the unsecured creditors would be disproportionate.

S 176A(1)

This sets out the circumstances in which the section is to apply, namely liquidation, administration, provisional liquidation and receivership.

S 176A(2)

This section introduces the concepts of the 'prescribed part' and 'net property' and sets out the basic rule. Net property is defined in IA 1986 s 176A(6). The Insolvency Act (Prescribed Part) Order 2003 reg. 3 provides that the prescribed part is calculated as follows:

(a)   where the company's net property does not exceed £10,000 in value, 50% of that property;

(b)   subject to paragraph (2), where the company's net property exceeds £10,000 in value the sum of—

   (i)   50% of the first £10,000 in value; and

   (ii)   20% of that part of the company's net property which exceeds £10,000 in value.

Further, the value of the prescribed part of the company's net property to be made available for the satisfaction of unsecured debts of the company pursuant to section IA 1986 176A shall not exceed £600,000.

S 176A(3)

This gives the office holder discretion in cases where the company's 'net property' (IA 1986 s 176A(6)) falls below the 'prescribed minimum' and he or she he takes the view that the cost of making a distribution to unsecured creditors would be disproportionate. The prescribed minimum is presently £10,000: Insolvency Act (Prescribed Part) Order 2003 reg. 2.

S 176A(4)

This allows contracting out under company voluntary arrangements and arrangements under CA 1985 s 425.

S 176A(5)

This provides for the court to disapply the section on grounds of proportionality. Such an application may only be made by the office holder and may not be made by the charge holder. The section is further disapplied in relation to charges created or otherwise arising under a financial collateral arrangement in connection with financial market transactions: Financial Collateral arrangements *(No 2)* Regulations 2003 (SI 2003/3226), reg 10(3).

S 176A(6)

This defines the company's net property as the property that would, but for this section, be available to satisfy the holders of debentures secured by or holders of any floating charge created by the company.

S 176A(9)

The present governing order is The Insolvency Act (Prescribed Part) Regulations 2003 (SI 2003/2097) and art 1(1) states the commencement date as 15 September 2003.

———

Special managers

1.201

177 Power to appoint special manager

(1) Where a company has gone into liquidation or a provisional liquidator has been appointed, the court may, on an application under this section, appoint any person to be the special manager of the business or property of the company.

(2) The application may be made by the liquidator or provisional liquidator in any case where it appears to him that the nature of the business or property of the company, or the interests of the company's creditors or contributories or members generally, require the appointment of another person to manage the company's business or property.

(3) The special manager has such powers as may be entrusted to him by the court.

(4) The court's power to entrust powers to the special manager includes power to direct that any provision of this Act that has effect in relation to the provisional liquidator or liquidator of a company shall have the like effect in relation to the special manager for the purposes of the carrying out by him of any of the functions of the provisional liquidator or liquidator.

(5) The special manager shall—
    (a)   give such security or, in Scotland, caution as may be prescribed;
    (b)   prepare and keep such accounts as may be prescribed; and
    (c)   produce those accounts in accordance with the rules to the Secretary of State or to such other persons as may be prescribed.

Notes

S 177(1)

This section enables the court on the application of a liquidator or provisional liquidator to appoint any person to manage the business or property of the company where the nature of the business or the interests of the creditors, contributories or members require the appointment of another person. This may be desirable, for example, where the business or property of the company is highly specialised. It should be borne in mind that a liquidator's power to carry on the business is limited to carrying on the business only so far as is necessary for the beneficial winding up of the company: see IA 1986 Sch 4 para 55. The special manager may be 'any person' and need not be a licensed insolvency practitioner. The special manager is an officer of the court (*Re Walter L Jacob & Son Ltd* (1989) 5 BCC 244) and his or her powers are limited by the order under which he or she is appointed. The relevant rules in relation to the special manager are in IR 1986 r 4.206–4.210.

1.202

178 Power to disclaim onerous property

(1) This and the next two sections apply to a company that is being wound up in England and Wales.

(2) Subject as follows, the liquidator may, by the giving of the prescribed notice, disclaim any onerous property and may do so notwithstanding that he has taken possession of it, endeavoured to sell it, or otherwise exercised rights of ownership in relation to it.

(3) The following is onerous property for the purposes of this section—
    (a)   any unprofitable contract, and
    (b)   any other property of the company which is unsaleable or not readily saleable or is such that it may give rise to a liability to pay money or perform any other onerous act.

(4) A disclaimer under this section—
    (a)   operates so as to determine, as from the date of the disclaimer, the rights, interests and liabilities of the company in or in respect of the property disclaimed; but
    (b)   does not, except so far as is necessary for the purpose of releasing the company from any liability, affect the rights or liabilities of any other person.

(5) A notice of disclaimer shall not be given under this section in respect of any property if—
    (a)   a person interested in the property has applied in writing to the liquidator or one of his predecessors as liquidator requiring the liquidator or that predecessor to decide whether he will disclaim or not, and
    (b)   the period of 28 days beginning with the day on which that application was made, or such longer period as the court may allow, has expired without a notice of disclaimer having been given under this section in respect of that property.

(6) Any person sustaining loss or damage in consequence of the operation of a disclaimer under this section is deemed a creditor of the company to the extent of the loss or damage and accordingly may prove for the loss or damage in the winding up.

1.203

Notes

S 178

IA 1986 s 178–182 deal with the liquidator's power to disclaim onerous property. These provisions widened the liquidator's power to disclaim property. In particular, the power to disclaim may now be exercised over a wider range of property. In liquidations commenced prior to 29 December 1986 a liquidator could not disclaim an onerous chattel: see for example *Re Potters Oils Ltd (In Liquidation)* [1985] BCLC 203. Under the present regime a liquidator can. A liquidator who is not the official receiver does not require the leave of the court to disclaim under IA 1986 whereas previously he or she did. Under the current regime there is no time limit within which the liquidator has to disclaim (although see section 178(5) which enables a party who is interested in property which may be disclaimed to put the liquidator to an election as to whether or not to disclaim).

S 178(1)

IA 1986 s 178–180 apply to a company that is being wound up, whether a members' or creditors' voluntarily liquidation or a compulsory winding up. The powers contained in these sections do not apply to receivership, administration or voluntary arrangements.

S 178(2)

The prescribed notice must contain such particulars of the property disclaimed as enable it to be easily identified: IR 1986 4.187(1). It must be filed in court: IR 1986 4.187(2). For the provisions relating to the persons on whom the prescribed notice must be served, see IR 1986 r 4.188. In addition, the liquidator may at any time give notice of the disclaimer to any person who in his or her opinion ought in the public interest or otherwise to be informed of it: IR 1986 r 4.189. The fact that a liquidator has taken possession of property or endeavoured to sell it or otherwise has exercised rights of ownership does not prevent him or her disclaiming. For example, a liquidator is entitled to apply for relief against forfeiture (*Re Brompton Securities (No 2)* (1988) 4 BCC 436) or pay off arrears of rent to prevent a lease being forfeited, in the hope of being able to assign the lease. If an assignment is not possible the liquidator may then disclaim the lease.

S 178(3)

Property is defined very widely by IA 1986 s 436 as including '*money, goods, things in action, land and every description of property wherever situated and also obligations and every description of interest, whether present or future or vested or contingent, arising out of, or incidental to property*'. Onerous property includes an unprofitable contract. Whether a contract is unprofitable is a question of fact and it is not unprofitable merely because the company could have made a better bargain or because it is financially disadvantageous. The crucial question was whether the performance of future obligations under the contract would be detrimental to creditors and whether the liquidator would be prejudiced in realising the company's assets and paying a dividend to creditors in a reasonable time *Re SSSL Realisations Ltd, Squires v AIG Europe (UK) Ltd* [2006] BCC 233. It has been held in respect of bankruptcy that the power does not enable a trustee in bankruptcy to disclaim a contract because it would be more beneficial to the estate to do so: *Re Bastable, ex p Trustee* [1901] 2 KB 518, and the same principle should apply to a disclaimer by a liquidator. Examples of property that may be disclaimed include most leases (as to which see the additional provisions of section 179 IA 1986), a periodic tenancy (*Alloway v Steere* (1882) 10 QBD 22), a continuation tenancy under Part II of the Landlord and Tenant Act 1954 (*Rothschild v Bell* [1999] EGCS 27), a contract for the sale of a lease provided that the lease is also disclaimed (*Re Bastable, ex p Trustee* [1901] 2 KB 518; *Capital Prime Properties plc v Worthgate Ltd* [1999] EGCS 112), shares which are subject to calls (*Re Hallett* (1894) 1 Mans 380) and a waste management licence (*Re Celtic Extraction Ltd; Re Bluestone Chemicals Ltd* [1999] 4 All ER 684). The chlorinated waste oil, the subject of the unsuccessful attempt to disclaim in *Re Potters Oils Ltd* [1985] BCLC 203, could now be disclaimed.

S 178(4)

On a disclaimer (apart from the operation of any vesting order made under IA 1986, s 181) the disclaimed property vests in the Crown as bona vacantia. In the case of land held in fee simple it vests in the Crown by escheat. On a disclaimer of a lease the liability of a guarantor or surety of future liabilities under the lease (which includes a former tenant) is not determined by the disclaimer: see *Hindcastle Ltd v Barbara Attenborough Associates Ltd* [1997] AC 70; *Scottish Widows plc v Tripipatkul* [2003] BPIR 1413; *Beegas Nominees Ltd v BHP Petroleum Ltd* (1998) 77 P&CR 14; *Warnford Investments Ltd v Duckworth* [1979] Ch 127.

Not only will the benefit of a surety covenant given by a surety to a landlord not cease on a disclaimer (*Active Estates v Parness* [2002] BPIR 865), but it will also be annexed to the freehold on a subsequent sale of the freehold and inure for the benefit of the purchaser of the freehold: *Scottish Widows plc and another v Tripipatkul* [2003] EWHC 1874, [2004] BCC 200. Note, however, that if a liquidator does not disclaim a lease, and following dissolution of the company the Crown disclaims (pursuant to section 656 CA 1985) the effect of such a disclaimer is to discharge a guarantor from liability under the lease: *Allied Dunbar Assurance plc v Fowle* [1994] 2 BCLC 197. This is so even though the effect of a Crown disclaimer is that the lease is deemed not to have been vested in the Crown and IA 1986 s 178(4) and 179–182 apply as if the liquidator had disclaimed the lease immediately before the dissolution of the company.

On a disclaimer of a head lease, a sub-tenant is allowed to occupy the premises for the remainder of the term of the sub-lease so long as the terms of the headlease are complied with. It is therefore possible that a sub-tenant could find himself paying an increased rent or being subject to more onerous covenants. The head landlord retains his or her rights in rem – that is the right to distrain for rent due under the lease and to forfeit for non-payment of rent or breach of covenant: *Re A E Realisations* [1987] 3 All ER 83.

If there has been a disclaimer of the headlease prior to forfeiture of the interest of the sub-tenant, the sub-tenant can not apply for relief against forfeiture pursuant to section 146(2) LPA 1925: *Barclays Bank plc v Prudential Assurance Co Ltd* [1998] BCC 928; however, the sub-tenant may still apply for a vesting order pursuant to LPA 1925 s 146(4).

Where a company which is being wound up is as a result of one or more assignments the tenant of part only of the premises demised by a tenancy, and the liquidator of the company exercises his power under IA 1986 s 178 to disclaim property demised by the tenancy, the power is exercisable only in relation to the part of the premises the subject of the assignment(s) to the company: Landlord and Tenant (Covenants) Act 1995 s 21(2).

Any disclaimer of property by the liquidator is presumed to be valid and effective, unless it is proved that the liquidator was in breach of the duty to give notice or any other provision of the IA 1986 or IR 1986 (IR 1986 r 4.193). The decision to disclaim cannot be interfered with by the court in the absence of bad faith or perversity: *Re Hans Place Ltd in liquidation* [1993] BCLC 768. Where third parties have acquired rights under the contract which is disclaimed, although the company is released from the date of disclaimer, those third party rights will generally be upheld: *Capital Prime Properties Ltd v Worthgate Ltd* [2000] BCC 525. If a liquidator does not disclaim a contract he or she does not become personally liable on it: *Stead, Hazel & Co v Cooper* [1933] 1 KB 840.

S 178(4)(b)

See *Hughes v Groveholt Ltd* [2005] BPIR 1345, 1368 para 106 per Jonathan Parker LJ (third party charge not affected by disclaimer).

S 178(5)

This sub-section allows a person interested in property (for example a sub-tenant, mortgagee or a party to a contract) to serve a notice putting the liquidator to an election as to whether or not to disclaim the property in question. The liquidator's initial period of 28 days within which he or she must serve a notice of disclaimer can be extended with the permission of the court. There is no such equivalent discretion on the part of the court in relation to the equivalent provisions relating to trustees in bankruptcy: see section IA 1986 316(1). The notice to elect should be in Form 4.54 (IR 1986 Sch 4) or a substantially similar form and must be delivered to the liquidator personally or by registered post: IR 1986 r 4.191.

S 178(6)

The right of compensation under IA 1986 s 178(6) is analogous to the right to claim damages for a statutory fault: *Re Park Air Services plc* [2000] AC 172. Where the effect of a disclaimer is that a landlord has regained possession of premises and has re-let them, the starting point for assessing loss is the difference between them for what would have been the remainder of the term or the earliest date at which the lease might have been determined at the tenant's option: *Re McEwan ex p Blake* (1879) 11 Ch D 572. The landlord can also claim for the rates and cost of any repairs needed to achieve the letting: *Re Park Air Services (above)*. If the landlord has not re-let he or she is entitled to the difference between the rent reserved by the disclaimed lease and the rent at which the premises are fairly worth: *Re Hide, ex p Llynvi Coal and Iron Co* (1871) 7 Ch App 28.

The effect of a vesting order made under IA 1986 s 181 needs to be taken into account in assessing the extent of any loss or damage: IA 1986 s 181(5). Any award made will be subject to a discount for accelerated receipt: *Re Park Air Services* (above) where the discount was fixed at 8.5% to reflect the yield at the time on gilt edged securities for an equivalent term of the disclaimed lease. Any award made may carry interest under IA 1986 s 189 from the date of the disclaimer: *Re Park Air Services* (above)). Persons other than the landlord (for example, a surety or sub-tenant) may also suffer loss through a disclaimer.

1.204

179 Disclaimer of leaseholds

(1) The disclaimer under section 178 of any property of a leasehold nature does not take effect unless a copy of the disclaimer has been served (so far as the liquidator is aware of their addresses) on every person claiming under the company as underlessee or mortgagee and either—

    (a)   no application under section 181 below is made with respect to that property before the end of the period of 14 days beginning with the day on which the last notice served under this subsection was served; or

    (b)   where such an application has been made, the court directs that the disclaimer shall take effect.

(2) Where the court gives a direction under subsection (1)(b it may also, instead of or in addition to any order it makes under section 181, make such orders with respect to fixtures, tenant's improvements and other matters arising out of the lease as it thinks fit.

Notes

S 179(1)

In the case of a disclaimer of a leasehold interest the disclaimer does not take effect unless a copy of the disclaimer has been served on every person claiming as underlessee or mortgagee and either no application has been made under IA 1986 s 181 for a vesting order within 14 days beginning with the day on which the last notice was served or an application has been made and the court directs that the disclaimer takes effect. See, however, IR 1986 r 4.194, which provides that an underlessee or mortgagee can apply for a vesting order within 3 months of the applicant becoming aware of the disclaimer.

The combined effect of IA 1986 s 179(1) and IR 1986 r 4.194 is that, if no application is made to the court within 14 days pursuant to IA 1986 s 179, the disclaimer has effect and the rights and obligations of the landlord and tenant cease. Notwithstanding this, the lease can be re-instated if a successful application is made for a vesting order within the 3-month time limit laid down by IR 1986 r 4.194. If a new interest is created in the land between the expiry of the 14-day time limit set out in IA 1986 s 179(1) and the making of a subsequent application for a vesting order, this may be a ground for refusing a vesting order. A lease may become ownerless following a disclaimer; however the disclaimer does not of itself cause the lease to cease to exist. It will only cease to exist on one of the normal methods of termination, namely effluxion of time, surrender or forfeiture by the landlord: *W H Smith Ltd v Wyndham Investments Ltd* [1994] BCC 699.

1.205

180 Land subject to rentcharge

(1) The following applies where, in consequence of the disclaimer under section 178 of any land subject to a rentcharge, that land vests by operation of law in the Crown or any other person (referred to in the next subsection as 'the proprietor').

(2) The proprietor and the successors in title of the proprietor are not subject to any personal liability in respect of any sums becoming due under the rentcharge except sums becoming due after the proprietor, or some person claiming under or through the proprietor, has taken possession or control of the land or has entered into occupation of it.

Notes

S 180(1)

For the meaning of 'land', see the Interpretation Act 1978, s 5, Sch 1.

1.206

181 Powers of court (general)

(1) This section and the next apply where the liquidator has disclaimed property under section 178.

(2) An application under this section may be made to the court by—
    (a)   any person who claims an interest in the disclaimed property, or
    (b)   any person who is under any liability in respect of the disclaimed property, not being a liability discharged by the disclaimer.

(3) Subject as follows, the court may on the application make an order, on such terms as it thinks fit, for the vesting of the disclaimed property in, or for its delivery to—
    (a)   a person entitled to it or a trustee for such a person, or
    (b)   a person subject to such a liability as is mentioned in subsection (2)(b) or a trustee for such a person.

(4) The court shall not make an order under subsection (3)(b) except where it appears to the court that it would be just to do so for the purpose of compensating the person subject to the liability in respect of the disclaimer.

(5) The effect of any order under this section shall be taken into account in assessing for the purpose of section 178(6) the extent of any loss or damage sustained by any person in consequence of the disclaimer.

(6) An order under this section vesting property in any person need not be completed by conveyance, assignment or transfer.

Notes

S 181(2)

In *Re Vedmay* [1994] 1 EGLR 74 it was held that a statutory tenant had an interest in disclaimed property since the term 'interest' was not restricted to a proprietary interest but extended to any financial interest in the subsistence or otherwise of the lease and included in particular any interest that would be adversely affected by the disclaimer. However in *Lloyds Bank SF Nominees v Aladdin Ltd* [1996] 1 BCLC 720 the Court of Appeal appeared to confine *Re Vedmay* (above) to statutory tenants having the 'status of irremovability'. The persons who may apply for a vesting order include original tenants, sureties, mortgagees, subtenants, the landlord him or herself (*Re Cock, ex p Shilson* (1887) 20 QBD 343) and a local authority seeking to recover the costs spent on a dangerous structure: *Hackney Borough Council v Crown Estates Commissioners* [1996] 1 EGLR 151. There is a 'pecking order' of persons entitled to make an application under IA 1986 s 181 (*A E Realisations Ltd* [1987] 3 All ER 83) which is as follows:

(a) underlesee or mortgagee;
(b) any person 'liable either personally or in a representative character and either alone or jointly' with the company or bankrupt e g surety or former tenant not released from liability;
(c) 'any person claiming an interest' in the lease or under any liability not discharged by it e g landlord.

The order cannot be altered by one party making an application in priority to another. For instance, if a landlord wishes to make an application that a lease be vested in itself, the court will only make an order if the sub-tenant indicates that it does not want to make an application itself (at which point the court can offer a lease which the sub-tenant can decline, thereby excluding themselves from the property and leaving the landlord without the benefit of the sub-leases (as happened in *Sterling Estates v Pickard UK Ltd* [1997] 2 EGLR 33)). See also *Re ITM Corporation Ltd (in liquidation)* [1997] BCC 554 where it was held that the need to clear off the interests of a person higher up in the 'pecking order' than the applicant landlord meant that a vesting order could not be made in favour of a landlord on terms subject to and with the benefit of existing sub-leases.

Note that in *A E Realisations* (above) the terms of the guarantee provided that in the event of the lease being disclaimed the guarantor would take a new lease from the landlord for the residue of the term at the same rent. In light of this provision the court declined to make a vesting order in favour of the guarantor.

S 181(5)

If a vesting order is made this must be taken in to account when assessing a landlord's loss for the purposes of section IA 1986 178(6). Notwithstanding the making of a vesting order a landlord may still suffer loss, for example:

(a) If the lease is vested in a sub-tenant, the landlord will lose the right to recover sub-rents under the Law of Distress Amendment Act 1908 s 6.
(b) If the lease is vested in a surety, the landlord will lose the benefit of having a surety.
(c) The court may on the making of a vesting order relieve the recipient of the lease from liability for past beaches of the lease: see IA 1986 s 182(1)(b).

S 181(6)

See also LPA 1925 s 52(2).

1.207

182 Powers of court (leaseholds)

(1) The court shall not make an order under section 181 vesting property of a leasehold nature in any person claiming under the company as underlessee or mortgagee except on terms making that person—

(a) subject to the same liabilities and obligations as the company was subject to under the lease at the commencement of the winding up, or

(b)   if the court thinks fit, subject to the same liabilities and obligations as that person would be subject to if the lease had been assigned to him at the commencement of the winding up.

(2) For the purposes of an order under section 181 relating to only part of any property comprised in a lease, the requirements of subsection (1) apply as if the lease comprised only the property to which the order relates.

(3) Where subsection (1) applies and no person claiming under the company as underlessee or mortgagee is willing to accept an order under section 181 on the terms required by virtue of that subsection, the court may, by order under that section, vest the company's estate or interest in the property in any person who is liable (whether personally or in a representative capacity, and whether alone or jointly with the company) to perform the lessee's covenants in the lease.

The court may vest that estate and interest in such a person freed and discharged from all estates, incumbrances and interests created by the company.

(4) Where subsection (1) applies and a person claiming under the company as underlessee or mortgagee declines to accept an order under section 181, that person is excluded from all interest in the property.

Notes

S 182(1)

If the court makes a vesting order it can do so either on terms that the applicant is subject to the same liabilities and obligations as the company was subject to at the commencement of the winding up (in which case the applicant will be liable for breaches of covenant which occurred before the commencement of the winding up) or if the court thinks fit to the same liabilities and obligations as the applicant would have been subject to if the lease has been assigned to it at the commencement of the winding up (in which case there may be no liability for breaches of covenant occurring before the commencement of the winding up). In either case the vesting of the lease will carry with it liability for breaches of covenant between the date of the commencement of the winding up and the date of the vesting order: *Re Walker, ex p Mills* (1895) 64 LJQB 783; *Re Carter & Ellis, ex p Savill Bros* [1905] 1 KB 735. The court does not have the jurisdiction to make a vesting order in favour of a landlord subject to and with the benefit of existing sub-leases (*Re ITM Corporation Ltd (In Liquidation)* [1997] BCC 544 and see also the notes to IA 1986 s 181(2) above.

S 182(4)

This provision allows a party to put an underlessee or mortgagee to an election as to whether or not to accept an order pursuant to IA 1986, s 181. If the person declines (and the application for a vesting order made has been made by another party, for example, the landlord) such person will be excluded from all interest in the property (and in the case of an underlessee in possession will become a trespasser). The section only applies to a person with a proprietary interest and cannot be invoked to determine a statutory tenancy: *Re Vedmay Ltd* [1994] 1 BCLC 676.

Execution, attachment and the Scottish equivalents

1.208

183 Effect of execution or attachment (England and Wales)

(1) Where a creditor has issued execution against the goods or land of a company or has attached any debt due to it, and the company is subsequently wound up, he is not entitled to retain the benefit of the execution or attachment against the liquidator unless he has completed the execution or attachment before the commencement of the winding up.

(2) However—

(a) if a creditor has had notice of a meeting having been called at which a resolution for voluntary winding up is to be proposed, the date on which he had notice is substituted, for the purpose of subsection (1), for the date of commencement of the winding up;

(b) a person who purchases in good faith under a sale by the enforcement officer or other officer charged with the execution of the writ any goods of a company on which execution has been levied in all cases acquires a good title to them against the liquidator; and

(c) the rights conferred by subsection (1) on the liquidator may be set aside by the court in favour of the creditor to such extent and subject to such terms as the court thinks fit.

(3) For the purposes of this Act—

(a) an execution against goods is completed by seizure and sale, or by the making of a charging order under section 1 of the Charging Orders Act 1979;

(b) an attachment of a debt is completed by receipt of the debt; and

(c) an execution against land is completed by seizure, by the appointment of a receiver, or by the making of a charging order under section 1 of the Act above-mentioned.

(4) In this section 'goods' includes all chattels personal; and 'enforcement officer' means an individual who is authorised to act as an enforcement officer under the Courts Act 2003.

(5) This section does not apply in the case of a winding up in Scotland.

Notes

S 183

Whereas IA 1986, s 128 applies only to compulsory liquidation and deals with '*any attachment, sequestration, distress or execution*' put in force after commencement of the winding up, this section applies to both compulsory and voluntary liquidations and deals with the position post-commencement of a winding up. It only applies to '*execution or attachment*'. In the case of a voluntary liquidation, the date of the commencement of the winding up is deemed to be the 'date' on which the creditor had notice of the meeting at which the resolution for the winding up was to be proposed: IA 1986 s 183(2)(a). The use of the word 'date' as opposed to 'time' (cf IA1986, s 86) means that it is the day of the notice and not the time of the actual receipt of it which matters: *Trow v Ind Coope (West Midlands) Ltd* [1967] 2 QB 899. The section does not deal with existing distress, which can therefore continue unless special reasons justify a stay: see IA 1986 s 126. The creditor who has not completed before commencement may not retain the benefit without an order from the court, even if he or she has completed the process by the date of the making of winding up order or the passing of the resolution. The section does not apply to distress by a landlord: *Re Bellaglade* [1977] 1 All ER 319; *Re Herbert Berry Associates v IRC* [1977] 1 WLR 1437 nor a distraint levied under the Taxes Management Act 1970 by walking possession in respect of unpaid Inland Revenue debts *Re Modern Jet Support Ltd* [2005] BPIR 1382, [2006] BCC 174.

Whilst the provision would catch a charge obtained by issue of execution or attachment (*Re Andrew* [1937] Ch 122) and the right to take further steps necessary to complete execution, it would not catch money already received before commencement (*Re Caribbean Products (Yam Importers) Ltd* [1966] Ch 331). Money paid to the sheriff to avoid a sale and still held by him is not a 'benefit of the execution' and accordingly not within s 183 *Re Walkden Sheet Metal Co Ltd* [1960] Ch 170, although see IA 1986 s 184(3).

Completion

Seizure of goods without sale is insufficient: *Re Standard Manufacturing Co* [1891] 1 Ch 627; *Re Opera Ltd* [1891] 3 Ch 260. Where a charging order is relied upon, it must be an order absolute since an order nisi is only a revocable order for security and would ordinarily be discharged if not made absolute before commencement of a liquidation: *Roberts Petroleum Ltd v Bernard Kenny Ltd* [1983] 2 AC 192. Similarly, garnishee proceedings require an order absolute: *Norton v Yates* [1906] 1 KB 112.

Discretion of the court

S 183(2)

The court has an unfettered discretion under IA 1986 s 183(2)(c) to allow all or part of an execution (*Re Aro Co Ltd* [1980] Ch 196) and to impose terms. It is a discretion exercised sparingly which requires 'weighty reasons' to disturb the general rule of rateable distribution to creditors which reflect the difficulty faced by the court in knowing whether or not other creditors could put up as good a case as the creditor concerned: *Re Caribbean Products (Yam Importers) Ltd* [1966] Ch 331.

Where as a result of deliberate conduct by the company a particular creditor has been persuaded or induced to hold off an intended execution, the court may be persuaded that it would be unfair not to allow the execution to proceed even though there was no actual fraud: *Re Grosvenor Metal Co Ltd* [1950] Ch 63; *Re Suidair International Airways Ltd* [1951] Ch 165); cf where all the creditors have been misled: *Re Redman (Builders) Ltd* [1964] 1 WLR 541; *Re Vron Colliery Co* (1882) 20 Ch D 442. Where a creditor has been the victim of fraud or trickery, the court will be all the more ready to allow execution: *Armourduct Manufacturing Co Ltd v General Incandescent Co Ltd* [1911] 2 KB 143; but the conduct in question is that after judgment has been obtained and not pre-judgment conduct: *Landau v Purvis, 15 June 1999, LTL 16/6/99*. Some guidance on pre-judgment conduct is provided in *Re Buckingham International Ltd, Mitchell v Buckingham International plc* [1998] 2 BCLC 369

Execution, attachment etc against foreign assets

S 183(3)

IA 1986 s 183 has no extra-territorial effect and cannot therefore apply to an execution process abroad once completed: *Re: Buckingham International Ltd, Mitchell v Buckingham International plc* [1998] 2 BCLC 369. Where, however, the execution process has not been completed (in that it has not yet begun or has begun but has not been completed), the court retains a discretion to intervene by restraining the initiating or completing the execution: *Re North Carolina Estate Co* (1889) 5 TLR 328; *Re Vocalion (Foreign) Ltd)* [1932] 2 Ch 196, see also *Re Buckingham International plc* [1997] BCC 71.

S 183(4)

Note that the definition of 'goods' goes wider than that provided by the Sale of Goods Act 1979 and includes intangible property such as choses in action.

I.209

184 Duties of officers charged with execution of writs and other processes (England and Wales)

(1) The following applies where a company's goods are taken in execution and, before their sale or the completion of the execution (by the receipt or recovery of the full amount of the levy), notice is served on the sheriff that a provisional liquidator has been appointed or that a winding-up order has been made, or that a resolution for voluntary winding up has been passed.

(2) The sheriff shall, on being so required, deliver the goods and any money seized or received in part satisfaction of the execution to the liquidator; but the costs of execution are a first charge on the goods or money so delivered, and the liquidator may sell the goods, or a sufficient part of them, for the purpose of satisfying the charge.

(3) If under an execution in respect of a judgment for a sum exceeding [£500] a company's goods are sold or money is paid in order to avoid sale, the enforcement officer or other officer shall deduct the costs of the execution from the proceeds of sale or the money paid and retain the balance for 14 days.

(4) If within that time notice is served on the enforcement officer or other officer of a petition for the winding up of the company having been presented, or of a meeting having been called at which there is to be proposed a resolution for voluntary winding up, and an order is made or a resolution passed (as the case may be), the enforcement officer or other officer shall pay the balance to the liquidator, who is entitled to retain it as against the execution creditor.

(5) The rights conferred by this section on the liquidator may be set aside by the court in favour of the creditor to such extent and subject to such terms as the court thinks fit.

(6) In this section, 'goods' includes all chattels personal; and 'enforcement officer' means an individual who is authorised to act as an enforcement officer under the Courts Act 2003.

(7) The money sum for the time being specified in subsection (3) is subject to increase or reduction by order under section 416 in Part XV.

(8) This section does not apply in the case of a winding up in Scotland.

Notes

S 184

The duties of the enforcement officer are governed by this section and by IR 1986 r 12.19. The enforcement officer's costs may be subjected to detailed assessment at the request of the insolvency practitioner under IR 1986 r 7.36.

S 184(1), (2)

These sub-sections apply where the company in respect of which notice is served is already wound up or subject to the control of a provisional liquidator when the notice is served on the enforcement officer. They ensure that the benefit of execution (subject to the enforcement officer's costs) passes to the liquidator. The costs of execution do not include a creditor's costs of issuing proceedings or serving a writ of *fi fa*: *Re Woods (Bristol) Ltd* [1931] 2 Ch 320. Nor does this provision apply to money paid to avoid sale: *Re Walkden Sheet Metal Co Ltd* [1960] Ch 170.

S 183(3), (4)

The requirement that the enforcement officer hold the proceeds of executions (or payments in lieu of sale) in respect of judgments over £500 for 14 days enables notice to be served on him or her during the period after a winding up petition has been presented or a meeting to consider a proposal for voluntary winding up has been called. Where such a notice is served the enforcement officer holds the relevant proceeds pending the outcome of the petition or meeting. If in due course a winding up order is made or a resolution passed, then unless the court orders otherwise under IA 1986 s 184(5) the monies pass to the liquidator (subject to the enforcement officer's costs). In the case of monies paid to avoid sale, the 14 day period runs from the time of receipt by the bailiff, not the date he or she passes it to the enforcement officer: *Marley Tile Co Ltd v Burrows* [1978] QB 241.

The notice, however, must relate to the actual form of liquidation, which in fact takes place; accordingly, notice of a petition does not invoke this section if the petition does not proceed because a resolution is passed and the company goes into voluntary liquidation. Similarly, the section is not invoked by service of a notice of a meeting of creditors to consider a proposal for voluntary winding up where the company is in fact wound up by the court: *Bluston and Bramley Ltd v Leigh* [1950] 2 KB 548. Although strictly the section requires a notice to members in the case of a proposal for voluntary liquidation, it is in fact satisfied by a notice to creditors: *Engineering Industry Training Board v Samuel Talbot (Engineers) Ltd* [1969] 2 QB 270) The notice, however, must be served within 14 days on the enforcement officer and not on his or her assistant: *Hellyer v Sheriff of Yorkshire* [1975] Ch 16; *Marley Tile Co Ltd v Burrows* [1978] QB 241. If the proceeds of an execution are in the enforcement officer's hands, it is not complete and whilst the sheriff is entitled to retain the costs of execution, he or she must account to the liquidator (*Re Andrew, ex p Official Receiver* [1937] Ch 122) who may insist on detailed taxation of those costs: IR 1986 r 7.36.

S 184(5), (6)

The court has a discretion to set aside the rights of the liquidator under this section, as under IA 1986 s 183(2)(c). As to the discretion of the court and the definition of 'goods', see commentaries under IA 1986 s 183(2)(c) and s 183(4) respectively.

1.209A

185 Effect of diligence (Scotland)

(1) In the winding up of a company registered in Scotland, the following provisions of the Bankruptcy (Scotland) Act 1985—

    (a)   subsections (1) to (6) of section 37 (effect of sequestration on diligence); and

    (b)   subsections (3), (4), (7) and (8) of section 39 (realisation of estate),

apply, so far as consistent with this Act, in like manner as they apply in the sequestration of a debtor's estate, with the substitutions specified below and with any other necessary modifications.

(2) The substitutions to be made in those sections of the Act of 1985 are as follows—

    (a)   for references to the debtor, substitute references to the company;

(b)   for references to the sequestration, substitute references to the winding up;

(c)   for references to the date of sequestration, substitute references to the commencement of the winding up of the company; and

(d)   for references to the permanent trustee, substitute references to the liquidator.

(3) In this section, 'the commencement of the winding up of the company' means, where it is being wound up by the court, the day on which the winding-up order is made.

(4) This section, so far as relating to any estate or effects of the company situated in Scotland, applies in the case of a company registered in England and Wales as in the case of one registered in Scotland.

Miscellaneous matters

1.210

186 Rescission of contracts by the court

(1) The court may, on the application of a person who is, as against the liquidator, entitled to the benefit or subject to the burden of a contract made with the company, make an order rescinding the contract on such terms as to payment by or to either party of damages for the non-performance of the contract, or otherwise as the court thinks just.

(2) Any damages payable under the order to such a person may be proved by him as a debt in the winding up.

Notes

S 186(1)

Liquidation may amount to an anticipatory breach of a contract: *Sale Continuation Ltd v Austin Taylor and Co Ltd* [1968] 2 QB 849; [1967] 2 All ER 1092. CA 1989 s 164 disapplies this section in relation to a 'market contract' and the Financial Markets and Insolvency (Settlement Finality) Regulations 1999 (SI 1999/2979) disapply this section in relation to a transfer order or a contract for the purpose of realising collateral security: see reg 16(1).

1.211

187 Power to make over assets to employees

(1) On the winding up of a company (whether by the court or voluntarily), the liquidator may, subject to the following provisions of this section, make any payment which the company has, before the commencement of the winding up, decided to make under section 719 of the Companies Act (power to provide for employees or former employees on cessation or transfer of business).

(2) The power which a company may exercise by virtue only of that section may be exercised by the liquidator after the winding up has commenced if, after the company's liabilities have been fully satisfied and provision has been made for the expenses of the winding up, the exercise of that power has been sanctioned by such a resolution of the company as

would be required of the company itself by section 719(3) before that commencement, if paragraph (b) of that subsection were omitted and any other requirement applicable to its exercise by the company had been met.

(3) Any payment which may be made by a company under this section (that is, a payment after the commencement of its winding up) may be made out of the company's assets which are available to the members on the winding up.

(4) On a winding up by the court, the exercise by the liquidator of his powers under this section is subject to the court's control, and any creditor or contributory may apply to the court with respect to any exercise or proposed exercise of the power.

(5) Subsections (1) and (2) above have effect notwithstanding anything in any rule of law or in section 107 of this Act (property of company after satisfaction of liabilities to be distributed among members).

Notes

S 187(2)

CA 1985 s 719 gives express power to a company by ordinary resolution to make provision for employees or former employees when it ceases to trade or transfers the whole or part of its business. In either a compulsory or voluntary liquidation where the company has already resolved to make a payment to employees the liquidator may implement that resolution provided the company's liabilities have been fully satisfied and sufficient provision has been made for the expenses of the winding-up.

S 187(3)

This provision limits the assets, which can be used for this purpose.

S 187(4)

This provision gives the court ultimate control over any exercise of this power by the liquidator.

1.212

188 Notification that company is in liquidation

(1) When a company is being wound up, whether by the court or voluntarily, every invoice, order for goods or business letter issued by or on behalf of the company, or a liquidator of the company, or a receiver or manager of the company's property, being a document on or in which the name of the company appears, shall contain a statement that the company is being wound up.

(2) If default is made in complying with this section, the company and any of the following persons who knowingly and wilfully authorises or

permits the default, namely, any officer of the company, any liquidator of the company and any receiver or manager, is liable to a fine.

Notes

S 188

This provision reflects the similar provisions in relation to managers and receivers in IA 1986, s 39 and in relation to administrators in IA 1986 Sch B1, para 45.

1.213

189 Interest on debts

(1) In a winding up interest is payable in accordance with this section on any debt proved in the winding up, including so much of any such debt as represents interest on the remainder.

(2) Any surplus remaining after the payment of the debts proved in a winding up shall, before being applied for any other purpose, be applied in paying interest on those debts in respect of the periods during which they have been outstanding since the company went into liquidation.

(3) All interest under this section ranks equally, whether or not the debts on which it is payable rank equally.

(4) The rate of interest payable under this section in respect of any debt ('the official rate' for the purposes of any provision of this Act in which that expression is used) is whichever is the greater of—
    (a)   the rate specified in section 17 of the Judgments Act 1838 on the day on which the company went into liquidation, and
    (b)   the rate applicable to that debt apart from the winding up.

(5) In the application of this section to Scotland—
    (a)   references to a debt proved in a winding up have effect as references to a claim accepted in a winding up, and
    (b)   the reference to section 17 of the Judgments Act 1838 has effect as a reference to the rules.

Notes

S 189(1), (2)

Interest is payable on all debts proved in the winding up in respect of the periods during which the debts have been outstanding since the company went into liquidation. Interest which arises on a debt prior to liquidation is itself provable as a debt in the liquidation subject to IR 1986 r 4.93. For a comparison of IR 1986 r 4.93 and IA 1986 s 189, see *Re Empire Paper Ltd (In Liq) Ch D* [1999] 406. Where a person sustains loss or damage as a consequence of the operation of a disclaimer under IA 1986 s 178(6) and thereby becomes a creditor, interest runs at the rate specified from the date of the disclaimer: *Re Park Air Services plc* [2000] 2 AC 172.

S 189(3)

Interest will only be payable as dividend in the event that all debts are paid in full, and all such interest ranks equally whether or not the debts in respect of which it is paid rank equally. The Inland Revenue does not as a normal rule treat such interest as annual interest and there is therefore no obligation to deduct tax.

1.214

190 Documents exempt from stamp duty

(1) In the case of a winding up by the court, or of a creditors' voluntary winding up, the following has effect as regards exemption from duties chargeable under the enactments relating to stamp duties.

(2) If the company is registered in England and Wales, the following documents are exempt from stamp duty—

(a)   every assurance relating solely to freehold or leasehold property, or to any estate, right or interest in, any real or personal property, which forms part of the company's assets and which, after the execution of the assurance, either at law or in equity, is or remains part of those assets, and

(b)   every writ, order, certificate, or other instrument or writing relating solely to the property of any company which is being wound up as mentioned in subsection (1), or to any proceeding under such a winding up.

'Assurance' here includes deed, conveyance, assignment and surrender.

(3) If the company is registered in Scotland, the following documents are exempt from stamp duty—

(a)   every conveyance relating solely to property which forms part of the company's assets and which, after the execution of the conveyance, is or remains the company's property for the benefit of its creditors,

(b)   any articles of roup or sale, submission and every other instrument and writing whatsoever relating solely to the company's property, and

(c)   every deed or writing forming part of the proceedings in the winding up.

'Conveyance' here includes assignation, instrument, discharge, writing and deed.

1.215

191 Company's books to be evidence

Where a company is being wound up, all books and papers of the company and of the liquidators are, as between the contributories of the company, prima facie evidence of the truth of all matters purporting to be recorded in them.

Notes

S 191

'Books and papers' are widely defined to include '*accounts, deeds writings, and documents*', with 'document' being further defined as including '*summons, notice, order, and other legal process, and registers*': CA 1985 s 744, IA 1986 s 251. A contributory may adduce evidence to show that the books are not correct but the burden of showing that they are incorrect lies on the contributory: *Re Baranagh Oil Refining Co, Arnot's Case* (1887) 36 Ch D 702 at 712; *Re Great Northern Salt and Chemical Works, ex p Kennedy* (1890) 44 Ch D 472 at 483. A creditor may rely upon entries in the minute book as a sufficient admission of the company's liability for his claim: *Re Teignmouth and General Mutual Shipping Association, Martin's Claim* (1872) LR 14 Eq 148.

1.216

192 Information as to pending liquidations

(1) If the winding up of a company is not concluded within one year after its commencement, the liquidator shall, at such intervals as may be prescribed, until the winding up is concluded, send to the registrar of companies a statement in the prescribed form and containing the pre-scribed particulars with respect to the proceedings in, and position of, the liquidation.

(2) If a liquidator fails to comply with this section, he is liable to a fine and, for continued contravention, to a daily default fine.

Notes

S 192

Further requirements in relation to such statements made to the registrar of companies are contained in IR 1986 r 4.223. The court may make an order under IA 1986 s 170 to secure compliance by the liquidator with his or her duties to maintain accounts and file documents and returns. In *Re S & A Conversions Ltd* (1988) 4 BCC 384 and in *Re Allan Ellis (Transport and Packing) Services Ltd* (1989) 5 BCC 835 liquidators received custodial sentences inter alia for failure to comply with this provision.

1.217

193 Unclaimed dividends (Scotland)

(1) The following applies where a company registered in Scotland has been wound up, and is about to be dissolved.

(2) The liquidator shall lodge in an appropriate bank or institution as defined in section 73(1) of the Bankruptcy (Scotland) Act 1985 (not being a bank or institution in or of which the liquidator is acting partner, manager, agent or cashier) in the name of the Accountant of Court the whole unclaimed dividends and unapplied or undistributable balances, and the deposit receipts shall be transmitted to the Accountant of Court.

(3) The provisions of section 58 of the Bankruptcy (Scotland) Act 1985 (so far as consistent with this Act and the Companies Act) apply with any necessary modifications to sums lodged in a bank or institution under this section as they apply to sums deposited under section 57 of the Act first mentioned.

1.218

194 Resolutions passed at adjourned meetings

Where a resolution is passed at an adjourned meeting of a company's creditors or contributories, the resolution is treated for all purposes as

> having been passed on the date on which it was in fact passed, and not as having been passed on any earlier date.

Notes

S 194

This section, which is self-explanatory, confirms that resolutions passed at an adjourned meeting within a liquidation are to be treated consistently with the general rule for company meetings provided by CA 1985, s 381.

1.219

195 Meetings to ascertain wishes of creditors or contributories

(1) The court may—
  (a) as to all matters relating to the winding up of a company, have regard to the wishes of the creditors or contributories (as proved to it by any sufficient evidence), and
  (b) if it thinks fit, for the purpose of ascertaining those wishes, direct meetings of the creditors or contributories to be called, held and conducted in such manner as the court directs, and appoint a person to act as chairman of any such meeting and report the result of it to the court.

(2) In the case of creditors, regard shall be had to the value of each creditor's debt.

(3) In the case of contributories, regard shall be had to the number of votes conferred on each contributory by the Companies Act or the articles.

Notes

S 195

With respect to all matters relating to the winding up of a company, the court will in general take into account the views of the creditors and contributories. Further, the bigger the debt or the bigger the interest in the company, the more weight the court will in general give to the view of any particular creditor or contributory. It should be noted, however, that the section is expressed in discretionary as opposed to mandatory terms ('may' as opposed to 'shall') and accordingly although in general the court will act as above (see for example *Re Falcon R J Developments Ltd* (1987) 3 BCC 146), in appropriate circumstances the court may depart from the general rule: *Re Bank of Credit and Commerce International SA (No 2)* (1992) BCC 715.

S 195(1)(b)

For the procedural rules governing any meeting, see IR 1986, r 4.54 to 4.71.

1.219A

196 Judicial notice of court documents

In all proceedings under this Part, all courts, judges and persons judicially acting, and all officers, judicial or ministerial, of any court, or employed in enforcing the process of any court shall take judicial notice—

(a) of the signature of any officer of the High Court or of a county court in England and Wales, or of the Court of Session or a sheriff court in Scotland, or of the High Court in Northern Ireland, and also

(b) of the official seal or stamp of the several offices of the High Court in England and Wales or Northern Ireland, or of the Court of Session, appended to or impressed on any document made, issued or signed under the provisions of this Act or the Companies Act, or any official copy of such a document.

1.220

197 Commission for receiving evidence

(1) When a company is wound up in England and Wales or in Scotland, the court may refer the whole or any part of the examination of witnesses—

(a) to a specified county court in England and Wales, or
(b) to the sheriff principal for a special sheriffdom in Scotland, or
(c) to the High Court in Northern Ireland or a specified Northern Ireland County Court,

('specified' meaning specified in the order of the winding-up court).

(2) Any person exercising jurisdiction as a judge of the court to which the reference is made (or, in Scotland, the sheriff principal to whom it is made) shall then, by virtue of this section, be a commissioner for the purpose of taking the evidence of those witnesses.

(3) The judge or sheriff principal has in the matter referred the same power of summoning and examining witnesses, of requiring the production and delivery of documents, of punishing defaults by witnesses, and of allowing costs and expenses to witnesses, as the court which made the winding-up order.

These powers are in addition to any which the judge or sheriff principal might lawfully exercise apart from this section.

(4) The examination so taken shall be returned or reported to the court which made the order in such manner as that court requests.

(5) This section extends to Northern Ireland.

1.221

198 Court order for examination of persons in Scotland

(1) The court may direct the examination in Scotland of any person for the time being in Scotland (whether a contributory of the company or not), in regard to the trade, dealings, affairs or property of any company in course of being wound up, or of any person being a contributory of the company, so far as the company may be interested by reason of his being a contributory.

(2) The order or commission to take the examination shall be directed to the sheriff principal of the sheriffdom in which the person to be examined is residing or happens to be for the time; and the sheriff principal shall summon the person to appear before him at a time and place to be

specified in the summons for examination on oath as a witness or as a haver, and to produce any books or papers called for which are in his possession or power.

(3) The sheriff principal may take the examination either orally or on written interrogatories, and shall report the same in writing in the usual form to the court, and shall transmit with the report the books and papers produced, if the originals are required and specified by the order or commission, or otherwise copies or extracts authenticated by the sheriff.

(4) If a person so summoned fails to appear at the time and place specified, or refuses to be examined or to make the production required, the sheriff principal shall proceed against him as a witness or haver duly cited; and failing to appear or refusing to give evidence or make production may be proceeded against by the law of Scotland.

(5) The sheriff principal is entitled to such fees, and the witness is entitled to such allowances, as sheriffs principal when acting as commissioners under appointment from the Court or Session and as witnesses and havers are entitled to in the like cases according to the law and practice of Scotland.

(6) If any objection is stated to the sheriff principal by the witness, either on the ground of his incompetency as a witness, or as to the production required, or on any other ground, the sheriff principal may, if he thinks fit, report the objection to the court, and suspend the examination of the witness until it has been disposed of by the court.

1.222

199 Costs of application for leave to proceed (Scottish companies)

Where a petition or application for leave to proceed with an action or proceeding against a company which is being wound up in Scotland is unopposed and is granted by the court, the costs of the petition or application shall, unless the court otherwise directs, be added to the amount of the petitioner's or applicant's claim against the company.

1.223

200 Affidavits etc in United Kingdom and overseas

(1) An affidavit required to be sworn under or for the purposes of this Part may be sworn in the United Kingdom, or elsewhere in Her Majesty's dominions, before any court, judge or person lawfully authorised to take and receive affidavits, or before any of Her Majesty's consuls or vice-consuls in any place outside Her dominions.

(2) All courts, judges, justices, commissioners and persons acting judicially shall take judicial notice of the seal or stamp or signature (as the case may be) of any such court, judge, person, consul or vice-consul attached, appended or subscribed to any such affidavit, or to any other document to be used for the purposes of this Part.

> **Chapter IX**
> **Dissolution of companies after winding Up**
>
> **Introduction**

Dissolution procedure

SS 201–205

This section set out the procedure for bringing an insolvent company's existence to an end after it has been wound up. A company can also be dissolved under CA 1985, s 652 and s 652A. The former provision entitles the registrar to strike a company off the register if it appears to be defunct, a power which is often used when a company fails to file its accounts. The latter provision allows the company itself to apply to be struck of the register.

Effect of dissolution

On dissolution the company ceases to exist so that for example it can no longer be a party to proceedings. It cannot own property and any property it owned at the time of dissolution passes to the Crown as bona vacantia.

Reinstatement of company after dissolution

CA 1985 s 651 empowers the court to declare the dissolution of a company void on the application of any person appearing to the court to be interested: *Re Forte's Manufacturing Ltd* [1994] BCC 84. This might be required in order to enable the liquidator to distribute an overlooked asset or to enable a creditor to obtain a judgment against the company so that he can enforce it against an insurer under the Third Parties (Rights against Insurers) Act 1930. The reinstatement application must be brought within two years of dissolution unless its purpose is to bring a personal injury claim against the company in which case special provisions apply (CA 1985, s 651(5)). Further, CA 1985 s 653 contains a procedure for restoring to the register companies which have been struck off under CA 1985 s 652 or 652A. Restoration under CA 1985 s 653 is retrospective in its effect unlike CA 1985 s 651: *Top Creative Ltd v St Albans District Council* [1999] BCC 999.

> **1.224**
>
> **201 Dissolution (voluntary winding up)**
>
> (1) This section applies, in the case of a company wound up voluntarily, where the liquidator has sent to the registrar of companies his final account and return under section 94 (members' voluntary) or section 106 (creditors' voluntary).
>
> (2) The registrar on receiving the account and return shall forthwith register them; and on the expiration of 3 months from the registration of the return the company is deemed to be dissolved.
>
> (3) However, the court may, on the application of the liquidator or any other person who appears to the court to be interested, make an order deferring the date at which the dissolution of the company is to take effect for such time as the court thinks fit.
>
> (4) It is the duty of the person on whose application an order of the court under this section is made within 7 days after the making of the order to deliver to the registrar an office copy of the order for registration; and if

that person fails to do so he is liable to a fine and, for continued contravention, to a daily default fine.

Notes

S 201

This provision contains the procedure applicable to both members' voluntary and creditors' voluntary liquidations. On receipt of the liquidator's final account and return, the registrar of companies must register the return and the company is automatically dissolved three months after such registration. The date of dissolution, however, can be deferred if an application is made under IA 1986 s 201(3).

I.225

202 Early dissolution (England and Wales)

(1) This section applies where an order for the winding up of a company has been made by the court in England and Wales.

(2) The official receiver, if—
    (a)   he is the liquidator of the company, and
    (b)   it appears to him—
        (i)   that the realisable assets of the company are insufficient to cover the expenses of the winding up, and
        (ii)   that the affairs of the company do not require any further investigation,
may at any time apply to the registrar of companies for the early dissolution of the company.

(3) Before making that application, the official receiver shall give not less than 28 days' notice of his intention to do so to the company's creditors and contributories and, if there is an administrative receiver of the company, to that receiver.

(4) With the giving of that notice the official receiver ceases (subject to any directions under the next section) to be required to perform any duties imposed on him in relation to the company, its creditors or contributories by virtue of any provision of this Act, apart from a duty to make an application under subsection (2) of this section.

(5) On the receipt of the official receiver's application under subsection (2) the registrar shall forthwith register it and, at the end of the period of 3 months beginning with the day of the registration of the application, the company shall be dissolved.

However, the Secretary of State may, on the application of the official receiver or any other person who appears to the Secretary of State to be interested, give directions under section 203 at any time before the end of that period.

I.226

203 Consequence of notice under s 202

(1) Where a notice has been given under section 202(3), the official receiver or any creditor or contributory of the company, or the administrative receiver of the company (if there is one) may apply to the Secretary of State for directions under this section.

(2) The grounds on which that application may be made are—

    (a)   that the realisable assets of the company are sufficient to cover the expenses of the winding up;

    (b)   that the affairs of the company do require further investigation; or

    (c)   that for any other reason the early dissolution of the company is inappropriate.

(3) Directions under this section—

    (a)   are directions making such provision as the Secretary of State thinks fit for enabling the winding up of the company to proceed as if no notice had been given under section 202(3), and

    (b)   may, in the case of an application under section 202(5), include a direction deferring the date at which the dissolution of the company is to take effect for such period as the Secretary of State thinks fit.

(4) An appeal to the court lies from any decision of the Secretary of State on an application for directions under this section.

(5) It is the duty of the person on whose application any directions are given under this section, or in whose favour an appeal with respect to an application for such directions is determined, within 7 days after the giving of the directions or the determination of the appeal, to deliver to the registrar of companies for registration such a copy of the directions or determination as is prescribed.

(6) If a person without reasonable excuse fails to deliver a copy as required by subsection (5), he is liable to a fine and, for continued contravention, to a daily default fine.

Notes

SS 202, 203

These provisions contain a procedure for early dissolution, which may be used if a company's realisable assets will not cover the costs of the usual winding up procedure. It only applies to winding up by the court and is only exercisable where the official receiver is the liquidator of the company. If the official receiver considers that the affairs of the company do not warrant further investigation (for example, misfeasance by directors, preferences etc) he or she can apply to the registrar of companies for early dissolution. The registrar must then register the application and the company is automatically dissolved three months after such registration. The official receiver has to notify creditors and shareholders who can apply to the Secretary of State with any objection. If he or she thinks appropriate, the Secretary of State can direct that the winding up proceed as normal.

1.227

204 Early dissolution (Scotland)

(1) This section applies where a winding-up order has been made by the court in Scotland.

(2) If after a meeting or meetings under section 138 (appointment of liquidator in Scotland) it appears to the liquidator that the realisable

assets of the company are insufficient to cover the expenses of the winding up, he may apply to the court for an order that the company be dissolved.

(3) Where the liquidator makes that application, if the court is satisfied that the realisable assets of the company are insufficient to cover the expenses of the winding up and it appears to the court appropriate to do so, the court shall make an order that the company be dissolved in accordance with this section.

(4) A copy of the order shall within 14 days from its date be forwarded by the liquidator to the registrar of companies, who shall forthwith register it; and, at the end of the period of 3 months beginning with the day of the registration of the order, the company shall be dissolved.

(5) The court may, on an application by any person who appears to the court to have an interest, order that the date at which the dissolution of the company is to take effect shall be deferred for such period as the court thinks fit.

(6) It is the duty of the person on whose application an order is made under subsection (5), within 7 days after the making of the order, to deliver to the registrar of companies such a copy of the order as is prescribed.

(7) If the liquidator without reasonable excuse fails to comply with the requirements of subsection (4), he is liable to a fine and, for continued contravention, to a daily default fine.

(8) If a person without reasonable excuse fails to deliver a copy as required by subsection (6), he is liable to a fine and, for continued contravention, to a daily default fine.

1.228

205 Dissolution otherwise than under ss 202–204

(1) This section applies where the registrar of companies receives—
- (a) a notice served for the purposes of section 172(8) (final meeting of creditors and vacation of office by liquidator), or
- (b) a notice from the official receiver that the winding up of a company by the court is complete.

(2) The registrar shall, on receipt of the notice, forthwith register it; and, subject as follows, at the end of the period of 3 months beginning with the day of the registration of the notice, the company shall be dissolved.

(3) The Secretary of State may, on the application of the official receiver or any other person who appears to the Secretary of State to be interested, give a direction deferring the date at which the dissolution of the company is to take effect for such period as the Secretary of State thinks fit.

(4) An appeal to the court lies from any decision of the Secretary of State on an application for a direction under subsection (3).

(5) Subsection (3) does not apply in a case where the winding-up order was made by the court in Scotland, but in such a case the court may, on an application by any person appearing to the court to have an interest,

order that the date at which the dissolution of the company is to take effect shall be deferred for such period as the court thinks fit.

(6) It is the duty of the person—

   (a)   on whose application a direction is given under subsection (3);

   (b)   in whose favour an appeal with respect to an application for such a direction is determined; or

   (c)   on whose application an order is made under subsection (5),

within 7 days after the giving of the direction, the determination of the appeal or the making of the order, to deliver to the registrar for registration such a copy of the direction, determination or order as is prescribed.

(7) If a person without reasonable excuse fails to deliver a copy as required by subsection (6), he is liable to a fine and, for continued contravention to a daily default fine.

Notes

S 205

This section contains the dissolution procedure applicable to compulsory liquidations. On receipt of a notice that the liquidator has vacated office or that the winding up is complete the registrar of companies must register the notice and the company is automatically dissolved three months after such registration. The date of dissolution, however, can be deferred if an application is made under IA 1986 s 205(3).

Chapter X
Malpractice before and during liquidation; Penalisation of companies and company officers; Investigations and prosecutions

Offences of fraud, deception, etc

1.229

206 Fraud, etc in anticipation of winding up

(1) When a company is ordered to be wound up by the court, or passes a resolution for voluntary winding up, any person, being a past or present officer of the company, is deemed to have committed an offence if, within the 12 months immediately preceding the commencement of the winding up, he has—

   (a)   concealed any part of the company's property to the value of £500 or more, or concealed any debt due to or from the company, or

   (b)   fraudulently removed any part of the company's property to the value of £500 or more, or

   (c)   concealed, destroyed, mutilated or falsified any book or paper affecting or relating to the company's property or affairs, or

   (d)   made any false entry in any book or paper affecting or relating to the company's property or affairs, or

(e) fraudulently parted with, altered or made any omission in any document affecting or relating to the company's property or affairs, or

(f) pawned, pledged or disposed of any property of the company which has been obtained on credit and has not been paid for (unless the pawning, pledging or disposal was in the ordinary way of the company's business).

(2) Such a person is deemed to have committed an offence if within the period above mentioned he has been privy to the doing by others of any of the things mentioned in paragraphs (c), (d) and (e) of subsection (1); and he commits an offence if, at any time after the commencement of the winding up, he does any of the things mentioned in paragraphs (a) to (f) of that subsection, or is privy to the doing by others of any of the things mentioned in paragraphs (c) to (e) of it.

(3) For purposes of this section, 'officer' includes a shadow director.

(4) It is a defence—

(a) for a person charged under paragraph (a) or (f) of subsection (1) (or under subsection (2) in respect of the things mentioned in either of those two paragraphs) to prove that he had no intent to defraud, and

(b) for a person charged under paragraph (c) or (d) of subsection (1) (or under subsection (2) in respect of the things mentioned in either of those two paragraphs) to prove that he had no intent to conceal the state of affairs of the company or to defeat the law.

(5) Where a person pawns, pledges or disposes of any property in circumstances which amount to an offence under subsection (1)(f), every person who takes in pawn or pledge, or otherwise receives, the property knowing it to be pawned, pledged or disposed of in such circumstances, is guilty of an offence.

(6) A person guilty of an offence under this section is liable to imprisonment or a fine, or both.

(7) The money sums specified in paragraphs (a) and (b) of subsection (1) are subject to increase or reduction by order under section 416 in Part XV.

Notes

S 206

This provision and s 207–211 contain provisions under which past or present officers of the company are made criminally liable for various acts and omissions in the run up to, or during, a liquidation. They do not provide for recovery by the liquidator but they impose criminal sanctions against the directors. This may be gratifying and in the public interest, but – unlike the misfeasance, wrongful trading and fraudulent trading provisions (ss 212–214) – is of little practical help to creditors. What is more, civil proceedings may be stayed if there are ongoing criminal proceedings: *Re DPR Futures Ltd* [1989] 1 WLR 778 (in which undertakings given by the liquidator obviated the need for a stay). For summary proceedings in respect of these offences, see s 431. For 'commencement of the winding up', see s 86, 129.

Section 206 provides for specific criminal liability in the case of frauds by past or present officers of the company within the 12 months immediately preceding the commencement of a voluntary or compulsory liquidation (or at any time thereafter: s 206(2)). 'Officer' is defined in CA s 1985 s 744 to include a director, manager or company secretary. A director '*includes any person occupying the position of director by whatever name called*' (CA 1985 s 744, IA 1986 s 251), and expressly includes a shadow director (s 206(3)). A shadow director is defined in s 251 as meaning a person in accordance with whose directions or instructions the directors are accustomed to act (but someone is not a shadow director merely because he gives professional advice that the directors follow). Accordingly s 206 applies to de jure directors, de facto directors (persons not actually appointed but who nevertheless act as directors) and shadow directors: for the meaning of 'director', and the difference between a shadow director and a de facto director, see *Re Lo-Line Electric Motors Ltd* [1988] Ch 477 at 488–490, and *Re Hydrodam (Corby) Ltd* [1994] 2 BCLC 180. See further on shadow directors the notes below on s 214, 'Comparison with fraudulent trading' and on IA 1986 s 249(a).

The precise ambit of the term 'manager' is unclear. 'Manager' includes someone who exercises a supervisory control which reflects the general policy of the company or which is related to general administration: *Re a Company (No 00996 of 1979)* [1980] Ch 138 at 144, *cf R v Boal* [1992] 1 QB 591. Liquidators, administrators and administrative receivers undoubtedly manage in this sense. However, it is unlikely that they are intended to be within the definition of an officer for the purpose of ss 206–219, since where a section is intended to apply to an office-holder as well as an officer, it is expressly stated (eg. ss 212(1) and 219(3)); it was held in *Re B Johnson & Co (Builders) Ltd* [1955] Ch 634 that a receiver and manager appointed by a debenture-holder was not an "officer" within the predecessor section to s 212. Accordingly, and notwithstanding that an administrator has been held to be an officer for the purpose of relief under s 727 CA 1985 (*Re Home Treat Ltd* [1991] BCLC 705), it is doubtful that such office-holders are 'officers' within s 206. Auditors are officers if formally appointed under the CA 1985, s 384, but not if they are merely retained to carry out a specific audit function without being appointed as auditors: *Mutual Reinsurance Co Ltd v Peat Marwick Mitchell & Co* [1997] 1 BCLC 1, *Re London and General Bank* [1895] 2 Ch 166.

S 206(1)(b)

This includes diverting money which should have been returned to the company into another's bank account, and also obtaining such monies properly but run fraudulently failing to return them to the company *R v Robinson* [1990] BCC 656.

S 206(2)

An offence is also committed by a past or present officer who, within the 12 months preceding the commencement of the liquidation or at any time thereafter, is privy to the commission by someone else, whether an officer or not, of an act referred to in s 206(1)(c) to (e). A person need not have an interest in something to be privy to it: 'privy' in this context means someone who 'knows about and does nothing to stop' the thing in question.

S 206(3)

See s 251 IA 1986.

S 206(4)

It is a defence for a person charged with commission of an act set out in s 206(1)(a) or (f) to prove that he had no intent to defraud. It is a defence for a person charged with commission of an act set out in ss (1)(c) or (d), or with being privy to such an act by another, that he had no intent to conceal the state of affairs of the company or to defeat the law. It was held in *R v Carass* [2002] 1 WLR 1714, CA, a case under s 206(1)(a), that to read s 206(4) so as to shift to the defendant the legal burden of proving that he had no intent to defraud would infringe Article 6(2) of the European Convention on Human Rights. Accordingly s 206(4) should be read down so as to reverse the evidential burden of proof only; its effect was therefore to provide that it was a defence for a person charged under s 206(1) to adduce evidence sufficient to raise an issue that he had no intent to defraud, unless, if he did so, the prosecution proved the contrary beyond reasonable doubt. In a bankruptcy context the same conclusion was reached in *Attorney-General's Reference (No 1 of 2004)* [2004] BPIR 1073.

S 206(6)

The penalty for anyone convicted under s 206 is 7 years' imprisonment or an unlimited fine or both if tried upon indictment, and 6 months' imprisonment or a fine limited to the statutory maximum or both if tried summarily: s 430 and Sch 10.

1.230

207 Transactions in fraud of creditors

(1) When a company is ordered to be wound up by the court or passes a resolution for voluntary winding up, a person is deemed to have committed an offence if he, being at the time an officer of the company—

   (a)   has made or caused to be made any gift or transfer of, or charge on, or has caused or connived at the levying of any execution against, the company's property, or

   (b)   has concealed or removed any part of the company's property since, or within 2 months before, the date of any unsatisfied judgment or order for the payment of money obtained against the company.

(2) A person is not guilty of an offence under this section—

   (a)   by reason of conduct constituting an offence under subsection (1)(a) which occurred more than 5 years before the commencement of the winding up, or

   (b)   if he proves that, at the time of the conduct constituting the offence, he had no intent to defraud the company's creditors.

(3) A person guilty of an offence under this section is liable to imprisonment or a fine, or both.

Notes

S 207

This provision imposes liability on any officer of a company in voluntary or compulsory liquidation who, within the period of 5 years immediately preceding the commencement of the winding up or at any time thereafter, does any of the acts set out in s 207(1)(a); or who, within 2 months immediately preceding the date of any unsatisfied judgment or order for payment against the company or at any time thereafter, does either of the acts set out in s 207(1)(b). However, such liability is avoided where the officer shows that he did not intend to defraud creditors. For 'officer', see notes under s 206: de facto directors are included in s 207, but not shadow directors (unlike under s 206). For 'commencement of the winding up', see s 86, 129.

S 207(1)(a)

It has been held that the procuring by a director of the cancellation by the company of a debt due to it by the director was not a transfer of property within this subsection: *R v Davies* [1955] 1 QB 71.

S 207(2)

As to the burden of proof, see notes under s 206(4).

S 207(3)

The penalty for anyone convicted under s 207 is 2 years' imprisonment or an unlimited fine or both if tried on indictment, or 6 months' imprisonment or the statutory maximum fine or both if tried summarily: s 430 and Sch 10.

_____

1.231

208 Misconduct in course of winding up

(1) When a company is being wound up, whether by the court or voluntarily, any person, being a past or present officer of the company, commits an offence if he—

(a) does not to the best of his knowledge and belief fully and truly discover to the liquidator all the company's property, and how and to whom and for what consideration and when the company disposed of any part of that property (except such part as has been disposed of in the ordinary way of the company's business), or

(b) does not deliver up to the liquidator (or as he directs) all such part of the company's property as is in his custody or under his control, and which he is required by law to deliver up, or

(c) does not deliver up to the liquidator (or as he directs) all books and papers in his custody or under his control belonging to the company and which he is required by law to deliver up, or

(d) knowing or believing that a false debt has been proved by any person in the winding up, fails to inform the liquidator as soon as practicable, or

(e) after the commencement of the winding up, prevents the production of any book or paper affecting or relating to the company's property or affairs.

(2) Such a person commits an offence if after the commencement of the winding up he attempts to account for any part of the company's property by fictitious losses or expenses; and he is deemed to have committed that offence if he has so attempted at any meeting of the company's creditors within the 12 months immediately preceding the commencement of the winding up.

(3) For purposes of this section, 'officer' includes a shadow director.

(4) It is a defence—

(a) for a person charged under paragraph (a), (b) or (c) of subsection (1) to prove that he had no intent to defraud, and

(b) for a person charged under paragraph (e) of that subsection to prove that he had no intent to conceal the state of affairs of the company or to defeat the law.

(5) A person guilty of an offence under this section is liable to imprisonment or a fine, or both.

_____

Notes

S 208(1)–(3)

See generally the notes under s 206 above. Shadow directors are included in this section: s 208(3). Persons within s 208 are under a continuing duty to co-operate actively in disclosing company property unknown to the liquidator, and not merely to be reactive: *R v McCredie* [2000] 2 BCLC 438, CA.

S 208(1)(e)

For 'commencement of the winding up', see s 86 129

S 208(4)

As to the burden of proof, see notes under s 206(4).

_____

1.232

209 Falsification of company's books

(1) When a company is being wound up, an officer or contributory of the company commits an offence if he destroys, mutilates, alters or falsifies any books, papers or securities, or makes or is privy to the making of any false or fraudulent entry in any register, book of account or document belonging to the company with intent to defraud or deceive any person.

(2) A person guilty of an offence under this section is liable to imprisonment or a fine, or both.

_____

Notes

S 209(1)

There is a substantial overlap, so far as officers are concerned, between s 209, and s 206(1)(c)–(e) and (2). However, liability under s 209 extends to contributories but does not extend to shadow directors (cf s 206(3)). It has to be proved that the officer or contributory intended to defraud or deceive, as opposed to the burden being on him to prove his innocence (but only in an evidential sense: see notes under s 206(4) above).

_____

1.233

210 Material omissions from statement relating to company's affairs

(1) When a company is being wound up, whether by the court or voluntarily, any person, being a past or present officer of the company, commits an offence if he makes any material omission in any statement relating to the company's affairs.

(2) When a company has been ordered to be wound up by the court, or has passed a resolution for voluntary winding up, any such person is deemed to have committed that offence if, prior to the winding up, he has made any material omission in any such statement.

(3) For purposes of this section, 'officer' includes a shadow director.

(4) It is a defence for a person charged under this section to prove that he had no intent to defraud.

(5) A person guilty of an offence under this section is liable to imprisonment or a fine, or both.

Notes

S 210

This section relates to omissions in a statement about the company's affairs (including but not limited to a 'statement of affairs' under IA 986 s 131), not to actual misstatements, which may be caught under s 207–209, 211. As in s 206, (as opposed to s 209), the burden of proof of lack of intention to defraud is on the officer. The penalties for an offence under this section are the same as under s 206. Shadow directors are included: s 210(3). For the meaning of 'officer' and 'shadow director', see notes under s 206.

1.234

211 False representations to creditors

(1) When a company is being wound up, whether by the court or voluntarily, any person, being a past or present officer of the company—
  (a) commits an offence if he makes any false representation or commits any other fraud for the purpose of obtaining the consent of the company's creditors or any of them to an agreement with reference to the company's affairs or to the winding up, and
  (b) is deemed to have committed that offence if, prior to the winding up, he has made any false representation, or committed any other fraud, for that purpose.

(2) For purposes of this section, 'officer' includes a shadow director.

(3) A person guilty of an offence under this section is liable to imprisonment or a fine, or both.

Notes

S 211

Unlike s 210 which deals solely with omissions, s 211 applies to misrepresentations and other acts of fraud. Shadow directors are included and for the meaning of 'officer' and 'shadow director', see the notes under s 206.

Penalisation of directors and officers

1.235

212 Summary remedy against delinquent directors, liquidators, etc

(1) This section applies if in the course of the winding up of a company it appears that a person who—

   (a)   is or has been an officer of the company,

   (b)   has acted as liquidator or administrative receiver of the company, or

   (c)   not being a person falling within paragraph (a) or (b), is or has been concerned, or has taken part, in the promotion, formation or management of the company,

has misapplied or retained, or become accountable for, any money or other property of the company, or been guilty of any misfeasance or breach of any fiduciary or other duty in relation to the company.

(2) The reference in subsection (1) to any misfeasance or breach of any fiduciary or other duty in relation to the company includes, in the case of a person who has acted as liquidator of the company, any misfeasance or breach of any fiduciary or other duty in connection with the carrying out of his functions as liquidator of the company.

(3) The court may, on the application of the official receiver or the liquidator, or of any creditor or contributory, examine into the conduct of the person falling within subsection (1) and compel him—

   (a)   to repay, restore or account for the money or property or any part of it, with interest at such rate as the court thinks just, or

   (b)   to contribute such sum to the company's assets by way of compensation in respect of the misfeasance or breach of fiduciary or other duty as the court thinks just.

(4) The power to make an application under subsection (3) in relation to a person who has acted as liquidator of the company is not exercisable, except with the leave of the court, after he has had his release.

(5) The power of a contributory to make an application under subsection (3) is not exercisable except with the leave of the court, but is exercisable notwithstanding that he will not benefit from any order the court may make on the application.

Notes

S 212

Prior to the amendments made by the EA 2002 this provision also applied to an administrator. The misfeasance provision in respect of an administrator is now contained in IA 1986 sch B1 para 76. In respect of administrations where the petition for administration was presented before 15 September 2003 s 212 in its pre EA 2002 form continues to apply to administrators (Enterprise Act 2002 (Commencement No 4) Order 2003 (SI 2003/2093) art 3. IA 1986 sch B1 para 75 thus provides a convenient and practical remedy for unsecured creditors against administrators who are alleged to have been negligent rather than allowing individual creditors to sue such administrators in ordinary claim proceedings *Kyrris v Oldham* [2003] BPIR 940.

Although s 212 is concerned with misfeasance by officers and others, it does not provide any new cause of action in respect of such misfeasance; it merely provides a speedy way (provided that the company is being wound up) of dealing with such matters as breach of fiduciary duty or negligence by a director which would normally be dealt with by way of issuing a claim form (see e g *Re DKG Contractors Ltd* [1990] BCC 903 at 905). Such causes of action are assets of the company and any realisations of the same by recovery under s 212 will be subject to any charges granted by the company *Re Anglo-Austrian Printing & Publishing Union* [1895] 2 Ch 891. Section 212 is not limited to claims against directors and claims can be made against sufficiently senior employees of a company who have been involved in the 'management' of the company (see note to s 206). A liquidator can choose whether to proceed in the name of the company by way of a claim form (as in *Bishopsgate Investment Ltd v Maxwell* [1993] BCLC 814, [1994] 1 All ER 261, CA), or in his own name by way of an application under s 212; no security for costs can be ordered in the latter case *Re Strand Wool Co Ltd* [1904] 2 Ch 1. A misfeasance claim can be made against the estate of a deceased director: *Re Sharpe* [1892] 1 Ch 154. The court has a discretion whether to grant relief or not under the section, which it would not have in an action begun by claim form. A claim under s 212 is initiated by an application supported by a witness statement. In complicated cases it is advisable to ask the Court for a direction for service of points of claim and defence. A respondent to a misfeasance application could not under the predecessor of s 212 initiate third party proceedings in relation to a party who was not already a party to the application (*Re B Johnson & Co Ltd* [1955] Ch 634) and it is likely that the same principle applies despite the advent of the Civil Procedure Rules (Part 20).

The reasonable prospect of a claim under s 213 (or under s 212 or 214) is one of the core factors which the court takes into account in exercising its discretion to wind up an unregistered company, in that there is a potential benefit to creditors of such a winding-up: s 221, *Re Latreefers Inc* [2001] BCC 174, CA, *Re DAP Holding NV* [2006] BCC 48.

Assignment

The liquidator may assign a cause of action which he might otherwise have pursued under s 212 in return for a share of recoveries; and this will not be objectionable on the ground of maintenance or champerty, because of the express right of sale of the company's property contained in para 6 Sch 4 (*Re Oasis Merchandising Services Ltd* [1998] Ch 170 at 179, CA). As stated above s 212 does not create any new cause of action; rather the liquidator is dealing with an asset of the company which existed prior to liquidation.

As to whether the liquidator can, sell a share of the recoveries in return for funding of the action instead of assigning the cause of action, Lightman J decided in *Grovewood Holdings plc v James Capel & Co Ltd* [1995] Ch 80 (a case on s 214 wrongful trading) that he could not, because this was champertous; and that although the fruits of an action were the property of the company within IA 1986 para 6 Sch 4, this paragraph did not confer the same exemption from the law of champerty upon the sale of the fruits of an action as it did upon the assignment of the cause of action. However in *Re Oasis Merchandising Services Ltd* (above) the Court of Appeal held (contrary to Lightman J's view) that neither the assignment of the cause of action under s 214, nor the assignment of the fruits of such an action, were authorised by IA 1986 sch 4 para 6 because the special nature of a wrongful trading action meant that they did not constitute property of the company within that paragraph; so that whether the paragraph conferred exemption on an agreement which was champertous was not a question which arose under s 214. The wrongful trading application can only be made by the liquidator; it is not a cause of action that belongs in any sense to the company prior to its liquidation. However the Court of Appeal stated that as a matter of policy there was much to be said for enabling a liquidator to sell the fruits of an action; see notes to IA 1986 s 214 under 'Assignment.'.

Limitation

The limitation period for an application under s 212 is normally 6 years from the date of the cause of action arising, that is, from the date of the misfeasance, not from the date of the commencement of the winding-up: *Re Lands Allotment Co Ltd* [1894] 1 Ch 616, a case in which proceedings were brought under a predecessor of s 212 eight years after the misfeasance (but only seven months into the liquidation), and were held statute-barred by the Court of Appeal. However, s 21 Limitation Act 1980 provides that no period of limitation applies to an action by a beneficiary in respect of a fraud or fraudulent breach of trust to which the trustee was party or privy, or to recover from the trustee trust property or the proceeds of trust property in the possession of the trustee, or previously received by the trustee and converted to his use. The ambit of this section was discussed by Millett LJ in *Paragon Finance plc v Thakerar & Co* [1999] 1 All ER 400 pp 408–409, in which he makes the distinction between, on the one hand, a real constructive trustee who obtains trust property by a legitimate transaction and then breaches the trust; and on the other hand someone whom equity holds liable to account as a constructive trustee because he obtains property by means of an unlawful transaction. Those who fall within the former category, 'real' constructive trustees, come within the ambit of s 21 Limitation Act 1980; those who fall within the latter category do not, and a six year limitation period therefore applies to them. A director (or insolvency practitioner) who breaches his pre-existing fiduciary duty to obtain the company's property for his own use is a 'real' constructive trustee of the first kind. Accordingly, where an application under section 212 is based upon a fraudulent breach of trust, or a breach of fiduciary duty involving the misappropriation of company assets, there is no statutory limitation period (though if there is serious delay, the equitable doctrine of laches may bar the claim): *Re Pantone 485 Ltd [2002] 1 BCLC 266.* In *Gwembe Valley Development v Koshy (No.3)* [2003] EWCA Civ 1048, [2004] 1 BCLC 131, CA, the court clarified the position further. It said that the starting assumption should be that a six-year limitation applies. If the fiduciary concerned is a 'real' trustee, the claim will be within s 21 Limitation Act 1980 and subject to a six year limitation period by virtue of s 21(3), unless the claim is excluded by virtue of s 21(1)(a) or (b).

S 212(1)

The section is most commonly used in respect of breaches of fiduciary duty: directors are required to act 'bona fide in what they consider – not what a court may consider – is in the interests of the company, and not for any collateral purpose' (*Re Smith & Fawcett Ltd* [1942] 1 All ER 542, 543, per Lord Greene MR). However, it is clear that a director must use his powers for a proper purpose, not place himself in a position of conflict of interest and duty, and generally act bona fide in the interests of the company. Note that the Companies Bill 2006 contains a codification of the duties of directors (clauses 171ff).

Where the directors have failed to have regard to the separate interests of the company but have acted in accordance with what they perceive to be in the interests of, for example, a group of companies, the test becomes objective, or whether 'an intelligent and honest man in the position of a director of the company concerned, could, in the whole of the existing circumstances, have reasonably believed that the transactions were for the benefit of the company' (*Charterbridge Corpn Ltd v Lloyds Bank Ltd* [1970] Ch 62 at 74). For a discussion of misfeasance in a group situation, see *Facia Footwear Ltd v Hinchcliffe* [1998] 1 BCLC 218. With an insolvent company, or one on the verge of insolvency (*Re MDA Investment Management Ltd* [2005] BCC 783) the same test applies but with the substitution of the word 'creditors' for the word 'company', since the interests of the company become the interests of the existing creditors: *Gwyer & Associates v London Wharf (Limehouse) Ltd* [2002] EWHC 2748 (Ch), [2003] 2 BCLC 153. A director of a solvent company does not owe a duty to creditors (*West Mercia Safetywear Ltd v Dodd* [1988] BCLC 250); but if the company is insolvent or is on the verge of insolvency, a duty is owed not to individual creditors but to creditors generally, and can be enforced by the liquidator (*Yukong Line Ltd of Korea v Rendsburg Investment Corpn of Liberia (No 2)* [1998] 1 WLR 294).

The section expressly covers other duties, such as the duty of care, provided that the negligence has caused loss: *Re Simmon Box (Diamonds) Ltd* [2002] BCC 82. For the scope of the duty of care owed by a director, see *Re D'Jan of London Ltd* [1994] 1 BCLC 561, in which the court had regard to the provisions of s 214(4) in defining the scope of the common law duty of care. In this case partial relief was granted under s 727 CA 1985 (see under 'Orders the court may make' below).

Though a claim for a debt owed to the company is outside s 212 (*Re Etic Ltd* [1928] Ch 861) as is a claim vested in a third party (*Re Hill's Waterfall Estate and Gold Mining Co* [1896] 1 Ch 947), there are many situations where an application may be considered. The following are examples of claims which are within s 212: for a secret profit made by a director (*Re North*

Australian Territory Co Archer's case [1892] 1 Ch 322); where a director makes gifts of the company's property for no proper trading purpose (Re Barton Manufacturing Co Ltd [1999] 1 BCLC 740, and Bishopsgate Investment Ltd v Maxwell [1993] BCLC 814, [1994] 1 All ER 261, CA); to recover money lost as a result of making unlawful payments to shareholders (Re National Funds Assurance Co (1878) 10 ChD 118 and Cmmrs of Inland Revenue v Richmond [2003] EWCA 999); in respect of some preferences (see below, and West Mercia Safetywear v Dodd (1988) 4 BCC 30); against a liquidator who trades a company in liquidation without sanction of the court or the liquidation committee, where it is clear that the assets of the company should have been realised quickly (Re Centralcrest Engineering Ltd [2000] BCC 727); and where a director diverts a contract and the opportunity to negotiate a licence (Re Westlowe Storage and Distribution Ltd [2000] 2 BCLC 590).

It is not always the case that a preference or a transaction at an undervalue falls within s 212, because the statutory presumption applicable to, for example, preference claims under s 239(6) cannot be relied upon under s 212 to reverse the burden of proof: Re Brian D Pierson (Contractors) Ltd [1999] BCC 26. The court will not allow s 212 to be used to avoid the problem of establishing the requisite motive for a preference claim: Re Continental Assurance Co of London plc [2001] BPIR 733 at 855. However where a preference within the meaning of s 239 has been committed that will be a misfeasance on the part of the responsible director and an application can be made against that person under s 212 in addition to a claim against the recipient of the preference (see notes under 'Orders the court may make' below'). If the conditions of the preference provision are not met then there is no misfeasance on the part of the director/s on that ground (Re Westlowe Storage and Distribution Ltd [2000] 2 BCLC 590 and Re Continental Assurance Co of London plc (above)).

For 'officer', see notes under s 206. 'Administrative receiver' is defined by s 29(2) and does not include court appointed or fixed charge receivers, or receivers appointed under floating charges but outside s 29(2) (nor are they 'officers': Re B Johnson & Co (Builders) Ltd [1955] Ch 634). A receiver and manager would however appear to come within s 212(1)(c), as would a supervisor of a voluntary arrangement. See notes below under s 212(2) for limitations on s 212 actions as against administrative receivers or receivers and managers.

S 212(2)

This provision refers only to liquidators despite the wider terms of s 212(1). The explanation for this is unclear, but reliance may be placed on the word 'includes' to catch other types of respondent; s 212(1) certainly seems to make s 212 available against administrative receivers, and receivers and managers, who breach their duties in relation to the company in carrying out their functions as such. However, it appears that the liability of administrative receivers or receivers and managers may be limited; in Downsview Nominees Ltd v First City Corporation Ltd [1993] 2 WLR 86, [1993] AC 295 the Privy Council held that a receiver and manager owed no general duty to use reasonable care in the exercise of his powers and in dealing with the assets of a mortgagor though it further held that equity implied on the receiver and manager specific duties including the duty to exercise his powers 'in good faith for the purpose of obtaining payment.'

S 212(3)

The application is made in accordance with IR 1986 r 7.2. In the first instance the application is listed before the registrar who would then normally give directions and the trial would in due course be heard by a judge IR 1986 r 7.6(2), Practice Note: The Hearing of Insolvency Proceedings [2005] BPIR 688, Re Ayala Holdings Ltd [1993] BCLC 256, Re Embassy Art Products Ltd [1988] BCLC 1. If a creditor wishes to apply, he should notify the liquidator to avoid the possibility of two sets of proceedings running at the same time. A contributory may also apply, but under s 212(5), only with the leave of the court. It was held in Re Loquitur Ltd [2003] 2 BCLC 442 that former directors of a company, against whom an application has been made under s 212 by a creditor, are not entitled to be heard on an application to the court by the liquidator under s 112 for permission to disclose the company's documents to the creditor.

Where proceedings are brought by the liquidator, an application for security for costs cannot be made against him: *Re Strand Wool Co* [1904] 2 Ch 1. Where he brings proceedings and fails, the costs awarded against him would usually be ordered to be paid out of the company's assets as an expense of the liquidation (IR 1986 Rule 4.218(1)(a)(i)), although this is by no means guaranteed. For instance, if the liquidator makes an application when he has no reasonable basis for doing so the court may order the liquidator to pay the costs himself without any indemnity from the company's assets: *Re Silver Valley Mines Ltd* (1882) 21 Ch D 381, *Re Wilson Lovatt & Sons Ltd* [1977] 1 All ER 274. Where a liquidator applied to discontinue misfeasance proceedings on terms that there should be no order as to costs, the court held that there was no reason to depart from the general rule and ordered that he pay the respondents' costs. The proceedings had been commercially worthless throughout and it would be unfair to leave the respondent with a substantial liability for costs: *Walker v Walker* [2005] BPIR 454, *RBG Resources plc v Rastogi* [2005] 2 BCLC 592.

Orders the court may make

Compensation is discretionary. *Gil v Baygreen Properties Ltd* [2005] BPIR 95 is an example of the court refusing to make an order under s 212 against a director even though he had been acting improperly. In that case involving a transaction at an undervalue, the court held that the applicant was sufficiently protected by an order under IA 1986 s 423. The director concerned had not been motivated by a desire to make a personal profit and in all the circumstances it was not right to make an order against him personally. It is generally stated that the court will only order a contribution where it is proved that the company has suffered a loss as a result of the misfeasance (*Re Derek Randall Enterprises Ltd* [1990] BCC 749); however it is clear that a director is misfeasant in allowing a company to commit a preference, (see notes s 212(1) *above*), yet it is difficult to appreciate what loss is caused to the company where a creditor is preferred by the repayment of a debt. Further it must be shown that the alleged breach caused the loss as opposed to (for example) generally bad trading conditions (*Re Continental Assurance Co of London plc* [2001] BPIR 733). Where the application is based on breach of duty of care, the court should only award compensation for such loss as was caused by the negligence: *Cohen v Selby* [2001] 1 BCLC 176, *Re Simmon Box (Diamonds) Ltd* [2002] BCC 82.

The court has power to apportion compensation among different respondents: *Re Morecambe Bowling Ltd* [1969] 1 All ER 753. A respondent cannot set off against an order under s 212(3) money owed to him by the company: *Re Leeds and Hanley Theatres of Varieties (No 2)* [1904] 2 Ch 45, *Re Anglo-French Co-operative Society, ex p Pelly* (1882) 21 Ch D 492, *Manson v Smith* [1997] 2 BCLC 161. However, unlike under s 213 or s 214, he can seek relief from liability under s 727 CA 1985 if he acted honestly and reasonably (*Re Welfab Engineers Ltd* [1990] BCLC 833; *Re Brian D Pierson (Contractors) Ltd* [1999] BCC 26); a director may be honest in transferring the company's monies to a third party but if it is not a reasonable act he may not claim relief under s 727, *Re MDA Investment Management Ltd* [2005] BCC 783. It would be an uphill struggle to persuade the court to grant relief to a misfeasant director where this would enable the director to retain a benefit at the expense of the creditors *Re Marini Ltd* [2005] BCC 172. Though a request for relief under s 727 CA 1985 should be expressly pleaded, the absence of such a plea should not debar the court from considering it at trial (*Re Kirby's Coaches* [1991] BCLC 414). Any contribution to the company's assets is compensatory only and not punitive: see notes to s 213 below under 'contributions to the company's assets'. If a respondent is liable under both s 212 and another section, eg s 214 or s 239, the compensation ordered under each section may be cumulative or not, depending on whether such liability would lead to double recovery: *Re DKO Contractors Ltd* [1990] BCC 903, and *Re Purpoint Ltd* [1991] BCC 121.

S 212(4)

The release of a liquidator (IA 1986 s 173, 174) is an important step which then obliges an aggrieved party to make an application for leave of court if a misfeasance application is to be made.

S 212(5)

A contributory needs the leave of the court to make an application but he may apply notwithstanding that he will not benefit from any order that the court may make on the application. Accordingly, *Cavendish Bentinck v Fenn* (1887) 12 App Cas 652 (HL), in which permission was denied to a fully paid up shareholder of an insolvent company on the ground that he had no pecuniary interest in the outcome, is no longer good law. A contributory cannot apply under s 212 until a winding-up order has been made: *Wightman v Bennett* [2005] BPIR 470.

1.236

213 Fraudulent trading

(1) If in the course of the winding up of a company it appears that any business of the company has been carried on with intent to defraud creditors of the company or creditors of any other person, or for any fraudulent purpose, the following has effect.

(2) The court, on the application of the liquidator may declare that any persons who were knowingly parties to the carrying on of the business in the manner above-mentioned are to be liable to make such contributions (if any) to the company's assets as the court thinks proper.

Notes

S 213

Given that an application under s 213 requires the liquidator to show intention to defraud, it has become less popular as a remedy since the introduction of a remedy under s 214, wrongful trading, which has a lower threshold of proof. Under s 213, actual dishonesty (which includes wilful blindness and reckless indifference) must be shown (*Morris v Bank of America National Trust* [2001] 1 BCLC 771, CA, *Re Bank of Credit and Commerce International SA v State Bank of India* [2003] BCC 735, *Re Patrick and Lyon Ltd* [1933] Ch 786; see the wide view of dishonesty expressed in *Re Leyland DAF Ltd (No 2)* [1994] 2 BCLC 760 at 771, and contrast *Re Sobam BV* [1996] 1 BCLC 446). The need to show dishonesty means that if liability under s 213 is established, plainly no relief is available under CA 1985 s 727 (nor is it available under s 214, unlike under s 212). Further no claim can be made for fraudulent trading in the period between the presentation of the winding up petition and the winding up order because the winding up commences on the presentation of the petition (IA 1986 s 129(2)) and dispositions of property in that period are void (IA 1986 s 127); thus the company is not carrying on business in that period *Carman v Cronos Group SA* [2005] EWHC 2403 (Ch), [2006] BCC 451.

Unlike s 214, s 213 is not confined to attacking directors or shadow directors or a person who has been such a director but extends to all those who have been parties to the carrying on of the business of the company with the specified intent (even if unconnected with the company or an 'outsider'), and not just to those who perform a managerial or controlling role: *Re BCCI SA, Banque Arabe v Morris* [2001] 1 BCLC 263. In *Bank of India v Morris* [2005] BCC 789 the Bank of India was held liable for fraudulent trading on the basis of being 'knowingly' a party to the carrying on by BCCI of its business with intent to defraud; the crucial question in establishing the liability of the Bank of India under s 213 was, whose knowledge counted as corporate knowledge of the Bank of India? It was observed that the policy of s 213 could be easily defeated if liability was restricted to situations where the board of the outsider company was actually privy to the fraud; in certain circumstances it was appropriate to attribute knowledge of fraud to an outsider even though a person with knowledge of the fraud was acting dishonestly and in breach of his duty to his employer. It was held in *Re Maidstone*

Building Provisions Ltd [1971] 1 WLR 1085 that mere inertia did not amount to being party to carrying on business; but acceptance of money from the business, knowing that it has been procured by carrying on the business with intent to defraud, may be (*Re Gerald Cooper Chemicals Ltd* [1978] Ch 262).

A claim under s 213, like a claim under s 214, survives the death of the respondent or intended respondent (*Re Sherborne Associates Ltd* [1995] BCC 40 (a case under s 214)). As to assignment of a cause of action under s 213, or of the fruits of such an action, see the introductory note under s 214 below; the same objections would apply to an application in respect of fraudulent trading as apply to an application in respect of wrongful trading. Fraudulent trading is also a criminal offence under CA 1985 s 458, and is a ground for disqualification under the CDDA 1986.

Limitation

Different limitation considerations apply to an application under s 213 to those which apply under s 212, because unlike the latter section, s 213 creates a cause of action. It was held in *Re Farmizer (Products) Ltd* [1997] 1 BCLC 589, CA (a case under s 214) that the appropriate limitation period was 6 years from the date of the winding-up order or resolution, because proceedings under s 213 are proceedings to recover a sum of money by virtue of an enactment, and are therefore governed by s 9(1) Limitation Act 1980.

S 213(1)

The provision only applies in a winding up, and only the liquidator can bring proceedings. Proceedings may be taken in respect of a foreign company being wound up as an unregistered company (as in *Re Howard Holdings Inc* [1998] BCC 549), or following a request for assistance from a foreign court (*Re BCCI* [1993] BCC 787). The reasonable prospect of a claim under s 213 (or under s 212 or 214) is one of the core factors which the court takes into account in exercising its discretion to wind up an unregistered company, in that there is a potential benefit to creditors of such a winding-up: s 221, *Re Latreefers Inc* [2001] BCC 174, CA. The carrying on of business does not necessarily mean actively carrying on a trade, but includes the collection of assets acquired in the course of business, and distribution of the proceeds in reduction of business liabilities: *Re Sarflax Ltd* [1979] Ch 592 (although no fraudulent intent was found in that case). However, it is not sufficient that a creditor has in fact been defrauded in the course of a business; the business must have been carried on with intent to achieve this, though if it has, the fact that only one creditor has been defrauded, and by a single transaction, is irrelevant (*Morphitis v Bernasconi* [2003] EWCA Civ 289, [2003] 2 WLR 1521).

S 213(2)

Contributions ordered are treated as general assets for the benefit of all creditors, not just for those creditors who have been defrauded: *Morphitis v Bernasconi* [2003] EWCA Civ 289, [2003] 2 WLR 1521. The contribution made is held by the liquidator for payment to creditors and it is not charged to a security holder *Re Oasis Merchandising Services Ltd* [1995] BCC 911, [1997] BCC 282. Although s 213 does not expressly refer to such payment being by way of compensation (unlike s 212), punitive damages will not be awarded, and the contribution ordered should reflect and compensate for the loss caused to the creditors (*Bank of India v Morris* [2005] BCC 739, *Morphitis v Bernasconi* (above)): see notes to s 214 below under 'Contribution to company's assets'. Double recovery will not be permitted, so that a compromise reached with one defendant may prevent further recovery against other defendants, if the compromise has fully compensated the company for its loss: *Morphitis v Bernasconi* (above). At the stage of an application for a freezing order connected to a fraudulent trading claim the court may be obliged to take a rather 'rough and ready' approach to the assessment of what compensation might be ordered: *Re Industrial Services Group Ltd (No 1)* [2003] BPIR 392. Under s 215, the court has wide powers to order relief following a finding of fraudulent trading under s 213, and can impose a charge in favour of the company on any debt owed by the company to the respondent, or order that any such debt shall rank in priority after all other debts owed by the company. If a respondent is liable under both s 213 and another section, eg s 212 or 239, the compensation ordered under each section may be cumulative or not, depending on whether such liability would lead to double recovery: *Re DKG Contractors Ltd* [1990] BCC 903, and *Re Purpoint Ltd* [1991] BCC 121.

1.237

214 Wrongful trading

(1) Subject to subsection (3) below, if in the course of the winding up of a company it appears that subsection (2) of this section applies in relation to a person who is or has been a director of the company, the court, on the application of the liquidator, may declare that that person is to be liable to make such contribution (if any) to the company's assets as the court thinks proper.

(2) This subsection applies in relation to a person if—
   (a)   the company has gone into insolvent liquidation,
   (b)   at some time before the commencement of the winding up of the company, that person knew or ought to have concluded that there was no reasonable prospect that the company would avoid going into insolvent liquidation, and
   (c)   that person was a director of the company at that time;
but the court shall not make a declaration under this section in any case where the time mentioned in paragraph (b) above was before 28 April 1986.

(3) The court shall not make a declaration under this section with respect to any person if it is satisfied that after the condition specified in subsection (2)(b) was first satisfied in relation to him that person took every step with a view to minimising the potential loss to the company's creditors as (assuming him to have known that there was no reasonable prospect that the company would avoid going into insolvent liquidation) he ought to have taken.

(4) For the purposes of subsections (2) and (3), the facts which a director of a company ought to know or ascertain, the conclusions which he ought to reach and the steps which he ought to take are those which would be known or ascertained, or reached or taken, by a reasonably diligent person having both—
   (a)   the general knowledge, skill and experience that may reasonably be expected of a person carrying out the same functions as are carried out by that director in relation to the company, and
   (b)   the general knowledge, skill and experience that that director has.

(5) The reference in subsection (4) to the functions carried out in relation to a company by a director of the company includes any functions which he does not carry out but which have been entrusted to him.

(6) For the purposes of this section a company goes into insolvent liquidation if it goes into liquidation at a time when its assets are insufficient for the payment of its debts and other liabilities and the expenses of the winding up.

(7) In this section 'director' includes a shadow director.

(8) This section is without prejudice to section 213.

Notes

S 214

Under s 213 (fraudulent trading), it is necessary to show a fraudulent intention or purpose. The Cork Committee recommended the introduction of a form of civil liability for mismanagement falling short of fraud; and accordingly under s 214, dishonesty is not required. The word 'trading' does not appear in the section but only in the heading. The provision is not limited to directors of companies that are actively trading, but would include the realising of assets with a view to winding up the company's affairs and, for example, the payment of unjustified directors' remuneration. An application for a disqualification order against a director may be brought at the same time as an application under s 214, as in *Official Receiver v Doshi* [2001] 2 BCLC 235. There is no liability under s 214 where the net deficiency at liquidation is less than the net deficiency as at the date the alleged wrongful trading began. Thus the incurring of new credit and/or the payment of cash from the company in the period in question (s 214(2)(b)) does not constitute wrongful trading in itself; first it must be shown that the net deficiency increased in the period from the beginning of the wrongful trading to the date of the liquidation: *Re Marini Ltd* [2004] BCC 172.

Like s 213, s 214 only applies where the company has entered insolvent liquidation . Further, it is only the liquidator who has locus to make application under s 214 with the sanction of creditors or of the court, whether in a voluntary or a compulsory liquidation: IA 1986 Sch 4 para 3A. This useful section is therefore not available, for example, to an administrator. Indeed, some administrations are ended in favour of insolvent liquidations in order that a liquidator may investigate conduct of possible respondents for contravention of s 214.

The liquidator's costs of such an application are an expense of the liquidation following the amendments made by EA 2002 (IR 1986 r 4.218(1)(a)(i) which deals with the problems caused by the decision in *Re Floor Fourteen Ltd*, *Lewis v IRC* [2002] BCC 198. Until the EA 2002 amendments it was not clear that a liquidator could recover his costs from the assets of the company even if a wrongful trading claim was successful; now the rule change effected in IR 1986 r 4.218(1)(a)(i) makes it clear that such costs may be paid out of the assets of the company as expenses.

An action under s 214 can only be brought against directors or former directors of the company and s 214(7) expressly includes shadow directors. A liquidator of a foreign company which is being wound up as an unregistered company may make an application against its directors: *Re Howard Holdings Ltd* [1998] BCC 549. A claim under s 214, like a claim under s 213, survives the death of the respondent or intended respondent (*Re Sherborne Associates Ltd* [1995] BCC 40); but the court will bear in mind the dangers of hindsight as well as the possibility that the director might have had reasonable explanations of his conduct had he been alive.

Assignment

A liquidator cannot obtain funding by assigning the cause of action under s 214 as such an assignment would be champertous, and is not expressly authorised by para 6 Sch 4; a cause of action under s 214 (unlike under s 212) is not 'the company's property' (*Re Oasis Merchandising Services Ltd* [1995] 2 BCLC 493, *affd* [1998] Ch 170, CA). However, the Court of Appeal commented that although the fruits of a s 214 application did not constitute the company's property (and so were not expressly authorised to be sold by para 6 Sch 4), as a matter of policy there was much to be said for allowing a liquidator to sell the fruits of a s 214 action provided that the purchaser did not have the right to influence the course of the litigation. Thus, where the sale of the fruits of a s 214 application is made to a creditor, it is arguable that such a sale is not champertous on the basis that: (i) the creditor has sufficient interest in the outcome; and (ii) he has no right to influence the litigation. Accordingly, a liquidator may in this way obtain funding to bring a s 214 (or s 213) from creditors. He may also choose to enter into a conditional fee arrangement backed by an appropriate insurance policy.

Comparison with fraudulent trading

There is no reason why one application alleging both fraudulent and wrongful trading cannot be made: s 214(8). Although wrongful trading is wider in some respects in that it encompasses conduct which is not dishonest, it is in other respects narrower: it is a civil offence only, and applies only to directors (including de facto directors (*Re Hydrodam (Corby) Ltd* [1994] 2 BCLC 180) and to shadow directors (s 214(7)) as defined in s 251. Section 213, on the other hand, applies to anyone who has carried on the business with the necessary intent.

Clearly, the identification of a 'shadow director' is a fact-sensitive decision. A bank which simply assists in guiding the company through commercial difficulties is unlikely to be a shadow director; but a bank which actively polices a fixed charge over book debts and exerts substantive control over the company in its own interests, may be: *Re a Company (No 005009 of 1987), ex p Copp* [1989] BCLC 13. In that case Knox J refused to strike out a claim against a bank that was alleged to be a shadow director because of its control over book debts. On the other hand, in *Re PFTZM Ltd* [1995] 2 BCLC 354 where the lender had required the payment of the company's receipts into an account in the name of the lender as a condition of continuing credit, it was held that there was no prima facie case made out for holding the lender to be a shadow director; the lender was merely acting in defence of its own interests and did not instruct the company to pay its receipts into such an account, but merely made this a term of its offer for the continuation of credit which the company was free to accept or reject. A controlling shareholder or parent company may also be held to be a shadow director if it interferes in the management of the company by giving instructions to the board, but not simply by nominating a minority of the board (*Kuwait Asia Bank EC v National Mutual Life Nominees Ltd* [1991] 1 AC 187).

Limitation

The limitation period is six years from the date of the winding-up order or resolution (*Re Farmizer (Products) Ltd* [1997] 1 BCLC 589, CA), proceedings under s 214 being proceedings to recover a sum of money by virtue of an enactment, and therefore governed by s 9(1) Limitation Act 1980.

Insolvent liquidation

S 214(2), (6)

This means that the company is balance sheet insolvent, rather than that it is simply cash-flow insolvent; a liquidation due to cash-flow problems, but where the balance sheet is healthy, is not an insolvent liquidation in the sense that all debts and liabilities and expenses of the winding up could have been paid when the company entered liquidation.

Knew or ought to know no reasonable prospect of avoiding insolvent liquidation

S 214(2)(b)

Usually, one of the more difficult aspects of a wrongful trading claim is to identify the date when the wrongful trading began. It is advisable to apply on the basis of more than one date as at trial, the court may not accept one of the pleaded dates but may be willing to accept another: see *Rubin v Gunner* [2004] 2 BCLC 110. However, some caution should be exercised. If the liquidator leaves the pleading of alternative dates to trial he may be too late to secure permission to amend the application to plead such dates; furthermore, pleading multiple alternative dates may be oppressive: *Re Sherborne Associates Ltd* [1995] BCC 40.

S 214(4)

Under s 214(4), the test for the director's knowledge, as well as for the steps which he ought to have taken, is both objective (what would a reasonably diligent person have done given the knowledge, skill, and experience which a person carrying out the functions of that director of that company ought to have had), and subjective (what would a reasonably diligent person have done had he had the knowledge, skill and experience which that director in fact possessed). Accordingly if a director is professionally qualified, a higher standard of behaviour may be expected under the subjective element. On the other hand, under the objective element, a non-executive director may be less strictly judged than an executive director who has day-to-day control (see *Re Continental Assurance Co of London plc* [2001] BPIR 733). A director of a small company with uncomplicated accounts will not be expected to know as much as a director of a substantial company (unless, in fact, he does know as much). Thus in *Re Produce Marketing Consortium Ltd (No 2)* [1989] BCLC 520 [1989] BCLC 520 the court was satisfied that the directors had actual knowledge of the company's general financial state notwithstanding the absence of written records, and moreover ought to have ascertained the results subsequently demonstrated by the (late) accounts, and so ought to have concluded that the company would go into insolvent liquidation. In *Re DKG Contractors Ltd* [1990] BCC 903 the pressure being applied to the company by creditors was such that the directors, who were not experienced enough for the purpose of running the business, should have introduced financial controls, and would then have concluded that there was no reasonable prospect of avoiding liquidation.

Defence

S 214(3)

The running of a successful defence by a director under s 214(3) (by showing that he had taken every step that he ought to have done to minimise the potential loss to creditors) might include evidence of the following: consultations with professional advisers, particularly a licensed insolvency practitioner, and following the advice given; calling a meeting of creditors; ceasing to trade (although a sudden cessation of trade may cause loss to creditors rather than improve their position); procuring a liquidation; appointing an administrator; holding regular directors' meetings to review the situation with up-to-date financial information; considering rationalisation programmes such as reducing the number of employees and cutting back on company perks; and considering resignation if the director's warnings are being ignored by the rest of the board. The keeping of up-to-date financial records and the introduction of financial controls are particularly important steps (see *Re Purpoint Ltd* [1991] BCC 121, and *Re DKG Contractors Ltd* [1990] BCC 903). A director who acquires the necessary knowledge of the company's imminent insolvency will not necessarily absolve himself by deciding immediately to liquidate the company (it may be that the company's trading life will thereby be ended too early), or by resigning. If, therefore, he genuinely believes on reasonable grounds that the best course for creditors is likely to be to carry on trading, he should do so, whilst introducing whatever controls may be desirable. However, a director should ensure that his reasons for carrying on trading are properly documented and that he is fully informed of the company's up-to-date financial position; he may well also take professional advice (as in *Re Continental Assurance Co of London plc* [2001] BPIR 733).

Contribution to company's assets

Where the deficiency to creditors is not larger at the date of liquidation than at the date the wrongful trading began, there can be no liability for wrongful trading: *Re Marini Ltd* [2004] BCC 172. The court will consider the making of a contribution order only where the financial position of the company has deteriorated on a balance-sheet basis. An order under s 214 is compensatory and not punitive and the court can reflect the relative seriousness of the conduct of co-directors in the size of the contribution ordered: see *Re Produce Marketing Consortium Ltd (No 2)* (1989) BCLC 520, and *Re Brian D Pierson Ltd* [1999] BCC 26, [2001] 1 BCLC 275. The liability of each of the directors to compensate the company has to be approached on a several rather than a joint basis: *Re Continental Assurance Co of London plc* [2001] BPIR 733. The first enquiry will be to determine by how much the net liabilities of the company have increased by trading after the date when it ought to have ceased trading. In *Re Purpoint Ltd* [1991] BCC 121 the lack of accounting records made it impossible to ascertain this, and accordingly it was held that the compensation payable was the amount of debt owed to creditors and incurred after a certain date which was unpaid when the company eventually ceased trading. It is likely that this approach will survive despite the recent confirmation of the compensatory nature of relief in *Morphitis v Bernasconi* [2003] 2 WLR 1521 (see notes under s 213 above), since the court will not allow a director to avoid liability through his own default in failing to keep proper records. See also the notes under s 213(2) above.

As with fraudulent trading under s 213, contributions ordered are treated as general assets for the benefit of all creditors: *Morphitis v Bernasconi* [2003] 2 WLR 1521. The contribution is held by the liquidator for payment to creditors as a whole and it is not charged to a security holder: *Re Oasis Merchandising Services Ltd* [1995] BCC 911, [1997] BCC 282. In response to an application under s 214, a director cannot rely on CA 1985 s 727, which requires a substantially subjective exercise to be carried out (has the director acted honestly and reasonably and ought he therefore fairly to be excused); the two sections cannot be applied in sequence: *Re Produce Marketing Consortium Ltd (No 2)* [1989] BCLC 520, *Re Brian D Pierson (Contractors) Ltd)* [1999] BCC 26, [2001] 1 BCLC 275. If a respondent is liable under both s 214 and another provision, e g 212 or 239, the compensation ordered under each section may be cumulative or not, depending on whether such liability would lead to double recovery: *DKG Contractors Ltd* [1990] BCC 903, and *Re Purpoint Ltd* [1991] BCC 121.

1.238

215 Proceedings under ss 213, 214

(1) On the hearing of an application under section 213 or 214, the liquidator may himself give evidence or call witnesses.

(2) Where under either section the court makes a declaration, it may give such further directions as it thinks proper for giving effect to the declaration; and in particular, the court may—
  (a) provide for the liability of any person under the declaration to be a charge on any debt or obligation due from the company to him, or on any mortgage or charge or any interest in a mortgage or charge on assets of the company held by or vested in him, or any person on his behalf, or any person claiming as assignee from or through the person liable or any person acting on his behalf, and
  (b) from time to time make such further order as may be necessary for enforcing any charge imposed under this subsection.

(3) For the purposes of subsection (2), 'assignee'—
  (a) includes a person to whom or in whose favour, by the directions of the person made liable, the debt, obligation, mortgage or charge was created, issued or transferred or the interest created, but
  (b) does not include an assignee for valuable consideration (not including consideration by way of marriage or the formation of a civil partnership) given in good faith and without notice of any of the matters on the ground of which the declaration is made.

(4) Where the court makes a declaration under either section in relation to a person who is a creditor of the company, it may direct that the whole or any part of any debt owed by the company to that person and any interest thereon shall rank in priority after all other debts owed by the company and after any interest on those debts.

(5) Sections 213 and 214 have effect notwithstanding that the person concerned may be criminally liable in respect of matters on the ground of which the declaration under the section is to be made.

———

Notes

S 215(4)

An order may be made under s 215(4) directing that a debt owed by the company to, for example, a director, ranks after the company's other debts. Such an order was made in *Re Purpoint Ltd* [1991] BCC 121, though such orders are not commonly encountered in practice.

———

1.239

216 Restriction on re-use of company names

(1) This section applies to a person where a company ('the liquidating company') has gone into insolvent liquidation on or after the appointed day and he was a director or shadow director of the company at any time in the period of 12 months ending with the day before it went into liquidation.

(2) For the purposes of this section, a name is a prohibited name in relation to such a person if—
  (a) it is a name by which the liquidating company was known at any time in that period of 12 months, or
  (b) it is a name which is so similar to a name falling within paragraph (a) as to suggest an association with that company.

(3) Except with leave of the court or in such circumstances as may be prescribed, a person to whom this section applies shall not at any time in the period of 5 years beginning with the day on which the liquidating company went into liquidation—
  (a) be a director of any other company that is known by a prohibited name, or
  (b) in any way, whether directly or indirectly, be concerned or take part in the promotion, formation or management of any such company, or
  (c) in any way, whether directly or indirectly, be concerned or take part in the carrying on of a business carried on (otherwise than by a company) under a prohibited name.

(4) If a person acts in contravention of this section, he is liable to imprisonment or a fine, or both.

(5) In subsection (3) 'the court' means any court having jurisdiction to wind up companies; and on an application for leave under that subsection, the Secretary of State or the official receiver may appear and call the attention of the court to any matters which seem to him to be relevant.

(6) References in this section, in relation to any time, to a name by which a company is known are to the name of the company at that time or to any name under which the company carries on business at that time.

> (7) For the purposes of this section a company goes into insolvent liquidation if it goes into liquidation at a time when its assets are insufficient for the payment of its debts and other liabilities and the expenses of the winding up.
>
> (8) In this section 'company' includes a company which may be wound up under Part V of this Act.

Notes

S 216

Section 216 aims to prevent those who previously controlled an insolvent company from setting up a new business with the same or a similar name as the insolvent one. Such 'phoenix companies' take advantage of an insolvent company's goodwill without bearing the burden of liability for its creditors. It is intrinsic to the new rescue culture that the courts distinguish between culpable and non-culpable business failure; it may therefore when dealing with a non-culpable director, grant him leave to use an otherwise prohibited name: see *Penrose v Official Receiver* [1996] 1 BCLC 389 and *Re Lightning Electrical Contractors Ltd* [1996] 2 BCLC 302, in which comment is made on the earlier case of *Re Bonus Breaks Ltd* [1991] BCC 546. The restrictions do not apply unless the company has gone into insolvent liquidation; thus if a company exits administration through a dissolution (IA 1986 Sch B1 para 84) then the restrictions do not apply.

S 216(2)

It should be noted that there is no requirement for an applicant to satisfy the court that the public was in fact confused by the similarity of names and the names in question should not be looked at in the abstract but rather in the context of all the circumstances in which they were actually used or likely to be used *Commssioners for HM Revenue & Customs v Walsh* [2006] BCC 431, *Commisioners of HM Revenue & Customs v Benton-Diggins* [2006] BCC 769. There is no restriction on the use of the name *per se*: an offence is only committed by those who were directors or shadow directors of the insolvent company.

S 216(2)(b)

An objective test is applied in determining the similarity of names: *Archer Structures Ltd v Griffiths* [2004] BCC 156.

S 216(3)

Section 216(3) is broadly drafted in order that former directors of insolvent companies do not escape liability for their subsequent direct or indirect involvement with companies or other businesses using prohibited names. Section 216(3)(c) prevents a director of an insolvent company from carrying on business in a partnership, or otherwise, under a prohibited name. Application may be made under section 216(3) for leave of the court to use a prohibited name. It appears that permission will be granted where there is (i) no risk to the creditors of the old company (such as the appropriation of its goodwill at a knock-down price), (ii) no more risk to new creditors than is inherent in the legislature permitting directors who are inexperienced to trade undercapitalised limited companies, and (iii) no other factors suggesting that the directors are unfit to manage a company. Such permission cannot be obtained retrospectively. It is wrong in principle to treat an applicant for leave under s 216(3) in the way the court would approach an application for leave under s 17 CDDA 1986; it is not appropriate therefore that factors such as the likely failure of a company due to undercapitalisation or lack of experience of directors are taken into account: *Penrose v Official Receiver* [1996] 1 BCLC 389.

S 216(4)

There is criminal liability for breach of the restrictions on re-use of company names (s 216(4)), and it is an offence of strict liability (*R v Doring* [2002] BCC 838 at p 842B, CA; *R v Cole* [1998] 2 BCLC 234). There is no jurisdiction for the court to excuse or limit the respondent's liability: *Ricketts v Ad Valorem Factors Ltd* [2004] BCC 164. A breach of s 216 can be taken into account in director's disqualification proceedings: *Re Migration Services Ltd* [2000] BCC 1095.

S 216(6)

Section 216 applies to company trade names as well as their registered names: *IRC v Nash* [2003] BPIR 1138. Section 216 applies in respect of any company which uses a prohibited name, regardless of its date of incorporation, unless it comes within the exception in IR 1986 4.230.

S 216(7)

As with s 214, 'insolvent liquidation' means balance sheet insolvent rather than being cash-flow insolvent.

S 216(8)

This refers to unregistered companies IA 1986 s 221ff.

Exceptions

Exceptions, in other words instances in which a person may act as referred to in s 216 without having first obtained leave to do so, are provided IR 1986 rr 4.226–4.230. There are three exceptions:

(1) where the whole or substantially the whole of the business of an insolvent company is acquired by another company under the supervision of a licensed insolvency practitioner and office holder, and 28 days' notice is given to creditors. A creditor could object by applying under s 112 or s 167(3));

(2) where a restricted person applies for the permission of the court within 7 days of liquidation, in which case he may for up to six weeks act in relation to the new company, pending the hearing of the application for permission;

(3) where the new company has been known by the prohibited name for the whole 12 months before the insolvent company went into liquidation, and has not been dormant. 'Dormant' is defined in CA 1985 s 249(AA)(4),(5) (by reference to IA 1986 s 251). If such a company has been dormant during that period, permission must be sought. Unless the company in question has actually filed at Companies House as a dormant company, there may well be arguments as to whether the company was dormant or not during the relevant period. For useful guidance on the court's approach to IA 1986 s 216, and the third exception in particular, see *ESS Productions Ltd (in administration) v Sully* [2005] BPIR 691, CA.

I.240

217 Personal liability for debts, following contravention of s 216

(1) A person is personally responsible for all the relevant debts of a company if at any time—

   (a) in contravention of section 216, he is involved in the management of the company, or

   (b) as a person who is involved in the management of the company, he acts or is willing to act on instructions given (without the leave of the court) by a person whom he knows at that time to be in contravention in relation to the company of section 216.

(2) Where a person is personally responsible under this section for the relevant debts of a company, he is jointly and severally liable in respect of those debts with the company and any other person who, whether under this section or otherwise, is so liable.

(3) For the purposes of this section the relevant debts of a company are—

(a)   in relation to a person who is personally responsible under paragraph (a) of subsection (1), such debts and other liabilities of the company as are incurred at a time when that person was involved in the management of the company, and

(b)   in relation to a person who is personally responsible under paragraph (b) of that subsection, such debts and other liabilities of the company as are incurred at a time when that person was acting or was willing to act on instructions given as mentioned in that paragraph.

(4) For the purposes of this section, a person is involved in the management of a company if he is a director of the company or if he is concerned, whether directly or indirectly, or takes part, in the management of the company.

(5) For the purposes of this section a person who, as a person involved in the management of a company, has at any time acted on instructions given (without the leave of the court) by a person whom he knew at that time to be in contravention in relation to the company of section 216 is presumed, unless the contrary is shown, to have been willing at any time thereafter to act on any instructions given by that person.

(6) In this section 'company' includes a company which may be wound up under Part V.

Notes

S 217

This section has the effect of rendering anyone who is involved in the management of the phoenix company, in contravention of s 216, personally liable for debts of the phoenix company incurred at the time that he was involved in management (*Thorne v Silverleaf* [1994] 1 BCLC 637, CA). He will be liable for those debts even if he is only involved in management of the phoenix company intermittently during the 5 years prescribed by s 216(3), as in *IRC v Nash* [2003] BPIR 1138.

S 217(1)(b)

Anyone who is involved in the management of a company and is willing to accept instructions from someone whom he knows is in breach of s 216 (ie a 'front' person) also becomes personally liable for such debts of the company as are incurred at a time when he was willing to accept such instructions; even though it is only directors or shadow directors who can be criminally liable under s 216. Such a person will be liable if he is aware of all the facts which render a person in breach of s 216; he need not know of the existence and terms of s 216 itself.

S 217(2)

This provision would not enable the liquidator of the indebted company to claim the 'relevant debts' directly from a director of the indebted company but it would enable him to claim a contribution from the director in certain circumstances *Re Prestige Grindlngs Ltd* [2006] BCC 421, *Commrs of the Inland Revenue v McEntaggart* [2006] BPIR 750 (a case on s 15 CDDA 1986).

S 217(3)

The liability of a person under s 217 is not only for debts of the new company but also for its other liabilities, such as damages claims. Liability under s 217 extends to all obligations incurred by the new company whilst the person was involved in management, and is not restricted to such obligations as were incurred by him. For guidance on the court's general approach to IA 1986 s 217, see *ESS Productions Ltd (in administration) v Sully* [2005] BPIR 691, CA.

Investigation and prosecution of malpractice

1.241

218 Prosecution of delinquent officers and members of company

(1) If it appears to the court in the course of a winding up by the court that any past or present officer, or any member, of the company has been guilty of any offence in relation to the company for which he is criminally liable, the court may (either on the application of a person interested in the winding up or of its own motion) direct the liquidator to refer the matter
    [(a) in the case of a winding up in England and Wales, to the Secretary of State, and
    (b) in the case of a winding up in Scotland, to the Lord Advocate].

(2) ...

(3) If in the case of a winding up by the court in England and Wales it appears to the liquidator, not being the official receiver, that any past or present officer of the company, or any member of it, has been guilty of an offence in relation to the company for which he is criminally liable, the liquidator shall report the matter to the official receiver.

(4) If it appears to the liquidator in the course of a voluntary winding up that any past or present officer of the company, or any member of it, has been guilty of an offence in relation to the company for which he is criminally liable, he shall [forthwith report the matter—
    (a) in the case of a winding up in England and Wales, to the Secretary of State, and
    (b) in the case of a winding up in Scotland, to the Lord Advocate,
and shall furnish to the Secretary of State or (as the case may be) the Lord Advocate such information and give to him such access to and facilities for inspecting and taking copies of documents (being information or documents in the possession or under the control of the liquidator and relating to the matter in question) as [the Secretary of State or (as the case may be) the Lord Advocate requires.

(5) Where a report is made to the Secretary of State under subsection (4) he may, for the purpose of investigating the matter reported to him and such other matters relating to the affairs of the company as appear to him

to require investigation, exercise any of the powers which are exercisable by inspectors appointed under section 431 or 432 of the Companies Act to investigate a company's affairs.

(6) If it appears to the court in the course of a voluntary winding up that—

(a) any past or present officer of the company, or any member of it, has been guilty as above-mentioned, and

(b) no report with respect to the matter has been made by the liquidator ... under subsection (4),

the court may (on the application of any person interested in the winding up or of its own motion) direct the liquidator to make such a report.

On a report being made accordingly, this section has effect as though the report had been made in pursuance of subsection (4).

Notes

S 218

This section and s 219 provide for the investigation and prosecution of malpractices of past and present officers of the company. In both compulsory and voluntary liquidations, a person interested in the winding-up can apply to the court for a direction to the liquidator to report the matter to the Secretary of State; or the court can so direct of its own motion (IA 1986 s 218(1)).

S 218(3)–(5)

In the absence of a direction from the court, in a compulsory winding-up in England and Wales, the liquidator must report any such matter to the official receiver (where the liquidator is not the official receiver): IA 1986 s 218(3). Where the official receiver receives information under this provision he is entitled to pass it on to the relevant prosecuting authority *R v Brady* [2005] BCC 357.

S 218(4), (5)

In England and Wales, in a voluntary winding-up (and in the absence of a direction from the court), the liquidator must report it to the Secretary of State (s 218(4)). In any investigation by the Secretary of State, he has the same power to demand co-operation as an inspector appointed under the CA 1985 to investigate the company's affairs: IA 1986 s 218(5). For 'officer', see the Introductory notes under s 206 above.

1.242–1.256

219 Obligations arising under s 218

(1) For the purpose of an investigation by the Secretary of State [in consequence of a report made to him under section 218(4)], any obligation imposed on a person by any provision of the Companies Act to produce documents or give information to, or otherwise to assist, inspectors appointed as mentioned in [section 218(5)] is to be regarded as an obligation similarly to assist the Secretary of State in his investigation.

(2) An answer given by a person to a question put to him in exercise of the powers conferred by section 218(5) may be used in evidence against him.

[(2A) However, in criminal proceedings in which that person is charged with an offence to which this subsection applies—
  (a) no evidence relating to the answer may be adduced, and
  (b) no question relating to it may be asked,
by or on behalf of the prosecution, unless evidence relating to it is adduced, or a question relating to it is asked, in the proceedings by or on behalf of that person.

(2B) Subsection (2A) applies to any offence other than—
  (a) an offence under section 2 or 5 of the Perjury Act 1911 (false statements made on oath otherwise than in judicial proceedings or made otherwise than on oath), or
  (b) an offence under section 44(1) or (2) of the Criminal Law (Consolidation) (Scotland) Act 1995 (false statements made on oath or otherwise than on oath).]

(3) Where criminal proceedings are instituted by [the Director of Public Prosecutions, the Lord Advocate] or the Secretary of State following any report or reference under section 218, it is the duty of the liquidator and every officer and agent of the company past and present (other than the defendant or defender) to give to [the Director of Public Prosecutions, the Lord Advocate] or the Secretary of State (as the case may be) all assistance in connection with the prosecution which he is reasonably able to give.

For this purpose 'agent' includes any banker or solicitor of the company and any person employed by the company as auditor, whether that person is or is not an officer of the company.

(4) If a person fails or neglects to give assistance in the manner required by subsection (3), the court may, on the application of the [Director of Public Prosecutions, the Lord Advocate] or the Secretary of State (as the case may be) direct the person to comply with that subsection; and if the application is made with respect to a liquidator, the court may (unless it appears that the failure or neglect to comply was due to the liquidator not having in his hands sufficient assets of the company to enable him to do so) direct that the costs shall be borne by the liquidator personally.

Notes

S 219

Although answers given by a person in response to the Secretary of State's investigation may be used in evidence against him in civil proceedings, the IA 2000 inserted s 219(2A), (2B), which prevent this happening in criminal proceedings (other than for perjury) save where the defendant himself adduces evidence about his answers or asks questions about them.

Part V
Winding up of Unregistered Companies

1.257

220 Meaning of 'unregistered company'

(1) For the purposes of this Part, the expression 'unregistered company' includes … any association and any company, with the following exceptions—

(a) ...

(b) a company registered in any part of the United Kingdom under the Joint Stock Companies Acts or under the legislation (past or present) relating to companies in Great Britain.

(2) On such day as the Treasury appoints by order under section 4(3) of the Trustee Savings Banks Act 1985, the words in subsection (1) from 'any trustee' to 'banks' cease to have effect and are hereby repealed.

Notes

S 220

Companies registered under the CA 1985 or earlier acts and unregistered companies may be wound up (IA 1986 s 221, 225, 73). The definition of 'company' under IA 1986 s 73(1) refers back to CA 1985 s 735; and see also CA 1985 s 675. An unregistered company includes any association and any company other than a registered company (*Re Normandy Markets Ltd* [1993] BCC 879). Despite the use of the word 'association', members' social clubs and other 'not for profit' associations are not associations for the purposes of IA 1986 s 220 and cannot be wound up as an unregistered company *Re St.James' Club* (1852) 2 De GM & G 383, *Re Witney Town Football and Social Club* [1994] 2 BCLC 487; but such associations can be wound up under the court's general equitable jurisdiction *Butts Park Ventures (Coventry) Ltd v Bryant Homes Central Ltd* [2004] BCC 207. An international organisation whose members were sovereign states is not an unregistered company: *Re International Tin Council* [1989] Ch 309 (see s 225). The Court of Appeal in *Re International Tin Council* (above) followed *Re St James Club* (above) in asking itself whether Parliament could reasonably have intended such an organisation to be subject to the winding up process. However the variety of organisations which are unregistered companies is wide including foreign companies which have been dissolved in their country of incorporation: *Russian and English Bank v Baring Bros & Co Ltd* [1936] AC 405, 432 per Lord Russell. Unregistered companies also include: a company incorporated under a private Act of Parliament (*Re South London Fish Market* (1888) LR 39 Ch D 324); in certain circumstances, a company registered in Northern Ireland (*Re a Company (No 007946 of 1993)* [1994] Ch 198; *Re Normandy Marketing Ltd* [1993] BCC 879); an insolvent partnership (Insolvent Partnerships Order 1994 SI 1994/2421); and, importantly, a 'foreign' company which is a company that is incorporated outside Great Britain, *In the Matter of Soverign Marine & General Insurance Company Ltd* [2006] EWHC 1335 (Ch).

Section 220(1)(b) prevents companies registered in other parts of the United Kingdom from being wound up outside the place of registration. However, it is clear from *Re Normandy Marketing* (above) that Northern Irish companies are not so excluded provided they have a principal place of business in England and Wales. Further there are a number of organisations that may be wound up under IA 1986 due to specific enabling provisions which are not unregistered companies e g Industrial and Provident Societies Act 1965 s 55, 56; *Re Norse Self Build Association Ltd* (1985) 1 BCC 99,436; Financial Services and Markets Act 2000 s 367).

1.258

221 Winding up of unregistered companies

(1) Subject to the provisions of this Part, any unregistered company may be wound up under this Act; and all the provisions of this Act and the Companies Act about winding up apply to an unregistered company with the exceptions and additions mentioned in the following subsections.

(2) If an unregistered company has a principal place of business situated in Northern Ireland, it shall not be wound up under this Part unless it has

a principal place of business situated in England and Wales or Scotland, or in both England and Wales and Scotland.

(3) For the purpose of determining a court's winding-up jurisdiction, an unregistered company is deemed—

    (a)   to be registered in England and Wales or Scotland, according as its principal place of business is situated in England and Wales or Scotland, or

    (b)   if it has a principal place of business situated in both countries, to be registered in both countries;

and the principal place of business situated in that part of Great Britain in which proceedings are being instituted is, for all purposes of the winding up, deemed to be the registered office of the company.

(4) No unregistered company shall be wound up under this Act voluntarily except in accordance with the EC Regulation

(5) The circumstances in which an unregistered company may be wound up are as follows—

    (a)   if the company is dissolved, or has ceased to carry on business, or is carrying on business only for the purpose of winding up its affairs;

    (b)   if the company is unable to pay its debts;

    (c)   if the court is of opinion that it is just and equitable that the company should be wound up.

(6) ...

(7) In Scotland, an unregistered company which the Court of Session has jurisdiction to wind up may be wound up by the court if there is subsisting a floating charge over property comprised in the company's property and undertaking, and the court is satisfied that the security of the creditor entitled to the benefit of the floating charge is in jeopardy.

For this purpose a creditor's security is deemed to be in jeopardy if the court is satisfied that events have occurred or are about to occur which render it unreasonable in the creditor's interests that the company should retain power to dispose of the property which is subject to the floating charge.

Notes

S 221

The main justification for winding up an unregistered company rests on the assumption that some benefit will accrue to it, the creditors or others; if no benefit will accrue the court will refuse to make an order. Where the court makes a winding up order it is effective against all the assets of the company whether in the jurisdiction or not *Re Bank of Credit and Commerce International SA. (No 2)* [1992] BCLC 570. The principles upon which the courts in the UK will now act in winding up foreign companies which have their 'centre of main interests' in a state of the European Union must now be read in the light of Art 3(1), (2) EC Regulation on Insolvency Proceedings 2000 which is separately annotated; this enables an English court inter alia to make a winding up order in relation to: (a) any company wherever registered so long as it has its centre of main interests in the UK or (b) any company with its centre of main interests in a Member State which has an establishment in the UK. Further in respect of a foreign company outside the EU or the Commonwealth (see as to the latter the notes on s 426) which is subject to some form of insolvency process in its place of incorporation it may be relevant to consider the Cross-Border Insolvency Regulations 2006 (which implement UNCI-TRAL Model Law on Cross Border Insolvency) under which a foreign insolvency representative can apply to the British court to start British insolvency proceedings or to participate in British insolvency proceedings and further to obtain recognition and relief for foreign insolvency proceedings; the Regulations came into force on 4 April 2006.

The court may wind up an unregistered company despite the fact that it has been dissolved (*Re Imperial Anglo-German Bank* (1872) 26 LT 229) or it is undergoing a liquidation process in its own country (*Re Federal Bank of Australia* [1893] WN 77). However where the company is undergoing a liquidation process in its seat of incorporation and there is no obvious benefit to creditors in this jurisdiction the court is likely to refuse a winding up order *New Hampshire Insurance Co v Rush and Tompkins* [1998] 2 BCLC 471; or if it is more appropriate that a liquidation should take place in another jurisdiction *Re Wallace Smith & Co Ltd* [1992] BC LC 970.

S 221(1)

There is no territorial restriction placed on the ability of the court to wind up an unregistered company by this provision; the principles on which the court generally acts in considering whether to wind up an unregistered company are not pre-conditions to the existence of the jurisdiction of the court to wind up rather they are matters that go to the court's discretion *Re Drax Holdings Ltd* [2004] BCC 334, *Re DAP Holding NV* [2006] BCC 48, *In the Matter of Sovereign Marine & General Insurance Company Ltd* [2006] EWHC 1335 (Ch). However an unregistered company can only be wound up on limited grounds IA 1986 s 221(5) and then only by the court IA 1986 s 221(4) (unless the EC Regulation on Insolvency Proceedings 2000 applies, *see Re TXU Europe German Finance BV* [2005] BPIR 209).

S 221(2)

Therefore a Northern Irish company with a principal place of business in England may be wound up in England Re Normandy Marketing Ltd [1993] BCC 879.

S 221(4)

Under the EC Regulation on Insolvency Proceedings 2000 a foreign company which has its centre of main interests in England may be wound up voluntarily; see *Re TXU Europe German Finance BV* [2005] BPIR 209.

S 221(5)

Before the court will wind up an unregistered company it must generally be established that the company has a proper or sufficient connection with the jurisdiction *International Westminster Bank plc v Okeanos Maritime Corpn* [1987] 3 All ER 137, 144 per Peter Gibson LJ; for instance the fact that the company carried on business in England *Re a Company (No 003102 of 1991), ex p.Nyckeln Finance Co Ltd* [1991] BCLC 539, *Re La Mutuelles du Man Assurances IARD* [2006] BCC 11 or because the company has a right of action with a reasonable possibility of success *Re Allobrogia SS Corpn* [1978] 3 All ER 423, *Re Latreefers Inc* [1999] 1 BCLC 271. Without such a connection and in the absence of any benefit to creditors it is unlikely the court will make a winding up order *Banco Nacional de Cuba v Cosmos Trading Corp* [2000] BCC 910. Unless the petition is wholly based on the past or present carrying on of business within the jurisdiction it is not necessary to prove the carrying of business by the unregistered company *Atlantic & General Investment Trust Ltd v Richbell Information Services Inc* [2000] BCC 111, *Re Real Estate Development Co* [1991] BCLC 210.

Discretion

The court retains its general discretion and a winding up order may be refused if it is more appropriate that the company is wound up in its seat of incorporation *Re Hibernian Merchants Ltd* [1958] Ch 76; or it is undesirable for a winding up order to be made whilst the company continued to trade in its country of incorporation and elsewhere *Banco Nacional de Cuba v*

Cosmos Trading Corpn [2000] BCLC 813. However the fact that the company does not have assets within the jurisdiction will not prevent the court winding it up; but before it will do so the court will normally need to be satisfied that there is a sufficient connection with the jurisdiction and a reasonable possibility of benefit for the creditors from the winding up and one or more persons interested in the distribution of assets of the company is a person over whom the court can exercise jurisdiction *Re Drax Holdings Ltd* [2004] BCC 334. For example winding up orders have been made to enable ex-employees of the company to claim compensation from the Department of Employment (*Re Eloc Electro-Optieck and Communicatie BV* [1982] Ch 43); to enable creditors to benefit from wrongful/fraudulent trading claims *International Westminster Bank Plc v Okeanos Maritime Corpn* [1987] 3 All ER 137; and to enable the company to bring an insurance claim in the UK *Re Compania Merabello San Nicholas SA* [1973] Ch 75.

1.259

222 Inability to pay debts: unpaid creditor for £750 or more

(1) An unregistered company is deemed (for the purposes of section 221) unable to pay its debts if there is a creditor, by assignment or otherwise, to whom the company is indebted in a sum exceeding £750 then due and—

    (a)   the creditor has served on the company, by leaving at its principal place of business, or by delivering to the secretary or some director, manager or principal officer of the company, or by otherwise serving in such manner as the court may approve or direct, a written demand in the prescribed form requiring the company to pay the sum due, and

    (b)   the company has for 3 weeks after the service of the demand neglected to pay the sum or to secure or compound for it to the creditor's satisfaction.

(2) The money sum for the time being specified in subsection (1) is subject to increase or reduction by regulations under section 417 in Part XV; but no increase in the sum so specified affects any case in which the winding-up petition was presented before the coming into force of the increase.

Notes

S 222

This provision is in substantially the same form as IA 1986 s 123(1)(a); see notes to s 123. Note that the demand must be left at the unregistered company's 'principal place of business'.

1.260

223 Inability to pay debts: debt remaining unsatisfied after action brought

An unregistered company is deemed (for the purposes of section 221) unable to pay its debts if an action or other proceeding has been instituted against any member for any debt or demand due, or claimed to be due, from the company, or from him in his character of member, and—

(a)   notice in writing of the institution of the action or proceeding has been served on the company by leaving it at the company's principal place of business (or by delivering it to the secretary, or some director, manager or principal officer of the company, or by otherwise serving it in such manner as the court may approve or direct), and

(b)   the company has not within 3 weeks after service of the notice paid, secured or compounded for the debt or demand, or procured the action or proceeding to be stayed or sisted, or indemnified the defendant or defender to his reasonable satisfaction against the action or proceeding, and against all costs, damages and expenses to be incurred by him because of it.

Notes

S 223

This method of proving insolvency is not mirrored in the provisions relating to registered companies. It requires the issue of proceedings against any member of the company for a debt or demand either due from the company or from the member himself qua member of the company. Provided the proceedings are issued and notice of the same is given in accordance with IA 1986 s 223(a) then the company is deemed to be insolvent in the circumstances stated. This provision does not demand that judgment in the proceedings is obtained.

1.261

224 Inability to pay debts: other cases

(1) An unregistered company is deemed (for purposes of section 221) unable to pay its debts—

(a)   if in England and Wales execution or other process issued on a judgment, decree or order obtained in any court in favour of a creditor against the company, or any member of it as such, or any person authorised to be sued as nominal defendant on behalf of the company, is returned unsatisfied;

(b)   if in Scotland the induciae of a charge for payment on an extract decree, or an extract registered bond, or an extract registered protest, have expired without payment being made;

(c)   if in Northern Ireland a certificate of unenforceability has been granted in respect of any judgment, decree or order obtained as mentioned in paragraph (a);

(d)   if it is otherwise proved to the satisfaction of the court that the company is unable to pay its debts as they fall due.

(2) An unregistered company is also deemed unable to pay its debts if it is proved to the satisfaction of the court that the value of the company's

> assets is less than the amount of its liabilities, taking into account its contingent and prospective liabilities.

───────

Notes

S 224

This provision is substantially the same as IA 1986 s 123(1)(b)–(e), (2) and reference should be made to those provisions.

───────

1.262

225 Overseas company may be wound up though dissolved

[(1) Where a company incorporated outside Great Britain which has been carrying on business in Great Britain ceases to carry on business in Great Britain, it may be wound up as an unregistered company under this Act, notwithstanding that it has been dissolved or otherwise ceased to exist as a company under or by virtue of the laws of the country under which it was incorporated.

[(2) This section is subject to the EC Regulation.]

───────

Notes

S 225

This is an independent power given to the court to wind up a company which has been carrying on business in Great Britain but it has ceased to do so nothwithstanding its dissolution or it has ceased to exist under its law of incorporation *Mazur Media Ltd v Mazur Media Gmbh* [2004] BPIR 1253. Thus there is no general bar on winding up a dissolved overseas company and if a winding up order is made the liquidator may bring proceedings in the name of the company to enforce causes of action in its name and may do so whether they accrued before or after the company's dissolution abroad: *Russian and English Bank v Baring Bros & Co* [1936] AC 405. On dissolution the assets of the overseas company vest in the Crown as bona vacantia: *Russian and English Bank v Baring Bros & Co* [1936] AC 405. On the making of the winding up order the liquidator must take possession of all the company's former assets (*Re Azoff-Don Commercial Bank* [1954] Ch 315) and it may assist the liquidator to obtain a vesting of the assets in his own name under IA 1986 s 145. Once the company's assets have been realised and the creditors paid, any surplus should be distributed among the former members of the company and not returned to the Crown *Re Banque des Marchands de Moscou (Koupet-schesky)* [1957] 3 All ER 182; cf *Re Banque Industrielle de Moscou* [1952] Ch 919. The English court has jurisdiction under this provision to wind up a company registered in Northern Ireland *Re Normandy Marketing Ltd* [1993] BCC 879.

S 225(2)

The ability of the court to make a winding up order in respect of an overseas company whose centre of main interests is in the UK or another member state must now be considered in the light of the EC Regulation on Insolvency Proceedings 2000 Art 3 which is separately annotated.

───────

1.263

226 Contributories in winding up of unregistered company

(1) In the event of an unregistered company being wound up, every person is deemed a contributory who is liable to pay or contribute to the payment of any debt or liability of the company, or to pay or contribute to the payment of any sum for the adjustment of the rights of members among themselves, or to pay or contribute to the payment of the expenses of winding up the company.

(2) Every contributory is liable to contribute to the company's assets all sums due from him in respect of any such liability as is mentioned above.

(3) In the case of an unregistered company engaged in or formed for working mines within the stannaries, a past member is not liable to contribute to the assets if he has ceased to be a member for 2 years or more either before the mine ceased to be worked or before the date of the winding-up order.

(4) In the event of the death, bankruptcy or insolvency of any contributory, the provisions of this Act with respect to the personal representatives, to the heirs and legatees of heritage of the heritable estate in Scotland of deceased contributories, and to the trustees of bankrupt or insolvent contributories, respectively apply.

Notes

S 226

A contributory is not synonymous with 'shareholder' or 'member' and reference should be made to the notes appearing under IA 1986 s 124(1) above.

S 226(4)

This provision should be read alongside IA 1986 s 81 and s 82. In effect the personal representative becomes a contributory and may exercise the rights of a contributory accordingly: *Re Bayswater Trading Co Ltd* [1970] 1 All ER 608.

1.264

227 Power of court to stay, sist or restrain proceedings

The provisions of this Part with respect to staying, sisting or restraining actions and proceedings against a company at any time after the presentation of a petition for winding up and before the making of a winding-up order extend, in the case of an unregistered company, where the application to stay, sist or restrain is presented by a creditor, to actions and proceedings against any contributory of the company.

Notes

S 227

Reference should be made to the notes to IA 1986 s 147.

1.264A

228 Actions stayed on winding-up order

Where an order has been made for winding up an unregistered company, no action or proceeding shall be proceeded with or commenced against any contributory of the company in respect of any debt of the company, except by leave of the court, and subject to such terms as the court may impose.

Notes

S 228

Reference should be made to the notes to IA 1986 s 130(2).

1.265

229 Provisions of this Part to be cumulative

(1) The provisions of this Part with respect to unregistered companies are in addition to and not in restriction of any provisions in Part IV with respect to winding up companies by the court; and the court or liquidator may exercise any powers or do any act in the case of unregistered companies which might be exercised or done by it or him in winding up companies formed and registered under the Companies Act.

(2) However, an unregistered company is not, except in the event of its being wound up, deemed to be a company under the Companies Act, and then only to the extent provided by this Part of this Act.

Part VI
Miscellaneous Provisions Applying to Companies which are Insolvent or in Liquidation

Office-holders

1.266

230 Holders of office to be qualified insolvency practitioners

'*(1) Where an administration order is made in relation to a company, the administrator must be a person who is qualified to act as an insolvency practitioner in relation to the company.*'

(2) Where an administrative receiver of a company is appointed, he must be a person who is so qualified.

(3) Where a company goes into liquidation, the liquidator must be a person who is so qualified.

(4) Where a provisional liquidator is appointed, he must be a person who is so qualified.

> (5) Subsections (3) and (4) are without prejudice to any enactment under which the official receiver is to be, or may be, liquidator or provisional liquidator.

Notes

S 230(1)

Though repealed by EA 2002 s 248(3), Sch 17 para 9, 19 this provision continues to apply to cases where a petition for administration has been presented prior to 15 September 2003 and also to 'special administration regimes' (EA 2002 s 249). However, under the provisions introduced by EA 2002 an administrator must vacate office if he ceases to be qualified to act as an insolvency practitioner in relation to the company (IA 1986 Sch B1 para 89) thus preventing unlicensed insolvency practitioners from holding appointments. The 'qualification' of an insolvency practitioner is dealt with in IA 1986 s 390 and 'acting' as an insolvency practitioner is defined in IA 1986 s 388. 'Person' in this context means an individual: neither a company nor a partnership can hold office as an administrator, administrative receiver or liquidator. Therefore proceedings brought against the firm in which joint administrative receivers were partners were struck out and, since the application was made outside the limitation period, could not be rescued by amendment or re-issue: *Ramsay & Maclain v Leonard Curtis (a firm)* 28 July 1999, LTL 28/7/99 CA. Neither the office of nominee nor that of supervisor is mentioned in this provision though each has to be a 'qualified insolvency practitioner' (IA 1986 s 1(2), 2(4), 4(2), 7(5)); a non administrative receiver such as a LPA receiver does not have to be a qualified insolvency practitioner.

S 230(2)

An administrative receiver can no longer be appointed by a floating chargeholder subject to certain exceptions the most important of which is the ability to appoint an administrative receiver under a floating charge created before 15 September 2003 IA 1986 s 72A, Enterprise Act 2002 (Commencement No 4 and Transitional Provisions and Savings) Order 2003 SI 2003/2093 art 3.

S 230(3)

An appointment as liquidator should not be taken by a person who as principal or employee of a practice previously acted as an administrative receiver or receiver in relation to the company in the three years prior to liquidation; such a liquidator may be removed from office: *Re Karamelli & Barnett Ltd* [1917] 1 Ch 203.

S 230(5)

An official receiver is not required to be qualified to act as an insolvency practitioner though he is an officer of the court and subject to the general directions of the Secretary of State IA 1986 s 400(2).

1.267

231 Appointment to office of two or more persons

(1) This section applies if an appointment or nomination of any person to the office of ...], administrative receiver, liquidator or provisional liquidator—

    (a)   relates to more than one person, or

    (b)   has the effect that the office is to be held by more than one person.

> (2) The appointment or nomination shall declare whether any act required or authorised under any enactment to be done by the administrator, administrative receiver, liquidator or provisional liquidator is to be done by all or any one or more of the persons for the time being holding the office in question.

Notes

S 231

Though this provision no longer includes administrators by virtue of EA 2002 s 248(3), s 278(2) Sch 17, para 9, 20 it continues to apply to cases where a petition for administration has been presented prior to 15 September 2003 and also to 'special administration regimes' (EA 2002 s 249).

S 231(1)

In many insolvencies (particularly in administrations and administrative receiverships) it is standard practice to make a joint appointment to avoid the practical difficulties that arise if a sole officeholder is appointed and that person is unavailable to execute documentation or otherwise unable to act; further, it is useful to make a joint appointment where the insolvency is substantial or one insolvency practitioner is to carry out investigatory work and the other is to carry out collection and realisation work. Though the provision does not expressly refer to voluntary arrangements it is clear that there may be a joint appointment (IA 1986 s 7(6)). Though repealed by EA 2002 s 248(3), Sch 17, para 9, 19 this provision continues to apply to cases where a petition for administration has been presented prior to 15 September 2003 and also to 'special administration regimes' (EA 2002 s 249).

S 231(2)

The effect of non-compliance with this provision is unclear: it may render the appointment invalid or, alternatively, it may mean that the acts of the officeholder are valid only if carried out jointly by both officeholders concerned. Usually the relevant court order or appointment documentation recites that any act can be done by all or any one of the appointees. There are now detailed provisions dealing with joint and concurrent appointments of administrators (IA 1986 Sch B1 para 100–103).

> **1.268**
>
> ### 232 Validity of office-holder's acts
>
> The acts of an individual as administrative receiver, liquidator or provisional liquidator of a company are valid notwithstanding any defect in his appointment, nomination or qualifications.

Notes

S 232

By virtue of this section, third parties dealing with any of the officeholders specified are protected and are not obliged to enquire into the validity of their appointment. A purchaser of property from a liquidator, for example, would get a good title even if it subsequently transpired that his appointment was defective (for the position in relation to an administrator, see IA 1986 Sch B1 para 104). Since neither a company nor a partnership can hold office protection is only available where the third party deals with an individual officeholder. Similarly, the section could not operate to validate an act that was outside the powers of an officeholder, even if validly appointed; nor would it apply where there was no appointment at all (*Morris v Kanssen* [1946] AC 459, *Dawson v African Consolidated Land Trading Co* [1898] 1 Ch 6) which would presumably include a purported appointment of an unlicensed insolvency practitioner in the cases where an insolvency practitioner has to be qualified to act (IA 1986 s 388, 389). In *OBG Ltd and OBG (Plant & Transport) Ltd v Allan, Stevenson and Raymond International Ltd* [2005] EWCA Civ 106, [2005] 1 BCLC 711, the Court of Appeal held by a majority (Mance LJ dissenting) that invalidly appointed receivers were not liable for the tort of interference with the company's contractual relations, on the basis that their interference had been with the company's business but without any intention to procure a breach of contract. This case is the subject of a pending appeal to the House of Lords, due to be heard in November 2006.

Though this provision no longer includes administrators by virtue of EA 2002 s 248(3), s 278(2) Sch 17, para 9, 21 it continues to apply to cases where a petition for administration has been presented prior to 15 September 2003 and also to 'special administration regimes' EA 2002 s 249.

Management by administrators, liquidators, etc

1.269

233 Supplies of gas, water, electricity, etc

(1) This section applies in the case of a company where—
    [(a) the company enters administration,] or
    (b) an administrative receiver is appointed, or
    [(ba) a moratorium under section 1A is in force, or]
    (c) a voluntary arrangement [approved under Part I], has taken effect, or
    (d) the company goes into liquidation, or
    (e) a provisional liquidator is appointed;
and 'the office-holder' means the administrator, the administrative receiver, [the nominee,] the supervisor of the voluntary arrangement, the liquidator or the provisional liquidator, as the case may be.

(2) If a request is made by or with the concurrence of the office-holder for the giving, after the effective date, of any of the supplies mentioned in the next subsection, the supplier—
    (a) may make it a condition of the giving of the supply that the office-holder personally guarantees the payment of any charges in respect of the supply, but
    (b) shall not make it a condition of the giving of the supply, or do anything which has the effect of making it a condition of the giving of the supply, that any outstanding charges in respect of a supply given to the company before the effective date are paid.

(3) The supplies referred to in subsection (2) are—
    [(a) a supply of gas by a gas supplier within the meaning of Part I of the Gas Act 1986;]
    [(b) a supply of electricity by an electricity supplier within the meaning of Part I of the Electricity Act 1989;]
    (c) a supply of water by [a water undertaker] or, in Scotland, a water authority,
    [(d) a supply of communications services by a provider of a public electronic communications service].

(4) 'The effective date' for the purposes of this section is whichever is applicable of the following dates—
 [(a) the date on which the company entered administration,]
 (b) the date on which the administrative receiver was appointed (or, if he was appointed in succession to another administrative receiver, the date on which the first of his predecessors was appointed),
 [(ba) the date on which the moratorium came into force,]
 (c) the date on which the voluntary arrangement [took effect],
 (d) the date on which the company went into liquidation,
 (e) the date on which the provisional liquidator was appointed.

(5) The following applies to expressions used in subsection (3)—
 (a) ...
 (b) ...
 (c) ..
 [(d) 'communications services' do not include electronic communications services to the extent that they are used to broadcast or otherwise transmit programme services (within the meaning of the Communications Act 2003)].

Notes

S 233

The purpose of this provision is to prevent certain utilities suppliers from securing an unfair advantage over other creditors by demanding that arrears of payment be met before the office holder is provided with a relevant supply. It is not all utility suppliers that are prevented from demanding payment of arrears before continuing to supply to the company. Only those suppliers falling within IA 1986 s 233(3) are prevented from doing so.

S 233(4)

The date of entry into administration is governed by IA 1986 Sch B1 para 13(2) (court appointment) or para 19, para 31 (out of court appointment). A voluntary arrangement has effect under IA 1986 s 5 when the proposal is approved at the meeting of creditors. A company goes into liquidation when it passes a resolution for a voluntary winding up or when a winding-up order is made: IA 1986 s 247(2).

1.270

234 Getting in the company's property

(1) This section applies in the case of a company where—
 [(a) the company enters administration,] or
 (b) an administrative receiver is appointed, or
 (c) the company goes into liquidation, or
 (d) a provisional liquidator is appointed;
and 'the office-holder' means the administrator, the administrative receiver, the liquidator or the provisional liquidator, as the case may be.

(2) Where any person has in his possession or control any property, books, papers or records to which the company appears to be entitled, the court may require that person forthwith (or within such period as the

court may direct) to pay, deliver, convey, surrender or transfer the property, books, papers or records to the office-holder.

(3) Where the office-holder—
    (a) seizes or disposes of any property which is not property of the company, and
    (b) at the time of seizure or disposal believes, and has reasonable grounds for believing, that he is entitled (whether in pursuance of an order of the court or otherwise) to seize or dispose of that property,
the next subsection has effect.

(4) In that case the office-holder—
    (a) is not liable to any person in respect of any loss or damage resulting from the seizure or disposal except in so far as that loss or damage is caused by the office-holder's own negligence, and
    (b) has a lien on the property, or the proceeds of its sale, for such expenses as were incurred in connection with the seizure or disposal.

Notes

S 234(1)

The application is made in the name of the office holder rather than the company; it enables the office holder to recover property of the company but not to sue in conversion which would be an action in the name of the company: *Smith v Bridgend County Borough Council* [2002] 1 AC 336; nor to assist a secured creditor of the company in a claim against a third party: *Sutton v GE Capital Commercial Finance Ltd* [2004] 2 BCLC 662. An application under this provision cannot be made in a voluntary arrangement. However a supervisor of a voluntary arrangement could perhaps apply under IA 1986 s 7(4) to obtain relevant property, books, papers or records from the debtor, albeit that the statutory protection afforded in IA 1986 s 234(3), (4) would not be available. IA 1986 s 234 should be read together with IA 1986 s 246 which applies only in an administration, liquidation and provisional liquidation and renders liens unenforceable in certain circumstances. In a winding up by the court or where a provisional liquidator is appointed the powers given to the court under this provision are exercisable by the liquidator or provisional liquidator as the case may be: IR 1986 r 4.185.

S 234(2)

This provides a summary remedy for the office holder to obtain delivery up of the company's property and documentation from 'any person', which includes another office holder: *Re First Express Ltd* [1991] BCC 782. 'Property' does not include a chose in action such as a debt despite the wide definition in IA 1986 s 436: *Welsh Development Agency Ltd v Export Finance Co* [1992] BCC 270. The office holder may make an application provided that satisfactory evidence can be produced that the company 'appears to be entitled' to the relevant property or documentation; it is not necessary for the office holder to show that the ownership of the property is undisputed: *Re Cosslett (Contractors) Ltd* [1998] Ch 495; *Euro Commercial Leasing Ltd v Cartwright & Lewis* [1995] BCC 830. However an application under IA 1986 s 234 will be refused in a case where the ownership of property has to be determined by a foreign court: *Re Leyland Daf Ltd* [1994] BCC 166. Where an order is made in favour of the office holder it is not appropriate for the respondent to demand that restrictions be placed on the office holder as to the use of the company's property or documentation: *Walker Morris v Khalastchi* [2001] 1 BCLC 1.

S 234(3), (4)

The office holder is protected from liability for wrongful seizure/disposal provided that he can show 'reasonable grounds' for his belief. In the case of a retention of title supplier who notifies the office holder of a claim to ownership of the goods it may be risky for the office holder to rely on these provisions to provide automatic protection. It would be wiser for the office holder to apply for directions from the court to determine ownership of the goods in cases of genuine doubt.

1.271

235 Duty to co-operate with office-holder

(1) This section applies as does section 234; and it also applies, in the case of a company in respect of which a winding-up order has been made by the court in England and Wales, as if references to the office-holder included the official receiver, whether or not he is the liquidator.

(2) Each of the persons mentioned in the next subsection shall—
  (a) give to the office-holder such information concerning the company and its promotion, formation, business, dealings, affairs or property as the office-holder may at any time after the effective date reasonably require, and
  (b) attend on the office-holder at such times as the latter may reasonably require.

(3) The persons referred to above are—
  (a) those who are or have at any time been officers of the company,
  (b) those who have taken part in the formation of the company at any time within one year before the effective date,
  (c) those who are in the employment of the company, or have been in its employment (including employment under a contract for services) within that year, and are in the office-holder's opinion capable of giving information which he requires,
  (d) those who are, or have within that year been, officers of, or in the employment (including employment under a contract for services) of, another company which is, or within that year was, an officer of the company in question, and
  (e) in the case of a company being wound up by the court, any person who has acted as administrator, administrative receiver or liquidator of the company.

(4) For the purposes of subsections (2) and (3), 'the effective date' is whichever is applicable of the following dates—
  [(a) the date on which the company entered administration,]
  (b) the date on which the administrative receiver was appointed or, if he was appointed in succession to another administrative receiver, the date on which the first of his predecessors was appointed,
  (c) the date on which the provisional liquidator was appointed, and
  (d) the date on which the company went into liquidation.

> (5) If a person without reasonable excuse fails to comply with any obligation imposed by this section, he is liable to a fine and, for contravention, to a daily default fine.

Notes

S 235(1)

This provision enables the office holder as defined in IA 1986 s 234(1) and including the official receiver in any event) to request information from a wide variety of persons and/or for any of them to meet the office holder.

S 235(3)(a)

For the definition of 'officer' see notes under IA 1986 s 206.

S 235(2)

A meeting can be called informally by the office holder who would normally offer a number of dates convenient to himself and the interviewee. The meeting itself can be informal or attended by the office holder's and interviewee's advisers. There is nothing to prevent it being recorded and the interviewee being asked to sign a record of the meeting which might prove useful if proceedings are issued. Any statements obtained under this provision can be used in disqualification proceedings (*Re Polly Peck International plc* [1994] BCC 15) without any breach of the Human Rights Act 1998 (*Re Westminster Property Management Ltd* [2000] 1 WLR 2230). Further, although information collected under s 235 is confidential it may be in the public interest for the information to be disclosed to a regulatory authority: *R v Brady* [2004] EWCA Crim 1763, [2004] BPIR 962, [2005] BCC 357.

S 235(5)(a)

The date of entry into administration is governed by IA 1986 Sch B1 para 13(2) court appointment) or para 19, para 31 (out of court appointment).

S 235(5)(d

IA 1986 s 247(2) defines what is meant by 'a company goes into liquidation'.

S 235(5)

The duty to comply with a request from the office holder or official receiver under this provision can also be enforced by order of the court: *Re Wallace Smith Trust Co. Ltd* [1992] BCC 707 and see IR 1986 r 7.20.

1.272

236 Inquiry into company's dealings, etc

(1) This section applies as does section 234; and it also applies in the case of a company in respect of which a winding-up order has been made by the court in England and Wales as if references to the office-holder included the official receiver, whether or not he is the liquidator.

(2) The court may, on the application of the office-holder, summon to appear before it—
    (a)   any officer of the company,

(b) any person known or suspected to have in his possession any property of the company or supposed to be indebted to the company, or

(c) any person whom the court thinks capable of giving information concerning the promotion, formation, business, dealings, affairs or property of the company.

(3) The court may require any such person as is mentioned in subsection (2)(a) to (c) to submit an affidavit to the court containing an account of his dealings with the company or to produce any books, papers or other records in his possession or under his control relating to the company or the matters mentioned in paragraph (c) of the subsection.

(4) The following applies in a case where—

(a) a person without reasonable excuse fails to appear before the court when he is summoned to do so under this section, or

(b) there are reasonable grounds for believing that a person has absconded, or is about to abscond, with a view to avoiding his appearance before the court under this section.

(5) The court may, for the purpose of bringing that person and anything in his possession before the court, cause a warrant to be issued to a constable or prescribed officer of the court—

(a) for the arrest of that person, and

(b) for the seizure of any books, papers, records, money or goods in that person's possession.

(6) The court may authorise a person arrested under such a warrant to be kept in custody, and anything seized under such a warrant to be held, in accordance with the rules, until that person is brought before the court under the warrant or until such other time as the court may order.

Notes

S 236

This provision may be used to secure the attendance of a wide variety of persons before the court to be examined; the Crown is also bound by IA 1986 s 236 (*Soden v Burns* [1996] 1 WLR 1512) and the provision should be read in conjunction with IR 1986 r 9.1ff. The relevant rules in relation to an application under this provision are IR 1986 r 9.1–9.6. The application is supported by a brief statement of the grounds on which it is made. Before an application is made under this provision for a private examination it is not incumbent on the office holder to provide the respondent with a list of questions or topics which may be put at the examination: *Re Embassy Art Products Ltd* (1987) 3 BCC 292; however it is advisable to make a request for compliance under IA 1986 s 235 before making an application under IA 1986 s 236 and often just as productive *Re Barlow Clowes Gilt Managers Ltd* [1992] Ch 208.

S 236(1)

The 'office holder' is defined in IA 1986 s 234(1) and includes the official receiver in any event. If the office holder vacates office any order made under IA 1986 s 236 falls away: *Re Kingscroft Insurance Co Ltd* [1994] BCC 343. An application may be made even where the sole purpose is to obtain information to support the issue of disqualification proceedings under the CDDA 1986: *Re Pantmaenog Timber Co Ltd* [2004] 1 AC 158.

S 236(2)

Only the office holder (or the official receiver in the case of a compulsory liquidation) may make an application: *Re James McHale Automobiles Ltd* [1997] BCC 202. In considering whether to make an order for a private examination the court will balance the need of the applicant to obtain information against the oppression which may be caused to the respondent: *Long v Farrer & Co* [2004] BPIR 1218. In general terms, a private examination will be ordered only where it is necessary in the interests of the relevant insolvency proceedings and it is not unduly oppressive or unfair to the respondent: *Re British & Commonwealth Holdings plc (No 2)* [1993] AC 426, *Bellmex International Ltd v Green* [2001] BCC 253. There are a number of specific matters which may be relevant to the court's approach on that balancing exercise:

(i)   Although the applicant's view that a private examination is necessary is of considerable weight it is by no means determinative and the onus of proving such a need remains on the applicant: *Joint Liquidators of Sasea Finance Ltd v KPMG* [1998] BCC 216;

(ii) It may be an abuse of process for the applicant to delay service of a statement of case in ordinary litigation by applying for orders under IA 1986 s 236 merely to obtain damaging admissions from a respondent for the purposes of that litigation: *Re Sasea Finance Ltd* [1999] BCC 103. The use of a private examination to consider a proof of debt is inappropriate: *Bellmex International Ltd v Green* [2001] BCC 253;

(iii) Although a private examination may still be ordered where the applicant has decided to commence litigation (*Re Cloverbay Ltd (No 2)* [1991] Ch 90), and even where criminal proceedings have been brought (*Re Arrows Ltd (No 2)* [1992] BCC 446, *Re an Inquiry into Mirror Group Newspapers plc* [2000] BCC 217), it is generally easier to obtain an order where no such decision has been made or proceedings brought. However the court's power to order a private examination is not restricted and, even where proceedings have been issued alleging fraud, the court may still decide on balance to make an such an order: *Shierson v Rastogi* [2003] BPIR 148; see also *Daltel Europe Ltd v Makki* [2005] 1 BCLC 594;

(iv) The court is more likely to make an order for a private examination where the respondent is an officer or ex officer of the company as opposed to a third party: *Re Westmead Consultants Ltd* [2002] 1 BCLC 384;

(v)   Although a respondent cannot refuse to answer questions at a private examination on the basis of self incrimination, this may be taken into account as a factor weighing against making an order: *Bishopsgate Investment Management Ltd v Maxwell* [1993] Ch 1. Where a respondent is privately examined the answers he has given cannot be used against him in subsequent criminal proceedings: *Saunders v United Kingdom* [1997] BCC 872; but may be used in disqualification proceedings: *R v Secretary of State for Trade and Industry, ex parte McCormick* [1998] BCC 37; and in an Inland Revenue investigation: *R v Brady* [2004] BPIR 962);

(vi) In circumstances where information has been provided in strict confidence, there may be a public interest in maintaining that confidence and not ordering production of documents. Where the company is in a members' voluntary liquidation, the court is unlikely to make an order: *Re Galileo Group Ltd* [1998] BCC 228.

S 236(2)(b)

This category is somewhat open ended: *Re Trading Partners Ltd v Lomas* [2002] 1 BCLC 655; and it includes a wider range of persons than those who are placed under a duty of co-operation by IA 1986 s 235(3).

S 236(3)

If a respondent is ordered to submit an affidavit then the evidence has to be produced in that form; a witness statement will not suffice: IR 1986 r 9.3, r 7.57(6). The court will be anxious to ensure that an order for production of documents goes no further than is necessary in the interests of the relevant insolvency proceedings: *Re Trading Partners Ltd* [2002] 1 BCLC. However the applicant is not restricted to applying for information sufficient only to reconstitute the knowledge of the company; an order may be made so long as the applicant reasonably requires the same to carry out his duties: *Re British & Commonwealth Holdings plc (No 2)* [1993] AC 426.

S 236(4)

It appears that an order under IA 1986 s 236 can be made against a person who is not resident in the UK: *McIsaac, Petitioners*; *Joint Liquidators of First Tokyo Index Trust Ltd* [1994] BCC 410; but there is doubt about whether or not an order can be made for the private examination in the UK of a foreign resident: *Re Casterbridge Properties Ltd* [2002] BCC 453. A safer course of action may, in appropriate circumstances, be for the office holder to ask the court under its inherent jurisdiction to issue letters of request to the relevant foreign court for the purposes of examining the foreign residents and/or obtaining documents from them: *Re Anglo American Insurance Co* [2002] BCC 715.

S 236(4)(b)

The court may restrain a person from leaving the jurisdiction until a private examination has been held: *Re a Company No 003318 of 1987* [1988] Ch 204.

S 236(5)(b)

A solicitor's lien cannot be asserted against an office holder seeking production of documentation under IA 1986 s 236 though the lien is not destroyed by an order for production: *Re Aveling Barford Ltd* [1989] 1 WLR 360.

S 236(6)

The court may attach conditions to an order such as ordering a respondent to provide security before leaving the jurisdiction: *Re Bank of Credit & Commerce International (No 7)* [1994] 1 BCLC 455.

I.273

237 Court's enforcement powers under s 236

(1) If it appears to the court, on consideration of any evidence obtained under section 236 or this section, that any person has in his possession any property of the company, the court may, on the application of the office-holder, order that person to deliver the whole or any part of the property to the office-holder at such time, in such manner and on such terms as the court thinks fit.

(2) If it appears to the court, on consideration of any evidence so obtained, that any person is indebted to the company, the court may, on the application of the office-holder, order that person to pay to the office-holder, at such time and in such manner as the court may direct, the whole or any part of the amount due, whether in full discharge of the debt or otherwise, as the court thinks fit.

(3) The court may, if it thinks fit, order that any person who if within the jurisdiction of the court would be liable to be summoned to appear before it under section 236 or this section shall be examined in any part of the United Kingdom where he may for the time being be, or in a place outside the United Kingdom.

(4) Any person who appears or is brought before the court under section 236 or this section may be examined on oath, either orally or

(except in Scotland) by interrogatories, concerning the company or the matters mentioned in section 236(2)(c).

_____

Notes

S 237(1)

A respondent solicitor who acted for the company cannot claim legal professional privilege against an office holder of the company where the relevant documents belonged to the company: *Re Brook Martin & Co (Nominees) Ltd* [1993] BCLC 328. Evidence obtained during the course of a private examination cannot be made available for purposes unconnected with the liquidation: *Re Barlow Clowes Gilt Managers Ltd* [1992] Ch 208. Generally the office holder is bound by a duty of confidentiality in relation to any information or documentation obtained under IA 1986 s 236 but this may be waived by the court in certain circumstances: *Re a Company No 005374 of 1993* [1993] BCC 734.

_____

Part VI
Miscellaneous Provisions Applying to Companies which are Insolvent or in Liquidation

Adjustment of prior transactions (administration and liquidation)

1.274

238 Transactions at an undervalue (England and Wales)

(1) This section applies in the case of a company where—
    (a)   the company enters administration, or
    (b)   the company goes into liquidation;
and 'the office-holder' means the administrator or the liquidator, as the case may be.

(2) Where the company has at a relevant time (defined in section 240) entered into a transaction with any person at an undervalue, the office-holder may apply to the court for an order under this section.

(3) Subject as follows, the court shall, on such an application, make such order as it thinks fit for restoring the position to what it would have been if the company had not entered into that transaction.

(4) For the purposes of this section and section 241, a company enters into a transaction with a person at an undervalue if—
    (a)   the company makes a gift to that person or otherwise enters into a transaction with that person on terms that provide for the company to receive no consideration, or
    (b)   the company enters into a transaction with that person for a consideration the value of which, in money or money's worth, is significantly less than the value, in money or money's worth, of the consideration provided by the company.

(5) The court shall not make an order under this section in respect of a transaction at an undervalue if it is satisfied—
    (a)   that the company which entered into the transaction did so in good faith and for the purpose of carrying on its business, and

> (b)   that at the time it did so there were reasonable grounds for believing that the transaction would benefit the company.

Notes

S 238

A liquidator needs sanction to bring a claim under IA 1986 s 238 IA 1986 Sch 4 para 3A and the expenses incurred in making the claim will be an expense of the liquidation IR 1986 r 4.218(1)(a)(i). An order may be made both against a person who has entered into a transaction caught by the section, and (subject to the provisions of IA 1986 s 241(2), see below) against a third party who has acquired a benefit as a result of the transaction. The court has jurisdiction where the transaction in question took place abroad even where the person who benefits is non-resident and out of the jurisdiction (eg a foreign company which does no business here); however any person against whom relief is sought must be 'sufficiently connected with England for it to be just and proper to make an order': *Re Paramount Airways Ltd (No 2)* [1992] BCC 416. Similar considerations will apply in relation to a preference claim under IA 1986 s 239. In sufficiently clear cases, summary judgment may be given: *Re Unigreg Ltd* [2005] BPIR 220); cf *Henderson v 3052775 Nova Scotia Ltd* [2006] UKHL 21.

An assignment by a liquidator or administrator of the right to pursue a claim under this section (or IA 1986 s 239) will fall foul of the rules against maintenance, and thus be invalid, because the right does not constitute property belonging to the company within the meaning of IA 1986 Sch 6 para 4: *Re Oasis Merchandising Services Ltd* [1997] BCC 282; see introductory notes to IA 1986 s 214. For guidance on the question of whether a 12 year or only a 6 year limitation period (pursuant to the provisions, respectively, of the Limitation Act 1980 s 8, s 9) applies to a claim brought under this section, see *Re Priory Garage (Walthamstow) Ltd* [2001] BPIR 144, *Re Yates* [2005] BPIR 476 and *Re Nurkowski* [2006] BPIR 789. In summary, where the applicant's primary relief is the unscrambling of the relevant transaction a 12 year period applies, whereas if the applicant's primary relief is for recovery of a money sum then a 6 year period applies. The cause of action accrues on the entry into administration or liquidation: see note to s 238(1), (2) below.

The application is made by originating application or ordinary application to the registrar, rather than the judge, in the first instance: see Practice Note: the Hearing of Insolvency Proceedings [2005] BPIR 688. The court's permission is required before such proceedings can be served out of the jurisdiction: see IR 1986 r 12.12(3). When considering potential claims under this section reference should also be made to the provisions (which are in several respects wider in their scope) of IA 1986 s 423 which concerns transactions at an undervalue which amount to transactions defrauding creditors.

S 238(1), (2)

Relief is only available after the company enters administration or '*goes into liquidation*' (see IA 1986 s 247(2)). This may be compared with the provisions of IA 1986 s 423(5), s 424 pursuant to which, aside from office holders, any person who has been a 'victim of the transaction' can bring proceedings, for example a creditor. It would be unusual (but possible) for a creditor to seek an order that the office holder is directed to bring proceedings under IA 1986 s 238 or any of the other provisions attacking prior transactions. Prior to the reforms of the administration procedure introduced by EA 2002, IA 1986 s 238(1)(a) read '*an administration order is made in relation to the company*' and that wording continues to apply to cases where a petition for administration has been presented prior to 15 September 2003 and also to 'special administration regimes': EA 2002 s 249.

S 238(2)

Transactions are only vulnerable to attack if they have been entered into at a 'relevant time'; by contrast there is no requirement under IA 1986 s 423 that a transaction must have occurred within a specified time prior to the insolvency. The 'relevant time' in relation to a transaction is determined by reference to several matters: first, transactions are capable of being caught if they were entered into within prescribed fixed periods prior to the 'onset of insolvency' (IA 1986 s 240(3)) and these periods vary according to whether or not there is a connection between the company and the other party to the transaction; alternatively they may be caught if entered into between the making of an application for administration and the order or between the filing of notice of intention to appoint an administrator and the appointment. In the case of a transaction entered into after the making of an administration application or a filing of a notice of intention to appoint an administrator (provided that an order is made on that application or an appointment is made pursuant to the notice) insolvency need not be proved: IA 1986 s 240(1)(c), (d), s 240(2). However a transaction entered into prior to the making of an application for administration or the filing of a notice of intention to appoint an administrator will not have been entered into at a 'relevant time' (even where it is within the prescribed fixed period) unless the company was at the time of the transaction, or became as a result of the transaction, unable to pay its debts within the meaning of IA 1986 s 123; see notes to IA 1986 s 240 below. There is a presumption of insolvency in the case of a transaction at an undervalue in respect of a connected person: IA 1986 s 240(2).

S 238(3)

Notwithstanding the use of the word 'shall', the court has a discretion whether to make any order at all (and if so then what form of order). It does not automatically follow that an order must be made in favour of the office holder once the transaction has been established to be within the scope of the section: *Re Paramount Airways* [1992] BCC 416. The power of the court is limited to restoring the position to what it would have been had the company not entered the transaction at all; the court cannot reconstruct the position on the basis that the company would have entered a different transaction: *Re MDA Investment Management Ltd* [2005] BCC 783. In that case the court refused to make an order under IA 1986 s 238(3), notwithstanding that the company did not get full value for what it parted with, because it would have been in a worse position if it had not entered into the transaction at all and its business would have closed. No order under IA 1986 s 238 may be made a time when the recipient of the 'tainted gift' is the subject of a restraint or confiscation order under POCA 2002: see POCA 2002 s 427.

S 238(4)(a)

For the purposes of the section a 'transaction', (which is expressed by IA 1986 s 436 to include a 'gift, agreement or arrangement'), may include any formal or informal dealing with the company. For an example of a case where there was found to be no sufficient dealing between the company and the respondent to constitute a transaction within the meaning of the section see *Re Taylor Sinclair (Capital) Ltd* [2002] BPIR 203. It would appear that there must have been some positive act on the part of the company, e g the making of a gift, and that a mere omission – such as failing to pursue a debtor – could not amount to a transaction at an undervalue, although it could amount to the giving of a preference under the provisions of IA 1986 s 239.

S 238(4)(b)

If consideration is given, then only if its value is 'significantly' less than the value of the consideration provided by the company will the transaction be vulnerable. There are no clear judicial pronouncements as to what 'significantly' means. It will be a matter of fact and degree turning on the particular facts of each case. In *Re Marini Ltd* [2004] BCC 172 it was observed that a 10% difference between the transfer price of an asset and an independent valuation could represent a genuine difference between valuers. In *Re London Local Residential Ltd (No 2)* [2005] BPIR 163 a sale of an asset at 7% less than an expert valuation was held not to be a substantial undervalue. In *Re Kumar* [1993] BCLC 548 it was stated that a 'substantial element of bounty' would bring the transaction within the scope of the provision. In *Barclays Bank v Eustice* [1995] 2 BCLC 630 it was indicated that the test could be satisfied where goods or assets are sold on terms whereby payment of the sale price (although reflecting the true value of what is being sold) is deferred without any provision for interest. Each case must be looked at on its own facts: *Re MDA Investment Management Ltd* [2004] BPIR 75; *Ramlort Ltd v Reid* [2004] BPIR 985. See also *Re Shapland Inc* [2000] BCC 106, 110 (a case primarily concerned with questions of preference).

The exercise (which is the same under this section as it is under IA 1986 s 423) of measuring one value against the other must be carried out as at the date of the transaction. The assessment will often be far from straightforward especially where one is having to weigh the 'value' of future or contingent benefits or liabilities or assess the value of certain assets such as goodwill: *Western Intelligence Ltd v KDO Label Printing Machines Ltd* [1998] BCC 472. As to the proper approach see *Phillips v Brewin Dolphin Bell Lawrie Ltd [2001] 1 WLR 143* (HL), which involved future payments for the sale of a business pursuant to a number of connected agreements. It is also apparent from that authority and *Defra v Feakin* [2005] BPIR 292 (a case under IA 1986 s 423) that the court adopts a commercial and pragmatic approach in considering the 'transaction' under attack and it is ready to read 'enters into a transaction' in IA 1986 s 238(4)(b) as 'participate in an arrangement' in appropriate circumstances.

The provision does not stipulate by which person the consideration must be provided, and a transaction will not be caught simply because the person receiving the benefit from the company is not the same as the person who provides the consideration. What is required is simply an assessment of the consideration (which might come from more than one source) for which the company has entered into the transaction, with the value of the consideration to be assessed at the date of the transaction: see *Phillips v Brewin Dolphin Bell Lawrie Ltd* (above). In *Re Thoars (Dec'd)* [2003] BPIR 489, an application to determine a preliminary issue, which sought to limit the valuation evidence to events subsequent to the transaction, was refused. However where the value of the consideration depends on the occurrence or non-occurrence of some event and that event happens before the valuation is complete then the valuer may take it into account. At the hearing of the substantive application in *Re Thoars (dec'd)* (above) the court, in considering all the circumstances surrounding the declaration of trust in question, held there was a significant difference in value between the consideration given and received: *Re Thoars (Dec'd)* [2003] BPIR 1444; the unsuccessful appeal is reported as *Reid v Ramlort Ltd* [2004] BPIR 985.

Prior to the decision of the Court of Appeal in *Re Nurkowski, Hill v Spread Trustee Company Ltd* [2006] BPIR 789, it could be confidently advised that the provision of security by a company could not constitute a transaction at undervalue because a company's financial position is not worsened merely because a debt is converted from an unsecured debt to a secured debt. The reasoning was that the state of the company's balance sheet remains the same, and, although it may have lost the right to deal freely with those assets over which security has been given, that loss cannot be given a value in money terms: see *Re M C Bacon Ltd (No 1)* [1990] BCC 78; *Re Mistral Finance Ltd* [2001] BCC 27. However, Arden LJ in *Re Nurkowski* (above) doubted that this remains good law, and was prepared to hold that the grant of security rights could constitute consideration. There appears therefore to be no reason to leave the value of such rights out of account in the balancing exercise under IA 1986 s 238(4)(b), though it is not clear whether this approach would only apply to a fixed as opposed to a floating charge. Provision of security can certainly constitute a preference within the meaning of IA 1986 s 239, but under that section the office holder will have to establish that the company was influenced in deciding to give the security by a desire to prefer the lender: see IA 1986 s 239(5) below.

There is no reported authority on the question of whether the giving of a guarantee is, of itself, an act capable of being caught by IA 1986 s 238(4)(b). The point is not necessarily only of academic interest: although the guarantor company will necessarily be insolvent for the issue to arise (and thus not good for its guarantee), the question of whether the creditor can claim in the liquidation may well be relevant. Giving a guarantee (and the consequent creation of a new liability – albeit only contingent) is quite different from the situation where a company gives security for a debt which it already owes. Prima facie it would seem that the company is, having given the guarantee, worse off in a balance sheet sense than it was before. However, it is arguable that where a guarantee is given for someone else's debt it is not possible to measure 'in money or money's worth' the consideration given – ie the guarantee. Nor, often, will it be possible to assess the value of the consideration received. Applying the analysis of *Millet J* in

Re M C Bacon Ltd (above) would then lead to the conclusion that the comparison exercise required by IA 1986 s 238(4)(b) cannot be undertaken, and there can be no transaction at an undervalue. Where cross guarantees are given by each of a number of companies in a group then further difficulties arise in assessing the relative value of the guarantees that a particular company is respectively giving and benefiting from: as to cross-guarantees: generally, see *Rolled Steel Products v British Steel Corpn* [1986] Ch 246. Of course, if it can be established that no consideration at all has been received by the company (which will not be the case where it has received the benefit of cross-guarantees but might well be so where there is no commercial connection between the company and the principal debtor) then IA 1986 s 238(4)(a) will apply, and it will be unnecessary to embark on the balancing exercise required by IA 1986 s 238(4)(b).

S 238(5)

Transactions will be upheld if they can be shown to have been entered into in good faith and for proper business reasons. The onus of satisfying the court is on the person seeking to uphold the transaction: *Re Barton Manufacturing Co Ltd* [1999] 1 BCLC 740. The exercise of considering good faith necessarily involves a subjective assessment of what has occurred. If there has been an intent to promote the interests of a particular person (especially someone who has a connection with the company or those responsible for running it) above those of other creditors then good faith is unlikely to be established: *Re Barton Manufacturing Co Ltd.* [1999] 1 BCLC 740. Even if good faith can be established a transaction will only be upheld pursuant to the provisions of IA 1986 s 238(5) if it can be shown that there was a benefit that the company could reasonably have expected to gain from the transaction which was, by definition (since IA 1986 s 238(5) would not otherwise need to be prayed in aid), effected at an undervalue. The test of whether there were 'reasonable grounds for believing ...' involves an objective consideration of what a reasonable director or board of directors would have thought and done: *Lord v Sinai Securities Ltd* [2004] BCC 986.

1.275

239 Preferences (England and Wales)

(1) This section applies as does section 238.

(2) Where the company has at a relevant time (defined in the next section) given a preference to any person, the office-holder may apply to the court for an order under this section.

(3) Subject as follows, the court shall, on such an application, make such order as it thinks fit for restoring the position to what it would have been if the company had not given that preference.

(4) For the purposes of this section and section 241, a company gives a preference to a person if—
    (a)   that person is one of the company's creditors or a surety or guarantor for any of the company's debts or other liabilities, and
    (b)   the company does anything or suffers anything to be done which (in either case) has the effect of putting that person into a position which, in the event of the company going into insolvent liquidation, will be better than the position he would have been in if that thing had not been done.

(5) The court shall not make an order under this section in respect of a preference given to any person unless the company which gave the preference was influenced in deciding to give it by a desire to produce in relation to that person the effect mentioned in subsection (4)(b).

> (6) A company which has given a preference to a person connected with the company (otherwise than by reason only of being its employee) at the time the preference was given is presumed, unless the contrary is shown, to have been influenced in deciding to give it by such a desire as is mentioned in subsection (5).
>
> (7) The fact that something has been done in pursuance of the order of a court does not, without more, prevent the doing or suffering of that thing from constituting the giving of a preference.

Notes

S 239

A liquidator needs sanction to bring a s 239 claim (IA 1986 Sch 4 para 3A) and the expenses incurred in making the claim will be an expense of the liquidation: IR 1986 r 4.218(1)(a)(i).

S 239(1)

The section applies (as does IA 1986 s 238) only where the company has gone into administration or liquidation, and proceedings can only be instituted by the administrator or liquidator as the case may be. As to the section's extra-territorial effect and the inability of the office holder to assign a claim under the section see the introductory note to IA 1986 s 238 above. In respect of the question whether a 12 year or only a 6 year limitation period applies (pursuant to the provisions, respectively, of the Limitation Act 1980 s 8, s 9) see *Re Priory Garage (Walthamstow) Ltd* [2001] BPIR 144, *Re Yates* [2005] BPIR 476 and *Re Nurkowski* [2006] BPIR 789. In summary where the applicant's primary relief is the unscrambling of the relevant transaction a 12 year period applies, whereas if the applicant's primary relief is for recovery of a money sum then a 6 year period applies. The cause of action accrues on the entry into administration or the liquidation.

The application to court is made by originating application or ordinary application to the registrar, rather than the Judge, in the first instance: see *Practice Note: the Hearing of Insolvency Proceedings* [2005] BPIR 688. The court's permission is required before such proceedings can be served out of the jurisdiction: see IR 1986 r 12.12(3). If an ordinary application is used instead of an originating application it is difficult to see how substantial injustice might be caused and it is likely that the court will not invalidate such proceedings: *Re Buildlead (No 2) Ltd* [2005] BCC 138; IR 1986 r 7.55.

S 239(2)

As in the case of transactions at an undervalue under IA 1986 s 238, preferences are only vulnerable to attack if they have been given at a 'relevant time', as defined in IA 1986 s 240. In *Re M C Bacon Ltd (No 1)* [1990] BCC 78, the court held that for the purposes of identifying the time when it is given a preference occurs not at the moment of completion of the transaction (in that case the execution of a debenture) but at the moment when the decision to benefit the other party (ie by giving the debenture) is made. It will often be difficult to ascertain precisely when a decision to make a payment (or confer any other benefit) was made, and it should be borne in mind that the implementation of a decision (or indeed an agreement) previously made can itself constitute a preference notwithstanding that the implementation might be said to be merely the honouring of an existing obligation. A straightforward, and common, example involves the situation where a number of creditors remain unpaid, including a director who has previously made a loan to the company: the loan from the director is then repaid immediately prior to liquidation, but all other liabilities remain outstanding. It may well be the case that the contractual payment date by which each of the creditors (including the director) was entitled to payment has long since passed. A preference claim in respect of the repayment to the director could not be successfully defended simply by means of a truthful assertion that the company had previously decided (at a time which would render the transaction unimpeachable if the matter was to be considered by reference to the moment of the decision) that it would repay its director at some particular date in the future, and that the repayment had indeed been made on that date. If a decision had previously been made to repay the director then it would be incumbent on the company to consider, as at the repayment date, whether it was proper for repayment to be made in the circumstances as they then were: see *Wills v Corfe Joinery Ltd* [1997] BCC 511, and *Re Brian Pierson Contractors Ltd* [1999] BCC 26. Where payment is made by a cheque to a creditor at a time that the company is solvent but it is insolvent at the time the cheque is cashed it might be argued that the payment was actually made at the time the cheque was delivered *Coltrane v Day* [2003] EWCA Civ 342) and therefore the payment was not made at a relevant time.

The 'relevant time' in relation to a preference is determined by reference to several matters: first, preferences are capable of being caught if they were entered into within prescribed fixed periods prior to the 'onset of insolvency' (IA 1986 s 240(3)) and these periods vary according to whether or not there is a connection between the company and the other party to the transaction; the prescribed periods applicable to this section are different from those applying in the context of a transaction at an undervalue under IA 1986 s 238. Alternatively, they may be caught if entered into between the making of an application for an administration order and the order or between the filing of a notice of intention to appoint an administrator and the appointment. In the case of a preference entered into after an administration application is made or the filing of a notice of intention to appoint an administrator (provided that an order is made on that application or an appointment is made pursuant to the notice) insolvency need not be proved: IA 1986 s 240(1)(c), (d), s 240(2). However, a preference within the prescribed fixed period (IA 1986 s 240) will not have been given at a 'relevant time' in the period prior to the making of an administration application or the filing of a notice of intention to appoint an administrator, unless the company was at the time of the preference, or became as a result of it, unable to pay its debts within the meaning of IA 1986 s 123 of the Act; see notes to IA 1986 s 240 below. Unlike a transaction at an undervalue in favour of a connected person (IA 1986 s 240(2)) there is no presumption of insolvency in the case of a preference.

S 239(3)

As with transactions at an undervalue under IA 1986 s 238, the court has a discretion, notwithstanding the use of the word 'shall', whether any order at all (and if so then what form of order) should be made. It does not automatically follow that an order must be made in favour of the office holder once the transaction has been established to be within the scope of the section: *Re Paramount Airways* [1992] BCC 416. However it is not relevant to the validity or otherwise of the preference that, after it has been given, the recipients assist the company by providing working capital: *Re Conegrade Ltd* [2003] BPIR 358. No order under s 239 may be made a time when the recipient of the 'tainted gift' is the subject of a restraint or confiscation order under POCA 2002 (see POCA 2002 s 427).

S 239(4)

The question whether there has been a preference is to be determined by an objective assessment of the position of the person receiving the payment or other benefit, as against other creditors and/or persons standing as sureties for the company's liabilities. A common case is the payment of the debt of an unsecured creditor who is thereby preferred over other creditors whose debts remain outstanding. Other examples are the discharge of a debt which has been guaranteed by a surety who is thus released from liability in circumstances where other creditors remain unpaid; the return of goods to a supplier in circumstances where title has already passed to the company; and the giving of security for an existing debt: see *Re Mistral Finance Ltd* [2001] BCC 27. As regards an omission on the part of the company (i.e. the situation where it 'suffers anything to be done ...') there is no direct authority on what constitutes a preference, but the provision would cover any failure to take steps which the company might reasonably be expected to take in the protection of its own interests, eg allowing a judgment to be entered in default in circumstances where there was plainly a defence to the claim. See also in this regard IA 1986 s 239(7) which provides that the mere fact that an act has been done or suffered in pursuance of a court order does not by itself mean that there cannot have been a preference.

It is the actual conferring of the benefit (as opposed to any agreement to confer it) which constitutes the preference; *Re Ledingham-Smith* [1993] BCLC 635; but as to the time when the preference is given see the notes to IA 1986 s 239(2) above and IA 1986 s 240 below. In reaching a conclusion on preference the court will look to the entire transaction entered into by the parties rather than isolated elements of the arrangement: *Damon v Widney plc* [2002] BPIR 465.

S 239(5)

No order will be made by the court in respect of a preference unless it is established that the company was influenced by a desire to improve the position of the creditor or surety (in the context of the company going into insolvent liquidation): *Doyle v Saville* [2002] BPIR 947. Where there has been a desire to prefer there must necessarily have been an intention to do so. The requirement under the old law (s 44 of the Bankruptcy Act 1914) was that the company had to be shown to have acted with the 'dominant intention' of giving a preference. It is now no longer necessary for the office holder to establish a dominant intention: it is sufficient that the decision was 'influenced' by the desire to prefer. The converse of this, however, is that it is no longer sufficient to establish an intention to prefer; there must be a desire to promote the interests of the recipient in the way described in the subsection: *Re M C Bacon (No 1)* [1990] BCC 78. In *Re Ledingham Smith* (above) it was said by Morritt J that 'desire' and 'influenced by' are 'ordinary English words which are not susceptible of further useful definition. It is a question of applying them to the facts of the case.' The application of pressure of one form or another by a particular creditor who has obtained payment or security may well provide a defence: see, for example, *Re Fairway Magazines Ltd* [1992] BCC 924, where it was said that the transaction will be upheld if the company has been motivated by 'proper commercial considerations' rather than a positive wish to improve the creditor's position.

S 239(6)

A connected person is a director or shadow director of the company, or an associate of such person, or an associate of the company: IA 1986 s 249, s 435; *Re Thirty Eight Building Ltd* [1999] BCC 260). The effect of the presumption of desire in respect of a 'connected person' is to transfer the evidential burden of proof onto the person seeking to uphold the transaction. From a practical point of view the shift of the burden is important and may be decisive: the difficulty that a connected person will have in satisfying the court that the preference to him was motivated by proper commercial considerations is self-evident. Although in a number of the reported cases attempts to rebut the presumption were unsuccessful: *Weisgard v Pilkington* [1995] BCC 1108; *Wills v Corfe Joinery Ltd* [1997] BCC 511; *Re Brian Pierson Contractors Ltd* [1999] BCC 26; *Katz v McNally* [1999] BCC 291; *Re Shapland Inc* [2000] BCC 106; *Re Conegrade Ltd* [2003] BPIR 358); it is apparent that the presumption can be rebutted and it is certainly not safe to rely on proving the desire wholly by reference to the presumption: *Re Beacon Leisure Ltd* [1991] BCC 213; *Re Fairway Magazines Ltd* (above).

S 239(7)

If a company allows a judgment or order to be obtained against it without taking steps that it could reasonably be expected to have taken in opposition, then not only is there the possibility that the omission involved in allowing the judgment or order to be made might be caught as a preference by IA 1986 s 239(4); but also the court could treat the satisfaction of the judgment or order (whether by a payment or by, for example, execution by the sheriff) as a preference in itself. The fact that the payment or execution was consequent upon the court's order may not afford a defence if the proceedings ought to have been defended in the first place.

1.276

240 'Relevant time' under ss 238, 239

(1) Subject to the next subsection, the time at which a company enters into a transaction at an undervalue or gives a preference is a relevant time if the transaction is entered into, or the preference given—

(a) in the case of a transaction at an undervalue or of a preference which is given to a person who is connected with the company (otherwise than by reason only of being its employee), at a time in the period of 2 years ending with the onset of insolvency (which expression is defined below),

(b) in the case of a preference which is not such a transaction and is not so given, at a time in the period of 6 months ending with the onset of insolvency,

(c) in either case, at a time between the making of an administration application in respect of the company and the making of an administration order on that application and

(d) in either case, at a time between the filing with the court of a copy of notice of intention to appoint an administrator under paragraph 14 or 22 of Schedule B1 and the making of an appointment under that paragraph.

(2) Where a company enters into a transaction at an undervalue or gives a preference at a time mentioned in subsection (1)(a) or (b), that time is not a relevant time for the purposes of section 238 or 239 unless the company—

(a) is at that time unable to pay its debts within the meaning of section 123 in Chapter VI of Part IV, or

(b) becomes unable to pay its debts within the meaning of that section in consequence of the transaction or preference;

but the requirements of this subsection are presumed to be satisfied, unless the contrary is shown, in relation to any transaction at an undervalue which is entered into by a company with a person who is connected with the company.

(3) For the purposes of subsection (1), the onset of insolvency is—

(a) in a case where section 238 or 239 applies by reason of an administrator of the company being appointed by administration order, the date on which the administration application is made,

(b) in a case where section 238 or 239 applies by reason of an administrator of a company being appointed under paragraph 14 or 22 of Schedule B1 following filing with the court of a copy of a notice of intention to appoint under that paragraph, the date on which the copy of the notice is filed

(c) in a case where section 238 or 239 applies by reason of an administrator of a company being appointed otherwise than as mentioned in paragraph (a) or (b), the date on which the appointment takes effect

(d) in a case where section 238 or 239 applies by reason of a company going into liquidation either following conversion of administration into winding up by virtue of Article 37 of the EC Regulation or at the time when the appointment of an administrator ceases to have effect, the date on which the company

> entered administration (or, if relevant, the date on which the application for the administration order was made or a copy of the notice of intention to appoint was filed), and
>
> (e) in a case where section 238 or 239 applies by reason of a company going into liquidation at any other time, the date of the commencement of the winding up.

Notes

S 240

This section contains detailed provision for determining what is 'a relevant time' in relation to both transactions at an undervalue (IA 1986 s 238) and preferences (IA 1986 s 239). In each case transactions are only vulnerable if they took place within specific periods and (excepting arrangements entered into between an administration application and the order or between the notice of intention to appoint and the appointment of an administrator s 240(1)(c) (d)) at a time (within the specific period) when the company was unable to pay its debts. The section was amended by EA 2002 subject to savings and transitional provisions to take account of the new out of court route enabling a company to enter administration (Enterprise Act 2002 (Commencement No 4 and Transitional Provisions and Savings) Order 2003, SI 2003/2093 Art 3.)

S 240(1)

The specified period applicable to a transaction at an undervalue is two years ending with the 'onset of insolvency': IA 1986 s 240(1)(a). The period between the making of an administration application and the order or between the notice of intention to appoint and the appointment of an administrator is a relevant time (IA 1986 s 240 (1)(c)) without the need to prove insolvency (IA 1986 s 240(2)).

The specific periods applicable to a preference are two years ending with the 'onset of insolvency' in the case of preference to a connected person: IA 1986 s 240(1)(a); and six months ending with the onset of insolvency in any other case: IA 1986 s 240(1)(b). Again, the period between the making of an administration application and the order or between the notice of intention to appoint and the appointment of an administrator is also a relevant time without the need to prove insolvency: IA 1986 s 240(1)(c).

As to the phrase 'onset of insolvency' see the notes to IA 1986 s 240(3) below. A connected person is a director or shadow director of the company, or an associate of such person, or an associate of the company: IA 1986 s 249. The definition of an associate is contained in IA 1986 s 435.

S 240(2)

The requirement of insolvency only applies in relation to a transaction or a preference entered into or given at the times stated in s 240(1)(a), (b); there is no requirement to prove insolvency in relation to a transaction or preference entered into or given at the times stated in s 240(1)(c), (d). A transaction (or preference) will not have been entered into at 'a relevant time' unless the company was either, at the time of the transaction, unable to pay its debts within the meaning of IA 1986 s 123, or it became unable to pay them as a consequence of the transaction; Under IA 1986 s 123 a company is deemed to be unable to pay its debts if (amongst other things) it is proved that debts are not being paid as they fall due, or that the value of its assets is less than the amount of its liabilities taking into account its contingent and prospective liabilities: see notes to IA 1986 s 123.

In relation to the question of whether a company can pay its debts as they fall due, the court is likely to be prepared to infer insolvency simply from the fact that the company has overdue invoices that it has not paid: *Re DKG Contractors Ltd* [1990] BCC 903. As to balance sheet insolvency, consideration was given to the proper approach as regards contingent and prospective liabilities in *Re a Company (No 6794 of 1983)* [1986] BCLC 261 (not a case which directly involved preferences or transactions at an undervalue). Further in *Byblos Bank SAL v Al-Khudhairy* (1986) 2 BCC 99, 549 it was indicated that (again not in the context of a claim under these sections) the court cannot weigh against contingent and prospective liabilities, prospective assets which the company hopes or expects to acquire in the future. In the case of a transaction at an undervalue (but not a preference) involving a connected person, there is a presumption that the company was unable to pay its debts at the time of the transaction.

S 240(3)

In the context of an administration under order, the 'onset of insolvency' is the date on which the administration application is made: IA 1986 s 240(3)(a); in the case of an administrator appointed out of court under IA 1986 Sch B1 para 14 (qualifying floating chargeholder) or Sch B1 para 22 (the company) it is the date of the filing of the notice of intention to appoint an administrator (IA 1986 s 240(3)(b). In other cases of appointment of an administrator (sch B1 paras 35,38) it is the date on which the appointment takes effect (IA 1986 s 240(3)(c)). Where a liquidation has occurred without following on an administration then the onset of insolvency means either the date of presentation of the winding up petition (IA 1986 s 129(2)) or, where the liquidation was voluntary, the date of the passing of the resolution for voluntary winding up: see IA 1986 s 86, s 129(1).

S 240 (3)(d)

Where a company goes into liquidation following a conversion from administration at the behest of a liquidator in the 'main proceedings' under EC Regulation on Insolvency Proceedings 2000 art 37, or a time when the appointment of an administrator ceases to have effect (eg IA 1986 Sch B1 para 83) the onset of insolvency is the date on which the company entered administration or if relevant the date on which the application for administration was made or a copy of the intention to appoint was filed as the case may be.

1.277

241 Orders under ss 238, 239

(1) Without prejudice to the generality of sections 238(3) and 239(3), an order under either of those sections with respect to a transaction or preference entered into or given by a company may (subject to the next subsection)—

   (a) require any property transferred as part of the transaction, or in connection with the giving of the preference, to be vested in the company,

   (b) require any property to be so vested if it represents in any person's hands the application either of the proceeds of sale of property so transferred or of money so transferred,

   (c) release or discharge (in whole or in part) any security given by the company,

   (d) require any person to pay, in respect of benefits received by him from the company, such sums to the office-holder as the court may direct,

   (e) provide for any surety or guarantor whose obligations to any person were released or discharged (in whole or in part) under the transaction, or by the giving of the preference, to be under such new or revived obligations to that person as the court thinks appropriate,

   (f) provide for security to be provided for the discharge of any obligation imposed by or arising under the order, for such an obligation to be charged on any property and for the security or charge to have the same priority as a security or charge released or discharged (in whole or in part) under the transaction or by the giving of the preference, and

(g) provide for the extent to which any person whose property is vested by the order in the company, or on whom obligations are imposed by the order, is to be able to prove in the winding up of the company for debts or other liabilities which arose from, or were released or discharged (in whole or in part) under or by, the transaction or the giving of the preference.

(2) An order under section 238 or 239 may affect the property of, or impose any obligation on, any person whether or not he is the person with whom the company in question entered into the transaction or (as the case may be) the person to whom the preference was given; but such an order—

(a) shall not prejudice any interest in property which was acquired from a person other than the company and was acquired [in good faith and for value], or prejudice any interest deriving from such an interest, and

(b) shall not require a person who received a benefit from the transaction or preference [in good faith and for value] to pay a sum to the office-holder, except where that person was a party to the transaction or the payment is to be in respect of a preference given to that person at a time when he was a creditor of the company.

(2A) Where a person has acquired an interest in property from a person other than the company in question, or has received a benefit from the transaction or preference, and at the time of that acquisition or receipt—

(a) he had notice of the relevant surrounding circumstances and of the relevant proceedings, or

(b) he was connected with, or was an associate of, either the company in question or the person with whom that company entered into the transaction or to whom that company gave the preference,

then, unless the contrary is shown, it shall be presumed for the purposes of paragraph (a) or (as the case may be) paragraph (b) of subsection (2) that the interest was acquired or the benefit was received otherwise than in good faith.

(3) For the purposes of subsection (2A)(a), the relevant surrounding circumstances are (as the case may require)—

(a) the fact that the company in question entered into the transaction at an undervalue; or

(b) the circumstances which amounted to the giving of the preference by the company in question;

and subsections (3A) to (3C) have effect to determine whether, for those purposes, a person has notice of the relevant proceedings.

(3A) In a case where section 238 or 239 applies by reason of a company's entering administration, a person has notice of the relevant proceedings if he has notice that—

(a) an administration application has been made,

(b) an administration order has been made,

(c) a copy of a notice of intention to appoint an administrator under paragraph 14 or 22 of Schedule B1 has been filed, or

(d) notice of the appointment of an administrator has been filed under paragraph 18 or 29 of that Schedule

(3B) In a case where section 238 or 239 applies by reason of the company in question going into liquidation when the appointment of an administrator of the company ceases to have effect, a person has notice of the relevant proceedings if he has notice that —

(a) an administration application has been made,

(b) an administration order has been made,

(c) a copy of a notice of intention to appoint an administrator under paragraph 14 or 22 of Schedule B1 has been filed,

(d) notice of the appointment of an administrator has been filed under paragraph 18 or 29 of that Schedule, or

(e) the company has gone into liquidation

(3C) In a case where section 238 or 239 applies by reason of the company in question going into liquidation at any other time, a person has notice of the relevant proceedings if he has notice—

(a) where the company goes into liquidation on the making of a winding-up order, of the fact that the petition on which the winding-up order is made has been presented or of the fact that the company has gone into liquidation;

(b) in any other case, of the fact that the company has gone into liquidation.

(4) The provisions of sections 238 to 241 apply without prejudice to the availability of any other remedy, even in relation to a transaction or preference which the company had no power to enter into or give.

Notes

S 241

The court has a wide discretion as to the orders it can make consequent upon a successful application by the office holder under IA 1986 s 238,239 including not making any order at all: *Re Paramount Airways Ltd* [1993] Ch 223, 239 per Nicholls VC. Careful consideration will often have to be given by the applicant to the appropriate consequential relief which is requested at the time of the issue of the application not least because of the limitation period which may differ according to whether the order requested is merely for a payment of a money sum or for the unscrambling of the arrangement under attack: *Re Priory Garage (Walthamstow) Ltd* [2001] BPIR 144 (see above). The court will not necessarily be deterred from making an order by the fact that a creditor cannot be restored to the position he was in immediately before the transaction concerned: *Lord v Sinai Securities Ltd* [2005] 1 BCLC 295. The section indicates the sort of orders the court may make but it does not contain an exhaustive list. More difficult questions as to the appropriate form of order are likely to arise where third parties have acquired interests or rights subsequent to the original transaction that has been impeached. Third parties who have acquired an interest bona fide and for value are, however, protected: see the note to IA 1986 s 238(2) below.

It may also be necessary to revive obligations of a third party which appeared to have been released (as, for example, where a surety had previously been released from his obligation as a consequence of a payment by the principal debtor, but the payment is then successfully attacked by the office holder under IA 1986 s 239). The court should (subject to the protection afforded to bona fide third parties) seek to restore the position to what it was before the transaction in question: *Chohan v Saggar* [1994] BCC 134 (which concerned the similar provisions of IA 1986 s 425). Where there has been a series of linked transactions the court will look at the overall effect in deciding upon the appropriate order: *Damon v Widney Plc* [2002] BPIR 465. There is no presumption under the section that the court will grant relief in respect of a transaction at an undervalue by requiring the recipient of the assets in question to pay monetary compensation rather than requiring the assets to be restored: *Walker v WA Personnel Ltd* [2002] BPIR 621.

S 241(2)–(3C)

Third parties are not afforded protection merely because the transaction at an undervalue was not made with them, or the preference was not given directly to them. It is clear from IA 1986 s 241(2) that in the case, for example, where a payment is made by the company of a debt in order that a guarantee given by a director of the company might be released, an order may be made directly against the director who had given the guarantee.

In the form originally enacted the section required that third parties (ie those who have acquired their interest from a person other than the company in question, or those who have indirectly benefited from a transaction to which they were not a party) must, if they were to be afforded protection in respect of any proprietary interest or benefit they had received, have acted in good faith, for value and 'without notice of the relevant circumstances'. But the requirement of absence of notice was subsequently dropped by the IA 1994. The change had no retrospective effect and cases where the relevant property was acquired or benefits received prior to 26 July 1994 will fall to be considered by reference to the original wording of the section. The position now is that third parties who have given value for the interest or benefit received by them are protected so long as they acted in good faith.

There is, however, a presumption that such a third party acted otherwise than in good faith if he had notice of both 'the relevant surrounding circumstances' (i.e. the fact of the transaction or preference: IA 1986 s 241(3)) and 'the relevant proceedings' (i.e. the fact of the liquidation or administration proceedings: IA 1986 s 241(3A)-3(C)). There is also a presumption against good faith if the third party was connected with or was an associate of either the company in question or of the person who transacted with or was preferred by the company. In either of those cases it will be for the third party to rebut the presumption by proving his bona fides.

It would seem, since these provisions are dealing with the notion of good faith, that 'notice' for these purposes is restricted to actual knowledge or knowledge that would have resulted had it not been for a wilful refusal to make obvious enquiry. But the point is not made expressly clear and it is perhaps arguable that constructive notice would be sufficient to trigger the statutory presumption that the benefit was received otherwise than in good faith. There is further practical difficulty with the notion of 'good faith': under IA 1986 s 241(2A) there is a presumption that a person who had notice of the 'relevant surrounding circumstances and of the relevant proceedings' is not acting in good faith; however it is only a presumption and therefore can be rebutted.

S 241(3A), (3B)

These provisions were amended by EA 2002 subject to savings and transitional provisions to take account of the new out of court route enabling a company to enter administration: (Enterprise Act 2002 (Commencement No 4 and Transitional Provisions and Savings) Order 2003, SI 2003/2093 Art 3.)

S 241(4)

Even in circumstances where the company had no power either to enter into the transaction at an undervalue or to give the preference (for instance where the doctrine of ultra vires might still apply or in the case of an illegal arrangement), that will not prevent the application of IA 1986 s 238–241 and accordingly the court's ability to make such order as may be appropriate will be unimpeded.

I.278

242 Gratuitous alienations (Scotland)

(1) Where this subsection applies and—
  (a) the winding up of a company has commenced, an alienation by the company is challengeable by—
    (i) any creditor who is a creditor by virtue of a debt incurred on or before the date of such commencement, or
    (ii) the liquidator;
  (b) [a company enters administration], an alienation by the company is challengeable by the administrator.

(2) Subsection (1) applies where—
  (a) by the alienation, whether before or after 1 April 1986 (the coming into force of section 75 of the Bankruptcy (Scotland) Act 1985), any part of the company's property is transferred or any claim or right of the company is discharged or renounced, and
  (b) the alienation takes place on a relevant day.

(3) For the purposes of subsection (2)(b), the day on which an alienation takes place is the day on which it becomes completely effectual; and in that subsection 'relevant day' means, if the alienation has the effect of favouring—
  (a) a person who is an associate (within the meaning of the Bankruptcy (Scotland) Act 1985) of the company, a day not earlier than 5 years before the date on which—
    (i) the winding up of the company commences, or
    (ii) as the case may be, [the company enters administration]; or
  (b) any other person, a day not earlier than 2 years before that date.

(4) On a challenge being brought under subsection (1), the court shall grant decree of reduction or for such restoration of property to the company's assets or other redress as may be appropriate; but the court shall not grant such a decree if the person seeking to uphold the alienation establishes—
  (a) that immediately, or at any other time, after the alienation the company's assets were greater than its liabilities, or
  (b) that the alienation was made for adequate consideration, or
  (c) that the alienation—
    (i) was a birthday, Christmas or other conventional gift, or
    (ii) was a gift made, for a charitable purpose, to a person who is not an associate of the company,
  which, having regard to all the circumstances, it was reasonable for the company to make;

Provided that this subsection is without prejudice to any right or interest acquired in good faith and for value from or through the transferee in the alienation.

(5) In subsection (4) above, 'charitable purpose' means any charitable, benevolent or philanthropic purpose, whether or not it is charitable within the meaning of any rule of law.

(6) For the purposes of the foregoing provisions of this section, an alienation in implementation of a prior obligation is deemed to be one for

302

which there was no consideration or no adequate consideration to the extent that the prior obligation was undertaken for no consideration or no adequate consideration.

(7) A liquidator and an administrator have the same right as a creditor has under any rule of law to challenge an alienation of a company made for no consideration or no adequate consideration.

(8) This section applies to Scotland only.

1.279

243 Unfair preferences (Scotland)

(1) Subject to subsection (2) below, subsection (4) below applies to a transaction entered into by a company, whether before or after 1 April 1986, which has the effect of creating a preference in favour of a creditor to the prejudice of the general body of creditors, being a preference created not earlier than 6 months before the commencement of the winding up of the company or [the company enters administration].

(2) Subsection (4) below does not apply to any of the following transactions—
- (a) a transaction in the ordinary course of trade or business;
- (b) a payment in cash for a debt which when it was paid had become payable, unless the transaction was collusive with the purpose of prejudicing the general body of creditors;
- (c) a transaction whereby the parties to it undertake reciprocal obligations (whether the performance by the parties of their respective obligations occurs at the same time or at different times) unless the transaction was collusive as aforesaid;
- (d) the granting of a mandate by a company authorising an arrestee to pay over the arrested funds or part thereof to the arrester where—
  - (i) there has been a decree for payment or a warrant for summary diligence, and
  - (ii) the decree or warrant has been preceded by an arrestment on the dependence of the action or followed by an arrestment in execution.

(3) For the purposes of subsection (1) above, the day on which a preference was created is the day on which the preference became completely effectual.

(4) A transaction to which this subsection applies is challengeable by—
- (a) in the case of a winding up—
  - (i) any creditor who is a creditor by virtue of a debt incurred on or before the date of commencement of the winding up, or
  - (ii) the liquidator, and
- (b) [where the company has entered administration], the administrator.

(5) On a challenge being brought under subsection (4) above, the court, if satisfied that the transaction challenged is a transaction to which this section applies, shall grant decree of reduction or for such restoration of property to the company's assets or other redress as may be appropriate:

Provided that this subsection is without prejudice to any right or interest acquired in good faith and for value from or through the creditor in whose favour the preference was created.

(6) A liquidator and an administrator have the same right as a creditor has under any rule of law to challenge a preference created by a debtor.

(7) This section applies to Scotland only.

1.280

244 Extortionate credit transactions

(1) This section applies as does section 238, and where the company is, or has been, a party to a transaction for, or involving, the provision of credit to the company.

(2) The court may, on the application of the office-holder, make an order with respect to the transaction if the transaction is or was extortionate and was entered into in the period of 3 years ending with the day on which the company entered administration or went into liquidation.

(3) For the purposes of this section a transaction is extortionate if, having regard to the risk accepted by the person providing the credit—
  (a) the terms of it are or were such as to require grossly exorbitant payments to be made (whether unconditionally or in certain contingencies) in respect of the provision of the credit, or
  (b) it otherwise grossly contravened ordinary principles of fair dealing;
and it shall be presumed, unless the contrary is proved, that a transaction with respect to which an application is made under this section is or, as the case may be, was extortionate.

(4) An order under this section with respect to any transaction may contain such one or more of the following as the court thinks fit, that is to say—
  (a) provision setting aside the whole or part of any obligation created by the transaction,
  (b) provision otherwise varying the terms of the transaction or varying the terms on which any security for the purposes of the transaction is held,
  (c) provision requiring any person who is or was a party to the transaction to pay to the office-holder any sums paid to that person, by virtue of the transaction, by the company,
  (d) provision requiring any person to surrender to the office-holder any property held by him as security for the purposes of the transaction,
  (e) provision directing accounts to be taken between any persons.

(5) The powers conferred by this section are exercisable in relation to any transaction concurrently with any powers exercisable in relation to that transaction as a transaction at an undervalue or under section 242 (gratuitous alienations in Scotland).

Notes

S 244(1), (2)

These provisions apply (like IA 1986 s 238 and 239) where the company has entered administration or the company has gone into liquidation. Transactions vulnerable to attack (at the instance of the office holder) are those made within a period of 3 years prior to the date the company entered administration or the date on which the company 'went into liquidation' (IA 1986 s 247(2)) and which involved the provision of credit to the company. The concept of 'credit' is a wide one and will encompass not only loans but also any agreement under which the time for payment for goods or services is extended beyond delivery or provision of the service (cf the definition of 'credit' in Consumer Credit Act 1974 s 9).

Only if the transaction was 'extortionate' can it be set aside. There is no requirement either that the transaction must have been entered into at a time when the company was insolvent, or that it should have been causative of the company's subsequent financial difficulties (cf transactions at an undervalue and preferences under IA 1986 s 238 and 239). Even if the transaction was extortionate the court has a complete discretion as to whether any, and if so what, order should be made. If the company has itself behaved improperly in procuring the grant of credit then that, for example, would be relevant to the exercise of the court's discretion.

S 244(2)

This provision was amended by EA 2002 subject to savings and transitional provisions to take account of the new out of court route enabling a company to enter administration: Enterprise Act 2002 (Commencement No 4 and Transitional Provisions and Savings) Order 2003, SI 2003/2093 Art 3.

S 244(3)

This provides a statutory presumption that any transaction which is the subject of an application under the section was extortionate. Accordingly it will always be for the provider of the credit to establish that the transaction was not extortionate. The definition of 'extortionate' is similar to that in Consumer Credit Act 1974 s 138, and decisions under that Act are likely – although there are differences in the two statutory schemes – to be relevant to applications by an office holder under the present section. The relative bargaining power of the creditor and debtor will always be a relevant consideration, as will the degree of risk that the lender is assuming by lending to the company. The cases decided under the provisions of the CCA indicate that very high rates of interest (the equivalent of 48% per annum in *Ketley Ltd v Scott* [1981] ICR 241) may be upheld so long as the lender has acted properly and the borrower has made a free and informed decision. Other reported decisions under the CCA are *Wills v Wood* (1984) 128 Sol Jo 222; *Coldunell v Gallon* [1986] QB 1184; *Davies v Directloans Ltd* [1986] 1 WLR 823; and *Nash v Paragon Finance Plc* [2002] 1 WLR 685.

It should be noted that a transaction to which the company is a party could not ordinarily be set aside under the CCA, which concerns agreements where the debtor is an individual (although an agreement where credit is given to two or more persons only one of whom is an individual does come within the scope of that Act).

S 244(4)

The list of possible forms of order set out is not exclusive. Even if the transaction was extortionate the Court has a discretion to make no order.

I.281

245 Avoidance of certain floating charges

(1) This section applies as does section 238, but applies to Scotland as well as to England and Wales.

(2) Subject as follows, a floating charge on the company's undertaking or property created at a relevant time is invalid except to the extent of the aggregate of—

   (a)   the value of so much of the consideration for the creation of the charge as consists of money paid, or goods or services supplied, to the company at the same time as, or after, the creation of the charge,

   (b)   the value of so much of that consideration as consists of the discharge or reduction, at the same time as, or after the creation of the charge, of any debt of the company, and

   (c)   the amount of such interest (if any) as is payable on the amount falling within paragraph (a) or (b) in pursuance of any agreement under which the money was so paid, the goods or services were so supplied or the debt was so discharged or reduced.

(3) Subject to the next subsection, the time at which a floating charge is created by a company is a relevant time for the purposes of this section if the charge is created—

   (a)   in the case of a charge which is created in favour of a person who is connected with the company, at a time in the period of 2 years ending with the onset of insolvency,

   (b)   in the case of a charge which is created in favour of any other person, at a time in the period of 12 months ending with the onset of insolvency..

   (c)   in either case, at a time between the making of an administration application in respect of the company and the making of an administration order on that application, or

   (d)   in either case, at a time between the filing with the court of a copy of a notice of intention to appoint an administrator under paragraph 14 or 22 of Schedule B1 and the making of an appointment under that paragraph

(4) Where a company creates a floating charge at a time mentioned in subsection (3)(b) and the person in favour of whom the charge is created is not connected with the company, that time is not a relevant time for the purposes of this section unless the company—

   (a)   is at that time unable to pay its debts within the meaning of section 123 in Chapter VI of Part IV, or

   (b)   becomes unable to pay its debts within the meaning of that section in consequence of the transaction under which the charge is created.

(5) For the purposes of subsection (3), the onset of insolvency is—

   (a)   in a case where this section applies by reason of an administrator of a company being appointed by administration order, the date on which the administration application is made,

   (b)   in a case where this section applies by reason of an administrator of a company being appointed under paragraph 14 or 22 of

Schedule B1 following filing with the court of a copy of notice of intention to appoint under that paragraph, the date on which the copy of the notice is filed,

(c) in a case where this section applies by reason of an administrator of a company being appointed otherwise than as mentioned in paragraph (a) or (b), the date on which the appointment takes effect, and

(d) in a case where this section applies by reason of a company going into liquidation, the date of the commencement of the winding up.

(6) For the purposes of subsection (2)(a) the value of any goods or services supplied by way of consideration for a floating charge is the amount in money which at the time they were supplied could reasonably have been expected to be obtained for supplying the goods or services in the ordinary course of business and on the same terms (apart from the consideration) as those on which they were supplied to the company.

Notes

S 245

The position prior to the coming into force of the IA 1986 was that floating charges which had been created within 1 year of the company's winding up were valid only to the extent of any cash advance made to the company at, or after, the date of creation of the charge and in consideration of its creation. The present section replaces those provisions (which appeared in CA 1985 s 617, and before that CA 1948 s 322). It applies only to charges created after IA 1986 came into force on 29 December 1986. The aim, as with the old law, is to prevent a creditor obtaining security for a pre-existing debt at a time when the company has (or potentially has) financial difficulties: it is an aspect of the more general principle that unsecured creditors should be treated equally in the event of insolvency. Under the section a floating charge in favour of a 'connected' person can now be challenged by the office holder if it was given within a period of two years prior to the administration or liquidation. Where the recipient of the charge is a person unconnected with the company then the period is one year. Moreover, in respect of a charge given in favour of a 'connected' person it is irrelevant that the company may have been solvent at the date of the charge. This is again to be contrasted with the position where the recipient of the charge is unconnected, in which case the solvency or otherwise of the company must be considered. The other major change from the earlier law is that a charge will be upheld to the extent that goods or services (in addition to money payments) were provided at the same time as, or after, the creation of the charge and in consideration for it. The provisions of the section were considered (in the context of a charge granted to an alleged 'associate') in *Unidare plc v Cohen & Power* [2005] BPIR 1472.

S 245(1)

The section applies to a company in administration as well as to a liquidation.

S 245(2)

The expression 'floating charge' appears in the definition section at IA 1986 s 251 but the only assistance given there is that the term means a charge 'which, as created, was a floating charge' (i.e. the critical moment is the date of creation of the charge (*Re Beam Tube Products Ltd* [2006] EWHC 486 (Ch), [2006] BCC 615) and it matters not that a charge which was a floating charge at that time might subsequently have become a fixed charge. The term 'floating charge' is not itself the subject of any statutory definition, but such charge has been said to be';

'... ambulatory and shifting in its nature, hovering over and so to speak floating with the property which it is intended to affect until some event occurs or some act is done which causes it to settle and fasten on the subject of the charge within its reach and grasp.'

(*Illingworth v Houldsworth* [1904] AC 355, 358 per Lord Macnaghten)

A floating charge can be created over future assets, but it remains essential (if the categorisation of floating charge is properly to be made) that the company should remain free, at least to some extent, to deal with the assets subject to the charge: see, for example, *Re Spectrum Plus Ltd* [2005] BCC 694 and *Smith (Administrator of Cosslett (Contractors) Ltd) v Bridgend County Borough Council* [2001] UKHL 58, [2002] 1 AC 336. The badge of a fixed charge is that the chargeholder not only has the power to control the charged asset, but also chargeholder actively 'polices' the charged asset: *Re Spectrum Plus Ltd* [2005] BCC 694.

It is only the payment of money or the supply of goods or services (and not, it appears, transfers of real property or choses in action) which can validate a floating charge that has been created at a 'relevant time'. The proper approach to the question whether the considera-tion was given '*at the same time as, or after, the creation of the charge*' (this being the requirement imposed in IA 1986 s 245(2)(a)(b)) was considered in *Re Shoe Lace Ltd, Power v Sharp Investments Ltd* [1994] 1 BCLC 111. In that case a rigorous approach was taken and even money clearly given in consideration of the charge would not be secured by the charge if that money was advanced to the company prior to the creation of the charge '*unless the interval is so short that it can be regarded as de minimis – for example a coffee-break*' per Sir Christopher Slade p 122; see also *Re Matthew Ellis Ltd* [1933] Ch 458.

S 245(3)–(5)

These provisions were amended by EA 2002 subject to savings and transitional provisions to take account of the new out of court route enabling a company to enter administration (Enterprise Act 2002 (Commencement No 4 and Transitional Provisions and Savings) Order 2003, SI 2003/2093 art 3.)

Where the charge holder is connected with the company (see IA 1986 s 249 and 435 below) the floating charge will be vulnerable (and value will have to be shown to have been provided if it is to be upheld) if it was given within the period of 2 years ending with the 'onset of insolvency'. It does not however have to be shown that the company was insolvent at the time of the creation of the charge: IA 1986 s 245(3)(a). The onset of insolvency is determined by reference to s 245(5).

Where the charge holder is not connected with the company then the floating charge will not have been given at a 'relevant time' unless, first, it was created in the period of 12 months ending with the onset of insolvency, and secondly, it was created at a time (within that 12 month period) when the company was either unable to pay its debts (within the meaning of IA 1986 s 123) or became unable to pay its debts in consequence of the transaction under which the charge was created: IA 1986 s 245(3)(b), (c), (4). It appears that it will be for the charge holder to establish solvency rather than for the liquidator or administrator to establish insolvency but this is not made expressly clear (as it was by the wording of the former provision: CA 1985 s 617).

S 245(6)

Where consideration is given in the form of goods or services their value is to be assessed by reference to the amount in money which could reasonably have been expected to be paid for those goods or services in the ordinary course of business and on the same terms (save for the consideration given) as those on which they were in fact supplied at the time when they were supplied. The test is objective and any value that might have been attributed by the parties to the transaction is irrelevant to the calculation of the value.

1.282

246 Unenforceability of liens on books, etc

(1) This section applies in the case of a company where—
  (a)   the company enters administration, or
  (b)   the company goes into liquidation, or
  (c)   a provisional liquidator is appointed;
and 'the office-holder' means the administrator, the liquidator or the provisional liquidator, as the case may be.

(2) Subject as follows, a lien or other right to retain possession of any of the books, papers or other records of the company is unenforceable to the extent that its enforcement would deny possession of any books, papers or other records to the office-holder.

(3) This does not apply to a lien on documents which give a title to property and are held as such.

Notes

S 246

The task of a liquidator or administrator could be made difficult or even impossible if he was unable to get hold of the company's books and records in consequence of a lien being claimed (most likely by the company's professional advisers such as solicitors or accountants). For this reason it is provided that such a lien is unenforceable to the extent that its enforcement would deny possession to the office holder.

S 246(1)

The section applies only in the context of administration, liquidation and provisional liquidation. For a discussion of the scope of the section (and its impact on the moratorium IA 1986 Sch B1 para 43(2), pursuant to which securities are generally unenforceable in an administration without the leave of the court) see *Re Paramount Airways Ltd* [1990] BCC 130, 150–151. IA 1986 section 246 was amended by EA 2002 subject to savings and transitional provisions to take account of the new out of court route enabling a company to enter administration (Enterprise Act 2002 (Commencement No 4 and Transitional Provisions and Savings) Order 2003, SI 2003/2093 art 3.)

S 246(3)

The section does not apply to documents which give title to property. Thus lenders who have taken security in the form of a deposit of title deeds cannot be deprived (by reliance on this section) of that security. The words 'as such' refer to the circumstances in which the relevant documents are held – ie they make clear that the documents must, if they are to be outside the scope of the section, be held in circumstances such as to give rise to a lien: *Re SEIL Trade Finance Ltd* [1992] BCC 538. In *Re Carter Commercial Developments Ltd*, 31 December 2002, LTL 18/3/2002 (Ch D), the company's former solicitors held title deeds to a property owned by the company as security for their unpaid fees and the proviso contained in IA 1986 s 246(3) applied. The company was then placed in administration, the viability of which was compromised by the solicitors' assertion of their rights. The court held that there was no reason for refusing the solicitors' application for permission to enforce that lien pursuant to the provisions of the IA 1986 s 11(3) (see now IA 1986 Sch B1 para 43(2)).

Part VII
Interpretation for First Group of Parts

1.283

247 'Insolvency' and 'go into liquidation'

(1) In this Group of Parts, except in so far as the context otherwise requires, 'insolvency', in relation to a company, includes the approval of a voluntary arrangement under Part I, or the appointment of an administrator or an administrative receiver or the appointment of an administrative receiver.

(2) For the purposes of any provision in this Group of Parts, a company goes into liquidation if it passes a resolution for voluntary winding up or an order for its winding up is made by the court at a time when it has not already gone into liquidation by passing such a resolution.

(3) The reference to a resolution for voluntary winding up in subsection (2) includes a reference to a resolution which is deemed to occur by virtue of –

   (a)   paragraph 83(6)(b) of Schedule B1, or

   (b)   an order made following conversion of administration or a voluntary arrangement into winding up by virtue of Article 37 of the EC Regulation

---

Notes

S 247(1)

'This Group of Parts' refers to the First Group of Parts, namely Parts I to VII which contain corporate insolvency provisions. The section was amended by EA 2002 subject to savings and transitional provisions to take account of the new out of court route enabling a company to enter administration (Enterprise Act 2002 (Commencement No 4 and Transitional Provisions and Savings) Order 2003, SI 2003/2093 art 3.)

S 247(2)

For a resolution for voluntary winding up see IA 1986 s 84–86; for a winding up order see IA 1986 s 117, 125, 129. The date of commencement of a liquidation (IA 1986 s 86 (voluntary), IA 1986 s 129 (compulsory)) may be different to the date the company 'goes into liquidation' within IA 1986 s 247(2): see *Re Walter L Jacob & Co Ltd* [1993] BCC 512; *Mettoy Pension Trustees Ltd v Evans* [1991] 2 All ER 513.

S 247(3)(a)

Under the new administration procedure a company may exit from administration into a creditors' voluntary liquidation where the administrator thinks inter alia that there will be a distribution to unsecured creditors (IA 1986 Sch B1 para 83(1)(b)). The procedure includes the filing of a notice with the court and sending it to creditors; and on registration of the notice with the Registrar of Companies the company is wound up as if a resolution had been passed: IA 1986 Sch B1 para 83(6)(b).

S 247(3)(b)

Under the new administration procedure Art 37 of the EC Regulation enables a liquidator in 'main proceedings' to request that proceedings previously opened in another member state be converted into a liquidation if this is proved to be in the interests of the creditors in the main proceedings. The EC Regulation is separately annotated.

1.284

248 'Secured creditor', etc

In this Group of Parts, except in so far as the context otherwise requires—

   (a) 'secured creditor', in relation to a company, means a creditor of the company who holds in respect of his debt a security over property of the company, and 'unsecured creditor' is to be read accordingly; and

   (b) 'security' means—

      (i) in relation to England and Wales, any mortgage, charge, lien or other security, and

     (ii) in relation to Scotland, any security (whether heritable or moveable), any floating charge and any right of lien or preference and any right of retention (other than a right of compensation or set off).

Notes

S 248

'This Group of Parts' refers to the First Group of Parts, namely Parts I to VII which contain corporate insolvency provisions. The definition of *'creditor'* and *'secured creditor'* for the purpose of bankruptcy is contained in IA 1986 s 383.

S 248(b)(i)

The right of a landlord to re-enter for non payment of rent is not a security: *Re Lomax Leisure Ltd* [2000] BCC 352. A statutory right to detain an aircraft under the Civil Aviation Act 1982 s 88 for non payment of charges was held to be a 'lien or other security': *Bristol Airport plc v Powdrill* [1990] Ch 744; however a right of set off under English law does not appear to fall within that phrase. See also the notes to IA 1986 Sch B1 para 43(2). A contractual lien is clearly a security within the meaning of this provision but it is not registrable under CA 1985 s 395 *Trident International Ltd v Barlow* [2000] BCC 602 (warehouseman's lien).

1.285

249 'Connected' with a company

For the purposes of any provision in this Group of Parts, a person is connected with a company if—

   (a) he is a director or shadow director of the company or an associate of such a director or shadow director, or

   (b) he is an associate of the company;

and 'associate' has the meaning given by section 435 in Part XVIII of this Act.

_____

Notes

S 249(a)

A 'shadow director' is defined as 'a person in accordance with whose directions or instructions the directors of the company are accustomed to act': IA 1986 s 251 and CA 1985 s 741(2). The clear purpose of the definition is to enable certain provisions to apply not only to those who have been formally appointed as officers of the company but also to those who effectively run the company but without such formal appointment. Whether a particular person is caught will turn on the facts of the case. In general, however, a single direction or instruction is unlikely to be sufficient; some pattern of the board following directions or instructions will generally be required: *Re Hydrodam (Corby) Ltd* [1994] 180; *Kuwait Asia Bank v National Mutual Life Nominees Ltd* [1990] 3 All ER 404. See also *Secretary of State for Trade and Industry v Deverell* [2001] Ch 340 where it was observed that it was not necessary to find that the giver/receiver of 'information' understands/accepts that it is a direction/instruction for a shadow directorship to be established. For a recent and full discussion of the concept of 'de facto' and 'shadow directors' and the authorities, see *Ultraframe (UK) Ltd v Fielding* [2005] EWHC 1638 (Ch) at paras 1254 to 1278, [2005] All ER (D) 397 (Jul).

S 249(b)

The definition of 'associate' in IA 1986 s 435 is relatively wide and, amongst others, includes a person's spouse, relative, spouse's relative and relative's spouse (section 435(2) with 'relative' being further defined in IA 1986 s 435(8)), a person's business partner, employer and employee.

_____

1.286

250 'Member' of a company

For the purposes of any provision in this Group of Parts, a person who is not a member of a company but to whom shares in the company have been transferred, or transmitted by operation of law, is to be regarded as a member of the company, and references to a member or members are to be read accordingly.

_____

Notes

S 250

'.. *this Group of Parts..*' refers to the First Group of Parts, namely Parts I to VII which contain corporate insolvency provisions. Under CA 1985 s 22 'member' is defined as a person who has agreed to become a member of a company and whose name is entered in its register of members. The purpose of IA 1986, s 250 is to cover not just those who satisfy the CA 1985 definition but also certain others such as (a) a person to whom shares have been transferred but where registration has not yet taken place and (b) a personal representative of a deceased member on whom shares have devolved by operation of law. Such persons may potentially have liability as contributories.

_____

I.287

251 Expressions used generally

In this Group of Parts, except in so far as the context otherwise requires—

'administrative receiver' means—

    (a)   an administrative receiver as defined by section 29(2) in Chapter I of Part III, or

    (b)   a receiver appointed under section 51 in Chapter II of that Part in a case where the whole (or substantially the whole) of the company's property is attached by the floating charge;

'business day' means any day other than a Saturday, a Sunday, Christmas Day, Good Friday or a day which is a bank holiday in any part of Great Britain;

'chattel leasing agreement' means an agreement for the bailment or, in Scotland, the hiring of goods which is capable of subsisting for more than 3 months;

'contributory' has the meaning given by section 79;

'director' includes any person occupying the position of director, by whatever name called;

'floating charge' means a charge which, as created, was a floating charge and includes a floating charge within section 462 of the Companies Act (Scottish floating charges);

'office copy', in relation to Scotland, means a copy certified by the clerk of court;

'the official rate', in relation to interest, means the rate payable under section 189(4);

'prescribed' means prescribed by the rules;

'receiver', in the expression 'receiver or manager', does not include a receiver appointed under section 51 in Chapter II of Part III;

'retention of title agreement' means an agreement for the sale of goods to a company, being an agreement—

    (a)   which does not constitute a charge on the goods, but

    (b)   under which, if the seller is not paid and the company is wound up, the seller will have priority over all other creditors of the company as respects the goods or any property representing the goods;

'the rules' means rules under section 411 in Part XV; and

'shadow director', in relation to a company, means a person in accordance with whose directions or instructions the directors of the company are accustomed to act (but so that a person is not deemed a shadow director by reason only that the directors act on advice given by him in a professional capacity);

and any expression for whose interpretation provision is made by Part XXVI of the Companies Act, other than an expression defined above in this section, is to be construed in accordance with that provision.

Notes

S 251

'… this Group of Parts' refers to the First Group of Parts, namely Parts I to VII which contain corporate insolvency provisions; therefore the definitions are not of general application.

'floating charge': In deciding whether a charge was fixed or floating the court has to carry out a two stage process. First, it has to construe the charge not by considering whether the parties had intended to create a fixed or floating charge but by considering what rights and obligations the parties has intended to create. Second, having considered such rights and obligations, the court then has to categorise the charge in question according to those rights and obligations; accordingly the approach in *In Re Bullas Trading Ltd* (1994) 1 BCLC 449 was wrong: *Agnew v Commissioner of Inland Revenue* [2001] 2 AC 710; *Re Spectrum Plus Ltd* [2005] 2 AC 680; *Re Beam Tube Products Ltd* [2006] EWHC 486, [2006] BCC 615.

'shadow director' : see note to IA 1986 s 249.

The Second Group of Parts
Insolvency of Individuals; Bankruptcy

Part VIII
Individual Voluntary Arrangements

Moratorium for insolvent debtor

1.288

252 Interim order of court

(1) In the circumstances specified below, the court may in the case of a debtor (being an individual) make an interim order under this section.

(2) An interim order has the effect that, during the period for which it is in force—

    (a)   no bankruptcy petition relating to the debtor may be presented or proceeded with,

    (aa)   no landlord or other person to whom rent is payable may exercise any right of forfeiture by peaceable re-entry in relation to premises let to the debtor in respect of a failure by the debtor to comply with any term or condition of his tenancy of such premises, except with the leave of the court and

    (b)   no other proceedings, and no execution or other legal process, may be commenced or continued [and no distress may be levied] against the debtor or his property except with the leave of the court.

Notes

S 252(1) The interim order

Until the introduction of the new IA 1986 s 256A by the Insolvency Act 2000, obtaining an interim order was the essential first step in any IVA. Without an interim order having been made, any subsequently approved arrangement would not have binding effect as an IVA under IA 1986: see *Fletcher v Vooght* [2000] BPIR 435 (although the arrangement might have contractual force amongst those who agreed to it, and it was left open whether or not it might be binding generally under principles of estoppel by convention).

A debtor may now proceed without obtaining the protection of an interim order under s 256A. However, it will still be important to ensure that the procedures prerequisite to the summoning of a creditors' meeting as stated in IA 1986 Part VIII are followed in order to ensure that the arrangement, if approved, is binding on all creditors as a valid IVA.

S 252(2) The effect of the interim order

During the period when it is in force, the interim order provides protection to the debtor and his assets, while he puts together an IVA proposal for consideration by his creditors:

- from bankruptcy proceedings
- from all other proceedings and forms of execution or other legal process, and from forfeiture by peaceable re-entry and distraint, without the leave of the court.

As originally enacted, the interim order did not prevent a landlord from exercising his right of forfeiture against his debtor tenant by peaceable re-entry: *Re a Debtor (No 13A-IO-1995)* [1995] 1 WLR 1127. Nor did it prevent a landlord from distraining on his debtor tenant's goods for unpaid rent: *McMullen & Sons Ltd v Cerrone* [1994] BCC 25. The effect of both these decisions has now been reversed by amendments to IA 1986 s 252(2) introduced by IA 2000 (in force from 1 January 2003). The prohibition introduced against the levying of distress is not in terms limited to distress for rent at common law, so may presumably also prohibit statutory rights of distress eg for non-payment of rates, non-payment of taxes, and non-payment of magistrates court fines. A charging order is not complete until the making of a final charging order. A judgment creditor with an existing interim charging order against a debtor who obtains an interim order must therefore obtain the leave of the court to make the order final: *Clarke v Coutts & Co* [2002] BPIR 916.

The wording 'no other proceedings, and no execution or other legal process' in s 252(2)(b) mirrors that under the former IA 1986 s 10(1)(c) and 11(3)(d) (limitations which applied on petitioning for and upon the making of an administration order in respect of a company under the pre EA 2002 regime), and decisions under that section may assist in its interpretation: see in particular:

- *Bristol Airport v Powdrill* [1990] Ch 744 ('other proceedings' means legal or quasi legal proceedings);
- *Re Olympia and York Canary Wharf Ltd* [1993] BCLC 453 ('proceedings' and 'legal process' together contemplate all steps in legal proceedings from initiating process to their final termination in the process of execution or other means of enforcement of a judgment, but do not include the taking of non-judicial steps such as the serving of a notice);
- In *re Rhondda Waste Disposal Ltd* [2001] Ch 57, CA ('other proceedings' includes criminal proceedings); but cf. *R v Barnet Magistrates Court ex parte Philippou* [1997] BPIR 134 (where, in rejecting an application for judicial review, the Divisional Court held that the debt created by a compensation order in criminal proceedings was akin to a fine the enforcement of which was not barred by an interim order).

Where proceedings or execution etc may be commenced or continued with the leave of the court, such leave may be obtained retrospectively, and may be obtained by the court in which the proceedings are being pursued, and not just the court in which the interim order has been made: see *Clarke v Coutts & Co* [2002] BPIR 916.

Leave will not generally be granted where that would enable an unsecured creditor to steal a march on other creditors and upset the statutory scheme for pari passu distribution, for instance, by commencing or continuing execution: see *Roberts Petroleum Ltd v Bernard Kenny Ltd* [1983] 2 AC 192. Contrast the position of a secured creditor, who will require leave to enforce its security by legal process (such as by a claim for possession or order for sale), but who may more readily be granted such leave, since no subsequently approved IVA can (except by consent) affect its security.

1.289

253 Application for interim order

(1) Application to the court for an interim order may be made where the debtor intends to make a proposal under this Part, that is, a proposal to his creditors for a composition in satisfaction of his debts or a scheme of arrangement of his affairs (from here on referred to, in either case, as a 'voluntary arrangement').

(2) The proposal must provide for some person ('the nominee') to act in relation to the voluntary arrangement either as trustee or otherwise for the purpose of supervising its implementation [and the nominee must be a person who is qualified to act as an insolvency practitioner, or author-ised to act as nominee, in relation to the voluntary arrangement].

(3) Subject as follows, the application may be made—

  (a)   if the debtor is an undischarged bankrupt, by the debtor, the trustee of his estate, or the official receiver, and

  (b)   in any other case, by the debtor.

(4) An application shall not be made under subsection (3)(a) unless the debtor has given notice of the proposal to the official receiver and, if there is one, the trustee of his estate.

(5) An application shall not be made while a bankruptcy petition pre-sented by the debtor is pending, if the court has, under section 273 below, appointed an insolvency practitioner to inquire into the debtor's affairs and report.

Notes

S 253(1) Definition of voluntary arrangement

For the meaning of the terms 'composition in satisfaction of his debts' and 'scheme of arrangement of his affairs', see the commentary to IA 1986 s 1(1) (the equivalent CVA provision). Where a release of the debts owed by a bankrupt has occurred due to an automatic discharge of the bankruptcy under IA 1986 s 281 there is nothing for the debtor to release and a proposal cannot be approved following the automatic discharge *Re Ravichandran* [2004] BPIR 814, *Demarco v Perkins and Bulley Davey* [2005] BPIR 1118 (on appeal [2006] BPIR 645) unless debts preserved by IA 1986 s 281 are concerned. For the meaning of 'creditors': see IA 1986 s 383(1) and IA s 382(3) which defines 'debt' and 'liability' as including 'debts or liabilities which are present or future, certain or contingent, or in respect of an amount which is fixed or liquidated or is capable of being ascertained by fixed rules or as a matter of opinion'.

S 253(2) The nominee

For discussion on the extension to the classes of person who may acts as nominee, and on the circumstances in which the nominee in supervising the arrangement acts 'as trustee', see commentary to IA 1986 s 1(2).

S 253(3) Who may apply for an interim order

An application for an interim order may be made in any case where it is intended to put an IVA proposal to creditors. The application may be made by the debtor himself, and, if he is an undischarged bankrupt, by his trustee in bankruptcy or the official receiver. However, under the new IA 1986 s 256A it is no longer necessary to apply for an interim order as a prerequisite to making an IVA proposal, and, in the majority of cases where the debtor is an undischarged bankrupt, there may well be no need to do so.

S 253(5) Restriction where IA 1986 s 273 applies

IA 1986 s 273 and s 274 make provision, in the case of a debtor who has presented a petition for his own bankruptcy and where the other conditions set out in s 273(1) are met, for an insolvency practitioner to be appointed by the court to report on the willingness of the debtor making an IVA proposal in lieu of bankruptcy, and on whether a meeting should be summoned to consider such a proposal.

For the procedure which applies to the making of the application for an interim order, and the court in which the application should be brought, see IR r 5.7 to 5.10 and the commentary thereto; for the rules which govern the contents and action upon the IVA proposal itself, see IR r 5.2–5.6 and commentary.

1.290

254 Effect of application

(1) At any time when an application under section 253 for an interim order is pending,

   (a)   no landlord or other person to whom rent is payable may exercise any right of forfeiture by peaceable re-entry in relation to premises let to the debtor in respect of a failure by the debtor to comply with any term or condition of his tenancy of such premises, except with the leave of the court, and

   (b)   the court may [forbid the levying of any distress on the debtor's property or its subsequent sale, or both, and] stay any action, execution or other legal process against the property or person of the debtor.

(2) Any court in which proceedings are pending against an individual may, on proof that an application under that section has been made in respect of that individual, either stay the proceedings or allow them to continue on such terms as it thinks fit.

Notes

S 254(1)

Where there is an imminent threat of enforcement action by a creditor, a debtor may apply for an order staying or preventing such action even before an interim order is made. IA 2000 extended the scope of this protection to introduce a new s 254(1)(a) – imposing an automatic prohibition on forfeiting a lease by peaceable re-entry without the leave of the court – and by introducing a new right within s 254(1)(b) for a debtor to apply for an order forbidding the levying of distress on his property. Presumably, the reason for distinguishing peaceable re-entry (to which an automatic prohibition applies) from distress and other enforcement procedures is that, unlike other procedures, peaceable re-entry is a once and for all process, rather than one which continues over a period of time. Further, it is a procedure and one (in the case of non-payment of rent) for which there is no requirement of prior notice.

S 254(2)

An application to stay proceedings must be made in the court in which those proceedings are pending, rather than the court in which the interim order application has been made. This contrasts with applications for leave under s 252(1) which may be made either in the court in which proceedings are pending or in the court in which the interim order has been made. For the meaning and scope of the expressions 'distress' and 'execution or other legal process' see further the commentary to s 252 above.

1.291

255 Cases in which interim order can be made

(1) The court shall not make an interim order on an application under section 253 unless it is satisfied—

    (a)   that the debtor intends to make [a proposal under this Part];

    (b)   that on the day of the making of the application the debtor was an undischarged bankrupt or was able to petition for his own bankruptcy;

    (c)   that no previous application has been made by the debtor for an interim order in the period of 12 months ending with that day; and

    (d)   that the nominee under the debtor's proposal is willing to act in relation to the proposal.

(2) The court may make an order if it thinks that it would be appropriate to do so for the purpose of facilitating the consideration and implementation of the debtor's proposal.

(3) Where the debtor is an undischarged bankrupt, the interim order may contain provision as to the conduct of the bankruptcy, and the administration of the bankrupt's estate, during the period for which the order is in force.

(4) Subject as follows, the provision contained in an interim order by virtue of subsection (3) may include provision staying proceedings in the bankruptcy or modifying any provision in this Group of Parts, and any provision of the rules in their application to the debtor's bankruptcy.

(5) An interim order shall not, in relation to a bankrupt, make provision relaxing or removing any of the requirements of provisions in this Group of Parts, or of the rules, unless the court is satisfied that that provision is unlikely to result in any significant diminution in, or in the value of, the debtor's estate for the purposes of the bankruptcy.

(6) Subject to the following provisions of this Part, and interim order made on an application under section 253 ceases to have effect at the end of the period of 14 days beginning with the day after the making of the order.

Notes

S 255

The scheme of this provision in effect provides that:

- the debtor must satisfy the pre-conditions set out in subsection (1); if he does not, the court has no power to make an interim order;
- the court then has a discretion under subsection (2) whether or not to make an order; the guiding principle is whether it would be 'appropriate for the purpose of facilitating the consideration and implementation of the debtor's proposal'.

S 255(1)

The mandatory pre-conditions:

(a) *intention to make proposal:* see IR r 5.7(2) which requires the debtor to exhibit to his affidavit in support of the interim order application a copy of the proposal which he has given to his nominee.

(b) *undischarged bankrupt:* this appears to rule out an application by a discharged bankrupt for an IVA in respect of his discharged bankruptcy debts (and see notes to IA 1986 s 253(1)); this may be a significant limitation e g in a case where a trustee in bankruptcy is threatening to realise a discharged bankrupt's interest in a property for the benefit of his bankruptcy creditors some time after discharge, taking advantage of the property's increase in value; but see now s 283A inserted by EA 2002 s 261(1)

(c) *able to petition for his own bankruptcy:* see IA 1986 s 265(1) (domicile and residence requirements) and s 272(1) (condition that debtor is unable to pay his debts)

(d) *no previous application in 12 months preceding:* this condition is designed to prevent abuse by a debtor obtaining repeated interim orders; the prohibition cannot be circumvented by an application for review under IA 1986 s 375: *Hurst v Bennett (No 2)* [2002] BPIR 102; even if the 12 month period is passed, the court may still take into account when exercising its discretion whether to grant a further interim order under s (2), the fact that a debtor has obtained previous interim orders for proposals which have come to nothing

(e) *nominee willing to act:* see IR 1986 r 5.7(1)(e)

S 255(2) the court's discretion

In exercising its discretion under s 255(2), the court should take into account whether the proposal is 'serious and viable': see *Shah v Cooper* [2003] BPIR 1018 and *Cooper v Fearnley* [1997] BPIR 20; *Hook v Jewson* [1997] 1 BCLC 664 (where Scott V-C emphasised that judges should be careful not to allow interim order applications to become a means of postponing a bankruptcy order where there is no apparent likelihood of benefit to creditors from such postponement). The court may also take into account a failure on the part of the debtor to be open and honest in his proposals where this can be clearly demonstrated (In *Re a Debtor (No 2389 of 1989)* [1991] Ch 326) and the fact (if it can be clearly demonstrated) that the proposal with or without modifications is bound to be rejected because of the opposition of one or more creditors with in excess of 25% of votes: see *Re a Debtor (No 83 of 1988)* [1990] 1 WLR 708; *Re a debtor (No 140 of 1995)* [1996] 2 BCLC 429. The court may properly refuse to make an interim order where the debtor has by his conduct shown that an IVA is unlikely to proceed in good faith: *Hurst v Kroll Buchler Phillips Ltd* [2003] BPIR 872; or the proposal of the debtor is not viable or bona fide, rather it s an *'essay in make believe' Davidson v Stanley* [2005] BPIR 279 para 42 per Blackburne J.

However, it must be borne in mind that whether or not the proposal provides a satisfactory alternative for creditors to the debtor's bankruptcy is ultimately a decision for the creditors at their meeting. The court should not intervene at the threshold stage of the interim order application to prevent consideration of the proposal by creditors merely because the antici-pated dividend under the proposal is small (*Knowles v Coutts & Co* [1998] BPIR 96) or offers a return less than that which might be achieved in bankruptcy (*Re a debtor (No 140 IO of 1995)* [1996] 2 BCLC 429 per Knox J at p. 435e). For a useful summary of the authorities, see *Re O'Sullivan* [2001] BPIR 534, pp 537–8. In that case, the court upheld the registrar's refusal to make an interim order on grounds that the nominee's fee was plainly and grossly excessive, and the nominee had been given the opportunity but had failed to provide justification for the fee.

S 255(3)–(5)

Where the debtor is an undischarged bankrupt, the court on making the interim order may stay proceedings in the bankruptcy or make other orders modifying the operation of IR 1986 as they apply to the bankruptcy. But the court can only make such orders where it is satisfied that it is unlikely to result in any significant diminution of the debtor's estate in the bankruptcy. This is an important safeguard against abuse.

S 255(6)

The interim order in the first instance operates for only 14 days within which period the nominee is required to submit his report to the court on the proposal under IA s 256(1). The order may however be extended to provide more time for the submission of such report under the provisions of IA s 256(3A) and (4). It may also be discharged prior to the submission of the report on the application of the nominee under IA s 256(6).

Where there is no bankruptcy petition pending, or bankruptcy order in place, and where the papers are in order and the nominee consents, the court may make 14 day interim order (or, in an appropriate case, a 'concertina' order – see notes to IA 1986 s 256) without requiring the attendance of any party: see Practice Direction – Insolvency Proceedings paragraph 16.1 (Vol 2, Civil Procedure, Section 3E).

1.292

256 Nominee's report on debtor's proposal

(1) Where an interim order has been made on an application under section 253, the nominee shall, before the order ceases to have effect, submit a report to the court stating—

    (a)   whether, in his opinion, the voluntary arrangement which the debtor is proposing has a reasonable prospect of being approved and implemented,

    (aa)   whether, in his opinion, a meeting of the debtor's creditors should be summoned to consider the debtor's proposal, and

    (b)   if in his opinion such a meeting should be summoned, the date on which, and time and place at which, he proposes the meeting should be held.

(2) For the purpose of enabling the nominee to prepare his report the debtor shall submit to the nominee—

    (a)   a document setting out the terms of the voluntary arrangement which the debtor is proposing, and

    (b)   a statement of his affairs containing—

        (i)   such particulars of his creditors and of his debts and other liabilities and of his assets as may be prescribed, and

        (ii)   such other information as may be prescribed.

(3) The court may—

    (a)   on an application made by the debtor in a case where the nominee has failed to submit the report required by this section or has died, or

    (b)   on an application made by the debtor or the nominee in a case where it is impracticable or inappropriate for the nominee to continue to act as such,

direct that the nominee shall be replaced as such by another person qualified to act as an insolvency practitioner, or authorised to act as nominee, in relation to the voluntary arrangement.

(3A) The court may, on an application made by the debtor in a case where the nominee has failed to submit the report required by this section, direct that the interim order shall continue, or (if it has ceased to have effect) be renewed, for such further period as the court may specify in the direction.

(4) The court may, on the application of the nominee, extend the period for which the interim order has effect so as to enable the nominee to have more time to prepare his report.

(5) If the court is satisfied on receiving the nominee's report that a meeting of the debtor's creditors should be summoned to consider the debtor's proposal, the court shall direct that the period for which the interim order has effect shall be extended, for such further period as it may specify in the direction, for the purpose of enabling the debtor's proposal to be considered by his creditors in accordance with the following provisions of this Part.

(6) The court may discharge the interim order if it is satisfied, on the application of the nominee—

(a) that the debtor has failed to comply with his obligations under subsection (2), or

(b) that for any other reason it would be inappropriate for a meeting of the debtor's creditors to be summoned to consider the debtor's proposal.

Notes

S 256

Timing apart, these provisions, together with IR 1986 r 5.2 to 5.6 and 5.11 mirror the investigation and reporting obligations imposed on the nominee under a non-moratorium CVA under IA 1986 s 2(2), (3) and IR r 1.2 to 1.7.

The stipulated procedure is as follows:

- the debtor is responsible for the preparation of the proposal in accordance with IR 1986 r 5.3;

- the debtor must, under IR 1986 r 5.4, give the intended nominee written notice of his proposal, accompanied by a copy of the proposal; the intended nominee must endorse the notice with date of receipt where he agrees to act;

- within 7 days after delivery of his proposal (which period can be extended by the nominee), the debtor must deliver to the nominee a statement of his affairs under IR 1986 r 5.5;

- by IA 1986 s 256(1) and IR 1986 r 5.7(1) the nominee must prepare a report for submission to the court to be delivered not less than two days before the interim order made under IA 1986 s 255 (and with such extensions as the court may grant under s 256(3) or (4)) ceases to have effect; in preparing that report, he may require the debtor to provide further information of the matters set out in IR 1986 r 5.6;

- in reporting to the court, the nominee must consider both whether the proposal has reasonable prospects of being approved and implemented and whether a creditors' meeting should be summoned, if he concludes both questions positively, he should so report to the court (annexing his comments on the proposal) and propose a time, date and place for the meetings (IA 1986 s 256(1) and IR 1986 r 5.11(3));

- if he concludes that the proposal should not proceed further, he should report to the court his reasons for reaching a negative conclusion (IR 1986 r 5.11(3).

As with CVA proposals, the nominee himself will in practice very often have been consulted by the debtor prior to preparation of the proposal, and will himself have formulated the proposal on the debtor's behalf in the light of the debtor's financial circumstances as disclosed to him. He will accordingly often already have considered both the viability of the proposal and its chances of being approved before the proposal has been formulated or the interim order obtained. This practice is recognised in Practice Direction – Insolvency Proceedings paragraph 16.1(3) (Vol 2, Civil Procedure, Section 3E) under which the nominee is permitted to file his report on the debtor's proposal at the same time and accompanying the initial application for the interim order. In such cases, if the papers are in order and the nominee so reports, the court may make a 'concertina' order, under which the court proceeds immediately to summon a creditors' meeting and to both make and extend the interim order to a date 7 weeks after the date of the proposed meeting.

The nominee's obligations / liabilities in investigating and reporting on the debtor's proposal are considered in detail in the commentary to IA 1986 s 2 above, to which reference should be made.

S 256(3) Replacement of the nominee

The court may replace the nominee on the application of the debtor where he has failed to submit his report within the time specified under IR 1986 r 5.11(1). Under IA 1986 s 256(3)(b), introduced by IA 2000, the court's powers to replace the nominee are extended to apply, on the application either of nominee or debtor, in any case where it is impractical or inappropriate for the debtor to continue to act. Under IR 1986 r 5.12, where the debtor makes such application, he must give at least seven days notice to the nominee, and must file the consent of the replacement nominee to act as such. In the meantime, where it is necessary to do so, an application can be made under IA 1986 s 256(3A) to extend the interim order.

S 256(3A), (4) Pre-report extensions of the interim order

An application may be made to extend the interim order where the nominee is unable to submit his report within the specified 12 day period under IR 1986 r 5.11(1) after the making of the initial interim order either by the debtor under IA 1986 s 256(3A) (whether or not the debtor also seeks the removal of the defaulting nominee) or by the nominee himself under IA 1986 s 256(4). The court may grant such extension as it sees fit, and may, where appropriate, grant more than one such extension.

The subsections do not lay down the criteria to be applied in determining whether or not to grant such extensions once the basic conditions under either subsection are satisfied (ie nominee has failed to submit report / nominee requires more time). The initial time period for reporting is short, in particular having regard to the requirement under IA 1986 s 256(1)(a) to reach an opinion on whether the proposal has reasonable prospects of being approved and implemented and the standards laid down in *Greystoke v Hamilton- Smith* [1996] 2 BCLC 429, [1997] BPIR 24. Accordingly where more time is with good reason required such extensions should be granted. But the interim order is an interference with creditors' rights of action against the debtor, and so should not be extended without good cause, or for an excessive period: see In *re a Debtor (No 83 of 1988)* [1990] 1 WLR 708.

S 256(5) Court's consideration of nominee's report

If satisfied that a creditors' meeting should be summoned, the court must extend the interim order for a further period to enable the debtor's proposal to be considered at such meeting; see also IA 1986 s 257(1). Where the court is not so satisfied no valid meeting under IA 1986 s 257 can be held to approve the proposal *Vlieland-Boddy v Dexter Ltd* [2004] BPIR 235.

In practice, IA 1986 s 256 operates as follows:
- in the case of debtor against whom there is no pending bankruptcy petition and who is not an undischarged bankrupt, the court may generally be satisfied that a meeting should be summoned where the nominee has given a positive report under IA 1986 s 256(1)(a), (aa) and (b), and has complied with IR 1986 r 5.11(2) and (3); apart from the debtor and nominee, no other person will have standing to be heard and to object (see IR 1986 r 5.13), and, in such circumstances, the court may make an order extending the interim order to a date 7 weeks after the date of the proposed meeting without any attendance: see Practice Direction – Insolvency Proceedings (Vol 2 Civil Procedure Section 3E) para 16.1(2);

- in the case of an undischarged bankrupt, or debtor against whom a bankruptcy petition is pending, the official receiver trustee or (as the case may be) the petitioning creditor will be entitled to attend and be heard at a hearing at which the court considers the report; where the nominee's report is positive, the onus will fall upon any such person attending who objects to show why a meeting should not be summoned, and the interim order extended; the objector would have to show that, despite the nominee's report, the proposal with or without modifications is bound to be rejected because of the opposition of one or more creditors with in excess of 25% of votes (*Re a Debtor (No 83 of 1988)* [1990] 1 WLR 708), or that the debtor had misrepresented or failed to disclose material information relating to his financial position or other material factors, such that required further investigation by the nominee before the proposal proceeded further.

S 256(6) Discharge of the interim order

Only the nominee has standing under this sub-section to apply for the discharge of the interim order. But the subsection provides an important bulwark against the abuse by a debtor of the protection afforded by an interim order. 'Any other reason' whereby it would be inappropriate for a meeting of creditors to be summoned may include circumstances where the debtor refuses to co-operate with the nominee's reasonable inquiries into his affairs (other than by failing to comply with his IA 1986 s 256(2) obligations), or where the debtor is dissipating assets or otherwise abusing his protection.

Procedure where no interim order made

1.293

256A Debtor's proposal and nominee's report

(1) This section applies where a debtor (being an individual)—
   (a) intends to make a proposal under this Part (but an interim order has not been made in relation to the proposal and no application for such an order is pending), and
   (b) if he is an undischarged bankrupt, has given notice of the proposal to the official receiver and, if there is one, the trustee of his estate,

unless a bankruptcy petition presented by the debtor is pending and the court has, under section 273, appointed an insolvency practitioner to inquire into the debtor's affairs and report.

(2) For the purpose of enabling the nominee to prepare a report to the court, the debtor shall submit to the nominee—
   (a) a document setting out the terms of the voluntary arrangement which the debtor is proposing, and
   (b) a statement of his affairs containing—
       (i) such particulars of his creditors and of his debts and other liabilities and of his assets as may be prescribed, and
       (ii) such other information as may be prescribed.

(3) If the nominee is of the opinion that the debtor is an undischarged bankrupt, or is able to petition for his own bankruptcy, the nominee shall, within 14 days (or such longer period as the court may allow) after receiving the document and statement mentioned in subsection (2), submit a report to the court stating—

(a) whether, in his opinion, the voluntary arrangement which the debtor is proposing has a reasonable prospect of being approved and implemented,

(b) whether, in his opinion, a meeting of the debtor's creditors should be summoned to consider the debtor's proposal, and

(c) if in his opinion such a meeting should be summoned, the date on which, and time and place at which, he proposes the meeting should be held.

(4) The court may—

(a) on an application made by the debtor in a case where the nominee has failed to submit the report required by this section or has died, or

(b) on an application made by the debtor or the nominee in a case where it is impracticable or inappropriate for the nominee to continue to act as such,

direct that the nominee shall be replaced as such by another person qualified to act as an insolvency practitioner, or authorised to act as nominee, in relation to the voluntary arrangement.

(5) The court may, on an application made by the nominee, extend the period within which the nominee is to submit his report.

Notes

S 256A

This section was introduced by the IA 2000 to allow a debtor to make IVA proposals without first obtaining the protection of an interim order: see the introductory note to IA 1986 Part VIII. With the exception of a debtor in respect of whom an order under IA 1986 s 273 has been made, any debtor may proceed under this new provision but it may in particular be used by the following (who either do not need, or are ineligible for, the protection of an interim order):

- an undischarged bankrupt, who does not require the protection of an interim order;
- a debtor with only few creditors who are not threatening enforcement;
- a debtor who is precluded from proceeding with the benefit of an interim order under IA 1986 s 255(1)(c) because he has already been granted an interim order in the past 12 months.

The procedure set out under the section is supplemented by IR 1986 r 5.2 to 5.6 (which apply equally to proposals preceded by an interim order) and by IR 1986 r 5.14 to 5.16 (which apply specifically to proposals without interim orders). It differs from the procedure that applies where an interim order is obtained only in the following respects:

- no application is made to the court by the debtor at the outset: the debtor initiates the process by submitting to the nominee a document setting out the terms of his proposed voluntary arrangement, followed by his statement of affairs containing the information prescribed in IR 1986 r 5.5;
- the nominee then has 14 days from receipt of these two documents to prepare and deliver to the court his report on the proposal; however, the matters required to be covered by the report are identical to those required under IA 1986 s 256(1) in respect of proposals preceded by an interim order;
- the court does not consider the nominee's report unless an application is made either by the debtor or by a creditor in relation to the proposal: see IR 1986 r 5.14(1); instead, where the nominee reports that a meeting should be summoned, the nominee proceeds under IA 1986 s 257 to summon that meeting without any judicial act or intervention.

S 256A(3) The nominee's report on the debtor's proposal

The nominee's obligation to report on the debtor's proposal is stated to be conditional upon him being of the opinion that the debtor is either an undischarged bankrupt, or is able to petition for his own bankruptcy (under IA 1986 s 272). Nowhere else in IA 1986 s 256A is this requirement stated as a pre-condition of a debtor's entitlement to proceed with IVA proposals where he does not first obtain an interim order, although it is one of the four pre-conditions which must be satisfied for the grant of an interim order under IA 1986 s 255.

See the commentary to IA 1986 s 2 for detailed consideration of the nominee's obligations and potential liabilities in investigating and reporting on the debtor's proposal

S 256(A), (4), (5) Replacement of nominee; extension of time for filing of report

See r 5.16 for the rules which apply to applications to replace the nominee under IA 1986 s 256(4). See also the commentary to IA 1986 s 2(4). Where a nominee is unable to file his report within the 14 day period stipulated, he may himself apply for time to be extended under IA 1986 s 256(5).

Creditors' meeting

1.294

257 Summoning of creditors' meeting

(1) Where it has been reported to the court under section 256 or 256A that a meeting of the debtor's creditors should be summoned, the nominee (or his replacement under section 256(3) or 256A(4)) shall, unless the court otherwise directs, summon that meeting for the time, date and place proposed in his report.

(2) The persons to be summoned to the meeting are every creditor of the debtor of whose claim and address the person summoning the meeting is aware.

(3) For this purpose the creditors of a debtor who is an undischarged bankrupt include—
  (a)   every person who is a creditor of the bankrupt in respect of a bankruptcy debt, and
  (b)   every person who would be such a creditor if the bankruptcy had commenced on the day on which notice of the meeting is given.

Notes

S 257(1) Summoning of meetings

Once the nominee has filed his report with the court stating that a meeting of the debtor's creditors should be summoned to consider the proposal, he is then required to summon it. Note that the nominee cannot summon any such meeting without having first reported to the court that one should be summoned, and any meeting summoned in such circumstances, and any IVA approved by such meeting, would be a nullity. *Fletcher v Vooght* [2000] BPIR 405. IA 1986 s 257(1) provides for the meeting to be summoned *unless the court otherwise directs*. The involvement of the court will differ depending on whether the debtor has obtained an interim order or not:–
• where the debtor has obtained an interim order, the court is required to be satisfied that a meeting should be summoned before extending the interim order under IA 1986 s 256(5): see the commentary to that subsection for details of how the court approaches this task;

- where the debtor has proceeded under IA 1986 s 256A without an interim order, under IR 1986 r 5.14 (1) the court will not consider the report in any judicial capacity at all at this stage unless an application is made either by the debtor himself (eg to replace the nominee under IA 1986 s 256(3)(b)), or by a creditor or his trustee or the official receiver for the purpose of seeking a direction that a meeting should not be held despite the positive report of the nominee to that effect. Neither IA 1986 nor IR 1986 set out the circumstances in which a court might direct that a meeting should not be held despite the positive report of the nominee, nor the classes of person who have locus standi to apply to the court for such a direction. It may be argued that since IR 1986 r 5.7(4) and r 5.13(1) prescribe the classes of person entitled to receive notice of and appear at a hearing for an interim order (namely, the debtor and the nominee, and any petitioning creditor or trustee and the official receiver), the court should be slow to entertain an application for a direction under IA 1986 s 257(1) in a non-interim order case by anyone from the debtor's wider class of creditors; see further the commentary to IA 1986 s 3(1).

For the rules relating to the summoning of the meeting of creditors, see IR 1986 r 5.17 and 5.18. If a meeting is summoned otherwise than in accordance with IA 1986 s 257 such a meeting cannot validly approve a proposal *Vlieland-Boddy v Dexter Ltd* [2004] BPIR 235.

S 257(3) Creditors to whom notice of the meeting should be given in proposals by undischarged bankrupt

An undischarged bankrupt may submit a proposal for an IVA in relation to both his bankruptcy debts and debts which have arisen after the date of the bankruptcy order. This subsection makes clear that a proposal by undischarged bankrupt may be made in respect of both classes of debt, and provides the mechanism by which post-bankruptcy creditors will be bound by such IVA. However, see IR 1986 r 5.21(2)(c) and the note thereto.

Consideration and implementation of debtor's proposal

1.295

258 Decisions of creditors' meeting

(1) A creditors' meeting summoned under section 257 shall decide whether to approve the proposed voluntary arrangement.

(2) The meeting may approve the proposed voluntary arrangement with modifications, but shall not do so unless the debtor consents to each modification.

(3) The modifications subject to which the proposed voluntary arrangement may be approved may include one conferring the functions proposed to be conferred on the nominee on another person qualified to act as an insolvency practitioner [or authorised to act as nominee, in relation to the voluntary arrangement].

But they shall not include any modification by virtue of which the proposal ceases to be a proposal under this Part.

(4) The meeting shall not approve any proposal or modification which affects the right of a secured creditor of the debtor to enforce his security, except with the concurrence of the creditor concerned.

(5) Subject as follows, the meeting shall not approve any proposal or modification under which—

    (a)   any preferential debt of the debtor is to be paid otherwise than in priority to such of his debts as are not preferential debts, or

> (b)   a preferential creditor of the debtor is to be paid an amount in respect of a preferential debt that bears to that debt a smaller proportion than is borne to another preferential debt by the amount that is to be paid in respect of that other debt.
>
> However, the meeting may approve such a proposal or modification with the concurrence of the preferential creditor concerned.
>
> (6) Subject as above, the meeting shall be conducted in accordance with the rules.
>
> (7) In this section 'preferential debt' has the meaning given by section 386 in Part XII; and 'preferential creditor' is to be construed accordingly.

Notes

S 258

The creditor's meeting summoned to consider the debtor's IVA proposal forms the keystone of the IVA procedure. When approved by the requisite majority at the meeting, the IVA becomes binding on every creditor. But where the meeting is not convened in accordance with the statutory scheme, any proposal therein approved may not take effect at all as a binding arrangement: see *Fletcher v Vooght* [2000] BPIR 405; *Re N (a debtor)* [2002] BPIR 1024. For the rules relating to the conduct of the creditors' meetings, see IR 1986 r 5.17 to 5.24.

S 258(2), (3) Modifications to the proposal

At any time before the nominee files his report with the court, a debtor's IVA proposal may be modified by the debtor himself with the written agreement of the nominee: see IR 1986 r 5.3(3). Otherwise, under these subsections, the proposal may be and frequently is modified at the creditors' meeting itself at the behest of one or more creditors and subject to the vote of the requisite majority. However, any such modification can only be effected with the consent of the debtor. Where an IVA is approved subject to a modification which the debtor has not agreed to, the approval is of no effect: see *Reid v Hamblin* [2001] BPIR 929, *Re Plummer* [2004] BPIR 767.

No modification may be made by which the proposal ceases to be a composition or a scheme of arrangement within IA 1986 s 253 (see the commentary to that section) or which affects the rights of secured and preferential creditors without their consent (see the commentary below).

Where modifications are proposed at the meeting which make substantial alterations to the proposed IVA, and of which creditors voting by proxy will have had no notice, the safest course will be for the chairman to adjourn the creditors' meeting in accordance with the procedure in IR 1986 r 5.24 to enable proxy voters to consider the proposed modifications before proceeding further: see, in a different context, *Somji v Cadbury Schweppes plc* [2001] 1 WLR 615 para 25.

For detailed commentary on the power to modify a proposal *after* the creditors' meeting has taken place and has been concluded, see the notes to IA 1986 s 4(2), the equivalent provision which applies in respect of CVA proposals.

S 258(4), (5) Limitations on approval

(i) Secured creditors

No IVA can affect the right of a secured creditor to enforce his security except where it gives its consent *Joseph Manuel Rey v FNCB Ltd* [2006] EWHC 1386 (Ch). A similar restriction applies in respect of CVAs under IA 1986 s 4(3). For detailed commentary on the question (a) who is a secured creditor, (b) circumstances in which a secured creditor may be found (unwittingly) to have consented to a provision affecting his rights, and (c) the position of secured creditors more generally, see the notes to IA 1986 s 4(3). See also the notes to IR 1986 r 1.19(3) (the equivalent CVA rule to IR 1986 r 5.23(3)) on the voting rights of secured creditors in respect of any unsecured shortfall.

(ii) Preferential creditors

Likewise, an IVA cannot affect the priority rights of preferential creditors, or their rights of equal treatment between themselves. Note that the preferential status of Crown creditors is abolished under s 251 EA 2002, leaving employee's remuneration, occupational pension scheme contributions and ECSC levies (all as defined and limited by IA 1986 Sch 6) as the only remaining preferential debts.

1.296

259 Report of decisions to court

(1) After the conclusion in accordance with the rules of the meeting summoned under section 257, the chairman of the meeting shall report the result of it to the court and, immediately after so reporting, shall give notice of the result of the meeting to such persons as may be prescribed.

(2) If the report is that the meeting has declined (with or without modifications) to approve the debtor's proposal, the court may discharge any interim order which is in force in relation to the debtor.

Notes

S 259(1)

The chairman of the meeting is required to report the outcome of the meeting to the court and give notice of the outcome to creditors. See IR 1986 r 5.27 for the prescribed contents of the report, and the persons to whom notice should be given. Time limits for applications to challenge the outcome of the meeting under IA 1986 s 262 run from the date the report is filed with the court.

Although there is no express provision in IA 1986 or IR 1986 for the convening of a hearing to consider the chairman's report, such a hearing is contemplated under IA 1986 s 259 (2) and it is the practice of the bankruptcy court to convene such a hearing as part of the order extending the interim order to enable to creditors' meeting to take place. Under the Practice Direction – Insolvency Proceedings (Vol 2, Civil Procedure, Section 3E) para 16.1(4), final orders made at such hearings can be made without the need for attendance of any party.

Where the proposed IVA has been approved, any interim order which has been made is continued under IA 1986 s 260(4) for a period of four weeks from the date the chairman's report is filed with the court, unless the court otherwise directs on any application challenging the decision of the meeting under IA 1986 s 262.

S 259(2)

Where the proposals have been rejected, under IA 1986 s 259(2) the court may in its discretion discharge any interim order with immediate effect, or, it seems, may allow the interim order to run its course to give the debtor a short breathing space in which to bring any application under IA 1986 s 262 to challenge the decision of the meeting, and, ancillary to that, to seek an extension of the interim order for the duration of such challenge under IA 1986 s 262(6): see *Kent Carpets v Symes* [1995] 2 BCLC 651 at 669i – 670c.

1.297

260 Effect of approval

(1) This section has effect where the meeting summoned under section 257 approves the proposed voluntary arrangement (with or without modifications).

(2) The approved arrangement—
  (a) takes effect as if made by the debtor at the meeting, and
  (b) binds every person who in accordance with the rules—
    (i) was entitled to vote at the meeting (whether or not he was present or represented at it), or
    (ii) would have been so entitled if he had had notice of it,
  as if he were a party to the arrangement.

(2A) If—
  (a) when the arrangement ceases to have effect any amount payable under the arrangement to a person bound by virtue of subsection (2)(b)(ii) has not been paid, and
  (b) the arrangement did not come to an end prematurely,
the debtor shall at that time become liable to pay to that person the amount payable under the arrangement.

(3) The Deeds of Arrangement Act 1914 does not apply to the approved voluntary arrangement.

(4) Any interim order in force in relation to the debtor immediately before the end of the period of 28 days beginning with the day on which the report with respect to the creditors' meeting was made to the court under section 259 ceases to have effect at the end of that period.

This subsection applies except to such extent as the court may direct for the purposes of any application under section 262 below.

(5) Where proceedings on a bankruptcy petition have been stayed by an interim order which ceases to have effect under subsection (4), the petition is deemed, unless the court otherwise orders, to have been dismissed.

Notes

S 260(2) The effect of the approval of the arrangement

Once approved by the requisite majority of creditors voting at the meeting under IA 1986 s 258, the IVA is binding on all creditors falling within its ambit whether or not such creditors voted in its favour; it is also binding on the debtor and time ceases to run for limitation purposes *Tanner v Everitt* [2004] BPIR 1026. As explained by the Court of Appeal in *Johnson v Davies* [1999] Ch 117 at pp. 131–2, this section (and in particular subsection 2 (b)) does not purport to impose the IVA directly on a dissenting creditor. Rather he is bound by the arrangement as a result of a statutory hypothesis which requires him to be treated as if he had consented. This has important consequences on the question of the effect of a voluntary arrangement on third parties liable to a creditor in respect of the same debt as the debtor entering into the arrangement. For a discussion of this topic, see the notes to IA 1986 s 5 (the equivalent CVA provision).

S 260(2)(b) Creditors bound by the arrangement

The present IA 1986 s 260(2)(b) was introduced by amendment effected by IA 2000 and has been in force since 1 January 2003. Where previously an arrangement only bound those creditors who had been given notice of and were entitled to vote at the creditor's meeting, under this new provision, a creditor is bound by an arrangement notwithstanding that he was not given notice of the proposal or the meeting at which the proposal was to be considered by creditors. Any injustice which may result from the failure to give him notice is addressed by a new right under s 262(3)(a) on the part of such creditor to apply to the court to set aside the arrangement on the basis that he was not given notice.

The former IA 1986 s 260(2)(b) remains in effect in respect of IVAs approved prior to 1 January 2003. For a discussion as to the position of creditors under the former provision who were not given notice of the meeting, see the notes to IA 1986 s 5(2).

The question whether a creditor had received proper notice of the meeting was crucial under the old IA 1986 s 260(2)(b) to the question whether he was bound. It also continues to be of some importance under the new provision to the right of a creditor who did not receive proper notice to challenge to an approval. See the notes to IA 1986 s 5(2) for commentary on the the the question of notice.

S 260(2A)

An omitted creditor who finds himself bound to the arrangement by virtue of the new IA 1986 s 260(2)(b) will be entitled to receive the same dividend or other payments as are due to other creditors falling within the same class. While the arrangement remains in effect (or while any trusts created thereunder under which the supervisor holds funds for the benefit of the IVA creditors remain in being), it is submitted that the omitted creditor should apply to the supervisor, who should meet his claim from funds in his hands pari passu with other creditors in the same class.

Section IA 1986 s 260(2A) contemplates the case where the arrangement has been successfully concluded but an omitted creditor has not received a dividend in common with other creditors in his class as he should have, presumably because he never became aware of the IVA or that he was bound by it. In such a case, the debtor is liable to meet the omitted creditor's claim to the dividend or payment to which he was entitled under the arrangement.

'The amount payable under the arrangement' is, it is submitted, the amount of the dividend or payment which he would actually have received as a creditor falling within his class in common with that actually received by other creditors within that class – rather than (if different) the amount of the dividend originally contemplated in the proposal.

Section IA 1986 s 260(2A) only applies where the arrangement did not 'come to an end prematurely'. The meaning of this phrase is set out in IA 1986 s 262C. An arrangement will have ended prematurely where, when it ceases to have effect, 'it has not been fully implemented in respect of all persons bound by the arrangement'. IA 1986 is silent on the position of the omitted creditor in such circumstances, but it is submitted:

- where, the supervisor holds funds on trust for the benefit of the IVA creditors which trust has survived the premature termination of the arrangement, the omitted creditor should have the same entitlement to a share of such funds as other IVA creditors within the same class;
- however, where such funds held on the IVA trusts have already been distributed by the supervisor to the IVA creditors before receiving notice of the omitted creditor's claim, he may find himself with little or no recourse.

S 260(4), (5)

Once an IVA is approved at the creditors' meeting:

- any interim order which has been made will automatically cease to have effect 28 days after the filing of the nominee's report of the outcome of the meeting with the court, unless the court otherwise directs for the purposes of any application to challenge the approval under IA 1986 s 262;

- any pending petition which has been stayed under IA 1986 s 252 as a result of the making of an interim order will be deemed dismissed once the interim order ceases to have effect unless the court otherwise orders.

Once a pending petition is deemed dismissed by the operation of IA 1986 s 260(5), there is no equivalent provision under IA 1986 or IR 1986 by which the petition may be revived in the event the approval of the IVA is subsequently successfully challenged on an application under IA 1986 s 262. Accordingly, a petitioning creditor who either intends himself to challenge the approval of the IVA, or who becomes aware that other creditors intend to mount such a challenge, would be well advised to seek a direction of the court under IA 1986 s 260(4) or (5) providing for the petition to remain in effect pending the determination of any challenge under IA 1986 s 262.

There is, furthermore, no provision under IA 1986 s 260(5) for the payment of a petitioning creditors' costs in the event of the deemed dismissal of the petition. Such a creditor should therefore protect his position by seeking the debtor's agreement for such costs to be provided for as a term of the arrangement itself. Otherwise the petitioning creditor might seek an order under IA 1986 s 260(5) to the effect that the petition should not be deemed dismissed under that subsection, but should instead actually be dismissed on terms that the debtor pays his costs of the petition.

1.298

261 Additional effect on undischarged bankrupt

(1) This section applies where-
    (a) the creditors' meeting summoned under section 257 approves the proposed voluntary arrangement (with or without modifications), and
    (b) the debtor is an undischarged bankrupt.

(2) Where this section applies the court shall annul the bankruptcy order on an application made-
    (a) by the bankrupt, or
    (b) where the bankrupt has not made an application within the prescribed period, by the official receiver.

(3) An application under subsection (2) may not be made-
    (a) during the period specified in section 262(3)(a) during which the decision of the creditors' meeting can be challenged by application under section 262,
    (b) while an application under that section is pending, or
    (c) while an appeal in respect of an application under that section is pending or may be brought.

(4) Where this section applies the court may give such directions about the conduct of the bankruptcy and the administration of the bankrupt's estate as it thinks appropriate for facilitating the implementation of the approved voluntary arrangement.

Notes

S 261

This section was inserted by the EA 2002 with effect from 1 April 2004, replacing the former IA 1986 s 261. It is supplemented by new chapters 8, 9 and 11 to Part 5 of the IR 1986 (IR 1986 r 5.51 to 5.53, 5.54 to 5.56 and 5.60 to 5.61) brought into force from the same date. Under this provision, where an IVA is approved in respect of an undischarged bankrupt, the court is obliged to annul the bankruptcy order. This contrasts with the former IA 1986 s 261 under which the court had power, but was not bound, to discharge the bankruptcy order. The directions under IA 1986 s 261(4) may include directions for the re-vesting of the bankrupt's estate where it has previously vested in the trustee. A former bankrupt may make an application for annulment under s 261, *Re Johnson* [2006] BPIR 987.

_____

I.299

262 Challenge of meeting's decision

(1) Subject to this section, an application to the court may be made, by any of the persons specified below, on one or both of the following grounds, namely—

    (a)   that a voluntary arrangement approved by a creditors' meeting summoned under section 257 unfairly prejudices the interests of a creditor of the debtor;

    (b)   that there has been some material irregularity at or in relation to such a meeting.

(2) The persons who may apply under this section are—

    (a)   the debtor;

    (b)   a person who—

        (i)   was entitled, in accordance with the rules, to vote at the creditors' meeting, or

        (ii)   would have been so entitled if he had had notice of it;

    (c)   the nominee (or his replacement under section 256(3), 256A(4) or 258(3)); and

    (d)   if the debtor is an undischarged bankrupt, the trustee of his estate or the official receiver.

(3) An application under this section shall not be made

    (a)   after the end of the period of 28 days beginning with the day on which the report of the creditors' meeting was made to the court under section 259 or

    (b)   in the case of a person who was not given notice of the creditors' meeting, after the end of the period of 28 days beginning with the day on which he became aware that the meeting had taken place,

but (subject to that) an application made by a person within subsection (2)(b)(ii) on the ground that the arrangement prejudices his interests may be made after the arrangement has ceased to have effect, unless it has come to an end prematurely.

(4) Where on an application under this section the court is satisfied as to either of the grounds mentioned in subsection (1), it may do one or both of the following, namely—

    (a)   revoke or suspend any approval given by the meeting;

    (b)   give a direction to any person for the summoning of a further meeting of the debtor's creditors to consider any revised proposal he may make or, in a case falling within subsection (1)(b), to reconsider his original proposal.

(5) Where at any time after giving a direction under subsection (4)(b) for the summoning of a meeting to consider a revised proposal the court is satisfied that the debtor does not intend to submit such a proposal, the court shall revoke the direction and revoke or suspend any approval given at the previous meeting.

(6) Where the court gives a direction under subsection (4)(b), it may also give a direction continuing or, as the case may require, renewing, for such period as may be specified in the direction, the effect in relation to the debtor of any interim order.

(7) In any case where the court, on an application made under this section with respect to a creditors' meeting, gives a direction under subsection (4)(b) or revokes or suspends an approval under subsection (4)(a) or (5), the court may give such supplemental directions as it thinks fit and, in particular, directions with respect to—

(a) things done since the meeting under any voluntary arrangement approved by the meeting, and

(b) such things done since the meeting as could not have been done if an interim order had been in force in relation to the debtor when they were done.

(8) Except in pursuance of the preceding provisions of this section, an approval given at a creditors' meeting summoned under section 257 is not invalidated by any irregularity at or in relation to the meeting.

Notes

S 262

Once approved, an IVA may be challenged under IA 1986 s 262 on grounds either (a) of unfair prejudice or (b) of material irregularity at or in relation to the meeting at which it was approved. Where a meeting has rejected a proposal, that decision may also be challenged on grounds (b) of material irregularity. There is in addition a parallel process for appealing decisions of the chairman relating to voting rights under IR 1986 r 5.22(3), (5)–(7).

IA 1986 s 262(8) expressly provides that an approval given at a meeting summoned under IA 1986 s 257 is not invalidated by an irregularity at or in relation to the meeting otherwise than by a challenge under s 262. Contrast the position where a meeting purportedly held to consider a IVA proposal is a nullity, together with any approval purportedly given, because the meeting has not been summoned under and in accordance with IA 1986 s 257 at all: *Fletcher v Vooght* [2000] BPIR 435.

In addition to creditors' right of challenge under s 262, both the supervisor and any creditor bound by the arrangement have power under IA 1986 s 264(1)(c) and s 276(1)(b) to petition for a debtor's bankruptcy on the grounds that the IVA was procured by false or misleading information (or omissions) contained in the proposal, statement of affairs or other document or otherwise made available by the debtor to his creditors at or in connection with the creditors' meeting. For an example of such a petition, see *Cadbury Schweppes plc v Oomji* [2001] 1 WLR 615, CA, *Re Bradburn v Kaye* [2006] BPIR 605.

Except as it applies to creditors who find themselves bound to a IVA of which they did not receive any notice, IA 1986 s 262 provides a short 28 day window after the filing by the chairman of his report of the meeting within which any challenge must be made. The aim, where an IVA has been approved, is that the IVA may thereafter proceed without fear of subsequent challenge. However, unlike the position in respect of CVAs, there is a limited power conferred by IA s 376 to extend time for the making of a challenge under s 262. The discretion to extend time will be exercised with caution: see *Re Timothy* [2006] BPIR 329 for a summary of the relevant principles and authorities.

S 262(1)(a) Grounds of challenge: unfair prejudice

A challenge under (a) can only be made in respect of prejudice to a creditor brought about by unfairness stemming from the actual terms of the scheme itself: *Re a Debtor (No 259 of 1990)* [1992] 1 WLR 226. It is not apt to cover complaints that the arrangement should not have been approved at all but was procured by misrepresentations or material non-disclosure within the proposal or the statement of affairs, or by the votes of sham creditors, which rather constitute material irregularities at or in connection with the meetings of creditors or the company falling within ground (b): See *Re a debtor (No 87 of 1993) (No 2)* [1996] 1 BCLC 63.

For a full discussion of the case law relating to challenges under ground (a), see the commentary to IA 1986 s 6(1)(a) (the equivalent CVA provision) and the review of the authorities in *Sisu Capital Trust Ltd v Tucker* [2006] BPIR 154.

S 262(1)(b) Grounds of challenge: material irregularity

A challenge may be brought on the grounds of material irregularities at or in relation to the creditors' meeting convened to consider the IVA proposal. Where under IA 1986 s 260(2)(b) a creditor finds himself bound by an IVA of which he received no notice, this ground provides the means by which he can challenge the arrangement. For a discussion of the case law relating to material irregularities, see the commentary to IA 1986 s 6(1)(b).

It is important to stress that for a challenge under ground (b) to succeed, the irregularity must be material in that it would or might have affected the outcome of the meeting. Where the irregularity consists in of significant misrepresentations or non-disclosure, it may not be difficult to satisfy a court that this may have affected the outcome of the meeting, and that it would be appropriate to set aside the existing approval and reconvene a further meeting to consider the proposal afresh. However, where the irregularity consists in a failure to notify one or more creditors, whose votes would not directly have affected the outcome of the meeting, it may be more difficult to establish materiality even allowing for the fact that other creditors' voting intentions may not have been fixed in advance of the meeting.

S 262(2)

Persons entitled to challenge: see the commentary to IA 1986 s 6(2).

S 262(3)(a): Time for challenge

The court has power to extend the time for bringing an application beyond the 28 day time limit here provided under IA 1986 s 376: see *Tager v Westpac Banking Corporation* [1997] BPIR 543, *Re Timothy* [2006] BPIR 329. In determining whether or not to extend time for appealing the chairman's decision, the court should take into account the length of the delay, the reasons for it, the apparent merits of the underlying application and the prejudice to each side other than the inevitable prejudice inherent in re-opening the matter: see *Tager* at p 555. An application some thirteen years out of time was described as 'hopeless' in *Tanner v Everitt* [2004] BPIR 1036 and in *Warley Continental Services Ltd v Johal* [2004] BPIR 353 the judge, in rejecting an application for an extension of time under IA 1986 s 376, relied inter alia on the fact that a very short time limit is imposed under IA 1986 s 262. For a recent review of the authorities, see *Re Timothy* [2006] BPIR 329. However where a debtor does not give consent to modifications of a proposal and no valid IVA came into existence at all such an IVA is a complete nullity and the time limit for challenge on the grounds of material irregularity did not apply *Re Plummer* [2004] BPIR 767.

S 262(3)(b) Time for challenge; omitted creditors

See the commentary to IA 1986 s 6(3)(b).

S 262(4), (5) Powers of the court

Where an approved arrangement is successfully challenged on either ground, the court may revoke or suspend any decision approving the arrangement. It may also give directions in such a case for the summoning of a further meeting, but may first require revised proposals to be submitted to see whether such proposals are free from objection, and may refuse to convene any further meeting where it is clear that any revised proposal has no reasonable prospects of success. For the relevant case law, see the commentary to IA 1986 s 6(4). Where a decision rejecting a proposal is successfully challenged, the court may direct a further meeting be summoned to consider the original proposal, but has no power to order that the arrangement stand approved.

S 262(6) Continuation / renewal of interim order

Where the court orders that a further meeting be summoned to consider the original or revised proposals, the court may continue or renew the interim order to provide the debtor with continuing protection. There is no equivalent power while a challenge under IA 1986 s 262 is pending to extend or renew an interim order which has ceased to have effect. Where the challenge is to an IVA which has been approved, the debtor will in any event continue to be protected against enforcement action under the IVA itself while the challenge is still pending. But where the debtor himself seeks to challenge a decision rejecting an IVA proposal, the court may allow an existing interim order to continue for its course and not immediately discharge the same under IA 1986 s 259(2). However once such interim order expires by effluxion of time the court will have no power to extend or renew it: see *Kent Carpets v Symes* [1995] 2 BCLC 651 at 669i–670c. The debtor is not however wholly without redress; in the event that the debtor successfully challenges the decision rejecting his proposal and the court directs that a further meeting be held, the court is empowered under IA 1986 s 262(7)(b) to give directions in relation to any things done since the meeting which could not have been done had an interim order been in force.

S 262(7) Consequential directions

This subsection makes provision for orders:
- validating acts done by a supervisor (or others) under and with the authority of an arrangement where that arrangement (and the authority) is subsequently revoked by an order under IA 1986 s 262(4) or (5)
- giving directions including, it would seem, directions invalidating acts done since the meeting which could not have been done had an interim order been in force (see also the note to IA 1986 s 262(6) above)

In either case, where any such proposed direction affects the rights of third parties, they may need to be joined before such direction is made.

Procedural matters and costs

These matters are considered in the notes to IA 1986 s 6.

———————

1.300

262A False representations etc

(1) If for the purpose of obtaining the approval of his creditors to a proposal for a voluntary arrangement, the debtor—
    (a)   makes any false representation, or
    (b)   fraudulently does, or omits to do, anything,
he commits an offence.

(2) Subsection (1) applies even if the proposal is not approved.

(3) A person guilty of an offence under this section is liable to imprisonment or a fine, or both.

Notes

S 262A(1)

This provision was added by the IA 2000. It enacts by primary legislation an offence which was contained in former IR 1986 r 5.30. As now enacted, the offence is made clearly to apply whether or not the voluntary arrangement proposal is in fact approved. The penalties for the offence are to be found in IA 1986 Schedule 10.

1.301

262B Prosecution of delinquent debtors

(1) This section applies where a voluntary arrangement approved by a creditors' meeting summoned under section 257 has taken effect.

(2) If it appears to the nominee or supervisor that the debtor has been guilty of any offence in connection with the arrangement for which he is criminally liable, he shall forthwith—

    (a) report the matter to the Secretary of State, and

    (b) provide the Secretary of State with such information and give the Secretary of State such access to and facilities for inspecting and taking copies of documents (being information or documents in his possession or under his control and relating to the matter in question) as the Secretary of State requires.

(3) Where a prosecuting authority institutes criminal proceedings following any report under subsection (2), the nominee or, as the case may be, supervisor shall give the authority all assistance in connection with the prosecution which he is reasonably able to give.

For this purpose, 'prosecuting authority' means the Director of Public Prosecutions or the Secretary of State.

(4) The court may, on the application of the prosecuting authority, direct a nominee or supervisor to comply with subsection (3) if he has failed to do so.

Notes

S 262B(1)

This section was inserted by the IA 2000 and came into force on 1 January 2003. Note that the section only applies where a voluntary arrangement has been approved and has taken effect. Where a debtor has acted in a fraudulent manner for the purpose of obtaining approval to a voluntary arrangement, but such arrangement is not in fact approved, IA 1986 s 262B has no application, even though the debtor may nevertheless have committed an offence under IA 1986 s 262A.

1.302

262C Arrangements coming to an end prematurely

For the purposes of this Part, a voluntary arrangement approved by a creditors' meeting summoned under section 257 comes to an end prematurely if, when it ceases to have effect, it has not been fully implemented in respect of all persons bound by the arrangement by virtue of section 260(2)(b)(i).

___

Notes

S 262C

This section, inserted by the IA 2000, supplements the new IA 1986 s 260(2A). See further the commentary to that subsection above.

___

1.303

263 Implementation and supervision of approved voluntary arrangement

(1) This section applies where a voluntary arrangement approved by a creditors' meeting summoned under section 257 has taken effect.

(2) The person who is for the time being carrying out, in relation to the voluntary arrangement, the functions conferred by virtue of the approval on the nominee (or his replacement under section [256(3), 256A(4)] or 258(3)) shall be known as the supervisor of the voluntary arrangement.

(3) If the debtor, any of his creditors or any other person is dissatisfied by any act, omission or decision of the supervisor, he may apply to the court; and on such an application the court may—
    (a)   confirm, reverse or modify any act or decision of the supervisor,
    (b)   give him directions, or
    (c)   make such other order as it thinks fit.

(4) The supervisor may apply to the court for directions in relation to any particular matter arising under the voluntary arrangement.

(5) The court may, whenever—
    (a)   it is expedient to appoint a person to carry out the functions of the supervisor, and
    (b)   it is inexpedient, difficult or impracticable for an appointment to be made without the assistance of the court,
make an order appointing a person who is qualified to act as an insolvency practitioner [or authorised to act as supervisor, in relation to the voluntary arrangement], either in substitution for the existing supervisor or to fill a vacancy.

This is without prejudice to section 41(2) of the Trustee Act 1925 (power of court to appoint trustees of deeds of arrangement).

(6) The power conferred by subsection (5) is exercisable so as to increase the number of persons exercising the functions of the supervisor or,

> where there is more than one person exercising those functions, so as to replace one or more of those persons.

Notes

S 263

See generally the commentary contained in the general note to IA 1986 s 7 above (the equivalent CVA provision).

S 263(3) Power of the court to give directions to supervisor

For commentary on the questions (a) who is entitled to apply to the court for directions under IA 1986 s 262(3) and (b) the powers of the court to intervene on such application, see the commentary to IA 1986 s 7(3) above.

S 263(4) Application by supervisor for directions

See again the commentary to IA 1986 s 7(4)(a) and (b) above. This deals in particular with the following issues:

- the scope of the court's jurisdiction under IA 1986 s 263(4) and s 7(4)(a), its CVA equivalent;
- the approach of the court to questions of construction of a voluntary arrangement, following *Welsby v Brelec Installations Ltd* [2000] 2 BCLC 576;
- the effect of a subsequent bankruptcy on the voluntary arrangement, following *Re N T Gallagher Ltd* [2002] 1 WLR 2380;
- the circumstances in which an arrangement may be said to have failed, and the question whether under the terms of any particular arrangement the supervisor is bound to present a bankruptcy petition against a debtor, in the light of the decisions in *Re Brelec Installations Ltd* and *Re Maple Environmental Services Ltd* [2000] BCC 93.

S 263(5)

Power to remove supervisor, or to add a further supervisor: see the commentary to IA 1986 s 7(5) above.

Fast-track voluntary arrangement

1.304

263A Availability

Section 263B applies where an individual debtor intends to make a proposal to his creditors for a voluntary arrangement and –
  (a) the debtor is an undischarged bankrupt,
  (b) the official receiver is specified in the proposal as the nominee in relation to the voluntary arrangement, and
  (c) no interim order is applied for under section 253.

Notes

S 263A

IA 1986 s 263A to 263G were introduced by the EA 2002 and brought into force with effect from 1 April 2004. They introduce a new variant of voluntary arrangement, the fast-track voluntary arrangement ('FTVA') available only to undischarged bankrupts who do not require the protection of an interim order pending approval of the voluntary arrangement. Under the FTVA procedure, as set out in these sections, and supplemented by a new chapter 7 of Part 5 of the IR 1986 (IR r 5.35 to 5.50):

- the undischarged bankrupt prepares a proposal to his creditors to pay part or all of his debts for submission to the official reciever with conduct of his bankruptcy; on request, the OR will provide standard forms which the bankrupt may complete to set out his proposal; the official receiver charges a fee of £300 for acting as nominee in respect of such proposal (as provided under the Insolvency Proceedings (Fees) Order 2004 (SI 2004/593)) which must be submitted, together with a £15 IVA registration fee, with the proposal;

- the Official Reviewer must then decide whether he agrees to act as nominee in respect of the proposal, based upon his assessment of whether the proposal has reasonable prospects of being approved and implemented;

- if the Official Reviewer agrees to act, he then submits the proposal to all known creditors; they are invited to approve or reject the proposal by postal vote which must be received by the Official Reviewer by a date specified by him within a short timeframe after the proposal is submitted;

- the proposal may be approved by a majority of creditors in excess of 75% in value submitting their vote; there is no power for the nominee or bankrupt to amend or modify the proposal, or for creditors to approve the proposal only subject to modifications;

- once approved, the arrangement is implemented much as a standard IVA; the official receiver becomes the supervisor of the arrangement (although he may be replaced by a private practitioner), and, while he acts as such, his fee for so acting is prescribed under the Insolvency Proceedings (Fees) Order 2004 (SI 2004/593)) as 15% of monies realised by him.

In its guidance leaflet on FTVAs, the Insolvency Service state that the procedure is designed to deal only with straightforward sales or disposals of assets and the collection of regular payments, and may not be appropriate where a bankrupt has many assets to be sold. It further states that the Official Reviewer may decline to act as nominee where the affairs of the bankrupt are complicated. In such cases, the bankrupt's affairs may better be administered in a standard post-bankruptcy IVA by a private insolvency practitioner who is not subject to the same fee constraints as the Official Reviewer.

1.305

263B Decision

(1) The debtor may submit to the official receiver-
- (a) a document setting out the terms of the voluntary arrangement which the debtor is proposing, and
- (b) a statement of his affairs containing such particulars as may be prescribed of his creditors, debts, other liabilities and assets and such other information as may be prescribed.

(2) If the official receiver thinks that the voluntary arrangement proposed has a reasonable prospect of being approved and implemented, he may make arrangements for inviting creditors to decide whether to approve it.

(3) For the purposes of subsection (2) a person is a 'creditor' only if-
- (a) he is a creditor of the debtor in respect of a bankruptcy debt, and
- (b) the official receiver is aware of his claim and his address.

(4) Arrangements made under subsection (2)-
- (a) must include the provision to each creditor of a copy of the proposed voluntary arrangement,

> (b)   must include the provision to each creditor of information about the criteria by reference to which the official receiver will determine whether the creditors approve or reject the proposed voluntary arrangement, and
>
> (c)   may not include an opportunity for modifications to the proposed voluntary arrangement to be suggested or made.
>
> (5) Where a debtor submits documents to the official receiver under subsection (1) no application under section 253 for an interim order may be made in respect of the debtor until the official receiver has-
>
> (a)   made arrangements as described in subsection (2), or
>
> (b)   informed the debtor that he does not intend to make arrangements (whether because he does not think the voluntary arrangement has a reasonable prospect of being approved and implemented or because he declines to act).

Notes

S 263B

This section provides the framework for the first three stages in the FTVA procedure – (i) preparation by debtor and submission of proposal to the official receiver, (ii) decision by the official receiver whether to agree to act as nominee, and (iii) if the official receiver agrees to act, the submission of the proposal by the official receiver to creditors.

S 263B(1) Stage One

For the matters which must be included within the proposal prepared by the bankrupt, see IR 1986 r 5.37(1)(b) and (2). Standard form proposals for completion by the bankrupt are available from the official receiver. As regards the form and contents of the statement of affairs referred to in IA 1986 s 263(B)(1)(b), there are presently no rules within Chapter 7 of Part 5 of the IR 1986 prescribing the particulars required (contrast, in the case of standard IVAs, IR 1986 r 5.5). The bankrupt should, in any event, already have submitted to the official receiver, or be in the course of submitting, a statement of affairs under IA 196 s 272 or s 288.

S 263B(2) Stage Two

It is a precondition to the official receiver agreeing to act as nominee that he is satisfied that the voluntary arrangement has reasonable prospects of being approved by creditors and implemented. This is a similar precondition to that imposed on nominees in standard IVAs under IA 1986 s 256 (1)(a) and s 256A(3)(a) when reporting whether a creditors' meeting should be summoned to consider a proposal. It appears that the official receiver, if satisfied of the above, nevertheless retains a discretion to refuse to act as nominee, and may refuse where, for instance, the affairs of the bankrupt are complicated, and, on costs or other grounds, a standard IVA overseen by a private insolvency practitioner would be more appropriate than a FTVA.

Under IR 1986 r 5.38, the official receiver has 28 days in which to make a decision based on the information supplied to him, but, where that information is insufficient, he may call upon the bankrupt to provide further information, and the 28 day period will then only run from the date the information is supplied.

S 263B(4) Stage Three

The arrangements for inviting creditors whether or not to approve the proposal are prescribed in IR 1986 r 5.39 and 5.40. Rules relating to creditors' entitlement to vote are contained in IR 1986 r 5.41–5.44. Unlike standard IVAs, no meeting is summoned to consider whether or not to approve the proposal with or without modifications. Instead, creditors are invited to submit postal votes in favour of or against the proposal, and have no opportunity to propose any modifications to the proposal.

S 263B(5)

The submission of a FTVA proposal to the official receiver precludes a bankrupt from then making an application for an interim order until such time as (i) the official receiver has consented to act, and submitted the proposal to creditors for them to vote upon or (ii) the official receiver has refused to act as nominee, with the result that the bankrupt, if he wishes to pursue the proposal, must proceed by way of standard IVA proposal with a private nominee. However, in the former case, it is difficult to see how an application for an interim order under IA 1986 s 253 could be pursued, since such application is predicated upon a debtor submitting a standard IVA proposal upon which a nominee is required to report to the court under IA 1986 s 256 and thereafter to summon a meeting to consider the proposal under IA 1986 s 257, all of which is inconsistent with the more simplified FTVA procedure.

1.306

263C Result

As soon as is reasonably practicable after the implementation of arrangements under IA 1986 s 263B(2) the official receiver shall report to the court whether the proposed voluntary arrangement has been approved or rejected.

Notes

S 263C

Although there are no rules which prescribe the contents of the official receiver's report to the court on the outcome of the vote (with the exception of IR 1986 r 5.44 which deals just with the application of the EC Regulation on Insolvency Proceedings 2000), the official receiver should set out in his report not only the percentage of votes received approving and rejecting the proposal, but also details of any decisions which he has made in his capacity as nominee to admit or reject contentious proofs of debt for voting purposes (under IR 1986 r 5.42(1)) or to place a value other than £1 on the amount of an unliquidated debt (under IR 1986 r 5.41(3)). Without such information, aggrieved creditors, or the bankrupt himself, may not know whether they can mount a challenge to the approval of the FTVA under IA 1986 s 263F(1)(b) below.

1.307

263D Approval of voluntary arrangement

(1) This section applies where the official receiver reports to the court under section 263C that a proposed voluntary arrangement has been approved.

(2) The voluntary arrangement-
  (a) takes effect,
  (b) binds the debtor, and
  (c) binds every person who was entitled to participate in the arrangements made under section 263B(2).

(3) The court shall annul the bankruptcy order in respect of the debtor on an application made by the official receiver.

(4) An application under subsection (3) may not be made-

    (a)   during the period specified in section 263F(3) during which the voluntary arrangement can be challenged by application under section 263F(2),

    (b)   while an application under that section is pending, or

    (c)   while an appeal in respect of an application under that section is pending or may be brought.

(5) The court may give such directions about the conduct of the bankruptcy and the administration of the bankrupt's estate as it thinks appropriate for facilitating the implementation of the approved voluntary arrangement.

(6) The Deeds of Arrangement Act 1914 (c. 47) does not apply to the voluntary arrangement.

(7) A reference in this Act or another enactment to a voluntary arrangement approved under this Part includes a reference to a voluntary arrangement which has effect by virtue of this section.

Notes

S 263D

This section contains provisions as to the effect of the voluntary arrangement as approved and as to the annulment of the bankruptcy similar in effect to those which apply to standard IVAs under IA 1986 s 260 and s 261.

1.308

263E Implementation

Section 263 shall apply to a voluntary arrangement which has effect by virtue of section 263D(2) as it applies to a voluntary arrangement approved by a creditors' meeting.

Notes

S 263E

This applies the provisions of IA 1986 s 263 to FTVAs as they apply to standard IVAs. See the commentary to that section above.

1.309

263F Revocation

(1) The court may make an order revoking a voluntary arrangement which has effect by virtue of section 263D(2) on the ground-

(a) that it unfairly prejudices the interests of a creditor of the debtor, or
(b) that a material irregularity occurred in relation to the arrangements made under section 263B(2).

(2) An order under subsection (1) may be made only on the application of-
(a) the debtor,
(b) a person who was entitled to participate in the arrangements made under section 263B(2),
(c) the trustee of the bankrupt's estate, or
(d) the official receiver.

(3) An application under subsection (2) may not be made after the end of the period of 28 days beginning with the date on which the official receiver makes his report to the court under section 263C.

(4) But a creditor who was not made aware of the arrangements under section 263B(2) at the time when they were made may make an application under subsection (2) during the period of 28 days beginning with the date on which he becomes aware of the voluntary arrangement.

Notes

S 263F

The FTVA as approved by creditors may be challenged on grounds of unfair prejudice or material irregularity under this section in much the same way as a standard IVA may be so challenged under IA 1986 s 262. See further the commentary to that section. However, there are important limitations on the scope of the relief available and in the powers of the court under this section as compared to IA 1986 s 262. In particular:

- there is no power under this section on the part of the bankrupt to challenge a decision of creditors *refusing* to approve a voluntary arrangement on grounds of material irregularity as there is under IA 1986 s 262 – although the lack of such a power is largely mitigated by the right of appeal which exists under IR 1986 r 5.42 in favour both of the bankrupt and creditors against the official receiver's decision on a creditor's entitlement to vote and the power of the court following a successful appeal against such a decision to order another vote to be held;
- if a successful challenge is made to the voluntary arrangement as approved on either of the grounds in IA 1986 s 263F(1), the court has no other powers available to it other than simply to revoke the voluntary arrangement – leaving the bankrupt to start the whole procedure again if he wishes to put forward a revised voluntary arrangement which meets the objections which led to the successful challenge.

1.310

263G Offences

(1) Section 262A shall have effect in relation to obtaining approval to a proposal for a voluntary arrangement under section 263D.

(2) Section 262B shall have effect in relation to a voluntary arrangement which has effect by virtue of section 263D(2) (for which purposes the words 'by a creditors' meeting summoned under section 257' shall be disregarded).

Notes

S 263G

This section applies to FTVAs the same criminal offences and statutory reporting duties in respect of such offences as apply to standard IVAs by IA 1986 s 262A and 262B. See the commentary to those sections.

Part IX
Bankruptcy

Chapter I
Bankruptcy Petitions; Bankruptcy Orders

Preliminary

1.311

264 Who may present a bankruptcy petition

(1) A petition for a bankruptcy order to be made against an individual may be presented to the court in accordance with the following provisions of this Part—
- (a) by one of the individual's creditors or jointly by more than one of them,
- (b) by the individual himself,
- (ba) by a temporary administrator (within the meaning of Article 38 of the EC Regulation),
- (bb) by a liquidator (within the meaning of Article 2(b) of the EC Regulation) appointed in proceedings by virtue of Article 3(1) of the EC Regulation,
- (c) by the supervisor of, or any person (other than the individual) who is for the time being bound by, a voluntary arrangement proposed by the individual and approved under Part VIII, *or*
- (d) *where a criminal bankruptcy order has been made against the individual, by the Official Petitioner or by any person specified in the order in pursuance of section 39(3)(b) of the Powers of Criminal Courts Act 1973.*

(2) Subject to those provisions, the court may make a bankruptcy order on any such petition.

Notes

S 264

The appropriate court in which to present a petition is detailed in IR 1986 r 6.9 (creditors' petitions) and IR 1986 r 6.40 (debtors' petitions). A deposit is payable on the presentation of a petition by a creditor (£390) or a debtor (£325) (Insolvency Proceedings (Fees) Order 2004) (as amended) excepting petitions under IA 1986 s 264(1)(ba),(bb). A petition is presented against an 'individual' therefore a single petition cannot seek to make more than one person bankrupt. The relevant rules in relation to the petition and the procedure following presentation are contained in IR 1986 r 6.6ff. For bankruptcy petitions against members of a partnership, see the Insolvent Partnerships Order 1994 which is separately annotated in this volume. For deceased individuals, see the Administration of Insolvent Estates of Deceased Persons Order 1986 which is also separately annotated.

S 264(1)(a)

This provision enables a petition to be presented by more than one creditor. Although it does not expressly state that more than one petitioner can present a petition based on separate debts due to each of them, it is not right to confine the statutory words so that they permit a petition by two or more creditors only in relation to one or more debts due to them jointly: see per Ferris J in *Re Allen* [1998] BPIR 319, 320. 'Creditor' is defined in IA 1986 s 383. A debt will found a petition even if it is a non-provable debt in a bankruptcy (*Levy v Legal Service Commission* [2000] BPIR 1065) although such petitions should only succeed in exceptional circumstances, of which the Court of Appeal in that case had considerable difficulty envisaging any except perhaps where a supporting creditor with a provable debt has obtained a change of carriage of the petition under IR 1986 r 6.31. Creditors' petitions are dealt with under IA 1986 s 267 to 271.

S 264(1)(b)

A debtor may petition for his own bankruptcy and such a petition is dealt with under IA 1986 s 272 to 275.

S 264(1)(c)

IVAs are dealt with in IA 1986 s 252 to 263. Special provisions apply to a petition presented by a supervisor or another person bound by an individual voluntary arrangement in respect of a default in that arrangement IA 1986 s 276.

S 264(1)(d)

This provision has been prospectively repealed by section 170(2) and Schedule 16, Criminal Justice Act 1988 as from a day to be appointed. However s 264(1)(d) will remain in force in respect of criminal bankruptcy orders which have already been made; the power to make such orders was abolished by s 101 of the Criminal Justice Act 1988 from 3 April 1989. Criminal bankruptcy orders have been replaced by confiscation orders.

Financial Services Authority petitions

Under s 372 of the Financial Services and Markets Act 2000 the FSA may present a petition under IA 1986 s 264 against an individual who is either an 'authorised person' within the meaning of FSMA 2000 or who is not so authorised but is nonetheless carrying out a regulated activity in contravention of the general prohibition in that act. Where someone other than the FSA presents a petition against such a person, the FSA is entitled to be heard both at the hearing of the petition and at any other hearing in relation to the individual under Part IX of IA 1986.

1.312

265 Conditions to be satisfied in respect of debtor

(1) A bankruptcy petition shall not be presented to the court under section 264(1)(a) or (b) unless the debtor—

    (a)   is domiciled in England and Wales,

> (b)　is personally present in England and Wales on the day on which the petition is presented, or
>
> (c)　at any time in the period of 3 years ending with that day—
>
> > (i)　has been ordinarily resident, or has had a place of residence, in England and Wales, or
> >
> > (ii)　has carried on business in England and Wales.
>
> (2) The reference in subsection (1)(c) to an individual carrying on business includes—
>
> > (a)　the carrying on of business by a firm or partnership of which the individual is a member, and
> >
> > (b)　the carrying on of business by an agent or manager for the individual or for such a firm or partnership.
>
> (3) This section is subject to Article 3 of the EC Regulation.

Notes

S 265

This provision deals with who can be made bankrupt under the IA 1986. It is essentially concerned with matters of jurisdiction. Section 265(3) expressly subjects the section to the regime found in the EC Regulation on Insolvency Proceedings 2000 where that is applicable- and the standard form petition requires the petitioner to consider the application of the EC Regulation and state inter alia whether the petition constitutes main or secondary proceedings. The jurisdiction tests in s 265 are only applicable in relation to creditors' and debtors' petitions. This is simply because, in the case of a petition presented by anyone else having power under s 264(1), the basis of the court's jurisdiction will already have been established.

S 265(1)(a)

The first test is that of the debtor's domicile, which is determined by the common-law test and not by the Civil Jurisdiction and Judgments Act 1982, as the Brussels Convention underlying the Act does not apply to insolvency proceedings (Article 1, Brussels Convention). A person cannot be without a domicile. On birth a person has a domicile of origin, which is determined by the domicile of a legitimate child's father, by an illegitimate child's mother or by the place of birth of a foundling (*Udny v Udny* (1869) LR 1 Sc & Div 441, HL). A person can change their domicile. Where someone lives permanently in a country other than his domicile of origin, that may become his place of domicile (*Whicher v Hume* (1858) 7 HL Cas 124). For a full treatment of this area, see Dicey and Morris, *The Conflict of Laws*.

S 265(1)(b)

The second basis of jurisdiction is physical presence within the jurisdiction. But this is subject to the rules governing the service of process, so if a person is improperly or fraudulently persuaded into the jurisdiction to facilitate service then the petition will be set aside (*Colt Industries Inc v Sarlie* [1966] 1 All ER 673).

S 265(1)(c)(i)

It is unclear what would suffice as having 'a place of residence' for the purpose of this provision. The wording contemplates a distinction between having a place of residence and being ordinarily resident. Presumably then, one can have been resident in the jurisdiction without having been ordinarily so and therefore any period of residence, however small, would suffice. That seems to suggest that anything more than a fleeting visit to the country could provide a ground for the court assuming jurisdiction.

S 265(1)(c)(ii)

'Carrying on a business' refers to a continuity of business by the debtor himself with some degree of management and control (*Graham v Lewis* (1888) 22 QBD 1) and business is defined by IA 1986 s 436 as including a trade or profession. A business continues until all the trading debts have been paid even if the activity of the business ceases (*Re a Debtor (No 784 of 1991)* [1992] Ch 554).

S 265(3)

The section is overridden where the debtor has his centre of main interests ('COMI') in a EU member state (Article 3, EC Regulation on Insolvency Proceedings 2000). For the meaning of 'centre of main interest' in a bankruptcy context see *Shierson v Vlieland-Boddy* [2005] BCC 416 (and on appeal [2005] BPIR 1170) where it was held that the centre of main interests was to be tested as at the date that the court was asked to open insolvency proceedings and it was acknowledged that a debtor could change his centre of main interests; see further the notes to the EC Regulation on Insolvency Proceedings 2000. Where the centre of main interests not in an EU member state then IA 1986 s 265 still provides the relevant test for jurisdiction.

1.313

266 Other preliminary conditions

(1) Where a bankruptcy petition relating to an individual is presented by a person who is entitled to present a petition under two or more paragraphs of section 264(1), the petition is to be treated for the purposes of this Part as a petition under such one of those paragraphs as may be specified in the petition.

(2) A bankruptcy petition shall not be withdrawn without the leave of the court.

(3) The court has a general power, if it appears to it appropriate to do so on the grounds that there has been a contravention of the rules or for any other reason, to dismiss a bankruptcy petition or to stay proceedings on such a petition; and, where it stays proceedings on a petition, it may do so on such terms and conditions as it thinks fit.

(4) *Without prejudice to subsection (3), where a petition under section 264(1)(a), (b) or (c) in respect of an individual is pending at a time when a criminal bankruptcy order is made against him, or is presented after such an order has been so made, the court may on the application of the Official Petitioner dismiss the petition if it appears to it appropriate to do so.*

Notes

S 266(1)

Where a person can present a petition in different capacities, the petitioner may choose which to proceed in.

S 266(2)

This important provision reflects the fact that bankruptcy is a collective remedy intended to benefit creditors as a whole. The purpose of requiring that the court give its permission for a petition to be withdrawn is to ensure that a petition, once presented, proceeds to its first hearing. Commonly, the petitioning creditor will be paid by the debtor before the hearing so as to avoid the making of a bankruptcy order. Were it not for this provision, the petitioner, once paid, could simply contact the court and say that he wants to withdraw the petition, with the effect that it is taken out of the court's hearing list. As things are, the petition will be heard in any event and, should the petitioner not want to proceed, other creditors will have the opportunity to apply for a change of carriage of the petition under IR 1986 r 6.31.

IR 1986 r 6.32 requires that an application for permission to withdraw a petition be supported by evidence in writing. In practice this rarely happens. Usually, where a petitioner has been paid, he simply invites the court to dismiss the petition on the basis that the court could not make a bankruptcy order because of IA 1986 s 271(1).

S 266(3)

The power of the court to dismiss or stay the petition under this provision is unfettered (*TSB Bank v Platts* [1997] BPIR 151, *Re Micklethwait* [2003] BPIR 101, *Society of Lloyd's v Beaumont* [2006] BPIR 1021); but it is not open to the court to take the view that pursuing bankruptcy proceedings, even on a small debt, is 'disproportionate': *John Lewis plc v Pearson Burton* [2004] BPIR 70.

Dismissal or stay

The court may dismiss or stay the petition if:

(i)   there has been abuse of process (see the discussion in *Re Ross (No2)* [2000] BPIR 636). However a collateral purpose behind the petition will not necessarily amount to an abuse of process (*Hicks v Gulliver* [2002] BPIR 518). Compare the comments made in the winding-up case, *Mann v Goldstein* [1968] 1 WLR 1091, at p 1095. Whether the petition is an abuse of process is a question of fact dependent on whether the creditor is acting in good faith (*Re Bebro* [1900] 2 QB 316, *Re Atkinson ex p Atkinson* (1892) 9 Morr 193). If the petition is dismissed as an abuse of process the creditor is barred from presenting a petition for the same debt (*Re Shaw* (1901) 53 LT 754). If the petition was presented maliciously then an action may lie for damages (*Quartz Hill Consolidated Gold Mining Co v Eyre* (1883) 11 QBD 674);

(ii)   there has been an unreasonable costs-demand by the petitioner (*Lilley v American Express Europe Ltd* [2000] BPIR 70; *Re a Debtor (883 of 1927)* [1928] 1 Ch 199);

(iii)   the petition debt is a non-provable debt; while the court clearly has jurisdiction to make a bankruptcy order, Jonathan Parker LJ in *Levy v Legal Services Commission* [2000] BPIR 1065 said that the only circumstance in which such an order could conceivably be made was where a creditor with a provable debt is given change of carriage of a petition based on a non-provable debt;

(iv)   the debt is statute-barred or there has been a want of prosecution (*TSB Bank v Platts* [1997] BPIR 151);

(v)   it appears that a judgment may have been obtained by fraud, collusion or miscarriage of justice (*Dawodu v American Express Bank* [2001] BPIR 983 – and see the notes under IA 1986 s 268 below);

(vi)   there is an appeal against a judgment which founds the petition and the court considers that the appeal has a real prospect of success (*Westminster City Council v Parkin* [2001] BPIR 1156).

It is common for creditors to agree that a defaulting debtor can clear a debt by instalments. This kind of arrangement is very common with Crown creditors. But an agreement to allow payment by instalments will not be binding on the creditor without consideration. In *Re Selectmove Ltd* [1995] 1 WLR 474 (a winding-up case), the debtor company sought to prevent the Inland Revenue from proceeding on a petition where there had been a 'time-to-pay' agreement. The court rejected the argument as there was no consideration for the indulgence. Therefore debtors who are making such agreements with their creditors would be well-advised to offer consideration, perhaps by agreeing to pay one pound more than the sum then outstanding.

Adjournment

The court will not allow repeated adjournments *Judd v Williams* [1998] BPIR 88. Where there is valid debt and the formalities have been complied with the court will generally only adjourn for a short time where there is a reasonable prospect that the debtor will come to terms with the creditor and will pay the debt (*Re Gilmartin (A Bankrupt)* [1989] 1 WLR 513). The debtor must provide evidence of an ability to pay (*Dickins v Inland Revenue* [2004] EWHC 852, [2004] BPIR 718). Where a debt is undisputed and has remained unpaid for a substantial time, it is not appropriate to adjourn or dismiss the petition on the basis that the debtor might be able to repay the petitioner if he is allowed to pursue claims which might lead to a recovery. A court will not assume that the debtor's estate will lose the benefit of any possible future claim as the court will assume that the trustee will take the appropriate steps: *Re Micklethwait* [2002] EWHC 1123, [2003] BPIR 101. Indeed a review of other proceedings by an independent trustee is a proper purpose for presenting and proceeding with a bankruptcy petition (*Shepherd v Legal Services Commission* [2003] BPIR 140). As to adjournments to allow the debtor to seek legal advice, see *Henry Butcher International Ltd v KG Engineering* [2006] BPIR 56.

S 266(4)

This provision has been prospectively repealed by s 170(2), Schedule 16 to the Criminal Justice Act 1988 from a day to be appointed.

Creditor's petition

1.314

267 Grounds of creditor's petition

(1) A creditor's petition must be in respect of one or more debts owed by the debtor, and the petitioning creditor or each of the petitioning creditors must be a person to whom the debt or (as the case may be) at least one of the debts is owed.

(2) Subject to the next three sections, a creditor's petition may be presented to the court in respect of a debt or debts only if, at the time the petition is presented—
  (a) the amount of the debt, or the aggregate amount of the debts, is equal to or exceeds the bankruptcy level,
  (b) the debt, or each of the debts, is for a liquidated sum payable to the petitioning creditor, or one or more of the petitioning creditors, either immediately or at some certain, future time, and is unsecured,
  (c) the debt, or each of the debts, is a debt which the debtor appears either to be unable to pay or to have no reasonable prospect of being able to pay, and
  (d) there is no outstanding application to set aside a statutory demand served (under section 268 below) in respect of the debt or any of the debts.

(3) A debt is not to be regarded for the purposes of subsection (2) as a debt for a liquidated sum by reason only that the amount of the debt is specified in a criminal bankruptcy order.

(4) 'The bankruptcy level' is £750; but the Secretary of State may by order in a statutory instrument substitute any amount specified in the

order for that amount or (as the case may be) for the amount which by virtue of such an order is for the time being the amount of the bankruptcy level.

(5) An order shall not be made under subsection (4) unless a draft of it has been laid before, and approved by a resolution of, each House of Parliament.

Notes

S 267(1)

See the note to IA 1986 s 264(1)(a). A creditor's petition can only be presented by someone to whom a debt is owed at the moment of presentation. Otherwise the petition will be dismissed, unless there is some other creditor who can be substituted as petitioner under IR 1986 r 6.30: *Coulter v Chief of Dorset Police (No 1)* [2005] BPIR 62. Note that it is possible for a petitioner to present a petition and then to immediately assign the debt to a third party. In that case, there is nothing in the act or rules to stop the petition proceeding in the ordinary way.

S 267(2)(a)

The debt, which must be at least £750 at the time of the presentation of the petition, (IA 1986 s 267(4)) need not be denominated in sterling (*Re a Debtor (No 51 SD of 1991)* [1992] 1 WLR 1294). However, if a foreign currency is used, the petitioner must be able to show that, at the date of presentation, using the official exchange rate, the debt equalled or exceeded £750. For the meaning of 'official exchange rate', see IR 1986 r 111(2). Contrast this with proof of debts, where the proof must be denominated in sterling. In any case, it is irrelevant if there is a cross claim or a dispute as to part of a debt provided that the net amount after deducting the maximum value of the cross-claims or the undisputed amount is equal to or greater than the bankruptcy level at the date of presentation (*TSB Bank v Platts (No 2)* [1998] BPIR 284). If by the hearing of the petition the debt is reduced to below £750 a bankruptcy order can still be made (*Lilley v American Express Europe Ltd* [2000] BPIR 70).

S 267(2)(b)

IA 1986 s 382 gives a very wide meaning to 'debt' for the purposes of the second group of parts to the act (IA 1986 s 252 to 385). It includes any debt or liability to which the bankrupt is subject at the commencement of the bankruptcy (IA 1986 s 382(1)(a)) and, for the purpose of references to a debt or liability in that group of parts, it is immaterial whether the debt or liability is present or future, whether it is certain or contingent, or whether it is fixed or liquidated in amount or whether it is capable of being ascertained by reference to fixed rules or capable of assessment only as a matter of opinion. Section 267(2)(b) is considerably narrower. A debt on which a creditor's petition is based must be for a liquidated sum. This means that the amount of the debt must be specific and fully and finally ascertained. If there is no such debt, then the court has no jurisdiction to make a bankruptcy order: *Hope v Premierspace (Europe) Ltd* [1999] BPIR 695. The debt must also be payable either immediately or at some *certain* future time. A contingent debt will not suffice. Undetermined damages for breach of contract are not generally a good petition debt: see *eg Re Miller* [1901] 1 KB 51. However, if damages can be calculated precisely, eg by reference to a liquidated damages clause (not being an unlawful penalty), then that is sufficient: *Re a Debtor, ex p Berkshire Finance Co* (1962) 106 Sol Jo 468. The mere fact that the debt arises under an agreement regulated by the Consumer Credit Act 1974 does not exclude the right to serve a statutory demand before judgment has been obtained: *Mills v Grove Securities Ltd* [1997] BPIR 243. A liability to pay legal costs is not a liquidated liability until those costs are assessed and either made subject of a court order or a final costs certificate: *Re a Debtor (No 20 of 1953)* [1954] 1 WLR 1190. See also *Galloppa v Galloppa* [1999] BPIR 352, where it was held that an assisted (legally aided) person had locus standi to serve a statutory demand despite not being beneficially entitled to the debt created by the costs order. Further a solicitors' bill that has not been assessed is not a liquidated debt which can found a petition *Klamer v Kyriakdes and Braier* [2005] BPIR 1142. A non-provable debt can found a bankruptcy petition (*Levy v Legal Services Commission* [2000] BPIR 1065) as can an interim payment order under CPR 1998 r 25.6 (*Maxwell v Bishopsgate Investment Management Ltd* [1994] 1 All ER 261).

A bankruptcy petition based on a judgment debt is not an 'action upon a judgment' within the meaning of the Limitation Act 1980 s 24(1), with the consequence that a judgment creditor may present a petition notwithstanding that it is more than six years old and can no longer be sued upon: *Ridgeway Motors (Isleworth) Ltd v Alts Ltd* [2005] BCC 496. Nonetheless, a non-judgment creditor cannot present a petition on a debt which can no longer be sued upon.

S 267(2)(c)

For the definition of 'inability to pay' see IA 1986 s 268.

S 267(2)(d)

There must be no application outstanding at the relevant time, that is to say an application that has been properly made and made within the time limits in IR 1986 r 6.4. The mere fact that an application to set aside the demand is made out of time does not mean that the requirement of para (d) is unfulfilled. An order extending the time for making a set-aside application does not alter the fact that there was no properly made application at the time of presentation and so will not invalidate a previously invalid petition: *Chohan v Times Newspapers Ltd* [2001] 1 WLR 184. As to whether a defect in the petition, in that it was presented at a time when there was an outstanding application, can be waived, contrast the view expressed by Anthony Mann QC in *Chohan* with that of Lindsay J in *HM Customs & Excise v Jack Baars Wholesale* [2004] BPIR 543. This provision does not prevent a petition being presented if there is an outstanding appeal of a set-aside application: *Hunt v Bennett, Independent April 9, 2001.*

IA 1986 s 267(2)(d) seeks to ensure that the debtor has the full period of three weeks (IA 1986 s *268*) under the statutory demand to consider the position before a petition may be presented. However IA 1986 s 270 overrides this grace period where there is a risk of the assets being diminished; in that situation a petition can be presented within the three week period after service of the statutory demand *Re a Debtor (no 22 of 1993)* [1994] 1 WLR 46.

S 267(3)

This provision has been prospectively repealed by section 170(2) of and Schedule 16 to the Criminal Justice Act 1988 from a day to be appointed.

1.315

268 Definition of 'inability to pay', etc; the statutory demand

(1) For the purposes of section 267(2)(c), the debtor appears to be unable to pay a debt if, but only if, the debt is payable immediately and either—

(a) the petitioning creditor to whom the debt is owed has served on the debtor a demand (known as 'the statutory demand') in the prescribed form requiring him to pay the debt or to secure or compound for it to the satisfaction of the creditor, at least 3 weeks have elapsed since the demand was served and the demand has been neither complied with nor set aside in accordance with the rules, or

(b) execution or other process issued in respect of the debt on a judgment or order of any court in favour of the petitioning creditor, or one or more of the petitioning creditors to whom the debt is owed, has been returned unsatisfied in whole or in part.

> (2) For the purposes of section 267(2)(c) the debtor appears to have no reasonable prospect of being able to pay a debt if, but only if, the debt is not immediately payable and—
>
> (a)   the petitioning creditor to whom it is owed has served on the debtor a demand (also known as 'the statutory demand') in the prescribed form requiring him to establish to the satisfaction of the creditor that there is a reasonable prospect that the debtor will be able to pay the debt when it falls due,
>
> (b)   at least 3 weeks have elapsed since the demand was served, and
>
> (c)   the demand has been neither complied with nor set aside in accordance with the rules.

Notes

S 268

This section sets out the procedure for demonstrating to the court that a debtor is unable to pay his debts, or that he will not realistically be able to pay them when they fall due. Ordinarily this would be a very difficult thing to prove as a creditor will not usually have access to complete information about the debtor's affairs. In order to get around this, following the procedures in this section triggers a statutory presumption of insolvency. This presumption is only really rebuttable to the extent that the debtor may be able to persuade the court to set aside a statutory demand, as to which see IR 1986 r 6.4–5, if that is the route that the creditor has taken. Where an application to set aside a statutory demand has been refused on its merits and a second statutory demand is served for technical reasons on the same debt a fresh application to set aside will be refused if it raises the same issues as were decided on the first application; or the debtor seeks to challenge evidence which could have been challenged on the first application *Coulter v Chief of Dorset Police (No 2)* [2005] BPIR 76.

The creditor who holds a debt payable immediately can either serve a statutory demand or, if he is a judgment creditor, he can seek to obtain an execution of the debt. If the debt is payable at some time in the future, then only a statutory demand can be used to prove the inability of the debtor to pay IA 1986 s 268(2).

A judgment creditor should always consider carefully whether it is in his best interests to serve a statutory demand or to attempt execution first. The advantage of the statutory demand route is speed and simplicity. Attempting execution involves costs and possible delays. However, the failed-execution route is not open to challenge by the debtor once established and the creditor may proceed quickly to a petition. Contrast this with the position under the statutory demand route. If the debtor applies to set the demand aside, as it is his application, he has control over the application process to some extent. A debtor determined to slow a creditor's pursuit of him can raise vast numbers of unmeritorious issues on the application and thereby delay matters. Remember also that a party may appeal an order in insolvency proceedings without permission. That means that the determined debtor can delay things yet further. The moral is 'know your debtor'.

S 268(1)(a)

Note that a statutory demand is document generated by the creditor himself, unlike the 'bankruptcy notice' that was issued by the court under the old law (BA 1914). Therefore it is nothing more than a demand by the creditor for payment that happens to take a particular form. For notes on the form of a statutory demand and on an application to set it aside see the notes to IR 1986 r 6.1 to 6.5. A statutory demand provides the debtor with three weeks to act. If during this time the debt is either not paid or the demand not set aside a petition can be presented. If there are errors in the statutory demand the court will consider whether prejudice has been caused to the debtor. If there has been no prejudice, the statutory demand will not be set aside (*Re a Debtor (No 1 of 1987)* [1989] 1 WLR 271; *Re a Debtor (No 490 SD of 1991)* [1992] 1 WLR 507).

S 268(1)(b)

If a creditor wishes to claim that execution has been returned unsatisfied, he must prove that a proper attempt was made and that still the debt was unsatisfied either in whole or in part (*Skarzynski v Chalford Property Company Ltd* [2001] BPIR 673). If the judgment is later impugned then the petition will be dismissed (*Re a Debtor ex p Berkshire Finance Co Ltd* (1962) 106 Sol Jo 468). Once judgment has been obtained a petition based on the judgment debt may be presented even if the claim was originally for unspecified damages (*Re a Debtor (No 975 of 1937)* [1938] 2 All ER 530).

The failed execution route to a petition does allow a petition to be presented without the opportunity to delay matters that is afforded by the statutory demand procedure. However, once a petition has been presented, the bankruptcy court is not completely bound to recognise the judgment. A bankruptcy court does have a greater jurisdiction to look behind judgments than other courts. But generally the court will only look into the substance of a judgment debt in cases where there appears to be fraud, collusion or a miscarriage of justice. The court will need to be shown something from which it can conclude that, had there been a properly conducted judicial process, it would have been found, or very likely would have been found, that nothing was due to the claimant: see *Dawodu v American Express Bank* [2001] BPIR 983, at p 990; and see also the summary of the law in *McCourt and Siequien v Baron Meats Ltd* [1997] BPIR 114, at pp 120–121. Even where there are no such circumstances, a judgment creditor is not entitled to a bankruptcy order as of right and, if the debtor can show that there is a genuine and serious cross claim overtopping the debt claimed, then the petition may be dismissed (*Popely v Popely* [2004] EWCA Civ 42, [2004] BPIR 778, *Re Bayoil SA* [1999] 1 WLR 147).

If an appeal is proposed but permission is required to appeal out of time it cannot be said that an appeal is pending (*Rehman v Boardman* [2004] BPIR 820). However where an appeal is pending the court will consider whether the appeal is serious and real raising a question of law or a relevant ground of appeal of substance and whether the appeal is being taken seriously (*Re a Debtor (No 799 of 1994) ex p Cobbs Property Services Ltd* [1995] 1 WLR 467). A determination of the General Commissioners of the Inland Revenue is final and the bankruptcy court will not interfere with that determination *Cullinane v Inland Revenue Commissioners* [2000] BPIR 996.

S 268(2)

A creditor who holds a debt that is payable at some time in the future may serve a demand requiring the debtor to establish to the creditor's satisfaction that he will be in position to pay the debt in due course. The prescribed form requires the creditor to first state why he thinks that the debtor will not be in position to pay (IR 1986, Sch 4, form 6.3). These kinds of demand are rare in practice and this is reflected in the almost total absence of any reported authority on this provision. A debtor who is served with this type of demand should set out to the creditor an explanation of why he thinks that he will be able to pay the debt. This explanation may involve a substantial amount of speculation. In practice it is likely to be difficult for the creditor to find serious grounds for doubting what the debtor says unless it is manifestly unbelievable or improbable. The debtor is also helped by the terms of IA 1986 s 271(4), which says that, for the purpose of deciding whether, at the date of the hearing of the petition, the debtor has a reasonable prospect of being able to pay the debt, the court is to presume that the prospect given by the facts and other matters known to the creditor at the time that he entered into the transaction under which the debt arose was a reasonable prospect. That means that the creditor will only be able to persuade the court to make a bankruptcy order if the prospects of payment have worsened since that time.

1.316

269 Creditor with security

(1) A debt which is the debt, or one of the debts, in respect of which a creditor's petition is presented need not be unsecured if either—

    (a)   the petition contains a statement by the person having the right to enforce the security that he is willing, in the event of a bankruptcy order being made, to give up his security for the benefit of all the bankrupt's creditors, or

    (b)   the petition is expressed not to be made in respect of the secured part of the debt and contains a statement by that person of the estimated value at the date of the petition of the security for the secured part of the debt.

(2) In a case falling within subsection (1)(b) the secured and unsecured parts of the debt are to be treated for the purposes of sections 267 and 270 as separate debts.

Notes

S 269

A debt on which a creditor's bankruptcy petition is based must be unsecured: IA 1986 s 267(2)(b). The reason for this is that a secured creditor – provided that his debt is fully secured – has no interest in the bankruptcy process because he is entitled to be paid out of the proceeds of the asset that is charged with the security. However, he can elect to surrender his security and be treated as an unsecured creditor. To the extent that his debt is unsecured, he is entitled to invoke and participate in the bankruptcy process.

A failure to disclose security in a statutory demand (IR 1986 r 6.2) or in a petition will invalidate it if the balance left after accounting for the security is less than £750. If the balance is greater than £750 the court can waive the failure in appropriate cases, taking into account the knowledge of the debtor and any prejudice which may have been caused, and merely direct the amendment of the petition (*Barclays Bank Plc v Mogg* [2003] EWHC 2645, [2004] BPIR 259). IA 1986 s 269 does not apply to insolvent partnerships.

S 269(1)(a)

'Security' is defined in IA 1986 s 383(2). It does not include a lien on papers, books or records save to the extent that the documents relate to title and are held as such (IA 1986 s 383(4)) nor does it include third-party security, such as a guarantee (*Re a Debtor (No 310 of 1988)* [1989] 1 WLR 452). Security may be waived to enable the presentation of a petition notwithstanding that the petitioner is the only creditor of the debtor *Zandfarid v BCCI* [1996] 1 WLR 1420. If a bankruptcy order is made on a petition brought under this provision then on the granting of the order the security is deemed to have been given up (IA 1986 s 383(3)). If the order is later annulled the security revives: this is because the effect of IA 1986 s 383(3) is that the security is deemed to be given up only for the purposes of the bankruptcy provisions in the IA 1986; once the bankruptcy order is annulled, unless the petition is restored for hearing, there are no purposes remaining for which the security is deemed to be given up.

S 269(1)(b)

The value placed on a security must be realistic as the value can only be revisited for the purpose of proving in the bankruptcy with the leave of the court IR 1986 r 6.115(2). Unless leave is given the trustee will redeem the security at the value given by the creditor IR 1986 r 6.117; the rules specifically deal with the position of a secured creditor in a bankruptcy (IR 1986 r 6.115 to 6.119).

1.317

270 Expedited petition

In the case of a creditor's petition presented wholly or partly in respect of a debt which is the subject of a statutory demand under section 268, the petition may be presented before the end of the 3-week period there mentioned if there is a serious possibility that the debtor's property or the value of any of his property will be significantly diminished during that period and the petition contains a statement to that effect.

Notes

S 270

This provision permits presentation of a petition notwithstanding that the three-week period for compliance has not yet elapsed. Unsurprisingly, though, the creditor should at least have served the demand before seeking to take advantage of this facility: *Wehmeyer v Wehmeyer* [2001] BPIR 548. A petition can be expedited even if there is a set aside application pending (*Re a Debtor (No 22 of 1993)* [1994] 1 WLR 46). Use of this provision is always exceptional and the petition must state that there is a serious possibility of property being significantly diminished during the three-week period and it must be proven that a statutory demand has been served. The possibility of the assets being diminished must be serious and substantial. If this is not shown then the petition can be dismissed (*Re a Debtor (No 22 of 1993)* [1994] 1 WLR 46). Although the petition can be expedited the bankruptcy order cannot be made on such a petition until three weeks after service of the statutory demand: see IA 1986 s 271(2).

1.318

271 Proceedings on creditor's petition

(1) The court shall not make a bankruptcy order on a creditor's petition unless it is satisfied that the debt, or one of the debts, in respect of which the petition was presented is either—

    (a)   a debt which, having been payable at the date of the petition or having since become payable, has been neither paid nor secured or compounded for, or

    (b)   a debt which the debtor has no reasonable prospect of being able to pay when it falls due.

(2) In a case in which the petition contains such a statement as is required by section 270, the court shall not make a bankruptcy order until at least 3 weeks have elapsed since the service of any statutory demand under section 268.

(3) The court may dismiss the petition if it is satisfied that the debtor is able to pay all his debts or is satisfied—

    (a)   that the debtor has made an offer to secure or compound for a debt in respect of which the petition is presented,

> (b)   that the acceptance of that offer would have required the dismissal of the petition, and
>
> (c)   that the offer has been unreasonably refused;
>
> and, in determining for the purposes of this subsection whether the debtor is able to pay all his debts, the court shall take into account his contingent and prospective liabilities.
>
> (4) In determining for the purposes of this section what constitutes a reasonable prospect that a debtor will be able to pay a debt when it falls due, it is to be assumed that the prospect given by the facts and other matters known to the creditor at the time he entered into the transaction resulting in the debt was a reasonable prospect.
>
> (5) Nothing in sections 267 to 271 prejudices the power of the court, in accordance with the rules, to authorise a creditor's petition to be amended by the omission of any creditor or debt and to be proceeded with as if things done for the purposes of those sections had been done only by or in relation to the remaining creditors or debts.

Notes

S 271(1)

Before making a bankruptcy order the court must be satisfied that the debt has not been paid, secured or compounded for or that there is no reasonable prospect of it being paid. Any payment must be unconditional; that means that where an offer of payment is dependent on the dismissal of the petition, as it would otherwise be avoided by IA 1986 s 284, the tender should not be treated as relevant for the purposes of this provision: *Smith v Ian Simpson & Co* [2000] BPIR 667. Even if the court is satisfied of those matters, it retains a discretion under IA 1986 s 266 not to make an order. Where a debt has not been paid in full, but it has been reduced to below the bankruptcy level, the court is entitled to take the view that the whole of the debt should have been paid by the time of the hearing and to make an order anyway: see *Lilley v American Express Europe Ltd* [2000] BPIR 70. If there has been no payment by the time of the hearing, the court may yet adjourn the petition if it considers that there is a reasonable prospect of payment being made in the near future: see *Re Gilmartin* [1989] 1 WLR 513. A debtor seeking an adjournment on that basis would be well-advised to have evidence of when and how he will be able to pay (*Dickins v IRC* [2004] BPIR 718). The court should not allow repeated adjournments: *Judd v Williams* [1998] BPIR 88. As to adjournments to allow the debtor to seek legal advice, see *Henry Butcher International Ltd v KG Engineering* [2006] BPIR 56.

If a debtor has disputed the petition debt in an application to set aside a statutory demand, he will not be allowed to raise the same arguments at the hearing of the petition: *Turner v Royal Bank of Scotland* [2000] BPIR 683. This principle is well established despite suggestions to the contrary in some commentaries on IA 1986. Two cases often put forward for the opposing view, *Eberhardt v Mair* [1995] 1 WLR 1180 and *Platts v Western Trust and Savings* [1996] BPIR 339, need to be understood in the light of subsequent statements of the principle: see, *eg Coulter v Chief of Dorset Police (No 2)* [2005] BPIR 76. Despite the principle now being beyond doubt, the basis of it is not clear. Some cases treat it as a matter of issue estoppel: *Brillouet v Hachette Magazines Ltd* [1996] BPIR 518; *Barnes v Whitehead* [2004] BPIR 693; *Coulter v Chief of Dorset Police (No 2)* [2005] BPIR 76. But other cases doubt whether issue estoppel has any part to play in the bankruptcy jurisdiction: *Re a Debtor (32-SD-1991)* [1993] 1 WLR 314 (a case under IA 1986 s 375); and *Maple Division Ltd v Wilson* [1999] BPIR 102. Whatever the juridical basis of the rule, it is clear that it does not completely relieve the court of its duty to make the enquiries required by IA 1986 s 271(1): see the comments of Chadwick LJ in *West Bromwich BS v Crammer* [2002] EWCA Civ 1924, quoted in *Adams v Mason Bullock* [2005] BPIR 241. The best view is probably just that the court is not obliged to waste its time going over matters that have already been adjudicated upon: see *Turner* (*above*) and *Coulter v Chief of Dorset Police (No 2)* [2006] BPIR 10, para 22. While the rule is not as strict as the issue estoppel doctrine, it certainly works in the same way. So a debtor cannot raise an issue again simply because he has found a better way of arguing it, or because he has more evidence to support it (unless that evidence was not available before): *Atherton v Ogunlende* [2003] BPIR 21. Matters that might have been raised in the application to set aside the statutory demand but were not will be examined carefully before being heard on the petition. But where there was no application to set aside the demand at all, the debtor can raise every argument he could have raised before: *Barnes v Whitehead* [2004] BPIR 693. And if the application to set aside the demand is dismissed without consideration of its merits, the debtor is not limited to matters not raised in it: *CIR v Lee-Phipps* [2003] BPIR 803.

See also IR 1986 r 6.25.

S 271(2)

A bankruptcy order cannot be made on an expedited petition (IA 1986 s 270) until three weeks after service of the statutory demand.

S 271(3)

A debtor may defeat a petition if he establishes to the court's satisfaction that he is able to pay all of his debts. For these purposes, the court must be concerned with *actual* ability to pay rather than inability to pay established under IA 1986 s 268, which expressly only applies for the purpose of establishing the right to present a petition under IA 1986 s 267(2). Presumably, then, it is open to a debtor to appear at the hearing of the petition and argue that he could pay the petition debt, and his other debts, if he wanted to but that he is just being awkward. This is not an advisable course of action in the absence of the very strongest evidence of solvency as many registrars and district judges are likely to take the view that non-payment in the face of a bankruptcy petition is good evidence of insolvency. And, given that showing an ability to pay one's debts, gives the court a *discretion* to dismiss the petition (rather than requiring it to do so), the court could make an order in any event.

A debtor may also seek to defeat a petition by showing that he has made an offer to compound or secure the debt that the creditor has unreasonably refused. There are a number of conceptual difficulties in this provision. The first is the requirement that the offer be one that, if accepted, would lead to the petition being dismissed. This is presumably a reference to IA 1986 s 271(1)(a), which requires the court to dismiss the petition if there has been full payment, a grant of full security or a composition of the debt. But it is hard to see how this adds anything to the test. Perhaps the only circumstance in which the requirement has any meaning is where payment or composition is proposed out of the debtor's own assets and a supporting creditor attends the hearing of the petition with a view to seeking a change of carriage of the petition under IR 1986 r 6.31. In those circumstances, had the offer been accepted, the court could have allowed the petition to continue with the supporter having carriage, with the possible consequence that a bankruptcy order is eventually made, the effect of which would be to avoid the payment or composition under IA 1986 s 284. The second problem is in understanding when it would be unreasonable not to accept an offer to secure or compound a debt. Reasonableness may be judged in two ways: as against the creditor's existing entitlement; and as against the likely outcome for the creditor in the event of the debtor being made bankrupt. In the former case, it is hard to see how it could ever be *unreasonable* for the creditor to insist on what he is entitled to and not to accept something less in terms of the amount he is paid, when he is paid or in how he extracts payment (*io* by having to enforce the security). In the latter case, the test is predicated on the debtor actually being insolvent and vulnerable to bankruptcy proceedings. If the creditor were to accept security in those circumstances, he risks having it set aside as a preference (IA 1986 s 340) if or when the inevitable happens. If he were to unreasonably refuse to accept a composition of the debt, it could only be because he would do worse on a *pari passu* distribution in the bankruptcy. In that case, it is hard to see why the scheme of the IA 1986 is encouraging him to take an advantage over the other creditors.

Unreasonable refusal of an offer means a refusal in circumstances where no reasonable creditor would have done so: *Re a Debtor (No 32 of 1993)* [1994] 1 WLR 899. A proposal of an individual voluntary arrangement is not an offer within the meaning of IA 1986 s 271(3) as it is not – in most cases – capable of acceptance by the petitioning creditor alone (*Re a Debtor (No 2389 of 1989)* [1991] Ch 326).

S 271(4)

This means that, where a petition is based on a debtor having no real prospect of paying a debt when it falls due, the creditor must demonstrate to the court not just that the prospects may be poor but that they have got worse since the transaction giving rise to the debt. See also the notes to IA 1986 s 268(2).

Debtor's petition

1.319

272 Grounds of debtor's petition

(1) A debtor's petition may be presented to the court only on the grounds that the debtor is unable to pay his debts.

(2) The petition shall be accompanied by a statement of the debtor's affairs containing—

    (a)   such particulars of the debtor's creditors and of his debts and other liabilities and of his assets as may be prescribed, and

    (b)   such other information as may be prescribed.

Notes

S 272(1)

This section sets out the only grounds upon which a person may apply for their own bankruptcy and the relevant rules appear at IR 1986 r 6.37 to 6.50. The presentation of such a petition does not effect a disposition under s 37 Matrimonial Causes Act 1973, *Woodley v Woodley (No 2)* [1994] 1 WLR 1167. In contrast to a creditor's petition inability to pay debts is not defined and there is no minimum debt level. Inability to pay debts can be tested on a cash flow basis or a balance sheet exercise but, for this section, the test is one of ability to pay debts as they fall due: *Re Coney (A Bankrupt)* [1998] BPIR 333. IA 1986 s 382 defines bankruptcy debts and it is clear from that section that the debts include future and contingent liabilities.

Aside from the specific circumstances where the court is directed not to make a bankruptcy order (IA 1986 s 273) the court has a general power to dismiss or stay a petition under IA 1986 s 266. The court may refuse to make an order if the petition is an abuse of process such as to avoid committal on a judgment summons (*Re Painter ex p Painter* [1895] 1 QB 85). However if the protection of an instalment order has already been obtained then the court may make the order (*Re a Debtor (No 17 of 1966) ex p Debtor v Allen* [1967] Ch 590). It is also an abuse to present a joint petition between two debtors where there are no joint assets or liabilities and in that situation the court will strike out one of the names (*Re Bond* (1888) 21 QBD 17).

S 272(2)

See IR 1986 r 6.38, 6.39 for further requirements as to the contents of the petition. A deposit of £325 is payable on the issue of the petition (Insolvency Proceedings (Fees) Order 2004) (as amended). Such requirements are not a breach of the right to access to the courts (*R v Lord Chancellor ex p Lightfoot* [2000] BPIR 120).

1.320

273 Appointment of insolvency practitioner by the court

(1) Subject to the next section, on the hearing of a debtor's petition the court shall not make a bankruptcy order if it appears to the court—

(a) that if a bankruptcy order were made the aggregate amount of the bankruptcy debts, so far as unsecured, would be less than the small bankruptcies level,

(b) that if a bankruptcy order were made, the value of the bankrupt's estate would be equal to or more than the minimum amount,

(c) that within the period of 5 years ending with the presentation of the petition the debtor has neither been adjudged bankrupt nor made a composition with his creditors in satisfaction of his debts or a scheme of arrangement of his affairs, and

(d) that it would be appropriate to appoint a person to prepare a report under section 274.

'The minimum amount' and 'the small bankruptcies level' mean such amounts as may for the time being be prescribed for the purposes of this section.

(2) Where on the hearing of the petition, it appears to the court as mentioned in subsection (1), the court shall appoint a person who is qualified to act as an insolvency practitioner in relation to the debtor—

(a) to prepare a report under the next section, and

(b) subject to section 258(3) in Part VIII, to act in relation to any voluntary arrangement to which the report relates either as trustee or otherwise for the purpose of supervising its implementation.

Notes

S 273

This provision enables a bankruptcy order to be avoided in certain circumstances in favour of use of the voluntary arrangement procedure.

S 273(1)

In order for the court to make an order under this section the total debts of the debtor must be less than £40,000 and the value of the debtor's estate must be equal to or more than £4,000 (Insolvency Proceedings (Monetary Limits) (Amendment) Order 2004, SI 2004/547). Further the debtor must not have been made either bankrupt in the past five years or been the subject of a composition with his creditors or a scheme of arrangement of his affairs. If these conditions are met the court has a discretion to seek a report from an insolvency practitioner under IA 1986 s 274 and if appropriate for that person to act as supervisor of the voluntary arrangement.

S 273(2)

The remuneration of the licensed insolvency practitioner involved is subject to scrutiny of the Court pursuant to the Practice Statement – the Fixing and Approval of the Remuneration of Appointees (2004) [2004] BPIR 953; and see *Re Cabletel Installations Ltd* [2005] BPIR 28.

1.321

274 Action on report of insolvency practitioner

(1) A person appointed under section 273 shall inquire into the debtor's affairs and, within such period as the court may direct, shall submit a report to the court stating whether the debtor is willing, for the purposes of Part VIII, to make a proposal for a voluntary arrangement.

(2) A report which states that the debtor is willing as above mentioned shall also state—

    (a)   whether, in the opinion of the person making the report, a meeting of the debtor's creditors should be summoned to consider the proposal, and

    (b)   if in that person's opinion such a meeting should be summoned, the date on which, and time and place at which, he proposes the meeting should be held.

(3) On considering a report under this section the court may—

    (a)   without any application, make an interim order under section 252, if it thinks that it is appropriate to do so for the purpose of facilitating the consideration and implementation of the debtor's proposal, or

    (b)   if it thinks it would be inappropriate to make such an order, make a bankruptcy order.

(4) An interim order made by virtue of this section ceases to have effect at the end of such period as the court may specify for the purpose of enabling the debtor's proposal to be considered by his creditors in accordance with the applicable provisions of Part VIII.

(5) Where it has been reported to the court under this section that a meeting of the debtor's creditors should be summoned, the person making the report shall, unless the court otherwise directs, summon that meeting for the time, date and place proposed in his report.

The meeting is then deemed to have been summoned under section 257 in Part VIII, and subsections (2) and (3) of that section, and sections 258 to 263 apply accordingly.

Notes

S 274(1)

If the court has made an order under IA 1986 s 273(2) the person appointed must investigate the circumstances surrounding the petition and make a report. The report is that of the court and it must pay the appointed person a fee of £310 including VAT in accordance with Insolvency Proceedings (Fees) Order 2004 SI 2004/593, Art 5.

S 274(2)

The report must specify whether the debtor is willing to make a proposal for a voluntary arrangement. Any proposal is still that of the debtor and not the court and the debtor can refuse to make a proposal. In such situation it must be assumed that the court will make a bankruptcy order.

S 274(3)

The report must then be submitted to the court, which will then assess the contents and determine how the matter should proceed. The court can either make an interim order for a period to be determined by the court or a bankruptcy order. Therefore if the court believes that a meeting should be called then the court can make an interim order under IA 1986 s 252 and the meeting should be called by the person who made the report.

S 274(5)

If a creditors' meeting is called then regard must be had to IA 1986 s 257 to 263 as such a meeting will be deemed to have occurred under those sections.

1.322

275 [repealed]

Notes

S 275

This section was repealed by s 269, 278(2) EA 2002 from 1 April 2004 subject to savings provisions Enterprise Act (2002) Commencement No 4 and Transitional Provisions and Savings) Order 2003, SI 2003/2093, art 8.

Other cases for special consideration

1.323

276 Default in connection with voluntary arrangement

(1) The court shall not make a bankruptcy order on a petition under section 264(1)(c) (supervisor of, or person bound by, voluntary arrangement proposed and approved) unless it is satisfied—
    (a) that the debtor has failed to comply with his obligations under the voluntary arrangement, or
    (b) that information which was false or misleading in any material particular or which contained material omissions—
        (i) was contained in any statement of affairs or other document supplied by the debtor under Part VIII to any person, or
        (ii) was otherwise made available by the debtor to his creditors at or in connection with a meeting summoned under that Part, or
    (c) that the debtor has failed to do all such things as may for the purposes of the voluntary arrangement have been reasonably required of him by the supervisor of the arrangement.

> (2) Where a bankruptcy order is made on a petition under section 264(1)(c), any expenses properly incurred as expenses of the administration of the voluntary arrangement in question shall be a first charge on the bankrupt's estate.

Notes

S 276

Where an individual voluntary arrangement ('IVA') (IA 1986 s 252 ff) has been made, the debtor's insolvency will already have been established. That means that the statutory demand procedure applicable to creditors' petitions need not be followed. Rather, the supervisor or IVA creditor can proceed straight to a petition provided that it can prove one of the grounds in s 276(1). The form of a petition under this section is Form 6.10.

Obviously, it is a pre-requisite to invoking this jurisdiction that there be a valid IVA in the first place. In *Re Plummer* [2004] BPIR 767, after an arrangement had been in place for a number of years, its supervisor presented a petition against the debtor on her default. But the petition was dismissed when it was established that the IVA was never properly constituted.

If a bankruptcy order is made following a failed IVA, then the question arises of what should happen to the monies already realised within the IVA – whether it should pass to the IVA creditors or to the bankruptcy creditors. The usual answer is that the money paid into the IVA will be held on trust for the IVA creditors and that, once constituted that trust continues. But this is subject any express provision in the IVA itself. For a full discussion see: *Re N T Gallagher & Son Ltd* [2002] 2 BCLC 133. And for the position as regards funds introduced into the IVA by third parties see: *Cooper v Official Receiver* [2003] BPIR 55.

S 276(1)

The petition must include within its particulars the grounds relied upon for the making of an order. It is the responsibility of the petitioner to establish the grounds and a failure to do so will lead to the petition being dismissed. It is nowhere required that the petition be presented during the period for which the IVA was to last: see *Harris v Gross* [2001] BPIR 586. But petitions brought long after the alleged default may well be less likely to result in an order. The court maintains a discretion to dismiss a petition brought under this provision even if the ground relied upon is made out; for example where the majority of creditors oppose the making of the order, or where the continuance of the IVA would still provide a better outcome for all concerned: see eg *Kaye v Bourne* [2005] BPIR 590.

S 276(1)(a)

The fact that the non-compliance is remedied by the debtor prior to the hearing of the petition is no bar to the making of a bankruptcy order *Carter-Knight v Peat* [2000] BPIR 968. In exercising its discretion on a petition, the court will have regard to the seriousness of the default and whether it was intentional: see eg *Re Keenan* [1998] BPIR 205.

S 276(1)(b)

If the petition is presented on the ground that material was false or misleading the court assesses whether the material was false or misleading by reference to whether if the true position had been presented the creditors would have considered the proposals differently; information may be misleading by omission: *Re Tack* [2000] BPIR 164. And if there is a material change of circumstance between the preparation of the proposal and its consideration at the meeting of creditors, then the debtor is bound to make the change known: *Somji v Cadbury Schweppes plc* [2001] BPIR 172.

S 276(1)(c)

This provides for the situation where the debtor is refusing to cooperate with the supervisor of the IVA. Often such a debtor will also make himself liable to a petition under s 276(1)(a), by breaching one of the IVA's express terms. But an example of pure non-cooperation is given by *Vadher v Weisgard* [1998] BPIR 295, in which Chadwick J referred to an IVA failing where the supervisor's time costs in dealing with a bothersome debtor absorbed all of the payments received.

S 276(2)

If the order is made any expenses properly incurred as expenses of the individual voluntary arrangement will be a first charge on the bankrupt's estate.

1.324

277 Petition based on criminal bankruptcy order

(1) *Subject to section 266(3), the court shall make a bankruptcy order on a petition under section 264(1)(d) on production of a copy of the criminal bankruptcy order on which the petition is based.*

This does not apply if it appears to the court that the criminal bankruptcy order has been rescinded on appeal.

(2) *Subject to the provisions of this Part, the fact that an appeal is pending against any conviction by virtue of which a criminal bankruptcy order was made does not affect any proceedings on a petition under section 264(1)(d) based on that order.*

(3) *For the purposes of this section, an appeal against a conviction is pending—*
   (a) *in any case, until the expiration of the period of 28 days beginning with the date of conviction;*
   (b) *if notice of appeal to the Court of Appeal is given during that period and during that period the appellant notifies the official receiver of it, until the determination of the appeal and thereafter for so long as an appeal to the House of Lords is pending within the meaning of section 40(5) of the Powers of Criminal Courts Act 1973.*

Notes

S 277

The power to make criminal bankruptcy orders has been abolished and they have been replaced by confiscation orders.

Commencement and duration of bankruptcy; discharge

1.325

278 Commencement and continuance

The bankruptcy of an individual against whom a bankruptcy order has been made—
   (a)   commences with the day on which the order is made, and

(b)   continues until the individual is discharged under the following
       provisions of this Chapter.

Notes

S 278

Unlike the compulsory winding-up of a company which commences at the time of the presentation of the petition for winding up (IA 1986 s 129(2)), the bankruptcy commences on the day of the order, and lasts until discharge. This provision should be read together with IR 1986 r 6.33, 6.34, 6.45 and 6.46. After discharge, the bankrupt continues to be subject to obligations owed to the trustee (see IA 1986 s 333 below). Discharge has no effect on the functions of the trustee or operation of Part IX (IA 1986 ss 264 -371) (see IA 1986 s 281(1)) and a bankrupt remains liable, under Chapter VI (IA 1986 s 350 to 362), for bankruptcy offences committed before discharge.

I.326

279 Duration

(1) A bankrupt is discharged from bankruptcy at the end of the period of one year beginning with the date on which the bankruptcy commences.

(2) If before the end of that period the official receiver files with the court a notice stating that investigation of the conduct and affairs of the bankrupt under section 289 is unnecessary or concluded, the bankrupt is discharged when the notice is filed.

(3) On the application of the official receiver or the trustee of a bankrupt's estate, the court may order that the period specified in subsection (1) shall cease to run until-
  (a)   the end of a specified period, or
  (b)   the fulfilment of a specified condition.

(4) The court may make an order under subsection (3) only if satisfied that the bankrupt has failed or is failing to comply with an obligation under this Part.

(5) In subsection (3)(b) 'condition' includes a condition requiring that the court be satisfied of something.

(6) In the case of an individual who is adjudged bankrupt on a petition under section 264(1)(d):
  (a)   subsections (1) to (5) shall not apply, and
  (b)   the bankrupt is discharged from bankruptcy by an order of the court under section 280.

(7) This section is without prejudice to any power of the court to annul a bankruptcy order.

Notes

S 279(I)

This provides for the automatic discharge of a bankrupt after one year. The provision was introduced by EA 2002 with effect from 1 April 2004. Prior to April 2004, the general position was that bankrupts (other than those subject to a criminal bankruptcy order or second bankruptcy within fifteen years) would be automatically discharged after three years. Time runs from the date of the bankruptcy order and not from the date of presentation of the petition. For transitional provisions see EA 2002 Schedule 19. Generally a person subject to the transitional provisions will be automatically discharged either on 1 April 2005 or three years after the bankruptcy order, whichever is earlier. A bankrupt may obtain a certificate of discharge, see IR 1986 r.6.220.

S 279(2)

This provides for a discharge to take place earlier than one year after the bankruptcy order in appropriate cases. The official receiver must notify the creditors and the trustee of his intention to file a notice (IR 1986 r 6.214A), and where the official receiver rejects any objections raised there may be an appeal under IR 1986 7.50(2).

S 279(3)

Either the official receiver or the trustee may apply for an order suspending the discharge and the relevant rules dealing with the evidence and procedure in relation to suspension are IR 1986 r 6.215, 6.216.

S 279(3)–(5)

The new provisions are sufficiently similar to the former provisions (set out in italics after the notes to this section) that it is likely that the former case law will still be of relevance.

In *Re Jacobs (A Bankrupt)* [1999] 1 WLR 619 it was held that there was jurisdiction for an interim order to be made by the court suspending the automatic discharge from bankruptcy where, despite the bankrupt's argument not being heard because of a shortage of time, the court was satisfied of the non-compliance by the undischarged bankrupt on the application of the official receiver. In such circumstances, and by virtue of the principles of natural justice, there ought ordinarily to be provision made for the term of the extension to be extremely short until such time as the matter can be fully argued.

In *Bagnall v Official Receiver (CA)* [2003] EWCA Civ 1925, [2004] BPIR 445 Arden LJ, considering the approach of Mr Michael Burton QC in *Re Jacobs*, held in relation to interim orders that a judge cannot decide all matters in dispute until the substantive hearing, but he must be satisfied that there are reasonable grounds for concluding that an order would be made on the substantive hearing on the material then placed before the court. Arden LJ considered that the court would ordinarily lean on the side of the official receiver because of the consequences of refusing an interim order (ie the automatic discharge cannot be reversed).

In *Hardy v Focus Insurance Co. Ltd (In Liquidation)* [1997] BPIR 77 Walker J held that in deciding whether to make an application under s 279(3) the official receiver was performing a pubic law function and neither s 303(1) nor s 302(2) IA 1986 could be used to give the court jurisdiction to give directions to the official receiver thereon.

S 279(6)

IA 1986 s 264(1)(d) relates to criminal bankruptcy orders.

S 279(7)

The court has the power to annul a bankruptcy order under IA 1986 s 282.

1.327

279 Duration

(1) Subject as follows, a bankrupt is discharged from bankruptcy—

(a) in the case of an individual who was adjudged bankrupt on a petition under section 264(1)(d) or who had been an undischarged bankrupt at any time in the period of 15 years ending with the commencement of the bankruptcy, by an order of the court under the section next following, and

(b) in any other case, by the expiration of the relevant period under this section.

(2) That period is as follows—

(a) where a certificate for the summary administration of the bankrupt's estate has been issued and is not revoked before the bankrupt's discharge, the period of 2 years beginning with the commencement of the bankruptcy, and

(b) in any other case, the period of 3 years beginning with the commence-ment of the bankruptcy.

(3) Where the court is satisfied on the application of the official receiver that an undischarged bankrupt in relation to whom subsection (1)(b) applies has failed or is failing to comply with any of his obligations under this Part, the court may order that the relevant period under this section shall cease to run for such period, or until the fulfilment of such conditions (including a condition requiring the court to be satisfied as to any matter), as may be specified in the order.

(4) This section is without prejudice to any power of the court to annul a bankruptcy order.

Notes

S 279

This is the former s 279; see the notes to IA 1986 s 279(1) above.

1.328

280 Discharge by order of the court

(1) An application for an order of the court discharging an individual from bankruptcy in a case falling within section 279(6) may be made by the bankrupt at any time after the end of the period of 5 years beginning with the date on which the bankruptcy commences.

(2) On an application under this section the court may—
(a) refuse to discharge the bankrupt from bankruptcy,
(b) make an order discharging him absolutely, or
(c) make an order discharging him subject to such conditions with respect to any income which may subsequently become due to him, or with respect to property devolving upon him, or acquired by him, after his discharge, as may be specified in the order.

(3) The court may provide for an order falling within subsection (2)(b) or (c) to have immediate effect or to have its effect suspended for such

> period, or until the fulfilment of such conditions (including a condition requiring the court to be satisfied as to any matter), as may be specified in the order.

Notes

S 280(1)

IA 1986 s 279(1) (automatic discharge) is not applicable to individuals who are adjudged bankrupt under IA 1986 s 264(1)(d). An application for discharge must be made; but not before the end of 5 years from the commencement of the bankruptcy. This provision should be read together with IR 1986 r 6.217i to 6.219.

S 280(2)

The Secretary of State may appeal against the grant of a discharge IR 1986 r 7.48(1).

S 280(3)

It is open to the court to suspend the effect of an order it makes under subsection (2)(b) or (c) either for a specified period or until any conditions imposed have been fulfilled.

1.329

281 Effect of discharge

(1) Subject as follows, where a bankrupt is discharged, the discharge releases him from all the bankruptcy debts, but has no effect—

   (a)   on the functions (so far as they remain to be carried out) of the trustee of his estate, or

   (b)   on the operation, for the purposes of the carrying out of those functions, of the provisions of this Part;

and, in particular, discharge does not affect the right of any creditor of the bankrupt to prove in the bankruptcy for any debt from which the bankrupt is released.

(2) Discharge does not affect the right of any secured creditor of the bankrupt to enforce his security for the payment of a debt from which the bankrupt is released.

(3) Discharge does not release the bankrupt from any bankruptcy debt which he incurred in respect of, or forbearance in respect of which was secured by means of, any fraud or fraudulent breach of trust to which he was a party.

(4) Discharge does not release the bankrupt from any liability in respect of a fine imposed for an offence or from any liability under a recognisance except, in the case of a penalty imposed for an offence under an enactment relating to the public revenue or of a recognisance, with the consent of the Treasury.

(4A) In subsection (4) the reference to a fine includes a reference to a confiscation order under Part 2,3 or 4 of the Proceeds of Crime Act 2002.

(5) Discharge does not, except to such extent and on such conditions as the court may direct, release the bankrupt from any bankruptcy debt which—

(a) consists in a liability to pay damages for negligence, nuisance or breach of a statutory, contractual or other duty, or to pay damages by virtue of Part I of the Consumer Protection Act 1987, being in either case damages in respect of personal injuries to any person, or

(b) arises under any order made in family proceedings or under a *maintenance assessment* [maintenance calculation] made under the Child Support Act 1991

(6) Discharge does not release the bankrupt from such other bankruptcy debts, not being debts provable in his bankruptcy, as are prescribed.

(7) Discharge does not release any person other than the bankrupt from any liability (whether as partner or co-trustee of the bankrupt or otherwise) from which the bankrupt is released by the discharge, or from any liability as surety for the bankrupt or as a person in the nature of such a surety.

(8) In this section—

'family proceedings' means—

(a) family proceedings within the meaning of the Magistrates' Courts Act 1980 and any proceedings which would be such proceedings but for section 65(1)(ii) of that Act (proceedings for variation of order for periodical payments); and

(b) family proceedings within the meaning of Part V of the Matrimonial and Family Proceedings Act 1984.

'fine' means the same as in the Magistrates' Courts Act 1980; and

'personal injuries' includes death and any disease or other impairment of a person's physical or mental condition.

Notes

S 281(1)

'Bankruptcy debts' are defined in s 382. The bankrupt's discharge from 'bankruptcy debts' under this section does not affect any remaining functions of the trustee or the rights of creditors to prove in the bankruptcy for debts from which the bankrupt has been released.

There is no provision in s 281 dealing with the effect that discharge has on a voluntary arrangement proposal which has not been approved by the creditors at the date of discharge. It is the essence of a voluntary arrangement that under it each creditor comprises or releases his rights against the debtor (see *Re Bradley-Hole (a Bankrupt)* [1995] 1 WLR 1097, at 1118–1119 per Rimer J). After discharge the rights of the bankrupt's creditors are against the bankrupt's estate and not the debtor himself. If the debtor is discharged the creditors no longer have anything to release and a valid IVA cannot be entered into *Re Ravichandran* [2004] BPIR 814. See also *Wright v Official Receiver* [2001] BPIR 196, Cty Ct.

S 281(2)

Existing rights of secured creditors of the bankrupt to enforce securities are not affected by the discharge.

S 281(3)

Discharge does not release the bankrupt from liability for debts related to fraud or fraudulent breaches of trust. In *Manders v Evans* [2001] 1 WLR 2378 it was stated by Ferris J that the natural meaning of the word 'fraud' is actual fraud in the *Derry v Peek* (1889) 14 App Cas 337 sense. In *Woodland-Ferrari v UCL Group Retirement Benefits Scheme* [2002] EWHC 1354

(Ch), [2002] 3 WLR 1154 Ferris J held that there was no reason for regarding 'fraudulent breach of trust' in IA 1986 s 281(3) as meaning anything different from what the same expression meant in s 28 of the 1914 Act. Dishonesty therefore remains an essential ingredient.

S 281(4)

A 'fine' includes confiscation orders by virtue of the Criminal Justice Act 1988.

S 281(5)(a)

The court has the discretion under this sub-section to release the bankrupt from debts arising from negligence, nuisance, breach of duty, personal injury and family proceedings. In *Anglo Manx Group Ltd v Aitken* [2002] BPIR 215, it was held that the court was bound by the Court of Appeal's decision *In re Benzon; Bower v Chetwynd* [1914] 2 Ch 68 that for the purposes of limitation time did not cease to run during the period of bankruptcy.

S 281(5)(b)

The words in italics are substituted for the words 'maintenance calculation' from a day to be appointed Child Support, Pensions and Social Security Act 2000 s 26 Sch 3.

S 281(6)

The bankrupt is not released from debts not provable in the bankruptcy as are prescribed in IA 1986 r 12.3, and the bankrupt's obligations arising under a confiscation order IR 1986 r 6.223 remain unaffected. Student loans which a bankrupt receives or is entitled to receive after commencement of his bankruptcy do not form part of his estate. The liability to repay the student loan remains despite discharge from bankruptcy where the bankruptcy order was made on or after 1 September 2004 (Education (Student Support) (No 2) Regulations 2002 (SI 2002/3200) (as amended).

> **1.330**
>
> **281A Post-discharge restrictions**
>
> Schedule 4A to this Act (bankruptcy restrictions order and bankruptcy restrictions undertaking) shall have effect.

Notes

S 281A

This provision was introduced by the EA 2002 with effect from 1 April 2004. Bankruptcy restriction orders ('BROs') and undertakings ('BRUs') are dealt with in detail under IA 1986 Sch 4A. A BRO is made for a minimum of 2 and a maximum of 15 years. Under the BRO regime the bankrupt is subject to a series of restrictions (*EA 2002, Sch 21, IA 1986 s 426A*). The provision applies to all undischarged bankrupts whenever the order was made; however in making a BRO the court cannot take into account behaviour of the bankrupt prior to 1 April 2004 (*Enterprise Act 2002* (*Commencement No 4 and Transitional Provisions and Savings*) *Order 2003 art 7, SI 2003/2093*).

1.331

282 Court's power to annul bankruptcy order

(1) The court may annul a bankruptcy order if it at any time appears to the court—

    (a)   that, on the grounds existing at the time the order was made, the order ought not to have been made, or

    (b)   that, to the extent required by the rules, the bankruptcy debts and the expenses of the bankruptcy have all, since the making of the order, been either paid or secured for to the satisfaction of the court.

(2) The court may annul a bankruptcy order made against an individual on a petition under paragraph (a), (b) or (c) of section 264(1) if it at any time appears to the court, on an application by the Official Petitioner—

    (a)   *that the petition was pending at a time when a criminal bankruptcy order was made against the individual or was presented after such an order was so made, and*

    (b)   *no appeal is pending (within the meaning of section 277) against the individual's conviction of any offence by virtue of which the criminal bankruptcy order was made;*

and the court shall annul a bankruptcy order made on a petition under section 264(1)(d) if it at any time appears to the court that the criminal bankruptcy order on which the petition was based has been rescinded in consequence of an appeal.

(3) The court may annul a bankruptcy order whether or not the bankrupt has been discharged from the bankruptcy.

(4) Where the court annuls a bankruptcy order (whether under this section or under section 261 or 263D in Part VIII)—

    (a)   any sale or other disposition of property, payment made or other thing duly done, under any provision in this Group of Parts, by or under the authority of the official receiver or a trustee of the bankrupt's estate or by the court is valid, but

    (b)   if any of the bankrupt's estate is then vested, under any such provision, in such a trustee, it shall vest in such person as the court may appoint or, in default of any such appointment, revert to the bankrupt on such terms (if any) as the court may direct;

and the court may include in its order such supplemental provisions as may be authorised by the rules.

(5) In determining for the purposes of section 279 whether a person was an undischarged bankrupt at any time, any time when he was a bankrupt by virtue of an order that was subsequently annulled is to be disregarded.

Notes

S 282

Where the court is satisfied that either of the two grounds for annulling a bankruptcy is established it may then exercise its discretion whether to grant an annulment. It is a two stage process: *Society of Lloyds v Waters* [2001] BPIR 698. The court will not exercise the discretion in favour of an annulment merely because the creditor who petitioned for the bankruptcy does not oppose the annulment: *Leicester v Plumtree Farms Ltd* [2004] BPIR 296.

S 282(1)

The relevant rules for annulment are contained in IR 1986 r 6.206 to 6.214 (for appeals and the court's power to rescind and review individual insolvency matters see IA s 375).The difference between appeal, rescission and annulment is sometimes missed. The distinctions are highlighted in *Hoare v IRC* [2002] BPIR 986.

Section 282 does not contain a prescribed list of applicants. It may be invoked by the debtor or petitioning creditor or even the spouse of the bankrupt where the bankruptcy order is being used to defeat an ancillary relief claim *F v F* [1994] 1 FLR 359, *Couvaras v Wolf* [2002] FLR 107. There are two grounds upon which an application for an annulment can be made; under s 282(1)(a) if it appears that on any grounds existing at the time the order was made, the order ought not to have been made; and under s 282(1)(b), where the bankruptcy debts and expenses of the bankruptcy have been paid or secured to the satisfaction of the court.

As to the issue of costs on an annulment application; in *Butterworth v Souter* [2000] BPIR 582 Neuberger J stated that there is normally a strong argument for saying that the petitioning creditor should pay the trustee's costs if the annulment is under s 282(1)(a), and a strong argument for saying that the bankrupt should pay the trustee's costs if the annulment is under s 282(1)(b). But see *Thornhill v Atherton* [2005] BPIR 437 where the Court of Appeal upheld an annulment under s 282(1)(a) which was conditional on the bankrupt paying the trustee's fees and disbursements because of delay on the part of the bankrupt.

S 282(1)(a)

The court may annul a bankruptcy order if it appears that *'on any grounds existing at the time the order was made, the order ought not to have been made ...'*

It is sufficient for the applicant to show that looking back to the time of the bankruptcy order it can be seen that grounds existed on which the bankruptcy order ought not have been made. It does not matter that the debtor did not put the grounds before the court at the earlier hearing of the petition. It is enough for him to put them before the court at the later time of the hearing of the annulment application, provided that they did exist at the earlier time of the hearing of the bankruptcy petition. The burden of proof is on the applicant. It is not sufficient for the applicant to say that at the time of the bankruptcy order grounds *may* have existed on which the bankruptcy order ought not to have been made. The applicant has to establish that at the time the bankruptcy order was made grounds *did* exist on which the bankruptcy order ought not to have been made: see *Society of Lloyds v Waters* [2001] BPIR 698 per Park J. For instance that there was no liquidated debt supporting the petition as is required by IA 1986 s 267; a demand under an unassessed solicitor's bill (in the absence of agreement or an admission that a certain sum is due) will not constitute a liquidated debt (*see Klamer v Kyriakides and Braier* [2005] BPIR 1142, a statutory demand case).

A court when asked to make an order under s 282(1)(a) should satisfy itself, by such investigation of the facts as it thinks necessary, that the bankruptcy order ought not have been made. Bankruptcy is a class remedy. A court should not annul a bankruptcy order by consent and without investigation: *Housiax v HM Customs and Excise* [2003] BPIR 858 per Chadwick LJ. In *Henwood v Customs and Excise* [1998] BPIR 339 the Court of Appeal referred to Nicholls LJ's observations in *Re a Debtor (No 1 of 1987)* [1989] 1 WLR 271 and gave leave to a bankrupt to appeal from a refusal to annul a bankruptcy order where the bankruptcy order had been made on the basis of a debt disputed on substantial grounds and in the debtor's absence due to a misunderstanding with his solicitors.

Where the grounds supporting an annulment application have already been considered at the statutory demand or petition stage the bankrupt ought not be able to revisit the issue on an annulment application *Atherton v Ogunlende* [2003] BPIR 21, *Balendran v The Law Society* [2004] BPIR 859; *cf Owo-Samson v Barclays Bank plc* [2003] BPIR 1373 where the grounds relied upon in the annulment application were not raised at an earlier stage and the bankrupt was permitted to rely on them on the annulment application.

The court retains a broad discretion as to whether or not to order an annulment; it is not automatic upon the court being satisfied that grounds existed at the time the order was made such that the order ought not to have been made. As to the exercise of the court's discretion see *Askew v Peter Dominic Ltd* [1997] BPIR 163; *Hope v Premierpace (Europe) Ltd* [1999] BPIR 695; *Howman v Jackson* [2005] EWHC 1114 (Ch). In many cases, the existence of a dispute about the amount of the debts or bankruptcy expenses will prevent the court being satisfied that the debts and expenses have actually been paid. Where the bankrupt can satisfy the court that the petition debt is genuinely disputed the court will annul the bankruptcy order unless there are special circumstances *Guinan III v Caldwell Associates Ltd* [2003] EWCH 3348 (Ch), [2004] BPIR 531.

S 282(1)(b)

In order to see what is meant by the words 'to the extent required by the rules' in 282(1)(b) one has to look at IR 1986 r 6.209 and 6.211 *Re Robertson (a Bankrupt)* [1989] 1 WLR 1139. Despite the apparent acceptance by Warner J in *Re Robertson* of a submission that there could be no application until debts have actually been proved, IR 1986 6.209 clearly contemplates that an application might be made in the face of unproved debts, and in effect provides a mechanism for compelling or accelerating or requiring a proof. *As to the meaning of 'bankruptcy debt' see IA 1986* s 382. Not less than 21 days before the date fixed for the hearing of s 282(1)(b) application a report has to be provided by the trustee or official receiver IR 1986 r 6.207.

There is no fixed time limit on making the annulment application, but the sooner it is made the better. The longer the delay, the greater the risk that records of and/or contact with creditors will have been lost. Bankrupts should not assume that they can wait for a long period and then hope to have the bankruptcy set aside by, in effect, paying off less than the debts because some creditors have disappeared or lost interest *Gill v Quinn* [2005] BPIR 129.

The jurisdiction to annul is discretionary and will not be exercised simply on proof that debts which have been proved and not proved have been paid. The approach of the court to an application on this ground has been usefully discussed in *Harper v Buchler* [2004] BPIR 724 where Deputy Registrar Barnett, having held that statutory interest was not a bankruptcy debt within the meaning of IA 1986 s 382, set out the following general principles:

(1) The grant of an annulment is a privilege. The court has a completely unfettered discretion in deciding whether or not to grant it; (2) In considering the exercise of its discretion the court may have regard to all the circumstances of the matter before it. The court is not limited to an analysis of the applicant's conduct; (3) The length of time between the date of the bankruptcy order and the date of the application for the annulment of the order is one such factor that the court may take into consideration. If an application for an annulment is made very promptly it may very well be that a court would disregard the issue of statutory interest. Equally, if the application was not made until some years later, the court may very well have regard to that; (4) The court would also have regard to the source of the funds being made available to discharge creditors and would doubtless have regard to the question of whether the bankruptcy, if realised, is sufficient to discharge both the principal debts and any statutory interest which would ordinarily accrue in the bankruptcy.

See also *Harper v Buchler (no 2)* [2005] BPIR 577 and *Wilcock v Duckworth* [2005] BPIR 682 for discussion of the circumstances in which statutory interest should be paid before an annulment will be granted. The Bankruptcy Court will normally require statutory interest to be paid by a debtor where he or she seeks an annulment in circumstances where there are sufficient assets in the bankruptcy estate to pay all liabilities, costs, fees and expenses. Third party funds may avoid the payment of DTI fees but that should not in principle deprive creditors of interest on their claims. However, in Protracted Realisation Unit (PRU) cases only, the payment of statutory interest should only be for the period from the date of the bankruptcy order whilst the estate is being handled by the official receiver until his release and then from the appointment of a trustee by the Secretary of State (through the PRU) to annulment, see *Wilcock*.

However, the concept that the debts and expenses may be 'secured for' is more flexible and if satisfied that the debts and expenses cannot exceed a particular amount and payment of this amount is fully secured, the court may be satisfied that the statutory conditions have been met

Engel v Peri [2002] EWHC 799 (Ch), [2002] BPIR 961. In *Engel* Ferris J held that the court could make a conditional order for annulment (ie conditional upon the payment into court of security for the costs and expenses of the bankruptcy to abide the determination of a pending application under IA 1986 s 303). However, such an order might lead to doubt about precisely when the annulment took place on the footing that the conditions were satisfied. A better way of dealing with the position is for the court to order that the annulment, in unconditional form, shall not be perfected by the court office until evidence has been produced showing that the trustee is satisfied that the requisite payments into court have been made.

Where a debtor cannot satisfy the stringent conditions established by s 282(1)(b) and the Insolvency Rules, he cannot then circumvent those conditions by invoking the provisions of IA 1986 s 375: *IRC v Robinson* [1999] BPIR 333.

S 282(2)

This sub-section is prospectively repealed by the Criminal Justice Act 1988, s 170(2), Sch 16, as from a day to be appointed.

S 282(5)

This provision has been repealed by the EA 2002 s 269, 278 as from 1 April 2004.

———

1.332

283 Definition of bankrupt's estate

(1) Subject as follows, a bankrupt's estate for the purposes of any of this Group of Parts comprises—
  (a) all property belonging to or vested in the bankrupt at the commencement of the bankruptcy, and
  (b) any property which by virtue of any of the following provisions of this Part is comprised in that estate or is treated as falling within the preceding paragraph.

(2) Subsection (1) does not apply to—
  (a) such tools, books, vehicles and other items of equipment as are necessary to the bankrupt for use personally by him in his employment, business or vocation;
  (b) such clothing, bedding, furniture, household equipment and provisions as are necessary for satisfying the basic domestic needs of the bankrupt and his family.

This subsection is subject to section 308 in Chapter IV (certain excluded property reclaimable by trustee).

(3) Subsection (1) does not apply to—
  (a) property held by the bankrupt on trust for any other person, or
  (b) the right of nomination to a vacant ecclesiastical benefice.

(3A) Subject to section 308A in Chapter IV, subsection (1) does not apply to—
  (a) a tenancy which is an assured tenancy or an assured agricultural occupancy, within the meaning of Part I of the Housing Act 1988, and the terms of which inhibit an assignment as mentioned in section 127(5) of the Rent Act 1977, or

(b) a protected tenancy, within the meaning of the Rent Act 1977, in respect of which, by virtue of any provision of Part IX of that Act, no premium can lawfully be required as a condition of assignment, or

(c) a tenancy of a dwelling-house by virtue of which the bankrupt is, within the meaning of the Rent (Agriculture) Act 1976, a protected occupier of the dwelling-house, and the terms of which inhibit an assignment as mentioned in section 127(5) of the Rent Act 1977, or

(d) a secure tenancy, within the meaning of Part IV of the Housing Act 1985, which is not capable of being assigned, except in the cases mentioned in section 91(3) of that Act.

(4) References in any of this Group of Parts to property, in relation to a bankrupt, include references to any power exercisable by him over or in respect of property except in so far as the power is exercisable over or in respect of property not for the time being comprised in the bankrupt's estate and—

(a) is so exercisable at a time after either the official receiver has had his release in respect of that estate under section 299(2) in Chapter III or a meeting summoned by the trustee of that estate under section 331 in Chapter IV has been held, or

(b) cannot be so exercised for the benefit of the bankrupt;

and a power exercisable over or in respect of property is deemed for the purposes of any of this Group of Parts to vest in the person entitled to exercise it at the time of the transaction or event by virtue of which it is exercisable by that person (whether or not it becomes so exercisable at that time).

(5) For the purposes of any such provision in this Group of Parts, property comprised in a bankrupt's estate is so comprised subject to the rights of any person other than the bankrupt (whether as a secured creditor of the bankrupt or otherwise) in relation thereto, but disregarding—

(a) any rights in relation to which a statement such as is required by section 269(1)(a) was made in the petition on which the bankrupt was adjudged bankrupt, and

(b) any rights which have been otherwise given up in accordance with the rules.

(6) This section has effect subject to the provisions of any enactment not contained in this Act under which any property is to be excluded from a bankrupt's estate.

Notes

S 283

The bankrupt's estate vests in the trustee immediately on his appointment taking effect or, in the case of the official receiver, on his becoming trustee: IA 1986 s 306. The commencement of the bankruptcy is the date of the order s 278(a) IA 1986. Note that the trustee may also claim after-acquired property (IA 1986 s 307), certain items of excess value (IA 1986 s 308), and certain tenancies (IA 1986 s 308A). Note also the availability of Income payments orders and Income payments agreements IA 1986 s 310, 310A.

'Property' includes money, goods, things in action, land and every description of property wherever situated and also obligations and every description of interest, whether present or future or vested or contingent, arising out of, or incidental to, property IA 1986 s 436. As Sir Nicholas Browne-Wilkinson V-C observed in *Bristol Airport plc v Powdrill* [1990] Ch 744, 759D: 'It is hard to think of a wider definition of property'.

The definition is not exhaustive. It does not say what 'property' means, but what it 'includes'. It may therefore be taken to imply that 'property' includes other things than those that are expressly mentioned. To some extent, the definition defines 'property' by reference to that word itself. The first limb of the definition states that property includes 'money, goods, things in action, land and every description of property wherever situated'. What does 'property' mean in that collocation of words? 'Property' is not a term of art, but takes its meaning from its context, see for instance per Nicholls LJ in *Kirby v Thorn EMI plc* [1988] 2 All ER 947 at 953 citing Lord Porter in *Nokes v Doncaster Amalgamated Collieries Ltd* [1940] AC 1014 at 1051. In the phrase 'every description of property wherever situated' the word 'property' connotes anything which is capable of being owned and of which ownership can be asserted or defined in legal proceedings, see *Re Rae* [1995] BCC 102 per Warner J at 110. In construing the definition of 'property' it is proper also to have regard to the purposes of the Insolvency Act 1986 *Re Rae* [1995] BCC 102; *Bristol Airport plc v Powdrill* [1990] Ch 744; *Re International Bulk Commodities Ltd* [1992] BCC 463.

'Property' has been held to include an interest under a lease of an aircraft *Bristol Airport plc v Powdrill* [1990] Ch 744 a right of pre-emption *Dear v Reeves* [2001] EWCA Civ 277, [2001] BPIR 577, goodwill *Hudson v Osborne* (1869) 39 LJ Ch 79, the benefit of an entitlement to apply for a sea fish licence *Re Rae* [1995] BCC 102, a milk quota *Swift v Dairywise Farms Ltd* [2000] 1 WLR 1177 and a waste management licence *Re Celtic Extraction Ltd* [2000] 2 WLR 991. However the passport of the bankrupt is not part of the estate as it belongs to the Crown *Re Suswalsky* [1928] B & CR 142 and neither is the *hope* that a bankrupt may have of receiving an award from the Criminal Injuries Compensation Board *Re Campbell* [1997] Ch 14. In *City of London Corporation v Brown* (1989) 22 HLR 32 (which preceded the insertion of IA 1986 s 283(3A) by the Housing Act 1988 s 117), the Court of Appeal held that a non-assignable secure tenancy under Pt IV of the Housing Act 1985 did not vest in the tenant's trustee in bankruptcy. The ratio of the decision was expressed by Dillon LJ (at pp 38–39): '... I take the view that the non-assignable secure periodic tenancy … is a mere personal right dependent on the terms of the statute. It is not an asset which the trustee in bankruptcy could realise for the benefit of the creditors and I see no reason therefore why it should be included in the property of the bankrupt which has vested, albeit without assignment, under section 306 of the Insolvency Act in the trustee in bankruptcy.'

S 283(1)(a)

Pensions

By s 11 Welfare Reform and Pensions Act 1999, certain pensions are excluded from the bankrupt's estate where the bankruptcy order is made on a petition presented on or after 29 May 2000. Those pensions are described as 'approved pension arrangements' (s 11(11) WRPA 1999) and they include an occupational pension scheme, a retirement annuity contract and a personal pension scheme where approval has been given under the relevant provisions of the Income and Corporation Taxes Act 1988. However the trustee may apply under IA 1986 s 342A ff for the recovery of excessive pension contributions in respect of such approved pension schemes.

In respect of other bankruptcies (e g pre–29 May 2000 bankruptcies) useful guidance is contained in *Malcolm v Mackenzie & Ors* [2005] BPIR 176. In that case, the Court of Appeal held that to construe s 283(1), s 436 IA 1986 so as to include in the bankruptcy estate contractual pension rights vested in the bankrupt at the commencement of the bankruptcy would not be inconsistent with the obligations imposed on the UK by art 14 of the European Convention on Human Rights.

Personal rights

Despite the breadth of the definition in IA 1986 s 436, certain personal rights do not fall within the definition of property, for example claims in which 'the damages are to be estimated by immediate reference to pain felt by the bankrupt in respect of his body mind or character, and without reference to his rights of property' *Beckham v Drake* (1849) 2 HL Cas 579 per Earl J at 604. Actions for defamation and assault are obvious examples, see *Vine ex parte. Re Wilson* (1878) 8 Ch D 364 (slander). However, money payable under an insurance policy as a result of the insured's permanent disablement falls within the definition of property vesting in the trustee *Cork v Rawlins* [2001] EWCA Civ 202, [2001] 3 WLR 300. As to the court's treatment of 'hybrid claims' (in part personal and in part relating to property) see *Ord v Upton* [2000] Ch 352 (loss of earnings and pain and suffering caused by negligent medical treatment), *Mulkerrins v Price Waterhouse Coopers* [2003] UKHL 41, [2003] 1 WLR 1937 (damages against a firm of accountants for negligence in failing to achieve an IVA), *Grady v HM Prison Service* [2003] EWCA Civ 527, [2003] 3 All ER 745 (unfair dismissal) and *Khan v Trident Safeguards Ltd* [2004] BPIR 881 (unfair dismissal, race discrimination and victimisation). The issue of whether or not the bankrupt is properly claiming a personal right is between the trustee and the bankrupt and the potential or actual defendant in the proceedings is not entitled to be heard *Mulkerrins v Price Waterhouse Coopers* [2003] UKHL 4, [2003] 1 WLR 1937. Personal correspondence falls outside the scope of the bankrupt's estate *Haig v Aitken* [2001] Ch 110.

Where the bankrupt is a defendant, there is of course usually no question of any cause of action having vested in the trustee. Unless the defence is set-off the bankrupt will not be asserting by way of defence any cause of action of his own. Nevertheless, since any claim for monetary relief or for the return of property will be a claim which will have to be brought against the trustee in bankruptcy, since the subject matter of the proceedings will have vested in the trustee in bankruptcy, the bankrupt has no continuing interest in defending the proceedings. IA 1986 285(3) (subject to IA 1986 s 346, 347) deprives the claimant of any remedy against the bankrupt's person or property and confines him to his right to prove in the bankruptcy. On the other hand, some actions seeking relief such as injunctions against the bankrupt personally which do not directly concern his estate can still be maintained against the bankrupt himself, and he is entitled to defend them and, if he loses, to appeal. This distinction was the basis of the decision of the Court of Appeal in *Dence v Mason* [1879] WN 31. A more modern exposition of these rules is given by Hoffman LJ in *Heath v Tang; Stevens v Peacock* [1993] 1 WLR 1421. See also *Church of Scientology v Scott* [1997] BPIR 418.

S 283(1)(b)

This property would include recovery of post petition pre vesting dispositions (IA 1986 s 284 IA) after-acquired property (IA 1986 s 307), certain items of excess value (IA 1986 s 308), certain tenancies (IA 1986 s 308A), monies under income payment orders (IA 1986 s 310) and monies recovered under the 'clawback' provisions (IA 1986 s 339, 340, 423).

S 283(2)

Where property is excluded by virtue of section 283(2) from the bankrupt's estate, and it appears to the trustee that its realisable value exceeds the cost of a reasonable replacement for that property, the trustee may by notice in writing claim the property for the bankrupt's estate (IA 1986 s 308). Where the excluded property is not in the possession of the bankrupt at the date of vesting it is questionable whether he holds the right to obtain possession (a mere chose in action and not the goods themselves) or whether that right forms part of his estate, see *Church of Scientology v Scott* [1997] BPIR 418.

S 283(3)

Property held by the bankrupt on trust for others does not fall within his estate, since he has no beneficial interest in it. See *Re Johnson, Shearman v Robinson* (1880) 15 ChD 548 (monies held in a solicitor's client account); *Abrahams v Trustee of Property of Abrahams* [1999] BPIR 637 (a lottery win); *Re Coath [2000] BPIR 981* (funds held on trust for IVA creditors); *Roberts v Nunn* [2004] BPIR 623 (certain family court orders which impose a trust). Where a bankrupt has agreed to hold funds separately for another, then unless such arrangement constitutes an assignment of book debts which is void against the trustee, a valid trust for the purpose of this subsection will be established, see *Re Kayford* [1975] 1 WLR 279, *Re Multi Guarantee Co Ltd* [1987] BCLC 257, *Re Branston & Gothard Ltd* [1999] BPIR 466. Similarly where money has been advanced for a special purpose, see *Gilbert v Barber* [1987] BCLC 646. However, where a bankrupt holds property on trust for himself and others, his own beneficial interest falls within the estate *Burn v Carvalho* (1834) 1 Ad & El 883.

S 283(3A)

A trustee may under IA 1986 s 308A claim any of the tenancies otherwise excluded from the estate by this subsection. Continuation tenancies under the Landlord and Tenant Act 1954 Part 1 are not excluded from the bankruptcy estate under IA 1986 s 283(3A), *Rothschild v Bell* [1999] BPIR 300. See *Harlow District Council v Hall* [2006] EWCA Civ 156, [2006] BPIR 712 concerning s 283(3A)(d) and the non vesting of secure tenancies.

S 283(4)

See *Clarkson v Clarkson* [1994] BCC 921 on IA 1986 s 283(4).

S 283(5)

The court will apply the usual equitable principles in determining the beneficial interests of any third parties whose rights over the bankrupt's property are preserved pursuant to s 283(5). In the case of a sale of property by the trustee, both equitable accounting as between the trustee and any co-owner (usually the bankrupt's spouse or partner) *Re Pavlou* [1993] 1 WLR 1046, *Re Gorman* [1990] 2 FLR 284, *Byford v Butler* [2003] EWHC 1267 (Ch) and any right of the co-owner to exoneration *Re Pittortou* [1985] 1 WLR 58 should also be considered.

'Secured creditor' is defined by reference to IA 1986 s 383, s 385 and such a creditor may be constituted by an order under s 37 Matrimonial Causes Act 1973 *Mordant v Halls* [1996] BPIR 302 or s 23 Matrimonial Causes Act 1973 *Platt v Platt* (1976) 6 Fam Law 107 (lump sum order secured by court order).

S 283(6)

Property which is subject to an order under the Proceeds of Crime Act 2002 s 417 is excluded from the bankruptcy estate. Student loans which a bankrupt receives or is entitled to receive after commencement of his bankruptcy do not form part of his estate. The liability to repay the student loan remains despite discharge from bankruptcy where the bankruptcy order was made on or after 1 September 2004 (Education (Student Support) (No 2) Regulations 2002 (SI 2002/3200) (as amended).

1.333

283A Bankrupt's home ceasing to form part of estate

(1) This section applies where property comprised in the bankrupt's estate consists of an interest in a dwelling-house which at the date of the bankruptcy was the sole or principal residence of—

   (a) the bankrupt,

   (b) the bankrupt's spouse [or civil partner], or

   (c) a former spouse [or former civil partner] of the bankrupt.

(2) At the end of the period of three years beginning with the date of the bankruptcy the interest mentioned in subsection (1) shall—

   (a) cease to be comprised in the bankrupt's estate, and

   (b) vest in the bankrupt (without conveyance, assignment or transfer).

(3) Subsection (2) shall not apply if during the period mentioned in that subsection—

   (a) the trustee realises the interest mentioned in subsection (1),

(b)   the trustee applies for an order for sale in respect of the dwelling-house,

(c)   the trustee applies for an order for possession of the dwelling-house,

(d)   the trustee applies for an order under section 313 in Chapter IV in respect of that interest, or

(e)   the trustee and the bankrupt agree that the bankrupt shall incur a specified liability to his estate (with or without the addition of interest from the date of the agreement) in consideration of which the interest mentioned in subsection (1) shall cease to form part of the estate.

(4) Where an application of a kind described in subsection (3)(b) to (d) is made during the period mentioned in subsection (2) and is dismissed, unless the court orders otherwise the interest to which the application relates shall on the dismissal of the application—

(a)   cease to be comprised in the bankrupt's estate, and

(b)   vest in the bankrupt (without conveyance, assignment or transfer).

(5) If the bankrupt does not inform the trustee or the official receiver of his interest in a property before the end of the period of three months beginning with the date of the bankruptcy, the period of three years mentioned in subsection (2)—

(a)   shall not begin with the date of the bankruptcy, but

(b)   shall begin with the date on which the trustee or official receiver becomes aware of the bankrupt's interest.

(6) The court may substitute for the period of three years mentioned in subsection (2) a longer period—

(a)   in prescribed circumstances, and

(b)   in such other circumstances as the court thinks appropriate.

(7) The rules may make provision for this section to have effect with the substitution of a shorter period for the period of three years mentioned in subsection (2) in specified circumstances (which may be described by reference to action to be taken by a trustee in bankruptcy).

(8) The rules may also, in particular, make provision—

(a)   requiring or enabling the trustee of a bankrupt's estate to give notice that this section applies or does not apply;

(b)   about the effect of a notice under paragraph (a);

(c)   requiring the trustee of a bankrupt's estate to make an application to the Chief Land Registrar.

(9) Rules under subsection (8)(b) may, in particular—

(a)   disapply this section;

(b)   enable a court to disapply this section;

(c)   make provision in consequence of a disapplication of this section;

(d)   enable a court to make provision in consequence of a disapplication of this section;

> (e)   make provision (which may include provision conferring juris-
>   diction on a court or tribunal) about compensation.

Notes

S 283A(1)

This provision was introduced by the EA 2002 s 261(1). It came into force on 1 April 2004 and it applies to all bankruptcies whether the petition was presented before or after that date. In order to redress the perceived unfairness of waiting for property values to rise before realising family homes, often after the bankruptcy in question had long been discharged, these provisions were included as a late amendment providing a three year period for the trustee to realise the interest of the bankrupt in the sole or principal residence (ie not second/investment homes) of the bankrupt, the bankrupt's spouse or former spouse. By virtue of EA 2002 s 261(7) where the bankruptcy petition was presented before 1 April 2004 the trustee has three years from the date IA 1986 s 283 came into force (1 April 2004) to take one of the actions listed in s 283(3) IA 1986. The DTI has established a Protracted Realisations Unit ('PRU') to ensure that the official receiver is replaced by trustees who are appointed to estates so that such interests can be quickly realised. See also the notes under IA 1986 s 313 (Charge on bankrupt's home), s 313A (Low value home: application for sale, possession or charge).

S 283A(1)(b), (c)

The words 'or civil partner', 'or former civil partner' were inserted by the Civil Partnership Act 2004, s 261(1), Sch 27, para 113.

S 283A(3)(b)

The trustee must make the application within the period stated in s 283(A)(2) but there is no requirement that the order should be obtained within a specific period.

S 283A(4)

Where the trustee's application for sale/possession/security is dismissed then the interest revest in the bankrupt on that dismissal unless the court orders otherwise; revesting may then take place earlier than three years from the date of the bankruptcy.

S 283A(5)

The three year period in which the trustee must take action commences on the date of bankruptcy so long as the bankrupt informs the trustee of his interest in the relevant property within 3 months of the date of the bankruptcy. Where the bankrupt does not inform the trustee until after the expiry of the 3 month period then the three year period for the trustee only commences when the trustee or official receiver becomes aware of the bankrupt's interest.

S 283A(6)

The three year period can be extended if the court thinks that it is 'just and reasonable' in all the circumstances of the case; see IR 1986 r 6.237C.

S 283A(7)

The relevant rule is IR 1986 r 6.237CA in which a period of one month is substituted for the three year period in cases where the trustee notifies the bankrupt that the continued vesting is of no benefit to creditors or the revesting will facilitate a more efficient administration of the bankrupt's estate.

S 283A(8)

The relevant rules are IR 1986 r 6.237, 6.237A and 6.237B.

Chapter II
Protection of Bankrupt's Estate and Investigation of His Affairs

1.334

284 Restrictions on dispositions of property

(1) Where a person is adjudged bankrupt, any disposition of property made by that person in the period to which this section applies is void except to the extent that it is or was made with the consent of the court, or is or was subsequently ratified by the court.

(2) Subsection (1) applies to a payment (whether in cash or otherwise) as it applies to a disposition of property and, accordingly, where any payment is void by virtue of that subsection, the person paid shall hold the sum paid for the bankrupt as part of his estate.

(3) This section applies to the period beginning with the day of the presentation of the petition for the bankruptcy order and ending with the vesting, under Chapter IV of this Part, of the bankrupt's estate in a trustee.

(4) The preceding provisions of this section do not give a remedy against any person—
    (a)   in respect of any property or payment which he received before the commencement of the bankruptcy in good faith, for value and without notice that the petition had been presented, or
    (b)   in respect of any interest in property which derives from an interest in respect of which there is, by virtue of this subsection, no remedy.

(5) Where after the commencement of his bankruptcy the bankrupt has incurred a debt to a banker or other person by reason of the making of a payment which is void under this section, that debt is deemed for the purposes of any of this Group of Parts to have been incurred before the commencement of the bankruptcy unless—
    (a)   that banker or person had notice of the bankruptcy before the debt was incurred, or
    (b)   it is not reasonably practicable for the amount of the payment to be recovered from the person to whom it was made.

(6) A disposition of property is void under this section notwithstanding that the property is not or, as the case may be, would not be comprised in the bankrupt's estate; but nothing in this section affects any disposition made by a person of property held by him on trust for any other person.

Notes

S.284

This section applies to dispositions by a bankrupt in the period between presentation of the bankruptcy petition and the vesting of his estate in the trustee under IA 1986 s 306. It therefore includes the period between the making of the order and the appointment of a trustee.

Matrimonial Proceedings

An order under the Matrimonial Causes Act 1973 section 24(1)(a) (property adjustment order) amounts to a decree of specific performance in favour of the spouse, conferring on the spouse an equitable interest in the property at the moment when the order takes effect *Mountney v Treharne* [2002] EWCA Civ 1174, [2002] BPIR 1126 (overruling *Beer v Higham* [1997] BPIR 349). See also *Re Flint (a Bankrupt)* [1993] Ch 319. In *Treharne v Forrester* [2003] EWHC 2784 (Ch), [2004] BPIR 338 Lindley J observed that the abovementioned cases were examples of the equitable doctrine of taking as done that which ought to have been done, and that applying the maxim, the identity of the disponor (for the purpose of IA 1986 s 284) was the bankrupt.

Financial Markets

This section does not apply to the same transactions as are excluded from the effect of IA 1986 s 127 by CA 1989 s 175(3)–(5).

SS 284(1)–(4), (6)

For the court's powers to validate transactions both prospectively and retrospectively see notes to IA 1986 s 127 above. The overriding principle of rateable distribution is as applicable to IA 1986 s 284 as it is to IA 1986 s 127. However there is no advertisement of a bankruptcy petition under IR 1986, and therefore in contrast to compulsory liquidations, many persons dealing with the bankrupt in the relevant period in good faith for value will not have notice of the presentation of the bankruptcy petition and will therefore escape avoidance of the transaction (IA 1986 s 284(4)(a)), as will someone taking an interest from that person (IA 1986 s 284(4)(b)). Where however a purchaser knows of an unsatisfied statutory demand, it may suggest that he was not acting in good faith: *Re Abbott (A Bankrupt)* [1983] Ch 45.

The court's discretion to validate could be exercised to allow payment of the debtor's legal costs in opposing the bankruptcy petition. However, the court would expect to have some evidence as to the financial position of the debtor and of the grounds for the petition: *Rio Properties v Al-Midani* [2003] BPIR 128.

S 284(5)

For banking transactions generally, see note under IA 1986 s 127. In addition, in bankruptcy, where after the making of an order the bankrupt incurs a debt to a bank or other person by making a payment which is void under this section that bank or other person can prove in the bankruptcy where it had no notice of the bankruptcy or cannot reasonably recover the amount from the person to whom it was made.

1.334A

285 Restriction on proceedings and remedies

(1) At any time when proceedings on a bankruptcy petition are pending or an individual has been adjudged bankrupt the court may stay any action, execution or other legal process against the property or person of the debtor or, as the case may be, of the bankrupt.

(2) Any court in which proceedings are pending against any individual may, on proof that a bankruptcy petition has been presented in respect of that individual or that he is an undischarged bankrupt, either stay the proceedings or allow them to continue on such terms as it thinks fit.

(3) After the making of a bankruptcy order no person who is a creditor of the bankrupt in respect of a debt provable in the bankruptcy shall—
  (a)   have any remedy against the property or person of the bankrupt in respect of that debt, or
  (b)   before the discharge of the bankrupt, commence any action or other legal proceedings against the bankrupt except with the leave of the court and on such terms as the court may impose.

This is subject to sections 346 (enforcement procedures) and 347 (limited right to distress).

(4) Subject as follows, subsection (3) does not affect the right of a secured creditor of the bankrupt to enforce his security.

(5) Where any goods of an undischarged bankrupt are held by any person by way of pledge, pawn or other security, the official receiver may, after giving notice in writing of his intention to do so, inspect the goods.

Where such a notice has been given to any person, that person is not entitled, without leave of the court, to realise his security unless he has given the trustee of the bankrupt's estate a reasonable opportunity of inspecting the goods and of exercising the bankrupt's right of redemption.

(6) References in this section to the property or goods of the bankrupt are to any of his property or goods, whether or not comprised in his estate.

Notes

S 285

'The purpose of section 285 is to protect the estate for the whole body of creditors and to prevent unsecured creditors, after the initiation of bankruptcy proceedings, from taking steps to obtain advantages over other creditors: *Re Smith (A Bankrupt)* [1990] 2 AC 215, 230 per Lord Jauncey of Tullichette. It does not affect the right of a secured creditor to enforce his security s 285(4), nor a landlord from re-entry *Razzaq v Pala* [1998] BCC 66, nor deductions at source by the Secretary of State of earlier overpayments of social security benefit *R v Secretary of State for Social Security ex p. Taylor* [1997] BPIR 505.

Financial Markets

Nothing in section 285 affects any action taken by an exchange or clearing house for the purpose of its default proceedings CA 1989 s 161(4).

S 285(1), (2)

Power to stay or impose terms

In *Re Smith (a Bankrupt) ex pa Braintree* [1990] 2 AC 215 the House of Lords held that the words 'or other legal process' in s 285(1) were wide enough to comprehend all the machinery provided by Part VI of the General Rate Act 1967 for the recovery of unpaid rates, including proceedings for the issue of a warrant of commitment. Where a stay is not granted, the court may impose conditions as in *Polly Peck International plc v Nadir* [1992] BCLC 746, where the court directed that interlocutory proceedings, if not in chambers, should be held in camera, and that the claimants should undertake not to disclose to third parties material provided such as pleadings (otherwise than for the purposes of the action). See also *Re Eileen Davies (A Bankrupt)* [1997] BPIR 619 on the imposition of conditions (in that case, a term as to the enforcement of any order for costs that might be made against the bankrupt in the proceedings was not imposed).

S 285(3)

Prevention of actions and legal proceedings to recover provable debts other than by enforcement of security

Note that s 285(3) is subject to IA 1986 s 346 (enforcement procedures), 347 (limited right to distress). Not all debts are provable debts (see IA 1986 s 382 and IR 1986 r 12.3) and this section only applies to provable debts.

In *Re Melinek (a bankrupt)* [1997] BPIR 358 David Young QC (sitting as a deputy judge of the High Court) in deciding whether to grant leave to commence proceedings against two bankrupt solicitors, was assisted by the principles taken from a judgment of Master Lee QC in *ex parte Walker* (1982) 6 ACLR 423 at 426 and the approach of Jonathan Parker J in *Re Bank of Credit and Commerce International SA (No 4)* [1994] BCLC 419 which were summarised as follows:

(1)   The court should not investigate the merits of the proposed claim under s 285(3) provided it is satisfied that it is not clearly unsustainable.

(2)   There must be no prejudice to creditors or to the orderly administration of the bankruptcy if the action is to proceed.

(3)   The claim must be of a type which should proceed by action rather than through the proofing procedure in bankruptcy.

(4)   Leave is more likely to be granted where there is an insurance company standing behind the respondent to pay any judgment debt the plaintiff might obtain. If successful such an action is unlikely to prejudice the creditors of the respondent. The section is not designed to protect an insurer.

(5)   A condition is often imposed that the plaintiff will not enforce any judgment against the respondent without the leave of the court. This ensures that the bankruptcy court retains ultimate control.

(6)   Mere delay itself in applying for leave will not prevent leave being granted. Leave is not to be withheld simply and solely as punishment.

(7)   Leave may be granted after the expiry of the relevant period of limitation to continue an action commenced within the limitation period without the leave of the court.

Consistent with a purposive construction of the section permission may be granted retrospectively in relation to existing proceedings *Re Saunders (a bankrupt)*; *Re Bearman (a bankrupt)* [1997] Ch 60.

1.335

286 Power to appoint interim receiver

(1) The court may, if it is shown to be necessary for the protection of the debtor's property, at any time after the presentation of a bankruptcy petition and before making a bankruptcy order, appoint the official receiver to be interim receiver of the debtor's property.

(2) Where the court has, on a debtor's petition, appointed an insolvency practitioner under section 273 and it is shown to the court as mentioned in subsection (1) of this section, the court may, without making a bankruptcy order, appoint that practitioner, instead of the official receiver, to be interim receiver of the debtor's property.

(3) The court may by an order appointing any person to be an interim receiver direct that his powers shall be limited or restricted in any respect; but, save as so directed, an interim receiver has, in relation to the debtor's property, all the rights, powers, duties and immunities of a receiver and manager under the next section.

(4) An order of the court appointing any person to be an interim receiver shall require that person to take immediate possession of the debtor's property or, as the case may be, the part of it to which his powers as interim receiver are limited.

(5) Where an interim receiver has been appointed, the debtor shall give him such inventory of his property and such other information, and shall attend on the interim receiver at such times, as the latter may for the purpose of carrying out his functions under this section reasonably require.

(6) Where an interim receiver is appointed, section 285(3) applies for the period between the appointment and the making of a bankruptcy order on the petition, or the dismissal of the petition, as if the appointment were the making of such an order.

(7) A person ceases to be interim receiver of a debtor's property if the bankruptcy petition relating to the debtor is dismissed, if a bankruptcy order is made on the petition or if the court by order otherwise terminates the appointment.

(8) References in this section to the debtor's property are to all his property, whether or not it would be comprised in his estate if he were adjudged bankrupt.

Notes

SS 286(1)–(2)

It is sometimes necessary to protect the property of the debtor between the presentation of the bankruptcy petition and the making of the bankruptcy order, for example where there is a legitimate fear of dissipation. In *Gibson Dunn & Crutcher v Rio Properties Inc* [2004] BPIR 1203 the Court of Appeal held that there was no intention by Parliament to limit the (in terms) unlimited jurisdiction in s 37(1) of the Supreme Court Act 1981 to appoint someone other than the official receiver as interim receiver, but that the Court would normally appoint the official receiver unless there were exceptional circumstances. See IR 1986 r 6.51–6.57 as to the application, order of appointment, deposit, security, remuneration and termination of appointment. Note that the Practice Statement – The Fixing and Approval of the Remuneration of Appointees (2004) [2004] BPIR 953 applies to interim receivers.

S 286(3), (5)

See *Re Baars* [2003] EWHC 2159 (Ch), [2003] BPIR 523 as to the rights and powers of the interim receiver and the relationship between the interim receiver and the debtor.

S 286(8)

The interim receiver is appointed over all of the debtor's property whether or not it would come within his estate as defined in s 283 IA 1986. However if any property of the debtor is subject to an order under POCA 2002 the interim receiver may not deal with that property (s 417(4) POCA 2002).

1.336

287 Receivership pending appointment of trustee

(1) Between the making of a bankruptcy order and the time at which the bankrupt's estate vests in a trustee under Chapter IV of this Part, the

official receiver is the receiver and (subject to section 370 (special manager)) the manager of the bankrupt's estate and is under a duty to act as such.

(2) The function of the official receiver while acting as receiver or manager of the bankrupt's estate under this section is to protect the estate; and for this purpose—

(a) he has the same powers as if he were a receiver or manager appointed by the High Court, and

(b) he is entitled to sell or otherwise dispose of any perishable goods comprised in the estate and any other goods so comprised the value of which is likely to diminish if they are not disposed of.

(3) The official receiver while acting as receiver or manager of the estate under this section—

(a) shall take all such steps as he thinks fit for protecting any property which may be claimed for the estate by the trustee of that estate,

(b) is not, except in pursuance of directions given by the Secretary of State, required to do anything that involves his incurring expenditure,

(c) may, if he thinks fit (and shall, if so directed by the court) at any time summon a general meeting of the bankrupt's creditors.

(4) Where—

(a) the official receiver acting as receiver or manager of the estate under this section seizes or disposes of any property which is not comprised in the estate, and

(b) at the time of the seizure or disposal the official receiver believes, and has reasonable grounds for believing, that he is entitled (whether in pursuance of an order of the court or otherwise) to seize or dispose of that property,

the official receiver is not to be liable to any person in respect of any loss or damage resulting from the seizure or disposal except in so far as that loss or damage is caused by his negligence; and he has a lien on the property, or the proceeds of its sale, for such of the expenses of the bankruptcy as were incurred in connection with the seizure or disposal.

(5) This section does not apply where by virtue of section 297 (appointment of trustee; special cases) the bankrupt's estate vests in a trustee immediately on the making of the bankruptcy order.

Notes

S 287(1)

The estate of the bankrupt does not vest in the trustee at commencement of the bankruptcy but only when the trustee's appointment takes effect or the official receiver becomes the trustee, see s 306 IA 1986. In the meantime the official receiver is the receiver and (subject to s 370 IA 1986 (special manager)) the manager of the bankrupt's estate. Note however IA 1986 s 297(4), 297(5) (appointment of trustee upon the making of a bankruptcy order where either (s 297(4)) the order is made in a case in which an insolvency practitioner's report has been submitted to the court under IA 1986 s 274 but no certificate for the summary administration of the estate is issued or: (s 297(5)) there is a supervisor of a voluntary arrangement approved in relation to the bankrupt under Part VIII).

S 287(3)

Where, under this section, the official receiver acts as receiver or manager he is required to take all steps as he thinks fit for protecting any property which may be claimed for the estate, but he should not do anything involving expenditure without directions from the Secretary of State, and if he does so without justification may be liable for that expenditure, see *Inland Revenue Commissions v Hamilton* [2003] EWHC 3198 (Ch), [2004] BPIR 264.

S 287(4)

The interim receiver is similarly protected when mistakenly dealing with property the subject of an order under POCA 2002 (s 432(2)).

1.337

288 Statement of affairs

(1) Where a bankruptcy order has been made otherwise than on a debtor's petition, the bankrupt shall submit a statement of his affairs to the official receiver before the end of the period of 21 days beginning with the commencement of the bankruptcy.

(2) The statement of affairs shall contain—
    (a)   such particulars of the bankrupt's creditors and of his debts and other liabilities and of his assets as may be prescribed, and
    (b)   such other information as may be prescribed.

(3) The official receiver may, if he thinks fit—
    (a)   release the bankrupt from his duty under subsection (1), or
    (b)   extend the period specified in that subsection;
and where the official receiver has refused to exercise a power conferred by this section, the court, if it thinks fit, may exercise it.

(4) A bankrupt who—
    (a)   without reasonable excuse fails to comply with the obligation imposed by this section, or
    (b)   without reasonable excuse submits a statement of affairs that does not comply with the prescribed requirements,
is guilty of a contempt of court and liable to be punished accordingly (in addition to any other punishment to which he may be subject).

Notes

S 288(2)

See IR 1986 r 6.58 to 6.66. Note the use of statements of affairs in evidence against any person making or concurring in making the statement pursuant to IA 1986 s 433.

S 288(3)

The official receiver may release the bankrupt from this obligation (see IR 1986 r 6.62, 6.76). For debtor's petitions see IA 1986 s 272(2).

I.338

289 Investigatory duties of official receiver

(1) The official receiver shall—
   (a) investigate the conduct and affairs of each bankrupt (including his conduct and affairs before the making of the bankruptcy order), and
   (b) make such report (if any) to the court as the official receiver thinks fit.

(2) Subsection (1) shall not apply to a case in which the official receiver thinks an investigation under that subsection unnecessary.

(3) Where a bankrupt makes an application for discharge under section 280—
   (a) the official receiver shall make a report to the court about such matters as may be prescribed, and
   (b) the court shall consider the report before determining the application.

(4) A report by the official receiver under this section shall in any proceedings be prima facie evidence of the facts stated in it.

Notes

S 289

This provision was introduced by the Enterprise Act 2002 and it applies to all bankruptcies commencing after 1 April 2004. It allows the official receiver to decide whether or not it is necessary to investigate the affairs of the bankrupt.

S 289(3)

The mandatory contents of the report are detailed in IR 1986 r 6.218.

I.339

290 Public examination of bankrupt

(1) Where a bankruptcy order has been made, the official receiver may at any time before the discharge of the bankrupt apply to the court for the public examination of the bankrupt.

(2) Unless the court otherwise orders, the official receiver shall make an application under subsection (1) if notice requiring him to do so is given to him, in accordance with the rules, by one of the bankrupt's creditors with the concurrence of not less than one-half, in value, of those creditors (including the creditor giving notice).

(3) On an application under subsection (1), the court shall direct that a public examination of the bankrupt shall be held on a day appointed by the court; and the bankrupt shall attend on that day and be publicly examined as to his affairs, dealings and property.

(4) The following may take part in the public examination of the bankrupt and may question him concerning his affairs, dealings and property and the causes of his failure, namely—

> (a)   the official receiver and, in the case of an individual adjudged bankrupt on a petition under section 264(1)(d), the Official Petitioner,
>
> (b)   the trustee of the bankrupt's estate, if his appointment has taken effect,
>
> (c)   any person who has been appointed as special manager of the bankrupt's estate or business,
>
> (d)   any creditor of the bankrupt who has tendered a proof in the bankruptcy.
>
> (5) If a bankrupt without reasonable excuse fails at any time to attend his public examination under this section he is guilty of a contempt of court and liable to be punished accordingly (in addition to any other punishment to which he may be subject).

Notes

SS 290(1), (2)

Public examinations are only held if requested by the official receiver, and such a request may result from a demand by the majority of creditors. If the requesting creditor's debt is sufficient, then the concurrence of other creditors is not required and he does not need to provide a list of concurring creditors, see IR 1986, r 6.173(1). The requisitioning creditor must deposit with the official receiver such sum as the official receiver considers sufficient for the expenses of the examination if ordered, see IR 1986 r 6.173(2). IR 1986 r 6.173(4) deals with the procedure where the official receiver considers the request is an unreasonable one in the circumstances.

S 290(3)

The court has jurisdiction to compel attendance even if a person is resident outside the jurisdiction *Re Seagull Manufacturing Co Ltd* [1993] Ch 345, and a bankrupt cannot invoke the privilege against self-incrimination when he is publicly examined, see *Bishopsgate Investment Management Ltd v Maxwell* [1992] BCLC 475 and *Re Paget ex p the Official Receiver [1927]* 2 Ch 85. A similar provision is made for public examinations in a corporate context (IA 1986 s 133, *Jeeves v Official Receiver* [2003] EWCA Civ 1246, [2004] BPIR 46).

S 290(4)

As to the use which can be made of the written record which must be made of the examination, the position in civil proceedings is that it is admissible, and the questions and answers can stand as evidence in chief. This includes proceedings under the Company Directors Disqualification Act 1986, but only to allow such evidence to be used against the bankrupt, and not against other persons, see *Official Receiver v Stern* [2000] 1 WLR 2230. In criminal proceedings by contrast, following the decision of the European Court of Human Rights in *Saunders v United Kingdom* (1996) 23 EHRR 313 the Insolvency Act was amended, so that by s 433(2) IA 1986 no evidence relating to the statement may be adduced in criminal proceedings except where they relate to specific offences in s 433(3) IA 1986; see also *Kansal v UK* [2004] BPIR 740. As to use of books papers and other records delivered up by the bankrupt in criminal proceedings, see general note under IA 1986 s 291 below.

S 290(5)

The public examination may be adjourned IR 1986 r 6.176.

1.340

291 Duties of bankrupt in relation to official receiver

(1) Where a bankruptcy order has been made, the bankrupt is under a duty—

(a) to deliver possession of his estate to the official receiver, and

(b) to deliver up to the official receiver all books, papers and other records of which he has possession or control and which relate to his estate and affairs (including any which would be privileged from disclosure in any proceedings).

(2) In the case of any part of the bankrupt's estate which consists of things possession of which cannot be delivered to the official receiver, and in the case of any property that may be claimed for the bankrupt's estate by the trustee, it is the bankrupt's duty to do all such things as may reasonably be required by the official receiver for the protection of those things or that property.

(3) Subsections (1) and (2) do not apply where by virtue of section 297 below the bankrupt's estate vests in a trustee immediately on the making of the bankruptcy order.

(4) The bankrupt shall give the official receiver such inventory of his estate and such other information, and shall attend on the official receiver at such times, as the official receiver may reasonably require—

(a) for a purpose of this Chapter, or

(b) in connection with the making of a bankruptcy restrictions order.

(5) Subsection (4) applies to a bankrupt after his discharge.

(6) If the bankrupt without reasonable excuse fails to comply with any obligation imposed by this section, he is guilty of a contempt of court and liable to be punished accordingly (in addition to any other punishment to which he may be subject).

Notes

S 291(1)

In *Attorney General's Reference (No 7 of 2000)* [2001] BPIR 953 the Court of Appeal held that books papers and records delivered up under the compulsion of IA 1986 s 291(6) were admissible in criminal proceedings subject to the exercise of discretion under s 78 PACE 1984. The court held that *Saunders v United Kingdom* (1996) 23 EHRR 313 was concerned with respecting the will of the accused person to remain silent and did not extend to use in criminal proceedings of material such as documents which had been obtained using compulsory powers and which had an existence independent of the will of the accused.

S 291(4)

This provision was introduced by the EA 2002 effective from 1 April 2004.

The Second Group of Parts
Insolvency of Individuals; Bankruptcy

Part IX
Bankruptcy

Chapter III
Trustees in Bankruptcy

Tenure of office as trustee

1.341

292 Power to make appointments

(1) The power to appoint a person as trustee of a bankrupt's estate (whether the first such trustee or a trustee appointed to fill any vacancy) is exercisable—

   (a)   *[except at a time when a certificate for the summary administration of the bankrupt's estate is in force]* by a general meeting of the bankrupt's creditors;

   (b)   under section 295(2), 296(2) or 300(6) below in this Chapter, by the Secretary of State; or

   (c)   under section 297, by the court.

(2) No person may be appointed as trustee of a bankrupt's estate unless he is, at the time of the appointment, qualified to act as an insolvency practitioner in relation to the bankrupt.

(3) Any power to appoint a person as trustee of a bankrupt's estate includes power to appoint two or more persons as joint trustees; but such an appointment must make provision as to the circumstances in which the trustees must act together and the circumstances in which one or more of them may act for the others.

(4) The appointment of any person as trustee takes effect only if that person accepts the appointment in accordance with the rules. Subject to this, the appointment of any person as trustee takes effect at the time specified in his certificate of appointment.

(5) This section is without prejudice to the provisions of this Chapter under which the official receiver is, in certain circumstances, to be trustee of the estate.

Notes

S 292(1)(a)

A 'summary administration' is defined in IA 1986 s 275 and in practice it refers to a bankruptcy at the 'small bankruptcies level' which is presently fixed by reference to unsecured bankruptcy debts of less than £20,000. The court may revoke a certificate for summary administration at any time if it appears that, on grounds existing at the time of issue, it ought not to have been issued IA 1986 s 275(3). From 1 April 2004 the words in italics are repealed subject to certain exceptions where a certificate of summary administration is in force as at that date (EA 2002 s 269 Sch 23 para 1,6, Enterprise Act 2002 (Commencement No 4 and Transitional Provisions and Savings) Order 2003 SI 2003/2093 art 8).

S 292(1)–(3)

It is the official receiver who has control of the bankrupt's estate during the interregnum between the making of the bankruptcy order and the appointment of a trustee in bankruptcy: see IA 1986 s 287, which provides that the official receiver is receiver and manager of the estate during that period and sets out his powers and functions. Although IA 1986 s 292(1) does enable the Secretary of State or the court to appoint the trustee in certain situations the decision to appoint is normally left to the creditors at the meeting summoned under the next section. IR 1986 makes specific provision for the appointment by the creditors (r 6.120) the court (r 6.121) and the Secretary of State (r 6.122).

S 292(4)

The rules relating to the certificate of appointment appear at IR 1986 r 6.120 to 6.123.

S 292(5)

There are a variety of situations where the official receiver becomes trustee of the estate; see IA 1986 s 293(3), 295(4), 297(1), 300(2).

1.342

293 Summoning of meeting to appoint first trustee

(1) Where a bankruptcy order has been made [*and no certificate for the summary administration of the bankrupt's estate has been issued]* it is the duty of the official receiver, as soon as practicable in the period of 12 weeks beginning with the day on which the order was made, to decide whether to summon a general meeting of the bankrupt's creditors for the purpose of appointing a trustee of the bankrupt's estate.

This section [does not apply where the bankruptcy order was made on a petition under section 264(1)(d) (criminal bankruptcy); and it] is subject to the provision made in sections 294(3) and 297(6) below.

(2) Subject to the next section, if the official receiver decides not to summon such a meeting, he shall, before the end of the period of 12 weeks above mentioned, give notice of his decision to the court and to every creditor of the bankrupt who is known to the official receiver or is identified in the bankrupt's statement of affairs.

(3) As from the giving to the court of a notice under subsection (2), the official receiver is the trustee of the bankrupt's estate.

Notes

S 293(1)

The provisions relating to the convening of a creditors' meeting under this provision may be found in IR 1986 r 6.79, 6.80. For provisions relating to creditors' meetings generally, see Chapter 7 of IR 1986. From 1 April 2004 the first set of words in italics are repealed subject to certain exceptions where a certificate of summary administration is in force as at that date (EA 2002 s 269 Sch 23 para 1, 7); the second set of words in italics are repealed by CJA 1988 s 170(2) from a day to be appointed.

S 293(3)

The appointment of the official receiver as trustee in bankruptcy is automatic on the giving of the notice under IA 1986 s 293(2). Prior to the giving of such a notice unless the creditors secure an appointment of a trustee following a meeting under IA 1986 s 294 the official receiver is the receiver and manager of the estate IA 1986 s 287.

1.343

294 Power of creditors to requisition meeting

(1) Where in the case of any bankruptcy—
- (a)   the official receiver has not yet summoned, or has decided not to summon, a general meeting of the bankrupt's creditors for the purpose of appointing the trustee, [*and*
- (b)   *a certificate for the summary administration of the estate is not for the time being in force,*]

any creditor of the bankrupt may request the official receiver to summon such a meeting for that purpose.

(2) If such a request appears to the official receiver to be made with the concurrence of not less than one-quarter, in value, of the bankrupt's creditors (including the creditor making the request), it is the duty of the official receiver to summon the requested meeting.

(3) Accordingly, where the duty imposed by subsection (2) has arisen, the official receiver is required neither to reach a decision for the purposes of section 293(1) nor (if he has reached one) to serve any notice under section 293(2).

Notes

S 294(1)

Any creditor can make such a request, though he/she should be aware that IR 1986 r 6.87 requires the creditor to deposit security for the expenses of the meeting. The meeting then has power to vote that the expenses of summoning and holding it are payable out of the estate as an expense of the bankruptcy (r 6.87(3)). From 1 April 2004 the words in italics are repealed subject to certain exceptions where a certificate of summary administration is in force as at that date (EA 2002 s 269 Sch 23 para 1,7).

S 294(2)

The official receiver only comes under a duty to summon the meeting if a creditor or creditors representing 25 per cent in value of the creditors make the request. IR 1986 r 6.83 deals with the formalities of the requisition and the fixing of the venue by the official receiver. The general provisions relating to meetings appear in IR 1986 Chapter 7.

S 294(3)

Clearly, if the official receiver is under a duty to call a meeting of creditors then he is released from his duties under IA 1986 s 293.

1.344

295 Failure of meeting to appoint trustee

(1) If a meeting summoned under section 293 or 294 is held but no appointment of a person as trustee is made, it is the duty of the official receiver to decide whether to refer the need for an appointment to the Secretary of State.

(2) On a reference made in pursuance of that decision, the Secretary of State shall either make an appointment or decline to make one.

(3) If—
   (a)   the official receiver decides not to refer the need for an appointment to the Secretary of State, or
   (b)   on such a reference the Secretary of State declines to make an appointment,
the official receiver shall give notice of his decision or, as the case may be, of the Secretary of State's decision to the court.

(4) As from the giving of notice under subsection (3) in a case in which no notice has been given under section 293(2), the official receiver shall be trustee of the bankrupt's estate.

Notes

S 295

The effect of this section is to ensure that no bankrupt's estate is without a trustee. In the absence of the appointment of a trustee by the creditors' meeting or a Secretary of State's appointment, the official receiver automatically assumes office as trustee by the giving of notice under IA 1986 s 293(5). See IR 1986 r 6.122.

1.345

296 Appointment of trustee by Secretary of State

(1) At any time when the official receiver is the trustee of a bankrupt's estate by virtue of any provision of this Chapter (other than section 297(1) below) he may apply to the Secretary of State for the appointment of a person as trustee instead of the official receiver.

(2) On an application under subsection (1) the Secretary of State shall either make an appointment or decline to make one.

(3) Such an application may be made notwithstanding that the Secretary of State has declined to make an appointment either on a previous application under subsection (1) or on a reference under section 295 or under section 300(4) below.

(4) Where the trustee of a bankrupt's estate has been appointed by the Secretary of State (whether under this section or otherwise), the trustee shall give notice to the bankrupt's creditors of his appointment or, if the court so allows, shall advertise his appointment in accordance with the court's directions.

(5) In that notice or advertisement the trustee shall—

> (a) state whether he proposes to summon a general meeting of the bankrupt's creditors for the purposes of establishing a creditor's committee under section 301, and
>
> (b) if he does not propose to summon such a meeting, set out the power of the creditors under this Part to require him to summon one.

Notes

S 296

The Secretary of State may also appoint a trustee under IA 1986 s 295(2) (no appointment at first creditors' meeting) and IA 1986 s 300(6) (appointment of trustee fails to take effect or there is otherwise a vacancy). See IR 1986 r 6.122, 6.124.

1.346

297 Special cases

(1) Where a bankruptcy order is made on a petition under section 264(1)(d) (criminal bankruptcy), the official receiver shall be trustee of the bankrupt's estate.

(2) Subject to the next subsection, where the court issues a certificate for the summary administration of a bankrupt's estate, the official receiver shall, as from the issue of that certificate, be the trustee.

(3) Where such a certificate is issued or is in force, the court may, if it thinks fit, appoint a person other than the official receiver as trustee.

(4) Where a bankruptcy order is made in a case in which an insolvency practitioner's report has been submitted to the court under section 274 [but no certificate for the summary administration of the estate is issued,] the court, if it thinks fit, may on making the order appoint the person who made the report as trustee.

(5) Where a bankruptcy order is made (whether or not on a petition under section 264(1)(c)) at a time when there is a supervisor of a voluntary arrangement approved in relation to the bankrupt under Part VIII, the court, if it thinks fit, may on making the order appoint the supervisor of the arrangement as trustee.

(6) Where an appointment is made under subsection (4) or (5) of this section, the official receiver is not under the duty imposed by section 293(1) (to decide whether or not to summon a meeting of creditors).

(7) Where the trustee of a bankrupt's estate has been appointed by the court, the trustee shall give notice to the bankrupt's creditors of his appointment or, if the court so allows, shall advertise his appointment in accordance with the directions of the court.

(8) In that notice or advertisement he shall—

> (a) state whether he proposes to summon a general meeting of the bankrupt's creditors for the purpose of establishing a creditor's committee under section 301 below, and

(b)   if he does not propose to summon such a meeting, set out the power of the creditors under this Part to require him to summon one.

Notes

S 297(1)

This provision has been repealed by CJA 1988 s 170(2) from a day to be appointed.

S 297(2), (3)

From 1 April 2004 these provisions are repealed subject to certain exceptions where a certificate of summary administration is in force as at that date (EA 2002 s 269 Sch 23 para 1, 9 Enterprise Act 2002 (Commencement No 4 and Transitional Provisions and Savings) Order 2003 SI 2003/2093 art 8).

1.347

298 Removal of trustee; vacation of office

(1) Subject as follows, the trustee of a bankrupt's estate may be removed from office only by an order of the court or by a general meeting of the bankrupt's creditors summoned specially for that purpose in accordance with the rules.

(2) Where the official receiver is trustee by virtue of section 297(1), he shall not be removed from office under this section.

(3) [*A general meeting of the bankrupt's creditors shall not be held for the purpose of removing the trustee at any time when a certificate for the summary administration of the estate is in force.*]

(4) Where the official receiver is trustee by virtue of section 293(3) or 295(4) or a trustee is appointed by the Secretary of State or (otherwise than under section 297(5)) by the court, a general meeting of the bankrupt's creditors shall be summoned for the purpose of replacing the trustee only if—

(a)   the trustee thinks fit, or
(b)   the court so directs, or
(c)   the meeting is requested by one of the bankrupt's creditors with the concurrence of not less than one-quarter, in value, of the creditors (including the creditor making the request).

(5) If the trustee was appointed by the Secretary of State, he may be removed by a direction of the Secretary of State.

(6) The trustee (not being the official receiver) shall vacate office if he ceases to be a person who is for the time being qualified to act as an insolvency practitioner in relation to the bankrupt.

(7) The trustee may, in the prescribed circumstances, resign his office by giving notice of his resignation to the court.

(8) The trustee shall vacate office on giving notice to the court that a final meeting has been held under section 331 in Chapter IV and of the decision (if any) of that meeting.

(9) The trustee shall vacate office if the bankruptcy order is annulled.

___

Notes

S 298(1)

Procedural aspects of the removal of a trustee by the court are detailed in IR 1986 r 6.132. The court could for instance remove a trustee because of a conflict of interest *Re Corbenstoke Ltd (No 2)* [1990] BCLC 60. However the court will not be quick to remove a trustee simply because he no longer has the confidence of the creditors; the trustee must be shown to have been acting in an unreasonable manner *AMP Enterprises Ltd v Hoffman* [2002] EWHC 1899 (Ch), [2003] 1 BCLC 319, *Re Edennote Ltd* [1996] 2 BCLC 389, *Re Keypak Homecare Ltd* [1987] BCLC 409.

The court's power to remove a trustee is also commonly invoked in cases where a 'bulk order' is required because, for example, the insolvency practitioner concerned is leaving the firm where the day to day administration of the estate is being carried out. In these circumstances, it is expensive and cumbersome to summon creditors' meetings for each of the bankruptcies and the court's jurisdiction under this section is invoked instead; see *Re Alt Landscapes Limited* [1999] BPIR 459 (in which the issue of safeguarding the interests of creditors was also considered) and the guidance offered in *Re Equity Nominees Ltd* [2000] BCC 84. A useful table of the statutory sources of jurisdiction is appended to *Supperstone v Auger* [1999] BPIR 152 and the Practice Direction: Insolvency Proceedings (Civil Procedure Vol 2 Section 3E) para 1.6 provides useful practical guidance on the making of a single application for a 'bulk transfer' where an insolvency practitioner wishes to retire from a number of appointments. Notice of an application to remove an insolvency practitioner and replace him should normally be given to that insolvency practitioner. However where the relief sought is so urgent that there is not enough time to give notification, or notifying the insolvency practitioner would jeopardise effective relief then the court can hear the application, see *Clements v Udal* [2002] 2 BCLC 606.

Where a creditors' meeting is to be called to remove a trustee it is necessary to have regard to the provisions relating to creditors' meetings generally, see IR 1986 r 6.79ff and in particular IR 1986 r 6.129, 6.132. A trustee who intends to vacate office, whether by resignation or otherwise must notify the official receiver and provide information relating to the bankrupt's estate. He is also under a duty to deliver up all books and records, etc to his successor IR 1986 r 6.145, 6.146. This duty can be enforced by court order IR 1986 6.149.

S 298(2)

The official receiver cannot be removed by the court or the creditors (cf IA 1986 s 297(3), pursuant to which the official receiver may be replaced in a summary administration).

S 298(3)

For the power to revoke a certificate of summary administration, see IA 1986 s 275(3). From 1 April 2004 these provisions are repealed subject to certain exceptions where a certificate of summary administration is in force as at that date (EA 2002 s 269 Sch 23 para 1,10 Enterprise Act 2002 (Commencement No 4 and Transitional Provisions and Savings) Order 2003 SI 2003/2093 art 8).

S 298(5)

This makes the replacement of a trustee who was appointed by the Secretary of State straightforward and comparatively quick; and see IR 1986 r 6.133.

S 298(6)

IR 1986 r 6.144 requires an insolvency practitioner who ceases to be qualified to act as such to give notice to the official receiver.

S 298(7)

IR 1986 r 6.126(3) sets out the circumstances in which a trustee may resign office. For provisions relating to the resignation and removal of trustees generally, see IR 1986 r 6.126 to IR 1986 r 6.135 and IR 1986 r 6.144.

1.348

299 Release of trustee

(1) Where the official receiver has ceased to be the trustee of a bankrupt's estate and a person is appointed in his stead, the official receiver shall have his release with effect from the following time, that is to say—
  (a) where that person is appointed by a general meeting of the bankrupt's creditors or by the Secretary of State, the time at which the official receiver gives notice to the court that he has been replaced, and
  (b) where that person is appointed by the court, such time as the court may determine.

(2) If the official receiver while he is the trustee gives notice to the Secretary of State that the administration of the bankrupt's estate in accordance with Chapter IV of this Part is for practical purposes complete, he shall have his release with effect from such time as the Secretary of State may determine.

(3) A person other than the official receiver who has ceased to be the trustee shall have his release with effect from the following time, that is to say—
  (a) in the case of a person who has been removed from office by a general meeting of the bankrupt's creditors that has not resolved against his release or who has died, the time at which notice is given to the court in accordance with the rules that that person has ceased to hold office;
  (b) in the case of a person who has been removed from office by a general meeting of the bankrupt's creditors that has resolved against his release, or by the court, or by the Secretary of State, or who has vacated office under section 298(6), such time as the Secretary of State may, on an application by that person, determine;
  (c) in the case of a person who has resigned, such time as may be prescribed;
  (d) in the case of a person who has vacated office under section 298(8)—
      (i) if the final meeting referred to in that subsection has resolved against that person's release, such time as the Secretary of State may, on an application by that person, determine; and
      (ii) if that meeting has not so resolved, the time at which the person vacated office.

(4) Where a bankruptcy order is annulled, the trustee at the time of the annulment has his release with effect from such time as the court may determine.

(5) Where the official receiver or the trustee has his release under this section, he shall, with effect from the time specified in the preceding provisions of this section, be discharged from all liability both in respect of acts or omissions of his in the administration of the estate and otherwise in relation to his conduct as trustee.

But nothing in this section prevents the exercise, in relation to a person who has had his release under this section, of the court's powers under section 304.

Notes

S 299(1)

For provisions relating to the trustee's release on vacation of office, see IR 1986 r 6.135-6.137.

S 299(2)

The official receiver unlike the trustee in bankruptcy does not hold a final meeting of creditors to determine a date of release (IA 1986 s 331(1)) and the Secretary of State notifies the release to the court rather than the creditors IR 1986 r 6.136.

S 299(5)

It is important for the trustee to obtain a release so that the trustee is free from liability except possibly for a breach of duty application under IA 1986 s 304; under that provision the leave of court must be first obtained before such an application can be made where a trustee has obtained a release.

1.349

300 Vacancy in office of trustee

(1) This section applies where the appointment of any person as trustee of a bankrupt's estate fails to take effect or, such an appointment having taken effect, there is otherwise a vacancy in the office of trustee.

(2) The official receiver shall be trustee until the vacancy is filled.

(3) The official receiver may summon a general meeting of the bankrupt's creditors for the purpose of filling the vacancy and shall summon such a meeting if required to do so in pursuance of section 314(7) (creditors' requisition).

(4) If at the end of the period of 28 days beginning with the day on which the vacancy first came to the official receiver's attention he has not summoned, and is not proposing to summon, a general meeting of creditors for the purpose of filling the vacancy, he shall refer the need for an appointment to the Secretary of State.

[(5) *Where a certificate for the summary administration of the estate is for the time being in force—*

    (a)   *the official receiver may refer the need to fill any vacancy to the court or, if the vacancy arises because a person appointed by the Secretary of State has ceased to hold office, to the court or the Secretary of State, and*

    (b)   *subsections (3) and (4) of this section do not apply.*]

(6) On a reference to the Secretary of State under subsection (4) [*or (5)*] the Secretary of State shall either make an appointment or decline to make one.

(7) If on a reference under subsection (4) [*or (5)*] no appointment is made, the official receiver shall continue to be trustee of the bankrupt's estate, but without prejudice to his power to make a further reference.

(8) References in this section to a vacancy include a case where it is necessary, in relation to any property which is or may be comprised in a bankrupt's estate, to revive the trusteeship of that estate after the holding of a final meeting summoned under section 331 or the giving by the official receiver of notice under section 299(2).

Notes

S 300(4)

See IR 1986 r 6.122.

S 300(5), (6), (7)

From 1 April 2004 the italicized provisions (and words) are repealed subject to certain exceptions where a certificate of summary administration is in force as at that date (EA 2002 s 269 Sch 23 para 1,11 Enterprise Act 2002 (Commencement No 4 and Transitional Provisions and Savings) Order 2003 SI 2003/2093 art 8).

S 300(8)

This provision is directed at the situation where further property becomes available for realisation after the administration of the estate had appeared to be complete.

1.350

301 Creditors' committee

(1) Subject as follows, a general meeting of a bankrupt's creditors (whether summoned under the preceding provisions of this Chapter or otherwise) may, in accordance with the rules, establish a committee (known as 'the creditors' committee') to exercise the functions conferred on it by or under this Act.

(2) A general meeting of the bankrupt's creditors shall not establish such a committee, or confer any functions on such a committee, at any time when the official receiver is the trustee of the bankrupt's estate, except in connection with an appointment made by that meeting of a person to be trustee instead of the official receiver.

Notes

S 301(1)

The committee is a body which may be consulted by the trustee from time to time. The committee itself can indicate to the trustee that it wants certain matters to be investigated but the trustee is not duty bound to investigate IR 1986 r 6.152. Detailed provisions relating to the establishment and membership of the creditors' committee, the conduct of its meetings and its relationship with the trustee are contained in IR 1986 r 6.150–166. Members of the creditors' committee stand in a fiduciary relationship to the bankrupt's estate, see *In re Bulmer* [1937] Ch 499, CA. IR 1986 r 6.165 contains detailed provisions concerning dealings by any member of the committee and the bankrupt estate. However, it seems clear from the *Bulmer* case that the express rules are not intended to dilute or limit the applicability of general equitable principles governing the relationship between a person in a fiduciary position and the person to whom he stands in that relation (in this case, the bankrupt's estate as represented by the trustee in bankruptcy).

S 301(2)

The Secretary of State exercises the functions of a creditors' committee (IA 1986 s 302) where the official receiver is trustee.

1.350A

302 Exercise by Secretary of State of functions of creditors' committee

(1) The creditors' committee is not to be able or required to carry out its functions at any time when the official receiver is trustee of the bankrupt's estate; but at any such time the functions of the committee under this Act shall be vested in the Secretary of State, except to the extent that the rules otherwise provide.

(2) Where in the case of any bankruptcy there is for the time being no creditors' committee and the trustee of the bankrupt's estate is a person other than the official receiver, the functions of such a committee shall be vested in the Secretary of State, except to the extent that the rules otherwise provide.

Notes

S 302(1)

Where the official receiver is trustee or where there is no creditors' committee the Secretary of State carries out the functions of the creditors' committee; for instance the giving of sanction for the exercise of the trustee's Sch 5 powers (IA 1986 s 314) such as the bringing of proceedings relating to the bankrupt's estate. See IR 1986 r 6.166.

S 302(2)

Where the official receiver is not the trustee and there is no creditors' committee the committee's functions are vested in the Secretary of State; however those functions can be exercised by the official receiver IR 1986 r 6.166(2).

1.351

303 General control of trustee by the court

(1) If a bankrupt or any of his creditors or any other person is dissatisfied by any act, omission or decision of a trustee of the bankrupt's estate, he may apply to the court; and on such an application the court may confirm,

reverse or modify any act or decision of the trustee, may give him directions or may make such other order as it thinks fit.

(2) The trustee of a bankrupt's estate may apply to the court for directions in relation to any particular matter arising under the bankruptcy.

(2A) Where at any time after a bankruptcy petition has been presented to the court against any person, whether under the provisions of the Insolvent Partnerships Order 1994 or not, the attention of the court is drawn to the fact that the person in question is a member of an insolvent partnership, the court may make an order as to the future conduct of the insolvency proceedings and any such order may apply any provisions of that Order with any necessary modifications.

(2B) Where a bankruptcy petition has been presented against more than one individual in the circumstances mentioned in subsection (2A) above, the court may give such directions for consolidating the proceedings, or any of them, as it thinks just.

(2C) Any order or directions under subsection (2A) or (2B) may be made or given on the application of the official receiver, any responsible insolvency practitioner, the trustee of the partnership or any other interested person and may include provisions as to the administration of the joint estate of the partnership, and in particular how it and the separate estate of any member are to be administered.

Notes

Under these provisions the trustee's conduct of the administration of the bankrupt's estate can be challenged or he can seek guidance as to a particular course of action. An application under this section would be made by ordinary application supported by a witness statement: IR 1986 r 7.2ff. However, in relation to such challenges, it should be borne in mind that the trustee's discretion is very wide and the court will not lightly interfere *Re a Debtor (400 of 1940)* [1949] Ch 236, *Mahomed v Morris (No 2)* [2000] 2 BCLC 536. The discretion has been held to allow the trustee to refuse a derisory offer for a cause of action forming part of the bankrupt's estate in circumstances in which the trustee himself has no funds with which to pursue the action *Khan v Official Receiver* [1997] BPIR 109, CA.

An annulment of the bankruptcy (IA 1986 s 282) does not prevent an application under this provision being made *Engel v Peri* [2002] BPIR 961. Similarly, a former bankrupt remains entitled to apply under the section following his or her discharge *Osborn v Cole* [1999] BPIR 251. This provision does not give the court jurisdiction to direct the official receiver as to the performance of his public law functions such as making an application under IA 1986 s 279 to delay the bankrupt's discharge *Hardy v Focus Insurance Co Ltd* [1997] BPIR 77.

S 303(1)

'A person dissatisfied' is wide enough to extend to a person who is placed in a position of uncertainty or potential prejudice by any action of the trustee *Re Cook* [1999] BPIR 881 (application of a solicitor for the bankrupt who was in difficulty over a question of privilege attaching to certain documents).

Where the person dissatisfied is the bankrupt himself, he must show that he has some substantial interest that has been adversely affected by the action complained of *Port v Auger* [1994] 1 WLR 862. Normally, he will not be able to show the requisite interest unless there will be a surplus in the bankruptcy after the bankruptcy debts and expenses have been paid in full *Re a Debtor, ex parte the Debtor v Dodwell* [1946] Ch 236. However, this is not a universal requirement and whether the bankrupt has standing will depend on the facts of the particular case *Engel v Peri* [2002] EWHC 799 (Ch), [2002] EWHC 799 (Ch), [2002] BPIR 961. In that case, a bankrupt was entitled to challenge the level of the trustee's charges in the context of an annulment application, since payment of the bankruptcy debts and all the costs was a condition of the annulment being granted and clearly he had an interest in the level of those costs. Doubt was expressed as to whether IA 1986 s 303 could be invoked for the purpose of fixing the trustee's remuneration, although the court could intervene under IA 1986 s 363 or its inherent jurisdiction. However the incurring of legal fees, if shown to be outside the wide ambit of his discretion, can be the subject of a challenge under IA 1986 s 303, since it involves an act or omission by the trustee. In *Woodbridge v Smith* [2004] BPIR 247 Registrar Baister held that whilst s 303(1) itself may not confer jurisdiction to assess or fix a trustee's remuneration (citing *Engel*), it does enable the court to give relief in relation to the manner of its being fixed and the trustee's conduct in relation to its being fixed.

S 303(2)

The power to apply for directions should not be used as a 'rubber stamp' provision by the trustee rather it ought to be used for situations of real difficulty and/or uncertainty *Re a Debtor (No 26A of 1975)* [1985] 1 WLR 6. See also *Re Omar (A Bankrupt)* [2000] BCC 434.

Removal from office

The jurisdiction under IA 1986 s 303(2) can be used to remove a trustee from multiple offices under IA 1986 s 298(1) and, where appropriate, to appoint his replacement *Re Bullard and Taplin Ltd* [1996] BCC 973 avoiding the difficulty and expense of the statutory resignation procedure. The jurisdiction is usually invoked where an insolvency practitioner is retiring from a partnership whose employees have the day to day conduct of the trusteeship. In those circumstances, it is convenient to deal with his removal and replacement by another insolvency practitioner within the partnership by this procedure. The Practice Direction: Insolvency Proceedings (Civil Procedure Vol 2 Section 3E), para 1.6, contains general procedural provisions for applications for 'bulk' transfer orders and see also *Re Equity Nominees Ltd* [2000] BCC 84.

1.352

304 Liability of trustee

(1) Where on an application under this section the court is satisfied—
   (a)   that the trustee of a bankrupt's estate has misapplied or retained, or become accountable for, any money or other property comprised in the bankrupt's estate, or
   (b)   that a bankrupt's estate has suffered any loss in consequence of any misfeasance or breach of fiduciary or other duty by a trustee of the estate in the carrying out of his functions,

the court may order the trustee, for the benefit of the estate, to repay, restore or account for money or other property (together with interest at such rate as the court thinks just) or, as the case may require, to pay such sum by way of compensation in respect of the misfeasance or breach of fiduciary or other duty as the court thinks just.

   This is without prejudice to any liability arising apart from this section.

(2) An application under this section may be made by the official receiver, the Secretary of State, a creditor of the bankrupt or (whether or not there is, or is likely to be, a surplus for the purposes of section 330(5) (final distribution)) the bankrupt himself.

But the leave of the court is required for the making of an application if it is to be made by the bankrupt or if it is to be made after the trustee has had his release under section 299.

(3) Where—
    (a)   the trustee seizes or disposes of any property which is not comprised in the bankrupt's estate, and
    (b)   at the time of the seizure or disposal the trustee believes, and has reasonable grounds for believing, that he is entitled (whether in pursuance of an order of the court or otherwise) to seize or dispose of that property,

the trustee is not liable to any person (whether under this section or otherwise) in respect of any loss or damage resulting from the seizure or disposal except in so far as that loss or damage is caused by the negligence of the trustee; and he has a lien on the property, or the proceeds of its sale, for such of the expenses of the bankruptcy as were incurred in connection with the seizure or disposal.

Notes

S 304(1), (2)

The bankrupt himself may apply under the section, whether or not there is likely to be a surplus (cf the notes under IA 1986 s 303(1) above) but the trustee is to some extent shielded by the requirement (in IA 1986 s 304(2)) to obtain the leave of the court, which will act as a filter for misconceived claims. As to the factors which the court must bear in mind in deciding whether or not to grant permission, see *Brown v Beat* [2002] BPIR 421. An application under this section would be made by application supported by a witness statement; see IR 7.1–7.10.

S 304(3)

References in sub-ss (3) and (4) of IA 1986 s 234 to seizing property only apply to tangible property, and do not apply to choses in action *Welsh Development Agency v Export Finance Co Ltd* [1992] BCLC 148.

The Third Group of Parts
Miscellaneous Matters Bearing on both Company and Individual Insolvency; General Interpretation;
Final Provisions

Chapter IV
Administration by Trustee

Preliminary

1.353

305 General functions of trustee

(1) This Chapter applies in relation to any bankruptcy where either—
    (a)   the appointment of a person as trustee of a bankrupt's estate takes effect, or
    (b)   the official receiver becomes trustee of a bankrupt's estate.

(2) The function of the trustee is to get in, realise and distribute the bankrupt's estate in accordance with the following provisions of this Chapter; and in the carrying out of that function and in the management of the bankrupt's estate the trustee is entitled, subject to those provisions, to use his own discretion.

(3) It is the duty of the trustee, if he is not the official receiver—
  (a) to furnish the official receiver with such information,
  (b) to produce to the official receiver, and permit inspection by the official receiver of, such books, papers and other records, and
  (c) to give the official receiver such other assistance,
as the official receiver may reasonably require for the purpose of enabling him to carry out his functions in relation to the bankruptcy.

(4) The official name of the trustee shall be 'the trustee of the estate of ... ..., a bankrupt' (inserting the name of the bankrupt); be he may be referred to as 'the trustee in bankruptcy' of the particular bankrupt.

Notes

S 305(2)

The function of the trustee is to gather in, realise and distribute the bankrupt's estate. A trustee in bankruptcy, governed by the rule in *ex parte James, Re Condon* (1874) LR 9 Ch App 609 (see annotation to Sch B1 para 5), must not allow his office to be used for any purpose other than the best administration of the estate of the bankrupt to whom, as well as his creditors, he owes a duty. If there are two classes of creditors with different interests the trustee cannot properly favour the interest of one class of creditor over the interest of another class *Judd v Brown* [1997] BPIR 470, 479. The trustee should not enable himself to accept engagement as a 'hired gun' and allow his position to be used for the benefit of a secured creditor only, unless there be a surrender of the security, see *Re Ng (A Bankrupt)* [1997] BPIR 267 per Lightman J at 269, and *ex parte Cooper, Re Zucco* (1875) 10 LR Ch App 510 per James LJ.

S 305(3)

The trustee has a duty to assist the official receiver in the ways set out in (a) to (c).

S 305(4)

This sub-section sets out the official name of the trustee which is the proper way in which to refer to the trustee in statements of case.

Acquisition, control and realisation of bankrupt's estate

1.354

306 Vesting of bankrupt's estate in trustee

(1) The bankrupt's estate shall vest in the trustee immediately on his appointment taking effect or, in the case of the official receiver, on his becoming trustee.

> (2) Where any property which is, or is to be, comprised in the bankrupt's estate vests in the trustee (whether under this section or under any other provision of this Part), it shall so vest without any conveyance, assignment or transfer.

Notes

S 306(1)

See IA 1986 s 283 for the definition of the bankrupt's estate and IA 1986 s 436 (and the annotation to s 283) for a definition of 'property'. In contrast, where a company is being wound up, it is only upon the application of the liquidator that the court may direct that all or any part of the property belonging to the company shall vest in the liquidator IA 1986 s 145. The vesting of property of a bankrupt in his trustee under IA 1986 is not to be equated with an assignment of that property, see In *Re Riggs; ex parte Lovell* [1901] 2 KB 16; In *re Landau (A Bankrupt)* [1998] Ch 223. However in the case of land in which the bankrupt holds an interest as landlord or tenant such vesting is an 'excluded assignment' for the purposes of the Landlord and Tenant (Covenants) Act 1995; see the notes to s 11 of that Act which is separately annotated.

S 306(2)

The bankrupt's estate vests immediately in the trustee upon his effective appointment or on the official receiver becoming trustee without any conveyance, assignment or transfer and the property vests wherever its location *Pollard v Ashurst* [2001] BPIR 131.

1.355

306A Property subject to restraint order

(1) This section applies where-
   (a) property is excluded from the bankrupt's estate by virtue of section 417(2)(a) of the Proceeds of Crime Act 2002 (property subject to a restraint order),
   (b) an order under section 50, 52, 128, 198 or 200 of that Act has not been made in respect of the property, and
   (c) the restraint order is discharged.

(2) On the discharge of the restraint order the property vests in the trustee as part of the bankrupt's estate.

(3) But subsection (2) does not apply to the proceeds of property realised by a management receiver under section 49(2)(d) or 197(2)(d) of that Act (realisation of property to meet receiver's remuneration and expenses).

Notes

S 306A

This provision and the following two sections provide that in certain situations assets that were excluded by virtue of s 417 POCA 2002 fall back into the estate.

1.356

306B Property in respect of which receivership or administration order is made

(1) This section applies where-
  (a) property is excluded from the bankrupt's estate by virtue of section 417(2)(b), (c) or (d) of the Proceeds of Crime Act 2002 (property in respect of which an order for the appointment of a receiver or administrator under certain provisions of that Act is in force),
  (b) a confiscation order is made under section 6, 92 or 156 of that Act,
  (c) the amount payable under the confiscation order is fully paid, and
  (d) any of the property remains in the hands of the receiver or administrator (as the case may be).

(2) The property vests in the trustee as part of the bankrupt's estate.

1.357

306C Property subject to certain orders where confiscation order discharged or quashed

(1) This section applies where-
  (a) property is excluded from the bankrupt's estate by virtue of section 417(2)(a), (b), (c) or (d) of the Proceeds of Crime Act 2002 (property in respect of which a restraint order or an order for the appointment of a receiver or administrator under that Act is in force),
  (b) a confiscation order is made under section 6, 92 or 156 of that Act, and
  (c) the confiscation order is discharged under section 30, 114 or 180 of that Act (as the case may be) or quashed under that Act or in pursuance of any enactment relating to appeals against conviction or sentence.

(2) Any such property in the hands of a receiver appointed under Part 2 or 4 of that Act or an administrator appointed under Part 3 of that Act vests in the trustee as part of the bankrupt's estate.

(3) But subsection (2) does not apply to the proceeds of property realised by a management receiver under section 49(2)(d) or 197(2)(d) of that Act (realisation of property to meet receiver's remuneration and expenses).

1.358

307 After-acquired property

(1) Subject to this section and section 309, the trustee may by notice in writing claim for the bankrupt's estate any property which has been acquired by, or has devolved upon, the bankrupt since the commencement of the bankruptcy.

(2) A notice under this section shall not be served in respect of—
  (a) any property falling within subsection (2) or (3) of section 283 in Chapter II,

(aa)   any property vesting in the bankrupt by virtue of section 283A in Chapter II

(b)   any property which by virtue of any other enactment is excluded from the bankrupt's estate, or

(c)   without prejudice to section 280(2)(c) (order of court on application for discharge), any property which is acquired by or, devolves upon, the bankrupt after his discharge.

(3) Subject to the next subsection, upon the service on the bankrupt of a notice under this section the property to which the notice relates shall vest in the trustee as part of the bankrupt's estate; and the trustee's title to that property has relation back to the time at which the property was acquired by, or devolved upon, the bankrupt.

(4) Where, whether before or after service of a notice under this section—

(a)   a person acquires property in good faith, for value and without notice of the bankruptcy, or

(b)   a banker enters into a transaction in good faith and without such notice,

the trustee is not in respect of that property or transaction entitled by virtue of this section to any remedy against that person or banker, or any person whose title to any property derives from that person or banker.

(5) References in this section to property do not include any property which, as part of the bankrupt's income, may be the subject of an income payments order under section 310.

Notes

S 307(1)

The trustee may claim property for the bankrupt's estate which was acquired by, or devolved upon, the bankrupt since the commencement of the bankruptcy (the bankruptcy commences on the day on which the bankruptcy order is made IA 1986 s 278(a)).

'Property' includes money, goods, things in action, land and every description of property wherever situated and also obligations and every description of interest, whether present or future or vested or contingent, arising out of, or incidental to, property IA 1986 436. As Sir Nicholas Browne-Wilkinson V-C observed in *Bristol Airport plc v Powdrill* [1990] Ch 744 at 759D: 'It is hard to think of a wider definition of property'.

Where at any time after the commencement of the bankruptcy any property is acquired by, or devolves upon, the bankrupt, he must within 21 days of becoming aware of the relevant facts, give the trustee notice of the property IA 1986 s 333(2), IR 1986 r 6.200(1). If the bankrupt fails to do so without reasonable excuse he is guilty of a contempt of court IA 1986 s 333(4). Having served the notice, the bankrupt must not, without the trustee's written consent, dispose of it within the period of 42 days beginning with the date of the notice IR 1986 r 6.200(2).

The trustee has 42 days (except with the leave of the court) from the day on which it first came to his knowledge that the property had been acquired by the bankrupt (IA 1986 s 309(1)) to serve the s 307 notice on the bankrupt and claim the property for the bankrupt's estate: see the notes to s 309 (below) and *Solomons v Williams* [2001] BPIR 1123, 1136.

S 307(2)

There is excluded from 'after-acquired property' property not falling within the estate (as defined in s 283(2), (3)) and, by virtue of the EA 2002, the interest of the bankrupt in his home which revests under s 283A; and there is further excluded property acquired after discharge. Further where a bankrupt receives or is entitled to receive a student loan after his bankruptcy this does not fall into the bankrupt's estate Regulation 39(1)(a) Education (Student Support) (No 2) Regulations 2002 (SI 2002/3200) (as amended).

S 307(3)

Once the trustee gives notice under s 307(1), title to the property under s 307(3) relates back to the date on which the bankrupt acquired the property; it is therefore open to a trustee to seize property then serve notice under s 307(1) correcting the original defective seizure *Pike (a bankrupt) v Cork Gully* [1997] BPIR 723 at 724C.

S 307(4)

This sub-section deprives the trustee of any remedy against those who acquire property from the bankrupt in good faith, for value and without notice, or as against bankers who enter transactions with the bankrupt in good faith and without notice. Where the recipient of the property is not protected by this provision the trustee may claim the property for the estate IR 1986 r 6.201. See also IR 1986 r 6.200(3).

S 307(5)

'After-acquired property' does not include that which may the subject of an income payments order under s 310 see *Supperstone v Lloyd's Names Working Party* [1999] BPIR 832.

1.359

308 Vesting in trustee of certain items of excess value

(1) Subject to section 309, where—
  (a) property is excluded by virtue of section 283(2) (tools of trade, household effects, etc) from the bankrupt's estate, and
  (b) it appears to the trustee that the realisable value of the whole or any part of that property exceeds the cost of a reasonable replacement for that property or that part of it,
the trustee may by notice in writing claim that property or, as the case may be, that part of it for the bankrupt's estate.

(2) Upon the service on the bankrupt of a notice under this section, the property to which the notice relates vests in the trustee as part of the bankrupt's estate; and, except against a purchaser in good faith, for value and without notice of the bankruptcy, the trustee's title to that property has relation back to the commencement of the bankruptcy.

(3) The trustee shall apply funds comprised in the estate to the purchase by or on behalf of the bankrupt of a reasonable replacement for any property vested in the trustee under this section; and the duty imposed by this subsection has priority over the obligation of the trustee to distribute the estate.

(4) For the purposes of this section property is a reasonable replacement for other property if it is reasonably adequate for meeting the needs met by the other property.

Notes

S 308(1)

See IR 1986 r 6.187, 6.188. The trustee may claim property for the estate which is excluded by s 283(2) if it appears to the trustee that the realisable value of the property exceeds the cost of a reasonable replacement.

S 308(2)

The trustee's service of notice in relation to property vests that property in the bankrupt's estate and, except against a purchaser for value without notice, the trustee's title to it has relation back to the commencement of the bankruptcy.

S 308(3)

The trustee must use funds from the estate to purchase a reasonable replacement in priority to his obligation to distribute the estate. However, the trustee is under no obligation to apply funds to the purchase of a replacement property until he has sufficient funds in the estate for that purpose IR 1986 r 6.187(2).

1.360

308A Vesting in trustee of certain tenancies

Upon the service on the bankrupt by the trustee of a notice in writing under this section, any tenancy—
(a) which is excluded by virtue of section 283(3A) from the bankrupt's estate, and
(b) to which the notice relates,
vests in the trustee as part of the bankrupt's estate; and, except against a purchaser in good faith, for value and without notice of the bankruptcy, the trustee's title to that tenancy has relation back to the commencement of the bankruptcy.

1.361

309 Time-limit for notice under s 307 or 308

(1) Except with the leave of the court, a notice shall not be served—
(a) under section 307, after the end of the period of 42 days beginning with the day on which it first came to the knowledge of the trustee that the property in question had been acquired by, or had devolved upon, the bankrupt;
(b) under section 308 [or section 308A], after the end of the period of 42 days beginning with the day on which the property [or tenancy] in question first came to the knowledge of the trustee.

(2) For the purposes of this section—
(a) anything which comes to the knowledge of the trustee is deemed in relation to any successor of his as trustee to have come to the knowledge of the successor at the same time; and
(b) anything which comes (otherwise than under paragraph (a)) to the knowledge of a person before he is the trustee is deemed to come to his knowledge on his appointment taking effect or, in the case of the official receiver, on his becoming trustee.

Notes

S 309(1)

This provides a time limit of 42 days (commencing on the day on which the after-acquired property or property under s 308 or tenancy under s 308A came to the trustee's knowledge) in which the trustee can serve a notice under s 307, 308 or 308A. Once the time limit has expired the trustee must apply to the court for leave to serve a notice. In *Solomon v Williams* [2001] BPIR 1123, Pumfrey J refused an extension of the time period under s 309 in relation to a s 307(1) notice, and held that in determining whether there was 'good cause' for such an extension, reference must be made to the circumstances of the bankruptcy including the period of delay both in serving the notice under s 307 and seeking an extension of time; the merits of the application having regard to the overall position of the bankrupt; the prejudice caused to the bankrupt by the lateness of the application; and the reasons for the delay. A substantial deficiency or a bankruptcy in which there is no dividend for the secured creditors is, on the face of it, a good reason for making an order under s 307. Such an order should not, however, be made if it causes prejudice to the bankrupt which is disproportionate to the advantage conferred on the creditors. See *Frances v Oomerjee* [2005] BPIR 1320 for another unsuccessful time extension application where over 7 years had elapsed between the bankrupt giving notice to the official receiver and the service of any notice.

S 309(2)(a)

This sub-section fixes a trustee with the knowledge of his predecessor at the times that his predecessor came to it.

S 309(2)(b)

Any person who has 'knowledge' and then becomes a trustee is deemed to come to that knowledge on his effective appointment or in the case of the official receiver, when he becomes trustee.

1.362

310 Income payments orders

(1) The court may, [on the application of the trustee], make an order ('an income payments order') claiming for the bankrupt's estate so much of the income of the bankrupt during the period for which the order is in force as may be specified in the order.

(1A) An income payments order may be made only on an application instituted –

    (a)   by the trustee, and

    (b)   before the discharge of the bankrupt

(2) The court shall not make an income payments order the effect of which would be to reduce the income of the bankrupt when taken together with any payments to which subsection (8) applies below what appears to the court to be necessary for meeting the reasonable domestic needs of the bankrupt and his family.

(3) An income payments order shall, in respect of any payment of income to which it is to apply, either—

    (a)   require the bankrupt to pay the trustee an amount equal to so much of that payment as is claimed by the order, or

    (b)   require the person making the payment to pay so much of it as is so claimed to the trustee, instead of to the bankrupt.

(4) Where the court makes an income payments order it may, if it thinks fit, discharge or vary any attachment of earnings order that is for the time being in force to secure payments by the bankrupt.

(5) Sums received by the trustee under an income payments order form part of the bankrupt's estate.

(6) An income payments order must specify the period during which it is to have effect, and that period—
- (a)   may end after the discharge of the bankrupt, but
- (b)   may not end after the period of three years beginning with the date on which the order is made.

(6A) An income payments order may (subject to subsection (6)(b)) be varied on the application of the trustee or the bankrupt (whether before or after discharge).

(6) An income payments order shall not be made after the discharge of the bankrupt, and if made before, shall not have effect after his discharge except—
- *(a)   in the case of a discharge under section 279(1)(a) (order of court), by virtue of a condition imposed by the court under section 280(2)(c) (income, etc after discharge), or*
- *(b)   in the case of a discharge under section 279(1)(b) (expiration of relevant period), by virtue of a provision of the order requiring it to continue in force for a period ending after the discharge but no later than 3 years after the making of the order.*

(7) For the purposes of this section the income of the bankrupt comprises every payment in the nature of income which is from time to time made to him or to which he from time to time becomes entitled, including any payment in respect of the carrying on of any business or in respect of any office or employment and (despite anything in section 11 or 12 of the Welfare Reform and Pensions Act 1999) any payment under a pension scheme but excluding any payment to which subsection (8) applies.

(8) This subsection applies to—
- (a)   payments by way of guaranteed minimum pension; and
- (b)   payments giving effect to the bankrupt's protected rights as a member of a pension scheme.

(9) In this section, 'guaranteed minimum pension' and 'protected rights' have the same meaning as in the Pension Schemes Act 1993.

Notes

S 310(1)

The trustee may apply to the court for an 'income payments order' for so much of the bankrupt's income during the period for which the order is in force. The words 'on the application of the trustee' were repealed by EA 2002 as from 1 April 2004: see now s 310(1A). The relevant rules are contained in IR 1986 r 6.189 to 6.193. See also 'income payments agreement' IA 1986 s 310A (below).

S 310(1A)

This provision was inserted by EA 2002 with effect from 1 April 2004.

S 310(2)

The income payments order must not have the effect of reducing the income of the bankrupt below what is necessary for meeting 'reasonable domestic needs of the bankrupt and his family' which might include private school fees *Re Scott* [2003] BPIR 1009, *Re Rayatt (A Bankrupt)* [1998] BPIR 495. 'Family', in relation to a bankrupt, means the persons (if any) who are living with him and are dependent on him IA 1986 s 385. However, even where a child does not fit into that definition, a Child Support Agency assessment or lump sum order made under para 5 of Sch 1 to the Children Act 1989 might well be viewed as falling within the reasonable demands on the bankrupt's income *Re X (a bankrupt)* [1996] BPIR 494. The court's approach to making an income payments order should be to achieve proportionality between the creditors and the bankrupt, whilst not creating a situation in which the bankrupt is the slave of the creditors *Kilvert v Flackett* [1998] BPIR 721. See *Albert v Albert (A Bankrupt)* [1996] BPIR 232 for the relationship between creditors and family members of the bankrupt in ancillary relief proceedings.

S 310(3)

The court may order the bankrupt to pay the trustee the amount specified in the income payment order, or it may order the person making the payment to pay such sum to the trustee.

S 310(4)

If the court makes an income payment order, it may discharge or vary any attachment of earnings order imposed on the bankrupt.

S 310(5)

Payments received by the trustee under the order form part of the estate of the bankrupt.

S 310(6), (6A)

These provisions were inserted by the EA 2002 effective from 1 April 2004. The former IA 1986 s 310(6) appears in italics.

S 310(7)

The 'income' of the bankrupt is broadly defined to include any payments in the nature of income including, inter alia, payments of salary, income earned as a self-employed person and some pension payments (see s 310(8), (9)). In *Re Landau (A Bankrupt)* [1998] Ch 223 Ferris J held that where the bankrupt held a life assurance policy and at the time of the bankruptcy order he had a present right to compel payment thereunder, that policy and the right to receive an annuity therefrom formed part of the bankrupt's estate and vested in the trustee in bankruptcy upon his appointment and could not be made subject to an income payments order. In *Krasner v Dennison, Lerrer v Lawrence* [2000] BPIR 410, the Court of Appeal approved *Re Landau* (supra), Chadwick LJ holding that s 310 applied to income to which the bankrupt had no entitlement at the date of the bankruptcy order. But the section is not intended to apply to income which the bankrupt receives by virtue of some right to which he was entitled at the date of the bankruptcy order. In such a case the right, and the income received by virtue of that right, forms part of the bankrupt's estate under the provisions of section 283(1)(a). See also the notes to IA 1986 s 283(1)(a) in relation to the position of pensions after the introduction of the Welfare Reform and Pensions Act 1999. In *Supperstone v Lloyd's Names Association Working Party* [1999] BPIR 832, it was accepted that 'from time to time' in s 310(7) means 'at any time'; therefore one-off payments made to the bankrupt fall within s 310(7) as well as periodic payments.

S 310(8), (9)

The Pensions Act 1995 introduced these sections.

1.363

310A Income payments agreement

(1) In this section 'income payments agreement' means a written agreement between a bankrupt and his trustee or between a bankrupt and the official receiver which provides-

(a) that the bankrupt is to pay to the trustee or the official receiver an amount equal to a specified part or proportion of the bankrupt's income for a specified period, or

(b) that a third person is to pay to the trustee or the official receiver a specified proportion of money due to the bankrupt by way of income for a specified period.

(2) A provision of an income payments agreement of a kind specified in subsection (1)(a) or (b) may be enforced as if it were a provision of an income payments order.

(3) While an income payments agreement is in force the court may, on the application of the bankrupt, his trustee or the official receiver, discharge or vary an attachment of earnings order that is for the time being in force to secure payments by the bankrupt.

(4) The following provisions of section 310 shall apply to an income payments agreement as they apply to an income payments order-

(a) subsection (5) (receipts to form part of estate), and

(b) subsections (7) to (9) (meaning of income).

(5) An income payments agreement must specify the period during which it is to have effect; and that period-

(a) may end after the discharge of the bankrupt, but

(b) may not end after the period of three years beginning with the date on which the agreement is made.

(6) An income payments agreement may (subject to subsection (5)(b)) be varied-

(a) by written agreement between the parties, or

(b) by the court on an application made by the bankrupt, the trustee or the official receiver.

(7) The court-

(a) may not vary an income payments agreement so as to include provision of a kind which could not be included in an income payments order, and

(b) shall grant an application to vary an income payments agreement if and to the extent that the court thinks variation necessary to avoid the effect mentioned in section 310(2).

Notes

S 310A(1)

This provision was introduced by the EA 2002 effective from 1 April 2004. It enables the bankrupt to make a written agreement with the trustee or official receiver to pay part of his income or direct third party monies for the benefit of creditors rather than facing an application for an income payments order. The relevant rules are contained in IR 1086 rr 6.103A C.

S 310(5)

The income payments agreement may survive discharge of the bankruptcy but it cannot last longer than 3 years after the date of the agreement.

S 310(7)(b)

Note the application of s 310(2) and the continued relevance of the bankrupt's reasonable domestic needs where an application to vary an income payments agreement is made to the court.

1.364

311 Acquisition by trustee of control

(1) The trustee shall take possession of all books, papers and other records which relate to the bankrupt's estate or affairs and which belong to him or are in his possession or under his control (including any which would be privileged from disclosure in any proceedings).

(2) In relation to, and for the purpose of acquiring or retaining possession of, the bankrupt's estate, the trustee is in the same position as if he were a receiver of property appointed by the High Court; and the court may, on his application, enforce such acquisition or retention accordingly.

(3) Where any part of the bankrupt's estate consists of stock or shares in a company, shares in a ship or any other property transferable in the books of a company, office or person, the trustee may exercise the right to transfer the property to the same extent as the bankrupt might have exercised it if he had not become bankrupt.

(4) Where any part of the estate consists of things in action, they are deemed to have been assigned to the trustee; but notice of the deemed assignment need not be given except in so far as it is necessary, in a case where the deemed assignment is from the bankrupt himself, for protecting the priority of the trustee.

(5) Where any goods comprised in the estate are held by any person by way of pledge, pawn or other security and no notice has been served in respect of those goods by the official receiver under subsection (5) of section 285 (restriction on realising security), the trustee may serve such a notice in respect of the goods; and whether or not a notice has been served under this subsection or that subsection, the trustee may, if he thinks fit, exercise the bankrupt's right of redemption in respect of any such goods.

(6) A notice served by the trustee under subsection (5) has the same effect as a notice served by the official receiver under section 285(5).

Notes

S 311(1)

See IA 1986 s 312(1) (below). 'Records' includes computer records and other non-documentary records IA 1986 s 436. The trustee is empowered to take possession of property which 'relates to the bankrupt's estate or affairs' even where such documents are not themselves comprised in the estate. Those documents which properly relate to the bankrupt's estate are those which are necessary for the trustee to carry out his functions in administering the estate. Therefore, in *Haig v Aitken* [2000] BPIR 462 it was held that the reference in s 311 to the bankrupt's 'affairs' is to his financial or other affairs which may be relevant to the carrying out of trustee in bankruptcy's duties under the Insolvency Act, or possibly even affairs relevant to the conduct of the official receiver's independent duties under the 1986 Act. In the circumstances, wholly private, personal correspondence would not normally be covered by s 311. As to the use by the trustee of privileged information in the performance of his duties, see *Re Konigsberg (A Bankrupt)* [1989] WLR 1257; *Re Ouvaroff (A Bankrupt)* [1997] 1 BPIR 712, *Trustee of the Estate of Omar (A Bankrupt) v Omar & Others* [2000] BCC 434.

S 311(3)

Where the bankrupt remains the registered proprietor of the shares (ie where the company refuses to register the trustee as holder of the shares), the bankrupt is entitled to exercise the votes which are attributable to that status, but he must exercise those votes in accordance with the direction of the trustee who is beneficially entitled to the shares *Morgan v Gray* [1953] Ch 83.

S 311(5)

The trustee may serve a notice in relation to goods held by a third party by way of security if notice has not already been served by the official receiver under s 285(5). Regardless of the service of notice under s 285(5) or 311(5), the trustee may exercise the bankrupt's right of redemption.

S 311(6)

A notice served under s 311(5) has the same effect as that served under s 285(1).

———————

1.365

312 Obligation to surrender control to trustee

(1) The bankrupt shall deliver up to the trustee possession of any property, books, papers or other records of which he has possession or control and of which the trustee is required to take possession.

This is without prejudice to the general duties of the bankrupt under section 333 in this Chapter.

(2) If any of the following is in possession of any property, books, papers or other records of which the trustee is required to take possession, namely—

    (a)   the official receiver,

    (b)   a person who has ceased to be trustee of the bankrupt's estate, or

    (c)   a person who has been the supervisor of a voluntary arrangement approved in relation to the bankrupt under Part VIII,

the official receiver or, as the case may be, that person shall deliver up possession of the property, books, papers or records to the trustee.

(3) Any banker or agent of the bankrupt or any other person who holds any property to the account of, or for, the bankrupt shall pay or deliver to the trustee all property in his possession or under his control which forms part of the bankrupt's estate and which he is not by law entitled to retain as against the bankrupt or trustee.

(4) If any person without reasonable excuse fails to comply with any obligation imposed by this section, he is guilty of a contempt of court and liable to be punished accordingly (in addition to any other punishment to which he may be subject).

Notes

S 312(1)

See IA 1986 s 311(1) (above). Without prejudice to the bankrupt's general duty under s. 333 to provide information etc, he must deliver up to the trustee any property, books, papers or other records of which he has possession or control and of which the trustee is required to take possession.

S 312(2)

The official receiver, former trustees and supervisors of voluntary arrangements are required to deliver up such property to the trustee. See also IR 1986 r 6.125 (hand-over of estate to trustee), 6.146 (trustee's duties on vacating office).

S 312(4)

Failure to comply with obligations imposed by this section is punishable as a contempt of court.

1.366

313 Charge on bankrupt's home

(1) Where any property consisting of an interest in a dwelling house which is occupied by the bankrupt or by his spouse or former spouse is comprised in the bankrupt's estate and the trustee is, for any reason, unable for the time being to realise that property, the trustee may apply to the court for an order imposing a charge on the property for the benefit of the bankrupt's estate.

(2) If on an application under this section the court imposes a charge on any property, the benefit of that charge shall be comprised in the bankrupt's estate and is enforceable, up to the charged value from time to time, for the payment of any amount which is payable otherwise than to the bankrupt out of the estate and of interest on that amount at the prescribed rate.

(2A) In subsection (2) the charged value means-
    (a)   the amount specified in the charging order as the value of the bankrupt's interest in the property at the date of the order, plus
    (b)   interest on that amount from the date of the charging order at the prescribed rate.

(2B) In determining the value of an interest for the purposes of this section the court shall disregard any matter which it is required to disregard by the rules.

(3) An order under this section made in respect of property vested in the trustee shall provide, in accordance with the rules, for the property to cease to be comprised in the bankrupt's estate and, subject to the charge (and any prior charge), to vest in the bankrupt.

> (4) Subsections (1) and (2) and (4) to (6) of section 3 of the Charging Orders Act 1979 (supplemental provisions with respect to charging orders) have effect in relation to orders under this section as in relation to charging orders under that Act.
>
> (5) But an order under section 3(5) of that Act may not vary a charged value.

Notes

S 313(1)

'Dwelling house' includes any building or part of a building which is occupied as a dwelling and any yard, garden, garage or outhouse belonging to the dwelling house and occupied with it IA 1986 s 385. If the trustee is unable to realise the bankrupt's interest in the dwelling house (occupied by the bankrupt or his spouse or former spouse or civil partner), then he may apply to the court to impose a charging order on the property for the benefit of the estate. The procedural aspects of the application are detailed in IR 1986 r 6.237D, 6.237E. Note that an application by the trustee for such a charging order within the period of three years from the commencement of the bankruptcy will prevent the property from re-vesting in the bankrupt pursuant to IA 1986 s 283A(2), see IA 1986 s 283(3). Instead, upon a successful application under this section, the property will re-vest in the bankrupt subject to the charge for the benefit of the bankrupt's estate. On the application of s 20 Limitation Act 1980 to claims based on charging orders obtained pursuant to s 313, see *Doodes v Gotham* [2006] EWCA Civ 1080, which held that such a charge secures a future obligation which becomes a present obligation only on the making of an order for sale. Thus time does not begin to run against the trustee until the order for sale is made.

S 313(2)

As to the rate of interest see IR 1986 r 6.237D(5).

S 313(2A)

The value of the charge amounts to the value of the bankrupt's interest in the property at the date of the order. The aim is to ensure that any subsequent increase in value of the bankrupt's interest accrues to the bankrupt rather than his creditors who instead will receive the benefit of interest at judgment rate.

S 313(2B)

See IR 1986 r 6.237D(10).

S 313(5)

Note the lack of power to vary the charged value by an order under s 3(5) of the Charging Orders Act 1979. This provision does not on the face of it preclude any other form of application under s 3(5) Charging Orders Act 1979 to vary or discharge the charge.

1.367

313A Low value home: application for sale, possession or charge

(1) This section applies where-
    (a)   property comprised in the bankrupt's estate consists of an interest in a dwelling-house which at the date of the bankruptcy was the sole or principal residence of-

> (i) the bankrupt,
> (ii) the bankrupt's spouse, or
> (iii) a former spouse of the bankrupt, and
>
> (b) the trustee applies for an order for the sale of the property, for an order for possession of the property or for an order under section 313 in respect of the property.
>
> (2) The court shall dismiss the application if the value of the interest is below the amount prescribed for the purposes of this subsection.
>
> (3) In determining the value of an interest for the purposes of this section the court shall disregard any matter which it is required to disregard by the order which prescribes the amount for the purposes of subsection (2).

Notes

S 313A(1)

This provision was introduced by the EA 2002 s 261(3) effective from 1 April 2004.

S 313A(2)

The minimum amount prescribed is presently £1000 art 2, Insolvency Proceedings (Monetary Limits) (Amendment) Order 2004 (SI 2004/547). See also art 3, Insolvency Proceedings (Monetary Limits) (Amendment) Order 2004 (SI 2004/547) as to the valuation of the property.

> **1.368**
>
> ### 314 Powers of trustee
>
> (1) The trustee may—
> (a) with the permission of the creditors' committee or the court, exercise any of the powers specified in Part I of Schedule 5 of this Act, and
> (b) without that permission, exercise any of the general powers specified in Part II of that Schedule.
>
> (2) With the permission of the creditors' committee or the court, the trustee may appoint the bankrupt—
> (a) to superintend the management of his estate or any part of it,
> (b) to carry on his business (if any) for the benefit of his creditors, or
> (c) in any other respect to assist in administering the estate in such manner and on such terms as the trustee may direct.
>
> (3) A permission given for the purposes of subsection (1)(a) or (2) shall not be a general permission but shall relate to a particular proposed exercise of the power in question; and a person dealing with the trustee in good faith and for value is not to be concerned to enquire whether any permission required in either case has been given.
>
> (4) Where the trustee has done anything without the permission required by subsection (1)(a) or (2), the court or the creditors' committee may, for the purpose of enabling him to meet his expenses out of the bankrupt's estate, ratify what the trustee has done.

But the committee shall not do so unless it is satisfied that the trustee has acted in a case of urgency and has sought its ratification without undue delay.

(5) Part III of Schedule 5 to this Act has effect with respect to the things which the trustee is able to do for the purposes of, or in connection with, the exercise of any of his powers under any of this Group of Parts.

(6) Where the trustee (not being the official receiver) in exercise of the powers conferred on him by any provision in this Group of Parts—
  (a) disposes of any property comprised in the bankrupt's estate to an associate of the bankrupt, or
  (b) employs a solicitor,
he shall, if there is for the time being a creditors' committee, give notice to the committee of that exercise of his powers.

(7) Without prejudice to the generality of subsection (5) and Part III of Schedule 5, the trustee may, if he thinks fit, at any time summon a general meeting of the bankrupt's creditors.

Subject to the preceding provisions in this Group of Parts, he shall summon such a meeting if he is requested to do so by a creditor of the bankrupt and the request is made with the concurrence of not less than one-tenth, in value, of the bankrupt's creditors (including the creditor making the request).

(8) Nothing in this Act is to be construed as restricting the capacity of the trustee to exercise any of his powers outside England and Wales.

Notes

S 314(1)(a), (b)

The trustee may exercise any of the powers set out in Part I of Schedule 5 with the permission of the creditors' committee or the court. He may exercise those general powers set out in Part II of that Schedule without permission.

S 314(2)

With permission from the court or the creditors' committee, the trustee may appoint the bankrupt in a number of capacities to assist the trustee in carrying his duties under Part I of Schedule 5.

S 314(3)

Permission granted to the trustee relates to a 'particular proposed exercise' of the power in question, and does not constitute a 'general permission'. A person dealing with the trustee in good faith and for value need not inquire as to whether the trustee has acquired permission or not.

S 314(4)

If the trustee acts without 'permission', the court or the creditors committee may ratify such conduct to enable him to meet his expenses out of the estate. The committee shall not ratify such acts unless they were performed in a case of urgency and the trustee sought ratification without undue delay.

S 314(6)

It appears from IR 1986 r 6.166(1) that where the creditors' committee's powers are vested in the Secretary of State under s 302(1), (2), no notices need be given under s 314 although the committee may require a report. The trustee may employ the petitioning creditor's solicitor *Re Schuppan (A Bankrupt) (No 1)* [1997] 1 BCLC 211; however, the trustee must consider whether there is a real risk of a conflict of interest in doing so, see also *Re Maxwell Communication Corpn plc* [1992] BCLC 465; *Re Baron Investments (holdings) Ltd* [2000] 1 BCLC 272.

S 314(7)

The trustee may at any time summon a general meeting of the bankrupt's creditors. However, he is obliged to do so if so requested by a creditor(s) of one tenth of the bankrupt's creditors.

S 314(8)

As to the exercise by the trustee of any of his powers outside England and Wales and the court's consideration of Article 16 of the Convention on Jurisdiction and the Enforcement of Judgments in Civil and Commercial Matters 1968, see *Re Hayward* [1997] Ch 45; *Pollard v Ashurst* [2001] BPIR 131.

The Second Group of Parts
Insolvency of Individuals; Bankruptcy

Part IX
Bankruptcy

Chapter IV
Administration by Trustee

Disclaimer of onerous property

1.369

315 Disclaimer (general power)

(1) Subject as follows, the trustee may, by the giving of the prescribed notice, disclaim any onerous property and may do so notwithstanding that he has taken possession of it, endeavoured to sell it or otherwise exercised rights of ownership in relation to it.

(2) The following is onerous property for the purposes of this section, that is to say—
  (a) any unprofitable contract, and
  (b) any other property comprised in the bankrupt's estate which is unsaleable or not readily saleable, or is such that it may give rise to a liability to pay money or perform any other onerous act.

(3) A disclaimer under this section—
  (a) operates so as to determine, as from the date of the disclaimer, the rights, interests and liabilities of the bankrupt and his estate in or in respect of the property disclaimed, and
  (b) discharges the trustee from all personal liability in respect of that property as from the commencement of his trusteeship,

but does not, except so far as is necessary for the purpose of releasing the bankrupt, the bankrupt's estate and the trustee from any liability, affect the rights or liabilities of any other person.

(4) A notice of disclaimer shall not be given under this section in respect of any property that has been claimed for the estate under section 307 (after-acquired property) or 308 (personal property of bankrupt exceeding reasonable replacement value) [or 308A], except with the leave of the court.

(5) Any person sustaining loss or damage in consequence of the operation of a disclaimer under this section is deemed to be a creditor of the bankrupt to the extent of the loss or damage and accordingly may prove for the loss or damage as a bankruptcy debt.

Notes

S 315

For the equivalent provisions relating to corporate insolvency see IA 1986 s 178 to 182. The provisions are in essence identical (save for the specific provisions relating to bankruptcy found in sections 315(4), 316(2) and 318) and the notes to s 178 to 182 should be referred to. For the rules relating to disclaimer see IR 1986 r 6.178 to 6.186. The consent of the court is no longer needed to serve a notice of disclaimer (save in the case of after acquired property or personal property of the bankrupt exceeding the reasonable replacement value – see section IA 1986 s 315(4)). For the definition of 'property' see IA 1986 s 436. As Sir Nicholas Browne-Wilkinson V-C observed in *Bristol Airport plc v Powdrill* [1990] Ch 744 at 759D: 'It is hard to think of a wider definition of property'. It is not possible to disclaim liabilities in respect of property but retain the property itself, see *MEPC plc v Scottish Amicable Life Assurance Society* (1994) 67 P & CR 314.

S 315(1)(2)

The notice of disclaimer should be in Form 6.61. Onerous property can include a cause of action *Ghavri v Dunbar Bank plc* [2001] BPIR 618.

S 315(3)

For more on the effect of disclaimer, see *Hindcastle Ltd v Barbara Attenborough Associates Ltd* [1997] AC 70, *Hughes v Groveholt* [2005] BPIR 1345 and the annotations to IA 1986 s 178.

S 315(4)

IR 1986 r 6.182 sets out the procedure in relation to such an application.

S 315(5)

See *Re Park Air Services plc* [2000] 2 AC 172 and the notes to IA 1986 s 178(6).

I.370

316 Notice requiring trustee's decision

(1) Notice of disclaimer shall not be given under section 315 in respect of any property if—

> (a) a person interested in the property has applied in writing to the trustee or one of his predecessors as trustee requiring the trustee or that predecessor to decide whether he will disclaim or not, and
>
> (b) the period of 28 days beginning with the day on which that application was made has expired without a notice of disclaimer having been given under section 315 in respect of that property.
>
> (2) The trustee is deemed to have adopted any contract which by virtue of this section he is not entitled to disclaim.

Notes

S 316(1)

This section allows a person interested in the property to put the trustee to election as to whether or not to disclaim. For the rules and relevant form see IR 1986 r 6.183 and Form 6.62. Note that IA 1986 r 6.184 allows a trustee to give any person who appears to claim an interest in property which the trustee has the right to disclaim, notice calling on that person to declare within 14 days whether he claims any such interest and, if so, the nature and extent of it.

S 316(2)

Where a notice to elect is served in respect of a contract and the trustee elects not to disclaim the contract, the trustee is deemed to have adopted the contract.

1.371

317 Disclaimer of leaseholds

(1) The disclaimer of any property of a leasehold nature does not take effect unless a copy of the disclaimer has been served (so far as the trustee is aware of their addresses) on every person claiming under the bankrupt as underlessee or mortgagee and either—

> (a) no application under section 320 below is made with respect to the property before the end of the period of 14 days beginning with the day on which the last notice served under this subsection was served, or
>
> (b) where such an application has been made, the court directs that the disclaimer is to take effect.

(2) Where the court gives a direction under subsection (1)(b) it may also, instead of or in addition to any order it makes under section 320, make such orders with respect to fixtures, tenant's improvements and other matters arising out of the lease as it thinks fit.

Notes

S 317(1)

A notice of disclaimer must be served on all underlessees and mortgagees (IA 1986 s 317(1) and IR 1986 r 6.179(2); reference can be made to the corporate equivalent of this provision (IA 1986 s 179) and the notes thereto. If the leasehold property is a dwelling house the notice of disclaimer must also be served on all persons in occupation or claiming a right to occupy the dwelling house (IA 1986 s 318 IA and IR 1986 r 6.179(3)). Sections 317 and 318 IA 1986 provide that the disclaimer of a leasehold property or any property in a dwelling house does not take effect until a copy of the disclaimer has been served upon the persons identified in those sections and either (i) no application has been made under section 320 IA 1986 for a vesting order within 14 days beginning with the day on which the last notice was served; or (ii) an application has been made and the court directs that the disclaimer takes effect. Note that IR 1986 r 6.186 provides that an application for a vesting order pursuant to IA 1986 s 320 may be made within three months of the applicant becoming aware of the disclaimer.

1.372

318 Disclaimer of dwelling house

Without prejudice to section 317, the disclaimer of any property in a dwelling house does not take effect unless a copy of the disclaimer has been served (so far as the trustee is aware of their addresses) on every person in occupation of or claiming a right to occupy the dwelling house and either—

  (a) no application under section 320 is made with respect to the property before the end of the period of 14 days beginning with the day on which the last notice served under this section was served, or

  (b) where such an application has been made, the court directs that the disclaimer is to take effect.

Notes

S 318

'Dwelling house' includes any building or part of a building which is occupied as a dwelling and any yard, garden, garage or outhouse belonging to the dwelling house and occupied with it IA 1986 s 385.

1.373

319 Disclaimer of land subject to rent charge

(1) The following applies where, in consequence of the disclaimer under section 315 of any land subject to a rent charge, that land vests by operation of law in the Crown or any other person (referred to in the next subsection as 'the proprietor').

(2) The proprietor, and the successors in title of the proprietor, are not subject to any personal liability in respect of any sums becoming due under the rentcharge, except sums becoming due after the proprietor, or some person claiming under or through the proprietor, has taken possession or control of the land or has entered into occupation of it.

1.374

320 Court order vesting disclaimed property

(1) This section and the next apply where the trustee has disclaimed property under section 315.

(2) An application may be made to the court under this section by—
- (a) any person who claims an interest in the disclaimed property,
- (b) any person who is under any liability in respect of the disclaimed property, not being a liability discharged by the disclaimer, or
- (c) where the disclaimed property is property in a dwelling-house, any person who at the time when the bankruptcy petition was presented was in occupation of or entitled to occupy the dwelling house.

(3) Subject as follows in this section and the next, the court may, on an application under this section, make an order on such terms as it thinks fit for the vesting of the disclaimed property in, or for its delivery to—
- (a) a person entitled to it or a trustee for such a person,
- (b) a person subject to such a liability as is mentioned in subsection (2)(b) or a trustee for such a person, or
- (c) where the disclaimed property is property in a dwelling-house, any person who at the time when the bankruptcy petition was presented was in occupation of or entitled to occupy the dwelling house.

(4) The court shall not make an order by virtue of subsection (3)(b) except where it appears to the court that it would be just to do so for the purpose of compensating the person subject to the liability in respect of the disclaimer.

(5) The effect of any order under this section shall be taken into account in assessing for the purposes of section 315(5) the extent of any loss or damage sustained by any person in consequence of the disclaimer.

(6) An order under this section vesting property in any person need not be completed by any conveyance, assignment or transfer.

Notes

S 320(1)

See IR 1986 r 6.186 for the procedure applying to such an application. Notice of the hearing of the application must be given to the trustee, and any other persons that the court may direct on the hearing of the application IR 1986 r 6.186(4), (5). Note also the 3 month time limit for any application, IR 1986 r 6.186(2).

S 320(a)

See *LB of Hackney v Crown Estates Commissioners* [1996] BPIR 428 as to whether a local authority to which property was charged for the cost of statutory works claimed an interest in the disclaimed property within the meaning of IA 1986 s 320(2)(a) and was a person entitled to the property within the meaning of IA 1986 s 320(3)(a).

S 320(3)

The court's power to make a vesting order is a discretionary one. The words 'on such terms as the court thinks fit' give the court a wide discretion as to the terms that it can impose on the making of a vesting order such as in relation to any surplus on sale, see *Lee v Lee (a Bankrupt)* [1999] BPIR 926.

S 320(6)

See also section 52(2) LPA 1925.

———

1.375

321 Order under s 320 in respect of leaseholds

(1) The court shall not make an order under section 320 vesting property of a leasehold nature in any person, except on terms making that person—
- (a) subject to the same liabilities and obligations as the bankrupt was subject to under the lease on the day the bankruptcy petition was presented, or
- (b) if the court thinks fit, subject to the same liabilities and obligations as that person would be subject to if the lease had been assigned to him on that day.

(2) For the purposes of an order under section 320 relating to only part of any property comprised in a lease, the requirements of subsection (1) apply as if the lease comprised only the property to which the order relates.

(3) Where subsection (1) applies and no person is willing to accept an order under section 320 on the terms required by that subsection, the court may (by order under section 320) vest the estate or interest of the bankrupt in the property in any person who is liable (whether personally or in a representative capacity and whether alone or jointly with the bankrupt) to perform the lessee's covenants in the lease.

The court may by virtue of this subsection vest that estate and interest in such a person freed and discharged from all estates, incumbrances and interests created by the bankrupt.

(4) Where subsection (1) applies and a person declines to accept any order under section 320, that person shall be excluded from all interest in the property.

Distribution of bankrupt's estate

1.376

322 Proof of debts

(1) Subject to this section and the next, the proof of any bankruptcy debt by a secured or unsecured creditor of the bankrupt and the admission or rejection of any proof shall take place in accordance with the rules.

(2) Where a bankruptcy debt bears interest, that interest is provable as part of the debt except in so far as it is payable in respect of any period after the commencement of the bankruptcy.

(3) The trustee shall estimate the value of any bankruptcy debt which, by reason of its being subject to any contingency or contingencies or for any other reason, does not bear a certain value.

> (4) Where the value of a bankruptcy debt is estimated by the trustee under subsection (3) or, by virtue of section 303 in Chapter III, by the court, the amount provable in the bankruptcy in respect of the debt is the amount of the estimate.

Notes

S 322(1)

'Bankruptcy debt' has the wide meaning given to it by s 382(1). The relevant rules are IR 1986 r 6.96 to 6.114. Not all debts are provable, see IR 1986 r 12.3. As to the definition of secured creditor see IA 1986 s 383.

S 322(2)

See IR 1986 r 6.113 (interest).

S 322(3)

IR 1986 r 6.105 provides that if a creditor is dissatisfied with the trustee's decision with respect to his proof (including any decision on the question of preference), he may apply to the court for the decision to be reversed or varied. Any such application is not a true appeal, and the court is not restricted to the evidence available to the trustee at the time of his decision *Cadwell v Jackson* [2001] BPIR 966.

> **I.377**
>
> ### 323 Mutual credit and set-off
>
> (1) This section applies where before the commencement of the bankruptcy there have been mutual credits, mutual debts or other mutual dealings between the bankrupt and any creditor of the bankrupt proving or claiming to prove for a bankruptcy debt.
>
> (2) An account shall be taken of what is due from each party to the other in respect of the mutual dealings and the sums due from one party shall be set off against the sums due from the other.
>
> (3) Sums due from the bankrupt to another party shall not be included in the account taken under subsection (2) if that other party had notice at the time they became due that a bankruptcy petition relating to the bankrupt was pending.
>
> (4) Only the balance (if any) of the account taken under subsection (2) is provable as a bankruptcy debt or, as the case may be, to be paid to the trustee as part of the bankrupt's estate.

Notes

S 323

The leading authority on s 323 is *Stein v Blake* [1996] AC 243, which established the following points:

(i)   Set-off under s 323 is mandatory and self-executing (that is, automatic); there can be no contracting out and it operates whether or not the trustee in fact makes any claim against the creditor. One practical result is that where a trustee rejects a proof and the claimant then appeals the trustee should put before the Court any claim which the trustee makes against the claimant; it is not appropriate to first determine the proof and then have separate litigation concerning the claim of the trustee;

(ii) Equally, operation of the set off does not depend upon a proof of debt being lodged; a creditor who does not lodge a proof because his cross-claim does not exceed that of the trustee will nonetheless have the benefit of the statutory set-off. Equally, it will apply where the trustee has made no claim against the creditor;

(iii) The account is taken retrospectively, as at the date of the commencement of the bankruptcy, even though the sums concerned may not yet be due or ascertained or remained contingent at the date of bankruptcy;

(iv) In carrying out the calculation for the purposes of s 323(2), everything that has actually happened between the date of the bankruptcy order and the date of calculation is taken into account and, where necessary, an estimated value will be put on a creditor's contingent or unascertained claim. (The same does not apply to contingent or unascertained claims *against* the creditor);

(v) The effect of the section is to extinguish the original causes of action and substitute a claim to a net balance;

(vi) If the net balance is a credit balance in favour of the bankrupt's estate, it is a chose in action capable of assignment by the trustee in bankruptcy;

(vii) The balance can be assigned before the calculation of the net balance has been undertaken, since this may only be capable of being achieved at the conclusion of the litigation, which is itself part of the process of taking the account. (In cases where the creditor asserts, as against the assignee, that there will be a net balance in his favour, it may be necessary to join the trustee to the proceedings to preclude him from subsequently rejecting the proof of debt for the balance).

In a case decided on the corporate equivalent of s 323 (IR 1986 r 4.90), the House of Lords held that insolvency set-off is available where the contingent liability arises by virtue of a statute rather than a contract and therefore contains no consensual element; and that a contingent debt owed by the company which did not become due until after the liquidation could be set off against a debt owed to the company under IR 1986 r 4.90 *Secretary of State for Trade and Industry v Frid* [2004] UKHL 24, [2004] 2 WLR 1279. Further, set-off was available in favour of the Secretary of State for Trade and Industry on a subrogated claim where the company's own claim was against HM Customs and Excise: both SSTI and HM Customs and Excise were emanations of the Crown. The House of Lords confirmed that the phrase 'mutual dealings' extends the scope of the section to include the commission of a tort or the imposition of a statutory obligation; all that is necessary for the operation of insolvency set-off is that the dealings should give rise to 'commensurable cross-claims', that is claims capable of being expressed in money terms.

S 323(3)

The phrase 'at the time they became due' in subsection (3) refers to the date at which the obligation concerned was created, not the date for payment of that obligation *Coe v Ashurst* [1999] BPIR 662.

I.378

324 Distribution by means of dividend

(1) Whenever the trustee has sufficient funds in hand for the purpose he shall, subject to the retention of such sums as may be necessary for the expenses of the bankruptcy, declare and distribute dividends among the creditors in respect of the bankruptcy debts which they have respectively proved.

(2) The trustee shall give notice of his intention to declare and distribute a dividend.

(3) Where the trustee has declared a dividend, he shall give notice of the dividend and of how it is proposed to distribute it; and a notice given under this subsection shall contain the prescribed particulars of the bankrupt's estate.

(4) In the calculation and distribution of a dividend the trustee shall make provision—

    (a)   for any bankruptcy debts which appear to him to be due to persons who, by reason of the distance of their place of residence, may not have had sufficient time to tender and establish their proofs,

    (b)   for any bankruptcy debts which are the subject of claims which have not yet been determined, and

    (c)   for disputed proofs and claims.

Notes

S 324(1)

The effect of the reference to creditors having proved their debts is that a creditor with a non-provable debt will receive no distributions in the bankruptcy and the trustee owes him no duties *Levy v Legal Services Commission* [2000] BPIR 1065.

S 324(2)

The trustee can distribute interim dividends. IA 1986 s 325(1) (below) deals with the effect on distributions which have taken place before a creditor submits a proof. IR 1986 r 11.1 to 11.13 detail the rules on the declaration and payment of dividends.

1.379

325 Claims by unsatisfied creditors

(1) A creditor who has not proved his debt before the declaration of any dividend is not entitled to disturb, by reason that he has not participated in it, the distribution of that dividend or any other dividend declared before his debt was proved, but—

    (a)   when he has proved that debt he is entitled to be paid, out of any money for the time being available for the payment of any further dividend, any dividend or dividends which he has failed to receive; and

    (b)   any dividend or dividends payable under paragraph (a) shall be paid before that money is applied to the payment of any such further dividend.

(2) No action lies against the trustee for a dividend, but if the trustee refuses to pay a dividend the court may, if it thinks fit, order him to pay it and also to pay, out of his own money—

    (a)   interest on the dividend, at the rate for the time being specified in section 17 of the Judgments Act 1838, from the time it was withheld, and

> (b)   the costs of the proceedings in which the order to pay is made.

Notes

S 325(1)

A dividend paid under this section cannot be disturbed in favour of a secured creditor who has realised his security and subsequently proves for any unsecured shortfall *Whitehead v Household Mortgage Corporation* [2002] EWCA Civ 1697, [2003] BPIR 1482, CA. Conversely, if it transpires on revaluation of the security that a secured creditor has been overpaid a dividend, he must repay the excess to the trustee: IR 1986 11.9.

1.380

326 Distribution of property in specie

(1) Without prejudice to sections 315 to 319 (disclaimer), the trustee may, with the permission of the creditors' committee, divide in its existing form amongst the bankrupt's creditors, according to its estimated value, any property which from its peculiar nature or other special circumstances cannot be readily or advantageously sold.

(2) A permission given for the purposes of subsection (1) shall not be a general permission but shall relate to a particular proposed exercise of the power in question; and a person dealing with the trustee in good faith and for value is not to be concerned to enquire whether any permission required by subsection (1) has been given.

(3) Where the trustee has done anything without the permission required by subsection (1), the court or the creditors' committee may, for the purpose of enabling him to meet his expenses out of the bankrupt's estate, ratify what the trustee has done.

But the committee shall not do so unless it is satisfied that the trustee acted in a case of urgency and has sought its ratification without undue delay.

1.381

327 Distribution in criminal bankruptcy

Where the bankruptcy order was made on a petition under section 264(1)(d) (criminal bankruptcy), no distribution shall be made under sections 324 to 326 so long as an appeal is pending (within the meaning of section 277) against the bankrupt's conviction of any offence by virtue of which the criminal bankruptcy order on which the petition was based was made.

Notes

S 327

This provision was prospectively repealed by the Criminal Justice Act 1988, s 170(2), Sch 16, as from a day to be appointed.

1.382

328 Priority of debts

(1) In the distribution of the bankrupt's estate, his preferential debts (within the meaning given by section 386 in Part XII) shall be paid in priority to other debts.

(2) Preferential debts rank equally between themselves after the expenses of the bankruptcy and shall be paid in full unless the bankrupt's estate is insufficient for meeting them, in which case they abate in equal proportions between themselves.

(3) Debts which are neither preferential debts nor debts to which the next section applies also rank equally between themselves and, after the preferential debts, shall be paid in full unless the bankrupt's estate is insufficient for meeting them, in which case they abate in equal proportions between themselves.

(4) Any surplus remaining after the payment of the debts that are preferential or rank equally under subsection (3) shall be applied in paying interest on those debts in respect of the periods during which they have been outstanding since the commencement of the bankruptcy; and interest on preferential debts ranks equally with interest on debts other than preferential debts.

(5) The rate of interest payable under subsection (4) in respect of any debt is whichever is the greater of the following—

    (a)   the rate specified in section 17 of the Judgments Act 1838 at the commencement of the bankruptcy, and

    (b)   the rate applicable to that debt apart from the bankruptcy.

(6) This section and the next are without prejudice to any provision of this Act or any other Act under which the payment of any debt or the making of any other payment is, in the event of bankruptcy, to have a particular priority or to be postponed.

Notes

S 328(1)

'Preferential debts' are detailed in IA 1986 s 386, Sch 6.

S 328(4)

This provision deals with the payment of post bankruptcy interest; pre bankruptcy interest is dealt with under IA 1986 s 322(2).

1.383

329 Debts to spouse or civil partner

(1) This section applies to bankruptcy debts owed in respect of credit provided by a person who (whether or not the bankrupt's spouse *or civil partner* at the time the credit was provided) was the bankrupt's spouse *or civil partner* at the commencement of the bankruptcy.

(2) Such debts—
  (a)   rank in priority after the debts and interest required to be paid in pursuance of section 328(3) and (4), and
  (b)   are payable with interest at the rate specified in section 328(5) in respect of the period during which they have been outstanding since the commencement of the bankruptcy;
and the interest payable under paragraph (b) has the same priority as the debts on which it is payable.

Notes

S 329(1)

This provision has been amended to include a 'civil partner' see Civil Partnership Act 2004, s 263(10)(b) from 5th December 2005.

1.384

330 Final distribution

(1) When the trustee has realised all the bankrupt's estate or so much of it as can, in the trustee's opinion, be realised without needlessly protracting the trusteeship, he shall give notice in the prescribed manner either—
  (a)   of his intention to declare a final dividend, or
  (b)   that no dividend, or further dividend, will be declared.

(2) The notice under subsection (1) shall contain the prescribed particulars and shall require claims against the bankrupt's estate to be established by a date ('the final date') specified in the notice.

(3) The court may, on the application of any person, postpone the final date.

(4) After the final date, the trustee shall—
  (a)   defray any outstanding expenses of the bankruptcy out of the bankrupt's estate, and
  (b)   if he intends to declare a final dividend, declare and distribute that dividend without regard to the claim of any person in respect of a debt not already proved in the bankruptcy.

(5) If a surplus remains after payment in full and with interest of all the bankrupt's creditors and the payment of the expenses of the bankruptcy, the bankrupt is entitled to the surplus.

(6) Subsection (5) is subject to Article 35 of the EC Regulation (surplus in secondary proceedings to be transferred to main proceedings).

Notes

S 330(5)

The bankrupt's right to any surplus is an equity that the bankrupt can deal with even before it has been ascertained; whether the dealing is effectual will depend on whether in fact there is a surplus following the completion of the administration of his bankrupt estate *Bird v Philpott* [1900] 1 Ch 822. In the case of a second bankruptcy, the surplus from the first bankruptcy will vest in the second trustee only to the extent that the bankrupt has not already disposed of it. 'Creditors' for the purpose of subsection (5) means those creditors who have proved in the bankruptcy. Accordingly, there may be a surplus for the bankrupt in a case where other creditors are known to exist but have not submitted any proof *Hammond v Official Receiver* [1942] Ch 294.

1.385

331 Final meeting

(1) Subject as follows in this section and the next, this section applies where—

    (a)   it appears to the trustee that the administration of the bankrupt's estate in accordance with this Chapter is for practical purposes complete, and

    (b)   the trustee is not the official receiver.

(2) The trustee shall summon a final general meeting of the bankrupt's creditors which—

    (a)   shall receive the trustee's report of his administration of the bankrupt's estate, and

    (b)   shall determine whether the trustee should have his release under section 299 in Chapter III.

(3) The trustee may, if he thinks fit, give the notice summoning the final general meeting at the same time as giving notice under section 330(1); but, if summoned for an earlier date, that meeting shall be adjourned (and, if necessary, further adjourned) until a date on which the trustee is able to report to the meeting that the administration of the bankrupt's estate is for practical purposes complete.

(4) In the administration of the estate it is the trustee's duty to retain sufficient sums from the estate to cover the expenses of summoning and holding the meeting required by this section.

Notes

S 331(1)

The relevant rules dealing with the final meeting and specific quorum provisions are in IR 1986 r 6.137, r 6.137A

S 331(2)(a)

The question of the trustee's release is important, as this is the date from which he is discharged from liability for acts or omissions in relation to the administration of the bankrupt's estate and his conduct as trustee (subject only to the possibility of proceedings under IA 1986 s 304: see IA 1986 s 299(5)).

S 331(2)(b)

If the trustee does not obtain his release at the final meeting he will have to await a decision by the Secretary of State IA 1986 s 299(3)(b).

I.386

332 Saving for bankrupt's home

(1) This section applies where—
- (a) there is comprised in the bankrupt's estate property consisting of an interest in a dwelling house which is occupied by the bankrupt or by his spouse or former spouse *or by his civil partner or former civil partner*, and
- (b) the trustee has been unable for any reason to realise that property.

(2) The trustee shall not summon a meeting under section 331 unless either—
- (a) the court has made an order under section 313 imposing a charge on that property for the benefit of the bankrupt's estate, or
- (b) the court has declined, on an application under that section, to make such an order, or
- (c) the Secretary of State has issued a certificate to the trustee stating that it would be inappropriate or inexpedient for such an application to be made in the case in question.

Notes

S 332(1)

This provision has been amended to include a civil partner or former civil partner of the bankruptcy from 5 December 2005, the Civil Partnership Act 2004, s 263(10)(b). 'Dwelling house' includes any building or part of a building which is occupied as a dwelling and any yard, garden or outhouse belonging to the dwelling house and occupied with it IA 1986 s 385.

Supplemental

I.387

333 Duties of bankrupt in relation to trustee

(1) The bankrupt shall—
- (a) give to the trustee such information as to his affairs,
- (b) attend on the trustee at such times, and
- (c) do all such other things,

as the trustee may for the purposes of carrying out his functions under any of this Group of Parts reasonably require

(2) Where at any time after the commencement of the bankruptcy any property is acquired by, or devolves upon, the bankrupt or there is an increase of the bankrupt's income, the bankrupt shall, within the prescribed period, give the trustee notice of the property or, as the case may be, of the increase.

(3) Subsection (1) applies to a bankrupt after his discharge.

(4) If the bankrupt without reasonable excuse fails to comply with any obligation imposed by this section, he is guilty of a contempt of court and liable to be punished accordingly (in addition to any other punishment to which he may be subject).

Notes

S 333(1)

This imposes upon the bankrupt a general duty to assist the trustee in the performance of his statutory functions in collecting in and realising the assets of the bankrupt's estate for the benefit of his creditors. The duty is widely drawn, not limited to the provision of information but including the performance of such other acts as may be reasonably required by the trustee for the purpose of carrying out his statutory functions. It is supplemented by the more specific duties for the delivery up to the trustee of the bankrupt's property, books and records under IA 1986 s 312. The bankrupt may not direct his bankers to refuse to provide information to the trustee *Christofi v Barclays Bank plc* [1998] BPIR 452. Note also the similar duties owed by the bankrupt to the official receiver in the period before a trustee is appointed under IA 1986 s 291.

S 333(2)

The bankrupt is placed under a specific duty to notify the trustee of his acquisition of any property or any increase in his income in the period after commencement of the bankruptcy to enable the trustee to discharge his functions under IA 1986 s 307, s 310. Under IR 1986 r 6.200(1), the prescribed period within which such notice must be given is 21 days of the bankrupt becoming aware of the relevant facts.

S 333(4)

Failure to comply with the above duties is punishable as a contempt of court and general guidelines in relation to civil contempt may be found in *R M (A Minor)* (1998) Times, 31 December. More usefully as summarised in *Morris v Murjani* [1996] 1 WLR 848, p 852–3, the duties may also be enforced through the court by the trustee by mandatory injunction or by requesting the court to execute documentation (*Savage v Norton* [1908] 1 Ch 290, s 39(1) Supreme Court Act 1981) or to obtain vacant possession (*Bell v Tuohy* [2002] EWCA Civ 423, [2003] BPIR 749, *Fryer and Thompson v Brook* [1998] BPIR 687); further the court may make orders under IA 1986 s 366, s 367, and where the bankrupt threatens to leave the jurisdiction pending an application for contempt he may be restrained from so doing. Failure to comply with his duties under IA 1986 s 333 also provides grounds for suspending the bankrupt's discharge under IA s 279 *Re Thorogood (No 3)* [2003] BPIR 1476.

1.388

334 Stay of distribution in case of second bankruptcy

(1) This section and the next apply where a bankruptcy order is made against an undischarged bankrupt; and in both sections—
  (a) 'the later bankruptcy' means the bankruptcy arising from that order,
  (b) 'the earlier bankruptcy' means the bankruptcy (or, as the case may be, most recent bankruptcy) from which the bankrupt has not been discharged at the commencement of the later bankruptcy, and
  (c) 'the existing trustee' means the trustee (if any) of the bankrupt's estate for the purposes of the earlier bankruptcy.

(2) Where the existing trustee has been given the prescribed notice of the presentation of the petition for the later bankruptcy, any distribution or other disposition by him of anything to which the next subsection applies, if made after the giving of the notice, is void except to the extent that it was made with the consent of the court or is or was subsequently ratified by the court.

This is without prejudice to section 284 (restrictions on dispositions of property following bankruptcy order).

(3) This subsection applies to—

    (a) any property which is vested in the existing trustee under section 307(3) (after-acquired property);

    (b) any money paid to the existing trustee in pursuance of an income payments order under section 310; and

    (c) any property or money which is, or in the hands of the existing trustee represents, the proceeds of sale or application of property or money falling within paragraph (a) or (b) of this subsection.

Notes

S 334

The heading to this section is somewhat misleading. In cases where an undischarged bankrupt is made the subject of a second bankruptcy order, this section operates not as a stay of distribution in respect of the generality of sums realised in the first bankruptcy, but only in respect of property or the proceeds of sale of property which has been acquired by the bankrupt and passed to his trustee in the period after commencement of the first bankruptcy – ie after-acquired property under IA 1986 s 307 and sums paid under an income payments order under IA 1986 s 310. The scheme of this section and IA 1986 s 335 is to provide that such assets should be available for benefit of the creditors of the second bankruptcy in priority to creditors of the first bankruptcy.

S 334(1)

Note that this provision and IA 1986 s 335 only apply where at the date of the second bankruptcy the bankrupt has not been discharged from the first bankruptcy.

S 334(2)

The prescribed notice by which a trustee in a first bankruptcy may be notified of the presentation of a petition for a second bankruptcy in order to put into effect this provision is Form 6.78. It is, presumably, the petitioning creditor in the later bankruptcy who it is contemplated should give such notice. For the relevant rules which apply specifically to cases of a second bankruptcy of an undischarged bankrupt, see IR 1986 r 6.225 to 6.228. It is not clear how IA 1986 s 284 can apply where the disposition is effected by the trustee as opposed to the person adjudged bankrupt.

1.389

335 Adjustment between earlier and later bankruptcy estates

(1) With effect from the commencement of the later bankruptcy anything to which section 334(3) applies which, immediately before the commencement of that bankruptcy, is comprised in the bankrupt's estate for the purposes of the earlier bankruptcy is to be treated as comprised in

the bankrupt's estate for the purposes of the later bankruptcy and, until there is a trustee of that estate, is to be dealt with by the existing trustee in accordance with the rules.

(2) Any sums which in pursuance of an income payments order under section 310 are payable after the commencement of the later bankruptcy to the existing trustee shall form part of the bankrupt's estate for the purposes of the later bankruptcy; and the court may give such consequential directions for the modification of the order as it thinks fit.

(3) Anything comprised in a bankrupt's estate by virtue of subsection (1) or (2) is so comprised subject to a first charge in favour of the existing trustee for any bankruptcy expenses incurred by him in relation thereto.

(4) Except as provided above and in section 334, property which is, or by virtue of section 308 (personal property of bankrupt exceeding reasonable replacement value) or section 308A (vesting in trustee of certain tenancies) is capable of being, comprised in the bankrupt's estate for the purposes of the earlier bankruptcy, or of any bankruptcy prior to it, shall not be comprised in his estate for the purposes of the later bankruptcy.

(5) The creditors of the bankrupt in the earlier bankruptcy and the creditors of the bankrupt in any bankruptcy prior to the earlier one, are not to be creditors of his in the later bankruptcy in respect of the same debts; but the existing trustee may prove in the later bankruptcy for—

    (a)   the unsatisfied balance of the debts (including any debt under this subsection) provable against the bankrupt's estate in the earlier bankruptcy;

    (b)   any interest payable on that balance; and

    (c)   any unpaid expenses of the earlier bankruptcy.

(6) Any amount provable under subsection (5) ranks in priority after all the other debts provable in the later bankruptcy and after interest on those debts and, accordingly, shall not be paid unless those debts and that interest have first been paid in full.

Notes

S 335(1)–(4)

See the notes to IA 1986 s 334 above for the general scheme which operates where a second bankruptcy order is made against an undischarged bankrupt. As IA 1986 s 335(1), (2), (4) confirm, of the assets falling within the bankrupt's estate under his first bankruptcy, it is only after-acquired property and sums paid or payable under income payment orders which are, on the making of a second bankruptcy order, to be treated as falling within the estate under the second bankruptcy, and to be applied for the benefit of creditors of that second bankruptcy in priority to creditors in the first bankruptcy.

S 335(3)

The trustee of the first bankruptcy has a first charge over such assets held by him for the benefit of the second bankruptcy for his expenses incurred in respect of such assets; see also IR 1986 r 6.228.

S 335(5), (6)

If creditors in the first bankruptcy are not paid in full, the trustee of the first bankruptcy may prove for the unsatisfied balance of their debts in the second bankruptcy, but such proof ranks in priority behind all other debts provable in the second bankruptcy. The right of the trustee in the first bankruptcy to prove in the second is a right belonging to him, not to the creditors, and does not arise for limitation purposes until the making of the second bankruptcy order *Re Cullwick, ex p Official Receiver* [1918] 1 KB 646.

Chapter V
Effect of Bankruptcy on Certain Rights, Transactions, Etc

[Rights under trusts of land]

1.390

335A Rights under trusts of land

(1) Any application by a trustee of a bankrupt's estate under section 14 of the Trusts of Land and Appointment of Trustees Act 1996 (powers of court in relation to trusts of land) for an order under that section for the sale of land shall be made to the court having jurisdiction in relation to the bankruptcy.

(2) On such an application the court shall make such order as it thinks just and reasonable having regard to—
    (a)   the interests of the bankrupt's creditors;
    (b)   where the application is made in respect of land which includes a dwelling house which is or has been the home of the bankrupt or the *bankrupt's spouse or former spouse* [bankrupt's spouse or civil partner or former spouse or former civil partner]—
        (i)   the conduct of the *spouse or former spouse* [spouse, civil partner, former spouse or former civil partner], so far as contributing to the bankruptcy,
        (ii)   the needs and financial resources of the *spouse or former spouse* [spouse, civil partner, former spouse or former civil partner], and
        (iii)   the needs of any children; and
    (c)   all the circumstances of the case other than the needs of the bankrupt.

(3) Where such an application is made after the end of the period of one year beginning with the first vesting under Chapter IV of this Part of the bankrupt's estate in a trustee, the court shall assume, unless the circumstances of the case are exceptional, that the interests of the bankrupt's creditors outweigh all other considerations.

(4) The powers conferred on the court by this s are exercisable on an application whether it is made before or after the commencement of this section..]

Notes

S 335A

Section 335A applies to an application by a trustee in bankruptcy for a sale of jointly owned property. It was inserted by s 25(1) and Sch 3, para 23 of the Trusts of Land and Appointment of Trustees Act 1996 with effect from 1 January 1997. Applications for orders for sale of jointly owned property are now governed by s 14 Trusts of Land and Appointment of Trustees Act 1996, which replaced s 30 LPA 1925. This provision has been amended to include a civil partner or former civil partner of the bankruptcy effective from 5 December 2005 by the Civil Partnership Act 2004.

Prior to 1 January 1997 applications for orders for sale in relation to jointly owned land were made pursuant to s 30 LPA 1925 and s 336(3) IA 1986. s 336(3) has been repealed and s 336 in its current form does not relate to applications for orders for sale of jointly owned property. Instead it applies solely to applications to bring to an end a spouse's statutory rights of occupation.

There is a plethora of pre-1997 case law under which the general principle was that when a trustee in bankruptcy brought an application under s 30 LPA 1925 for an order for sale, the court would normally make an order (although it would consider family interests) – see for example *Re Citro (a Bankrupt)* [1991] Ch 142 and *Re Ng* [1997] BCC 507. In *Mortgage Corporation v Shaire* [2001] Ch 743 Neuberger J held that pre–1996 cases should be treated with caution in relation to an application by a creditor for an order for sale under s 14 Trusts of Land and Appointment of Trustees Act 1996. There must therefore be some doubt about whether case law relating to applications by trustees under s 30 LPA 1925 is of any great value, although it is of note that s 335A(4) re-enacts the previous provisions relating to jointly owned property found in s 336(5). There is therefore some force in the argument that the pre-1997 cases on 'exceptional circumstances' may continue to be of some relevance. See also notes to s 283A IA 1986.

S 335A(2)

Section 335A(2) sets out the criteria that the court should take into account when deciding whether it is just and reasonable to make an order for sale. These criteria are wide. There is however a statutory assumption that after the expiry of one year of the vesting of the property in the trustee in bankruptcy the interests of the creditors shall outweigh all other considerations (s 335A(3)) and in practice most applications are brought after the expiry of this period. There is nothing to prevent a trustee issuing an application before the expiry of the one year period and it coming on for hearing after the expiry, thereby affording the trustee the benefit of s 335A(3). Notwithstanding the references to the bankrupt's 'spouse' and 'civil partner', the section applies to any property held jointly with the bankrupt, whatever the relationship between those interested.

S 335(A)(3)

'Creditors' in s 335A(3) means secured and unsecured creditors and a trustee can make an application for an order for sale even if it is only likely to benefit a secured creditor (*Judd v Brown* [1999] BPIR 517). However, a trustee must be careful of not entering into some form of agreement with a secured creditor because if he does so he runs the risk of the court finding that the application is an abuse of process; see *Re Ng* [1997] BPIR 267, where the secured creditor gave an indemnity to the trustee for his costs and agreed to pay a fee to the trustee for his assistance. Note however that the court still made an order for sale on the basis that the secured creditor would succeed if it brought an application itself.

The fact that the entirety of the net proceeds of sale may be swallowed up in paying the expenses of the bankruptcy is not an exceptional circumstance (*Trustee of the Estate of Eric Bowe (a Bankrupt) v Bowe* [1997] BPIR 747, a case decided under s 336(5) prior to the coming into force of s 335A; nor are the ordinary 'melancholy consequences of debt and improvidence' (see *Re Citro* [1991] Ch 142, at 157). *Harrington v Bennett* [2000] BPIR 630, sets out some clear and valuable guidance at pages 633–634 on 'exceptional circumstances', as does *Dean v Stout* [2005] BPIR 1113. The fact that the bankrupt's wife had cancer (together with medical evidence that an order for sale might impeded her chances of recovery) was held to be exceptional circumstances which merited a refusal to make even a suspended order for sale (*Judd v Brown* [1997] BPIR 470, this decision was overturned in part on appeal, but not on this part of the judgment). The bankrupt's wife being aged and infirm was held to be exceptional circumstances in *Claughton v Charalombous* [1998] BPIR 228, where the court declined to make any order. In *Hosking v Michaelides* [2004] All ER (D) 147 the court was persuaded that the wife's illnesses did constitute 'exceptional circumstances'. Note however that a finding of exceptional circumstances does not necessarily mean that an order for sale will not be made (although it may be suspended for an appropriate length of time) – see *Re D.R. Raval* [1998] BPIR 389.

Following the Human Rights Act 1998, the impact of Art 8 of the European Convention on Human Rights and Fundamental Freedoms 1950 must be considered. In particular it was suggested in *Barca v Mears* [2005] BPIR 15 that following Art 8, there might need to be a change in emphasis and 'exceptional circumstances' may exist notwithstanding that the consequences of making an order under *s 335A* are nothing more than the 'usual' conse-quences of bankruptcy; see *Donohoe v Ingram* [2006] BPIR 417, paras 19–21. However in *Hosking v Michaelides* [2004] All ER (D) 147 (concerning an application under the similarly worded s 336(5)) the court after being persuaded that the wife's illnesses did constitute exceptional circumstances nevertheless took the opportunity to state that the approach in *Re Citro* (above) to the determination of such circumstances was not incompatible with Art 8. Further in *Nicholls v Lan* [2006] EWHC 1255 the court doubted that Art 8 was inconsistent with s 335A.

Rights of occupation

1.391

336 Rights of occupation etc of bankrupt's spouse or civil partner

(1) Nothing occurring in the initial period of the bankruptcy (that is to say, the period beginning with the day of the presentation of the petition for the bankruptcy order and ending with the vesting of the bankrupt's estate in a trustee) is to be taken as having given rise to any *matrimonial home rights* [home rights] under Part IV of the Family Law Act 1996 in relation to a dwelling house comprised in the bankrupt's estate.

(2) Where *a spouse's matrimonial home rights* [home rights] under the Act of 1996 are a charge on the estate or interest of the other spouse [or civil partner], or of trustees for the other spouse [or civil partner], and the other spouse [or civil partner] is adjudged bankrupt—

   (a) the charge continues to subsist notwithstanding the bankruptcy and, subject to the provisions of that Act, binds the trustee of the bankrupt's estate and persons deriving title under that trustee, and

   (b) any application for an order under section 33 of that Act shall be made to the court having jurisdiction in relation to the bank-ruptcy.

(3) ...

(4) On such an application as is mentioned in subsection (2) ... the court shall make such order under section 33 of the Act of 1996 ... as it thinks just and reasonable having regard to—

   (a) the interests of the bankrupt's creditors,

   (b) the conduct of the spouse or former spouse [or civil partner or former civil partner], so far as contributing to the bankruptcy,

   (c) the needs and financial resources of the spouse or former spouse [or civil partner or former civil partner],

   (d) the needs of any children, and

> (e)   all the circumstances of the case other than the needs of the bankrupt.
>
> (5) Where such an application is made after the end of the period of one year beginning with the first vesting under Chapter IV of this Part of the bankrupt's estate in a trustee, the court shall assume, unless the circumstances of the case are exceptional, that the interests of the bankrupt's creditors outweigh all other considerations.

Notes

S 336

This provision deals with the statutory rights of a spouse or civil partner to occupy a matrimonial home. Such rights arise pursuant to s 30 Family Law Act 1996. Where such rights constitute a charge on the interest of the other spouse (and they usually do – see s 31 Family Law Act 1996) they will in the first instance bind a trustee in bankruptcy. Section 336 does not apply to the rights of co-owning cohabitees (to which see s 335A and the notes above). This provision has been amended to include a civil partner or former civil partner of the bankruptcy effective from 5 December 2005 by the Civil Partnership Act 2004.

S 336(2)

A spouse's right to occupy a matrimonial home survives the bankruptcy of the other spouse subject to the court's power on an application under s 33 Family Law Act 1996 to terminate it. The criteria that the court will take into account when deciding whether to terminate the interest are set out in sub-sections (4) and (5).

S 336(5)

There is no reason why the principles set out in the cases relating to 'exceptional circumstances' under s 335A(3) should not also apply to this section; see the notes to that provision. In *Re Bremner (a bankrupt)* [1999] BPIR 185 a trustee brought an application under s 336 to terminate a wife's right of occupation and sought an order for sale. It was held that the fact that the bankrupt was terminally ill and his 74 year old wife was caring for him at home were 'exceptional circumstances' for the purposes of s 336(5). The court postponed an order for sale until 3 months after the death of the bankrupt.

> **1.392**
>
> ### 337 Rights of occupation of bankrupt
>
> (1) This section applies where—
> (a)   a person who is entitled to occupy a dwelling house by virtue of a beneficial estate or interest is adjudged bankrupt, and
> (b)   any persons under the age of 18 with whom that person had at some time occupied that dwelling house had their home with that person at the time when the bankruptcy petition was presented and at the commencement of the bankruptcy.
>
> (2) Whether or not the bankrupt's *spouse (if any) has matrimonial home rights* [spouse or civil partner (if any) has home rights] under Part IV of the Family Law Act 1996—
> (a)   the bankrupt has the following rights as against the trustee of his estate—

> (i) if in occupation, a right not to be evicted or excluded from the dwelling house or any part of it, except with the leave of the court,
>
> (ii) if not in occupation, a right with the leave of the court to enter into and occupy the dwelling house, and
>
> (b) the bankrupt's rights are a charge, having the like priority as an equitable interest created immediately before the commencement of the bankruptcy, on so much of his estate or interest in the dwelling house as vests in the trustee.
>
> (3) The Act of 1996 has effect, with the necessary modifications, as if—
>
> (a) the rights conferred by paragraph (a) of subsection (2) were *matrimonial home rights* [home rights] under that Act,
>
> (b) any application for such leave as is mentioned in that paragraph were an application for an order under section 33 of that Act, and
>
> (c) any charge under paragraph (b) of that subsection on the estate or interest of the trustee were a charge under that Act on the estate or interest of a spouse.
>
> (4) Any application for leave such as is mentioned in subsection (2)(a) or otherwise by virtue of this section for an order under section 33 of the Act of 1996 shall be made to the court having jurisdiction in relation to the bankruptcy.
>
> (5) On such an application the court shall make such order under [section 33 of the Act of 1996] as it thinks just and reasonable having regard to the interests of the creditors, to the bankrupt's financial resources, to the needs of the children and to all the circumstances of the case other than the needs of the bankrupt.
>
> (6) Where such an application is made after the end of the period of one year beginning with the vesting (under Chapter IV of this Part) of the bankrupt's estate in a trustee, the court shall assume, unless the circumstances of the case are exceptional, that the interests of the bankrupt's creditors outweigh all other considerations.

Notes

S 337

This provision applies where a person who is living in a dwelling house by virtue of a beneficial estate or interest resides at the dwelling house with dependent children both at the date of presentation of the petition *and* when the bankruptcy order is made (which is when the bankruptcy commences). In such a case, the bankrupt has the right not to be evicted or excluded from the dwelling house except with the leave of the court. In addition, if the bankrupt is not in possession there is a power in s 337(2)(a)(ii) to apply to the court for leave to enter into and occupy the dwelling house. This provision has been amended to include a civil partner or former civil partner of the bankruptcy effective from 5 December 2005 by the Civil Partnership Act 2004.

S 337(2)–(3)

Section 337(3) applies the Family Law Act 1996, with the necessary modifications, to the rights conferred on the bankrupt under s 337(2). Note that these rights are treated, with the necessary modifications, as if they were matrimonial home rights under Family Law Act 1996. A trustee seeking to terminate such rights would need to make an application under s 337 IA 1986 and s 33 Family Law Act 1996.

S 337(4)–(6)

An application under s 33 Family Law Act 1996 must be made to the court having jurisdiction in relation to the bankruptcy (to which see s 373, 374 IA 1986). Section 337(5) sets out the criteria the court will apply on such an application and as with s 335A, 336 IA 1986 there is a statutory assumption in favour of the creditors once the property has been vested in the trustee for more than 12 months. On 'exceptional circumstances' see the notes to s 335A above.

1.393

338 Payments in respect of premises occupied by bankrupt

Where any premises comprised in a bankrupt's estate are occupied by him (whether by virtue of the preceding section or otherwise) on condition that he makes payments towards satisfying any liability arising under a mortgage of the premises or otherwise towards the outgoings of the premises, the bankrupt does not, by virtue of those payments, acquire any interest in the premises.

Notes

S 338

This provision prevents any argument by the bankrupt that by virtue of paying the mortgage instalments after the bankruptcy he has thereby acquired any interest in the relevant premises as against his bankrupt estate.

Chapter V
Effect of Bankruptcy on Certain Rights, Transactions, etc

Adjustment of prior transactions, etc

1.394

339 Transactions at an undervalue

(1) Subject as follows in this section and sections 341 and 342, where an individual is adjudged bankrupt and he has at a relevant time (defined in section 341) entered into a transaction with any person at an undervalue, the trustee of the bankrupt's estate may apply to the court for an order under this section

(2) The court shall, on such an application, make such order as it thinks fit for restoring the position to what it would have been if that individual had not entered into that transaction.

(3) For the purposes of this section and sections 341 and 342, an individual enters into a transaction with a person at an undervalue if—

> (a) he makes a gift to that person or he otherwise enters into a transaction with that person on terms that provide for him to receive no consideration,
>
> (b) he enters into a transaction with that person in consideration of marriage, or the formation of a civil partnership or
>
> (c) he enters into a transaction with that person for a consideration the value of which, in money or money's worth, is significantly less than the value, in money or money's worth, of the consideration provided by the individual.

Notes

S 339

A trustee needs the sanction of the creditors' committee or the court to make an application under this section (IA 1986 s 314, Sch 5 para 2A); in suitable circumstances the sanction can be obtained retrospectively but it is obvious that sanction should be sought first (*Associated Travel Leisure Services Ltd* [1978] 2 All ER 273).

This section replaced s 42 of the Bankruptcy Act 1914, which concerned 'settlements of property' made prior to bankruptcy. No assistance as to the operation of the present provisions can be gained from decisions based on the old law because the relevant concepts and language have been entirely recast. The purpose of the section together with IA 1986 s 340, is to prevent a debtor with actual or potential financial difficulties from disposing of his assets and thereby frustrating the legitimate expectations of his creditors.

The provisions in IA 1986 s 339–341 substantively mirror (subject to changes to reflect the difference between corporations and individuals) those in IA 1986 s 238–240 in relation to corporate insolvency. Thus as to the extra-territorial effect of the provisions see *Re Paramount Airways Ltd (No 2)* [1992] BCC 416; and for guidance on the question of whether a 12 year or only a 6 year limitation period applies to a claim brought under IA 1986 s 339 see the notes to IA 1986 s 238 and s 212 (*Re Priory Garage (Walthamstow) Ltd* [2001] BPIR 144 – the cause of action accrues on the making of the bankruptcy order and the limitation period runs from that time). *Re Nurkowski* [2006] BPIR 789 considered limitation periods in the context of IA 1986 s 423; in summary, where the applicant's primary relief is the unscrambling of the relevant transaction a 12 year period applies whereas if the applicant's primary relief is for recovery of a money sum then a 6 year period applies. However, even if brought within the limitation period, inordinate/inexcusable delay can lead to the application being struck out, see *Re Farmizer (Products) Ltd* [1997] 1 BCLC 589 and *Hamblin v Field* [2000] BPIR 671.

The application to court is made by ordinary application to the registrar, rather than the judge, in the first instance: para 9.2 Practice Direction Insolvency Proceedings, Civil Procedure Vol 2 Section 3E. In a suitable case the court may be willing to give interim relief by injunction and/or appointing a receiver *Dept of Environment v Feakins and Hawkins* [2002] BPIR 281, *Walker v WA Personnel Ltd* [2002] BPIR 621 or ordering summary judgment (*Re Unigreg Ltd* [2005] BPIR 220).

S 339(1)

It must first be shown that a 'transaction' has occurred between the bankrupt and another person; if the bankrupt has transferred property which did not belong to him to another party it would be difficult to show that there had been a 'transaction' with that other party as the word 'transaction' connotes a dealing between parties which results in a depletion of the bankrupt's assets: see *Re Taylor Sinclair (Capital) Ltd* [2002] BPIR 203, *Pozzuto v Iacovides* [2003] BPIR 999. In *Mears v Naema Latif* [2006] BPIR 80, the trustee failed to have an alleged transaction set aside where the bankrupt was not the real owner of property at the time of its transfer. See further notes to s 339(3) as to what is meant by 'transaction'.

Transactions are only vulnerable to attack if they have been entered into at a 'relevant time' (compare the provisions of IA 1986 s 423 for which there is no requirement that the transaction should have occurred at any particular time prior to bankruptcy). The 'relevant time' in relation to any transaction is determined by reference to two matters (see IA 1986 s 341 below). First, transactions are only capable of being caught if they were entered into within the prescribed fixed period of five years prior to the presentation of the bankruptcy petition; secondly, unless the transaction occurred within two years before the presentation of the petition, a transaction will not have been entered into at a 'relevant time' unless the bankrupt was insolvent at the time of the transaction, or became so as a result of the transaction IA 1986 s 341(2). Where the transaction occurred within two years before the presentation of the petition it is not necessary to show that the bankrupt was insolvent.

S 339(2)

It does not automatically follow that an order must be made in favour of the trustee once the transaction has been established to be within the scope of the provision *Re Paramount Airways* [1992] BCC 416. The court has a discretion, notwithstanding the use of the word 'shall', as to whether any order should be made at all, and, if it decides to do so, as to the terms of the order it makes, and will so far as practical and just restore the position, see *Ramlort Ltd v Reid* [2005] 1 BCLC 331 (there is no presumption in favour of monetary compensation); see also notes to s 342. The transaction will only be vulnerable if effected by the bankrupt rather than, for example, his mortgagee: see *Re Brabon* [2001] BCLC 11 (compare dishonest schemes under IA 1986 s 423 *DEFRA v Feakins and Hawkins* [2002] BPIR 281).

S 339(3)

For the purposes of the section a 'transaction', which is expressed by IA 1986 s 436 to include a 'gift, agreement or arrangement', covers any formal or informal dealing. This will obviously include the provision of any goods or services. Moreover, the fact that assets may have been transferred in order to comply with a property adjustment order or other order made for financial relief in the context of matrimonial proceedings does not mean that the transaction will be immune from attack under the section; the point is made expressly clear in relation to property adjustment orders by s 39 of the Matrimonial Causes Act 1973. As to whether the principle (ie that compliance with a court order is not necessarily a defence to a claim under the section) is of general application, see *Jackson v Bell* [2001] EWCA Civ 387, [2001] BPIR 612 where permission was given for an appeal to the Court of Appeal. The Vice-Chancellor said in that case that the dividing line between the Family Division on the one hand and the insolvency regime on the other was something that required consideration by the Court of Appeal but the appeal did not proceed.

S 339(3)(c)

If consideration is provided by the other party to the transaction then only if its value is 'significantly' less than the value of the consideration that was provided by the bankrupt will the transaction be vulnerable *Doyle v Saville* [2002] BPIR 947. There are no clear judicial pronouncements as to what 'significantly' means. It will be a matter of fact and degree turning on the particular facts of each case. In *Re Kumar* [1993] BCLC 458 it was said that a 'substantial element of bounty' would bring the transaction within the scope of the equivalent provision (IA 1986 s 238) in the corporate insolvency regime: see also *Barclays Bank v Eustice* [1995] 2 BCLC 630 and *Re Shapland Inc* [2000] BCC 106, 110 (though the case was primarily concerned with questions of preference in the corporate context). In a corporate case involving an alleged transaction at an undervalue it was observed that a difference of 10% in the transfer value and the alleged market value might be explained by a genuine difference between valuers *Re Marini Ltd* [2004] BCC 172.

The exercise of measuring one value against the other must be carried out as at the date of the transaction. The assessment will often not be straightforward especially where one is having to weigh the 'value' of future or contingent benefits or liabilities. As to the proper approach see *Phillips v Brewin Dolphin Bell Lawrie Ltd* [2001] UKHL 2, [2001] BCC 864, a case under IA 1986 s 238 which involved future payments for the sale of a business pursuant to a number of connected agreements. A number of other authorities have considered the assessment of *'value'* including *National Westminster Bank v Jones* [2001] EWCA Civ 1541, [2000] BPIR 1092; *Walker & WA Personnel* [2002] BPIR 621; *Re Share* [2002] BPIR 194; and *Ramlort Ltd v Reid* [2004] EWCA Civ 800, [2004] BPIR 985 where it was held that expert evidence was required as to the value of a life assurance policy. The subsection does not stipulate by whom the consideration must be provided, and a transaction will not be caught merely because the person receiving the benefit from the bankrupt is not the same as the person who provides the consideration. What is required is simply an assessment of the consideration (which might come from more than one source) for which the bankrupt has entered into the transaction: see *Brewin Dolphin* above.

Prior to the decision of the Court of Appeal in *Re Nurkowski, Hill v Spread Trustee Company Ltd* [2006] BPIR 789 it could be confidently advised that the provision of security by an individual could not constitute a transaction at an undervalue as an individual's financial position was not worsened merely because a debt was converted from an unsecured debt to a secured debt (although it may constitute a voidable preference under s 340). The reasoning being that in balance sheet terms, the individual's financial position was unaltered and although he may have lost the right to deal freely with assets over which security had been given, that loss could not be given a value in money terms: see *Re M C Bacon Ltd (No 1)* [1990] BCC 827, and *Re Mistral Finance Ltd* [2001] BCC 27. However Arden LJ in *Re Nurkowski* doubted that remained good law and was prepared to hold that the grant of security rights could constitute consideration; therefore there appears to be no reason to leave the value of such rights out of account in the balancing exercise under IA 1986 s 339(3)(c). It has been held to follow from the reasoning in *M C Bacon* that where a property is sold subject to a prior charge given by the seller (which charge continues to secure a debt for which the seller remains liable), the consideration in money's worth given by the seller is the value of the property free from the charge: *Re Brabon* [2001] 1 BCLC 11.

1.395

340 Preferences

(1) Subject as follows in this and the next two sections, where an individual is adjudged bankrupt and he has at a relevant time (defined in section 341) given a preference to any person, the trustee of the bankrupt's estate may apply to the court for an order under this section.

(2) The court shall, on such an application, make such order as it thinks fit for restoring the position to what it would have been if that individual had not given that preference.

(3) For the purposes of this and the next two sections, an individual gives a preference to a person if—
    (a) that person is one of the individual's creditors or a surety or guarantor for any of his debts or other liabilities, and
    (b) the individual does anything or suffers anything to be done which (in either case) has the effect of putting that person into a position which, in the event of the individual's bankruptcy, will be better than the position he would have been in if that thing had not been done.

(4) The court shall not make an order under this section in respect of a preference given to any person unless the individual who gave the preference was influenced in deciding to give it by a desire to produce in relation to that person the effect mentioned in subsection (3)(b) above.

(5) An individual who has given a preference to a person who, at the time the preference was given, was an associate of his (otherwise than by reason only of being his employee) is presumed, unless the contrary is shown, to have been influenced in deciding to give it by such a desire as is mentioned in subsection(4).

(6) The fact that something has been done in pursuance of the order of a court does not, without more, prevent the doing or suffering of that thing from constituting the giving of a preference.

Notes

S 340

A trustee needs the sanction of the creditors' committee or the court to make an application to set aside a preference (IA 1986 s 314, Sch 5 para 2A); in suitable circumstances the sanction can be obtained retrospectively but it is obvious that sanction should ordinarily be sought first (*Associated Travel Leisure Services Ltd* [1978] 2 All ER 273).

This section is the bankruptcy equivalent of IA 1986 s 239 (which applies to insolvent companies). Prior to the IA 1986 the preference provisions were contained in s 44 Bankruptcy Act 1914 pursuant to which payments made or acts done 'with a view of giving' a creditor preference over other creditors were deemed fraudulent and thus were void against a trustee. The present section replaces those provisions and, as with IA 1986 s 339 above, decisions on the old law now have no direct relevance because the statutory language and concepts have been entirely recast. As to extra-territorial effect, the position on limitation and the procedure for making an application under IA 1986 s 340 see the notes to IA 1986 s 339 above.

S 340(1)

As in the case of transactions at an undervalue under IA 1986 s 339, preferences are only vulnerable to attack if they have been given at a 'relevant time', (see below) as defined in IA 1986 s 341. In *Re M C Bacon Ltd (No 1)* [1990] BCC 78, the court held that for the purposes of identifying the time when it is given a preference occurs not at the moment of completion of the transaction (in that case the execution of a debenture) but at the moment when the decision to benefit the other party was made. It may be difficult to ascertain precisely when a decision to make a payment (or confer any other benefit) was made; it should be borne in mind that the implementation of a decision (or indeed an agreement) previously made can constitute a preference notwithstanding that the implementation might be said to be merely the honouring of an existing obligation.

The 'relevant time' in relation to a preference is determined by reference to two matters (IA 1986 s 341). First, preferences are only capable of being caught if they were given within prescribed fixed periods prior to the presentation of the bankruptcy petition: these periods vary according to whether or not there is a connection between the bankrupt and the other party to the transaction; the prescribed periods applicable to this section are different from those applying in the context of a transaction at an undervalue under IA 1986 s 339. Secondly, a preference will not have been given at a 'relevant time', even where it is within the relevant fixed period unless the bankrupt was insolvent at the time of the preference, or became so as a result of making it; see IA 1986 s 341 below.

S 340(2)

The court has a discretion, notwithstanding the use of the word 'shall', as to whether to make any order at all and if so as to its form. It does not automatically follow that an order must be made in favour of the office holder once the transaction has been established to be within the scope of the section *Re Paramount Airways* [1992] BCC 416.

S 340(3)

The question whether there has been a preference 'in fact' is to be determined by an objective assessment of the position of the person receiving the payment or other benefit, as against other creditors and/or persons standing as sureties for the bankrupt's liabilities. The most common case is the payment of the debt of an unsecured creditor who is thereby preferred over other creditors whose debts remain outstanding. Other examples are the giving of security for an existing debt, the discharge of a debt which has been guaranteed by a surety who is thus released from liability in circumstances where other creditors remain unpaid, and the return of goods to a supplier in circumstances where title has already passed. As regards an omission on the part of the individual subsequently made bankrupt (ie the situation where he 'suffers anything to be done') there is no direct authority on what constitutes a preference but the provision would cover any failure to take steps which might reasonably be expected to have been taken in the protection of his own interests, eg allowing a judgment to be entered in default in circumstances where there was plainly a defence to the claim (see also in this regard, s 340(6) which provides that the mere fact that an act has been done or suffered in pursuance of a court order does not by itself mean that there cannot have been a preference). It is the actual conferring of the benefit (as opposed to any agreement to confer it) which constitutes the preference: *Re Ledingham-Smith* [1993] BCLC 635; see also *Doyle v Saville* [2002] BPIR 947. There is authority for the proposition that when payment is made by a cheque and the cheque clears that payment is actually made at the time the cheque was delivered (*Day v Coltrane* [2003] 1 WLR 1379, [2003] EWCA Civ 342); this might be used to argue that the payment was not made at a relevant time under s 341 if the company was solvent when the cheque was delivered.

S 340(4)

No order will be made by the court in respect of a preference unless it is established that the individual subsequently made bankrupt was influenced by a desire to improve the position (in the context of the prospective bankruptcy) of the creditor or surety. Where there has been a desire to prefer there must necessarily have been an intention to do so. The requirement under the former law (s 44 Bankruptcy Act 1914) was that the bankrupt had to be shown to have acted with the 'dominant intention' of giving a preference. It is now no longer necessary for the trustee to establish a dominant intention: it is sufficient that the decision was 'influenced' by the desire to prefer. The converse of this, however, is that it is no longer sufficient to establish an intention to prefer. What must be shown is a desire to promote the interests of the recipient in the way described in the subsection; for a conceptual analysis see *Re M C Bacon (No 1)* [1990] BCC 78.

In the *Ledingham Smith* case it was said by Morritt J that 'desire' and 'influenced by' are 'ordinary English words which are not susceptible of further useful definition. It is a question of applying them to the facts of the case.' The application of pressure of one form or another by a particular creditor who has obtained payment or security may well provide a defence: see, for example, *Re Fairway Magazines Ltd* [1992] BCC 924, where it was said that the transaction will be upheld if the company has been influenced by 'proper commercial considerations' rather than a positive wish to improve the creditor's position.

S 340(5)

The definition of an associate is contained in s 435. The effect of the presumption is to transfer the evidential burden of proof onto the person seeking to uphold the transaction. From a practical point of view the shift of the burden is a matter of importance (see *Re Conegrade Ltd* [2002] EWHC 2411 (Ch), [2003] BPIR 358 in a corporate context) but it is not decisive and a trustee making a preference application ought to seek positive evidence of desire rather than simply relying on the statutory presumption (see *Re Beacon Leisure Ltd* [1991] BCC 213 – presumption rebutted). Nevertheless, the difficulty that a connected person will have in satisfying the court that the preference to him was motivated by proper commercial considerations is self-evident. For corporate insolvency cases dealing with the impact of the presumption see the notes to s 239(6).

S 340(6)

If the prospective bankrupt allows a judgment or order to be obtained against him (without taking steps that he or she could reasonably be expected to have taken in opposition) then not only is there the possibility that the omission involved in allowing the judgment or order to be made might be caught as a preference by s 340(4), but also that the court could treat the satisfaction of the judgment or order (whether by a payment or by, for example, execution by the sheriff) as a preference in itself. The fact that the payment or execution was consequent upon the court's order may not provide a defence if the proceedings ought to have been properly defended in the first place. In any event the fact that a particular creditor has a judgment debt (and there is therefore an order of the court requiring payment) will not, in itself, prevent a payment to that creditor from constituting a preference under the section.

1.395A

341 'Relevant time' under ss 339, 340

(1) Subject as follows, the time at which an individual enters into a transaction at an undervalue or gives a preference is a relevant time if the transaction is entered into or the preference given—

    (a)   in the case of a transaction at an undervalue, at a time in the period of 5 years ending with the day of the presentation of the bankruptcy petition on which the individual is adjudged bankrupt,

    (b)   in the case of a preference which is not a transaction at an undervalue and is given to a person who is an associate of the individual (otherwise than by reason only of being his employee), at a time in the period of 2 years ending with that day, and

    (c)   in any other case of a preference which is not a transaction at an undervalue, at a time in the period of 6 months ending with that day.

(2) Where an individual enters into a transaction at an undervalue or gives a preference at a time mentioned in paragraph (a), (b) or (c) of subsection (1) (not being, in the case of a transaction at an undervalue, a time less than 2 years before the end of the period mentioned in paragraph (a)), that time is not a relevant time for the purposes of s.s 339 and 340 unless the individual—

    (a)   is insolvent at that time, or

    (b)   becomes insolvent in consequence of the transaction or preference;

but the requirements of this subsection are presumed to be satisfied, unless the contrary is shown, in relation to any transaction at an undervalue which is entered into by an individual with a person who is an associate of his (otherwise than by reason only of being his employee).

(3) For the purposes of subsection (2), an individual is insolvent if—

    (a)   he is unable to pay his debts as they fall due, or

    (b)   the value of his assets is less than the amount of his liabilities, taking into account his contingent and prospective liabilities.

(4) A transaction entered into or preference given by a person who is subsequently adjudged bankrupt on a petition under section 264(1)(d) (criminal bankruptcy) is to be treated as having been entered into or given at a relevant time for the purposes of s.s 339 and 340 if it was entered into

or given at any time on or after the date specified for the purposes of this subsection in the criminal bankruptcy order on which the petition was based.

(5) No order shall be made under section 339 or 340 by virtue of subsection (4) of this section where an appeal is pending (within the meaning of section 277) against the individual's conviction of any offence by virtue of which the criminal bankruptcy order was made.

Notes

S 341

The section contains detailed provision for determining what is 'a relevant time' in relation to both transactions at an undervalue (s 339) and preferences (s 340). In each case transactions are only vulnerable if they took place within specified fixed periods and also at a time (which is within the relevant fixed period) when the prospective bankrupt was insolvent or became (as a result of the transaction) insolvent. However, where one is dealing with a transaction at an undervalue within two years of the presentation of the bankruptcy petition, there is no requirement to prove insolvency at the time (s 341(2)).

S 341(1)

The fixed period applicable to a transaction at an undervalue (s 339) is 5 years ending with the date of presentation of the bankruptcy petition on which the bankruptcy order was made (s 341(1)(a)). The fixed periods applicable to a preference are 2 years ending with the date of presentation of the bankruptcy petition in the case of preference to an associate and 6 months ending with that date in any other case (s 341(b), (c)). The definition of an associate is contained in s 435.

S 341(2)–(3)

Except where a transaction at an undervalue occurs within two years before the presentation of the petition, a transaction at an undervalue or a preference will not have taken place at a 'relevant time' unless the prospective bankrupt was either insolvent then, or became insolvent as a consequence of the transaction. Insolvent means, in this context, being unable to pay debts as they fall due, or having liabilities (including contingent and prospective liabilities) which exceed the value of assets. For an analysis of the circumstances in which insolvency has been inferred in the corporate context see *Re DKG Contractors Ltd* [1990] BCC 903; *Re a Company (No 6794 of 1983)* [1986] BCLC 261; and *Byblos Bank SAL v Al-Khudhairy* (1986) 2 BCC 99, 549 which indicates that the court cannot weigh against contingent and prospective liabilities, prospective assets which it is hoped or expected will be acquired in the future. In the case of a transaction at an undervalue (but not a preference) involving an associate, there is a rebuttable presumption that the prospective bankrupt was insolvent at the time of the transaction. Where a transaction at an undervalue occurs within two years before the presentation of the petition the trustee does not have to show that the bankrupt was insolvent or became insolvent as a result of the transaction.

S 341(4)–(5)

Where the bankruptcy order was made pursuant to the provisions of s 264(1)(d) the question of whether a transaction was entered into or a preference was given at a relevant time is to be determined by reference to the date specified in the criminal bankruptcy order. No order is to be made under s 339 or s 440 whilst an appeal is pending against conviction of the offence by virtue of which the bankruptcy order was made. These two subsections are to be repealed by the Criminal Justice Act 1988 (see s 170(2) and Schedule 16 of that Act) but no day has yet been appointed under s 171(1) of that Act.

1.396

342 Orders under ss 339, 340

(1) Without prejudice to the generality of section 339(2) or 340(2), an order under either of those sections with respect to a transaction or preference entered into or given by an individual who is subsequently adjudged bankrupt may (subject as follows)—

(a) require any property transferred as part of the transaction, or in connection with the giving of the preference, to be vested in the trustee of the bankrupt's estate as part of that estate;

(b) require any property to be so vested if it represents in any person's hands the application either of the proceeds of sale of property so transferred or of money so transferred;

(c) release or discharge (in whole or in part) any security given by the individual;

(d) require any person to pay, in respect of benefits received by him from the individual, such sums to the trustee of his estate as the court may direct;

(e) provide for any surety or guarantor whose obligations to any person were released or discharged (in whole or in part) under the transaction or by the giving of the preference to be under such new or revived obligations to that person as the court thinks appropriate;

(f) provide for security to be provided for the discharge of any obligation imposed by or arising under the order, for such an obligation to be charged on any property and for the security or charge to have the same priority as a security or charge released or discharged (in whole or in part) under the transaction or by the giving of the preference; and

(g) provide for the extent to which any person whose property is vested by the order in the trustee of the bankrupt's estate, or on whom obligations are imposed by the order, is to be able to prove in the bankruptcy for debts or other liabilities which arose from, or were released or discharged (in whole or in part) under or by, the transaction or the giving of the preference.

(2) An order under section 339 or 340 may affect the property of, or impose any obligation on, any person whether or not he is the person with whom the individual in question entered into the transaction or, as the case may be, the person to whom the preference was given; but such an order—

(a) shall not prejudice any interest in property which was acquired from a person other than that individual and was acquired [in good faith and for value], or prejudice any interest deriving from such an interest, and

(b) shall not require a person who received a benefit from the transaction or preference [in good faith and for value] to pay a sum to the trustee of the bankrupt's estate, except where he was a party to the transaction or the payment is to be in respect of a preference given to that person at a time when he was a creditor of that individual.

(2A) Where a person has acquired an interest in property from a person other than the individual in question, or has received a benefit from the transaction or preference, and at the time of that acquisition or receipt—

(a)   he had notice of the relevant surrounding circumstances and of the relevant proceedings, or

(b)   he was an associate of, or was connected with, either the individual in question or the person with whom that individual entered into the transaction or to whom that individual gave the preference,

then, unless the contrary is shown, it shall be presumed for the purposes of paragraph (a) or (as the case may be) paragraph (b) of subsection (2) that the interest was acquired or the benefit was received otherwise than in good faith.

(3) Any sums required to be paid to the trustee in accordance with an order under section 339 or 340 shall be comprised in the bankrupt's estate.

(4) For the purposes of subsection (2A)(a), the relevant surrounding circumstances are (as the case may require)—

(a)   the fact that the individual in question entered into the transaction at an undervalue; or

(b)   the circumstances which amounted to the giving of the preference by the individual in question.

(5) For the purposes of subsection (2A)(a), a person has notice of the relevant proceedings if he has notice—

(a)   of the fact that the petition on which the individual in question is adjudged bankrupt has been presented; or

(b)   of the fact that the individual in question has been adjudged bankrupt.

(6) S 249 in Part VII of this Act shall apply for the purposes of subsection (2A)(b) as it applies for the purposes of the first Group of Parts.

Notes

S 342

The court has a wide discretion as to the orders it can make consequent upon a successful application by the trustee under s 339 and s 340. Section 342 indicates the sort of orders the court may make but it does not contain an exhaustive list. Any property or money ordered to be paid to the trustee will form part of the bankrupt's estate. It should also be noted that the court is not obliged to make any order: see the note to s 339(2) above. In a corporate context the court has refused to make an order restoring the position to what it would have been if the company had not entered a transaction at an undervalue because the company's only alternative would have been to collapse into liquidation in the absence of the transfer (*Re MDA Investment Management Ltd* [2003] EWHC 2177 (Ch), [2004] BPIR 75); thus it might be argued in the case of an individual that had he not transferred his business (at an alleged undervalue) he would have petitioned for bankruptcy and his business would have been worthless.

The more difficult questions as to the appropriate form of order are likely to arise where third parties have acquired interests or rights subsequent to the original transaction that has been impeached. Third parties who have acquired an interest bona fide and for value are protected: see the note to s 342(2) below.

The court should (subject to the protection afforded to bona fide third parties) seek to restore the position to what it was before the transaction in question took place: *Chohan v Saggar* [1994] BCC 134 (which concerned the similar provisions of s 425); and see *Ramlort Ltd v Reid* [2004] EWCA Civ 800, [2004] BPIR 985. See also the corporate insolvency case of *Damon v Widney plc* [2002] BPIR 465 where there were a series of linked transactions and the court looked at the substantive overall effect when deciding upon the appropriate form of order. There is no presumption under s 342 that the court will grant relief in respect of a transaction at an undervalue by requiring the recipient of the assets in question to pay monetary compensation rather than requiring the assets to be restored: *Walker v Jade Corporate Group Ltd* (Lawtel 9/4/2002).

S 342(2), (2A), (4), (5)

A third party is not afforded protection merely because the transaction at an undervalue was not made with it or the preference was not given to it directly. In the form originally enacted the section required that third parties (ie those acquiring their interest from a person other than the individual in question) should, if they were to be afforded protection, have acted in good faith, for value and 'without notice of the relevant circumstances'. But the requirement as to absence of notice was subsequently dropped by the Insolvency Act 1994. The position now is that third parties who have given value for the interest or benefit received by them are protected so long as they acted in good faith.

There is, however, a presumption (see s 342(2A)) that such a third party acted otherwise than in good faith if at the time of the acquisition of the interest or receipt of the benefit he had notice of both 'the relevant surrounding circumstances' (that is, the facts relating to the transaction or preference – s 342(4)) and 'the relevant proceedings (that is, the fact that a bankruptcy petition had been presented or a bankruptcy order made – s 342(5)). It is apparent therefore that this presumption does not apply merely because the recipient knows of the existence of a bankruptcy petition; he must also know of the fact that the individual in question entered a transaction at an undervalue or gave a preference IA 1986 s 342(4).

There is also a presumption against good faith if the third party was connected with or was an associate of either the bankrupt or of the person who transacted with or was preferred by the bankrupt. In either of those cases it will be for the third party to rebut the presumption by proving his bona fides. It would seem, since these provisions are dealing with the notion of good faith, that 'notice' for these purposes is restricted to actual knowledge or knowledge that would have resulted had it not been for a wilful refusal to make obvious enquiry. But the point is not made expressly clear and it is perhaps arguable that constructive notice would be sufficient to trigger the statutory presumption that the benefit was received otherwise than in good faith.

The above changes came into effect on 26 July 1994: they have no retrospective effect and property acquired and benefits received before 26 July 1994 will be considered by reference to the original wording of the section.

S 342(6)

The subsection incorporates the definitions of connected persons and associates (see s 249 and s 435).

1.397

342A Recovery of excessive pension contributions

(1) Where an individual who is adjudged bankrupt—
    (a)   has rights under an approved pension arrangement, or
    (b)   has excluded rights under an unapproved pension arrangement,
the trustee of the bankrupt's estate may apply to the court for an order under this section

(2) If the court is satisfied—
    (a)   that the rights under the arrangement are to any extent, and whether directly or indirectly, the fruits of relevant contributions, and
    (b)   that the making of any of the relevant contributions ('the excessive contributions') has unfairly prejudiced the individual's creditors,
the court may make such order as it thinks fit for restoring the position to what it would have been had the excessive contributions not been made.

(3) Subsection (4) applies where the court is satisfied that the value of the rights under the arrangement is, as a result of rights of the individual under the arrangement or any other pension arrangement having at any time become subject to a debit under section 29(1)(a) of the Welfare Reform and Pensions Act 1999 (debits giving effect to pension-sharing), less than it would otherwise have been.

(4) Where this subsection applies—
    (a)   any relevant contributions which were represented by the rights which became subject to the debit shall, for the purposes of subsection (2), be taken to be contributions of which the rights under the arrangement are the fruits, and
    (b)   where the relevant contributions represented by the rights under the arrangement (including those so represented by virtue of paragraph (a)) are not all excessive contributions, relevant contributions which are represented by the rights under the arrangement otherwise than by virtue of paragraph (a) shall be treated as excessive contributions before any which are so represented by virtue of that paragraph.

(5) In subsections (2) to (4) 'relevant contributions' means contributions to the arrangement or any other pension arrangement—
    (a)   which the individual has at any time made on his own behalf, or
    (b)   which have at any time been made on his behalf.

(6) The court shall, in determining whether it is satisfied under subsection (2)(b), consider in particular—
    (a)   whether any of the contributions were made for the purpose of putting assets beyond the reach of the individual's creditors or any of them, and
    (b)   whether the total amount of any contributions—
        (i)   made by or on behalf of the individual to pension arrangements, and
        (ii)   represented (whether directly or indirectly) by rights under approved pension arrangements or excluded rights under unapproved pension arrangements,
    is an amount which is excessive in view of the individual's circumstances when those contributions were made.

(7) For the purposes of this section and sections 342B and 342C ('the recovery provisions'), rights of an individual under an unapproved pension arrangement are excluded rights if they are rights which are excluded from his estate by virtue of regulations under section 12 of the Welfare Reform and Pensions Act 1999.

(8) In the recovery provisions—

'approved pension arrangement' has the same meaning as in section 11 of the Welfare Reform and Pensions Act 1999;
'unapproved pension arrangement' has the same meaning as in section 12 of that Act.]

Notes

S 342A

Part II of the Welfare Reform and Pensions Act 1999 ('the 1999 Act') introduced a new regime governing bankrupt's pension schemes. 'Approved pension arrangements' (as defined by s 11 of the 1999 Act) are now excluded from the bankrupt's estate in cases where the bankruptcy order was made on a petition presented on or after 29 May 2000 when the relevant provisions of the 1999 Act came into force. Furthermore, rights enjoyed in 'unapproved pension arrangements' (as defined by s 12 of the 1999 Act) will now also be excluded from a bankrupt's estate if they are rights which the Secretary of State has determined, pursuant to his regulatory powers, should be excluded (as to which see the note to ss(6) below). In order to prevent a situation where creditors are unfairly prejudiced as a result of a prospective bankrupt putting excessive sums in protected pension schemes, Parliament has put in place a mechanism by which the trustee can recover such contributions (see below).

The section applies only to rights which (as a result of the provisions of the 1999 Act) do not form part of the bankrupt's estate. Rights in 'unapproved pension arrangements' which are not 'excluded rights' continue to form part of the bankrupt's estate and fall to be dealt with in accordance with the decisions in cases such as *Re Landau* [1998] Ch 223, *Krasner v Dennison* [2001] Ch 76, and *Patel v Jones* [2001] EWCA Civ 779, [2001] BPIR 919.

S 342A(2)

If the court finds that creditors have been prejudiced by the making of 'excessive contributions' into a protected pension scheme (ie one which is, apart from an order under this section, immune from attack by the trustee) then it may make such order as it thinks fit for restoring the position to what it would have been had the excessive contributions not been made. Section 342B sets out the sort of orders the court may make but it does not contain an exhaustive list.

S 342A(3), (4)

Section 29 of the 1999 Act contains provisions whereby the bankrupt's rights may become subject to a debit (to give effect to a pension sharing order as between husband and wife), with the result that the value of those rights will be reduced. Subsections (3) and (4) provide that the court shall take into account all relevant contributions even where those contributions may be represented by rights which have become subject to a debit, and which the bankrupt therefore no longer enjoys. But where not all contributions were 'excessive contributions' the court will treat those rights which the bankrupt still enjoys as representing the excessive contributions before it looks to rights that have been transferred.

S 342(A)(5)

Any contributions, whether made by the bankrupt or on his behalf, are vulnerable to attack as being excessive contributions.

S 342A(6)

This subsection sets out the factors to which the court should give particular weight in deciding whether creditors have been unfairly prejudiced. The reference to the contributions being 'made for the purpose of putting assets beyond the reach of ... creditors' mirrors the wording of s 423 and it is not necessary to establish that this was a substantial purpose: see *IRC v Hashmi* [2002] EWCA Civ 981, [2002] BPIR 271. However in many cases under IA 1986 s 423 the evidence often shows that the defeat of creditors was a substantial motivation *Habib Bank Ltd v Ahmed* [2004] BPIR 35, *Re Brabon* [2004] EWHC 1697 (Ch), [2001] 1 BCLC 11.

S 342(A)(7)

The regulations that have been made under s 12 of 1999 Act are the Occupational and Personal Pensions Schemes (Bankruptcy) (No 2) Regulations 2002 (SI No 836 of 2002).

I.398

342B Orders under s 342A

(1) Without prejudice to the generality of section 342A(2), an order under section 342A may include provision—

(a) requiring the person responsible for the arrangement to pay an amount to the individual's trustee in bankruptcy,

(b) adjusting the liabilities of the arrangement in respect of the individual,

(c) adjusting any liabilities of the arrangement in respect of any other person that derive, directly or indirectly, from rights of the individual under the arrangement,

(d) for the recovery by the person responsible for the arrangement (whether by deduction from any amount which that person is ordered to pay or otherwise) of costs incurred by that person in complying in the bankrupt's case with any requirement under section 342C(1) or in giving effect to the order.

(2) In subsection (1), references to adjusting the liabilities of the arrangement in respect of a person include (in particular) reducing the amount of any benefit or future benefit to which that person is entitled under the arrangement.

(3) In subsection (1)(c), the reference to liabilities of the arrangement does not include liabilities in respect of a person which result from giving effect to an order or provision falling within section 28(1) of the Welfare Reform and Pensions Act 1999 (pension sharing orders and agreements).

(4) The maximum amount which the person responsible for an arrangement may be required to pay by an order under section 342A is the lesser of—

(a) the amount of the excessive contributions, and

(b) the value of the individual's rights under the arrangement (if the arrangement is an approved pension arrangement) or of his excluded rights under the arrangement (if the arrangement is an unapproved pension arrangement).

(5) An order under section 342A which requires the person responsible for an arrangement to pay an amount ('the restoration amount') to the individual's trustee in bankruptcy must provide for the liabilities of the arrangement to be correspondingly reduced.

(6) For the purposes of subsection (5), liabilities are correspondingly reduced if the difference between—

(a) the amount of the liabilities immediately before the reduction, and

(b) the amount of the liabilities immediately after the reduction, is equal to the restoration amount.

(7) An order under section 342A in respect of an arrangement—
- (a) shall be binding on the person responsible for the arrangement, and
- (b) overrides provisions of the arrangement to the extent that they conflict with the provisions of the order.

Notes

S 342B

Subsection (1) lists orders which it is open to the court to make. That list is not exhaustive. The aim will be to restore the position to what it would have been if the excessive contributions had not been made. Subsections (4)–(7) contain further detail as to the nature and impact of orders that the court is empowered to make.

S 342(B)(3)

Although s 1(c) provides that the court's order may adjust any liabilities of the arrangement in respect of any other person which derive directly or indirectly from the rights of the bankrupt, ss (3) makes clear that there shall be no interference with liabilities that have arisen from a pension order or agreement made for the benefit of that other person pursuant to the provisions of the Welfare Reform and Pensions Act 1999 Act. This provision is subject to the provisions of s 342D-F (see below) which enable the trustee to attack the prior transfer of pension rights – following the making of a pension sharing order or a pension sharing agreement – as being either a transaction at an undervalue (under s 339) or a preference (under s 340).

1.399

342C Orders under section 342A: supplementary

(1) The person responsible for—
- (a) an approved pension arrangement under which a bankrupt has rights,
- (b) an unapproved pension arrangement under which a bankrupt has excluded rights, or
- (c) a pension arrangement under which a bankrupt has at any time had rights,

shall, on the bankrupt's trustee in bankruptcy making a written request, provide the trustee with such information about the arrangement and rights as the trustee may reasonably require for, or in conn. with, the making of applications under section 342A.

(2) Nothing in—
- (a) any provision of section 159 of the Pension Schemes Act 1993 or section 91 of the Pensions Act 1995 (which prevent assignment and the making of orders that restrain a person from receiving anything which he is prevented from assigning),
- (b) any provision of any enactment (whether passed or made before or after the passing of the Welfare Reform and Pensions Act 1999) corresponding to any of the provisions mentioned in paragraph (a), or

(c)   any provision of the arrangement in question corresponding to any of those provisions,

applies to a court exercising its powers under section 342A.

(3) Where any sum is required by an order under section 342A to be paid to the trustee in bankruptcy, that sum shall be comprised in the bankrupt's estate.

(4) Regulations may, for the purposes of the recovery provisions, make provision about the calculation and verification of—
(a)   any such value as is mentioned in section 342B(4)(b);
(b)   any such amounts as are mentioned in section 342B(6)(a) and (b).

(5) The power conferred by subsection (4) includes power to provide for calculation or verification—
(a)   in such manner as may, in the particular case, be approved by a prescribed person; or
(b)   in accordance with guidance—
    (i)   from time to time prepared by a prescribed person, and
    (ii) approved by the Secretary of State.

(6) References in the recovery provisions to the person responsible for a pension arrangement are to—
(a)   the trustees, managers or provider of the arrangement, or
(b)   the person having functions in relation to the arrangement corresponding to those of a trustee, manager or provider.

(7) In this section and sections 342A and 342B—
'prescribed' means prescribed by regulations;
'the recovery provisions' means this section and sections 342A and 342B;
'regulations' means regulations made by the Secretary of State.

(8) Regulations under the recovery provisions may—
(a)   make different provision for different cases;
(b)   contain such incidental, supplemental and transitional provisions as appear to the Secretary of State necessary or expedient.

(9) Regulations under the recovery provisions shall be made by statutory instrument subject to annulment in pursuance of a resolution of either House of Parliament.]

Notes

S 342(C)(1)

The trustee is given powers enabling him to obtain such information about the bankrupt's pension arrangements as will enable him to assess the merits of a claim under s 342A. The 'person responsible' is defined in ss (6).

S 342(C)(2)

Section 159 Pension Schemes Act 1993, and s 91 Pensions Act 1995 contain provisions preventing the assignment of rights enjoyed under pension schemes. This subsection makes it clear that those provisions (and any equivalent provisions) do not prevent the making of an order under s 342A of the IA 1986, requiring the transfer of such rights.

S 342(C)(4)

The current regulation made pursuant to this provision is regulation 7 of the Occupational and Personal Pensions Schemes (Bankruptcy) (No 2) Regulations 2002 (SI No 836 of 2002).

1.400

342D Recovery of excessive contributions in pension-sharing cases

(1) For the purposes of sections 339, 341 and 342, a pension-sharing transaction shall be taken—

    (a)   to be a transaction, entered into by the transferor with the transferee, by which the appropriate amount is transferred by the transferor to the transferee; and

    (b)   to be capable of being a transaction entered into at an undervalue only so far as it is a transfer of so much of the appropriate amount as is recoverable.

(2) For the purposes of sections 340 to 342, a pension-sharing transaction shall be taken—

    (a)   to be something (namely a transfer of the appropriate amount to the transferee) done by the transferor; and

    (b)   to be capable of being a preference given to the transferee only so far as it is a transfer of so much of the appropriate amount as is recoverable.

(3) If on an application under section 339 or 340 any question arises as to whether, or the extent to which, the appropriate amount in the case of a pension-sharing transaction is recoverable, the question shall be determined in accordance with subsections (4) to (8).

(4) The court shall first determine the extent (if any) to which the transferor's rights under the shared arrangement at the time of the transaction appear to have been (whether directly or indirectly) the fruits of contributions ('personal contributions')—

    (a)   which the transferor has at any time made on his own behalf, or

    (b)   which have at any time been made on the transferor's behalf,

to the shared arrangement or any other pension arrangement.

(5) Where it appears that those rights were to any extent the fruits of personal contributions, the court shall then determine the extent (if any) to which those rights appear to have been the fruits of personal contributions whose making has unfairly prejudiced the transferor's creditors ('the unfair contributions').

(6) If it appears to the court that the extent to which those rights were the fruits of the unfair contributions is such that the transfer of the appropriate amount could have been made out of rights under the shared arrangement which were not the fruits of the unfair contributions, then the appropriate amount is not recoverable.

(7) If it appears to the court that the transfer could not have been wholly so made, then the appropriate amount is recoverable to the extent to which it appears to the court that the transfer could not have been so made.

(8) In making the determination mentioned in subsection (5) the court shall consider in particular—
- (a) whether any of the personal contributions were made for the purpose of putting assets beyond the reach of the transferor's creditors or any of them, and
- (b) whether the total amount of any personal contributions represented, at the time the pension-sharing transaction was made, by rights under pension arrangements is an amount which is excessive in view of the transferor's circumstances when those contributions were made.

(9) In this section and sections 342E and 342F—
'appropriate amount', in relation to a pension-sharing transaction, means the appropriate amount in relation to that transaction for the purposes of section 29(1) of the Welfare Reform and Pensions Act 1999 (creation of pension credits and debits);
'pension-sharing transaction' means an order or provision falling within section 28(1) of the Welfare Reform and Pensions Act 1999 (orders and agreements which activate pension-sharing);
'shared arrangement', in relation to a pension-sharing transaction, means the pension arrangement to which the transaction relates;
'transferee', in relation to a pension-sharing transaction, means the person for whose benefit the transaction is made;
'transferor', in relation to a pension-sharing transaction, means the person to whose rights the transaction relates.

Notes

S 342D

It is provided by s 342(B)(3) (see above) that an order under s 342(A) shall not affect any liabilities that have arisen from a pension sharing transaction entered into for the benefit of a third party pursuant to the provisions of the 1999 Act. That provision is subject, however, to this and the following two sections (s 342E and s 342F) which enable the trustee to attack the prior transfer of pension rights – following the making of a pension sharing order or a pension sharing agreement – as being either a transaction at an undervalue (under s 339) or a preference (under s 340).

S 342(D)(1), (2)

These provisions explain the extent to which a pension-sharing transaction is within the scope of, respectively, the transaction at an undervalue provisions in s 339 and the preference provisions in s 340.

S 342(D)(3)–(8)

These provisions govern the approach to be adopted by the court in determining whether an order under s 339 or s 340 ought to be made. The essential question is whether the rights transferred pursuant to the pension-sharing transaction are the fruits of personal contributions which were made in such a way as to unfairly prejudice the bankrupt's creditors. The court must consider, in particular, whether the contributions were made for the purpose of putting assets beyond the reach of the transferor's creditors, and whether the amount of the contributions that had been made by the time of the pension-sharing transaction was excessive in view of the bankrupt's circumstances.

I.401

342E Orders under section 339 or 340 in respect of pension-sharing transactions

(1) This section and section 342F apply if the court is making an order under section 339 or 340 in a case where—
  (a) the transaction or preference is, or is any part of, a pension-sharing transaction, and
  (b) the transferee has rights under a pension arrangement ('the destination arrangement', which may be the shared arrangement or any other pension arrangement) that are derived, directly or indirectly, from the pension-sharing transaction.

(2) Without prejudice to the generality of section 339(2) or 340(2), or of section 342, the order may include provision—
  (a) requiring the person responsible for the destination arrangement to pay an amount to the transferor's trustee in bankruptcy,
  (b) adjusting the liabilities of the destination arrangement in respect of the transferee,
  (c) adjusting any liabilities of the destination arrangement in respect of any other person that derive, directly or indirectly, from rights of the transferee under the destination arrangement,
  (d) for the recovery by the person responsible for the destination arrangement (whether by deduction from any amount which that person is ordered to pay or otherwise) of costs incurred by that person in complying in the transferor's case with any requirement under section 342F(1) or in giving effect to the order,
  (e) for the recovery, from the transferor's trustee in bankruptcy, by the person responsible for a pension arrangement, of costs incurred by that person in complying in the transferor's case with any requirement under section 342F(2) or (3).

(3) In subsection (2), references to adjusting the liabilities of the destination arrangement in respect of a person include (in particular) reducing the amount of any benefit or future benefit to which that person is entitled under the arrangement.

(4) The maximum amount which the person responsible for the destination arrangement may be required to pay by the order is the smallest of—
  (a) so much of the appropriate amount as, in accordance with section 342D, is recoverable,
  (b) so much (if any) of the amount of the unfair contributions (within the meaning given by section 342D(5)) as is not recoverable by way of an order under section 342A containing provision such as is mentioned in section 342B(1)(a), and
  (c) the value of the transferee's rights under the destination arrangement so far as they are derived, directly or indirectly, from the pension-sharing transaction.

(5) If the order requires the person responsible for the destination arrangement to pay an amount ('the restoration amount') to the transferor's trustee in bankruptcy it must provide for the liabilities of the arrangement to be correspondingly reduced.

(6) For the purposes of subsection (5), liabilities are correspondingly reduced if the difference between—

(a) the amount of the liabilities immediately before the reduction, and

(b) the amount of the liabilities immediately after the reduction,

is equal to the restoration amount.

(7) The order—

(a) shall be binding on the person responsible for the destination arrangement, and

(b) overrides provisions of the destination arrangement to the extent that they conflict with the provisions of the order.

Notes

S 342E

The court has a wide discretion as to the orders it can make consequent upon a successful application by the trustee under s 339 or s 340 (see the note to s 342 above). This section indicates the sort of orders the court may make where a successful application has been made in relation to a pension-sharing transaction but it does not contain an exhaustive list. The court is not obliged to make any order. The objective of any order will be to restore the position to what it would have been had the offending transaction not taken place.

1.401A

342F Orders under section 339 or 340 in pension-sharing cases: supplementary

(1) On the transferor's trustee in bankruptcy making a written request to the person responsible for the destination arrangement, that person shall provide the trustee with such information about—

(a) the arrangement,

(b) the transferee's rights under it, and

(c) where the destination arrangement is the shared arrangement, the transferor's rights under it,

as the trustee may reasonably require for, or in connection with, the making of applications under sections 339 and 340.

(2) Where the shared arrangement is not the destination arrangement, the person responsible for the shared arrangement shall, on the transferor's trustee in bankruptcy making a written request to that person, provide the trustee with such information about—

(a) the arrangement, and

(b) the transferor's rights under it,

as the trustee may reasonably require for, or in connection with, the making of applications under sections 339 and 340.

(3) On the transferor's trustee in bankruptcy making a written request to the person responsible for any intermediate arrangement, that person shall provide the trustee with such information about—

(a) the arrangement, and

(b) the transferee's rights under it,

as the trustee may reasonably require for, or in connection with, the making of applications under sections 339 and 340.

(4) In subsection (3) 'intermediate arrangement' means a pension arrangement, other than the shared arrangement or the destination arrangement, in relation to which the following conditions are fulfilled—
  (a) there was a time when the transferee had rights under the arrangement that were derived (directly or indirectly) from the pension-sharing transaction, and
  (b) the transferee's rights under the destination arrangement (so far as derived from the pension-sharing transaction) are to any extent derived (directly or indirectly) from the rights mentioned in paragraph (a).

(5) Nothing in—
  (a) any provision of section 159 of the Pension Schemes Act 1993 or section 91 of the Pensions Act 1995 (which prevent assignment and the making of orders which restrain a person from receiving anything which he is prevented from assigning),
  (b) any provision of any enactment (whether passed or made before or after the passing of the Welfare Reform and Pensions Act 1999) corresponding to any of the provisions mentioned in paragraph (a), or
  (c) any provision of the destination arrangement corresponding to any of those provisions,
applies to a court exercising its powers under section 339 or 340.

(6) Regulations may, for the purposes of sections 339 to 342, sections 342D and 342E and this section, make provision about the calculation and verification of—
  (a) any such value as is mentioned in section 342E(4)(c);
  (b) any such amounts as are mentioned in section 342E(6)(a) and (b).

(7) The power conferred by subsection (6) includes power to provide for calculation or verification—
  (a) in such manner as may, in the particular case, be approved by a prescribed person; or
  (b) in accordance with guidance—
      (i) from time to time prepared by a prescribed person, and
      (ii) approved by the Secretary of State.

(8) In section 342E and this section, references to the person responsible for a pension arrangement are to—
  (a) the trustees, managers or provider of the arrangement, or
  (b) the person having functions in relation to the arrangement corresponding to those of a trustee, manager or provider.

(9) In this section—
  'prescribed' means prescribed by regulations;
  'regulations' means regulations made by the Secretary of State.

(10) Regulations under this section may—
  (a) make different provision for different cases;
  (b) contain such incidental, supplemental and transitional provisions as appear to the Secretary of State necessary or expedient.

(11) Regulations under this section shall be made by statutory instrument subject to annulment in pursuance of a resolution of either House of Parliament.

Notes

S 342F(1), (2), (3)

The trustee is given powers enabling him to obtain such information about the pension-sharing transaction and the transferee's resulting rights as will enable him to assess the merits of a claim under s 339 or s 340. The person responsible is defined in s 342(8).

S 342(5)

Section 159 of the Pension Schemes Act 1993, and s 91 of the Pensions Act 1995 contain provisions preventing the assignment of rights enjoyed under pension schemes. This subsection makes it clear that those provisions (and any equivalent provisions) do not apply to the making of an order under s 339 or s 340 of the IA 1986.

S 342(6)

The current regulation made pursuant to this provision is regulation 24 of the Occupational and Personal Pensions Schemes (Bankruptcy) (No 2) Regulations 2002 (SI 836/2002).

1.402

343 Extortionate credit transactions

(1) This section applies where a person is adjudged bankrupt who is or has been a party to a transaction for, or involving, the provision to him of credit.

(2) The court may, on the application of the trustee of the bankrupt's estate, make an order with respect to the transaction if the transaction is or was extortionate and was not entered into more than 3 years before the commencement of the bankruptcy.

(3) For the purposes of this section a transaction is extortionate if, having regard to the risk accepted by the person providing the credit—

    (a)   the terms of it are or were such as to require grossly exorbitant payments to be made (whether unconditionally or in certain contingencies) in respect of the provision of the credit, or

    (b)   it otherwise grossly contravened ordinary principles of fair dealing;

and it shall be presumed, unless the contrary is proved, that a transaction with respect to which an application is made under this s is or, as the case may be, was extortionate.

(4) An order under this section with respect to any transaction may contain such one or more of the following as the court thinks fit, that is to say—

    (a)   provision setting aside the whole or part of any obligation created by the transaction;

    (b)   provision otherwise varying the terms of the transaction or varying the terms on which any security for the purposes of the transaction is held;

(c)   provision requiring any person who is or was party to the transaction to pay to the trustee any sums paid to that person, by virtue of the transaction, by the bankrupt;

(d)   provision requiring any person to surrender to the trustee any property held by him as security for the purposes of the transaction;

(e)   provision directing accounts to be taken between any persons.

(5) Any sums or property required to be paid or surrendered to the trustee in accordance with an order under this section shall be comprised in the bankrupt's estate.

(6) Neither the trustee of a bankrupt's estate nor an undischarged bankrupt is entitled to make an application under section 139(1)(a) of the Consumer Credit Act 1974 (re-opening of extortionate credit agreements) for any agreement by which credit is or has been provided to the bankrupt to be re-opened.

But the powers conferred by this s are exercisable in relation to any transaction concurrently with any powers exercisable under this Act in relation to that transaction as a transaction at an undervalue.

Notes

S 343

Transactions vulnerable to attack by the trustee are those made within a period of 3 years prior to the date of the bankruptcy order (IA 1986 s 278). The concept of 'credit' is a wide one and will encompass not only loans but also any agreement under which the time for payment for goods or services is extended beyond delivery or provision of the service (cf the definition of 'credit' in s 9 of the Consumer Credit Act 1974). Only if the transaction was 'extortionate' can it be set aside. There is no requirement either that the transaction must have been entered into at a time when the bankrupt was insolvent, or that it should have been causative of his subsequent financial difficulties (contrast transactions at an undervalue under s 339 and preferences under s 340).

Even if the transaction was extortionate the court has a complete discretion as to whether any, and if so what, order should be made. If the bankrupt has himself behaved improperly in procuring the grant of credit then that would impact on the exercise of the court's discretion.

S 343(3)

There is a statutory presumption that any transaction which is the subject of an application under the section was extortionate. Accordingly it will always be for the provider of the credit to establish that the transaction was not extortionate.

The definition of 'extortionate' is similar to that in s 138 of the Consumer Credit Act 1974 ('CCA'), and decisions under the CCA are likely – although there are differences in the statutory structure – to be relevant to applications by the trustee under the present section. The relative bargaining power of the creditor and debtor will always be a relevant consideration, as will the degree of risk that the lender is assuming. The cases decided under the provisions of the CCA indicate that very high rates of interest (the equivalent of 48% per annum in *Ketley Ltd v Scott* [1981] ICR 241) may be upheld so long as the lender has acted properly and the borrower has made a free and informed decision. Other reported decisions under the CCA are *Wills v Wood* (1984) 128 Sol Jo 222; *Coldunell v Gallon* [1986] QB 1184; *Davies v Directloans Ltd* [1986] 1 WLR 823; and *Paragon Finance plc v Nash* [2001] EWCA Civ 1466, [2002] 1 WLR 685.

S 343(4)

The list of possible forms of order set out is not exhaustive. Even if the transaction was extortionate the court has a discretion to make no order. The period of limitation will be 6 years if the relief claimed is simply repayment of monies to the estate (s 9(1) Limitation Act 1980); if other relief is claimed the application is likely be an action on a specialty and a period of 12 years will apply (s 8(1) Limitation Act 1980); see the discussion of limitation periods in *Re Priory Garage (Walthamstow) Ltd* [2001] BPIR 144, *Re Nurkowski* [2006] BPIR 789 and the notes under s 339 above. The period of limitation is dated from the bankruptcy order.

I.403

344 Avoidance of general assignment of book debts

(1) The following applies where a person engaged in any business makes a general assignment to another person of his existing or future book debts, or any class of them, and is subsequently adjudged bankrupt.

(2) The assignment is void against the trustee of the bankrupt's estate as regards book debts which were not paid before the presentation of the bankruptcy petition, unless the assignment has been registered under the Bills of Sale Act 1878.

(3) For the purposes of subsections (1) and (2)—
   (a) 'assignment' includes an assignment by way of security or charge on book debts, and
   (b) 'general assignment' does not include—
      (i) an assignment of book debts due at the date of the assignment from specified debtors or of debts becoming due under specified contracts, or
      (ii) an assignment of book debts included either in a transfer of a business made in good faith and for value or in an assignment of assets for the benefit of creditors generally.

(4) For the purposes of registration under the Act of 1878 an assignment of book debts is to be treated as if it were a bill of sale given otherwise than by way of security for the payment of a sum of money; and the provisions of that Act with respect to the registration of bills of sale apply accordingly with such necessary modifications as may be made by rules under that Act.

Notes

S 344

This section replaces, without substantive alteration to the law, the postion under s 43 of the Bankruptcy Act 1914. Its provisions are considered in *Hill v Alex Lawrie Factors* [2001] BPIR 1038. The meaning of 'book debts' (essentially debts accruing in the course of trade which would ordinarily be entered in the trader's books) was considered in *Independent Automatic Sales Ltd v Knowles & Foster* [1962] 1 WLR 974, 983; and in *Re Brightlife Ltd* [1987] Ch 200 where it was held that monies in a company's bank account which were in credit were not book debts of the company.

It is only a 'general assignment' which must be registered under the Bills of Sale Act 1878. This does not include (see ss (3)(b)) an assignment of book debts due (at the date of assignment) from specified debtors or of debts becoming due under specified contracts; nor does it include an assignment included in a transfer of a business made in good faith and for value, or an assignment of assets for the benefit of creditors generally. If the registration provisions have not been complied with then the assignment will be void against the trustee as regards book debts which remained outstanding as at the date of presentation of the bankruptcy petition.

S 344(4)

The provisions of the Bills of Sale Act 1878 relating to the method of registration of a bill of sale are to apply to the registration of a general assignment of book debts – i e the assignment is to be treated as if it were a bill of sale for the purposes of registration. The mechanics of registration are set out in Schedule 1 to the Civil Procedure Rules, at RSC Order 95 r 6.

1.404

345 Contracts to which bankrupt is a party

(1) The following applies where a contract has been made with a person who is subsequently adjudged bankrupt.

(2) The court may, on the application of any other party to the contract, make an order discharging obligations under the contract on such terms as to payment by the applicant or the bankrupt of damages for non-performance or otherwise as appear to the court to be equitable.

(3) Any damages payable by the bankrupt by virtue of an order of the court under this section are provable as a bankruptcy debt.

(4) Where an undischarged bankrupt is a contractor in respect of any contract jointly with any person, that person may sue or be sued in respect of the contract without the joinder of the bankrupt.

Notes

S 345

The provisions of this section apply to any contract (save for a 'market contract' or other agreement referred to in s 164(1) of the Companies Act 1989) unlike s 315 (disclaimer) which applies only to unprofitable contracts. It is the non-bankrupt party who is intended to benefit from the ability to make an application to the court, which has a discretion as to whether or not to make an order and a discretion as to the terms of any order which may include the discharge of obligations and/or the award of damages. Any damages determined by the court to be payable by the bankrupt are provable as a bankruptcy debt.

S 345(4)

This subsection replaces s 118 of the Bankruptcy Act 1914. Its purpose is simply to obviate the need for joinder of the bankrupt in proceedings being brought or defended by a person who originally contracted jointly with the bankrupt.

1.405

346 Enforcement procedures

(1) Subject to section 285 in Chapter II (restrictions on proceedings and remedies) and to the following provisions of this section, where the creditor of any person who is adjudged bankrupt has, before the commencement of the bankruptcy—

(a)   issued execution against the goods or land of that person, or

(b)   attached a debt due to that person from another person,

that creditor is not entitled, as against the official receiver or trustee of the bankrupt's estate, to retain the benefit of the execution or attachment, or any sums paid to avoid it, unless the execution or attachment was completed, or the sums were paid, before the commencement of the bankruptcy.

(2) Subject as follows, where any goods of a person have been taken in execution, then, if before the completion of the execution notice is given to the enforcement officer or other officer charged with the execution that that person has been adjudged bankrupt—

(a)   the enforcement officer or other officer shall on request deliver to the official receiver or trustee of the bankrupt's estate the goods and any money seized or recovered in part satisfaction of the execution, but

(b)   the costs of the execution are a first charge on the goods or money so delivered and the official receiver or trustee may sell the goods or a sufficient part of them for the purpose of satisfying the charge.

(3) Subject to subsection (6) below, where—

(a)   under an execution in respect of a judgment for a sum exceeding such sum as may be prescribed for the purposes of this subs., the goods of any person are sold or money is paid in order to avoid a sale, and

(b)   before the end of the period of 14 days beginning with the day of the sale or payment the enforcement officer or other officer charged with the execution is given notice that a bankruptcy petition has been presented in relation to that person, and

(c)   a bankruptcy order is or has been made on that petition,

the balance of the proceeds of sale or money paid, after deducting the costs of execution, shall (in priority to the claim of the execution creditor) be comprised in the bankrupt's estate.

(4) Accordingly, in the case of an execution in respect of a judgment for a sum exceeding the sum prescribed for the purposes of subsection (3), the enforcement officer or other officer charged with the execution—

(a)   shall not dispose of the balance mentioned in subsection (3) at any time within the period of 14 days so mentioned or while there is pending a bankruptcy petition of which he has been given notice under that subs., and

(b)   shall pay that balance, where by virtue of that subsection it is comprised in the bankrupt's estate, to the official receiver or (if there is one) to the trustee of that estate.

(5) For the purposes of this section—

(a)   an execution against goods is completed by seizure and sale, or by the making of a charging order under section 1 of the Charging Orders Act 1979;

(b)   an execution against land is completed by seizure, by the appointment of a receiver or by the making of a charging order under that section;

(c)   an attachment of a debt is completed by the receipt of the debt.

(6) The rights conferred by subsections (1) to (3) on the official receiver or the trustee may, to such extent and on such terms as it thinks fit, be set aside by the court in favour of the creditor who has issued the execution or attached the debt.

(7) Nothing in this section entitles the trustee of a bankrupt's estate to claim goods from a person who has acquired them in good faith under a sale by an enforcement officer or other officer charged with an execution.

(8) Neither subsection (2) nor subsection (3) applies in relation to any execution against property which has been acquired by or has devolved upon the bankrupt since the commencement of the bankruptcy, unless, at the time the execution is issued or before it is completed—

    (a)   the property has been or is claimed for the bankrupt's estate under section 307 (after-acquired property), and

    (b)   a copy of the notice given under that section has been or is served on the sheriff or other officer charged with the execution.

(9) In this section 'enforcement officer' means an individual who is authorised to act as an enforcement officer under the Courts Act 2003

Notes

S 346

The principle behind the provisions of the section is that all creditors of the same class should be treated equally. IA 1986 s 285 provides that the court may stay any action, execution or other process at any time after a bankruptcy petition has been presented or a person has been made bankrupt and it can be used in addition to s 346 to stay executions.

S 346(1)

A creditor who has begun enforcement proceedings against the prospective bankrupt but who has not 'completed' either his execution of goods (or land) or his attachment of a debt due from a third party before the date of the bankruptcy order will not be entitled to retain the benefit of that execution or attachment. Where sums have been paid to the creditor to avoid the execution or attachment then he will be entitled to retain them only if they were paid before the date of the bankruptcy order. The question of whether execution or attachment has been 'completed' must be answered by reference to the definitions in ss (5). The court is not prevented from setting aside the attachment order itself (*Industrial Diseases Compensation Ltd v Marrons* [2001] BPIR 600).

S 346(2)

Where a sheriff has taken goods in execution and before the execution is completed he is notified of the bankruptcy order, those goods and any money taken in part satisfaction of the execution must be delivered up (on request) to the trustee or official receiver. There will be a first charge over the money or goods delivered up for the enforcement officer's costs, and the goods may be sold for the purpose of satisfying the charge: see also IR 1986 r 7.36, r 12.19.

S 346(3), (4)

If the debtor's goods are sold in execution, or money is paid to avoid a sale, in respect of a judgment debt exceeding £1000 (this is currently the sum prescribed by the Insolvency Proceedings (Monetary Limits) (Amendment) Order 2004 (SI 2004/547)) and within 14 days after such sale the sheriff is given notice that a bankruptcy petition has been presented against the debtor, then the balance of the proceeds after deducting the costs of execution shall form part of the bankrupt's estate following the making of a bankruptcy order. To give effect to the foregoing provision the enforcement officer, or other officer charged with the execution, must hold the proceeds of sale or money paid for a period of 14 days and then for any further period whilst a bankruptcy petition of which he has been given notice remains pending.

S 346(5)

The reference to the making of a charging order in s 346(5)(a) is a reference to the final charging order and not merely the interim order – see *Roberts Petroleum Ltd v Bernard Kenny Ltd* [1983] 2 AC 192. An execution by the appointment of a receiver by the court is complete when the order is made even if required security has not at that point been given: see the *Roberts Petroleum* case. As regards the attachment of a debt, the receipt must be actual before attachment is completed. Constructive receipt is insufficient: see *Butler v Wearing* (1885) 17 QBD 182. It will be for the creditor to establish that the execution or attachment was completed before the date of the bankruptcy order.

S 346(6)

The court may allow the creditor to retain the benefit of an incomplete execution or attachment to such extent and on such terms as it thinks fit. But this is a discretion that is likely to be exercised only in exceptional circumstances because to do so will invariably contravene the overriding principle that the bankrupt's assets should be distributed equally between creditors: see *Re Redman (Builders) Ltd* [1964] 1 WLR 541, *Roberts Petroleum Ltd v Bernard Kenny Ltd* [1983] 2 AC 192, and *Re Buckingham Inernational plc* [1998] BCC 943.

S 346(7)

Protection is given to persons who have bought goods in 'good faith' from the enforcement officer or other officer charged with execution. It is not clear whether a purchaser who knew of the bankruptcy proceedings would be found to lack good faith in all cases.

S 346(8)

The provisions set out in s 346(2), (3) do not apply to an execution against property acquired after the date of the bankruptcy order unless the property is claimed for the estate under s 307 and a copy of the notice given under that section is served on the enforcement officer. This does not mean that judgment creditors with debts provable in the bankruptcy are at liberty to execute against after-acquired property: see s 285(3) above.

1.406

347 Distress, etc

(1) The right of any landlord or other person to whom rent is payable to distrain upon the goods and effects of an undischarged bankrupt for rent due to him from the bankrupt is available (subject to sections 252(2)(b) and 254(1) above and subsection (5) below) against goods and effects comprised in the bankrupt's estate, but only for 6 months' rent accrued due before the commencement of the bankruptcy.

(2) Where a landlord or other person to whom rent is payable has distrained for rent upon the goods and effects of an individual to whom a bankruptcy petition relates and a bankruptcy order is subsequently made on that petition, any amount recovered by way of that distress which—

    (a)   is in excess of the amount which by virtue of subsection (1) would have been recoverable after the commencement of the bankruptcy, or

    (b)   is in respect of rent for a period or part of a period after the distress was levied, shall be held for the bankrupt as part of his estate.

(3) Where any person (whether or not a landlord or person entitled to rent) has distrained upon the goods or effects of an individual who is adjudged bankrupt before the end of the period of 3 months beginning with the distraint, so much of those goods or effects, or of the proceeds of their sale, as is not held for the bankrupt under subsection (2) shall be charged for the benefit of the bankrupt's estate with the preferential debts of the bankrupt to the extent that the bankrupt's estate is for the time being insufficient for meeting those debts.

(4) Where by virtue of any charge under subsection (3) any person surrenders any goods or effects to the trustee of a bankrupt's estate or makes a payment to such a trustee, that person ranks, in respect of the amount of the proceeds of the sale of those goods or effects by the trustee or, as the case may be, the amount of the payment, as a preferential creditor of the bankrupt, except as against so much of the bankrupt's estate as is available for the payment of preferential creditors by virtue of the surrender or payment.

(5) A landlord or other person to whom rent is payable is not at any time after the discharge of a bankrupt entitled to distrain upon any goods or effects comprised in the bankrupt's estate.

(6) Where in the case of any execution—
   (a) a landlord is (apart from this s.) entitled under section 1 of the Landlord and Tenant Act 1709 or section 102 of the county courts Act 1984 (claims for rent where goods seized in execution) to claim for an amount not exceeding one year's rent, and
   (b) the person against whom the execution is levied is adjudged bankrupt before the notice of claim is served on the enforcement officer or other officer charged with the execution,
the right of the landlord to claim under that s is restricted to a right to claim for an amount not exceeding 6 months' rent and does not extend to any rent payable in respect of a period after the notice of claim is so served.

(7) Nothing in subsection (6) imposes any liability on a sheriff or other officer charged with an execution to account to the official receiver or the trustee of a bankrupt's estate for any sums paid by him to a landlord at any time before the enforcement officer or other officer was served with notice of the bankruptcy order in question.

But this subsection is without prejudice to the liability of the landlord.

(8) Subject to sections 252(2)(b) and 254(1) above nothing in this Group of Parts affects any right to distrain otherwise than for rent; and any such right is at any time exercisable without restriction against property comprised in a bankrupt's estate, even if that right is expressed by any enactment to be exercisable in like manner as a right to distrain for rent.

(9) Any right to distrain against property comprised in a bankrupt's estate is exercisable notwithstanding that the property has vested in the trustee.

(10) The provisions of this section are without prejudice to a landlord's right in a bankruptcy to prove for any bankruptcy debt in respect of rent.

> (11) In this section 'enforcement officer' means an individual who is authorised to act as an enforcement officer under the Courts Act 2003

Notes

S 347

Pursuant to the provisions of this section a landlord retains limited rights to distrain against his tenant's goods notwithstanding the tenant's bankruptcy. To this extent a landlord is placed in a better position than the general body of unsecured creditors.

S 347(1), (9)

The bankruptcy of a tenant does not disentitle his landlord from distraining upon goods and effects comprised in his estate, but distraint can only be made for a maximum of six months worth of rent accrued due before the date of the bankruptcy order. The landlord does not disable himself from restraining merely because he has put in a proof claiming the unpaid rent. But at the point when a dividend is paid the landlord is effectively put to his election and will no longer be able to distrain if he accepts the dividend: see *Holmes v Watt* [1935] 2 KB 300.

S 347(2)

Where distress has been levied against a tenant against whom a bankruptcy petition has been presented and on which petition an order is subsequently made, the landlord can retain only that amount to which he would be entitled under s 347(1) above – ie six months rent accrued due before the bankruptcy order. Any amount which is in excess of that sum, and any amount in respect of rent for a period after the distress was levied, forms part of the bankrupt's estate. The reference to distress for rent for a period after the distraint is a reference to leases under which rent is payable in advance. In those cases, the landlord can distrain for the rent as soon as it is payable, notwithstanding that it relates to a future period.

S 347(3), (4)

These subsections deal with a situation where distress is levied by any person whether or not the distress relates to rent (this would include for example the Commissioners of Customs & Excise) against a person who is then adjudged bankrupt before the end of 3 months from the distraint. Any amount held by the distrainor which is not held for the benefit of the bankrupt's estate under ss (2) stands charged with the bankrupt's preferential debts. The distrainor is then in effect subrogated to the position of those preferential creditors, having a claim that is preferential as against the bankrupt's estate but which does not rank pari passu with the other preferential creditors until after they have received the value of the surrender or payment.

S 347(5)

Once the bankrupt has been discharged the landlord can no longer levy distress.

S 347(6), (7)

Where a debtor's goods are seized in execution by an enforcement officer, they cannot be removed from the premises unless the execution creditor pays to the landlord any rent then outstanding, up to a maximum of one year's rent: see s 1 Landlord and Tenant Act 1709; s 102 of the County Courts Act 1984 applies a similar provision to execution by the county court bailiff. The effect of s 347(6) is to limit that right to six months of pre-bankruptcy order rent. Section 347(7) affords the execution officer a measure of protection against paying money out in breach of this rule.

S 347(8)

The right of any person to distrain otherwise than for rent is unaffected by the provisions of Part III of the Act.

1.407

348 Apprenticeships, etc

(1) This section applies where—
- (a) a bankruptcy order is made in respect of an individual to whom another individual was an apprentice or articled clerk at the time when the petition on which the order was made was presented, and
- (b) the bankrupt or the apprentice or clerk gives notice to the trustee terminating the apprenticeship or articles.

(2) Subject to subsection (6) below, the indenture of apprenticeship or, as the case may be, the articles of agreement shall be discharged with effect from the commencement of the bankruptcy.

(3) If any money has been paid by or on behalf of the apprentice or clerk to the bankrupt as a fee, the trustee may, on an application made by or on behalf of the apprentice or clerk, pay such sum to the apprentice or clerk as the trustee thinks reasonable, having regard to—
- (a) the amount of the fee,
- (b) the proportion of the period in respect of which the fee was paid that has been served by the apprentice or clerk before the commencement of the bankruptcy, and
- (c) the other circumstances of the case.

(4) The power of the trustee to make a payment under subsection (3) has priority over his obligation to distribute the bankrupt's estate.

(5) Instead of making a payment under subsection (3), the trustee may, if it appears to him expedient to do so on an application made by or on behalf of the apprentice or clerk, transfer the indenture or articles to a person other than the bankrupt.

(6) Where a transfer is made under subsection (5), subsection (2) has effect only as between the apprentice or clerk and the bankrupt.

Notes

S 348

Where a person has been apprenticed or articled to the individual who is made bankrupt and notice is given (by the bankrupt or the apprentice) to the trustee terminating the apprenticeship or articles then the apprenticeship or articles will be determined with effect from the date of the bankruptcy order. If the apprentice has previously paid a fee to the bankrupt then the trustee may (on the apprentice's application) repay such sum as the trustee thinks reasonable having regard to the matters set out in ss(3). Any payment under the s 348(3) has priority over the trustee's obligation to distribute the estate, and accordingly comes before any payment even to preferential creditors.

1.408

349 Unenforceability of liens on books, etc

(1) Subject as follows, a lien or other right to retain possession of any of the books, papers or other records of a bankrupt is unenforceable to the extent that its enforcement would deny possession of any books, papers or other records to the official receiver or the trustee of the bankrupt's estate.

(2) Subsection (1) does not apply to a lien on documents which give a title to property and are held as such.

Notes

S 349(1)

Subject to the exception contained in s 349(2) no lien or other right to retain possession of a bankrupt's books papers or other records can be asserted in denial of the entitlement which the official receiver or trustee has to take possession of them.

S 349(2)

The wording of this subsection is identical to that used in the context of liens asserted over insolvent companies in s 246(3). In *Re SEIL Trade Finance Ltd* [1992] BCC 538 the court decided that it was not necessary that the holder of the document in question had to enjoy a proprietary interest in the underlying property; rather the requirement that the documents are held 'as such' refers to the circumstances, manner or capacity in which the documents are held. Therefore a solicitor holding a debenture, counterpart lease and share certificates of a company which went into liquidation leaving an unpaid bill was in a position to assert a lien successfully.

1.409

349A Arbitration agreements to which bankrupt is party

(1) This section applies where a bankrupt had become party to a contract containing an arbitration agreement before the commencement of his bankruptcy.

(2) If the trustee in bankruptcy adopts the contract, the arbitration agreement is enforceable by or against the trustee in relation to matters arising from or connected with the contract.

(3) If the trustee in bankruptcy does not adopt the contract and a matter to which the arbitration agreement applies requires to be determined in connection with or for the purposes of the bankruptcy proceedings—
    (a)   the trustee with the consent of the creditors' committee, or
    (b)   any other party to the agreement,
may apply to the court which may, if it thinks fit in all the circumstances of the case, order that the matter be referred to arbitration in accordance with the arbitration agreement.

(4) In this section.—
    'arbitration agreement' has the same meaning as in Part I of the Arbitration Act 1996; and

'the court' means the court which has jurisdiction in the bankruptcy proceedings.

Notes

S 349A

The section does not apply to proceedings or applications made before 31 January 1997, on which date it came into force. A trustee faced with the choice of whether or not to adopt a contract to which the bankrupt was a party will have to give consideration to the impact that any arbitration provision in the contract may have. If he adopts the contract then he will be bound by the arbitration provision contained in it. If he does not adopt it but it nevertheless becomes necessary, in the context of the bankruptcy, to determine a matter to which the arbitration agreement applies then application may be made to the court in accordance with the provisions of ss (3), and the court may order that the matter be referred to arbitration.

Chapter VI
Bankruptcy Offences

Preliminary

1.410

350 Scheme of this Chapter

(1) Subject to section 360(3) below, this Chapter applies where the court has made a bankruptcy order on a bankruptcy petition.

(2) This Chapter applies whether or not the bankruptcy order is annulled, but proceedings for an offence under this Chapter shall not be instituted after the annulment.

(3) Without prejudice to his liability in respect of a subsequent bankruptcy, the bankrupt is not guilty of an offence under this Chapter in respect of anything done after his discharge; but nothing in this Group of Parts prevents the institution of proceedings against a discharged bankrupt for an offence committed before his discharge.

(3A) Subsection (3) is without prejudice to any provision of this Chapter which applies to a person in respect of whom a bankruptcy restrictions order is in force

(4) It is not a defence in proceedings for an offence under this Chapter that anything relied on, in whole or in part, as constituting that offence was done outside England and Wales.

(5) Proceedings for an offence under this Chapter or under the rules shall not be instituted except by the Secretary of State or by or with the consent of the Director of Public Prosecutions.

(6) A person guilty of an offence under this Chapter is liable to imprisonment or a fine, or both.

Notes

S 350

Chapter VI (ss 350–362) deals with bankruptcy offences. s 350 sets out the general scheme of the chapter, s 351 sets out various definitions, s 352 sets out a defence and s 353–362 set out the various offences themselves.

S 350(1)

With one exception (s 360(3)) this chapter applies only where a bankruptcy order has been made.

S 350(2)

Proceedings cannot be started after the bankruptcy order has been annulled. Where, however, proceedings have already been started, they may continue even after the annulment.

S 350(3)

Proceedings can be started either before or after the bankruptcy order has been discharged. Such proceedings, however, can only relate to things done before the discharge.

S 350(6)

For provisions relating to the punishment of offences, see s 430 and Schedule 10.

1.411

351 Definitions

In the following provisions of this Chapter—

(a) references to property comprised in the bankrupt's estate or to property possession of which is required to be delivered up to the official receiver or the trustee of the bankrupt's estate include any property which would be such property if a notice in respect of it were given under section 307 (after-acquired property), section 308 (personal property and effects of bankrupt having more than replacement value) [or section 308A (vesting in trustee of certain tenancies);

(b) 'the initial period' means the period between the presentation of the bankruptcy petition and the commencement of the bankruptcy; and

(c) a reference to a number of months or years before petition is to that period ending with the presentation of the bankruptcy petition.

Notes

S 351(a)

This definition along with the definitions in (b) and (c) is relevant to s 352 to 359 only.

S 351(b)

The initial period is defined as the period between the date that the petition is presented and the commencement of the bankruptcy. The commencement of the bankruptcy is itself defined as the date on which the bankruptcy order is made: s 278(a).

1.411A

352 Defence of innocent intention

Where in the case of an offence under any provision of this Chapter it is stated that this section applies, a person is not guilty of the offence if he proves that, at the time of the conduct constituting the offence, he had no intent to defraud or to conceal the state of his affairs.

Notes

S 352

The defence does not apply to all bankruptcy offences appearing in the chapter but only to those which expressly provide that it so applies. In particular, therefore, it does not apply to the offences created by s 354(3), 356(2), 359(2) and 360(1).

The burden of proving the defence is expressly stated to lie on the person relying on it, that is the bankrupt. For pre-Human Rights Act 1998 matters, the burden imposed is the legal burden of proof. For post-HRA 1998 matters, however, interpretation is now governed by HRA 1998, s 3(1) so that the section has to be read and given effect to compatibly with the presumption of innocence in article 6(2) of the European Convention on Human Rights. Accordingly, for such matters the burden imposed is not the legal burden of proof but is evidential only: *R v Daniel* [2002] BPIR 1193 and see also *Attorney General's Reference (No 1 of 2004)* [2004] 1 WLR 2111.

Wrongdoing by the bankrupt before and after bankruptcy

1.412

353 Non-disclosure

(1) The bankrupt is guilty of an offence if—
   (a) he does not to the best of his knowledge and belief disclose all the property comprised in his estate to the official receiver or the trustee, or
   (b) he does not inform the official receiver or the trustee of any disposal of any property which but for the disposal would be so comprised, stating how, when, to whom and for what consideration the property was disposed of.

(2) Subsection (1)(b) does not apply to any disposal in the ordinary course of a business carried on by the bankrupt or to any payment of the ordinary expenses of the bankrupt or his family.

(3) Section 352 applies to this offence.

Notes

S 353(1)(a)

This imposes a positive obligation on the bankrupt to disclose to the official receiver or trustee all property comprised in his estate. 'Property' is defined in s 351(a).

S 353(1)(b)

This imposes a positive obligation on the bankrupt to inform the official receiver or trustee of certain disposals of property, except where such disposals are in the ordinary course of business or payments of the ordinary expenses of the bankrupt or his family (s 353(2)).

1.413

354 Concealment of property

(1) The bankrupt is guilty of an offence if—
  (a) he does not deliver up possession to the official receiver or trustee, or as the official receiver or trustee may direct, of such part of the property comprised in his estate as is in his possession or under his control and possession of which he is required by law so to deliver up,
  (b) he conceals any debt due to or from him or conceals any property the value of which is not less than the prescribed amount and possession of which he is required to deliver up to the official receiver or trustee, or
  (c) in the 12 months before petition, or in the initial period, he did anything which would have been an offence under paragraph (b) above if the bankruptcy order had been made immediately before he did it.

Section 352 applies to this offence.

(2) The bankrupt is guilty of an offence if he removes, or in the initial period removed, any property the value of which was not less than the prescribed amount and possession of which he has or would have been required to deliver up to the official receiver or the trustee.

Section 352 applies to this offence.

(3) The bankrupt is guilty of an offence if he without reasonable excuse fails, on being required to do so by the official receiver the trustee or the court—
  (a) to account for the loss of any substantial part of his property incurred in the 12 months before petition or in the initial period, or
  (b) to give a satisfactory explanation of the manner in which such a loss was incurred.

Notes

S 354(1)

For the definition of property, see s 351(a).

S 354(1)(b)

The prescribed amount referred to (and in s 354(2)) is currently £500: Insolvency Proceedings (Monetary Limits) Order 1986 (SI 1986/1996); see also s 384(2) and 418(1).

S 354(3)

The requirement to account for a loss under s 354(3)(a) does not contravene article 6 of the European Convention on Human Rights. The implied rights to remain silent and not to incriminate oneself are not rights of an absolute character but can be qualified or restricted if there is proper justification and if the restriction is appropriate. The public interest that the affairs of bankrupts should be investigated provides ample justification for the limited restriction imposed by s 354(3)(a) and accordingly the section is not incompatible with article 6: *R v Kearns* [2002] EWCA Crim 748, [2002] 1 WLR 2815.

S 354(3)(b)

On the question of when an explanation is satisfactory, see *R v Salter* [1968] 2 QB 793, a case under the predecessor to this provision.

1.414

355 Concealment of books and papers; falsification

(1) The bankrupt is guilty of an offence if he does not deliver up possession to the official receiver or the trustee, or as the official receiver or trustee may direct, of all books, papers and other records of which he has possession or control and which relate to his estate or his affairs.

Section 352 applies to this offence.

(2) The bankrupt is guilty of an offence if—
- (a)   he prevents, or in the initial period prevented, the production of any books, papers or records relating to his estate or affairs;
- (b)   he conceals, destroys, mutilates or falsifies, or causes or permits the concealment, destruction, mutilation or falsification of, any books, papers or other records relating to his estate or affairs;
- (c)   he makes, or causes or permits the making of, any false entries in any book, document or record relating to his estate or affairs; or
- (d)   in the 12 months before petition, or in the initial period, he did anything which would have been an offence under paragraph (b) or (c) above if the bankruptcy order had been made before he did it.

Section 352 applies to this offence.

(3) The bankrupt is guilty of an offence if—
- (a)   he disposes of, or alters or makes any omission in, or causes or permits the disposal, altering or making of any omission in, any book, document or record relating to his estate or affairs, or
- (b)   in the 12 months before petition, or in the initial period, he did anything which would have been an offence under paragraph (a) if the bankruptcy order had been made before he did it.

Section 352 applies to this offence.

(4) In their application to a trading record subsections 2(d) and (3)(b) shall have effect as if the reference to 12 months were a reference to two years

(5) In subsection (4) 'trading record' means a book, document or record which shows or explains the transactions or financial position of a person's business, including -

> (a)   a periodic record of cash paid and received,
> (b)   a statement of periodic stock-taking, and
> (c)   except in the case of goods sold by way of retail trade, a record of goods sold and purchased which identifies the buyer and seller or enables them to be identified.

Notes

S 355(1)

This section creates a number of wide ranging offences relating to the books, papers and other records of the bankrupt. In particular, it is an offence to fail to produce any such documents as directed by the official receiver or trustee (s 355(1)), to prevent the production of such documents (s 355(2)(a)), to conceal, destroy, mutilate or falsify such documents (s 355(2)(b)), to make false entries in such documents (s 355(2)(c)), and to dispose or alter such documents (s 355(3)).

S 355(4), (5)

These provisions were introduced by the EA 2002 as from 1 April 2004.

1.415

356 False statements

(1) The bankrupt is guilty of an offence if he makes or has made any material omission in any statement made under any provision in this Group of Parts and relating to his affairs.

Section 352 applies to this offence.

(2) The bankrupt is guilty of an offence if—
   (a)   knowing or believing that a false debt has been proved by any person under the bankruptcy, he fails to inform the trustee as soon as practicable; or
   (b)   he attempts to account for any part of his property by fictitious losses or expenses; or
   (c)   at any meeting of his creditors in the 12 months before petition or (whether or not at such a meeting) at any time in the initial period, he did anything which would have been an offence under paragraph (b) if the bankruptcy order had been made before he did it; or
   (d)   he is, or at any time has been, guilty of any false representation or other fraud for the purpose of obtaining the consent of his creditors, or any of them, to an agreement with reference to his affairs or to his bankruptcy.

Notes

S 356(1)

The offence created relates to material omissions. No particular *mens rea* or state of mind is specifically required by the provision; it is, however, subject to the innocent intention defence set out in s 352.

S 356(2)

The offences created relate to various positive acts on the part of the bankrupt. The offences themselves require, either expressly or by their very nature, a certain state of mind; accordingly, unlike s 356(1), it is not subject to the innocent intention defence set out in s 352.

1.416

357 Fraudulent disposal of property

(1) The bankrupt is guilty of an offence if he makes or causes to be made, or has in the period of 5 years ending with the commencement of the bankruptcy made or caused to be made, any gift or transfer of, or any charge on, his property.

Section 352 applies to this offence.

(2) The reference to making a transfer of or charge on any property includes causing or conniving at the levying of any execution against that property.

(3) The bankrupt is guilty of an offence if he conceals or removes, or has at any time before the commencement of the bankruptcy concealed or removed, any part of his property after, or within 2 months before, the date on which a judgment or order for the payment of money has been obtained against him, being a judgment or order which was not satisfied before the commencement of the bankruptcy.

Section 352 applies to this offence.

Notes

S 357(1)

This offence relates to gifts, transfers or charges on property within a period of 5 years leading up to the bankruptcy; the innocent intention defence in s 352 applies. In practice, only transactions which were intended to defraud creditors will be caught.

S 357(3)

This offence relates to the concealment or removal of property for the purposes of avoiding a judgment debt; the innocent intention defence in s 352 applies.

For provisions relating to the punishment of offences, see s 430 and schedule 10. For an example where a custodial sentence was appropriate, see *R v Mungroo,* [1998] BPIR 784. The commencement of the bankruptcy is defined as the day on which the bankruptcy order is made s 278(a) and 'property' is defined in s 351(a).

1.417

358 Absconding

The bankrupt is guilty of an offence if—
    (a) he leaves, or attempts or makes preparations to leave, England and Wales with any property the value of which is not less than

> the prescribed amount and possession of which he is required to deliver up to the official receiver or the trustee, or
>
> (b) in the 6 months before petition, or in the initial period, he did anything which would have been an offence under paragraph (a) if the bankruptcy order had been made immediately before he did it.
>
> Section 352 applies to this offence.

Notes

For the definition of property see s 351(a). The 'prescribed amount' is currently £1000: Insolvency Proceedings (Monetary Limits) Order 2004 (SI 2004/547) and see also s 384(2) and 418(1).

1.418

359 Fraudulent dealing with property obtained on credit

(1) The bankrupt is guilty of an offence if, in the 12 months before petition, or in the initial period, he disposed of any property which he had obtained on credit and, at the time he disposed of it, had not paid for.

Section 352 applies to this offence.

(2) A person is guilty of an offence if, in the 12 months before petition or in the initial period, he acquired or received property from the bankrupt knowing or believing—

(a) that the bankrupt owed money in respect of the property, and

(b) that the bankrupt did not intend, or was unlikely to be able, to pay the money he so owed.

(3) A person is not guilty of an offence under subsection (1) or (2) if the disposal, acquisition or receipt of the property was in the ordinary course of a business carried on by the bankrupt at the time of the disposal, acquisition or receipt.

(4) In determining for the purposes of this section whether any property is disposed of, acquired or received in the ordinary course of a business carried on by the bankrupt, regard may be had, in particular, to the price paid for the property.

(5) In this section references to disposing of property include pawning or pledging it; and references to acquiring or receiving property shall be read accordingly.

Notes

S 359(1)

This offence relates to the bankrupt disposing of assets that he has not paid for and it is subject to the innocent intention defence in s 352 and the specific defence in s 359(3) (disposals in the ordinary course of business). 'Property' is defined in s 351(a).

S 359(2)

This provision makes it an offence to receive or acquire property from the bankrupt while believing that he owed money in respect of it and that he intended not to, or was unlikely to be able to pay the money owed. There is no s 352 defence of innocent intention to this offence. The effect of this is that the offence is extremely broad in its reach. It appears that the offence would be committed even if the person acquiring or receiving the property had a false belief.

1.419

360 Obtaining credit; engaging in business

(1) The bankrupt is guilty of an offence if—
- (a) either alone or jointly with any other person, he obtains credit to the extent of the prescribed amount or more without giving the person from whom he obtains it the relevant information about his status; or
- (b) he engages (whether directly or indirectly) in any business under a name other than that in which he was adjudged bankrupt without disclosing to all persons with whom he enters into any business transaction the name in which he was so adjudged.

(2) The reference to the bankrupt obtaining credit includes the following cases—
- (a) where goods are bailed to him under a hire-purchase agreement, or agreed to be sold to him under a conditional sale agreement, and
- (b) where he is paid in advance (whether in money or otherwise) for the supply of goods or services.

(3) A person whose estate has been sequestrated in Scotland, or who has been adjudged bankrupt in Northern Ireland, is guilty of an offence if, before his discharge, he does anything in England and Wales which would be an offence under subsection (1) if he were an undischarged bankrupt and the sequestration of his estate or the adjudication in Northern Ireland were an adjudication under this Part.

(4) For the purposes of subsection (1)(a), the relevant information about the status of the person in question is the information that he is an undischarged bankrupt or, as the case may be, that his estate has been sequestrated in Scotland and that he has not been discharged.

(5) This section applies to the bankrupt after discharge while a bankruptcy restrictions order is in force in respect of him.

(6) For the purposes of subsection (1)(a) as it applies by virtue of subsection (5), the relevant information about the status of a person in question is the information that a bankruptcy restrictions order is in force in respect of him.

Notes

S 360(1)

This section makes it an offence for a bankrupt to obtain credit (subsection(1)(a)) or engage in a business (subsection 1(b)) without revealing his status as a bankrupt. Not only does the section not require any particular *mens rea* or state of mind, it is not subject to the defence of innocent intention in s 352. For provisions relating to the punishment of offences, see s 430 and Schedule 10. For sentencing considerations under s 360, see *R v Theivendran* (1992) 13 Cr App R 601.

The 'prescribed amount' is currently £500: Insolvency Proceedings (Monetary Limits) Order 2004 (SI 2004/547); see also sub-section 384(2) and 418(1). The prescribed amount may be reached by either a single transaction or by a number of smaller transactions over several separate occasions: *R v Hartley* [1972] 2 QB 1.

S 360(2)

In a number of cases, the predecessor of s 360 (s 155(a) of the Bankruptcy Act 1914) had been given a restricted definition. In *Fisher v Raven* [1964] AC 210 it was held that the section was limited by its context to credit in respect of the payment or repayment of a sum of money and accordingly did not cover the situation where the bankrupt agreed to provide certain services having taken part payment in advance. Similarly, in *R v Miller* [1977] 3 All ER 986 it was held that obtaining credit meant obtaining some benefit from another under an agreement which postponed payment of the consideration for the benefit and accordingly did not cover a hire-purchase agreement. s 360(2), however, sets out an expanded definition of obtaining credit, covering both the supply of goods or services following payment in advance (sub-section 2(b)) and also hire-purchase and conditional sale agreements (sub-section 2(a)). Accordingly, the previous limitations no longer apply and the above authorities are of no application to cases to be decided under IA 1986.

S 360(5)–(6)

These provisions were introduced by the EA 2002 from 1 April 2004 to take account of the effect of bankruptcy restrictions orders (IA 1986 Sch 4A).

1.420

[361 Failure to keep proper accounts of business

(1) Where the bankrupt has been engaged in any business for any of the period of 2 years before petition, he is guilty of an offence if he—

    (a) has not kept proper accounting records throughout that period and throughout any part of the initial period in which he was so engaged, or

    (b) has not preserved all the accounting records which he has kept.

(2) The bankrupt is not guilty of an offence under subsection (1)—

    (a) if his unsecured liabilities at the commencement of the bankruptcy did not exceed the prescribed amount, or

    (b) if he proves that in the circumstances in which he carried on business the omission was honest and excusable.

(3) For the purposes of this section a person is deemed not to have kept proper accounting records if he has not kept such records as are necessary to show or explain his transactions and financial position in his business, including—

    (a) records containing entries from day to day, in sufficient detail, of all cash paid and received,

    (b) where the business involved dealings in goods, statements of annual stock-takings, and

    (c) except in the case of goods sold by way of retail trade to the actual customer, records of all goods sold and purchased showing the buyers and sellers in sufficient detail to enable the goods and the buyers and sellers to be identified.

(4) In relation to any such records as are mentioned in subsection (3), subsections (2)(d) and (3)(b) of section 355 apply with the substitution of 2 years for 12 months.

Notes

S 361

This provision was repealed by the EA 2002 effective from 1 April 2004.

1.421

[362 Gambling

(1) The bankrupt is guilty of an offence if he has—
- *(a)*   *in the 2 years before petition, materially contributed to, or increased the extent of, his insolvency by gambling or by rash and hazardous speculations, or*
- *(b)*   *in the initial period, lost any part of his property by gambling or by rash and hazardous speculations.*

(2) In determining for the purposes of this section whether any speculations were rash and hazardous, the financial position of the bankrupt at the time when he entered into them shall be taken into consideration.]

Notes

S 362

This provision was repealed by the EA 2002 effective from 1 April 2004.

CHAPTER VII
Powers of court in bankruptcy

1.421A

363 General control of court

(1) Every bankruptcy is under the general control of the court and subject to the provisions in this Group of Parts, the court has full power to decide all questions of priorities and all other questions, whether of law or fact, arising in any bankruptcy.

(2) Without prejudice to any other provision in this Group of Parts, an undischarged bankrupt or a discharged bankrupt whose estate is still being administered under Chapter VI of this Part shall do all such things as he may be directed to by the court for the purposes of his bankruptcy, or as the case may be, the administration of estate.

(3) The official receiver or the trustee of a bankrupt's estate may at any time apply to the court for a direction under subsection (2).

> (4) If any person without reasonable excuse fails to comply with any obligation imposed on him by subsection (2), he is guilty of a contempt of court and liable to be punished accordingly (in addition to any other punishment to which he may be subject).

Notes

S 363(1)

The breadth of this provision enables the court for instance to review (*Engel v Peri* [2002] BPIR 961) or fix (*Re Colgate* [1986] 2 WLR 137) the remuneration of the trustee; or to appoint a temporary additional trustee (*Clements v Udal* [2001] BPIR 454); or to decide whether statutory interest has to be paid to secure an annulment *Harper v Buchler* [2004] BPIR 724. The power of the court to control and make directions in relation to matters arising in the bankruptcy can be regarded as similar to its supervisory powers over trustees more generally see IA 1986 s 303. The 'court' means the High Court and the county court, as appropriate, see IA 1986 s 385(1), s 373.

S 363(2)

For an example of the width of the orders that may be made under this provision see *Buchler v Al-Midani* [2006] BPIR 881. The court may make an order despite the bankrupt having been discharged under IA 1986 s 279. The qualification is that the bankrupt's estate is still being administered.

S 363(3)

The official receiver may make an application under this provision despite not being the trustee. However, persons who can apply to the court for a direction of this kind are not limited to the trustee and the official receiver: see *Hardy v Buchler* [1997] BPIR 643.

S 363(4)

Clearly a refusal to obey the instructions of the court is likely to lead to contempt proceedings *Official Receiver v Cummings-John* [2000] BPIR 320. The official receiver is an officer of the court (IA 1986 s 400(2)) as is a trustee in bankruptcy (*Re Condon, Ex.parte James*(1874) 9 Ch App 609) and non compliance with their requests may also give rise to contempt proceedings (IA 1986 s 291, s 333).

1.422

364 Power of arrest

(1) In the cases specified in the next subsection the court may cause a warrant to be issued to a constable or prescribed officer of the court—

   (a)   for the arrest of a debtor to whom a bankruptcy petition relates or of an undischarged bankrupt, or of a discharged bankrupt whose estate is still being administered under Chapter IV of this Part, and

   (b)   for the seizure of any books, papers, records, money or goods in the possession of a person arrested under the warrant,

and may authorise a person arrested under such a warrant to be kept in custody, and anything seized under such a warrant to be held, in accordance with the rules, until such time as the court may order.

(2) The powers conferred by subsection (1) are exercisable in relation to a debtor or undischarged or discharged bankrupt if, at any time after the presentation of the bankruptcy petition relating to him or the making of the bankruptcy order against him, it appears to the court—

(a) that there are reasonable grounds for believing that he has absconded, or is about to abscond, with a view to avoiding or delaying the payment of any of his debts or his appearance to a bankruptcy petition or to avoiding, delaying or disrupting any proceedings in bankruptcy against him or any examination of his affairs, or

(b) that he is about to remove his goods with a view to preventing or delaying possession being taken of them by the official receiver or the trustee of his estate, or

(c) that there are reasonable grounds for believing that he has concealed or destroyed, or is about to conceal or destroy, any of his goods or any books, papers or records which might be of use to his creditors in the course of his bankruptcy or in connection with the administration of his estate, or

(d) that he has, without the leave of the official receiver or the trustee of his estate, removed any goods in his possession which exceed in value such sum as may be prescribed for the purposes of this paragraph, or

(e) that he has failed, without reasonable excuse, to attend any examination ordered by the court.

Notes

S 364(1)

The power of the court to issue a warrant is subject to the safeguards of Article 5 (right to liberty and security) and Article 8 (right to respect for private and family life) Human Rights Act 1998 Sch 1 and it is a power used sparingly. IR 1986 r 7.21 details the officers of the High Court or county court who may exercise the warrant and IR 1986 r 7.22 directs what should be done with the debtor or bankrupt and the property in that person's possession following the arrest.

S 364(2)(c)

'*records*' include computer and other non-documentary records (IA 1986 s 436).

S 364(2)(d)

'*sum as may be prescribed*' is £1000 from 1 April 2004 (Insolvency Proceedings (Monetary Limits) (Amendment) Order 2004).

1.423

365 Seizure of bankrupt's property

(1) At any time after a bankruptcy order has been made, the court may, on the application of the official receiver or the trustee of the bankrupt's estate, issue a warrant authorising the person to whom it is directed to seize any property comprised in the bankrupt's estate which is, or any books, papers or records relating to the bankrupt's estate or affairs which

are, in the possession or under the control of the bankrupt or any other person who is required to deliver the property, books, papers or records to the official receiver or trustee.

(2) Any person executing a warrant under this section may, for the purpose of seizing any property comprised in the bankrupt's estate or any books, papers or records relating to the bankrupt's estate or affairs, break open any premises where the bankrupt or anything that may be seized under the warrant is or is believed to be and any receptacle of the bankrupt which contains or is believed to contain anything that may be so seized.

(3) If, after a bankruptcy order has been made, the court is satisfied that any property comprised in the bankrupt's estate is, or any books, papers or records relating to the bankrupt's estate or affairs are, concealed in any premises not belonging to him, it may issue a warrant authorising any constable or prescribed officer of the court to search those premises for the property, books, papers or records.

(4) A warrant under subsection (3) shall not be executed except in the prescribed manner and in accordance with its terms.

Notes

S 365(1)

The burden of persuading the court that such an order should be made is not light and it would usually be necessary to establish that there is real risk that property or books, papers or records of the bankruptcy estate are likely to be lost to the trustee.

S 365(2)

The court has to be satisfied that the property or books, papers or records are at the relevant premises or that there is a reasonable basis for believing that they are.

S 365(4)

See IR 1986 r 7.21, 7.25.

1.424

366 Inquiry into bankrupt's dealings and property

(1) At any time after a bankruptcy order has been made the court may, on the application of the official receiver or the trustee of the bankrupt's estate, summon to appear before it—

(a) the bankrupt or the bankrupt's spouse or former spouse [or civil partner or former civil partner],

(b) any person known or believed to have any property comprised in the bankrupt's estate in his possession or to be indebted to the bankrupt,

(c) any person appearing to the court to be able to give information concerning the bankrupt or the bankrupt's dealings, affairs or property.

The court may require any such person as is mentioned in paragraph (b) or (c) to submit an affidavit to the court containing an account of his dealings with the bankrupt or to produce any documents in his possession or under his control relating to the bankrupt or the bankrupt's dealings, affairs or property.

(2) Without prejudice to section 364, the following applies in a case where—

(a) a person without reasonable excuse fails to appear before the court when he is summoned to do so under this section, or

(b) there are reasonable grounds for believing that a person has absconded, or is about to abscond, with a view to avoiding his appearance before the court under this section.

(3) The court may, for the purpose of bringing that person and anything in his possession before the court, cause a warrant to be issued to a constable or prescribed officer of the court—

(a) for the arrest of that person, and

(b) for the seizure of any books, papers, records, money or goods in that person's possession.

(4) The court may authorise a person arrested under such a warrant to be kept in custody, and anything seized under such a warrant to be held, in accordance with the rules, until that person is brought before the court under the warrant or until such other time as the court may order.

Notes

S 366

IA 1986 s 366 is similar to the corporate provision for private examination in IA 1986 s 236 both in terms and substance and many of the authorities on the latter provision may be referred to in considering the former. The court retains a discretion whether to make an order under IA 1986 s 366 even where the conditions for the exercise of the discretion are fulfilled, *Buchler v Al-Midani (No 2)* [2006] BPIR 867. The rules relating to the procedure of the private examination are found in IR 1986 r 9.1 to 9.6 and reference should be made to those rules and the accompanying notes in conjunction with IA 1986 s 366.

The application should not be made without notice unless there are urgent circumstances *Re Murjani (a Bankrupt)* [1996] 1 WLR 1498, *Re Maxwell Communications Corporation plc* [1995] 1 BCLC 521. The private examination in a bankruptcy enables the court to assist the official receiver or trustee in obtaining information for the better administration of the estate. It applies notwithstanding the bankrupt has been discharged *Oakes v Simms* [1997] BPIR 499 and it also applies against the *Crown Soden v Burns* [1996] 2 BCLC 636, IA 1986 s 434(a). Where the respondent is a company the order should require it to attend or furnish information/documents by a proper officer *Re Murjani (a Bankrupt)* [1996] 1 BCLC 272.

S 366(1)

Though it may be financed by a particular creditor (*Re Adlards Motor Group Holdings Ltd* [1990] BCLC 68) only the official receiver or the trustee may make the application. Where the documents sought from the respondent are documents belonging to third parties which have been seized by the respondent acting under powers to compel the production of evidence or are transcripts of evidence given by third parties under compulsion, the order for production should not be made until those third parties have been notified and given an opportunity to make representations *Morris v Director of the Serious Fraud Office* [1993] Ch 372 (seized documents), *Soden v Burns* [1996] 2 BCLC 636 (transcripts); such representations were made in *Re Atlantic Computers plc* [1998] BCC 200. The court will not order documents to be produced which are subject to legal professional privilege (*Re Ouvaroff* [1997] BPIR 712 (privilege waived)) but mere possession of documents by a solicitor on behalf of a client does not mean that legal professional privilege applies *Re Murjani (a Bankrupt)* [1996] 1 BCLC 272, 279.

The court's discretion to order an examination or the production of documents is general *British and Commonwealth Holdings plc v Spicer and Oppenheim* [1993] AC 426 and the court may order that the costs of producing the relevant documents are borne by the applicant *Re Bank of Credit and Commerce International SA* [1997] BCC 561 (see further IR 1986 r 9.6). The task of the court is to strike a balance between the importance to the applicant of obtaining the relevant information and the possible oppression to the respondent *Sasea Finance Ltd v KPMG* [1998] BCC 216. Though it would be unusual to apply for an order after the decision has been taken to sue, an order for examination will not be refused on that ground alone *Re Cloverbay Ltd (No 3)* [1991] Ch 90.

In appropriate circumstances an order can be made notwithstanding the respondent is at risk of being sued (*Re BCCI (No 12)*, *Morris v Bank of America National Trust and Savings Association* [1997] 1 BCLC 526, *Re Castle New Homes* [1979] 1 WLR 1075,1089) or the respondent is facing charges in relation to the matters that are the subject of the intended examination *Re Arrows (No 2)* [1994] 1 BCLC 355. The respondent is not entitled to refuse to answer questions in a private examination on the ground that he may incriminate himself *Bishopsgate Investment Management Ltd v Maxwell* [1992] BCLC 475.

Though substantial difficulties will be faced in obtaining and enforcing orders for examination of unwilling respondents outside the UK (see *Re Tucker (a Bankrupt)* [1988] 1 All ER 603) the phrase '*any person*' is potentially wide enough to include non resident respondents where there is a parallel application under IA 1986 s 426 *McIsaac, Petitioners (Joint liquidators of First Tokyo Index Trust Ltd)* [1994] BCC 410. In such circumstances the court could order service out of the jurisdiction under IR 1986 r 12.12(3).

Where the production of a document will infringe a statutory prohibition the court will not make an order for production though the provision of a redacted version may be ordered *Re Galileo Group Ltd* [1999] Ch 100. The court may order production of documents held outside the jurisdiction *Re Mid-East Trading Ltd* [1998] 1 BCLC 240.

S 366(2)

An order may be made restraining a person from leaving the jurisdiction pending an examination being held or concluded *Re a Company (No 3318 of 1987)* (1987) 3 BCC 564.

S 366(3), (4)

The rules relating to the prescribed officers and procedure following arrest are in IR 1986 r 7.21, 7.23.

1.425

367 Court's enforcement powers under s 366

(1) If it appears to the court, on consideration of any evidence obtained under section 366 or this section, that any person has in his possession any property comprised in the bankrupt's estate, the court may, on the application of the official receiver or the trustee of the bankrupt's estate, order that person to deliver the whole or any part of the property to the official receiver or the trustee at such time, in such manner and on such terms as the court thinks fit.

(2) If it appears to the court, on consideration of any evidence obtained under section 366 or this section, that any person is indebted to the bankrupt, the court may, on the application of the official receiver or the trustee of the bankrupt's estate, order that person to pay to the official receiver or trustee, at such time and in such manner as the court may direct, the whole or part of the amount due, whether in full discharge of the debt or otherwise as the court thinks fit.

(3) The court may, if it thinks fit, order that any person who if within the jurisdiction of the court would be liable to be summoned to appear before it under section 366 shall be examined in any part of the United Kingdom where he may be for the time being, or in any place outside the United Kingdom.

(4) Any person who appears or is brought before the court under section 366 or this section may be examined on oath, either orally or by interrogatories, concerning the bankrupt or the bankrupt's dealings, affairs and property.

Notes

S 367(1), (2)

The court has the power to make summary orders for delivery up of property and payment of debts.

S 367(4)

The rules dealing with private examinations are IR 1986 r 9.1 to 9.6.

1.426

368 Provision corresponding to s 366, where interim receiver appointed

Sections 366 and 367 apply where an interim receiver has been appointed under section 286 as they apply where a bankruptcy order has been made, as if—
  (a) references to the official receiver or the trustee were to the interim receiver, and
  (b) references to the bankrupt and to his estate were (respectively) to the debtor and his property.

Notes

S 368

This provision enables an interim receiver to use the examination powers under IA 1986 s 366, 367. An interim receiver is a person appointed under IA 1986 s 286 following the presentation of a bankruptcy petition and before the making of a bankruptcy order where it is necessary to protect the debtor's property.

I.427

369 Order for production of documents by inland revenue

(1) For the purposes of an examination under section 290 (public examination of bankrupt) or proceedings under sections 366 to 368, the court may, on the application of the official receiver or the trustee of the bankrupt's estate, order an inland revenue official to produce to the court—

    (a)   any return, account or accounts submitted (whether before or after the commencement of the bankruptcy) by the bankrupt to any inland revenue official,

    (b)   any assessment or determination made (whether before or after the commencement of the bankruptcy) in relation to the bankrupt by any inland revenue official, or

    (c)   any correspondence (whether before or after the commencement of the bankruptcy) between the bankrupt and any inland revenue official.

(2) Where the court has made an order under subsection (1) for the purposes of any examination or proceedings, the court may, at any time after the document to which the order relates is produced to it, by order authorise the disclosure of the document, or of any part of its contents, to the official receiver, the trustee of the bankrupt's estate or the bankrupt's creditors.

(3) The court shall not address an order under subsection (1) to an inland revenue official unless it is satisfied that that official is dealing, or has dealt, with the affairs of the bankrupt.

(4) Where any document to which an order under subsection (1) relates is not in the possession of the official to whom the order is addressed, it is the duty of that official to take all reasonable steps to secure possession of it and, if he fails to do so, to report the reasons for his failure to the court.

(5) Where any document to which an order under subsection (1) relates is in the possession of an inland revenue official other than the one to whom the order is addressed, it is the duty of the official in possession of the document, at the request of the official to whom the order is addressed, to deliver it to the official making the request.

(6) In this section 'inland revenue official' means any inspector or collector of taxes appointed by the Commissioners of Inland Revenue or any person appointed by the Commissioners to serve in any other capacity.

(7) This section does not apply for the purposes of an examination under sections 366 and 367 which takes place by virtue of section 368 (interim receiver).

Notes

S 369(1)

This provision enables the court to order the Inland Revenue official who is dealing or has dealt with the affairs of the bankrupt to produce to the court the relevant tax documentation of the bankrupt including correspondence. The power is only exercised to assist in a public examination of the bankrupt or a private examination under IA 1986 s 366–368. The relevant rules are IR 1986 r 6.194 to 6.196.

S 369(7)

The power of the court to order production of documents by the Inland Revenue does not apply in the period when an interim receiver is appointed (IA 1986 s 286).

1.428

370 Power to appoint special manager

(1) The court may, on an application under this section, appoint any person to be the special manager—
- (a) of a bankrupt's estate, or
- (b) of the business of an undischarged bankrupt, or
- (c) of the property or business of a debtor in whose case the official receiver has been appointed interim receiver under section 286.

(2) An application under this section may be made by the official receiver or the trustee of the bankrupt's estate in any case where it appears to the official receiver or trustee that the nature of the estate, property or business, or the interests of the creditors generally, require the appointment of another person to manage the estate, property or business.

(3) A special manager appointed under this section has such powers as may be entrusted to him by the court.

(4) The power of the court under subsection (3) to entrust powers to a special manager includes power to direct that any provision in this Group of Parts that has effect in relation to the official receiver, interim receiver or trustee shall have the like effect in relation to the special manager for the purposes of the carrying out by the special manager of any of the functions of the official receiver, interim receiver or trustee.

(5) A special manager appointed under this section shall—
- (a) give such security as may be prescribed,
- (b) prepare and keep such accounts as may be prescribed, and
- (c) produce those accounts in accordance with the rules to the Secretary of State or to such other persons as may be prescribed.

Notes

S 370

The purpose of this provision is to enable the trustee or official receiver to appoint someone to manage the bankrupt's estate or certain parts of it. This will be necessary where the estate comprises assets which are unusual or which require ongoing management to preserve their value. Typically, an application will be made where the assets require management by someone with specialist industry knowledge.

S 370(1)

This provision should be read in conjunction with s 286 IA 1986 (appointment of interim receiver) and IA 1986 s 287 (appointment of receiver/ manager) and IR 1986 r 6.167 to 6.171 which deal inter alia with the remuneration of the special manager and the security to be given in respect of the appointment. The order appointing the special manager must either specify the duration of the appointment which may be for a fixed period or until the happening of a specified event; or specify that the appointment is subject to a further order of the court IR 1986 r 6.167(2). However the appointment will terminate in the circumstances which are set out in IR 1986 r 6.171 which appear to override whatever may have been specified in the order of appointment.

S 370(2)

The applicant for the appointment must therefore satisfy the court that the appointment is necessary because the official receiver or trustee cannot adequately protect or administer the property over which the appointment is made. The application must be supported by a report setting out the reasons for the application. The report must include the applicant's estimate of the value of the estate, property or business in respect of which the special manager is to be appointed (IR 1986 r 6.167(1)). It is important that the estimate should be as accurate as possible because the minimum amount of security which the special manager must give is set by reference to that estimate (IR 1986 r 6.168(3)).

S 370(3)

The scope of the powers given to the special manager will be set out in the court order which appoints him. Care should be taken to ensure that the powers are extensive enough to allow the manager to discharge his intended function.

S 370(5)

The security to be given is detailed in IR 1986 r 6.168 and the rules relating to the keeping of accounts are detailed in IR 1986 r 6.170(1).

1.429

371 Re-direction of bankrupt's letters, etc

(1) Where a bankruptcy order has been made, the court may from time to time, on the application of the official receiver or the trustee of the bankrupt's estate, order [a postal operator (within the meaning of the Postal Services Act 2000)] to re-direct and send or deliver to the official receiver or trustee or otherwise any postal packet (within the meaning of [that Act]) which would otherwise be sent or delivered by [the operator concerned] to the bankrupt at such place or places as may be specified in the order.

(2) An order under this section has effect for such period, not exceeding 3 months, as may be specified in the order.

Notes

S 371(1)

A redirection can only take place in a bankruptcy. An application under this provision must be supported by a report from the official receiver (IR 1986 r 7.9) or an affidavit/witness statement from the trustee (IR 1986 r 7.8, r 7.57) setting out substantial grounds for the redirection. In *Singh v Official Receiver* [1997] BPIR 530 the court was unimpressed by the without-notice nature of an application made by the official receiver supported only by a letter.

An application for redirection may fall foul of the protection afforded by art 8 European Convention on Human Rights. In *Foxley v United Kingdom* [2000] BPIR 1009 it was accepted that s 371 was an interference by a public authority with the art 8 right but such interference was justified. Subject to one exception the European Court of Human Rights held that the redirection was justified. The exception related to privileged communications between the bankrupt and his lawyers which the trustee had read and copied. The court held that there was no justification for such action and that was a violation of art 8. In practice, before applying for a redirection of post the trustee should consider whether it is possible to obtain the relevant information by less intrusive means.

S 371(2)

There does not appear to be any ban on applying for further periods of restriction whilst the bankruptcy order is in force.

Part X
Individual Insolvency: General Provisions

1.430

372 Supplies of gas, water, electricity, etc

(1) This section applies where on any day ('the relevant day')—
  (a) a bankruptcy order is made against an individual or an interim receiver of an individual's property is appointed, or
  (b) a voluntary arrangement proposed by an individual is approved under Part VIII, or
  (c) a deed of arrangement is made for the benefit of an individual's creditors;
and in this section 'the office-holder' means the official receiver, the trustee in bankruptcy, the interim receiver, the supervisor of the voluntary arrangement or the trustee under the deed of arrangement, as the case may be.

(2) If a request falling within the next subsection is made for the giving after the relevant day of any of the supplies mentioned in subsection (4), the supplier—
  (a) may make it a condition of the giving of the supply that the office-holder personally guarantees the payment of any charges in respect of the supply, but
  (b) shall not make it a condition of the giving of the supply, or do anything which has the effect of making it a condition of the giving of the supply, that any outstanding charges in respect of a supply given to the individual before the relevant day are paid.

(3) A request falls within this subsection if it is made—
  (a) by or with the concurrence of the office-holder, and
  (b) for the purposes of any business which is or has been carried on by the individual, by a firm or partnership of which the individual is or was a member, or by an agent or manager for the individual or for such a firm or partnership.

(4) The supplies referred to in subsection (2) are—
  [(a) a supply of gas by a gas supplier within the meaning of Part I of the Gas Act 1986;]
  [(b) a supply of electricity by an electricity supplier within the meaning of Part I of the Electricity Act 1989;]

> (c) a supply of water by [a water undertaker],
> [(d) a supply of communications services by a provider of a public electronic communications service].
>
> (5) The following applies to expressions used in subsection (4)—
> (a) ...
> (b) ... and
> [(c) 'communications services' do not include electronic communications services to the extent that they are used to broadcast or otherwise transmit programme services (within the meaning of the Communications Act 2003)].

Notes

S 372(1)

The aim of this provision is to ensure that essential supplies of gas, electricity, water and communications are maintained notwithstanding the entry of an individual into a formal insolvency procedure as detailed in sub paragraphs s 372(1)(a)–(c).

S 372(2), (3)

The request for the supplies must be made by or with the concurrence of the relevant office holder (s 372(1)) and for the purpose of any business which is or has been carried on by the relevant individual. The office holder cannot be forced to pay arrears as a condition for being provided with the relevant supply (s 372(2)(b)), but may be made to personally guarantee the payment of any charges in respect of the supply (s 372(2)(a)).

1.431

373 Jurisdiction in relation to insolvent individuals

(1) The High Court and the county courts have jurisdiction throughout England and Wales for the purposes of the Parts in this Group.

(2) For the purposes of those Parts, a county court has, in addition to its ordinary jurisdiction, all the powers and jurisdiction of the High Court; and the orders of the court may be enforced accordingly in the prescribed manner.

(3) Jurisdiction for the purposes of those Parts is exercised—
(a) by the High Court in relation to the proceedings which, in accordance with the rules, are allocated to the London insolvency district, and
(b) by each county court in relation to the proceedings which are so allocated to the insolvency district of that court.

(4) Subsection (3) is without prejudice to the transfer of proceedings from one court to another in the manner prescribed by the rules; and nothing in that subsection invalidates any proceedings on the grounds that they were initiated or continued in the wrong court.

Notes

S 373(1)

In England and Wales the courts possessing bankruptcy jurisdiction are the High Court and certain county courts, and these courts have jurisdiction for the purposes of IA 1986 s 252 to

385. A bankruptcy petition should be presented in the High Court in the circumstances set out in IR 1986 r 6.9(1). In any other case it should be presented in the county court for the insolvency district (see IA 1986 s 374) in which the debtor has resided or carried on business for the longest period during the 6 months preceding the presentation of the petition; however there are circumstances where a debtor outside the London insolvency district may present a petition in an alternative county court (IR 1986 6.40(3)).

S 373(2)

The county court has all the powers of the High Court in exercising its bankruptcy jurisdiction and this would include the county court reviewing an order of the High Court in a case transferred to the county court *Re a Debtor (No 2A of 1980)* [1981] Ch 148.

S 373(3)

Though each bankruptcy court has jurisdiction throughout England and Wales (IA 1986s 373(1)) they primarily exercise jurisdiction in relation to those proceedings which are allocated to their own 'insolvency district', see IA 1986 s 374.

S 373(4)

Bankruptcy proceedings are not invalidated by reason of the fact that they are commenced in the wrong bankruptcy court and they may be transferred between courts having insolvency jurisdiction. This does not permit validation of proceedings commenced in a court without any bankruptcy jurisdiction at all *Re Southsea Garage Ltd* (1911) 27 TLR 295. Detailed rules on the transfer of proceedings are contained in IR 1986 r 7.11 to 7.15. Reference in those rules to the transfer of *proceedings* has the effect that the transfer relates to the whole proceedings, and it is not possible to transfer individual claims within the proceedings (IR 1986 r 7.11, r 7.15(2), *Re Kou Youmdjian, ex parte The Trustee v Lord* [1956] 1 WLR 558). Further where an order is made by a bankruptcy county court it may be enforced and/or dealt with by another county court even if the latter county court does not have bankruptcy jurisdiction IR 1986 r 7.19(2).

1.432

374 Insolvency districts

(1) The Lord Chancellor may[, with the concurrence of the Lord Chief Justice,] by order designate the areas which are for the time being to be comprised, for the purposes of the Parts in this Group, in the London Insolvency district and the insolvency district of each county court; and an order under this section may—

    (a)   exclude any county court from having jurisdiction for the purposes of those Parts, or

    (b)   confer jurisdiction for those purposes on any county court which has not previously had that jurisdiction.

(2) An order under this section may contain such incidental, supplemental and transitional provisions as may appear to the Lord Chancellor [and the Lord Chief Justice] necessary or expedient.

(3) An order under this section shall be made by statutory instrument and, after being made, shall be laid before each House of Parliament.

(4) Subject to any order under this section—

    (a)   the district which, immediately before the appointed day, is the London bankruptcy district becomes, on that day, the London insolvency district;

> (b) any district which immediately before that day is the bankruptcy district of a county court becomes, on that day, the insolvency district of that court, and
>
> (c) any county court which immediately before that day is excluded from having jurisdiction in bankruptcy is excluded, on and after that day, from having jurisdiction for the purposes of the Parts in this Group.
>
> [(5) The Lord Chief Justice may nominate a judicial office holder (as defined in section 109(4) of the Constitutional Reform Act 2005) to exercise his functions under this section.]

Notes

S 374

The county courts presently within the London insolvency district are Barnet, Bloomsbury, Bow, Brentford, Central London, Clerkenwell, Edmonton, Lambeth, Mayor's & City of London, Shoreditch, Wandsworth, West London and Willesden. The county courts having bankruptcy jurisdiction are set out in Vol 2 Civil Procedure Para 11–7 referring to Civil Courts Order 1983 (SI 1983/713) (as amended); and IR 1986 Sch 2 lists those bankruptcy county courts with alternative courts for a debtor who wishes to expedite his petition (IR 1986 r 6.40(3)).

> **1.433**
>
> **375 Appeals etc from courts exercising insolvency jurisdiction**
>
> (1) Every court having jurisdiction for the purposes of the Parts in this Group may review, rescind or vary any order made by it in the exercise of that jurisdiction.
>
> (2) An appeal from a decision made in the exercise of jurisdiction for the purposes of those Parts by a county court or by a registrar in bankruptcy of the High Court lies to a single judge of the High Court; and an appeal from a decision of that judge on such an appeal lies ... to the Court of Appeal.
>
> (3) A county court is not, in the exercise of its jurisdiction for the purposes of those Parts, to be subject to be restrained by the order of any other court, and no appeal lies from its decision in the exercise of that jurisdiction except as provided by this section.

Notes

S 375(1)

Review, rescind, vary

In *Papanicola v Humphreys* [2005] EWHC 335 (Ch), [2005] 2 All ER 418 Laddie J formulated the following propositions in relation to IA 1986 s 375:
1   The section gives the court a wide discretion to review, vary or rescind any order made in the exercise of the bankruptcy jurisdiction.
2   The onus is on the applicant to demonstrate the existence of circumstances which justify exercise of the discretion in his favour.

3   Those circumstances must be exceptional (see also *Fitch v Official Receiver* [1996] 1 WLR 242).

4   The circumstances relied on must involve a material difference to what was before the court which made the original order. In other words there must be something new to justify the overturning of the original order.

5   There is no limit to the factors which may be taken into account. They can include, for example, changes which have occurred since the making of the original order and significant facts which, although in existence at the time of the original order, were not brought to the court's attention at that time.

6   Where the new circumstances relied on consist of or include new evidence which could have been made available at the original hearing, that, and any explanation the applicant gives for the failure to produce it then or any lack of such explanation, are factors which can be taken into account in the exercise of the discretion.

It would be particularly difficult to secure the review of a consent order *Boorer v Trustee in Bankruptcy of Boorer* [2002] BPIR 21. Further, it is not appropriate to seek to use the jurisdiction to review in order to evade the express prohibition in IA 1986 s 255(1)(c) against making a second application for an interim order within 12 months of the first application *Hurst v Bennett (No 2)* [2001] EWCA Civ 1398, [2002] BPIR 102; nor to prolong an exhausted appeal process *Egleton v IRC* [2003] EWHC 3226 (Ch), [2004] BPIR 476. Similarly, where a debtor cannot satisfy the stringent conditions established by s 282(1)(b) (annulment) and the Insolvency Rules, he cannot then circumvent those conditions by invoking the provisions of IA 1986 s 375: *IRC v Robinson* [1999] BPIR 329.

Normally a review should be carried out by the same judge who made the original order, but a judge of co-ordinate jurisdiction has jurisdiction to conduct the review *Mond v Hammond Suddards* [2000] Ch 40. A judge also has jurisdiction to review a decision of an inferior court *O'Brien v Commrs of Inland Revenue* [2000] BPIR 306; *Re Picadilly Property Management Ltd* [1999] BPIR 260; however, where possible, a review should be carried out by the same judge in the same court as made the original order.

Where a bankruptcy order is rescinded the Secretary of State although not a party has standing to appeal IR 1986 r 7.48(1)

S 375(2)

Appeals

Subject to certain modifications the procedure and practice of the Supreme Court relating to appeals to the Court of Appeal applies to appeals in bankruptcy proceedings (IR 1986 r 7.49(1)). That procedure and practice is contained in CPR Part 52 and its Practice Direction; they need to be read in the light of the Practice Direction Insolvency Proceedings (Civil Procedure Vol 2 Section 3E ('PDIP') para 17 (CPR r 52.1(4)). In the case of 'first appeals' (see below) the application of CPR Part 52 is restricted. Though the provisions of the PDIP are annotated separately it is important to note that the time for filing the appellant's notice is 14 days after the decision of the lower court unless another period is directed by the lower court (PDIP para 17.11(2)).

In the case of an order made by a county court (whether district judge or circuit judge) or by a registrar of the High Court, appeal lies to a single judge of the High Court (IR 1986 r 7.48(2)). Such an appeal is referred to in the PDIP para 17.2(1) (PDIP is already defined above) as a 'first appeal' and no permission is required to make such an appeal (PDIP para 17.6).

Decisions by judges of the High Court fall into two categories: (i) decisions made on appeals from a decision of a county court or a bankruptcy registrar, that is decisions made on first appeal; and (ii) decisions at first instance. From a decision made by a judge of the High Court on a first appeal, a further appeal to the Court of Appeal may only be made with the permission of the Court of Appeal (PDIP para 17.3). From a decision made by a High Court judge at first instance an appeal may be made to the Court of Appeal (Supreme Court Act 1981 s 16(1)) with the permission of either the judge or the Court of Appeal

(CPR r 52.3(1)). Although such an appeal will be the first to be made in such a case it is not a 'first appeal' within the meaning of the PDIP para 17.3(3).

New evidence not before the lower court may be admitted on appeal if permission is given (*Sadrolashrafi v Marvel International Food Logistics Ltd* [2004] BPIR 834, CPR r 52.11(2)) and although it is not a requirement that 'special grounds' be shown (*Ladd v Marshall* [1954] 1 WLR 1489) the principles in *Ladd v Marshall* remain relevant to the exercise by the court of its discretion *Hertfordshire Investments v Bubb* [2000] 1 WLR 2318, *Lombard Natwest Factors Ltd v Arbis* [2000] BPIR 79l. See also *Salvage v Hussein* [1999] BPIR 410 (admission of fresh evidence on appeal against the dismissal of an application to set aside a statutory demand).

1.434

376 Time-limits

Where by any provision in this Group of Parts or by the rules the time for doing anything is limited, the court may extend the time, either before or after it has expired, on such terms, if any, as it thinks fit.

Notes

S 376

The provisions of CPR r 2.8 apply as regards the computation of time to anything required or authorised to be done under the Insolvency Rules IR 1986 r 12.9. Reference should be made to CPR r 2.8 but, in general, it provides that where a period of time is expressed as a number of days it should be computed as clear days. That means that in computing the number of days, the day on which the period begins and, if the end of the period is defined by reference to an event, the day on which that even occurs, are not included. The court is also authorised to extend or shorten the time for compliance with any rule or practice direction under CPR r 3.1(2)(a) which applies by virtue of IR 1986 r 12.9. IA 1986 s 376 can be used to extend the period for challenging the approval of an individual voluntary arrangement *Tager v Westpac Banking Corpn* [1997] 1 BCLC 313. The power to extend time is unlimited and involves balancing such considerations as the length of the delay, the reasons for the delay, the merits of the underlying complaint and the prejudice to the parties (other than that inevitably involved in extending the time limit) *Warley Continental Services Ltd v Johal* [2004] BPIR 353.

1.435

377 Formal defects

The acts of a person as the trustee of a bankrupt's estate or as a special manager, and the acts of the creditors' committee established for any bankruptcy, are valid notwithstanding any defect in the appointment, election or qualifications of the trustee or manager or, as the case may be, of any member of the committee.

Notes

S 377

This provision validates the acts of a person as the trustee of a bankrupt's estate or as a special manager, and the acts of the creditors' committee established for any bankruptcy, notwithstanding any procedural defect in appointment, election or qualification. It is difficult to see how it would apply where in law there was no appointment at all (*Morris v Kannsen* [1946] AC 459 and see IA 1986 s 232). This provision should also be read alongside IR 1986 r 7.55 which saves insolvency proceedings from being invalidated by any formal defect or irregularity in certain circumstances.

1.436

378 Exemption from stamp duty

Stamp duty shall not be charged on—

   (a)   any document, being a deed, conveyance, assignment, surrender, admission or other assurance relating solely to property which is comprised in a bankrupt's estate and which, after the execution of that document, is or remains at law or in equity the property of the bankrupt or of the trustee of that estate,

   (b)   any writ, order, certificate or other instrument relating solely to the property of a bankrupt or to any bankruptcy proceedings.

1.436A

379 Annual report

As soon as practicable after the end of 1986 and each subsequent calendar year, the Secretary of State shall prepare and lay before each House of Parliament a report about the operation during that year of so much of this Act as is comprised in this Group of Parts, and about proceedings in the course of that year under the Deeds of Arrangement Act 1914.

Part XI
Interpretation for Second Group of Parts

1.437

380 Introductory

The next five sections have effect for the interpretation of the provisions of this Act which are comprised in this Group of Parts; and where a definition is provided for a particular expression, it applies except so far as the context otherwise requires.

Notes

S 380

The relevant interpretation provisions for individual voluntary arrangements and bankruptcy are contained in s 381 to 385; there are further interpretation provisions of general application in s 435 to 437 and corporate interpretation provisions in s 247 to 251.

1.438

381 'Bankrupt' and associated terminology

(1) 'Bankrupt' means an individual who has been adjudged bankrupt and, in relation to a bankruptcy order, it means the individual adjudged bankrupt by that order.

(2) 'Bankruptcy order' means an order adjudging an individual bankrupt.

(3) 'Bankruptcy petition' means a petition to the court for a bankruptcy order.

1.438A

382 'Bankruptcy debt', etc

(1) 'Bankruptcy debt', in relation to a bankrupt, means (subject to the next subsection) any of the following—
  (a)   any debt or liability to which he is subject at the commencement of the bankruptcy,
  (b)   any debt or liability to which he may become subject after the commencement of the bankruptcy (including after his discharge from bankruptcy) by reason of any obligation incurred before the commencement of the bankruptcy,
  (c)   *any amount specified in pursuance of section 39(3)(c) of the Powers of Criminal Courts Act 1973 in any criminal bankruptcy order made against him before the commencement of the bankruptcy, and*
  (d)   any interest provable as mentioned in section 322(2) in Chapter IV of Part IX.

(2) In determining for the purposes of any provision in this Group of Parts whether any liability in tort is a bankruptcy debt, the bankrupt is deemed to become subject to that liability by reason of an obligation incurred at the time when the cause of action accrued.

(3) For the purposes of references in this Group of Parts to a debt or liability, it is immaterial whether the debt or liability is present or future, whether it is certain or contingent or whether its amount is fixed or liquidated, or is capable of being ascertained by fixed rules or as a matter of opinion; and references in this Group of Parts to owing a debt are to be read accordingly.

(4) In this Group of Parts, except in so far as the context otherwise requires, 'liability' means (subject to subsection (3) above) a liability to pay money or money's worth, including any liability under an enactment, any liability for breach of trust, any liability in contract, tort or bailment and any liability arising out of an obligation to make restitution.

Notes

S 382

In general terms all debts and liabilities, present or future, certain or contingent to which the debtor was actually or prospectively liable at the commencement of the bankruptcy are provable in the debtor's bankruptcy. However there is a distinction between '*bankruptcy debts*' and '*provable debts*' (IR 1986 r 12.3) and there are debts which are not provable although they are '*bankruptcy debts*' (see IR 1986 r 12.3(2), (2A)(3)). The importance of the distinction is that a creditor's bankruptcy petition is based on a bankruptcy debt not a provable debt (see IA 1986 ss 264(a), 383(b), 383(a)); therefore a creditor with a non provable debt can still petition for bankruptcy *Russell v Russell* [1998] BPIR 259, *Levy v Legal Services Commission* [2001] 1 All ER 895. However, in the absence of some special circumstances, as a matter of discretion, it will not usually be appropriate to make a bankruptcy order on such a petition, see *Russell*, and *Wehmeyer v Wehmeyer* [2001] BPIR 548.

S 382(1)

The commencement of the bankruptcy is the date of the bankruptcy order s 278.

S 382(1)(c)

This provision is prospectively repealed by Criminal Justice Act 1988 s 170(2) Sch 16 from a date to be appointed.

S 382(1)(d)

Although statutory interest is not a 'bankruptcy debt' the court will generally require its payment on an annulment where there are enough assets to meet all liabilities, expenses and costs *Wilcock v Duckworth* [2005] BPIR 682.S 382(2).

An unliquidated liability in tort may be a bankruptcy debt; see notes IR 1986 r 13.12.

S 382(3)

A claim for costs does not constitute a contingent liability, see *Glenister v Rowe* [2000] Ch 76. Costs of legal proceedings are in the discretion of the court. Until an order for payment of costs is made there is no obligation or liability to pay them and there is no right to recover them.

1.439

383 'Creditor', 'security', etc

(1) 'Creditor'—
   (a)   in relation to a bankrupt, means a person to whom any of the bankruptcy debts is owed (*being, in the case of an amount falling within paragraph (c) of the definition in section 382(1) of 'bankruptcy debt', the person in respect of whom that amount is specified in the criminal bankruptcy order in question*), and
   (b)   in relation to an individual to whom a bankruptcy petition relates, means a person who would be a creditor in the bankruptcy if a bankruptcy order were made on that petition.

(2) Subject to the next two subsections and any provision of the rules requiring a creditor to give up his security for the purposes of proving a debt, a debt is secured for the purposes of this Group of Parts to the extent that the person to whom the debt is owed holds any security for the debt (whether a mortgage, charge, lien or other security) over any property of the person by whom the debt is owed.

(3) Where a statement such as is mentioned in section 269(1)(a) in Chapter I of Part IX has been made by a secured creditor for the purposes of any bankruptcy petition and a bankruptcy order is subsequently made on that petition, the creditor is deemed for the purposes of the Parts in this Group to have given up the security specified in the statement.

(4) In subsection (2) the reference to a security does not include a lien on books, papers or other records, except to the extent that they consist of documents which give a title to property and are held as such.

Notes

S 383(1)(a)

The words in brackets are repealed from a day to be appointed by the Criminal Justice Act 1988 s 170(2), Sch 16. For 'bankruptcy debts' see notes under IA 1986 s 382 above.

S 383(2)

This only relates to security granted by the debtor to the creditor and not to security provided by others. 'Security' is widely defined and it would include money paid into court as a condition of defending or as an offer to settle under CPR Part 36, or into an out of court account for the same purpose; in those circumstances a charge is created over the monies *Re Mordant* [1996] 1 FLR 334. However a freezing order does not create a charge over the frozen assets in favour of the claimant *Flightline Ltd v Edwards* [2003] EWCA Civ 63, [2003] 1 WLR 1200. A peaceable re-entry by a landlord does not create a security *Razzaq v Pala* [1998] BCC 66.

S 383(3)

This refers to a petitioning creditor making a statement in his petition that he is willing to give up his security for the benefit of all the creditors (IA 1986 s 269).

1.440

384 'Prescribed' and 'the rules'

(1) Subject to the next subsection [and sections 342C(7) and 342F(9) in Chapter V of Part IX], 'prescribed' means prescribed by the rules; and 'the rules' means rules made under section 412 in Part XV.

(2) References in this Group of Parts to the amount prescribed for the purposes of any of the following provisions—
    section 273;
    [section 313A;]
    section 346(3);
    section 354(1) and (2);
    section 358;
    section 360(1);
    section 361(2); and
    section 364(2)(d),
and references in those provisions to the prescribed amount are to be read in accordance with section 418 in Part XV and orders made under that section.

1.441

385 Miscellaneous definitions

(1) The following definitions have effect—
    'the court', in relation to any matter, means the court to which, in accordance with section 373 in Part X and the rules, proceedings with respect to that matter are allocated or transferred;

'creditor's petition' means a bankruptcy petition under section 264(1)(a);

'criminal bankruptcy order' means an order under section 39(1) of the Powers of Criminal Courts Act 1973;

'debt' is to be construed in accordance with section 382(3);

'the debtor'—

    (a)   in relation to a proposal for the purposes of Part VIII, means the individual making or intending to make that proposal, and

    (b)   in relation to a bankruptcy petition, means the individual to whom the petition relates;

'debtor's petition' means a bankruptcy petition presented by the debtor himself under section 264(1)(b);

'dwelling house' includes any building or part of a building which is occupied as a dwelling and any yard, garden, garage or outhouse belonging to the dwelling house and occupied with it;

'estate', in relation to a bankrupt is to be construed in accordance with section 283 in Chapter II of Part IX;

'family', in relation to a bankrupt, means the persons (if any) who are living with him and are dependent on him;

['insolvency administration order' means an order for the administration in bankruptcy of the insolvent estate of a deceased debtor (being an individual at the date of his death);

'insolvency administration petition' means a petition for an insolvency administration order;

'the Rules' means the Insolvency Rules 1986.]

'secured' and related expressions are to be construed in accordance with section 383; and

'the trustee', in relation to a bankruptcy and the bankrupt, means the trustee of the bankrupt's estate.

(2) References in this Group of Parts to a person's affairs include his business, if any.

The Third Group of Parts
Miscellaneous Matters Bearing on both Company and Individual Insolvency; General Interpretation; Final Provisions

Part XII
Preferential Debts in Company and Individual Insolvency

1.442

386 Categories of preferential debts

(1) A reference in this Act to the preferential debts of a company or an individual is to the debts listed in Schedule 6 to this Act [(contributions to occupational pension schemes; remuneration, &c of employees; levies on coal and steel production)]; and references to preferential creditors are to be read accordingly.

(2) In that Schedule 'the debtor' means the company or the individual concerned.

(3) Schedule 6 is to be read with Schedule 4 to the Pension Schemes Act 1993 (occupational pension scheme contributions).

Notes

S 386

This provision should be read in conjuction with IA 1986 Sch 6 and the notes thereto. The words in square brackets in IA 1986 s 386(1) were inserted by the EA 2002 s 251(3) subject to transitional provisions in cases beginning before 15 September 2003. Generally preferential debts rank in priority to a floating charge but not a fixed charge: IA 1986 s 175; *Re Lewis Merthyr Consolidated Collieries Ltd* [1929] 1 Ch 498. Priority may be affected by a priority agreement amongst the chargeholders: *Re Portbase (Clothing) Ltd* [1993] Ch 388. In considering which debts are preferential debts reference should be made not only to this provision and to IA 1986 Sch 6 but also to IA 1986 s 176(3) which provides that in a compulsory winding up a creditor who has levied distress within a period of three months ending with the making of the winding up order will be treated as a preferential creditor to the extent of the proceeds of sale of the assets that were the subject of the distress.

Prior to the coming into force of the relevant parts of the EA 2002 on 15 September 2003, the main classes of preferential debts could be broadly described as 'Crown debts' (ie debts due to the Inland Revenue and HM Customs and Excise and Class 1 Class 2 and Class 4 National Insurance contributions), contributions to occupational pension schemes and employees' remuneration. In addition, with effect from 1 January 1988, levies in respect of coal and steel production under the ECSC Treaty were also given preferential status under the Insolvency ESCS Levy Debts) Regulations 1987 (SI 1987/2093). Following the coming into force of the amendments made under the EA 2002 Crown debts have not enjoyed preferential status since 15 September 2003.

1.443

387 'The relevant date'

(1) This section explains references in Schedule 6 to the relevant date (being the date which determines the existence and amount of a preferential debt).

(2) For the purposes of section 4 in Part I (meetings to consider company voluntary arrangement), the relevant date in relation to a company which is not being wound up is—

    (a) if the company is in administration, the date on which it entered administration, and

    (b) if the company is not in administration, the date on which the voluntary arrangement takes effect.

(2A) For the purposes of paragraph 31 of Schedule A1 (meetings to consider company voluntary arrangement where a moratorium under section 1A is in force), the relevant date in relation to a company is the date of filing.

(3) In relation to a company which is being wound up, the following applies—

(a)   if the winding up is by the court, and the winding-up order was made immediately upon the discharge of an administration order, the relevant date is the date on which the company entered administration;

(aa) if the winding up is by the court and the winding-up order was made following conversion of administration into winding up by virtue of Article 37 of the EC Regulation, the relevant date is the date on which the company entered administration;

(ab) if the company is deemed to have passed a resolution for voluntary winding up by virtue of an order following conversion of administration into winding up under Article 37 of the EC Regulation, the relevant date is the date on which the company entered administration;

(b)   if the case does not fall within paragraph (a)[, (aa) or (ab)] and the company—

    (i)   is being wound up by the court, and

    (ii) had not commenced to be wound up voluntarily before the date of the making of the winding-up order,

the relevant date is the date of the appointment (or first appointment) of a provisional liquidator or, if no such appointment has been made, the date of the winding-up order;

(ba) if the case does not fall within paragraph (a), (aa), (ab) or (b) and the company is being wound up following administration pursuant to paragraph 83 of Schedule B1, the relevant date is the date on which the company entered administration;

(c)   if the case does not fall within paragraph (a), (aa), (ab), (b) or (ba), the relevant date is the date of the passing of the resolution for the winding up of the company.

(3A) In relation to a company which is in administration (and to which no other provision of this section applies) the relevant date is the date on which the company enters administration.

(4) In relation to a company in receivership (where section 40 or, as the case may be, section 59 applies), the relevant date is—

(a)   in England and Wales, the date of the appointment of the receiver by debenture-holders, and

(b)   in Scotland, the date of the appointment of the receiver under section 53(6) or (as the case may be) 54(5).

(5) For the purposes of section 258 in Part VIII (individual voluntary arrangements), the relevant date is, in relation to a debtor who is not an undischarged bankrupt—

(a)   where an interim order has been made under section 252 with respect to his proposal, the date of that order, and

(b)   in any other case, the date on which the voluntary arrangement takes effect.

(6) In relation to a bankrupt, the following applies—

(a)   where at the time the bankruptcy order was made there was an interim receiver appointed under section 286, the relevant date is the date on which the interim receiver was first appointed after the presentation of the bankruptcy petition;

(b)   otherwise, the relevant date is the date of the making of the bankruptcy order.

Notes

S 387

Care must be taken in considering this section in relation to insolvency proceedings commenced before 15 September 2003 because of the reforms introduced by the EA 2002 s 248(3). These provisions are self explanatory and the 'relevant date' for ascertaining whether a debt is a preferential debt clearly varies according to the nature of the insolvency proceedings in question.

Part XIII
Insolvency Practitioners and their Qualification

Restrictions on unqualified persons acting as liquidator, trustee in bankruptcy, etc

1.444

388 Meaning of 'act as insolvency practitioner'

(1) A person acts as an insolvency practitioner in relation to a company by acting—

(a)   as its liquidator, provisional liquidator, administrator or administrative receiver, or

(b)   where a voluntary arrangement in relation to the company is proposed or approved under Part I, as nominee or supervisor.

(2) A person acts as an insolvency practitioner in relation to an individual by acting—

(a)as his trustee in bankruptcy or interim receiver of his property or as permanent or interim trustee in the sequestration of his estate; or

(b)   as trustee under a deed which is a deed of arrangement made for the benefit of his creditors or, in Scotland, a trust deed for his creditors; or

(c)   where a voluntary arrangement in relation to the individual is proposed or approved under Part VIII, as nominee or supervisor

(d)   in the case of a deceased individual to the administration of whose estate this section applies by virtue of an order under section 421 (application of provisions of this Act to insolvent estates of deceased persons), as administrator of that estate.

(2A) A person acts as an insolvency practitioner in relation to an insolvent partnership by acting—

(a)   as its liquidator, provisional liquidator or administrator, or

as trustee of the partnership under article 11 of the Insolvent Partnerships Order 1994, or

(c)   as supervisor of a voluntary arrangement approved in relation to it under Part I of this Act.

(2B) In relation to a voluntary arrangement proposed under Part I or VIII, a person acts as nominee if he performs any of the functions conferred on nominees under the Part in question.

(3) References in this section to an individual include, except in so far as the context otherwise requires, references ...... to any debtor within the meaning of the Bankruptcy (Scotland) Act 1985.

(4) In this section—
'administrative receiver' has the meaning given by section 251 in Part VII;
'company' means a company within the meaning given by section 735(1) of the Companies Act or a company which may be wound up under Part V of this Act (unregistered companies); and
'interim trustee' and 'permanent trustee' mean the same as in the Bankruptcy (Scotland) Act 1985.

(5) Nothing in this section applies to anything done by—
(a) the official receiver; or
(b) the Accountant in Bankruptcy (within the meaning of the Bankruptcy (Scotland) Act 1985).

(6) Nothing in this section applies to anything done (whether in the United Kingdom or elsewhere) in relation to insolvency proceedings under the EC Regulation in a member State other than the United Kingdom

---

1.445

389 Acting without qualification an offence

(1) A person who acts as an insolvency practitioner in relation to a company or an individual at a time when he is not qualified to do so is liable to imprisonment or a fine, or to both.

(1A) This section is subject to section 389A.

(2) This section does not apply to the official receiver [or the Accountant in Bankruptcy (within the meaning of the Bankruptcy (Scotland) Act 1985.]

1.446

389A Authorisation of nominees and supervisors

(1) Section 389 does not apply to a person acting, in relation to a voluntary arrangement proposed or approved under Part I or Part VIII, as nominee or supervisor if he is authorised so to act.

(2) For the purposes of subsection (1) and those Parts, an individual to whom subsection (3) does not apply is authorised to act as nominee or supervisor in relation to such an arrangement if—
(a) he is a member of a body recognised for the purpose by the Secretary of State, and

(b) there is in force security (in Scotland, caution) for the proper performance of his functions and that security or caution meets the prescribed requirements with respect to his so acting in relation to the arrangement.

(3) This subsection applies to a person if—
    (a) he has been adjudged bankrupt or sequestration of his estate has been awarded and (in either case) he has not been discharged,
    (b) he is subject to a disqualification order made or a disqualification undertaking accepted under the Company Directors Disqualification Act 1986 or to a disqualification order made under Part II of the Companies (Northern Ireland) Order 1989, or
    (c) he is a patient within the meaning of Part VII of the Mental Health Act 1983 or section 125(1) of the Mental Health (Scotland) Act 1984.
    (d) he lacks capacity (within the meaning of the Mental Capacity Act 2005) to act as nominee or supervisor.

(4) The Secretary of State may by order declare a body which appears to him to fall within subsection (5) to be a recognised body for the purposes of subsection (2)(a).

(5) A body may be recognised if it maintains and enforces rules for securing that its members—
    (a) are fit and proper persons to act as nominees or supervisors, and
    (b) meet acceptable requirements as to education and practical training and experience.

(6) For the purposes of this section, a person is a member of a body only if he is subject to its rules when acting as nominee or supervisor (whether or not he is in fact a member of the body).

(7) An order made under subsection (4) in relation to a body may be revoked by a further order if it appears to the Secretary of State that the body no longer falls within subsection (5).

(8) An order of the Secretary of State under this section has effect from such date as is specified in the order; and any such order revoking a previous order may make provision for members of the body in question to continue to be treated as members of a recognised body for a specified period after the revocation takes effect.]

Notes

S 389A(2)

So far no bodies have been recognised by the Secretary of State. The rationale is to introduce 'turnaround' professionals to appointments as nominees/supervisors who need not be licensed insolvency practitioners, but this has not yet been acted upon.

1.447

389B Official Receiver as nominee or supervisor

(1) The official receiver is authorised to act as nominee or supervisor in relation to a voluntary arrangement approved under Part VIII provided that the debtor is an undischarged bankrupt when the arrangement is proposed.

(2) The Secretary of State may by order repeal the proviso in subsection (1)

(3) An order under subsection (2)-
  (a) must be made by statutory instrument, and
  (b) shall be subject to annulment in pursuance of either House of Parliament.

Notes

S 389B(1)

This provision came into force on 1 April 2004 and it allows the official receiver to act as a nominee/supervisor of an individual voluntary arrangement where the debtor is an undischarged bankrupt. Its aim is to encourage the use of 'fast track IVAs' (IA 1986 s 263A to 263G). There is no exemption from obtaining an interim order IA 1986 s 253(3)(a). Presumably the official receiver will be taking the relevant appointment in his office as official receiver by analogy with liquidation IA 1986 s 136(2); thus retirement of a particular individual as official receiver will not require a transfer of office application.

S 389B(2)

It is therefore contemplated that the official receiver will also be allowed to act as a nominee/supervisor where the debtor is not an undischarged bankrupt.

The requisite qualification, and the means of obtaining it

1.448

390 Persons not qualified to act as insolvency practitioners

(1) A person who is not an individual is not qualified to act as an insolvency practitioner.

(2) A person is not qualified to act as an insolvency practitioner at any time unless at that time—
  (a) he is authorised so to act by virtue of membership of a professional body recognised under section 391 below, being permitted so to act by or under the rules of that body, or
  (b) he holds an authorisation granted by a competent authority under section 393.

(3) A person is not qualified to act as an insolvency practitioner in relation to another person at any time unless—
  (a) there is in force at that time security or, in Scotland, caution for the proper performance of his functions, and
  (b) that security or caution meets the prescribed requirements with respect to his so acting in relation to that other person.

(4) A person is not qualified to act as an insolvency practitioner at any time if at that time—
  (a) he has been adjudged bankrupt or sequestration of his estate has been awarded and (in either case) he has not been discharged,

> (b) he is subject to a disqualification order made [or a disqualification undertaking accepted] under the Company Directors Disqualification Act 1986 [or to a disqualification order made under Part II of the Companies (Northern Ireland) Order 1989], or
>
> (c) he is a patient within the meaning of Part VII of the Mental Health Act 1983 or section 125(1) of the Mental Health (Scotland) Act 1984 [or has had a guardian appointed to him under the Adults with Incapacity (Scotland) Act 2000 (asp 4)].
>
> (d) he lacks capacity (within the meaning of the Mental Capacity Act 2005) to act as nominee or supervisor.
>
> (5) A person is not qualified to act as an insolvency practitioner while a bankruptcy restriction order is in force in respect of him.

Notes

S 390(1)

The effect is that a company cannot be or act as an insolvency practitioner. Further, where an insolvency practitioner who is a partner of a firm is appointed the appointment is nonetheless personal to that partner. Accordingly, proceedings brought by or against him in his capacity as insolvency practitioner must be issued in his individual name, not the name of the firm. For an example of a case in which this error was fatal, see *Ramsay v Leonard Curtis (a firm) 28 July 1999, LTL 28/7/99 (CA)*.

S 390(2)

Where a professional body removes a member's licence to act as an insolvency practitioner it may take immediate effect *R (on the application of Eliades) v Institute of Chartered Accountants* [2001] BPIR 363.

S 390(3)

This provision deals with the mandatory bonding requirements for insolvency practitioners which are dealt with in detail by the Insolvency Practitioners Regulations 2005 (SI 2005/524); those Regulations also set out detailed provisions on the educational and practical experience which is required for an individual to be 'qualified' to act as an insolvency practitioner.

S 390(4)

Where any of these circumstances occur then the individual is immediately disqualified from acting as an insolvency practitioner.

1.449

391 Recognised professional bodies

(1) The Secretary of State may by order declare a body which appears to him to fall within subsection (2) below to be a recognised professional body for the purposes of this section.

(2) A body may be recognised if it regulates the practice of a profession and maintains and enforces rules for securing that such of its members as are permitted by or under the rules to act as insolvency practitioners—

    (a) are fit and proper persons so to act, and

(b) meet acceptable requirements as to education and practical training and experience.

(3) References to members of a recognised professional body are to persons who, whether members of that body or not, are subject to its rules in the practice of the profession in question.

The reference in section 390(2) above to membership of a professional body recognised under this section is to be read accordingly.

(4) An order made under subsection (1) in relation to a professional body may be revoked by a further order if it appears to the Secretary of State that the body no longer falls within subsection (2).

(5) An order of the Secretary of State under this section has effect from such date as is specified in the order; and any such order revoking a previous order may make provision whereby members of the body in question continue to be treated as authorised to act as insolvency practitioners for a specified period after the revocation takes effect.

Notes

S 391(1)

Various bodies have been recognised under the Insolvency Practitioners (Recognised Professional Bodies) Order 1986, SI 1986/1764 (as amended). They are as follows: The Chartered Association of Certified Accountants, The Insolvency Practitioners Assocation, The Institute of Chartered Accountants in England and Wales, The Institute of Chartered Accountants in Ireland, The Institute of Chartered Accountants in Scotland, The Law Society and The Law Society of Scotland. The Insolvency Practitioners Regulations 2005 (SI 2005/524) contain detailed provisions relating to the determination of whether an applicant is a fit and proper person, his educational qualifications, training and experience. For a decision on disciplinary proceedings against an insolvency practitioner see *Mond v The Association of Chartered Certified Accountants* [2006] BPIR 94.

S 391(4)

The Secretary of State has no express power to direct a recognised professional body as to how to discipline its members nor to discipline those members directly; however this provision enables the Secretary of State to revoke the authority of the body to license its members.

1.450

392 Authorisation by competent authority

(1) Application may be made to a competent authority for authorisation to act as an insolvency practitioner.

(2) The competent authorities for this purpose are—
  (a) in relation to a case of any description specified in directions given by the Secretary of State, the body or person so specified in relation to cases of that description, and
  (b) in relation to a case not falling within paragraph (a), the Secretary of State.

(3) The application—

(a) shall be made in such manner as the competent authority may direct,

(b) shall contain or be accompanied by such information as that authority may reasonably require for the purpose of determining the application, and

(c) shall be accompanied by the prescribed fee;

and the authority may direct that notice of the making of the application shall be published in such manner as may be specified in the direction.

(4) At any time after receiving the application and before determining it the authority may require the applicant to furnish additional information.

(5) Directions and requirements given or imposed under subsection (3) or (4) may differ as between different applications.

(6) Any information to be furnished to the competent authority under this section shall, if it so requires, be in such form or verified in such manner as it may specify.

(7) An application may be withdrawn before it is granted or refused.

(8) Any sums received under this section by a competent authority other than the Secretary of State may be retained by the authority; and any sums so received by the Secretary of State shall be paid into the Consolidated Fund.

(9) Subsection (3)(c) shall not have effect in respect of an application made to the Secretary of State (but this subsection is without prejudice to section 415A).

Notes

S 392(1)

Presently the only 'competent authority' is the Secretary of State.

S 392(9)

IA 1986 s 415A enables the Secretary of State to prescribe fees to be paid in a variety of circumstances.

1.451

393 Grant, refusal and withdrawal of authorisation

(1) The competent authority may, on an application duly made in accordance with section 392 and after being furnished with all such information as it may require under that section, grant or refuse the application.

(2) The authority shall grant the application if it appears to it from the information furnished by the applicant and having regard to such other information, if any, as it may have—

(a) that the applicant is a fit and proper person to act as an insolvency practitioner, and

(b) that the applicant meets the prescribed requirements with respect to education and practical training and experience.

(3) An authorisation granted under this section, if not previously withdrawn, continues in force for such period not exceeding the prescribed maximum as may be specified in the authorisation.

(4) An authorisation so granted may be withdrawn by the competent authority if it appears to it—
    (a)   that the holder of the authorisation is no longer a fit and proper person to act as an insolvency practitioner, or
    (b)   without prejudice to paragraph (a), that the holder—
        (i)   has failed to comply with any provision of this Part or of any regulations made under this Part or Part XV, or
        (ii)   in purported compliance with any such provision, has furnished the competent authority with false, inaccurate or misleading information.

(5) An authorisation granted under this section may be withdrawn by the competent authority at the request or with the consent of the holder of the authorisation.

Notes

S 393(1), (2)

Presently the only 'competent authority' is the Secretary of State. The Insolvency Practitioners Regulations 2005 (SI 2005/524) contain detailed provisions relating to the determination of whether an applicant is a fit and proper person including, amongst other matters, his educational qualifications, training and experience.

1.452

394 Notices

(1) Where a competent authority grants an authorisation under section 393, it shall give written notice of that fact to the applicant, specifying the date on which the authorisation takes effect.

(2) Where the authority proposes to refuse an application, or to withdraw an authorisation under section 393(4), it shall give the applicant or holder of the authorisation written notice of its intention to do so, setting out particulars of the grounds on which it proposes to act.

(3) In the case of a proposed withdrawal the notice shall state the date on which it is proposed that the withdrawal should take effect.

(4) A notice under subsection (2) shall give particulars of the rights exercisable under the next two sections by a person on whom the notice is served.

1.453

395 Right to make representations

(1) A person on whom a notice is served under section 394(2) may within 14 days after the date of service make written representations to the competent authority.

(2) The competent authority shall have regard to any representations so made in determining whether to refuse the application or withdraw the authorisation, as the case may be.

Notes

S 395(1)

The right to make representations is in addition to the right to require the matter to be referred to the Insolvency Practitioners Tribunal IA 1986 s 396(2).

1.454

396 Reference to Tribunal

(1) The Insolvency Practitioners Tribunal ('the Tribunal') continues in being; and the provisions of Schedule 7 apply to it.

(2) Where a person is served with a notice under section 394(2), he may—
   (a)   at any time within 28 days after the date of service of the notice, or
   (b)   at any time after the making by him of representations under section 395 and before the end of the period of 28 days after the date of the service on him of a notice by the competent authority that the authority does not propose to alter its decision in consequence of the representations,
give written notice to the authority requiring the case to be referred to the Tribunal.

(3) Where a requirement is made under subsection (2), then, unless the competent authority—
   (a)   has decided or decides to grant the application or, as the case may be, not to withdraw the authorisation, and
   (b)   within 7 days after the date of the making of the requirement, gives written notice of that decision to the person by whom the requirement was made,
it shall refer the case to the Tribunal.

1.455

397 Action of Tribunal on reference

(1) On a reference under section 396 the Tribunal shall—
   (a)   investigate the case, and
   (b)   make a report to the competent authority stating what would in their opinion be the appropriate decision in the matter and the reasons for that opinion,
and it is the duty of the competent authority to decide the matter accordingly.

(2) The Tribunal shall send a copy of the report to the applicant or, as the case may be, the holder of the authorisation; and the competent authority shall serve him with a written notice of the decision made by it in accordance with the report.

(3) The competent authority may, if he thinks fit, publish the report of the Tribunal.

Notes

S 397(1)

The Tribunal reports what in its opinion would be the 'appropriate' decision to make, together with its reasons for that opinion. It is however the competent authority which actually makes the decision; presently the only 'competent authority' is the Secretary of State see IA 1986 s 392.

1.456

398 Refusal or withdrawal without reference to Tribunal

Where in the case of any proposed refusal or withdrawal of an authorisation either—

(a) the period mentioned in section 396(2)(a) has expired without the making of any requirement under that subsection or of any representations under section 395, or

(b) the competent authority has given a notice such as is mentioned in section 396(2)(b) and the period so mentioned has expired without the making of any such requirement,

the competent authority may give written notice of the refusal or withdrawal to the person concerned in accordance with the proposal in the notice given under section 394(2).

Part XIV
Public Administration (England and Wales)

Official receivers

1.457

399 Appointment, etc of official receivers

(1) For the purposes of this Act the official receiver, in relation to any bankruptcy winding up or individual voluntary arrangement is any person who by virtue of the following provisions of this section or section 401 below is authorised to act as the official receiver in relation to that bankruptcy winding up or individual voluntary arrangement.

(2) The Secretary of State may (subject to the approval of the Treasury as to numbers) appoint persons to the office of official receiver, and a person appointed to that office (whether under this section or section 70 of the Bankruptcy Act 1914)—

(a) shall be paid out of money provided by Parliament such salary as the Secretary of State may with the concurrence of the Treasury direct,

(b) shall hold office on such other terms and conditions as the Secretary of State may with the concurrence of the Treasury direct, and

(c) may be removed from office by a direction of the Secretary of State.

(3) Where a person holds the office of official receiver, the Secretary of State shall from time to time attach him either to the High Court or to a county court having jurisdiction for the purposes of the second Group of Parts of this Act.

(4) Subject to any directions under subsection (6) below, an official receiver attached to a particular court is the person authorised to act as the official receiver in relation to every bankruptcy winding up or individual voluntary arrangement falling within the jurisdiction of that court.

(5) The Secretary of State shall ensure that there is, at all times, at least one official receiver attached to the High Court and at least one attached to each county court having jurisdiction for the purposes of the second Group of Parts; but he may attach the same official receiver to two or more different courts.

(6) The Secretary of State may give directions with respect to the disposal of the business of official receivers, and such directions may, in particular—

(a) authorise an official receiver attached to one court to act as the official receiver in relation to any case or description of cases falling within the jurisdiction of another court;

(b) provide, where there is more than one official receiver authorised to act as the official receiver in relation to cases falling within the jurisdiction of any court, for the distribution of their business between or among themselves.

(7) A person who at the coming into force of section 222 of the Insolvency Act 1985 (replaced by this section) is an official receiver attached to a court shall continue in office after the coming into force of that section as an official receiver attached to that court under this section.

Notes

S 399(1)

The office of official receiver is a statutory office which confers upon the holders of that office the power to bring proceedings in their own name and a right of audience before the court. Accordingly, when the official receiver brings proceedings personally, he does so as a litigant in person and is entitled to recover costs. Such costs are not limited to the official receiver's disbursements and will be assessed on a similar basis to those of an employed solicitor: *Re Minotaur Data Systems Ltd, Official Receiver v Brunt and others* [1999] 2 BCLC 766, CA which authority also contains a useful historical analysis of the nature of the office of official receiver.

An official receiver enjoys immunity from suit in respect of statements made by him while performing his duty as such and in the course of bankruptcy proceedings. The immunity extends to statements made preparatory to or for the purpose of proceedings: *Mond v Hyde* [1998] 2 BCLC 340, CA. In that case, a trustee in bankruptcy had accepted office for the purpose of recovering an asset for the estate in reliance upon a negligent statement by the official receiver to the effect that the right to issue the proceedings concerned had not been disclaimed by the receiver. In fact, the contrary was the case and the trustee in bankruptcy incurred substantial costs which he was unable to recover from the official receiver by reason of the immunity.

At the same time, the official receiver is an officer of the court (see IA 1986 s 400(2),) and as such subject to the rule in *ex parte James (1874) Re Condon* LR 9 Ch App 609, requiring him to act with utmost fairness. The effect of the rule applies between the estate and third parties and has no application in situations such as arose in *Mond v Hyde* (above). Although the official receiver is 'attached' to the court (IA 1986 s 399(5)) this is in an administrative rather than a substantive sense. It is unlikely that any claim that the court to which the official receiver is 'attached' cannot be an independent tribunal (for the purposes of the human rights legislation) would succeed on the basis that the official receiver is a regular litigant before the court.

S 399(2)

The remuneration of the official receiver is dealt with in detail in Insolvency Regulations 1994 para 33–36, Sch 2 SI 1994/2507 (as amended); those provisions establish that the remuneration is determined by reference to a 'realisation scale' and a 'distribution scale'.

1.458

400 Functions and status of official receivers

(1) In addition to any functions conferred on him by this Act, a person holding the office of official receiver shall carry out such other functions as may from time to time be conferred on him by the Secretary of State.

(2) In the exercise of the functions of his office a person holding the office of official receiver shall act under the general directions of the Secretary of State and shall also be an officer of the court in relation to which he exercises those functions.

(3) Any property vested in his official capacity in a person holding the office of official receiver shall, on his dying, ceasing to hold office or being otherwise succeeded in relation to the bankruptcy or winding up in question by another official receiver, vest in his successor without any conveyance, assignment or transfer.

1.459

401 Deputy official receivers and staff

(1) The Secretary of State may, if he thinks it expedient to do so in order to facilitate the disposal of the business of the official receiver attached to any court, appoint an officer of his department to act as deputy to that official receiver.

(2) Subject to any directions given by the Secretary of State under section 399 or 400, a person appointed to act as deputy to an official receiver has, on such conditions and for such period as may be specified in

the terms of his appointment, the same status and functions as the official receiver to whom he is appointed deputy.

Accordingly, references in this Act (except section 399(1) to (5)) to an official receiver include a person appointed to act as his deputy.

(3) An appointment made under subsection (1) may be terminated at any time by the Secretary of State.

(4) The Secretary of State may, subject to the approval of the Treasury as to numbers and remuneration and as to the other terms and conditions of the appointments, appoint officers of his department to assist official receivers in the carrying out of their functions.

The Official Petitioner

1.460

402 Official Petitioner

(1) There continues to be an officer known as the Official Petitioner for the purpose of discharging, in relation to cases in which a criminal bankruptcy order is made, the functions assigned to him by or under this Act; and the Director of Public Prosecutions continues, by virtue of his office, to be the Official Petitioner.

(2) The functions of the Official Petitioner include the following—
- (a) to consider whether, in a case in which a criminal bankruptcy order is made, it is in the public interest that he should himself present a petition under section 264(1)(d) of this Act;
- (b) to present such a petition in any case where he determines that it is in the public interest for him to do so;
- (c) to make payments, in such cases as he may determine, towards expenses incurred by other persons in connection with proceedings in pursuance of such a petition; and
- (d) to exercise, so far as he considers it in the public interest to do so, any of the powers conferred on him by or under this Act.

(3) Any functions of the Official Petitioner may be discharged on his behalf by any person acting with his authority.

(4) Neither the Official Petitioner nor any person acting with his authority is liable to any action or proceeding in respect of anything done or omitted to be done in the discharge, or purported discharge, of the functions of the Official Petitioner.

(5) In this section 'criminal bankruptcy order' means an order under section 39(1) of the Powers of Criminal Courts Act 1973.

Notes

S 402

This provision is repealed from a day to be appointed (*CJA 1988 s 170(2) Sch 16*).

Insolvency Service finance, accounting and investment

1.461

403 Insolvency Services Account

(1) All money received by the Secretary of State in respect of proceedings under this Act as it applies to England and Wales shall be paid into the Insolvency Services Account kept by the Secretary of State with the Bank of England; and all payments out of money standing to the credit of the Secretary of State in that account shall be made by the Bank of England in such manner as he may direct.

(2) Whenever the cash balance standing to the credit of the Insolvency Services Account is in excess of the amount which in the opinion of the Secretary of State is required for the time being to answer demands in respect of bankrupts' estates or companies' estates, the Secretary of State shall—
    (a)   notify the excess to the National Debt Commissioners, and
    (b)   pay into the Insolvency Services Investment Account ('the Investment Account') kept by the Commissioners with the Bank of England the whole or any part of the excess as the Commissioners may require for investment in accordance with the following provisions of this Part.

(3) Whenever any part of the money so invested is, in the opinion of the Secretary of State, required to answer any demand in respect of bankrupt's estates or companies' estates, he shall notify to the National Debt Commissioners the amount so required and the Commissioners—
    (a)   shall thereupon repay to the Secretary of State such sum as may be required to the credit of the Insolvency Services Account, and
    (b)   for that purpose may direct the sale of such part of the securities in which the money has been invested as may be necessary.

Notes

S 403

The section regulates the use of sums received in respect of proceedings under the Act. Such sums are to be paid into the Insolvency Services Account. Insofar as sums held in that account exceed the amount which the Secretary of State considers necessary for the purposes of answering demands in respect of bankrupts' or companies' estates, then the excess is to be invested according to the provisions of IA 1986 s 403(2). If the money that has been invested is subsequently required for the purpose of answering such demands then it shall be repaid back into the ordinary Insolvency Services Account in accordance with the provisions of IA 1986 s 403(3).

1.462

404 Investment Account

Any money standing to the credit of the Investment Account (including any money received by the National Debt Commissioners by way of interest on or proceeds of any investment under this section) may be invested by the Commissioners, in accordance with such directions as may be given by the Treasury, in any manner for the time being specified in part II of schedule 1 to the Trustee Investments Act 1961.

Notes

S 404

The section makes provision, by reference to the investment powers contained in part II of Schedule 1 to the Trustee Investments Act 1961, as to what may be done with money in the 'Investment Account' referred to in s 403(2) above.

1.463

[405 Application of income in Investment Account; adjustment of balances

(1) Where the annual account to be kept by the National Debt Commissioners under section 409 below shows that in the year for which it is made up the gross amount of the interest accrued from the securities standing to the credit of the Investment Account exceeded the aggregate of—

(a) a sum, to be determined by the Treasury, to provide against the depreciation in the value of the securities, and

(b) the sums paid into the Insolvency Services Account in pursuance of the next section together with the sums paid in pursuance of that section to the Commissioners of Inland Revenue,

the National Debt Commissioners shall, within 3 months after the account is laid before Parliament, cause the amount of the excess to be paid out of the Investment Account into the Consolidated Fund in such manner as may from time to time be agreed between the Treasury and the Commissioners.

(2) Where the said annual account shows that in the year for which it is made up the gross amount of interest accrued from the securities standing to the credit of the Investment Account was less than the aggregate mentioned in subsection (1), an amount equal to the deficiency shall, at such times as the Treasury direct, be paid out of the Consolidated Fund into the Investment Account.

(3) If the Investment Account is insufficient to meet its liabilities the Treasury may, on being informed of the insufficiency by the National Debt Commissioners, issue the amount of the deficiency out of the Consolidated Fund and the Treasury shall certify the deficiency to Parliament.]

Notes

S 405

This section was repealed by the Enterprise Act 2002 s 272(1), 278(2) as from 1 April 2004.

1.464

406 Interest on money received by liquidators or trustees in bankruptcy and invested

Where under rules made by virtue of paragraph 16 of Schedule 8 to this Act (investment of money received by company liquidators) [or paragraph 21 of Schedule 9 to this Act (investment of money received by trustee in bankruptcy) a company or a bankrupt's estate] has become entitled to any sum by way of interest, the Secretary of State shall certify that sum and the amount of tax payable on it to the National Debt Commissioners; and the Commissioners shall pay, out of the Investment Account—

(a)   into the Insolvency Services Account, the sum so certified less the amount of tax so certified, and

(b)   to the Commissioners of Inland Revenue, the amount of tax so certified.

Notes

S 406

The section makes provision for either a company in liquidation or a bankrupt's estate to benefit from any interest (less the appropriate tax payable on that interest) earned on sums which the liquidator or trustee has received and then paid into the Insolvency Services Account.

1.465

407 Unclaimed dividends and undistributed balances

(1) The Secretary of State shall from time to time pay into the Consolidated Fund out of the Insolvency Services Account so much of the sums standing to the credit of that Account as represents—

(a)   dividends which were declared before such date as the Treasury may from time to time determine and have not been claimed, and

(b)   balances ascertained before that date which are too small to be divided among the persons entitled to them.

(2) For the purposes of this section the sums standing to the credit of the Insolvency Services Account are deemed to include any sums paid out of that Account and represented by any sums or securities standing to the credit of the Investment Account.

(3) The Secretary of State may require the National Debt Commissioners to pay out of the Investment Account into the Insolvency Services Account the whole or part of any sum which he is required to pay out of that account under subsection (1); and the Commissioners may direct the sale of such securities standing to the credit of the Investment Account as may be necessary for that purpose.

Notes

S 407

The section makes provision for dividends and other amounts that remain unclaimed to be transferred into the Consolidated Fund, from where they will be used for the general purposes of Government.

1.466

408 Adjustment of balances

(1) The Treasury may direct the payment out of the Consolidated Fund of sums into–
- (a) Insolvency Services Account
- (b) Investment Account.

(2) The Treasury shall certify to the House of Commons the reason for any payment under subsection (1).

(3) The Secretary of State may pay sums out of the Insolvency Services Account into the Consolidated Fund.

(4) The National Debt Commissioners may pay sums out of the Investment Account into the Consolidated Fund.

1.467

409 Annual financial statement and audit

(1) The National Debt Commissioners shall for each year ending on 31 March prepare a statement of the sums credited and debited to the Investment Account in such form and manner as the Treasury may direct and shall transmit it to the Comptroller and Auditor General before the end of November next following the year.

(2) The Secretary of State shall for each year ending 31 March prepare a statement of the sums received or paid by him under section 403 above in such form and manner as the Treasury may direct and shall transmit each statement to the Comptroller and Auditor General before the end of November next following the year.

(3) Every such statement shall include such additional information as the Treasury may direct.

(4) The Comptroller and Auditor General shall examine, certify and report on every such statement and shall lay copies of it, and of his report, before Parliament.

Notes

S 409

Annual statements must be prepared detailing the activity on the Investment Account and the sums paid to or by the Secretary of State under section 403 above.

Supplementary

1.468

410 Extent of this Part

This Part of this Act extends to England and Wales only.

Part XV
Subordinate Legislation
General insolvency rules

1.469

411 Company insolvency rules

(1) Rules may be made—
  (a)   in relation to England and Wales, by the Lord Chancellor with the concurrence of the Secretary of State [and in the case of rules that affect court procedure, with the concurrence of the Lord Chief Justice], or
  (b)   in relation to Scotland, by the Secretary of State,
for the purpose of giving effect to Parts I to VII of this Act or the EC Regulation

(2) Without prejudice to the generality of subsection (1), or to any provision of those Parts by virtue of which rules under this section may be made with respect to any matter, rules under this section may contain—
  (a)   any such provision as is specified in Schedule 8 to this Act or corresponds to provision contained immediately before the coming into force of section 106 of the Insolvency Act 1985 in rules made, or having effect as if made, under section 663(1) or (2) of the Companies Act (old winding-up rules), and
  (b)   such incidental, supplemental and transitional provisions as may appear to the Lord Chancellor or, as the case may be, the Secretary of State necessary or expedient.

(2A) For the purpose of subsection (2), a reference in Schedule 8 to this Act to doing anything under or for the purposes of a provision of this Act includes a reference to doing anything under or for the purposes of the EC Regulation (in so far as the provision of this Act relates to a matter to which the EC Regulation applies).

(2B) Rules under this section for the purpose of giving effect to the EC Regulation may not create an offence of a kind referred to in paragraph (1)(1)(d) of Schedule 2 to the European Communities Act 1972.

(3) In Schedule 8 to this Act 'liquidator' includes a provisional liquidator; and references above in this section to Parts I to VII of this Act are to be read as including the Companies Act so far as relating to, and to matters connected with or arising out of, the insolvency or winding up of companies.

(4) Rules under this section shall be made by statutory instrument subject to annulment in pursuance of a resolution of either House of Parliament.

(5) Regulations made by the Secretary of State under a power conferred by rules under this section shall be made by statutory instrument and, after being made, shall be laid before each House of Parliament.

(6) Nothing in this section prejudices any power to make rules of court.

Notes

S 411

The section provides for the making of the subordinate legislation relating to company winding up. The main source of such provisions is SI No 1925 of 1986 which contains IR 1986 but numerous other rules and regulations have been made pursuant to the power given by this section. The words in square brackets in IA 1986 s 411(1) were inserted by the Constitutional Reform Act 2005 s 15(1) and come into force on a day to be appointed.

1.470

412 Individual insolvency rules (England and Wales)

(1) The Lord Chancellor may, with the concurrence of the Secretary of State State [and in the case of rules that affect court procedure, with the concurrence of the Lord Chief Justice], make rules for the purpose of giving effect to Parts VIII to XI of this Act or the EC Regulation.

(2) Without prejudice to the generality of subsection (1), or to any provision of those Parts by virtue of which rules under this section may be made with respect to any matter, rules under this section may contain—

(a) any such provision as is specified in Schedule 9 to this Act or corresponds to provision contained immediately before the appointed day in rules made under section 132 of the Bankruptcy Act 1914; and

(b) such incidental, supplemental and transitional provisions as may appear to the Lord Chancellor necessary or expedient.

(2A) For the purpose of subsection (2), a reference in Schedule 9 to this Act to doing anything under or for the purposes of a provision of this Act includes a reference to doing anything under or for the purposes of the EC Regulation (in so far as the provision of this Act relates to a matter to which the EC Regulation applies.

(2B) Rules under this section for the purpose of giving effect to the EC Regulation may not create an offence of a kind referred to in paragraph (1)(1)(d) of Schedule 2 to the European Communities Act 1972.

(3) Rules under this section shall be made by statutory instrument subject to annulment in pursuance of a resolution of either House of Parliament.

(4) Regulations made by the Secretary of State under a power conferred by rules under this section shall be made by statutory instrument and, after being made, shall be laid before each House of Parliament.

(5) Nothing in this section prejudices any power to make rules of court.

(6) The Lord Chief Justice may nominate a judicial office holder (as defined in section 109(4) of the Constitutional Reform Act 2005) to exercise his functions under this section

---

Notes

S 412(1)

The words in square brackets were inserted by the Constitutional Reform Act 2005 s 15(1) and come into force on a day to be appointed.

1.471

413 Insolvency Rules Committee

(1) The committee established under section 10 of the Insolvency Act 1976 (advisory committee on bankruptcy and winding-up rules) continues to exist for the purpose of being consulted under this section.

(2) The Lord Chancellor shall consult the committee before making any rules under section 411 or 412 other than rules which contain a statement that the only provision made by the rules is provision applying rules made under section 411, with or without modifications, for the purposes of provision made by [any of sections 23 to 26 of the Water Industry Act 1991 or Schedule 3 to that Act or by any of sections 59 to 65 of, or Schedule 6 or 7 to, the Railways Act 1993.

(3) Subject to the next subsection, the committee shall consist of—
  (a)   a judge of the High Court attached to the Chancery Division;
  (b)   a circuit judge;
  (c)   a registrar in bankruptcy of the High Court;
  (d)   the registrar of a county court;
  (e)   a practising barrister;
  (f)   a practising solicitor; and
  (g)   a practising accountant;
and the appointment of any person as a member of the committee shall be made by *the Lord Chancellor* [in accordance with subsection (3A) or (3B)].
[(3A) The Lord Chief Justice must appoint the persons referred to in paragraphs (a) to (d) of subsection (3) after consulting the Lord Chancellor
(3B)The Lord Chancellor must appoint the persons referred to in paragraphs (e) to (g) of subsection (3), after consulting the Lord Chief Justice]

(4) The Lord Chancellor may appoint as additional members of the committee any persons appearing to him to have qualifications or experience that would be of value to the committee in considering any matter with which it is concerned.

[(5) The Lord Chief Justice may nominate a judicial office holder (as defined in section 109(4) of the Constitutional Reform Act 2005) to exercise his functions under the scheme]

Notes

S 413

The Insolvency Rules Committee (the composition of which is as prescribed by IA 1986 s 413(3) and (4)) exists as a consultative body. It gives advice and makes recommendations to the Lord Chancellor who is charged with making the rules pursuant to s 411 (company insolvency) and s 412 (personal insolvency). In *Woodley v Woodley (No 2)* [1994] 1 WLR 1167 the court invited the Insolvency Rules Committee to consider whether certain debts should fall under the definition of provable debts under IR 1986 r 12.3. The words in square brackets in s 413 were inserted by the Consitutional Reform Act 2005 and they are effective from a day to be appointed; as regards IA 1986 s 413(3) the words in square brackets will replace the words in italics from a day to be appointed.

Fees orders

1.472

414 Fees orders (company insolvency proceedings)

(1) There shall be paid in respect of—
    (a) proceedings under any of Parts I to VII of this Act, and
    (b) the performance by the official receiver or the Secretary of State of functions under those Parts,
such fees as the competent authority may with the sanction of the Treasury by order direct.

(2) That authority is—
    (a) in relation to England and Wales, the Lord Chancellor, and
    (b) in relation to Scotland, the Secretary of State.

(3) The Treasury may by order direct by whom and in what manner the fees are to be collected and accounted for.

(4) The Lord Chancellor may, with the sanction of the Treasury, by order provide for sums to be deposited, by such persons, in such manner and in such circumstances as may be specified in the order, by way of security for fees payable by virtue of this section.

(5) An order under this section may contain such incidental, supplemental and transitional provisions as may appear to the Lord Chancellor, the Secretary of State or (as the case may be) the Treasury necessary or expedient.

(6) An order under this section shall be made by statutory instrument and, after being made, shall be laid before each House of Parliament.

(7) Fees payable by virtue of this section shall be paid into the Consolidated Fund.

(8) References in subsection (1) to Parts I to VII of this Act are to be read as including the Companies Act so far as relating to, and to matters connected with or arising out of, the insolvency or winding up of companies.

(9) Nothing in this section prejudices any power to make rules of court; and the application of this section to Scotland is without prejudice to section 2 of the Courts of Law Fees (Scotland) Act 1895.

Notes

S 414

The section makes provision for the setting of fees relating to company insolvency proceedings: see the Insolvency Proceedings (Fees) Order 2004 which revokes the Insolvency Fees Order 1986 almost wholly.

1.473

415 Fees orders (individual insolvency proceedings in England and Wales)

(1) There shall be paid in respect of—

(a) proceedings under Parts VIII to XI of this Act, and

(b) the performance by the official receiver or the Secretary of State of functions under those Parts,

such fees as the Lord Chancellor may with the sanction of the Treasury by order direct.

(2) The Treasury may by order direct by whom and in what manner the fees are to be collected and accounted for.

(3) The Lord Chancellor may, with the sanction of the Treasury, by order provide for sums to be deposited, by such persons, in such manner and in such circumstances as may be specified in the order, by way of security for—

(a) fees payable by virtue of this section, and

(b) fees payable to any person who has prepared an insolvency practitioner's report under section 274 in Chapter I of Part IX.

(4) An order under this section may contain such incidental, supplemental and transitional provisions as may appear to the Lord Chancellor or, as the case may be, the Treasury, necessary or expedient.

(5) An order under this section shall be made by statutory instrument and, after being made, shall be laid before each House of Parliament.

(6) Fees payable by virtue of this section shall be paid into the Consolidated Fund.

(7) Nothing in this section prejudices any power to make rules of court.

Notes

S 415

The section makes provision for the setting of fees relating to personal insolvency proceedings: see the Insolvency Proceedings (Fees) Order 2004 which revokes the Insolvency Fees Order 1986 almost wholly.

1.473A

415A Fees orders (general)

(1) The Secretary of State:

(a) may by order require a body to pay a fee in connection with the grant or maintenance of recognition of the body under section 391, and

(b) may refuse recognition, or revoke an order of recognition under section 391(1) by a further order, where a fee is not paid.

(2) The Secretary of State:

(a) may by order require a person to pay a fee in connection with the grant or maintenance of authorisation of the person under section 393, and

(b) may disregard an application or withdraw an authorisation where a fee is not paid.

(3) The Secretary of State may by order require the payment of fees in respect of:

(a) the operation of the Insolvency Services Account,
(b) payments into and out of that Account.

(4) The following provisions of section 414 apply to fees under this section as they apply to fees under that section:
(a) subsection (3) (manner of payment)
(b) subsection (5) (additional provision)
(c) subsection (6) (statutory instrument)
(d) subsection (7) (payment into Consolidated Fund), and
(e) subsection (9) (saving for rules of court).

Specification, increase and reduction of money sums relevant in the operation of this Act

1.474

416 Monetary limits (companies winding up)

(1) The Secretary of State may by order in a statutory instrument increase or reduce any of the money sums for the time being specified in the following provisions in the first Group of Parts—

section 117(2) (amount of company's share capital determining whether county court has jurisdiction to wind it up);

section 120(3) (the equivalent as respects sheriff court jurisdiction in Scotland);

section 123(1)(a) (minimum debt for service of demand on company by unpaid creditor);

section 184(3) (minimum value of judgment, affecting sheriff's duties on levying execution);

section 206(1)(a) and (b) (minimum value of company property concealed or fraudulently removed, affecting criminal liability of company's officer).

(2) An order under this section may contain such transitional provisions as may appear to the Secretary of State necessary or expedient.

(3) No order under this section increasing or reducing any of the money sums for the time being specified in section 117(2), 120(3), or 123(1)(a) shall be made unless a draft of the order has been laid before and approved by a resolution of each House of Parliament.

(4) A statutory instrument containing an order under this section, other than an order to which subsection (3) applies, is subject to annulment in pursuance of a resolution of either House of Parliament.

Notes

S 416

Changes in the various monetary amounts specified in the various sections referred to at IA 1986 ss (1) may be made by way of statutory instrument. This avoids the need for the passing of further Acts of Parliament in order to alter threshold amounts that may, by reason of inflation, have become outdated.

1.475

417 Money sum in s 222

The Secretary of State may by regulations in a statutory instrument increase or reduce the money sum for the time being specified in section 222(1) (minimum debt for service of demand on unregistered company by unpaid creditor); but such regulations shall not be made unless a draft of the statutory instrument containing them has been approved by resolution of each House of Parliament.

Notes

S 417

The minimum debt in respect of which a statutory demand can be served on an unregistered company is, at present, £750. This section provides that that amount may be changed by statutory instrument.

1.476

417A Money sums (company moratorium)

(1) The Secretary of State may by order increase or reduce any of the money sums for the time being specified in the following provisions of Schedule A1 to this Act—

paragraph 17(1) (maximum amount of credit which company may obtain without disclosure of moratorium);

paragraph 41(4) (minimum value of company property concealed or fraudulently removed, affecting criminal liability of company's officer).

(2) An order under this section may contain such transitional provisions as may appear to the Secretary of State necessary or expedient.

(3) An order under this section shall be made by statutory instrument subject to annulment in pursuance of a resolution of either House of Parliament.

Notes

S 417A

The section was introduced by IA 2000 and came into force on 1 January 2003. It empowers the Secretary of State to alter, by statutory instrument, the specified monetary limits set out in IA 1986 Sch A1.

1.477

418 Monetary limits (bankruptcy)

(1) The Secretary of State may by order prescribe amounts for the purposes of the following provisions in the second Group of Parts—

section 273 (minimum value of debtor's estate determining whether immediate bankruptcy order should be made; small bankruptcies level);

section 313A (value of property below which application for sale, possession or charge to be dismissed);

section 346(3) (minimum amount of judgment, determining whether amount recovered on sale of debtor's goods is to be treated as part of his estate in bankruptcy);

section 354(1) and (2) (minimum amount of concealed debt, or value of property concealed or removed, determining criminal liability under the s.);

section 358 (minimum value of property taken by a bankrupt out of England and Wales, determining his criminal liability);

section 360(1) (maximum amount of credit which bankrupt may obtain without disclosure of his status);

section 361(2) (exemption of bankrupt from criminal liability for failure to keep proper accounts, if unsecured debts not more than the prescribed minimum);

section 364(2)(d) (minimum value of goods removed by the bankrupt, determining his liability to arrest);

and references in the second Group of Parts to the amount prescribed for the purposes of any of those provisions, and references in those provisions to the prescribed amount, are to be construed accordingly.

(2) An order under this section may contain such transitional provisions as may appear to the Secretary of State necessary or expedient.

(3) An order under this section shall be made by statutory instrument subject to annulment in pursuance of a resolution of either House of Parliament.

Notes

S 418

This is the bankruptcy equivalent of IA 1986 s 416. Changes in the various monetary amounts specified in the various sections referred to at ss (1) may be made by way of statutory instrument. Again, this avoids the need for the passing of further Acts of Parliament in order to alter threshold amounts that may, by reason of inflation, have become outdated. The insertion of the reference to IA 1986 s 313A was made by EA 2002 and it came into force as from 1 April 2004.

Insolvency practice

I.478

419 Regulations for purposes of Part XIII

(1) The Secretary of State may make regulations for the purpose of giving effect to Part XIII of this Act; and 'prescribed' in that Part means prescribed by regulations made by the Secretary of State.

(2) Without prejudice to the generality of sub section (1) or to any provision of that Part by virtue of which regulations may be made with respect to any matter, regulations under this section may contain—

(a)   provision as to the matters to be taken into account in determining whether a person is a fit and proper person to act as an insolvency practitioner;

(b)   provision prohibiting a person from so acting in prescribed cases, being cases in which a conflict of interest will or may arise;

(c)   provision imposing requirements with respect to—

    (i)   the preparation and keeping by a person who acts as an insolvency practitioner of prescribed books, accounts and other records, and

    (ii)   the production of those books, accounts and records to prescribed persons;

(d)   provision conferring power on prescribed persons—

    (i)   to require any person who acts or has acted as an insolvency practitioner to answer any inquiry in relation to a case in which he is so acting or has so acted, and

    (ii)   to apply to a court to examine such a person or any other person on oath concerning such a case;

(e)   provision making non-compliance with any of the regulations a criminal offence; and

(f)   such incidental, supplemental and transitional provisions as may appear to the Secretary of State necessary or expedient.

(3) Any power conferred by Part XIII or this Part to make regulations, rules or orders is exercisable by statutory instrument subject to annulment by resolution of either House of Parliament.

(4) Any rule or regulation under Part XIII or this Part may make different provision with respect to different cases or descriptions of cases, including different provision for different areas.

Notes

S 419

The provisions of IA 1986 Part XIII, in relation to which this section gives the Secretary of State power to make regulations, govern insolvency practitioners and the qualifications which they must have.

Other order-making powers

1.479

420 Insolvent partnerships

(1) The Lord Chancellor may, by order made with the concurrence of the Secretary of State [and the Lord Chief Justice], provide that such provisions of this Act as may be specified in the order shall apply in relation to insolvent partnerships with such modifications as may be so specified.

(1A) An order under this section may make provision in relation to the EC Regulation.

(1B) But provision made by virtue of this section in relation to the EC Regulation may not create an offence of a kind referred to in paragraph 1(1)(d) of Schedule 2 to the European Communities Act 1972.

(2) An order under this section may make different provision for different cases and may contain such incidental, supplemental and transitional provisions as may appear to the Lord Chancellor [and the Lord Chief Justice] necessary or expedient.

(3) An order under this section shall be made by statutory instrument subject to annulment in pursuance of a resolution of either House of Parliament.

[(4) The Lord Chief Justice may nominate a judicial officer holder (as defined in section 109(4) of the Constitutional Reform Act 2005) to exercise his functions under this section]

Notes

S 420

The relevant order dealing with insolvent partnerships is the Insolvent Partnerships Order 1994 (as amended) which treats such a partnership as an unregistered company. The Insolvent Partnerships Order is separately annotated. The words in square brackets were inserted by the Constitutional Reform Act 2005 effective from a date to be appointed.

1.480

421 Insolvent estates of deceased persons

(1) The Lord Chancellor may, by order made with the concurrence of the Secretary of State [and the Lord Chief Justice], provide that such provisions of this Act as may be specified in the order shall apply in relation to the administration of the insolvent estates of deceased persons with such modifications as may be so specified.

(1A) An order under this section may make provision in relation to the EC Regulation.

(1B) But provision made by virtue of this section in relation to the EC Regulation may not create an offence of a kind referred to in paragraph 1(1)(d) of Schedule 2 to the European Communities Act 1972.

(2) An order under this section may make different provision for different cases and may contain such incidental, supplemental and transitional provisions as may appear to the Lord Chancellor [and the Lord Chief Justice] necessary or expedient.

(3) An order under this section shall be made by statutory instrument subject to annulment in pursuance of a resolution of either House of Parliament.

(4) For the purposes of this section the estate of a deceased person is insolvent if, when realised, it will be insufficient to meet in full all the debts and other liabilities to which it is subject.

[(5) The Lord Chief Justice may nominate a judicial officer holder (as defined in section 109(4) of the Constitutional Reform Act 2005) to exercise his functions under this section]

Notes

S 421

The relevant order is the Administration of Insolvent Estates of Deceased Persons Order 1986 (as amended) which is separately annotated. Though it is not encountered often in practice the Court of Appeal considered its terms in relation to an insolvency administration order in *Re Palmer* [1994] Ch 316. The effect of the decision in *Re Palmer* was reversed by the insertion of IA 1986 s 421A by IA 2000. The words in square brackets were inserted by the Constitutional Reform Act 2005 effective from a date to be appointed.

1.481

421A Insolvent estates: joint tenancies

(1) This section applies where—
- (a) an insolvency administration order has been made in respect of the insolvent estate of a deceased person,
- (b) the petition for the order was presented after the commencement of this section and within the period of five years beginning with the day on which he died, and
- (c) immediately before his death he was beneficially entitled to an interest in any property as joint tenant.

(2) For the purpose of securing that debts and other liabilities to which the estate is subject are met, the court may, on an application by the trustee appointed pursuant to the insolvency administration order, make an order under this section requiring the survivor to pay to the trustee an amount not exceeding the value lost to the estate.

(3) In determining whether to make an order under this section, and the terms of such an order, the court must have regard to all the circumstances of the case, including the interests of the deceased's creditors and of the survivor; but, unless the circumstances are exceptional, the court must assume that the interests of the deceased's creditors outweigh all other considerations.

(4) The order may be made on such terms and conditions as the court thinks fit.

(5) Any sums required to be paid to the trustee in accordance with an order under this section shall be comprised in the estate.

(6) The modifications of this Act which may be made by an order under section. 421 include any modifications which are necessary or expedient in consequence of this section.

(7) In this section, 'survivor' means the person who, immediately before the death, was beneficially entitled as joint tenant with the deceased or, if the person who was so entitled dies after the making of the insolvency administration order, his personal representatives.

(8) If there is more than one survivor—
   (a) an order under this section may be made against all or any of them, but
   (b) no survivor shall be required to pay more than so much of the value lost to the estate as is properly attributable to him.

(9) In this section.—
   'insolvency administration order' has the same meaning as in any order under section 421 having effect for the time being,
   'value lost to the estate' means the amount which, if paid to the trustee, would in the court's opinion restore the position to what it would have been if the deceased had been adjudged bankrupt immediately before his death.

Notes

S 421A

This provision was enacted to deal with the effect of the decision of the Court of Appeal in *Re Palmer* [1994] Ch 316. The Court of Appeal held that where a joint tenant was insolvent at the date of death his interest passed to the other joint tenant rather than being made available for the creditors of the insolvent joint tenant. The Court now has under IA 1986 s 421A a wide discretion to order the surviving joint tenant to pay to the trustee an amount not exceeding the value lost to the estate of the insolvent joint tenant.

1.482

422 Recognised banks, etc

(1) The Secretary of State may by order made with the concurrence of the Treasury and after consultation with the Financial Services Authority provide that specified provisions in the first Group of Parts shall apply with modifications in relation to any person who-

(a) has a liability in respect of a deposit which he has accepted in accordance with the Banking Act 1979 (c.37) or 1987 (c.22) but

(b) does not have permission inder Part IV of the Financial Services and Markets Act 200 (c.8) (regulated activities) to accept deposits.

(1A) Subsection 1(b) shall be construed in accordance with-
   (a) section 22 of the Financial Services and Markets Act 2000 (classes of regulated activity and categories of investment),
   (b) any relevant order under that section, and
   (c) Schedule 2 to that Act (regulated activities).

(2) An order under this section may make different provision for different cases and may contain such incidental, supplemental and transitional provisions as may appear to the Secretary of State necessary or expedient.

(3) An order under this section shall be made by statutory instrument subject to annulment in pursuance of a resolution of either House of Parliament.

Notes

S 422

Power is given to the Secretary of State to determine (by statutory instrument) that the provisions of IA 1986 Parts I to VII (i.e. those Parts relating to company insolvency) shall apply – with any specified modifications – in relation to persons or bodies having liabilities in respect of deposits held by them in accordance with the Banking Acts.

Part XVI
Provisions Against Debt Avoidance (England and Wales only)

1.483

423 Transactions defrauding creditors

(1) This section relates to transactions entered into at an undervalue; and a person enters into such a transaction with another person if—
- (a) he makes a gift to the other person or he otherwise enters into a transaction with the other on terms that provide for him to receive no consideration;
- (b) he enters into a transaction with the other in consideration of marriage [or the formation of a civil partnership]; or
- (c) he enters into a transaction with the other for a consideration the value of which, in money or money's worth, is significantly less than the value, in money or money's worth, of the consideration provided by himself.

(2) Where a person has entered into such a transaction, the court may, if satisfied under the next subsection, make such order as it thinks fit for—
- (a) restoring the position to what it would have been if the transaction had not been entered into, and
- (b) protecting the interests of persons who are victims of the transaction.

(3) In the case of a person entering into such a transaction, an order shall only be made if the court is satisfied that it was entered into by him for the purpose—
- (a) of putting assets beyond the reach of a person who is making, or may at some time make, a claim against him, or
- (b) of otherwise prejudicing the interests of such a person in relation to the claim which he is making or may make.

(4) In this section 'the court' means the High Court or—
- (a) if the person entering into the transaction is an individual, any other court which would have jurisdiction in relation to a bankruptcy petition relating to him;

> (b)   if that person is a body capable of being wound up under Part IV or V of this Act, any other court having jurisdiction to wind it up.
>
> (5) In relation to a transaction at an undervalue, references here and below to a victim of the transaction are to a person who is, or is capable of being, prejudiced by it; and in the following two sections the person entering into the transaction is referred to as 'the debtor'.

———

Notes

S 423

This is an important provision enabling certain transactions to be attacked whether or not the person who enters the transaction is in an insolvency procedure or not. The burden of proof is on the applicant *Habib Bank Ltd v Ahmed* [2004] BPIR 35 and the application should be made by claim form rather than an originating/ordinary application *Banca Carige SPA v Banco Nactional de Cuba* [2001] BPIR 407 although in practice the court would not normally regard that as a substantive issue. In general terms, s 423 entitles the court to grant appropriate relief where it appears that a transaction at an undervalue has taken place for the purpose of putting assets beyond the reach of an actual or potential claimant or otherwise prejudicing that person's interests. It is a provision which is dependent on the applicant satisfying the court of the fraudulent purpose of the transaction (s 423(3)) and the court may put aside professional privilege to ascertain the true purpose of the transaction *Barclays Bank v Eustice* [1995] 1 WLR 1238. It is not necessary to prove that the transaction under scrutiny was a risky or hazardous one *Sands v Clitheroe* [2006] BPIR 1000. While superficially similar to other anti-avoidance provision (eg s 238, s 339 IA 1986), it has a number of important differences including: (1) it applies to both companies and individuals; (2) it applies whether or not there is an insolvency; (*Trowbridge v Trowbridge* [2002] EWHC 3114 (Ch), [2003] BPIR 258).

Limitation

The questions of whether there is any statutory limitation period for an application under s 423, and if so when time begins to run, were considered by the Court of Appeal in *Re Nurkowski* [2006] BPIR 789. The position is that Limitation Act 1980 does apply, and that the period will be either 6 or 12 years depending on whether the relief sought is substantively a sum of money (6 years under s 9 LA 1980) or other relief (12 years for a specialty: s 8 LA 1980). See also *Re Priory Garage (Walthamstow) Ltd* [2001] BPIR 144 distinguishing *Re Farmizer Products Ltd* [1995] 2 BCLC 462, [1997] 1 BCLC 589) and analysing s 8, 9 Limitation Act 1980 and the discussion in *Re Yates* [2005] BPIR 476. As to the question of when time starts to run, the majority of the Court of Appeal in *Re Nurkowski* (above) held that there was no inherent objection to separate limitation periods for different applicants. In the case of a trustee in bankruptcy this would presumably be from the date of his appointment except where the official receiver was appointed earlier in which case it would be the date of that appointment. In the case of a claim by a liquidator it would be the date of the winding up order or winding up resolution; in a claim by an administrator the date of the commencement of the administration; and in respect of a supervisor the date the proposals were approved.

S 423(1)

The definition of 'transaction at an undervalue' is the same as appears in s 339 (transactions at an undervalue: individual insolvency) and differs from s 238 (transactions at an undervalue: corporate insolvency) only in that it also covers transactions in consideration of marriage (something which for obvious reasons cannot apply to a company). In short, it covers (a) a gift or transaction for no consideration, (b) a transaction in consideration of marriage, and (c) a transaction for a consideration worth significantly less than that provided by the person. It has been held that the giving of a security cannot constitute a transaction at an undervalue (*Re MC Bacon Ltd (No 1)* [1990] BCLC 324, *Agricultural Mortgage Corpn Plc v Woodward* [1995] 1

BCLC 1, *Re Brabon* [2001] 1 BCLC 11). However this was doubted in *Hill, (as Trustee in Bankruptcy of Nurkowski) v Spread Trustee Company Ltd and another* [2006] BPIR 789, 821 per Arden LJ.

The word 'transaction' connotes a dealing between the parties and would not include the transfer of property in which the transferor does not have a beneficial interest (*Re Taylor Sinclair (Capital) Ltd* [2002] BPIR 203, *Pozzuto v Iacovides* [2003] EWHC 431 (Ch), [2003] BPIR 999, *Mears v Latif* [2006] BPIR 80). In assessing whether or not a transaction has occurred the court takes a realistic approach in analysing the relevant arrangements and the court is willing to 'link' arrangements to constitute a 'transaction' within the provision *Phillips v Brewin Dolphin Bell Lawrie Ltd* [2001] UKHL 2, [2001] 1 WLR 143 and *National Westminster Bank plc v Jones* [2001] EWCA Civ 1541, [2000] BPIR 1092, [2002] BPIR 361; see also *Defra v Feakins* [2006] BPIR 895 where the court was prepared to read '*enter into .. a transaction* ' as meaning '*participate in an arrangement*' to bring within s 423(1) an arrangement amongst several family members and a company controlled by family members.

A liquidator or a trustee in bankruptcy needs sanction before making a s 423 application (ss 165, 167 Sch 4 para 3A and s 314, Sch 5 para 2A respectively). Although as stated above it is not necessary to prove that a person was insolvent when he entered into a transaction to defraud creditors it is clearly helpful evidentially if he can be proved to have been or become insolvent at that time.

S 423(1)(b)

This provision was amended by the Civil Partnership Act 2004 effective from 5 December 2005

S 423(1)(c)

As to what constitutes an 'undervalue' reference should be made to the notes under s 238, 339; a substantial amount of 'bounty' is usually involved and in a corporate case under s 238 it was observed that a difference in the sale price and a valuation of 10% could be explained by reference to a genuine difference in view between different valuers *Re Marini Ltd* [2004] BCC 172.

S 423(2)

Though the burden of proof of fraud under s 423(3) is heavy the applicant should consider an interim application for relief under s 423 in cases of real urgency *Walker v WA Personnel Ltd* [2002] BPIR 621, (injunction/appointment of receiver under s 238) *Dept of Environment v Feakins and Hawkins* [2002] BPIR 281 (freezing order under s 423).

S 423(2)(a)

An order for restoration would normally take account of the value of any interest which the respondent had in property prior to it being involved in a transaction defrauding creditors, *Chohan v Saggar* [1994] BCC 134 and *Kubiangha v Ekpenyong* [2003] BPIR 623; in the latter case a wife to whom the matrimonial home was transferred for no consideration was able to claim a share in its equity due to her contributions over the years although she had never been registered as an owner. For specific orders capable of being made on such an application, see s 425(1). However the court will not make an order restoring the position to what it would have been if the transaction had not occurred where the person entering the transaction would have been no better off had the transaction not occurred; for instance the transaction in question is a transfer of a business and the individual/corporate transferor was on the verge of entering bankruptcy/liquidation and the business would have been worthless in such an event *Re MDA Investment Management Ltd* [2004] BPIR 75. Similarly an order under s 423(2) cannot put the applicant in a better position than he would have been if the transaction had not occurred *Ram v Ram* [2005] BPIR 616

S 423(3)

In addition, to establishing a transaction at an undervalue, it must be shown that the person entered into the transaction for the purpose of putting assets beyond the reach of an actual or potential claimant or otherwise prejudicing such a person and the evidence of that purpose should be specific not speculative (*Law Society v Southall* [2002] BPIR 336); the motivation of the transferee in entering the transaction is not relevant in establishing the requisite purpose *Moon v Franklin* [1996] BPIR 196. However the court has not been slow to take a purposive and realistic approach to unscrambling transactions at an undervalue which clearly prejudice creditors *Agricultural Mortgage Corporation plc v Woodward* [1995] 1 BCLC 1, *National Westminster Bank plc v Jones* [2001] EWCA Civ 1541, [2002] 1 BCLC 55. The relevant purpose relates to the intention of the person making the transaction and it is tested subjectively *Pagemanor Ltd v Ryan* [2002] BPIR 593 and the fact that the respondent was acting on legal advice does not exclude him/her from having the relevant purpose *Arbuthnot Leasing International Ltd v Havelet Leasing Ltd (No 2)* [1990] BCC 636. The purpose or intention of the other party to the transaction is not relevant at the liability stage (see *Moon v Franklin* [1996] BPIR 196), although it may be relevant at the later stage of determining the appropriate relief to be granted: see s 425(2).

As to the appropriate test at first instance in *Chohan v Saggar* [1992] BCC 306 (on appeal [1994] BCC 134) it was held that that purpose had to be the dominant one; in *Royscot Spa Leasing Ltd v Lovett* [1995] BCC 502, however, it was held that it would be sufficient if the purpose was a substantial one. The matter was finally resolved by the Court of Appeal in *IRC v Hashmi* [2002] BPIR 974 which held that the dominant purpose test was no longer appropriate. Instead, as Arden LJ said at page 981 paragraph 25:

> '... for something to be a purpose it must be a real substantial purpose; it is not sufficient to quote something which is a by-product of the transaction under consideration, or to show that it was simply a result of it ...or an element which made no contribution of importance to the debtor's purpose of carrying out the transaction under consideration ...'.

That ruling was confirmed in *Habib Bank Ltd v Ahmed* [2003] EWHC 1697 (Ch), [2004] BPIR 35.

S 423(5)

A 'victim' is defined as a person who is (or is capable of being) prejudiced by the transaction in question; it would include a creditor of an insolvent company *Re Ayala Holdings Ltd* [1993] BCLC 256. The significance of being such a victim is that it entitles such a person to apply for relief under s 423: see s 424(1)(c). Although the section applies whether or not there is an insolvency, for the purposes of s 423–425 the person entering the transaction is referred to as the 'debtor'. The victim need not necessarily be the person referred to in s 423(3)(a), (b). Thus one can still be a 'victim' of the transaction though the debtor enters the transaction with the purpose of putting assets beyond the reach or otherwise prejudicing the interests of a person different to the 'victim'; see *Re Nurkowski* [2006] BPIR 789, 812ff per Arden LJ, *Sands v Clitheroe* [2006] BPIR 1000.

I.484

424 Those who may apply for an order under s 423

(1) An application for an order under section 423 shall not be made in relation to a transaction except—

    (a)   in a case where the debtor has been adjudged bankrupt or is a body corporate which is being wound up or is in administration, by the official receiver, by the trustee of the bankrupt's estate or the liquidator or administrator of the body corporate or (with the leave of the court) by a victim of the transaction;

> (b)   in a case where a victim of the transaction is bound by a voluntary arrangement approved under Part I or Part VIII of this Act, by the supervisor of the voluntary arrangement or by any person who (whether or not so bound) is such a victim; or
>
> (c)   in any other case, by a victim of the transaction.
>
> (2) An application made under any of the paragraphs of subsection (1) is to be treated as made on behalf of every victim of the transaction.

S 424(1)

This section deals with the categories of person who may bring an application under section 423; (under s 375 Financial Services and Markets Act 2000 in certain circumstances an application can be made by the Financial Services Authority). In short, where the debtor (the person whose transaction is being challenged) is not insolvent, the application must be made by either a victim of the transaction (as defined in section 423(5)), or where the victim is bound by a voluntary arrangement, such victim's supervisor: section 424(1)(b), (c). Where, however, the debtor is insolvent, in general the application must be made by the relevant insolvency practitioner (the liquidator, administrator, official receiver or trustee in bankruptcy as the case may be), although a victim of the transaction may also bring such an application with the leave of the court: s 424(1)(a); the court probably has jurisdiction to grant leave retrospectively *Dora v Simper* [1999] BCC 836.

S 424(2)

Importantly, however, whoever brings the application, it is deemed to have been brought on behalf of every victim of the transaction and where an order for payment of money is requested by the applicant steps may have to be taken to establish the identity of all the victims of the transaction so that they may benefit from the order.

1.485

425 Provision which may be made by order under s 423

(1) Without prejudice to the generality of section 423, an order made under that section with respect to a transaction may (subject as follows)—

> (a)   require any property transferred as part of the transaction to be vested in any person, either absolutely or for the benefit of all the persons on whose behalf the application for the order is treated as made;
>
> (b)   require any property to be so vested if it represents, in any person's hands, the application either of the proceeds of sale of property so transferred or of money so transferred;
>
> (c)   release or discharge (in whole or in part) any security given by the debtor;
>
> (d)   require any person to pay to any other person in respect of benefits received from the debtor such sums as the court may direct;
>
> (e)   provide for any surety or guarantor whose obligations to any person were released or discharged (in whole or in part) under the transaction to be under such new or revived obligations as the court thinks appropriate;
>
> (f)   provide for security to be provided for the discharge of any obligation imposed by or arising under the order, for such an

obligation to be charged on any property and for such security or charge to have the same priority as a security or charge released or discharged (in whole or in part) under the transaction.

(2) An order under section 423 may affect the property of, or impose any obligation on, any person whether or not he is the person with whom the debtor entered into the transaction; but such an order—

(a) shall not prejudice any interest in property which was acquired from a person other than the debtor and was acquired in good faith, for value and without notice of the relevant circumstances, or prejudice any interest deriving from such an interest, and

(b) shall not require a person who received a benefit from the transaction in good faith, for value and without notice of the relevant circumstances to pay any sum unless he was a party to the transaction.

(3) For the purposes of this section the relevant circumstances in relation to a transaction are the circumstances by virtue of which an order under section 423 may be made in respect of the transaction.

(4) In this section 'security' means any mortgage, charge, lien or other security.

S 425(1)

The court may make an order with extra territorial effect *Jyske Bank (Gibraltar) Ltd v Spjeldnaes (No 2)* [1999] BPIR 525. The overriding provision for relief is contained in s 423(2) which gives the court wide powers to restore the position to what it would have been if the transaction had not been entered into and protect the interests of the victims of the transaction. Without prejudice to the above, however, s 425(1) goes on to give specific examples of orders which might be made; reference can be made to the notes on the similar order making powers of the court under s 241(1) and s 342(1).

S 425(2)

Relief granted under s 423(2) may include relief which affects third parties. Where, however, the third party has acquired property in good faith and for value, s 425(2) offers some limited protection.

S 425(3)

Knowledge of the relevant circumstances would presumably include knowledge of the fact that the transaction was at an undervalue (s 423(1)) and that it was carried out with the purpose stated in s 423(3); this may present a difficult evidential burden for the applicant.

S 425(4)

See notes to *IA 1986 s 248*.

Part XVII
Miscellaneous and General

1.486

426 Co-operation between courts exercising jurisdiction in relation to insolvency

(1) An order made by a court in any part of the United Kingdom in the exercise of jurisdiction in relation to insolvency law shall be enforced in

any other part of the United Kingdom as if it were made by a court exercising the corresponding jurisdiction in that other part.

(2) However, without prejudice to the following provisions of this section, nothing in subsection (1) requires a court in any part of the United Kingdom to enforce, in relation to property situated in that part, any order made by a court in any other part of the United Kingdom.

(3) The Secretary of State, with the concurrence in relation to property situated in England and Wales of the Lord Chancellor, may by order make provision for securing that a trustee or assignee under the insolvency law of any part of the United Kingdom has, with such modifications as may be specified in the order, the same rights in relation to any property situated in another part of the United Kingdom as he would have in the corresponding circumstances if he were a trustee or assignee under the insolvency law of that other part.

(4) The courts having jurisdiction in relation to insolvency law in any part of the United Kingdom shall assist the courts having the corresponding jurisdiction in any other part of the United Kingdom or any relevant country or territory.

(5) For the purposes of subsection (4) a request made to a court in any part of the United Kingdom by a court in any other part of the United Kingdom or in a relevant country or territory is authority for the court to which the request is made to apply, in relation to any matters specified in the request, the insolvency law which is applicable by either court in relation to comparable matters falling within its jurisdiction.

In exercising its discretion under this subsection, a court shall have regard in particular to the rules of private international law.

(6) Where a person who is a trustee or assignee under the insolvency law of any part of the United Kingdom claims property situated in any other part of the United Kingdom (whether by virtue of an order under subsection (3) or otherwise), the submission of that claim to the court exercising jurisdiction in relation to insolvency law in that other part shall be treated in the same manner as a request made by a court for the purpose of subsection (4).

(7) Section 38 of the Criminal Law Act 1977 (execution of warrant of arrest throughout the United Kingdom) applies to a warrant which, in exercise of any jurisdiction in relation to insolvency law, is issued in any part of the United Kingdom for the arrest of a person as it applies to a warrant issued in that part of the United Kingdom for the arrest of a person charged with an offence.

(8) Without prejudice to any power to make rules of court, any power to make provision by subordinate legislation for the purpose of giving effect in relation to companies or individuals to the insolvency law of any part of the United Kingdom includes power to make provision for the purpose of giving effect in that part to any provision made by or under the preceding provisions of this section.

(9) An order under subsection (3) shall be made by statutory instrument subject to annulment in pursuance of a resolution of either House of Parliament.

(10) In this section 'insolvency law' means—
  (a) in relation to England and Wales, provision extending to England and Wales and] made by or under this Act or sections 1A, 6 to 10, 12 to 15, 19(c) and 20 (with Schedule 1) of the Company Directors Disqualification Act 1986 and sections 1 to 17 of that Act as they apply for the purposes of those provisions of that Act;
  (b) in relation to Scotland, provision extending to Scotland and made by or under this Act, sections 1A, 6 to 10, 12 to 15, 19(c) and 20 (with Schedule 1) of the Company Directors Disqualification Act 1986 and sections 1 to 17 of that Act as they apply for the purposes of those provisions of that Act, Part XVIII of the Companies Act or the Bankruptcy (Scotland) Act 1985;
  (c) in relation to Northern Ireland, provision made by or under the Insolvency (Northern Ireland) Order 1989 [*or Part II of the Companies (Northern Ireland) Order 1989] [not yet in force]*.
  (d) in relation to any relevant country or territory, so much of the law of that country or territory as corresponds to provisions falling within any of the foregoing paragraphs;
and references in this subsection to any enactment include, in relation to any time before the coming into force of that enactment the corresponding enactment in force at that time.

(11) In this section 'relevant country or territory' means—
  (a) any of the Channel Islands or the Isle of Man, or
  (b) any country or territory designated for the purposes of this section by the Secretary of State by order made by statutory instrument.

[(12) In the application of this section to Northern Ireland—
  (a) for any reference to the Secretary of State there is substituted a reference to the Department of Economic Development in Northern Ireland;
  (b) in subsection (3) for the words 'another part of the United Kingdom' and the words 'that other part' there are substituted the words 'Northern Ireland';
  (c) for subsection (9) there is substituted the following subsection—

'(9) An order made under subsection (3) by the Department of Economic Development in Northern Ireland shall be a statutory rule for the purposes of the Statutory Rules (Northern Ireland) Order 1979 and shall be subject to negative resolution within the meaning of section 41(6) of the Interpretation Act (Northern Ireland) 1954.'] [*not yet in force so far as amends sub-section (11)(b)].*

Notes

Introduction

IA 1986 s 426 provides a statutory means by which the English court may recognise and act in aid of foreign insolvency procedures. It is limited to procedures taking place in certain designated countries; mainly Commonwealth countries which may be expected to have similar systems, principles, procedures and legal traditions. It stands alongside, and in certain respects supplements:

- The common law, as to which see *Re HIH Casualty and General Insurance Limited* [2006] 2 All ER 671 (David Richards J); [2006] EWCA Civ 732; *Cambridge Gas Transport Corporation v The Official Committee of Unsecured Creditors of Navigator Holdings plc and others* [2006] UKPC 26.
- The Cross-Border Insolvency Regulations 2006 (which implement the UNCITRAL Model Law on Cross Border Insolvency) under which a foreign insolvency representative can apply to the British court to start British insolvency proceedings or to participate in British insolvency proceedings and further to obtain recognition and relief for foreign insolvency proceedings.
- The EC Regulation on Insolvency Proceedings 2000 (which is separately annotated) which provides for the mutual recognition of insolvency proceedings as between members of the EU.

S 426(1), (2)

The effect of these subsections is that court orders in insolvency matters are enforceable throughout the UK, even if they originated in another part of the UK, unless they relate to property in the part of the UK where enforcement is sought. Thus an order by a court in England under IA 1986 s 241(1)(d) requiring a person to repay money in respect of a preference or transaction at an undervalue can be enforced in Scotland or Northern Ireland.

'any part of the United Kingdom' This refers to the three jurisdictions or law districts which the UK includes: England and Wales, Scotland, and Northern Ireland. Subsections (1) and (2) only have effect with respect to the UK, in contrast to subsections (4) and (5), discussed below, which extend to other countries as well. The UK does not include the Isle of Man or the Channel Islands.

'insolvency law' This is defined, widely, in subsection (10). s 426 applies to limited liability partnerships with certain modifications Limited Liability Partnerships Regulations 2001 reg 5(1)(b)

S 426(3), (9)

No order has been made pursuant to this subsection to date.

S 426(4), (5)

These subsections give the English court a discretion to assist courts in any other part of the UK (see notes to IA 1986 s 426(1)) and specified foreign countries: see note to IA 1986 s 426(11)). IA 1986 s 426 does not concern 'insolvency proceedings' as defined in IR 1986 r 13.7. Accordingly, IR 1986 r 12.12 (service outside jurisdiction) is not applicable and CPR Part 6.20 applies in respect of serving proceedings outside the jurisdiction: *Fourie v Le Roux* [2005] BPIR 723.

In order to give the English court jurisdiction the letter of request must be specific and in particular spell out what the English court is being asked to do: *Fourie v Le Roux* [2005] BPIR 723. The English courts having jurisdiction in relation to insolvency law (as widely defined in subsection IA 1986 s 426(10)) are obliged to assist 'the courts having the corresponding jurisdiction' abroad. It follows that the request has to come from a court, not (directly at least) from a foreign office holder. It is clear from authorities such as *Hughes v Hannover-Ruckversicherungs AG* [1997] 1 BCLC 49, *England v Smith* [2001] Ch 419 and *Re HIH Casualty and General Insurance Ltd* (above) that the English courts have a discretion whether to give the assistance requested, despite the use of mandatory words in IA 1986 s 426(4) ('..shall assist..'). However the discretion should be exercised in favour of assistance unless there is a good reason to the contrary and the existence of the request is a highly material factor in favour of granting assistance: *Re Bank of Credit and Commerce International SA (No 9)* [1994] 3 All ER 764, 785; *Duke Group Ltd v Carver* [2001] BCC 144. A good reason to the contrary would include a material change in circumstances since a request was made by the foreign court: *Hughes v Hannover-Ruckversicherungs AG* [1997] BCC 921; *Re Focus Insurance Co Ltd* [1996] BCC 659; or where the court is satisfied that the making of an order would be oppressive: *Re Southern Equities Corp Ltd*; *England v Smith* [2000] 2 BCLC 21.

'the corresponding jurisdiction' This means jurisdiction in relation to insolvency matters, rather than jurisdiction in the foreign country to do precisely what is asked in England: *Re Television Trade Rentals Ltd* [2002] BCC 807. The English courts can assist by applying English insolvency law, their general powers under English law, or the insolvency law of the foreign country in question: IA 1986 s 426(5); *Hughes v Hannover-Ruckversicherungs AG* (above). The English courts can apply English insolvency law even if, in the absence of a request under IA 1986 s 426(1), the relevant provision of the IA 1986 would not have applied; for example because the company in question was an overseas company: *Re Television Trade Rentals Ltd* [2002] BCC 807.

'have regard ... to the rules of private international law' This provision has been described as obscure and ill thought out: *Re Television Trade Rentals Ltd* [2002] BCC 807; *Re HIH Casualty and General Insurance Ltd* (above). It appears to mean at least that the court should take into account the foreign element when deciding which law to apply, such as the connections of the parties with England and with the foreign country: *Re Television Trade Rentals Ltd* (above).

Examples of the application of English insolvency law include: (i) making an administration order in respect of a foreign company: *Re Dallhold Estates (UK) Pty Ltd* [1992] BCLC 621; (ii) applying the provisions of the IA 1986 relating to fraudulent and wrongful trading: *Re Bank of Credit and Commerce International SA (No 9)* [1994] 3 All ER 764; (iii) ordering the production of documentation: *Re J.N.Taylor Finance Pty Ltd* [1999] 2 BCLC 256; *Re Trading Partners Ltd* [2002] BPIR 606; (iv) giving effect to a foreign scheme of arrangement: *Re Business City Express Ltd* [1997] BCC 826 (v) obtaining an order seeking the aid of a foreign court in realising a bankruptcy estate: *Dick v McIntosh* [2002] BPIR 290. *Hughes v Hannover-Ruckversicherungs (above)* was a case where the English court was asked to assist by exercising one of its general powers under English law, namely to grant an injunction.

An example of the English court assisting by applying foreign insolvency law is *England v Smith* (above). In that case the Court of Appeal made an order for the examination of an individual pursuant to an Australian provision, even though such an examination would not have been ordered under IA 1986 s 236.

S 426(6)

For *'any part of the United Kingdom'* see the notes to IA 1986 s 426(1), (2) above; thus a trustee or assignee under the insolvency law of any part of the UK claims property in another part of the UK he can apply to the court in which the property is situated to deal with the claim notwithstanding that there has not been a request from a court for assistance.

S 426(11)

'relevant country or territory' subsections (4) and (5) provide for assistance to courts in 'any relevant country or territory'. This means the Channel Islands, the Isle of Man, and countries designated by statutory instrument. The Channel Islands, that is Jersey, Guernsey, Sark and Alderney, are each separate jurisdictions.

Statutory instruments have been made under this provision as follows:

- Cooperation of Insolvency Courts (Designation of Relevant Countries and Territories) Order 1986 (SI 1986/2123), designating Anguilla, Australia, the Bahamas, Bermuda, Botswana, Canada, Cayman Islands, Falkland Islands, Gibraltar, Hong Kong, the Republic of Ireland, Montserrat, New Zealand, St Helena, Turks and Caicos Islands, Tuvalu, and the Virgin Islands;
- Cooperation of Insolvency Courts (Designation of Relevant Countries) Order 1996 (SI 1996/253), designating Malaysia and South Africa;
- Cooperation of Insolvency Courts (Designation of Relevant Country) Order 1998 (SI 1998/2766), designating Brunei Darussalam.

I.487

426A Disqualification from Parliament (England and Wales)

(1) A person in respect of whom a bankruptcy restrictions order has effect shall be disqualified—

(a)   from membership of the House of Commons,

(b)   from sitting or voting in the House of Lords, and

(c)   from sitting or voting in a committee of the House of Lords or a joint committee of both Houses.

(2) If a member of the House of Commons becomes disqualified under this section, his seat shall be vacated.

(3) If a person who is disqualified under this section is returned as a member of the House of Commons, his return shall be void.

(4) No writ of summons shall be issued to a member of the House of Lords who is disqualified under this section.

(5) If a court makes a bankruptcy restrictions order or interim order in respect of a member of the House of Commons or the House of Lords the court shall notify the Speaker of that House.

(6) If the Secretary of State accepts a bankruptcy restrictions undertaking made by a member of the House of Commons or the House of Lords, the Secretary of State shall notify the Speaker of that House.

Notes

S 426A

This provision was inserted by the Enterprise Act 2002, s 266(1) and came into force on 1 April 2004: see SI 2003/2093, art 2(2), Sch 2.

1.488

426B Devolution

(1) If a court makes a bankruptcy restrictions order or interim order in respect of a member of the Scottish Parliament, the Northern Ireland Assembly or the National Assembly for Wales, the court shall notify the presiding officer of that body.

(2) If the Secretary of State accepts a bankruptcy restrictions undertaking made by a member of the Scottish Parliament, the Northern Ireland Assembly or the National Assembly for Wales, the Secretary of State shall notify the presiding officer of that body.]

Notes

S 426B

This provision was inserted by the Enterprise Act 2002, s 266(1) and came into force on 1 April 2004: see SI 2003/2093, art 2(2), Sch 2.

1.489

426C Irrelevance of privilege

(1) An enactment about insolvency applies in relation to a member of the House of Commons or the House of Lords irrespective of any Parliamentary privilege.

(2) In this section 'enactment' includes a provision made by or under—
(a)   an Act of the Scottish Parliament, or
(b)   Northern Ireland legislation.

Notes

S 426C

This provision was inserted by the Enterprise Act 2002, s 266(1) and came into force on 1 April 2004: see SI 2003/2093, art 2(2), Sch 2.

I.490

427 Disqualification from Parliament (Scotland and Northern Ireland)

(1) Where a court in Northern Ireland adjudges an individual bankrupt or a court in Scotland awards sequestration of an individual's estate, the individual is disqualified—
(a)   for sitting or voting in the House of Lords,
(b)   for being elected to, or sitting or voting in, the House of Commons, and
(c)   for sitting or voting in a committee of either House.

(2) Where an individual is disqualified under this section, the disqualification ceases—
(a)   except where the adjudication is annulled or the award recalled or reduced without the individual having been first discharged, on the discharge of the individual, and
(b)   in the excepted case, on the annulment, recall or reduction, as the case may be.

(3) No writ of summons shall be issued to any lord of Parliament who is for the time being disqualified under this section for sitting and voting in the House of Lords.

(4) Where a member of the House of Commons who is disqualified under this section continues to be so disqualified until the end of the period of 6 months beginning with the day of the adjudication or award, his seat shall be vacated at the end of that period.

(5) A court which makes an adjudication or award such as is mentioned in subsection (1) in relation to any lord of Parliament or member of the House of Commons shall forthwith certify the adjudication or award to the Speaker of the House of Lords or, as the case may be, to the Speaker of the House of Commons.

(6) Where a court has certified an adjudication or award to the Speaker of the House of Commons under subsection (5), then immediately after it becomes apparent which of the following certificates is applicable, the court shall certify to the Speaker of the House of Commons—
(a)   that the period of 6 months beginning with the day of the adjudication or award has expired without the adjudication or award having been annulled, recalled or reduced, or

(b)   that the adjudication or award has been annulled, recalled or reduced before the end of that period.

(6A) Subsections (4) to (6) have effect in relation to a member of the Scottish Parliament but as if—
    (a)   references to the House of Commons were to the Parliament and references to the Speaker were to the Presiding Officer, and
    (b)   in subsection (4), for 'under this section' there were substituted 'under section 15(1)(b) of the Scotland Act 1998 by virtue of this section'.

(6B) Subsections (4) to (6) have effect in relation to a member of the National Assembly for Wales but as if—
    (a)   references to the House of Commons were to the Assembly and references to the Speaker were to the presiding officer, and
    (b)   in subsection (4), for 'under this section' there were substituted 'under section 12(2) of the Government of Wales Act 1998 by virtue of this section'.

(6C) Subsection (1), as applied to a member of the Northern Ireland Assembly by virtue of section 36(4) of the Northern Ireland Act 1998, has effect as if 'or Northern Ireland' were omitted; and subsections (4) to (6) have effect in relation to such a member as if—
    (a)   references to the House of Commons were to the Assembly and references to the Speaker were to the Presiding Officer; and
    (b)   in subsection (4), for 'under this section' there were substituted 'under section 36(4) of the Northern Ireland Act 1998 by virtue of this section'.

(7) …

1.491

428 Exemptions from Restrictive Trade Practices Act

(1) …

(2) …

(3) In this section 'insolvency services' means the services of persons acting as insolvency practitioners or carrying out under the law of Northern Ireland functions corresponding to those mentioned in section 388(1) or (2) in Part XIII, in their capacity as such …

1.492

429 Disabilities on revocation of administration order against an individual

(1) The following applies where a person fails to make any payment which he is required to make by virtue of an administration order under Part VI of the County Courts Act 1984.

(2) The court which is administering that person's estate under the order may, if it thinks fit—
    (a)   revoke the administration order, and

(b)   make an order directing that this section and section 12 of the Company Directors Disqualification Act 1986 shall apply to the person for such period, not exceeding one year, as may be specified in the order.

(3) A person to whom this section so applies shall not—
   (a)   either alone or jointly with another person, obtain credit to the extent of the amount prescribed for the purposes of section 360(1)(a) or more, or
   (b)   enter into any transaction in the course of or for the purposes of any business in which he is directly or indirectly engaged,
without disclosing to the person from whom he obtains the credit, or (as the case may be) with whom the transaction is entered into, the fact that this section applies to him.

(4) The reference in subsection (3) to a person obtaining credit includes—
   (a)   a case where goods are bailed or hired to him under a hire-purchase agreement or agreed to be sold to him under a conditional sale agreement, and
   (b)   a case where he is paid in advance (whether in money or otherwise) for the supply of goods or services.

(5) A person who contravenes this section is guilty of an offence and liable to imprisonment or a fine, or both.

1.493

430 Provision introducing Schedule of punishments

(1) Schedule 10 to this Act has effect with respect to the way in which offences under this Act are punishable on conviction.

(2) In relation to an offence under a provision of this Act specified in the first column of the Schedule (the general nature of the offence being described in the second column), the third column shows whether the offence is punishable on conviction on indictment, or on summary conviction, or either in the one way or the other.

(3) The fourth column of the Schedule shows, in relation to an offence, the maximum punishment by way of fine or imprisonment under this Act which may be imposed on a person convicted of the offence in the way specified in relation to it in the third column (that is to say, on indictment or summarily) a reference to a period of years or months being to a term of imprisonment of that duration.

(4) The fifth column shows, (in relation to an offence for which there is an entry in that column) that a person convicted of the offence after continued contravention is liable to a daily default fine; that is to say, he is liable on a second or subsequent conviction of the offence to the fine specified in that column for each day on which the contravention is continued (instead of the penalty specified for the offence in the fourth column of the Schedule).

(5) For the purpose of any enactment in this Act whereby an officer of a company who is in default is liable to a fine or penalty, the expression 'officer who is in default' means any officer of the company who

knowingly and wilfully authorises or permits the default, refusal or contravention mentioned in the enactment.

_____

Notes

S 430

See IR 1986, r 12.21 and Sch 5 for offences and punishments under the IR 1986.

S 430(5)

The definition of 'officer who is in default' is the same as in CA 1985 s 730(5).

_____

1.494

431 Summary proceedings

(1) Summary proceedings for any offence under any of Parts I to VII of this Act may (without prejudice to any jurisdiction exercisable apart from this subsection) be taken against a body corporate at any place at which the body has a place of business, and against any other person at any place at which he is for the time being.

(2) Notwithstanding anything in section 127(1) of the Magistrates' Courts Act 1980, an information relating to such an offence which is triable by a magistrates' court in England and Wales may be so tried if it is laid at any time within 3 years after the commission of the offence and within 12 months after the date on which evidence sufficient in the opinion of the Director of Public Prosecutions or the Secretary of State (as the case may be) to justify the proceedings comes to his knowledge.

(3) Summary proceedings in Scotland for such an offence shall not be commenced after the expiration of 3 years from the commission of the offence.

Subject to this (and notwithstanding anything in [section 136 of the Criminal Procedure (Scotland) Act 1995]), such proceedings may (in Scotland) be commenced at any time within 12 months after the date on which evidence sufficient in the Lord Advocate's opinion to justify the proceedings came to his knowledge or, where such evidence was reported to him by the Secretary of State, within 12 months after the date on which it came to the knowledge of the latter; and subsection (3) of that section applies for the purpose of this subsection as it applies for the purpose of that section.

(4) For purposes of this section, a certificate of the Director of Public Prosecutions, the Lord Advocate or the Secretary of State (as the case may be) as to the date on which such evidence as is referred to above came to his knowledge is conclusive evidence.

1.495

432 Offences by bodies corporate

(1) This section applies to offences under this Act other than those excepted by subsection (4).

(2) Where a body corporate is guilty of an offence to which this section applies and the offence is proved to have been committed with the consent or connivance of, or to be attributable to any neglect on the part of, any director, manager, secretary or other similar officer of the body corporate or any person who was purporting to act in any such capacity he, as well as the body corporate, is guilty of the offence and liable to be proceeded against and punished accordingly.

(3) Where the affairs of a body corporate are managed by its members, subsection (2) applies in relation to the acts and defaults of a member in connection with his functions of management as if he were a director of the body corporate.

(4) The offences excepted from this section are those under sections 30, 39, 51, 53, 54, 62, 64, 66, 85, 89, 164, 188, 201, 206, 207, 208, 209, 210 and 211 [and those under paragraphs 16(2), 17(3)(a), 18(3)(a), 19(3)(a), 22(1) and 23(1)(a) of Schedule A1].

1.496

433 Admissibility in evidence of statements of affairs, etc

(1) In any proceedings (whether or not under this Act)—
   (a)   a statement of affairs prepared for the purposes of any provision of this Act which is derived from the Insolvency Act 1985, and
   (b)   any other statement made in pursuance of a requirement imposed by or under any such provision or by or under rules made under this Act,
may be used in evidence against any person making or concurring in making the statement.

(2) However, in criminal proceedings in which any such person is charged with an offence to which this subsection applies—
   (a)   no evidence relating to the statement may be adduced, and
   (b)   no question relating to it may be asked,
by or on behalf of the prosecution, unless evidence relating to it is adduced, or a question relating to it is asked, in the proceedings by or on behalf of that person.

(3) Subsection (2) applies to any offence other than—
   (a)   an offence under section 22(6), 47(6), 48(8), 66(6), 67(8), 95(8), 98(6), 99(3)(a), 131(7), 192(2), 208(1)(a) or (d) or (2), 210, 235(5), 353(1), 354(1)(b) or (3) or 356(1) or (2)(a) or (b) or paragraph 4(3)(a) of Schedule 7;
   (b)   an offence which is—
      (i)   created by rules made under this Act, and
      (ii) designated for the purposes of this subsection by such rules or by regulations made by the Secretary of State,
   (c)   an offence which is—
      (i)   created by regulations made under any such rules, and
      (ii) designated for the purposes of this subsection by such regulations;
   (d)   an offence under section 1, 2 or 5 of the Perjury Act 1911 (false statements made on oath or made otherwise than on oath); or

(e)   an offence under section 44(1) or (2) of the Criminal Law (Consolidation) (Scotland) Act 1995 (false statements made on oath or otherwise than on oath).

(4) Regulations under subsection (3)(b)(ii) shall be made by statutory instrument and, after being made, shall be laid before each House of Parliament.

1.497

434 Crown application

For the avoidance of doubt it is hereby declared that provisions of this Act which derive from the Insolvency Act 1985 bind the Crown so far as affecting or relating to the following matters, namely—
    (a)   remedies against, or against the property of, companies or individuals;
    (b)   priorities of debts;
    (c)   transactions at an undervalue or preferences;
    (d)   voluntary arrangements approved under Part I or Part VIII, and
    (e)   discharge from bankruptcy.

Part XVIII
Interpretation

1.498

435 Meaning of 'associate'

(1) For the purposes of this Act any question whether a person is an associate of another person is to be determined in accordance with the following provisions of this section (any provision that a person is an associate of another person being taken to mean that they are associates of each other).

(2) A person is an associate of an individual if that person is the individual's husband or wife, or is a relative, or the husband or wife of a relative, of the individual or of the individual's husband or wife.

(3) A person is an associate of any person with whom he is in partnership, and of the husband or wife or a relative of any individual with whom he is in partnership; and a Scottish firm is an associate of any person who is a member of the firm.

(4) A person is an associate of any person whom he employs or by whom he is employed.

(5) A person in his capacity as trustee of a trust other than—
    (a)   a trust arising under any of the second Group of Parts or the Bankruptcy (Scotland) Act 1985, or
    (b)   a pension scheme or an employees' share scheme (within the meaning of the Companies Act),
is an associate of another person if the beneficiaries of the trust include, or the terms of the trust confer a power that may be exercised for the benefit of, that other person or an associate of that other person.

(6) A company is an associate of another company—

(a)   if the same person has control of both, or a person has control of one and persons who are his associates, or he and persons who are his associates, have control of the other, or

(b)   if a group of two or more persons has control of each company, and the groups either consist of the same persons or could be regarded as consisting of the same persons by treating (in one or more cases) a member of either group as replaced by a person of whom he is an associate.

(7) A company is an associate of another person if that person has control of it or if that person and persons who are his associates together have control of it.

(8) For the purposes of this section a person is a relative of an individual if he is that individual's brother, sister, uncle, aunt, nephew, niece, lineal ancestor or lineal descendant, treating—

(a)   any relationship of the half blood as a relationship of the whole blood and the stepchild or adopted child of any person as his child, and

(b)   an illegitimate child as the legitimate child of his mother and reputed father;

and references in this section to a husband or wife include a former husband or wife and a reputed husband or wife.

(9) For the purposes of this section any director or other officer of a company is to be treated as employed by that company.

(10) For the purposes of this section a person is to be taken as having control of a company if—

(a)   the directors of the company or of another company which has control of it (or any of them) are accustomed to act in accordance with his directions or instructions, or

(b)   he is entitled to exercise, or control the exercise of, one third or more of the voting power at any general meeting of the company or of another company which has control of it;

and where two or more persons together satisfy either of the above conditions, they are to be taken as having control of the company.

(11) In this section 'company' includes any body corporate (whether incorporated in Great Britain or elsewhere); and references to directors and other officers of a company and to voting power at any general meeting of a company have effect with any necessary modifications.

Notes

S 435(1)

This section sets out a detailed definition of 'associate' IA 1986 s 435 itself is expressly referred to in IA 1986 s 249; in addition the term 'associate' is referred to in IA 1986 s 314(6) and 340(5).The definition is wide and includes spouses, relatives, spouse's relatives and relatives' spouses (IA 1986 s 435(2) with 'relative being further defined in section 435(8)), business partners (s 435(3)), employers or employees (IA 1986 s 435(4)) and certain trust relationships (IA 1986 s 435(5)).

S 435(6)

A company may be an associate of another company and/or an individual (IA 1986 s 435(6), (7), (9), (10)).

S 435(10)(b)

A registered member of a company holding shares on a bare trust under which the beneficial owner directs the voting rights cannot be said to '... *control the exercise of ... the voting power ... of the company*': *Unidare plc v Cohen and Power* [2005] BPIR 1472.

1.499

436 Expressions used generally

In this Act, except in so far as the context otherwise requires (and subject to Parts VII and XI)—

'the appointed day' means the day on which this Act comes into force under section 443;

'associate' has the meaning given by section 435;

'business' includes a trade or profession;

'the Companies Act' means the Companies Act 1985;

'conditional sale agreement' and 'hire-purchase agreement' have the same meanings as in the Consumer Credit Act 1974;

'modifications' includes additions, alterations and omissions and cognate expressions shall be construed accordingly;

'property' includes money, goods, things in action, land and every description of property wherever situated and also obligations and every description of interest, whether present or future or vested or contingent, arising out of, or incidental to, property;

'records' includes computer records and other non-documentary records;

'subordinate legislation' has the same meaning as in the Interpretation Act 1978; and

'transaction' includes a gift, agreement or arrangement, and references to entering into a transaction shall be construed accordingly.

Notes

S 436

This section defines various expressions and terms which appear in the IA 1986. It applies to IA 1986 as a whole: (1) 'except in so far as the context otherwise requires', (2) 'subject to Part VII' (Interpretation for First Group of Parts corporate insolvency) and (3) 'subject to ...Part XI' (Interpretation for Second Group of Parts individual insolvency).

'the appointed day' The IA 1986 came into force on 29 December 1986: see Insolvency Act 1985 (Commencement Order) 1986 (SI 1986/1924). See also IA 1986 s 443.

'associate'; see the notes to IA 1986 s 435.

'conditional sale agreement ..'; see Consumer Credit Act 1974 s 189.

'property'; Sir Nicholas Browne-Wilkinson V-C observed in *Bristol Airport plc v Powdrill* [1990] Ch 744, 759D that 'It is hard to think of a wider definition of property'. As a general rule, a right of action will be covered by the expression 'things in action' and therefore will be property for the purpose of IA 1986 s 436 as will beneficial interests in a right of action: *Farmer v Moseley (Holdings) Ltd* [2002] BPIR 473. As an exception to the general rule, however, certain rights of action of a particularly personal nature, such as defamation or assault, are not caught: *Heath v Tang* [1993] 1 WLR 1421; and the right to be reinstated following a finding of unfair dismissal (but arguably not the compensation award): *Grady v HM Prison Service* [2003] BPIR 823. For

similar reasons, correspondence of a personal nature is also not deemed to be property for these purposes: *Haig v Aitken* [2001] Ch 110. However, where a single claim was both for damages for loss of earning and also for damages for pain, suffering and loss of amenity, that claim was property for the purposes of IA 1986 s 436 and accordingly would vest in the trustee in bankruptcy who would hold the right to recover damages under the latter head on constructive trust for the bankrupt: *Ord v Upton* [2000] Ch 352. Further see the notes to IA 1986 s 283.

Further, in order to constitute a thing in action the thing must be a right as opposed to a mere expectation; accordingly, an anticipated award from the Criminal Injuries Compensation Boards was not property for the purpose of IA 1986 s 436: In *Re Campbell (A Bankrupt) (No 145 of 1995)* [1997] Ch 14. On the other hand, monies received under an insurance policy was property despite the fact that the same was payable as a result of personal injuries: *Cork v Rawlins* [2001] Ch 792.

Other things which have been held to be property include a pre-emption right: *Dear v Reeves* [2002] Ch 1; [2001] 1 BCLC 643; a waste disposal licence: In *Re Celtic Extraction Ltd* [2001] Ch 475; but see In *Re Wilmott Trading Ltd* [1999] 2 BCLC 541 where the matter was considered for the purposes of the CA 1985 s 654; and rights in respect of a pension policy: *Re L (A Bankrupt)* [1997] 2 FLR 660.

'subordinate legislation'; see Interpretation Act 1978 s 21(1).

———

Part XIX
Final Provisions

1.500

437 Transitional provisions, and savings

The transitional provisions and savings set out in Schedule 11 to this Act shall have effect, the Schedule comprising the following Parts—

Part I: company insolvency and winding up (matters arising before appointed day, and continuance of proceedings in certain cases as before that day);

Part II: individual insolvency (matters so arising, and continuance of bankruptcy proceedings in certain cases as before that day);

Part III: transactions entered into before the appointed day and capable of being affected by orders of the court under Part XVI of this Act;

Part IV: insolvency practitioners acting as such before the appointed day; and

Part V: general transitional provisions and savings required consequentially on, and in connection with, the repeal and replacement by this Act and the Company Directors Disqualification Act 1986 of provisions of the Companies Act, the greater part of the Insolvency Act 1985 and other enactments.

1.501

438 Repeals

The enactments specified in the second column of Schedule 12 to this Act are repealed to the extent specified in the third column of that Schedule.

1.502

439 Amendment of enactments

(1) The Companies Act is amended as shown in Parts I and II of Schedule 13 to this Act, being amendments consequential on this Act and the Company Directors Disqualification Act 1986.

(2) The enactments specified in the first column of Schedule 14 to this Act (being enactments which refer, or otherwise relate, to those which are repealed and replaced by this Act or the Company Directors Disqualification Act 1986) are amended as shown in the second column of that Schedule.

(3) The Lord Chancellor may by order make such consequential modifications of any provision contained in any subordinate legislation made before the appointed day and such transitional provisions in connection with those modifications as appear to him necessary or expedient in respect of—

    (a)   any reference in that subordinate legislation to the Bankruptcy Act 1914;

    (b)   any reference in that subordinate legislation to any enactment repealed by Part III or IV of Schedule 10 to the Insolvency Act 1985; or

    (c)   any reference in that subordinate legislation to any matter provided for under the Act of 1914 or under any enactment so repealed.

(4) An order under this section shall be made by statutory instrument subject to annulment in pursuance of a resolution of either House of Parliament.

1.503

440 Extent (Scotland)

(1) Subject to the next subsection, provisions of this Act contained in the first Group of Parts extend to Scotland except where otherwise stated.

(2) The following provisions of this Act do not extend to Scotland—

    (a)   in the first Group of Parts—
        section 43;
        sections 238 to 241; and
        section 246;

    (b)   the second Group of Parts;

    (c)   in the third Group of Parts—
        sections 399 to 402,
        sections 412, 413, 415, [415A(3),] 418, 420 and 421,
        sections 423 to 425, and
        section 429(1) and (2); and

    (d)   in the Schedules—
        Parts II and III of Schedule 11; and
        Schedules 12 and 14 so far as they repeal or amend enactments which extend to England and Wales only.

1.504

441 Extent (Northern Ireland)

(1) The following provisions of this Act extend to Northern Ireland—

(a)   sections 197, 426, 427 and 428; and
(b)   so much of section 439 and Schedule 14 as relates to enactments which extend to Northern Ireland.

(2) Subject as above, and to any provision expressly relating to companies incorporated elsewhere than in Great Britain, nothing in this Act extends to Northern Ireland or applies to or in relation to companies registered or incorporated in Northern Ireland.

Notes

S 441(2)

A company incorporated in Northern Ireland can be wound up as an unregistered company under IA 1986 s 221, *Re Normandy Marketing Ltd* [1993] BCC 879.

1.505

442 Extent (other territories)

Her Majesty may, by Order in Council, direct that such of the provisions of this Act as are specified in the Order, being provisions formerly contained in the Insolvency Act 1985, shall extend to any of the Channel Islands or any colony with such modifications as may be so specified.

1.506

443 Commencement

This Act comes into force on the day appointed under section 236(2) of the Insolvency Act 1985 for the coming into force of Part III of that Act (individual insolvency and bankruptcy), immediately after that Part of that Act comes into force for England and Wales.

1.507

444 Citation

This Act may be cited as the Insolvency Act 1986.

SCHEDULE A1
Moratorium where Directors Propose Voluntary Arrangement

Part I
Introductory

Interpretation

1.508

1

In this Schedule—
   'the beginning of the moratorium' has the meaning given by paragraph 8(1),

'the date of filing' means the date on which the documents for the time being referred to in paragraph 7(1) are filed or lodged with the court,

'hire-purchase agreement' includes a conditional sale agreement, a chattel leasing agreement and a retention of title agreement,

'market contract' and 'market charge' have the meanings given by Part VII of the Companies Act 1989,

'moratorium' means a moratorium under section 1A,

'the nominee' includes any person for the time being carrying out the functions of a nominee under this Schedule,

'the settlement finality regulations' means the Financial Markets and Insolvency (Settlement Finality) Regulations 1999,

'system-charge' has the meaning given by the Financial Markets and Insolvency Regulations 1996.

Eligible companies

1.509

2

(1) A company is eligible for a moratorium if it meets the requirements of paragraph 3, unless—
- (a)   it is excluded from being eligible by virtue of paragraph 4, or
- (b)   it falls within sub-paragraph (2).

(2) A company falls within this sub-paragraph if—
- (a)   it effects or carries out contracts of insurance, but is not exempt from the general prohibition, within the meaning of section 19 of the Financial Services and Markets Act 2000 in relation to that activity
- (b)   it has permission under Part IV of that Act to accept deposits,
- (bb)   it has a liability in respect of a deposit which it accepted in accordance with the banking Act 1979 (c37) or 1987 (c22)
- (c)   it is a party to a market contract or any of its property is subject to a market charge or a system-charge, or
- (d)   it is a participant (within the meaning of the settlement finality regulations) or any of its property is subject to a collateral security charge (within the meaning of those regulations).

(3) Paragraphs (a), (b) and (bb) of sub-paragraph (2) must be read with –
- (a)   section 22 of the Financial Services and Markets Act 2000;
- (b)   any relevant order; and
- (c)   Schedule 2 to that Act

Notes

Para 2

See the general note after Paragraph 5.

1.510

3

(1) A company meets the requirements of this paragraph if the qualifying conditions are met—

(a) in the year ending with the date of filing, or

(b) in the financial year of the company which ended last before that date.

(2) For the purposes of sub-paragraph (1)—

(a) the qualifying conditions are met by a company in a period if, in that period, it satisfies two or more of the requirements for being a small company specified for the time being in section 247(3) of the Companies Act 1985, and

(b) a company's financial year is to be determined in accordance with that Act.

(3) Subsections (4), (5) and (6) of section 247 of that Act apply for the purposes of this paragraph as they apply for the purposes of that section.

(4) A company does not meet the requirements of this paragraph if it is a holding company of a group of companies which does not qualify as a small group or medium –sized group in respect of the financial year of the company which ended last before the date of filing.

(5) For the purposes of sub-paragraph (4) 'group' has the meaning given by section 262 of the Companies Act 1985 (c6) (definitions for Part VII) and a group qualifies as small or medium sized if it qualifies as such under section 249 of the Companies Act 1985 (qualification of group as small or medium sized).

_____

Notes

Para 3

See the general note after Paragraph 5.

_____

1.511

4

(1) A company is excluded from being eligible for a moratorium if, on the date of filing—

(a) the company is in administration,

(b) the company is being wound up,

(c) there is an administrative receiver of the company,

(d) a voluntary arrangement has effect in relation to the company,

(e) there is a provisional liquidator of the company,

(f) a moratorium has been in force for the company at any time during the period of 12 months ending with the date of filing and—

(i) no voluntary arrangement had effect at the time at which the moratorium came to an end, or

(ii) a voluntary arrangement which had effect at any time in that period has come to an end prematurely,

(fa) an administrator appointed under paragraph 22 of Schedule B1 has held office in the period of 12 months ending with the date of filing or

(g) a voluntary arrangement in relation to the company which had effect in pursuance of a proposal under section 1(3) has come to an end prematurely and, during the period of 12 months ending with the date of filing, an order under section 5(3)(a) has been made.

(2) Sub-paragraph (1)(b) does not apply to a company which, by reason of a winding-up order made after the date of filing, is treated as being wound up on that date.

Notes

Para 4

See the general note after paragraph 5.

Capital market arrangement

1.512

4A

A company is also excluded from being eligible for a moratorium if, on the date of filing, it is a party to an agreement which is or forms part of a capital market arrangement under which-

(i) a party has incurred, or when the agreement was entered into was expected to incur, a debt of at least £10 million under the arrangement, and

(ii) the arrangement involves the issue of a capital market investment.

Public private partnership

1.513

4B

A company is also excluded from being eligible for a moratorium if, on the date of filing, it is a project company of a project which-

(i) is a public-private partnership project, and

(ii) includes step-in rights.

Liability under an arrangement.

1.514

4C

(1) A company is also excluded from being eligible for a moratorium if, on the date of filing, it has incurred a liability under an agreement of £10 million or more.

(2) Where the liability in sub-paragraph (1) is a contingent liability under or by virtue of a guarantee or an indemnity or security provided on behalf

of another person, the amount of that liability is the full amount of the liability in relation to which the guarantee, indemnity or security is provided.

(3) In this paragraph –
  (a)   the reference to 'liability' includes a present or future liability whether, in either case, it is certain or contingent,
  (b)   the reference to 'liability' includes a reference to a liability to be paid wholly or partly in foreign currency (in which case the sterling equivalent shall be calculated as at the time when the liability is incurred).

Interpretation of capital market arrangement

1.515

4D

(1) For the purposes of paragraph 4A an arrangement is a capital market arrangement if –
  (a)   it involves a grant of security to a person holding it as trustee for a person who holds a capital market investment issued by a party to the arrangement, or
  (b)   at least one party guarantees the performance of obligations of another party, or
  (c)   at least one party provides security in respect of the performance of obligations of another party, or
  (d)   the arrangement involves an investment of a kind described in articles 83 to 85 of the Financial Services and Markets Act 2000 (Regulated Activities) Order 2001 (SI 2001/544) (options, futures and contracts for differences).

(2) For the purposes of sub-paragraph (1) –
  (a)   a reference to holding as trustee includes a reference to holding as nominee or agent,
  (b)   a reference to holding for a person who holds a capital market investment includes a reference to holding for a number of persons at least one of whom holds a capital market investment, and
  (c)   a person holds a capital market investment if he has a legal or beneficial interest in it.

(3) In paragraph 4A, 4C, 4J and this paragraph –
  'agreement' includes an agreement or undertaking effected by –
        (a)   contract,
        (b)   deed, or
        (c)   any other instrument intended to have effect in accordance with the law of England and Wales, Scotland or another jurisdiction, and
  'party' to an arrangement includes a party to an agreement which-
        (a)   forms part of the arrangement,
        (b)   provides for the raising of finance as part of the arrange-ment, or
        (c)   is necessary for the purposes of implementing the arrange-ment.

Capital market investment

1.516

4E

(1) For the purposes of paragraphs 4A and 4D, an investment is a capital market investment if–
- (a) it is within article 77 of the Financial Services and Markets Act 2000 (Regulated Activities) Order 2001 (SI 2001/544) (debt instruments) and
- (b) it is rated, listed or traded or designed to be rated, listed or traded.

(2) In sub-paragraph (1) –
'listed' means admitted to the official list within the meaning given by section 103(1) of the Financial Services and Markets Act 2000 (c. 8) (interpretation),
'rated' means rated for the purposes of investment by an internationally recognised rating agency,
'traded' means admitted to trading on a market established under the rules of a recognised investment exchange or on a foreign market.

(3) In sub-paragraph (2) –
'foreign market' has the same meaning as 'relevant market' in article 67(2) of the Financial Services and Markets Act 2000 (Financial Promotion) Order 2001 (SI 2001/1335) (foreign markets),
'recognised investment exchange' has the meaning given by section 285 of the Financial Services and Markets Act 2000 (recognised investment exchange).

1.517

4F

(1) For the purposes of paragraphs 4A and 4D an investment is also a capital market investment if it consists of a bond or commercial paper issued to one or more of the following-
- (a) an investment professional within the meaning of article 19(5) of the Financial Services and Markets Act 2000 (Financial Promotion) Order 2001,
- (b) a person who is, when the agreement mentioned in paragraph 4A is entered into, a certified high net worth individual in relation to a communication within the meaning of article 48(2) of that order,
- (c) a person to whom article 49(2) of that order applies (high net worth company, &c.),
- (d) a person who is, when the agreement mentioned in paragraph 4A is entered into, a certified sophisticated investor in relation to a communication within the meaning of article 50(1) of that order, and
- (e) a person in a State other than the United Kingdom who under the law of that State is not prohibited from investing in bonds or commercial paper.

(2) For the purposes of sub-paragraph (1) –

(a) in applying article 19(5) of the Financial Services and Markets Act 2000 (Financial Promotion) Order 2001 for the purposes of sub-paragraph (1)(a) –
  (i) in article 19(5)(b), ignore the words after 'exempt person',
  (ii) in article 19(5)(c)(i), for the words from 'the controlled activity' to the end substitute 'a controlled activity', and
  (iii) in article 19(5)(e) ignore the words from 'where the communication' to the end, and
(b) in applying article 49(2) of that order for the purposes of sub-paragraph (1)(c), ignore article 49(2)(e).

(3) In sub-paragraph (1) –
'bond' shall be construed in accordance with article 77 of the Financial Services and Markets Act 2000 (Regulated Activities) Order 2001 (SI 2001/544), and
'commercial paper' has the meaning given by article 9(3) of that order.

Debt

1.518

4G

The debt of at least £10 million referred to in paragraph 4A –
(a) may be incurred at any time during the life of the capital market arrangement, and
(b) may be expressed wholly or partly in a foreign currency (in which case the sterling equivalent shall be calculated as at the time when the arrangement is entered into).

Interpretation of project company

1.519

4H

(1) For the purposes of paragraph 4B a company is a 'project company' of a project if –
(a) it holds property for the purpose of the project,
(b) it has sole or principal responsibility under an agreement for carrying out all or part of the project,
(c) it is one of a number of companies which together carry out the project,
(d) it has the purpose of supplying finance to enable the project to be carried out, or
(e) it is the holding company of a company within any of paragraphs (a) to (d).

(2) But a company is not a 'project company' of a project if –
(a) it performs a function within sub-paragraph (1)(a) to (d) or is within sub-paragraph (1)(e), but
(b) it also performs a function which is not –
  (i) within sub-paragraph (1)(a) to (d),
  (ii) related to a function within sub-paragraph (1)(a) to (d), or
  (iii) related to the project.

(3) For the purposes of this paragraph a company carries out all or part of a project whether or not it acts wholly or partly through agents.

Public-private partnership project

1.520

4I

(1) In paragraph 4B 'public-private partnership project' means a project –
   (a) the resources for which are provided partly by one or more public bodies and partly by one or more private persons, or
   (b) which is designed wholly or mainly for the purpose of assisting a public body to discharge a function.

(2) In sub-paragraph (1) 'resources' includes –
   (a) funds (including payment for the provision of services or facilities),
   (b) assets,
   (c) professional skill,
   (d) the grant of a concession or franchise, and
   (e) any other commercial resource.

(3) In sub-paragraph (1) 'public body' means –
   (a) a body which exercises public functions,
   (b) a body specified for the purposes of this paragraph by the Secretary of State, and
   (c) a body within a class specified for the purposes of this paragraph by the Secretary of State.

(4) A specification under sub-paragraph (3) may be –
   (a) general, or
   (b) for the purpose of the application of paragraph 4B to a specified case.

Step-in rights

1.521

4J

(1) For the purposes of paragraph 4B a project has 'step-in rights' if a person who provides finance in connection with the project has a conditional entitlement under an agreement to –
   (i) assume sole or principal responsibility under an agreement for carrying out all or part of the project, or
   (ii) make arrangements for carrying out all or part of the project.

(2) In sub-paragraph (1) a reference to the provision of finance includes a reference to the provision of an indemnity.

'Person'

1.522

4K

For the purposes of paragraphs 4A to 4J, a reference to a person includes a reference to a partnership or another unincorporated group of persons.

1.523

5

The Secretary of State may by regulations modify the qualifications for eligibility of a company for a moratorium.

Notes

Introductory

The introduction of a moratorium to enable a company to consider proposals for a voluntary arrangement was long overdue. IA 1986 Sch A1 was introduced by the IA 2000; however it did not come into force until 1 January 2003. In practice the companies which have taken advantage of the moratorium procedure are few and far between. There are two major problems with the procedure. First there is a considerable onus placed on the nominee to express opinions as a condition of obtaining a moratorium (Paragraph 6(2)) and to monitor the company's affairs and form further opinions (Paragraph 24). Secondly there is no encouragement for lenders to fund a company through a moratorium; indeed if a security is granted by a company in a moratorium it is subject to a test of it being proved that there were reasonable grounds for believing that the grant of the security would benefit the company (Paragraph 14).

Para 2 to 5

Qualifying conditions for eligibility

Unless excluded under the provisions referred to below, under paragraph 3 a company is eligible for a moratorium if for the relevant period it meets two out of the three of the conditions for being a small company specified under CA 1985 s 247(3). Those conditions are:
- turnover not exceeding £5.6m;
- balance sheet total (as defined in CA 1985 s 247(5) not more than £2.8m;
- number of employees not more than 50.

The relevant period for which those conditions must be met is either:
- the year ending with the 'date of filing' (as defined in paragraph 1); or
- the financial year of the company (as determined under CA 1985 s 223) which ended last before the date of filing.

Companies excluded from eligibility

The following categories of company are excluded from eligibility:
- under paragraph 3(4)–(5) the holding company of a group of companies which does not qualify as a small or medium sized group for the last financial year ending last before the date of filing (see CA 1985 s 249 for the qualifying conditions for a group to be a small or medium sized group);
- under paragraph 2(2)–(3) banks, insurance companies and companies operating in the financial markets (as more specifically defined in those sub-paragraphs);
- under paragraph 4(1)(a)–(e) companies in respect of which insolvency procedures are already in place; this includes where a company is in administration or liquidation. A company which is merely subject to a winding up petition is not excluded from being eligible (paragraph 4(2));
- under paragraph 4(1)(f), (g) a company in respect of which a moratorium has been obtained in the 12 month period preceding the date of filing following which either no company voluntary arrangement ('CVA') came into effect, or any CVA which did come into effect came to an end prematurely (as defined by IA 1986 s 7B); or a company which in the 12 month period preceding the date of filing has had the benefit of a stay of an administration or liquidation after entering into a CVA under IA 1986 s 1(3) and where that CVA subsequently came to an end prematurely;
- under paragraph 4A a company which is a party to a capital market arrangement as defined by paragraph 4A, 4D and 4E–4G;

- under paragraph 4B a company which is a project company of a public-private partnership ('PPP') project which includes step-in rights; the expressions 'project company', 'PPP project' and 'step in rights' are defined in paragraphs 4H, 4I and 4J respectively. Power for a fimancier to appoint an administrative receiver does not amount to step-in rights: *Cabvision Ltd v Feetum* [2005] EWCA Civ 1601, [2006] BCC 340 (a case decided under identically worded provisions of Sch 2A);
- under paragraph 4C a company which at the date of filing has incurred liability under an agreement of £10 million or more, whether that liability is present or future, or actual or contingent.

Under Paragraph 5 the Secretary of State has power to modify the eligibility qualifications by regulation.

Part II
Obtaining a Moratorium

Nominee's statement

1.524

6

(1) Where the directors of a company wish to obtain a moratorium, they shall submit to the nominee—
- (a) a document setting out the terms of the proposed voluntary arrangement,
- (b) a statement of the company's affairs containing—
  - (i) such particulars of its creditors and of its debts and other liabilities and of its assets as may be prescribed, and
  - (ii) such other information as may be prescribed, and
- (c) any other information necessary to enable the nominee to comply with sub-paragraph (2) which he requests from them.

(2) The nominee shall submit to the directors a statement in the prescribed form indicating whether or not, in his opinion—
- (a) the proposed voluntary arrangement has a reasonable prospect of being approved and implemented,
- (b) the company is likely to have sufficient funds available to it during the proposed moratorium to enable it to carry on its business, and
- (c) meetings of the company and its creditors should be summoned to consider the proposed voluntary arrangement.

(3) In forming his opinion on the matters mentioned in sub-paragraph (2), the nominee is entitled to rely on the information submitted to him under sub-paragraph (1) unless he has reason to doubt its accuracy.

(4) The reference in sub-paragraph (2)(b) to the company's business is to that business as the company proposes to carry it on during the moratorium.

Notes

Introductory

As with CVAs where a moratorium is not possible or sought the first stage in the CVA moratorium procedure is for the directors of the company to prepare and submit to the nominee the CVA proposal and, within seven days thereafter, a statement of the company's affairs. However the nominee is then required to report in the first instance to the directors, on his opinion as to the prospects of the proposal being approved and implemented, on the question whether the company will have sufficient funds to enable it to carry on its proposed business during the period of the moratorium, and (depending on his opinion to the first two questions) whether or not meetings should be summoned to consider the proposals. To enable the directors to obtain a moratorium, this statement must give a positive opinion on each of the three questions, and must be filed by the directors with the court: see paragraph 7(1)(e) below.

Despite the formal terms of the procedure as set out above, it is likely in practice that the directors will have approached an insolvency practitioner at a rather earlier stage to advise on appropriate insolvency procedures, and, if appropriate, to formulate the CVA proposal. As a result, unless the insolvency practitioner has already satisfied himself of the matters on which he is required to report to the directors under paragraph 6(2), it is unlikely that any proposal will have been prepared in the first place.

Para 6(1)(a)

Under IR 1986 r 1.35, the proposal must contain the substantively the same information as is prescribed for non-moratorium CVAs under IR 1986 r 1.3(1), (2). See further the note to that rule.

Para 6(1)(b)

Under IR 1986 r 1.37, the statement of affairs must be delivered to the nominee no later than 7 days after delivery of the proposal, and must contain the same particulars as prescribed by IR 1986 r 1.5(2) for non-moratorium CVAs. See further the note to that rule.

Para 6(2)

Under IR 1986 r 1.38, the nominee has 28 days from the submission to him of the CVA proposal to prepare the statement dealing with each of the three matters specified in Paragraph 6(2). The first and the third matters replicate the nominee's reporting requirements in a non-moratorium proposal under IA 1986 s 2(2).

However, the second matter is new. It requires the nominee to form an opinion as to whether the company has sufficient funds to carry on the business which it proposes to carry on during the proposed moratorium. In practical terms, this may require the nominee to consult with the company's funders and its key suppliers, and to obtain written confirmation from such persons of their willingness to provide the requisite support, and the terms on which they are prepared to do so. At this stage, the nominee is reporting to the directors on his opinion on the three matters (whether it is positive or negative). However, unless he has formed a positive opinion, the moratorium will not be able to proceed under the pre-conditions set out in Paragraph 7(1) below.

Although Paragraph 6(2) does not in terms require the nominee's statement to be in any prescribed form, the nominee's statement which must be filed with the court under paragraph 7(1)(e) in order to obtain the moratorium is required to be in prescribed form: see paragraph 7(2). This prescribed form is Form 1.5 and describes itself as 'Nominee's statement of opinion pursuant to paragraph 6.2 of Schedule A1 to the Insolvency Act 1986'. Accordingly, it seems to be envisaged that the statement under paragraph 6.2 and that under paragraph 7(1)(e) will be one and the same document, and in a prescribed form.

It should be noted that under IR 1986 r 1.38 the nominee is obliged at the same time as submitted his statement also to annex to it his comments on the proposal, or, where he forms a negative opinion on any of the three matters, his reasons for that opinion.

Para 6(3)

The nominee is entitled to rely on the information supplied to him by the company's directors, unless he has reason to doubt its accuracy. This provision should be read in conjunction with the dicta of Lindsay J in the '*Greystoke*' case (*Re a debtor (No 140 IO of 1995)* [1996] 2 BCLC

429) as to the obligations of a nominee where the fullness or candour of the information supplied by a debtor has come into question). For a full discussion of this topic, see the notes under IA 1986 s 2.

Documents to be submitted to court

1.525

7

(1) To obtain a moratorium the directors of a company must file (in Scotland, lodge) with the court—
  (a) a document setting out the terms of the proposed voluntary arrangement,
  (b) a statement of the company's affairs containing—
      (i) such particulars of its creditors and of its debts and other liabilities and of its assets as may be prescribed, and
      (ii) such other information as may be prescribed,
  (c) a statement that the company is eligible for a moratorium,
  (d) a statement from the nominee that he has given his consent to act, and
  (e) a statement from the nominee that, in his opinion—
      (i) the proposed voluntary arrangement has a reasonable prospect of being approved and implemented,
      (ii) the company is likely to have sufficient funds available to it during the proposed moratorium to enable it to carry on its business, and
      (iii) meetings of the company and its creditors should be summoned to consider the proposed voluntary arrangement.

(2) Each of the statements mentioned in sub-paragraph (1)(b) to (e), except so far as it contains the particulars referred to in paragraph (b)(i), must be in the prescribed form.

(3) The reference in sub-paragraph (1)(e)(ii) to the company's business is to that business as the company proposes to carry it on during the moratorium.

(4) The Secretary of State may by regulations modify the requirements of this paragraph as to the documents required to be filed (in Scotland, lodged) with the court in order to obtain a moratorium.

Notes

Introductory

Unlike the court-ordered moratoria (so-called interim orders) obtained by individuals who are proposing to submit IVA proposals for consideration by their creditors under IA 1986 s 252 to 255, the new moratoria available to small companies are obtained automatically on the filing with the court of the five required documents set out in paragraph 7(1); there is no judicial consideration of whether a moratorium is appropriate or proper. This is in part a recognition of the practice which has developed with respect to interim orders whereby such orders may be made where there is no pending bankruptcy petition on the filing of the requisite documents without the requirement for the debtor or nominee to attend. But, in contrast to the practice developed with interim orders, a company moratorium is automatically obtained on filing of documents even where there is a pending winding up petition against the company.

Paragraph 7 is supplemented by IR 1986 r 1.39 which stipulates a time limit of 3 working days for the filing of the requisite documents with the court after the submission to the directors of the nominee's statement under paragraph 6(2) above.

Para 7(1)

For relevant notes see:

(a) The CVA Proposal: see paragraph 6(1)(a) above;
(b) Statement of Affairs (Prescribed Form 1.6) see paragraph 6(1)(b) above;
(c) Statement of Eligibility (Prescribed Form 1.7) for the eligibility requirements, see paragraphs 2 to 5 above;
(d) Statement of Nominee's Consent to Act (Prescribed Form 1.8) the nominee must include this with his statement submitted to the directors under paragraph 6(2); see IR 1986 r 1.38(2)(b);
(e) Nominee's Statement of Opinion (Prescribed Form 1.5) see paragraph 6(2) above;

Note that under IR 1986 r 1.39(2) the directors must also file with the court

- a copy of any statement of reasons made by the nominee under r 1.37(3) in allowing the directors to prepare the company's statement of affairs to a date more than 2 weeks before the date of delivery of the proposal;
- a copy of the nominee's comments on the proposal made under r 1.38(2)

Para 7(2)

The prescribed forms for each of the documents in (b) to (e) above are the forms noted above. These Forms are included within the IR 1986 Schedule 4 (as inserted by paragraph 8 and part 5 of the Schedule to The Insolvency (Amendment) (No 2) Rules 2002 (SI 2002/2712)).

Duration of moratorium

1.526

8

(1) A moratorium comes into force when the documents for the time being referred to in paragraph 7(1) are filed or lodged with the court and references in this Schedule to 'the beginning of the moratorium' shall be construed accordingly.

(2) A moratorium ends at the end of the day on which the meetings summoned under paragraph 29(1) are first held (or, if the meetings are held on different days, the later of those days), unless it is extended under paragraph 32.

(3) If either of those meetings has not first met before the end of the period of 28 days beginning with the day on which the moratorium comes into force, the moratorium ends at the end of the day on which those meetings were to be held (or, if those meetings were summoned to be held on different days, the later of those days), unless it is extended under paragraph 32.

(4) If the nominee fails to summon either meeting within the period required by paragraph 29(1), the moratorium ends at the end of the last day of that period.

(5) If the moratorium is extended (or further extended) under paragraph 32, it ends at the end of the day to which it is extended (or further extended).

(6) Sub-paragraphs (2) to (5) do not apply if the moratorium comes to an end before the time concerned by virtue of—

(a) paragraph 25(4) (effect of withdrawal by nominee of consent to act),

(b) an order under paragraph 26(3), 27(3) or 40 (challenge of actions of nominee or directors), or

(c) a decision of one or both of the meetings summoned under paragraph 29.

(7) If the moratorium has not previously come to an end in accordance with sub-paragraphs (2) to (6), it ends at the end of the day on which a decision under paragraph 31 to approve a voluntary arrangement takes effect under paragraph 36.

(8) The Secretary of State may by order increase or reduce the period for the time being specified in sub-paragraph (3).

Notes

Para 8(1)–(3)

As noted under Paragraph 7, the moratorium comes into force as soon as the requisite documents are filed with the court. The nominee is then obliged under Paragraph 29 to convene meetings of creditors and the company to consider the proposals within 28 days thereafter. The moratorium is initially to remain in force for a period up until the end of the day when those meetings are first held (or, if the meetings are held on different days, the later of the meetings). In the event that either meeting does not on its first date make a decision on the proposal, but instead resolves that it be adjourned (under Paragraph 30) for further consideration, the meeting can further resolve under Paragraph 32 to extend the moratorium for a maximum period of not more than two months from the date of the first meeting (or later of the two first meetings). Any extended moratorium will terminate automatically once a decision to approve the CVA has taken effect.

Para 8(4), (5)

In the event the nominee fails to summon the meetings to take place within the requisite 28 day period, the moratorium comes to an end at the end of that period. If, in contrast, the nominee summons meetings to take place within the period, but one or both meetings do not take place as summoned, the moratorium comes to an end at the end of the day on which the meetings were to be held (or, if summoned for different days, at the end of the day of the later of the meetings). But in this latter case, the moratorium can again be extended under Paragraph 32.

Para 8(6)

The initial or any extended moratorium may be terminated prematurely in one of three ways:

- by the nominee withdrawing his consent to act under Paragraph 25(2) (which he can only do, but is obliged to do in the circumstances set out in that paragraph);
- by an order of the court made on a challenge by a dissatisfied creditor, director, member or other person affected by a moratorium to an act or decision either of the nominee, or of the directors during the course of the moratorium;
- by a decision of either meeting.

Para 8(7)

Unless ended prematurely the moratorium ends at the end of the day on which the decision of the creditors and members to approve proposals for a voluntary arrangement takes effect under Paragraph 36; the company is then in a CVA.

Notification of beginning of moratorium

1.527

9

(1) When a moratorium comes into force, the directors shall notify the nominee of that fact forthwith.

(2) If the directors without reasonable excuse fail to comply with sub-paragraph (1), each of them is liable to imprisonment or a fine, or both.

Notes

Para 9

The directors are required to notify the nominee that a moratorium has come into force. Under IR 1986 r 1.40(1) they must do this by delivering to the nominee two copies of the schedule setting out the documents filed with the court (Form 1.9) duly endorsed by the court (under IR 1986 r 1.39(3)).

1.528

10

(1) When a moratorium comes into force, the nominee shall, in accordance with the rules—
  (a)   advertise that fact forthwith, and
  (b)   notify the registrar of companies, the company and any petitioning creditor of the company of whose claim he is aware of that fact.

(2) In sub-paragraph (1)(b), 'petitioning creditor' means a creditor by whom a winding-up petition has been presented before the beginning of the moratorium, as long as the petition has not been dismissed or withdrawn.

(3) If the nominee without reasonable excuse fails to comply with sub-paragraph (1)(a) or (b), he is liable to a fine.

Notes

Para 10

The nominee is then required to publicise the moratorium:
*   by advertisement – under IR 1986 r 1.40(2) this must be in the London Gazette and in one other newspaper appropriate for ensuring that the moratorium comes to the notice of the company's creditors;

- by notifying the persons specified in Paragraph 10(1)(b), giving details of the date on which the moratorium came into force: see IR 1986 r 1.40(3).

Further under IR 1986 r 1.40(4) the nominee must further notify any sheriff or officer who to his knowledge is charged with execution or other legal process against the company, and any person who to his knowledge has distrained against the company or its property.

Notification of end of moratorium

1.529

11

(1) When a moratorium comes to an end, the nominee shall, in accordance with the rules—
   (a)   advertise that fact forthwith, and
   (b)   notify the court, the registrar of companies, the company and any creditor of the company of whose claim he is aware of that fact.

(2) If the nominee without reasonable excuse fails to comply with sub-paragraph (1)(a) or (b), he is liable to a fine.

Notes

Para 11(1)

See IR 1986 r 1.42 for provisions relating to advertisement and notification of the termination of the moratorium.

Part III
Effects of Moratorium

Effect on creditors, etc

1.530

12

(1) During the period for which a moratorium is in force for a company—
   (a)   no petition may be presented for the winding up of the company,
   (b)   no meeting of the company may be called or requisitioned except with the consent of the nominee or the leave of the court and subject (where the court gives leave) to such terms as the court may impose,
   (c)   no resolution may be passed or order made for the winding up of the company,
   (d)   no administration application may be made in respect of the company,
   (da) no administrator of the company may be appointed under paragraph 14 or 22 of Schedule B1,
   (e)   no administrative receiver of the company may be appointed,

> (f)   no landlord or other person to whom rent is payable may exercise any right of forfeiture by peaceable re-entry in relation to premises let to the company in respect of a failure by the company to comply with any term or condition of its tenancy of such premises, except with the leave of the court and subject to such terms as the court may impose,
>
> (g)   no other steps may be taken to enforce any security over the company's property, or to repossess goods in the company's possession under any hire-purchase agreement, except with the leave of the court and subject to such terms as the court may impose, and
>
> (h)   no other proceedings and no execution or other legal process may be commenced or continued, and no distress may be levied, against the company or its property except with the leave of the court and subject to such terms as the court may impose.
>
> (2) Where a petition, other than an excepted petition, for the winding up of the company has been presented before the beginning of the moratorium, section 127 shall not apply in relation to any disposition of property, transfer of shares or alteration in status made during the moratorium or at a time mentioned in paragraph 37(5)(a).
>
> (3) In the application of sub-paragraph (1)(h) to Scotland, the reference to execution being commenced or continued includes a reference to diligence being carried out or continued, and the reference to distress being levied is omitted.
>
> (4) Paragraph (a) of sub-paragraph (1) does not apply to an excepted petition and, where such a petition has been presented before the beginning of the moratorium or is presented during the moratorium, paragraphs (b) and (c) of that sub-paragraph do not apply in relation to proceedings on the petition.
>
> (5) For the purposes of this paragraph, 'excepted petition' means a petition under—
>
> (a)   section 124A of this Act,
>
> (b)   section 72 of the Financial Services Act 1986 on the ground mentioned in subsection (1)(b) of that section, or
>
> (c)   section 92 of the Banking Act 1987 on the ground mentioned in subsection (1)(b) of that section.
>
> (d)   section 367 of the Financial services and Markets Act 2000 on the ground mentioned in subsection (30(b) of that section

Notes

Introductory

Paragraph 12(1) imposes restrictions on enforcement action by creditors similar in terms to those previously imposed under the former administration regime (IA 1986 s 10, 11) and now contained in IA 1986 Sch B1 para 42 -44. Decisions under those provisions may therefore be persuasive in the interpretation of paragraph 12(1).

Para 12(1)(a), (c); para 12(2)

While the moratorium is in place, no petition may be presented, and no winding up order made or resolution for voluntary winding up passed. Importantly, where a winding up petition has been presented before the moratorium comes into effect, Paragraph 12(2) disapplies IA 1986 s 127 for both the duration of the moratorium and a further period of 28 days after the result of the meetings summoned to consider the CVA proposal has been reported to the court.

A company will therefore be able to continue business during the moratorium without the need to apply to the Companies Court for an order under s 127 validating payments in and out of its bank account and other transactions; however there are certain restrictions on the company's transactions during the moratorium period (see Paragraphs 15 to 23 below). Contravention of those restrictions does not make the transaction void or unenforceable (Paragraph 15(2)), but renders any officer responsible liable to criminal prosecution. Whilst the schedule does not expressly provide for civil liability an officer who causes or permits any contravention is likely to be found to have been in breach of his obligations to the company.

Neither sub-paragraphs (a) nor (c) of Paragraph 12 in terms prevent a petitioning creditor from advertising a petition during the moratorium. In *Re a Company (No 1992 of 1988)* [1989] BCLC 9, the Companies Court restrained advertisement of winding up petition where an administration petition was pending in the light of the damage that such step could cause the company. The court in that case appeared to accept that advertisement itself would be prohibited by IA 1986 s 10(1)(c) which was in the same terms as Paragraph 12(1)(h).

Para 12(1), (d), (da), (e)

However if the company is already in administration or an administrative receiver has already been appointed, the company will not be entitled to obtain a moratorium: see paragraph 4(1), (a), (c). The holder of a floating charge enabling the appointment of an administrator or an administrative receiver is not entitled to any prior notice of the company's intention to obtain a moratorium, and so will not be able to block the moratorium. For further restrictions on the rights of holders of floating charges, see Paragraph 13 and Paragraph 43 below.

Para 12(1)(f)–(h)

The various restrictions under these three paragraphs all apply unless the court grants leave. The principles which may apply to the grant of leave are not set out in the paragraph, and have not yet been considered by the courts in any reported decision. However, since, in contrast to administrations, the moratorium is to last only for a short period pending consideration of the CVA proposals at the creditors' and company meeting, it may be unusual for leave to be sought or given. By analogy with interim orders, leave may probably be obtained retrospectively where proceedings are commenced or continued without it: see *Clarke v Coutts & Co* [2002] BPIR 916.

Para 12(1)(g)

For the meaning of 'security' see IA 1986 s 248. The refusal by the holder of a lien to hand over property the subject of the lien to its owner constitutes steps taken to enforce a security: see *Bristol Airport v Powdrill* [1990] Ch 744. The expression *'hire purchase agreement'* does not in terms have the extended definition (to include conditional sale agreements, chattel leasing agreement and retention of title agreements) which the equivalent expression in IA 1986 Sch B1 para 72 has by virtue of IA 1986 Sch B1 para 111.

Para 12(1)(h)

For the meaning of *'no other proceedings, and no execution or other legal process'* it may be useful to refer to decisions under the former administration regime (IA 1986 s 10(1)(c), 11(3))including:

- *Re a Company (No 1992 of 1988)* [1989] BCLC 9 (advertisement of winding up petition was prohibited);
- *Bristol Airport v Powdrill* [1990] Ch 744 ('other proceedings' means legal or quasi legal proceedings); this includes statutory adjudication procedures: *A Straume (UK) Ltd v Bradlor Developments Ltd* [2000] BCC 333;
- *Re Olympia and York Canary Wharf Ltd* [1993] BCLC 453 ('proceedings' and 'legal process' together contemplate all steps in legal proceedings from initiating process to

their final termination in the process of execution or other means of enforcement of a judgment, but do not include the taking of non-judicial steps such as the serving of a notice;

- *Biosource Technologies Inc v Axis Genetics plc* [2000] 1 BCLC 286 ('other proceedings' includes not just claims brought by a company's creditors, but also proceedings brought by its competitors, in this case, a claim for the revocation of a patent held by the company);
- In *re Rhondda Waste Disposal Ltd* [2001] Ch 57 (CA) ('other proceedings' includes criminal proceedings);
- *Re Railtrack plc, Winsor v Bloom* [2002] EWCA Civ 955, [2003] BPIR 507 (power of railway regulator to give regulatory directions was not prohibited).

Para 12(4)

The general prohibition against presenting or proceeding with a winding up petition, (and the disapplication of section IA 1986 s 127), does not apply in respect of 'excepted petitions' as defined in Paragraph 12(5). These include petitions brought by the Secretary of State on public interest grounds, and petitions brought under other regulatory regimes.

1.531

13

(1) This paragraph applies where there is an uncrystallised floating charge on the property of a company for which a moratorium is in force.

(2) If the conditions for the holder of the charge to give a notice having the effect mentioned in sub-paragraph (4) are met at any time, the notice may not be given at that time but may instead be given as soon as practicable after the moratorium has come to an end.

(3) If any other event occurs at any time which (apart from this sub-paragraph) would have the effect mentioned in sub-paragraph (4), then—

   (a) the event shall not have the effect in question at that time, but

   (b) if notice of the event is given to the company by the holder of the charge as soon as is practicable after the moratorium has come to an end, the event is to be treated as if it had occurred when the notice was given.

(4) The effect referred to in sub-paragraphs (2) and (3) is—

   (a) causing the crystallisation of the floating charge, or

   (b) causing the imposition, by virtue of provision in the instrument creating the charge, of any restriction on the disposal of any property of the company.

(5) Application may not be made for leave under paragraph 12(1)(g) or (h) with a view to obtaining—

   (a) the crystallisation of the floating charge, or

   (b) the imposition, by virtue of provision in the instrument creating the charge, of any restriction on the disposal of any property of the company.

Notes

Para 13

Paragraph 13 must be read in conjunction with paragraph 43. Together they operate to suspend for the duration of the moratorium the crystallisation of any floating charge, or the imposition of any restrictions in favour of such charge holder on the disposal of the property of the company. Paragraph 43 renders void any provision in a floating charge instrument which provides that the obtaining of a moratorium (or anything done with a view to obtaining such moratorium) is an event which either causes the charge to crystallise, or imposes restrictions which would not otherwise apply on the disposal or property by the company, or provides grounds for the appointment of an administrative receiver.

In the event that Paragraph 43 does not avoid the relevant provisions of the floating charge Paragraph 13 operates to prevent the crystallisation of any floating charge or the imposition of restrictions on the disposal of any property of the company for the duration of the moratorium by:

- prohibiting the giving of any notice which the chargee would be entitled to give under the floating charge instrument which would have that effect until after the moratorium has come to an end; and
- disapplying for the duration of the moratorium any provision under the floating charge which causes that effect without the requirement for notice on the occurrence of any event.

1.532

14

Security granted by a company at a time when a moratorium is in force in relation to the company may only be enforced if, at that time, there were reasonable grounds for believing that it would benefit the company.

Notes

Para 14

This provision may be designed broadly to protect a company pressured to give security to creditors in respect of existing debt as a condition for the provision of further credit in the moratorium, while permitting security to be taken in respect of new credit provided to enable the company to continue trading. However it remains to be seen the extent to which any bank would be prepared to provide such facilities where a security may be tested under Paragraph 14.

Effect on company

1.533

15

(1) Paragraphs 16 to 23 apply in relation to a company for which a moratorium is in force.

(2) The fact that a company enters into a transaction in contravention of any of paragraphs 16 to 22 does not—
    (a)   make the transaction void, or
    (b)   make it to any extent unenforceable against the company.

Notes

Paras 15–23

For the duration of the moratorium, control of the company and its business remains vested in its directors. The nominee is obliged under Paragraph 24 to monitor the company's affairs during the moratorium but only for the purpose of forming an opinion as to whether the CVA has reasonable prospects of being approved and implemented, and whether the company is likely to have sufficient funds for the remainder of the moratorium to enable it to continue to carry on its business. Paragraphs 16 to 19 and 23 are designed to provide creditors with some additional protection from abuse of the moratorium by the company's directors by restricting the directors' freedom:

- to enter into contracts or obtain credit without disclosing the existence of the moratorium (paras 16, 17);
- to pay pre-moratorium debts or dispose of the company's property otherwise than in the ordinary course of business unless there are reasonable grounds for believing this will be for the benefit of the company, and approval has been obtained by the nominee or any moratorium committee (paras 18, 19);
- to enter into any of the financial market transactions set out in paragraph 23.

Any contravention of these restrictions on the part of the company constitutes an offence rendering the company and any defaulting officer liable to a fine, or in certain cases, imprisonment; see IA 1986 s 430 and schedule 10 for details of the manner in which the offence is punishable and the maximum fine or term of imprisonment. However, it does not render the offending transaction void or unenforceable, or directly impose any personal liability on the defaulting directors to the company or its creditors in respect of the transaction.

Paragraphs 20 to 22 in contrast provide the company with a freedom it would not otherwise enjoy, subject to obtaining the leave of the court, to dispose of property subject to a security or in the possession of the company under a hire-purchase agreement. These rights are analogous to those enjoyed by an administrator under IA 1986 Sch B1 para 70–72.

It is relevant to note that under paragraph 26 a creditor who is dissatisfied by any act, omission or decision of nominee during moratorium may apply to court; in addition a creditor has a right to apply to court under paragraph 40 on the grounds that the company's affairs/business are being managed by the directors in a manner unfairly prejudicial to the interest of creditors etc, or that any actual or proposed act or omission of the directors would be so prejudicial.

Company invoices, etc

1.534

16

(1) Every invoice, order for goods or business letter which—
  (a)   is issued by or on behalf of the company, and
  (b)   on or in which the company's name appears,
shall also contain the nominee's name and a statement that the moratorium is in force for the company.

(2) If default is made in complying with sub-paragraph (1), the company and (subject to sub-paragraph (3)) any officer of the company is liable to a fine.

(3) An officer of the company is only liable under sub-paragraph (2) if, without reasonable excuse, he authorises or permits the default.

Obtaining credit during moratorium

1.535

17

(1) The company may not obtain credit to the extent of £250 or more from a person who has not been informed that a moratorium is in force in relation to the company.

(2) The reference to the company obtaining credit includes the following cases—

    (a)   where goods are bailed (in Scotland, hired) to the company under a hire-purchase agreement, or agreed to be sold to the company under a conditional sale agreement, and

    (b)   where the company is paid in advance (whether in money or otherwise) for the supply of goods or services.

(3) Where the company obtains credit in contravention of sub-paragraph (1)—

    (a)   the company is liable to a fine, and

    (b)   if any officer of the company knowingly and wilfully authorised or permitted the contravention, he is liable to imprisonment or a fine, or both.

(4) The money sum specified in sub-paragraph (1) is subject to increase or reduction by order under section 417A in Part XV.

Disposals and payments

I.536

18

(1) Subject to sub-paragraph (2), the company may only dispose of any of its property if—

    (a)   there are reasonable grounds for believing that the disposal will benefit the company, and

    (b)   the disposal is approved by the committee established under paragraph 35(1) or, where there is no such committee, by the nominee.

(2) Sub-paragraph (1) does not apply to a disposal made in the ordinary way of the company's business.

(3) If the company makes a disposal in contravention of sub-paragraph (1) otherwise than in pursuance of an order of the court—

    (a)   the company is liable to a fine, and

    (b)   if any officer of the company authorised or permitted the contravention, without reasonable excuse, he is liable to imprisonment or a fine, or both.

Notes

See the commentary to paragraph 15 and paragraph 20.

I.537

19

(1) Subject to sub-paragraph (2), the company may only make any payment in respect of any debt or other liability of the company in existence before the beginning of the moratorium if—

    (a)   there are reasonable grounds for believing that the payment will benefit the company, and

(b)   the payment is approved by the committee established under paragraph 35(1) or, where there is no such committee, by the nominee.

(2) Sub-paragraph (1) does not apply to a payment required by paragraph 20(6).

(3) If the company makes a payment in contravention of sub-paragraph (1) otherwise than in pursuance of an order of the court—
(a)   the company is liable to a fine, and
(b)   if any officer of the company authorised or permitted the contravention, without reasonable excuse, he is liable to imprisonment or a fine, or both.

Disposal of charged property, etc

I.538

20

(1) This paragraph applies where—
(a)   any property of the company is subject to a security, or
(b)   any goods are in the possession of the company under a hire-purchase agreement.

(2) If the holder of the security consents, or the court gives leave, the company may dispose of the property as if it were not subject to the security.

(3) If the owner of the goods consents, or the court gives leave, the company may dispose of the goods as if all rights of the owner under the hire-purchase agreement were vested in the company.

(4) Where property subject to a security which, as created, was a floating charge is disposed of under sub-paragraph (2), the holder of the security has the same priority in respect of any property of the company directly or indirectly representing the property disposed of as he would have had in respect of the property subject to the security.

(5) Sub-paragraph (6) applies to the disposal under sub-paragraph (2) or (as the case may be) sub-paragraph (3) of–
(a)   any property subject to a security other than a security which, as created, was a floating charge, or
(b)   any goods in the possession of the company under a hire-purchase agreement.

(6) It shall be a condition of any consent or leave under sub-paragraph (2) or (as the case may be) sub-paragraph (3) that—
(a)   the net proceeds of the disposal, and
(b)   where those proceeds are less than such amount as may be agreed, or determined by the court, to be the net amount which would be realised on a sale of the property or goods in the open market by a willing vendor, such sums as may be required to make good the deficiency,
shall be applied towards discharging the sums secured by the security or payable under the hire-purchase agreement.

(7) Where a condition imposed in pursuance of sub-paragraph (6) relates to two or more securities, that condition requires—

>   (a)   the net proceeds of the disposal, and
>   (b)   where paragraph (b) of sub-paragraph (6) applies, the sums
>   mentioned in that paragraph,
> to be applied towards discharging the sums secured by those securities in
> the order of their priorities.
>
> (8) Where the court gives leave for a disposal under sub-paragraph (2) or
> (3), the directors shall, within 14 days after leave is given, send an office
> copy of the order giving leave to the registrar of companies.
>
> (9) If the directors without reasonable excuse fail to comply with sub-
> paragraph (8), they are liable to a fine.

Notes

Paras 20–22

These paragraphs supplement the provisions of paragraph 18 above. Paragraph 18 restricts the power of the company to dispose of its property otherwise than in the usual course of business during the moratorium (for instance by a sale of the business) except where there are reasonable grounds for believing the disposal will benefit the company, and the disposal is approved either by a moratorium committee or the nominee. Where the conditions of paragraph 18 are met, paragraph 20 then confers a further power on the company to dispose of charged property, subject to the company obtaining the consent of the chargee or the leave of the court, which the company would not enjoy outside a moratorium.

The power mirrors that conferred on an administrator under IA 1986 Sch B1 para 70ff. Such a power is useful in an administration to enable an administrator to dispose of the company's business (or any part of that business) as a going concern, and is presumably envisaged to be used for similar purposes in moratoria cases. In an administration, the court will only grant leave where the disposal in question would be likely to promote the objective of the administration. In a moratorium, it will be necessary at least to satisfy the 'benefit' test in Paragraph 18(1)(a) (presumably this would include a better result for the creditors as whole than would otherwise be effected), but it remains to be seen what principles will be developed on the exercise of the court's discretion; see *Re A R V Aviation Ltd* (1988) 4 BCC 708 for an example of the operation of similar provisions under the former administration regime.

Para 20(6)

This provision is almost identical in wording to former IA 1986 s 15(5). In *Re A R V Aviation Ltd* (1988) 4 BCC 708, the expression 'sums secured by the security ...' was construed to cover not only the capital sum secured but also interest and any costs which the chargee was entitled to add to his security under the general law and the terms of the charge.

Applications for leave

See IR 1986 r 1.43 for the rules relating to applications for leave under paragraph 20.

> **1.539**
>
> **21**
>
> (1) Where property is disposed of under paragraph 20 in its application
> to Scotland, the company shall grant to the disponee an appropriate
> document of transfer or conveyance of the property, and
>   (a)   that document, or

(b) where any recording, intimation or registration of the document is a legal requirement for completion of title to the property, that recording, intimation or registration,

has the effect of disencumbering the property of, or (as the case may be) freeing the property from, the security.

(2) Where goods in the possession of the company under a hire-purchase agreement are disposed of under paragraph 20 in its application to Scotland, the disposal has the effect of extinguishing, as against the disponee, all rights of the owner of the goods under the agreement.

1.540

22

(1) If the company—
  (a) without any consent or leave under paragraph 20, disposes of any of its property which is subject to a security otherwise than in accordance with the terms of the security,
  (b) without any consent or leave under paragraph 20, disposes of any goods in the possession of the company under a hire-purchase agreement otherwise than in accordance with the terms of the agreement, or
  (c) fails to comply with any requirement imposed by paragraph 20 or 21,

it is liable to a fine.

(2) If any officer of the company, without reasonable excuse, authorises or permits any such disposal or failure to comply, he is liable to imprisonment or a fine, or both.

Market contracts, etc

1.541

23

(1) If the company enters into any transaction to which this paragraph applies—
  (a) the company is liable to a fine, and
  (b) if any officer of the company, without reasonable excuse, authorised or permitted the company to enter into the transaction, he is liable to imprisonment or a fine, or both.

(2) A company enters into a transaction to which this paragraph applies if it—
  (a) enters into a market contract, a money market contract,
  (b) gives a transfer order,
  (c) grants a market charge, or a system-charge, or
  (d) provides any collateral security.

(3) The fact that a company enters into a transaction in contravention of this paragraph does not—
  (a) make the transaction void, or
  (b) make it to any extent unenforceable by or against the company.

(4) Where during the moratorium a company enters into a transaction to which this paragraph applies, nothing done by or in pursuance of the transaction is to be treated as done in contravention of paragraphs 12(1)(g), 14 or 16 to 22.

(5) Paragraph 20 does not apply in relation to any property which is subject to a market charge, a system-charge or a collateral security charge.

(6) In this paragraph, 'transfer order', 'collateral security' and 'collateral security charge' have the same meanings as in the settlement finality regulations.

Part IV
Nominees

Monitoring of company's activities

1.542

24

(1) During a moratorium, the nominee shall monitor the company's affairs for the purpose of forming an opinion as to whether—
  (a) the proposed voluntary arrangement or, if he has received notice of proposed modifications under paragraph 31(7), the proposed arrangement with those modifications has a reasonable prospect of being approved and implemented, and
  (b) the company is likely to have sufficient funds available to it during the remainder of the moratorium to enable it to continue to carry on its business.

(2) The directors shall submit to the nominee any information necessary to enable him to comply with sub-paragraph (1) which he requests from them.

(3) In forming his opinion on the matters mentioned in sub-paragraph (1), the nominee is entitled to rely on the information submitted to him under sub-paragraph (2) unless he has reason to doubt its accuracy.

(4) The reference in sub-paragraph (1)(b) to the company's business is to that business as the company proposes to carry it on during the remainder of the moratorium.

Notes

Para 24(1)

This is an important provision providing some protection to creditors against the possibility of abuse of the moratorium by the company and its directors. The nominee must have been satisfied of the two matters set out in paragraph 24(1) in order for the moratorium to be put in place (see paragraphs 6(2), 7(1)(e) above); and he is under a continuing monitoring duty for the duration of the moratorium for the purposes of forming an opinion on those two matters. Where he is no longer satisfied on one or both of those matters, he must withdraw his consent to act as nominee in the moratorium under paragraph 25(2)(a), thereby bringing the moratorium to an end.

Para 24(2)

The directors are under an obligation to provide the nominee with such information as he requires in order to undertake this assessment. Where they fail to comply with that obligation, the nominee must again withdraw his consent to act under paragraph 25(2)(c).

Withdrawal of consent to act

1.543

25

(1) The nominee may only withdraw his consent to act in the circumstances mentioned in this paragraph.

(2) The nominee must withdraw his consent to act if, at any time during a moratorium—

    (a)   he forms the opinion that—

        (i)   the proposed voluntary arrangement or, if he has received notice of proposed modifications under paragraph 31(7), the proposed arrangement with those modifications no longer has a reasonable prospect of being approved or implemented, or

        (ii)   the company will not have sufficient funds available to it during the remainder of the moratorium to enable it to continue to carry on its business,

    (b)   he becomes aware that, on the date of filing, the company was not eligible for a moratorium, or

    (c)   the directors fail to comply with their duty under paragraph 24(2).

(3) The reference in sub-paragraph (2)(a)(ii) to the company's business is to that business as the company proposes to carry it on during the remainder of the moratorium.

(4) If the nominee withdraws his consent to act, the moratorium comes to an end.

(5) If the nominee withdraws his consent to act he must, in accordance with the rules, notify the court, the registrar of companies, the company and any creditor of the company of whose claim he is aware of his withdrawal and the reason for it.

(6) If the nominee without reasonable excuse fails to comply with sub-paragraph (5), he is liable to a fine.

Notes

Para 25(2)

Where the nominee fails to withdraw his consent to act in circumstances where he is obliged to do so under paragraph 25(2), any creditor, director or member may mount a challenge to that failure under paragraph 26 below, and/or a creditor may seek an order under paragraph 27 requiring the company to pursue a claim against the nominee or authorising him to bring the claim on the company's behalf.

Para 25(5)

See IR 1986 r 1.44 for the provision governing the giving of notice of withdrawal.

___

Challenge of nominee's actions, etc

1.544

26

(1) If any creditor, director or member of the company, or any other person affected by a moratorium, is dissatisfied by any act, omission or decision of the nominee during the moratorium, he may apply to the court.

(2) An application under sub-paragraph (1) may be made during the moratorium or after it has ended.

(3) On an application under sub-paragraph (1) the court may—
  (a)   confirm, reverse or modify any act or decision of the nominee,
  (b)   give him directions, or
  (c)   make such other order as it thinks fit.

(4) An order under sub-paragraph (3) may (among other things) bring the moratorium to an end and make such consequential provision as the court thinks fit.

___

Notes

Para 26

As noted in the commentary to paragraph 15 above, during the moratorium control of the company and its business remains with the directors. Any challenge to the way in which the business is being managed by the directors should be brought by a creditor or member under paragraph 40 below where that creditor/member can show unfair prejudice. See IR 1986 r 1.47 for provisions governing applications under paragraph 26.

Para 26(1)

The role of the nominee during the moratorium is two-fold. First he is required to monitor the company's affairs to assess whether or not the proposed CVA has reasonable prospects of being approved and implemented and whether the company has sufficient funds available to it to continue its business for the remainder of the moratorium (see paragraph 24); where he is not satisfied, he is required to withdraw his consent to act, thereby bringing the moratorium to an end (see paragraph 25). Secondly, he is required to adjudicate on any request by the company to dispose of its property otherwise than in the ordinary course of business or to settle pre-moratorium debts (see paragraphs 18, 19). Accordingly, any challenge to an act, omission or decision of the nominee under paragraph 26 is likely to be connected with one of these two functions.

Any challenge to a decision of the nominee made in his function as chairman of the meetings of creditors and members summoned to consider the CVA proposals should be brought under paragraph 38 below.

___

1.545

27

(1) Where there are reasonable grounds for believing that—
  (a) as a result of any act, omission or decision of the nominee during the moratorium, the company has suffered loss, but
  (b) the company does not intend to pursue any claim it may have against the nominee,
any creditor of the company may apply to the court.

(2) An application under sub-paragraph (1) may be made during the moratorium or after it has ended.

(3) On an application under sub-paragraph (1) the court may—
  (a) order the company to pursue any claim against the nominee,
  (b) authorise any creditor to pursue such a claim in the name of the company, or
  (c) make such other order with respect to such a claim as it thinks fit,
unless the court is satisfied that the act, omission or decision of the nominee was in all the circumstances reasonable.

(4) An order under sub-paragraph (3) may (among other things)—
  (a) impose conditions on any authority given to pursue a claim,
  (b) direct the company to assist in the pursuit of a claim,
  (c) make directions with respect to the distribution of anything received as a result of the pursuit of a claim,
  (d) bring the moratorium to an end and make such consequential provision as the court thinks fit.

(5) On an application under sub-paragraph (1) the court shall have regard to the interests of the members and creditors of the company generally.

Notes

Para 27(1)

This paragraph does not appear in its terms to create any new statutory cause of action in favour of a company, or its creditors, against a nominee. It appears that the company must have a pre-existing cause of action against the nominee (e g for breach of contract, negligence or, perhaps, breach of fiduciary duty) arising from any act, omission or decision of his during the moratorium. In such circumstances paragraph 27(1) provides a means whereby a creditor can either require the company to pursue such a claim or authorise the creditor to pursue the claim in the name of and on the company's behalf.

Para 27(3)

This provides protection against vexatious attempts on the part of creditors to pursue claims against the nominee in the company's name; where the court is satisfied that the act, omission or decision of the nominee was in all the circumstances reasonable it may refuse to make an order in favour of the creditors.

Para 27(4)

The court may inter alia give directions for the distribution of any proceeds of any claim. If, as suggested above, this paragraph does not create any new causes of action in favour of creditors, but simply provides a procedure by which any causes of action which the company may have against the nominee may be pursued on the company's behalf by a creditor (or by which the company may itself be required to pursue the claim), this provision is presumably designed to provide a means by which any creditor bringing or funding such a claim may be indemnified for his costs of so doing from the proceeds of the claim.

See IR 1986 r 1.47 governing applications under this paragraph.

_____

Replacement of nominee by court

1.546

28

(1) The court may—
  (a) on an application made by the directors in a case where the nominee has failed to comply with any duty imposed on him under this Schedule or has died, or
  (b) on an application made by the directors or the nominee in a case where it is impracticable or inappropriate for the nominee to continue to act as such,
direct that the nominee be replaced as such by another person qualified to act as an insolvency practitioner, or authorised to act as nominee, in relation to the voluntary arrangement.

(2) A person may only be appointed as a replacement nominee under this paragraph if he submits to the court a statement indicating his consent to act.

_____

Notes

Para 28

The power of the court to replace a nominee conferred by this paragraph should be read in conjunction with paragraph 33 which empowers the creditors' meeting and the company meeting to require the replacement of the nominee as a condition of any decision by those meetings to extend the moratorium beyond its initial period. See IR 1986 r 1.45 and 1.46 for the rules which apply to applications under paragraph 28.

Para 28(1)(a)

Unlike paragraphs 26 and 27 which apply in terms only to acts, omissions or decisions of the nominee during the moratorium, paragraph 28 provides a remedy in the event of a nominee's failure to comply with any duty both during and prior to the moratorium; for instance it would be relevant in the event of a failure by a nominee to produce a paragraph 6(2) statement within the 28 day period after submission to him of the proposal.

Para 28(1)(b)

A similar power to replace the nominee where it is impracticable or inappropriate for him to continue to act exists under IA 1986 s 2(4)(b) (non-moratorium CVAs) and s 256(3)(b) and s 256A (4)(b) (IVAs).

_____

Part V
Consideration and Implementation of Voluntary Arrangement

Summoning of meetings

1.547

29

(1) Where a moratorium is in force, the nominee shall summon meetings of the company and its creditors for such a time, date (within the period for the time being specified in paragraph 8(3)) and place as he thinks fit.

(2) The persons to be summoned to a creditors' meeting under this paragraph are every creditor of the company of whose claim the nominee is aware.

Notes

Para 29(1)

Where the nominee has given a positive opinion on the matters he is required to consider under paragraph 6(2), and the directors have accordingly filed the requisite documents with the court to obtain a moratorium under paragraph 7, the nominee is then required to summon the meetings of creditors and the company within a 28 day period from the beginning of the moratorium. This time limit is confirmed by IR 1986 r 1.48, and, coupled with the requirement to give creditors and members 14 days notice of the meeting, imposes a tight timetable on the nominee.

See paragraph 8 for provisions relating to the termination of the moratorium in the event the meetings are not summoned to take place within the 28 day period. See also paragraph 32 on the power of one or both meetings to extend the moratorium on any adjournment of such meeting when it is first held, or subsequently.

Conduct of meetings

1.548

30

(1) Subject to the provisions of paragraphs 31 to 35, the meetings summoned under paragraph 29 shall be conducted in accordance with the rules.

(2) A meeting so summoned may resolve that it be adjourned (or further adjourned).

(3) After the conclusion of either meeting in accordance with the rules, the chairman of the meeting shall report the result of the meeting to the court, and, immediately after reporting to the court, shall give notice of the result of the meeting to such persons as may be prescribed.

Notes

Para 30(1)

For the rules governing the conduct of meetings, see IR 1986 r 1.49 to 1.53.

Approval of voluntary arrangement

1.549

31

(1) The meetings summoned under paragraph 29 shall decide whether to approve the proposed voluntary arrangement (with or without modifications).

(2) The modifications may include one conferring the functions proposed to be conferred on the nominee on another person qualified to act as an insolvency practitioner, or authorised to act as nominee, in relation to the voluntary arrangement.

(3) The modifications shall not include one by virtue of which the proposal ceases to be a proposal such as is mentioned in section 1.

(4) A meeting summoned under paragraph 29 shall not approve any proposal or modification which affects the right of a secured creditor of the company to enforce his security, except with the concurrence of the creditor concerned.

(5) Subject to sub-paragraph (6), a meeting so summoned shall not approve any proposal or modification under which—

    (a)   any preferential debt of the company is to be paid otherwise than in priority to such of its debts as are not preferential debts, or

    (b)   a preferential creditor of the company is to be paid an amount in respect of a preferential debt that bears to that debt a smaller proportion than is borne to another preferential debt by the amount that is to be paid in respect of that other debt.

(6) The meeting may approve such a proposal or modification with the concurrence of the preferential creditor concerned.

(7) The directors of the company may, before the beginning of the period of seven days which ends with the meetings (or either of them) summoned under paragraph 29 being held, give notice to the nominee of any modifications of the proposal for which the directors intend to seek the approval of those meetings.

(8) References in this paragraph to preferential debts and preferential creditors are to be read in accordance with section 386 in Part XII of this Act.

Notes

Para 31

This paragraph is in substantially the same terms as IA 1986 s 4 (the equivalent provision which applies to non-moratorium CVAs); see the detailed commentary to that section.

Para 31(7)

This is different to the substantially similar provisions of IA 1986 s 4. Under paragraph 31(7) the directors 'may' give notice to the nominee of any modification to the proposal for which the directors intend to seek the approval of the meeting not less than 7 days before the meeting. It appears that this is not merely permissive but in fact requires the directors to notify the nominee of any such proposed modifications within the stipulated time. This will ensure that the nominee has time to notify creditors, including in particular those intending to vote by proxy, of any such proposed modifications; further it will enable the nominee to comply with his duty under paragraph 24 to assess whether the CVA subject to the proposed modifications has reasonable prospects of being approved and implemented.

Extension of moratorium

1.550

32

(1) Subject to sub-paragraph (2), a meeting summoned under paragraph 29 which resolves that it be adjourned (or further adjourned) may resolve that the moratorium be extended (or further extended), with or without conditions.

(2) The moratorium may not be extended (or further extended) to a day later than the end of the period of two months which begins—
    (a)   where both meetings summoned under paragraph 29 are first held on the same day, with that day,
    (b)   in any other case, with the day on which the later of those meetings is first held.

(3) At any meeting where it is proposed to extend (or further extend) the moratorium, before a decision is taken with respect to that proposal, the nominee shall inform the meeting—
    (a)   of what he has done in order to comply with his duty under paragraph 24 and the cost of his actions for the company, and
    (b)   of what he intends to do to continue to comply with that duty if the moratorium is extended (or further extended) and the expected cost of his actions for the company.

(4) Where, in accordance with sub-paragraph (3)(b), the nominee informs a meeting of the expected cost of his intended actions, the meeting shall resolve whether or not to approve that expected cost.

(5) If a decision not to approve the expected cost of the nominee's intended actions has effect under paragraph 36, the moratorium comes to an end.

(6) A meeting may resolve that a moratorium which has been extended (or further extended) be brought to an end before the end of the period of the extension (or further extension).

(7) The Secretary of State may by order increase or reduce the period for the time being specified in sub-paragraph (2).

Notes

Para 32(1)

This provision confers on the creditors' meeting, and the company meeting, summoned to consider the CVA proposal, the power to extend the moratorium beyond its initial term which under paragraph 8 expires at the earlier of (i) the end of the day on which the meetings are first held (or if held on different days, the day on which the later of the meetings is held) and (ii) 28 days after the moratorium comes into force. Note that there is no equivalent power for the court to extend the moratorium.

Para 32(3)–(5)

The nominee is under a duty to inform any meeting considering extending the moratorium of the steps undertaken in monitoring the company pursuant to his duty under paragraph 24 and of the further steps he intends to take to comply with that duty for the period of the extended moratorium. He is also under a duty to inform the meeting of the costs already incurred and the anticipated future costs, and the meeting correspondingly must decide whether to approve such costs, or otherwise bring the moratorium to an immediate end.

1.551

33

(1) The conditions which may be imposed when a moratorium is extended (or further extended) include a requirement that the nominee be replaced as such by another person qualified to act as an insolvency practitioner, or authorised to act as nominee, in relation to the voluntary arrangement.

(2) A person may only be appointed as a replacement nominee by virtue of sub-paragraph (1) if he submits to the court a statement indicating his consent to act.

(3) At any meeting where it is proposed to appoint a replacement nominee as a condition of extending (or further extending) the moratorium—
    (a)   the duty imposed by paragraph 32(3)(b) on the nominee shall instead be imposed on the person proposed as the replacement nominee, and
    (b)   paragraphs 32(4) and (5) and 36(1)(e) apply as if the references to the nominee were to that person.

Notes

Para 33

This provision complements paragraph 28 which enables an application to be made to court to replace a nominee. Paragraph 33 enables either meeting to resolve to replace the nominee without any application to court as a condition of extending the moratorium on any adjournment of such meeting.

1.552

34

(1) If a decision to extend, or further extend, the moratorium takes effect under paragraph 36, the nominee shall, in accordance with the rules, notify the registrar of companies and the court.

(2) If the moratorium is extended, or further extended, by virtue of an order under paragraph 36(5), the nominee shall, in accordance with the rules, send an office copy of the order to the registrar of companies.

(3) If the nominee without reasonable excuse fails to comply with this paragraph, he is liable to a fine.

Moratorium committee

1.553

35

(1) A meeting summoned under paragraph 29 which resolves that the moratorium be extended (or further extended) may, with the consent of the nominee, resolve that a committee be established to exercise the functions conferred on it by the meeting.

(2) The meeting may not so resolve unless it has approved an estimate of the expenses to be incurred by the committee in the exercise of the proposed functions.

(3) Any expenses, not exceeding the amount of the estimate, incurred by the committee in the exercise of its functions shall be reimbursed by the nominee.

(4) The committee shall cease to exist when the moratorium comes to an end.

Notes

Para 35

The only function specifically envisaged by Sch A1 for a moratorium committee is to adjudicate during the course of the moratorium upon any intended disposal of the company's property otherwise than in the ordinary course of business or on any intended payment of pre-moratorium debts under paragraphs 18 and 19. The consent of the nominee is specifically required before any resolution can be passed for the establishment of such a committee, and, in general terms, such a committee might be expected to undertake a monitoring function in parallel to that which the nominee is required to undertake under paragraph 24.

Effectiveness of decisions

1.554

36

(1) Sub-paragraph (2) applies to references to one of the following decisions having effect, that is, a decision, under paragraph 31, 32 or 35, with respect to—
- (a) the approval of a proposed voluntary arrangement,
- (b) the extension (or further extension) of a moratorium,
- (c) the bringing of a moratorium to an end,
- (d) the establishment of a committee, or
- (e) the approval of the expected cost of a nominee's intended actions.

(2) The decision has effect if, in accordance with the rules—

(a) it has been taken by both meetings summoned under paragraph 29, or

(b) (subject to any order made under sub-paragraph (5)) it has been taken by the creditors' meeting summoned under that paragraph.

(3) If a decision taken by the creditors' meeting under any of paragraphs 31, 32 or 35 with respect to any of the matters mentioned in sub-paragraph (1) differs from one so taken by the company meeting with respect to that matter, a member of the company may apply to the court.

(4) An application under sub-paragraph (3) shall not be made after the end of the period of 28 days beginning with—

(a) the day on which the decision was taken by the creditors' meeting, or

(b) where the decision of the company meeting was taken on a later day, that day.

(5) On an application under sub-paragraph (3), the court may—

(a) order the decision of the company meeting to have effect instead of the decision of the creditors' meeting, or

(b) make such other order as it thinks fit.

Notes

Para 36

This provision adopts and extends similar provisions conferring primacy of decisions of the creditors' meeting over that of the company meeting as were introduced in respect of non-moratorium CVAs by the new IA 1986 s 4A; see the notes to IA 1986 s 4A.

Effect of approval of voluntary arrangement

1.555

37

(1) This paragraph applies where a decision approving a voluntary arrangement has effect under paragraph 36.

(2) The approved voluntary arrangement—

(a) takes effect as if made by the company at the creditors' meeting, and

(b) binds every person who in accordance with the rules—

(i) was entitled to vote at that meeting (whether or not he was present or represented at it), or

(ii) would have been so entitled if he had had notice of it,

as if he were a party to the voluntary arrangement.

(3) If—

(a) when the arrangement ceases to have effect any amount payable under the arrangement to a person bound by virtue of sub-paragraph (2)(b)(ii) has not been paid, and

(b) the arrangement did not come to an end prematurely,

the company shall at that time become liable to pay to that person the amount payable under the arrangement.

(4) Where a petition for the winding up of the company, other than an excepted petition within the meaning of paragraph 12, was presented before the beginning of the moratorium, the court shall dismiss the petition.

(5) The court shall not dismiss a petition under sub-paragraph (4)—
- (a) at any time before the end of the period of 28 days beginning with the first day on which each of the reports of the meetings required by paragraph 30(3) has been made to the court, or
- (b) at any time when an application under paragraph 38 or an appeal in respect of such an application is pending, or at any time in the period within which such an appeal may be brought.

Notes

Para 37(1)–(3)

These provisions are identical to IA 1986 s 5(1)–(2A) (which apply to non-moratorium CVAs); see the notes to IA 1986 s 5.

Para 37(4)–(5)

Once the CVA is approved the moratorium comes to an end at the end of the day on which the decision approving the CVA takes effect under paragraph 36: see paragraph 8(7). The court must dismiss any petition presented before the moratorium came into force, other than an excepted petition, but may not do so until the 28 day period for challenging the approval under paragraph 38 has expired, or, if an application is made mounting such a challenge, while that application, or any appeal therefrom is pending.

Challenge of decisions

1.556

38

(1) Subject to the following provisions of this paragraph, any of the persons mentioned in sub-paragraph (2) may apply to the court on one or both of the following grounds—
- (a) that a voluntary arrangement approved at one or both of the meetings summoned under paragraph 29 and which has taken effect unfairly prejudices the interests of a creditor, member or contributory of the company,
- (b) that there has been some material irregularity at or in relation to either of those meetings.

(2) The persons who may apply under this paragraph are—
- (a) a person entitled, in accordance with the rules, to vote at either of the meetings,
- (b) a person who would have been entitled, in accordance with the rules, to vote at the creditors' meeting if he had had notice of it, and
- (c) the nominee.

(3) An application under this paragraph shall not be made—

(a) after the end of the period of 28 days beginning with the first day on which each of the reports required by paragraph 30(3) has been made to the court, or

(b) in the case of a person who was not given notice of the creditors' meeting, after the end of the period of 28 days beginning with the day on which he became aware that the meeting had taken place,

but (subject to that) an application made by a person within sub-paragraph (2)(b) on the ground that the arrangement prejudices his interests may be made after the arrangement has ceased to have effect, unless it came to an end prematurely.

(4) Where on an application under this paragraph the court is satisfied as to either of the grounds mentioned in sub-paragraph (1), it may do any of the following—

(a) revoke or suspend—
   (i) any decision approving the voluntary arrangement which has effect under paragraph 36, or
   (ii) in a case falling within sub-paragraph (1)(b), any decision taken by the meeting in question which has effect under that paragraph,

(b) give a direction to any person—
   (i) for the summoning of further meetings to consider any revised proposal for a voluntary arrangement which the directors may make, or
   (ii) in a case falling within sub-paragraph (1)(b), for the summoning of a further company or (as the case may be) creditors' meeting to reconsider the original proposal.

(5) Where at any time after giving a direction under sub-paragraph (4)(b)(i) the court is satisfied that the directors do not intend to submit a revised proposal, the court shall revoke the direction and revoke or suspend any decision approving the voluntary arrangement which has effect under paragraph 36.

(6) Where the court gives a direction under sub-paragraph (4)(b), it may also give a direction continuing or, as the case may require, renewing, for such period as may be specified in the direction, the effect of the moratorium.

(7) Sub-paragraph (8) applies in a case where the court, on an application under this paragraph—

(a) gives a direction under sub-paragraph (4)(b), or

(b) revokes or suspends a decision under sub-paragraph (4)(a) or (5).

(8) In such a case, the court may give such supplemental directions as it thinks fit and, in particular, directions with respect to—

(a) things done under the voluntary arrangement since it took effect, and

(b) such things done since that time as could not have been done if a moratorium had been in force in relation to the company when they were done.

> (9) Except in pursuance of the preceding provisions of this paragraph, a decision taken at a meeting summoned under paragraph 29 is not invalidated by any irregularity at or in relation to the meeting.

Notes

Para 38

This provision sets out the grounds on which a creditor or member, or the nominee, may challenge a decision of the meetings to approve or reject the CVA proposal. It is nearly identical in its terms to IA 1986 s 6 (the equivalent provision applying in respect of non-moratorium CVAs); see the notes to s 6.

Para 38(6)–(8)

Where, on a successful challenge to a decision either approving the CVA proposal under paragraph 38(1)(a) or because of some material irregularity under paragraph 38–(1)(b), the court orders that a further meeting is summoned to consider the original or revised proposals, the court may continue or renew the moratorium for a further period. There is no equivalent power while a challenge under paragraph 38 is pending to extend or renew a moratorium which has already come to an end. Where the challenge is to a CVA which has been approved, the company may in any event continue to be protected against enforcement action under the CVA itself while the challenge is still pending.

Implementation of voluntary arrangement

1.557

39

(1) This paragraph applies where a voluntary arrangement approved by one or both of the meetings summoned under paragraph 29 has taken effect.

(2) The person who is for the time being carrying out in relation to the voluntary arrangement the functions conferred—
- (a) by virtue of the approval of the arrangement, on the nominee, or
- (b) by virtue of paragraph 31(2), on a person other than the nominee,

shall be known as the supervisor of the voluntary arrangement.

(3) If any of the company's creditors or any other person is dissatisfied by any act, omission or decision of the supervisor, he may apply to the court.

(4) On an application under sub-paragraph (3) the court may—
- (a) confirm, reverse or modify any act or decision of the supervisor,
- (b) give him directions, or
- (c) make such other order as it thinks fit.

(5) The supervisor—
- (a) may apply to the court for directions in relation to any particular matter arising under the voluntary arrangement, and
- (b) is included among the persons who may apply to the court for the winding up of the company or for an administration order to be made in relation to it.

(6) The court may, whenever—
  (a) it is expedient to appoint a person to carry out the functions of the supervisor, and
  (b) it is inexpedient, difficult or impracticable for an appointment to be made without the assistance of the court,
make an order appointing a person who is qualified to act as an insolvency practitioner, or authorised to act as supervisor, in relation to the voluntary arrangement, either in substitution for the existing supervisor or to fill a vacancy.

(7) The power conferred by sub-paragraph (6) is exercisable so as to increase the number of persons exercising the functions of supervisor or, where there is more than one person exercising those functions, so as to replace one or more of those persons.

Notes

Para 39

This provision is identical to IA 1986 s 7 (which applies to non-moratorium CVAs); see notes to IA 1986 s 7.

Part VI
Miscellaneous

Challenge of directors' actions

1.558

40

(1) This paragraph applies in relation to acts or omissions of the directors of a company during a moratorium.

(2) A creditor or member of the company may apply to the court for an order under this paragraph on the ground—
  (a) that the company's affairs, business and property are being or have been managed by the directors in a manner which is unfairly prejudicial to the interests of its creditors or members generally, or of some part of its creditors or members (including at least the petitioner), or
  (b) that any actual or proposed act or omission of the directors is or would be so prejudicial.

(3) An application for an order under this paragraph may be made during or after the moratorium.

(4) On an application for an order under this paragraph the court may—
  (a) make such order as it thinks fit for giving relief in respect of the matters complained of,
  (b) adjourn the hearing conditionally or unconditionally, or
  (c) make an interim order or any other order that it thinks fit.

(5) An order under this paragraph may in particular—

(a) regulate the management by the directors of the company's affairs, business and property during the remainder of the moratorium,

(b) require the directors to refrain from doing or continuing an act complained of by the petitioner, or to do an act which the petitioner has complained they have omitted to do,

(c) require the summoning of a meeting of creditors or members for the purpose of considering such matters as the court may direct,

(d) bring the moratorium to an end and make such consequential provision as the court thinks fit.

(6) In making an order under this paragraph the court shall have regard to the need to safeguard the interests of persons who have dealt with the company in good faith and for value.

(7) Sub-paragraph (8) applies where –

(a) the appointment of an administrator has effect in relation to the company and that appointment was in pursuance of –

(i) an administration application made, or

(ii) a notice of intention to appoint filed

before the moratorium came into force or

(b) the company is being wound up in pursuance of a petition presented before the moratorium came into force

(8) No application for an order under this paragraph may be made by a creditor or member of the company; but such an application may be made instead by the administrator or (as the case may be) the liquidator.

Notes

Para 40

This provision enables a creditor or member to apply to court on the grounds that the affairs or business of the company has been managed by the directors during the moratorium in a manner unfairly prejudicial to one or more creditors/members and it is similar language to that used in the former administration regime (IA 1986 s 27.)

Para 40(1)

An application under this paragraph must relate to the conduct of the directors in their management of the company during the moratorium; where a creditor or member is dissatisfied with an act, omission or decision of the nominee in the moratorium, his remedy is an application under paragraph 26; where a creditor or member contends that the terms of the CVA itself as approved are unfairly prejudicial, his remedy is an application under paragraph 38; and where a creditor or member is dissatisfied with an act, omission or decision of the supervisor in the implementation or operation of the CVA itself once approved, his remedy is an application under paragraph 39.

Para 40(2)

Any creditor or member has potential standing to apply under this paragraph, but as the sub-paragraph suggests, a creditor or member bringing an application must show that his interests personally have been unfairly prejudiced by the directors' management of the company's affairs. An applicant must have an interest in the outcome of his application, and for that reason, a member may have difficulty in obtaining relief under the paragraph unless he can show that the company is or would, but for the unfairly prejudicial conduct complained of, be solvent.

The reference to 'petitioner' in paragraph 40(2) appears to be a drafting error for 'applicant' since, there is no requirement for an application under Paragraph 40 to be brought by petition.

The considering the phrase 'unfairly prejudicial' it is important to distinguish between misconduct consisting of negligent conduct or conduct in breach of a director's fiduciary duties owed to the company (and through the company to its creditors where the company is insolvent) on the one hand, and unfairly prejudicial conduct on the other hand. In *Re Charnley Davies (No 2)* [1990] BCLC 760 (a claim brought under the former administration regime IA 1986 s 27), creditors complained that an administrator had sold the company's business too hastily and at an undervalue during the course of the administration. Millett J at p 782d–784c rejected an attempt to equate unfairly prejudicial conduct with tortious or unlawful conduct, which should per se be pursued by an ordinary claim by the company against the directors, utilising if necessary the provisions of IA 1986 s 212 to enable such claim to be brought by a liquidator or creditor in the company's liquidation. Conduct which is actionable may also be 'unfairly prejudicial' but it has a wider connotation and will also include conduct, whether lawful or not, in disregard of the interest of the creditors or the members generally, or of a class of creditors or members, for the benefit of or in preference to the interests of another class or body. See also *MTI Trading Systems v Winter* [1998] BCC 591 (again a decision under IA 1986 s 27) where the court expressed reluctance to interfere in what was essentially a commercial decision of the administrators in negotiating the sale of the company's business.

The wording of paragraph 40(2) is similar to that in s 459 CA 1985 and reference could be made to the discussion of unfair prejudice in *O'Neil v Phillips* [1999] 1 WLR 1092 (HL) with the caveat that a shareholders' dispute under s 459 is substantially different to a creditors' complaint in a CVA.

Paras 40(4), (5)

The list of remedies tat the court may make is not exhaustive. The court has power to make such order as it thinks fit for giving relief in respect of the matters complained of. The possibility of financial compensation is therefore left open.

Para 40(7), (8)

In these circumstances the decision of whether or not to apply on grounds of unfair prejudice rests with the administrator or the liquidator as the case may be. In relation to administration petitions presented prior to 15 September 2003 reference should be made to the former paragraph 40(7) (Enterprise Act 2002 Commencement No 4 and Transitional Provisions and Savings) Order 2003 Art 3).

Offences

1.559

41

(1) This paragraph applies where a moratorium has been obtained for a company.

(2) If, within the period of 12 months ending with the day on which the moratorium came into force, a person who was at the time an officer of the company—

    (a)   did any of the things mentioned in paragraphs (a) to (f) of sub-paragraph (4), or

    (b)   was privy to the doing by others of any of the things mentioned in paragraphs (c), (d) and (e) of that sub-paragraph,

he is to be treated as having committed an offence at that time.

(3) If, at any time during the moratorium, a person who is an officer of the company—

(a) does any of the things mentioned in paragraphs (a) to (f) of sub-paragraph (4), or

(b) is privy to the doing by others of any of the things mentioned in paragraphs (c), (d) and (e) of that sub-paragraph,

he commits an offence.

(4) Those things are—

(a) concealing any part of the company's property to the value of £500 or more, or concealing any debt due to or from the company, or

(b) fraudulently removing any part of the company's property to the value of £500 or more, or

(c) concealing, destroying, mutilating or falsifying any book or paper affecting or relating to the company's property or affairs, or

(d) making any false entry in any book or paper affecting or relating to the company's property or affairs, or

(e) fraudulently parting with, altering or making any omission in any document affecting or relating to the company's property or affairs, or

(f) pawning, pledging or disposing of any property of the company which has been obtained on credit and has not been paid for (unless the pawning, pledging or disposal was in the ordinary way of the company's business).

(5) For the purposes of this paragraph, 'officer' includes a shadow director.

(6) It is a defence—

(a) for a person charged under sub-paragraph (2) or (3) in respect of the things mentioned in paragraph (a) or (f) of sub-paragraph (4) to prove that he had no intent to defraud, and

(b) for a person charged under sub-paragraph (2) or (3) in respect of the things mentioned in paragraph (c) or (d) of sub-paragraph (4) to prove that he had no intent to conceal the state of affairs of the company or to defeat the law.

(7) Where a person pawns, pledges or disposes of any property of a company in circumstances which amount to an offence under sub-paragraph (2) or (3), every person who takes in pawn or pledge, or otherwise receives, the property knowing it to be pawned, pledged or disposed of in circumstances which—

(a) would, if a moratorium were obtained for the company within the period of 12 months beginning with the day on which the pawning, pledging or disposal took place, amount to an offence under sub-paragraph (2), or

(b) amount to an offence under sub-paragraph (3),

commits an offence.

(8) A person guilty of an offence under this paragraph is liable to imprisonment or a fine, or both.

(9) The money sums specified in paragraphs (a) and (b) of sub-paragraph (4) are subject to increase or reduction by order under section 417A in Part XV.

1.560

42

(1) If, for the purpose of obtaining a moratorium, or an extension of a moratorium, for a company, a person who is an officer of the company—
    (a)   makes any false representation, or
    (b)   fraudulently does, or omits to do, anything,
he commits an offence.

(2) Sub-paragraph (1) applies even if no moratorium or extension is obtained.

(3) For the purposes of this paragraph, 'officer' includes a shadow director.

(4) A person guilty of an offence under this paragraph is liable to imprisonment or a fine, or both.

Void provisions in floating charge documents

1.561

43

(1) A provision in an instrument creating a floating charge is void if it provides for—
    (a)   obtaining a moratorium, or
    (b)   anything done with a view to obtaining a moratorium (including any preliminary decision or investigation),
to be an event causing the floating charge to crystallise or causing restrictions which would not otherwise apply to be imposed on the disposal of property by the company or a ground for the appointment of a receiver.

(2) In sub-paragraph (1), 'receiver' includes a manager and a person who is appointed both receiver and manager.

Notes

Para 43

See the notes to paragraph 13 above.

Functions of the Financial Services Authority

1.562

44

(1) This Schedule has effect in relation to a moratorium for a regulated company with the modifications in sub-paragraphs (2) to (16) below.

(2) Any notice or other document required by virtue of this Schedule to be sent to a creditor of a regulated company must also be sent to the Authority.

(3) The Authority is entitled to be heard on any application to the court for leave under paragraph 20(2) or 20(3) (disposal of charged property, etc).

(4) Where paragraph 26(1) (challenge of nominee's actions, etc) applies, the persons who may apply to the court include the Authority.

(5) If a person other than the Authority applies to the court under that paragraph, the Authority is entitled to be heard on the application.

(6) Where paragraph 27(1) (challenge of nominee's actions, etc) applies, the persons who may apply to the court include the Authority.

(7) If a person other than the Authority applies to the court under that paragraph, the Authority is entitled to be heard on the application.

(8) The persons to be summoned to a creditors' meeting under paragraph 29 include the Authority.

(9) A person appointed for the purpose by the Authority is entitled to attend and participate in (but not to vote at)—
  (a)   any creditors' meeting summoned under that paragraph,
  (b)   any meeting of a committee established under paragraph 35 (moratorium committee).

(10) The Authority is entitled to be heard on any application under paragraph 36(3) (effectiveness of decisions).

(11) Where paragraph 38(1) (challenge of decisions) applies, the persons who may apply to the court include the Authority.

(12) If a person other than the Authority applies to the court under that paragraph, the Authority is entitled to be heard on the application.

(13) Where paragraph 39(3) (implementation of voluntary arrangement) applies, the persons who may apply to the court include the Authority.

(14) If a person other than the Authority applies to the court under that paragraph, the Authority is entitled to be heard on the application.

(15) Where paragraph 40(2) (challenge of directors' actions) applies, the persons who may apply to the court include the Authority.

(16) If a person other than the Authority applies to the court under that paragraph, the Authority is entitled to be heard on the application.

(17) This paragraph does not prejudice any right the Authority has (apart from this paragraph) as a creditor of a regulated company.

(18) In this paragraph—
  'the Authority' means the Financial Services Authority, and
  'regulated company' means a company which—
      (a)   is, or has been, an authorised person within the meaning given by section 31 of the Financial Services and Markets Act 2000,
      (b)   is, or has been, an appointed representative within the meaning given by section 39 of that Act, or
      (c)   is carrying on, or has carried on, a regulated activity, within the meaning given by section 22 of that Act, in contravention of the general prohibition within the meaning given by section 19 of that Act.

Subordinate legislation

1.563–1.584

45

(1) Regulations or an order made by the Secretary of State under this Schedule may make different provision for different cases.

(2) Regulations so made may make such consequential, incidental, supplemental and transitional provision as may appear to the Secretary of State necessary or expedient.

(3) Any power of the Secretary of State to make regulations under this Schedule may be exercised by amending or repealing any enactment contained in this Act (including one contained in this Schedule) or contained in the Company Directors Disqualification Act 1986.

(4) Regulations (except regulations under paragraph 5) or an order made by the Secretary of State under this Schedule shall be made by statutory instrument subject to annulment in pursuance of a resolution of either House of Parliament.

(5) Regulations under paragraph 5 of this Schedule are to be made by statutory instrument and shall only be made if a draft containing the regulations has been laid before and approved by resolution of each House of Parliament.

[SCHEDULE B1
Administration]

Section 8

1.585

[Arrangement of Schedule

Nature of administration	Paragraphs 1 to 9
Appointment of administrator by court	Paragraphs 10 to 13
Appointment of administrator by holder of floating charge	Paragraphs 14 to 21
Appointment of administrator by company or directors	Paragraphs 22 to 34
Administration application: special cases	Paragraphs 35 to 39
Effect of administration	Paragraphs 40 to 45
Process of administration	Paragraphs 46 to 58
Functions of administrator	Paragraphs 59 to 75
Ending administration	Paragraphs 76 to 86
Replacing administrator	Paragraphs 87 to 99
General	Paragraphs 100 to 116

Notes

Part II (the new IA 1986 s 8 and IA 1986 Sch B1) and the new IR 1986 Part 2 were brought into effect with effect from 15 September 2003 by the Enterprise Act 2002 (Commencement No 4 and Transitional Provisions and Savings) Order 2003 (SI 2003/2093) and the Insolvency (Amendment) Rules 2003 (SI 2003/1730). The provisions of the former IR 1986 Part 2 continue to apply to all administrations which either were or continue to be subject to the provisions of the former IA 1986 Part II: Art 5(3) of the Insolvency (Amendment) Rules 2003, SI 2003/1730.

From 15 September 2003, the existing provisions of Part II of the 1986 Act ceased to have effect save as follows:
- Where the petition for the administration order was presented before 15 September 2003: art 3(2) of the Enterprise Act 2002 (Commencement No 4 and Transitional Provisions and Savings) Order 2003 (SI 2003/2093). Thus, all pre-existing administrations, plus any administration commenced by an order made on or after 15 September 2003 but pursuant to a petition presented before that date, continue to be governed by the old regime.
- Undertakings carrying on business of the type identified in EA 2002 s 249 are excluded from the provisions of the new Part II. Those undertakings are:
  - Water and sewage undertakers within Chapter 1 of Part II of the Water Industry Act 1991,
  - Protected railway companies within section 59 of the Railways Act 1993 as extended,
  - Air traffic service companies within section 26 of the Transport Act 2000,
  - Public private partnerships within section 210 of the Greater London Authority Act 1999, and
  - Building societies within section 119 of the Building Societies Act 1986.

In these cases, the exclusionary provisions of EA 2002 s 249(2) may be modified by order of the Treasury (building societies) or the Secretary of State (all other cases); at present, no such orders have been made.

By art 3 Enterprise Act 2002 (Commencement No 4 and Transitional Provisions and Savings) Order 2003, SI 2003/2093, the provisions of the old Part II continued to apply to administrations in relation to the following undertakings:
- Insolvent partnerships.
- Limited liability partnerships.
- Insurers within the Financial Services and Markets Act 2000 (Administration Orders relating to Insurers) Order 2002.

However from 1 July 2005 the Insolvent Partnerships (Amendment) Order 2005 (SI 2005 No. 1516) extended the new administration regime (with certain modifications) to partnerships including importantly the ability to make an out of court appointment of an administrator to an insolvent partnership. Further amendments effective from 6 April 2006 were made to the insolvent partnership regime under the Insolvent Partnerships (Amendment) Order 2006 (SI 2006 No 622). The Insolvency Service website is a useful source for checking for checking the chronology of those recent changes (www.insolvency.gov.uk.) As from 1st October 2005 the new administration regime was also extended to limited liability partnerships under the Limited Liability Partnerships (Amendment) Regulations 2005 (SI 2005 No 1989).

'Company'

The definition of 'company' is in IA 1986 Sch B1 para 111A. It should be noted that EA 2002 s 254 gives the Secretary of State the power by order to provide for the application of provisions of IA 1986 to foreign companies but unfortunately no such order has yet been made. There has been considerable confusion whether the term 'company' in IA 1986 was capable of extending to foreign corporations: see *Re Dallhold Estates (UK) Ltd* [1992] BCC

394. The position was made a little clearer as result of the EC Regulation on Insolvency Proceedings 2000 art 3. This extended the definition of 'company' so that certain unregistered companies could fall within the company voluntary arrangement/administration provisions: *Re Salvage Association* [2003] BCC 504. However, the Insolvency Act 1986 (Amendment) Regulations 2005 (SI 2005/879) para 2 amended the definition of 'company' in IA 1986 s 1(4) and Sch B1 para 111 to reverse *Re Salvage Association* (above) so that companies such as those incorporated by charter and other bodies falling outside the definition in this provision cannot now enter administration or propose a voluntary arrangement unless there is a specific statutory power to do so. The definition of company in summary now covers only: (a) companies registered under the Companies Acts; (b) companies incorporated in European Economic Association states other than the UK (this would include Danish companies); and (c) companies registered outside the European Union but with a centre of main interest in an European Union member state (other than Denmark): see for example *Re Brac Rent-a-Car International Inc* [2004] BCC 248, *Re Sendo Ltd* [2006] 1 BCLC 395.

It should further be noted that EA 2002 s .255 gives the Treasury, with the concurrence of the Secretary of State, the power by order to provide for the application of the provisions relating to company arrangements and administration to the following:
- Societies registered under the Industrial and Provident Societies Act 1965.
- Societies registered under the Friendly Societies Act 1974, societies within the Friendly Societies Act 1992 and unregistered Friendly Societies.

Nature of Administration

Administration

1.586

1

(1) For the purposes of this Act 'administrator' of a company means a person appointed under this Schedule to manage the company's affairs, business and property.

(2) For the purposes of this Act—

    (a)   a company is 'in administration' while the appointment of an administrator of the company has effect,

    (b)   a company 'enters administration' when the appointment of an administrator takes effect,

    (c)   a company ceases to be in administration when the appointment of an administrator of the company ceases to have effect in accordance with this Schedule, and

    (d)   a company does not cease to be in administration merely because an administrator vacates office (by reason of resignation, death or otherwise) or is removed from office.

Notes

Para 1

The 'old' regime defined administration and its period by reference to orders of the court, the period of administration commencing when the order was made and ending on its discharge. With the introduction of out of court appointments, it was necessary to re-define the administration period which is achieved by IA 1986 Sch B1 para 1.

Para 1(2)(b)

The entry into administration is defined as 'when the appointment of an administrator takes effect'; if the appointment is by the court this time is defined in IA 1986 Sch B1 para 13(2); in the case of an out of court appointment by a qualifying floating chargeholder in IA 1986 Sch B1 para 19; and by the company or directors in IA 1986 Sch B1 para 31. The complex provisions relating to appointment are dealt with below. A failure to observe those provisions may lead to an appointment, considered by those concerned to be valid, not taking effect in accordance with IA 1986 Sch B1. This has potentially serious consequences for, in particular, the purported administrators who may act for some time before discovering the problem. Their position, in this regard, is the same or similar to invalidly appointed receivers (e g *Ford & Carter Ltd v Midland Bank Ltd* [1979] NLJ 543) though IA 1986 Sch B1 contains provisions which afford a measure of protection: IA 1986 Sch B1 paras 21, 34.

Para 1(2)(d)

Vacation of office and removal from the office of administrator are dealt with in IA 1986 Sch B1 paras 87–99.

I.587

2

A person may be appointed as administrator of a company—
  (a)   by administration order of the court under paragraph 10,
  (b)   by the holder of a floating charge under paragraph 14, or
  (c)   by the company or its directors under paragraph 22.

Notes

Para 2

This provision sets out the three ways in which administrators may be appointed under the new regime. They are:

By administration order under Sch B1 para 10.

- IR 1986 Part 2 Ch 1 governs applications for administration orders. Those who are entitled to present an administration application are set out in IA 1986 Sch B1 para 12(1). Although out of court appointments seem likely to be the norm, applications to court still have a part to play.
- IA 1986 Sch B1 para 8 contains a general prohibition on the appointment of administrators where the company is already in voluntary or compulsory liquidation. However, in such cases, the holder of a qualifying floating charge or the liquidator may apply for the appointment of administrators under IA 1986 Sch B1 paras 37, 38 respectively.
- The power of the holder of a qualifying floating charge to appoint an administrator under IA 1986 Sch B1 para 14 is subject to the restrictions contained in IA 1986 Sch B1 paras 15–17 and in those cases, an application for an order might be an option.
- Similarly, although the directors or a company may make an out of court appointment under IA 1986 Sch B1 para 22, such an appointment may not be made if the case falls within IA 1986 Sch B1 paras 23–25. Again, in such cases, an application for an order would be necessary if an administration is desired.

By the holder of a qualifying floating charge under IA 1986 Sch B1 para 14.

- What counts as a holder of a qualifying floating charge is set out in IA 1986 Sch B1 para 14(2), (3).

- The holder must hold one or more debentures secured by:
  - A qualifying floating charge or charges over the whole or substantially the whole of the property of the company; or
  - Charges or other forms of security which together relate to the whole or substantially the whole of the company's property and of which one is a qualifying floating charge.
- To qualify, the floating charge must:
  - State that IA 1986 Sch B1 para 14 applies; or
  - Purport to authorise the holder to appoint an administrator or;
  - Purport to authorise the holder to make an appointment that, under the old regime, would have been the appointment of an administrative receiver under IA 1986 s 29(2).

By the company or its directors under IA 1986 Sch B1 para 22.
- As noted, there are restrictions on the power to appoint which, if they apply, will necessitate an application for an administration order.

Purpose of administration

1.588

3

(1) The administrator of a company must perform his functions with the objective of—
  - (a) rescuing the company as a going concern, or
  - (b) achieving a better result for the company's creditors as a whole than would be likely if the company were wound up (without first being in administration), or
  - (c) realising property in order to make a distribution to one or more secured or preferential creditors.

(2) Subject to sub-paragraph (4), the administrator of a company must perform his functions in the interests of the company's creditors as a whole.

(3) The administrator must perform his functions with the objective specified in sub-paragraph (1)(a) unless he thinks either—
  - (a) that it is not reasonably practicable to achieve that objective, or
  - (b) that the objective specified in sub-paragraph (1)(b) would achieve a better result for the company's creditors as a whole.

(4) The administrator may perform his functions with the objective specified in sub-paragraph (1)(c) only if—
  - (a) he thinks that it is not reasonably practicable to achieve either of the objectives specified in sub-paragraph (1)(a) and (b), and
  - (b) he does not unnecessarily harm the interests of the creditors of the company as a whole.

Notes

Para 3

Under the old regime, there were independent statutory purposes of equal ranking. IA 1986 Sch B1 para 3 introduces a new single purpose for administrations. However, that single purpose comprises a number of objectives which are ranked in order of priority. The objectives are:

- rescue of the company as a going concern;
- better result for creditors than would otherwise be likely to be achieved if the company were wound up;
- realisation to make a distribution to secured and preferential creditors;

Administration is justified only for so long as the administration purpose remains reasonably capable of achievement. Before an administration order is made, the court must be satisfied that the administration purpose is reasonably likely to be achieved: IA 1986 Sch B1 para 11(b). It would not be a proper use of the procedure to apply for an administration and obtain the moratorium simply for the directors to prevent a secured creditor taking action in order to obtain a higher sale price for the assets; *Re Doltable Ltd* [2006] 1 BCLC 384.

In out of court appointments, the notice of appointment must include a statement from the administrator that in his opinion the administration purpose is reasonably likely to be achieved IA 1986 Sch B1 paras 18(3)(b), 29(3)(b). If an administrator believes that the administration purpose cannot be achieved, he is under a duty to make an application to court IA 1986 Sch B1 (para 79(2)). If the administration purpose has been sufficiently achieved, he must apply to court in cases where the administration was as a result of a court order IA 1986 Sch B1 para 79(3), or file a notice in a case of an out of court appointments IA 1986 Sch B1 para 80(2).

There is a hierarchy of objectives created under para 3. The primary objective for which an administrator must perform his functions is rescuing the company as a going concern. This objective must be pursued unless the administrator thinks that rescue is not reasonably practicable, or that the secondary objective – achieving a better result for creditors as a whole than would be achieved on a winding up – would achieve a better result for the creditors as a whole IA 1986 Sch B1 para 3(3). The third objective – a realisation of assets in order to make a distribution to secured or preferential creditors – may be resorted to only if (a) the administrator thinks that it is not reasonably practicable to achieve the primary and secondary objectives and (b) it does not unnecessarily harm the interests of the creditors of the company as a whole IA 1986 Sch B1 para 3(4).

The administrator is required to perform his functions (a) in the interests of the creditors as a whole IA 1986 Sch B1 para 3(2) and (b) as quickly and efficiently as reasonably practicable IA 1986 Sch B1 para 4.

The Objectives

The primary objective refers to the rescue of 'the company as a going concern'. This is similar to the IA 1986 Sch B1 s 8(3)(a) purpose under the old regime – 'survival of the company, and the whole or any part of its undertaking, as a going concern'. It envisages that the company will emerge from administration with the whole or at least a substantial part of its business as a going concern, possibly by utilisation of a company voluntary arrangement or a scheme of arrangement. Formerly, these were the subject of separate statutory purposes. Now, they are simply tools for the achievement of the primary, and indeed the secondary, objectives.

An administrator is not required to pursue the primary objective merely because it is capable of achievement. A sale on a going concern basis of the whole, or substantially the whole, of the company's undertaking might well produce a better financial result for creditors than a rescue of the company. Such a sale would fall within the secondary objective, which an administrator would be justified in pursuing because of its favourable outcome so far as the creditors were concerned ie under IA 1986 Sch B1 para 3(b).

An administrator may be justified in pursuing the secondary objective even where a sale of the whole or a part of the undertaking as a going concern is not reasonably practicable. This is because the secondary objective is expressed in terms of the result for creditors. There was no equivalent under the old regime. The 'better realisation' purpose under that regime referred, not to the result, but to the process by which a particular result was achieved. Thus, without more, it was not permissible to prolong an administration to realise assets in circumstances when it could not be said that the administration was producing better realisations than could be achieved in a liquidation. Now, provided that it can be said that the creditors are likely to achieve a better result at the end of the administration process than could otherwise be achieved, the administration is justified. It is usually the case therefore that the court must be provided with evidence that the result in an administration will be better than that in a liquidation and a comparative estimated outcome statement should be provided (*see notes to* IR 1986 r 2.4(2)).

Where the primary and secondary objectives are not reasonably capable of achievement, the administrator may resort to the third objective: realisation for the purposes of making a distribution to secured or preferential creditors.

Selecting Objectives

Although IA 1986 Sch B1 para 3 ranks the three objectives in order of priority, it is left to the administrator to decide whether the specified circumstances, which justify him pursuing the secondary or tertiary objectives, exist. This follows from the fact that neither the order (in a court appointment) nor the notice of appointment (in an out of court appointment) specify the objectives to be pursued, and also from the use of the verb 'thinks' in IA 1986 Sch B1 para 3. This introduces a subjective test and it is likely that the court will interfere with an administrator's decision to pursue a particular objective only if it can be demonstrated that the decision was one made in bad faith or irrationally. What is involved is assessing the evidence to ascertain whether there has been a rational thought process on the part of the administrator but that does not require the administrator's thought to be '.. *subject to any form of test by reference to an objective standard' Unidare plc v Cohen and Power* [2005] BPIR 1472, 1489. This is consistent with the large numbers of cases in which the courts have declined to interfere with the decisions taken by insolvency practitioners. That said, however, the administrator clearly owes duties which go beyond a mere duty not to act in bad faith or irrationally. It does not follow, from the fact that a court will not interfere with a decision, that a court will not hold the administrator to account if it turns out that the decision, whilst not made in bad faith or irrationally, was negligent and has caused loss.

1.589

4

The administrator of a company must perform his functions as quickly and efficiently as is reasonably practicable.

Notes

Para 4

The existence of such a duty then enables a creditor or member to complain to the court if it is breached IA 1986 Sch B1 para 74(2); the administrator must respond promptly to the queries and requests of third parties *Re Sabre International Products Ltd* [1991] BCLC 470.

Status of Administrator

1.590

5

An administrator is an officer of the court (whether or not he is appointed by the court).

Notes

Para 5

Administrators, like liquidators in a compulsory winding-up and court appointed receivers, are officers of the court; additionally an administrator is an 'officer' of the company within CA 1985 s 744 *Re Home Treat Ltd* [1991] BCC 165. This carries with it the rarely used protection of the law of contempt as it is a contempt to interfere with the performance by an officer of the court of his duties: see *Bristol Airport plc v Powdrill* [1990] Ch. 744; *Re Sabre International Products Ltd* [1991] BCC 694. It also renders the administrator subject to special responsibilities; the administrator must act honourably and fairly, in accordance with the rule in *ex p James* (1874) 9 C App 609, *Re Designer Room Ltd* [2004] BCC 904. This rule is of discretionary application where the court finds that an officer of the court has taken unfair advantage in dealings with a third party which results in unjust enrichment to the company *Re Mirror Group (Holdings) Ltd* [1993] BCLC 538. In circumstances where statute prevented an administrator from acting in a particular manner either expressly or by implication he is unlikely to be able to rely on the rule in *ex parte James* (above) to engage in such conduct *Collins & Aikman Europe SA* [2006] BCC 606. Note that even out of court appointed administrators are officers of the court.

General restrictions

1.591

6

A person may be appointed as administrator of a company only if he is qualified to act as an insolvency practitioner in relation to the company.

Notes

Para 6

A 'person qualified to act as an insolvency practitioner in relation to the company' is a person qualified in accordance with the provisions of Part XIII IA 1986 ss 388–398.

1.592

7

A person may not be appointed as administrator of a company which is in administration (subject to the provisions of paragraphs 90 to 97 and 100 to 103 about replacement and additional administrators).

Notes

Para 7

The general rule is that there can be no appointment where the company is already is administration. Such an appointment can be made, however, where it is made:

- under IA 1986 Sch B1 para 91–95, to fill a vacancy caused by the death, resignation and removal of, or vacation of office by, an existing administrator;
- under IA 1986 Sch B1 para 96 – the replacement, by the holder of a prior qualifying floating charge, of an administrator appointed by a qualifying floating charge-holder;
- under IA 1986 Sch B1 para 97 – the replacement, by the creditors, of an administrator appointed by the company or its directors;
- under IA 1986 Sch B1 para 103 – the power to appoint additional administrators to act jointly or concurrently with the existing administrator.

1.593

8

(1) A person may not be appointed as administrator of a company which is in liquidation by virtue of—
  (a)   a resolution for voluntary winding up, or
  (b)   a winding-up order.

(2) Sub-paragraph (1)(a) is subject to paragraph 38.

(3) Sub-paragraph (1)(b) is subject to paragraphs 37 and 38.

Notes

Para 8

The general rule is that there can be no appointment of administrator where the company is already in liquidation. To this, there are two exceptions:
- Where the company is in compulsory or voluntary liquidation, the liquidator may apply for an administration order. If the order is made, the court will discharge the liquidation and give directions: see IA 1986 Sch B1 para 38;
- Where the company is in compulsory liquidation, the holder of a qualifying floating charge may apply for an administration order. Again, if the order is made, the court will discharge the administration and give directions: see IA 1986 Sch B1 para 37. No such application can be made where the company is being wound up voluntarily.

1.594

9

(1) A person may not be appointed as administrator of a company which—
  (a)   has a liability in respect of a deposit which it accepted in accordance with the Banking Act 1979 (c 37) or 1987 (c 22), but
  (b)   is not an authorised deposit taker.

(2) A person may not be appointed as administrator of a company which effects or carries out contracts of insurance.

(3) But sub-paragraph (2) does not apply to a company which—
  (a)   is exempt from the general prohibition in relation to effecting or carrying out contracts of insurance, or
  (b)   is an authorised deposit taker effecting or carrying out contracts of insurance in the course of a banking business.

(4) In this paragraph—
'authorised deposit taker' means a person with permission under Part IV of the Financial Services and Markets Act 2000 (c 8) to accept deposits, and
'the general prohibition' has the meaning given by section 19 of that Act.

(5) This paragraph shall be construed in accordance with—
(a) section 22 of the Financial Services and Markets Act 2000 (classes of regulated activity and categories of investment),
(b) any relevant order under that section, and
(c) Schedule 2 to that Act (regulated activities).

Notes

Para 9

The former administration regime was extended, with modifications, to banking and insurance companies by the Banks (Administration Proceedings) Order 1989 (SI 1989/1276) and the Financial Services and Markets Act 2000 (Administration Orders Relating to Insurers) Order 2002 (SI 2002/1242). By art 3(3) of the Enterprise Act 2002 (Commencement No 4 and Transitional Provisions and Savings) Order 2003 (SI 2003/2093), the former administration regime continued so far as insurance companies are concerned until 18 February 2004 when the new regime with modifications was applied Financial Services and Markets Act 2000 (Administration Orders Relating to Insurers) Order 2002 (SI 2002/1242) art 3 (as amended). Significantly an insurance company cannot be put into administration out of court.

Appointment of Administrator by court

Administration order

1.595

10

An administration order is an order appointing a person as the administrator of a company.

Notes

Para 10

There is a standard (pre-printed) form for use (Form 2.4B, IR 1986 r 2.12(2)) but the court is often provided at the hearing with a draft order compiled by the applicant.

Conditions for making order

1.596

11

The court may make an administration order in relation to a company only if satisfied—

> (a) that the company is or is likely to become unable to pay its debts, and
>
> (b) that the administration order is reasonably likely to achieve the purpose of administration.

Notes

Para 11

There are two jurisdictional requirements which are similar to those to be found in the original IA 1986 s 8. The court must be 'satisfied':
- that the company is or is likely to become unable to pay its debts, and
- that an administration order is reasonably likely to achieve the purpose of administration.

Under the original IA 1986 s 8(1), the jurisdictional requirements were that the court had:
- to be 'satisfied' that the company was insolvent and
- to 'consider' that the making of an order would be 'likely to achieve one or more of the [statutory] purposes ...'.

The use of the word 'satisfied' in relation to the insolvency requirement meant that it was one which had to be proved on the balance of probabilities: see *Re Colt Telecom (No 2)* [2003] BPIR 324; and the position appears to be the same under the new administration regime in IA 1986 Sch B1: *Re AA Mutual International Insurance Co Ltd* [2005] 2 BCLC 8.

The second requirement – likelihood of achievement of the statutory purposes – required the court to be satisfied that there was a 'real prospect', as opposed to a mere hope or possibility: *Re Harris Simons Construction Ltd* [1989] 1 WLR 368; cf *Re Consumer & Industrial Press Ltd* (1988) 4 BCC 68 where Peter Gibson J suggested that this requirement also had to be established on a balance of probabilities. However, in *Re Lomax Leisure Ltd* [2000] BCC 352, Peter Gibson J followed the Harris Simons approach. It appears that IA 1986 Sch B1 para 11 has not effected any material change to the 'real prospect' test *Re Redman Construction Ltd* [2005] EWHC 1850 (Ch), [2004] All ER (D) 146 (Jun).

It would not be a proper use of the procedure to apply for an administration and obtain the moratorium simply for the directors to prevent a secured creditor taking action in order to obtain a higher sale price for the assets: *Re Doltable Ltd* [2006] 1 BCLC 384. In *Re Logitext UK Ltd* [2005] 1 BCLC 326 it was held that an administration order was more appropriate than a liquidation as it would produce a better result for creditors where a creditor agreed to fund claims against the directors if the company went into administration. It would be helpful for the evidence in such a case to show that the proposed funding is definitely not available in a liquidation. However each situation is fact sensitive and a different conclusion was reached in *Re AMCD (Property Holdings) Ltd* [2004] All ER (D) 125 (Jun) where the only ground relied upon for administration was to recover a debt due from a third party.

Insolvency

The term 'unable to pay its debts' has the meaning ascribed to it by IA 1986 s 123: see IA 1986 Sch B1 para 111(1). It covers both want of liquidity (ie cash flow insolvency) and balance sheet insolvency. In assessing balance sheet insolvency, the court is required to have regard to prospective and contingent liabilities (*Re a Company* [1986] BCLC 261, *Re AA Mutual International Insurance Co Ltd* [2006] 2 BCLC 8; on this exercise, see *Re Stonegate Securities Ltd v Gregory* [1980] Ch 576 and balance sheet insolvency includes taking into account contingent and prospective liabilities (IA 1986, s 123(2)) but not contingent and prospective assets (*Byblos Bank SAL v Al-Khudhairy* [1987] BCLC 232). Cash flow and balance sheet insolvency are alternatives. The test has been held to have been satisfied where the court was satisfied that the company was balance sheet insolvent: *Re Dianoor Jewels Ltd* [2001] 1 BCLC

450, and where it was satisfied of cash flow insolvency even though the company appeared to be solvent on a balance sheet basis: *Re Business Properties Ltd* (1988) 4 BCC 684; *Re Imperial Motors (UK) Ltd* (1989) 5 BCC 214.

Likelihood of achievement of purpose of administration

IR 1986 r 2.3(5) requires there to be attached to an application for an administration order a statement in prescribed form by the proposed administrator stating inter alia that in his opinion it is reasonably likely that the purpose of administration will be achieved. In the ordinary case, this statement alone might be thought sufficient but it would be optimistic to approach the court without some credible evidence from the proposed administrator or at least a letter addressed to the company containing a favourable analysis of the proposed administration. In more complex or contested cases, something more akin to the old 'Rule 2.2 ' report is likely to be required. In giving even the limited statement required by IR 1986 r 2.3(5), the proposed administrator is an expert witness and subject therefore to the provisions of Part 35 of the Civil Procedure Rules and the Code of Guidance on Expert Evidence: *Re Colt Telecom (No 2)* [2003] BPIR 324. In all cases, proposed administrators should have regard to those provisions. Further, and particularly in contested cases, the proposed administrator should have regard to the potential conflict which exists between his role as expert and his interest in securing an appointment.

Discretion

As before, once the jurisdictional requirements are satisfied, the court has a discretion whether or not to make an administration order and this can be exercised in favour of making the order despite evidence that the board of the applicant company were influenced in making the application for non-corporate purposes *Re Dianoor Jewels Ltd* [2001] 1 BCLC 450. However the court is unlikely to make an order as a means of resolving a shareholder dispute or to break a deadlock of a balance sheet solvent company *Re Business Properties Ltd* (1988) 4 BCC 684. It is likely that the views of the secured creditors carry less weight than those of the unsecured creditors in particular where the secured creditors are fully secured *Re Consumer and Industrial Press Ltd* [1988] BCLC 177, *Re Imperial Motors (UK) Ltd* [1990] BCLC 29. Under the old law, a court which was only just satisfied as to the second of the jurisdictional requirements would take this into account when exercising its discretion. Again, if it appears to the court that the majority of creditors are opposed to an administration, so that it is unlikely that the administrator's proposals will be passed, this is likely to lead the court to refuse the order *Re Land & Property Trust Co plc (No 2)* [1991] BCLC 849, *Re Stallton Distribution Ltd* [2002] BCC 486; but this is certainly not a foregone conclusion because the court may consider that the majority creditor may change its stance following the preparation of the administrator's proposals *Re Structures and Computers Ltd* [1998] 1 BCLC 292.

Administration application

1.597

12

(1) An application to the court for an administration order in respect of a company (an 'administration application') may be made only by—

    (a)   the company,

    (b)   the directors of the company,

    (c)   one or more creditors of the company,

    (d)   the [designated officer] for a magistrates' court in the exercise of the power conferred by section 87A of the Magistrates' Courts Act 1980 (c 43) (fine imposed on company), or

    (e)   a combination of persons listed in paragraphs (a) to (d).

(2) As soon as is reasonably practicable after the making of an administration application the applicant shall notify—

    (a)   any person who has appointed an administrative receiver of the company,

    (b)   any person who is or may be entitled to appoint an administrative receiver of the company,

    (c)   any person who is or may be entitled to appoint an administrator of the company under paragraph 14, and

    (d)   such other persons as may be prescribed.

(3) An administration application may not be withdrawn without the permission of the court.

(4) In sub-paragraph (1) 'creditor' includes a contingent creditor and a prospective creditor.

[(5) Sub-paragraph (1) is without prejudice to section 7(4)(b).]

Notes

Persons with standing to apply

The persons entitled to apply for the administration order are the same as those listed in the old law (IA 1986 s 9(1)). Individual members may not apply for an administration order *Re Chelmsford City Football Club (1980) Ltd* [1991] BCC 133 but the company clearly can despite the fact that the members themselves do not directly benefit *Re Land and Property Trust Co plc* [1991] BCLC 845. A creditor includes a contingent or prospective creditor: see IA 1986 Sch B1 para 12(4). Where there is a genuine and substantial dispute whether the applicant is a creditor the court will not make an administration order *Re British American Racing (Holdings) Ltd* [2005] BCC 110. A supervisor of a voluntary arrangement may also apply for an administration order pursuant to IA 1986 s 7(4)(b). Under the old law, applications by directors had to be made by all of the directors (*Re Instrumentation Electrical Services Ltd* (1988) 4 BCC 301) or by a majority pursuant to a resolution of the board (*Re Equiticorp International plc* [1989] 1 WLR 1010). Now IA 1986 Sch B1 para 105 expressly provides that something done by a majority of the directors is sufficient even where, apparently, it is done informally.

Form of evidence in support and filing of the application

The form and filing of the administration application, and the evidence in support, is governed by IR 1986 r 2.2 to 2.5. Reference should be made to the notes to those provisions but in outline:

- The application is required to be in Form 2.1B. It should be supported by an affidavit complying with IR 1986 r 2.4 which should be prepared and sworn with a view to its being filed with the application IR 1986 r 2.2(1); a witness statement may be used instead of an affidavit IR 1986 r 7.57(5);

- The affidavit should be sworn by a director of the secretary (if the application is made by the directors or the company), or by a person having authority to make the affidavit (if the application is made by creditors), IR 1986 r 2.2(2),(3);

- If the application is made by a supervisor under IA 1986 s 7(4)(b), it will be treated as an application by the company: IR 1986 r 2.2(4);

- If the application is made by the directors, it must state that it is so made, but once made is treated as an application by the company: IR 1986 r 2.3(2);

- If the application is made by more than one creditor, it must state that it is so made and identify the creditors, but once made is to be treated as the application of one of them who is to be named in the application as applying on behalf of himself and the other creditors: IR 1986 r 2.3(4);

- There must be attached to the application a statement from the proposed administrator stating that he consents to being appointed, setting out details of any prior professional relationships which he has had with the company and stating that in his opinion it is reasonably likely that the administration purpose will be achieved: IR 1986 r 2.3(5);

- Unless the application is made by a qualifying floating charge holder pursuant to para 35, the administration application must contain a statement of the applicant's belief that the company is insolvent: IR 1986 r 2.4(1).

The affidavit in support must contain the following (IR 1986 r 2.4(2):

- a statement of the company's financial position;
- details of securities and whether any of them confer a power to appoint an administrative receiver or administrator pursuant to IA 1986 Sch B1 para 14;
- details of the appointment of any administrative receiver;
- details of any insolvency proceedings in relation the company;
- details regarding the exercise of their functions by joint administrators, where it is proposed to appoint more than one;
- all other matters which might assist the court is determining whether or not to make an administration order;
- Where the application is made by the holder of a qualifying floating charge pursuant to para 35, details sufficient to satisfy the court that he is entitled to appoint an administrator under IA 1986 Sch B1 para 14: IR 1986 r 2.4(3).
- The affidavit must give details regarding the application of the EC Regulation on Insolvency Proceedings 2000: IR 1986 r 2.4(4).
- The application and supporting documents are filed in court with sufficient copies for service and use as provided by IR 1986 r 2.6. They are then sealed, endorsed with a time and date of filing and a venue fixed for hearing: IR 1986 r 2.5(1)–(3).
- After filing, it is the duty of the applicant to notify the court of any insolvency proceedings and any change in the application of the EC Regulation as soon as the applicant becomes aware of them: IR 1986 r 2.5(4).

Notification of application

IA 1986 Sch B1 para 12(2) lists the persons to whom notice of the application must be given as soon as is reasonably practicable after it has been made:

- Any person who has appointed or may be entitled to appoint an administrative receiver. That person effectively has a right of veto, unless the charge in question is challenge-able as a transaction at an undervalue or preference or a void floating charge: IA 1986 Sch B1 para 39.
- Any person who may be entitled to appoint an administrator under IA 1986 Sch B1 para 14, that is to say, the holder of a qualifying floating charge. Such a person may then intervene by making an application under IA 1986 Sch B1 para 36(1)(b) to have his own nominee appointed administrator, an application which the court must accede to unless the particular circumstances of the case dictate otherwise: IA 1986 Sch B1 para 36(2).
- Such other persons as may be prescribed. These are identified in IR 1986 r 2.7 and are:
  - any enforcement officer or other officer who is to the knowledge of the applicant charged with an execution or other legal process against the company or its property, and
  - any person who has distrained against the company or its property.

Notification for the purposes of IA 1986 Sch B1 para 12(2) is by way of service in accordance with the provisions of IR 1986 r 2.8, r 2.6(2).

Service and proof of service of application

Service of the application, the documents attached to it and the affidavit in support is regulated by IR 1986 r 2.6, 2.8, 2.9.

In addition to those persons who are to be notified in accordance with para 12(2), service is to be effected (in the prescribed manner and not less than 5 days before the date fixed for the hearing: IR 1986 r 2.8) upon the following persons listed in IR 1986 r 2.6(3):

- An administrative receiver, if appointed;

- Any person who has petitioned for a winding up order, and a provisional liquidator if one has been appointed;
- Any member State liquidator, if appointed;
- The proposed administrator;
- The company (unless the application is made by the company);
- Any supervisor (*Re Leisure Study Group Ltd* [1994] 2 BCLC 65), if appointed.

Proof of service is way of affidavit in the prescribed form which must be filed in court as soon as reasonably practicable and in any event not less than the day before the hearing: IR 1986 r 2.9.

Withdrawal of application

An application may not be withdrawn without the permission of the court: IA 1986 Sch B1 para 12(3). The effect on creditors of merely issuing an application is dramatic as a moratorium is imposed IA 1986 Sch B1 paras 44, 42, 43; and where the applicant decides not to proceed with the application he will have to provide a full explanation to the court.

Powers of the Court

1.598

13

(1) On hearing an administration application the court may—
    (a)   make the administration order sought;
    (b)   dismiss the application;
    (c)   adjourn the hearing conditionally or unconditionally;
    (d)   make an interim order;
    (e)   treat the application as a winding-up petition and make any order which the court could make under section 125;
    (f)   make any other order which the court thinks appropriate.

(2) An appointment of an administrator by administration order takes effect—
    (a)   at a time appointed by the order, or
    (b)   where no time is appointed by the order, when the order is made.

(3) An interim order under sub-paragraph (1)(d) may, in particular—
    (a)   restrict the exercise of a power of the directors or the company;
    (b)   make provision conferring a discretion on the court or on a person qualified to act as an insolvency practitioner in relation to the company.

(4) This paragraph is subject to paragraph 39.

Notes

Para 13

The 'court' is defined by reference to IA 1986 s 251 and CA 1985 s 744 as the court having the jurisdiction to wind up the company (IA 1986 s 117 – see notes to that provision and to IR 1986 r 2.2(1)). The persons entitled to appear or be represented at the hearing of the application are listed in IA 1986 r 2.12(1). There is no general requirement to notify/serve the general body of creditors of the application (*see* IA 1986 Sch B1 para 12(2), IR 1986 r 2.6(3)) but in practice it is usually an uphill struggle for the applicant to persuade the court not to hear an interested creditor. Where the company is obviously insolvent on a balance sheet basis the court is unlikely to agree to hear from members of the company *Re Chelmsford City Football Club (1980) Ltd* [1991] BCC 133.The applicant must be conscious of its duty of disclosure to the court *Cornhill Insurance plc v Cornhill Financial Services Ltd* [1992] BCC 818 and if relevant matters have not been disclosed to the court it may be necessary to seek directions and/or a termination of the administration (IA 1986 Sch B1 para 79, 81) *Re West Park Golf & Country Club* [1997] 1 BCLC 20. In those circumstances a creditor may alternatively apply for a recission of the order under IR 1986 r 7.47 (*Cornhill Insurance plc v Cornhill Financial Services Ltd* [1993] BCLC 914) though where the administration is in the best interests of the creditors it is unlikely to order recission *Re MTI Trading Systems Ltd* [1998] BCC 400. If an administration order is made it must state expressly what time the administrator is appointed and the pre-printed Form 2.8B contains a specific paragraph for that purpose; otherwise the appointment takes effect when the court makes the order IA 1986 Sch B1 para 13(2).

Orders which may be made

Para 13(1)

This provision sets out the orders which may be made by the court on the hearing of the application. The court may also treat the application as the hearing of a winding up petition possibly without requiring the presentation of a petition (see notes *to* para 79(4)(d) dealing with the circumstances where a termination of the administration is sought). Where, at the hearing, it is apparent that the company is insolvent and the court is not satisfied that the administration purpose will be achieved, or would achieve only marginal benefits for creditors, the making of a winding up order may well be the best way of protecting the interests of creditors and ensuring that the affairs of the company are independently investigated *El-Ajou v Dollar Land (Manhattan) Ltd* [2005] EWHC 2861 (Ch); further the court may prefer a liquidation because the affairs of the company demand a comprehensive examination *Re West-Tech International* [1989] BCLC 600. IA 1986 Sch B1 para 13 is expressly made subject to IA 1986 Sch B1 para 39 (para 13(4)), which confers a right of veto upon a person entitled to appoint an administrative receiver unless the charge under which the right to appoint arises is voidable on one of the grounds set out in that paragraph (preference, transaction at an undervalue or void floating charge); where the relevant charge is attackable on other grounds (for instance failure to register under CA 1985 s 395) the court may also be persuaded to exercise its discretion not to make an order.

Where there is a conflict between the company's nominee for administrator and another party's nominee then the court has a discretion. It is not a discretion that is expressly weighted in favour of the company's nomination nor the creditors' nomination. The court will be concerned to ensure that the nominee will be capable of acting independently and competently. The relevant factors for the court to consider include the knowledge of the nominee of the affairs of the company, how much work the nominee had already done in investigating the company's affairs and the resources of the nominee. It may be that where overwhelming preference is shown by the creditors for one nominee rather than another then the court may be persuaded to appoint their nominee *Re Maxwell Communication Corporation plc* [1992] BCLC 465, *Re World Class Homes Ltd* [2005] 2 BCLC 1.

Para 13(1)(c)

Even in cases of urgency the court may decide to adjourn the application to assess the evidence and/or consider fresh evidence *Cornhill Insurance plc v Cornhill Financial Services Ltd* [1992] BCC 818.

Para 13(3)

It should be noted that though there is no express power to appoint an interim administrator (*Re Gallidoro Trawlers Ltd* [1991] BCLC 411) IA 1986 Sch B1 para 13(1)(d) gives the court a power to make an interim order. What might be ordered on an interim basis is then set out in IA 1986 Sch B1 para 13(3); the description of the interim orders which may be made is not exhaustive.

Costs

IR 1986 r 2.12(3) provides that, if an administration order is made, the costs of the applicant are to be payable as an expense of the administration. The costs of other persons appearing (IR 1986 r 2.12(1)(k) are also to be payable as an expense if the court allows those persons their costs. The court may well view the input of even an opposing creditor as helpful on the hearing of the application, for instance to fill in evidential gaps and therefore give such a creditor its costs *Re Structures & Computers Ltd* [1998] 1 BCLC 292. It is possible though unusual for the court to order the directors of an applicant company to pay the costs of a failed administration application *Re Land and Property Trust Co plc (No 2)* [1993] BCC 462. Any winding up petitioner will also obtain an order for its costs as an expense of the administration; on the making of an administration order by the court the winding up petition is dismissed IA 1986 Sch B1 para 40(1)(a). Where the winding up petition has been issued in a court different to the court making the administration order it may be convenient to transfer the winding up petition so that the court making the administration order can also dismiss the winding up petition. Alternatively on the hearing of the winding up petition the court will be informed that an administration order has been made and the court will formally confirm the dismissal of the winding up petition accordingly.

Notice and advertisement of administration order

Where an administration order is made, provision is made for notice and advertisement by IR 1986 r 2.14; the equivalent provision in respect of an out of court appointment of an administrator is IR 1986 r 2.27.In *Re Sporting Options plc* [2005] BCC 88 the court refused an application to enable administrators to notify their appointment by email.

Appointment of Administrator by Holder of Floating Charge

Power to appoint

1.599

14

(1) The holder of a qualifying floating charge in respect of a company's property may appoint an administrator of the company.

(2) For the purposes of sub-paragraph (1) a floating charge qualifies if created by an instrument which—

    (a)   states that this paragraph applies to the floating charge,

    (b)   purports to empower the holder of the floating charge to appoint an administrator of the company,

    (c)   purports to empower the holder of the floating charge to make an appointment which would be the appointment of an administrative receiver within the meaning given by section 29(2), or

    (d)   purports to empower the holder of a floating charge in Scotland to appoint a receiver who on appointment would be an administrative receiver.

(3) For the purposes of sub-paragraph (1) a person is the holder of a qualifying floating charge in respect of a company's property if he holds one or more debentures of the company secured—

    (a)   by a qualifying floating charge which relates to the whole or substantially the whole of the company's property,

> (b)   by a number of qualifying floating charges which together relate to the whole or substantially the whole of the company's property, or
>
> (c)   by charges and other forms of security which together relate to the whole or substantially the whole of the company's property and at least one of which is a qualifying floating charge.

Notes

Introduction

IA 1986 Sch B1 paras 14–21, IR 1986 r 2.15–2.19 provide for and regulate out of court appointments of administrators by holders of qualifying floating charges:

- The appointment must be by the holder of a qualifying floating charge, as defined by IA 1986 Sch B1 para 14(2), (3);
- IA 1986 Sch B1 paras 15–17 impose certain restrictions on the power to appoint;
- Notice of the appointment must be given in accordance with the provisions of para 18;
- Upon notice being given in the prescribed form, the appointment takes effect in accordance with the provisions of IA 1986 Sch B1 para 19;

A floating charge is somewhat unhelpfully defined in IA 1986 s 251 and the debate as to whether a particular security is fixed or floating reached the House of Lords in *Re Spectrum Plus Ltd* [2005] 2 AC 680 and its analysis was applied in *Re Beam Tube Products Ltd* [2006] BCC 615. It is clear that simply labelling a charge a 'fixed charge' is not conclusive: *Re Keenan Bros Ltd* [1986] BCLC 242, *Re Spectrum Plus Ltd* (above)). The court is concerned with establishing the nature of the rights that have been given to the chargeholder or reserved to the company. The court will look to the way in which these rights are expressed in the security documentation and what has actually happened in practice by way of the control exerted by the chargeholder. A debenture in the 'Siebe Gorman' form (*Re Siebe Gorman & Co Ltd* [1979] 2 Lloyd's Rep 142) creates a floating charge rather than a fixed charge over book debts: *Re Spectrum Plus Ltd* (above). The main characteristic of a floating charge is that it leaves the company the freedom to control and deal with the assets subject to the charge without reference to the charegeholder: *Agnew v IRC* [2001] 2 AC 710; *Smith (Administrator of Cosslet (Contractors) Ltd v Brigend County Borough Council* [2002] AC 336; a legal possessory lien conferred by a contract coupled with a right to sell the goods subject to the lien is not a floating charge: *Trident International Ltd v Barlow* [2000] BCC 602.

Qualifying floating charge

A floating charge qualifies if created by an instrument which satisfies one of the requirements set out in IA 1986 Sch B1 para 14(2). Those requirements are that the instrument:

- states that IA 1986 Sch B1 para 14 applies to the floating charge;
- purports to empower the holder to appoint an administrator;
- purports to empower the holder to make an appointment which would if made be the appointment of an administrative receiver under IA 1986 s 29(2).

The first two requirements envisage that debentures granted after the passing of the Enterprise Act 2002 will be drafted to reflect the new regime. For the standard form power to appoint an administrative receiver, there will be substituted either a reference to IA 1986 Sch B1 para 14 or a power to appoint an administrator.

The third requirement covers two poooibilitioo.

- Holders of pre-EA 2002 floating charges may, if they wish, appoint administrators under the new regime rather than appoint administrative receivers.
- Loose drafting or error, where a post-EA 2002 floating charge has not taken into account the new regime.

Thus a pre 15 September 2003 security can be a qualifying floating charge that but there is no requirement to serve such a security holder with notice that the company is to pass a resolution for voluntary winding up (IA 1986 s 84(2A)). The requirement to give such notice only applies in favour of *'any qualifying floating charge to which section 72A applies'* and IA 1986 s 72A clearly applies only to floating charges created on after 15 September 2003.

Holder of a qualifying floating charge

In addition, to make an appointment, the holder must satisfy the requirements of IA 1986 Sch B1 para 14(3). Those requirements are that the holder must hold one or more debentures of the company secured:

- by a qualifying floating charge which relates to the whole or substantially the whole of the assets of the company,
- by a number of qualifying floating charges which together relate to the whole or substantially the whole of the assets of the company,
- by charges, at least one of which must be a qualifying floating charge, which together relate to the whole or substantially the whole of the assets of the company.

There are some similarities between these requirements and the provisions of IA 1986 s 29(2), which defined what constituted an administrative receiver for the purposes of IA 1986. IA 1986 Sch B1 para 14(3) refers to the extent of the security conferred upon the debenture holder; IA 1986 s 29(2) referred to the extent of the property over which a receiver had been appointed. The first is a condition for appointment; the second describes the effect of an appointment and the status of the appointee. Both, however, use the concept of the 'whole or substantially the whole' of the company's assets or property. Whether a charge, or a series of charges (including at least one floating charge), relate to the whole or substantially the whole of the company's assets is a question to be determined at the time of the purported appointment and by reference to the value of the assets in question.

Restrictions on power to appoint

1.600

15

(1) A person may not appoint an administrator under paragraph 14 unless—

    (a)   he has given at least two business days' written notice to the holder of any prior floating charge which satisfies paragraph 14(2), or

    (b)   the holder of any prior floating charge which satisfies paragraph 14(2) has consented in writing to the making of the appointment.

(2) One floating charge is prior to another for the purposes of this paragraph if—

    (a)   it was created first, or

    (b)   it is to be treated as having priority in accordance with an agreement to which the holder of each floating charge was party.

(3) Sub-paragraph (2) shall have effect in relation to Scotland as if the following were substituted for paragraph (a)—

    '(a)   it has priority of ranking in accordance with section 464(4)(b) of the Companies Act 1985 (c 6),'.

Notes

Para 15

This provision deals with a case where an appointment is to be made, but there are floating charges 'prior to' the floating charge, the holder of which is proposing to make the appointment. In such cases, the holder of the prior floating charge may effectively veto the appointment by making his own appointment (of an administrator, or an administrative receiver in the case of the pre-Enterprise Act 2002 debenture).

For the purposes of this paragraph, a relevant prior floating charge must satisfy two requirements:

- It must be a qualifying floating charge within the meaning of IA 1986 Sch B1 para 14(2).
- It must be 'prior' either because it was created first, or because it is afforded priority by virtue of some agreement between the holders of the floating charges.

It should be noted that priority, for the purposes of IA 1986 Sch B1 para 15(2), is expressly defined and is more limited than the sense in which that term is ordinarily understood. A qualifying charge which would have priority over a prior floating charge under the general law may not be a 'prior floating charge' for the purposes of IA 1986 Sch B1 para 15(2).

If there is a prior floating charge, as defined, one of two requirements must be satisfied before the appointment can be made:

- The appointor must give written notice of the proposed appointment at least two business days before the proposed appointment; or
- The holder of the prior floating charge must have given his consent to the proposed appointment.

The requirement that notice be given, or consent sought, applies whether or not the holder of the prior floating charge is a relevant holder (that is, someone who satisfies the requirement of IA 1986 Sch B1 para 14(3)) or is otherwise able to appoint an administrator or administrative receiver. This is because the holder to whom notice must be given is defined solely by reference to the charge itself – that is to say, whether it is a qualifying floating charge for the purposes of IA 1986 Sch B1 para 14(2) – and not to the ability of the holder to make an appointment.

1.601

16

An administrator may not be appointed under paragraph 14 while a floating charge on which the appointment relies is not enforceable.

Notes

Para 16

The holder of the qualifying floating charge must be entitled to call in its security and exercise its remedies. For example, if formal demand is a prerequisite for the enforcement of the security, such a demand must be made before an appointment may be made under IA 1986 Sch B1 para 14(1). Where it is alleged that the charge is not enforceable this does not prevent an administrator being appointed but the appointment will be invalidated if it is later determined that the charge was not enforceable: *BCPMS (Europe) Ltd v GMAC Commercial Finance plc* [2006] All ER (I) 285.

1.602

17

An administrator of a company may not be appointed under paragraph 14 if—

> (a)   a provisional liquidator of the company has been appointed under section 135, or
> (b)   an administrative receiver of the company is in office.

Notes

Para 17

No appointment may be made under IA 1986 Sch B1 para 14(1) if a provisional liquidator (IA 1986 s 135) has been appointed or an administrative receiver (IA 1986 s 29(2)) is in office. There is no provision enabling the consent of the appointor of the administrative receiver to be given to enable an out of court appointment of an administrator to proceed. Where the company is already in liquidation, an out of court appointment may not be made but an administrator can be appointed by the court in the circumstances set out in IA 1986 Sch B1 para 37, 38. Note however that the mere existence of a winding up petition does not prevent an appointment being made by a qualifying floating chargeholder under para 14; if an appointment is made then the winding up petition is suspended, IA 1986 Sch B1 para 40(1)(b).

Where the company is in compulsory liquidation, the holder of a qualifying charge, who would have been entitled to make an out of court appointment under IA 1986 Sch B1 para 14(1) but for the liquidation, may make an administration application: IA 1986 Sch B1 para 37. In that event, an administration order may be made under para 13, but that order must deal with the matters set out in IA 1986 Sch B1 para 37(3). Where the company is in voluntary liquidation, the holder of a qualifying charge may not make an administration application. In this case, the only person who may make an administration application is the voluntary liquidator, under IA 1986 Sch B1 para 38. If an administration order is made, the order must deal with the matters set out in IA 1986 Sch B1 para 38(2). A liquidator in a compulsory liquidation is also entitled to make an administration application under para 38. Although the holder of a qualifying charge may not make an administration application where the company is in voluntary liquidation, he has the right to nominate the liquidator IA 1986 s 100(4).

Notice of appointment

1.603

18

(1) A person who appoints an administrator of a company under paragraph 14 shall file with the court—
   (a)   a notice of appointment, and
   (b)   such other documents as may be prescribed.

(2) The notice of appointment must include a statutory declaration by or on behalf of the person who makes the appointment—
   (a)   that the person is the holder of a qualifying floating charge in respect of the company's property,
   (b)   that each floating charge relied on in making the appointment is (or was) enforceable on the date of the appointment, and
   (c)   that the appointment is in accordance with this Schedule.

(3) The notice of appointment must identify the administrator and must be accompanied by a statement by the administrator—
   (a)   that he consents to the appointment,
   (b)   that in his opinion the purpose of administration is reasonably likely to be achieved, and

> (c)   giving such other information and opinions as may be prescribed.
>
> (4) For the purpose of a statement under sub-paragraph (3) an adminis-
> trator may rely on information supplied by directors of the company
> (unless he has reason to doubt its accuracy).
>
> (5) The notice of appointment and any document accompanying it must
> be in the prescribed form.
>
> (6) A statutory declaration under sub-paragraph (2) must be made during
> the prescribed period.
>
> (7) A person commits an offence if in a statutory declaration under
> sub-paragraph (2) he makes a statement—
> (a)   which is false, and
> (b)   which he does not reasonably believe to be true.

Notes

Formalities: appointments during business hours

Para 18

This provision and IR 1986 r 2.16–2.19 set out the formalities which must be observed following the making of an out of court appointment under IA 1986 Sch B1 para 14(1). An appointment takes effect, not from the time at which it is made, but from the time at which the requirements of IA 1986 Sch B1 para 18 are satisfied: para 19. The appointor must file with the court a notice of appointment: IA 1986 Sch B1 para 18(1)(a). The notice must be in Form 2.6B: para 18(5) and IR 1986 r 2.16. Three copies must be filed: IR 1986 r 2.17(1).

The notice of appointment must contain a statutory declaration that the appointor is the holder of a qualifying floating charge, that the relevant charge was enforceable at the date of the appointment and that the appointment was in accordance with the schedule: IA 1986 Sch B1 para 18(2). The statutory declaration must be made not more than 5 business days before the notice is filed with the court: IA 1986 Sch B1 para 18(6) and IR 1986 r 2.16(3).

The notice of appointment must identify the administrator and be accompanied by a written statement by the administrator that he consents to the appointment and that in his opinion the purpose of administration is reasonably likely to be achieved: IA 1986 Sch B1 para 18(3). The statement must be in Form 2.2B: para 18(5) and IR 1986 r 2.16(2)(a).

In giving the statement required by IA 1986 Sch B1 para 18(3) as to the likelihood of achievement of the purpose of administration, the administrator is acting as an expert. He ought therefore to have regard to the provisions of Part 35 of the Civil Procedure Rules and the Code of Guidance on Expert Evidence: *Re Colt Telecom (No 2)* [2003] BPIR 324. In giving the statement, however, the administrator is entitled to rely on information given to him by the directors, unless he has reason to doubt its accuracy: IA 1986 Sch B1 para 18(4). There is no express provision enabling an out of court appointed administrator to charge his pre-appointment costs as an expense of the administration (*see* IR 1986 r 2.67); although it will not be determinative it would be helpful to obtain creditors' approval of such costs following the appointment.

Where there is the holder of a prior qualifying floating charge to whom notice must be given or whose consent must be obtained under IA 1986 Sch B1 para 15(1), evidence that the requisite notice has been given, or copies of the written consent should be filed. Written consent may be given by completion of the relevant section of the notice of intention to appoint given in accordance with IA 1986 Sch B1 para 44(2) and IR 1986 r 2.15 and returning a copy of the form to the appointor: IR 1986 r 2.16(4). Where consent is not given in this way, the written consent of the holder of the prior qualifying floating charge must include the details specified in IR 1986 r 2.16(5).

Where a number of persons are appointed as administrator, the notice must be accompanied by a statement specifying how those persons are to perform their functions: IA 1986 Sch B1 para 100(2) and IR 1986 r 2.16(2)(c). When filed with the court, the copies of the notice of appointment are sealed and endorsed with the date and time of filing: IR 1986 r 2.17(1). Two copies are issued to the appointor who must send one of them to the administrator: IR 1986 r 2.17(2). If the appointment is made after receipt by the appointor of notice of an administration application, a copy of the notice must be send as soon as reasonably practicable to the person who has made the application and the court where the application has been made: IR 1986 r 2.18.

Formalities: appointments out of hours

Where an appointment is made out of hours, the appointor must follow the requirements set out in IR 1986 r 2.19 which includes using a particular form of notice of appointment: Form 2.7B. That notice must be faxed to a designated telephone number which is available on the Insolvency Service website (www.insolvency.gov.uk) IR 1986 r 2.19(3), and a record created of the transmission. In these cases, the appointment takes effect from the date and time of the transmission: IR 1986 r 2.19(5). The appointor must as soon as reasonably practicable notify the administrator and forward copies of the notice of appointment and the transmission report to the court having jurisdiction in the case. On the next day on which the court is open to business, three copies of the notice of appointment must be taken to the court, together with the fax transmission report, the documents accompanying the notice of appointment and a statement giving full reasons for the out of hours appointment. The copies of the notice of appointment will be sealed by the court and endorsed with the date and time of the fax transmission and the date on which the notice and accompanying documents were delivered to the court. Two sealed copies are sent to the appointor who must send one to the administrator.

If the appointor fails to observe the requirements of IR 1986 r 2.19(7) (delivery of copies of the notice of appointment, accompanying documents, fax transmission report and statement of reasons), the appointment will cease to have effect: IR 1986 r 2.19(10).

Commencement of appointment

1.604

19

The appointment of an administrator under IA 1986 Sch B1 paragraph 14 takes effect when the requirements of paragraph 18 are satisfied.

Notes

Para 19

As noted above, the appointment takes effect only from the time at which the requirements of IA 1986 Sch B1 para 18 are satisfied. Until this happens, the administrator may not exercise his powers.

1.605

20

A person who appoints an administrator under paragraph 14—

> (a) shall notify the administrator and such other persons as may be prescribed as soon as is reasonably practicable after the requirements of paragraph 18 are satisfied, and
> (b) commits an offence if he fails without reasonable excuse to comply with paragraph (a).

Notes

Para 20

Once those requirements are satisfied, the appointor must inform the administrator and prescribed persons (IR 1986 r 2.27(2)) of this fact.

Invalid appointment: indemnity

1.606

21

(1) This paragraph applies where—
  (a) a person purports to appoint an administrator under paragraph 14, and
  (b) the appointment is discovered to be invalid.

(2) The court may order the person who purported to make the appointment to indemnify the person appointed against liability which arises solely by reason of the appointment's invalidity.

Notes

Para 21

An invalidly appointed administrator who takes possession of the company's property, or otherwise intervenes in its business, may find himself liable in tort for any damage resulting from those activities and/or subject to a misfeasance application under IA 1986 Sch B1 para 75. IA 1986 Sch B1 para 21, which is based on IA 1986 s 34, enables to court to order the appointor to indemnify the purported administrator against such liability. This paragraph must be read in conjunction with IA 1986 Sch B1 para 104, which is based on IA 1986 s 232. Para 21 covers a wholly invalid appointment *Morris v Kanssen* [1946] AC 459; for example, where the power to appoint had not arisen at all. It is probable that para 104, which validates the acts of an administrator where there was some defect in the appointment, applies to a narrower range of circumstances; for example, where there was a failure to comply with the provisions of IA 1986 Sch B1 para 18. An application to challenge the validity of an administrator's appointment should be made promptly following discovery of the alleged grounds of invalidity *Fliptex Ltd v Hogg* [2004] BCC 870.

Appointment of Administrator by Company or Directors

Power to appoint

1.607

22

(1) A company may appoint an administrator.

(2) The directors may appoint an administrator.

Notes

Paras 22ff

IA 1986 Sch B1 paras 22–34 and IR 1986 r 2.20 to 2.26 regulate out of court appointments by the company or its directors. A company or its directors may make an out of court of appointment, but this right is subject to the restrictions contained in IA 1986 Sch B1 para 23 and the formalities set out in para 24–30 and IR 1986 r 2.20–2.27. Importantly the out of court procedure cannot be used by the company or the directors where a winding up petition has been presented but it is not yet disposed of IA 1986 Sch B1 para 25; however a qualifying floating chargeholder is not prevented from making an out of court appointment either in those circumstances (IA 1986 Sch B1 para 15) or where an administration application has been made to the court IA 1986 Sch B1 para 44(7)(b). Note that an out of court appointed administrator is also an officer of the court IA 1986 Sch B1 para 5.

Para 22

The directors may act by majority without the need for a resolution passed at at a board meeting IA 1986 Sch B1 para 105 (*see also* IR 1986 r 2.22). Appointment by the company (by contrast with appointment by the directors) appears to envisage that there will be either a resolution of the company in general meeting, or an informal but unanimous decision by the shareholders that such an appointment should be made. Under the old law, petitions for administration orders by directors had to be presented by all of the directors *Re Instrumentation Electrical Services Ltd* (1988) 4 BCC 301 or by a majority pursuant to a resolution of the board *Re Equiticorp International plc* [1989] 1 WLR 1010; IA 1986 Sch B1 para 105 now expressly provides that something done by a majority of the directors is sufficient even where, apparently, it is done informally.

Restrictions on power to appoint

1.609

23

(1) This paragraph applies where an administrator of a company is appointed—
    (a)   under paragraph 22, or
    (b)   on an administration application made by the company or its directors.

(2) An administrator of the company may not be appointed under paragraph 22 during the period of 12 months beginning with the date on which the appointment referred to in sub-paragraph (1) ceases to have effect.

Notes

Para 23

Where there has been a previous out of court appointment under IA 1986 Sch B1 para 22, or on an administration application made by the company or its directors, no further appointment may be made under IA 1986 Sch B1 para 22 within the period of 12 months from the time at which the appointment of the administrator ceased to have effect. It is only an out of court appointment under IA 1986 Sch B1 para 22 that is prohibited by this provision; the company or the directors are free to seek an appointment of an administrator pursuant to an administration application made under IA 1986 Sch B1 para 12 within the stated period.

1.610

24

(1) If a moratorium for a company under Schedule A1 ends on a date when no voluntary arrangement is in force in respect of the company, this paragraph applies for the period of 12 months beginning with that date.

(2) This paragraph also applies for the period of 12 months beginning with the date on which a voluntary arrangement in respect of a company ends if—
    (a)   the arrangement was made during a moratorium for the company under Schedule A1, and
    (b)   the arrangement ends prematurely (within the meaning of section 7B).

(3) While this paragraph applies, an administrator of the company may not be appointed under paragraph 22.

Notes

Para 24

Where the directors of the company have obtained a moratorium under the provisions of IA 1986 Sch B1 Part II Sch A1, but either: that moratorium has ended with no voluntary arrangement in force; or an arrangement was made, but terminated prematurely within the meaning of IA 1986 s 7B (that is to say, ceased to have effect without having been fully implemented as regards the persons bound by its terms); then no out of court appointment may be made under IA 1986 Sch B1 para 22 for a period of 12 months following the end of the moratorium, or the date on which the arrangement ceased to have effect.

1.611

25

An administrator of a company may not be appointed under paragraph 22 if—

> (a) a petition for the winding up of the company has been presented and is not yet disposed of,
> (b) an administration application has been made and is not yet disposed of, or
> (c) an administrative receiver of the company is in office.

Notes

Para 25(a)

Where there is an extant winding up petition and the company or the directors wish the company to go into administration an application to court is necessary: IA 1986 Sch B1 para 12; an out of court appointment by the company or the directors cannot be made. A petition for unfair prejudice under s 459 Companies Act 1985 sometimes contains a prayer for winding up but it is not clear that the inclusion of such a prayer in a s 459 petition would constitute a winding up petition. At first sight it appears not. However the Practice Direction – Applications under the Companies Act 1985 (Civil Procedure Vol 2 section 2G – 1, para 9) requires that a s 459 CA 1985 petition must state whether the petitioner consents to a validation order under IA 1986 s 127 and that latter provision only applies where a winding up petition has been presented.

Para 25(c)

There is no provision enabling the consent of the appointor of the administrative receiver to be given to enable an out of court appointment of an administrator to proceed; *cf* where an administration application is made to court IA 1986 Sch B1 para 39.

Notice of intention to appoint

1.612

26

(1) A person who proposes to make an appointment under paragraph 22 shall give at least five business days' written notice to—
  (a) any person who is or may be entitled to appoint an administrative receiver of the company, and
  (b) any person who is or may be entitled to appoint an administrator of the company under paragraph 14.

(2) A person who proposes to make an appointment under paragraph 22 shall also give such notice as may be prescribed to such other persons as may be prescribed.

(3) A notice under this paragraph must—
  (a) identify the proposed administrator, and
  (b) be in the prescribed form.

Notes

Para 26

Under this provision a notice of intention to appoint must be served where there is a person who is or may be entitled to appoint an administrative receiver, or where there is a qualifying floating chargeholder who is or may be entitled to appoint an administrator under IA 1986

Sch B1 para 14. The notice of intention to appoint must be in Form 2.8B and must identify the proposed administrator: IA 1986 Sch B1 para 26(3) and IR 1986 r 2.20(1). It must be served on the person or persons entitled to appoint an administrative receiver or an administrator (para 26(1)) and those listed in IR 1986 r 2.20(2) (para 26(2)), namely any enforcement officer who is charged with execution or legal process against the company, any person who has distrained against the company or its property, any supervisor of a voluntary arrangement and the company (if it is not the company making the appointment). Service must be at least 5 business days prior to appointment and it must be effected in accordance with the provisions of IR 1986 r 2.8(2)–(6). On the face of it there does not appear to be any express provision preventing consecutive notices of intention to be filed which each initiate an interim moratorium under IA 1986 Sch B1 para 44

1.613

27

(1) A person who gives notice of intention to appoint under paragraph 26 shall file with the court as soon as is reasonably practicable a copy of—
  (a) the notice, and
  (b) any document accompanying it.

(2) The copy filed under sub-paragraph (1) must be accompanied by a statutory declaration made by or on behalf of the person who proposes to make the appointment—
  (a) that the company is or is likely to become unable to pay its debts,
  (b) that the company is not in liquidation, and
  (c) that, so far as the person making the statement is able to ascertain, the appointment is not prevented by paragraphs 23 to 25, and
  (d) to such additional effect, and giving such information, as may be prescribed.

(3) A statutory declaration under sub-paragraph (2) must—
  (a) be in the prescribed form, and
  (b) be made during the prescribed period.

(4) A person commits an offence if in a statutory declaration under sub-paragraph (2) he makes a statement—
  (a) which is false, and
  (b) which he does not reasonably believe to be true.

Notes

Para 27

As soon as reasonably practicable after service of a notice of intention to appoint, the person giving such notice must file a copy of the notice with the court, together with any document accompanying. The form itself contains a statutory declaration, the contents of which are described in IA 1986 Sch B1 para 27(2). That statutory declaration is in Form 2.8B and must be made not more than 5 business days before the notice is filed in court: IA 1986 Sch B1 para 27(3), IR 1986 r 2.21. By the statutory declaration, the maker confirms that the company is insolvent, that it is not in liquidation and that the restrictions in IA 1986 Sch B1 para 23–25 do not apply. With the form there must be filed either a copy of the resolution of the company or a record of the decision of the directors. The making of a false statement, known to the maker of the statement to be so, or not reasonably believed by him to be true, is an offence.

1.614

28

(1) An appointment may not be made under paragraph 22 unless the person who makes the appointment has complied with any requirement of paragraphs 26 and 27 and—
  (a) the period of notice specified in paragraph 26(1) has expired, or
  (b) each person to whom notice has been given under paragraph 26(1) has consented in writing to the making of the appointment.

(2) An appointment may not be made under paragraph 22 after the period of ten business days beginning with the date on which the notice of intention to appoint is filed under paragraph 27(1).

Notes

Para 28

Where a notice of intention to appoint is necessary, an appointment may not be made until the requirements of IA 1986 Sch B1 para 26, 27 have been complied with and either (a) the 5 business days have elapsed or (b) the written consent of the person or persons entitled to appoint an administrative receiver or administrator has been secured: IA 1986 Sch B1 para 28(1). Further, it may not be made after the expiry of 10 business days from the date on which the notice of intention to appoint has been filed in court.

Notice of appointment

1.615

29

(1) A person who appoints an administrator of a company under paragraph 22 shall file with the court—
  (a) a notice of appointment, and
  (b) such other documents as may be prescribed.

(2) The notice of appointment must include a statutory declaration by or on behalf of the person who makes the appointment—
  (a) that the person is entitled to make an appointment under paragraph 22,
  (b) that the appointment is in accordance with this Schedule, and
  (c) that, so far as the person making the statement is able to ascertain, the statements made and information given in the statutory declaration filed with the notice of intention to appoint remain accurate.

(3) The notice of appointment must identify the administrator and must be accompanied by a statement by the administrator—

> (a) that he consents to the appointment,
> (b) that in his opinion the purpose of administration is reasonably likely to be achieved, and
> (c) giving such other information and opinions as may be prescribed.
>
> (4) For the purpose of a statement under sub-paragraph (3) an administrator may rely on information supplied by directors of the company (unless he has reason to doubt its accuracy).
>
> (5) The notice of appointment and any document accompanying it must be in the prescribed form.
>
> (6) A statutory declaration under sub-paragraph (2) must be made during the prescribed period.
>
> (7) A person commits an offence if in a statutory declaration under sub-paragraph (2) he makes a statement—
> (a) which is false, and
> (b) which he does not reasonably believe to be true.

Notes

Para 29

Following the appointment, a notice of appointment must be filed with the court: IA 1986 Sch B1 para 29(1)(a). The notice of appointment must be in the prescribed form: IA 1986 Sch B1 para 29(5). There are two prescribed forms: Form 2.9B and 2.10B: IR 1986 r 2.23. The first must be used where a notice of intention to appoint has been served; the second where there has been no such notice. The appointor must also file the documents specified in IR 1986 r 2.23, 2.25. IR 1986 r 2.23 requires the following documents to be filed in all cases: (a) the administrator's written statement in Form 2.2B dealing with the matters set out in IA 1986 Sch B1 para 29(3); (b) the written consent of all persons on whom a notice of intention to appoint has been served (unless the period of notice has expired); and (c) (where there are joint administrators) a statement dealing with the manner in which they will exercise their functions.

In cases where there has been no notice of intention to appoint, a copy of the company resolution, or a written record of the directors' decision, to appoint must also be filed: IR 1986 r 2.25. Forms 2.9B and 2.10B contain the statutory declarations required to be made by or on behalf of the appointor pursuant to IA 1986 Sch B1 para 29(2), 30. Where a notice of intention to appoint has been served, a statutory declaration will already have been made confirming that the company is insolvent, that it is not in liquidation and that the restrictions in IA 1986 Sch B1 para 23–25 do not apply (the requirements set out in IA 1986 Sch B1 para 27(2)). Para 29(2) requires the maker of the declaration to confirm that the earlier declaration remains accurate. The maker must also confirm that the person making the appointment was entitled to make the appointment under IA 1986 Sch B1 para 22, and that the appointment was made in accordance with IA 1986 Sch B1.

Where there has been no notice of intention to appoint, and no earlier statutory declaration, the statutory declaration filed with the notice of appointment must satisfy the requirements of IA 1986 Sch B1 para 27(2), as well as those of IA 1986 Sch B1 para 29(2)(a),(b); para 30. The statutory declarations must be made not more than 5 business days before the notice of appointment is filed in court: IA 1986 Sch B1 para 29(6) and IR 1986 r 2.24. The making of false statements, knowingly or without reasonable belief in the statement's truth, is an offence: IA 1986 Sch B1 para 29(7). Three copies of the notice of appointment must be filed. They are sealed and endorsed with the date and time of filing. One copy is retained and two returned. One of the sealed copies must then be sent to the administrator: IR 1986 r 2.26.

1.616

30

In a case in which no person is entitled to notice of intention to appoint under paragraph 26(1) (and paragraph 28 therefore does not apply)—
- (a) the statutory declaration accompanying the notice of appointment must include the statements and information required under paragraph 27(2), and
- (b) paragraph 29(2)(c) shall not apply.

Notes

Para 30

See the notes to IA 1986 Sch B1 para 29 above.

Commencement of appointment

1.617

31

The appointment of an administrator under paragraph 22 takes effect when the requirements of paragraph 29 are satisfied.

Notes

Paras 31–33

The appointment takes effect only once the requirements of IA 1986 Sch B1 para 29 are satisfied: IA 1986 Sch B1 para 31. As soon as reasonably practicable after the requirements of IA 1986 Sch B1 para 29 are satisfied, the appointor must notify the administrator and the other persons prescribed IR 1986 r 2.27(2): IA 1986 Sch B1 para 32(a). If, before the requirements are satisfied, an administration order is made, the IA 1986 Sch B1 para 22 appointment will not take effect and the appointor is relieved from his IA 1986 Sch B1 para 32 obligations: IA 1986 Sch B1 para 33.

1.618

32

A person who appoints an administrator under paragraph 22—
- (a) shall notify the administrator and such other persons as may be prescribed as soon as is reasonably practicable after the requirements of paragraph 29 are satisfied, and
- (b) commits an offence if he fails without reasonable excuse to comply with paragraph (a).

Notes

Para 32

See notes to IA 1986 Sch B1 para 31 above.

1.619

33

If before the requirements of paragraph 29 are satisfied the company enters administration by virtue of an administration order or an appointment under paragraph 14—
(a) the appointment under paragraph 22 shall not take effect, and
(b) paragraph 32 shall not apply.

Notes

Para 33

See notes to IA 1986 Sch B1 para 31 above.

Invalid appointment: indemnity

1.620

34

(1) This paragraph applies where—
(a) a person purports to appoint an administrator under paragraph 22, and
(b) the appointment is discovered to be invalid.

(2) The court may order the person who purported to make the appointment to indemnify the person appointed against liability which arises solely by reason of the appointment's invalidity.

Notes

Para 34

An invalidly appointed administrator who takes possession of the company's property, or otherwise intervenes in its business, may find himself liable in tort for any damage resulting from those activities and/or subject to a misfeasance application under IA 1986 Sch B1 para 75. This provision, which is based on IA 1986 s 34, enables to court to order the appointor to indemnify the purported administrator against such liability and it must be read in conjunction with IA 1986 Sch B1 para 104, which is based on IA 1986 s 232. IA 1986 Sch B1 para 34 covers a wholly invalid appointment; *Morris v Kannsen* [1946] AC 459; for example, where the power to appoint had not arisen at all. It is possible that IA 1986 Sch B1 para 104, which validates the acts of an administrator where there was some defect in the appointment, applies to a narrower range of circumstances; for example, where there was a failure to comply with the provisions of IA 1986 Sch B1 para 29; see notes to IA 1986 Sch B1 para 104.

Administration Application – Special Cases

Application by holder of floating charge

1.621

35

(1) This paragraph applies where an administration application in respect of a company—

> (a) is made by the holder of a qualifying floating charge in respect of the company's property, and
> (b) includes a statement that the application is made in reliance on this paragraph.
>
> (2) The court may make an administration order—
> (a) whether or not satisfied that the company is or is likely to become unable to pay its debts, but
> (b) only if satisfied that the applicant could appoint an administrator under paragraph 14.

Notes

Para 35

This provision enables the holder of a qualifying floating charge to make an administration application. If the application is made in reliance on this paragraph, there is no need to establish insolvency. However, the applicant must establish that he could appoint an administrator under IA 1986 Sch B1 para 14. It is difficult to foresee a situation (unless there is an administrative receiver or provisional liquidator in office IA 1986 Sch B1 para 17) in which such a chargeholder would become involved in an application to court rather than making an out of court appointment; unless perhaps the chargeholder desires the benefit of a court order to prevent a contemplated challenge to the appointment.

Intervention by holder of floating charge

1.622

36

(1) This paragraph applies where—
> (a) an administration application in respect of a company is made by a person who is not the holder of a qualifying floating charge in respect of the company's property, and
> (b) the holder of a qualifying floating charge in respect of the company's property applies to the court to have a specified person appointed as administrator (and not the person specified by the administration applicant).

(2) The court shall grant an application under sub-paragraph (1)(b) unless the court thinks it right to refuse the application because of the particular circumstances of the case.

Notes

Para 36

Where an application for an administration order has been made, the holder of a qualifying floating charge may intervene and seek the appointment of his own nominee. The court must accede to this application unless the circumstances of the case are such as to persuade it to take a different course. As noted above under IA 1986 Sch B1 para 35, it is somewhat difficult to see why such a charge holder would go down the court route unless there is an administrative receiver or provisional liquidator in office: IA 1986 Sch B1 para 17. Normally the easiest course for the chargeholder would be to appoint out of court (IA 1986 Sch B1 para 14) despite the existence of an administration application (IA 1986 Sch B1 para 44(7)(b)). Once the IA 1986 Sch B1 para 14 appointment out of court is made the court cannot make an administration order IA 1986 Sch B1 para 7.

Application where company in liquidation

1.623

37

(1) This paragraph applies where the holder of a qualifying floating charge in respect of a company's property could appoint an administrator under paragraph 14 but for paragraph 8(1)(b).

(2) The holder of the qualifying floating charge may make an administration application.

(3) If the court makes an administration order on hearing an application made by virtue of sub-paragraph (2)—
  (a) the court shall discharge the winding-up order,
  (b) the court shall make provision for such matters as may be prescribed,
  (c) the court may make other consequential provision,
  (d) the court shall specify which of the powers under this Schedule are to be exercisable by the administrator, and
  (e) this Schedule shall have effect with such modifications as the court may specify.

Notes

Para 37

There is a general prohibition on the appointment of an administrator where the company is in liquidation, whether voluntary or compulsory: IA 1986 Sch B1 para 8(1). However where the company is in compulsory liquidation, the holder of a qualifying floating charge may apply for an administration order under this provision. He must be able to establish that he would have been entitled to appoint an administrator but for the liquidation: IA 1986 Sch B1 para 37(2). If the court accedes to the application, it will discharge the winding-up order and make consequential orders dealing with the matters specified in IA 1986 Sch B1 para 37(3). The prescribed matters referred to in IA 1986 Sch B1 para 37(3)(b) are those set out in IR 1986 r 2.13. They deal with the matters required to bring the liquidation to an end.

1.624

38

(1) The liquidator of a company may make an administration application.

(2) If the court makes an administration order on hearing an application made by virtue of sub-paragraph (1)—
  (a) the court shall discharge any winding-up order in respect of the company,
  (b) the court shall make provision for such matters as may be prescribed,

> (c)   the court may make other consequential provision,
> (d)   the court shall specify which of the powers under this Schedule are to be exercisable by the administrator, and
> (e)   this Schedule shall have effect with such modifications as the court may specify.

Notes

Para 38

A liquidator of the company, whether it is in compulsory or voluntary liquidation, may make an administration application. Again as under IA 1986 Sch B1 para 37, if the court accedes to the application, it will discharge the winding-up order and make consequential orders dealing with the matters specified in IA 1986 Sch B1 para 38(2). The prescribed matters referred to in IA 1986 Sch B1 para 38(2)(b) are those set out in IR 1986 r 2.13. They deal with the matters required to bring the liquidation to an end.

Effect of administrative receivership

1.625

39

(1) Where there is an administrative receiver of a company the court must dismiss an administration application in respect of the company unless—

> (a)   the person by or on behalf of whom the receiver was appointed consents to the making of the administration order,
> (b)   the court thinks that the security by virtue of which the receiver was appointed would be liable to be released or discharged under sections 238 to 240 (transaction at undervalue and preference) if an administration order were made,
> (c)   the court thinks that the security by virtue of which the receiver was appointed would be avoided under section 245 (avoidance of floating charge) if an administration order were made, or
> (d)   the court thinks that the security by virtue of which the receiver was appointed would be challengeable under section 242 (gratuitous alienations) or 243 (unfair preferences) or under any rule of law in Scotland.

(2) Sub-paragraph (1) applies whether the administrative receiver is appointed before or after the making of the administration application.

Notes

Para 39(1)(a)

Where an administrative receiver is in office an administration application must be dismissed unless the qualifying floating chargeholder consents to the administration *Chesterton International Group plc v Deka Immobilien Inv Gmbh* [2005] BPIR 1103. Where an administrative receiver is appointed, the court must dismiss the administration application unless one of the conditions set out in IA 1986 Sch B1 para 39(1) is satisfied. This is so, whether the administrative receiver was appointed before or after the making of the administration application. There is no provision enabling the consent of the appointor of the administrative receiver to be given to enable an out of court appointment of an administrator to proceed (see IA 1986 Sch B1 para 14, 22, 17(b), 25(c)).

Para 39(1)(b), (c)

Aside from these specific grounds under the former law challenges could be made, for instance on the grounds that: the administrative receiver was invalidly appointed because the appointor failed to fulfil the 'mechanics of payment' test (*Bank of Baroda v Panessar* [1987] Ch 335, [1986] 3 All ER 751, or the qualifying floating charge had not been registered under CA 1985 s 395 or the appointment was made contrary to an express contractual provision (*Sheppard & Cooper Ltd v TSB Bank plc* [1997] 2 BCLC 222; or the security was given in contravention of the financial assistance provisions (CA 1985, s 151 to 158), or the grant of the security was ultra vires.

Para 39(2)

The veto given to the holder of the qualifying floating charge is exercisable whether the administrative receiver is appointed before or after the administration application is issued.

Effect of Administration

Notes

Introduction

Paras 40–44

These paragraphs provide for the moratorium which is at the heart of the administration process. IA 1986 Sch B1 para 40–43 define the extent of the moratorium when a company in administration following the making of an administration order, or an out of court appointment. These paragraphs provide for:

- the dismissal of pending winding-up petitions in most cases: IA 1986 Sch B1 para 40;
- the dismissal of administrative and other receivers: IA 1986 Sch B1 para 41;
- a moratorium on other insolvency proceedings: IA 1986 Sch B1 para 42; and
- a moratorium on other legal process: IA 1986 Sch B1 para 43.

Para 44 provides for an interim moratorium in the following circumstances:

- When an administration application has been made but not yet granted or dismissed, or when an administration order has been made, but not yet taken effect: IA 1986 Sch B1 para 44(1)(a);
- When a notice of intention to appoint has been filed with the court by the holder of a qualifying floating charge: IA 1986 Sch B1 para 44(1)(b);
- When a notice of intention to appointed has been filed by the company or its directors: IA 1986 Sch B1 para 44(4).

On the face of it there does not appear to be any express provision preventing the filing of consecutive notices of intention to appoint each of which initiates an interim moratorium though this may lead to an application by an aggrieved creditor. During the period of the interim moratorium, the provisions of IA 1986 Sch B1 para 42,43 apply, but with certain important exceptions and modifications. These are as follows:

- The interim moratorium does not automatically apply where an administration application is made at a time when an administrative receiver is in place. It applies only if and when the person by or on behalf of whom the administrative receiver was appointed consents to the making of an administrative order: IA 1986 Sch B1 para 44(6). In such cases, an administration order may not be made without that consent: IA 1986 Sch B1 para 39(1). The consent is a necessary condition of the administration order. Whilst that condition remains unsatisfied, it would be wrong to prevent creditors from exercising the remedies available to them. Hence this limit on the application of the interim moratorium;

- Again, the interim moratorium does not prevent (a) the appointment of an administrative receiver, or (b) the exercise by such a receiver of his functions: IA 1986 Sch B1 para 44(7)(c),(d). The holder of a charge having a right to appoint an administrative receiver still has an effective right of veto exercisable by appointment even after the making of an administration application: IA 1986 Sch B1 para 39(1). That right is retained notwithstanding the making of the application. The exercise of at least some of such an administrative receiver's functions are capable of being affected by the interim moratorium; hence, the exception contained in IA 1986 Sch B1 para 44(7)(d);
- The holder of a qualifying floating charge appointing an administrator under IA 1986 Sch B1 para 14; IA 1986 Sch B1 para 44(7)(b);
- The presentation of a public interest winding up petition under IA 1986 s 124A or a Financial Services Authority petition under FSMA 2000 s 367; IA 1986 Sch B1 para 44(7)(a).

Dismissal of pending winding-up petition

1.626

40

(1) A petition for the winding up of a company—
 (a) shall be dismissed on the making of an administration order in respect of the company, and
 (b) shall be suspended while the company is in administration following an appointment under paragraph 14.

(2) Sub-paragraph (1)(b) does not apply to a petition presented under—
 (a) section 124A (public interest),
 [(aa) section 124B (SEs),] or
 (b) section 367 of the Financial Services and Markets Act 2000 (c 8) (petition by Financial Services Authority).

(3) Where an administrator becomes aware that a petition was presented under a provision referred to in sub-paragraph (2) before his appointment, he shall apply to the court for directions under paragraph 63.

Notes

Para 40(1)(a)

A winding up petitioner will also normally obtain an order for its costs as an expense of the administration; on the making of an administration order by the court the winding up petition is dismissed. Where the winding up petition has been issued in a court different to the court making the administration order it is usually appropriate to transfer the winding up petition so that the court making the administration order can also dismiss the winding up petition. Otherwise on the hearing of the winding up petition the court will be informed that an administration order has been made and the court will confirm the dismissal of the winding up petition accordingly.

Para 40(1)(b)

This deals with the situation where a qualifying floating chargeholder has made an appointment out of court (IA 1986 Sch B1 para 14) despite the existence of a winding up petition; such a chargeholder is not restricted from making an appointment out of court by the existence of a winding up petition: IA 1986 Sch B1 paras 15–17. The suspension of the petition carries with it the suspension of the operation of IA 1986 s 127 which avoids dispositions of property of the company in the hiatus between winding up petition and winding up order IA 1986 s 127(2). The suspension of the winding up will be brought to an end either upon the administrator's proposals not being approved by creditors and the court making an order on the suspended petition: IA 1986 Sch B1 para 55(2)(d); or when the company exits administration. There is no statutory provision under which the acceptance of the administrator's proposals by creditors itself results in the winding up petition being dismissed. It may be that the proposals themselves could contain a term requiring the administrator to apply for dismissal of the petition in defined circumstances; but such a term has yet to be tested.

Para 40(3)

The administrator is directed (IA 1986 Sch B1 para 40(3)) to make an application for directions under IA 1986 Sch B1 para 63 only in the case of the petitions listed in IA 1986 Sch B1 para 40(2).

1.627

41

(1) When an administration order takes effect in respect of a company any administrative receiver of the company shall vacate office.

(2) Where a company is in administration, any receiver of part of the company's property shall vacate office if the administrator requires him to.

(3) Where an administrative receiver or receiver vacates office under sub-paragraph (1) or (2)—

   (a)   his remuneration shall be charged on and paid out of any property of the company which was in his custody or under his control immediately before he vacated office, and

   (b)   he need not take any further steps under section 40 or 59.

(4) In the application of sub-paragraph (3)(a)—

   (a)   'remuneration' includes expenses properly incurred and any indemnity to which the administrative receiver or receiver is entitled out of the assets of the company,

   (b)   the charge imposed takes priority over security held by the person by whom or on whose behalf the administrative receiver or receiver was appointed, and

   (c)   the provision for payment is subject to paragraph 43.

Notes

Para 41(1)

When there is an administrative receiver in office no out of court appointment of an administrator can be made IA 1986 Sch B1 paras 17(b), 25(c) but the court can still make an administration order. The mere presentation of an administration application to court does not prevent the appointment of an administrative receiver IA 1986 Sch B1 para 44(7)(c) nor the carrying out of his functions IA 1986 Sch B1 para 44(7)(d); if an administrative receiver is in office when the application is made the moratorium on insolvency proceedings and other legal process does not apply until the person by or on whose behalf the administrative receiver was appointed consents to the making of the administration order IA 1986 Sch B1 para 44(6).

Para 41(3)

Though the administrative receiver is entitled to his remuneration the moratorium on legal process under IA 1986 Sch B1 para 43 prevents him from taking recovery action unless the consent of the administrator or the permission of the court is obtained IA 1986 Sch B1 para 41(4)(c).

Moratorium on insolvency proceedings

1.628

42

(1) This paragraph applies to a company in administration.

(2) No resolution may be passed for the winding up of the company.

(3) No order may be made for the winding up of the company.

(4) Sub-paragraph (3) does not apply to an order made on a petition presented under—
    (a)   section 124A (public interest),
    [(aa) section 124B (SEs),] or
    (b)   section 367 of the Financial Services and Markets Act 2000 (c 8) (petition by Financial Services Authority).

(5) If a petition presented under a provision referred to in sub-paragraph (4) comes to the attention of the administrator, he shall apply to the court for directions under paragraph 63.

Notes

Para 42(1)

A company is 'in administration' while the appointment of an administrator has effect but it does not cease to be in administration merely because an administrator vacates or is removed from office IA 1986 Sch B1 para 1(2)(a), (d). An interim moratorium also applies prior to the company being in administration in the circumstances stated in IA 1986 Sch B1 para 44 which inter alia restricts the ability to put a company into liquidation: IA 1986 Sch B1 para 44(5).

Paras 42(2), (3)

Thus once the company is in administration it cannot pass into a liquidation by resolution of the company nor by order of the court save in the latter case in the circumstances stated in IA 1986 Sch B1 para 42(4). However on termination of the administration the company may be put into a creditors' voluntary liquidation by registration of a notice sent by the administrator to the registrar of companies under IA 1986 Sch B1 para 83; or wound up by the court if a winding up petition is presented by the administrator on an application to court for termination: IA 1986 Sch B1 para 79, para 60; IA 1986 Sch 1 para 21.

Moratorium on other legal process

1.629

43

(1) This paragraph applies to a company in administration.

(2) No step may be taken to enforce security over the company's property except—
(a)   with the consent of the administrator, or
(b)   with the permission of the court.

(3) No step may be taken to repossess goods in the company's possession under a hire-purchase agreement except—
(a)   with the consent of the administrator, or
(b)   with the permission of the court.

(4) A landlord may not exercise a right of forfeiture by peaceable re-entry in relation to premises let to the company except—
(a)   with the consent of the administrator, or
(b)   with the permission of the court.

(5) In Scotland, a landlord may not exercise a right of irritancy in relation to premises let to the company except—
(a)   with the consent of the administrator, or
(b)   with the permission of the court.

(6) No legal process (including legal proceedings, execution, distress and diligence) may be instituted or continued against the company or property of the company except—
(a)   with the consent of the administrator, or
(b)   with the permission of the court.

[(6A) An administrative receiver of the company may not be appointed.]

(7) Where the court gives permission for a transaction under this paragraph it may impose a condition on or a requirement in connection with the transaction.

(8) In this paragraph 'landlord' includes a person to whom rent is payable.

Notes

Para 43(1)

A company is '*in administration*' while the appointment of an administrator has effect but it does not cease to be in administration merely because an administrator vacates or is removed from office IA 1986 Sch B1 para 1(2)(a),(d). An interim moratorium also applies in the circumstances stated in IA 1986 Sch B1 para 44 to restrict other legal process

Para 43(2)

'Security' is given a wide definition in the IA 1986, s 248 meaning 'any mortgage, charge, lien or other security' which therefore includes security arising by operation of law as well as consensual security: *Re Euro Commercial Leasing Ltd v Cartwright & Lewis* [1995] BCC 830. 'Other security' is to be given its ordinary meaning, and in *Bristol Airport plc v Powdrill* [1990] Ch 744,760 the Court of Appeal was content to accept a wide definition suggested by counsel, the gist of which was a right to look to another's property to secure the payment of a debt. A right of set off is unlikely to be categorised as 'other security'; in Scotland such a right is specifically excluded from the definition of 'security' (IA 1986 s 248(b)(ii)). The 'taking of steps' is a sufficiently vague concept to cause some confusion and it is discussed at some length in *Bristol Airport plc v Powdrill* [1990] Ch 744; in the context of a lien it was stated in that case that there must be something in the nature of an unqualified refusal to give up the goods to the administrator (at p 768).

It is unclear whether a demand for payment from the company is the 'taking of steps' to enforce a security over the company's property *Re Olympia & York Canary Wharf Ltd* [1993] BCLC 453, cf *Barclays Mercantile Business Finance Ltd v Sibec Developments Ltd* [1992] 1 WLR 1253.

Para 43(2)(b)

In deciding whether or not to give permission the court will be guided by the principles stated by Nicholls LJ in *Re Atlantic Computer Systems plc* [1992] Ch 505, 542ff; it is necessary to consider carefully each one of those principles if an application for permission is to be made. In giving permission the court should not prefer the interests of one unsecured creditor over another *Re TBL Realisations plc* [2004] BCC 81 and where the appointment of a receiver would be more likely to produce a better return for creditors than an administrator then the court will permit the appointment of the former *Sinai Securities Ltd v Hooper* [2004] BCC 973. The burden of obtaining permission is on the applicant and as a practical matter such a person faces an uphill struggle in the face of opposition from the administrator (if the company is in administration) or from the company in the case of a proposed appointment in the periods stated in IA 1986 Sch B1 para 44(1)–(4). Where the applicant shows that the giving of permission will not impede the objective of the administration then permission should be given, otherwise it is a question of the court carrying out a balancing exercise and great weight is attached to the proprietary interests of the creditor. Where a significant loss can be proved by the creditor if permission is not given this will normally be sufficient ground for giving leave, but it is not automatic (*Scottish Exhibition Centre Ltd v Mirestop Ltd* [1993] BCC 529). Each case must be looked at individually as many factors may influence the court's decision; for instance in *Bristol Airport plc v Powdrill* the conduct of the applicants in initially appearing to consent to the administration, and enjoying the fruits of the administration, and then seeking to enforce security rights at a later date was a factor which resulted in the court refusing leave. In *Re David Meek Access Ltd* [1994] 1 BCLC 680 after a thorough consideration of the evidence the court refused permission to re-possess to a number of finance companies which had supplied the company with goods on hire purchase. However, permission was given to two companies which had sought to re-possess the day before the presentation of the administration petition; it is difficult to determine when and where such a dividing line will be drawn in future cases.

Para 43(6)

For the meaning of *'No legal process (including legal proceedings, execution ..',* it is helpful to refer to decisions under the former administration regime (IA 1986 s 10(1)(c), 11(3)) including:

- *Re a Company (No 1992 of 1988)* [1989] BCLC 9 – advertisement of winding up petition was prohibited;
- *Bristol Airport v Powdrill* [1990] Ch 744 – 'other proceedings' means legal or quasi legal proceedings which includes statutory adjudication procedures: *A Straume (UK) Ltd v Bradlor Developments Ltd* [2000] BCC 333;
- Employment tribunal claims *Re Divine Solutions (UK) Ltd* [2004] BCC 325, *Carr v British International Helicopters Ltd* [1994] 2 BCLC 474;
- *Re Olympia and York Canary Wharf Ltd* [1993] BCLC 453 'proceedings' and 'legal process' together contemplate all steps in legal proceedings from initiating process to their final termination in the process of execution or other means of enforcement of a judgment, but do not include the taking of non-judicial steps such as the serving of a notice;
- *Biosource Technologies Inc v Axis Genetics plc* [2000] 1 BCLC 286 – 'other proceedings' includes not just claims brought by a company's creditors, but also proceedings brought by its competitors, in this case, a claim for the revocation of a patent held by the company;

- In *Re Rhondda Waste Disposal Ltd* [2001] Ch 57, CA – 'other proceedings' includes criminal proceedings;
- *Re Railtrack plc v Winsor v Bloom* [2003] BPIR 507 – the power of the railway regulator to give regulatory directions was not prohibited

Para 43(7)

A wide definition is given to 'transaction' IA 1986 s 436.

Interim moratorium

1.630

44

(1) This paragraph applies where an administration application in respect of a company has been made and—
- (a) the application has not yet been granted or dismissed, or
- (b) the application has been granted but the administration order has not yet taken effect.

(2) This paragraph also applies from the time when a copy of notice of intention to appoint an administrator under paragraph 14 is filed with the court until—
- (a) the appointment of the administrator takes effect, or
- (b) the period of five business days beginning with the date of filing expires without an administrator having been appointed.

(3) Sub-paragraph (2) has effect in relation to a notice of intention to appoint only if it is in the prescribed form.

(4) This paragraph also applies from the time when a copy of notice of intention to appoint an administrator is filed with the court under paragraph 27(1) until—
- (a) the appointment of the administrator takes effect, or
- (b) the period specified in paragraph 28(2) expires without an administrator having been appointed.

(5) The provisions of paragraphs 42 and 43 shall apply (ignoring any reference to the consent of the administrator).

(6) If there is an administrative receiver of the company when the administration application is made, the provisions of paragraphs 42 and 43 shall not begin to apply by virtue of this paragraph until the person by or on behalf of whom the receiver was appointed consents to the making of the administration order.

(7) This paragraph does not prevent or require the permission of the court for—
- (a) the presentation of a petition for the winding up of the company under a provision mentioned in paragraph 42(4),
- (b) the appointment of an administrator under paragraph 14,
- (c) the appointment of an administrative receiver of the company, or

643

> (d) the carrying out by an administrative receiver (whenever appointed) of his functions.

Notes

Para 44(1)(b)

Under IA 1986 Sch B1 para 13(2)(a) the court can make an administration order and appoint a time when the order takes effect; until it takes effect the interim moratorium applies.

Para 44(2), (4)

A qualifying floating chargeholder must file and serve a notice of intention to appoint where there is in existence a prior floating charge IA 1986 Sch B1 para 15, IR 1986 r 2.15, see notes to para 15; otherwise providing none of the other restrictions apply (paras 16, 17) he may proceed straight to an appointment under IA 1986 Sch B1 para 14, IR 1986 r 2.16. There does not appear to be an express restriction on successive notices of intention to appoint being filed by the qualifying floating chargeholder, company or directors albeit that such behaviour may quickly attract criticism from the creditors. Obviously the advantage of an extant notice of intention to appoint is the imposition of the interim moratorium.

Para 44(5)

Given that IA 1986 Sch B1 para 44 contemplates that the appointment of the administrator has not taken effect it is only the court that may permit the lifting of the moratorium.

Para 44(6)

Clearly this provision does not apply where the appointment of an administrator is made out of court under IA 1986 Sch B1 para 14 or IA 1986 Sch B1 para 22; it only applies in the case of an application to court being made for an administrator and there is at that time an administrative receiver in office. Thus the appointor of an administrative receiver must consent to the making of an administration order before the interim moratorium can take effect. Further under IA 1986 Sch B1 para 39 the application must be dismissed unless the appointor consents or the court thinks that the security under which the administrative receiver has been appointed can be attacked in the specific circumstances listed in IA 1986 Sch B1 para 39.

Para 44(7)(b)

The holder of the qualifying floating charge must send a copy of the notice of appointment of an administrator under IA 1986 Sch B1 para 14 as soon as reasonably practicable to the applicant for the administration and to the court in which the application was made IR 1986 r 2.18. The administrator is under a separate duty to notify his appointment IR 1986 r 2.27.

> ## Publicity
>
> **1.631**
>
> **45**
>
> (1) While a company is in administration every business document issued by or on behalf of the company or the administrator must state—
>
> (a) the name of the administrator, and
>
> (b) that the affairs, business and property of the company are being managed by him.

(2) Any of the following commits an offence if without reasonable excuse he authorises or permits a contravention of sub-paragraph (1)—
    (a)   the administrator,
    (b)   an officer of the company, and
    (c)   the company.

(3) In sub-paragraph (1) 'business document' means—
    (a)   an invoice,
    (b)   an order for goods or services, and
    (c)   a business letter.

Notes

Para 45

The administrator is under a separate duty to notify and advertise his appointment see IA 1986 Sch B1 para 46 below and IR 1986 r 2.27.

Para 45(3)

In exercising his functions an administrator acts as its agent (IA 1986 Sch B1 para 69) and it is usual for an administrator to exclude personal liability and refer to his status as an agent in business documents.

Process of Administration

Announcement of administrator's appointment

1.632

46

(1) This paragraph applies where a person becomes the administrator of a company.

(2) As soon as is reasonably practicable the administrator shall—
    (a)   send a notice of his appointment to the company, and
    (b)   publish a notice of his appointment in the prescribed manner.

(3) As soon as is reasonably practicable the administrator shall—
    (a)   obtain a list of the company's creditors, and
    (b)   send a notice of his appointment to each creditor of whose claim and address he is aware.

(4) The administrator shall send a notice of his appointment to the registrar of companies before the end of the period of 7 days beginning with the date specified in sub-paragraph (6).

(5) The administrator shall send a notice of his appointment to such persons as may be prescribed before the end of the prescribed period beginning with the date specified in sub-paragraph (6).

(6) The date for the purpose of sub-paragraphs (4) and (5) is—
    (a)   in the case of an administrator appointed by administration order, the date of the order,
    (b)   in the case of an administrator appointed under paragraph 14, the date on which he receives notice under paragraph 20, and

> (c) in the case of an administrator appointed under paragraph 22, the date on which he receives notice under paragraph 32.
>
> (7) The court may direct that sub-paragraph (3)(b) or (5)—
>   (a) shall not apply, or
>   (b) shall apply with the substitution of a different period.
>
> (8) A notice under this paragraph must—
>   (a) contain the prescribed information, and
>   (b) be in the prescribed form.
>
> (9) An administrator commits an offence if he fails without reasonable excuse to comply with a requirement of this paragraph.

Notes

Para 46(3)

This provision should be read together with IR 1986 r 2.27. In *Re Sporting Options plc* [2005] BCC 88 the court refused an application to enable administrators to notify their appointment by email. However the court was prepared to direct that the proposals of the administrators under IA 1986 Sch B1 para 49 could be served in the letter notifying their appointment by referring the creditors to a relevant web site where the proposals could be viewed. See also the notes to IR 1986 r 12.4(1).

Para 46(5)

The prescribed persons are listed in IR 1986 r 2.27(2).

> **Statement of company's affairs**
>
> **1.633**
>
> **47**
>
> (1) As soon as is reasonably practicable after appointment the administrator of a company shall by notice in the prescribed form require one or more relevant persons to provide the administrator with a statement of the affairs of the company.
>
> (2) The statement must—
>   (a) be verified by a statement of truth in accordance with Civil Procedure Rules,
>   (b) be in the prescribed form,
>   (c) give particulars of the company's property, debts and liabilities,
>   (d) give the names and addresses of the company's creditors,
>   (e) specify the security held by each creditor,
>   (f) give the date on which each security was granted, and
>   (g) contain such other information as may be prescribed.
>
> (3) In sub-paragraph (1) 'relevant person' means—
>   (a) a person who is or has been an officer of the company,
>   (b) a person who took part in the formation of the company during the period of one year ending with the date on which the company enters administration,
>   (c) a person employed by the company during that period, and

(d) a person who is or has been during that period an officer or employee of a company which is or has been during that year an officer of the company.

(4) For the purpose of sub-paragraph (3) a reference to employment is a reference to employment through a contract of employment or a contract for services.

(5) In Scotland, a statement of affairs under sub-paragraph (1) must be a statutory declaration made in accordance with the Statutory Declarations Act 1835 (c 62) (and sub-paragraph (2)(a) shall not apply).

Notes

Para 47

This provision should be read together with IR 1986 r 2.28 to 2.32; IR 1986 r 7.20 enables the administrator to apply to court to enforce the obligations under IA 1986 Sch B1 para 47. If the administrator thinks that it would prejudice the conduct of the administration for the whole or part of the statement of affairs to be disclosed he may apply to the court for an order limiting its disclosure IR 1986 r 2.30.

Para 47(3)(a)

'Officer' is widely defined by reference to CA 1985 s 744 and IA 1986 s 251 and includes a director, manager or secretary.

1.634

48

(1) A person required to submit a statement of affairs must do so before the end of the period of 11 days beginning with the day on which he receives notice of the requirement.

(2) The administrator may—
(a) revoke a requirement under paragraph 47(1), or
(b) extend the period specified in sub-paragraph (1) (whether before or after expiry).

(3) If the administrator refuses a request to act under sub-paragraph (2)—
(a) the person whose request is refused may apply to the court, and
(b) the court may take action of a kind specified in sub-paragraph (2).

(4) A person commits an offence if he fails without reasonable excuse to comply with a requirement under paragraph 47(1).

Notes

Para 48

This provision should be read together with IR 1986 r 2.31.

Administrator's proposals

1.635

49

(1) The administrator of a company shall make a statement setting out proposals for achieving the purpose of administration.

(2) A statement under sub-paragraph (1) must, in particular—
- (a) deal with such matters as may be prescribed, and
- (b) where applicable, explain why the administrator thinks that the objective mentioned in paragraph 3(1)(a) or (b) cannot be achieved.

(3) Proposals under this paragraph may include—
- (a) a proposal for a voluntary arrangement under Part I of this Act (although this paragraph is without prejudice to section 4(3));
- (b) a proposal for a compromise or arrangement to be sanctioned under section 425 of the Companies Act (compromise with creditors or members).

(4) The administrator shall send a copy of the statement of his proposals—
- (a) to the registrar of companies,
- (b) to every creditor of the company of whose claim and address he is aware, and
- (c) to every member of the company of whose address he is aware.

(5) The administrator shall comply with sub-paragraph (4)—
- (a) as soon as is reasonably practicable after the company enters administration, and
- (b) in any event, before the end of the period of eight weeks beginning with the day on which the company enters administration.

(6) The administrator shall be taken to comply with sub-paragraph (4)(c) if he publishes in the prescribed manner a notice undertaking to provide a copy of the statement of proposals free of charge to any member of the company who applies in writing to a specified address.

(7) An administrator commits an offence if he fails without reasonable excuse to comply with sub-paragraph (5).

(8) A period specified in this paragraph may be varied in accordance with paragraph 107.

Notes

Para 49

This provision should be read together with IR 1986 r 2.33 which lists matters which must be included aside from the information required by IA 1986 Sch B1 para 49(2)(b). Importantly the obligation imposed on the administrator to send out his proposals to the relevant parties must be fulfilled within the 8 weeks beginning with the entry of the company into administration (para 49(5)) though this period can be extended by the court IA 1986 Sch B1 para 49(8), 107 or by the administrator with the consent of the creditors IA 1986 Sch B1 para 108. A company enters administration when the appointment of the administrator takes effect (IA 1986 Sch B1 para 1(2)(b)) which varies depending on the manner of appointment (IA 1986 Sch B1 paras 13(2), 19, 31).

Para 49(2)(a)

The relevant matters are prescribed in IR 1986 r 2.33(2). The proposals may not include any action which affects the right of a secured creditor to enforce his security nor preferential creditors in the manner set out and subject to the exceptions contained in IA 1986 Sch B1 para 73.

Creditors' meeting

1.636

50

(1) In this Schedule 'creditors' meeting' means a meeting of creditors of a company summoned by the administrator—
  (a) in the prescribed manner, and
  (b) giving the prescribed period of notice to every creditor of the company of whose claim and address he is aware.

(2) A period prescribed under sub-paragraph (1)(b) may be varied in accordance with paragraph 107.

(3) A creditors' meeting shall be conducted in accordance with the rules.

Notes

Para 50

This provision should be read together with IR 1986 rr 2.34–2.48. Generally there is no necessity to hold a formal meeting as anything that is required or permitted to be done at a creditors' meeting can be done by correspondence between the creditors and the administrator: IA 1986 Sch B1 para 58; 'correspondence' includes the telephone or other electronic means: IA 1986 Sch B1 para 111. There is no obligation on the administrator to call a meeting of members but the administrator might consider doing so in the case of a solvent administration and if he does so it must be summoned and held in accordance with IR 1986 r 2.49.

Para 50(1)(b)

The period of notice which is prescribed is at least 14 days IR 1986 r 2.35(4).

Para 50(2)

The period may be varied under IA 1986 Sch B1 para 107 by the court or by the administrator with the consent of the creditors under IA 1986 Sch B1 para 108.

Requirement for initial creditors' meeting

1.637

51

(1) Each copy of an administrator's statement of proposals sent to a creditor under paragraph 49(4)(b) must be accompanied by an invitation to a creditors' meeting (an 'initial creditors' meeting').

(2) The date set for an initial creditors' meeting must be—
   (a) as soon as is reasonably practicable after the company enters administration, and
   (b) in any event, within the period of ten weeks beginning with the date on which the company enters administration.

(3) An administrator shall present a copy of his statement of proposals to an initial creditors' meeting.

(4) A period specified in this paragraph may be varied in accordance with paragraph 107.

(5) An administrator commits an offence if he fails without reasonable excuse to comply with a requirement of this paragraph.

Notes

Para 51(1)

This provision should be read together with IR 1986 r 2.34 dealing with the notice of the initial creditors' meeting. There is no requirement to hold an initial creditors' meeting in the circumstances stated in IA 1986 Sch B1 para 52; nor where he adopts either the procedure under IA 1986 Sch B1 para 80 to terminate the administration before he has sent out proposals to creditors (IR 1986 r 2.33(6)) or the dissolution procedure under IA 1986 Sch B1 para 84.

Para 51(2)(b)

The period may be varied (even after expiry of the period) under IA 1986 Sch B1 para 107 by the court (IA 1986 Sch B1 para 51(4)) or by the administrator with the consent of the creditors under IA 1986 Sch B1 para 108.

1.638

52

(1) Paragraph 51(1) shall not apply where the statement of proposals states that the administrator thinks—
   (a) that the company has sufficient property to enable each creditor of the company to be paid in full,
   (b) that the company has insufficient property to enable a distribution to be made to unsecured creditors other than by virtue of section 176A(2)(a), or
   (c) that neither of the objectives specified in paragraph 3(1)(a) and (b) can be achieved.

(2) But the administrator shall summon an initial creditors' meeting if it is requested—
   (a) by creditors of the company whose debts amount to at least 10% of the total debts of the company,
   (b) in the prescribed manner, and
   (c) in the prescribed period.

(3) A meeting requested under sub-paragraph (2) must be summoned for a date in the prescribed period.

> (4) The period prescribed under sub-paragraph (3) may be varied in accordance with paragraph 107.

Notes

Para 52(1)

In these circumstances the unsecured creditors are unlikely to have any substantive interest in having a meeting although a meeting can be requisitioned under IA 1986 Sch B1 para 52(2) below.

Para 52(2)

This provision should be read together with IR 1986 r 2.37 which deals with the procedure for the requisition and holding of an initial creditors' meeting.

> ## Business and result of initial creditors' meeting
>
> **1.639**
>
> **53**
>
> (1) An initial creditors' meeting to which an administrator's proposals are presented shall consider them and may—
> - (a) approve them without modification, or
> - (b) approve them with modification to which the administrator consents.
>
> (2) After the conclusion of an initial creditors' meeting the administrator shall as soon as is reasonably practicable report any decision taken to—
> - (a) the court,
> - (b) the registrar of companies, and
> - (c) such other persons as may be prescribed.
>
> (3) An administrator commits an offence if he fails without reasonable excuse to comply with sub-paragraph (2).

Notes

Para 53(1)

The procedure at the meeting is governed by IR 1986 r 2.34 to 2.48. Once approved then the administrator subject to any directions of the court must manage the company's affairs, business and property subject to those proposals IA 1986 Sch B1 para 68. Although not expressly stated clearly the creditors can vote to reject the proposals.

Para 53(2)(c)

The persons prescribed are listed in IR 1986 r 2.46. A resolution of the creditors is invalid if those voting against it include more than half in value of the creditors to whom notice of the meeting was given and are not connected to the company; 'connected' is defined in IA 1986 s 249.

Revision of administrator's proposals

1.640

54

(1) This paragraph applies where—
  (a) an administrator's proposals have been approved (with or without modification) at an initial creditors' meeting,
  (b) the administrator proposes a revision to the proposals, and
  (c) the administrator thinks that the proposed revision is substantial.

(2) The administrator shall—
  (a) summon a creditors' meeting,
  (b) send a statement in the prescribed form of the proposed revision with the notice of the meeting sent to each creditor,
  (c) send a copy of the statement, within the prescribed period, to each member of the company of whose address he is aware, and
  (d) present a copy of the statement to the meeting.

(3) The administrator shall be taken to have complied with sub-paragraph (2)(c) if he publishes a notice undertaking to provide a copy of the statement free of charge to any member of the company who applies in writing to a specified address.

(4) A notice under sub-paragraph (3) must be published—
  (a) in the prescribed manner, and
  (b) within the prescribed period.

(5) A creditors' meeting to which a proposed revision is presented shall consider it and may—
  (a) approve it without modification, or
  (b) approve it with modification to which the administrator consents.

(6) After the conclusion of a creditors' meeting the administrator shall as soon as is reasonably practicable report any decision taken to—
  (a) the court,
  (b) the registrar of companies, and
  (c) such other persons as may be prescribed.

(7) An administrator commits an offence if he fails without reasonable excuse to comply with sub-paragraph (6).

Notes

Para 54

This provision should be read with IR 1986 r 2.45 and the general rules on creditors' meetings IR 1986 r 2.35ff.

Para 54(1)(c)

The obligation to consult with creditors' only arises where the proposed revision is '*substantial*'; in cases of doubt or urgency then an application should be made for directions IA 1986 Sch B1 para 63, para 68(3)(c).

Failure to obtain approval of administrator's proposals

1.641

55

(1) This paragraph applies where an administrator reports to the court that—

(a) an initial creditors' meeting has failed to approve the administrator's proposals presented to it, or

(b) a creditors' meeting has failed to approve a revision of the administrator's proposals presented to it.

(2) The court may—

(a) provide that the appointment of an administrator shall cease to have effect from a specified time;

(b) adjourn the hearing conditionally or unconditionally;

(c) make an interim order;

(d) make an order on a petition for winding up suspended by virtue of paragraph 40(1)(b);

(e) make any other order (including an order making consequential provision) that the court thinks appropriate.

Notes

Para 55

The report to the court would be made by an application to court coupled with seeking directions underIA 1986 Sch B1 para 63 and/or presenting a winding up petition or otherwise ensuring that the claims of creditors will be dealt with appropriately (see notes to IA 1986 Sch B1 para 79(4)(d) below.)

Para 55(2)(d)

A winding up petition is suspended if the respondent company enters administration pursuant to an out of court appointment by a qualifying floating chargeholder under IA 1986 Sch B1 para 14; if the respondent company enters administration by any other route the winding up petition is dismissed (IA 1986 Sch B1 para 40(1)(a)). This provision deals only with the situation where the proposals are not approved by the creditors. If they are approved Sch B1 does not contain any express provision under which the acceptance of the administrator's proposals by creditors results in the winding up petition being dismissed. It may be that the proposals themselves could contain a term requiring the administrator to apply for dismissal of the petition in such circumstances but such a term has yet to be tested.

Further creditors' meetings

1.642

56

(1) The administrator of a company shall summon a creditors' meeting if—

(a) it is requested in the prescribed manner by creditors of the company whose debts amount to at least 10% of the total debts of the company, or

(b)   he is directed by the court to summon a creditors' meeting.

(2) An administrator commits an offence if he fails without reasonable excuse to summon a creditors' meeting as required by this paragraph.

Notes

Para 56

This provision should be read with the general rules on creditors' meetings IR 1986 r 2.35ff and in particular r 2.37.

Creditors' committee

1.643

57

(1) A creditors' meeting may establish a creditors' committee.

(2) A creditors' committee shall carry out functions conferred on it by or under this Act.

(3) A creditors' committee may require the administrator—
    (a)   to attend on the committee at any reasonable time of which he is given at least seven days' notice, and
    (b)   to provide the committee with information about the exercise of his functions.

Notes

Para 57

This provision should be read with the general rules on the creditors' committee IR 1986 r 2.50 to 2.65.

Correspondence instead of creditors' meeting

1.644

58

(1) Anything which is required or permitted by or under this Schedule to be done at a creditors' meeting may be done by correspondence between the administrator and creditors—
    (a)   in accordance with the rules, and
    (b)   subject to any prescribed condition.

(2) A reference in this Schedule to anything done at a creditors' meeting includes a reference to anything done in the course of correspondence in reliance on sub-paragraph (1).

> (3) A requirement to hold a creditors' meeting is satisfied by conducting correspondence in accordance with this paragraph.

Notes

Para 58

This provision should be read together with IR 1986 r 2.48. 'Correspondence' includes correspondence by telephonic or other electronic means IA 1986 Sch B1 para 111.

Functions of Administrator

General powers

1.645

59

(1) The administrator of a company may do anything necessary or expedient for the management of the affairs, business and property of the company.

(2) A provision of this Schedule which expressly permits the administrator to do a specified thing is without prejudice to the generality of sub-paragraph (1).

(3) A person who deals with the administrator of a company in good faith and for value need not inquire whether the administrator is acting within his powers.

Notes

Para 59

A list of specific powers is given to the administrator under IA 1986 Sch B1 para 60 by reference to IA 1986 Sch 1.

Para 59(1)

Although widely worded this provision does not empower the administrator to disclaim onerous property or leaseholds (cf IA 1986 s 178,179 in a liquidation) nor to make distributions to members: *Re Business Properties Ltd* (1988) 4 BCC 684.

1.646

60

The administrator of a company has the powers specified in Schedule 1 to this Act.

Notes

Para 60

Aside from the general powers given under IA 1986 Sch B1 para 59 and the listed powers in IA 1986 Sch 1 an administrator is given a number of specific powers under a variety of provisions, for instance IA 1986 Sch B1 para 61–63, 65, 66.

1.647

61

The administrator of a company—
   (a)   may remove a director of the company, and
   (b)   may appoint a director of the company (whether or not to fill a
         vacancy).

Notes

Para 61

Unless the director has a service contract entitling him to sue for damages for loss of office he would have no claim against the company as the administrator is exercising his statutory rights: *Newtherapeutics Ltd v Katz* [1991] Ch 226.

1.648

62

The administrator of a company may call a meeting of members or creditors of the company.

Notes

Para 62

The relevant rules relating to the calling of creditors' meetings appear at IR 1986 r 2.35ff; members' meetings are dealt with in IR 1986 r 2.49.

1.649

63

The administrator of a company may apply to the court for directions in connection with his functions.

Notes

Para 63

This provision enables an administrator to apply to court for directions but it does not oblige him to do so: *Unidare plc v Cohen* [2005] BPIR 1472. It is a wide ranging provision which may for instance be used to determine difficult legal issues (*Re T & N Ltd* [2005] BCC 982) but it should not be used to obtain a 'rubber stamping' of a commercial decision; for instance a 'run of the mill' sale of assets by the administrator: *Re T & D Industries plc* [2000] BCC 956, *Re Transbus International Ltd* [2004] Ch 401, *MTI Trading Systems Ltd v Winter* [1998] BCC 591. Nor it is suggested could it be used to obtain an authority for the payment of pre appointment fees for an out of court administrator. The administrator may make an application for directions where he has been appointed out of court by a qualifying floating chargeholder under IA 1986 Sch B1 para 14 at a time when there was a winding up petition presented against the company; the effect of the appointment is not to dismiss the petition (as in the case of other types of appointment of an administrator: IA 1986 Sch B1 para 40(1)(a)), but rather to suspend it: IA 1986 Sch B1 para 40(1)(b). An application for directions should be specific and it will be dismissed if it is too vague: *Re Synthetic Technology Ltd* [1990] BCLC 378.

1.650

64

(1) A company in administration or an officer of a company in administration may not exercise a management power without the consent of the administrator.

(2) For the purpose of sub-paragraph (1)—
  (a) 'management power' means a power which could be exercised so as to interfere with the exercise of the administrator's powers,
  (b) it is immaterial whether the power is conferred by an enactment or an instrument, and
  (c) consent may be general or specific.

Notes

Para 64(1)

The consent may be given generally or in relation to particular cases *Re P & C and R & T (Stockport) Ltd* [1991] BCLC 366.

Distribution

1.651

65

(1) The administrator of a company may make a distribution to a creditor of the company.

(2) Section 175 shall apply in relation to a distribution under this paragraph as it applies in relation to a winding up.

(3) A payment may not be made by way of distribution under this paragraph to a creditor of the company who is neither secured nor preferential unless the court gives permission.

Notes

Para 65

This provision should be read together with IR 1986 r 2.68–2.105. There is no power given to an administrator to make a distribution to a member *Re Business Properties Ltd* (1988) 4 BCC 684. The court will need to be satisfied that the distribution is in the best interests of the creditors as a whole in accordance with the objective of the administration stated in IA 1986 Sch B1 para 3; further relevant factors may include that the administrator's proposals under IA 1986 Sch B1 para 49 (or as revised) contemplate the making of a distribution, the company has sufficient monies to effect the distribution and that it is not proposed to exit the administration through a creditors' voluntary liquidation *Re GHE Realisations Ltd* [2005] BCC 139.

Para 65(1)

Under the former regime the ability of an administrator to make a distribution to creditors was very limited *Re Designer Room Ltd* [2004] BCC 904; often a company voluntary arrangement would be promoted merely to effect a distribution. This provision enables an administrator to make a distribution without resorting to such a mechanism.

Para 65(2)

Preferential creditors are given priority over floating chargeholders under IA 1986 s 175 (and see IA 1986 s 387(3)(A) for the 'relevant date'). The operation of IA 1986 s 175 was considered by the House of Lords in *Buchler v Talbot* [2004] 2 AC 298, where it was made clear that whilst that section made a significant incursion into the proprietary rights of floating charge holders this was limited to the payment of preferential debts and did not extend to payment of other costs and expenses of the liquidation ahead of the rights of the charge holder and *Re Barleycorn Enterprises* [1970] Ch 465 was overruled. Nor does IA 1986 s 115 or any other statutory provision allow a liquidator to claim the costs and expenses of the winding up out of assets caught by a floating charge. This is because the proprietary rights of the charge holder mean that the assets in question are not 'the company's assets' for the purposes of that section *Buchler v Talbot* [2004] 2 AC 298. The position however is different in an administration given the express provisions of IA 1986 Sch B1 para 99(3); an administrator may charge his remuneration and expenses on the floating charge assets. Note it is presently proposed (under cl 1246 Companies Bill 2006 inserting new IA 1986 s 176ZA) that the costs and expenses of the liquidation may be paid out of floating charge property to bring the position into line with administrations.

Para 65(3)

Thus a distribution to secured or preferential creditors may be made without the court's permission. In respect of other creditors an application to court is necessary and it appears that the court must authorise specific *'payments'* rather than giving an administrator a general authority to make distributions and leaving the administrator to decide the quantum.

1.652

66

The administrator of a company may make a payment otherwise than in accordance with paragraph 65 or paragraph 13 of Schedule 1 if he thinks it likely to assist achievement of the purpose of administration.

Notes

Para 66

It is difficult to draw a dividing line between payments authorised under this provision and those under para 13 Sch 1 ('.. *necessary or incidental to the performance of his functions'*, *Re TXU UK Ltd* [2003] 2 BCLC 341). However it is clear that an administrator may rely on this provision to pay unsecured pre administration creditors if that is '*likely to assist the achievement of the purpose of the administration'*, for instance to obtain continuing supplies to the company in administration and the administrator's power under para 66 is stated in the widest terms *Re MG Rover Espana* [2005] BPIR 1162, [2006] BCC 599. There is no restriction imposed by the provision on the administrator to pay secured or preferential creditors before making distributions to other creditors *Re Collins & Aikman Europe SA* [2006] BCC 606.

General duties

1.653

67

The administrator of a company shall on his appointment take custody or control of all the property to which he thinks the company is entitled.

Notes

Para 67

In case of a challenge the administrator should therefore evidence why he 'thinks' that the company is entitled to the relevant property; although it is a subjective matter for the administrator to determine it is obviously helpful if that determination is made on the basis of relevant information and on reasonable grounds; see notes to IA 1986 Sch B1 para 3 'Selecting Objectives'.

1.654

68

(1) Subject to sub-paragraph (2), the administrator of a company shall manage its affairs, business and property in accordance with—
  (a) any proposals approved under paragraph 53,
  (b) any revision of those proposals which is made by him and which he does not consider substantial, and
  (c) any revision of those proposals approved under paragraph 54.

(2) If the court gives directions to the administrator of a company in connection with any aspect of his management of the company's affairs, business or property, the administrator shall comply with the directions.

(3) The court may give directions under sub-paragraph (2) only if—
  (a) no proposals have been approved under paragraph 53,
  (b) the directions are consistent with any proposals or revision approved under paragraph 53 or 54,
  (c) the court thinks the directions are required in order to reflect a change in circumstances since the approval of proposals or a revision under paragraph 53 or 54, or
  (d) the court thinks the directions are desirable because of a misunderstanding about proposals or a revision approved under paragraph 53 or 54.

Notes

Para 68(1)

Following the creditors' approval of the proposals and/or revised proposals (and/or any insubstantial revisions) the administrator's management of the affairs business and property of the company is governed by the content of those proposals and by the directions of the court under IA 1986 Sch B1 para 68(3). Prior to the consideration of the proposals by the creditors the administrator may exercise all of his powers subject only to directions from the court *Re T & D Industries plc* [2000] BCC 956.

Para 68(2)

An administrator should consider carefully whether or not to apply for directions. Where a commercial decision ought to be made by the administrator (for example to sell assets) he will not generally be justified in applying for directions from the court *Re Transbus International Ltd* [2004] BCC 401.

Para 68(3)(b)

This restriction on the ability of the court to give directions is tempered by the court's powers under IA 1986 Sch B1 para 68(3)(c) and (d).

Administrator as agent of company

1.655

69

In exercising his functions under this Schedule the administrator of a company acts as its agent.

Notes

Para 69

Absent a special relationship which has been created between the administrator and a creditor/s no general duty of care is owed by an administrator to the creditors *Oldham v Kyrris* [2004] BCC 111. The duties owed by an administrator are akin to those presently owed by directors to the shareholders in the context of a solvent company and he is subject to fiduciary duties *Re Sheridan Securities Ltd* (1988) 4 BCC 200 and duties of care and skill *Re Charnley Davies Ltd (No 2)* [1990] BCC 605; a misfeasance application can be brought against the administrator and any recovery is for the benefit of the creditors/members as a whole rather than individual creditors/members IA 1986 Sch B1 para 75, *Oldham v Kyrris* [2004] BCC 111. As agent the administrator can have no greater power than his principal to act beyond the scope of its objects clause *Re Home Treat Ltd* [1991] BCC 165 though third parties dealing with the administrator are protected in any event by IA 1986 Sch B1 para 59(3) and CA 1985 s 35.

Charged property: floating charge

1.656

70

(1) The administrator of a company may dispose of or take action relating to property which is subject to a floating charge as if it were not subject to the charge.

> (2) Where property is disposed of in reliance on sub-paragraph (1) the holder of the floating charge shall have the same priority in respect of acquired property as he had in respect of the property disposed of.
>
> (3) In sub-paragraph (2) 'acquired property' means property of the company which directly or indirectly represents the property disposed of.

Notes

Para 70

In practice this provision is not relied upon frequently as the administrator would normally wish to proceed by way of agreement with the chargeholder rather than a contested application. IA 1986 s 251 defines a floating charge. This provision does not apply to 'market charges' EA 2002, Sch 17 para 47, s 173 CA 1989. The distinction in treatment between property subject to the floating charge under this paragraph and that subject to a fixed charge under IA 1986 Sch B1 para 71 below will inevitably add fuel to the debate as to whether a particular security is fixed or floating; simply calling a charge a 'fixed charge' does not prevent the court declaring it to be floating (*Re Keenan Bros Ltd* [1986] BCLC 242, *Re Spectrum Plus Ltd* [2005] 3 WLR 58, *Re Beam Tube Products Ltd* [2006] BCC 615). The court is concerned with establishing the nature of the rights that have been given to the chargeholder or reserved to the company. The court will look to the way in which these rights are expressed in the security documentation and what has actually happened in practice by way of the control exerted by the chargeholder; it is clear that a debenture in the '*Siebe Gorman*' form (*Re Siebe Gorman & Co Ltd* [1979] 2 Lloyd's Rep 142) creates a floating charge rather than a fixed charge over book debts *Re Spectrum Plus Ltd* [2005] 3 WLR 58. A legal possessory lien conferred by a contract coupled with a right to sell the goods subject to the lien is not a floating charge and does not require registration under CA 1985 s 395, *Trident International Ltd v Barlow* [2000] BCC 602.

Charged property: non-floating charge

1.657

71

(1) The court may by order enable the administrator of a company to dispose of property which is subject to a security (other than a floating charge) as if it were not subject to the security.

(2) An order under sub-paragraph (1) may be made only—
    (a)   on the application of the administrator, and
    (b)   where the court thinks that disposal of the property would be likely to promote the purpose of administration in respect of the company.

(3) An order under this paragraph is subject to the condition that there be applied towards discharging the sums secured by the security—
    (a)   the net proceeds of disposal of the property, and
    (b)   any additional money required to be added to the net proceeds so as to produce the amount determined by the court as the net amount which would be realised on a sale of the property at market value.

(4) If an order under this paragraph relates to more than one security, application of money under sub-paragraph (3) shall be in the order of the priorities of the securities.

> (5) An administrator who makes a successful application for an order under this paragraph shall send a copy of the order to the registrar of companies before the end of the period of 14 days starting with the date of the order.
>
> (6) An administrator commits an offence if he fails to comply with sub-paragraph (5) without reasonable excuse.

Notes

Para 71

This provision (which does not apply to 'market charges' EA 2002, Sch 17 para 47, s 173 CA 1989) should be read together with IR 1986 r 2.66 which deals with the procedure for the application. It relates only to property subject to a security which is not a floating charge (see notes to IA 1986 Sch B1 para 14, para 70 above); 'security' is widely defined in IA 1986 s 248(b)(i). Where the administrator contends that the security is invalid he should make an application for that issue to be determined first rather than seek to obtain an order under para 71 and challenge the security at a later date *Re Newman Shopfitters (Cleveland) Ltd* [1991] BCLC 407.

Para 71(2)

Such an order would appear to be useful in an administration to enable an administrator to dispose of the company's business (or any part of that business) as a going concern; however such applications are rare as they would inevitably involve a contested hearing. The court will only grant permission where the disposal in question would be likely to promote the objective of the administration and this exercise will involve considering the prejudice to the security holder if the order is made and the prejudice to the administration if it is not; see *Re A R V Aviation Ltd* (1988) 4 BCC 708 for an example of the operation of similar provisions under the former administration regime.

Para 71(3)

This provision is similar to the former IA 1986 s 15(5). In *Re A R V Aviation Ltd* (1988) 4 BCC 708, the expression 'sums secured by the security ...' was construed to cover not only the capital sum secured but also interest and any costs which the chargee was entitled to add to his security under the general law and the terms of the charge. 'Market value' is defined in IA 1986 Sch B1 para 111(1) as the amount which would be realised upon a sale of property in the open market by a willing vendor and in the event of a dispute the court can make an order under para 71 coupled with an order for an inquiry as to the market value *Re A R V Aviation Ltd* (1988) 4 BCC 708.

Para 71(5)

The fact that an administrator makes a successful application under IA 1986 Sch B1 para 71 does not prevent an aggrieved secured creditor challenging the conduct of the administrator as causing unfair harm to his interests IA 1986 Sch B1 para 74(5).

Hire-purchase property

1.658

72

(1) The court may by order enable the administrator of a company to dispose of goods which are in the possession of the company under a

hire-purchase agreement as if all the rights of the owner under the agreement were vested in the company.

(2) An order under sub-paragraph (1) may be made only—
 (a) on the application of the administrator, and
 (b) where the court thinks that disposal of the goods would be likely to promote the purpose of administration in respect of the company.

(3) An order under this paragraph is subject to the condition that there be applied towards discharging the sums payable under the hire-purchase agreement—
 (a) the net proceeds of disposal of the goods, and
 (b) any additional money required to be added to the net proceeds so as to produce the amount determined by the court as the net amount which would be realised on a sale of the goods at market value.

(4) An administrator who makes a successful application for an order under this paragraph shall send a copy of the order to the registrar of companies before the end of the period of 14 days starting with the date of the order.

(5) An administrator commits an offence if he fails without reasonable excuse to comply with sub-paragraph (4).

Notes

Para 72

This provision (which does not apply to 'market charges' EA 2002, Sch 17 para 47, s 173 CA 1989) should be read together with IR 1986 r 2.66 dealing with the procedure for the application 'Hire purchase agreement' is defined in IA 1986 Sch B1 para 111 as including 'a conditional sale agreement, a chattel leasing agreement and a retention of title agreement.'

Para 72(2), (3)

Reference should be made to the notes under IA 1986 Sch B1 para 71(2), (3) which are substantially similar provisions. The 'sums payable' under IA 1986 Sch B1 para 72(3) would include sums payable under the hire purchase agreement both at the date of the disposal of the relevant goods and following the disposal.

Para 72(4)

The fact that an administrator makes a successful application under IA 1986 Sch B1 para 71 does not prevent an aggrieved secured creditor challenging the conduct of the administrator as causing unfair harm to his interests IA 1986 Sch B1 para 74(5).

Protection for secured or preferential creditor

1.659

73

(1) An administrator's statement of proposals under paragraph 49 may not include any action which—

(a) affects the right of a secured creditor of the company to enforce his security,

(b) would result in a preferential debt of the company being paid otherwise than in priority to its non-preferential debts, or

(c) would result in one preferential creditor of the company being paid a smaller proportion of his debt than another.

(2) Sub-paragraph (1) does not apply to—

(a) action to which the relevant creditor consents,

(b) a proposal for a voluntary arrangement under Part I of this Act (although this sub-paragraph is without prejudice to section 4(3)), or

(c) a proposal for a compromise or arrangement to be sanctioned under section 425 of the Companies Act (compromise with creditors or members).

(3) The reference to a statement of proposals in sub-paragraph (1) includes a reference to a statement as revised or modified.

Notes

Para 73

'Secured creditor' is defined in IA 1986 s 248(a) as a creditor who holds a 'security'; 'security' is defined in IA 1986 s 248(b)(i) as 'any mortgage, charge, lien or other security'. 'Preferential creditors' are defined in IA 1986 s 386, Sch 6. Para 73 itself is similar to the provision in the context of company voluntary arrangements which preserves the rights of a secured/preferential creditor to veto proposals which affect those rights; reference should be made to the notes under IA 1986 s 4(3),(4).

Challenge to administrator's conduct of company

1.660

74

(1) A creditor or member of a company in administration may apply to the court claiming that—

(a) the administrator is acting or has acted so as unfairly to harm the interests of the applicant (whether alone or in common with some or all other members or creditors), or

(b) the administrator proposes to act in a way which would unfairly harm the interests of the applicant (whether alone or in common with some or all other members or creditors).

(2) A creditor or member of a company in administration may apply to the court claiming that the administrator is not performing his functions as quickly or as efficiently as is reasonably practicable.

(3) The court may—

(a) grant relief;

(b) dismiss the application;

(c) adjourn the hearing conditionally or unconditionally;

(d) make an interim order;

> (e)　make any other order it thinks appropriate.
>
> (4)　In particular, an order under this paragraph may—
> (a)　regulate the administrator's exercise of his functions;
> (b)　require the administrator to do or not do a specified thing;
> (c)　require a creditors' meeting to be held for a specified purpose;
> (d)　provide for the appointment of an administrator to cease to have effect;
> (e)　make consequential provision.
>
> (5)　An order may be made on a claim under sub-paragraph (1) whether or not the action complained of—
> (a)　is within the administrator's powers under this Schedule;
> (b)　was taken in reliance on an order under paragraph 71 or 72.
>
> (6)　An order may not be made under this paragraph if it would impede or prevent the implementation of—
> (a)　a voluntary arrangement approved under Part I,
> (b)　a compromise or arrangement sanctioned under section 425 of the Companies Act (compromise with creditors and members), or
> (c)　proposals or a revision approved under paragraph 53 or 54 more than 28 days before the day on which the application for the order under this paragraph is made.

Notes

Para 74

An administrator's conduct amounting to a breach of duty or negligence ought to be challenged under IA 1986 Sch B1 para 75 (misfeasance) rather than para 74 (see *Re Charnley Davies Ltd (No 2)* [1990] BCLC 760); similarly where the complaint is that the administrator is refusing to consent to the lifting of the moratorium an application should be made to court under IA 1986 Sch B1 para 43(2) rather than IA 1986 Sch B1 para 74.

Para 74(1)

A 'member' is defined by s 22 CA 1985, (IA 1986 s 251) and so the register of members is the starting point to confirm that the intended applicant is a member; if necessary a rectification application may have to be made. Presumably a member would only consider making an application where the company is solvent or would be solvent were it not for the conduct of the administrator. A member state liquidator under EC Regulation on Insolvency Proceedings 2000 art 32(3) may also make an application under IA 1986 Sch B1 para 74. The application under IA 1986 Sch B1 para 74 must be made whilst the company is 'in administration' which is so long as the appointment of an administrator has effect IA 1986 Sch B1 para 1(2(a); but a company does not cease to be 'in administration' merely because an administrator vacates or is removed from office, see notes to IA 1986 Sch B1 para 42(1).

Para 74(1)(a), (b)

The application is based on satisfying the court that the administrator is or has acted or proposes to act in a way which causes unfair harm to the applicant or the applicant and others. It is not sufficient to prove 'harm' which is presumably conduct prejudicial to the financial interests of the applicant or the applicant and others; rather the 'harm' must be 'unfair', that is it prejudices the applicant or the applicant and others in a manner which is different from the remaining creditors or members as the case may be. It is tempting to refer to authorities under s 459 CA 1985 on 'unfair prejudice' in considering 'unfair harm' (for example, *O'Neill v Phillips*

[1999] 1 WLR 1092) so that an applicant under IA 1986 Sch B1 para 74 could complain where it is appropriate to subject the strict legal rights relied upon by the administrator to equitable considerations on the part of the applicant. However IA 1986 Sch B1 para 74 and s 459 CA 1985 are markedly different in their terms and reliance on the s 459 cases may be dangerous particularly where mismanagement on the part of the administrator is being alleged which should properly be the subject of a IA 1986 Sch B1 para 75 misfeasance application. An application under IA 1986 Sch B1 para 74 may in suitable circumstances be coupled with an application to remove the administrator under para 88, *Sisu Capital Fund Ltd v Tucker* [2006] BPIR 154, 176.

Para 74(2)

This is a specific ground of complaint based on the duty expressed in IA 1986 Sch B1 para 4; the administrator must respond promptly to the queries and requests of third parties *Re Sabre International Products Ltd* [1991] BCLC 470.

Para 74(3), (4)

Though the breadth of the possible orders that the court may make is obvious the court is limited in the relief it might order by IA 1986 Sch B1 para 74(6).

Para 74(5)(b)

Thus a court order permitting the disposal of fixed charge or hire purchase property does not insulate the administrator from challenge on the basis of causing unfair harm under IA 1986 Sch B1 para 74.

Para 74(6)

However a voluntary arrangement can itself be challenged inter alia on the grounds of unfair prejudice under IA 1986 s 6 and 'fairness' is a consideration for the approval of the court to a CA 1985 s 425 scheme of arrangement.

Misfeasance

1.661

75

(1) The court may examine the conduct of a person who—
    (a)   is or purports to be the administrator of a company, or
    (b)   has been or has purported to be the administrator of a company.

(2) An examination under this paragraph may be held only on the application of—
    (a)   the official receiver,
    (b)   the administrator of the company,
    (c)   the liquidator of the company,
    (d)   a creditor of the company, or
    (e)   a contributory of the company.

(3) An application under sub-paragraph (2) must allege that the administrator—
    (a)   has misapplied or retained money or other property of the company,
    (b)   has become accountable for money or other property of the company,

(c)   has breached a fiduciary or other duty in relation to the company, or

(d)   has been guilty of misfeasance.

(4) On an examination under this paragraph into a person's conduct the court may order him—

(a)   to repay, restore or account for money or property;

(b)   to pay interest;

(c)   to contribute a sum to the company's property by way of compensation for breach of duty or misfeasance.

(5) In sub-paragraph (3) 'administrator' includes a person who purports or has purported to be a company's administrator.

(6) An application under sub-paragraph (2) may be made in respect of an administrator who has been discharged under paragraph 98 only with the permission of the court.

Notes

Para 75

An application can be made against an administrator for misfeasance under this provision; there is no requirement that the company must be in liquidation. IA 1986 Sch B1 para 75 is substantially similar to IA 1986 s 212 and reference should be made to the notes under that provision.

Para 75(1)

'*Purports to be ..*' makes it clear that invalidly appointed administrators or a person whose appointment as administrator was void may the subject of a misfeasance application; see notes to IA 1986 Sch B1 para 21,34.

Para 75(4)

Any recovery ordered is for the benefit of the creditors/members as a whole rather than individual creditors/members *Oldham v Kyrris* [2004] BCC 111.

Ending Administration

Automatic end of administration

1.662

76

(1) The appointment of an administrator shall cease to have effect at the end of the period of one year beginning with the date on which it takes effect.

(2) But—

(a)   on the application of an administrator the court may by order extend his term of office for a specified period, and

> (b) an administrator's term of office may be extended for a specified
> period not exceeding six months by consent.

___

Notes

Para 76

This provision does not however prevent the court making an administration order for a shorter period than one year to enable the court to monitor the administration if felt necessary; the court can make a variety of consequential directions on the hearing of the application IA 1986 Sch B1 para 13(1). IA 1986 Sch B1 para 76 does not expressly tie in with IA 1986 Sch B1 para 83 which enables the company to pass from administration to creditors' voluntary liquidation upon *registration* of a notice sent by the administrator rather than the *sending* of the notice. Therefore there may be a period of 'limbo' where the administrator's appointment has automatically ceased under IA 1986 Sch B1 para 76(1) but the notice has not yet been registered; see notes to IA 1986 para 83(6) below.

Para 76(1)

When a step has to be taken within a period described as 'beginning with' a specified day then that day is included in the period *Zoan v Rouamba* [2000] 1 WLR 1509. The one year period of an administration beginning on 14 January 2005 therefore will end at midnight on 13 January 2006 being 365 days including the day of the appointment taking effect rather than the calendar anniversary; thus the 13 January 2006 would be the last day on which the administrator could send a notice under IA 1986 Sch B1 para 83(3) necessary to pass the company from administration into creditors' voluntary liquidation.

Para 76(2)(a)

There are little guidelines on the exercise of the discretion by the court but an application to court must be accompanied by a progress report IR 1986 r 2.112(1), r 2.47. See notes to IA 1986 Sch B1 para 77 below.

Para 76(2)(b)

The requisite consent is defined in IA 1986 Sch B1 para 78 and it may only be given once and prior to any extension granted by the court: IA 1986 Sch B1 para 78(4).

___

1.663

77

(1) An order of the court under paragraph 76—
>   (a) may be made in respect of an administrator whose term of office has already been extended by order or by consent, but
>   (b) may not be made after the expiry of the administrator's term of office.

(2) Where an order is made under paragraph 76 the administrator shall as soon as is reasonably practicable notify the registrar of companies.

(3) An administrator who fails without reasonable excuse to comply with sub-paragraph (2) commits an offence.

___

Notes

Para 77(1)(b)

It is imperative that the administrator monitors carefully the progress of the administration and the date of the expiry of his office as administrator. Once the office has expired then the court cannot make an extension order unless the application for extension was made before the expiry and it is shown that the way in which the court dealt with hearing/listing of the application had been responsible for the failure to extend the administration: *Re TT Industries Ltd* [2006] BPIR 597, [2006] BCC 372.

1.664

78

(1) In paragraph 76(2)(b) 'consent' means consent of—
  (a)   each secured creditor of the company, and
  (b)   if the company has unsecured debts, creditors whose debts amount to more than 50% of the company's unsecured debts, disregarding debts of any creditor who does not respond to an invitation to give or withhold consent.

(2) But where the administrator has made a statement under paragraph 52(1)(b) 'consent' means—
  (a)   consent of each secured creditor of the company, or
  (b)   if the administrator thinks that a distribution may be made to preferential creditors, consent of—
      (i)   each secured creditor of the company, and
      (ii)   preferential creditors whose debts amount to more than 50% of the preferential debts of the company, disregarding debts of any creditor who does not respond to an invitation to give or withhold consent.

(3) Consent for the purposes of paragraph 76(2)(b) may be—
  (a)   written, or
  (b)   signified at a creditors' meeting.

(4) An administrator's term of office—
  (a)   may be extended by consent only once,
  (b)   may not be extended by consent after extension by order of the court, and
  (c)   may not be extended by consent after expiry.

(5) Where an administrator's term of office is extended by consent he shall as soon as is reasonably practicable—
  (a)   file notice of the extension with the court, and
  (b)   notify the registrar of companies.

(6) An administrator who fails without reasonable excuse to comply with sub-paragraph (5) commits an offence.

Notes

Para 78

This provision details the consent that is required from creditors for an extension of the administrator's term of office under IA 1986 Sch B1 para 76(2)(b). The consent required varies according to whether or not the administrator has stated in his proposals to creditors (IA 1986 Sch B1 para 52(1)(b)) that the company has insufficient property to enable a distribution to be made to creditors other than under the 'prescribed part' provisions of IA 1986 s 176A; if he has so stated then the relevant consent is defined by IA 1986 Sch B1 para 78(2); if he has not made such a statement then the relevant consent is defined by IA 1986 Sch B1 para 78(1). Note in the former case that the consent is either that of each secured creditor of the company or if the administrator forms the relevant thought the consent of each secured creditor and the preferential creditors stated in IA 1986 Sch B1 para 78(2)(b).

Para 78(4)

It is important to note these restrictions on the ability of the creditors to consent to an extension of the administrator's term of office.

_____

Court ending administration on application of administrator

1.665

79

(1) On the application of the administrator of a company the court may provide for the appointment of an administrator of the company to cease to have effect from a specified time.

(2) The administrator of a company shall make an application under this paragraph if—

   (a) he thinks the purpose of administration cannot be achieved in relation to the company,

   (b) he thinks the company should not have entered administration, or

   (c) a creditors' meeting requires him to make an application under this paragraph.

(3) The administrator of a company shall make an application under this paragraph if—

   (a) the administration is pursuant to an administration order, and

   (b) the administrator thinks that the purpose of administration has been sufficiently achieved in relation to the company.

(4) On an application under this paragraph the court may—

   (a) adjourn the hearing conditionally or unconditionally;

   (b) dismiss the application;

   (c) make an interim order;

   (d) make any order it thinks appropriate (whether in addition to, in consequence of or instead of the order applied for).

_____

Notes

Para 79

This provision should be read together with IR 1986 r 2.114, 2.116. If an order is made then the court must also discharge the administration order if the administration was pursuant to an administration order IA 1986 Sch B1 para 85(2). If the relevant conditions are fulfilled to move the company into a creditors' voluntary liquidation under IA 1986 Sch B1 para 83 no application under IA Sch B1 para 79 is necessary *Re Ballast plc* [2005] BCC 96.

Para 79(1)

The circumstances in which the administrator may apply to the court for his appointment to cease to have effect are not limited; once the appointment ceases to have effect so too does the administration IA 1986 Sch B1 para 1(2)(c).

Para 79(2)

Albeit that the language appears mandatory the court held in *Re Ballast plc* [2005] BCC 96 that no application to court is necessary where the administrator wishes to exit the administration under IA 1986 Sch B1 para 83 (creditors' voluntary liquidation) or IA 1986 Sch B1 para 84 (dissolution).

Para 79(3)

In the case of an out of court appointment of administrator where the objective of the administration has been achieved then the administrator can follow the IA 1986 Sch B1 para 80 procedure.

Para 79(4)(d)

Although it is not mandatory to seek any order from the court other than for termination of the administration it is strongly advisable in the case of an insolvent administration to provide some method of dealing with creditors' claims following the termination and this would normally be achieved by a liquidation *Re Barrow Borough Transport Ltd* [1990] Ch 227, *Oakley Smith v Greenberg* [2003] BPIR 709, 721. Where the company is to move into a compulsory liquidation on the cesser of the administrator's appointment it is usual for the administrator to present a winding up petition rather than simply rely on the court making a winding up order under the 'catch all' language of IA 1986 Sch B1 para 79(4)(d); the administrator must also notify the creditors if he is seeking to be appointed as liquidator of the company by the court IR 1986 r 2.114(4), IA 1986 s 140, IR 1986 r 4.7(10). The court in exceptional circumstances may of its own motion order a winding up in the absence of a winding up petition (*Lancefield v Lancefield* [2002] BPIR 1108, (cf *Re Brooke Marine Ltd* [1988] BCLC 546 and *Re Synthetic Technology Ltd* [1990] BCLC 378) but it would be unwise to rely on the court exercising such a power on a IA 1986 Sch B1 para 79 application; a winding up petition should be presented. Commonly the administrator will also make an application for his discharge from liability under IA 1986 Sch B1 para 98(2)(c) at the same as the application for termination of his office and the creditors should be specifically informed of the discharge application in the final progress report IA 1986 Sch B1, IR 1986 r 2.114.

Termination of administration where objective achieved

1.666

80

(1) This paragraph applies where an administrator of a company is appointed under paragraph 14 or 22.

(2) If the administrator thinks that the purpose of administration has been sufficiently achieved in relation to the company he may file a notice in the prescribed form—

    (a)   with the court, and

    (b)   with the registrar of companies.

(3) The administrator's appointment shall cease to have effect when the requirements of sub-paragraph (2) are satisfied.

(4) Where the administrator files a notice he shall within the prescribed period send a copy to every creditor of the company of whose claim and address he is aware.

(5) The rules may provide that the administrator is taken to have complied with sub-paragraph (4) if before the end of the prescribed period he publishes in the prescribed manner a notice undertaking to provide a copy of the notice under sub-paragraph (2) to any creditor of the company who applies in writing to a specified address.

(6) An administrator who fails without reasonable excuse to comply with sub-paragraph (4) commits an offence.

Notes

Para 80

This provision relating only to an out of court appointment of administrator should be read together with IR 1986 r 2.113, 2.110.

Para 80(2)

Alternatively where the administrator thinks that the purpose of the administration cannot be achieved an application to end the administration should be made to court under IA 1986 Sch B1 para 79.

Para 80(3)

Once the appointment as administrator ceases to have effect so too does the administration IA 1986 Sch B1 para 1(2)(c). The administrator may obtain his discharge from liability from the creditors or the court IA 1986 Sch B1 para 98(2)(b), (c).

Para 80(4)

The creditors may therefore discover that the administration has ended only after the notice under IA 1986 Sch B1 para 80(2) has been filed and without having had an opportunity to consider the same. However pursuant to IA 1986 Sch B1 para 98(4) notwithstanding that the administrator obtains his discharge from liability a creditor retains a right to make a misfeasance application under IA 1986 Sch B1 para 75.

Court ending administration on application of creditor

1.667

81

(1) On the application of a creditor of a company the court may provide for the appointment of an administrator of the company to cease to have effect at a specified time.

(2) An application under this paragraph must allege an improper motive—

    (a)   in the case of an administrator appointed by administration order, on the part of the applicant for the order, or

    (b)   in any other case, on the part of the person who appointed the administrator.

(3) On an application under this paragraph the court may—

> (a) adjourn the hearing conditionally or unconditionally;
> (b) dismiss the application;
> (c) make an interim order;
> (d) make any order it thinks appropriate (whether in addition to, in consequence of or instead of the order applied for).

Notes

Para 81

This provision should be read together with IR 1986 r 2.115. It provides a creditor with limited scope inter alia to bring an administration to an end whether the company has entered administration by court order or otherwise. Alternatively where the court has made an administration order a creditor may apply for a recission of the order: IR 1986 r 7.47, *Cornhill Insurance plc v Cornhill Financial Services Ltd* [1993] BCLC 914 though where the administration is in the best interests of the creditors it is unlikely to order recission *Re MTI Trading Systems Ltd* [1998] BCC 400.

Para 81(1)

A company ceases to be in administration when the appointment of the administrator ceases to have effect IA 1986 Sch B1 para 1(2)(c) but not merely because an administrator is removed from office (IA 1986 Sch B1 para 1(2)(d)). Therefore it appears to be contemplated that on the application of a creditor an order could be made under IA 1986 Sch B1 para 81(3)(d) enabling the company to remain in administration albeit with a replacement administrator.

Para 81(2)

The application must at least include some evidence of 'improper motive' on the part of the applicant or appointor as the case may be to justify the court making an order to end the administration. This is an evidential exercise requiring the applicant first to satisfy the court of the motive involved and secondly that the motive was improper. The improper motive must have existed at the time of and/or leading up to the administration order or appointment of administrator. The use of the word 'motive' indicates that the court is concerned with a subjective rather than objective test. Further in using the phrase ' *must allege an improper motive*' it is unlikely that the applicant will need to prove that the applicant or appointor had only an improper motive in making the application or appointment to succeed. Where the court has made an administration order notwithstanding allegations of the application being an abuse of process and made for private advantage (*Re Dianoor Jewels Ltd* [2001] 1 BCLC 450) it is unlikely that the court would consider that an improper motive existed within this provision if such an application was based on the same evidence on the hearing of the administration application.

Para 81(3)

Where the court has made an administration order and an order is made providing for the appointment of the administrator to cease to have effect then the court must also discharge the administration order IA 1986 Sch B1 para 85(2). As a separate matter the administrator may wish to apply for his discharge from liability under IA 1986 Sch B1 para 98(2)(c) unless the administrator was appointed out of court and the discharge has already been authorised under IA 1986 Sch B1 para 98(2)(b).

Public interest winding-up

1.668

82

(1) This paragraph applies where a winding-up order is made for the winding up of a company in administration on a petition presented under—

   (a)   section 124A (public interest),

   [(aa) section 124B (SEs),] or

   (b)   section 367 of the Financial Services and Markets Act 2000 (c 8) (petition by Financial Services Authority).

(2) This paragraph also applies where a provisional liquidator of a company in administration is appointed following the presentation of a petition under any of the provisions listed in sub-paragraph (1).

(3) The court shall order—

   (a)   that the appointment of the administrator shall cease to have effect, or

   (b)   that the appointment of the administrator shall continue to have effect.

(4) If the court makes an order under sub-paragraph (3)(b) it may also—

   (a)   specify which of the powers under this Schedule are to be exercisable by the administrator, and

   (b)   order that this Schedule shall have effect in relation to the administrator with specified modifications.

Notes

Para 82

The moratorium on making a winding up order does not apply to such orders made pursuant to petitions presented under IA 1986 s 124A nor FMSA 200 s 367, IA 1986 Sch B1 para 42(4), para 40(2).

Para 82(3)(b)

It is thus contemplated that an administrator and a liquidator may be in office at the same time.

Moving from administration to creditors' voluntary liquidation

1.669

83

(1) This paragraph applies in England and Wales where the administrator of a company thinks—

   (a)   that the total amount which each secured creditor of the company is likely to receive has been paid to him or set aside for him, and

   (b)   that a distribution will be made to unsecured creditors of the company (if there are any).

(2) This paragraph applies in Scotland where the administrator of a company thinks—

- (a) that each secured creditor of the company will receive payment in respect of his debt, and
- (b) that a distribution will be made to unsecured creditors (if there are any).

(3) The administrator may send to the registrar of companies a notice that this paragraph applies.

(4) On receipt of a notice under sub-paragraph (3) the registrar shall register it.

(5) If an administrator sends a notice under sub-paragraph (3) he shall as soon as is reasonably practicable—

- (a) file a copy of the notice with the court, and
- (b) send a copy of the notice to each creditor of whose claim and address he is aware.

(6) On the registration of a notice under sub-paragraph (3)—

- (a) the appointment of an administrator in respect of the company shall cease to have effect, and
- (b) the company shall be wound up as if a resolution for voluntary winding up under section 84 were passed on the day on which the notice is registered.

(7) The liquidator for the purposes of the winding up shall be—

- (a) a person nominated by the creditors of the company in the prescribed manner and within the prescribed period, or
- (b) if no person is nominated under paragraph (a), the administrator.

(8) In the application of Part IV to a winding up by virtue of this paragraph—

- (a) section 85 shall not apply,
- (b) section 86 shall apply as if the reference to the time of the passing of the resolution for voluntary winding up were a reference to the beginning of the date of registration of the notice under sub-paragraph (3),
- (c) section 89 does not apply,
- (d) sections 98, 99 and 100 shall not apply,
- (e) section 129 shall apply as if the reference to the time of the passing of the resolution for voluntary winding up were a reference to the beginning of the date of registration of the notice under sub-paragraph (3), and
- (f) any creditors' committee which is in existence immediately before the company ceases to be in administration shall continue in existence after that time as if appointed as a liquidation committee under section 101.

Notes

Para 83

This provision should be read together with IR 1986 r 2.117, r 4.1(6); it aims to provide a simple, seamless procedure for passing the company from administration into a creditors' voluntary liquidation *Re E Squared Ltd* [2006] BCC 379. An exit from administration under this provision does not depend on the manner in which the company entered administration. So long as the conditions set out in the provision are met then the administration can be ended without any application to court *Re Ballast plc* [2005] BCC 96.

Para 83(1)

After the IA 1986 Sch B1 para 83 procedure has been followed and the company goes into liquidation it may transpire that evidence is produced to show that the administrator was wrong in his thinking at the relevant time. However so long as the administrator formed the necessary thought (which is a subjective matter) at that time it will not be possible to argue that the company did not go into liquidation. The court will assess the evidence to ascertain whether there has been a rational thought process on the part of the administrator but that does not require the administrator's thought to be '.. *subject to any form of test by reference to an objective standard' Unidare plc v Cohen and Power* [2005] BPIR 1472, 1489 per Lewison J.

Para 83(3)

In order to use the IA 1986 Sch B1 para 83 procedure the sender of the notice must be 'the administrator' not the former administrator. Under IA 1986 Sch B1 para 76 the appointment of an administrator ceases to have effect '*at the end of the period of one year beginning with the date on which it takes effect*'. When a step has to be taken within a period described as 'beginning with' a specified day then that day is included in the period *Zoan v Rouamba* [2000] 1 WLR 1509. Thus in order to initiate the IA 1986 Sch B1 para 83 process the administrator must send the notice at the latest at the end of that one year period and this is not the calendar anniversary of the appointment taking effect, *see notes to* IA 1986 Sch B1 para 76. Thus it is important for an administrator to leave himself sufficient time both to send the notice and ensure its registration under IA 1986 Sch B1 para 83(6) before his term of office automatically expires under IA 1986 Sch B1 para 76. There is nothing in IA 1986 Sch B1 para 83 or IR 1986 which requires the administrator to give the notice a minimum period before the end of the administrator's period of appointment. In practice Companies House may take up to 5 working days from receipt of the notice to effect its registration.

Para 83(6)

In the absence of an extension the administrator's appointment ceases automatically under IA 1986 Sch B1 para 76 one year after the appointment took effect. Where an administrator sends the IA 1986 Sch B1 para 83(3) notice to Companies House it may be that it is not registered until after the administrator's appointment has ceased. In that situation Para 83(6)(a) appears to have no effect but IA 1986 Sch B1 para 83(6)(b) still has effect and the company goes into liquidation on the date of the registration of the notice *Re E Squared Ltd* [2006] BCC 379. The administrator may also wish to apply for his discharge from liability under IA 1986 Sch B1 para 98(2)(c) unless the administrator was appointed out of court and the discharge has already been authorised under IA 1986 Sch B1 para 98(2)(b).

Para 83(7)

The creditors are alerted to the nomination of liquidator in the administrator's proposals under IA 1986 Sch B1 para 49, IR 1986 r 2.117(3), r 2.33(2)(m), r 2.45(2)(g) and their ability to choose someone other than the administrator to become liquidator

Para 83(8)

The relevant date for determining preferential creditors is the date the company entered administration IA 1986 s 387(3)(ba).

Moving from administration to dissolution

1.670

84

(1) If the administrator of a company thinks that the company has no property which might permit a distribution to its creditors, he shall send a notice to that effect to the registrar of companies.

(2) The court may on the application of the administrator of a company disapply sub-paragraph (1) in respect of the company.

(3) On receipt of a notice under sub-paragraph (1) the registrar shall register it.

(4) On the registration of a notice in respect of a company under sub-paragraph (1) the appointment of an administrator of the company shall cease to have effect.

(5) If an administrator sends a notice under sub-paragraph (1) he shall as soon as is reasonably practicable—
- (a) file a copy of the notice with the court, and
- (b) send a copy of the notice to each creditor of whose claim and address he is aware.

(6) At the end of the period of three months beginning with the date of registration of a notice in respect of a company under sub-paragraph (1) the company is deemed to be dissolved.

(7) On an application in respect of a company by the administrator or another interested person the court may—
- (a) extend the period specified in sub-paragraph (6),
- (b) suspend that period, or
- (c) disapply sub-paragraph (6).

(8) Where an order is made under sub-paragraph (7) in respect of a company the administrator shall as soon as is reasonably practicable notify the registrar of companies.

(9) An administrator commits an offence if he fails without reasonable excuse to comply with sub-paragraph (5).

Notes

Para 84

This provision should be read together with IR 1986 r 2.118. An exit from administration under IA 1986 Sch B1 para 84 does not depend on the manner in which the company entered administration. So long as the conditions set out in the provision are met then the administration can be ended without any application to court *Re Ballast plc* [2005] BCC 96. Where a dissolution is used as an exit mechanism from administration the restrictions on the re-use of company names in a 'phoenix' situation do not apply as the company has been dissolved rather than liquidated; see IA 1986 s 216.

Para 84(1)

An administrator can move the company into dissolution under this procedure notwithstanding that he has distributed all of the company's property *Re GHE Realisations Ltd* [2006] BCC 139, *Re Preston & Duckworth Ltd* [2006] BCC 133. It is the duty of the administrator to send the notice to the registrar of companies if he forms the relevant thought; however the court can disapply that duty on an application by the administrator under IA 1986 Sch B1 para 84(2).

Para 84(4)

There is no power to recall the notice once it has been registered nor to restore the company to administration.

Para 84(6)

Following dissolution the company might be restored to the register under CA 1985 s 651 if for instance there is an asset which might be claimed for the company.

Para 84(7)

The dissolution of the company can therefore be delayed. As a separate matter the administrator may wish to apply for his discharge from liability under IA 1986 Sch B1 para 98(2)(c) unless the administrator was appointed out of court and the discharge has already been authorised under IA 1986 Sch B1 para 98(2)(b).

Discharge of administration order where administration ends

1.671

85

(1) This paragraph applies where—
  (a)   the court makes an order under this Schedule providing for the appointment of an administrator of a company to cease to have effect, and
  (b)   the administrator was appointed by administration order.

(2) The court shall discharge the administration order.

Notes

Para 85(1)

Such an order might be made under IA 1986 Sch B1 para 79 on the application of the administrator or IA 1986 Sch B1 para 81 on the application of a creditor or where a winding up order has been made under IA 1986 Sch B1 para 82.

Para 85(2)

The administrator may also wish to apply for his discharge from liability under IA 1986 Sch B1 para 98(2)(c).

Notice to Companies Registrar where administration ends

1.672

86

(1) This paragraph applies where the court makes an order under this Schedule providing for the appointment of an administrator to cease to have effect.

(2) The administrator shall send a copy of the order to the registrar of companies within the period of 14 days beginning with the date of the order.

(3) An administrator who fails without reasonable excuse to comply with sub-paragraph (2) commits an offence.

Notes

Para 86

The court makes such orders on the application of the administrator under IA 1986 Sch B1 para 79, a creditor under IA 1986 Sch B1 para 81 and where a winding up order has been made under IA 1986 Sch B1 para 82.

Para 86(2)

This provision should be read together with IR 1986 r 2.116 which requires the order to be accompanied by a final progress report.

Replacing Administrator

Resignation of administrator

1.673

87

(1) An administrator may resign only in prescribed circumstances.

(2) Where an administrator may resign he may do so only—
- (a) in the case of an administrator appointed by administration order, by notice in writing to the court,
- (b) in the case of an administrator appointed under paragraph 14, by notice in writing to the [holder of the floating charge by virtue of which the appointment was made],
- (c) in the case of an administrator appointed under paragraph 22(1), by notice in writing to the company, or
- (d) in the case of an administrator appointed under paragraph 22(2), by notice in writing to the directors of the company.

Notes

Para 87(1)

The prescribed circumstances are listed in IR 1986 r 2.119; if the administrator applies to court the circumstances in which he may resign are not limited. IR 1986 r 2.120, 2.121 deal with the requirement to give a notice of intention to resign and the filing of the notice of intention to resign and IR 1986 r 2.129 details the administrator's duty on vacating office.

Para 87(2)

The company does not cease to be in administration merely because an administrator resigns from office IA 1986 Sch B1 para 1(2)(d).

Removal of administrator from office

1.674

88

The court may by order remove an administrator from office.

Notes

Para 88

This provision should be read together with IR 1986 r 2.122. An application under IA 1986 Sch B1 para 88 to remove an administrator may in suitable circumstances be coupled with an application under IA 1986 Sch B1 para 74: *Sisu Capital Fund Limited v Tucker* [2006] BPIR 154, 176. The company does not cease to be in administration merely because an administrator is removed from office IA 1986 Sch B1 para 1(2)(d); see notes to IA 1986 Sch B1 para 42(1). The power of the court to remove the administrator is not limited to 'cause shown' but the application must state the grounds upon which the removal is sought IR 1986 r 2.122(1). Commonly an application is made as part of a 'block transfer' of insolvency appointments where a licensed insolvency practitioner changes firm para 1(6) Practice Direction: Insolvency Proceedings (Civil Procedure 2006, Vol 2, Sec 3E; *Re A & C Supplies Ltd* [1998] 1 BCLC 603; *HM Customs & Excise v Allen* [2003] BPIR 830. The court may also remove an administrator on analogous grounds to other insolvency practitioners such as misconduct, misfeasance or bias (see IA 1986 s 108, *Sisu Capital Fund Limited v Tucker* (above) at 176; *Re Buildlead Ltd (No 2)* [2005] BCC 138). Presumably an administrator could also be removed if he has not performed his functions as quickly or as efficiently as is reasonably practicable: IA 1986 Sch B1 para 74(2).

Administrator ceasing to be qualified

1.675

89

(1) The administrator of a company shall vacate office if he ceases to be qualified to act as an insolvency practitioner in relation to the company.

(2) Where an administrator vacates office by virtue of sub-paragraph (1) he shall give notice in writing—

    (a)   in the case of an administrator appointed by administration order, to the court,

    (b)   in the case of an administrator appointed under paragraph 14, to the [holder of the floating charge by virtue of which the appointment was made],

    (c)   in the case of an administrator appointed under paragraph 22(1), to the company, or

    (d)   in the case of an administrator appointed under paragraph 22(2), to the directors of the company.

(3) An administrator who fails without reasonable excuse to comply with sub-paragraph (2) commits an offence.

Notes

Para 89

This provision should be read together with IR 1986 r 2.123 and IA 1986 s 390 which states the circumstances in which a person is not qualified to act as an insolvency practitioner in relation to the company. The company does not cease to be in administration merely because an administrator vacates office IA 1986 Sch B1 para 1(2)(d).

Supplying vacancy in office of administrator

1.676

90

Paragraphs 91 to 95 apply where an administrator—
  (a) dies,
  (b) resigns,
  (c) is removed from office under paragraph 88, or
  (d) vacates office under paragraph 89.

Notes

Para 90

The stated provisions only apply in the circumstances listed in IA 1986 Sch B1 para 90.

1.677

91

(1) Where the administrator was appointed by administration order, the court may replace the administrator on an application under this sub-paragraph made by—
  (a) a creditors' committee of the company,
  (b) the company,
  (c) the directors of the company,
  (d) one or more creditors of the company, or
  (e) where more than one person was appointed to act jointly or concurrently as the administrator, any of those persons who remains in office.

(2) But an application may be made in reliance on sub-paragraph (1)(b) to (d) only where—
  (a) there is no creditors' committee of the company,
  (b) the court is satisfied that the creditors' committee or a remaining administrator is not taking reasonable steps to make a replacement, or
  (c) the court is satisfied that for another reason it is right for the application to be made.

Notes

Para 91

This provision only applies where the court has made an administration order in relation to the company and it should be read together with IR 1986 r 2.125. Further the vacancy can only be filled if it has arisen in the circumstances stated in IA 1986 Sch B1 para 90.

1.678

92

Where the administrator was appointed under paragraph 14 the holder of the floating charge by virtue of which the appointment was made may replace the administrator.

Notes

Para 92

The vacancy can only be filled if it has arisen in the circumstances stated in IA 1986 Sch B1 para 90.

1.679

93

(1) Where the administrator was appointed under paragraph 22(1) by the company it may replace the administrator.

(2) A replacement under this paragraph may be made only—
    (a)   with the consent of each person who is the holder of a qualifying floating charge in respect of the company's property, or
    (b)   where consent is withheld, with the permission of the court.

Notes

Para 93

Under IA 1986 Sch B1 para 22(1) the administrator is appointed by the company out of court. The vacancy can only be filled if it has arisen in the circumstances stated in IA 1986 Sch B1 para 90.

1.680

94

(1) Where the administrator was appointed under paragraph 22(2) the directors of the company may replace the administrator.

(2) A replacement under this paragraph may be made only—
    (a)   with the consent of each person who is the holder of a qualifying floating charge in respect of the company's property, or
    (b)   where consent is withheld, with the permission of the court.

Notes

Para 94

Under IA 1986 Sch B1 para 22(2) the administrator is appointed by the directors out of court. The vacancy can only be filled if it has arisen in the circumstances stated in IA 1986 Sch B1 para 90.

1.681

95

The court may replace an administrator on the application of a person listed in paragraph 91(1) if the court—
- (a) is satisfied that a person who is entitled to replace the administrator under any of paragraphs 92 to 94 is not taking reasonable steps to make a replacement, or
- (b) that for another reason it is right for the court to make the replacement.

Notes

Para 95

The vacancy can only be filled if it has arisen in the circumstances stated in IA 1986 Sch B1 para 90. This provision should be read together with IR 1986 r 2.125.

Substitution of administrator: competing floating charge-holder

1.682

96

(1) This paragraph applies where an administrator of a company is appointed under paragraph 14 by the holder of a qualifying floating charge in respect of the company's property.

(2) The holder of a prior qualifying floating charge in respect of the company's property may apply to the court for the administrator to be replaced by an administrator nominated by the holder of the prior floating charge.

(3) One floating charge is prior to another for the purposes of this paragraph if—
- (a) it was created first, or
- (b) it is to be treated as having priority in accordance with an agreement to which the holder of each floating charge was party.

(4) Sub-paragraph (3) shall have effect in relation to Scotland as if the following were substituted for paragraph (a)—
- '(a) it has priority of ranking in accordance with section 464(4)(b) of the Companies Act 1985 (c 6),'.

Notes

Para 96(2)

This provision should be read together with IR 1986 r 2.126 r 2.129 and IA 1986 Sch B1 para 14 the latter provision defining a '*qualifying floating charge*'. The court has a discretion whether or not to substitute the administrator and this is likely to involve consideration of the cost and expense of making the substitution and how the interests of the creditors are best served. It would be unusual for the holder of a prior qualifying floating charge not to appoint its own nominee on being served with the required notice of intention to appoint by the holder of the later ranking qualifying floating charge (IA 1986 Sch B1 para 15(1)(a), IR 1986 r 2.15), rather than leave the matter until after an appointment has been made by the latter floating charge holder. However such a situation might arise where the holder of the prior qualifying floating charge has not actually become aware of the notice of intention to appoint which has been served.

Substitution of administrator appointed by company or directors: creditors' meeting

1.683

97

(1) This paragraph applies where—
- (a) an administrator of a company is appointed by a company or directors under paragraph 22, and
- (b) there is no holder of a qualifying floating charge in respect of the company's property.

(2) A creditors' meeting may replace the administrator.

(3) A creditors' meeting may act under sub-paragraph (2) only if the new administrator's written consent to act is presented to the meeting before the replacement is made.

Notes

Para 97(1)

This provision should be read together with IR 1986 r 2.126 r 2.129.

Para 97(2)

Thus no application to court is required. The procedure in relation to creditors' meetings held under a variety of specific provisions is contained in IR 1986 r 2.35ff; however a creditors' meeting under IA 1986 Sch B1 para 97(2) is not one of those specific provisions. In Sch B1 'creditors' meeting' is defined in IA 1986 Sch B1 para 50 and it is advisable to follow the IR 1986 r 2.35ff procedure in calling and holding a creditors' meeting to consider replacing the administrator.

Vacation of office: discharge from liability

1.684

98

(1) Where a person ceases to be the administrator of a company (whether because he vacates office by reason of resignation, death or otherwise, because he is removed from office or because his appointment ceases to have effect) he is discharged from liability in respect of any action of his as administrator.

(2) The discharge provided by sub-paragraph (1) takes effect—

(a)   in the case of an administrator who dies, on the filing with the court of notice of his death,

(b)   in the case of an administrator appointed under paragraph 14 or 22, at a time appointed by resolution of the creditors' committee or, if there is no committee, by resolution of the creditors, or

(c)   in any case, at a time specified by the court.

(3) For the purpose of the application of sub-paragraph (2)(b) in a case where the administrator has made a statement under paragraph 52(1)(b), a resolution shall be taken as passed if (and only if) passed with the approval of—

(a)   each secured creditor of the company, or

(b)   if the administrator has made a distribution to preferential creditors or thinks that a distribution may be made to preferential creditors—

    (i)   each secured creditor of the company, and

    (ii)   preferential creditors whose debts amount to more than 50% of the preferential debts of the company, disregarding debts of any creditor who does not respond to an invitation to give or withhold approval.

(4) Discharge—

(a)   applies to liability accrued before the discharge takes effect, and

(b)   does not prevent the exercise of the court's powers under paragraph 75.

Notes

Para 98(1)

Under the former law the administrator applied for *'release'* (IA 1986 s 20); under the new provisions the administrator applies for *'discharge'* from liability. It is important for the administrator to obtain the discharge because he is then insulated from a misfeasance application unless the court gives permission for such an application (IA 1986 Sch B1 para 75(6)).

Para 98(2)(b)

In the case of an out of court appointment it is necessary for the administrator to obtain the consent of the creditors' committee (IR 1986 r 2.50ff) or the creditors. The procedure in relation to creditors' meetings held under a variety of specific provisions is contained in IR 1986 r 2.35ff; however a creditors' meeting under IA 1986 Sch B1 para 98 is not one of those specific provisions. In IA 1986 Sch B1 'creditors' meeting' is defined in IA 1986 Sch B1 para 50 and it is advisable to follow the IR 1986 r 2.35ff procedure in calling and holding a creditors' meeting to consider replacing the administrator.

Para 98(2)(c)

The discharge may be postponed to allow for investigation of the administrator's actions *Re Sibec Developments Ltd* [1993] BCC 148.The power of the court to specify the time that the discharge takes effect appears to apply in all administrations. This provision could therefore be used by an aggrieved creditor to override the time of the discharge decided by the creditors' committee or meeting under IA 1986 Sch B1 para 98(2)(b).

Para 98(3)

The relevant statement is made in the administrator's proposals and states that the administrator thinks that the company has insufficient property to enable a distribution to be made to unsecured creditors other than from the 'prescribed part' under IA 1986 s 176A(2)(a).

Para 98(4)

Thus following discharge from liability the former administrator may still find himself facing a misfeasance application under IA 1986 Sch B1 para 75 but only if the court gives permission for such an application IA 1986 Sch B1 para 75(6).

Vacation of office: charges and liabilities

1.685

99

(1) This paragraph applies where a person ceases to be the administrator of a company (whether because he vacates office by reason of resignation, death or otherwise, because he is removed from office or because his appointment ceases to have effect).

(2) In this paragraph—
'the former administrator' means the person referred to in sub-paragraph (1), and
'cessation' means the time when he ceases to be the company's administrator.

(3) The former administrator's remuneration and expenses shall be—
   (a) charged on and payable out of property of which he had custody or control immediately before cessation, and
   (b) payable in priority to any security to which paragraph 70 applies.

(4) A sum payable in respect of a debt or liability arising out of a contract entered into by the former administrator or a predecessor before cessation shall be—
   (a) charged on and payable out of property of which the former administrator had custody or control immediately before cessation, and
   (b) payable in priority to any charge arising under sub-paragraph (3).

(5) Sub-paragraph (4) shall apply to a liability arising under a contract of employment which was adopted by the former administrator or a predecessor before cessation; and for that purpose—
   (a) action taken within the period of 14 days after an administrator's appointment shall not be taken to amount or contribute to the adoption of a contract,
   (b) no account shall be taken of a liability which arises, or in so far as it arises, by reference to anything which is done or which occurs before the adoption of the contract of employment, and
   (c) no account shall be taken of a liability to make a payment other than wages or salary.

(6) In sub-paragraph (5)(c) 'wages or salary' includes—

> (a)   a sum payable in respect of a period of holiday (for which purpose the sum shall be treated as relating to the period by reference to which the entitlement to holiday accrued),
>
> (b)   a sum payable in respect of a period of absence through illness or other good cause,
>
> (c)   a sum payable in lieu of holiday,
>
> (d)   in respect of a period, a sum which would be treated as earnings for that period for the purposes of an enactment about social security, and
>
> (e)   a contribution to an occupational pension scheme.

Notes

Para 99(1)

Although it is stated that IA 1986 Sch B1 para 99 applies where a person ceases to be the administrator it is clear that the administrator may make the payments contemplated and in the order of the stated priority during the course of the administration *Re Salmet International Ltd* [2001] BCC 796, *Re Paramount Airways (No 3)* [1994] BCC 172.

Para 99(3)

This provision has the effect that remuneration and expenses of the administrator are payable ahead of floating charge realisations; but IA 1986 Sch B1 para 99(4) then provides that debts or liabilities under contracts entered into by the administrator are charged on and paid out of the assets in priority to remuneration and expenses. 'Remuneration' is dealt with in IR 1986 r 2.106 to 2.109 and the priority of expenses is listed in IR 1986 r 2.67. There is no express provision dealing with the situation where the administrator trades the administration at a loss and there is insufficient to pay both his remuneration and the administration expenses. In such a situation the administrator should avoid paying himself remuneration without first applying to the court.

Para 99(3)(b)

IA 1986 Sch B1 para 70 refers to a floating charge which is defined in para 111. An administrator's remuneration and expenses rank prior to a floating charge and may therefore be deducted from the realisations of property and assets subject to the floating charge; *Re Leyland Daf Ltd (No 2)* [2004] BCC 214 (*Buchler v Talbot* [2004] 2 AC 298) which generally has the effect of preventing a liquidator charging remuneration and liquidation expenses against floating charge assets does not apply in an administration context; see notes to IA 1986 s 175. It is proposed that the position in liquidation is to be changed to be same as in an administration: (cl 1246 Companies Bill 2006).

Para 99(4)–(6)

These provisions create a priority over the administration expenses in favour of liabilities which have been adopted by the administrator 14 days after appointment and which consist of 'wages or salary' IA 1986 Sch B1 para 99(5)(c); such liabilities do not include unfair dismissal/redundancy payments, *Re Allders Department Stores Ltd* [2005] BCC 289, nor payments in lieu of notice (save for certain garden leave payments) or protective awards, *Re Ferrotech Ltd*, *Re Granville Technology Group Ltd* [2005] BCC 905, *Re Huddersfield Fine Worsteds Ltd* [2005] BCC 915). Also unfair dismissal/redundancy payments do not qualify as 'necessary disbursements' within IR 1986 r 2.67(1)(f) (*administration expenses*) and therefore rank as unsecured claims in the administration. The provisions are not dealing with pre administration contracts made by the company *Re Salmet International Ltd* [2001] BCC 796.

General

Joint and concurrent administrators

1.686

100

(1) In this Schedule—
- (a) a reference to the appointment of an administrator of a company includes a reference to the appointment of a number of persons to act jointly or concurrently as the administrator of a company, and
- (b) a reference to the appointment of a person as administrator of a company includes a reference to the appointment of a person as one of a number of persons to act jointly or concurrently as the administrator of a company.

(2) The appointment of a number of persons to act as administrator of a company must specify—
- (a) which functions (if any) are to be exercised by the persons appointed acting jointly, and
- (b) which functions (if any) are to be exercised by any or all of the persons appointed.

Notes

Para 100(1)

Where an additional person is appointed as administrator following an initial appointment then notice and advertisement of the appointment must be given in accordance with IR 1986 r 2.127, r 2.128.

Para 100(2)

It is important to ensure that the administration order is drafted to ensure compliance with this provision where two or more persons are appointed as administrators.

1.687

101

(1) This paragraph applies where two or more persons are appointed to act jointly as the administrator of a company.

(2) A reference to the administrator of the company is a reference to those persons acting jointly.

(3) But a reference to the administrator of a company in paragraphs 87 to 99 of this Schedule is a reference to any or all of the persons appointed to act jointly.

(4) Where an offence of omission is committed by the administrator, each of the persons appointed to act jointly—
- (a) commits the offence, and
- (b) may be proceeded against and punished individually.

(5) The reference in paragraph 45(1)(a) to the name of the administrator is a reference to the name of each of the persons appointed to act jointly.

(6) Where persons are appointed to act jointly in respect of only some of the functions of the administrator of a company, this paragraph applies only in relation to those functions.

1.688

102

(1) This paragraph applies where two or more persons are appointed to act concurrently as the administrator of a company.

(2) A reference to the administrator of a company in this Schedule is a reference to any of the persons appointed (or any combination of them).

1.689

103

(1) Where a company is in administration, a person may be appointed to act as administrator jointly or concurrently with the person or persons acting as the administrator of the company.

(2) Where a company entered administration by administration order, an appointment under sub-paragraph (1) must be made by the court on the application of—
    (a)   a person or group listed in paragraph 12(1)(a) to (e), or
    (b)   the person or persons acting as the administrator of the company.

(3) Where a company entered administration by virtue of an appointment under paragraph 14, an appointment under sub-paragraph (1) must be made by—
    (a)   the holder of the floating charge by virtue of which the appointment was made, or
    (b)   the court on the application of the person or persons acting as the administrator of the company.

(4) Where a company entered administration by virtue of an appointment under paragraph 22(1), an appointment under sub-paragraph (1) above must be made either by the court on the application of the person or persons acting as the administrator of the company or—
    (a)   by the company, and
    (b)   with the consent of each person who is the holder of a qualifying floating charge in respect of the company's property or, where consent is withheld, with the permission of the court.

(5) Where a company entered administration by virtue of an appointment under paragraph 22(2), an appointment under sub paragraph (1) must be made either by the court on the application of the person or persons acting as the administrator of the company or—
    (a)   by the directors of the company, and
    (b)   with the consent of each person who is the holder of a qualifying floating charge in respect of the company's property or, where consent is withheld, with the permission of the court.

(6) An appointment under sub-paragraph (1) may be made only with the consent of the person or persons acting as the administrator of the company.

Presumption of validity

1.690

104

An act of the administrator of a company is valid in spite of a defect in his appointment or qualification.

Notes

Para 104

This is similar to the provision applicable to other types of insolvency practitioners under IA 1986 s 232.

Majority decision of directors

1.691

105

A reference in this Schedule to something done by the directors of a company includes a reference to the same thing done by a majority of the directors of a company.

Notes

Para 105

This provision enables the directors to act by majority without the need for a resolution passed at a formal board meeting. It is an important relaxation of the general principle that the directors make decisions by way of a resolution passed at a board meeting unanimously or by majority (*Re Equitcorp International plc* [1989] 1 WLR 1010) or if no formal board meeting is held then by the individual assent of each director (*Re Instrumentation Electrical Services Ltd* (1988) 4 BCC 301).

Penalties

1.692

106

(1) A person who is guilty of an offence under this Schedule is liable to a fine (in accordance with section 430 and Schedule 10).

(2) A person who is guilty of an offence under any of the following paragraphs of this Schedule is liable to a daily default fine (in accordance with section 430 and Schedule 10)—
    (a)   paragraph 20,

(b) paragraph 32,
(c) paragraph 46,
(d) paragraph 48,
(e) paragraph 49,
(f) paragraph 51,
(g) paragraph 53,
(h) paragraph 54,
(i) paragraph 56,
(j) paragraph 71,
(k) paragraph 72,
(l) paragraph 77,
(m) paragraph 78,
(n) paragraph 80,
(o) paragraph 84,
(p) paragraph 86, and
(q) paragraph 89.

Extension of time limit

1.692A

107

(1) Where a provision of this Schedule provides that a period may be varied in accordance with this paragraph, the period may be varied in respect of a company—
(a) by the court, and
(b) on the application of the administrator.

(2) A time period may be extended in respect of a company under this paragraph—
(a) more than once, and
(b) after expiry.

Notes

Para 107

The relevant provisions referring to variation under IA 1986 Sch B1 para 107 are IA 1986 Sch B1 para 49(8) (proposals of administrator's proposals), 50(2) (notice of creditors' meeting) and 51(4) (notice of initial creditors' meeting). Under IA 1986 Sch B1 para 108 other time limits can be varied with consent.

1.693

108

(1) A period specified in paragraph 49(5), 50(1)(b) or 51(2) may be varied in respect of a company by the administrator with consent.

(2) In sub-paragraph (1) 'consent' means consent of—
(a) each secured creditor of the company, and
(b) if the company has unsecured debts, creditors whose debts amount to more than 50% of the company's unsecured debts,

disregarding debts of any creditor who does not respond to an invitation to give or withhold consent.

(3) But where the administrator has made a statement under paragraph 52(1)(b) 'consent' means—
    (a)   consent of each secured creditor of the company, or
    (b)   if the administrator thinks that a distribution may be made to preferential creditors, consent of—
        (i)   each secured creditor of the company, and
        (ii)   preferential creditors whose debts amount to more than 50% of the total preferential debts of the company, disregarding debts of any creditor who does not respond to an invitation to give or withhold consent.

(4) Consent for the purposes of sub-paragraph (1) may be—
    (a)   written, or
    (b)   signified at a creditors' meeting.

(5) The power to extend under sub-paragraph (1)—
    (a)   may be exercised in respect of a period only once,
    (b)   may not be used to extend a period by more than 28 days,
    (c)   may not be used to extend a period which has been extended by the court, and
    (d)   may not be used to extend a period after expiry.

1.694

109

Where a period is extended under paragraph 107 or 108, a reference to the period shall be taken as a reference to the period as extended.

Amendment of provision about time

1.695

110

(1) The Secretary of State may by order amend a provision of this Schedule which—
    (a)   requires anything to be done within a specified period of time,
    (b)   prevents anything from being done after a specified time, or
    (c)   requires a specified minimum period of notice to be given.

(2) An order under this paragraph—
    (a)   must be made by statutory instrument, and
    (b)   shall be subject to annulment in pursuance of a resolution of either House of Parliament.

Interpretation

1.696

111

(1) In this Schedule—
    'administrative receiver' has the meaning given by section 251,
    'administrator' has the meaning given by paragraph 1 and, where the context requires, includes a reference to a former administrator,

...

'correspondence' includes correspondence by telephonic or other electronic means,

'creditors' meeting' has the meaning given by paragraph 50,

'enters administration' has the meaning given by paragraph 1,

'floating charge' means a charge which is a floating charge on its creation,

'in administration' has the meaning given by paragraph 1,

'hire-purchase agreement' includes a conditional sale agreement, a chattel leasing agreement and a retention of title agreement,

'holder of a qualifying floating charge' in respect of a company's property has the meaning given by paragraph 14,

'market value' means the amount which would be realised on a sale of property in the open market by a willing vendor,

'the purpose of administration' means an objective specified in paragraph 3, and

'unable to pay its debts' has the meaning given by section 123.

[(1A) In this Schedule, 'company' means—

(a)   a company within the meaning of section 735(1) of the Companies Act 1985,

(b)   a company incorporated in an EEA State other than the United Kingdom, or

(c)   a company not incorporated in an EEA State but having its centre of main interests in a member State other than Denmark.

(1B) In sub-paragraph (1A), in relation to a company, 'centre of main interests' has the same meaning as in the EC Regulation and, in the absence of proof to the contrary, is presumed to be the place of its registered office (within the meaning of that Regulation).]

(2) A reference in this Schedule to a thing in writing includes a reference to a thing in electronic form.

(3) In this Schedule a reference to action includes a reference to inaction.

Notes

Para 111(1)

The definition of 'company' that previously appeared has been deleted by Insolvency Act 1986 (Amendment) Regulations 2005 (SI 2005/879).

Para 111(1A)

This provision was introduced by Insolvency Act 1986 (Amendment) Regulations 2005 (SI 2005/879) reg 2. The effect of the amendment is to reverse *Re Salvage Association* [2003] BCC 504 so that companies such as those incorporated by charter and other bodies falling outside the definition in this provision cannot now enter administration or voluntary arrangement unless there is a specific statutory authority to enter administration. The definition of company in summary now covers only: (a) registered companies under the Companies Acts; (b) companies incorporated in European Economic Association states other than the UK (this would include Danish companies); and (c) companies registered outside the European Union but with a centre of main interest in an European Union member state (other than Denmark), see for instance *Re Brac Rent-a-Car International Inc* [2004] BCC 248, *Re Sendo Ltd* [2006] 1 BCLC 395.

Para 111(3)

The administrator has a general power to do anything necessary or expedient for the management of the affairs, business and property of the company would under IA 1986 Sch B1 para 59 and given the definition in IA 1986 Sch B1 para 111(3) this would include not carrying out any action in suitable circumstances.

[Non-UK companies

1.697

111A

A company incorporated outside the United Kingdom that has a principal place of business in Northern Ireland may not enter administration under this Schedule unless it also has a principal place of business in England and Wales or Scotland (or both in England and Wales and in Scotland).]

Notes

Para 111A

See now The Insolvency (Northern Ireland) Order 2005 (SI 2005/1455) introducing the new regime for company administration.

Scotland

1.698

112

In the application of this Schedule to Scotland—
  (a)   a reference to filing with the court is a reference to lodging in court, and
  (b)   a reference to a charge is a reference to a right in security.

1.699

113

Where property in Scotland is disposed of under paragraph 70 or 71, the administrator shall grant to the disponee an appropriate document of transfer or conveyance of the property, and—
  (a)   that document, or
  (b)   recording, intimation or registration of that document (where recording, intimation or registration of the document is a legal requirement for completion of title to the property),
has the effect of disencumbering the property of or, as the case may be, freeing the property from, the security.

1.700

114

In Scotland, where goods in the possession of a company under a hire-purchase agreement are disposed of under paragraph 72, the disposal has the effect of extinguishing as against the disponee all rights of the owner of the goods under the agreement.

1.701

115

(1) In Scotland, the administrator of a company may make, in or towards the satisfaction of the debt secured by the floating charge, a payment to the holder of a floating charge which has attached to the property subject to the charge.

(2) In Scotland, where the administrator thinks that the company has insufficient property to enable a distribution to be made to unsecured creditors other than by virtue of section 176A(2)(a), he may file a notice to that effect with the registrar of companies.

(3) On delivery of the notice to the registrar of companies, any floating charge granted by the company shall, unless it has already so attached, attach to the property which is subject to the charge and that attachment shall have effect as if each floating charge is a fixed security over the property to which it has attached.

1.702

116

In Scotland, the administrator in making any payment in accordance with paragraph 115 shall make such payment subject to the rights of any of the following categories of persons (which rights shall, except to the extent provided in any instrument, have the following order of priority)—

   (a)   the holder of any fixed security which is over property subject to the floating charge and which ranks prior to, or pari passu with, the floating charge,

   (b)   creditors in respect of all liabilities and expenses incurred by or on behalf of the administrator,

   (c)   the administrator in respect of his liabilities, expenses and remuneration and any indemnity to which he is entitled out of the property of the company,

   (d)   the preferential creditors entitled to payment in accordance with paragraph 65,

   (e)   the holder of the floating charge in accordance with the priority of that charge in relation to any other floating charge which has attached, and

   (f)   the holder of a fixed security, other than one referred to in paragraph (a), which is over property subject to the floating charge.

SCHEDULE 1
Powers of Administrator or Administrative Receiver
Sections 14, 42

1.703

1

Power to take possession of, collect and get in the property of the company and, for that purpose, to take such proceedings as may seem to him expedient.

2

Power to sell or otherwise dispose of the property of the company by public auction or private contract or, in Scotland, to sell, ... hire out or otherwise dispose of the property of the company by public group or private bargain.

3

Power to raise or borrow money and grant security therefor over the property of the company.

4

Power to appoint a solicitor or accountant or other professionally qualified person to assist him in the performance of his functions.

5

Power to bring or defend any action or other legal proceedings in the name and on behalf of the company.

6

Power to refer to arbitration any question affecting the company.

7

Power to effect and maintain insurances in respect of the business and property of the company.

8

Power to use the company's seal.

9

Power to do all acts and to execute in the name and on behalf of the company any deed, receipt or other document.

10

Power to draw, accept, make and endorse any bill of exchange or promissory note in the name and on behalf of the company.

11

Power to appoint any agent to do any business which he is unable to do himself or which can more conveniently be done by an agent and power to employ and dismiss employees.

12

Power to do all such things (including the carrying out of works) as may be necessary for the realisation of the property of the company.

13

Power to make any payment which is necessary or incidental to the performance of his functions.

14

Power to carry on the business of the company.

15

Power to establish subsidiaries of the company.

16

Power to transfer to subsidiaries of the company the whole or any part of the business and property of the company.

17

Power to grant or accept a surrender of a lease or tenancy of any of the property of the company, and to take a lease or tenancy of any property required or convenient for the business of the company.

18

Power to make any arrangement or compromise on behalf of the company.

19

Power to call up any uncalled capital of the company.

20

Power to rank and claim in the bankruptcy, insolvency, sequestration or liquidation of any person indebted to the company and to receive dividends, and to accede to trust deeds for the creditors of any such person.

21

Power to present or defend a petition for the winding up of the company.

22

Power to change the situation of the company's registered office.

23

Power to do all other things incidental to the exercise of the foregoing powers.

SCHEDULE 2
Powers of a Scottish Receiver (Additional to Those Conferred on him by the Instrument of Charge)
Section 55

1.704

1

Power to take possession of, collect and get in the property from the company or a liquidator thereof or any other person, and for that purpose, to take such proceedings as may seem to him expedient.

2

Power to sell, ... hire out or otherwise dispose of the property by public group or private bargain and with or without advertisement.

3

Power to raise or borrow money and grant security therefor over the property.

4

Power to appoint a solicitor or accountant or other professionally qualified person to assist him in the performance of his functions.

5

Power to bring or defend any action or other legal proceedings in the name and on behalf of the company.

6

Power to refer to arbitration all questions affecting the company.

7

Power to effect and maintain insurances in respect of the business and property of the company.

8

Power to use the company's seal.

9

Power to do all acts and to execute in the name and on behalf of the company any deed, receipt or other document.

10

Power to draw, accept, make and endorse any bill of exchange or promissory note in the name and on behalf of the company.

11

Power to appoint any agent to do any business which he is unable to do himself or which can more conveniently be done by an agent, and power to employ and dismiss employees.

12

Power to do all such things (including the carrying out of works), as may be necessary for the realisation of the property.

13

Power to make any payment which is necessary or incidental to the performance of his functions.

14

Power to carry on the business of the company or any part of it.

15

Power to grant or accept a surrender of a lease or tenancy of any of the property, and to take a lease or tenancy of any property required or convenient for the business of the company.

16

Power to make any arrangement or compromise on behalf of the company.

17

Power to call up any uncalled capital of the company.

18

Power to establish subsidiaries of the company.

19

Power to transfer to subsidiaries of the company the business of the company or any part of it and any of the property.

20

Power to rank and claim in the bankruptcy, insolvency, sequestration or liquidation of any person or company indebted to the company and to receive dividends, and to accede to trust deeds for creditors of any such person.

21

Power to present or defend a petition for the winding up of the company.

22

Power to change the situation of the company's registered office.

23

Power to do all other things incidental to the exercise of the powers mentioned in section 55(1) of this Act or above in this Schedule.

[SCHEDULE 2A
Exceptions to Prohibition on Appointment of Administrative
Receiver: Supplementary Provisions]

[Capital market arrangement

1.705

1

(1) For the purposes of section 72B an arrangement is a capital market
arrangement if—
- (a) it involves a grant of security to a person holding it as trustee for
a person who holds a capital market investment issued by a party
to the arrangement, or
- [(aa) it involves a grant of security to—
  - (i) a party to the arrangement who issues a capital market
  investment, or
  - (ii) a person who holds the security as trustee for a party to the
  arrangement in connection with the issue of a capital
  market investment, or
- (ab) it involves a grant of security to a person who holds the security
as trustee for a party to the arrangement who agrees to provide
finance to another party, or]
- (b) at least one party guarantees the performance of obligations of
another party, or
- (c) at least one party provides security in respect of the performance
of obligations of another party, or
- (d) the arrangement involves an investment of a kind described in
articles 83 to 85 of the Financial Services and Markets Act 2000
(Regulated Activities) Order 2001 (SI 2001/544) (options, futures
and contracts for differences).

(2) For the purposes of sub-paragraph (1)—
- (a) a reference to holding as trustee includes a reference to holding
as nominee or agent,
- (b) a reference to holding for a person who holds a capital market
investment includes a reference to holding for a number of
persons at least one of whom holds a capital market investment,
and
- (c) a person holds a capital market investment if he has a legal or
beneficial interest in it[; and
- (d) the reference to the provision of finance includes the provision of
an indemnity].

(3) In section 72B(1) and this paragraph 'party' to an arrangement
includes a party to an agreement which—
- (a) forms part of the arrangement,
- (b) provides for the raising of finance as part of the arrangement, or
- (c) is necessary for the purposes of implementing the arrangement.

Capital market investment

1.706

2

(1) For the purposes of section 72B an investment is a capital market investment if it—
- (a) is within article 77 of the Financial Services and Markets Act 2000 (Regulated Activities) Order 2001 (SI 2001/544) (debt instruments), and
- (b) is rated, listed or traded or designed to be rated, listed or traded.

(2) In sub-paragraph (1)—
'rated' means rated for the purposes of investment by an internationally recognised rating agency,
'listed' means admitted to the official list within the meaning given by section 103(1) of the Financial Services and Markets Act 2000 (c 8) (interpretation), and
'traded' means admitted to trading on a market established under the rules of a recognised investment exchange or on a foreign market.

(3) In sub-paragraph (2)—
'recognised investment exchange' has the meaning given by section 285 of the Financial Services and Markets Act 2000 (recognised investment exchange), and
'foreign market' has the same meaning as 'relevant market' in article 67(2) of the Financial Services and Markets Act 2000 (Financial Promotion) Order 2001 (SI 2001/1335) (foreign markets).

1.706A

3

(1) An investment is also a capital market investment for the purposes of section 72B if it consists of a bond or commercial paper issued to one or more of the following—
- (a) an investment professional within the meaning of article 19(5) of the Financial Services and Markets Act 2000 (Financial Promotion) Order 2001,
- (b) a person who is, when the agreement mentioned in section 72B(1) is entered into, a certified high net worth individual in relation to a communication within the meaning of article 48(2) of that order,
- (c) a person to whom article 49(2) of that order applies (high net worth company, &c),
- (d) a person who is, when the agreement mentioned in section 72B(1) is entered into, a certified sophisticated investor in relation to a communication within the meaning of article 50(1) of that order, and
- (e) a person in a State other than the United Kingdom who under the law of that State is not prohibited from investing in bonds or commercial paper.

(2) In sub-paragraph (1)—

'bond' shall be construed in accordance with article 77 of the Financial Services and Markets Act 2000 (Regulated Activities) Order 2001 (SI 2001/544), and

'commercial paper' has the meaning given by article 9(3) of that order.

(3) For the purposes of sub-paragraph (1)—

    (a)   in applying article 19(5) of the Financial Promotion Order for the purposes of sub-paragraph (1)(a)—

        (i)   in article 19(5)(b), ignore the words after 'exempt person',

        (ii) in article 19(5)(c)(i), for the words from 'the controlled activity' to the end substitute 'a controlled activity', and

        (iii) in article 19(5)(e) ignore the words from 'where the communication' to the end, and

    (b)   in applying article 49(2) of that order for the purposes of sub-paragraph (1)(c), ignore article 49(2)(e).

'Agreement'

1.707

4

For the purposes of sections 72B and 72E and this Schedule 'agreement' includes an agreement or undertaking effected by—

    (a)   contract,

    (b)   deed, or

    (c)   any other instrument intended to have effect in accordance with the law of England and Wales, Scotland or another jurisdiction.

Debt

1.708

5

The debt of at least £50 million referred to in section 72B(1)(a) or 72E(2)(a)—

    (a)   may be incurred at any time during the life of the capital market arrangement or financed project, and

    (b)   may be expressed wholly or partly in foreign currency (in which case the sterling equivalent shall be calculated as at the time when the arrangement is entered into or the project begins).

Step-in rights

1.709

6

(1) For the purposes of sections 72C to 72E a project has 'step-in rights' if a person who provides finance in connection with the project has a conditional entitlement under an agreement to—

    (a)   assume sole or principal responsibility under an agreement for carrying out all or part of the project, or

    (b)   make arrangements for carrying out all or part of the project.

(2) In sub-paragraph (1) a reference to the provision of finance includes a reference to the provision of an indemnity.

Project company

1.710

7

(1) For the purposes of sections 72C to 72E a company is a 'project company' of a project if—
 (a) it holds property for the purpose of the project,
 (b) it has sole or principal responsibility under an agreement for carrying out all or part of the project,
 (c) it is one of a number of companies which together carry out the project,
 (d) it has the purpose of supplying finance to enable the project to be carried out, or
 (e) it is the holding company of a company within any of paragraphs (a) to (d).

(2) But a company is not a 'project company' of a project if—
 (a) it performs a function within sub-paragraph (1)(a) to (d) or is within sub-paragraph (1)(e), but
 (b) it also performs a function which is not—
  (i) within sub-paragraph (1)(a) to (d),
  (ii) related to a function within sub-paragraph (1)(a) to (d), or
  (iii) related to the project.

(3) For the purposes of this paragraph a company carries out all or part of a project whether or not it acts wholly or partly through agents.

'Resources'

1.711

8

In section 72C 'resources' includes—
 (a) funds (including payment for the provision of services or facilities),
 (b) assets,
 (c) professional skill,
 (d) the grant of a concession or franchise, and
 (e) any other commercial resource.

'Public body'

1.712

9

(1) In section 72C 'public body' means—
 (a) a body which exercises public functions,
 (b) a body specified for the purposes of this paragraph by the Secretary of State, and
 (c) a body within a class specified for the purposes of this paragraph by the Secretary of State.

(2) A specification under sub-paragraph (1) may be—
 (a) general, or

(b)   for the purpose of the application of section 72C to a specified case.

Regulated business

I.713

10

(1) For the purposes of section 72D a business is regulated if it is carried on—

(a)   ...

(b)   in reliance on a licence under section 7 or 7A of the Gas Act 1986 (c 44) (transport and supply of gas),

(c)   in reliance on a licence granted by virtue of section 41C of that Act (power to prescribe additional licensable activity),

(d)   in reliance on a licence under section 6 of the Electricity Act 1989 (c 29) (supply of electricity),

(e)   by a water undertaker,

(f)   by a sewerage undertaker,

(g)   by a universal service provider within the meaning given by section 4(3) and (4) of the Postal Services Act 2000 (c 26),

(h)   by the Post Office company within the meaning given by section 62 of that Act (transfer of property),

(i)   by a relevant subsidiary of the Post Office Company within the meaning given by section 63 of that Act (government holding),

(j)   in reliance on a licence under section 8 of the Railways Act 1993 (c 43) (railway services),

(k)   in reliance on a licence exemption under section 7 of that Act (subject to sub-paragraph (2) below),

(l)   by the operator of a system of transport which is deemed to be a railway for a purpose of Part I of that Act by virtue of section 81(2) of that Act (tramways, &c), ...

(m)   by the operator of a vehicle carried on flanged wheels along a system within paragraph (l) [or

(n)   in reliance on a European licence granted pursuant to a provision contained in any instrument made for the purpose of implementing Council Directive 1995/18/EC dated 19 June 1995 on the licensing of railway undertakings, as amended by Directive 2001/13/EC dated 26 February 2001 and Directive 2004/49/EC dated 29 April 2004, both of the European Parliament and of the Council, or pursuant to any action taken by an EEA State for that purpose].

(2) Sub-paragraph (1)(k) does not apply to the operator of a railway asset on a railway unless on some part of the railway there is a permitted line speed exceeding 40 kilometres per hour.

[(2A) For the purposes of section 72D a business is also regulated to the extent that it consists in the provision of a public electronic communications network or a public electronic communications service.]

[(2B) In sub-paragraph (1)(n), an 'EEA State' means a member State, Norway, Iceland or Liechtenstein.]

'Person'

1.714

11

A reference to a person in this Schedule includes a reference to a partnership or another unincorporated group of persons.]

SCHEDULE 3
Orders in Course of Winding Up Pronounced in Vacation (Scotland)
Section 162

1.715

Part I
Orders which are to be final

Orders under section 153, as to the time for proving debts and claims.

Orders under section 195 as to meetings for ascertaining wishes of creditors or contributories.

Orders under section 198, as to the examination of witnesses in regard to the property or affairs of a company.

Part II
Orders which are to take effect until matter disposed of by Inner House

1.716

Orders under section 126(1), 130(2) or (3), 147, 227 or 228, restraining or permitting the commencement or the continuance of legal proceedings.

Orders under section 135(5), limiting the powers of provisional liquidators.

Orders under section 108, appointing a liquidator to fill a vacancy.

Orders under section 167 or 169, sanctioning the exercise of any powers by a liquidator, other than the powers specified in paragraphs 1, 2 and 3 of Schedule 4 to this Act.

Orders under section 158, as to the arrest and detention of an absconding contributory and his property.

SCHEDULE 4
Powers of Liquidator in a Winding Up
Sections 165, 167

Introductory

This is the specific list of powers granted to a liquidator referred to in IA 1986 ss 165–167 and the notes to those sections should be consulted. The powers are not granted to a provisional liquidator though the court can confer such IA 1986 Sch 4 powers as may be necessary pursuant to IA 1986 s 135(4); *Re Hawk Insurance Co Ltd* [2001] BCC 57. Where sanction is needed for the exercise of a power, such sanction can be obtained retrospectively; *Re Associated Travel and Leisure Services Ltd* [1978] 1 WLR 547.

Part I
Powers Exercisable with Sanction

1.717

1

Power to pay any class of creditors in full.

2

Power to make any compromise or arrangement with creditors or persons claiming to be creditors, or having or alleging themselves to have any claim (present or future, certain or contingent, ascertained or sounding only in damages) against the company, or whereby the company may be rendered liable.

3

Power to compromise, on such terms as may be agreed—
  (a) all calls and liabilities to calls, all debts and liabilities capable of resulting in debts, and all claims (present or future, certain or contingent, ascertained or sounding only in damages) subsisting or supposed to subsist between the company and a contributory or alleged contributory or other debtor or person apprehending liability to the company, and
  (b) all questions in any way relating to or affecting the assets or the winding up of the company,
and take any security for the discharge of any such call, debt, liability or claim and give a complete discharge in respect of it.

[3A

Power to bring legal proceedings under section 213, 214, 238, 239, 242, 243 or 423.]

Notes

Para I

Sanction is not required to pay preferential creditors as IA 1986 s 175 of the Act imposes a duty to pay the preferential debts ahead of other creditors

Para 2

This paragraph appears to allow the liquidator to enter into a scheme or compromise that would involve a departure from the statutory scheme of pari passu distribution, provided that the company could itself have entered into the arrangement. In *Re BCCI (No 3)* [1993] BCLC 1490 the court allowed an arrangement whereby assets in different jurisdictions were pooled and all creditors were paid out under the scheme. This power also allows a liquidator to reach settlement of claims by individual creditors. For an example of where the court refused to sanction a compromise see: *Re Greenhaven Motors Ltd* [1999] BCC 463.

Para 3

Where the liquidator applies for sanction from the court it is advisable for him to consider notifying interested parties if it appears that the proposed compromise might prove controversial: *Re Greenhaven Motors Ltd* [1999] BCC 463. The court has to be satisfied that the compromise is for the benefit and in the interests of the creditors for it to be approved: *Re Edennote Ltd (No 2)* [1997] 2 BCLC 89. Where a right of action vested in the company is being sold by the liquidator the main concern is to achieve the best result for creditors even if that has the effect of stifling a claim for breach of duty by the company against the purchaser of the claim; it is the duty of the liquidator to market the cause of action appropriately: *Re Edennote Ltd (No 2) (above)*.

Para 3A

This paragraph was introduced by the EA 2002 s 253 as part of a number of provisions to ensure that a liquidator who takes such proceedings is properly authorised and therefore may charge the costs of such proceedings as an expense of the liquidation: IR 1986 r 4.218(1)(a)(i). Prior to these reforms a liquidator had no clear entitlement to claim such costs as expenses of the liquidation; *Lewis v Inland Revenue Commissioners* [2001] 3 All ER 499.

Part II
Powers Exercisable without Sanction in Voluntary Winding Up, with Sanction in Winding Up by the Court

1.718

4

Power to bring or defend any action or other legal proceeding in the name and on behalf of the company.

Note

Para 4

This paragraph does not govern proceedings which are brought in the liquidator's own name such as proceedings for wrongful or fraudulent trading under IA 1986 ss 213 or 214, or to set aside preferences or transactions at an undervalue under IA 1986 ss 238, 239 or 423 which require sanction under para 3A above; and see the notes thereunder. In some situations (for example a breach of duty by a director) the liquidator will have a choice of whether or not to litigate in his own name (under IA 1986 s 212 which is not subject to sanction under para 3A above) or rely on this provision to take proceedings in the company's name. If the latter course is chosen, the defendant may obtain security for costs; if the former course is chosen security for costs cannot be obtained (*Re Strand Wool Co Ltd* [1904] 2 Ch 1) but the liquidator will be personally liable for costs. The liquidator should always carefully consider his involvement in proceedings as he may incur personal liability despite acting reasonably if he decides to discontinue proceedings: *Walker v Walker* [2005] BPIR 454; *RBG Resources plc v Rastogi* [2005] 2 BCLC 592. Further a liquidator who commences an action in the name of the company may be the subject of a non-party costs order, Supreme Court Act 1981 s 51(1), *Aiden Shipping Co Ltd v Interbulk Ltd* [1986] AC 965.

1.719

5

Power to carry on the business of the company so far as may be necessary for its beneficial winding up.

Note

Para 5

If a liquidator in a winding up by the court is contemplating trading, it is imperative to obtain sanction before trading begins. Although sanction may be obtained retrospectively for an exercise of powers under IA 1986 Sch 4 it would be dangerous in practice to trade without sanction see *Re Centralcrest Engineering Ltd* [2000] BCC 727, where a liquidator was found liable in misfeasance for trading the company without sanction.

The power is limited to trading only so far as is necessary for the beneficial winding up of the company. It is not a power to be exercised to carry on business with the hope of making a profit and in any event any permission granted is likely to be for a short period: *Re Wreck Recovery and Salvage Co* (1880) 15 Ch D 353. The court will not interfere if the liquidator, acting in good faith, reasonably forms the view that the carrying on of the business is necessary for the beneficial winding up; nor in those circumstances will a liquidator be held liable if his/her view turns out to be mistaken: *Re Great Eastern Electric Co Ltd* [1941] Ch 241. The burden of showing that the carrying on of trade by a liquidator is not beneficial is on the party making the objection: *Hire Purchase Co v Richens* (1887) 20 QBD 387.

Part III
Powers Exercisable Without Sanction in any Winding Up

1.720

6

Power to sell any of the company's property by public auction or private contract with power to transfer the whole of it to any person or to sell the same in parcels.

Note

Para 6

The court will only interfere to restrain a sale by a liquidator where he has acted fraudulently, displayed a lack of bona fides or acted in a totally unreasonable manner: *Harold M Pitman & Co v Top Business Systems (Nottingham) Ltd* (1985) 1 BCC 99, 435.

'Property' is widely defined in IA 1986 s 436 and includes choses in action. The liquidator accordingly has power to assign the company's causes of action, and the express power in this paragraph confers an exemption from the common law rules of champerty: see eg *Empire Resolution Ltd v MPW Insurance Brokers Ltd* [1999] BPIR 486.

Claims for wrongful or fraudulent trading (IA 1986 ss 213, 214), and to set aside preferences or transactions at an undervalue (IA 1986 ss 238, 238 and 423), or to recover payments rendered void by IA 1986 s 127 are claims which the liquidator brings in his own right and are not the company's property. They therefore do not fall within this paragraph. Although such claims cannot be assigned, the proceeds of such claims may be assigned in whole or in part to a person who has a genuine interest in the outcome; eg in consideration of that person funding the litigation, provided that the liquidator retains control of the proceedings: see eg *Re Oasis Merchandising Services Ltd* [1998] Ch 170 and *Katz v McNally* [1997] BCC 784. In *ANC Ltd v Clark Goldring & Page Ltd* [2001] BCC 479 Robert Walker LJ accepted the following argument as a valuable aid to clarifying the law in this area:

(1)   The power of sale under IA 1986 ch 4 para 6 gives rise to an exemption from the rules of champerty;

(2)   A legal assignment of a cause of action consists of the right to prosecute the action, to be named as a party and to give a good discharge to the judgment debtor;

(3)   An assignment of the fruits of a cause of action is an equitable assignment, being an agreement to assign such fruits as and when they arise. The assignee has no right to conduct the action or any beneficial interest in the action itself;

(4)   Since an assignment of the fruits of an action does not confer any right in the action itself, no question of champerty (or the scope of the liquidator's exemption) arises;

(5)   (The court expressing no view as to whether this particular point is correct) an agreement that an equitable assignee of the fruits of an action should have conduct of the action is separate from an independent assignment of the fruits of the action and amounts to no more than a funding arrangement and is therefore subject to the usual champerty rules.

In *Katz v McNally* (above) the Court of Appeal observed that in the cases where assignments of the fruits of an action had been held unlawful, the assignee had had control of the action and the liquidator had been reduced to a mere puppet. It was held that an agreement that the fruits of an action should be used first to repay a creditor who funded the action was unobjectionable. If a contract contains a prohibition against assignment, that will be binding on the liquidator: *Quadmost Ltd v Reprotech (Pebsham) Ltd* [2001] BPIR 349. An assignment to a director who might be entitled to pursue a claim with the benefit of public funding is not in itself unlawful: *Norglen Ltd v Reeds Rains Prudential Ltd* [1999] 2 AC 1.

1.721

7

Power to do all acts and execute, in the name and on behalf of the company, all deeds, receipts and other documents and for that purpose to use, when necessary, the company's seal.

8

Power to prove, rank and claim in the bankruptcy, insolvency or seques- tration of any contributory for any balance against his estate, and to receive dividends in the bankruptcy, insolvency or sequestration in respect of that balance, as a separate debt due from the bankrupt or insolvent, and rateably with the other separate creditors.

9

Power to draw, accept, make and indorse any bill of exchange or promissory note in the name and on behalf of the company, with the same

> effect with respect to the company's liability as if the bill or note had been drawn, accepted, made or indorsed by or on behalf of the company in the course of its business.

Note

Para 9

This provision enables a liquidator to draw a cheque on the company's bank account. The liquidator should sign as agent of the company using the official style as 'liquidator of X Limited' IA 1986 s 163: *Dutton v Marsh* (1871) LR 6 QB 361; *Rolfe Lubell & Co v Keith* [1979] 1 All ER 860.

1.722

10

Power to raise on the security of the assets of the company any money requisite.

Note

Para 10

This power might be exercised where a liquidator is considering carrying on the business of the company in liquidation. Though a liquidator has this power, there is no provision under which the security holder is given some form of 'super priority' over other creditors of the company: *Re Regent's Canal Ironworks Co* [1875] 3 Ch D 411.

1.723

11

Power to take out in his official name letters of administration to any deceased contributory, and to do in his official name any other act necessary for obtaining payment of any money due from a contributory or his estate which cannot conveniently be done in the name of the company.

In all such cases the money due is deemed, for the purpose of enabling the liquidator to take out the letters of administration or recover the money, to be due to the liquidator himself.

12

Power to appoint an agent to do any business which the liquidator is unable to do himself.

Note

Para 12

This provision enables the liquidator to employ advisers for a variety of purposes but it may not be relied upon to effect a total delegation of duty: *Re Great Eastern Electric Co Ltd* [1941] Ch 241.

> **1.724**
>
> **13**
>
> Power to do all such other things as may be necessary for winding up the company's affairs and distributing its assets.

Note

Para 13

This is a wide power which allows the liquidator to do anything expeditious for the purpose of the beneficial winding up of the company: *Re Cambrian Mining Co* (1881) 20 Ch D 376. This would include the presentation of a winding up petition by a voluntary liquidator *Re Zoedene Co Ltd* (1884) 49 LT 654 but it does not enable a liquidator to avoid conditions that are imposed on the exercise of a specific power *Re Phoenix Oil and Transport Co Ltd (No 2)* [1958] Ch 565. If the liquidator has doubt about whether a particular act falls within this power an application ought to be made to court for sanction *Re Banque des Marchands de Moscou* [1953] 1 All ER 278 (*approval of ex gratia payment to adviser*).

> ## SCHEDULE 4A
> Bankruptcy Restrictions Order and Undertaking]

Notes

See the notes to IA 1986 s 281A and EA 2002 Sch 21 and IR 1986 rr 6.240–6.244 for the procedure for making a bankruptcy restrictions order and IR 1986 rr 6.245–6.248 for an interim bankruptcy restrictions order (see para 6 below); and IR 1986 rr 6.249, 6.250 for giving a bankruptcy restrictions undertaking (see para 7 below).

> ## Bankruptcy restrictions order
>
> **1.725**
>
> **1**
>
> (1) A bankruptcy restrictions order may be made by the court.
>
> (2) An order may be made only on the application of—
>   (a)   the Secretary of State, or
>   (b)   the official receiver acting on a direction of the Secretary of State.
>
> ## Grounds for making order
>
> **2**
>
> (1) The court shall grant an application for a bankruptcy restrictions order if it thinks it appropriate having regard to the conduct of the bankrupt (whether before or after the making of the bankruptcy order).
>
> (2) The court shall, in particular, take into account any of the following kinds of behaviour on the part of the bankrupt—

(a) failing to keep records which account for a loss of property by the bankrupt, or by a business carried on by him, where the loss occurred in the period beginning 2 years before petition and ending with the date of the application;

(b) failing to produce records of that kind on demand by the official receiver or the trustee;

(c) entering into a transaction at an undervalue;

(d) giving a preference;

(e) making an excessive pension contribution;

(f) a failure to supply goods or services which were wholly or partly paid for which gave rise to a claim provable in the bankruptcy;

(g) trading at a time before commencement of the bankruptcy when the bankrupt knew or ought to have known that he was himself to be unable to pay his debts;

(h) incurring, before commencement of the bankruptcy, a debt which the bankrupt had no reasonable expectation of being able to pay;

(i) failing to account satisfactorily to the court, the official receiver or the trustee for a loss of property or for an insufficiency of property to meet bankruptcy debts;

(j) carrying on any gambling, rash and hazardous speculation or unreasonable extravagance which may have materially contributed to or increased the extent of the bankruptcy or which took place between presentation of the petition and commencement of the bankruptcy;

(k) neglect of business affairs of a kind which may have materially contributed to or increased the extent of the bankruptcy;

(l) fraud or fraudulent breach of trust;

(m) failing to cooperate with the official receiver or the trustee.

(3) The court shall also, in particular, consider whether the bankrupt was an undischarged bankrupt at some time during the period of six years ending with the date of the bankruptcy to which the application relates.

(4) For the purpose of sub-paragraph (2)—
'before petition' shall be construed in accordance with section 351(c),
'excessive pension contribution' shall be construed in accordance with section 342A,
'preference' shall be construed in accordance with section 340, and
'undervalue' shall be construed in accordance with section 339.

Timing of application for order

3

(1) An application for a bankruptcy restrictions order in respect of a bankrupt must be made—

(a) before the end of the period of one year beginning with the date on which the bankruptcy commences, or

(b) with the permission of the court.

(2) The period specified in sub-paragraph (1)(a) shall cease to run in respect of a bankrupt while the period set for his discharge is suspended under section 279(3).

Duration of order

4

(1) A bankruptcy restrictions order—
- (a) shall come into force when it is made, and
- (b) shall cease to have effect at the end of a date specified in the order.

(2) The date specified in a bankruptcy restrictions order under sub-paragraph (1)(b) must not be—
- (a) before the end of the period of two years beginning with the date on which the order is made, or
- (b) after the end of the period of 15 years beginning with that date.

Interim bankruptcy restrictions order

5

(1) This paragraph applies at any time between—
- (a) the institution of an application for a bankruptcy restrictions order, and
- (b) the determination of the application.

(2) The court may make an interim bankruptcy restrictions order if the court thinks that—
- (a) there are prima facie grounds to suggest that the application for the bankruptcy restrictions order will be successful, and
- (b) it is in the public interest to make an interim order.

(3) An interim order may be made only on the application of—
- (a) the Secretary of State, or
- (b) the official receiver acting on a direction of the Secretary of State.

(4) An interim order—
- (a) shall have the same effect as a bankruptcy restrictions order, and
- (b) shall come into force when it is made.

(5) An interim order shall cease to have effect—
- (a) on the determination of the application for the bankruptcy restrictions order,
- (b) on the acceptance of a bankruptcy restrictions undertaking made by the bankrupt, or
- (c) if the court discharges the interim order on the application of the person who applied for it or of the bankrupt.

6

(1) This paragraph applies to a case in which both an interim bankruptcy restrictions order and a bankruptcy restrictions order are made.

(2) Paragraph 4(2) shall have effect in relation to the bankruptcy restrictions order as if a reference to the date of that order were a reference to the date of the interim order.

Bankruptcy restrictions undertaking

7

(1) A bankrupt may offer a bankruptcy restrictions undertaking to the Secretary of State.

(2) In determining whether to accept a bankruptcy restrictions undertaking the Secretary of State shall have regard to the matters specified in paragraph 2(2) and (3).

8

A reference in an enactment to a person in respect of whom a bankruptcy restrictions order has effect (or who is 'the subject of' a bankruptcy restrictions order) includes a reference to a person in respect of whom a bankruptcy restrictions undertaking has effect.

9

(1) A bankruptcy restrictions undertaking—
- (a) shall come into force on being accepted by the Secretary of State, and
- (b) shall cease to have effect at the end of a date specified in the undertaking.

(2) The date specified under sub-paragraph (1)(b) must not be—
- (a) before the end of the period of two years beginning with the date on which the undertaking is accepted, or
- (b) after the end of the period of 15 years beginning with that date.

(3) On an application by the bankrupt the court may—
- (a) annul a bankruptcy restrictions undertaking;
- (b) provide for a bankruptcy restrictions undertaking to cease to have effect before the date specified under sub-paragraph (1)(b).

Effect of annulment of bankruptcy order

10

Where a bankruptcy order is annulled under section 282(1)(a) or (2)—
- (a) any bankruptcy restrictions order, interim order or undertaking which is in force in respect of the bankrupt shall be annulled,
- (b) no new bankruptcy restrictions order or interim order may be made in respect of the bankrupt, and
- (c) no new bankruptcy restrictions undertaking by the bankrupt may be accepted.

11

Where a bankruptcy order is annulled under section 261, 263D or 282(1)(b)—
- (a) the annulment shall not affect any bankruptcy restrictions order, interim order or undertaking in respect of the bankrupt,
- (b) the court may make a bankruptcy restrictions order in relation to the bankrupt on an application instituted before the annulment,
- (c) the Secretary of State may accept a bankruptcy restrictions undertaking offered before the annulment, and

> (d) an application for a bankruptcy restrictions order or interim order in respect of the bankrupt may not be instituted after the annulment.
>
> ## Registration
>
> **12**
>
> The Secretary of State shall maintain a register of—
> (a) bankruptcy restrictions orders,
> (b) interim bankruptcy restrictions orders, and
> (c) bankruptcy restrictions undertakings.]

> ## SCHEDULE 5
> ## Powers of Trustee in Bankruptcy
> *Section 314*

Notes

Part I sets out the powers exercisable by the trustee with sanction of the court or the creditors' committee (IA 1986 s 314). However, the absence of such sanction may not render a transaction void: see *Weddell v J.A. Pearce & Major and anor* [1988] Ch 26.

> ## Part I
> ## Powers Exercisable with Sanction
>
> **1.726**
>
> **1**
>
> Power to carry on any business of the bankrupt so far as may be necessary for winding it up beneficially and so far as the trustee is able to do so without contravening any requirement imposed by or under any enactment.
>
> **2**
>
> Power to bring, institute or defend any action or legal proceedings relating to the property comprised in the bankrupt's estate.

Notes

Para 2

Ordinarily causes of action belonging to the bankrupt prior to his bankruptcy vest in the trustee as property of the estate *Heath v Tang* [1993] 1 WLR 1421;and see notes to IA 1986 s 283 under 'Personal rights'. The trustee may decide to continue with the cause of action in which case it is at his own risk as to costs including the pre-bankruptcy costs which have arisen *Watson v Holliday* (1882) 20 Ch D 780. Further, where a trustee by taking steps in the litigation even though he is not formally a party to the proceeding's costs may be ordered against him *Vickery v Modern Security Systems Ltd* [1998] BPIR 164. Where a trustee makes an application within the bankruptcy then he does so at his own risk as to costs and if there are not sufficient assets in the estate he will be personally liable to make up the shortfall.

1.727

[2A

Power to bring legal proceedings under section 339, 340 or 423.]

Notes

Para 2A

This provision was introduced by EA 2002 s 262 but it does not apply to proceedings issued prior to 15 September 2003 Enterprise Act (Commencement No 4 etc) Order 2003 art 6.

1.728

3

Power to accept as the consideration for the sale of any property comprised in the bankrupt's estate a sum of money payable at a future time subject to such stipulations as to security or otherwise as the creditors' committee or the court thinks fit.

4

Power to mortgage or pledge any part of the property comprised in the bankrupt's estate for the purpose of raising money for the payment of his debts.

5

Power, where any right, option or other power forms part of the bankrupt's estate, to make payments or incur liabilities with a view to obtaining, for the benefit of the creditors, any property which is the subject of the right, option or power.

6

Power to refer to arbitration, or compromise on such terms as may be agreed on, any debts, claims or liabilities subsisting or supposed to subsist between the bankrupt and any person who may have incurred any liability to the bankrupt.

7

Power to make such compromise or other arrangement as may be thought expedient with creditors, or persons claiming to be creditors, in respect of bankruptcy debts.

8

Power to make such compromise or other arrangement as may be thought expedient with respect to any claim arising out of or incidental to the bankrupt's estate made or capable of being made on the trustee by any person or by the trustee on any person.

Part II
General Powers

Notes

Part II sets out the 'General Powers' exercisable by the trustee without sanction.

1.729

9

Power to sell any part of the property for the time being comprised in the bankrupt's estate, including the goodwill and book debts of any business.

Notes

Para 9

The trustee is not bound to dispose of an asset at the only price offered to him if that price is a derisory one; however, the court may interfere with the trustee's decision regarding assignment if it considers that the decision-making process employed was flawed: *Khan v Official Receiver* [1997] BPIR 109; *Faryab v Smith* [2001] BPIR 246.

The trustee may sell the bankrupt's cause of action to the bankrupt or a creditor: see *Ramsey v Hartley* [1977] 1 WLR 686; *Weddell and anor v J.A. Pearce & Major and anor* [1988] Ch 26; *Guy v Churchill* [1888] 40 Ch D 481; *Grovewood Holdings plc v James Capel & Co Ltd* [1995] Ch 80; *Re Oasis Merchandising Services Ltd* [1995] 2 BCLC 493; *Farmer v Moseley (Holdings) Ltd* [2002] BPIR 473; *Re Papaloizou* [1999] BPIR 106.

The trustee may also assign a cause of action to the bankrupt or a creditor on the condition that he receives a share of any sums awarded therein, if the terms of the assignment are 'proper' and 'fair' to the creditors: see *Norglen Ltd (In Liquidation) v Reeds Rains Prudential* [1999] 2 AC 1; *Bankruptcy Estate of Cirillo, ex.p Official Trustee in Bankruptcy* [1997] BPIR 574.

1.730

10

Power to give receipts for any money received by him, being receipts which effectually discharge the person paying the money from all responsibility in respect of its application.

11

Power to prove, rank, claim and draw a dividend in respect of such debts due to the bankrupt as are comprised in his estate.

12

Power to exercise in relation to any property comprised in the bankrupt's estate any powers the capacity to exercise which is vested in him under Parts VIII to XI of this Act.

13

Power to deal with any property comprised in the estate to which the bankrupt is beneficially entitled as tenant in tail in the same manner as the bankrupt might have dealt with it.

Part III
Ancillary Powers

Notes

Part III lists the 'Ancillary Powers' available to the trustee to be exercised for the purposes of, or in connection with, the exercise of any of his powers under Parts VIII to XI of this Act. The trustee is also empowered to do any other act which is necessary or expedient for the purposes of or in connection with the exercise of those powers.

1.731

14

For the purposes of, or in connection with, the exercise of any of his powers under Parts VIII to XI of this Act, the trustee may, by his official name—
  (a) hold property of every description,
  (b) make contracts,
  (c) sue and be sued,
  (d) enter into engagements binding on himself and, in respect of the bankrupt's estate, on his successors in office,
  (e) employ an agent,
  (f) execute any power of attorney, deed or other instrument;
and he may do any other act which is necessary or expedient for the purposes of or in connection with the exercise of those powers.

SCHEDULE 6
The Categories of Preferential Debts
Section 386

Notes

Prior to the coming into force of the relevant parts of the EA 2002 on 15 September 2003, the main classes of preferential debts could be broadly described as Crown debts (ie debts due to the Inland Revenue and HM Customs and Excise and Class 1, Class 2 and Class 4 National Insurance contributions), contributions to occupational pension schemes, and employees' remuneration. In addition, with effect from 1 January 1988, levies in respect of coal and steel production under the ECSC Treaty were also given preferential status under the Insolvency (ECSC Levy Debts) Regulations 1987 (SI 1987/2093). Following the coming into force of the amendments made under the EA 2002, Crown debts have not enjoyed preferential status in liquidations occurring since 15 September 2003. The list of preferential debts must be settled as at a 'relevant date,' defined in IA 1986 s 387, which varies according to the type of insolvency process concerned.

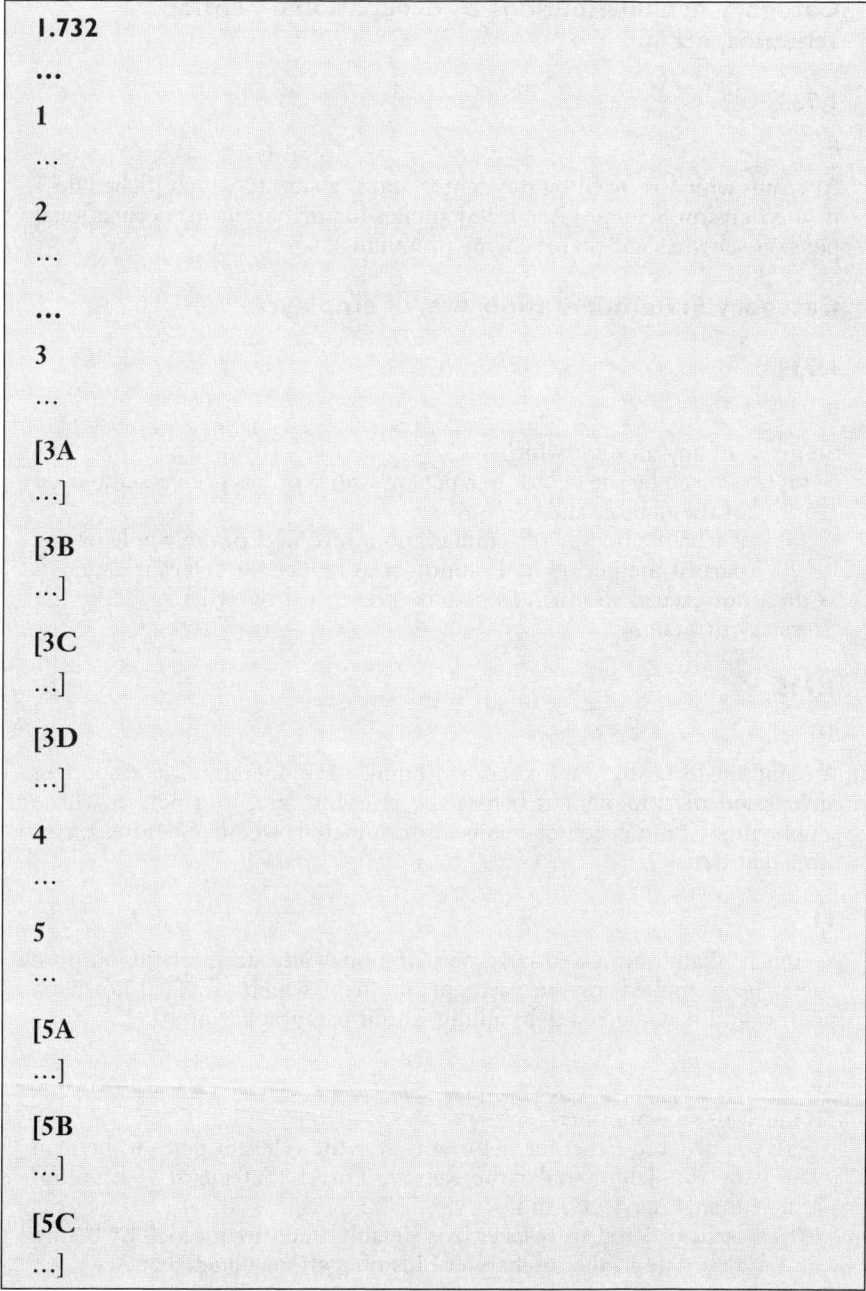

1.732

...

1

...

2

...

...

3

...

[3A

...]

[3B

...]

[3C

...]

[3D

...]

4

...

5

...

[5A

...]

[5B

...]

[5C

...]

...

6

...

7

...

Category 4: Contributions to occupational pension schemes, etc

1.733

8

Any sum which is owed by the debtor and is a sum to which [Schedule 4 to the Pension Schemes Act 1993] applies (contributions to occupational pension schemes and state scheme premiums).

Category 5: Remuneration, etc, of employees

1.734

9

So much of any amount which—
- (a) is owed by the debtor to a person who is or has been an employee of the debtor, and
- (b) is payable by way of remuneration in respect of the whole or any part of the period of 4 months next before the relevant date,

as does not exceed so much as may be prescribed by order made by the Secretary of State.

1.735

10

An amount owed by way of accrued holiday remuneration, in respect of any period of employment before the relevant date, to a person whose employment by the debtor has been terminated, whether before, on or after that date.

11

So much of any sum owed in respect of money advanced for the purpose as has been applied for the payment of a debt which, if it had not been paid, would have been a debt falling within paragraph 9 or 10.

12

So much of any amount which—
- (a) is ordered (whether before or after the relevant date) to be paid by the debtor under the Reserve Forces (Safeguard of Employment) Act 1985, and
- (b) is so ordered in respect of a default made by the debtor before that date in the discharge of his obligations under that Act,

as does not exceed such amount as may be prescribed by order made by the Secretary of State.

Notes

Paras 9, 12

The 'prescribed' amount is £800: Insolvency Proceedings (Monetary Limits) Order 1986 (SI 1986/1996).

Interpretation for Category 5

1.736

13

(1) For the purposes of paragraphs 9 to 12, a sum is payable by the debtor to a person by way of remuneration in respect of any period if—

    (a)   it is paid as wages or salary (whether payable for time or for piece work or earned wholly or partly by way of commission) in respect of services rendered to the debtor in that period, or

    (b)   it is an amount falling within the following sub-paragraph and is payable by the debtor in respect of that period.

[(2) An amount falls within this sub-paragraph if it is—

    (a)   a guarantee payment under Part III of the Employment Rights Act 1996 (employee without work to do);

    (b)   any payment for time off under section 53 (time off to look for work or arrange training) or section 56 (time off for ante-natal care) of that Act or under section 169 of the Trade Union and Labour Relations (Consolidation) Act 1992 (time off for carrying out trade union duties etc);

    (c)   remuneration on suspension on medical grounds, or on maternity grounds, under Part VII of the Employment Rights Act 1996; or

    (d)   remuneration under a protective award under section 189 of the Trade Union and Labour Relations (Consolidation) Act 1992 (redundancy dismissal with compensation).]

Notes

Para 13

Sums payable by way of redundancy pay or compensation for unfair dismissal are not ' wages or salary ' and are therefore not preferential debts: *Re Allders Department Stores Ltd* [2005] All ER 231 and see notes to IA 1986 Sch B1 para 99.

1.737

14

(1) This paragraph relates to a case in which a person's employment has been terminated by or in consequence of his employer going into

liquidation or being adjudged bankrupt or (his employer being a company not in liquidation) by or in consequence of—

(a)   a receiver being appointed as mentioned in section 40 of this Act (debenture-holders secured by floating charge), or

(b)   the appointment of a receiver under section 53(6) or 54(5) of this Act (Scottish company with property subject to floating charge), or

(c)   the taking of possession by debenture-holders (so secured), as mentioned in section 196 of the Companies Act.

(2) For the purposes of paragraphs 9 to 12, holiday remuneration is deemed to have accrued to that person in respect of any period of employment if, by virtue of his contract of employment or of any enactment that remuneration would have accrued in respect of that period if his employment had continued until he became entitled to be allowed the holiday.

(3) The reference in sub-paragraph (2) to any enactment includes an order or direction made under an enactment.

15

Without prejudice to paragraphs 13 and 14—

(a)   any remuneration payable by the debtor to a person in respect of a period of holiday or of absence from work through sickness or other good cause is deemed to be wages or (as the case may be) salary in respect of services rendered to the debtor in that period, and

(b)   references here and in those paragraphs to remuneration in respect of a period of holiday include any sums which, if they had been paid, would have been treated for the purposes of the enactments to social security as earnings in respect of that period.

Category 6: Levies on coal and steel production

1.738

15A

Any sums due at the relevant date from the debtor in respect of—

(a)   the levies on the production of coal and steel referred to in Articles 49 and 50 of the E.C.S.C. Treaty, or

(b)   any surcharge for delay provided for in Article 50(3) of that Treaty and Article 6 of Decision 3/52 of the High Authority of the Coal and Steel Community.]

Orders

1.739

16

An order under paragraph 9 or 12—

(a)   may contain such transitional provisions as may appear to the Secretary of State necessary or expedient;

(b)   shall be made by statutory instrument subject to annulment in pursuance of a resolution of either House of Parliament.

SCHEDULE 7
Insolvency Practitioners Tribunal
Section 396

Panels of members

1.740

1

(1) The Secretary of State shall draw up and from time to time revise—
  (a)   a panel of persons who
    [(i)   have a 7 year general qualification, within the meaning of section 71 of the Courts and Legal Services Act 1990;
    (ii)   are advocates or solicitors in Scotland of at least 7 years' standing,]
    and are nominated for the purpose by the Lord Chancellor or the Lord President of the Court of Session, and
  (b)   a panel of persons who are experienced in insolvency matters;
and the members of the Tribunal shall be selected from those panels in accordance with this Schedule.

(2) The power to revise the panels includes power to terminate a person's membership of either of them, and is accordingly to that extent subject to [section 7 of the Tribunals and Inquiries Act 1992] (which makes it necessary to obtain the concurrence of the Lord Chancellor and the Lord President of the Court of Session to dismissals in certain cases).

Remuneration of members

1.741

2

The Secretary of State may out of money provided by Parliament pay to members of the Tribunal such remuneration as he may with the approval of the Treasury determine; and such expenses of the Tribunal as the Secretary of State and the Treasury may approve shall be defrayed by the Secretary of State out of money so provided.

Sittings of Tribunal

1.742

3

(1) For the purposes of carrying out their functions in relation to any cases referred to them, the Tribunal may sit either as a single tribunal or in two or more divisions.

(2) The functions of the Tribunal in relation to any case referred to them shall be exercised by three members consisting of—
  (a)   a chairman selected by the Secretary of State from the panel drawn up under paragraph 1(1)(a) above, and
  (b)   two other members selected by the Secretary of State from the panel drawn up under paragraph 1(1)(b).

Procedure of Tribunal

1.743

4

(1) Any investigation by the Tribunal shall be so conducted as to afford a reasonable opportunity for representations to be made to the Tribunal by or on behalf of the person whose case is the subject of the investigation.

(2) For the purposes of any such investigation, the Tribunal—
  (a) may by summons require any person to attend, at such time and place as is specified in the summons, to give evidence or to produce any books, papers and other records in his possession or under his control which the Tribunal consider it necessary for the purposes of the investigation to examine, and
  (b) may take evidence on oath, and for the purpose administer oaths, or may, instead of administering an oath, require the person examined to make and subscribe a declaration of the truth of the matter respecting which he is examined;

but no person shall be required, in obedience to such a summons, to go more than ten miles from his place of residence, unless the necessary expenses of his attendance are paid or tendered to him.

(3) Every person who—
  (a) without reasonable excuse fails to attend in obedience to a summons issued under this paragraph, or refuses to give evidence, or
  (b) intentionally alters, suppresses, conceals or destroys or refuses to produce any document which he may be required to produce for the purpose of an investigation by the Tribunal,

is liable to a fine.

(4) Subject to the provisions of this paragraph, the Secretary of State may make rules for regulating the procedure on any investigation by the Tribunal.

(5) In their application to Scotland, sub-paragraphs (2) and (3) above have effect as if for any reference to a summons there were substituted a reference to a notice in writing.

SCHEDULE 8
Provisions Capable of Inclusion in Company Insolvency Rules
Section 411

Courts

1.744

1

Provision for supplementing, in relation to the insolvency or winding up of companies, any provision made by or under section 117 of this Act (jurisdiction in relation to winding up).

2

[(1)] Provision for regulating the practice and procedure of any court exercising jurisdiction for the purposes of Parts I to VII of this Act or the Companies Act so far as relating to, and to matters connected with or arising out of, the insolvency or winding up of companies, being any provision that could be made by rules of court.

[(2) Rules made by virtue of this paragraph about the consequence of failure to comply with practice or procedure may, in particular, include provision about the termination of administration.]

Notices, etc

1.745

3

Provision requiring notice of any proceedings in connection with or arising out of the insolvency or winding up of a company to be given or published in the manner prescribed by the rules.

4

Provision with respect to the form, manner of serving, contents and proof of any petition, application, order, notice, statement or other document required to be presented, made, given, published or prepared under any enactment or subordinate legislation relating to, or to matters connected with or arising out of, the insolvency or winding up of companies.

5

Provisions specifying the persons to whom any notice is to be given.

Registration of voluntary arrangements

1.746

6

Provision for the registration of voluntary arrangements approved under Part I of this Act, including provision for the keeping and inspection of a register.

Provisional liquidator

1.747

7

Provision as to the manner in which a provisional liquidator appointed under section 135 is to carry out his functions.

Conduct of insolvency

1.748

8

Provision with respect to the certification of any person as, and as to the proof that a person is, the liquidator, administrator or administrative receiver of a company.

9

The following provision with respect to meetings of a company's creditors, contributories or members—

(a) provision as to the manner of summoning a meeting (including provision as to how any power to require a meeting is to be exercised, provision as to the manner of determining the value of any debt or contribution for the purposes of any such power and provision making the exercise of any such power subject to the deposit of a sum sufficient to cover the expenses likely to be incurred in summoning and holding a meeting);

(b) provision specifying the time and place at which a meeting may be held and the period of notice required for a meeting;

(c) provision as to the procedure to be followed at a meeting (including the manner in which decisions may be reached by a meeting and the manner in which the value of any vote at a meeting is to be determined);

(d) provision for requiring a person who is or has been an officer of the company to attend a meeting;

(e) provision creating, in the prescribed circumstances, a presumption that a meeting has been duly summoned and held;

(f) provision as to the manner of proving the decisions of a meeting.

10

(1) Provision as to the functions, membership and proceedings of a committee established under [section 49, 68, 101, 141 or 142 of, or paragraph 57 of Schedule B1 to, this Act].

(2) The following provision with respect to the establishment of a committee under section 101, 141 or 142 of this Act, that is to say—

(a) provision for resolving differences between a meeting of the company's creditors and a meeting of its contributories or members;

(b) provision authorising the establishment of the committee without a meeting of contributories in a case where a company is being wound up on grounds including its inability to pay its debts; and

(c) provision modifying the requirements of this Act with respect to the establishment of the committee in a case where a winding-up order has been made immediately upon the discharge of an administration order.

11

Provision as to the manner in which any requirement that may be imposed on a person under any of Parts I to VII of this Act by the official receiver, the liquidator, administrator or administrative receiver of a company or a special manager appointed under section 177 is to be so imposed.

12

Provision as to the debts that may be proved in a winding up, as to the manner and conditions of proving a debt and as to the manner and expenses of establishing the value of any debt or security.

13

Provision with respect to the manner of the distribution of the property of a company that is being wound up, including provision with respect to unclaimed funds and dividends.

14

Provision which, with or without modifications, applies in relation to the winding up of companies any enactment contained in Parts VIII to XI of this Act or in the Bankruptcy (Scotland) Act 1985.

[14A

Provision about the application of section 176A of this Act which may include, in particular—
    (a)   provision enabling a receiver to institute winding up proceedings;
    (b)   provision requiring a receiver to institute winding up proceedings.]

[Administration

1.749

14B

Provision which—
    (a)   applies in relation to administration, with or without modifications, a provision of Parts IV to VII of this Act, or
    (b)   serves a purpose in relation to administration similar to a purpose that may be served by the rules in relation to winding up by virtue of a provision of this Schedule.]

Financial provisions

1.750

15

Provision as to the amount, or manner of determining the amount, payable to the liquidator, administrator or administrative receiver of a company or a special manager appointed under section 177, by way of remuneration for the carrying out of functions in connection with or arising out of the insolvency or winding up of a company.

16

Provision with respect to the manner in which moneys received by the liquidator of a company in the course of carrying out his functions as such are to be invested or otherwise handled and with respect to the payment of interest on sums which, in pursuance of rules made by virtue of this paragraph, have been paid into the Insolvency Services Account.

[16A

Provision enabling the Secretary of State to set the rate of interest paid on sums which have been paid into the Insolvency Services Account.]

17

Provision as to the fees, costs, charges and other expenses that may be treated as the expenses of a winding up.

18

Provision as to the fees, costs, charges and other expenses that may be treated as properly incurred by the administrator or administrative receiver of a company.

19

Provision as to the fees, costs, charges and other expenses that may be incurred for any of the purposes of Part I of this Act or in the administration of any voluntary arrangement approved under that Part.

Information and records

1.751

20

Provision requiring registrars and other officers of courts having jurisdiction in England and Wales in relation to, or to matters connected with or arising out of, the insolvency or winding up of companies—
(a) to keep books and other records with respect to the exercise of that jurisdiction, and
(b) to make returns to the Secretary of State of the business of those courts.

21

Provision requiring a creditor, member or contributory, or such a committee as is mentioned in paragraph 10 above, to be supplied (on payment in prescribed cases of the prescribed fee) with such information and with copies of such documents as may be prescribed.

22

Provision as to the manner in which public examinations under sections 133 and 134 of this Act and proceedings under sections 236 and 237 are to be conducted, as to the circumstances in which records of such examinations or proceedings are to be made available to prescribed persons and as to the costs of such examinations and proceedings.

23

Provision imposing requirements with respect to—
(a) the preparation and keeping by the liquidator, administrator or administrative receiver of a company, or by the supervisor of a voluntary arrangement approved under Part I of this Act, of prescribed books, accounts and other records;
(b) the production of those books, accounts and records for inspection by prescribed persons;
(c) the auditing of accounts kept by the liquidator, administrator or administrative receiver of a company, or the supervisor of such a voluntary arrangement; and

(d)   the issue by the administrator or administrative receiver of a company of such a certificate as is mentioned in section 22(3)(b) of the Value Added Tax Act 1983 (refund of tax in cases of bad debts) and the supply of copies of the certificate to creditors of the company.

24

Provision requiring the person who is the supervisor of a voluntary arrangement approved under Part I, when it appears to him that the voluntary arrangement has been fully implemented and that nothing remains to be done by him under the arrangement—

(a)   to give notice of that fact to persons bound by the voluntary arrangement, and

(b)   to report to those persons on the carrying out of the functions conferred on the supervisor of the arrangement.

25

Provision as to the manner in which the liquidator of a company is to act in relation to the books, papers and other records of the company, including provision authorising their disposal.

26

Provision imposing requirements in connection with the carrying out of functions under section 7(3) of the Company Directors Disqualification Act 1986 (including, in particular, requirements with respect to the making of periodic returns).

General

1.752

27

Provision conferring power on the Secretary of State to make regulations with respect to so much of any matter that may be provided for in the rules as relates to the carrying out of the functions of the liquidator, administrator or administrative receiver of a company.

28

Provision conferring a discretion on the court.

29

Provision conferring power on the court to make orders for the purpose of securing compliance with obligations imposed by or under [section 47, 66, 131, 143(2) or 235 of, or paragraph 47 of Schedule B1 to, this Act] or section 7(4) of the Company Directors Disqualification Act 1986.

30

Provision making non-compliance with any of the rules a criminal offence.

31

Provision making different provision for different cases or descriptions of cases, including different provisions for different areas.

SCHEDULE 9
Provisions Capable of Inclusion in Individual Insolvency Rules
Section 412

Courts

1.753

1

Provision with respect to the arrangement and disposition of the business under Parts VIII to XI of this Act of courts having jurisdiction for the purpose of those Parts, including provision for the allocation of proceedings under those Parts to particular courts and for the transfer of such proceedings from one court to another.

2

Provision for enabling a registrar in bankruptcy of the High Court or a registrar of a county court having jurisdiction for the purposes of those Parts to exercise such of the jurisdiction conferred for those purposes on the High Court or, as the case may be, that county court as may be prescribed.

3

Provision for regulating the practice and procedure of any court exercising jurisdiction for the purposes of those Parts, being any provision that could be made by rules of court.

4

Provision conferring rights of audience, in courts exercising jurisdiction for the purposes of those Parts, on the official receiver and on solicitors.

Notices, etc

1.754

5

Provision requiring notice of any proceedings under Parts VIII to XI of this Act or of any matter relating to or arising out of a proposal under Part VIII or a bankruptcy to be given or published in the prescribed manner.

6

Provision with respect to the form, manner of serving, contents and proof of any petition, application, order, notice, statement or other document required to be presented, made, given, published or prepared under any enactment contained in Parts VIII to XI or subordinate legislation under those Parts or Part XV (including provision requiring prescribed matters to be verified by affidavit).

7

Provision specifying the persons to whom any notice under Parts VIII to XI is to be given.

Registration of voluntary arrangements

1.755

8

Provision for the registration of voluntary arrangements approved under Part VIII of this Act, including provision for the keeping and inspection of a register.

Official receiver acting on voluntary arrangement

1.756

8A

Provision about the official receiver acting as nominee or supervisor in relation to a voluntary arrangement under Part VIII of this Act, including—

(a)   provision requiring the official receiver to act in specified circumstances;

(b)   provision about remuneration;

(c)   provision prescribing terms or conditions to be treated as forming part of a voluntary arrangement in relation to which the official receiver acts as nominee or supervisor;

(d)   provision enabling those terms or conditions to be varied or excluded, in specified circumstances or subject to specified conditions, by express provision in an arrangement.]

Interim receiver

1.757

9

Provision as to the manner in which an interim receiver appointed under section 286 is to carry out his functions, including any such provision as is specified in relation to the trustee of a bankrupt's estate in paragraph 21 or 27 below.

Receiver or manager

1.758

10

Provision as to the manner in which the official receiver is to carry out his functions as receiver or manager of a bankrupt's estate under section 287, including any such provision as is specified in relation to the trustee of a bankrupt's estate in paragraph 21 or 27 below.

Administration of individual insolvency

1.759

11

Provision with respect to the certification of the appointment of any person as trustee of a bankrupt's estate and as to the proof of that appointment.

12

The following provision with respect to meetings of creditors—
 (a) provision as to the manner of summoning a meeting (including provision as to how any power to require a meeting is to be exercised, provision as to the manner of determining the value of any debt for the purposes of any such power and provision making the exercise of any such power subject to the deposit of a sum sufficient to cover the expenses likely to be incurred in summoning and holding a meeting);
 (b) provision specifying the time and place at which a meeting may be held and the period of notice required for a meeting;
 (c) provision as to the procedure to be followed at such a meeting (including the manner in which decisions may be reached by a meeting and the manner in which the value of any vote at a meeting is to be determined);
 (d) provision for requiring a bankrupt or debtor to attend a meeting;
 (e) provision creating, in the prescribed circumstances, a presumption that a meeting has been duly summoned and held; and
 (f) provision as to the manner of proving the decisions of a meeting.

13

Provision as to the functions, membership and proceedings of a creditors' committee established under section 301.

14

Provision as to the manner in which any requirement that may be imposed on a person under Parts VIII to XI of this Act by the official receiver, the trustee of a bankrupt's estate or a special manager appointed under section 370 is to be so imposed and, in the case of any requirement imposed under section 305(3) (information etc to be given by the trustee to the official receiver), provision conferring power on the court to make orders for the purpose of securing compliance with that requirement.

15

Provision as to the manner in which any requirement imposed by virtue of section 310(3) (compliance with income payments order) is to take effect.

16

Provision as to the terms and conditions that may be included in a charge under section 313 (dwelling house forming part of bankrupt's estate).

17

Provision as to the debts that may be proved in any bankruptcy, as to the manner and conditions of proving a debt and as to the manner and expenses of establishing the value of any debt or security.

18

Provision with respect to the manner of the distribution of a bankrupt's estate, including provision with respect to unclaimed funds and dividends.

19

Provision modifying the application of Parts VIII to XI of this Act in relation to a debtor or bankrupt who has died.

Financial provisions

1.760

20

Provision as to the amount, or manner of determining the amount, payable to an interim receiver, the trustee of a bankrupt's estate or a special manager appointed under section 370 by way of remuneration for the performance of functions in connection with or arising out of the bankruptcy of any person.

21

Provision with respect to the manner in which moneys received by the trustee of a bankrupt's estate in the course of carrying out his functions as such are to be [invested or otherwise handled and with respect to the payment of interest on sums which, in pursuance of rules made by virtue of this paragraph, have been paid into the Insolvency Services Account].

[21A

Provision enabling the Secretary of State to set the rate of interest paid on sums which have been paid into the Insolvency Services Account.]

22

Provision as to the fees, costs, charges and other expenses that may be treated as the expenses of a bankruptcy.

23

Provision as to the fees, costs, charges and other expenses that may be incurred for any of the purposes of Part VIII of this Act or in the administration of any voluntary arrangement approved under that Part.

Information and records

1.761

24

Provision requiring registrars and other officers of courts having juris-diction for the purposes of Parts VIII to XI—

(a)   to keep books and other records with respect to the exercise of that jurisdiction and of jurisdiction under the Deeds of Arrangement Act 1914, and

(b)   to make returns to the Secretary of State of the business of those courts.

25

Provision requiring a creditor or a committee established under section 301 to be supplied (on payment in prescribed cases of the prescribed fee) with such information and with copies of such documents as may be prescribed.

26

Provision as to the manner in which public examinations under section 290 and proceedings under sections 366 to 368 are to be conducted, as to the circumstances in which records of such examinations and proceedings are to be made available to prescribed persons and as to the costs of such examinations and proceedings.

27

Provision imposing requirements with respect to—

(a)   the preparation and keeping by the trustee of a bankrupt's estate, or the supervisor of a voluntary arrangement approved under Part VIII, of prescribed books, accounts and other records;

(b)   the production of those books, accounts and records for inspection by prescribed persons; and

(c)   the auditing of accounts kept by the trustee of a bankrupt's estate or the supervisor of such a voluntary arrangement.

28

Provision requiring the person who is the supervisor of a voluntary arrangement approved under Part VIII, when it appears to him that the voluntary arrangement has been fully implemented and that nothing remains to be done by him under it—

(a)   to give notice of that fact to persons bound by the voluntary arrangement, and

(b)   to report to those persons on the carrying out of the functions conferred on the supervisor of it.

29

Provision as to the manner in which the trustee of a bankrupt's estate is to act in relation to the books, papers and other records of the bankrupt, including provision authorising their disposal.

Bankruptcy restrictions orders and undertakings

1.762

29A

Provision about bankruptcy restrictions orders, interim orders and undertakings, including—

(a)   provision about evidence;

(b) provision enabling the amalgamation of the register mentioned in paragraph 12 of Schedule 4A with another register;

(c) provision enabling inspection of that register by the public.]

General

1.763

30

Provision conferring power on the Secretary of State to make regulations with respect to so much of any matter that may be provided for in the rules as relates to the carrying out of the functions of an interim receiver appointed under section 286, of the official receiver while acting as a receiver or manager under section 287 or of a trustee of a bankrupt's estate.

31

Provision conferring a discretion on the court.

32

Provision making non-compliance with any of the rules a criminal offence.

33

Provision making different provision for different cases, including different provision for different areas.

SCHEDULE 10
Punishment of Offences under this Act

Section 430

1.764

< ... >

Section (Section of Act creating offence)	General nature of offence	Mode of prosecution	Punish-ment	Daily default fine (where applicable)
[6A(1)	False representation or fraud for purpose of obtaining members' or creditors' approval of proposed voluntary arrangement.	1 On indictment	7 years or a fine, or both.	

Section (Section of Act creating offence)	General nature of offence	Mode of prosecution	Punishment	Daily default fine (where applicable)
		2 Summary	6 months or the statutory maximum, or both.]	
12(2)	...	...	...	
15(8)	...	...	...	...
18(5)	...	...	...	...
21(3)	...	...	...	...
22(6)	...	...	...	
		...	...	...
23(3)	...	...	...	...
24(7)	...	...	...	...
27(6)	...	...	...	< ... >
30	Body corporate acting as receiver.	1 On indictment	A fine.	
		2 Summary	The statutory maximum.	
31	... Bankrupt acting as receiver or manager.	1 On indictment	2 years or a fine, or both.	
		2 Summary	6 months or the statutory maximum, or both.	
38(5)	Receiver failing to deliver accounts to registrar.	Summary	One-fifth of the statutory maximum.	One-fiftieth of the statutory maximum.
39(2)	Company and others failing to state in correspondence that receiver appointed.	Summary	One-fifth of the statutory maximum.	
43(6)	Administrative receiver failing to file office copy of order permitting disposal of charged property.	Summary	One-fifth of the statutory maximum.	One-fiftieth of the statutory maximum.

Section (Section of Act creating offence)	General nature of offence	Mode of prosecution	Punishment	Daily default fine (where applicable)
45(5)	Administrative receiver failing to file notice of vacation of office.	Summary	One-fifth of the statutory maximum.	One-fiftieth of the statutory maximum.
46(4)	Administrative receiver failing to give notice of his appointment.	Summary	One-fifth of the statutory maximum.	One-fiftieth of the statutory maximum.
47(6)	Failure to comply with provisions relating to statement of affairs, where administrative receiver appointed.	1 On indictment	A fine.	
		2 Summary	The statutory maximum.	One-tenth of the statutory maximum.
48(8)	Administrative receiver failing to comply with requirements as to his report.	Summary	One-fifth of the statutory maximum.	One-fiftieth of the statutory maximum.
51(4)	Body corporate or Scottish firm acting as receiver.	1 On indictment	A fine.	
		2 Summary	The statutory maximum.	
51(5)	Undischarged bankrupt acting as receiver (Scotland).	1 On indictment	2 years or a fine, or both.	
		2 Summary	6 months or the statutory maximum, or both.	
53(2)	Failing to deliver to registrar copy of instrument of appointment of receiver.	Summary	One-fifth of the statutory maximum.	*One-fiftieth of the statutory maximum.*
54(3)	Failing to deliver to registrar the court's interlocutor appointing receiver.	Summary	One-fifth of the statutory maximum.	*One-fiftieth of the statutory maximum.*

Section (Section of Act creating offence)	General nature of offence	Mode of prosecution	Punish-ment	Daily default fine (where applicable)
61(7)	Receiver failing to send to registrar certified copy of court order authorising disposal of charged property.	Summary	One-fifth of the statutory maximum.	One-fiftieth of the statutory maximum.
62(5)	Failing to give notice to registrar of cessation or removal of receiver.	Summary	One-fifth of the statutory maximum.	*One-fiftieth of the statutory maximum.*
64(2)	Company and others failing to state on correspondence etc that receiver appointed.	Summary	One-fifth of the statutory maximum.	
65(4)	Receiver failing to send or publish notice of his appointment.	Summary	One-fifth of the statutory maximum.	One-fiftieth of the statutory maximum.
66(6)	Failing to comply with provisions concerning statement of affairs, where receiver appointed.	1 On indictment	A fine.	
		2 Summary	The statutory maximum.	One-tenth of the statutory maximum.
67(8)	Receiver failing to comply with requirements as to his report.	Summary	One-fifth of the statutory maximum.	One-fiftieth of the statutory maximum.
85(2)	Company failing to give notice in Gazette of resolution for voluntary winding up.	Summary	One-fifth of the statutory maximum.	One-fiftieth of the statutory maximum.

Section (Section of Act creating offence)	General nature of offence	Mode of prosecution	Punishment	Daily default fine (where applicable)
89(4)	Director making statutory declaration of company's solvency without reasonable grounds for his opinion.	1 On indictment	2 years or a fine, or both.	
		2 Summary	6 months or the statutory maximum, or both.	
89(6)	Declaration under section 89 not delivered to registrar within prescribed time.	Summary	One-fifth of the statutory maximum.	One-fiftieth of the statutory maximum.
93(3)	Liquidator failing to summon general meeting of company at each year's end.	Summary	One-fifth of the statutory maximum.	
94(4)	Liquidator failing to send to registrar a copy of account of winding up and return of final meeting.	Summary	One-fifth of the statutory maximum.	One-fiftieth of the statutory maximum.
94(6)	Liquidator failing to call final meeting.	Summary	One-fifth of the statutory maximum.	
95(8)	Liquidator failing to comply with s 95, where company insolvent.	Summary	The statutory maximum.	
98(6)	Company failing to comply with s 98 in respect of summoning and giving notice of creditors' meeting.	1 On indictment	A fine.	
		2 Summary	The statutory maximum.	

Section (Section of Act creating offence)	General nature of offence	Mode of prosecution	Punish-ment	Daily default fine (where applicable)
99(3)	Directors failing to attend and lay statement in prescribed form before creditors' meeting.	1 On indictment	A fine.	
		2 Summary	The statutory maximum.	
105(3)	Liquidator failing to summon company general meeting and creditors' meeting at each year's end.	Summary	One-fifth of the statutory maximum.	
106(4)	Liquidator failing to send to registrar account of winding up and return of final meetings.	Summary	One-fifth of the statutory maximum.	One-fiftieth of the statutory maximum.
106(6)	Liquidator failing to call final meeting of company or creditors.	Summary	One-fifth of the statutory maximum.	
109(2)	Liquidator failing to publish notice of his appointment.	Summary	One-fifth of the statutory maximum.	One-fiftieth of the statutory maximum.
114(4)	Directors exercising powers in breach of s 114, where no liquidator.	Summary	The statutory maximum.	
131(7)	Failing to comply with requirements as to statement of affairs, where liquidator appointed.	1 On indictment	A fine.	
		2. Summary	The statutory maximum.	One-tenth of the statutory maximum.
164	Giving, offering etc corrupt inducement affecting appointment of liquidator.	1 On indictment	A fine.	

Section (Section of Act creating offence)	General nature of offence	Mode of prosecution	Punish- ment	Daily default fine (where applicable)
		2 Summary	The statutory maximum.	
166(7)	Liquidator failing to comply with requirements of s 166 in creditors' voluntary winding up.	Summary	The statutory maximum.	
188(2)	Default in compliance with s 188 as to notification that company being wound up.	Summary	One-fifth of the statutory maximum.	
192(2)	Liquidator failing to notify registrar as to progress of winding up.	Summary	One-fifth of the statutory maximum.	One-fiftieth of the statutory maximum.
201(4)	Failing to deliver to registrar office copy of court order deferring dissolution.	Summary	One-fifth of the statutory maximum.	One-fiftieth of the statutory maximum.
203(6)	Failing to deliver to registrar copy of directions or result of appeal under s 203.	Summary	One-fifth of the statutory maximum.	One-fiftieth of the statutory maximum.
204(7)	Liquidator failing to deliver to registrar copy of court order for early dissolution.	Summary	One-fifth of the statutory maximum.	One-fiftieth of the statutory maximum.
204(8)	Failing to deliver to registrar copy of court order deferring early dissolution.	Summary	One-fifth of the statutory maximum.	One-fiftieth of the statutory maximum.
205(7)	Failing to deliver to registrar copy of Secretary of State's directions or court order deferring dissolution.	Summary	One-fifth of the statutory maximum.	One-fiftieth of the statutory maximum.

Section (Section of Act creating offence)	General nature of offence	Mode of prosecution	Punish- ment	Daily default fine (where applicable)
206(1)	Fraud etc in anticipation of winding up.	1 On indictment	7 years or a fine, or both.	
		2 Summary	6 months or the statutory maximum, or both.	
206(2)	Privity to fraud in anticipation of winding up; fraud, or privity to fraud, after commencement of winding up.	1 On indictment	7 years or a fine, or both.	
		2 Summary	6 months or the statutory maximum, or both.	
206(5)	Knowingly taking in pawn or pledge, or otherwise receiving, company property.	1 On indictment	7 years or a fine, or both.	
		2 Summary	6 months or the statutory maximum, or both.	
207	Officer of company entering into transaction in fraud of company's creditors.	1 On indictment	2 years or a fine, or both.	
		2 Summary	6 months or the statutory maximum, or both.	
208	Officer of company misconducting himself in course of winding up.	1 On indictment	7 years or a fine, or both.	

Section (Section of Act creating offence)	General nature of offence	Mode of prosecution	Punish-ment	Daily default fine (where applicable)
		2 Summary	6 months or the statutory maximum, or both.	
209	Officer or contributory destroying, falsifying, etc company's books.	1 On indictment	7 years or a fine, or both.	
		2 Summary	6 months or the statutory maximum, or both.	
210	Officer of company making material omission from statement relating to company's affairs.	1 On indictment	7 years or a fine, or both.	
		2 Summary	6 months or the statutory maximum, or both.	
211	False representation or fraud for purpose of obtaining creditors' consent to an agreement in connection with winding up.	1 On indictment	7 years or a fine, or both.	
		2 Summary	6 months or the statutory maximum, or both.	
216(4)	Contravening restrictions on re-use of name of company in insolvent liquidation.	1 On indictment	2 years or a fine, or both.	

743

Section (Section of Act creating offence)	General nature of offence	Mode of prosecution	Punish-ment	Daily default fine (where applicable)
		2 Summary	6 months or the statutory maximum, or both.	
235(5)	Failing to co-operate with office-holder.	1 On indictment.	A fine.	
		2 Summary	The statutory maximum.	One-tenth of the statutory maximum.
[262A(1)	False representation or fraud for purpose of obtaining creditors' approval of proposed voluntary arrangement.	1 On indictment	7 years or a fine, or both.	
		2 Summary	6 months or the statutory maximum, or both.]	
353(1)	Bankrupt failing to disclose property or disposals to official receiver or trustee.	1 On indictment	7 years or a fine, or both.	
		2 Summary	6 months or the statutory maximum, or both.	
354(1)	Bankrupt failing to deliver property to, or concealing property from, official receiver or trustee.	1 On indictment	7 years or a fine, or both.	
		2 Summary	6 months or the statutory maximum, or both.	

Section (Section of Act creating offence)	General nature of offence	Mode of prosecution	Punish-ment	Daily default fine (where applicable)
354(2)	Bankrupt removing property which he is required to deliver to official receiver or trustee.	1 On indictment	7 years or a fine, or both.	
		2 Summary	6 months or the statutory maximum, or both.	
354(3)	Bankrupt failing to account for loss of substantial part of property.	1 On indictment	2 years or a fine, or both.	
		2 Summary	6 months or the statutory maximum, or both.	
355(1)	Bankrupt failing to deliver books, papers and records to official receiver or trustee.	1 On indictment	7 years or a fine, or both.	
		2 Summary	6 months or the statutory maximum, or both.	
355(2)	Bankrupt concealing, destroying etc books, papers or records, or making false entries in them.	1 On indictment	7 years or a fine, or both.	
		2 Summary	6 months or the statutory maximum, or both.	
355(3)	Bankrupt disposing of, or altering, books, papers or records relating to his estate or affairs.	1 On indictment	7 years or a fine, or both.	

Section (Section of Act creating offence)	General nature of offence	Mode of prosecution	Punish- ment	Daily default fine (where applicable)
		2 Summary	6 months or the statutory maximum, or both.	
356(1)	Bankrupt making material omission in statement relating to his affairs.	1 On indictment	7 years or a fine, or both.	
		2 Summary	6 months or the statutory maximum, or both.	
356(2)	Bankrupt making false statement, or failing to inform trustee, where false debt proved.	1 On indictment	7 years or a fine, or both.	
		2 Summary	6 months or the statutory maximum, or both.	
357	Bankrupt fraudulently disposing of property.	1 On indictment	2 years or a fine, or both.	
		2 Summary	6 months or the statutory maximum, or both.	
358	Bankrupt absconding with property he is required to deliver to official receiver or trustee.	1 On indictment	2 years or a fine, or both.	
		2 Summary	6 months or the statutory maximum, or both.	

Section (Section of Act creating offence)	General nature of offence	Mode of prosecution	Punish-ment	Daily default fine (where applicable)
359(1)	Bankrupt disposing of property obtained on credit and not paid for.	1 On indictment	7 years or a fine, or both.	
		2 Summary	6 months or the statutory maximum, or both.	
359(2)	Obtaining property in respect of which money is owed by a bankrupt.	1 On indictment	7 years or a fine, or both.	
		2 Summary	6 months or the statutory maximum, or both.	
360(1)	Bankrupt obtaining credit or engaging in business without disclosing his status or name in which he was made bankrupt.	1 On indictment	2 years or a fine, or both.	
		2 Summary	6 months or the statutory maximum, or both.	
360(3)	Person made bankrupt in Scotland or Northern Ireland obtaining credit, etc in England and Wales.	1 On indictment	2 years or a fine, or both.	
		2 Summary	6 months or the statutory maximum, or both.	
361(1)	...	...	...	
		...	...	
362	...	...	...	
		...	...	

Section (Section of Act creating offence)	General nature of offence	Mode of prosecution	Punish-ment	Daily default fine (where applicable)
389	Acting as insolvency practitioner when not qualified.	1 On indictment	2 years or a fine, or both.	
		2 Summary	6 months or the statutory maximum or both.	
429(5)	Contravening s 429 in respect of disabilities imposed by county court on revocation of administration order.	1 On indictment	2 years or a fine, or both.	
		2 Summary	6 months or the statutory maximum, or both.	
[Sch A1, para 9(2)	Directors failing to notify nominee of beginning of moratorium.	1 On indictment	2 years or a fine, or both.	
		2 Summary	6 months or the statutory maximum, or both.	
Sch A1, para 10(3)	Nominee failing to advertise or notify beginning of moratorium.	Summary	One-fifth of the statutory maximum.	
Sch A1, para 11(2)	Nominee failing to advertise or notify end of moratorium.	Summary	One-fifth of the statutory maximum.	
Sch A1, para 16(2)	Company and officers failing to state in correspondence etc that moratorium in force.	Summary	One-fifth of the statutory maximum.	

Section (Section of Act creating offence)	General nature of offence	Mode of prosecution	Punish-ment	Daily default fine (where applicable)
Sch A1, para 17(3)(a)	Company obtaining credit without disclosing existence of moratorium.	1 On indictment	A fine.	
		2 Summary	The statutory maximum.	
Sch A1, para 17(3)(b)	Obtaining credit for company without disclosing existence of moratorium.	1 On indictment	2 years or a fine, or both.	
		2 Summary	6 months or the statutory maximum, or both.	
Sch A1, para 18(3)(a)	Company disposing of property otherwise than in ordinary way of business.	1 On indictment	A fine.	
		2 Summary	The statutory maximum.	
Sch A1, para 18(3)(b)	Authorising or permitting disposal of company property.	1 On indictment	2 years or a fine, or both.	
		2 Summary	6 months or the statutory maximum, or both.	
Sch A1, para 19(3)(a)	Company making payments in respect of liabilities existing before beginning of moratorium.	1 On indictment	A fine.	
		2 Summary	The statutory maximum.	
Sch A1, para 19(3)(b)	Authorising or permitting such a payment.	1 On indictment	2 years or a fine, or both.	

Section (Section of Act creating offence)	General nature of offence	Mode of prosecution	Punish-ment	Daily default fine (where applicable)
		2 Summary	6 months or the statutory maximum, or both.	
Sch A1, para 20(9)	Directors failing to send to registrar office copy of court order permitting disposal of charged property.	Summary	One-fifth of the statutory maximum.	
Sch A1, para 22(1)	Company disposing of charged property.	1 On indictment	A fine.	
		2 Summary	The statutory maximum.	
Sch A1, para 22(2)	Authorising or permitting such a disposal.	1 On indictment	2 years or a fine, or both.	
		2 Summary	6 months or the statutory maximum, or both.	
Sch A1, para 23(1)(a)	Company entering into market contract, etc	1 On indictment	A fine.	
		2 Summary	The statutory maximum.	
Sch A1, para 23(1)(b)	Authorising or permitting company to do so.	1 On indictment	2 years or a fine, or both.	
		2 Summary	6 months or the statutory maximum, or both.	
Sch A1, para 25(6)	Nominee failing to give notice of withdrawal of consent to act.	Summary	One-fifth of the statutory maximum.	
Sch A1, para 34(3)	Nominee failing to give notice of extension of moratorium.	Summary	One-fifth of the statutory maximum.	

Section (Section of Act creating offence)	General nature of offence	Mode of prosecution	Punish-ment	Daily default fine (where applicable)
Sch A1, para 41(2)	Fraud or privity to fraud in anticipation of moratorium.	1 On indictment	7 years or a fine, or both.	
		2 Summary	6 months or the statutory maximum, or both.	
Sch A1, para 41(3)	Fraud or privity to fraud during moratorium.	1 On indictment	7 years or a fine, or both.	
		2 Summary	6 months or the statutory maximum, or both.	
Sch A1, para 41(7)	Knowingly taking in pawn or pledge, or otherwise receiving, company property.	1 On indictment	7 years or a fine, or both.	
		2 Summary	6 months or the statutory maximum, or both.	
Sch A1, para 42(1)	False representation or fraud for purpose of obtaining or extending moratorium.	1 On indictment	7 years or a fine, or both.	
		2 Summary	6 months or the statutory maximum, or both.]	
[Sch B1, para 18(7)	Making false statement in statutory declaration where administrator appointed by holder of floating charge.	1 On indictment	2 years, or a fine or both.	

Section (Section of Act creating offence)	General nature of offence	Mode of prosecution	Punish-ment	Daily default fine (where applicable)
		2 Summary	6 months, or the statutory maximum or both.	
Sch B1, para 20	Holder of floating charge failing to notify administrator or others of commencement of appointment.	1 On indictment	2 years, or a fine or both.	
		2 Summary	6 months, or the statutory maximum or both.	One-tenth of the statutory maximum.
Sch B1, para 27(4)	Making false statement in statutory declaration where appointment of administrator proposed by company or directors.	1 On indictment	2 years, or a fine or both.	
		2 Summary	6 months, or the statutory maximum or both.	
Sch B1, para 29(7)	Making false statement in statutory declaration where administrator appointed by company or directors.	1 On indictment	2 years, or a fine or both.	
		2 Summary	6 months, or the statutory maximum or both.	
Sch B1, para 32	Company or directors failing to notify administrator or others of commencement of appointment.	1 On indictment	2 years, or a fine or both.	One-tenth of the statutory maximum.

Section (Section of Act creating offence)	General nature of offence	Mode of prosecution	Punish-ment	Daily default fine (where applicable)
		2 Summary	6 months, or the statutory maximum or both.	
Sch B1, para 45(2)	Administrator, company or officer failing to state in business document that administrator appointed.	Summary	One-fifth of the statutory maximum.	
Sch B1, para 46(9)	Administrator failing to give notice of his appointment.	Summary	One-fifth of the statutory maximum.	One-fiftieth of the statutory maximum.
Sch B1, para 48(4)	Failing to comply with provisions about statement of affairs where administrator appointed.	1 On indictment	A fine.	
		2 Summary	The statutory maximum.	One-tenth of the statutory maximum.
Sch B1, para 49(7)	Administrator failing to send out statement of his proposals.	Summary	One-fifth of the statutory maximum.	One-fiftieth of the statutory maximum.
Sch B1, para 51(5)	Administrator failing to arrange initial creditors' meeting.	Summary	One-fifth of the statutory maximum.	One-fiftieth of the statutory maximum.
Sch B1, para 53(3)	Administrator failing to report decision taken at initial creditors' meeting.	Summary	One-fifth of the statutory maximum.	One-fiftieth of the statutory maximum.
Sch B1, para 54(7)	Administrator failing to report decision taken at creditors' meeting summoned to consider revised proposal.	Summary	One-fifth of the statutory maximum.	One-fiftieth of the statutory maximum.
Sch B1, para 56(2)	Administrator failing to summon creditors' meeting.	Summary	One-fifth of the statutory maximum.	One-fiftieth of the statutory maximum.

753

Section (Section of Act creating offence)	General nature of offence	Mode of prosecution	Punishment	Daily default fine (where applicable)
Sch B1, para 71(6)	Administrator failing to file court order enabling disposal of charged property.	Summary	One-fifth of the statutory maximum.	One-fiftieth of the statutory maximum.
Sch B1, para 72(5)	Administrator failing to file court order enabling disposal of hire-purchase property.	Summary	One-fifth of the statutory maximum.	One-fiftieth of the statutory maximum.
Sch B1, para 77(3)	Administrator failing to notify Registrar of Companies of automatic end of administration.	Summary	One-fifth of the statutory maximum.	One-fiftieth of the statutory maximum.
Sch B1, para 78(6)	Administrator failing to give notice of extension by consent of term of office.	Summary	One-fifth of the statutory maximum.	One-fiftieth of the statutory maximum.
Sch B1, para 80(6)	Administrator failing to give notice of termination of administration where objective achieved.	Summary	One-fifth of the statutory maximum.	One-fiftieth of the statutory maximum.
Sch B1, para 84(9)	Administrator failing to comply with provisions where company moves to dissolution.	Summary	One-fifth of the statutory maximum.	One-fiftieth of the statutory maximum.
Sch B1, para 86(3)	Administrator failing to notify Registrar of Companies where court terminates administration.	Summary	One-fifth of the statutory maximum.	One-fiftieth of the statutory maximum.
Sch B1, para 89(3)	Administrator failing to give notice on ceasing to be qualified.	Summary	One-fifth of the statutory maximum.	One-fiftieth of the statutory maximum.]

Section (Section of Act creating offence)	General nature of offence	Mode of prosecution	Punishment	Daily default fine (where applicable)
Sch 7, para 4(3)	Failure to attend and give evidence to Insolvency Practitioners Tribunal; suppressing, concealing, etc relevant documents.	Summary	Level 3 on the standard scale within the meaning given by section 75 of the Criminal Justice Act 1982.	

SCHEDULE 11
Transitional Provisions and Savings

Section 437

Part I
Company Insolvency and Winding Up

Administration orders

1.765

1

(1) Where any right to appoint an administrative receiver of a company is conferred by any debentures or floating charge created before the appointed day, the conditions precedent to the exercise of that right are deemed to include the presentation of a petition applying for an administration order to be made in relation to the company.

(2) 'Administrative receiver' here has the meaning assigned by section 251.

Receivers and managers (England and Wales)

1.766

2

(1) In relation to any receiver or manager of a company's property who was appointed before the appointed day, the new law does not apply; and the relevant provisions of the former law continue to have effect.

(2) 'The new law' here means Chapter I of Part III, and Part VI, of this Act; and 'the former law' means the Companies Act and so much of this Act as replaces provisions of that Act (without the amendments in paragraphs 15 to 17 of Schedule 6 to the Insolvency Act 1985, or the

associated repeals made by that Act), and any provision of the Insolvency Act 1985 which was in force before the appointed day.

(3) This paragraph is without prejudice to the power conferred by this Act under which rules under section 411 may make transitional provision in connection with the coming into force of those rules; and such provision may apply those rules in relation to the receiver or manager of a company's property notwithstanding that he was appointed before the coming into force of the rules or section 411.

Receivers (Scotland)

1.767

3

(1) In relation to any receiver appointed under section 467 of the Companies Act before the appointed day, the new law does not apply and the relevant provisions of the former law continue to have effect.

(2) 'The new law' here means Chapter II of Part III, and Part VI, of this Act; and 'the former law' means the Companies Act and so much of this Act as replaces provisions of that Act (without the amendments in paragraphs 18 to 22 of Schedule 6 to the Insolvency Act 1985 or the associated repeals made by that Act), and any provision of the Insolvency Act 1985 which was in force before the appointed day.

(3) This paragraph is without prejudice to the power conferred by this Act under which rules under section 411 may make transitional provision in connection with the coming into force of those rules; and such provision may apply those rules in relation to a receiver appointed under section 467 notwithstanding that he was appointed before the coming into force of the rules or section 411.

Winding up already in progress

1.768

4

(1) In relation to any winding up which has commenced, or is treated as having commenced, before the appointed day, the new law does not apply, and the former law continues to have effect, subject to the following paragraphs.

(2) 'The new law' here means any provisions in the first Group of Parts of this Act which replace sections 66 to 87 and 89 to 105 of the Insolvency Act 1985; and 'the former law' means Parts XX and XXI of the Companies Act (without the amendments in paragraphs 23 to 52 of Schedule 6 to the Insolvency Act 1985, or the associated repeals made by that Act).

Statement of affairs

1.769

5

(1) Where a winding up by the court in England and Wales has commenced, or is treated as having commenced, before the appointed

day, the official receiver or (on appeal from a refusal by him) the court may, at any time on or after that day—

    (a)   release a person from an obligation imposed on him by or under section 528 of the Companies Act (statement of affairs), or

    (b)   extend the period specified in subsection (6) of that section.

(2) Accordingly, on and after the appointed day, section 528(6) has effect in relation to a winding up to which this paragraph applies with the omission of the words from 'or within' onwards.

Provisions relating to liquidator

1.770

6

(1) This paragraph applies as regards the liquidator in the case of a winding up by the court in England and Wales commenced, or treated as having commenced, before the appointed day.

(2) The official receiver may, at any time when he is liquidator of the company, apply to the Secretary of State for the appointment of a liquidator in his (the official receiver's) place; and on any such application the Secretary of State shall either make an appointment or decline to make one.

(3) Where immediately before the appointed day the liquidator of the company has not made an application under section 545 of the Companies Act (release of liquidators), then—

    (a)   except where the Secretary of State otherwise directs, sections 146(1) and (2) and 172(8) of this Act apply, and section 545 does not apply, in relation to any liquidator of that company who holds office on or at any time after the appointed day and is not the official receiver;

    (b)   section 146(3) applies in relation to the carrying out at any time after that day by any liquidator of the company of any of his functions; and

    (c)   a liquidator in relation to whom section 172(8) has effect by virtue of this paragraph has his release with effect from the time specified in section 174(4)(d) of this Act.

(4) Subsection (6) of section 174 of this Act has effect for the purposes of sub-paragraph (3)(c) above as it has for the purposes of that section, but as if the reference to section 212 were to section 631 of the Companies Act.

(5) The liquidator may employ a solicitor to assist him in the carrying out of his functions without the permission of the committee of inspection; but if he does so employ a solicitor he shall inform the committee of inspection that he has done so.

Winding up under supervision of the court

1.771

7

The repeals in Part II of Schedule 10 to the Insolvency Act 1985 of references (in the Companies Act and elsewhere) to a winding up under the supervision of the court do not affect the operation of the enactments in which the references are contained in relation to any case in which an order under section 606 of the Companies Act (power to order winding up under supervision) was made before the appointed day.

Saving for power to make rules

1.772

8

(1) Paragraphs 4 to 7 are without prejudice to the power conferred by this Act under which rules made under section 411 may make transitional provision in connection with the coming into force of those rules.

(2) Such provision may apply those rules in relation to a winding up notwithstanding that the winding up commenced, or is treated as having commenced, before the coming into force of the rules or section 411.

Setting aside of preferences and other transactions

1.773

9

(1) Where a provision in Part VI of this Act applies in relation to a winding up or in relation to a case in which an administration order has been made, a preference given, floating charge created or other transaction entered into before the appointed day shall not be set aside under that provision except to the extent that it could have been set aside under the law in force immediately before that day, assuming for this purpose that any relevant administration order had been a winding-up order.

(2) The references above to setting aside a preference, floating charge or other transaction include the making of an order which varies or reverses any effect of a preference, floating charge or other transaction.

Part II
Individual Insolvency

Bankruptcy (general)

1.774

10

(1) Subject to the following provisions of this Part of this Schedule, so much of this Act as replaces Part III of the Insolvency Act 1985 does not apply in relation to any case in which a petition in bankruptcy was presented, or a receiving order or adjudication in bankruptcy was made, before the appointed day.

(2) In relation to any such case as is mentioned above, the enactments specified in Schedule 8 to that Act, so far as they relate to bankruptcy, and those specified in Parts III and IV of Schedule 10 to that Act, so far as they so relate, have effect without the amendments and repeals specified in those Schedules.

(3) Where any subordinate legislation made under an enactment referred to in sub-paragraph (2) is in force immediately before the appointed day, that subordinate legislation continues to have effect on and after that day in relation to any such case as is mentioned in sub-paragraph (1).

11

(1) In relation to any such case as is mentioned in paragraph 10(1) the references in any enactment or subordinate legislation to a petition, order or other matter which is provided for under the Bankruptcy Act 1914 and corresponds to a petition, order or other matter provided for under provisions of this Act replacing Part III of the Insolvency Act 1985 continue on and after the appointed day to have effect as references to the petition, order or matter provided for by the Act of 1914; but otherwise those references have effect on and after that day as references to the petition, order or matter provided for by those provisions of this Act.

(2) Without prejudice to sub-paragraph (1), in determining for the purposes of section 279 of this Act (period of bankruptcy) or paragraph 13 below whether any person was an undischarged bankrupt at a time before the appointed day, an adjudication in bankruptcy and an annulment of a bankruptcy under the Act of 1914 are to be taken into account in the same way, respectively, as a bankruptcy order under the provisions of this Act replacing Part III of the Insolvency Act 1985 and the annulment under section 282 of this Act of such an order.

12

Transactions entered into before the appointed day have effect on and after that day as if references to acts of bankruptcy in the provisions for giving effect to those transactions continued to be references to acts of bankruptcy within the meaning of the Bankruptcy Act 1914, but as if such acts included failure to comply with a statutory demand served under section 268 of this Act.

Discharge from old bankruptcy

1.775

13

(1) Where a person—
    (a) was adjudged bankrupt before the appointed day or is adjudged bankrupt on or after that day on a petition presented before that day, and
    (b) that person was not an undischarged bankrupt at any time in the period of 15 years ending with the adjudication,
that person is deemed (if not previously discharged) to be discharged from his bankruptcy for the purposes of the Bankruptcy Act 1914 at the end of the discharge period.

(2) Subject to sub-paragraph (3) below, the discharge period for the purposes of this paragraph is—
    (a) in the case of a person adjudged bankrupt before the appointed day, the period of 3 years beginning with that day, and

(b)   in the case of a person who is adjudged bankrupt on or after that day on a petition presented before that day, the period of 3 years beginning with the date of the adjudication.

(3) Where the court exercising jurisdiction in relation to a bankruptcy to which this paragraph applies is satisfied, on the application of the official receiver, that the bankrupt has failed, or is failing, to comply with any of his obligations under the Bankruptcy Act 1914, any rules made under that Act or any such rules as are mentioned in paragraph 19(1) below, the court may order that the discharge period shall cease to run for such period, or until the fulfilment of such conditions (including a condition requiring the court to be satisfied as to any matter) as may be specified in the order.

Provisions relating to trustee

1.776

14

(1) This paragraph applies as regards the trustee in the case of a person adjudged bankrupt before the appointed day, or adjudged bankrupt on or after that day on a petition presented before that day.

(2) The official receiver may at any time when he is the trustee of the bankrupt's estate apply to the Secretary of State for the appointment of a person as trustee instead of the official receiver; and on any such application the Secretary of State shall either make an appointment or decline to make one.

(3) Where on the appointed day the trustee of a bankrupt's estate has not made an application under section 93 of the Bankruptcy Act 1914 (release of trustee), then—

(a)   except where the Secretary of State otherwise directs, sections 298(8), 304 and 331(1) to (3) of this Act apply, and section 93 of the Act of 1914 does not apply, in relation to any trustee of the bankrupt's estate who holds office on or at any time after the appointed day and is not the official receiver;

(b)   section 331(4) of this Act applies in relation to the carrying out at any time on or after the appointed day by the trustee of the bankrupt's estate of any of his functions; and

(c)   a trustee in relation to whom section 298(8) of this Act has effect by virtue of this paragraph has his release with effect from the time specified in section 299(3)(d).

(4) Subsection (5) of section 299 has effect for the purposes of sub-paragraph (3)(c) as it has for the purposes of that section.

(5) In the application of subsection (3) of section 331 in relation to a case by virtue of this paragraph, the reference in that subsection to section 330(1) has effect as a reference to section 67 of the Bankruptcy Act 1914.

(6) The trustee of the bankrupt's estate may employ a solicitor to assist him in the carrying out of his functions without the permission of the committee of inspection; but if he does so employ a solicitor, he shall inform the committee of inspection that he has done so.

Copyright

1.777

15

Where a person who is adjudged bankrupt on a petition presented on or after the appointed day is liable, by virtue of a transaction entered into before that day, to pay royalties or a share of the profits to any person in respect of any copyright or interest in copyright comprised in the bankrupt's estate, section 60 of the Bankruptcy Act 1914 (limitation on trustee's powers in relation to copyright) applies in relation to the trustee of that estate as it applies in relation to a trustee in bankruptcy under the Act of 1914.

Second bankruptcy

1.778

16

(1) Sections 334 and 335 of this Act apply with the following modifications where the earlier bankruptcy (within the meaning of section 334) is a bankruptcy in relation to which the Act of 1914 applies instead of the second Group of Parts in this Act, that is to say—
- (a) references to property vested in the existing trustee under section 307(3) of this Act have effect as references to such property vested in that trustee as was acquired by or devolved on the bankrupt after the commencement (within the meaning of the Act of 1914) of the earlier bankruptcy; and
- (b) references to an order under section 310 of this Act have effect as references to an order under section 51 of the Act of 1914.

(2) Section 39 of the Act of 1914 (second bankruptcy) does not apply where a person who is an undischarged bankrupt under that Act is adjudged bankrupt under this Act.

Setting aside of preferences and other transactions

1.779

17

(1) A preference given, assignment made or other transaction entered into before the appointed day shall not be set aside under any of sections 339 to 344 of this Act except to the extent that it could have been set aside under the law in force immediately before that day.

(2) References in sub-paragraph (1) to setting aside a preference, assignment or other transaction include the making of any order which varies or reverses any effect of a preference, assignment or other transaction.

Bankruptcy offences

1.780

18

(1) Where a bankruptcy order is made under this Act on or after the appointed day, a person is not guilty of an offence under Chapter VI of

Part IX in respect of anything done before that day; but, notwithstanding the repeal by the Insolvency Act 1985 of the Bankruptcy Act 1914, is guilty of an offence under the Act of 1914 in respect of anything done before the appointed day which would have been an offence under that Act if the making of the bankruptcy order had been the making of a receiving order under that Act.

(2) Subsection (5) of section 350 of this Act applies (instead of sections 157(2), 158(2), 161 and 165 of the Act of 1914) in relation to proceedings for an offence under that Act which are instituted (whether by virtue of sub-paragraph (1) or otherwise) after the appointed day.

Power to make rules

I.781

19

(1) The preceding provisions of this Part of this Schedule are without prejudice to the power conferred by this Act under which rules under section 412 may make transitional provision in connection with the coming into force of those rules; and such provision may apply those rules in relation to a bankruptcy notwithstanding that it arose from a petition presented before either the coming into force of the rules or the appointed day.

(2) Rules under section 412 may provide for such notices served before the appointed day as may be prescribed to be treated for the purposes of this Act as statutory demands served under section 268.

Part III
Transitional Effect of Part XVI

I.782

20

(1) A transaction entered into before the appointed day shall not be set aside under Part XVI of this Act except to the extent that it could have been set aside under the law in force immediately before that day.

(2) References above to setting aside a transaction include the making of any order which varies or reverses any effect of a transaction.

Part IV
Insolvency Practitioners

I.783

21

Where an individual began to act as an insolvency practitioner in relation to any person before the appointed day, nothing in section 390(2) or (3) prevents that individual from being qualified to act as an insolvency practitioner in relation to that person.

Part V
General Transitional Provisions and Savings

Interpretation for this Part

I.784

22

In this Part of this Schedule, 'the former enactments' means so much of the Companies Act as is repealed and replaced by this Act, the Insolvency Act 1985 and the other enactments repealed by this Act.

General saving for past acts and events

I.785

23

So far as anything done or treated as done under or for the purposes of any provision of the former enactments could have been done under or for the purposes of the corresponding provision of this Act, it is not invalidated by the repeal of that provision but has effect as if done under or for the purposes of the corresponding provision; and any order, regulation, rule or other instrument made or having effect under any provision of the former enactments shall, insofar as its effect is preserved by this paragraph, be treated for all purposes as made and having effect under the corresponding provision.

Periods of time

I.786

24

Where any period of time specified in a provision of the former enactments is current immediately before the appointed day, this Act has effect as if the corresponding provision had been in force when the period began to run; and (without prejudice to the foregoing) any period of time so specified and current is deemed for the purposes of this Act—
  (a)   to run from the date or event from which it was running immediately before the appointed day, and
  (b)   to expire (subject to any provision of this Act for its extension) whenever it would have expired if this Act had not been passed;
and any rights, priorities, liabilities, reliefs, obligations, requirements, powers, duties or exemptions dependent on the beginning, duration or end of such a period as above mentioned shall be under this Act as they were or would have been under the former enactments.

Internal cross-references in this Act

I.787

25

Where in any provision of this Act there is a reference to another such provision, and the first-mentioned provision operates, or is capable of operating, in relation to things done or omitted, or events occurring or not occurring, in the past (including in particular past acts of compliance with any enactment, failures of compliance, contraventions, offences and convictions of offences), the reference to the other provision is to be read as including a reference to the corresponding provision of the former enactments.

Punishment of offences

1.788

26

(1) Offences committed before the appointed day under any provision of the former enactments may, notwithstanding any repeal by this Act, be prosecuted and punished after that day as if this Act had not passed.

(2) A contravention of any provision of the former enactments committed before the appointed day shall not be visited with any severer punishment under or by virtue of this Act than would have been applicable under that provision at the time of the contravention; but where an offence for the continuance of which a penalty was provided has been committed under any provision of the former enactments, proceedings may be taken under this Act in respect of the continuance of the offence on and after the appointed day in the like manner as if the offence had been committed under the corresponding provision of this Act.

References elsewhere to the former enactments

1.789

27

(1) A reference in any enactment, instrument or document (whether express or implied, and in whatever phraseology) to a provision of the former enactments (including the corresponding provision of any yet earlier enactment) is to be read, where necessary to retain for the enactment, instrument or document the same force and effect as it would have had but for the passing of this Act, as, or as including, a reference to the corresponding provision by which it is replaced in this Act.

(2) The generality of the preceding sub-paragraph is not affected by any specific conversion of references made by this Act, nor by the inclusion in any provision of this Act of a reference (whether express or implied, and in whatever phraseology) to the provision of the former enactments corresponding to that provision, or to a provision of the former enactments which is replaced by a corresponding provision of this Act.

Saving for power to repeal provisions in section 51

1.790

28

The Secretary of State may by order in a statutory instrument repeal subsections (3) to (5) of section 51 of this Act and the entries in Schedule 10 relating to subsections (4) and (5) of that section.

Saving for Interpretation Act 1978 ss 16, 17

1.791

29

Nothing in this Schedule is to be taken as prejudicing sections 16 and 17 of the Interpretation Act 1978 (savings from, and effect of, repeals); and for the purposes of section 17(2) of that Act (construction of references to enactments repealed and replaced, etc), so much of section 18 of the Insolvency Act 1985 as is replaced by a provision of this Act is deemed to have been replaced by this Act and not by the Company Directors Disqualification Act 1986.

SCHEDULE 12
Enactments Repealed
Section 438

1.792

Chapter	Short title	Extent of repeal
1970 c 8	The Insolvency Services (Accounting and Investment) Act 1970	The whole Act.
1976 c 60	The Insolvency Act 1976	Section 3.
1985 c 6	The Companies Act 1985	In section 463(4), the words 'Subject to section 617'.
		Sections 467 to 485.
		In section 486, in the definition of 'company' the words 'other than in Chapter II of this Part'; and the definitions of 'instrument of appointment', 'prescribed', 'receiver' and 'register of charges'.
		Sections 488 to 650.
		Sections 659 to 664.
		Sections 665 to 674.
		Section 709(4).
		Section 710(4).
		Section 724.
		Schedule 16.
		In Schedule 24, the entries relating to section 467; all entries thereafter up to and including section 641(2); and the entry relating to section 710(4).
1985 c 65	The Insolvency Act 1985	Sections 1 to 11.
		Section 15.
		Section 17.
		Section 19.

		Sections 20 to 107.
		Section 108(1) and (3) to (7).
		Sections 109 to 211.
		Sections 212 to 214.
		Section 216.
		Section 217(1) to (3).
		Sections 221 to 234.
		In section 235, subsections (2) to (5).
		In section 236, subsections (3) to (5).
		In Schedule 1, paragraphs 1 to 4, and sub-paragraph (4) of paragraph 5.
		Schedules 3 to 5.
		In Schedule 6, paragraphs 5, 6, 9, 15 to 17, 20 to 22, 25 to 44 and 48 to 52.
		Schedule 7.
		In Schedule 9, paragraphs 1 and 4 to 24.
		Schedule 10.
1985 c 66	The Bankruptcy (Scotland) Act 1985	In Schedule 7, paragraphs 19 to 22.
1986 c 44	The Gas Act 1986	In Schedule 7, paragraph 31.

SCHEDULE 13
Consequential Amendments of Companies Act 1985
Section 439(1)

Part I
Internal and Other Section References Amended or Re-amended

1.793

< ... >

1.794

Part II
Amendment of Part XXVI (Interpretation)

...

SCHEDULE 14
Consequential Amendments of other Enactments
Section 439(2)

1.795

...

Insolvency Rules 1986

(SI 1986/1925)

Made: 10 November 1986.

Authority: Insolvency Act 1986, ss 411, 412.

Commencement: 29 December 1986.
Arrangement of Rules

Chapter 5
Proceedings On a Proposal Made By the Directors,
Or By the Administrator, Or By the Liquidator

Chapter 6
General

Chapter 7
EC Regulation—Conversion of Voluntary
Arrangement Into Winding Up

Chapter 8
EC Regulation—Member State Liquidator

Chapter 9
Obtaining a Moratorium
Proceedings During a Moratorium
Nominees
Consideration of Proposals Where Moratorium Obtained

Part 2
Administration Procedure

Chapter 1
Preliminary

Chapter 2
Appointment of Administrator By Court

Chapter 13
Replacing Administrator

Chapter 14
EC Regulation: Conversion of Administration Into Winding Up

Chapter 15
EC Regulation: Member State Liquidator

Part 3
Administrative Receivership

Chapter 1
Appointment of Administrative Receiver

Chapter 2
Statement of Affairs and Report to Creditors

Chapter 3
Creditors' Meeting

Chapter 6
Statement of Affairs and Other Information

Chapter 7
Information to Creditors and Contributories

Chapter 8
Meetings of Creditors and Contributories

Section A: Rules of General Application

Chapter 14
Collection and Distribution of Company's Assets By Liquidator

Chapter 15
Disclaimer

Chapter 16
Settlement of List of Contributories

Chapter 17
Calls

Chapter 18
Special Manager

Chapter 19
Public Examination of Company Officers and Others

Chapter 20
Order of Payment of Costs, Etc, Out of Assets

Chapter 21
Miscellaneous Rules

Section A: Return of Capital
(No CVL Application)

Section B: Conclusion of Winding Up

Section C: Dissolution After Winding Up

Chapter 22
Leave to Act As Director, Etc, of Company with Prohibited Name
(Section 216 of the Act)

Chapter 23
EC Regulation—Member State Liquidator

The Second Group of Parts
Individual Insolvency; Bankruptcy

Part 5
Individual Voluntary Arrangements

Chapter 1
Preliminary

Chapter 2
Preparation of the Debtor's Proposal

Chapter 3
Cases in Which an Application for an Interim Order Is Made

Chapter 4
Cases Where No Interim Order Is to Be Obtained

Chapter 5
Creditors' Meetings

Chapter 6
Implementation of the Arrangement

Chapter 10
Application By Official Receiver to Annul
a Bankruptcy Order Under Section 263D(3)

Chapter 11
Other Matters Arising On Annulments Under
Sections 261(2)(A), 261(2)(B) Or 263D(3)

Chapter 12
EC Regulation: Conversion of Voluntary
Arrangement Into Bankruptcy

Part 6
Bankruptcy

Chapter 1
The Statutory Demand

Chapter 2
Bankruptcy Petition (Creditor's)

The Third Group of Parts

Part 7
Court Procedure and Practice

Chapter 1
Applications

Chapter 2
Transfer of Proceedings Between Courts

Chapter 3
Shorthand Writers

Chapter 4
Enforcement Procedures

Chapter 5
Court Records and Returns

Chapter 10
EC Regulation—Creditor's Voluntary Winding Up —Confirmation by the Court

Chapter 11
EC Regulation—member State Liquidator

Part 8
Proxies and Company Representation

Part 9
Examination of Persons Concerned in Company and Individual Insolvency

Part 10
Official Receivers

Part 11
Declaration and Payment of Dividend (Winding Up and Bankruptcy)

Insolvency Rules 1986

Introductory Provisions

2.1

0.1 Citation and commencement

These Rules may be cited as the Insolvency Rules 1986 and shall come into force on 29 December 1986.

0.2 Construction and interpretation

[(1) In these Rules—
'the Act' means the Insolvency Act 1986 (any reference to a numbered section being to a section of that Act);
'the Companies Act' means the Companies Act 1985;
'CPR' means the Civil Procedure Rules 1998 and 'CPR' followed by a Part or rule by number means the Part or rule with that number in those Rules;
'RSC' followed by an Order by number means the Order with that number set out in Schedule 1 to the CPR; and
'the Rules' means the Insolvency Rules 1986.

(2) References in the Rules to ex parte hearings shall be construed as references to hearings without notice being served on any other party; references to applications made ex parte as references to applications made without notice being served on any other party and other references which include the expression 'ex parte' shall be similarly construed.

(3) Subject to paragraphs (1) and (2), Part 13 of the Rules has effect for their interpretation and application.]

0.3 Extent

(1) Parts 1, 2 and 4 of the Rules, and Parts 7 to 13 as they relate to company insolvency, apply in relation to companies which the courts in England and Wales have jurisdiction to wind up.

[(2) Rule 3.1 applies to all receivers to whom Part III of the Act applies, Rule 3.39 and 3.40 apply to all receivers who are not administrative receivers, and the remainder of Part 3 of the Rules applies to administrative receivers appointed otherwise than under section 51 (Scottish Receivership).]

(3) Parts 5 and 6 of the Rules, and Parts 7 to 13 as they relate to individual insolvency, extend to England and Wales only.

The First Group of Parts
Company Insolvency; Companies Winding Up

Part I
Company Voluntary Arrangements

Chapter I
Preliminary

2.2

1.1 Scope of this Part; interpretation

(1) The Rules in this Part apply where, pursuant to Part I of the Act, it is intended to make, and there is made, a proposal to a company and its creditors for a voluntary arrangement, that is to say, a composition in satisfaction of its debts or a scheme of arrangement of its affairs.

(2) In this Part—
    (a)   Chapter 2 applies where the proposal for the voluntary arrangement is made by the directors of the company and
        (i)   the company is neither in liquidation nor is the company in administration; and
        (ii) no steps have been taken to obtain a moratorium under Schedule A1 to the Act in connection with the proposal;
    (b)   Chapter 3 applies where the company is in liquidation or the company is in administration, and the proposal is made by the liquidator or (as the case may be) the administrator, he in either case being the nominee for the purposes of the proposal;
    (c)   Chapter 4 applies in the same case as Chapter 3, but where the nominee is not the liquidator or administrator;
    (d)   Chapter 5 applies in all the three cases mentioned in sub-paragraphs (a) to (c) above;
    (e)   Chapters 7 and 8 apply to all voluntary arrangements with or without a moratorium; and
    (f)   Chapter 9 applies where the proposal is made by the directors of an eligible company with a view to obtaining a moratorium.

(3) In Chapters 3, 4 and 5, the liquidator or the administrator is referred to as 'the responsible insolvency practitioner'.

(4) In this Part, a reference to an 'eligible company' is to a company that is eligible for a moratorium in accordance with paragraph 2 of Schedule A1 to the Act.

Notes

R 1.1

This provision was amended with effect from 1 January 2003 as a result of the introduction of the moratorium for eligible companies (IA 1986 Sch A1) and from 15 September 2003 because of the new administration procedure (IA 1986 Sch B1). Certain transitional provisions apply in relation to the former amendments: Insolvency (Amendment)(No 2) Rules 2002 (SI 2002/2712) r 3.

Chapter 2
Proposal by Directors

2.3

1.2 Preparation of proposal

The directors shall prepare for the intended nominee a proposal on which (with or without amendments to be made under Rule 1.3 below) to make his report to the court under section 2.

Notes

R 1.2

The obligation on the directors to 'prepare' a proposal does not mean that they have to draft it themselves: *Tanner v Everitt* [2004] EWHC 1130 (Ch), [2004] BPIR 1026. They are entitled to use professional advisers to draft the proposal.

2.4

1.3 Contents of proposal

(1) The directors' proposal shall provide a short explanation why, in their opinion, a voluntary arrangement under Part I of the Act is desirable, and give reasons why the company's creditors may be expected to concur with such an arrangement.

(2) The following matters shall be stated, or otherwise dealt with, in the directors' proposal—
    (a)   the following matters, so far as within the directors' immediate knowledge—
        (i)   the company's assets, with an estimate of their respective values,
        (ii)   the extent (if any) to which the assets are charged in favour of creditors,
        (iii)   the extent (if any) to which particular assets are to be excluded from the voluntary arrangement;

(b) particulars of any property, other than assets of the company itself, which is proposed to be included in the arrangement, the source of such property and the terms on which it is to be made available for inclusion;

(c) the nature and amount of the company's liabilities (so far as within the directors' immediate knowledge), the manner in which they are proposed to be met, modified, postponed or otherwise dealt with by means of the arrangement, and (in particular)—

    (i) how it is proposed to deal with preferential creditors (defined in section 4(7)) and creditors who are, or claim to be, secured,

    (ii) how persons connected with the company (being creditors) are proposed to be treated under the arrangement, and

    (iii) whether there are, to the directors' knowledge, any circumstances giving rise to the possibility, in the event that the company should go into liquidation, of claims under—

        section 238 (transactions at an undervalue),

        section 239 (preferences),

        section 244 (extortionate credit transactions), or

        section 245 (floating charges invalid);

    and, where any such circumstances are present, whether, and if so how, it is proposed under the voluntary arrangement to make provision for wholly or partly indemnifying the company in respect of such claims;

(ca) an estimate (to the best of the directors' knowledge and belief and subject to paragraph (4)) of –

    (i) the value of the prescribed part, should the company go into liquidation if the proposal for the voluntary arrangement is not accepted, whether or not section 176A is to be disapplied; and

    (ii) the value of the company's net property on the date that the estimate is made

(d) whether any, and if so what, guarantees have been given of the company's debts by other persons, specifying which (if any) of the guarantors are persons connected with the company;

(e) the proposed duration of the voluntary arrangement;

(f) the proposed dates of distributions to creditors, with estimates of their amounts;

(fa) how it is proposed to deal with the claim of any person who is bound by the arrangement by virtue of section 5(2)(b)(ii);

(g) the amount proposed to be paid to the nominee (as such) by way of remuneration and expenses;

(h) the manner in which it is proposed that the supervisor of the arrangement should be remunerated, and his expenses defrayed;

(j) whether, for the purposes of the arrangement, any guarantees are to be offered by directors, or other persons, and whether (if so) any security is to be given or sought;

(k) the manner in which funds held for the purposes of the arrangement are to be banked, invested or otherwise dealt with pending distribution to creditors;

> (l)   the manner in which funds held for the purpose of payment to creditors, and not so paid on the termination of the arrangement, are to be dealt with;
>
> (m)   the manner in which the business of the company is proposed to be conducted during the course of the arrangement;
>
> (n)   details of any further credit facilities which it is intended to arrange for the company, and how the debts so arising are to be paid;
>
> (o)   the functions which are to be undertaken by the supervisor of the arrangement;
>
> (p)   the name, address and qualification of the person proposed as supervisor of the voluntary arrangement, and confirmation that he is either qualified to act as an insolvency practitioner in relation to the company or is an authorised person in relation to the company; and
>
> (q)   whether the EC Regulation will apply and, if so, whether the proceedings will be main proceedings, secondary proceedings or territorial proceedings.
>
> (3) With the agreement in writing of the nominee, the directors' proposal may be amended at any time up to delivery of the former's report to the court under section 2(2).
>
> (4) Nothing in paragraph (2)(ca) is to be taken as requiring the estimate referred to in that paragraph to include any information, the disclosure of which could seriously prejudice the commercial interests of the company. If such information is excluded from the calculation the estimate shall be accompanied by a statement to that effect

---

Notes

R 1.3

Although both IA 1986 and IR 1986 envisage the directors preparing the proposal for submission to the intended nominee who then reports on the proposal to the court, in the majority of cases it will be the intended nominee who in fact prepares the proposal; and this is all the more so given the amount of detailed information which is required to be included under this rule.

It is important to ensure that the proposal deals with each of the 17 prescribed matters set out under this rule. Failure to do so, even where the omissions are immaterial, may result in the proposal being returned by the court office in which it is to be filed, or in a challenge under IA 1986 s 6 (although in an appropriate case, such a challenge might be met by invoking IR 1986 r 7.55): see *Re a debtor (No 87 of 1993) (No 2)* [1996] 1 BCLC 63; *Bradburn v Kaye [2006] BPIR 605* and the notes to IA 1986 s 6. Note that the nominee may be expected to draw the court's attention in his report to any failure to comply with the requirements of this rule: see *Re a Debtor (No 222 of 1990)* [1992] BCLC 137.

A properly drafted proposal will be tailored to the precise circumstances and needs of the debtor company, and will include detailed provisions ranging beyond the matters prescribed under this rule. It is also common practice for proposals drafted by insolvency practitioners to incorporate their firm's standard CVA terms and conditions. The Association of Business Recovery Professionals (R3) produces Standard Conditions for IVAs and anticipates producing Standard Conditions for CVAs.

In preparing the proposal, the directors for their part are required to be open and honest and to put all relevant facts before the creditors: see In *re a Debtor (No 2389 of 1989)* [1991] Ch 326.

The provision of false information or fraudulent non-disclosure of material facts is now an offence under IA 1986 s 6A. Note however that, in the proposal itself, the directors are required to provide information as to the company's assets under IR 1986 r 1.3(2)(a) only so far as this is 'within the directors' immediate knowledge' and compare this with the language of IR 1986 r 1.5 (2) (the particulars which the directors are required to provide to the nominee in the statement of the company's affairs).

R 1.3(1)

The desirability of a proposed CVA will often be based on it resulting in a better anticipated return to creditors than would be available under other insolvency procedures. This may reflect the cost advantages which a CVA offers over other procedures – for instance in avoiding DTI fees and other realisation costs which would be payable in a company's liquidation.

R 1.3(2)(c)(iii)

The provisions of IA 1986 relating to the adjustment of prior transactions do not apply in a CVA (likewise the provisions of IA 1986 for claims against directors for wrongful trading and misfeasance). This may operate to the disadvantage of creditors, and may be a reason why liquidation (allowing full investigation of the company's affairs by the liquidator) may in any particular case be more appropriate – at least unless the beneficiaries of such transactions (or others) are prepared voluntarily within the CVA to have the potentially voidable transaction set aside. Oddly, however, the disclosure of such potential claims is here required as part of the general requirement to set out 'the nature and amount of the company's liabilities' rather than for the purpose of notifying creditors of potential benefits which may be afforded in liquidation but not under the CVA.

R 1.3(2)(ca)

This provision was introduced following the coming into force of the EA 2002 on 15 September 2003. The 'value of the prescribed part' is a reference to the fund which a liquidator under IA 1986 s 176A is required to ring-fence out of net realisations of the company's property in a liquidation to be made available to unsecured creditors. It is important for this information to be available to creditors considering whether or not to approve a CVA proposal (where the alternative is liquidation) because it will affect the estimated dividend which they might receive in a liquidation. However, where the disclosure of such information could be commercially damaging within the test set out in IR 1986 r 1.3(4), the directors are at liberty to exclude it from the proposal provided they include a statement to that effect.

R 1.3(2)(j)

It is not unusual as part of a proposal for one or more directors to offer a 'guarantee' to creditors of payment of a minimum dividend under the CVA. In order to ensure such guarantee is binding and enforceable against the director(s), it is important that the guarantee is made in writing within or annexed to the proposal and is signed by the intended guarantor.

R 1(3)(3)

The directors may amend the terms of the proposal with the written agreement of the nominee at any time up to the delivery by the nominee of his report to the court. Given the nominee's obligation to report to the court on the question as to whether or not the proposal has a reasonable prospect of being approved (and he or she must for that purpose have canvassed the views of the company's creditors), this provision is a useful tool to enable amendments to be made to the proposal such as may be required by the company's creditors as a condition of their likely approval.

2.5

1.4 Notice to intended nominee

(1) The directors shall give to the intended nominee written notice of their proposal.

(2) The notice, accompanied by a copy of the proposal, shall be delivered either to the nominee himself, or to a person authorised to take delivery of documents on his behalf.

(3) If the intended nominee agrees to act, he shall cause a copy of the notice to be endorsed to the effect that it has been received by him on a specified date; and the period of 28 days referred to in section 2(2) then runs from that date.

(4) The copy of the notice so endorsed shall be returned by the nominee forthwith to the directors at an address specified by them in the notice for that purpose.

2.6

1.5 Statement of affairs

(1) The directors shall, within 7 days after their proposal is delivered to the nominee, or within such longer time as he may allow, deliver to him a statement of the company's affairs.

(2) The statement shall comprise the following particulars (supplementing or amplifying, so far as is necessary for clarifying the state of the company's affairs, those already given in the directors' proposal)—

  (a) a list of the company's assets, divided into such categories as are appropriate for easy identification, with estimated values assigned to each category;
  (b) in the case of any property on which a claim against the company is wholly or partly secured, particulars of the claim and its amount, and of how and when the security was created;
  (c) the names and addresses of the company's preferential creditors (defined in section 4(7)), with the amounts of their respective claims;
  (d) the names and addresses of the company's unsecured creditors, with the amounts of their respective claims;
  (e) particulars of any debts owed by or to the company to or by persons connected with it;
  (f) the names and addresses of the company's members, with details of their respective shareholdings;
  (g) such other particulars (if any) as the nominee may in writing require to be furnished for the purposes of making his report to the court on the directors' proposal.

(3) The statement of affairs shall be made up to a date not earlier than 2 weeks before the date of the notice to the nominee under Rule 1.4.

However, the nominee may allow an extension of that period to the nearest practicable date (not earlier than 2 months before the date of the notice under Rule 1.4); and if he does so, he shall give his reasons in his report to the court on the directors' proposal.

(4) The statement shall be certified as correct, to the best of their knowledge and belief, by two or more directors of the company, or by the company secretary and at least one director (other than the secretary himself).

Notes

R 1.5

The particulars of assets and liabilities required to be provided to the nominee by the directors in the statement of affairs duplicate to some degree information already required to be provided in the proposal itself. But note that, whereas in the proposal the directors are required to provide details of assets (IR 1986 r 1.3(2)(a) and liabilities (IR 1986 r 1.3(2)(c)) so far as this was 'within the directors' immediate knowledge', there is no such qualification in this rule.

R 1.5(2)(g)

This provision covers much of the same ground as IR 1986 r 1.6(1)(c) below. See further the general note to IA 1986 s 2 for the nominee's obligations in preparing his report to the court.

2.7

1.6 Additional disclosure for assistance of nominee

(1) If it appears to the nominee that he cannot properly prepare his report on the basis of information in the directors' proposal and statement of affairs, he may call on the directors to provide him with—

   (a)   further and better particulars as to the circumstances in which, and the reasons why, the company is insolvent or (as the case may be) threatened with insolvency;

   (b)   particulars of any previous proposals which have been made in respect of the company under Part I of the Act;

   (c)   any further information with respect to the company's affairs which the nominee thinks necessary for the purposes of his report.

(2) The nominee may call on the directors to inform him, with respect to any person who is, or at any time in the 2 years preceding the notice under Rule 1.4 has been, a director or officer of the company, whether and in what circumstances (in those 2 years or previously) that person—

   (a)   has been concerned in the affairs of any other company (whether or not incorporated in England and Wales) which has become insolvent, or

   (b)   has himself been adjudged bankrupt or entered into an arrangement with his creditors.

(3) For the purpose of enabling the nominee to consider their proposal and prepare his report on it, the directors must give him access to the company's accounts and records.

Notes

R 1.6

For general discussion of the nominee's obligations in reporting to the court, see the commentary to IA 1986 s 2.

R 1.6(1)(a)

It is not a formal precondition to a CVA that the company is either insolvent or even threatened with insolvency. However, it is unlikely that a CVA proposal would be submitted or approved except in circumstances of actual or threatened insolvency. The reasons for the company's financial predicament may plainly be relevant in assisting the nominee to determine whether or not the proposal has reasonable prospects of being successfully implemented and is serious and viable.

R 1.6(1)(b)

There is no limitation on the number of CVAs which a company can enter into or on the timescale for such successive CVAs; contrast the position as regards the CVAs brought under the new moratorium procedure under IA 1986 Sch A1 para 4(1)(f). However the existence of prior CVAs is plainly relevant in enabling the nominee to determine the viability of the current proposal and its prospects of being approved.

2.8

1.7 Nominee's report on the proposal

(1) With his report to the court under section 2 the nominee shall deliver—

    (a)   a copy of the directors' proposal (with amendments, if any, authorised under Rule 1.3(3)); and

    (b)   a copy or summary of the company's statement of affairs.

(2) If the nominee makes known his opinion [that the directors' proposal has a reasonable prospect of being approved and implemented and] that meetings of the company and its creditors should be summoned under section 3, his report shall have annexed to it his comments on the proposal.

If his opinion is otherwise, he shall give his reasons for that opinion.

(3) The court shall cause the nominee's report to be endorsed with the date on which it is filed in court. Any director, member or creditor of the company is entitled, at all reasonable times on any business day, to inspect the file.

(4) The nominee shall send a copy of his report, and of his comments (if any), to the company.

Notes

R 1.7

For a general discussion of the nominee's reporting obligations, see the commentary to IA 1986 s 2. For discussion of the role of the court, see the commentary to IA 1986 s 2 and 3.

2.9

1.8 Replacement of nominee

(1) Where a person other than the nominee intends to apply to the court under section 2(4) for the nominee to be replaced, (except in any case where the nominee has died) he shall give to the nominee at least 7 days' notice of his application.

(2) Where the nominee intends to apply to the court under section 2(4) of the Act to be replaced, he shall give at least 7 days' notice of his application to the person intending to make the proposal.

(3) No appointment of a replacement nominee shall be made by the court unless there is filed in court a statement by the replacement nominee—
   (a)   indicating his consent to act, and
   (b)   that he is qualified to act as an insolvency practitioner in relation to the company or is an authorised person in relation to the company.

Notes

R 1.8(3)(b)

So far no additional class of persons has been authorised to act as nominees in relation to the company; only licensed insolvency practitioners may presently act as nominees (IA 1986 s 388(2B)).

2.10

1.9 Summoning of meetings under s 3

(1) If in his report the nominee states that in his opinion meetings of the company and its creditors should be summoned to consider the directors' proposal, the date on which the meetings are to be held shall be not less than 14, nor more than 28, days from that on which the nominee's report is filed in court under Rule 1.7.

(2) Notices calling the meetings shall be sent by the nominee, at least 14 days before the day fixed for them to be held—
   (a)   in the case of the creditors' meeting, to all the creditors specified in the statement of affairs, and any other creditors of the company of whom he is otherwise aware; and
   (b)   in the case of the meeting of members of the company, to all persons who are, to the best of the nominee's belief, members of it.

(3) Each notice sent under this Rule shall specify the court to which the nominee's report under section 2 has been delivered and shall state the effect of Rule 1.19(1), (3) and (4) (requisite majorities (creditors)); and with each notice there shall be sent—
   (a)   a copy of the directors' proposal;
   (b)   a copy of the statement of affairs or, if the nominee thinks fit, a summary of it (the summary to include a list of creditors and the amount of their debts); and
   (c)   the nominee's comments on the proposal.

Notes

R 1.9(1)

The nominee is required to specify the date, time and place at which the meetings of creditors and members are to be held in his report to the court – which must be not less than 14 days and not more than 28 days after filing his report: see IA 1986 s 2(2)(b). He is then required under IA 1986 s 3 to summon the meeting for the date, time and place so specified, unless the court otherwise orders.

R 1.9(2)

See the commentary to IA 1986 s 5(2)(b) for a survey of the rules and reported decisions relating to the giving of notice. In brief:

- 14 days notice means 14 days clear notice (ie excluding the day of sending and the day of the meeting).
- Notices must be delivered (rather than merely posted) at least 14 clear days before the meeting.
- Notices must be sent to creditors at their address for service or (where no such address has been given) at the place specified in the table at CPR r 6.2: see IR 1986 r 12.11 incorporating the provisions of CPR Part 6.
- Where sent by post, notices are treated as being served two days (in the case of first class post) and four days (in the case of second class post) after posting, unless the contrary is shown: IR 1986 r 12.10.

IA 1986 and IR 1986 therefore impose a tight timetable within which notices must be sent. Where the nominee is, for whatever reason, unable to effect service on the creditors and members within the stipulated timescale, his safest course may be to apply to the court to extend the time for the holding of the meeting to a new date. Otherwise, if the meeting is convened for a date other than that specified in the report in order to accommodate the 14 day notice requirement, the meeting, and any approval given thereat, may be found to be invalid: see *Re N (a Debtor)* [2002] BPIR 1024.

The failure to give due notice to one or more creditors will not in itself invalidate the meeting: see IR 1986 r 12.16. Creditors who do not receive due notice will be bound by any CVA approved at the meeting, but will have a right of challenge to the approval under IA 1986 s 6(2). Where a challenge is successful in circumstances where the nominee is at fault, he may be liable for the costs of such challenge: see *Re a Debtor (No 222 of 1990) ex p Bank of Ireland (No 2)* [1993] BCLC 233; *Harmony Carpets v Chaffin-Laird* [2001] BPIR 61; *Smurthwaite v Simpson-Smith*, 25 July 2006, LTL 25/07/06, CA.

Chapter 3
Proposal by Administrator or Liquidator (Himself the Nominee)

2.11

1.10 Preparation of proposal

(1) The responsible insolvency practitioner's proposal shall specify—
   (a) all such matters as under Rule 1.3 (subject to paragraph (3) below) in Chapter 2 the directors of the company would be required to include in a proposal by them, with the addition, where the company is in administration, of the names and addresses of the company's preferential creditors (defined in section 4(7)), with the amounts of their respective claims, and
   (b) such other matters (if any) as the insolvency practitioner considers appropriate for ensuring that members and creditors of the company are enabled to reach an informed decision on the proposal.

(2) Where the company is being wound up by the court, the insolvency practitioner shall give notice of the proposal to the official receiver.

(3) The administrator or liquidator shall include, in place of the estimate required by Rule 1.3(2)(ca), a statement which contains –

(a) to the best of the administrator or liquidator's knowledge and belief –

(i) an estimate of the value of the prescribed part (whether or not he proposes to make an application to court under section 176A(5) or section 176A(3) applies), and

(ii) an estimate of the value of the company's net property, and

(b) whether, and, if so, why, the administrator or liquidator proposes to make an application to court under section 176A(5).

(4) Nothing in this Rule is to be taken as requiring any such estimate to include any information, the disclosure of which could seriously prejudice the commercial interests of the company. If such information is excluded from the calculation the estimate shall be accompanied by a statement to that effect.

2.12

1.11 Summoning of meetings under s 3

(1) The responsible insolvency practitioner shall fix a venue for the creditors' meeting and the company meeting, and give at least 14 days' notice of the meetings—

(a) in the case of the creditors' meeting, to all the creditors specified in the company's statement of affairs, and to any other creditors of whom the insolvency practitioner is aware; and

(b) in the case of the company meeting, to all persons who are, to the best of his belief, members of the company.

(2) Each notice sent out under this Rule shall state the effect of Rule 1.19(1), (3) and (4) (requisite majorities (creditors)); and with it there shall be sent—

(a) a copy of the responsible insolvency practitioner's proposal, and

(b) a copy of the statement of affairs or, if he thinks fit, a summary of it (the summary to include a list of creditors and the amounts of their debts).

Notes

R 1.11

IR 1986 r 1.10 and 1.11 apply in cases where an administrator or liquidator makes the proposal, and is himself to be the nominee. In such cases, there is no requirement to report to the court before summoning meetings of creditors and members, which may be done as soon as the proposal has been formulated. Although there is no requirement for the responsible insolvency practitioner to report to the court on the proposal, he is required under IR 1986 r 1.10(1)(b) to include within the proposal such information as he considers appropriate to enable members and creditors to reach an informed decision on the proposal.

Chapter 4
Proposal by Administrator or Liquidator (Another Insolvency Practitioner the Nominee)

2.13

1.12 Preparation of proposal and notice to nominee

(1) The responsible insolvency practitioner shall give notice to the intended nominee, and prepare his proposal for a voluntary arrangement, in the same manner as is required of the directors, in the case of a proposal by them, under Chapter 2.

(2) Rule 1.2 applies to the responsible insolvency practitioner as it applies to the directors; and Rule 1.4 applies as regards the action to be taken by the nominee.

(3) The content of the proposal shall be as required by Rule 1.3 (and, where relevant, Rule 1.10), reading references to the directors as referring to the responsible insolvency practitioner.

(4) Rule 1.6 applies in respect of the information to be furnished to the nominee, reading references to the directors as referring to the responsible insolvency practitioner.

(5) With the proposal the responsible insolvency practitioner shall provide a copy of the company's statement of affairs.

(6) Where the company is being wound up by the court, the responsible insolvency practitioner shall send a copy of the proposal to the official receiver, accompanied by the name and address of the insolvency practitioner [or authorised person] who has agreed to act as nominee.

(7) Rules 1.7 to 1.9 apply as regards a proposal under this Chapter as they apply to a proposal under Chapter 2.

Notes

R 1.12

Where an administrator or liquidator submits the proposal, but is not himself to be the nominee, the stipulated procedure largely incorporates the procedure that applies where the directors submit the proposal.

Chapter 5
Proceedings on a Proposal made by the Directors, or by the Administrator, or by the Liquidator

Section A: Meetings of Company's Creditors and Members

2.14

1.13 Summoning of meetings

(1) Subject as follows, in fixing the venue for the creditors' meeting and the company meeting, the person summoning the meeting ('the convener') shall have regard primarily to the convenience of the creditors.

(2) Meetings shall in each case be summoned for commencement between 10.00 and 16.00 hours on a business day.

(3) The meetings may be held on the same day or on different days. If held on the same day, the meetings shall be held in the same place, but in either case the creditors' meeting shall be fixed for a time in advance of the company meeting.

(4) Where the meetings are not held on the same day, they shall be held within 7 days of each other.

(5) With every notice summoning either meeting there shall be sent out forms of proxy.

Notes

R 1.13(3)

Previously it was a requirement that the meetings were held on the same day and in the same place. IR 1986 r 1.13 was substituted by the Insolvency (Amendment) Rules 2003 r 4 (SI 2003/1730) subject to certain savings. See also IR 1986 r 1.21 which provides (notwithstanding the wording of IR 1986 r 1.13 (3)) that the chairman of the two meetings may in his discretion hold the two meetings together.

2.15

1.14 The chairman at meetings

(1) Subject as follows, at both the creditors' meeting and the company meeting, and at any combined meeting, the convener shall be chairman.

(2) If for any reason he is unable to attend, he may nominate another person to act as chairman in his place; but a person so nominated must be.

  [(a)   a person qualified to act as an insolvency practitioner in relation to the company;
  (b)   an authorised person in relation to the company; or
  (c)   an employee of the convenor or his firm who is experienced in insolvency matters].

2.16

1.15 The chairman as proxy-holder

The chairman shall not by virtue of any proxy held by him vote to increase or reduce the amount of the remuneration or expenses of the nominee or the supervisor of the proposed arrangement, unless the proxy specifically directs him to vote in that way.

2.17

1.16 Attendance by company officers

(1) At least 14 days' notice to attend the meetings shall be given by the convener—
  (a)   to all directors of the company, and

(b)   to any persons in whose case the convener thinks that their presence is required as being officers of the company, or as having been directors or officers of it at any time in the 2 years immediately preceding the date of the notice.

(2) The chairman may, if he thinks fit, exclude any present or former director or officer from attendance at a meeting, either completely or for any part of it; and this applies whether or not a notice under this Rule has been sent to the person excluded.

Section B: Voting Rights and Majorities

2.18

1.17 Entitlement to vote (creditors)

(1) Subject as follows, every creditor who has notice of the creditors' meeting is entitled to vote at the meeting or any adjournment of it.

(2) Votes are calculated according to the amount of the creditor's debt as at the date of the meeting or, where the company is being wound up or is in administration, the date of its going into liquidation or (as the case may be) when the company entered administration.

(3) A creditor may vote in respect of a debt for an unliquidated amount or any debt whose value is not ascertained and for the purposes of voting (but not otherwise) his debt shall be valued at £1 unless the chairman agrees to put a higher value on it.

Notes

R 1.17

Under IA 1986 s 5(2)(b) (as amended by IA 2000) all creditors entitled to notice of the meeting are bound by the arrangement whether or not they received notice.

The status of a creditor who has received notice of the meeting but has not received the prescribed 14 clear days notice, or has received notice informally (for example, through a third party), is unclear. Under the old IA 1986 s 5(2)(b), a creditor who did not receive notice of the meeting *in accordance with the rules* was not bound by the arrangement, and this rule was interpreted by the courts in a literal fashion so that creditors who had been given notice of the meeting which was less than the prescribed 14 clear days notice were not bound by the arrangement: see *Mytre Investments v Reynolds (No 2)* [1996] BPIR 464. It might be argued that such creditor may, equally, not be entitled to vote even if he wishes to do so. However, this would be unduly formalistic and it is submitted that the better view is that a creditor who receives less than the prescribed notice, or only informal notice, may at his option waive the inadequacy of notice and attend at the meeting in person or by proxy to vote, or may insist on the inadequacy of the notice and instead mount a challenge to any approval under IA 1986 s 6(3). However, in determining whether or not to allow any challenge under s 6(3), in a case where an omitted creditor had notice but not the prescribed notice of the meeting, a court might take into account whether the omitted creditor was able to attend the meeting in person or by proxy notwithstanding the inadequate notice, and, if he was, why he did not. Note also *Beverley Group plc v McClue* [1995] 2 BCLC 407.

Although neither IA 1986 nor IR 1986 define 'creditor' or 'debt' for the purpose of IA 1986 Part I, it is clear that 'debt' encompasses both liquidated and unliquidated claims, and both present, future and contingent liabilities: see the commentary to IA 1986 s 1.

R 1.17(2)

It is incumbent on a creditor who wishes to vote in respect of his debt to state to the best of his ability the total amount which is owed to him by the debtor, and, if the value of the whole or some part is unascertained, so to state and to supply the chairman with as much information as possible to enable him to put an estimated minimum value on it: see *Re Hoare* [1997] BPIR 683.

R 1.17(3)

This sub-rule sets out the machinery which applies in dealing, for voting purposes, with claims for sums which are unliquidated or unascertained. The machinery is distinct from that which applies to debts which are disputed, which are governed by r 1.17A (4): see In *re Cranley Mansions Ltd* [1994] 1 WLR 1610, 1625B-E; *Re Sweatfield Ltd* [1997] BCC 744.

The sub-rule formerly provided that a creditor should not be entitled to vote in respect of a debt for an unliquidated or unascertained amount, unless the chairman agreed to put an estimated minimum value on the debt. Because only those creditors who were entitled to vote at the meeting were bound by the CVA, this provision potentially excluded completely creditors with unliquidated or contingent claims from the CVA which could in turn frustrate the operation of the CVA. This problem does not arise under the current IR 1986 r 1.17(3) which was introduced by the Insolvency (Amendment) (No 2) Rules 2002 (SI 2002/2712) r 3 subject to transitional provisions.

Although IR 1986 r 1.17(3) refers to the chairman 'agreeing' to put a higher value on an unliquidated claim, this process is not consensual in requiring the agreement of the creditor to the valuation: *Doorbar v Alltime Securities Ltd* [1996] 1 WLR 456 overruling *Re Cranley Mansions Ltd* [1994] 1 WLR 1610 on this point. The rule itself makes clear that the attribution of a £1 or other value for unascertained or unliquidated claims is for voting purposes only. So creditors with such claims will not be prejudiced by the valuation on the subsequent payment of dividends in the CVA. It will be difficult to complain that the chairman has not put an estimated value on a debt where the creditor has decided not to attend the meeting: *Beverley Group plc v McClue* [1995] BCC 407.

In putting a value to such claims for voting purposes, a chairman may face a difficult task where the outcome of the vote at the meeting may depend on his determination of the value. Allowing for the fact he is not a lawyer, or a valuer or actuary, he is, however, obliged to take reasonable steps to undertake some assessment of a claim's value: see Knox J *Doorbar v Alltime Securities Ltd (No 2)* [1995] 2 BCLC 513 at p 526 (a decision based on the old r 5.17(3) and *Fender v IRC* [2003] BPIR 1304, 1313). However, he should not speculate, and nor should he investigate the creditor's claim. He should examine the evidence put forward by the creditor, and by any other person, and if '*the totality of that evidence leads him to the conclusion that he can safely attribute to the claim a minimum value higher than £1 then he should do so*': *Re Newlands (Seaford Educational Trust* [2006] EWHC 1511 (Ch), [2006] All ER (D) 299 (Jun).

Where a creditor disagrees with the value placed on his claim by the chairman, he may appeal the chairman's decision to the court under r 1.17A(3) and/or apply under IA 1986 s 6(1) – as, it seems may any member of the company or other creditor. In *Doorbar v Alltime Securities Ltd (No 1 & 2)* [1996] 1 WLR 456, CA the court upheld a chairman's decision valuing a landlord's claim for future rent in respect of a lease which had seven years to run on the basis of only one year's rent; the chairman properly took into account what was likely to happen, and in particular the possibility that the landlord would exercise his power of re-entry thereby terminating the lease before its term date. Similar reasoning was applied in *Re Sweatfield Ltd* [1997] BCC 744. See also *Re Newlands (Seaford Educational Trust* [2006] EWHC 1511 (Ch), [2006] All ER (D) 299 (Jun) where the court upheld the chairman's refusal to place a higher value on a claim for future rent and dilapidations.

2.19

1.17A Procedure for admission of creditors' claims for voting purposes

(1) Subject as follows, at any creditors' meeting the chairman shall ascertain the entitlement of persons wishing to vote and shall admit or reject their claims accordingly.

(2) The chairman may admit or reject a claim in whole or in part.

(3) The chairman's decision on any matter under this Rule or under paragraph (3) of Rule 1.17 is subject to appeal to the court by any creditor or member of the company.

(4) If the chairman is in doubt whether a claim should be admitted or rejected, he shall mark it as objected to and allow votes to be cast in respect of it, subject to such votes being subsequently declared invalid if the objection to the claim is sustained.

(5) If on an appeal the chairman's decision is reversed or varied, or votes are declared invalid, the court may order another meeting to be summoned, or make such order as it thinks just.

The court's power to make an order under this paragraph is exercisable only if it considers that the circumstances giving rise to the appeal give rise to unfair prejudice or material irregularity.

(6) An application to the court by way of appeal against the chairman's decision shall not be made after the end of the period of 28 days beginning with the first day on which the report required by section 4(6) has been made to the court.

(7) The chairman is not personally liable for any costs incurred by any person in respect of an appeal under this Rule.

Notes

R 1.17A(1), (2), (4)

These provisions set out the procedure which the chairman should follow in determining whether or not to admit a creditor's claim for voting purposes. Note that there is a different procedure under r 1.17(3) which applies for the purpose of attributing a value for voting purposes on unliquidated or unascertained claims.

Where a creditor's claim is disputed – either by the company itself, or by other creditors – the chairman should look at the claim; if it is plain or obvious that it is good, he should admit it; if it is plain or obvious that it is bad, he should reject it; if there is a question or doubt about the claim, under r 1.17A(4) he should admit it but mark it as objected to. It is not the role of the chairman in the case of a disputed debt to undertake any lengthy quasi-judicial inquiry into the status of the debt, which is a task better suited to the Companies Court on an appeal: see the dicta of Harman J in *Re a Debtor (No 222 of 1990)* [1992] BCLC 137, 144 (cited with approval in *Re a Debtor (No 574 of 1995)* [1998] 2 BCLC 124). For rules governing the votes of secured creditors, see r 1.19 (3) and commentary below.

R 1.17A(3), (5), (7)

An appeal lies to the court with jurisdiction over the CVA against a chairman's decision:
- to admit or reject a claim (under IR 1986 r 1.17A(1), (2), (4) above;

- on the value put on an unliquidated / unascertained claim (under IR 1986 r 1.17(3) above);

• on whether a vote falls to be left out of account under r 1.19(3) or (4) or otherwise under IR 1986 r 1.19 below for the purpose of calculating whether the requisite majority of creditors is achieved, and whether the resolution is valid.

Such an appeal may be brought by any creditor or member of the company. This appeal procedure runs in parallel with an aggrieved creditor's or member's right to apply to the court under IA 1986 s 6(1) for an order revoking the decision of a meeting on grounds of material irregularity. On an appeal from a chairman's decision, the court may consider the validity of the debt, or its proper valuation (as the case may be) afresh and unfettered by the decision of the chairman; it may examine all the evidence before it and conclude whether on balance the claim is established and/or its appropriate value for voting purposes: see *Re a Debtor (No 574 of 1995)* [1998] 2 BCLC 124 p 127h – 128c (also reported at [1998] BPIR 224 under *National Westminster Bank v Scher*). See also *Fender v IRC* [2003] BPIR 1304, 1313.

Where the court reverses or varies the decision of the chairman, it has power under r 1.17A(5) to order another meeting to be summoned, or make such order as it thinks just. This must include a power in appropriate circumstances to revoke the approval of a CVA itself where such approval was obtained only by reason of the decision of the chairman on voting entitlement which has been overturned. These powers, however, are only exercisable where the impugned decision has resulted in unfair prejudice or material irregularity (IA 1986 s 6). This will, in general, only be the case where the decision has affected the outcome of the vote.

R 1.17A(6)

This imposes a 28–day time limit from the date of filing of the chairman's report with the court for appealing a decision on voting. It appears that this time limit may be extended under IR 1986 r 12.9 (importing CPR r 3.1(2)). In *Re Bournemouth & Boscombe Athletic Football Club Co Ltd* [1998] BPIR 183, it was held that there was no power under r 12.9 to extend the 28 day time limit under IA 1986 s 6(3) for challenging the decision of meetings. However, this was on the footing that s 6(3) was a limitation period imposed by statute to which IR 1986 r 12.9 did not apply. By contrast it does so apply to the time limit here imposed by the rules.

In determining whether or not to extend time for appealing the chairman's decision, the court should take into account, the length of the delay, the reasons for it, the apparent merits of the underlying application and the prejudice to each side other than the inevitable prejudice inherent in re-opening the matter: *Tager v Westpac Banking Corporation* [1997] BPIR 543, 555.

R 1.17A(7)

The chairman is protected from adverse costs orders in relation to any appeal against his decision brought under IR 1986 r 1.17A(3). But there is no such protection where an aggrieved creditor or member applies instead or at the same time to the court under IA 1986 s 6(1) for an order revoking the decision of the meeting on grounds of material irregularity. In *Re a debtor (No 222 of 1990) (No 2)* [1993] BCLC 233, Harman J ordered a nominee to pay the costs of an application under IA 1986 s 262 to revoke approval of an IVA where the approval was revoked as a result of a material irregularity arising from a failure by the nominee to discharge his duties under the IR 1986 and where, in so failing, the nominee had fallen significantly below the standards required of a licensed insolvency practitioner. See also *Fender v IRC* [2003] BPIR 1304, 1320, *Smurthwaite v Simpson-Smith*, 25 July 2006, LTL 25/07/06, CA.

2.20

1.18 Voting rights (members)

(1) Subject as follows, members of the company at their meeting vote according to the rights attaching to their shares respectively in accordance with the articles.

(2) ...

(3) References in this Rule to a person's shares include any other interest which he may have as a member of the company.

Notes

R 1.18(2)

This sub rule previously entitled members whose shares carried no voting rights to vote on the proposal, although their votes were discounted in determining whether a majority was achieved for any resolution (under the previous IR r 1.20(2)). Both these provisions were removed by the Insolvency (Amendment) (No 2) Rules 2002 with effect from 1 January 2003.

2.21

1.19 Requisite majorities (creditors)

(1) Subject as follows, at the creditors' meeting for any resolution to pass approving any proposal or modification there must be a majority in excess of three-quarters in value of the creditors present in person or by proxy and voting on the resolution.

(2) The same applies in respect of any other resolution proposed at the meeting, but substituting one-half for three-quarters.

(3) In the following cases there is to be left out of account a creditor's vote in respect of any claim or part of a claim—
- (a) where written notice of the claim was not given, either at the meeting or before it, to the chairman or convener of the meeting;
- (b) where the claim or part is secured;
- (c) where the claim is in respect of a debt wholly or partly on, or secured by, a current bill of exchange or promissory note, unless the creditor is willing—
  - (i) to treat the liability to him on the bill or note of every person who is liable on it antecedently to the company, and against whom a bankruptcy order has not been made (or in the case of a company, which has not gone into liquidation), as a security in his hands, and
  - (ii) to estimate the value of the security and (for the purpose of entitlement to vote, but not of any distribution under the arrangement) to deduct it from his claim.

(4) Any resolution is invalid if those voting against it include more than half in value of the creditors, counting in these latter only those—
- (a) to whom notice of the meeting was sent;
- (b) whose votes are not to be left out of account under paragraph (3); and
- (c) who are not, to the best of the chairman's belief, persons connected with the company.

(5) It is for the chairman of the meeting to decide whether under this Rule—
- (a) a vote is to be left out of account in accordance with paragraph (3), or

> (b) a person is a connected person for the purposes of para-
>   graph (4)(c);
> and in relation to the second of these two cases the chairman is entitled to
> rely on the information provided by the company's statement of affairs or
> otherwise in accordance with this Part of the Rules.
>
> (6) If the chairman uses a proxy contrary to Rule 1.15, his vote with that
> proxy does not count towards any majority under this Rule.
>
> (7) The chairman's decision on any matter under this Rule is subject to
> appeal to the court by any creditor or member and paragraphs (5) to (7) of
> Rule 1.17A apply as regards such an appeal.

Notes

R 1.19

This rule imposes a two-stage process for determining whether or not a proposal obtains the approval of creditors:

- any resolution to approve the CVA must be passed with a majority in excess of three-quarters in value of the creditors present at the meeting in person or by proxy and voting on the resolution (r 1.19(1)). R 1.19(3) provides that certain votes to be left out of account.
- if the resolution achieves the necessary majority, it is nevertheless invalid under IR 1986 r 1.19(4) if more than half in value of the creditors who have been given notice of the meeting (excluding those who are connected with the company as well as those whose votes do not count under IR 1986 r 1.19(3)) have voted against it.

The purpose of the process is to prevent a CVA being imposed upon independent creditors against their will by the weight of votes cast by persons connected with the company.

R 1.19(3)

A creditor's vote is to be left out of account for the purpose of calculating majorities where it falls within one of the three categories in r 1.19(3). It is for the chairman to decide whether it does, subject to an appeal under the provisions of r 1.17A(5)–(7). A creditor whose vote is left out of account is still bound by the arrangement as a creditor entitled to vote.

R 1.19(3)(a)

This requires a vote to be left out of account in respect of a debt where no written notice of claim has been given. However, it appears that the submission by a creditor of a written proxy is itself sufficient notice under this rule even if the proxy does not state the amount of the debt the subject of the claim: see *Roberts v Pinnacle Entertainment Ltd* [2003] EWHC 2394 (Ch), [2004] BPIR 208 at paras 16 and 17.

R 1.19(3)(b)

For details of those included within the phrase 'secured creditors' see notes to IA 1986 s 4(3). Secured creditors are entitled to vote at the creditors' meeting, but their vote falls to be left out of account to the extent that it relates to claim which is in whole or part secured. In *Calor Gas v Piercy* [1994] 2 BCLC 321, it was held that where the value of creditor's security is less than its debt, the creditor's vote should not be left out of account in its entirety, but should be taken into account in respect of the unsecured balance. Further a creditor may be able to waive part of its secured claim to enable its vote to be counted insofar as it has been waived: *Swindon Town Properties v Swindon Town Football Co Ltd* [2003] BPIR 253. It falls to the chairman to put an estimated value on the security at the date of the meeting in order to determine the value (for voting purposes) of the unsecured balance.

Unless the CVA itself so provides, there is no reason in principle why the estimate made by the chairman for voting purposes should subsequently be binding on the secured creditor or the supervisor in the subsequent determination of the amount of a creditor's unsecured balance in respect of which a dividend may be payable in the course of or at the conclusion of the CVA.

R 1.19(4)

For the meaning of creditors *'connected with the company'* see IA 1986 s 249. Whether a person falls within this category is for the chairman to determine. The directors are required to identify such persons both within the proposal (IR 1986 r 1.3(2)(c)) and in the statement of affairs (IR 1986 r 1.5(2), (3)) and the chairman is entitled to rely upon such information in making his determination. His decision is again subject to appeal to the court under r 1.17A(5)–(7).

2.22

1.20 Requisite majorities (members)

(1) Subject as follows, and to any express provision made in the articles, at a company meeting any resolution is to be regarded as passed if voted for by more than one-half in value of the members present in person or by proxy and voting on the resolution.

The value of members is determined by reference to the number of votes conferred on each member by the company's articles.

(2) ...

(3) If the chairman uses a proxy contrary to Rule 1.15, his vote with that proxy does not count towards any majority under this Rule.

2.23

1.21 Proceedings to obtain agreement on the proposal

(1) If the chairman thinks fit, the creditors' meeting and the company meeting may be held together.

(2) The chairman may, and shall if it is so resolved at the meeting in question, adjourn that meeting for not more than 14 days.

(3) If there are subsequently further adjournments, the final adjournment shall not be to a day later than 14 days after the date on which the meeting in question was originally held.

(4) In the case of a proposal by the directors, if the meetings are adjourned under paragraph (2), notice of the fact shall be given by the nominee forthwith to the court.

(5) If following the final adjournment of the creditors' meeting the proposal (with or without modifications) has not been approved by the creditors, it is deemed rejected.

Notes

R 1.21

There is provision only for one meeting of creditors and one company meeting (see r 1.20 above). Such meetings may be adjourned for up to 14 days and can be held on different days (see IR 1986 r 1.13(3)) rather than together. Where a meeting has come to a final conclusion, there is no power to call a further meeting to reconsider the proposal in a modified form: *Re Symes* [1995] 2 BCLC 651 (an IVA case).

As with the summoning of meetings, the rules impose a tight 14–day timetable within which the creditors' meeting and the company meeting must reach a conclusion. If the creditors' meeting fails to approve the proposal within this timescale, it is deemed to have been rejected. It is unclear on its strict wording whether IR 1986 r 12.9 could be invoked in order to extend time for concluding the meeting beyond the stipulated period; (see notes to IR 1986 r 1.17(A)(6) above).

Section C: Implementation of the Arrangement

2.24

1.22 Resolutions to follow approval

(1) If the voluntary arrangement is approved (with or without modifications) by the creditors' meeting, a resolution may be taken by the creditors, where two or more supervisors are appointed, on the question whether acts to be done in connection with the arrangement may be done by any one or more of them, or must be done by all of them.]

(2) ...

(3) If at either meeting a resolution is moved for the appointment of some person other than the nominee to be supervisor of the arrangement, there must be produced to the chairman, at or before the meeting—
> (a) that person's written consent to act (unless he is present and then and there signifies his consent), and
> (b) his written confirmation that he is qualified to act as an insolvency practitioner in relation to the company [or is an authorised person in relation to the company.

2.25

1.22A Notice of order made under section 4A(6)

(1) This Rule applies where the court makes an order under section 4A(6).

(2) The member of the company who applied for the order shall serve sealed copies of it on—
> (a) the supervisor of the voluntary arrangement; and
> (b) the directors of the company.

(3) Service on the directors may be effected by service of a single copy on the company at its registered office.

(4) The directors or (as the case may be) the supervisor shall forthwith after receiving a copy of the court's order, give notice of it to all persons who were sent notice of the creditors' or company meetings or who, not having been sent such notice, are affected by the order.

(5) The person on whose application the order of the court was made shall, within 7 days of the order, deliver an office copy to the registrar of companies.

2.26

1.23 Hand-over of property etc to supervisor

(1) [Where the decision approving the voluntary arrangement has effect under section 4A—]
  (a)   the directors, or
  (b)   where the company is in liquidation or is in administration, and a person other than the responsible insolvency practitioner is appointed as supervisor of the voluntary arrangement, the insolvency practitioner,
shall forthwith do all that is required for putting the supervisor into possession of the assets included in the arrangement.

(2) Where the company is in liquidation or is in administration, the supervisor shall on taking possession of the assets discharge any balance due to the insolvency practitioner by way of remuneration or on account of—
  (a)   fees, costs, charges and expenses properly incurred and payable under the Act or the Rules, and
  (b)   any advances made in respect of the company, together with interest on such advances at the rate specified in section 17 of the Judgments Act 1838 at the date on which the company went into liquidation or (as the case may be) entered administration.

(3) Alternatively, the supervisor must, before taking possession, give the responsible insolvency practitioner a written undertaking to discharge any such balance out of the first realisation of assets.

(4) The insolvency practitioner has a charge on the assets included in the voluntary arrangement in respect of any sums due as above until they have been discharged, subject only to the deduction from realisations by the supervisor of the proper costs and expenses of such realisations.

(5) The supervisor shall from time to time out of the realisation of assets discharge all guarantees properly given by the responsible insolvency practitioner for the benefit of the company, and shall pay all the insolvency practitioner's expenses.

(6) References in this Rule to the responsible insolvency practitioner include, where a company is being wound up by the court, the official receiver, whether or not in his capacity as liquidator; and any sums due to the official receiver take priority over those due to a liquidator.

Notes

R 1.23(2)–(4)

These provisions apply in cases where a company in liquidation or administration enters into a voluntary arrangement and operate to give the liquidator/administrator priority for his fees and costs properly incurred and payable under the IA 1986 or IR 1986. This priority extends to all such costs incurred up to the date when the supervisor takes possession from the liquidator or administrator of the assets included within the arrangement, but does not extend to any costs which the liquidator or administrator may subsequently incur: *Rooney v Cardona* [1999] BPIR 954 (an IVA case based on the similarly worded provisions of what is now IR 1986 r 5.26).

2.27

1.24 Report of meetings

(1) A report of the meetings shall be prepared by the person who was chairman of them.

(2) The report shall—

(a) state whether the proposal for a voluntary arrangement was approved by the creditors of the company alone or by both the creditors and members of the company and in either case whether such approval was with any modifications;

(b) set out the resolutions which were taken at each meeting, and the decision on each one;

(c) list the creditors and members of the company (with their respective values) who were present or represented at the meetings, and how they voted on each resolution;

(ca) state whether, in the opinion of the supervisor, (i) the EC Regulation applies to the voluntary arrangement and (ii) if so, whether the proceedings are main proceedings, secondary proceedings or territorial proceedings; and

(d) include such further information (if any) as the chairman thinks it appropriate to make known to the court.

(3) A copy of the chairman's report shall, within 4 days of the meetings being held, be filed in court; and the court shall cause that copy to be endorsed with the date of filing.

(4) In respect of each of the meetings, the persons to whom notice of its result is to be sent by the chairman under section 4(6) are all of those who were sent notice of the meeting under this Part of the Rules.

The notice shall be sent immediately after a copy of the chairman's report is filed in court under paragraph (3).

(5) If the decision approving the voluntary arrangement has effect under section 4A (whether or not in the form proposed), the supervisor shall forthwith send a copy of the chairman's report to the registrar of companies.

Notes

R 1.24

This rule supplements IA 1986 s 4(6). The date of filing by the chairman of his report with the court (rather than the date on which notice is received by any creditor of the result of the meetings) is the trigger date for any challenge under IA 1986 s 6 to the arrangement (where approved) or the conduct of the meetings. The further information contemplated under IR 1986 r 1.24(2) (d) should include details of all determinations on voting entitlement etc made by the chairman under IR 1986 r 1.17(3), r 1.17A(1), (2), (4) and r 1.19(3), (4) which may be the subject of any appeal to the court.

2.28

1.25 Revocation or suspension of the arrangement

(1) This Rule applies where the court makes an order of revocation or suspension under section 6.

(2) The person who applied for the order shall serve sealed copies of it—
    (a)   on the supervisor of the voluntary arrangement, and
    (b)   on the directors of the company or the administrator or liquidator (according to who made the proposal for the arrangement).

Service on the directors may be effected by service of a single copy of the order on the company at its registered office.

(3) If the order includes a direction by the court under section 6(4)(b) for any further meetings to be summoned, notice shall also be given (by the person who applied for the order) to whoever is, in accordance with the direction, required to summon the meetings.

(4) The directors or (as the case may be) the administrator or liquidator shall—
    (a)   forthwith after receiving a copy of the court's order, give notice of it to all persons who were sent notice of the creditors' and company meetings or who, not having been sent that notice, appear to be affected by the order;
    (b)   within 7 days of their receiving a copy of the order (or within such longer period as the court may allow), give notice to the court whether it is intended to make a revised proposal to the company and its creditors, or to invite re-consideration of the original proposal.

(5) The person on whose application the order of revocation or suspension was made shall, within 7 days after the making of the order, deliver a copy of the order to the registrar of companies.

Notes

R 1.25

This rule sets out the notification requirements in a case where a successful challenge is made under IA 1986 s 6 to a CVA which has been approved. Curiously, the rule does not appear in terms to apply in cases where a successful challenge, on grounds of material irregularity, is made to the decision of a creditors' meeting to reject a CVA proposal. In such cases, the court may give directions for the summoning of a further creditors' meeting to reconsider the proposal but will, *ex hypothesi*, not make any order revoking or suspending the CVA (so as to fall within the terms of paragraph (1)).

2.29

1.26 Supervisor's accounts and reports

(1) Where the voluntary arrangement authorises or requires the supervisor—
    (a)   to carry on the business of the company or trade on its behalf or in its name, or
    (b)   to realise assets of the company, or
    (c)   otherwise to administer or dispose of any of its funds,
he shall keep accounts and records of his acts and dealings in and in connection with the arrangement, including in particular records of all receipts and payments of money.

(2) The supervisor shall, not less often than once in every 12 months beginning with the date of his appointment, prepare an abstract of such receipts and payments, and send copies of it, accompanied by his comments on the progress and efficacy of the arrangement, to—

    (a)   the court,

    (b)   the registrar of companies,

    (c)   the company,

    (d)   all those of the company's creditors who are bound by the arrangement,

    (e)   subject to paragraph (5) below, the members of the company who are so bound, and

    (f)   if the company is not in liquidation, the company's auditors for the time being.

If in any period of 12 months he has made no payments and had no receipts, he shall at the end of that period send a statement to that effect to all those specified in sub-paragraphs (a) to (f) above.

(3) An abstract provided under paragraph (2) shall relate to a period beginning with the date of the supervisor's appointment or (as the case may be) the day following the end of the last period for which an abstract was prepared under this Rule; and copies of the abstract shall be sent out, as required by paragraph (2), within the 2 months following the end of the period to which the abstract relates.

(4) If the supervisor is not authorised as mentioned in paragraph (1), he shall, not less often than once in every 12 months beginning with the date of his appointment, send to all those specified in paragraph (2)(a) to (f) a report on the progress and efficacy of the voluntary arrangement.

(5) The court may, on application by the supervisor—

    (a)   dispense with the sending under this Rule of abstracts or reports to members of the company, either altogether or on the basis that the availability of the abstract or report to members is to be advertised by the supervisor in a specified manner;

    (b)   vary the dates on which the obligation to send abstracts or reports arises.

Notes

R 1.26

This rule sets out important provisions requiring the supervisor every 12 months during the currency of the arrangement to keep (above all) creditors informed of the progress and efficacy of the arrangement. This requirement applies to all CVAs, whether or not the supervisor is authorised to do any of the matters set out in IR 1986 r 1.26(1): see r 1.26(2), (4). Where the supervisor is so authorised under r 1.26(1), he must in addition keep the creditors informed of the financial status of the arrangement, by an abstract of receipts and payments. See further the commentary to IA 1986 s 7 on questions relating to the 'failure' of a CVA.

2.30

1.27 Production of accounts and records to Secretary of State

(1) The Secretary of State may at any time during the course of the voluntary arrangement or after its completion or termination require the supervisor to produce for inspection—

(a) his records and accounts in respect of the arrangement, and
(b) copies of abstracts and reports prepared in compliance with Rule 1.26.

(2) The Secretary of State may require production either at the premises of the supervisor or elsewhere; and it is the duty of the supervisor to comply with any requirement imposed on him under this Rule.

(3) The Secretary of State may cause any accounts and records produced to him under this Rule to be audited; and the supervisor shall give to the Secretary of State such further information and assistance as he needs for the purposes of his audit.

2.31

1.28 Fees, costs, charges and expenses

(1) The fees, costs, charges and expenses that may be incurred for any of the purposes of the voluntary arrangement are—
(a) any disbursements made by the nominee prior to the [decision approving the arrangement taking effect under section 4A], and any remuneration for his services as such agreed between himself and the company (or, as the case may be, the administrator or liquidator);
(b) any fees, costs, charges or expenses which—
    (i) are sanctioned by the terms of the arrangement, or
    (ii) would be payable, or correspond to those which would be payable, in an administration or winding up.

2.32

1.29 Completion or termination of the arrangement

(1) Not more than 28 days after the final completion or termination of the voluntary arrangement, the supervisor shall send to creditors and members of the company who are bound by it a notice that the voluntary arrangement has been fully implemented or (as the case may be) has terminated.

(2) With the notice there shall be sent to each creditor and member a copy of a report by the supervisor summarising all receipts and payments made by him in pursuance of the arrangement, and explaining in relation to implementation of the arrangement any departure from the proposals as they originally took effect, or (in the case of termination of the arrangement) explaining the reasons why the arrangement has terminated.

(3) The supervisor shall, within the 28 days mentioned above, send to the registrar of companies and to the court a copy of the notice to creditors and members under paragraph (1), together with a copy of the report under paragraph (2), and the supervisor shall not vacate office until after such copies have been sent.

(4) In the report under paragraph (2), the supervisor shall include a statement as to the amount paid, if any, to unsecured creditors by virtue of the application of section 176A (prescribed part).

_____

Notes

R 1.29

Again, the supervisor is required on the completion or early termination of the arrangement not only to provide a final receipts and payments account but also to explain to creditors and members the reasons for any departure in the implementation of the arrangement from its terms as approved and the reason for its early termination. Any creditor or member dissatisfied with such explanation may apply to the court under IA 1986 s 7(3).

_____

2.33

1.30 False representations etc

...

_____

Notes

R 1.30

This provision was revoked by the Insolvency (Amendment) No 2 Rules 2002, SI 2002/2712 r 3 and replaced in substance by IA 1986 s 6A.

_____

Chapter 7
EC Regulation—Conversion of Voluntary Arrangement into Winding up

2.34

1.31 Application for conversion into winding up

(1) Where a member State liquidator proposes to apply to the court for the conversion under Article 37 of the EC Regulation (conversion of earlier proceedings) of a voluntary arrangement into a winding up, an affidavit complying with Rule 1.32 must be prepared and sworn, and filed in court in support of the application.

(2) An application under this Rule shall be by originating application.

(3) The application and the affidavit required under this Rule shall be served upon—
    (a)   the company; and
    (b)   the supervisor.

2.35

1.32 Contents of affidavit

(1) The affidavit shall state—
    (a)   that main proceedings have been opened in relation to the company in a member State other than the United Kingdom;

(b) the deponent's belief that the conversion of the voluntary arrangement into a winding up would prove to be in the interests of the creditors in the main proceedings;

(c) the deponent's opinion as to whether the company ought to enter voluntary winding up or be wound up by the court; and

(d) all other matters that, in the opinion of the member State liquidator, would assist the court—

(i) in deciding whether to make such an order, and

(ii) if the court were to do so, in considering the need for any consequential provision that would be necessary or desirable.

(2) An affidavit under this Rule shall be sworn by, or on behalf of, the member State liquidator.

2.36

1.33 Power of court

(1) On hearing the application for conversion into winding up the court may make such order as it thinks fit.

(2) If the court makes an order for conversion into winding up the order may contain all such consequential provisions as the court deems necessary or desirable.

(3) Without prejudice to the generality of paragraph (1), an order under that paragraph may provide that the company be wound up as if a resolution for voluntary winding up under section 84 were passed on the day on which the order is made.

(4) Where the court makes an order for conversion into winding up under paragraph (1), any expenses properly incurred as expenses of the administration of the voluntary arrangement in question shall be a first charge on the company's assets.

Notes

R 1.33

IR 1986 r 1.31 to 1.33 above (and IR 1986 1.34 below) were introduced by the Insolvency (Amendment) Regulations 2002 (SI 2002/1307) with effect from 31 May 2002 pursuant to the implementation of the Council Regulation (EC) 1346/2000 on Insolvency Proceedings. They set out the procedure for applications under Article 37 of the EC Regulation to convert the voluntary arrangement into a winding up. This applies (i) where the insolvent debtor is subject to insolvency proceedings in another member state which is its centre of main interests–the 'main proceedings' – as well as 'secondary proceedings' (the voluntary arrangement) in England and Wales and (ii) where the liquidator in the main proceedings considers that it would be in the interests of the creditors in the main proceedings to convert the voluntary arrangement into a winding up.

Chapter 8
EC Regulation—Member State Liquidator

2.37

1.34 Interpretation of creditor and notice to member State liquidator

(1) This Rule applies where a member State liquidator has been appointed in relation to the company.

(2) Where the supervisor is obliged to give notice to, or provide a copy of a document (including an order of court) to, the court, the registrar of companies or the official receiver, the supervisor shall give notice or provide copies, as appropriate, to the member State liquidator.

(3) Paragraph (2) is without prejudice to the generality of the obligations imposed by Article 31 of the EC Regulation (duty to cooperate and communicate information).

———

Notes

R 1.34

Again, this rule was introduced by the Insolvency (Amendment) Rules 2002 with effect from 31 May 2002 following the implementation of the EC Regulation. Where the supervisor is under a duty to give notice etc to the court, the registrar of companies or the official receiver of any matter under the various sections of Part 1 of IA 1986 and Part 1 of IR 1986, this rule simply extends the supervisor's notification obligation in circumstances where insolvency proceedings relating to the company are also taking place in another member state to include the liquidator in those proceedings.

———

Chapter 9
Obtaining a Moratorium

Proceedings during a Moratorium
Nominees
Consideration of Proposals where Moratorium Obtained

Section A: Obtaining a Moratorium

2.38

1.35 Preparation of proposal by directors and submission to nominee

(1) The document containing the proposal referred to in paragraph 6(1)(a) of Schedule A1 to the Act shall—
    (a)   be prepared by the directors;
    (b)   comply with the requirements of paragraphs (1) and (2) of Rule 1.3 (save that the reference to preferential creditors shall be to preferential creditors within the meaning of paragraph 31(8) of Schedule A1 to the Act); and
    (c)   state the address to which notice of the consent of the nominee to act and the documents referred to in Rule 1.38 shall be sent.

(2) With the agreement in writing of the nominee, the directors may amend the proposal at any time before submission to them by the nominee of the statement required by paragraph 6(2) of Schedule A1 to the Act.

Notes

R 1.35

This rule supplements Schedule A1 para 6(1)(a). It applies the provisions of IR 1986 r 1.3 (prescribing the contents of CVA proposals in cases not involving a moratorium) to proposals submitted under the moratorium procedure. See further the notes to IR 1986 r 1.3.

2.39

1.36 Delivery of documents to the intended nominee etc

(1) The documents required to be delivered to the nominee pursuant to paragraph 6(1) of Schedule A1 to the Act shall be delivered to the nominee himself or to a person authorised to take delivery of documents on his behalf.

(2) On receipt of the documents, the nominee shall forthwith issue an acknowledgement of receipt of the documents to the directors which shall indicate the date on which the documents were received.

2.40

1.37 Statement of affairs

(1) The statement of the company's affairs required to be delivered to the nominee pursuant to paragraph 6(1)(b) of Schedule A1 to the Act shall be delivered to the nominee no later than 7 days after the delivery to him of the document setting out the terms of the proposed voluntary arrangement or such longer time as he may allow.

(2) The statement of affairs shall comprise the same particulars as required by Rule 1.5(2) (supplementing or amplifying, so far as is necessary for clarifying the state of the company's affairs, those already given in the directors' proposal).

(3) The statement of affairs shall be made up to a date not earlier than 2 weeks before the date of the delivery of the document containing the proposal for the voluntary arrangement to the nominee under Rule 1.36(1).

However, the nominee may allow an extension of that period to the nearest practicable date (not earlier than 2 months before the date of delivery of the documents referred to in Rule 1.36(1)) and if he does so, he shall give a statement of his reasons in writing to the directors.

(4) The statement of affairs shall be certified as correct, to the best of their knowledge and belief, by two or more directors of the company, or by the company secretary and at least one director (other than the secretary himself).

Notes

R 1.37

This rule supplements Schedule A1 paragraph 6(1)(b). It applies the provisions of IR 1986 r 1.5(2) (prescribing the contents of the statement of affairs required in non-moratorium proposals) to proposals submitted under the moratorium procedure, and is otherwise in similar terms to that rule; see further the notes to IR 1986 r 1.5.

2.41

1.38 The nominee's statement

(1) The nominee shall submit to the directors the statement required by paragraph 6(2) of Schedule A1 to the Act within 28 days of the submission to him of the document setting out the terms of the proposed voluntary arrangement.

(2) The statement shall have annexed to it—
    (a) the nominee's comments on the proposal, unless the statement contains an opinion in the negative on any of the matters referred to in paragraph 6(2)(a) and (b) of Schedule A1 to the Act, in which case he shall instead give his reasons for that opinion, and
    (b) where he is willing to act in relation to the proposed arrangement, a statement of his consent to act.

Notes

R 1.38

This rule supplements Schedule A1 paragraph 6(2). See generally the notes to that sub-paragraph. The 28 day time limit imposed under r 1.38(1) runs from the date of 'submission to' the nominee of the proposal. It is not clear whether this date is the date of receipt by the nominee of the proposal, or (if different) the date the proposal is sent by the directors. However, the terms of IR 1986 r 1.36(2) suggest it is the date of receipt.

R 1.38(2)(b)

Under Schedule A1 paragraph 7(1)(d), in order to obtain a moratorium the directors are required to file with the court the nominee's statement of consent to act in the prescribed form (Form 1.8). Although this rule does not in terms require the nominee to annex his statement of consent in such prescribed form, the nominee should do so to avoid delay.

2.42

1.39 Documents submitted to the court to obtain moratorium

(1) Where pursuant to paragraph 7 of Schedule A1 to the Act the directors file the document and statements referred to in that paragraph

in court, those documents shall be delivered together with 4 copies of a schedule listing them within 3 working days of the date of the submission to them of the nominee's statement under paragraph 6(2) of Schedule A1 to the Act.

(2) When the directors file the document and statements referred to in paragraph (1), they shall also file—
  (a) a copy of any statement of reasons made by the nominee pursuant to Rule 1.37(3); and
  (b) a copy of the nominee's comments on the proposal submitted to them pursuant to Rule 1.38(2).

(3) The copies of the schedule shall be endorsed by the court with the date on which the documents were filed in court and 3 copies of the schedule sealed by the court shall be returned by the court to the person who filed the documents in court.

(4) The statement of affairs required to be filed under paragraph 7(1)(b) of Schedule A1 to the Act shall comprise the same particulars as required by Rule 1.5(2).

Notes

R 1.39

This rule supplements Schedule A1 paragraph 7. Note that it introduces a time limit of 3 working days from submission of the nominee's statement under paragraph 6(2) for delivering to the court the documents required under paragraph 7 in order to obtain a moratorium.

R 1.39(1)

The documents required to be filed under Schedule A1 paragraph 7 must be accompanied by a Schedule listing those documents. That Schedule can be found as Form 1.9 in IR 1986 Sch 4.

R 1.39(2)

Note the requirement for the filing of these additional documents in addition to those required under Schedule A1 paragraph 7.

R 1.39(4)

This provision appears to cover ground already covered under IR 1986 r 1.37(2).

2.43

1.40 Notice and advertisement of beginning of a moratorium

(1) After receiving the copies of the schedule endorsed by the court under Rule 1.39(3), the directors shall forthwith serve 2 of them on the nominee and one on the company.

(2) Forthwith after receiving the copies of the schedule pursuant to paragraph (1) the nominee shall advertise the coming into force of the moratorium once in the Gazette, and once in such newspaper as he thinks most appropriate for ensuring that its coming into force comes to the notice of the company's creditors.

(3) The nominee shall forthwith notify the registrar of companies, the company and any petitioning creditor of the company of whose claim he is aware of the coming into force of the moratorium and such notification shall specify the date on which the moratorium came into force.

(4) The nominee shall give notice of the coming into force of the moratorium specifying the date on which it came into force to—

(a) any enforcement officer or other officer who, to his knowledge, is charged with an execution or other legal process against the company or its property; and

(b) any person who, to his knowledge, has distrained against the company or its property.

Notes

R 1.40

This rule supplements Schedule A1 paragraphs 9, 10; see the commentary to those paragraphs.

2.44

1.41 Notice of extension of moratorium

(1) The nominee shall forthwith notify the registrar of companies and the court of a decision taking effect pursuant to paragraph 36 of Schedule A1 to the Act to extend or further extend the moratorium and such notice shall specify the new expiry date of the moratorium.

(2) Where an order is made by the court extending or further extending or renewing or continuing a moratorium, the nominee shall forthwith after receiving a copy of the same give notice to the registrar of companies and with the notice shall send an office copy of the order.

2.45

1.42 Notice and advertisement of end of moratorium

(1) After the moratorium comes to an end, the nominee shall forthwith advertise its coming to an end once in the Gazette, and once in such newspaper as he thinks most appropriate for ensuring that its coming to an end comes to the notice of the company's creditors, and such notice shall specify the date on which the moratorium came to an end.

(2) The nominee shall forthwith give notice of the ending of the moratorium to the registrar of companies, the court, the company and any creditor of the company of whose claim he is aware and such notice shall specify the date on which the moratorium came to an end.

Section B: Proceedings during a Moratorium

2.46

1.43 Disposal of charged property etc during a moratorium

(1) This Rule applies in any case where the company makes an application to the court under paragraph 20 of Schedule A1 to the Act for leave

to dispose of property of the company which is subject to a security, or goods in possession of the company under an agreement to which that paragraph relates.

(2) The court shall fix a venue for the hearing of the application and the company shall forthwith give notice of the venue to the person who is the holder of the security or, as the case may be, the owner under the agreement.

(3) If an order is made, the company shall forthwith give notice of it to that person or owner.

(4) The court shall send 2 sealed copies of the order to the company, who shall send one of them to that person or owner.

Section C: Nominees

2.47

1.44 Withdrawal of nominee's consent to act

Where the nominee withdraws his consent to act he shall, pursuant to paragraph 25(5) of Schedule A1 to the Act, forthwith give notice of his withdrawal and the reason for withdrawing his consent to act to—
    (a)   the registrar of companies;
    (b)   the court;
    (c)   the company; and
    (d)   any creditor of the company of whose claim he is aware.

2.48

1.45 Replacement of nominee by the court

(1) Where the directors intend to make an application to the court under paragraph 28 of Schedule A1 to the Act for the nominee to be replaced, they shall give to the nominee at least 7 days' notice of their application.

(2) Where the nominee intends to make an application to the court under that paragraph to be replaced, he shall give to the directors at least 7 days' notice of his application.

(3) No appointment of a replacement nominee shall be made by the court unless there is filed in court a statement by the replacement nominee indicating his consent to act.

2.49

1.46 Notification of appointment of a replacement nominee

Where a person is appointed as a replacement nominee, he shall forthwith give notice of his appointment to—
    (a)   the registrar of companies;
    (b)   the court (in any case where he was not appointed by the court); and
    (c)   the person whom he has replaced as nominee.

2.50

1.47 Applications to court under paragraphs 26 or 27 of Schedule A1 to the Act

Where any person intends to make an application to the court pursuant to paragraph 26 or 27 of Schedule A1 to the Act, he shall give to the nominee at least 7 days' notice of his application.

Section D: Consideration of proposals where Moratorium obtained

2.51

1.48 Summoning of meetings; procedure at meetings etc

(1) Where the nominee summons meetings of creditors and the company pursuant to paragraph 29(1) of Schedule A1 to the Act, each of those meetings shall be summoned for a date that is not more than 28 days from the date on which the moratorium came into force.

(2) Notices calling the creditors' meetings shall be sent by the nominee to all creditors specified in the statement of affairs and any other creditors of the company of whose address he is aware at least 14 days before the day fixed for the meeting.

(3) Notices calling the company meeting shall be sent by the nominee to all persons who are, to the best of the nominee's belief, members of the company at least 14 days before the day fixed for the meeting.

(4) Each notice sent under this Rule shall specify the court in which the documents relating to the obtaining of the moratorium were filed and state the effect of paragraphs (1), (3) and (4) of Rule 1.52 (requisite majorities (creditors)) and with each notice there shall be sent—
    (a)   a copy of the directors' proposal;
    (b)   a copy of the statement of the company's affairs or, if the nominee thinks fit, a summary of it (the summary to include a list of creditors and the amount of their debts); and
    (c)   the nominee's comments on the proposal.

(5) The provisions of Rules 1.13 to 1.16 shall apply.

Notes

R 1.48

This rule is similar in terms to IR 1986 r 1.9 (the corresponding rule in respect of non-moratorium CVAs) see the commentary to that rule.

2.52

1.49 Entitlement to vote (creditors)

(1) Subject as follows, every creditor who has notice of the creditors' meeting is entitled to vote at the meeting or any adjournment of it.

(2) Votes are calculated according to the amount of the creditor's debt as at the beginning of the moratorium, after deducting any amounts paid in respect of that debt after that date.

(3) A creditor may vote in respect of a debt for an unliquidated amount or any debt whose value is not ascertained and for the purposes of voting (but not otherwise) his debt shall be valued at £1 unless the chairman agrees to put a higher value on it.

Notes

R 1.49

This rule, and IR 1986 r 1.50 and 1.52 following are almost identical to IR 1986 r 1.17, 1.17A and r 1.19 (the equivalent rules which apply to non-moratorium CVAs); see the detailed commentary to those rules.

2.53

1.50 Procedure for admission of creditors' claims for voting purposes

(1) Subject as follows, at any creditors' meeting the chairman shall ascertain the entitlement of persons wishing to vote and shall admit or reject their claims accordingly.

(2) The chairman may admit or reject a claim in whole or in part.

(3) The chairman's decision on any matter under this Rule or under paragraph (3) of Rule 1.49 is subject to appeal to the court by any creditor or member of the company.

(4) If the chairman is in doubt whether a claim should be admitted or rejected, he shall mark it as objected to and allow votes to be cast in respect of it, subject to such votes being subsequently declared invalid if the objection to the claim is sustained.

(5) If on an appeal the chairman's decision is reversed or varied, or votes are declared invalid, the court may order another meeting to be summoned, or make such order as it thinks just.

The court's power to make an order under this paragraph is exercisable only if it considers that the circumstances giving rise to the appeal are such as give rise to unfair prejudice or material irregularity.

(6) An application to the court by way of appeal against the chairman's decision shall not be made after the end of the period of 28 days beginning with the first day on which the report required by paragraph 30(3) of Schedule A1 to the Act has been made to the court.

(7) The chairman is not personally liable for any costs incurred by any person in respect of an appeal under this Rule.

Notes

R 1.50

See the note to IR 1986 r 1.49 above

2.54

1.51 Voting rights (members)

Rule 1.18 shall apply.

2.55

1.52 Requisite majorities (creditors)

(1) Subject as follows, at the creditors' meeting for any resolution to pass approving any proposal or modification there must be a majority in excess of three-quarters in value of the creditors present in person or by proxy and voting on the resolution.

(2) The same applies in respect of any other resolution proposed at the meeting, but substituting one-half for three-quarters.

(3) At a meeting of the creditors for any resolution to pass extending (or further extending) a moratorium, or to bring a moratorium to an end before the end of the period of any extension, there must be a majority in excess of three quarters in value of the creditors present in person or by proxy and voting on the resolution. For this purpose paragraph (4)(b) below shall not apply and a secured creditor is entitled to vote in respect of the amount of his claim without deducting the value of his security.

(4) In the following cases there is to be left out of account a creditor's vote in respect of any claim or part of a claim—
    (a)   where written notice of the claim was not given, either at the meeting or before it, to the chairman or convenor of the meeting;
    (b)   where the claim or part is secured;
    (c)   where the claim is in respect of a debt wholly or partly on, or secured by, a current bill of exchange or promissory note, unless the creditor is willing—
        (i)   to treat the liability to him on the bill or note of every person who is liable on it antecedently to the company, and against whom a bankruptcy order has not been made (or, in the case of a company, which has not gone into liquidation), as a security in his hands, and
        (ii)   to estimate the value of the security and (for the purpose of entitlement to vote, but not of any distribution under the arrangement) to deduct it from his claim.

(5) Any resolution is invalid if those voting against it include more than half in value of the creditors, counting in these latter only those—
    (a)   who have notice of the meeting;
    (b)   whose votes are not to be left out of account under paragraph (4); and
    (c)   who are not, to the best of the chairman's belief, persons connected with the company.

(6) It is for the chairman of the meeting to decide whether under this Rule—
    (a)   a vote is to be left out of account in accordance with paragraph (4), or
    (b)   a person is a connected person for the purposes of paragraph (5)(c);

and in relation to the second of these two cases the chairman is entitled to rely on the information provided by the statement of the company's affairs or otherwise in accordance with this Part of the Rules.

(7) If the chairman uses a proxy contrary to Rule 1.15 as it applies by virtue of Rule 1.48(5), his vote with that proxy does not count towards any majority under this Rule.

(8) The chairman's decision on any matter under this Rule is subject to appeal to the court by any creditor or member and paragraphs (5) to (7) of Rule 1.50 apply as regards such an appeal.

Notes

R 1.52

See the note to IR 1986 r 1.49 above.

2.56

1.53 Requisite majorities (members) and proceedings to obtain agreement on the proposal

(1) Rule 1.20 shall apply.

(2) If the chairman thinks fit, the creditors' meeting and the company meeting may be held together.

(3) The chairman may, and shall if it is so resolved at the meeting in question, adjourn that meeting, but any adjournment shall not be to a day which is more than 14 days after the date on which the moratorium (including any extension) ends.

(4) If the meetings are adjourned under paragraph (3), notice of the fact shall be given by the nominee forthwith to the court.

(5) If following the final adjournment of the creditors' meeting the proposal (with or without modifications) has not been approved by the creditors, it is deemed rejected.

Notes

R 1.53

There is provision for one meeting of creditors and one company meeting only. Such meetings may be adjourned to a date up to 14 days after the moratorium when any extension expires. But where such a meeting has come to a final conclusion, there is no power to call a further meeting to reconsider the proposal in a modified form: *Re Symes* [1995] 2 BCLC 651 (an IVA case). If the creditors' meeting fails to approve the proposal within the timescale provided, the proposal is deemed rejected.

2.57

1.54 Implementation of the arrangement

(1) Where a decision approving the arrangement has effect under paragraph 36 of Schedule A1 to the Act, the directors shall forthwith do all that is required for putting the supervisor into possession of the assets included in the arrangement.

(2) Subject to paragraph (3), Rules 1.22, 1.22A and 1.24 to 1.29 apply.

(3) The provisions referred to in paragraph (2) are modified as follows—

(a) in paragraph (1) of Rule 1.22A the reference to section 4A(6) is to be read as a reference to paragraph 36(5) of Schedule A1 to the Act;

(b) in paragraph (4) of Rule 1.24 the reference to section 4(6) is to be read as a reference to paragraph 30(3) of Schedule A1 to the Act;

(c) in paragraph (5) of Rule 1.24 the reference to section 4A is to be read as a reference to paragraph 36 of Schedule A1 to the Act;

(d) in paragraph (1) of Rule 1.25 the reference to section 6 is to be read as a reference to paragraph 38 of Schedule A1 to the Act and the references in paragraphs (2) and (4) to the administrator or liquidator shall be ignored;

(e) in paragraph (3) of Rule 1.25 the reference to section 6(4)(b) is to be read as a reference to paragraph 38 (4)(b) of Schedule A1 to the Act; and

(f) in sub-paragraph (a) of paragraph (1) of Rule 1.28 the reference to section 4A is to be read as a reference to paragraph 36 of Schedule A1 to the Act.

**[Part 2
Administration Procedure]**

Notes

IR 1986 r 2.1 to 2.133 contain the rules supporting the administration regime introduced by the EA 2002 Sch B1 effective from 15 September 2003. The former regime applies where the petition for the administration order was presented before 15 September 2003: art 3(2) of the Enterprise Act 2002 (Commencement No 4 and Transitional Provisions and Savings) Order 2003, SI 2003/2093. Thus, all pre-existing administrations, plus any administration commenced by an order made on or after 15 September 2003 but pursuant to a petition presented before that date, continue to be governed by the old provisions (IA 1986 s 8–27; and the former IR 1986 r 2.1–2.62, Insolvency (Amendment) Rules 2003 SI 2003/1730 r 5.1). The former IR 1986 r 2.1–2.62 are set out below.

2.57.1

2.1 Affidavit to support petition

(1) Where it is proposed to apply to the court by petition for an administration order to be made in relation to a company, an affidavit complying with Rule 2.3 below must be prepared and sworn, with a view to its being filed in court in support of the petition.

(2) *If the petition is to be presented by the company or by the directors, the affidavit must be made by one of the directors, or the secretary of the company, stating himself to make it on behalf of the company or, as the case may be, on behalf of the directors.*

(3) *If the petition is to be presented by creditors, the affidavit must be made by a person acting under the authority of them all, whether or not himself one of their number. In any case there must be stated in the affidavit the nature of his authority and the means of his knowledge of the matters to which the affidavit relates.*

(4) *If the petition is to be presented by the supervisor of a voluntary arrangement under Part I of the Act, it is to be treated as if it were a petition by the company.*

2.57.2

2.2 Independent report on company's affairs

(1) *There may be prepared, with a view to its being exhibited to the affidavit in support of the petition, a report by an independent person to the effect that the appointment of an administrator for the company is expedient.*

(2) *The report may be by the person proposed as administrator, or by any other person having adequate knowledge of the company's affairs, not being a director, secretary, manager, member, or employee of the company.*

(3) *The report shall specify the purposes which, in the opinion of the person preparing it, may be achieved for the company by the making of an administration order, being purposes particularly specified in section 8(3).*

2.57.3

2.3 Contents of affidavit

(1) *The affidavit shall state—*
  (a) *the deponent's belief that the company is, or is likely to become, unable to pay its debts and the grounds of that belief; and*
  (b) *which of the purposes specified in section 8(3) is expected to be achieved by the making of an administration order.*
  (c) *whether in the opinion of the deponent, (i) the EC Regulation will apply and (ii) if so, whether the proceedings will be main proceedings, secondary proceedings or territorial proceedings.]*

(2) *There shall in the affidavit be provided a statement of the company's financial position, specifying (to the best of the deponent's knowledge and belief) assets and liabilities, including contingent and prospective liabilities.*

(3) *Details shall be given of any security known or believed to be held by creditors of the company, and whether in any case the security is such as to confer power on the holder to appoint an administrative receiver. If an administrative receiver has been appointed, that fact shall be stated.*

(4) *If any petition has been presented for the winding up of the company, details of it shall be given in the affidavit, so far as within the immediate knowledge of the deponent.*

(5) *If there are other matters which, in the opinion of those intending to present the petition for an administration order, will assist the court in deciding whether to make such an order, those matters (so far as lying within the knowledge or belief of the deponent) shall also be stated.*

(6) If a report has been prepared for the company under Rule 2.2, that fact shall be stated. If not, an explanation shall be provided why not.

2.57.4

2.4 Form of petition

(1) If presented by the company or by the directors, the petition shall state the name of the company and its address for service, which (in the absence of special reasons to the contrary) is that of the company's registered office.

(2) If presented by a single creditor, the petition shall state his name and address for service.

(3) If the petition is presented by the directors, it shall state that it is so presented under section 9; but from and after presentation it is to be treated for all purposes as the petition of the company.

(4) If the petition is presented by two or more creditors, it shall state that it is so presented (naming them); but from and after presentation it is to be treated for all purposes as the petition of one only of them, named in the petition as petitioning on behalf of himself and other creditors. An address for service for that one shall be specified.

(5) The petition shall specify the name and address of the person proposed to be appointed as administrator; and it shall be stated that, to the best of the petitioner's knowledge and belief, the person is qualified to act as an insolvency practitioner in relation to the company.

(6) There shall be exhibited to the affidavit in support of the petition—

    (a) a copy of the petition;
    (b) a written consent by the proposed administrator to accept appointment, if an administration order is made; and
    (c) if a report has been prepared under Rule 2.2, a copy of it.

2.57.5

2.5 Filing of petition

(1) The petition and affidavit shall be filed in court, with a sufficient number of copies for service and use as provided by Rule 2.6.

(2) Each of the copies delivered shall have applied to it the seal of the court and be issued to the petitioner; and on each copy there shall be endorsed the date and time of filing.

(3) The court shall fix a venue for the hearing of the petition and this also shall be endorsed on each copy of the petition issued under paragraph (2).

(4) After the petition is filed, it is the duty of the petitioner to notify the court in writing of any winding-up petition presented against the company, as soon as he becomes aware of it.

2.57.6

2.6 Service of petition

(1) In the following paragraphs of this Rule, references to the petition are to a copy of the petition issued by the court under Rule 2.5(2) together with the affidavit in support of it and the documents (other than the copy petition) exhibited to the affidavit.

(2) The petition shall be served—
- [(a) on any person who has appointed, or is or may be entitled to appoint, an administrative receiver of the company;]
- (b) if an administrative receiver has been appointed, on him;
- [(ba) if a member State liquidator has been appointed in main proceedings in relation to the company, on him;]
- (c) if there is pending a petition for the winding up of the company, on the petitioner (and also on the provisional liquidator, if any); and
- (d) on the person proposed as administrator.

(3) If the petition for the making of an administration order is presented by creditors of the company, the petition shall be served on the company.

2.57.7

[2.6A Notice to sheriff, etc]

[The petitioner shall forthwith after filing the petition give notice of its presentation to—
- (a) any sheriff or other officer who to his knowledge is charged with an execution or other legal process against the company or its property, and
- (b) any person who to his knowledge has distrained against the company or its property.]

2.57.8

2.7 Manner in which service to be effected

(1) Service of the petition in accordance with Rule 2.6 shall be effected by the petitioner, or his solicitor, or by a person instructed by him or his solicitor, not less than 5 days before the date fixed for the hearing.

(2) Service shall be effected as follows—
- (a) on the company (subject to paragraph (3) below), by delivering the documents to its registered office;
- (b) on any other person (subject to paragraph (4)), by delivering the documents to his proper address;
- (c) in either case, in such other manner as the court may direct.

(3) If delivery to the company's registered office is not practicable, service may be effected by delivery to its last known principal place of business in England and Wales.

(4) [Subject to paragraph (4A),] for the purposes of paragraph (2)(b), a person's proper address is any which he has previously notified as his address for service; but if he has not notified any such address, service may be effected by delivery to his usual or last known address.

[(4A) in the case of a person who—
- (a) is an authorised institution or former authorised institution within the meaning of the Banking Act 1987,
- (h) has appointed, or is or may be entitled to appoint, an administrative receiver of the company, and
- (c) has not notified an address for service,
the proper address is the address of an office of that person where, to the knowledge of the petitioner, the company maintains a bank account or, where no such office is known to the petitioner, the registered office of that person, or, if there is no such office, his usual or last known address.]

(5) *Delivery of documents to any place or address may be made by leaving them there, or sending them by first class post.*

2.57.9

2.8 Proof of service

(1) *Service of the petition shall be verified by affidavit, specifying the date on which, and the manner in which, service was effected.*

(2) *The affidavit, with a sealed copy of the petition exhibited to it, shall be filed in court forthwith after service, and in any event not less than one day before the hearing of the petition.*

2.57.10

2.9 The hearing

(1) *At the hearing of the petition, any of the following may appear or be represented—*
  (a)   *the petitioner;*
  (b)   *the company;*
  [(c)   *any person who has appointed, or is or may be entitled to appoint, an administrative receiver of the company;]*
  (d)   *if an administrative receiver has been appointed, he;*
  (e)   *any person who has presented a petition for the winding up of the company;*
  (f)   *the person proposed for appointment as administrator; and*
  [(fa)   *if a member State liquidator has been appointed in main proceedings in relation to the company, he;]*
  (g)   *with the leave of the court, any other person who appears to have an interest justifying his appearance.*

(2) *If the court makes an administration order, the costs of the petitioner, and of any person appearing whose costs are allowed by the court, are payable as an expense of the administration.*

2.57.11

2.10 Notice and advertisement of administration order

(1) *If the court makes an administration order, it shall forthwith give notice to the person appointed as administrator.*

(2) *Forthwith after the order is made, the administrator shall advertise its making once in the Gazette, and once in such newspaper as he thinks most appropriate for ensuring that the order comes to the notice of the company's creditors.*

(3) *The administrator shall also forthwith give notice of the making of the order—*
  [(a)   *to any person who has appointed, or is or may be entitled to appoint, an administrative receiver of the company;]*
  (b)   *if an administrative receiver has been appointed, to him;*
  (c)   *if there is pending a petition for the winding up of the company, to the petitioner (and also to the provisional liquidator, if any); and*
  (d)   *to the registrar of companies.*

(4) Two sealed copies of the order shall be sent by the court to the administrator, one of which shall be sent by him to the registrar of companies in accordance with section 21(2).

(5) If under section 9(4) the court makes any other order, it shall give directions as to the persons to whom, and how, notice of it is to be given.

2.57.12

Chapter 2
Statement of Affairs and Proposals to Creditors

2.11 Notice requiring statement of affairs

(1) [Where] the administrator determines to require a statement of the compa-ny's affairs to be made out and submitted to him in accordance with section 22, he shall send notice to each of the persons whom he considers should be made responsible under that section, requiring them to prepare and submit the statement.

(2) The persons to whom the notice is sent are referred to in this Chapter as "the deponents".

(3) The notice shall inform each of the deponents—
  (a) of the names and addresses of all others (if any) to whom the same notice has been sent;
  (b) of the time within which the statement must be delivered;
  (c) of the effect of section 22(6) (penalty for non-compliance); and
  (d) of the application to him, and to each of the other deponents, of section 235 (duty to provide information, and to attend on the administrator if required).

(4) The administrator shall, on request, furnish each deponent with [the forms required for the preparation of the statement of affairs].

2.57.13

2.12 Verification and filing

(1) The statement of affairs shall be in Form 2.9, shall contain all the particulars required by that form and shall be verified by affidavit by the deponents (using the same form).

(2) The administrator may require any of the persons mentioned in sec-tion 22(3) to submit an affidavit of concurrence, stating that he concurs in the statement of affairs.

(3) An affidavit of concurrence may be qualified in respect of matters dealt with in the statement of affairs, where the maker of the affidavit is not in agreement with the deponents, or he considers the statement to be erroneous or misleading, or he is without the direct knowledge necessary for concurring with it.

(4) The statement of affairs shall be delivered to the administrator by the deponent making the affidavit of verification (or by one of them, if more than one), together with a copy of the verified statement.

(5) Every affidavit of concurrence shall be delivered by the person who makes it, together with a copy.

(6) *The administrator shall file the verified copy of the statement, and the affidavits of concurrence (if any) in court.*

2.57.14

2.13 Limited disclosure

(1) *Where the administrator thinks that it would prejudice the conduct of the administration for the whole or part of the statement of affairs to be disclosed, he may apply to the court for an order of limited disclosure in respect of the statement, or any specified part of it.*

(2) *The court may on the application order that the statement or, as the case may be, the specified part of it, be not filed in court, or that it is to be filed separately and not be open to inspection otherwise than with leave of the court.*

(3) *The court's order may include directions as to the delivery of documents to the registrar of companies and the disclosure of relevant information to other persons.*

2.57.15

2.14 Release from duty to submit statement of affairs; extension of time

(1) *The power of the administrator under section 22(5) to give a release from the obligation imposed by that section, or to grant an extension of time, may be exercised at the administrator's own discretion, or at the request of any deponent.*

(2) *A deponent may, if he requests a release or extension of time and it is refused by the administrator, apply to the court for it.*

(3) *The court may, if it thinks that no sufficient cause is shown for the application, dismiss it; but it shall not do so unless the applicant has had an opportunity to attend the court for an ex parte hearing, of which he has been given at least 7 days' notice.*

If the application is not dismissed under this paragraph, the court shall fix a venue for it to be heard, and give notice to the deponent accordingly.

(4) *The deponent shall, at least 14 days before the hearing, send to the administrator a notice stating the venue and accompanied by a copy of the application, and of any evidence which he (the deponent) intends to adduce in support of it.*

(5) *The administrator may appear and be heard on the application; and, whether or not he appears, he may file a written report of any matters which he considers ought to be drawn to the court's attention.*

If such a report is filed, a copy of it shall be sent by the administrator to the deponent, not later than 5 days before the hearing.

(6) *Sealed copies of any order made on the application shall be sent by the court to the deponent and the administrator.*

(7) *On any application under this Rule the applicant's costs shall be paid in any event by him and, unless the court otherwise orders, no allowance towards them shall be made out of the assets.*

2.57.16

2.15 Expenses of statement of affairs

(1) A deponent making the statement of affairs and affidavit shall be allowed, and paid by the administrator out of his receipts, any expenses incurred by the deponent in so doing which the administrator considers reasonable.

(2) Any decision by the administrator under this Rule is subject to appeal to the court.

(3) Nothing in this Rule relieves a deponent from any obligation with respect to the preparation, verification and submission of the statement of affairs, or to the provision of information to the administrator.

2.57.17

2.16 Statement to be annexed to proposals

[(1)] There shall be annexed to the administrator's proposals, when sent to the registrar of companies under section 23 and laid before the creditors' meeting to be summoned under that section, a statement by him showing—

- (a) *details relating to his appointment as administrator, the purposes for which an administration order was applied for and made, and any subsequent variation of those purposes;*
- (b) *the names of the directors and secretary of the company;*
- (c) *an account of the circumstances giving rise to the application for an administration order;*
- (d) *if a statement of affairs has been submitted, a copy or summary of it, with the administrator's comments, if any;*
- (e) *if no statement of affairs has been submitted, details of the financial position of the company at the latest practicable date (which must, unless the court otherwise orders, be a date not earlier than that of the administration order);*
- [(f) *the manner in which the affairs and business of the company—*
  - (i) *have, since the date of the administrator's appointment, been managed and financed, and*
  - (ii) *will, if the administrator's proposals are approved, continue to be managed and financed; ...]*
- [(fa) *whether (i) of the EC Regulation applies and (ii) if so, whether the proceedings are main proceedings, secondary proceedings or territorial proceedings; and]*
- (g) *such other information (if any) as the administrator thinks necessary to enable creditors to decide whether or not to vote for the adoption of the proposals.*

[(2) Where the administrator intends to apply to the court under section 18 for the administration order to be discharged at a time before he has sent a statement of his proposals to creditors in accordance with section 23(1), he shall, at least 10 days before he makes such an application, send to all creditors of the company (so far as he is aware of their addresses) a report containing the information required by paragraph (1)(a)–(f)(i) of this Rule.]

2.57.18

2.17 Notice to members of proposals to creditors

The manner of publishing—

>   *(a)   under section 23(2)(b), notice to members of the administrator's propos-*
>   *als to creditors, and*
>   *(b)   under section 25(3)(b), notice to members of the substantial revisions of*
>   *the proposals,*
> *shall be by gazetting; and the notice shall also in either case be advertised once in*
> *the newspaper in which the administration order was advertised.*

Chapter 3
Creditors' and Company Meetings

Section A: Creditors' Meetings

2.57.19

2.18 Meeting to consider administrator's proposals

(1) Notice of the creditors' meeting to be summoned under section 23(1) shall be given to all the creditors of the company who are identified in the statement of affairs, or are known to the administrator and had claims against the company at the date of the administration order.

(2) Notice of the meeting shall also (unless the court otherwise directs) be given by advertisement in the newspaper in which the administration order was advertised.

(3) Notice to attend the meeting shall be sent out at the same time to any directors or officers of the company (including persons who have been directors or officers in the past) whose presence at the meeting is, in the administrator's opinion, required.

(4) If at the meeting there is not the requisite majority for approval of the administrator's proposals (with modifications, if any), the chairman may, and shall if a resolution is passed to that effect, adjourn the meeting for not more than 14 days.

2.57.20

2.19 Creditors' meetings generally

(1) This Rule applies to creditors' meetings summoned by the administrator under—
    (a)   section 14(2)(b) (general power to summon meetings of creditors);
    (b)   section 17(3) (requisition by creditors; direction by the court);
    (c)   section 23(1) (to consider administrator's proposals); or
    (d)   section 25(2)(b) (to consider substantial revisions).

(2) In fixing the venue for the meeting, the administrator shall have regard to the convenience of creditors.

(3) The meeting shall be summoned for commencement between 10.00 and 16.00 hours on a business day, unless the court otherwise directs.

(4) ... notice of the meeting shall be given to all creditors who are known to the administrator and had claims against the company at the date of the administration order; and the notice shall specify the purpose of the meeting and contain a statement of the effect of Rule 2.22(1) (entitlement to vote).

[(4A) Except in relation to a meeting summoned under section 23(1) or 25(2), at least 21 days' notice of the meeting shall be given.]

(5) With the notice summoning the meeting there shall be sent out forms of proxy.

(6) If within 30 minutes from the time fixed for commencement of the meeting there is no person present to act as chairman, the meeting stands adjourned to the same time and place in the following week or, if that is not a business day, to the business day immediately following.

(7) The meeting may from time to time be adjourned, if the chairman thinks fit, but not for more than 14 days from the date on which it was fixed to commence.

2.57.21

2.20 The chairman at meetings

(1) At any meeting of creditors summoned by the administrator, either he shall be chairman, or a person nominated by him in writing to act in his place.

(2) A person so nominated must be either—
  (a) *one who is qualified to act as an insolvency practitioner in relation to the company, or*
  (b) *an employee of the administrator or his firm who is experienced in insolvency matters.*

2.57.22

2.21 Meeting requisitioned by creditors

(1) Any request by creditors to the administrator for a meeting of creditors to be summoned shall be accompanied by—
  (a) *a list of the creditors concurring with the request, showing the amounts of their respective claims in the administration;*
  (b) *from each creditor concurring, written confirmation of his concurrence; and*
  (c) *a statement of the purpose of the proposed meeting.*

This paragraph does not apply if the requisitioning creditor's debt is alone sufficient, without the concurrence of other creditors.

(2) The administrator shall, if he considers the request to be properly made in accordance with section 17(3), fix a venue for the meeting, not more than 35 days from his receipt of the request, and give at least 21 days' notice of the meeting to creditors.

(3) The expenses of summoning and holding a meeting at the instance of any person other than the administrator shall be paid by that person, who shall deposit with the administrator security for their payment.

(4) The sum to be deposited shall be such as the administrator may determine, and he shall not act without the deposit having been made.

(5) The meeting may resolve that the expenses of summoning and holding it are to be payable out of the assets of the company, as an expense of the administration.

(6) To the extent that any deposit made under this Rule is not required for the payment of expenses of summoning and holding the meeting, it shall be repaid to the person who made it.

2.57.23

2.22 Entitlement to vote

(1) Subject as follows, at a meeting of creditors in administration proceedings a person is entitled to vote only if—
- *(a) he has given to the administrator, not later than 12.00 hours on the business day before the day fixed for the meeting, details in writing of the debt which—*
  - *[(i) he claims to be due to him from the company, or*
  - *(ii) in relation to a member State liquidator, is claimed to be due to creditors in proceedings in relation to which he holds office], and the claim has been duly admitted under the following provisions of this Rule, and*
- *(b) there has been lodged with the administrator any proxy which he intends to be used on his behalf.*

Details of the debt must include any calculation for the purposes of Rules 2.24 to 2.27.

(2) The chairman of the meeting may allow a creditor to vote, notwithstanding that he has failed to comply with paragraph (1)(a), if satisfied that the failure was due to circumstances beyond the creditor's control.

(3) The administrator or, if other, the chairman of the meeting may call for any document or other evidence to be produced to him, where he thinks it necessary for the purpose of substantiating the whole or any part of the claim.

(4) Votes are calculated according to the amount of a creditor's debt as at the date of the administration order, deducting any amounts paid in respect of the debt after that date.

(5) A creditor shall not vote in respect of a debt for an unliquidated amount, or any debt whose value is not ascertained, except where the chairman agrees to put upon the debt an estimated minimum value for the purpose of entitlement to vote and admits the claim for that purpose.

[(6) No vote shall be cast by virtue of a claim more than once on any resolution put to the meeting.

(7) Where—
- *(a) a creditor is entitled to vote under this Rule,*
- *(b) has lodged his claim in one or more sets of other proceedings, and*
- *(c) votes (either in person or by proxy) on a resolution put to the meeting, only the creditors' vote shall be counted.*

(8) Where—
- *(a) a creditor has lodged his claim in more than one set of other proceedings, and*
- *(b) more than one member State liquidator seeks to vote by virtue of that claim,*

the entitlement to vote by virtue of that claim is not excersiable by the member State liquidator in main proceedings, whether or not the creditor has lodged his claim in the main proceedings.

(9) For the purposes of paragraph (6), the claim of a creditor and of any member State liquidator in relation to the same debt are a single claim.

(10) For the purposes of paragraphs (7) and (8), 'other proceedings' means main proceedings, secondary proceedings or territorial proceedings in another member State.]

2.57.24

2.23 Admission and rejection of claims

(1) At any creditors' meeting the chairman has power to admit or reject a creditor's claim for the purpose of his entitlement to vote; and the power is exercisable with respect to the whole or any part of the claim.

(2) The chairman's decision under this Rule, or in respect of any matter arising under Rule 2.22, is subject to appeal to the court by any creditor.

(3) If the chairman is in doubt whether a claim should be admitted or rejected, he shall mark it as objected to and allow the creditor to vote, subject to his vote being subsequently declared invalid if the objection to the claim is sustained.

(4) If on an appeal the chairman's decision is reversed or varied, or a creditor's vote is declared invalid, the court may order that another meeting be summoned, or make such other order as it thinks just.

(5) In the case of the meeting summoned under section 23 to consider the administrator's proposals, an application to the court by way of appeal under this Rule against a decision of the chairman shall not be made later than 28 days after the delivery of the administrator's report in accordance with section 24(4).

(6) Neither the administrator nor any person nominated by him to be chairman is personally liable for costs incurred by any person in respect of an appeal to the court under this Rule, unless the court makes an order to that effect.

2.57.25

2.24 Secured creditors

At a meeting of creditors a secured creditor is entitled to vote only in respect of the balance (if any) of his debt after deducting the value of his security as estimated by him.

2.57.26

2.25 Holders of negotiable instruments

A creditor shall not vote in respect of a debt on, or secured by, a current bill of exchange or promissory note, unless he is willing—
   (a)   to treat the liability to him on the bill or note of every person who is liable on it antecedently to the company, and against whom a bankruptcy order has not been made (or, in the case of a company, which has not gone into liquidation), as a security in his hands, and
   (b)   to estimate the value of the security and, for the purpose of his entitlement to vote, to deduct it from his claim.

2.57.27

2.26 Retention of title creditors

For the purpose of entitlement to vote at a creditors' meeting in administration proceedings, a seller of goods to the company under a retention of title agreement shall deduct from his claim the value, as estimated by him, of any rights arising under that agreement in respect of goods in possession of the company.

2.57.28

2.27 Hire-purchase, conditional sale and chattel leasing agreements

(1) Subject as follows, an owner of goods under a hire-purchase or chattel leasing agreement, or a seller of goods under a conditional sale agreement, is entitled to vote in respect of the amount of the debt due and payable to him by the company as at the date of the administration order.

(2) In calculating the amount of any debt for this purpose, no account shall be taken of any amount attributable to the exercise of any right under the relevant agreement, so far as the right has become exercisable solely by virtue of the presentation of the petition for an administration order or any matter arising in consequence of that, or of the making of the order.

2.57.29

2.28 Resolutions and minutes

(1) [Subject to paragraph (1A),] at a creditors' meeting in administration proceedings, a resolution is passed when a majority (in value) of those present and voting, in person or by proxy, have voted in favour of it.

[(1A) Any resolution is invalid if those voting against it include more than half in value of the creditors to whom notice of the meeting was sent and who are not, to the best of the chairman's belief, persons connected with the company.]

(2) The chairman of the meeting shall cause minutes of its proceedings to be entered in the company's minute book.

(3) The minutes shall include a list of the creditors who attended (personally or by proxy) and, if a creditors' committee has been established, the names and addresses of those elected to be members of the committee.

2.57.30

[2.29 Reports and notices under sections 23 and 25]

[Any report or notice by the administrator of the result of a creditors' meeting held under section 23 or 25 shall have annexed to it details of the proposals which were considered by the meeting and of the revisions and modifications to the proposals which were so considered.]

2.57.31

2.30 Notices to creditors

(1) Within 14 days of the conclusion of a meeting of creditors to consider the administrator's proposals or revised proposals, the administrator shall send notice of the result of the meeting (including, where appropriate, details of the proposals as approved) to every creditor who received notice of the meeting under the Rules, and to any other creditor of whom the administrator has since become aware.

(2) Within 14 days of the end of every period of 6 months beginning with the date of approval of the administrator's proposals or revised proposals, the administrator shall send to all creditors of the company a report on the progress of the administration.

(3) On vacating office the administrator shall send to creditors a report on the administration up to that time.

This does not apply where the administration is immediately followed by the company going into liquidation, nor when the administrator is removed from office by the court or ceases to be qualified as an insolvency practitioner.

Section B: Company Meetings

2.57.32

2.31 Venue and conduct of company meeting

(1) Where the administrator summons a meeting of members of the company, he shall fix a venue for it having regard to their convenience.

(2) The chairman of the meeting shall be the administrator or a person nominated by him in writing to act in his place.

(3) A person so nominated must be either—
  (a) one who is qualified to act as an insolvency practitioner in relation to the company, or
  (b) an employee of the administrator or his firm who is experienced in insolvency matters.

(4) If within 30 minutes from the time fixed for commencement of the meeting there is no person present to act as chairman, the meeting stands adjourned to the same time and place in the following week or, if that is not a business day, to the business day immediately following.

(5) Subject as above, the meeting shall be summoned and conducted as if it were a general meeting of the company summoned under the company's articles of association, and in accordance with the applicable provisions of the Companies Act.

[(5A) Paraagraph (5) does not apply where the laws of a member State and not the laws of England and Wales apply in relation to the conduct of the meeting.

[(5B) Where paragraph (5A) applies, subject as above, the meeting shall be summoned and conducted in accordance with the constitution of the company and the laws of the member State referred to in that paragraph shall apply to the conduct of the meeting.]

(6) The chairman of the meeting shall cause minutes of its proceedings to be entered in the company's minute book.

Chapter 4
The Creditors' Committee

2.57.33

2.32 Constitution of committee

(1) Where it is resolved by a creditors' meeting to establish a creditors' committee for the purposes of the administration, the committee shall consist of at least 3 and not more than 5 creditors of the company elected at the meeting.

(2) Any creditor of the company is eligible to be a member of the committee, so long as his claim has not been rejected for the purpose of his entitlement to vote.

(3) A body corporate may be a member of the committee, but it cannot act as such otherwise than by a representative appointed under Rule 2.37 below.

2.57.34

2.33 Formalities of establishment

(1) The creditors' committee does not come into being, and accordingly cannot act, until the administrator has issued a certificate of its due constitution.

[(2) No person may act as a member of the committee unless and until he has agreed to do so and, unless the relevant proxy or authorisation contains a statement to the contrary, such agreement may be given by his proxy-holder or representative under section 375 of the Companies Act present at the meeting establishing the committee.

(2A) The administrator's certificate of the committee's due constitution shall not issue unless and until at least 3 of the persons who are to be members of the committee have agreed to act.]

(3) As and when the others (if any) agree to act, the administrator shall issue an amended certificate.

(4) The certificate, and any amended certificate, shall be filed in court by the administrator.

(5) If after the first establishment of the committee there is any change in its membership, the administrator shall report the change to the court.

2.57.35

2.34 Functions and meetings of the committee

(1) The creditors' committee shall assist the administrator in discharging his functions, and act in relation to him in such manner as may be agreed from time to time.

(2) Subject as follows, meetings of the committee shall be held when and where determined by the administrator.

(3) The administrator shall call a first meeting of the committee not later than 3 months after its first establishment; and thereafter he shall call a meeting—

    (a) if so requested by a member of the committee or his representative (the meeting then to be held within 21 days of the request being received by the administrator), and

    (b) for a specified date, if the committee has previously resolved that a meeting be held on that date.

(4) The administrator shall give 7 days' written notice of the venue of any meeting to every member of the committee (or his representative designated for that purpose), unless in any case the requirement of notice has been waived by or on behalf of any member.

Waiver may be signified either at or before the meeting.

2.57.36

2.35 The chairman at meetings

(1) Subject to Rule 2.44(3), the chairman at any meeting of the creditors' committee shall be the administrator or a person nominated by him in writing to act.

(2) *A person so nominated must be either—*

    (*a*)   *one who is qualified to act as an insolvency practitioner in relation to the company, or*

    (*b*)   *an employee of the administrator or his firm who is experienced in insolvency matters.*

2.57.37

2.36 Quorum

A meeting of the committee is duly constituted if due notice of it has been given to all the members, and at least 2 members are present or represented.

2.57.38

2.37 Committee-members' representatives

(1) *A member of the committee may, in relation to the business of the committee, be represented by another person duly authorised by him for that purpose.*

(2) *A person acting as a committee-member's representative must hold a letter of authority entitling him so to act (either generally or specially) and signed by or on behalf of the committee-member [, and for this purpose any proxy or any authorisation under section 375 of the Companies Act in relation to any meeting of creditors of the company shall, unless it contains a statement to the contrary, be treated as a letter of authority to act generally signed by or on behalf of the committee-member].*

(3) *The chairman at any meeting of the committee may call on a person claiming to act as a committee-member's representative to produce his letter of authority, and may exclude him if it appears that his authority is deficient.*

(4) *No member may be represented by a body corporate, or by a person who is an undischarged bankrupt, or is subject to a composition or arrangement with his creditors.*

(5) *No person shall—*

    (*a*)   *on the same committee, act at one and the same time as representative of more than one committee-member, or*

    (*b*)   *act both as a member of the committee and as representative of another member.*

(6) *Where a member's representative signs any document on the member's behalf, the fact that he so signs must be stated below his signature.*

2.57.39

2.38 Resignation

A member of the committee may resign by notice in writing delivered to the administrator.

2.57.40

2.39 Termination of membership

(1) *Membership of the creditors' committee is automatically terminated if the member—*

    (*a*)   *becomes bankrupt, or compounds or arranges with his creditors, or*

> (*b*)   at 3 consecutive meetings of the committee is neither present nor represented (*unless at the third of those meetings it is resolved that this Rule is not to apply in his case*), or
>
> (*c*)   ceases to be, or is found never to have been, a creditor.

(2) *However, if the cause of termination is the member's bankruptcy, his trustee in bankruptcy replaces him as a member of the committee.*

2.57.41

2.40 Removal

A member of the committee may be removed by resolution at a meeting of creditors, at least 14 days' notice having been given of the intention to move that resolution.

2.57.42

2.41 Vacancies

(1) *The following applies if there is a vacancy in the membership of the creditors' committee.*

(2) *The vacancy need not be filled if the administrator and a majority of the remaining members of the committee so agree, provided that the total number of members does not fall below the minimum required under Rule 2.32.*

(3) *The administrator may appoint any creditor (being qualified under the Rules to be a member of the committee) to fill the vacancy, if a majority of the other members of the committee agree to the appointment, and the creditor concerned consents to act.*

2.57.43

2.42 Procedure at meetings

(1) *At any meeting of the creditors' committee, each member of it (whether present himself, or by his representative) has one vote; and a resolution is passed when a majority of the members present or represented have voted in favour of it.*

(2) *Every resolution passed shall be recorded in writing, either separately or as part of the minutes of the meeting.*

(3) *A record of each resolution shall be signed by the chairman and placed in the company's minute book.*

2.57.44

2.43 Resolutions by post

(1) *In accordance with this Rule, the administrator may seek to obtain the agreement of members of the creditors' committee to a resolution by sending to every member (or his representative designated for the purpose) a copy of the proposed resolution.*

(2) *Where the administrator makes use of the procedure allowed by this Rule, he shall send out to members of the committee or their representatives (as the case may be) [a copy of any proposed resolution on which a decision is sought, which shall be set out in such a way that agreement with or dissent from each separate resolution may be indicated by the recipient on the copy so sent].*

(3) *Any member of the committee may, within 7 business days from the date of the administrator sending out a resolution, require him to summon a meeting of the committee to consider the matters raised by the resolution.*

(4) *In the absence of such a request, the resolution is deemed to have been passed by the committee if and when the administrator is notified in writing by a majority of the members that they concur with it.*

(5) *A copy of every resolution passed under this Rule, and a note that the committee's concurrence was obtained, shall be placed in the company's minute book.*

2.57.45

2.44 Information from administrator

(1) *Where the committee resolves to require the attendance of the administrator under section 26(2), the notice to him shall be in writing signed by the majority of the members of the committee for the time being. A member's representative may sign for him.*

(2) *The meeting at which the administrator's attendance is required shall be fixed by the committee for a business day, and shall be held at such time and place as he determines.*

(3) *Where the administrator so attends, the members of the committee may elect any one of their number to be chairman of the meeting, in place of the administrator or a nominee of his.*

2.57.46

2.45 Expenses of members

(1) *Subject as follows, the administrator shall out of the assets of the company defray any reasonable travelling expenses directly incurred by members of the creditors' committee or their representatives in relation to their attendance at the committee's meetings, or otherwise on the committee's business, as an expense of the administration.*

(2) *Paragraph (1) does not apply to any meeting of the committee held within 3 months of a previous meeting, unless the meeting in question is summoned at the instance of the administrator.*

2.57.47

2.46 Members' dealings with the company

(1) *Membership of the committee does not prevent a person from dealing with the company while the administration order is in force, provided that any transactions in the course of such dealings are in good faith and for value.*

(2) *The court may, on the application of any person interested, set aside any transaction which appears to it to be contrary to the requirements of this Rule, and may give such consequential directions as it thinks fit for compensating the company for any loss which it may have incurred in consequence of the transaction.*

2.57.48

[2.46A Formal defects]

[The acts of the creditors' committee established for any administration are valid notwithstanding any defect in the appointment, election or qualifications of any member of the committee or any committee-member's representative or in the formalities of its establishment.]

Chapter 5
The Administrator

2.57.49

2.47 Fixing of remuneration

(1) The administrator is entitled to receive remuneration for his services as such.

(2) The remuneration shall be fixed either—
  (a) as a percentage of the value of the property with which he has to deal, or
  (b) by reference to the time properly given by the insolvency practitioner (as administrator) and his staff in attending to matters arising in the administration.

(3) It is for the creditors' committee (if there is one) to determine whether the remuneration is to be fixed under paragraph (2)(a) or (b) and, if under paragraph (2)(a), to determine any percentage to be applied as there mentioned.

(4) In arriving at that determination, the committee shall have regard to the following matters—
  (a) the complexity (or otherwise) of the case,
  (b) any respects in which, in connection with the company's affairs, there falls on the administrator any responsibility of an exceptional kind or degree,
  (c) the effectiveness with which the administrator appears to be carrying out, or to have carried out, his duties as such, and
  (d) the value and nature of the property with which he has to deal.

(5) If there is no creditors' committee, or the committee does not make the requisite determination, the administrator's remuneration may be fixed (in accordance with paragraph (2)) by a resolution of a meeting of creditors; and paragraph (4) applies to them as it does to the creditors' committee.

(6) If not fixed as above, the administrator's remuneration shall, on his application, be fixed by the court.

[(7) Where there are joint administrators, it is for them to agree between themselves as to how the remuneration payable should be apportioned. Any dispute arising between them may be referred—
  (a) to the court, for settlement by order, or
  (b) to the creditors' committee or a meeting of creditors, for settlement by resolution.

(8) If the administrator is a solicitor and employs his own firm, or any partner in it, to act on behalf of the company, profit costs shall not be paid unless this is authorised by the creditors' committee, the creditors or the court.]

2.57.50

2.48 Recourse to meeting of creditors

If the administrator's remuneration has been fixed by the creditors' committee, and he considers the rate or amount to be insufficient, he may request that it be increased by resolution of the creditors.

2.57.51

2.49 Recourse to the court

(1) If the administrator considers that the remuneration fixed for him by the creditors' committee, or by resolution of the creditors, is insufficient, he may apply to the court for an order increasing its amount or rate.

(2) The administrator shall give at least 14 days' notice of his application to the members of the creditors' committee; and the committee may nominate one or more members to appear or be represented, and to be heard, on the application.

(3) If there is no creditors' committee, the administrator's notice of his application shall be sent to such one or more of the company's creditors as the court may direct, which creditors may nominate one or more of their number to appear or be represented.

(4) The court may, if it appears to be a proper case, order the costs of the administrator's application, including the costs of any member of the creditors' committee appearing [or being represented] on it, or any creditor so appearing [or being represented], to be paid as an expense of the administration.

2.57.52

2.50 Creditors' claim that remuneration is excessive

(1) Any creditor of the company may, with the concurrence of at least 25 per cent in value of the creditors (including himself), apply to the court for an order that the administrator's remuneration be reduced, on the grounds that it is, in all the circumstances, excessive.

(2) The court may, if it thinks that no sufficient cause is shown for a reduction, dismiss the application; but it shall not do so unless the applicant has had an opportunity to attend the court for an ex parte hearing, of which he has been given at least 7 days' notice.

If the application is not dismissed under this paragraph, the court shall fix a venue for it to be heard, and give notice to the applicant accordingly.

(3) The applicant shall, at least 14 days before the hearing, send to the administrator a notice stating the venue and accompanied by a copy of the application, and of any evidence which the applicant intends to adduce in support of it.

(4) If the court considers the application to be well-founded, it shall make an order fixing the remuneration at a reduced amount or rate.

(5) Unless the court orders otherwise, the costs of the application shall be paid by the applicant, and are not payable as an expense of the administration.

2.57.53

2.51 Disposal of charged property, etc

(1) The following applies where the administrator applies to the court under section 15(2) for authority to dispose of property of the company which is subject to a security, or goods in the possession of the company under an agreement, to which that subsection relates.

(2) The court shall fix a venue for the hearing of the application, and the administrator shall forthwith give notice of the venue to the person who is the holder of the security or, as the case may be, the owner under the agreement.

(3) If an order is made under section 15(2), the administrator shall forthwith give notice of it to that person or owner.

(4) The court shall send 2 sealed copies of the order to the administrator, who shall send one of them to that person or owner.

2.57.54

2.52 Abstract of receipts and payments

(1) The administrator shall—
  (a)   within 2 months after the end of 6 months from the date of his appointment, and of every subsequent period of 6 months, and
  (b)   within 2 months after he ceases to act as administrator,
send to the court, and to the registrar of companies, and to each member of the creditors' committee, the requisite accounts of the receipts and payments of the company.

(2) The court may, on the administrator's application, extend the period of 2 months mentioned above.

(3) The accounts are to be in the form of an abstract showing—
  (a)   receipts and payments during the relevant period of 6 months, or
  (b)   where the administrator has ceased to act, receipts and payments during the period from the end of the last 6 month period to the time when he so ceased (alternatively, if there has been no previous abstract, receipts and payments in the period since his appointment as administrator).

(4) If the administrator makes default in complying with this Rule, he is liable to a fine and, for continued contravention, to a daily default fine.

2.57.55

2.53 Resignation

(1) The administrator may give notice of his resignation on grounds of ill health or because—
  (a)   he intends ceasing to be in practice as an insolvency practitioner, or
  (b)   there is some conflict of interest, or change of personal circumstances, which precludes or makes impracticable the further discharge by him of the duties of administrator.

(2) The administrator may, with the leave of the court, give notice of his resignation on grounds other than those specified in paragraph (1).

(3) The administrator must give to the persons specified below at least 7 days' notice of his intention to resign, or to apply for the court's leave to do so—
  (a)   if there is a continuing administrator of the company, to him;

(b)   if there is no such administrator, to the creditors' committee; and

(c)   if there is no such administrator and no creditors' committee, to the company and its creditors.

[(4) Where the administrator gives notice under paragraph (3), he must also give notice to a member State liquidator, if such a person has been appointed in relation to the company.]

2.57.56

2.54 Administrator deceased

(1) Subject as follows, where the administrator has died, it is the duty of his personal representatives to give notice of the fact to the court, specifying the date of the death.

This does not apply if notice has been given under any of the following paragraphs of this Rule.

(2) If the deceased administrator was a partner in a firm, notice may be given by a partner in the firm who is qualified to act as an insolvency practitioner, or is a member of any body recognised by the Secretary of State for the authorisation of insolvency practitioners.

(3) Notice of the death may be given by any person producing to the court the relevant death certificate or a copy of it.

2.57.57

2.55 Order filling vacancy

Where the court makes an order filling a vacancy in the office of administrator, the same provisions apply in respect of giving notice of, and advertising, the order as in the case of the [administration order].

Chapter 6
VAT Bad Debt Relief

2.57.58

2.56 Issue of certificate of insolvency

(1) In accordance with this Rule, it is the duty of the administrator to issue a certificate in the terms of paragraph (b) of section 22(3) of the Value Added Tax Act 1983 (which specifies the circumstances in which a company is deemed insolvent for the purposes of that section) forthwith upon his forming the opinion described in that paragraph.

(2) There shall in the certificate be specified—

(a)   *the name of the company and its registered number;*

(b)   *the name of the administrator and the date of his appointment;*

(c)   *the date on which the certificate is issued.*

(3) The certificate shall be intituled "CERTIFICATE OF INSOLVENCY FOR THE PURPOSES OF SECTION 22(3)(b) OF THE VALUE ADDED TAX ACT 1983".

2.57.59

2.57 Notice to creditors

(1) Notice of the issue of the certificate shall be given by the administrator within 3 months of his appointment or within 2 months of issuing the certificate, whichever is the later, to all of the company's unsecured creditors of whose address he is then aware and who have, to his knowledge, made supplies to the company, with a charge to value added tax, at any time before his appointment.

(2) Thereafter, he shall give the notice to any such creditor of whose address and supplies to the company he becomes aware.

(3) He is not under obligation to provide any creditor with a copy of the certificate.

2.57.60

2.58 Preservation of certificate with company's records

(1) The certificate shall be retained with the company's accounting records, and section 222 of the Companies Act (where and for how long records are to be kept) shall apply to the certificate as it applies to those records.

(2) It is the duty of the administrator, on vacating office, to bring this Rule to the attention of the directors or (as the case may be) any successor of his as administrator.

Chapter 7
EC Regulation – Conversion of Administration into winding up

2.57.61

2.59 Application for conversion into winding up

(1) Where a member State liquidator proposes to apply to the court for the conversion under Article 37 of the EC Regulation (conversion of earlier proceedings) of an administration into a winding up, an affidavit complying with Rule 2.60 must be prepared and sworn, and filed in court in support of the application..

(2) An application under this Rule shall be originating application.

(3) The application and the affidavit required under this Rule shall be served upon—
  (a)   the company; and
  (b)   the administrator.]

2.57.62

2.60 Contents of affidavit

(1) The affidavit shall state—
  (a)   that main proceedings have been opened in relation to the company in a member State other than the United Kingdom;
  (b)   the deponent's belief that the conversion of the administration into a winding up would prove to be in the interests of the creditors in the main proceedings;

    (c)   *the deponent's opinion as to whether the company ought to enter voluntary winding up or be wound up by the court; and*

    (d)   *all other matters that, in the opinion of the member State liquidator, would assist the court—*

         (i)   *in deciding whether to make such an order, and*

        (ii)   *if the court were to do so, in considering the need for any consequential provision that would be necessary or desirable.*

(2) An Affidavit under this Rule shall be sworn by, or on behalf of the member State liquidator.'

2.57.63

2.61 Power of court

(1) On hearing the application for conversion into winding up the court may make such order as it thinks fit.

(2) If the court makes an order for conversion into winding up the order may contain all such consequential provisions as the court deems necessary and desirable.

(3) Without prejudice to the generality of paragraph (1), an order under that paragraph may provide that the company be wound up as if a resolution for voluntary winding up under section 84 were passed on the day on which the order is made.]

Chapter 8
EC Regulation – Member State Liquidator

2.57.64

2.62 Interpretation of creditor and notice to member State Liquidator

(1) This Rule applies where a member State liquidator has been appointed in relation to the company.

(2) For the purposes of the Rules referred to in paragraph (3) the member State liquidator is deemed to be a creditor

(3) The Rules referred to in paragraph (2) are Rules 2.18(1) (notice of creditors' meeting), 2.19(4) (creditors' meeting), 2.21 (requisitioning of creditors' meeting), 2.22 (entitlement to vote), 2.23 (admission and rejection of claims), 2.24 (secured creditors), 2.25 (holders of negotiable instruments), 2.26 (retention of title creditors), 2.27 (hire-purchase, conditional sale and chattel leasing agreements), 2.30 (notice of result of creditors' meeting), 2.32(2) (creditors' committee), 2.39(1)(b) and (c) (termination of membership of creditors' committee), 2.41(3) (vacancies in creditors' committee) 2.49(3) (administration of membership of creditors' committee), and 2.50 (challenge to administrator's remuneration).

(4) Paragraphs (2) and (3) are without prejudice to the generality of the right to participate referred to in paragraph 3 of Article 32 of the EC Regulation (exercise of creditors' rights).

(5) Where the administrator is obliged to give notice to, or provide a copy of a document (including an order of court) to the court, the registrar of companies or

the official receiver, the administrator shall give notice or provide copies, as the case may be, to the member State liquidator.

(6) Paragraph (5) is without prejudice to the generality of the obligations imposed by Article 31 of the EC Regulation (duty to cooperate and communicate information).

[Chapter 1
Preliminary

2.58

[2.1 Introductory and interpretation]

[(1) In this Part—
- (a) Chapter 2 applies in relation to the appointment of an administrator by the court;
- (b) Chapter 3 applies in relation to the appointment of an administrator by the holder of a qualifying floating charge under paragraph 14;
- (c) Chapter 4 applies in relation to the appointment of an administrator by the company or the directors under paragraph 22;
- (d) The following Chapters apply in all the cases mentioned in sub-paragraphs (a)–(c) above:
  —Chapter 5: Process of administration;
  —Chapter 6: Meetings and reports;
  —Chapter 7: The creditors' committee;
  —Chapter 8: Disposal of charged property;
  —Chapter 9: Expenses of the administration;
  —Chapter 10: Distributions to creditors;
  —Chapter 11: The administrator;
  —Chapter 12: Ending administration;
  —Chapter 13: Replacing administrator;
  —Chapter 14: EC Regulation—conversion of administration into winding up;
  —Chapter 15: EC Regulation—member State liquidator.

(2) In this Part of these Rules a reference to a numbered paragraph shall, unless otherwise stated, be to the paragraph so numbered in Schedule B1 to the Act.]

Notes

R 2.1(2)

The former substantive provisions (IA 1986 ss 8–27) have been repealed from 15 September 2003 except in the case where the administration petition was presented before that date: Enterprise Act 2002 (Commencement No 4 and Transitional Provisions and Savings) Order 2003 SI 2003/2093 para 3; the new substantive provisions are contained in IA 1986 Sch B1.

**[Chapter 2
Appointment of Administrator by Court]**

2.59

[2.2 Affidavit in support of administration application]

[(1) Where it is proposed to apply to the court for an administration order to be made in relation to a company, the administration application shall be in Form 2.1B and an affidavit complying with Rule 2.4 must be prepared and sworn, with a view to its being filed with the court in support of the application.

(2) If the administration application is to be made by the company or by the directors, the affidavit shall be made by one of the directors, or the secretary of the company, stating himself to make it on behalf of the company or, as the case may be, on behalf of the directors.

(3) If the application is to be made by creditors, the affidavit shall be made by a person acting under the authority of them all, whether or not himself one of their number. In any case there must be stated in the affidavit the nature of his authority and the means of his knowledge of the matters to which the affidavit relates.

(4) If the application is to be made by the supervisor of a voluntary arrangement under Part I of the Act, it is to be treated as if it were an application by the company.]

Notes

R 2.2(1)

Form 2.1B is the required form of application which must be completed; it would be unwise to use a 'homemade' application. The 'court' is the High Court; or the county court where the company's paid up capital does not exceed £120,000 and it has insolvency jurisdiction IA 1986 s 251, CA 1985 s 744, IA 1986 s 117 – see notes to s 117. A witness statement may be used instead of an affidavit IR 1986 r 7.57(6). Form 2.1B is the standard form which can be amended according to the relevant circumstances. It was possible under the former regime to obtain an administration order in an emergency on an undertaking to present a petition (*Re Shearing and Loader Ltd* [1991] BCLC 764, *Re Chancery plc* [1991] BCLC 712).

R 2.2(2)

It is important to evidence the authority of the maker of the witness statement/ affidavit usually by reference to a board resolution (or a record of the majority directors' decision IA 1986 Sch B1 para 105) approving an application to court and nominating an individual to make the witness statement/affidavit.

R 2.2(4)

A supervisor may apply for an administration under IA 1986 s 7(4)(b).

2.60

[2.3 Form of application]

[(1) If made by the company or by the directors, the application shall state the name of the company and its address for service, which (in the absence of special reasons to the contrary) is that of the company's registered office.

(2) If the application is made by the directors, it shall state that it is so made under paragraph 12(1)(b); but from and after making it is to be treated for all purposes as the application of the company.

(3) If made by a single creditor, the application shall state his name and address for service.

(4) If the application is made by two or more creditors, it shall state that it is so made (naming them); but from and after making it is to be treated for all purposes as the application of only one of them, named in the application as applying on behalf of himself and other creditors. An address for service for that one shall be specified.

(5) There shall be attached to the application a written statement which shall be in Form 2.2B by each of the persons proposed to be administrator stating—
(a) that he consents to accept appointment;
(b) details of any prior professional relationship(s) that he has had with the company to which he is to be appointed as administrator; and
(c) his opinion that it is reasonably likely that the purpose of administration will be achieved.]

Notes

R 2.3(1)

In the case of a foreign company whose centre of main interests under the EC Regulation Insolvency Proceedings 2000 is in the United Kingdom it would be appropriate to use the principal business address in the United Kingdom. Form 2.1B which is the required form of application (IR 1986 r 2.2(1)) obliges the applicant to state whether the EC Regulation applies and if so whether the proceedings will be 'main proceedings'; see notes to the EC Regulation Insolvency Proceedings 2000.

R 2.3(5)(c)

The proposed administrator must therefore express a favourable opinion in Form 2.2B. It is important that the proposed administrator considers the matter carefully as he may be the subject of criticism for giving that opinion if the administration is later challenged (eg IA 1986 Sch B1 para 81). There is no suggestion that the proposed administrator should file an independent report as under the former administration regime (former IR 1986 r 2.2) or that he has to explain the reasons why he formed the necessary opinion *Re Redman Construction Ltd* [2004] All ER 146; but see the notes to IR 1986 r 2.4(2)(e) below.

2.61

[2.4 Contents of application and affidavit in support]

[(1) The administration application shall contain a statement of the applicant's belief that the company is, or is likely to become, unable to pay its debts, except where the applicant is the holder of a qualifying floating charge and is making the application in reliance on paragraph 35.

(2) There shall be attached to the application an affidavit in support which shall contain—

> (a) a statement of the company's financial position, specifying (to the best of the applicant's knowledge and belief) the company's assets and liabilities, including contingent and prospective liabilities;
>
> (b) details of any security known or believed to be held by creditors of the company, and whether in any case the security is such as to confer power on the holder to appoint an administrative receiver or to appoint an administrator under paragraph 14. If an administrative receiver has been appointed, that fact shall be stated;
>
> (c) details of any insolvency proceedings in relation to the company including any petition that has been presented for the winding up of the company so far as within the immediate knowledge of the applicant;
>
> (d) where it is intended to appoint a number of persons as administrators, details of the matters set out in paragraph 100(2) regarding the exercise of the function of the administrators; and
>
> (e) any other matters which, in the opinion of those intending to make the application for an administration order, will assist the court in deciding whether to make such an order, so far as lying within the knowledge or belief of the applicant.
>
> (3) Where the application is made by the holder of a qualifying floating charge in reliance on paragraph 35, he shall give sufficient details in the affidavit in support to satisfy the court that he is entitled to appoint an administrator under paragraph 14.
>
> (4) The affidavit shall state whether, in the opinion of the person making the application, (i) the EC Regulation will apply and (ii) if so, whether the proceedings will be main proceedings or territorial proceedings.]

Notes

R 2.4(1)

Thus a qualifying floating chargeholder (IA 1986 Sch B1 para 14(2)) does not have to prove to the court that the company is insolvent so long as the application for administration is made under IA 1986 Sch B1 para 35. Where such a chargeholder cannot fulfil all the conditions set out in that provision he will have to make an application as a creditor under IA 1986 IA 1986 Sch B1 para 12(1)(c) and prove insolvency IA 1986 Sch B1 para 11. A qualifying floating chargeholder might be advised to apply to court for an administrator rather than appoint out of court under IA 1986 Sch B1 para 14 where for instance there could be debate about the location of the 'centre of main interests' of the company under the EC Regulation on Insolvency Proceedings 2000 for the purposes of opening 'main proceedings'; in those circumstances it would be safer to obtain a court order which might carry more weight in the relevant foreign jurisdiction. Further he may be obliged to make an application to court because of the restrictions on the power to appoint imposed in IA 1986 Sch B1 paras 15–17.

R 2.4(2)(a)

It would be usual to produce a comparison of the estimated realisations in an administration and a liquidation/forced sale situation including the costs of the respective procedures. *Re C E King Ltd* [2000] 2 BCLC 297; and in a trading administration it would be helpful to include a cash flow statement and an explanation of how the administration is to be funded.

R 2.4(2)(e)

There is no longer any express provision allowing a report to be made by an independent person (usually the proposed administrator) as there was under the former administration regime (former IR 1986 r 2.2). However it is preferable to have some evidence before the court from the proposed administrator explaining the reasons for the favourable opinion he has formed under IR 1986 r 2.3(5)(c); this should be in the form of a witness statement or a report/letter addressed to the company and exhibited to a witness statement. In any event the duty of disclosure of relevant information is strict: *Re West Park Golf & Country Club* [1997] 1 BCLC 20.

R 2.4(4)

The standard form of application for administration (Form 2.1B IR 1986 r 2.2(1)) also contains an obligation to state these details. Where a company has its centre of main interests in the United Kingdom then 'main proceedings' under the EC Regulation on Insolvency Proceedings 2000 can be opened in the United Kingdom; see the notes to IR 1986 r 2.4(1) above.

2.62

[2.5 Filing of application]

[(1) The application (and all supporting documents) shall be filed with the court, with a sufficient number of copies for service and use as provided by Rule 2.6.

(2) Each of the copies filed shall have applied to it the seal of the court and be issued to the applicant; and on each copy there shall be endorsed the date and time of filing.

(3) The court shall fix a venue for the hearing of the application and this also shall be endorsed on each copy of the application issued under paragraph (2).

(4) After the application is filed, it is the duty of the applicant to notify the court in writing of the existence of any insolvency proceedings, and any insolvency proceedings under the EC Regulation, in relation to the company, as soon as he becomes aware of them.]

Notes

R 2.5(1)

Once presented the application cannot be withdrawn without leave of the court IA 1986 Sch B1 para 12(3). An application for administration should not be presented simply to 'buy time' to achieve a higher price on a proposed sale of property: *Re Doltable Limited* [2006] 1 BCLC 384..

R 2.5(4)

There is therefore a continuing duty of disclosure in relation to the existence of 'insolvency proceedings' IR 1986 r 13.

2.63

[2.6 Service of application]

[(1) In the following paragraphs of this Rule, references to the application are to a copy of the application issued by the court under Rule 2.5(2) together with the affidavit in support of it and the documents attached to the application.

(2) Notification for the purposes of paragraph 12(2) shall be by way of service in accordance with Rule 2.8, verified in accordance with Rule 2.9.

(3) The application shall be served in addition to those persons referred to in paragraph 12(2)—

(a) if an administrative receiver has been appointed, on him;

(b) if there is pending a petition for the winding-up of the company, on the petitioner (and also on the provisional liquidator, if any);

(c) if a member State liquidator has been appointed in main pro-ceedings in relation to the company, on him;

(d) on the person proposed as administrator;

(e) on the company, if the application is made by anyone other than the company;

(f) if a supervisor of a voluntary arrangement under Part I of the Act has been appointed, on him.]

Notes

R 2.6(2)

Under IA 1986 Sch B1 para 12(2) those who have appointed or may appoint an administrative receiver or who is or may be entitled to appoint an administrator under IA 1986 Sch B1 para 14 must be notified of the application.

R 2.6(3)

The 'application' includes the application itself and the evidence in support and it must be served on the parties stated in addition to those listed in IA 1986 Sch B1 para 12(2).

2.64

[2.7 Notice to [officers charged with execution of writs or other process.], etc]

[The applicant shall as soon as reasonably practicable after filing the application give notice of its being made to—

(a) any [enforcement officer] or other officer who to his knowledge is charged with an execution or other legal process against the company or its property; and

(b) any person who to his knowledge has distrained against the company or its property.]

Notes

R 2.7

These parties must be given notice of the application but there is no requirement to serve them with the application and supporting evidence. Where such a party is not given notice the court may be prepared to make an administration order in any event and give the relevant party liberty to apply.

2.65

[2.8 Manner in which service to be effected]

[(1) Service of the application in accordance with Rule 2.6 shall be effected by the applicant, or his solicitor, or by a person instructed by him or his solicitor, not less than 5 days before the date fixed for the hearing.

(2) Service shall be effected as follows—

    (a)   on the company (subject to paragraph (3) below), by delivering the documents to its registered office;

    (b)   on any other person (subject to paragraph (4) below), by delivering the documents to his proper address.;

    (c)   in either case, in such other manner as the court may direct.

(3) If delivery to a company's registered office is not practicable, service may be effected by delivery to its last known principal place of business in England and Wales.

(4) Subject to paragraph (5), for the purposes of paragraph (2)(b) above, a person's proper address is any which he has previously notified as his address for service; but if he has not notified any such address service may be effected by delivery to his usual or last known address..

(5) In the case of a person who—

    (a)   is an authorised deposit-taker or former authorised deposit-taker;

    (b)

        (i)   has appointed, or is or may be entitled to appoint, an administrative receiver of the company, or

        (ii) is, or may be, entitled to appoint an administrator of the company under paragraph 14; and

    (c)   has not notified an address for service,

the proper address is the address of an office of that person where, to the knowledge of the applicant, the company maintains a bank account or, where no such office is known to the applicant, the registered office of that person, or, if there is no such office, his usual or last known address..

(6) Delivery of documents to any place or address may be made by leaving them there, or sending them by first class post.]

Notes

R 2.8(1)

The court may abridge time: *Re a Company (No 00175 of 1987)* [1987] BCLC 467; and the applicant should in those circumstances obtain letters of consent from the relevant parties to short service IR 1986 r 12.9(2). If the court is not willing to abridge time it may be possible to persuade it to make an interim order IA 1986 Sch B1 para 13(1)(d).

2.66

[2.9 Proof of service]

[(1) Service of the application shall be verified by an affidavit of service in Form 2.3B, specifying the date on which, and the manner in which, service was effected.

(2) The affidavit of service, with a sealed copy of the application exhibited to it, shall be filed with the court as soon as reasonably practicable after service, and in any event not less than 1 day before the hearing of the application.]

2.67

[2.10 Application to appoint specified person as administrator by holder of qualifying floating charge]

[(1) Where the holder of a qualifying floating charge applies to the court under paragraph 36(1)(b), he shall produce to the court—
 (a) the written consent of all holders of any prior qualifying floating charge;
 (b) a written statement in the Form 2.2B made by the specified person proposed by him as administrator; and
 (c) sufficient evidence to satisfy the court that he is entitled to appoint an administrator under paragraph 14.

(2) If an administration order is made appointing the specified person, the costs of the person who made the administration application and the applicant under paragraph 36(1)(b) shall, unless the court otherwise orders, be paid as an expense of the administration.]

Notes

R 2.10(1)

It is unlikely that this provision will be much relied upon in practice. Where a qualifying floating chargeholder is notified of an administration application and the chargeholder wishes to appoint its nominee then an appointment can be made under IA 1986 Sch B1 para 14 without applying to court; this is so even though a winding up petition may have been presented IA 1986 Sch B1 para 17, 40(1)(b). It is difficult to foresee a situation in which it would be preferable for such a chargeholder to become involved in a contested appointment in court; unless perhaps the chargeholder desires the benefit of a court order to prevent a contemplated challenge to the appointment; or he is restricted from making an appointment under IA 1986 Sch B1 para 14 by the restrictions in IA 1986 Sch B1 para 15–17.

R 2.10(2)

The priority of administration expenses is dealt with in IR 1986 r 2.67.

Chapter 2

2.68

[2.11 Application where company in liquidation]

[(1) Where an administration application is made under paragraph 37 or paragraph 38, the affidavit in support of the administration application shall contain—
 (a) full details of the existing insolvency proceedings, the name and address of the liquidator, the date he was appointed and by whom;

(b)   the reasons why it has subsequently been considered appropriate that an administration application should be made;

(c)   all other matters that would, in the opinion of the applicant, assist the court in considering the need to make provisions in respect of matters arising in connection with the liquidation; and

(d)   the details required in Rules 2.4(2) and (4).

(2) Where the application is made by the holder of a qualifying floating charge he shall set out sufficient evidence in the affidavit to satisfy the court that he is entitled to appoint an administrator under paragraph 14.]

Notes

R 2.11(1)

Though it would be unusual to leave the possibility of an administration until after the company has gone into liquidation under IA 1986 Sch B1 para 37 a qualifying floating chargeholder can apply for an administration order where a company is in a compulsory liquidation; and under IA 1986 Sch B1 para 38 a liquidator in any type of liquidation may also make such an application.

R 2.11(2)

Such a chargeholder must satisfy the court (IA 1986 Sch B1 para 37(1)) that were it not for the ban imposed by IA 1986 Sch B1 para 8(1)(b) the conditions for an out of court appointment under IA 1986 Sch B1 para 14 are met.

2.69

[2.12 The hearing]

[(1) At the hearing of the administration application, any of the following may appear or be represented—

(a)   the applicant;

(b)   the company;

(c)   one or more of the directors;

(d)   if an administrative receiver has been appointed, that person;

(e)   any person who has presented a petition for the winding-up of the company;

(f)   the person proposed for appointment as administrator;

(g)   if a member State liquidator has been appointed in main proceedings in relation to the company, that person;

(h)   any person that is the holder of a qualifying floating charge;

(j)   any supervisor of a voluntary arrangement under Part I of the Act;

(k)   with the permission of the court, any other person who appears to have an interest justifying his appearance.

(2) If the court makes an administration order, it shall be in Form 2.4B.

> (3) If the court makes an administration order, the costs of the applicant, and of any person whose costs are allowed by the court, are payable as an expense of the administration.]

Notes

R 2.12(1)

It is normally not difficult to persuade the court that an interested party should be heard *Re Farnborough-Aircraft.com Ltd* [2002] 2 BCLC 641.

R 2.12(1)(k)

The most obvious group of persons with an interest in the application will be creditors; members may also have an interest if the company is or may be solvent but if it is clear that the company is insolvent on a balance sheet basis the court would usually refuse to hear members: *Re Chelmsford City Football Club (1980) Ltd* [1991] BCC 133.

R 2.12(2)

The name of the administrator appears on the face of the order in Form 2.4B.

R 2.12(3)

The court would normally order that the costs of parties attending the hearing are paid as an expense of the administration even where a party has opposed the making of an order: *Re Structures & Computers Ltd* [1998] 1 BCLC 292. In the event that there are insufficient funds to pay all the expenses the court can make an order prioritising the different expenses: *Re a Company (No 005174 of 1999)* [2000] 1 BCLC 593, IR 1986 r 2.67(3). The costs ought to include the costs of the proposed administrator in reaching his opinion under IR 1986 r 2.3(5)(c); it is doubtful whether other costs of the proposed administrator (such as time costs in giving actual insolvency advice) would be regarded as an administration expense. The court may order the directors to pay the costs of a failed application personally but this would require exceptional circumstances: *Re Land and Property Trust Co plc (No 2)* [1993] BCC 462.

> **2.70**
>
> **[2.13**
>
> [Where the court makes an administration order in relation to a company upon an application under paragraph 37 or 38, the court shall include in the order—
> - (a) in the case of a liquidator appointed in a voluntary winding-up, his removal from office;
> - (b) details concerning the release of the liquidator;
> - (c) provision for payment of the expenses of the liquidation;
> - (d) provisions regarding any indemnity given to the liquidator;
> - (e) provisions regarding the handling or realisation of any of the company's assets in the hands of or under the control of the liquidator;
> - (f) such provision as the court thinks fit with respect to matters arising in connection with the liquidation; and

> (g)   such other provisions as the court shall think fit.]

Notes

R 2.13

An application for administration under IA 1986 Sch B1 para 37 or para 38 occurs when the company is in a liquidation; see the notes to IR 1986 r 2.11 above.

2.71

[2.14 Notice of administration order]

[(1) If the court makes an administration order, it shall as soon as reasonably practicable send two sealed copies of the order to the person who made the application.

(2) The applicant shall send a sealed copy of the order as soon as reasonably practicable to the person appointed as administrator.

(3) If the court makes an order under paragraph 13(1)(d) or any other order under paragraph 13(1)(f), it shall give directions as to the persons to whom, and how, notice of that order is to be given.]

Notes

R 2.14(3)

Such orders refer to interim or other orders made on the hearing of an administration application aside from those specifically listed in IA 1986 Sch B1 para 13(1)(a)–(c) or (e).

**[Chapter 3
Appointment of Administrator by Holder of Floating Charge]**

2.72

[2.15 Notice of intention to appoint]

[(1) The prescribed form for the notice of intention to appoint for the purposes of paragraph 44(2) is Form 2.5B.

(2) For the purposes of paragraph 44(2), a copy of Form 2.5B shall be filed with the court at the same time as it is sent in accordance with paragraph 15(1) to the holder of any prior qualifying floating charge.

(3) The provisions of Rule 2.8(2) to 2.8(6) shall apply to the sending of a notice under this Rule as they apply to the manner in which service of an administration application is effected under that Rule.]

Notes

R 2.15(1)

An interim moratorium applies under IA 1986 Sch B1 para 44(2) on the filing at court of the notice of intention to appoint (Form 2.5B) by the holder of a qualifying floating charge under IA

1986 Sch B1 para 14. The moratorium is detailed in IA 1986 Sch B1 paras 42, 43. However there is no obligation to file such a notice on the part of the holder of the qualifying floating charge unless there is a prior floating charge in existence (IA 1986 Sch B1 para 15). In the absence of a prior floating charge the holder of a qualifying floating charge may proceed directly to make an appointment under IA 1986 Sch B1 para 14 unless any of the other restrictions on the power to appoint apply: IA 1986 Sch B1 paras 16, 17. The advantage of filing a notice of intention to appoint is the imposition of the interim moratorium (IA 1986 Sch B1 para 44(2)) prior to the satisfaction of the IA 1986 Sch B1 para 18 conditions. An appointment of an administrator under IA 1986 Sch B1 para 14 only takes effect when those conditions have been satisfied: IA 1986 Sch B1 para 19. There does not appear to be an express restriction on filing consecutive notices of intention to appoint although such conduct might be challenged by aggrieved creditors on an application to lift the interim moratorium: IA 1986 Sch B1 para 44(5), 43(6).

R 2.15(2)

For the definition of 'the court' see the notes to IR 1986 r 2.2(1).

2.73

[2.16 Notice of appointment]

[(1) The notice of appointment for the purposes of an appointment under paragraph 14 shall be in Form 2.6B.

(2) The copies of the notice filed with the court, shall be accompanied by—

    (a) the administrator's written statement in Form 2.2B; and

    (b) either—

        (i) evidence that the person making the appointment has given such notice as may be required by paragraph 15(1)(a); or

        (ii) copies of the written consent of all those required to give consent in accordance with paragraph 15(1)(b); and

    (c) a statement of those matters provided for in paragraph 100(2), if applicable.

(3) The statutory declaration on Form 2.6B shall be made not more than 5 business days before the form is filed with the court.

(4) Written consent may be given by the holder of a prior qualifying floating charge where a notice of intention to appoint an administrator has been given and filed with the court in accordance with Rule 2.15 above, by completing the section provided on Form 2.5B and returning to the appointor a copy of the form.

(5) Where the holder of a prior qualifying floating charge does not choose to complete the section provided on Form 2.5B to indicate his consent, or no such form has been sent to him, his written consent shall include—

    (a) details of the name, address of registered office and registered number of the company in respect of which the appointment is proposed to be made;

    (b) details of the charge held by him including the date it was registered and, where applicable, any financial limit and any deeds of priority;

    (c) his name and address.;

 (d) the name and address of the holder of the qualifying floating charge who is proposing to make the appointment;
 (e) the date that notice of intention to appoint was given;
 (f) the name of the proposed administrator;
 (g) a statement of consent to the proposed appointment,
and it shall be signed and dated.

(6) This Rule and the following Rule are subject to Rule 2.19, the provisions of which apply when an appointment is to be made out of court business hours.]

Notes

R 2.16(2)

Under IA 1986 Sch B1 para 15 an appointment of an administrator cannot be made by a qualifying floating chargeholder under IA 1986 Sch B1 para 14 unless at least two business days' written notice is given to any prior qualifying floating chargeholder; or such a chargeholder gives its written consent to the appointment.

2.74

[2.17

[(1) Three copies of the notice of appointment shall be filed with the court and shall have applied to them the seal of the court and be endorsed with the date and time of filing.

(2) The court shall issue two of the sealed copies of the notice of appointment to the person making the appointment, who shall as soon as reasonably practicable send one of the sealed copies to the administrator.]

Chapter 3

2.75–2.76

[2.18

[Where, after receiving notice that an administration application has been made, the holder of a qualifying floating charge appoints an administrator in reliance on paragraph 14, he shall as soon as reasonably practicable send a copy of the notice of appointment to the person making the administration application and to the court in which the application has been made.]

2.77

[2.19 Appointment taking place out of court business hours]

[(1) The holder of a qualifying floating charge may file a notice of appointment with the court, notwithstanding that the court is not open for public business When the court is closed (and only when it is closed) a notice of appointment may be filed with the court by faxing that form in accordance with paragraph (3). The notice of appointment shall be in Form 2.7B.

(2) The filing of a notice in accordance with this Rule shall have the same effect for all purposes as a notice of appointment filed in accordance with Rule 2.16 with the court specified in the notice as having jurisdiction in the case.

(3) The notice shall be faxed to a designated telephone number which shall be provided by the Court Service for that purpose. The Secretary of State shall publish the telephone number of the relevant fax machine on The Insolvency Service website and on request to The Insolvency Service, make it available in writing.

(4) The appointor shall ensure that a fax transmission report detailing the time and date of the fax transmission and containing a copy of the first page (in part or in full) of the document faxed is created by the fax machine that is used to fax the form.

(5) The appointment shall take effect from the date and time of that fax transmission. The appointor shall notify the administrator, as soon as reasonably practicable, that the notice has been filed.

(6) The copy of the faxed notice of appointment received by the Court Service fax machine shall be forwarded as soon as reasonably practicable to the court specified in the notice as the court having jurisdiction in the case, to be placed on the relevant court file.

(7) The appointor shall take three copies of the notice of appointment that was faxed to the designated telephone number, together with the transmission report showing the date and time that the form was faxed to the designated telephone number and all the necessary supporting documents listed on Form 2.7B, to the court on the next day that the court is open for business

(8) The appointor shall attach to the notice a statement providing full reasons for the out of hours filing of the notice of appointment, including why it would have been damaging to the company and its creditors not to have so acted.

(9) The copies of the notice shall be sealed by the court and shall be endorsed with the date and time when, according to the appointor's fax transmission report, the notice was faxed and the date when the notice and accompanying documents were delivered to the court.

(10) The administrator's appointment shall cease to have effect if the requirements of paragraph (7) are not completed within the time period indicated in that paragraph.

(11) Where any question arises in respect of the date and time that the notice of appointment was filed with the court it shall be a presumption capable of rebuttal that the date and time shown on the appointor's fax transmission report is the date and time at which the notice was so filed.

(12) The court shall issue two of the sealed copies of the notice of appointment to the person making the appointment, who shall, as soon as reasonably practicable, send one of the copies to the administrator.]

Notes

R 2.19

This procedure enables an appointment by fax to be made out of court by a qualifying floating chargeholder outside normal court office hours. It is not a provision to be used lightly and the appointor must provide full reasons for such a course of action under IR 1986 r 2.19(8).

R 2.19(1)

The procedure may not be used if the court office is open. The fax number is presently 0207 947 6607. Form 2.7B must be used by the appointor with a statement attached as required by IR 1986 r 2.19(8).

R 2.19(7)

The obligation to attend the court office the next day it is open for business is expressly stated. If the appointor does not for whatever reason comply with that obligation the administrator's appointment ceases to have effect.

R 2.19(8)

It is important for the appointor to provide a full explanation of the required matters which places a heavy burden on the appointor to justify the urgency of an out of hours appointment. An administration can be challenged by a creditor (eg IA 1986 Sch B1 para 81) and non compliance with this rule would support such a challenge.

R 2.19(10)

It is difficult to contemplate circumstances in which the court could be persuaded to use its power to extend time limits (IR 1986 r 12.9(2)) where the appointor has failed to attend the court on the next day it is open for business.

[Chapter 4
Appointment of Administrator by Company or Directors]

2.78

[2.20 Notice of intention to appoint]

[(1) The notice of intention to appoint an administrator for the purposes of paragraph 26 shall be in Form 2.8B.

(2) A copy of the notice of intention to appoint must, in addition to the persons specified in paragraph 26, be given to—

    (a)   any [enforcement officer] who, to the knowledge of the person giving the notice, is charged with execution or other legal process against the company;

    (b)   any person who, to the knowledge of the person giving the notice, has distrained against the company or its property;

    (c)   any supervisor of a voluntary arrangement under Part I of the Act; and

> (d) the company, if the company is not intending to make the appointment.
>
> (3) The provisions of Rule 2.8(2) to 2.8(6) shall apply to the sending or giving of a notice under this Rule as they apply to the manner in which service of an administration application is effected under that Rule.]

Notes

R 2.20(1)

An interim moratorium applies under IA 1986 Sch B1 para 44(4) on the filing at court of the notice of intention to appoint by the company or the directors under para 22. The moratorium is detailed in IA 1986 Sch B1 paras 42, 43. There does not appear to be an express restriction on filing consecutive notices of intention to appoint although such conduct might be challenged by aggrieved creditors on an application to lift the interim moratorium: IA 1986 Sch B1 para 44(5), 43(6).

R 2.20(2)

The persons specified under IA 1986 Sch B1 para 26 are those who are or may be entitled to appoint an administrative receiver or an administrator under IA 1986 Sch B1 para 14.

2.79

[2.21

[The statutory declaration on Form 2.8B shall be made not more than 5 business days before the notice is filed with the court.]

2.80

[2.22

[The notice of intention to appoint shall be accompanied by either a copy of the resolution of the company to appoint an administrator (where the company intends to make the appointment) or a record of the decision of the directors (where the directors intend to make the appointment).]

Notes

R 2.22

Where the directors intend to make the appointment a formal board resolution is not required simply a 'record' of the directors' decision (see also IA 1986 Sch B1 para 105); in practice a board resolution should be obtained for the avoidance of doubt.

2.81

[2.23 Notice of appointment]

[(1) The notice of appointment for the purposes of an appointment under paragraph 22 shall be in Form 2.9B or Form 2.10B, as appropriate.

(2) The copies of the notice filed with the court shall be accompanied by—
(a) the administrator's written statement in Form 2.2B;
(b) the written consent of all those persons to whom notice was given in accordance with paragraph 26(1) unless the period of notice set out in paragraph 26(1) has expired; and
(c) a statement of the matters provided for in paragraph 100(2), where applicable.]

Notes

R 2.23(2)

For the definition of 'the court' see the notes to IR 1986 r 2.2(1), IA 1986 s 117).

R 2.23(2)(b)

The persons listed in IA 1986 Sch B1 para 26 (those who are or may be entitled to appoint an administrative receiver or an administrator under IA 1986 Sch B1 para 14) must be given a copy of the notice of intention to appoint at least five business days before the appointment: IR 1986 r 2.20, IA 1986 Sch B1 para 26.

2.82

[2.24

[The statutory declaration on Form 2.9B or Form 2.10B shall be made not more than 5 business days before the notice is filed with the court.]

2.83

[2.25

[Where a notice of intention to appoint an administrator has not been given, the notice of appointment shall be accompanied by the documents specified in Rule 2.22 above.]

Notes

R 2.25

This deals with the situation where the company is appointing the administrator and none of the parties listed in IA 1986 Sch B1 para 26 or IR 1986 r 2.20(2) are involved.

2.84

[2.26

[(1) Three copies of the notice of appointment shall be filed with the court and shall have applied to them the seal of the court and be endorsed with the date and time of filing.

(2) The court shall issue two of the sealed copies of the notice of appointment to the person making the appointment who shall as soon as reasonably practicable send one of the sealed copies to the administrator.]

[Chapter 5
Process of Administration]

2.85

[2.27 Notification and advertisement of administrator's appointment]

[(1) The administrator shall advertise his appointment once in the Gazette, and once in such newspaper as he thinks most appropriate for ensuring that the appointment comes to the notice of the company's creditors. The advertisement shall be in Form 2.11B.

(2) The administrator shall, as soon as reasonably practicable after the date specified in paragraph 46(6), give notice of his appointment—
-   (a)   if a receiver or an administrative receiver has been appointed, to him;
-   (b)   if there is pending a petition for the winding up of the company, to the petitioner (and also to the provisional liquidator, if any);
-   (c)   to any [enforcement officer] who, to the administrator's knowledge, is charged with execution or other legal process against the company;
-   (d)   to any person who, to the administrator's knowledge, has distrained against the company or its property; and
-   (e)   any supervisor of a voluntary arrangement under Part I of the Act.

(3) Where, under a provision of Schedule B1 to the Act or these Rules, the administrator is required to send a notice of his appointment to any person he shall do so in Form 2.12B.]

2.86

[2.28 Notice requiring statement of affairs]

[(1) In this Chapter 'relevant person' shall have the meaning given to it in paragraph 47(3).

(2) The administrator shall send notice in Form 2.13B to each relevant person whom he determines appropriate requiring him to prepare and submit a statement of the company's affairs.

(3) The notice shall inform each of the relevant persons—
-   (a)   of the names and addresses of all others (if any) to whom the same notice has been sent;
-   (b)   of the time within which the statement must be delivered;
-   (c)   of the effect of paragraph 48(4) (penalty for non-compliance); and
-   (d)   of the application to him, and to each other relevant person, of section 235 (duty to provide information, and to attend on the administrator, if required).

(4) The administrator shall furnish each relevant person to whom he has sent notice in Form 2.13B with the forms required for the preparation of the statement of affairs.]

2.87

[2.29 Verification and filing]

[(1) The statement of the company's affairs shall be in Form 2.14B, contain all the particulars required by that form and be verified by a statement of truth by the relevant person.

(2) The administrator may require any relevant person to submit a statement of concurrence in Form 2.15B stating that he concurs in the statement of affairs. Where the administrator does so, he shall inform the person making the statement of affairs of that fact.

(3) The statement of affairs shall be delivered by the relevant person making the statement of truth, together with a copy, to the administrator. The relevant person shall also deliver a copy of the statement of affairs to all those persons whom the administrator has required to make a statement of concurrence.

(4) A person required to submit a statement of concurrence shall do so before the end of the period of 5 business days (or such other period as the administrator may agree) beginning with the day on which the statement of affairs being concurred with is received by him.

(5) A statement of concurrence may be qualified in respect of matters dealt with in the statement of affairs, where the maker of the statement of concurrence is not in agreement with the relevant person, or he considers the statement of affairs to be erroneous or misleading, or he is without the direct knowledge necessary for concurring with it.

(6) Every statement of concurrence shall be verified by a statement of truth and be delivered to the administrator by the person who makes it, together with a copy of it.

(7) Subject to Rule 2.30 below, the administrator shall as soon as reasonably practicable send to the registrar of companies and file with the court a Form 2.16B together with a copy of the statement of affairs and any statement of concurrence.]

Notes

R 2.29(7)

An order of limited disclosure can be made in respect of the filing with the registrar of companies under IR 1986 r 2.30 below; such an application may also be accompanied by a request to restrict disclosure of material on the court file under IR 1986 r 7.31(5).

2.88

[2.30 Limited disclosure]

[(1) Where the administrator thinks that it would prejudice the conduct of the administration for the whole or part of the statement of the company's affairs to be disclosed, he may apply to the court for an order of limited disclosure in respect of the statement, or any specified part of it.

(2) The court may, on such application, order that the statement or, as the case may be, the specified part of it, shall not be filed with the registrar of companies.

(3) The administrator shall as soon as reasonably practicable send to the registrar of companies a Form 2.16B together with a copy of the order and the statement of affairs (to the extent provided by the order) and any statement of concurrence.

(4) If a creditor seeks disclosure of a statement of affairs or a specified part of it in relation to which an order has been made under this Rule, he may apply to the court for an order that the administrator disclose it or a specified part of it. The application shall be supported by written evidence in the form of an affidavit.

(5) The applicant shall give the administrator notice of his application at least 3 days before the hearing.

(6) The court may make any order for disclosure subject to any conditions as to confidentiality, duration, the scope of the order in the event of any change of circumstances, or other matters as it sees fit.

(7) If there is a material change in circumstances rendering the limit on disclosure or any part of it unnecessary, the administrator shall, as soon as reasonably practicable after the change, apply to the court for the order or any part of it to be rescinded.

(8) The administrator shall, as soon as reasonably practicable after the making of an order under paragraph (7) above, file with the registrar of companies Form 2.16B together with a copy of the statement of affairs to the extent provided by the order.

(9) When the statement of affairs is filed in accordance with paragraph (8), the administrator shall, where he has sent a statement of proposals under paragraph 49, provide the creditors with a copy of the statement of affairs as filed, or a summary thereof.

(10) The provisions of Part 31 of the CPR shall not apply to an application under this Rule.]

Notes

R 2.30(10)

Part 31 CPR contains provisions relating to disclosure and inspection.

2.89

[2.31 Release from duty to submit statement of affairs; extension of time]

[(1) The power of the administrator under paragraph 48(2) to give a release from the obligation imposed by paragraph 47(1), or to grant an extension of time, may be exercised at the administrator's own discretion, or at the request of any relevant person.

(2) A relevant person may, if he requests a release or extension of time and it is refused by the administrator, apply to the court for it.

(3) The court may, if it thinks that no sufficient cause is shown for the application, disMiss it without a hearing but it shall not do so without giving the relevant person at least 7 days' notice, upon receipt of which the relevant person may request the court to list the application for a without notice hearing. If the application is not dismissed the court shall fix a venue for it to be heard, and give notice to the relevant person accordingly.

(4) The relevant person shall, at least 14 days before the hearing, send to the administrator a notice stating the venue and accompanied by a copy of the application and of any evidence which he (the relevant person) intends to adduce in support of it.

(5) The administrator may appear and be heard on the application and, whether or not he appears, he may file a written report of any matters which he considers ought to be drawn to the court's attention.

If such a report is filed, a copy of it shall be sent by the administrator to the relevant person, not later than 5 days before the hearing.

(6) Sealed copies of any order made on the application shall be sent by the court to the relevant person and the administrator.

(7) On any application under this Rule the relevant person's costs shall be paid in any event by him and, unless the court otherwise orders, no allowance towards them shall be made out of the assets.]

Chapter 4

2.90

[2.32 Expenses of statement of affairs]

[(1) A relevant person making the statement of the company's affairs or statement of concurrence shall be allowed, and paid by the administrator out of his receipts, any expenses incurred by the relevant person in so doing which the administrator considers reasonable.

(2) Any decision by the administrator under this Rule is subject to appeal to the court.

(3) Nothing in this Rule relieves a relevant person from any obligation with respect to the preparation, verification and submission of the statement of affairs, or to the provision of information to the administrator.]

2.91

[2.33 Administrator's proposals]

[(1) The administrator shall, under paragraph 49, make a statement which he shall send to the registrar of companies attached to Form 2.17B.

(2) The statement shall include, in addition to those matters set out in paragraph 49—

(a)   details of the court where the proceedings are and the relevant court reference number;

(b)   the full name, registered address registered number and any other trading names of the company;

(c)   details relating to his appointment as administrator, including the date of appointment and the person making the application or appointment and, where there are joint administrators, details of the matters set out in paragraph 100(2);

(d)   the names of the directors and secretary of the company and details of any shareholdings in the company they may have;

(e)   an account of the circumstances giving rise to the appointment of the administrator;

(f)   if a statement of the company's affairs has been submitted, a copy or summary of it, with the administrator's comments, if any;

(g)   if an order limiting the disclosure of the statement of affairs (under Rule 2.30) has been made, a statement of that fact, as well as—

    (i)   details of who provided the statement of affairs;

    (ii) the date of the order of limited disclosure; and

    (iii) the details or a summary of the details that are not subject to that order;

(h)   if a full statement of affairs is not provided, the names, addresses and debts of the creditors including details of any security held;

(j)   if no statement of affairs has been submitted, details of the financial position of the company at the latest practicable date (which must, unless the court otherwise orders, be a date not earlier than that on which the company entered administration), a list of the company's creditors including their names, addresses and details of their debts, including any security held, and an explanation as to why there is no statement of affairs;

(k)   the basis upon which it is proposed that the administrator's remuneration should be fixed under Rule 2.106;

(l)   (except where the administrator proposes a voluntary arrangement in relation to the company and subject to paragraph (3))—

    (i)   to the best of the administrator's knowledge and belief—

        (aa) an estimate of the value of the prescribed part (whether or not he proposes to make an application to court under section 176A(5) or section 176A(3) applies); and

        (bb) an estimate of the value of the company's net property; and

    (ii) whether, and, if so, why, the administrator proposes to make an application to court under section 176A(5);

(m)   how it is envisaged the purpose of the administration will be achieved and how it is proposed that the administration shall end. If a creditors' voluntary liquidation is proposed, details of the proposed liquidator must be provided, and a statement that, in accordance with paragraph 83(7) and Rule 2.117(3), creditors may nominate a different person as the proposed liquidator, provided that the nomination is made after the receipt of the proposals and before the proposals are approved;

(n) where the administrator has decided not to call a meeting of creditors, his reasons;

(o) the manner in which the affairs and business of the company—
   (i) have, since the date of the administrator's appointment, been managed and financed, including, where any assets have been disposed of, the reasons for such disposals and the terms upon which such disposals were made; and
   (ii) will, if the administrator's proposals are approved, continue to be managed and financed;

(p) whether—
   (i) the EC Regulation applies; and
   (ii) if so, whether the proceedings are main proceedings or territorial proceedings; and

(q) such other information (if any) as the administrator thinks necessary to enable creditors to decide whether or not to vote for the adoption of the proposals.

(3) Nothing in paragraph (2)(l) is to be taken as requiring any such estimate to include any information, the disclosure of which could seriously prejudice the commercial interests of the company. If such information is excluded from the calculation the estimate shall be accompanied by a statement to that effect.

(4) Where the court orders, upon an application by the administrator under paragraph 107, an extension of the period of time in paragraph 49(5), the administrator shall notify in Form 2.18B all the persons set out in paragraph 49(4) as soon as reasonably practicable after the making of the order.

(5) Where the administrator has made a statement under paragraph 52(1) and has not called an initial meeting of creditors, the proposals sent out under this Rule and paragraph 49 will (if no meeting has been requisitioned under paragraph 52(2) within the period set out in Rule 2.37(1)) be deemed to have been approved by the creditors.

(6) Where the administrator intends to apply to the court (or file a notice under paragraph 80(2)) for the administration to cease at a time before he has sent a statement of his proposals to creditors in accordance with paragraph 49, he shall, at least 10 days before he makes such an application (or files such a notice), send to all creditors of the company (so far as he is aware of their addresses) a report containing the information required by paragraphs (2)(a)–(p) of this Rule.

(7) Where the administrator wishes to publish a notice under paragraph 49(6) he shall publish the notice once in such newspaper as he thinks most appropriate for ensuring that the notice comes to the attention of the company's members. The notice shall—

(a) state the full name of the company;
(b) state the full name and address of the administrator;
(c) give details of the administrator's appointment; and
(d) specify an address to which members can write for a copy of the statement of proposals.

> (8) This notice must be published as soon as reasonably practicable after the administrator sends his statement of proposals to the company's creditors but no later than 8 weeks (or such other period as may be agreed by the creditors or as the court may order) from the date that the company entered administration.]

Notes

R 2.33

This provision demands that a number of specific matters are included in the proposals aside from the information required in the 'catch all' provision in IR r 2.33(2)(q). The proposals may not include any action which affects the right of a secured creditor to enforce his security nor preferential creditors in the manner set out and subject to the exceptions contained in IA 1986 Sch B1 para 73.

R 2.33(1)

Under IA 1986 Sch B1 para 49(5) the administrator must send a statement of his proposals as soon as reasonably practicable (and in any event within 8 weeks) after the company enters administration; the period can be extended under IA 1986 Sch B1 para 107 by the court and under IA 1986 Sch B1 para 108 by the administrator with the consent of the creditors.

R 2.33(2)(j)

Although this provision contemplates that no statement of affairs may be submitted there is no express power given to the administrator to relieve a person from providing a statement of affairs under IA 1986 Sch B1 para 47; cf IA 1986 s 131(5) in a liquidation.

R 2.33(2)(m)

Where it is envisaged that the exit route shall be a compulsory liquidation there is no requirement to inform the creditors of alternative appointees. This is because either the incumbent administrator is appointed under IA 1986 s 140 (and there is a chance for creditors to object under IR 1986 r 4.7(10)); or the official receiver becomes liquidator and a meeting of creditors may be held in the compulsory liquidation to appoint an alternative liquidator. It is important that the administrator expresses the relevant proposals concerning exit from administration carefully as he/she may be criticised if a change in the exit route is required later.

R 2.33(4)

Thus it is envisaged that an application to court by the administrator for an extension of time is on a without notice basis.

R 2.33(6)

Where before the IA 1986 Sch B1 para 49 proposals are sent out an administrator applies for the cesser of the administration (IA 1986 Sch B1 para 79), or in respect of an out of court administration its objective has been sufficiently achieved (IA 1986 Sch B1 para 80) the administrator is not obliged to provide the information contemplated by IR 1986 r 2.33(2)(q).

[Chapter 6
Meetings and Reports]

[Section A: Creditors' Meetings]

2.92

[2.34 Meetings to consider administrator's proposals]

[(1) Notice of an initial creditors' meeting shall (unless the court otherwise directs) be given by notice in the newspaper in which the administrator's appointment was advertised and, if he considers it appropriate to do so, in such other newspaper as he thinks most appropriate for ensuring that the notice comes to the attention of the company's creditors.

(2) Notice in Form 2.19B to attend the meeting shall be sent out at the same time to any directors or officers of the company (including persons who have been directors or officers in the past) whose presence at the meeting is, in the administrator's opinion, required.

(3) Where the court orders an extension to the period set out in paragraph 51(2)(b) the administrator shall send a notice in Form 2.18B to each person to whom he is required to send notice by paragraph 49(4).

(4) If at the meeting there is not the requisite majority for approval of the administrator's proposals (with modifications, if any), the chairman may, and shall if a resolution is passed to that effect, adjourn the meeting for not more than 14 days and may only adjourn once (subject to any direction by the court).]

2.93

[2.35 Creditors' meetings generally]

[(1) This Rule applies to creditors' meetings summoned by the administrator under—
  (a)   paragraph 51 (initial creditors' meeting);
  (b)   paragraph 52(2) (at the request of the creditors);
  (c)   paragraph 54(2) (to consider revision to the administrator's proposals);
  (d)   paragraph 56(1) (further creditors' meetings); and
  (e)   paragraph 62 (general power to summon meetings of creditors).

(2) Notice of any of the meetings set out in paragraph (1) above shall be in Form 2.20B.

(3) In fixing the venue for the meeting, the administrator shall have regard to the convenience of creditors and the meeting shall be summoned for commencement between 10.00 and 16.00 hours on a business day, unless the court otherwise directs.

(4) Subject to paragraphs (6) and (7) below, at least 14 days' notice of the meeting shall be given to all creditors who are known to the administrator and had claims against the company at the date when the company entered administration unless that creditor has subsequently been paid in full; and the notice shall—
  (a)   specify the purpose of the meeting;

(b)   contain a statement of the effect of Rule 2.38 (entitlement to vote); and

(c)   contain the forms of proxy.

(5) If within 30 minutes from the time fixed for commencement of the meeting there is no person present to act as chairman, the meeting stands adjourned to the same time and place in the following week or, if that is not a business day, to the business day immediately following.

(6) The meeting may be adjourned once, if the chairman thinks fit, but not for more than 14 days from the date on which it was fixed to commence, subject to the direction of the court.

(7) If a meeting is adjourned the administrator shall as soon as reasonably practicable notify the creditors of the venue of the adjourned meeting.]

Notes

R 2.35(4)

This period may be varied by consent or court order: IA 1986 Sch B1 para 50(2), para 107, para 108); also reliance could be placed on the general power to extend or shorten time limits IR 1986 r 12.9.

R 2.35(6)

If the chairman does adjourn the meeting more than once this may prompt an application on the basis of IA 1986 Sch B1 para 74, para 75; presumably a new meeting should be called.

2.94

[2.36 The chairman at meetings]

[(1) At any meeting of creditors summoned by the administrator, either he shall be chairman, or a person nominated by him in writing to act in his place.

(2) A person so nominated must be either—

(a)   one who is qualified to act as an insolvency practitioner in relation to the company; or

(b)   an employee of the administrator or his firm who is experienced in insolvency matters.]

2.95

[2.37 Meeting requisitioned by creditors]

[(1) The request for a creditors' meeting under paragraph 52(2) or 56(1) shall be in Form 2.21B. A request for an initial creditors' meeting shall be made within 12 days of the date on which the administrator's statement of proposals is sent out. A request under paragraph 52(2) or 56(1) shall include—

(a)   a list of the creditors concurring with the request, showing the amounts of their respective debts in the administration;

(b)   from each creditor concurring, written confirmation of his concurrence; and

(c)   a statement of the purpose of the proposed meeting,
but sub-paragraph (a) does not apply if the requisitioning creditor's debt
is alone sufficient without the concurrence of other creditors.

(2) A meeting requested under paragraph 52(2) or 56(1) shall be held
within 28 days of the administrator's receipt of the notice requesting the
meeting.

(3) The expenses of summoning and holding a meeting at the request of
a creditor shall be paid by that person, who shall deposit with the
administrator security for their payment.

(4) The sum to be deposited shall be such as the administrator may
determine, and he shall not act without the deposit having been made.

(5) The meeting may resolve that the expenses of summoning and
holding it are to be payable out of the assets of the company as an expense
of the administration.

(6) To the extent that any deposit made under this Rule is not required
for the payment of expenses of summoning and holding the meeting, it
shall be repaid to the person who made it.]

Notes

R 2.37(1)

Creditors constituting at least 10% of the total debts of the company may requisition a
creditors' meeting; presumably the total debts will be those detailed in the full statement of
affairs that must be contained within the IA 1986 Sch B1 para 49 proposals; see also IR 1986
r 2.33(2)(h).

2.96

[2.38 Entitlement to vote]

[(1) Subject as follows, at a meeting of creditors in administration
proceedings a person is entitled to vote only if—
  (a)   he has given to the administrator, not later than 12.00 hours on
         the business day before the day fixed for the meeting, details in
         writing of the debt which—
         (i)   he claims to be due to him from the company; or
         (ii) in relation to a member State liquidator, is claimed to be
               due to creditors in proceedings in relation to which he
               holds office;
  (b)   the claim has been duly admitted under the following provisions
         of this Rule; and
  (c)   there has been lodged with the administrator any proxy which he
         intends to be used on his behalf,
and details of the debt must include any calculation for the purposes of
Rules 2.40 to 2.42.

(2) The chairman of the meeting may allow a creditor to vote, notwithstanding that he has failed to comply with paragraph (1)(a), if satisfied
that the failure was due to circumstances beyond the creditor's control.

(3) The chairman of the meeting may call for any document or other evidence to be produced to him, where he thinks it necessary for the purpose of substantiating the whole or any part of the claim.

(4) Votes are calculated according to the amount of a creditor's claim as at the date on which the company entered administration, less any payments that have been made to him after that date in respect of his claim and any adjustment by way of set-off in accordance with Rule 2.85 as if that Rule were applied on the date that the votes are counted.

(5) A creditor shall not vote in respect of a debt for an unliquidated amount, or any debt whose value is not ascertained, except where the chairman agrees to put upon the debt an estimated minimum value for the purpose of entitlement to vote and admits the claim for that purpose.

(6) No vote shall be cast by virtue of a claim more than once on any resolution put to the meeting.

(7) Where—
  (a) a creditor is entitled to vote under this Rule;
  (b) has lodged his claim in one or more sets of other proceedings; and
  (c) votes (either in person or by proxy) on a resolution put to the meeting; and
  (d) the member State liquidator casts a vote in respect of the same claim,
only the creditor's vote shall be counted.

(8) Where—
  (a) a creditor has lodged his claim in more than one set of other proceedings; and
  (b) more than one member State liquidator seeks to vote by virtue of that claim,
the entitlement to vote by virtue of that claim is exercisable by the member State liquidator in main proceedings, whether or not the creditor has lodged his claim in the main proceedings.

(9) For the purposes of paragraph (6), the claim of a creditor and of any member State liquidator in relation to the same debt are a single claim.

(10) For the purposes of paragraphs (7) and (8), 'other proceedings' means main proceedings, secondary proceedings or territorial proceedings in another member State.]

Notes

R 2.38(1)(c)

A proxy must be lodged before the vote is taken but not necessarily before the meeting itself *Re Philip Alexander Securities & Futures Ltd* [1999] 1 BCLC 124.

R 2.38(4)

A company enters administration when the appointment of the administrator takes effect IA 1986 Sch B1 para 1(2)(b).

R 2.38(5)

The chairman's agreement under this provision does not mean that he has to reach a consensus with the creditor: *Doorbar v Alltime Securities Ltd* [1996] 1 WLR 456. For a discussion of voting at creditor's meetings, see the notes to creditor's meetings to consider proposals for a company voluntary arrangement under IR 1986 r 1.17.

2.97

[2.39 Admission and rejection of claims]

[(1) At any creditors' meeting the chairman has power to admit or reject a creditor's claim for the purpose of his entitlement to vote; and the power is exercisable with respect to the whole or any part of the claim.

(2) The chairman's decision under this Rule, or in respect of any matter arising under Rule 2.38, is subject to appeal to the court by any creditor.

(3) If the chairman is in doubt whether a claim should be admitted or rejected, he shall mark it as objected to and allow the creditor to vote, subject to his vote being subsequently declared invalid if the objection to the claim is sustained.

(4) If on an appeal the chairman's decision is reversed or varied, or a creditor's vote is declared invalid, the court may order that another meeting be summoned, or make such other order as it thinks fit.

(5) In the case of the meeting summoned under paragraph 51 to consider the administrator's proposals, an application to the court by way of appeal under this Rule against a decision of the chairman shall not be made later than 14 days after the delivery of the administrator's report in accordance with paragraph 53(2).

(6) Neither the administrator nor any person nominated by him to be chairman is personally liable for costs incurred by any person in respect of an appeal to the court under this Rule, unless the court makes an order to that effect.]

Notes

R 2.39

See the notes to the equivalent rule in liquidation: IR 1986 r 4.70

R 2.39(4)

On an appeal from the chairman's decision the court may take into account material that was not available to the chairman: *Re a Company (No 004539 of 1993)* [1995] 1 BCLC 459.

R 2.39(5)

This is a short time period in which to consider an appeal; the court could be asked to extend time under IR 1986 r 12.9.

2.98

[2.40 Secured creditors]

[(1) At a meeting of creditors a secured creditor is entitled to vote only in respect of the balance (if any) of his debt after deducting the value of his security as estimated by him.

(2) However, in a case where the administrator has made a statement under paragraph 52(1)(b) and an initial creditors' meeting has been requisitioned under paragraph 52(2) then a secured creditor is entitled to vote in respect of the full value of his debt without any deduction of the value of his security.]

Notes

R 2.40(2)

This provision contemplates the situation where the administrator does not wish to hold a creditors' meeting because there will be no distribution to unsecured creditors (other than 'ring fenced' monies under IA 1986 s 176A) but he is obliged to hold a meeting on a creditors' requisition. The secured creditor (see IA 1986 s 248) may then vote for the full amount of his debt.

2.99

[2.41 Holders of negotiable instruments]

[A creditor shall not vote in respect of a debt on, or secured by, a current bill of exchange or promissory note, unless he is willing—
   (a)   to treat the liability to him on the bill or note of every person who is liable on it antecedently to the company, and against whom a bankruptcy order has not been made (or, in the case of a company, which has not gone into liquidation), as a security in his hands; and
   (b)   to estimate the value of the security and, for the purpose of his entitlement to vote, to deduct it from his claim.]

2.100

[2.42 Hire-purchase, conditional sale and chattel leasing agreements]

[(1) Subject as follows, an owner of goods under a hire-purchase or chattel leasing agreement, or a seller of goods under a conditional sale agreement, is entitled to vote in respect of the amount of the debt due and payable to him by the company on the date that the company entered administration.

(2) In calculating the amount of any debt for this purpose, no account shall be taken of any amount attributable to the exercise of any right under the relevant agreement, so far as the right has become exercisable solely by virtue of the making of an administration application, a notice of

intention to appoint an administrator or any matter arising as a consequence, or of the company entering administration.]

Notes

R 2.42(1)

A reference to 'hire purchase agreement' in IA 1986 Sch B1 includes a conditional sale
agreement, a chattel leasing agreement and a retention of title agreement: IA 1986 Sch B1
para 111.

2.101

[2.43 Resolutions]

[(1) Subject to paragraph (2), at a creditors' meeting in administration
proceedings, a resolution is passed when a majority (in value) of those
present and voting, in person or by proxy, have voted in favour of it.

(2) Any resolution is invalid if those voting against it include more than
half in value of the creditors to whom notice of the meeting was sent and
who are not, to the best of the chairman's belief, persons connected with
the company.]

Notes

R 2.43(2)

A 'connected' person is defined by reference to IA 1986 s 249, 435; whether a person falls
within this category is for the chairman to determine and his decision can be challenged under
IR 1986 r 2.39 and/or IA 1986 Sch B1 para 74.

2.102

[2.44 Minutes]

[(1) The chairman of the meeting shall cause minutes of its proceedings
to be entered in the company's minute book.

(2) The minutes shall include a list of the names and addresses of
creditors who attended (personally or by proxy) and, if a creditors'
committee has been established, the names and addresses of those elected
to be members of the committee.]

2.103

[2.45 Revision of the administrator's proposals]

[(1) The administrator shall, under paragraph 54, make a statement
setting out the proposed revisions to his proposals which he shall attach
to Form 2.22B and send to all those to whom he is required to send a
copy of his revised proposals.

(2) The statement of revised proposals shall include—

(a) details of the court where the proceedings are and the relevant court reference number;

(b) the full name, registered address registered number and any other trading names of the company;

(c) details relating to his appointment as administrator, including the date of appointment and the person making the administration application or appointment;

(d) the names of the directors and secretary of the company and details of any shareholdings in the company they may have;

(e) a summary of the initial proposals and the reason(s) for proposing a revision;

(f) details of the proposed revision including details of the administrator's assessment of the likely impact of the proposed revision upon creditors generally or upon each class of creditors (as the case may be);

(g) where a proposed revision relates to the ending of the administration by a creditors' voluntary liquidation and the nomination of a person to be the proposed liquidator of the company, a statement that, in accordance with paragraph 83(7) and Rule 2.117(3), creditors may nominate a different person as the proposed liquidator, provided that the nomination is made after the receipt of the revised proposals and before those revised proposals are approved; and

(h) any other information that the administrator thinks necessary to enable creditors to decide whether or not to vote for the proposed revisions.

(3) Subject to paragraph 54(3), within 5 days of sending out the statement in paragraph (1) above, the administrator shall send a copy of the statement to every member of the company.

(4) When the administrator is acting under paragraph 54(3), the notice shall be published once in such newspaper as he thinks most appropriate for ensuring that the notice comes to the attention of the company's members. The notice shall—

(a) state the full name of the company;

(b) state the name and address of the administrator;

(c) specify an address to which members can write for a copy of the statement; and

(d) be published as soon as reasonably practicable after the administrator sends the statement to creditors.]

2.104

[2.46 Notice to creditors]

[As soon as reasonably practicable after the conclusion of a meeting of creditors to consider the administrator's proposals or revised proposals, the administrator shall

(a) send notice in Form 2.23B of the result of the meeting (including details of any modifications to the proposals that were approved) to every creditor who received notice of the meeting and any other person who received a copy of the original proposals; and

(b) file with the court, and send to the registrar of companies, and any creditors who did not receive notice of the meeting (of whose claim he has become subsequently aware), a copy of Form 2.23B, attaching a copy of the proposals considered at the meeting.]

2.105

[2.47 Reports to creditors]

[(1) 'Progress report' means a report which includes—
  (a) details of the court where the proceedings are and the relevant court reference number;
  (b) full details of the company's name, address of registered office and registered number;
  (c) full details of the administrator's name and address date of appointment and name and address of appointor, including any changes in office-holder, and, in the case of joint administrators, their functions as set out in the statement made for the purposes of paragraph 100(2);
  (d) details of any extensions to the initial period of appointment;
  (e) details of progress during the period of the report, including a receipts and payments account (as detailed in paragraph (2) below);
  (f) details of any assets that remain to be realised; and
  (g) any other relevant information for the creditors.

(2) A receipts and payments account shall state what assets of the company have been realised, for what value, and what payments have been made to creditors or others. The account is to be in the form of an abstract showing receipts and payments during the period of the report and where the administrator has ceased to act, the receipts and payments account shall include a statement as to the amount paid to unsecured creditors by virtue of the application of section 176A (prescribed part).

(3) The progress report shall cover—
  (a) the period of 6 months commencing on the date that the company entered administration, and every subsequent period of 6 months; and
  (b) when the administrator ceases to act, any period from the date of the previous report, if any, and from the date that the company entered administration if there is no previous report, until the time that the administrator ceases to act.

(4) The administrator shall send a copy of the progress report, attached to Form 2.24B, within 1 month of the end of the period covered by the report, to—
  (a) the creditors;
  (b) the court; and
  (c) the registrar of companies.

(5) The court may, on the administrator's application, extend the period of 1 month mentioned in paragraph (4) above, or make such other order in respect of the content of the report as it thinks fit.

> (6) If the administrator makes default in complying with this Rule, he is liable to a fine and, for continued contravention, to a daily default fine.]

Notes

R 2.47(1)

Where commercially sensitive information is contained in the progress report an application can be made for a closure order under IR 1986 r 7.31(5).

R 2.47(3)(a)

Where an administrator makes an application to court during the course of an administration it is clearly advisable to include a report on the progress of the administration though technically a 'progress report' may not be required under this rule. Where an application is made to court for an extension of the administration (IA 1986 Sch B1 para 76) a progress report has to be produced for the period since the last progress report (if any) was filed IR 1986 r 2.112.

R 2.47(3)(b)

The discharge of the administrator from liability (IA 1986 Sch B1 para 98) is likely to be delayed by the court until some time after the filing of the final progress report to enable creditors to make their objections if any known: see IR 1986 r 2.110); a progress report is also required on an application to court for extension of an administration: IR 1986 r 2.112. Inevitably the court will have to be provided with a draft final progress report where an administrator applies to court for his discharge from liability under IA 1986 Sch B1 para 98 and he has not yet ceased to act until the company enters a liquidation or dissolution (see IR 1986 rr 2.117, 2.118).

2.106

[2.48 Correspondence instead of creditors' meetings]

[(1) The administrator may seek to obtain the passing of a resolution by the creditors by sending a notice in Form 2.25B to every creditor who is entitled to be notified of a creditors' meeting under Rule 2.35(4).

(2) In order to be counted, votes must be received by the administrator by 12.00 hours on the closing date specified on Form 2.25B and must be accompanied by the statement in writing on entitlement to vote required by Rule 2.38.

(3) If any votes are received without the statement as to entitlement, or the administrator decides that the creditor is not entitled to vote according to Rules 2.38 and 2.39, then that creditor's votes shall be disregarded.

(4) The closing date shall be set at the discretion of the administrator. In any event it must not be set less than 14 days from the date of issue of the Form 2.25B.

(5) For any business to be transacted the administrator must receive at least 1 valid Form 2.25B by the closing date specified by him.

(6) If no valid Form 2.25B is received by the closing date specified then the administrator shall call a meeting of the creditors in accordance with Rule 2.35.

(7) Any single creditor, or a group of creditors, of the company whose debt(s) amount to at least 10% of the total debts of the company may,

within 5 business days from the date of the administrator sending out a resolution or proposals, require him to summon a meeting of creditors to consider the matters raised therein in accordance with Rule 2.37. Any meeting called under this Rule shall be conducted in accordance with Rule 2.35.

(8) If the administrator's proposals or revised proposals are rejected by the creditors pursuant to this Rule, the administrator may call a meeting of creditors.

(9) A reference in these Rules to anything done, or required to be done, at, or in connection with, or in consequence of, a creditors' meeting includes a reference to anything done in the course of correspondence in accordance with this Rule.]

Notes

R 2.48

Correspondence has an extended definition in IA 1986 Sch B1 para 11 and 'includes correspondence by telephonic or other electronic means'; see also IA 1986 Sch B1 para 58.

R 2.48(6)

This provision emphasises the importance of using the stated Form 2.25B. If no valid Form 2.25B is received by the administrator (IR 1986 r 2.48(5)) then a meeting of creditors must be called and the general rules as to meetings apply: IR 1986 rr 2.35ff.

[Section B: Company Meetings]

2.107

[2.49 Venue and conduct of company meeting]

[(1) Where the administrator summons a meeting of members of the company, he shall fix a venue for it having regard to their convenience.

(2) The chairman of the meeting shall be the administrator or a person nominated by him in writing to act in his place.

(3) A person so nominated must be either—
    (a)   one who is qualified to act as an insolvency practitioner in relation to the company; or
    (b)   an employee of the administrator or his firm who is experienced in insolvency matters.

(4) If within 30 minutes from the time fixed for commencement of the meeting there is no person present to act as chairman, the meeting stands adjourned to the same time and place in the following week or, if that is not a business day, to the business day immediately following.

(5) Subject as above, the meeting shall be summoned and conducted as if it were a general meeting of the company summoned under the company's articles of association, and in accordance with the applicable provisions of the Companies Act.

(6) Paragraph (5) does not apply where the laws of a member State and not the laws of England and Wales apply in relation to the conduct of the meeting. The meeting shall be summoned and conducted in accordance with the constitution of the company and the laws of the member State referred to in this paragraph shall apply to the conduct of the meeting.

(7) The chairman of the meeting shall cause minutes of its proceedings to be entered in the company's minute book.]

Notes

R 2.49

It would be rare for an administrator to call a meeting of members; presumably the administrator might consider doing so in the case of a solvent administration. An administrator does not have the power to make a distribution to members: *Re Business Properties Ltd (1988) 4 BCC 684.*

[Chapter 7
The Creditors' Committee]

2.108

[2.50 Constitution of committee]

[(1) Where it is resolved by a creditors' meeting to establish a creditors' committee for the purposes of the administration, the committee shall consist of at least 3 and not more than 5 creditors of the company elected at the meeting.

(2) Any creditor of the company is eligible to be a member of the committee, so long as his claim has not been rejected for the purpose of his entitlement to vote.

(3) A body corporate may be a member of the committee, but it cannot act as such otherwise than by a representative appointed under Rule 2.55 below.]

Notes

R 2.50ff

A number of the provisions dealing with a creditors' committee in an administration are similar to those in a liquidation and reference can be made to the notes under IR 1986 r 4.151ff.

R 2.50(1)

A creditors' committee may be formed pursuant to IA 1986 Sch B1 para 57 and a member of the committee is a fiduciary: *Re F T Hawkins & Co Ltd* [1952] Ch 881.

2.109

[2.51 Formalities of establishment]

[(1) The creditors' committee does not come into being, and accordingly cannot act, until the administrator has issued a certificate in Form 2.26B of its due constitution.

(2) No person may act as a member of the committee unless and until he has agreed to do so and, unless the relevant proxy or authorisation contains a statement to the contrary, such agreement may be given by his proxy-holder or representative under section 375 of the Companies Act present at the meeting establishing the committee.

(3) The administrator's certificate of the committee's due constitution shall not be issued unless and until at least 3 of the persons who are to be members of the committee have agreed to act and shall be issued as soon as reasonably practicable thereafter.

(4) As and when the others (if any) agree to act, the administrator shall issue an amended certificate in Form 2.26B.

(5) The certificate, and any amended certificate, shall be filed with the court and a copy sent to the registrar of companies by the administrator, as soon as reasonably practicable.

(6) If after the first establishment of the committee there is any change in its membership, the administrator shall as soon as reasonably practicable report the change to the court and the registrar of companies in Form 2.27B.]

2.110

[2.52 Functions and meetings of the committee]

[(1) The creditors' committee shall assist the administrator in discharging his functions, and act in relation to him in such manner as may be agreed from time to time.

(2) Subject as follows, meetings of the committee shall be held when and where determined by the administrator.

(3) The administrator shall call a first meeting of the committee not later than 6 weeks after its first establishment, and thereafter he shall call a meeting—
  (a) if so requested by a member of the committee or his representative (the meeting then to be held within 14 days of the request being received by the administrator); and
  (b) for a specified date, if the committee has previously resolved that a meeting be held on that date.

(4) The administrator shall give 7 days' written notice of the venue of any meeting to every member of the committee (or his representative designated for that purpose), unless in any case the requirement of notice has been waived by or on behalf of any member. Waiver may be signified either at or before the meeting.]

———

Notes

R 2.52(1)

The court may regard the views expressed by the creditors' committee as influential in determining the views of the creditors as a whole: *Re WSBL Realisations 1992 Ltd* [1995] 2 BCLC 576; *Re C E King Ltd* [2000] 2 BCLC 297.

———

2.111

[2.53 The chairman at meetings]

[(1) Subject to Rule 2.62(3), the chairman at any meeting of the creditors' committee shall be the administrator or a person nominated by him in writing to act.

(2) A person so nominated must be either—
    (a)   one who is qualified to act as an insolvency practitioner in relation to the company; or
    (b)   an employee of the administrator or his firm who is experienced in insolvency matters.]

2.112

[2.54 Quorum]

[A meeting of the committee is duly constituted if due notice of it has been given to all the members, and at least 2 members are present or represented.]

2.113

[2.55 Committee-members' representatives]

[(1) A member of the committee may, in relation to the business of the committee, be represented by another person duly authorised by him for that purpose.

(2) A person acting as a committee-member's representative must hold a letter of authority entitling him so to act (either generally or specially) and signed by or on behalf of the committee-member, and for this purpose any proxy or any authorisation under section 375 of the Companies Act in relation to any meeting of creditors of the company shall, unless it contains a statement to the contrary, be treated as a letter of authority to act generally signed by or on behalf of the committee-member.

(3) The chairman at any meeting of the committee may call on a person claiming to act as a committee-member's representative to produce his letter of authority, and may exclude him if it appears that his authority is deficient.

(4) No member may be represented by a body corporate, a person who is an undischarged bankrupt [or], a disqualified director or a person who is subject to a [bankruptcy restrictions order, bankruptcy restrictions undertaking or interim bankruptcy restrictions order].

(5) No person shall on the same committee, act at one and the same time as representative of more than one committee-member.

(6) Where a member's representative signs any document on the member's behalf, the fact that he so signs must be stated below his signature.]

2.114

[2.56 Resignation]

[A member of the committee may resign by notice in writing delivered to the administrator.]

2.115

[2.57 Termination of membership]

[(1) Membership of the creditors' committee is automatically terminated if the member—
    (a)   becomes bankrupt …; or
    (b)   at 3 consecutive meetings of the committee is neither present nor represented (unless at the third of those meetings it is resolved that this Rule is not to apply in his case); or
    (c)   ceases to be, or is found never to have been, a creditor.

(2) However, if the cause of termination is the member's bankruptcy, his trustee in bankruptcy replaces him as a member of the committee.]

2.116

[2.58 Removal]

[A member of the committee may be removed by resolution at a meeting of creditors' at least 14 days' notice having been given of the intention to move that resolution.]

2.117

[2.59 Vacancies]

[(1) The following applies if there is a vacancy in the membership of the creditors' committee.

(2) The vacancy need not be filled if the administrator and a majority of the remaining members of the committee so agree, provided that the total number of members does not fall below the minimum required under Rule 2.50(1).

(3) The administrator may appoint any creditor (being qualified under the Rules to be a member of the committee) to fill the vacancy, if a

majority of the other members of the committee agree to the appointment, and the creditor concerned consents to act.]

2.118

[2.60 Procedure at meetings]

[(1) At any meeting of the creditors' committee, each member of it (whether present himself, or by his representative) has one vote; and a resolution is passed when a majority of the members present or represented have voted in favour of it.

(2) Every resolution passed shall be recorded in writing, either separately or as part of the minutes of the meeting.

(3) A record of each resolution shall be signed by the chairman and placed in the company's minute book.]

2.119

[2.61 Resolutions of creditors' committee by post]

[(1) In accordance with this Rule, the administrator may seek to obtain the agreement of members of the creditors' committee to a resolution by sending to every member (or his representative designated for the purpose) a copy of the proposed resolution.

(2) Where the administrator makes use of the procedure allowed by this Rule, he shall send out to members of the committee or their representatives (as the case may be) a copy of any proposed resolution on which a decision is sought, which shall be set out in such a way that agreement with or dissent from each separate resolution may be indicated by the recipient on the copy so sent.

(3) Any member of the committee may, within 7 business days from the date of the administrator sending out a resolution, require him to summon a meeting of the committee to consider matters raised by the resolution.

(4) In the absence of such a request, the resolution is deemed to have been passed by the committee if and when the administrator is notified in writing by a majority of the members that they concur with it.

(5) A copy of every resolution passed under this Rule, and a note that the committee's concurrence was obtained, shall be placed in the company's minute book.]

Notes

R 2.61

This provision may be compared with IA 1986 Sch B1 para 58 which enables anything which is required or permitted to be done at a creditors' meeting under IA 1986 Sch B1 to be done by correspondence between the administrator and the creditors. 'Correspondence' includes correspondence by telephone or other electronic means: IA 1986 Sch B1 para 111. Whether IR 1986 r 2.61 would enable a creditors' committee resolution to be done by telephone or other electronic means is not clear.

2.120

[2.62 Information from administrator]

[(1) Where the committee resolves to require the attendance of the administrator under paragraph 57(3)(a), the notice to him shall be in writing signed by the majority of the members of the committee for the time being. A member's representative may sign for him.

(2) The meeting at which the administrator's attendance is required shall be fixed by the committee for a business day, and shall be held at such time and place as he determines.

(3) Where the administrator so attends, the members of the committee may elect any one of their number to be chairman of the meeting, in place of the administrator or a nominee of his.]

2.121

[2.63 Expenses of members]

[(1) Subject as follows, the administrator shall, out of the assets of the company, defray any reasonable travelling expenses directly incurred by members of the creditors' committee or their representatives in relation to their attendance at the committee's meetings, or otherwise on the committee's business as an expense of the administration.

(2) Paragraph (1) does not apply to any meeting of the committee held within 6 weeks of a previous meeting, unless the meeting in question is summoned at the instance of the administrator.]

2.122

[2.64 Members' dealing with the company]

[(1) Membership of the committee does not prevent a person from dealing with the company while the company is in administration, provided that any transactions in the course of such dealings are in good faith and for value.

(2) The court may, on the application of any person interested, set aside any transaction which appears to it to be contrary to the requirements of this Rule, and may give such consequential directions as it thinks fit for compensating the company for any loss which it may have incurred in consequence of the transaction.]

Notes

R 2.64(1)

There is no definition of 'value' in IR 1986.

2.123

[2.65 Formal defects]

[The acts of the creditors' committee established for any administration are valid notwithstanding any defect in the appointment, election or qualifications of any member of the committee or any committee-member's representative or in the formalities of its establishment.]

Notes

R 2.65

However this provision is unlikely to validate the acts of the committee where a member has not been appointed to the committee at all: *cf Morris v Kannsen* [1946] AC 459; CA 1985 s 285.

[Chapter 8
Disposal of Charged Property]

2.124

[2.66

[(1) The following applies where the administrator applies to the court under paragraphs 71 or 72 for authority to dispose of property of the company which is subject to a security (other than a floating charge), or goods in the possession of the company under a hire purchase agreement.

(2) The court shall fix a venue for the hearing of the application, and the administrator shall as soon as reasonably practicable give notice of the venue to the person who is the holder of the security or, as the case may be, the owner under the agreement.

(3) If an order is made under paragraphs 71 or 72 the court shall send two sealed copies to the administrator.

(4) The administrator shall send one of them to that person who is the holder of the security or owner under the agreement.

(5) The administrator shall send a Form 2.28B to the registrar of companies with a copy of the sealed order.]

Notes

R 2.66(1)

In the absence of the agreement of the security holder an administrator under IA 1986 Sch B1 para 71 must apply to the court to dispose of property which is subject to a security other than a floating charge. 'Security' has an extended definition: IA 1986 s 248(b). It is similarly the case with property subject to a hire purchase agreement under IA 1986 Sch B1 para 72. 'Hire purchase agreement' is given an extended definition in IA 1986 Sch B1 para 111 to include conditional sale, chattel leasing and retention of title agreements.

[Chapter 9
Expenses of the Administration]

2.125

[2.67

[(1) The expenses of the administration are payable in the following order of priority—

(a) expenses properly incurred by the administrator in performing his functions in the administration of the company;

(b) the cost of any security provided by the administrator in accordance with the Act or the Rules;

(c) where an administration order was made, the costs of the applicant and any person appearing on the hearing of the application and where the administrator was appointed otherwise than by order of the court, any costs and expenses of the appointor in connection with the making of the appointment and the costs and expenses incurred by any other person in giving notice of intention to appoint an administrator;

(d) any amount payable to a person employed or authorised, under Chapter 5 of this Part of the Rules, to assist in the preparation of a statement of affairs or statement of concurrence;

(e) any allowance made, by order of the court, towards costs on an application for release from the obligation to submit a statement of affairs or statement of concurrence;

(f) any necessary disbursements by the administrator in the course of the administration (including any expenses incurred by members of the creditors' committee or their representatives and allowed for by the administrator under Rule 2.63, but not including any payment of corporation tax in circumstances referred to in sub-paragraph (j) below);

(g) the remuneration or emoluments of any person who has been employed by the administrator to perform any services for the company, as required or authorised under the Act or the Rules;

(h) the remuneration of the administrator agreed under Chapter 11 of this Part of the Rules;

(j) the amount of any corporation tax on chargeable gains accruing on the realisation of any asset of the company (without regard to whether the realisation is effected by the administrator, a secured creditor, or a receiver or manager appointed to deal with a security).

(2) The priorities laid down by paragraph (1) of this Rule are subject to the power of the court to make orders under paragraph (3) of this Rule where the assets are insufficient to satisfy the liabilities.

(3) The court may, in the event of the assets being insufficient to satisfy the liabilities, make an order as to the payment out of the assets of the expenses incurred in the administration in such order of priority as the court thinks just.]

[(4) For the purposes of paragraph 99(3), the former administrator's remuneration and expenses shall comprise all those items set out in paragraph (1) of this Rule.]

Notes

R 2.67

This list of expenses is similar to the list which appears in a liquidation context: IR 1986 r 4.218; but unlike the liquidation regime it is not of general application. IR 1986 r 2.67 only applies where the administrator is proposing to make a distribution (IR 1986 r 2.68(3)(c)) or he ceases to be the administrator (IA 1986 Sch B1 para 99(3)). The expenses may be the subject of a detailed assessment in the absence of agreement: IR 1986 r 7.34.

R 2.67(1)(a)

This provision is substantially the same as its liquidation counterpart IR 1986 r 4.218(1)(r). However the principle that where a company in liquidation remains in occupation of a leasehold property which is used to benefit for the benefit of the liquidation then rent should be paid as an expense (*Re Toshuku Finance UK plc* [2002] 1 WLR 671) does not automatically apply in an administration. Whether or not a liability is paid as an expense of the administration within this provision is still a matter for judicial discretion applying the principles in *Re Atlantic Computer Systems plc* [1992] Ch 505.

R 2.67(1)(f)

This provision is substantially the same as its liquidation counterpart: IR 1986 r 4.218(1)(m). In a liquidation context it has been held that the payment of community charge and tax are 'necessary' disbursements: *Re Toshuku Finance UK plc* [2002] 1 WLR 671. In *Re Allders Department Stores Ltd* [2005] 1 All ER 231 directions were sought by administrators to determine first whether unfair dismissal and redundancy payments had to be paid as expenses of the administration as '*necessary disbursements*'; and secondly whether such payments were '*wages or salary*'. Under IA 1986 Sch B1 para 99(4), (5), priority is conferred over administration expenses in favour of liabilities which have been adopted by the administrator 14 days after appointment, and which consist of '*wages or salary*': IA 1986 Sch B1 para 99(5)(c). It was held on the latter point that unfair dismissal/redundancy payments were not '*wages or salary*' so they did not take in priority to administration expenses; unfair dismissal/redundancy payments are statutory payments rather than contractual payments and they would not ordinarily be considered as '*wages or salary*': *Re Huddersfield Fine Worsteds Ltd*, *Re Granville Technology Group Ltd* [2005] BCC 915; see notes to IA 1986 IA 1986 Sch B1 para 99). On the former point it was held that such payments did not qualify as '*necessary disbursements*' within IR 1986 r 2.67(1)(f) and *Re Toshuku Finance UK plc* [2002] 1 WLR 671 was distinguished as being a liquidation rather than an administration case. Further it was held that it could not have been intended to have elevated redundancy/unfair dismissal payments to an 'expense' of the administration whilst leaving certain unpaid wages as merely preferential under IA 1986 Sch 6.

R 2.67(3)

Where there are insufficient assets to meet the expenses the court may alter the priority set out in this provision; presumably this would only apply in the context of a cessation of the administrator's appointment as the administrator would not be making a distribution if there were insufficient funds to pay the expenses in full.

R 2.67(4)

This provision was inserted by Insolvency (Amendment) Rules 2005 SI 2005/527, r 8 effective from 1 April 2005: transitional provisions apply in relation to any case where a company has entered administration made before that date, see r 3(1) thereof.

[Chapter 10
Distributions to Creditors]

[Section A: Application of Chapter and General]

2.126

[2.68

[(1) This Chapter applies where the administrator makes, or proposes to make, a distribution to any class of creditors. Where the distribution is to a particular class of creditors, references in this Chapter to creditors shall, in so far as the context requires, be a reference to that class of creditors only.

(2) The administrator shall give notice to the creditors of his intention to declare and distribute a dividend in accordance with Rule 2.95.

(3) Where it is intended that the distribution is to be a sole or final dividend, the administrator shall, after the date specified in the notice referred to in paragraph (2)—

(a) defray any outstanding expenses of a liquidation (including any of the items mentioned in Rule 4.218) or provisional liquidation that immediately preceded the administration;

(b) defray any items payable in accordance with the provisions of paragraph 99;

(c) defray any amounts (including any debts or liabilities and his own remuneration and expenses) which would, if the administrator were to cease to be the administrator of the company, be payable out of the property of which he had custody or control in accordance with the provisions of paragraph 99; and

(d) declare and distribute that dividend without regard to the claim of any person in respect of a debt not already proved.

(4) The court may, on the application of any person, postpone the date specified in the notice.]

Notes

R 2.68

Such a distribution would include a distribution to secured or preferential creditors. This provision must be read together with IA 1986 Sch B1 para 99. The combined effect is to provide that the general costs and expenses of an administration are paid ahead of preferential creditors and floating chargeholders. This is a markedly different position to that in liquidation where generally liquidation expenses are not payable out of the floating charge assets: *Buchler v Talbot* [2004] 2 AC 298; and see Statement on behalf of HM Revenue & Customs and the DTI Insolvency Service 7 June 2005. An exception occurs in a liquidation where the liquidation expenses relate to protecting and realising the floating charge assets in which case such expenses are payable out of floating charge assets. It is proposed that the position in liquidation is to be changed to be same as in an administration: cl 1246 Companies Bill 2006 inserting new IA 1986 s 176ZA.

R 2.68(3)(a)

This provision will assist the liquidator where the liquidation is followed by an administration. The effect of *Buchler v Talbot* [2004] 2 AC 298 is to create two distinct funds in this context: (a) the company's 'free assets' and (b) the floating charge assets. Each fund has its own costs and expenses. Liquidation expenses are not generally payable out of the latter fund; (see also notes to IA 1986 s 175(2)(b)) although it is proposed that the position in liquidation is to be changed to be same as in an administration: cl 1246 Companies Bill 2006. Where the liquidation is immediately followed by an administration IR 1986 r 2.68(3)(a) has the effect of obliging the administrator to meet any unpaid liquidation expenses when the administrator decides to make a distribution.

R 2.68(3)(c)

The administrator's expenses are also charged on and payable out of the company's property when his appointment ceases to have effect and they must be paid before any return is made to the holder of a floating charge: IA 1986 Sch B1 para 99(3). However the administrator is not duty bound to wait for the administration to end before paying administration expenses: *Re Paramount Airways Ltd* [1994] BCC 172.

2.127

[2.69 Debts of insolvent company to rank equally]

[Debts other than preferential debts rank equally between themselves in the administration and, after the preferential debts, shall be paid in full unless the assets are insufficient for meeting them, in which case they abate in equal proportions between themselves.]

2.128

[2.70 Supplementary provisions as to dividend]

[(1) In the calculation and distribution of a dividend the administrator shall make provision for—
- (a) any debts which appear to him to be due to persons who, by reason of the distance of their place of residence, may not have had sufficient time to tender and establish their proofs;
- (b) any debts which are the subject of claims which have not yet been determined; and
- (c) disputed proofs and claims.

(2) A creditor who has not proved his debt before the declaration of any dividend is not entitled to disturb, by reason that he has not participated in it, the distribution of that dividend or any other dividend declared before his debt was proved, but—
- (a) when he has proved that debt he is entitled to be paid, out of any money for the time being available for the payment of any further dividend, any dividend or dividends which he has failed to receive; and
- (b) any dividends payable under sub-paragraph (a) shall be paid before the money is applied to the payment of any such further dividend.

(3) No action lies against the administrator for a dividend; but if he refuses to pay a dividend the court may, if it thinks fit, order him to pay it and also to pay, out of his own money—
- (a) interest on the dividend, at the rate for the time being specified in section 17 of the Judgments Act 1838, from the time when it was withheld; and
- (b) the costs of the proceedings in which the order to pay is made.]

2.129

[2.71 Division of unsold assets]

[The administrator may, with the permission of the creditors' committee, or if there is no creditors' committee, the creditors, divide in its existing form amongst the company's creditors, according to its estimated value, any property which from its peculiar nature or other special circumstances cannot be readily or advantageously sold.]

[Section B: Machinery of Proving a Debt]

2.130

[2.72 Proving a debt]

[(1) A person claiming to be a creditor of the company and wishing to recover his debt in whole or in part must (subject to any order of the court to the contrary) submit his claim in writing to the administrator.

(2) A creditor who claims is referred to as 'proving' for his debt and a document by which he seeks to establish his claim is his 'proof'.

(3) Subject to the next paragraph, a proof must—
    (a)   be made out by, or under the direction of, the creditor and signed by him or a person authorised in that behalf; and
    (b)   state the following matters—
        (i)   the creditor's name and address;
        (ii) the total amount of his claim as at the date on which the company entered administration, less any payments that have been made to him after that date in respect of his claim and any adjustment by way of set-off in accordance with Rule 2.85;
        (iii) whether or not the claim includes outstanding uncapitalised interest;
        (iv) whether or not the claim includes value added tax;
        (v) whether the whole or any part of the debt falls within any, and if so, which categories of preferential debts under section 386;
        (vi) particulars of how and when the debt was incurred by the company;
        (vii) particulars of any security held, the date on which it was given and the value which the creditor puts on it;
        (viii) details of any reservation of title in respect of goods to which the debt refers; and
        (ix) the name, address and authority of the person signing the proof (if other than the creditor himself).

(4) There shall be specified in the proof details of any documents by reference to which the debt can be substantiated; but (subject as follows) it is not essential that such document be attached to the proof or submitted with it.

(5) The administrator may call for any document or other evidence to be produced to him, where he thinks it necessary for the purpose of substantiating the whole or any part of the claim made in the proof.]

Notes

RR 2.72ff

The provisions in relation to proof of a debt in an administration are modelled on the provisions which apply in a liquidation and it may be helpful to refer to the notes to IR 1986 4.73ff.

R 2.72(1)

Although the claim must be put in writing no specific form is required.

___

2.131

[2.73 Claim established by affidavit]

[(1) The administrator may, if he thinks it necessary, require a claim of debt to be verified by means of an affidavit in Form 2.29B.

(2) An affidavit may be required notwithstanding that a proof of debt has already been lodged.]

2.132

[2.74 Costs of proving]

[Unless the court otherwise orders—
- (a) every creditor bears the cost of proving his own debt, including costs incurred in providing documents or evidence under Rule 2.72(5); and
- (b) costs incurred by the administrator in estimating the quantum of a debt under Rule 2.81 are payable out of the assets as an expense of the administration.]

2.133

[2.75 Administrator to allow inspection of proofs]

[The administrator shall, so long as proofs lodged with him are in his hands, allow them to be inspected, at all reasonable times on any business day, by any of the following persons—
- (a) any creditor who has submitted a proof of debt (unless his proof has been wholly rejected for purposes of dividend or otherwise);
- (b) any contributory of the company; and
- (c) any person acting on behalf of either of the above.]

2.134

[2.76 New administrator appointed]

[(1) If a new administrator is appointed in place of another, the former administrator shall transmit to him all proofs which he has received, together with an itemised list of them.

(2) The new administrator shall sign the list by way of receipt for the proofs, and return it to his predecessor.]

2.135

[2.77 Admission and rejection of proofs for dividend]

[(1) A proof may be admitted for dividend either for the whole amount claimed by the creditor, or for part of that amount.

> (2) If the administrator rejects a proof in whole or in part, he shall prepare a written statement of his reasons for doing so, and send it as soon as reasonably practicable to the creditor.]

Notes

R 2.77(1)

The administrator in admitting or rejecting a proof is acting in a quasi judicial capacity; and even in the case of a proof based on a judgment debt the administrator is not limited to the evidence that was before the court when it gave its judgment: *Re Menastar Finance Ltd* [2003] BCC 404; *Re Trepca Mines Ltd* [1960] 1 WLR 1273.

2.136

[2.78 Appeal against decision on proof]

[(1) If a creditor is dissatisfied with the administrator's decision with respect to his proof (including any decision on the question of preference), he may apply to the court for the decision to be reversed or varied. The application must be made within 21 days of his receiving the statement sent under Rule 2.77(2).

(2) Any other creditor may, if dissatisfied with the administrator's decision admitting or rejecting the whole or any part of a proof, make such an application within 21 days of becoming aware of the administrator's decision.

(3) Where application is made to the court under this Rule, the court shall fix a venue for the application to be heard, notice of which shall be sent by the applicant to the creditor who lodged the proof in question (if it is not himself) and the administrator.

(4) The administrator shall, on receipt of the notice, file with the court the relevant proof, together (if appropriate) with a copy of the statement sent under Rule 2.77(2).

(5) After the application has been heard and determined, the proof shall, unless it has been wholly disallowed, be returned by the court to the administrator.

(6) The administrator is not personally liable for costs incurred by any person in respect of an application under this Rule unless the court otherwise orders.]

Notes

R 2.78

This rule is modelled on IR 1986 r 4.83 which applies in a liquidation and reference should be made to the notes under that provision.

R 2.78(1)

The burden on proof rests on the creditor who is challenging the administrator's decision: *Bellmex International Ltd v British American Tobacco Ltd* [2001] 1 BCLC 91.

_____

2.137

[2.79 Withdrawal or variation of proof]

[A creditor's proof may at any time, by agreement between himself and the administrator, be withdrawn or varied as to the amount claimed.]

2.138

[2.80 Expunging of proof by the court]

[(1) The court may expunge a proof or reduce the amount claimed—
  (a) on the administrator's application, where he thinks that the proof has been improperly admitted, or ought to be reduced; or
  (b) on the application of a creditor, if the administrator declines to interfere in the matter.

(2) Where application is made to the court under this Rule, the court shall fix a venue for the application to be heard, notice of which shall be sent by the applicant—
  (a) in the case of an application by the administrator, to the creditor who made the proof; and
  (b) in the case of an application by a creditor, to the administrator and to the creditor who made the proof (if not himself).]

_____

Notes

R 2.80(1)(b)

Thus where an administrator refuses to act a creditor can make an application.

R 2.80(2)

The court has a discretion whether or not to make an order and it is not necessary for the administrator to show that he had made a mistake of fact although that is a relevant factor: *Re Globe Legal Services Ltd* [2002] BCC 858.

_____

[Section C: Quantification of Claims]

2.139

[2.81 Estimate of quantum]

[(1) The administrator shall estimate the value of any debt which, by reason of its being subject to any contingency or for any other reason, does not bear a certain value; and he may revise any estimate previously made, if he thinks fit by reference to any change of circumstances or to information becoming available to him. He shall inform the creditor as to his estimate and any revision of it.

(2) Where the value of a debt is estimated under this Rule, the amount provable in the administration in the case of that debt is that of the estimate for the time being.]

2.140

[2.82 Negotiable instruments, etc]

[Unless the administrator allows, a proof in respect of money owed on a bill of exchange, promissory note, cheque or other negotiable instrument or security cannot be admitted unless there is produced the instrument or security itself or a copy of it, certified by the creditor or his authorised representative to be a true copy.]

2.141

[2.83 Secured creditors]

[(1) If a secured creditor realises his security, he may prove for the balance of his debt, after deducting the amount realised.

(2) If a secured creditor voluntarily surrenders his security for the general benefit of creditors, he may prove for his whole debt, as if it were unsecured.]

2.142

[2.84 Discounts]

[There shall in every case be deducted from the claim all trade and other discounts which would have been available to the company but for its administration except any discount for immediate, early or cash settlement.]

2.143

[2.85 Mutual credits and set-off]

[(1) This Rule applies where the administrator, being authorised to make the distribution in question, has, pursuant to Rule 2.95 given notice that he proposes to make it.

(2) In this Rule 'mutual dealings' means mutual credits, mutual debts or other mutual dealings between the company and any creditor of the company proving or claiming to prove for a debt in the administration but does not include any of the following—
- (a) any debt arising out of an obligation incurred after the company entered administration;
- (b) any debt arising out of an obligation incurred at a time when the creditor had notice that—
  - (i) an application for an administration order was pending; or
  - (ii) any person had given notice of intention to appoint an administrator;
- (c) any debt arising out of an obligation where—
  - (i) the administration was immediately preceded by a winding up; and

      (ii) at the time the obligation was incurred the creditor had notice that a meeting of creditors had been summoned under section 98 or a petition for the winding up of the company was pending;

(d) any debt arising out of an obligation incurred during a winding up which immediately preceded the administration; or

(e) any debt which has been acquired by a creditor by assignment or otherwise, pursuant to an agreement between the creditor and any other party where that agreement was entered into—
    (i) after the company entered administration;
    (ii) at a time when the creditor had notice that an application for an administration order was pending;
    (iii) at a time when the creditor had notice that any person had given notice of intention to appoint an administrator;
    (iv) where the administration was immediately preceded by a winding up, at a time when the creditor had notice that a meeting of creditors had been summoned under section 98 or that a winding up petition was pending; or
    (v) during a winding up which immediately preceded the administration.

(3) An account shall be taken as at the date of the notice referred to in paragraph (1) of what is due from each party to the other in respect of the mutual dealings and the sums due from one party shall be set off against the sums due from the other.

(4) A sum shall be regarded as being due to or from the company for the purposes of paragraph (3) whether—
(a) it is payable at present or in the future;
(b) the obligation by virtue of which it is payable is certain or contingent; or
(c) its amount is fixed or liquidated, or is capable of being ascertained by fixed rules or as a matter of opinion.

(5) Rule 2.81 shall apply for the purposes of this Rule to any obligation to or from the company which, by reason of its being subject to any contingency or for any other reason, does not bear a certain value;

(6) Rules 2.86 to 2.88 shall apply for the purposes of this Rule in relation to any sums due to the company which—
(a) are payable in a currency other than sterling;
(b) are of a periodical nature; or
(c) bear interest.

(7) Rule 2.105 shall apply for the purposes of this Rule to any sum due to or from the company which is payable in the future.

(8) Only the balance (if any) of the account owed to the creditor is provable in the administration. Alternatively the balance (if any) owed to the company shall be paid to the administrator as part of the assets except where all or part of the balance results from a contingent or prospective debt owed by the creditor and in such a case the balance (or that part of it which results from the contingent or prospective debt) shall be paid if and when that debt becomes due and payable.

> (9) In this Rule 'obligation' means an obligation however arising, whether by virtue of an agreement, rule of law or otherwise.]

Notes

R 2.85

This provision was introduced by Insolvency (Amendment) Rules 2005 SI 2005/527, r 9 effective from 1 April 2005. For transitional provisions in relation to any case where a company has entered administration before that date see r 3(1) thereof. IR 1986 r 2.85 is substantially in the same form as the set off rule in liquidation: IR 1986 r 4.90. The set off rules are important not only for the purpose of proving in the administration but also voting in the administration: IR 1986 r 2.38(4). The main change effected in the administration regime is to ensure that actual, contingent and future debts owed both to and by the company will be brought into the account that must be taken: *Stein v Blake* [1996] AC 243.

R 2.85(1)

The special set off rule in administration does not apply unless the administrator has given the relevant 28 day notice of a proposed distribution: IR 1986 r 2.95; IA 1986 Sch B1 para 65; *Re GHE Realisations Ltd* [2005] BCC 139. Until that point the normal rules of set off apply.

R 2.85(2)

This provision lists debts which cannot form the basis of 'mutual dealings'. The term 'mutual debts' does not require '.. anything more than commensurable cross obligations between the same people in the same capacity. How those debts arose – whether by contract, statute or tort, voluntarily or by compulsion- is not material': *Secretary of State for Trade and Industry v Frid* [2004] 2 AC 506 at 513 per Lord Hoffmann.

R 2.85(2)(c), (d)

These provisions assist in ensuring each separate insolvency regime achieves an exclusion from set off of certain sums due both to and from the company arising in the relevant time.

R 2.85(2)(e)

Certain dealings therefore are not to be brought into the account being debts acquired by a creditor under an agreement entered into after the specified times; this aims to prevent assignments of debts for the purpose of unfairly improving the position of a claimant by giving a right of set off. Where the debts are acquired by a creditor under an agreement entered into prior to those specified times a mutual dealing occurs.

R 2.85(4)

This provision can be compared with the definition of 'debt' and 'liability' under IR 1986 r 13.12(5). Thus not only contingent and future debts owed by the company are to be taken into account but also such debts owed to the company. Under the earlier version of IR 1986 r 2.85 contingent debts owed by a third party to the company were not brought into account whilst they remained contingent; the position has now changed. Although the contingent debt is brought into the account this does not mean that the third party is obliged to pay the contingent/prospective liability earlier than its due date: IR 1986 r 2.85(8).

R 2.85(5)

Contingent debts are valued using the procedure set out in IR 1986 r 2.81.

R 2.85(6)

Reference should be made to IR 1986 r 2.86–2.88.

R 2.85(7)

Thus future debts owed to the company are to be discounted adopting the statutory formula which applies to future debts owed by the company IR 1986 r 2.105; that provision was amended effective from 1 April 2005 to take into account the criticisms made in *Re Park Air Services Ltd* [2000] 2 AC 172, 187 per Lord Millett, see notes to IR 1986 r 2.105.

R 2.85(8)

The third party is not therefore obliged to make any balancing payment to the administrator in respect of a contingent/future debt owed to the company until the contingency or due date falls in; the new provisions ensure that the contingent/future debts owed to the company are taken into account but they do not force the third party to make an earlier payment.

2.144

[2.86 Debt in foreign currency]

[(1) For the purpose of proving a debt incurred or payable in a currency other than sterling, the amount of the debt shall be converted into sterling at the official exchange rate prevailing on the date when the company entered administration [or, if the administration was immediately preceded by a winding up, on the date that the company went into liquidation].

(2) 'The official exchange rate' is the middle exchange rate on the London Foreign Exchange Market at the close of business as published for the date in question. In the absence of any such published rate, it is such rate as the court determines.]

Notes

R 2.86(1)

This provision was amended by Insolvency (Amendment) Rules 2005 SI 2005/527, r 10 effective from 1 April 2005. For transitional provisions in relation to any case where a company has entered administration before that date see r 3(1) thereof.

2.145

[2.87 Payments of a periodical nature]

[(1) In the case of rent and other payments of a periodical nature, the creditor may prove for any amounts due and unpaid up to the date when the company entered administration [or, if the administration was immediately preceded by a winding up, up to the date that the company went into liquidation].

(2) Where at that date any payment was accruing due, the creditor may prove for so much as would have fallen due at that date, if accruing from day to day.]

———

Notes

R 2.87(1)

This provision was amended by Insolvency (Amendment) Rules 2005 SI 2005/527, r 11 effective from 1 April 2005. For transitional provisions in relation to any case where a company has entered administration prior to that date see r 3(1) thereof.

———

2.146

[2.88 Interest]

[(1) Where a debt proved in the administration bears interest, that interest is provable as part of the debt except in so far as it is payable in respect of any period after the company entered administration [or, if the administration was immediately preceded by a winding up, any period after the date that the company went into liquidation].

(2) In the following circumstances the creditor's claim may include interest on the debt for periods before the company entered administration, although not previously reserved or agreed.

(3) If the debt is due by virtue of a written instrument, and payable at a certain time, interest may be claimed for the period from that time to the date when the company entered administration.

(4) If the debt is due otherwise, interest may only be claimed if, before that date, a demand for payment of the debt was made in writing by or on behalf of the creditor, and notice given that interest would be payable from the date of the demand to the date of payment.

(5) Interest under paragraph (4) may only be claimed for the period from the date of the demand to that of the company's entering administration and for all the purposes of the Act and the Rules shall be chargeable at a rate not exceeding that mentioned in paragraph (6).

(6) The rate of interest to be claimed under paragraphs (3) and (4) is the rate specified in section 17 of the Judgments Act 1838 on the date when the company entered administration.

(7) Any surplus remaining after payment of the debts proved shall, before being applied for any purpose, be applied in paying interest on those debts in respect of the periods during which they have been outstanding since the company entered administration.

(8) All interest payable under paragraph (7) ranks equally whether or not the debts on which it is payable rank equally.

(9) The rate of interest payable under paragraph (7) is whichever is the greater of the rate specified under paragraph (6) or the rate applicable to the debt apart from the administration.]

Notes

R 2.88(1)

This provision was amended by Insolvency (Amendment) Rules 2005 SI 2005/527, r 12a effective from 1 April 2005. For transitional provisions in relation to any case where a company has entered administration prior to that date see r 3(1) thereof.

2.147

[2.89 Debt payable at future time]

[A creditor may prove for a debt of which payment was not yet due on the date when the company entered administration, [or, if the administration was immediately preceded by a winding up, up to the date that the company went into liquidation] subject to Rule 2.105 (adjustment of dividend where payment made before time).]

Notes

R 2.89(1)

This provision was amended by Insolvency (Amendment) Rules 2005 SI 2005/527, r 10 effective from 1 April 2005 to take account of the criticisms made by Lord Millett in *Re Park Air Services* [2000] 2 AC 172, 187 of the former rule. For transitional provisions in relation to any case where a company has entered administration before that date see r 3(1) thereof.

2.148

[2.90 Value of security]

[(1) A secured creditor may, with the agreement of the administrator or the leave of the court, at any time alter the value which he has, in his proof of debt, put upon his security.

(2) However, if a secured creditor—
    (a)   being the applicant for an administration order or the appointor of the administrator, has in the application or the notice of appointment put a value on his security; or
    (b)   has voted in respect of the unsecured balance of his debt,
he may re-value his security only with permission of the court.]

2.149

[2.91 Surrender for non-disclosure]

[(1) If a secured creditor omits to disclose his security in his proof of debt, he shall surrender his security for the general benefit of creditors, unless the court, on application by him, relieves him from the effect of this Rule on the ground that the omission was inadvertent or the result of honest mistake.

(2) If the court grants that relief, it may require or allow the creditor's proof of debt to be amended, on such terms as may be just.

(3) Nothing in this Rule or the following two Rules may affect the rights in rem of creditors or third parties protected under Article 5 of the EC Regulation (third parties' rights in rem).]

2.150

[2.92 Redemption by administrator]

[(1) The administrator may at any time give notice to a creditor whose debt is secured that he proposes, at the expiration of 28 days from the date of the notice, to redeem the security at the value put upon it in the creditor's proof.

(2) The creditor then has 21 days (or such longer period as the administrator may allow) in which, if he so wishes, to exercise his right to revalue his security (with the permission of the court, where Rule 2.90(2) applies).

If the creditor re-values his security, the administrator may only redeem at the new value.

(3) If the administrator redeems the security, the cost of transferring it is payable out of the assets.

(4) A secured creditor may at any time, by a notice in writing, call on the administrator to elect whether he will or will not exercise his power to redeem the security at the value then placed on it; and the administrator then has 3 months in which to exercise the power or determine not to exercise it.]

2.151

[2.93 Test of security's value]

[(1) Subject as follows, the administrator, if he is dissatisfied with the value which a secured creditor puts on his security (whether in his proof or by way of re-valuation under Rule 2.90), may require any property comprised in the security to be offered for sale.

(2) The terms of sale shall be such as may be agreed, or as the court may direct; and if the sale is by auction, the administrator on behalf of the company, and the creditor on his own behalf, may appear and bid.]

2.152

[2.94 Realisation of security by creditor]

[If a creditor who has valued his security subsequently realises it (whether or not at the instance of the administrator)—
  (a)   the net amount realised shall be substituted for the value previously put by the creditor on the security; and
  (b)   that amount shall be treated in all respects as an amended valuation made by him.]

2.153

[2.95 Notice of proposed distribution]

[(1) Where an administrator is proposing to make a distribution to creditors he shall give 28 days' notice of that fact.

(2) The notice given pursuant to paragraph (1) shall—
  (a) be sent to—
    (i) all creditors whose addresses are known to the administrator; and
    (ii) where a member State liquidator has been appointed in relation to the company, to the member State liquidator;
  (b) state whether the distribution is to preferential creditors or preferential creditors and unsecured creditors; and
  (c) where the administrator proposes to make a distribution to unsecured creditors, state the value of the prescribed part, except where the court has made an order under section 176A(5).

(3) Subject to paragraph (5), the administrator shall not declare a dividend unless he has by public advertisement invited creditors to prove their debts.

(4) A notice pursuant to paragraphs (1) or (3) shall—
  (a) state that it is the intention of the administrator to make a distribution to creditors within the period of 2 months from the last date for proving;
  (b) specify whether the proposed dividend is interim or final;
  (c) specify a date up to which proofs may be lodged being a date which—
    (i) is the same date for all creditors; and
    (ii) is not less than 21 days from that of the notice.

(5) A notice pursuant to paragraph (1) where a dividend is to be declared for preferential creditors, need only be given to those creditors in whose case he has reason to believe that their debts are preferential and public advertisement of the intended dividend need only be given if the administrator thinks fit.]

Notes

R 2.95

An administrator needs the permission of the court to make distribution to a creditor who is not secured or preferential: IA 1986 Sch B1 para 65(3); there is no power for an administrator to make a distribution to a member: *Re Business Properties Ltd* (1988) 4 BCC 684. The court should be informed of the amount of the payment which the administrator intends to make to the creditors: IA 1986 Sch B1 para 65(3).

2.154

[2.96 Admission or rejection of proofs]

[(1) Unless he has already dealt with them, within 7 days of the last date for proving, the administrator shall—

(a)   admit or reject proofs submitted to him; or
(b)   make such provision in respect of them as he thinks fit.

(2) The administrator is not obliged to deal with proofs lodged after the last date for proving, but he may do so, if he thinks fit.

(3) In the declaration of a dividend no payment shall be made more than once by virtue of the same debt.

(4) Subject to Rule 2.104, where—
(a)   a creditor has proved; and
(b)   a member State liquidator has proved in relation to the same debt,
payment shall only be made to the creditor.]

2.155

[2.97 Declaration of dividend]

[(1) Subject to paragraph (2), within the 2 month period referred to in Rule 2.95(4)(a) the administrator shall proceed to declare the dividend to one or more classes of creditor of which he gave notice.

(2) Except with the permission of the court, the administrator shall not declare a dividend so long as there is pending any application to the court to reverse or vary a decision of his on a proof, or to expunge a proof or to reduce the amount claimed.]

2.156

[2.98 Notice of declaration of a dividend]

[(1) Where the administrator declares a dividend he shall give notice of that fact to all creditors who have proved their debts and, where a member State liquidator has been appointed in relation to the company, to the member State liquidator.

(2) The notice shall include the following particulars relating to the administration—
(a)   amounts raised from the sale of assets, indicating (so far as practicable) amounts raised by the sale of particular assets;
(b)   payments made by the administrator when acting as such;
(c)   where the administrator proposed to make a distribution to unsecured creditors, the value of the prescribed part, except where the court has made an order under section 176A(5);
(d)   provision (if any) made for unsettled claims, and funds (if any) retained for particular purposes;
(e)   the total amount of dividend and the rate of dividend;
(f)   how he proposes to distribute the dividend; and
(g)   whether, and if so when, any further dividend is expected to be declared.]

2.157

[2.99 Payments of dividends and related matters]

[(1) The dividend may be distributed simultaneously with the notice declaring it.

(2) Payment of dividend may be made by post, or arrangements may be made with any creditor for it to be paid to him in another way, or held for his collection.

(3) Where a dividend is paid on a bill of exchange or other negotiable instrument, the amount of the dividend shall be endorsed on the instrument, or on a certified copy of it, if required to be produced by the holder for that purpose.]

2.158

[2.100 Notice of no dividend, or no further dividend]

[If the administrator gives notice to creditors that he is unable to declare any dividend or (as the case may be) any further dividend, the notice shall contain a statement to the effect either—
  (a)   that no funds have been realised; or
  (b)   that the funds realised have already been distributed or used or allocated for defraying the expenses of administration.]

2.159

[2.101 Proof altered after payment of dividend]

[(1) If after payment of dividend the amount claimed by a creditor in his proof is increased, the creditor is not entitled to disturb the distribution of the dividend; but he is entitled to be paid, out of any money for the time being available for the payment of any further dividend, any dividend or dividends which he has failed to receive.

(2) Any dividend or dividends payable under paragraph (1) shall be paid before the money there referred to is applied to the payment of any such further dividend.

(3) If, after a creditor's proof has been admitted, the proof is withdrawn or expunged, or the amount is reduced, the creditor is liable to repay to the administrator any amount overpaid by way of dividend.]

2.160

[2.102 Secured creditors]

[(1) The following applies where a creditor re-values his security at a time when a dividend has been declared.

(2) If the revaluation results in a reduction of his unsecured claim ranking for dividend, the creditor shall forthwith repay to the administrator, for the credit of the administration, any amount received by him as dividend in excess of that to which he would be entitled having regard to the revaluation of the security.

(3) If the revaluation results in an increase of his unsecured claim, the creditor is entitled to receive from the administrator, out of any money for the time being available for the payment of a further dividend, before any such further dividend is paid, any dividend or dividends which he has failed to receive, having regard to the revaluation of the security.

However, the creditor is not entitled to disturb any dividend declared (whether or not distributed) before the date of the revaluation.]

2.161

[2.103 Disqualification from dividend]

[If a creditor contravenes any provision of the Act or the Rules relating to the valuation of securities, the court may, on the application of the administrator, order that the creditor be wholly or partly disqualified from participation in any dividend.]

2.162

[2.104 Assignment of right to dividend]

[(1) If a person entitled to a dividend gives notice to the administrator that he wishes the dividend to be paid to another person, or that he has assigned his entitlement to another person, the administrator shall pay the dividend to that other accordingly.

(2) A notice given under this Rule must specify the name and address of the person to whom payment is to be made.]

2.163

[2.105 Debt payable at future time]

[(1) Where a creditor has proved for a debt of which payment is not due at the date of the declaration of dividend, he is entitled to dividend equally with other creditors, but subject as follows.

[(2) For the purpose of dividend (and no other purpose) the amount of the creditor's admitted proof (or, if a distribution has previously been made to him, the amount remaining outstanding in respect of his admitted proof) shall be reduced by applying the following formula—

$$X/1.05n$$

where—
   (a) 'X' is the value of the admitted proof; and
   (b) 'n' is the period beginning with the relevant date and ending with the date on which the payment of the creditor's debt would otherwise be due expressed in years and months in a decimalised form.

(3) In paragraph (2) 'relevant date' means—
   (a) in the case of an administration which was not immediately preceded by a winding up, the date that the company entered administration;
   (b) in the case of an administration which was immediately preceded by a winding up, the date that the company went into liquidation.]

Notes

R 2.105

This provision was substantially amended by Insolvency (Amendment) Rules 2005 SI 2005/527, r 14 effective from 1 April 2005; for transitional provisions in relation to any case where a company has entered administration prior to that date see r 3(1) thereof. Under the former regime the debt was discounted at 5% per annum on the full amount. This was criticised in *Re Park Air Services Ltd* [200] 2 AC 172, 187 per Lord Millett who pointed out that, after 20 years, the debt would be reduced to nothing. Under the new regime the debt is discounted on a reducing balance to avoid such an illogical result: see also IR 1986 r 11.13.

[Chapter 11
The Administrator]

2.164

[2.106 Fixing of remuneration]

[(1) The administrator is entitled to receive remuneration for his services as such.

(2) The remuneration shall be fixed either—
  (a) as a percentage of the value of the property with which he has to deal; or
  (b) by reference to the time properly given by the insolvency practitioner (as administrator) and his staff in attending to matters arising in the administration.

(3) It is for the creditors' committee (if there is one) to determine whether the remuneration is to be fixed under paragraph (2)(a) or (b) and, if under paragraph (2)(a), to determine any percentage to be applied as there mentioned.

(4) In arriving at that determination, the committee shall have regard to the following matters—
  (a) the complexity (or otherwise) of the case;
  (b) any respects in which, in connection with the company's affairs, there falls on the administrator any responsibility of an exceptional kind or degree;
  (c) the effectiveness with which the administrator appears to be carrying out, or to have carried out, his duties as such; and
  (d) the value and nature of the property with which he has to deal.

(5) If there is no creditors' committee, or the committee does not make the requisite determination, the administrator's remuneration may be fixed (in accordance with paragraph (2)) by a resolution of a meeting of creditors; and paragraph (4) applies to them as it does to the creditors' committee.

[(5A) In a case where the administrator has made a statement under paragraph 52(1)(b), if there is no creditors' committee, or the committee does not make the requisite determination, the administrator's remuneration may be fixed (in accordance with paragraph (2)) by the approval of—
  (a) each secured creditor of the company: or
  (b) if the administrator has made or intends to make a distribution to preferential creditors
    (i) each secured creditor of the company; and
    (ii) preferential creditors whose debts amount to more than 50% of the preferential debts of the company, disregarding debts of any creditor who does not respond to an invitation to give or withhold approval;
and paragraph (4) applies to them as it does to the creditors' committee.]

(6) If not fixed as above, the administrator's remuneration shall, on his application, be fixed by the court.

(7) Where there are joint administrators, it is for them to agree between themselves as to how the remuneration payable should be apportioned. Any dispute arising between them may be referred—
    (a)   to the court, for settlement by order; or
    (b)   to the creditors' committee or a meeting of creditors, for settlement by resolution.

(8) If the administrator is a solicitor and employs his own firm, or any partner in it, to act on behalf of the company, profit costs shall not be paid unless this is authorised by the creditors' committee, the creditors or the court.

(9) ......

Notes

R 2.106

This provision was amended by Insolvency (Amendment) Rules 2005 SI 2005/527, r 15(1) effective from 1 April 2005. For transitional provisions in relation to any case where a company has entered administration prior to that date see r 3(1) thereof.

R. 2.106(2)

Where fixed properly the remuneration can be paid during rather than at the end of the administration: *Re Salmet International Ltd* [2001] BCC 796.

R. 2.106(6)

Particular regard should be paid to Practice Statement – The Fixing and Approval of the Remuneration of Appointees [2004] BPIR 953 and *Re Cabletel Installations Ltd* [2005] BPIR 28. The court may require the assistance of an expert assessor in fixing the remuneration: *Re Independent Insurance Co Ltd* [2003] 1 BCLC 640.

Where the administrator has dealt with assets that the company in administration holds on trust for others an application can be made to the court to charge some or all of the administrator's remuneration on those assets: *Re Berkeley Applegate (Investment Consultants) Ltd (No 2)* (1988) 4 BCC 279; *Re Berkeley Applegate (Investment Consultants) Ltd (No 3)* (1989) 5 BCC 803; cf *Tom Wise Ltd v Fillimore* [1999] BCC 129; *Re Local London Residential Ltd* [2004] 2 BCLC 72.

Where an administrator is appointed out of court (IA 1986 Sch B1 paras 14, 22) there is no express authority in the IR 1986 to enable payment of pre-appointment costs of the person who becomes administrator. It is unlikely that a board resolution authorising payment of such costs as an 'administration expense' would be determinative. The putative administrator should therefore secure payment for pre-appointment services from the board personally; or provide for payment by the purchaser of the business in the sale/purchase agreement in a 'pre-pack' case. It might be argued on behalf of the administrator that the work required to form an 'opinion' under IA 1986 Sch B1 para 18(3), 29(3) for an out of court appointment ought to be treated as an expense but such an argument has yet to be tested. In a number of liquidation cases it has been recognised that some work must necessarily be done prior to a liquidation to ensure the company successfully enters liquidation: *Re A V Sorge & Co Ltd* (1986) 2 BCC 99, 306; *Re Sandwell Copiers Ltd* [1988] BCLC 209.

2.165

[2.107 Recourse to meeting of creditors]

[(1)] [If the administrator's remuneration has been fixed by the creditors' committee, and he considers the rate or amount to be insufficient, he may request that it be increased by resolution of the creditors.]

[(2) In a case where the administrator has made a statement under paragraph 52(1)(b), if the administrator's remuneration has been fixed by the creditors' committee, and he considers the rate or amount to be insufficient, he may request that it be increased by the approval of—
  (a)   each secured creditor of the company: or
  (b)   if the administrator has made or intends to make a distribution to preferential creditors—
    (i)   each secured creditor of the company; and
    (ii) preferential creditors whose debts amount to more than 50% of the preferential debts of the company, disregarding debts of any creditor who does not respond to an invitation to give or withhold approval.]

Notes

R 2.107

This provision was amended by Insolvency (Amendment) Rules 2005 SI 2005/527, r 16 effective from 1 April 2005. For transitional provisions in relation to any case where a company has entered administration before that date see r 3(1) thereof.

2.166

[2.108 Recourse to the court]

[(1) If the administrator considers that the remuneration fixed for him by the creditors' committee, or by resolution of the creditors, is insufficient, he may apply to the court for an order increasing its amount or rate.

[(1A) In a case where the administrator has made a statement under paragraph 52(1)(b), if the administrator considers that the remuneration fixed by the approval of the creditors in accordance with Rule 2.107(2) is insufficient, he may apply to the court for an order increasing its amount or rate.]

(2) The administrator shall give at least 14 days' notice of his application to the members of the creditors' committee; and the committee may nominate one or more members to appear, or be represented, and to be heard on the application.

(3) If there is no creditors' committee, the administrator's notice of his application shall be sent to such one or more of the company's creditors as the court may direct, which creditors may nominate one or more of their number to appear or be represented.

(4) The court may, if it appears to be a proper case, order the costs of the administrator's application, including the costs of any member of the

> creditors' committee appearing or being represented on it, or any creditor so appearing or being represented, to be paid as an expense of the administration.]

Notes

R 2.108

This provision was amended by Insolvency (Amendment) Rules 2005 SI 2005/527, r 17 effective from 1 April 2005; for transitional provisions in relation to any case where a company has entered administration prior to that date see r 3(1) thereof.

2.167

[2.109 Creditors' claim that remuneration is excessive]

[(1) Any creditor of the company may, with the concurrence of at least 25% in value of the creditors (including himself), apply to the court for an order that the administrator's remuneration be reduced, on the grounds that it is, in all the circumstances, excessive.

(2) The court may, if it thinks that no sufficient cause is shown for a reduction, disMiss it without a hearing but it shall not do so without giving the applicant at least 7 days' notice, upon receipt of which the applicant may require the court to list the application for a without notice hearing. If the application is not dismissed, the court shall fix a venue for it to be heard, and give notice to the applicant accordingly.

(3) The applicant shall, at least 14 days before the hearing, send to the administrator a notice stating the venue and accompanied by a copy of the application, and of any evidence which the applicant intends to adduce in support of it.

(4) If the court considers the application to be well-founded, it shall make an order fixing the remuneration at a reduced amount or rate.

(5) Unless the court orders otherwise, the costs of the application shall be paid by the applicant, and are not payable as an expense of the administration.]

Notes

R 2.109

The creditor will inevitably refer to the guidance given in the Practice Statement – The Fixing and Approval of the Remuneration of Appointees [2004] BPIR 953 and *Re Cabletel Installations Ltd* [2005] BPIR 28; see notes to IR 1986 r 2.106.

[Chapter 12
Ending Administration]

2.168

[2.110 Final progress reports]

[(1) In this Chapter reference to a progress report is to a report in the form specified in Rule 2.47.

> (2) The final progress report means a progress report which includes a summary of—
> (a)   the administrator's proposals;
> (b)   any major amendments to, or deviations from, those proposals;
> (c)   the steps taken during the administration; and
> (d)   the outcome.]

Notes

R 2.110

When an administrator applies for his discharge from liability under IA 1986 Sch B1 para 98 it is common to request that discharge takes place a stated period after the filing of the final progress report. At the hearing of the application for discharge the court should be provided with a draft final progress report.

2.169

[2.111 Notice of automatic end of administration]

[(1) Where the appointment of an administrator has ceased to have effect, and the administrator is not required by any other Rule to give notice of that fact, he shall, as soon as reasonably practicable, and in any event within 5 business days of the date when the appointment has ceased, file a notice of automatic end of administration in Form 2.30B with the court. The notice shall be accompanied by a final progress report.

(2) A copy of the notice and accompanying document shall be sent as soon as reasonably practicable to the registrar of companies, and to all persons who received a copy of the administrator's proposals.

(3) If the administrator makes default in complying with this Rule, he is liable to a fine and, for continued contravention, to a daily default fine.]

Notes

R 2.111

Unless extended an administration is automatically ended one year beginning with the date the appointment of the administrator has taken effect: IA 1986 Sch B1 para 76. An administration beginning on 14 January 2005 will end at midnight on 13 January 2006, as the one year period means 365 days including the day of the appointment taking effect rather than the calendar anniversary. It is obviously important to diarise the end of the administration; for instance under IA 1986 Sch B1 para 83(3) the administrator may send a notice to the Registrar of Companies which upon registration puts the company into a creditors' voluntary liquidation. However if the administration has ceased prior to the sending of the notice (and consequently there is no administrator in office at the time the notice is sent) the company does not enter a creditors' voluntary liquidation under IA 1986 Sch B1 para 83. Where the notice is sent whilst the administrator is in office then the company will enter liquidation on registration of the notice by the Registrar despite the administration ceasing prior to the registration: *Re E-Squared Ltd* [2006] BCC 379.

2.170

[2.112 Applications for extension of administration]

[(1) An application to court for an extension of administration shall be accompanied by a progress report for the period since the last progress report (if any) or the date the company entered administration.

(2) When the administrator requests an extension of the period of the administration by consent of creditors, his request shall be accompanied by a progress report for the period since the last progress report (if any) or the date the company entered administration.

(3) The administrator shall use the notice of extension of period of administration in Form 2.31B in all circumstances where he is required to give such notice.]

Notes

R 2.112

The period of administration can be extended under IA 1986 Sch B1 para 76(2) by the court and the evidence in support must contain a progress report: IR 1986 r 2.47. The court should be provided with an adequate explanation of what tasks the administrator has yet to carry out and the reasons why it is not possible to carry them out without an extension of the administration. An application for extension should be considered where the administrator contemplates being unable to send the relevant notices to exit administration under IA 1986 Sch B1 para 83 (creditors' voluntary liquidation) or para 84 (dissolution): see notes to IR 1986 R2.111 above.

2.171

[2.113 Notice of end of administration]

[(1) Where an administrator who was appointed under paragraph 14 or 22 gives notice that the purpose of administration has been sufficiently achieved he shall use Form 2.32B. The notice shall be accompanied by a final progress report.

(2) The administrator shall send a copy of the notice to the registrar of companies.

(3) Two copies of the notice shall be filed with the court and shall contain a statement that a copy of the notice has been sent to the registrar of companies. The court shall endorse each copy with the date and time of filing. The appointment shall cease to have effect from that date and time.

(4) The court shall give a sealed copy of the notice to the administrator.

(5) The administrator shall, as soon as reasonably practicable, and within 5 business days, send a copy of the notice of end of administration (and the accompanying report) to every creditor of the company of whose claim and address he is aware, to all those persons who were notified of his appointment and to the company.

(6) The administrator shall be taken to have complied with the requirements of paragraph 80(5) if, within 5 business days of filing the notice of

end of administration with the court, he publishes once in the same newspaper as he published his notice of appointment, and in the Gazette, a notice undertaking to provide a copy of the notice of end of administration to any creditor of the company.

(7) The notice must—
  (a) state the full name of the company;
  (b) state the name and address of the administrator;
  (c) state the date that the administration ended; and
  (d) specify an address to which the creditors can write for a copy of the notice of end of administration.]

2.172–2.173

[2.114 Application to court by administrator]

[(1) An application to court under paragraph 79 for an order ending an administration shall have attached to it a progress report for the period since the last progress report (if any) or the date the company entered administration and a statement indicating what the administrator thinks should be the next steps for the company (if applicable).

(2) Where the administrator applies to the court because the creditors' meeting has required him to, he shall also attach a statement to the application in which he shall indicate (giving reasons) whether or not he agrees with the creditors' requirement to him to make the application.

(3) When the administrator applies other than at the request of a creditors' meeting, he shall—
  (a) give notice in writing to the applicant for the administration order under which he was appointed, or the person by whom he was appointed and the creditors of his intention to apply to court at least 7 days before the date that he intends to makes his application; and
  (b) attach to his application to court a statement that he has notified the creditors, and copies of any response from creditors to that notification.

(4) Where the administrator applies to court under paragraph 79 in conjunction with a petition under section 124 for an order to wind up the company, he shall, in addition to the requirements of paragraph (3), notify the creditors whether he intends to seek appointment as liquidator.]

2.174

[2.115 Application to court by creditor]

[(1) Where a creditor applies to the court to end the administration a copy of the application shall be served on the administrator and the person who either made the application for the administration order or made the appointment. Where the appointment was made under paragraph 14, a copy of the application shall be served on the holder of the floating charge by virtue of which the appointment was made.

(2) Service shall be effected not less than 5 business days before the date fixed for the hearing. The administrator, applicant or appointor, or holder of the floating charge by virtue of which the appointment was made may appear at the hearing of the application.

(3) Where the court makes an order to end the administration, the court shall send a copy of the order to the administrator.]

Notes

R 2.115

A creditor can apply to end an administration under IA 1986 Sch B1 para 81 on the basis of improper motive on the part of the applicant or appointor of the administrator.

2.175

[2.116 Notification by administrator of court order]

[Where the court makes an order to end the administration, the administrator shall notify the registrar of companies in Form 2.33B, attaching a copy of the court order and a copy of his final progress report.]

Notes

R 2.116

Presumably this provision would apply when an administration order is rescinded (IR 1986 r 7.47; *Cornhill Insurance plc v Cornhill Financial Services Ltd* [1993] BCLC 914) as well as where specific orders are made to end the administration under a variety of express provisions: for example, IA 1986 Sch B1 paras 79, 81, 82).

2.176

[2.117 Moving from administration to creditors' voluntary liquidation]

[(1) Where for the purposes of paragraph 83(3) the administrator sends a notice of moving from administration to creditors' voluntary liquidation to the registrar of companies, he shall do so in Form 2.34B and shall attach to that notice a final progress report which must include details of the assets to be dealt with in the liquidation.

(2) As soon as reasonably practicable the administrator shall send a copy of the notice and attached document to all those who received notice of the administrator's appointment.

(3) For the purposes of paragraph 83(7) a person shall be nominated as liquidator in accordance with the provisions of Rule 2.33(2)(m) or Rule 2.45(2)(g) and his appointment takes effect by the creditors' approval, with or without modification, of the administrator's proposals or revised proposals.]

Notes

R 2.117(1)

Where an administrator sends the para 83(3) notice to Companies House it may be that it is not registered until after the administrator's appointment has ceased. In that situation para 83(6)(a) appears to have no effect but para 83(6)(b) still has effect and the company goes into liquidation on the date of the registration of the notice *Re E Squared Ltd* [2006] BCC 379. See notes to IR 1986 R2.111 above.

R 2.117(2)

This provision does not require that the notice and the final progress report to be given to all third parties who have dealt with the administrator during the course of the administration.

R 2.117(3)

Certain rules under IR 1986 Part 4 are disapplied in the case of a creditors' voluntary liquidation initiated under IA 1986 Sch B1 para 83: IR 1986 r 4.1(6).

2.177

[2.118 Moving from administration to dissolution]

[(1) Where, for the purposes of paragraph 84(1), the administrator sends a notice of moving from administration to dissolution to the registrar of companies, he shall do so in Form 2.35B and shall attach to that notice a final progress report.

(2) As soon as reasonably practicable a copy of the notice and the attached document shall be sent to all those who received notice of the administrator's appointment.

(3) Where a court makes an order under paragraph 84(7) it shall, where the applicant is not the administrator, give a copy of the order to the administrator.

(4) The administrator shall use Form 2.36B to notify the registrar of companies in accordance with paragraph 84(8) of any order made by the court under paragraph 84(7).]

Notes

R 2.118(1)

An administrator can move the company into dissolution under IA 1986 Sch B1 para 84 following a distribution of all the company's property: *Re GHE Realisations Ltd* [2005] BCC 139; *Re Preston & Duckworth Ltd* [2006] BCC 133; see notes to IA 1986 Sch B1 para 84.

[Chapter 13
Replacing Administrator]

2.170–2.101

[2.119 Grounds for resignation]

[(1) The administrator may give notice of his resignation on grounds of ill health or because—
    (a)   he intends ceasing to be in practice as an insolvency practitioner; or

(b) there is some conflict of interest, or change of personal circumstances, which precludes or makes impracticable the further
discharge by him of the duties of administrator.

(2) The administrator may, with the permission of the court, give notice
of his resignation on grounds other than those specified in paragraph (1).]

[2.120 Notice of intention to resign]

[(1) The administrator shall in all cases give at least 7 days' notice in
Form 2.37B of his intention to resign, or to apply for the court's
permission to do so, to the following persons—
   (a) if there is a continuing administrator of the company, to him; and
   (b) if there is a creditors' committee to it; but
   (c) if there is no such administrator and no creditors' committee, to
       the company and its creditors.

(2) Where the administrator gives notice under paragraph (1), he shall
also give notice to a member State liquidator, if such a person has been
appointed in relation to the company.

(3) Where the administrator was appointed by the holder of a qualifying
floating charge under paragraph 14, the notice of intention to resign shall
also be sent to all holders of prior qualifying floating charges, and to the
person who appointed the administrator. A copy of the notice shall also be
sent to the holder of the floating charge by virtue of which the appointment was made.

(4) Where the administrator was appointed by the company or the
directors of the company under paragraph 22, a copy of the notice of
intention to resign shall also be sent to the appointor and all holders of a
qualifying floating charge.]

2.183

[2.121 Notice of resignation]

[(1) The notice of resignation shall be in Form 2.38B.

(2) Where the administrator was appointed under an administration
order, the notice shall be filed with the court, and a copy sent to the
registrar of companies. A copy of the notice of resignation shall be sent
not more than 5 business days after it has been filed with the court to all
those to whom notice of intention to resign was sent.

(3) Where the administrator was appointed by the holder of a qualifying
floating charge under paragraph 14, a copy of the notice of resignation
shall be filed with the court and sent to the registrar of companies, and
anyone else who received a copy of the notice of intention to resign,
within 5 business days of the notice of resignation being sent to the
holder of the floating charge by virtue of which the appointment was
made.

(4) Where the administrator was appointed by the company or the
directors under paragraph 22, a copy of the notice of resignation shall be
filed with the court and sent to the registrar of companies and to anyone
else who received notice of intention to resign within 5 business days of
the notice of resignation being sent to either the company or the directors
that made the appointment.]

2.184

[2.122 Application to court to remove administrator from office]

[(1) Any application under paragraph 88 shall state the grounds on which it is requested that the administrator should be removed from office.

(2) Service of the notice of the application shall be effected on the administrator, the person who made the application for the administration order or the person who appointed the administrator, the creditors' committee (if any), the joint administrator (if any), and where there is neither a creditors' committee or joint administrator, to the company and all the creditors, including any floating charge holders not less than 5 business days before the date fixed for the application to be heard. Where the appointment was made under paragraph 14, the notice shall be served on the holder of the floating charge by virtue of which the appointment was made.

(3) Where a court makes an order removing the administrator it shall give a copy of the order to the applicant who as soon as reasonably practicable shall send a copy to the administrator.

(4) The applicant shall also within 5 business days of the order being made send a copy of the order to all those to whom notice of the application was sent.

(5) A copy of the order shall also be sent to the registrar of companies in Form 2.39B within the same time period.]

2.185

[2.123 Notice of vacation of office when administrator ceases to be qualified to act]

[Where the administrator who has ceased to be qualified to act as an insolvency practitioner in relation to the company gives notice in accordance with paragraph 89, he shall also give notice to the registrar of companies in Form 2.39B.]

2.186

[2.124 Administrator deceased]

[(1) Subject as follows, where the administrator has died, it is the duty of his personal representatives to give notice of the fact to the court, specifying the date of the death. This does not apply if notice has been given under either paragraph (2) or (3) of this Rule.

(2) If the deceased administrator was a partner in a firm, notice may be given by a partner in the firm who is qualified to act as an insolvency practitioner, or is a member of any body recognised by the Secretary of State for the authorisation of insolvency practitioners.

(3) Notice of the death may be given by any person producing to the court the relevant death certificate or a copy of it.

(4) Where a person gives notice to the court under this Rule, he shall also give notice to the registrar of companies in Form 2.39B.]

2.187

[2.125 Application to replace]

[(1) Where an application is made to court under paragraphs 91(1) or 95 to appoint a replacement administrator, the application shall be accompanied by a written statement in Form 2.2B by the person proposed to be the replacement administrator.

(2) Where the original administrator was appointed under an administration order, a copy of the application shall be served, in addition to those persons listed in paragraph 12(2) and Rule 2.6(3), on the person who made the application for the administration order.

(3) Where the application to court is made under paragraph 95, the application shall be accompanied by an affidavit setting out the applicant's belief as to the matters set out in that paragraph.

(4) Rule 2.8 shall apply to the service of an application under paragraphs 91(1) and 95 as it applies to service in accordance with Rule 2.6.

(5) Rules 2.9, 2.10, 2.12 and 2.14(1) and (2) apply to an application under paragraphs 91(1) and 95.]

2.188

[2.126 Notification and advertisement of appointment of replacement administrator]

[Where a replacement administrator is appointed, the same provisions apply in respect of giving notice of, and advertising, the replacement appointment as in the case of the appointment (subject to Rule 2.128), and all statements, consents etc as are required shall also be required in the case of the appointment of a replacement. All forms and notices shall clearly identify that the appointment is of a replacement administrator.]

2.189

[2.127 Notification and advertisement of appointment of joint administrator]

[Where, after an initial appointment has been made, an additional person or persons are to be appointed as joint administrator the same Rules shall apply in respect of giving notice of and advertising the appointment as in the case of the initial appointment, subject to Rule 2.128.]

2.190

[2.128

[The replacement or additional administrator shall send notice of the appointment in Form 2.40B to the registrar of companies.]

Notes

RR 2.119–2.128

For a detailed consideration of the law relating to the removal of office holders, see the notes to IA 1986 s 108(2) and the helpful summary of the principles and authorities in *Sisu Capital Fund Ltd v Tucker* [2006] BPIR 154, paras 82ff.

The power to appoint an additional administrator is in IA 1986 Sch B1 para 103.

———

2.191

[2.129 Administrator's duties on vacating office]

[(1) Where the administrator ceases to be in office as such, in consequence of removal, resignation or cesser of qualification as an insolvency practitioner, he is under obligation as soon as reasonably practicable to deliver up to the person succeeding him as administrator the assets (after deduction of any expenses properly incurred and distributions made by him) and further to deliver up to that person—
   (a)   the records of the administration, including correspondence, proofs and other related papers appertaining to the administration while it was within his responsibility; and
   (b)   the company's books, papers and other records.

(2) If the administrator makes default in complying with this Rule, he is liable to a fine and, for continued contravention, to a daily default fine.]

[Chapter 14
EC Regulation: Conversion of Administration into Winding Up]

2.192

[2.130 Application for conversion into winding up]

[(1) Where a member State liquidator proposes to apply to the court for the conversion under Article 37 of the EC Regulation (conversion of earlier proceedings) of an administration into a winding up, an affidavit complying with Rule 2.131 must be prepared and sworn, and filed with the court in support of the application.

(2) An application under this Rule shall be by originating application.

(3) The application and the affidavit required under this Rule shall be served upon—
   (a)   the company; and
   (b)   the administrator.]

2.193

[2.131 Contents of affidavit]

[(1) The affidavit shall state—
   (a)   that main proceedings have been opened in relation to the company in a member State other than the United Kingdom;
   (b)   the deponent's belief that the conversion of the administration into a winding up would prove to be in the interests of the creditors in the main proceedings;
   (c)   the deponent's opinion as to whether the company ought to enter voluntary winding up or be wound up by the court; and
   (d)   all other matters that, in the opinion of the member State liquidator, would assist the court—
        (i)   in deciding whether to make such an order; and

(ii) if the court were to do so, in considering the need for any consequential provision that would be necessary or desirable.

(2) An affidavit under this rule shall be sworn by, or on behalf of, the member State liquidator.]

2.194

[2.132 Power of court]

[(1) On hearing the application for conversion into winding up the court may make such order as it thinks fit.

(2) If the court makes an order for conversion into winding up the order may contain all such consequential provisions as the court deems necessary or desirable.

(3) Without prejudice to the generality of paragraph (1), an order under that paragraph may provide that the company be wound up as if a resolution for voluntary winding up under section 84 were passed on the day on which the order is made.]

Notes

RR 2.130–2.132

These provisions deal with the situation under the EC Regulation on Insolvency Proceedings 2000 where main insolvency proceedings are brought in another member state after an administration has occurred in England; see IR 1986 r 13.13(11) for the definition of 'Member State liquidator'. Article 37 of the EC Regulation entitles the foreign liquidator to apply for the conversion of the English administration to winding up proceedings and IR 1986 r 2.130–2.132 contain the procedure for such an application. It seems from the wording of IR 1986 r 2.132(1) that the court has a wide discretion when dealing with such an application.

[Chapter 15
EC Regulation: Member State Liquidator]

2.195

[2.133 Interpretation of creditor and notice to member State liquidator]

[(1) This Rule applies where a member State liquidator has been appointed in relation to the company.

(2) For the purposes of the Rules referred to in paragraph (3) the member State liquidator is deemed to be a creditor.

(3) The Rules referred to in paragraph (2) are Rules 2.34 (notice of creditors' meeting), 2.35(4) (creditors' meeting), 2.37 (requisitioning of creditors' meeting), 2.38 (entitlement to vote), 2.39 (admission and rejection of claims), 2.40 (secured creditors), 2.41 (holders of negotiable instruments), 2.42 (hire-purchase, conditional sale and chattel leasing agreements), 2.46 (notice to creditors), 2.47 (reports to creditors), 2.48

(correspondence instead of creditors' meeting), 2.50(2) (creditors' committee), 2.57(1)(b) and (c) (termination of membership of creditors' committee), 2.59(3) (vacancies in creditors' committee), 2.108(3) (administrator's remuneration—recourse to court) and 2.109 (challenge to administrator's remuneration).

(4) Paragraphs (2) and (3) are without prejudice to the generality of the right to participate referred to in paragraph 3 of Article 32 of the EC Regulation (exercise of creditor's rights).

(5) Where the administrator is obliged to give notice to, or provide a copy of a document (including an order of court) to, the court, the registrar of companies or the official receiver, the administrator shall give notice or provide copies, as the case may be, to the member State liquidator.

(6) Paragraph (5) is without prejudice to the generality of the obligations imposed by Article 31 of the EC Regulation (duty to co-operate and communicate information).]

Notes

R 2.133

EC Regulation on Insolvency Proceedings 2000, art 32 entitles the foreign liquidator to lodge claims in the English administration on behalf of creditors who have lodged claims with him, and to participate in the English administration on the same basis as a creditor and IR 1986 r 2.133 contains the detailed machinery in this respect.

Part 3
Administrative Receivership

Chapter 1

Appointment of Administrative Receiver

2.196

[3.1 Acceptance and confirmation of acceptance of appointment

[(1) Where two or more persons are appointed as joint receivers or managers of a company's property under powers contained in an instrument, the acceptance of such an appointment shall be made by each of them in accordance with section 33 as if that person were a sole appointee, but the joint appointment takes effect only when all such persons have so accepted and is then deemed to have been made at the time at which the instrument of appointment was received by or on behalf of all such persons.

(2) Subject to the next paragraph, where a person is appointed as the sole or joint receiver of a company's property under powers contained in an instrument, the appointee shall, if he accepts the appointment, within 7 days confirm his acceptance in writing to the person appointing him.

(3) Paragraph (2) does not apply where an appointment is accepted in writing.

(4) Any acceptance or confirmation of acceptance of appointment as a receiver or manager of a company's property, whether under the Act or the Rules, may be given by any person (including, in the case of a joint appointment, any joint appointee) duly authorised for that purpose on behalf of the receiver or manager.

(5) In confirming acceptance the appointee or person authorised for that purpose shall state—
- (a) the time and date of receipt of the instrument of appointment, and
- (b) the time and date of acceptance.]

Notes

R 3.1

Note that this provision applies not just to administrative receivers as defined in IA 1986 s 29(2) but to all receivers or managers of a company's property appointed under powers contained in an instrument.

2.197

3.2 Notice and advertisement of appointment

(1) This Rule relates to the notice which a person is required by section 46(1) to send and publish, when appointed as administrative receiver.

(2) The following matters shall be stated in the [notices sent to the company and the creditors]—
- (a) the registered name of the company, as at the date of the appointment, and its registered number;
- (b) any other name with which the company has been registered in the 12 months preceding that date;
- (c) any name under which the company has traded at any time in those 12 months, if substantially different from its then registered name;
- (d) the name and address of the administrative receiver, and the date of his appointment;
- (e) the name of the person by whom the appointment was made;
- (f) the date of the instrument conferring the power under which the appointment was made, and a brief description of the instrument;
- (g) a brief description of the assets of the company (if any) in respect of which the person appointed is not made the receiver.

(3) The administrative receiver shall cause notice of his appointment to be advertised once in the Gazette, and once in such newspaper as he thinks most appropriate for ensuring that it comes to the notice of the company's creditors.

(4) The advertisement shall state all the matters specified in sub-paragraphs (a) to (e) of paragraph (2) above.

Notes

R 3.2

The receiver is required to cause the notice to be advertised forthwith on his appointment: IA 1986 s 46(1)).

Chapter 2
Statement of Affairs and Report to Creditors

2.198

3.3 Notice requiring statement of affairs

(1) [Where] the administrative receiver determines to require a statement of the company's affairs to be made out and submitted to him in accordance with section 47, he shall send notice to each of the persons whom he considers should be made responsible under that section, requiring them to prepare and submit the statement.

(2) The persons to whom the notice is sent are referred to in this Chapter as 'the deponents'.

(3) The notice shall inform each of the deponents—
  (a) of the names and addresses of all others (if any) to whom the same notice has been sent;
  (b) of the time within which the statement must be delivered;
  (c) of the effect of section 47(6) (penalty for non-compliance); and
  (d) of the application to him, and to each of the other deponents, of section 235 (duty to provide information, and to attend on the administrative receiver if required).

(4) The administrative receiver shall, on request, furnish each deponent with [the forms required for the preparation of the statement of affairs].

Notes

R 3.3

IA 1986 s 47 requires the administrative receiver to require at least one of the persons listed in s 47(3) referred to in this rule as 'the deponents' to provide a statement of affairs and this rule provides that the request must be in writing and that the administrative receiver must provide the necessary form (Form 3.2) for the preparation of the statement of affairs. Both failure by the administrative receiver to require a statement of affairs and failure by a deponent to comply with a notice requiring him to do so are punishable by fine.

2.199

3.4 Verification and filing

(1) The statement of affairs shall be in Form 3.2, shall contain all the particulars required by that form and shall be verified by affidavit by the deponents (using the same form).

(2) The administrative receiver may require any of the persons mentioned in section 47(3) to submit an affidavit of concurrence, stating that he concurs in the statement of affairs.

(3) An affidavit of concurrence may be qualified in respect of matters dealt with in the statement of affairs, where the maker of the affidavit is not in agreement with the deponents, or he considers the statement to be erroneous or misleading, or he is without the direct knowledge necessary for concurring with it.

(4) The statement of affairs shall be delivered to the receiver by the deponent making the affidavit of verification (or by one of them, if more than one), together with a copy of the verified statement.

(5) Every affidavit of concurrence shall be delivered by the person who makes it, together with a copy.

(6) The administrative receiver shall retain the verified copy of the statement and the affidavits of concurrence (if any) as part of the records of the receivership.

Notes

R 3.4

The statement of affairs must be in Form 3.2 and must be verified by affidavit. A mere statement of truth such is commonly found in witness statements is not sufficient for any purpose provided for in this rule (eg an affidavit of concurrence): see r 7.57(6)

2.200

3.5 Limited disclosure

(1) Where the administrative receiver thinks that it would prejudice the conduct of the receivership for the whole or part of the statement of affairs to be disclosed, he may apply to the court for an order of limited disclosure in respect of the statement or a specified part of it.

(2) The court may on the application order that the statement, or, as the case may be, the specified part of it, be not open to inspection otherwise than with leave of the court.

(3) The court's order may include directions as to the delivery of documents to the registrar of companies and the disclosure of relevant information to other persons.

Notes

R 3.5

The statement of affairs or part of it may only be suppressed by order of the court. The only ground for an order is that disclosure would prejudice the conduct of the receivership.

2.201

3.6 Release from duty to submit statement of affairs; extension of time

(1) The power of the administrative receiver under section 47(5) to give a release from the obligation imposed by that section, or to grant an extension of time, may be exercised at the receiver's own discretion, or at the request of any deponent.

(2) A deponent may, if he requests a release or extension of time and it is refused by the receiver, apply to the court for it.

(3) The court may, if it thinks that no sufficient cause is shown for the application, disMiss it; but it shall not do so unless the applicant has had an opportunity to attend the court for an *ex parte* hearing, of which he has been given at least 7 days' notice.

If the application is not dismissed under this paragraph, the court shall fix a venue for it to be heard, and give notice to the deponent accordingly.

(4) The deponent shall, at least 14 days before the hearing, send to the receiver a notice stating the venue and accompanied by a copy of the application, and of any evidence which he (the deponent) intends to adduce in support of it.

(5) The receiver may appear and be heard on the application; and, whether or not he appears, he may file a written report of any matters which he considers ought to be drawn to the court's attention.

If such a report is filed, a copy of it shall be sent by the receiver to the deponent, not later than 5 days before the hearing.

(6) Sealed copies of any order made on the application shall be sent by the court to the deponent and the receiver.

(7) On any application under this Rule the applicant's costs shall be paid in any event by him and, unless the court otherwise orders, no allowance towards them shall be made out of the assets under the administrative receiver's control.

Notes

R 3.6

Where a deponent seeks an extension of time or release from his obligation to provide a statement of affairs and is refused by the administrative receiver he may apply to the court. The court can dismiss the application summarily but only after giving the deponent an opportunity to be heard. The administrative receiver is not heard on that occasion. If the application is not summarily dismissed then it is listed to be heard inter partes in the usual way. The onus is then on the deponent to notify the administrative receiver of the time and venue for the hearing and to serve his evidence not less than 14 days before the hearing. The administrative receiver may respond not less the 5 days before the hearing and may attend and be heard at the hearing.

2.202

3.7 Expenses of statement of affairs

(1) A deponent making the statement of affairs and affidavit shall be allowed, and paid by the administrative receiver out of his receipts, any expenses incurred by the deponent in so doing which the receiver thinks reasonable.

(2) Any decision by the receiver under this Rule is subject to appeal to the court.

(3) Nothing in this Rule relieves a deponent from any obligation with respect to the preparation, verification and submission of the statement of affairs, or to the provision of information to the receiver.

Notes

R 3.7

The deponent is entitled to be paid his expenses of preparing the statement of affairs out of the administrative receiver's receipts, but non payment or the absence of sufficient assets does not relieve the deponent of his obligations.

2.203

3.8 Report to creditors

(1) If under section 48(2) the administrative receiver determines not to send a copy of his report to creditors, but to publish notice under paragraph (b) of that subsection, the notice shall be published in the newspaper in which the receiver's appointment was advertised.

(2) If he proposes to apply to the court to dispense with the holding of the meeting of unsecured creditors (otherwise required by section 48(2)), he shall in his report to creditors or (as the case may be) in the notice published as above, state the venue fixed by the court for the hearing of the application.

(3) Subject to any order of the court under Rule 3.5, the copy of the receiver's report which under section 48(1) is to be sent to the registrar of companies shall have attached to it a copy of any statement of affairs under section 47, and copies of any affidavits of concurrence.

(4) If the statement of affairs or affidavits of concurrence, if any, have not been submitted to the receiver by the time he sends a copy of his report to the registrar of companies, he shall send a copy of the statement and any affidavits of concurrence as soon thereafter as he receives them.

[(5) The receiver's report under section 48(1) shall state, to the best of his knowledge and belief—
    (a)   an estimate of the value of the prescribed part (whether or not he proposes to make an application under section 176A(5) or whether section 176A(3) applies); and
    (b)   an estimate of the value of the company's net property.

(6) Nothing in this Rule is to be taken as requiring any such estimate to include any information, the disclosure of which could seriously prejudice the commercial interests of the company.

If such information is excluded from the calculation the estimate shall be accompanied by a statement to that effect.

(7) The report shall also state whether, and if so why, the receiver proposes to make an application to court under section 176A(5).]

Notes

R 3.8

Paras (5) and (6) of this rule were introduced following the changes effected by the EA 2002 under which a prescribed part of the assets caught by a floating charge are to be made available to satisfy the claims of unsecured creditors unless either the company's assets are less than the minimum prescribed under s 176A or the administrative receiver applies under s 176A(5) for exemption on the grounds that the costs of making a distribution to unsecured creditors would be disproportionate. However, para (5) of this rule applies whether or not the assets exceed the prescribed minimum or the administrative receiver intends to make an application. He must therefore state in his report what the value of the prescribed part would be, even if there will be no distribution to unsecured creditors. The report must also state the grounds of any proposed application under s 176A(5).

See also r 3.39 and 3.40 post.

Chapter 3
Creditor's Meeting

2.204

Note

Chapter 3 deals with the procedure for the summoning and the conduct of creditors' meetings under IA 1986 s 48(2). The provisions are substantially similar to those relating, for example, to meetings summoned to consider proposals for a CVA. Reference should be made to the commentary on those provisions for a discussion of the giving of notices and the admission, rejection and quantification of claims for voting purposes.

2.205

3.9 Procedure for summoning meeting under s 48(2)

(1) In fixing the venue for a meeting of creditors summoned under section 48(2), the administrative receiver shall have regard to the convenience of the persons who are invited to attend.

(2) The meeting shall be summoned for commencement between 10.00 and 16.00 hours on a business day, unless the court otherwise directs.

(3) At least 14 days' notice of the venue shall be given to all creditors of the company who are identified in the statement of affairs, or are known to the receiver and had claims against the company at the date of his appointment.

(4) With the notice summoning the meeting there shall be sent out forms of proxy.

(5) The notice shall include a statement to the effect that creditors whose claims are wholly secured are not entitled to attend or be represented at the meeting.

(6) Notice of the venue shall also be published in the newspaper in which the receiver's appointment was advertised.

(7) The notice to creditors and the newspaper advertisement shall contain a statement of the effect of Rule 3.11(1) below (voting rights).

2.206

3.10 The chairman at the meeting

(1) The chairman at the creditors' meeting shall be the receiver, or a person nominated by him in writing to act in his place.

(2) A person so nominated must be either—
  (a)   one who is qualified to act as an insolvency practitioner in relation to the company, or
  (b)   an employee of the receiver or his firm who is experienced in insolvency matters.

2.207

3.11 Voting rights

(1) Subject as follows, at the creditors' meeting a person is entitled to vote only if—
  (a)   he has given to the receiver, not later than 12.00 hours on the business day before the day fixed for the meeting, details in writing of the debt that he claims to be due to him from the company, and the claim has been duly admitted under the following provisions of this Rule, and
  (b)   there has been lodged with the administrative receiver any proxy which the creditor intends to be used on his behalf.

(2) The chairman of the meeting may allow a creditor to vote, notwithstanding that he has failed to comply with paragraph (1)(a), if satisfied that the failure was due to circumstances beyond the creditor's control.

(3) The receiver or (if other) the chairman of the meeting may call for any document or other evidence to be produced to him where he thinks it necessary for the purpose of substantiating the whole or any part of the claim.

(4) Votes are calculated according to the amount of a creditor's debt as at the date of the appointment of the receiver, after deducting any amounts paid in respect of that debt after that date.

(5) A creditor shall not vote in respect of a debt for an unliquidated amount, or any debt whose value is not ascertained, except where the

chairman agrees to put upon the debt an estimated minimum value for the purpose of entitlement to vote and admits the claim for that purpose.

(6) A secured creditor is entitled to vote only in respect of the balance (if any) of his debt after deducting the value of his security as estimated by him.

(7) A creditor shall not vote in respect of a debt on, or secured by, a current bill of exchange or promissory note, unless he is willing—

    (a)   to treat the liability to him on the bill or note of every person who is liable on it antecedently to the company, and against whom a bankruptcy order has not been made (or, in the case of a company, which has not gone into liquidation), as a security in his hands, and

    (b)   to estimate the value of the security and, for the purpose of his entitlement to vote, to deduct it from his claim.

2.208

3.12 Admission and rejection of claim

(1) At the creditors' meeting the chairman has power to admit or reject a creditor's claim for the purpose of his entitlement to vote; and the power is exercisable with respect to the whole or any part of the claim.

(2) The chairman's decision under this Rule, or in respect of any matter arising under Rule 3.11, is subject to appeal to the court by any creditor.

(3) If the chairman is in doubt whether a claim should be admitted or rejected, he shall mark it as objected to and allow the creditor to vote, subject to his vote being subsequently declared invalid if the objection to the claim is sustained.

(4) If on an appeal the chairman's decision is reversed or varied, or a creditor's vote is declared invalid, the court may order that another meeting be summoned, or make such other order as it thinks just.

(5) Neither the receiver nor any person nominated by him to be chairman is personally liable for costs incurred by any person in respect of an appeal to the court under this Rule, unless the court makes an order to that effect.

2.209

3 .13 (**Revoked**)

2.210

3.14 Adjournment

(1) The creditors' meeting shall not be adjourned, even if no quorum is present, unless the chairman decides that it is desirable; and in that case he shall adjourn it to such date, time and place as he thinks fit.

(2) Rule 3.9(1) and (2) applies, with necessary modifications, to any adjourned meeting.

> (3) If there is no quorum, and the meeting is not adjourned, it is deemed to have been duly summoned and held.

Notes

The rules for ascertaining whether a quorum is present are now found in IR 1986 r 12.4A. A quorum is now one creditor. IR 1986 r 3.14(1) allows the chairman to proceed even if there is no quorum, and the presumption is that an inquorate meeting shall proceed unless the chairman considers that an adjournment is desirable.

2.211

3.15 Resolution and minutes

(1) At the creditors' meeting, a resolution is passed when a majority (in value) of those present and voting in person or by proxy have voted in favour of it.

(2) The chairman of the meeting shall cause a record to be made of the proceedings, and kept as part of the records of the receivership.

(3) The record shall include a list of the creditors who attended (personally or by proxy) and, if a creditors' committee has been established, the names and addresses of those elected to be members of the committee.

Chapter 4
The Creditors' Committee

2.212

3.16 Constitution of committee

(1) Where it is resolved by the creditors' meeting to establish a creditors' committee, the committee shall consist of at least 3 and not more than 5 creditors of the company elected at the meeting.

(2) Any creditor of the company is eligible to be a member of the committee, so long as his claim has not been rejected for the purpose of his entitlement to vote.

(3) A body corporate may be a member of the committee, but it cannot act as such otherwise than by a representative appointed under Rule 3.21 below.

2.213

3.17 Formalities of establishment

(1) The creditors' committee does not come into being, and accordingly cannot act, until the administrative receiver has issued a certificate of its due constitution.

[(2) No person may act as a member of the committee unless and until he has agreed to do so and, unless the relevant proxy or authorisation contains a statement to the contrary, such agreement may be given by his proxy-holder or representative under section 375 of the Companies Act present at the meeting establishing the committee.

(2A) The receiver's certificate of the committee's due constitution shall not issue unless and until at least 3 of the persons who are to be members of the committee have agreed to act.]

(3) As and when the others (if any) agree to act, the receiver shall issue an amended certificate.

(4) The certificate, and any amended certificate, shall be sent by the receiver to the registrar of companies.

(5) If, after the first establishment of the committee, there is any change in its membership, the receiver shall report the change to the registrar of companies.

2.214

3.18 Functions and meetings of the committee

(1) The creditors' committee shall assist the administrative receiver in discharging his functions, and act in relation to him in such manner as may be agreed from time to time.

(2) Subject as follows, meetings of the committee shall be held when and where determined by the receiver.

(3) The receiver shall call a first meeting of the committee not later than 3 months after its establishment; and thereafter he shall call a meeting—

    (a)   if requested by a member of the committee or his representative (the meeting then to be held within 21 days of the request being received by the receiver), and

    (b)   for a specified date, if the committee has previously resolved that a meeting be held on that date.

(4) The receiver shall give 7 days' written notice of the venue of any meeting to every member (or his representative designated for that purpose), unless in any case the requirement of notice has been waived by or on behalf of any member.

Waiver may be signified either at or before the meeting.

2.215

3.19 The chairman at meetings

(1) Subject to Rule 3.28(3), the chairman at any meeting of the creditors' committee shall be the administrative receiver, or a person nominated by him in writing to act.

(2) A person so nominated must be either—

    (a)   one who is qualified to act as an insolvency practitioner in relation to the company, or

    (b)   an employee of the receiver or his firm who is experienced in insolvency matters.

2.216

3.20 Quorum

A meeting of the committee is duly constituted if due notice has been given to all the members, and at least 2 members are present or represented.

2.217

3.21 Committee–members' representatives

(1) A member of the committee may, in relation to the business of the committee, be represented by another person duly authorised by him for that purpose.

(2) A person acting as a committee-member's representative must hold a letter of authority entitling him so to act (either generally or specially) and signed by or on behalf of the committee-member [, and for this purpose any proxy or any authorisation under section 375 of the Companies Act in relation to any meeting of creditors of the company shall, unless it contains a statement to the contrary, be treated as a letter of authority to act generally signed by or on behalf of the committee-member].

(3) The chairman at any meeting of the committee may call on a person claiming to act as a committee-member's representative to produce his letter of authority, and may exclude him if it appears that his authority is deficient.

(4) No member may be represented by a body corporate, or by a person who is an undischarged bankrupt, [or a disqualified director,] or is subject to a [bankruptcy restrictions order, bankruptcy restrictions undertaking or interim bankruptcy restrictions order].

(5) No person shall—
  (a)   on the same committee, act at one and the same time as representative of more than one committee-member, or
  (b)   act both as a member of the committee and as representative of another member.
  (6)   Where a member's representative signs any document on the member's behalf, the fact that he so signs must be stated below his signature.

2.218

3.22 Resignation

A member of the committee may resign by notice in writing delivered to the administrative receiver.

2.219

3.23 Termination of membership

(1) Membership of the creditors' committee is automatically terminated if the member—
  (a)   becomes bankrupt<... >, or
  (b)   at 3 consecutive meetings of the committee is neither present nor represented (unless at the third of those meetings it is resolved that this Rule is not to apply in his case), or
  (c)   ceases to be, or is found never to have been, a creditor.
  (2)   However, if the cause of termination is the member's bankruptcy, his trustee in bankruptcy replaces him as a member of the committee.

2.220

3.24 Removal

A member of the committee may be removed by resolution at a meeting of creditors, at least 14 days' notice having been given of the intention to move that resolution.

2.221

3.25 Vacancies

(1) The following applies if there is a vacancy in the membership of the creditors' committee.

(2) The vacancy need not be filled if the administrative receiver and a majority of the remaining members of the committee so agree, provided that the total number of members does not fall below the minimum required under Rule 3.16.

(3) The receiver may appoint any creditor (being qualified under the Rules to be a member of the committee) to fill the vacancy, if a majority of the other members of the committee agree to the appointment and the creditor concerned consents to act.

2.222

3.26 Procedure at meetings

(1) At any meeting of the committee, each member of it (whether present himself or by his representative) has one vote; and a resolution is passed when a majority of the members present or represented have voted in favour of it.

(2) Every resolution passed shall be recorded in writing, either separately or as part of the minutes of the meeting.

(3) A record of each resolution shall be signed by the chairman and kept as part of the records of the receivership.

2.223

3.27 Resolutions by post

(1) In accordance with this Rule, the administrative receiver may seek to obtain the agreement of members of the creditors' committee to a resolution by sending to every member (or his representative designated for the purpose) a copy of the proposed resolution.

(2) Where the receiver makes use of the procedure allowed by this Rule, he shall send out to members of the committee or their representatives (as the case may be) [a copy of any proposed resolution on which a decision is sought, which shall be set out in such a way that agreement with or dissent from each separate resolution may be indicated by the recipient on the copy so sent].

(3) Any member of the committee may, within 7 business days from the date of the receiver sending out a resolution, require him to summon a meeting of the committee to consider the matters raised by the resolution.

(4) In the absence of such a request, the resolution is deemed to have been passed by the committee if and when the receiver is notified in writing by a majority of the members that they concur with it.

(5) A copy of every resolution passed under this Rule, and a note that the committee's concurrence was obtained, shall be kept with the records of the receivership.

2.224

3.28 Information from receiver

(1) Where the committee resolves to require the attendance of the administrative receiver under section 49(2), the notice to him shall be in writing signed by the majority of the members of the committee for the time being. A member's representative may sign for him.

(2) The meeting at which the receiver's attendance is required shall be fixed by the committee for a business day, and shall be held at such time and place as he determines.

(3) Where the receiver so attends, the members of the committee may elect any one of their number to be chairman of the meeting, in place of the receiver or any nominee of his.

2.225

3.29 Expenses of members

(1) Subject as follows, the administrative receiver shall out of the assets of the company defray any reasonable travelling expenses directly incurred by members of the creditors' committee or their representatives in relation to their attendance at the committee's meetings, or otherwise on the committee's business as an expense of the receivership.

(2) Paragraph (1) does not apply to any meeting of the committee held within 3 months of a previous meeting, unless the meeting in question is summoned at the instance of the administrative receiver.

2.226

3.30 Members' dealings with the company

(1) Membership of the committee does not prevent a person from dealing with the company while the receiver is acting, provided that any transactions in the course of such dealings are entered into in good faith and for value.

(2) The court may, on the application of any person interested, set aside a transaction which appears to it to be contrary to the requirements of this Rule, and may give such consequential directions as it thinks fit for compensating the company for any loss which it may have incurred in consequence of the transaction.

2.227

[3.30A Formal defects

The acts of the creditors' committee established for any administrative receivership are valid notwithstanding any defect in the appointment, election or qualifications of any member of the committee or any committee-member's representative or in the formalities of its establishment.]

Chapter 5
The Administrative Receiver (Miscellaneous)

2.228

3.31 Disposal of charged property

(1) The following applies where the administrative receiver applies to the court under section 43(1) for authority to dispose of property of the company which is subject to a security.

(2) The court shall fix a venue for the hearing of the application, and the receiver shall forthwith give notice of the venue to the person who is the holder of the security.

(3) If an order is made under section 43(1), the receiver shall forthwith give notice of it to that person.

(4) The court shall send 2 sealed copies of the order to the receiver, who shall send one of them to that person.

2.229

3.32 Abstract of receipts and payments

(1) The administrative receiver shall—
   (a)   within 2 months after the end of 12 months from the date of his appointment, and of every subsequent period of 12 months, and
   (b)   within 2 months after he ceases to act as administrative receiver,
send to the registrar of companies, to the company and to the person by whom he was appointed, and to each member of the creditors' committee (if there is one), the requisite accounts of his receipts and payments as receiver.

(2) The court may, on the receiver's application, extend the period of 2 months referred to in paragraph (1).

(3) The accounts are to be in the form of an abstract showing—
   (a)   receipts and payments during the relevant period of 12 months, or
   (b)   where the receiver has ceased to act, receipts and payments during the period from the end of the last 12 month period to the time when he so ceased (alternatively, if there has been no previous abstract, receipts and payments in the period since his appointment as administrative receiver).

(4) This Rule is without prejudice to the receiver's duty to render proper accounts required otherwise than as above.

(5) If the administrative receiver makes default in complying with this Rule, he is liable to a fine and, for continued contravention, to a daily default fine.

2.230

3.33 Resignation

(1) Subject as follows, before resigning his office the administrative receiver shall give at least 7 days' notice of his intention to do so to—
    (a)   the person by whom he was appointed, <... >
    (b)   the company or, if it is then in liquidation, its liquidator [, and
    (c)   in any case, to the members of the creditors' committee (if any)].

(2) A notice given under this Rule shall specify the date on which the receiver intends his resignation to take effect.

(3) No notice is necessary if the receiver resigns in consequence of the making of an administration order.

2.231

3.34 Receiver deceased

If the administrative receiver dies, the person by whom he was appointed shall, forthwith on his becoming aware of the death, give notice of it to—
    (a)   the registrar of companies, <... >
    (b)   the company or, if it is in liquidation, the liquidator [, and
    (c)   in any case, to the members of the creditors' committee (if any)].

2.232

3.35 Vacation of office

(1) The administrative receiver, on vacating office on completion of the receivership, or in consequence of his ceasing to be qualified as an insolvency practitioner, shall forthwith give notice of his doing so—
    [(a)   to the company or, if it is in liquidation, the liquidator, and]
    (b)   to the members of the creditors' committee (if any).

(2) Where the receiver's office is vacated, the notice to the registrar of companies which is required by section 45(4) may be given by means of an endorsement on the notice required by section 405(2) of the Companies Act (notice for the purposes of the register of charges).

Chapter 6
VAT Bad Debt Relief

2.233

3.36 Issue of certificate of insolvency

(1) In accordance with this Rule, it is the duty of the administrative receiver to issue a certificate in the terms of paragraph (b) of section 22(3) of the Value Added Tax Act 1983 (which specifies the circumstances in which a company is deemed insolvent for the purposes of that section) forthwith upon his forming the opinion described in that paragraph.

(2) There shall in the certificate be specified—
    (a)   the name of the company and its registered number;
    (b)   the name of the administrative receiver and the date of his appointment; and

(c)   the date on which the certificate is issued.

(3) The certificate shall be intituled 'CERTIFICATE OF INSOL-VENCY FOR THE PURPOSES OF SECTION 22(3)(b) OF THE VALUE ADDED TAX ACT 1983'.

2.234

3.37 Notice to creditors

(1) Notice of the issue of the certificate shall be given by the administrative receiver within 3 months of his appointment or within 2 months of issuing the certificate, whichever is the later, to all of the company's unsecured creditors of whose address he is then aware and who have, to his knowledge, made supplies to the company, with a charge to value added tax, at any time before his appointment.

(2) Thereafter, he shall give the notice to any such creditor of whose address and supplies to the company he becomes aware.

(3) He is not under obligation to provide any creditor with a copy of the certificate.

2.235

3.38 Preservation of certificate with company's records

(1) The certificate shall be retained with the company's accounting records, and section 222 of the Companies Act (where and for how long records are to be kept) shall apply to the certificate as it applies to those records.

(2) It is the duty of the administrative receiver, on vacating office, to bring this Rule to the attention of the directors or (as the case may be) any successor of his as receiver.

Chapter 7

Section 176A:– The Prescribed Part

2.236

3.39 Report to creditors

[(1) This Rule applies where—
  (a)   a receiver (other than an administrative receiver) is appointed by the court or otherwise under a charge which as created was a floating charge; and
  (b)   section 176A applies.

(2) Within 3 months (or such longer period as the court may allow) of the date of his appointment the receiver shall send to creditors, details of whose names and addresses are available to him, notice of his appointment and a report which will include the following matters—
  (a)   to the best of the receiver's knowledge and belief—

(i) an estimate of the value of the prescribed part (whether or not he proposes to make an application to the court under section 176A(5) or section 176A(3) applies); and

(ii) an estimate of the value of company's net property;

(b) whether, and if so, why, he proposes to make an application to court under section 176A(5); and

(c) whether he proposes to present a petition for the winding up of the company.

(3) Nothing in this Rule is to be taken as requiring any such estimate to include any information, the disclosure of which could seriously prejudice the commercial interests of the company. If such information is excluded from the calculation the estimate shall be accompanied by a statement to that effect.

(4) Where the receiver thinks that it is impracticable to send the report required under paragraph (2) or where full details of the unsecured creditors of the company are not available to him, he may, instead of sending a report as required by this Rule, publish a notice to the same effect in such newspaper as he thinks most appropriate for ensuring that it comes to the notice of the company's unsecured creditors.]

Notes

R 3.39

This provision was introduced by the Insolvency (Amendment) Rules 2003 (SI 2003/1730) with effect from 15 September 2003 to oblige a receiver to report on the operation of the 'prescribed part' provisions under IA 1986 s 176A in a receivership other than an administrative receivership; reference should be made to the notes under that section. An administrative receiver has a wider ranging reporting obligation under IA 1986 s 48.

2.237

3.40 Receiver to deal with prescribed part

[Where Rule 3.39 applies—

(a) the receiver may present a petition for the winding up of the company if the ground of the petition is that in section 122(1)(f);

(b) where a liquidator or administrator has been appointed to the company, the receiver shall deliver up the sums representing the prescribed part to him;

(c) in any other case, the receiver shall apply to the court for directions as to the manner in which he is to discharge his duty under section 176A(2)(a) and shall act in accordance with such directions as are given by the court.]

Part 4
Companies Winding Up

Chapter 1
The Scheme of this Part of the Rules

2.238

4.1 Voluntary winding up; winding up by the court

[(1) In a members' voluntary winding up, the Rules in this Part do not apply, except as follows—
- (a) Rule 4.3 applies in the same way as it applies in a creditors' voluntary winding up;
- (b) Rule 4.72 (additional provisions concerning meetings in relation to [the Financial Services Authority] and [the scheme manager]) applies in the winding up of [authorised deposit-takers or former authorised deposit-takers], whether members' or creditors' voluntary or by the court;
- (c) Chapters 9 (proof of debts in a liquidation), 10 (secured creditors), 15 (disclaimer) and 18 (special manager) apply wherever, and in the same way as, they apply in a creditors' voluntary winding up;
- (d) Section F of Chapter 11 (the liquidator) applies only in a members' voluntary winding up, and not otherwise;
- (e) Section G of that Chapter (court's power to set aside certain transactions; rule against solicitation) applies in any winding up, whether members' or creditors' voluntary or by the court;
- (f) Rule 4.182A applies only in a members' voluntary winding up, and not otherwise; and
- (g) Rule 4.223–CVL (liquidator's statements) applies in the same way as it applies in a creditors' voluntary winding up.]

(2) Subject as follows, the Rules in this Part apply both in a creditors' voluntary winding up and in a winding up by the court; and for this purpose a winding up is treated as a creditors' voluntary [winding up] if, and from the time when, the liquidator forms the opinion that the company will be unable to pay its debts in full, and determines accordingly to summon a creditors' meeting under section 95.

(3) The following Chapters, or Sections of Chapters, of this Part do not apply in a creditors' voluntary winding up—
Chapter 2—The statutory demand;
Chapter 3—Petition to winding-up order;
Chapter 4—Petition by contributories;
Chapter 5—Provisional liquidator;
[Chapter 11 (Section F)—The Liquidator in a members' voluntary winding up;]
Chapter 13 The liquidation committee where winding up follows immediately on administration;
Chapter 16—Settlement of list of contributories;
Chapter 17—Calls;
Chapter 19—Public examination of company officers and others; and
Chapter 21 (Section A)—Return of capital.
[Chapter 21 (Section C)—Dissolution after winding up].

(4) Where at the head of any Rule, or at the end of any paragraph of a Rule, there appear the words '(NO CVL APPLICATION)', this signifies that the Rule or, as the case may be, the paragraph does not apply in a creditors' voluntary winding up.

However, this does not affect the court's power to make orders under section 112 (exercise in relation to voluntary winding up of powers available in winding up by the court).

(5) Where to any Rule or paragraph there is given a number incorporating the letters 'CVL', that signifies that the Rule or (as the case may be) the paragraph applies in a creditors' voluntary winding up, and not in a winding up by the court.

[(6) In a voluntary winding up which is commenced by the registration of a notice under paragraph 83(3) of Schedule B1 to the Act, the following provisions of this Part shall not apply—
    Rules 4.34, 4.38, 4.49, 4.51, 4.53, 4.62, 4.101, 4.103, 4.106, 4.152, 4.153, 4.206–4.210.]

2.239

4.2 Winding up by the court: the various forms of petition [(No CVL Application)]

(1) Insofar as the Rules in this Part apply to winding up by the court, they apply (subject as follows) whether the petition for winding up is presented under any of the several paragraphs of section 122(1), namely—
    paragraph (a)—company special resolution for winding up by the court;
    paragraph (b)—public company without certificate under section 117 of the Companies Act;
    paragraph (c)—old public company;
    paragraph (d)—company not commencing business after formation, or suspending business;
    paragraph (e)—number of company's members reduced below 2;
    paragraph (f)—company unable to pay its debts;
    paragraph (fa) – end of moratorium without approval of voluntary arrangement;
    paragraph (g)—court's power under the 'just and equitable' rule,

or under any enactment enabling the presentation of a winding-up petition.

(2) Except as provided by the following two paragraphs or by any particular Rule, the Rules apply whether the petition for winding up is presented by the company, the directors, one or more creditors, one or more contributories, the Secretary of State, the official receiver, or any person entitled under any enactment to present such a petition.

(3) Chapter 2 (statutory demand) has no application except in relation to an unpaid creditor of the company satisfying section 123(1)(a) (the first of the two cases specified, in relation to England and Wales, of the company being deemed unable to pay its debts within section 122(1)(f) or section 222(1) (the equivalent provision in relation to unregistered companies).

> (4) Chapter 3 (petition to winding-up order) has no application to a petition for winding up presented by one or more contributories; and in relation to a petition so presented Chapter 4 has effect.

Notes

R 4.2(1)

The rules relating to compulsory liquidation in IR 1986 r 4.1–4.231 apply irrespective of the ground upon which a petition is presented and whether or not the petition is presented under IA 1986 or another statute enabling the presentation of a winding up petition.

R 4.2(2)

Unless otherwise provided IR 1986 apply irrespective of the identity of the petitioner.

R 4.2(3)

The statutory demand procedure set out in IR 1986 r 4.4–4.6 only applies in relation to the petition of an unpaid creditor seeking to satisfy the court of the company's insolvency for winding up purposes.

R 4.2(4)

Generally IR 1986 r 4.7–4.21, which set out the procedure from the presentation of the petition to the making of the order, do not apply to a contributory's petition which follows its own course: IR 1986 r 4.22–4.24. However the effect of IR 1986 r 4.24 is to apply several of the rules in IR 1986 r 4.7–4.21 to a contributory's petition. The main difference is that the return day fixed for hearing a contributory's petition is used as a directions hearing (IR 1986 r 4.22(2)); whereas at the first hearing of a creditor's petition the company may be wound up.

2.240

4.3 Time-limits

Where by any provision of the Act or the Rules about winding up, the time for doing anything is limited, the court may extend the time, either before or after it has expired, on such terms, if any, as it thinks fit.

Notes

R 4.3

This is a useful and wide ranging power to extend time limits imposed in a liquidation by any provision of IA 1986 or IR 1986. This provision should be read alongside IR 1986 r 12.9(2) which applies the court's general powers of management under CPR Part 3.1(2)(a) to time limits under IR 1986; thus time can not only be extended under that provision but also abridged.

Chapter 2
The Statutory Demand (No CVL Application)

Notes

These rules relating to statutory demands should be read alongside IA 1986 s 123(1)(a) (and the accompanying notes) and enable a petitioning creditor to prove insolvency. It is important for the creditor to act immediately the three week period for complying the statutory demand has elapsed: IA 1986 s 123(1)(a). If insolvency is to be proved in a petition by reference to an unsatisfied statutory demand then the petition ought to be presented quickly and not allowed to go 'stale'.

2.241

4.4 Preliminary

(1) This Chapter does not apply where a petition for the winding up of a company is presented under section 124 on or after the date on which the Rules come into force and the petition is based on failure to comply with a written demand served on the company before that date.

(2) A written demand served by a creditor on a company under section 123(1)(a) (registered companies) or 222(1)(a) (unregistered companies) is known in winding-up proceedings as 'the statutory demand'.

(3) The statutory demand must be dated, and be signed either by the creditor himself or by a person stating himself to be authorised to make the demand on the creditor's behalf.

Notes

R 4.4(1)

This provision is no longer of relevance.

R 4.4(2)

Reference should be made to the notes under IA 1986 s 123(1)(a) for detail of the use and effect of a statutory demand. Under that provision it must be made in the *'prescribed form'* (Form 4.1, IR 1986 Sch 4) which in practice rules out the use of 'home made' demands if IA 1986 s 123(1)(a) is to be relied upon.

R 4.4(3)

Though time limits in relation to winding up can be extended/shortened (IR 1986 r 4.3, r 12.9) it is unlikely that a court would find that an undated statutory demand was acceptable. Further, a petition should not be presented within the three weeks after service of a statutory demand. In calculating time limits the day on which the demand is served is excluded or any part of a day: *Trow v Ind Coope (West Midlands) Ltd* [1967] 2 QB 899.

2.242

4.5 Form and content of statutory demand

(1) The statutory demand must state the amount of the debt and the consideration for it (or, if there is no consideration, the way in which it arises).

(2) If the amount claimed in the demand includes—
    (a)   any charge by way of interest not previously notified to the company as included in its liability, or
    (b)   any other charge accruing from time to time,

> the amount or rate of the charge must be separately identified, and the grounds on which payment of it is claimed must be stated.
>
> In either case the amount claimed must be limited to that which has accrued due at the date of the demand.

Notes

R 4.5(1)

The length of explanation of these details given in statutory demands varies considerably but the aim should always be to state the required information as clearly as possible.

R 4.5(2)

It would be unusual though possible to issue a series of statutory demands so as to ensure that the largest possible unpaid debt is before the court on any application which might be made by the company to restrain the petition or its advertisement.

2.243

4.6 Information to be given in statutory demand

(1) The statutory demand must include an explanation to the company of the following matters—

    (a)   the purpose of the demand, and the fact that, if the demand is not complied with, proceedings may be instituted for the winding up of the company;

    (b)   the time within which it must be complied with, if that consequence is to be avoided; and

    (c)   the methods of compliance which are open to the company.

(2) Information must be provided for the company as to how an officer or representative of it may enter into communication with one or more named individuals, with a view to securing or compounding for the debt to the creditor's satisfaction.

In the case of any individual so named in the demand, his address and telephone number (if any) must be given.

Notes

R 4.6(1)

These details appear on the prescribed form itself (Form 4.1 IR 1986 Sch 4).

Chapter 3
Petition to Winding-up Order (No CVL Application) (No Application to Petition by Contributories)

Notes

IR 1986 rr 4.7–4.21A do not apply in voluntary liquidations nor where the petitioner is a contributory; a contributory's petition follows the course set out in IR 1986 rr 4.22–4.24. The rules apply to a petition whether presented in the High Court or the county court and similarly the designated forms are used in both courts IR 1986 r 12.7, Sch 4. The rules themselves are supplemented by Practice Direction: Insolvency Proceedings, Civil Procedure 2006, Vol 2 Sect 3E paras 1–6. The form of the petition is set out in Form 4.2 IR 1986 Sch 4 and it should be followed with such variations as circumstances may require IR 1986 r 12.7(1), (2). If the company's name is misstated the court will generally dismiss the petition unless the mistake is very minor and unlikely to cause confusion: *Re Vidiofusion Ltd* [1974] 1 WLR 1548; in relation to errors in a petition discovered after a winding up order has been made see Practice Direction: Insolvency Proceedings, Civil Procedure 2006, Vol 2 Sect 3E para 4. Where a creditor seeks to wind up a number of companies in a group then separate petitions should be presented and directions can then be obtained for consolidation if thought appropriate: *Re a Company* [1984] BCLC 307; *cf Re William Pickles plc* [1996] 1 BCLC 681 in relation to an originating application issued under IA 1986 s 112 by the liquidator of a group of companies.

Before presenting a petition it is advisable to check that a petition has not already been presented against the debtor company by telephoning the Companies Court search facility (0906 754 0043). Theoretically every petition presented in a county court should be notified to the Companies Court and entered on the central database maintained by the Companies Court, 'the Central Registry of Winding up Petitions': Chancery Guide, October 2005, Civil Procedure 2006, Vol 2 Section 1 para 1A-166. On rare occasions the system may fail: see notes to IA 1986 s 117 on the priority of petitions in that circumstance.

2.244

4.7 Presentation and filing of petition

(1) The petition, verified by affidavit in accordance with Rule 4.12 below, shall be filed in court.

(2) No petition shall be filed unless there is produced with it the receipt for the deposit payable on presentation.

(2A) This paragraph applies in any case where the Secretary of State has given written notice to the court that the petitioner has made suitable alternative arrangements for the payment of the deposit to the official receiver and such notice has not been revoked in relation to the petitioner in accordance with paragraph (2B)

(2B) A notice of the kind referred to in paragraph (2A) may be revoked in relation to the petitioner in whose favour it is given by a further notice in writing to the court stating that the earlier notice is revoked in relation to the petitioner.

(3) If the petitioner is other than the company itself, there shall be delivered with the petition—
    (a)   one copy for service on the company, and
    (b)   one copy to be exhibited to the affidavit verifying service.

(4) There shall in any case be delivered with the petition—
    (a)   if the company is in course of being wound up voluntarily, and a liquidator has been appointed, one copy of the petition to be sent to him;
    (b)   if the company is in administration, one copy to be sent to the administrator;
    (c)   if an administrative receiver has been appointed in relation to the company, one copy to be sent to him;

> (d) if there is in force for the company a voluntary arrangement under Part I of the Act, one copy for the supervisor of the arrangement; and
>
> (da) if a member State liquidator has been appointed in main proceedings in relation to the company, one copy to be sent to him; and
>
> (e) if the company is an authorised deposit-taker or a former authorised deposit-taker and the petitioner is not the Bank of England, one copy to be sent to the Bank.
>
> (5) Each of the copies delivered shall have applied to it the seal of the court, and shall be issued to the petitioner.
>
> (6) The court shall fix a venue for the hearing of the petition; and this shall be endorsed on any copy issued to the petitioner under paragraph (5).
>
> (7) Where a petition is filed at the instance of a company's administrator the petition shall—
>
> (a) be expressed to be the petition of the company by its administrator,
>
> (b) state the name of the administrator, the court case number and the date that the company entered administration, and
>
> (c) where applicable, contain an application under paragraph 79 of Schedule B1 requesting that the appointment of the administrator shall cease to have effect.
>
> (8) Any petition filed in relation to a company in respect of which there is in force a voluntary arrangement under Part I of the Act or which is in administration shall be presented to the court to which the nominee's report under section 2 was submitted or the court having jurisdiction for the administration
>
> (9) Any petition such as is mentioned in paragraph (7) above or presented by the supervisor of a voluntary arrangement under Part I of the Act in force for the company shall be treated as if it were a petition filed by contributories, and Chapter 4 in this Part of the Rules shall apply accordingly.
>
> (10) Where a petition contains a request for the appointment of a person as liquidator in accordance with section 140 (appointment of former administrator or supervisor as liquidator) the person whose appointment is sought shall, not less than 2 days before the return day for the petition, file in court a report including particulars of—
>
> (a) a date on which he notified creditors of the company, either in writing or at a meeting of creditors, of the intention to seek his appointment as liquidator, such date to be at least 10 days before the day on which the report under this paragraph is filed, and
>
> (b) details of any response from creditors to that notification, including any objections to his appointment.

Notes

R 4.7(1)

The petition is in Form 4.2. It must state whether the EC Regulation on Insolvency Proceedings 2000 applies and whether the proceedings are main or other proceedings as defined in EC

Regulation art 3. The failure to state whether the EC Regulation applies and if so, what type of proceedings is involved is a substantive defect which is unlikely to be waived under IR 1986 r 7.55 ; see also former Insolvency Proceedings – Practice Note 1/2002, 10th May 2002. A witness statement can be used instead of an affidavit (IR 1986 r 7.57(5)) to verify the petition in the manner set out in IR 1986 r 4.12. The affidavit/witness statement should follow Form 4.3 IR 1986 Sch 4 but it may be varied as circumstances require, IR 1986 r 12.7. Solicitors asked to make such a witness statement on behalf of a client should be wary given the dramatic costs consequences of verifying the insolvency of the company named in the petition without adequate grounds for doing so: *Re a Company (No 006798 of 1995)* [1996] 1 WLR 491; *Philex plc v Golban* [1994] BCC 390.

R 4.7(2)

The deposit is currently £655: Insolvency Fees Order 2004 (SI 2004/593) art 6 (as amended). If the company is wound up the deposit is paid to the official receiver; if the winding up petition is dismissed the deposit is returned to the petitioner: Insolvency Fees Order 2004 (SI 2004/593).

R 4.7(3)–(5)

Additionally a director, contributory or creditor is entitled to a copy of the petition within 2 days of requiring it (IR 1986 r 4.13) on the payment of a fee which is calculated by reference to page size: IR 1986 r 13.11.

R 4.7(6)

'Venue' has an extended meaning IR 1986 r 13.6; the sealed petition will inform the company of the time, date and place of the hearing of the petition.

R 4.7(7)

An administrator files a petition as an agent of the company in pursuance of an express. power to present a petition: IA 1986 s 14(1), (5), Sch 1 para 21 (former administration procedure); IA 1986 Sch B1 paras 60, 69 Sch 1 para 21 (new administration procedure); see notes to IR 1986 r 4.7(10) below. It is not generally possible under either the former or new administration procedure for the court to make a winding up order unless the administrator has presented a petition: *Re Brook Marine Ltd* [1988] BCLC 546 However in *Lancefield v Lancefield* [2002] BPIR 1108 the court held that it had jurisdiction to wind a company of its own motion though it would require a thoroughly exceptional case before it would consider doing so.

R 4.7(8)

The general power of transfer in IR 1986 r 7.11 ff applies to winding up proceedings. If the petition is presented in the 'wrong' court it may be transferred to the correct court, continued in the 'wrong' court or struck out: IR 1986 r 7.12; and see notes to IA 1986 s 117.

R 4.7(9)

A petition presented by an administrator or a supervisor theoretically follows the course of a contributory's petition. On presentation of the petition the court fixes a 'return day' for the petition which is supposed to be used as a directions hearing IR 1986 r 4.22(2). However frequently under the former administration regime the court would dispense with service and advertisement and make a winding up order on the hearing of the application of the administrator to discharge the administration order: see further the notes to IR 1986 r 4.7(1) below. In the case of a creditor's petition the venue for the hearing of the petition is stated on the face of the petition IR 1986 r 4.7(6) and a winding up order can be made at that hearing.

R 4.7(10)

Former administration procedure (administration order made on a petition presented prior to 15th September 2003)

Under the former administration procedure an administrator who desired to be appointed liquidator immediately upon discharge of the order (see IA 1986 s 140 prior to amendment by the EA 2002) would normally present an application for a discharge together with the winding up petition. In practice the prayer for winding up could be included in the application for discharge although some practitioners preferred to issue a separate application for discharge and a winding up petition. Directions would then be obtained on the petition whether it was included in the application or presented separately. The usual directions on such a petition would include dispensing with advertisement of the petition and service on the company. Under IR 1986 r 4.7(1), the administrator would have publicised to creditors his intention to exit from administration by a liquidation and the creditors would have been informed of the intention of the administrator to seek appointment as liquidator.

New administration procedure (company enters administration out of court or pursuant to an application made on or after 15 September 2003)

Under the new administration procedure there are express provisions dealing with a discharge of an administration order (IA 1986 Sch B1 para 85) and the ending of administrations in general (IA 1986 Sch B1 paras 79ff); see also *Re Ballast plc* [2005] 1 BCLC 446. Whether appointed in or out of court an administrator whose appointment ceases to have effect may apply for appointment as liquidator under IA 1986 s 140 and IR 1986 r 4.7(10) must be observed. IA 1986 Sch B1 provides a number of exit routes from administration aside from a compulsory liquidation: IA 1986 Sch B1 para 83 (creditors' voluntary liquidation); para 84 (dissolution). The proposed exit route from administration must be contained in the administrator's proposals: IR 1986 r 2.33(2)(m).

2.245

4.8 Service of petition

(1) The following paragraphs apply as regards service of the petition on the company (where the petitioner is other than the company itself); and references to the petition are to a copy of the petition bearing the seal of the court in which it is presented.

(2) Subject as follows, the petition shall be served at the company's registered office, that is to say—

   (a)   the place which is specified, in the company's statement delivered under section 10 of the Companies Act as the intended situation of its registered office on incorporation, or

   (b)   if notice has been given by the company to the registrar of companies under section 287 of that Act (change of registered office), the place specified in that notice or, as the case may be, in the last such notice.

(3) Service of the petition at the registered office may be effected in any of the following ways—

   (a)   it may be handed to a person who there and then acknowledges himself to be, or to the best of the server's knowledge, information and belief is, a director or other officer, or employee, of the company; or

   (b)   it may be handed to a person who there and then acknowledges himself to be authorised to accept service of documents on the company's behalf; or

   (c)   in the absence of any such person as is mentioned in sub-paragraph (a) or (b), it may be deposited at or about the

> registered office in such a way that it is likely to come to the notice of a person attending at the office.
>
> (4) If for any reason service at the registered office is not practicable, or the company has no registered office or is an unregistered company, the petition may be served on the company by leaving it at the company's last known principal place of business in such a way that it is likely to come to the attention of a person attending there, or by delivering it to the secretary or some director, manager or principal officer of the company, wherever that person may be found.
>
> (5) In the case of an overseas company, service may be effected in any manner provided for by section 695 of the Companies Act.
>
> (6) If for any reason it is impracticable to effect service as provided by paragraphs (2) to (5), the petition may be served in such other manner as the court may [approve or] direct.
>
> (7) Application for leave of the court under paragraph (6) may be made *ex parte*, on affidavit stating what steps have been taken to comply with paragraphs (2) to (5), and the reasons why it is impracticable to effect service as there provided.

Notes

R 4.8(2)

An action in negligence against a petitioner who served a winding up petition at the wrong address was struck out in *Business Computers International Ltd v Registrar of Companies* [1987] BCLC 621.

R 4.8(3)

The effect of these provisions is that a petition can be lawfully served in a variety of ways. For instance a receptionist at the registered office who states that he is an employee of the respondent company could be left with an envelope enclosing the petition and that would be effective service under IR 1986 r 4.8(3)(a). Where a petition is served by depositing it 'at or about' the registered office it should be left in a prominent place in the registered office itself; if that is not possible then it should be put through the letter box for the registered office or fixed to the door rather than just being pushed under the door. In those circumstances the affidavit/witness statement of service should explain the manner of service in detail: IR 1986 r 4.9, r 7.57(5)

R 4.8(4)

The 'last known principal place of business' may be used for service of the petition by 'leaving' it at that place. Under the statutory demand procedure there was debate about whether posting the demand constituted 'leaving' it at the registered office (see notes to IA 1986 s 23(1)(a) above); to avoid potential difficulties it is wiser to use a process server to effect service and reference should be made to the notes in the above paragraph. Alternatively the process server can effect service on a variety of individuals wherever they may be found.

R 4.8(5)

This is straightforward enough if the company has nominated a person and address to accept service on its behalf and notified that to the Registrar of Companies; the petition is posted to that person or else left at the notified address. Where no such notification has been made or if the notified person is dead, ceased to reside or refuses to accept service then the petition may be served by leaving it at or sending it by post to any place of business which the company has established in Great Britain: CA 1985 ss 695, 694A.

R 4.8(6), (7)

The application is made to the Court Manager of the Companies Court or a District Judge in a District Registry: Practice Direction: Insolvency Proceedings, Civil Procedure 2006, Vol 2 Sect 3E para 5.4(2); the usual order is to place an advertisement in the London Gazette. As IR 1986 r 4.8(7) indicates such an application must be supported by detailed evidence.

2.246

4.9 Proof of service

(1) Service of the petition shall be proved by affidavit, specifying the manner of service.

(2) The affidavit shall have exhibited to it—
  (a) a sealed copy of the petition, and
  (b) if substituted service has been ordered, a sealed copy of the order;

and it shall be filed in court immediately after service.

Notes

R 4.9(1)

A witness statement can be used instead of an affidavit: IR 1986 r 7.57(5)

R 4.9(2)

Though *'immediately'* does not carry the same urgency as *'forthwith'* evidence of service should be provided within a business day of service; it is important for the petitioner to confirm that it has properly served not least because it is relevant in calculating the period for advertisement: IR 1986 r 4.11.

2.247

4.10 Other persons to receive copies of petition

(1) If to the petitioner's knowledge the company is in course of being wound up voluntarily, a copy of the petition shall be sent by him to the liquidator.

(2) If to the petitioner's knowledge an administrative receiver has been appointed in relation to the company, or the company is in administration, a copy of the petition shall be sent by him to the receiver or, as the case may be, the administrator.

(3) If to the petitioner's knowledge there is in force for the company a voluntary arrangement under Part I of the Act, a copy of the petition shall be sent by him to the supervisor of the voluntary arrangement.

(3A) If to the petitioner's knowledge, there is a member State liquidator appointed in main proceedings in relation to the company, a copy of the petition shall be sent by him to that person.

This does not apply if the petitioner referred to in this paragraph is a member State liquidator.

(4) If the company is an authorised institution or former authorised institution within the meaning of the Banking Act 1987 a copy of the petition shall be sent by the petitioner to the Bank of England.

This does not apply if the petitioner is the Bank of England itself.

(5) A copy of the petition which is required by this Rule to be sent shall be despatched on the next business day after the day on which the petition is served on the company.

Notes

R 4.10

Other persons listed in IR 1986 r 4.13 are entitled to a copy of the petition on the payment of a fee. Entitlement to a copy of the petition would include a copy of the affidavit/witness statement verifying the petition as the court will not seal the petition without such verification: IR 1986 r 4.7(1).

R 4.10(3)(A)

See the notes to the EC Regulation on Insolvency Proceedings 2000.

2.248–2.249

4.11 Advertisement of petition

(1) Unless the court otherwise directs, the petition shall be advertised once in the Gazette.

(2) The advertisement must be made to appear—
  (a) if the petitioner is the company itself, not less than 7 business days before the day appointed for the hearing, and
  (b) otherwise, not less than 7 business days after service of the petition on the company, not less than 7 business days before the day so appointed.

(3) The court may, if compliance with paragraph (2) is not reasonably practicable, direct that advertisement of the petition be made to appear in a specified ... newspaper, instead of in the Gazette.

(4) The advertisement of the petition must state—
  (a) the name and registered number of the company and the address of its registered office, or—
    (i) in the case of an unregistered company, the address of its principal place of business;
    (ii) in the case of an oversea company, the address at which service of the petition was effected;
  (b) the name and address of the petitioner;

> (c)   where the petitioner is the company itself, the address of its registered office or, in the case of an unregistered company, of its principal place of business;
>
> (d)   the date on which the petition was presented;
>
> (e)   the venue fixed for the hearing of the petition;
>
> (f)   the name and address of the petitioner's solicitor (if any); and
>
> (g)   that any person intending to appear at the hearing (whether to support or oppose the petition) must give notice of his intention in accordance with Rule 4.16.
>
> (5) If the petition is not duly advertised in accordance with this Rule, the court may disMiss it.

Notes

R 4.11

The advertisement rules should be complied with strictly otherwise the petition may be dismissed as not having been duly advertised: IR 1986 r 4.11(5); *Re Signland Ltd* [1982] 2 All ER 609. The petitioning creditor will not obtain an order for costs where the petition is dismissed before advertisement: *Re Shusella Ltd* [1983] BCLC 505. The aim of advertisement is to inform third parties of the petition and its hearing date: *Re a Company (No 007923 of 1994)* [1995] 1 WLR 953, 958. The advertisement itself gives constructive notice of the existence of the petition: *Re London, Hamburg and Continental Exchange Bank* (1866) LR 2 Eq 231.

The court will not grant repeated adjournments of the petition to allow for advertisement to take place. Though practice may vary somewhat a petitioner who mistakenly fails to advertise or advertise properly will normally be granted one adjournment but should assume that it will be difficult to secure any further adjournment. Failure to advertise at all is a fundamental error which would justify dismissal of the petition Practice Direction: Insolvency Proceedings, Civil Procedure 2006, Vol 2 Sect 3E para 2.1. However in the case of a failure to advertise when the company is already in liquidation the court may be persuaded not to dismiss the petition: *Re Roselmar Properties Ltd (No 2)* (1986) 2 BCC 99,156.

R 4.11(1)

'*Unless the court otherwise directs* ...' The advertisement rule is concerned primarily with advertisement in the Gazette. It is unusual for the court to direct that a petition be not advertised. However in a number of cases involving public interest petitions (IA 1986 s 124A) such a direction has been made: *Re a Company (No 007923 of 1994)* [1995] 1 WLR 953; *Re Golden Chemical Products Ltd* [1976] Ch 300; *cf Applied Data Base Ltd v Secretary of State for Trade and Industry* [1995] 1 BCLC 272 (application for direction not to advertise refused). Advertisement may also be restrained when the court is persuaded that this may assist with the presentation of an application for administration: *Re a Company (No 001448 of 1989)* [1989] BCLC 715; or the holding of a creditors' meeting to consider a proposal for a voluntary arrangement. A dispensation from advertisement may also be applied for when an administrator presents a winding up petition (IA 1986 s 140) as a prelude to obtaining discharge of the administration order and it is considered that the creditors have already been sufficiently informed of the impending liquidation of the company (see notes to IR 1986 r 4 7(10) above).

R 4.11(2)

'Business day' means a clear business day and therefore the day the advertisement appears and the day of the hearing are excluded; in addition weekends, bank holidays, Christmas Day and Good Friday are excluded (IR 1986 r 13.13). The court will usually waive short advertisement if it is short by one or two days (IR 1986 r 4.4) otherwise the petition will require re-advertisement. Where a petition is advertised prematurely in the Gazette the court can order the petition to be struck out: *Re a Company (No 007020 of 1996)* [1998] 2 BCLC 54.

R 4.11(3)

The London Gazette is a newspaper published on weekdays and can be contacted on 0207 394 4580 or at www.london-gazette.co.uk. In practice the advertisement is placed in the Gazette rather than another newspaper; however where for instance the Gazette is not being printed then advertisement in a specified newspaper can be ordered. An advertisement can be withdrawn if written instructions to that effect are given to the Gazette not later than 3.30 pm the day before it is due to appear.

R 4.11(4), (5)

If there are minor misstatements or omissions in the advertisement the court will waive the defect at the hearing. However where a mistake is made in the name of the company or its registered office which is regarded as more than trivial the court will order readvertisement of the petition to take place. Where the breach of the rules consists of something less than failure to advertise at all and the breach is not due to the fault of the petitioner (*Re Corbenstoke Ltd* (1989) 5 BCC 197) and it is not otherwise an abuse of process (*Re Garton (Western) Ltd* (1989) 5 BCC 198) the court may allow the petition to proceed.

It is not 'best practice' to advertise the existence of a petition otherwise than by advertisement in the Gazette in accordance with the rules. However it is not uncommon for a petitioner to have informed third parties of the petition either mistakenly or deliberately. Though there is authority which treats such 'informal' advertisement as a breach of IR 1986 r 4.11 (*Re a Company (No 001127 of 1992)* [1992] BCC 477), the weight of authority appears to treat the rule as dealing only with advertisement in the Gazette; therefore advertisement by other means and at whatever time is not actually a breach of IR 1986 r 4.11: *SN Group plc v Barclays Bank plc* [1993] BCC 506; *Secretary of State for Trade and Industry v North West Holdings plc* [1999] 1 BCLC 425; *Re a Company (No 0013925 of 1991) ex parte Rousell* [1992] BCLC 562). However in those cases the existence of the inherent jurisdiction of the court to strike out a petition as an abuse of process was emphasised; for instance where the 'informal' advertisement is designed to pressurise the company the court is very likely to strike out the petition whether it is a creditor's or contributory's petition: *Re Doreen Boards Ltd* [1996] 1 BCLC 501.

Restraint of advertisement

The delay in advertising until seven business days have elapsed from service of the petition gives the company the opportunity to pay the debt or apply to restrain advertisement. If restraint is sought then the petitioner should first be approached by the company for an undertaking not to advertise pending the hearing of the restraint application. If no suitable undertaking is given then an ordinary application should be made without notice or on short notice to the Judge (not the Registrar – Practice Note on the Hearing of Insolvency Proceedings [2005] BPIR 688) in open court: Practice Direction: Insolvency Proceedings, Civil Procedure 2006, Vol 2 Sect 3E para 8.1; *Holt Southey Ltd v Catric Components Ltd* [1978] 1 WLR 630; *Re Druce & Co* [1993] BCLC 964; *Coulon Sanderson & Ward Ltd v Ward* (1985) 2 BCC 99, 207). If the court does make a restraint order in the usual terms ('the petitioner be restrained whether by itself its servants or agents or otherwise howsoever from advertising or proceeding further on the petition; the petition be removed from the file') then any communication or publication of the petition is banned: *Re a Company* [1986] BCLC 127, *Re a Company* [1894] 2 Ch 349.

The court will restrain the advertisement of a petition where:
(a)   the petition constitutes an abuse of process in that the petition debt is disputed bona fide on substantial grounds (*Re a Company (No 003079 of 1990)* [1991] BCC 683, *Greenacre Publishing Group v The Manson Group* [2000] BCC 111, *Re a Company (No 0044502 of 1988) ex p Johnson* [1992] BCLC 701, *Re a Company (No 0012209 of 1991)* [1992] 1 WLR 351); and/or

(b)   there is a genuine and serious cross claim by the company which is for a greater amount than claimed by the creditor, the company has been unable to litigate the cross claim and there are no 'special circumstances' which would justify letting the petition proceed *Re Bayoil SA* [1998] BCC 988, *Marchands Associates LLP v The Thompson Partnership (CA)* 28/06/04 (Lawtel, No AC 9200240). However it is not clear whether the 'inability to litigate' condition is actually crucial to the restraint application (*Popely v Popely* [2004] EWCA Civ 4463, [2004] BPIR 778, 812 para 123, *Southern Cross v Deka Immobilien* [2005] BPIR 1010). For a consideration of 'special circumstances' see the notes below.

So far as (a) is concerned the court will investigate whether or not there are substantial grounds for disputing the debt and it will be alive to the possibility of an unwilling debtor company raising a '*cloud of objections .. and then to claim that because a dispute of fact cannot be decided without cross examination, the petition should not be heard at all ...' Re a Company (No 006685 of 1996)* [1997] BCC 830, 835E per Chadwick J.

So far as (b) is concerned the court will need to be satisfied that the evidence supporting the cross claim is substantive and detailed: *Orion Media Marketing Ltd v Media Brook Ltd* [2002] 1 BCLC 184. It is dangerous for the company to rely on unsubstantiated assertions by the directors and/or the directors' 'best estimate' of what value there is in any particular aspect of the cross claim.

Though it would be unusual to restrain advertisement outside the situations outlined in (a) and (b) above the court has been prepared to direct that there should be no advertisement in some cases concerning a public interest petition. The court would only make such a direction in exceptional circumstances (*Applied Data Base Ltd v Secretary of State for Trade and Industry* [1995] 1 BCLC 272) where the company is not alleged to be insolvent and the company opposes the petition. In those cases the court has to be satisfied that the potential damage to the company in advertising the petition outweighs the interests of those who want the company wound up; to meet the court's concerns the company would have to produce cogent evidence of the serious prejudice which would be caused by advertisement (*Re Golden Chemical Products Ltd [1976] Ch 300, Re a Company (No 007923 of 1994)* [1995] 1 WLR 953).

Restraint of Presentation

An application to restrain presentation of a petition is made by originating application (Practice Direction Insolvency Proceedings Civil Procedure Vol 2 Section 3E para 8.1, r 7.1 IR 1986 Form 7.1).The distinction between the test employed by the court for restraint of presentation and that for restraint of advertisement of a petition is sometimes difficult to discern. If the presentation of a petition would constitute an abuse of process then the court has no discretion; it must restrain the presentation of the petition. However once the petition is presented then under IR 1986 r 4.11(1) the court has a discretion to restrain advertisement which discretion would not arise in a case of abuse of process; to that extent the tests are different: *Re a Company (No 007923 of 1994)* [1995] BCC 634, *Southern Cross v Deka Immobilien* [2005] BPIR 1010. The court may restrain advertisement in situations other than an abuse of process at its discretion; for instance as noted in public interest petitions it is possible to restrain advertisement where the company is solvent and wishes to oppose the petition (see above under 'Restraint of Advertisement').

The most frequently encountered type of abuse of process is the use of the winding up procedure to secure payment of a debt in respect of which there is a substantial and/or genuine dispute of the debt being claimed; if that abuse is established then the court will restrain presentation or advertisement as the case may be. If an application to restrain the presentation of the petition is unsuccessful the company should ask the court for a short period of grace to pay the petition debt (or so much of it as the court finds undisputed/not the subject of a genuine and serious cross claim) to ensure that no petition is presented *Orion Media Marketing Ltd v Media Brook Ltd* [2002] 1 BCLC 184. Where mutual disclosure and cross examination is essential to resolve a dispute the court will restrain presentation of the petition; *Abbey National plc v JSF Finance and Currency Exchange Co Ltd* [2006] EWCA Civ 328.

'Special circumstances' and petitions based on judgments/dishonoured cheques/statutory provisions

It is trite law that the Companies Court may not be used as a debt collection agency. If there is a genuine and serious cross claim it should be tried through claim proceedings: *Re Portman Provincial Cinemas Ltd* [1999] 1 WLR 157. As noted above in 'special circumstances' the court may allow a petition to proceed despite the existence of such a cross claim. For a recent discussion of the principles applicable in disputed debt and cross-claim cases, see *Re VP Developments Ltd* [2005] BCC 393. In a number of cases it has been argued by the petitioner that 'special circumstances' exist because the petition was based on: (i) a judgment debt: *Re LHF Wools Ltd* [1970] Ch 27; (ii) dishonoured cheques coupled with mandatory payment provisions: *Marchands Associates LLP v The Thompson Partnership, 28 June 2004, LTL 28/06/04* (CA) ; and (iii) binding arbitration awards: *Re Bayoil SA* [1998] BCC 988. In none of those cases was the court prepared to hold that such circumstances were so special that the petition should be allowed to proceed.

Further, where there is a mandatory rule of 'no set off' under statute, there are a series of authorities which hold that, though the provision is contained in statute rather than imposed by common law, this does not qualify as a 'special circumstance'. Thus under s 111 Housing Grants, Construction and Regeneration Act 1996 a party to a construction contract under the Act may not withhold payment after the final date for payment of a sum due under the contract unless he has given an effective notice of intention to withhold payment. In summary the Act creates a 'pay now, litigate later' regime. However notwithstanding the absence of a withholding notice a company is allowed to assert the existence of a genuine and serious cross claim which prevents the petition proceeding: *Re a Company (No 1229 of 2001)* (2001) CILL 1745; see also www.adjudication.co.uk/cases/company). In *Re a Company (No 1229 of 2001)* (above), however, the court on the facts allowed the petition to proceed because the company had had a reasonable opportunity to litigate the cross claim but it had not done so. In *Re Environmental Services Ltd*, 14 November 2001, LTL 18/1/2002 (ChD), Hart J approved of the reasoning in *Re a Company (No 1229 of 2001)* (above) and dismissed the petition albeit that no withholding notice had been served by the company under the Act.

In *Re a Company (No 1229 of 2001)* (above) there had been an adjudication under the Act whereas in *Re Environmental Services Ltd* (above) no adjudication had taken place. However it is difficult to see what purpose is served by not allowing a creditor to progress a petition where there could be no defence at all to a claim in the absence of a withholding notice under the Act and in particular where an adjudication has taken place. This appears to be the view taken by the court in *Guido Shoes Limited v Datum Contracts* (28 October 2002, unreported) where the court refused to restrain advertisement of the petition in the absence of a withholding notice. There the court appeared to treat the provisions of the construction contract and the provisions of the Act as constituting 'special circumstances'.

2.250

4.12 Verification of petition

(1) The petition shall be verified by an affidavit that the statements in the petition are true, or are true to the best of the deponent's knowledge, information and belief.

(2) If the petition is in respect of debts due to different creditors, the debts to each creditor must be separately verified.

(3) The petition shall be exhibited to the affidavit verifying it.

(4) The affidavit shall be made—
    (a)   by the petitioner (or if there are two or more petitioners, any one of them), or

    (b)   by some person such as a director, company secretary or similar company officer, or a solicitor, who has been concerned in the matters giving rise to the presentation of the petition, or

    (c)   by some responsible person who is duly authorised to make the affidavit and has the requisite knowledge of those matters.

(5) Where the deponent is not the petitioner himself, or one of the petitioners, he must in the affidavit identify himself and state—

    (a)   the capacity in which, and the authority by which, he makes it, and

    (b)   the means of his knowledge of the matters sworn to in the affidavit.

(6) The affidavit is prima facie evidence of the statements in the petition to which it relates.

(7) An affidavit verifying more than one petition shall include in its title the names of the companies to which it relates and shall set out, in respect of each company, the statements relied on by the petitioner; and a clear and legible photocopy of the affidavit shall be filed with each petition which it verifies.

(8) The affidavit shall state whether, in the opinion of the person making the application, (i) the EC Regulation will apply and (ii) if so, whether the proceedings will be main proceedings or territorial proceedings.

Notes

R 4.12(1)

A witness statement can be used instead of an affidavit: IR 1986 r 7.57(5).

R 4.12(4)(b)

Given the potential costs implications of verifying a petition on client instructions it is unwise for a solicitor to verify a petition for a client *Re a Company (No 006798 of 1995)* [1996] 1 WLR 491, *Philex plc v Golban* [1994] BCC 390.

R 4.12(6)

The evidence may and often does refer to hearsay *Re Koscot Interplanetary (UK) Ltd* [1972] 3 All ER 829.

2.251

4.13 Persons entitled to copy of petition

Every director, contributory or creditor of the company is entitled to be furnished by the solicitor for the petitioner (or by the petitioner himself, if acting in person) with a copy of the petition within 2 days after requiring it, on payment of the appropriate fee.

Notes

R 4.13

The appropriate fee is defined in IR 1986 r 13.11 but hardly ever asked for in practice; other persons are entitled to a copy of the petition free of charge: IR 1986 r 4.10.

2.252

4.14 Certificate of compliance

(1) The petitioner or his solicitor shall, at least 5 days before the hearing of the petition, file in court a certificate of compliance with the Rules relating to service and advertisement.

(2) The certificate shall show—
   (a)   the date of presentation of the petition,
   (b)   the date fixed for the hearing, and
   (c)   the date or dates on which the petition was served and advertised in compliance with the Rules.

A copy of the advertisement of the petition shall be filed in court with the certificate.

(3) Non-compliance with this Rule is a ground on which the court may, if it thinks fit, disMiss the petition.

Notes

R 4.14(1)

The filing of the certificate (IR 1986 Sch 4 Form 4.7) should not be regarded as a 'technicality'. However there is a relaxation of the time limit imposed for filing the certificate and a copy of the advertisement in Practice Direction: Insolvency Proceedings, Civil Procedure 2006, Vol 2 Sect 3E para 3 which enables the filing to take place not later than 4.30 pm on the Friday preceding the day on which the petition is to be heard. If that is not complied with an application to file after that time will only be allowed if some good reason for the delay is shown.

R 4.14(3)

Failure to file a certificate at all may well result in a dismissal of the petition although the court is not bound to order dismissal.

2.253

4.15 Leave for petitioner to withdraw

If at least 5 days before the hearing the petitioner, on an *ex parte* application, satisfies the court that—

(a) the petition has not been advertised, and

(b) no notices (whether in support or in opposition) have been received by him with reference to the petition, and

(c) the company consents to an order being made under this Rule,

the court may order that the petitioner has leave to withdraw the petition on such terms as to costs as the parties may agree.

Notes

R 4.15

This is a useful provision which enables the parties to settle the petition without the respondent company suffering the dramatic effects of advertisement of the petition on its business and banking facilities. Some difficulty may be encountered if the parties settle the dispute but the petitioner fails to reach an agreement on costs with the respondent company. The latter will be anxious to avoid advertisement but there will be no pressure on the petitioner to agree costs. The respondent company should offer costs to be assessed if not agreed; if that is refused then the respondent company would have to apply to the Judge to restrain advertisement or list the matter before the Registrar in the Companies Court or a District Judge in a district registry on a withdrawal application: Practice Note on the Hearing of Insolvency Proceedings [2005] BPIR 688. In either case the respondent company should inform the court of the unreasonableness of the petitioner not agreeing a standard costs order and ask that the court summarily assesses the costs.

2.254

4.16 Notice of appearance

(1) Every person who intends to appear on the hearing of the petition shall give to the petitioner notice of his intention in accordance with this Rule.

(2) The notice shall specify—
   (a)   the name and address of the person giving it, and any telephone number and reference which may be required for communication with him or with any other person (to be also specified in the notice) authorised to speak or act on his behalf;
   (b)   whether his intention is to support or oppose the petition; and
   (c)   the amount and nature of his debt.

(3) The notice shall be sent to the petitioner at the address shown for him in the court records, or in the advertisement of the petition required by Rule 4.11; or it may be sent to his solicitor.

(4) The notice shall be sent so as to reach the addressee not later than 16.00 hours on the business day before that which is appointed for the hearing (or, where the hearing has been adjourned, for the adjourned hearing).

(5) A person failing to comply with this Rule may appear on the hearing of the petition only with the leave of the court.

Notes

R 4.16(1)

The requirement to notify an appearance also applies to a contributory's petition: IR 1986 r 4.24.

R 4.16(5)

It is unlikely that a person who fails to notify (IR 1986 Sch 4 Form 4.9) the petitioner will be prevented from appearing at the hearing which then allows a party a right of audience: *Re Piccadilly Property Management Ltd* [2000] BCC 44. When leave is given the details of the person granted leave is added to the list of appearances under IR 1986 r 4.17.

2.255

4.17 List of appearances

(1) The petitioner shall prepare for the court a list of the persons (if any) who have given notice under Rule 4.16, specifying their names and addresses and (if known to him) their respective solicitors.

(2) Against the name of each creditor in the list it shall be stated whether his intention is to support the petition, or to oppose it.

(3) On the day appointed for the hearing of the petition, a copy of the list shall be handed to the court before the commencement of the hearing.

(4) If any leave is given under Rule 4.16(5), the petitioner shall add to the list the same particulars in respect of the person to whom leave has been given.

Notes

R 4.17(1)

This rule also applies to a contributory's petition: IR 1986 r 4.24.

R 4.17(3)

Usually just before the court begins to hear the list of petitions the associate of the court is handed the list of appearances (IR 1986 Sch 4 Form 4.10) which is frequently described as 'negative' when the court is asked for the winding up order; this means that nobody has indicated support or opposition to the petition.

2.256

4.18 Affidavit in opposition

(1) If the company intends to oppose the petition, its affidavit in opposition shall be filed in court not less than 7 days before the date fixed for the hearing.

(2) A copy of the affidavit shall be sent by the company to the petitioner, forthwith after filing.

Notes

R 4.18(1)

A witness statement may be used instead of an affidavit IR 1986 r 7.57(5); if it is not filed in time this is a point which will be taken by the petitioner but at most it will lead to an adjournment of the petition. The rules do not expressly provide for the petitioner to file evidence in reply nor for supporting/opposing parties to file evidence. In practice the petitioner is very likely to file evidence in reply because the affidavit/witness statement verifying the petition is likely to be short: IR 1986 Sch 4 Form 4.3. Evidence in opposition to a contributory's petition is dealt with on the return day of the petition IR 1986 r 4.23.

R 4.18(2)

'Forthwith' rather than 'immediately' stresses the urgency of dealing with this requirement.

2.257

4.19 Substitution of creditor or contributory for petitioner

(1) This Rule applies where a person petitions and is subsequently found not entitled to do so, or where the petitioner—

   (a)   fails to advertise his petition within the time prescribed by the Rules or such extended time as the court may allow, or

   (b)   consents to withdraw his petition, or to allow it to be dismissed, consents to an adjournment, or fails to appear in support of his petition when it is called on in court on the day originally fixed for the hearing, or on a day to which it is adjourned, or

   (c)   appears, but does not apply for an order in the terms of the prayer of his petition.

(2) The court may, on such terms as it thinks just, substitute as petitioner any creditor or contributory who in its opinion would have a right to present a petition, and who is desirous of prosecuting it.

(2A) Where a member State liquidator has been appointed in main proceedings in relation to the company, without prejudice to paragraph (2), the court may, on such terms as it thinks just, substitute the member State liquidator as petitioner, where he is desirous of prosecuting the petition.

(3) An order of the court under this Rule may, where a petitioner fails to advertise his petition within the time prescribed by these Rules, or consents to withdraw his petition, be made at any time.

Notes

R 4.19(1)

Substitution allows a person the carriage of the petition and the court will give directions including an order allowing an amendment and re-verification of the petition. Re-service of the petition will be ordered unless the company appears at the hearing and re-advertisement is dispensed with if the petition was duly advertised earlier. Where one class of petitioner is seeking substitution for a different class of petitioner it is likely that re-advertisement will be ordered (*Re Creative Handbook Ltd* [1985] BCLC 1) unless there is no opposition to the winding up: *Re Commercial and Industrial Insulations Ltd* (1986) 2 BCC 98, 901.

Where a respondent company offers to pay the petition debt it is important for the petitioner to accept payment via third party funds if possible in settlement of the debt. If it is not possible to withdraw the petition (IR 1986 r 4.15), or another creditor learns of the petitioner's consent to a withdrawal or it goes to a hearing, then substitution may occur and if the company has paid off the debt with its own funds, that disposition is void by virtue of IA 1986 s 127: *Re Western Welsh International System Buildings Ltd* (1985) 1 BCC 99, 296. It is to be remembered that when a winding up order is made the commencement of the liquidation is back dated to the date of the presentation of the petition, not the date of substitution: IA 1986 s 129.

R 4.19(2)

Usually an application for substitution occurs at the hearing of the petition. If there are a number of creditors vying for substitution the creditor with the largest undisputed debt will usually be substituted. The discretion of the court is wide and it can even be exercised after a winding up order has been set aside (*Re Goldthorpe & Lacey Ltd* (1987) 3 BCC 595) or to substitute an assignee of the petition debt even though assignment has taken place after the date of the presentation of the petition: *Perak Pioneer Ltd v Petroliam Nasional Bhd* [1986] AC

849. However it is more difficult for one class of petitioner to be substituted for a different class: *Re Xyllyx plc (No 1)* [1992] BCLC 376. In order to obtain substitution as a creditor it is necessary for the applicant to show that it was a creditor at the time of the presentation of the petition: *Re Elgar Heights Pty Ltd* (1985) 3 ACLC 480; *Deputy Commissioner of Taxation v Sun Heating Pty Ltd* (1983) 8 ACLR 314.

R 4.19(3)

Where the petitioner fails to advertise or consents to a withdrawal of the petition an order for substitution does not have to await the hearing of the petition; however it may be difficult to discover whether the petitioner has consented to a withdrawal of the petition prior to an order for withdrawal actually being made under IR 1986 r 4.15.

2.258

4.20 Notice and settling of winding-up order

(1) When a winding-up order has been made, the court shall forthwith give notice of the fact to the official receiver.

(2) The petitioner and every other person who has appeared on the hearing of the petition shall, not later than the business day following that on which the order is made, leave at the court all the documents required for enabling the order to be completed forthwith.

(3) It is not necessary for the court to appoint a venue for any person to attend to settle the order, unless in any particular case the special circumstances make an appointment necessary.

Notes

R 4.20(1)

This rule also applies to a contributory's petition IR 1986 r 4.24.

R 4.20(3)

The standard order is made (IR 1986 Sch 4 Form 4.11) which is often referred to as 'the usual compulsory order'. In the High Court the order is not sealed until eight days after it is made so that an application for recission can be made if relevant within the time period of within seven days of the making of the order: IR 1986 r 7.47(4).

2.259

4.21 Transmission and advertisement of order

(1) When the winding-up order has been made, 3 copies of it, sealed with the seal of the court, shall be sent forthwith by the court to the official receiver.

(2) The official receiver shall cause a sealed copy of the order to be served on the company by prepaid letter addressed to it at its registered office (if any) or, if there is no registered office, at its principal or last known principal place of business

Alternatively, the order may be served on such other person or persons, or in such other manner, as the court directs.

(3) The official receiver shall forward to the registrar of companies the copy of the order which by section 130(1) is directed to be so forwarded by the company.

(4) The official receiver shall forthwith—
  (a) cause the order to be gazetted, and
  (b) advertise the order in such ... newspaper as the official receiver may select.

Notes

R 4.21(1)

This rule also applies to a contributory's petition IR 1986 r 4.24. Where a petition is dismissed an order is not usually drawn up unless it is requested or it contains a costs order.

R 4.21(4)

The requirement to gazette is imposed by CA 1985 s.42, s 711. Until the advertisement of the order appears the company cannot rely on the making of the order against persons who were not actually aware of it: *Official Custodian for Charities v Parway Estates Developments Ltd* [1985] Ch 151.

2.260

4.21A Expenses of voluntary arrangement

Where a winding-up order is made and there is at the time of the presentation of the petition in force for the company a voluntary arrangement under Part I of the Act, any expenses properly incurred as expenses of the administration of the arrangement in question shall be a first charge on the company's assets.

Notes

R 4.21A

The charge will only arise if there is no trust of the assets in favour of the creditors in the voluntary arrangement upon termination/discharge of the voluntary arrangement; if there is such a trust then the assets remain dedicated to the creditors in the voluntary arrangement rather than being passed to the liquidator *Re NT Gallagher & Sons Ltd* [2002] BPIR 56].

This rule also applies to a contributory's petition: IR 1986 r 4.24.

Chapter 4
Petition by Contributories (No CVL Application)

2.261

4.22 Presentation and service of petition

(1) The petition shall specify the grounds on which it is presented ... and shall be filed in court with one copy for service under this Rule.

(1A) No petition shall be filed unless there is produced with it the receipt for the deposit payable on presentation.

(2) The court shall fix a hearing for a day ('the return day') on which, unless the court otherwise directs, the petitioner and the company shall attend before the registrar in chambers for directions to be given in relation to the procedure on the petition.

(3) On fixing the return day, the court shall return to the petitioner a sealed copy of the petition for service, endorsed with the return day and time of hearing.

(4) The petitioner shall, at least 14 days before the return day, serve a sealed copy of the petition on the company.

(5) Where a member State liquidator has been appointed in main proceedings in relation to the company, the petitioner shall send a copy of the petition to him.

Notes

R 4.22(1)

Usually a contributory's petition relies on the 'just and equitable' ground for winding up arising from a shareholders' dispute: IA 1986 s 122(1)(g). The petition is not supported by an affidavit/witness statement on filing. IR 1986 r 4.7–4.21A do not apply to a petition presented by a contributory: see heading to Chapter 3.

R 4.22(1A)

The deposit is currently £655 and it is generally returned if the petition is dismissed or withdrawn: Insolvency Proceedings (Fees) Order 2004 (SI 593/2004) art 6.

R 4.22(2)

The directions are given by a district judge in a district registry Practice Direction: Insolvency Proceedings, Civil Procedure, Vol 2 Sect 3E para 5.2Directions are made by the registrar or district judge in chambers.

R 4.22(4)

It is in the court's discretion on the return day to direct that other parties should be served with a copy of the petition: IR 1986 r 4.23(2). It is regarded as an abuse of process for the petitioner to inform creditors and/or third parties of the petition's existence without an order of the court: *Re Doreen Boards Ltd* [1996] 1 BCLC 501.

2.262

4.23 Return of petition

(1) On the return day, or at any time after it, the court shall give such directions as it thinks appropriate with respect to the following matters—
- (a) service of the petition, whether in connection with the venue for a further hearing, or for any other purpose;
- (b) whether particulars of claim and defence are to be delivered, and generally as to the procedure on the petition;
- (c) whether and if so by what means, the petition is to be advertised;

(d) the manner in which any evidence is to be adduced at any hearing before the judge and in particular (but without prejudice to the generality of the above) as to—
    (i) the taking of evidence wholly or in part by affidavit or orally;
    (ii) the cross-examination of any deponents to affidavits;
    (iii) the matters to be dealt with in evidence;
(e) any other matter affecting the procedure on the petition or in connection with the hearing and disposal of the petition.

(2) In giving directions under paragraph (1)(a), the court shall have regard to whether any of the persons specified in Rule 4.10 should be served with a copy of the petition.

Notes

R 4.23(1)

The parties should attempt to agree directions prior to the return day so that all necessary directions can be made on that occasion. However, the parties can apply to court for further directions following the return day. It is important to obtain a direction for particulars/points of claim and subsequent statements of case on the return day rather than progressing the proceedings by way of contested affidavit/witness statement evidence: *Re a Company (No 005134 of 1986) ex p Harries* [1989] BCLC 383, 390(g) per Peter Gibson LJ. It is also important to ensure by the return day that the respondent members are aware that they are not allowed to use company monies to defend the petition. If they refuse to give a suitable undertaking an injunction can be obtained: *Re a Company (No 004502 of 1988) ex p Johnson* [1991] BCC 234; *Corbett v Corbett* [1998] BCC 93. The company may only pay for the costs of matters directly concerning the company, for instance disclosure obligations and validation applications (IA 1986 s 127) if required: *Re Milgate Developments Ltd* [1991] BCC 24.

R 4.23(2)

On the return day it may become apparent that parties other than the company should be served with a copy of the petition.

2.263

4.24 Application of Rules in Chapter 3

The following Rules in Chapter 3 apply, with the necessary modifications—
Rule 4.16 (notice of appearance);
Rule 4.17 (list of appearances);
Rule 4.20 (notice and settling of winding-up order);...
Rule 4.21 (transmission and advertisement of order)[; and
Rule 4.21A (expenses of voluntary arrangement)].

The First Group of Parts
Company Insolvency; Companies Winding Up

Part 4
Companies Winding Up

Chapter 5
Provisional Liquidator (No CVL Application)

2.264

4.25 Appointment of provisional liquidator

(1) An application to the court for the appointment of a provisional liquidator under section 135 may be made by—
- (a) the petitioner;
- (b) a creditor of the company;
- (c) a contributory;
- (d) the company;
- (e) the Secretary of State;
- (f) a temporary administrator;
- (g) a member State liquidator appointed in main proceedings; or
- (h) any person who under any enactment would be entitled to present a petition for the winding up of the company.

(2) The application must be supported by an affidavit stating—
- (a) the grounds on which it is proposed that a provisional liquidator should be appointed;
- (b) if some person other than the official receiver is proposed to be appointed, that the person has consented to act and, to the best of the applicant's belief, is qualified to act as an insolvency practitioner in relation to the company;
- (c) whether or not the official receiver has been informed of the application and, if so, has been furnished with a copy of it;
- (d) whether to the applicant's knowledge—
  - (i) there has been proposed or is in force for the company a voluntary arrangement under Part I of the Act, or
  - (ii) an administrator or administrative receiver is acting in relation to the company, or
  - (iii) a liquidator has been appointed for its voluntary winding up; and
- (e) the applicant's estimate of the value of the assets in respect of which the provisional liquidator is to be appointed.

(3) The applicant shall send copies of the application and of the affidavit in support to the official receiver, who may attend the hearing and make any representations which he thinks appropriate.

If for any reason it is not practicable to comply with this paragraph, the official receiver must be informed of the application in sufficient time for him to be able to attend.

(4) The court may on the application, if satisfied that sufficient grounds are shown for the appointment, make it on such terms as it thinks fit.

Notes

R 4.25(1)

An application for the appointment of a provisional liquidator whose function will generally be to safeguard assets of the company which are perceived to be in jeopardy until a winding up order has been made and a liquidator appointed see IA 1986 s 135; *Re Namco UK Ltd* [2003] 2 [BCLC] 78; *MHMH Ltd v Carwood Barker Holdings Ltd [2005] BCC 536)* may be made by the company itself or any of the persons listed.

IR 1986 r 4.25(1) was substituted with effect from 31 May 2002 subject to certain savings for anything done prior to that date: Insolvency (Amendment) Rules 2002 (SI 2002/1307).

R 4.25(2)

The application should be made a to a Judge of the Companies Court and (unless the court otherwise orders) is heard in public: Practice Direction: Insolvency Proceedings, Civil Procedure 2006, Vol 2 Sect 3E para 5.1(4). The application (if made by, for example, the Secretary of State or a creditor) may be made without notice to the company and its directors and shareholders, but the official receiver must be put on notice.

2.265

4.25A Notice of Appointment

(1) Where a provisional liquidator has been appointed the court shall forthwith give notice of the fact to the official receiver.

(2) A copy of that notice shall at the same time be sent by the court to the provisional liquidator where he is not the official receiver.

2.266

4.26 Order of appointment

(1) The order appointing the provisional liquidator shall specify the functions to be carried out by him in relation to the company's affairs.

(2) The court shall, forthwith after the order is made, send sealed copies of the order as follows—
    (a)   if the official receiver is appointed, three copies to him;
    (b)   if a person other than the official receiver is appointed—
        (i)   three copies to that person, and
        (ii) one copy to the official receiver;
    (c)   if there is an administrative receiver acting in relation to the company, one copy to him.

(3) Of the three copies of the order sent to the official receiver under paragraph (2)(a), or to another person under paragraph (2)(b)(i)—
        (i)   one shall in each case be sent by the recipient to the company, or if a liquidator has been appointed for the company's voluntary winding-up, to him; and

> (ii) one shall be sent with Form 4.15A to the registrar of companies.

Notes

R 4.26

The powers of a provisional liquidator will typically include powers to enter the company's premises, take possession of assets, and authority to give instructions to, for example, its bankers, but they may be more limited. In *Re Goodwill Merchant Financial Services Ltd* [2001] 1 BCLC 259 the court gave authority to the provisional liquidator to dispose of assets but subject to obtaining leave of the court. It refused to authorise the provisional liquidators to draw their remuneration. It may also be useful to ask the court for a specific power to initiate proceedings in the name of the company if it is intended to recover assets. This rule was the subject of minor amendments under Insolvency (Amendment) Rules 2005 (SI 2005/527).

2.267

4.27 Deposit

(1) Before an order appointing the official receiver as provisional liquidator is issued, the applicant for it shall deposit with him, or otherwise secure to his satisfaction, such sum as the court directs to cover the official receiver's remuneration and expenses.

(2) If the sum deposited or secured subsequently proves to be insufficient, the court may, on application by the official receiver, order that an additional sum be deposited or secured. If the order is not complied with within 2 days after service of it on the person to whom it is directed, the court may discharge the order appointing the provisional liquidator.

(3) If a winding-up order is made after a provisional liquidator has been appointed, any money deposited under this Rule shall (unless it is required by reason of insufficiency of assets for payment of remuneration and expenses of the provisional liquidator) be repaid to the person depositing it (or as that person may direct) out of the assets, in the prescribed order of priority.

Notes

R 4.27

The amount of the deposit required is likely to depend on the official receiver's view as to the likely costs and expenses of the provisional liquidation.

2.268

4.28 Security

(1) The following applies where an insolvency practitioner is appointed to be provisional liquidator under section 135.

(2) The cost of providing the security required under the Act shall be paid in the first instance by the provisional liquidator; but—
- (a) if a winding-up order is not made, the person so appointed is entitled to be reimbursed out of the property of the company, and the court may make an order on the company accordingly, and
- (b) if a winding-up order is made, he is entitled to be reimbursed out of the assets in the prescribed order of priority.

Notes

R 4.28(2)(b)

As to the prescribed order of priority see IR 1986 r 4.218(1)(e) below.

2.269

4.29 Failure to give or keep up security

(1) If the provisional liquidator fails to give or keep up his security, the court may remove him, and make such order as it thinks fit as to costs.

(2) If an order is made under this Rule removing the provisional liquidator, or discharging the order appointing him, the court shall give directions as to whether any, and if so what, steps should be taken for the appointment of another person in his place.

2.270

4.30 Remuneration

(1) The remuneration of the provisional liquidator (other than the official receiver) shall be fixed by the court from time to time on his application.

(2) In fixing his remuneration, the court shall take into account—
- (a) the time properly given by him (as provisional liquidator) and his staff in attending to the company's affairs;
- (b) the complexity (or otherwise) of the case;
- (c) any respects in which, in connection with the company's affairs, there falls on the provisional liquidator any responsibility of an exceptional kind or degree;
- (d) the effectiveness with which the provisional liquidator appears to be carrying out, or to have carried out, his duties; and
- (e) the value and nature of the property with which he has to deal.

(3) Without prejudice to any order the court may make as to costs, the provisional liquidator's remuneration (whether the official receiver or another) shall be paid to him, and the amount of any expenses incurred by him (including the remuneration and expenses of any special manager appointed under section 177) reimbursed—
- (a) if a winding-up order is not made, out of the property of the company, and
- (b) if a winding-up order is made, out of the assets, in the prescribed order of priority,

or, in either case (the relevant funds being insufficient), out of the deposit under Rule 4.27.

(3A) Unless the court otherwise directs, in a case falling within paragraph (3)(a) above the provisional liquidator may retain out of the company's property such sums or property as are or may be required for meeting his remuneration and expenses.

(4) Where a person other than the official receiver has been appointed provisional liquidator, and the official receiver has taken any steps for the purpose of obtaining a statement of affairs or has performed any other duty under the Rules, he shall pay the official receiver such sum (if any) as the court may direct.

Notes

R 4.30(1)

The court may order that the petitioner pays the remuneration of the provisional liquidator instead of being met out of company assets (*Re Secure & Provide plc* [1992] BCC 405) where it is not satisfied after an on notice hearing that the evidence in support of the appointment was sufficient: *cf Re Walter L Jacob & Co Ltd* (1987) 3 BCC 532 (court refused to order the petitioning creditor to pay the provisional liquidator's remuneration although the petition was ultimately dismissed)

R 4.30(3)(b)

Provision is made in IR 1986 r 4.218, which governs priorities of expenses and costs in a liquidation, for the remuneration of a provisional liquidator, but no provision is made for expenses incurred by him. In *Re Grey Marlin Ltd* [2000] BCC 410, it was held that the provisional liquidator's expenses of preserving, realising or getting in any of the assets of the company should have priority to the expenses and costs referred to in IR 1986 r 4.218(1)(a) (being the liquidator's expenses of preserving etc the company's assets) but should come after tax liabilities that had been incurred in order to preserve the company's business.

In *Re Independent Insurance Co Ltd* [2002] 2 BCLC 709 it was directed that an assessor should be appointed (pursuant to s 70 of the Supreme Court Act 1981 and r 35.15 of the CPR) to consider the remuneration of provisional liquidators in a 'mega-insolvency'. In the event the remuneration claimed was reduced by only a very small amount: see *Re Independent Insurance Co Ltd (No 2)* [2003] 1 BCLC 640. In assessing the remuneration payable to a provisional liquidator regard must now be had to the Practice Statement – the Fixing and Approval of the Remuneration of Appointees [2004] BPIR 953 which came into effect on 1 October 2004.

2.271

4.31 Termination of appointment

(1) The appointment of the provisional liquidator may be terminated by the court on his application, or on that of any of the persons specified in Rule 4.25(1).

(2) If the provisional liquidator's appointment terminates, in consequence of the dismissal of the winding-up petition or otherwise, the court may give such directions as it thinks fit with respect to the accounts of his administration or any other matters which it thinks appropriate.

> (3) ...

Notes

R 4.31

As to the exercise of the court's powers to make orders in respect of the remuneration of a provisional liquidator whose appointment was terminated prior to the hearing of the winding up petition, see *Alipour v UOC Corporation* [1998] BCC 191.

Chapter 6
Statement of Affairs and other Information

2.272

4.32 Notice requiring statement of affairs (No CVL Application)

(1) The following applies where the official receiver determines to require a statement of the company's affairs to be made out and submitted to him in accordance with section 131.

(2) He shall send notice to each of the persons whom he considers should be made responsible under that section, requiring them to prepare and submit the statement.

(3) The persons to whom that notice is sent are referred to in this Chapter as 'the deponents'.

(4) The notice shall inform each of the deponents—
  (a) of the names and addresses of all others (if any) to whom the same notice has been sent;
  (b) of the time within which the statement must be delivered;
  (c) of the effect of section 131(7) (penalty for non-compliance); and
  (d) of the application to him, and to each of the other deponents, of section 235 (duty to provide information, and to attend on the official receiver if required).

(5) The official receiver shall, on request, furnish a deponent with instructions for the preparation of the statement and with the forms required for that purpose.

Notes

R 4.32

Following a winding-up order it is the invariable practice of the official receiver to require a statement of affairs verified by affidavit (as envisaged by IA 1986 s 131, and in Form 4.17 as required by IR 1986 r 4.33 below) from the directors, or former directors, in order that he has sufficient information about the company's affairs to make decisions as to the future conduct of the liquidation.

2.273

4.33 Verification and filing (No CVL Application)

(1) The statement of affairs shall be in Form 4.17, shall contain all the particulars required by that form and shall be verified by affidavit by the deponents (using the same form).

(2) The official receiver may require any of the persons mentioned in section 131(3) to submit an affidavit of concurrence, stating that he concurs in the statement of affairs.

(3) An affidavit of concurrence made under paragraph (2) may be qualified in respect of matters dealt with in the statement of affairs, where the maker of the affidavit is not in agreement with the deponents, or he considers the statement to be erroneous or misleading, or he is without the direct knowledge necessary for concurring in the statement.

(4) The statement of affairs shall be delivered to the official receiver by the deponent making the affidavit of verification (or by one of them, if more than one), together with a copy of the verified statement.

(5) Every affidavit of concurrence shall be delivered to the official receiver by the person who makes it, together with a copy.

(6) The official receiver shall file the verified copy of the statement and the affidavits of concurrence (if any) in court.

(7) The affidavit may be sworn before an official receiver or a deputy official receiver, or before an officer of the Department or the court duly authorised in that behalf.

Notes

R 4.33

Verification must be by way of affidavit rather than witness statement: IR 1986 r 7.57(6).

2.274

4.34 Statement of affairs—CVL

(1) This Rule applies with respect to the statement of affairs made out by the liquidator under section 95(3) or (as the case may be) by the directors under section 99(1).

(2) Where it is made out by the liquidator, the statement of affairs shall be delivered by him to the registrar of companies within 7 days after the creditors' meeting summoned under section 95(2).

(3) Where it is made out by the directors under section 99(1) the statement of affairs shall be delivered by them to the liquidator in office following the creditors' meeting summoned under section 98 forthwith after that meeting has been held; and he shall, within 7 days, deliver it to the registrar of companies.

> (4) A statement of affairs under section 99(1) may be made up to a date not more than 14 days before that on which the resolution for voluntary winding up is passed by the company.

Notes

R 4.34

In the case of a creditors' voluntary liquidation (as opposed to a compulsory liquidation), the statement of affairs will either have been prepared by the liquidator already appointed (IA 1986 s 95(3)); or by the directors: IA 1986 s 99(1).

2.275

4.34A Copy Statement of affairs—CVL

Where a liquidator is nominated by the company at a general meeting held on a day prior to that on which the creditors' meeting summoned under section 98 is held, the directors shall forthwith after his nomination or the making of the statement of affairs, whichever is the later, deliver to him a copy of the statement of affairs.

2.276

4.35 Limited disclosure (No CVL Application)

(1) Where the official receiver thinks that it would prejudice the conduct of the liquidation for the whole or part of the statement of affairs to be disclosed, he may apply to the court for an order of limited disclosure in respect of the statement, or any specified part of it.

(2) The court may on the application order that the statement or, as the case may be, the specified part of it be not filed, or that it is to be filed separately and not be open to inspection otherwise than with leave of the court.

Notes

R 4.35

An application by the official receiver for limited disclosure of the statement of affairs (or part of it) may be made to the court manager of the Companies Court pursuant to the provisions of IR 1986 r 13.2(2) below: see Practice Direction: Insolvency Proceedings, Civil Procedure 2006, Vol 2 Sect 3E para 5.4(5).

2.277

4.36 Release from duty to submit statement of affairs; extension of time (No CVL Application)

(1) The power of the official receiver under section 131(5) to give a release from the obligation imposed by that section, or to grant an

extension of time, may be exercised at the official receiver's own discretion, or at the request of any deponent.

(2) A deponent may, if he requests a release or extension of time and it is refused by the official receiver, apply to the court for it.

(3) The court may, if it thinks that no sufficient cause is shown for the application, dismiss it; but it shall not do so unless the applicant has had an opportunity to attend the court for an *ex parte* hearing, of which he has been given at least 7 days' notice.

If the application is not dismissed under this paragraph, the court shall fix a venue for it to be heard, and give notice to the deponent accordingly.

(4) The deponent shall, at least 14 days before the hearing, send to the official receiver a notice stating the venue and accompanied by a copy of the application, and of any evidence which he (the deponent) intends to adduce in support of it.

(5) The official receiver may appear and be heard on the application; and, whether or not he appears, he may file a written report of any matters which he considers ought to be drawn to the court's attention.

If such a report is filed, a copy of it shall be sent by the official receiver to the deponent, not later than 5 days before the hearing.

(6) Sealed copies of any order made on the application shall be sent by the court to the deponent and the official receiver.

(7) On any application under this Rule the applicant's costs shall be paid in any event by him and, unless the court otherwise orders, no allowance towards them shall be made out of the assets.

Notes

R 4.36

This rule deals with the official receiver's discretionary power either to release the company's officers or employees from the obligation to submit a statement of affairs, or to grant an extension of time for the submission of that document. If a request for release or an extension of time is refused by the official receiver, then application may be made to the court in accordance with the procedure prescribed in sub-paragraphs (3)–(7).

2.278

4.37 Expenses of statement of affairs (No CVL Application)

(1) If any deponent cannot himself prepare a proper statement of affairs, the official receiver may, at the expense of the assets, employ some person or persons to assist in the preparation of the statement.

(2) At the request of any deponent, made on the grounds that he cannot himself prepare a proper statement, the official receiver may authorise an allowance, payable out of the assets, towards expenses to be incurred by the deponent in employing some person or persons to assist him in preparing it.

(3) Any such request by the deponent shall be accompanied by an estimate of the expenses involved; and the official receiver shall only authorise the employment of a named person or a named firm, being in either case approved by him.

(4) An authorisation given by the official receiver under this Rule shall be subject to such conditions (if any) as he thinks fit to impose with respect to the manner in which any person may obtain accessto relevant books and papers.

(5) Nothing in this Rule relieves a deponent from any obligation with respect to the preparation, verification and submission of the statement of affairs, or to the provision of information to the official receiver or the liquidator.

(6) Any payment out of the assets under this Rule shall be made in the prescribed order of priority.

(7) Paragraphs (2) to (6) of this Rule may be applied, on application to the official receiver by any deponent, in relation to the making of an affidavit of concurrence.

Notes

R 4.37

Since the preparation of a statement of affairs may require, for example, accounting expertise, the official receiver is empowered to provide assistance to the person obliged to prepare it.

R 4.37(6)

As to the prescribed order of priority: IR 1986 r 4.218(1)(k) below.

2.279

4.38 Expenses of statement of affairs—CVL

(1) Payment may be made out of the company's assets, either before or after the commencement of the winding up, of any reasonable and necessary expenses of preparing the statement of affairs under section 99.

Any such payment is an expense of the liquidation.

(2) Where such a payment is made before the commencement of the winding up, the director presiding at the creditors' meeting held under section 98 shall inform the meeting of the amount of the payment and the identity of the person to whom it was made.

(3) The liquidator appointed under section 100 may make such a payment (subject to the next paragraph); but if there is a liquidation committee, he must give the committee at least 7 days' notice of his intention to make it.

(4) Such a payment shall not be made by the liquidator to himself, or to any associate of his, otherwise than with the approval of the liquidation committee, the creditors, or the court.

(5) This Rule is without prejudice to the powers of the court under Rule 4.219 (voluntary winding up superseded by winding up by the court).

Notes

R 4.38

Under IA 1986 s 99, the obligation to prepare the statement of affairs is imposed on the directors of the company and it must be verified by some or all of the directors: IA 1986 s 99(2). As to the prescribed order of priority of payment of the reasonable and necessary expenses of preparing a statement of affairs (in a case, for example, where the directors require professional assistance), see IR 1986 r 4.218(1)(k) below.

2.280

4.39 Submission of accounts (No CVL Application)

(1) Any of the persons specified in section 235(3) shall, at the request of the official receiver, furnish him with accounts of the company of such nature, as at such date, and for such period, as he may specify.

(2) The period specified may begin from a date up to 3 years preceding the date of the presentation of the winding-up petition, or from an earlier date to which audited accounts of the company were last prepared.

(3) The court may, on the official receiver's application, require accounts for any earlier period.

(4) Rule 4.37 applies (with the necessary modifications) in relation to accounts to be furnished under this Rule as it applies in relation to the statement of affairs.

(5) The accounts shall, if the official receiver so requires, be verified by affidavit and (whether or not so verified) delivered to him within 21 days of the request under paragraph (1), or such longer period as he may allow.

(6) Two copies of the accounts and (where required) the affidavit shall be delivered to the official receiver by whoever is required to furnish them; and the official receiver shall file one copy in court (with the affidavit, if any).

Notes

R 4.39

The official receiver will consider making a request pursuant to the provisions of this rule in cases where there has been a failure on the part of those responsible for the management of the company to comply with the statutory obligations to keep proper accounting records (see CA 1985 s 221) and to prepare annual accounts: see CA 1985 s 226.

2.281

4.40 Submission of accounts—CVL

(1) Any of the persons specified in section 235(3) shall, at the request of the liquidator, furnish him with accounts of the company of such nature, as at such date, and for such period, as he may specify.

(2) The specified period for the accounts may begin from a date up to 3 years preceding the date of the resolution for winding up, or from an earlier date to which audited accounts of the company were last prepared.

(3) The accounts shall, if the liquidator so requires, be verified by affidavit and (whether or not so verified) delivered to him, with the affidavit if required, within 21 days from the request under paragraph (1), or such longer period as he may allow.

2.282

4.41 Expenses of preparing accounts—CVL

(1) Where a person is required under Rule 4.40—CVL to furnish accounts, the liquidator may, with the sanction of the liquidation committee (if there is one) and at the expense of the assets, employ some person or persons to assist in the preparation of the accounts.

(2) At the request of the person subject to the requirement, the liquidator may, with that sanction, authorise an allowance, payable out of the assets, towards expenses to be incurred by that person in employing others to assist him in preparing the accounts.

(3) Any such request shall be accompanied by an estimate of the expenses involved; and the liquidator shall only authorise the employment of a named person or a named firm, being in either case approved by him.

Notes

R 4.41

As to the prescribed order of priority of payment of expenses of obtaining assistance for the preparation of accounts, see IR 1986 r 4.218(1)(k).

2.283

4.42 Further disclosure (No CVL Application)

(1) The official receiver may at any time require the deponents, or any one or more of them, to submit (in writing) further information amplifying, modifying or explaining any matter contained in the statement of affairs, or in accounts submitted in pursuance of the Act or the Rules.

(2) The information shall, if the official receiver so directs, be verified by affidavit, and (whether or not so verified) delivered to him within 21 days of the requirement under paragraph (1), or such longer period as he may allow.

(3) Two copies of the documents containing the information and (where verification is directed) the affidavit shall be delivered by the deponent to the official receiver, who shall file one copy in court (with the affidavit, if any).

Notes

R 4.42

A request for further disclosure may follow the submission of a statement of affairs (as to which see IA 1986 s 131, and IR 1986 r 4.32, 4,33) or accounts (IR 1986 r 4.39) previously requested by the official receiver.

Chapter 7
Information to Creditors and Contributories

2.284

4.43 Reports by official receiver (No CVL Application)

(1) The official receiver shall, at least once after the making of the winding-up order, send a report to creditors and contributories with respect to the proceedings in the winding up, and the state of the company's affairs.

(1A) The official receiver shall also include in the report under paragraph (1)—
    (a)   to the best of his knowledge and belief—
        (i)   an estimate of the value of the prescribed part (whether or not he proposes to make an application to the court under section 176A(5) or section 176A(3) applies);
        (ii) an estimate of the value of the company's net property; and
    (b)   whether, and if so, why, he proposes to make an application to court under section 176A(5).

(1B) Nothing in this Rule is to be taken as requiring any such estimate to include any information, the disclosure of which could seriously prejudice the commercial interests of the company. If such information is excluded from the calculation the estimate shall be accompanied by a statement to that effect.

(2) The official receiver shall file in court a copy of any report sent under this Chapter.

2.285

4.44 Meaning of 'creditors'

Any reference in this Chapter to creditors is to creditors of the company who are known to the official receiver or (as the case may be) the

> liquidator or, where a statement of the company's affairs has been submitted, are identified in the statement.

Notes

IR 4.44

There is no all -embracing definition of 'creditors' under IA 1986; rather, there are several definitions for different purposes within the insolvency legislation: see for example, IA 1986 ss 248, 383 and IR 1986 rr 12.3 and 13.12.

2.286

4.45 Report where statement of affairs lodged (No CVL Application)

(1) Where a statement of affairs has been submitted and filed in court, the official receiver shall send out to creditors and contributories a report containing a summary of the statement [(if he thinks fit, as amplified, modified or explained by virtue of Rule 4.42)] and such observations (if any) as he thinks fit to make with respect to it, or to the affairs of the company in general.

(2) The official receiver need not comply with paragraph (1) if he has previously reported to creditors and contributories with respect to the company's affairs (so far as known to him) and he is of opinion that there are no additional matters which ought to be brought to their attention.

2.287

4.46 Statement of affairs dispensed with (No CVL Application)

(1) This Rule applies where, in the company's case, release from the obligation to submit a statement of affairs has been granted by the official receiver or the court.

(2) As soon as may be after the release has been granted, the official receiver shall send to creditors and contributories a report containing a summary of the company's affairs (so far as within his knowledge), and his observations (if any) with respect to it, or to the affairs of the company in general.

(3) The official receiver need not comply with paragraph (2) if he has previously reported to creditors and contributories with respect to the company's affairs (so far as known to him) and he is of opinion that there are no additional matters which ought to be brought to their attention.

2.288

4.47 General rule as to reporting (No CVL Application)

(1) The court may, on the official receiver's application, relieve him of any duty imposed on him by this Chapter, or authorise him to carry out the duty in a way other than there required.

(2) In considering whether to act under this Rule, the court shall have regard to the cost of carrying out the duty, to the amount of the assets available, and to the extent of the interest of creditors or contributories, or any particular class of them.

2.289

4.48 Winding up stayed (No CVL Application)

(1) If proceedings in the winding up are stayed by order of the court, any duty of the official receiver to send reports under the preceding Rules in this Chapter ceases.

(2) Where the court grants a stay, it may include in its order such requirements on the company as it thinks fit with a view to bringing the stay to the notice of creditors and contributories.

Notes

IR 4.48(1)

A stay is granted under IA 1986 s 147 and it may be granted either 'altogether', which effectively means that the company is returned to the control of the directors, or for a 'limited time'.

2.290

4.49 Information to creditors and contributories—CVL

(1) The liquidator shall, within 28 days of a meeting held under section 95 or 98, send to creditors and contributories of the company—
    (a)   a copy or summary of the statement of affairs, and
    (b)   a report of the proceedings at the meeting.

(2) The report under paragraph (1) shall also include—
    (a)   to the best of the liquidator's knowledge and belief—
        (i)   an estimate of the value of the prescribed part (whether or not he proposes to make an application to court under section 176A(5) or section 176A(3) applies); and
        (ii)   an estimate of the value of the company's net property; and
    (b)   whether, and if so, why, the liquidator proposes to make an application to court under section 176A(5).

(3) Nothing in this Rule is to be taken as requiring any such estimate to include any information, the disclosure of which could seriously prejudice the commercial interests of the company. If such information is excluded from the calculation the estimate shall be accompanied by a statement to that effect.

Notes

IR 4.49(2)

In particular the report must give the required details relating to the 'prescribed part' set aside for unsecured creditors under IA 1986 s 176A.

2.291

4.49A Further information where liquidation follows administration

Where under section 140 the court appoints as the company's liquidator a person who was formerly its administrator or a person is appointed as liquidator upon the registration of a notice under paragraph 83(3) of Schedule B1 to the Act and that person becomes aware of creditors not formerly known to him in his capacity as administrator, he shall send to those creditors a copy of any statement or report sent by him to creditors under Rule 2.33, so noted as to indicate that it is being sent under this Rule.

Notes

IR 4.49A

This provision deals with both the pre–15th September 2003 (IA 1986 ss 8–27) and post–15th September 2003 (IA 1986 Sch B1) administration regimes.

Chapter 8
Meetings of Creditors and Contributories

Section A: Rules of General Application

2.292

4.50 First meetings (No CVL Application)

(1) If under section 136(5) the official receiver decides to summon meetings of the company's creditors and contributories for the purpose of nominating a person to be liquidator in place of himself, he shall fix a venue for each meeting, in neither case more than 4 months from the date of the winding-up order.

(2) When for each meeting a venue has been fixed, notice of the meetings shall be given to the court and—
  (a) in the case of the creditors' meeting, to every creditor who is known to the official receiver or is identified in the company's statement of affairs; and
  (b) in the case of the contributories' meeting, to every person appearing (by the company's books or otherwise) to be a contributory of the company.

(3) Notice to the court shall be given forthwith, and the other notices shall be given at least 21 days before the date fixed for each meeting respectively.

(4) The notice to creditors shall specify a time and date, not more than 4 days before the date fixed for the meeting, by which they must lodge proofs and (if applicable) proxies, in order to be entitled to vote at the meeting; and the same applies in respect of contributories and their proxies.

(5) Notice of the meetings shall also be given by public advertisement.

(6) Where the official receiver receives a request by creditors under section 136(5)(c) for meetings of creditors and contributories to be summoned, and it appears to him that the request is properly made in accordance with the Act, he shall—

    (a)   withdraw any notices previously given by him under section 136(5)(b) (that he has decided not to summon such meetings),

    (b)   fix the venue of each meeting for not more than 3 months from his receipt of the creditors' request, and

    (c)   act in accordance with paragraphs (2) to (5) above, as if he had decided under section 136 to summon the meetings.

(7) Meetings summoned by the official receiver under this Rule are known respectively as 'the first meeting of creditors' and 'the first meeting of contributories', and jointly as 'the first meetings in the liquidation'.

(8) Where the company is [an authorised deposit-taker or a former authorised deposit-taker], additional notices are required by Rule 4.72.

Notes

R 4.50

The rules in this chapter deal with the mechanics of meetings of creditors and contributories. 'Creditors' are not comprehensively defined for the purpose of winding up but reference can be made to IR 1986 r 13.12; 'contributories' are defined by IA 1986 s 79.

R 4.50(1)

The official receiver has a discretion whether or not to summon meetings: IA 1986 s 136(5).

2.293

4.51 First meeting of creditors—CVL

(1) This Rule applies in the case of a meeting of creditors summoned by the liquidator under section 95 (where, in what starts as a members' voluntary winding up, he forms the opinion that the company will be unable to pay its debts) or a meeting under section 98 (first meeting of creditors in a creditors' voluntary winding up).

(2) The notice summoning the meeting shall state the name of the company and the registered number of the company, and] specify a venue for the meeting and the time (not earlier than 12.00 hours on the business day before the day fixed for the meeting) by which, and the place at which, creditors must lodge any proxies necessary to entitle them to vote at the meeting.

(3) Where the company is an authorised deposit-taker or a former authorised deposit-taker, additional notices are required by Rule 4.72.

Notes

R 4.51(2)

Minor amendments were made to this provision by Insolvency (Amendment) Rules 2005 SI 2005/527.

2.294

4.52 Business at first meetings in the liquidation (No CVL Application)

(1) At the first meeting of creditors, no resolutions shall be taken other than the following—
- (a) a resolution to appoint a named insolvency practitioner to be liquidator, or two or more insolvency practitioners as joint liquidators;
- (b) a resolution to establish a liquidation committee;
- (c) (unless it has been resolved to establish a liquidation committee) a resolution specifying the terms on which the liquidator is to be remunerated, or to defer consideration of that matter;
- (d) (if, and only if, two or more persons are appointed to act jointly as liquidator) a resolution specifying whether acts are to be done by both or all of them, or by only one;
- (e) (where the meeting has been requisitioned under section 136), a resolution authorising payment out of the assets, as an expense of the liquidation, of the cost of summoning and holding the meeting and any meeting of contributories so requisitioned and held;
- (f) a resolution to adjourn the meeting for not more than 3 weeks;
- (g) any other resolution which the chairman thinks it right to allow for special reasons.

(2) The same applies as regards the first meeting of contributories, but that meeting shall not pass any resolution to the effect of paragraph (1)(c) or (e).

(3) At neither meeting shall any resolution be proposed which has for its object the appointment of the official receiver as liquidator.

2.295

4.53 Business at meeting under s 95 or 98—CVL

Rule 4.52(1), except sub-paragraph (e), applies to a creditors' meeting under section 95 or 98.

2.296

4.53A Effect of adjournment of company meeting—CVL

Where a company meeting at which a resolution for voluntary winding up is to be proposed is adjourned, any resolution passed at a meeting under section 98 held before the holding of the adjourned company meeting only has effect on and from the passing by the company of a resolution for winding up.

Notes

R 4.53A

This presupposes that the meeting of members was quorate and properly adjourned; without the relevant members' resolution the company is not in voluntary liquidation and in that event the meeting of creditors would not be a meeting pursuant to IA 1986 s 98.

2.297

4.53B Report by director, etc—CVL

(1) At any meeting held under section 98 where the statement of affairs laid before the meeting does not state the company's affairs as at the date of the meeting, the directors of the company shall cause to be made to the meeting, either by the director presiding at the meeting or by another person with knowledge of the relevant matters, a report (written or oral) on any material transactions relating to the company occurring between the date of the making of the statement of affairs and that of the meeting.

(2) Any such report shall be recorded in the minutes of the meeting kept under Rule 4.71.

Notes

R 4.53B

This provision is intended to avoid the practical problem created by the fact that a statement of affairs may well be produced before the IA 1986 s 98 creditors' meeting, at a time when the status of the company concerned may be changing daily.

2.298

4.54 General power to call meetings

(1) The official receiver or the liquidator may at any time summon and conduct meetings of creditors or of contributories for the purpose of ascertaining their wishes in all matters relating to the liquidation; and in relation to any meeting summoned under the Act or the Rules, the person summoning it is referred to as 'the convener'.

(2) When (in either case) a venue for the meeting has been fixed, notice of it shall be given by the convener—

    (a)   in the case of a creditors' meeting, to every creditor who is known to him or is identified in the company's statement of affairs; and

    (b)   in the case of a meeting of contributories, to every person appearing (by the company's books or otherwise) to be a contributory of the company.

(3) Notice of the meeting shall be given at least 21 days before the date fixed for it, and shall specify the purpose of the meeting.

(4) The notice shall specify a time and date, not more than 4 days before the date fixed for the meeting, by which, and the place at which, creditors must lodge proofs and proxies, in order to be entitled to vote at the meeting; and the same applies in respect of contributories and their proxies.

(NO CVL APPLICATION)

(5–CVL) The notice shall specify a time and date, not more than 4 days before that fixed for the meeting, by which, and the place at which, creditors (if not individuals attending in person) must lodge proxies, in order to be entitled to vote at the meeting.

(6) Additional notice of the meeting may be given by public advertisement if the convener thinks fit, and shall be so given if the court orders.

2.299

4.55 The chairman at meetings (**No CVL Application**)

(1) This Rule applies both to a meeting of creditors and to a meeting of contributories.

(2) Where the convener of the meeting is the official receiver, he, or a person nominated by him, shall be chairman.

A nomination under this paragraph shall be in writing, unless the nominee is another official receiver or a deputy official receiver.

(3) Where the convener is other than the official receiver, the chairman shall be he, or a person nominated in writing by him.

A person nominated under this paragraph must be either—
  (a)   one who is qualified to act as an insolvency practitioner in relation to the company, or
  (b)   an employee of the liquidator or his firm who is experienced in insolvency matters.

2.300

4.56 The chairman at meetings—CVL

(1) This rule applies both to a meeting of creditors (except a meeting under section 95 or 98) and to a meeting of contributories.

(2) The liquidator, or a person nominated by him in writing to act, shall be chairman of the meeting.

A person nominated under this paragraph must be either—
  (a)   one who is qualified to act as an insolvency practitioner in relation to the company, or
  (b)   an employee of the liquidator or his firm who is experienced in insolvency matters.

2.301

4.57 Requisitioned meetings

(1) Any request by creditors to the liquidator (whether or not the official receiver) for a meeting of creditors or contributories, or meetings of both, to be summoned shall be accompanied by—

   (a)   a list of the creditors concurring with the request and the amount of their respective claims in the winding up;

   (b)   from each creditor concurring, written confirmation of his concurrence; and

   (c)   a statement of the purpose of the proposed meeting.

Sub-paragraphs (a) and (b) do not apply if the requisitioning creditor's debt is alone sufficient, without the concurrence of other creditors.

(2) The liquidator shall, if he considers the request to be properly made in accordance with the Act, fix a venue for the meeting, not more than 35 days from his receipt of the request.

(3) The liquidator shall give 21 days' notice of the meeting, and the venue for it, to creditors.

(4) Paragraphs (1) to (3) above apply to the requisitioning by contributories of contributories' meetings, with the following modifications—

   (a)   for the reference in paragraph (1)(a) to the creditors' respective claims substitute the contributories' respective values (being the amounts for which they may vote at any meeting); and

   (b)   the persons to be given notice under paragraph (3) are those appearing (by the company's books or otherwise) to be contributories of the company.

(NO CVL APPLICATION)

Notes

R 4.57

Under IA 1986 s 168(2) the liquidator has an obligation to call a meeting when requested by creditors or contributories. The request must be made by 10% by value of creditors or contributories as the case may be. The value of contributories is ascertained by reference to voting rights under the company's articles of association (IR 1986 r 4.63(1), 4.69).

R 4.57(1)(c)

This provision requires that there be a statement of the purpose of the meeting, but that there is no such requirement under IA 1986 s 168 itself.

2.302

4.58 Attendance at meetings of company's personnel

(1) This Rule applies to meetings of creditors and to meetings of contributories.

(2) Whenever a meeting is summoned, the convener shall give at least 21 days' notice to such of the company's personnel as he thinks should be told of, or be present at, the meeting.

'The company's personnel' means the persons referred to in paragraphs (a) to (d) of section 235(3) (present and past officers, employees, etc).

(3) If the meeting is adjourned, the chairman of the meeting shall, unless for any reason he thinks it unnecessary or impracticable, give notice of the adjournment to such (if any) of the company's personnel as he considers appropriate, being persons who were not themselves present at the meeting.

(4) The convener may, if he thinks fit, give notice to any one or more of the company's personnel that he is, or they are, required to be present at the meeting, or to be in attendance.

(5) In the case of any meeting, any one or more of the company's personnel, and any other persons, may be admitted, but—
   (a) they must have given reasonable notice of their wish to be present, and
   (b) it is a matter for the chairman's discretion whether they are to be admitted or not, and his decision is final as to what (if any) intervention may be made by any of them.

(6) If it is desired to put questions to any one of the company's personnel who is not present, the chairman may adjourn the meeting with a view to obtaining his attendance.

(7) Where one of the company's personnel is present at a meeting, only such questions may be put to him as the chairman may in his discretion allow.

2.303

4.59 Notice of meetings by advertisement only

(1) In the case of any meeting of creditors or contributories to be held under the Act or the Rules, the court may order that notice of the meeting be given by public advertisement, and not by individual notice to the persons concerned.

(2) In considering whether to act under this Rule, the court shall have regard to the cost of public advertisement, to the amount of the assets available, and to the extent of the interest of creditors or of contributories, or any particular class of either of them.

2.304

4.60 Venue

(1) In fixing the venue for a meeting of creditors or contributories, the convener shall have regard to the convenience of the persons (other than whoever is to be chairman) who are invited to attend

(2) Meetings shall in all cases be summoned for commencement between the hours of 10.00 and 16.00 hours on a business day, unless the court otherwise directs.

(3) With every notice summoning a meeting of creditors or contributories there shall be sent out forms of proxy.

2.305

4.61 Expenses of summoning meetings

(1) Subject as follows, the expenses of summoning and holding a meeting of creditors or contributories at the instance of any person other than the official receiver or the liquidator shall be paid by that person, who shall deposit with the liquidator security for their payment.

(2) The sum to be deposited shall be such as the official receiver or liquidator (as the case may be) determines to be appropriate; and neither shall act without the deposit having been made.

(3) Where a meeting of creditors is so summoned, it may vote that the expenses of summoning and holding it, and of summoning and holding any meeting of contributories requisitioned at the same time, shall be payable out of the assets, as an expense of the liquidation.

(4) Where a meeting of contributories is summoned on the requisition of contributories, it may vote that the expenses of summoning and holding it shall be payable out of the assets, but subject to the right of creditors to be paid in full, with interest.

(5) To the extent that any deposit made under this Rule is not required for the payment of expenses of summoning and holding a meeting, it shall be repaid to the person who made it.

2.306

4.62 Expenses of meeting under s 98—CVL

(1) Payment may be made out of the company's assets, either before or after the commencement of the winding up, of any reasonable and necessary expenses incurred in connection with the summoning, advertisement and holding of a creditors' meeting under section 98.

Any such payment is an expense of the liquidation.

(2) Where such payments are made before the commencement of the winding up, the director presiding at the creditors' meeting shall inform the meeting of their amount and the identity of the persons to whom they were made.

(3) The liquidator appointed under section 100 may make such a payment (subject to the next paragraph); but if there is a liquidation committee, he must give the committee at least 7 days' notice of his intention to make the payment.

(4) Such a payment shall not be made by the liquidator to himself, or to any associate of his, otherwise than with the approval of the liquidation committee, the creditors, or the court.

(5) This Rule is without prejudice to the powers of the court under Rule 4.219 (voluntary winding up superseded by winding up by the court).

2.307

4.63 Resolutions

(1) Subject as follows, at a meeting of creditors or contributories, a resolution is passed when a majority (in value) of those present and voting, in person or by proxy, have voted in favour of the resolution.

The value of contributories is determined by reference to the number of votes conferred on each contributory by the company's articles.

(2) In the case of a resolution for the appointment of a liquidator—
- (a) subject to paragraph (2A), if on any vote there are two nominees for appointment, the person who obtains the most support is appointed;
- (b) if there are three or more nominees, and one of them has a clear majority over both or all the others together, that one is appointed; and
- (c) in any other case, the chairman of the meeting shall continue to take votes (disregarding at each vote any nominee who has withdrawn and, if no nominee has withdrawn, the nominee who obtained the least support last time), until a clear majority is obtained for any one nominee.

(2A) In a winding up by the court the support referred to in paragraph (2)(a) must represent a majority in value of all those present (in person or by proxy) at the meeting and entitled to vote.

(NO CVL APPLICATION).

(3) The chairman may at any time put to the meeting a resolution for the joint appointment of any two or more nominees.

(4) Where a resolution is proposed which affects a person in respect of his remuneration or conduct as liquidator, or as proposed or former liquidator, the vote of that person, and of any partner or employee of his, shall not be reckoned in the majority required for passing the resolution.

This paragraph applies with respect to a vote given by a person (whether personally or on his behalf by a proxy-holder) either as creditor or contributory or as proxy-holder for a creditor or a contributory (but subject to Rule 8.6 in Part 8 of the Rules).

Notes

R 4.63(1)

IR 1986 r 8.6 places restrictions on the actions of a proxy-holder with a financial interest in the matter to be voted upon.

2.308

4.64 Chairman of meeting as proxy-holder

Where the chairman at a meeting of creditors or contributories holds a proxy which requires him to vote for a particular resolution, and no other person proposes that resolution—
- (a) he shall himself propose it, unless he considers that there is good reason for not doing so, and
- (b) if he does not propose it, he shall forthwith after the meeting notify his principal of the reason why not.

2.309

4.65 Suspension and adjournment

(1) This Rule applies to meetings of creditors and to meetings of contributories.

(2) Once only in the course of any meeting, the chairman may, in his discretion and without an adjournment, declare the meeting suspended for any period up to one hour.

(3) The chairman at any meeting may in his discretion, and shall if the meeting so resolves, adjourn it to such time and place as seems to him to be appropriate in the circumstances.

This is subject to Rule 4.113(3) or, as the case may be, 4.144—CVL (3), in a case where the liquidator or his nominee is chairman, and a resolution has been proposed for the liquidator's removal.

(4) If within a period of 30 minutes from the time appointed for the commencement of a meeting a quorum is not present, then the chairman may, at his discretion, adjourn the meeting to such time and place as he may appoint.

(5) An adjournment under this Rule shall not be for a period of more than 21 days; and Rule 4.60(1) and (2) applies.

(6) If there is no person present to act as chairman, some other person present (being entitled to vote) may make the appointment under paragraph (4), with the agreement of others present (being persons so entitled).

Failing agreement, the adjournment shall be to the same time and place in the next following week or, if that is not a business day, to the business day immediately following.

(7) Where a meeting is adjourned under this Rule, proofs and proxies may be used if lodged at any time up to midday on the business day immediately before the adjourned meeting.

4.66 (Revoked)

2.310

4.67 Entitlement to vote (creditors)

(1) Subject as follows in this Rule and the next, at a meeting of creditors a person is entitled to vote as a creditor only if—
    (a) there has been duly lodged (in a winding up by the court by the time and date stated in the notice of the meeting) a proof of the debt
        (i) claimed to be due to him from the company, or
        (ii) in relation to a member State liquidator, is claimed to be due to creditors in proceedings in relation to which he holds office, and the claim has been admitted under Rule 4.70 for the purpose of entitlement to vote, and
    (b) there has been lodged, by the time and date stated in the notice of the meeting, any proxy requisite for that entitlement.

(2) The court may, in exceptional circumstances, by order declare the creditors, or any class of them, entitled to vote at creditors' meetings, without being required to prove their debts.

Where a creditor is so entitled, the court may, on the application of the liquidator, make such consequential orders as it thinks fit (as for example an order treating a creditor as having proved his debt for the purpose of permitting payment of dividend).

(3) A creditor shall not vote in respect of a debt for an unliquidated amount, or any debt whose value is not ascertained, except where the chairman agrees to put upon the debt an estimated minimum value for the purpose of entitlement to vote and admits his proof for that purpose.

(4) A secured creditor is entitled to vote only in respect of the balance (if any) of his debt after deducting the value of his security as estimated by him.

(5) A creditor shall not vote in respect of a debt on, or secured by, a current bill of exchange or promissory note, unless he is willing—
- (a) to treat the liability to him on the bill or note of every person who is liable on it antecedently to the company, and against whom a bankruptcy order has not been made (or, in the case of a company, which has not gone into liquidation), as a security in his hands, and
- (b) to estimate the value of the security and (for the purpose of entitlement to vote, but not for dividend) to deduct it from his proof.

(6) No vote shall be cast by virtue of a debt more than once on any resolution put to the meeting.

(7) Where—
- (a) a creditor is entitled to vote under this Rule and Rule 4.70 (admission of proof),
- (b) has lodged his claim in one or more sets of other proceedings, and
- (c) votes (either in person or by proxy) on a resolution put to the meeting, only the creditor's vote shall be counted.

(8) Where—
- (a) a creditor has lodged his claim in more than one set of other proceedings, and
- (b) more than one member State liquidator seeks to vote by virtue of that claim,

the entitlement to vote by virtue of that claim is exercisable by the member State liquidator in main proceedings, whether or not the creditor has lodged his claim in the main proceedings.

> (9) For the purposes of paragraphs (7) and (8), 'other proceedings' means main proceedings, secondary proceedings or territorial proceedings in another member State.

Notes

R 4.67(2)

Clearly such an order will not be made lightly. In *Re Theo Garvin Ltd* [1969] 1 Ch 624 proofs were dispensed with where the creditors' claims were in respect of interest on money accepted as deposit.

R 4.67(3)

For a commentary on the equivalent or nearly equivalent provisions for creditors' meetings called to consider proposals for a company or individual voluntary arrangement, see the notes to IR 1986 r 1.17 and 5.17.

R 4.67(6)–(9)

These sub-rules are intended to ensure that no debt is counted twice in the voting procedures, and to clarify who may cast the vote in respect of any particular debt where there is more than one set of insolvency proceedings. They came into force on 31 May 2002 subject to savings provisions: Insolvency (Amendment) Rules 2002 (SI 2002/1307).

2.311

4.68 Chairman's discretion to allow vote—CVL

At a creditors' meeting, the chairman may allow a creditor to vote, notwithstanding that he has failed to comply with Rule 4.67(1)(a), if satisfied that the failure was due to circumstances beyond the creditor's control.

Notes

R 4.68

The fact that the chairman allows a creditor to vote for a particular amount and an appeal against his decision is dismissed is not conclusive on the issue of whether the creditor is owed that particular amount: *Re Assico Engineering Ltd* [2002] BCC 481.

2.312

4.69 Entitlement to vote (contributories)

At a meeting of contributories, voting rights are as at a general meeting of the company, subject to any provision in the articles affecting entitlement to vote, either generally or at a time when the company is in liquidation.

2.313

4.70 Admission and rejection of proof (creditors' meeting)

(1) At any creditors' meeting the chairman has power to admit or reject a creditors' proof for the purpose of his entitlement to vote; and the power is exercisable with respect to the whole or any part of the proof.

(2) The chairman's decision under this Rule, or in respect of any matter arising under Rule 4.67, is subject to appeal to the court by any creditor or contributory.

(3) If the chairman is in doubt whether a proof should be admitted or rejected, he shall mark it as objected to and allow the creditor to vote, subject to his vote being subsequently declared invalid if the objection to the proof is sustained.

(4) If on an appeal the chairman's decision is reversed or varied, or a creditor's vote is declared invalid, the court may order that another meeting be summoned, or make such other order as it thinks just.

(5) Neither the official receiver, nor any person nominated by him to be chairman, is personally liable for costs incurred by any person in respect of an application under this Rule; and the chairman (if other than the official receiver or a person so nominated) is not so liable unless the court makes an order to that effect.

(NO CVL APPLICATION)

(6–CVL) The liquidator or his nominee as chairman is not personally liable for costs incurred by any person in respect of an application under this Rule, unless the court makes an order to that effect.

Notes

R 4.70(3)

It is useful to compare this provision with the wording of IR 1986 5.22(4) dealing with individual voluntary arrangements (which replaces the former IR 1986 5.17(6) referred to in the cases cited below). If in doubt the chairman should admit the proof for voting purposes but mark it as objected to: *In re a Debtor (no 222 of 1990), ex parte the Bank of Ireland* [1992] BCLC 137, and In *Re a Debtor, the Debtors v UCB Bank plc*, 16 December 1998, LTL 16/12/98 (Ch D). The fact that a proof is admitted under this rule for the purpose of a voting does not necessarily mean that the person voting is a creditor for other purposes: *Re Assico Engineering Limited* [2002] BCC 481.

R 4.70(4)

On any appeal the court is not confined to the evidence that was before the chairman at the time of his decision, but can consider any admissible evidence the parties choose to place before the court: *Re a Company (No 004539 of 1993)* [1995] BCC 116.

2.314

4.71 Record of proceedings

(1) At any meeting, the chairman shall cause minutes of the proceedings to be kept. The minutes shall be signed by him, and retained as part of the records of the liquidation.

(2) The chairman shall also cause to be made up and kept a list of all the creditors or, as the case may be, contributories who attended the meeting.

(3) The minutes of the meeting shall include a record of every resolution passed.

(4) It is the chairman's duty to see to it that particulars of all such resolutions, certified by him, are filed in court not more than 21 days after the date of the meeting.

(NO CVL APPLICATION)

2.315

4.72 Additional provisions as regards certain meetings

(1) This Rule applies where a company goes, or proposes to go, into liquidation and it is [an authorised deposit-taker or a former authorised deposit-taker].

(2) Notice of any meeting of the company at which it is intended to propose a resolution for its winding up shall be given by the directors to the [Financial Services Authority] and [to the scheme manager established under section 212(1) of the Financial Services and Markets Act 2000].

(3) Notice to the [Authority] and [the scheme manager] shall be the same as given to members of the company.

(4) Where a creditors' meeting is summoned by the liquidator under section 95 or, in a creditors' voluntary winding up, is summoned under section 98, the same notice of the meeting must be given to the [Authority] and [the scheme manager] as is given to creditors under Rule 4.51—CVL.

(5) Where the company is being wound up by the court, notice of the first meetings of creditors and contributories shall be given to the [Authority] and [the scheme manager] by the official receiver.

(6) Where in the winding up (whether voluntary or by the court) a meeting of creditors or contributories or of the company is summoned for the purpose of—
   (a)   receiving the liquidator's resignation, or
   (b)   removing the liquidator, or
   (c)   appointing a new liquidator,
the person summoning the meeting and giving notice of it shall also give notice to the [Authority] and [the scheme manager].

(7) [The scheme manager] is entitled to be represented at any meeting of which it is required by this Rule to be given notice; and Schedule 1 to the Rules has effect with respect to the voting rights of [the scheme manager] at such a meeting.

Chapter 9
Proof of Debts in a Liquidation

Section A: Procedure for Proving

2.315A

4.73 Meaning of 'prove'

(1) Where a company is being wound up by the court, a person claiming to be a creditor of the company and wishing to recover his debt in whole

or in part must (subject to any order of the court under Rule 4.67(2)) submit his claim in writing to the liquidator. (NO CVL APPLICATION)

(2–CVL) In a voluntary winding up (whether members' or creditors') the liquidator may require a person claiming to be a creditor of the company and wishing to recover his debt in whole or in part, to submit the claim in writing to him.

(3) A creditor who claims (whether or not in writing) is referred to as 'proving' for his debt; and a document by which he seeks to establish his claim is his 'proof'.

(4) Subject to the next paragraph, a proof must be in the form known as 'proof of debt' (whether the form prescribed by the Rules, or a substantially similar form), which shall be made out by or under the directions of the creditor, and signed by him or a person authorised in that behalf. (NO CVL APPLICATION)

(5) Where a debt is due to a Minister of the Crown or a Government Department, the proof need not be in that form, provided that there are shown all such particulars of the debt as are required in the form used by other creditors, and as are relevant in the circumstances. (NO CVL APPLICATION)

(6–CVL) The creditor's proof may be in any form.

(7) In certain circumstances, specified below in this Chapter, the proof must be in the form of an affidavit.

(8) Where a winding up is immediately preceded by an administration, a creditor proving in the administration shall be deemed to have proved in the winding up

---

Notes

R 4.73(1)

No time for proving is specified. However the court under IA 1986 s 153 may fix a time or times within which creditors are to prove their debts or claims failing which they may be excluded from any distribution (including a distribution to contributories: *Butler v Broadhead* [1975] Ch 97)) made before debts are proved. The court's power may be delegated to the liquidator: IA 1986 s 160(1)(e), IR 1986 r 11.2. The normal practice is not to reject a late proof but to allow the creditor to prove on terms that dividends already made are not disturbed and on terms as to costs: *Harrison v Kirk* [1904] AC 1.

R 4.73(2)

However unless the creditor submits a proof he will not be able to vote at a creditors' meeting (IR 1986 r 4.67(1)) subject to the chairman's discretion to allow the vote: IR 1986 r 4.68

R 4.73(8)

This provision was introduced due to the reforms of the EA 2002 which enable creditors to prove and receive distributions in an administration: IR 1986 rr 2.72ff.

2.316

4.74 Supply of forms (No CVL Application)

[A form of proof shall be sent to any creditor of the company by the liquidator where the creditor so requests.]

Notes

R 4.74(1)

If the liquidator is aware of a debt in respect of which the creditor has not submitted a claim it is his duty (provided he can communicate with the creditor) to invite the creditor to prove *Re Compania de Electricidad de la Provincia de Buenos Aires Ltd* [1980] Ch 146.

2.317

4.75 Contents of proof (No CVL Application)

(1) Subject to Rule 4.73(5), the following matters shall be stated in a creditor's proof of debt—
- (a) the creditor's name and address, and, if a company its company registration number;
- (b) the total amount of his claim (including any Value Added Tax) as at the date on which the company went into liquidation;
- (c) whether or not that amount includes outstanding uncapitalised interest;
- (d) particulars of how and when the debt was incurred by the company;
- (e) particulars of any security held, the date when it was given and the value which the creditor puts upon it;
- (f) details of any reservation of title in respect of goods to which the debt refers; and
- (g) the name, address and authority of the person signing the proof (if other than the creditor himself).

(2) There shall be specified in the proof any documents by reference to which the debt can be substantiated; but (subject as follows) it is not essential that such documents be attached to the proof or submitted with it.

(3) The liquidator, or the chairman or convener of any meeting, may call for any document or other evidence to be produced to him, where he thinks it necessary for the purpose of substantiating the whole or any part of the claim made in the proof.

Notes

R 4.75(1)(f)

Thus a claimant may assert that he owns goods which have been supplied to the company and for which he has not been paid and submit a proof of debt (as an ordinary creditor) without waiving any retention of title claim. It is advisable for the claimant to mark the proof 'without prejudice to retention of title rights' or words to that effect.

_____

2.318

4.76 Particulars of creditor's claim—CVL

The liquidator, or the convener or chairman of any meeting, may, if he thinks it necessary for the purpose of clarifying or substantiating the whole or any part of a creditor's claim made in his proof, call for details of any matter specified in paragraphs (a) to (h) of Rule 4.75(1), or for the production to him of such documentary or other evidence as he may require.

2.319

4.77 Claim established by affidavit

(1) The liquidator may, if he thinks it necessary, require a claim of debt to be verified by means of an affidavit, for which purpose there shall be used the form known as 'affidavit of debt', or a substantially similar form.

(2) An affidavit may be required notwithstanding that a proof of debt has already been lodged.

(3) The affidavit may be sworn before an official receiver or deputy official receiver, or before an officer of the Department or of the court duly authorised in that behalf. (NO CVL APPLICATION)

2.320

4.78 Cost of proving

(1) Subject as follows, every creditor bears the cost of proving his own debt, including such as may be incurred in providing documents or evidence under Rule 4.75(3) or 4.76—CVL.

(2) Costs incurred by the liquidator in estimating the quantum of a debt under Rule 4.86 (debts not bearing a certain value) are payable out of the assets, as an expense of the liquidation.

(3) Paragraphs (1) and (2) apply unless the court otherwise orders.

2.321

4.79 Liquidator to allow inspection of proofs

The liquidator shall, so long as proofs lodged with him are in his hands, allow them to be inspected, at all reasonable times on any business day, by any of the following persons—
   (a)   any creditor who has submitted his proof of debt (unless his proof has been wholly rejected for purposes of dividend or otherwise);
   (b)   any contributory of the company;
   (c)   any person acting on behalf of either of the above.

2.322

4.80 Transmission of proofs to liquidator (No CVL Application)

(1) Where a liquidator is appointed, the official receiver shall forthwith transmit to him all the proofs which he has so far received, together with an itemised list of them.

(2) The liquidator shall sign the list by way of receipt for the proofs, and return it to the official receiver.

(3) From then on, all proofs of debt shall be sent to the liquidator, and retained by him.

2.323

4.81 New liquidator appointed

(1) If a new liquidator is appointed in place of another, the former liquidator shall transmit to him all proofs which he has received, together with an itemised list of them.

(2) The new liquidator shall sign the list by way of receipt for the proofs, and return it to his predecessor.

2.324

4.82 Admission and rejection of proofs for dividend

(1) A proof may be admitted for dividend either for the whole amount claimed by the creditor, or for part of that amount.

(2) If the liquidator rejects a proof in whole or in part, he shall prepare a written statement of his reasons for doing so, and send it forthwith to the creditor.

Notes

R 4.82(1)

The liquidator should examine every proof and consider the validity of the grounds of the debt being proved: *Re Home and Colonial Insurance Co* [1930] 1 Ch 102; and this is the case notwithstanding that the proof is based on a judgment, covenant or account stated: *Re Van Laun* [1907] 2 KB 23. The liquidator must consider any set off to ascertain the proper sum in which the proof may be admitted: *Re National Wholemeal Bread and Biscuit Co* [1892] 2 Ch 457; and he or she is duty bound to assess the true value of the claim: *Re Exchange Securities and Commodities Ltd* [1988] Ch 46.

R 4.82(2)

The liquidator is not under any particular time constraint in dealing with the admission and rejection of proofs. However once the creditor receives the written statement he or she has 21 days to apply to court under IR 1986 r 4.83 below.

2.325

4.83 Appeal against decision on proof

(1) If a creditor is dissatisfied with the liquidator's decision with respect to his proof (including any decision on the question of preference), he may apply to the court for the decision to be reversed or varied.

The application must be made within 21 days of his receiving the statement sent under Rule 4.82(2).

(2) A contributory or any other creditor may, if dissatisfied with the liquidator's decision admitting or rejecting the whole or any part of a proof, make such an application within 21 days of becoming aware of the liquidator's decision.

(3) Where application is made to the court under this Rule, the court shall fix a venue for the application to be heard, notice of which shall be sent by the applicant to the creditor who lodged the proof in question (if it is not himself) and to the liquidator.

(4) The liquidator shall, on receipt of the notice, file in court the relevant proof, together (if appropriate) with a copy of the statement sent under Rule 4.82(2).

(5) After the application has been heard and determined, the proof shall, unless it has been wholly disallowed, be returned by the court to the liquidator.

(6) The official receiver is not personally liable for costs incurred by any person in respect of an application under this Rule; and the liquidator (if other than the official receiver) is not so liable unless the court makes an order to that effect.

Notes

R 4.83(5)

The court will decide the issue on the merits on the evidence before it; its function is not that of deciding merely whether the rejection was right or wrong on the evidence which was available to the liquidator: *Re Kentwood Construction Ltd* [1960] 2 All ER 655. Accordingly the liquidator is not restricted before the court to the reasons he had given for rejecting the proof and provided it is fairly taken the court may uphold the liquidator's decision on the basis of a ground that was not in the statement of reasons under IR 1986 r 4.82(2): *Re Thomas Christy Ltd* [1994] 2 BCLC 527. In appropriate cases the court may make orders for disclosure and cross examination in order to determine the application: *Re BCCI SA (No 6), Mahfouz v Morris* [1994] 1 BCLC 450, 454. As cross examination can be ordered on the application it would be unusual to make an order under IA 1986 s 236 for the purpose of determining a disputed proof: *Re BCCI SA (No 7)* [1994] 1 BCLC 455.

R 4.83(6)

The court would be slow to make the liquidator who wrongly rejects a proof liable for costs but it is within its power to do so. Further the court may make an order that the applicant give security for the liquidator's costs: *Re Pretoria Pietersburg Rly Co* [1904] 2 Ch 359.

2.326

4.84 Withdrawal or variation of proof

A creditor's proof may at any time, by agreement between himself and the liquidator, be withdrawn or varied as to the amount claimed.

2.327

4.85 Expunging of proof by the court

(1) The court may expunge a proof or reduce the amount claimed—
- (a) on the liquidator's application, where he thinks that the proof has been improperly admitted, or ought to be reduced; or
- (b) on the application of a creditor, if the liquidator declines to interfere in the matter.

(2) Where application is made to the court under this Rule, the court shall fix a venue for the application to be heard, notice of which shall be sent by the applicant—
- (a) in the case of an application by the liquidator, to the creditor who made the proof, and
- (b) in the case of an application by a creditor, to the liquidator and to the creditor who made the proof (if not himself).

Notes

R 4.85(1)

In *Re Global Legal Services Ltd* [2002] BCC 858 it was held that, in determining whether a proof was properly admitted, the test is the civil test. It is not necessary to satisfy the court beyond all reasonable doubt that it ought not to have been admitted. Further there is no 'moral opprobium' in the words 'improperly admitted' or 'ought to be reduced'. A mistake on the part of the liquidator does not automatically mean that the proof was improperly admitted. In *Re Menastar Finance Ltd* [2003] BCC 404 it was held, applying *McCourt v Baron Meats Ltd* [1997] BPIR 114, that the court could in limited circumstances look behind a creditor's proof based on a judgment , for instance where the judgment was obtained through fraud or it would be unjust.

R 4.85(2)

In *Re Allard Holdings Ltd* [2001] BCLC 404, it was held that, if there are any complaints that the liquidator has delayed considering whether a proof should be expunged, that is a matter which the court can take into account in determining whether the burden of proof on the liquidator is actually discharged. No time limit for an application is set by the rules and mere lapse of time does not bar the court's right to expunge or reduce a proof: *Re Tait* (1882) 21 Ch D 537. If a proof is expunged or reduced a creditor may retain any dividend previously received but he is not entitled to receive any further dividend without giving credit for the overpayment in respect of his original proof: *Re Browne* [1960] 1 WLR 692.

Section B: Quantification of Claim

2.328

4.86 Estimate of quantum

(1) The liquidator shall estimate the value of any debt which, by reason of its being subject to any contingency or for any other reason, does not bear a certain value; and he may revise any estimate previously made, if he thinks fit by reference to any change of circumstances or to information becoming available to him.

He shall inform the creditor as to his estimate and any revision of it.

> (2) Where the value of a debt is estimated under this Rule, or by the court under section 168(3) or (5), the amount provable in the winding up in the case of that debt is that of the estimate for the time being.

Notes

R 4.86(1)

It may be difficult for the liquidator to estimate a debt subject to a contingency and he may, therefore, revise previous estimates as appropriate. Where, for example, there are claims for future breaches of covenant, the liquidator should make a just estimate so far as possible of their value: *Re Luciana Temperance Billiard Halls (London) Ltd* [1966] Ch 98. However no practical guidance was offered in that case as to how to go about that task. In the event that a contingent debt becomes ascertained during the liquidation then the ascertained amount should be admitted to proof in substitution of the amount previously assessed; however dividends already paid should not be disturbed following the substitution *Re English Assurance Co* (1872) LR 14 Eq 72; and see in particular *Stein v Blake* [1996] AC 243 at 252–253 for Lord Hoffmann's explanation of the operation of the 'hindsight' principle.

R 4.86(2)

The liquidator should have regard to relevant events which have happened since the commencement of the liquidation in valuing the claim: *MS Fashions Ltd v BCCI (No 2)* [1993] Ch 425; *Stein v Blake* (above). If a claimant is dissatisfied he may apply to the court and the court will estimate the value.

2.329

4.87 Negotiable instruments, etc

Unless the liquidator allows, a proof in respect of money owed on a bill of exchange, promissory note, cheque or other negotiable instrument or security cannot be admitted unless there is produced the instrument or security itself or a copy of it, certified by the creditor or his authorised representative to be a true copy.

Notes

R 4.87

Where bills bearing the company's and other names are indorsed by the company to a creditor the test whether they should be valued as securities or not is whether the indorsement was intended to make the company liable as indorser of the bills: *Re Firth ex p Schofield* (1879) 12 Ch D 337. Generally where a bill bearing the names of third parties is indorsed and handed to a creditor he may proceed against all the parties to the bill until he receives full payment and interest; and until he has been paid in full the creditor may prove in the liquidation without reference to sums he may receive but has not yet received from other indorsers: *Re Fowler ex p Martin* (1814) 2 Rose 87. The liquidator will have an interest in any surplus received by the creditor *Re Morris* [1899] 1 Ch 485.

2.330

4.88 Secured creditors

(1) If a secured creditor realises his security, he may prove for the balance of his debt, after deducting the amount realised.

> (2) If a secured creditor voluntarily surrenders his security for the general benefit of creditors, he may prove for his whole debt, as if it were unsecured.

Notes

R 4.88

The following principles apply in relation to secured creditors in a liquidation:

- if the secured creditor has a number of claims against the company he may appropriate the proceeds of realisation of his security as he thinks fit including between provable and non provable claims: *Re William Hall (Contractors) Ltd* [1967] 1 WLR 948;
- the net proceeds of the realisation may not be applied to interest accrued after the date of the liquidation *Re William Hall (Contractors) Ltd* [1967] 1 WLR 948; however profits made from an unrealised security may be applied to meet such interest: *Re Savin* (1872) 7 Ch App 760;
- if a secured creditor has realised his security for a particular debt and has a balance in his hands when the company goes into liquidation he may set off this balance against another unsecured debt due to him by the company: *Re H E Thorne and Son* [1914] 2 Ch 438;
- a creditor who holds several securities in respect of different debts must apply the proceeds of each security to its particular debt and the surplus funds of one security may not be applied to make good the deficiency of another: *Re Newton ex p Bignold* (1836) 2 Deac 66;
- IR 1986 r 4.88 does not constitute an exception to the 'hotchpot rule' which ensures that the assets of a liquidation are divided pari passu among unsecured creditors by requiring creditors who have acquired liquidation assets by participating in a distribution in a foreign jurisdiction, to bring that share into the hotchpot before it can receive any dividend in the English jurisdiction. The hotchpot rule only extends to assets that were part of the liquidation estate, and not to assets that the creditor has received from a third party *Cleaver v Delta American Reinsurance Co (In Liquidation)* [2001] 1 BCLC 482; and see the discussion of the rule in *Re HIH Casualty and General Insurance Ltd* [2006] 2 All ER 671 paras 157–165.

2.331

4.89 Discounts

There shall in every case be deducted from the claim all trade and other discounts which would have been available to the company but for its liquidation, except any discount for immediate, early or cash settlement.

2.332

4.90 Mutual credits and set–off

(1) This Rule applies where, before the company goes into liquidation there have been mutual credits, mutual debts or other mutual dealings between the company and any creditor of the company proving or claiming to prove for a debt in the liquidation.

(2) The reference in paragraph (1) to mutual credits, mutual debts or other mutual dealings does not include –

    (a)   any debt arising out of an obligation incurred at a time when the creditor had notice that –

(i) a meeting of creditors had been summoned under section 98; or

(ii) a petition for the winding up of the company was pending;

(b) any debt arising out of an obligation where –

(i) the liquidation was immediately preceded by an administration; and

(ii) at the time the obligation was incurred, the creditor had notice that an application for an administration order was pending or a person had given notice of intention to appoint an administrator;

(c) any debt arising out of an obligation incurred during an administration which immediately preceded the liquidation; or

(d) any debt which has been acquired by a creditor by assignment or otherwise, pursuant to an agreement between the creditor and any other party where that agreement was entered into –

(i) after the company went into liquidation;

(ii) at a time when the creditor had notice that a meeting of creditors had been summoned under section 98;

(iii) at a time when the creditor had notice that a winding up petition was pending;

(iv) where the liquidation was imediately preceded by an administration, at a time when the creditor had notice that an application for an administration order was pending or a person had given notice of intention to appoint an administrator; or

(v) during an administration which immediately preceded the liquidation.

(3) An account shall be taken of what is due from each party to the other in respect of the mutual dealings, and the sums due from one party shall be set off against the sums due from the other.

(4) A sum shall be regarded as being due to or from the company for the purposes of paragraph (3) whether –

(a) it is payable at present or in the future;

(b) the obligation by virtue of which it is payable is certain or contingent; or

(c) its amount is fixed or liquidated, or is capable of being ascertained by fixed rules or as a matter of opinion.

(5) Rule 4.86 shall also apply for the purposes of this Rule to any obligation to or from the company which, by reason of its being subject to any contingency or for any other reason, does not bear a certain value.

(6) Rules 4.91 to 4.93 shall apply for the purposes of this Rule in relation to any sums due to the company which –

(a) are payable in a currency other than sterling;

(b) are of a periodical nature; or

(c) bear Interest.

(7) Rule 11.13 shall apply for the purposes of this Rule to any sum due to or from the company which is payable in the future.

(8) Only the balance (if any) of the account owed to the creditor is provable in the liquidation. Alternatively the balance (if any) owed to the company shall be paid to the liquidator as part of the assets except where

> all (or part of the balance results from a contingent or prospective debt which results from the contingent or prospective debt) shall be paid if and when the debt becomes due and payable.
>
> (9) In this Rule 'obligation' means an obligation however arising, whether by virtue of an agreement, rule or law or otherwise.

Notes

IR 1986 r 4.90 was amended and extended by the Insolvency (Amendment) Rules 2005 with effect from 1 April 2005. The amendment was intended to take account of case law and to iron out certain difficulties associated with the former rule. It mirrors IR 1986 r 2.85 which applies in company administrations. For the equivalent provision which applies in cases of bankruptcy, see IA 1986 s 323. Where the conditions for set–off under r 4.90(1) are met, the rule operates automatically as at the date of liquidation to set off, pound for pound, sums due from a creditor to the company as against sums due from the company to that creditor, leaving only the net balance, as the case may be, recoverable from the creditor or provable by the creditor in the liquidation. This avoids the injustice of a creditor having to pay in full the sums due from it to the company, while being able only to prove in the liquidation for the sums due to it from the company. For an authoritative explanation of the operation of the rule (and perhaps the best introduction to the subject), see the speech of Lord Hoffmann in *Stein v Blake* [1996] AC 243, 251ff.

Claims in respect of which set–off is available

Set–off is available not only in cases where sums have actually fallen due for payment, either way between company and creditor, before the company goes into liquidation. Instead, as now made explicit by paragraph (4), it applies more widely to all claims between creditor and company which arise out of mutual dealings which took place before the date of liquidation. So it applies:

- In respect of debts which are payable in the future;
- In respect of claims of a monetary nature which are at the date of liquidation unliquidated or unascertained in amount;
- In respect of claims which are only contingent at the date of liquidation; eg claims for breach of contract where the contract was made before the date of liquidation, but the breach occurred afterwards: *Re Asphaltic Wood Pavement Co Ltd* (1885) LR 30 Ch 216; or claims for an indemnity by a guarantor where the guarantee was given before the date of liquidation, but the guarantee was called upon and paid afterwards: *Jones v Mossop* (1884) 3 Hare 568. And see *Secretary of State for Trade and Industry v Frid* [2004] 2 AC 506 para 9 per Lord Hoffman who said of contingent claims: 'It is sufficient that there should have been an obligation arising out of the terms of a contract or statute [entered into or in existence at the date of liquidation] by which a debt sounding in money would become payable upon the occurrence of some future event or events';
- In respect of debts or pecuniary claims arising under statute: see *Secretary of State for Trade and Industry v Frid* (above);
- In respect of claims arising from the commission of a tort: *Gye v McIntyre* (1991) 171 CLR 609; *Re T&N Ltd* [2006] BPIR 532;
- However, set–off is not available as between a debt due to a misfeasant director and his liability to repay moneys which he is liable to pay in misfeasance proceedings: *Manson v Smith* [1997] 2 BCLC 161.

However, there are two important provisos to the operation of the set-off rule:
- The obligations in respect of which the right of set–off can operate must be ones which have given rise or may (subject to any contingency) give rise to a monetary liability; an obligation simply to transfer or deliver up property in kind cannot be the subject of a set–off: see *Eberle's Hotel v Jonas* (1887) LR 18 QBD 459; cf. *Rolls Razor Ltd v Cox* [1967] 1 QB 552;

- Although there is no requirement that the creditor should have actually submitted a proof, the creditor's claim must have been one which was provable in the liquidation: see *Stein v Blake* (above) per Lord Hoffman at p 253B–E.

For the rules on provable claims, see IR 1986 r 12.3 and r 13.12. For an example of an unprovable claim, see *Re Glen Express Ltd* [2000] BPIR 456 (claim unprovable as contrary to the law against double proof). A creditor having submitted a proof which has been rejected by the liquidator, cannot then use the debt by way of set off: see *BCCI (Overseas) Ltd v Habib Bank Ltd* [1998] 2 BCLC 459. The creditor in such circumstances should appeal against the rejection of his proof under IR 1986 r 4.83. A creditor whose debt is secured cannot prove for that debt to the extent of such security unless he surrenders his security (see IR 1986 r 4.88) and for that reason at least the secured part of debt is not subject to set–off: see *Re Norman Holding Co Ltd* [1991] 1 WLR 10.

Requirement for mutuality

The requirement for there to have been mutual debts, credits or dealings between the company and the creditor has sometimes been misunderstood as a requirement that the respective claims must arise out of or be referable to the same transaction. That is a fallacy: see Lord Hoffman in *Secretary of State for Trade and Industry v Frid* (above) at para 25.

Instead the requirement for mutuality is that the obligations the subject of the set–off were incurred by the same parties in the same right or capacity. For example, claims brought by or against A in his capacity as executor cannot be set–off against claims brought by or against A in his personal capacity. However, the beneficial owner of a debt held for him by a third party as nominee or on bare trust may set that off against an obligation due to the debtor provided that the beneficial owner's right is absolute and can be established without further enquiry: *ex parte Morier* (1879) 12 Ch D 491; *BCCI v Al-Saud* [1997] BCC 63.

Where monies belonging to A have been transferred to B for use for a specific purpose, B's obligation to repay those monies (or any surplus thereof) to A on failure or completion of the purpose has been held in a line of 19th century cases not to be subject to a right of set–off against sums due personally from A to B on grounds of lack of mutuality: see e g *in re Pollitt* [1893] 1 QB 455; *In re Mid Kent Fruit Factory* [1896] 1 Ch 567. In *National Westminster Bank v Halesowen Presswork and Assemblies Ltd* [1972] AC 785, it was held by Lord Simon that the exclusion of mutuality in such cases may be explained on the grounds that the monies were held subject to a *Quistclose* type trust.

A debt is not excluded from set–off for lack of mutuality merely because it is secured: *ex parte Barnett* (1874) [LR 9 Ch App 293; *Re ILG Travel Ltd* [1996] BCC 21; cf *Re Norman Holding Ltd* (above).

R 4.90(2): Obligations incurred before liquidation to which the right of set off does not apply

As noted above, set–off is generally available under IR 1986 r 4.90(1) in respect of debts or claims arising from obligations incurred or entered into before the company went into liquidation. However, r 4.90(2) introduces a number of exceptions to this:

- In cases where liquidation has been immediately preceded by an administration, the relevant date is the date the company went into administration; claims arising from obligations incurred during the administration are not available for set off: see IR 1986 r 4.90(2)(c);
- A creditor cannot set off claims arising from obligations incurred by the company at a time when the creditor had notice of the company's pending administration or liquidation, as defined in IR 1986 r 4.90(2)(a) and (b);
- Debts acquired by a creditor by assignment during the company's liquidation or any preceding administration, or at a time when the creditor had notice of the company's pending liquidation or administration: IR 1986 r 4.90(d).

The operation of the set–off; the taking of the account and quantification of the cross–claims

The set–off operates automatically at the date of liquidation to extinguish the cross–claims, and to create a single claim in respect of the net balance due after setting off one against the other: *Stein v Blake* (above) at p 255A–B. However, the accounting process under IR 1986 r 4.90(3) by which the amount of such net balance is ascertained may not take place until some months or years after the date of liquidation. Such process may only be activated at the time either the company or its creditor seeks to assert its claim against the other by lodging a proof of debt or instituting legal proceedings.

To determine the net balance due, it is necessary on the taking of the account to ascertain the value of the cross–claims as the date of liquidation. In respect of liabilities which are contingent or unascertained at the date of liquidation, two principles should be applied (see *Stein v Blake* (above) at p 252E–253A):

- First, under the 'hindsight' principle, account can and should be taken of everything which has happened since the date of liquidation; so if the contingency has since occurred and the liability quantified, the claim should be valued at the date of the liquidation in the amount so quantified;
- Second, in cases where either of the liabilities remains contingent or payable in the future at the time the account the is taken, the liquidator is required to estimate its value pursuant to IR 1986 r 4.86 and r 4.90(5) (contingent liabilities) or IR 1986 r 4.90(7) and r 11.13 (future liabilities).

Although claims of the company which remain contingent at the date the account is taken can now be included in the set–off account under the new IR 1986 r 4.90(5) (in a change to the previous law as set out in *Stein v Blake (above)* at p 714F), the new IR 1986 r 4.90(8) provides that in the event that, on taking the account, a net balance is found due from the creditor to the company arising from a contingent debt or a debt payable at a future time, such balance only has to be paid by the creditor to the liquidator if and when that debt becomes due and payable. This counters the injustice which would otherwise arise from a creditor's liability to the company under a contingent or future debt being advanced merely because of the company's liquidation.

Contracting out of (and into) the rule

The set–off rule is mandatory and cannot be excluded by contract: *National Westminster Bank Ltd v Halesowen Presswork Assemblies* [1972] AC 785. But equally, parties cannot by contract confer a right of set–off between claims in the event of insolvency where the conditions for the operation of the rule are not met as this would contravene the fundamental principle of *pari passu* distribution: see Lord Hoffman in *Re BCCI (No 8)* [1998] AC 214 at 223C–D. For further discussion on this, see commentary to IR r 4.181.

2.333

4.91 Debt in foreign currency

(1) For the purpose of proving a debt incurred or payable in a currency other than sterling, the amount of the debt shall be converted into sterling at the official exchange rate prevailing on the date when the company went into liquidation [or, if the liquidation was immediately preceded by an administration, on the date that the company entered administration.]

(2) 'The official exchange rate' is the middle market rate at the Bank of England, as published for the date in question. In the absence of any such published rate, it is such rate as the court determines.

Notes

R 4.91(1)

For an example see *Re Lines Bros* [1983] Ch 1.

That part of the rule which appears in square brackets was added by Insolvency (Amendment) Rules 2005 (SI 2005/527). The amendment does not apply where a company has entered administration or gone into liquidation before 1 April 2005.

2.334

4.92 Payments of a periodical nature

(1) In the case of rent and other payments of a periodical nature, the creditor may prove for any amounts due and unpaid up to the date when the company went into liquidation [or if the liquidation was immediately preceded by an administration, up to the date that the company entered administration.]

(2) Where at that date any payment was accruing due, the creditor may prove for so much as would have fallen due at that date, if accruing from day to day.

Notes

R 4.92

That part of the rule which appears in square brackets was added by Insolvency (Amendment) Rules 2005 (SI 2005/527). The amendment does not apply where a company has entered administration or gone into liquidation before 1 April 2005.

2.335

4.93 Interest

(1) Where a debt proved in the liquidation bears interest, that interest is provable as part of the debt except in so far as it is payable in respect of any period after the company went into liquidation [or, if the liquidation was immediately preceded by an administration, any period after the date that the company entered administration.]

(2) In the following circumstances the creditor's claim may include interest on the debt for periods before the company went into liquidation, although not previously reserved or agreed.

(3) If the debt is due by virtue of a written instrument, and payable at a certain time, interest may be claimed for the period from that time to the date when the company went into liquidation.

(4) If the debt is due otherwise, interest may only be claimed if, before that date, a demand for payment of the debt was made in writing by or on behalf of the creditor, and notice given that interest would be payable from the date of the demand to the date of payment.

(5) Interest under paragraph (4) may only be claimed for the period from the date of the demand to that of the company's going into liquidation [and for all the purposes of the Act and the Rules shall be chargeable at a rate not exceeding that mentioned in paragraph (6)].

(6) The rate of interest to be claimed under paragraphs (3) and (4) is the rate specified in section 17 of the Judgments Act 1838 on the date when the company went into liquidation.

Notes

R 4.93

Where the contract in question contains provisions for the capitalisation of interest falling due before winding up these are to be applied in the quantification of a creditor's claim but such provisions cannot be applied to interest payments falling due after the winding up: *Re Amalgamated Investment and Property Co Ltd* [1985] Ch 349.

That part of IR 1986 r 4.93(1) which appears in square brackets was added by Insolvency (Amendment) Rules 2005 (SI 2005/527). The amendment does not apply where a company has entered administration or gone into liquidation before 1 April 2005.

2.336

4.94 Debt payable at future time

A creditor may prove for a debt of which payment was not yet due on the date when the company went into liquidation, [or, if the liquidation was immediately preceded by an administration, on the date that the company entered administration] but subject to Rule 11.13 in Part II of the Rules (adjustment of dividend where payment made before time).

Notes

R 4.94

This provision permits a creditor to prove for a debt of which payment was not due at the date of liquidation; and see IR 1986 r 13.12. The amount of the claim will be subject to the provisions for the adjustment of dividends where payment is made before time (IR 1986 r 4.94) and a discount at a the rate of 5% per annum will be made in respect of each day by which any dividend paid in respect of the debt is earlier than the due date: IR 1986 r 11.13(2).

That part of the rule which appears in square brackets was added by Insolvency (Amendment) Rules 2005 (SI 2005/527). The amendment does not apply where a company has entered administration or gone into liquidation before 1 April 2005.

Chapter 10
Secured Creditors

2.337

4.95 Value of security

(1) A secured creditor may, with the agreement of the liquidator or the leave of the court, at any time alter the value which he has, in his proof of debt, put upon his security.

(2) However, if a secured creditor—
  (a) being the petitioner, has in the petition put a value on his security, or
  (b) has voted in respect of the unsecured balance of his debt,

he may re-value his security only with leave of the court. (NO CVL APPLICATION)

———

Notes

R 4.95(1)

A secured creditor is defined in IA 1986 s 248(a).

———

2.338

4.96 Surrender for non-disclosure

(1) If a secured creditor omits to disclose his security in his proof of debt, he shall surrender his security for the general benefit of creditors, unless the court, on application by him, relieves him for the effect of this Rule on the ground that the omission was inadvertent or the result of honest mistake.

(2) If the court grants that relief, it may require or allow the creditor's proof of debt to be amended, on such terms as may be just.

(3) Nothing in this rule or the following two Rules may affect the rights in rem of creditors or third parties protected under Article 5 of the EC Regulation (third parties' rights in rem).

———

Notes

R 4.96(1)

A surrender of a security does not discharge a surety: *Rainbow v Juggins* (1880) 5 QBD 422. Inadvertence covers a case where the omission is accidental but not where the omission was made deliberately: *Re Safety Explosives Ltd* [1904] 1 Ch 226 or where the omission is not explained appropriately *LCP Retail Ltd v Richard Andrew Segal* [2006] EWHC 2087 (Ch).

———

2.339

4.97 Redemption by liquidator

(1) The liquidator may at any time give notice to a creditor whose debt is secured that he proposes, at the expiration of 28 days from the date of the notice, to redeem the security at the value put upon it in the creditor's proof.

(2) The creditor then has 21 days (or such longer period as the liquidator may allow) in which, if he so wishes, to exercise his right to revalue his security (with the leave of the court, where Rule 4.95(2) applies).

If the creditor re-values his security, the liquidator may only redeem at the new value.

(3) If the liquidator redeems the security, the cost of transferring it is payable out of the assets.

(4) A secured creditor may at any time, by a notice in writing, call on the liquidator to elect whether he will or will not exercise his power to redeem the security at the value then placed on it; and the liquidator then has 6 months in which to exercise the power or determine not to exercise it.

2.340

4.98 Test of security's value

(1) Subject as follows, the liquidator, if he is dissatisfied with the value which a secured creditor puts on his security (whether in his proof or by way of re-valuation under Rule 4.97), may require any property comprised in the security to be offered for sale.

(2) The terms of sale shall be such as may be agreed, or as the court may direct; and if the sale is by auction, the liquidator on behalf of the company, and the creditor on his own behalf, may appear and bid.

2.341

4.99 Realisation of security by creditor

If a creditor who has valued his security subsequently realises it (whether or not at the instance of the liquidator)—

   (a)   the net amount realised shall be substituted for the value previously put by the creditor on the security, and

   (b)   that amount shall be treated in all respects as an amended valuation made by him.

Chapter 11
The Liquidator

Section A: Appointment and Associated Formalities

2.342

4.100 Appointment by creditors or contributories (No CVL Application)

(1) This Rule applies where a person is appointed as liquidator either by a meeting of creditors or by a meeting of contributories.

(2) The chairman of the meeting shall certify the appointment, but not unless and until the person appointed has provided him with a written statement to the effect that he is an insolvency practitioner, duly qualified under the Act to be the liquidator, and that he consents so to act.

(3) The liquidator's appointment is effective from the date on which the appointment is certified, that date to be endorsed on the certificate.

(4) The chairman of the meeting (if not himself the official receiver) shall send the certificate to the official receiver.

(5) The official receiver shall in any case send the certificate to the liquidator and file a copy of it in court.

Notes

R 4.100(2)

A liquidator cannot be appointed without his consent: *Charles Petitioner* [1964] SC 1. A person is not qualified to act as a liquidator unless there is in force a security which meets the prescribed requirements: IA 1986 s 390(3)(b). In summary a general insurance bond of £250,000 must be held and a 'specific penalty sum' in a sum not less than the value of the assets to which he is appointed: Insolvency Practitioners Regulations 2005 (SI 2005/524) reg 12 Sch 2 (as amended). Without complying with the bonding requirements the liquidator's appointment should not be certified.

2.343

4.101 Appointment by creditors or by the company—CVL

(1) This Rule applies where a person is appointed as liquidator either by a meeting of creditors or by a meeting of the company.

(2) Subject as follows, the chairman of the meeting shall certify the appointment, but not unless and until the person appointed has provided him with a written statement to the effect that he is an insolvency practitioner, duly qualified under the Act to be the liquidator, and that he consents so to act; the liquidator's appointment takes effect upon the passing of the resolution for that appointment.

(3) The chairman shall send the certificate forthwith to the liquidator, who shall keep it as part of the records of the liquidation.

(4) Paragraphs (2) and (3) need not be complied with in the case of a liquidator appointed by a company meeting and replaced by another liquidator appointed on the same day by a creditors' meeting.

Notes

R 4.101(2)

See note to IR 1986 r 4.100(2) above.

2.344

4.101A Power to fill vacancy in office of liquidator—CVL

Where a vacancy in the office of liquidator occurs in the manner mentioned in section 104 a meeting of creditors to fill the vacancy may be convened by any creditor or, if there were more liquidators than one, by the continuing liquidators.

Notes

R 4.101A

Under s 104 the creditors can appoint a new liquidator unless the former liquidator was appointed by the court under IA 1986 s 100(3) (application for court appointment following creditors/contributories meetings) or IA 1986 s 108 (removal of liquidator by the court for cause).

2.345

4.102 Appointment by the court (No CVL Application)

(1) This Rule applies where the liquidator is appointed by the court under section 139(4) (different persons nominated by creditors and contributories) or section 140 (liquidation following administration or voluntary arrangement).

(2) The court's order shall not issue unless and until the person appointed has filed in court a statement to the effect that he is an insolvency practitioner, duly qualified under the Act to be the liquidator, and that he consents so to act.

(3) Thereafter, the court shall send 2 copies of the order to the official receiver. One of the copies shall be sealed, and this shall be sent to the person appointed as liquidator.

(4) The liquidator's appointment takes effect from the date of the order.

(5) The liquidator shall, within 28 days of his appointment, give notice of it to all creditors and contributories of the company of whom he is aware in that period. Alternatively, if the court allows, he may advertise his appointment in accordance with the court's directions.

(6) In his notice or advertisement under this Rule the liquidator shall—
  (a) state whether he proposes to summon meetings of creditors and contributories for the purpose of establishing a liquidation committee, or proposes to summon only a meeting of creditors for that purpose, and
  (b) if he does not propose to summon any such meeting, set out the powers of the creditors under the Act to require him to summon one.

Notes

R 4.102(2)

See note to IR 1986 r 4.100(2) above.

2.346

4.103 Appointment by the court—CVL

(1) This Rule applies where the liquidator is appointed by the court under section 100(3) or 108.

(2) The court's order shall not issue unless and until the person appointed has filed in court a statement to the effect that he is an insolvency practitioner, duly qualified under the Act to be the liquidator, and that he consents so to act.

(3) Thereafter, the court shall send a sealed copy of the order to the liquidator, whose appointment takes effect from the date of the order.

(4) Not later than 28 days from his appointment, the liquidator shall give notice of it to all creditors of the company of whom he is aware in that period. Alternatively, if the court allows, he may advertise his appointment in accordance with the court's directions.

Notes

R 4.103(1)

Such appointments take place following an application for a court appointment following a dispute at the creditors/contributories meetings (IA 1986 s 100(3)) or the removal of liquidator by the court for cause (IA 1986 s 108).

R 4.103(4)

The liquidator must also publish his appointment in the Gazette within 14 days of it being made and deliver a notice to the Registrar of Companies: IA 1986 s 109.

2.347

4.104 Appointment by Secretary of State (No CVL Application)

(1) This Rule applies where the official receiver applies to the Secretary of State to appoint a liquidator in place of himself, or refers to the Secretary of State the need for an appointment.

(2) If the Secretary of State makes an appointment, he shall send two copies of the certificate of appointment to the official receiver, who shall transmit one such copy to the person appointed, and file the other in court.

(3) The certificate shall specify the date from which the liquidator's appointment is to be effective.

2.348

4.105 Authentication of liquidator's appointment

A copy of the certificate of the liquidator's appointment or (as the case may be) a sealed copy of the court's order or a copy of the notice registered in accordance with paragraph 83(3) of Schedule B1 to the Act,

> may in any proceedings be adduced as proof that the person appointed is duly authorised to exercise the powers and perform the duties of liquidator in the company's winding up.

Notes

R 4.105

An appointment under IA 1986 para 83 Sch B1 occurs because the administrator wishes to move the company from administration into a creditors' voluntary liquidation. This can be done without the need for a resolution; instead, the administrator registers the appropriate notice with the Registrar of Companies.

2.349

4.106 Appointment to be advertised and registered

(1) Subject as follows, where the liquidator is appointed by a creditors' or contributories' meeting, or by a meeting of the company, he shall, on receiving his certificate of appointment, give notice of his appointment in such newspaper as he thinks most appropriate for ensuring that it comes to the notice of the company's creditors and contributories.

(2–CVL) Paragraph (1) need not be complied with in the case of a liquidator appointed by a company meeting and replaced by another liquidator appointed on the same day by a creditors' meeting.

(3) The expense of giving notice under this Rule shall be borne in the first instance by the liquidator; but he is entitled to be reimbursed out of the assets, as an expense of the liquidation.

The same applies also in the case of the notice or advertisement required where the appointment is made by the court or the Secretary of State.

(4) In the case of a winding up by the court, the liquidator shall also forthwith notify his appointment to the registrar of companies.

This applies however the liquidator is appointed. [(NO CVL APPLICATION)]

Notes

R 4.106(1)

The liquidator must also publish notice of his appointment in the Gazette: see IA 1986 s 109. For the priority of expenses in a liquidation, see IR 1986 r 4.218.

2.350

4.107 Hand-over of assets to liquidator (No CVL Application)

(1) This Rule applies only where the liquidator is appointed in succession to the official receiver acting as liquidator.

(2) When the liquidator's appointment takes effect, the official receiver shall forthwith do all that is required for putting him into possession of the assets.

(3) On taking possession of the assets, the liquidator shall discharge any balance due to the official receiver on account of—

    (a)   expenses properly incurred by him and payable under the Act or the Rules, and

    (b)   any advances made by him in respect of the assets, together with interest on such advances at the rate specified in section 17 of the Judgments Act 1838 at the date of the winding-up order.

(4) Alternatively, the liquidator may (before taking office) give to the official receiver a written undertaking to discharge any such balance out of the first realisation of assets.

(5) The official receiver has a charge on the assets in respect of any sums due to him under paragraph (3). But, where the liquidator has realised assets with a view to making those payments, the official receiver's charge does not extend in respect of sums deductible by the liquidator from the proceeds of realisation, as being expenses properly incurred therein.

(6) The liquidator shall from time to time out of the realisation of assets discharge all guarantees properly given by the official receiver for the benefit of the estate, and shall pay all the official receiver's expenses.

(7) The official receiver shall give to the liquidator all such information relating to the affairs of the company and the course of the winding up as he (the official receiver) considers to be reasonably required for the effective discharge by the liquidator of his duties as such.

(8) The liquidator shall also be furnished with a copy of any report made by the official receiver under Chapter 7 of this Part of the Rules.

Notes

R 4.107(1)

A liquidator may be appointed following from the official receiver under IA 1986 s 136, 137 and 139.

Section B: Resignation and Removal; Vacation of Office

2.351

4.108 Creditors' meeting to receive liquidator's resignation

(1) Before resigning his office, the liquidator must call a meeting of creditors for the purpose of receiving his resignation. The notice summoning the meeting shall indicate that this is the purpose, or one of the purposes, of it, and shall draw the attention of creditors to Rule 4.121 or, as the case may be, Rule 4.122—CVL with respect to the liquidator's release.

(2) A copy of the notice shall at the same time also be sent to the official receiver. (NO CVL APPLICATION)

(3) The notice to creditors under paragraph (1) must be accompanied by an account of the liquidator's administration of the winding up, including—
    (a)   a summary of his receipts and payments, and
    (b)   a statement by him that he has reconciled his account with that which is held by the Secretary of State in respect of the winding up.

(4) Subject as follows, the liquidator may only proceed under this Rule on grounds of ill health or because—
    (a)   he intends ceasing to be in practice as an insolvency practitioner, or
    (b)   there is some conflict of interest or change of personal circumstances which precludes or makes impracticable the further discharge by him of the duties of liquidator.

(5) Where two or more persons are acting as liquidator jointly, any one of them may proceed under this Rule (without prejudice to the continuation in office of the other or others) on the ground that, in his opinion and that of the other or others, it is no longer expedient that there should continue to be the present number of joint liquidators.

(6) If there is no quorum present at the meeting summoned to receive the liquidator's resignation, the meeting is deemed to have been held, a resolution is deemed to have been passed that the liquidator's resignation be accepted and the creditors are deemed not to have resolved against the liquidator having his release.

(7) Where paragraph (6) applies any reference in the Rules to a resolution that the liquidator's resignation be accepted is replaced by a reference to the making of a written statement, signed by the person who, had there been a quorum present, would have been chairman of the meeting, that no quorum was present and that the liquidator may resign.

Notes

R 4.108(1)

Where a liquidator wishes to resign from numerous appointments without going through the detailed procedures set out in this and following rules in respect of each and every company, the court has jurisdiction to make block orders replacing the resigning liquidator: *Re Equity Nominees Ltd* [2000] BCC 84; *Supperstone v Auger* [1999] BPIR 152; and see IA 1986 s 108 (voluntary liquidations), IA 1986 s 168(3) and 172(2) (compulsory liquidations). The court will give directions as to the notification of creditors. Further the Practice Direction: Insolvency Proceedings, Civil Procedure 2006, Vol 2, Sec 3E, para 1.6ff sets down a procedure under which a block order can be made on paper.

The grounds on which a liquidator may resign are limited. A liquidator is, of course, in a fiduciary relationship to the company, and so must not allow a conflict of interests to arise, and must resign if one does: *Re Corbenstoke Ltd (No 2)* (1989) 5 BCC 767.

2.352

4.109 Action following acceptance of resignation (No CVL Application)

(1) This Rule applies where a meeting is summoned to receive the liquidator's resignation.

(2) If the chairman of the meeting is other than the official receiver, and there is passed at the meeting any of the following resolutions—
    (a)   that the liquidator's resignation be accepted,
    (b)   that a new liquidator be appointed,
    (c)   that the resigning liquidator be not given his release,
the chairman shall, within 3 days, send to the official receiver a copy of the resolution.

If it has been resolved to accept the liquidator's resignation, the chairman shall send to the official receiver a certificate to that effect.

(3) If the creditors have resolved to appoint a new liquidator, the certificate of his appointment shall also be sent to the official receiver within that time; and Rule 4.100 shall be complied with in respect of it.

(4) If the liquidator's resignation is accepted, the notice of it required by section 172(6) shall be given by him forthwith after the meeting; and he shall send a copy of the notice to the official receiver.

The notice shall be accompanied by a copy of the account sent to creditors under Rule 4.108(3).

(5) The official receiver shall file a copy of the notice in court.

(6) The liquidator's resignation is effective as from the date on which the official receiver files the copy notice in court, that date to be endorsed on the copy notice.

2.353

4.110 Action following acceptance of resignation—CVL

(1) This Rule applies where a meeting is summoned to receive the liquidator's resignation.

(2) If his resignation is accepted, the notice of it required by section 171(5) shall be given by him forthwith after the meeting.

(3) Where a new liquidator is appointed in place of the one who has resigned, the certificate of his appointment shall be delivered forthwith by the chairman of the meeting to the new liquidator.

2.354

4.111 Leave to resign granted by the court

(1) If at a creditors' meeting summoned to accept the liquidator's resignation it is resolved that it be not accepted, the court may, on the liquidator's application, make an order giving him leave to resign.

(2) The court's order may include such provision as it thinks fit with respect to matters arising in connection with the resignation, and shall determine the date from which the liquidator's release is effective.

(3) The court shall send two sealed copies of the order to the liquidator, who shall send one of the copies forthwith to the official receiver. (NO CVL APPLICATION)

(4–CVL) The court shall send two sealed copies of the order to the liquidator, who shall forthwith send one of them to the registrar of companies.

(5) On sending notice of his resignation to the court, the liquidator shall send a copy of it to the official receiver. (NO CVL APPLICATION)

2.355

4.112 Advertisement of resignation

Where a new liquidator is appointed in place of one who has resigned, the former shall, in giving notice of his appointment, state that his predecessor has resigned and (if it be the case) that he has been given his release.

2.356

4.113 Meeting of creditors to remove liquidator (No CVL Application)

(1) Where a meeting of creditors is summoned for the purpose of removing the liquidator, the notice summoning it shall indicate that this is the purpose, or one of the purposes, of the meeting; and the notice shall draw the attention of creditors to section 174(4) with respect to the liquidator's release.

(2) A copy of the notice shall at the same time also be sent to the official receiver.

(3) At the meeting, a person other than the liquidator or his nominee may be elected to act as chairman; but if the liquidator or his nominee is chairman and a resolution has been proposed for the liquidator's removal, the chairman shall not adjourn the meeting without the consent of at least one-half (in value) of the creditors present (in person or by proxy) and entitled to vote.

(4) Where the chairman of the meeting is other than the official receiver, and there is passed at the meeting any of the following resolutions—
    (a)   that the liquidator be removed,
    (b)   that a new liquidator be appointed,
    (c)   that the removed liquidator be not given his release,
the chairman shall, within 3 days, send to the official receiver a copy of the resolution.

If it has been resolved to remove the liquidator, the chairman shall send to the official receiver a certificate to that effect.

(5) If the creditors have resolved to appoint a new liquidator, the certificate of his appointment shall also be sent to the official receiver within that time; and Rule 4.100 above shall be complied with in respect of it.

2.357

4.114 Meeting of creditors to remove liquidator—CVL

(1) A meeting held under section 171(2)(b) for the removal of the liquidator shall be summoned by him if requested by 25% in value of the company's creditors, excluding those who are connected with it.

(2) The notice summoning the meeting shall indicate that the removal of the liquidator is the purpose, or one of the purposes, of the meeting; and the notice shall draw the attention of creditors to section 173(2) with respect to the liquidator's release.

(3) At the meeting, a person other than the liquidator or his nominee may be elected to act as chairman; but if the liquidator or his nominee is chairman and a resolution has been proposed for the liquidator's removal, the chairman shall not adjourn the meeting without the consent of at least one-half (in value) of the creditors present (in person or by proxy) and entitled to vote.

2.358

4.115 Court's power to regulate meetings under Rules 4.113, 4.114—CVL

Where a meeting under Rule 4.113 or 4.114—CVL is to be held, or is proposed to be summoned, the court may, on the application of any creditor, give directions as to the mode of summoning it, the sending out and return of forms of proxy, the conduct of the meeting, and any other matter which appears to the court to require regulation or control under this Rule.

2.359

4.116 Procedure on removal (No CVL Application)

(1) Where the creditors have resolved that the liquidator be removed, the official receiver shall file in court the certificate of removal.

(2) The resolution is effective as from the date on which the official receiver files the certificate of removal in court, and that date shall be endorsed on the certificate.

(3) A copy of the certificate, so endorsed, shall be sent by the official receiver to the liquidator who has been removed and, if a new liquidator has been appointed, to him.

(4) The official receiver shall not file the certificate in court unless and until the Secretary of State has certified to him that the removed liquidator has reconciled his account with that held by the Secretary of State in respect of the winding up.

2.360

4.117 Procedure on removal—CVL

Where the creditors have resolved that the liquidator be removed, the chairman of the creditors' meeting shall forthwith—
  (a) if at the meeting another liquidator was not appointed, send the certificate of the liquidator's removal to the registrar of companies, and
  (b) otherwise, deliver the certificate to the new liquidator, who shall send it to the registrar.

2.361

4.118 Advertisement of removal

Where a new liquidator is appointed in place of one removed, the former shall, in giving notice of his appointment, state that his predecessor has been removed and (if it be the case) that he has been given his release.

2.362

4.119 Removal of liquidator by the court (No CVL Application)

(1) This Rule applies where application is made to the court for the removal of the liquidator, or for an order directing the liquidator to summon a meeting of creditors for the purpose of removing him.

(2) The court may, if it thinks that no sufficient cause is shown for the application, disMiss it; but it shall not do so unless the applicant has had an opportunity to attend the court for an *ex parte* hearing, of which he has been given at least 7 days' notice.

If the application is not dismissed under this paragraph, the court shall fix a venue for it to be heard.

(3) The court may require the applicant to make a deposit or give security for the costs to be incurred by the liquidator on the application.

(4) The applicant shall, at least 14 days before the hearing, send to the liquidator and the official receiver a notice stating the venue and accompanied by a copy of the application, and of any evidence which he intends to adduce in support of it.

(5) Subject to any contrary order of the court, the costs of the application are not payable out of the assets.

(6) Where the court removes the liquidator—
  (a)   it shall send copies of the order of removal to him and to the official receiver;
  (b)   the order may include such provision as the court thinks fit with respect to matters arising in connection with the removal; and
  (c)   if the court appoints a new liquidator, Rule 4.102 applies.

2.363

4.120 Removal of liquidator by the court—CVL

(1) This Rule applies where application is made to the court for the removal of the liquidator, or for an order directing the liquidator to summon a creditors' meeting for the purpose of removing him.

(2) The court may, if it thinks that no sufficient cause is shown for the application, dismiss it; but it shall not do so unless the applicant has had an opportunity to attend the court for an *ex parte* hearing, of which he has been given at least 7 days' notice.

If the application is not dismissed under this paragraph, the court shall fix a venue for it to be heard.

(3) The court may require the applicant to make a deposit or give security for the costs to be incurred by the liquidator on the application.

(4) The applicant shall, at least 14 days before the hearing, send to the liquidator a notice stating the venue and accompanied by a copy of the application, and of any evidence which he intends to adduce in support of it.

(5) Subject to any contrary order of the court, the costs of the application are not payable out of the assets.

(6) Where the court removes the liquidator—
  (a) it shall send 2 copies of the order of removal to him, one to be sent by him forthwith to the registrar of companies, with notice of his ceasing to act;
  (b) the order may include such provision as the court thinks fit with respect to matters arising in connection with the removal; and
  (c) if the court appoints a new liquidator, Rule 4.103–CVL applies.

Notes

RR 4.113–4.120

For the removal of liquidators see IA 1986 s 171 (voluntary winding up) and IA 1986 s 172 (compulsory winding up). For a recent review of the authorities on removal of office holders, see *Sisu Capital Fund Ltd v Tucker* [2006] BPIR 154. Generally a liquidator is only removed by the court 'on cause shown': *Re A & C Supplies Ltd* [1998] BCC 708; *Deloitte and Touche AG v Johnson* [2000] 1 BCLC 485. The liquidator must be given the opportunity to attend court (IR 1986 rr. 4.120(4), 4.143(4), 4.119(4)) and he has the right to appeal against his removal: *Re New De Kaap Ltd* [1908] 1 Ch 589. The applicant will succeed in obtaining an order for removal if the liquidator has been acting mala fide or in an improper manner (*Re Ryder Installation Ltd* [1966] 1 All ER 453), or he fails to act in an even handed and independent manner (*Re Rubber and Produce Investment Trust* [1915] 1 Ch 382) or if there is a conflict of interest: *Re Karamelli & Barnett Ltd* [1917] 1 Ch 203; or where it is in the general interests of the creditors in an insolvent liquidation that a different liquidator is appointed because it is less costly: *Re Sankey Furniture Ltd* [1995] 2 BCLC 594. Clearly a liquidator will run the risk of being removed if he adopts a complacent attitude to the winding up of the company's affairs: *Re AMF International Ltd* [1995] 2 BCLC 529. The court should only use its power under IR 1986 r 4.120(3) where the applicant's case, whist arguable, seems likely to fail: *Re Buildlead Ltd* [2005] BCC 133.

R 4.120(3)

The appropriate approach to whether or not the court will make an order for security for costs was 'merits based', so that the court would order security to be given where an application to remove a liquidator was arguable but likely to fail: *Re Buildlead Ltd* [2005] BCC 134.

2.364

4.121 Release of resigning or removed liquidator (No CVL Application)

(1) Where the liquidator's resignation is accepted by a meeting of creditors which has not resolved against his release, he has his release from when his resignation is effective under Rule 4.109.

(2) Where the liquidator is removed by a meeting of creditors which has not resolved against his release, the fact of his release shall be stated in the certificate of removal.

(3) Where—
  (a) the liquidator resigns, and the creditors' meeting called to receive his resignation has resolved against his release, or
  (b) he is removed by a creditors' meeting which has so resolved, or is removed by the court,
he must apply to the Secretary of State for his release.

(4) When the Secretary of State gives the release, he shall certify it accordingly, and send the certificate to the official receiver, to be filed in court.

(5) A copy of the certificate shall be sent by the Secretary of State to the former liquidator, whose release is effective from the date of the certificate.

Notes

R 4.121(1)

The obtaining of a release is important because it discharges the liquidator from liability for acts and omissions in the course of the liquidation and enables him to avoid a claim for breach of duty by creditors or contributories unless the court gives leave: IA 1986 s 212(4), s 173(4), s 174(6).

2.365

4.122 Release of resigning or removed liquidator—CVL

(1) Where the liquidator's resignation is accepted by a meeting of creditors which has not resolved against his release, he has his release from when he gives notice of his resignation to the registrar of companies.

(2) Where the liquidator is removed by a creditors' meeting which has not resolved against his release, the fact of his release shall be stated in the certificate of removal.

(3) Where—
  (a) the liquidator resigns, and the creditors' meeting called to receive his resignation has resolved against his release, or
  (b) he is removed by a creditors' meeting which has so resolved, or is removed by the court,
he must apply to the Secretary of State for his release.

(4) When the Secretary of State gives the release, he shall certify it accordingly, and send the certificate to the registrar of companies.

(5) A copy of the certificate shall be sent by the Secretary of State to the former liquidator, whose release is effective from the date of the certificate.

2.366

4.123 Removal of liquidator by Secretary of State (No CVL Application)

(1) If the Secretary of State decides to remove the liquidator, he shall before doing so notify the liquidator and the official receiver of his

decision and the grounds of it, and specify a period within which the liquidator may make representations against implementation of the decision.

(2) If the Secretary of State directs the removal of the liquidator, he shall forthwith—
  (a) file notice of his decision in court, and
  (b) send notice to the liquidator and the official receiver.

(3) If the liquidator is removed by direction of the Secretary of State—
  (a) Rule 4.121 applies as regards the liquidator obtaining his release, as if he had been removed by the court, and
  (b) the court may make any such order in his case as it would have power to make if he had been so removed.

Notes

R 4.123

If the Secretary of State appointed the liquidator he may remove him IA 1986 s 172(4).

Section C: Release on Completion of Administration

2.367

4.124 Release of official receiver (No CVL Application)

(1) The official receiver shall, before giving notice to the Secretary of State under section 174(3) (that the winding up is for practical purposes complete), send out notice of his intention to do so to all creditors of which he is aware.

(2) The notice shall in each case be accompanied by a summary of the official receiver's receipts and payments as liquidator.

(2A) The summary of receipts and payments referred to in paragraph (2) shall also include a statement as to the amount paid to unsecured creditors by virtue of the application of section 176A (prescribed part).

(3) The Secretary of State, when he has determined the date from which the official receiver is to have his release, shall give notice to the court that he has done so. The notice shall be accompanied by the summary referred to in paragraph (2).

Notes

R 4.124(2A)

This was introduced by the Insolvency Amendment Rules 2003 (SI 2003/1730) to detail the prescribed part (or 'ring fenced') monies that have been used to pay the unsecured creditors.

2.368

4.125 Final meeting (No CVL Application)

(1) Where the liquidator is other than the official receiver, he shall give at least 28 days' notice of the final meeting of creditors to be held under section 146. The notice shall be sent to all creditors of which he is aware; and the liquidator shall cause it to be gazetted at least one month before the meeting is to be held.

(2) The liquidator's report laid before the meeting under that section shall contain an account of the liquidator's administration of the winding up, including—

    (a)   a summary of his receipts and payments, and

    (b)   a statement by him that he has reconciled his account with that which is held by the Secretary of State in respect of the winding up.

(2A) The liquidator's report shall also contain a statement as to the amount paid to unsecured creditors by virtue of the application of section 176A (prescribed part).

(3) At the final meeting, the creditors may question the liquidator with respect to any matter contained in his report, and may resolve against him having his release.

(4) The liquidator shall give notice to the court that the final meeting has been held; and the notice shall state whether or not he has been given his release, and be accompanied by a copy of the report laid before the final meeting. A copy of the notice shall be sent by the liquidator to the Secretary of State.

(5) If there is no quorum present at the final meeting, the liquidator shall report to the court that a final meeting was summoned in accordance with the Rules, but there was no quorum present; and the final meeting is then deemed to have been held, and the creditors not to have resolved against the liquidator having his release.

(6) If the creditors at the final meeting have not so resolved, the liquidator is released when the notice under paragraph (4) is filed in court. If they have so resolved, the liquidator must obtain his release from the Secretary of State and Rule 4.121 applies accordingly.

Notes

R 4.125(2A)

This was introduced by the Insolvency Amendment Rules 2003 (SI 2003/1730) 2003 to detail the prescribed part (or 'ring fenced') monies that have been used to pay the unsecured creditors.

2.369

4.125A Rule as to reporting]

[(1) The court may, on the liquidator or official receiver's application, relieve him of any duty imposed on him by Rule 4.124 or 4.125, or authorise him to carry out the duty in a way other than there required.

(2) In considering whether to act under this Rule, the court shall have regard to the cost of carrying out the duty, to the amount of the assets available, and to the extent of the interest of creditors or contributories, or any particular class of them.]

2.370

4.126 Final meeting—CVL

(1) The liquidator shall give at least 28 days' notice of the final meeting of creditors to be held under section 106. The notice shall be sent to all creditors who have proved their debts.

(2) At the final meeting, the creditors may question the liquidator with respect to any matter contained in the account required under the section or paragraph (4) of this Rule, and may resolve against the liquidator having his release.

(3) Where the creditors have so resolved, he must obtain his release from the Secretary of State; and Rule 4.122—CVL applies accordingly.

(4) The account of the winding up required under section 106 shall also include a statement as to the amount paid to unsecured creditors by virtue of the application of section 176A (prescribed part)

Section D: Remuneration

2.371

4.127 Fixing of remuneration

(1) The liquidator is entitled to receive remuneration for his services as such.

(2) The remuneration shall be fixed either—
    (a) as a percentage of the value of the assets which are realised or distributed, or of the one value and the other in combination, or
    (b) by reference to the time properly given by the insolvency practitioner (as liquidator) and his staff in attending to matters arising in the winding up.

(3) Where the liquidator is other than the official receiver, it is for the liquidation committee (if there is one) to determine whether the remuneration is to be fixed under paragraph (2)(a) or (b) and, if under paragraph (2)(a), to determine any percentage to be applied as there mentioned.

(4) In arriving at that determination, the committee shall have regard to the following matters—
    (a) the complexity (or otherwise) of the case,
    (b) any respects in which, in connection with the winding up, there falls on the insolvency practitioner (as liquidator) any responsibility of an exceptional kind or degree,
    (c) the effectiveness with which the insolvency practitioner appears to be carrying out, or to have carried out, his duties as liquidator, and
    (d) the value and nature of the assets with which the liquidator has to deal.

(5) If there is no liquidation committee, or the committee does not make the requisite determination, the liquidator's remuneration may be fixed (in accordance with paragraph (2)) by a resolution of a meeting of creditors; and paragraph (4) applies to them as it does to the liquidation committee.

(6) Where the liquidator is not the official receiver and his remuneration is not fixed as above, the liquidator shall be entitled to remuneration fixed in accordance with the provisions of Rule 4.127A

Notes

R 4.127(2)

In practice a liquidator will charge on a time basis rather than a percentage basis and sometimes the liquidator will charge a fixed fee. For the fixing of remuneration, see Practice Statement – Fixing and Approval of the Remuneration of Appointees [2004] BPIR 953; *Re Cabletel Instalations Ltd* [2005] BPIR 28.

2.372

[4.127A Liquidator's entitlement to remuneration where it is not fixed under Rule 4.127]

[(1) This Rule applies where the liquidator is not the official receiver and his remuneration is not fixed in accordance with Rule 4.127.

(2) The liquidator shall be entitled by way of remuneration for his services as such, to such sum as is arrived at by—
- (a) first applying the realisation scale set out in Schedule 6 to the monies received by him from the realisation of the assets of the company (including any Value Added Tax thereon but after deducting any sums paid to secured creditors in respect of their securities and any sums spent out of money received in carrying on the business of the company); and
- (b) then by adding to the sum arrived at under sub-paragraph (a) such sum as is arrived at by applying the distribution scale set out in Schedule 6 to the value of assets distributed to creditors of the company (including payments made in respect of preferential debts) and to contributories.]

2.373

[4.127B Liquidator's remuneration where he realises assets on behalf of chargeholder]

[(1) This Rule applies where the liquidator is not the official receiver and realises assets on behalf of a secured creditor.

(2) Where the assets realised for a secured creditor are subject to a charge which when created was a mortgage or a fixed charge, the liquidator shall be entitled to such sum by way of remuneration as is arrived at by applying the realisation scale set out in Schedule 6 to the monies received by him in respect of the assets realised (including any sums received in

respect of Value Added Tax thereon but after deducting any sums spent out of money received in carrying on the business of the company).

(3) Where the assets realised for a secured creditor are subject to a charge which when created was a floating charge, the liquidator shall be entitled to such sum by way of remuneration as is arrived at by—

    (a)   first applying the realisation scale set out in Schedule 6 to monies received by him from the realisation of those assets (including any Value Added Tax thereon but ignoring any sums received which are spent in carrying on the business of the company); and

    (b)   then by adding to the sum arrived at under sub-paragraph (a) such sum as is arrived at by applying the distribution scale set out in Schedule 6 to the value of the assets distributed to the holder of the charge] and payments made in respect of preferential debts.

2.374

4.128 Other matters affecting remuneration

(1) (*revoked*)

(2) Where there are joint liquidators, it is for them to agree between themselves as to how the remuneration payable should be apportioned. Any dispute arising between them may be referred—

    (a)   to the court, for settlement by order, or

    (b)   to the liquidation committee or a meeting of creditors, for settlement by resolution.

(3) If the liquidator is a solicitor and employs his own firm, or any partner in it, to act on behalf of the company, profit costs shall not be paid unless this is authorised by the liquidation committee, the creditors or the court.

2.375

4.129 Recourse of liquidator to meeting of creditors

If the liquidator's remuneration has been fixed by the liquidation committee, and he considers the rate or amount to be insufficient, he may request that it be increased by resolution of the creditors.

2.376

4.130 Recourse to the court

(1) If the liquidator considers that the remuneration fixed for him by the liquidation committee, or by resolution of the creditors, or as under Rule 4.127(6), is insufficient, he may apply to the court for an order increasing its amount or rate.

(2) The liquidator shall give at least 14 days' notice of his application to the members of the liquidation committee; and the committee may nominate one or more members to appear or be represented, and to be heard, on the application.

(3) If there is no liquidation committee, the liquidator's notice of his application shall be sent to such one or more of the company's creditors as

the court may direct, which creditors may nominate one or more of their number to appear or be represented.

(4) The court may, if it appears to be a proper case, order the costs of the liquidator's application, including the costs of any member of the liquidation committee appearing or being represented on it, or any creditor so appearing or being represented, to be paid out of the assets.

2.377

4.131 Creditors' claim that remuneration is excessive

(1) Any creditor of the company may, with the concurrence of at least 25% in value of the creditors (including himself), apply to the court for an order that the liquidator's remuneration be reduced, on the grounds that it is, in all the circumstances, excessive.

(2) The court may, if it thinks that no sufficient cause is shown for a reduction, dismiss the application; but it shall not do so unless the applicant has had an opportunity to attend the court for an *ex parte* hearing, of which he has been given at least 7 days' notice.

If the application is not dismissed under this paragraph, the court shall fix a venue for it to be heard, and give notice to the applicant accordingly.

(3) The applicant shall, at least 14 days before the hearing, send to the liquidator a notice stating the venue and accompanied by a copy of the application, and of any evidence which the applicant intends to adduce in support of it.

(4) If the court considers the application to be well-founded, it shall make an order fixing the remuneration at a reduced amount or rate.

(5) Unless the court orders otherwise, the costs of the application shall be paid by the applicant, and are not payable out of the assets.

Notes

R 4.131

The principal points in relation to remuneration are as follows:

- A liquidator may not set his own remuneration: *Re Salters Hall School Ltd* [1998] BCC 503.
- With the permission of the court a liquidator may be paid out of the assets of a trust where he has done work benefiting the trust assets: *Re Berkeley Applegate (Investment Consultants) Ltd (No 2)* (1988) 4 BCC 279; *Re Berkeley Applegate (Investment Consultants) Ltd (No 3)* (1989) 5 BCC 803; *Rye v Ashfield Nominees Ltd*, 6 Aug 2001, LTL 23/11/2001 (Ch D); *cf Tom Wise Ltd v Fillimore* [1999] BCC 129; *Re Local London Residential Ltd* [2004] 2 BCLC 72.
- For the priority in which a liquidator's remuneration is paid see IR 1986 r 4.218.

In an application under IR 1986 r 4.130 the court will need to have evidence that the rates allowed are genuinely insufficient before it will increase a liquidator's remuneration: *Re Tony Rowse NMC Ltd* [1996] BCC 196. In practice there were increasing numbers of challenges to the remuneration of office holders in the recent past applying the taxation provisions of Civil Procedure Rules. However, the court will now be guided by the principles set out in Practice Statement – Fixing and Approval of the Remuneration of Appointees (2004) [2004] BPIR 953 and *Re Cabletel Installations Ltd* [2005] BPIR. The court generally becomes involved in the task of assessing the remuneration when an appeal is made to it that the remuneration to be charged is excessive: *Re Independent Insurance Co Ltd (No 1)* [2003] BPIR 562. The experience of costs judges is growing in this area, but the court may still need an expert assessor to assist as in the *Re Independent Insurance Co Ltd* (above).

Section E: Supplementary Provisions

2.378

4.132 Liquidator deceased (No CVL Application)

(1) Subject as follows, where the liquidator (other than the official receiver) has died, it is the duty of his personal representatives to give notice of the fact to the official receiver, specifying the date of the death.

This does not apply if notice has been given under any of the following paragraphs of this Rule.

(2) If the deceased liquidator was a partner in a firm, notice may be given to the official receiver by a partner in the firm who is qualified to act as an insolvency practitioner, or is a member of any body recognised by the Secretary of State for the authorisation of insolvency practitioners.

(3) Notice of the death may be given by any person producing to the official receiver the relevant death certificate or a copy of it.

(4) The official receiver shall give notice to the court, for the purpose of fixing the date of the deceased liquidator's release.

2.379

4.133 Liquidator deceased—CVL

(1) Subject as follows, where the liquidator has died, it is the duty of his personal representatives to give notice of the fact, and of the date of death, to the registrar of companies and to the liquidation committee (if any) or a member of that committee.

(2) In the alternative, notice of the death may be given—
   (a)   if the deceased liquidator was a partner in a firm, by a partner qualified to act as an insolvency practitioner or who is a member of any body approved by the Secretary of State for the authorisation of insolvency practitioners, or
   (b)   by any person, if he delivers with the notice a copy of the relevant death certificate.

2.380

4.134 Loss of qualification as insolvency practitioner (No CVL Application)

(1) This Rule applies where the liquidator vacates office on ceasing to be qualified to act as an insolvency practitioner in relation to the company.

(2) He shall forthwith give notice of his doing so to the official receiver, who shall give notice to the Secretary of State.

The official receiver shall file in court a copy of his notice under this paragraph.

(3) Rule 4.121 applies as regards the liquidator obtaining his release, as if he had been removed by the court.

2.381

4.135 Loss of qualification as insolvency practitioner—CVL

(1) This Rule applies where the liquidator vacates office on ceasing to be qualified to act as an insolvency practitioner in relation to the company.

(2) He shall forthwith give notice of his doing so to the registrar of companies and the Secretary of State.

(3) Rule 4.122—CVL applies as regards the liquidator obtaining his release, as if he had been removed by the court.

2.382

4.136 Vacation of office on making of winding-up order—CVL

Where the liquidator vacates office in consequence of the court making a winding-up order against the company, Rule 4.122—CVL applies as regards his obtaining his release, as if he had been removed by the court.

2.383

4.137 Notice to official receiver of intention to vacate office (No CVL Application)

[(1) Where the liquidator intends to vacate office, whether by resignation or otherwise, he shall give notice of his intention to the official receiver together with notice of any creditors' meeting to be held in respect of his vacation of office, including any meeting to receive his resignation.

(2) The notice to the official receiver must be given at least 21 days before any such creditors' meeting.

(3) Where there remains any property of the company which has not been realised, applied, distributed or otherwise fully dealt with in the winding up, the liquidator shall include in his notice to the official receiver details of the nature of that property, its value (or the fact that it has no value), its location, any action taken by the liquidator to deal with that property or any reason for his not dealing with it, and the current position in relation to it.]

2.384

4.138 Liquidator's duties on vacating office

(1) Where the liquidator ceases to be in office as such, in consequence of removal, resignation or cesser of qualification as an insolvency practitioner, he is under obligation forthwith to deliver up to the person succeeding him as liquidator the assets (after deduction of any expenses properly incurred, and distributions made, by him) and further to deliver up to that person—
  (a) the records of the liquidation, including correspondence, proofs and other related papers appertaining to the administration while it was within his responsibility, and
  (b) the company's books, papers and other records.

(2) *(revoked)*

[(3) Where the liquidator vacates office under section 172(8) (final meeting of creditors), he shall deliver up to the official receiver the company's books, papers and other records which have not already been disposed of in accordance with general regulations in the course of the liquidation. (NO CVL APPLICATION)].

Section F: The Liquidator in a Members' Voluntary Winding Up

2.385

4.139 Appointment by the company

(1) This Rule applies where the liquidator is appointed by a meeting of the company.

(2) Subject as follows, the chairman of the meeting shall certify the appointment, but not unless and until the person appointed has provided him with a written statement to the effect that he is an insolvency practitioner, duly qualified under the Act to be the liquidator, and that he consents so to act.

(3) The chairman shall send the certificate forthwith to the liquidator, who shall keep it as part of the records of the liquidation.

(4) Not later than 28 days from his appointment, the liquidator shall give notice of it to all creditors of the company of whom he is aware in that period.

2.386

4.140 Appointment by the court

(1) This Rule applies where the liquidator is appointed by the court under section 108.

(2) The court's order shall not issue unless and until the person appointed has filed in court a statement to the effect that he is an insolvency practitioner, duly qualified under the Act to be the liquidator, and that he consents so to act.

(3) Thereafter, the court shall send a sealed copy of the order to the liquidator, whose appointment takes effect from the date of the order.

(4) Not later than 28 days from his appointment, the liquidator shall give notice of it to all creditors of the company of whom he is aware in that period.

2.387

4.141 Authentication of liquidator's appointment

A copy of the certificate of the liquidator's appointment or (as the case may be) a sealed copy of the court's order appointing him may in any proceedings be adduced as proof that the person appointed is duly authorised to exercise the powers and perform the duties of liquidator in the company's winding up.

2.388

4.142 Company meeting to receive liquidator's resignation

(1) Before resigning his office, the liquidator must call a meeting of the company for the purpose of receiving his resignation. The notice summoning the meeting shall indicate that this is the purpose, or one of the purposes, of it.

(2) The notice under paragraph (1) must be accompanied by an account of the liquidator's administration of the winding up, including—
    (a)   a summary of his receipts and payments, and
    (b)   a statement by him that he has reconciled his account with that which is held by the Secretary of State in respect of the winding up.

(3) Subject as follows, the liquidator may only proceed under this Rule on grounds of ill health or because—
    (a)   he intends ceasing to be in practice as an insolvency practitioner, or
    (b)   there is some conflict of interest or change of personal circumstances which precludes or makes impracticable the further discharge by him of the duties of liquidator.

(4) Where two or more persons are acting as liquidator jointly, any one of them may proceed under this Rule (without prejudice to the continuation in office of the other or others) on the ground that, in his opinion or that of the other or others, it is no longer expedient that there should continue to be the present number of joint liquidators.

(4A) If there is no quorum present at the meeting summoned to receive the liquidator's resignation, the meeting is deemed to have been held.

(5) The notice of the liquidator's resignation required by section 171(5) shall be given by him forthwith after the meeting.

(6) Where a new liquidator is appointed in place of one who has resigned, the former shall, in giving notice of his appointment, state that his predecessor has resigned.

2.389

4.143 Removal of liquidator by the court

(1) This Rule applies where application is made to the court for the removal of the liquidator, or for an order directing the liquidator to summon a company meeting for the purpose of removing him.

(2) The court may, if it thinks that no sufficient cause is shown for the application, disMiss it; but it shall not do so unless the applicant has had an opportunity to attend the court for an *ex parte* hearing, of which he has been given at least 7 days' notice.

If the application is not dismissed under this paragraph, the court shall fix a venue for it to be heard.

(3) The court may require the applicant to make a deposit or give security for the costs to be incurred by the liquidator on the application.

(4) The applicant shall, at least 14 days before the hearing, send to the liquidator a notice stating the venue and accompanied by a copy of the application, and of any evidence which he intends to adduce in support of it.

Subject to any contrary order of the court, the costs of the application are not payable out of the assets.

(5) Where the court removes the liquidator—

   (a)   it shall send 2 copies of the order of removal to him, one to be sent by him forthwith to the registrar of companies, with notice of his ceasing to act;

   (b)   the order may include such provision as the court thinks fit with respect to matters arising in connection with the removal; and

   (c)   if the court appoints a new liquidator, Rule 4.140 applies.

Notes

R 4.143(1)

See the notes to IR 1986 rr 4.113– 4.120 above.

R 4.143(4)

For an example of a case where the liquidator was required to pay costs personally see *Re AMF International Ltd* [1996] 1 WLR 77.

2.390

4.144 Release of resigning or removed liquidator

(1) Where the liquidator resigns, he has his release from the date on which he gives notice of his resignation to the registrar of companies.

(2) Where the liquidator is removed by a meeting of the company, he shall forthwith give notice to the registrar of companies of his ceasing to act.

(3) Where the liquidator is removed by the court, he must apply to the Secretary of State for his release.

(4) When the Secretary of State gives the release, he shall certify it accordingly, and send the certificate to the registrar of companies.

(5) A copy of the certificate shall be sent by the Secretary of State to the former liquidator, whose release is effective from the date of the certificate.

Notes

R 4.144

See the note to IA 1986 r 4.121(1).

2.391

4.145 Liquidator deceased

(1) Subject as follows, where the liquidator has died, it is the duty of his personal representatives to give notice of the fact, and of the date of death, to the company's directors, or any one of them, and to the registrar of companies.

(2) In the alternative, notice of the death may be given—

    (a)   if the deceased liquidator was a partner in a firm, by a partner qualified to act as an insolvency practitioner or who is a member of any body approved by the Secretary of State for the authorisation of insolvency practitioners, or

    (b)   by any person, if he delivers with the notice a copy of the relevant death certificate.

2.392

4.146 Loss of qualification as insolvency practitioner

(1) This Rule applies where the liquidator vacates office on ceasing to be qualified to act as an insolvency practitioner in relation to the company.

(2) He shall forthwith give notice of his doing so to the registrar of companies and the Secretary of State.

(3) Rule 4.144 applies as regards the liquidator obtaining his release, as if he had been removed by the court.

2.393

4.147 Vacation of office on making of winding-up order

Where the liquidator vacates office in consequence of the court making a winding-up order against the company, Rule 4.144 applies as regards his obtaining his release, as if he had been removed by the court.

2.394

4.148 Liquidator's duties on vacating office

Where the liquidator ceases to be in office as such, in consequence of removal, resignation or cesser of qualification as an insolvency practitioner, he is under obligation forthwith to deliver up to the person succeeding him as liquidator the assets (after deduction of any expenses properly incurred, and distributions made, by him) and further to deliver up to that person—

    (a)   the records of the liquidation, including correspondence, proofs and other related papers appertaining to the administration while it was within his responsibility, and

    (b)   the company's books, papers and other records.

2.395

4.148A Remuneration of liquidator in members' voluntary winding up

(1) The liquidator is entitled to receive remuneration for his services as such.

(2) The remuneration shall be fixed either—
  (a)   as a percentage of the value of the assets which are realised or distributed, or of the one value and the other in combination, or
  (b)   by reference to the time properly given by the insolvency practitioner (as liquidator) and his staff in attending to matters arising in the winding up;
and the company in general meeting shall determine whether the remuneration is to be fixed under subparagraph (a) or (b) and, if under subparagraph (a), the percentage to be applied as there mentioned.

(3) In arriving at that determination the company in general meeting shall have regard to the matters set out in paragraph (4) of Rule 4.127.

(4) Where the liquidator's remuneration is not fixed as above, the liquidator shall be entitled to remuneration calculated in accordance with the provisions of Rule 4.148B

(5) Rule 4.128 [and Rule 4.127B] shall apply in relation to the remuneration of the liquidator in respect of the matters there mentioned and for this purpose references in that Rule to 'the liquidation committee' and 'a meeting of creditors' shall be read as references to the company in general meeting.

(6) If the liquidator considers that the remuneration fixed for him by the company in general meeting, or as under paragraph (4), is insufficient, he may apply to the court for an order increasing its amount or rate.

(7) The liquidator shall give at least 14 days' notice of an application under paragraph (6) to the company's contributories, or such one or more of them as the court may direct, and the contributories may nominate any one or more of their number to appear or be represented.

(8) The court may, if it appears to be a proper case, order the costs of the liquidator's application, including the costs of any contributory appearing or being represented on it, to be paid out of the assets.

Notes

R 4.148A

See the notes to IR 1986 r 4.131(1).

2.396

[4.148B Liquidator's remuneration in members' voluntary liquidation where it is not fixed under Rule 4.148A]

[(1) This Rule applies where the liquidator's remuneration is not fixed in accordance with Rule 4.148A.

(2) The liquidator shall be entitled by way of remuneration for his services as such, to such sum as is arrived at by—
  (a)   first applying the realisation scale set out in Schedule 6 to the monies received by him from the realisation of the assets of the company (including any Value Added Tax thereon but after deducting any sums paid to secured creditors in respect of their

securities and any sums spent out of money received in carrying on the business of the company); and

(b) then by adding to the sum arrived at under sub-paragraph (a) such sum as is arrived at by applying the distribution scale set out in Schedule 6 to the value of assets distributed to creditors of the company (including payments made in respect of preferential debts) and to contributories.]

Notes

R 4.148B

This provision was introduced by Insolvency (Amendment) Rules 2004 (SI 2004/584), from 1 April 2004.

Section G: Rules applying in every winding up, whether voluntary or by the Court

2.397

4.149 Power of court to set aside certain transactions

(1) If in the administration of the estate the liquidator enters into any transaction with a person who is an associate of his, the court may, on the application of any person interested, set the transaction aside and order the liquidator to compensate the company for any loss suffered in consequence of it.

(2) This does not apply if either—
(a) the transaction was entered into with the prior consent of the court, or
(b) it is shown to the court's satisfaction that the transaction was for value, and that it was entered into by the liquidator without knowing, or having any reason to suppose, that the person concerned was an associate.

(3) Nothing in this Rule is to be taken as prejudicing the operation of any rule of law or equity with respect to a liquidator's dealings with trust property, or the fiduciary obligations of any person.

Notes

R 4.149(1)

'Associate' is defined by IA 1986 s 435.

2.398

4.150 Rule against solicitation

(1) Where the court is satisfied that any improper solicitation has been used by or on behalf of the liquidator in obtaining proxies or procuring

his appointment, it may order that no remuneration out of the assets be allowed to any person by whom, or on whose behalf, the solicitation was exercised.

(2) An order of the court under this Rule overrides any resolution of the liquidation committee or the creditors, or any other provision of the Rules relating to the liquidator's remuneration.

Chapter 12
The Liquidation Committee

2.399

4.151 Preliminary (No CVL Application)

For the purposes of this Chapter—
  (a) an 'insolvent winding up' is where the company is being wound up on grounds which include inability to pay its debts, and
  (b) a 'solvent winding up' is where the company is being wound up on grounds which do not include that one.

Notes

R 4.151(a)

The meaning of 'inability to pay its debts' is set out in IA 1986 s 123.

R 4.151(b)

Thus any winding up by the court which is not on the grounds of IA 1986 s 122(1)(f) is a 'solvent' winding up for the purposes of the rules in Chapter 12.

2.400

4.152 Membership of committee

(1) Subject to Rule 4.154 below, the liquidation committee shall consist as follows—
  (a) in any case of at least 3, and not more than 5, creditors of the company, elected by the meeting of creditors held under section 141 of the Act, and
  (b) also, in the case of a solvent winding up, where the contributories' meeting held under that section so decides, of up to 3 contributories, elected by that meeting.

(NO CVL APPLICATION)

(2–CVL) The committee must have at least 3 members before it can be established.

(3) Any creditor of the company (other than one whose debt is fully secured) is eligible to be a member of the committee, so long as—
  (a) he has lodged a proof of his debt, and
  (b) his proof has neither been wholly disallowed for voting purposes, nor wholly rejected for purposes of distribution or dividend.

(4) No person can be a member as both a creditor and a contributory.

(5) A body corporate may be a member of the committee, but it cannot act as such otherwise than by a representative appointed under Rule 4.159.

(6) Members of the committee elected or appointed to represent the creditors are called 'creditor members'; and those elected or appointed to represent the contributories are called 'contributory members'.

(7) The following categories of person are to be regarded as additional creditor members—

(a)   a representative of the Financial Services Authority who exercises the right under section 371 (4)(b) of the Financial Services and Markets Act 2000 to be a member of the committee;

(b)   a representative of the scheme manager who exercises the right under section 215(4) of that Act to be a member of the committee.

Notes

R 4.152

The purpose of the liquidation committee is to assist and supervise in the orderly administration of the assets in liquidation. It cannot give instructions to the liquidator. It is established under IA 1986 s 141 at the first meeting of creditors and contributories in the liquidation or at any other time by a meeting of creditors/contributories: IA 1986 s 141(2). Where there is no liquidation committee and the official receiver is not the liquidator, its functions are vested in the Secretary of State: IA 1986 s 141(4); for instance the Secretary of State could be approached to permit the exercise of certain powers by a liquidator under IA 1986 s 167(1)(a) or s 165(2)(b). Where a winding up order follows on from an administration special rules relating to the liquidation committee apply: IR 1986 rr. 4.173–4.178.

2.401

4.153 Formalities of establishment

(1) The liquidation committee does not come into being, and accordingly cannot act, until the liquidator has issued a certificate of its due constitution.

(2) If the chairman of the meeting which resolves to establish the committee is not the liquidator, he shall forthwith give notice of the resolution to the liquidator (or, as the case may be, the person appointed as liquidator by that same meeting), and inform him of the names and addresses of the persons elected to be members of the committee.

(3) No person may act as a member of the committee unless and until he has agreed to do so and, unless the relevant proxy or authorisation contains a statement to the contrary, such agreement may be given by his proxy-holder or representative under section 375 of the Companies Act present at the meeting establishing the committee.

(3A) The liquidator's certificate of the committee's due constitution shall not issue before the minimum number of persons (in accordance with Rule 4.152) who are to be members of the committee have agreed to act.

(4) As and when the others (if any) agree to act, the liquidator shall issue an amended certificate.

(5) The certificate, and any amended certificate, shall be filed in court by the liquidator.

(NO CVL APPLICATION)

(6–CVL) The certificate, and any amended certificate, shall be sent by the liquidator to the registrar of companies.

(7) If after the first establishment of the committee there is any change in its membership, the liquidator shall report the change to the court. (NO CVL APPLICATION)

(8–CVL) If after the first establishment of the committee there is any change in its membership, the liquidator shall report the change to the registrar of companies.

Notes

R 4.153

The committee only comes into being once the liquidator has issued a certificate of due constitution. Only once this certificate has been issued can the committee act. The certificate has to be filed at court and sent to the Registrar of Companies.

2.402

4.154 Committee established by contributories (No CVL Application)

(1) The following applies where the creditors' meeting under section 141 does not decide that a liquidation committee should be established, or decides that a committee should not be established.

(2) The meeting of contributories under that section may appoint one of their number to make application to the court for an order to the liquidator that a further creditors' meeting be summoned for the purpose of establishing a liquidation committee; and—

    (a)   the court may, if it thinks that there are special circumstances to justify it, make that order, and

    (b)   the creditors' meeting summoned by the liquidator in compliance with the order is deemed to have been summoned under section 141.

(3) If the creditors' meeting so summoned does not establish a liquidation committee, a meeting of contributories may do so.

(4) The committee shall then consist of at least 3, and not more than 5, contributories elected by that meeting; and Rule 4.153 applies, [substituting for the reference in paragraph (3A) of that Rule to Rule 4.152 a reference to this paragraph].

Notes

R 4.154

This rule contains an important qualification to IA 1986 s 141(3). Where a meeting of contributories resolves that a liquidation committee should be established, but a meeting of creditors does not, the contributories cannot proceed to establish such a committee without first obtaining an order of the court for the summoning of a creditors' meeting. The court will only order such further meeting where there are special circumstances to justify it.

2.403

4.155 Obligations of liquidator to committee

(1) Subject as follows, it is the duty of the liquidator to report to the members of the liquidation committee all such matters as appear to him to be, or as they have indicated to him as being, of concern to them with respect to the winding up.

(2) In the case of matters so indicated to him by the committee, the liquidator need not comply with any request for information where it appears to him that—

    (a)   the request is frivolous or unreasonable, or

    (b)   the cost of complying would be excessive, having regard to the relative importance of the information, or

    (c)   there are not sufficient assets to enable him to comply.

(3) Where the committee has come into being more than 28 days after the appointment of the liquidator, he shall report to them, in summary form, what actions he has taken since his appointment, and shall answer all such questions as they may put to him regarding his conduct of the winding up hitherto.

(4) A person who becomes a member of the committee at any time after its first establishment is not entitled to require a report to him by the liquidator, otherwise than in summary form, of any matters previously arising.

(5) Nothing in this Rule disentitles the committee, or any member of it, from having access to the liquidator's records of the liquidation, or from seeking an explanation of any matter within the committee's responsibility.

Notes

R 4.155

Whilst the liquidator has a duty to report to members of the committee all matters which may be of concern to this them with respect to the winding-up (subject to the proviso in IR 1986 r 4.155(2)), the liquidator cannot be obliged by the committee to disclose reports he has made under the CDDA 1986: *Re W and A Glaser* [1994] BCC 199. This is because the committee has no right to inspect or ask any questions concerning such documents. See also IR 1986 R4.168 for the liquidator's general reporting duty to the liquidation committee.

2.404

4.156 Meetings of the committee

(1) Subject as follows, meetings of the liquidation committee shall be held when and where determined by the liquidator.

(2) The liquidator shall call a first meeting of the committee to take place within 3 months of his appointment or of the committee's establishment (whichever is the later); and thereafter he shall call a meeting—

    (a)   if so requested by a creditor member of the committee or his representative (the meeting then to be held within 21 days of the request being received by the liquidator), and

    (b)   for a specified date, if the committee has previously resolved that a meeting be held on that date.

(3) The liquidator shall give 7 days' written notice of the venue of a meeting to every member of the committee (or his representative, if designated for that purpose), unless in any case the requirement of the notice has been waived by or on behalf of any member.

Waiver may be signified either at or before the meeting.

Notes

R 4.156

The committee meets as and when determined by the liquidator, save that (i) the liquidator is required to call a meeting within three months of his appointment or following the establishment of the committee, whichever is later, and (ii) any creditor member can requisition a meeting and (iii) the liquidation committee itself can fix further meetings.

2.405

4.157 The chairman at meetings

(1) The chairman at any meeting of the liquidation committee shall be the liquidator, or a person nominated by him to act.

(2) A person so nominated must be either—

    (a)   one who is qualified to act as an insolvency practitioner in relation to the company, or

    (b)   an employee of the liquidator or his firm who is experienced in insolvency matters.

2.406

4.158 Quorum

(1) A meeting of the committee is duly constituted if due notice of it has been given to all the members, and at least 2 creditor members are present or represented.

(NO CVL APPLICATION)

(2–CVL) A meeting of the committee is duly constituted if due notice of it has been given to all the members, and at least 2 members are present or represented.

Notes

R 4.158

The quorum at meetings of the committee is two creditor members present or represented. Presumably if the committee does not have creditor members because it is established under IR 1986 r 4.154(4) the quorum is two contributory members; see also IR 1986 r 4.165(3).

2.407

4.159 Committee-members' representatives

(1) A member of the liquidation committee may, in relation to the business of the committee, be represented by another person duly authorised by him for that purpose.

(2) A person acting as a committee-member's representative must hold a letter of authority entitling him so to act (either generally or specially) and signed by or on behalf of the committee-member, and for this purpose any proxy or any authorisation under section 375 of the Companies Act in relation to any meeting of creditors (or, as the case may be, members or contributories) of the company shall, unless it contains a statement to the contrary, be treated as such a letter of authority to act generally signed by or on behalf of the committee-member.

(3) The chairman at any meeting of the committee may call on a person claiming to act as a committee-member's representative to produce his letter of authority, and may exclude him if it appears that his authority is deficient.

(4) No member may be represented by a body corporate, or by a person who is an undischarged bankrupt [or a disqualified director,] or is subject to a bankruptcy restrictions order, bankruptcy restrictions undertaking or an interim bankruptcy restrictions order.

(5) No person shall—
   (a) on the same committee, act at one and the same time as representative of more than one committee-member, or
   (b) act both as a member of the committee and as representative of another member.

(6) Where a member's representative signs any document on the member's behalf, the fact that he so signs must be stated below his signature.

Notes

R 4.159(4)

This provision was amended by Insolvency (Amendment) Rules 2004 SI 2004/584 from 1 April 2004 to take into account the reforms in insolvency introduced by EA 2002.

2.408

4.160 Resignation

A member of the liquidation committee may resign by notice in writing delivered to the liquidator.

2.409

4.161 Termination of membership

(1) A person's membership of the liquidation committee is automatically terminated if—
   (a) he becomes bankrupt, or

(b)   at 3 consecutive meetings of the committee he is neither present nor represented (unless at the third of those meetings it is resolved that this Rule is not to apply in his case).

(2) However, if the cause of termination is the member's bankruptcy, his trustee in bankruptcy replaces him as a member of the committee.

(3) The membership of a creditor member is also automatically terminated if he ceases to be, or is found never to have been, a creditor.

2.410

4.162 Removal

(1) A creditor member of the committee may be removed by resolution at a meeting of creditors; and a contributory member may be removed by a resolution of a meeting of contributories.

(2) In either case, 14 days' notice must be given of the intention to move the resolution.

2.411

4.163 Vacancy (creditor members)

(1) The following applies if there is a vacancy among the creditor members of the committee.

(2) The vacancy need not be filled if the liquidator and a majority of the remaining creditor members so agree, provided that the total number of members does not fall below the minimum required by Rule 4.152.

(3) The liquidator may appoint any creditor (being qualified under the Rules to be a member of the committee) to fill the vacancy, if a majority of the other creditor members agree to the appointment, and the creditor concerned consents to act.

(4) Alternatively, a meeting of creditors may resolve that a creditor be appointed (with his consent) to fill the vacancy. In this case, at least 14 days' notice must have been given of the resolution to make such an appointment (whether or not of a person named in the notice).

(5) Where the vacancy is filled by an appointment made by a creditors' meeting at which the liquidator is not present, the chairman of the meeting shall report to the liquidator the appointment which has been made.

2.412

4.164 Vacancy (contributory members)

(1) The following applies if there is a vacancy among the contributory members of the committee.

(2) The vacancy need not be filled if the liquidator and a majority of the remaining contributory members so agree, provided that, in the case of a committee of contributory members only, the total number of members does not fall below the minimum required by Rule 4.154(4) or, as the case may be, 4.171(5).

(3) The liquidator may appoint any contributory member (being qualified under the Rules to be a member of the committee) to fill the vacancy,

if a majority of the other contributory members agree to the appointment, and the contributory concerned consents to act.

(4) Alternatively, a meeting of contributories may resolve that a contributory be appointed (with his consent) to fill the vacancy. In this case, at least 14 days' notice must have been given of the resolution to make such an appointment (whether or not of a person named in the notice).

(5–CVL) Where the contributories make an appointment under paragraph (4), the creditor members of the committee may, if they think fit, resolve that the person appointed ought not to be a member of the committee; and—

(a) that person is not then, unless the court otherwise directs, qualified to act as a member of the committee, and

(b) on any application to the court for a direction under this paragraph the court may, if it thinks fit, appoint another person (being a contributory) to fill the vacancy on the committee.

(6) Where the vacancy is filled by an appointment made by a contributories' meeting at which the liquidator is not present, the chairman of the meeting shall report to the liquidator the appointment which has been made.

2.413

4.165 Voting rights and resolutions (No CVL Application)

(1) At any meeting of the committee, each member of it (whether present himself, or by his representative) has one vote; and a resolution is passed when a majority of the creditor members present or represented have voted in favour of it.

(2) Subject to the next paragraph, the votes of contributory members do not count towards the number required for passing a resolution, but the way in which they vote on any resolution shall be recorded.

(3) Paragraph (2) does not apply where, by virtue of Rule 4.154 or 4.171, the only members of the committee are contributories. In that case the committee is to be treated for voting purposes as if all its members were creditors.

(4) Every resolution passed shall be recorded in writing, either separately or as part of the minutes of the meeting. The record shall be signed by the chairman and kept with the records of the liquidation.

2.414

4.166 Voting rights and resolutions—CVL

(1) At any meeting of the committee, each member of it (whether present himself, or by his representative) has one vote; and a resolution is passed when a majority of the members present or represented have voted in favour of it.

(2) Every resolution passed shall be recorded in writing, either separately or as part of the minutes of the meeting. The record shall be signed by the chairman and kept with the records of the liquidation.

2.415

4.167 Resolutions by post

(1) In accordance with this Rule, the liquidator may seek to obtain the agreement of members of the liquidation committee to a resolution by sending to every member (or his representative designated for the purpose) a copy of the proposed resolution.

(2) Where the liquidator makes use of the procedure allowed by this Rule, he shall send out to members of the committee or their representatives (as the case may be) [a copy of any proposed resolution on which a decision is sought, which shall be set out in such a way that agreement with or dissent from each separate resolution may be indicated by the recipient on the copy so sent].

(3) Any creditor member of the committee may, within 7 business days from the date of the liquidator sending out a resolution, require him to summon a meeting of the committee to consider the matters raised by the resolution. (NO CVL APPLICATION)

(4–CVL) Any member of the committee may, within 7 business days from the date of the liquidator sending out a resolution, require him to summon a meeting of the committee to consider the matters raised by the resolution.

(5) In the absence of such a request, the resolution is deemed to have been passed by the committee if and when the liquidator is notified in writing by a majority of the creditor members that they concur with it. (NO CVL APPLICATION)

(6–CVL) In the absence of such a request, the resolution is deemed to have been passed by the committee if and when the liquidator is notified in writing by a majority of the members that they concur with it.

(7) A copy of every resolution passed under this Rule, and a note that the committee's concurrence was obtained, shall be kept with the records of the liquidation.

2.416

4.168 Liquidator's reports

(1) The liquidator shall, as and when directed by the liquidation committee (but not more often than once in any period of 2 months), send a written report to every member of the committee setting out the position generally as regards the progress of the winding up and matters arising in connection with it, to which he (the liquidator) considers the committee's attention should be drawn.

(2) In the absence of such directions by the committee, the liquidator shall send such a report not less often than once in every period of 6 months.

(3) The obligations of the liquidator under this Rule are without prejudice to those imposed by Rule 4.155.

2.417

4.169 Expenses of members, etc

The liquidator shall defray out of the assets, in the prescribed order of priority, any reasonable travelling expenses directly incurred by members of the liquidation committee or their representatives in respect of their attendance at the committee's meetings, or otherwise on the committee's business.

Notes

R.4.169

See IR 1986 r 4.218(1)(m) for the priority of such expenses.

2.418

4.170 Dealings by committee-members and others

(1) This Rule applies to—
   (a)   any member of the liquidation committee,
   (b)   any committee-member's representative,
   (c)   any person who is an associate of a member of the committee or a committee-member's representative, and
   (d)   any person who has been a member of the committee at any time in the last 12 months.

(2) Subject as follows, a person to whom this Rule applies shall not enter into any transaction whereby he—
   (a)   receives out of the company's assets any payment for services given or goods supplied in connection with the administration, or
   (b)   obtains any profit from the administration, or
   (c)   acquires any asset forming part of the estate.

(3) Such a transaction may be entered into by a person to whom this Rule applies—
   (a)   with the prior leave of the court, or
   (b)   if he does so as a matter of urgency, or by way of performance of a contract in force before the date on which the company went into liquidation, and obtains the court's leave for the transaction, having applied for it without undue delay, or
   (c)   with the prior sanction of the liquidation committee, where it is satisfied (after full disclosure of the circumstances) that the person will be giving full value in the transaction.

(4) Where in the committee a resolution is proposed that sanction be accorded for a transaction to be entered into which, without that sanction or the leave of the court, would be in contravention of this Rule, no member of the committee, and no representative of a member, shall vote if he is to participate directly or indirectly in the transaction.

(5) The court may, on the application of any person interested—

(a) set aside a transaction on the ground that it has been entered into in contravention of this Rule, and

(b) make with respect to it such other order as it thinks fit, including (subject to the following paragraph) an order requiring a person to whom this Rule applies to account for any profit obtained from the transaction and compensate the estate for any resultant loss..

(6) In the case of a person to whom this Rule applies as an associate of a member of the committee or of a committee-member's representative, the court shall not make any order under paragraph (5), if satisfied that he entered into the relevant transaction without having any reason to suppose that in doing so he would contravene this Rule.

(7) The costs of an application to the court for leave under this Rule are not payable out of the assets, unless the court so orders.

Notes

R 4.170

Members of the liquidation committee are fiduciaries with respect to the company's assets, and may not be involved in any transaction involving the company assets without the permission of the court or the liquidation committee: *Re F T Hawkins & Co Ltd* [1952] Ch 881. Usually permission should be obtained prior to the committee member entering into the transaction in question, but in cases of urgency the court's permission may be obtained after the event provided that the application seeking permission is made promptly. 'Associate' is defined in IA 1986 s 435.

2.419

4.171 Composition of committee when creditors paid in full

(1) This Rule applies if the liquidator issues a certificate that the creditors have been paid in full, with interest in accordance with section 189.

(2) The liquidator shall forthwith file the certificate in court. (NO CVL APPLICATION)

(3–CVL) The liquidator shall forthwith send a copy of the certificate to the registrar of companies.

(4) The creditor members of the liquidation committee cease to be members of the committee.

(5) The committee continues in being unless and until abolished by decision of a meeting of contributories, and (subject to the next paragraph) so long as it consists of at least 3 contributory members.

(6) The committee does not cease to exist on account of the number of contributory members falling below 3, unless and until 28 days have elapsed since the issue of the liquidator's certificate under paragraph (1).

But at any time when the committee consists of less than 3 contributory members, it is suspended and cannot act.

(7) Contributories may be co-opted by the liquidator, or appointed by a contributories' meeting, to be members of the committee; but the maximum number of members is 5.

(8) The foregoing Rules in this Chapter continue to apply to the liquidation committee (with any necessary modifications) as if all the members of the committee were creditor members.

2.420

4.172 Committee's functions vested in Secretary of State (No CVL Application)

(1) At any time when the functions of the liquidation committee are vested in the Secretary of State under section 141(4) or (5), requirements of the Act or the Rules about notices to be given, or reports to be made, to the committee by the liquidator do not apply, otherwise than as enabling the committee to require a report as to any matter.

(2) Where the committee's functions are so vested under section 141(5), they may be exercised by the official receiver.

2.421

4.172A Formal defects

The acts of the liquidation committee established for any winding up are valid notwithstanding any defect in the appointment, election or qualifications of any member of the committee or any committee-member's representative or in the formalities of its establishment.

Notes

R 4.172A

However this provision is unlikely to validate the acts of the committee where a member has not been appointed to the committee at all: see *Morris v Kannsen* [1946] AC 459, *a case concerning the validity of acts of a company director under what is now* CA 1985 s 285.

Chapter 13
The Liquidation Committee Where Winding Up Follows Immediately on Administration (No CVL Application)

2.422

4.173 Preliminary

(1) The Rules in this Chapter apply where—
    (a)   the winding-up order has been made by the court upon an application under paragraph 79 of Schedule B1 to the Act, and
    (b)   the court makes an order under section 140(1) of the Act appointing as liquidator the person who was previously the administrator.

> (2) In this Chapter, 'insolvent winding up', 'solvent winding up', 'creditor member' and 'contributory member' mean the same as in Chapter 12.

Notes

R 4.173–4.178

In cases where a winding up order is made following a company's administration, the rules in Chapter 13 apply to the establishment and composition of the liquidation committee in place of those which apply to other liquidations under IR 1986 rr. 4.152–4.154. The references to Schedule B1 throughout these rules reflect the changes that were made as a result of the new administration regime with effect from 15 September 2003: Insolvency (Amendment) Rules 2003 SI 2003/1730. The general principle is that the creditors' committee already established in the administration should continue as the liquidation committee, unless in the case of a solvent winding-up, the contributories decide to elect their own members: see IR 1986 r 4.175(2). Otherwise, the rules relating to the proceedings of liquidation committees which are set out in IR 1986 r 4.155–4.172A apply to post-administration compulsory liquidations as they do to compulsory liquidations generally: IR 1986 r 4.178.

2.423

4.174 Continuation of creditors' committee

(1) If under paragraph 57 of Schedule B1 to the Act a creditors' committee has been established for the purposes of the administration, then (subject as follows in this Chapter) that committee continues in being as the liquidation committee for the purposes of the winding up, and—

    (a)   it is deemed to be a committee established as such under section 141, and

    (b)   no action shall be taken under subsections (1) to (3) of that section to establish any other.

(2) This Rule does not apply if, at the time when the court's order under section 140(1) is made, the committee under paragraph 57 of Schedule B1 to the Act consists of less than 3 members; and a creditor who was, immediately before that date, a member of it, ceases to be a member on the making of the order if his debt is fully secured.

2.424

4.175 Membership of committee

(1) Subject as follows, the liquidation committee shall consist of at least 3, and not more than 5, creditors of the company, elected by the creditors' meeting held under paragraph 57 of Schedule B1 to the Act or (in order to make up numbers or fill vacancies) by a creditors' meeting summoned by the liquidator after the company goes into liquidation.

(2) In the case of a solvent winding up, the liquidator shall, on not less than 21 days' notice, summon a meeting of contributories, in order to elect (if it so wishes) contributory members of the liquidation committee, up to 3 in number.

2.425

4.176 Liquidator's certificate

(1) The liquidator shall issue a certificate of the liquidation committee's continuance, specifying the persons who are, or are to be, members of it.

(2) It shall be stated in the certificate whether or not the liquidator has summoned a meeting of contributories under Rule 4.175(2), and whether (if so) the meeting has elected contributories to be members of the committee.

(3) Pending the issue of the liquidator's certificate, the committee is suspended and cannot act.

(4) No person may act, or continue to act, as a member of the committee unless and until he has agreed to do so; and the liquidator's certificate shall not issue until at least the minimum number of persons required under Rule 4.175 to form a committee have signified their agreement.

(5) As and when the others signify their agreement, the liquidator shall issue an amended certificate.

(6) The liquidator's certificate (or, as the case may be, the amended certificate) shall be filed by him in court.

(7) If subsequently there is any change in the committee's membership, the liquidator shall report the change to the court.

2.426

4.177 Obligations of liquidator to committee

(1) As soon as may be after the issue of the liquidator's certificate under Rule 4.176, the liquidator shall report to the liquidation committee what actions he has taken since the date on which the company went into liquidation.

(2) A person who becomes a member of the committee after that date is not entitled to require a report to him by the liquidator, otherwise than in a summary form, of any matters previously arising.

(3) Nothing in this Rule disentitles the committee, or any member of it, from having access to the records of the liquidation (whether relating to the period when he was administrator, or to any subsequent period), or from seeking an explanation of any matter within the committee's responsibility.

Notes

R 4.177

The reporting obligations of the liquidator in post-administration compulsory liquidations set out under this rule supplement rather than replace those placed upon the liquidator in other compulsory liquidations under IR 1986 r 4.155.

2.427

4.178 Application of Chapter 12

Except as provided above in this Chapter, Rules 4.155 to 4.172A in Chapter 12 apply to the liquidation committee following the issue of the liquidator's certificate under Rule 4.176, as if it had been established under section 141.

Chapter 14
Collection and Distribution of Company's Assets by Liquidator

2.428

4.179 General duties of liquidator (No CVL Application)

(1) The duties imposed on the court by the Act with regard to the collection of the company's assets and their application in discharge of its liabilities are discharged by the liquidator as an officer of the court subject to its control.

(2) In the discharge of his duties the liquidator, for the purposes of acquiring and retaining possession of the company's property, has the same powers as a receiver appointed by the High Court, and the court may on his application enforce such acquisition or retention accordingly.

Notes

R 4.179

This provision confirms the long-established rule that in exercising the functions conferred upon him, the liquidator in a compulsory winding-up acts as an officer of the court (*Re Contract Corpn, Gooch's case* (1872) 7 Ch App 207; *ex parte James In re Condon* (1874) 9 Ch App 609) and is subject to the court's control (in particular by the procedure provided for under IA 1986 s 168). Further it confers upon him the same powers as a court-appointed receiver for the purposes of acquiring or retaining possession of the company's property. The general function of the liquidator to collect in and realise the company's assets and to distribute such realisations rateably amongst creditors in satisfaction of their debts is set out in IA 1986 s 143. In so acting, he owes duties both of a fiduciary nature and to exercise reasonable care and skill, for which he may be held to account under an application under IA 1986 s 212.

2.429

4.180 Manner of distributing assets

(1) Whenever the liquidator has sufficient funds in hand for the purpose he shall, subject to the retention of such sums as may be necessary for the expenses of the winding up, declare and distribute dividends among the creditors in respect of the debts which they have respectively proved.

(2) The liquidator shall give notice of his intention to declare and distribute a dividend.

(3) Where the liquidator has declared a dividend, he shall give notice of it to the creditors, stating how the dividend is proposed to be distributed.

> The notice shall contain such particulars with respect to the company, and to its assets and affairs, as will enable the creditors to comprehend the calculation of the amount of the dividend and the manner of its distribution.

Notes

R 4.180(1)

The general scheme for the ascertainment by the liquidator of creditors and the distribution of the company's assets to them in their proper order is governed by IA 1986 s 148 (1), s 160 (1)(b), s 175 and s 386. This rule, which is similar to the provisions to IA 1986 s 324 as applies in bankruptcy, provides for the declaration of dividends by the liquidator for distribution to creditors in accordance with the statutory rules of priority whenever sufficient funds are available. The rule must be read in conjunction with Part 11 of the Insolvency Rules which contains provisions of general application to the declaration and payment of dividends.

R 4.180(2)

In giving notice of intended dividend, the liquidator must comply with the provisions of IR 1986 r 11.2. In particular, before declaring a first dividend, the liquidator must give notice of intended dividend by public advertisement unless he has previously invited creditors to prove their debts by public advertisement (IR 1986 r 11.2(1A). Such advertisement must specify a date (not less than 21 days thereafter) by which proofs must be lodged (IR 1986 r 11.2(2)). The notice must also specify such date and must state the liquidator's intention to declare a dividend within a 4 month period from the last date for creditors to lodge their proofs of debt (IR 1986 r 11.2(3)). Unless the liquidator has had cause within that 4 month period to postpone or cancel the dividend, he should declare it within that period: IR 1986 r 11.5(1); but cf. IR 1986 r 11.5(2)).

R 4.180(3)

The particulars required in the notice of declaration of dividend are supplemented by the provisions of IR 1986 r 11.6(2).

> **2.430**
>
> **4.181 Debts of insolvent company to rank equally (No CVL Application)**
>
> (1) Debts other than preferential debts rank equally between themselves in the winding up and, after the preferential debts, shall be paid in full unless the assets are insufficient for meeting them, in which case they abate in equal proportions between themselves.
>
> (2) Paragraph (1) applies whether or not the company is unable to pay its debts.

Notes

R 4.181

The principle that the assets of the company after prior satisfaction of liquidation expenses and preferential debts should be distributed *pari passu* amongst the company's unsecured creditors has traditionally been regarded as fundamental to insolvency law, and not capable of being contracted out of: see *British Eagle International Airlines v Compagnie Nationale Air France*

[1975] 1 WLR 758. In the case of compulsory liquidation, the principle is no longer to be found in IA 1986, but in this rule alone; see, in contrast IA 1986 s 107 for the principle as it is enacted in the case of voluntary liquidations, and, as regard bankruptcy, IA 1986 s 328.

Under IA 1986 s 167(1) schedule 4 Part 1, the liquidator does have power with the sanction of the court or liquidation committee to pay any class of creditors in full, although the circumstances in which such sanction might be given or approved by the court (in the absence of the universal consent of creditors or a scheme of arrangement or voluntary arrangement) are extremely limited: see *Re Trix Ltd* [1970] 1 WLR 1421.

The *pari passu* rule does not invalidate a debt subordination agreement by which one creditor agrees that his debt should rank in priority after those of other creditors: *Re Maxwell Communications Corporation Ltd* [1993] 1 WLR 1402. There is no reason why a particular creditor should not waive his right to prove altogether or save to the extent of assets remaining after another creditor is satisfied, whether in the insolvency of his debtor or in advance of it. Such an agreement is valid even where the creditor himself subsequently becomes insolvent, unless there are grounds independently for challenging the agreement in the creditor's insolvency eg as a preference or transaction at an undervalue: see *Re SSSL Realisations (2002) Ltd* [2005] BCLC 1 (Ch D); [2006] 2 WLR 1369, [2006] BCC 233, CA.

2.431

4.182 Supplementary provisions as to dividend

(1) In the calculation and distribution of a dividend the liquidator shall make provision—
- (a) for any debts which appear to him to be due to persons who, by reason of the distance of their place of residence, may not have had sufficient time to tender and establish their proofs,
- (b) for any debts which are the subject of claims which have not yet been determined, and
- (c) for disputed proofs and claims.

(2) A creditor who has not proved his debt before the declaration of any dividend is not entitled to disturb, by reason that he has not participated in it, the distribution of that dividend or any other dividend declared before his debt was proved, but—
- (a) when he has proved that debt he is entitled to be paid, out of any money for the time being available for the payment of any further dividend, any dividend or dividends which he has failed to receive, and
- (b) any dividend or dividends payable under sub-paragraph (a) shall be paid before that money is applied to the payment of any such further dividend.

(3) No action lies against the liquidator for a dividend; but if he refuses to pay a dividend the court may, if it thinks fit, order him to pay it and also to pay, out of his own money—
- (a) interest on the dividend, at the rate for the time being specified in section 17 of the Judgments Act 1838, from the time when it was withheld, and

(b)   the costs of the proceedings in which the order to pay is made.

Notes

R 4.182

The three paragraphs of this rule are identical in form, respectively, to IA 1986 s 324(4), 325(1) and 325(2) as apply in the case of bankruptcy.

R 4.182(1)

In paying dividends, the liquidator must make provision for debts which appear to him due but which for good reason have not yet been proved and for claims which are as yet undetermined or disputed. See also IR 1986 r 11.5(2) which prohibits the declaration of dividend where there is any pending application challenging a liquidator's decision on any proof of debt except with the leave of the court and subject to such provision in respect of such proof as the court directs.

R 4.182(2)

A creditor who fails to prove his debt before a dividend is declared will be entitled to payment of his due out of monies as they become available before payment of any further dividend. A similar rule applies in the event he subsequently increases the amount claimed in his proof under IR 1986 r 11.8(1), (2). If, in contrast, an admitted proof is subsequently withdrawn or expunged, or the amount of the debt reduced, the creditor in question is liable to repay the overpaid dividend: IR 1986 r 11.8(3).

R 4.182(3)

This rule prevents a dissatisfied creditor from bringing a claim by ordinary action against the liquidator in respect of a dividend. But such a creditor may seek the directions of the court in the liquidation and on such application the liquidator may be ordered personally to pay both interest and costs. An action may also lie against the liquidator for breach of statutory duty: *Pulsford v Devenish* [1903] 2 Ch 604; *James Smith & Sons (Norwood) Ltd v Goodman* [1936] Ch 216.

2.432

4.182A Distribution in members' voluntary winding up (No CVL Application)

(1) In a member's voluntary winding up the liquidator may give notice in such newspaper as he considers most appropriate for the purpose of drawing the matter to the attention of the company's creditors that he intends to make a distribution to creditors.

(2) The notice shall specify a date ('the last date for proving') up to which proofs may be lodged. The date shall be the same for all creditors and not less than 21 days from that of the notice.

(3) The liquidator is not obliged to deal with proofs lodged after the last date for proving; but he may do so, if he thinks fit.

(4) A creditor who has not proved his debt before the last date for proving or after that date increases the claim in his proof is not entitled to disturb, by reason that he has not participated in it, either at all or, as the case may be, to the extent that his increased claim would allow, that

distribution or any other distribution made before his debt was proved or his claim increased; but when he has proved his debt or, as the case may be, increased his claim, he is entitled to be paid, out of any money for the time being available for the payment of any further distribution, any distribution or distributions which he has failed to receive.

(5) Where the distribution proposed to be made is to be the only or the final distribution in that winding up, the liquidator may, subject to paragraph (6), make that distribution without regard to the claim of any person in respect of a debt not already proved.

(6) Where the distribution proposed to be made is one specified in paragraph (5), the notice given under paragraph (1) shall state the effect of paragraph (5).

Notes

R 4.182A

This rule sets out the procedure for distribution in cases of members' voluntary liquidation in similar terms to those set out in IA 1986 r 4.180 to 4.182. It may be that a contingency fund has to be set up to provide for future claimants before any final distribution can be made to members: *Tombs v Moulinex* [2004] 2 BCLC 397.

2.433

4.183 Division of unsold assets

Without prejudice to provisions of the Act about disclaimer, the liquidator may, with the permission of the liquidation committee, divide in its existing form amongst the company's creditors, according to its estimated value, any property which from its peculiar nature or other special circumstances cannot be readily or advantageously sold.

Notes

R 4.183

The liquidator's power to distribute assets *in specie* under this rule may only be exercised with the permission of the liquidation committee. The circumstances in which resort to the rule will be required will be rare.

2.434

4.184 General powers of liquidator

(1) Any permission given by the liquidation committee (or if there is no such committee, a meeting of the company's creditors) or the court under section 165(2) or section 167(1)(a), or under the Rules, shall not be a general permission but shall relate to a particular proposed exercise of the liquidator's power in question; and a person dealing with the liquidator in good faith and for value is not concerned to enquire whether any such permission has been given.

> (2) Where the liquidator has done anything without that permission, the court or the liquidation committee may, for the purpose of enabling him to meet his expenses out of the assets, ratify what he has done; but neither shall do so unless it is satisfied that the liquidator has acted in a case of urgency and has sought ratification without undue delay.

Notes

R 4.184

This rule contains important provisions relating, in particular, to the exercise by the liquidator of those powers under IA 1986 s 167 (1) (a) which require the prior sanction of the court or liquidation committee. This rule has been amended by the Insolvency (Amendment) Rules 2005 to expressly include voluntary winding up under IA 1986 s 165. For the equivalent bankruptcy provision, see IA 1986 s 314 (3), (4).

R 4.184(1)

The second limb of this provision confers protection on persons dealing in good faith and for value with the liquidator, absolving them from any need to enquire as to whether any proposed transaction requires the sanction of or has been sanctioned by either the court or liquidation committee. In such circumstances, the absence of the requisite sanction is actionable by disgruntled creditors against the liquidator alone.

R 4.184(2)

Regardless of any steps which may be taken by disgruntled creditors, where the liquidator acts without the requisite sanction, he is at risk in respect of the expenses incurred in so doing, unless he can justify his actions on grounds of urgency.

> **2.435**
>
> **4.185 Enforced delivery up of company's property (No CVL Application)**
>
> (1) The powers conferred on the court by section 234 (enforced delivery of company property) are exercisable by the liquidator or, where a provisional liquidator has been appointed, by him.
>
> (2) Any person on whom a requirement under section 234(2) is imposed by the liquidator or provisional liquidator shall, without avoidable delay, comply with it.

Notes

R 4.185

This is an important provision delegating to the liquidator all the powers conferred by IA 1986 s 234 on the court to require any person in possession of the company's property, books or records to hand such items over to the liquidator. See further commentary to that section. See also IA 1986 s 160(1)(c) for the provision authorising such delegation of power.

2.436

4.186 Final distribution

(1) When the liquidator has realised all the company's assets or so much of them as can, in his opinion, be realised without needlessly protracting the liquidation, he shall give notice, under Part 11 of the Rules, either—

   (a)   of his intention to declare a final dividend, or

   (b)   that no dividend, or further dividend, will be declared.

(2) The notice shall contain all such particulars as are required by Part 11 of the Rules and shall require claims against the assets to be established by a date specified in the notice.

(3) After that date, the liquidator shall—

   (a)   defray any outstanding expenses of the winding up out of the assets, and

   (b)   if he intends to declare a final dividend, declare and distribute that dividend without regard to the claim of any person in respect of a debt not already proved.

(4) The court may, on the application of any person, postpone the date specified in the notice.

Notes

R 4.186(1)

Notwithstanding his duty to collect in and realise the company's assets, the liquidator is not bound to prolong the liquidation for the purposes of pursuing debts or assets which cannot in his opinion practicably be realised either at all or to their full potential value within any reasonable time. This will generally be an exercise of commercial judgment with which the court would be reluctant to interfere. The provisions of this rule relating to the final distribution which then follows should be read in conjunction with Part 11 of the IR 1986. Where future claimants might appear the liquidator would be advised to apply to the court to set up a contingency fund before making final distribution to creditors *Tombs v Moulinex* [2004] 2 BCLC 397.

R 4.186(2)

The particulars required to be given by a notice of intention to declare a final dividend are set out in IR 1986 r 11(2). As with interim dividends (see commentary to IR 1986 r 4.180 above), the liquidator must specify a date not less than 21 days from the date of notice within which proofs may be lodged, and must state his intention to declare the dividend within the period of 4 months from the last date of proving. In addition, however, the notice should require 'claims against the assets to be established by a date specified in the notice'. Although inelegantly drafted, this must refer to the proving of debts (rather than any proprietary claim to the company's assets which will at this stage in most cases have been realised). The provision is supplemented by IR 1986 r 11.3 which stipulates that every creditor's proof, if not already dealt with, must finally be admitted or rejected within 7 days of the last date for proving the debt. However by IR 1986 r 4.186(4) the court has power to postpone the final date for proving a debt. Where no (further) dividend is to be declared, the particulars required are set out in IR 1986 r 11.7.

R 4.186(3)

By IR 1986 r 11.5, the declaration of final dividend should follow within 4 months after the date specified, unless the liquidator has had cause to postpone or cancel the dividend (e g following an application under paragraph 4 of this rule), or there is a pending application challenging his decision on a proof. Although this provision does not stipulate any notice accompanies the declaration of final dividend, the notice requirements of IR 1986 r 11.6 appear of general application.

2.437

4.187 Liquidator's notice of disclaimer

(1) Where the liquidator disclaims property under section 178, the notice of disclaimer shall contain such particulars of the property disclaimed as enable it to be easily identified.

(2) The notice shall be signed by the liquidator and filed in court, with a copy. The court shall secure that both the notice and the copy are sealed and endorsed with the date of filing.

(3) The copy notice, so sealed and endorsed, shall be returned by the court to the liquidator as follows—
  (a) if the notice has been delivered at the offices of the court by the liquidator in person, it shall be handed to him,
  (b) if it has been delivered by some person acting on the liquidator's behalf, it shall be handed to that person, for immediate transmission to the liquidator, and
  (c) otherwise, it shall be sent to the liquidator by first class post.

The court shall cause to be endorsed on the original notice, or otherwise recorded on the file, the manner in which the copy notice was returned to the liquidator.

(4) For the purposes of section 178, the date of the prescribed notice is that which is endorsed on it, and on the copy, in accordance with this Rule.

Notes

RR 4.187–4.194

These set out the procedure in relation to the service of notices of disclaimer and the making of an application for a vesting order. For the relevant sections of the IA 1986 see ss 178–182.

R 4.187(1)

In *MEPC plc v Scottish Amicable Life Assurance Society* [1993] 2 EGLR 93 the court construed a disclaimer of an interest in a licence to assign a lease as a disclaimer of the lease itself. It was impossible to disclaim the assignment without disclaiming the lease, and it was clear from the notice of disclaimer that it was the intention of the bankrupt's trustee to rid himself of continuing liability in respect of such property.

2.438

4.188 Communication of disclaimer to persons interested

(1) Within 7 days after the day on which the copy of the notice of disclaimer is returned to him under Rule 4.187, the liquidator shall send

or give copies of the notice (showing the date endorsed as required by that Rule) to the persons mentioned in paragraphs (2) to (4) below.

(2) Where the property disclaimed is of a leasehold nature, he shall send or give a copy to every person who (to his knowledge) claims under the company as underlessee or mortgagee.

(3) He shall in any case send or give a copy of the notice to every person who (to his knowledge)—
  (a)   claims an interest in the disclaimed property, or
  (b)   is under any liability in respect of the property, not being a liability discharged by the disclaimer.

(4) If the disclaimer is of an unprofitable contract, he shall send or give copies of the notice to all such persons as, to his knowledge, are parties to the contract or have interests under it.

(5) If subsequently it comes to the liquidator's knowledge, in the case of any person, that he has such an interest in the disclaimed property as would have entitled him to receive a copy of the notice of disclaimer in pursuance of paragraphs (2) to (4), the liquidator shall then forthwith send or give to that person a copy of the notice.

But compliance with this paragraph is not required if—
  (a)   the liquidator is satisfied that the person has already been made aware of the disclaimer and its date, or
  (b)   the court, on the liquidator's application, orders that compliance is not required in that particular case.

Notes

R 4.188(3)

Guarantors of the company's obligations in respect of the property disclaimed or of the obligations of others liable in respect of such obligations in addition to the company will come within this class: *Maurice Tempany v Royal Liver Trustees Ltd* [1984] BCLC 568; *Hindcastle Ltd v Barbara Attenborough Associates Ltd* [1997] AC 70.

2.439

4.189 Additional notices

The liquidator disclaiming property may, without prejudice to his obligations under sections 178 to 180 and Rules 4.187 and 4.188, at any time give notice of the disclaimer to any persons who in his opinion ought, in the public interest or otherwise, to be informed of it.

2.440

4.190 Duty to keep court informed

The liquidator shall notify the court from time to time as to the persons to whom he has sent or given copies of the notice of disclaimer under the two preceding Rules, giving their names and addresses, and the nature of their respective interests.

2.441

4.191 Application by interested party under s 178(5)

Where, in the case of any property, application is made to the liquidator by an interested party under section 178(5) (request for decision whether the property is to be disclaimed or not), the application—

   (a)   shall be delivered to the liquidator personally or by registered post, and

   (b)   shall be made in the form known as 'notice to elect', or a substantially similar form.

2.442

4.192 Interest in property to be declared on request

(1) If, in the case of property which the liquidator has the right to disclaim, it appears to him that there is some person who claims, or may claim, to have an interest in the property, he may give notice to that person calling on him to declare within 14 days whether he claims any such interest and, if so, the nature and extent of it.

(2) Failing compliance with the notice, the liquidator is entitled to assume that the person concerned has no such interest in the property as will prevent or impede its disclaimer.

2.443

4.193 Disclaimer presumed valid and effective

Any disclaimer of property by the liquidator is presumed valid and effective, unless it is proved that he has been in breach of his duty with respect to the giving of notice of disclaimer, or otherwise under sections 178 to 180, or under this Chapter of the Rules.

2.444

4.194 Application for exercise of court's powers under s 181

(1) This Rule applies with respect to an application by any person under section 181 for an order of the court to vest or deliver disclaimed property.

(2) The application must be made within 3 months of the applicant becoming aware of the disclaimer, or of his receiving a copy of the liquidator's notice of disclaimer sent under Rule 4.188, whichever is the earlier.

(3) The applicant shall with his application file in court an affidavit—

   (a)   stating whether he applies under paragraph (a) of section 181(2) (claim of interest in the property) or under paragraph (b) (liability not discharged);

   (b)   specifying the date on which he received a copy of the liquidator's notice of disclaimer, or otherwise became aware of the disclaimer; and

   (c)   specifying the grounds of his application and the order which he desires the court to make under section 181.

(4) The court shall fix a venue for the hearing of the application; and the applicant shall, not later than 7 days before the date fixed, give to the

liquidator notice of the venue, accompanied by copies of the application and the affidavit under paragraph (3).

(5) On the hearing of the application, the court may give directions as to other persons (if any) who should be sent or given notice of the application and the grounds on which it is made.

(6) Sealed copies of any order made on the application shall be sent by the court to the applicant and the liquidator.

(7) In a case where the property disclaimed is of a leasehold nature, and section 179 applies to suspend the effect of the disclaimer, there shall be included in the court's order a direction giving effect to the disclaimer.

This paragraph does not apply if, at the time when the order is issued, other applications under section 181 are pending in respect of the same property.

Notes

R 4.194(2)

The time limit of 3 months stated in IR 1986 r 4.194(2) may be extended at the discretion of the court: *W H Smith Ltd v Wyndham Investments Ltd* [1994] BCC 699.

Chapter 16
Settlement of List of Contributories (No CVL Application)

2.445

4.195 Preliminary

The duties of the court with regard to the settling of the list of contributories are, by virtue of the Rules, delegated to the liquidator.

Notes

R 4.195

The duty of the court is set out in IA 1986 s 148, and the power to delegate is found in IA 1986 s 160(1)(b).

2.446

4.196 Duty of liquidator to settle list

(1) Subject as follows, the liquidator shall, as soon as may be after his appointment, exercise the court's power to settle a list of the company's contributories for the purposes of section 148 and, with the court's approval, rectify the register of members.

(2) The liquidator's duties under this Rule are performed by him as an officer of the court subject to the court's control.

The liquidator may only rectify the register with special leave of the court: section 160(2).

Notes

R 4.196

The liquidator may only rectify the register with special leave of the court: IA 1986 s 160(2).

2.447

4.197 Form of list

(1) The list shall identify—
  (a) the several classes of the company's shares (if more than one), and
  (b) the several classes of contributories, distinguishing between those who are contributories in their own right and those who are so as representatives of, or liable for the debts of, others.

(2) In the case of each contributory there shall in the list be stated—
  (a) his address.
  (b) the number and class of shares, or the extent of any other interest to be attributed to him, and
  (c) if the shares are not fully paid up, the amounts which have been called up and paid in respect of them (and the equivalent, if any, where his interest is other than shares).

2.448

4.198 Procedure for settling list

(1) Having settled the list, the liquidator shall forthwith give notice, to every person included in the list, that he has done so.

(2) The notice given to each person shall state—
  (a) in what character, and for what number of shares or what interest, he is included in the list,
  (b) what amounts have been called up and paid up in respect of the shares or interest, and
  (c) that in relation to any shares or interest not fully paid up, his inclusion in the list may result in the unpaid capital being called.

(3) The notice shall inform any person to whom it is given that, if he objects to any entry in, or omission from, the list, he should so inform the liquidator in writing within 21 days from the date of the notice.

(4) On receipt of any such objection, the liquidator shall within 14 days give notice to the objector either—
  (a) that he has amended the list (specifying the amendment), or
  (b) that he considers the objection to be not well-founded and declines to amend the list.

The notice shall in either case inform the objector of the effect of Rule 4.199.

2.449

4.199 Application to court for variation of the list

(1) If a person objects to any entry in, or exclusion from, the list of contributories as settled by the liquidator and, notwithstanding notice by the liquidator declining to amend the list, maintains his objection, he may apply to the court for an order removing the entry to which he objects or (as the case may be) otherwise amending the list.

(2) The application must be made within 21 days of the service on the applicant of the liquidator's notice under Rule 4.198(4).

2.450

4.200 Variation of, or addition to, the list

The liquidator may from time to time vary or add to the list of contributories as previously settled by him, but subject in all respects to the preceding Rules in this Chapter.

2.451

4.201 Costs not to fall on official receiver

The official receiver is not personally liable for any costs incurred by a person in respect of an application to set aside or vary his act or decision in settling the list of contributories, or varying or adding to the list; and the liquidator (if other than the official receiver) is not so liable unless the court makes an order to that effect.

Chapter 17
Calls (No CVL Application)

2.452

4.202 Calls by liquidator

Subject as follows, the powers conferred by the Act with respect to the making of calls on contributories are exercisable by the liquidator as an officer of the court subject to the court's control.

Notes

R 4.202

The power vested in the court to make calls on contributories under IA 1986 s 150 is delegated to the liquidator by virtue of IA 1986 s 160(1)(a) and this provision. However the liquidator may only exercise the power with the special leave of the court or sanction of the liquidation committee' see IA 1986 s 160(2).

2.453

4.203 Control by liquidation committee

(1) Where the liquidator proposes to make a call, and there is a liquidation committee, he may summon a meeting of the committee for the purpose of obtaining its sanction.

(2) At least 7 days' notice of the meeting shall be given by the liquidator to each member of the committee.

(3) The notice shall contain a statement of the proposed amount of the call, and the purpose for which it is intended to be made.

2.454

4.204 Application to court for leave to make a call

(1) For the purpose of obtaining the leave of the court for the making of a call on any contributories of the company, the liquidator shall apply *ex parte*, supporting his application by affidavit.

(2) There shall in the application be stated the amount of the proposed call, and the contributories on whom it is to be made.

(3) The court may direct that notice of the order be given to the contributories concerned, or to other contributories, or may direct that the notice be publicly advertised.

2.455

4.205 Making and enforcement of the call

(1) Notice of the call shall be given to each of the contributories concerned, and shall specify—
    (a) the amount or balance due from him in respect of it, and
    (b) whether the call is made with the sanction of the court or the liquidation committee.

(2) Payment of the amount due from any contributory may be enforced by order of the court.

Chapter 18
Special Manager

2.456

4.206 Appointment and remuneration

(1) An application made by the liquidator under section 177 for the appointment of a person to be special manager shall be supported by a report setting out the reasons for the application.

The report shall include the applicant's estimate of the value of the assets in respect of which the special manager is to be appointed.

(2) This Chapter applies also with respect to an application by the provisional liquidator, where one has been appointed, and references to the liquidator are to be read accordingly as including the provisional liquidator. (NO CVL APPLICATION)

(3) The court's order appointing the special manager shall specify the duration of his appointment, which may be for a period of time, or until the occurrence of a specified event. Alternatively, the order may specify that the duration of the appointment is to be subject to a further order of the court.

(4) The appointment of a special manager may be renewed by order of the court.

(5) The special manager's remuneration shall be fixed from time to time by the court.

(6) The acts of the special manager are valid notwithstanding any defect in his appointment or qualifications.

___

Notes

R 4.206

A special manager does not have to be a licensed insolvency practitioner and is usually appointed because he has expertise necessary for the continued trading of the business of the company: *Re US Ltd* (1984) 1 BCC 98, 985*; Re Pinstripe Farming Co Ltd* [1996] BCC 913. The court can grant the special manager such powers as it thinks fit: IA 1986 s 177(3). He is an officer of the court: *Re Walter L Jacob Co Ltd* (1989) 5 BCC 244, 255A.

___

2.457

4.207 Security

(1) The appointment of the special manager does not take effect until the person appointed has given (or, being allowed by the court to do so, undertaken to give) security to the person who applies for him to be appointed.

(2) It is not necessary that security shall be given for each separate company liquidation; but it may be given either specially for a particular liquidation, or generally for any liquidation in relation to which the special manager may be employed as such.

(3) The amount of the security shall be not less than the value of the assets in respect of which he is appointed, as estimated by the applicant in his report under Rule 4.206.

(4) When the special manager has given security to the person applying for his appointment, that person shall file in court a certificate as to the adequacy of the security.

(5) The cost of providing the security shall be paid in the first instance by the special manager; but—
    (a)   where a winding-up order is not made, he is entitled to be reimbursed out of the property of the company, and the court may make an order on the company accordingly, and
    (b)   where a winding-up order is made, he is entitled to be reimbursed out of the assets in the prescribed order of priority.

(NO CVL APPLICATION)

(6–CVL) The cost of providing the security shall be paid in the first instance by the special manager; but he is entitled to be reimbursed out of the assets, in the prescribed order of priority.

2.458

4.208 Failure to give or keep up security

(1) If the special manager fails to give the required security within the time stated for that purpose by the order appointing him, or any extension of that time that may be allowed, the liquidator shall report the failure to the court, which may thereupon discharge the order appointing the special manager.

(2) If the special manager fails to keep up his security, the liquidator shall report his failure to the court, which may thereupon remove the special manager, and make such order as it thinks fit as to costs.

(3) If an order is made under this Rule removing the special manager, or discharging the order appointing him, the court shall give directions as to whether any, and if so what, steps should be taken for the appointment of another special manager in his place.

2.459

4.209 Accounting

(1) The special manager shall produce accounts, containing details of his receipts and payments, for the approval of the liquidator.

(2) The accounts shall be in respect of 3–month periods for the duration of the special manager's appointment (or for a lesser period, if his appointment terminates less than 3 months from its date, or from the date to which the last accounts were made up).

(3) When the accounts have been approved, the special manager's receipts and payments shall be added to those of the liquidator.

2.460

4.210 Termination of appointment

(1) The special manager's appointment terminates if the winding-up petition is dismissed or if, a provisional liquidator having been appointed, the latter is discharged without a winding-up order having been made. (NO CVL APPLICATION)

(2) If the liquidator is of opinion that the employment of the special manager is no longer necessary or profitable for the company, he shall apply to the court for directions, and the court may order the special manager's appointment to be terminated.

(3) The liquidator shall make the same application if a resolution of the creditors is passed, requesting that the appointment be terminated.

Chapter 19
Public Examination of Company Officers and Others

2.461

4.211 Order for public examination

(1) If the official receiver applies to the court under section 133 for the public examination of any person, a copy of the court's order shall, forthwith after its making, be served on that person.

(2) Where the application relates to a person falling within section 133(1)(c) (promoters, past managers, etc), it shall be accompanied by a report by the official receiver indicating—
    (a)   the grounds on which the person is supposed to fall within that paragraph, and
    (b)   whether, in the official receiver's opinion, it is likely that service of the order on the person can be effected by post at a known address..

(3) If in his report the official receiver gives it as his opinion that, in a case to which paragraph (2) applies, there is no reasonable certainty that service by post will be effective, the court may direct that the order be served by some means other than, or in addition to, post.

(4) In a case to which paragraphs (2) and (3) apply, the court shall rescind the order if satisfied by the person to whom it is directed that he does not fall within section 133(1)(c).

Notes

R 4.211

See notes to IA 1986 s 133. It is a rarely used procedure in practice; usually the liquidator would proceed with a private examination under IA 1986 s.236. Where the court makes an order for a public examination, it must be served as soon as reasonably practicable on that person: see *Re Seagull Manufacturing Co Ltd (In liquidation)* [1993] Ch 345, 359 construing IR 1986 r 4.211(1). An order for a public examination may be made by a Registrar: see Practice Direction: Insolvency Proceedings, Civil Procedure 2006, Vol 2 Sect 3E, para 5.2. *An order for public examination will be made if the statutory conditions are satisfied unless no useful purpose is served by it. The court will consider whether there is any foreign jurisdiction (in relation to a foreign company) that might make it difficult or oppressive for the proposed examinee to be required to answer the questions: see Jeeves v Official Receiver* [2004] BPIR 46 *regarding a BVI company.*

2.462

4.212 Notice of hearing

(1) The court's order shall appoint a venue for the examination of the person to whom it is directed ('the examinee'), and direct his attendance thereat.

(2) The official receiver shall give at least 14 days' notice of the hearing—
    (a)   if a liquidator has been nominated or appointed, to him;
    (b)   if a special manager has been appointed, to him; and

    (c)   subject to any contrary direction of the court, to every creditor and contributory of the company who is known to the official receiver or is identified in the company's statement of affairs.

(3) The official receiver may, if he thinks fit, cause notice of the order to be given, by advertisement in one or more newspapers, at least 14 days before the date fixed for the hearing; but, unless the court otherwise directs, there shall be no such advertisement before at least 7 days have elapsed since the examinee was served with the order.

2.463

4.213 Order on request by creditors or contributories

(1) A request to the official receiver by creditors or contributories under section 133(2) shall be made in writing and be accompanied by—
    (a)   a list of the creditors concurring with the request and the amounts of their respective claims in the liquidation or (as the case may be) of the contributories so concurring, with their respective values, and
    (b)   from each creditor or contributory concurring, written confirmation of his concurrence.

This paragraph does not apply if the requisitioning creditor's debt or, as the case may be, requisitioning contributory's shareholding is alone sufficient, without the concurrence of others.

(2) The request must specify the name of the proposed examinee, the relationship which he has, or has had, to the company and the reasons why his examination is requested.

(3) Before an application to the court is made on the request, the requisitionists shall deposit with the official receiver such sum as the latter may determine to be appropriate by way of security for the expenses of the hearing of a public examination, if ordered.

(4) Subject as follows, the official receiver shall, within 28 days of receiving the request, make the application to the court required by section 133(2).

(5) If the official receiver is of opinion that the request is an unreasonable one in the circumstances, he may apply to the court for an order relieving him from the obligation to make the application otherwise required by that subsection.

(6) If the court so orders, and the application for the order was made *ex parte*, notice of the order shall be given forthwith by the official receiver to the requisitionists. If the application for an order is dismissed, the official receiver's application under section 133(2) shall be made forthwith on conclusion of the hearing of the application first mentioned.

2.464

4.214 Witness unfit for examination

(1) Where the examinee is suffering from any mental disorder or physical affliction or disability rendering him unfit to undergo or attend for public examination, the court may, on application in that behalf, either stay the

order for his public examination or direct that it shall be conducted in such manner and at such place as it thinks fit.

(2) Application under this Rule shall be made—
- (a) by a person who has been appointed by a court in the United Kingdom or elsewhere to manage the affairs of, or to represent, the examinee, or
- (b) by a relative or friend of the examinee whom the court considers to be a proper person to make the application, or
- (c) by the official receiver.

(3) Where the application is made by a person other than the official receiver, then—
- (a) it shall, unless the examinee is a patient within the meaning of the Mental Health Act 1983, be supported by the affidavit of a registered medical practitioner as to the examinee's mental and physical condition;
- (b) at least 7 days' notice of the application shall be given to the official receiver and the liquidator (if other than the official receiver); and
- (c) before any order is made on the application, the applicant shall deposit with the official receiver such sum as the latter certifies to be necessary for the additional expenses of any examination that may be ordered on the application.

An order made on the application may provide that the expenses of the examination are to be payable, as to a specified proportion, out of the deposit under sub-paragraph (c), instead of out of the assets.

(4) Where the application is made by the official receiver it may be made *ex parte*, and may be supported by evidence in the form of a report by the official receiver to the court.

2.465

4.215 Procedure at hearing

(1) The examinee shall at the hearing be examined on oath; and he shall answer all such questions as the court may put, or allow to be put, to him.

(2) Any of the persons allowed by section 133(4) to question the examinee may, with the approval of the court (made known either at the hearing or in advance of it), appear by solicitor or counsel; or he may in writing authorise another person to question the examinee on his behalf.

(3) The examinee may at his own expense employ a solicitor with or without counsel, who may put to him such questions as the court may allow for the purpose of enabling him to explain or qualify any answers given by him, and may make representations on his behalf.

(4) There shall be made in writing such record of the examination, as the court thinks proper. The record shall be read over either to or by the examinee, signed by him, and verified by affidavit at a venue fixed by the court.

(5) The written record may, in any proceedings (whether under the Act or otherwise) be used as evidence against the examinee of any statement made by him in the course of his public examination.

> If criminal proceedings have been instituted against the examinee, and the court is of opinion that the continuance of the hearing would be calculated to prejudice a fair trial of those proceedings, the hearing may be adjourned.

Notes

R 4.215

It is a matter for the judge presiding at the examination to decide whether or not a question is proper, or oppressive, see *Re Richbell Strategic Holdings Ltd* [2001] BCC 409.

2.466

4.216 Adjournment

(1) The public examination may be adjourned by the court from time to time, either to a fixed date or generally.

(2) Where the examination has been adjourned generally, the court may at any time on the application of the official receiver or of the examinee—
- (a)   fix a venue for the resumption of the examination, and
- (b)   give directions as to the manner in which, and the time within which, notice of the resumed public examination is to be given to persons entitled to take part in it.

(3) Where application under paragraph (2) is made by the examinee, the court may grant it on terms that the expenses of giving the notices required by that paragraph shall be paid by him and that, before a venue for the resumed public examination is fixed, he shall deposit with the official receiver such sum as the latter considers necessary to cover those expenses.

2.467

4.217 Expenses of examination

(1) Where a public examination of the examinee has been ordered by the court on a creditors' or contributories' requisition under Rule 4.213, the court may order that the expenses of the examination are to be paid, as to a specified proportion, out of the deposit under Rule 4.213(3), instead of out of the assets.

(2) In no case do the costs and expenses of a public examination fall on the official receiver personally.

Chapter 20
Order of Payment of Costs, etc, Out of Assets

2.468

4.218 General rule as to priority

(1) The expenses of the liquidation are payable out of the assets in the following order of priority—

[(a) expenses or costs which—
  (i) are properly chargeable or incurred by the official receiver or the liquidator in preserving, realising or getting in any of the assets of the company or otherwise relating to the conduct of any legal proceedings which he has power to bring or defend whether in his own name or the name of the company;
  (ii) relate to the employment of a shorthand writer, if appointed by an order of the court made at the instance of the official receiver in connection with an examination; or
  (iii) are incurred in holding an examination under Rule 4.214 (examinee unfit) where the application for it was made by the official receiver;]
(b) any other expenses incurred or disbursements made by the official receiver or under his authority, including those incurred or made in carrying on the business of the company;
[(c) the fees payable under any order made under section 414 [or section 415A], including those payable to the official receiver (other than the fee referred to in sub-paragraph (d)(i) below), and any remuneration payable to him under general regulations;
(d)
  (i) the fee payable under any order made under section 414 for the performance by the official receiver of his general duties as official receiver;
  (ii) any repayable deposit lodged under any such order as security for the fee mentioned in sub-paragraph (i);]
(e) the cost of any security provided by a provisional liquidator, liquidator or special manager in accordance with the Act or the Rules;
(f) the remuneration of the provisional liquidator (if any);
(g) any deposit lodged on an application for the appointment of a provisional liquidator;
(h) the costs of the petitioner, and of any person appearing on the petition whose costs are allowed by the court;
(j) the remuneration of the special manager (if any);
(k) any amount payable to a person employed or authorised, under Chapter 6 of this Part of the Rules, to assist in the preparation of a statement of affairs or of accounts;
(l) any allowance made, by order of the court, towards costs on an application for release from the obligation to submit a statement of affairs, or for an extension of time for submitting such a statement;
[(la) the costs of employing a shorthand writer in any case other than one appointed by an order of the court at the instance of the official receiver in connection with an examination;]
(m) any necessary disbursements by the liquidator in the course of his administration (including any expenses incurred by members of the liquidation committee or their representatives and allowed by the liquidator under Rule 4.169, but not including any payment of [corporation] tax in circumstances referred to in sub-paragraph (p) below);

(n) the remuneration or emoluments of any person who has been employed by the liquidator to perform any services for the company, as required or authorised by or under the Act or the Rules;

(o) the remuneration of the liquidator, up to any amount not exceeding that which is payable under Schedule 6;

(p) the amount of any [corporation] tax on chargeable gains accruing on the realisation of any asset of the company (without regard to whether the realisation is effected by the liquidator, a secured creditor, or a receiver or manager appointed to deal with a security);

(q) the balance, after payment of any sums due under sub-paragraph (o) above, of any remuneration due to the liquidator[;

(r) any other expenses properly chargeable by the liquidator in carrying out his functions in the liquidation].

(2) <...>

(3) <...>

Notes

R 4.218

This provision lists the categories of expenses payable in all liquidations (IR 1986 r 4.1(2)) and dictates a strict priority amongst the expenses though it does not define exactly what constitutes an 'expense'. The list was amended by the Insolvency (Amendment) (No 2) Rules 2002 (SI 2002/2712) and the Insolvency (Amendment) Rules 2004 (SI 2004/584). If in doubt as to whether or not any particular item of expenditure will be recoverable as an expense or cost for the purposes of IR 1986 r 4.218(a), a prudent liquidator will seek the directions of the court: see for example *Re Demaglass Ltd* [2003] 1 BCLC 412 where, on the applications of two liquidators, directions were given as to what was and was not permissible under the rules; and *Re SSSL Realisations* (2002) Ltd [2005] 1 BCLC 1 where it was held that damages for breach of contract were not 'expenses or costs' under IR 1986 r 4.218(1)(a).

In *Re Leyland DAF Ltd, Buchler v Talbot* [2004] 2 AC 298 the House of Lords held that where a company went into receivership and then liquidation, the assets comprised in the floating charge were not 'assets' for the purposes of IR 1986 r 4.218(1) and accordingly the costs and expenses of the liquidation were not payable out of the same; and see HM Revenue & Customs and DTI statement 6 June 2005 on *Re Leyland DAF Ltd (above). However the Companies* Bill 2006 cl 1246 proposes *to reverse the effect of the ruling in Re Leyland Daf (above) on this issue; see further the notes to IA 1986 s 175.*

Since IR r 4.218(1) gives the remuneration of a provisional liquidator a significantly higher priority than that of a liquidator, it follows that the expenses incurred by the provisional liquidator should also be given priority to those incurred by the liquidator: *Re Grey Marlin Ltd* [1999].

Formerly it had been held that a liquidator's costs in pursuing claims under the avoidance provisions (such as IA 1986 ss 214, 238, 239) were not payable out of the company's assets: see *Re MC Bacon Ltd (No 2)* [1991] Ch 127; *Re Floor Fourteen Ltd* [2001] 3 All ER 449. The Insolvency (Amendment) (No 2) Rules 2002 (SI 2002/2712), however, reversed the above by amending this provision with effect from 1 January 2003 so as to expressly provide that such costs are recoverable. As a quid pro quo, since 15 September 2003 the power to bring such proceedings can now only be exercised with the sanction of the liquidation committee or court: IA 1986, schedule 4, para 3A.

Under the former law the court had jurisdiction to order the costs incurred in an administration petition down to the date of the first hearing to be paid in the winding up together with the company's costs on the winding up petition where the administration petition was presented in good faith, reasonably and on professional advice: *Re Gosscott (Groundworks) Ltd* (1988) 4 BCC 372. See also *Re WF Fearman Ltd (No 2)* (1988) 4 BCC 141 cited in *Re Goscott* (above).

Where rent is paid by a liquidator in order to avoid the forfeiture of a lease so as to enable him to realise the lease advantageously the payment of rent may be regarded as an expense incurred in preserving an asset of the company: see *Linda Marie Ltd (in liquidation)* (1988) 4 BCC 463.

In *Re Toshoku Finance (UK) plc* [2002] 1 WLR 671 it was held that since it was expressly enacted by statute that a company was chargable to corporation tax on profits or gains arising in the winding up, the tax was post-liquidation liability which the liquidator was bound to discharge and it was therefore a 'necessary disbursement' within the meaning of the rule; notwithstanding that the interest upon which the tax was assessed was not actually received by the company, it was payable as a priority under paragraph (m). See also *Alders Department Stores Ltd* [2005] 1 All ER 231 which concerned the similar expenses provision in an administration (IR 1986 r 2.67); *Re Huddersfield Fine Worsteds Ltd, Re Granville Technology Group Ltd* [2005] 4 All ER 886).

Any costs order made against liquidators in relation to civil proceedings undertaken by them has priority over the general expenses of the liquidation: see *London Metallurgical Co* [1895] 1 CL 758, *Re MT Realisations Ltd* [2004] 1 WLR 1678. The liquidator will however first be able to claim the costs of realising the assets to pay those costs: see *Re Movitex Ltd* [1990] BCC 491.

2.469

4.219 Winding up commencing as voluntary

In a winding up by the court which follows immediately on a voluntary winding up (whether members' voluntary or creditors' voluntary), such remuneration of the voluntary liquidator and costs and expenses of the voluntary liquidation as the court may allow are to rank in priority with the expenses specified in Rule 4.218(1)(a).

Notes

R 4.219

In *Re Tony Rowse NMC Ltd* [1996] BCC 196 it was held that this provision conferred on the court a discretion to allow and, a fortiori, to review and disallow all or some part of the voluntary liquidator's remuneration, costs and expenses. It is doubtful, however, whether an application for an increase in the liquidator's remuneration can be made under this rule; such an application should instead be made under IR 1986 r 4.130.

2.470

4.220 Saving for powers of the court

(1) In a winding up by the court, the priorities laid down by Rules 4.218 and 4.219 are subject to the power of the court to make orders under section 156, where the assets are insufficient to satisfy the liabilities.

(2) Nothing in those Rules applies to or affects the power of any court, in proceedings by or against the company, to order costs to be paid by the

> company, or the liquidator; nor do they affect the rights of any person to whom such costs are ordered to be paid.

Notes

R 4.220(2)

Costs which are payable as a result of a court order made against liquidators who engage in liquidation are not 'expenses incurred in the winding up'. Therefore it is not open to the court to use IA 1986 s 156 to change the normal precedence afforded to costs made payable by court order: *Re MT Realisations Ltd* [2004] 1 WCR 1678.

Chapter 21
Miscellaneous Rules

Section A: Return of Capital (No CVL Application)

2.471

4.221 Application to court for order authorising return

(1) This Rule applies where the liquidator intends to apply to the court for an order authorising a return of capital.

(2) The application shall be accompanied by a list of the persons to whom the return is to be made.

(3) The list shall include the same details of those persons as appears in the settled list of contributories, with any necessary alterations to take account of matters after settlement of the list, and the amount to be paid to each person.

(4) Where the court makes an order authorising the return, it shall send a sealed copy of the order to the liquidator.

2.472

4.222 Procedure for return

(1) The liquidator shall inform each person to whom a return is made of the rate of return per share, and whether it is expected that any further return will be made.

(2) Any payments made by the liquidator by way of the return may be sent by post, unless for any reason another method of making the payment has been agreed with the payee.

Section B: Conclusion of Winding Up

2.473

4.223 Statements to registrar of companies under s 192—CVL

(1) Subject to paragraphs (3) and (3A), the statement which section 192 requires the liquidator to send to the registrar of companies, if the winding up is not concluded within one year from its commencement,

shall be sent not more than 30 days after the expiration of that year, and thereafter 6–monthly until the winding up is concluded.

(2) For this purpose the winding up is concluded at the date of the dissolution of the company, except that if at that date any assets or funds of the company remain unclaimed or undistributed in the hands or under the control of the liquidator or any former liquidator, the winding up is not concluded until those assets or funds have either been distributed or paid into the Insolvency Services Account.

(3) Subject as above, the liquidator's final statement shall be sent forthwith after the conclusion of the winding up.

(3A) No statement shall be required to be delivered under this Rule where the return of the final meeting in respect of the company under sections 94 or 106 is delivered before the date at which the statement is to be delivered and that return shows that no assets or funds of the company remain unclaimed or undistributed in the hands or under the control of the liquidator or any former liquidator; but where this paragraph applies, the liquidator shall deliver a copy of that return to the Secretary of State.

Notes

R 4.223

Under IA 1986 s 192 it is provided that if the winding up of a company is not concluded within one year after its commencement, the liquidator shall at such intervals as may be prescribed until the winding up is concluded send to the registrar of companies a statement in the prescribed form summarising the status of the liquidation. This provision sets out the prescribed period, which apply in a voluntary winding up, providing that the first such statement is to be sent within 30 days after the expiration of the initial year, with further statements to follow at 6 monthly intervals until the conclusion of the winding up.

Section C: Dissolution after Winding Up

2.474

4.224 Secretary of State's directions under ss 203, 205

(1) Where the Secretary of State gives a direction under—
- (a) section 203 (where official receiver applies to registrar of companies for a company's early dissolution), or
- (b) section 205 (application by interested person for postponement of dissolution),

he shall send two copies of the direction to the applicant for it.

(2) Of those copies one shall be sent by the applicant to the registrar of companies, to comply with section 203(5) or, as the case may be 205(6).

2.475

4.225 Procedure following appeal under s 203(4) or 205(4)

Following an appeal under section 203(4) or 205(4) (against a decision of the Secretary of State under the applicable section) the court shall send two sealed copies of its order to the person in whose favour the appeal was determined; and that party shall send one of the copies to the registrar of companies to comply with section 203(5) or, as the case may be, 205(6).

Notes

RR 4.224, 4.225

The official receiver is entitled under IA 1986 s 202 in certain circumstances to apply to the registrar of companies for the early dissolution of a company. Where such an application is made, the official receiver or any creditor or contributory of the company may apply under IA 1986 s 203 to the Secretary of State for directions, including a direction for the deferring of the dissolution. Similarly, in a dissolution other than an early dissolution, directions for deferral can be sought from the Secretary of State under IA 1986 s 205. In respect of both procedures, the relevant machinery for the service of such directions and of any appeal from the same are set out in IR 1986 r 4.224, 4.225.

Chapter 22
Leave to act as Director, etc, of Company with Prohibited Name
(Section 216 of the Act)

2.476

4.226 Preliminary

The Rules in this Chapter—
- (a) relate to the leave required under section 216 (restriction on re-use of name of company in insolvent liquidation) for a person to act as mentioned in section 216(3) in relation to a company with a prohibited name,
- (b) prescribe the cases excepted from that provision, that is to say, those in which a person to whom the section applies may so act without that leave [, and
- (c) apply to all windings up to which section 216 applies, whether or not the winding up commenced before the coming into force of the Rules].

Notes

R 4.226

Control is placed over the rise of 'phoenix' companies by IA 1986 s 216 which prevents a former director or shadow director from using a prohibited company name 'except with the leave of the court or in such circumstances as may be prescribed'. This provision introduces the relevant rules: IR 1986 r 4.227 relates to the giving of leave, while IR 1986 rr. 4.228–4.230 set out with various exceptions where leave is not required. These rules must be interpreted in conjunction with IA 1986 s 216 so as to create a coherent and rational scheme: see *ESS Productions Ltd v Sully* [2005] 2 BCLC 547, para 61.

2.477

4.227 Application for leave under s 216(3)

When considering an application for leave under section 216, the court may call on the liquidator, or any former liquidator, of the liquidating company for a report of the circumstances in which that company became insolvent, and the extent (if any) of the applicant's apparent responsibility for its doing so.

Notes

R 4.227

See also IA 1986 s 216(5) under which both the Secretary of State and the official receiver have locus to appear on the application and call the court's attention to any relevant matter. Under the present rule, the court is enabled to investigate and consider the conduct of the applicant as regards his stewardship of the liquidated company, and if there is prima facie evidence of that misconduct or lack of skill on his part led to its insolvency, either to refuse leave on these grounds, or to grant leave only subject to the kinds of restriction which may be imposed under CDDA 1986 s 1.

2.478

4.228 First excepted case

(1) Where a company ('the successor company') acquires the whole, or substantially the whole, of the business of an insolvent company, under arrangements made by an insolvency practitioner acting as its liquidator, administrator or administrative receiver, or as supervisor of a voluntary arrangement under Part I of the Act, the successor company may for the purposes of section 216 give notice under this Rule to the insolvent company's creditors.

(2) To be effective, the notice must be given within 28 days from the completion of the arrangements, to all creditors of the insolvent company of whose addresses the successor company is aware in that period; and it must specify—
  (a) the name and registered number of the insolvent company and the circumstances in which its business has been acquired by the successor company,
  (b) the name which the successor company has assumed, or proposes to assume for the purpose of carrying on the business, if that name is or will be a prohibited name under section 216, and
  (c) any change of name which it has made, or proposes to make, for that purpose under section 28 of the Companies Act.

(3) The notice may name a person to whom section 216 may apply as having been a director or shadow director of the insolvent company, and give particulars as to the nature and duration of that directorship, with a view to his being a director of the successor company or being otherwise associated with its management.

(4) If the successor company has effectively given notice under this Rule to the insolvent company's creditors, a person who is so named in the

> notice may act in relation to the successor company in any of the ways
> mentioned in section 216(3), notwithstanding that he has not the leave of
> the court under that section.

Notes

R 4.228

The first exception where leave is not required relates to the transfer by the relevant insolvency practitioner of an insolvent company's business to a successor company and requires the service of notice specifying the prescribed information on all creditors. This rule both identifies and addresses the mischief to which IA 1986 s 216 is directed, namely the danger: (i) that the business and assets of the liquidated company might be transferred to the phoenix company at an undervalue, to the detriment of creditors; and (ii) that creditors of the liquidated company might be misled into believing there is no change in the corporate vehicle, see *Penrose v Official Receiver* [1996] 1 WLR 489; *ESS Productions Ltd v Sully* [2005] 2 BCLC 547. For a case which came close to fulfilling the above requirements, see *Re Lightning Electrical Contractors Ltd* [1996] BCLC 302. There is no express provision enabling a creditor to challenge the permission then given to the director to act in relation to the successor company but doubtless the court would entertain an application against the insolvency practitioner's decision to give the notice.

2.479

4.229 Second excepted case

(1) Where a person to whom section 216 applies as having been a director or shadow director of the liquidating company applies for leave of the court under that section not later than 7 days from the date on which the company went into liquidation, he may, during the period specified in paragraph (2) below, act in any of the ways mentioned in section 216(3), notwithstanding that he has not the leave of the court under that section.

(2) The period referred to in paragraph (1) begins with the day on which the company goes into liquidation and ends either on the day falling six weeks after that date or on the day on which the court disposes of the application for leave under section 216, whichever of those days occurs first.

Notes

R 4.229

This second exception allows a person who applies promptly for leave to act pending the determination of that application or within 6 weeks of the insolvency (whichever is the sooner).

2.480

4.230 Third excepted case

The court's leave under section 216(3) is not required where the company there referred to, though known by a prohibited name within the meaning of the section—

> (a)   has been known by that name for the whole of the period of 12 months ending with the day before the liquidating company went into liquidation, and
>
> (b)   has not at any time in those 12 months been dormant within the meaning of section 252(5) of the Companies Act.

Notes

R 4.230

This third exception applies to established companies, to which the mischief at which IA 1986 s 216 is aimed (as identified in *Penrose v Official Receiver* [1996] 1 WLR 489) does not apply: see the general discussion in *ESS Productions Ltd v Sully* [2005] 2 BCLC 547. However, it is necessary to show that the company has not been dormant at any time within the relevant 12 month period. A dormant company is defined by CA 1985 s 249AA(4) as one which has had no significant accounting transactions during the relevant period. For IR 1986 r 4.230 to apply it is not necessary to show that the prohibited name is the only name by which the company has been known or carried on business during the relevant 12 month period, or that it used that name for the whole (as opposed to merely a part) of its business: see *ESS Productions Ltd v Sully* [2005] 2 BCLC 547.

Chapter 23
EC Regulation—Member State Liquidator

2.481

4.231 Interpretation of creditor and notice to member State liquidator

(1) This Rule applies where a member State liquidator has been appointed in relation to the company.

(2) For the purposes of the Rules referred to in paragraph (3) the member State liquidator is deemed to be a creditor.

(3) The Rules referred to in paragraph (2) are Rules 4.43(1) (official receiver's report), 4.45(1) (report on statement of affairs), 4.46(2) (report where no statement of affairs), 4.47(2) (general rule on reporting), 4.48(2) (winding up stayed), 4.49 (information to creditors), 4.50(2) (notice of meetings), 4.51(2) (notice of creditors' meeting—CVL), 4.54 (power to call meetings), 4.57(1) (requisitioned meetings), 4.57(3), 4.67 (entitlement to vote (creditors)), 4.68 (chairman's discretion to allow vote—CVL), 4.70 (admission and rejection of proof (creditors' meeting)), 4.73 (meaning of 'prove'), 4.74 (supply of forms), 4.75 (contents of proof), 4.76 (particulars of creditor's claim), 4.77 (claim established by affidavit), 4.78 (cost of proving), 4.79 (inspection of proofs), 4.82 (admission and rejection of proofs for dividend), 4.83(1) (appeal against decision in relation to proof), 4.83(2), 4.84 (withdrawal or variation of proof), 4.85(1) (expunging of proof), 4.86 (estimate of quantum), 4.87 (negotiable instruments, etc), 4.88 (secured creditors), 4.89 (discounts), 4.90 (mutual credit and set-off), 4.91 (debt in foreign currency), 4.92 (payment of a periodical nature), 4.93 (interest), 4.94 (debt payable at future time), 4.101A (power to fill vacancy in office of liquidator), 4.102(5) (appointment by court), 4.103(4)

(appointment by court), 4.113(1) (meeting of creditors to remove liquidator), 4.114(1) (meeting of creditors to remove liquidator), 4.115 (regulation of meetings), 4.124(1) (release of official receiver), 4.125(1) (final meeting), [4.125A(2) (rule on reporting),] 4.126(1) (final meeting), 4.131(1) (challenge to liquidator's remuneration), 4.152(1) (liquidation committee), 4.152(3) (eligibility for liquidation committee), 4.163(3) (vacancy on liquidation committee), 4.175(1) (liquidation committee), 4.180 (notice of dividend) and 4.212(2) (notice of public examination hearing).

(4) Paragraphs (2) and (3) are without prejudice to the generality of the right to participate referred to in paragraph 3 of Article 32 of the EC Regulation (exercise of creditor's rights).

(5) Where the liquidator is obliged to give notice to, or provide a copy of a document (including an order of court) to, the court, the registrar of companies or the official receiver, the liquidator shall give notice or provide copies, as the case may be, to the member State liquidator.

(6) Paragraph (5) is without prejudice to the generality of the obligations imposed by Article 31 of the EC Regulation (duty to cooperate and communicate information).

Notes

R 4.231

This provision deals with the situation where insolvency proceedings are brought in another member state before or after a winding up in England; see IR 1986 r 13.13(11) for the definition of 'Member State liquidator'. Article 32 of the EC Regulation on Insolvency Proceedings 2000 entitles the foreign liquidator to lodge claims in the English winding up on behalf of creditors who have lodged claims with him, and to participate in the English insolvency proceedings on the same basis as a creditor; this provision contains the detailed machinery in this respect.

The Second Group of Parts
Individual Insolvency; Bankruptcy

Part 5
Individual Voluntary Arrangements

Notes

Part 5 of IR 1986 was substantially redrafted and revised by the Insolvency (Amendment) (No 2) Rules 2002 (SI 2002/2712) and in their revised form they came into effect on 1 January 2003. The former Part 5 rules (IR 1986 r 5.1–5.34) appear immediately below in italicised form.

2.482

5.1 Introductory

(1) The Rules in this Part apply where a debtor, with a view to an application for an interim order under Part VIII of the Act, makes a proposal to his creditors

for a voluntary arrangement, that is to say, a composition in satisfaction of his debts or a scheme of arrangement of his affairs.

(2) The Rules apply whether the debtor is an undischarged bankrupt ('Case 1'), or he is not ('Case 2').

Section A: The Debtor's Proposal

2.483

5.2 Preparation of proposal

The debtor shall prepare for the intended nominee a proposal on which (with or without amendments to be made under Rule 5.3(3) below) to make his report to the court under section 256.

2.484

5.3 Contents of proposal

(1) The debtor's proposal shall provide a short explanation why, in his opinion, a voluntary arrangement under Part VIII is desirable, and give reasons why his creditors may be expected to concur with such an arrangement.

(2) The following matters shall be stated, or otherwise dealt with, in the proposal—

   (a)   *the following matters, so far as within the debtor's immediate knowledge—*

      (i)   *his assets, with an estimate of their respective values,*

      (ii)   *the extent (if any) to which the assets are charged in favour of creditors,*

      (iii)   *the extent (if any) to which particular assets are to be excluded from the voluntary arrangement;*

   (b)   *particulars of any property, other than assets of the debtor himself, which is proposed to be included in the arrangement, the source of such property and the terms on which it is to be made available for inclusion;*

   (c)   *the nature and amount of the debtor's liabilities (so far as within his immediate knowledge), the manner in which they are proposed to be met, modified, postponed or otherwise dealt with by means of the arrangement and (in particular)—*

      (i)   *how it is proposed to deal with preferential creditors (defined in section 258(7)) and creditors who are, or claim to be, secured,*

      (ii)   *how associates of the debtor (being creditors of his) are proposed to be treated under the arrangement, and*

     [(iii)   *in Case 1 whether, to the debtor's knowledge, claims have been made under section 339 (transactions at an undervalue), section 340 (preferences) or section 343 (extortionate credit transactions), or there are circumstances giving rise to the possibility of such claims, and in Case 2 whether there are circumstances which would give rise to the possibility of such claims in the event that he should be adjudged bankrupt,]*

    and, where any such circumstances are present, whether, and if so how, it is proposed under the voluntary arrangement to make provision for wholly or partly indemnifying the insolvent estate in respect of such claims;

(d)   *whether any, and if so what, guarantees have been given of the debtor's debts by other persons, specifying which (if any) of the guarantors are associates of his;*

(e)   *the proposed duration of the voluntary arrangement;*

(f)   *the proposed dates of distributions to creditors, with estimates of their amounts;*

(g)   *the amount proposed to be paid to the nominee (as such) by way of remuneration and expenses;*

(h)   *the manner in which it is proposed that the supervisor of the arrangement should be remunerated, and his expenses defrayed;*

(j)   *whether, for the purposes of the arrangement, any guarantees are to be offered by any persons other than the debtor, and whether (if so) any security is to be given or sought;*

(k)   *the manner in which funds held for the purposes of the arrangement are to be banked, invested or otherwise dealt with pending distribution to creditors;*

(l)   *the manner in which funds held for the purpose of payment to creditors, and not so paid on the termination of the arrangement, are to be dealt with;*

(m)   *if the debtor has any business the manner in which it is proposed to be conducted during the course of the arrangement;*

(n)   *details of any further credit facilities which it is intended to arrange for the debtor, and how the debts so arising are to be paid;*

(o)   *the functions which are to be undertaken by the supervisor of the arrangement;*

(p)   *the name, address and qualification of the person proposed as supervisor of the voluntary arrangement, and confirmation that he is (so far as the debtor is aware) qualified to act as an insolvency practitioner in relation to him.*

(q)   *whether the EC Regulation will apply and, if so, whether the proceedings will be main proceedings, secondary proceedings or territorial proceedings..*

(3) With the agreement in writing of the nominee, the debtor's proposal may be amended at any time up to the delivery of the former's report to the court under section 256.

2.485

5.4 Notice to intended nominee

(1) The debtor shall give to the intended nominee written notice of his proposal.

(2) The notice, accompanied by a copy of the proposal, shall be delivered either to the nominee himself, or to a person authorised to take delivery of documents on his behalf.

(3) If the intended nominee agrees to act, he shall cause a copy of the notice to be endorsed to the effect that it has been received by him on a specified date.

(4) The copy of the notice so endorsed shall be returned by the nominee forthwith to the debtor at an address specified by him in the notice for that purpose.

(5) Where (in Case 1) the debtor gives notice of his proposal to the official receiver and (if any) the trustee, the notice must contain the name and address of the insolvency practitioner who has agreed to act as nominee.

2.486

5.5 Application for interim order

(1) An application to the court for an interim order under Part VIII of the Act shall be accompanied by an affidavit of the following matters—

(a) *the reasons for making the application;*

(b) *particulars of any execution or other legal process which, to the debtor's knowledge, has been commenced against him;*

(c) *that he is an undischarged bankrupt or (as the case may be) that he is able to petition for his own bankruptcy;*

(d) *that no previous application for an interim order has been made by or in respect of the debtor in the period of 12 months ending with the date of the affidavit; and*

(e) *that the nominee under the proposal (naming him) is a person who is qualified to act as an insolvency practitioner in relation to the debtor, and is willing to act in relation to the proposal.*

(2) A copy of the notice to the intended nominee under Rule 5.4, endorsed to the effect that he agrees so to act [and a copy of the debtor's proposal given to the nominee under that Rule], shall be exhibited to the affidavit.

(3) On receiving the application and affidavit, the court shall fix a venue for the hearing of the application.

(4) The applicant shall give at least 2 days' notice of the hearing—

(a) *in Case 1, to the bankrupt, the official receiver and the trustee (whichever of those three is not himself the applicant),*

(b) *in Case 2, to any creditor who (to the debtor's knowledge) has presented a bankruptcy petition against him, and*

(c) *in either case, to the nominee who has agreed to act in relation to the debtor's proposal.*

2.487

[5.5A Court in which application to be made]

[(1) Except in the case of a bankrupt, an application to the court under Part VIII of the Act shall be made to a court in which the debtor would be entitled to present his own petition in bankruptcy under Rule 6.40.

(2) The application shall contain sufficient information to establish that it is brought in the appropriate court.

(3) In the case of a bankrupt such an application shall be made to the court having the conduct of his bankruptcy and shall be filed with those bankruptcy proceedings.]

2.488

5.6 Hearing of the application

(1) Any of the persons who have been given notice under Rule 5.5(4) may appear or be represented at the hearing of the application.

(2) The court, in deciding whether to make an interim order on the application, shall take into account any representations made by or on behalf of any of those persons (in particular, whether an order should be made containing such provision as is referred to in section 255(3) and (4)).

(3) *If the court makes an interim order, it shall fix a venue for consideration of the nominee's report. Subject to the following paragraph, the date for that consideration shall be not later than that on which the interim order ceases to have effect under section 255(6).*

(4) *If under section 256(4) an extension of time is granted for filing the nominee's report, the court shall, unless there appear to be good reasons against it, correspondingly extend the period for which the interim order has effect.*

2.489

5.7 Action to follow making of order

(1) *Where an interim order is made, at least 2 sealed copies of the order shall be sent by the court forthwith to the person who applied for it; and that person shall serve one of the copies on the nominee under the debtor's proposal.*

(2) *The applicant shall also forthwith give notice of the making of the order to any person who was given notice of the hearing pursuant to Rule 5.5(4) and was not present or represented at it.*

2.490

5.8 Statement of affairs

(1) *In Case 1, if the debtor has already delivered a statement of affairs under section 272 (debtor's petition) or 288 (creditor's petition), he need not deliver a further statement unless so required by the nominee, with a view to supplementing or amplifying the former one.*

(2) *In Case 2, the debtor shall, within 7 days after his proposal is delivered to the nominee, or within such longer time as the latter may allow, deliver to the nominee a statement of his (the debtor's) affairs.*

(3) *The statement shall comprise the following particulars (supplementing or amplifying, so far as is necessary for clarifying the state of the debtor's affairs, those already given in his proposal)—*

    (a)   *a list of his assets, divided into such categories as are appropriate for easy identification, with estimated values assigned to each category;*

    (b)   *in the case of any property on which a claim against the debtor is wholly or partly secured, particulars of the claim and its amount, and of how and when the security was created;*

    (c)   *the names and addresses of the debtor's preferential creditors (defined in section 258(7)), with the amounts of their respective claims;*

    (d)   *the names and addresses of the debtor's unsecured creditors, with the amounts of their respective claims;*

    (e)   *particulars of any debts owed by or to the debtor to or by persons who are associates of his;*

    (f)   *such other particulars (if any) as the nominee may in writing require to be furnished for the purposes of making his report to the court on the debtor's proposal.*

(4) *The statement of affairs shall be made up to a date not earlier than 2 weeks before the date of the notice to the nominee under Rule 5.4.*

However, the nominee may allow an extension of that period to the nearest practicable date (not earlier than 2 months before the date of the notice under Rule 5.4); and if he does so, he shall give his reasons in his report to the court on the debtor's proposal.

(5) *The statement shall be certified by the debtor as correct, to the best of his knowledge and belief.*

2.491

5.9 Additional disclosure for assistance of nominee

(1) *If it appears to the nominee that he cannot properly prepare his report on the basis of information in the debtor's proposal and statement of affairs, he may call on the debtor to provide him with—*

    (a)   *further and better particulars as to the circumstances in which, and the reasons why, he is insolvent or (as the case may be) threatened with insolvency;*

    (b)   *particulars of any previous proposals which have been made by him under Part VIII of the Act;*

    (c)   *any further information with respect to his affairs which the nominee thinks necessary for the purposes of his report.*

(2) *The nominee may call on the debtor to inform him whether and in what circumstances he has at any time—*

    (a)   *been concerned in the affairs of any company (whether or not incorporated in England and Wales) which has become insolvent, or*

    (b)   *been adjudged bankrupt, or entered into an arrangement with his creditors.*

(3) *For the purpose of enabling the nominee to consider the debtor's proposal and prepare his report on it, the latter must give him access to his accounts and records.*

2.492

5.10 Nominee's report on the proposal

(1) *The nominee's report shall be delivered by him to the court not less than 2 days before the interim order ceases to have effect.*

(2) *With his report the nominee shall deliver—*

    (a)   *a copy of the debtor's proposal (with amendments, if any, authorised under Rule 5.3(3)); and*

    (b)   *a copy or summary of any statement of affairs provided by the debtor.*

(3) *If the nominee makes known his opinion that a meeting of the debtor's creditors should be summoned under section 257, his report shall have annexed to it his comments on the debtor's proposal.*

If his opinion is otherwise, he shall give his reasons for that opinion.

(4) *The court shall cause the nominee's report to be endorsed with the date on which it is filed in court. Any creditor of the debtor is entitled, at all reasonable times on any business day, to inspect the file.*

(5) *In Case 1, the nominee shall send to the official receiver [and (if any) the trustee]—*

    (a)   *a copy of the debtor's proposal,*

    (b)   *a copy of his (the nominee's) report and his comments accompanying it (if any), and*

    (c)   *a copy or summary of the debtor's statement of affairs.*

In Case 2, the nominee shall send a copy of each of those documents to any person who has presented a bankruptcy petition against the debtor.

2.493

5.11 Replacement of nominee

Where the debtor intends to apply to the court under section 256(3) for the nominee to be replaced, he shall give to the nominee at least 7 days' notice of his application.

Section B: Action on the Proposal; Creditors' Meeting

2.494

5.12 Consideration of nominee's report

(1) At the hearing by the court to consider the nominee's report, any of the persons who have been given notice under Rule 5.5(4) may appear or be represented.

(2) Rule 5.7 applies to any order made by the court at the hearing.

2.495

5.13 Summoning of creditors' meeting

(1) If in his report the nominee states that in his opinion a meeting of creditors should be summoned to consider the debtor's proposal, the date on which the meeting is to be held shall be not less than 14... days from that on which the nominee's report is filed in court under Rule 5.10 [, nor more than 28 days from that on which that report is considered by the court under Rule 5.12].

(2) Notices calling the meeting shall be sent by the nominee, at least 14 days before the day fixed for it to be held, to all the creditors specified in the debtor's statement of affairs, and any other creditors of whom the nominee is otherwise aware.

(3) Each notice sent under this Rule shall specify the court to which the nominee's report on the debtor's proposal has been delivered and shall state the effect of Rule 5.18(1), (3) and (4) (requisite majorities); and with it there shall be sent—

    (a)   a copy of the proposal,

    (b)   a copy of the statement of affairs or, if the nominee thinks fit, a summary of it (the summary to include a list of the creditors and the amounts of their debts), and

    (c)   the nominee's comments on the proposal.

2.496

5.14 Creditors' meeting: supplementary

(1) Subject as follows, in fixing the venue for the creditors' meeting, the nominee shall have regard to the convenience of creditors.

(2) The meeting shall be summoned for commencement between 10.00 and 16.00 hours on a business day.

(3) With every notice summoning the meeting there shall be sent out forms of proxy.

2.497

5.15 The chairman at the meeting

(1) Subject as follows, the nominee shall be chairman of the creditors' meeting.

(2) *If for any reason the nominee is unable to attend, he may nominate another person to act as chairman in his place; but a person so nominated must be either—*

    (a)   *a person qualified to act as an insolvency practitioner in relation to the debtor; or*

    (b)   *an employee of the nominee or his firm who is experienced in insolvency matters.*

2.498

5.16 The chairman as proxy-holder

The chairman shall not by virtue of any proxy held by him vote to increase or reduce the amount of the remuneration or expenses of the nominee or the supervisor of the proposed arrangement, unless the proxy specifically directs him to vote in that way.

2.499

5.17 Voting rights

(1) *Subject as follows, every creditor who was given notice of the creditors' meeting is entitled to vote at the meeting or any adjournment of it.*

(2) *In Case 1, votes are calculated according to the amount of the creditor's debt as at the date of the bankruptcy order, and in Case 2 according to the amount of the debt as at the date of the meeting.*

(3) *A creditor shall not vote in respect of a debt for an unliquidated amount, or any debt whose value is not ascertained, except where the chairman agrees to put upon the debt an estimated minimum value for the purpose of entitlement to vote.*

(4) *The chairman has power to admit or reject a creditor's claim for the purpose of his entitlement to vote, and the power is exercisable with respect to the whole or any part of the claim.*

(5) *The chairman's decision on entitlement to vote is subject to appeal to the court by any creditor, or by the debtor.*

(6) *If the chairman is in doubt whether a claim should be admitted or rejected, he shall mark it as objected to and allow the creditor to vote, subject to his vote being subsequently declared invalid if the objection to the claim is sustained.*

(7) *If on an appeal the chairman's decision is reversed or varied, or a creditor's vote is declared invalid, the court may order another meeting to be summoned, or make such other order as it thinks just.*

The court's power to make an order under this paragraph is exercisable only if it considers that the matter is such as to give rise to unfair prejudice or a material irregularity.

(8) *An application to the court by way of appeal under this Rule against the chairman's decision shall not be made after the end of the period of 28 days beginning with the day on which the chairman's report to the court is made under section 259.*

(9) *The chairman is not personally liable for any costs incurred by any person in respect of an appeal under this Rule.*

2.500

5.18 Requisite majorities

(1) Subject as follows, at the creditors' meeting for any resolution to pass approving any proposal or modification there must be a majority in excess of three-quarters in value of the creditors present in person or by proxy and voting on the resolution.

(2) The same applies in respect of any other resolution proposed at the meeting, but substituting one-half for three-quarters.

(3) In the following cases there is to be left out of account a creditor's vote in respect of any claim or part of a claim—

    (a)   where written notice of the claim was not given, either at the meeting or before it, to the chairman or the nominee;

    (b)   where the claim or part is secured;

    (c)   where the claim is in respect of a debt wholly or partly on, or secured by, a current bill of exchange or promissory note, unless the creditor is willing—

        (i)   to treat the liability to him on the bill or note of every person who is liable on it antecedently to the debtor, and against whom a bankruptcy order has not been made (or, in the case of a company, which has not gone into liquidation), as a security in his hands, and

        (ii)   to estimate the value of the security and (for the purpose of entitlement to vote, but not of any distribution under the arrangement) to deduct it from his claim.

(4) Any resolution is invalid if those voting against it include more than half in value of the creditors, counting in these latter only those—

    (a)   to whom notice of the meeting was sent;

    (b)   whose votes are not to be left out of account under paragraph (3); and

    (c)   who are not, to the best of the chairman's belief, associates of the debtor.

(5) It is for the chairman of the meeting to decide whether under this Rule—

    (a)   a vote is to be left out of account in accordance with paragraph (3), or

    (b)   a person is an associate of the debtor for the purposes of paragraph (4)(c);

and in relation to the second of these two cases the chairman is entitled to rely on the information provided by the debtor's statement of affairs or otherwise in accordance with this Part of the Rules.

(6) If the chairman uses a proxy contrary to Rule 5.16, his vote with that proxy does not count towards any majority under this Rule.

(7) Paragraphs (5) to (9) of Rule 5.17 apply as regards an appeal against the decision of the chairman under this Rule.

2.501

5.19 Proceedings to obtain agreement on the proposal

(1) On the day on which the creditors' meeting is held, it may from time to time be adjourned.

(2) If on that day the requisite majority for the approval of the voluntary arrangement (with or without modifications) has not been obtained, the chairman may, and shall if it is so resolved, adjourn the meeting for not more than 14 days.

(3) If there are subsequently further adjournments, the final adjournment shall not be to a day later than 14 days after that on which the meeting was originally held.

(4) If the meeting is adjourned under paragraph (2), notice of the fact shall be given by the chairman forthwith to the court.

(5) If following any final adjournment of the meeting the proposal (with or without modifications) is not agreed to, it is deemed rejected.

Section C: Implementation of the Arrangement

2.502

5.20 Resolutions to follow approval

(1) If the voluntary arrangement is approved (with or without modifications), a resolution may be taken by the creditors, where two or more insolvency practitioners are appointed to act as supervisor, on the question whether acts to be done in connection with the arrangement may be done by any one of them, or must be done by both or all.

(2) If at the creditors' meeting a resolution is moved for the appointment of some person other than the nominee to be supervisor of the arrangement, there must be produced to the chairman, at or before the meeting—

    (a)   that person's written consent to act (unless he is present and then and there signifies his consent), and

    (b)   his written confirmation that he is qualified to act as an insolvency practitioner in relation to the debtor.

2.503

5.21 Hand-over of property, etc to supervisor

(1) Forthwith after the approval of the voluntary arrangement, the debtor in Case 2, and the official receiver or trustee in Case 1, shall do all that is required for putting the supervisor into possession of the assets included in the arrangement.

(2) On taking possession of the assets in Case 1, the supervisor shall discharge any balance due to the official receiver and (if other) the trustee by way of remuneration or on account of—

    (a)   fees, costs, charges and expenses properly incurred and payable under the Act or the Rules, and

    (b)   any advances made in respect of the insolvent estate, together with interest on such advances at the rate specified in section 17 of the Judgments Act 1838 at the date of the bankruptcy order.

(3) Alternatively in Case 1, the supervisor must, before taking possession, give the official receiver or the trustee a written undertaking to discharge any such balance out of the first realisation of assets.

(4) The official receiver and (if other) the trustee has in Case 1 a charge on the assets included in the voluntary arrangement in respect of any sums due as above until they have been discharged, subject only to the deduction from realisations by the supervisor of the proper costs and expenses of realisation.

Any sums due to the official receiver take priority over those due to a trustee.

(5) The supervisor shall from time to time out of the realisation of assets discharge all guarantees properly given by the official receiver or the trustee for the benefit of the estate, and shall pay all their expenses.

2.504

5.22 Report of creditors' meeting

(1) A report of the creditors' meeting shall be prepared by the chairman of the meeting.

(2) The report shall—
- *(a) state whether the proposal for a voluntary arrangement was approved or rejected and, if approved, with what (if any) modifications;*
- *(b) set out the resolutions which were taken at the meeting, and the decision on each one;*
- *(c) list the creditors (with their respective values) who were present or represented at the meeting, and how they voted on each resolution; and*
- *(d) include such further information (if any) as the chairman thinks it appropriate to make known to the court.*

(3) A copy of the chairman's report shall, within 4 days of the meeting being held, be filed in court; and the court shall cause that copy to be endorsed with the date of filing.

(4) The persons to whom notice of the result is to be given, under section 259(1), are all those who were sent notice of the meeting under this Part of the Rules [and, in Case 1, the official receiver and (if any) the trustee].

The notice shall be sent immediately after a copy of the chairman's report is filed in court under paragraph (3).

2.505

5.23 Register of voluntary arrangements

(1) The Secretary of State shall maintain a register of individual voluntary arrangements, and shall enter in it all such matters as are reported to him in pursuance of [Rules 5.24, 5.25 and 5.29] [and orders of suspension made under section 262 reported to him in pursuance of Rule 5.25].

[(1A) Where the Secretary of State has received notice of the making of a revocation order or that an arrangement has been fully implemented in pursuance of Rules 5.25 or 5.29 or has otherwise received written notice of the termination of an arrangement from the supervisor and –
- (a) the revocation order under section 262 was made prior to 22 March 1999, or
- (b) the final completion or termination of the arrangement from the supervisor and–

The Secretary of state shall delete from the register all matters entered in it relating to such arrangement.

[(1B) Where the Secretary of State receives notice under Rule 5.25(5) of fthe making of a revocation order on respect of an individual voluntary arrangement of which entry is made in the register the Secretary of State shall delete from the register all matters entered in it relating to that arrangement.

[(1C) Where the Secretary of State receives notice under Rule 5.29(3) of the full implementation or termination of an individual voluntary arrangement of

which entry is made in the register the Secretary of State shall, on the expiry of two years after the final completion or termination of such individual voluntary arrangement, delete from the register all matters in it relating to that arrangement.]

(2) The register shall be open to public inspection.

2.506

5.24 Reports to Secretary of State

(1) Immediately after the chairman of the creditors' meeting has filed in court a report that the meeting has approved the voluntary arrangement, he shall report to the Secretary of State the following details of the arrangement—
- *(a) the name and address of the debtor;*
- *(b) the date on which the arrangement was approved by the creditors;*
- *(c) the name and address of the supervisor; and*
- *(d) the court in which the chairman's report has been filed.*

(2) A person who is appointed to act as supervisor of an individual voluntary arrangement (whether in the first instance or by way of replacement of another person previously appointed) shall forthwith give written notice to the Secretary of State of his appointment.

If he vacates office as supervisor, he shall forthwith give written notice of that fact also to the Secretary of State.

2.507

5.25 Revocation or suspension of the arrangement

(1) This Rule applies where the court makes an order of revocation or suspension under section 262.

(2) The person who applied for the order shall serve sealed copies of it—
- *(a) in Case 1, on the debtor, the official receiver and the trustee;*
- *(b) in Case 2, on the debtor; and*
- *(c) in either case on the supervisor of the voluntary arrangement.*

(3) If the order includes a direction by the court under section 262(4)(b) for any further creditors' meeting to be summoned, notice shall also be given (by the person who applied for the order) to whoever is, in accordance with the direction, required to summon the meeting.

(4) The debtor (in Case 2) and the [trustee, or if there is no trustee, the official receiver] (in Case 1) shall—
- *(a) forthwith after receiving a copy of the court's order, give notice of it to all persons who were sent notice of the creditors' meeting which approved the voluntary arrangement or who, not having been sent that notice, appear to be affected by the order;*
- *(b) within 7 days of their receiving a copy of the order (or within such longer period as the court may allow), give notice to the court whether it is intended to make a revised proposal to creditors, or to invite re-consideration of the original proposal.*

(5) The person on whose application the order of revocation or suspension was made shall, within 7 days after the making of the order, give written notice of it to the Secretary of State.

2.508

5.26 Supervisor's accounts and reports

(1) Where the voluntary arrangement authorises or requires the supervisor—

    (a)   to carry on the debtor's business or to trade on his behalf or in his name, or

    (b)   to realise assets of the debtor or (in Case 1) belonging to the estate, or

    (c)   otherwise to administer or dispose of any funds of the debtor or the estate,

he shall keep accounts and records of his acts and dealings in and in connection with the arrangement, including in particular records of all receipts and payments of money.

(2) The supervisor shall, not less often than once in every 12 months beginning with the date of his appointment, prepare an abstract of such receipts and payments, and send copies of it, accompanied by his comments on the progress and efficacy of the arrangement, to—

    (a)   the court,

    (b)   the debtor, and

    (c)   all those of the debtor's creditors who are bound by the arrangement.

If in any period of 12 months he has made no payments and had no receipts, he shall at the end of that period send a statement to that effect to all who are specified in sub-paragraphs (a) to (c) above.

(3) An abstract provided under paragraph (2) shall relate to a period beginning with the date of the supervisor's appointment or (as the case may be) the day following the end of the last period for which an abstract was prepared under this Rule; and copies of the abstract shall be sent out, as required by paragraph (2), within the 2 months following the end of the period to which the abstract relates.

(4) If the supervisor is not authorised as mentioned in paragraph (1), he shall, not less often than once in every 12 months beginning with the date of his appointment, send to all those specified in paragraph (2)(a) to (c) a report on the progress and efficacy of the voluntary arrangement.

(5) The court may, on application by the supervisor, vary the dates on which the obligation to send abstracts or reports arises.

2.509

5.27 Production of accounts and records to Secretary of State

(1) The Secretary of State may at any time during the course of the voluntary arrangement or after its completion require the supervisor to produce for inspection—

    (a)   his records and accounts in respect of the arrangement, and

    (b)   copies of abstracts and reports prepared in compliance with Rule 5.26.

(2) The Secretary of State may require production either at the premises of the supervisor or elsewhere; and it is the duty of the supervisor to comply with any requirement imposed on him under this Rule.

(3) The Secretary of State may cause any accounts and records produced to him under this Rule to be audited; and the supervisor shall give to the Secretary of State such further information and assistance as he needs for the purposes of his audit.

2.510

5.28 Fees, costs, charges and expenses

The fees, costs, charges and expenses that may be incurred for any purposes of the voluntary arrangement are—
  (*a*)   *any disbursements made by the nominee prior to the approval of the arrangement, and any remuneration for his services as such agreed between himself and the debtor, the official receiver or the trustee;*
  (*b*)   *any fees, costs, charges or expenses which—*
      (*i*)   *are sanctioned by the terms of the arrangement, or*
      (*ii*) *would be payable, or correspond to those which would be payable, in the debtor's bankruptcy.*

2.511

5.29 Completion or termination of the arrangement

(1) Not more than 28 days after the final completion [or termination] of the voluntary arrangement, the supervisor shall send to all creditors of the debtor who are bound by the arrangement, and to the debtor, a notice that the arrangement has been fully implemented [or (as the case may be) terminated].

(2) With the notice there shall be sent to each of those persons a copy of a report by the supervisor summarising all receipts and payments made by him in pursuance of the arrangement, and explaining any difference in the actual implementation of it as compared with the proposal as approved by the creditors' meeting [or (in the case of termination of the arrangement) explaining the reasons why the arrangement has not been implemented in accordance with the proposal as approved by the creditors' meeting]..

(3) The supervisor shall, within the 28 days mentioned above, send to the Secretary of State and to the court a copy of the notice under paragraph (1), together with a copy of the report under paragraph (2) [and he shall not vacate office until after such copies have been sent].

(4) The court may, on application by the supervisor, extend the period of 28 days under paragraphs (1) and (3).

Section D: General

2.512

5.30 False representations, etc

(*1*) *The debtor commits an offence if he makes any false representation or commits any other fraud for the purpose of obtaining the approval of his creditors to a proposal for a voluntary arrangement under Part VIII of the Act.*

(2) A person guilty of an offence under this Rule is liable to imprisonment or a fine, or both.

2.512A

5.31 Application for conversion into bankruptcy

(*1*) *Where a member State liquidator proposes to apply to the court for the conversion under Article 37 of the EC Regulation (conversion of earlier proceedings) of a voluntary arrangement into bankruptcy, an affidavit complying with Rule 5.32 must be prepared and sworn, and filed in court in support of the application.*

(2) An application under this Rule shall be by originating application.

(3) The application and the affidavit required under this Rule shall be served upon
- (a)   the debtor; and
- (b)   the supervisor.

2.512B

5.32 Contents of affidavit

(1) The affidavit shall state–
- (*a*)   *that main proceedings have been opened in relation to the debtor in a member State other than the United Kingdom;*
- (*b*)   *the deponent's belief that the conversion of the voluntary arrangement into a bankruptcy would prove to be in the interests of the creditors in the main proceedings; and*
- (*c*)   *all other matters that, in the opinion of the member State liquidator, would assist the court–*
    - (*i*)   *in deciding whether to make an order under Rule 5.33, and*
    - (*ii*)   *if the court were to do so, in considering the need for any consequential provision that would be necessary or desirable.*

(2) An affidavit under this Rule shall be sworn by, or on behalf of, the member State liquidator.

2.512C

5.33 Power of court

(1) On hearing the application for conversion into bankruptcy the court may make such order as it thinks fit.

(2) If the court makes an order for conversion into bankruptcy the order may contain all such consequential provisions as the court deems necessary or desirable.

(3) Where the court makes an order for conversion into bankruptcy under paragraph (1), any expenses properly incurred as expenses of the administration of the voluntary arrangement in question shall be a first charge on the bankrupt's estate.

Section F: EC Regulation – Member State Liquidator

2.512D

5.34 Interpretation of creditor and notice to member State liquidator

(1) This Rule applies where a member State liquidator has been appointed in relation to the debtor.

(2) Where the supervisor is obliged to give notice to, or provide a copy of a document (including an order of court) to, the court or the official receiver, the supervisor shall give notice or provide copies, as appropriate, to the member State liquidator.

> *(3) Paragraph (2) is without prejudice to the generality of the obligations imposed by Article 31 of the EC Regulation (duty to cooperate and communicate information).*

Chapter 1
Preliminary

Notes

Part 5 of the IR 1986 was substantially redrafted and revised by the Insolvency (Amendment) (No 2) Rules 2002 (SI 2002/2712) to take into account the provisions for entering into IVAs without first obtaining an interim order which were introduced by the IA 2000. The rules in their revised form came into effect on 1 January 2003. Further amendments and additions to IR 1986 Part 5 were subsequently made by the Insolvency (Amendment) Rules 2003 (SI 2003/1730) to take into account the annulment provisions of the new IA 1986 s 261 and the provisions for 'Fast Track' Voluntary Arrangements ('FTVAs') introduced by the EA 2002, which came into effect on 1 April 2004; the Insolvency (Amendment) Rules 2004 (SI 2004/584), and the Insolvency (Amendment) Rules 2005 (SI 2005/527) also effected some minor changes.

As IR 1986 Part 5 now stands, different chapters apply to the different types of voluntary arrangement.

Chapters 2 to 6 and 8 and 9 apply only to the two types of standard IVAs (ones with and without an interim order) as follows:-
* Chapter 2 (IR 1986 r 5.2 to 5.6) contains provisions relating to the preparation of the debtor's proposal which apply to both types of standard IVAs;
* Chapter 3 (IR 1986 r 5.7 to 5.13) contains provisions relating to applications for interim orders, for the nominee's report on proposals and for the court's consideration of that report at the hearing convened to consider whether or not to extend the interim order to enable the report to be considered at any meeting of the debtor's creditors recommended by the nominee;
* Chapter 4 (IR 1986 r 5.14 to 5.16) sets out the alternative procedure which applies in respect of the nominee's report where no interim order has been applied for;
* Chapters 5 and 6 (IR 1986 r 5.17 to 5.34) dealing with the creditors' meeting itself and the implementation of any IVA approved at such meeting apply equally to both types of standard IVA;
* Chapters 8 and 9 (IR 1986 r 5.51 to 5.56) dealing with annulment of bankruptcy orders apply to both types of standard IVAs where entered into by an undischarged bankrupt.
* Chapter 7 (general provisions) and Chapter 10 (provisions for annulment of bankruptcy order) apply only to FTVAs.
* Chapter 11 (consequential provisions following annulment of bankruptcy order) and Chapter 12 (EC Regulation) apply to all variants of voluntary arrangement.

2.513

5.1 Introductory

(1) The Rules in this Part apply in relation to a voluntary arrangement under Part VIII of the Act, except in relation to voluntary arrangements under section 263A, in relation to which only Chapters 7, 10, 11 and 12 of this Part apply.

(2) In this Part, in respect of voluntary arrangements other than voluntary arrangements under section 263A –

(a) Chapter 2 applies in all cases;

(b) Chapter 3 applies in cases where an application for an interim is order is made;

(c) Chapter 4 applies in cases where no application for an interim order is or is to be made;

(d) except where otherwise stated, Chapters 5 and 6 apply in all cases;

(e) Chapter 8 applies where a bankrupt makes an application under section 261(2)(a); and

(f) Chapter 9 applies where the official receiver makes an application under section 261(2)(b).

(3) In this Part, in respect of voluntary arrangements under section 263A

—

(a) Chapter 7 applies in all cases; and

(b) Chapter 10 applies where the official receiver makes an application under section 263D(3).

(4) In this Part, Chapters 11 and 12 apply in all cases.

Chapter 2
Preparation of the Debtor's Proposal

2.514

5.2 Preparation of proposal

The debtor shall prepare for the intended nominee a proposal on which (with or without amendments to be made under Rule 5.3(3) below) to make his report to the court under section 256 or section 256A.

2.515

5.3 Contents of proposal

(1) The debtor's proposal shall provide a short explanation why, in his opinion, a voluntary arrangement under Part VIII is desirable, and give reasons why his creditors may be expected to concur with such an arrangement.

(2) The following matters shall be stated, or otherwise dealt with, in the proposal—

(a) the following matters, so far as within the debtor's immediate knowledge—

(i) his assets, with an estimate of their respective values,

(ii) the extent (if any) to which the assets are charged in favour of creditors,

(iii) the extent (if any) to which particular assets are to be excluded from the voluntary arrangement;

(b) particulars of any property, other than assets of the debtor himself, which is proposed to be included in the arrangement, the source of such property and the terms on which it is to be made available for inclusion;

(c)   the nature and amount of the debtor's liabilities (so far as within his immediate knowledge), the manner in which they are proposed to be met, modified, postponed or otherwise dealt with by means of the arrangement and (in particular)—

     (i)   how it is proposed to deal with preferential creditors (defined in section 258(7)) and creditors who are, or claim to be, secured,

    (ii)   how associates of the debtor (being creditors of his) are proposed to be treated under the arrangement, and

   (iii)   in any case where the debtor is an undischarged bankrupt, whether, to the debtor's knowledge, claims have been made under section 339 (transactions at an undervalue), section 340 (preferences) or section 343 (extortionate credit transactions), or where the debtor is not an undischarged bankrupt, whether there are circumstances which would give rise to the possibility of such claims in the event that he should be adjudged bankrupt,

and, where any such circumstances are present, whether, and if so how, it is proposed under the voluntary arrangement to make provision for wholly or partly indemnifying the insolvent estate in respect of such claims;

(d)   whether any, and if so what, guarantees have been given of the debtor's debts by other persons, specifying which (if any) of the guarantors are associates of his;

(e)   the proposed duration of the voluntary arrangement;

(f)   the proposed dates of distributions to creditors, with estimates of their amounts;

(g)   how it is proposed to deal with the claims of any person who is bound by the arrangement by virtue of section 260(2)(b)(ii);

(h)   the amount proposed to be paid to the nominee (as such) by way of remuneration and expenses;

(j)   the manner in which it is proposed that the supervisor of the arrangement should be remunerated, and his expenses defrayed;

(k)   whether, for the purposes of the arrangement, any guarantees are to be offered by any persons other than the debtor, and whether (if so) any security is to be given or sought;

(l)   the manner in which funds held for the purposes of the arrangement are to be banked, invested or otherwise dealt with pending distribution to creditors;

(m)   the manner in which funds held for the purpose of payment to creditors, and not so paid on the termination of the arrangement, are to be dealt with;

(n)   if the debtor has any business the manner in which it is proposed to be conducted during the course of the arrangement;

(o)   details of any further credit facilities which it is intended to arrange for the debtor, and how the debts so arising are to be paid;

(p)   the functions which are to be undertaken by the supervisor of the arrangement;

(q)   the name, address and qualification of the person proposed as supervisor of the voluntary arrangement, and confirmation that he is, so far as the debtor is aware, qualified to act as an insolvency practitioner in relation to him or is an authorised person in relation to him; and

(r) whether the EC Regulation will apply and, if so, whether the proceedings will be main proceedings or territorial proceedings.

(3) With the agreement in writing of the nominee, the debtor's proposal may be amended at any time up to the delivery of the former's report to the court under section 256 or section 256A.

Notes

R 5.3

The provisions replicate almost exactly the provisions of IR 1986 r 1.3 prescribing the matters which are required to be included within a proposal for a CVA; for detailed commentary thereon, see the notes to IR 1986 r 1.3. It is important for the debtor to take his obligations of disclosure under this provision seriously *Stanley v Phillips* [2004] BPIR 632. The presence of defects within the proposal do not invalidate it: *Tanner v Everitt* [2004] BPIR 1026.

2.516

5.4 Notice to the intended nominee

(1) The debtor shall give to the intended nominee written notice of his proposal.

(2) The notice, accompanied by a copy of the proposal, shall be delivered either to the nominee himself, or to a person authorised to take delivery of documents on his behalf.

(3) If the intended nominee agrees to act, he shall cause a copy of the notice to be endorsed to the effect that it has been received by him on a specified date.

(4) The copy of the notice so endorsed shall be returned by the nominee forthwith to the debtor at an address specified by him in the notice for that purpose.

(5) Where the debtor is an undischarged bankrupt and he gives notice of his proposal to the official receiver and (if any) the trustee, the notice must contain the name and address of the insolvency practitioner or (as the case may be) authorised person who has agreed to act as nominee.

2.517

5.5 Statement of Affairs

(1) Subject to paragraph (2), the debtor shall, within 7 days after his proposal is delivered to the nominee, or such longer time as the latter may allow, deliver to the nominee a statement of his (the debtor's) affairs.

(2) Paragraph (1) shall not apply where the debtor is an undischarged bankrupt and he has already delivered a statement of affairs under section 272 (debtor's petition) or 288 (creditor's petition) but the nominee may require the debtor to submit a further statement supplementing or amplifying the statement of affairs already submitted.

(3) The statement of affairs shall comprise the following particulars (supplementing or amplifying, so far as is necessary for clarifying the state of the debtor's affairs, those already given in his proposal)—

(a)   a list of his assets, divided into such categories as are appropriate for easy identification, with estimated values assigned to each category;

(b)   in the case of any property on which a claim against the debtor is wholly or partly secured, particulars of the claim and its amount, and of how and when the security was created;

(c)   the names and addresses of the debtor's preferential creditors (defined in section 258(7)), with the amounts of their respective claims;

(d)   the names and addresses of the debtor's unsecured creditors, with the amounts of their respective claims;

(e)   particulars of any debts owed by or to the debtor to or by persons who are associates of his;

(f)   such other particulars (if any) as the nominee may in writing require to be furnished for the purposes of making his report to the court on the debtor's proposal.

(4) The statement of affairs shall be made up to a date not earlier than 2 weeks before the date of the notice to the nominee under Rule 5.4.

However, the nominee may allow an extension of that period to the nearest practicable date (not earlier than 2 months before the date of the notice under Rule 5.4); and if he does so, he shall give his reasons in his report to the court on the debtor's proposal.

(5) The statement shall be certified by the debtor as correct, to the best of his knowledge and belief.

Notes

R 5.5

This provision sets out the prescribed information which must be included within the statement of affairs which the debtor is required to submit to the nominee under IA 1986 s 256(2) (in cases where an interim order is obtained) or IA 1986 s 256A(2) (where no interim order is sought). Again, the requirements replicate those relating to statements of affairs that are required to be submitted in proposed CVA; see the commentary to IR 1986 r 1.5.

R 5.5(2)

Where the debtor is an undischarged bankrupt, he is not automatically required to submit a further statement of affairs where he has already delivered such a statement in his bankruptcy. However, the nominee can require him to do so, and, in a case where the debtor has incurred further trading or other debts after his bankruptcy, such further statement is likely to be necessary.

2.518

5.6 Additional disclosure for assistance of nominee

(1) If it appears to the nominee that he cannot properly prepare his report on the basis of information in the debtor's proposal and statement of affairs, he may call on the debtor to provide him with—

> (a) further and better particulars as to the circumstances in which, and the reasons why, he is insolvent or (as the case may be) threatened with insolvency;
> (b) particulars of any previous proposals which have been made by him under Part VIII of the Act;
> (c) any further information with respect to his affairs which the nominee thinks necessary for the purposes of his report.
>
> (2) The nominee may call on the debtor to inform him whether and in what circumstances he has at any time—
> (a) been concerned in the affairs of any company (whether or not incorporated in England and Wales) which has become insolvent, or
> (b) been adjudged bankrupt, or entered into an arrangement with his creditors.
>
> (3) For the purpose of enabling the nominee to consider the debtor's proposal and prepare his report on it, the latter must give him access to his accounts and records.

───────

Notes

R 5.6

This provision replicates IR 1986 r 1.6 as applies in CVAs; see the commentary to that rule.

R 5.6(1)(a)

It is a pre-condition to the grant of an interim order under IA 1986 s 255(1) that the debtor is either an undischarged bankrupt or able to present a petition for his own bankruptcy (IA 1986 s 272 requires for this purpose that the debtor is 'unable to pay his debts'). These also appear to be pre-conditions to a debtor proceeding with an IVA proposal without an interim order under IA 1986 s 256A(3). The wording of this rule is different, and does not sit happily with those sections.

R 5.6(1)(b)

Under IA 1986 s 255(1)(c) a debtor is barred from obtaining an interim order where he has made a prior application for an interim order within the previous 12 months. There is no similar limitation on the debtor submitting proposals for an IVA without the protection of an interim order under IA 1986 s 256A, but in this latter case, the fact that a debtor has made previous applications for interim orders may well be relevant in enabling the nominee to determine the viability of the proposal and its prospects of being approved.

───────

Chapter 3
Cases in which an Application for an Interim Order is made

2.519

5.7 Application for interim order

(1) An application to the court for an interim order under Part VIII of the Act shall be accompanied by an affidavit of the following matters—
  (a) the reasons for making the application;

(b) particulars of any execution or other legal process or levying of any distress which, to the debtor's knowledge, has been commenced against him;

(c) that he is an undischarged bankrupt or (as the case may be) that he is able to petition for his own bankruptcy;

(d) that no previous application for an interim order has been made by or in respect of the debtor in the period of 12 months ending with the date of the affidavit;

(e) that the nominee under the proposal (naming him) is willing to act in relation to the proposal and is a person who is either qualified to act as an insolvency practitioner in relation to the debtor or is authorised to act as nominee in relation to him; and

(f) that the debtor has not submitted to the official receiver either the document referred to at section 263B (1) (a) or the statement referred to at section 263B (1) (b).

(2) A copy of the notice to the intended nominee under Rule 5.4, endorsed to the effect that he agrees so to act, and a copy of the debtor's proposal given to the nominee under that Rule, shall be exhibited to the affidavit.

(3) On receiving the application and affidavit, the court shall fix a venue for the hearing of the application.

(4) The applicant shall give at least 2 days' notice of the hearing—

(a) where the debtor is an undischarged bankrupt, to the bankrupt, the official receiver and the trustee (whichever of those three is not himself the applicant),

(b) where the debtor is not an undischarged bankrupt, to any creditor who (to the debtor's knowledge) has presented a bankruptcy petition against him, and

(c) in either case, to the nominee who has agreed to act in relation to the debtor's proposal.

Notes

R 5.7

This rule supplements IA 1986 s 253 (application for interim order). It sets out the manner in which the debtor is to prove the four pre-conditions to the making of an interim order stipulated in IA 1986 s 255(1). It also requires the debtor to set out particulars of any execution or other legal process, or the levying of distress, which has to his knowledge been commenced against him. Although creditors pursuing such remedies will clearly be affected by the making of an interim order, no such creditors with the exception of a creditor who has presented a bankruptcy petition, are entitled to notice of the application for an interim order, and it is not clear how the fact that creditors are (or are not) pursuing such remedies is relevant to the decision of the court whether or not to make an interim order under IA 1986 s 255.

2.520

5.8 Court in which application to be made

(1) Except in the case of an undischarged bankrupt, an application to the court under Part VIII of the IA 1986 shall be made to a court in which the debtor would be entitled to present his own petition in bankruptcy under IR 1986 r 6.40.

(2) The application shall contain sufficient information to establish that it is brought in the appropriate court.

(3) In the case of an undischarged bankrupt, such an application shall be made to the court having the conduct of his bankruptcy and shall be filed with the bankruptcy proceedings.

Notes

R 5.8

The High Court however has power to transfer to itself voluntary arrangement proceedings taking place in the county court: *Re Bullard & Taplin Ltd* [1996] BPIR 526, *County Courts Act 1984 s 41(1)*.

2.521

5.9 Hearing of the application

(1) Any of the persons who have been given notice under Rule 5.7(4) may appear or be represented at the hearing of the application.

(2) The court, in deciding whether to make an interim order on the application, shall take into account any representations made by or on behalf of any of those persons (in particular, whether an order should be made containing such provision as is referred to in section 255(3) and (4)).

(3) If the court makes an interim order, it shall fix a venue for consideration of the nominee's report. Subject to the following paragraph, the date for that consideration shall be not later than that on which the interim order ceases to have effect under section 255(6).

(4) If under section 256(4) an extension of time is granted for filing the nominee's report, the court shall, unless there appear to be good reasons against it, correspondingly extend the period for which the interim order has effect.

Notes

R 5.9

This provision restricts the entitlement of creditors or others who may be affected by the making of an interim order to appear or be represented at the hearing of the application. Only those entitled to notice of the application under IR 1986 r 5.7(4) have *locus standi* to appear at the hearing. This excludes all creditors, except those who have already presented a bankruptcy petition; it therefore excludes creditors who are proceeding by other means to enforce their debt and so would be directly affected by the making of an interim order.

Under para 16.1 Practice Direction Insolvency Proceedings (Civil Procedure, Vol 2, Section 3E) the court may make an interim order without the attendance of any party where:

- the application is made by a debtor who is not an undischarged bankrupt and against whom (so far as is known) there is no pending bankrutpcy petition; and
- the nominee's signed consent to act includes a waiver of notice of the application or his consent to the making of an interim order without attendance.

2.522

5.10 Action to follow making of order

(1) Where an interim order is made, at least 2 sealed copies of the order shall be sent by the court to the person who applied for it; and that person shall serve one of the copies on the nominee under the debtor's proposal.

(2) The applicant shall also forthwith give notice of the making of the order to any person who was given notice of the hearing pursuant to Rule 5.7(4) and was not present or represented at it.

2.523

5.11 Nominee's report on the proposal

(1) Where the nominee makes his report to the court under section 256, he shall deliver 2 copies of it to the court not less than 2 days before the interim order ceases to have effect.

(2) With his report the nominee shall deliver—
  (a) a copy of the debtor's proposal (with amendments, if any, authorised under Rule 5.3(3)); and
  (b) a copy or summary of any statement of affairs provided by the debtor.

(3) If the nominee makes known his opinion that the debtor's proposal has a reasonable prospect of being approved and implemented, and that a meeting of the debtor's creditors should be summoned under section 257, his report shall have annexed to it his comments on the debtor's proposal.

If his opinion is otherwise, he shall give his reasons for that opinion.

(4) The court shall upon receipt of the report cause one copy of the report to be endorsed with the date of its filing in court and returned to the nominee.

(5) Any creditor of the debtor is entitled, at all reasonable times on any business day, to inspect the file.

(6) Where the debtor is an undischarged bankrupt, the nominee shall send to the official receiver and (if any) the trustee—
  (a) a copy of the debtor's proposal,
  (b) a copy of his (the nominee's) report and his comments accompanying it (if any), and
  (c) a copy or summary of the debtor's statement of affairs.

(7) Where the debtor is not an undischarged bankrupt, the nominee shall send a copy of each of the documents referred to in paragraph (6) to any person who has presented a bankruptcy petition against the debtor.

Notes

R 5.11

This provision supplements IA 1986 s 256(1). The nominee's report is required to be filed with the court not less than two days before the initial 14 day interim order (or any extension thereto) ceases to have effect. For a general discussion of the nominee's duties and liabilities in reporting to the court on the debtor's proposals, see the commentary to IA 1986 s 2 which concerns the nominee's duties in a CVA.

2.524

5.12 Replacement of nominee

(1) Where the debtor intends to apply to the court under section 256(3) for the nominee to be replaced, he shall give to the nominee at least 7 days' notice of his application.

(2) No appointment of a replacement nominee shall be made by the court unless there is filed in court a statement by the replacement nominee indicating his consent to act.

2.525

5.13 Consideration of nominee's report

(1) At the hearing by the court to consider the nominee's report, any of the persons who have been given notice under Rule 5.7(4) may appear or be represented.

(2) Rule 5.10 applies to any order made by the court at the hearing.

Notes

R 5.13

This rule supplements the provisions in IA 1986 s 256(5) for the consideration by the court of the nominee's report to which reference should be made. The only persons entitled to be heard at the hearing to consider the nominee's report are those who were entitled to receive notice of the interim order application, namely the debtor's nominee and, in the case of undischarged bankrupt his trustee or the official receiver, and in other cases any creditor who has presented a bankruptcy petition. This rule contemplates that no meeting should be held unless and until the court has positively considered the report: *Vlieland-Boddy v Dexter Ltd* [2004] BPIR 235.

Under para 16.1 Practice Direction Insolvency Proceedings (Civil Procedure, Vol 2 section 3E) where the debtor is not an undischarged bankrupt, and there is no pending petition against him, the court may, in an appropriate case, make an order extending the interim order to a date seven weeks after the date of the creditors meeting without the need for the attendance of any party at the hearing convened to consider the nominee's report. See also para 16(3) Practice Direction Insolvency Proceedings (Civil Procedure, Vol 2 section 3E) for the making of so-called 'concertina' orders.

Chapter 4
Cases where no Interim Order is to be Obtained

2.526

5.14 Nominee's report to the court

(1) The nominee shall deliver 2 copies of his report to the court (as defined in Rule 5.15) under section 256A within 14 days (or such longer period as the court may allow) after receiving from the debtor the

document and statement mentioned in section 256A(2) but the court shall not consider the report unless an application is made under the Act or these Rules in relation to the debtor's proposal.

(2) With his report the nominee shall deliver—
- (a) a copy of the debtor's proposal (with amendments, if any, authorised under Rule 5.3(3));
- (b) a copy or summary of any statement of affairs provided by the debtor; and
- (c) a copy of the notice referred to in Rule 5.4(3),

together with 2 copies of Form 5.5 listing the documents referred to in (a) to (c) above and containing a statement that no application for an interim order under section 252 is to be made.

(3) If the nominee makes known his opinion that the debtor's proposal has a reasonable prospect of being approved and implemented, and that a meeting of the debtor's creditors should be summoned under section 257, his report shall have annexed to it his comments on the debtor's proposal.

If his opinion is otherwise, he shall give his reasons for that opinion.

(4) The court shall upon receipt of the report and Form 5.5 cause one copy of the form to be endorsed with the date of its filing in court and returned to the nominee.

(5) Any creditor of the debtor is entitled, at all reasonable times on any business day, to inspect the file.

(6) Where the debtor is an undischarged bankrupt, the nominee shall send to the official receiver and (if any) the trustee—
- (a) a copy of the debtor's proposal,
- (b) a copy of his (the nominee's) report and his comments accompanying it (if any), and
- (c) a copy or summary of the debtor's statement of affairs.

(7) Where the debtor is not an undischarged bankrupt, the nominee shall send a copy of each of the documents referred to in paragraph (6) to any person who has presented a bankruptcy petition against the debtor.

(8) The filing in court of the report under section 256A shall constitute an insolvency proceeding for the purpose of Rule 7.27 and Rule 7.30.

Notes

R 5.14

This provision supplements IA 1986 s 256A (nominee's report to the court on debtor's proposal in case where no interim order is applied for) and IA 1986 s 257(1) (summoning of creditor's meeting).

R 5.14(1)

This provision makes clear that although the nominee is required to submit his report to the court, the court does not and should not have any judicial role to play in determining whether or not a meeting should be summoned, and should not consider the report at all unless an application is made in relation to the debtor's proposal. The rule does not set out specifically the 'application(s)' which will require the court to consider the report, but it seems to contemplate, amongst other matters, an application for a direction that a meeting should not be summoned notwithstanding a positive recommendation to that effect by the nominee; see further the commentary to IA 1986 s 257(1).

R 5.14(5)–(8)

These provisions are aimed at ensuring that interested parties either receive copies of the nominee's report and the basic material upon which it is based (the trustee / official receiver in a proposal by an undischarged bankrupt and any petitioning creditor in other cases); or at least are able to access such documents by inspection of a court file (in the case of the general body of the debtor's creditors).

2.527

5.15 Filing of reports made under section 256A—appropriate court

(1) Except where the debtor is an undischarged bankrupt, the court in which the nominee's report under section 256A is to be filed is the court in which the debtor would be entitled to present his own petition in bankruptcy under Rule 6.40.

(2) The report shall contain sufficient information to establish that it is filed in the appropriate court.

(3) Where the debtor is an undischarged bankrupt, such report shall be filed in the court having the conduct of his bankruptcy and shall be filed with the bankruptcy proceedings.

2.528

5.16 Applications to the court

(1) Any application to court in relation to any matter relating to a voluntary arrangement or a proposal for a voluntary arrangement shall be made in the court in which the nominee's report was filed.

(2) Where the debtor intends to apply to the court under section 256A(4)(a) or (b) for the nominee to be replaced, he shall give to the nominee at least 7 days' notice of the application.

(3) Where the nominee intends to apply to the court under section 256A(4)(b) for his replacement as nominee, he shall give to the debtor at least 7 days' notice of the application.

(4) No appointment of a replacement nominee shall be made by the court unless there is filed in court a statement by the replacement nominee indicating his consent to act.

Notes

R 5.16

This provision and IR 1986 r 5.14(8) and 5.15 set out the basic framework for issue of court process in non-interim order IVAs. There is a distinction between cases where the debtor is an undischarged banrkupt and where he is not. Where the debtor is an undischarged bankrupt:

- the report is filed in the court which has conduct of the debtor's bankruptcy in the existing bankruptcy proceedings; the report should be headed with the case reference number for those proceedings;
- any applications relating to the debtor's proposal should be made by ordinary application in the existing bankruptcy proceedings;

In contrast, where the debtor is not an undischarged bankrupt:
- the nominee must file his report with the court at which the debtor would be entitled to present his own petition in bankruptcy;
- insolvency proceedings come into being on the filing by the nominee of his report at that court;
- all applications relating to the debtor's proposals must be made to that court.

Although IR 1986 r 5.16(1) refers in terms to applications made subsequent to the filing of the report, it must apply equally to any application which has to be made before the filing of the nominee's report, including in particular any application under IA 1986 s 256A(4) or (5) either to replace the nominee, or to extend time for the filing of the nominee's report.

Chapter 5
Creditors' Meetings

2.529

5.17 Summoning of creditors' meeting

(1) If in his report the nominee states that in his opinion a meeting of creditors should be summoned to consider the debtor's proposal, the date on which the meeting is to be held shall be—

(a) in a case where an interim order has not been obtained, not less than 14 days and not more than 28 days from that on which the nominee's report is filed in court under Rule 5.14; and

(b) in a case where an interim order is in force, not less than 14 days from the date on which the nominee's report is filed in court nor more than 28 days from that on which the report is considered by the court.

(2) Notices calling the meeting shall be sent by the nominee, at least 14 days before the day fixed for it to be held, to all the creditors specified in the debtor's statement of affairs, and any other creditors of whom the nominee is otherwise aware.

(3) Each notice sent under this Rule shall specify the court to which the nominee's report on the debtor's proposal has been delivered and shall state the effect of Rule 5.23(1), (3) and (4) (requisite majorities); and with it there shall be sent—

(a) a copy of the proposal,

(b) a copy of the statement of affairs or, if the nominee thinks fit, a summary of it (the summary to include a list of the creditors and the amounts of their debts), and

(c) the nominee's comments on the proposal.

Notes

R 5.17

This rule supplements:

- the provisions of IA 1986 s 256(1) (interim order IVAs) and IA 1986 s 256A(3) (non interim order IVAs) under which the nominee is required, if he reports that a meeting of creditors be summoned to consider the debtor's proposals, to set a date, time and place for the meeting;
- the provisions of IA 1986 s 257 under which the nominee, where he has reported that such a meeting be summoned, is required to summon the meeting for the date, time and place suggested unless the court otherwise directs.

R 5.17(2)

In order to prevent possible challenges to the decision of a meeting by creditors who contend that they did not receive due notice of the meeting, it is important to ensure that the 14 day notice requirement in this rule is complied with. For a detailed survey of the rules and reported decisions relating to the sending of notices in respect of both CVA and IVA cases, see the commentary to IA 1986 s 5(2)(b) and IR 1986 r 1.9(2).

2.530

5.18 Creditors' meeting: supplementary

(1) Subject as follows, in fixing the venue for the creditors' meeting, the nominee shall have regard to the convenience of creditors.

(2) The meeting shall be summoned for commencement between 10.00 and 16.00 hours on a business day.

(3) With every notice summoning the meeting there shall be sent out forms of proxy.

2.531

5.19 The chairman at the meeting

(1) Subject as follows, the nominee shall be chairman of the creditors' meeting.

(2) If for any reason the nominee is unable to attend, he may nominate another person to act as chairman in his place; but a person so nominated must be—
    (a) a person qualified to act as an insolvency practitioner in relation to the debtor;
    (b) an authorised person in relation to the debtor; or
    (c) an employee of the nominee or his firm who is experienced in insolvency matters.

2.532

5.20 The chairman as proxy-holder

The chairman shall not by virtue of any proxy held by him vote to increase or reduce the amount of the remuneration or expenses of the nominee or the supervisor of the proposed arrangement, unless the proxy specifically directs him to vote in that way.

2.533

5.21 Entitlement to vote

(1) Subject as follows, every creditor who has notice of the creditors' meeting is entitled to vote at the meeting or any adjournment of it.

> (2) A creditor's entitlement to vote is calculated as follows—
>
>   (a)   where the debtor is not an undischarged bankrupt and an interim order is in force, by reference to the amount of the debt owed to him as at the date of the interim order;
>
>   (b)   where the debtor is not an undischarged bankrupt and an interim order is not in force, by reference to the amount of the debt owed to him at the date of the meeting; and
>
>   (c)   where the debtor is an undischarged bankrupt, by reference to the amount of the debt owed to him as at the date of the bankruptcy order.
>
> (3) A creditor may vote in respect of a debt for an unliquidated amount or any debt whose value is not ascertained, and for the purposes of voting (but not otherwise) his debt shall be valued at £1 unless the chairman agrees to put a higher value on it.

Notes

R 5.21(1)

Only those creditors who have been given notice of the meeting are entitled to vote at the meeting. However, under IA 1986 s 260(2)(b) (as amended by IA 2000) all creditors entitled to notice of the meeting are bound by the arrangement whether or not they received notice; see the commentary to that subsection. For a discussion as to the status of a creditor who has received notice of the meeting, but not the prescribed 14 days notice, see the general note to IR 1986 r 1.17 (the equivalent CVA rule). It is submitted that such a creditor would be entitled at his option to waive the inadequacy of any notice and vote at the meeting, although he may instead rely upon the inadequacy of notice and seek to challenge any approval under s 262(3) on that basis.

R 5.21(2)

It is incumbent on a creditor who wishes to vote in respect of his debt to state to the best of his ability the **total amount** which is owed to him by the debtor, and, if the value of the whole or some part is unascertained, to so state and to supply the chairman with as much information as possible to enable him to put an estimated minimum value on it: see *Re Kenneth George Hoare* [1997] BPIR 683.

R 5.21(2)(c)

In the case of undischarged bankrupts, a creditor is only entitled to vote in the amount of the debt owed to him at the date of the bankruptcy order. This appears inconsistent with IA 1986 s 257(3) under which both pre-bankruptcy and post-bankruptcy creditors are entitled to notice of the meeting.

R 5.21(3)

This sub-rule sets out the machinery which applies in dealing, for voting purposes, with claims for sums which are unliquidated or unascertained. The machinery is distinct from that which applies to debts which are disputed, which are governed by IR 1986 r 5.22(4): see *Re Cranley Mansions Ltd* [1994] 1 WLR 1010, 1025D-E; *Re Sweatfield Ltd* [1997] BCC 744.

Although IR 1986 r 5.21(3) refers to the chairman 'agreeing' to put a higher value on an unliquidated claim, this process is not consensual in requiring the agreement of the creditor to the valuation: *Doorbar v Alltime Securities Ltd* [1996] 1 WLR 456 overruling *Re Cranley Mansions Ltd* [1994] 1 WLR 1610 on this point. The rule itself makes clear that the attribution of a £1 or other value for unascertained or unliquidated claims is for voting purposes only. So creditors with such claims will not be prejudiced by the valuation on the subsequent payment of dividends in the CVA. It will be difficult to complain that the chairman has not put an estimated value on a debt where the creditor has decided not to attend the meeting: *Beverley Group plc v McClue* [1995] BCLC 407.

In putting a value to such claims for voting purposes, a chairman may face a difficult task where the outcome of the vote at the meeting may depend on his determination of the value. Allowing for the fact he is not a lawyer, or a valuer or actuary, he is, however, obliged to take reasonable steps to undertake some assessment of a claim's value: see Knox J *Doorbar v Alltime Securities Ltd No 2* [1995] 2 BCLC 513 at p 526 (a decision based on the old IR 1986 r 5.17(3) and *Fender v IRC* [2003] BPIR 1304, 1313). However, he should not speculate, and nor should he investigate the creditor's claim. He should examine the evidence put forward by the creditor, and by any other person, and if '*the totality of that evidence leads him to the conclusion that he can safely attribute to the claim a minimum value higher than £1 then he should do so*': *Re Newlands (Seaford Educational Trust* [2006] EWHC 1511 (Ch), [2006] All ER (D) 299 (Jun).

Where a creditor disagrees with the value placed on his claim by the chairman, he may appeal the chairman's decision to the court under r 5.22(3) and/or apply under IA 1986 s 266 (1). For further commentary on the appeal process, see the notes to IR 1986 r 5.22(3) below.

2.534

5.22 Procedure for admission of creditors' claims for voting purposes

(1) Subject as follows, at the creditors' meeting the chairman shall ascertain the entitlement of persons wishing to vote and shall admit or reject their claims accordingly.

(2) The chairman may admit or reject a claim in whole or in part.

(3) The chairman's decision on any matter under this Rule or under paragraph (3) of Rule 5.21 is subject to appeal to the court by any creditor or by the debtor.

(4) If the chairman is in doubt whether a claim should be admitted or rejected, he shall mark it as objected to and allow votes to be cast in respect of it, subject to such votes being subsequently declared invalid if the objection to the claim is sustained.

(5) If on an appeal the chairman's decision is reversed or varied, or votes are declared invalid, the court may order another meeting to be summoned, or make such order as it thinks just.

The court's power to make an order under this paragraph is exercisable only if it considers that the circumstances giving rise to the appeal are such as give rise to unfair prejudice or material irregularity.

(6) An application to the court by way of appeal against the chairman's decision shall not be made after the end of the period of 28 days beginning with the first day on which the report required by section 259 is made to the court.

(7) The chairman is not personally liable for any costs incurred by any person in respect of an appeal under this Rule.

Notes

R 5.22(1), (2), (4) Admission of creditor's claims

These provisions set out the procedure that the chairman should follow in determining whether or not to admit a creditor's claim for voting purposes. Note that there is a distinct procedure under IR 1986 r 5.21(3) which applies for the purpose of attributing a value for voting purposes on unliquidated or unascertained claims. Where a creditor's claim is disputed – either by the debtor himself or by other creditors – the chairman should look at the claim; if it is plain or obvious that it is good, he should admit it; if it is plain or obvious that it is bad, he should reject it; if there is a question or doubt about the claim, under IR 1986 r 5.22(4) he should admit it but mark it as objected to. The chairman has a duty to investigate the claim of a creditor (*Roberts v Pinnacle Entertainment Ltd* [2004] BPIR 208) but it is not the role of the chairman in the case of a disputed debt to undertake any lengthy quasi-judicial inquiry into the status of the debt, which is a task better suited to the court on an appeal: see the dicta of Harman J in *Re a debtor (No 222 of 1990)* [1992] BCLC 137, 144 (cited with approval in *Re a Debtor (No 574 of 1995)* [1998] 2 BCLC 124). For further rules governing the votes of secured creditors, see IR 1986 r 5.23(3) and commentary below.

R 5.22(3)

An appeal lies to the court with jurisdiction over the IVA against a chairman's decision:
- to admit or reject a claim (under IR 1986 r 5.22(1), (2), (4) above;
- on the value put on an unliquidated / unascertained claim (under IR 1986 r 5.21(3) above);
- on whether a vote falls to be left out of account under IR 1986 r 5.23(3) or (4) or otherwise under IR 1986 r 5.23 below for the purpose of calculating whether the requisite majority of creditors is achieved, and whether the resolution is valid;

Such an appeal may be brought by any creditor or by the debtor. This appeal procedure runs in parallel with an aggrieved creditor's or debtor's right to apply to the court under IA 1986 s 262(1) for an order revoking the decision of the creditors' meeting on grounds of material irregularity.

On an appeal from a chairman's decision, the court may consider the validity of the debt, or its proper valuation (as the case may be) afresh and unfettered by the decision of the chairman; it may examine all the evidence before it and conclude whether on balance the claim is established and / or its appropriate value for voting purposes: see *Re a debtor (No 574 of 1995)* [1998] 2 BCLC 124 at p 127h–128c (also reported at [1998] BPIR 224 under the name *National Westminster Bank v Scher*). See also *Fender v IRC* [2003] BPIR 1304, para 20 which emphasises the distinction between the task of the chairman at the meeting, who might have to make robust and speedy decisions, and the role of the court on appeal from such decisions, which had to be satisfied on the basis of a proper standard of evidence that the claim was a good one.

R 5.22(5)

Where the court reverses or varies the decision of the chairman, it has power under this provision to order another meeting to be summoned, or make such order as it thinks just. It is submitted that this includes a power in appropriate circumstances to revoke the approval of the IVA where such approval was obtained only by reason of the decision of the chairman on voting entitlement which has been overturned. These powers, however, are only exercisable where the impugned decision has resulted in unfair prejudice or material irregularity. This will, in general, only be the case where the decision has directly (or perhaps indirectly) affected the outcome of the vote.

R 5.22(6)

This provision imposes a 28 day time limit from the date of filing of the chairman's report with the court for appealing a decision on voting. This time limit may be extended under IR 1986 r 12.9 (importing CPR r 3.1(2)) or IA 1986 s 376: *UK Hydroslides Ltd v Stem*, 9 July 2004, LTL 9/7/2004 (Ch D). In determining whether or not to extend time for appealing the chairman's decision, the court should take into account the length of the delay, the reasons for it, the apparent merits of the underlying application and the prejudice to each side other than the inevitable prejudice inherent in re-opening the matter: *Tager v Westpac Banking Corporation* [1997] BPIR 543 at p 555. In *Re Timothy* [2006] BPIR 329 (which contains a review of the relevant authorities) an application for an extension of the 28 day time limit under IA 1986 s 262 for challenging the decision of the creditors' meeting was refused where a period of nine months had elapsed since the meeting, the application was only arguable and prejudice would be caused by the delay in making the application.

R 5.22(7)

The chairman is protected from adverse costs orders in relation to any appeal against his decision brought under IR 1986 r 5.22(3). But there is no such protection where an aggrieved creditor or debtor applies instead or at the same time to the court under IA 1986 s 262(1) for an order revoking the decision of the meeting on grounds of material irregularity. In *Re a debtor (No 222 of 1990) (No 2)* [1993] BCLC 233 the nominee was ordered to pay the costs of an application under IA 1986 s 262(1)(b) where a material irregularity had arisen because the nominee had failed to discharge his duties under the rules and had thereby fallen significantly below the standards required of a licensed insolvency practitioner; also *Fender v IRC* [2003] BPIR 1304 paras 36, 37. *Smurthwaite v Simpson-Smith*, 25 July 2006, LTL 25/07/06 (CA).

2.535

5.23 Requisite majorities

(1) Subject as follows, at the creditors' meeting for any resolution to pass approving any proposal or modification there must be a majority in excess of three-quarters in value of the creditors present in person or by proxy and voting on the resolution.

(2) The same applies in respect of any other resolution proposed at the meeting, but substituting one-half for three-quarters.

(3) In the following cases there is to be left out of account a creditor's vote in respect of any claim or part of a claim—
   (a)   where written notice of the claim was not given, either at the meeting or before it, to the chairman or the nominee;
   (b)   where the claim or part is secured;
   (c)   where the claim is in respect of a debt wholly or partly on, or secured by, a current bill of exchange or promissory note, unless the creditor is willing—
      (i)   to treat the liability to him on the bill or note of every person who is liable on it antecedently to the debtor, and against whom a bankruptcy order has not been made (or, in the case of a company, which has not gone into liquidation), as a security in his hands, and
      (ii)   to estimate the value of the security and (for the purpose of entitlement to vote, but not of any distribution under the arrangement) to deduct it from his claim.

(4) Any resolution is invalid if those voting against it include more than half in value of the creditors, counting in these latter only those—
   (a)   who have notice of the meeting;
   (b)   whose votes are not to be left out of account under paragraph (3); and
   (c)   who are not, to the best of the chairman's belief, associates of the debtor.

(5) It is for the chairman of the meeting to decide whether under this Rule—

> (a)   a vote is to be left out of account in accordance with the
>   paragraph (3), or
> (b)   a person is an associate of the debtor for the purposes of
>   paragraph (4)(c);
> and in relation to the second of these cases the chairman is entitled to rely
> on the information provided by the debtor's statement of affairs or
> otherwise in accordance with this Part of the Rules.
>
> (6) If the chairman uses a proxy contrary to Rule 5.20, his vote with that
> proxy does not count towards any majority under this Rule.
>
> (7) The chairman's decision on any matter under this Rule is subject to
> appeal to the court by any creditor or by the debtor and paragraphs (5) to
> (7) of Rule 5.22 apply as regards such an appeal.

Notes

R 5.23

This provision imposes a two-stage process for determining whether or not a proposal obtains the approval of creditors:

(1)   any resolution to approve the IVA must be passed with a majority in excess of three-quarters in value of the creditors present at the meeting in person or by proxy and voting on the resolution (IR 1986 r 5.23(1)); in counting votes for this purpose, certain votes fall to be left out of account as defined in IR 1986 r 5.23(3))

(2)   if the resolution achieves this majority, it is nevertheless invalid under IR 1986 r 5.23(4) if more than half in value of the creditors who have been given notice of the meeting (excluding those who are associates of the debtor as well as those whose votes do not count under IR 1986 r 5.23(3)) have voted against it.

R 5.23(3)

A creditor's vote is to be left out of account for the purpose of calculating majorities where it falls within one of the three categories in IR 1986 r 5.23(3). It is for the chairman to decide whether it does, subject to an appeal under the provisions of IR 1986 r 5.22(5)–(7). A creditor whose vote is left out of account is still bound by the arrangement as a creditor entitled to vote. All creditors must have given written notice of their claim to the chairman at or prior to the meeting for their vote to count. It is good practice for a proof of debt form to be sent out with the notice and proxy form to enable creditors to comply with this requirement. However, it appears that the submission by a creditor of a written proxy is sufficient notice under this rule even if the proxy does not state the amount of the debt the subject of the claim, provided that the chairman was already aware of the amount of the debt for other information: see *Roberts v Pinnacle Entertainment Ltd* [2004] BPIR 208, paras 16, 17.

Secured creditors are entitled to vote at a creditors' meeting, but their vote falls to be left out of account to the extent that it relates to claim which is in whole or part secured. In *Calor Gas v Piercy* [1994] 2 BCLC 321, it was held that where the value of creditor's security is less than its debt, the creditor's vote should not be left out of account in its entirety, but should be taken into account in respect of the unsecured balance. A creditor may be able to waive part of its secured claim to enable its vote to be counted insofar as it has been waived: *Swindon Town Properties v Swindon Town Football Co Ltd* [2003] BPIR 253. It falls to the chairman to put an estimated value on the security at the date of the meeting in order to determine the value (for voting purposes) of the unsecured balance.

R 5.23(4)

For the meaning of 'associates' of the debtor, see IA 1986 s 435. Whether a person falls within this category is for the chairman to determine. The debtor is required to identify such persons both within the proposal (IR 1986 r 5.3(2)(c)) and in the statement of affairs (IR 1986 r 5.5(3)) and the chairman is entitled to rely upon such information in making his determination. His decision is again subject to appeal to the court under IR 1986 r 5.22(5)–(7).

2.536

5.24 Proceedings to obtain agreement on the proposal

(1) On the day on which the creditors' meeting is held, it may from time to time be adjourned.

(2) If on that day the requisite majority for the approval of the voluntary arrangement (with or without modifications) has not been obtained, the chairman may, and shall if it is so resolved, adjourn the meeting for not more than 14 days.

(3) If there are subsequently further adjournments, the final adjournment shall not be to a day later than 14 days after that on which the meeting was originally held.

(4) If the meeting is adjourned under paragraph (2), notice of the fact shall be given by the chairman forthwith to the court.

(5) If following any final adjournment of the meeting the proposal (with or without modifications) is not agreed to, it is deemed rejected.

Notes

R 5.24(2)

There is provision only for one meeting of creditors. Such meetings may be adjourned for up to 14 days. But where such a meeting has come to a final conclusion, there is no power to call a further meeting to reconsider the proposal in a modified form: *Re Symes* [1995] 2 BCLC 651. As with the summoning of meetings, the rules impose a tight 14 day timetable within which the creditors' meeting must reach a conclusion. If the creditors' meeting fails to come to approve the proposal within this timescale, it is deemed rejected: *Re Plummer* [2004] BPIR 767. However, in an appropriate case, time for concluding the meeting beyond the stipulated period could probably be extended under IA 1986 s 376.

Chapter 6
Implementation of the Arrangement

2.537

5.25 Resolutions to follow approval

(1) If the voluntary arrangement is approved (with or without modifications), a resolution may be taken by the creditors, where two or more individuals are appointed to act as supervisor, on the question whether acts to be done in connection with the arrangement may be done by any one of them, or must be done by both or all.

(2) If at the creditors' meeting a resolution is moved for the appointment of some person other than the nominee to be supervisor of the arrangement, there must be produced to the chairman, at or before the meeting—
- (a)   that person's written consent to act (unless he is present and then and there signifies his consent), and
- (b)   his written confirmation that he is qualified to act as an insolvency practitioner in relation to the debtor or is an authorised person in relation to the debtor.

2.538

5.26 Hand-over of property, etc to supervisor

(1) Forthwith after the approval of the voluntary arrangement, the debtor or, where the debtor is an undischarged bankrupt, the official receiver or the debtor's trustee, shall do all that is required for putting the supervisor into possession of the assets included in the arrangement.

(2) On taking possession of the assets in any case where the debtor is an undischarged bankrupt, the supervisor shall discharge any balance due to the official receiver and (if other) the trustee by way of remuneration or on account of—
- (a)   fees, costs, charges and expenses properly incurred and payable under the Act or the Rules, and
- (b)   any advances made in respect of the insolvent estate, together with interest on such advances at the rate specified in section 17 of the Judgments Act 1838 at the date of the bankruptcy order.

(3) Alternatively where the debtor is an undischarged bankrupt, the supervisor must, before taking possession, give the official receiver or the trustee a written undertaking to discharge any such balance out of the first realisation of assets.

(4) Where the debtor is an undischarged bankrupt, the official receiver and (if other) the trustee has a charge on the assets included in the voluntary arrangement in respect of any sums due as above until they have been discharged, subject only to the deduction from realisations by the supervisor of the proper costs and expenses of realisation.

Any sums due to the official receiver take priority over those due to a trustee.

(5) The supervisor shall from time to time out of the realisation of assets discharge all guarantees properly given by the official receiver or the trustee for the benefit of the estate, and shall pay all their expenses.

Notes

R 5.26(2)–(4)

These provisions operate in cases where an undischarged bankrupt enters into a voluntary arrangement to give the official receiver or trustee priority for his fees and costs properly incurred and payable under IA 1986 or IR 1986. This priority extends to all such costs incurred up to the date when the supervisor takes possession from the trustee of the assets included within the arrangement, but does not extend to any costs which the trustee may subsequently incur: *Rooney v Cardona* [1999] BPIR 954.

2.539

5.27 Report of creditors' meeting

(1) A report of the creditors' meeting shall be prepared by the chairman of the meeting.

(2) The report shall—

    (a)   state whether the proposal for a voluntary arrangement was approved or rejected and, if approved, with what (if any) modifications;

    (b)   set out the resolutions which were taken at the meeting, and the decision on each one;

    (c)   list the creditors (with their respective values) who were present or represented at the meeting, and how they voted on each resolution;

    (d)   whether in the opinion of the supervisor,

        (i)   the EC Regulation applies to the voluntary arrangement, and

        (ii)   if so, whether the proceedings are main proceedings or territorial proceedings; and

    (e)   include such further information (if any) as the chairman thinks it appropriate to make known to the court.

(3) A copy of the chairman's report shall, within 4 days of the meeting being held, be filed in court; and the court shall cause that copy to be endorsed with the date of filing.

(4) The persons to whom notice of the result is to be given, under section 259(1), are all those who were sent notice of the meeting under this Part of the Rules and any other creditor of whom the chairman is aware, and where the debtor is an undischarged bankrupt, the official receiver and (if any) the trustee.

The notice shall be sent immediately after a copy of the chairman's report is filed in court under paragraph (3).

(5) In a case where no interim order has been obtained the court shall not consider the chairman's report unless an application is made to the court under the Act or the Rules in relation to it.

Notes

R 5.27

This provision supplements IA 1986 s 259 and reference should be made to that section. The further information contemplated under IR 1986 r 5.27(2)(e) should include details of all determinations on voting entitlement etc made by the chairman under IR 1986 r 5. 21(3), r 5.22(1), (2) and (4), r 5.23(3) and (4) which may be the subject of any appeal to the court.

2.540

5.28 Register of voluntary arrangements (*revoked as from 1 April 2004*)

5.29 Reports to Secretary of State

(1) Immediately after the chairman of the creditors' meeting has filed in court a report that the meeting has approved the voluntary arrangement, he shall report to the Secretary of State the following details of the arrangement—
  (a) the name and address of the debtor;
  (b) the date on which the arrangement was approved by the creditors;
  (c) the name and address of the supervisor; and
  (d) the court in which the chairman's report has been filed.

(2) A person who is appointed to act as supervisor of an individual voluntary arrangement (whether in the first instance or by way of replacement of another person previously appointed) shall forthwith give written notice to the Secretary of State of his appointment.

If he vacates office as supervisor, he shall forthwith give written notice of that fact also to the Secretary of State.

2.541

5.30 Revocation or suspension of the arrangement

(1) This Rule applies where the court makes an order of revocation or suspension under section 262.

(2) The person who applied for the order shall serve sealed copies of it—
  (a) in a case where the debtor is an undischarged bankrupt, on the debtor, the official receiver and the trustee;
  (b) in any other case, on the debtor; and
  (c) in either case, on the supervisor of the voluntary arrangement.

(3) If the order includes a direction by the court under section 262(4)(b) for any further creditors' meeting to be summoned, notice shall also be given (by the person who applied for the order) to whoever is, in accordance with the direction, required to summon the meeting.

(4) The debtor or (where the debtor is an undischarged bankrupt) the trustee or (if there is no trustee) the official receiver shall—
  (a) forthwith after receiving a copy of the court's order, give notice of it to all persons who were sent notice of the creditors' meeting which approved the voluntary arrangement or who, not having been sent that notice, are affected by the order;
  (b) within 7 days of their receiving a copy of the order (or within such longer period as the court may allow), give notice to the court whether it is intended to make a revised proposal to creditors, or to invite reconsideration of the original proposal.

(5) The person on whose application the order of revocation or suspension was made shall, within 7 days after the making of the order, give written notice of it to the Secretary of State and shall, in the case of an

> order of suspension, within 7 days of the expiry of any suspension order, given written notice of such expiry to the Secretary of State.

Notes

R 5.30

This provision sets out the notification requirements in a case where a successful challenge is made under IA 1986 s 262 to an IVA which has been approved. Curiously, the rule does not appear in terms to apply in cases where a successful challenge, on grounds of material irregularity, is made to the decision of a creditors' meeting to reject an IVA proposal, where the court may give directions for the summoning of a further creditors' meeting to reconsider the proposal but will, *ex hypothesi*, not make any order revoking or suspending the IVA (so as to fall within the terms of IR 1986 r 5.30(1)).

2.542

5.31 Supervisor's accounts and reports

(1) Where the voluntary arrangement authorises or requires the supervisor—
    (a)   to carry on the debtor's business or to trade on his behalf or in his name, or
    (b)   to realise assets of the debtor or (in a case where the debtor is an undischarged bankrupt) belonging to the estate, or
    (c)   otherwise to administer or dispose of any funds of the debtor or the estate,
he shall keep accounts and records of his acts and dealings in and in connection with the arrangement, including in particular records of all receipts and payments of money.

(2) The supervisor shall, not less often than once in every 12 months beginning with the date of his appointment, prepare an abstract of such receipts and payments, and send copies of it, accompanied by his comments on the progress and efficacy of the arrangement, to—
    (a)   the court,
    (b)   the debtor, and
    (c)   all those of the debtor's creditors who are bound by the arrangement.

If in any period of 12 months he has made no payments and had no receipts, he shall at the end of that period send a statement to that effect to all who are specified in sub-paragraphs (a) to (c) above.

(3) An abstract provided under paragraph (2) shall relate to a period beginning with the date of the supervisor's appointment or (as the case may be) the day following the end of the last period for which an abstract was prepared under this Rule; and copies of the abstract shall be sent out, as required by paragraph (2), within the 2 months following the end of the period to which the abstract relates.

(4) If the supervisor is not authorised as mentioned in paragraph (1), he shall, not less often than once in every 12 months beginning with the date of his appointment, send to all those specified in paragraph 2(a) to (c) a report on the progress and efficacy of the voluntary arrangement.

(5) The court may, on application by the supervisor, vary the dates on which the obligation to send abstracts or reports arises.

―――――

Notes

R 5.31

This rule sets out important provisions requiring the supervisor every 12 months during the currency of the arrangement to keep creditors (and others) informed of the progress and efficacy of the arrangement. This requirement applies to all IVAs – whether or not the supervisor is authorised to do any of the matters set out in paragraph (1): see paragraph (2) and (4). Where the supervisor is so authorised under paragraph (1), he must in addition keep the creditors informed of the financial status of the arrangement, by an abstract of receipts and payments.

―――――

2.543

5.32 Production of accounts and records to Secretary of State

(1) The Secretary of State may at any time during the course of the voluntary arrangement or after its completion require the supervisor to produce for inspection—
   (a)   his records and accounts in respect of the arrangement, and
   (b)   copies of abstracts and reports prepared in compliance with Rule 5.31.

(2) The Secretary of State may require production either at the premises of the supervisor or elsewhere; and it is the duty of the supervisor to comply with any requirement imposed on him under this Rule.

(3) The Secretary of State may cause any accounts and records produced to him under this Rule to be audited; and the supervisor shall give to the Secretary of State such further information and assistance as he needs for the purposes of his audit.

2.544

5.33 Fees, costs, charges and expenses

The fees, costs, charges and expenses that may be incurred for any purposes of the voluntary arrangement are—
   (a)   any disbursements made by the nominee prior to the approval of the arrangement, and any remuneration for his services as such agreed between himself and the debtor, the official receiver or the trustee;
   (b)   any fees, costs, charges or expenses which—
      (i)   are sanctioned by the terms of the arrangement, or
      (ii)   would be payable, or correspond to those which would be payable, in the debtor's bankruptcy.

2.545

5.34 Completion or termination of the arrangement

(1) Not more than 28 days after the final completion or termination of the voluntary arrangement, the supervisor shall send to all creditors of the

debtor who are bound by the arrangement, and to the debtor, a notice that the arrangement has been fully implemented or (as the case may be) terminated.

(2) With the notice there shall be sent to each of those persons a copy of a report by the supervisor summarising all receipts and payments made by him in pursuance of the arrangement, and explaining any difference in the actual implementation of it as compared with the proposal as approved by the creditors' meeting or (in the case of termination of the arrangement) explaining the reasons why the arrangement has not been implemented in accordance with the proposal as approved by the creditors' meeting.

(3) The supervisor shall, within the 28 days mentioned above, send to the Secretary of State and to the court a copy of the notice under paragraph (1), together with a copy of the report under paragraph (2), and he shall not vacate office until after such copies have been sent.

(4) The court may, on application by the supervisor, extend the period of 28 days under paragraphs (1) and (3).

Notes

R 5.34

The supervisor is required on the completion or early termination of the arrangement not only to provide a final receipts and payments account but also to explain to creditors and the debtor the reasons for any departure in the implementation of the arrangement from its terms as approved and the reason for its early termination. Any creditor or member dissatisfied with such explanation may apply to the court under IA 1986 s 263(3).

Chapter 7
Fast-Track Voluntary Arrangement

2.546

5.35 Application of Chapter

The Rules in this Chapter apply in relation to an individual debtor who intends to submit a proposal for a voluntary arrangement with his creditors to the official receiver in accordance with the provisions of section 263B.

Notes

R 5.35

For general commentary on the new fast track voluntary arrangement procedure ('FTVA'), see the notes to IA 1986 s 263A. The detailed machinery of the FTVA is to be found in the following rules which make up Chapter 7.

2.547

5.36 Interpretation

In this Chapter –
  'voluntary arrangement' means an individual voluntary arrangement under section 263A;
  'proposal' means the document setting out the terms of the voluntary arrangement which the debtor is proposing.

2.548

5.37 Contents of proposal

(1) The debtor's proposal submitted under section 263B(1) shall –
  (a) be accompanied by any fee payable to the official receiver for acting as nominee; and
  (b) contain –
     (i) a statement that the debtor is eligible to propose a voluntary arrangement;
     (ii) a short explanation why, in his opinion, a voluntary arrangement is desirable, and give reasons why his creditors may be expected to concur with such an arrangement; and
     (iii) a statement that the debtor is aware that he commits an offence under section 262A if, for the purpose of obtaining the approval of his creditors to his proposal, he makes any false representation, or fraudulently does, or omits to do, anything.

(2) The following matters shall be stated, or otherwise dealt with, in the proposal –
  (a) the following matters, so far as within the debtor's immediate knowledge –
     (i) his assets, with an estimate of their respective values;
     (ii) the extent (if any) to which the assets are charged in favour of creditors; and
     (iii) the extent (if any) to which particular assets are to be excluded from the voluntary arrangement;
  (b) particulars of any property, other than assets of the debtor himself, which is proposed to be included in the voluntary arrangement, the source of such property and the terms on which it is to be made available for inclusion;
  (c) the nature and amount of the debtor's liabilities (so far as within his immediate knowledge), the manner in which they are proposed to be met, modified, postponed or otherwise dealt with by means of the voluntary arrangement and (in particular) –
     (i) how it is proposed to deal with preferential creditors (defined in section 258(7)) and creditors who are, or claim to be, secured;
     (ii) how associates of the debtor (being creditors of his) are proposed to be treated under the voluntary arrangement; and
     (iii) whether, to the debtor's knowledge, claims have been made under section 339 (transactions at an undervalue), section 340 (preferences), section 343 (extortionate credit

transactions), or whether there are circumstances giving rise to the possibility of such claims,

and, where any such circumstances are present, whether, and if so how, it is proposed under the voluntary arrangement to make provision for wholly or partly indemnifying the insolvent estate in respect of such claims;

(d) whether any, and if so what, guarantees have been given of the debtor's debts by other persons, specifying which (if any) of the guarantors are associates of his;

(e) the proposed duration of the voluntary arrangement;

(f) the proposed dates of distributions to creditors, with estimates of their amounts;

(g) how it is proposed to deal with the claims of any person who is bound by the arrangement by virtue of section 263D(2)(c);

(h) an estimate of the fees and expenses that will be incurred in connection with the approval and implementation of the voluntary arrangement;

(j) whether, for the purposes of the voluntary arrangement, any guarantees are to be offered by any persons other than the debtor, and whether (if so) any security is to be given or sought;

(k) the manner in which funds held for the purpose of payment to creditors, and not so paid on the termination of the voluntary arrangement, are to be dealt with;

(l) the functions which are to be undertaken by the supervisor of the voluntary arrangement;

(m) an address of the official receiver to which correspondence with the official receiver is to be sent;

(n) the names and addresses of all the debtor's creditors so far as within his immediate knowledge; and

(o) whether the EC Regulation will apply and, if so, whether the proceedings will be main proceedings or territorial proceedings,

and the proposal shall be signed and dated by the debtor.

(3) The official receiver shall on request supply to the debtor the address referred to in paragraph (2)(m).

Notes

R 5.37

This rule sets out the information that must be included within the proposal for FTVA submitted by the debtor to the official receiver. Its requirements are very similar to those for a proposal for a standard IVA contained in IR 1986 r 5.3. For detailed commentary, see the notes to IR 1986 r 1.3, which deals with the mirror provisions in a CVA.

R 5.37(1)(a)

The fee payable to the official receiver for acting as nominee is £300. In addition a sum of £35 is payable for registering the FTVA with the Secretary of State. Although this rule refers only to the nominee's fee, both sums are in fact payable when the proposal is submitted to the official receiver by virtue of Article 7 Insolvency Proceedings (Fees) Order 2004 (SI 2004/593). In the event that the official receiver declines to act as nominee, the two fees are to be returned to 'the person entitled to it' under Article 8 Insolvency Proceedings (Fees) Order 2004 (SI 2004/593). The official receiver's practice, as set out in the Insolvency Service's Guidance

Notes, will be initially to credit the refunded fees to the bankrupt's estate, presumably pending a decision whether the monies in question properly form part of the bankrupt's estate or should be returned to the bankrupt or other person who provided the monies.

R 5.37(2)

Standard forms of proposal for completion by the bankrupt are to be provided by the official receiver. The Insolvency Service's Guidance Notes suggest that these will already be partially completed with the details of the assets that the bankrupt has already provided to the official receiver, further simplifying the process for the bankrupt.

2.549

5.38 Requirement for the official receiver's decision

(1) Where the official receiver receives a proposal for a voluntary arrangement in accordance with Rule 5.37 he shall, within 28 days of its receipt, serve a notice on the debtor stating that–
   (a)   he agrees to act as nominee in relation to the proposal;
   (b)   he declines to act as nominee in relation to the proposal and specifying reasons for his decision; or
   (c)   on the basis of the information supplied to him he is unable to reach a decision as to whether to act and specifying what further information he requires.

(2) Where the debtor, pursuant to a request under paragraph (1)(c), supplies the information requested, the official receiver shall, within 28 days of the receipt of the information, serve a notice on the debtor in accordance with paragraph (1).

Notes

R 5.38

This rule supplements IA 1986 s 263B(2). Under that provision, the official receiver should only agree to act as nominee if he is satisfied that the proposal has a reasonable prospect of being approved and implemented, and, even if so satisfied, he appears to have a residual discretion to decline to act if he considers it would be not be appropriate for him to do so. The Insolvency Service's Guidance Notes suggest that the official receiver will decline to act where the affairs of the bankrupt are complicated – where it may be more appropriate for the bankrupt to make a standard IVA proposal with a private IP acting as nominee and supervisor. This rule prescribes the time period with within the official receiver must reach a decision and, where the information supplied is insufficient to enable the official receiver to reach such decision empowers him to request further information from the bankrupt.

2.550

5.39 Arrangements for approval of fast-track voluntary arrangement

(1) As soon as reasonably practicable after the official receiver agrees to act as nominee, he shall send to the creditors and any trustee who is not the official receiver –
   (a)   a copy of the proposal; and

(b) a notice inviting creditors to vote to approve or reject the debtor's proposal and stating that –

    (i) if a majority in excess of three-quarters in value of creditors who vote approve the proposal, the official receiver will, as soon as reasonably practicable, report to the court that the proposal has been approved;

    (ii) under section 263F –

        (aa) the debtor, a person who was entitled to participate in the arrangements made under section 263B(2), any trustee who is not the official receiver, or the official receiver, has 28 days from the date the official receiver reports to the court under section 263C that the proposal has been approved to apply to the court to have the proposal set aside on the grounds set out in section 263F(1);

        (bb) a creditor, who was not made aware of the arrangements under section 263B(2) at the time when they were made, has 28 days from the date on which he becomes aware of the voluntary arrangement, to apply to have the proposal set aside on the grounds set out in section 263F(1); and

    (iii) creditors cannot propose modifications to the debtor's proposal; and

(c) for the creditors, a copy of Form 5.6 for their use.

(2) The notice shall include a date specified by the official receiver as the final date on which he will accept votes from creditors, being a date not less than 14 days and not more than 28 days from the date of the notice.

Notes

R 5.39

This provision supplements IA 1986 s 263B(4) in prescribing the arrangements that the official receiver must make for inviting creditors to decide whether to approve the bankrupt's proposal.

2.551

5.40 Approval by creditors

(1) All creditors who wish to vote shall give notice in Form 5.6 to the official receiver of their decision whether to accept or reject the debtor's proposal. Such notification shall be sent to the official receiver at the address specified in the notice.

(2) Votes may be signed by a representative of a creditor.

(3) Votes from a representative of a creditor shall be accompanied by written authority for that representation signed and dated by the creditor.

Notes

R 5.40

The FTVA procedure differs from that for consideration of standard IVAs in that no creditors' meeting is held to consider the proposal. Instead, creditors are invited to approve or reject the proposal simply by giving notice to the official receiver on the form provided by him (Form 5.6). This must be 'sent' by the creditor to the official receiver at the address specified in the notice. The rules do not prescribe the means by which the notice must be sent, and transmission by fax is presumably effective: see, in the context of proxy forms, *Re a Debtor (No 2021 of 1995)* [1996] 2 All ER 345 (also reported as *IRC v Conbeer* [1996] BPIR 398).

2.552

5.41 Entitlement to vote

(1) Subject as follows, any creditor who is sent a notice by the official receiver is entitled to vote for the approval or rejection of the proposal.

(2) A creditor's entitlement to vote is calculated by reference to the amount of the creditor's debt at the date of the bankruptcy order.

(3) A creditor may vote in respect of a debt for an unliquidated amount or any debt whose value is not ascertained, and for the purposes of voting (but not otherwise) his debt shall be valued at £1 unless the official receiver agrees to put a higher value on it.

Notes

R 5.41

This rule is modelled on and substantially follows IR 1986 *r* 5.21 – the equivalent rule which applies to standard IVAs. See the commentary thereto above.

2.553

5.42 Procedure for admission of creditors' claims for voting purposes.

(1) The official receiver has the power to admit or reject a creditor's claim for the purpose of his entitlement to vote, and the power is exercisable with respect to the whole or part of the claim.

(2) The official receiver's decision on entitlement to vote is subject to appeal to the court by any creditor or the debtor.

(3) If on appeal the official receiver's decision is reversed or varied, or votes are declared invalid, the court may order another vote to be held, or make such order as it thinks just.
The court's power to make an order under this paragraph is exercisable only if it considers that the circumstances giving rise to the appeal are such as give rise to unfair prejudice or material irregularity.

(4) An application to the court by way of appeal against the official receiver's decision shall not be made after the end of the period of 28 days beginning with the day on which the report required by section 263C is made to the court.

(5) The official receiver is not personally liable for any costs incurred by any person in respect of an appeal under this Rule.

Notes

R 5.42

This rule sets out the procedure to be followed by the official receiver in deciding whether or not to admit a creditor's claim for voting purposes, and the right of, and procedure for, appealing a decision of the official receiver on entitlement to vote to the court. It substantially mirrors IR 1986 *r* 5.22, the equivalent rule which applies in standard IVAs, and for further commentary, see the notes to that rule.

2.554

5.43 Requisite majorities

(1) A proposal is approved by the creditors if a majority in excess of three-quarters in value of the creditors who vote approve the proposal.

(2) In the following cases there is to be left out of account a creditor's vote in respect of any claim or part of a claim –
    (a)   where the claim or part is secured;
    (b)   where the claim is in respect of a debt wholly or partly on, or secured by, a current bill of exchange or promissory note, unless the creditor is willing –
        (i)   to treat the liability to him on the bill or note of every person who is liable on it antecedently to the debtor, and against whom a bankruptcy order has not been made (or in the case of a company, which has not gone into liquidation), as a security in his hands; and
        (ii)   to estimate the value of the security and (for the purpose of entitlement to vote, but not of any distribution under the arrangement) to deduct it from his claim.

(3) A proposal is not approved if those voting against include more than half in value of the creditors in the latter onnly those
    (a)   who gave notice to the official receiver in accordance with Rule 5.40;
    (b)   whose votes are not to be left out of account under paragraph (2); and
    (c)   who are not, to the best of the official receiver's belief, associates of the debtor.

(4) It is for the official receiver to decide whether, under this Rule a person is an associate of the debtor for the purposes of paragraph (3)(c) and in relation to this he is entitled to rely on the information provided by the debtor's statement of affairs or otherwise in accordance with this Part of the Rules.

Notes

R 5.43

As with standard IVAs, a three-quarters majority of those voting (excluding secured creditors as defined in the rule) must approve the proposal in order for it to go forward; and at least half of the votes approving the proposal must come from creditors who are not associates of the bankrupt. See further the commentary to IR 1986 *r* 5.23.

2.555

5.44 Notification to the court

The official receiver shall, in his report to court for the purposes of section 263C, include a statement whether, in his opinion –
    (a)   the EC Regulation applies to the voluntary arrangement; and
    (b)   if so, whether the proceedings are main proceedings or territorial proceedings.

Notes

R 5.44

See the commentary to IA 1986 s 263C.

2.556

5.45 Notice of appointment as supervisor etc

(1) Where the official receiver is appointed to act as supervisor of a voluntary arrangement, he shall, as soon as reasonably practicable, give written notice of his appointment to the Secretary of State, and all creditors of whom he is aware, and the trustee (if any) who is not the official receiver.

(2) If the official receiver vacates office as supervisor he shall give written notice of that fact to the Secretary of State.

2.557

5.46 Revocation of the fast-track voluntary arrangement

(1) This Rule applies where the court makes an order of revocation under section 263F.

(2) Where the person who applied for the order is –
    (a)   the debtor, he shall serve a sealed copy of the order on the supervisor and any trustee of his estate who is not the official receiver;
    (b)   the supervisor, he shall serve a sealed copy of the order on the debtor, and any trustee who is not the official receiver;
    (c)   a trustee who is not the official receiver, he shall serve a sealed copy of the order on the debtor and the supervisor; and
    (d)   a creditor, he shall serve a sealed copy of the order on the debtor, the supervisor and any trustee who is not the official receiver.

(3) The supervisor shall, as soon as reasonably practicable after receiving a copy of the order, give notice of it, to all persons who were sent a copy of the debtor's proposal under Rule 5.39 and all other persons who are affected by the order.

(4) The person on whose application the order was made shall, within 7 days after the making of the order, give written notice of it to the Secretary of State.

2.558

5.47 Supervisor's accounts and reports

(1) The supervisor shall keep accounts and records of his acts and dealings in and in connection with the arrangement, including in particular records of all receipts and payments of money.

(2) The supervisor shall, not less often than once in every 12 months beginning with the date of his appointment –
    (a)   prepare a report on the progress of the voluntary arrangement, including a summary of receipts and payments; and
    (b)   send copies of it to –
        (i)   the debtor; and
        (ii)   all of the debtor's creditors of whom he is aware,
and if in any period of 12 months he has made no payments and had no receipts, he shall at the end of that period send a statement to that effect to those specified in sub-paragraphs (a) and (b) above.

(3) A report provided under paragraph (2) shall relate to a period beginning with the date of the supervisor's appointment or (as the case may be) the day following the end of the last period for which a report was prepared under this Rule; and copies of the report shall be sent, as required by paragraph (2), within the 2 months following the end of the period to which the report relates.

2.559

5.48 Fees, costs and expenses in respect of the performance of the functions of the official receiver

The fees, costs and expenses in respect of the performance by the official receiver of his functions in relation to the bankruptcy and those of the trustee who is not the official receiver (including those in connection with the employment of agents) shall be a first charge on any sums realised under the terms of the voluntary arrangement, and those of the official receiver in relation to the voluntary arrangement, shall be a second charge.

2.560

5.49 Employment of agents by the supervisor

The supervisor may employ agents in connection with the realisation of any assets subject to the terms of the voluntary arrangement.

2.561

5.50 Completion or termination of the fast-track voluntary arrangement

(1) Not more than 28 days after the final completion or termination of the voluntary arrangement, the supervisor shall send to all creditors of the

debtor who are bound by the arrangement, and to the debtor, a notice that the voluntary arrangement has been fully implemented, (or as the case may be) terminated.

(2) With the notice there shall be sent to each of those persons a copy of a report by the supervisor summarising all receipts and payments made by him in pursuance of the voluntary arrangement, and explaining any difference in the actual implementation of it compared with the proposal as approved by the creditors.

(3) The supervisor shall, within the 28 days mentioned above, send to the Secretary of State a copy of the notice under paragraph (1), together with a copy of the report under paragraph (2), and he shall not vacate office until after such copies have been sent.

(4) The court may, on application by the supervisor, extend the period of 28 days under paragraphs (1) and (3).

Chapter 8
Application by a bankrupt to annul a bankruptcy order under Section 261 (2) (a)

2.562

5.51 Application of this Chapter

The following Rules apply where a bankrupt applies for an annulment of a bankruptcy order under section 261(2)(a).

2.563

5.52 Application to court

(1) An application to the court to annul a bankruptcy order under section 261(2)(a) shall specify the section under which it is made.

(2) The application shall be supported by an affidavit stating–
    (a)   that the voluntary arrangement has been approved at a meeting of creditors;
    (b)   the date of the approval by the creditors; and
    (c)   that the 28 day period in section 262(3)(a) for applications to be made under section 262(1) has expired and no applications or appeal remain to be disposed of.

(3) The application and supporting affidavit shall be filed in court; and the court shall give to the bankrupt notice of the venue fixed for the hearing.

(4) The bankrupt shall give notice of the venue, accompanied by copies of the application and affidavit to the official receiver, any trustee who is not the official receiver, and the supervisor of the voluntary arrangement not less than 7 days before the date of the hearing.

(5) The official receiver, the supervisor of the voluntary arrangement and any trustee who is not the official receiver may attend the hearing or be represented and call to the attention of the court any matters which seem to him to be relevant.

(6) Where the court annuls a bankruptcy order, it shall send sealed copies of the order of annulment in Form 5.7 to the bankrupt, the official receiver, the supervisor of the voluntary arrangement and any trustee who is not the official receiver.

2.564

5.53 Notice to creditors

(1) Where the official receiver has notified creditors of the debtor's bankruptcy, and the bankruptcy order is annulled, he shall, as soon as reasonably practicable, notify them of the annulment.

(2) Expenses incurred by the official receiver in giving notice under this Rule are a charge in his favour on the property of the former bankrupt, whether or not actually in his hands.

(3) Where any property is in the hands of a trustee or any person other than the former bankrupt himself, the official receiver's charge is valid subject only to any costs that may be incurred by the trustee or that other person in effecting realisation of the property for the purpose of satisfying the charge.

Notes

RR 5.51–5.53

The rules in Chapter 8 set out the procedure that applies on a bankrupt's application under IA 1986 s 261(2)(a) to annul his bankruptcy order following the approval by his creditors of his IVA. The rules in Chapter 9 below set out the almost identical procedure which applies where the application to annul the bankruptcy is not made by the bankrupt himself but rather by the official receiver under IA 1986 s 261(2)(b) following the failure by the bankrupt to make the application himself.

The bankrupt may apply for the annulment of his bankruptcy at any time after the time for challenging the approval of his IVA under IA 1986 s 262 has expired – that is on the expiry of 28 days from the date the report is made to the court of the decision of the creditor's meeting approving the IVA, or, in the event a challenge is made within that period, following the disposal of the application and of any appeal against the decision on the application. Such an application may be made notwithstanding that the bankrupt has been discharged from his bankruptcy: see *Re Johnson* [2006] BPIR 987. Note:

- the bankrupt can apply if no challenge is made within the 28 day time period notwithstanding the fact that the 28 day time-limit for challenging the approval of the IVA may itself subsequently be extended; in the event that a challenge out of time is sought to be made to the approval of the IVA while an annulment application is pending, it is submitted that the application should be adjourned until the IVA challenge is finally disposed of.
- where a challenge under IA 1986 s 262 is made and dismissed, it is submitted that no application to annul can be made during the 14 day period within which the complainant has a right to bring an appeal against the order dismissing the challenge (under IA 1986 s 375), since, during that period there may be an appeal which 'remains to be disposed of': compare the wording of IA 1986 s 263D(4)(c) (the analogous annulment provision which applies following approval of a fast-track voluntary arrangement) where this is made rather more explicit; however, if no appeal is brought within that 14 day period, the annulment application can then be brought notwithstanding the fact that time for bringing an appeal against the order may subsequently be extended.

The official receiver may apply for the annulment of the bankruptcy under IA 1986 s 261(2)(b) in the event that the bankrupt has not made such application within 14 days after the time for challenging the approval of the IVA has expired, and where there is no application or appeal which, to the official receiver's knowledge, remains to be disposed of. See IR 1986 r 5.54 to 5.56 below.

Chapter 9
Application by Official Receiver to annul a bankruptcy order under section 261(2)(b)

2.565

5.54 Application of this Chapter

The following Rules apply where the official receiver applies for an annulment of a bankruptcy order under section 261(2)(b).

2.566

5.55 Application to court

(1) An application to the court to annul a bankruptcy order under section 261(2)(b) shall specify the section under which it is made.

(2) An application under section 261(2)(b) shall not be made before the expiry of 14 days from the date that the time period in section 262(3)(a) for applications under section 262(1) has expired.

(3) The application shall be supported by a report stating the grounds on which it is made. It shall also state that –
    (a)   the time period for application in paragraph (2) above has expired; and
    (b)   the official receiver is not aware that any application or appeal remains to be disposed of.

(4) The application and the report shall be filed in court and the court shall give to the official receiver notice of the venue fixed for the hearing.

(5) The official receiver shall give notice of the venue, accompanied by copies of the application and the report to the bankrupt not less than 7 days before the date of the hearing.

(6) Where the court annuls a bankruptcy order, it shall send sealed copies of the order of annulment in Form 5.7 to the official receiver, any trustee who is not the official receiver, the supervisor of the voluntary arrangement and the bankrupt.

2.567

5.56 Notice to creditors

(1) Where the bankruptcy order is annulled, the official receiver shall notify all creditors of whom he is aware of the annulment.

(2) Expenses incurred by the official receiver in giving notice under this Rule are a charge in his favour on the property of the former bankrupt, whether or not actually in his hands.

(3) Where any property is in the hands of a trustee or any person other than the former bankrupt himself, the official receiver's charge is valid subject only to any costs that may be incurred by the trustee or that other person in effecting realisation of the property for the purpose of satisfying the charge.

───────

Notes

RR 5.54–5.56

See the notes to IR 1986 r 5.51 to 5.53 above.

───────

Chapter 10
Application by Official Receiver to annul a bankruptcy order under section 263D(3)

2.568

5.57 Application of this Chapter

The following Rules apply where the official receiver applies for an annulment of a bankruptcy order under section 263D(3).

2.569

5.58 Application to court

(1) An application to the court to annul a bankruptcy order under section 263D(3) shall specify the section under which it is made.

(2) An application under section 263D(3) shall be made within 21 days of the expiry of the relevant period set out in section 263D(4).

(3) The application shall be supported by a report stating the grounds on which it is made and a statement by the official receiver that he is not aware that any application or appeal under section 263F remains to be disposed of.

(4) The report shall be accompanied by a copy of the proposal for the voluntary arrangement and a copy of the report under section 263C.

(5) The application, together with the report and the documents in support, shall be filed in court and the court shall give to the official receiver notice of the venue fixed for the hearing.

(6) The official receiver shall give notice of the venue, accompanied by copies of the application and the report, to the bankrupt not less than 7 days before the date of the hearing.

(7) Where the court annuls a bankruptcy order, it shall send sealed copies of the order of annulment in Form 5.8 to the official receiver and the bankrupt.

2.570

5.59 Notice to creditors

(1) Where the official receiver has notified creditors of the debtor's bankruptcy, and the bankruptcy order is annulled, he shall, as soon as reasonably practicable, notify them of the annulment.

(2) Expenses incurred by the official receiver in giving notice under this Rule are a charge in his favour on the property of the former bankrupt, whether or not actually in his hands.

(3) Where any property is in the hands of a trustee or any person other than the former bankrupt himself, the official receiver's charge is valid subject only to any costs that may be incurred by the trustee or that other person in effecting realisation of the property for the purpose of satisfying the charge.

Notes

RR 5.57–5.59

Chapter 10 sets out the rules which apply specifically to application to annul a bankruptcy by the official receiver under IA 1986 s 263D(3) following the approval of a FTVA. The procedure is similar to that which applies to annulment applications where a standard IVA has been approved under Chapters 8 and 9 above. The noteworthy differences are as follows:

- in contrast with standard IVAs, only the official receiver can make the application to annul the bankruptcy order following approval of a FTVA in respect of a bankrupt;
- the official receiver must make the annulment application within 21 days after the 28 day time period for challenging approval of the FTVA, or, as the case may be, the time for appealing any dismissal of any such application, has expired;
- since, in the case of a FTVA, neither the proposal nor any document will previously have been filed with the court, the official receiver is required to file the proposal together with his report of the outcome of the creditor's' vote on the proposal with the annulment application.

Chapter 11
Other matters arising on annulments under sections 261(2)(a), 261(2)(b) or 263D(3)

2.571

5.60

(1) In an order under section 261(2)(a), 261(2)(b) or 263D(3) the court shall include provision permitting vacation of the registration of the bankruptcy petition as a pending action, and of the bankruptcy order, in the register of writs and orders affecting land.

(2) The court shall as soon as reasonably practicable give notice of the making of the order to the Secretary of State.

(3) The former bankrupt may, in writing, within 28 days of the date of the order, require the Secretary of State to give notice of the making of the order –
    (a)   in the Gazette;

> (b) in any newspaper in which the bankruptcy order was advertised; or
>
> (c) in both.
>
> (4) [deleted].
>
> (5) Where the former bankrupt has died, or is a person incapable of managing his affairs (within the meaning of Chapter 7 in Part 7 of the Rules), the references to him in paragraph (3) is to be read as referring to his personal representative or, as the case may be, a person appointed by the court to represent or act for him.

Notes

R 5.60

This rule contains consequential provisions on the annulment of a bankruptcy order and replicates IR 1986 r 6.213, which applies to annulments under IA 1986 s 282(1) (and which formerly also applied to annulments under IA 1986 s 261). Note that it is a matter for the bankrupt whether he wishes the annulment of his bankruptcy to be advertised.

2.572

5.61 Trustee's final account

(1) Where a bankruptcy order is annulled under section 261(2)(a), 261(2)(b) or 263D(3), this does not of itself release the trustee from any duty or obligation, imposed on him by or under the Act or the Rules, to account for all his transactions in connection with the former bankrupt's estate.

(2) The trustee shall submit a copy of his final account to the Secretary of State as soon as reasonably practicable after the court's order annulling the bankruptcy order; and he shall file a copy of the final account in court.

(3) The final account must include a summary of the trustee's receipts and payments in the administration, and contain a statement to the effect that he has reconciled his account with that held by the Secretary of State in respect of the bankruptcy.

(4) The trustee is released from such time as the court may determine, having regard to whether paragraph (2) of this Rule has been complied with.

Notes

R 5.61

This rule replicates IR 1986 r 6.214, which applies to annulments under IA 1986 s 282(1) (and which used also to apply to annulments under IA 1986 s 261 before the introduction of this rule).

Chapter 12
EC Regulation: Conversion of Voluntary Arrangement into Bankruptcy

2.573

5.62 Application for conversion of voluntary arrangement into bankruptcy

(1) Where a member State liquidator proposes to apply to the court for conversion under Article 37 of the EC Regulation (conversion of earlier proceedings) of a voluntary arrangement into a bankruptcy, an affidavit complying with Rule 5.63 must be prepared and sworn, and filed in court in support of the application.

(2) The application and the affidavit required under this Rule shall be served upon–
    (a) the debtor; and
    (b) the supervisor.

2.574

5.63 Contents of affidavit

(1) The affidavit shall state –
  (a)   that the main proceedings have been opened in relation to the debtor in a member State other than the United Kingdom;
  (b)   the deponent's belief that the conversion of the voluntary arrangement into a bankruptcy would prove to be in the interests of the creditors in the main proceedings; and
  (c)   all other matters that, in the opinion of the member State liquidator, would assist the court –
    (i)   in deciding whether to make an order under Rule 5.64; and
    (ii) if the court were to do so, in considering the need for any consequential provision that would be necessary or desirable.

(2) An affidavit under this Rule shall be sworn by, or on behalf of, the member State liquidator.

2.575

5.64 Power of court

(1) On hearing an application for conversion of a voluntary arrangement into a bankruptcy, the court may make such order as it thinks fit.

(2) If the court makes an order for conversion of a voluntary arrangement into a bankruptcy under paragraph (1), the order may contain all such consequential provisions as the court deems necessary or desirable.

(3) Where the court makes an order for conversion of a voluntary arrangement into a bankruptcy under paragraph (1), any expenses properly incurred as expenses of the administration of the voluntary arrangement in question shall be a first charge on the bankrupt's estate.

2.575A

5.65 Notices to be given to State liquidator

(1) This Rule applies where a member State liquidator has been appointed in relation to the debtor.

(2) Where the supervisor is obliged to give notice to, or provide a copy of a document (including an order of the court) to, the court, or the official receiver, the supervisor shall give notice or provide copies, as appropriate, to the member State liquidator.]

Notes

S 5.62–5.65

These provisions were first introduced by the Insolvency (Amendment) Rules 2002 (SI 2002/1307) with effect from 31 May 2002 pursuant to the implementation of the EC Regulation on Insolvency Proceedings 2000. They provide for the procedure for applications under Article 37 of the EC Regulation for the conversion of a voluntary arrangement into a bankruptcy. This applies: (i) where the insolvent debtor is subject to insolvency proceedings in another member state which is its centre of main interests – the 'main proceedings' – as well as 'secondary proceedings' – the voluntary arrangement – in England and Wales; and (ii) where the liquidator in those proceedings considers that it would be in the interests of the creditors in the main proceedings to convert the voluntary arrangement into a bankruptcy. See the notes to the EC Regulation.

Part 6
Bankruptcy

Chapter 1
The Statutory Demand

2.576

6.1 Form and content of statutory demand

(1) A statutory demand under section 268 must be dated, and be signed either by the creditor himself or by a person stating himself to be authorised to make the demand on the creditor's behalf.

(2) The statutory demand must specify whether it is made under section 268(1) (debt payable immediately) or section 268(2) (debt not so payable).

(3) The demand must state the amount of the debt, and the consideration for it (or, if there is no consideration, the way in which it arises) and—

    (a)   if made under section 268(1) and founded on a judgment or order of a court, it must give details of the judgment or order, and

    (b)   if made under section 268(2), it must state the grounds on which it is alleged that the debtor appears to have no reasonable prospect of paying the debt.

(4) If the amount claimed in the demand includes—

> (a) any charge by way of interest not previously notified to the debtor as a liability of his, or
>
> (b) any other charge accruing from time to time,
>
> the amount or rate of the charge must be separately identified, and the grounds on which payment of it is claimed must be stated.
>
> In either case the amount claimed must be limited to that which has accrued due at the date of the demand.
>
> (5) If the creditor holds any security in respect of the debt, the full amount of the debt shall be specified, but—
>
> (a) there shall in the demand be specified the nature of the security, and the value which the creditor puts upon it as at the date of the demand, and
>
> (b) the amount of which payment is claimed by the demand shall be the full amount of the debt, less the amount specified as the value of the security.

Notes

R 6.1

For statutory demands generally see the notes to IA 1986 s 268. A statutory demand is a document produced and served by a creditor himself. It is not a court document – unlike the bankruptcy notices that were issued by the court under the former regime – and so leave to serve out of the jurisdiction is not needed (para 10 Practice Direction Insolvency Proceedings Civil Procedure Vol 2 Section 3*E*). IA 1986 s 268 requires that a statutory demand be 'in the prescribed form'. This is a reference to Forms 6.1–3 in the IR 1986. The use of these forms is mandatory (IR 1986 r 12.7(1); *Practice Note (Bankruptcy: prescribed forms)* [1988] 1 WLR 557). However, where appropriate, the forms can be modified (IR 1986 r 12.7(2)). The purpose of requiring that the prescribed form be used is to ensure that the demand contains the prescribed information warning the debtor of the consequences of non-compliance with it. However, a defective form may not necessarily be invalid. The court will always ask whether the defect caused actual prejudice to the debtor: *Re a Debtor (No 1 of 1987)* [1989] 1 WLR 271. See further the notes to IR 1986 r 6.5. Because serving a statutory demand not amount to a step in 'insolvency proceedings', the general saving provision in IR 1986 r 7.55 is of no application: *Re a Debtor (No 190 of 1987)*, Times, 21 May 1988.

R 6.1(1)

If the creditor is not preparing the demand and signing it himself, care should be taken. There are two issues to remember: authority and the form of signature. If the person preparing and signing the demand is not authorised to do so, it is not the creditor's demand and so falls outside IA 1986 s 268 (although query whether that could be ratified by the creditor). But if the person signing on the creditor's behalf does not state that he is so authorised, there is a risk that the debtor will not take it to be the creditor's demand – hence the requirement of this rule: see *Horne v Dacorum BC* [2000] BPIR 1047.

R 6.1(2)

Three forms of statutory demand are provided. Form 6.1 relates to debts which are payable immediately. Form 6.2 relate to claims for debts founded on a judgment or order of a court which are payable immediately. Form 6.3 relates to debts payable in the future – note that this form requires that the creditor state why he thinks that the debtor will not be in position to pay the debt (see also the notes to s 268(2) IA 1986). The use of the wrong form should not be fatal to the statutory demand provided that no substantial confusion is caused as a result: *Cartwright v Staffordshire and Moorlands DC* [1998] BPIR 328.

R 6.1(3)

The forms of statutory demand contain a number of instructions to assist with their completion. Regard should be had to those instructions. In particular the description of the debt and when it is payable should be clear and understandable and supported by a reference to any relevant statutory provision. If the debt has come to the creditor by way of an assignment, it is particularly important to fill out the part of the form dealing with the assignment. Otherwise, there is a risk that the debtor will not recognise the debt being referred to. If this causes genuine confusion, the demand could be set aside.

R 6.1(4)

The amount of the debt and interest if claimed must be stated. Interest must only be calculated to the date of the demand. The grounds upon which interest is claimed must also be set out. Whilst every attempt should be made to state the amount of the debt correctly a misstatement of the debt should not be fatal to the demand unless it causes actual prejudice: see the notes to IR 1986 r 6.5(4)(d).

R 6.1(5)

Any security held should be stated. Here, security has the same meaning as it does in the IA 1986: see s 383. The security must be held by the creditor over the debtor's property rather than that of a third party (*Re a Debtor (No 310 of 1988)* [1989] 1 WLR 452 and it must relate to the debt in question. If the statutory demand does not mention security or incorrectly states the security then the demand should be set aside if prejudice has been caused by the omission; but absent prejudice then the statutory demand may stand (*Re a Debtor (No 106 of 1992)* [1996] BPIR 190). If the debt demanded is completely secured, that in itself can provide a ground for setting the demand aside: IR 1986 r 6.5(4)(c).

2.577

6.2 Information to be given in statutory demand

(1) The statutory demand must include an explanation to the debtor of the following matters—
  (a) the purpose of the demand, and the fact that, if the debtor does not comply with the demand, bankruptcy proceedings may be commenced against him;
  (b) the time within which the demand must be complied with, if that consequence is to be avoided;
  (c) the methods of compliance which are open to the debtor; and
  (d) his right to apply to the court for the statutory demand to be set aside.

(2) The demand must specify one or more named individuals with whom the debtor may, if he wishes, enter into communication with a view to securing or compounding for the debt to the satisfaction of the creditor or (as the case may be) establishing to the creditor's satisfaction that there is a reasonable prospect that the debt will be paid when it falls due.

In the case of any individual so named in the demand, his address and telephone number (if any) must be given.

Notes

R 6.2(1)

These provisions are important and must be complied with. They set out the information to be provided in the demand informing the debtor of his rights and duties as regards the demand.

Therefore any failure as regards these requirements is likely to cause injustice to a debtor. In relation to the time limits see IR 1986 r 6.4 and IA 1986 s 268. But, provided that the proper forms are used, there should be no such failure.

R 6.2(2)

The individual to contact need not be the creditor but can be a person authorised on the creditor's behalf and the individual must be named. It is not enough to state a corporate name. This is clearly due to the use of the word 'individual' rather than 'person' in accordance with the Interpretation Act 1978.

Financial Services Authority demands

IR 1986 r 6.1 to 6.2 are modified where a demand is made by the Financial Services Authority (under the Financial Services and Markets Act 2000, s 372(4)(a)): see the Bankruptcy (Financial Services and Markets Act 2000) Rules 2001, SI 2001/3634, r 3, 5.

2.578

6.3 Requirements as to service

(1) Rule 6.11 in Chapter 2 below has effect as regards service of the statutory demand, and proof of that service by affidavit to be filed with a bankruptcy petition.

(2) The creditor is, by virtue of the Rules, under an obligation to do all that is reasonable for the purpose of bringing the statutory demand to the debtor's attention and, if practicable in the particular circumstances, to cause personal service of the demand to be effected.

(3) Where the statutory demand is for payment of a sum due under a judgment or order of any court and the creditor knows, or believes with reasonable cause—

    (a)   that the debtor has absconded or is keeping out of the way with a view to avoiding service, and

    (b)   there is no real prospect of the sum due being recovered by execution or other process.

the demand may be advertised in one or more newspapers; and the time limited for compliance with the demand runs from the date of the advertisement's appearance or (as the case may be) its first appearance.

Notes

R 6.3(1)

This provision deals with service of the demand. It is supplemented by the provisions of IR 1986 r 6.11 which deals with proof of service, and by para 11 Practice Direction : Insolvency Proceedings Civil Procedure Vol 2 Sect 3E, which should be followed to the letter. If a demand needs to be served out of the jurisdiction the procedure set out in para 10 Practice Direction: Insolvency Proceedings (Civil Procedure Vol 2, Sect 3E) must be followed.

R 6.3(2)

The usual practice is that the demand is to be personally served such that the demand is handed to the debtor. This means that if service cannot be affected at the residential premises of the debtor then attempts should be made to serve the demand at both the residential premises and the business premises of the debtor (*Regional Collection Services v Heald* [2000] BPIR 661). As a matter of practicality, the person serving the demand should always keep detailed notes of the personal service, and in particular a description of the person served. This evidence can be invaluable if a petition is later contested on service grounds.

If personal service cannot be effected then service can be effected by other means (para 11.1 Practice Direction: Insolvency Proceedings (Civil Procedure Vol 2 Sect 3E) so long as the creditor can show on the evidence that he has done all that is reasonably practicable to effect personal service; this is a stringent test (*Anderson v Kas Bank NV* [2004] BPIR 685, *Takavarasha v Newham Borough Council* [2006] BPIR 311). Guidance on what a creditor needs to show to prove he has taken all reasonable steps can be found in the provisions on substituted service of a petition in para 11.4 Practice Direction: Insolvency Proceedings (Civil Procedure Vol 2, Sect 3E). The means adopted (which can include by post, insertion through a letter box or – in appropriate cases – by advertisement) must on the balance of probabilities be likely to bring the petition to the attention of the debtor. For example in *Lilly v Davison* [1999] BPIR 81 advertisement was permitted in the Evening Standard once it was shown that the debtor lived in London. Service can be affected on a debtor's solicitor provided that the claimant has been notified that the solicitor is entitled to accept service (*Re a Debtor (Nos 234 and 236)* The Independent June 29 1992).

R 6.3(3)

Advertisement as a means of service is only allowed in the circumstances set out in this rule. The risks of the debtor not becoming aware of a demand in this form are plain. But, at least, a judgment debtor can be expected to know or have notice of his debt. Where this method of 'service' is used, the creditor must be able to show how he comes to believe that the two further conditions are made out: see IR 1986 R 6.11(8). As the creditor would need to be able to show that execution will not bear fruit, and the best way of showing that is by attempting it and failing, in many cases the creditor will prefer to avoid a statutory demand altogether and to petition on failed-execution grounds under s 268(1)(b) IA 1986. The form of advertisement set out in para 11.2 Practice Direction: Insolvency Proceedings (Civil Procedure Vol 2, Sect 3E) should be used and the guidance there followed.

2.579

6.4 Application to set aside statutory demand

(1) The debtor may, within the period allowed by this Rule, apply to the appropriate court for an order setting the statutory demand aside.

That period is 18 days from the date of the service on him of the statutory demand or, where the demand is advertised in a newspaper pursuant to Rule 6.3, from the date of the advertisement's appearance or (as the case may be) its first appearance.

(2) Where the creditor issuing the statutory demand is a Minister of the Crown or a Government Department, and—

   (a) the debt in respect of which the demand is made, or a part of it equal to or exceeding the bankruptcy level (within the meaning of section 267), is the subject of a judgment or order of any court, and

   (b) the statutory demand specifies the date of the judgment or order and the court in which it was obtained, but indicates the creditor's intention to present a bankruptcy petition against the debtor in the High Court, the appropriate court under this Rule is the High Court; and in any other case it is that to which the debtor would, in accordance with paragraphs (1) and (2) of Rule 6.40 in Chapter 3 below, present his own bankruptcy petition.

(3) As from (inclusive) the date on which the application is filed in court, the time limited for compliance with the statutory demand ceases to run, subject to any order of the court under Rule 6.5(6).

(4) The debtor's application shall be supported by an affidavit—
  (a) specifying the date on which the statutory demand came into his hands, and
  (b) stating the grounds on which he claims that it should be set aside.

The affidavit shall have exhibited to it a copy of the statutory demand.

Notes

R 6.4(1)

This provision deals with the mechanics by which an application to set aside a statutory demand is to be made. The test applicable on such an application is set out in IR 1986 r 6.5 below. Though it was said in *Barnes v Whitehead* [2004] BPIR 693 that the correct time to challenge a demand is at the set aside hearing stage it was also said that the debtor can instead wait for a petition to be presented and then raise a dispute. In practice though, there is unlikely ever to be a good reason for waiting. The only reason could be that the debtor's grounds for his application are complex and need a lot of time to be prepared. Because a failure to set aside a demand will usually prevent the same arguments being run at the petition stage (see the notes to IA 1986 s 271(1)), the debtor will want to ensure that he gets it right first time. However, this is really a reason for seeking appropriate directions under IR 1986 r 6.5(3).

How to make the application

R 6.4(1) should be read in conjunction with para 12 Practice Direction: Insolvency Proceedings (Civil Procedure Vol 2, Sect 3E). Forms are prescribed for use in such an application; Form 6.4 for the application which sets out the grounds on which the application can be founded and Form 6.5 which sets out the affidavit in support. The forms prescribed must be used and any fee paid (*Ariyo v Sovereign Leasing plc* [1998] BPIR 177). The application should be made to the court which is stated on the statutory demand. Three copies of the demand and all documents must be lodged with the court so as to enable service of the application para 12 Practice Direction: Insolvency Proceedings (Civil Procedure Vol 2, Sect 3E).

When to make the application

Any application must be made within 18 days from service or from first advertisement. The 18 days means 18 clear days in accordance with CPR Part 2.8(2). Consideration needs to be given where substituted service is effected as to when time starts to run and this is dealt with under the provisions of CPR Part 6.7. Once an application is made time ceases to run. If the application is made outside the 18 day time period then the evidence must explain the reason for this and the application must include a request for an extension of time. Such a request will be dealt with under IA 1986 s 376. In the event of a late application then the creditor is entitled to present a petition unless the debtor makes an application for an order to restrain such presentation pending determination of his application. The additional details in relation to either application are set out in para 12 Practice Direction:Insolvency Proceedings (Civil Procedure Vol 2, Sect 3E). The test on an application for an order restraining presentation is the balance of convenience unless it is clear that the application to set aside the demand should be dismissed.

Dealing with the application

If the application to set aside discloses no case then the application can be dismissed without a hearing or notice to the creditor. Otherwise, there will be a hearing in accordance with IR 1986 r 6.5. Seven days' notice of the hearing must be given to the creditor, the debtor and the persons named in the demand. When the demand is being made by the Financial Services Authority (under the Financial Services and Markets Act 2000, s 372(4)(a)) then this provision is modified by the Bankruptcy (Financial Services and Markets Act 2000) Rules 2001, SI 2001/3634, r 3, 7.

2.580

6.5 Hearing of application to set aside

(1) On receipt of an application under Rule 6.4, the court may, if satisfied that no sufficient cause is shown for it, disMiss it without giving notice to the creditor. As from (inclusive) the date on which the application is dismissed, the time limited for compliance with the statutory demand runs again.

(2) If the application is not dismissed under paragraph (1), the court shall fix a venue for it to be heard, and shall give at least 7 days' notice of it to—

    (a)   the debtor or, if the debtor's application was made by a solicitor acting for him, to the solicitor,

    (b)   the creditor, and

    (c)   whoever is named in the statutory demand as the person with whom the debtor may enter into communication with reference to the demand (or, if more than one person is so named, the first of them).

(3) On the hearing of the application, the court shall consider the evidence then available to it, and may either summarily determine the application or adjourn it, giving such directions as it thinks appropriate.

(4) The court may grant the application if—

    (a)   the debtor appears to have a counterclaim, set-off or cross demand which equals or exceeds the amount of the debt or debts specified in the statutory demand; or

    (b)   the debt is disputed on grounds which appear to the court to be substantial; or

    (c)   it appears that the creditor holds some security in respect of the debt claimed by the demand, and either Rule 6.1(5) is not complied with in respect of it, or the court is satisfied that the value of the security equals or exceeds the full amount of the debt; or

    (d)   the court is satisfied, on other grounds, that the demand ought to be set aside.

(5) Where the creditor holds some security in respect of his debt, and Rule 6.1(5) is complied with in respect of it but the court is satisfied that the security is under-valued in the statutory demand, the creditor may be required to amend the demand accordingly (but without prejudice to his right to present a bankruptcy petition by reference to the original demand).

> (6) If the court dismisses the application, it shall make an order authoris-
> ing the creditor to present a bankruptcy petition either forthwith, or on
> or after a date specified in the order.
>
> A copy of the order shall be sent by the court forthwith to the creditor.

Notes

R 6.5

This provision sets out how the court will deal with the application to set aside the statutory demand. Reference should be made to para 12, para 16.3(1) Practice Direction: Insolvency Proceedings (Civil Procedure Vol 2, Sect 3E).

R 6.5(1)

This power allows the court to weed out applications which are obviously bound to fail. It is also commonly used where the statutory demand is based on a judgment debt and, under para 12.3 Practice Direction: Insolvency Proceedings (Civil Procedure Vol 2, Sect 3E), where the court declines to deal with the debtor's arguments. The fact that the court has summarily dismissed the application on this ground will not mean that the arguments cannot be raised again at the petition stage. For a discussion of when arguments raised on the statutory demand will prevent their being reargued on the petition, see the notes to s 271(1) IA 1986 in this work.

R 6.5(2)

The specified parties must be given 7 days notice of the hearing. This includes details of the date, time and location of the hearing. In accordance with CPR Part 2.8(2) the 7 days must be 7 clear days.

R 6.5(3)

At the first hearing of the application, the court may decide to deal with it there and then. In many cases this will be possible. However, in other cases, it will be appropriate to give directions, for example as to further evidence and, in some cases, disclosure. Often it is impractical to deal with these applications at a first hearing simply because of insufficient time. The need to attend the first hearing may be avoided if the parties can agree directions and present them to the court in advance. However, parties should beware that agreeing directions does not displace the court's power to deal with the matter substantively or the obligation expressly imposed by this rule on the court to consider the merits of the application. The risk is that the court may decline to make the directions as sought and can dismiss the application. But this should only happen in plain and obvious cases: for a discussion see *Jay Benning Peltz v Deutsch* [2001] BPIR 510.

R 6.5(4)

The four grounds set out in this part of the rule provide the only bases on which a statutory demand can be set aside. The court cannot enquire into the broad justice of the matter. Matters going to unfairness – if they are to be relevant at all – *must fall into the principles that apply to* ground (d). Although determination of the application is a summary procedure, the court can nonetheless determine matters of law, rather than being bound to find that there is a triable issue as to what the law is: see *Global Financial Recoveries Ltd v Jones* [2000] BPIR 1029. But the court's role is not to resolve matters of fact (although see the notes to R 6.5(4)(c)). Rather it must determine whether any of the four grounds is made out. Therefore a 'mini-trial' of disputed issues of fact will be inappropriate – for a discussion of 'mini-trials' in the context of CPR Part 24, see *Swain v Hillman* [2001] 1 All ER 91.

Having heard the application, the court must either allow it or dismiss it. It cannot make an order on conditions, e g on making a payment into court of the sum claimed in the demand: see *Higgins v Valambia* [2004] EWHC 429 (Ch), [2004] BPIR 876. An appeal against the decision of the Registrar is a 'true appeal' and the appeal court must be satisfied that the Registrar was wrong if the appeal is to be allowed, *Union Bank v Pathak* [2006] BPIR 1062, *Williamson v Governor of the Bank of Scotland* [2006] BPIR 1085. Practice Direction: Insolvency Proceedings para 17.8, Civil Procedure Vol 2 Section 3E.

R 6.5(4)(a)

The requirement that the debtor has a counterclaim, set-off or cross demand does not mean the claim asserted by the debtor must have any particular relationship to the claim made in the statutory demand. Para 12.4 of the Practice Direction: Insolvency Proceedings (Civil Procedure Vol 2 Section 3E) makes this clear as indeed does the reference to a 'cross demand': compare *Popely v Popely* [2004] BPIR 778. But it is necessary that the counterclaim or cross demand exist between the parties in the same capacities as the debt claimed in the statutory demand: see *Hurst v Bennett* [2001] BPIR 287. Often the relationship between debtor and creditor will be subject to a 'no set-off clause' in the agreement between them. The effect of this type of clause – if in the right form – is to prevent one party raising set-off defences to sums due to the other. The courts generally give effect to these on applications for summary judgment or when one party seeks to execute a judgment debt against the other. But such a clause does not prevent the court from considering a set-off on an application to set aside a statutory demand and nor is it a matter that it will necessarily take into account in exercising its discretion: see *McAllister v Society of Lloyds* [1999] BPIR 548. This reflects the fact that set-off is essentially a procedural remedy, which allows claims to be heard together with the court giving judgment for the net amount. No-set-off clauses are primarily concerned with the order in which the parties are to be paid, ie whether someone with an admitted claim must wait for another dispute to be resolved before getting judgment. So too is the 'cheque rule', which excludes set-off as a defence to an action on a cheque (as to which see *Hofer v Strawson* [1999] BPIR 501). This concept of set-off as a procedural matter has no place in these kinds of application, where the main issue for the court (subject to the terms of the rules) is whether the facts of the case are such that non-payment of the sum demanded should fairly lead to the statutory inference that the debtor is insolvent (see the comments of Nicholls LJ in *Re a Debtor (No 1 of 1987)* [1989] 1 WLR 271). One can see that in some cases the non-payment of an admitted debt on the basis of an assertion of a cross-demand will fall on one side of the line and other cases on the other. It will all depend on the surrounding circumstances. For example the court may wonder why a cross-claim has not been asserted or made in other proceedings or otherwise before the service of the statutory demand: for a discussion in the context of winding-up petitions see *Southern Cross Group plc v Deka Immobilien Investments* [2005] BPIR 1010.

The standard to which the debtor must prove his counterclaim, set-off or cross demand is given in para 12.4 of the Practice Direction:Insolvency Proceedings (Civil Procedure Vol 2 Section 3E). The court must be satisfied on the evidence that there is 'a triable issue'. This standard is somewhat lower than the real prospect of success prescribed by CPR Part 24 *Wilson v Edwards* [2006] BPIR 367. It is rather closer to the old summary judgment test under *RSC Order 14*: see the discussion in *Kellar v BBR Graphic Engineers (Yorks) Ltd* [2002] BPIR 544. The fact that the debtor's claim has previously been dismissed summarily in other proceedings does not preclude the court from finding that there is a triable issue, although it should be slow to grant the application in these circumstances: see *Society of Lloyds v Bowman* [2004] BPIR 324. Clearly, the debtor must produce all available evidence to show that there is such a triable issue. It will not be sufficient simply to make bare assertions. Nor will it be sufficient merely to indicate how a triable issue could arise and claim that the matter needs further investigation; see *Bank of Scotland v Williamson* [2006] EWHC 1289 (Ch), citing *Lady Anne Tennant v Associated Newspapers Group Ltd* [1979] FSR 298. In resisting an application on this ground, the creditor cannot set up another claim against the debtor, which has not been demanded in the statutory demand, with a view to demonstrating that the debtor still owes him money on aggregate: *Bennett v Filmer* [1998] BPIR 444.

If the debtor's claim does not exceed the amount of the demand, or if it cannot be shown to do so to the requisite standard, then the debtor must pay enough of the balance to reduce the debt below the bankruptcy level. If he does not then his application will fail.

R 6.5(4)(b)

This ground applies where the debtor can demonstrate that the debt is disputed on substantial grounds. Provided the debt is not a judgment debt – in which case it will usually dismiss the application (Practice Direction:Insolvency Proceedings (Civil Procedure Vol 2, Sect 3E) para 12.3 – the court will set the demand aside if it finds that there is a triable issue on the dispute: see para 12.4 Practice Direction: Insolvency Proceedings (Civil Procedure Vol 2, Sect 3E). As to what that involves, see the note to r 6.5(4)(a) above.

In establishing this ground it is essential that the dispute relates to the whole of the debt demanded or enough of it so that the undisputed part is less than £750. A dispute that leaves more than that amount unchallenged will not suffice. The court will not set aside a demand simply because the amount of debt in it is overstated: see e g *Re a Debtor (No 1 of 1987)* [1989] 1 WLR 271. But if the debtor can show that the overstatement has somehow caused him genuine prejudice, then this may provide a basis for setting aside the demand under r 6.5(4)(d) – see below.

R 6.5(4)(c)

In this ground, 'security' has the same meaning as in r 6.1(5) IR1986 and in s 383(2) IA 1986. It will be made out either where the security has not been disclosed, or where the debt is fully secured. This reflects the policy that secured creditors cannot initiate bankruptcy proceedings without giving up their security, as strictly they have no interest in it.

While the ground is satisfied if there is some undeclared security, it is hard to see why the demand should be set aside if the unsecured amount is equal to or exceeds the bankruptcy level – £750. The court will only set the demand aside in those circumstances if the debtor can show that the non-disclosure has caused the debtor real prejudice: *Re a Debtor (No 106 of 1992)* [1996] BPIR 190. Where the security is merely under-valued, and the unsecured amount exceeds the bankruptcy level, then provided that there has been no real prejudice, the appropriate thing for the court to do would be to direct that the demand be amended under r 6.5(5) IR 1986.

Where there is a dispute as to the value of the security, the court must be 'satisfied' that its value equals or exceeds the debt. This indicates that the court needs to satisfy itself on the balance of probabilities what the value is. Where there is a dispute as to the basis of valuation, it will usually be appropriate to value it on a forced sale basis: see *Platts v Western Trust & Savings* [1996] BPIR 339. That case also highlights the need for the debtor to ensure that appropriate directions are given both as to expert valuation evidence and the possibility of cross-examination of experts.

R 6.5(4)(d)

This is a sweeping-up provision which allows the court to set aside statutory demands where there is some other good reason why the creditor should not be allowed be proceed to a petition. The courts have deliberately declined to set out all of the circumstances where this ground might apply. But the overriding test was explained in *Re a Debtor (No 1 of 1987)* [1989] 1 WLR 271, where Nichols LJ explained that, as non-compliance with a statutory demand leads to the statutory presumption of insolvency, this ground requires that there be something that makes it unfair for the court to draw that inference. A classic example is the defective demand. But, as explained in that case, the practice that applied to the old bankruptcy notice procedure under BA 1914 does not apply to the new procedure. Formerly, demands that were defective in some respect would often be taken to be ineffective without further enquiry. But now, in considering defective demands, the court will ask whether the defect has caused the debtor actual prejudice. This question is asked not as at the time of service, but as at the time of the hearing. Therefore a demand that fails to set out the basis of the debt may be set aside if the debtor was genuinely confused by it, and he could not decide whether he was legally liable to pay it. But if, notwithstanding the defect, he knew what the debt was for, or he had no means or intention to pay, then he has suffered no prejudice and the demand will stand. In practice then, defective demands – as opposed demands which cannot be characterised as statutory demands at all because, for example, they omit to demand payment or contain some other fundamental mistake – will rarely lead to actual prejudice as at the date of the hearing because the creditor will usually have remedied the omission or in clarity by serving evidence in response to the application to set aside. In those circumstances, the court may only be required to decide whether the debtor should be given more time to pay (under r 6.5(6) IR 1986). An interesting example of these principles in action is *Coulter v Chief of Dorset Police* [2005] BPIR 62.

It is worth noting that r 7.55 IR 1986, which saves any formally defective insolvency proceedings as long as the defect has not caused any prejudice, does not apply to statutory demands, as these are not insolvency proceedings but rather the unilateral act of the creditor: see *Re a Debtor (190 of 1987)* (1988) Times, 21 May.

The other circumstances where the court may find that r 6.5(4)(d) is made out cannot be exhaustively listed because of the deliberately open-ended terms of the provision. But in *Budge v Budge (Contractors) Ltd* [1997] BPIR 366 the court said that the circumstances must disclose something as substantial as in grounds 6.5(4)(a)–(c). It also approved a passage from *Muir Hunter on Personal Insolvency* (para 7–204) which points to the possible relevance of the marginal notes on the pro-forma affidavit for setting aside the demand. These mention an offer to compound the debt, a stay of execution of a judgment debt and non-compliance with the Insolvency Rules. An example of a setting-aside under ground 6.5(4)(d) is *Re a Debtor (Nos 49 and 50 of 1992)* [1995] Ch 66 where a bona fide dispute was found as to part of the debt, leaving less than £750 undisputed. While this would not have allowed the demand to be set aside under r 6.5(4)(b), it was appropriate to set the demand aside under ground (d), because the demand could not have supported a bankruptcy petition. Compare *City Electrical Factors v Hardingham* [1996] BPIR 541 where, at the hearing of the application to set aside the demand, the debtor offered to pay enough of the debt to reduce it below the bankruptcy level.

R 6.5(6)

When an application to set aside a statutory demand is filed at court, the debtor's time for compliance with it ceases to run: r 6.4(3) IR 1986. The effect of r 6.5(6) is to allow the court to authorise the presentation of a bankruptcy petition notwithstanding that the debtor has not had his full 21 days to pay. The terms of the rule direct the court to set a date in any event. The purpose of this is clear – to underline for the debtor when he must pay by. In most cases, the application will have taken months from the date of filing to be finally determined and so the court may take the view that the debtor has had ample time to pay, or at least to raise the money to pay in the event that the application failed. The court may also take the view that immediate presentation is appropriate where there is a likelihood that the debtor's trustee in bankruptcy will want to apply to set aside pre-bankruptcy transactions. This is because, with certain applications of this kind, transactions can only be set aside if they took place within a certain period before the presentation of the petition: see s 341 IA 1986. For a discussion of this rule see *Neely v IRC* [1996] BPIR 632.

That case indicates that it may be appropriate to postpone the presentation of the petition if the debtor can show a reasonable prospect of being able to pay the debt within a short time, or if he has an appeal with a reasonable prospect of success. However, it is submitted, it will rarely be appropriate to postpone presentation pending the determination of an appeal. This is for two reasons. First, in most cases where a debtor seeks to set aside a statutory demand, he is seeking to raise triable issues of fact and, if the court thinks that he has a reasonable prospect of successfully appealing the way that it has approached these issues, it probably ought to have set the demand aside. Second, there is a practical problem in that the rule requires the court to set a date for presentation of the petition. But, usually, the court will have no way of knowing how long it will take to prepare, list and hear an appeal. In all save unusual cases, the best course is to leave it to the debtor to apply to the appeal court for an order restraining presentation of the petition pending the appeal. The creditor would have to take a view on whether to oppose that application or not.

The power to postpone presentation under this rule may also be used to substantive effect on the application to set aside the demand. Where the debtor is complaining about some defect or irregularity which is remedied before the hearing, the court may dismiss the application but postpone the date for presentation long enough so that the debtor has had three weeks to pay after the defect was remedied: see *Coulter v Chief of Dorset Police* [2005] BPIR 62, para 27.

Financial Services Authority demands

IR 1986 r 6.5 is modified in relation to a statutory demand by the Financial Services Authority (under the Financial Services and Markets Act 2000, s 372(4)(a)), by the Bankruptcy (Financial Services and Markets Act 2000) Rules 2001, SI 2001/3634, r 3, 6.

Chapter 2
Bankruptcy Petition (Creditor's)

2.581

6.6 Preliminary

The Rules in this Chapter relate to a creditor's petition, and the making of a bankruptcy order thereon; and in those Rules 'the debt' means, except where the context otherwise requires, the debt (or debts) in respect of which the petition is presented.

Those Rules also apply to a petition under section 264(1)(c) (supervisor of, or person bound by, voluntary arrangement), with any necessary modifications.

2.582

6.7 Identification of debtor

(1) The petition shall state the following matters with respect to the debtor, so far as they are within the petitioner's knowledge—
   (a) his name, place of residence and occupation (if any);
   (b) the name or names in which he carries on business if other than his true name, and whether, in the case of any business of a specified nature, he carries it on alone or with others;
   (c) the nature of his business and the address or addresses at which he carries it on;
   (d) any name or names, other than his true name, in which he has carried on business at or after the time when the debt was incurred, and whether he has done so alone or with others;
   (e) any address or addresses at which he has resided or carried on business at or after that time, and the nature of that business;
   (f) whether the debtor has his centre of main interests or an establishment in another member State.

(2) The particulars of the debtor given under this Rule determine the full title of the proceedings.

(3) If to the petitioner's personal knowledge the debtor has used any name other than the one specified under paragraph (1)(a), that fact shall be stated in the petition.

Notes

R 6.7

Under IR 1986 r 7.55 no insolvency proceedings shall be invalidated by any formal defect or irregularity unless the court considers that substantial injustice has been caused by the defect or irregularity and that injustice cannot be remedied by any order of the court. The failure to deal with the applicability of the EC Regulation on Insolvency Proceedings in the standard form petitions is a substantive defect and it is unlikely to be waived; see former Insolvency Proceedings – Practice Note 1/2002, 10 May 2002. The court may amend the title of the proceedings to correct inaccuracies in naming the debtor: r 6.35 IR 1986. The unusual case of *Sadrolashrafi v Marvel International Food Logistics Ltd* [2004] EWHC 777 (Ch), [2004] BPIR 834 demonstrates the importance of getting names right in the demand and the petition.

R 6.7(3)

Failure to list aliases in the petition will not automatically invalidate the petition *Michael Yee Fun Chu v Price* [2004] BPIR 603.

2.583

6.8 Identification of debt

(1) There shall be stated in the petition, with reference to every debt in respect of which it is presented—
  (a) the amount of the debt, the consideration for it (or, if there is no consideration, the way in which it arises) and the fact that it is owed to the petitioner;
  (b) when the debt was incurred or became due;
  (c) if the amount of the debt includes—
    (i) any charge by way of interest not previously notified to the debtor as a liability of his, or
    (ii) any other charge accruing from time to time,
  the amount or rate of the charge (separately identified) and the grounds on which it is claimed to form part of the debt[, provided that such amount or rate must, in the case of a petition based on a statutory demand, be limited to that claimed in that demand];
  (d) either—
    (i) that the debt is for a liquidated sum payable immediately, and the debtor appears to be unable to pay it, or
    (ii) that the debt is for a liquidated sum payable at some certain, future time (that time to be specified), and the debtor appears to have no reasonable prospect of being able to pay it,
and, in either case (subject to section 269) that the debt is unsecured.

(2) Where the debt is one for which, under section 268, a statutory demand must have been served on the debtor—
  (a) there shall be specified the date and manner of service of the statutory demand, and
  (b) it shall be stated that, to the best of the creditor's knowledge and belief—
    (i) the demand has been neither complied with nor set aside in accordance with the Rules, and
    (ii) no application to set it aside is outstanding.

> (3) If the case is within section 268(1)(b) (debt arising under judgment or order of court; execution returned unsatisfied), the court from which the execution or other process issued shall be specified, and particulars shall be given relating to the return.

Notes

R 6.8

The debt on which the petition is based must be the same debt as was the subject of the statutory demand: see para 15.3 Practice Direction: Insolvency Proceedings (Civil Procedure Vol 2, Sect 3E). As to when formal defects in the petition will invalidate it, see IR 1986 r 7.55.

R 6.8(1)(d)(ii)

Where the basis of the petition is a debt for a liquidated sum payable at some certain, future time (and the debtor appears to have no reasonable prospect of being able to pay it) the debtor can apply for an order for security for costs under IR 1986 r 6.17.

2.584

6.9 Court in which petition to be presented

(1) In the following cases, the petition shall be presented to the High Court—

    (a)   if the petition is presented by a Minister of the Crown or a Government Department, and either in any statutory demand on which the petition is based the creditor has indicated the intention to present a bankruptcy petition to that Court, or the petition is presented under section 268(1)(b), or

    (b)   if the debtor has resided or carried on business within the London insolvency district for the greater part of the 6 months immediately preceding the presentation of the petition, or for a longer period in those 6 months than in any other insolvency district, or

    (c)   if the debtor is not resident in England and Wales, or

    (d)   if the petitioner is unable to ascertain the residence of the debtor, or his place of business.

(2) In any other case the petition shall be presented to the county court for the insolvency district in which the debtor has resided or carried on business for the longest period during those 6 months.

(3) If the debtor has for the greater part of those 6 months carried on business in one insolvency district and resided in another, the petition shall be presented to the court for the insolvency district in which he has carried on business.

(4) If the debtor has during those 6 months carried on business in more than one insolvency district, the petition shall be presented to the court for the insolvency district in which is, or has been for the longest period in those 6 months, his principal place of business.

(4A) Notwithstanding any other provision of this Rule, where there is in force for the debtor a voluntary arrangement under Part VIII of the Act, the petition shall be presented to the court to which the nominee's report under section 256 or section 256A or 263C was submitted.

(5) The petition shall contain sufficient information to establish that it is brought in the appropriate court.

Notes

R 6.9(1)(a)

Where a demand is made by the Financial Services Authority under s 372(4)(a) Financial Services and Markets Act 2000 then IR 1986 r 6.9 does not apply Bankruptcy (Financial Services and Markets Act 2000) Rules 2001 (SI 2001/3634).

R 6.9(4)(A)

This will ordinarily be the court to which the debtor would be entitled to present his own petition in bankruptcy IR 1986 r 5.8, r 6.40.

2.585

6.10 Procedure for presentation and filing

(1) The petition, verified by affidavit in accordance with Rule 6.12(1) below, shall be filed in court.

(2) No petition shall be filed unless there is produced on presentation of the petition a receipt for the deposit payable or paragraph (2A) applies.

(2A) This paragraph applies in any case where the Secretary of State has given written notice to the court that the petitioner has made suitable alternative arrangements for the payment of the deposit to the official receiver and such notice has not been revoked in relation to the petitioner in accordance with paragraph (2B).

(2B) A notice of the kind referred to in paragraph (2A) may be revoked in relation to the petitioner in whose favour it is given by a further notice in writing to the court stating that the earlier notice is revoked in relation to the petitioner.

(3) The following copies of the petition shall also be delivered to the court with the petition—
  (a)   one for service on the debtor, ...
  (b)   one to be exhibited to the affidavit verifying that service, and
  (c)   if there is in force for the debtor a voluntary arrangement under Part VIII of the Act, and the petitioner is not the supervisor of the arrangement, one copy for him.

Each of these copies shall have applied to it the seal of the court, and shall be issued to the petitioner.

(4) The date and time of filing the petition shall be endorsed on the petition and on any copy issued under paragraph (3).

(5) The court shall fix a venue for hearing the petition, and this also shall be endorsed on the petition and on any copy so issued.

(6) Where a petition contains a request for the appointment of a person as trustee in accordance with section 297(5) (appointment of former supervisor as trustee) the person whose appointment is sought shall, not less than 2 days before the day appointed for hearing the petition, file in court a report including particulars of—

(a) a date on which he gave written notification to creditors bound by the arrangement of the intention to seek his appointment as trustee, such date to be at least 10 days before the day on which the report under this paragraph is filed, and

(b) details of any response from creditors to that notice, including any objections to his appointment.

2.586

6.11 Proof of service of statutory demand

(1) Where under section 268 the petition must have been preceded by a statutory demand, there must be filed in court, with the petition, an affidavit or affidavits proving service of the demand.

(2) Every affidavit must have exhibited to it a copy of the demand as served.

(3) Subject to the next paragraph, if the demand has been served personally on the debtor, the affidavit must be made by the person who effected that service.

(4) If service of the demand (however effected) has been acknowledged in writing either by the debtor himself, or by some person stating himself in the acknowledgement to be authorised to accept service on the debtor's behalf, the affidavit must be made either by the creditor or by a person acting on his behalf, and the acknowledgement of service must be exhibited to the affidavit.

(5) If neither paragraph (3) nor paragraph (4) applies, the affidavit or affidavits must be made by a person or persons having direct personal knowledge of the means adopted for serving the statutory demand, and must—

(a) give particulars of the steps which have been taken with a view to serving the demand personally, and

(b) state the means whereby (those steps having been ineffective) it was sought to bring the demand to the debtor's attention, and

(c) specify a date by which, to the best of the knowledge, information and belief of the person making the affidavit, the demand will have come to the debtor's attention.

(6) The steps of which particulars are given for the purposes of paragraph (5)(a) must be such as would have sufficed to justify an order for substituted service of a petition.

(7) If the affidavit specifies a date for the purposes of compliance with paragraph (5)(c), then unless the court otherwise orders, that date is deemed for the purposes of the Rules to have been the date on which the statutory demand was served on the debtor.

(8) Where the creditor has taken advantage of Rule 6.3(3) (newspaper advertisement), the affidavit must be made either by the creditor himself

or by a person having direct personal knowledge of the circumstances; and there must be specified in the affidavit—

    (a)   the means of the creditor's knowledge or (as the case may be) belief required for the purposes of that Rule, and

    (b)   the date or dates on which, and the newspaper in which, the statutory demand was advertised under that Rule;

and there shall be exhibited to the affidavit a copy of any advertisement of the statutory demand.

(9) The court may decline to file the petition if not satisfied that the creditor has discharged the obligation imposed on him by Rule 6.3(2).

Notes

R 6.11(1)

See generally para 13, Practice Direction: Insolvency Proceedings (Civil Procedure Vol 2 Section 3E). A witness statement can be used in place of an affidavit: see IR 1986 r 7.57(5).

R 6.11(3)

If personal service was effected, the affidavit should be in Form 6.11. Copies of this form can be found in pdf and Microsoft Word format at www.insolvency.gov.uk. In the event that substituted service is effected, the affidavit should be in Form 6.12. Guidance on service of statutory demands is given in Practice Direction: Insolvency Proceedings (Civil Procedure Vol 2, Sect 3E).

2.587

6.12 Verification of petition

(1) The petition shall be verified by an affidavit that the statements in the petition are true, or are true to the best of the deponent's knowledge, information and belief.

(2) If the petition is in respect of debts to different creditors, the debts to each creditor must be separately verified.

(3) The petition shall be exhibited to the affidavit verifying it.

(4) The affidavit shall be made—

    (a)   by the petitioner (or if there are two or more petitioners, any one of them), or

    (b)   by some person such as a director, company secretary or similar company officer, or a solicitor, who has been concerned in the matters giving rise to the presentation of the petition, or

    (c)   by some responsible person who is duly authorised to make the affidavit and has the requisite knowledge of those matters.

(5) Where the maker of the affidavit is not the petitioner himself, or one of the petitioners, he must in the affidavit identify himself and state—

    (a)   the capacity in which, and the authority by which, he makes it, and

    (b)   the means of his knowledge of the matters sworn to in the affidavit.

(6) The affidavit is prima facie evidence of the truth of the statements in the petition to which it relates.

(7) If the petition is based upon a statutory demand, and more than 4 months have elapsed between the service of the demand and the presentation of the petition, the affidavit must also state the reasons for the delay.

Notes

R 6.12

The affidavit should be in Form 6.13. Copies of this form can be found in pdf format at www.insolvency.gov.uk. Rather than an affidavit being sworn a witness statement can be made IR 1986 r 7.57(5).

R 6.12(7)

It is important to provide an adequate explanation of the delay and it is not advisable for the creditor to rely on a 'stale' statutory demand. There is no requirement otherwise that the petition be presented within four months of the service of the demand but the court could still dismiss the petition under IA 1986 s 266(3). One presumes that the delay would need to have caused the debtor actual prejudice before it would contemplate such a course.

2.588

6.13 Notice to Chief Land Registrar

When the petition is filed, the court shall forthwith send to the Chief Land Registrar notice of the petition together with a request that it may be registered in the register of pending actions.

Notes

R 6.13

The notice should be in Form 6.14. Where the land is registered the further step of entering a creditor's notice against the title will be taken as soon as practicable by the registrar. The purpose of this is to ensure that the debtor's real property assets are protected from the date of presentation of the petition. From that date, all dispositions of the debtor's property are prima facie void: see s 284 IA 1986.

2.589

6.14 Service of petition

(1) Subject ao follows, the petition shall be served personally on the debtor by an officer of the court, or by the petitioning creditor or his solicitor, or by a person instructed by the creditor or his solicitor for that purpose; and service shall be effected by delivering to him a sealed copy of the petition.

(2) If the court is satisfied by affidavit or other evidence on oath that prompt personal service cannot be effected because the debtor is keeping

out of the way to avoid service of the petition or other legal process, or for any other cause, it may order substituted service to be effected in such manner as it thinks fit.

(3) Where an order for substituted service has been carried out, the petition is deemed duly served on the debtor.

(4) If to the petitioner's knowledge there is in force for the debtor a voluntary arrangement under Part VIII of the Act, and the petitioner is not himself the supervisor of the arrangement, a copy of the petition shall be sent by him to the supervisor.

(5) If to the petitioner's knowledge, there is a member State liquidator appointed in main proceedings in relation to the bankrupt, a copy of the petition shall be sent by him to the member State liquidator.

Notes

R 6.14

The petition must be served personally unless the court authorises substituted service. Before applying for substituted service, efforts must have been made to serve personally. As to what efforts the court will regard as sufficient, see para 11.4 Practice Direction: Insolvency Proceedings (Civil Procedure Vol 2, Sect 3E). When applying for an order allowing substituted service, the creditor should always consider whether he also needs to apply for an order extending the time for hearing the petition: see r 6.28 IR 1986.

Substituted service may take a number of forms eg service by first class post or insertion through a letterbox or by advertisement. The order for substituted service should be made in Form 6.15. In the event that the court orders substituted service by advertisement in the Gazette, the advert should be in Form 6.16.

Where service has been effected personally, it is always worth ensuring that the person effecting the service keeps detailed contemporaneous notes of the service, including a physical description of the person served. Should the debtor say that he never received the petition, it is immensely useful for the process server or outdoor clerk to refer to their notes, rather than trying to remember the event which may have taken place months before and with many other petitions having been served by them in the meantime.

2.590

6.15 Proof of service

(1) Service of the petition shall be proved by affidavit.

(2) The affidavit shall have exhibited to it—
    (a)   a sealed copy of the petition, and
    (b)   if substituted service has been ordered, a sealed copy of the order;
and it shall be filed in court immediately after service.

Notes

R 6.15

The affidavit should be in Form 6.15–18 as appropriate. Copies of the forms can be found in pdf and Microsoft Word format at www.insolvency.gov.uk. Rather than an affidavit being sworn a witness statement can be made IR 1986 r 7.57(5). The rules on service (including proof of service) must be followed exactly. Missing proof of service is not a procedural defect which the court will waive under r 7.55 IR 1986: see *Re Awan* [2000] BPIR 241.

2.591

6.16 Death of debtor before service

If the debtor dies before service of the petition, the court may order service to be effected on his personal representatives, or on such other persons as it thinks fit.

2.592

6.17 Security for costs (s 268(2) only)

(1) This Rule applies where the debt in respect of which the petition is presented is for a liquidated sum payable at some future time, it being claimed in the petition that the debtor appears to have no reasonable prospect of being able to pay it.

(2) The petitioning creditor may, on the debtor's application, be ordered to give security for the debtor's costs.

(3) The nature and amount of the security to be ordered is in the court's discretion.

(4) If an order is made under this Rule, there shall be no hearing of the petition until the whole amount of the security has been given.

Notes

R 6.17

The purpose of this rule is to protect the debtor-to-be where he is forced to incur costs in demonstrating his future ability to pay – which may require detailed financial evidence – in circumstances where the creditor-to-be does not appear to be good for those costs. It appears to be intended to strike a balance between the interests of the debtor and creditor in cases where the debtor has not (yet) done anything wrong but is nonetheless forced to resist bankruptcy proceedings. There appears to be no reported authority on how this provision works in practice, presumably because applications, and petitions, of this kind are very rare. Guidance may be obtained by analogy with CPR r 25.12ff.

2.593

6.18 Hearing of petition

(1) Subject as follows, the petition shall not be heard until at least 14 days have elapsed since it was served on the debtor.

(2) The court may, on such terms as it thinks fit, hear the petition at an earlier date, if it appears that the debtor has absconded, or the court is satisfied that it is a proper case for an expedited hearing, or the debtor consents to a hearing within the 14 days.

(3) Any of the following may appear and be heard, that is to say, the petitioning creditor, the debtor, the supervisor of any voluntary arrangement under Part VIII of the Act in force for the debtor and any creditor who has given notice under Rule 6.23 below.

Notes

See also s 270 IA 1986 and the notes to that section.

2.593A

6.19

(Revoked by the Insolvency (Amendment) Rules 1987, SI 1987/1919, r 3(1), Schedule Pt 1, para 97.)

2.594

6.20 Petition by moneylender

A petition in respect of a money-lending transaction made before 27 January 1980 of a creditor who at the time of the transaction was a licensed moneylender shall at the hearing of the petition be supported by an affidavit incorporating a statement setting out in detail the particulars mentioned in section 9(2) of the Moneylenders Act 1927.

Notes

R 6.20

The details referred to in s 9(2) Moneylenders Act 1927 (repealed by Consumer Credit Act 1974 s 192(3)(b)(4)) include details about the amount lent, the date when the sum(s) in question was advanced, the amount and date of any repayment, the amount outstanding, and details in relation to interest.

2.595

6.21 Petition opposed by debtor

Where the debtor intends to oppose the petition, he shall not later than 7 days before the day fixed for the hearing—
(a) file in court a notice specifying the grounds on which he will object to the making of a bankruptcy order, and
(b) send a copy of the notice to the petitioning creditor or his solicitor.

Notes

R 6.21

The notice to oppose should be in Form 6.19. In practice, this rule is often not adhered to and the debtor will just file a witness statement in opposition to the petition; failure to comply with this provision does not prevent the debtor opposing the petition at the hearing *Barclays Bank plc v Mogg* [2003] EWHC 2645 (Ch), [2004] BPIR 259.

2.596

6.22 Amendment of petition

With the leave of the court (given on such terms, if any, as the court thinks fit to impose), the petition may be amended at any time after presentation by the omission of any creditor or any debt.

Notes

The court has general power to allow amendment of a bankruptcy petition under the CPR: see *Aspinalls Club Ltd v Simone Halabi* [1998] BPIR 322. Whilst the court can under IR 1986 r 6.22 amend the petition to omit any debt, the petition can only be based on a debt included in the statutory demand: see para 15.3 Practice Direction : Insolvency Proceedings (Civil Procedure Vol 2 Section 3E).

2.597

6.23 Notice by persons intending to appear

(1) Every creditor who intends to appear on the hearing of the petition shall give to the petitioning creditor notice of his intention in accordance with this Rule.

(2) The notice shall specify—
   (a) the name and address of the person giving it, and any telephone number and reference which may be required for communication with him or with any other person (to be also specified in the notice) authorised to speak or act on his behalf;
   (b) whether his intention is to support or oppose the petition; and
   (c) the amount and nature of his debt.

(3) The notice shall be sent so as to reach the addressee not later than 16.00 hours on the business day before that which is appointed for the hearing (or, where the hearing has been adjourned, for the adjourned hearing).

(4) A person failing to comply with this Rule may appear on the hearing of the petition only with the leave of the court.

Notes

The notice should be in Form 6.20.

2.598

6.24 List of appearances

(1) The petitioning creditor shall prepare for the court a list of the creditors (if any) who have given notice under Rule 6.23, specifying their names and addresses and (if known to him) their respective solicitors.

(2) Against the name of each creditor in the list it shall be stated whether his intention is to support the petition, or to oppose it.

(3) On the day appointed for the hearing of the petition, a copy of the list shall be handed to the court before the commencement of the hearing.

(4) If any leave is given under Rule 6.23(4), the petitioner shall add to the list the same particulars in respect of the person to whom leave has been given.

Notes

The list should be in Form 6.21.

2.599

6.25 Decision on the hearing

(1) On the hearing of the petition, the court may make a bankruptcy order if satisfied that the statements in the petition are true, and that the debt on which it is founded has not been paid, or secured or compounded for.

(2) If the petition is brought in respect of a judgment debt, or a sum ordered by any court to be paid, the court may stay or dismiss the petition on the ground that an appeal is pending from the judgment or order, or that execution of the judgment has been stayed.

(3) A petition preceded by a statutory demand shall not be dismissed on the ground only that the amount of the debt was over-stated in the demand, unless the debtor, within the time allowed for complying with the demand, gave notice to the creditor disputing the validity of the demand on that ground; but, in the absence of such notice, the debtor is deemed to have complied with the demand if he has, within the time allowed, paid the correct amount.

Notes

R 6.25(1)

Once the petitioner has proved the facts in the petition, and the court is satisfied that there is nothing to prevent the making of an order (as specified in this rule and in s 271(1) IA 1986), it should be slow to adjourn the petition. But the court is required to enquire into these matters, although this duty is somewhat lighter if the debtor is raising matters which have already been determined on any application to set aside the statutory demand: see the notes to s 271(1) IA 1986 in this work. Once the court is satisfied that it has jurisdiction to make a bankruptcy order, it must then decide whether, in its discretion, it will do so. It may take into account any cross-claim that the debtor has against the creditor or even the general state of account between them: see *TSB v Platts (No 2)* [1997] BPIR 302.

R 6.25(2)

On the hearing of the petition the court will only investigate the judgment debt if it was obtained by fraud, collusion or represents a miscarriage of justice, and then it will consider whether an appeal from the order would have a reasonable prospect of success: see *Dawodu v American*

Express Bank [2001] BPIR 983. Where the judgment on which the petition debt is based is stayed the court cannot make a bankruptcy order and must either stay or dismiss the petition: *Legal Services Commission v Leonard* [2002] EWCA Civ 744, [2002] BPIR 994. Where the Court of Appeal had not yet decided to extend the time for making an appeal and had not granted permission to appeal no appeal could be 'pending' *Rehman v Boardman* [2004] BPIR 820.

R 6.25(3)

This curious provision, which is derived from the old BA 1914, in which it had some role to play, confirms the position stated in the modern case-law, ie that a mere overstatement of the debt in a statutory demand will not invalidate the demand itself (see the notes to r 6.5 IR 1986). But the rule allows the debtor to take that kind of technical point at the hearing of the petition provided he has served the notice referred to. Then the court 'may' dismiss the petition. However, it is hard to see that the court would think it appropriate to do so for that reason alone when it would not have set the demand aside. This rule is likely only to relevant where the debtor can demonstrate that he has suffered some real prejudice as a result of the overstatement.

2.600

6.26 Non-appearance of creditor

If the petitioning creditor fails to appear on the hearing of the petition, no subsequent petition against the same debtor, either alone or jointly with any other person, shall be presented by the same creditor in respect of the same debt, without the leave of the court to which the previous petition was presented.

Notes

R 6.26

The applicable principles when an application is made under this provision are set out in *Omgate Limited v Gordon* [2001] BPIR 909.

2.601

6.27 Vacating registration on dismissal of petition

If the petition is dismissed or withdrawn by leave of the court, an order shall be made at the same time permitting vacation of the registration of the petition as a pending action; and the court shall send to the debtor two sealed copies of the order.

Notes

See IR 1986 r 6.13 and Form 6.27.

2.602

6.28 Extension of time for hearing

(1) The petitioning creditor may, if the petition has not been served, apply to the court to appoint another venue for the hearing.

(2) The application shall state the reasons why the petition has not been served.

(3) No costs occasioned by the application shall be allowed in the proceedings except by order of the court.

(4) If the court appoints another day for the hearing, the petitioning creditor shall forthwith notify any creditor who has given notice under Rule 6.23.

Notes

R 6.28

Where the application is made less than two clear working days before the hearing date the costs of the application will not be allowed; where an application for extension is made it should state the date currently fixed for the hearing of the petition. The petitioning creditor must attend the court on or before the hearing date to check that the extension has been given and should not assume that the extension will be given as a matter of course para 14.1–14.3 Practice Direction: Insolvency Proceedings (Civil Procedure Vol 2, Sect 3E).

2.603

6.29 Adjournment

(1) If the court adjourns the hearing of the petition, the following applies.

(2) Unless the court otherwise directs, the petitioning creditor shall forthwith send—
    (a)   to the debtor, and
    (b)   where any creditor has given notice under Rule 6.23 but was not present at the hearing, to him,
notice of the making of the order of adjournment. The notice shall state the venue for the adjourned hearing.

Notes

R 6.29(1)

It is essential to establish that a debtor has had notice of an adjourned hearing. In the absence of such proof, any bankruptcy order made at the adjourned hearing may well be annulled under IA 1986 s 282(1) if it is challenged by the debtor/bankrupt: *Skarzynski v Chalford Property Company Ltd* [2001] BPIR 673.

The practice of the bankruptcy registrars at the Royal Courts of Justice, where all petitions within the London insolvency district are heard, is to require the person attending from or on behalf of the petitioning creditor to certify that a notice of the adjourned hearing has been served on the debtor. The certificate is on the attendance sheet, together with the certificate of continuing debt (see para 15.9 Practice Direction:Insolvency Proceedings (Civil Procedure

Vol 2, Sect 3E). The person attending will need to state when the notice was sent and to what address. It essential that advocates in petition hearings have this information.

R 6.29(2)

The order of the court adjourning the hearing should be made in the form of Form 6.23 and the notice of adjournment to the debtor in Form 6.24.

———

2.604

6.30 Substitution of petitioner

(1) This Rule applies where a creditor petitions and is subsequently found not entitled to do so, or where the petitioner—
  (a) consents to withdraw his petition or to allow it to be dismissed, or consents to an adjournment, or fails to appear in support of his petition when it is called on in court on the day originally fixed for the hearing, or on a day to which it is adjourned, or
  (b) appears, but does not apply for an order in the terms of the prayer of his petition.

(2) The court may, on such terms as it thinks just, order that there be substituted as petitioner any creditor who—
  (a) has under Rule 6.23 given notice of his intention to appear at the hearing,
  (b) is desirous of prosecuting the petition, and
  (c) was, at the date on which the petition was presented, in such a position in relation to the debtor as would have enabled him (the creditor) on that date to present a bankruptcy petition in respect of a debt or debts owed to him by the debtor [(or in the case of the member State liquidator, owed to creditors in proceedings in relation to which he holds office)], paragraphs (a) to (d) of section 267(2) being satisfied in respect of that debt or those debts.

———

Notes

R 6.30

An order for substitution should be in Form 6.24A and an order dismissing or withdrawing the petition should follow Form 6.22.

———

2.604A

6.31 Change of carriage of petition

(1) On the hearing of the petition, any person who claims to be a creditor of the debtor, and who has given notice under Rule 6.23 of his intention to appear at the hearing, may apply to the court for an order giving him carriage of the petition in place of the petitioning creditor, but without requiring any amendment of the petition.

(2) The court may, on such terms as it thinks just, make a change of carriage order if satisfied that—
   (a)   the applicant is an unpaid and unsecured creditor of the debtor, and
   (b)   the petitioning creditor either—
      (i)   intends by any means to secure the postponement, adjournment or withdrawal of the petition, or
      (ii)   does not intend to prosecute the petition, either diligently or at all.

(3) The court shall not make the order if satisfied that the petitioning creditor's debt has been paid, secured or compounded for by means of—
   (a)   a disposition of property made by some person other than the debtor, or
   (b)   a disposition of the debtor's own property made with the approval of, or ratified by, the court.

(4) A change of carriage order may be made whether or not the petitioning creditor appears at the hearing.

(5) If the order is made, the person given the carriage of the petition is entitled to rely on all evidence previously adduced in the proceedings (whether by affidavit or otherwise).

Notes

R 6.31

The court can make an order for change of carriage under this provision even where the petition was originally based on a non-provable debt: *Levy v Legal Services Commission* [2000] BPIR 1065. Formal amendment of the petition is not necessary: *Re Purvis* [1998] BPIR 153. The order is made in Form 6.24B.

2.605

6.32 Petitioner seeking dismissal or leave to withdraw

(1) Where the petitioner applies to the court for the petition to be dismissed, or for leave to withdraw it, he must, unless the court otherwise orders, file in court an affidavit specifying the grounds of the application and the circumstances in which it is made.

(2) If, since the petition was filed, any payment has been made to the petitioner by way of settlement (in whole or in part) of the debt or debts in respect of which the petition was brought, or any arrangement has been entered into for securing or compounding it or them, the affidavit must state—
   (a)   what dispositions of property have been made for the purposes of the settlement or arrangement, and
   (b)   whether, in the case of any disposition, it was property of the debtor himself, or of some other person, and
   (c)   whether, if it was property of the debtor, the disposition was made with the approval of, or has been ratified by, the court (if so, specifying the relevant court order).

(3) No order giving leave to withdraw a petition shall be given before the petition is heard.

———

Notes

R 6.32(1)

This provision is not often complied with. Its purpose is to allow the court to consider whether other creditors who appear on the petition should be given a change of carriage or substitution. However, where there are no supporting creditors in attendance, the practice is usually to dismiss the petition if it has not been served, or to allow it to be withdrawn if it has been, notwithstanding that this rule has not been complied with.

R 6.32(2)

The court will be particularly concerned to consider the position of the other creditors *Smith v Ian Simpson* [2001] Ch 239.

———

2.606

6.33 Settlement and content of bankruptcy order

(1) The bankruptcy order shall be settled by the court.

(2) The order shall—
- (a) state the date of the presentation of the petition on which the order is made, and the date and time of the making of the order, and
- (b) contain a notice requiring the bankrupt, forthwith after service of the order on him, to attend on the official receiver at the place stated in the order.

(3) Subject to section 346 (effect of bankruptcy on enforcement procedures), the order may include provision staying any action or proceeding against the bankrupt.

(4) Where the petitioning creditor is represented by a solicitor, the order shall be endorsed with the latter's name, address telephone number and reference (if any).

———

Notes

The order is in Form 6.25.

———

2.607

6.34 Action to follow making of order

(1) At least two sealed copies of the bankruptcy order shall be sent forthwith by the court to the official receiver, who shall forthwith send one of them to the bankrupt.

(2) Subject to the next paragraph, the official receiver shall—

> (a) send notice of the making of the order to the Chief Land Registrar, for registration in the register of writs and orders affecting land,
> (b) cause the order to be advertised in such [newspaper] as the official receiver thinks fit, and
> (c) cause the order to be gazetted.
>
> (3) The court may, on the application of the bankrupt or a creditor, order the official receiver to suspend action under paragraph (2) and Rule 6.A.4(2), pending a further order of the court.
>
> An application under this paragraph shall be supported by an affidavit stating the grounds on which it is made.
>
> (4) Where an order is made under paragraph (3), the applicant for the order shall forthwith deliver a copy of it to the official receiver.

———

Notes

The courts will not generally grant a stay of action on a bankruptcy order just because there is a pending appeal of it: see *Official Receiver v Turner* [1998] BPIR 636.

———

2.608

6.35 Amendment of title of proceedings

(1) At any time after the making of a bankruptcy order, the official receiver or the trustee may apply to the court for an order amending the full title of the proceedings.

(2) Where such an order is made, the official receiver shall forthwith send notice of it to the Chief Land Registrar, for corresponding amendment of the register; and, if the court so directs he shall also cause notice of the order to be gazetted, and to be advertised in such ... newspaper as the official receiver thinks fit.

———

Notes

R 6.35

See for example *Michael Yee Fun Chu v Price* [2004] BPIR 603.

———

2.609

6.36 Old bankruptcy notices

(1) Subject as follows, a person who has before the appointed day for the purposes of the Act served a bankruptcy notice under the Bankruptcy Act 1914 may, on or after that day, proceed on the notice as if it were a statutory demand duly served under Chapter 1 of this Part of the Rules.

(2) The conditions of the application of this Rule are that—

> (a) the debt in respect of which the bankruptcy notice was served has not been paid, secured or compounded for in the terms of the notice and the Act of 1914;
> (b) the date by which compliance with the notice was required was not more than 3 months before the date of presentation of the petition; and
> (c) there has not, before the appointed day, been presented any bankruptcy petition with reference to an act of bankruptcy arising from non-compliance with the bankruptcy notice.
>
> (3) If before, on or after the appointed day, application is made (under the Act of 1914) to set the bankruptcy notice aside, that application is to be treated, on and after that day, as an application duly made (on the date on which it was in fact made) to set aside a statutory demand duly served on the date on which the bankruptcy notice was in fact served.

Notes

R 6.36(1)

The *'appointed day'* is 29 December 1986.

Chapter 3
Bankruptcy Petition (Debtor's)

2.610

6.37 Preliminary

The Rules in this Chapter relate to a debtor's petition, and the making of a bankruptcy order thereon.

Notes

A petition is presented by a debtor pursuant to IA 1986 s 264(1)(b) and the grounds and procedure relating to the petition are contained in IA 1986 s 272ff.

2.611

6.38 Identification of debtor

(1) The petition shall state the following matters with respect to the debtor—
> (a) his name, place of residence and occupation (if any);
> (b) the name or names in which he carries on business if other than his true name, and whether, in the case of any business of a specified nature, he carries it on alone or with others;
> (c) the nature of his business and the address or addresses at which he carries it on;
> (d) any name or names, other than his true name, in which he has carried on business in the period in which any of his bankruptcy

debts were incurred and, in the case of any such business whether he has carried it on alone or with others; and

(e) any address or addresses at which he has resided or carried on business during that period, and the nature of that business.

(2) The particulars of the debtor given under this Rule determine the full title of the proceedings.

(3) If the debtor has at any time used a name other than the one given under paragraph (1)(a), that fact shall be stated in the petition.

Notes

R 6.38(2)

The 'full title of the proceedings' includes the details required by IR 1986 r 7.26

2.612

6.39 Admission of insolvency

(1) The petition shall contain the statement that the petitioner is unable to pay his debts, and a request that a bankruptcy order be made against him.

(2) If within the period of 5 years ending with the date of the petition the petitioner has been adjudged bankrupt, or has made a composition with his creditors in satisfaction of his debts or a scheme of arrangement of his affairs, or he has entered into any voluntary arrangement or been subject to an administration order under Part VI of the county courts Act 1984, particulars of these matters shall be given in the petition.

(3) If there is at the date of the petition in force for the debtor a voluntary arrangement under Part VIII of the Act, the particulars required by paragraph (2) above shall contain a statement to that effect and the name and address of the supervisor of the arrangement.

2.613

6.40 Court in which petition to be filed

(1) In the following cases, the petition shall be presented to the High Court—
(a) if the debtor has resided or carried on business in the London insolvency district for the greater part of the 6 months immediately preceding the presentation of the petition, or for a longer period in those 6 months than in any other insolvency district, or
(b) if the debtor is not resident in England and Wales.

(2) In any other case, the petition shall (subject to paragraph (3) below), be presented to the debtor's own county court, which is—
(a) the county court for the insolvency district in which he has resided or carried on business for the longest period in those 6 months, or

(b) if he has for the greater part of those 6 months carried on business in one insolvency district and resided in another, the county court for that in which he has carried on business or

(c) if he has during those 6 months carried on business in more than one insolvency district, the county court for that in which is, or has been for the longest period in those 6 months, his principal place of business.

(3) If, in a case not falling within paragraph (1), it is more expedient for the debtor with a view to expediting his petition—

(a) it may in any case be presented to whichever court is specified by Schedule 2 to the Rules as being, in relation to the debtor's own court, the nearest full-time court, and

(b) it may alternatively, in a case falling within paragraph (2)(*b*), be presented to the court for the insolvency district in which he has resided for the greater part of the 6 months there referred to.

(3A) Notwithstanding any other provision of this Rule, where there is in force for the debtor a voluntary arrangement under Part VIII of the Act the petition shall be presented to the court to which the nominee's report under section 256 or section 256A or 263C was submitted.

(4) The petition shall contain sufficient information to establish that it is brought in the appropriate court.

Notes

R 6.40(3)

Where the debtor is residing or carrying on business outside the London insolvency district but within England and Wales this provision gives the debtor a certain choice of courts in which to present his petition.

2.614

6.41 Statement of affairs

(1) The petition shall be accompanied by a statement of the debtor's affairs, verified by affidavit.

(2) Section B of Chapter 5 below applies with respect to the statement of affairs.

Notes

R 6.41(2)

Section B refers to IR 1986 r 6.67–6.72. See Form 6.28.

2.615

6.42 Procedure for presentation and filing

(1) The petition and the statement of affairs shall be filed in court, together with three copies of the petition, and one copy of the statement. No petition shall be filed unless there is produced with it the receipt for the deposit payable on presentation.

(2) Subject to paragraph (2A), the court may hear the petition forthwith. If it does not do so, it shall fix a venue for the hearing.

(2A) If the petition contains particulars of a voluntary arrangement under Part VIII of the Act in force for the debtor, the court shall fix a venue for the hearing and give at least 14 days' notice of it to the supervisor of the arrangement; the supervisor may appear and be heard on the petition.

(3) Of the three copies of the petition delivered—

    (a)   one shall be returned to the petitioner, endorsed with any venue fixed;

    (b)   another, so endorsed, shall be [sent by the court to the official receiver; and]

    (c)   the remaining copy shall be retained by the court, to be sent to an insolvency practitioner (if appointed under section 273(2)).

(4) The copy of the statement of affairs shall be sent by the court to the official receiver.

(5) The affidavit verifying the debtor's statement of affairs may be sworn before an officer of the court duly authorised in that behalf.

(6) Where the court hears a petition forthwith, or it will in the opinion of the court otherwise expedite the delivery of any document to the official receiver, the court may, instead of sending that document to the official receiver, direct the bankrupt forthwith to deliver it to him.

(7) Where a petition contains a request for the appointment of a person as trustee in accordance with section 297(5) (appointment of former supervisor as trustee) the person whose appointment is sought shall, not less than 2 days before the day appointed for hearing the petition, file in court a report including particulars of—

    (a)   a date on which he gave written notification to creditors bound by the arrangement of the intention to seek his appointment as trustee, such date to be at least 10 days before the day on which the report under this paragraph is filed, and

    (b)   details of any response from creditors to that notice, including any objections to his appointment.

Notes

R 6.42(1)

There is no constitutional right to petition for one's own bankruptcy and, even if there were, the requirement of a deposit under IR 1986 6.42(1) does not amount to an infringement of such right: *Lightfoot v Lord Chancellor* [2000] BPIR 120. The deposit for a debtor's petition is £325 and for a creditor's petition it is £390 (Insolvency Proceedings (Fees) Order 2004) (as amended with effect from 1 April 2006).

R 6.42(2)

The Court cannot make a bankruptcy order if the conditions specified in IA 1986 s 273 are fulfilled; the maximum level of unsecured bankruptcy debts on a debtor's petition for a case to be referred to an insolvency practitioner to assess the possibility of a voluntary arrangement under s 273 is increased to £40,000 and the minimum amount of the estate's value is increased to £4000: Insolvency Proceedings (Monetary Limits) (Amendment) Order 2004.

2.616

6.43 Notice to Chief Land Registrar

When the petition is filed, the court shall forthwith send to the Chief Land Registrar notice of the petition, for registration in the register of pending actions.

Notes

R 6.43

Although this falls far short of the advertising of a winding up petition in relation to a company (IR 1986 r 4.11) it provides some publicity that a bankruptcy petition has been filed and protects the debtor's real property assets pending the making of the bankruptcy order. See also s 284 IA 1986.

2.617

6.44 Report of insolvency practitioner

(1) If the court under section 273(2) appoints an insolvency practitioner to act in the debtor's case, it shall forthwith—
 (a) send to the person appointed—
  (i) a sealed copy of the order of appointment, and
  (ii) copies of the petition and statement of affairs,
 (b) fix a venue for the insolvency practitioner's report to be considered, and
 (c) send notice of the venue to the insolvency practitioner and the debtor.

(2) The insolvency practitioner shall file his report in court ... and send one copy of it to the debtor, so as to be in his hands not less than 3 days before the date fixed for consideration of the report, and a further copy to the official receiver.

(3) The debtor is entitled to attend when the report is considered, and shall attend if so directed by the court. If he attends, the court shall hear any representations which he makes with respect to any of the matters dealt with in the report.

2.618

6.45 Settlement and content of bankruptcy order

(1) The bankruptcy order shall be settled by the court.

(2) The order shall—
 (a) state the date of the presentation of the petition on which the order is made, and the date and time of the making of the order, and
 (b) contain a notice requiring the bankrupt, forthwith after the service of the order on him, to attend on the official receiver at the place stated in the order.

(3) Subject to section 346 (effect of bankruptcy on enforcement procedures), the order may include provision staying any action or proceeding against the bankrupt.

(4) Where the bankrupt is represented by a solicitor, the order shall be endorsed with the latter's name, address telephone number and reference.

———

Notes

R 6.45

See Form 6.30 for the form of order.

———

2.619

6.46 Action to follow making of order

(1) At least two sealed copies of the bankruptcy order shall be sent forthwith by the court to the official receiver, who shall forthwith send one of them to the bankrupt.

(2) Subject to the next paragraph, the official receiver shall—
  (a) send notice of the making of the order to the Chief Land Registrar, for registration in the register of writs and orders affecting land,
  (b) cause the order to be advertised in such newspaper as the official receiver thinks fit, and
  (c) cause notice of the order to be gazetted.

(3) The court may, on the application of the bankrupt or a creditor, order the official receiver to suspend action under paragraph (2) and Rule 6A.4(2), pending a further Order of the court.

An application under this paragraph shall be supported by an affidavit stating the grounds on which it is made.

(4) Where an order is made under paragraph (3), the applicant shall forthwith deliver a copy of it to the official receiver.

———

Notes

R 6.46(3)

A stay pending an appeal against the bankruptcy order is likely only to be granted where there are special circumstances; it is vital that there should be no undue delay in putting the official receiver in a position to take appropriate steps to preserve the estate: see *Official Receiver v Turner* [1998] BPIR 636.

———

2.620

6.46A Expenses of Voluntary arrangement

Where a bankruptcy order is made on a debtor's petition and there is at the time of the petition in force for the debtor a voluntary arrangement under Part VIII of the Act, any expenses properly incurred as expenses of the administration of the arrangement in question shall be a first charge on the bankrupt's estate.

2.621

6.47 Amendment of title of proceedings

(1) At any time after the making of the bankruptcy order, the official receiver or the trustee may apply to the court for an order amending the full title of the proceedings.

(2) Where such an order is made, the official receiver shall forthwith send notice of it to the Chief Land Registrar, for corresponding amendment of the register; and, if the court so directs, he shall also—
  (a) cause notice of the order to be gazetted, and
  (b) cause notice of the order to be advertised in such [newspaper] as the official receiver thinks appropriate.

———

Notes

R.6.47

The 'full title of the proceedings' includes the details required by IR 1986 r 7.26; and see IR 1986 r 6.38(2) above.

———

2.622

6.48 Certificate of summary administration

(1) If the court under section 275 issues a certificate for the summary administration of the bankrupt's estate, the certificate may be included in the bankruptcy order.

(2) If the certificate is not so included, the court shall forthwith send copies of it to the official receiver and the bankrupt.

2.623

6.49 Duty of official receiver in summary administration

(1) Where a trustee has been appointed, the official receiver shall send a copy of the certificate of summary administration (whether or not included in the bankruptcy order) to him.

(2) Within 12 weeks after the issue of the certificate the official receiver shall (insofar as he has not already done so) give notice to creditors of the making of the bankruptcy order.

2.624

6.50 Revocation of certificate of summary administration

(1) The court may under section 275(3) revoke a certificate for summary administration, either of its own motion or on the application of the official receiver.

> (2) *If the official receiver applies for the certificate to be revoked, he shall give at least 14 days' notice of the application to the bankrupt.*
>
> (3) *If the court revokes the certificate, it shall forthwith give notice to the official receiver and the bankrupt.*
>
> (4) *If at the time of revocation there is a trustee other than the official receiver, the official receiver shall send a copy of the court's notice to him.*

Notes

RR 6.48–6.50

These provisions were revoked from 1 April 2004.

Chapter 4
The Interim Receiver

2.625

6.51 Application for appointment of interim receiver

(1) An application to the court for the appointment of an interim receiver under section 286 may be made by—
  (a)   a creditor;
  (b)   the debtor;
  (c)   an insolvency practitioner appointed under section 273(2);
  (d)   a temporary administrator, or
  (e)   a member State liquidator appointed in main proceedings.

(2) The application must be supported by an affidavit stating—
  (a)   the grounds on which it is proposed that the interim receiver should be appointed,
  (b)   whether or not the official receiver has been informed of the application and, if so, has been furnished with a copy of it,
  (c)   whether to the applicant's knowledge there has been proposed or is in force a voluntary arrangement under Part VIII of the Act, and
  (d)   the applicant's estimate of the value of the property or business in respect of which the interim receiver is to be appointed.

(3) If an insolvency practitioner has been appointed under section 273, and it is proposed that he (and not the official receiver) should be appointed interim receiver, and it is not the insolvency practitioner himself who is the applicant under this Rule, the affidavit under paragraph (2) must state that he has consented to act.

(4) The applicant shall send copies of the application and the affidavit to the person proposed to be appointed interim receiver. If that person is the official receiver and an insolvency practitioner has been appointed under section 273 (and he is not himself the applicant), copies of the application and affidavit shall be sent by the applicant to the insolvency practitioner.

If, in any case where a copy of the application is to be sent to a person under this paragraph, it is for any reason not practicable to send a copy, that person must be informed of the application in sufficient time to enable him to be present at the hearing.

(5) The official receiver and (if appointed) the insolvency practitioner may attend the hearing of the application and make representations.

(6) The court may on the application, if satisfied that sufficient grounds are shown for the appointment, make it on such terms as it thinks fit.

Notes

R 6.51(1)

The court may appoint the official receiver (IA 1986 s 286(1)) or in certain circumstances a licensed insolvency practitioner (IA 1986 s 286(2)) as an interim receiver. However the provisions of IA 1986 s 286 do not prevent the Court from appointing other persons as interim receivers in exceptional circumstances: see *Gibson Dunn & Crutcher v Rio Properties Inc* [2004] BPIR 1203.

2.626

6.52 Order of appointment

(1) The order appointing the interim receiver shall state the nature and a short description of the property of which the person appointed is to take possession, and the duties to be performed by him in relation to the debtor's affairs.

(2) The court shall, forthwith after the order is made, send 2 sealed copies of it to the person appointed interim receiver (one of which shall be sent by him forthwith to the debtor).

Notes

The order should be in Form 6.32.

2.627

6.53 Deposit

(1) Before an order appointing the official receiver as interim receiver is issued, the applicant for it shall deposit with him, or otherwise secure to his satisfaction, such sum as the court directs to cover his remuneration and expenses.

(2) If the sum deposited or secured subsequently proves to be insufficient, the court may, on application by the official receiver, order that an additional sum be deposited or secured. If the order is not complied with within 2 days after service on the person to whom the order is directed, the court may discharge the order appointing the interim receiver.

(3) If a bankruptcy order is made after an interim receiver has been appointed, any money deposited under this Rule shall (unless it is required by reason of insufficiency of assets for payment of remuneration

and expenses of the interim receiver, or the deposit was made by the debtor out of his own property) be repaid to the person depositing it (or as that person may direct) out of the bankrupt's estate, in the prescribed order of priority.

2.628

6.54 Security

(1) The following applies where an insolvency practitioner is appointed to be interim receiver under section 286(2).

(2) The cost of providing the security required under the Act shall be paid in the first instance by the interim receiver; but—

    (a)   if a bankruptcy order is not made, the person so appointed is entitled to be reimbursed out of the property of the debtor, and the court may make an order on the debtor accordingly, and

    (b)   if a bankruptcy order is made, he is entitled to be reimbursed out of the estate in the prescribed order of priority.

2.629

6.55 Failure to give or keep up security

(1) If the interim receiver fails to give or keep up his security, the court may remove him, and make such order as it thinks fit as to costs.

(2) If an order is made under this Rule removing the interim receiver, or discharging the order appointing him, the court shall give directions as to whether any, and if so what, steps should be taken for the appointment of another person in his place.

2.630

6.56 Remuneration

(1) The remuneration of the interim receiver (other than the official receiver) shall be fixed by the court from time to time on his application.

(2) In fixing the interim receiver's remuneration, the court shall take into account—

    (a)   the time properly given by him (as interim receiver) and his staff in attending to the debtor's affairs,

    (b)   the complexity (or otherwise) of the case,

    (c)   any respects in which, in connection with the debtor's affairs, there falls on the interim receiver any responsibility of an exceptional kind or degree,

    (d)   the effectiveness with which the interim receiver appears to be carrying out, or to have carried out, his duties as such, and

    (e)   the value and nature of the property with which he has to deal.

(3) Without prejudice to any order the court may make as to costs, the interim receiver's remuneration (whether the official receiver or another) shall be paid to him, and the amount of any expenses incurred by him (including the remuneration and expenses of any special manager appointed under section 370) reimbursed—

(a) if a bankruptcy order is not made, out of the property of the debtor], and

(b) if a bankruptcy order is made, out of the estate in the prescribed order of priority,

or, in either case (the relevant funds being insufficient), out of the deposit under Rule 6.53.

(4) Unless the court otherwise directs, in a case falling within paragraph (3)(a) above the interim receiver may retain out of the debtor's property such sums or property as are or may be required for meeting his remuneration and expenses.

Notes

R 6.56

The Court will now take into account in fixing the remuneration the guidance provided by *Practice Statement – the Fixing and Approval of the Remuneration of Appointees* which came into force on 1 October 2004, and see *Re Cabletel Installations Ltd* [2005] BPIR 28.

2.631

6.57 Termination of appointment

(1) The appointment of the interim receiver may be terminated by the court on his application, or on that of the official receiver, the debtor or any creditor.

(2) If the interim receiver's appointment terminates, in consequence of the dismissal of the bankruptcy petition or otherwise, the court may give such directions as it thinks fit with respect to the accounts of his administration and any other matters which it thinks appropriate.

(3) ...

Chapter 5
Disclosure by Bankrupt with Respect to the State of his Affairs

Section A: Creditor's Petition

2.632

6.58 Preliminary

The Rules in this Section apply with respect to the statement of affairs required by section 288(1) to be submitted by the bankrupt, following a bankruptcy order made on a creditor's petition, and the further and other disclosure which is required of him in that case.

2.633

6.59 The statement of affairs

The bankrupt's statement of affairs shall be in Form 6.33, and contain all the particulars required by that form.

2.634

6.60 Verification and filing

(1) The bankrupt shall be furnished by the official receiver with instructions for the preparation of his statement of affairs, and the forms required for that purpose.

(2) The statement of affairs shall be verified by affidavit and delivered to the official receiver, together with one copy.

(3) The official receiver shall file the verified statement in court.

(4) The affidavit may be sworn before an official receiver or a deputy official receiver, or before an officer of the Department or the court duly authorised in that behalf.

Notes

RR 6.58–6.60

A person who has been made bankrupt otherwise than on his own petition must under IA 1986 s 288 submit a statement of affairs in the approved form (form 6.33) to the official receiver (unless the official receiver or the court releases him from this obligation: IA 1986 s 288(3)). These rules deal with that statement of affairs and any other disclosure made of the bankrupt under s 291 IA 1986 and IR 1986 r 6.66; see also IR 1986 r 6.75.

2.635

6.61 Limited disclosure

(1) Where the official receiver thinks that it would prejudice the conduct of the bankruptcy for the whole or part of the statement of affairs to be disclosed, he may apply to the court for an order of limited disclosure in respect of the statement, or any specified part of it.

(2) The court may on the application order that the statement or, as the case may be, the specified part of it be not filed in court, or that it is to be filed separately and not be open to inspection otherwise than with leave of the court.

2.636

6.62 Release from duty to submit statement of affairs; extension of time

(1) The power of the official receiver under section 288(3) to release the bankrupt from his duty to submit a statement of affairs, or to grant an extension of time, may be exercised at the official receiver's own discretion, or at the bankrupt's request.

(2) The bankrupt may, if he requests a release or extension of time and it is refused by the official receiver, apply to the court for it.

(3) The court may, if it thinks that no sufficient cause is shown for the application, disMiss it; but it shall not do so unless the bankrupt has had an opportunity to attend the court for an *ex parte* hearing, of which he has been given at least 7 days' notice.

If the application is not dismissed under this paragraph, the court shall fix a venue for it to be heard, and give notice to the bankrupt accordingly.

(4) The bankrupt shall, at least 14 days before the hearing, send to the official receiver a notice stating the venue and accompanied by a copy of the application, and of any evidence which he (the bankrupt) intends to adduce in support of it.

(5) The official receiver may appear and be heard on the application; and, whether or not he appears, he may file a written report of any matters which he considers ought to be drawn to the court's attention.

If such a report is filed, a copy of it shall be sent by the official receiver to the bankrupt, not later than 5 days before the hearing.

(6) Sealed copies of any order on the application shall be sent by the court to the bankrupt and the official receiver.

(7) On any application under this Rule the bankrupt's costs shall be paid in any event by him and, unless the court otherwise orders, no allowance towards them shall be made out of the estate.

Notes

R 6.62

Under IA 1986 s 288(3) the official receiver or the court may release the bankrupt from the obligation to file a statement of affairs. This rule sets out the procedure for the grant of such release; see also IR 1986 r 6.76.

2.637

6.63 Expenses of statement of affairs

(1) If the bankrupt cannot himself prepare a proper statement of affairs, the official receiver may, at the expense of the estate, employ some person or persons to assist in the preparation of the statement.

(2) At the request of the bankrupt, made on the grounds that he cannot himself prepare a proper statement, the official receiver may authorise an allowance payable out of the estate (in accordance with the prescribed order of priority) towards expenses to be incurred by the bankrupt in employing some person or persons to assist him in preparing it.

(3) Any such request by the bankrupt shall be accompanied by an estimate of the expenses involved; and the official receiver shall only authorise the employment of a named person or a named firm, being in either case approved by him.

(4) An authorisation given by the official receiver under this Rule shall be subject to such conditions (if any) as he thinks fit to impose with respect to the manner in which any person may obtain access to relevant books and papers.

(5) Nothing in this Rule relieves the bankrupt from any obligation with respect to the preparation, verification and submission of his statement of affairs, or to the provision of information to the official receiver or the trustee.

Notes

R 6.63

The general order of priority of expenses is dealt with in IR 1986 r 6.224.

2.638

6.64 Requirement to submit accounts

(1) The bankrupt shall, at the request of the official receiver, furnish him with accounts relating to his affairs of such nature, as at such date and for such period as he may specify.

(2) The period specified may begin from a date up to 3 years preceding the date of the presentation of the bankruptcy petition.

(3) The court may, on the official receiver's application, require accounts in respect of any earlier period.

(4) Rule 6.63 applies (with the necessary modifications) in relation to accounts to be furnished under this Rule as it applies in relation to the statement of affairs.

2.639

6.65 Submission and filing of accounts

(1) The accounts to be furnished under Rule 6.64 shall, if the official receiver so requires, be verified by affidavit, and (whether or not so verified) delivered to him within 21 days of the request under Rule 6.64(1), or such longer period as he may allow.

(2) Two copies of the accounts and (where required) the affidavit shall be delivered by the bankrupt to the official receiver, who shall file one copy in court (with the affidavit, if any).

2.640

6.66 Further disclosure

(1) The official receiver may at any time require the bankrupt to submit (in writing) further information amplifying, modifying or explaining any matter contained in his statement of affairs, or in accounts submitted in pursuance of the Act or the Rules.

(2) The information shall, if the official receiver so directs, be verified by affidavit, and (whether or not so verified) delivered to him within 21 days of the requirement under this Rule, or such longer period as he may allow.

(3) Two copies of the documents containing the information and (where verification is directed) the affidavit shall be delivered by the bankrupt to the official receiver, who shall file one copy in court (with the affidavit, if any).

Notes

See also IA 1986 s 291.

Section B: Debtor's Petition

2.641

6.67 Preliminary

The Rules in this Section apply with respect to the statement of affairs required in the case of a person petitioning for a bankruptcy order to be made against him, and the further disclosure which is required of him in that case.

2.642

6.68 Contents of statement

The statement of affairs required by Rule 6.41 to accompany the debtor's petition shall be in Form 6.28, and contain all the particulars required by that form.

2.643

6.69 Requirement to submit accounts

(1) The bankrupt shall, at the request of the official receiver, furnish him with accounts relating to his affairs of such nature, as at such date and for such period as he may specify.

(2) The period specified may begin from a date up to 3 years preceding the date of the presentation of the bankruptcy petition.

(3) The court may, on the official receiver's application, require accounts in respect of any earlier period.

2.644

6.70 Submission and filing of accounts

(1) The accounts to be furnished under Rule 6.69 shall, if the official receiver so requires, be verified by affidavit, and (whether or not so verified) delivered to him within 21 days of the request under Rule 6.69, or such longer period as he may allow.

(2) Two copies of the accounts and (where required) the affidavit shall be delivered by the bankrupt to the official receiver, who shall file one copy in court (with the affidavit, if any).

2.645

6.71 Expenses of preparing accounts

(1) If the bankrupt cannot himself prepare proper accounts under Rule 6.69, the official receiver may, at the expense of the estate, employ some person or persons to assist in their preparation.

(2) At the request of the bankrupt, made on the grounds that he cannot himself prepare the accounts, the official receiver may authorise an allowance payable out of the estate (in accordance with the prescribed order of priority) towards expenses to be incurred by the bankrupt in employing some person or persons to assist him in their preparation.

(3) Any such request by the bankrupt shall be accompanied by an estimate of the expenses involved; and the official receiver shall only authorise the employment of a named person or a named firm, being in either case approved by him.

(4) An authorisation given by the official receiver under this Rule shall be subject to such conditions (if any) as he thinks fit to impose with respect to the manner in which any person may obtain access to relevant books and papers.

(5) Nothing in this Rule relieves the bankrupt from any obligation with respect to the preparation and submission of accounts, or to the provision of information to the official receiver or the trustee.

2.646

6.72 Further disclosure

(1) The official receiver may at any time require the bankrupt to submit (in writing) further information amplifying, modifying or explaining any matter contained in his statement of affairs, or in accounts submitted in pursuance of the Act or the Rules.

(2) The information shall, if the official receiver so directs, be verified by affidavit, and (whether or not so verified) delivered to him within 21 days from the date of the requirement under paragraph (1), or such longer period as he may allow.

(3) Two copies of the documents containing the information and (where verification is directed) the affidavit shall be delivered by the bankrupt to the official receiver, who shall file one copy in court, with the affidavit (if any).

Chapter 6
Information to Creditors

2.647

6.73 General duty of official receiver

(1) In accordance with this Chapter, the official receiver shall, at least once after the making of the bankruptcy order, send a report to creditors with respect to the bankruptcy proceedings, and the state of the bankrupt's affairs.

(2) The official receiver shall file in court a copy of any report sent under this Chapter.

2.648

6.74 Those entitled to be informed

Any reference in this Chapter to creditors is to creditors of the bankrupt who are known to the official receiver or, where the bankrupt has submitted a statement of affairs, are identified in the statement.

2.649

6.75 Report where statement of affairs lodged

(1) Where the bankrupt has submitted a statement of affairs, and it has been filed in court, the official receiver shall send out to creditors a report containing a summary of the statement [(if he thinks fit, as amplified, modified or explained by virtue of Rule 6.66 or 6.72)] and such observations (if any) as he thinks fit to make with respect to it or to the bankrupt's affairs generally.

(2) The official receiver need not comply with paragraph (1) if he has previously reported to creditors with respect to the bankrupt's affairs (so far as known to him) and he is of opinion that there are no additional matters which ought to be brought to their attention.

Notes

R 6.75

On the statement of affairs, see generally IA 1986 s 288 and IR 1986 r 6.59 to 6.72.

2.650

6.76 Statement of affairs dispensed with

(1) This Rule applies where the bankrupt has been released from the obligation to submit a statement of affairs.

(2) As soon as may be after the release has been granted, the official receiver shall send to creditors a report containing a summary of the bankrupt's affairs (so far as within his knowledge), and his observations (if any) with respect to it or the bankrupt's affairs generally.

(3) The official receiver need not comply with paragraph (2) if he has previously reported to creditors with respect to the bankrupt's affairs (so far as known to him) and he is of opinion that there are no additional matters which ought to be brought to their attention.

2.651

6.77 General rule as to reporting

(1) The court may, on the official receiver's application, relieve him of any duty imposed on him by this Chapter of the Rules, or authorise him to carry out the duty in a way other than there required.

(2) In considering whether to act as above, the court shall have regard to the cost of carrying out the duty, to the amount of the funds available in the estate, and to the extent of the interest of creditors or any particular class of them.

Notes

RR 6.76, 6.77

On release from the obligation to submit a statement of affairs, see IA 1986 s 288(3) and IR 1986 r 6.62.

2.652

6.78 Bankruptcy order annulled

If the bankruptcy order is annulled, the duty of the official receiver to send reports under the preceding Rules in this Chapter ceases.

Notes

R 6.78

The court may annul a bankruptcy under IA 1986 s 282.

Chapter 7
Creditors' Meetings

Notes

This chapter sets out the procedures for calling creditors' meetings in a bankruptcy and the rules are fairly self explanatory and do not call for detailed comment. Decisions at creditors' meetings are made by ordinary resolution, with the majority being determined according to the value of the creditors' respective debts. Part 8 contains provisions dealing with proxy voting which should be in Form 8.4. Certain terms are defined in Chapter 13, notably 'venue' which is given an extended meaning to encompass the time and date as well as place of the meeting (IR 1986 r 13.6) and 'business day' (IR 1986 r 13.13(1)). This chapter is amended as regards criminal bankruptcy orders by IR 1986 r 6.233.

2.653

6.79 First meeting of creditors

(1) If under section 293(1) the official receiver decides to summon a meeting of creditors, he shall fix a venue for the meeting, not more than 4 months from the date of the bankruptcy order.

(2) When a venue has been fixed, notice of the meeting shall be given—
    (a)   to the court, and

   (b)   to every creditor of the bankrupt who is known to the official receiver or is identified in the bankrupt's statement of affairs.

(3) Notice to the court shall be given forthwith; and the notice to creditors shall be given at least 21 days before the date fixed for the meeting.

(4) The notice to creditors shall specify a time and date, not more than 4 days before the date fixed for the meeting, by which they must lodge proofs and (if applicable) proxies, in order to be entitled to vote at the meeting.

(5) Notice of the meeting shall also be given by public advertisement.

(6) Where the official receiver receives a request by a creditor under section 294 for a meeting of creditors to be summoned, and it appears to him that the request is properly made in accordance with the Act, he shall—
   (a)   withdraw any notice already given by him under section 293(2) (that he has decided not to summon such a meeting), and
   (b)   fix the venue of the meeting for not more than 3 months from his receipt of the creditor's request, and
   (c)   act in accordance with paragraphs (2) to (5) above, as if he had decided under section 293(1) to summon the meeting.

(7) A meeting summoned by the official receiver under section 293 or 294 is known as 'the first meeting of creditors'.

2.654

6.80 Business at first meeting

(1) At the first meeting of creditors, no resolutions shall be taken other than the following—
   (a)   a resolution to appoint a named insolvency practitioner to be trustee in bankruptcy or two or more named insolvency practitioners as joint trustees;
   (b)   a resolution to establish a creditors' committee;
   (c)   (unless it has been resolved to establish a creditors' committee) a resolution specifying the terms on which the trustee is to be remunerated, or to defer consideration of that matter;
   (d)   (if, and only if, two or more persons are appointed to act jointly as trustee) a resolution specifying whether acts are to be done by both or all of them, or by only one;
   (e)   (where the meeting has been requisitioned under section 294) a resolution authorising payment out of the estate, as an expense of the bankruptcy, of the cost of summoning and holding the meeting;
   (f)   a resolution to adjourn the meeting for not more than 3 weeks;
   (g)   any other resolution which the chairman thinks it right to allow for special reasons.

(2) No resolution shall be proposed which has for its object the appointment of the official receiver as trustee.

Notes

R 6.80(1)(b)

See IR 1986 r 6.150ff for provisions concerning the creditors' committee.

2.655

6.81 General power to call meetings

(1) The official receiver or the trustee may at any time summon and conduct meetings of creditors for the purpose of ascertaining their wishes in all matters relating to the bankruptcy.

In relation to any meeting of creditors, the person summoning it is referred to as 'the convener'.

(2) When a venue for the meeting has been fixed, notice of the meeting shall be given by the convener to every creditor who is known to him or is identified in the bankrupt's statement of affairs.

The notice shall be given at least 21 days before the date fixed for the meeting.

(3) The notice to creditors shall specify the purpose for which the meeting is summoned, and a time and date (no more than 4 days before the meeting) by which creditors must lodge proxies and those who have not already lodged proofs must do so, in order to be entitled to vote at the meeting.

(4) Additional notice of the meeting may be given by public advertisement if the convener thinks fit, and shall be so given if the court so orders.

2.656

6.82 The chairman at a meeting

(1) Where the convener of a meeting is the official receiver, he, or a person nominated by him, shall be chairman.

A nomination under this paragraph shall be in writing, unless the nominee is another official receiver or a deputy official receiver.

(2) Where the convener is other than the official receiver, the chairman shall be he, or a person nominated by him in writing to act.

A person nominated under this paragraph must be either—
    (a) one who is qualified to act as an insolvency practitioner in relation to the bankrupt, or
    (b) an employee of the trustee or his firm who is experienced in insolvency matters.

2.657

6.83 Requisitioned meetings

(1) A request by creditors to the official receiver for a meeting of creditors to be summoned shall be accompanied by—
  (a)   a list of the creditors concurring with the request and the amount of their respective claims in the bankruptcy,
  (b)   from each creditor concurring, written confirmation of his concurrence, and
  (c)   a statement of the purpose of the proposed meeting.

Sub-paragraphs (a) and (b) do not apply if the requisitioning creditor's debt is alone sufficient, without the concurrence of other creditors.

(2) The official receiver, if he considers the request to be properly made in accordance with the Act, shall—
  (a)   fix a venue for the meeting, to take place not more than 35 days from the receipt of the request, and
  (b)   give 21 days' notice of the meeting, and of the venue for it, to creditors.

(3) Where a request for a creditors' meeting is made to the trustee, this Rule applies to him as it does to the official receiver.

(4) This Rule shall not apply to voluntary arrangements under section 263A.

_____

Notes

R 6.83(1)

Creditors have the power to requisition a meeting under IA 1986 s 294 using Form 6.34. Any single creditor can requisition a meeting to appoint a trustee where the official receiver fails to do so and the official receiver must do so if the requisition has the support of a quarter of the creditors by value.

_____

2.658

6.84 Attendance at meetings of bankrupt, etc

(1) Whenever a meeting of creditors is summoned, the convener shall give at least 21 days' notice of the meeting to the bankrupt.

(2) If the meeting is adjourned, the chairman of the meeting shall (unless for any reason it appears to him to be unnecessary or impracticable) give notice of the fact to the bankrupt, if the latter was not himself present at the meeting.

(3) The convener may, if he thinks fit, give notice to the bankrupt that he is required to be present, or in attendance.

(4) In the case of any meeting, the bankrupt or any other person may, if he has given reasonable notice of his wish to be present, be admitted; but this is at the discretion of the chairman.

The chairman's decision is final as to what (if any) intervention may be made by the bankrupt, or by any other person admitted to the meeting under this paragraph.

(5) If the bankrupt is not present, and it is desired to put questions to him, the chairman may adjourn the meeting with a view to obtaining his attendance.

(6) Where the bankrupt is present at a creditors' meeting, only such questions may be put to him as the chairman may in his discretion allow.

2.659

6.85 Notice of meetings by advertisement only

(1) In the case of any meeting to be held under the Act or the Rules, the court may order that notice of it be given by public advertisement, and not by individual notice to the persons concerned.

(2) In considering whether to act under this Rule, the court shall have regard to the cost of public advertisement, to the amount of the funds available in the estate, and to the extent of the interest of creditors or any particular class of them.

2.660

6.86 Venue of meetings

(1) In fixing the venue for a meeting of creditors, the person summoning the meeting shall have regard to the convenience of the creditors.

(2) Meetings shall in all cases be summoned for commencement between the hours of 10.00 and 16.00 hours on a business day, unless the court otherwise directs.

(3) With every notice summoning a creditors' meeting there shall be sent out forms of proxy.

Notes

R 6.86

Notices shall be in Form 6.35 or 6.36.

2.661

6.87 Expenses of summoning meetings

(1) Subject to paragraph (3) below, the expenses of summoning and holding a meeting of creditors at the instance of any person other than the official receiver or the trustee shall be paid by that person, who shall deposit security for their payment with the trustee or, if no trustee has been appointed, with the official receiver.

(2) The sum to be deposited shall be such as the trustee or (as the case may be) the official receiver determines to be appropriate; and neither shall act without the deposit having been made.

(3) Where a meeting is so summoned, it may vote that the expenses of summoning and holding it shall be payable out of the estate, as an expense of the bankruptcy.

(4) To the extent that any deposit made under this Rule is not required for the payment of expenses of summoning and holding the meeting, it shall be repaid to the person who made it.

2.662

6.88 Resolutions

(1) Subject as follows, at a meeting of creditors, a resolution is passed when a majority (in value) of those present and voting, in person or by proxy, have voted in favour of the resolution.

(2) In the case of a resolution for the appointment of a trustee—
- (a) if on any vote there are two nominees for appointment, the person who obtains the most support is appointed, provided that such support represents a majority in value of all those present (in person or by proxy) at the meeting and entitled to vote;
- (b) if there are three or more nominees, and one of them has a clear majority over both or all the others together, that one is appointed; and
- (c) in any other case the chairman shall continue to take votes (disregarding at each vote any nominee who has withdrawn and, if no nominee has withdrawn, the nominee who obtained the least support last time), until a clear majority is obtained for any one nominee.

(3) The chairman may at any time put to the meeting a resolution for the joint appointment of any two or more nominees.

(4) Where a resolution is proposed which affects a person in respect of his remuneration or conduct as trustee, or as proposed or former trustee, the vote of that person, and of any partner or employee of his, shall not be reckoned in the majority required for passing the resolution.

This paragraph applies with respect to a vote given by a person (whether personally or on his behalf by a proxy-holder) either as creditor or as proxy-holder for a creditor (but subject to Rule 8.6 in Part 8 of the Rules).

2.663

6.89 Chairman of meeting as proxy-holder

Where the chairman at a meeting holds a proxy for a creditor, which requires him to vote for a particular resolution, and no other person proposes that resolution—
- (a) he shall himself propose it, unless he considers that there is good reason for not doing so, and
- (b) if he does not propose it, he shall forthwith after the meeting notify his principal of the reason why not.

2.664

6.90 Suspension of meeting

Once only in the course of any meeting, the chairman may, in his discretion and without an adjournment, declare the meeting suspended for any period up to one hour.

2.665

6.91 Adjournment

(1) The chairman at any meeting may, in his discretion, and shall if the meeting so resolves, adjourn it to such time and place as seems to him to be appropriate in the circumstances.

This is subject to Rule 6.129(3) in a case where the trustee or his nominee is chairman and a resolution has been proposed for the trustee's removal.

(2) If within a period of 30 minutes from the time appointed for the commencement of a meeting a quorum is not present, then [the chairman may, at his discretion, adjourn the meeting to such time and place as he may appoint].

(3) An adjournment under this Rule shall not be for a period of more than 21 days; and Rule 6.86(1) and (2) applies with regard to the venue of the adjourned meeting.

(4) If there is no person present to act as chairman, some other person present (being entitled to vote) may make the appointment under paragraph (2), with the agreement of others present (being persons so entitled).

Failing agreement, the adjournment shall be to the same time and place in the next following week or, if that is not a business day, to the business day immediately following.

(5) Where a meeting is adjourned under this Rule, proofs and proxies may be used if lodged at any time up to midday on the business day immediately before the adjourned meeting.

2.666

6.92 Quorum

(Revoked)

2.666A

6.93 Entitlement to vote

(1) Subject as follows, at a meeting of creditors a person is entitled to vote as a creditor only if—
  (a) there has been duly lodged, by the time and date stated in the notice of the meeting, a proof of the debt
    [(i) claimed to be due to him from the bankrupt, or
    (ii) in relation to a member State liquidator, is claimed to be due to creditors in proceedings in relation to which he holds office], and the claim has been admitted under Rule 6.94 for the purpose of entitlement to vote, and
  (b) there has been lodged, by that time and date, any proxy requisite for that entitlement.
  (2) The court may, in exceptional circumstances, by order declare the creditors, or any class of them, entitled to vote at creditors' meetings, without being required to prove their debts.

Where a creditor is so entitled, the court may, on the application of the trustee, make such consequential orders as it thinks fit (as for example an order treating a creditor as having proved his debt for the purpose of permitting payment of dividend).

(3) A creditor shall not vote in respect of a debt for an unliquidated amount, or any debt whose value is not ascertained, except where the chairman agrees to put upon the debt an estimated minimum value for the purpose of entitlement to vote and admits his proof for that purpose.

(4) A secured creditor is entitled to vote only in respect of the balance (if any) of his debt after deducting the value of his security as estimated by him.

(5) A creditor shall not vote in respect of a debt on, or secured by, a current bill of exchange or promissory note, unless he is willing—

(a)   to treat the liability to him on the bill or note of every person who is liable on it antecedently to the bankrupt, and against whom a bankruptcy order has not been made (or, in the case of a company, which has not gone into liquidation), as a security in his hands, and

(b)   to estimate the value of the security and (for the purpose of entitlement to vote, but not for dividend) to deduct it from his proof.

[(6) No vote shall be cast by virtue of a debt more than once on any resolution put to the meeting.

(7) Where—

(a)   a creditor is entitled to vote under this Rule and Rule 6.94 (admission of proof),

(b)   has lodged his claim in one or more sets of other proceedings, and

(c)   votes (either in person or by proxy) on a resolution put to the meeting, only the creditor's vote shall be counted.

(8) Where—

(a)   a creditor has lodged his claim in more than one set of other proceedings, and

(b)   more than one member State liquidator seeks to vote by virtue of that claim,

the entitlement to vote by virtue of that claim is exercisable by the member State liquidator in main proceedings, whether or not the creditor has lodged his claim in the main proceedings.

(9) For the purposes of paragraphs (7) and (8), 'other proceedings' means main proceedings, secondary proceedings or territorial proceedings in another member State.]

Notes

R 6.93(1)(a)

Until a creditor's proof is rejected he is entitled to vote and challenge the admission of other creditors to vote: see *Re a Company (004539 of 1993)* [1995] 1 BCLC 459.

2.667

6.94 Admission and rejection of proof

(1) At any creditors' meeting the chairman has power to admit or reject a creditor's proof for the purpose of his entitlement to vote; and the power is exercisable with respect to the whole or any part of the proof.

(2) The chairman's decision under this Rule, or in respect of any matter arising under Rule 6.93, is subject to appeal to the court by any creditor, or by the bankrupt.

(3) If the chairman is in doubt whether a proof should be admitted or rejected, he shall mark it as objected to and allow the creditor to vote, subject to his vote being subsequently declared invalid if the objection to the proof is sustained.

(4) If on an appeal the chairman's decision is reversed or varied, or a creditor's vote is declared invalid, the court may order that another meeting be summoned, or make such other order as it thinks just.

(5) Neither the official receiver nor any person nominated by him to be chairman is personally liable for costs incurred by any person in respect of an application to the court under this Rule; and the chairman (if other than the official receiver or a person so nominated) is not so liable unless the court makes an order to that effect.

Notes

R 6.94(2)

See *Re Gunningham* [2002] BPIR 302 for an example of an appeal from a chairman's decision. The court on hearing the appeal is not restricted to considering only the evidence that was before the chairman at the time he made his decision *National Westminster Bank plc v Scher* [1998] BPIR 224.

2.668

6.95 Record of proceedings

(1) The chairman at any creditors' meeting shall cause minutes of the proceedings at the meeting, signed by him, to be retained by him as part of the records of the bankruptcy.

(2) He shall also cause to be made up and kept a list of all the creditors who attended the meeting.

(3) The minutes of the meeting shall include a record of every resolution passed; and it is the chairman's duty to see to it that particulars of all such resolutions, certified by him, are filed in court not more than 21 days after the date of the meeting.

Chapter 8
Proof of Bankruptcy Debts

Section A: Procedure for Proving

2.669

6.96 Meaning of 'prove'

(1) A person claiming to be a creditor of the bankrupt and wishing to recover his debt in whole or in part must (subject to any order of the court under Rule 6.93(2)) submit his claim in writing to the official receiver, where acting as receiver and manager, or to the trustee.

(2) The creditor is referred to as 'proving' for his debt; and the document by which he seeks to establish his claim is his 'proof'.

(3) Subject to the next two paragraphs, the proof must be in the form known as 'proof of debt' (whether the form prescribed by the Rules, or a substantially similar form), which shall be made out by or under the directions of the creditor, and signed by him or a person authorised in that behalf.

(4) Where a debt is due to a Minister of the Crown or a Government Department, the proof need not be in that form, provided that there are shown all such particulars of the debt as are required in the form used by other creditors, and as are relevant in the circumstances.

(5) Where an existing trustee proves in a later bankruptcy under section 335(5), the proof must be in Form 6.38.

(6) In certain circumstances, specified below in this Chapter, the proof must be in the form of an affidavit.

Notes

R 6.96

The rule details the procedure to be followed by a creditor when proving for a debt in the bankruptcy (see IA 1986 s 322 which requires that any proof be submitted in accordance with the rules). The general form in which the proof should be submitted is Form 6.37, but note that Form 6.38 is required (IR 1986 r 6.96(5)) where an existing trustee proves in a later bankruptcy of the same individual. Note also that the trustee may require the debt to be verified by an affidavit (rather than, or in addition to, the general form which needs only to be signed by the creditor 'or a person authorised by him'): see IR 1986 r 6.99 below.

2.670

6.97 Supply of forms

A form of proof shall be sent to any creditor of the bankrupt by the official receiver or trustee where the creditor so requests.

2.671

6.98 Contents of proof

(1) Subject to Rule 6.96(4), the following matters shall be stated in a creditor's proof of debt—

(a) the creditor's name and address and, if a company, its company registration number;

(b) the total amount of his claim (including any Value Added Tax) as at the date of the bankruptcy order;

(c) whether or not that amount includes outstanding uncapitalised interest;

(d) particulars of how and when the debt was incurred by the debtor;

(e) particulars of any security held, the date when it was given and the value which the creditor puts upon it

(f) details of any reservation of title in respect of goods to which the debt refers; and

(g) the name, and address and authority of the person signing the proof (if other than the creditor himself).]

(2) There shall be specified in the proof any documents by reference to which the debt can be substantiated; but (subject as follows) it is not essential that such documents be attached to the proof or submitted with it.

(3) The trustee, the official receiver, acting as receiver and manager or the convener or chairman of any meeting, may call for any document or other evidence to be produced to him, where he thinks it necessary for the purpose of substantiating the whole or any part of the claim made in the proof.

Notes

R 6.98(1)

The various matters that are required by this provision to be stated in the proof of debt are identified in Form 6.37 (the prescribed general form for proof). If the debt in question has not fallen due by the date of the bankruptcy order (a possibility not catered for in Form 6.37 but envisaged by IR 1986 r 6.114) then this would need to be made clear to the trustee and the calculation provided for by IR 1986 r 11.13 would then be applied to reduce the amount payable. There is no specified time limit for submission of proofs of debt, but a creditor who has not submitted a proof will not be able to vote at meetings. The trustee can seek a direction from the court requiring proofs to be lodged by a particular time (IA 1986 s 363).

2.672

6.99 Claim established by affidavit

(1) The trustee or the official receiver, acting as receiver and manager may, if he thinks it necessary, require a claim of debt to be verified by affidavit, for which purpose there shall be used the form known as 'affidavit of debt'.

(2) An affidavit may be required notwithstanding that a proof of debt has already been lodged.

(3) The affidavit may be sworn before an official receiver or a deputy official receiver, or before an officer of the Department or of the court duly authorised in that behalf.

Notes

R 6.99(1)

There is no restriction on the power of the trustee, or the official receiver, to require an affidavit (which should be in Form 6.39) verifying the debt instead of, or in addition to, a proof in the general form.

2.673

6.100 Cost of proving

(1) Subject as follows, every creditor bears the cost of proving his own debt, including such as may be incurred in providing documents or evidence under Rule 6.98(3).

(2) Costs incurred by the trustee in estimating the value of a bankruptcy debt under section 322(3) (debts not bearing a certain value) fall on the estate, as an expense of the bankruptcy.

(3) Paragraphs (1) and (2) apply unless the court otherwise orders.

2.674

6.101 Trustee to allow inspection of proofs

The trustee shall, so long as proofs lodged with him are in his hands, allow them to be inspected, at all reasonable times on any business day, by any of the following persons—
 (a) any creditor who has submitted his proof of debt (unless his proof has been wholly rejected for purposes of dividend or otherwise),
 (b) the bankrupt, and
 (c) any person acting on behalf of either of the above.

Notes

R 6.101

Creditors (as well as the bankrupt) may inspect all proofs that have been lodged with the trustee.

2.675

6.102 Proof of licensed moneylender

A proof of debt in respect of a money-lending transaction made before 27th January 1980, where the creditor was at the time of the transaction a licensed moneylender, shall have endorsed on or annexed to it a statement setting out in detail the particulars mentioned in section 9(2) of the Moneylenders Act 1927.

Notes

R 6.102

The details referred to in s 9(2) of the Moneylenders Act 1927 (repealed) include details about the amount lent, the date when the sum(s) in question was advanced, the amount and date of any repayment, the amount outstanding, and details in relation to interest.

2.676

6.103 Transmission of proofs to trustee

(1) Where a trustee is appointed, the official receiver shall forthwith transmit to him all the proofs which he has so far received, together with an itemised list of them.

(2) The trustee shall sign the list by way of receipt for the proofs, and return it to the official receiver.

(3) From then on, all proofs of debt shall be sent to the trustee and retained by him.

2.677

6.104 Admission and rejection of proofs for dividend

(1) A proof may be admitted for dividend either for the whole amount claimed by the creditor, or for part of that amount.

(2) If the trustee rejects a proof in whole or in part, he shall prepare a written statement of his reasons for doing so, and send it forthwith to the creditor.

Notes

R 6.104(1)

This is not simply an administrative function. The trustee should examine every proof and consider its validity even where it is based on a judgment or account stated: see *Re Lupkovics [1954] 1 WLR 1234*.

R 6.104(2)

If the trustee does reject the creditor's proof then there is a right of appeal which must be exercised in accordance with the provisions of IR 1986 r 6.105 below.

2.678

6.105 Appeal against decision on proof

(1) If a creditor is dissatisfied with the trustee's decision with respect to his proof (including any decision on the question of preference), he may apply to the court for the decision to be reversed or varied.

The application must be made within 21 days of his receiving the statement sent under Rule 6.104(2).

(2) The bankrupt or any other creditor may, if dissatisfied with the trustee's decision admitting or rejecting the whole or any part of a proof, make such an application within 21 days of becoming aware of the trustee's decision.

(3) Where application is made to the court under this Rule, the court shall fix a venue for the application to be heard, notice of which shall be sent by the applicant to the creditor who lodged the proof in question (if it is not himself) and to the trustee.

(4) The trustee shall, on receipt of the notice, file in court the relevant proof, together (if appropriate) with a copy of the statement sent under Rule 6.104(2).

(5) After the application has been heard and determined, the proof shall, unless it has been wholly disallowed, be returned by the court to the trustee.

(6) The official receiver is not personally liable for costs incurred by any person in respect of an application under this Rule; and the trustee (if other than the official receiver) is not so liable unless the court makes an order to that effect.

Notes

R 6.105(1)

The court has the power to extend the 21 day time limit for contesting the trustee's decision pursuant to the provisions of IA 1986 s 376.

R 6.105(2)

The application under this rule is not a true appeal: it involves a fresh consideration of the matter and the court is not restricted to the evidence that was available to the trustee *Re Trepca Mines Ltd [1960] 1 WLR 1273*. The court will approach the question of whether the proof should be admitted by reference to the evidence and arguments put before it (irrespective of the way in which the issues were put before the trustee). However a claim which was unliquidated at the time of a creditors' meeting under IA 1986 s 98 cannot be treated retrospectively as a liquidated claim when after the meeting it was converted to a judgment *Re Shruth Limited [2005] BPIR 1455. .* The court may reverse or vary the trustee's decision in any way it thinks fit: see *In re Kentwood Construction Ltd [1960] 1 WLR 646*, and *Cadwell v Jackson [2001] BPIR 966*. The court may also uphold the trustee's decision on the basis of a ground not included in his statement of reasons under IR 1986 r 6.104(2): see *Re Thomas Christy Ltd [1994] 2 BCLC 527*.

R 6.105(3)

In appropriate cases the court can make orders for statements of case, disclosure and cross examination (see *Mahfouz v Morris* [1994] 1 BCLC 450) rather than allow the proof to be tested by the private examination procedure under *IA 1986 s 366*: see *Re BCCI SA (No 7)* [1994] 1 BCLC 455.

2.679

6.106 Withdrawal or variation of proof

A creditor's proof may at any time, by agreement between himself and the trustee, be withdrawn or varied as to the amount claimed.

2.680

6.107 Expunging of proof by the court

(1) The court may expunge a proof or reduce the amount claimed—
    (a)   on the trustee's application, where he thinks that the proof has been improperly admitted, or ought to be reduced; or
    (b)   on the application of a creditor, if the trustee declines to interfere in the matter.

(2) Where application is made to the court under this Rule, the court shall fix a venue for the application to be heard, notice of which shall be sent by the applicant—
    (a)   in the case of an application by the trustee, to the creditor who made the proof, and
    (b)   in the case of an application by a creditor, to the trustee and to the creditor who made the proof (if not himself).

Notes

R 6.107(1)

The court will admit the evidence as it is at the date of the hearing, whatever the basis on which the trustee has considered matters: see the note to IR 1986 R 6.105 above. No time limit for an application is stated and mere lapse of time does not bar the court's right to expunge or reduce a proof *Re Tait (1882) 21 Ch D 537*.

R 6.107(2)

If a proof is expunged or reduced a creditor may retain any dividend previously received but he is not entitled to any further dividend without giving credit for the overpayment in respect of his original proof *Re Browne (A bankrupt) [1960] 1 WLR 692*.

Section B: Quantification of Claim

2.681

6.108 Negotiable instruments, etc

Unless the trustee allows, a proof in respect of money owed on a bill of exchange, promissory note, cheque or other negotiable instrument or security cannot be admitted unless there is produced the instrument or security itself or a copy of it, certified by the creditor or his authorised representative to be a true copy.

Notes

R 6.108

Relevant documentation need not generally be attached to the proof (IR 1986 r 6.98(2)), but where the debt is owed on a negotiable instrument, the document, or a certified copy of it, will be required unless the trustee agrees that it need not be produced.

2.682

6.109 Secured creditors

(1) If a secured creditor realises his security, he may prove for the balance of his debt, after deducting the amount realised.

(2) If a secured creditor voluntarily surrenders his security for the general benefit of creditors, he may prove for his whole debt, as if it were unsecured.

Notes

R 6.109(1)

A creditor cannot prove for interest after the date of the bankruptcy order (but see IA 1986 s 328(4) for the circumstances in which interest might be recovered) and accordingly a secured creditor cannot apply the proceeds of any security in discharge of interest for a period after the bankruptcy. The proceeds of the security should be applied in discharge of the amount due at the date of bankruptcy, and a proof submitted for the balance: see *Re London, Windsor and Greenwich Hotels Co [1892] 1 Ch 639.*

2.683

6.110 Discounts

There shall in every case be deducted from the claim all trade and other discounts which would have been available to the bankrupt but for his bankruptcy, except any discount for immediate, early or cash settlement.

2.604

6.111 Debt in foreign currency

(1) For the purpose of proving a debt incurred or payable in a currency other than sterling, the amount of the debt shall be converted into sterling at the official exchange rate prevailing on the date of the bankruptcy order.

> (2) 'The official exchange rate' is the middle exchange rate on the London Foreign Exchange Market at the close of business as published for the date in question. In the absence of any such published rate, it is such rate as the court determines.
>
> **2.685**
>
> **6.112 Payments of a periodical nature**
>
> (1) In the case of rent and other payments of a periodical nature, the creditor may prove for any amounts due and unpaid up to the date of the bankruptcy order.
>
> (2) Where at that date any payment was accruing due, the creditor may prove for so much as would have fallen due at that date, if accruing from day to day.

Notes

R 6.112(1)

Where a lease is continuing the landlord cannot prove for future rent (or other prospective amounts), but only for such amount as has become due at the date of the bankruptcy order. The position may be otherwise if the landlord is prepared to accept that the lease is terminated: see *Re Panther Lead Co [1896] Ch 978*. See also IA 1986 s 378 for the provisions governing disclaimer of an onerous lease by the trustee, and the House of Lords decision in *Re Park Air Services plc [2000] AC 172*, regarding the calculation of the landlord's loss (for which he can prove) if disclaimer takes place; in that case the appropriate discount rate used was the yield on gilt edged securities for the appropriate term which was 8.5%.

> **2.686**
>
> **6.113 Interest**
>
> (1) In the following circumstances the creditor's claim may include interest on the debt for periods before the bankruptcy order; although not previously reserved or agreed.
>
> (2) If the debt is due by virtue of a written instrument and payable at a certain time, interest may be claimed for the period from that time to the date of the bankruptcy order.
>
> (3) If the debt is due otherwise, interest may only be claimed if, before the presentation of the bankruptcy petition, a demand for payment was made in writing by or on behalf of the creditor, and notice given that interest would be payable from the date of the demand to the date of payment [and for all the purposes of the Act and the Rules shall be chargeable at a rate not exceeding that mentioned in paragraph (5)].
>
> (4) Interest under paragraph (3) may only be claimed for the period from the date of the demand to that of the bankruptcy order.

> (5) The rate of interest to be claimed under paragraphs (2) and (3) is the rate specified in section 17 of the Judgments Act 1838 on the date of the bankruptcy order.

Notes

R 6.113

The judgment debt rate is presently 8% per annum: Judgment Debts (Rate of Interest) Order 1993, SI 1993/564. As regards the possibility of creditors receiving interest in relation to the period after the date of the bankruptcy order, see IA 1986 s 328(4). Where a contract contains provisions for the capitalisation of interest falling due before the bankruptcy these are to be applied in the quantification of a creditors' claim, but such provisions cannot be applied to interest payments falling due after the commencement of the bankruptcy *Re Amalgamated Investment and Property Co Ltd [1984] BCLC 341.*

2.687

6.114 Debt payable at future time

A creditor may prove for a debt of which payment was not yet due at the date of the bankruptcy order, but subject to Rule 11.13 in Part 11 of the Rules (adjustment of dividend where payment made before time).

Notes

R 6.114

The formula to be applied for the purposes of discounting a debt that has not fallen due by the date of the bankruptcy order is provided in IR 1986 r 11.13 which was amended by the Insolvency (Amendment) Rules 2005 (SI 2005/527).

Chapter 9
Secured Creditors

2.688

6.115 Value of security

(1) A secured creditor may, with the agreement of the trustee or the leave of the court, at any time alter the value which he has, in his proof of debt, put upon his security.

(2) However, if a secured creditor—
    (a)   being the petitioner, has in the petition put a value on his security, or
    (b)   has voted in respect of the unsecured balance of his debt,

> he may re-value his security only with leave of the court.

Notes

R 6.115(2)

Once a secured creditor has either put a value on his security for the purposes of petitioning or has voted in respect of the unsecured balance of the debt, a re-valuation of the security may only be effected with the permission of the court; and see *Joseph Manuel Key v FNCB Ltd* [2006] EWHC 1386 (Ch) in the context of a term in a voluntary arrangement which was unsuccessfully asserted as preventing a secured creditor from enforcing its security. See also IR 1986 r 6.119, below, which provides that once the creditor has realised the security the actual amount shall replace the valuation previously put on it, and IR 1986 r 11.9, below, which provides for such monetary adjustment as may then be necessary in respect of the dividend received by the creditor. These provisions were considered in *Khan v Mortgage Express* [2000] BPIR 473.

2.689

6.116 Surrender for non-disclosure

(1) If a secured creditor omits to disclose his security in his proof of debt, he shall surrender his security for the general benefit of creditors, unless the court, on application by him, relieves him from the effect of this Rule on the ground that the omission was inadvertent or the result of honest mistake.

(2) If the court grants that relief, it may require or allow the creditor's proof of debt to be amended, on such terms as may be just.

(3) Nothing in this Rule or the following two Rules may affect the rights in rem of creditors or third parties protected under Article 5 of the EC Regulation (third parties' rights in rem).

Notes

R 6.116(1)

A secured creditor will forfeit his security if he does not disclose it in the proof of debt. The court's power to grant relief from that forfeiture is dependent on the finding that the failure was inadvertent or an honest mistake.

2.690

6.117 Redemption by trustee

(1) The trustee may at any time give notice to a creditor whose debt is secured that he proposes, at the expiration of 28 days from the date of the notice, to redeem the security at the value put upon it in the creditor's proof.

(2) The creditor then has 21 days (or such longer period as the trustee may allow) in which, if he so wishes, to exercise his right to re-value his security (with the leave of the court, where Rule 6.115(2) applies).

If the creditor re-values his security, the trustee may only redeem at the new value.

(3) If the trustee redeems the security, the cost of transferring it is borne by the estate.

(4) A secured creditor may at any time, by a notice in writing, call on the trustee to elect whether he will or will not exercise his power to redeem the security at the value then placed on it; and the trustee then has 6 months in which to exercise the power or determine not to exercise it.

Notes

R 6.117

This and the following rule make provision for the trustee to effect a release of security held over the bankrupt's assets either on terms agreed with the secured creditor or directed by the Court.

2.691

6.118 Test of security's value

(1) Subject as follows, the trustee, if he is dissatisfied with the value which a secured creditor puts on his security (whether in his proof or by way of re-valuation under Rule 6.117), may require any property comprised in the security to be offered for sale.

(2) The terms of sale shall be such as may be agreed, or as the court may direct; and if the sale is by auction, the trustee on behalf of the estate, and the creditor on his own behalf, may appear and bid.

(3) This Rule does not apply if the security has been re-valued and the re-valuation has been approved by the court.

2.692

6.119 Realisation of security by creditor

If a creditor who has valued his security subsequently realises it (whether or not at the instance of the trustee)—
    (a)   the net amount realised shall be substituted for the value previously put by the creditor on the security; and
    (b)   that amount shall be treated in all respects as an amended valuation made by him.

Notes

R 6.119

Once a creditor has realised his security the actual amount shall replace the valuation previously put on it; see also IR 1986 r 6.115.

Chapter 10
The Trustee in Bankruptcy

Section A: Appointment and Associated Formalities

2.693

6.120 Appointment by creditors' meeting

(1) This Rule applies where a person has been appointed trustee by resolution of a creditors' meeting.

(2) The chairman of the meeting shall certify the appointment, but not unless and until the person to be appointed has provided him with a written statement to the effect that he is an insolvency practitioner, duly qualified under the Act to act as trustee in relation to the bankrupt, and that he consents so to act.

[(3) The trustee's appointment is effective from the date on which the appointment is certified, that date to be endorsed on the certificate.

(4) The chairman of the meeting (if not himself the official receiver) shall send the certificate to the official receiver.

(5) The official receiver shall in any case send the certificate to the trustee and file a copy of it in court.]

Notes

R 6.120

The relevant forms are Forms 6.40 or 6.41.

2.694

6.121 Appointment by the court

(1) This Rule applies where the court under section 297(3), (4) or (5) appoints the trustee.

(2) The court's order shall not issue unless and until the person appointed has filed in court a statement to the effect that he is an insolvency practitioner, duly qualified under the Act to be the trustee, and that he consents so to act.

(3) Thereafter, the court shall send 2 copies of the order to the official receiver. One of the copies shall be sealed, and this shall be sent by him to the person appointed as trustee.

(4) The trustee's appointment takes effect from the date of the order.

Notes

R 6.121

The relevant forms are Forms 6.42 and 6.43.

2.695

6.122 Appointment by Secretary of State

(1) This Rule applies where the official receiver—
  (a) under section 295 or 300, refers to the Secretary of State the need for an appointment of a trustee, or
  (b) under section 296, applies to the Secretary of State to make the appointment.

(2) If the Secretary of State makes an appointment he shall send two copies of the certificate of appointment to the official receiver, who shall transmit one such copy to the person appointed, and file the other copy in court.

The certificate shall specify the date from which the trustee's appointment is to be effective.

2.696

6.123 Authentication of trustee's appointment

Where a trustee is appointed under any of the 3 preceding Rules, a sealed copy of the order of appointment or (as the case may be) a copy of the certificate of his appointment may in any proceedings be adduced as proof that he is duly authorised to exercise the powers and perform the duties of trustee of the bankrupt's estate.

2.697

6.124 Advertisement of appointment

(1) Where the trustee is appointed by a creditors' meeting, he shall, forthwith after receiving his certificate of appointment, give notice of his appointment in such newspaper as he thinks most appropriate for ensuring that it comes to the notice of the bankrupt's creditors.

(2) The expense of giving the notice shall be borne in the first instance by the trustee; but he is entitled to be reimbursed by the estate, as an expense of the bankruptcy.

The same applies also in the case of the notice or advertisement under section 296(4) (appointment of trustee by Secretary of State), and of the notice or advertisement under section 297(7) (appointment by the court).

2.698

6.125 Hand-over of estate to trustee

(1) This Rule applies only where—
  (a) the bankrupt's estate vests in the trustee under Chapter IV of Part IX of the Act, following a period in which the official receiver is the receiver and manager of the estate according to section 287, or
  (b) the trustee is appointed in succession to the official receiver acting as trustee.

(2) When the trustee's appointment takes effect, the official receiver shall forthwith do all that is required for putting him into possession of the estate.

(3) On taking possession of the estate, the trustee shall discharge any balance due to the official receiver on account of—

   (a) expenses properly incurred by him and payable under the Act or the Rules, and

   (b) any advances made by him in respect of the estate, together with interest on such advances at the rate specified in section 17 of the Judgments Act 1838 on the date of the bankruptcy order.

(4) Alternatively, the trustee may (before taking office) give to the official receiver a written undertaking to discharge any such balance out of the first realisation of assets.

(5) The official receiver has a charge on the estate in respect of any sums due to him under paragraph (3). But, where the trustee has realised assets with a view to making those payments, the official receiver's charge does not extend in respect of sums deductible by the trustee from the proceeds of realisation, as being expenses properly incurred therein.

(6) The trustee shall from time to time out of the realisation of assets discharge all guarantees properly given by the official receiver for the benefit of the estate, and shall pay all the official receiver's expenses.

(7) The official receiver shall give to the trustee all such information, relating to the affairs of the bankrupt and the course of the bankruptcy, as he (the official receiver) considers to be reasonably required for the effective discharge by the trustee of his duties in relation to the estate.

(8) The trustee shall also be furnished with any report of the official receiver under Chapter 6 of this Part of the Rules.

Section B: Resignation and Removal; Vacation of Office

2.699

6.126 Creditors' meeting to receive trustee's resignation

(1) Before resigning his office, the trustee must call a meeting of creditors for the purpose of receiving his resignation. Notice of the meeting shall be sent to the official receiver at the same time as it is sent to creditors.

(2) The notice to creditors must be accompanied by an account of the trustee's administration of the bankrupt's estate, including—

   (a) a summary of his receipts and payments and

   (b) a statement by him that he has reconciled his account with that which is held by the Secretary of State in respect of the bankruptcy.

(3) Subject as follows, the trustee may only proceed under this Rule on grounds of ill health or because—

   (a) he intends ceasing to be in practice as an insolvency practitioner, or

   (b) there is some conflict of interest or change of personal circumstances which precludes or makes impracticable the further discharge by him of the duties of trustee.

(4) Where two or more persons are acting as trustee jointly, any one of them may proceed under this Rule (without prejudice to the continuation

in office of the other or others) on the ground that, in his opinion and that of the other or others, it is no longer expedient that there should continue to be the present number of joint trustees.

[(5) If there is no quorum present at the meeting summoned to receive the trustee's resignation, the meeting is deemed to have been held, a resolution is deemed to have been passed that the trustee's resignation be accepted and the creditors are deemed not to have resolved against the trustee having his release.

(6) Where paragraph (5) applies any reference in the Rules to a resolution that the trustee's resignation be accepted is replaced by a reference to the making of a written statement, signed by the person who, had there been a quorum present, would have been chairman of the meeting, that no quorum was present and that the trustee may resign.]

Notes

R 6.126(1)

A trustee may resign in accordance with IA 1986 s 298. Notice must also be given to the official receiver if there are unrealised assets (IR 1986 r 6.145).

R 6.126(5)

As to quorum see IR 1986 r 12.4A.

2.700

6.127 Action following acceptance of resignation

(1) Where a meeting of creditors is summoned for the purpose of receiving the trustee's resignation, the notice summoning it shall indicate that this is the purpose, or one of the purposes, of the meeting; and the notice shall draw the attention of creditors to Rule 6.135 with respect to the trustee's release.

(2) A copy of the notice shall at the same time also be sent to the official receiver.

(3) Where the chairman of the meeting is other than the official receiver, and there is passed at the meeting any of the following resolutions—
    (a)   that the trustee's resignation be accepted,
    (b)   that a new trustee be appointed,
    (c)   that the resigning trustee be not given his release,
the chairman shall, within 3 days, send to the official receiver a copy of the resolution

If it has been resolved to accept the trustee's resignation, the chairman shall send to the official receiver a certificate to that effect.

(4) If the creditors have resolved to appoint a new trustee, the certificate of his appointment shall also be sent to the official receiver within that time; and Rule 6.120 above shall be complied with in respect of it.

(5) If the trustee's resignation is accepted, the notice of it required by section 298(7) shall be given by him forthwith after the meeting; and he shall send a copy of the notice to the official receiver.

The notice shall be accompanied by a copy of the account sent to creditors under Rule 6.126(2).

(6) The official receiver shall file a copy of the notice in court.

(7) The trustee's resignation is effective as from the date on which the official receiver files the copy notice in court, that date to be endorsed on the copy notice.

2.701

6.128 Leave to resign granted by the court

(1) If at a creditors' meeting summoned to accept the trustee's resignation it is resolved that it be not accepted, the court may, on the trustee's application, make an order giving him leave to resign.

(2) The court's order under this Rule may include such provision as it thinks fit with respect to matters arising in connection with the resignation, and shall determine the date from which the trustee's release is effective.

(3) The court shall send two sealed copies of the order to the trustee, who shall send one of the copies forthwith to the official receiver.

(4) On sending notice of his resignation to the court, as required by section 298(7), the trustee shall send a copy of it to the official receiver.

Notes

R 6.128

The relevant forms are Forms 6.45, 6.46.

2.702

6.129 Meeting of creditors to remove trustee

(1) Where a meeting of creditors is summoned for the purpose of removing the trustee, the notice summoning it shall indicate that this is the purpose, or one of the purposes, of the meeting; and the notice shall draw the attention of creditors to section 299(3) with respect to the trustee's release.

(2) A copy of the notice shall at the same time also be sent to the official receiver.

(3) At the meeting, a person other than the trustee or his nominee may be elected to act as chairman; but if the trustee or his nominee is chairman and a resolution has been proposed for the trustee's removal, the chairman shall not adjourn the meeting without the consent of at least one-half (in value) of the creditors present (in person or by proxy) and entitled to vote.

(4) Where the chairman of the meeting is other than the official receiver, and there is passed at the meeting any of the following resolutions—
  (a)   that the trustee be removed,
  (b)   that a new trustee be appointed,
  (c)   that the removed trustee be not given his release,
the chairman shall, within 3 days, send to the official receiver a copy of the resolution.

If it has been resolved to remove the trustee, the chairman shall send to the official receiver a certificate to that effect.

(5) If the creditors have resolved to appoint a new trustee, the certificate of his appointment shall also be sent to the official receiver within that time; and rule 6.120 shall be complied with in respect of it.

Notes

R 6.129

The notice in para (1) should be in Form 6.35 and in para (4) in Form 6.47. The notice in para (1) should be in Form 6.35. The notice in paragraph 4 should be in Form 6.47.

2.703

6.130 Court's power to regulate meeting under Rule 6.129

Where a meeting under Rule 6.129 is to be held, or is proposed to be summoned, the court may on the application of any creditor give directions as to the mode of summoning it, the sending out and return of forms of proxy, the conduct of the meeting, and any other matter which appears to the court to require regulation or control.

2.704

6.131 Procedure on removal

(1) Where the creditors have resolved that the trustee be removed, the official receiver shall file the certificate of removal in court.

(2) The resolution is effective as from the date on which the official receiver files the certificate of removal in court, and that date shall be endorsed on the certificate.

(3) A copy of the certificate, so endorsed, shall be sent by the official receiver to the trustee who has been removed and, if a new trustee has been appointed, to him.

(4) The official receiver shall not file the certificate in court until the Secretary of State has certified to him that the removed trustee has reconciled his account with that held by the Secretary of State in respect of the bankruptcy.

2.705

6.132 Removal of trustee by the court

(1) This Rule applies where application is made to the court for the removal of the trustee, or for an order directing the trustee to summon a meeting of creditors for the purpose of removing him.

(2) The court may, if it thinks that no sufficient cause is shown for the application, disMiss it; but it shall not do so unless the applicant has had an opportunity to attend the court for an *ex parte* hearing, of which he has been given at least 7 days' notice.

If the application is not dismissed under this paragraph, the court shall fix a venue for it to be heard.

(3) The applicant shall, at least 14 days before the hearing, send to the trustee and the official receiver notice stating the venue so fixed; and the notice shall be accompanied by a copy of the application, and of any evidence which the applicant intends to adduce in support of it.

(4) Subject to any contrary order of the court, the costs of the application do not fall on the estate.

(5) Where the court removes the trustee—
   (a)   it shall send copies of the order of removal to him and to the official receiver;
   (b)   the order may include such provision as the court thinks fit with respect to matters arising in connection with the removal; and
   (c)   if the court appoints a new trustee, Rule 6.121 applies.

2.706

6.133 Removal of trustee by Secretary of State

(1) If the Secretary of State decides to remove the trustee, he shall before doing so notify the trustee and the official receiver of his decision and the grounds of it, and specify a period within which the trustee may make representations against implementation of the decision.

(2) If the Secretary of State directs the removal of the trustee, he shall forthwith—
   (a)   file notice of his decision in court, and
   (b)   send notice to the trustee and the official receiver.

(3) If the trustee is removed by direction of the Secretary of State, the court may make any such order in his case as it would have power to make if he had been removed by itself.

2.707

6.134 Advertisement of resignation or removal

Where a new trustee is appointed in place of one who has resigned or been removed, the new trustee shall, in the advertisement of his appointment, state that his predecessor has resigned or, as the case may be, been removed and (if it be the case) that he has been given his release.

2.708

6.135 Release of resigning or removed trustee

(1) Where the trustee's resignation is accepted by a meeting of creditors which has not resolved against his release, he has his release from when his resignation is effective under Rule 6.127.

(2) Where the trustee is removed by a meeting of creditors which has not resolved against his release, the fact of his release shall be stated in the certificate of removal.

(3) Where—
  (a) the trustee resigns, and the creditors' meeting called to receive his resignation has resolved against his release, or
  (b) he is removed by a creditors' meeting which has so resolved, or is removed by the court,
he must apply to the Secretary of State for his release.

(4) When the Secretary of State gives the release, he shall certify it accordingly, and send the certificate to the official receiver, to be filed in court.

(5) A copy of the certificate shall be sent by the Secretary of State to the former trustee, whose release is effective from the date of the certificate.

Section C: Release on Completion of Administration

2.709

6.136 Release of official receiver

(1) The official receiver shall, before giving notice to the Secretary of State under section 299(2) (that the administration of the estate is for practical purposes complete), send out notice of his intention to do so to all creditors who have proved their debts, and to the bankrupt.

(2) The notice shall in each case be accompanied by a summary of the official receiver's receipts and payments as trustee.

(3) The Secretary of State, when he has under section 299(2) determined the date from which the official receiver is to have his release, shall give notice to the court that he has done so. The notice shall be accompanied by the summary referred to in paragraph (2).

2.710

6.137 Final meeting of creditors

(1) Where the trustee is other than the official receiver, he shall give at least 28 days' notice of the final meeting of creditors to be held under section 331. The notice shall be sent to all creditors who have proved their debts, and to the bankrupt.

(2) The trustee's report laid before the meeting under that section shall include—
  (a) a summary of his receipts and payments, and
  (b) a statement by him that he has reconciled his account with that which is held by the Secretary of State in respect of the bankruptcy.

(3) At the final meeting, the creditors may question the trustee with respect to any matter contained in his report, and may resolve against him having his release.

(4) The trustee shall give notice to the court that the final meeting has been held; and the notice shall state whether or not he has been given his release, and be accompanied by a copy of the report laid before the final meeting. A copy of the notice shall be sent by the trustee to the Secretary of State.

(5) If there is no quorum present at the final meeting, the trustee shall report to the court that a final meeting was summoned in accordance with the Rules, but there was no quorum present; and the final meeting is then deemed to have been held, and the creditors not to have resolved against the trustee having his release.

(6) If the creditors at the final meeting have not so resolved, the trustee is released when the notice under paragraph (4) is filed in court. If they have so resolved, the trustee must obtain his release from the Secretary of State, as provided by Rule 6.135.

2.711

6.137A Rule as to reporting

[(1) The court may, on the trustee or official receiver's application, relieve him of any duty imposed on him by Rules 6.136 or 6.137, or authorise him to carry out the duty in a way other than there required.

(2) In considering whether to act as above, the court shall have regard to the cost of carrying out the duty, to the amount of the funds available in the estate, and to the extent of the interest of creditors or any particular class of them.]

Section D: Remuneration

2.712

6.138 Fixing of remuneration

(1) The trustee is entitled to receive remuneration for his services as such.

(2) The remuneration shall be fixed either—
    (a) as a percentage of the value of the assets in the bankrupt's estate which are realised or distributed, or of the one value and the other in combination, or
    (b) by reference to the time properly given by the insolvency practitioner (as trustee) and his staff in attending to matters arising in the bankruptcy.

(3) Where the trustee is other than the official receiver, it is for the creditors' committee (if there is one) to determine whether his remuneration is to be fixed under paragraph (2)(a) or (b) and, if under paragraph (2)(a), to determine any percentage to be applied as there mentioned.

(4) In arriving at that determination, the committee shall have regard to the following matters—
    (a) the complexity (or otherwise) of the case,
    (b) any respects in which, in connection with the administration of the estate, there falls on the insolvency practitioner (as trustee) any responsibility of an exceptional kind or degree,
    (c) the effectiveness with which the insolvency practitioner appears to be carrying out, or to have carried out, his duties as trustee, and

(d)   the value and nature of the assets in the estate with which the trustee has to deal.

(5) If there is no creditors' committee, or the committee does not make the requisite determination, the trustee's remuneration may be fixed (in accordance with paragraph (2)) by a resolution of a meeting of creditors; and paragraph (4) applies to them as it does to the creditors' committee.

(6) Where the trustee is not the official receiver and his remuneration is not fixed as above, the trustee shall be entitled to remuneration calculated in accordance with Rule 6.138A.].

Notes

R 6.138

The fixing of the trustee's; remuneration must now be considered in the light of the Practice Statement – The Fixing and Approval of the Remuneration of Appointees [2004] BPIR 953 and *Re Cabletel Installations Ltd* [2005] BPIR 28; see the notes to the Practice Statement.

2.713

6.138A Trustees remuneration where it is not fixed in accordance with Rule 6.138

[(1) This Rule applies where the trustee is not the official receiver and his remuneration is not fixed in accordance with Rule 6.138.

(2) Subject to paragraph (3), the trustee shall be entitled by way of remuneration for his services as such, to such sum as is arrived at by—
  (a)   first applying the realisation scale set out in Schedule 6 to the monies received by him from the realisation of the assets of the bankrupt (including any Value Added Tax thereon but after deducting any sums paid to secured creditors in respect of their securities and any sums spent out of money received in carrying on the business of the bankrupt); and
  (b)   then by adding to the sum arrived at under sub-paragraph (a) such sum as is arrived at by applying the distribution scale set out in Schedule 6 to the value of assets distributed to creditors of the bankrupt (including sums paid in respect of preferential debts).

(3) That part of the trustee's remuneration calculated by reference to the realisation scale shall not exceed such sum as is arrived at by applying the realisation scale to such part of the bankrupt's assets as are required to pay the items referred to in paragraph (4).

(4) The items referred to in paragraph (3) are—
  (a)   the bankruptcy debts (including any interest payable by virtue of section 328(4)) to the extent required to be paid by these Rules (ignoring those debts paid otherwise than out of the proceeds of the realisation of the bankrupt's assets or which have been secured to the satisfaction of the court);
  (b)   the expenses of the bankruptcy other than—
      (i)   fees or the remuneration of the official receiver; and

      (ii)   any sums spent out of money received in carrying on the business of the bankrupt;

  (c)   fees payable by virtue of any order made under section 415; and

  (d)   the remuneration of the official receiver.]

2.714

6.139 Other matters affecting remuneration

[(1) Where the trustee (not being the official receiver) realises assets on behalf of a secured creditor, the trustee is entitled to such sum by way of remuneration as is arrived at by applying the realisation scale set out in Schedule 6 to the monies received by him in respect of the assets realised (including any Value Added Tax thereon).]

(2) Where there are joint trustees, it is for them to agree between themselves as to how the remuneration payable should be apportioned. Any dispute arising between them may be referred—

  (a)   to the court, for settlement by order, or

  (b)   to the creditors' committee or a meeting of creditors, for settlement by resolution.

(3) If the trustee is a solicitor and employs his own firm, or any partner in it, to act on behalf of the estate, profit costs shall not be paid unless this is authorised by the creditors' committee, the creditors or the court.

2.715

6.140 Recourse of trustee to meeting of creditors

If the trustee's remuneration has been fixed by the creditors' committee, and he considers the rate or amount to be insufficient, he may request that it be increased by resolution of the creditors.

2.716

6.141 Recourse to the court

(1) If the trustee considers that the remuneration fixed for him by the creditors' committee, or by resolution of the creditors, or as under Rule 6.138(6), is insufficient, he may apply to the court for an order increasing its amount or rate.

(2) The trustee shall give at least 14 days' notice of his application to the members of the creditors' committee; and the committee may nominate one or more members to appear or be represented, and to be heard, on the application.

(3) If there is no creditors' committee, the trustee's notice of his application shall be sent to such one or more of the bankrupt's creditors as the court may direct, which creditors may nominate one or more of their number to appear or be represented.

(4) The court may, if it appears to be a proper case, order the costs of the trustee's application, including the costs of any member of the creditors' committee appearing [or being represented] on it, or any creditor so appearing [or being represented], to be paid out of the estate.

2.717

6.142 Creditor's claim that remuneration is excessive

(1) Any creditor of the bankrupt may, with the concurrence of at least 25% in value of the creditors (including himself), apply to the court for an order that the trustee's remuneration be reduced, on the grounds that it is, in all the circumstances, excessive.

(2) The court may, if it thinks that no sufficient cause is shown for the application, disMiss it; but it shall not do so unless the applicant has had an opportunity to attend the court for an *ex parte* hearing, of which he has been given at least 7 days' notice.

If the application is not dismissed under this paragraph, the court shall fix a venue for it to be heard.

(3) The applicant shall, at least 14 days before the hearing, send to the trustee a notice stating the venue so fixed; and the notice shall be accompanied by a copy of the application, and of any evidence which the applicant intends to adduce in support of it.

(4) If the court considers the application to be well-founded, it shall make an order fixing the remuneration at a reduced amount or rate.

(5) Unless the court orders otherwise, the costs of the application shall be paid by the applicant, and do not fall on the estate.

Section E: Supplementary Provisions

2.718

6.143 Trustee deceased

(1) Subject as follows, where the trustee (other than the official receiver) has died, it is the duty of his personal representatives to give notice of the fact to the official receiver, specifying the date of the death.

This does not apply if notice has been given under any of the following paragraphs of this Rule.

(2) If the deceased trustee was a partner in a firm, notice may be given to the official receiver by a partner in the firm who is qualified to act as an insolvency practitioner, or is a member of any body recognised by the Secretary of State for the authorisation of insolvency practitioners.

(3) Notice of the death may be given by any person producing to the official receiver the relevant death certificate or a copy of it.

(4) The official receiver shall give notice to the court, for the purpose of fixing the date of the deceased trustee's release in accordance with section 299(3)(a).

2.719

6.144 Loss of qualification as insolvency practitioner

(1) This Rule applies where the trustee vacates office, under section 298(6), on his ceasing to be qualified to act as an insolvency practitioner in relation to the bankrupt.

(2) The trustee vacating office shall forthwith give notice of his doing so to the official receiver, who shall give notice to the Secretary of State.

The official receiver shall file in court a copy of his notice under this paragraph.

(3) Rule 6.135 applies as regards the trustee obtaining his release, as if he had been removed by the court.

2.720

[6.145 Notice to official receiver of intention to vacate office]

[(1) Where the trustee intends to vacate office, whether by resignation or otherwise, he shall give notice of his intention to the official receiver together with notice of any creditors' meeting to be held in respect of his vacation of office, including any meeting to receive his resignation.

(2) The notice to the official receiver must given at least 21 days before any such creditors' meeting.

(3) Where there remains in the bankrupt's estate any property which has not been realised, applied, distributed or otherwise fully dealt with in the bankruptcy, the trustee shall include in his notice to the official receiver details of the nature of that property, its value (or the fact that it has no value), its location, any action taken by the trustee to deal with that property or any reason for his not dealing with it, and the current position in relation to it.]

2.721

6.146 Trustee's duties on vacating office

(1) Where the trustee ceases to be in office as such, in consequence of removal, resignation or cesser of qualification as an insolvency practitioner, he is under obligation forthwith to deliver up to the person succeeding him as trustee the assets of the estate (after deduction of any expenses properly incurred, and distributions made, by him) and further to deliver up to that person—

   (a)   the records of the bankruptcy, including correspondence, proofs and other related papers appertaining to the bankruptcy while it was within his responsibility, and

   (b)   the bankrupt's books, papers and other records.

(2) ...

Notes

R 6.146

This rule supplements IA 1986 s 298.

R 6.146(2)

This provision was deleted from 1 April 2004 by Insolvency (Amendment) Rules 2004 (SI 2004/584).

2.722

6.147 Power of court to set aside certain transactions

(1) If in the administration of the estate the trustee enters into any transaction with a person who is an associate of his, the court may, on the application of any person interested, set the transaction aside and order the trustee to compensate the estate for any loss suffered in consequence of it.

(2) This does not apply if either—
  (a) the transaction was entered into with the prior consent of the court, or
  (b) it is shown to the court's satisfaction that the transaction was for value, and that it was entered into by the trustee without knowing, or having any reason to suppose, that the person concerned was an associate.

(3) Nothing in this Rule is to be taken as prejudicing the operation of any rule of law or equity with respect to a trustee's dealings with trust property, or the fiduciary obligations of any person.

2.723

6.148 Rule against solicitation

(1) Where the court is satisfied that any improper solicitation has been used by or on behalf of the trustee in obtaining proxies or procuring his appointment, it may order that no remuneration out of the estate be allowed to any person by whom, or on whose behalf, the solicitation was exercised.

(2) An order of the court under this Rule overrides any resolution of the creditors' committee or the creditors, or any other provision of the Rules relating to the trustee's remuneration.

2.724

6.149 Enforcement of trustee's obligations to official receiver

(1) The court may, on the application of the official receiver, make such orders as it thinks necessary for enforcement of the duties of the trustee under section 305(3) (information and assistance to be given; production and inspection of books and records relating to the bankruptcy).

(2) An order of the court under this Rule may provide that all costs of and incidental to the official receiver's application shall be borne by the trustee.

Chapter 11
The Creditors' Committee

2.725

6.150 Membership of creditors' committee

(1) The creditors' committee shall consist of at least 3, and not more than 5, members.

(2) All the members of the committee must be creditors of the bankrupt; and any creditor (other than one who is fully secured) may be a member, so long as—

    (a)   he has lodged a proof of his debt, and

    (b)   his proof has neither been wholly disallowed for voting purposes, nor wholly rejected for the purposes of distribution or dividend.

(3) A body corporate may be a member of the committee, but it cannot act as such otherwise than by a representative appointed under Rule 6.156.

Notes

R 6.150

The general meeting of a bankrupt's creditors may establish a creditors' committee in certain circumstances, IA 1986 s 301. This provision sets out the requirements for membership of such a committee.

2.726

6.151 Formalities of establishment

(1) The creditors' committee does not come into being, and accordingly cannot act, until the trustee has issued a certificate of its due constitution.

(2) If the chairman of the creditors' meeting which resolves to establish the committee is not the trustee, he shall forthwith give notice of the resolution to the trustee (or, as the case may be, the person appointed as trustee by that same meeting), and inform him of the names and addresses of the persons elected to be members of the committee.

(3) No person may act as a member of the committee unless and until he has agreed to do so and, unless the relevant proxy contains a statement to the contrary, such agreement may be given by his proxy-holder present at the meeting establishing the committee.

(3A) The trustee's certificate of the committee's due constitution shall not issue before at least 3 persons elected to be members of the committee have agreed to act.

(4) As and when the others (if any) agree to act, the trustee shall issue an amended certificate.

(5) The certificate, and any amended certificate, shall be filed in court by the trustee.

(6) If after the first establishment of the committee there is any change in its membership, the trustee shall report the change to the court.

Notes

R 6.151

This provision sets out the formalities of establishment of a creditors' committee pursuant to IA 1986 s 301. The certificate shall be in Form 6.52. The report shall be in Form 6.53.

2.727

6.152 Obligations of trustee to committee

(1) Subject as follows, it is the duty of the trustee to report to the members of the creditors' committee all such matters as appear to him to be, or as they have indicated to him as being, of concern to them with respect to the bankruptcy.

(2) In the case of matters so indicated to him by the committee, the trustee need not comply with any request for information where it appears to him that—
  (a)   the request is frivolous or unreasonable, or
  (b)   the cost of complying would be excessive, having regard to the relative importance of the information, or
  (c)   the estate is without funds sufficient for enabling him to comply.

(3) Where the committee has come into being more than 28 days after the appointment of the trustee, the latter shall report to them, in summary form, what actions he has taken since his appointment, and shall answer such questions as they may put to him regarding his conduct of the bankruptcy hitherto.

(4) A person who becomes a member of the committee at any time after its first establishment is not entitled to require a report to him by the trustee, otherwise than in summary form, of any matters previously arising.

(5) Nothing in this Rule disentitles the committee, or any member of it, from having access to the trustee's records of the bankruptcy, or from seeking an explanation of any matter within the committee's responsibility.

Notes

R 6.152(1)

This provision obliges the trustee to report to the creditor's committee.

R 6.152(2)

It appears that the exceptions allowing for non-compliance by the trustee with his duty to report to the creditor's committee set out this provision apply only to concerns expressed by the committee under IR 1986 r 6.152(1) and not to the powers given to it under IR 1986 r 6.152(5).

2.728

6.153 Meetings of the committee

(1) Subject as follows, meetings of the creditors' committee shall be held when and where determined by the trustee.

(2) The trustee shall call a first meeting of the committee to take place within 3 months of his appointment or of the committee's establishment (whichever is the later); and thereafter he shall call a meeting—

> (a)   if so requested by a member of the committee or his representative (the meeting then to be held within 21 days of the request being received by the trustee), and
>
> (b)   for a specified date, if the committee has previously resolved that a meeting be held on that date.
>
> (3) The trustee shall give 7 days' notice in writing of the venue of any meeting to every member of the committee (or his representative, if designated for that purpose), unless in any case the requirement of the notice has been waived by or on behalf of any member.
>
> Waiver may be signified either at or before the meeting.

Notes

RR 6.153–6.156

These provisions relate to meetings of the creditors' committee. IR 1986 r 6.153 relates to the calling of the meeting, IR 1986 r 6.154 to the chairing of the meeting, IR 1986 r 6.155 to the quorum of the meeting and IR 1986 r 6.156 to representation at the meeting.

2.729

6.154 The chairman at meetings

(1) The chairman at any meeting of the creditors' committee shall be the trustee, or a person appointed by him in writing to act.

(2) A person so nominated must be either—

> (a)   one who is qualified to act as an insolvency practitioner in relation to the bankrupt, or
>
> (b)   an employee of the trustee or his firm who is experienced in insolvency matters.

2.730

6.155 Quorum

A meeting of the committee is duly constituted if due notice of it has been given to all the members and at least two of the members are present or represented.

2.731

6.156 Committee-members' representatives

(1) A member of the creditors' committee may, in relation to the business of the committee, be represented by another person duly authorised by him for that purpose.

(2) A person acting as a committee-member's representative must hold a letter of authority entitling him so to act (either generally or [specially) and signed by or on behalf of the committee-member, and for this purpose any proxy in relation to any meeting of creditors of the bankrupt shall, unless it contains a statement to the contrary, be treated as such a letter of authority to act generally signed by or on behalf of the committee-member.

(3) The chairman at any meeting of the committee may call on a person claiming to act as a committee-member's representative to produce his letter of authority, and may exclude him if it appears that his authority is deficient.

(4) No member may be represented by a body corporate, or by a person who is an undischarged bankrupt or a disqualified director, or is subject to a bankruptcy restrictions order, bankruptcy restrictions undertaking or an interim bankruptcy restrictions order.

(5) No person shall—
  (a) on the same committee, act at one and the same time as representative of more than one committee-member, or
  (b) act both as a member of the committee and as representative of another member.

(6) Where the representative of a committee-member signs any document on the latter's behalf, the fact that he so signs must be stated below his signature.

(7) The acts of the committee are valid notwithstanding any defect in the appointment or qualifications of any committee-member's representative.

Notes

R 6.156(4)

Since 1 April 2004 disqualified directors and those subject to bankruptcy restrictions orders have been unable to act as authorised representatives.

2.732

6.157 Resignation

A member of the creditors' committee may resign by notice in writing delivered to the trustee.

2.733

6.158 Termination of membership

(1) A person's membership of the creditors' committee is automatically terminated if—
  (a) he becomes bankrupt, or
  (b) at 3 consecutive meetings of the committee he is neither present nor represented (unless at the third of those meetings it is resolved that this Rule is not to apply in his case), or
  (c) he ceases to be, or is found never to have been, a creditor.

(2) However, if the cause of termination is the member's bankruptcy, his trustee in bankruptcy replaces him as a member of the committee.

2.734

6.159 Removal

A member of the creditors' committee may be removed by resolution at a meeting of creditors, at least 14 days' notice having been given of the intention to move that resolution.

2.735

6.160 Vacancies

(1) The following applies if there is a vacancy in the membership of the creditors' committee.

(2) The vacancy need not be filled if the trustee and a majority of the remaining committee-members so agree, provided that the number of members does not fall below the minimum required by Rule 6.150(1).

(3) The trustee may appoint any creditor (being qualified under the Rules to be a member of the committee) to fill the vacancy, if a majority of the other members of the committee agree to the appointment and the creditor concerned consents to act.

(4) Alternatively, a meeting of creditors may resolve that a creditor be appointed (with his consent) to fill the vacancy. In this case at least 14 days' notice must have been given of a resolution to make such an appointment (whether or not of a person named in the notice).

(5) Where the vacancy is filled by an appointment made by a creditors' meeting at which the trustee is not present, the chairman of the meeting shall report to the trustee the appointment which has been made.

2.736

6.161 Voting rights and resolutions

(1) At any meeting of the committee, each member (whether present himself, or by his representative) has one vote; and a resolution is passed when a majority of the members present or represented have voted in favour of it.

(2) Every resolution passed shall be recorded in writing, either separately or as part of the minutes of the meeting. The record shall be signed by the chairman and kept with the records of the bankruptcy.

Notes

R 6.161(1)

Each member of the creditors' committee has a single vote regardless of the size of the debt due. For the quorum, see IR 1986 r 6.155. Note also that there is no provision for the chairman to have a casting vote in the event that there is no majority and the vote may be deadlocked.

2.737

6.162 Resolutions by post

(1) In accordance with this Rule, the trustee may seek to obtain the agreement of members of the creditors' committee to a resolution by sending to every member (or his representative designated for the purpose) a copy of the proposed resolution.

(2) Where the trustee makes use of the procedure allowed by this Rule, he shall send out to members of the committee or their representatives (as the case may be) a copy of any proposed resolution on which a decision is

sought, which shall be set out in such a way that agreement with or dissent from each separate resolution may be indicated by the recipient on the copy so sent.

(3) Any member of the committee may, within 7 business days from the date of the trustee sending out a resolution, require the trustee to summon a meeting of the committee to consider the matters raised by the resolution.

(4) In the absence of such a request, the resolution is deemed to have been carried in the committee if and when the trustee is notified in writing by a majority of the members that they concur with it.

(5) A copy of every resolution passed under this Rule, and a note that the concurrence of the committee was obtained, shall be kept with the records of the bankruptcy.

Notes

R 6.162

This provision sets out a procedure designed to simplify and speed up the carrying out of business.

2.738

6.163 Trustee's reports

(1) The trustee shall, as and when directed by the creditors' committee (but not more often than once in any period of 2 months), send a written report to every member of the committee setting out the position generally as regards the progress of the bankruptcy and matters arising in connection with it, to which he (the trustee) considers the committee's attention should be drawn.

(2) In the absence of any such directions by the committee, the trustee shall send such a report not less often than once in every period of 6 months.

(3) The obligations of the trustee under this Rule are without prejudice to those imposed by Rule 6.152.

Notes

R 6.163

The net effect of this provision is that a trustee is obliged to send a report to the creditors' committee at intervals of between two and six months.

2.739

6.164 Expenses of members etc

The trustee shall defray out of the estate, in the prescribed order of priority, any reasonable travelling expenses directly incurred by members of the creditors' committee or their representatives in respect of their attendance at the committee's meetings, or otherwise on the committee's business.

2.740

6.165 Dealings by committee—members and others

(1) This Rule applies to—
  (a)   any member of the creditors' committee,
  (b)   any committee-member's representative,
  (c)   any person who is an associate of a member of the committee or a committee-member's representative, and
  (d)   any person who has been a member of the committee at any time in the last 12 months.

(2) Subject as follows, a person to whom this Rule applies shall not enter into any transaction whereby he—
  (a)   receives out of the estate any payment for services given or goods supplied in connection with the estate's administration, or
  (b)   obtains any profit from the administration, or
  (c)   acquires any asset forming part of the estate.

(3) Such a transaction may be entered into by a person to whom this Rule applies—
  (a)   with the prior leave of the court, or
  (b)   if he does so as a matter of urgency, or by way of performance of a contract in force before the commencement of the bankruptcy, and obtains the court's leave for the transaction, having applied for it without undue delay, or
  (c)   with the prior sanction of the creditors' committee, where it is satisfied (after full disclosure of the circumstances) that the person will be giving full value in the transaction.

(4) Where in the committee a resolution is proposed that sanction be accorded for a transaction to be entered into which, without that sanction or the leave of the court, would be in contravention of this Rule, no member of the committee, and no representative of a member, shall vote if he is to participate directly or indirectly in the transaction.

(5) The court may, on the application of any person interested—
  (a)   set aside a transaction on the ground that it has been entered into in contravention of this Rule, and
  (b)   make with respect to it such other order as it thinks fit, including (subject to the following paragraph) an order requiring a person to whom this Rule applies to account for any profit obtained from the transaction and compensate the estate for any resultant loss..

(6) In the case of a person to whom this Rule applies as an associate of a member of the committee or of a committee-member's representative, the court shall not make any order under paragraph (5), if satisfied that he entered into the relevant transaction without having any reason to suppose that in doing so he would contravene this Rule.

> (7) The costs of an application to the court for leave under this Rule do not fall on the estate, unless the court so orders.

Notes

R 6.165

This provision restricts dealings involving members and former members of the creditors' committee and/or their authorised representatives; see *Re Bulmer* [1937] Ch 499.

2.741

6.166 Committee's functions vested in Secretary of State

(1) At any time when the functions of the creditors' committee are vested in the Secretary of State under section 302(1) or (2), requirements of the Act or the Rules about notices to be given, or reports to be made, to the committee by the trustee do not apply, otherwise than as enabling the committee to require a report as to any matter.

(2) Where the committee's functions are so vested under section 302(2), they may be exercised by the official receiver.

Notes

R 6.166(1)

This provision supplements IA 1986 s 302 under which the functions of the creditors' committee are effectively suspended during any period when the official receiver acts as trustee.

R 6.166(2)

Thus where there is no creditors' committee available to give sanction for the commencement of legal proceedings this may be obtained from the official receiver (IA 1986 s 314, Sch 5).

Chapter 12
Special Manager

2.742

6.167 Appointment and remuneration

(1) An application made by the official receiver or trustee under section 370 for the appointment of a person to be special manager shall be supported by a report setting out the reasons for the application.

The report shall include the applicant's estimate of the value of the estate, property or business in respect of which the special manager is to be appointed.

(2) The court's order appointing the special manager shall specify the duration of his appointment, which may be for a period of time, or until

the occurrence of a specified event. Alternatively, the order may specify that the duration of the appointment is to be subject to a further order of the court.

(3) The appointment of a special manager may be renewed by order of the court.

(4) The special manager's remuneration shall be fixed from time to time by the court.

Notes

R 6.167

The court under IA 1986 s 370 may appoint a special manager over a bankrupt's property. The appointment should be in Form 6.54. Chapter 12 supplements the above provision by setting out mechanisms for the appointment and remuneration of the special manager, the giving of security (IR 1986 r 6.168, 6.169), the provision of accounts (IR 1986 r 6.170) and the termination of the appointment (IR 1986 r 6.171).

2.743

6.168 Security

(1) The appointment of the special manager does not take effect until the person appointed has given (or, being allowed by the court to do so, undertaken to give) security to the person who applies for him to be appointed.

(2) It is not necessary that security shall be given for each separate bankruptcy; but it may be given either specially for a particular bankruptcy, or generally for any bankruptcy in relation to which the special manager may be employed as such.

(3) The amount of the security shall be not less than the value of the estate, property or business in respect of which he is appointed, as estimated by the applicant in his report under Rule 6.167(1).

(4) When the special manager has given security to the person applying for his appointment, that person's certificate as to the adequacy of the security shall be filed in court.

(5) The cost of providing the security shall be paid in the first instance by the special manager; but—
    (a)   where a bankruptcy order is not made, he is entitled to be reimbursed out of the property of the debtor, and the court may make an order on the debtor accordingly, and
    (b)   where a bankruptcy order is made, he is entitled to be reimbursed out of the estate in the prescribed order of priority.

Notes

R 6.168(1)

For further on the giving of security, see the Insolvency Practitioners Regulations 2005 (SI 2005/524).

2.744

6.169 Failure to give or keep up security

(1) If the special manager fails to give the required security within the time stated for that purpose by the order appointing him, or any extension of that time that may be allowed, the official receiver or trustee (as the case may be) shall report the failure to the court, which may thereupon discharge the order appointing the special manager.

(2) If the special manager fails to keep up his security, the official receiver or trustee shall report his failure to the court, which may thereupon remove the special manager, and make such order as it thinks fit as to costs.

(3) If an order is made under this Rule removing the special manager, or discharging the order appointing him, the court shall give directions as to whether any, and if so what, steps should be taken for the appointment of another special manager in his place.

2.745

6.170 Accounting

(1) The special manager shall produce accounts, containing details of his receipts and payments, for the approval of the trustee.

(2) The accounts shall be in respect of 3–month periods for the duration of the special manager's appointment (or for a lesser period, if his appointment terminates less than 3 months from its date, or from the date to which the last accounts were made up).

(3) When the accounts have been approved, the special manager's receipts and payments shall be added to those of the trustee.

2.746

6.171 Termination of appointment

(1) The special manager's appointment terminates if the bankruptcy petition is dismissed or if, an interim receiver having been appointed, the latter is discharged without a bankruptcy order having been made.

(2) If the official receiver or the trustee is of opinion that the employment of the special manager is no longer necessary or profitable for the estate, he shall apply to the court for directions, and the court may order the special manager's appointment to be terminated.

(3) The official receiver or the trustee shall make the same application if a resolution of the creditors is passed, requesting that the appointment be terminated.

Chapter 13
Public Examination of Bankrupt

2.747

6.172 Order for public examination

(1) If the official receiver applies to the court, under section 290, for the public examination of the bankrupt, a copy of the court's order shall, forthwith after its making, be sent by the official receiver to the bankrupt.

(2) The order shall appoint a venue for the hearing, and direct the bankrupt's attendance thereat.

(3) The official receiver shall give at least 14 days' notice of the hearing—
  (a) if a trustee has been nominated or appointed, to him;
  (b) if a special manager has been appointed, to him; and
  (c) subject to any contrary direction of the court, to every creditor of the bankrupt who is known to the official receiver or is identified in the bankrupt's statement of affairs.

(4) The official receiver may, if he thinks fit, cause notice of the order to be given, by public advertisement in one or more newspapers, at least 14 days before the day fixed for the hearing.

Notes

R 6.172

The official receiver may apply to the court for the public examination of the bankrupt under IA 1986 s 290 and IR 1986 r 6.172–6.177 set out the detailed procedure in respect of the same. As for the application to the court by the official receiver, see Form 6.55.

2.748

6.173 Order on request by creditors

(1) A request by a creditor to the official receiver, under section 290(2), for the bankrupt to be publicly examined shall be made in writing and be accompanied by—
  (a) a list of the creditors concurring with the request and the amount of their respective claims in the bankruptcy,
  (b) from each creditor concurring, written confirmation of his concurrence, and
  (c) a statement of the reasons why the examination is requested.

Sub-paragraphs (a) and (b) do not apply if the requisitioning creditor's debt is alone sufficient, without the concurrence of others.

(2) Before an application to the court is made on the request, the requisitionist shall deposit with the official receiver such sum as the latter may determine to be appropriate by way of security for the expenses of the hearing of a public examination, if ordered.

(3) Subject as follows, the official receiver shall, within 28 days of receiving the request, make the application to the court required by section 290(2).

(4) If the official receiver is of opinion that the request is an unreasonable one in the circumstances, he may apply to the court for an order relieving him from the obligation to make the application otherwise required by that subsection.

(5) If the court so orders, and the application for the order was made *ex parte*, notice of the order shall be given forthwith by the official receiver to the requisitionist. If the application for an order is dismissed, the

official receiver's application under section 290(2) shall be made forthwith on conclusion of the hearing of the application first mentioned.

Notes

R 6.173

Under IA 1986 s 290(2), a creditor with the concurrence of not less than one-half in value of the bankrupt's creditors can request the official receiver to make an application to the court for a public examination: see Form 6.56.

2.749

6.174 Bankrupt unfit for examination

(1) Where the bankrupt is suffering from any mental disorder or physical affliction or disability rendering him unfit to undergo or attend for public examination, the court may, on application in that behalf, either stay the order for his public examination or direct that it shall be conducted in such manner and at such place as it thinks fit.

(2) Application under this Rule shall be made—
- (a) by a person who has been appointed by a court in the United Kingdom or elsewhere to manage the affairs of, or to represent, the bankrupt, or
- (b) by a relative or friend of the bankrupt whom the court considers to be a proper person to make the application, or
- (c) by the official receiver.

(3) Where the application is made by a person other than the official receiver, then—
- (a) it shall, unless the bankrupt is a patient within the meaning of the Mental Health Act 1983, be supported by the affidavit of a registered medical practitioner as to the bankrupt's mental and physical condition;
- (b) at least 7 days' notice of the application shall be given to the official receiver and the trustee (if any); and
- (c) before any order is made on the application, the applicant shall deposit with the official receiver such sum as the latter certifies to be necessary for the additional expenses of any examination that may be ordered on the application.

An order made on the application may provide that the expenses of the examination are to be payable, as to a specified proportion, out of the deposit under sub-paragraph (c), instead of out of the estate.

(4) Where the application is made by the official receiver, it may be made *ex parte*, and may be supported by evidence in the form of a report by the official receiver to the court.

2.750

6.175 Procedure at hearing

(1) The bankrupt shall at the hearing be examined on oath; and he shall answer all such questions as the court may put, or allow to be put, to him.

(2) Any of the persons allowed by section 290(4) to question the bankrupt may, with the approval of the court (made known either at the hearing or in advance of it), appear by solicitor or counsel; or he may in writing authorise another person to question the bankrupt on his behalf.

(3) The bankrupt may at his own expense employ a solicitor with or without counsel, who may put to him such questions as the court may allow for the purpose of enabling him to explain or qualify any answers given by him, and may make representations on his behalf.

(4) There shall be made in writing such record of the examination as the court thinks proper. The record shall be read over either to or by the bankrupt, signed by him, and verified by affidavit at a venue fixed by the court.

(5) The written record may, in any proceedings (whether under the Act or otherwise) be used as evidence against the bankrupt of any statement made by him in the course of his public examination.

(6) If criminal proceedings have been instituted against the bankrupt, and the court is of opinion that the continuance of the hearing would be calculated to prejudice a fair trial of those proceedings, the hearing may be adjourned.

Notes

R 6.175

This provision together with Practice Direction Insolvency Proceedings para 9.3 sets out the procedure to be adopted at the public examination itself and in particular those who may appear and/or be represented at the hearing.

R 6.175(4)

The affidavit of verification is in Form 6.58.

R 6.175(5)

The privilege against self-incrimination is expressly abrogated subject only to the discretion of the court under IR 1986 r 6.175(6) see *R v Kansal* [1993] QB 244.

2.751

6.176 Adjournment

(1) The public examination may be adjourned by the court from time to time, either to a fixed date or generally.

(2) Where the examination has been adjourned generally, the court may at any time on the application of the official receiver or of the bankrupt—
  (a) fix a venue for the resumption of the examination, and
  (b) give directions as to the manner in which, and the time within which, notice of the resumed public examination is to be given to persons entitled to take part in it.

(3) Where application under paragraph (2) is made by the bankrupt, the court may grant it on terms that the expenses of giving the notices

required by that paragraph shall be paid by him and that, before a venue for the resumed public examination is fixed, he shall deposit with the official receiver such sum as the latter considers necessary to cover those expenses.

(4) Where the examination is adjourned generally, the official receiver may, there and then, make application under section 279(3) (suspension of automatic discharge).

[(5) If, on the hearing of an application pursuant to paragraph (4), the court makes an order suspending the bankrupt's discharge, copies of such order shall be sent by the court to the official receiver, the trustee and the bankrupt.]

2.752

6.177 Expenses of examination

(1) Where a public examination of the bankrupt has been ordered by the court on a creditors' requisition under Rule 6.173, the court may order that the expenses of the examination are to be paid, as to a specified proportion, out of the deposit under Rule 6.173(2), instead of out of the estate.

(2) In no case do the costs and expenses of a public examination fall on the official receiver personally.

Notes

R 6.177

In general, the costs of the public examination will be borne by the bankrupt's estate. Under this provision however, where the public examination has been ordered at the request of a creditor, the court may direct some or all of the costs to be borne out of the relevant deposit; see also IR 1986 r 6.173(2).

2.753

6.178 Trustee's notice of disclaimer

(1) Where the trustee disclaims property under section 315, the notice of disclaimer shall contain such particulars of the property disclaimed as enable it to be easily identified.

(2) The notice shall be signed by the trustee and filed in court, with a copy. The court shall secure that both the notice and the copy are sealed and endorsed with the date of filing.

(3) The copy notice, so sealed and endorsed, shall be returned by the court to the trustee as follows—
  (a) if the notice has been delivered at the offices of the court by the trustee in person, it shall be handed to him,
  (b) if it has been delivered by some person acting on the trustee's behalf, it shall be handed to that person, for immediate transmission to the trustee, and
  (c) otherwise, it shall be sent to the trustee by first class post.

> The court shall cause to be endorsed on the original notice, or otherwise recorded on the file, the manner in which the copy notice was returned to the trustee.
>
> (4) For the purposes of section 315, the date of the prescribed notice is that which is endorsed on it, and on the copy, in accordance with this Rule.

Notes

R 6.178–6.186

These provisions should be read in conjunction with IA 1986 s 315 to 321 dealing with disclaimer of onerous property.

R 6.178(1)

A notice of disclaimer should be in Form 6.61. In *MEPC plc v Scottish Amicable Life Assurance Society* [1993] 2 EGLR 93 the court construed a disclaimer of an interest in a licence to assign a lease as a disclaimer of the lease itself given that the intention to disclaim and the property concerned were clearly identified.

2.754

6.179 Communication of disclaimer to persons interested

(1) Within 7 days after the day on which a copy of the notice of disclaimer is returned to him, the trustee shall send or give copies of the notice (showing the date endorsed as required by Rule 6.178) to the persons mentioned in paragraphs (2) to (5) below.

(2) Where the property disclaimed is of a leasehold nature, he shall send or give a copy to every person who (to his knowledge) claims under the bankrupt as underlessee or mortgagee.

(3) Where the disclaimer is of property in a dwelling-house, he shall send or give a copy to every person who (to his knowledge) is in occupation of, or claims a right to occupy, the house.

(4) He shall in any case send or give a copy of the notice to every person who (to his knowledge)—
  (a) claims an interest in the disclaimed property, or
  (b) is under any liability in respect of the property, not being a liability discharged by the disclaimer.

(5) If the disclaimer is of an unprofitable contract, he shall send or give copies of the notice to all such persons, as, to his knowledge, are parties to the contract or have interests under it.

(6) If subsequently it comes to the trustee's knowledge, in the case of any person, that he has such an interest in the disclaimed property as would have entitled him to receive a copy of the notice of disclaimer in pursuance of paragraphs (2) to (5), the trustee shall then forthwith send or give to that person a copy of the notice.

But compliance with this paragraph is not required if—

(a)   the trustee is satisfied that the person has already been made aware of the disclaimer and its date, or

(b)   the court, on the trustee's application, orders that compliance is not required in that particular case.

(7) A notice or copy notice to be served on any person under the age of 18 in relation to the disclaimer of property in a dwelling-house is sufficiently served if sent or given to the parent or guardian of that person.

Notes

R 6.179(4)

Guarantors of the bankrupt's obligations in respect of the property disclaimed or of the obligations of others liable in respect of such obligations in addition to the bankrupt will come within this class *Maurice Tempany v Royal Liver Trustees Ltd* [1984] BCLC 568, *Hindcastle Ltd v Barbara Attenborough Associates Ltd* [1997] AC 70.

2.755

6.180 Additional notices

The trustee disclaiming property may, without prejudice to his obligations under sections 315 to 319 and Rules 6.178 and 6.179, at any time give notice of the disclaimer to any persons who in his opinion ought, in the public interest or otherwise, to be informed of it.

2.756

6.181 Duty to keep court informed

The trustee shall notify the court from time to time as to the persons to whom he has sent or given copies of the notice of disclaimer under the two preceding Rules, giving their names and addresses, and the nature of their respective interests.

2.757

6.182 Application for leave to disclaim

(1) Where under section 315(4) the trustee requires the leave of the court to disclaim property claimed for the bankrupt's estate under section 307 or 308, he may apply for that leave *ex parte*.

(2) The application must be accompanied by a report—

(a)   giving such particulars of the property proposed to be disclaimed as enable it to be easily identified,

(b)   setting out the reasons why, the property having been claimed for the estate, the court's leave to disclaim is now applied for, and

(c)   specifying the persons (if any) who have been informed of the trustee's intention to make the application.

(3) If it is stated in the report that any person's consent to the disclaimer has been signified, a copy of that consent must be annexed to the report.

(4) The court may, on consideration of the application, grant the leave applied for; and it may, before granting leave—
  (a) order that notice of the application be given to all such persons who, if the property is disclaimed, will be entitled to apply for a vesting or other order under section 320, and
  (b) fix a venue for the hearing of the application under section 315(4).

2.758

6.183 Application by interested party under s 316

(1) The following applies where, in the case of any property, application is made to the trustee by an interested party under section 316 (request for decision whether the property is to be disclaimed or not).

(2) The application—
  (a) shall be delivered to the trustee personally or by registered post, and
  (b) shall be made in the form known as 'notice to elect', or a substantially similar form.

(3) This paragraph applies in a case where the property concerned cannot be disclaimed by the trustee without the leave of the court.

If within the period of 28 days mentioned in section 316(1) the trustee applies to the court for leave to disclaim, the court shall extend the time allowed by that section for giving notice of disclaimer to a date not earlier than the date fixed for the hearing of the application.

2.759

6.184 Interest in property to be declared on request

(1) If, in the case of property which the trustee has the right to disclaim, it appears to him that there is some person who claims, or may claim, to have an interest in the property, he may give notice to that person calling on him to declare within 14 days whether he claims any such interest and, if so, the nature and extent of it.

(2) Failing compliance with the notice, the trustee is entitled to assume that the person concerned has no such interest in the property as will prevent or impede its disclaimer.

Notes

R 6.184(1)

The notice should be in Form 6.63.

2.760

6.185 Disclaimer presumed valid and effective

Any disclaimer of property by the trustee is presumed valid and effective, unless it is proved that he has been in breach of his duty with respect to the giving of notice of disclaimer, or otherwise under sections 315 to 319, or under this Chapter of the Rules.

2.761

6.186 Application for exercise of court's powers under s 320

(1) This Rule applies with respect to an application by any person under section 320 for an order of the court to vest or deliver disclaimed property.

(2) The application must be made within 3 months of the applicant becoming aware of the disclaimer, or of his receiving a copy of the trustee's notice of disclaimer sent under Rule 6.179, whichever is the earlier.

(3) The applicant shall with his application file an affidavit—
- (a) stating whether he applies under paragraph (a) of section 320(2) (claim of interest in the property), under paragraph (b) (liability not discharged) or under paragraph (c) (occupation of dwelling-house);
- (b) specifying the date on which he received a copy of the trustee's notice of disclaimer, or otherwise became aware of the disclaimer; and
- (c) specifying the grounds of his application and the order which he desires the court to make under section 320.

(4) The court shall fix a venue for the hearing of the application; and the applicant shall, not later than 7 days before the date fixed, give to the trustee notice of the venue, accompanied by copies of the application and the affidavit under paragraph (3).

(5) On the hearing of the application, the court may give directions as to other persons (if any) who should be sent or given notice of the application and the grounds on which it is made.

(6) Sealed copies of any order made on the application shall be sent by the court to the applicant and the trustee.

(7) In a case where the property disclaimed is of a leasehold nature, or is property in a dwelling-house, and section 317 or (as the case may be) section 318 applies to suspend the effect of the disclaimer, there shall be included in the court's order a direction giving effect to the disclaimer.

This paragraph does not apply if, at the time when the order is issued, other applications under section 320 are pending in respect of the same property.

Chapter 15
Replacement of Exempt Property

2.762

6.187 Purchase of replacement property

(1) A purchase of replacement property under section 308(3) may be made either before or after the realisation by the trustee of the value of the property vesting in him under the section.

(2) The trustee is under no obligation, by virtue of the section, to apply funds to the purchase of a replacement for property vested in him, unless and until he has sufficient funds in the estate for that purpose.

Notes

R 6.187(1)

A trustee may not set off funds set aside to purchase replacement property against money owed by the bankrupt to the trustee, for example pursuant to an income payment order, nor can he retain it in order to recoup expenditure on legal costs (*Re Rayatt* [1998] BPIR 495).

2.763

6.188 Money provided in lieu of sale

(1) The following applies where a third party proposes to the trustee that he (the former) should provide the estate with a sum of money enabling the bankrupt to be left in possession of property which would otherwise be made to vest in the trustee under section 308.

(2) The trustee may accept that proposal, if satisfied that it is a reasonable one, and that the estate will benefit to the extent of the value of the property in question less the cost of a reasonable replacement.

Chapter 16
Income Payments Orders

2.764

6.189 Application for order

(1) Where the trustee applies for an income payments order under section 310, the court shall fix a venue for the hearing of the application.

(2) Notice of the application, and of the venue, shall be sent by the trustee to the bankrupt at least 28 days before the day fixed for the hearing, together with a copy of the trustee's application and a short statement of the grounds on which it is made.

(3) The notice shall inform the bankrupt that—
  (a) unless at least 7 days before the date fixed for the hearing he sends to the court and to the trustee written consent to an order being made in the terms of the application, he is required to attend the hearing, and
  (b) if he attends, he will be given an opportunity to show cause why the order should not be made, or an order should be made otherwise than as applied for by the trustee.

Notes

R 6.189

An application under IA 1986 s 310 for an income payment order should be made in Form 6.64. Any order made should be in the form of either Form 6.65 (if the order is made under IA

1986 s 310(3)(a) or Form 6.66 (if the order is made under IA 1986 s 310(3)(b)). Such an application should not be made by the trustee simply to ensure payment of his own remuneration: *Boyden v Watson* [2004] BPIR 1131.

2.765

6.190 Action to follow making of order

(1) Where the court makes an income payments order, a sealed copy of the order shall, forthwith after it is made, be sent by the trustee to the bankrupt.

(2) If the order is made under section 310(3)(b), a sealed copy of the order shall also be sent by the trustee to the person to whom the order is directed.

2.766

6.191 Variation of order

(1) If an income payments order is made under section 310(3)(a), and the bankrupt does not comply with it, the trustee may apply to the court for the order to be varied, so as to take effect under section 310(3)(b) as an order to the payor of the relevant income.

(2) The trustee's application under this Rule may be made *ex parte*.

(3) Sealed copies of any order made on the application shall, forthwith after it is made, be sent by the court to the trustee and the bankrupt.

(4) In the case of an order varying or discharging an income payments order made under section 310(3)(b), an additional sealed copy shall be sent to the trustee, for transmission forthwith to the payor of the relevant income.

Notes

R 6.191

This provision applies if the bankrupt has not complied with the income payments order. If the trustee wants to seek a variation of the amount (for instance because the bankrupt's financial circumstances have improved) the application should be made under IR 1986 r 6.193 and not under this provision. The most common form of application under this rule is to convert an order that the bankrupt make income payments to the trustee to one that a third party (*e g* the bankrupt's employer) make such payments. In such a case, it is recommended that before issuing an application under IR 1986 r 6.191 the trustee asks the bankrupt for up to date details of the bankrupt's income and expenditure, because the court is likely to want to know whether this information has been obtained.

R 6.191(1)

A trustee can not set off any sums due to the bankrupt, for instance to purchase cheaper replacement items the originals of which were sold by the trustee, against any arrears due under the income payment order: *Rayatt v Official Receiver and another* [1998] BPIR 495.

R 6.191(3)

An order made under this rule converting an income payments order made under IA 1986 s 310(1)(a) to one under IA 1986 s 310(1)(b) should be made in the form of Form 6.67.

_____

2.767

6.192 Order to payor of income: administration

(1) Where a person receives notice of an income payments order under section 310(3)(b), with reference to income otherwise payable by him to the bankrupt, he shall make the arrangements requisite for immediate compliance with the order.

(2) When making any payment to the trustee, he may deduct the appropriate fee towards the clerical and administrative costs of compliance with the income payments order.

He shall give to the bankrupt a written statement of any amount deducted by him under this paragraph.

(3) Where a person receives notice of an income payments order imposing on him a requirement under section 310(3)(b), and either—
- (a) he is then no longer liable to make to the bankrupt any payment of income, or
- (b) having made payments in compliance with the order, he ceases to be so liable,

he shall forthwith give notice of that fact to the trustee.

_____

Notes

R 6.192(2)

The appropriate fee is currently 50p: see IR 1986 r 13.11(a).

_____

2.768

6.193 Review of order

(1) Where an income payments order is in force, either the trustee or the bankrupt may apply to the court for the order to be varied or discharged.

(2) If the application is made by the trustee, Rule 6.189 applies (with any necessary modification) as in the case of an application for an income payments order.

(3) If the application is made by the bankrupt, it shall be accompanied by a short statement of the grounds on which it is made.

(4) The court may, if it thinks that no sufficient cause is shown for the application, disMiss it; but it shall not do so unless the applicant has had an opportunity to attend the court for an *ex parte* hearing, of which he has been given at least 7 days' notice.

If the application is not dismissed under this paragraph, the court shall fix a venue for it to be heard.

(5) At least 28 days before the date fixed for the hearing, the applicant shall send to the trustee or the bankrupt (whichever of them is not himself the applicant) notice of the venue, accompanied by a copy of the application.

Where the applicant is the bankrupt, the notice shall be accompanied by a copy of the statement of grounds under paragraph (3).

(6) The trustee may, if he thinks fit, appear and be heard on the application; and, whether or not he intends to appear, he may, not less than 7 days before the date fixed for the hearing, file a written report of any matters which he considers ought to be drawn to the court's attention.

If such a report is filed, a copy of it shall be sent by the trustee to the bankrupt.

(7) Sealed copies of any order made on the application shall, forthwith after the order is made, be sent by the court to the trustee, the bankrupt and the payor (if other than the bankrupt).

Notes

R 6.193

The power to alter the amount payable should only be exercised where there has been a substantial change in circumstances: *Jones v Patel* [1999] BPIR 509. An order made under this provision varying or discharging an income payments order should be made in the form of Form 6.68.

[Chapter 16A
Income Payments Agreements]

Notes

RR 6.193A–6.193C

A legally binding income payments agreement can be put into place under IA 1986 s 310A without the need for a court order. IR 1986 r 6.193A to 6.193C deal with the mechanisms for entering into such an agreement. As with income payments orders an income payments agreement may extend beyond the date of the discharge of the bankruptcy but may not be for a longer period than 3 years.

2.769

[6.193A Approval of income payments agreements]

[(1) An income payments agreement can only be entered into prior to the discharge of the bankrupt.

(2) Where an income payments agreement is to be entered into between the official receiver or trustee and the bankrupt under section 310A(1),

the official receiver or trustee shall provide an income payments agreement to the bankrupt for his approval.

(3) Within 14 days or such longer period as may be specified by the official receiver or trustee (whichever is appropriate) from the date on which the income payments agreement was sent, the bankrupt shall—

(a) if he decides to approve the draft income payments agreement, sign the agreement and return it to the official receiver or trustee (whichever is appropriate); or

(b) if he decides not to approve the agreement, notify the official receiver or trustee (whichever is appropriate) in writing of his decision.]

2.770

[6.193B Acceptance of income payments agreements]

[(1) On receipt by the official receiver or trustee of the signed income payments agreement, the official receiver or trustee shall sign and date it.

(2) When the official receiver or the trustee signs and dates the income payments agreement, it shall come into force. A copy shall be sent to the bankrupt.

(3) Where the agreement provides for payments by a third person to the official receiver or trustee who is not the official receiver in accordance with section 310A(1)(b), a notice of the agreement shall be sent by the official receiver or trustee to that person.

(4) The notice shall contain—

(a) the full name and address of the bankrupt;

(b) a statement that an income payments agreement has been made, the date of it, and that it provides for the payment by the third person of sums owed to the bankrupt (or a part thereof) to be paid to the official receiver or trustee;

(c) the full name and address of the third person;

(d) a statement of the amount of money to be paid to the official receiver or trustee from the bankrupt's income, the period over which the payments are to be made, and the intervals at which the sums are to be paid; and

(e) the full name and address of the official receiver or trustee and the address or details of where the sums are to be paid.

(5) When making any payment to the official receiver or the trustee a person who has received notice of an income payments agreement with reference to income otherwise payable by him to the bankrupt may deduct the appropriate fee towards the clerical and administrative costs of compliance with the income payments agreement. He shall give to the bankrupt a written statement of any amount deducted by him under this paragraph.]

2.771

[6.193C Variation of income payments agreements]

[(1) Where an application is made to court for variation of an income payments agreement, the application shall be accompanied by a copy of the agreement.

(2) Where the bankrupt applies to the court for variation of an income payments agreement under section 310A(6)(b), he shall send a copy of the application and notice of the venue to the official receiver or trustee (whichever is appropriate) at least 28 days before the date fixed for the hearing.

(3) When the official receiver or trustee applies to the court for variation of an income payments agreement under section 310A(6)(b), he shall send a copy of the application and notice of the venue to the bankrupt at least 28 days before the date fixed for the hearing.

(4) The court may order in Form 6.81 the variation of an income payments agreement under section 310A.

(5) Where the court orders an income payments agreement under section 310A(1)(a) to be varied, so as to take the form of an agreement under section 310A(1)(b) as an agreement providing that a third person is to make payments to the trustee or the official receiver, the official receiver or trustee shall send a notice in accordance with Rule 6.193B(3).

(6) When making any payment to the official receiver or the trustee a person who has received notice of an income payments agreement with reference to income otherwise payable by him to the bankrupt may deduct the appropriate fee towards the clerical and administrative costs of compliance with the income payments agreement. He shall give to the bankrupt a written statement of any amount deducted by him under this paragraph.]

Notes

R 6.193C

If either the bankrupt or the official receiver or trustee wish to vary the income payments agreement they can do so by agreement or, if agreement cannot be reached, by making an application to the court under IA 1986 310A(6)(b).

Chapter 17
Action by Court under Section 369; Order to Inland Revenue Official

2.772

6.194 Application for order

(1) An application by the official receiver or the trustee for an order under section 369 (order to inland revenue official to produce documents) shall specify (with such particularity as will enable the order, if made, to be most easily complied with) the documents whose production to the court is desired, naming the official to whom the order is to be addressed.

(2) The court shall fix a venue for the hearing of the application.

(3) Notice of the venue, accompanied by a copy of the application, shall be sent by the applicant to the Commissioners of Inland Revenue ('the Commissioners') at least 28 days before the hearing.

(4) The notice shall require the Commissioners, not later than 7 days before the date fixed for the hearing of the application, to inform the court whether they consent or object to the making of an order under the section.

(5) If the Commissioners consent to the making of an order, they shall inform the court of the name of the official to whom it should be addressed, if other than the one named in the application.

(6) If the Commissioners object to the making of an order, they shall secure that an officer of theirs attends the hearing of the application and, not less than 7 days before it, deliver to the court a statement in writing of their grounds of objection.

A copy of the statement shall be sent forthwith to the applicant.

2.773

6.195 Making and service of the order

(1) If on the hearing of the application it appears to the court to be a proper case, the court may make the order applied for, with such modifications (if any) as appear appropriate having regard to any representations made on behalf of the Commissioners.

(2) The order—
  (a) may be addressed to an inland revenue official other than the one named in the application,
  (b) shall specify a time, not less than 28 days after service on the official to whom the order is addressed, within which compliance is required, and
  (c) may include requirements as to the manner in which documents to which the order relates are to be produced.

(3) A sealed copy of the order shall be served by the applicant on the official to whom it is addressed.

(4) If the official is unable to comply with the order because he has not the relevant documents in his possession, and has been unable to obtain possession of them, he shall deliver to the court a statement in writing as to the reasons for his non-compliance.

A copy of the statement shall be sent forthwith by the official to the applicant.

2.774

6.196 Custody of documents

Where in compliance with an order under section 369 original documents are produced, and not copies, any person who, by order of the court under section 369(2) (authorised disclosure to persons with right of inspection), has them in his possession or custody is responsible to the court for their safe keeping and return as and when directed.

Chapter 18
Mortgaged Property

2.775

6.197 Claim by mortgagee of land

(1) Any person claiming to be the legal or equitable mortgagee of land belonging to the bankrupt may apply to the court for an order directing that the land be sold.

'Land' includes any interest in, or right over, land.

(2) The court, if satisfied as to the applicant's title, may direct accounts to be taken and enquiries made to ascertain—
   (a)   the principal, interest and costs due under the mortgage, and
   (b)   where the mortgagee has been in possession of the land or any part of it, the rents and profits, dividends, interest, or other proceeds received by him or on his behalf.

Directions may be given by the court under this paragraph with respect to any mortgage (whether prior or subsequent) on the same property, other than that of the applicant.

(3) For the purpose of those accounts and enquiries, and of making title to the purchaser, any of the parties may be examined by the court, and shall produce on oath before the court all such documents in their custody or under their control relating to the estate of the bankrupt as the court may direct.

The court may under this paragraph order any of the parties to clarify any matter which is in dispute in the proceedings or give additional information in relation to any such matter and CPR Part 18 (further information) shall apply to any such order.

(4) In any proceedings between a mortgagor and mortgagee, or the trustee of either of them, the court may order accounts to be taken and enquiries made in like manner as in the Chancery Division of the High Court.

Notes

R 6.197

This rule allows a mortgagee to apply for an order for sale on the basis that the mortgagor is bankrupt. Whilst it does not say so in terms, this rule must be in addition to the mortgagee's powers of sale found in s 101 to 103 LPA 1925 and/or the mortgage deed. In practice, a bankrupt mortgagor is likely to fall into arrears and possession will be sought on the basis of the arrears rather than the mere fact of the mortgagor's bankruptcy.

2.776

6.198 Power of court to order sale

(1) The court may order that the land, or any specified part of it, be sold; and any party bound by the order and in possession of the land or part, or

in receipt of the rents and profits from it, may be ordered to deliver up possession or receipt to the purchaser or to such other person as the court may direct.

(2) The court may permit the person having the conduct of the sale to sell the land in such manner as he thinks fit. Alternatively, the court may direct that the land be sold as directed by the order.

(3) The court's order may contain directions—
  (a)   appointing the persons to have the conduct of the sale;
  (b)   fixing the manner of sale (whether by contract conditional on the court's approval, private treaty, public auction, or otherwise);
  (c)   settling the particulars and conditions of sale;
  (d)   obtaining evidence of the value of the property, and fixing a reserve or minimum price;
  (e)   requiring particular persons to join in the sale and conveyance;
  (f)   requiring the payment of the purchase money into court, or to trustees or others;
  (g)   if the sale is to be by public auction, fixing the security (if any) to be given by the auctioneer, and his remuneration.

(4) The court may direct that, if the sale is to be by public auction, the mortgagee may appear and bid on his own behalf.

(5) Nothing in this Rule or the following Rule may affect the rights in rem of creditors or third parties protected under Article 5 of the EC Regulation (third parties rights in rem).

Notes

R 6.198(1)

The court has a discretion as to whether or not to make an order for sale on an application made pursuant to IR 1986 r 6.197. If it does so, the directions that the court might include in an order for sale (see IR 1986 r 6.198(3)) are similar to those that a court might make when ordering a sale pursuant to s 14 Trusts of Land and Appointment of Trustees Act 1996.

R 6.198(5)

See the notes to the EC Regulation.

2.777

6.199 Proceeds of sale

(1) The proceeds of sale shall be applied—
  (a)   first, in payment of the expenses of the trustee, of and occasioned by the application to the court, of the sale and attendance thereat, and of any costs arising from the taking of accounts, and making of enquiries, as directed by the court under Rule 6.197; and
  (b)   secondly, in payment of the amount found due to any mortgagee, for principal, interest and costs;
and the balance (if any) shall be retained by or paid to the trustee.

> (2) Where the proceeds of the sale are insufficient to pay in full the amount found due to any mortgagee, he is entitled to prove as a creditor for any deficiency, and to receive dividends rateably with other creditors, but not so as to disturb any dividend already declared.

Notes

R 6.199

This sets out the priority of claims against the proceeds of any sale made pursuant to IR 1986 r 6.198.

> ## Chapter 19
> ## After-Acquired Property
>
> **2.778**
>
> **6.200 Duties of bankrupt in respect of after-acquired property**
>
> (1) The notice to be given by the bankrupt to the trustee, under section 333(2), of property acquired by, or devolving upon, him, or of any increase of his income, shall be given within 21 days of his becoming aware of the relevant facts.
>
> (2) Having served notice in respect of property acquired by or devolving upon him, the bankrupt shall not, without the trustee's consent in writing, dispose of it within the period of 42 days beginning with the date of the notice.
>
> (3) If the bankrupt disposes of property before giving the notice required by this Rule or in contravention of paragraph (2), it is the duty forthwith to disclose to the trustee the name and address of the disponee, and to provide any other information which may be necessary to enable the trustee to trace the property and recover it for the estate.
>
> (4) Subject as follows, paragraphs (1) to (3) do not apply to property acquired by the bankrupt in the ordinary course of a business carried on by him.
>
> (5) If the bankrupt carries on a business he shall, not less often than 6–monthly, furnish to the trustee information with respect to it, showing the total of goods bought and sold (or, as the case may be, services supplied) and the profit or loss arising from the business.
>
> The trustee may require the bankrupt to furnish fuller details (including accounts) of the business carried on by him.

Notes

R 6.200(1)

The bankrupt has a duty under IA 1986 s 333(2) to inform the trustee in bankruptcy about any property which he either acquires or which devolves to him after the commencement of the bankruptcy (including any increase in the bankrupt's income). The mechanism by which the bankrupt must give notice is set out in IR 6.200 and IR 6.200(1) requires the bankrupt to give notice within 21 days of him becoming aware of the relevant facts relating to after-acquired property or increase in income. A failure to give such notice within the 21 day prescribed period without reasonable excuse is a contempt of court under IA 1986 s 333(4).

R 6.200(2)

Once the bankrupt has served notice on the trustee he must not dispose of the property within the period of 42 days from the date of the notice without first obtaining the written consent of the trustee. The trustee therefore has 42 days in which to claim the property under IA 1986 s 307 after which the bankrupt is free to dispose of the property. After the expiration of 42 days the trustee cannot make a claim under IA 1986 s 307 without the permission of the court – see IA1986 s 309(1)(a). When considering an application by the trustee for permission to serve out of time a notice claiming after acquired property the court will have regard to (i) the period of delay both in serving the notice and seeking an extension; (ii) the merits of the application having regard to the overall position of the bankruptcy; (iii) the prejudice caused to the bankrupt; and (iv) the reasons for the delay – *Solomons v Williams* [2001] BPIR 1123. After acquired property will only vest in the trustee upon the service of notice – see IA 1986 s 307. The Trustee may also use the information for the purposes of applying for an income payments order under IA 1986 s 310A.

R 6.200(3)

Where property is disposed of without first giving notice to the trustee or without the written consent of the trustee within the 42 day notice period under IR 1986 r 6.200(2), the bankrupt has a duty to forthwith disclose to the trustee the name and address of the disponee together with any other relevant information. Such information will enable the trustee to trace the property for the benefit of the estate. However, see notes to IA 1986 s 307(4) concerning a disposition to a third party without notice of the bankruptcy in good faith.

R 6.200(4)–(5)

These rules do not apply to property acquired by the bankrupt in the ordinary course of his business provided that he supplies the trustee with information showing the total goods or services bought and sold by the business together with profit and loss not less than every six months. It is open to the trustee to request fuller details including the accounts of the business carried on by the bankrupt.

2.779

6.201 Trustee's recourse to disponee of property

(1) Where property has been disposed of by the bankrupt, before giving the notice required by Rule 6.200 or otherwise in contravention of that Rule, the trustee may serve notice on the disponee, claiming the property as part of the estate by virtue of section 307(3).

(2) The trustee's notice under this Rule must be served within 28 days of his becoming aware of the disponee's identity and an address at which he can be served.

Notes

R 6.201

The trustee may serve notice on the disponee of property within 28 days of his becoming aware of the disponee's identity and address claiming that the property is part of the bankrupt's estate. This time limit may be extended pursuant to IA 1986 s 376. The trustees right to trace the property arises by virtue of IA 1986 s 307(3) which vests the property in the trustee upon notice being given under IA 1986 s 307(1) and backdates the trustee's title to the time when the property was acquired by or devolved upon the bankrupt ie being prior to the bankrupts disposal to the disponee. See notes to IA 1986 s 307(4) in relation to disposals to third parties and bankers without notice of the bankruptcy and in good faith against whom the trustee is not entitled to any remedy.

2.780

6.202 Expenses of getting in property for the estate

Any expenses incurred by the trustee in acquiring title to after-acquired property shall be paid out of the estate, in the prescribed order of priority.

Notes

R 6.202

Expenses incurred by the trustee in relation to the acquisition of after-acquired property are expenses in the bankruptcy. The order of priority of expenses is set out in IR 1986 r 6.224(1) below.

Chapter 20
Leave to Act as Director, etc

2.781

6.202A

In this Chapter a reference to a bankrupt includes a reference to a person in respect of whom a bankruptcy restrictions order is in force.

Notes

R 6.202A

This provision was introduced by IAR 2003 to complement the new bankruptcy regime introduced by EA 2002.

2.782

6.203 Application for leave

(1) An application by the bankrupt for leave, under section 11 of the Company Directors Disqualification Act 1986, to act as director of, or to take part or be concerned in the promotion, formation or management of a company, shall be supported by an affidavit complying with this Rule.

(2) The affidavit must identify the company and specify—
    (a)   the nature of its business or intended business and the place or places where that business is, or is to be, carried on,
    (b)   whether it is, or is to be, a private or a public company,

(c) the persons who are, or are to be, principally responsible for the conduct of its affairs (whether as directors, shadow directors, managers or otherwise),

(d) the manner and capacity in which the applicant proposes to take part or be concerned in the promotion or formation of the company or, as the case may be, its management, and

(e) the emoluments and other benefits to be obtained from the directorship.

(3) If the company is already in existence, the affidavit must specify the date of its incorporation and the amount of its nominal and issued share capital; and if not, it must specify the amount, or approximate amount, of its proposed commencing share capital, and the sources from which that capital is to be obtained.

(4) Where the bankrupt intends to take part or be concerned in the promotion or formation of a company, the affidavit must contain an undertaking by him that he will, within not less than 7 days of the company being incorporated, file in court a copy of its memorandum of association and certificate of incorporation under section 13 of the Companies Act.

(5) The court shall fix a venue for the hearing of the bankrupt's application, and give notice to him accordingly.

Notes

R 6.203

Such applications are likely to be rare in practice and likely to be unsuccessful: see *Re McQuillan* (1989) 5 BCC 137.

2.783

6.204 Report of official receiver

(1) The bankrupt shall, not less than 28 days before the date fixed for the hearing, give to the official receiver and the trustee notice of the venue, accompanied by copies of the application and the affidavit under Rule 6.203.

(2) The official receiver may, not less than 14 days before the date fixed for the hearing, file in court a report of any matters which he considers ought to be drawn to the court's attention. A copy of the report shall be sent by him, forthwith after it is filed, to the bankrupt and to the trustee.

(3) The bankrupt may, not later than 7 days before the date of the hearing, file in court a notice specifying any statements in the official receiver's report which he intends to deny or dispute.

If he gives notice under this paragraph, he shall send copies of it, not less than 4 days before the date of the hearing, to the official receiver and the trustee.

(4) The official receiver and the trustee may appear on the hearing of the application, and may make representations and put to the bankrupt such questions as the court may allow.

Notes

R 6.204

Under s 11(3) CDDA 1986 the official receiver is duty bound to attend and oppose the application by the bankrupt if he is of the opinion that it would be contrary to the public interest that the application should be granted.

2.784

6.205 Court's order on application

(1) If the court grants the bankrupt's application for leave under section 11 of the Company Directors Disqualification Act 1986, its order shall specify that which by virtue of the order the bankrupt has leave to do.

(2) The court may at the same time, having regard to any representations made by the trustee on the hearing of the application—
  (a) include in the order provision varying an income payments order [or an income payments agreement] already in force in respect of the bankrupt, or
  (b) if no income payments order is in force, make one.

(3) Whether or not the application is granted, copies of the order shall be sent by the court to the bankrupt, the trustee and the official receiver.

The Second Group of Parts
Individual Insolvency; Bankruptcy

Part 6
Bankruptcy

Chapter 21
Annulment of Bankruptcy Order

2.785

6.206 Application for annulment

(1) An application to the court under section 282(1) for the annulment of a bankruptcy order shall specify whether it is made—
  (a) under subsection (1)(a) of the section (claim that the order ought not to have been made), or
  (b) under subsection (1)(b) (debts and expenses of the bankruptcy all paid or secured).

(2) The application shall, in either case, be supported by an affidavit stating the grounds on which it is made; and, where it is made under

section 282(1)(b), there shall be set out in the affidavit all the facts by reference to which the court is, under the Act and the Rules, required to be satisfied before annulling the bankruptcy order.

(3) A copy of the application and supporting affidavit shall be filed in court; and the court shall give to the applicant notice of the venue fixed for the hearing.

(4) The applicant shall ... give to the official receiver and (if other) the trustee notice of the venue, accompanied by copies of the application and the affidavit under paragraph (2)

(a) where the application is made under section 282(1)(a), in sufficient time to enable them to be present at the hearing, and

(b) where the application is made under section 282(1)(b), not less than 28 days before the hearing.

(5) Where the application is made under section 282(1)(a), paragraph (4) shall additionally be complied with in relation to the person on whose petition the bankruptcy order was made.

(6) In this Chapter, where the applicant is not the bankrupt all notices, documents and affidavits required to be given, sent or delivered to another party by the applicant shall also be given, sent or delivered to the bankrupt.

Notes

R 6.206

The general circumstances in which a bankruptcy order may be annulled are set out in s 282(1) IA 1986. This rule prescribes the relevant procedure. An annulment shall also be ordered under IA 1986 s 261 where an application is made by an undischarged bankrupt and the creditors have approved proposals for an individual voluntary arrangement. An application for annulment is made to the registrar (rather than the Judge) in the first instance: paragraph 9.2 of Practice Direction: Insolvency Proceedings (Civil Procedure Vol 2, Sect 3E), Practice Note on the Hearing of Insolvency Proceeedings [2005] BPIR 688.

R 6.206(2)

Though the application can be combined with an attack on the level of the costs and remuneration of the trustee it is often advisable to approach them as separate matters: see *Hirani v Rendle* [2004] BPIR 274. The trustee should be careful before opposing an annulment on the ground that the bankrupt desires the court to assess his costs: see *Engel v Peri* [2002] BPIR 961.

IR 6.206(5)

The petitioning creditor must be served where it is alleged the bankruptcy order ought not have been made at all; albeit that the petitioning creditor is not given the express right to attend the annulment hearing and address the court it is probable that permission would be given in any event.

IR 6.206(6)

This provision was added by IAR 2003 to ensure that the bankrupt receives the relevant documents.

2.786

6.207 Report by trustee

(1) The following applies where the application is made under section 282(1)(b) (debts and expenses of the bankruptcy all paid or secured).

(2) Not less than 21 days before the date fixed for the hearing, the trustee or, if no trustee has been appointed, the official receiver shall file in court a report with respect to the following matters—

  (a) the circumstances leading to the bankruptcy;

  (b) (in summarised form) the extent of the bankrupt's assets and liabilities at the date of the bankruptcy order and at the date of the present application;

  (c) details of creditors (if any) who are known to him to have claims, but have not proved; and

  (d) such other matters as the person making the report considers to be, in the circumstances, necessary for the information of the court.

(3) The report shall include particulars of the extent (if any) to which, and the manner in which, the debts and expenses of the bankruptcy have been paid or secured.

In so far as debts and expenses are unpaid but secured, the person making the report shall state in it whether and to what extent he considers the security to be satisfactory.

(4) A copy of the report shall be sent to the applicant at least 14 days before the date fixed for the hearing; and he may, if he wishes, file further affidavits in answer to statements made in the report.

Copies of any such affidavits shall be sent by the applicant to the official receiver and (if other) the trustee.

(5) If the trustee is other than the official receiver, a copy of his report shall be sent to the official receiver at least 21 days before the hearing. The official receiver may then file an additional report, a copy of which shall be sent to the applicant at least 7 days before the hearing.

Notes

R 6.207

These provisions apply only where the application for annulment is made under 282(1)(b) that is on the basis that all bankruptcy debts and expenses have, since the order was made, been paid or secured for to the satisfaction of the Court.

R 6.207(2)

A trustee is not automatically appointed on the making of a bankruptcy order IA 1986 s 293. The report of the official receiver will inevitably detail the course of the bankruptcy and the actions and/or omissions of the bankrupt.

R 6.207(4)

There is no obligation on the official receiver to attend the annulment hearing unless he has provided a report under IR 1986 r 6.207, 6.210(2).

2.787

6.208 Power of court to stay proceedings

(1) The court may, in advance of the hearing, make an interim order staying any proceedings which it thinks ought, in the circumstances of the application, to be stayed.

(2) Except in relation to an application for an order staying all or any part of the proceedings in the bankruptcy, application for an order under this Rule may be made *ex parte*.

(3) Where application is made under this Rule for an order staying all or any part of the proceedings in the bankruptcy, the applicant shall send copies of the application to the official receiver and (if other) the trustee in sufficient time to enable them to be present at the hearing and (if they wish to do so) make representations.

(4) Where the court makes an order under this Rule staying all or any part of the proceedings in the bankruptcy, the rules in this Chapter nevertheless continue to apply to any application for, or other matters in connection with, the annulment of the bankruptcy order.

(5) If the court makes an order under this Rule, it shall send copies of the order to the applicant, the official receiver and (if other) the trustee.

Notes

R 6.208

The rule gives power to the court to order a stay, pending the substantive hearing of the application to annul, on any proceedings which are ongoing at the time when the annulment application is made. The purpose of the rule is to prevent prejudice and/or a potential waste of costs in circumstances where the bankruptcy order consequent upon which proceedings are ongoing might ultimately be annulled.

R 6.208(2)

Though this provision allows an application to be made without notice it would be inadvisable to do so without very good reason.

2.788

6.209 Notice to creditors who have not proved

Where the application for annulment is made under section 282(1)(b) and it has been reported to the court under Rule 6.207 that there are known creditors of the bankrupt who have not proved, the court may—

(a) direct the trustee [or, if no trustee has been appointed, the official receiver] to send notice of the application to such of those creditors as the court thinks ought to be informed of it, with a view to their proving their debts (if they so wish) within 21 days, and

(b) direct the trustee [or, if no trustee has been appointed, the official receiver] to advertise the fact that the application has been made, so that creditors who have not proved may do so within a specified time, and

> (c) adjourn the application meanwhile, for any period not less than 35 days.

Notes

R 6.209

In *Re Robertson* [1989] 1 WLR 1139 Warner J held that a bankruptcy order could be annulled under s 282(1)(b) only where all the bankruptcy debts had been proved and paid or secured in accordance with the rules: where there were debts that had not yet been proved then the power to annul could not arise. The latter point was doubted in *Gill v Quinn* [2005] BPIR 129, 133 para 16 per Mann J. The present rule is intended to ensure that creditors who have not submitted proofs are contacted and given a chance to act before a decision is made on the application to annul.

2.789

6.210 The hearing

(1) The trustee shall attend the hearing of the application.

(2) The official receiver, if he is not the trustee, may attend, but is not required to do so unless he has filed a report under Rule 6.207.

(3) If the court makes an order on the application, it shall send copies of the order to the applicant, the official receiver and (if other) the trustee.

Notes

R 6.210

The trustee is bound to attend the hearing. The official receiver (if he is not the trustee) is required to do so only if he has filed a report under IR 1986 r 6.207.

2.790

6.211 Matters to be proved under s 282(1)(b)

(1) This rule applies with regard to the matters which must, in an application under section 282(1)(b), be proved to the satisfaction of the court.

(2) Subject to the following paragraph, all bankruptcy debts which have been proved must have been paid in full.

(3) If a debt is disputed, or a creditor who has proved can no longer be traced, the bankrupt must have given such security (in the form of money paid into court, or a bond entered into with approved sureties) as the court considers adequate to satisfy any sum that may subsequently be proved to be due to the creditor concerned and (if the court thinks fit) costs.

(4) Where under paragraph (3) security has been given in the case of an untraced creditor, the court may direct that particulars of the alleged debt, and the security, be advertised in such manner as it thinks fit.

If advertisement is ordered under this paragraph, and no claim on the security is made within 12 months from the date of the advertisement (or the first advertisement, if more than one), the court shall, on application in that behalf, order the security to be released.

2.791

6.212 Notice to creditors

(1) Where the official receiver has notified creditors of the debtor's bankruptcy, and the bankruptcy order is annulled, he shall forthwith notify them of the annulment.

(2) Expenses incurred by the official receiver in giving notice under this Rule are a charge in his favour on the property of the former bankrupt, whether or not actually in his hands.

(3) Where any property is in the hands of a trustee or any person other than the former bankrupt himself, the official receiver's charge is valid subject only to any costs that may be incurred by the trustee or that other person in effecting realisation of the property for the purpose of satisfying the charge.

Notes

R 6.212(2), (3)

The official receiver's costs of notification will be secured by a charge. It is only the costs incurred by a trustee or any third party in realising property which he holds and which is subject to the official receiver's charge that will take priority to the entitlement of the official receiver.

2.792

[6 .212A Annulment under section 261]

[Rules 6.206 to 6.212 *apply to an application for annulment under section 261 as they apply to such an application under section 282(1)(a).]*

Notes

R 6.212A

Revoked by the Insolvency (Amendment) Rules 2003 r 9(1) as from 1 April 2004 subject to a saving provision (r 9(3)) for bankruptcies commenced prior to that date.

2.793

6.213 Other matters arising on annulment

(1) In an order under section 282 the court shall include provision permitting vacation of the registration of the bankruptcy petition as a pending action, and of the bankruptcy order, in the register of writs and orders affecting land.

(2) The court shall forthwith give notice of the making of the order to the Secretary of State.

(3) The former bankrupt may require within 28 days of the order the Secretary of State to give notice of the making of the order—
  (a) in the Gazette, or
  (b) in any newspaper in which the bankruptcy order was advertised, or
  (c) in both.

(4) Any requirement by the former bankrupt under paragraph (3) shall be addressed to the Secretary of State in writing.

(5) Where the former bankrupt has died, or is a person incapable of managing his affairs (within the meaning of Chapter 7 in Part 7 of the Rules), the references to him in paragraphs (3) and (4) are to be read as referring to his personal representative or, as the case may be, a person appointed by the court to represent or act for him.

Notes

R 6.213

The rule deals with matters that arise on annulment of an order pursuant to the provisions of s 282 (the order ought never to have been made, or satisfaction or securing of bankruptcy debts and expenses).

R 6.213(1)

This rule also formerly applied to annulments following the approval of a voluntary arrangement under IA 1986 s 261. The Insolvency Amendment Rules 2003 revoked its application to s 261 though in relation to bankruptcies commenced prior to 1 April 2004 it still applies (IAR 2003 r 9(3)(b)).

R 6.213(3)–(4)

It is the bankrupt who can now decide whether he wishes to have notice of the making of the annulment order published. The time limit of 28 days was introduced by the Insolvency (Amendment) Rules 2004.

2.794

6.214 Trustee's final account

(1) Where a bankruptcy order is annulled under section [261 or] 282, this does not of itself release the trustee from any duty or obligation, imposed on him by or under the Act or the Rules, to account for all his transactions in connection with the former bankrupt's estate.

(2) The trustee shall submit a copy of his final account to the Secretary of State, as soon as practicable after the court's order annulling the bankruptcy order; and he shall file a copy of the final account in court.

(3) The final account must include a summary of the trustee's receipts and payments in the administration, and contain a statement to the effect that he has reconciled his account with that which is held by the Secretary of State in respect of the bankruptcy.

(4) The trustee is released from such time as the court may determine, having regard to whether—
(a)   paragraph (2) of this Rule has been complied with, and
(b)   any security given under Rule 6.211(3) has been, or will be, released.

Notes

R 6.214

Following an annulment order the trustee is released only from such time as the court may determine: the relevant considerations for the court will be whether the trustee has filed his final account of the bankruptcy (which account can be challenged by a dissatisfied former bankrupt pursuant to the general provisions of s 303 and IR 6.214 *Hirani v Rendle* [2004] EWHC 2538 (Ch), [2004] BPIR 274, and whether any security given (pursuant to the provisions of r 6.211(3)) to satisfy amounts due to any untraced creditors has been or will be released.

R 6.214(1)

This rule also formerly applied to annulments following the approval of a voluntary arrangement under IA 1986 s 261. The Insolvency Amendment Rules 2003 revoked its application to s 261 though in relation to bankruptcies commenced prior to 1 April 2004 it still applies (IAR 2003 r 9(3)(b)).

Chapter 21A
Notice under section 279(2)

2.795

6.214A Notice under section 279(2) that an investigation of the conduct and affairs of the bankrupt is unnecessary or concluded

(1) Where the official receiver intends to file a notice that an investigation of the conduct and affairs of the bankrupt is unnecessary or concluded under section 279(2), he shall give notice in writing to all creditors of which he is aware and any trustee of his intention to file such a notice.

(2) Where a creditor or a trustee receives written notice of the official receiver's intention to file a notice under section 279(2) and he has any objection to the official receiver filing such a notice, he may, within 28 days of the date of such written notice, inform the official receiver in writing of his objection and give reasons for that objection.

(3) The official receiver shall not file a notice under section 279(2) until the period allowed for creditors or a trustee to object under paragraph (2) has expired.

(4) Where the official receiver receives no objection from either a creditor or a trustee he may file a notice under section 279(2) by sending to the court two copies of Form 6.82. The court shall endorse each copy with the date of filing and shall return one copy to the official receiver. The official receiver shall send a copy of the endorsed form to the bankrupt.

(5) Where the official receiver receives an objection under this Rule and he rejects that objection, he shall not file the notice under section 279(2) until he has-
    (a)   given notice of the rejection (and his reasons) to the complainant; and
    (b)   the period of time for an appeal by the complainant under Rule 7.50(2) has expired,
or an appeal under that Rule has been determined by the court.

Notes

R 6.214A

This provision does not apply to bankruptcies commenced prior to 1 April 2004 (IAR 2003 r 9(3)(c)). Its aim is to supplement the provision which enables a bankrupt to obtain his discharge from bankruptcy within one year from the commencement of bankruptcy (IA 1986 s 279(2)). The recent reforms to personal insolvency aim to differentiate between culpable bankrupts and others; it is the latter group which should be discharged from bankruptcy as soon as possible. The provision is silent as to what occurs if a creditor is not served with a notice and the discharge then takes place; presumably the discharge will remain unaffected.

Chapter 22
Discharge

2.796

6.215 Application for suspension of discharge

(1) The following applies where the official receiver or any trustee who is not the official receiver applies to the court for an order under section 279(3) (suspension of automatic discharge), but not where the official receiver makes that application, pursuant to Rule 6.176(4), on the adjournment of the bankrupt's public examination.

(2) The official receiver or any trustee shall, with his application, file evidence in support setting out the reasons why it appears to him that such an order should be made.

(3) The court shall fix a venue for the hearing of the application, and give notice of it to the official receiver, the trustee who is not the official receiver, and the bankrupt.

(4) Copies of the official receiver's report under this Rule shall be sent by him to the bankrupt and any trustee who is not the official receiver so as to reach them at least 21 days before the date fixed for the hearing.

(5) Copies of the trustee's evidence in support under this Rule shall be sent by him to the official receiver and the bankrupt, so as to reach them at least 21 days before the date fixed for the hearing.

(6) The bankrupt may, not later than 7 days before the date of the hearing, file in court a notice specifying any statements in the official receiver's or trustee's evidence in support which he intends to deny or dispute.

(7) If the bankrupt files notice under paragraph (6), he shall send copies of it, not less than 4 days before the date of the hearing, to the official receiver and any trustee who is not the official receiver

(8) If the court makes an order suspending the bankrupt's discharge, copies of the order shall be sent by the court to the official receiver, any trustee who is not the official receiver and the bankrupt.

Notes

R 6.215

This provision applies both to bankruptcies commenced prior to and after 1 April 2004 (IAR 2003 r 9(4)). The circumstances in which an order may be made to suspend the automatic discharge from bankruptcy are set out in IA 1986 s 279(3). This rule sets out the relevant procedure. The application is made to the registrar (rather than the Judge) in the first instance: paragraph 9.2 of Practice Direction: Insolvency Proceedings Civil Procedure Vol 2, Sect 3E.

Once the statutory period of one year has expired (IA 1986 s 279(1)) without a continuation, then it cannot be restarted. Accordingly the application for suspension must be brought on or before the end of the statutory period and the application must be based on the failure of the bankrupt to comply with his bankruptcy obligations (IA 1986 s 279(4)). If the application cannot be substantively determined before the end of the period then it may be appropriate for the court to order (before the period has expired) an interim suspension until the full hearing has taken place: see *Re Jacobs* [1999] 1 WLR 619.

R 6.215(4)

In cases of urgency the court may hear a without notice application (IR 1986 r 7.4(6)) and in a suitable case this would include making an interim order suspending an automatic discharge before the provisions of IR 6.215(4) can be complied with *Bagnall v Official Receiver* [2003] BPIR 1080.

2.797

6.216 Lifting of suspension of discharge

(1) Where the court has made an order under section 279(3) that the period specified in section 279(1) shall cease to run, the bankrupt may apply to it for the order to be discharged.

(2) The court shall fix a venue for the hearing of the application; and the bankrupt shall, not less than 28 days before the date fixed for hearing, give notice of the venue to the official receiver and any trustee who is not the official receiver, accompanied in each case by a copy of the application.

(3) The official receiver and the trustee may appear and be heard on the bankrupt's application; and, whether or not they appear, the official receiver and trustee may file in court evidence in support of any matters which either of them considers ought to be drawn to the court's attention.

(4) If the court made an order under section 279(3)(b) the court may request a report from the official receiver or the trustee as to whether the conditions specified in the order have or have not been fulfilled.

(5) If a report is filed under paragraph (3) or (4), copies of it shall be sent by the official receiver or trustee to the bankrupt and to either the official receiver or trustee (depending on which has filed the report), not later than 14 days before the hearing.

(6) The bankrupt may, not later than 7 days before the date of the hearing, file in court a notice specifying any statements in the official receiver's or trustee's report which he intends to deny or dispute.

If he files a notice under this paragraph, he shall send copies of it, not less than 4 days before the date of the hearing, to the official receiver and the trustee.

(7) If on the bankrupt's application the court discharges the order under section 279(3) (being satisfied that the period specified in section 279(1) should begin to run again), it shall issue to the bankrupt a certificate that it has done so, with effect from a specified date and shall send copies of the certificate to the official receiver and the trustee.

Notes

R 6.216

At any time after the court has ordered a suspension of the bankrupt's discharge he may make an application for that order to be discharged. Plainly the bankrupt will have to show that the position has changed since the court thought it appropriate to order a suspension. Ordinarily this will involve establishing, at least, that he has now co-operated with the trustee and complied with his obligations under the Act.

2.798

6.217 Application by bankrupt for discharge

(1) If the bankrupt applies under section 280 for an order discharging him from bankruptcy, he shall give to the official receiver notice of the application, and deposit with him such sum as the latter may require to cover his costs of the application.

(2) The court, if satisfied that paragraph (1) has been complied with, shall fix a venue for the hearing of the application, and give at least 42 days' notice of it to the official receiver and the bankrupt.

(3) The official receiver shall give notice accordingly—
    (a)   to the trustee, and
    (b)   to every creditor who, to the official receiver's knowledge, has a claim outstanding against the estate which has not been satisfied.

(4) Notices under paragraph (3) shall be given not later than 14 days before the date fixed for the hearing of the bankrupt's application.

Notes

R 6.217

Section 280 concerns the discharge from bankruptcy of criminal bankrupts and any person who was an undischarged bankrupt (pursuant to an earlier order) during the period of 15 years prior to the date of the extant bankruptcy order. In such cases there is no automatic discharge and such bankrupts have to make application to court.

R 6.217(1)

The Insolvency Fees Order 1986 has been substantially revoked by The Insolvency Proceedings (Fees) Order 2004 (art 3, Sch 1) and therefore there is no longer a set fee for the official receiver's attendance and report (see Insolvency Fees Order 1986 Part 2 Fee 7); however the revocation does not affect cases where a bankruptcy order was made before 1 April 2004.

2.799

6.218 Report of official receiver

(1) Where the bankrupt makes an application under section 280, the official receiver shall, at least 21 days before the date fixed for the hearing of the application, file in court a report containing the following information with respect to the bankrupt—

    (a)   any failure by him to comply with his obligations under Parts VIII to XI of the Act;

    (b)   the circumstances surrounding the present bankruptcy, and those surrounding any previous bankruptcy of his;

    (c)   the extent to which, in the present and in any previous bankruptcy, his liabilities have exceeded his assets; and

    (d)   particulars of any distribution which has been, or is expected to be, made to creditors in the present bankruptcy or, if such is the case, that there has been and is to be no distribution;

and the official receiver shall include in his report any other matters which in his opinion ought to be brought to the court's attention.

(2) The official receiver shall send a copy of the report to the bankrupt and the trustee, so as to reach them at least 14 days before the date of the hearing of the application under section 280.

(3) The bankrupt may, not later than 7 days before the date of the hearing, file in court a notice specifying any statements in the official receiver's report which he intends to deny or dispute.

If he gives notice under this paragraph, he shall send copies of it, not less than 4 days before the date of the hearing, to the official receiver and the trustee.

(4) The official receiver, the trustee and any creditor may appear on the hearing of the bankrupt's application, and may make representations and put to the bankrupt such questions as the court may allow.

Notes

R 6.218

The rule details the matters which must be covered by the official receiver's report in a case where application has been made by the bankrupt under s 280 for discharge of the bankruptcy order; see also the preceding rule and the note thereto. The bankrupt must file a notice, not later than 7 days before the hearing, identifying any statements in the official receiver's report that he intends to deny or dispute. Such notice must be served on the official receiver and trustee not less than 4 days before the hearing.

R 6.218(4)

A creditor may appear on the bankrupt's hearing for a discharge without forewarning and cross-examine the bankrupt. However it is advisable for the creditor to liaise with the official receiver and the bankrupt to ensure that the hearing is going to be effective.

2.800

6.219 Order of discharge on application

(1) An order of the court under section 280(2)(b) (discharge absolutely) or (c) (discharge subject to conditions with respect to income or property) shall bear the date on which it is made, but does not take effect until such time as it is drawn up by the court.

(2) The order then has effect retrospectively to the date on which it was made.

(3) Copies of any order made by the court on an application by the bankrupt for discharge under section 280 shall be sent by the court to the bankrupt, the trustee and the official receiver.

Notes

R 6.219

The rule identifies the moment at which an order for discharge will take effect.

2.801

6.220 Certificate of discharge

(1) Where it appears to the court that a bankrupt is discharged, whether by expiration of time or otherwise, the court shall, on his application, issue to him a certificate of his discharge, and the date from which it is effective.

(2) The discharged bankrupt may require the Secretary of State to give notice of the discharge—
   (a)   in the Gazette, or
   (b)   in any newspaper in which the bankruptcy was advertised, or
   (c)   in both.

(3) Any requirement by the former bankrupt under paragraph (2) shall be addressed to the Secretary of State in writing. The Secretary of State shall notify him forthwith as to the cost of the advertisement, and is under no obligation to advertise until that sum has been paid.

(4) Where the former bankrupt has died, or is a person incapable of managing his affairs (within the meaning of Chapter 7 in Part 7 of the Rules), the references to him in paragraphs (2) and (3) are to be read as

> referring to his personal representative or, as the case may be, a person appointed by the court to represent or act for him.

Notes

R 6.220

The former bankrupt may, by application to the court, obtain a certificate of his discharge. He may also require the Secretary of State to publish notice of his discharge subject to the costs of that exercise being paid by him.

2.802

6.221 Deferment of issue of order pending appeal

An order made by the court on an application by the bankrupt for discharge under section 280 shall not be issued or gazetted until the time allowed for appealing has expired or, if an appeal is entered, until the appeal has been determined.

Notes

R 6.221

The time allowed for appealing is 14 days from the date on which the order was made unless the court whose decision is being appealed has directed some other period: see r 7.49; CPR r 52.4(2); and paragraph 17.11(2) of Practice Direction: Insolvency Proceedings Civil Procedure Vol 2, Sect 3E.

2.803

6.222 Costs under this Chapter

In no case do any costs or expenses arising under this Chapter fall on the official receiver personally.

2.804

6.223 Bankrupt's debts surviving discharge

Discharge does not release the bankrupt from any obligation arising under a confiscation order made under section 1 of the Drug Trafficking Offences Act 1986 or section 1 of the Criminal Justice (Scotland) Act 1987 or section 71 of the Criminal Justice Act 1988 or under Parts 2,3 or 4 of the Proceeds of Crime Act 2002.

Notes

R 6.223

The confiscation provisions referred to in the rule contain wide powers enabling orders to be made against a convicted person's property and assets.

[Chapter 22(A)
Register of Bankruptcy Orders]

Notes

R 6.223(A)–(C)

The Rules in this Chapter have been revoked by IAR 2003 r 9(1) as from 1 April 2004; for convenience sake they appear in italicised form below.

2.805

[6.223(A) Register of Bankruptcy Orders]

[(1) The Secretary of State shall maintain a register of bankruptcy orders ('the register') which shall contain the specified bankruptcy information entered in it by the official receiver in pursuance of Rule 6.223(B), any information entered in it by the official receiver in pursuance of Rule 6.223(C) and the information set out in paragraphs (2) and (3).

(2) The Secretary of State shall cause to be entered in the register notice of the making of an annulment order under section 261(1)(a) or 282(1)(b) given to him in pursuance of Rule 6.213(2).

(3) The Secretary of State shall cause to be entered in the register such of the specified bankruptcy information and notice of the making of any annulment order under section 261(1)(a) or 282(1)(b) relating to any bankruptcy order where such bankruptcy order was made in the period of five years prior to 22nd March 1999 as is in the possession of the Secretary of State on that date but excluding information relating to—

   (a) any bankruptcy order which has been annulled under section 282(1)(a) or which has been rescinded under section 375,

   (b) any bankruptcy order which has been annulled under section 261(1)(a) or 282(1)(b) more than two years prior to 22nd March 1999, and

   (c) any bankruptcy order in respect of which an order made under Rule 6.34(3) or 6.46(3) is in force on that date and a copy of which has been delivered to the official receiver under Rule 6.34(4) or 6.46(4), provided that where after that date the order under Rule 6.34(3) or 6.46(3) expires, the Secretary of State shall enter in the register such of the specified bankruptcy information relating to the bankruptcy order previously the subject of the order under Rule 6.34(3) or 6.46(3) as is in his possession as at the date of expiry of such order, except where the official receiver receives a copy of any further order of the court under Rule 6.34(3) or 6.46(3) in respect of such bankruptcy order, in which event the Secretary of State shall not enter such specified bankruptcy information in the register until the expiry of such further order.

(4) Where a bankrupt in respect of whom specified bankruptcy information has been entered in the register is discharged from the bankruptcy or obtains an annulment order under section 261(1)(a) or 282(1)(b) in respect of the bankruptcy order, the Secretary of State shall, on the expiry of two years after the date of such discharge or annulment order (or where a certificate for the summary administration of the bankrupt's estate has been issued under section 275(1), on

the expiry of three years after the date on which the bankrupt is discharged from the bankruptcy) delete from the register the specified bankruptcy information and any other information entered in the register in respect of such bankruptcy order.

(5) If a bankruptcy order in respect of which specified bankruptcy information has been entered in the register is annulled by the court under section 282(1)(a), the Secretary of State shall delete from the register the specified bankruptcy information and any other information entered in the register in respect of such bankruptcy order upon receiving notice of such annulment under Rule 6.213(2).

(6) If a bankruptcy order in respect of which specified bankruptcy information has been entered in the register is rescinded by the court under section 375 the Secretary of State shall delete from the register the specified bankruptcy information and any other information entered in the register in respect of such bankruptcy order upon receiving a copy of the order of the court rescinding the bankruptcy order.

(7) The register shall be open to public inspection.]

2.806

[6.223(B) Specified Bankruptcy Information]

[(1) Following the receipt by the official receiver pursuant to Rule 6.34 or 6.46 of a copy of the bankruptcy order from the court, the official receiver shall cause to be entered in the register the information listed in paragraph (5)(a) and shall cause to be entered in the register the information listed in paragraph 5(b) upon receipt by him of such information.

(2) Following the receipt by the official receiver—
- *(a)   pursuant to Rule 6.50(3), of notice of the revocation of a certificate for summary administration,*
- *(b)   pursuant to Rule 6.176(5), of a copy of an order suspending the bankrupt's discharge,*
- *(c)   pursuant to Rule 6.215(6), of a copy of an order suspending the bankrupt's discharge,*
- *(d)   pursuant to Rule 6.216(7), of a copy of a certificate certifying the discharge of an order under section 279(3), or*
- *(e)   pursuant to Rule 6.219(3), of a copy of an order discharging the bankrupt absolutely or subject to conditions,*

the official receiver shall cause the information listed in paragraph (5)(c) to be entered in the register.

(3) Where an order referred to in paragraph 2(d) is subsequently rescinded by the court the official receiver shall cause the specified bankruptcy information relating to such bankruptcy to be amended to record the fact that the bankrupt is not discharged and, where the information in respect of such bankruptcy has been deleted from the register pursuant to paragraph (4) of Rule 6.223(A), shall cause such information to be restored to the register.

(4) Where a bankrupt is discharged from bankruptcy under section 279(1)(b) the official receiver shall cause the fact and date of such discharge to be entered in the register.

(5) In this Chapter 'specified bankruptcy information' means the following information—
- *(a)*

     (i)   *the matters listed in Rules 6.7 and 6.38 with respect to the debtor as stated in the bankruptcy petition;*

     (ii) *the bankruptcy order date, the court and court reference number;*

(b)

     (i)   *the name, gender, occupation (if any) and date of birth of the bankrupt;*

     (ii) *the bankrupt's last known address.;*

     (iii) *where the bankrupt has been an undischarged bankrupt at any time in the period of 15 years ending with the date of the bankruptcy order in question, the date of the most recent of any previous bankruptcy orders (but excluding an order annulled under section 282(1)(a) or rescinded under section 375);*

     (iv) *any name by which the bankrupt is known other than his true name;*

     (v) *the name or names in which he carries on business if other than his true name and any address at which he carries on business;*

     (vi) *the contact address of the official receiver's office;*

     (vii) *the name and address of the insolvency practitioner (where appointed);*

     (viii) *the automatic discharge date under section 279(1)(b) or, where section 279(1)(a) applies, a statement that there is no automatic discharge date;*

     (ix) *where a certificate for summary administration has been issued, a statement to that effect; and*

(c)

     (i)   *the revised automatic discharge date where— (aa) the court has revoked a certificate for the summary administration of a bankrupt's estate under section 275(3), (bb) the court has made an order under section 279(3) that the relevant period under that section shall cease to run for the period specified in the order, or (cc) the court has discharged an order under section 279(3) being satisfied that the relevant period should begin to run again;*

     (ii) *a statement that discharge has been suspended where the court has made an order under section 279(3) that the relevant period under that section shall cease to run until the fulfilment of such conditions as may be specified in the order;*

     (iii) *the fact that and date on which the bankrupt is discharged.]*

2.807

[6.223(C) Notification of Changes]

[(1) If the official receiver becomes aware that the information which has been entered in the register is inaccurate he shall rectify the information entered in the register.

(2) If the official receiver receives notice of the date of death of a bankrupt in respect of whom specified bankruptcy information has been entered in the register he shall cause such date to be entered in the register.]

Chapter 23
Order of Payment of Costs, etc, Out of Estate

2.808

6.224 General rule as to priority

(1) The expenses of the bankruptcy are payable out of the estate in the following order of priority—

- (a) expenses or costs which—
    - (i) are properly chargeable or incurred by the official receiver or the trustee in preserving, realising or getting in any of the assets of the bankrupt or otherwise relating to the conduct of any legal proceedings which he has power to bring (whether the claim on which the proceedings are based forms part of the estate or otherwise) or defend;
    - (ii) relate to the employment of a shorthand writer, if appointed by an order of the court made at the instance of the official receiver in connection with an examination; or
    - (iii) are incurred in holding an examination under Rule 6.174 (examinee unfit) where the application was made by the official receiver;
- (b) any other expenses incurred or disbursements made by the official receiver or under his authority, including those incurred or made in carrying on the business of a debtor or bankrupt;
- (c) the fees payable under any order made under section 415 or 415A, including those payable to the official receiver (other than the fee referred to in sub-paragraph (d)(i) below), and any remuneration payable to him under general regulations;
- (d)
    - (i) the fee payable under any order made under section 415 for the performance by the official receiver of his general duties as official receiver;
    - (ii) any repayable deposit lodged under any such order as security for the fee mentioned in sub-paragraph (i) (except where the deposit is applied to the payment of the remuneration of an insolvency practitioner appointed under section 273 (debtor's petition));
- (e) the cost of any security provided by an interim receiver, trustee or special manager in accordance with the Act or the Rules;
- (f) the remuneration of the interim receiver (if any);
- (g) any deposit lodged on an application for the appointment of an interim receiver;
- (h) the costs of the petitioner, and of any person appearing on the petition whose costs are allowed by the court;
- (j) the remuneration of the special manager (if any);
- (k) any amount payable to a person employed or authorised, under Chapter 5 of this Part of the Rules, to assist in the preparation of a statement of affairs or of accounts;
- (l) any allowance made, by order of the court, towards costs on an application for release from the obligation to submit a statement of affairs, or for an extension of time for submitting such a statement;

(la) the costs of employing a shorthand writer in any case other than one appointed by an order of the court at the instance of the official receiver in connection with an examination;

(m) any necessary disbursements by the trustee in the course of his administration (including any expenses incurred by members of the creditors' committee or their representatives and allowed by the trustee under Rule 6.164, but not including any payment of capital gains tax in circumstances referred to in sub-paragraph (p) below);

(n) the remuneration or emoluments of any person (including the bankrupt) who has been employed by the trustee to perform any services for the estate, as required or authorised by or under the Act or the Rules;

(o) the remuneration of the trustee, up to any amount not exceeding that which is payable under Schedule 6;

(p) the amount of any capital gains tax on chargeable gains accruing on the realisation of any asset of the bankrupt (without regard to whether the realisation is effected by the trustee, a secured creditor, or a receiver or manager appointed to deal with a security);

(q) the balance, after payment of any sums due under sub-paragraph (o) above, of any remuneration due to the trustee[;

(r) any other expenses properly chargeable by the trustee in carrying out his functions in the bankruptcy.

(2) ...

(3) ...

Notes

R 6.224(1)

Assets which are available to the general body of creditors are to be distributed in the order set out in IA 1986 s 328. The expenses of the bankruptcy are to be paid first and prior to the payment of preferential debts. IR 1986 r 6.224 sets out the order of priority in which the items comprising the expenses of the bankruptcy are to be paid.

R 6.224(1)(a)

This provision was amended by the Insolvency (Amendment) (No 2) Rules 2002 to clarify that expenses and costs incurred in all legal proceedings which the trustee has the power to bring or defend are bankruptcy expenses. It had been previously doubted that proceedings brought under the preference and transaction at an undervalue provisions were liquidation expenses – see *Lewis v Inland Revenue Commissioners & Others, Re Floor Fourteen Ltd* [2001] 3 All ER 499. Expenses under this provision also include proceedings brought in relation to after acquired property IR 1986 r 6.202.

R 6.224(1)(h)

The petitioning creditor and any other creditor who gave notice to appear on the petition and who was awarded costs have the same priority.

R 6.224(1)(k)

This provision relates to expenses incurred by employing persons to assist a bankrupt in preparing his statement of affairs pursuant to IA 1986 s 288(1) and accounts if so required by the official receiver where the bankruptcy was based on a creditor's petition: see IR 6.58–6.66, and in relation to expenses incurred by employing persons to assist with the bankrupt's accounts on a debtor's petition: see IR 1986 r 6.71.

R 6.224(1)(m)

See by way of analogy the equivalent corporate provision IR 1986 4.218(m); *Re Toshoku Finance UK plc (in liquidation)* [2002] UKHL 6, [2002] 1 WLR 671 and *Re Mesco Properties Ltd* [1980] 1 WLR 96 classifying corporation tax on a company's post liquidation profits as a 'necessary disbursement' albeit the company had not been paid and was not likely to be paid the income which was taxable.

Chapter 24
Second Bankruptcy

Notes

RR 6.225–6.228

These rules only apply where a second or subsequent bankruptcy order is made against an undischarged bankrupt. The occurrence of second bankruptcies is likely to diminish since the coming into force of the EA 2002 and the revision of IA 1986 s 279. A second bankruptcy would have to occur within one year of the first unless the discharge period in relation to the first bankruptcy had been postponed or the bankruptcy was a criminal bankruptcy. The provisions aim to avoid any conflict between the powers and duties of the existing and subsequent trustees and further to avoid any potential conflict over property which may form part of the second estate but could also be regarded as after acquired property in relation to the first estate. The rules supplement IA 1986 s 334. In brief any distribution or disposition of after-acquired property, money from any income payment order or any proceeds thereof by the existing trustee after he receives notice of the second bankruptcy petition is void unless such distribution or disposition is made with the consent of the court. IA 1986 s 334(2) refers to the notice of the presentation of the petition being the 'prescribed notice' and should be in Form 6.78. Such notice should presumably be given to the existing trustee by the petitioning creditor on the second petition. Any property referred to in IA 1986 s 334(3) must be treated as part of the second bankruptcy on the commencement of the second bankruptcy pursuant to IA 1986 335(1)–(3).

2.809

6.225 Scope of this Chapter

(1) The Rules in this Chapter relate to the manner in which, in the case of a second bankruptcy, the trustee in the earlier bankruptcy is to deal with property and money to which section 334(3) applies, until there is a trustee of the estate in the later bankruptcy.

(2) 'The earlier bankruptcy', 'the later bankruptcy' and 'the existing trustee' have the meanings given by section 334(1).

2.810

6.226 General duty of existing trustee

(1) Subject as follows, the existing trustee shall take into his custody or under his control all such property and money, in so far as he has not already done so as part of his duties as trustee in the earlier bankruptcy.

(2) Where any of that property consists of perishable goods, or goods the value of which is likely to diminish if they are not disposed of, the existing trustee has power to sell or otherwise dispose of those goods.

(3) The proceeds of any such sale or disposal shall be held, under the existing trustee's control, with the other property and money comprised in the bankrupt's estate.

Notes

R 6.226(2)

This provision gives the existing trustee power to dispose of property comprising perishable goods or goods of value which are likely to diminish. The existing trustee must hold the proceeds of such a sale with the other property comprised in the bankrupt's estate and they must be delivered up to the later trustee as and when requested by him for the purposes of the later bankruptcy under IR 1986 r 6.227.

2.811

6.227 Delivery up to later trustee

The existing trustee shall, as and when requested by the trustee for the purposes of the later bankruptcy, deliver up to the latter all such property and money as is in his custody or under his control in pursuance of Rule 6.226.

2.812

6.228 Existing trustee's expenses

Any expenses incurred by the existing trustee in compliance with section 335(1) and this Chapter of the Rules shall be defrayed out of, and are a charge on, all such property and money as is referred to in section 334(3), whether in the hands of the existing trustee or of the trustee for the purposes of the later bankruptcy.

Chapter 25
Criminal Bankruptcy

2.813

6.229 Presentation of petition

(1) In criminal bankruptcy, the petition under section 264(1)(d) shall be presented to the High Court, and accordingly Rule 6.9 in Chapter 2 (court in which other petitions to be presented) does not apply.

(2) This does not affect the High Court's power to order that the proceedings be transferred.

Notes

R 6.229(1)

In general, the presentation of bankruptcy petitions is governed by IR 1986 r 6.9, which provides for the petition to be presented in either the High Court or the appropriate county court depending on the relevant circumstances. Where, however, the bankruptcy is a criminal bankruptcy, IR 1986 r 6.9 does not apply and the petition must be presented in the High Court.

R 6.229(2)

The general power to transfer is dealt with in CPR Part 30.2, section 65 of the Supreme Court Act 1981 (Civil Procedure 2005 Vol 2, para 9A–309), section 40 of the County Courts Act 1984 (Civil Procedure 2005 Vol 2 para 9A–548) and the High Court and County Court Jurisdiction Order 1991 (Civil Procedure 2005 Vol 2 para 9B–138 to 9B–160).

2.814

6.230 Status and functions of Official Petitioner

(1) Subject as follows, the Official Petitioner is to be regarded for all purposes of the Act and the Rules as a creditor of the bankrupt.

(2) He may attend or be represented at any meeting of creditors, and is to be given any notice under the Act or the Rules which is required or authorised to be given to creditors; and the requirements of the Rules as to the lodging or use of proxies do not apply.

Notes

R 6.230

The role and function of the Official Petitioner are set out in IA 1986 s 402 which is to be repealed from a day to be appointed (Criminal Justice Act 1988 s 170(2), Sch 16).

2.815

6.231 Interim receivership

Chapter 4 of this Part of the Rules applies in criminal bankruptcy only in so far as it provides for the appointment of the official receiver as interim receiver.

2.816

6.232 Proof of bankruptcy debts and notice of order

(1) The making of a bankruptcy order on a criminal bankruptcy petition does not affect the right of creditors to prove for their debts arising otherwise than in consequence of the criminal proceedings.

(2) A person specified in a criminal bankruptcy order as having suffered loss or damage shall be treated as a creditor of the bankrupt; and a copy of the order is sufficient evidence of his claim, subject to its being shown by any party to the bankruptcy proceedings that the loss or damage actually suffered was more or (as the case may be) less than the amount specified in the order.

(3) The requirements of the Rules with respect to the proof of debts do not apply to the Official Petitioner.

(4) In criminal bankruptcy, forms of proof shall be sent out by the official receiver within 12 weeks from the making of the bankruptcy order, to every creditor who is known to him, or is identified in the bankrupt's statement of affairs.

(5) The official receiver shall, within those 12 weeks, send to every such creditor notice of the making of the bankruptcy order.

Notes

R 6.232

This rule sets out the procedure for proofs of debt in relation to a criminal bankruptcy. Note in particular that the requirements do not apply to the Official Petitioner: r 6.232(3).

2.817

6.233 Meetings under the Rules

(1) The following Rules in Chapter 6 of this Part do not apply in criminal bankruptcy—
  Rules 6.79 and 6.80 (first meeting of creditors, and business thereat);
  Rule 6.82(2) (the chairman, if other than the official receiver);
  Rule 6.88(2) and (3) (resolution for appointment of trustee).

(2) Rule 6.97 (supply of forms for proof of debts) does not apply.

2.818

6.234 Trustee in bankruptcy; creditors' committee; annulment of bankruptcy order

(1) Chapter 10 of this Part of the Rules does not apply in criminal bankruptcy, except Rules 6.136 (release of official receiver) and 6.147 (power of court to set aside transactions).

(2) Chapter 11 (creditors' committee) does not apply.

(3) Chapter 21 (annulment of bankruptcy order) applies to an application to the court under section 282(2) as it applies to an application under section 282(1), with any necessary modifications.

Notes

R 6.234(1)–(2)

These sub-rules detail certain provisions which do not apply to criminal bankruptcies.

R 6.234(3)

The jurisdiction for the court to annul a bankruptcy order is contained in IA 1986 s 282. S 282(1) relates to non criminal bankruptcies, while s 282(2) relates to criminal bankruptcies. Chapter 21 of the IR 1986 sets out the relevant procedure for 'an application to the court under s 282(1)', in other words for non criminal bankruptcies. IR 1986 r 6.234(3) makes it clear that the Chapter 21 procedure equally applies to criminal bankruptcies subject to any necessary modifications.

Chapter 26
Miscellaneous Rules in Bankruptcy

2.819

6.235 Bankruptcy of solicitors

Where a bankruptcy order is made against a solicitor, or such an order made against a solicitor is rescinded or annulled, the court shall forthwith give notice to the Secretary of the Law Society of the order that it has made.

2.820

6.235A Application for redirection order

[(1) This Rule applies where the official receiver or trustee in bankruptcy applies to the court under section 371(1) (re-direction of bankrupt's letters etc).

(2) The application shall be made without notice to the bankrupt or any other person, unless the court directs otherwise.

(3) The applicant shall with his application, where he is the official receiver, file a report, and where he is the trustee in bankruptcy, an affidavit, setting out the reasons why such an order is sought.

(4) The court shall fix a venue for the hearing of the application if the court thinks fit and give notice to the applicant.

(5) The court may make an order on such conditions as it thinks fit.

(6) The order shall identify the person on whom it is to be served, and need not be served on the bankrupt unless the court directs otherwise.]

Notes

R 6.235A

An application for a redirection order under IA 1986 s 371 should be accompanied by evidence detailing the 'chapter and verse' of the non-cooperation relied upon which can then be provided to the bankrupt respondent *Singh v The Official Receiver* [1997] BPIR 530.

2.821

6.236 Consolidation of petitions

Where two or more bankruptcy petitions are presented against the same debtor, the court may order the consolidation of the proceedings, on such terms as it thinks fit.

2.822

6.237 Bankrupt's dwelling-house and home

(1) This Rule applies where the trustee applies to the court under section 313 for an order imposing a charge on property consisting of an interest in a dwelling-house.

(2) *The bankrupt's spouse or former spouse shall be made respondent to the application; and the court may, if it thinks fit, direct other persons to be made respondents also, in respect of any interest which they may have in the property.*

(3) *The trustee shall make a report to the court, containing the following particulars—*

    (a)   *the extent of the bankrupt's interest in the property which is the subject of the application; and*

    (b)   *the amount which, at the date of the application, remains owing to unsecured creditors of the bankrupt.*

(4) *The terms of the charge to be imposed shall be agreed between the trustee and the bankrupt or, failing agreement, shall be settled by the court.*

(5) *The rate of interest applicable under section 313(2) is the rate specified in section 17 of the Judgments Act 1838 on the day on which the charge is imposed, and the rate so applicable shall be stated in the court's order imposing the charge.*

(6) *The court's order shall also—*

    (a)   *describe the property to be charged;*

    (b)   *state whether the title to the property is registered and, if it is, specify the title number;*

    (c)   *set out the extent of the bankrupt's interest in the property which has vested in the trustee;*

    [(d)   *indicate, by reference to any, or the total, amount which is payable otherwise than to the bankrupt out of the estate and of interest on that amount, how the amount of the charge to be imposed is to be ascertained;]*

    (e)   *set out the conditions (if any) imposed by the court under section 3(1) of the Charging Orders Act 1979;*

    [(f)   *identify when any property charged under section 313 shall cease to be comprised in the bankrupt's estate and, subject to the charge (and any prior charge), to vest in the bankrupt.]*

(7) *Unless the court is of the opinion that a different date is appropriate, the date under paragraph (6)(f) shall be that of the registration of the charge in accordance with section 3(2) of the Charging Orders Act 1979.*

(8) *The trustee shall, forthwith after the making of the court's order, send notice of it and its effect to the Chief Land Registrar.*

Notes

R 6.237

This provision was replaced by r 6.237 and r 6.237A–E below from 1 April 2004.

2.823

[6.237 Bankrupt's Home—Notification of property falling within section 283A]

[(1) Where it appears to a trustee that section 283A(1) applies, the trustee shall give notice in Form 6.83 as soon as reasonably practicable to—

    (a)   the bankrupt;

> (b) the bankrupt's spouse (in a case falling within section 283A(1)(b));
> and
> (c) a former spouse of the bankrupt (in a case falling within sec-
> tion 283A(1)(c)).
>
> (2) A notice under paragraph (1) shall contain—
> (a) the name of the bankrupt;
> (b) the address of the dwelling-house; and
> (c) if the dwelling-house is registered land, the title number.
>
> (3) A trustee shall not give notice under paragraph (1) any later than 14
> days before the expiry of the three year period under section 283A(2) or
> 283A(5).]

───────

Notes

R 6.237

This provision and IR 6.237A–E took effect as from 1 April 2004 under the Insolvency
(Amendment) Rules 2003, SI 2003/1730.

───────

> **2.824**
>
> **[6.237A Application in respect of the vesting of an interest in a
> dwelling-house (registered land)]**
>
> [(1) Paragraph (2) applies where—
> (a) property comprised in the bankrupt's estate consists of an interest
> in a dwelling-house which at the date of bankruptcy was the sole
> or principal residence of—
> (i) the bankrupt;
> (ii) the bankrupt's spouse; or
> (iii) a former spouse of the bankrupt; and
> (b) the dwelling-house is registered land; and
> (c) an entry has been made, or entries have been made, in the
> individual register or registers of the dwelling-house relating to
> the bankrupt's bankruptcy or the individual register or registers
> has or have been altered to reflect the vesting of the bankrupt's
> interest in a trustee in bankruptcy.
>
> (2) Where an interest of a kind mentioned in paragraph (1) ceases to be
> comprised in the bankrupt's estate and vests in the bankrupt under either
> section 283A(2) or 283A(4) of the Act, or under section 261(8) of the
> Enterprise Act 2002, the trustee shall, within 7 days of the vesting, make
> such application or applications to the Chief Land Registrar as shall be
> necessary to show in the individual register or registers of the dwelling-
> house that the interest has vested in the bankrupt.
>
> (3) An application under paragraph (2) shall be made in accordance with
> the Land Registration Act 2002 and shall be accompanied by—
> (a) evidence of the trustee's appointment (where not previously
> provided to the Chief Land Registrar); and

(b) a certificate from the trustee stating that the interest has vested in the bankrupt under section 283A(2) or 283A(4) of the Act or section 261(8) of the Enterprise Act 2002 (whichever is appropriate).

(4) As soon as reasonably practicable after making an application under paragraph (2), the trustee shall notify the bankrupt and if the dwelling-house was the sole or principal residence of his spouse or former spouse, such person, that the application has been made.

(5) The trustee shall notify every person who (to his knowledge) either claims an interest in the dwelling-house, or is under any liability in respect of the dwelling-house that an application has been made.]

2.825

[6.237B Vesting of bankrupt's interest (unregistered land)]

[(1) Where an interest in a dwelling-house which at the date of the bankruptcy was the sole or principal residence of—
(a) the bankrupt;
(b) the bankrupt's spouse; or
(c) a former spouse of the bankrupt,
ceases to be comprised in the bankrupt's estate and vests in the bankrupt under either section 283A(2) or 283A(4) of the Act or section 261(8) of the Enterprise Act 2002 and the dwelling-house is unregistered land, the trustee shall issue the bankrupt with a certificate as to the vesting in Form 6.84 as soon as reasonably practicable.

(2) A certificate issued under paragraph (1) shall be conclusive proof that the interest mentioned in paragraph (1) has vested in the bankrupt.

(3) As soon as reasonably practicable after issuing the certificate under paragraph (1) the trustee shall, if the dwelling-house was the sole or principal residence of the bankrupt's spouse or former spouse, notify such person, that the application has been made.

(4) The trustee shall notify every person who (to his knowledge) either claims an interest in the dwelling-house, or is under any liability in respect of the dwelling-house that an application has been made.]

2.826

[6.237C

The court may substitute for the period of three years mentioned in section 283A(2) such longer period as the court thinks just and reasonable in all the circumstances of the case.

2.827

[6.237CA Vesting of bankrupt's estate—substituted period]

[For the purposes of section 283A(2) for the period of three years set out therein there shall be substituted, where the trustee in bankruptcy has sent notice to the bankrupt that he considers—
(a) the continued vesting of the property in the bankrupt's estate to be of no benefit to creditors; or

> (b) the re-vesting to the bankrupt will facilitate a more efficient
> administration of the bankrupt's estate,
> the period of one month from the date of that notice.]

Notes

R 6.237CA

The new regime obliging the trustee to realise the family home within three years, or not at all is set out in IA 1986 s 283A. IR 1986 r 6.237 to 6.237CA contain provisions inter alia for notification to the bankrupt, registration of the bankrupt's interest and extension of the three year period.

2.828

6.237D Charging Order

(1) This Rule applies where the trustee applies to the court under section 313 for an order imposing a charge on property consisting of an interest in a dwelling-house.

(2) The respondents to the application shall be—
    (a) any spouse or former spouse of the bankrupt having or claiming to have an interest in the property;
    (b) any other person appearing to have an interest in the property; and
    (c) such other persons as the court may direct.

(3) The trustee shall make a report to the court, containing the following particulars—
    (a) the extent of the bankrupt's interest in the property which is the subject of the application;
    (b) the amount which, at the date of the application, remains owing to unsecured creditors of the bankrupt; and
    (c) an estimate of the cost of realising the interest.

(4) The terms of the charge to be imposed shall be agreed between the trustee and the bankrupt or, failing agreement, shall be settled by the court.

(5) The rate of interest applicable under section 313(2) is the rate specified in section 17 of the Judgments Act 1838 on the day on which the charge is imposed, and the rate so applicable shall be stated in the court's order imposing the charge.

(6) The court's order shall also—
    (a) describe the property to be charged;
    (b) state whether the title to the property is registered and, if it is, specify the title number;
    (c) set out the extent of the bankrupt's interest in the property which has vested in the trustee;
    (d) indicate, by reference to any, or the total, amount which is payable otherwise than to the bankrupt out of the estate and of interest on that amount, how the amount of the charge to be imposed is to be ascertained;

(e)   set out the conditions (if any) imposed by the court under section 3(1) of the Charging Orders Act 1979; and

(f)   identify the date any property charged under section 313 shall cease to be comprised in the bankrupt's estate and shall, subject to the charge (and any prior charge), vest in the bankrupt.

(7) Unless the court is of the opinion that a different date is appropriate, the date referred to in paragraph (6)(f) shall be that of the registration of the charge in accordance with section 3(2) of the Charging Orders Act 1979.

(8) Where the court order is capable of giving rise to an application or applications under the Land Charges Act 1972 or the Land Registration Act 2002, the trustee shall, as soon as reasonably practicable after the making of the court order or at the appropriate time, make the appropriate application or applications to the Chief Land Registrar.

(9) In paragraph (8) an 'appropriate application' is—

(a)   an application under section 6(1)(a) of the Land Charges Act 1972 (application for registration in the register of writs and orders affecting land); or

(b)   an application under the Land Registration Act 2002 for an entry in the register in respect of the charge imposed by the order; and such application under that Act as shall be necessary to show in the individual register or registers of the dwelling-house that the interest has vested in the bankrupt.

(10) In determining the value of the bankrupt's interest for the purposes of paragraph (6)(c), the court shall disregard that part of the value of the property in which the bankrupt's interest subsists which is equal to the value of—

(a)   any loans secured by mortgage or other charge against the property;

(b)   any other third party interest; and

(c)   the reasonable costs of sale.]

2.829

[6.237E Interpretation]

[(1) In Rules 6.237 and 6.237A, 'registered land' has the same meaning as in section 132(1) of the Land Registration Act 2002.

(2) In Rules 6.237A and 6.237D, 'individual register' has the same meaning as in the Land Registration Rules 2003.]

Chapter 27
EC Regulation—Member State Liquidator

2.830

6.238 Interpretation of creditor and notice to member State liquidator

(1) This Rule applies where a member State liquidator has been appointed in relation to the bankrupt.

(2) For the purposes of the Rules referred to in paragraph (3) a member State liquidator is deemed to be a creditor.

(3) The Rules referred to in paragraph (2) are Rules 6.73(1) (duty of official receiver), 6.75(1) (report of official receiver), 6.76(2) (report of official receiver), 6.79(2) (creditors' meeting), 6.81 (power to call creditors' meeting), 6.83 (requisitioned meetings), 6.93 (entitlement to vote), 6.94 (admission and rejection of proof), 6.96 (meaning of 'prove'), 6.97 (supply of forms), 6.98 (contents of proof), 6.99 (claim established by affidavit), 6.100 (cost of proving), 6.101 (inspection of proofs), 6.104 (admission and rejection of proofs for dividend), 6.105(1) (appeal against decision on proof), 6.105(2), 6.106 (withdrawal or variation of proofs), 6.107(1) (expunging of proof), 6.108 (negotiable instruments, etc), 6.109 (secured creditors), 6.110 (discounts), 6.111 (debts in foreign currency), 6.112 (payments of a periodical nature), 6.113 (interest), 6.114 (debt payable at future time), 6.126(1) (resignation of trustee), 6.136(1) (release of official receiver), 6.137(1) (final meeting), 6.142(1) (challenge to remuneration), 6.150(2) (creditors' committee), 6.160(3) (vacancy on creditors' committee), 6.172(3) (request for public examination), 6.212(1) (notice of annulment) and 6.217(3) (application by bankrupt for discharge).

(4) Paragraphs (2) and (3) are without prejudice to the generality of the right to participate referred to in paragraph 3 of Article 32 of the EC Regulation (exercise of creditor's rights).

(5) Where the trustee is obliged to give notice to, or provide a copy of a document (including an order of court) to, the court or the official receiver, the trustee shall give notice or provide copies, as the case may be, to the member State liquidator.

(6) Paragraph (5) is without prejudice to the generality of the obligations imposed by Article 31 of the EC Regulation (duty to cooperate and communicate information).

2.831

6.239 Interpretation of creditor and notice to member State liquidator appointed in main proceedings

[(1) This Rule applies, in addition to Rule 6.238, where a member State liquidator has been appointed in main proceedings in relation to the bankrupt.

(2) For the purposes of the Rules referred to in paragraph (3) the member State liquidator is deemed to be a creditor.

(3) The Rules referred to in paragraph (2) are Rules 6.18(3) (hearing of petition), 6.23(1) (notice of intention to appear), 6.28(4) (extension of time), 6.30(2) (substitution of petitioner), 6.31(1) (change of carriage of petition) and 6.218(4) (report of official receiver).

(4) Paragraphs (2) and (3) are without prejudice to the generality of the right to participate referred to in paragraph 3 of Article 32 of the EC Regulation (exercise of creditor's rights).]

———

Notes

RR 6.238–6.239

These provisions deal with the situation where insolvency proceedings are brought in another member state before or after a bankruptcy order in England; see IR 1986 r 13.13(11) for the definition of 'Member State liquidator'. Article 32 of the EC Regulation on Insolvency Proceedings entitles the foreign liquidator to lodge claims in the English bankruptcy on behalf of creditors who have lodged claims with him, and to participate in the English bankruptcy on the same basis as a creditor.

———

Chapter 28
Bankruptcy Restrictions Order

2.832

[6.240

[In this and the following two Chapters, 'Secretary of State' includes the official receiver acting in accordance with paragraph 1(2)(b) of Schedule 4A to the Act.]

2.833

[6.241 Application for bankruptcy restrictions order]

[(1) Where the Secretary of State applies to the court for a bankruptcy restrictions order under paragraph 1 of Schedule 4A to the Act, the application shall be supported by a report by the Secretary of State.

(2) The report shall include—
   (a)   a statement of the conduct by reference to which it is alleged that it is appropriate for a bankruptcy restrictions order to be made; and
   (b)   the evidence on which the Secretary of State relies in support of the application.

(3) Any evidence in support of an application for a bankruptcy restrictions order provided by persons other than the Secretary of State shall be by way of affidavit.

(4) The date for the hearing shall be no earlier than 8 weeks from the date when the court fixes the venue for the hearing.

(5) For the purposes of hearing an application under this Rule by a registrar, Rule 7.6(1) shall not apply and the application shall be heard in public.]

2.834

[6.242 Service on the defendant]

[(1) The Secretary of State shall serve notice of the application and the venue fixed by the court on the bankrupt not more than 14 days after the application is made at court.

(2) Service shall be accompanied by a copy of the application, together with copies of the report by the Secretary of State, any other evidence filed with the court in support of the application, and an acknowledgement of service.

(3) The defendant shall file in court an acknowledgement of service of the application indicating whether or not he contests the application not more than 14 days after service on him of the application.

(4) Where the defendant has failed to file an acknowledgement of service and the time period for doing so has expired, the defendant may attend the hearing of the application but may not take part in the hearing unless the court gives permission.]

2.835

[6.243 The bankrupt's evidence]

[(1) If the bankrupt wishes to oppose the application, he shall within 28 days of the service of the application and evidence of the Secretary of State, file in court any evidence which he wishes the court to take into consideration, and shall serve a copy of such evidence upon the Secretary of State within 3 days of filing it at court.

(2) The Secretary of State shall, within 14 days from receiving the copy of the bankrupt's evidence, file in court any further evidence in reply he wishes the court to take into consideration and shall as soon as reasonably practicable serve a copy of that evidence upon the bankrupt.]

2.836

[6.244 Making a bankruptcy restrictions order]

[(1) The court may make a bankruptcy restrictions order against the bankrupt, whether or not the latter appears, and whether or not he has filed evidence in accordance with Rule 6.243.

(2) Where the court makes a bankruptcy restrictions order, it shall send two sealed copies to the Secretary of State.

(3) As soon as reasonably practicable after receipt of the sealed copy of the order, the Secretary of State shall send a sealed copy of the order to the bankrupt.]

[Chapter 29
Interim Bankruptcy Restrictions Order]

2.837

[6.245 Application for interim bankruptcy restrictions order]

[(1) Where the Secretary of State applies for an interim bankruptcy restrictions order under paragraph 5 of Schedule 4A to the Act, the court shall fix a venue for the hearing.

(2) Notice of an application for an interim bankruptcy restrictions order shall be given to the bankrupt at least 2 business days before the date set for the hearing unless the court directs otherwise.

(3) For the purposes of hearing an application under this Rule by a registrar, Rule 7.6(1) shall not apply and the application shall be heard in public.]

2.838

[6.246 The case against the defendant]

[(1) The Secretary of State shall file a report in court as evidence in support of any application for an interim bankruptcy restrictions order.

(2) The report shall include evidence of the bankrupt's conduct which is alleged to constitute the grounds for the making of an interim bankruptcy restrictions order and evidence of matters which relate to the public interest in making the order.

(3) Any evidence by persons other than the Secretary of State in support of an application for an interim bankruptcy restrictions order shall be by way of affidavit.]

2.839

[6.247 Making an interim bankruptcy restrictions order]

[(1) The bankrupt may file in court any evidence which he wishes the court to take into consideration and may appear at the hearing for an interim bankruptcy restrictions order.

(2) The court may make an interim bankruptcy restrictions order against the bankrupt, whether or not the latter appears, and whether or not he has filed evidence.

(3) Where the court makes an interim bankruptcy restrictions order, it shall send two sealed copies of the order shall be sent, as soon as reasonably practicable, to the Secretary of State.

(4) As soon as reasonably practicable after receipt of the sealed copies of the order, the Secretary of State shall send a copy of the order to the bankrupt.]

2.840

[6.248 Application to set aside an interim bankruptcy restrictions order]

[(1) A bankrupt may apply to the court to set aside an interim bankruptcy restrictions order.

(2) An application by the bankrupt to set aside an interim bankruptcy restrictions order shall be supported by an affidavit stating the grounds on which the application is made.

(3) Where a bankrupt applies to set aside an interim bankruptcy restrictions order under paragraph (1), he shall send to the Secretary of State, not less than 7 days before the hearing—
  (a) notice of his application;
  (b) notice of the venue;

(c)   a copy of his application; and

(d)   a copy of the supporting affidavit.

(4) The Secretary of State may attend the hearing and call the attention of the court to any matters which seem to him to be relevant, and may himself give evidence or call witnesses.

(5) Where the court sets aside an interim bankruptcy restrictions order two sealed copies of the order shall be sent, as soon as reasonably practicable, to the Secretary of State by the court.

(6) As soon as reasonably practicable after receipt of the sealed copies of the order, the Secretary of State shall send a sealed copy of the order to the bankrupt.]

[Chapter 30
Bankruptcy Restrictions Undertaking]

2.841

[6.249 Acceptance of the bankruptcy restrictions undertaking]

[A bankruptcy restrictions undertaking signed by the bankrupt shall be deemed to have been accepted by the Secretary of State for the purposes of paragraph 9 of Schedule 4A of the Act when the undertaking is signed by the Secretary of State.]

2.842

[6.250 Notification to the court]

[As soon as reasonably practicable after a bankruptcy restrictions undertaking has been accepted by the Secretary of State, a copy shall be sent to the bankrupt and filed in court and sent to the official receiver if he is not the applicant.]

2.843

[6.251 Application under paragraph 9(3) of Schedule 4A to the Act to annul a bankruptcy restrictions undertaking]

[(1) An application under paragraphs 9(3)(a) or (b) of Schedule 4A to the Act shall be supported by an affidavit stating the grounds on which it is made.

(2) The bankrupt shall give notice of the application and the venue, together with a copy of the affidavit supporting his application to the Secretary of State at least 28 days before the date fixed for the hearing.

(3) The Secretary of State may attend the hearing and call the attention of the court to any matters which seem to him to be relevant, and may himself give evidence or call witnesses.

(4) The court shall send a sealed copy of any order annulling or varying the bankruptcy restrictions undertaking to the Secretary of State and the bankrupt.]

> ## Chapter 1
> ## General

Notes

This new Part 6A brings together rules about the various registers that are to be maintained in relation to individual insolvencies in England and Wales and adds rules to deal with the new bankruptcy restriction orders and undertakings introduced by the Enterprise Act 2002. The rules that are replaced are r 5.28 and r 6.223A–C. The changes came into force on 1 April 2004 and were created by the Insolvency (Amendment) Rules 2003 (SI 2003/1730).

> ## [Part 6A]
>
> *[Chapter 1*
> *General]*
>
> **2.844**
>
> **6A.1 The individual insolvency register; the bankruptcy restrictions register**
>
> (1) The Secretary of State shall create and maintain a register of matters relating to bankruptcies and individual voluntary arrangements in accordance with the provisions of this Part (referred to in this Part as 'the individual insolvency register').
>
> (2) The register referred to in paragraph 12 of Schedule 4A to the Act (referred to in this Part as 'the bankruptcy restrictions register') shall be maintained in accordance with the provisions of this Part.
>
> (3) In this Part the 'registers' means the registers referred to in paragraphs (1) and (2).
>
> (4) The registers shall be open to public inspection on any business day between the hours of 9.00 am and 5.00 pm.
>
> (5) Where an obligation to enter information onto, or delete information from, the registers arises under this Part, that obligation shall be performed as soon as is reasonably practicable after it arises.]

Notes

R 6A.1

This rule obliges the Secretary of State to maintain the register relating to individual insolvencies and provides that it shall be open to public inspection in the manner set out. The language of the rule suggests that the register is only to be open to physical inspection. However, it can be searched on-line from the Insolvency Service's website: http://www.insolvency.gov.uk/guidanceleaflets/registerfrontpage.htm. This site also sets out the other ways that the register can be searched. The Secretary of State is obliged to keep the register accurate by updating it as soon as reasonably practicable.

Chapter 2
Individual Insolvency Register

2.845

6A.2 Entry of information onto the individual insolvency register—individual voluntary arrangements

(1) The Secretary of State shall enter onto the individual insolvency register—

    (a)   as regards any voluntary arrangement other than a voluntary arrangement under section 263A any information—

        (i)   that was required to be held on the register of individual voluntary arrangements maintained by the Secretary of State immediately prior to the coming into force of this Rule and which relates to a voluntary arrangement which has not been completed or has not terminated on or before the date on which this Rule comes into force; or

        (ii) that is sent to him in pursuance of Rule 5.29 or Rule 5.34; and

    (b)   as regards any voluntary arrangement under section 263A of which notice is given to him pursuant to Rule 5.45—

        (i)   the name and address of the debtor;

        (ii) the date on which the arrangement was approved by the creditors; and

        (iii) the court in which the official receiver's report has been filed.

    and,

    (c) in the circumstances set out in (a) and (b) above, the debtor's gender, date of birth and any name by which he was known, not being the name in which he has entered into the voluntary arrangement.

(2) This Rule is subject to Rule 6A.3.

Notes

R 6A.2

This rule sets out how a person comes to be on the individual insolvency register by entering into an IVA and the details to be recorded.

R 6A.2(C)

This provision was inserted by the Insolvency (Amendment) Rules 2005 SI 2005/527 with effect from 1 April 2005.

2.846

6A.3 Deletion of information from the individual insolvency register—individual voluntary arrangements

The Secretary of State shall delete from the individual insolvency register all information concerning an individual voluntary arrangement where—

(a) he receives notice under Rule 5.30(5) or Rule 5.46(4) of the making of a revocation order in respect of the arrangement; or

(b) he receives notice under Rule 5.34(3) or Rule 5.50(3) of the full implementation or termination of the arrangement.

Notes

R 6A.3

This provision states how those who were on the register by entering into an individual voluntary arrangement come to be removed from it.

2.847

6A.4 Entry of information onto the individual insolvency register—bankruptcy orders

(1) The Secretary of State shall enter onto the individual insolvency register any information that was required to be held on the register of bankruptcy orders maintained by the Secretary of State immediately prior to the coming into force of this Rule and which relates to a bankrupt who—

(a) has not received his discharge on or before the date that this Rule comes into force; or

(b) was discharged in the period of 3 months immediately preceding the coming into force of this Rule.

(2) Where the official receiver receives pursuant to Rule 6.34 or Rule 6.46 a copy of a bankruptcy order from the court, he shall cause to be entered onto the individual insolvency register—

(a) the matters listed in Rules 6.7 and 6.38 with respect to the debtor as they are stated in the bankruptcy petition;

(b) the date of the making of the bankruptcy order;

(c) the name of the court that made the order; and

(d) the court reference number as stated on the order.

(3) The official receiver shall cause to be entered onto the individual insolvency register as soon as reasonably practicable after receipt by him, the following information—

(a) the name, gender, occupation (if any) and date of birth of the bankrupt;

(b) the bankrupt's last known address.;

(c) the date of any bankruptcy order (or if more than one the latest of them) made in the period of 6 years immediately prior to the date of the latest bankruptcy order made against the bankrupt (excluding for these purposes any order that was annulled);

(d) any name by which the bankrupt was known, not being the name in which he was adjudged bankrupt;

(e) the address of any business carried on by the bankrupt and the name in which that business was carried on if carried on in a name other than the name in which the bankrupt was adjudged bankrupt;

(f)   the name and address of any insolvency practitioner appointed to act as trustee in bankruptcy;

(g)   the address at which the official receiver may be contacted; and

(h)   the automatic discharge date under section 279.

(4) Where pursuant to Rule 6.176(5) or Rule 6.215(8) the official receiver receives a copy of an order suspending the bankrupt's discharge he shall cause to be entered onto the individual insolvency register—

(a)   the fact that such an order has been made; and

(b)   the period for which the discharge has been suspended or that the relevant period has ceased to run until the fulfilment of conditions specified in the order.

(5) Where pursuant to Rule 6.216(7) a copy of a certificate certifying the discharge of an order under section 279(3) is received by the official receiver, he shall cause to be entered onto the individual insolvency register—

(a)   that the court has discharged the order made under section 279(3); and

(b)   the new date of discharge of the bankrupt,

but where the order discharging the order under section 279(3) is subsequently rescinded by the court, the official receiver shall cause the register to be amended accordingly.

(6) Where a bankrupt is discharged from bankruptcy under section 279(1) or section 279(2), the official receiver shall cause the fact and date of such discharge to be entered in the individual insolvency register.

(7) This Rule is subject to Rule 6A.5.

———

Notes

R 6A.4

This deals with the obligation to register those individuals who are subject to a bankruptcy order. It is subject to the following rule, which deals with how one comes off the register.

———

2.848

6A.5 Deletion of information from the individual insolvency register—bankruptcy orders

... The Secretary of State shall delete from the individual insolvency register all information concerning a bankruptcy where—

(a)   the bankruptcy order has been annulled pursuant to section 261(2)(a), 261(2)(b), 263D(3) or section 282(1)(b);

(b)   the bankrupt has been discharged from the bankruptcy and a period of 3 months has elapsed from the date of discharge;

(c)   the bankruptcy order is annulled pursuant to section 282(1)(a) and he has received notice of the annulment under Rule 6.213(2); or

(d) the bankruptcy order is rescinded by the court under section 375 and the Secretary of State has received a copy of the order made by the court.

___

Notes

R 6A.5

This provides that all information concerning a bankruptcy is to be removed from the register where the bankruptcy is annulled or rescinded or three months after it is discharged.

___

Chapter 3
Bankruptcy Restrictions Register

2.849

6A.6 Bankruptcy restrictions orders and undertakings—entry of information onto the bankruptcy restrictions register

(1) Where an interim bankruptcy restrictions order or a bankruptcy restrictions order is made against a bankrupt, the Secretary of State shall enter onto the bankruptcy restrictions register—

(a) the name, gender, occupation (if any) and date of birth of the bankrupt;

(aa) the bankrupt's last known address.;

(b) a statement that an interim bankruptcy restrictions order or, as the case may be, a bankruptcy restrictions order has been made against him;

(c) the date of the making of the order, the court and the court reference number; and

(d) the duration of the order.

(2) Where a bankruptcy restrictions undertaking is given by a bankrupt, the Secretary of State shall enter onto the bankruptcy restrictions register—

(a) the name, gender, occupation (if any) and date of birth of the bankrupt;

(aa) the bankrupt's last known address.;

(b) a statement that a bankruptcy restrictions undertaking has been given;

(c) the date of the acceptance of the bankruptcy restrictions undertaking by the Secretary of State; and

(d) the duration of the bankruptcy restrictions undertaking.

(3) This Rule is subject to Rule 6A.7.

2.850

6A.7 Deletion of information from the bankruptcy restrictions register—bankruptcy restrictions orders and undertakings

In any case where an interim bankruptcy restrictions order or a bankruptcy restrictions order is made or a bankruptcy restrictions undertaking has been accepted, the Secretary of State shall remove from the bankruptcy restrictions register all information regarding that order or, as the case may be, undertaking after—

(a) receipt of notification that the order or, as the case may be, the undertaking has ceased to have effect; or

(b) the expiry of the order or, as the case may be, undertaking.

Notes

R 6A.7

At the end of the period of the bankruptcy restriction order or bankruptcy restriction undertaking, the corresponding entry on the register is to be removed.

Chapter 4
Rectification of Registers

2.851

6A.8 Rectification of the registers

(1) Where the Secretary of State becomes aware that there is any inaccuracy in any information maintained on the registers he shall rectify the inaccuracy as soon as reasonably practicable.

(2) Where the Secretary of State receives notice of the date of the death of a bankrupt in respect of whom information is held on the register, he shall cause the fact and date of the bankrupt's death to be entered onto the individual insolvency register and bankruptcy restrictions register.

Notes

R 6A.8

This puts the Secretary of State under an obligation to rectify the registers as soon as reasonably practicable after he becomes aware of the error. It also provides that the death of someone who appears on the register is to be noted.

The Third Group of Parts

Part 7
Court Procedure and Practice

Chapter 1
Applications

2.852

7.1 Preliminary

This Chapter applies to any application made to the court under the Act or Rules except —

> (a)   an application for an administration order under Part II,
> (b)   a petition for a winding-up order under Part IV, or
> (c)   a petition for a bankruptcy order under Part IX
> of the Act.

Notes

R 7.1

All proceedings under IA 1986 or IR 1986 are governed by the IR 1986 except where it is otherwise provided (IR 1986 R13.14). Part 7 therefore applies to all applications under IA 1986 or IR 1986 other than the three stated types of proceedings in R7.1. However IR 1986 does not provide a complete procedural code for insolvency applications. IR 1986 r 7.51 provides that the Civil Procedure Rules apply to insolvency proceedings except so far as inconsistent with IR 1986. A number of forms are prescribed for use under IR 1986 which are to be found in IR 1986 Sch 4. Applications for administration orders are dealt with in IR 1986 rr 2.2ff; winding up petitions in IR 1986 rr 4.7ff; and bankruptcy petitions IR 1986 rr 6.6ff.

2.853

7.2 Interpretation

(1) In this Chapter, except in so far as the context otherwise requires—
   'originating application' means an application to the court which is not an application in pending proceedings before the court; and
   'ordinary application' means any other application to the court.

(2) Every application shall be in the form appropriate to the application concerned.

Notes

R 7.2(1)

The only types of application that can be made are: (i) originating (IR 1986 Sch 4 Form 7.1); and (ii) ordinary (IR 1986 Sch 4 Form 7.2). An originating application is an application that is made to the court which is not an application in pending proceedings; whereas an ordinary application is an application that is made in pending proceedings. The fact that there are proceedings in existence in relation to the company whether before or after a winding up order has been made does not mean that any further proceedings should be commenced by an ordinary application. The question is whether the further proceeding is an application in the existing proceedings *Port v Auger* [1994] 1 WLR 862. For example an application to restrain the presentation of a winding up petition must be made by originating application (para 8.1 Practice Direction: Insolvency Proceedings, Civil Procedure Vol 2, Sect 3E) whereas an application to restrain advertisement of or a stay of a petition which has been presented should be made by ordinary application. Once a winding up order has been made there will be no existing proceedings and an application for relief within the winding up and each separate such application should be made by originating application. In practice it is unlikely to be a substantive problem if an originating application has been used rather than an ordinary application or vice versa *Re Buildlead Ltd (No 2)* [2005] BCC 138. Unless the court considers that '.. substantial injustice has been caused by the defect or irregularity and that the injustice cannot be remedied by order of the court ...' then 'any formal defect ... or irregularity..' (IR 1986 r 7.55) can be ignored *Re Buildlead Ltd (No 2)* [2005] BCC 138.

R 7.2(2)

In *Port v Auger* [1994] 1 WLR 862 it was held that an ordinary application was not a 'pleading' within the then applicable striking out provisions (see now CPR r 3.4); though it could be struck out under the inherent jurisdiction of the court.

———

2.854

7.3 Form and contents of application

(1) Each application shall be in writing and shall state—
- (a) the names of the parties;
- (b) the nature of the relief or order applied for or the directions sought from the court;
- (c) the names and addresses of the persons (if any) on whom it is intended to serve the application or that no person is intended to be served;
- (d) where the Act or Rules require that notice of the application is to be given to specified persons, the names and addresses of all those persons (so far as known to the applicant); and
- (e) the applicant's address for service.

(2) An originating application shall set out the grounds on which the applicant claims to be entitled to the relief or order sought.

(3) The application must be signed by the applicant if he is acting in person or, when he is not so acting, by or on behalf of his solicitor.

———

Notes

R 7.3(1)

Every application should be headed (upper case) 'IN THE MATTER OF [*name of company*] AND IN THE MATTER OF THE INSOLVENCY ACT 1986', IR 1986 r 7.26. There is no requirement that a company in liquidation should be so described in the heading of an application although this is frequently done; (cf IA 1986 s 188 in relation to publicising the liquidation in other documents). Traditionally the court out of which the application is issued is set out in the top left hand corner. Where the liquidator is party to the application he/she should be described by the style '*Liquidator of [...] Limited*' or where the official receiver is liquidator '*the Official Receiver and Liquidator of [...] Limited*' IA 1986 s 163; in practice it is common to see a liquidator using his/her own name.

R 7.3(2)

Though this requirement is only applicable to an originating application the guidance notes appearing on an ordinary application indicate that the Applicant should '*state nature and grounds of application*'.

———

2.855

Application under section 176A(5) to disapply section 176A

7.3A (1) An application under section 176A(5) shall be accompanied by an affidavit of truth prepared and sworn by the liquidator, administrator or receiver

(2) The affidavit shall state –
- (a) the type of insolvency proceedings in which the application arises;
- (b) a summary of the financial position of the company;
- (c) the information substantiating the applicant's view that the cost of making a distribution to unsecured creditors would be disproportionate to the benefits; and
- (d) whether any other insolvency practitioner is acting in relation to the company and if so his address.

Notes

R 7.3A

The Enterprise Act 2002 introduced the notion of the 'prescribed part' (IA 1986 s 176A) which is concerned with setting aside monies in certain insolvency proceedings for the unsecured creditors that would otherwise go to the holders of floating charges. The amount of the monies known as the 'prescribed part' is calculated in accordance with The Insolvency Act 1986 (Prescribed Part) Order 2003. There is no obligation to make the prescribed part available where the liquidator applies to court on the ground that the cost of making a distribution to unsecured creditors would be disproportionate to the benefits (IA 1986 s 176A(5)) and this provision details the contents of the evidence that is required to support such an application.

2.856

7.4 Filing and service of application

(1) The application shall be filed in court, accompanied by one copy and a number of additional copies equal to the number of persons who are to be served with the application.

(2) Subject as follows in this Rule and the next, or unless the Rule under which the application is brought provides otherwise, or the court otherwise orders, upon the presentation of the documents mentioned in paragraph (1) above, the court shall fix a venue for the application to be heard.

(3) Unless the court otherwise directs, the applicant shall serve a sealed copy of the application, endorsed with the venue for the hearing, on the respondent named in the application (or on each respondent if more than one).

(4) The court may give any of the following directions—
- (a) that the application be served upon persons other than those specified by the relevant provision of the Act or Rules;
- (b) that the giving of notice to any person may be dispensed with;
- (c) that notice be given in some way other than that specified in paragraph (3).

(5) Unless the provision of the Act or Rules under which the application is made provides otherwise, and subject to the next paragraph, the application must be served at least 14 days before the date fixed for the hearing.

> (6) Where the case is one of urgency, the court may (without prejudice to its general power to extend or abridge time limits)—
>
> (a) hear the application immediately, either with or without notice to, or the attendance of, other parties, or
>
> (b) authorise a shorter period of service than that provided for by paragraph (5);
>
> and any such application may be heard on terms providing for the filing or service of documents, or the carrying out of other formalities, as the court thinks fit.

Notes

R 7.4(1)

'.. *filed in court..*' means delivered to the court for filing IR 1986 r 13.1, r 13.13(3).

R 7.4(2)

'.. *venue'* means the time, date and place for the application to be heard IR 1986 r 13.1, r 13.6.

R 7.4(3)

There are specific rules dealing with service by post (IR 1986 r 12.10, r 13.3(1)), personal service (IR 1986 r 13.3(3)) and provision requiring notices to be given in writing unless otherwise ordered (IR 1986 r 12.4). IR 1986 r 12.11 applies CPR Part 6 (service of documents) in insolvency proceedings.

R 7.4(5), (6)

The general rule is that applications have to served not later than 14 days before the hearing date. However where the case is one of urgency the court may without prejudice to its general power to extend or abridge time limits (CPR r 3.1(2)(a), IR 1986 r 12.9(2)) hear the application immediately or authorise a shorter period of notice. The court may impose terms for the filing or service of documents *Re W F Fearman Ltd* (1988) 4 BCC 139.

2.857

7.4A Notice of application under section 176A(5)

An application under section 176A(5) may be made without the application being served upon or notice being given to any other party, save that notice of the application shall be given to any other insolvency practitioner who acts as such in relation to the company including any member State liquidator.

Notes

R 7.4A

In relation to such an application see the notes to IR 1986 r 7.3A above. The phrase '.. *acts as such in relation to the company'* is widely worded and it may be necessary for the liquidator to enquire of the directors of the company whether they have been taking any advice from an insolvency practitioner following the liquidation.

2.858

7.5 Other hearings ex parte

(1) Where the relevant provisions of the Act or Rules do not require service of the application on, or notice of it to be given to, any person, the court may hear the application *ex parte*.

(2) Where the application is properly made *ex parte*, the court may hear it forthwith, without fixing a venue as required by Rule 7.4(2).

(3) Alternatively, the court may fix a venue for the application to be heard, in which case Rule 7.4 applies (so far as relevant).

Notes

R 7.5

The terminology of *'without notice'* does not appear to have made its way into IR 1986 as yet. An application to review an ex parte order can be made under IR 1986 r 7.47, *Re Casterbridge Properties* [2002] BPIR 428.

R 7.5(2)

The basic rule for an applicant on an ex parte application is to provide full and frank disclosure *Re First Express Ltd* [1991] BCC 782; also see the notes in Civil Procedure Vol 1 CPR Part 25.3.5.

2.859

7.6 Hearing of application

(1) Unless allowed or authorised to be made otherwise, every application before the registrar shall, and every application before the judge may, be heard in chambers.

(2) Unless either—
    (a)   the judge has given a general or special direction to the contrary, or
    (b)   it is not within the registrar's power to make the order required,

the jurisdiction of the court to hear and determine the application may be exercised by the registrar, and the application shall be made to the registrar in the first instance.

(3) Where the application is made to the registrar he may refer to the judge any matter which he thinks should properly be decided by the judge, and the judge may either dispose of the matter or refer it back to the registrar with such directions as he thinks fit.

(4) Nothing in this Rule precludes an application being made directly to the judge in a proper case.

Notes

R 7.6(1)

Solicitors have long had a right of audience in insolvency applications but in exercising their rights under s 27 Courts and Legal Services Act 1990 they have to comply with the Law

Society requirements. A company may appear by a duly authorised employee with the court's permission (Civil Procedure Vol 1 CPR 39.6). The court has been reluctant to allow a company to appear without a solicitor (*Arbuthnot Leasing International Ltd v Havelet Leasing Ltd* [1990] BCLC 802, *Re a Company (No 001029 of 1990)* [1991] BCLC 567). Official receivers have a right of audience in insolvency proceedings IR 1986 r 7.52.

R 7.6(2)

See Practice Note on the Hearing of Insolvency Proceedings [2005] BPIR 668, para 9 Practice Direction: Insolvency Proceedings (Civil Procedure Vol 2, Sect 3E) headed 'Distribution of Business' which provides for the types of cases in which an application should be made direct to the Judge as opposed to the Registrar.

2.860

7.7 Use of affidavit evidence

(1) In any proceedings evidence may be given by affidavit unless by any provision of the Rules it is otherwise provided or the court otherwise directs; but the court may, on the application of any party, order the attendance for cross-examination of the person making the affidavit.

(2) Where, after such an order has been made, the person in question does not attend, his affidavit shall not be used in evidence without the leave of the court.

Notes

R 7.7(1)

Evidence is normally given by affidavit/witness statement in insolvency applications but the court may in exceptional circumstances (*Re Colt Telecom Group plc (No 1)* [2003] BPIR 311) order the attendance for cross examination of the deponent on the application of any party; but such an application should be made promptly *Re Ultra Motorhomes International Ltd* [2006] BCC 57. The form and contents of affidavits in insolvency proceedings follow the rules and practice of the High Court IR 1986 r 7.57. Where proceedings are of a final nature the court will usually order the cross examination of deponents *Re Lifecare International plc* [1990] BCLC 222, 225 *cf Re Cloverbay Ltd (No 2)* [1990] BCLC 449, 451 (cross examination will rarely be allowed in interim proceedings and then only where an issue of fact is raised). A witness statement may be used as an alternative to an affidavit in all cases except those listed in IR 1986 r 7.57(6).

R 7.7(2)

However if a deponent is not cross examined the court is unlikely to disbelieve their evidence *Re Smith and Fawcett Ltd* [1942] Ch 304, *Re a Debtor (No 574 of 1995)* [1998] 2 BCLC 124, 131, *Wilkinson v IRC* [1998] BPIR 418.

2.861

7.8 Filing and service of affidavits

(1) Unless the provision of the Act or Rules under which the application is made provides otherwise, or the court otherwise allows—

> (a) if the applicant intends to rely at the first hearing on affidavit evidence, he shall file the affidavit or affidavits (if more than one) in court and serve a copy or copies on the respondent, not less than 14 days before the date fixed for the hearing, and
>
> (b) where a respondent to an application intends to oppose it and to rely for that purpose on affidavit evidence, he shall file the affidavit or affidavits (if more than one) in court and serve a copy or copies on the applicant, not less than 7 days before the date fixed for the hearing.
>
> (2) Any affidavit may be sworn by the applicant or by the respondent or by some other person possessing direct knowledge of the subject matter of the application.

Notes

R 7.8

Where these time limits are ignored the party in default runs the risk of the hearing being adjourned with the possibility of adverse costs consequences.

> **2.862**
>
> **7.9 Use of reports**
>
> (1) A report may be filed in court instead of an affidavit—
> (a) in any case, by the official receiver (whether or not he is acting in any capacity mentioned in sub-paragraph (b)), or a deputy official receiver, or
> (b) unless the application involves other parties or the court otherwise orders, by—
>   (i) an administrator, a liquidator or a trustee in bankruptcy,
>   (ii) a provisional liquidator or an interim receiver,
>   (iii) a special manager, or
>   (iv) an insolvency practitioner appointed under section 273(2).
>
> (2) In any case where a report is filed instead of an affidavit, the report shall be treated for the purposes of Rule 7.8(1) and any hearing before the court as if it were an affidavit.
>
> (3) Any report filed by the official receiver in accordance with the Act or the Rules is prima facie evidence of any matter contained in it.

Notes

R 7.9(3)

Clearly the report is not conclusive evidence *Re ABC Coupler & Engineering Co* [1962] 1 WLR 1236.

2.863

7.10 Adjournment of hearing; directions

(1) The court may adjourn the hearing of an application on such terms (if any) as it thinks fit.

(2) The court may at any time give such directions as it thinks fit as to—

   (a)   service or notice of the application on or to any person, whether in connection with the venue of a resumed hearing or for any other purpose;

   (b)   whether particulars of claim and defence are to be delivered and generally as to the procedure on the application;

   (c)   the manner in which any evidence is to be adduced at a resumed hearing and in particular (but without prejudice to the generality of this sub-paragraph) as to—

      (i)   the taking of evidence wholly or in part by affidavit or orally;

      (ii)   the cross-examination either before the judge or registrar on the hearing in court or in chambers, of any deponents to affidavits;

      (iii)   any report to be given by the official receiver or any person mentioned in Rule 7.9(1)(b);

   (d)   the matters to be dealt with in evidence.

Notes

R 7.10(2)(c)

This rule (along with the rest of Part 7) does not apply to winding up petitions (IR 1986 r 7.1) and it would be highly unusual for an order for cross examination to be made in winding up proceedings

Chapter 2
Transfer of Proceedings between Courts

2.864

7.11 General power of transfer

(1) Where winding-up or bankruptcy proceedings are pending in the High Court, the court may order them to be transferred to a specified county court.

(2) Where winding-up or bankruptcy proceedings are pending in a county court, the court may order them to be transferred either to the High Court or to another county court.

(3) In any case where proceedings are transferred to a county court, the transfer must be to a court which has jurisdiction to wind up companies or, as the case may be, jurisdiction in bankruptcy.

(4) Where winding-up or bankruptcy proceedings are pending in a county court, a judge of the High Court may order them to be transferred to that Court.

(5) A transfer of proceedings under this Rule may be ordered—
  (a)   by the court of its own motion, or
  (b)   on the application of the official receiver, or
  (c)   on the application of a person appearing to the court to have an interest in the proceedings.

(6) A transfer of proceedings under this Rule may be ordered notwithstanding that the proceedings commenced before the coming into force of the Rules.

Notes

R 7.11(1)

The power to transfer appears to be exercisable only in relation to the whole file of the proceedings rather than a specific matter or cause within proceedings (*Re Kouyoumdjian* [1956] 1 WLR 558, IR 1986 r 7.14, r 7.30). The fact that the company has a paid up share capital in excess of the county court jurisidiction (IA 1986 s 117(2), presently £120,000) is immaterial; provided that the county court has winding up jurisdiction it may be 'specified' to deal with the winding up proceedings *Re Vernon Heaton Co Ltd* [1936] Ch 289.

R 7.11(2)

A transfer could occur from the county court to the High Court because there is a difficult point of law involved and it would be pointless to put the parties to an expense of hearing the case in the county court only for the matter to be appealed to the High Court *Woodland-Ferrari v UCL Group Retirment Benefits Scheme* [2002] BPIR 1270. In the unusual situation where a petitioner has presented a winding up petition in a county court and another petitioner presents a petition against the same company in the High Court the proceedings will continue in both courts until the High Court has determined which court should deal with the matter *Re Filby Bros (Provender) Ltd* [1958] 1 WLR 683. Where a petition in the High Court was due to be heard earlier than a petition in the county court an order was made in the High Court that the county court petition be transferred to the High Court and all proceedings on it were stayed *Re Audio Systems Ltd* [1965] 1 WLR 1096.

R 7.11(3)

Again the county court to which the proceedings are to be transferred must have winding up jurisdiction *Re Real Estates Co* [1893] 1 Ch 398.

R 7.11(4)

A transfer of proceedings to the High Court will be ordered where a difficult question of law is involved *Re Laxon & Co* [1892] Ch 31 or where the procedure in the High Court is more suitable to the conduct of the particular proceedings being transferred as in the case of misfeasance proceedings *Re Vestal Hosiery Co* (1922) 91 LJ Ch 627.

R 7.11(5)

An order for transfer may be made even after the petition has been opened at a hearing (*Re East Dulwich No 295 Starr-Bowkett Building Society* (1890) 39 WR 32). It is possible to transfer proceedings from one court to another for a single purpose, eg for the removal and replacement of an office-holder in circumstances where there are multiple appointments in various courts *Re Equity Nominees Ltd* [2000] BCC 84, para 1.6(7) Practice Direction: Insolvency Proceedings Civil Procedure Vol 2, Sect 3E.

2.865

7.12 Proceedings commenced in wrong court

Where winding-up or bankruptcy proceedings are commenced in a court which is, in relation to those proceedings, the wrong court, that court may—

(a) order the transfer of the proceedings to the court in which they ought to have been commenced;

(b) order that the proceedings be continued in the court in which they have been commenced; or

(c) order the proceedings to be struck out.

Notes

R 7.12

The High Court has jurisdiction to wind up any company registered in England and Wales (IA 1986 s 117); of the District Registries of the High Court, only those in Birmingham, Bristol, Cardiff, Leeds, Liverpool and Manchester, Newcastle upon Tyne and Preston may take winding up proceedings as it is only in those registries that the district registrar has power to act in insolvency matters (IR 1986 r 13.2). County courts with an insolvency jurisidiction (Civil Courts Order 1983 SI 1983/713 Sch 3 (as amended)) have jurisdiction to wind up companies where the amount of the company's share capital, paid up or credited as paid up, does not exceed £120,000 (IA 1986 s 117(2)). Though IA 1986 s 118(2) specifically authorises proceedings to be retained in a court other than that in which they should have been commenced proceedings are likely to be dismissed if it appears that the petition has been issued in the wrong court for tactical considerations *Re Brightmore, ex p May* (1884) 14 QBD 37, *Re French* (1889) 24 QBD 63.

2.866

7.13 Applications for transfer

(1) An application by the official receiver for proceedings to be transferred shall be made with a report by him—

(a) setting out the reasons for the transfer, and

(b) including a statement either that the petitioner consents to the transfer, or that he has been given at least 14 days' notice of the official receiver's application.

(2) If the court is satisfied from the official receiver's report that the proceedings can be conducted more conveniently in another court, the proceedings shall be transferred to that court.

(3) Where an application for the transfer of proceedings is made otherwise than by the official receiver, at least 14 days' notice of the application shall be given by the applicant—

(a) to the official receiver attached to the court in which the proceedings are pending, and

> (b) to the official receiver attached to the court to which it is proposed that they should be transferred.

Notes

R 7.13(3)

Though the official receiver is '*attached*' to the relevant court (IA 1986 s 399(3) it is unlikely to be arguable that the right of a person to be tried by an independent and impartial tribunal is infringed under The Human Rights Act 1998 Sch 1 art 6 where proceedings are taken in that court involving the official receiver *Smith v Secretary of State for Trade and Industry* [2000] IRLR 6.

2.867

7.14 Procedure following order for transfer

(1) Subject as follows, the court making an order under Rule 7.11 shall forthwith send to the transferee court a sealed copy of the order, and the file of the proceedings.

(2) On receipt of these, the transferee court shall forthwith send notice of the transfer to the official receivers attached to that court and the transferor court respectively.

(3) Paragraph (1) does not apply where the order is made by the High Court under Rule 7.11(4). In that case—
  (a) the High Court shall send sealed copies of the order to the county court from which the proceedings are to be transferred, and to the official receivers attached to that court and the High Court respectively, and
  (b) that county court shall send the file of the proceedings to the High Court.

(4) Following compliance with this Rule, if the official receiver attached to the court to which the proceedings are ordered to be transferred is not already, by virtue of directions given by the Secretary of State under section 399(6)(a), the official receiver in relation to those proceedings, he becomes, in relation to those proceedings, the official receiver in place of the official receiver attached to the other court concerned.

Notes

R 7.14(1)

The '*file*' means the whole of the insolvency proceedings rather than a specific matter or cause within proceedings (*Re Kouyoumdjian* [1956] 1 WLR 558, IR 1986 r 7.30, *Re a Debtor (264 of 1975)* [1985] 1 WLR 6.

R 7.14(2)

If the county court refuses to deal with the case the proper remedy is to apply for an order of mandamus *Re Vernon Heaton Co Ltd* [1936] Ch 289.

2.868

7.15 Consequential transfer of other proceedings

(1) This Rule applies where—
  (a) an order for the winding up of a company, or a bankruptcy order in the case of an individual, has been made by the High Court, or
  (b) in either such case, a provisional liquidator or (as the case may be) an interim receiver has been appointed, or
  (c) winding-up or bankruptcy proceedings have been transferred to that Court from a county court.

(2) A judge of any Division of the High Court may, of his own motion, order the transfer to that Division of any such proceedings as are mentioned below and are pending against the company or individual concerned ('the insolvent') either in another Division of the High Court or in a court in England and Wales other than the High Court.

(3) Proceedings which may be so transferred are those brought by or against the insolvent for the purpose of enforcing a claim against the insolvent estate, or brought by a person other than the insolvent for the purpose of enforcing any such claim (including in either case proceedings of any description by a debenture-holder or mortgagee).

(4) Where proceedings are transferred under this Rule, the registrar may (subject to general or special directions of the judge) dispose of any matter arising in the proceedings which would, but for the transfer, have been disposed of in chambers or, in the case of proceedings transferred from a county court, by the registrar of that court.

Chapter 3
Shorthand Writers

2.869

7.16 Nomination and appointment of shorthand writers

(1) In the High Court the judge and, in a county court, the registrar may in writing nominate one or more persons to be official shorthand writers to the court.

(2) The court may, at any time in the course of insolvency proceedings, appoint a shorthand writer to take down the evidence of a person examined under section 133, 236, 290 or 366.

(3) Where the official receiver applies to the court for an order appointing a shorthand writer, he shall name the person he proposes for appointment; and that appointment shall be made, unless the court otherwise orders.

2.870

7.17 Remuneration

(1) The remuneration of a shorthand writer appointed in insolvency proceedings shall be paid by the party at whose instance the appointment was made, or out of the insolvent estate, or otherwise, as the court may direct.

[(2) Any question arising as to the rates of remuneration payable under this Rule shall be determined by the court in its discretion.]

2.871

7.18 Cost of shorthand note

Where in insolvency proceedings the court appoints a shorthand writer on the application of the official receiver, in order that a written record may be taken of the evidence of a person to be examined, the cost of the written record is deemed an expense of the official receiver in the proceedings.

Chapter 4
Enforcement Procedures

2.872

7.19 Enforcement of court orders

(1) In any insolvency proceedings, orders of the court may be enforced in the same manner as a judgment to the same effect.

(2) Where an order in insolvency proceedings is made, or any process is issued, by a county court ('the primary court'), the order or process may be enforced, executed and dealt with by any other county court ('the secondary court'), as if it had been made or issued for the enforcement of a judgment or order to the same effect made by the secondary court.

This applies whether or not the secondary court has jurisdiction to take insolvency proceedings.

Notes

R 7.19

There is no special procedure for enforcing orders of the courts made in relation to 'insolvency proceedings' (see IR 1986 r 13.7). A party wishing to enforce an order may use any relevant enforcement method that would be available in other types of proceedings. The designation of 'insolvency districts' under IA 1986, s 374 does not restrict the jurisdiction of other courts to enforce orders in the appropriate way.

2.873

7.20 Orders enforcing compliance with the Rules

(1) The court may, on application by the competent person, make such orders as it thinks necessary for the enforcement of obligations falling on any person in accordance with—
  (a) [paragraph 47 of Schedule B1 to the Act or section] 47 or 131 (duty to submit statement of affairs in administration, administrative receivership or winding up),
  (b) section 143(2) (liquidator to furnish information, books, papers, etc), or

(c)   section 235 (duty of various persons to co-operate with office-holder).

(2) The competent person for this purpose is—
    (a)   under [paragraph 47 of Schedule B1 to the Act], the administrator,
    (b)   under section 47, the administrative receiver,
    (c)   under section 131 or 143(2), the official receiver, and
    (d)   under section 235, the official receiver, the administrator, the administrative receiver, the liquidator or the provisional liquidator, as the case may be.

(3) An order of the court under this Rule may provide that all costs of and incidental to the application for it shall be borne by the person against whom the order is made.

Notes

R 7.20

This provision enables the court to make any order it thinks fit for the purpose of enforcing compliance with various duties created under the IA 1986. The *locus* to apply for such orders is restricted to the 'competent person', who is identified in each case.

2.874

7.21 Warrants (general provisions)

(1) A warrant issued by the court under any provision of the Act shall be addressed to such officer of the High Court or of a county court (whether or not having jurisdiction in insolvency proceedings) as the warrant specifies, or to any constable.

(2) The persons referred to in sections 134(2), 236(5), 364(1), 365(3) and 366(3) (court's powers of enforcement) as the prescribed officer of the court are—
    (a)   in the case of the High Court, the tipstaff and his assistants of the court, and
    (b)   in the case of a county court, the registrar and the bailiffs.

(3) In this Chapter references to property include books, papers and records.

Notes

R 7.21

This provision sets out the form of the warrant that the court may issue under the powers given by the IA 1986.

2.875

7.22 Warrants under ss 134, 364

When a person is arrested under a warrant issued by the court under section 134 (officer of company failing to attend for public examination), or section 364 (arrest of debtor or bankrupt)—
  (a) the officer apprehending him shall give him into the custody of the governor of the prison named in the warrant, who shall keep him in custody until such time as the court otherwise orders and shall produce him before the court as it may from time to time direct; and
  (b) any property in the arrested person's possession which may be seized shall be—
    (i) lodged with, or otherwise dealt with as instructed by, whoever is specified in the warrant as authorised to receive it, or
    (ii) kept by the officer seizing it pending the receipt of written orders from the court as to its disposal,
  as may be directed by the court in the warrant.

Notes

R 7.22

See Forms 7.6 and 7.7 for forms of warrant and Form 7.14 for the form of order for discharge from custody. It would be usual practice for certain undertakings to be given before the person arrested is released from prison including securing that person's attendance for interview, co-operation with the official receiver, disclosure of relevent documentation and attendance at a re-scheduled public examination under s 134(g).

2.876

7.23 Warrants under ss 236, 366

(1) When a person is arrested under a warrant issued under section 236 (inquiry into insolvent company's dealings) or 366 (the equivalent in bankruptcy), the officer arresting him shall forthwith bring him before the court issuing the warrant in order that he may be examined.

(2) If he cannot immediately be brought up for examination, the officer shall deliver him into the custody of the governor of the prison named in the warrant, who shall keep him in custody and produce him before the court as it may from time to time direct.

(3) After arresting the person named in the warrant, the officer shall forthwith report to the court the arrest or delivery into custody (as the case may be) and apply to the court to fix a venue for the person's examination.

(4) The court shall appoint the earliest practicable time for the examination, and shall—
  (a) direct the governor of the prison to produce the person for examination at the time and place appointed, and

(b) forthwith give notice of the venue to the person who applied for the warrant.

(5) Any property in the arrested person's possession which may be seized shall be—
(a) lodged with, or otherwise dealt with as instructed by, whoever is specified in the warrant as authorised to receive it, or
(b) kept by the officer seizing it pending the receipt of written orders from the court as to its disposal,
as may be directed by the court.

Notes

R 7.23

This provision is similar to IR 1986 r 7.22 although the provisions under which the jurisdiction to issue the warrant is granted envisage that the persons summoned to appear may not have an independent duty to cooperate in the investigation of the company's or bankrupt's affairs. The persons summoned to attend must be tendered a sum of money for their travelling expenses (IR 1986, r 9.6(4)).

2.877

7.24 Execution of warrants outside court's district

(1) This Rule applies where a warrant for a person's arrest has been issued in insolvency proceedings by a county court ('the primary court') and is addressed to another county court ('the secondary court') for execution in its district.

(2) The secondary court may send the warrant to the registrar of any other county court (whether or not having jurisdiction to take insolvency proceedings) in whose district the person to be arrested is or is believed to be, with a notice to the effect that the warrant is transmitted to that court under this Rule for execution in its district at the request of the primary court.

(3) The court receiving a warrant transmitted by the secondary court under this Rule shall apply its seal to the warrant, and secure that all such steps are taken for its execution as would be appropriate in the case of a warrant issued by itself.

Notes

R 7.24

This provision enables a court selected for enforcement of an order, which is not itself the 'primary court', to pass the warrant to another, more appropriate court; as such, it complements IR 1986, r 7.19(2).

2.878

7.25 Warrants under s 365

(1) A warrant issued under section 365(3) (search of premises not belonging to the bankrupt) shall authorise any person executing it to seize any property of the bankrupt found as a result of the execution of the warrant.

(2) Any property seized under a warrant issued under section 365(2) or (3) shall be—
  (a) lodged with, or otherwise dealt with as instructed by, whoever is specified in the warrant as authorised to receive it, or
  (b) kept by the officer seizing it pending the receipt of written orders from the court as to its disposal,
as may be directed by the warrant.

Chapter 5
Court Records and Returns

2.879

7.26 Title of proceedings

(1) Every proceeding under Parts I to VII of the Act shall, with any necessary additions, be intituled 'IN THE MATTER OF ... .. (naming the company to which the proceedings relate) AND IN THE MATTER OF THE INSOLVENCY ACT 1986'.

(2) Every proceeding under Parts IX to XI of the Act shall be intituled 'IN BANKRUPTCY'.

Notes

R 7.26

This provision sets out how proceedings under Parts I to VII and Parts IX to XI of IA 1986 should be headed. It applies whether the proceedings are in the county court or in the High Court.

2.880

7.27 Court records

The court shall keep records of all insolvency proceedings, and shall cause to be entered in the records the taking of any step in the proceedings, and such decisions of the court in relation thereto, as the court thinks fit.

Notes

R 7.27

These records are distinct from the court file, which is dealt with in IR 1986 r 7.30, 7.31. The records amount to a skeletal history of the proceedings.

2.881

7.28 Inspection of records

(1) Subject as follows, the court's records of insolvency proceedings shall be open to inspection by any person.

(2) If in the case of a person applying to inspect the records the registrar is not satisfied as to the propriety of the purpose for which inspection is required, he may refuse to allow it. The person may then apply forthwith and *ex parte* to the judge, who may refuse the inspection, or allow it on such terms as he thinks fit.

(3) The judge's decision under paragraph (2) is final.

Notes

R 7.28(2)

It is necessary that the registrar be satisfied that the inspection be sought for a proper purpose. If he is not, he may refuse inspection. There is then a right to apply to the judge. Note that this is not an appeal in the strict sense. Where a court gives permission for multiple searches of the court records it is important that any undertakings given to the court are strictly complied with *Re Haines Watts* [2005] BPIR 798.

R 7.28(3)

Once the judge has made his decision, there is no right of appeal; see *ex parte Austintel* [1997] 1 WLR 616 (CA) which also deals with the question of whether inspecting the records for a commercial purpose is a proper purpose and the propriety of certain types of searches. See also *Re Creditnet Ltd* [1996] 2 BCLC 133 (the same case at first instance), *Re an Application pursuant to Rule 7.28* [1997] 1 BCLC 233.

2.882

7.29 Returns to Secretary of State

(1) The court shall from time to time send to the Secretary of State the following particulars relating to winding-up and bankruptcy proceedings—

    (a)   the full title of the proceedings, including the number assigned to each case;

    (b)   where a winding-up or bankruptcy order has been made, the date of the order.

(2) The Secretary of State may, on the request of any person, furnish him with particulars sent by the court under this Rule.

2.883

7.30 File of court proceedings

(1) In respect of all insolvency proceedings, the court shall open and maintain a file for each case; and (subject to directions of the registrar) all documents relating to such proceedings shall be placed on the relevant file.

(2) No proceedings shall be filed in the Central Office of the High Court.

Notes

R 7.30(1)

The court is obliged to open and maintain a file for each set of insolvency proceedings. The file contains all documents relating to the matter. This is the file that will be before the judge or registrar in many types of hearing in such proceedings. For guidance in relation to Chancery procedure, one should consult the latest edition of the *Chancery Guide*, which is reproduced in Civil Procedure Vol 2 para 1–1. A transfer of proceedings can take place under IR 1986 r 7.11 and the reference to transferring the proceedings means the whole file and not just a part of the proceedings IR 1986 r 7.14, *Re Kouyououmdjian* [1956] 1 WLR 558, *Re a Debtor (26A of 1975)* [1985] 1 WLR 6.

2.884

7.31 Right to inspect the file

(1) In the case of any insolvency proceedings, the following have the right, at all reasonable times, to inspect the court's file of the proceedings—
- (a) the person who, in relation to those proceedings, is the responsible insolvency practitioner;
- (b) any duly authorised officer of the Department; and
- (c) any person stating himself in writing to be a creditor of the company to which, or the individual to whom, the proceedings relate.

(2) The same right of inspection is exercisable—
- (a) in proceedings under Parts I to VII of the Act, by every person who is, or at any time has been, a director or officer of the company to which the proceedings relate, or who is a member of the company or a contributory in its winding up;
- (b) in proceedings with respect to a voluntary arrangement proposed by a debtor under Part VIII of the Act, by the debtor;
- (c) in bankruptcy proceedings, by—
  - (i) the bankrupt,
  - (ii) any person against whom, or by whom, a bankruptcy petition has been presented, and
  - (iii) any person who has been served, in accordance with Chapter 1 of Part 6 of the Rules, with a statutory demand.

(3) The right of inspection conferred as above on any person may be exercised on his behalf by a person properly authorised by him.

(4) Any person may, by special leave of the court, inspect the file.

(5) The right of inspection conferred by this Rule is not exercisable in the case of documents, or parts of documents, as to which the court directs (either generally or specially) that they are not to be made open to inspection without the court's leave.

An application for a direction of the court under this paragraph may be made by the official receiver, by the person who in relation to any proceedings is the responsible insolvency practitioner, or by any party appearing to the court to have an interest.

(6) If, for the purpose of powers conferred by the Act or the Rules, the Secretary of State, the Department or the official receiver requires to inspect the file of any insolvency proceedings, and requests the transmission of the file, the court shall comply with the request (unless the file is for the time being in use for the court's own purposes).

(7) Paragraphs (2) and (3) of Rule 7.28 apply in respect of the court's file of any proceedings as they apply in respect of court records.

Notes

R 7.31(1), (2)

These provisions confer an absolute right of inspection on the persons listed. This right can be curtailed by a direction of the court under IR 1986 r 7.31(5). If such an order is made that person is in the same position as a member of the public and must apply for inspection under IR 1986 r 7.31(4); see *Astor Chemical Ltd v Synthetic Technology Ltd* [1990] BCC 97.

R 7.31(7)

This provision is somewhat unclear. It imports the restrictions found in paragraphs IR 1986 r 7.28(2), (3). The latter provides that the decision of a judge will be final but the former provides that the registrar may refuse to allow inspection if he is not satisfied that the inspection is being sought for a proper purpose. This apparently conflicts with the absolute right that seems to have been intended by the terms of IR 1986 r 7.31(1), (2). However this is not likely to cause problems in practice as an application to inspect made by the persons listed in IR 1986 r 7.31(1), (2) is always likely to be made for a proper purpose in the sense of a purpose connected to their role in the insolvency; see also the note to IR 1986 r 7.28.

2.885

7.32 Filing of Gazette notices and advertisements

(1) In any court in which insolvency proceedings are pending, an officer of the court shall file a copy of every issue of the Gazette which contains an advertisement relating to those proceedings.

(2) Where there appears in a newspaper an advertisement relating to insolvency proceedings pending in any court, the person inserting the advertisement shall file a copy of it in that court.

The copy of the advertisement shall be accompanied by, or have endorsed on it, such particulars as are necessary to identify the proceedings and the date of the advertisement's appearance.

(3) An officer of any court in which insolvency proceedings are pending shall from time to time file a memorandum giving the dates of, and other particulars relating to, any notice published in the Gazette, and any newspaper advertisements, which relate to proceedings so pending.

The officer's memorandum is prima facie evidence that any notice or advertisement mentioned in it was duly inserted in the issue of the newspaper or the Gazette which is specified in the memorandum.

Chapter 6
Costs and Detailed Assessment

2.886

7.33 Application of the CPR

Subject to provision to inconsistent effect made as follows in this Chapter, CPR Part 43 (scope of costs rules and definitions), Part 44 (general rules about costs), Part 45 (fixed costs), Part 47 (procedure for detailed assessment of costs and default provisions) and Part 48 (costs special cases) shall apply to insolvency proceedings with any necessary modifications.

Notes

R 7.33

All 'insolvency proceedings' (IR 1986 r 13.7) are allocated to the multi-track thus CPR Part 46 (fast track costs) does not apply.

2.887

7.34 Requirement to assess costs by the detailed procedure

(1) Subject as follows, where the costs, charges or expenses of any person are payable out of the insolvent estate, the amount of those costs, charges or expenses shall be decided by detailed assessment unless agreed between the responsible insolvency practitioner and the person entitled to payment, and in the absence of such agreement the responsible insolvency practitioner may serve notice in writing requiring that person to commence detailed assessment proceedings in accordance with CPR Part 47 (procedure for detailed assessment of costs and default provisions) in the court to which the insolvency proceedings are allocated or, where in relation to a company there is no such court, that in relation to any court having jurisdiction to wind up the company.

(2) If a liquidation or creditors' committee established in insolvency proceedings (except administrative receivership) resolves that the amount of any such costs, charges or expenses should be decided by detailed assessment, the insolvency practitioner shall require detailed assessment in accordance with CPR Part 47.

(3) Where the amount of the costs, charges or expenses of any person employed by an insolvency practitioner in insolvency proceedings are required to be decided by detailed assessment or fixed by order of the court this does not preclude the insolvency practitioner from making payments on account to such person on the basis of an undertaking by that person to repay immediately any money which may, when detailed

assessment is made, prove to have been overpaid, with interest at the rate specified in section 17 of the Judgments Act 1838 on the date payment was made and for the period from the date of payment to that of repayment.

(4) In any proceedings before the court, including proceedings on a petition, the court may order costs to be decided by detailed assessment.

(5) Unless otherwise directed or authorised, the costs of a trustee in bankruptcy or a liquidator are to be allowed on the standard basis for which provision is made in CPR rule 44.4 (basis of assessment) and rule 44.5 (factors to be taken into account in deciding the amount of costs).

(6) This Rule applies additionally (with any necessary modifications) to winding-up and bankruptcy proceedings commenced before the coming into force of the Rules.

2.888

7.35 Procedure where detailed assessment required

(1) Before making a detailed assessment of the costs of any person employed in insolvency proceedings by a responsible insolvency practitioner, the costs officer shall require a certificate of employment, which shall be endorsed on the bill and signed by the insolvency practitioner.

(2) The certificate shall include—
    (a)   the name and address of the person employed,
    (b)   details of the functions to be carried out under the employment, and
    (c)   a note of any special terms of remuneration which have been agreed.

(3) Every person whose costs in insolvency proceedings are required to be decided by detailed assessment shall, on being required in writing to do so by the insolvency practitioner, commence detailed assessment proceedings in accordance with CPR Part 47 (procedure for detailed assessment of costs and default provisions).

(4) If that person does not commence detailed assessment proceedings within 3 months of the requirement under paragraph (3), or within such further time as the court, on application, may permit, the insolvency practitioner may deal with the insolvent estate without regard to any claim by that person, whose claim is forfeited by such failure to commence proceedings.

(5) Where in any such case such a claim lies additionally against an insolvency practitioner in his personal capacity, that claim is also forfeited by such failure to commence proceedings.

(6) Where costs have been incurred in insolvency proceedings in the High Court and those proceedings are subsequently transferred to a county court, all costs of those proceedings directed by the court or otherwise required to be assessed may nevertheless, on the application of the person who incurred the costs, be ordered to be decided by detailed assessment in the High Court.

2.889

7.36 Costs of officers charged with execution of writs or other process.

(1) Where an enforcement officer, or other officer charged with execution of the writs or other process.—

    (a)   is required under section 184(2) or 346(2) to deliver up goods or money, or

    (b)   has under section 184(3) or 346(3) deducted costs from the proceeds of an execution or money paid to him,

the responsible insolvency practitioner may require in writing that the amount of the enforcement officer's or other officer's bill of costs be decided by detailed assessment.'

(2) Where such a requirement is made, Rule 7.35(4) applies.

(3) Where, in the case of a deduction under paragraph (1)(b), any amount deducted is disallowed at the conclusion of the detailed assessment proceedings, the enforcement officer shall forthwith pay a sum equal to that disallowed to the insolvency practitioner for the benefit of the insolvent estate.

2.890

7.37 Petitions presented by insolvents

(1) In any case where a petition is presented by a company or individual ('the insolvent') against himself, any solicitor acting for the insolvent shall in his bill of costs give credit for any sum or security received from the insolvent as a deposit on account of the costs and expenses to be incurred in respect of the filing and prosecution of the petition; and the deposit shall be noted by the costs officer on the final costs certificate.

(2) Paragraph (3) applies where a petition is presented by a person other than the insolvent to whom the petition relates and before it is heard the insolvent presents a petition for the same order, and that order is made.

(3) Unless the court considers that the insolvent estate has benefited by the insolvent's conduct, or that there are otherwise special circumstances justifying the allowance of costs, no costs shall be allowed to the insolvent or his solicitor out of the insolvent estate.

2.891

7.38 Costs paid otherwise than out of the insolvent estate

Where the amount of costs is decided by detailed assessment under an order of the court directing that those costs are to be paid otherwise than out of the insolvent estate, the costs officer shall note on the final costs certificate by whom, or the manner in which, the costs are to be paid.

2.892

7.39 Award of costs against official receiver or responsible insolvency practitioner

Without prejudice to any provision of the Act or Rules by virtue of which the official receiver is not in any event to be liable for costs and expenses, where the official receiver or a responsible insolvency practitioner is made a party to any proceedings on the application of another party to the proceedings, he shall not be personally liable for costs unless the court otherwise directs.

———

Notes

R 7.39

Thus the general rule is that neither the official receiver nor the responsible insolvency practitioner is liable for costs when joined to proceedings *Re Mordant (A Bankrupt)* [1995] 2 BCLC 647. Provided that the official receiver is acting in the course of the bankruptcy proceedings and within the scope of his powers and duties he has immunity from suit in respect of his actions and any statements that are relied upon by others *Mond v Hyde* [1999] 2 WLR 499.

———

2.893

7.40 Applications for costs

(1) This Rule applies where a party to, or person affected by, any proceedings in an insolvency—
- (a) applies to the court for an order allowing his costs, or part of them, incidental to the proceedings, and
- (b) that application is not made at the time of the proceedings.

(2) The person concerned shall serve a sealed copy of his application on the responsible insolvency practitioner, and, in winding up by the court or bankruptcy, on the official receiver.

(3) The insolvency practitioner and, where appropriate, the official receiver may appear on the application.

(4) No costs of or incidental to the application shall be allowed to the applicant unless the court is satisfied that the application could not have been made at the time of the proceedings.

2.894

7.41 Costs and expenses of witnesses

(1) Except as directed by the court, no allowance as a witness in any examination or other proceedings before the court shall be made to the bankrupt or an officer of the insolvent company to which the proceedings relate.

(2) A person presenting any petition in insolvency proceedings shall not be regarded as a witness on the hearing of the petition, but the costs officer may allow his expenses of travelling and subsistence.

2.895

7.42 Final costs certificate

(1) A final costs certificate of the costs officer is final and conclusive as to all matters which have not been objected to in the manner provided for under the rules of the court.

(2) Where it is proved to the satisfaction of a costs officer that a final costs certificate has been lost or destroyed, he may issue a duplicate.

Chapter 7
Persons Incapable of managing their affairs

2.896

7.43 Introductory

(1) The Rules in this Chapter apply where in insolvency proceedings it appears to the court that a person affected by the proceedings is one who is incapable of managing and administering his property and affairs either—
    (a)   by reason of mental disorder within the meaning of the Mental Health Act 1983, or
    (b)   due to physical affliction or disability.

(2) The person concerned is referred to as 'the incapacitated person'.

2.897

7.44 Appointment of another person to act

(1) The court may appoint such person as it thinks fit to appear for, represent or act for the incapacitated person.

(2) The appointment my be made either generally or for the purpose of any particular application or proceeding, or for the exercise of particular rights or powers which the incapacitated person might have excercised but for his incapacity.

(3) The court may make the appointemnt either of its own motion or on application by–
    (a)   a person who has been appointed by a court in the United Kingdom or elsewhere to manage the affairs of, or to represent, the incapacitated person, or
    (b)   any relative or friend of the incapacitated person who appears to the court to be a proper person to make the application, or
    (c)   the official receiver, or
    (d)   the person who, in relation to the proceedings, is the responsible insolvency practitioner.

(4) Application under paragraph (3) may be made ex parte; but the court may require such notice of the application as it thinks necessary to be given to the person alleged to be incapacitated, or any other person, and may adjourn the hearing of the application to enable the notice to be given.

2.897A

7.45 Affidavit in support of application

(1) Except where made by the official reciever, an application under Rule 7.44(3) shall be supported by an affidavit of a registered medical practitioner as to the mental or physical condition of the incapacitated person.

(2) In the excepted case, a report made by the official receiver is sufficient.

Notes

R 7.45(1)

A witness statement may be used instead of an affidavit IR 1986 r 7.57(5),(6).

R 7.45(2)

Given the need to establish a mental disorder with the Mental Health Act 1983 or physical affliction or disability (IR 1986 r 7.43) it is unlikely that such a report could in fact be sufficient unless it at least exhibits a further report by a registered medical practitioner.

2.898

7.46 Service of Notices following appointment

Any notice served on, or sent to, a person appointed under Rule 7.44 has the same effect as if it had been served on, or given to, the incapacitated person.

Chapter 8
Appeals in Insolvency Proceedings

2.899

7.47 Appeals and reviews of court orders (winding up)

(1) Every court having jurisdiction under the Act to wind up companies may review, rescind or vary any order made by it in the exercise of that jurisdiction.

(2) An appeal from a decision made in the exercise of that jurisdiction by a county court or by a registrar of the High Court lies to a single judge of the High Court; and an appeal from a decision of that judge on such an appeal lies, with the leave of that judge or the Court of Appeal, to the Court of Appeal.

(3) A county court is not, in the exercise of its jurisdiction to wind up companies, subject to be restrained by the order of any other court, and no appeal lies from its decision in the exercise of that jurisdiction except as provided by this Rule.

(4) Any application for the rescission of a winding-up order shall be made within 7 days after the date on which the order was made.

Notes

R 7.47(1)

A review involves a revisiting of the matter by the same court (but not necessarily the same judge *Re Casterbridge Properties* [2002] BPIR 428) and any order including a winding up order may be reviewed (*Re Portedge Ltd* [1997] BCC 23). The appropriate test on a review is whether in view of the facts and circumstances known at the time of the review the court would still have made the order the subject of the review *HM Customs and Excise v Allen* [2003] BPIR 830. Reference should also be made to the principles formulated by Laddie J in *Papanicola v Humphreys* [2005] 2 All ER 418. That case involved s 375 IA 1986, which is a comparable provision in relation to personal insolvency. The principles may be summarised as follows:

(i)   The court has a wide discretion to review, vary or rescind any order made in the exercise of the bankruptcy jurisdiction;

(ii)   The onus is on the applicant to demonstrate the existence of circumstances which justify exercise of the discretion in his favour;

(iii)   Those circumstances must be exceptional (see also *Fitch v Official Receiver* [1996] 1 WLR 242);

(iv)   The circumstances relied on must involve a material difference to what was before the court which made the original order. In other words there must be something new to justify the overturning of the original order;

(v)   There is no limit to the factors which may be taken into account. They can include, for example, changes which have occurred since the making of the original order and significant facts which, although in existence at the time of the original order, were not brought to the court's attention at that time;

(vi) Where the new circumstances relied on consist of or include new evidence which could have been made available at the original hearing, and any explanation the applicant gives for the failure to produce it then or any lack of such explanation, are factors which can be taken into account in the exercise of the discretion. (In winding-up cases, however, new evidence will not be necessary where it is clear that the winding up order was made on a petition which was misconceived for example where the wrong company was named (*Re Calmex Ltd* [1989] BCLC 299; as to evidence in winding-up cases, see *RWH Enterprises Ltd v Portedge* [1998] BCC 566).

The power to review may be used alongside the 'slip rule' (Civil Procedure Vol 1 CPR 40.12; *Re Brian Sheridan Cars Ltd* [1995] BCC 1035).

The jurisdiction to review should not be used to mount an appeal out of time (*Re Mid East Trading Ltd* [1997] 3 All ER 481). Though the power to review should not be narrowly confined (*Re Dollar Land (Feltham) Ltd* [1995] BCC 740, 748) very cogent reasons are needed to support a review (*Re Piccadilly Management Ltd* [1999] 2 BCLC 145, *Re R S & M Engineering Co Ltd* [2000] BCC 445). Save in exceptional cases where it might be necessary to correct an obvious injustice review is confined to those cases of changed circumstances or the introduction of fresh evidence (*Re Thirty Eight Building Ltd (No 2)* [2000] 1 BCLC 201, *Re a Debtor* [1993] 1 WLR 314, *Re Turnstem Ltd* [2005] 1 BCLC 388.

A review of an order made by a registrar should ordinarily be undertaken by the registrar and not the judge. It has been stated that a challenge to a registrar's order to a judge should be by way of an appeal including where appropriate an appeal against the registrar's decision to refuse to review his original decision (*Re SN Group plc* [1993] BCC 808); however the better view is a judge has jurisdiction to review an order of the registrar (*Re Casterbridge Properties* [2002] BPIR 428, *Re W & A Glaser Ltd* [1994] BCC 199, *Re Dollar Land (Feltham) Ltd* [1995] 2 BCLC 370) and this jurisdiction may be exercised together with an appeal though such 'double barrelled' applications are discouraged *Re Piccadilly Management Ltd* [1999] 2 BCLC 145.

The power to vary was used in *Re Roches Leisure Services Ltd* [2006] [BPIR] 453 to make a retrospective order extending an administration order which had been made for a limited period.

R 7.47(2)

An appeal from a Registrar's or District Judge's decision is heard by a single High Court Judge ('a first appeal') and it does not require permission (para 17.6 Practice Direction: Insolvency Proceedings (Civil Procedure Vol 2, Sect 3E). An appeal from a decision on a first appeal by a

High Court Judge lies to the Court of Appeal with the permission of the Court of Appeal (para 17.3(1) Practice Direction: Insolvency Proceedings). An appeal from a High Court Judge which is not a decision on a first appeal lies to the Court of Appeal with the permission of the Judge or the Court of Appeal (para 17.3(2) Practice Direction: Insolvency Proceedings.). Para 17 Practice Direction: Insolvency Proceedings generally sets out the procedure for appeals in insolvency proceedings as from 2 May 2000. The form for an appellant's notice is Form PDIP 1 (para 17.9). The appeal is true appeal. An exercise of discretion cannot be challenged unless it can be shown that the wrong principles were applied or there was an error of law *Re Industrial and Commercial Securities plc* (1989) 5 BCC 320, *Re Probe Data Systems Ltd (No 3)* [1991] BCLC 586, para 17.18(3) Practice Direction: Insolvency Proceedings (Civil Procedure Vol 2, Sect 3E).

R 7.47(4)

The application to rescind must be made within 7 days of the winding up order but in appropriate cases the court may extend the time CPR 3.1(2)(a), IR 1986 R 12.9, *Re Virgo Systems Ltd* (1989) 5 BCC 833 (*company unaware of winding up order for several days*) *Re Calmex Ltd* [1989] BCLC 299 (*winding up order made against wrong company*). If there is a substantial period of delay then it will have to be shown that there has been an 'obvious injustice' *Leicester v Stevenson* [2003] 2 BCLC 97 *and Re Oakwood Storage Services Ltd* [2004] 2 BCLC 404. There is no need to issue an application as the petition is simply restored before the court para 7.5 Practice Direction Insolvency Proceedings (Civil Procedure Vol 2, Section 3E). Reference should be made to para 7 Practice Direction Insolvency Proceedings (Civil Procedure Vol 2 Section 3E) which sets out who should join in making the application, the evidential requirements and the costs implications.

A winding up order can be rescinded where the petition debt is disputed on bona fide grounds and the company is able to give a satisfactory explanation of how the winding up order came to be made. In cases where the petition debt is not disputed but the company claims to be solvent and wishes to resume trading the court will require: (a) the petition debt and any supporting creditors to be paid; (b) proof that the company is solvent; (c) the official receiver to be satisfied that the company's affairs do not require investigation; (d) the official receiver's costs to be paid *Re Dollar Land (Feltham) Ltd* [1995] BCC 740.

2.900

7.48 Appeals in bankruptcy

(1) In bankruptcy proceedings, an appeal lies at the instance of the Secretary of State from any order of the court made on an application for the rescission or annulment of a bankruptcy order, or for a bankrupt's discharge.

(2) In the case of an order made by a county court or by a registrar of the High Court, the appeal lies to a single judge of the High Court; and an appeal from a decision of that judge on such an appeal lies, with the leave of that judge or the Court of Appeal, to the Court of Appeal.

Notes

R 7.48(1)

The appeal is a true appeal and not a fresh hearing *Re Gilmartin* [1989] 1 WLR 513.

R 7.48(2)

See the notes to IR 1986 7.47(2) above. Again a decision from a High Court Judge made on a 'first appeal' lies to the Court of Appeal with the permission of the Court of Appeal rather than the permission of the High Court Judge (para 17.3(1) Practice Direction Insolvency Proceedings (Civil Procedure Vol 2 Section 3E)).

2.901

7.49 Procedure on appeal

(1) Subject as follows, the procedure and practice of the Supreme Court relating to appeals to the Court of Appeal apply to appeals in insolvency proceedings.

(2) In relation to any appeal to a single judge of the High Court under section 375(2) (individual insolvency) or Rule 7.47(2) above (company insolvency), any reference in the CPR to the Court of Appeal is replaced by a reference to that judge and any reference to the registrar of civil appeals is replaced by a reference to the registrar of the High Court who deals with insolvency proceedings of the kind involved.

(3) In insolvency proceedings, the procedure under RSC Order 59 (appeals to the Court of Appeal) is by ordinary application and not by application notice.

Notes

R 7.49(2)

The time for appealing is 14 days after the date of the decision that is appealed unless a longer period is ordered by the lower court para 17.11(1) Practice Direction Insolvency Proceedings (Civil Procedure Vol 2 Section 3E, CPR Part 52.4. An appeal against a refusal to extend the time for appealing can be heard by the Court of Appeal but not an appeal against a refusal of leave to appeal CPR Part 52.6, *Foenander v Bond Lewis & Co* [2002] 1 WLR 525. The detailed procedural rules for appeals are set out in para 17 Practice Direction Insolvency Proceedings (Civil Procedure Vol 2 Section 3E.

2.902

7.50 Appeal against decision of Secretary of State or official receiver

(1) An appeal under the Act or the Rules against a decision of the Secretary of State or the official receiver shall be brought within 28 days of the notification of the decision.

(2) In respect of a decision under Rule 6.214A(5)(b) and appeal shall be brought within 14 days of the notification of the decision

Chapter 9
General

2.903

7.51 Principal court rules and practice to apply

(1) The CPR, the practice and procedure of the High Court and of the county court (including any practice direction) apply to insolvency proceedings in the High Court and county court as the case may be, in either case with any necessary modifications, except so far as inconsistent with the Rules.

(2) All insolvency proceedings shall be allocated to the multi-track for which CPR Part 29 (the multi-track) makes provision, accordingly those provisions of the CPR which provide for allocation questionnaires and track allocation will not apply.

Notes

R 7.51(1)

This is a useful and wide ranging provision. For instance it would allow an applicant to ask the court for a direction that the detailed costs assessment rules (CPR Part 47) should apply to an insolvency practitioner's bill so as to allow a challenge to be made to that bill; or that the factors to be taken into account under CPR 44.3 on a costs application should be taken into account *Cork v Gill* [2005] BPIR 272. The provision has also been used to apply the CPR Part 35 rules on expert evidence to the making of an independent report for an administration petition (*Re Colt Telecom Group plc (No 2)* [2003] BPIR 324) under the former administration provisions.

2.904

7.52 Right of audience

(1) Official receivers and deputy official receivers have right of audience in insolvency proceedings, whether in the High Court or a county court.

(2) Subject as above, rights of audience in insolvency proceedings are the same as obtained before the coming into force of the Rules.

Notes

R 7.52(1)

See the notes to IR 1986 r 10.1ff dealing with the position and status of the official receiver and *Re Minotaur Data Systems Ltd* [1999] 2 BCLC 766.

2.905

7.53 Right of attendance (company insolvency)

(1) Subject as follows, in company insolvency proceedings any person stating himself in writing, in records kept by the court for that purpose, to be a creditor or member of the company or, where the company is being

wound up, a contributory, is entitled, at his own cost, to attend in court or in chambers at any stage of the proceedings.

(2) Attendance may be by the person himself, or his solicitor.

(3) A person so entitled may request the court in writing to give him notice of any step in the proceedings; and, subject to his paying the costs involved and keeping the court informed as to his address, the court shall comply with the request.

(4) If the court is satisfied that the exercise by a person of his rights under this Rule has given rise to costs for the insolvent estate which would not otherwise have been incurred and ought not, in the circumstances, to fall on that estate, it may direct that the costs be paid by the person concerned, to an amount specified.

The person's rights under this Rule are in abeyance so long as those costs are not paid.

(5) The court may appoint one or more persons to represent the creditors, the members or the contributories of an insolvent company, or any class of them, to have the rights conferred by this Rule, instead of the rights being exercisable by any or all of them individually.

If two or more persons are appointed under this paragraph to represent the same interest, they must (if at all) instruct the same solicitor.

2.906

7.54 Insolvency practitioner's solicitor

Where in any proceedings the attendance of the responsible insolvency practioner's solicitor is required, whether in court or in chambers, the insolvency practitioner himself need not attend, unless directed by the court.

2.907

7.55 Formal defects

No insolvency proceedings shall be invalidated by any formal defect or by any irregularity, unless the court before which objection is made considers that substantial injustice has been caused by the defect or irregularity, and that the injustice cannot be remedied by any order of the court.

Notes

R 7.55

This is a useful provision which may be used to prevent a party taking a 'technical' objection to proceedings *Skarzynski v Chalford Property Company Ltd* [2001] BPIR 673. For instance a creditor's failure to state that no application to set aside the demand is outstanding (as required by IR 1986 r 6.8(2)(b)(ii))) does not automatically invalidate the petition and may be waived under this rule, *Re a Debtor (No 22 of 1993)* [1994] 1 WLR 46; or where an ordinary application is used rather than an originating application and no substantial injustice had been done *Re Buildlead Ltd (No 2)* [2005] BCC 138; see notes to IR 1986 r 7.2. However where a statement that no application to set aside the demand is outstanding was missing from the petition and it was not correct to state that the debtor had no reasonable prospect of paying a debt the court held that these defects could not be cured under this rule (*Hoare v Commissioners of Inland Revenue* [2002] BPIR 986, IA 1986 s 267(2)(c).

The absence of evidence of service of a bankruptcy petition is not a defect that can be waived by an application under this rule, *Re Awan* [2000] BPIR 241 and the fact that there are defects in the petition may result in the petitioner being unable to obtain an order for costs against the debtor, *Oben v Blackman* [2000] BPIR 302. Another example of a substantive defect is the failure to state in a winding up or bankruptcy petition whether the EC Regulation Insolvency Proceedings 2000 applies and if so what type of proceedings is concerned; see also former Insolvency Proceedings – Practice Note 1/2002, 10 May 2002. This rule applies to formal defects and irregularities in 'insolvency proceedings'; (defined in IR 1986 r 13.7). Therefore this rule does apply to defects or irregularities in statutory demands.

2.908

7.56 Restriction on concurrent proceedings and remedies

Where in insolvency proceedings the court makes an order staying any action, execution or other legal process against the property of a company, or against the property or person of an individual debtor or bankrupt, service of the order may be effected by sending a sealed copy of the order to whatever is the address for service of the plaintiff or other party having the carriage of the proceedings to be stayed.

2.909

7.57 Affidavits

(1) Subject to the following paragraphs of this Rule the practice and procedure of the High Court with regard to affidavits, their form and contents and the procedure governing their use are to apply to all insolvency proceedings.

(2) Where, in insolvency proceedings, an affidavit is made by the official receiver or the responsible insolvency practitioner, the deponent shall state the capacity in which he makes it, the position which he holds, and the address at which he works.

(3) A creditor's affidavit of debt may be sworn before his own solicitor.

(4) The official receiver, any deputy official receiver, or any officer of the court duly authorised in that behalf, may take affidavits and declarations.

(5) Subject to paragraph (6), where the Rules provide for the use of an affidavit, a witness statement verified by a statement of truth may be used as an alternative.

(6) Paragraph (5) does not apply to Rules 3.4, 4.33, 6.60 (statement of affairs), 4.42, 6.66, 6.72 (further disclosure), 4.39, 4.40, 6.65; 6.70 (accounts), 4.73, 4.77, 6.96; 6.99 (claims) and 9.3, 9.4 (examinations).

(7) Where paragraph (5) applies any form prescribed by Rule 12.7 of these Rules shall be modified as necessary.

Notes

R 7.57(1)

See the notes to IR 1986 r 7.7 above. There is express provision in IA 1986 s 200 as to the swearing of affidavits both in the United Kingdom and overseas.

R 7.57(5)

Witness statements are now commonly used instead of affidavits; however note the exceptions in IR 1986 r 7.57(6).

2.910

7.58 Security in court

(1) Where security has to be given to the court (otherwise than in relation to costs), it may be given by guarantee, bond or the payment of money into court.

(2) A person proposing to give a bond as security shall give notice to the party in whose favour the security is required, and to the court, naming those who are to be sureties to the bond.

(3) The court shall forthwith give notice to both the parties concerned of a venue for the execution of the bond and the making of any objection to the sureties.

(4) The sureties shall make an affidavit of their sufficiency (unless dispensed with by the party in whose favour the security is required) and shall, if required by the court, attend the court to be cross-examined.

2.911

7.59 Payment into court

The CPR relating to payment into and out of court of money lodged in court as security for costs apply to money lodged in court under the Rules.

2.912

7.60 Further Information and Disclosure

(1) Any party to insolvency proceedings may apply to the court for an order—
    (a)   that any other party
        (i)   clarify any matter which is in dispute in the proceedings, or
        (ii) give additional information in relation to any such matter;
        in accordance with CPR Part 18 (further information); or
    (b)   to obtain disclosure from any other party in accordance with CPR Part 31 (disclosure and inspection of documents).

(2) An application under this Rule may be made without notice being served on any other party.

Notes

R 7.60

For examples of discovery being given in cases decided before the CPR see *Re Primlaks (UK) Ltd (No 2)* [1990] BCLC 234 (*creditor alleging company voluntary arrangement was unfairly prejudicial*) and *Re BCC SA (No 6)* [1991] BCLC 450 (*appeal against rejection of proof by liquidators*).

2.913

7.61 Office copies of documents

(1) Any person who has under the Rules the right to inspect the court file of insolvency proceedings may require the court to provide him with an office copy of any document from the file.

(2) A person's rights under this Rule may be exercised on his behalf by his solicitor.

(3) An office copy provided by the court under this Rule shall be in such form as the registrar thinks appropriate, and shall bear the court's seal.

Chapter 10
EC Regulation—Creditors' Voluntary Winding up—Confirmation by
the Court

2.914

7.62 Application for confirmation

(1) Where a company has passed a resolution for voluntary winding up, and no declaration under section 89 has been made, the liquidator may apply to court for an order confirming the creditors' voluntary winding up for the purposes of the EC Regulation.

(2) The application shall be in writing and verified by affidavit by the liquidator (using FORM 7.20 the same form) and shall state—
- (a) the name of the applicant,
- (b) the name of the company and its registered number,
- (c) the date on which the resolution for voluntary winding up was passed,
- (d) that the application is accompanied by all of the documents required under paragraph (3) which are true copies of the documents required, and
- (e) that the EC Regulation will apply to the company and whether the proceedings will be main proceedings, territorial proceedings or secondary proceedings.

(3) The liquidator shall file in court two copies of the application, together with one copy of the following—
- (a) a copy of the resolution for voluntary winding up referred to by section 84(3),
- (b) evidence of his appointment as liquidator of the company, and
- (c) a copy of the statement of affairs required under section 99.

(4) It shall not be necessary to serve the application on, or give notice of it to, any person.

(5) On an application under this Rule the court may confirm the creditors' voluntary winding up.

(6) If the court confirms the creditor's voluntary winding up—
- (a) it may do so without a hearing,
- (b) it shall affix its seal to the application.

(7) A member of the court staff may deal with an application under this Rule.

(8) This Rule shall also apply where a company has moved to a voluntary liquidation in accordance with paragraph 83 of Schedule B1 to the Act.

2.915

7.63 Notice to member State liquidator and creditors in member States

Where the court has confirmed the creditors' voluntary winding up, the liquidator shall forthwith give notice—
  (a)   if there is a member State liquidator in relation to the company, to the member State liquidator;
  (b)   in accordance with Article 40 of the EC Regulation (duty to inform creditors).

Notes

RR 7.62, 7.63

The EC Regulation on Insolvency Proceedings 2000 is directed primarily at insolvency proceedings conducted by the courts: Virgos-Schmit Report, para 52. However it was apparently considered appropriate for creditors' voluntary liquidation proceedings to be brought within the EC Regulation, provided they were subject to confirmation by the court. These provisions contain the machinery for such confirmation. No hearing is required, and somewhat surprisingly the matter can be dealt with by a member of the court staff. This confirmation will be required if the liquidator wished to take advantage of the EC Regulation, in order, for example, to have his authority recognised in another EC state. For an example of a case where the court refused to make an order without a hearing see, *Re TXU Europe German Finance BV* [2005] BCC 90.

[Chapter 11
EC Regulation—Member State Liquidator]

2.916

7.64 Interpretation of creditor

(1) This Rule applies where a member State liquidator has been appointed in relation to a person subject to insolvency proceedings.

(2) For the purposes of the Rules referred to in paragraph (3) a member State liquidator appointed in main proceedings is deemed to be a creditor.

(3) The Rules referred to in paragraph (2) are Rules 7.31(1) (right to inspect court file) and 7.53(1) (right of attendance).

(4) Paragraphs (2) and (3) are without prejudice to the generality of the right to participate referred to in paragraph 3 of Article 32 of the EC Regulation (exercise of creditor's rights).

Notes

R 7.64

This provision deals with the situation where insolvency proceedings are brought in another EC member state before or after proceedings in England; See IR 1986 r 13.13(11) for the definition of 'Member State liquidator'. Article 32 of the EC Regulation entitles the foreign liquidator to participate in the English proceedings on the same basis as a creditor. IR 1986 r 7.64 entitles the liquidator to inspect the court file and attend hearings. There are further rules dealing with the rights of a foreign liquidator in the various different types of English insolvency proceedings, i e administration (IR 1986 r 2.130 to 2.133); winding up (IR 1986 r 4.231); and bankruptcy (IR 1986 r 6.238 to 6.239).

Part 8
Proxies and Company Representation

2.917

8.1 Definition of 'proxy'

(1) For the purposes of the Rules, a proxy is an authority given by a person ('the principal') to another person ('the proxy-holder') to attend a meeting and speak and vote as his representative.

(2) Proxies are for use at creditors', company or contributories' meetings summoned or called under the Act or the Rules.

(3) Only one proxy may be given by a person for any one meeting at which he desires to be represented; and it may only be given to one person, being an individual aged 18 or over. But the principal may specify one or more other such individuals to be proxy-holder in the alternative, in the order in which they are named in the proxy.

(4) Without prejudice to the generality of paragraph (3), a proxy for a particular meeting may be given to whoever is to be the chairman of the meeting; and for a meeting held as part of the proceedings in a winding up by the court, or in a bankruptcy, it may be given to the official receiver.

(5) A person given a proxy under paragraph (4) cannot decline to be the proxy-holder in relation to that proxy.

(6) A proxy requires the holder to give the principal's vote on matters arising for determination at the meeting, or to abstain, or to propose, in the principal's name, a resolution to be voted on by the meeting, either as directed or in accordance with the holder's own discretion.

Notes

RR 8.1ff

These rules provide a comprehensive code for the use of proxies at creditors' meetings. A faxed proxy may be used at the meeting *IRC v Conbeer, Re a Debtor 2021 of 1995* [1996] 1 BCLC 538 and the proxy may be varied or revoked or replaced at any time prior to the meeting: *Re Cardona* [1997] BCC 697.

2.918

8.2 Issue and use of forms

(1) When notice is given of a meeting to be held in insolvency proceedings, and forms of proxy are sent out with the notice, no form so sent out shall have inserted in it the name or description of any person.

(2) No form of proxy shall be used at any meeting except that which is sent out with the notice summoning the meeting, or a substantially similar form.

(3) A form of proxy shall be signed by the principal, or by some person authorised by him (either generally or with reference to a particular meeting). If the form is signed by a person other than the principal, the nature of the person's authority shall be stated.

2.919

8.3 Use of proxies at meetings

(1) A proxy given for a particular meeting may be used at any adjournment of that meeting.

(2) Where the official receiver holds proxies for use at any meeting, his deputy, or any other official receiver, may act as proxy-holder in his place.

Alternatively, the official receiver may in writing authorise another officer of the Department to act for him at the meeting and use the proxies as if that other officer were himself proxy-holder.

(3) Where the responsible insolvency practitioner holds proxies to be used by him as chairman of a meeting, and some other person acts as chairman, the other person may use the insolvency practitioner's proxies as if he were himself proxy-holder.

(4) Where a proxy directs a proxy-holder to vote for or against a resolution for the nomination or appointment of a person as the responsible insolvency practitioner, the proxy-holder may, unless the proxy states otherwise, vote for or against (as he thinks fit) any resolution for the nomination or appointment of that person jointly with another or others.

(5) A proxy-holder may propose any resolution which, if proposed by another, would be a resolution in favour of which by virtue of the proxy he would be entitled to vote.

(6) Where a proxy gives specific directions as to voting, this does not, unless the proxy states otherwise, preclude the proxy-holder from voting at his discretion on resolutions put to the meeting which are not dealt with in the proxy.

2.920

8.4 Retention of proxies

(1) Subject as follows, proxies used for voting at any meeting shall be retained by the chairman of the meeting.

(2) The chairman shall deliver the proxies, forthwith after the meeting, to the responsible insolvency practitioner (where that is someone other than himself).

2.921

8.5 Right of inspection

(1) The responsible insolvency practitioner shall, so long as proxies lodged with him are in his hands, allow them to be inspected, at all reasonable times on any business day, by—

(a) the creditors, in the case of proxies used at a meeting of creditors, and

(b) a company's members or contributories, in the case of proxies used at a meeting of the company or of its contributories.

(2) The reference in paragraph (1) to creditors is—

(a) in the case of a company in liquidation or of an individual's bankruptcy, those creditors who have proved their debts, and

(b) in any other case, persons who have submitted in writing a claim to be creditors of the company or individual concerned;

but in neither case does it include a person whose proof or claim has been wholly rejected for purposes of voting, dividend or otherwise.

(3) The right of inspection given by this Rule is also exercisable—

(a) in the case of an insolvent company, by its directors, and

(b) in the case of an insolvent individual, by him.

(4) Any person attending a meeting in insolvency proceedings is entitled, immediately before or in the course of the meeting, to inspect proxies and associated documents (including proofs) sent or given, in accordance with directions contained in any notice convening the meeting, to the chairman of that meeting or to any other person by a creditor, member or contributory for the purpose of that meeting.

2.922

8.6 Proxy-holder with financial interest

(1) A proxy-holder shall not vote in favour of any resolution which would directly or indirectly place him, or any associate of his, in a position to receive any remuneration out of the insolvent estate, unless the proxy specifically directs him to vote in that way.

(1A) Where a proxy-holder has signed the proxy as being authorised to do so by his principal and the proxy specifically directs him to vote in the way mentioned in paragraph (1), he shall nevertheless not vote in that way unless he produces to the chairman of the meeting written authorisation from his principal sufficient to show that the proxy-holder was entitled so to sign the proxy.

(2) This Rule applies also to any person acting as chairman of a meeting and using proxies in that capacity under Rule 8.3; and in its application to him, the proxy-holder is deemed an associate of his.

2.923

8.7 Company representation

(1) Where a person is authorised under section 375 of the Companies Act to represent a corporation at a meeting of creditors or of the company or its contributories, he shall produce to the chairman of the meeting a copy of the resolution from which he derives his authority.

(2) The copy resolution must be under the seal of the corporation, or certified by the secretary or a director of the corporation to be a true copy.

(3) Nothing in this Rule requires the authority of a person to sign a proxy on behalf of a principal which is a corporation to be in the form of a resolution of that corporation.

2.924

8.8 Interpretation of creditor

(1) This Rule applies where a member State liquidator has been appointed in relation to a person subject to insolvency proceedings.

(2) For the purposes of rule 8.5(1) (right of inspection of proxies) a member State liquidator appointed in main proceedings is deemed to be a creditor.

(3) Paragraph (2) is without prejudice to the generality of the right to participate referred to in paragraph 3 of Article 32 of the EC Regulation (exercise of creditor's rights).

Part 9
Examination of Persons Concerned in Company and Individual Insolvency

2.925

9.1 Preliminary

(1) The Rules in this Part relate to applications to the court for an order under—
- (a) section 236 (inquiry into company's dealings when it is, or is alleged to be, insolvent), or
- (b) section 366 (inquiry in bankruptcy, with respect to the bankrupt's dealings).

(2) The following definitions apply—
- (a) the person in respect of whom an order is applied for is 'the respondent';
- (b) 'the applicable section' is section 236 or section 366, according to whether the affairs of a company or those of a bankrupt or (where the application under section 366 is made by virtue of section 368) a debtor are in question;
- (c) the company or, as the case may be, the bankrupt or debtor concerned is 'the insolvent'.

Notes

R 9.1

Under IA 1986 s 236 the relevant office-holder may apply to the court for an order summoning any officer of the company, any person known or suspected to have in his possession property of the company or supposed to be indebted to the company, or any person thought to be capable of giving information concerning the dealings of the company. Similarly, under IA 1986 s 366 a trustee may apply for equivalent relief in respect of a bankrupt's estate. Reference should be made to the notes under both those provisions. IR 1986 r 9.1 to 9.6 set out the detailed procedure in relation to such applications.

2.926

9.2 Form and contents of application

(1) The application shall be in writing, and be accompanied by a brief statement of the grounds on which it is made.

(2) The respondent must be sufficiently identified in the application.

(3) It shall be stated whether the application is for the respondent—
- (a)   to be ordered to appear before the court, or
- (b)   to be ordered to clarify any matter which is in dispute in the proceedings or to give additional information in relation to any such matter and if so CPR Part 18 (further information) shall apply to any such order, or
- (c)   to submit affidavits (if so, particulars to be given of the matters to which he is required to swear), or
- (d)   to produce books, papers or other records (if so, the items in question to be specified),

or for any two or more of those purposes.

(4) The application may be made *ex parte*.

Notes

R 9.2(1)

The previous practice was to put a 'confidential' statement before the court (*Re Murjani* [1996] 1 WLR 1498, *Re Aveling Barford Ltd* [1989] 1 WLR 360). However the better practice is not to make the statement 'confidential' as this runs the risk of being challenged on human rights grounds as offending the 'equality of arms' principle enshrined in the right to a fair trial (art 6(1) European Convention on Human Rights). Before making an application for an order for a private examination it is worth considering whether an 'informal' examination by the office holder assisted by legal advisers would achieve the same or a more productive result as a court ordered private examination; such a request could be made under IA 1986 s 235, s 363(2), s 312. If an informal examination is held then the person to be interviewed should be allowed legal representation and the interview should be recorded and the record signed by the interviewee.

R 9.2(3)

The powers of the court under IA 1986 s 236, s 366 are wide and accordingly the office-holder must clarify the precise purpose of the application (ie whether to appear for private examination, submit an affidavit or produce documents etc). Insufficient particularly may leave the application open to challenge: *Re Aveling Barford Ltd* [1989] 1 WLR 360.

R 9.2(4)

Although it is clear that the application may be made without notice, in general it should be made on notice: *Re Murjani (a bankrupt)* [1996] 1 WLR 1498.

2.927

9.3 Order for examination, etc

(1) The court may, whatever the purpose of the application, make any order which it has power to make under the applicable section.

(2) The court, if it orders the respondent to appear before it, shall specify a venue for his appearance, which shall be not less than 14 days from the date of the order.

(3) If he is ordered to submit affidavits, the order shall specify—
    (a)   the matters which are to be dealt with in his affidavits, and
    (b)   the time within which they are to be submitted to the court.

(4) If the order is to produce books, papers or other records, the time and manner of compliance shall be specified.

(5) The order must be served forthwith on the respondent; and it must be served personally, unless the court otherwise orders.

Notes

R 9.3(2)

Where the court orders a person to appear before the examination is a private examination (as opposed to a public examination under IA 1986 s 133, s 290). 'Venue' is defined in IR 1986 r 13.6.

2.928

9.4 Procedure for examination

(1) At any examination of the respondent, the applicant may attend in person, or be represented by a solicitor with or without counsel, and may put such questions to the respondent as the court may allow.

(2) Any other person who could have applied for an order under the applicable section in respect of the insolvent's affairs may, with the leave of the court and if the applicant does not object, attend the examination and put questions to the respondent (but only through the applicant).

(3) If the respondent is ordered to clarify any matter or to give additional information, the court shall direct him as to the questions which he is required to answer, and as to whether his answers (if any) are to be made on affidavit.

(4) Where application has been made under the applicable section on information provided by a creditor of the insolvent, that creditor may, with the leave of the court and if the applicant does not object, attend the examination and put questions to the respondent (but only through the applicant).

(5) The respondent may at his own expense employ a solicitor with or without counsel, who may put to him such questions as the court may allow for the purpose of enabling him to explain or qualify any answers given by him, and may make representations on his behalf.

(6) There shall be made in writing such record of the examination as the court thinks proper. The record shall be read over either to or by the respondent and signed by him at a venue fixed by the court.

> (7) The written record may, in any proceedings (whether under the Act
> or otherwise) be used as evidence against the respondent of any statement
> made by him in the course of his examination.

Notes

R 9.4(5)

Though the court will not allow a general 're-examination' the respondent's advisers may in practice take an active part in the private examination.

R 9.4(6)

It is the responsibility of the office holder to arrange for a stenographer to be present.

2.929

9.5 Record of examination

(1) Unless the court otherwise directs, the written record of the respondent's examination, and any answer given by him to interrogatories, and any affidavits submitted by him in compliance with an order of the court under the applicable section, shall not be filed in court.

(2) The written record, answers and affidavits shall not be open to inspection, without an order of the court, by any person other than—
    (a)   the applicant for an order under the applicable section, or
    (b)   any person who could have applied for such an order in respect of the affairs of the same insolvent.

(3) Paragraph (2) applies also to so much of the court file as shows the grounds of the application for an order under the applicable section and to any copy of proposed interrogatories.

(4) The court may from time to time give directions as to the custody and inspection of any documents to which this Rule applies, and as to the furnishing of copies of, or extracts from, such documents.

Notes

R 9.5(1)

Under the previous practice, the record of the private examination was kept on the court file and was only protected from public inspection in the event of the court making a 'stop order.' Under the current practice, the position is effectively reversed.

R 9.5(3), (4)

For obvious reasons, the restrictions apply not only to the record of the examination itself but also to the documents filed in support of the application: *Re Arrows Ltd (No 4), Hamilton v Naviede* [1995] 2 AC 75.

> **2.930**
>
> ### 9.6 Costs of proceedings under ss 236, 366
>
> (1) Where the court has ordered an examination of any person under the applicable section, and it appears to it that the examination was made necessary because information had been unjustifiably refused by the respondent, it may order that the costs of the examination be paid by him.
>
> (2) Where the court makes an order against a person under—
>
>   (a)   section 237(1) or 367(1) (to deliver up property in his possession which belongs to the insolvent), or
>
>   (b)   section 237(2) or 367(2) (to pay any amount in discharge of a debt due to the insolvent),
>
> the costs of the application for the order may be ordered by the court to be paid by the respondent.
>
> (3) Subject to paragraphs (1) and (2) above, the applicant's costs shall, unless the court otherwise orders, be paid out of the insolvent estate.
>
> (4) A person summoned to attend for examination under this Chapter shall be tendered a reasonable sum in respect of travelling expenses incurred in connection with his attendance. Other costs falling on him are at the court's discretion.
>
> (5) Where the examination is on the application of the official receiver otherwise than in the capacity of liquidator or trustee, no order shall be made for the payment of costs by him.

Notes

R 9.6(1), (2)

As an exception to the general rule (IR 1986 r 9.6(3)) in appropriate circumstances the court may order costs to be borne by the respondent to the application.

R 9.6(3)

In general, the costs of the office-holder's application are to be paid by the insolvent company or from the bankrupt's estate, as the case may be.

R 9.6(4)

Witnesses attending for examination must be offered a reasonable sum in respect of travelling expenses and may be awarded further costs in the court's discretion, although there is no presumption that such further costs should be awarded: *Re Aveling Barford Ltd* [1989] 1 WLR 360. In addition, it would appear that the jurisdiction to award such costs under this provision is not limited to persons summoned to attend for examination but may also apply to those required to provide information by the other methods provided by IA 1986 s 236 (ie submitting an affidavit, producing documents etc): *Re Aveling Barford Ltd (above)*.

Part 10
Official Receivers

2.931

10.1 Appointment of official receivers

Judicial notice shall be taken of the appointment under sections 399 to 401 of official receivers and deputy official receivers.

Notes

R 10.1

Each person holding the office of official receiver is attached by the Secretary of State from time to time either to the High Court or to a county court having bankruptcy jurisdiction IA s 399(3); and see IR 1986 Sch 2 for a list of alternative courts for a debtor's petition for bankruptcy. Subject to directions by the Secretary of State an official receiver attached to a particular court is the person authorised to act as the official receiver in relation to every bankruptcy or winding up falling within the jurisidiction of that court. It is doubtful whether a successful 'human rights' challenge could be made by a bankrupt under art 6(1) European Convention on Human Rights against an official receiver on the basis that the bankrupt could not have a fair trial because the official receiver is 'attached' to the relevant court in which proceedings are being brought by the official receiver.

2.932

10.2 Persons entitled to act on official receiver's behalf

(1) In the absence of the official receiver authorised to act in a particular case, an officer authorised in writing for the purpose by the Secretary of State, or by the official receiver himself, may, with the leave of the court, act on the official receiver's behalf and in his place—

    (a)   in any examination under section 133, 236, 290 or 366, and

    (b)   in respect of any application to the court.

(2) In case of emergency, where there is no official receiver capable of acting, anything to be done by, to or before the official receiver may be done by, to or before the registrar of the court.

Notes

R 10.2

It is the Department of Trade and Industry that has overall responsibility for the administration of insolvency in England and Wales. Within the Department the relevant work is undertaken by the Insolvency Service. The Insolvency Service is presided over by the Inspector General who has a supervisory responsibility over all official receivers and qualified insolvency practitioners. The headquarters of the Insolvency Service is 21 Bloomsbury Street London WC1B 3QW. The addresses of the various offices of the official receivers are given in the '*Guide to the Insolvency Services*' obtainable on the Insolvency Service website (www.insolvency.gov.uk).

2.933

10.3 Application for directions

The official receiver may apply to the court for directions in relation to any matter arising in insolvency proceedings.

Notes

R 10.3

'Insolvency proceedings' are defined in IR 1986 r 13.7 as any proceedings under IA 1986 or IR 1986. In carrying out his duties the official receiver is performing a public law function and is not susceptible to control by the court (*Hardy v Focus Insurance Co Ltd* [1997] BPIR 77). As holder of a statutory office the official receiver is empowered to bring proceedings in his own name and is accorded by law a right of audience before the court to which he or she is attached *Re Minotaur Data Systems Ltd* [1999] 2 BCLC 766.

2.934

10.4 Official receiver's expenses

(1) Any expenses incurred by the official receiver (in whatever capacity he may be acting) in connection with proceedings taken against him in insolvency proceedings are to be treated as expenses of the insolvency proceedings.

'Expenses' includes damages.

(2) In respect of any sums due to him under paragraph (1), the official receiver has a charge on the insolvent estate.

Notes

R 10.4

When bringing proceedings the official receiver is entitled to have his costs assessed as a litigant in person and the fact that he or she is salaried does not result in his costs being limited to disbursements *Re Minotaur Data Systems Ltd* [1999] 2 BCLC 766. Provided that the official receiver is acting in the course of the bankruptcy proceedings and within the scope of his powers and duties he has immunity from suit in respect of his actions and any statements that are relied upon by others *Mond v Hyde* [1999] QB 1097.

R 10.1

The Department of Trade and Industry has overall responsibility for the administration of insolvency in England and Wales. Within the Department the relevant work is undertaken by the Insolvency Service. The Insolvency Service is presided over by the Inspector General who has a supervisory responsibility over all official receivers and qualified insolvency practitioners. The headquarters of the Insolvency Service is 21 Bloomsbury Street London WC1B 3QW. The addresses of the various offices of the official receivers are given in the '*Guide to the Insolvency Services*' obtainable on the Insolvency Service website (www.insolvency.gov.uk).

R 10.3

An official receiver is an officer of the court IA 1986 s 400(2). Further under IA 1986 s 399(3) each official receiver is 'attached' to a High Court or county court. The attachment is purely administrative and it is unlikely that a claim or application brought by an official receiver in the court to which he is attached would give rise to any successful challenge under Human Rights Act 1998 Article 6 (right to a fair trial) on the basis that the court is not independent.

R 10.4(1)

Insolvency proceedings are widely defined under IR 1986 r 13.7. All fees, costs charges and other expenses incurred in the course of winding up or bankruptcy proceedings (IR 1986 r 12.2) are expenses of the winding up or bankruptcy as the case may be. It is to be noted that 'expenses' includes damages.

Part 11
Declaration and Payment of Dividend (Winding Up and Bankruptcy)

2.935

11.1 Preliminary

(1) The Rules in this Part relate to the declaration and payment of dividends in companies winding up and in bankruptcy.

(2) The following definitions apply—

    (a)   'the insolvent' means the company in liquidation or, as the case may be, the bankrupt; and

    (b)   'creditors' means those creditors of the insolvent of whom the responsible insolvency practitioner is aware, or who are identified in the insolvent's statement of affairs.

(3) For the purposes of this Part, a member State liquidator appointed in relation to an insolvent is deemed to be a creditor.

2.936

11.2 Notice of intended dividend

(1) Before declaring a dividend, the responsible insolvency practitioner shall give notice of his intention to do so

    (a)   to all creditors whose addresses are known to him and who have not proved their debts, and

    (b)   where a member State liquidator has been appointed in relation to the insolvent, to that person

(1A) Before declaring a first dividend, the responsible insolvency practitioner shall, unless he has previously by public advertisement invited creditors to prove their debts, give notice of the intended dividend by public advertisement.

(2) Any notice under paragraph (1) and any notice of a first dividend under paragraph (1A) shall specify a date ('the last date for proving') up to which proofs may be lodged. The date shall be the same for all creditors, and not less than 21 days from that of the notice.

(3) The insolvency practitioner shall in the notice state his intention to declare a dividend (specified as interim or final, as the case may be) within the period of 4 months from the last date for proving.

2.937

11.3 Final admission/rejection of proofs

(1) The responsible insolvency practitioner shall, within 7 days from the last date for proving, deal with every creditor's proof (in so far as not already dealt with) by admitting or rejecting it in whole or in part, or by making such provision as he thinks fit in respect of it.

(2) The insolvency practitioner is not obliged to deal with proofs lodged after the last date for proving; but he may do so, if he thinks fit.

(3) In the declaration of a dividend no payment shall be made more than once by virtue of the same debt.

(4) Subject to Rule 11.11, where—
    (a)   a creditor has proved, and
    (b)   a member State liquidator has proved in relation to the same debt,
payment shall only be made to the creditor.

2.938

11.4 Postponement or cancellation of dividend

If in the period of 4 months referred to in Rule 11.2(3)—
    (a)   the responsible insolvency practitioner has rejected a proof in whole or in part and application is made to the court for his decision to be reversed or varied, or
    (b)   application is made to the court for the insolvency practitioner's decision on a proof to be reversed or varied, or for a proof to be expunged, or for a reduction of the amount claimed,
the insolvency practitioner may postpone or cancel the dividend.

2.939

11.5 Decision to declare dividend

(1) If the responsible insolvency practitioner has not, in the 4–month period referred to in Rule 11.2(3), had cause to postpone or cancel the dividend, he shall within that period proceed to declare the dividend of which he gave notice under that Rule.

(2) Except with the leave of the court, the insolvency practitioner shall not declare the dividend so long as there is pending any application to the court to reverse or vary a decision of his on a proof, or to expunge a proof or to reduce the amount claimed.

If the court gives leave under this paragraph, the insolvency practitioner shall make such provision in respect of the proof in question as the court directs.

2.940

11.6 Notice of declaration

(1) The responsible insolvency practitioner shall give notice of the dividend to
    (a)   all creditors who have proved their debts, and

    (b)   where a member State liquidator has been appointed in relation to the insolvent, to that person.

(2) The notice shall include the following particulars relating to the insolvency and the administration of the insolvent estate–
- (a) amounts realised from the sale of assets, indicating (so far as practicable) amounts raised by the sale of particular assets;
- (b) payments made by the insolvency practitioner in the administration of the insolvent estate;
- (c) provision (if any) made for unsettled claims, and funds (if any) retained for particular purposes;
- (d) the total amount to be distributed, and the rate of dividend;
- (e) whether, and if so when, any further dividend is expected to be declared.

(3) The dividend may be distributed simultaneously with the notice declaring it.

(4) Payment of dividend may be made by post, or arrangements may be made with any creditor for it to be paid to him in another way, or held for his collection.

(5) Where a dividend is paid on a bill of exchange or other negotiable instrument, the amount of the dividend shall be endorsed on the instrument, or on a certified copy of it, if required to be produced by the holder for that purpose.

2.941

11.7 Notice of no, or no further, dividend

If the responsible insolvency practitioner gives notice to creditors that he is unable to declare any dividend or (as the case may be) any further dividend, the notice shall contain a statement to the effect either—
- (a) that no funds have been realised, or
- (b) that the funds realised have already been distributed or used or allocated for defraying the expenses of administration.

2.942

11.8 Proof altered after payment of dividend

(1) If after payment of dividend the amount claimed by a creditor in his proof is increased, the creditor is not entitled to disturb the distribution of the dividend; but he is entitled to be paid, out of any money for the time being available for the payment of any further dividend, any dividend or dividends which he has failed to receive.

(2) Any dividend or dividends payable under paragraph (1) shall be paid before the money there referred to is applied to the payment of any such further dividend.

(3) If, after a creditor's proof has been admitted, the proof is withdrawn or expunged, or the amount of it is reduced, the creditor is liable to repay to the responsible insolvency practitioner, for the credit of the insolvent estate, any amount overpaid by way of dividend.

2.943

11.9 Secured creditors

(1) The following applies where a creditor re-values his security at a time when a dividend has been declared.

(2) If the revaluation results in a reduction of his unsecured claim ranking for dividend, the creditor shall forthwith repay to the responsible insolvency practitioner, for the credit of the insolvent estate, any amount received by him as dividend in excess of that to which he would be entitled having regard to the revaluation of the security.

(3) If the revaluation results in an increase of his unsecured claim, the creditor is entitled to receive from the insolvency practitioner, out of any money for the time being available for the payment of a further dividend, before any such further dividend is paid, any dividend or dividends which he has failed to receive, having regard to the revaluation of the security.

However, the creditor is not entitled to disturb any dividend declared (whether or not distributed) before the date of the revaluation.

2.944

11.10 Disqualification from dividend

If a creditor contravenes any provision of the Act or the Rules relating to the valuation of securities, the court may, on the application of the responsible insolvency practitioner, order that the creditor be wholly or partly disqualified from participation in any dividend.

2.945

11.11 Assignment of right to dividend

(1) If a person entitled to a dividend gives notice to the responsible insolvency practitioner that he wishes the dividend to be paid to another person, or that he has assigned his entitlement to another person, the insolvency practitioner shall pay the dividend to that other accordingly.

(2) A notice given under this Rule must specify the name and address of the person to whom payment is to be made.

2.946

11.12 Preferential creditors

(1) Subject as follows, the Rules in this Part apply with respect to any distribution made in the insolvency to preferential creditors, with such adaptations as are appropriate considering that such creditors are of a limited class

(2) The notice by the responsible insolvency practitioner under Rule 11.2, where a dividend is to be declared for preferential creditors, need only be given to those creditors in whose case he has reason to believe that their debts are preferential [and public advertisement of the intended dividend need only be given if the insolvency practitioner thinks fit].

2.947

11.13 Debt payable at future time

(1) Where a creditor has proved for a debt of which payment is not due at the date of the declaration of dividend, he is entitled to dividend equally with other creditors, but subject as follows.

(2) For the purpose of dividend (and no other purpose) the amount of the creditor's admitted proof (or, if a distribution has previously been made to him, the amount remaining outstanding in respect of his admitted proof) shall be reduced by applying the following formula—

$X / 1.05n$
where—
  (a) 'X' is the value of the admitted proof; and
  (b) 'n' is the period beginning with the relevant date and ending with the date on which the payment of the creditor's debt would otherwise be due expressed in years and months in a decimalised form.

(3) In paragraph (2) 'relevant date' means—
  (a) in the case of a winding up which was not immediately preceded by an administration, the date that the company went into liquidation;
  (b) in the case of a winding up which was immediately preceded by an administration, the date that the company entered administration; and
  (c) in the case of a bankruptcy, the date of the bankruptcy order.

Notes

R 11.13

This provision was amended by Insolvency (Amendment) Rules 2005 with effect from 1st April 2005 and subject to transitional provisions in relation to any case where a company has entered administration or gone into liquidation, or a bankruptcy order has been made before that date: see Insolvency (Amendment) Rules 2005 SI 2005/527, r 1(2). Under the former rule where a creditor had proved in respect of a debt which was payable at a future time and had his debt discounted in accordance with IR 1986 r 11.13 then he was entitled to be paid his debt in full before any other creditor was entitled to interest. The drafting of the former rule was described as 'seriously defective' by the House of Lords in *Re Park Air Services Ltd, Christopher Moran Holdings v Bairstow* [2000] 2 AC 172.

Part 12
Miscellaneous and General

2.948

12.1 Power of Secretary of State to regulate certain matters

(1) Pursuant to paragraph 27 of Schedule 8 to the Act, and paragraph 30 of Schedule 9 to the Act, the Secretary of State may, subject to the Act and the Rules, make regulations with respect to any matter provided for in the Rules as relates to the carrying out of the functions of a liquidator,

provisional liquidator, administrator or administrative receiver of a company, an interim receiver appointed under section 286, of the official receiver while acting as receiver or manager under section 287 or of a trustee of a bankrupt's estate, including, without prejudice to the generality of the foregoing, provision with respect to the following matters arising in companies winding up and individual bankruptcy—

(a) the preparation and keeping by liquidators, trustees, provisional liquidators, interim receivers and the official receiver, of books, accounts and other records, and their production to such persons as may be authorised or required to inspect them;

(b) the auditing of liquidators' and trustees' accounts;

(c) the manner in which liquidators and trustees are to act in relation to the insolvent company's or bankrupt's books, papers and other records, and the manner of their disposal by the responsible insolvency practitioner or others;

(d) the supply—

   (i) in company insolvency, by the liquidator to creditors and members of the company, contributories in its winding up and the liquidation committee, and

   (ii) in individual insolvency, by the trustee to creditors and the creditors' committee,

of copies of documents relating to the insolvency and the affairs of the insolvent company or individual (on payment, in such cases as may be specified by the regulations, of the specified fee);

(e) the manner in which insolvent estates are to be distributed by liquidators and trustees, including provision with respect to unclaimed funds and dividends;

(f) the manner in which moneys coming into the hands of a liquidator or trustee in the course of his administration are to be handled and ... invested, and the payment of interest on sums which, in pursuance of regulations made by virtue of this sub-paragraph, have been paid into the Insolvency Services Account;

(g) the amount (or the manner of determining the amount) to be paid to the official receiver by way of remuneration when acting as provisional liquidator, liquidator, interim receiver or trustee.

(2) Any reference in paragraph (1) to a trustee includes a reference to the official receiver when acting as receiver and manager under section 287.

(3) Regulations made pursuant to paragraph (1) may—

(a) confer a discretion on the court;

(b) make non-compliance with any of the regulations a criminal offence;

(c) make different provision for different cases, including different provision for different areas[; and

(d) contain such incidental, supplemental and transitional provisions as may appear to the Secretary of State necessary or expedient].

2.949

12.2 Costs, expenses, etc

(1) All fees, costs, charges and other expenses incurred in the course of winding up, administration] or bankruptcy proceedings are to be regarded as expenses of the winding up or the administration or, as the case may be, of the bankruptcy.

(2) The costs associated with the prescribed part shall be paid out of the prescribed part.

2.950

12.3 Provable debts

(1) Subject as follows, in administration, winding up and bankruptcy, all claims by creditors are provable as debts against the company or, as the case may be, the bankrupt, whether they are present or future, certain or contingent, ascertained or sounding only in damages.

(2) The following are not provable—

    (a)   in bankruptcy, any fine imposed for an offence, and any obligation (other than an obligation to pay a lump sum or to pay costs) arising under an order made in family proceedings or any obligation arising under a maintenance assessment made under the Child Support Act 1991;

    (b)   in administration, winding up or bankruptcy, any obligation arising under a confiscation order made under section 1 of the Drug Trafficking Offences Act 1986 or section 1 of the Criminal Justice (Scotland) Act 1987 or section 71 of the Criminal Justice Act 1988 or under Parts 2, 3 or 4 of the Proceeds of Crime Act 2002.

'Fine' <...> and 'family proceedings' have the meanings given by section 281(8) of the Act (which applies the Magistrates' Courts Act 1980 and the Matrimonial and Family Proceedings Act 1984.)

(2A) The following are not provable except at a time when all other claims of creditors in the insolvency proceedings (other than any of a kind mentioned in this paragraph) have been paid in full with interest under section 189(2), Rule 2.88 or, as the case may be, section 328(4)—

    (a)   in an administration, a winding up or a bankruptcy, any claim arising by virtue of section 382(1)(a) of the Financial Services and Markets Act 2000, not being a claim also arising by virtue of section 382(1)(b) of that Act;

    (c)   in an administration or a winding up, any claim which by virtue of the Act or any other enactment is a claim the payment of which in a bankruptcy, an administration or a winding up is to be postponed.

(3) Nothing in this Rule prejudices any enactment or rule of law under which a particular kind of debt is not provable, whether on grounds of public policy or otherwise.

Notes

Introduction

This rule is based on the provisions of CA 1948 s 316 and describes, for administration, winding up and bankruptcy, what claims are provable. It must be read together with the provisions of IA 1986 s 382 (bankruptcy) and the equivalent provisions for winding up contained in IR 1986 r 13.12.

For the purposes of proof, claims by creditors are defined in the widest possible terms. This is consistent with the 'basic principle of the law of insolvency that every debt or liability capable of being expressed in money terms should be eligible for proof in the insolvency proceedings, so that the insolvency administration should deal comprehensively with, and in one way oranother discharge, all such debts and liabilities': see paragraph 1289 of the Final Report of the Insolvency Law Review Committee, 'Insolvency Law and Practice', Cmnd 8558; Goode, Principles of Corporate Insolvency Law', 3rd Ed (2005) at paragraph 12–13.

This inclusionary principle can clearly be seen from the successive amendments which were made to the bankruptcy and companies legislation in the nineteenth century and in judicial observations on those amendments: see *Re Hide, ex p Llynvi Coal and Iron Co* (1871) 7 Ch App 28 at 31; *Re Sneezum* (1876) 3 Ch D 463 at 472, *Morgan v Hardy* (1887) QBD 646 at 653–657, *Hardy v Fothergill* (1883) 13 App Cas 351 at 355, *Flint v Barnard* (1882) 22 QBD 90 at 92, *Re Law Car & General Insurance Corp* [1913] 2 Ch 103 at 120–121.

The principle is particularly important in company winding up. The final objective of any winding up is the dissolution of the company. A creditor excluded from proof in a winding up is effectively denied recourse against the company. By contrast, the purpose of bankruptcy is the rehabilitation of the debtor. To the extent that a claim against a bankrupt is not provable, the bankrupt remains liable.

For a detailed consideration of these points, and IA 1986 s 382 and IR 1986 r 12.3 and 13.12, see *Re T&N Limited* [2006] BPIR 532.

Provable Claims

IA 1986 r 12.3 defines claims which are prima facie provable in an insolvency. However, r 12.3 claims may nevertheless not be provable if they do not also satisfy the requirements of IA 1986 s 382 or IR 1986 r 13.12. Thus, future tort claims (claims in tort where the wrongful act or omission has occurred, but no material damage has been suffered and therefore no cause of action has accrued) are contingent claims within r 12.3, but are excluded from proof by IA 1986 s 382(2) and IR 1986 r 13.12(2): see *Re T&N Limited* (see above). Note that IA 1986 r 13.12 has now been amended to permit such claims to be proved in a winding up.

Re T&N Limited (see above) contains an extensive consideration of the meaning of contingent liabilities for the purposes of proof. It was held that future tort claimants (as described above) were contingent creditors for the purposes of IR 1986 r 12.3, and creditors for the purposes of schemes of arrangement and CVAs. Contrast, however, *R on the application of Steele v Birmingham City Council* [2005] EWCA Civ 1824, where Arden LJ adopted a different approach to the meaning of contingent creditor for the purposes of IR r 12.3 and IA s 382. It is arguable that her approach is itself inconsistent with the decision of the House of Lords in *Secretary of State for Trade and Industry v Frid* [2004] 2 AC 506, a case which David Richards J (In *Re T&N Limited* (see above)) relied on. Further, Arden LJ made it clear that her approach was confined to the meaning of the term contingent creditor for the purposes of proof and locus to petition for a winding up order. It does not undermine, therefore, David Richards J's approach so far as schemes of arrangement and CVAs are concerned. Sir Martin Nourse's judgment in *Steele* is consistent with that of David Richards J. The third member of the Court of Appeal, May LJ, simply gave a short judgment agreeing with the other two. *In Re T&N Ltd* [2006] EWHC 1447 (Ch) David Richards J confirmed his earlier decision after considering *Steele*.

Claims Excluded from Proof

The most significant debts which are *not* provable (in bankruptcy) are fines and orders in family proceedings; see also the notes to IA 1986 s 283 in relation to student loans. The latter includes costs orders in such proceedings: see *Levy v Legal Services Commission* [2000] BPIR 1065, *Wehmeyer v Wehmeyer* [2001] BPIR 548; but to be a non provable debt the order must be made in 'family proceedings' *Cadwell v Jackson* [2001] BPIR 966. The words '(other than an obligation to pay a lump sum or to pay costs)' and 'any obligation arising' were inserted by Insolvency (Amendment) Rules SI 2005/527, r 44. as from 1 April 2005; for transitional provisions in relation to any case where a company has entered administration or gone into liquidation, or a bankruptcy order has been made before that date see r 3(1) thereof IR 1986 r 12.3(2)(a) was held not be ultra vires in *Woodley v Woodley (No 2)* [1994] 1 WLR 1167.

IR 1986 r 12.3(3) preserves various public policy rules whereby certain debts are not provable. There is such a rule with respect to foreign tax claims (*Government of India v Taylor* [1955] AC 491), though this has now been abrogated in EC cases by Article 39 of the EC Insolvency Regulation; and in relation to debts which are unenforceable in the United Kingdom (*Cartwright v Cartwright* [2002] BPIR 895 (*foreign matrimonial periodic payment order subject to variation by foreign court*). This provision is most commonly encountered in the case of statute barred debts (*Cotterell v Price* [1960] 1 WLR 1097). In the case of a provable debt time ceases to run after the making of the bankruptcy order but not in respect of taking remedies outside the bankruptcy proceedings (*Anglo Manx Group Ltd v Aitken* [2002] BPIR 215); however time continues to run in respect of a debt owed to the bankrupt *Re Mansel* (1892) 9 Morr 198.

A further instance of a rule of law preventing the lodging of a proof concerns the rule against 'double proof'. A creditor may not prove in respect of every claim which he has against a debtor if by doing so he submits more than one proof in respect of the same debt or liability. The reason for this is that a debtor ought not to pay two dividends in respect of the same debt (*Re Oriental Commercial Bank* (1871) 7 Ch App 99, 103 per Mellish LJ). A surety will have a contingent claim against an insolvent principal debtor in the event that the surety pays the debt to the creditor, but the surety may not make that claim until the debt is paid in full. Therefore the surety may not prove in the debtor's bankruptcy or liquidation in any way which is in competition with the creditor but where the surety has guaranteed part only of a debt he may prove once he has paid that part in full *Re Sass* [1896] 2 QB 12, *Barclays Bank v TSOG Fund Ltd* [1984] AC 626. A useful analysis of the rule against double proof is contained in *Re Polly Peck International plc* [1996] BCC 486.

2.951

12.4 Notices

(1) All notices required or authorised by or under the Act or the Rules to be given must be in writing, unless it is otherwise provided, or the court allows the notice to be given in some other way.

(2) Where in any proceedings a notice is required to be sent or given by the official receiver or by the responsible insolvency practitioner, the sending or giving of it may be proved by means of a certificate—

    (a)   in the case of the official receiver, by him or a member of his staff, and

    (b)   in the case of the insolvency practitioner, by him, or his solicitor, or a partner or an employee of either of them,

that the notice was duly posted.

(3) In the case of a notice to be sent or given by a person other than the official receiver or insolvency practitioner, the sending or giving of it may be proved by means of a certificate by that person that he posted the notice, or instructed another person (naming him) to do so.

(4) A certificate under this Rule may be endorsed on a copy or specimen of the notice to which it relates.

Notes

R 12.4(1)

Although an administrator's notice of appointment must be sent by post (*Re Sporting Options plc* [2005] BCC 88) the court will allow copies of proposals and progress reports to be sent by email or be made available on a web site in appropriate cases under this provision.

2.952

12.4A Quorum at meeting of creditors or contributories

(1) Any meeting of creditors or contributories in insolvency proceedings is competent to act if a quorum is present.

(2) Subject to the next paragraph, a quorum is—
- (a) in the case of a creditors' meeting, at least one creditor entitled to vote;
- (b) in the case of a meeting of contributories, at least 2 contributories so entitled, or all the contributories, if their number does not exceed 2.

(3) For the purposes of this Rule, the reference to the creditor or contributories necessary to constitute a quorum is to those persons present or represented by proxy by any person (including the chairman) and in the case of any proceedings under Parts I–VII of the Act includes persons duly represented under section 375 of the Companies Act.

(4) Where at any meeting of creditors or contributories—
- (a) the provisions of this Rule as to a quorum being present are satisfied by the attendance of—
  - (i) the chairman alone, or
  - (ii) one other person in addition to the chairman, and
- (b) the chairman is aware, by virtue of proofs and proxies received or otherwise, that one or more additional persons would, if attending, be entitled to vote,

the meeting shall not commence until at least the expiry of 15 minutes after the time appointed for its commencement.

2.953

12.5 Evidence of proceedings at meetings

(1) A minute of proceedings at a meeting (held under the Act or the Rules) of a person's creditors, or of the members of a company, or of the contributories in a company's liquidation, signed by a person describing himself as, or appearing to be, the chairman of that meeting is admissible in insolvency proceedings without further proof.

(2) The minute is prima facie evidence that—
- (a) the meeting was duly convened and held,
- (b) all resolutions passed at the meeting were duly passed, and
- (c) all proceedings at the meeting duly took place.

2.954

12.6 Documents issuing from Secretary of State

(1) Any document purporting to be, or to contain, any order, directions or certificate issued by the Secretary of State shall be received in evidence and deemed to be or (as the case may be) contain that order or certificate, or those directions, without further proof, unless the contrary is shown.

(2) Paragraph (1) applies whether the document is signed by the Secretary of State himself or an officer on his behalf.

(3) Without prejudice to the foregoing, a certificate signed by the Secretary of State or an officer on his behalf and confirming—

(a) the making of any order,
(b) the issuing of any document, or
(c) the exercise of any discretion, power or obligation arising or imposed under the Act or the Rules,

is conclusive evidence of the matters dealt with in the certificate.

2.955

12.7 Forms for use in insolvency proceedings

(1) The forms contained in Schedule 4 to the Rules shall be used in and in connection with, insolvency proceedings, whether in the High Court or a county court.

(2) The forms shall be used with such variations, if any, as the circumstances may require.

(3) Where any form contained in Schedule 4 is substantially the same as one used for a corresponding purpose under either—
(a) the law and practice obtaining before the coming into force of the Rules; or
(b) if the form was first required to be used after the coming into force of the Rules, the law and practice obtaining before the making of the requirement,

whichever shall be appropriate in any case, the latter may continue to be used (with the necessary modifications) until 1 March 1988.

2.956

12.8 Insolvency practitioner's security

(1) Wherever under the Rules any person has to appoint, or certify the appointment of, an insolvency practitioner to any office, he is under a duty to satisfy himself that the person appointed or to be appointed has security for the proper performance of his functions.

(2) It is the duty—
(a) of the creditors' committee in companies administration, administrative receivership and bankruptcy,
(b) of the liquidation committee in companies winding up, and
(c) of any committee of creditors established for the purposes of a voluntary arrangement under Part I or VIII of the Act,

to review from time to time the adequacy of the responsible insolvency practitioner's security.

(3) In any insolvency proceedings the cost of the responsible insolvency practitioner's security shall be defrayed as an expense of the proceedings.

Notes

R 12.8

The requirement to provide security is contained in IA 1986 s 390(3).

2.957

12.9 Time-Limits

(1) The provisions of CPR rule 2.8 (time) apply, as regards computation of time, to anything required or authorised to be done by the Rules.

(2) The provisions of CPR rule 3.1(2)(a) (the court's general powers of management) apply so as to enable the court to extend or shorten the time for compliance with anything required or authorised to be done by the Rules.

Notes

R 12.9(2)

This provision is often relied upon to shorten the period of notice required to be given by an applicant for an administration order *Re a Company (00175 of 1987)* (1987) 3 BCC 124, and to extend the period of 7 days allowed to make an application for rescission of a winding up order *Re Virgo Systems Ltd* [1990] BCLC 34. However the provision cannot be relied upon to extend the time required or authorised by IA 1986, such as extending the time of an administration after its expiry *Re TT Ltd* [2006] BPIR 597; however on the proper construction of IA 1986 Sch B1 para 77(1)(b) the court did extend time.

2.958

12.10 Service by post

(1) For a document to be properly served by post, it must be contained in an envelope addressed to the person on whom service is to be effected, and pre-paid for either first or second class post.

(1A) A document to be served by post may be sent to the last known address of the person to be served.

(2) Where first class post is used, the document is treated as served on the second business day after the date of posting, unless the contrary is shown.

(3) Where second class post is used, the document is treated as served on the fourth business day after the date of posting, unless the contrary is shown.

(4) The date of posting is presumed, unless the contrary is shown, to be the date shown in the post-mark on the envelope in which the document is contained.

Notes

R 12.10

This must be read in conjunction with IR 1986 rr 12.11 and 12.12. These rules (together with those parts of CPR Part 6 which are incorporated by IR 1986 r 12.11) provide a code for the service of documents. The code clearly applies to documents relating to court proceedings. It has been held that it also applies to the giving of notices summoning creditors' meetings for the purposes of considering proposals for IVAs and CVAs: see *Re a Debtor (No 64 of 1992)* [1994] 1 WLR 264; *Beverley Group plc v McClue* [1995] 2 BCLC 405; *Skipton Building Society v*

Collins [1998] BPIR 267. The burden of proving 'the contrary' for the purposes of IR 12.10 is on the person to whom the document was sent *Skipton Building Society v Collins* [1998] BPIR 267.

2.959

12.11 General provisions as to service

Subject to Rule 12.10 and Rule 12.12, CPR Part 6 (service of documents) applies as regards any matter relating to the service of documents and the giving of notice in insolvency proceedings.

Notes

R 12.11

The words 'and Rule 12.12' were inserted by Insolvency (Amendment) Rules SI 2005/527, SI 2005/527, r 45 from 1 April 2005.

2.960

12.12 Service outside the jurisdiction

(1) CPR Part 6, paragraphs 6.17 to 6.35 (service of process, etc, out of the jurisdiction) do not apply in insolvency proceedings.

(2) A bankruptcy petition may, with the leave of the court, be served outside England and Wales in such manner as the court may direct.

(3) Where for the purposes of insolvency proceedings any process or order of the court, or other document, is required to be served on a person who is not in England and Wales, the court may order service to be effected within such time, on such person, at such place and in such manner as it thinks fit, and may also require such proof of service as it thinks fit.

(4) An application under this Rule shall be supported by an affidavit stating—
  (a) the grounds on which the application is made, and
  (b) in what place or country the person to be served is, or probably may be found.

(5) Leave of the court is not required to serve anything referred to in this Rule on a member State liquidator.

Notes

R 12.12

This rule contains a self-contained regime for service out of the jurisdiction in insolvency proceedings. 'Insolvency proceedings' are defined in IR 1986 r 13.7 and do not include statutory claims arising under foreign law which are not '..*proceedings under*' IA 1986 or IR 1986, *Fourie & Ors v Le Roux* [2005] BPIR 779. In *Re T&N Limited* [2006] EWHC 842 (Ch) David Richards J accepted that IR 1986 rr 12.10 to 12.11 applied to the giving of notices of meeting under IA 1986 s 3. However, he held that IR 1986 r 12.12, which deals with service out of the jurisdiction did not, so that it was not necessary for the court to give leave for the giving notice to overseas creditors.

In *Re T&N Limited* [2006] EWHC 842 (Ch) David Richards J accepted that IR 1986 r 12.10 to 12.11 applied to the giving of notices of meeting under IA 1986 s 3. However he held that IR 1986 r 12.12 did not so that it was not necessary for the court to give leave for the giving of notice to overseas creditors.

R 12.12(1)

This provision was amended by Insolvency (Amendment) Rules SI 2005/527, SI 2005/527, r 46 from 1 April 2005 to refer to the CPR rather than the former provision dealing with service abroad (RSC Order 11) 'Insolvency proceedings' are defined by IR 1986 r 13.7 as '*any proceedings under the Act or the Rules*'. However this only means proceedings under Parts I to XI of the Insolvency Act 1986: *Jyske Bank (Gibraltar) Ltd v Spjeldnaes* [2000] BCC 16. So preference, undervalue and wrongful trading claims are subject to IR 1986 r 12.12, but not transactions defrauding creditors under IA 1986 s 423.

R 12.12(3)

Service pursuant to IR 1986 r 12.12 is a matter for the discretion of the court, and there are no complex provisions relating to the subject matter of the proceedings of the type found in CPR Part 6. In exercising its discretion the court has to be satisfied that there is a real issue between the parties, and that England is the proper place for that issue to be determined: *Re Howard Holdings Inc* [1999] BCC 549. The court has for instance been willing to make such orders to enable a public examination to be held (*Re Seagull Manufacturing Co Ltd* [1993] Ch 345); a private examination to be conducted (*McIsaac, Petitioners* [1994] BCC 91) and for misfeasance proceedings under IA 1986 s 212 to be served by a liquidator (*Miller v Bain* [2003] BPIR 959). It is presumed that, where service is to be effected in an EU member state, the manner of service has to be one permitted by the EC Service Regulation (Council Regulation No 1348/2000 of May 29, 2000). Where non EU states are concerned it is important for the applicant to comply with the local service rules after obtaining an order for service outside the jurisdiction; otherwise the proceedings may later be challenged on the grounds of lack of proper service in the local jurisdiction.

2.961

12.13 Confidentiality of documents

(1) Where in insolvency proceedings the responsible insolvency practitioner considers, in the case of a document forming part of the records of the insolvency, that—

(a) it should be treated as confidential, or

(b) it is of such a nature that its disclosure would be calculated to be injurious to the interests of the insolvent's creditors or, in the case of a company's insolvency, its members or the contributories in its winding up,

he may decline to allow it to be inspected by a person who would otherwise be entitled to inspect it.

(2) The persons to whom the insolvency practitioner may under this Rule refuse inspection include the members of a liquidation committee or a creditors' committee.

(3) Where under this Rule the insolvency practitioner determines to refuse inspection of a document, the person wishing to inspect it may

apply to the court for that determination to be overruled; and the court may either overrule it altogether, or sustain it subject to such conditions (if any) as it thinks fit to impose.

(4) Nothing in this Rule entitles the insolvency practitioner to decline to allow the inspection of any proof or proxy.

2.962

12.14 Notices sent simultaneously to the same person

Where under the Act or the Rules a document of any description is to be sent to a person (whether or not as a member of a class of persons to whom that same document is to be sent), it may be sent as an accompaniment to any other document or information which the person is to receive, with or without modification or adaptation of the form applicable to that document.

2.963

12.15 Right to copy documents

Where the Act or the Rules confer a right for any person to inspect documents, the right includes that of taking copies of those documents, on payment—

   (a)   in the case of documents on the court's file of proceedings, of the fee chargeable under any order made under section 92 of the Courts Act 2003, and

   (b)   otherwise, of the appropriate fee.

Notes

R 12.15

This provision was slightly amended by Insolvency (Amendment) Rules 2005 from 1 April 2005 in that it now refers to the Courts Act 2003.

2.964

12.15A Charge for copy documents

Where the responsible insolvency practitioner or the official receiver is requested by a creditor, member, contributory or member of a liquidation or creditors' committee to supply copies of any documents he is entitled to require the payment of the appropriate fee in respect of the supply of the documents.

Notes

R 12.15A

The 'appropriate fee' is defined in IR 1986 r 13.11.

2.965

12.16 Non-receipt of notice of meeting

Where in accordance with the Act or the Rules a meeting of creditors or other persons is summoned by notice, the meeting is presumed to have been duly summoned and held, notwithstanding that not all those to whom the notice is to be given have received it.

Notes

This does not cure defective service of a notice, but ensures that a meeting is not invalid by reason of such defective service: see *Re a Debtor (No 64 of 1992)* [1994] 1 WLR 264.

2.966

12.17 Right to have list of creditors

(1) This Rule applies in any of the following proceedings—
   (a)   proceedings under Part II of the Act (company administration),
   (b)   a creditors' voluntary winding up, or a winding up by the court, and
   (c)   proceedings in bankruptcy.

(2) In any such proceedings a creditor who under the Rules has the right to inspect documents on the court file also has the right to require the responsible insolvency practitioner to furnish him with a list of the insolvent's creditors and the amounts of their respective debts.

This does not apply if a statement of the insolvent's affairs has been filed in court or, in the case of a creditors' voluntary winding up, been delivered to the registrar of companies.

(2A) For the purpose of this Rule a member State liquidator appointed in main proceedings in relation to a person is deemed to be a creditor.

(3) The insolvency practitioner, on being required by any person to furnish the list, shall send it to him, but is entitled to charge the appropriate fee for doing so.

Notes

R 12.17(1)(b)

This provision does not apply where there is a provisional liquidation in progress *Equitas Limited v Jacob* [2005] BPIR 1312 as in that case there has not yet been a winding up order made (see notes to IA 1986 s 135).

R 12.17(3)

The 'appropriate fee' is defined in IR 1986 r 13.11.

2.967

12.18 False claim of status as creditor, etc

(1) Where the Rules provide for creditors, members of a company or contributories in a company's winding up a right to inspect any documents, whether on the court's file or in the hands of a responsible insolvency practitioner or other person, it is an offence for a person, with the intention of obtaining a sight of documents which he has not under the Rules any right to inspect, falsely to claim a status which would entitle him to inspect them.

(2) A person guilty of an offence under this Rule is liable to imprisonment or a fine, or both.

2.968

12.19 Execution overtaken by judgment debtor's insolvency

(1) This Rule applies where execution has been taken out against property of a judgment debtor, and notice is given to the enforcement officer or other officer charged with the execution—

    (a)   under section 184(1) (that a winding-up order has been made against the debtor, or that a provisional liquidator has been appointed, or that a resolution for voluntary winding up has been passed); or

    (b)   under section 184(4) (that a winding-up petition has been presented or a winding-up order made, or that a meeting has been called at which there is to be proposed a resolution for voluntary winding up, or that such a resolution has been passed); or

    (c)   under section 346(2) (that the judgment debtor has been adjudged bankrupt); or

    (d)   under section 346(3)(b) (that a bankruptcy petition has been presented in respect of him).

(2) Subject as follows, the notice shall be in writing and be delivered by hand at, or sent by recorded delivery to, the office of the enforcement officer or (as the case may be) of the officer charged with the execution.

(3) Where the execution is in a county court, and the officer in charge of it is the registrar of that court, then if—

    (a)   there is filed in that court in respect of the judgment debtor a winding-up or bankruptcy petition, or

    (b)   there is made by that court in respect of him a winding-up order or an order appointing a provisional liquidator, or a bankruptcy order or an order appointing an interim receiver,

section 184 or (as the case may be) 346 is deemed satisfied as regards the requirement of a notice to be served on, or given to, the officer in charge of the execution.

Notes

R 12.19

This provision was slightly amended by Insolvency (Amendment) Rules 2005 from 1 April 2005 to reflect the language of the CPR, so that 'Sheriff' and 'under-sheriff' become 'enforcement officer.'

2.969

12.20 The Gazette

(1) A copy of the Gazette containing any notice required by the Act or the Rules to be gazetted is evidence of any facts stated in the notice.

(2) In the case of an order of the court notice of which is required by the Act or the Rules to be gazetted, a copy of the Gazette containing the notice may in any proceedings be produced as conclusive evidence that the order was made on the date specified in the notice.

(3) Where an order of the court which is gazetted has been varied, and where any matter has been erroneously or inaccurately gazetted, the person whose responsibility it was to procure the requisite entry in the Gazette shall forthwith cause the variation of the order to be gazetted or, as the case may be, a further entry to be made in the Gazette for the purpose of correcting the error or inaccuracy.

Notes

R 12.20

Gazetting information does not provide notice to the whole world *Official Custodian for Charities v Parway Estates* [1985] Ch 151, *Rooney v Cardona* [1999] 1 WLR 1388.

2.970

12.21 Punishment of offences

(1) Schedule 5 to the Rules has effect with respect to the way in which contraventions of the Rules are punishable on conviction.

(2) In relation to an offence under a provision of the Rules specified in the first column of the Schedule (the general nature of the offence being described in the second column), the third column shows whether the offence is punishable on conviction on indictment, or on summary conviction, or either in the one way or the other.

(3) The fourth column shows, in relation to an offence, the maximum punishment by way of fine or imprisonment which may be imposed on a person convicted of the offence in the way specified in relation to it in the third column (that is to say, on indictment or summarily), a reference to a period of years or months being to a term of imprisonment of that duration.

(4) The fifth column shows (in relation to an offence for which there is an entry in that column) that a person convicted of the offence after continued contravention is liable to a daily default fine; that is to say, he is liable on a second or subsequent conviction of the offence to the fine specified in that column for each day on which the contravention is continued (instead of the penalty specified for the offence in the fourth column of the Schedule).

(5) Section 431 (summary proceedings), as it applies to England and Wales, has effect in relation to offences under the Rules as to offences under the Act.

2.971

12.22 Notice of order under section 176A(5)

(1) Where the court makes an order under section 176A(5), it shall as soon as reasonably practicable send two sealed copies of the order to the applicant and a sealed copy to any other insolvency practitioner who holds office in relation to the company.

(2) Where the court has made an order under section 176A(5), the liquidator, administrator or receiver, as the case may be, shall, as soon as reasonably practicable, send a sealed copy of the order to the company.

(3) Where the court has made an order under section 176A(5), the liquidator, administrator or receiver, as the case may be, shall as soon as reasonably practicable, give notice to each creditor of whose claim and address he is aware.

(4) Paragraph (3) shall not apply where the court directs otherwise.

(5) The court may direct that the requirement in paragraph (3) is complied with by the liquidator, administrator or receiver, as the case may be, publishing a notice in such newspaper as he thinks most appropriate for ensuring that it comes to the notice of the company's unsecured creditors stating that the court has made an order disapplying the requirement to set aside the prescribed part.

(6) The liquidator, administrator or receiver shall send a copy of the order to the registrar of companies as soon as reasonably practicable after the making of the order.

The Third Group of Parts

Part 13
Interpretation and application

2.972

13.1 Introductory

This Part of the Rules has effect for their interpretation and application; and any definition given in this Part applies except, and in so far as, the context otherwise requires.

Notes

R 13.1

Rule 13 contains definitions of expressions of general application in IR 1986 and IA 1986. With the important exception of r 13.12 (which defines 'debt' and 'liability') these relate primarily to procedural matters. Other definitions, in particular of expressions of more limited application, are to be found elsewhere in IR 1986. The most important interpretation provisions in IA 1986 itself are as follows:

SS 247–251

These contain definitions for the First Group of Parts–corporate insolvency.

SS 380–385

These contain definitions for the Second Group of Parts–individual insolvency.

SS 435–6

These contain definitions generally applicable to the IA 1986.

The rules for the calculation of periods of time in CPR r 2.8 are incorporated into IR 1986 by r 12.9(1); however the expression 'Business day' is separately defined by r 13.13(1). Rule 13.13 also adopts various definitions contained in the EC Regulation, which deals with cross-border matters.

2.973

13.2 'The court'; 'the registrar'

(1) Anything to be done under or by virtue of the Act or the Rules by, to or before the court may be done by, to or before a judge or the registrar.

(2) The registrar may authorise any act of a formal or administrative character which is not by statute his responsibility to be carried out by the chief clerk or any other officer of the court acting on his behalf, in accordance with directions given by the Lord Chancellor.

(3) In individual insolvency proceedings, 'the registrar' means a Registrar in Bankruptcy of the High Court, or the registrar or deputy registrar of a county court.

(4) In company insolvency proceedings in the High Court, 'the registrar' means—

    (a)   subject to the following paragraph, a Registrar in Bankruptcy of the High Court;

    (b)   where the proceedings are in the District Registry of Birmingham, Bristol, Cardiff, Leeds, Liverpool, Manchester, Newcastle-upon-Tyne or Preston, the District Registrar.

(5) In company insolvency proceedings in a county court, 'the registrar' means the officer of the court whose duty it is to exercise the functions which in the High Court are exercised by a registrar.

Notes

R 13.2

Insolvency jurisdiction is vested in both the county court and the High Court: see IA 1986 s 117 (corporate insolvency) and IR 1986 r. 6.9 (personal insolvency). The Practice Note: the Hearing of Insolvency Proceedings [2005] BPIR 688 stipulates which matters are to be dealt with by 'the judge' and which can be heard by the 'registrar or the district judge'. The latter deal with most routine matters, and in particular the winding up lis. It is clear from the context that 'the judge' means a county court judge in the case of proceedings in the county court, and a High Court judge (including a deputy or judge authorised under s 9 Supreme Court Act 1981) in the case of the High Court. The only registrars now remaining are the bankruptcy and Companies Court registrars who sit in the High Court in London. Subordinate insolvency jurisdiction outside London is exercised by district judges. This rule, which has not been brought up to date to refer to district judges, should be interpreted accordingly.

2.974

13.3 'Give notice', etc

(1) A reference in the Rules to giving notice, or to delivering, sending or serving any document, means that the notice or document may be sent by post, unless under a particular Rule personal service is expressly required.

(2) Any form of post may be used, unless under a particular Rule a specified form is expressly required.

(3) Personal service of a document is permissible in all cases.

(4) Notice of the venue fixed for an application may be given by service of the sealed copy of the application under Rule 7.4(3).

Notes

R 13.3(1)

The court is not however precluded from ordering the sending of documents by email (see notes to IR 1986 r 12.4)

2.975

13.4 Notice, etc to solicitors

Where under the Act or the Rules a notice or other document is required or authorised to be given to a person, it may, if he has indicated that his solicitor is authorised to accept service on his behalf, be given instead to the solicitor.

Notes

For a consideration of this rule, see *Re T&N Ltd* [2006] EWHC 842 (Ch).

2.976

13.5 Notice to joint liquidators, joint trustees, etc

Where two or more persons are acting jointly as the responsible insolvency practitioner in any proceedings, delivery of a document to one of them is to be treated as delivery to them all.

2.977

13.6 'Venue'

References to the 'venue' for any proceeding or attendance before the court, or for a meeting, are to the time, date and place for the proceeding, attendance or meeting.

2.978

13.7 'Insolvency proceedings'

'Insolvency proceedings' means any proceedings under the Act or the Rules.

Notes

R 13(7)

It was held by Evans Lombe in *Jyske bank (Gibraltar) Ltd v Spjeldnaes & ors* [2006] BCC 16 that this expression only covers proceedings under the parts of the Insolvency Act covered by s 411 and 412, that is Parts I to XI. Consequently proceedings under s 423 (transactions defrauding creditors) are not 'insolvency proceedings' see *TSB Bank plc v Katz* [1997] BPIR 147. It would follow for example that service out of the jurisdiction of s 423 proceedings would be governed by CPR r 6.17 et seq rather than IR 1986. The same reasoning applies to the service of statutory claims arising under South African law pursuant to a request under s 426, *Fourie v Le Roux* [2005] BPIR 723 as s 426 is contained in Part XVII of IA 1986. However service of s 238 proceedings (transactions at an undervalue) would be subject to IR 1986 r 12.12. In *Re a Debtor (190 of 1987)* The Times, 26 April 1988 *it was* held that a statutory demand was not an 'insolvency proceeding' and therefore cannot be amended under IR 1986 r 7.55.

2.979

13.8 'Insolvent estate'

References to 'the insolvent estate' are—
- (a) in relation to a company insolvency, the company's assets, and
- (b) in relation to an individual insolvency, the bankrupt's estate or (as the case may be) the debtor's property.

2.980

13.9 'Responsible insolvency practitioner', etc

(1) In relation to any insolvency proceedings, 'the responsible insolvency practitioner' means—
- (a) the person acting in a company insolvency, as supervisor of a voluntary arrangement under Part I of the Act, or as administrator, administrative receiver, liquidator or provisional liquidator;
- (b) the person acting in an individual insolvency, as the supervisor of a voluntary arrangement under Part VIII of the Act, or as trustee or interim receiver;
- (c) the official receiver acting as receiver and manager of a bankrupt's estate.

(2) Any reference to the liquidator, provisional liquidator, trustee or interim receiver includes the official receiver when acting in the relevant capacity.

(3) A reference to an 'authorised person' is a reference to a person who is authorised pursuant to section 389A of the Act to act as nominee or supervisor of a voluntary arrangement proposed or approved under Part I or Part VIII of the Act.

2.981

13.10 'Petitioner'

In winding-up and bankruptcy, references to 'the petitioner' or 'the petitioning creditor' include any person who has been substituted as such, or been given carriage of the petition.

2.982

13.11 'The appropriate fee'

'The appropriate fee' means—
  (a)   in Rule 6.192(2) (payor under income payments order entitled to clerical etc costs), 50 pence; and
  (b)   in other cases, 15 pence per A4 or A5 page, and 30 pence per A3 page.

2.983

13.12 'Debt', 'liability' (winding up)

(1) 'Debt', in relation to the winding up of a company, means (subject to the next paragraph) any of the following—
  (a)   any debt or liability to which the company is subject at the date on which it goes into liquidation;
  (b)   any debt or liability to which the company may become subject after that date by reason of any obligation incurred before that date; and
  (c)   any interest provable as mentioned in Rule 4.93(1).

(2) For the purposes of any provision of the Act or the Rules about winding up, any liability in tort is a debt provable in the winding up, if either—
  (a)   the cause of action has accrued at the date on which the company goes into liquidation; or
  (b)   all the elements necessary to establish the cause of action exist at that date except for actionable damage.

(3) For the purposes of references in any provision of the Act or the Rules about winding up to a debt or liability, it is immaterial whether the debt or liability is present or future, whether it is certain or contingent, or whether its amount is fixed or liquidated, or is capable of being ascertained by fixed rules or as a matter of opinion; and references in any such provision to owing a debt are to be read accordingly.

(4) In any provision of the Act or the Rules about winding up, except in so far as the context otherwise requires, 'liability' means (subject to paragraph (3) above) a liability to pay money or money's worth, including any liability under an enactment, any liability for breach of trust, any liability in contract, tort or bailment, and any liability arising out of an obligation to make restitution.

> (5) This Rule shall apply where a company is in administration and shall be read as if references to winding-up were a reference to administration'.

Notes

Introduction

For a detailed consideration of this rule prior to the amendment of IR 1986 r 13.12(2), see *Re T&N Limited* [2006] BPIR 532.

Although described as an interpretative provision, IR 1986 r 13.12 is in fact a substantive and important provision, which reflects IA 1986 s 382 which applies in bankruptcy. Its purpose is to define 'debt' by reference to a point in time – commencement of the liquidation – and it therefore restricts the class of claims otherwise provable under IR 1986 r 12.3. It requires debts either to exist at that time, or to arise by reason of an obligation incurred before that date. In focusing on that date, r 13.12 is consistent with the basic theory of insolvency law, that of theoretical ascertainment of claims and distribution of assets as at the commencement of the winding up: see *Wight v Eckhardt Marine GmbH* [2003] UKPC 37, [2004] 1 AC 147.

R 13.12(1) 'Debt'

This definition applies to winding up and administration (by virtue of paragraph 5). With respect to personal insolvency, there is a definition of 'Bankruptcy debt' in Insolvency Act s 382.

The definition in IR 1986 r 13.12 is important for two reasons in particular.

- First it identifies what debts are capable of forming the basis of a petition to wind up: IA 1986 s 122(1)(f). There is no statutory definition of 'creditor'and in *Tottenham Hotspur plcv Edennote plc* [1994] BCC 681 the court accepted that in the absence of such a definition it must be taken to mean a person to whom a debt is owed as defined in this rule.
- It defines what are provable debts: see above.

Post liquidation debts

IR 1986 r 13.12 was considered in *Re Kentish Homes Ltd* [1993] BCC 212. This company became liable to pay community charge after it had gone into liquidation. Nicholls V–C held that this was not a provable debt since the liability did not exist when the company went into liquidation (r. 13.12(1)(a)); and was not a liability to which the company became subject by reason of an obligation incurred before liquidation (r. 13.12(1)(b)). The judge further held that the liability to community charge was not an expense of the liquidation. However in the last respect the case was held to be wrongly decided by the House of Lords in In *re Toshoku Finance UK plc* [2002] 1 WLR 671.

Claims in Tort

Before the changes made by IA 1986 and IR 1986, claims in tort were not provable unless they had been liquidated by judgment or agreement prior to the commencement of the bankruptcy or winding up. For a criticism of the rule, and an attempt to escape some of its rigours, see *Re Berkeley Securities (Property) Ltd* [1980] 1 WLR 1589; not followed in *Re Islington Metal & Plating Works Ltd* [1984] 1 WLR 14.

The Cork Committee recommended that claims in tort should be provable, provided that they were liquidated by the time that they came into proof. However, this recommendation was not followed. Instead, IA 1986 s 382(2) and IR 1986 r 13.12(2) provides that an unliquidated claim in tort is provable provided that it arose from an obligation which was incurred prior to bankruptcy or winding up, and that such an obligation is deemed to arise when the cause of action accrued. This means that it is necessary for the cause of action to have accrued before the relevant date, and future tort claimants (as described above) are excluded from proof: see *Re Kentish Homes Ltd* [1993] BCC 212 *and Re T&N Limited [2006] BPIR 532.*

IR 1986 r 13.12(2) has now been replaced to reverse the effect of *Re T&N Ltd* (above) and to permit future claims in tort to be proved: see the Insolvency (Amendment) Rules 2006 (SI 2006/1272). The amendments made apply to all companies which:

(a) go into a voluntary liquidation initiated by a resolution to wind up passed on or after the commencement date (1 June 2006);

(b) go into a voluntary liquidation following an exit from administration under IA 1986 Sch B1 para 83 except where the administration commenced before 1 June 2006 or where it commenced by an administration order made on an administration application presented before 1 June 2006;

(c) go into a compulsory liquidation on a petition presented on or after 1 June 2006 except where the liquidation is immediately preceded by (i) an administration order made on an administration application presented before 1 June 2006, (ii) an out of court administration under IA 1986 para 14 or para 22 Sch B1 which took effect prior to 1 June 2006, or (iii) a voluntary liquidation where the resolution to wind up was passed prior to 1 June 2006;

(d) on or after 1 June 2006 enter administration except where (i) such entry is by virtue of an administration order made on an administration application presented before 1 June 2006, (ii) the administration is immediately preceded by a voluntary liquidation where the resolution to wind up was passed before 1 June 2006, or (iii) the administration is immediately preceded by a compulsory liquidation on a petition presented prior to 1 June 2006.

Future and unascertained debts

As a result of IR 1986 r 13.12(3), for winding up purposes debts can be future, contingent or unascertained. They can therefore include a liability under a costs order where the amount of costs has not yet been assessed: *Tottenham Hotspur plc v Edennote plc* [1994] BCC 681.

Administration

R 13.12(5)

This provision was added by the IAR 2003 so that the definitions contained in this provision could be applied in administration. Under the administration procedure introduced by the EA 2002 creditors will prove in the administration where the administrator intends to make a distribution (IR 1986 r 2.68ff) and therefore it is necessary to ascertain the debts and liabilities of the company.

2.984

13.12A 'Authorised deposit-taker and former authorised deposit-taker

[(1) 'Authorised deposit-taker' means a person with permission under Part 4 of the Financial Services and Markets Act 2000 to accept deposits.

(2) 'Former authorised deposit-taker' means a person who—
(a) is not an authorised deposit-taker,
(b) was formerly an authorised institution under the Banking Act 1987, or a recognised bank or a licensed institution under the Banking Act 1979, and
(c) continues to have liability in respect of any deposit for which it had a liability at a time when it was an authorised institution, recognised bank or licensed institution.

(3) Paragraphs (1) and (2) must be read with—
(a) section 22 of the Financial Services and Markets Act 2000;

   (b)   any relevant order under that section; and

(c) Schedule 22 to that Act.]

2.985

13.13 Expressions used generally

(1) 'Business day' means any day other than a Saturday, a Sunday, Christmas Day, Good Friday or a day which is a bank holiday in any part of Great Britain under or by virtue of the Banking and Financial Dealings Act 1971 except in Rules 1.7, 4.10, 4.11, 4.16, 4.20, 5.10 and 6.23 where 'business day' shall include any day which is a bank holiday in Scotland but not in England and Wales.

(2) 'The Department' means the Department of Trade and Industry.

(3) 'File in court' and 'file with the court' means deliver to the court for filing.

(4) 'The Gazette' means the London Gazette.

(5) 'General regulations' means regulations made by the Secretary of State under Rule 12.1.

(6) 'Practice direction' means a direction as to the practice and procedure of any court within the scope of the CPR.

(7) 'Prescribed order of priority' means the order of priority of payments laid down by Chapter 20 of Part 4 of the Rules, or Chapter 23 of Part 6.

(8) 'Centre of main interests' has the same meaning as in the EC Regulation

(9) 'Establishment' has the meaning given by Article 2(h) of the EC Regulation

(10) 'Main proceedings' means proceedings opened in accordance with Article 3(1) of the EC Regulation and falling within the definition of insolvency proceedings in Article 2(a) of the EC Regulation and
   (a)   in relation to England and Wales and Scotland set out in Annex A to the EC Regulation under the heading 'United Kingdom', and
   (b)   in relation to another member State, set out in Annex A to the EC Regulation under the heading relating to that member State.

(11) 'Member State liquidator' means a person falling within the definition of liquidator in Article 2(b) of the EC Regulation appointed in proceedings to which it applies in a member State other than the United Kingdom.

(12) 'Secondary proceedings' means proceedings opened in accordance with Articles 3(2) and 3(3) of the EC Regulation and falling within the definition of winding-up proceedings in Article 2(c) of the EC Regulation, and
   (a)   in relation to England and Wales and Scotland, set out in Annex B to the EC Regulation under the heading 'United Kingdom', and
   (b)   in relation to another member State, set out in Annex B to the EC Regulation under the heading relating to that member State.

(13) 'Temporary administrator' means a temporary administrator referred to by Article 38 of the EC Regulation.

(14) 'Territorial proceedings' means proceedings opened in accordance with Articles 3(2) and 3(4) of the EC Regulation and falling within the definition of insolvency proceedings in Article 2(a) of the EC Regulation, and
  (a)   in relation to England and Wales and Scotland, set out in Annex A to the EC Regulation under the heading 'United Kingdom', and
  (b)   in relation to another member State, set out in Annex A to the EC Regulation under the heading relating to that member State.

(15) 'Prescribed part' has the same meaning as it does in section 176A(2)(a).

2.986

13.14 Application

(1) Subject to paragraph (2) of this Rule, and save where otherwise expressly provided, the Rules apply—
  (a)   to ... receivers appointed on or after the day on which the Rules come into force,
  (b)   to bankruptcy proceedings where the bankruptcy petition is presented on or after the day on which the Rules come into force, and
  (c)   to all other insolvency proceedings commenced on or after that day.

(2) The Rules also apply to winding-up and bankruptcy proceedings commenced before that day to which provisions of the Act are applied by Schedule 11 to the Act, to the extent necessary to give effect to those provisions.

SCHEDULE 1
[Scheme Manager's] Voting Rights
Rule 4.72(7)

2.987

1

This Schedule applies as does Rule 4.72.

2

In relation to any meeting at which the [scheme manager] is under Rule 4.72 entitled to be represented, the [scheme manager] may submit in the liquidation, instead of a proof, a written statement of voting rights ('the statement').

3

The statement shall contain details of—

(a) the names of creditors of the company in respect of whom an obligation of the [scheme manager] has arisen or may reasonably be expected to arise as a result of the liquidation or proposed liquidation;

(b) the amount of the obligation so arising; and

(c) the total amount of all such obligations specified in the statement.

4

The [scheme manager's] statement shall, for the purpose of voting at a meeting (but for no other purpose), be treated in all respects as if it were a proof.

5

Any voting rights which a creditor might otherwise exercise at a meeting in respect of a claim against the company are reduced by a sum equal to the amount of that claim in relation to which the [scheme manager], by virtue of its having submitted a statement, is entitled to exercise voting rights at that meeting.

6

The [scheme manager] may from time to time submit a further statement, and, if it does so, that statement supersedes any statement previously submitted.

[SCHEDULE 2
Alternative Courts for Debtors' Petitions in Bankruptcy]
Rule 6.40(3)

2.988

[Debtor's own county court	Nearest full-time court
ABERDARE	CARDIFF
ABERYSTWYTH	CARDIFF
AYLESBURY	LUTON
BANBURY	LUTON or GLOUCESTER or READING
BANGOR	BIRKENHEAD or CHESTER
BARNSLEY	SHEFFIELD
BARNSTAPLE	EXETER
BARROW IN FURNESS	BLACKPOOL or PRESTON
BATH	BRISTOL
BEDFORD	LUTON
BLACKBURN	PRESTON
BLACKWOOD	CARDIFF
BOSTON	NOTTINGHAM

[Debtor's own county court	Nearest full-time court
BRIDGEND	CARDIFF
BRIDGWATER	BRISTOL
BURNLEY	BOLTON or PRESTON
BURTON ON TRENT	LEICESTER or DERBY or NOTTINGHAM
BURY ST EDMUNDS	CAMBRIDGE
CANTERBURY	CROYDON or THE HIGH COURT (LONDON)
CARLISLE	PRESTON or BLACKPOOL
CARMARTHEN	CARDIFF
CHELMSFORD	SOUTHEND or THE HIGH COURT (LONDON)
CHELTENHAM	GLOUCESTER
CHESTERFIELD	SHEFFIELD
COLCHESTER	SOUTHEND or THE HIGH COURT (LONDON)
COVENTRY	BIRMINGHAM
CREWE	STOKE or CHESTER
DARLINGTON	MIDDLESBOROUGH
DEWSBURY	LEEDS
DONCASTER	SHEFFIELD
DUDLEY	BIRMINGHAM
DURHAM	NEWCASTLE
EASTBOURNE	BRIGHTON
GREAT GRIMSBY	HULL
GREAT YARMOUTH	NORWICH
GUILDFORD	CROYDON
HALIFAX	LEEDS
HARROGATE	LEEDS
HASTINGS	BRIGHTON
HAVERFORDWEST	CARDIFF
HEREFORD	GLOUCESTER
HERTFORD	LUTON
HUDDERSFIELD	LEEDS
IPSWICH	NORWICH or SOUTHEND
KENDAL	BLACKPOOL or PRESTON
KIDDERMINSTER	BIRMINGHAM
KING'S LYNN	NORWICH or CAMBRIDGE
LANCASTER	BLACKPOOL or PRESTON

[Debtor's own county court	Nearest full-time court
LINCOLN	NOTTINGHAM
MACCLESFIELD	STOKE or MANCHESTER
MAIDSTONE	CROYDON or THE HIGH COURT (LONDON)
MEDWAY	CROYDON or THE HIGH COURT (LONDON)
MERTHYR TYDFIL	CARDIFF
MILTON KEYNES	LUTON
NEATH	CARDIFF
NEWBURY	READING
NEWPORT (GWENT)	CARDIFF
NEWPORT (IOW)	SOUTHAMPTON or PORTSMOUTH
NORTHAMPTON	LUTON
OXFORD	READING
PETERBOROUGH	CAMBRIDGE
PONTYPRIDD	CARDIFF
PORTMADOC	BIRKENHEAD or STOKE or CHESTER
RHYL	BIRKENHEAD or CHESTER
ROCHDALE	OLDHAM or MANCHESTER
SALISBURY	BOURNEMOUTH or SOUTHAMPTON
SCARBOROUGH	YORK or HULL or MIDDLESBOROUGH
SCUNTHORPE	HULL or SHEFFIELD
SHREWSBURY	STOKE
ST. ALBANS	LUTON
STAFFORD	STOKE
STOCKTON ON TEES	MIDDLESBOROUGH
STOCKPORT	MANCHESTER
STOURBRIDGE	BIRMINGHAM
SUNDERLAND	NEWCASTLE
SWANSEA	CARDIFF
SWINDON	GLOUCESTER or READING
TAMESIDE	MANCHESTER
TAUNTON	EXETER or BRISTOL
TORQUAY	EXETER
TRURO	PLYMOUTH
TUNBRIDGE WELLS	CROYDON

[Debtor's own county court	Nearest full-time court
WAKEFIELD	LEEDS
WARRINGTON	CHESTER or LIVERPOOL or MANCHESTER
WARWICK	BIRMINGHAM
WELSHPOOL	STOKE or CHESTER
WEST BROMWICH	BIRMINGHAM
WEYMOUTH	BOURNEMOUTH
WIGAN	BOLTON or MANCHESTER or PRESTON
WINCHESTER	SOUTHAMPTON
WORCESTER	GLOUCESTER
WORKINGTON	PRESTON or BLACKPOOL
WREXHAM	BIRKENHEAD or STOKE or CHESTER
YEOVIL	EXETER or BRISTOL]

NOTES

Amendment

Substituted by SI 1987/1919, r 3(1), Schedule, Part 2, para 153, Part 3.

SCHEDULE 4
Forms
Rule 12.7

2.989

Forms index

Part 1: Company Voluntary Arrangements

FORM NO / TITLE

[1.1 Notice to registrar of companies of voluntary arrangement taking effect]

[1.2 Notice to registrar of companies of order of revocation or suspension of voluntary arrangement

1.3 Notice to registrar of companies of supervisor's abstract of receipts and payments

1.4 Notice to registrar of companies of completion or termination of voluntary arrangement

1.5 Nominee's statement of opinion

2.15B Statement of concurrence

2.16B Notice of statement of affairs

2.17B Statement of administrator's proposals

2.18B Notice of extension of time period

2.19B Notice to attend meeting of creditors

2.20B Notice of a meeting of creditors

2.21B Creditor's request for a meeting

2.22B Statement of administrator's revised proposals

2.23B Notice of result of meeting of creditors

2.24B Administrator's progress report

2.25B Notice of conduct of business by correspondence

2.26B [Amended] Certificate of constitution of creditors' committee

2.27B Notice by administrator of a change in committee membership

2.28B Notice of order to deal with charged property

2.29B Affidavit of debt

2.30B Notice of automatic end of administration

2.31B Notice of extension of period of administration

2.32B Notice of end of administration

2.33B Notice of court order ending administration

2.34B Notice of move from administration to creditors' voluntary liquidation

2.35B Notice of move from administration to dissolution

2.36B Notice to registrar of companies in respect of date of dissolution

2.37B Notice of intention to resign as administrator

2.38B Notice of resignation by administrator

2.39B Notice of vacation of office by administrator

2.40B Notice of appointment of replacement/additional administrator]

Part 3: Administrative Receivership

3.1 [Written acceptance of appointment by receiver]

3.1A [Notice of appointment of administrative receiver (for newspaper or London Gazette)]

3.1B [Notice requiring preparation and submission of administrative receivership statement of affairs]

3.2 Statement of affairs

3.3 Statement of affairs in administrative receivership following report to creditors

3.4 Certificate of constitution (amended certificate) of creditors' committee

3.5 Administrative receiver's report as to change in membership of creditors' committee

3.6 Receiver or manager or administrative receiver's abstract of receipts and payments

3.7 Notice of administrative receiver's death

3.8 Notice of order to dispose of charged property

3.9 Notice of resignation of administrative receiver pursuant to section 45(1) of Insolvency Act 1986

3.10 Administrative receiver's report

Part 4: Companies Winding Up

4.1 [Statutory demand under section 123(1)(a) or 222(1)(a) of the Insolvency Act 1986]

4.2 Winding-up petition

4.3 ...

4.4 Affidavit of service of winding-up petition at registered office

4.5 Affidavit of service of winding-up petition other than at registered office or on an oversea company

4.6 Advertisement of winding-up petition

4.7 Certificate that relevant provisions of Rules have been complied with

4.8 Order for leave to withdraw winding-up petition

4.9 Notice of intention to appear on petition

4.10 List of persons intending to appear on the hearing of the petition

4.11 Order for winding up by the court

[4.12 Order for Winding Up by the Court following upon the cessation of the appointment of an administrator]

4.13 [Notice to official receiver of winding-up order]

4.14 [Petition by contributory]

4.14A [Notice to official receiver of appointment of provisional liquidator]

4. 15 Order of appointment of provisional liquidator

[4.15A Notice of appointment of provisional liquidator in winding up by the court]

4.16 [Notice requiring preparation and submission of statement of company's affairs]

4.17 Statement of affairs (s 131 IA86—winding up by court)

4.18 Statement of affairs (s 95 IA86—voluntary liquidator)

4. 19 Statement of affairs (s 99 IA86—creditors' voluntary winding up)

4.20 Statement of company's affairs

4.21 Request by creditors for a meeting of the company's creditors (and contributories)

4.22 Notice to creditors of meeting of creditors

4.23 Notice to contributories of meeting of contributories

4.24 Request by contributory/contributories for a meeting of the company's contributories

4.25 Proof of debt—general form

4.26 Affidavit of debt

4.27 Certificate of appointment of liquidator by meeting

4.28 Certificate of appointment of two or more liquidators by meeting

4.29 Order of court appointing liquidator

4.30 Order of court appointing two or more liquidators

4.31 Notice of appointment of liquidator in winding up by the court (for registrar of companies)

4.32 Notice to court of resignation of liquidator following meeting of creditors

4.33 Notice of resignation as voluntary liquidator under s 171(5) of the Insolvency Act 1986

4.34 Order of court giving liquidator leave to resign

4.35 Order of court granting voluntary liquidator leave to resign

4.36 Notice to court of resignation of liquidator following leave of the court

4.37 Certificate of removal of liquidator

4.38 Certificate of removal of voluntary liquidator

4.39 Order of court removing liquidator or directing liquidator to summon a meeting of creditors for purpose of his removal

4.40 Notice of ceasing to act as voluntary liquidator

4.41 Liquidator's application to the Secretary of State for his release

4.42 Notice to court of final meeting of creditors

4.43 Notice to registrar of companies of final meeting of creditors

4.44 Notice of death of liquidator

4.45 Notice to official receiver or Secretary of State by liquidator on loss of qualification as insolvency practitioner

4.46 Notice of vacation of office by voluntary liquidator

4.47 Certificate of constitution (amended certificate) of liquidation committee

4.48 Notice of constitution of liquidation committee

4.49 Report by liquidator of any change in membership of liquidation committee

4.50 Liquidator's certificate that creditors paid in full

4.51 Certificate that creditors have been paid in full

4.52 Liquidator's certificate of continuance of liquidation committee

4.53 [Notice of disclaimer under section 178 of the Insolvency Act 1986]

4.54 Notice to elect

4.55 Notice of intended disclaimer to interested party

4.56 Affidavit of liquidator in support of application for call

4.57 Order giving leave to make a call

4.58 Notice of call sanctioned by the court or the liquidation committee to be sent to contributory

4.59 Order for payment of call due from contributory

4.60 Order of appointment of special manager

4.61 [Order of public examination]

4.62 Notice to official receiver by creditor requesting him to make application for the holding of a public examination

4.63 Notice to official receiver by contributory requesting him to make application for the holding of a public examination

4.64 [Order as to examination of person who is suffering from mental disorder or physical affliction or disability]

4.65 Affidavit of verification of record of the public examination

4.66 [Order of adjournment of public examination]

4.67 [Order appointing time for proceeding with public examination adjourned generally]

4.68 [Liquidator's statement of receipts and payments]

4.69 Order of court on appeal against Secretary of State's decision under section 203(4) or 205(4) of the Insolvency Act 1986

4.70 [Members' voluntary winding up declaration of solvency embodying a statement of assets and liabilities]

4.71 Return of final meeting in a members' voluntary winding up

4.72 Return of final meeting in a creditors' voluntary winding up

Part 5: Individual Voluntary Arrangements

5.1 [Order for stay pending hearing of application for interim order]

5.2 [Interim order of court under section 252 of the Insolvency Act 1986]

5.3 [Order extending effect of interim order]

5.4 [Alternative orders to be made at hearing to consider chairman's report]

[5.5 Documents to be submitted to court under Rule 5.14]

[5.6 Voting form in relation to a proposal for a voluntary arrangement under section 263A of the Insolvency Act 1986

5.7 Order of annulment under section 261 of the Insolvency Act 1986

5.8 Order of annulment under section 263D of the Insolvency Act 1986]

Part 6: Bankruptcy

6.1 [Statutory demand under section 268(1)(a) of the Insolvency Act 1986—debt for liquidated sum payable immediately]

6.2 [Statutory demand under section 268(1)(a) of the Insolvency Act 1986—debt for liquidated sum payable immediately following a judgment or order of the court]

6.3 [Statutory demand under section 268(2) of the Insolvency Act 1986—debt payable at future date]

6.4 Application to set aside statutory demand

6.5 Affidavit in support of application to set aside statutory demand

6.6 Order setting aside statutory demand

6.7 Creditor's bankruptcy petition on failure to comply with a statutory demand for a liquidated sum payable immediately

6.8 Creditor's bankruptcy petition on failure to comply with a statutory demand for a liquidated sum payable at a future date

6.9 Creditor's bankruptcy petition where execution or other process on a judgment has been returned unsatisfied in whole or part

6.10 Bankruptcy petition for default in connection with voluntary arrangement

6.11 [Affidavit of personal service of statutory demand]

6.12 Affidavit of substituted service of statutory demand

6.13 Affidavit of truth of statements in bankruptcy petition

6.14 [Application for registration of a petition in bankruptcy against an individual under Land Charges Act 1972]

6.15 Order for substituted service of a bankruptcy petition

6.16 Substituted service of bankruptcy petition—notice in Gazette

6.17 Affidavit of personal service of bankruptcy petition

6.18 Affidavit of substituted service of bankruptcy petition

6.19 Notice by debtor of intention to oppose bankruptcy petition

6.20 Notice of intention to appear on bankruptcy petition

6.21 List of creditors intending to appear on hearing of the bankruptcy petition

6.22 Dismissal of bankruptcy petition

6.23 Order of adjournment of bankruptcy petition

6.24 Notice to debtor and creditors of order of adjournment of bankruptcy petition

6.24A [Order for substitution of petitioner on creditor's petition]

6.24B [Change of carriage order]

6.25 Bankruptcy order on creditor's petition

6.26 [Application for registration of a bankruptcy order against an individual under Land Charges Act 1972]

6.27 Debtor's bankruptcy petition

6.28 Statement of affairs—debtor's petition

6.29 Order of appointment of insolvency practitioner to prepare a report under section 274(1) of the Insolvency Act 1986

6.30 [Bankruptcy order on debtor's petition]

6.31 ...

6.32 Order of appointment of interim receiver

6.33 Statement of affairs—creditor's petition

6.34 Request by creditor(s) for a meeting of the bankrupt's creditors

6.35 Notice to creditors of meeting of creditors

6.36 Notice to bankrupt of meeting of creditors

6.37 Proof of debt—general form

6.38 Proof by existing trustee as a claim in later bankruptcy

6.39 Affidavit of debt

6.40 Certificate of appointment of trustee by creditors' meeting

6.41 Certificate of appointment of two or more trustees by creditors' meeting

6.42 Order of court appointing trustee

6.43 Order of court appointing two or more trustees

6.44 Notice to court of resignation of trustee following meeting of creditors

6.45 Order of court giving trustee leave to resign

6.46 Notice to court of resignation of trustee following leave of the court

6.47 Certificate of removal of trustee

6.48 Order of court removing trustee or directing trustee to summon a meeting of creditors for the purpose of his removal

6.49 Trustee's application to the Secretary of State for his release

6.50 Notice to court of final meeting of creditors

6.51 Notice to official receiver by trustee on loss of qualification as insolvency practitioner

6.52 Certificate of constitution (amended certificate) of creditors' committee

6.53 Report by trustee of any change in membership of creditors' committee

6.54 Order of appointment of special manager

6.55 [Order for public examination of bankrupt]

6.56 Request by creditor(s) for the holding of a public examination of the bankrupt

6.57 [Order as to examination of bankrupt who is suffering from mental disorder or physical affliction or disability]

6.58 Affidavit of verification of record of the public examination of the bankrupt

6.59 [Order of adjournment of public examination of bankrupt]

6.60 [Order appointing time for proceeding with public examination of bankrupt adjourned generally]

6.61 [Notice of disclaimer under section 315 of the Insolvency Act 1986]

6.62 Notice to elect

6.63 Notice of intended disclaimer to interested party

6.64 Notice to bankrupt of an application under section 310 of the Insolvency Act 1986 for an income payments order

6.65 Order for income claimed under section 310(3)(a) of the Insolvency Act 1986

6.66 Order for income claimed under section 310(3)(b) of the Insolvency Act 1986

6.67 Order converting income payments order made under section 310(1)(a) to an order under section 310(3)(b) of the Insolvency Act 1986

6.68 Discharge or variation of order for income claimed under section 310 of the Insolvency Act 1986

6.69 Order under section 369(l) of the Insolvency Act 1986

6.70 Order under section 369(2) of the Insolvency Act 1986

6.71 Order of annulment under section 282 of the Insolvency Act 1986

6.72 Order of suspension of discharge under section 279(3) of the Insolvency Act 1986

6.73 Order of court lifting suspension of discharge

6.74 Certificate that order suspending discharge has been lifted

6.75 Notice to court by bankrupt that he intends to dispute statements made by official receiver in his report under section 289(2) of the Insolvency Act 1986

6.76 Order granting absolute/suspended discharge under section 280(2)(b) or (c) of the Insolvency Act 1986

6.77 Certificate of discharge

6.78 [Notice to existing trustee of the presentation of a petition for a later bankruptcy]

6.79 Criminal bankruptcy petition

6.79A [Charging order under section 313 of the Insolvency Act 1986]

6.80 Order to [postal operator] under section 371 of the Insolvency Act 1986

[6.81 Variation of income payments agreement under section 310A of the Insolvency Act 1986

6.82 Notice under section 279(2) of the Insolvency Act 1986

6.83 Notice to interested parties of a dwelling-house falling within section 283A of the Insolvency Act 1986

6.84 Certificate issued pursuant to Rule 6.237B(1) of the Insolvency Rules 1986]

Part 7: Court Procedure and Practice

7.1 Originating application

7.2 Ordinary application

7.3 Declaration by official shorthand writer

7.4 Appointment of shorthand writer to take examination under the Insolvency Act 1986

7.5 Declaration by shorthand writer

7.6 Warrant for failure to attend examination under section 133 of the Insolvency Act 1986

7.7 Warrant of arrest etc under section 364 of the Insolvency Act 1986

7.8 Warrant of arrest etc under section 236 or 366 of the Insolvency Act 1986

7.9 [Order for production of person arrested under warrant issued under section 134, 236, 364 or 366 of the Insolvency Act 1986]

7.10 Warrant to registrar of court in whose district a person against whom a warrant of arrest has been issued is believed to be

7. 11 Endorsement of warrant of arrest issued by a court to which the same has been sent for execution by the court which originally issued it

7.12 Warrant of seizure of property under section 365 of the Insolvency Act 1986

7.13 Search warrant under section 365 of the Insolvency Act 1986

7.14 Order of discharge from custody under the Insolvency Act 1986 (General)

7.15 [Affidavit in support of application for committal for contempt of court]

7.16 ...

7.17 Warrant of committal for contempt

7.18 Order of discharge from custody on contempt

7.19 Order appointing person to act for incapacitated person

[7.20 Application, affidavit and order confirming creditors' voluntary winding up]

Part 8: Proxies and Company Representation

8.1 Proxy—company or individual voluntary arrangements

8.2 Proxy—administration

8.3 Proxy—administrative receivership

8.4 Proxy—winding up by the court or bankruptcy

8.5 Proxy—members' or creditors' voluntary winding up

Part 9: Examination of Persons Concerned in Company and Individual Insolvency

9.1 Order under section 236 or 366 of the Insolvency Act 1986

[Part 12: Miscellaneous and General

12.1 Notice to the Registrar of Companies in respect of order under section 176A]

SCHEDULE 5
Punishment of Offences under the Rules
Rule 12.21

2.990

Note: In the fourth and fifth columns of this Schedule, 'the statutory maximum' means the prescribed sum under section 32 of the Magistrates' Courts Act 1980 (c 43).

Rule creating offence	General nature of offence	Mode of prosecution	Punishment	Daily default fine (where applicable)
	< ... >			
		2 Summary	6 months or the statutory maximum, or both	
In Part 2, [Rule 2.47(6)]	Administrator failing to send notification as to progress of administration	Summary	One-fifth of the statutory maximum	One-fiftieth of the statutory maximum
[Rule 2.111(3)	Administrator failing to file a notice of automatic end of administration	Summary	One-fifth of the statutory maximum	One-fiftieth of the statutory maximum
Rule 2.129(2)	Administrator's duties on vacating office	Summary	One-fifth of the statutory maximum	One-fiftieth of the statutory maximum]
In Part 3, Rule 3.32(5)	Administrative receiver failing to send notification as to progress of receivership	Summary.	One-fifth of the statutory maximum	One-fiftieth of the statutory maximum

Rule creating offence	General nature of offence	Mode of prosecution	Punishment	Daily default fine (where applicable)
In Part 12, Rule 12.18	False representation of status for purpose of inspecting documents	2 Summary	6 months or the statutory maximum, or both	
		1 On indictment	2 years or a fine, or both	
		2 Summary	6 months or the statutory maximum, or both	

[SCHEDULE 6
Determination of Insolvency Office Holder's Remuneration]

2.991

[As regards the determination of the remuneration of trustees and liquidators the realisation and distribution scales are as set out in the table below—

The realisation scale		
(i)	on the first £5000 or fraction thereof	20%
(ii)	on the next £5000 or fraction thereof	15%
(iii)	on the next £90000 or fraction thereof	10%
(iv)	on all further sums realised	5%
The distribution scale		
(i)	on the first £5000 or fraction thereof	10%
(ii)	on the next £5000 or fraction thereof	7.5%
(iii)	on the next £90000 or fraction thereof	5%
(iv)	on all further sums distributed	2.5%.]

1994 No 2421

Insolvent Partnerships Order 1994

Made: 13th September 1994

The Lord Chancellor, in exercise of the powers conferred on him by section 420(1) and (2) of the Insolvency Act 1986 and section 21(2) of the Company Directors Disqualification Act 1986 and of all other powers enabling him in that behalf, with the concurrence of the Secretary of State, hereby makes the following Order

Part I
General

3.1

1 Citation, commencement and extent

(1) This Order may be cited as the Insolvent Partnerships Order 1994 and shall come into force on 1st December 1994.

(2) This Order—
- (a) in the case of insolvency proceedings in relation to companies and partnerships, relates to companies and partnerships which the courts in England and Wales have jurisdiction to wind up; and
- (b) in the case of insolvency proceedings in relation to individuals, extends to England and Wales only.

(3) In paragraph (2) the term 'insolvency proceedings' has the meaning ascribed to it by article 2 below.

Notes

The Insolvent Partnerships Order 1994 ('IPO 1994 ') replaced the Insolvent Partnership Order 1986 in its entirety. Like the 1986 Order, the IPO 1994 makes amendments to the IA 1986 and applies them to partnerships. It is, however, more user-friendly as the schedules to the IPO 1994 reproduce the whole of the text of the relevant parts of the IA 1986 as amended. The annotations are not intended to be a comprehensive discussion of all of the procedures laid out in the IPO 1994 but are intended to state particular points of significance for partnerships. For general guidance on the procedures in the IPO 1994 reference should be made to the annotations to the relevant parts of the IA 1986.

The annotations assume a certain knowledge of the law of partnership. In understanding the IPO 1994 and the way that it works, it is important to have in mind the distinction between the partnership or 'joint' estate and the estate of each of the individual partners. Much of the complexity of the law relating to insolvent partnerships derives from the interaction of the joint and separate liabilities. In the very briefest of terms, the partnership's assets and liabilities are jointly held by the partners; and their assets and liabilities held by them separately from their role as partners in the firm are notionally separate. See further the definitions in Article 2 below.

1387

The basic rule in an insolvency is that the assets in the joint estate are to be applied in the discharge of the liabilities accruing to the joint estate. Correspondingly, a partner's separate assets are to be applied in discharging his separate liabilities. It is impossible to make sense of the IPO 1994 without this is mind.

Before the IPO 1994 it had been the rule that, where the partnership is being wound up at the same time as the separate estates of the partners, there had to be a surplus in a separate estate before a joint estate creditor could benefit from assets in a separate estate. Now, pursuant to Articles 8, 10 or 11 of the IPO 1994, the liquidator of the joint estate may prove for the amount of the deficit of assets over liabilities in the bankruptcy or liquidation of the separate estates: see Schedules 4 and 7 below.

The IPO 1994 has been amended a number of times most recently with effect from 6 April 2006 (Insolvent Partnerships (Amendment) Order 2006 SI 2006/622). The amendments relating to the administration of insolvent partnerships only apply where an administration application has been presented after 1 July 2005 (Insolvent Partnerships (Amendment) Order 2005 (SI 2005/1516).

3.2

2 Interpretation: definitions

(1) In this Order, except in so far as the context otherwise requires—
'the Act' means the Insolvency Act 1986;
'agricultural charge' has the same meaning as in the Agricultural Credits Act 1928;
'agricultural receiver' means a receiver appointed under an agricultural charge;
'corporate member' means an insolvent member which is a company;
'the court', in relation to an insolvent partnership, means the court which has jurisdiction to wind up the partnership;
'individual member' means an insolvent member who is an individual;
'insolvency order' means—
    (a) in the case of an insolvent partnership or a corporate member, a winding-up order; and
    (b) in the case of an individual member, a bankruptcy order;
'insolvency petition' means, in the case of a petition presented to the court—
    (a) against a corporate member, a petition for its winding up by the court;
    (b) against an individual member, a petition for a bankruptcy order to be made against that individual,
where the petition is presented in conjunction with a petition for the winding up of the partnership by the court as an unregistered company under the Act;
'insolvency proceedings' means any proceedings under the Act, this Order or the Insolvency Rules 1986;
'insolvent member' means a member of an insolvent partnership, against whom an insolvency petition is being or has been presented;
'joint bankruptcy petition' means a petition by virtue of article 11 of this Order;
'joint debt' means a debt of an insolvent partnership in respect of which an order is made by virtue of Part IV or V of this Order;

'joint estate' means the partnership property of an insolvent partnership in respect of which an order is made by virtue of Part IV or V of this Order;

'joint expenses' means expenses incurred in the winding up of an insolvent partnership or in the winding up of the business of an insolvent partnership and the administration of its property;

'limited partner' has the same meaning as in the Limited Partnerships Act 1907;

'member' means a member of a partnership and any person who is liable as a partner within the meaning of section 14 of the Partnership Act 1890;

'officer', in relation to an insolvent partnership, means—
    (a)   a member; or
    (b)   a person who has management or control of the partnership business;

'partnership property' has the same meaning as in the Partnership Act 1890;

'postponed debt' means a debt the payment of which is postponed by or under any provision of the Act or of any other enactment;

'responsible insolvency practitioner' means—
    (a)   in winding up, the liquidator of an insolvent partnership or corporate member; and
    (b)   in bankruptcy, the trustee of the estate of an individual member,
and in either case includes the official receiver when so acting;

'separate debt' means a debt for which a member of a partnership is liable, other than a joint debt;

'separate estate' means the property of an insolvent member against whom an insolvency order has been made;

'separate expenses' means expenses incurred in the winding up of a corporate member, or in the bankruptcy of an individual member; and

'trustee of the partnership' means a person authorised by order made by virtue of article 11 of this Order to wind up the business of an insolvent partnership and to administer its property.

(2) The definitions in paragraph (1), other than the first definition, shall be added to those in section 436 of the Act.

(3) References in provisions of the Act applied by this Order to any provision of the Act so applied shall, unless the context otherwise requires, be construed as references to the provision as so applied.

(4) Where, in any Schedule to this Order, all or any of the provisions of two or more sections of the Act are expressed to be modified by a single paragraph of the Schedule, the modification includes the combination of the provisions of those sections into the one or more sections set out in that paragraph.

Notes

'insolvency order'

Para (a) of the definition of 'insolvency order' refers to a 'winding-up order'. This is the terminology employed by the IA 1986. This should be contrasted with the terminology employed by the Partnership Act 1890 which contrasts 'dissolution' with 'winding up'. In the context of a solvent partnership, dissolution may be ordered by the court, effected by the partners or arise automatically on certain events; winding up is then the process of applying the firm's assets to the discharge of its liabilities and then distributing the surplus. See also Article 3(1) below in relation to *'expressions appropriate to companies'*

'member'

The definition in the IPO 1994 is wider than previously and includes those persons liable as a partner under s 14 Partnership Act 1890, persons held out as partners. This would therefore include the 'salaried partner'. The consequences of this are important for certain parts of the IPO 1994. It should be noted, however, that there is more to liability under s 14 Partnership Act 1890 than simply a holding out. There is a further requirement that such holding out has been relied upon in the giving of credit to the firm by another person: see s 14(1). The section only imposes liability as against that creditor. It is to be noted that there is a considerable amount of law of the question of when liability under s 14 can be imposed, (see generally Blackett-Ord Partnership (2nd edition) chapter 5) and that there is no presumption that any creditor of the firm has placed any reliance on the holding out: *Nationwide BS v Lewis* [1998] Ch 482. It follows that determining who is and who is not a member of a firm that has 'non-equity' partners may be a difficult matter and that may increase the complexity of many aspects of the insolvency of such a firm.

3.3

3 Interpretation: expressions appropriate to companies

(1) This article applies for the interpretation in relation to insolvent partnerships of expressions appropriate to companies in provisions of the Act and of the Company Directors Disqualification Act 1986 applied by this Order, unless the contrary intention appears.

(2) References to companies shall be construed as references to insolvent partnerships and all references to the registrar of companies shall be omitted.

(3) References to shares of a company shall be construed—
    (a) in relation to an insolvent partnership with capital, as references to rights to share in that capital; and
    (b) in relation to an insolvent partnership without capital, as references to interests—
        (i) conferring any right to share in the profits or liability to contribute to the losses of the partnership, or
        (ii) giving rise to an obligation to contribute to the debts or expenses of the partnership in the event of a winding up.

(4) Other expressions appropriate to companies shall be construed, in relation to an insolvent partnership, as references to the corresponding persons, officers, documents or organs (as the case may be) appropriate to a partnership.

Notes

Articles 2 and 3 above provide the definitions that will be used in and the constructions that should be placed upon the relevant parts of the IA 1986.

Part II
Voluntary Arrangements

3.4

4 Voluntary arrangement of insolvent partnership

[(1) The provisions of Part I of, and Schedule A1 to, the Act shall apply in relation to an insolvent partnership, certain of those provisions being modified in such manner that, after modification, they are as set out in Schedule 1 to this Order.]

(2) For the purposes of the provisions of the Act applied by paragraph (1), the provisions of the Act specified in paragraph (3) below, insofar as they relate to company voluntary arrangements, shall also apply in relation to insolvent partnerships.

(3) The provisions referred to in paragraph (2) are—
   (a) section 233 in Part VI,
   (b) Part VII, with the exception of section 250,
   (c) Part XII,
   (d) Part XIII,
   (e) sections 411, 413, 414 and 419 in Part XV, and
   (f) Parts XVI to XIX.

Notes

Article 4

This provides for the Partnership Voluntary Arrangement. There was no such provision in the IPO 1986: voluntary arrangements of partnerships could only be achieved by means of each partner proposing an IVA and each IVA being approved by all of the joint and separate creditors. The PVA was introduced by the IPO 1994 and introduced a procedure based on the CVA procedure in Part I of the IA 1986.

Moratorium

As a result of the Insolvent Partnerships (Amendment) (No 2) Order 2002 the changes implemented for companies by the IA 2000 were applied to PVAs from 1 January 2003; for the transitional provisions, see art 11(1) and (3) of that Order. The partnership is still treated as an unregistered company for the purposes of proposing a voluntary arrangement. Under the previous regime the partnership could not benefit from an interim order (as for IVAs) while the voluntary arrangement proposal was being prepared and considered by the creditors; now under the new provisions a partnership may take advantage of the moratorium that is available to companies under the CVA procedure (IA 1986 Sch A1). The availability of the moratorium could cause creditors to pursue the individual members and this could lead to difficulties in ascertaining what out of the partnership's property (loosely) is and is not subject to the moratorium as many partnerships are relatively lax in distinguishing between the property of the partnership and that of the members.

The new provisions in relation to CVAs are applied with appropriate changes. These are all self-explanatory; reference should be made to Schedule 1 below.

Who proposes the PVA?

The PVA should be proposed by the partners. However, where the partnership is in administration, is being wound up as an unregistered company or where there has been an order made on a joint bankruptcy petition, the proper person to propose the PVA is the administrator, liquidator or trustee as the case may be.

Authority to propose the PVA

It is essential that those who are making the proposal have the necessary authority to do so. Unless there is express provision in the partnership deed as to authority to make a PVA proposal, it is thought that a unanimous resolution would be required (as a PVA is presumably not an 'ordinary matter connected with the partnership business' within the meaning of s 24(8) Partnership Act 1890). Problems may arise from the definition of 'member' for the purposes of the IPO 1994. It includes not just actual partners but also those liable as partners under s 14 Partnership Act 1890: that is, someone who has allowed himself to be held out as a partner. An obvious category of such 'members' is that of salaried partners. The problem could arise when the 'member' concerned will not want to concede that he could be liable under s 14 Partnership Act 1890 (as the consequences are serious in the case of an insolvent partnership) and so will not want to agree to the proposal.

Interlocking PVA and members' VAs

As noted above, care should be taken to ensure that a PVA and the IVA or CVA of a member fit together in an appropriate way. In many cases the partnership creditor will only approve the PVA if the members enter into IVAs and CVAs as the case may be.

3.5

5 Voluntary arrangements of members of insolvent partnership

(1) Where insolvency orders are made against an insolvent partnership and an insolvent member of that partnership in his capacity as such, Part I of the Act shall apply to corporate members and Part VIII to individual members of that partnership, with the modification that any reference to the creditors of the company or of the debtor, as the case may be, includes a reference to the creditors of the partnership.

(2) Paragraph (1) is not to be construed as preventing the application of Part I or (as the case may be) Part VIII of the Act to any person who is a member of an insolvent partnership (whether or not a winding-up order has been made against that partnership) and against whom an insolvency order has not been made under this Order or under the Act.

Notes

The purpose of Article 5 is to clarify the position as regards joint liabilities where either the partnership or a member has had an insolvency order made against him/it. In those circumstances, a member may still propose an IVA or CVA (as appropriate) but the joint creditors are still to be treated as creditors for the purpose of that VA. This has been enacted from an abundance of caution: the joint debts would have had to have been included in any event – cf *Re Cupit [1996] BPIR 560*; *Schooler v Commissioners of Customs and Excise [1995] 2 BCLC 610*.

[Part III
Administration]

3.6

[6 Administration in relation to insolvent partnership]

[(1) The provisions of Part II of, and Schedule B1 to, the Act shall apply in relation to an insolvent partnership, certain of those provisions being modified in such manner that, after modification, they are as set out in Schedule 2 to this Order.

(2) In its application to insolvent partnerships, Part II of, and Schedule B1 to, the Act (as modified as set out in Schedule 2 to this Order) shall be read subject to paragraph (3).

(3) For every reference to—
   (a) 'administrative receiver' there shall be substituted 'agricultural receiver'; and
   (b) 'floating charge' there shall be substituted 'agricultural floating charge'.

(4) For the purposes of the provisions of the Act applied by paragraph (1), the provisions of the Act specified in paragraph (5) below, insofar as they relate to the appointment of an administrator, shall also apply in relation to insolvent partnerships.

(5) The provisions referred to in paragraph (4) are—
   (a) Part VI,
   (b) Part VII (with the exception of section 250),
   (c) Part XII,
   (d) Part XIII,
   (e) sections 411, 413, 414 and 419 in Part XV, and
   (f) Parts XVI to XIX.

(6) For the purposes of this Article and the provisions of the Act applied by paragraph (1), 'agricultural floating charge' shall be construed as a reference to a floating charge created under section 5 of the Agricultural Credits Act 1928.]

Notes

This Article applies the new administration procedure under IA 1986 Part II, Sch B1 to insolvent partnerships with appropriate changes. The new procedure applies except where a petition for an administration was presented before 1 July 2005; in that event the former procedure under the former IA 1986 s 8 to 27 will apply. Under the new procedure in relation to insolvent partnerships an administrator may be appointed by a court order; or by the holder of an agricultural floating charge; or by the members of the insolvent partnership (Sch 2 para 2).

Floating Charges

A difference between administration for companies and partnerships is that usually there will be no floating chargeholder who can veto the administration. A partnership cannot create a floating charge as a company can: see, *Re West Park Golf and Country Club* [1997] 1 BCLC 20. However, a farming partnership may create a floating charge over its assets under s 28 Agricultural Credits Act 1928. Accordingly, the provisions applicable in relation to those entitled to appoint administrative receivers in company administrations are changed so that, with partnerships, the relevant provisions refer to agricultural chargeholders

Duty of administrator

In *Oldham v Kyrris* [2004] BPIR 165 the Court of Appeal has held that an administrator of an insolvent partnership does not in general owe a duty of care to individual unsecured creditors.

Part IV
Creditors' etc Winding-up Petitions

3.7

7 Winding up of insolvent partnership as unregistered company on petition of creditor etc where no concurrent petition presented against member

(1) Subject to paragraph (2) below, the provisions of Part V of the Act shall apply in relation to the winding up of an insolvent partnership as an unregistered company on the petition of a creditor, [of a liquidator (within the meaning of Article 2(b) of the EC Regulation) appointed in proceedings by virtue of Article 3(1) of the EC Regulation, of a temporary administrator (within the meaning of Article 38 of the EC Regulation),] of a responsible insolvency practitioner[, of the Secretary of State or of any other person other than a member,] where no insolvency petition is presented by the petitioner against a member or former member of that partnership in his capacity as such.

(2) Certain of the provisions referred to in paragraph (1) are modified in their application in relation to insolvent partnerships which are being wound up by virtue of that paragraph in such manner that, after modification, they are as set out in Part I of Schedule 3 to this Order.

(3) The provisions of the Act specified in Part II of Schedule 3 to this Order shall apply as set out in that Part for the purposes of section 221(5) of the Act, as modified by Part I of that Schedule.

Notes

Article 7

This makes provision for a creditor's petition for the winding up of a partnership as an unregistered company without concurrently petitioning for the bankruptcy or winding up of the members of the partnership. The winding up of unregistered companies is dealt with in IA 1986 s 220 to 229. The consequence of an order for the winding up of the firm alone is that the joint estate will be wound up and that the individual members will be liable to contribute to any shortfall in joint assets over joint debts. The alternative course for a creditor is to petition for the winding up of the partnership and also concurrently petition against the members. This latter course might be thought to be preferable as the joint and single estate can all be administered together. However, there are circumstances where an Article 7 petition is preferable, for example, where the members are participating in a profitable business outside the partnership and the creditor does not want to prevent them from earning the money that will enable the creditor to be repaid but it is desired to prevent the partnership from incurring any more debts. Another circumstance where the facility to present an Article 7 petition is essential is where one member is bankrupt and his trustee wants to realise any value in the bankrupt's share of the partnership assets.

3.8

8 [Winding up of insolvent partnership as unregistered company on the petition of creditor etc where concurrent petitions presented against one or more members]

(1) Subject to paragraph (2) below, the provisions of Part V of the Act (other than sections 223 and 224), shall apply in relation to the winding

up of an insolvent partnership as an unregistered company on [the petition of a creditor, of a liquidator (within the meaning of Article 2(b) of the EC Regulation) appointed in proceedings by virtue of Article 3(1) of the EC Regulation, or of a temporary administrator (within the meaning of Article 38 of the EC Regulation)] where insolvency petitions are presented by the petitioner against the partnership and against one or more members or former members of the partnership in their capacity as such.

(2) Certain of the provisions referred to in paragraph (1) are modified in their application in relation to insolvent partnerships which are being wound up by virtue of that paragraph in such manner that, after modification, they are as set out in Part I of Schedule 4 to this Order.

(3) The provisions of the Act specified in Part II of Schedule 4 to this Order shall apply as set out in that Part for the purposes of section 221(5) of the Act, as modified by Part I of that Schedule.

(4) The provisions of the Act specified in paragraph (5) below, insofar as they relate to winding up of companies by the court in England and Wales on a creditor's petition, shall apply in relation to the winding up of a corporate member or former corporate member (in its capacity as such) of an insolvent partnership which is being wound up by virtue of paragraph (1).

(5) The provisions referred to in paragraph (4) are—
    (a)   Part IV,
    (b)   Part VI,
    (c)   Part VII, and
    (d)   Parts XII to XIX.

(6) The provisions of the Act specified in paragraph (7) below, insofar as they relate to the bankruptcy of individuals in England and Wales on a petition presented by a creditor, shall apply in relation to the bankruptcy of an individual member or former individual member (in his capacity as such) of an insolvent partnership which is being wound up by virtue of paragraph (1).

(7) The provisions referred to in paragraph (6) are—
    (a)   Part IX (other than sections 269, 270, 287 and 297), and
    (b)   Parts X to XIX.

(8) Certain of the provisions referred to in paragraphs (4) and (6) are modified in their application in relation to the corporate or individual members or former corporate or individual members of insolvent partnerships in such manner that, after modification, they are as set out in Part II of Schedule 4 to this Order.

(9) The provisions of the Act applied by this Article shall further be modified so that references to a corporate or individual member include any former such member against whom an insolvency petition is being or has been presented by virtue of this Article.

Notes

A creditor's petition against the partnership and against one or more of the members will generally be regarded as the most effective way of maximising returns where there is no reason why it would be better for the members not to be bankrupt or in liquidation. It allows the process of allocating debts between the joint and single estates to be dealt with however. It is therefore unsurprising that this is the most common way of winding up a partnership on a creditor's petition.

The fact that the petitions are concurrent makes for a slightly more complicated procedure (as to which refer to the provisions of Schedule 4 below). In summary, the petitions must be presented to the same court and on the same day (unless otherwise directed). Each petition must have particulars of the other petitions. The petition against the partnership will be heard first, usually in the companies winding up list for the court in question. At that hearing the petitioner will have to notify the court of the progress of the other petitions.

The hearings against the individual members will take place separately. The current practice in the Royal Courts of Justice in London is for the partners' bankruptcy petition list to be heard in the afternoon following the morning winding up list. At that hearing, the court will need to be informed of what has happened to the petition against the partnership. However, the court hearing the individual petitions will not be bound to follow the decision in relation to the petition against the partnership: if the petition against the firm is dismissed, the petitions against the members can still proceed in the ordinary way; likewise, if no insolvency order is made against a member within 28 days of a winding up order against the firm, then the partnership winding up will proceed as though under Article 7. In deciding how to proceed on the individual petitions, the court will have regard to all of the circumstances, and to whether they have changed since the hearing of the partnership petition; for a case where the petition debt was paid between the petitions see *Re Marr* [1990] Ch 773 (CA).

Note that in Article 8(5)(a) the words '(other than section 176A)' were deleted from 6 April 2006 by the Insolvent Partnerships (Amendment) Order 2006 (SI 2006/622).

Part V
Members' Petitions

3.9

9 Winding up of insolvent partnership as unregistered company on member's petition where no concurrent petition presented against member

The following provisions of the Act shall apply in relation to the winding up of an insolvent partnership as an unregistered company on the petition of a member where no insolvency petition is presented by the petitioner against a member of that partnership in his capacity as such—

    (a)   sections 117 and 221, modified in such manner that, after modification, they are as set out in Schedule 5 to this Order; and

    (b)   the other provisions of Part V of the Act, certain of those provisions being modified in such manner that, after modification, they are as set out in Part I of Schedule 3 to this Order.

Notes

Article 9

This provides for a member's petition to wind the partnership up as an unregistered company where there are no petitions against the petitioning or any other member. A member may petition under Article 9 if there are 8 members or more (Schedule 5 s 221A), otherwise the permission of the court is required (on the petitioner's without notice application). The grounds for petitioning are that the partnership has ceased trading, that it is insolvent or on the just and equitable ground.

For the purposes of Article 9, 'member' includes the trustee in bankruptcy or liquidator of a member.

3.10

10 Winding up of insolvent partnership as unregistered company on member's petition where concurrent petitions presented against all members

(1) The following provisions of the Act shall apply in relation to the winding up of an insolvent partnership as an unregistered company on a member's petition where insolvency petitions are presented by the petitioner against the partnership and against all its members in their capacity as such—

(a) sections 117, 124, 125, 221, 264, 265, 271 and 272 of the Act, modified in such manner that, after modification, they are as set out in Schedule 6 to this Order; and

(b) sections 220, 225 and 227 to 229 in Part V of the Act, section 220 being modified in such manner that, after modification, it is as set out in Part I of Schedule 4 to this Order.

(2) The provisions of the Act specified in paragraph (3) below, insofar as they relate to winding up of companies by the court in England and Wales on a member's petition, shall apply in relation to the winding up of a corporate member (in its capacity as such) of an insolvent partnership which is wound up by virtue of paragraph (1).

(3) The provisions referred to in paragraph (2) are—

(a) Part IV,
(b) Part VI,
(c) Part VII, and
(d) Parts XII to XIX.

(4) The provisions of the Act specified in paragraph (5) below, insofar as they relate to the bankruptcy of individuals in England and Wales where a bankruptcy petition is presented by a debtor, shall apply in relation to the bankruptcy of an individual member (in his capacity as such) of an insolvent partnership which is being wound up by virtue of paragraph (1).

(5) The provisions referred to in paragraph (4) are—

(a) Part IX (other than sections 273, 274, 287 and 297), and
(b) Parts X to XIX.

[(6) Certain of the provisions referred to in paragraphs (2) and (4) are modified in their application in relation to the corporate or individual members of insolvent partnerships in such manner that, after modification, they are as set out in Part II of Schedule 4 to this Order.]

Notes

This provides for petitions against the partnership in circumstances where there are petitions against all of the members (including the petitioner) and all of the members consent to an insolvency order being made against them. Like other provisions under the IPO 1994 that allow for more than one related petition, the proper procedure needs to be followed (as to which see Schedule 6). In short, the petitions will usually need to be presented to the same court on the same day. The partnership petition will be heard first and then the individual petitions will need to be heard in the next 28 days. The court will not necessarily make the same order on the partnership and individual petitions.

Note that in Article 10(3)(a) the words '(other than section 176A)' were deleted from 6 April 2006 by the Insolvent Partnerships (Amendment) Order 2006 (SI 2006/622).

3.11

11 Insolvency proceedings not involving winding up of insolvent partnership as unregistered company where individual members present joint bankruptcy petition

(1) The provisions of the Act specified in paragraph (2) below shall apply in relation to the bankruptcy of the individual members of an insolvent partnership where those members jointly present a petition to the court for orders to be made for the bankruptcy of each of them in his capacity as a member of the partnership, and the winding up of the partnership business and administration of its property, without the partnership being wound up as an unregistered company under Part V of the Act.

(2) The provisions referred to in paragraph (1) are—
  (a)   Part IX (other than sections 273, 274 and 287), and
  (b)   Parts X to XIX,
insofar as they relate to the insolvency of individuals in England and Wales where a bankruptcy petition is presented by a debtor.

(3) Certain of the provisions referred to in paragraph (1) are modified in their application in relation to the individual members of insolvent partnerships in such manner that, after modification, they are as set out in Schedule 7 to this Order.

Notes

Article 11 provides for the members of a partnership to wind up their affairs without petitioning for the winding up of the firm. The members jointly present a petition in the prescribed form and request that the trustee winds up and administers the partnership's affairs without it being wound up as an unregistered company. The sole ground on which an Article 11 petition may be presented is that the partnership is unable to pay its debts.

Part VI
Provisions Applying in Insolvency Proceedings in Relation to Insolvent Partnerships

3.12

12 Winding up of unregistered company which is a member of insolvent partnership being wound up by virtue of this Order

Where an insolvent partnership or other body which may be wound up under Part V of the Act as an unregistered company is itself a member of

> an insolvent partnership being so wound up, articles 8 and 10 above shall apply in relation to the latter insolvent partnership as though the former body were a corporate member of that partnership.

Notes

The purpose of Article 12 is to provide for the separation of estates in the species of partnership known as a 'group partnership'. A group partnership may be described as a partnership between members one of which is itself a partnership. The proper analysis of the structure of these partnerships is that all of the members of the member firms are equally members of the group partnership. Article 12 provides that the member firm in a group partnership is to be treated as a corporate member for the purposes of Articles 8 and 10. The effect of that is that the joint estate of the group partnership is kept distinct from those of members being firms themselves. Note though that Article 12 does not alter the basis of the winding up of the member firm.

The group partnership should be distinguished from the 'sub-partnership'. A sub-partnership arises in the situation where one member of a partnership agrees to divide his share in that partnership with other persons. The relationship between that partner and the other persons may then satisfy the conditions in the Partnership Act 1890 for the existence of a partnership. However, those other persons will not be partners with the other members of the main partnership. This kind of situation is relatively rare as many partnership deeds prohibit sub-partnerships. It is not clear but the better view is that Article 12 does not apply in cases of sub-partnership: see *Lindley & Banks on Partnership* (18th edition) paragraph 27–32, n39.

The distinction between the two types of partnership may not be obvious. For example, the case of a firm with different regional offices where each office takes a share of the firm's profit which is then divided between the partners based there may be difficult to analyse.

3.13

13 Deposit on petitions

(1) Where an order under section 414(4) or 415(3) of the Act (security for fees) provides for any sum to be deposited on presentation of a winding-up or bankruptcy petition, that sum shall, in the case of petitions presented by virtue of articles 8 and 10 above, only be required to be deposited in respect of the petition for winding up the partnership, but shall be treated as a deposit in respect of all those petitions.

(2) Production of evidence as to the sum deposited on presentation of the petition for winding up the partnership shall suffice for the filing in court of an insolvency petition against an insolvent member.

Notes

IA 1900 s 414 provides for the making of fees orders in relation to corporate insolvency and IA 1986 s 415 deals with individual insolvency. The petitioner must deposit a sum on the presentation of a winding-up or bankruptcy petition (see Insolvency Proceedings (Fees) Order 2004 SI 2004/593).

Article 13 applies in cases where there is either a member's or creditor's petition for the winding up of the partnership and concurrent petitions in relation to one or more members. It allows the petitioner to lodge a deposit in relation to the petition in respect of the partnership only. Without this, initiating insolvency proceedings under Articles 8 and 10 could be prohibitively expensive, especially in the case of a partnership with many members.

3.14

14 Supplemental powers of court

...

Notes

This article inserts the Insolvency Act 1986, s 168(5A) to (5C), 303(2A) to (2C).

3.15

15 Meaning of 'act as insolvency practitioner'

...

Notes

This article inserts the Insolvency Act 1986, s 388(2A) and amends s 388(3).

Part VII
Disqualification

3.16

16 Application of Company Directors Disqualification Act 1986

Where an insolvent partnership is wound up as an unregistered company under Part V of the Act, the provisions of [sections 1, 1A, 6 to 10, 13 to 15, 17], 19(c) and 20 of, and Schedule 1 to, the Company Directors Disqualification Act 1986 shall apply, certain of those provisions being modified in such manner that, after modification, they are as set out in Schedule 8 to this Order.

Notes

This provision applies certain of the provisions of the CDDA 1986 to insolvent partnerships. Broadly, a partner in an insolvent partnership is liable to be disqualified if his conduct is found to be such as to make him unfit to be concerned in the management of a company. This part of the IPO 1994 is interesting as a matter of policy. At first glance the policy behind the CDDA 1986 is to prevent and punish the abuse of limited liability. As a partner (save as part of a LLP) one does not enjoy limited liability. See Schedule 8 below and the notes to it for the parts of the CDDA 1986 that apply with modifications and see also the notes to the CDDA 1986 elsewhere in this work.

Part VIII
Miscellaneous

3.17

17 Forms

(1) The forms contained in Schedule 9 to this Order shall be used in and in connection with proceedings by virtue of this Order, whether in the High Court or a county court.

(2) The forms shall be used with such variations, if any, as the circumstances may require.

Notes

See Schedule 9 below for the forms. The forms may be adapted to fit the circumstances of the individual case.

3.18

18 Application of subordinate legislation

(1) The subordinate legislation specified in Schedule 10 to this Order shall apply as from time to time in force and with such modifications as the context requires for the purpose of giving effect to the provisions of the Act and of the Company Directors Disqualification Act 1986 which are applied by this Order.

(2) In the case of any conflict between any provision of the subordinate legislation applied by paragraph (1) and any provision of this Order, the latter provision shall prevail.

Notes

See Schedule 10 for a list of the relevant subordinate legislation. There is a wider range of subordinate legislation than under the IPO 1986. The legislation referred to must be read with such modifications as the context requires for giving effect to the provisions of the IA 1986 and the CDDA 1986. Given the fact that the affairs of companies are more closely regulated than those of partnerships, there will be considerable scope for argument about what modifications are required by the context in each case when the legislation in question was intended to take effect primarily in relation to companies.

3.19

19 Supplemental and transitional provisions

(1) This Order does not apply in relation to any case in which a winding-up or a bankruptcy order was made under the Insolvent Partnerships Order 1986 in relation to a partnership or an insolvent member of a partnership, and where this Order does not apply the law in force immediately before this Order came into force continues to have effect.

(2) Where winding-up or bankruptcy proceedings commenced under the provisions of the Insolvent Partnerships Order 1986 were pending in relation to a partnership or an insolvent member of a partnership immediately before this Order came into force, either—

(a) those proceedings shall be continued, after the coming into force of this Order, in accordance with the provisions of this Order, or

(b) if the court so directs, they shall be continued under the provisions of the 1986 Order, in which case the law in force immediately before this Order came into force continues to have effect.

(3) For the purpose of paragraph (2) above, winding-up or bankruptcy proceedings are pending if a statutory or written demand has been served or a winding-up or bankruptcy petition has been presented.

[(4) Nothing in this Order is to be taken as preventing a petition being presented against an insolvent partnership under section 367 of the Financial Services and Markets Act 2000, or any other enactment [except where paragraph 12 of Schedule A1 to the Act, as applied by this Order, has the effect of preventing a petition being so presented].]

(5) Nothing in this Order is to be taken as preventing any creditor or creditors owed one or more debts by an insolvent partnership from presenting a petition under the Act against one or more members of the partnership liable for that debt or those debts (as the case may be) without including the others and without presenting a petition for the winding up of the partnership as an unregistered company.

(6) Bankruptcy proceedings may be consolidated by virtue of article 14(2) above irrespective of whether they were commenced under the Bankruptcy Act 1914 or the Insolvency Act 1986 or by virtue of the Insolvent Partnerships Order 1986 or this Order, and the court shall, in the case of proceedings commenced under or by virtue of different enactments, make provision for the manner in which the consolidated proceedings are to be conducted.

3.20

20 Revocation

...

Notes

This article revokes The Insolvent Partnerships Order 1986 (SI 1986/2142).

[SCHEDULE 1
Modified Provisions of Part I of, and Schedule A1 to, the Act
(Company Voluntary Arrangements) as Applied by Article 4]

Notes

This Schedule was substituted by Insolvent Partnerships (Amendment) (No 2) Order 2002, art 6 Sch 1 SI 2002/2708 and came into force on 1 January 2003 subject to transitional provisions; Article 11(1), (3).

[Part I
Modified Provisions of Sections 1 to 7B of the Act]

[For sections 1 to 7B of the Act there shall be substituted:—

'Part I
Partnership Voluntary Arrangements

The proposal

3.21

1 Those who may propose an arrangement

(1) The members of an insolvent partnership (other than one [which is in administration], or which is being wound up as an unregistered company, or in respect of which an order has been made by virtue of article 11 of the Insolvent Partnerships Order 1994) may make a proposal under this Part to the partnership's creditors for a composition in satisfaction of the debts of the partnership or a scheme of arrangement of its affairs (from here on referred to, in either case, as a 'voluntary arrangement').

(2) A proposal under this Part is one which provides for some person ('the nominee') to act in relation to the voluntary arrangement either as trustee or otherwise for the purpose of supervising its implementation; and the nominee must be a person who is qualified to act as an insolvency practitioner or authorised to act as nominee, in relation to the voluntary arrangement.

(3) Such a proposal may also be made—
  (a) where [the partnership is in administration], by the administrator,
  (b) where the partnership is being wound up as an unregistered company, by the liquidator, and
  (c) where an order has been made by virtue of article 11 of the Insolvent Partnerships Order 1994, by the trustee of the partnership.

(4) ...

————

Notes

This deals with who may propose the PVA and in what circumstances; and see the notes to Article 4 above.

————

3.22

1A Moratorium

(1) Where the members of an eligible insolvent partnership intend to make a proposal for a voluntary arrangement, they may take steps to obtain a moratorium for the insolvent partnership.

(2) Subject to subsections (3), (4), (5), (6) and (7), the provisions of Schedule A1 to this Act have effect with respect to—

(a)   insolvent partnerships eligible for a moratorium under this section,

(b)   the procedure for obtaining such a moratorium,

(c)   the effects of such a moratorium, and

(d)   the procedure applicable (in place of sections 2 to 6 and 7) in relation to the approval and implementation of a voluntary arrangement where such a moratorium is or has been in force.

(3) Certain of the provisions applied in relation to insolvent partnerships by virtue of subsection (2) are modified in their application in relation to insolvent partnerships in such manner that, after modification, they are as set out in Part II of Schedule 1 to the Insolvent Partnerships Order 1994.

(4) Paragraphs 4A, 4B, 4C, 4D, 4E, 4F, 4G, 4H, 4I, 4J, 4K, 5, 7(4), 8(8), 32(7), 34(2), 41(5) and 45 of Schedule A1 to this Act shall not apply.

(5) An insolvent partnership is not liable to a fine under paragraphs 16(2), 17(3), 18(3), 19(3), 22 or 23(1) of Schedule A1 to the Act.

(6) Notwithstanding subsection (5) an officer of an insolvent partnership may be liable to imprisonment or a fine under the paragraphs referred to in that subsection in the same manner as an officer of a company.

(7) In the application of Schedule A1, and the application of the entries in Schedule 10 relating to offences under Schedule A1, to insolvent partnerships—

(a)   references to the directors or members of a company shall be construed as references to the members of an insolvent partnership,

(b)   references to officers of a company shall be construed as references to the officers of an insolvent partnership,

(c)   references to a meeting of a company shall be construed as references to a meeting of the members of an insolvent partnership, and

(d)   references to a floating charge shall be construed as references to a floating charge created under section 5 of the Agricultural Credits Act 1928.

Notes

This provision modifies the moratorium provisions so as to make them suitable for application to insolvent partnerships. The fines that are imposed on a company that is in breach of the restrictions on its activities set out in IA 1986 Sch A1 are not applied to the insolvent partnership. However, the provisions as to fining and imprisoning a company's officers are applied.

3.23

2 Procedure where nominee is not the liquidator, administrator or trustee

(1) This section applies where the nominee under section 1 is not the liquidator, administrator or trustee of the insolvent partnership and the

members of the partnership do not propose to take steps to obtain a moratorium under section 1A for the insolvent partnership.

(2) The nominee shall, within 28 days (or such longer period as the court may allow) after he is given notice of the proposal for a voluntary arrangement, submit a report to the court stating—

(a) whether, in his opinion, the proposed voluntary arrangement has a reasonable prospect of being approved and implemented,

(b) whether, in his opinion, meetings of the members of the partnership and of the partnership's creditors should be summoned to consider the proposal, and

(c) if in his opinion such meetings should be summoned, the date on which, and time and place at which, he proposes the meetings should be held.

(3) The nominee shall also state in his report whether there are in existence any insolvency proceedings in respect of the insolvent partnership or any of its members.

(4) For the purposes of enabling the nominee to prepare his report, the person intending to make the proposal shall submit to the nominee—

(a) a document setting out the terms of the proposed voluntary arrangement, and

(b) a statement of the partnership's affairs containing—

(i) such particulars of the partnership's creditors and of the partnership's debts and other liabilities and of the partnership property as may be prescribed, and

(ii) such other information as may be prescribed.

(5) The court may—

(a) on an application made by the person intending to make the proposal, in a case where the nominee has failed to submit the report required by this section or has died, or

(b) on an application made by that person or the nominee, in a case where it is impracticable or inappropriate for the nominee to continue to act as such,

direct that the nominee be replaced as such by another person qualified to act as an insolvency practitioner, or authorised to act as nominee, in relation to the voluntary arrangement.

Notes

This provision will necessarily apply where the proposal is made by the members.

3.24

3 Summoning of meetings

(1) Where the nominee under section 1 is not the liquidator, administrator or trustee of the insolvent partnership, and it has been reported to the court that such meetings as are mentioned in section 2(2) should be summoned, the person making the report shall (unless the court otherwise directs) summon those meetings for the time, date and place proposed in the report.

(2) Where the nominee is the liquidator, administrator or trustee of the insolvent partnership, he shall summon meetings of the members of the partnership and of the partnership's creditors to consider the proposal for such a time, date and place as he thinks fit.

(3) The persons to be summoned to a creditors' meeting under this section are every creditor of the partnership of whose claim and address the person summoning the meeting is aware.

Consideration and implementation of proposal

3.25

4 Decisions of meetings

(1) The meetings under section 3 shall decide whether to approve the proposed voluntary arrangement (with or without modifications).

(2) The modifications may include one conferring the functions proposed to be conferred on the nominee on another person qualified to act as an insolvency practitioner, or authorised to act as nominee, in relation to the voluntary arrangement.

But they shall not include any modification by virtue of which the proposal ceases to be a proposal such as is mentioned in section 1.

(3) A meeting so summoned shall not approve any proposal or modification which affects the right of a secured creditor of the partnership to enforce his security, except with the concurrence of the creditor concerned.

(4) Subject as follows, a meeting so summoned shall not approve any proposal or modification under which—
- (a) any preferential debt of the partnership is to be paid otherwise than in priority to such of its debts as are not preferential debts, or
- (b) a preferential creditor of the partnership is to be paid an amount in respect of a preferential debt that bears to that debt a smaller proportion than is borne to another preferential debt by the amount that is to be paid in respect of that other debt.

However, the meeting may approve such a proposal or modification with the concurrence of the preferential creditor concerned.

(5) Subject as above, each of the meetings shall be conducted in accordance with the rules.

(6) After the conclusion of either meeting in accordance with the rules, the chairman of the meeting shall report the result of the meeting to the court, and, immediately after reporting to the court, shall give notice of the result of the meeting to all those who were sent notice of the meeting in accordance with the rules.

(7) References in this section to preferential debts and preferential creditors are to be read in accordance with section 386 in Part XII of this Act.

3.26

4A Approval of arrangement

(1) This section applies to a decision, under section 4, with respect to the approval of a proposed voluntary arrangement.

(2) The decision has effect if, in accordance with the rules—
- (a) it has been taken by both meetings summoned under section 3, or
- (b) (subject to any order made under subsection (6)) it has been taken by the creditors' meeting summoned under that section.

(3) If the decision taken by the creditors' meeting differs from that taken by the meeting of the members of the partnership, a member of the partnership may apply to court.

(4) An application under subsection (3) shall not be made after the end of the period of 28 days beginning with—
- (a) the day on which the decision was taken by the creditors' meeting, or
- (b) where the decision of the meeting of the members of the partnership was taken on a later day, that day.

(5) Where a member of an insolvent partnership which is regulated applies to the court under subsection (3), the Financial Services Authority is entitled to be heard on the application.

(6) On an application under subsection (3), the court may—
- (a) order the decision of the meeting of the members of the partnership to have effect instead of the decision of the creditors' meeting, or
- (b) make such other order as it thinks fit.

(7) In this section 'regulated' in relation to an insolvent partnership means a person who—
- (a) is, or has been, an authorised person within the meaning given by section 31 of the Financial Services and Markets Act 2000,
- (b) is, or has been, an appointed representative within the meaning given by section 39 of that Act, or
- (c) is carrying on, or has carried on, a regulated activity, within the meaning given by section 22 of that Act, in contravention of the general prohibition within the meaning given by section 19 of that Act.

3.27

5 Effect of approval

(1) This section applies where a decision approving a voluntary arrangement has effect under section 4A.

(2) The voluntary arrangement—
- (a) takes effect as if made by the members of the partnership at the creditors' meeting, and
- (b) binds every person who in accordance with the rules—
  - (i) was entitled to vote at that meeting (whether or not he was present or represented at it), or
  - (ii) would have been so entitled if he had had notice of it,

as if he were a party to the voluntary arrangement.

(2A) If—
- (a) when the arrangement ceases to have effect any amount payable under the arrangement to a person bound by virtue of subsection 2(b)(ii) has not been paid, and
- (b) the arrangement did not come to an end prematurely,

the insolvent partnership shall at that time become liable to pay to that person the amount payable under the arrangement.

(3) Subject as follows, if the partnership is being wound up as an unregistered company, or [is in administration] or an order by virtue of article 11 of the Insolvent Partnerships Order 1994 is in force, the court may do one or both of the following, namely—
- (a) by order—
  - (i) stay all proceedings in the winding up or in the proceedings under the order made by virtue of the said article 11 (as the case may be), including any related insolvency proceedings of a member of the partnership in his capacity as such, or
  - (ii) [provide for the appointment of the administrator to cease to have effect];
- (b) give such directions as it thinks appropriate for facilitating the implementation of the voluntary arrangement with respect to—
  - (i) the conduct of the winding up, the proceedings by virtue of the said article 11 or the administration (as the case may be), and
  - (ii) the conduct of any related insolvency proceedings as referred to in paragraph (a)(i) above.

(4) The court shall not make an order under subsection (3)(a)—
- (a) at any time before the end of the period of 28 days beginning with the first day on which each of the reports required by section 4(6) has been made to the court, or
- (b) at any time when an application under the next section or an appeal in respect of such an application is pending, or at any time in the period within which such an appeal may be brought.

3.28

6 Challenge of decisions

(1) Subject to this section, an application to the court may be made, by any of the persons specified below, on one or both of the following grounds, namely—
- (a) that a voluntary arrangement which has effect under section 4A unfairly prejudices the interests of a creditor, member or contributory of the partnership;
- (b) that there has been some material irregularity at or in relation to either of the meetings.

(2) The persons who may apply under this section are—
- (a) a person entitled, in accordance with the rules, to vote at either of the meetings;
- (b) a person who would have been entitled, in accordance with the rules, to vote at the creditors' meeting if he had had notice of it;

- (c) the nominee or any person who has replaced him under section 2(5) or 4(2); and
- (d) if the partnership is being wound up as an unregistered company or [is in administration or an] order by virtue of article 11 of the Insolvent Partnerships Order 1994 is in force, the liquidator, administrator or trustee of the partnership.

(3) An application under this section shall not be made—
- (a) after the end of the period of 28 days beginning with the first day on which each of the reports required by section 4(6) has been made to the court, or
- (b) in the case of a person who was not given notice of the creditors' meeting, after the end of the period of 28 days beginning with the day on which he became aware that the meeting had taken place,

but (subject to that) an application made by a person within subsection (2)(b) on the ground that the voluntary arrangement prejudices his interests may be made after the voluntary arrangement has ceased to have effect, unless it came to an end prematurely.

(4) Where on such an application the court is satisfied as to either of the grounds mentioned in subsection (1), it may do one or both of the following, namely—
- (a) revoke or suspend any decision approving the voluntary arrangement which has effect under section 4A or, in a case falling within subsection (1)(b), any decision taken by the meeting in question which has effect under that section;
- (b) give a direction to any person for the summoning of further meetings to consider any revised proposal the person who made the original proposal may make or, in a case falling within subsection (1)(b), a further meeting of the members of the partnership or (as the case may be) of the partnership's creditors to reconsider the original proposal.

(5) Where at any time after giving a direction under subsection (4)(b) for the summoning of meetings to consider a revised proposal the court is satisfied that the person who made the original proposal does not intend to submit a revised proposal, the court shall revoke the direction and revoke or suspend any decision approving the voluntary arrangement which has effect under section 4A.

(6) In a case where the court, on an application under this section with respect to any meeting—
- (a) gives a direction under subsection (4)(b), or
- (b) revokes or suspends an approval under subsection (4)(a) or (5),

the court may give such supplemental directions as it thinks fit, and, in particular, directions with respect to things done under the voluntary arrangement since it took effect.

(7) Except in pursuance of the preceding provisions of this section, a decision taken at a meeting summoned under section 3 is not invalidated by any irregularity at or in relation to the meeting.

3.29

6A False representations, etc

(1) If, for the purpose of obtaining the approval of the members or creditors of an insolvent partnership or of the members or creditors of any of its members to a proposal for a voluntary arrangement in relation to the partnership or any of its members, a person who is an officer of the partnership or an officer (which for this purpose includes a shadow director) of a corporate member in relation to which a voluntary arrangement is proposed—

(a)   makes a false representation, or

(b)   fraudulently does, or omits to do, anything,

he commits an offence.

(2) Subsection (1) applies even if the proposal is not approved.

(3) A person guilty of an offence under this section is liable to imprisonment or a fine, or both.

3.30

7 Implementation of proposal

(1) This section applies where a voluntary arrangement has effect under section 4A.

(2) The person who is for the time being carrying out in relation to the voluntary arrangement the functions conferred—

(a)   on the nominee by virtue of the approval given at one or both of the meetings summoned under section 3, or

(b)   by virtue of section 2(5) or 4(2) on a person other than the nominee,

shall be known as the supervisor of the voluntary arrangement.

(3) If any of the partnership's creditors or any other person is dissatisfied by any act, omission or decision of the supervisor, he may apply to the court; and on the application the court may—

(a)   confirm, reverse or modify any act or decision of the supervisor,

(b)   give him directions, or

(c)   make such other order as it thinks fit.

(4) The supervisor—

(a)   may apply to the court for directions in relation to any particular matter arising under the voluntary arrangement, and

(b)   is included among the persons who may apply to the court for the winding up of the partnership as an unregistered company or for an administration order to be made in relation to it.

(5) The court may, whenever—

(a)   it is expedient to appoint a person to carry out the functions of the supervisor, and

(b)   it is inexpedient, difficult or impracticable for an appointment to be made without the assistance of the court,

make an order appointing a person who is qualified to act as an insolvency practitioner or authorised to act as supervisor, in relation to the voluntary arrangement, either in substitution for the existing supervisor or to fill a vacancy.

(6) The power conferred by subsection (5) is exercisable so as to increase the number of persons exercising the functions of supervisor or, where there is more than one person exercising those functions, so as to replace one or more of those persons.

3.31

7A Prosecution of delinquent officers of partnership

(1) This section applies where a moratorium under section 1A has been obtained for an insolvent partnership or the approval of a voluntary arrangement in relation to an insolvent partnership has taken effect under section 4A or paragraph 36 of Schedule A1.

(2) If it appears to the nominee or supervisor that any past or present officer of the insolvent partnership has been guilty of any offence in connection with the moratorium or, as the case may be, voluntary arrangement for which such officer is criminally liable, the nominee or supervisor shall forthwith—
(a) report the matter to the Secretary of State, and
(b) provide the Secretary of State with such information and give him such access to and facilities for inspecting and taking copies of documents (being information or documents in the possession or under the control of the nominee or supervisor and relating to the matter in question) as the Secretary of State requires.

(3) Where a prosecuting authority institutes criminal proceedings following any report under subsection (2), the nominee or supervisor, and every officer and agent of the insolvent partnership past or present (other than the defendant), shall give the authority all assistance in connection with the prosecution which he is reasonably able to give.

For this purpose—
'agent' includes any banker or solicitor of the insolvent partnership and any person employed by the insolvent partnership as auditor, whether that person is or is not an officer of the insolvent partnership,
'prosecuting authority' means the Director of Public Prosecutions or the Secretary of State.

(4) The court may, on the application of the prosecuting authority, direct any person referred to in subsection (3) to comply with that subsection if he has failed to do so.

3.32

7B Arrangements coming to an end prematurely

For the purposes of this Part, a voluntary arrangement the approval of which has taken effect under section 4A or paragraph 36 of Schedule A1 comes to an end prematurely if, when it ceases to have effect, it has not been fully implemented in respect of all persons bound by the arrangement by virtue of section 5(2)(b)(i) or, as the case may be, paragraph 37(2)(b)(i) of Schedule A1'.'.]

[Part II
Modified Provisions of Schedule A1 to the Act]

Notes

This Schedule was substituted by Insolvent Partnerships (Amendment) (No 2) Order, art 6 Sch 1 SI 2002/2708 and came into force on 1 January 2003 subject to transitional provisions; Article 11(1), (3).

3.33

[The following provisions of Schedule A1 to the Act are modified so as to read as follows:

'**3**

(1) An insolvent partnership meets the requirements of this paragraph if the qualifying conditions are met—
    (a)   in the year ending with the date of filing, or
    (b)   in the tax year of the insolvent partnership which ended last before that date.

(2) For the purposes of sub-paragraph (1) the qualifying conditions are met by an insolvent partnership in a period if, in that period, it satisfies two or more of the requirements set out in sub-paragraph (3).

(3) The qualifying conditions referred to in this paragraph are—
    (a)   turnover of not more than [£5.6] million,
    (b)   assets of not more than [£2.8] million, and
    (c)   no more than 50 employees.

(4) For the purposes of sub-paragraph (3)—
    (a)   the total of turnover is the amount which is or would be, as the case may be, entered as turnover in the partnership's tax return,
    (b)   the total of assets is the amount which—
        (i)   in the case of the period referred to in paragraph 3(1)(a), is entered in the partnership's statement of affairs which must be filed with the court under paragraph 7(1)(b), or
        (ii)   in the case of the period referred to in paragraph 3(1)(b), would be entered in the partnership's statement of affairs had it prepared such a statement on the last day of the period to which the amount for turnover is calculated for the purposes of paragraph 3(4)(a),
    (c)   the number of employees is the average number of persons employed by the insolvent partnership—
        (i)   in the case of the period referred to in paragraph 3(1)(a), in the period ending with the date of filing,
        (ii)   in the case of the period referred to in paragraph 3(1)(b), in the period to which the amount for turnover is calculated for the purposes of paragraph 3(4)(a).

(5) Where the period covered by the qualifying conditions in respect of the insolvent partnership is not a year the total of turnover referred to in paragraph 3(3)(a) shall be proportionately adjusted.

(6) The average number of persons employed by the insolvent partnership shall be calculated as follows—
  (a) by ascertaining the number of persons employed by it under contracts of service for each month of the year (whether throughout the month or not),
  (b) by adding those figures together, and
  (c) by dividing the resulting figure by the number of months during which persons were so employed by it during the year.

(7) In this paragraph—
'tax return' means a return under section 12AA of the Taxes Management Act 1970,
'tax year' means the 12 months beginning with 6th April in any year.

Notes

This sets out which partnerships are eligible for the moratorium. The provisions in the IA 1986 are applicable only to companies; accordingly, this provision applies a test that is appropriate in the partnership context.

3.34

4

(1) An insolvent partnership is excluded from being eligible for a moratorium if, on the date of filing—
  (a) [the partnership is in administration],
  (b) the insolvent partnership is being wound up as an unregistered company,
  (c) there is an agricultural receiver of the insolvent partnership,
  (d) a voluntary arrangement has effect in relation to the insolvent partnership,
  (e) there is a provisional liquidator of the insolvent partnership,
  (f) a moratorium has been in force for the insolvent partnership at any time during the period of 12 months ending with the date of filing and—
    (i) no voluntary arrangement had effect at the time at which the moratorium came to an end, or
    (ii) a voluntary arrangement which had effect at any time in that period has come to an end prematurely,
  (g) a voluntary arrangement in relation to the insolvent partnership which had effect in pursuance of a proposal under section 1(3) has come to an end prematurely and, during the period of 12 months ending with the date of filing, an order under section 5(3)(a) has been made, or
  (h) an order has been made by virtue of article 11 of the Insolvent Partnerships Order 1994.

(2) Sub-paragraph (1)(b) does not apply to an insolvent partnership which, by reason of a winding-up order made after the date of filing, is treated as being wound up on that date.

Effect on creditors, etc

3.35

12

(1) During the period for which a moratorium is in force for an insolvent partnership—

(a) no petition may be presented for the winding-up of the insolvent partnership as an unregistered company,

(b) no meeting of the members of the partnership may be called or requisitioned except with the consent of the nominee or the leave of the court and subject (where the court gives leave) to such terms as the court may impose,

(c) no order may be made for the winding-up of the insolvent partnership as an unregistered company,

[(d) no administration application may be made in respect of the partnership,

(da) no administrator of the partnership may be appointed under paragraph 14 or 22 of Schedule B1,]

(e) no agricultural receiver of the partnership may be appointed except with the leave of the court and subject to such terms as the court may impose,

(f) no landlord or other person to whom rent is payable may exercise any rights of forfeiture by peaceable re-entry in relation to premises forming part of the partnership property or let to one or more officers of the partnership in their capacity as such in respect of a failure by the partnership or one or more officers of the partnership to comply with any term or condition of the tenancy of such premises, except with the leave of the court and subject to such terms as the court may impose,

(g) no other steps may be taken to enforce any security over the partnership property, or to repossess goods in the possession, under any hire-purchase agreement, of one or more officers of the partnership in their capacity as such, except with the leave of the court and subject to such terms as the court may impose,

(h) no other proceedings and no execution or other legal process may be commenced or continued, and no distress may be levied, against the insolvent partnership or the partnership property except with the leave of the court and subject to such terms as the court may impose,

(i) no petition may be presented, and no order may be made, by virtue of article 11 of the Insolvent Partnerships Order 1994, and

(j) no application or order may be made under section 35 of the Partnership Act 1890 in respect of the insolvent partnership.

(2) Where a petition, other than an excepted petition, for the winding-up of the insolvent partnership has been presented before the beginning of the moratorium, section 127 shall not apply in relation to any disposition of partnership property, any transfer of an interest in the insolvent partnership or alteration in status of a member of the partnership made during the moratorium or at a time mentioned in paragraph 37(5)(a).

(3) Paragraph (a) of sub-paragraph (1) does not apply to an excepted petition and, where such a petition has been presented before the

beginning of the moratorium or is presented during the moratorium, paragraphs (b) and (c) of that sub-paragraph do not apply in relation to proceedings on the petition.

(4) For the purposes of this paragraph, 'excepted petition' means a petition under—
- (a) article 7(1) of the Insolvent Partnerships Order 1994 presented by the Secretary of State on the grounds mentioned in subsections (b), (c) and (d) of section 124A of this Act,
- (b) section 72 of the Financial Services Act 1986 on the ground mentioned in subsection (1)(b) of that section,
- (c) section 92 of the Banking Act 1987 on the ground mentioned in subsection (1)(b) of that section, or
- (d) section 367 of the Financial Services and Markets Act 2000 on the ground mentioned in subsection (3)(b) of that section.

Disposal of charged property, etc

3.36

20

(1) This paragraph applies where—
- (a) any partnership property of the insolvent partnership is subject to a security, or
- (b) any goods are in possession of one or more officers of the partnership in their capacity as such under a hire-purchase agreement.

(2) If the holder of the security consents, or the court gives leave, the insolvent partnership may dispose of the property as if it were not subject to the security.

(3) If the owner of the goods consents, or the court gives leave, the insolvent partnership may dispose of the goods as if all rights of the owner under the hire-purchase agreement were vested in the members of the partnership.

(4) Where property subject to a security which, as created, was a floating charge is disposed of under sub-paragraph (2), the holder of the security has the same priority in respect of any partnership property directly or indirectly representing the property disposed of as he would have had in respect of the property subject to the security.

(5) Sub-paragraph (6) applies to the disposal under sub-paragraph (2) or (as the case may be) sub-paragraph (3) of—
- (a) any property subject to a security other than a security which, as created, was a floating charge, or
- (b) any goods in the possession of one or more officers of the partnership in their capacity as such under a hire-purchase agreement.

(6) It shall be a condition of any consent or leave under sub-paragraph (2) or (as the case may be) sub-paragraph (3) that—
- (a) the net proceeds of the disposal, and
- (b) where those proceeds are less than such amount as may be agreed, or determined by the court, to be the net amount which

would be realised on a sale of the property or goods in the open market by a willing vendor, such sums as may be required to make good the deficiency,

shall be applied towards discharging the sums secured by the security or payable under the hire-purchase agreement.

(7) Where a condition imposed in pursuance of sub-paragraph (6) relates to two or more securities, that condition requires—

(a) the net proceeds of the disposal, and

(b) where paragraph (b) of sub-paragraph (6) applies, the sums mentioned in that paragraph,

to be applied towards discharging the sums secured by those securities in the order of their priorities.

(8) In this paragraph 'floating charge' means a floating charge created under section 5 of the Agricultural Credits Act 1928.

Effect of approval of voluntary arrangement

3.37

37

(1) This paragraph applies where a decision approving a voluntary arrangement has effect under paragraph 36.

(2) The approved voluntary arrangement—

(a) takes effect as if made by the members of the partnership at the creditors' meeting, and

(b) binds every person who in accordance with the rules—

(i) was entitled to vote at that meeting (whether or not he was present or represented at it), or

(ii) would have been so entitled if he had had notice of it,

as if he were a party to the voluntary arrangement.

(3) If—

(a) when the arrangement ceases to have effect any amount payable under the arrangement to a person bound by virtue of sub-paragraph (2)(b)(ii) has not been paid, and

(b) the arrangement did not come to an end prematurely,

the insolvent partnership shall at that time become liable to pay to that person the amount payable under the arrangement.

(4) Where a petition for the winding-up of the insolvent partnership as an unregistered company or a petition by virtue of article 11 of the Insolvent Partnerships Order 1994, other than an excepted petition within the meaning of paragraph 12, was presented before the beginning of the moratorium, the court shall dismiss the petition.

(5) The court shall not dismiss a petition under sub-paragraph (4)—

(a) at any time before the end of the period of 28 days beginning with the first day on which each of the reports of the meetings required by paragraph 30(3) has been made to the court, or

(b) at any time when an application under paragraph 38 or an appeal in respect of such an application is pending, or at any time in the period within which such an appeal may be brought.

Challenge of actions of officers of insolvent partnership

3.38

40

(1) This paragraph applies in relation to acts or omissions of the officers of a partnership during a moratorium.

(2) A creditor or member of the insolvent partnership may apply to the court for an order under this paragraph on the ground—
  (a) that the partnership's affairs and business and partnership property are being or have been managed by the officers of the partnership in a manner which is unfairly prejudicial to the interests of its creditors or members generally, or of some part of its creditors or members (including at least the petitioner), or
  (b) that any actual or proposed act or omission of the officers of the partnership is or would be so prejudicial.

(3) An application for an order under this paragraph may be made during or after the moratorium.

(4) On an application for an order under this paragraph the court may—
  (a) make such order as it thinks fit for giving relief in respect of the matters complained of,
  (b) adjourn the hearing conditionally or unconditionally, or
  (c) make an interim order or any other order that it thinks fit.

(5) An order under this paragraph may in particular—
  (a) regulate the management by the officers of the partnership of the partnership's affairs and business and partnership property during the remainder of the moratorium,
  (b) require the officers of the partnership to refrain from doing or continuing an act complained of by the petitioner, or to do an act which the petitioner has complained they have omitted to do,
  (c) require the summoning of a meeting of creditors or members of the partnership for the purpose of considering such matters as the court may direct,
  (d) bring the moratorium to an end and make such consequential provision as the court thinks fit.

(6) In making an order under this paragraph the court shall have regard to the need to safeguard the interests of persons who have dealt with the insolvent partnership in good faith and for value.

[(7) Sub-paragraph (8) applies where—
  (a) the appointment of an administrator has effect in relation to the insolvent partnership and the appointment took effect before the moratorium came into force, or
  (b) the insolvent partnership is being wound up as an unregistered company or an order by virtue of article 11 of the Insolvent Partnerships Order 1994 has been made, in pursuance of a petition presented before the moratorium came into force.

(8) No application for an order under this paragraph may be made by a creditor or member of the insolvent partnership; but such an application may be made instead by the administrator (or as the case may be) the liquidator.]

3.39

42

(1) If, for the purpose of obtaining a moratorium, or an extension of a moratorium, for an insolvent partnership or any of its members (a moratorium meaning in the case of an individual the effect of an application for, or the making of, an interim order under Part VIII of the Act), a person who is an officer of an insolvent partnership or an officer (which for this purpose includes a shadow director) of a corporate member in relation to which a voluntary arrangement is proposed—
    (a)   makes any false representation, or
    (b)   fraudulently does, or omits to do, anything,
he commits an offence.

(2) Sub-paragraph (1) applies even if no moratorium or extension is obtained.

(3) A person guilty of an offence under this paragraph is liable to imprisonment or a fine, or both']

[SCHEDULE 2
Modified Provisions of Part II of, and Schedule B1 to, the Act
(Administration) as Applied by Article 6]

Notes

The new administration procedure under IA 1986, Sch B1 applies to insolvent partnerships with the changes stated in this Schedule 2. The new procedure applies except where a petition for an administration was presented before 1 July 2005; in that event the former procedure under the former IA 1986 s 8 to 27 will apply. Under the new procedure in relation to insolvent partnerships an administrator may be appointed by a court order; or by the holder of an agricultural floating charge; or by the members of the insolvent partnership (sch 2 para 2 below).

3.40

[1

The following provisions of Schedule B1 and Schedule 1 to the Act are modified as follows.

2

Paragraph 2 is modified so as to read as follows—

'2

A person may be appointed as administrator of a partnership—
    (a)   by administration order of the court under paragraph 10,
    (b)   by the holder of an agricultural floating charge under paragraph 14, or
    (c)   by the members of the insolvent partnership in their capacity as such under paragraph 22'.

3

Paragraph 7 is modified so as to read as follows—

'7

A person may not be appointed as administrator of a partnership which is in administration (subject to the provisions of paragraphs 90 to 93, 95 to 97, and 100 to 103 about replacement and additional administrators)'.

4

Paragraph 8 is modified so as to read as follows—

'8

(1) A person may not be appointed as administrator of a partnership after—
    (a)   an order has been made in relation to it by virtue of Article 11 of the Insolvent Partnerships Order 1994; or
    (b)   an order has been made for it to be wound up by the court as an unregistered company.

(2) Sub-paragraph (1)(a) is subject to paragraph 38.

(3) Sub-paragraph (1)(b) is subject to paragraphs 37 and 38'.

5

Paragraph 11 is modified so as to read as follows—

'11

The court may make an administration order in relation to a partnership only if satisfied—
    (a)   that the partnership is unable to pay its debts, and
    (b)   that the administration order is reasonably likely to achieve the purpose of administration'.

3.41

Notes

It is essential that an applicant for an administration order in relation to the insolvent partnership is able to demonstrate that the partnership is unable to pay its debts; this condition does not however apply if the application is made by the holder of a qualifying agricultural floating charge (see Sch B1 para 35 as modified below). Where insolvency has to be proved it is not enough to show that the company may become insolvent. Insolvency can be demonstrated in three ways: unsatisfied statutory demand (s 222); unpaid debt after action brought (s 223); and balance sheet insolvency (s 224). It is important to note that when the court is considering whether the partnership is insolvent, it will not take into account the assets of the members, notwithstanding that the members assets will, ultimately, be available to the partnership's creditors on a winding up: see *Re H S Smith & Sons*, The Times, 7 January 1999.

It must next be shown that one or more of the statutory purposes is achievable; see Sch B1 para 3 and thereafter, whether to make an administration order in respect of the partnership is a matter of the court's discretion. Where it is shown that an administration is likely to achieve a better result for the creditors as a whole than would be likely in a liquidation, a request by the firm for an adjournment to allow it to sell its assets itself is likely to be refused: see *Re Kyrris*

(No 1) [1998] BPIR 103. The court may dismiss an application if it concludes that it was improperly presented: see *Re West Park Golf and Country Club* [1997] 1 BCLC 20.

3.42

6

Paragraph 12 is modified so as to read as follows—

'12

(1) An application to the court for an administration order in respect of a partnership ('an administration application') shall be by application in Form 1 in Schedule 9 to the Insolvent Partnerships Order 1994 and may be made only by—
    (a)   the members of the insolvent partnership in their capacity as such;
    (b)   one or more creditors of the partnership; or
    (c)   a combination of persons listed in paragraphs (a) and (b).

(2) As soon as is reasonably practicable after the making of an administration application the applicant shall notify—
    (a)   any person who has appointed an agricultural receiver of the partnership;
    (b)   any person who is or may be entitled to appoint an agricultural receiver of the partnership;
    (c)   any person who is or may be entitled to appoint an administrator of the partnership under paragraph 14; and
    (d)   such other persons as may be prescribed.

(3) An administration application may not be withdrawn without the permission of the court.

(4) In sub-paragraph (1) 'creditor' includes a contingent creditor and a prospective creditor.

(5) Sub-paragraph (1) is without prejudice to section 7(4)(b)'.

Notes

As to the question of whether the petition is required to be presented jointly by all of the members, the position is the same as with the question of who may propose a PVA: see the notes to Article 4 above. In short, the petition should either be made by all of the members (in the broad sense employed by the IPO 1994) or by some of the members indicating the consent of the other members. As to the reference to agricultural receivers, see the notes to Article 6 and the definition in Article 2.

3.43

7

Paragraph 14 is modified so as to read as follows—

'14

(1) The holder of a qualifying agricultural floating charge in respect of partnership property may appoint an administrator of the partnership.

(2) For the purposes of sub-paragraph (1) an agricultural floating charge qualifies if created by an instrument which—
- (a) states that this paragraph applies to the agricultural floating charge,
- (b) purports to empower the holder of the agricultural floating charge to appoint an administrator of the partnership or,
- (c) purports to empower the holder of the agricultural floating charge to make an appointment which would be the appointment of an agricultural receiver.

(3) For the purposes of sub-paragraph (1) a person is the holder of a qualifying agricultural floating charge in respect of partnership property if he holds one or more charges of the partnership secured—
- (a) by a qualifying agricultural floating charge which relates to the whole or substantially the whole of the partnership property,
- (b) by a number of qualifying agricultural floating charges which together relate to the whole or substantially the whole of the partnership property, or
- (c) by charges and other forms of security which together relate to the whole or substantially the whole of the partnership property and at least one of which is a qualifying agricultural floating charge'.

8

Paragraph 15 is modified so as to read as follows—

'15

(1) A person may not appoint an administrator under paragraph 14 unless—
- (a) he has given at least two business days' written notice to the holder of any prior agricultural floating charge which satisfies paragraph 14(2); or
- (b) the holder of any prior agricultural floating charge which satisfies paragraph 14(2) has consented in writing to the making of the appointment.

(2) For the purposes of this paragraph, one agricultural floating charge is prior to another in accordance with the provisions of section 8(2) of the Agricultural Credits Act 1928.

9

Paragraph 22 is modified so as to read as follows—

'22

The members of the insolvent partnership may appoint an administrator'.

10

Paragraph 23 is modified so as to read as follows—

'23

(1) This paragraph applies where an administrator of a partnership is appointed—

    (a)   under paragraph 22, or

    (b)   on an administration application made by the members of the partnership.

(2) An administrator of the partnership may not be appointed under paragraph 22 during the period of 12 months beginning with the date on which the appointment referred to in sub-paragraph (1) ceases to have effect'.

11

Paragraph 26 is modified so as to read as follows—

'26

(1) A person who proposes to make an appointment under paragraph 22 shall give at least five business days' written notice to—

    (a)   any person who is or may be entitled to appoint an agricultural receiver of the partnership, and

    (b)   any person who is or may be entitled to appoint an administrator of the partnership under paragraph 14.

(2) A person who proposes to make an appointment under paragraph 22 shall also give such notice as may be prescribed to such other persons as may be prescribed.

(3) A notice under this paragraph must—

    (a)   identify the proposed administrator, and

    (b)   be in Form 1A in Schedule 9 to the Insolvent Partnerships Order 1994'.

12

Paragraph 27 is modified so as to read as follows—

'27

(1) A person who gives notice of intention to appoint under paragraph 26 shall file with the court as soon as is reasonably practicable a copy of—

    (a)   the notice, and

    (b)   any document accompanying it.

(2) The copy filed under sub-paragraph (1) must be accompanied by a statutory declaration made by or on behalf of the person who proposes to make the appointment—

    (a)   that the partnership is unable to pay its debts,

    (b)   that the partnership is not in liquidation, and

    (c)   that, so far as the person making the statement is able to ascertain, the appointment is not prevented by paragraphs 23 to 25, and

    (d)   to such additional effect, and giving such information, as may be prescribed.

(3) A statutory declaration under sub-paragraph (2) must—

    (a)   be in the prescribed form, and

(b)   be made during the prescribed period.

(4) A person commits an offence if in a statutory declaration under sub-paragraph (2) he makes a statement—
  (a)   which is false, and
  (b)   which he does not reasonably believe to be true'.

13

Paragraph 29 is modified so as to read as follows—

'29

(1) A person who appoints an administrator of a partnership under paragraph 22 shall file with the court—
  (a)   a notice of appointment, and
  (b)   such other documents as may be prescribed.

(2) The notice of appointment must include a statutory declaration by or on behalf of the person who makes the appointment—-
  (a)   that the person is entitled to make an appointment under paragraph 22,
  (b)   that the appointment is in accordance with this Schedule, and
  (c)   that, so far as the person making the statement is able to ascertain, the statements made, and information given in the statutory declaration filed with the notice of intention to appoint remain accurate.

(3) The notice of appointment must identify the administrator and must be accompanied by a statement by the administrator—
  (a)   that he consents to the appointment,
  (b)   that in his opinion the purpose of administration is reasonably likely to be achieved, and
  (c)   giving such other information and opinions as may be prescribed.

(4) For the purpose of a statement under sub-paragraph (3) an administrator may rely on information supplied by members of the partnership (unless he has reason to doubt its accuracy).

(5) The notice of appointment must be in Form 1B in Schedule 9 to the Insolvent Partnerships Order 1994 and any document accompanying it must be in the prescribed form.

(6) A statutory declaration under sub-paragraph (2) must be made during the prescribed period.

(7) A person commits an offence if in a statutory declaration under sub-paragraph (2) he makes a statement—
  (a)   which is false, and
  (b)   which he does not reasonably believe to be true'.

14

Paragraph 35 is modified so as to read as follows—

'35

(1) This paragraph applies where an administration application in respect of a partnership—

(a) is made by the holder of a qualifying agricultural floating charge in respect of the partnership property, and

(b) includes a statement that the application is made in reliance on this paragraph.

(2) The court may make an administration order—

(a) whether or not satisfied that the partnership is unable to pay its debts; but

(b) only if satisfied that the applicant could appoint an administrator under paragraph 14'.

15

Paragraph 39 is modified so as to read as follows—

'**39**

(1) Where there is an agricultural receiver of a partnership the court must dismiss an administration application in respect of the partnership unless—

(a) the person by or on behalf of whom the agricultural receiver was appointed consents to the making of the administration order,

(b) the court thinks that the security by virtue of which the agricultural receiver was appointed would be liable to be released or discharged under sections 238 to 240 (transaction at undervalue and preference) if an administration order were made, or

(c) the court thinks that the security by virtue of which the agricultural receiver was appointed would be avoided under section 245 (avoidance of floating charge) if an administration order were made.

(2) Sub-paragraph (1) applies whether the agricultural receiver is appointed before or after the making of the administration application'.

16

Paragraph 41 is modified so as to read as follows—

'**41**

(1) When an administration order takes effect in respect of a partnership any agricultural receiver of the partnership shall vacate office.

(2) Where a partnership is in administration, any receiver of part of the partnership property shall vacate office if the administrator requires him to.

(3) Where an agricultural receiver vacates office under sub-paragraph (1) or (2), his remuneration shall be charged on and paid out of any partnership property which was in his custody or under his control immediately before he vacated office.

(4) In the application of sub-paragraph (3)—

(a) 'remuneration' includes expenses properly incurred and any indemnity to which the agricultural receiver is entitled out of the partnership property,

(b) the charge imposed takes priority over security held by the person by whom or on whose behalf the agricultural receiver was appointed, and

(c)   the provision for payment is subject to paragraph 43'.

17

Paragraph 42 is modified so as to read as follows—

'**42**

(1) This paragraph applies to a partnership in administration.

(2) No order may be made for the winding up of the partnership.

(3) No order may be made by virtue of Article 11 of the Insolvent Partnerships Order 1994 in respect of the partnership.

(4) No order may be made under section 35 of the Partnership Act 1890 in respect of the partnership.

(5) Sub-paragraph (2) does not apply to an order made on a petition presented under—
(a)   section 124A(public interest); or
(b)   section 367 of the Financial Services and Markets Act 2000 (c 8)(petition by Financial Services Authority).

(6) If a petition presented under a provision referred to in sub-paragraph (5) comes to the attention of the administrator, he shall apply to the court for directions under paragraph 63'.

Notes

Para 42 Sch B1

IA 1986 Sch B1 para 42 is amended so as to also prevent the court from decreeing a dissolution of the partnership under s 35 Partnership Act 1890 and from making the members bankrupt on their own petition under Article 11. The prohibitions in Sch B1 para 42 apply only to the partnership and to the partnership assets. This distinction is, in a sense, artificial as the partnership is nothing more than the joint assets and liabilities of the individual members. It appears that nothing in this provision or the next would prevent a creditor pursuing a member for a joint debt and perhaps making him bankrupt. This could have a significant effect on the course of the administration as it may render the objective of the administration less achievable. It may be that a member who is being so pursued may be in a position to propose an IVA and so benefit from the interim order under Part VIII of the IA 1986.

Further problems could arise in distinguishing what is and what is not partnership property for the purpose of the protection afforded by this provision and the next. Many partnerships have an informal attitude to distinguishing between the property of the partnership and that of the individual members.

3.44

18

Paragraph 43 is modified so as to read as follows—

'**43**

(1)
This paragraph applies to a partnership in administration.

(2) No step may be taken to enforce security over the partnership property except—
    (a)   with the consent of the administrator, or
    (b)   with the permission of the court.

(3) No step may be taken to repossess goods in the partnership's possession under a hire-purchase agreement except—
    (a)   with the consent of the administrator, or
    (b)   with the permission of the court.

(4) A landlord may not exercise a right of forfeiture by peaceable re-entry in relation to premises forming part of the partnership property or let to one or more officers of the partnership in their capacity as such except—
    (a)   with the consent of the administrator, or
    (b)   with the permission of the court.

(5) No legal process (including legal proceedings, execution, distress and diligence) may be instituted or continued against the partnership or partnership property except—
    (a)   with the consent of the administrator, or
    (b)   with the permission of the court.

(6) An agricultural receiver of the partnership may not be appointed.

(7) Where the court gives permission for a transaction under this paragraph it may impose a condition on or a requirement in connection with the transaction.

(8) In this paragraph 'landlord' includes a person to whom rent is payable'.

Notes

See the note to para 17 of this Schedule above

3.45

19

Paragraph 47 is modified so as to read as follows—

'**47**

(1) As soon as is reasonably practicable after appointment the administrator of a partnership shall by notice in the prescribed form require one or more relevant persons to provide the administrator with a statement of the affairs of the partnership.

(2) The statement must—
    (a)   be verified by a statement of truth in accordance with Civil Procedure Rules,
    (b)   be in the prescribed form,
    (c)   give particulars of the partnership property, debts and liabilities,
    (d)   give the names and addresses of the creditors of the partnership,
    (e)   specify the security held by each creditor,
    (f)   give the date on which each security was granted, and

    (g)   contain such other information as may be prescribed.

(3) In sub-paragraph (1) 'relevant person' means—
    (a)   a person who is or has been an officer of the partnership,
    (b)   a person who took part in the formation of the partnership during the period of one year ending with the date on which the partnership enters administration,
    (c)   a person employed by the partnership during that period, and
    (d)   a person who is or has been during that period an officer or employee of a partnership which is or has been during that year an officer of the partnership.

(4) For the purpose of sub-paragraph (3) a reference to employment is a reference to employment through a contract of employment or a contract for services'.

20

Paragraph 49 is modified so as to read as follows—

'49

(1) The administrator of a partnership shall make a statement setting out proposals for achieving the purpose of administration.

(2) A statement under sub-paragraph (1) must, in particular—
    (a)   deal with such matters as may be prescribed, and
    (b)   where applicable, explain why the administrator thinks that the objective mentioned in paragraph 3(1)(a) or (b) cannot be achieved.

(3) Proposals under this paragraph may include a proposal for a voluntary arrangement under Part I of this Act (although this paragraph is without prejudice to section 4(3)).

(4) The administrator shall send a copy of the statement of his proposals—
    (a)   to the court,
    (b)   to every creditor of the partnership of whose claim and address he is aware, and
    (c)   to every member of the partnership of whose address he is aware.

(5) The administrator shall comply with sub-paragraph (4)—
    (a)   as soon as is reasonably practicable after the partnership enters administration, and
    (b)   in any event, before the end of the period of eight weeks beginning with the day on which the partnership enters administration.

(6) The administrator shall be taken to comply with sub-paragraph (4)(c) if he publishes in the prescribed manner a notice undertaking to provide a copy of the statement of proposals free of charge to any member of the partnership who applies in writing to a specified address.

(7) An administrator commits an offence if he fails without reasonable excuse to comply with sub-paragraph (5).

(8) A period specified in this paragraph may be varied in accordance with paragraph 107'.

21

Paragraph 52 is modified so as to read as follows—

'52

(1) Paragraph 51(1) shall not apply where the statement of proposals states that the administrator thinks—
  (a)   that the partnership has sufficient property to enable each creditor of the partnership to be paid in full,
  (b)   that the partnership has insufficient property to enable a distribution to be made to unsecured creditors, or
  (c)   that neither of the objectives specified in paragraph 3(1)(a) and (b) can be achieved.

(2) But the administrator shall summon an initial creditors' meeting if it is requested—
  (a)   by creditors of the partnership whose debts amount to at least 10% of the total debts of the partnership,
  (b)   in the prescribed manner, and
  (c)   in the prescribed period.

(3) A meeting requested under sub-paragraph (2) must be summoned for a date in the prescribed period.

(4) The period prescribed under sub-paragraph (3) may be varied in accordance with paragraph 107'.

22

Paragraph 61 is modified so as to read as follows—

'61

The administrator of a partnership—
  (a)   may prevent any person from taking part in the management of the partnership business, and
  (b)   may appoint any person to be a manager of that business'.

23

Paragraph 65 is modified so as to read as follows—

'65

(1) The administrator of a partnership may make a distribution to a creditor of the partnership.

(2) Section 175(1) and (2)(a) shall apply in relation to a distribution under this paragraph as it applies in relation to a winding up.

(3) A payment may not be made by way of distribution under this paragraph to a creditor of the partnership who is neither secured nor preferential unless the court gives permission'.

24

Paragraph 69 is modified so as to read as follows:—

'69

(1) Subject to sub-paragraph (2) below, in exercising his function under this Schedule the administrator of a partnership acts as the agent of the members of the partnership in their capacity as such.

(2) An officer of the partnership shall not, unless he otherwise consents, be personally liable for the debts and obligations of the partnership incurred during the period when the partnership is in administration'.

25

Paragraph 73 is modified so as to read as follows—

'73

(1) An administrator's statement of proposals under paragraph 49 may not include any action which—
  (a) affects the right of a secured creditor of the partnership to enforce his security,
  (b) would result in a preferential debt of the partnership being paid otherwise than in priority to its non-preferential debts, or
  (c) would result in one preferential creditor of the partnership being paid a smaller proportion of his debt than another.

(2) Sub-paragraph (1) does not apply to—
  (a) action to which the relevant creditor consents, or
  (b) a proposal for a voluntary arrangement under Part I of this Act (although this sub-paragraph is without prejudice to section 4(3)).

(3) The reference to a statement of proposals in sub-paragraph (1) includes a reference to a statement as revised or modified'.

26

Paragraph 74 is modified so as to read as follows—

'74

(1) A creditor or member of a partnership in administration may apply to the court claiming that—
  (a) the administrator is acting or has acted so as unfairly to harm the interests of the applicant (whether alone or in common with some or all other members or creditors), or
  (b) the administrator proposes to act in a way which would unfairly harm the interests of the applicant (whether alone or in common with some or all other members or creditors).

(2) A creditor or member of a partnership in administration may apply to the court claiming that the administrator is not performing his functions as quickly or as efficiently as is reasonably practicable.

(3) The court may—
  (a) grant relief;
  (b) dismiss the application;
  (c) adjourn the hearing conditionally or unconditionally;
  (d) make an interim order;
  (e) make any other order it thinks appropriate.

(4) In particular, an order under this paragraph may—
  (a)   regulate the administrator's exercise of his functions;
  (b)   require the administrator to do or not do a specified thing;
  (c)   require a creditors' meeting to be held for a specified purpose;
  (d)   provide for the appointment of an administrator to cease to have effect;
  (e)   make consequential provision.

(5) An order may be made on a claim under sub-paragraph (1) whether or not the action complained of—
  (a)   is within the administrator's powers under that Schedule;
  (b)   was taken in reliance on an order under paragraph 71 or 72.

(6) An order may not be made under this paragraph if it would impede or prevent the implementation of—
  (a)   a voluntary arrangement approved under Part I, or
  (b)   proposals or a revision approved under paragraph 53 or 54 more than 28 days before the day on which the application for the order under this paragraph is made'.

27

Omit paragraph 83.

28

Paragraph 84 is modified so as to read as follows—

'84

(1) If the administrator of a partnership thinks that the partnership has no property which might permit a distribution to its creditors, he shall file a notice to that effect with the court.

(2) The court may on the application of the administrator of a partnership disapply sub-paragraph (1) in respect of the partnership.

(3) On the filing of a notice in respect of a partnership under sub-paragraph (1) the appointment of an administrator of the partnership shall cease to have effect.

(4) If an administrator files a notice under sub-paragraph (1) he shall as soon as is reasonably practicable send a copy of the notice to each creditor of whose claim and address he is aware.

(5) At the end of the period of three months beginning with the date of filing of a notice in respect of a partnership under sub-paragraph (1) the partnership is deemed to be dissolved.

(6) On an application in respect of a partnership by the administrator or another interested person the court may—
  (a)   extend the period specified in sub-paragraph (5);
  (b)   suspend that period; or
  (c)   disapply sub-paragraph (5).

(7) An administrator commits an offence if he fails without reasonable excuse to comply with sub-paragraph (4)'.

29

Paragraph 87 is modified to read as follows—

'87

(1) An administrator may resign only in prescribed circumstances.

(2) Where an administrator may resign he may do so only—
   (a)   in the case of an administrator appointed by administration order, by notice in writing to the court,
   (b)   in the case of an administrator appointed under paragraph 14, by notice in writing to the holder of the agricultural floating charge by virtue of which the appointment was made, or
   (c)   in the case of an administrator appointed under paragraph 22, by notice in writing to the members of the insolvent partnership'.

30

Paragraph 89 is modified so as to read as follows—

'89

(1) The administrator of a partnership shall vacate office if he ceases to be qualified to act as an insolvency practitioner in relation to the partnership.

(2) Where an administrator vacates office by virtue of sub-paragraph (1) he shall give notice in writing—
   (a)   in the case of an administrator appointed by administration order, to the court,
   (b)   in the case of an administrator appointed under paragraph 14, to the holder of the agricultural floating charge by virtue of which the appointment was made, or
   (c)   in the case of an administrator appointed under paragraph 22, to the members of the insolvent partnership.

(3) An administrator who fails without reasonable excuse to comply with sub-paragraph (2) commits an offence'.

31

Paragraph 90 is modified so as to read as follows—

'90

Paragraphs 91 to 93 and 95 apply where an administrator—
   (a)   dies
   (b)   resigns
   (c)   is removed from office under paragraph 88, or
   (d)   vacates office under paragraph 89'.

32

Paragraph 91 is modified so as to read as follows—

'91

(1) Where the administrator was appointed by administration order, the court may replace the administrator on an application under this sub-paragraph made by—
   (a)   a creditors' committee of the partnership,
   (b)   the members of the partnership,
   (c)   one or more creditors of the partnership, or

(d) where more than one person was appointed to act jointly or concurrently as the administrator, any of those persons who remains in office.

(2) But an application may be made in reliance on sub-paragraph (1)(b) and (c) only where—

(a) there is no creditors' committee of the partnership,

(b) the court is satisfied that the creditors' committee or a remaining administrator is not taking reasonable steps to make a replacement, or

(c) the court is satisfied that for another reason it is right for the application to be made'.

33

Paragraph 93 is modified so as to read as follows—

'93

(1) Where the administrator was appointed under paragraph 22 by the members of the partnership they may replace the administrator.

(2) A replacement under this paragraph may be made only—

(a) with the consent of each person who is the holder of a qualifying agricultural floating charge in respect of the partnership property, or

(b) where consent is withheld, with the permission of the court'.

34

Omit paragraph 94.

35

Paragraph 95 is modified so as to read as follows—

'95

The court may replace an administrator on the application of a person listed in paragraph 91(1) if the court—

(a) is satisfied that a person who is entitled to replace the administrator under any of paragraphs 92 and 93 is not taking reasonable steps to make a replacement, or

(b) that for another reason it is right for the court to make the replacement'.

36

Paragraph 96 is modified so as to read as follows—

'96

(1) This paragraph applies where an administrator of a partnership is appointed under paragraph 14 by the holder of a qualifying agricultural floating charge in respect of the partnership property.

(2) The holder of a prior qualifying agricultural floating charge in respect of the partnership property may apply to the court for the administrator to be replaced by an administrator nominated by the holder of the prior agricultural floating charge.

(3) One agricultural floating charge is prior to another for the purposes of this paragraph if—
   (a) it was created first, or
   (b) it is to be treated as having priority in accordance with an agreement to which the holder of each agricultural floating charge was party'.

37

Paragraph 97 is modified so as to read as follows—

'97

(1) This paragraph applies where—
   (a) an administrator of a partnership is appointed by the members of the partnership under paragraph 22, and
   (b) there is no holder of a qualifying agricultural floating charge in respect of the partnership property.

(2) A creditor's meeting may replace the administrator.

(3) A creditors' meeting may act under sub-paragraph (2) only if the new administrator's written consent to act is presented to the meeting before the replacement is made'.

38

Paragraph 103 is modified so as to read as follows—

'103

(1) Where a partnership is in administration, a person may be appointed to act as administrator jointly or concurrently with the person or persons acting as the administrator of the partnership.

(2) Where a partnership entered administration by administration order, an appointment under sub-paragraph (1) must be made by the court on the application of—
   (a) a person or group listed in paragraph 12(1)(a) to (c), or
   (b) the person or persons acting as the administrator of the partnership.

(3) Where a partnership entered administration by virtue of an appointment under paragraph 14, an appointment under sub-paragraph (1) must be made by—
   (a) the holder of the agricultural floating charge by virtue of which the appointment was made, or
   (b) the court on the application of the person or persons acting as the administrator of the partnership.

(4) Where a partnership entered administration by virtue of an appointment under paragraph 22, an appointment under sub-paragraph (1) above must be made either by the court on the application of the person or persons acting as the administrator of the partnership or—
   (a) by the members of the partnership, and
   (b) with the consent of each person who is the holder of a qualifying agricultural floating charge in respect of the partnership property or, where consent is withheld, with the permission of the court.

(5) An appointment under sub-paragraph (1) may be made only with the consent of the person or persons acting as the administrator of the partnership'.

39

Omit paragraph 105.

40

Paragraph 106 is modified so as to read as follows—

'106

(1) A person who is guilty of an offence under this Schedule is liable to a fine (in accordance with section 430 and Schedule 10).

(2) A person who is guilty of an offence under any of the following paragraphs of this Schedule is liable to a daily default fine (in accordance with section 430 and Schedule 10)—

    (a)   paragraph 20,
    (b)   paragraph 32,
    (c)   paragraph 46,
    (d)   paragraph 48,
    (e)   paragraph 49,
    (f)   paragraph 51,
    (g)   paragraph 53,
    (h)   paragraph 54,
    (i)   paragraph 56,
    (j)   paragraph 78,
    (k)   paragraph 80,
    (l)   paragraph 84, and
    (m)   paragraph 89'.

41

Paragraph 111 is modified so as to read as follows—

'111

(1) In this Schedule—
    'administrator' has the meaning given by paragraph 1 and, where the context requires, includes a reference to a former administrator,
    'agricultural floating charge' means a charge which is an agricultural floating charge on its creation,
    'correspondence' includes correspondence by telephonic or other electronic means,
    'creditors' meeting' has the meaning given by paragraph 50,
    'enters administration' has the meaning given by paragraph 1,
    'in administration' has the meaning given by paragraph 1,
    'hire-purchase agreement' includes a conditional sale agreement, a chattel leasing agreement and a retention of title agreement,
    'holder of a qualifying agricultural floating charge' in respect of partnership property has the meaning given by paragraph 14,
    'market value' means the amount which would be realised on a sale of property in the open market by a willing vendor,

'the purpose of administration' means an objective specified in paragraph 3, and
'unable to pay its debts' has the meaning given by sections 222, 223, and 224.

(2) A reference in this Schedule to a thing in writing includes a reference to a thing in electronic form.

(3) In this Schedule a reference to action includes a reference to inaction'.

42

Omit paragraphs 112–116.

43

Schedule 1 is modified to read as follows:—

'SCHEDULE 1
Powers of Administrator
Paragraph 60 of Schedule B1

3.46

1

Power to take possession of, collect and get in the partnership property and, for that purpose, to take such proceedings as may seem to him expedient.

2

Power to sell or otherwise dispose of the partnership property by public auction or private auction or private contract or, in Scotland, to sell, feu, hire out or otherwise dispose of the partnership property by public roup or private bargain.

3

Power to raise or borrow money and grant security therefor over the partnership property.

4

Power to appoint a solicitor or accountant or other professionally qualified person to assist him in the performance of his functions.

5

Power to bring or defend any action or other legal proceedings in the name and on behalf of any member of the partnership in his capacity as such or of the partnership.

6

Power to refer to arbitration any question affecting the partnership.

7

Power to effect and maintain insurances in respect of the partnership business and property.

8

Power to do all acts and execute, in the name and on behalf of the partnership or of any member of the partnership in his capacity as such, any deed, receipt or other document.

9

Power to draw, accept, make and endorse any bill of exchange or promissory note in the name and on behalf of any member of the partnership in his capacity as such or of the partnership.

10

Power to appoint any agent to do any business which he is unable to do himself or which can more conveniently be done by an agent and power to employ and dismiss employees.

11

Power to do all such things (including the carrying out of works) as may be necessary for the realisation of the partnership property.

12

Power to make any payment which is necessary or incidental to the performance of his functions.

13

Power to carry on the business of the partnership.

14

Power to establish subsidiary undertakings of the partnership.

15

Power to transfer to subsidiary undertakings of the partnership the whole or any part of the business of the partnership or of the partnership property.

16

Power to grant or accept a surrender of a lease or tenancy of any of the partnership property, and to take a lease or tenancy of any property required or convenient for the business of the partnership.

17

Power to make any arrangement or compromise on behalf of the partnership or of its members in their capacity as such.

18

Power to rank and claim in the bankruptcy, insolvency, sequestration or liquidation of any person indebted to the partnership and to receive dividends, and to accede to trust deeds for the creditors of any such person.

19

Power to present or defend a petition for the winding up of the partnership under the Insolvent Partnerships Order 1994.

20

Power to do all other things incidental to the exercise of the foregoing powers.]

Notes

The reference to proceedings, arrangements or compromises in relation to members of the partnership 'in their capacity as such' in paragraphs 5 and 17 must be a reference to situations where something is held by or in the name of the member but for the partnership.

'Schedule 2
Modified Provisions of Part II of the Act (Administration Orders) as Applied by Article 6'
Article 6

Notes

Prior to being substituted Schedule 2 read as set out below.

3.46A

"Schedule 2
Modified Provisions of Part II of the Act (Administration Orders) As Applied By Article 6
Article 6

1

Sections 8 to 15 of and Schedule 1 to, the Act are set out as modified in this Schedule.

2 Section 8: Power of court to make order

Section 8 is modified so as to read as follows:—

"8 —

(1) Subject to this section, if the court—

(a)   is satisfied that a partnership is unable to pay its debts (within the meaning given to that expression by section 222, 223 or 224 of this Act [or subsection (1A) below]), and

(b)   considers that the making of an order under this section would be likely to achieve one or more of the purposes mentioned below,

the court may make an administration order in relation to the partnership.

[(1A) An authorised deposit taker which defaults on an obligation to pay any sum due and payable in respect of a relevant deposit is deemed to be unable to pay its debts.

(1B) In subsection (1A)—

(a)   "authorised deposit taker" means a person (being a partnership) which has permission under Part 4 of the Financial Services and Markets Act 2000 to accept deposits, other than a person who has such permission only for the purpose of carrying on another regulated activity in accordance with that permission, and

(b)   "relevant deposit" must be read with—

(i)   section 22 of the Financial Services and Markets Act 2000;

(ii)   any relevant order under that section; and

(iii)   Schedule 2 to that Act,

but any restriction on the meaning of deposit which arises from the identity of the person making it is to be disregarded.]

(2) An administration order is an order directing that, during the period for which the order is in force, the affairs and business of the partnership and the partnership property shall be managed by a person ("the administrator") appointed for the purpose by the court.

(3) The purposes for whose achievement an administration order may be made are—

(a)   the survival of the whole or any part of the undertaking of the partnership as a going concern;

(b)   the approval of a voluntary arrangement under Part I; and

(c)   a more advantageous realisation of the partnership property than would be effected on a winding up;

and the order shall specify the purpose or purposes for which it is made.

[(4) An administration order shall not be made in relation to a partnership after an order has been made for it to be wound up by the court as an unregistered company, nor after an order has been made in relation to it by virtue of article 11 of the Insolvent Partnerships Order 1994.

(5) An administration order shall not be made against a partnership if—

(a)   it has permission under Part 4 of the Financial Services and Markets Act 2000 to effect or carry out contracts of insurance in the United Kingdom;

(b)   it continues to have a liability in respect of a deposit which was held by it in accordance with the Banking Act 1979 or the Banking Act 1987[, but is not an authorised deposit taker, within the meaning given by subsection (1B)].

(6) The definition of "authorised deposit taker" in subsection (1B)(a) and subsection (5)(a) must be read with—

(a)   section 22 of the Financial Services and Markets Act 2000;

(b)   any relevant order under that section; and

    (c)   *Schedule 2 to that Act.]*

[(7) In this Part a reference to an insolvent partnership includes a reference to an insolvent partnership in relation to which an administration order may be made by virtue of Article 3 of the EC Regulation.]".

3 Section 9: Application for order

Section 9 is modified so as to read as follows:—

"9 —

(1) An application to the court for an administration order shall be by petition in Form 1 in Schedule 9 to the Insolvent Partnerships Order 1994 presented either by the members of the insolvent partnership in their capacity as such, or by a creditor or creditors (including any contingent or prospective creditor or creditors), or by all or any of those parties, together or separately.

(2) Where a petition is presented to the court—
    (a)   *notice of the petition shall be given forthwith to any person who has appointed, or is or may be entitled to appoint, an agricultural receiver of the partnership, and to such other persons as may be prescribed, and*
    (b)   *the petition shall not be withdrawn except with the leave of the court.*

(3) Where the court is satisfied that there is an agricultural receiver of the partnership, the court shall dismiss the petition unless it is also satisfied either—
    (a)   *that the person by whom or on whose behalf the receiver was appointed has consented to the making of the order, or*
    (b)   *that, if an administration order were made, any security by virtue of which the receiver was appointed would—*
        (i)   *be liable to be released or discharged under sections 238 to 240 in Part VI (transactions at an undervalue and preferences),*
        (ii)   *be avoided under section 245 in that Part (avoidance of floating charges), or*
        (iii)   *be challengeable under section 242 (gratuitous alienations) or 243 (unfair preferences) in that Part, or under any rule of law in Scotland.*

(4) Subject to subsection (3), on hearing a petition the court may dismiss it, or adjourn the hearing conditionally or unconditionally, or make an interim order or any other order that it thinks fit.

(5) Without prejudice to the generality of subsection (4), an interim order under that subsection may restrict the exercise of any powers of the officers of the partnership (whether by reference to the consent of the court or of a person qualified to act as an insolvency practitioner in relation to the partnership, or otherwise).".

4 Section 10: Effect of application

Section 10 is modified so as to read as follows:—

"10 —

(1) During the period beginning with the presentation of a petition for an administration order and ending with the making of such an order or the dismissal of the petition—
    (a)   *no order may be made for the winding up of the insolvent partnership, nor may any order be made by virtue of article 11 of the Insolvent*

Partnerships Order 1994 or under section 35 of the Partnership Act 1890 in respect of the partnership;

[(aa) no landlord or other person to whom rent is payable may exercise any right of forfeiture by peaceable re-entry in relation to premises forming part of the partnership property or let to one or more officers of the partnership in their capacity as such in respect of a failure by the partnership or one or more officers of the partnership to comply with any term or condition of the tenancy of such premises, except with the leave of the court and subject to such terms as the court may impose;]

(b) no steps may be taken to enforce any security over the partnership property, or to repossess goods in the possession, under any hire-purchase agreement, of one or more of the officers of the partnership in their capacity as such, except with the leave of the court and subject to such terms as the court may impose; and

(c) no other proceedings and no execution or other legal process may be commenced or continued, and no distress may be levied, against the partnership or the partnership property except with the leave of the court and subject to such terms as aforesaid.

(2) Nothing in subsection (1) requires the leave of the court—

(a) for the presentation of a petition for the winding up of the partnership,

(b) for the presentation of a petition by virtue of article 11 of the Insolvent Partnerships Order 1994 in respect of the partnership,

(c) for the appointment of an agricultural receiver of the partnership, or

(d) for the carrying out by such a receiver (whenever appointed) of any of his functions.

(3) Where—

(a) a petition for an administration order is presented at a time when there is an agricultural receiver of the partnership, and

(b) the person by or on whose behalf the receiver was appointed has not consented to the making of the order,

the period mentioned in subsection (1) is deemed not to begin unless and until that person so consents.

(4) References in this section and the next to hire-purchase agreements include conditional sale agreements, chattel leasing agreements and retention of title agreements.

(5) In the application of this section and the next to Scotland, references to execution being commenced or continued include references to diligence being carried out or continued, and references to distress being levied shall be omitted.".

5 Section 11: Effect of order

Section 11 is modified so as to read as follows:—

"11 —

(1) On the making of an administration order, any petition for the winding up of the insolvent partnership and any petition for an order to be made by virtue of article 11 of the Insolvent Partnerships Order 1994 shall be dismissed.

(2) Where an administration order has been made, any agricultural receiver of the partnership and any receiver of the partnership property shall vacate office on being required to do so by the administrator.

(3) During the period for which an administration order is in force—

(*a*) no order may be made for the winding up of the partnership;

(*b*) no order may be made by virtue of article 11 of the Insolvent Partnerships Order 1994 in respect of the partnership;

(*c*) no order may be made under section 35 of the Partnership Act 1890 in respect of the partnership;

(*d*) no agricultural receiver of the partnership may be appointed except with the consent of the administrator or the leave of the court and subject (where the court gives leave) to such terms as the court may impose;

[(*da*) no landlord or other person to whom rent is payable may exercise any right of forfeiture by peaceable re-entry in relation to premises forming part of the partnership property or let to one or more officers of the partnership in their capacity as such in respect of a failure by the partnership or one or more officers of the partnership to comply with any term or condition of the tenancy of such premises, except with the consent of the administrator or the leave of the court and subject (where the court gives leave) to such terms as the court may impose;]

(*e*) no other steps may be taken to enforce any security over the partnership property, or to repossess goods in the possession, under any hire-purchase agreement, of one or more of the officers of the partnership in their capacity as such, except with the consent of the administrator or the leave of the court and subject (where the court gives leave) to such terms as the court may impose; and

(*f*) no other proceedings and no execution or other legal process may be commenced or continued, and no distress may be levied, against the partnership or the partnership property except with the consent of the administrator or the leave of the court and subject (where the court gives leave) to such terms as aforesaid.

(*4*) Where at any time an agricultural receiver or a receiver of part of the partnership property has vacated office under subsection (2)—

(*a*) his remuneration and any expenses properly incurred by him, and

(*b*) any indemnity to which he is entitled out of the partnership property,

shall be charged on and (subject to subsection (3) above) paid out of any partnership property which was in his custody or under his control at that time in priority to any security held by the person by or on whose behalf he was appointed.".

6 Section 12: Notification of order

Section 12 is modified so as to read as follows:—

"12 —

(1) Every invoice, order for goods or business letter which, at a time when an administration order is in force in relation to an insolvent partnership, is issued by or on behalf of the partnership or the administrator, being a document on or in which the name under which the partnership carries on business appears, shall also contain the administrator's name and a statement that the affairs and business of the partnership and the partnership property are being managed by the administrator.

(2) If default is made in complying with this section, any of the following persons who without reasonable excuse authorises or permits the default, namely, the administrator and any officer of the partnership, is liable to a fine.".

7 Section 13: Appointment of administrator

Section 13 is modified so as to read as follows:—

"13 —

(1) The administrator of a partnership shall be appointed either by the administration order or by an order under the next subsection.

(2) If a vacancy occurs by death, resignation or otherwise in the office of the administrator, the court may by order fill the vacancy.

(3) An application for an order under subsection (2) may be made—
    (a)   by any continuing administrator of the partnership; or
    (b)   where there is no such administrator, by a creditors' committee established under section 26 below; or
    (c)   where there is no such administrator and no such committee, by the members of the partnership or by any creditor or creditors of the partnership.".

8 Section 14: General powers

Section 14 is modified so as to read as follows:—

"14 —

(1) The administrator of an insolvent partnership—
    (a)   may do all such things as may be necessary for the management of the affairs and business of the partnership and of the partnership property, and
    (b)   without prejudice to the generality of paragraph (a), has the powers specified in Schedule 1 to this Act;
and in the application of that Schedule to the administrator of a partnership the words "he" and "him" refer to the administrator.

(2) The administrator also has power—
    (a)   to prevent any person from taking part in the management of the partnership business and to appoint any person to be a manager of that business, and
    (b)   to call any meeting of the members or creditors of the partnership.

(3) The administrator may apply to the court for directions in relation to any particular matter arising in connection with the carrying out of his functions.

(4) Any power exercisable by the officers of the partnership, whether under the Partnership Act 1890, the partnership agreement or otherwise, which could be exercised in such a way as to interfere with the exercise by the administrator of his powers is not exercisable except with the consent of the administrator, which may be given either generally or in relation to particular cases.

(5) Subject to subsection (6) below, in exercising his powers the administrator is deemed to act as the agent of the members of the partnership in their capacity as such.

(6) An officer of the partnership shall not, unless he otherwise consents, be personally liable for the debts and obligations of the partnership incurred during the period when the administration order is in force.

(7) A person dealing with the administrator in good faith and for value is not concerned to inquire whether the administrator is acting within his powers.".

9 Section 15: Power to deal with charged property, etc

Section 15 is modified so as to read as follows:—

"15 —

(1) The administrator of a partnership may dispose of or otherwise exercise his powers in relation to any partnership property which is subject to a security to which this subsection applies as if the property were not subject to the security.

(2) Where, on an application by the administrator, the court is satisfied that the disposal (with or without other assets) of—

    (a)   any partnership property subject to a security to which this subsection applies, or

    (b)   any goods in the possession of one or more officers of the partnership in their capacity as such under a hire-purchase agreement,

would be likely to promote the purpose or one or more of the purposes specified in the administration order, the court may by order authorise the administrator to dispose of the property as if it were not subject to the security or to dispose of the goods as if all rights of the owner under the hire-purchase agreement were vested in the members of the partnership.

(3) Subsection (1) applies to any security which, as created, was a floating charge unless an agricultural receiver has been appointed under that security; and subsection (2) applies to any other security.

(4) Where property is disposed of under subsection (1), the holder of the security has the same priority in respect of any partnership property directly or indirectly representing the property disposed of as he would have had in respect of the property subject to the security.

(5) It shall be a condition of an order under subsection (2) that—

    (a)   the net proceeds of the disposal, and

    (b)   where those proceeds are less than such amount as may be determined by the court to be the net amount which would be realised on a sale of the property or goods in the open market by a willing vendor, such sums as may be required to make good the deficiency,

shall be applied towards discharging the sums secured by the security or payable under the hire-purchase agreement.

(6) Where a condition imposed in pursuance of subsection (5) relates to two or more securities, that condition requires the net proceeds of the disposal and, where paragraph (b) of that subsection applies, the sums mentioned in that paragraph to be applied towards discharging the sums secured by those securities in the order of their priorities.

(7) References in this section to hire-purchase agreements include conditional sale agreements, chattel leasing agreements and retention of title agreements.".

10

Schedule 1 is modified so as to read as follows:—

"Schedule 1
Powers of Administrator

Section 14

1.

Power to take possession of, collect and get in the partnership property and, for that purpose, to take such proceedings as may seem to him expedient.

2.

Power to sell or otherwise dispose of the partnership property by public auction or private auction or private contract or, in Scotland, to sell, feu, hire out or otherwise dispose of the partnership property by public group or private bargain.

3.

Power to raise or borrow money and grant security therefor over the partnership property.

4.

Power to appoint a solicitor or accountant or other professionally qualified person to assist him in the performance of his functions.

5.

Power to bring or defend any action or other legal proceedings in the name and on behalf of any member of the partnership in his capacity as such or of the partnership.

6.

Power to refer to arbitration any question affecting the partnership.

7.

Power to effect and maintain insurances in respect of the partnership business and property.

8.

Power to do all acts and execute, in the name and on behalf of the partnership or of any member of the partnership in his capacity as such, any deed, receipt or other document.

9.

Power to draw, accept, make and endorse any bill of exchange or promissory note in the name and on behalf of any member of the partnership in his capacity as such or of the partnership.

10.

Power to appoint any agent to do any business which he is unable to do himself or which can more conveniently be done by an agent and power to employ and dismiss employees.

11.

Power to do all such things (including the carrying out of works) as may be necessary for the realisation of the partnership property.

12.

Power to make any payment which is necessary or incidental to the performance of his functions.

13.

Power to carry on the business of the partnership.

14.

Power to establish subsidiary undertakings of the partnership.

15.

Power to transfer to subsidiary undertakings of the partnership the whole or any part of the business of the partnership or of the partnership property.

16.

Power to grant or accept a surrender of a lease or tenancy of any of the partnership property, and to take a lease or tenancy of any property required or convenient for the business of the partnership.

17.

Power to make any arrangement or compromise on behalf of the partnership or of its members in their capacity as such.

18.

Power to rank and claim in the bankruptcy, insolvency, sequestration or liquidation of any person indebted to the partnership and to receive dividends, and to accede to trust deeds for the creditors of any such person.

19.

Power to present or defend a petition for the winding up of the partnership under the Insolvent Partnerships Order 1994.

20.

Power to do all other things incidental to the exercise of the foregoing powers.".

Notes

Para 2: in s 8 of the Act (as set out above) words in square brackets in sub-s (1)(a) and the whole of sub-ss (1A), (1B) inserted, and sub-ss (4)–(6) substituted for original sub-s (4), by the Financial Services and Markets Act 2000 (Consequential Amendments and Repeals) Order 2001, SI 2001/3649, art 468; words in square brackets in sub-s (5) inserted by the Financial Services and Markets Act 2000 (Consequential Amendments) Order 2002, SI 2002/1555, art 36; sub-s (7) added by the Insolvent Partnerships (Amendment) (No 2) Order 2002, SI 2002/2708, art 7(1), (2), except in relation to a petition for an administration order in relation to an insolvent partnership presented before 1 January 2003 (see SI 2002/2708, art 11(2), (3)).

Para 4: in s 10 of the Act (as set out above) sub-s (1)(aa) inserted by the Insolvent Partnerships (Amendment) (No 2) Order 2002, SI 2002/2708, art 7(1), (3), except in relation to a petition for an administration order in relation to an insolvent partnership presented before 1 January 2003 (see SI 2002/2708, art 11(2), (3)).

Para 5: in s 11 of the Act (as set out above) sub-s (3)(da) inserted by the Insolvent Partnerships (Amendment) (No 2) Order 2002, SI 2002/2708, art 7(1), (4), except in relation to a petition for an administration order in relation to an insolvent partnership presented before 1 January 2003 (see SI 2002/2708, art 11(2), (3)).

SCHEDULE 3
Provisions of the Act which Apply with Modifications for the Purposes of Article 7 to Winding up of Insolvent Partnership on Petition of Creditor etc Where no Concurrent Petition Presented Against Member

Article 7

Part I
Modified Provisions of Part V of the Act

3.47

1

Sections 220 to 223 of the Act are set out as modified in Part I of this Schedule, and sections 117, 131, 133, 234 and Schedule 4 are set out as modified in Part II.

2 Section 220: Meaning of 'unregistered company'

Section 220 is modified so as to read as follows:—

'220

For the purposes of this Part, the expression 'unregistered company' includes any insolvent partnership'.

3 Section 221: Winding up of unregistered companies

Section 221 is modified so as to read as follows:—

'221

(1) Subject to subsections (2) and (3) below and to the provisions of this Part, any insolvent partnership may be wound up under this Act if it has, or at any time had, in England and Wales either—
   (a)   a principal place of business, or
   (b)   a place of business at which business is or has been carried on in the course of which the debt (or part of the debt) arose which forms the basis of the petition for winding up the partnership.

(2) Subject to subsection (3) below, an insolvent partnership shall not be wound up under this Act if the business of the partnership has not been carried on in England and Wales at any time in the period of 3 years ending with the day on which the winding-up petition is presented.

(3) If an insolvent partnership has a principal place of business situated in Scotland or in Northern Ireland, the court shall not have jurisdiction to wind up the partnership unless it had a principal place of business in England and Wales—
   (a)   in the case of a partnership with a principal place of business in Scotland, at any time in the period of 1 year, or
   (b)   in the case of a partnership with a principal place of business in Northern Ireland, at any time in the period of 3 years,
ending with the day on which the winding-up petition is presented.

[(3A) The preceding subsections are subject to Article 3 of the EC Regulation (jurisdiction under the EC Regulation).]

(4) No insolvent partnership shall be wound up under this Act voluntarily.

(5) To the extent that they are applicable to the winding up of a company by the court in England and Wales on the petition of a creditor or of the Secretary of State, all the provisions of this Act and the Companies Act about winding up apply to the winding up of an insolvent partnership as an unregistered company—
  (a)   with the exceptions and additions mentioned in the following subsections of this section and in section 221A, and
  (b)   with the modifications specified in Part II of Schedule 3 to the Insolvent Partnerships Order 1994.

(6) Sections 73(1), 74(2)(a) to (d) and (3), 75 to 78, 83, 122, 123, 176A, 202, 203, 205 and 250 shall not apply.

(7) The circumstances in which an insolvent partnership may be wound up as an unregistered company are as follows—
  (a)   if the partnership is dissolved, or has ceased to carry on business, or is carrying on business only for the purpose of winding up its affairs;
  (b)   if the partnership is unable to pay its debts;
  (c)   if the court is of the opinion that it is just and equitable that the partnership should be wound up[;
  (d)   at the time at which a moratorium for the insolvent partnership under section 1A comes to an end, no voluntary arrangement approved under Part I of this Act has effect in relation to the insolvent partnership.

(7A) A winding-up petition on the ground set out in section 221(7)(d) may only be presented by one or more creditors.]

(8) Every petition for the winding up of an insolvent partnership under Part V of this Act shall be verified by affidavit in Form 2 in Schedule 9 to the Insolvent Partnerships Order 1994.

221A Petition by liquidator, administrator, trustee or supervisor to wind up insolvent partnership as unregistered company

(1) A petition in Form 3 in Schedule 9 to the Insolvent Partnerships Order 1994 for winding up an insolvent partnership may be presented by—
  (a)   the liquidator or administrator of a corporate member or of a former corporate member, or
  (b)   the administrator of the partnership, or
  (c)   the trustee of an individual member's, or of a former individual member's, estate, or
  (d)   the supervisor of a voluntary arrangement approved under Part I of this Act in relation to a corporate member or the partnership, or under Part VIII of this Act in relation to an individual member,
if the ground of the petition is one of the circumstances set out in section 221(7).

(2) In this section 'petitioning insolvency practitioner' means a person who has presented a petition under subsection (1).

(3) If the ground of the petition presented under subsection (1) is that the partnership is unable to pay its debts and the petitioning insolvency practitioner is able to satisfy the court that an insolvency order has been made against the member whose liquidator or trustee he is because of that member's inability to pay a joint debt, that order shall, unless it is proved otherwise to the satisfaction of the court, be proof for the purposes of section 221(7) that the partnership is unable to pay its debts.

(4) Where a winding-up petition is presented under subsection (1), the court may appoint the petitioning insolvency practitioner as provisional liquidator of the partnership under section 135 (appointment and powers of provisional liquidator).

(5) Where a winding-up order is made against an insolvent partnership after the presentation of a petition under subsection (1), the court may appoint the petitioning insolvency practitioner as liquidator of the partnership; and where the court makes an appointment under this subsection, section 140(3) (official receiver not to become liquidator) applies as if an appointment had been made under that section.

(6) Where a winding-up petition is presented under subsection (1), in the event of the partnership property being insufficient to satisfy the costs of the petitioning insolvency practitioner the costs may be paid out of the assets of the corporate or individual member, as the case may be, as part of the expenses of the liquidation, administration, bankruptcy or voluntary arrangement of that member, in the same order of priority as expenses properly chargeable or incurred by the practitioner in getting in any of the assets of the member'.

4 Section 222: Inability to pay debts: unpaid creditor for £750 or more

Section 222 is modified so as to read as follows:—

'**222**

(1) An insolvent partnership is deemed (for the purposes of section 221) unable to pay its debts if there is a creditor, by assignment or otherwise, to whom the partnership is indebted in a sum exceeding £750 then due and—

  (a)   the creditor has served on the partnership, in the manner specified in subsection (2) below, a written demand in the prescribed form requiring the partnership to pay the sum so due, and

  (b)   the partnership has for 3 weeks after the service of the demand neglected to pay the sum or to secure or compound for it to the creditor's satisfaction.

(2) Service of the demand referred to in subsection (1)(a) shall be effected—

  (a)   by leaving it at a principal place of business of the partnership in England and Wales, or

(b) by leaving it at a place of business of the partnership in England and Wales at which business is carried on in the course of which the debt (or part of the debt) referred to in subsection (1) arose, or

(c) by delivering it to an officer of the partnership, or

(d) by otherwise serving it in such manner as the court may approve or direct.

(3) The money sum for the time being specified in subsection (1) is subject to increase or reduction by regulations under section 417 in Part XV; but no increase in the sum so specified affects any case in which the winding-up petition was presented before the coming into force of the increase'.

5 Section 223: Inability to pay debts: debt remaining unsatisfied after action brought

Section 223 is modified so as to read as follows:—

'223

(1) An insolvent partnership is deemed (for the purposes of section 221) unable to pay its debts if an action or other proceeding has been instituted against any member for any debt or demand due, or claimed to be due, from the partnership, or from him in his character of member, and—

(a) notice in writing of the institution of the action or proceeding has been served on the partnership in the manner specified in subsection (2) below, and

(b) the partnership has not within 3 weeks after service of the notice paid, secured or compounded for the debt or demand, or procured the action or proceeding to be stayed or sisted, or indemnified the defendant or defender to his reasonable satisfaction against the action or proceeding, and against all costs, damages and expenses to be incurred by him because of it.

(2) Service of the notice referred to in subsection (1)(a) shall be effected—

(a) by leaving it at a principal place of business of the partnership in England and Wales, or

(b) by leaving it at a place of business of the partnership in England and Wales at which business is carried on in the course of which the debt or demand (or part of the debt or demand) referred to in subsection (1) arose, or

(c) by delivering it to an officer of the partnership, or

(d) by otherwise serving it in such manner as the court may approve or direct'.

Notes

Part I of Schedule 3 applies the provisions of Part V of IA 1986 with certain modifications. These are largely self-explanatory and make the necessary changes for the different context.

Note that, while 'unregistered company' is replaced with 'insolvent partnership', insolvency is not the only ground for winding up. Where the court has the jurisdiction to wind up an insolvent partnership it may do so of its own motion and without a winding up petition being presented *Launcefield v Launcefield* [2002] BPIR 1108. IA 1986 s 224, also applies: this allows for a petition on the basis that insolvency can be proved in a number of ways, for instance the firm's liabilities are greater than its assets. This additional ground is likely to be of little consequence because of the relative lack of availability of financial information about partnerships.

Carried on business

The carrying on of business under s 221(7) (*above*) continues until all obligations of the partnership are completed and debts paid *Re a Debtor [1992] Ch 554*.

Inability to pay

As with unregistered companies under Part V of the IA 1986, inability to pay debts may be proved by the usual statutory demand route (s 222 above) and also by showing that an action for the recovery of a joint debt has been commenced against a member and, having notice of the action, the partnership has failed to pay the debt in 3 weeks, to stay it or to indemnify the member in relation to the claim (see s 233 above).

Insolvency practitioner's petition

There is a further ground for petitioning provided for trustees, liquidators, administrators and supervisors of members of the partnership (s 221A(3)). Where there has been an insolvency order in respect of a member and that order can be proved to have been in relation to a joint debt, that will be conclusive of the partnership's inability to pay its debts under s 221(7) above.

Service

Note that the provisions for service of petitions under this Schedule (s 222(2) above) differ from those in relation to registered companies (ie, IR 1986, r 4.8). There is likely to be little difference in practice but care should be taken to ensure that the chosen method is within the provisions above.

Part II
Other Modified Provisions of the Act about Winding up by the Court

3.48

6 Section 117: High Court and county court jurisdiction

Section 117 is modified so as to read as follows:—

'**117**

(1) Subject to subsections (3) and (4) below, the High Court has jurisdiction to wind up any insolvent partnership as an unregistered company by virtue of article 7 of the Insolvent Partnerships Order 1994 if the partnership has, or at any time had, in England and Wales either—
   (a)   a principal place of business, or
   (b)   a place of business at which business is or has been carried on in the course of which the debt (or part of the debt) arose which forms the basis of the petition for winding up the partnership.

(2) Subject to subsections (3) and (4) below, a petition for the winding up of an insolvent partnership by virtue of the said article 7 may be presented to a county court in England and Wales if the partnership has, or at any time had, within the insolvency district of that court either—
   (a)   a principal place of business, or

(b)   a place of business at which business is or has been carried on in the course of which the debt (or part of the debt) arose which forms the basis of the winding-up petition.

(3) Subject to subsection (4) below, the court only has jurisdiction to wind up an insolvent partnership if the business of the partnership has been carried on in England and Wales at any time in the period of 3 years ending with the day on which the petition for winding it up is presented.

(4) If an insolvent partnership has a principal place of business situated in Scotland or in Northern Ireland, the court shall not have jurisdiction to wind up the partnership unless it had a principal place of business in England and Wales—

(a)   in the case of a partnership with a principal place of business in Scotland, at any time in the period of 1 year, or

(b)   in the case of a partnership with a principal place of business in Northern Ireland, at any time in the period of 3 years,

ending with the day on which the petition for winding it up is presented.

(5) The Lord Chancellor [may, with the concurrence of the Lord Chief Justice, by order] in a statutory instrument exclude a county court from having winding-up jurisdiction, and for the purposes of that jurisdiction may attach its district, or any part thereof, to any other county court, and may by statutory instrument revoke or vary any such order.

In exercising the powers of this section, the Lord Chancellor shall provide that a county court is not to have winding-up jurisdiction unless it has for the time being jurisdiction for the purposes of Parts VIII to XI of this Act (individual insolvency).

(6) Every court in England and Wales having winding-up jurisdiction has for the purposes of that jurisdiction all the powers of the High Court; and every prescribed officer of the court shall perform any duties which an officer of the High Court may discharge by order of a judge of that court or otherwise in relation to winding up.

[(7) This section is subject to Article 3 of the EC Regulation (jurisdiction under the EC Regulation).]

[(8) The Lord Chief Justice may nominate a judicial office holder (as defined in section 109(4) of the Constitutional Reform Act 2005) to exercise his functions under this section.]'.

7 Section 131: Statement of affairs of insolvent partnership

Section 131 is modified so as to read as follows:—

'131

(1) Where the court has, by virtue of article 7 of the Insolvent Partnerships Order 1994, made a winding-up order or appointed a provisional liquidator in respect of an insolvent partnership, the official receiver may require some or all of the persons mentioned in subsection (3) below to make out and submit to him a statement in the prescribed form as to the affairs of the partnership.

(2) The statement shall be verified by affidavit by the persons required to submit it and shall show—

(a) particulars of the debts and liabilities of the partnership and of the partnership property;

(b) the names and addresses of the partnership's creditors;

(c) the securities held by them respectively;

(d) the dates when the securities were respectively given; and

(e) such further or other information as may be prescribed or as the official receiver may require.

(3) The persons referred to in subsection (1) are—

(a) those who are or have been officers of the partnership;

(b) those who have taken part in the formation of the partnership at any time within one year before the relevant date;

(c) those who are in the employment of the partnership, or have been in its employment within that year, and are in the official receiver's opinion capable of giving the information required;

(d) those who are or have been within that year officers of, or in the employment of, a company which is, or within that year was, an officer of the partnership.

(4) Where any persons are required under this section to submit a statement of affairs to the official receiver, they shall do so (subject to the next subsection) before the end of the period of 21 days beginning with the day after that on which the prescribed notice of the requirement is given to them by the official receiver.

(5) The official receiver, if he thinks fit, may—

(a) at any time release a person from an obligation imposed on him under subsection (1) or (2) above; or

(b) either when giving the notice mentioned in subsection (4) or subsequently, extend the period so mentioned;

and where the official receiver has refused to exercise a power conferred by this subsection, the court, if it thinks fit, may exercise it.

(6) In this section—

'employment' includes employment under a contract for services; and

'the relevant date' means—

(a) in a case where a provisional liquidator is appointed, the date of his appointment; and

(b) in a case where no such appointment is made, the date of the winding-up order.

(7) If a person without reasonable excuse fails to comply with any obligation imposed under this section, he is liable to a fine and, for continued contravention, to a daily default fine'.

8 Section 133: Public examination of officers of insolvent partnerships

Section 133 is modified so as to read as follows:—

'133

(1) Where an insolvent partnership is being wound up by virtue of article 7 of the Insolvent Partnerships Order 1994, the official receiver may at any time before the winding up is complete apply to the court for the public examination of any person who—

(a) is or has been an officer of the partnership; or

(b) has acted as liquidator or administrator of the partnership or as receiver or manager or, in Scotland, receiver of its property; or

(c) not being a person falling within paragraph (a) or (b), is or has been concerned, or has taken part, in the formation of the partnership.

(2) Unless the court otherwise orders, the official receiver shall make an application under subsection (1) if he is requested in accordance with the rules to do so by one-half, in value, of the creditors of the partnership.

(3) On an application under subsection (1), the court shall direct that a public examination of the person to whom the application relates shall be held on a day appointed by the court; and that person shall attend on that day and be publicly examined as to the formation or management of the partnership or as to the conduct of its business and affairs, or his conduct or dealings in relation to the partnership.

(4) The following may take part in the public examination of a person under this section and may question that person concerning the matters mentioned in subsection (3), namely—

(a) the official receiver;

(b) the liquidator of the partnership;

(c) any person who has been appointed as special manager of the partnership's property or business;

(d) any creditor of the partnership who has tendered a proof in the winding up'.

9 Section 234: Getting in the partnership property

Section 234 is modified so as to read as follows:—

'234

(1) This section applies where, by virtue of article 7 of the Insolvent Partnerships Order 1994—

(a) an insolvent partnership is being wound up, or

(b) a provisional liquidator of an insolvent partnership is appointed; and 'the office-holder' means the liquidator or the provisional liquidator, as the case may be.

(2) Any person who is or has been an officer of the partnership, or who is an executor or administrator of the estate of a deceased officer of the partnership, shall deliver up to the office-holder, for the purposes of the exercise of the office-holder's functions under this Act and (where applicable) the Company Directors Disqualification Act 1986, possession of any partnership property which he holds for the purposes of the partnership.

(3) Where any person has in his possession or control any property, books, papers or records to which the partnership appears to be entitled, the court may require that person forthwith (or within such period as the court may direct) to pay, deliver, convey, surrender or transfer the property, books, papers or records to the office-holder or as the court may direct.

(4) Where the office-holder—

(a) seizes or disposes of any property which is not partnership property, and

(b)   at the time of seizure or disposal believes, and has reasonable grounds for believing, that he is entitled (whether in pursuance of an order of the court or otherwise) to seize or dispose of that property,

the next subsection has effect.

(5) In that case the office-holder—

(a)   is not liable to any person in respect of any loss or damage resulting from the seizure or disposal except in so far as that loss or damage is caused by the office-holder's own negligence, and

(b)   has a lien on the property, or the proceeds of its sale, for such expenses as were incurred in connection with the seizure or disposal'.

10

Schedule 4 is modified so as to read as follows:—

Schedule 4
Powers of Liquidator in a Winding Up
Section 167

Part I
Powers Exercisable With Sanction

3.49

1

Power to pay any class of creditors in full.

2

Power to make any compromise or arrangement with creditors or persons claiming to be creditors, or having or alleging themselves to have any claim (present or future, certain or contingent, ascertained or sounding only in damages) against the partnership, or whereby the partnership may be rendered liable.

3

Power to compromise, on such terms as may be agreed—

(a)   all debts and liabilities capable of resulting in debts, and all claims (present or future, certain or contingent, ascertained or sounding only in damages) subsisting or supposed to subsist between the partnership and a contributory or alleged contributory or other debtor or person apprehending liability to the partnership, and

(b)   all questions in any way relating to or affecting the partnership property or the winding up of the partnership,

and take any security for the discharge of any such debt, liability or claim and give a complete discharge in respect of it.

[3A

Power to bring legal proceedings under section 213, 214, 238, 239 or 423.]

4

Power to bring or defend any action or other legal proceeding in the name and on behalf of any member of the partnership in his capacity as such or of the partnership.

5

Power to carry on the business of the partnership so far as may be necessary for its beneficial winding up.

Part II
Powers Exercisable Without Sanction

3.50

6

Power to sell any of the partnership property by public auction or private contract, with power to transfer the whole of it to any person or to sell the same in parcels.

7

Power to do all acts and execute, in the name and on behalf of the partnership or of any member of the partnership in his capacity as such, all deeds, receipts and other documents.

8

Power to prove, rank and claim in the bankruptcy, insolvency or sequestration of any contributory for any balance against his estate, and to receive dividends in the bankruptcy, insolvency or sequestration in respect of that balance, as a separate debt due from the bankrupt or insolvent, and rateably with the other separate creditors.

9

Power to draw, accept, make and endorse any bill of exchange or promissory note in the name and on behalf of any member of the partnership in his capacity as such or of the partnership, with the same effect with respect to the liability of the partnership or of any member of the partnership in his capacity as such as if the bill or note had been drawn, accepted, made or endorsed in the course of the partnership's business.

10

Power to raise on the security of the partnership property any money requisite.

11

Power to take out in his official name letters of administration to any deceased contributory, and to do in his official name any other act necessary for obtaining payment of any money due from a contributory or his estate which cannot conveniently be done in the name of the partnership.

In all such cases the money due is deemed, for the purpose of enabling the liquidator to take out the letters of administration or recover the money, to be due to the liquidator himself.

12

Power to appoint an agent to do any business which the liquidator is unable to do himself.

13

Power to do all such other things as may be necessary for winding up the partnership's affairs and distributing its property'.

Notes

The modifications to the provisions set up above are self-explanatory. For commentary on the unmodified parts of the IA 1986 and for the rest of the provisions applicable to Article 7 petitions, see the notes elsewhere in this work.

SCHEDULE 4
Provisions of the Act which apply with Modifications for the Purposes of Article 8 to Winding up of Insolvent Partnership on Creditor's Petition Where Concurrent Petitions are Presented Against One or More Members
Article 8

Part I
Modified Provisions of Part V of the Act

3.51

1

(1) Sections 220 to 222 of the Act are set out as modified in Part I of this Schedule, and the provisions of the Act specified in sub-paragraph (2) below are set out as modified in Part II.

(2) The provisions referred to in sub-paragraph (1) are sections 117, 122 to 125, 131, 133, 136, 137, 139 to 141, 143, 146, 147, 168, 172, 174, 175, 189, 211, 230, 231, 234, 264, 265, 267, 268, 271, 283, [283A,] 284, 288, 292 to 296, 298 to 303, 305, [313A,] 314, 328, 331 and 356, and Schedule 4.

2 Section 220: Meaning of 'unregistered company'

Section 220 is modified so as to read as follows:—

'**220**

For the purposes of this Part, the expression 'unregistered company' includes any insolvent partnership'.

3 Section 221: Winding up of unregistered companies

Section 221 is modified so as to read as follows:—

'**221**

(1) Subject to subsections (2) and (3) below and to the provisions of this Part, any insolvent partnership may be wound up under this Act if it has, or at any time had, in England and Wales either—
  (a) a principal place of business, or
  (b) a place of business at which business is or has been carried on in the course of which the debt (or part of the debt) arose which forms the basis of the petition for winding up the partnership.

(2) Subject to subsection (3) below, an insolvent partnership shall not be wound up under this Act if the business of the partnership has not been carried on in England and Wales at any time in the period of 3 years ending with the day on which the winding-up petition is presented.

(3) If an insolvent partnership has a principal place of business situated in Scotland or in Northern Ireland, the court shall not have jurisdiction to wind up the partnership unless it had a principal place of business in England and Wales—
  (a) in the case of a partnership with a principal place of business in Scotland, at any time in the period of 1 year, or
  (b) in the case of a partnership with a principal place of business in Northern Ireland, at any time in the period of 3 years,
ending with the day on which the winding-up petition is presented.

[(3A) The preceding subsections are subject to Article 3 of the EC Regulation (jurisdiction under the EC Regulation).]

(4) No insolvent partnership shall be wound up under this Act voluntarily.

(5) To the extent that they are applicable to the winding up of a company by the court in England and Wales on a creditor's petition, all the provisions of this Act and the Companies Act about winding up apply to the winding up of an insolvent partnership as an unregistered company—
  (a) with the exceptions and additions mentioned in the following subsections of this section, and
  (b) with the modifications specified in Part II of Schedule 4 to the Insolvent Partnerships Order 1994.

(6) Sections 73(1), 74(2)(a) to (d) and (3), 75 to 78, 83, 154, 176A, 202, 203, 205 and 250 shall not apply.

(7) Unless the contrary intention appears, a member of a partnership against whom an insolvency order has been made by virtue of article 8 of the Insolvent Partnerships Order 1994 shall not be treated as a contributory for the purposes of this Act.

[(8) The circumstances in which an insolvent partnership may be wound up as an unregistered company are as follows—
  (a) the partnership is unable to pay its debts,
  (b) at the time at which a moratorium for the insolvent partnership under section 1A comes to an end, no voluntary arrangement approved under Part I of this Act has effect in relation to the insolvent partnership.]

(9) Every petition for the winding up of an insolvent partnership under Part V of this Act shall be verified by affidavit in Form 2 in Schedule 9 to the Insolvent Partnerships Order 1994'.

4 Section 222: Inability to pay debts: unpaid creditor for £750 or more

Section 222 is modified so as to read as follows:—

'**222**

(1) An insolvent partnership is deemed (for the purposes of section 221) unable to pay its debts if there is a creditor, by assignment or otherwise, to whom the partnership is indebted in a sum exceeding £750 then due and—
  (a) the creditor has served on the partnership, in the manner specified in subsection (2) below, a written demand in Form 4 in Schedule 9 to the Insolvent Partnerships Order 1994 requiring the partnership to pay the sum so due,
  (b) the creditor has also served on any one or more members or former members of the partnership liable to pay the sum due (in the case of a corporate member by leaving it at its registered office and in the case of an individual member by serving it in accordance with the rules) a demand in Form 4 in Schedule 9 to that Order, requiring that member or those members to pay the sum so due, and
  (c) the partnership and its members have for 3 weeks after the service of the demands, or the service of the last of them if served at different times, neglected to pay the sum or to secure or compound for it to the creditor's satisfaction.

(2) Service of the demand referred to in subsection (1)(a) shall be effected—
  (a) by leaving it at a principal place of business of the partnership in England and Wales, or
  (b) by leaving it at a place of business of the partnership in England and Wales at which business is carried on in the course of which the debt (or part of the debt) referred to in subsection (1) arose, or
  (c) by delivering it to an officer of the partnership, or
  (d) by otherwise serving it in such manner as the court may approve or direct.

(3) The money sum for the time being specified in subsection (1) is subject to increase or reduction by regulations under section 417 in

> Part XV; but no increase in the sum so specified affects any case in which the winding-up petition was presented before the coming into force of the increase'.

Notes

This Part modifies the provisions of Part V of IA 1986 for the purpose of Article 8 petitions. Note that s 223, 224 are disapplied by Article 8. It follows that the means of proving insolvency allowed in those sections do not apply. Indeed the only grounds for a petition are inability to pay debts proved by failure to comply with a statutory demand and, post IA 2000, the failure of the partnership's creditors to approve a voluntary arrangement after a moratorium.

S 221(1)(b)

The 'carrying on' of business under s 221 continues until all obligations of the partnership are completed and debts paid *Re a Debtor* [1992] Ch 554.

S 221(7)

This provides that a member against whom an insolvency order is made under Article 8 shall not be treated as a contributory unless a contrary intention appears. This does not mean that the other members will not be so treated. The member against whom an order is made need not be treated as a contributory because his separate estate will be applied to any shortfall in the joint estate by virtue of the provisions of s 175A–C as modified.

Part II
Other Modified Provisions of the Act About Winding up by the Court and Bankruptcy of Individuals

3.52

5 Sections 117 and 265: High Court and county court jurisdiction

Sections 117 and 265 are modified so as to read as follows:—

'117

(1) Subject to the provisions of this section, the High Court has jurisdiction to wind up any insolvent partnership as an unregistered company by virtue of article 8 of the Insolvent Partnerships Order 1994 if the partnership has, or at any time had, in England and Wales either—
    (a) a principal place of business, or
    (b) a place of business at which business is or has been carried on in the course of which the debt (or part of the debt) arose which forms the basis of the petition for winding up the partnership.

(2) Subject to subsections (3) and (4) below, a petition for the winding up of an insolvent partnership by virtue of the said article 8 may be presented to a county court in England and Wales if the partnership has, or at any time had, within the insolvency district of that court either—
    (a) a principal place of business, or
    (b) a place of business at which business is or has been carried on in the course of which the debt (or part of the debt) arose which forms the basis of the winding-up petition.

(3) Subject to subsection (4) below, the court only has jurisdiction to wind up an insolvent partnership if the business of the partnership has been carried on in England and Wales at any time in the period of 3 years ending with the day on which the petition for winding it up is presented.

(4) If an insolvent partnership has a principal place of business situated in Scotland or in Northern Ireland, the court shall not have jurisdiction to wind up the partnership unless it had a principal place of business in England and Wales—

    (a)   in the case of a partnership with a principal place of business in Scotland, at any time in the period of 1 year, or

    (b)   in the case of a partnership with a principal place of business in Northern Ireland, at any time in the period of 3 years,

ending with the day on which the petition for winding it up is presented.

(5) Subject to subsection (6) below, the court has jurisdiction to wind up a corporate member or former corporate member, or make a bankruptcy order against an individual member or former individual member, of a partnership against which a petition has been presented by virtue of article 8 of the Insolvent Partnerships Order 1994 if it has jurisdiction in respect of the partnership.

(6) Petitions by virtue of the said article 8 for the winding up of an insolvent partnership and the bankruptcy of one or more members or former members of that partnership may not be presented to a district registry of the High Court.

(7) The Lord Chancellor [may, with the concurrence of the Lord Chief Justice, by order] in a statutory instrument exclude a county court from having winding-up jurisdiction, and for the purposes of that jurisdiction may attach its district, or any part thereof, to any other county court, and may by statutory instrument revoke or vary any such order.

In exercising the powers of this section, the Lord Chancellor shall provide that a county court is not to have winding-up jurisdiction unless it has for the time being jurisdiction for the purposes of Parts VIII to XI of this Act (individual insolvency).

(8) Every court in England and Wales having winding-up jurisdiction has for the purposes of that jurisdiction all the powers of the High Court; and every prescribed officer of the court shall perform any duties which an officer of the High Court may discharge by order of a judge of that court or otherwise in relation to winding up.

[(9) This section is subject to Article 3 of the EC Regulation (jurisdiction under the EC Regulation).]

[(10) The Lord Chief Justice may nominate a judicial office holder (as defined in section 109(4) of the Constitutional Reform Act 2005) to exercise his functions under this section.]'.

6 Circumstances in which members of insolvent partnerships may be wound up or made bankrupt by the court:
Section 122—corporate member; Section 267—individual member

(a) Section 122 is modified so as to read as follows:—

['122

A corporate member or former corporate member of an insolvent partnership may be wound up by the court if—
  (a) it is unable to pay its debts,
  (b) there is a creditor, by assignment or otherwise, to whom the insolvent partnership is indebted and the corporate member or former corporate member is liable in relation to that debt and at the time at which a moratorium for the insolvent partnership under section 1A comes to an end, no voluntary arrangement approved under Part I of this Act has effect in relation to the insolvent partnership.'].

(b) Section 267 is modified so as to read as follows:-

'267

(1) Where a petition for the winding up of an insolvent partnership has been presented to the court by virtue of article 8 of the Insolvent Partnerships Order 1994, a creditor's petition against any individual member or former individual member of that partnership by virtue of that article must be in respect of one or more joint debts owed by the insolvent partnership, and the petitioning creditor or each of the petitioning creditors must be a person to whom the debt or (as the case may be) at least one of the debts is owed.

(2) Subject to [subsection (2A) below and] section 268, a creditor's petition may be presented to the court in respect of a joint debt or debts only if, at the time the petition is presented—
  (a) the amount of the debt, or the aggregate amount of the debts, is equal to or exceeds the bankruptcy level,
  (b) the debt, or each of the debts, is for a liquidated sum payable to the petitioning creditor, or one or more of the petitioning creditors, immediately, and is unsecured,
  (c) the debt, or each of the debts, is a debt for which the individual member or former member is liable and which he appears to be unable to pay, and
  (d) there is no outstanding application to set aside a statutory demand served (under section 268 below) in respect of the debt or any of the debts.

[(2A) A creditor's petition may be presented to the court in respect of a joint debt or debts if at the time at which a moratorium for the insolvent partnership under section 1A comes to an end, no voluntary arrangement approved under Part I of this Act has effect in relation to the insolvent partnership.]

(3) 'The bankruptcy level' is £750; but the Secretary of State may by order in a statutory instrument substitute any amount specified in the order for that amount or (as the case may be) for the amount which by virtue of such an order is for the time being the amount of the bankruptcy level.

(4) An order shall not be made under subsection (3) unless a draft of it has been laid before, and approved by a resolution of, each House of Parliament'.

_____

Notes

Paragraph 6 sets out the grounds for petitioning against the member of the partnership where there are concurrent petitions against the partnership and one or more members. There are two grounds: inability to pay debts – service of a statutory demand which has gone unheeded for 3 weeks (see paragraph 7 below); and the failure of the firm's creditors to approve a voluntary arrangement after a moratorium. In this latter case, the petitioner has to show that he is a creditor of the joint estate and the member in question is liable for that joint debt. In most cases this will be straightforward. But, in others, this may cause problems, especially where the member has left the partnership or in 'holding out' cases.

_____

7 Definition of inability to pay debts: Section 123—corporate member; Section 268—individual member

(a) Section 123 is modified so as to read as follows:—

'123

(1) A corporate member or former member is deemed unable to pay its debts if there is a creditor, by assignment or otherwise, to whom the partnership is indebted in a sum exceeding £750 then due for which the member or former member is liable and—

  (a) the creditor has served on that member or former member and the partnership, in the manner specified in subsection (2) below, a written demand in Form 4 in Schedule 9 to the Insolvent Partnerships Order 1994 requiring that member or former member and the partnership to pay the sum so due, and

  (b) the corporate member or former member and the partnership have for 3 weeks after the service of the demands, or the service of the last of them if served at different times, neglected to pay the sum or to secure or compound for it to the creditor's satisfaction.

(2) Service of the demand referred to in subsection (1)(a) shall be effected, in the case of the corporate member or former corporate member, by leaving it at its registered office, and, in the case of the partnership—

  (a) by leaving it at a principal place of business of the partnership in England and Wales, or

  (b) by leaving it at a place of business of the partnership in England and Wales at which business is carried on in the course of which the debt (or part of the debt) referred to in subsection (1) arose, or

  (c) by delivering it to an officer of the partnership, or

  (d) by otherwise serving it in such manner as the court may approve or direct.

(3) The money sum for the time being specified in subsection (1) is subject to increase or reduction by order under section 416 in Part XV'.

(b) Section 268 is modified so as to read as follows:—

'268

(1) For the purposes of section 267(2)(c), an individual member or former individual member appears to be unable to pay a joint debt for which he is liable if the debt is payable immediately and the petitioning creditor to whom the insolvent partnership owes the joint debt has served—

    (a) on the individual member or former individual member in accordance with the rules a demand (known as 'the statutory demand'), in Form 4 in Schedule 9 to the Insolvent Partnerships Order 1994, and

    (b) on the partnership in the manner specified in subsection (2) below a demand (known as 'the written demand') in the same form,

requiring the member or former member and the partnership to pay the debt or to secure or compound for it to the creditor's satisfaction, and at least 3 weeks have elapsed since the service of the demands, or the service of the last of them if served at different times, and neither demand has been complied with nor the demand against the member set aside in accordance with the rules.

(2) Service of the demand referred to in subsection (1)(b) shall be effected—

    (a) by leaving it at a principal place of business of the partnership in England and Wales, or

    (b) by leaving it at a place of business of the partnership in England and Wales at which business is carried on in the course of which the debt (or part of the debt) referred to in subsection (1) arose, or

    (c) by delivering it to an officer of the partnership, or

    (d) by otherwise serving it in such manner as the court may approve or direct'.

Notes

This paragraph sets out the provisions relating to proof of a member's inability to pay – the statutory demand. Note the requirements to use the standard forms in Schedule 9 and the provisions as to service.

3.53

8 Sections 124 and 264: Applications to wind up insolvent partnership and to wind up or bankrupt insolvent member

Sections 124 and 264 are modified so as to read as follows:—

'124

(1) An application to the court by virtue of article 8 of the Insolvent Partnerships Order 1994 for the winding up of an insolvent partnership as an unregistered company and the winding up or bankruptcy (as the case may be) of at least one of its members or former members shall—

(a)   in the case of the partnership, be by petition in Form 5 in Schedule 9 to that Order,

(b)   in the case of a corporate member or former corporate member, be by petition in Form 6 in that Schedule, and

(c)   in the case of an individual member or former individual member, be by petition in Form 7 in that Schedule.

(2) Each of the petitions mentioned in subsection (1) may be presented by [a liquidator (within the meaning of Article 2(b) of the EC Regulation) appointed in proceedings by virtue of Article 3(1) of the EC Regulation, a temporary administrator (within the meaning of Article 38 of the EC Regulation) or] any creditor or creditors to whom the partnership and the member or former member in question is indebted in respect of a liquidated sum payable immediately.

(3) The petitions mentioned in subsection (1)—

(a)   shall all be presented to the same court and, except as the court otherwise permits or directs, on the same day, and

(b)   except in the case of the petition mentioned in subsection (1)(c), shall be advertised in Form 8 in the said Schedule 9.

(4) At any time after presentation of a petition under this section the petitioner may, with the leave of the court obtained on application and on such terms as it thinks just, add other members or former members of the partnership as parties to the proceedings in relation to the insolvent partnership.

(5) Each petition presented under this section shall contain particulars of other petitions being presented in relation to the partnership, identifying the partnership and members concerned.

(6) The hearing of the petition against the partnership fixed by the court shall be in advance of the hearing of any petition against an insolvent member.

(7) On the day appointed for the hearing of the petition against the partnership, the petitioner shall, before the commencement of the hearing, hand to the court Form 9 in Schedule 9 to the Insolvent Partnerships Order 1994, duly completed.

(8) Any member of the partnership or any person against whom a winding-up or bankruptcy petition has been presented in relation to the insolvent partnership is entitled to appear and to be heard on any petition for the winding up of the partnership.

(9) A petitioner under this section may at the hearing withdraw a petition if—

(a)   subject to subsection (10) below, he withdraws at the same time every other petition which he has presented under this section; and

(b)   he gives notice to the court at least 3 days before the date appointed for the hearing of the relevant petition of his intention to withdraw the petition.

(10) A petitioner need not comply with the provisions of subsection (9)(a) in the case of a petition against an insolvent member if the court is satisfied on application made to it by the petitioner that, because of difficulties in serving the petition or for any other reason, the continuance

of that petition would be likely to prejudice or delay the proceedings on the petition which he has presented against the partnership or on any petition which he has presented against any other insolvent member.

(11) Where notice is given under subsection (9)(b), the court may, on such terms as it thinks just, substitute as petitioner, both in respect of the partnership and in respect of each insolvent member against whom a petition has been presented, any creditor of the partnership who in its opinion would have a right to present the petitions, and if the court makes such a substitution the petitions in question will not be withdrawn.

(12) Reference in subsection (11) to substitution of a petitioner includes reference to change of carriage of the petition in accordance with the rules'.

9 Sections 125 and 271: Powers of court on hearing of petitions against insolvent partnership and members

Sections 125 and 271 are modified so as to read as follows:—

'125

(1) Subject to the provisions of section 125A, on hearing a petition under section 124 against an insolvent partnership or any of its insolvent members, the court may dismiss it, or adjourn the hearing conditionally or unconditionally or make any other order that it thinks fit; but the court shall not refuse to make a winding-up order against the partnership or a corporate member on the ground only that the partnership property or (as the case may be) the member's assets have been mortgaged to an amount equal to or in excess of that property or those assets, or that the partnership has no property or the member no assets.

(2) An order under subsection (1) in respect of an insolvent partnership may contain directions as to the future conduct of any insolvency proceedings in existence against any insolvent member in respect of whom an insolvency order has been made.

125A Hearing of petitions against members

(1) On the hearing of a petition against an insolvent member the petitioner shall draw the court's attention to the result of the hearing of the winding-up petition against the partnership and the following subsections of this section shall apply.

(2) If the court has neither made a winding-up order, nor dismissed the winding-up petition, against the partnership the court may adjourn the hearing of the petition against the member until either event has occurred.

(3) Subject to subsection (4) below, if a winding-up order has been made against the partnership, the court may make a winding-up order against the corporate member in respect of which, or (as the case may be) a bankruptcy order against the individual member in respect of whom, the insolvency petition was presented.

(4) If no insolvency order is made under subsection (3) against any member within 28 days of the making of the winding-up order against the partnership, the proceedings against the partnership shall be conducted as

if the winding-up petition against the partnership had been presented by virtue of article 7 of the Insolvent Partnerships Order 1994 and the proceedings against any member shall be conducted under this Act without the modifications made by that Order (other than the modifications made to sections 168 and 303 by article 14).

(5) If the court has dismissed the winding-up petition against the partnership, the court may dismiss the winding-up petition against the corporate member or (as the case may be) the bankruptcy petition against the individual member. However, if an insolvency order is made against a member, the proceedings against that member shall be conducted under this Act without the modifications made by the Insolvent Partnerships Order 1994 (other than the modifications made to sections 168 and 303 of this Act by article 14 of that Order).

(6) The court may dismiss a petition against an insolvent member if it considers it just to do so because of a change in circumstances since the making of the winding-up order against the partnership.

(7) The court may dismiss a petition against an insolvent member who is a limited partner, if—

(a) the member lodges in court for the benefit of the creditors of the partnership sufficient money or security to the court's satisfaction to meet his liability for the debts and obligations of the partnership; or

(b) the member satisfies the court that he is no longer under any liability in respect of the debts and obligations of the partnership.

(8) Nothing in sections 125 and 125A or in sections 267 and 268 prejudices the power of the court, in accordance with the rules, to authorise a creditor's petition to be amended by the omission of any creditor or debt and to be proceeded with as if things done for the purposes of those sections had been done only by or in relation to the remaining creditors or debts'.

Notes

This sets out the procedure for the hearing of the petition against the partnership and the concurrent petitions against the members and is self-explanatory. Under s 124(3), (5) the petitions must be presented to the same court and on the same day unless otherwise permitted *Smith and Williamson v Sims Pipes* [2001] BPIR 401 and each petition must give particulars of the other. It is implicit from s 125A(2)–(3) that the court should not make a final order on the petitions against the members until a final order has been made on the petition against the partnership. It is also implicit that the court hearing the member's petition should follow the result of that against the firm. Though that is usually the case an example of a case where that did not happen is *Re Marr* [1990] Ch 773 (CA).

3.54

10 Sections 131 and 288: Statements of affairs—Insolvent partnerships; corporate members; individual members

Sections 131 and 288 are modified so as to read as follows:—

'131

(1) This section applies where the court has, by virtue of article 8 of the Insolvent Partnerships Order 1994—

    (a)   made a winding-up order or appointed a provisional liquidator in respect of an insolvent partnership, or

    (b)   made a winding-up order or appointed a provisional liquidator in respect of any corporate member of that partnership, or

    (c)   made a bankruptcy order in respect of any individual member of that partnership.

(2) The official receiver may require some or all of the persons mentioned in subsection (4) below to make out and submit to him a statement as to the affairs of the partnership or member in the prescribed form.

(3) The statement shall be verified by affidavit by the persons required to submit it and shall show—

    (a)   particulars of the debts and liabilities of the partnership or of the member (as the case may be), and of the partnership property and member's assets;

    (b)   the names and addresses of the creditors of the partnership or of the member (as the case may be);

    (c)   the securities held by them respectively;

    (d)   the dates when the securities were respectively given; and

    (e)   such further or other information as may be prescribed or as the official receiver may require.

(4) The persons referred to in subsection (2) are—

    (a)   those who are or have been officers of the partnership;

    (b)   those who are or have been officers of the corporate member;

    (c)   those who have taken part in the formation of the partnership or of the corporate member at any time within one year before the relevant date;

    (d)   those who are in the employment of the partnership or of the corporate member, or have been in such employment within that year, and are in the official receiver's opinion capable of giving the information required;

    (e)   those who are or have been within that year officers of, or in the employment of, a company which is, or within that year was, an officer of the partnership or an officer of the corporate member.

(5) Where any persons are required under this section to submit a statement of affairs to the official receiver, they shall do so (subject to the next subsection) before the end of the period of 21 days beginning with the day after that on which the prescribed notice of the requirement is given to them by the official receiver.

(6) The official receiver, if he thinks fit, may—

    (a)   at any time release a person from an obligation imposed on him under subsection (2) or (3) above; or

    (b)   either when giving the notice mentioned in subsection (5) or subsequently, extend the period so mentioned;

and where the official receiver has refused to exercise a power conferred by this subsection, the court, if it thinks fit, may exercise it.

(7) In this section—

'employment' includes employment under a contract for services; and
'the relevant date' means—

    (a)   in a case where a provisional liquidator is appointed, the
date of his appointment; and

    (b)   in a case where no such appointment is made, the date of
the winding-up order.

(8) Any person who without reasonable excuse fails to comply with any
obligation imposed under this section (other than, in the case of an
individual member, an obligation in respect of his own statement of
affairs), is liable to a fine and, for continued contravention, to a daily
default fine.

(9) An individual member who without reasonable excuse fails to comply
with any obligation imposed under this section in respect of his own
statement of affairs, is guilty of a contempt of court and liable to be
punished accordingly (in addition to any other punishment to which he
may be subject)'.

11 Section 133: Public examination of officers of insolvent partnerships

Section 133 is modified so far as insolvent partnerships are concerned so
as to read as follows:—

'133

(1) Where an insolvent partnership is being wound up by virtue of
article 8 of the Insolvent Partnerships Order 1994, the official receiver
may at any time before the winding up is complete apply to the court for
the public examination of any person who—

    (a)   is or has been an officer of the partnership; or

    (b)   has acted as liquidator or administrator of the partnership or as
receiver or manager or, in Scotland, receiver of its property;

    (c)   not being a person falling within paragraph (a) or (b), is or has
been concerned, or has taken part, in the formation of the
partnership.

(2) Unless the court otherwise orders, the official receiver shall make an
application under subsection (1) if he is requested in accordance with the
rules to do so by one-half, in value, of the creditors of the partnership.

(3) On an application under subsection (1), the court shall direct that a
public examination of the person to whom the application relates shall be
held on a day appointed by the court; and that person shall attend on that
day and be publicly examined as to the formation or management of the
partnership or as to the conduct of its business and affairs, or his conduct
or dealings in relation to the partnership.

(4) The following may take part in the public examination of a person
under this section and may question that person concerning the matters
mentioned in subsection (3), namely—

    (a)   the official receiver;

    (b)   the liquidator of the partnership;

    (c)   any person who has been appointed as special manager of the
partnership's property or business;

(d) any creditor of the partnership who has tendered a proof in the winding up.

(5) On an application under subsection (1), the court may direct that the public examination of any person under this section in relation to the affairs of an insolvent partnership be combined with the public examination of any person under this Act in relation to the affairs of a corporate member of that partnership against which, or an individual member of the partnership against whom, an insolvency order has been made'.

12 Sections 136, 293 and 294: Functions of official receiver in relation to office of responsible insolvency practitioner

Sections 136, 293 and 294 are modified so as to read as follows:—

'136

(1) The following provisions of this section and of section 136A have effect, subject to section 140 below, where insolvency orders are made in respect of an insolvent partnership and one or more of its insolvent members by virtue of article 8 of the Insolvent Partnerships Order 1994.

(2) The official receiver, by virtue of his office, becomes the responsible insolvency practitioner of the partnership and of any insolvent member and continues in office until another person becomes responsible insolvency practitioner under the provisions of this Part.

(3) The official receiver is, by virtue of his office, the responsible insolvency practitioner of the partnership and of any insolvent member during any vacancy.

(4) At any time when he is the responsible insolvency practitioner of the insolvent partnership and of any insolvent member, the official receiver may summon a combined meeting of the creditors of the partnership and the creditors of such member, for the purpose of choosing a person to be responsible insolvency practitioner in place of the official receiver.

136A Duty of official receiver to summon meetings

(1) It is the duty of the official receiver—
  (a) as soon as practicable in the period of 12 weeks beginning with the day on which the insolvency order was made against the partnership, to decide whether to exercise his power under section 136(4) to summon a meeting, and
  (b) if in pursuance of paragraph (a) he decides not to exercise that power, to give notice of his decision, before the end of that period, to the court and to the creditors of the partnership and the creditors of any insolvent member against whom an insolvency order has been made, and
  (c) (whether or not he has decided to exercise that power) to exercise his power to summon a meeting under section 136(4) if he is at any time requested to do so in accordance with the rules by one-quarter, in value, of either—
    (i) the partnership's creditors, or
    (ii) the creditors of any insolvent member against whom an insolvency order has been made,

and accordingly, where the duty imposed by paragraph (c) arises before the official receiver has performed a duty imposed by paragraph (a) or (b), he is not required to perform the latter duty.

(2) A notice given under subsection (1)(b) to the creditors shall contain an explanation of the creditors' power under subsection (1)(c) to require the official receiver to summon a combined meeting of the creditors of the partnership and of any insolvent member.

(3) If the official receiver, in pursuance of subsection (1)(a), has decided to exercise his power under section 136(4) to summon a meeting, he shall hold that meeting in the period of 4 months beginning with the day on which the insolvency order was made against the partnership.

(4) If (whether or not he has decided to exercise that power) the official receiver is requested, in accordance with the provisions of subsection (1)(c), to exercise his power under section 136(4) to summon a meeting, he shall hold that meeting in accordance with the rules.

(5) Where a meeting of creditors of the partnership and of any insolvent member has been held under section 136(4), and an insolvency order is subsequently made against a further insolvent member by virtue of article 8 of the Insolvent Partnerships Order 1994—

    (a)   any person chosen at that meeting to be responsible insolvency practitioner in place of the official receiver shall also be the responsible insolvency practitioner of the member against whom the subsequent order is made, and

    (b)   subsection (1) of this section shall not apply'.

Notes

This provides that the Official Receiver will be the responsible insolvency practitioner in relation to the insolvencies of the partnership and the member(s).

3.55

13 Sections 137, 295, 296 and 300: Appointment of responsible insolvency practitioner by Secretary of State

Sections 137, 295, 296 and 300 are modified so as to read as follows:—

'137

(1) This section and the next apply where the court has made insolvency orders in respect of an insolvent partnership and one or more of its insolvent members by virtue of article 8 of the Insolvent Partnerships Order 1994.

(2) The official receiver may, at any time when he is the responsible insolvency practitioner of the partnership and of any insolvent member, apply to the Secretary of State for the appointment of a person as responsible insolvency practitioner of both the partnership and of such member in his place.

(3) If a meeting is held in pursuance of a decision under section 136A(1)(a), but no person is chosen to be responsible insolvency

practitioner as a result of that meeting, it is the duty of the official receiver to decide whether to refer the need for an appointment to the Secretary of State.

137A Consequences of section 137 application

(1) On an application under section 137(2), or a reference made in pursuance of a decision under section 137(3), the Secretary of State shall either make an appointment or decline to make one.

(2) If on an application under section 137(2), or a reference made in pursuance of a decision under section 137(3), no appointment is made, the official receiver shall continue to be responsible insolvency practitioner of the partnership and its insolvent member or members, but without prejudice to his power to make a further application or reference.

(3) Where a responsible insolvency practitioner has been appointed by the Secretary of State under subsection (1) of this section, and an insolvency order is subsequently made against a further insolvent member by virtue of article 8 of the Insolvent Partnerships Order 1994, then the practitioner so appointed shall also be the responsible insolvency practitioner of the member against whom the subsequent order is made.

(4) Where a responsible insolvency practitioner has been appointed by the Secretary of State under subsection (1), or has become responsible insolvency practitioner of a further insolvent member under subsection (3), that practitioner shall give notice of his appointment or further appointment (as the case may be) to the creditors of the insolvent partnership and the creditors of the insolvent member or members against whom insolvency orders have been made or, if the court so allows, shall advertise his appointment in accordance with the directions of the court.

(5) Subject to subsection (6) below, in that notice or advertisement the responsible insolvency practitioner shall—

    (a)   state whether he proposes to summon, under section 141 below, a combined meeting of the creditors of the insolvent partnership and of the insolvent member or members against whom insolvency orders have been made, for the purpose of determining whether a creditors' committee should be established under that section, and

    (b)   if he does not propose to summon such a meeting, set out the power under that section of the creditors of the partnership and of the insolvent member or members to require him to summon one.

(6) Where in a case where subsection (3) applies a meeting has already been held under section 141 below, the responsible insolvency practitioner shall state in the notice or advertisement whether a creditors' committee was established at that meeting and—

    (a)   if such a committee was established, shall state whether he proposes to appoint additional members of the committee under section 141A(3), and

    (b)   if such a committee was not established, shall set out the power under section 141 of the creditors of the partnership and of the insolvent member or members to require him to summon a

> meeting for the purpose of determining whether a creditors' committee should be established under that section'.

Notes

The Official Receiver can apply to the Secretary of State to appoint someone else in his place as the responsible insolvency practitioner for the insolvencies of the partnership and the members. There is separate provision for a change of insolvency practitioner where the one in place feels that there is a conflict between the different roles: see paragraph 26 below (s 230A).

3.56

14 Section 139: Rules applicable to meetings of creditors

Section 139 is modified so as to read as follows:—

'**139**

(1) This section applies where the court has made insolvency orders against an insolvent partnership and one or more of its insolvent members by virtue of article 8 of the Insolvent Partnerships Order 1994.

(2) Subject to subsection (4) below, the rules relating to the requisitioning, summoning, holding and conducting of meetings on the winding up of a company are to apply (with the necessary modifications) to the requisitioning, summoning, holding and conducting of—

   (a)   separate meetings of the creditors of the partnership or of any corporate member against which an insolvency order has been made, and

   (b)   combined meetings of the creditors of the partnership and the creditors of the insolvent member or members.

(3) Subject to subsection (4) below, the rules relating to the requisitioning, summoning, holding and conducting of meetings on the bankruptcy of an individual are to apply (with the necessary modifications) to the requisitioning, summoning, holding and conducting of separate meetings of the creditors of any individual member against whom an insolvency order has been made.

(4) Any combined meeting of creditors shall be conducted as if the creditors of the partnership and of the insolvent member or members were a single set of creditors'.

15 Section 140: Appointment by the court following administration or voluntary arrangement

Section 140 is modified so as to read as follows:—

'**140**

(1) This section applies where insolvency orders are made in respect of an insolvent partnership and one or more of its insolvent members by virtue of article 8 of the Insolvent Partnerships Order 1994.

(2) Where the orders referred to in subsection (1) are made immediately upon the [appointment of an administrator in respect of the partnership ceasing to have effect], the court may appoint as responsible insolvency practitioner the person [whose appointment as administrator has ceased to have effect].

(3) Where the orders referred to in subsection (1) are made at a time when there is a supervisor of a voluntary arrangement approved in relation to the partnership under Part I, the court may appoint as responsible insolvency practitioner the person who is the supervisor at the time when the winding-up order against the partnership is made.

(4) Where the court makes an appointment under this section, the official receiver does not become the responsible insolvency practitioner as otherwise provided by section 136(2), and he has no duty under section 136A(1)(a) or (b) in respect of the summoning of creditors' meetings'.

Notes

The occasions where s 140 applies will be rare: an administrator of a partnership can only petition for its winding up under Article 7.

3.57

16 Sections 141, 301 and 302: Creditors' Committee: Insolvent partnership and members

Sections 141, 301 and 302 are modified so as to read as follows:—

'141

(1) This section applies where—
  (a) insolvency orders are made in respect of an insolvent partnership and one or more of its insolvent members by virtue of article 8 of the Insolvent Partnerships Order 1994, and
  (b) a combined meeting of creditors has been summoned for the purpose of choosing a person to be responsible insolvency practitioner of the partnership and of any such insolvent member or members.

(2) The meeting of creditors may establish a committee ('the creditors' committee') which shall consist of creditors of the partnership or creditors of any insolvent member against whom an insolvency order has been made, or both.

(3) The responsible insolvency practitioner of the partnership and of its insolvent member or members (not being the official receiver) may at any time, if he thinks fit, summon a combined general meeting of the creditors of the partnership and of such member or members for the purpose of determining whether a creditors' committee should be established and, if it is so determined, of establishing it.

The responsible insolvency practitioner (not being the official receiver) shall summon such a meeting if he is requested, in accordance with the rules, to do so by one-tenth, in value, of either—

(a) the partnership's creditors, or

(b) the creditors of any insolvent member against whom an insolvency order has been made.

141A Functions and membership of creditors' committee

(1) The committee established under section 141 shall act as liquidation committee for the partnership and for any corporate member against which an insolvency order has been made, and as creditors' committee for any individual member against whom an insolvency order has been made, and shall as appropriate exercise the functions conferred on liquidation and creditors' committees in a winding up or bankruptcy by or under this Act.

(2) The rules relating to liquidation committees are to apply (with the necessary modifications and with the exclusion of all references to contributories) to a committee established under section 141.

(3) Where the appointment of the responsible insolvency practitioner also takes effect in relation to a further insolvent member under section 136A(5) or 137A(3), the practitioner may appoint any creditor of that member (being qualified under the rules to be a member of the committee) to be an additional member of any creditors' committee already established under section 141, provided that the creditor concerned consents to act.

(4) The court may at any time, on application by a creditor of the partnership or of any insolvent member against whom an insolvency order has been made, appoint additional members of the creditors' committee.

(5) If additional members of the creditors' committee are appointed under subsection (3) or (4), the limit on the maximum number of members of the committee specified in the rules shall be increased by the number of additional members so appointed.

(6) The creditors' committee is not to be able or required to carry out its functions at any time when the official receiver is responsible insolvency practitioner of the partnership and of its insolvent member or members; but at any such time its functions are vested in the Secretary of State except to the extent that the rules otherwise provide.

(7) Where there is for the time being no creditors' committee, and the responsible insolvency practitioner is a person other than the official receiver, the functions of such a committee are vested in the Secretary of State except to the extent that the rules otherwise provide.'

Notes

SS 141, 141A

These make provision for the establishment of a creditors committee. It can be made up from the creditors of either the partnership or the member(s): see s 140(2).

3.58

17 Sections 143, 168(4) and 305: General functions of responsible insolvency practitioner

Sections 143, 168(4) and 305 are modified so as to read as follows:—

'**143**

(1) The functions of the responsible insolvency practitioner of an insolvent partnership and of its insolvent member or members against whom insolvency orders have been made by virtue of article 8 of the Insolvent Partnerships Order 1994, are to secure that the partnership property and the assets of any such corporate member, and the estate of any such individual member, are got in, realised and distributed to their respective creditors and, if there is a surplus of such property or assets or in such estate, to the persons entitled to it.

(2) In the carrying out of those functions, and in the management of the partnership property and of the assets of any corporate member and of the estate of any individual member, the responsible insolvency practitioner is entitled, subject to the provisions of this Act, to use his own discretion.

(3) It is the duty of the responsible insolvency practitioner, if he is not the official receiver—

    (a)   to furnish the official receiver with such information,

    (b)   to produce to the official receiver, and permit inspection by the official receiver of, such books, papers and other records, and

    (c)   to give the official receiver such other assistance,

as the official receiver may reasonably require for the purposes of carrying out his functions in relation to the winding up of the partnership and any corporate member or the bankruptcy of any individual member.

(4) The official name of the responsible insolvency practitioner in his capacity as trustee of an individual member shall be 'the trustee of the estate of ... ..., a bankrupt' (inserting the name of the individual member); but he may be referred to as 'the trustee in bankruptcy' of the particular member'.

18 Sections 146 and 331: Duty to summon final meeting of creditors

Sections 146 and 331 are modified so as to read as follows:—

'**146**

(1) This section applies, subject to subsection (3) of this section and section 332 below, if it appears to the responsible insolvency practitioner of an insolvent partnership which is being wound up by virtue of article 8 of the Insolvent Partnerships Order 1994 and of its insolvent member or members that the winding up of the partnership or of any corporate member, or the administration of any individual member's estate, is for practical purposes complete and the practitioner is not the official receiver.

(2) The responsible insolvency practitioner shall summon a final general meeting of the creditors of the partnership or of the insolvent member or

members (as the case may be) or a combined final general meeting of the creditors of the partnership and of the insolvent member or members which—

(a) shall as appropriate receive the practitioner's report of the winding up of the insolvent partnership or of any corporate member or of the administration of the estate of any individual member, and

(b) shall determine whether the practitioner should have his release under section 174 in Chapter VII of this Part in respect of the winding up of the partnership or of the corporate member, or the administration of the individual member's estate (as the case may be).

(3) The responsible insolvency practitioner may, if he thinks fit, give the notice summoning the final general meeting at the same time as giving notice of any final distribution of the partnership property or the property of the insolvent member or members; but, if summoned for an earlier date, that meeting shall be adjourned (and, if necessary, further adjourned) until a date on which the practitioner is able to report to the meeting that the winding up of the partnership or of any corporate member, or the administration of any individual member's estate, is for practical purposes complete.

(4) In the carrying out of his functions in the winding up of the partnership and of any corporate member and the administration of any individual member's estate, it is the duty of the responsible insolvency practitioner to retain sufficient sums from the partnership property and the property of any such insolvent member to cover the expenses of summoning and holding any meeting required by this section'.

19 Section 147: Power of court to stay proceedings

Section 147 is modified, so far as insolvent partnerships are concerned, so as to read as follows:—

'**147**

(1) The court may, at any time after an order has been made by virtue of article 8 of the Insolvent Partnerships Order 1994 for winding up an insolvent partnership, on the application either of the responsible insolvency practitioner or the official receiver or any creditor or contributory, and on proof to the satisfaction of the court that all proceedings in the winding up of the partnership ought to be stayed, make an order staying the proceedings, either altogether or for a limited time, on such terms and conditions as the court thinks fit.

(2) If, in the course of hearing an insolvency petition presented against a member of an insolvent partnership, the court is satisfied that an application has been or will be made under subsection (1) in respect of a winding-up order made against the partnership, the court may adjourn the petition against the insolvent member, either conditionally or unconditionally.

(3) Where the court makes an order under subsection (1) staying all proceedings on the order for winding up an insolvent partnership—

> (a) the court may, on hearing any insolvency petition presented against an insolvent member of the partnership, dismiss that petition; and
>
> (b) if any insolvency order has already been made by virtue of article 8 of the Insolvent Partnerships Order 1994 in relation to an insolvent member of the partnership, the court may make an order annulling or rescinding that insolvency order, or may make any other order that it thinks fit.
>
> (4) The court may, before making any order under this section, require the official receiver to furnish to it a report with respect to any facts or matters which are in his opinion relevant to the application'.

Notes

This modifies the power to stay winding up proceedings that the court derives from s 147 IA 1986 in order to apply it to partnerships. The basic purpose of the provision is to allow a firm to continue to trade where it appears that it will be able to discharge all of its debts. See the notes to s 147 IA 1986 for a discussion of the principles applicable to this power.

3.59

20 Sections 168, 303 and 314(7): Supplementary powers of responsible insolvency practitioner

Sections 168(1) to (3) and (5), 303 and 314(7) are modified so as to read as follows:—

'**168**

(1) This section applies where the court has made insolvency orders in respect of an insolvent partnership and one or more of its insolvent members by virtue of article 8 of the Insolvent Partnerships Order 1994.

(2) The responsible insolvency practitioner of the partnership and of such member or members may at any time summon either separate or combined general meetings of—

> (a) the creditors or contributories of the partnership, and
> (b) the creditors or contributories of the member or members,

for the purpose of ascertaining their wishes.

(3) It is the duty of the responsible insolvency practitioner—

> (a) to summon separate meetings at such times as the creditors of the partnership or of the member (as the case may be), or the contributories of any corporate member, by resolution (either at the meeting appointing the responsible insolvency practitioner or otherwise) may direct, or whenever requested in writing to do so by one-tenth in value of such creditors or contributories (as the case may be); and
>
> (b) to summon combined meetings at such times as the creditors of the partnership and of the member or members by resolution (either at the meeting appointing the responsible insolvency practitioner or otherwise) may direct, or whenever requested in writing to do so by one-tenth in value of such creditors.

(4) The responsible insolvency practitioner may apply to the court (in the prescribed manner) for directions in relation to any particular matter arising in the winding up of the insolvent partnership or in the winding up or bankruptcy of an insolvent member.

(5) If any person is aggrieved by an act or decision of the responsible insolvency practitioner, that person may apply to the court; and the court may confirm, reverse or modify the act or decision complained of, and make such order in the case as it thinks just'.

3.60

21 Sections 172 and 298: Removal etc of responsible insolvency practitioner or of provisional liquidator

Sections 172 and 298 are modified so as to read as follows:—

'**172**

(1) This section applies with respect to the removal from office and vacation of office of—
  (a) the responsible insolvency practitioner of an insolvent partnership which is being wound up by virtue of article 8 of the Insolvent Partnerships Order 1994 and of its insolvent member or members against whom insolvency orders have been made, or
  (b) a provisional liquidator of an insolvent partnership, and of any corporate member of that partnership, against which a winding-up petition is presented by virtue of that article,
and, subject to subsections (6) and (7) below, any removal from or vacation of office under this section relates to all offices held in the proceedings relating to the partnership.

(2) Subject as follows, the responsible insolvency practitioner or provisional liquidator may be removed from office only by an order of the court.

(3) If appointed by the Secretary of State, the responsible insolvency practitioner may be removed from office by a direction of the Secretary of State.

(4) A responsible insolvency practitioner or provisional liquidator, not being the official receiver, shall vacate office if he ceases to be a person who is qualified to act as an insolvency practitioner in relation to the insolvent partnership or any insolvent member of it against whom an insolvency order has been made.

(5) The responsible insolvency practitioner may, with the leave of the court (or, if appointed by the Secretary of State, with the leave of the court or the Secretary of State), resign his office by giving notice of his resignation to the court.

(6) Where a final meeting has been held under section 146 (final meeting of creditors of insolvent partnership or of insolvent members), the responsible insolvency practitioner whose report was considered at the meeting shall vacate office as liquidator of the insolvent partnership or of any corporate member or as trustee of the estate of any individual member (as the case may be) as soon as he has given notice to the court

(and, in the case of a corporate member, to the registrar of companies) that the meeting has been held and of the decisions (if any) of the meeting.

(7) The responsible insolvency practitioner shall vacate office as trustee of the estate of an individual member if the insolvency order against that member is annulled'.

3.61

22 Sections 174 and 299: Release of responsible insolvency practitioner or of provisional liquidator

Sections 174 and 299 are modified so as to read as follows:—

'**174**

(1) This section applies with respect to the release of—
    (a)   the responsible insolvency practitioner of an insolvent partnership which is being wound up by virtue of article 8 of the Insolvent Partnerships Order 1994 and of its insolvent member or members against whom insolvency orders have been made, or
    (b)   a provisional liquidator of an insolvent partnership, and of any corporate member of that partnership, against which a winding-up petition is presented by virtue of that article.

(2) Where the official receiver has ceased to be the responsible insolvency practitioner and a person is appointed in his stead, the official receiver has his release with effect from the following time, that is to say—
    (a)   in a case where that person was nominated by a combined general meeting of creditors of the partnership and of any insolvent member or members, or was appointed by the Secretary of State, the time at which the official receiver gives notice to the court that he has been replaced;
    (b)   in a case where that person is appointed by the court, such time as the court may determine.

(3) If the official receiver while he is a responsible insolvency practitioner gives notice to the Secretary of State that the winding up of the partnership or of any corporate member or the administration of the estate of any individual member is for practical purposes complete, he has his release as liquidator or trustee (as the case may be) with effect from such time as the Secretary of State may determine.

(4) A person other than the official receiver who has ceased to be a responsible insolvency practitioner has his release with effect from the following time, that is to say—
    (a)   in the case of a person who has died, the time at which notice is given to the court in accordance with the rules that that person has ceased to hold office;
    (b)   in the case of a person who has been removed from office by the court or by the Secretary of State, or who has vacated office under section 172(4), such time as the Secretary of State may, on an application by that person, determine;
    (c)   in the case of a person who has resigned, such time as may be directed by the court (or, if he was appointed by the Secretary of

State, such time as may be directed by the court or as the Secretary of State may, on an application by that person, determine);

(d) in the case of a person who has vacated office under section 172(6)—

(i) if the final meeting referred to in that subsection has resolved against that person's release, such time as the Secretary of State may, on an application by that person, determine, and

(ii) if that meeting has not so resolved, the time at which that person vacated office.

(5) A person who has ceased to hold office as a provisional liquidator has his release with effect from such time as the court may, on an application by him, determine.

(6) Where a bankruptcy order in respect of an individual member is annulled, the responsible insolvency practitioner at the time of the annulment has his release with effect from such time as the court may determine.

(7) Where the responsible insolvency practitioner or provisional liquidator (including in both cases the official receiver when so acting) has his release under this section, he is, with effect from the time specified in the preceding provisions of this section, discharged from all liability both in respect of acts or omissions of his in the winding up of the insolvent partnership or any corporate member or the administration of the estate of any individual member (as the case may be) and otherwise in relation to his conduct as responsible insolvency practitioner or provisional liquidator.

But nothing in this section prevents the exercise, in relation to a person who has had his release under this section, of the court's powers under section 212 (summary remedy against delinquent directors, liquidators, etc) or section 304 (liability of trustee)'.

3.62

23 Sections 175 and 328: Priority of expenses and debts

Sections 175 and 328(1) to (3) and (6) are modified so as to read as follows:-

175 'Priority of expenses

(1) The provisions of this section shall apply in a case where article 8 of the Insolvent Partnerships Order 1994 applies, as regards priority of expenses incurred by a responsible insolvency practitioner of an insolvent partnership, and of any insolvent member of that partnership against whom an insolvency order has been made.

(2) The joint estate of the partnership shall be applicable in the first instance in payment of the joint expenses and the separate estate of each insolvent member shall be applicable in the first instance in payment of the separate expenses relating to that member.

(3) Where the joint estate is insufficient for the payment in full of the joint expenses, the unpaid balance shall be apportioned equally between

the separate estates of the insolvent members against whom insolvency orders have been made and shall form part of the expenses to be paid out of those estates.

(4) Where any separate estate of an insolvent member is insufficient for the payment in full of the separate expenses to be paid out of that estate, the unpaid balance shall form part of the expenses to be paid out of the joint estate.

(5) Where after the transfer of any unpaid balance in accordance with subsection (3) or (4) any estate is insufficient for the payment in full of the expenses to be paid out of that estate, the balance then remaining unpaid shall be apportioned equally between the other estates.

(6) Where after an apportionment under subsection (5) one or more estates are insufficient for the payment in full of the expenses to be paid out of those estates, the total of the unpaid balances of the expenses to be paid out of those estates shall continue to be apportioned equally between the other estates until provision is made for the payment in full of the expenses or there is no estate available for the payment of the balance finally remaining unpaid, in which case it abates in equal proportions between all the estates.

(7) Without prejudice to subsections (3) to (6) above, the responsible insolvency practitioner may, with the sanction of any creditors' committee established under section 141 or with the leave of the court obtained on application—

(a) pay out of the joint estate as part of the expenses to be paid out of that estate any expenses incurred for any separate estate of an insolvent member; or

(b) pay out of any separate estate of an insolvent member any part of the expenses incurred for the joint estate which affects that separate estate.

Notes

This important provision deals with how the expenses of the different insolvencies resulting from an Article 8 petition should be paid. The section is self-explanatory. As for priority between the various different costs which may be incurred in any insolvency, the usual rules apply by virtue of Article 18, that is, IR 1986 r 4.128 (partnership and corporate member) and r 6.224 (individual member).

3.63

175A Priority of debts in joint estate

(1) The provisions of this section and the next (which are subject to the provisions of section 9 of the Partnership Act 1890 as respects the liability of the estate of a deceased member) shall apply as regards priority of debts in a case where article 8 of the Insolvent Partnerships Order 1994 applies.

(2) After payment of expenses in accordance with section 175 and subject to section 175C(2), the joint debts of the partnership shall be paid out of its joint estate in the following order of priority—

(a) the preferential debts;
(b) the debts which are neither preferential debts nor postponed debts;
(c) interest under section 189 on the joint debts (other than postponed debts);
(d) the postponed debts;
(e) interest under section 189 on the postponed debts.

(3) The responsible insolvency practitioner shall adjust the rights among themselves of the members of the partnership as contributories and shall distribute any surplus to the members or, where applicable, to the separate estates of the members, according to their respective rights and interests in it.

(4) The debts referred to in each of paragraphs (a) and (b) of subsection (2) rank equally between themselves, and in each case if the joint estate is insufficient for meeting them, they abate in equal proportions between themselves.

(5) Where the joint estate is not sufficient for the payment of the joint debts in accordance with paragraphs (a) and (b) of subsection (2), the responsible insolvency practitioner shall aggregate the value of those debts to the extent that they have not been satisfied or are not capable of being satisfied, and that aggregate amount shall be a claim against the separate estate of each member of the partnership against whom an insolvency order has been made which—
(a) shall be a debt provable by the responsible insolvency practitioner in each such estate, and
(b) shall rank equally with the debts of the member referred to in section 175B(1)(b) below.

(6) Where the joint estate is sufficient for the payment of the joint debts in accordance with paragraphs (a) and (b) of subsection (2) but not for the payment of interest under paragraph (c) of that subsection, the responsible insolvency practitioner shall aggregate the value of that interest to the extent that it has not been satisfied or is not capable of being satisfied, and that aggregate amount shall be a claim against the separate estate of each member of the partnership against whom an insolvency order has been made which—
(a) shall be a debt provable by the responsible insolvency practitioner in each such estate, and
(b) shall rank equally with the interest on the separate debts referred to in section 175B(1)(c) below.

(7) Where the joint estate is not sufficient for the payment of the postponed joint debts in accordance with paragraph (d) of subsection (2), the responsible insolvency practitioner shall aggregate the value of those debts to the extent that they have not been satisfied or are not capable of being satisfied, and that aggregate amount shall be a claim against the separate estate of each member of the partnership against whom an insolvency order has been made which—
(a) shall be a debt provable by the responsible insolvency practitioner in each such estate, and
(b) shall rank equally with the postponed debts of the member referred to in section 175B(1)(d) below.

(8) Where the joint estate is sufficient for the payment of the postponed joint debts in accordance with paragraph (d) of subsection (2) but not for the payment of interest under paragraph (e) of that subsection, the responsible insolvency practitioner shall aggregate the value of that interest to the extent that it has not been satisfied or is not capable of being satisfied, and that aggregate amount shall be a claim against the separate estate of each member of the partnership against whom an insolvency order has been made which—

(a) shall be a debt provable by the responsible insolvency practitioner in each such estate, and

(b) shall rank equally with the interest on the postponed debts referred to in section 175B(1)(e) below.

(9) Where the responsible insolvency practitioner receives any distribution from the separate estate of a member in respect of a debt referred to in paragraph (a) of subsection (5), (6), (7) or (8) above, that distribution shall become part of the joint estate and shall be distributed in accordance with the order of priority set out in subsection (2) above.

3.64

175B Priority of debts in separate estate

(1) The separate estate of each member of the partnership against whom an insolvency order has been made shall be applicable, after payment of expenses in accordance with section 175 and subject to section 175C(2) below, in payment of the separate debts of that member in the following order of priority—

(a) the preferential debts;

(b) the debts which are neither preferential debts nor postponed debts (including any debt referred to in section 175A(5)(a));

(c) interest under section 189 on the separate debts and under section 175A(6);

(d) the postponed debts of the member (including any debt referred to in section 175A(7)(a));

(e) interest under section 189 on the postponed debts of the member and under section 175A(8).

(2) The debts referred to in each of paragraphs (a) and (b) of subsection (1) rank equally between themselves, and in each case if the separate estate is insufficient for meeting them, they abate in equal proportions between themselves.

(3) Where the responsible insolvency practitioner receives any distribution from the joint estate or from the separate estate of another member of the partnership against whom an insolvency order has been made, that distribution shall become part of the separate estate and shall be distributed in accordance with the order of priority set out in subsection (1) of this section.

Notes

SS 175A, 175B

These provisions deal with the order of payment of debts in the joint estate and the separate estates. Importantly, they deal with how debts in the one rank in the other.

Both sections are expressly made subject to s 9 of the Partnership Act 1890. In essence, this provides that each member will be liable jointly for the debts of the firm but that, where one of the members has died, his estate will remain jointly liable for the firm's debts but subject to the prior payment of the separate creditors of his estate. Therefore, the principle that the claims of joint creditors which cannot be met out of the joint estate rank equally with separate creditors in the insolvency of the separate estate does not apply.

Note the special treatment given to postponed debts. Postponed debts are those referred to in s 3 Partnership Act 1890 and include debts like loans in consideration of a share of the partnership's profits. Section 3 of PA 1890 provides that postponed debts shall not be recoverable in the event of insolvency until all of the other claims have been satisfied. This then explains their treatment in s 175A and 175B above, the effect of which is to ensure that postponed debts can only compete for payment with other postponed debts: see s 175A(2), (7) and (8) and s 175B(1). However, where a postponed creditor holds security for his debt, he will not be prevented from enforcing his security ahead of the rights of other, unsecured creditors: see *Re Vince ex p Baxter* [1892] 2 QB 478. Nor will a postponed creditor be prevented from setting off his debt against a partnership debt under the insolvency set-off provisions: see *Re Lonergan* (1877) 4 Ch D 789.

Note that under s 175A(3), where there is a surplus, the responsible insolvency practitioner should distribute the surplus of joint assets over joint liabilities to the members (as contributories) or the separate estates as the case may be. The distribution will be subject to the rights of the members inter se under the partnership agreement. A partner's lien will bind the insolvency practitioner and so take priority over the separate creditors of the other members' estates: see *Re Butterworth* (1835) 4 Deac & Ch 160.

3.65

175C Provisions generally applicable in distribution of joint and separate estates

(1) Distinct accounts shall be kept of the joint estate of the partnership and of the separate estate of each member of that partnership against whom an insolvency order is made.

(2) No member of the partnership shall prove for a joint or separate debt in competition with the joint creditors, unless the debt has arisen—
    (a)   as a result of fraud, or
    (b)   in the ordinary course of a business carried on separately from the partnership business.

(3) For the purpose of establishing the value of any debt referred to in section 175A(5)(a) or (7)(a), that value may be estimated by the responsible insolvency practitioner in accordance with section 322 or (as the case may be) in accordance with the rules.

(4) Interest under section 189 on preferential debts ranks equally with interest on debts which are neither preferential debts nor postponed debts.

(5) Sections 175A and 175B are without prejudice to any provision of this Act or of any other enactment concerning the ranking between themselves of postponed debts and interest thereon, but in the absence of any such provision postponed debts and interest thereon rank equally between themselves.

(6) If any two or more members of an insolvent partnership constitute a separate partnership, the creditors of such separate partnership shall be

deemed to be a separate set of creditors and subject to the same statutory provisions as the separate creditors of any member of the insolvent partnership.

(7) Where any surplus remains after the administration of the estate of a separate partnership, the surplus shall be distributed to the members or, where applicable, to the separate estates of the members of that partnership according to their respective rights and interests in it.

(8) Neither the official receiver, the Secretary of State nor a responsible insolvency practitioner shall be entitled to remuneration or fees under the Insolvency Rules 1986, the Insolvency Regulations 1986 or the Insolvency Fees Order 1986 for his services in connection with—

    (a)   the transfer of a surplus from the joint estate to a separate estate under section 175A(3),

    (b)   a distribution from a separate estate to the joint estate in respect of a claim referred to in section 175A(5), (6), (7) or (8), or

    (c)   a distribution from the estate of a separate partnership to the separate estates of the members of that partnership under subsection (7) above'.

Notes

S 175C(2)

A member of an insolvent partnership cannot prove in the winding up of the partnership in competition with its joint creditors. The reason for this long established rule is that the joint creditors are also his own creditors. There are two exceptions: where there has been fraud and where the member is not proving for a debt incurred as member but as a party trading with the partnership.

S 175C(3)

This provides the responsible insolvency practitioner with a useful means of ensuring that the administration of the separate estates is not delayed unduly if the administration of the joint estate is long and complex (as it often is).

S 175C(6)

Note the provisions of Article 12 above.

3.66

24 Sections 189 and 328: Interest on debts

Sections 189 and 328(4) and (5) are modified so as to read as follows:—

'189

(1) In the winding up of an insolvent partnership or the winding up or bankruptcy (as the case may be) of any of its insolvent members interest is payable in accordance with this section, in the order of priority laid down by sections 175A and 175B, on any debt proved in the winding up or bankruptcy, including so much of any such debt as represents interest on the remainder.

(2) Interest under this section is payable on the debts in question in respect of the periods during which they have been outstanding since the winding-up order was made against the partnership or any corporate member (as the case may be) or the bankruptcy order was made against any individual member.

(3) The rate of interest payable under this section in respect of any debt ('the official rate' for the purposes of any provision of this Act in which that expression is used) is whichever is the greater of—

    (a)   the rate specified in section 17 of the Judgments Act 1838 on the day on which the winding-up or bankruptcy order (as the case may be) was made, and

    (b)   the rate applicable to that debt apart from the winding up or bankruptcy'.

3.67

25 Sections 211 and 356: False representations to creditors

Sections 211 and 356(2)(d) are modified so as to read as follows:—

'**211**

(1) This section applies where insolvency orders are made against an insolvent partnership and any insolvent member or members of it by virtue of article 8 of the Insolvent Partnerships Order 1994.

(2) Any person, being a past or present officer of the partnership or a past or present officer (which for these purposes includes a shadow director) of a corporate member against which an insolvency order has been made—

    (a)   commits an offence if he makes any false representation or commits any other fraud for the purpose of obtaining the consent of the creditors of the partnership (or any of them) or of the creditors of any of its members (or any of such creditors) to an agreement with reference to the affairs of the partnership or of any of its members or to the winding up of the partnership or of a corporate member, or the bankruptcy of an individual member, and

    (b)   is deemed to have committed that offence if, prior to the winding up or bankruptcy (as the case may be), he has made any false representation, or committed any other fraud, for that purpose.

(3) A person guilty of an offence under this section is liable to imprisonment or a fine, or both'.

3.68

26 Sections 230, 231 and 292: Appointment to office of responsible insolvency practitioner or provisional liquidator

Sections 230, 231 and 292 are modified so as to read as follows:—

'**230**

(1) This section applies with respect to the appointment of—

    (a)   the responsible insolvency practitioner of an insolvent partnership which is being wound up by virtue of article 8 of the Insolvent Partnerships Order 1994 and of one or more of its insolvent members, or

    (b)   a provisional liquidator of an insolvent partnership, or of any of its corporate members, against which a winding-up petition is presented by virtue of that article,

but is without prejudice to any enactment under which the official receiver is to be, or may be, responsible insolvency practitioner or provisional liquidator.

(2) No person may be appointed as responsible insolvency practitioner unless he is, at the time of the appointment, qualified to act as an insolvency practitioner both in relation to the insolvent partnership and to the insolvent member or members.

(3) No person may be appointed as provisional liquidator unless he is, at the time of the appointment, qualified to act as an insolvency practitioner both in relation to the insolvent partnership and to any corporate member in respect of which he is appointed.

(4) If the appointment or nomination of any person to the office of responsible insolvency practitioner or provisional liquidator relates to more than one person, or has the effect that the office is to be held by more than one person, then subsection (5) below applies.

(5) The appointment or nomination shall declare whether any act required or authorised under any enactment to be done by the responsible insolvency practitioner or by the provisional liquidator is to be done by all or any one or more of the persons for the time being holding the office in question.

(6) The appointment of any person as responsible insolvency practitioner takes effect only if that person accepts the appointment in accordance with the rules. Subject to this, the appointment of any person as responsible insolvency practitioner takes effect at the time specified in his certificate of appointment.

3.69

230A Conflicts of interest

(1) If the responsible insolvency practitioner of an insolvent partnership being wound up by virtue of article 8 of the Insolvent Partnerships Order 1994 and of one or more of its insolvent members is of the opinion at any time that there is a conflict of interest between his functions as liquidator of the partnership and his functions as responsible insolvency practitioner of any insolvent member, or between his functions as responsible insolvency practitioner of two or more insolvent members, he may apply to the court for directions.

(2) On an application under subsection (1), the court may, without prejudice to the generality of its power to give directions, appoint one or more insolvency practitioners either in place of the applicant to act as

responsible insolvency practitioner of both the partnership and its insolvent member or members or to act as joint responsible insolvency practitioner with the applicant'.

Notes

This is an important provision: it allows the insolvency practitioner responsible in the various insolvencies to apply for directions in cases where he perceives that there may be a conflict of interest between the different roles. The court may appoint other insolvency practitioners in appropriate cases.

3.70

27 Section 234: Getting in the partnership property

Section 234 is modified, so far as insolvent partnerships are concerned, so as to read as follows:—

'234

(1) This section applies where—
   (a) insolvency orders are made by virtue of article 8 of the Insolvent Partnerships Order 1994 in respect of an insolvent partnership and its insolvent member or members, or
   (b) a provisional liquidator of an insolvent partnership and any of its corporate members is appointed by virtue of that article;
and 'the office-holder' means the liquidator or the provisional liquidator, as the case may be.

(2) Any person who is or has been an officer of the partnership, or who is an executor or administrator of the estate of a deceased officer of the partnership, shall deliver up to the office-holder, for the purposes of the exercise of the office-holder's functions under this Act and (where applicable) the Company Directors Disqualification Act 1986, possession of any partnership property which he holds for the purposes of the partnership.

(3) Where any person has in his possession or control any property, books, papers or records to which the partnership appears to be entitled, the court may require that person forthwith (or within such period as the court may direct) to pay, deliver, convey, surrender or transfer the property, books, papers or records to the office-holder or as the court may direct.

(4) Where the office-holder—
   (a) seizes or disposes of any property which is not partnership property, and
   (b) at the time of seizure or disposal believes, and has reasonable grounds for believing, that he is entitled (whether in pursuance of an order of the court or otherwise) to seize or dispose of that property,
the next subsection has effect.

(5) In that case the office-holder—

(a)   is not liable to any person in respect of any loss or damage resulting from the seizure or disposal except in so far as that loss or damage is caused by the office-holder's own negligence, and

(b)   has a lien on the property, or the proceeds of its sale, for such expenses as were incurred in connection with the seizure or disposal'.

3.71

28 Section 283: Definition of individual member's estate

Section 283 is modified so as to read as follows:—

'283

(1) Subject as follows, the estate of an individual member for the purposes of this Act comprises—

(a)   all property belonging to or vested in the individual member at the commencement of the bankruptcy, and

(b)   any property which by virtue of any of the provisions of this Act is comprised in that estate or is treated as falling within the preceding paragraph.

(2) Subsection (1) does not apply to—

(a)   such tools, books, vehicles and other items of equipment as are not partnership property and as are necessary to the individual member for use personally by him in his employment, business or vocation;

(b)   such clothing, bedding, furniture, household equipment and provisions as are not partnership property and as are necessary for satisfying the basic domestic needs of the individual member and his family.

This subsection is subject to section 308 in Chapter IV (certain excluded property reclaimable by trustee).

(3) Subsection (1) does not apply to—

(a)   property held by the individual member on trust for any other person, or

(b)   the right of nomination to a vacant ecclesiastical benefice.

(4) References in any provision of this Act to property, in relation to an individual member, include references to any power exercisable by him over or in respect of property except in so far as the power is exercisable over or in respect of property not for the time being comprised in the estate of the individual member and—

(a)   is so exercisable at a time after either the official receiver has had his release in respect of that estate under section 174(3) or a meeting summoned by the trustee of that estate under section 146 has been held, or

(b)   cannot be so exercised for the benefit of the individual member; and a power exercisable over or in respect of property is deemed for the purposes of any provision of this Act to vest in the person entitled to exercise it at the time of the transaction or event by virtue of which it is exercisable by that person (whether or not it becomes so exercisable at that time).

(5) For the purposes of any such provision of this Act, property comprised in an individual member's estate is so comprised subject to the rights of any person other than the individual member (whether as a secured creditor of the individual member or otherwise) in relation thereto, but disregarding any rights which have been given up in accordance with the rules.

(6) This section has effect subject to the provisions of any enactment not contained in this Act under which any property is to be excluded from a bankrupt's estate'.

3.72

28A [Section 283A: Individual member's home ceasing to form part of estate

Section 283A is modified so as to read as follows:—

'283A

(1) This section applies where property comprised in the estate of an individual member consists of an interest in a dwelling-house which at the date of the bankruptcy was the sole or principal residence of—
- (a)   the individual member;
- (b)   the individual member's spouse [or civil partner], or
- (c)   a former spouse [or former civil partner] of the individual member.

(2) At the end of the period of three years beginning with the date of the bankruptcy the interest mentioned in subsection (1) shall—
- (a)   cease to be comprised in the individual member's estate, and
- (b)   vest in the individual member (without conveyance, assignment or transfer).

(3) Subsection (2) shall not apply if during the period mentioned in that subsection—
- (a)   the trustee realises the interest mentioned in subsection (1),
- (b)   the trustee applies for an order for sale in respect of the dwelling-house,
- (c)   the trustee applies for an order for possession of the dwelling-house,
- (d)   the trustee applies for an order under section 313 in Chapter IV in respect of that interest, or
- (e)   the trustee and the individual member agree that the individual member shall incur a specified liability to his estate (with or without the addition of interest from the date of the agreement) in consideration of which the interest mentioned in subsection (1) shall cease to form part of the estate.

(4) Where an application of a kind described in subsection (3)(b) to (d) is made during the period mentioned in subsection (2) and is dismissed, unless the court orders otherwise the interest to which the application relates shall on the dismissal of the application—
- (a)   cease to be comprised in the individual member's estate, and
- (b)   vest in the individual member (without conveyance, assignment or transfer).

(5) If the individual member does not inform the trustee or the official receiver of his interest in a property before the end of the period of three months beginning with the date of the bankruptcy, the period of three years mentioned in subsection (2)—

    (a)   shall not begin with the date of the bankruptcy, but

    (b)   shall begin with the date on which the trustee or official receiver becomes aware of the individual member's interest.

(6) The court may substitute for the period of three years mentioned in subsection (2) a longer period—

    (a)   in prescribed circumstances, and

    (b)   in such other circumstances as the court thinks appropriate.

(7) The rules may make provision for this section to have effect with the substitution of a shorter period for the period of three years mentioned in subsection (2) in specified circumstances (which may be described by reference to action to be taken by a trustee in bankruptcy).

(8) The rules may also, in particular, make provision—

    (a)   requiring or enabling the trustee of an individual member's estate to give notice that this section applies or does not apply;

    (b)   about the effect of a notice under paragraph (a);

    (c)   requiring the trustee of an individual member's estate to make an application to the Chief Land Registrar.

(9) Rules under subsection (8)(b) may, in particular—

    (a)   disapply this section;

    (b)   enable a court to disapply this section;

    (c)   make provision in consequence of a disapplication of this section;

    (d)   enable a court to make provision in consequence of a disapplication of this section;

    (e)   make provision (which may include provision conferring jurisdiction on a court or tribunal) about compensation'.]

3.73

29 Section 284: Individual member: Restrictions on dispositions of property

Section 284 is modified so as to read as follows:—

'284

(1) Where an individual member is adjudged bankrupt by virtue of article 8 of the Insolvent Partnerships Order 1994, any disposition of property made by that member in the period to which this section applies is void except to the extent that it is or was made with the consent of the court, or is or was subsequently ratified by the court.

(2) Subsection (1) applies to a payment (whether in cash or otherwise) as it applies to a disposition of property and, accordingly, where any payment is void by virtue of that subsection, the person paid shall hold the sum paid for the individual member as part of his estate.

(3) This section applies to the period beginning with the day of the presentation of the petition for the bankruptcy order and ending with the vesting, under Chapter IV of this Part, of the individual member's estate in a trustee.

(4) The preceding provisions of this section do not give a remedy against any person—

  (a) in respect of any property or payment which he received before the commencement of the bankruptcy in good faith, for value and without notice that the petition had been presented, or

  (b) in respect of any interest in property which derives from an interest in respect of which there is, by virtue of this subsection, no remedy.

(5) Where after the commencement of his bankruptcy the individual member has incurred a debt to a banker or other person by reason of the making of a payment which is void under this section, that debt is deemed for the purposes of any provision of this Act to have been incurred before the commencement of the bankruptcy unless—

  (a) that banker or person had notice of the bankruptcy before the debt was incurred, or

  (b) it is not reasonably practicable for the amount of the payment to be recovered from the person to whom it was made.

(6) A disposition of property is void under this section notwithstanding that the property is not or, as the case may be, would not be comprised in the individual member's estate; but nothing in this section affects any disposition made by a person of property held by him on trust for any other person other than a disposition made by an individual member of property held by him on trust for the partnership'.

29A [Section 313A: Low value home: application for sale, possession or charge

Section 313A is modified so as to read as follows:—

'313A

(1) This section applies where—

  (a) property comprised in the individual member's estate consists of an interest in a dwelling-house which at the date of the bankruptcy was the sole or principal residence of—

    (i)   the individual member,

    (ii) the individual member's spouse [or civil partner], or

    (iii) a former spouse [or former civil partner] of the individual member, and

  (b) the trustee applies for an order for the sale of the property, for an order for possession of the property or for an order under section 313 in respect of the property.

(2) The court shall dismiss the application if the value of the interest is below the amount prescribed for the purposes of this subsection.

(3) In determining the value of an interest for the purposes of this section the court shall disregard any matter which it is required to disregard by the order which prescribes the amount for the purposes of subsection (2)'.]

30

Schedule 4 is modified so as to read as follows:—

Schedule 4
Powers of Liquidator in a Winding Up
Section 167

Part I
Powers Exercisable With Sanction

3.74

1

Power to pay any class of creditors in full.

2

Power to make any compromise or arrangement with creditors or persons claiming to be creditors, or having or alleging themselves to have any claim (present or future, certain or contingent, ascertained or sounding only in damages) against the partnership, or whereby the partnership may be rendered liable.

3

Power to compromise, on such terms as may be agreed—
(a) all debts and liabilities capable of resulting in debts, and all claims (present or future, certain or contingent, ascertained or sounding only in damages) subsisting or supposed to subsist between the partnership and a contributory or alleged contributory or other debtor or person apprehending liability to the partnership, and
(b) all questions in any way relating to or affecting the partnership property or the winding up of the partnership,
and take any security for the discharge of any such debt, liability or claim and give a complete discharge in respect of it.

[3A

Power to bring legal proceedings under section 213, 214, 238, 239 or 423.]

4

Power to bring or defend any action or other legal proceeding in the name and on behalf of any member of the partnership in his capacity as such or of the partnership.

5

Power to carry on the business of the partnership so far as may be necessary for its beneficial winding up.

Part II
Powers Exercisable Without Sanction

3.75

6

Power to sell any of the partnership property by public auction or private contract, with power to transfer the whole of it to any person or to sell the same in parcels.

7

Power to do all acts and execute, in the name and on behalf of the partnership or of any member of the partnership in his capacity as such, all deeds, receipts and other documents.

8

Power to prove, rank and claim in the bankruptcy, insolvency or sequestration of any contributory for any balance against his estate, and to receive dividends in the bankruptcy, insolvency or sequestration in respect of that balance, as a separate debt due from the bankrupt or insolvent, and rateably with the other separate creditors.

9

Power to draw, accept, make and endorse any bill of exchange or promissory note in the name and on behalf of any member of the partnership in his capacity as such or of the partnership, with the same effect with respect to the liability of the partnership or of any member of the partnership in his capacity as such as if the bill or note had been drawn, accepted, made or endorsed in the course of the partnership's business.

10

Power to raise on the security of the partnership property any money requisite.

11

Power to take out in his official name letters of administration to any deceased contributory, and to do in his official name any other act necessary for obtaining payment of any money due from a contributory or his estate which cannot conveniently be done in the name of the partnership.

In all such cases the money due is deemed, for the purpose of enabling the liquidator to take out the letters of administration or recover the money, to be due to the liquidator himself.

12

Power to appoint an agent to do any business which the liquidator is unable to do himself.

13

Power to do all such other things as may be necessary for winding up the partnership's affairs and distributing its property'.

SCHEDULE 5
Provisions of the Act which Apply with Modifications for the Purposes of Article 9 to Winding up of Insolvent Partnership on Member's Petition where no Concurrent Petition Presented Against Member

Article 9

3.76

1 Section 117: High Court and county court jurisdiction

Section 117 is modified so as to read as follows:—

'117

(1) Subject to subsections (3) and (4) below, the High Court has jurisdiction to wind up any insolvent partnership as an unregistered company by virtue of article 9 of the Insolvent Partnerships Order 1994 if the partnership has, or at any time had, a principal place of business in England and Wales.

(2) Subject to subsections (3) and (4) below, a petition for the winding up of an insolvent partnership by virtue of the said article 9 may be presented to a county court in England and Wales if the partnership has, or at any time had, a principal place of business within the insolvency district of that court.

(3) Subject to subsection (4) below, the court only has jurisdiction to wind up an insolvent partnership if the business of the partnership has been carried on in England and Wales at any time in the period of 3 years ending with the day on which the petition for winding it up is presented.

(4) If an insolvent partnership has a principal place of business situated in Scotland or in Northern Ireland, the court shall not have jurisdiction to wind up the partnership unless it had a principal place of business in England and Wales—
    (a)   in the case of a partnership with a principal place of business in Scotland, at any time in the period of 1 year, or
    (b)   in the case of a partnership with a principal place of business in Northern Ireland, at any time in the period of 3 years,
ending with the day on which the petition for winding it up is presented.

(5) The Lord Chancellor [may, with the concurrence of the Lord Chief Justice, by order] in a statutory instrument exclude a county court from having winding-up jurisdiction, and for the purposes of that jurisdiction may attach its district, or any part thereof, to any other county court, and may by statutory instrument revoke or vary any such order.

In exercising the powers of this section, the Lord Chancellor shall provide that a county court is not to have winding-up jurisdiction unless it has for the time being jurisdiction for the purposes of Parts VIII to XI of this Act (individual insolvency).

(6) Every court in England and Wales having winding-up jurisdiction has for the purposes of that jurisdiction all the powers of the High Court; and every prescribed officer of the court shall perform any duties which an officer of the High Court may discharge by order of a judge of that court or otherwise in relation to winding up.

[(7) This section is subject to Article 3 of the EC Regulation (jurisdiction under the EC Regulation).]

[(8) The Lord Chief Justice may nominate a judicial office holder (as defined in section 109(4) of the Constitutional Reform Act 2005) to exercise his functions under this section.]'

3.77

2 Section 221: Winding up of unregistered companies

Section 221 is modified so as to read as follows:—

'**221**

(1) Subject to subsections (2) and (3) below and to the provisions of this Part, any insolvent partnership which has, or at any time had, a principal place of business in England and Wales may be wound up under this Act.

(2) Subject to subsection (3) below an insolvent partnership shall not be wound up under this Act if the business of the partnership has not been carried on in England and Wales at any time in the period of 3 years ending with the day on which the winding-up petition is presented.

(3) If an insolvent partnership has a principal place of business situated in Scotland or in Northern Ireland, the court shall not have jurisdiction to wind up the partnership unless it had a principal place of business in England and Wales—
  (a)   in the case of a partnership with a principal place of business in Scotland, at any time in the period of 1 year, or
  (b)   in the case of a partnership with a principal place of business in Northern Ireland, at any time in the period of 3 years,
ending with the day on which the winding-up petition is presented.

[(3A) The preceding subsections are subject to Article 3 of the EC Regulation (jurisdiction under the EC Regulation).]

(4) No insolvent partnership shall be wound up under this Act voluntarily.

(5) To the extent that they are applicable to the winding up of a company by the court in England and Wales on a member's petition or on a petition by the company, all the provisions of this Act and the Companies Act about winding up apply to the winding up of an insolvent partnership as an unregistered company—
  (a)   with the exceptions and additions mentioned in the following subsections of this section and in section 221A, and

(b)   with the modifications specified in Part II of Schedule 3 to the Insolvent Partnerships Order 1994.

(6) Sections 73(1), 74(2)(a) to (d) and (3), 75 to 78, 83, 122, 123, 124(2) and (3), 176A, 202, 203, 205 and 250 shall not apply.

(7) The circumstances in which an insolvent partnership may be wound up as an unregistered company are as follows—

(a)   if the partnership is dissolved, or has ceased to carry on business, or is carrying on business only for the purpose of winding up its affairs;

(b)   if the partnership is unable to pay its debts;

(c)   if the court is of the opinion that it is just and equitable that the partnership should be wound up.

(8) Every petition for the winding up of an insolvent partnership under Part V of this Act shall be verified by affidavit in Form 2 in Schedule 9 to the Insolvent Partnerships Order 1994.

3.78

221A Who may present petition

(1) A petition for winding up an insolvent partnership may be presented by any member of the partnership if the partnership consists of not less than 8 members.

(2) A petition for winding up an insolvent partnership may also be presented by any member of it with the leave of the court (obtained on his application) if the court is satisfied that—

(a)   the member has served on the partnership, by leaving at a principal place of business of the partnership in England and Wales, or by delivering to an officer of the partnership, or by otherwise serving in such manner as the court may approve or direct, a written demand in Form 10 in Schedule 9 to the Insolvent Partnerships Order 1994 in respect of a joint debt or debts exceeding £750 then due from the partnership but paid by the member, other than out of partnership property;

(b)   the partnership has for 3 weeks after the service of the demand neglected to pay the sum or to secure or compound for it to the member's satisfaction; and

(c)   the member has obtained a judgment, decree or order of any court against the partnership for reimbursement to him of the amount of the joint debt or debts so paid and all reasonable steps (other than insolvency proceedings) have been taken by the member to enforce that judgment, decree or order.

(3) Subsection (2)(a) above is deemed included in the list of provisions specified in subsection (1) of section 416 of this Act for the purposes of the Secretary of State's order-making power under that section'.

Notes

This Schedule sets out the circumstances in which a member may petition for the winding of the partnership without any concurrent petitions against himself or other members. It is essentially a modification to the provisions of Schedule 3 above.

S 221A

This is the main difference in that the ground for petitioning in this section is available to the member who wants to petition. The necessary circumstances will be fairly unusual. The member will have to have paid a partnership debt out of his own assets and then demanded reimbursement from the partnership (in the appropriate form) and this demand has gone unsatisfied. The member will then have to have gone to court for an order that the partnership reimburse him.

SCHEDULE 6
Provisions of the Act which Apply with Modifications for the Purposes of Article 10 to Winding up of Insolvent Partnership on Member's Petition where Concurrent Petitions are Presented Against all the Members

Article 10

3.79

1 Sections 117 and 265: High Court and county court jurisdiction

Sections 117 and 265 are modified so as to read as follows:—

'117

(1) Subject to the provisions of this section, the High Court has jurisdiction to wind up any insolvent partnership as an unregistered company by virtue of article 10 of the Insolvent Partnerships Order 1994 if the partnership has, or at any time had, a principal place of business in England and Wales.

(2) Subject to the provisions of this section, a petition for the winding up of an insolvent partnership by virtue of the said article 10 may be presented to a county court in England and Wales if the partnership has, or at any time had, a principal place of business within the insolvency district of that court.

(3) Subject to subsection (4) below, the court only has jurisdiction to wind up an insolvent partnership if the business of the partnership has been carried on in England and Wales at any time in the period of 3 years ending with the day on which the petition for winding it up is presented.

(4) If an insolvent partnership has a principal place of business situated in Scotland or in Northern Ireland, the court shall not have jurisdiction to wind up the partnership unless it had a principal place of business in England and Wales—
  (a)   in the case of a partnership with a principal place of business in Scotland, at any time in the period of 1 year, or
  (b)   in the case of a partnership with a principal place of business in Northern Ireland, at any time in the period of 3 years,
ending with the day on which the petition for winding it up is presented.

(5) Subject to subsection (6) below, the court has jurisdiction to wind up a corporate member, or make a bankruptcy order against an individual member, of a partnership against which a petition has been presented by

virtue of article 10 of the Insolvent Partnerships Order 1994 if it has jurisdiction in respect of the partnership.

(6) Petitions by virtue of the said article 10 for the winding up of an insolvent partnership and the bankruptcy of one or more members of that partnership may not be presented to a district registry of the High Court.

(7) The Lord Chancellor [may, with the concurrence of the Lord Chief Justice, by order] in a statutory instrument exclude a county court from having winding-up jurisdiction, and for the purposes of that jurisdiction may attach its district, or any part thereof, to any other county court, and may by statutory instrument revoke or vary any such order.

In exercising the powers of this section, the Lord Chancellor shall provide that a county court is not to have winding-up jurisdiction unless it has for the time being jurisdiction for the purposes of Parts VIII to XI of this Act (individual insolvency).

(8) Every court in England and Wales having winding-up jurisdiction has for the purposes of that jurisdiction all the powers of the High Court; and every prescribed officer of the court shall perform any duties which an officer of the High Court may discharge by order of a judge of that court or otherwise in relation to winding up.

[(9) This section is subject to Article 3 of the EC Regulation (jurisdiction under the EC Regulation).]

[(10) The Lord Chief Justice may nominate a judicial office holder (as defined in section 109(4) of the Constitutional Reform Act 2005) to exercise his functions under this section.]'.

3.80

2 Sections 124, 264 and 272: Applications to wind up insolvent partnership and to wind up or bankrupt insolvent members

Sections 124, 264 and 272 are modified so as to read as follows:—

'124

(1) An application to the court by a member of an insolvent partnership by virtue of article 10 of the Insolvent Partnerships Order 1994 for the winding up of the partnership as an unregistered company and the winding up or bankruptcy (as the case may be) of all its members shall—
  (a) in the case of the partnership, be by petition in Form 11 in Schedule 9 to that Order,
  (b) in the case of a corporate member, be by petition in Form 12 in that Schedule, and
  (c) in the case of an individual member, be by petition in Form 13 in that Schedule.

(2) Subject to subsection (3) below, a petition under subsection (1)(a) may only be presented by a member of the partnership on the grounds that the partnership is unable to pay its debts and if—
  (a) petitions are at the same time presented by that member for insolvency orders against every member of the partnership (including himself or itself); and

(b)   each member is willing for an insolvency order to be made against him or it and the petition against him or it contains a statement to this effect.

(3) If the court is satisfied, on application by any member of an insolvent partnership, that presentation of petitions under subsection (1) against the partnership and every member of it would be impracticable, the court may direct that petitions be presented against the partnership and such member or members of it as are specified by the court.

(4) The petitions mentioned in subsection (1)—
(a)   shall all be presented to the same court and, except as the court otherwise permits or directs, on the same day, and
(b)   except in the case of the petition mentioned in subsection (1)(c) shall be advertised in Form 8 in the said Schedule 9.

(5) Each petition presented under this section shall contain particulars of the other petitions being presented in relation to the partnership, identifying the partnership and members concerned.

(6) The hearing of the petition against the partnership fixed by the court shall be in advance of the hearing of the petitions against the insolvent members.

(7) On the day appointed for the hearing of the petition against the partnership, the petitioner shall, before the commencement of the hearing, hand to the court Form 9 in Schedule 9 to the Insolvent Partnerships Order 1994, duly completed.

(8) Any person against whom a winding-up or bankruptcy petition has been presented in relation to the insolvent partnership is entitled to appear and to be heard on any petition for the winding up of the partnership.

(9) A petitioner under this section may at the hearing withdraw the petition if—
(a)   subject to subsection (10) below, he withdraws at the same time every other petition which he has presented under this section; and
(b)   he gives notice to the court at least 3 days before the date appointed for the hearing of the relevant petition of his intention to withdraw the petition.

(10) A petitioner need not comply with the provisions of subsection (9)(a) in the case of a petition against a member, if the court is satisfied on application made to it by the petitioner that, because of difficulties in serving the petition or for any other reason, the continuance of that petition would be likely to prejudice or delay the proceedings on the petition which he has presented against the partnership or on any petition which he has presented against any other insolvent member'.

Notes

Note the procedural requirements in this section. It is open to any member to argue that the proposed course of presenting petitions against the firm and all members is impracticable. It is hard to see when this could be invoked. It might be invoked where one of the members of the firm has disappeared thus making it impossible to effect personal service of the bankruptcy petition on him. But, in that case, the court could simply direct service by another method. Obviously, where there are no assets in the separate estate of one member, that will not, of itself, render the petition and bankruptcy against 'impracticable'.

3.81

3 Sections 125 and 271: Powers of court on hearing of petitions against insolvent partnership and members

Sections 125 and 271 are modified so as to read as follows:—

'125

(1) Subject to the provisions of section 125A, on hearing a petition under section 124 against an insolvent partnership or any of its insolvent members, the court may dismiss it, or adjourn the hearing conditionally or unconditionally or make any other order that it thinks fit; but the court shall not refuse to make a winding-up order against the partnership or a corporate member on the ground only that the partnership property or (as the case may be) the member's assets have been mortgaged to an amount equal to or in excess of that property or those assets, or that the partnership has no property or the member no assets.

(2) An order under subsection (1) in respect of an insolvent partnership may contain directions as to the future conduct of any insolvency proceedings in existence against any insolvent member in respect of whom an insolvency order has been made.

3.82

125A Hearing of petitions against members

(1) On the hearing of a petition against an insolvent member the petitioner shall draw the court's attention to the result of the hearing of the winding-up petition against the partnership and the following subsections of this section shall apply.

(2) If the court has neither made a winding-up order, nor dismissed the winding-up petition, against the partnership the court may adjourn the hearing of the petition against the member until either event has occurred.

(3) Subject to subsection (4) below, if a winding-up order has been made against the partnership, the court may make a winding-up order against the corporate member in respect of which, or (as the case may be) a bankruptcy order against the individual member in respect of whom, the insolvency petition was presented.

(4) If no insolvency order is made under subsection (3) against any member within 28 days of the making of the winding-up order against the partnership, the proceedings against the partnership shall be conducted as if the winding-up petition against the partnership had been presented by virtue of article 7 of the Insolvent Partnerships Order 1994, and the proceedings against any member shall be conducted under this Act without the modifications made by that Order (other than the modifications made to sections 168 and 303 by article 14).

(5) If the court has dismissed the winding-up petition against the partnership, the court may dismiss the winding-up petition against the corporate member or (as the case may be) the bankruptcy petition against the individual member. However, if an insolvency order is made against a member, the proceedings against that member shall be conducted under this Act without the modifications made by the Insolvent Partnerships Order 1994 (other than the modifications made to sections 168 and 303 of this Act by article 14 of that Order).

(6) The court may dismiss a petition against an insolvent member if it considers it just to do so because of a change in circumstances since the making of the winding-up order against the partnership.

(7) The court may dismiss a petition against an insolvent member who is a limited partner, if—

(a) the member lodges in court for the benefit of the creditors of the partnership sufficient money or security to the court's satisfaction to meet his liability for the debts and obligations of the partnership; or

(b) the member satisfies the court that he is no longer under any liability in respect of the debts and obligations of the partnership'.

Notes

Compare the equivalent provisions for Article 9 petitions above.

3.83

4 Section 221: Winding up of unregistered companies

Section 221 is modified so as to read as follows:—

'221

(1) Subject to subsections (2) and (3) below and to the provisions of this Part, any insolvent partnership which has, or at any time had, a principal place of business in England and Wales may be wound up under this Act.

(2) Subject to subsection (3) below, an insolvent partnership shall not be wound up under this Act if the business of the partnership has not been carried on in England and Wales at any time in the period of 3 years ending with the day on which the winding-up petition is presented.

(3) If an insolvent partnership has a principal place of business situated in Scotland or in Northern Ireland, the court shall not have jurisdiction to wind up the partnership unless it had a principal place of business in England and Wales—

(a) in the case of a partnership with a principal place of business in Scotland, at any time in the period of 1 year, or

(b) in the case of a partnership with a principal place of business in Northern Ireland, at any time in the period of 3 years,

ending with the day on which the winding-up petition is presented.

[(3A) The preceding subsections are subject to Article 3 of the EC Regulation (jurisdiction under the EC Regulation).]

(4) No insolvent partnership shall be wound up under this Act voluntarily.

(5) To the extent that they are applicable to the winding up of a company by the court in England and Wales on a member's petition, all the provisions of this Act and the Companies Act about winding up apply to the winding up of an insolvent partnership as an unregistered company—
   (a)   with the exceptions and additions mentioned in the following subsections of this section, and
   (b)   with the modifications specified in Part II of Schedule 4 to the Insolvent Partnerships Order 1994.

(6) Sections 73(1), 74(2)(a) to (d) and (3), 75 to 78, 83, 124(2) and (3), 154, 176A, 202, 203, 205 and 250 shall not apply.

(7) Unless the contrary intention appears, the members of the partnership against whom insolvency orders are made by virtue of article 10 of the Insolvent Partnerships Order 1994 shall not be treated as contributories for the purposes of this Act.

(8) The circumstances in which an insolvent partnership may be wound up as an unregistered company are that the partnership is unable to pay its debts.

(9) Every petition for the winding up of an insolvent partnership under Part V of this Act shall be verified by affidavit in Form 2 in Schedule 9 to the Insolvent Partnerships Order 1994'.

SCHEDULE 7
Provisions of the Act which Apply with Modifications for the Purposes of Article 11 Where Joint Bankruptcy Petition Presented by Individual Members without Winding up Partnership as Unregistered Company

Article 11

3.84

1

(1) The provisions of the Act specified in sub-paragraph (2) below, are set out as modified in this Schedule.

(2) The provisions referred to in sub-paragraph (1) above are sections 264 to 266, 272,... 283, 284, 290, 292 to 301, 305, 312, 328, 331 and 387.

2 Section 264: Presentation of joint bankruptcy petition

Section 264 is modified so as to read as follows:—

'264

(1) Subject to section 266(1) below, a joint bankruptcy petition may be presented to the court by virtue of article 11 of the Insolvent Partnerships

Order 1994 by all the members of an insolvent partnership in their capacity as such provided that all the members are individuals and none of them is a limited partner.

(2) A petition may not be presented under paragraph (1) by the members of an insolvent partnership [if the partnership—

   (a)   has permission under Part 4 of the Financial Services and Markets Act 2000 to accept deposits, other than such a permission only for the purpose of carrying on another regulated activity in accordance with that permission, or

   (b)   continues to have a liability in respect of a deposit which was held by it in accordance with the Banking Act 1979 or the Banking Act 1987].

[(2A) Subsection 2(a) must be read with—

   (a)   section 22 of the Financial Services and Markets Act 2000;

   (b)   any relevant order under that section; and

   (c)   Schedule 2 to that Act.]

(3) The petition—

   (a)   shall be in Form 14 in Schedule 9 to the Insolvent Partnerships Order 1994; and

   (b)   shall contain a request that the trustee shall wind up the partnership business and administer the partnership property without the partnership being wound up as an unregistered company under Part V of this Act.

(4) The petition shall either—

   (a)   be accompanied by an affidavit in Form 15 in Schedule 9 to the Insolvent Partnerships Order 1994 made by the member who signs the petition, showing that all the members are individual members (and that none of them is a limited partner) and concur in the presentation of the petition, or

   (b)   contain a statement that all the members are individual members and be signed by all the members.

(5) On presentation of a petition under this section, the court may make orders in Form 16 in Schedule 9 to the Insolvent Partnerships Order 1994 for the bankruptcy of the members and the winding up of the partnership business and administration of its property'.

3.85

3 Section 265: Conditions to be satisfied in respect of members

Section 265 is modified so as to read as follows:—

'**265**

(1) Subject to the provisions of this section, a joint bankruptcy petition by virtue of article 11 of the Insolvent Partnerships Order 1994 may be presented—

   (a)   to the High Court (other than to a district registry of that Court) if the partnership has, or at any time had, a principal place of business in England and Wales, or

   (b)   to a county court in England and Wales if the partnership has, or at any time had, a principal place of business within the insolvency district of that court.

(2) A joint bankruptcy petition shall not be presented to the court by virtue of article 11 unless the business of the partnership has been carried on in England and Wales at any time in the period of 3 years ending with the day on which the joint bankruptcy petition is presented'.

4 Section 266: Other preliminary conditions

Section 266 is modified so as to read as follows:—

'266

(1) If the court is satisfied, on application by any member of an insolvent partnership, that the presentation of the petition under section 264(1) by all the members of the partnership would be impracticable, the court may direct that the petition be presented by such member or members as are specified by the court.

(2) A joint bankruptcy petition shall not be withdrawn without the leave of the court.

(3) The court has a general power, if it appears to it appropriate to do so on the grounds that there has been a contravention of the rules or for any other reason, to dismiss a joint bankruptcy petition or to stay proceedings on such a petition; and, where it stays proceedings on a petition, it may do so on such terms and conditions as it thinks fit'.

Notes

S 266(1)

As to impracticability, see the note to s 125(3) in Schedule 6 above

3.86

5 Section 272: Grounds of joint bankruptcy petition

Section 272 is modified so as to read as follows:—

'272

(1) A joint bankruptcy petition may be presented to the court by the members of a partnership only on the grounds that the partnership is unable to pay its debts.

(2) The petition shall be accompanied by—
  (a) a statement of each member's affairs in Form 17 in Schedule 9 to the Insolvent Partnerships Order 1994, and
  (b) a statement of the affairs of the partnership in Form 18 in that Schedule, sworn by one or more members of the partnership.

(3) The statements of affairs required by subsection (2) shall contain—
  (a) particulars of the member's or (as the case may be) partnership's creditors, debts and other liabilities and of their assets, and

> (b)   such other information as is required by the relevant form'.

_____

Notes

In the case of an Article 11 petition, each member must demonstrate his insolvency by filing a statement of affairs on the standard form (as to which see Form 17 of Schedule 9).

_____

3.87

6

...

3.88

7 Section 283: Definition of member's estate

Section 283 is modified so as to read as follows:—

'283

(1) Subject as follows, a member's estate for the purposes of this Act comprises—
   (a)   all property belonging to or vested in the member at the commencement of the bankruptcy, and
   (b)   any property which by virtue of any of the provisions of this Act is comprised in that estate or is treated as falling within the preceding paragraph.

(2) Subsection (1) does not apply to—
   (a)   such tools, books, vehicles and other items of equipment as are not partnership property and as are necessary to the member for use personally by him in his employment, business or vocation;
   (b)   such clothing, bedding, furniture, household equipment and provisions as are not partnership property and as are necessary for satisfying the basic domestic needs of the member and his family.

This subsection is subject to section 308 in Chapter IV (certain excluded property reclaimable by trustee).

(3) Subsection (1) does not apply to—
   (a)   property held by the member on trust for any other person, or
   (b)   the right of nomination to a vacant ecclesiastical benefice.

(4) References in any provision of this Act to property, in relation to a member, include references to any power exercisable by him over or in respect of property except insofar as the power is exercisable over or in respect of property not for the time being comprised in the member's estate and—
   (a)   is so exercisable at a time after either the official receiver has had his release in respect of that estate under section 299(2) in Chapter III or a meeting summoned by the trustee of that estate under section 331 in Chapter IV has been held, or
   (b)   cannot be so exercised for the benefit of the member;

and a power exercisable over or in respect of property is deemed for the purposes of any provision of this Act to vest in the person entitled to exercise it at the time of the transaction or event by virtue of which it is exercisable by that person (whether or not it becomes so exercisable at that time).

(5) For the purposes of any such provision of this Act, property comprised in a member's estate is so comprised subject to the rights of any person other than the member (whether as a secured creditor of the member or otherwise) in relation thereto, but disregarding any rights which have been given up in accordance with the rules.

(6) This section has effect subject to the provisions of any enactment not contained in this Act under which any property is to be excluded from a bankrupt's estate'.

Notes

The purpose of this provision is to ensure that the category of assets ordinarily excluded from the bankruptcy does not include any property of the partnership.

3.89

7A [Section 283A: Bankrupt's home ceasing to form part of estate

Section 283A is modified so as to read as follows:—

'**283A**

(1) This section applies where property comprised in the estate of an individual member consists of an interest in a dwelling-house which at the date of the bankruptcy was the sole or principal residence of—
  (a)   the individual member;
  (b)   the individual member's spouse [or civil partner], or
  (c)   a former spouse [or former civil partner] of the individual member.

(2) At the end of the period of three years beginning with the date of the bankruptcy the interest mentioned in subsection (1) shall—
  (a)   cease to be comprised in the individual member's estate, and
  (b)   vest in the individual member (without conveyance, assignment or transfer).

(3) Subsection (2) shall not apply if during the period mentioned in that subsection—
  (a)   the trustee realises the interest mentioned in subsection (1),
  (b)   the trustee applies for an order for sale in respect of the dwelling-house,
  (c)   the trustee applies for an order for possession of the dwelling-house,
  (d)   the trustee applies for an order under section 313 in Chapter IV in respect of that interest, or
  (e)   the trustee and the individual member agree that the individual member shall incur a specified liability to his estate (with or

without the addition of interest from the date of the agreement) in consideration of which the interest mentioned in subsection (1) shall cease to form part of the estate.

(4) Where an application of a kind described in subsection (3)(b) to (d) is made during the period mentioned in subsection (2) and is dismissed, unless the court orders otherwise the interest to which the application relates shall on the dismissal of the application—

    (a)   cease to be comprised in the individual member's estate, and

    (b)   vest in the individual member (without conveyance, assignment or transfer).

(5) If the individual member does not inform the trustee or the official receiver of his interest in a property before the end of the period of three months beginning with the date of the bankruptcy, the period of three years mentioned in subsection (2)—

    (a)   shall not begin with the date of the bankruptcy, but

    (b)   shall begin with the date on which the trustee or official receiver becomes aware of the individual member's interest.

(6) The court may substitute for the period of three years mentioned in subsection (2) a longer period—

    (a)   in prescribed circumstances, and

    (b)   in such other circumstances as the court thinks appropriate.

(7) The rules may make provision for this section to have effect with the substitution of a shorter period for the period of three years mentioned in subsection (2) in specified circumstances (which may be described by reference to action to be taken by a trustee in bankruptcy).

(8) The rules may also, in particular, make provision—

    (a)   requiring or enabling the trustee of an individual member's estate to give notice that this section applies or does not apply;

    (b)   about the effect of a notice under paragraph (a);

    (c)   requiring the trustee of an individual member's estate to make an application to the Chief Land Registrar.

(9) Rules under subsection (8)(b) may, in particular—

    (a)   disapply this section;

    (b)   enable a court to disapply this section;

    (c)   make provision in consequence of a disapplication of this section;

    (d)   enable a court to make provision in consequence of a disapplication of this section;

    (e)   make provision (which may include provision conferring jurisdiction on a court or tribunal) about compensation'.]

3.90

8 Section 284: Restrictions on dispositions of property

Section 284 is modified so as to read as follows:—

'**284**

(1) Where a member is adjudged bankrupt on a joint bankruptcy petition, any disposition of property made by that member in the period to

which this section applies is void except to the extent that it is or was made with the consent of the court, or is or was subsequently ratified by the court.

(2) Subsection (1) applies to a payment (whether in cash or otherwise) as it applies to a disposition of property and, accordingly, where any payment is void by virtue of that subsection, the person paid shall hold the sum paid for the member as part of his estate.

(3) This section applies to the period beginning with the day of the presentation of the joint bankruptcy petition and ending with the vesting, under Chapter IV of this Part, of the member's estate in a trustee.

(4) The preceding provisions of this section do not give a remedy against any person—
    (a)   in respect of any property or payment which he received before the commencement of the bankruptcy in good faith, for value, and without notice that the petition had been presented, or
    (b)   in respect of any interest in property which derives from an interest in respect of which there is, by virtue of this subsection, no remedy.

(5) Where after the commencement of his bankruptcy the member has incurred a debt to a banker or other person by reason of the making of a payment which is void under this section, that debt is deemed for the purposes of any provision of this Act to have been incurred before the commencement of the bankruptcy unless—
    (a)   that banker or person had notice of the bankruptcy before the debt was incurred, or
    (b)   it is not reasonably practicable for the amount of the payment to be recovered from the person to whom it was made.

(6) A disposition of property is void under this section notwithstanding that the property is not or, as the case may be, would not be comprised in the member's estate; but nothing in this section affects any disposition made by a person of property held by him on trust for any other person other than a disposition made by a member of property held by him on trust for the partnership'.

Notes

This amends the ordinary avoidance provision in the IA 1986. The amendment makes clear that a transaction would be avoided whether or not it affects the individual or joint estate.

3,91

9 Section 290: Public examination of member

Section 290 is modified so as to read as follows:—

'**290**

(1) Where orders have been made against the members of an insolvent partnership on a joint bankruptcy petition, the official receiver may at any time before the discharge of any such member apply to the court for the public examination of that member.

(2) Unless the court otherwise orders, the official receiver shall make an application under subsection (1) if notice requiring him to do so is given to him, in accordance with the rules, by one of the creditors of the member concerned with the concurrence of not less than one-half, in value, of those creditors (including the creditor giving notice).

(3) On an application under subsection (1), the court shall direct that a public examination of the member shall be held on a day appointed by the court; and the member shall attend on that day and be publicly examined as to his affairs, dealings and property and as to those of the partnership.

(4) The following may take part in the public examination of the member and may question him concerning the matters mentioned in subsection (3), namely—
    (a)   the official receiver,
    (b)   the trustee of the member's estate, if his appointment has taken effect,
    (c)   any person who has been appointed as special manager of the member's estate or business or of the partnership property or business,
    (d)   any creditor of the member who has tendered a proof in the bankruptcy.

(5) On an application under subsection (1), the court may direct that the public examination of a member under this section be combined with the public examination of any other person.

(6) If a member without reasonable excuse fails at any time to attend his public examination under this section he is guilty of a contempt of court and liable to be punished accordingly (in addition to any other punishment to which he may be subject)'.

3.92

10 Section 292: Power to appoint trustee

Section 292 is modified so as to read as follows:—

'**292**

(1) The power to appoint a person as both trustee of the estates of the members of an insolvent partnership against whom orders are made on a joint bankruptcy petition and as trustee of the partnership is exercisable—
    (a)   by a combined general meeting of the creditors of the members and of the partnership;
    (b)   under section 295(2), 296(2) or 300(3) below in this Chapter, by the Secretary of State.

(2) No person may be appointed as trustee of the members' estates and as trustee of the partnership unless he is, at the time of the appointment, qualified to act as an insolvency practitioner both in relation to the insolvent partnership and to each of the members.

(3) Any power to appoint a person as trustee of the members' estates and of the partnership includes power to appoint two or more persons as joint trustees; but such an appointment must make provision as to the circumstances in which the trustees must act together and the circumstances in which one or more of them may act for the others.

(4) The appointment of any person as trustee of the members' estates and of the partnership takes effect only if that person accepts the appointment in accordance with the rules. Subject to this, the appointment of any person as trustee takes effect at the time specified in his certificate of appointment.

(5) This section is without prejudice to the provisions of this Chapter under which the official receiver is, in certain circumstances, to be trustee of the members' estates and of the partnership.

Notes

Note that the creditors may choose the trustee on a vote at a meeting. This means that some of those concerned in the partnership, eg former partners or salaried partners with indemnity claims, may be entitled to vote. However, in the ordinary case, this will be of little consequence

3.93

292A Conflicts of interest

(1) If the trustee of the members' estates and of the partnership is of the opinion at any time that there is a conflict of interest between his functions as trustee of the members' estates and his functions as trustee of the partnership, or between his functions as trustee of the estates of two or more members, he may apply to the court for directions.

(2) On an application under subsection (1), the court may, without prejudice to the generality of its power to give directions, appoint one or more insolvency practitioners either in place of the applicant to act both as trustee of the members' estates and as trustee of the partnership, or to act as joint trustee with the applicant'.

Notes

In cases where there is a conflict of interest between the trustee's different roles under Article 11, the court may appoint another insolvency practitioner to act in order to resolve the conflict

3.94

11 Sections 293 and 294: Summoning of meeting to appoint trustee

Sections 293 and 294 are modified so as to read as follows:—

'293

(1) Where orders are made by virtue of article 11 of the Insolvent Partnerships Order 1994, the official receiver, by virtue of his office, becomes the trustee of the estates of the members and the trustee of the partnership and continues in office until another person becomes trustee under the provisions of this Part.

(2) The official receiver is, by virtue of his office, the trustee of the estates of the members and the trustee of the partnership during any vacancy.

(3) At any time when he is trustee, the official receiver may summon a combined meeting of the creditors of the members and the creditors of the partnership, for the purpose of appointing a trustee in place of the official receiver.

(4) It is the duty of the official receiver—

    (a)   as soon as practicable in the period of 12 weeks beginning with the day on which the first order was made by virtue of article 11 of the Insolvent Partnerships Order 1994, to decide whether to exercise his power under subsection (3) to summon a meeting, and

    (b)   if in pursuance of paragraph (a) he decides not to exercise that power, to give notice of his decision, before the end of that period, to the court and to those creditors of the members and those of the partnership who are known to the official receiver or identified in a statement of affairs submitted under section 272, and

    (c)   (whether or not he has decided to exercise that power) to exercise his power to summon a meeting under subsection (3) if he is at any time requested to do so by one-quarter, in value, of either—

        (i)   the creditors of any member against whom an insolvency order has been made, or

        (ii) the partnership's creditors,

and accordingly, where the duty imposed by paragraph (c) arises before the official receiver has performed a duty imposed by paragraph (a) or (b), he is not required to perform the latter duty.

(5) A notice given under subsection (4)(b) to the creditors shall contain an explanation of the creditors' power under subsection (4)(c) to require the official receiver to summon a combined meeting of the creditors of the partnership and of the members against whom insolvency orders have been made.

(6) If the official receiver, in pursuance of subsection (4)(a), has decided to exercise his power under subsection (3) to summon a meeting, he shall hold that meeting in the period of 4 months beginning with the day on which the first order was made by virtue of article 11 of the Insolvent Partnerships Order 1994.

(7) If (whether or not he has decided to exercise that power) the official receiver is requested, in accordance with the provisions of subsection (4)(c), to exercise his power under subsection (3) to summon a meeting, he shall hold that meeting in accordance with the rules.

(8) Where a meeting of creditors of the partnership and of the members has been held, and an insolvency order is subsequently made against a further insolvent member by virtue of article 11 of the Insolvent Partnerships Order 1994—

    (a)   any person chosen at the meeting to be responsible insolvency practitioner in place of the official receiver shall also be the responsible insolvency practitioner of the member against whom the subsequent order is made, and

(b)   subsection (4) of this section shall not apply'.

3.95

12 Section 295: Failure of meeting to appoint trustee

Section 295 is modified so as to read as follows:—

'**295**

(1) If a meeting of creditors summoned under section 293 is held but no appointment of a person as trustee is made, it is the duty of the official receiver to decide whether to refer the need for an appointment to the Secretary of State.

(2) On a reference made in pursuance of that decision, the Secretary of State shall either make an appointment or decline to make one.

(3) If—
   (a)   the official receiver decides not to refer the need for an appointment to the Secretary of State, or
   (b)   on such a reference the Secretary of State declines to make an appointment,
the official receiver shall give notice of his decision or, as the case may be, of the Secretary of State's decision to the court'.

3.96

13 Section 296: Appointment of trustee by Secretary of State

Section 296 is modified so as to read as follows:—

'**296**

(1) At any time when the official receiver is the trustee of the members' estates and of the partnership by virtue of any provision of this Chapter he may apply to the Secretary of State for the appointment of a person as trustee instead of the official receiver.

(2) On an application under subsection (1) the Secretary of State shall either make an appointment or decline to make one.

(3) Such an application may be made notwithstanding that the Secretary of State has declined to make an appointment either on a previous application under subsection (1) or on a reference under section 295 or under section 300(2) below.

(4) Where a trustee has been appointed by the Secretary of State under subsection (2) of this section, and an insolvency order is subsequently made against a further insolvent member by virtue of article 11 of the Insolvent Partnerships Order 1994, then the trustee so appointed shall also be the trustee of the member against whom the subsequent order is made.

(5) Where the trustee of the members' estates and of the partnership has been appointed by the Secretary of State (whether under this section or otherwise) or has become trustee of a further insolvent member under subsection (4), the trustee shall give notice of his appointment or further appointment (as the case may be) to the creditors of the members and the

creditors of the partnership or, if the court so allows, shall advertise his appointment in accordance with the court's directions.

(6) Subject to subsection (7) below, in that notice or advertisement the trustee shall—

    (a)   state whether he proposes to summon a combined general meeting of the creditors of the members and of the creditors of the partnership for the purpose of establishing a creditors' committee under section 301, and

    (b)   if he does not propose to summon such a meeting, set out the power of the creditors under this Part to require him to summon one.

(7) Where in a case where subsection (4) applies a meeting referred to in subsection (6)(a) has already been held, the trustee shall state in the notice or advertisement whether a creditors' committee was established at that meeting and—

    (a)   if such a committee was established, shall state whether he proposes to appoint additional members of the committee under section 301A(3), and

    (b)   if such a committee was not established, shall set out the power of the creditors to require him to summon a meeting for the purpose of determining whether a creditors' committee should be established'.

3.97

14 Section 297: Rules applicable to meetings of creditors

Section 297 is modified so as to read as follows:—

'297

(1) This section applies where the court has made orders by virtue of article 11 of the Insolvent Partnerships Order 1994.

(2) Subject to subsection (3) below, the rules relating to the requisitioning, summoning, holding and conducting of meetings on the bankruptcy of an individual are to apply (with the necessary modifications) to the requisitioning, summoning, holding and conducting of separate meetings of the creditors of each member and of combined meetings of the creditors of the partnership and the creditors of the members.

(3) Any combined meeting of creditors shall be conducted as if the creditors of the members and of the partnership were a single set of creditors'.

3.98

15 Section 298: Removal of trustee; vacation of office

Section 298 is modified so as to read as follows:—

'298

(1) Subject as follows, the trustee of the estates of the members and of the partnership may be removed from office only by an order of the court.

(2) If the trustee was appointed by the Secretary of State, he may be removed by a direction of the Secretary of State.

(3) The trustee (not being the official receiver) shall vacate office if he ceases to be a person who is for the time being qualified to act as an insolvency practitioner in relation to any member or to the partnership.

(4) The trustee may, with the leave of the court (or, if appointed by the Secretary of State, with the leave of the court or the Secretary of State), resign his office by giving notice of his resignation to the court.

(5) Subject to subsections (6) and (7) below, any removal from or vacation of office under this section relates to all offices held in the proceedings by virtue of article 11 of the Insolvent Partnerships Order 1994.

(6) The trustee shall vacate office on giving notice to the court that a final meeting has been held under section 331 in Chapter IV (final meeting of creditors of insolvent partnership or of members) and of the decision (if any) of that meeting.

(7) The trustee shall vacate office as trustee of a member if the order made by virtue of article 11 of the Insolvent Partnerships Order 1994 in relation to that member is annulled'.

3.99

16 Section 299: Release of trustee

Section 299 is modified so as to read as follows:—

'**299**

(1) Where the official receiver has ceased to be the trustee of the members' estates and of the partnership and a person is appointed in his stead, the official receiver shall have his release with effect from the following time, that is to say—

   (a)   where that person is appointed by a combined general meeting of creditors of the members and of the partnership or by the Secretary of State, the time at which the official receiver gives notice to the court that he has been replaced, and

   (b)   where that person is appointed by the court, such time as the court may determine.

(2) If the official receiver while he is the trustee gives notice to the Secretary of State that the administration of the estate of any member, or the winding up of the partnership business and administration of its affairs, is for practical purposes complete, he shall have his release as trustee of any member or as trustee of the partnership (as the case may be) with effect from such time as the Secretary of State may determine.

(3) A person other than the official receiver who has ceased to be the trustee of the estate of any member or of the partnership shall have his release with effect from the following time, that is to say—

   (a)   in the case of a person who has died, the time at which notice is given to the court in accordance with the rules that that person has ceased to hold office;

   (b)   in the case of a person who has been removed from office by the court or by the Secretary of State, or who has vacated office under section 298(3), such time as the Secretary of State may, on an application by that person, determine;

(c) in the case of a person who has resigned, such time as may be directed by the court (or, if he was appointed by the Secretary of State, such time as may be directed by the court or as the Secretary of State may, on an application by that person, determine);

(d) in the case of a person who has vacated office under section 298(6)—

   (i) if the final meeting referred to in that subsection has resolved against that person's release, such time as the Secretary of State may, on an application by that person, determine; and

   (ii) if that meeting has not so resolved, the time at which the person vacated office.

(4) Where an order by virtue of article 11 of the Insolvent Partnerships Order 1994 is annulled in so far as it relates to any member, the trustee at the time of the annulment has his release in respect of that member with effect from such time as the court may determine.

(5) Where the trustee (including the official receiver when so acting) has his release under this section, he shall, with effect from the time specified in the preceding provisions of this section, be discharged from all liability both in respect of acts or omissions of his in the administration of the estates of the members and in the winding up of the partnership business and administration of its affairs and otherwise in relation to his conduct as trustee.

But nothing in this section prevents the exercise, in relation to a person who has had his release under this section, of the court's powers under section 304 (liability of trustee)'.

Notes

The position in relation to the removal and release of the trustee is different to that which applies in ordinary bankruptcy cases. The trustee may be removed only by the court and not by a meeting of the creditors; where the trustee was appointed by the Secretary of State, he or she can remove the trustee.

3.100

17 Section 300: Vacancy in office of trustee

Section 300 is modified so as to read as follows:—

'300

(1) This section applies where the appointment of any person as trustee of the members' estates and of the partnership fails to take effect or, such an appointment having taken effect, there is otherwise a vacancy in the office of trustee.

(2) The official receiver may refer the need for an appointment to the Secretary of State and shall be trustee until the vacancy is filled.

(3) On a reference to the Secretary of State under subsection (2) the Secretary of State shall either make an appointment or decline to make one.

(4) If on a reference under subsection (2) no appointment is made, the official receiver shall continue to be trustee, but without prejudice to his power to make a further reference.

(5) References in this section to a vacancy include a case where it is necessary, in relation to any property which is or may be comprised in a member's estate, to revive the trusteeship of that estate after the holding of a final meeting summoned under section 331 or the giving by the official receiver of notice under section 299(2)'.

3.101

18 Section 301: Creditors' committee

Section 301 is modified so as to read as follows:—

'**301**

(1) Subject as follows, a combined general meeting of the creditors of the members and of the partnership (whether summoned under the preceding provisions of this Chapter or otherwise) may establish a committee (known as 'the creditors' committee') to exercise the functions conferred on it by or under this Act.

(2) A combined general meeting of the creditors of the members and of the partnership shall not establish such a committee, or confer any functions on such a committee, at any time when the official receiver is the trustee, except in connection with an appointment made by that meeting of a person to be trustee instead of the official receiver.

3.102

301A Functions and membership of creditors' committee

(1) The committee established under section 301 shall act as creditors' committee for each member and as liquidation committee for the partnership, and shall as appropriate exercise the functions conferred on creditors' and liquidation committees in a bankruptcy or winding up by or under this Act.

(2) The rules relating to liquidation committees are to apply (with the necessary modifications and with the exclusion of all references to contributories) to a committee established under section 301.

(3) Where the appointment of the trustee also takes effect in relation to a further insolvent member under section 293(8) or 296(4), the trustee may appoint any creditor of that member (being qualified under the rules to be a member of the committee) to be an additional member of any creditors' committee already established under section 301, provided that the creditor concerned consents to act.

(4) The court may at any time, on application by a creditor of any member or of the partnership, appoint additional members of the creditors' committee.

(5) If additional members of the creditors' committee are appointed under subsection (3) or (4), the limit on the maximum number of members of the committee specified in the rules shall be increased by the number of additional members so appointed'.

3.103

19 Section 305: General functions and powers of trustee

Section 305 is modified so as to read as follows:—

'**305**

(1) The function of the trustee of the estates of the members and of the partnership is to get in, realise and distribute the estates of the members and the partnership property in accordance with the following provisions of this Chapter.

(2) The trustee shall have all the functions and powers in relation to the partnership and the partnership property that he has in relation to the members and their estates.

(3) In the carrying out of his functions and in the management of the members' estates and the partnership property the trustee is entitled, subject to the following provisions of this Chapter, to use his own discretion.

(4) It is the duty of the trustee, if he is not the official receiver—
    (a)   to furnish the official receiver with such information,
    (b)   to produce to the official receiver, and permit inspection by the official receiver of, such books, papers and other records, and
    (c)   to give the official receiver such other assistance,
as the official receiver may reasonably require for the purpose of enabling him to carry out his functions in relation to the bankruptcy of the members and the winding up of the partnership business and administration of its property.

(5) The official name of the trustee in his capacity as trustee of a member shall be 'the trustee of the estate of ... ..., a bankrupt' (inserting the name of the member concerned); but he may be referred to as 'the trustee in bankruptcy' of the particular member.

(6) The official name of the trustee in his capacity as trustee of the partnership shall be 'the trustee of a partnership' (inserting the name of the partnership concerned)'.

3.104

20 Section 312: Obligation to surrender control to trustee

Section 312 is modified so as to read as follows:—

'**312**

(1) This section applies where orders are made by virtue of article 11 of the Insolvent Partnerships Order 1994 and a trustee is appointed.

(2) Any person who is or has been an officer of the partnership in question, or who is an executor or administrator of the estate of a deceased officer of the partnership, shall deliver up to the trustee of the

partnership, for the purposes of the exercise of the trustee's functions under this Act, possession of any partnership property which he holds for the purposes of the partnership.

(3) Each member shall deliver up to the trustee possession of any property, books, papers or other records of which he has possession or control and of which the trustee is required to take possession.

This is without prejudice to the general duties of the members as bankrupts under section 333 in this Chapter.

(4) If any of the following is in possession of any property, books, papers or other records of which the trustee is required to take possession, namely—
  (a) the official receiver,
  (b) a person who has ceased to be trustee of a member's estate,
  (c) a person who has been the administrator of the partnership or supervisor of a voluntary arrangement approved in relation to the partnership under Part I,
  (d) a person who has been the supervisor of a voluntary arrangement approved in relation to a member under Part VIII,
the official receiver or, as the case may be, that person shall deliver up possession of the property, books, papers or records to the trustee.

(5) Any banker or agent of a member or of the partnership, or any other person who holds any property to the account of, or for, a member or the partnership shall pay or deliver to the trustee all property in his possession or under his control which forms part of the member's estate or which is partnership property and which he is not by law entitled to retain as against the member, the partnership or the trustee.

(6) If any person without reasonable excuse fails to comply with any obligation imposed by this section, he is guilty of a contempt of court and liable to be punished accordingly (in addition to any other punishment to which he may be subject)'.

3.105

20A [Section 313A: Low value home: application for sale, possession or charge

Section 313A is modified so as to read as follows:—

'313A

(1) This section applies where—
  (a) property comprised in the individual member's estate consists of an interest in a dwelling-house which at the date of the bankruptcy was the sole or principal residence of—
    (i)   the individual member,
    (ii) the individual member's spouse [or civil partner], or
    (iii) a former spouse [or former civil partner] of the individual member, and
  (b) the trustee applies for an order for the sale of the property, for an order for possession of the property or for an order under section 313 in respect of the property.

(2) The court shall dismiss the application if the value of the interest is below the amount prescribed for the purposes of this subsection.

(3) In determining the value of an interest for the purposes of this section the court shall disregard any matter which it is required to disregard by the order which prescribes the amount for the purposes of subsection (2)'.]

21 Section 328: Priority of expenses and debts

Section 328 is modified so as to read as follows:—

3.106

328 'Priority of expenses

(1) The provisions of this section shall apply in a case where article 11 of the Insolvent Partnerships Order 1994 applies, as regards priority of expenses incurred by a person acting as trustee of the estates of the members of an insolvent partnership and as trustee of that partnership.

(2) The joint estate of the partnership shall be applicable in the first instance in payment of the joint expenses and the separate estate of each insolvent member shall be applicable in the first instance in payment of the separate expenses relating to that member.

(3) Where the joint estate is insufficient for the payment in full of the joint expenses, the unpaid balance shall be apportioned equally between the separate estates of the insolvent members against whom insolvency orders have been made and shall form part of the expenses to be paid out of those estates.

(4) Where any separate estate of an insolvent member is insufficient for the payment in full of the separate expenses to be paid out of that estate, the unpaid balance shall form part of the expenses to be paid out of the joint estate.

(5) Where after the transfer of any unpaid balance in accordance with subsection (3) or (4) any estate is insufficient for the payment in full of the expenses to be paid out of that estate, the balance then remaining unpaid shall be apportioned equally between the other estates.

(6) Where after an apportionment under subsection (5) one or more estates are insufficient for the payment in full of the expenses to be paid out of those estates, the total of the unpaid balances of the expenses to be paid out of those estates shall continue to be apportioned equally between the other estates until provision is made for the payment in full of the expenses or there is no estate available for the payment of the balance finally remaining unpaid, in which case it abates in equal proportions between all the estates.

(7) Without prejudice to subsections (3) to (6) above, the trustee may, with the sanction of any creditors' committee established under section 301 or with the leave of the court obtained on application—

    (a)   pay out of the joint estate as part of the expenses to be paid out of that estate any expenses incurred for any separate estate of an insolvent member; or

    (b)   pay out of any separate estate of an insolvent member any part of the expenses incurred for the joint estate which affects that separate estate.

3.107

328A Priority of debts in joint estate

(1) The provisions of this section and the next (which are subject to the provisions of section 9 of the Partnership Act 1890 as respects the liability of the estate of a deceased member) shall apply as regards priority of debts in a case where article 11 of the Insolvent Partnerships Order 1994 applies.

(2) After payment of expenses in accordance with section 328 and subject to section 328C(2), the joint debts of the partnership shall be paid out of its joint estate in the following order of priority—
    (a)   the preferential debts;
    (b)   the debts which are neither preferential debts nor postponed debts;
    (c)   interest under section 328D on the joint debts (other than postponed debts);
    (d)   the postponed debts;
    (e)   interest under section 328D on the postponed debts.

(3) The responsible insolvency practitioner shall adjust the rights among themselves of the members of the partnership as contributories and shall distribute any surplus to the members or, where applicable, to the separate estates of the members, according to their respective rights and interests in it.

(4) The debts referred to in each of paragraphs (a) and (b) of subsection (2) rank equally between themselves, and in each case if the joint estate is insufficient for meeting them, they abate in equal proportions between themselves.

(5) Where the joint estate is not sufficient for the payment of the joint debts in accordance with paragraphs (a) and (b) of subsection (2), the responsible insolvency practitioner shall aggregate the value of those debts to the extent that they have not been satisfied or are not capable of being satisfied, and that aggregate amount shall be a claim against the separate estate of each member of the partnership against whom an insolvency order has been made which—
    (a)   shall be a debt provable by the responsible insolvency practitioner in each such estate, and
    (b)   shall rank equally with the debts of the member referred to in section 328B(1)(b) below.

(6) Where the joint estate is sufficient for the payment of the joint debts in accordance with paragraphs (a) and (b) of subsection (2) but not for the payment of interest under paragraph (c) of that subsection, the responsible insolvency practitioner shall aggregate the value of that interest to the extent that it has not been satisfied or is not capable of being satisfied, and that aggregate amount shall be a claim against the separate estate of each member of the partnership against whom an insolvency order has been made which—

(a) shall be a debt provable by the responsible insolvency practitioner in each such estate, and

(b) shall rank equally with the interest on the separate debts referred to in section 328B(1)(c) below.

(7) Where the joint estate is not sufficient for the payment of the postponed joint debts in accordance with paragraph (d) of subsection (2), the responsible insolvency practitioner shall aggregate the value of those debts to the extent that they have not been satisfied or are not capable of being satisfied, and that aggregate amount shall be a claim against the separate estate of each member of the partnership against whom an insolvency order has been made which—

(a) shall be a debt provable by the responsible insolvency practitioner in each such estate, and

(b) shall rank equally with the postponed debts of the member referred to in section 328B(1)(d) below.

(8) Where the joint estate is sufficient for the payment of the postponed joint debts in accordance with paragraph (d) of subsection (2) but not for the payment of interest under paragraph (e) of that subsection, the responsible insolvency practitioner shall aggregate the value of that interest to the extent that it has not been satisfied or is not capable of being satisfied, and that aggregate amount shall be a claim against the separate estate of each member of the partnership against whom an insolvency order has been made which—

(a) shall be a debt provable by the responsible insolvency practitioner in each such estate, and

(b) shall rank equally with the interest on the postponed debts referred to in section 328B(1)(e) below.

(9) Where the responsible insolvency practitioner receives any distribution from the separate estate of a member in respect of a debt referred to in paragraph (a) of subsection (5), (6), (7) or (8) above, that distribution shall become part of the joint estate and shall be distributed in accordance with the order of priority set out in subsection (2) above.

3.108

328B Priority of debts in separate estate

(1) The separate estate of each member of the partnership against whom an insolvency order has been made shall be applicable, after payment of expenses in accordance with section 328 and subject to section 328C(2) below, in payment of the separate debts of that member in the following order of priority—

(a) the preferential debts;

(b) the debts which are neither preferential debts nor postponed debts (including any debt referred to in section 328A(5)(a));

(c) interest under section 328D on the separate debts and under section 328A(6);

(d) the postponed debts of the member (including any debt referred to in section 328A(7)(a));

(e) interest under section 328D on the postponed debts of the member and under section 328A(8).

(2) The debts referred to in each of paragraphs (a) and (b) of subsection (1) rank equally between themselves, and in each case if the separate estate is insufficient for meeting them, they abate in equal proportions between themselves.

(3) Where the responsible insolvency practitioner receives any distribution from the joint estate or from the separate estate of another member of the partnership against whom an insolvency order has been made, that distribution shall become part of the separate estate and shall be distributed in accordance with the order of priority set out in subsection (1) of this section.

3.109

328C Provisions generally applicable in distribution of joint and separate estates

(1) Distinct accounts shall be kept of the joint estate of the partnership and of the separate estate of each member of that partnership against whom an insolvency order is made.

(2) No member of the partnership shall prove for a joint or separate debt in competition with the joint creditors, unless the debt has arisen—
   (a)   as a result of fraud, or
   (b)   in the ordinary course of a business carried on separately from the partnership business.

(3) For the purpose of establishing the value of any debt referred to in section 328A(5)(a) or (7)(a), that value may be estimated by the responsible insolvency practitioner in accordance with section 322.

(4) Interest under section 328D on preferential debts ranks equally with interest on debts which are neither preferential debts nor postponed debts.

(5) Sections 328A and 328B are without prejudice to any provision of this Act or of any other enactment concerning the ranking between themselves of postponed debts and interest thereon, but in the absence of any such provision postponed debts and interest thereon rank equally between themselves.

(6) If any two or more members of an insolvent partnership constitute a separate partnership, the creditors of such separate partnership shall be deemed to be a separate set of creditors and subject to the same statutory provisions as the separate creditors of any member of the insolvent partnership.

(7) Where any surplus remains after the administration of the estate of a separate partnership, the surplus shall be distributed to the members or, where applicable, to the separate estates of the members of that partnership according to their respective rights and interests in it.

(8) Neither the official receiver, the Secretary of State nor a responsible insolvency practitioner shall be entitled to remuneration or fees under the Insolvency Rules 1986, the Insolvency Regulations 1986 or the Insolvency Fees Order 1986 for his services in connection with—
   (a)   the transfer of a surplus from the joint estate to a separate estate under section 328A(3),

> (b)   a distribution from a separate estate to the joint estate in respect of a claim referred to in section 328A(5), (6), (7) or (8), or
>
> (c)   a distribution from the estate of a separate partnership to the separate estates of the members of that partnership under subsection (7) above.

Notes

The provisions of this Schedule in relation to the priority of expenses and debts and their apportionment as between the joint and separate estates are the same as for Article 8 petitions: see the notes to s 175 to 175C in Schedule 4 above.

3.110

328D Interest on debts

(1) In the bankruptcy of each of the members of an insolvent partnership and in the winding up of that partnership's business and administration of its property, interest is payable in accordance with this section, in the order of priority laid down by sections 328A and 328B, on any debt proved in the bankruptcy including so much of any such debt as represents interest on the remainder.

(2) Interest under this section is payable on the debts in question in respect of the periods during which they have been outstanding since the relevant order was made by virtue of article 11 of the Insolvent Partnerships Order 1994.

(3) The rate of interest payable under this section in respect of any debt ('the official rate' for the purposes of any provision of this Act in which that expression is used) is whichever is the greater of—

> (a)   the rate specified in section 17 of the Judgments Act 1838 on the day on which the relevant order was made, and
>
> (b)   the rate applicable to that debt apart from the bankruptcy or winding up'.

3.111

22 Section 331: Final meeting

Section 331 is modified so as to read as follows:—

'331

(1) Subject as follows in this section and the next, this section applies where—

> (a)   it appears to the trustee of the estates of the members and of the partnership that the administration of any member's estate or the winding up of the partnership business and administration of the partnership property is for practical purposes complete, and
>
> (b)   the trustee is not the official receiver.

(2) The trustee shall summon a final general meeting of the creditors of any such member or of the partnership (as the case may be) or a

combined final general meeting of the creditors of any such members or (as the case may be) the creditors of any such members and of the partnership which—

    (a)   shall as appropriate receive the trustee's report of the administration of the estate of the member or members or of the winding up of the partnership business and administration of the partnership property, and

    (b)   shall determine whether the trustee should have his release under section 299 in Chapter III in respect (as the case may be) of the administration of the estate of the member or members, or of the winding up of the partnership business and administration of the partnership property.

(3) The trustee may, if he thinks fit, give the notice summoning the final general meeting at the same time as giving notice under section 330(1); but, if summoned for an earlier date, that meeting shall be adjourned (and, if necessary, further adjourned) until a date on which the trustee is able to report that the administration of the estate of the member or members or the winding up of the partnership business and administration of the partnership property is for practical purposes complete.

(4) In the administration of the members' estates and the winding up of the partnership business and administration of the partnership property it is the trustee's duty to retain sufficient sums from the property of the members and of the partnership to cover the expenses of summoning and holding any meeting required by this section'.

3.112

23 Section 387: The 'relevant date'

Section 387 is modified so as to read as follows:—

'387

Where an order has been made in respect of an insolvent partnership by virtue of article 11 of the Insolvent Partnerships Order 1994, references in Schedule 6 to this Act to the relevant date (being the date which determines the existence and amount of a preferential debt) are to the date on which the said order was made'.

SCHEDULE 8
Modified Provisions of Company Directors Disqualification Act 1986 for the Purposes of Article 16

Notes

The modifications made to the CDDA 1986 by Schedule 8 are largely self-explanatory and the reader is referred to the annotation of the CDDA 1986 that appears elsewhere in this work. However, there are features that should be noted.

The first is that, in an apparent oversight, s 22 CDDA 1986, the definitions section, is not applied by Article 16. That means that the CDDA as applied to insolvent partnerships does not define 'company'. It therefore appears that, applying Article 3(2) IPO 1994, the reference to a company in s 1 CDDA 1986, which sets out the effect of a disqualification order, should be construed as a reference to an insolvent partnership. It would therefore appear that the effect of a disqualification order would be to prevent the person concerned being a partner in (the appropriate term (art 3(4) IPO 1994 of 'director' in s 1 CDDA 1986) or concerned in the management of an insolvent partnership; this would be an absurd result.

The alternative is that the reference to a company in s 1 CDDA 1986 should be construed according to the definition in s 22(2)(b) CDDA 1986, which includes any company liable to wound up under Part V of IA 1986 (ie unregistered companies). This itself creates a problem because, by virtue of the IPO 1994, an insolvent partnership may be so wound up in any event. It seems that the problem could be avoided by the fact that s 22(2)(b) CDDA 1986 includes a company that may be would up under Part V: a partnership is not a company. However, the argument could continue as the reasoning is circular.

The issue is important because, if it can be argued that a disqualification order would prohibit a connection with an insolvent partnership, it might be suggested that the disqualified partner is prohibited from being a partner or otherwise concerned in the management of a partnership during the currency of the order. An answer is suggested by a case involving the disqualification of a director. In *Re Probe Data Systems (No 3) [1991] BCLC 586*, Harman J thought that a disqualified director would not be prevented from setting up as a partner in a business.

Another feature of the parts of the CDDA 1986 applied by this Schedule that should be noted is that many of the matters in Schedule 1 CDDA 1986 are not applicable to a partnership context in a straightforward manner. There is no authority that sets out what the approach of the court should be to these matters.

Article 16

3.113

The following provisions of the Company Directors Disqualification Act 1986 are modified so as to read as follows:—

6 'Section 6: Duty of court to disqualify unfit officers of insolvent partnerships

(1) The court shall make a disqualification order against a person in any case where, on an application under this section, it is satisfied—

    (a)   that he is or has been an officer of a partnership which has at any time become insolvent (whether while he was an officer or subsequently), and

    (b)   that his conduct as an officer of that partnership (either taken alone or taken together with his conduct as an officer of any other partnership or partnerships, or as a director of any company or companies) makes him unfit to be concerned in the management of a company.

(2) For the purposes of this section and the next—

    (a)   a partnership becomes insolvent if—

        (i)   the court makes an order for it to be wound up as an unregistered company at a time when its assets are insufficient for the payment of its debts and other liabilities and the expenses of the winding up; or

        (ii)   [the partnership enters administration]; and

    (b)   a company becomes insolvent if—

        (i)   the company goes into liquidation at a time when its assets are insufficient for the payment of its debts and other liabilities and the expenses of the winding up,

      (ii) [the company enters administration], or
      (iii) an administrative receiver of the company is appointed.

(3) For the purposes of this section and the next, references to a person's conduct as an officer of any partnership or partnerships, or as a director of any company or companies, include, where the partnership or company concerned or any of the partnerships or companies concerned has become insolvent, that person's conduct in relation to any matter connected with or arising out of the insolvency of that partnership or company.

[(4) In this section and section 7(2), 'the court' means—
    (a) where the partnership in question is being or has been wound up as an unregistered company by the court, that court,
    (b) where the preceding paragraph does not apply but [an administrator has at any time been appointed] in relation to the partnership in question, any court which has jurisdiction to wind it up.

(4A) Section 117 of the Insolvency Act 1986 (High Court and county court jurisdiction), as modified and set out in Schedule 5 to the 1994 Order, shall apply for the purposes of subsection (4) as if in a case within paragraph (b) of that subsection the references to the presentation of the petition for winding up in sections 117(3) and 117(4) of the Insolvency Act 1986, as modified and set out in that Schedule, were references to the making of the administration order.

(4B) Nothing in subsection (4) invalidates any proceedings by reason of their being taken in the wrong court; and proceedings—
    (a) for or in connection with a disqualification order under this section, or
    (b) in connection with a disqualification undertaking accepted under section 7,
may be retained in the court in which the proceedings were commenced, although it may not be the court in which they ought to have been commenced.

(4C) In this section and section 7, 'director' includes a shadow director.]

(5) Under this section the minimum period of disqualification is 2 years, and the maximum period is 15 years.

3.114

7 [Section 7: Disqualification order or undertaking; and reporting provisions]

(1) If it appears to the Secretary of State that it is expedient in the public interest that a disqualification order under section 6 should be made against any person, an application for the making of such an order against that person may be made—
    (a) by the Secretary of State, or
    (b) if the Secretary of State so directs in the case of a person who is or has been an officer of a partnership which is being [or has been] wound up by the court as an unregistered company, by the official receiver.

(2) Except with the leave of the court, an application for the making under that section of a disqualification order against any person shall not

be made after the end of the period of 2 years beginning with the day on which the partnership of which that person is or has been an officer became insolvent.

[(2A) If it appears to the Secretary of State that the conditions mentioned in section 6(1) are satisfied as respects any person who has offered to give him a disqualification undertaking, he may accept the undertaking if it appears to him that it is expedient in the public interest that he should do so (instead of applying, or proceeding with an application, for a disqualification order).]

(3) If it appears to the office-holder responsible under this section, that is to say—

(a) in the case of a partnership which is being wound up by the court as an unregistered company, the official receiver, or

(b) in the case of a partnership [which is in administration], the administrator,

that the conditions mentioned in section 6(1) are satisfied as respects a person who is or has been an officer of that partnership, the office-holder shall forthwith report the matter to the Secretary of State.

(4) The Secretary of State or the official receiver may require any of the persons mentioned in subsection (5) below—

(a) to furnish him with such information with respect to any person's conduct as an officer of a partnership or as a director of a company, and

(b) to produce and permit inspection of such books, papers and other records relevant to that person's conduct as such an officer or director,

as the Secretary of State or the official receiver may reasonably require for the purpose of determining whether to exercise, or of exercising, any function of his under this section.

(5) The persons referred to in subsection (4) are—

(a) the liquidator or administrator, or former liquidator or administrator of the partnership,

(b) the liquidator, administrator or administrative receiver, or former liquidator, administrator or administrative receiver, of the company.

3.115

8 Section 8: Disqualification after investigation

[(1) If it appears to the Secretary of State from—

(a) a report made by an inspector or person appointed to conduct an investigation under a provision mentioned in subsection (1A), or

(b) information or documents obtained under a provision mentioned in subsection (1B),

that it is expedient in the public interest that a disqualification order should be made against any person who is or has been an officer of an insolvent partnership, he may apply to the court for such an order to be made against that person.

(1A) The provisions are—

(a) section 437 of the Companies Act,

   (b)   section 167, 168, 169(1)(b) or 284 of the Financial Services and Markets Act 2000, or

   (c)   regulations made as a result of section 262(2)(k) of that Act.

(1B) The provisions are—
   (a)   section 447 or 448 of the Companies Act,
   (b)   section 2 of the Criminal Justice Act 1987,
   (c)   section 52 of the Criminal Justice (Scotland) Act 1987,
   (d)   section 83 of the Companies Act 1989, or
   (e)   section 171 or 173 of the Financial Services and Markets Act 2000.]

(2) The court may make a disqualification order against a person where, on an application under this section, it is satisfied that his conduct in relation to the partnership makes him unfit to be concerned in the management of a company.

[(2A) Where it appears to the Secretary of State from such report, information or documents that, in the case of a person who has offered to give him a disqualification undertaking—
   (a)   the conduct of the person in relation to an insolvent partnership of which the person is or has been an officer makes him unfit to be concerned in the management of a company, and
   (b)   it is expedient in the public interest that he should accept the undertaking (instead of applying, or proceeding with an application, for a disqualification order),
he may accept the undertaking.]

(3) In this section 'the court' means the High Court.

(4) The maximum period of disqualification under this section is 15 years.

3.116

9 Section 9: Matters for determining unfitness of officers of partnerships

(1) This section applies where it falls to a court to determine whether a person's conduct as an officer of a partnership (either taken alone or taken together with his conduct as an officer of any other partnership or partnerships or as a director ... of any company or companies) makes him unfit to be concerned in the management of a company.

[(1A) In determining whether he may accept a disqualification undertaking from any person the Secretary of State shall, as respects the person's conduct as an officer of any partnership or a director of any company concerned, have regard in particular—
   (a)   to the matters mentioned in Part I of Schedule 1 to this Act, and
   (b)   where the partnership or the company (as the case may be) has become insolvent, to the matters mentioned in Part II of that Schedule;
and references in that Schedule to the officer and the partnership or, as the case may be, to the director and the company are to be read accordingly.]

(2) The court shall, as respects that person's conduct as an officer of that partnership or each of those partnerships or as a director of that company or each of those companies, have regard in particular—
  (a) to the matters mentioned in Part I of Schedule 1 to this Act, and
  (b) where the partnership or company (as the case may be) has become insolvent, to the matters mentioned in Part II of that Schedule;
and references in that Schedule to the officer and the partnership or, as the case may be, to the director and the company, are to be read accordingly [and in this section and that Schedule 'director' includes a shadow director].

(3) Subsections (2) and (3) of section 6 apply for the purposes of this section and Schedule 1 as they apply for the purposes of sections 6 and 7.

(4) Subject to the next subsection, any reference in Schedule 1 to an enactment contained in the Companies Act or the Insolvency Act includes, in relation to any time before the coming into force of that enactment, the corresponding enactment in force at that time.

(5) The Secretary of State may by order modify any of the provisions of Schedule 1; and such an order may contain such transitional provisions as may appear to the Secretary of State necessary or expedient.

(6) The power to make orders under this section is exercisable by statutory instrument subject to annulment in pursuance of a resolution of either House of Parliament.

3.117

13 [Section 13: Criminal penalties

If a person acts in contravention of a disqualification order or disqualification undertaking he is liable—
  (a) on conviction on indictment, to imprisonment for not more than 2 years or a fine or both; and
  (b) on summary conviction, to imprisonment for not more than 6 months or a fine not exceeding the statutory maximum, or both.

3.118

14 Section 14: Offences by body corporate

(1) Where a body corporate is guilty of an offence of acting in contravention of a disqualification order or disqualification undertaking and it is proved that the offence occurred with the consent or connivance of, or was attributable to any neglect on the part of any director, manager, secretary or other similar officer of the body corporate, or any person who was purporting to act in any such capacity he, as well as the body corporate, is guilty of the offence and liable to be proceeded against and punished accordingly.

(2) Where the affairs of a body corporate are managed by its members, subsection (1) applies in relation to the acts and defaults of a member in connection with his functions of management as if he were a director of the body corporate.

3.119

15 Section 15: Personal liability for company's debts where person acts while disqualified

(1) A person is personally responsible for all the relevant debts of a company if at any time—
  (a) in contravention of a disqualification order or disqualification undertaking he is involved in the management of the company, or
  (b) as a person who is involved in the management of the company, he acts or is willing to act on instructions given without the leave of the court by a person whom he knows at that time to be the subject of a disqualification order or disqualification undertaking or a disqualification order under Part II of the Companies (Northern Ireland) Order 1989 or to be an undischarged bankrupt.

(2) Where a person is personally responsible under this section for the relevant debts of a company, he is jointly and severally liable in respect of those debts with the company and any other person who, whether under this section or otherwise, is so liable.

(3) For the purposes of this section the relevant debts of a company are—
  (a) in relation to a person who is personally responsible under paragraph (a) of subsection (1), such debts and other liabilities of the company as are incurred at a time when that person was involved in the management of the company, and
  (b) in relation to a person who is personally responsible under paragraph (b) of that subsection, such debts and other liabilities of the company as are incurred at a time when that person was acting or was willing to act on instructions given as mentioned in that paragraph.

(4) For the purposes of this section, a person is involved in the management of a company if he is a director of the company or if he is concerned, whether directly or indirectly, or takes part, in the management of the company.

(5) For the purposes of this section a person who, as a person involved in the management of a company, has at any time acted on instructions given without the leave of the court by a person whom he knew at that time to be the subject of a disqualification order or disqualification undertaking or a disqualification order under Part II of the Companies (Northern Ireland) Order 1989 or to be an undischarged bankrupt is presumed, unless the contrary is shown, to have been willing at any time thereafter to act on any instructions given by that person.

3.120

17 Section 17: Application for leave under an order or undertaking

(1) Where a person is subject to a disqualification order made by a court having jurisdiction to wind up partnerships, any application for leave for the purposes of section 1(1)(a) shall be made to that court.

(2) Where a person is subject to a disqualification undertaking accepted at any time under section 7 or 8, any application for leave for the purposes

of section 1A(1)(a) shall be made to any court to which, if the Secretary of State had applied for a disqualification order under the section in question at that time, his application could have been made.

(3) But where a person is subject to two or more disqualification orders or undertakings (or to one or more disqualification orders and to one or more disqualification undertakings), any application for leave for the purposes of section 1(1)(a) or 1A(1)(a) shall be made to any court to which any such application relating to the latest order to be made, or undertaking to be accepted, could be made.

(4) On the hearing of an application for leave for the purposes of section 1(1)(a) or 1A(1)(a), the Secretary of State shall appear and call the attention of the court to any matters which seem to him to be relevant, and may himself give evidence or call witnesses.]

Schedule 1
Matters for Determining Unfitness of Officers of Partnerships
Section 9

Part 1
Matters Applicable in All Cases

3.121

1

Any misfeasance or breach of any fiduciary or other duty by the officer in relation to the partnership or, as the case may be, by the director in relation to the company.

2

Any misapplication or retention by the officer or the director of, or any conduct by the officer or the director giving rise to an obligation to account for, any money or other property of the partnership or, as the case may be, of the company.

3

The extent of the officer's or the director's responsibility for the partnership or, as the case may be, the company entering into any transaction liable to be set aside under Part XVI of the Insolvency Act (provisions against debt avoidance).

4

The extent of the director's responsibility for any failure by the company to comply with any of the following provisions of the Companies Act, namely—
    (a)   section 221 (companies to keep accounting records);
    (b)   section 222 (where and for how long records to be kept);
    (c)   section 288 (register of directors and secretaries);
    (d)   section 352 (obligation to keep and enter up register of members);

(e)   section 353 (location of register of members);
(f)   section 363 (duty of company to make annual returns); and
(g)   sections 399 and 415 (company's duty to register charges it creates).

5

The extent of the director's responsibility for any failure by the directors of the company to comply with—
(a)   section 226 or 227 of the Companies Act (duty to prepare annual accounts), or
(b)   section 233 of that Act (approval and signature of accounts).

6

Any failure by the officer to comply with any obligation imposed on him by or under any of the following provisions of the Limited Partnerships Act 1907—
(a)   section 8 (registration of particulars of limited partnership);
(b)   section 9 (registration of changes in particulars);
(c)   section 10 (advertisement of general partner becoming limited partner and of assignment of share of limited partner).

Part II
Matters Applicable Where Partnership or Company has Become Insolvent

3.122

7

The extent of the officer's or the director's responsibility for the causes of the partnership or (as the case may be) the company becoming insolvent.

8

The extent of the officer's or the director's responsibility for any failure by the partnership or (as the case may be) the company to supply any goods or services which have been paid for (in whole or in part).

9

The extent of the officer's or the director's responsibility for the partnership or (as the case may be) the company entering into any transaction or giving any preference, being a transaction or preference—
(a)   liable to be set aside under section 127 or sections 238 to 240 of the Insolvency Act, or
(b)   challengeable under section 242 or 243 of that Act or under any rule of law in Scotland.

10

The extent of the director's responsibility for any failure by the directors of the company to comply with section 98 of the Insolvency Act (duty to call creditors' meeting in creditors' voluntary winding up).

11

Any failure by the director to comply with any obligation imposed on him by or under any of the following provisions of the Insolvency Act—
(a) section 47 (statement of affairs to administrative receiver);
(b) section 66 (statement of affairs in Scottish receivership);
(c) section 99 (directors' duty to attend meeting; statement of affairs in creditors' voluntary winding up).

12

Any failure by the officer or the director to comply with any obligation imposed on him by or under any of the following provisions of the Insolvency Act (both as they apply in relation to companies and as they apply in relation to insolvent partnerships by virtue of the provisions of the Insolvent Partnerships Order 1994)—
(a) [paragraph 48 of Schedule B1] (statement of affairs in administration);
(b) section 131 (statement of affairs in winding up by the court);
(c) section 234 (duty of any one with property to deliver it up);
(d) section 235 (duty to co-operate with liquidator, etc)'.

SCHEDULE 9
Forms
Article 17

Arrangement of Forms

Form No	Description
1	*Petition for administration order* [Administration application].
[1A	Notice of intention to appoint an administrator by the members of the partnership
1B	Notice of an appointment of an administrator by the members of the partnership (where a notice of intention to appoint has not been issued)]
2	Affidavit verifying petition to wind up partnership.
3	Petition to wind up partnership by liquidator, administrator, trustee or supervisor.
4	Written/statutory demand by creditor.
5	Creditor's petition to wind up partnership (presented in conjunction with petitions against members).
6	Creditor's petition to wind up corporate member (presented in conjunction with petition against partnership).
7	Creditor's bankruptcy petition against individual member (presented in conjunction with petition against partnership).
8	Advertisement of winding-up petition(s) against partnership (and any corporate members).
9	Notice to court of progress on petitions presented.
10	Demand by member.

Form No	Description
11	Members' petition to wind up partnership (presented in conjunction with petitions against members).
12	Members' petition to wind up corporate member (presented in conjunction with petition against partnership).
13	Member's bankruptcy petition against individual member (presented in conjunction with petition against partnership).
14	Joint bankruptcy petition against individual members.
15	Affidavit of individual member(s) as to concurrence of all members in presentation of joint bankruptcy petition against individual members.
16	Bankruptcy orders on joint bankruptcy petition presented by individual members.
17	Statement of affairs of member of partnership.
18	Statement of affairs of partnership.

Notes

These forms are for use in proceedings brought under this Order. The forms themselves are omitted from this work.

SCHEDULE 10
Subordinate Legislation Applied

Article 18

The Insolvency Practitioners Tribunal (Conduct of Investigations) Rules 1986

The Insolvency Practitioners (Recognised Professional Bodies) Order 1986

The Insolvency Rules 1986

[The Insolvency Regulations 1994]

The Insolvency Proceedings (Monetary Limits) Order 1986

The Administration of Insolvent Estates of Deceased Persons Order 1986

The Insolvency (Amendment of Subordinate Legislation) Order 1986

...

[The Companies (Disqualification Orders) Regulations 2001]

The Co-operation of Insolvency Courts (Designation of Relevant Countries and Territories) Order 1986

[The Insolvent Companies (Reports on Conduct of Directors) Rules 1996]

The Insolvent Companies (Disqualification of Unfit Directors) Proceedings Rules 1987

[The Insolvency Practitioners Regulations 2005]

[The Insolvency Practitioners and Insolvency Services Accounts (Fees) Order 2003

The Insolvency Proceedings (Fees) Order 2004]

EC Council Regulation 1346/2000/EC on Insolvency Proceedings

of 29 May 2000

(1346/2000/EC)

Introductory

Purpose of the Regulation

The Council Regulation 1346/2000 on Insolvency Proceedings 2000 ('EC Regulation') came into force (without any retrospective effect) on 31 May 2002 (see art 47 below). Its primary object is to establish a rational regime, throughout the European Union, for the allocation of jurisdiction in insolvency matters. The EC Regulation also contains rules for the applicable law, in such matters, and the cross-border recognition and enforcement of judgments in insolvency proceedings. What the EC Regulation does not attempt, however, is the harmonisation of substantive insolvency law as amongst EU member states.

The Brussels Convention/Judgments Regulation

The EC Regulation is complementary to the 1968 Brussels Convention on jurisdiction and the enforcement of judgments in civil and commercial matters ('the Brussels Convention'), and therefore to the similar EU regulation, Council Regulation (EC) 44/2001 of 22 December 2000 ('the Judgments Regulation'), which has largely superseded the Brussels Convention. These instruments expressly exclude insolvency from their scope.

Jurisdiction and applicable law

The basic principle of the EC Regulation is that the 'main' insolvency proceedings must be brought in the state where the 'centre of [the] debtor's main interests is situated'. However subordinate insolvency proceedings may be brought in another state (or states), if the debtor has an 'establishment' there, but such proceedings can only affect assets situated in that other state. In most cases the applicable law is that of the Member State where the proceedings are opened (see art 4 below).

Member States

The EC Regulation only applies if the centre of the debtor's main interests is situated in a Member State, apart from Denmark which has opted out. It therefore applies with respect to Austria, Belgium, Finland, France, Germany, Greece, Ireland, Italy, Luxembourg, the Netherlands, Portugal, Spain, Sweden, and the United Kingdom. It also applies to the 10 states which joined the EU with effect from 1 May 2004; see EC Council Regulation 603/2005 [2005] OJ L100/1. The EC Regulation has no effect on insolvencies relating to debtors whose centre of main interests are not situated in a Member State, even if they have assets in a Member State.

Types of insolvency

Both corporate and personal insolvencies are covered by the EC Regulation. It does not apply to insurance companies, banks or certain other financial institutions. It extends to most types of insolvency proceedings brought in England and Wales, including winding up by the court (excepting liquidations based on public interest petitions), creditors' voluntary liquidation, administration, voluntary arrangements, and bankruptcy. However it does not cover administrative or other receiverships nor schemes of arrangement under CA 1985 s 425.

Direct effect

The EC Regulation has direct effect in England and Wales, and the other countries where it applies. Nevertheless certain specific changes were required to IA 1986, and the IR 1986, including the introduction of prescribed forms and these changes were effected by statutory instrument.

Interpretation

Since the EC Regulation is an EC instrument its provisions should be interpreted purposively and not necessarily literally. Its long preamble ('the Preamble') containing 33 recitals is the most important guide to its purpose. Further interpretative assistance may be obtained from the Virgos-Schmit Report on the 1995 Convention on Insolvency Proceedings, on which the EC Regulation was based: see *Geveran Trading Company Limited v Skjevesland (No 3)* [2003] BCC 209 (upheld on appeal [2003] BPIR 924).

4.1

THE COUNCIL OF THE EUROPEAN UNION,

Having regard to the Treaty establishing the European Community, and in particular Articles 61(c) and 67(1) thereof,

Having regard to the initiative of the Federal Republic of Germany and the Republic of Finland,

Having regard to the opinion of the European Parliament,[1]

Having regard to the opinion of the Economic and Social Committee,[2]

Whereas:

(1) The European Union has set out the aim of establishing an area of freedom, security and justice.

(2) The proper functioning of the internal market requires that cross-border insolvency proceedings should operate efficiently and effectively and this Regulation needs to be adopted in order to achieve this objective which comes within the scope of judicial cooperation in civil matters within the meaning of Article 65 of the Treaty.

(3) The activities of undertakings have more and more cross-border effects and are therefore increasingly being regulated by Community law. While the insolvency of such undertakings also affects the proper functioning of the internal market, there is a need for a Community act requiring coordination of the measures to be taken regarding an insolvent debtor's assets.

(4) It is necessary for the proper functioning of the internal market to avoid incentives for the parties to transfer assets or judicial proceedings from one Member State to another, seeking to obtain a more favourable legal position (forum shopping).

(5) These objectives cannot be achieved to a sufficient degree at national level and action at Community level is therefore justified.

(6) In accordance with the principle of proportionality this Regulation should be confined to provisions governing jurisdiction for opening insolvency proceedings and judgments which are delivered directly on the basis of the insolvency proceedings and are closely connected with such proceedings. In addition, this Regulation should contain provisions regarding the recognition of those judgments and the applicable law which also satisfy that principle.

(7) Insolvency proceedings relating to the winding-up of insolvent companies or other legal persons, judicial arrangements, compositions and analogous proceedings are excluded from the scope of the 1968 Brussels Convention on Jurisdiction and the Enforcement of Judgments in Civil and Commercial Matters,[3] as amended by the Conventions on Accession to this Convention.[4]

(8) In order to achieve the aim of improving the efficiency and effectiveness of insolvency proceedings having cross-border effects, it is necessary, and appropriate, that the provisions on jurisdiction, recognition and applicable law in this area should be contained in a Community law measure which is binding and directly applicable in Member States.

(9) This Regulation should apply to insolvency proceedings, whether the debtor is a natural person or a legal person, a trader or an individual. The insolvency proceedings to which this Regulation applies are listed in the Annexes. Insolvency proceedings concerning insurance undertakings, credit institutions, investment undertakings holding funds or securities for third parties and collective investment undertakings should be excluded from the scope of this Regulation. Such undertakings should not be covered by this Regulation since they are subject to special arrangements and, to some extent, the national supervisory authorities have extremely wide-ranging powers of intervention.

(10) Insolvency proceedings do not necessarily involve the intervention of a judicial authority; the expression 'court' in this Regulation should be given a broad meaning and include a person or body empowered by national law to open insolvency proceedings. In order for this Regulation to apply, proceedings (comprising acts and formalities set down in law) should not only have to comply with the provisions of this Regulation, but they should also be officially recognised and legally effective in the Member State in which the insolvency proceedings are opened and should be collective insolvency proceedings which entail the partial or total divestment of the debtor and the appointment of a liquidator.

(11) This Regulation acknowledges the fact that as a result of widely differing substantive laws it is not practical to introduce insolvency proceedings with universal scope in the entire Community. The application without exception of the law of the State of opening of proceedings would, against this background, frequently lead to difficulties. This applies, for example, to the widely differing laws on security interests to be found in the Community. Furthermore, the preferential rights enjoyed by some creditors in the insolvency proceedings are, in some cases, completely different. This Regulation should take account of this in two different ways. On the one hand, provision should be made for special rules on applicable law in the case of particularly significant rights and legal relationships (eg rights in rem and contracts of employment). On

the other hand, national proceedings covering only assets situated in the State of opening should also be allowed alongside main insolvency proceedings with universal scope.

(12) This Regulation enables the main insolvency proceedings to be opened in the Member State where the debtor has the centre of his main interests. These proceedings have universal scope and aim at encompassing all the debtor's assets. To protect the diversity of interests, this Regulation permits secondary proceedings to be opened to run in parallel with the main proceedings. Secondary proceedings may be opened in the Member State where the debtor has an establishment. The effects of secondary proceedings are limited to the assets located in that State. Mandatory rules of coordination with the main proceedings satisfy the need for unity in the Community.

(13) The 'centre of main interests' should correspond to the place where the debtor conducts the administration of his interests on a regular basis and is therefore ascertainable by third parties.

(14) This Regulation applies only to proceedings where the centre of the debtor's main interests is located in the Community.

(15) The rules of jurisdiction set out in this Regulation establish only international jurisdiction, that is to say, they designate the Member State the courts of which may open insolvency proceedings. Territorial jurisdiction within that Member State must be established by the national law of the Member State concerned.

(16) The court having jurisdiction to open the main insolvency proceedings should be enabled to order provisional and protective measures from the time of the request to open proceedings. Preservation measures both prior to and after the commencement of the insolvency proceedings are very important to guarantee the effectiveness of the insolvency proceedings. In that connection this Regulation should afford different possibilities. On the one hand, the court competent for the main insolvency proceedings should be able also to order provisional protective measures covering assets situated in the territory of other Member States. On the other hand, a liquidator temporarily appointed prior to the opening of the main insolvency proceedings should be able, in the Member States in which an establishment belonging to the debtor is to be found, to apply for the preservation measures which are possible under the law of those States.

(17) Prior to the opening of the main insolvency proceedings, the right to request the opening of insolvency proceedings in the Member State where the debtor has an establishment should be limited to local creditors and creditors of the local establishment or to cases where main proceedings cannot be opened under the law of the Member State where the debtor has the centre of his main interest. The reason for this restriction is that cases where territorial insolvency proceedings are requested before the main insolvency proceedings are intended to be limited to what is absolutely necessary. If the main insolvency proceedings are opened, the territorial proceedings become secondary.

(18) Following the opening of the main insolvency proceedings, the right to request the opening of insolvency proceedings in a Member State

where the debtor has an establishment is not restricted by this Regulation. The liquidator in the main proceedings or any other person empowered under the national law of that Member State may request the opening of secondary insolvency proceedings.

(19) Secondary insolvency proceedings may serve different purposes, besides the protection of local interests. Cases may arise where the estate of the debtor is too complex to administer as a unit or where differences in the legal systems concerned are so great that difficulties may arise from the extension of effects deriving from the law of the State of the opening to the other States where the assets are located. For this reason the liquidator in the main proceedings may request the opening of secondary proceedings when the efficient administration of the estate so requires.

(20) Main insolvency proceedings and secondary proceedings can, however, contribute to the effective realisation of the total assets only if all the concurrent proceedings pending are coordinated. The main condition here is that the various liquidators must cooperate closely, in particular by exchanging a sufficient amount of information. In order to ensure the dominant role of the main insolvency proceedings, the liquidator in such proceedings should be given several possibilities for intervening in secondary insolvency proceedings which are pending at the same time. For example, he should be able to propose a restructuring plan or composition or apply for realisation of the assets in the secondary insolvency proceedings to be suspended.

(21) Every creditor, who has his habitual residence, domicile or registered office in the Community, should have the right to lodge his claims in each of the insolvency proceedings pending in the Community relating to the debtor's assets. This should also apply to tax authorities and social insurance institutions. However, in order to ensure equal treatment of creditors, the distribution of proceeds must be coordinated. Every creditor should be able to keep what he has received in the course of insolvency proceedings but should be entitled only to participate in the distribution of total assets in other proceedings if creditors with the same standing have obtained the same proportion of their claims.

(22) This Regulation should provide for immediate recognition of judgments concerning the opening, conduct and closure of insolvency proceedings which come within its scope and of judgments handed down in direct connection with such insolvency proceedings. Automatic recognition should therefore mean that the effects attributed to the proceedings by the law of the State in which the proceedings were opened extend to all other Member States. Recognition of judgments delivered by the courts of the Member States should be based on the principle of mutual trust. To that end, grounds for non-recognition should be reduced to the minimum necessary. This is also the basis on which any dispute should be resolved where the courts of two Member States both claim competence to open the main insolvency proceedings. The decision of the first court to open proceedings should be recognised in the other Member States without those Member States having the power to scrutinise the court's decision.

(23) This Regulation should set out, for the matters covered by it, uniform rules on conflict of laws which replace, within their scope of

application, national rules of private international law. Unless otherwise stated, the law of the Member State of the opening of the proceedings should be applicable (lex concursus). This rule on conflict of laws should be valid both for the main proceedings and for local proceedings; the lex concursus determines all the effects of the insolvency proceedings, both procedural and substantive, on the persons and legal relations concerned. It governs all the conditions for the opening, conduct and closure of the insolvency proceedings.

(24) Automatic recognition of insolvency proceedings to which the law of the opening State normally applies may interfere with the rules under which transactions are carried out in other Member States. To protect legitimate expectations and the certainty of transactions in Member States other than that in which proceedings are opened, provisions should be made for a number of exceptions to the general rule.

(25) There is a particular need for a special reference diverging from the law of the opening State in the case of rights in rem, since these are of considerable importance for the granting of credit. The basis, validity and extent of such a right in rem should therefore normally be determined according to the lex situs and not be affected by the opening of insolvency proceedings. The proprietor of the right in rem should therefore be able to continue to assert his right to segregation or separate settlement of the collateral security. Where assets are subject to rights in rem under the lex situs in one Member State but the main proceedings are being carried out in another Member State, the liquidator in the main proceedings should be able to request the opening of secondary proceedings in the jurisdiction where the rights in rem arise if the debtor has an establishment there. If a secondary proceeding is not opened, the surplus on sale of the asset covered by rights in rem must be paid to the liquidator in the main proceedings.

(26) If a set-off is not permitted under the law of the opening State, a creditor should nevertheless be entitled to the set-off if it is possible under the law applicable to the claim of the insolvent debtor. In this way, set-off will acquire a kind of guarantee function based on legal provisions on which the creditor concerned can rely at the time when the claim arises.

(27) There is also a need for special protection in the case of payment systems and financial markets. This applies for example to the position-closing agreements and netting agreements to be found in such systems as well as to the sale of securities and to the guarantees provided for such transactions as governed in particular by Directive 98/26/EC of the European Parliament and of the Council of 19 May 1998 on settlement finality in payment and securities settlement systems.[5] For such transactions, the only law which is material should thus be that applicable to the system or market concerned. This provision is intended to prevent the possibility of mechanisms for the payment and settlement of transactions provided for in the payment and set-off systems or on the regulated financial markets of the Member States being altered in the case of insolvency of a business partner. Directive 98/26/EC contains special provisions which should take precedence over the general rules in this Regulation.

(28) In order to protect employees and jobs, the effects of insolvency proceedings on the continuation or termination of employment and on the rights and obligations of all parties to such employment must be determined by the law applicable to the agreement in accordance with the general rules on conflict of law. Any other insolvency-law questions, such as whether the employees' claims are protected by preferential rights and what status such preferential rights may have, should be determined by the law of the opening State.

(29) For business considerations, the main content of the decision opening the proceedings should be published in the other Member States at the request of the liquidator. If there is an establishment in the Member State concerned, there may be a requirement that publication is compulsory. In neither case, however, should publication be a prior condition for recognition of the foreign proceedings.

(30) It may be the case that some of the persons concerned are not in fact aware that proceedings have been opened and act in good faith in a way that conflicts with the new situation. In order to protect such persons who make a payment to the debtor because they are unaware that foreign proceedings have been opened when they should in fact have made the payment to the foreign liquidator, it should be provided that such a payment is to have a debt-discharging effect.

(31) This Regulation should include Annexes relating to the organisation of insolvency proceedings. As these Annexes relate exclusively to the legislation of Member States, there are specific and substantiated reasons for the Council to reserve the right to amend these Annexes in order to take account of any amendments to the domestic law of the Member States.

(32) The United Kingdom and Ireland, in accordance with Article 3 of the Protocol on the position of the United Kingdom and Ireland annexed to the Treaty on European Union and the Treaty establishing the European Community, have given notice of their wish to take part in the adoption and application of this Regulation.

(33) Denmark, in accordance with Articles 1 and 2 of the Protocol on the position of Denmark annexed to the Treaty on European Union and the Treaty establishing the European Community, is not participating in the adoption of this Regulation, and is therefore not bound by it nor subject to its application,

HAS ADOPTED THIS REGULATION—

Chapter I
General Provisions

4.2

1 Scope

1 This Regulation shall apply to collective insolvency proceedings which entail the partial or total divestment of a debtor and the appointment of a liquidator.

> 2 This Regulation shall not apply to insolvency proceedings concerning insurance undertakings, credit institutions, investment undertakings which provide services involving the holding of funds or securities for third parties, or to collective investment undertakings.

Notes

Art 1(1) – Scope of Regulation

Article 1 defines the type of insolvency proceedings to which the EC Regulation applies *Eurofood IFSC Ltd Case C-341/04*, [2006] BPIR 661, 692. The definition in art 1(1) is amplified in Annex A to the EC Regulation (referred to in art 2(a)) which specifically lists the insolvency proceedings covered in each Member State. The list includes in the UK compulsory and creditors' voluntary liquidations, administration and voluntary arrangements and bankruptcy; it does not include receivership, administrative or otherwise, nor does it include schemes of arrangement. That is because such procedures are not regarded as 'collective' for the benefit of all creditors. The list in Annex A does not include the winding up of insolvent partnerships and the administration of the insolvent estates of deceased persons. Nevertheless it is clear that the EC Regulation applies to such proceedings since specific statutory instruments have been made amending the relevant procedures and forms to take account of the EC Regulation (SI 2002/1308 and SI 2002/1309). The EC Regulation does not apply to Denmark which has exercised its right of opt out.

Creditors' voluntary liquidation

Annex A refers to a 'Creditors' voluntary winding up (with confirmation by the court)'. IR 1986 r 7.62 contains the procedure for obtaining such confirmation which is a novel concept in a voluntary liquidation *Re TXU Europe German Finance BV* [2005] BPIR 209. It is therefore arguable that the creditors' voluntary liquidation proceedings have only been opened, and are only entitled to recognition, when this confirmation has been obtained; however the Virgos-Schmit Report, para 68 (see Introductory notes 'Interpretation' above) suggests the contrary.

'Insolvency proceedings'

It is clear from art 1(1) that the EC Regulation only applies to *insolvency proceedings* (see notes to art 2(a) *below*). It does not therefore cover a members' voluntary liquidation, since this requires the company to be solvent (IA 1986 s 89). Similarly, it does not cover proceedings by the Secretary of State under IA 1986 s 124A to wind a company up on public interest grounds even where the company is insolvent: *Re Marann Brooks CSV Limited* [2003] BCC 239. *The Brussels Convention however (see Introductory notes 'The Brussels Convention/Judgments Regulation') does apply to solvent liquidations Re Cover Europe Ltd* [2002] BCLC 61.

Ancillary actions

Another question is whether 'insolvency proceedings' includes the ancillary actions which liquidators often bring, eg to enforce preference claims, or breach of duty claims against directors. The answer is to be found in the case law on the Brussels Convention (*see Introductory notes 'The Brussels Convention/Judgments Regulation'* above). It is apparent from the Preamble to the EC Regulation (Recitals 3, 7) that it is intended to complement the Brussels Convention (and therefore the Judgments Regulation which has now largely replaced it). Consequently the EC Regulation deals with jurisdiction over matters which are not covered by the Brussels Convention. Art 1(2) of the Brussels Convention states that it does not apply to: '*bankruptcy, proceedings relating to the winding up of insolvent companies or other legal persons, judicial arrangements, compositions and analogous proceedings*'. It was held in Case 133/78 *Gourdain v Nadler* [1979] ECR 733, [1979] 3 CMLR 180 that this exclusion only extends to ancillary actions which derive directly from the bankruptcy or winding up and are closely connected with the insolvency proceedings. On this basis, preference and wrongful trading claims appear to be outside the Judgments Regulation, but are covered by the EC

Regulation. Conversely claims by a liquidator to recover debts due to the company, and breach of duty claims against directors, are covered by the Judgments Regulation, and are outside the scope of the EC Regulation. Similarly where a liquidator claims that a third party holds an asset on trust for a company this would not be a claim governed by the EC Regulation *Oakley v Ultra Vehicle Design Ltd* [2006] BPIR 115.

'Appointment of a liquidator'

Although art 1(1) refers to proceedings which entail the appointment of a 'liquidator', this term is widely defined in art 2(b) and Annex C to include: liquidator; supervisor; administrator; official receiver; trustee; provisional liquidator; and in Scotland, judicial factor.

Art 1(2)

Although excluded from the EC Regulation such undertakings/institutions can be wound up as unregistered companies under IA 1986 s 221, *Re La Mutuelles du Mans Assurances IARD* [2006] BCC 11, *Re DAP Holding NV* [2006] BCC 48.

4.3

2 Definitions

For the purposes of this Regulation—
  (a) 'insolvency proceedings' shall mean the collective proceedings referred to in Article 1(1). These proceedings are listed in Annex A;
  (b) 'liquidator' shall mean any person or body whose function is to administer or liquidate assets of which the debtor has been divested or to supervise the administration of his affairs. Those persons and bodies are listed in Annex C;
  (c) 'winding-up proceedings' shall mean insolvency proceedings within the meaning of point (a) involving realising the assets of the debtor, including where the proceedings have been closed by a composition or other measure terminating the insolvency, or closed by reason of the insufficiency of the assets. Those proceedings are listed in Annex B;
  (d) 'court' shall mean the judicial body or any other competent body of a Member State empowered to open insolvency proceedings or to take decisions in the course of such proceedings;
  (e) 'judgment' in relation to the opening of insolvency proceedings or the appointment of a liquidator shall include the decision of any court empowered to open such proceedings or to appoint a liquidator;
  (f) 'the time of the opening of proceedings' shall mean the time at which the judgment opening proceedings becomes effective, whether it is a final judgment or not;
  (g) 'the Member State in which assets are situated' shall mean, in the case of:
    — tangible property, the Member State within the territory of which the property is situated,
    — property and rights ownership of or entitlement to which must be entered in a public register, the Member State under the authority of which the register is kept,

> — claims, the Member State within the territory of which the third party required to meet them has the centre of his main interests, as determined in Article 3(1);
>
> (h) 'establishment' shall mean any place of operations where the debtor carries out a non-transitory economic activity with human means and goods.

Notes

Definitions

Note that art 2 does not contain a definition of 'centre of a debtor's main interests'; see the notes under art 3 for a discussion of this key expression.

Art 2(a)

'insolvency proceedings'

See notes to art 1(1) under *'insolvency proceedings'*.

Art 2(b)

'liquidator'

See notes to art 1(1) under *'appointment of liquidator'*.

Art 2(c)

'winding up proceedings'

Such proceedings are listed in Annex B. In respect of the UK they include *'Winding up through administration, including appointments made by filing prescribed documents with the court'*; thus secondary proceedings which *'must be winding up proceedings'* (art 3.2, art 3.3) include a liquidation following an administration though traditionally administration is regarded as a rescue rather than a winding up proceeding.

Arts 2(d), (e)

'court', 'judgment'

The definitions are much wider than the ordinary meaning of these words. For instance 'court' includes a company's members acting together in passing a resolution for its voluntary winding up and thereby commencing a creditors' winding up (see Recital 10 Preamble.) It was also held to include a meeting of creditors to consider proposals to approve a company voluntary arrangement of a company incorporated by Royal Charter *Re The Salvage Association* [2003] BCC 504; *however the definition of 'company' for the purposes of the company voluntary arrangement provisions (IA 1986, s 1(4)) was amended in 2005 to take unregistered companies out of the company voluntary arrangement regime*; see notes to art 3(1); 'Unregistered companies' The reason for the wide definitions of 'court' and 'judgment' is to be found in Articles 16–25 dealing with cross-border recognition of insolvency proceedings. Their width reflects the fact that in the insolvency context it is not merely judicial bodies which make the key decisions which merit recognition in Member States.

Art 2(f)

'the time of the opening of proceedings'

This definition is important because many issues turn on the point in time when the proceedings are opened. For instance the question of whether or not the court can open main proceedings is determined by reference to the location of the centre of main interests of the debtor at the time the court is asked to decide whether to open proceedings *Shierson v*

Vlieland Boddy [2005] BCC 949; see notes to art 3(2) below. Other issues include whether 'secondary' or 'territorial' proceedings can be brought (see art 3), and which in rem, set off and reservation of title rights are preserved (see arts 5, 6 and 7).

The 'time of the opening of proceedings" is:

(a) in the case of a bankruptcy normally the date of the hearing of the bankruptcy petition. However where an application is made prior to the hearing of the bankruptcy petition such as an application to appoint an interim receiver (IA 1986 s 286) or to serve the petition outside the jurisdiction the *'time of the opening of proceedings'* would be the date when the court hears that application *Shierson v Vlieland Boddy* [2005] BCC 949;

(b) in the case of a compulsory liquidation normally the date of the hearing of the winding up petition unless there is an interim application (for instance to restrain advertisement of the petition or for the appointment of a provisional liquidator *Eurofood IFSC Ltd Case C-341/04* [2006] BPIR 661 in which case it is the time of the hearing of that interim application (*Shierson v Vlieland Boddy* [2005] BCC 949, 966 para 55(1)). The *Eurofood IFSC Ltd* judgment did not consider in the context of the *'time of the opening of the proceedings'* the effect of the relation back of the commencement of a compulsory winding up (IA 1986 s 129(2)) to the date of the petition; however the Advocate General in his Opinion referred favourably to the recognition in the Virgos-Schmidt report of the doctrine of relation back (*Eurofood IFSC Ltd* [2006] BCC 621, 679 para 95. Thus there is no clear guidance on the point as yet and where this might be an issue an application to appoint a provisional liquidator on the presentation of the petition should be considered;

(c) in the case of a creditors' voluntary liquidation the date of the passing of the members' resolution to liquidate (see notes to arts 2 (d), (e) above);

(d) in the case of an administration in court be the date of the hearing of the administration application unless there is an interim application (for instance to appoint a manager IA 1986 Sch B1 para 13(1)(d), (3)) in which case it would be the time of the hearing of that interim application;

(e) 'in the case of an administration out of court the date the appointment of the administrator takes effect (IA 1986 Sch B1 para 19, para 31)';

(f) in the case of voluntary arrangement the date of the approval of the proposals.

'judgment opening proceedings'

See *Eurofood IFSC Ltd Case C-341/04* [2006] BPIR 661 699ff and the commentary on art 2(e) for the wide meaning of this expression. Where an office holder in an insolvency as described in Annex C of the EC Regulation is appointed and this involves the office holder taking control of the assets to the exclusion of the debtor this will amount to a decision to open proceedings *Eurofood IFSC Ltd Case C-341/04* [2006] BPIR 661, 700, para 58. As yet there is no central register of the opening of insolvency proceedings under the EC Regulation in Member States so as to avoid parallel filings in different Member States of main proceedings and practitioners are reliant on web sites maintained by interested parties (eg www.eir.database.com, www.ci-mejes.com).

Art 2(g)

'the Member State in which assets are situated'

This has to be defined for a number of reasons. In particular, territorial and secondary proceedings only affect assets situated in the Member State where those proceedings are opened. Arts 5 and 7 respectively preserve rights in rem and reservation of title rights over assets situated in Member States other than the Member State where the main proceedings are opened. The definitions seem clear, and avoid the need to investigate the conflicts rules of individual Member States as to the *situs* of assets.

'Member State'

The Member States are the Member States of the EC, apart from Denmark which opted out of the EC Regulation; (see Introductory notes under 'Member States').

Art 2(h)

'establishment'

Although the basic principle of the EC Regulation is that the main insolvency proceedings are to be brought in the Member State where the debtor has the 'centre of its main interests', art 3(2) permits more limited proceedings to be brought in Member States where the debtor has an 'establishment': see notes to art 3(2) and art 27. Thus for example there may be 'secondary proceedings' (see notes to art 3(3)) taken in one or more Member States at the same time.

Art 2(h) defines 'establishment' though the 'centre of main interests' is not defined. It is clear from the Virgos-Schmit Report (para 70) that the reference to the carrying out of 'non-transitory economic activity' requires something more than the existence of a bank account or the mere presence of other assets in a Member State before such proceedings may be taken. In Telia AB v Hilcourt (Docklands) Ltd [2002] EWHC 2377 (Ch), [2003] BCC 856 the court considered that the English business premises of a subsidiary company of Telia AB (the centre of whose main interests was in Sweden) did not amount to an 'establishment' of Telia AB within the meaning of art 2(h); the separate legal personality of Telia AB and its English subsidiary was thus respected. However in Shierson v Vlieland-Boddy [2005] BCC 949 the veil of incorporation was lifted and it was stated that an individual who carried on a letting and management business through a front or nominee company was himself carrying out a 'non-transitory economic activity with human means and goods' and thus constituted an establishment within the EC Regulation which enabled a bankruptcy order to be made. There was no discussion in the Court of Appeal of how mere ownership of property constitutes a 'place of operations' of the debtor within the definition of art 2(h).

Whether a debtor has an establishment must be determined at the time of the opening of the proceedings in the relevant Member State; see notes to art 3(2) and Shierson v Vlieland-Boddy [2005] BCC 949, Staubitz-Schreiber (Case C-1/04) [2006] BPIR 510.

Comparison with 'Branch etc' in the Brussels Convention/Judgments Regulation

According to the Virgos-Schmit report, para 70 (see Introductory notes ' Interpretation' above), 'establishment', as defined in art 2(h), is intended to have a wider meaning than the expression 'branch, agency or other establishment' in the Brussels Convention, as defined in Somafer SA v Saar-Ferngas AG [1978] ECR 2183 and Etablissements A de Bloos Sprl V Societe en ammandite par Actons Bouyer: 14/76 [1976] ECR 1497, ECJ.

4.4

3 International jurisdiction

1. The courts of the Member State within the territory of which the centre of a debtor's main interests is situated shall have jurisdiction to open insolvency proceedings. In the case of a company or legal person, the place of the registered office shall be presumed to be the centre of its main interests in the absence of proof to the contrary.

2. Where the centre of a debtor's main interests is situated within the territory of a Member State, the courts of another Member State shall have jurisdiction to open insolvency proceedings against that debtor only if he possesses an establishment within the territory of that other Member

State. The effects of those proceedings shall be restricted to the assets of the debtor situated in the territory of the latter Member State.

3. Where insolvency proceedings have been opened under paragraph 1, any proceedings opened subsequently under paragraph 2 shall be secondary proceedings. These latter proceedings must be winding-up proceedings.

4. Territorial insolvency proceedings referred to in paragraph 2 may be opened prior to the opening of main insolvency proceedings in accordance with paragraph 1 only:

(a) where insolvency proceedings under paragraph 1 cannot be opened because of the conditions laid down by the law of the Member State within the territory of which the centre of the debtor's main interests is situated; or

(b) where the opening of territorial insolvency proceedings is requested by a creditor who has his domicile, habitual residence or registered office in the Member State within the territory of which the establishment is situated, or whose claim arises from the operation of that establishment.

Notes

International jurisdiction

Art 3 sets out the fundamental jurisdictional rules of the EC Regulation: the main insolvency proceedings have to be brought in the Member State where the centre of the debtor's main interests is situated, but 'secondary' or 'territorial' proceedings can be brought in another Member State where the debtor has an establishment. Such proceedings will only cover assets situated in that State and they cannot be opened by the court of its own motion *Eco Jet Ltd v Selafa MJA* [2005] BCC 979. It is noteworthy that where insolvency proceedings are first opened by a court in a Member State in which a company's registered office is situated and in which the company conducts the administration of its interests on a regular basis in a manner ascertainable by third parties (*Recital (13) Preamble, 'main proceedings'*), the courts of other Member States do not have jurisdiction to open main proceedings though there remains no substantive guidance on what is meant by '*administration*' notwithstanding the recent decision of the ECJ in *Eurofood IFSC Ltd (Case C-341/04)* [2006] BPIR 661.

It is of obvious importance that the court which hears the application for the opening of main proceedings considers the question of the centre of main interests carefully and with due regard to the necessity for a fair legal process *Eurofood IFSC Ltd (Case C-341/04)* [2006] BPIR 661, 698, 702, paras 41, 66. In practice this could mean that on the hearing of an administration application in England it may be advisable to serve unsecured creditors (or certain of them) with the application albeit that in a purely domestic context this would not be required (IR 1986 r 2.6, IA 1986 Sch B1 para 12(2)). The EC Regulation itself does not require that unsecured creditors generally are served with an administration application, and see notes to art 17(1) below.

Debtors outside the EU

If the debtor's centre of main interests is not situated in a Member State, if for example it is situated in the USA, then the EC Regulation has no application (Recital 14, Preamble). Whether insolvency proceedings against such a debtor can be brought in England is governed by the ordinary English law principles, in the case of winding up to be found primarily in IA 1986 s 221. However if the debtor's centre of main interests is in a Member State of the EU, the EC Regulation does apply even though the debtor is a company formed and/or registered outside the EU: *Re BRAC Rent-a Car International Inc* [2003] BCC 248.

Art 3(1)

Main insolvency proceedings

Proceedings opened in accordance with art 3(1) are generally referred to as 'main insolvency proceedings' or 'main proceedings', though art 3 does not actually use the word 'main'. However Recital 12, Preamble refers to the proceedings opened where the debtor has the centre of his main interests as the 'main insolvency proceedings', and IR 1986 r 13.13(10) defines 'main proceedings' as those opened in accordance with art 3(1). The important advantage of main proceedings is that collective insolvency proceedings are initiated throughout Member States and the substantive law of the Member State opening the main proceedings normally applies; see notes to art 4. Further in appropriate circumstances an administrator in the main proceedings may apply for directions enabling him to apply the law of other Member States instead of the law of the main proceedings; Re Collins & Aikman Europe SA [2006] BCC 606, Re MG Rover Espana [2005] BPIR 1162.

Scope of main insolvency proceedings

Art 3(1) itself does not define the scope of the main proceedings. However Recital 12, Preamble states that they 'have universal scope and aim at encompassing all the debtor's assets'. It follows that art 3(1) proceedings apply to assets within all other member states, except to the extent that such assets are affected by territorial or secondary proceedings in those other states, or by arts 5, 6 or 7. The powers of the liquidator in the main proceedings, and these limitations, are dealt with expressly in art 18.

Assets in non-member states

Whether the main proceedings cover these is probably determined by ordinary, pre-EC Regulation principles. An English winding up order in theory extends to a company's foreign assets (Dicey & Morris on The Conflict of Laws (13th ed) 30–072) but whether it does normally depends on the law of those states, since the office holder may have to bring proceedings there to recover the assets.

'centre of the debtor's main interests'

This concept is crucial, because on it depends jurisdiction over the main insolvency proceedings Eurofood IFSC Ltd (Case C-341/04) [2006] BPIR 661, Telia Sonera AB v Hilcourt (Docklands) Ltd [2003] BCC 856. It is not formally defined in the EC Regulation, but Recital 13, Preamble states that it 'should correspond to the place where the debtor conducts the administration of his interests on a regular basis and is therefore ascertainable by third parties'. A debtor may change his/its centre of main interests Shierson v Vlieland-Boddy [2005] BCC 949. According to the Virgos-Schmit Report (para 75) (see Introductory notes under 'Interpretation' above), 'interests' means not only commercial, industrial or professional activities, but also general economic activities so as to include the activities of private individuals. In Geveran Trading Company Limited v Skjevesland [2003] BCC 209, Mr Registrar Jacques stressed the importance of ascertaining the place where the debtor conducts the administration of his interests on a regular basis, which is therefore ascertainable by third parties. He stated that it was the need for third parties to ascertain the debtor's centre of main interests which was paramount. In that case the court drew a distinction between a debtor who was not a professional whose usual centre of main interests would be the place of his habitual residence; and a professional where the fundamental factor would be the 'professional domicile'; the decision was upheld on appeal: [2003] BPIR 924.

In Shierson v Vlieland-Boddy [2005] BCC 971 there was a divergence in opinion in the approach to be taken to the standard proof required in dealing with the question of the centre of main interests of an individual; one judge left open the point of whether a balance of probabilities test or 'good arguable case' standard was required, whereas another of the judges pointed out that the case was argued on the basis of a balance of probabilities test ([2005] BCC 971 para 72 cf para 75). As with a company the determination of an individual's centre of main interest is a facts sensitive decision, see: Cross Construction Sussex Ltd v Tseliki [2006] BPIR 888.

Centre of a company's main interests

This phrase was considered by the European Court of Justice in *Eurofood IFSC Ltd (Case C-341/04)* [2006] BPIR 661 in the context of a group of companies based in different member states. Art 3(1) sets out a rebuttable presumption that the centre of a company's main interests will be the registered office, in the case of a company or legal person. In some English cases it has been stated that there is no reason to suppose that the presumption is particularly strong *Re Parkside Flexibles SA* [2006] BCC 589, *Re Ci4Net.com Inc* [2005] BCC 277; whereas in the Irish Supreme Court it was stated that to defeat the presumption the burden was on a party to produce 'cogent proof' *Re Eurofood IFSC Ltd* [2005] BCC 999, 1011G. The Virgos-Schmit Report (para 75) (see Introductory notes *'Interpretation'* above) indicates that the presumption arises because the registered office normally corresponds to the debtor's head office, which suggests that what matters is the place where head office functions are carried out. This was an approach which the Advocate General appeared to approve in his Opinion in *Eurofood IFSC Ltd* [2005] BCC 999, 1039F although he did not entirely explain what was meant by the *'head office functions test'*; the approach of the Advocate General on this matter was simply not discussed by the European Court of Justice in its subsequent decision in *Eurofood IFSC Ltd (Case C-341/04)* [2006] BPIR 661.

The centre of main interests requirement was considered in *Re Daisytek–ISA Ltd* [2003] BCC 562: the court in that case was provided with detailed evidence of the way in which the affairs of a large group of companies including a number of French and German subsidiaries were managed. The court was persuaded that the more important management, financial and trading functions of the subsidiaries were actually carried out from Bradford, England. The court was particularly concerned to identify the scale and importance of the interests carried out in Bradford so that could be compared with what actually occurred at other places which might be considered the 'centre of main interests'. The most important question was whether the fact that a particular place was the centre of main interests of the company was ascertainable by third parties, in particular creditors of the company. *Re Daisytek–ISA Ltd* is an instructive example of the substantive evidence that must be produced so that the court may determine the centre of main interests which is therefore ascertainable by third parties such as creditors and suppliers (*see Recital 13 Preamble*). In *Re Parkside Flexibles SA* [2006] BCC 589, the court observed that the identification of a company's centre of main interests was a 'facts sensitive' decision. The court was dealing with a Polish registered company and after a thorough review of the evidence and balancing the factors favouring Poland and those favouring England the court decided by the 'narrowest of margins' that the centre of main interests was England. In *Re BRAC Rent-A-Car International Inc* [2003] BCC 248, the debtor company was incorporated in Delaware, but its operations were conducted almost exclusively in England. Lloyd J held that the debtor's centre of main interests was in England, and so the court could make an administration order notwithstanding the company was a foreign company registered outside the EU.

COMI in the ECJ

The question of a company's 'centre of main interests' was considered by the European Court of Justice in *Eurofood IFSC Ltd (Case C-341/04)* [2006] BPIR 661 and the following points emerge from that decision:

(i) the concept of the 'centre of main interests' is peculiar to the EC Regulation. It has an *'autonomous meaning and must therefore be interpreted in a uniform way, independently of national legislation'* p 697 para 31;

(ii) in determining the centre of main interests of a company the presumption in favour of the registered office *'can be rebutted only if factors which are both objective and ascertainable by third parties enable it to be established that an actual situation exists which is different from that locating it at that registered office is deemed to reflect'* p 697, para 34. The ECJ thus emphasised that the evidence before the court needs to detail such factors but it did not otherwise comment on the strength or otherwise of the presumption in favour of the registered office. It would therefore appear that the control operated by a parent company over its subsidiary will remain a relevant factor to the determination of the centre of main interests of a company if it is *'objective and ascertainable by third parties'*;

(iii)   the ECJ did not discuss the 'head office functions' test adopted by the Advocate General in his Opinion which preceded the decision of the ECJ *(Eurofood IFSC Ltd (Case C-341/04)* [2005] BCC 1021) and arguably would have made the rebuttal of the presumption in favour of the registered office a more difficult exercise;

(iv)   there is no such concept as a 'group COMI' in the EC Regulation and it is necessary to determine the centre of main interests of each debtor company in a group regarding each debtor as a separate legal personality. It is therefore important when an application is made involving a group of companies that the position of each company is addressed separately in the evidence but inevitably there has to be analysis and evidence relating to the 'group' entity as well as dealing with each company in the group;

(v)   the mere fact that a UK parent company can or does control the economic choices of a subsidiary in another Member State is not sufficient to rebut the presumption in favour of the registered office as being the centre of a company's main interests;

(vi)   the determination of a company's centre of main interests remains a 'facts sensitive' decision (see above *(Re Parkside Flexibles SA* [2006] BCC 589).

(vii)   the ECJ's approach requires that an applicant seeking to open main proceedings discloses to the court both the factors for and against the UK being the centre of main interests. In England there is wide scope for challenging a decision to open main proceedings on the basis of non disclosure and if a decision is taken not to serve potentially interested creditors with the application to open proceedings the risk is run that the decision is later challenged *Eurofood IFSC Ltd (Case C-341/04)* [2006] BPIR 661, p 698 para 41, p 702 para 66; *see notes under* 'International Jurisdiction' above

Unregistered companies

In *Re The Salvage Association* [2003] BCC 504 the court made an administration order in respect of a company created by Royal Charter on the basis that art 3(1) referred merely to a 'company or legal person'. Clearly the Salvage Association was a company; it had its centre of main interests in England and therefore an administration order could be made. This decision extended the application of the administration regime to unregistered companies. However as a result of The Insolvency Act 1986 (Amendment) Regulations 2005 the IA 1986 definitions of 'company' for the purposes of a CVA (s 1(4)) and administration (sch B1 para 111(1A)) were amended to exclude such unregistered companies from the CVA and administration regimes.

Individuals and professionals

The Virgos-Schmit Report (para 75) states that, in principle, the centre of main interests will in the case of professionals be the place of their professional domicile, and for natural persons in general, the place of their habitual residence. In *Geveran Trading Company Limited v Skjevesland* [2003] BCC 209, Mr Registrar Jacques who was upheld on appeal [2003] BPIR 924) stated that this was because such was the place where the debtor could be contacted. Ascertaining a debtor's professional domicile required consideration of where his home was, where he conducted his business, where his emotional ties were and what time he spent in various places. Amendments were made to the standard form bankruptcy petition in 2002 to ensure that the petitioner considered the impact of the EC Regulation when presenting a petition (IA 1986 s 265(3); see Insolvency Proceedings – Practice Note 1/2002..

Rival proceedings in different states

It is implicit in the wording of arts 3(1) and 3(2), and expressly stated in the Virgos-Schmit Report (para 73), that there can be only one set of main insolvency proceedings. The EC Regulation contains no express provisions dealing with rival proceedings in different Member States. However Recital 22, Preamble, states that the decision of the first 'court' (in the wide sense given by art 2(d)) to open proceedings should be recognised in other Member States without those other States having the power to scrutinise the original court's decision. Recital 22, Preamble is based on the principle of mutual trust and if any objection is to be taken to the decision to open main proceedings it should be taken in the Member State which made the decision and under its law *Eurofood IFSC Ltd (Case C-341/04)* [2006] BPIR 661, paras 39, 43. In England there is wide scope for challenging a decision to open main proceedings on the basis of non disclosure and if a decision is taken not to serve potentially interested creditors with the application to open proceedings a risk is run that the decision is later challenged *Eurofood IFSC Ltd (Case C-341/04)* [2006] BPIR 661, 702, 698, paras 66, 41; *see notes under 'International Jurisdiction'* above be recognised in France.

Jurisdiction within the UK

Where jurisdiction is conferred on the UK by art 3(1), the EC Regulation does not stipulate which part of the UK, Recital 15, Preamble. The UK consists of three separate jurisdictions, England and Wales, Scotland, and Northern Ireland. Jurisdiction as between those jurisdictions is determined by the normal pre- EC Regulation rules.

Art 3(2)

Although the EC Regulation requires that the main insolvency proceedings be brought in the Member State where the debtor has the centre of its main interests, subordinate proceedings can be brought in other Member States in respect of the debtor; art 3(2) sets out the basic principles in this respect. It should be noted that although recognition is afforded throughout the EU to such subordinate proceedings any restrictions of creditor rights relating to the assets of the debtor in such other Member States only apply if the creditors give their consent; see art 17(2).

'establishment'

The key requirement is that the debtor should have an *'establishment'* in the other Member State. This expression is defined, quite broadly, in art 2(h) (*see notes to art 2(h)*). It is clear from the wording of art 3(2) that the debtor must have an establishment in the other Member State at *'the time of the opening of proceedings'* in that Member State. Similarly a debtor's centre of main interests is determined at the time that the court is required to decide whether to open insolvency proceedings: *Shierson v Vlieland-Boddy* [2005] BCC 949; *see notes to art 2(f) under 'the time of opening proceedings'*.

In the context of considering the centre of main interests of a debtor it has been held that the court of a Member State through which the application for the opening of insolvency proceedings has been made is the competent court to open those proceedings; this remains the case notwithstanding that the defendant has moved the centre of his main interests to the territory of another Member State after the application was brought but before the proceedings were opened: *Staubitz-Schreiber (Case C-1/04)* [2006] BPIR 510. It is not clear whether the same reasoning would apply in the context of considering the 'establishment' of the debtor where for instance at the time of filing a petition to wind up the debtor has an establishment but at the time of hearing of the petition there is no such establishment in the relevant Member State. In circumstances where there are grounds for suspicion that a debtor has intentionally changed his centre of main interests in order to change the insolvency rules applicable to him in respect of existing debts, the court will need to be satisfied that the change was based on substance, was not illusory and had a lasting element of permanence: (*Shierson v Vlieland-Boddy (above)*).

Assets situated in the Member State

The proceedings referred to in art 3(2) can only affect assets situated in the Member State where the debtor has the establishment. Art 2(g) sets out rules for determining where the various types of assets are situated (see art 2(g)).

Further restrictions

There are further restrictions (set out in arts 3(3) and 3(4)) depending on whether the proceedings are 'opened' before or after the main proceedings. Art 2(f) explains what is meant by the 'opening' of proceedings.

Multiple proceedings

It must be the case that several sets of proceedings may be brought pursuant to art 3(2), in different Member States, if the debtor has an establishment in each. The Virgos-Schmit Report (para 83) states this expressly with respect to secondary proceedings, that is those brought after the main proceedings. Logically the same should apply to territorial proceedings, that is, those opened before the main proceedings.

Art 3(3)
Secondary Proceedings

This paragraph deals with proceedings pursuant to art 3(2) 'opened' (see art 2(f)) after the main proceedings. Such proceedings are given the name 'secondary proceedings' and can only be winding up proceedings (see also the notes to art 27 below). 'Winding up proceedings' are defined in art 2(c) and listed in respect of each Member State in Annex B. They comprise winding up by the court, creditors' voluntary liquidation, bankruptcy and also administration albeit that an administration is not otherwise regarded as a 'winding up' proceeding.

Art 3(4)
Territorial Proceedings

This paragraph deals with proceedings pursuant to art 3(2) 'opened' (see art 2(f)) before the main proceedings. Confusingly, the expression 'territorial insolvency proceedings' seems to be used at the beginning of art 3(4) to refer to such proceedings whether opened before or after the main proceedings. However *'territorial proceedings'* has come to refer to the former only, and indeed IR 1986 r 13.13(14) defines *'Territorial proceedings'* as those opened in accordance with art 3(4). Unlike 'secondary proceedings' pursuant to art 3(3), territorial proceedings can be any sort of insolvency proceedings, not just winding up proceedings.

Restrictions on territorial proceedings

Such proceedings can only be brought in two situations:
(1)   if main insolvency proceedings cannot be brought where the debtor has the centre of his/its main interests because of conditions laid down by the law of that Member State. An example of this is where that law stipulates that the debtor cannot be subjected to insolvency proceedings because he is not a trader (Virgos-Schmit Report, para 85).
(2)   if the opening of the proceedings is requested by a creditor who is based in the Member State where the debtor has his/its establishment, or whose claim arises from the operation of that establishment.

The latter situation will usually be the basis for opening territorial proceedings; however the requirement that the request is made by a creditor appears to rule out, in this context, a petition by a debtor for his own bankruptcy, or a winding up or administration initiated by the company itself. Further the court of its own motion cannot initiate territorial proceedings *Eco Jet Ltd v Selafa MJA* [2005] BCC 979.

4.5

4 Law applicable

1 Save as otherwise provided in this Regulation, the law applicable to insolvency proceedings and their effects shall be that of the Member State within the territory of which such proceedings are opened, hereafter referred to as the 'State of the opening of proceedings'.

2 The law of the State of the opening of proceedings shall determine the conditions for the opening of those proceedings, their conduct and their closure. It shall determine in particular:

(a) against which debtors insolvency proceedings may be brought on account of their capacity;

(b) the assets which form part of the estate and the treatment of assets acquired by or devolving on the debtor after the opening of the insolvency proceedings;

(c) the respective powers of the debtor and the liquidator;

(d) the conditions under which set-offs may be invoked;

(e) the effects of insolvency proceedings on current contracts to which the debtor is party;

(f) the effects of the insolvency proceedings on proceedings brought by individual creditors, with the exception of lawsuits pending;

(g) the claims which are to be lodged against the debtor's estate and the treatment of claims arising after the opening of insolvency proceedings;

(h) the rules governing the lodging, verification and admission of claims;

(i) the rules governing the distribution of proceeds from the realisation of assets, the ranking of claims and the rights of creditors who have obtained partial satisfaction after the opening of insolvency proceedings by virtue of a right in rem or through a set-off;

(j) the conditions for and the effects of closure of insolvency proceedings, in particular by composition;

(k) creditors' rights after the closure of insolvency proceedings;

(l) who is to bear the costs and expenses incurred in the insolvency proceedings;

(m) the rules relating to the voidness, voidability or unenforceability of legal acts detrimental to all the creditors.

(n) the Convention between the Federative People's Republic of Yugoslavia and the Kingdom of Greece on the Mutual Judicial Cooperation in Civil and Administrative Matters, signed at Rome on 3 December 1960;

(o) the Agreement between the Socialist Federative Republic of Yugoslavia and the Kingdom of Belgium on Judicial Cooperation in Civil and Commercial Matters, signed at Belgrade on 24 September 1971;

(p) the Convention between the Governments of Yugoslavia and France on the Recognition and Enforcement of Judgments in Civil and Commercial Matters, signed at Paris on 18 May 1971;

(q) the Agreement between the Czechoslovak Socialist Republic and the Hellenic Republic on Legal Aid in Civil and Criminal Matters, signed at Athens on 22 October 1980, still in force between the Czech Republic and Greece;

(r) the Agreement between the Czechoslovak Socialist Republic and the Republic of Cyprus on Legal Aid in Civil and Criminal Matters, signed at Nicosia on 23 April 1982, still in force between the Czech Republic and Cyprus;

(s) the Treaty between the Czechoslovak Socialist Republic and the Government of the Republic of France on Legal Aid and the

> Recognition and Enforcement of Judgments in Civil, Family and Commercial Matters, signed at Paris on 10 May 1984, still in force between the Czech Republic and France;
>
> (t) the Treaty between the Czechoslovak Socialist Republic and the Italian Republic on Legal Aid in Civil and Criminal Matters, signed at Prague on 6 December 1985, still in force between the Czech Republic and Italy; signed at Tallinn on 27 November 1998;
>
> (w) the Agreement between the Republic of Lithuania and the Republic of Poland on Legal Assistance and Legal Relations in Civil, Family, Labour and Criminal Matters, signed in Warsaw on 26 January 1993.

Notes

Law applicable

As a result of art 4 the EC Regulation not only stipulates which Member States have jurisdiction in insolvency proceedings; but also it provides which law is to be applied to the proceedings and their effects. Article 4 applies to the main proceedings, and also to any secondary or territorial proceedings.

Art 4(1)

Applicable law

The general rule stated here is that the applicable law is that of the Member State where the proceedings are opened. Thus art 4 provides a general rule as to applicable law which replaces any conflict rules of the various Member States though there are exceptions to the general rule stated in arts 5–15. However where administrators appointed in main proceedings in the UK had given assurances to creditors in various Member States that their rights under local laws would be respected so far as possible (if they did not issue secondary proceedings) the court was prepared to direct the administrators to fulfil those assurances pursuant to IA 1986 Sch B1 para 66 and the inherent jurisdiction of the court; this was despite the possibility that the direction would result in a departure from the rules under English law being the law of the main proceedings *Re Collins & Aikman Europe SA* [2006] EWHC 1343, [2006] BCC 606.

Position prior to the EC Regulation

Prior to the EC Regulation, the English courts applied English law to matters of both substance and procedure when winding up a company, generally speaking (*Dicey & Morris on The Conflict of Laws* (13th ed) 30–075).

'Save as otherwise provided'

Art 4 is subject to various exceptions derived from other provisions of the EC Regulation. These are to be found in arts 5–15. In particular various rights including security, set off and reservation of title rights are expressly not affected by the opening of the insolvency proceedings, and will therefore continue to be governed by the law under which those rights exist. Other exceptions relate to contracts relating to land, payment systems and financial markets, employment contracts, rights subject to registration, community patents, void transactions, and pending lawsuits.

Art 4(2)

This paragraph sets out a non-exhaustive list of 'standard' insolvency issues determined by the law of the Member State of the opening of proceedings. It is clear from the list that this law covers both procedural and substantive matters.

Art 4(2)(m)

Void transactions

If for example main insolvency proceedings were brought in England, under art 4(2)(m) English law would generally determine whether transactions could be attacked as preferences or on the basis of a transaction at an undervalue *Becheret Thierry v Industrie Guido Malvestio SpA* [2005] BCC 974; see the notes to art 13 below for an exception to this general rule.

4.6

5 Third parties' rights in rem

1. The opening of insolvency proceedings shall not affect the rights in rem of creditors or third parties in respect of tangible or intangible, moveable or immovable assets—both specific assets and collections of indefinite assets as a whole which change from time to time—belonging to the debtor which are situated within the territory of another Member State at the time of the opening of proceedings.

2. The rights referred to in paragraph 1 shall in particular mean:
   (a) the right to dispose of assets or have them disposed of and to obtain satisfaction from the proceeds of or income from those assets, in particular by virtue of a lien or a mortgage;
   (b) the exclusive right to have a claim met, in particular a right guaranteed by a lien in respect of the claim or by assignment of the claim by way of a guarantee;
   (c) the right to demand the assets from, and/or to require restitution by, anyone having possession or use of them contrary to the wishes of the party so entitled;
   (d) a right in rem to the beneficial use of assets.

3. The right, recorded in a public register and enforceable against third parties, under which a right in rem within the meaning of paragraph 1 may be obtained, shall be considered a right in rem.

4. Paragraph 1 shall not preclude actions for voidness, voidability or unenforceability as referred to in Article 4(2)(m).

Notes

Art 5(1)

Rights of secured creditors

Art 5 contains one of the most significant exceptions to the rule that the main insolvency proceedings cover all the debtor's assets, wherever situated. It provides that 'rights in rem' over assets situated in another Member State are not affected by the opening of insolvency proceedings and it is clear that assets subject to a floating charge are included.

Jurisdiction and applicable law

Art 5 affects both jurisdiction and applicable law. The courts of the Member State where the asset is situated will retain the jurisdiction they would normally have over proceedings relating to the right over the asset, and the applicable law will continue to be that which would apply to the right apart from the EC Regulation. Normally this will be the law of the Member State where the asset is situated (see art 2(g)).

Limitations on art 5

Three limitations should be noted:

(1)   the assets themselves (as opposed to the rights in rem over them) remain covered by the main proceedings. Consequently any surplus after the security has been satisfied can be claimed by the liquidator in the main proceedings;

(2)   Art 5 only covers rights in rem created before the opening of the main proceedings (Virgos-Schmit Report, para 96);

(3)   Issues about whether the security is void for any reason are subject to the law of the Member State where the main proceedings are opened (see art 4(2)(m) and art 5(4)) unless the security cannot be impugned under the law otherwise applicable to the security (Art. 13). However the Virgos-Schmit Report, para 135 suggests that jurisdiction over such issues also lies with the court where the main proceedings are opened but this is not entirely clear.

Art 5(2)

Definition of rights in rem

Art 5(2) provides a non exclusive definition of such rights; the most significant English law rights generally falling within the definition are mortgages, fixed charges, liens, and floating charges. Art 2(g) sets out rules for determining where the various types of assets are situated (see notes to art 2(g)).

4.7

6 Set-off

1. The opening of insolvency proceedings shall not affect the right of creditors to demand the set-off of their claims against the claims of the debtor, where such a set-off is permitted by the law applicable to the insolvent debtor's claim.

2. Paragraph 1 shall not preclude actions for voidness, voidability or unenforceability as referred to in Article 4(2)(m).

Notes

Art 6(1)

Set-off

Art 4(2)(d) states that the conditions under which set-offs may be invoked are determined by the law of the Member State where the insolvency proceedings are opened. However art 6 preserves a creditor's rights of set off which arise under the law applicable to the debtor's claim. This may be useful because rights of set-off are wider under some legal systems than others.

4.8

7 Reservation of title

1. The opening of insolvency proceedings against the purchaser of an asset shall not affect the seller's rights based on a reservation of title where

at the time of the opening of proceedings the asset is situated within the territory of a Member State other than the State of opening of proceedings.

2. The opening of insolvency proceedings against the seller of an asset, after delivery of the asset, shall not constitute grounds for rescinding or terminating the sale and shall not prevent the purchaser from acquiring title where at the time of the opening of proceedings the asset sold is situated within the territory of a Member State other than the State of the opening of proceedings.

3. Paragraphs 1 and 2 shall not preclude actions for voidness, voidability or unenforceability as referred to in Article 4(2)(m).

4.9

8 Contracts relating to immoveable property

The effects of insolvency proceedings on a contract conferring the right to acquire or make use of immoveable property shall be governed solely by the law of the Member State within the territory of which the immoveable property is situated.

4.10

9 Payment systems and financial markets

1 Without prejudice to Article 5, the effects of insolvency proceedings on the rights and obligations of the parties to a payment or settlement system or to a financial market shall be governed solely by the law of the Member State applicable to that system or market.

2 Paragraph 1 shall not preclude any action for voidness, voidability or unenforceability which may be taken to set aside payments or transactions under the law applicable to the relevant payment system or financial market.

4.11

10 Contracts of employment

The effects of insolvency proceedings on employment contracts and relationships shall be governed solely by the law of the Member State applicable to the contract of employment.

Notes

Contracts of employment

Under English law, the Rome Convention on the Law applicable to Contractual Obligations (incorporated into English law by the Contracts (Applicable Law) Act 1990) determines which country's law governs a contract of employment. Normally, in the absence of express choice, it will be the law of the country where the employee carries out the work.

'effects of insolvency proceedings on employment contracts'

This is the only area that the applicable law under the Rome Convention continues to cover. Other matters, such as whether employment claims get preference, will be governed by the law of the Member State of the opening of the proceedings, pursuant to art 4.

4.12

11 Effects on rights subject to registration

The effects of insolvency proceedings on the rights of the debtor in immoveable property, a ship or an aircraft subject to registration in a public register shall be determined by the law of the Member State under the authority of which the register is kept.

4.13

12 Community patents and trade marks

For the purposes of this Regulation, a Community patent, a Community trade mark or any other similar right established by Community law may be included only in the proceedings referred to in Article 3(1).

4.14

13 Detrimental acts

Article 4(2)(m) shall not apply where the person who benefited from an act detrimental to all the creditors provides proof that:
— the said act is subject to the law of a Member State other than that of the State of the opening of proceedings, and
— that law does not allow any means of challenging that act in the relevant case.

Notes

Void transactions

This provision refers back to art 4(2)(m) which provides that the law of the Member State where the proceedings are opened governs the voidness etc of acts detrimental to creditors *Becheret Thierry v Industrie Guido Malvestio SpA* [2005] BCC 974. Art 13 contains an exception to this rule if the act cannot be impugned under the law otherwise applicable. If for example main insolvency proceedings were brought in England, under art 4(2)(m) English law would determine whether transactions could be attacked as preferences or on the basis of a transaction at an undervalue. Art 13 modifies this rule so that if the transaction was subject to a foreign law (such as a mortgage of foreign land) which did not allow the particular transaction to be challenged, it could not be challenged under English preference or transaction at an undervalue rules.

4.15

14 Protection of third-party purchasers

Where, by an act concluded after the opening of insolvency proceedings, the debtor disposes, for consideration, of:

— an immoveable asset, or
— a ship or an aircraft subject to registration in a public register, or
— securities whose existence presupposes registration in a register laid down by law,

the validity of that act shall be governed by the law of the State within the territory of which the immoveable asset is situated or under the authority of which the register is kept.

4.16

15 Effects of insolvency proceedings on lawsuits pending

The effects of insolvency proceedings on a lawsuit pending concerning an asset or a right of which the debtor has been divested shall be governed solely by the law of the Member State in which that lawsuit is pending.

Notes

Pending lawsuits

This provision preserves the existing rules about actions pending when insolvency proceedings begin: so if an action is pending in England against a Spanish company and insolvency proceedings are commenced against it in Spain, English law will determine whether the action should be stayed. This will be a matter of discretion. In *Banque Indosuez SA v Ferromet Resources Inc* [1993] BCLC 112, Hoffman J stated that the English court would do its utmost to avoid action which would disturb the orderly administration of a foreign insolvency. This suggests that a stay will often be appropriate.

Chapter II
Recognition of Insolvency Proceedings

4.17

16 Principle

1. Any judgment opening insolvency proceedings handed down by a court of a Member State which has jurisdiction pursuant to Article 3 shall be recognised in all the other Member States from the time that it becomes effective in the State of the opening of proceedings.

This rule shall also apply where, on account of his capacity, insolvency proceedings cannot be brought against the debtor in other Member States.

2. Recognition of the proceedings referred to in Article 3(1) shall not preclude the opening of the proceedings referred to in Article 3(2) by a court in another Member State. The latter proceedings shall be secondary insolvency proceedings within the meaning of Chapter III.

Notes

Art 16(1)

Automatic recognition of foreign insolvency proceedings

Art 16 has the effect that insolvency proceedings in one Member State must be recognised automatically, without further formalities, in all other Member States and art 19 provides for a standard method of evidencing the office-holder's appointment. Although art 16(1) provides for automatic recognition it is helpful in practice for the court opening the main proceedings to 'spell out' the status of the proceedings and/or the powers of the appointed insolvency practitioners *Re MG Rover Espana SA* [2005] BPIR 1162. For example on obtaining an administration order in main proceedings it is important to recite in the sealed order (as appears in the standard form of order, Form 2.4B) that the court has determined the centre of main interests as being the UK ('*AND UPON the Court being satisfied on the evidence before it that the EC Regulation on Insolvency Proceedings 2000 does apply and that the proceedings herein are Main Proceedings as within Article 3 of the said Regulation*'). Though art 16(1) refers to the court '*handing down*' a judgment opening proceedings it is apparent from the width of the definition of the '*court*' and '*judgment*' (see notes to arts 2(d), (e)) and the inclusion of administrations (Annex A) and creditors' voluntary liquidations (Annex B) that the recognition of insolvency proceedings throughout the EU is not confined by reference to orders made by a court following a hearing. Art 16 covers main, secondary and territorial insolvency proceedings (see art 3). However since the last two categories only affect assets in the Member State where the proceedings are brought the question of their recognition in other Member States will arise much less frequently.

'judgment' and 'court'

These terms are used in the wide sense employed generally in the EC Regulation (see notes to arts 2(d), (e) above).

Creditors' voluntary liquidation

As discussed in the note to art 1(1) above, it is arguable that the creditors' voluntary liquidation proceedings have only been opened, and are only entitled to recognition, when they have been confirmed by the court; see IR 1986 r 7.62.

4.18

17 Effects of recognition

1 The judgment opening the proceedings referred to in Article 3(1) shall, with no further formalities, produce the same effects in any other Member State as under this law of the State of the opening of proceedings, unless this Regulation provides otherwise and as long as no proceedings referred to in Article 3(2) are opened in that other Member State.

2 The effects of the proceedings referred to in Article 3(2) may not be challenged in other Member States. Any restriction of the creditors' rights, in particular a stay or discharge, shall produce effects vis-à-vis assets situated within the territory of another Member State only in the case of those creditors who have given their consent.

Notes

Art 17(1)

Effect of recognition

Art 17(1) means that the main insolvency proceedings have the same effect in other Member States as in the Member State where they are opened. In particular, therefore, the debtor's assets devolve in the same way, and creditors have the same rights. The position of the liquidator is dealt with expressly in art 18. Following the decision of the European Court of Justice in *Eurofood IFSC Ltd (Case C-341/04)* [2006] BPIR 661, 702, para 67 a Member State may only refuse to recognise insolvency proceedings opened in another Member State '...

where the decision to open the proceedings was taken in flagrant breach of the fundamental right to be heard, which a person concerned by such proceedings enjoys'. In England an administration application must be served or notified to a variety of stated parties (IR 1986 r 2.6(3), IA 1986 Sch B1 para 12(2)) but there is no obligation to serve or advertise the application generally to unsecured creditors. The lack of notification in respect of such creditors is therefore a matter that is encountered routinely on an administration application however in the context of a possible argument about the location of the centre of main interests of the company it is important to consider carefully the duty of disclosure owed to the court. Part of that duty is to draw the attention of the court to the matters which indicate that the centre of main interests is somewhere other than the UK and the evidence in support of the application and the submissions at the hearing itself should ensure that the court is apprised of factors that might influence the determination of the location of a company's centre of main interests.

'unless this Regulation provides otherwise ...'

Art 17 is expressly subject to other provisions of the EC Regulation, such as arts 5–15, which in essence preserve local rights in various cases, such as secured claims, reservation of title, and employment. It is also subject to any secondary or territorial proceedings (see art 3) in the other Member State.

Art 17(2)

Although the EC Regulation requires that the main insolvency proceedings be brought in the Member State where the debtor has the centre of his/its main interests, subordinate proceedings can be brought in other Member States in respect of the debtor and art 3(2) sets out the basic principles in this respect. It should be noted that although recognition is afforded throughout the EU to such subordinate proceedings any restrictions of creditor rights relating to the assets of the debtor in such other Member States only apply if the creditors give their consent. Creditors who have not consented are therefore free to claim against assets of the debtor in those other Member States.

4.19

18 Powers of the liquidator

1 The liquidator appointed by a court which has jurisdiction pursuant to Article 3(1) may exercise all the powers conferred on him by the law of the State of the opening of proceedings in another Member State, as long as no other insolvency proceedings have been opened there nor any preservation measure to the contrary has been taken there further to a request for the opening of insolvency proceedings in that State. He may in particular remove the debtor's assets from the territory of the Member State in which they are situated, subject to Articles 5 and 7.

2 The liquidator appointed by a court which has jurisdiction pursuant to Article 3(2) may in any other Member State claim through the courts or out of court that moveable property was removed from the territory of the State of the opening of proceedings to the territory of that other Member State after the opening of the insolvency proceedings. He may also bring any action to set aside which is in the interests of the creditors.

3 In exercising his powers, the liquidator shall comply with the law of the Member State within the territory of which he intends to take action, in

particular with regard to procedures for the realisation of assets. Those powers may not include coercive measures or the right to rule on legal proceedings or disputes.

Notes

Art 18(1)

Powers of the Liquidator

Art 18(1) is one of the key provisions of the EC Regulation. Its effect is that the liquidator in the main insolvency proceedings has the same powers in other Member States as in the Member State where the main proceedings are brought. However this does not apply if other insolvency proceedings have been brought in the other member state. This refers to the 'territorial' or 'secondary' proceedings which might have been brought under art 3(3) or art 3(4) respectively, and which will affect assets in the Member State where they are brought. It is useful to obtain an order from the court detailing the powers of the appointed insolvency practitioner to assist the recognition of the practitioner in other Member States *Re MG Rover Espana SA* [2005] BPIR 1162; see notes to art 19 below.

Power to remove assets

Art 18(1) refers in particular to the liquidator's powers to remove assets from the Member States where they are situated. This is expressly subject to arts 5 and 7, which preserve security and reservation of title rights over assets situated in other Member States.

Art 18(2)

Secondary proceedings

This provision enables the liquidator in the secondary proceedings (see note to art 3(3), art 27) to reclaim assets which have been moved to another Member State provided that the assets have been removed after the opening of the secondary proceedings. The liquidator could presumably make preference or transaction at an undervalue claims under the power to '*bring any action to set aside ...*'.

Art 18(3)

It is not clear what exactly is covered by '*coercive measures*', for instance whether it would cover a demand made of the directors of a company incorporated in France to co-operate with an English liquidator appointed in main proceedings in England to that French company (IA 1986 s 235).

4.20

19 Proof of the liquidator's appointment

The liquidator's appointment shall be evidenced by a certified copy of the original decision appointing him or by any other certificate issued by the court which has jurisdiction.

A translation into the official language or one of the official languages of the Member State within the territory of which he intends to act may be required. No legalisation or other similar formality shall be required.

Notes

Art 19

'Liquidator'

The 'Liquidator' has the extended definition given in art 2(b) and see notes to art 1(1) *'appointment of liquidator'*. There has sometimes been difficulty faced by an administrator appointed in the UK in main proceedings to ensure that his appointment is accepted in other Member States. Thus on obtaining an administration order in main proceedings it is important to recite in the sealed order that the court has determined the centre of main interests as being the UK (*'AND UPON the Court being satisfied on the evidence before it that the EC Regulation on Insolvency Proceedings 2000 does apply and that the proceedings herein are Main Proceedings as within Article 3 of the said Regulation'*) as appears in the standard order (Form 2.4B); this will normally assist recognition of the administrator in other Member States, The proper route for interested parties in other Member States to challenge the determination of the court opening the main proceedings is to apply to that court rather than to litigate the matter in the courts of other Member State *Klempka v ISA Daisytek SA* [2003] BCC 984, *Eurofood IFSC Ltd (Case C-341/04)* [2006] BPIR 661.

4.21

20 Return and imputation

1 A creditor who, after the opening of the proceedings referred to in Article 3(1) obtains by any means, in particular through enforcement, total or partial satisfaction of his claim on the assets belonging to the debtor situated within the territory of another Member State, shall return what he has obtained to the liquidator, subject to Articles 5 and 7.

2 In order to ensure equal treatment of creditors a creditor who has, in the course of insolvency proceedings, obtained a dividend on his claim shall share in distributions made in other proceedings only where creditors of the same ranking or category have, in those other proceedings, obtained an equivalent dividend.

4.22

21 Publication

1 The liquidator may request that notice of the judgment opening insolvency proceedings and, where appropriate, the decision appointing him, be published in any other Member State in accordance with the publication procedures provided for in that State. Such publication shall also specify the liquidator appointed and whether the jurisdiction rule applied is that pursuant to Article 3(1) or Article 3(2).

2 However, any Member State within the territory of which the debtor has an establishment may require mandatory publication. In such cases, the liquidator or any authority empowered to that effect in the Member

> State where the proceedings referred to in Article 3(1) are opened shall take all necessary measures to ensure such publication.

Notes

Art 21(1)

Publication

Art 21(1) entitles the liquidator to publicise the proceedings in other Member States. This may be important in order to notify persons who owe obligations to the debtor and to enforce the company's rights and take enforcement action. If such a person is unaware of the proceedings he will be deemed by art 24 to have discharged the obligation by payment to the debtor, even if he should have paid the liquidator. Furthermore, art 24 provides that publication under art 21 gives rise to a presumption of notice, and vice versa.

4.23

22 Registration in a public register

1 The liquidator may request that the judgment opening the proceedings referred to in Article 3(1) be registered in the land register, the trade register and any other public register kept in the other Member States.

2 However, any Member State may require mandatory registration. In such cases, the liquidator or any authority empowered to that effect in the Member State where the proceedings referred to in Article 3(1) have been opened shall take all necessary measures to ensure such registration.

4.24

23 Costs

The costs of the publication and registration provided for in Articles 21 and 22 shall be regarded as costs and expenses incurred in the proceedings.

4.25

24 Honouring of an obligation to a debtor

1 Where an obligation has been honoured in a Member State for the benefit of a debtor who is subject to insolvency proceedings opened in another Member State, when it should have been honoured for the benefit of the liquidator in those proceedings, the person honouring the obligation shall be deemed to have discharged it if he was unaware of the opening of proceedings.

2 Where such an obligation is honoured before the publication provided for in Article 21 has been effected, the person honouring the obligation shall be presumed, in the absence of proof to the contrary, to have been unaware of the opening of insolvency proceedings; where the obligation is honoured after such publication has been effected, the person honouring the obligation shall be presumed, in the absence of proof to the contrary, to have been aware of the opening of proceedings.

4.26

25 Recognition and enforceability of other judgments

1 Judgments handed down by a court whose judgment concerning the opening of proceedings is recognised in accordance with Article 16 and which concern the course and closure of insolvency proceedings, and compositions approved by that court shall also be recognised with no further formalities. Such judgments shall be enforced in accordance with Articles 31 to 51, with the exception of Article 34(2), of the Brussels Convention on Jurisdiction and the Enforcement of Judgments in Civil and Commercial Matters, as amended by the Conventions of Accession to this Convention.

The first subparagraph shall also apply to judgments deriving directly from the insolvency proceedings and which are closely linked with them, even if they were handed down by another court.

The first subparagraph shall also apply to judgments relating to preservation measures taken after the request for the opening of insolvency proceedings.

2 The recognition and enforcement of judgments other than those referred to in paragraph 1 shall be governed by the Convention referred to in paragraph 1, provided that that Convention is applicable.

3 The Member States shall not be obliged to recognise or enforce a judgment referred to in paragraph 1 which might result in a limitation of personal freedom or postal secrecy.

Notes

Art 25(1)

Recognition and enforceability of judgments in the course of insolvency proceedings

Art 16 provides for the recognition in other Member States of the judgment opening the insolvency proceedings; see notes to art 2(f) above. Art 25 provides for the recognition, and enforcement of judgments in the course of, and concerning the closure of, those proceedings.

Recognition and enforcement

These are different concepts. Enforcement means the execution or carrying out of the judgment as against the person against whom it is given. A judgment setting aside a transaction at an undervalue might well order a third party to transfer property or pay money to the liquidator. The liquidator may need to enforce this order against the third party.

The Brussels Convention/Judgments Regulation machinery

Art 25(1) provides the machinery for enforcement in other Member States: it states that the judgments will be enforced in accordance with Articles 31–51, with the exception of Article 34(2), of the Brussels Convention. In fact the Brussels Convention has now been largely superseded by the similar Judgments Regulation (*see Introductory notes above*). Art 25 of the EC Regulation should therefore be regarded as referring to Articles 38–58, with the exception of Article 45(2), of the Judgments Regulation. Articles 38–58 of the Judgments Regulation contain a tried and tested mechanism for enforcing judgments of other member states, and art 25 therefore extends this mechanism to judgments arising in insolvency matters.

Enforcement procedure

Articles 38–58 of the Judgments Regulation do require fresh proceedings to be brought in the enforcing country, but its courts will be unable to review the substance of the original judgment or the jurisdiction of the original court (Virgos-Schmit report, para 202 –*see Introductory notes* ' above). The relevant English procedure is set out in CPR Part 74.

'judgments handed down by another court'

Art 25 covers judgments of a different court, if they derive directly from the insolvency proceedings and are closely connected with them. It would therefore cover a judgment setting aside a transaction at an undervalue on the application of a liquidator in a creditors' voluntary liquidation. Such a judgment would be made by a different 'court' from that opening the creditors' voluntary liquidation, since the latter would in fact be the meeting passing the original liquidation resolution – see note to art 2(d) and (e).

Art 25(2)

Enforcement of other judgments

This paragraph relates to judgments which are not covered by art 25(1). This presumably means judgments connected with insolvencies but which do not derive directly from them, such as judgments against misfeasant directors or third party debtors of an insolvent company. Such judgments *were* previously enforceable under the Brussels Convention/Judgments Regulation (*see note to art* 1(1) 'Ancillary actions') and art 25(2) makes it clear that this remains the case.

> **4.27**
>
> **26 Public policy**
>
> Any Member State may refuse to recognise insolvency proceedings opened in another Member State or to enforce a judgment handed down in the context of such proceedings where the effects of such recognition or enforcement would be manifestly contrary to that State's public policy, in particular its fundamental principles or the constitutional rights and liberties of the individual.

Notes

Public policy

This is likely to be interpreted restrictively, and invoked rarely (Virgos-Schmit report, paras 204–6) though it was relied on in *Re Eurofood IFSC Ltd* [2004] BCC 383 where the Irish High Court refused to recognise a decision of the Italian court to put a company into an extraordinary administration in Italy as the opening of main proceedings. The emphasis following the decision of the European Court of Justice in *Eurofood IFSC Ltd (Case C-341/04)* [2006] BCC 661, 702, para 67 is that this exception will only be applicable '... *where the decision to open the proceedings was taken in flagrant breach of the fundamental right to be heard, which a person concerned by such proceedings enjoys*'. In England ordinarily an unsecured creditor does not have to be served with an administration application (IR 1986 r 2.6(3), IA 1986 Sch B1 para 12(2)). Though the EC Regulation does not have the effect of demanding that such a creditor is heard on an administration application seeking to open main proceedings, the English court will be ready to investigate whether full and proper disclosure has been made on the determination of the 'centre of main interests' of the company; see notes to art 17 above. It is apparent from *Eurofood IFSC Ltd (Case C-341/04)* [2006] BCC 661, 698, 702, paras 41, 66 that the European Court of Justice emphasised the necessity for the court to examine this matter '... *in such a way as to comply with the essential procedural guarantees required for a fair legal process ...*'.

Chapter III
Secondary Insolvency Proceedings

4.28

27 Opening of proceedings

The opening of the proceedings referred to in Article 3(1) by a court of a Member State and which is recognised in another Member State (main proceedings) shall permit the opening in that other Member State, a court of which has jurisdiction pursuant to Article 3(2), of secondary insolvency proceedings without the debtor's insolvency being examined in that other State. These latter proceedings must be among the proceedings listed in Annex B. Their effects shall be restricted to the assets of the debtor situated within the territory of that other Member State.

Notes

Secondary insolvency proceedings

Art 27 deals with the first of the two types of subordinate proceedings which the EC Regulation allows to be opened in Member States other than the Member State where the main proceedings have been opened. The first are 'secondary insolvency proceedings' which are those which are opened after the main proceedings (see note to art 3(3)) and must be winding up proceedings; the second are 'territorial proceedings' (see art 36) which are opened before the main proceedings and may be winding up or rescue proceedings.

Restrictions on secondary proceedings

Such proceedings can only be brought if the debtor has an 'establishment' in the other Member State (see notes to art 3(3) and art 2(h)). Furthermore they can only be winding up, that is not rescue, proceedings (Art 3(3)). Annex B specifically lists such proceedings in the various Member States (see note to art 3(3)) and in the case of the UK it includes 'winding up through administration, including appointments made by filing prescribed documents with the court' which would therefore include an administration which is often in fact required as a rescue rather than a winding up proceeding.

Assets covered by secondary proceedings

Such proceedings only affect assets situated within the other Member State (see note to art 3(3)). However art 18(2) empowers the liquidator appointed in the Member State in which the secondary proceedings have been opened to claim, in any other member state, assets removed from the Member State in which the secondary proceedings have been opened and after they have been opened. Art 18(2) also enables the liquidator to bring 'any action to set aside', which presumably refers to actions attacking preferences or transactions at an undervalue.

Insolvency to be presumed

Art 27 stipulates that the debtor's insolvency is not to be examined in the Member State where the secondary proceedings are brought. Obviously such insolvency is presumed from the fact that main proceedings have been opened elsewhere. It will not necessarily be clear from the wording of a foreign document opening insolvency proceedings that they are main proceedings. However in the case of English insolvency proceedings, the Insolvency Amendment Rules 2002, SI 2002/1307, introduced new forms of petition and order which make this clear; (see also the former Insolvency Proceedings – Practice Note 1/2002, 10 May 2002).

4.29

28 Applicable law

Save as otherwise provided in this Regulation, the law applicable to secondary proceedings shall be that of the Member State within the territory of which the secondary proceedings are opened.

4.30

29 Right to request the opening of proceedings

The opening of secondary proceedings may be requested by:
(a)   the liquidator in the main proceedings;
(b)   any other person or authority empowered to request the opening of insolvency proceedings under the law of the Member State within the territory of which the opening of secondary proceedings is requested.

Notes

Request to open the secondary proceedings

The liquidator (as broadly defined in art 2(b)) in the main proceedings, as well as local creditors, may wish to open secondary proceedings in another member state. The object might be to take advantage of remedies available under the law of that other member state, which will govern the secondary proceedings (Art 28), or simply because this makes the debtor's affairs easier to administer: see Recital 19, Preamble IA 1986 s 124(1) and IR 1986 (r 6.238, r 6.239, r 4.231, r 2.133) have been amended accordingly, to enable a liquidator in another Member State to bring secondary proceedings in England.

4.31

30 Advance payment of costs and expenses

Where the law of the Member State in which the opening of secondary proceedings is requested requires that the debtor's assets be sufficient to cover in whole or in part the costs and expenses of the proceedings, the court may, when it receives such a request, require the applicant to make an advance payment of costs or to provide appropriate security.

4.32

31 Duty to cooperate and communicate information

1 Subject to the rules restricting the communication of information, the liquidator in the main proceedings and the liquidators in the secondary proceedings shall be duty bound to communicate information to each other. They shall immediately communicate any information which may

be relevant to the other proceedings, in particular the progress made in lodging and verifying claims and all measures aimed at terminating the proceedings.

2 Subject to the rules applicable to each of the proceedings, the liquidator in the main proceedings and the liquidators in the secondary proceedings shall be duty bound to cooperate with each other.

3 The liquidator in the secondary proceedings shall give the liquidator in the main proceedings an early opportunity of submitting proposals on the liquidation or use of the assets in the secondary proceedings.

Notes

Cooperation of liquidators with each other

Where there is more than one set of proceedings underway, the respective liquidators are obliged to cooperate with each other; there may be more than one set of secondary proceedings in existence at the same time. Amendments to IR 1986 inserted by the Insolvency Amendment Rules 2002, SI 2002/1307, place specific obligations on office holders in English insolvencies to give information to liquidators in other Member States; see IR 1986 r 6.238, r 6.239, r 4.231, r 2.133.

Assets in secondary proceedings

The liquidator in the main proceedings enjoys a primacy in the secondary proceedings (eg arts 33–35) which includes the opportunity to submit proposals in the secondary proceedings (Art 31(3)) and in certain circumstances he may request a stay of those proceedings, art 33.

4.33

32 Exercise of creditors' rights

1 Any creditor may lodge his claim in the main proceedings and in any secondary proceedings.

2 The liquidators in the main and any secondary proceedings shall lodge in other proceedings claims which have already been lodged in the proceedings for which they were appointed, provided that the interests of creditors in the latter proceedings are served thereby, subject to the right of creditors to oppose that or to withdraw the lodgement of their claims where the law applicable so provides.

3 The liquidator in the main or secondary proceedings shall be empowered to participate in other proceedings on the same basis as a creditor, in particular by attending creditors' meetings.

Notes

Art 32(3)

Exercise of creditors' rights by liquidator

It is not clear from this provision whether the foreign liquidator is entitled to exercise the voting rights attaching to the claims which he lodges in proceedings in another Member State;

para 240 of the Virgos-Schmit Report stated that provisions to this effect were rejected during negotiations. However under IR 1986 r 2.133 for the purposes of a variety of rules relating to administration (including entitlement to vote) the foreign liquidator is treated as being a creditor entitled to vote and this is stated to be '*without prejudice to the generality of the right to participate referred to in paragraph 3 of Article 32 of the EC Regulation...*'; see also IR 1986 r 7.64.

4.34

33 Stay of liquidation

1 The court, which opened the secondary proceedings, shall stay the process of liquidation in whole or in part on receipt of a request from the liquidator in the main proceedings, provided that in that event it may require the liquidator in the main proceedings to take any suitable measure to guarantee the interests of the creditors in the secondary proceedings and of individual classes of creditors. Such a request from the liquidator may be rejected only if it is manifestly of no interest to the creditors in the main proceedings. Such a stay of the process of liquidation may be ordered for up to three months. It may be continued or renewed for similar periods.

2 The court referred to in paragraph 1 shall terminate the stay of the process of liquidation:
— at the request of the liquidator in the main proceedings,
— of its own motion, at the request of a creditor or at the request of the liquidator in the secondary proceedings if that measure no longer appears justified, in particular, by the interests of creditors in the main proceedings or in the secondary proceedings.

Notes

Art 33

See the notes under art 31 above; in particular a stay may be requested to enable the liquidator in the main proceedings to submit proposals as to the liquidation or use of assets in the secondary proceedings, art 31(3).

4.35

34 Measures ending secondary insolvency proceedings

1 Where the law applicable to secondary proceedings allows for such proceedings to be closed without liquidation by a rescue plan, a composition or a comparable measure, the liquidator in the main proceedings shall be empowered to propose such a measure himself.

Closure of the secondary proceedings by a measure referred to in the first subparagraph shall not become final without the consent of the liquidator in the main proceedings; failing his agreement, however, it may become final if the financial interests of the creditors in the main proceedings are not affected by the measure proposed.

2 Any restriction of creditors' rights arising from a measure referred to in paragraph 1 which is proposed in secondary proceedings, such as a stay of payment or discharge of debt, may not have effect in respect of the debtor's assets not covered by those proceedings without the consent of all the creditors having an interest.

3 During a stay of the process of liquidation ordered pursuant to Article 33, only the liquidator in the main proceedings or the debtor, with the former's consent, may propose measures laid down in paragraph 1 of this Article in the secondary proceedings; no other proposal for such a measure shall be put to the vote or approved.

Notes

Art 34(1)

Such measures include a company or individual voluntary arrangement.

4.36

35 Assets remaining in the secondary proceedings

If by the liquidation of assets in the secondary proceedings it is possible to meet all claims allowed under those proceedings, the liquidator appointed in those proceedings shall immediately transfer any assets remaining to the liquidator in the main proceedings.

4.37

36 Subsequent opening of the main proceedings

Where the proceedings referred to in Article 3(1) are opened following the opening of the proceedings referred to in Article 3(2) in another Member State, Articles 31 to 35 shall apply to those opened first, in so far as the progress of those proceedings so permits.

Notes

Coordination of territorial proceedings with subsequent main proceedings

Art 36 refers to 'territorial' proceedings, which are subordinate insolvency proceedings that have been opened before the main proceedings; also see notes to art 27. Arts 31–35 (which seek to coordinate main and subordinate insolvency proceedings) are only applied to such proceedings so far as their progress permits. This is because the territorial proceeding might be so far advanced that the provisions of arts 31–35 are unworkable or inappropriate.

4.38

37 Conversion of earlier proceedings

The liquidator in the main proceedings may request that proceedings listed in Annex A previously opened in another Member State be

> converted into winding-up proceedings if this proves to be in the interests of the creditors in the main proceedings.
>
> The court with jurisdiction under Article 3(2) shall order conversion into one of the proceedings listed in Annex B.

Notes

Conversion of territorial to secondary proceedings

'Territorial' proceedings, which are subordinate insolvency proceedings that have been opened before the main proceedings can be either winding up or rescue proceedings. Art 37 enables the liquidator in the main proceedings to apply for the conversion of rescue-type territorial proceedings into winding up/bankruptcy proceedings. IR 1986 has been amended to provide for such applications: rr 1.31–1.33; 2.130–2.132; 5.62–5.65.

> **4.39**
>
> **38 Preservation measures**
>
> Where the court of a Member State which has jurisdiction pursuant to Article 3(1) appoints a temporary administrator in order to ensure the preservation of the debtor's assets, that temporary administrator shall be empowered to request any measures to secure and preserve any of the debtor's assets situated in another Member State, provided for under the law of that State, for the period between the request for the opening of insolvency proceedings and the judgment opening the proceedings.

Notes

Preservation measures in another Member State

This provision enables a temporary administrator appointed in the Member State with jurisdiction over the main insolvency proceedings to request measures available under the law of another Member State to secure assets in that state. This should enable him to preserve those assets until the main proceedings are actually opened, when they will take effect in all Member States pursuant to art 17.

'temporary administrator'

This would include a provisional liquidator, or interim manager appointed under English winding up (IA 1986 s 135) and administration (IA 1986 Sch B1 para 13(1)(d), (3)) procedures respectively.

> ## Chapter IV
> ## Provision of Information for Creditors and Lodgement of Their Claims
>
> **4.40**
>
> **39 Right to lodge claims**
>
> Any creditor who has his habitual residence, domicile or registered office in a Member State other than the State of the opening of proceedings,

> including the tax authorities and social security authorities of Member States, shall have the right to lodge claims in the insolvency proceedings in writing.

Notes

Foreign creditors' right to lodge claims

The object of this provision is to outlaw any discrimination as between Member States. It does not exclude non–EU creditors from lodging claims, if they are entitled to under the law of the Member State where the proceedings are brought.

'tax authorities'

Art 39 expressly allows tax authorities to bring claims in another Member State, contrary to the traditional refusal to enforce foreign tax laws.

> **4.41**
>
> **40 Duty to inform creditors**
>
> 1 As soon as insolvency proceedings are opened in a Member State, the court of that State having jurisdiction or the liquidator appointed by it shall immediately inform known creditors who have their habitual residences, domiciles or registered offices in the other Member States.
>
> 2 That information, provided by an individual notice, shall in particular include time limits, the penalties laid down in regard to those time limits, the body or authority empowered to accept the lodgement of claims and the other measures laid down. Such notice shall also indicate whether creditors whose claims are preferential or secured in rem need lodge their claims.

Notes

Informing creditors of insolvency proceedings

Further art 42 states that the notice containing this information must have a heading in all the official EU languages.

> **4.42**
>
> **41 Content of the lodgement of a claim**
>
> A creditor shall send copies of supporting documents, if any, and shall indicate the nature of the claim, the date on which it arose and its

amount, as well as whether he alleges preference, security in rem or a reservation of title in respect of the claim and what assets are covered by the guarantee he is invoking.

Notes

Contents of creditors' claim

New forms of proof of debt have been prescribed (Forms 4.25 and 6.37) to reflect the requirements of art 41. Art 42(2) contains stipulations about the languages to be used in proofs of debt which are lodged in other Member States.

4.43

42 Languages

1 The information provided for in Article 40 shall be provided in the official language or one of the official languages of the State of the opening of proceedings. For that purpose a form shall be used bearing the heading 'Invitation to lodge a claim. Time limits to be observed' in all the official languages of the institutions of the European Union.

2 Any creditor who has his habitual residence, domicile or registered office in a Member State other than the State of the opening of proceedings may lodge his claim in the official language or one of the official languages of that other State. In that event, however, the lodgement of his claim shall bear the heading 'Lodgement of claim' in the official language or one of the official languages of the State of the opening of proceedings. In addition, he may be required to provide a translation into the official language or one of the official languages of the State of the opening of proceedings.

Chapter V
Transitional and Final Provisions

4.44

43 Applicability in time

The provisions of this Regulation shall apply only to insolvency proceedings opened after its entry into force. Acts done by a debtor before the entry into force of this Regulation shall continue to be governed by the law which was applicable to them at the time they were done.

Notes

Regulation not retrospective

The EC Regulation came into force on 31 May 2002 (art 47). Art 43 makes it clear that it is not retrospective. However it would potentially apply to winding up/bankruptcy proceedings where the petition was presented before 31 May 2002, providing the order was made after that date. This was the situation in a bankruptcy context in *Geveran Trading Company Limited v*

Skjevesland [2003] BCC 209 (upheld on appeal [2003] BPIR 924); see the definition of '*the time of the opening of proceedings*' in art 2(f) and the notes thereto.

4.45

44 Relationship to Conventions

1 After its entry into force, this Regulation replaces, in respect of the matters referred to therein, in the relations between Member States, the Conventions concluded between two or more Member States, in particular:

(a) the Convention between Belgium and France on Jurisdiction and the Validity and Enforcement of Judgments, Arbitration Awards and Authentic Instruments, signed at Paris on 8 July 1899;

(b) the Convention between Belgium and Austria on Bankruptcy, Winding-up, Arrangements, Compositions and Suspension of Payments (with Additional Protocol of 13 June 1973), signed at Brussels on 16 July 1969;

(c) the Convention between Belgium and the Netherlands on Territorial Jurisdiction, Bankruptcy and the Validity and Enforcement of Judgments, Arbitration Awards and Authentic Instruments, signed at Brussels on 28 March 1925;

(d) the Treaty between Germany and Austria on Bankruptcy, Winding-up, Arrangements and Compositions, signed at Vienna on 25 May 1979;

(e) the Convention between France and Austria on Jurisdiction, Recognition and Enforcement of Judgments on Bankruptcy, signed at Vienna on 27 February 1979;

(f) the Convention between France and Italy on the Enforcement of Judgments in Civil and Commercial Matters, signed at Rome on 3 June 1930;

(g) the Convention between Italy and Austria on Bankruptcy, Winding-up, Arrangements and Compositions, signed at Rome on 12 July 1977;

(h) the Convention between the Kingdom of the Netherlands and the Federal Republic of Germany on the Mutual Recognition and Enforcement of Judgments and other Enforceable Instruments in Civil and Commercial Matters, signed at The Hague on 30 August 1962;

(i) the Convention between the United Kingdom and the Kingdom of Belgium providing for the Reciprocal Enforcement of Judgments in Civil and Commercial Matters, with Protocol, signed at Brussels on 2 May 1934;

(j) the Convention between Denmark, Finland, Norway, Sweden and Iceland on Bankruptcy, signed at Copenhagen on 7 November 1933;

(k) the European Convention on Certain International Aspects of Bankruptcy, signed at Istanbul on 5 June 1990;

[(l) the Convention between the Federative People's Republic of Yugoslavia and the Kingdome of Greece on the Mutual Recognition and Enforcement of Judgments, signed at Athens on 18 June 1959;

   (m)   the Agreement between the Federative People's Republic of Yugoslavia and the Republic of Austria on the Mutual Recognition and Enforcement of Arbitral Awards and Arbitral Settlements in Commercial Matters, signed at Belgrade on 18 March 1960;

   (n)   the Convention between the Federative People's Republic of Yugoslavia and the Republic of Italy on Mutual Judicial Cooperation in Civil and Administrative Matters, signed at Rome on 3 December 1960;

   (o)   the Agreement between the Socialist Federative People's Republic of Yugoslavia and the Kingdom of Belgium on Judicial Cooperation in Civil and Commercial Matters, signed at Belgrade on 24 September 1971

   (p)   the Convention between the Governments of Yugoslavia and France on the Recognition and Enforcement of Judgments in Civil and Commercial Matters, signed at Paris on 18 May 1971

   (q)   the Agreement between Czechoslovak Socialist Republic and the Hellenic Republic on Legal Aid in Civil and Criminal Matters, signed at Athens on 22 October 1980, still in force between the Czech Republic and Greece;

   (r)   the Agreement between the Czechoslovak Socialist Republic and the Republic of Cyprus on Legal Aid in Civil and Criminal Matters, signed at Nicosia on 23 April 1982, still in force between Czech Republic and Cyprus;

   (s)   the Treaty between the Government of the Czechoslovak Socialist Republic and the Government of the Republic of France on Legal Aid and the Recognition and Enforcement of Judgments in Civil, Family and Commercial Matters, signed at Paris on 10 May 1984, still in force between the Czech Republic and France;

   (t)   the Treaty between the Czechoslovak Socialist Republic and the Italian Republic on Legal Aid in Civil and Criminal Matters, signed at Prague on 6 December 1985, still in force between the Czech Republic and Italy; signed at Tallinn on 27 November 1998;

   (w)   the Agreement between the Republic of Lithuania and the Republic of Poland on Legal Assistance and Legal Relations in Civil, Family, Labour and Criminal Matters, signed at Warsaw on 26 January 1993.]

2. The Conventions referred to in paragraph 1 shall continue to have effect with regard to proceedings opened before the entry into force of this Regulation.

3. This Regulation shall not apply:
   (a)   in any Member State, to the extent that it is irreconcilable with the obligations arising in relation to bankruptcy from a convention concluded by that State with one or more third countries before the entry into force of this Regulation;
   (b)   in the United Kingdom of Great Britain and Northern Ireland, to the extent that is irreconcilable with the obligations arising in

> relation to bankruptcy and the winding-up of insolvent companies from any arrangements with the Commonwealth existing at the time this Regulation enters into force.

Notes

Art 44(3)(b)

Without prejudice to Commonwealth arrangements

The purpose of art 44(3)(b) is unclear. It is probably directed at IA 1986 s 426 which provides for international co-operation between insolvency courts, including those in many Commonwealth countries.

4.46

45 Amendment of the Annexes

The Council, acting by qualified majority on the initiative of one of its members or on a proposal from the Commission, may amend the Annexes.

4.47

46 Reports

No later than 1 June 2012, and every five years thereafter, the Commission shall present to the European Parliament, the Council and the Economic and Social Committee a report on the application of this Regulation. The report shall be accompanied if need be by a proposal for adaptation of this Regulation.

4.48

47 Entry into force

This Regulation shall enter into force on 31 May 2002.

This Regulation shall be binding in its entirety and directly applicable in the Member States in accordance with the Treaty establishing the European Community.

Done at Brussels, 29 May 2000.

Notes

Art 47

Thus proceedings cannot be opened for the purposes of the EC Regulation where the relevant insolvency proceeding were opened prior to 31 May 2002 *Oakley v Ultra Vehicle Design Ltd* [2006] BPIR 115.

4.49

Annex A
Insolvency proceedings referred to in Article 2(a)

BELGIË—BELGIQUE
— Het faillissement/La faillite
— Het gerechtelijk akkoord/Le concordat judiciaire
— De collectieve schuldenregeling/Le règlement collectif de dettes
— De vrijwillige vreffening/La liquidation volontaire
— De gerechteliijke vereffening/La liquidation judiciaire
— De voorlopige ontneming van beheer, bepaald in artikel 8 van de faillissementswet/Le dessaisissement provisoire, visé à l'article 8 de la loi sur les faillites

ČESKÁ REPUBLIKA
— Konkurs
— Nucené vyrovnání
— Vyrovnání

DEUTSCHLAND
— Das Konkursverfahren
— Das gerichtliche Vergleichsverfahren
— Das Gesamtvollstreckungsverfahren
— Das Insolvenzverfahren

EESTI
— Pankrotimenetlus

ΕΛΛΑΣ
— Η πτώχευση
— Η ειδική εκκαθάριση
— Η προσωρινή διαχείριση εταιρείας. Η διοίκηση και διαχείριση τωνπιστωτών
— Η υπαγωγή επιχείρησης υπό επίτροπο με σκοπό τη σύναψη συμβιβασμούμε τους πιστωτές

ESPAÑA
— Concurso

FRANCE
— Sauvegarde
— Redressement judiciaire
— Liquidation judiciaire

IRELAND
— Compulsory winding up by the court
— Bankruptcy
— The administration in bankruptcy of the estate of persons dying insolvent
— Winding-up in bankruptcy of partnerships
— Creditors' voluntary winding up (with confirmation of a Court)
— Arrangements under the control of the court which involve the vesting of all or part of the property of the debtor in the Official Assignee for realisation and distribution
— Company examinership

ITALIA
— Fallimento
— Concordato preventivo
— Liquidazione coatta amministrativa
— Amministrazione straordinaria

ΚΥΠΡΟΣ
— Υποχρεωτική εκκαθάριση από το Δικαστήριο
— Εκούσια εκκαθάριση από πιστωτές κατόπιν Δικαστικού Διατάγματος
— Εκούσια εκκαθάριση από μέλη
— Εκκαθάριση με την εποπτεία του Δικαστηρίου
— Πτώχευση κατόπιν Δικαστικού Διατάγματος
— Διαχείριση της περιουσίας προσώπων που απεβίωσαν αφερέγγυα

LATVIJA
— Bankrots
— Izlīgums
— Sanācija

LIETUVA
— įmonės restrukt rizavimo byla
— įmonės bankroto byla
— įmonės bankroto procesas ne teismo tvarka

LUXEMBOURG
— Faillite
— Gestion contrôlée
— Concordat préventif de faillite (par abandon d' actif)
— Régime spécial de liquidation du notariat

MAGYARORSZÁG
— Csódeljárás
— Felszámolási eljárás

MALTA
— Xoljiment
— Amministrazzjoni
— Stralċvolontarju mill-membri jew mill-kredituri
— Stralċmill-Qorti
— Falliment f'każ ta' negozjant

NEDERLAND
— Het faillissement
— De surséance van betaling
— De schuldsaneringsregeling natuurlijke personen

ÖSTERREICH
— Das Konkursverfahren
— Das Ausgleichsverfahren

POLSKA
— Postępowanie upadłościowe
— Postępowanie ukladowe
— Upadłość obejmująca likwidację
— Upadłość z możliwością zawarcia ukladu

PORTUGAL
— O processo de insolvência
— O processo de falência
— Os processos especiais de recuperação de empresa, ou seja:
    — A concordata
    — A reconstituição empresarial
    — A reestruturação financeira
    — A gestão controlada

SLOVENIJA
— Stečajni postopek
— Skrajšani stečajni postopek
— Postopek prisilne poravnave
— Prisilna poravnava v stečaju

SLOVENSKO
— Konkurzné konanie
— Reštrukturalizačné konanie

SUOMI/FINLAND
— Konkurssi/konkurs
— Yrityssaneeraus/företagssanering

SVERIGE
— Konkurs
— Företagsrekonstruktion

UNITED KINGDOM
— Winding up by or subject to the supervision of the court
— Creditors' voluntary winding up (with confirmation by the court)
— Administration, including appointments made by filing prescribed documents with the court
— Voluntary arrangements under insolvency legislation
— Bankruptcy or sequestration.]

4.50

Annex B
Winding up proceedings referred to in Article 2(c)

BELGIË/BELGIQUE
— Het faillissement/La faillite
— De vrijwillige vereffening/La liquidation volontaire
— De gerechtelijke vereffening/La liquidation judiciaire

ČESKÁ REPUBLIKA
— Konkurs
— Nucené vyrovnání

DEUTSCHLAND
— Das Konkursverfahren
— Das Gesamtvollstreckungsverfahren
— Das Insolvenzverfahren

EESTI
— Pankrotimenetlus

ΕΛΛΑΣ
— Η πτώχευση
— Η ειδική εκκαθάριση

ESPAÑA
— Concurso

FRANCE
— Liquidation judiciaire

IRELAND
— Compulsory winding up
— Bankruptcy
— The administration in bankruptcy of the estate of persons dying insolvent
— Winding-up in bankruptcy of partnerships
— Creditors' voluntary winding up (with confirmation of a court)
— Arrangements under the control of the court which involve the vesting of all or part of the property of the debtor in the Official Assignee for realisation and distribution

ITALIA
— Fallimento
— Liquidazione coatta amministrativa
— Concordato preventivo con cessione dei beni

ΚΥΠΡΟΣ
— Υποχρεωτική εκκαθάριση από το Δικαστήριο
— Εκκαθάριση με την εποπτεία του Δικαστηρίου
— Εκούσια εκκαθάριση από πιστωτές (με την επικύρωση του Δικαστηρίου)
— Πτώχευση
— Διαχείριση της περιουσίας προσώπων που απεβίωσαν αφερέγγυα

LATVIJA
— Bankrots

LIETUVA
— įmonės bankroto byla
— įmonės bankroto procesas ne teismo tvarka

LUXEMBOURG
— Faillite
— Régime spécial de liquidation du notariat

MAGYARORSZÁG
— Felszámolási eljárás

MALTA
— Stralċvolontarju
— Stralċmill-Qorti
— Falliment inkluż il-hruġta' mandat ta' qbid mill-Kuratur f'każ ta' negozjant fallut

NEDERLAND
— Het faillissement
— De schuldsaneringsregeling natuurlijke personen

ÖSTERREICH
— Das Konkursverfahren

POLSKA
— Postępowanie upadłościowe
— Upadłość obejmująca likwidację

PORTUGAL
— O processo de insolvência
— O processo de falência

SLOVENIJA
— Stečajni postopek
— Skrajšani stečajni postopek

SLOVENSKO
— Konkurzné konanie
— Reštrukturalizačné konanie

SUOMI/FINLAND
— Konkurssi/konkurs

SVERIGE
— Konkurs

UNITED KINGDOM
— Winding up by or subject to the supervision of the court
— Winding up through administration, including appointments made by filing prescribed documents with the court
— Creditors' voluntary winding up (with confirmation by the court)
— Bankruptcy or sequestration.]

4.51

Annex C
Liquidators referred to in Article 2(b)

BELGIË/BELGIQUE
— De curator/Le curateur
— De commissaris inzake opschorting/Le commissaire au sursis
— De schuldbemiddelaar/Le médiateur de dettes
— De vereffenaar/Le liquidateur
— De voorlopige bewindvoerder/L' administrateur provisoire

ČESKÁ REPUBLIKA
— Správce podstaty
— Předběžní správce
— Vyrovnací správce
— Zvláštní správce
— Zástupce správce

DEUTSCHLAND
— Konkursverwalter
— Vergleichsverwalter
— Sachwalter (nach der Vergleichsordnung)
— Verwalter
— Insolvenzverwalter

— Sachwalter (nach der Insolvenzordnung)
— Treuhänder
— Vorläufiger Insolvenzverwalter

EESTI
— Pankrotihaldur
— Ajutine pankrotihaldur
— Usaldusisik

ΕΛΛΑΣ
— Ο σύνδικος
— Ο προσωρινός διαχειριστής. Η διοικούσα επιτροπή των πιστωτών
— Ο ειδικός εκκαθαριστής
— Ο επίτροπος

ESPAÑA
— Administradores concursales

FRANCE
— Mandataire judiciaire
— Liquidateur
— Administrateur judiciaire
— Commissaire à l'exécution du plan

IRELAND
— Liquidator
— Official Assignee
— Trustee in bankruptcy
— Provisional Liquidator
— Examiner

ITALIA
— Curatore
— Commissario
— Liquidatore giudiziale

ΚΥΠΡΟΣ
— Εκκαθαριστής και Προσωρινός Εκκαθαριστής
— Επίσημος Παραλήπτης
— Διαχειριστής της Πτώχευσης
— Εξεταστής

LATVIJA
— Maksātnespējas procesa administrators

LIETUVA
— Bankrutuojančių įmonių administratorius
— Restruktūrizuojamų įmonių administratorius

LUXEMBOURG
— Le curateur
— Le commissaire
— Le liquidateur
— Le conseil de gérance de la section d' assainissement du notariat

MAGYARORSZÁG
— Csódeljárás
— Felszámolási eljárás

1585

MALTA
— Amministratur Proviżorju
— Riċevitur Uffiċjali
— Stralċjarju
— Manager Speċjali
— Kuraturi f'każ ta' proċeduri ta' falliment

NEDERLAND
— De curator in het faillissement
— De bewindvoerder in de surséance van betaling
— De bewindvoerder in de schuldsaneringsregeling natuurlijke personen

ÖSTERREICH
— Masseverwalter
— Ausgleichsverwalter
— Sachverwalter
— Treuhänder
— Besondere Verwalter
— Konkursgericht

POLSKA
— Syndyk
— Nadzorca sądowy
— Zarządca

PORTUGAL
— Administrador da insolvência
— Gestor judicial
— Liquidatário judicial
— Comissão de credores

SLOVENIJA
— Upravitelj prisilne poravnave
— Stečajni upravitelj
— Sodišče, pristojno za postopek prisilne poravnave
— Sodišče, pristojno za stečajni postopek

SLOVENSKO
— Predbežný správca
— Správca

SUOMI/FINLAND
— Pesänhoitaja/boförvaltare
— Selvittäjä/utredare

SVERIGE
— Förvaltare
— God man
— Rekonstruktör

UNITED KINGDOM
— Liquidator
— Supervisor of a voluntary arrangement
— Administrator
— Official Receiver
— Trustee

—   Provisional Liquidator
—   Judicial factor.]

Part Two

Company Directors Disqualification Act 1986

1986 CHAPTER 46

An Act to consolidate certain enactments relating to the disqualification of persons from being directors of companies, and from being otherwise concerned with a company's affairs

[25th July 1986]

BE IT ENACTED by the Queen's most Excellent Majesty, by and with the advice and consent of the Lords Spiritual and Temporal, and Commons, in this present Parliament assembled, and by the authority of the same, as follows:–

Notes

Introduction

Under the Company Directors Disqualification Act 1986 ('CDDA') the court has the power to disqualify a person from acting as a director of a company, a receiver of a company's property or from being concerned or taking part (in any way directly or indirectly) in the management, promotion or formation of a company for the period specified in the order without the permission of the court. The CDDA should be read together with The Insolvent Companies (Disqualification of Unfit Directors) Proceedings Rules 1987 and the Practice Direction: Directors Disqualification Proceedings (the latter is reproduced in Civil Procedure, Vol 2).

Substantial amendments were made to the CDDA by the Insolvency Act 2000, which introduced the concept of disqualification undertakings; see the notes to section 1A below. More recently, the CDDA has been amended by the Enterprise Act 2002 which introduced a new ground for disqualification where a person is a director of a company which has breached competition law.

It should be noted that the CDDA not only applies to companies incorporated under the Companies Act 1985 but under section 22(2)(b) to any 'company' which may be wound up under Part V of the Insolvency Act 1986, e g unregistered companies incorporated by private act of parliament / Royal Charter, and foreign companies carrying on business within the jurisdiction. Article 16 of the Insolvent Partnerships Order 1994 confirms that certain sections of the CDDA are applicable to insolvent partnerships wound up as unregistered companies. For the application of the CDDA to limited liability partnerships see the Limited Liability Partnership Regulations 2001 Regulation 4. For the application of the CDDA to building societies, incorporated friendly societies and NHS foundation trusts see sections 22A to 22C.

References in these notes to sections are to those of the CDDA unless otherwise stated.

Preliminary

5.1

1 Disqualification orders: general

(1) In the circumstances specified below in this Act a court may, and under [sections 6 and 9A] shall, make against a person a disqualification order, that is to say an order that [for a period specified in the order—

    (a)   he shall not be a director of a company, act as receiver of a company's property or in any way, whether directly or indirectly, be concerned or take part in the promotion, formation or management of a company unless (in each case) he has the leave of the court, and

    (b)   he shall not act as an insolvency practitioner].

(2) In each section of this Act which gives to a court power or, as the case may be, imposes on it the duty to make a disqualification order there is specified the maximum (and, in section 6, the minimum) period of disqualification which may or (as the case may be) must be imposed by means of the order [and, unless the court otherwise orders, the period of disqualification so imposed shall begin at the end of the period of 21 days beginning with the date of the order].

(3) Where a disqualification order is made against a person who is already subject to such an order [or to a disqualification undertaking], the periods specified in those orders [or, as the case may be, in the order and the undertaking] shall run concurrently.

(4) A disqualification order may be made on grounds which are or include matters other than criminal convictions, notwithstanding that the person in respect of whom it is to be made may be criminally liable in respect of those matters.

Notes

S 1(1)

The court has a discretion as to whether or not to make an order in all cases apart from where proceedings are successfully brought under sections 6 or 9A, in which case the respondent must be disqualified. The effect of a disqualification order is that a person must not act as a director of a company or act as receiver of a company's property, or in any way, whether directly or indirectly, be concerned or take part in the promotion, formation or management of a company. A person may, however, seek the leave of the court under s 17 to act as or do any of the aforesaid , although there are no circumstances in which a disqualified person may act as an insolvency practitioner.

S 1(2)

See notes to section 6(4) below on periods of disqualification.

S 1(3)

Where the person disqualified was already subject to a period of disqualification (including a criminal disqualification order), the periods of disqualification will run concurrently; see also s 1A(3).

5.2

[1A Disqualification undertakings: general]

[(1) In the circumstances specified in sections 7 and 8 the Secretary of State may accept a disqualification undertaking, that is to say an undertaking by any person that, for a period specified in the undertaking, the person—

(a) will not be a director of a company, act as receiver of a company's property or in any way, whether directly or indirectly, be concerned or take part in the promotion, formation or management of a company unless (in each case) he has the leave of a court, and

(b) will not act as an insolvency practitioner.

(2) The maximum period which may be specified in a disqualification undertaking is 15 years; and the minimum period which may be specified in a disqualification undertaking under section 7 is two years.

(3) Where a disqualification undertaking by a person who is already subject to such an undertaking or to a disqualification order is accepted, the periods specified in those undertakings or (as the case may be) the undertaking and the order shall run concurrently.

(4) In determining whether to accept a disqualification undertaking by any person, the Secretary of State may take account of matters other than criminal convictions, notwithstanding that the person may be criminally liable in respect of those matters.]

Notes

S 1A(1)

If it appears to the Secretary of State that the conditions for 'unfitness' are satisfied under either section s 6(1) or section 8(2A)(a), and he considers that it is expedient in the public interest to do so, the Secretary of State may accept a disqualification undertaking instead of pursuing court proceedings. In making that decision he must have regard to the matters in Schedule 1, in accordance with section 9(1) below.

Section 1A was inserted by the Insolvency Act 2000. Prior to the commencement of the IA 2000 on 2 April 2001, there were no provisions in the CDDA for the applicant and respondent to agree a disqualification order (and its period) by consent. In the absence of a statutory mechanism, the court developed a summary procedure whereby the parties could agree a statement of agreed (or not opposed) facts and ask the court to make a disqualification order for an agreed period or within an agreed range – this became known as the 'Carecraft Procedure'. It was held by Ferris J in *Re Carecraft Construction Limited* [1994] 1 WLR 172 that the court had to itself be satisfied that a director was unfit to be concerned in the management of a company before there was jurisdiction to make the order (and it remained for the court to decide the period of any disqualification). However, in order to be so satisfied, the court was entitled to take into account the agreement of the parties and if it concurred with the parties it could make an order on that summary procedure.

The 'Carecraft Procedure' has largely fallen into disuse since section 1A came into force in April 2001; the Secretary of State may accept an undertaking from a person not to act as a director or be concerned with the management of a company for a certain period. Indeed, undertakings may also be accepted prior to the commencement of proceedings so as to minimise costs. The effect of an undertaking is the same as an order for disqualification and the sanctions for breach are the same.

S 1A(2)

As with disqualification orders, undertakings may be given and accepted for a maximum of 15 years and where proceedings are brought under section 6, such that an undertaking is given under section 7, the minimum period is two years.

S 1A(3)

Where an undertaking is accepted by a person who is already subject to a disqualification order or undertaking, the periods of disqualification shall run concurrently.

Disqualification for general misconduct in connection with companies

5.3

2 Disqualification on conviction of indictable offence

(1) The court may make a disqualification order against a person where he is convicted of an indictable offence (whether on indictment or summarily) in connection with the promotion, formation, management[, liquidation or striking off] of a company, [with the receivership of a company's property or with his being an administrative receiver of a company].

(2) 'The court' for this purpose means—
   (a) any court having jurisdiction to wind up the company in relation to which the offence was committed, or
   (b) the court by or before which the person is convicted of the offence, or
   (c) in the case of a summary conviction in England and Wales, any other magistrates' court acting [in the same local justice] area;
and for the purposes of this section the definition of 'indictable offence' in Schedule 1 to the Interpretation Act 1978 applies for Scotland as it does for England and Wales.

(3) The maximum period of disqualification under this section is—
   (a) where the disqualification order is made by a court of summary jurisdiction, 5 years, and
   (b) in any other case, 15 years.

Notes

S 2

This gives the court the power to disqualify a person convicted of an indictable offence in connection with the promotion, formation, management, liquidation or striking off of a company or in connection with the receivership of a company's property or with being an administrative receiver of a company. Unlike sections 6 and 8 below section 2 does not only apply to directors but to 'a person' so could include other officers such as the company secretary. Where the disqualification is made by a court of summary jurisdiction the maximum period of disqualification is 5 years and in any other case 15 years. For Court of Appeal guidance on the breadth of section 2 see *R v Goodman* [1993] 2 All ER 789. Proceedings under section 2 may be brought against a person by the Secretary of State, the Official Receiver, or the liquidator or any past or present member or creditor of any company in relation to which the person has committed or is alleged to have committed an offence or other default – see section 16(2).

_____

5.4

3 Disqualification for persistent breaches of companies legislation

(1) The court may make a disqualification order against a person where it appears to it that he has been persistently in default in relation to provisions of the companies legislation requiring any return, account or other document to be filed with, delivered or sent, or notice of any matter to be given, to the registrar of companies.

(2) On an application to the court for an order to be made under this section, the fact that a person has been persistently in default in relation to such provisions as are mentioned above may (without prejudice to its proof in any other manner) be conclusively proved by showing that in the 5 years ending with the date of the application he has been adjudged guilty (whether or not on the same occasion) of three or more defaults in relation to those provisions.

(3) A person is to be treated under subsection (2) as being adjudged guilty of a default in relation to any provision of that legislation if—

    (a)   he is convicted (whether on indictment or summarily) of an offence consisting in a contravention of or failure to comply with that provision (whether on his own part or on the part of any company), or

    (b)   a default order is made against him, that is to say an order under any of the following provisions—

        (i)   [section 242(4)] of the Companies Act (order requiring delivery of company accounts),

       [(ia) section 245B of that Act (order requiring preparation of revised accounts),]

       (ii) section 713 of that Act (enforcement of company's duty to make returns),

      (iii) section 41 of the Insolvency Act (enforcement of receiver's or manager's duty to make returns), or

      (iv) section 170 of that Act (corresponding provision for liquidator in winding up),

in respect of any such contravention of or failure to comply with that provision (whether on his own part or on the part of any company).

(4) In this section 'the court' means any court having jurisdiction to wind up any of the companies in relation to which the offence or other default has been or is alleged to have been committed.

(5) The maximum period of disqualification under this section is 5 years.

_____

Notes

S 3(1)

As with section 2 above, section 3 is not restricted to directors of a company but applies to any 'person' who has been persistently in default in relation to provisions of the companies legislation. For instance the provision applies to an insolvency practitioner who has failed to file returns on behalf of a company – see *Re Arctic Engineering Ltd (No 2)* [1986] 1 WLR 686 . 'The companies legislation' means the Companies Act 1985, the Companies Consolidation (Consequential Provisions) Act 1985 and the Insolvency Act 1986 Parts I to VII and sections 411, 413, 414, 416 and 417: see section 22(7) CDDA. Section 3 is extremely broad, applying to any notice, return, account or other document to be given to, filed with, delivered or sent to the Registrar of Companies. Proceedings under section 3 may be brought against a person by the Secretary of State, the Official Receiver, or the liquidator or any past or present member or creditor of any company in relation to which the person has committed or is alleged to have committed an offence or other default – see section 16(2) below.

S 3(2)

'Persistently in default' can be conclusively proved by showing that, in the 5 years ending with the date of the application, a person been adjudged guilty of at least 3 defaults under 'the companies legislation', whether or not on the same occasion. However, persistent default may also be proved in other ways. Once persistent default is established on the facts, the court will exercise its discretion as to whether or not to make an order; disqualification is not mandatory upon proof of persistent default.

S 3(3)

A person can be shown to have been 'adjudged guilty' if he has been convicted of an offence (whether on his own part or on the part of any company) or if a default order has been made against him under the provisions set out in section 3(3)(b).

S 3(4)

An application under section 3 can only be made to the court having the jurisdiction to wind up any of the companies in relation to which the offence or default has been or is alleged to have been committed. Such an order can therefore only be obtained in civil as opposed to criminal courts.

S 3(5)

There is no minimum disqualification period, although the maximum is 5 years.

5.5

4 Disqualification for fraud, etc, in winding up

(1) The court may make a disqualification order against a person if, in the course of the winding up of a company, it appears that he—

    (a)   has been guilty of an offence for which he is liable (whether he has been convicted or not) under section 458 of the Companies Act (fraudulent trading), or

    (b)   has otherwise been guilty, while an officer or liquidator of the company [receiver of the company's property or administrative receiver of the company], of any fraud in relation to the company or of any breach of his duty as such officer, liquidator, [receiver or administrative receiver].

(2) In this section 'the court' means any court having jurisdiction to wind up any of the companies in relation to which the offence or other default has been or is alleged to have been committed; and 'officer' includes a shadow director.

> (3) The maximum period of disqualification under this section is 15 years.

Notes

S 4(1)

Section 4 will only apply where a company is being or has been wound up. This section applies not only to directors but to any 'person' who has been guilty (whether or not convicted) of fraudulent trading or otherwise guilty (while acting as an officer, liquidator, receiver or administrative receiver of a company or its property) of any fraud in relation to the company or any breach of duty. Proceedings under section 4 may be brought against a person by the Secretary of State, the Official Receiver, or by the liquidator or any past or present member or creditor of any company in relation to which the person has committed or is alleged to have committed an offence or other default – see section 16(2).

S 4(2)

An application under section 4 can only be made to the court having the jurisdiction to wind up any of the companies in relation to which the offence or default has been (or is alleged to have been) committed. Such an order can therefore only be obtained in civil as opposed to criminal courts. In this section 'officer' explicitly includes a shadow director.

S 4(3)

There is no minimum disqualification period under this section however the maximum period is 15 years.

5.6

5 Disqualification on summary conviction

(1) An offence counting for the purposes of this section is one of which a person is convicted (either on indictment or summarily) in consequence of a contravention of, or failure to comply with, any provision of the companies legislation requiring a return, account or other document to be filed with, delivered or sent, or notice of any matter to be given, to the registrar of companies (whether the contravention or failure is on the person's own part or on the part of any company).

(2) Where a person is convicted of a summary offence counting for those purposes, the court by which he is convicted (or, in England and Wales, any other magistrates' court acting [in the same local justice] area) may make a disqualification order against him if the circumstances specified in the next subsection are present.

(3) Those circumstances are that, during the 5 years ending with the date of the conviction, the person has had made against him, or has been convicted of, in total not less than 3 default orders and offences counting for the purposes of this section; and those offences may include that of which he is convicted as mentioned in subsection (2) and any other offence of which he is convicted on the same occasion.

(4) For the purposes of this section—

> (a) the definition of 'summary offence' in Schedule 1 to the Interpretation Act 1978 applies for Scotland as for England and Wales, and
>
> (b) 'default order' means the same as in section 3(3)(b).
>
> (5) The maximum period of disqualification under this section is 5 years.

Notes

S 5

This provision is similar to section 3. It provides for discretionary disqualification where, as a result of specified breaches of the companies legislation, a person is convicted of a summary offence and that person has incurred three or more default orders and convictions for such breaches within the last five years (including this and any other offence he is convicted of on the same occasion). The maximum period of disqualification under this section is 5 years.

Disqualification for unfitness

5.7

6 Duty of court to disqualify unfit directors of insolvent companies

(1) The court shall make a disqualification order against a person in any case where, on an application under this section, it is satisfied—

> (a) that he is or has been a director of a company which has at any time become insolvent (whether while he was a director or subsequently), and
>
> (b) that his conduct as a director of that company (either taken alone or taken together with his conduct as a director of any other company or companies) makes him unfit to be concerned in the management of a company.

(2) For the purposes of this section and the next, a company becomes insolvent if—

> (a) the company goes into liquidation at a time when its assets are insufficient for the payment of its debts and other liabilities and the expenses of the winding up,
>
> [(b) the company enters administration, or]
>
> (c) an administrative receiver of the company is appointed;

and references to a person's conduct as a director of any company or companies include, where that company or any of those companies has become insolvent, that person's conduct in relation to any matter connected with or arising out of the insolvency of that company.

[(3) In this section and section 7(2), 'the court' means—

> (a) where the company in question is being or has been wound up by the court, that court,
>
> (b) where the company in question is being or has been wound up voluntarily, any court which has or (as the case may be) had jurisdiction to wind it up,

[(c) where neither paragraph (a) nor (b) applies but an administrator or administrative receiver has at any time been appointed in respect of the company in question, any court which has jurisdiction to wind it up].

(3A) Sections 117 and 120 of the Insolvency Act 1986 (jurisdiction) shall apply for the purposes of subsection (3) as if the references in the definitions of 'registered office' to the presentation of the petition for winding up were references—

(a) in a case within paragraph (b) of that subsection, to the passing of the resolution for voluntary winding up,

[(b) in a case within paragraph (c) of that subsection, to the appointment of the administrator or (as the case may be) administrative receiver].

(3B) Nothing in subsection (3) invalidates any proceedings by reason of their being taken in the wrong court; and proceedings—

(a) for or in connection with a disqualification order under this section, or

(b) in connection with a disqualification undertaking accepted under section 7,

may be retained in the court in which the proceedings were commenced, although it may not be the court in which they ought to have been commenced.

(3C) In this section and section 7, 'director' includes a shadow director.]

(4) Under this section the minimum period of disqualification is 2 years, and the maximum period is 15 years.

Notes

S 6(1)

This is a ground for mandatory disqualification. It must be established that a person was a director of a company which has at any time become insolvent and further that his conduct makes him unfit to be concerned in the management of a company. Once the court is satisfied that these matters are made out it has a duty to make a disqualification order. For the purposes of establishing unfit conduct, a person's conduct as a director of any other company may be taken into account, although it is not necessary for any of these companies to have become insolvent. For matters determining unfitness see the notes to section 9 below and part 1 and 2 of Schedule 1.Only the Secretary of State for Trade and Industry or the Official Receiver may bring proceedings on the basis of section 6 – see section 7(1) below.

The ground is restricted to directors (or former directors) as opposed to other officers of a company. Pursuant to section 22(4), 'director' includes any person occupying the position of a director, by whatever name called. For the purposes of sections 6 and 7 this expressly includes a shadow director (see section 6(3C)) and the sections have equally been held to apply to *de facto* directors – see *Re Kaytech International plc* [1999] 2 BCLC 351.

S 6(2)

Section 6 can only be invoked where a company (of which the respondent has been a director) has at any time been 'insolvent'. A company is defined as being 'insolvent' where it goes into liquidation when its assets are insufficient for the payment of its debts, other liabilities and expenses of the winding up or when the company enters administration or an administrative receiver is appointed.

S 6(3)

This sets out the court where proceedings should be issued. Proceedings are not however invalidated by being issued in the wrong court: see section 6(3B).

S 6(4)

Once the court is satisfied that that a director's conduct makes him unfit to be concerned in the management of the company, it must disqualify him for a period between 2 and 15 years. The Court of Appeal has endorsed the division of the potential 15 year disqualification period into three brackets in the context of an application under section 6 – see *Re Sevenoaks Stationers (Retail) Limited* [1991] Ch 164:

(1) A top bracket for periods over 10 years which should be reserved for particularly serious cases, such as a director who has already had one period of disqualification imposed against him or cases involving fraud – see for example *The Official Receiver v Ohayon* LTL 6/09/04 (unreported elsewhere) and *Re Westminster Property Management Ltd* [2002] 1 BCLC 119;

(2) a middle bracket from 6 to 10 years for serious cases which do not merit the top bracket – see for example *Secretary of State v Amiss* [2003] EWHC 932 (Ch) [2003] 2 BCLC 206 (a case involving dishonesty by the director to the considerable benefit of the company. leading to a 9 year disqualification order); and

(3) a minimum bracket of 2 to 5 years where though the disqualification is mandatory the case is relatively not very serious – see for example *GSAR Realisations Ltd* [1993] BCLC 409 (three year disqualification for continuing to trade after the company had become insolvent. bearing in mind the director had gained no personal benefit from the conduct had suffered loss from the collapse and that the other charges would not of themselves have demonstrated unfitness).

It is of course for the trial judge to apply the principles governing the court's powers in the individual case before him; the citation of authorities as to the correct period of disqualification is generally unnecessary and inappropriate: see below, *Re Westmid Packaging Services Ltd (No 2)* [1998] 2 BCLC 646, [1998] 2 All ER 124. The length of the period of disqualification is a matter with which an appeal court will not interfere, unless it can be shown that the judge erred in principle – see *Secretary of State for Trade and Industry v McTighe (No 2)* [1996] 2 BCLC 477 and *Re Grayan Building Services Ltd* [1995] Ch 241. *Re Sevenoaks* was reviewed by Lord Woolf MR in *Re Westmid Packing Services Ltd* [1998] 2 BCLC 646, where the Court of Appeal gave the following further guidance on the approach to periods of disqualification:

(1) It is of the greatest importance that anyone who undertakes the statutory and fiduciary duties of being a company director should realise that these are inescapable personal responsibilities.

(2) the power to grant leave under section 17 is irrelevant to determining the proper period of disqualification. The fact that there is a pending application under section 17 which the court is minded to grant is no reason for the court to impose the minimum period of disqualification; that is a separate matter to be considered after the period has been fixed.

(3) as the staring point, the period of disqualification must reflect the gravity of the offence (the exercise being similar to a criminal sentencing exercise). The court will consider factors other than just the facts of the offence, since one of the primary purposes of disqualification is the protection of the public and every period of disqualification must contain deterrent elements.

(4) once the starting point has been established, mitigating factors may be taken into account to reduce the proposed period of disqualification. Again, the court is again not limited simply to consideration of the facts of the offence [as to which see the notes to section 9 below]. A wide variety of other matters may be relevant, including: the director's general professional reputation; whether he has shown himself unlikely to re-offend; his age and health; whether he has admitted the offence; his general conduct both before and after the offence; and the periods of disqualification of his co-directors that may have been ordered by other courts. A pending section 17 application is not a mitigating factor.

(5)   in fixing the period of disqualification, the court should adopt a broad brush approach and confine the evidence to that necessary for it to deal with the matter in a summary way.

5.8

7 [Disqualification order or undertaking; and reporting provisions]

(1) If it appears to the Secretary of State that it is expedient in the public interest that a disqualification order under section 6 should be made against any person, an application for the making of such an order against that person may be made—

(a)   by the Secretary of State, or

(b)   if the Secretary of State so directs in the case of a person who is or has been a director of a company which is being [or has been] wound up by the court in England and Wales, by the official receiver.

(2) Except with the leave of the court, an application for the making under that section of a disqualification order against any person shall not be made after the end of the period of 2 years beginning with the day on which the company of which that person is or has been a director became insolvent.

[(2A) If it appears to the Secretary of State that the conditions mentioned in section 6(1) are satisfied as respects any person who has offered to give him a disqualification undertaking, he may accept the undertaking if it appears to him that it is expedient in the public interest that he should do so (instead of applying, or proceeding with an application, for a disqualification order).]

(3) If it appears to the office-holder responsible under this section, that is to say—

(a)   in the case of a company which is being wound up by the court in England and Wales, the official receiver,

(b)   in the case of a company which is being wound up otherwise, the liquidator,

[(c)   in the case of a company which is in administration, the administrator, or]

(d)   in the case of a company of which there is an administrative receiver, that receiver,

that the conditions mentioned in section 6(1) are satisfied as respects a person who is or has been a director of that company, the office-holder shall forthwith report the matter to the Secretary of State.

(4) The Secretary of State or the official receiver may require the liquidator, administrator or administrative receiver of a company, or the former liquidator, administrator or administrative receiver of a company—

(a)   to furnish him with such information with respect to any person's conduct as a director of the company, and

(b)   to produce and permit inspection of such books, papers and other records relevant to that person's conduct as such a director,

> as the Secretary of State or the official receiver may reasonably require for the purpose of determining whether to exercise, or of exercising, any function of his under this section.

Notes

S 7(1)

This prescribes the circumstances in which an application based on section 6 may be made. Applications for disqualification under section 6 can only be made by the Secretary of State for Trade and Industry, or if the Secretary of State directs in the case of a company in compulsory liquidation, by the Official Receiver. Official Receivers and Deputy Official Receivers have rights of audience to appear on applications whether brought by themselves or the Secretary of State, and whether in the High Court or the County Court.

S 7(2)

Disqualification proceedings under section 6 should be commenced within two years of the company becoming 'insolvent', as defined by section 6(2). Failing that, an application must be made for leave to bring the proceedings .The procedure for such an application is contained in Part 3 of the Practice Direction: Directors Disqualification Proceedings (see Civil Procedure, Vol 2). The applicant must demonstrate a good reason for the necessary extension of time and to that end the court will consider: the length of delay; the reasons for the delay; the strength of the case against the director; and the degree of prejudice caused to him by the delay: *Re Polly Peck International plc (No 2)* [1994] 1 BCLC 574.

S 7(2A)

The Secretary of State may accept a disqualification undertaking under section 6 if it appears to him that the conditions in section 6(1) are satisfied and that it is expedient in the public interest that he should do so, rather than proceeding with the application for a disqualification order – see the notes to section 1A CDDA above and section 9(1A) below.

S 7(3)

Subsection (3) imposes a mandatory reporting obligation on office-holders (whether the liquidator, official receiver, administrator or administrative receiver of a company – but not, it seems, the supervisor of a voluntary arrangements) to report a director to the Secretary of State if it appears to the office-holder that the conditions in section 6(1) are fulfilled. The Official Receiver will make the report in the case of a company in compulsory liquidation. Otherwise the Insolvent Companies (Reports on Conduct of Directors) Rules 1986 apply, and require a return (or if applicable a report) in respect of every director within 6 months of taking office. This reporting procedure is crucial to the Secretary of State acquiring knowledge in order to decide whether to bring proceedings, hence its mandatory nature.

S 7(4)

This subsection gives the Secretary of State and Official Receiver the power to demand, from-office holders (or former office-holders) of a company, information regarding the conduct of any person as a director of that company and the production and inspection of books, papers and other records which they may reasonably require for the purposes of deciding whether to exercise or in exercising his functions under this section. For the procedure on applications under section 7(4), see paragraphs 18 – 19 of the Practice Direction: Directors Disqualification Proceedings (see Civil Procedure, Vol 2). In relation to the power of the Official Receiver to make an application under the Insolvency Act 1986 s 236 for the purposes of obtaining evidence for disqualification proceedings see *Re Pantmaenog Timber Co Ltd* [2003] UKHL 49, [2004] 1 AC 158. The liquidator (or the Official Receiver) is not precluded from invoking the court's wide powers of inquiry under section 236 Insolvency Act 1986 in order to comply with a request made of him under section 7(4) or solely to obtain evidence for use in disqualification proceedings: see *Re Pantmaenog Timber Co Ltd* [2003] UKHL 49, [2004] 1 AC 158.

———

5.9

8 Disqualification after investigation of company

[(1) If it appears to the Secretary of State from investigative material that it is expedient in the public interest that a disqualification order should be made against a person who is, or has been, a director or shadow director of a company, he may apply to the court for such an order.

(1A) 'Investigative material' means—
   (a)   a report made by inspectors under—
         (i)   section 437 of the Companies Act 1985;
         (ii) section 167, 168, 169 or 284 of the Financial Services and Markets Act 2000; or
         (iii) where the company is an open-ended investment company (within the meaning of that Act) regulations made as a result of section 262(2)(k) of that Act; and
   (b)   information or documents obtained under—
         (i)   section 447[, 448 or 453A] of the Companies Act 1985;
         (ii) section 2 of the Criminal Justice Act 1987;
         (iii) section 28 of the Criminal Law (Consolidation) (Scotland) Act 1995;
         (iv) section 83 of the Companies Act 1989; or
         (v)   section 165, 171, 172, 173 or 175 of the Financial Services and Markets Act 2000.]

(2) The court may make a disqualification order against a person where, on an application under this section, it is satisfied that his conduct in relation to the company makes him unfit to be concerned in the management of a company.

[(2A) Where it appears to the Secretary of State from such report, information or documents that, in the case of a person who has offered to give him a disqualification undertaking—
   (a)   the conduct of the person in relation to a company of which the person is or has been a director or shadow director makes him unfit to be concerned in the management of a company, and
   (b)   it is expedient in the public interest that he should accept the undertaking (instead of applying, or proceeding with an application, for a disqualification order),
he may accept the undertaking.]

(3) In this section 'the court' means the High Court or, in Scotland, the Court of Session.

(4) The maximum period of disqualification under this section is 15 years.

Notes

S 8

Proceedings under section 8 may only be brought by the Secretary of State for Trade and Industry. Unlike section 6 proceedings, disqualification is discretionary and follows a two stage process the court must first make a finding of unfitness and then exercise its discretion as to whether or not to disqualify. Furthermore section 8 proceedings are not limited to companies which have become insolvent. For matters determining unfitness see section 9 and Part 1 of Schedule 1. Section 8 was amended by the Insolvency Act 2000 to provide for disqualification undertakings to be given: see the notes to section 1A(1) above.

5.10

[8A Variation etc of disqualification undertaking]

[(1) The court may, on the application of a person who is subject to a disqualification undertaking—
 (a) reduce the period for which the undertaking is to be in force, or
 (b) provide for it to cease to be in force.

(2) On the hearing of an application under subsection (1), the Secretary of State shall appear and call the attention of the court to any matters which seem to him to be relevant, and may himself give evidence or call witnesses.

[(2A) Subsection (2) does not apply to an application in the case of an undertaking given under section 9B, and in such a case on the hearing of the application whichever of the OFT or a specified regulator (within the meaning of section 9E) accepted the undertaking—
 (a) must appear and call the attention of the court to any matters which appear to it or him (as the case may be) to be relevant;
 (b) may give evidence or call witnesses.]

[(3) In this section 'the court'—
 (a) in the case of an undertaking given under section 9B means the High Court or (in Scotland) the Court of Session;
 (b) in any other case has the same meaning as in section 7(2) or 8 (as the case may be).]]

Notes

S 8A

By section 8A the court retains a degree of control over the undertaking procedure. On the respondent's application, the court can reduce or completely remove the period of disqualification *Re INS Realisations Ltd* [2006] BCC 307.

5.11

9 Matters for determining unfitness of directors

(1) Where it falls to a court to determine whether a person's conduct as a director ... of any particular company or companies makes him unfit to be concerned in the management of a company, the court shall, as respects his conduct as a director of that company or, as the case may be, each of those companies, have regard in particular—
  (a) to the matters mentioned in Part I of Schedule 1 to this Act, and
  (b) where the company has become insolvent, to the matters mentioned in Part II of that Schedule;
and references in that Schedule to the director and the company are to be read accordingly.

[(1A) In determining whether he may accept a disqualification undertaking from any person the Secretary of State shall, as respects the person's conduct as a director of any company concerned, have regard in particular—
  (a) to the matters mentioned in Part I of Schedule 1 to this Act, and
  (b) where the company has become insolvent, to the matters mentioned in Part II of that Schedule;
and references in that Schedule to the director and the company are to be read accordingly.]

(2) Section 6(2) applies for the purposes of this section and Schedule 1 as it applies for the purposes of sections 6 and 7 [and in this section and that Schedule 'director' includes a shadow director].

(3) Subject to the next subsection, any reference in Schedule 1 to an enactment contained in the Companies Act or the Insolvency Act includes, in relation to any time before the coming into force of that enactment, the corresponding enactment in force at that time.

(4) The Secretary of State may by order modify any of the provisions of Schedule 1; and such an order may contain such transitional provisions as may appear to the Secretary of State necessary or expedient.

(5) The power to make orders under this section is exercisable by statutory instrument subject to annulment in pursuance of a resolution of either House of Parliament.

Notes

S 9

The court must be satisfied that a director's conduct makes him unfit to be involved in the management of a company. The matters to which the court must have particular regard when considering the question of unfitness are those set out in Schedule 1. Part 1 of the Schedule applies in all cases (whether or not that company has become insolvent) and includes matters such as: any misfeasance or breach of duty by the director; and the extent of his responsibility for the company's failure to comply with accounting, filing and record-keeping obligations under the Companies Act 1985. Part 2 applies when a company has become insolvent, and includes matters such as: the director's responsibility for the company's insolvency; his responsibility for the company entering into transactions at an undervalue or preferences; and any failure to co-operate with an office holder.

The list in Schedule 1 is not exhaustive and the court may take other matters into account. Common grounds for a finding of unfitness include: insolvent trading; a failure to keep proper books, records and accounts (see *Re Bath Glass Ltd* [1988] BCLC 329, *Re Promwalk Services* [2002] EWHC 2688 (Ch), [2003] 2 BCLC 305); trading through a succession of failed companies including the use of phoenix companies (see *Re Swift 736 Ltd* [1993] BCC 312); and discrimination between creditors. The respondent's conduct as a director can also include his conduct in the disqualification proceedings themselves: see *Reynard v Secretary of State* [2002] EWCA Civ 497, [2002] 2 BCLC 625, where the court took account of the director's deceitful conduct in the witness box.

Crown debts

Crown debts are not in a special class; the failure to pay HM Revenue and Customs (in respect of VAT or other tax liabilities, including PAYE and NI) is not a matter included in the Schedule as something to which the court must have particular regard. The fact that the unpaid creditor is the Crown does not, without more, mean that the failure can automatically be treated as evidence of unfitness; rather the court must examine the significance of non-payment in each case. If there was a deliberate policy of failing to pay creditors who were not pressing for payment, such as the Crown (which faces obvious administrative difficulties in this regard), despite knowing that the company lacked sufficient reserves to discharge those debts, any continuing trade by the company will be at the risk of those creditors, and this can commonly amount to unfitness. Such a policy can also be characterised as unfair discrimination between creditors. A prolonged period of deliberately not paying crown debts may amount to unfitness on this basis, whether or not other grounds are made out. For cases on this issue, see: *Re Bath Glass* [1988] BCLC 329; *Re Sevenoaks Stationers (Retail) Ltd* [1991] Ch 164; *Re GSAR Realisations Ltd* [1993] BCLC 409; *Re Verby Print for Advertising Ltd* [1998] 2 BCLC 23; *Re Structural Concrete Ltd* [2001] BCC 578; *Secretary of State v Lewis* [2003] BCC 611; but cf *Official Receiver v Dhaliwall [2006] 1 BCLC 285*.

Commercial Misjudgement

Commercial misjudgement does not (by itself) make a person unfit to be concerned in the management of a company: *Re McNulty's Interchange Ltd* [1989] BCLC 709; there must have been culpability, whether by a sufficient degree of incompetence or some breach of commercial morality, which was serious enough to merit disqualification. The court must consider the evidence and decide whether, viewed cumulatively, the respondent has fallen below the appropriate standards of competence. It is not necessary to show that the director is unfit for *any* management role in a company; it will suffice if the conduct displayed in his actual or specific role shows him to be unfit. Nor is a finding of a breach of duty necessary or indeed sufficient for a finding of unfitness: see also *Re Barings Plc (No 5)* [2000] 1 BCLC 523.

Passive directors

A director has a duty to concern himself with the affairs of a company. It is no defence for a director to say that he was a director in name only and was not concerned with the day to day running of the company or indeed with the company's general financial state. Nor can a director rely on his ignorance of accountancy or delegation of those functions to others or the collective responsibility of directors as a defence to unfitness; a director is expected to have a prudent businessman's sense of reality: see *Re Queens Moat Houses Plc* [2004] EWHC 1730 (Ch), [2005] 1 BCLC 136 (cf *Re Northstar Multimedia Ltd* LTL 19/07/2001 where a director, who concentrated on the sales side of the business and was unaware of the company's financial difficulties, escaped disqualification).

Mitigating factors

The following factors may be taken into consideration by the court in determining the period of disqualification: lack of dishonesty (*Re Burnham Marketing Services Ltd* [1993] BCC 518); loss of the director's own money in the company and the absence of personal gain or excessive remuneration (*Re GSAR Realisations Ltd* [1993] BCLC 409); reliance on professional advice provided that it is reasonable to do so (see *Re Bradcrown Ltd* [2001] 1 BCLC 547; *Secretary of*

State v Lewis [2003] BCC 611); and the director's efforts to retrieve the situation (*Re Burnham Marketing Services Ltd* above; *Re Uno Plc & World of Leather Plc* [2006] BCC 725.

_____

[Disqualification for competition infringements]

5.12

[9A Competition disqualification order]

[(1) The court must make a disqualification order against a person if the following two conditions are satisfied in relation to him.

(2) The first condition is that an undertaking which is a company of which he is a director commits a breach of competition law.

(3) The second condition is that the court considers that his conduct as a director makes him unfit to be concerned in the management of a company.

(4) An undertaking commits a breach of competition law if it engages in conduct which infringes any of the following—
   (a)   the Chapter 1 prohibition (within the meaning of the Competition Act 1998) (prohibition on agreements, etc preventing, restricting or distorting competition);
   (b)   the Chapter 2 prohibition (within the meaning of that Act) (prohibition on abuse of a dominant position);
   (c)   Article 81 of the Treaty establishing the European Community (prohibition on agreements, etc preventing, restricting or distorting competition);
   (d)   Article 82 of that Treaty (prohibition on abuse of a dominant position).

(5) For the purpose of deciding under subsection (3) whether a person is unfit to be concerned in the management of a company the court—
   (a)   must have regard to whether subsection (6) applies to him;
   (b)   may have regard to his conduct as a director of a company in connection with any other breach of competition law;
   (c)   must not have regard to the matters mentioned in Schedule 1.

(6) This subsection applies to a person if as a director of the company—
   (a)   his conduct contributed to the breach of competition law mentioned in subsection (2);
   (b)   his conduct did not contribute to the breach but he had reasonable grounds to suspect that the conduct of the undertaking constituted the breach and he took no steps to prevent it;
   (c)   he did not know but ought to have known that the conduct of the undertaking constituted the breach

(7) For the purposes of subsection (6)(a) it is immaterial whether the person knew that the conduct of the undertaking constituted the breach.

(8) For the purposes of subsection (4)(a) or (c) references to the conduct of an undertaking are references to its conduct taken with the conduct of one or more other undertakings.

(9) The maximum period of disqualification under this section is 15 years.

(10) An application under this section for a disqualification order may be made by the OFT or by a specified regulator.

(11) Section 60 of the Competition Act 1998 (c 41) (consistent treatment of questions arising under United Kingdom and Community law) applies in relation to any question arising by virtue of subsection (4)(a) or (b) above as it applies in relation to any question arising under Part 1 of that Act.]

[9B Competition undertakings]

[(1) This section applies if—
  (a) the OFT or a specified regulator thinks that in relation to any person an undertaking which is a company of which he is a director has committed or is committing a breach of competition law,
  (b) the OFT or the specified regulator thinks that the conduct of the person as a director makes him unfit to be concerned in the management of a company, and
  (c) the person offers to give the OFT or the specified regulator (as the case may be) a disqualification undertaking.

(2) The OFT or the specified regulator (as the case may be) may accept a disqualification undertaking from the person instead of applying for or proceeding with an application for a disqualification order.

(3) A disqualification undertaking is an undertaking by a person that for the period specified in the undertaking he will not—
  (a) be a director of a company;
  (b) act as receiver of a company's property;
  (c) in any way, whether directly or indirectly, be concerned or take part in the promotion, formation or management of a company;
  (d) act as an insolvency practitioner.

(4) But a disqualification undertaking may provide that a prohibition falling within subsection (3)(a) to (c) does not apply if the person obtains the leave of the court.

(5) The maximum period which may be specified in a disqualification undertaking is 15 years.

(6) If a disqualification undertaking is accepted from a person who is already subject to a disqualification undertaking under this Act or to a disqualification order the periods specified in those undertakings or the undertaking and the order (as the case may be) run concurrently.

(7) Subsections (4) to (8) of section 9A apply for the purposes of this section as they apply for the purposes of that section but in the application of subsection (5) of that section the reference to the court must be construed as a reference to the OFT or a specified regulator (as the case may be).]

[9C Competition investigations]

[(1) If the OFT or a specified regulator has reasonable grounds for suspecting that a breach of competition law has occurred it or he (as the case may be) may carry out an investigation for the purpose of deciding whether to make an application under section 9A for a disqualification order.

(2) For the purposes of such an investigation sections 26 to 30 of the Competition Act 1998 (c 41) apply to the OFT and the specified regulators as they apply to the OFT for the purposes of an investigation under section 25 of that Act.

(3) Subsection (4) applies if as a result of an investigation under this section the OFT or a specified regulator proposes to apply under section 9A for a disqualification order.

(4) Before making the application the OFT or regulator (as the case may be) must—

(a) give notice to the person likely to be affected by the application, and

(b) give that person an opportunity to make representations.]

[9D Co-ordination]

[(1) The Secretary of State may make regulations for the purpose of co-ordinating the performance of functions under sections 9A to 9C (relevant functions) which are exercisable concurrently by two or more persons.

(2) Section 54(5) to (7) of the Competition Act 1998 (c 41) applies to regulations made under this section as it applies to regulations made under that section and for that purpose in that section—

(a) references to Part 1 functions must be read as references to relevant functions;

(b) references to a regulator must be read as references to a specified regulator;

(c) a competent person also includes any of the specified regulators.

(3) The power to make regulations under this section must be exercised by statutory instrument subject to annulment in pursuance of a resolution of either House of Parliament.

(4) Such a statutory instrument may—

(a) contain such incidental, supplemental, consequential and transitional provision as the Secretary of State thinks appropriate;

(b) make different provision for different cases.]

[9E Interpretation]

[(1) This section applies for the purposes of sections 9A to 9D.

(2) Each of the following is a specified regulator for the purposes of a breach of competition law in relation to a matter in respect of which he or it has a function—

[(a) the Office of Communications;]

(b) the Gas and Electricity Markets Authority;

(c) *the Director General of Water Services;*

[(c) the Water Services Regulation Authority;]

(d) [the Office of Rail Regulation];

(e) the Civil Aviation Authority.

(3) The court is the High Court or (in Scotland) the Court of Session.

(4) Conduct includes omission.

(5) Director includes shadow director.]

———

Notes

SS 9A-9E

Sections 9A to 9E relate to competition infringements and are outside the ambit of this work, although it should be noted that proceedings under section 9A may only be brought by the Office of Fair Trading or by specified regulators.

———

Other cases of disqualification

5.13

10 Participation in wrongful trading

(1) Where the court makes a declaration under section 213 or 214 of the Insolvency Act that a person is liable to make a contribution to a company's assets, then, whether or not an application for such an order is made by any person, the court may, if it thinks fit, also make a disqualification order against the person to whom the declaration relates.

(2) The maximum period of disqualification under this section is 15 years.

———

Notes

S 10

This section permits the court to make a disqualification order of its own motion where it finds a person liable for fraudulent trading (under section 213 IA 1986) or wrongful trading (under section 214 IA 1986) and declares him personally liable to contribute to the company's assets. The liquidator who brought the application under section 213 or 214 may also apply for a disqualification order. There is no minimum period of disqualification but a maximum period of 15 years.

———

5.14

11 Undischarged bankrupts

[(1) It is an offence for a person to act as director of a company or directly or indirectly to take part in or be concerned in the promotion, formation or management of a company, without the leave of the court, at a time when—

    (a)   he is an undischarged bankrupt, or

    (b)   a bankruptcy restrictions order is in force in respect of him.]

(2) 'The court' for this purpose is the court by which the person was adjudged bankrupt or, in Scotland, sequestration of his estates was awarded.

(3) In England and Wales, the leave of the court shall not be given unless notice of intention to apply for it has been served on the official receiver; and it is the latter's duty, if he is of opinion that it is contrary to the public interest that the application should be granted, to attend on the hearing of the application and oppose it.

Notes

S 11

This provision prohibits an undischarged bankrupt from acting as a director of a company or from otherwise being involved with its promotion, formation or management *Hill v Secretary of State for the Environment, Food and Naval Affairs* [2006] 1 BCLC 601. The prohibition is automatic upon a bankruptcy order being made and applies equally to a person against whom a bankruptcy restriction order is in force or a person who has given a bankruptcy restriction undertaking.

5.15

12 Failure to pay under county court administration order

(1) The following has effect where a court under section 429 of the Insolvency Act revokes an administration order under Part VI of the County Courts Act 1984.

(2) A person to whom that section applies by virtue of the order under section 429(2)(b) shall not, except with the leave of the court which made the order, act as director or liquidator of, or directly or indirectly take part or be concerned in the promotion, formation or management of, a company.

[12A Northern Irish disqualification orders]

[A person subject to a disqualification order under Part II of the Companies (Northern Ireland) Order 1989—
  (a)   shall not be a director of a company, act as receiver of a company's property or in any way, whether directly or indirectly, be concerned or take part in the promotion, formation or management of a company unless (in each case) he has the leave of the High Court of Northern Ireland, and
  (b)   shall not act as an insolvency practitioner.]

[12B Northern Irish disqualification undertakings]

[A person subject to a disqualification undertaking under the Company Directors Disqualification (Northern Ireland) Order 2002—
  (a)   shall not be a director of a company, act as receiver of a company's property or in any way, whether directly or indirectly, be concerned or take part in the promotion, formation or management of a company unless (in each case) he has the leave of the High Court of Northern Ireland, and
  (b)   shall not act as an insolvency practitioner.]

Consequences of contravention

5.16

13 Criminal penalties

(1) If a person acts in contravention of a disqualification order or [disqualification undertaking or in contravention] of section 12(2)[, 12A or 12B], or is guilty of an offence under section 11, he is liable—
- (a) on conviction on indictment, to imprisonment for not more than 2 years or a fine, or both; and
- (b) on summary conviction, to imprisonment for not more than 6 months or a fine not exceeding the statutory maximum, or both.

14 Offences by body corporate

(1) Where a body corporate is guilty of an offence of acting in contravention of a disqualification order [or disqualification undertaking or in contravention of section 12A] [or 12B], and it is proved that the offence occurred with the consent or connivance of, or was attributable to any neglect on the part of any director, manager, secretary or other similar officer of the body corporate, or any person who was purporting to act in any such capacity he, as well as the body corporate, is guilty of the offence and liable to be proceeded against and punished accordingly.

(2) Where the affairs of a body corporate are managed by its members, subsection (1) applies in relation to the acts and defaults of a member in connection with his functions of management as if he were a director of the body corporate.

15 Personal liability for company's debts where person acts while disqualified

(1) A person is personally responsible for all the relevant debts of a company if at any time—
- (a) in contravention of a disqualification order or [disqualification undertaking or in contravention] of section 11[, 12A or 12B] of this Act he is involved in the management of the company, or
- (b) as a person who is involved in the management of the company, he acts or is willing to act on instructions given without the leave of the court by a person whom he knows at that time to be the subject of a disqualification order [or disqualification undertaking or a disqualification order under Part II of the Companies (Northern Ireland) Order 1989] [or disqualification undertaking under the Company Directors Disqualification (Northern Ireland) Order 2002] or to be an undischarged bankrupt.

(2) Where a person is personally responsible under this section for the relevant debts of a company, he is jointly and severally liable in respect of those debts with the company and any other person who, whether under this section or otherwise, is so liable.

(3) For the purposes of this section the relevant debts of a company are—
- (a) in relation to a person who is personally responsible under paragraph (a) of subsection (1), such debts and other liabilities of the company as are incurred at a time when that person was involved in the management of the company, and

> (b) in relation to a person who is personally responsible under paragraph (b) of that subsection, such debts and other liabilities of the company as are incurred at a time when that person was acting or was willing to act on instructions given as mentioned in that paragraph.
>
> (4) For the purposes of this section, a person is involved in the management of a company if he is a director of the company or if he is concerned, whether directly or indirectly, or takes part, in the management of the company.
>
> (5) For the purposes of this section a person who, as a person involved in the management of a company, has at any time acted on instructions given without the leave of the court by a person whom he knew at that time to be the subject of a disqualification order [or disqualification undertaking or a disqualification order under Part II of the Companies (Northern Ireland) Order 1989] [or disqualification undertaking under the Company Directors Disqualification (Northern Ireland) Order 2002] or to be an undischarged bankrupt is presumed, unless the contrary is shown, to have been willing at any time thereafter to act on any instructions given by that person.

Notes

S 15

In addition to the criminal liability set out in section 13 above, a person who contravenes a disqualification order or undertaking (or an undischarged bankrupt who acts in contravention of section 11) incurs a civil liability for all the 'relevant debts' of the company. A liability for company debts is also imposed on anyone involved in the management of the company who acts or is willing to act on instructions from a person whom he knows at that time to be the subject of a disqualification order or undertaking, unless the person disqualified has obtained leave from the court to act under section 17. In relation to a person who acts in breach of his own disqualification (or an undischarged bankrupt who acts in breach of section 11), 'relevant debts' are defined as such debts and other liabilities of the company as are incurred at a time when that person was involved in the management of the company. In relation to a person who acts on the instructions of a disqualified person within subsection 1(b), the 'relevant debts' will be those incurred at a time when that person was acting or was willing to act on the such instructions.

Liability under this section is joint and several with the company and any other person who is liable under this section or otherwise. The creditor may claim the whole amount of its debt from either the company or the disqualified person. The company itself (ie the liquidator) can claim a contribution from the director by virtue of his joint and several liability, but section 15 does not enable the liquidator to claim the relevant debts directly from the director: *Re Prestige Grindings* [2006] BCC 421; *IRC v McEntaggart* [2006] BCLC 476. A director cannot plead relief under section 727 Companies Act 1985 in an action brought against him under section 15 for recovery of the debt: *IRC v McEntaggart* (above).

Supplementary provisions

S.17

16 Application for disqualification order

(1) A person intending to apply for the making of a disqualification order by the court having jurisdiction to wind up a company shall give not less

than 10 days' notice of his intention to the person against whom the order is sought; and on the hearing of the application the last-mentioned person may appear and himself give evidence or call witnesses.

(2) An application to a court with jurisdiction to wind up companies for the making against any person of a disqualification order under any of sections 2 to [4] may be made by the Secretary of State or the official receiver, or by the liquidator or any past or present member or creditor of any company in relation to which that person has committed or is alleged to have committed an offence or other default.

(3) On the hearing of any application under this Act made by [a person falling within subsection (4)], the applicant shall appear and call the attention of the court to any matters which seem to him to be relevant, and may himself give evidence or call witnesses.

[(4) The following fall within this subsection—
    (a)   the Secretary of State;
    (b)   the official receiver;
    (c)   the OFT;
    (d)   the liquidator;
    (e)   a specified regulator (within the meaning of section 9E).]

Notes

S 16

Prior to the issue of proceedings a 'section 16 letter' or notice must be sent to the person against whom a disqualification order is sought. Such a letter is a letter before action *Re City Truck Group Ltd* [2006] BCC 384.Unlike applications under sections 7 and 8, applications under sections 2 to 4 may be brought not only by the Secretary of State or Official Receiver but also by the liquidator or any past or present member or creditor of a company, being any company in relation to which that person has committed or is alleged to have committed an offence or other default.

5.18

[17 Application for leave under an order or undertaking]

[(1) Where a person is subject to a disqualification order made by a court having jurisdiction to wind up companies, any application for leave for the purposes of section 1(1)(a) shall be made to that court.

(2) Where—
    (a)   a person is subject to a disqualification order made under section 2 by a court other than a court having jurisdiction to wind up companies, or
    (b)   a person is subject to a disqualification order made under section 5,
any application for leave for the purposes of section 1(1)(a) shall be made to any court which, when the order was made, had jurisdiction to wind up the company (or, if there is more than one such company, any of the companies) to which the offence (or any of the offences) in question related.

(3) Where a person is subject to a disqualification undertaking accepted at any time under section 7 or 8, any application for leave for the purposes of section 1A(1)(a) shall be made to any court to which, if the Secretary of State had applied for a disqualification order under the section in question at that time, his application could have been made.

[(3A) Where a person is subject to a disqualification undertaking accepted at any time under section 9B any application for leave for the purposes of section 9B(4) must be made to the High Court or (in Scotland) the Court of Session.]

(4) But where a person is subject to two or more disqualification orders or undertakings (or to one or more disqualification orders and to one or more disqualification undertakings), any application for leave for the purposes of section 1(1)(a)[, 1A(1)(a) or 9B(4)] shall be made to any court to which any such application relating to the latest order to be made, or undertaking to be accepted, could be made.

(5) On the hearing of an application for leave for the purposes of section 1(1)(a) or 1A(1)(a), the Secretary of State shall appear and call the attention of the court to any matters which seem to him to be relevant, and may himself give evidence or call witnesses.]

[(6) Subsection (5) does not apply to an application for leave for the purposes of section 1(1)(a) if the application for the disqualification order was made under section 9A.

(7) In such a case and in the case of an application for leave for the purposes of section 9B(4) on the hearing of the application whichever of the OFT or a specified regulator (within the meaning of section 9E) applied for the order or accepted the undertaking (as the case may be)—
   (a) must appear and draw the attention of the court to any matters which appear to it or him (as the case may be) to be relevant;
   (b) may give evidence or call witnesses.]

Notes

S 17

There is no guidance within section 17 itself as to what matters the court should take into account on an application for leave to act, but the court must be satisfied both: (1) that there is a need for leave to be granted; and more importantly (2) that the public would be adequately protected if permission to act were given: *Re Gibson Davies Ltd* [1995] BCC 11 and see also *Re Tech Textiles Ltd* [1998] 1 BCLC 259. As to the first point both the needs of the individual respondent and those of the company can be considered – in some cases the involvement of the applicant may be vital to customer or investor confidence. As to the issue of public protection the court has power to grant leave on a conditional basis and may allow him to act if he agrees to comply with certain safeguards such as requiring that no cheque shall be signed on behalf of the company by him alone and that the company institutes a system for producing regular financial information. In *Re Tech Textiles Ltd.* Arden J. said that the court must look at: the grounds on which unfitness was found (in particular if they involved misappropriation of assets or knowing breach of duty); the applicant's character; and whether there was a potential for the matters giving rise to his disqualification to recur. The director's previous career and any other disqualifications would also be relevant. The 'public' for these purposes would include shareholders, employees, lenders, customers and other creditors, therefore it was necessary to consider the particular nature and size of the company and its business.

The fact that a person has applied for leave under section 17 is irrelevant to the exercise of determining the length of any disqualification: see *Re Westmid Packaging Services Ltd (No 2)* [1998] 2 BCLC 646 and the notes to section 6 above. As to whether granting leave under section 17 undermines the disqualification procedure see *Re Tech Textiles Ltd* (above) and *Re TLL Realisations Ltd* [2000] BCC 998 in relation to section 17 applications generally see.

The procedure under section 17 is dealt with generally in Part 4 of the Practice Direction: Directors Disqualification Proceedings (Civil Procedure, Vol 2). The Court of Appeal has stated that it is desirable that applications for permission to act are made at the hearing of the disqualification proceedings: *Re TLL Realisations Ltd* [2000] BCC 998. The director should also provide clear evidence as to the precise role he intends to play in the company and up-to-date information about the company.

5.19

18 [Register of disqualification orders and undertakings]

(1) The Secretary of State may make regulations requiring officers of courts to furnish him with such particulars as the regulations may specify of cases in which—

(a) a disqualification order is made, or

(b) any action is taken by a court in consequence of which such an order [or a disqualification undertaking] is varied or ceases to be in force, or

(c) leave is granted by a court for a person subject to such an order to do any thing which otherwise the order prohibits him from doing[, or

(d) leave is granted by a court for a person subject to such an undertaking to do anything which otherwise the undertaking prohibits him from doing];

and the regulations may specify the time within which, and the form and manner in which, such particulars are to be furnished.

(2) The Secretary of State shall, from the particulars so furnished, continue to maintain the register of orders, and of cases in which leave has been granted as mentioned in subsection (1)(c), which was set up by him under section 29 of the Companies Act 1976 and continued under section 301 of the Companies Act 1985.

[(2A) The Secretary of State must include in the register such particulars as he considers appropriate of—

(a) disqualification undertakings accepted by him under section 7 or 8;

(b) disqualification undertakings accepted by the OFT or a specified regulator under section 9B;

(c) cases in which leave has been granted as mentioned in subsection (1)(d).]

(3) When an order [or undertaking] of which entry is made in the register ceases to be in force, the Secretary of State shall delete the entry from the register and all particulars relating to it which have been furnished to him under this section or any previous corresponding provision [and, in the case of a disqualification undertaking, any other particulars he has included in the register].

(4) The register shall be open to inspection on payment of such fee as may be specified by the Secretary of State in regulations.

[(4A) Regulations under this section may extend the preceding provisions of this section, to such extent and with such modifications as may be specified in the regulations, to disqualification orders made under Part II of the Companies (Northern Ireland) Order 1989] [or disqualification undertakings made under the Company Directors Disqualification (Northern Ireland) Order 2002].

(5) Regulations under this section shall be made by statutory instrument subject to annulment in pursuance of a resolution of either House of Parliament.

Notes

S 18

Following the making of a disqualification order or the giving of an undertaking the fact of the order or undertaking is usually advertised by the Official Receiver in a newspaper local to the respondent.

5.20

19 Special savings from repealed enactments

(1) Schedule 2 to this Act has effect—
   (a)   in connection with certain transitional cases arising under sections 93 and 94 of the Companies Act 1981, so as to limit the power to make a disqualification order, or to restrict the duration of an order, by reference to events occurring or things done before the sections came into force,
   (b)   to preserve orders made under section 28 of the Companies Act 1976 (repealed by the Act of 1981), and
   (c)   to preclude any applications for a disqualification order under section 6 or 8, where the relevant company went into liquidation before 28th April 1986.

Miscellaneous and general

5.21

20 Admissibility in evidence of statements

[(1)] In any proceedings (whether or not under this Act), any statement made in pursuance of a requirement imposed by or under sections 6 to 10, 15 or 19(c) of, or Schedule 1 to, this Act, or by or under rules made for the purposes of this Act under the Insolvency Act, may be used in evidence against any person making or concurring in making the statement.

[(2) However, in criminal proceedings in which any such person is charged with an offence to which this subsection applies—
   (a)   no evidence relating to the statement may be adduced, and
   (b)   no question relating to it may be asked,

by or on behalf of the prosecution, unless evidence relating to it is adduced, or a question relating to it is asked, in the proceedings by or on behalf of that person.

(3) Subsection (2) applies to any offence other than—
    (a)   an offence which is—
        (i)   created by rules made for the purposes of this Act under the Insolvency Act, and
        (ii) designated for the purposes of this subsection by such rules or by regulations made by the Secretary of State;
    (b)   an offence which is—
        (i)   created by regulations made under any such rules, and
        (ii) designated for the purposes of this subsection by such regulations;
    (c)   an offence under section 5 of the Perjury Act 1911 (false statements made otherwise than on oath); or
    (d)   an offence under section 44(2) of the Criminal Law (Consolidation) (Scotland) Act 1995 (false statements made otherwise than on oath).

(4) Regulations under subsection (3)(a)(ii) shall be made by statutory instrument and, after being made, shall be laid before each House of Parliament.]

21 Interaction with Insolvency Act

(1) References in this Act to the official receiver, in relation to the winding up of a company or the bankruptcy of an individual, are to any person who, by virtue of section 399 of the Insolvency Act, is authorised to act as the official receiver in relation to that winding up or bankruptcy; and, in accordance with section 401(2) of that Act, references in this Act to an official receiver includes a person appointed as his deputy.

(2) Sections [1A][,] 6 to 10, [13, 14,] 15, 19(c) and 20 of, and Schedule 1 to, this Act [and sections 1 and 17 of this Act as they apply for the purposes of those provisions] are deemed included in Parts I to VII of the Insolvency Act for the purposes of the following sections of that Act—
    section 411 (power to make insolvency rules);
    section 414 (fees orders);
    section 420 (orders extending provisions about insolvent companies to insolvent partnerships);
    section 422 (modification of such provisions in their application to recognised banks); <... >
    ...

(3) Section 434 of that Act (Crown application) applies to sections [1A,] 6 to 10, [13, 14,] 15, 19(c) and 20 of, and Schedule 1 to, this Act [and sections 1 and 17 of this Act as they apply for the purposes of those provisions] as it does to the provisions of that Act which are there mentioned.

[(4) For the purposes of summary proceedings in Scotland, section 431 of that Act applies to summary proceedings for an offence under section 11 or 13 of this Act as it applies to summary proceedings for an offence under Parts I to VII of that Act.]

22 Interpretation

(1) This section has effect with respect to the meaning of expressions used in this Act, and applies unless the context otherwise requires.

(2) The expression 'company'—
  (a) in section 11, includes an unregistered company and a company incorporated outside Great Britain which has an established place of business in Great Britain, and
  (b) elsewhere, includes any company which may be wound up under Part V of the Insolvency Act.

(3) Section 247 in Part VII of the Insolvency Act (interpretation for the first Group of Parts to that Act) applies as regards references to a company's insolvency and to its going into liquidation; and 'administrative receiver' has the meaning given by section 251 of that Act [and references to acting as an insolvency practitioner are to be read in accordance with section 388 of that Act].

(4) 'Director' includes any person occupying the position of director, by whatever name called ...

(5) 'Shadow director', in relation to a company, means a person in accordance with whose directions or instructions the directors of the company are accustomed to act (but so that a person is not deemed a shadow director by reason only that the directors act on advice given by him in a professional capacity).

(6) Section 740 of the Companies Act applies as regards the meaning of 'body corporate'; and 'officer' has the meaning given by section 744 of that Act.

(7) In references to legislation other than this Act—
'the Companies Act' means the Companies Act 1985;
'the Companies Acts' has the meaning given by section 744 of that Act; and
'the Insolvency Act' means the Insolvency Act 1986;
and in sections 3(1) and 5(1) of this Act 'the companies legislation' means the Companies Acts (except the Insider Dealing Act), Parts I to VII of the Insolvency Act and, in Part XV of that Act, sections 411, 413, 414, 416 and 417.

(8) Any reference to provisions, or a particular provision, of the Companies Acts or the Insolvency Act includes the corresponding provisions or provision of the former Companies Acts (as defined by section 735(1)(c) of the Companies Act, but including also that Act itself) or, as the case may be, the Insolvency Act 1985.

(9) Any expression for whose interpretation provision is made by Part XXVI of the Companies Act (and not by subsections (3) to (8) above) is to be construed in accordance with that provision.

[(10) Any reference to acting as receiver—
  (a)   includes acting as manager or as both receiver and manager, but
  (b)   does not include acting as administrative receiver;
and 'receivership' is to be read accordingly.]

[22A Application of Act to building societies]

[(1) This Act applies to building societies as it applies to companies.

(2) References in this Act to a company, or to a director or an officer of a company include, respectively, references to a building society within the meaning of the Building Societies Act 1986 or to a director or officer, within the meaning of that Act, of a building society.

(3) In relation to a building society the definition of 'shadow director' in section 22(5) applies with the substitution of 'building society' for 'company'.

(4) In the application of Schedule 1 to the directors of a building society, references to provisions of the Insolvency Act or the Companies Act include references to the corresponding provisions of the Building Societies Act 1986.]

[22B Application of Act to incorporated friendly societies]

[(1) This Act applies to incorporated friendly societies as it applies to companies.

(2) References in this Act to a company, or to a director or an officer of a company include, respectively, references to an incorporated friendly society within the meaning of the Friendly Societies Act 1992 or to a member of the committee of management or officer, within the meaning of the Act, of an incorporated friendly society.

(3) In relation to an incorporated friendly society every reference to a shadow director shall be omitted.

(4) In the application of Schedule 1 to the members of the committee of management of an incorporated friendly society, references to provisions of the Insolvency Act or the Companies Act include references to the corresponding provisions of the Friendly Societies Act 1992.]

[22C Application of Act to NHS foundation trusts]

[(1) This Act applies to NHS foundation trusts as it applies to companies within the meaning of this Act.

(2) References in this Act to a company, or to a director or officer of a company, include, respectively, references to an NHS foundation trust or to a director or officer of the trust; but references to shadow directors are omitted.

(3) In the application of Schedule 1 to the directors of an NHS foundation trust, references to the provisions of the Insolvency Act or the Companies Act include references to the corresponding provisions of Part 1 of the Health and Social Care (Community Health and Standards) Act 2003.]

23 Transitional provisions, savings, repeals

(1) The transitional provisions and savings in Schedule 3 to this Act have effect, and are without prejudice to anything in the Interpretation Act 1978 with regard to the effect of repeals.

(2) The enactments specified in the second column of Schedule 4 to this Act are repealed to the extent specified in the third column of that Schedule.

24 Extent

(1) This Act extends to England and Wales and to Scotland.

(2) Nothing in this Act extends to Northern Ireland.

25 Commencement

This Act comes into force simultaneously with the Insolvency Act 1986.

26 Citation

This Act may be cited as the Company Directors Disqualification Act 1986.

SCHEDULE 1
Matters for Determining Unfitness of Directors
Section 9

Part I
Matters applicable in all cases

5.22

1

Any misfeasance or breach of any fiduciary or other duty by the director in relation to the company.

2

Any misapplication or retention by the director of, or any conduct by the director giving rise to an obligation to account for, any money or other property of the company.

3

The extent of the director's responsibility for the company entering into any transaction liable to be set aside under Part XVI of the Insolvency Act (provisions against debt avoidance).

4

The extent of the director's responsibility for any failure by the company to comply with any of the following provisions of the Companies Act, namely—

    (a)   section 221 (companies to keep accounting records);
    (b)   section 222 (where and for how long records to be kept);
    (c)   section 288 (register of directors and secretaries);
    (d)   section 352 (obligation to keep and enter up register of members);
    (e)   section 353 (location of register of members);
    [(f)   section 363 (duty of company to make annual returns);]

(*b*)   *sections 399 and 415 (company's duty to register charges it creates).*
[(h)   sections 398 and 703D (duty of company to deliver particulars of charges on its property)].

[5

The extent of the director's responsibility for any failure by the directors of the company to comply with—
   (a)   section 226 or 227 of the Companies Act (duty to prepare annual accounts), or
   (b)   section 233 of that Act (approval and signature of accounts).]

[5A

In the application of this Part of this Schedule in relation to any person who is a director of an open-ended investment company, any reference to a provision of the Companies Act is to be taken to be a reference to the corresponding provision of the Open-Ended Investment Companies Regulations 2001 or of any rules made under regulation 6 of those Regulations (Financial Services Authority rules).]

Part II
Matters applicable where company has become insolvent

5.23

6

The extent of the director's responsibility for the causes of the company becoming insolvent.

7

The extent of the director's responsibility for any failure by the company to supply any goods or services which have been paid for (in whole or in part).

8

The extent of the director's responsibility for the company entering into any transaction or giving any preference, being a transaction or preference—
   (a)   liable to be set aside under section 127 or sections 238 to 240 of the Insolvency Act, or
   (b)   challengeable under section 242 or 243 of that Act or under any rule of law in Scotland.

9

The extent of the director's responsibility for any failure by the directors of the company to comply with section 98 of the Insolvency Act (duty to call creditors' meeting in creditors' voluntary winding up).

10

Any failure by the director to comply with any obligation imposed on him by or under any of the following provisions of the Insolvency Act—

(a) [paragraph 47 of Schedule B1] (company's statement of affairs in administration);
(b) section 47 (statement of affairs to administrative receiver);
(c) section 66 (statement of affairs in Scottish receivership);
(d) section 99 (directors' duty to attend meeting; statement of affairs in creditors' voluntary winding up);
(e) section 131 (statement of affairs in winding up by the court);
(f) section 234 (duty of any one with company property to deliver it up);
(g) section 235 (duty to co-operate with liquidator, etc).

Enterprise Act 2002

(2002 c 40)

Arrangement of Sections

Part 10
Insolvency

Companies, etc

SCHEDULES:

Establish and provide for the functions of the Office of Fair Trading, the Competition Appeal Tribunal and the Competition Service; to make provision about mergers and market structures and conduct; to amend the constitution and functions of the Competition Commission; to create an offence for those entering into certain anti-competitive agreements, to provide for the disqualification of directors of companies engaging in certain anti-competitive practices; to make other provision about competition law; to amend the law relating to the protection of the collective interests of consumers; to make further provision about the disclosure of information obtained under competition and consumer legislation; to amend the Insolvency Act 1986 and make other provision about insolvency; and for connected purposes

Part 10
Insolvency

Companies, etc

6.1

248 Replacement of Part II of Insolvency Act 1986

(1), (2) (*Substitute the IA 1986, Pt II at* **1.14** *and insert* Sch B1 at **1.585**.)

(3) Schedule 17 (minor and consequential amendments relating to administration) shall have effect.

(4) The Secretary of State may by order amend an enactment in consequence of this section.

(5) An order under subsection (4)—
  (a) must be made by statutory instrument, and
  (b) shall be subject to annulment in pursuance of a resolution of either House of Parliament.

6.2

249 Special administration regimes

(1) Section 248 shall have no effect in relation to—
  (a) a company holding an appointment under Chapter I of Part II of the Water Industry Act 1991 (c 56) (water and sewerage undertakers),
  (b) a protected railway company within the meaning of section 59 of the Railways Act 1993 (c 43) (railway administration order) (including that section as it has effect by virtue of section 19 of the Channel Tunnel Rail Link Act 1996 (c 61) (administration)),
  (c) a licence company within the meaning of section 26 of the Transport Act 2000 (c 38) (air traffic services),
  (d) a public-private partnership company within the meaning of section 210 of the Greater London Authority Act 1999 (c 29) (public-private partnership agreement), or
  (e) a building society within the meaning of section 119 of the Building Societies Act 1986 (c 53) (interpretation).

(2) A reference in an Act listed in subsection (1) to a provision of Part II of the Insolvency Act 1986 (or to a provision which has effect in relation to a provision of that Part of that Act) shall, in so far as it relates to a company or society listed in subsection (1), continue to have effect as if it referred to Part II as it had effect immediately before the coming into force of section 248.

(3) But the effect of subsection (2) in respect of a particular class of company or society may be modified by order of—
  (a) the Treasury, in the case of building societies, or
  (b) the Secretary of State, in any other case.

(4) An order under subsection (3) may make consequential amendment of an enactment.

(5) An order under subsection (3)—
   (a)   must be made by statutory instrument, and
   (b)   may not be made unless a draft has been laid before and approved by resolution of each House of Parliament.

(6) An amendment of the Insolvency Act 1986 (c 45) made by this Act is without prejudice to any power conferred by Part VII of the Companies Act 1989 (c 40) (financial markets) to modify the law of insolvency.

6.3

250–253

6.4

254 Application of insolvency law to foreign company

(1) The Secretary of State may by order provide for a provision of the Insolvency Act 1986 to apply (with or without modification) in relation to a company incorporated outside Great Britain.

(2) An order under this section—
   (a)   may make provision generally or for a specified purpose only,
   (b)   may make different provision for different purposes, and
   (c)   may make transitional, consequential or incidental provision.

(3) An order under this section—
   (a)   must be made by statutory instrument, and
   (b)   shall be subject to annulment in pursuance of a resolution of either House of Parliament.

6.5

255 Application of law about company arrangement or administration to non-company

(1) The Treasury may with the concurrence of the Secretary of State by order provide for a company arrangement or administration provision to apply (with or without modification) in relation to—
   (a)   a society registered under the Industrial and Provident Societies Act 1965 (c 12),
   (b)   a society registered under section 7(1)(b), (c), (d), (e) or (f) of the Friendly Societies Act 1974 (c 46),
   (c)   a friendly society within the meaning of the Friendly Societies Act 1992 (c 40), or
   (d)   an unregistered friendly society.

(2) In subsection (1) "company arrangement or administration provision" means—
   (a)   a provision of Part I of the Insolvency Act 1986 (company voluntary arrangements),
   (b)   a provision of Part II of that Act (administration), and
   (c)   section 425 of the Companies Act 1985 (c 6) (compromise or arrangement with creditors).

(3) An order under this section may not provide for a company arrangement or administration provision to apply in relation to a society which is registered as a social landlord under Part I of the Housing Act 1996 (c 52) or under Part 3 of the Housing (Scotland) Act 2001 (asp 10).

(4) An order under this section—
(a) may make provision generally or for a specified purpose only,
(b) may make different provision for different purposes, and
(c) may make transitional, consequential or incidental provision.

(5) Provision by virtue of subsection (4)(c) may, in particular—
(a) apply an enactment (with or without modification);
(b) amend an enactment.

(6) An order under this section—
(a) must be made by statutory instrument, and
(b) shall be subject to annulment in pursuance of a resolution of either House of Parliament.

Individuals

6.6

256 Duration of bankruptcy

(1) (*Substitutes IA 1986, s 279 at* **1.326.**)

(2) Schedule 19 (which makes transitional provision in relation to this section)—
(a) shall have effect, and
(b) is without prejudice to the generality of section 276.

6.7

257–260

6.8

261 Bankrupt's home

(1)–(6) (*Inserts IA 1986, ss 283A, 313A at* **1.333**, **1.367**, *amend ss 307(2), 313, 384(2), 418(1) of that Act at* **1.358**, **1.366**, **1.440**, **1.477.**)

(7) In subsection (8)—
(a) "pre-commencement bankrupt" means an individual who is adjudged bankrupt on a petition presented before subsection (1) above comes into force, and
(b) "the transitional period" is the period of three years beginning with the date on which subsection (1) above comes into force.

(8) If a pre-commencement bankrupt's estate includes an interest in a dwelling-house which at the date of the bankruptcy was the sole or principal residence of him, his spouse or a former spouse of his, at the end of the transitional period that interest shall—
(a) cease to be comprised in the estate, and
(b) vest in the bankrupt (without conveyance, assignment or transfer).

(9) But subsection (8) shall not apply if before or during the transitional period—

(a) any of the events mentioned in section 283A(3) of the Insolvency Act 1986 (c 45) (inserted by subsection (1) above) occurs in relation to the interest or the dwelling-house, or

(b) the trustee obtains any order of a court, or makes any agreement with the bankrupt, in respect of the interest or the dwelling-house.

(10) Subsections 283A(4) to (9) of that Act shall have effect, with any necessary modifications, in relation to the provision made by subsections (7) to (9) above; in particular—

(a) a reference to the period mentioned in section 283A(2) shall be construed as a reference to the transitional period,

(b) in the application of section 283A(5) a reference to the date of the bankruptcy shall be construed as a reference to the date on which subsection (1) above comes into force, and

(c) a reference to the rules is a reference to rules made under section 412 of the Insolvency Act 1986 (for which purpose this section shall be treated as forming part of Parts VIII to XI of that Act).

6.9

264 Individual voluntary arrangement

(1) ...

(2) The Secretary of State may by order amend the Insolvency Act 1986 so as to extend the provisions of sections 263B to 263G (which are inserted by Schedule 22 and provide a fast-track procedure for making an individual voluntary arrangement) to some or all cases other than those specified in section 263A as inserted by Schedule 22.

(3) An order under subsection (2)—

(a) must be made by statutory instrument, and

(b) may not be made unless a draft has been laid before and approved by each House of Parliament.

(4) An order under subsection (2) may make—

(a) consequential provision (which may include provision amending the Insolvency Act 1986 or another enactment);

(b) transitional provision.

6.10

265

6.11

266 Disqualification from office: Parliament

(1), (2) (*Inserts IA 1986, ss 426A–426C at* **1.487** **1.189**; *amends s 427 of that Act at* **1.490**.)

(3) The Secretary of State may by order—

(a) provide for section 426A or 426B of that Act (as inserted by subsection (1) above) to have effect in relation to orders made or undertakings accepted in Scotland or Northern Ireland under a system which appears to the Secretary of State to be equivalent to the system operating under Schedule 4A to that Act (as inserted by section 257 of this Act);

(b) make consequential amendment of section 426A or 426B of that Act (as inserted by subsection (1) above);

(c) make other consequential amendment of an enactment.

(4) An order under this section may make transitional, consequential or incidental provision.

(5) An order under this section—

(a) must be made by statutory instrument, and

(b) may not be made unless a draft has been laid before and approved by resolution of each House of Parliament.

6.12

267

6.13

268 Disqualification from office: general

(1) The Secretary of State may make an order under this section in relation to a disqualification provision.

(2) A "disqualification provision" is a provision which disqualifies (whether permanently or temporarily and whether absolutely or conditionally) a bankrupt or a class of bankrupts from—

(a) being elected or appointed to an office or position,

(b) holding an office or position, or

(c) becoming or remaining a member of a body or group.

(3) In subsection (2) the reference to a provision which disqualifies a person conditionally includes a reference to a provision which enables him to be dismissed.

(4) An order under subsection (1) may repeal or revoke the disqualification provision.

(5) An order under subsection (1) may amend, or modify the effect of, the disqualification provision—

(a) so as to reduce the class of bankrupts to whom the disqualification provision applies;

(b) so as to extend the disqualification provision to some or all individuals who are subject to a bankruptcy restrictions regime;

(c) so that the disqualification provision applies only to some or all individuals who are subject to a bankruptcy restrictions regime;

(d) so as to make the application of the disqualification provision wholly or partly subject to the discretion of a specified person, body or group.

(6) An order by virtue of subsection (5)(d) may provide for a discretion to be subject to—

(a) the approval of a specified person or body;

(b) appeal to a specified person or body.

(7) An order by virtue of subsection (5)(d) made with the concurrence of the Lord Chancellor may provide for a discretion to be subject to appeal to a specified court or tribunal.

(8) The Secretary of State may specify himself for the purposes of subsection (5)(d) or (6)(a) or (b).

(9) In this section "bankrupt" means an individual—
   (a)   who has been adjudged bankrupt by a court in England and Wales or in Northern Ireland,
   (b)   whose estate has been sequestrated by a court in Scotland, or
   (c)   who has made an agreement with creditors of his for a composition of debts, for a scheme of arrangement of affairs, for the grant of a trust deed or for some other kind of settlement or arrangement.

(10) In this section "bankruptcy restrictions regime" means an order or undertaking—
   (a)   under Schedule 4A to the Insolvency Act 1986 (c 45) (bankruptcy restrictions orders), or
   (b)   under any system operating in Scotland or Northern Ireland which appears to the Secretary of State to be equivalent to the system operating under that Schedule.

(11) In this section—
"body" includes Parliament and any other legislative body, and
"provision" means—
   (a)   a provision made by an Act of Parliament passed before or in the same Session as this Act, and
   (b)   a provision made, before or in the same Session as this Act, under an Act of Parliament.

(12) An order under this section—
   (a)   may make provision generally or for a specified purpose only,
   (b)   may make different provision for different purposes, and
   (c)   may make transitional, consequential or incidental provision.

(13) An order under this section—
   (a)   must be made by statutory instrument, and
   (b)   may not be made unless a draft has been laid before and approved by resolution of each House of Parliament.

(14) A reference in this section to the Secretary of State shall be treated as a reference to the National Assembly for Wales in so far as it relates to a disqualification provision which—
   (a)   is made by the National Assembly for Wales, or
   (b)   relates to a function of the National Assembly.

(15) Provision made by virtue of subsection (7) is subject to any order of the Lord Chancellor under section 56(1) of the Access to Justice Act 1999 (c 22) (appeals: jurisdiction).

6.14

269

Money

6.15

270 Fees

(1) (*Inserts IA 1986, s 415A at* **1.473.**)

(2) An order made by virtue of subsection (1) may relate to the maintenance of recognition or authorisation granted before this section comes into force.

(3), (4) *(Inserts IA 1986, s 392(9) at* **1.450**; *amends 440(2) at* **1.503**.)

6.16

271, 272

**Part 11
Supplementary**

6.17

273–278

6.18

279 Commencement

The preceding provisions of this Act shall come into force on such day as the Secretary of State may by order made by statutory instrument appoint; and different days may be appointed for different purposes.

6.19

280 Extent

(1) Sections 256 to 265, 267, 269 and 272 extend only to England and Wales.

(2) Sections 204, 248 to 255 and 270 extend only to England and Wales and Scotland (but subsection (3) of section 415A as inserted by section 270 extends only to England and Wales).

(3) Any other modifications by this Act of an enactment have the same extent as the enactment being modified.

(4) Otherwise, this Act extends to England and Wales, Scotland and Northern Ireland.

6.20

281 Short title

This Act may be cited as the Enterprise Act 2002.

Schedules

Schedule 17
Administration: Minor and Consequential Amendments
Section 248

General

6.21

1

In any instrument made before section 248(1) to (3) of this Act comes into force—

(a) a reference to the making of an administration order shall be treated as including a reference to the appointment of an administrator under paragraph 14 or 22 of Schedule B1 to the Insolvency Act 1986 (c 45) (inserted by section 248(2) of this Act), and

(b) a reference to making an application for an administration order by petition shall be treated as including a reference to making an administration application under that Schedule, appointing an administrator under paragraph 14 or 22 of that Schedule or giving notice under paragraph 15 or 26 of that Schedule.

2–59

Schedule 19
Duration of Bankruptcy: Transitional Provisions
Section 256

Introduction

6.22

1

This Schedule applies to an individual who immediately before commencement—
(a) has been adjudged bankrupt, and
(b) has not been discharged from the bankruptcy.

2

In this Schedule—
"commencement" means the date appointed under section 279 for the commencement of section 256, and
"pre-commencement bankrupt" means an individual to whom this Schedule applies.

Neither old law nor new law to apply

6.23

3

Section 279 of the Insolvency Act 1986 (c 45) (bankruptcy: discharge) shall not apply to a pre-commencement bankrupt (whether in its pre-commencement or its post-commencement form).

General rule for discharge from pre-commencement bankruptcy

6.24

4

(1) A pre-commencement bankrupt is[, subject to sub-paragraphs (2) and (3),] discharged from bankruptcy at whichever is the earlier of—
(a) the end of the period of one year beginning with commencement, and

(b)   the end of the relevant period applicable to the bankrupt under section 279(1)(b) of the Insolvency Act 1986 (duration of bankruptcy) as it had effect immediately before commencement.

(2) An order made under section 279(3) of that Act before commencement—

(a)   shall continue to have effect in respect of the pre-commencement bankrupt after commencement, and

(b)   may be varied or revoked after commencement by an order under section 279(3) as substituted by section 256 of this Act.

(3) Section 279(3) to (5) of that Act as substituted by section 256 of this Act shall have effect after commencement in relation to the period mentioned in sub-paragraph (1)(a) or (b) above.

Second-time bankruptcy

6.25

5

(1) This paragraph applies to a pre-commencement bankrupt who was an undischarged bankrupt at some time during the period of 15 years ending with the day before the date on which the pre-commencement bankruptcy commenced.

(2) The pre-commencement bankrupt shall not be discharged from bankruptcy in accordance with paragraph 4 above.

(3) An order made before commencement under section 280(2)(b) or (c) of the Insolvency Act 1986 (c 45) (discharge by order of the court) shall continue to have effect after commencement (including any provision made by the court by virtue of section 280(3)).

(4) A pre-commencement bankrupt to whom this paragraph applies (and in respect of whom no order is in force under section 280(2)(b) or (c) on commencement) is discharged—

(a)   at the end of the period of five years beginning with commencement, or

(b)   at such earlier time as the court may order on an application under section 280 of the Insolvency Act 1986 (discharge by order) heard after commencement.

(5) Section 279(3) to (5) of the Insolvency Act 1986 as substituted by section 256 of this Act shall have effect after commencement in relation to the period mentioned in sub-paragraph (4)(a) above.

(6) A bankruptcy annulled under section 282 shall be ignored for the purpose of sub-paragraph (1).

Criminal bankruptcy

6.26

6

A pre-commencement bankrupt who was adjudged bankrupt on a petition under section 264(1)(d) of the Insolvency Act 1986 (criminal bankruptcy)—

(a) shall not be discharged from bankruptcy in accordance with paragraph 4 above, but

(b) may be discharged from bankruptcy by an order of the court under section 280 of that Act.

Income payments order

6.27

7

(1) This paragraph applies where—

(a) a pre-commencement bankrupt is discharged by virtue of paragraph 4(1)(a), and

(b) an income payments order is in force in respect of him immediately before his discharge.

(2) If the income payments order specifies a date after which it is not to have effect, it shall continue in force until that date (and then lapse).

(3) But the court may on the application of the pre-commencement bankrupt—

(a) vary the income payments order;

(b) provide for the income payments order to cease to have effect before the date referred to in sub-paragraph (2).

Bankruptcy restrictions order or undertaking

6.28

8

A provision of this Schedule which provides for an individual to be discharged from bankruptcy is subject to—

(a) any bankruptcy restrictions order (or interim order) which may be made in relation to that individual, and

(b) any bankruptcy restrictions undertaking entered into by that individual.

Environmental Protection Act 1990

1990 CHAPTER 43

7.1

An Act to make provision for the improved control of pollution arising from certain industrial and other processes; to re-enact the provisions of the Control of Pollution Act 1974 relating to waste on land with modifications as respects the functions of the regulatory and other authorities concerned in the collection and disposal of waste and to make further provision in relation to such waste; to restate the law defining statutory nuisances and improve the summary procedures for dealing with them, to provide for the termination of the existing controls over offensive trades or businesses and to provide for the extension of the Clean Air Acts to prescribed gases; to amend the law relating to litter and make further provision imposing or conferring powers to impose duties to keep public places clear of litter and clean; to make provision conferring powers in relation to trolleys abandoned on land in the open air; to amend the Radioactive Substances Act 1960; to make provision for the control of genetically modified organisms; to make provision for the abolition of the Nature Conservancy Council and for the creation of councils to replace it and discharge the functions of that Council and, as respects Wales, of the Countryside Commission; to make further provision for the control of the importation, exportation, use, supply or storage of prescribed substances and articles and the importation or exportation of prescribed descriptions of waste; to confer powers to obtain information about potentially hazardous substances; to amend the law relating to the control of hazardous substances on, over or under land; to amend section 107(6) of the Water Act 1989 and sections 31(7)(a), 31A(c)(i) and 32(7)(a) of the Control of Pollution Act 1974; to amend the provisions of the Food and Environment Protection Act 1985 as regards the dumping of waste at sea; to make further provision as respects the prevention of oil pollution from ships; to make provision for and in connection with the identification and control of dogs; to confer powers to control the burning of crop residues; to make provision in relation to financial or other assistance for purposes connected with the environment; to make provision as respects superannuation of employees of the Groundwork Foundation and for remunerating the chairman of the Inland Waterways Amenity Advisory Council; and for purposes connected with those purposes

Part II
Waste on Land

Waste Management Licences

7.2

35 Waste management licences: general

(1) A waste management licence is a licence granted by a waste regulation authority authorising the treatment, keeping or disposal of any specified description of controlled waste in or on specified land or the treatment or disposal of any specified description of controlled waste by means of specified mobile plant.

(2) A licence shall be granted to the following person, that is to say—
  (a) in the case of a licence relating to the treatment, keeping or disposal of waste in or on land, to the person who is in occupation of the land; and
  (b) in the case of a licence relating to the treatment or disposal of waste by means of mobile plant, to the person who operates the plant.

(3) A licence shall be granted on such terms and subject to such conditions as appear to the waste regulation authority to be appropriate and the conditions may relate—
  (a) to the activities which the licence authorises, and
  (b) to the precautions to be taken and works to be carried out in connection with or in consequence of those activities;
and accordingly requirements may be imposed in the licence which are to be complied with before the activities which the licence authorises have begun or after the activities which the licence authorises have ceased.

(4) Conditions may require the holder of a licence to carry out works or do other things notwithstanding that he is not entitled to carry out the works or to do the thing and any person whose consent would be required shall grant, or join in granting, the holder of the licence such rights in relation to the land as will enable the holder of the licence to comply with any requirements imposed on him by the licence.

(5) Conditions may relate, where waste other than controlled waste is to be treated, kept or disposed of, to the treatment, keeping or disposal of that other waste.

(6) The Secretary of State may, by regulations, make provision as to the conditions which are, or are not, to be included in a licence; and regulations under this subsection may make different provision for different circumstances.

(7) The Secretary of State may, as respects any licence for which an application is made to a waste regulation authority, give to the authority directions as to the terms and conditions which are, or are not, to be included in the licence; and it shall be the duty of the authority to give effect to the directions.

(7A) In any case where—
  (a) an entry is required under this section to be made in any record as to the observance of any condition of a licence, and

(b)   the entry has not been made,
that fact shall be admissible as evidence that condition has not been observed.

(7B) Any person who
(a)   intentionally makes a false entry in any record required to be kept under any condition of a licence, or
(b)   with intent to deceive, forges or uses a licence or makes or has in his possession a document so closely resembling a licence as to be likely to deceive,
shall be guilty of an offence.

(7C) A person guilty of an offence under subsection (7B) above shall be liable—
(a)   on summary conviction, to a fine not exceeding the statutory maximum;
(b)   on conviction on indictment, to a fine or to imprisonment for a term not exceeding two years, or to both.

(8) It shall be the duty of waste regulation authorities to have regard to any guidance issued to them by the Secretary of State with respect to the discharge of their functions in relation to licences.

(9) A licence may not be surrendered by the holder except in accordance with section 39 below.

(10) A licence is not transferable by the holder but the waste regulation authority may transfer it to another person under section 40 below.

(11) A licence shall continue in force until [it ceases to have effect under subsection (11A) below,] it is revoked entirely by the waste regulation authority under section 38 below or it is surrendered or its surrender is accepted under section 39 below.

(11A) A licence shall cease to have effect if and to the extent that the treatment, keeping or disposal of waste authorised by the licence is authorised by a permit granted under regulations under section 2 of the Pollution Prevention and Control Act 1999.

(12) In this Part "licence" means a waste management licence and "site licence" and "mobile plant licence" mean, respectively, a licence authorising the treatment, keeping or disposal of waste in or on land and a licence authorising the treatment or disposal of waste by means of mobile plant.

Notes

S 35

A waste disposal licence is "property" for the purposes of IA 1986, s 436 and accordingly is capable of being disclaimed by the official receiver under IA 1986, 178: In *Re Celtic Extraction Ltd* [2001] Ch 475 (overruling in part *in re Mineral Resources Ltd* [1999] 1 All ER 746; [1999] 2 BCLC 516). For the purposes of CA s 654(1) (property of dissolved company to be bona vacantia), however, such a waste disposal licence may not be "property": *In re Wilmott Trading Ltd (No 2)* [1999] 2 BCLC 541.

Part IIA
Contaminated Land

7.3

78X Supplementary provisions

(1) ....

(2) ....

(3) A person acting in a relevant capacity–
  (a) shall not thereby be personally liable, under this Part, to bear the whole or any part of the cost of doing any thing by way of remediation, unless that thing is to any extent referable to substances whose presence in, on or under the contaminated land in question is a result of any act done or omission made by him which it was unreasonable for a person acting in that capacity to do or make; and
  (b) shall not thereby be guilty of an offence under or by virtue of section 78M above unless the requirement which has not been complied with is a requirement to do some particular thing for which he is personally liable to bear the whole or any part of the cost.

(4) In subsection (3) above, "person acting in a relevant capacity" means–
  (a) a person acting as an insolvency practitioner, within the meaning of section 388 of the Insolvency Act 1986 (including that section as it applies in relation to an insolvent partnership by virtue of any order made under section 421 of that Act);
  (b) the official receiver acting in a capacity in which he would be regarded as acting as an insolvency practitioner within the meaning of section 388 of the Insolvency Act 1986 if subsection (5) of that section were disregarded;
  (c) the official receiver acting as receiver or manager;
  (d) a person acting as a special manager under section 177 or 370 of the Insolvency Act 1986;
  (e) the Accountant in Bankruptcy acting as permanent or interim trustee in a sequestration (within the meaning of the Bankruptcy (Scotland) Act 1985);
  (f) a person acting as a receiver or receiver and manager–
    (i) under or by virtue of any enactment; or
    (ii) by virtue of his appointment as such by an order of a court or by any other instrument.

(5) ....

Notes

Part IIA

This Part sets out the procedures for dealing with contaminated land. In general terms, it imposes on the local authority (and in some cases, the Secretary of State) a duty to identify contaminated land (section 78B) and to require remediation of the same (section 78E) by the person determined to be responsible (section 78F). Non-compliance without reasonable excuse of a remediation notice is an offence (section 78M). In the event of non-compliance the enforcing authority may carry out the remediation itself (section 78N) and recover the cost of the same from the person responsible (section 78P).

S 78X

The relevance of Part IIA to insolvency law appears in section 78X, which contains various supplementary provisions. In short, it limits the potential civil and criminal liabilities of a person acting as an insolvency practitioner, of the official receiver and of various other similar persons as set out in section 78X(4). Where it applies, the insolvency practitioner (or other relevant person, as the case may be) cannot be personally liable to bear any part of the cost of the remediation, except to the extent that the remediation is referable to an act or omission of the insolvency practitioner: section 78X(3)(a). Similarly, such a person cannot be guilty of an offence, except to the extent that the requirement which has not been complied with is a requirement to do something for which he or she is personally liable to bear any part of the cost: section 78X(3)(b).

Housing Act 1996

Insolvency, &c of registered social landlord

Introductory Notes

SS 39–50

The Housing Act 1996 set out a scheme relating to the insolvency of a registered social landlord. For the purposes of the Act registered social landlords fall within three categories:

(a) Industrial and Provident Societies which satisfy the conditions set out in section 2(2) HA 1996;

(b) Companies registered under the Companies Act 1985 which satisfy such conditions;

(c) Registered charities that are housing associations and that are not companies.

The Housing Act 1996 affords an important role to the 'Relevant Authority', which means the Housing Corporation or the Secretary of State (if the industrial and provident society, company or charity has its registered office or address for the purposes of registration by the Charity Commissioners in Wales) – see section 56 HA 1996. The Housing Corporation is constituted by the Housing Association Act 1985 s 74, schedule 6. The Relevant Authority can petition for the winding up of an industrial and provident society or company on the grounds that (a) the landlord is failing properly to carry out its purposes or objects or (b) it is unable to pay its debts within the meaning of section 123 IA 1986 (HA 1996 schedule 1 paragraphs 14(1) & (2)). In addition, there are constraints placed on persons other than the Relevant Authority who wish to enforce a security against a registered social landlord or institute insolvency proceedings. Sections 39–50 HA 1996 deal with these situations and ensures the intervention of the Relevant Authority. The purpose of the provisions is to provide the Relevant Authority with an early opportunity to deal with assets that have been funded by social housing money to ensure their continued use for social housing.

8.1

39 Insolvency, &c of registered social landlord: scheme of provisions

(1) The following sections make provision—

(a) for notice to be given to the Relevant Authority of any proposal to take certain steps in relation to a registered social landlord (section 40), and for further notice to be given when any such step is taken (section 41),

(b) for a moratorium on the disposal of land, and certain other assets, held by the registered social landlord (sections 42 and 43),

(c) for proposals by the Relevant Authority as to the future ownership and management of the land held by the landlord (section 44), which are binding if agreed (section 45),

(d) for the appointment of a manager to implement agreed proposals (section 46) and as to the powers of such a manager (sections 47 and 48),

(e) for the giving of assistance by the Relevant Authority (section 49), and

(f) for application to the court to secure compliance with the agreed proposals (section 50).

(2) In those sections—
'disposal' means sale, lease, mortgage, charge or any other disposition, and includes the grant of an option;
'secured creditor' means a creditor who holds a mortgage or charge (including a floating charge) over land held by the landlord or any existing or future interest of the landlord in rents or other receipts from land; and
'security' means any mortgage, charge or other security.

(3) The Secretary of State may make provision by order defining for the purposes of those sections what is meant by a step to enforce security over land.

Any such order shall be made by statutory instrument which shall be subject to annulment in pursuance of a resolution of either House of Parliament.

Notes

S 39(3)

The Secretary of State has the power to make provision by means of a statutory instrument defining what is meant by 'a step to enforce security over land.' This power has not been exercised.

8.2

40 Initial notice to be given to the Relevant Authority

(1) Notice must be given to the [Relevant Authority] before any of the steps mentioned below is taken in relation to a registered social landlord.

The person by whom the notice must be given is indicated in the second column.

(2) Where the registered social landlord is an industrial and provident society, the steps and the person by whom notice must be given are—

Any step to enforce any security over land held by the landlord.	The person proposing to take the step.
Presenting a petition for the winding up of the landlord.	The petitioner.
Passing a resolution for the winding up of the landlord.	The landlord.

(3) Where the registered social landlord is a company registered under the Companies Act 1985 (including a registered charity), the steps and the person by whom notice must be given are—

Any step to enforce any security over land held by the landlord	The person proposing to take the step.
Applying for an administration order.	The applicant.

Presenting a petition for the winding up of the landlord	The petitioner.
Passing a resolution for the winding up of the landlord.	The landlord.

(4) Where the registered social landlord is a registered charity (other than a company registered under the Companies Act 1985), the steps and the person by whom notice must be given are—

Any step to enforce any security over land held by the landlord.	The person proposing to take the step.

(5) Notice need not be given under this section in relation to a resolution for voluntary winding up where the consent of the [Relevant Authority] is required (see paragraphs 12(4) and 13(6) of schedule 1).

(6) Any step purportedly taken without the requisite notice being given under this section is ineffective.

(7) Subsections (8) and (9) apply in relation to the reference in subsection (3) to applying for an administration order.

(8) In a case where an administrator is appointed under paragraph 14 or 22 of schedule B1 to the Insolvency Act 1986 (appointment by floating charge holder, company or directors)—
   (a)   the reference includes a reference to appointing an administrator under that paragraph, and
   (b)   in respect of an appointment under either of those paragraphs the reference to the applicant shall be taken as a reference to the person making the appointment.

(9) In a case where a copy of a notice of intention to appoint an administrator under either of those paragraphs is filed with the court—
   (a)   the reference shall be taken to include a reference to the filing of the copy of the notice, and
   (b)   in respect of the filing of a copy of a notice of intention to appoint under either of those paragraphs the reference to the applicant shall be taken as a reference to the person giving the notice.

8.3

41 Further notice to be given to the Relevant Authority

(1) Notice must be given to the Relevant Authority as soon as may be after any of the steps mentioned below is taken in relation to a registered social landlord.

The person by whom the notice must be given is indicated in the second column.

(2) Where the registered social landlord is an industrial and provident society, the steps and the person by whom notice must be given are—

The taking of a step to enforce any security over land held by the landlord.	The person taking the step.
The making of an order for the winding up of the landlord.	The petitioner.
The passing of a resolution for the winding up of the landlord.	The landlord.

(3) Where the registered social landlord is a company registered under the Companies Act 1985 (including a registered charity), the steps and the person by whom notice must be given are—

The taking of a step to enforce any security over land held by the landlord.	The making of an administration order.
The making of an order for the winding up of the landlord.	The passing of a resolution for the winding up of the landlord.

(4) Where the registered social landlord is a registered charity (other than a company registered under the Companies Act 1985), the steps and the person by whom notice must be given are—

The taking of a step to enforce any security over land held by the landlord.	The person taking the step.
The making of an administration order.	The person who applied for the order.
The making of an order for the winding up of the landlord.	The petitioner.
The passing of a resolution for the winding up of the landlord.	The landlord.

(5) Failure to give notice under this section does not affect the validity of any step taken; but the period of 28 days mentioned in section 43(1) (period after which moratorium on disposal of land, &c ends) does not begin to run until any requisite notice has been given under this section.

(6) In subsection (3)—

    (a)   the reference to the making of an administration order includes a reference to appointing an administrator under paragraph 14 or 22 of schedule B1 to the Insolvency Act 1986 (administration), and

    (b)   in respect of an appointment under either of those paragraphs the reference to the applicant shall be taken as a reference to the person making the appointment.

Notes

SS 40, 41

These sections require that any party that wishes to take enforcement action in respect of any security over land or commence insolvency proceedings against a social landlord must first serve a notice on the Relevant Authority of the intention to take such a step and then serve a second notice as soon as reasonably practicable to inform the Relevant Authority of the action taken. Security means any mortgage, charge or other security (s 39(2) HA 1996). The table set out below indicates who should serve what notice in respect of the stipulated steps.

Type of registered social landlord	Enforcement of security	Administration order	Petition for winding up	Resolution for winding up
Industrial and Provident Society	Person wishing to enforce the security must serve: 1. First notice that proposing to enforce the security (section 40(2) HA 1996) 2. Second notice that security enforced (section 41(2) HA 1996)		Petitioner must serve: 1. First notice of intention to present a winding up petition (section 40(2) HA 1996) 2. Second notice that winding up order has been made (section 41(2) HA 1996)	Landlord (I&PS) must serve: 1. First notice of intention to present a petition for the winding up of the landlord (section 40(2) HA 1996) 2. Second notice of the passing of a resolution for the winding up of the landlord (section 41(2) HA 1996)

Type of registered social landlord	Enforcement of security	Administration order	Petition for winding up	Resolution for winding up
Company	Person wishing to enforce – same as for Industrial and Provident Society (see sections 40(3) and 41(3) HA 1996)	Applicant for an administration order (including where order is sought by the holder of a floating charge, the company or a director, the person making the appointment) must serve: 1. First notice of intention to apply for an administration order or to file a notice of intention to appoint an administrator as the case may be (section 40(3) HA 1996) 2. Second notice that an order has been made or an administrator appointed as the case may be (section 41(3) HA 1996)	Petitioner must serve notices as above (see section 40(3) HA 1996)	Landlord (company) must serve: 1. First notice of intention to present a petition for the winding up of the landlord (section 40(2) HA 1996) 2. Second notice of the passing of a resolution for the winding up of the landlord (section 41(2) HA 1996)
Registered charity that is not a company	Person wishing to enforce – as above (see section 40(4) and 41(4) HA 1996)			

Note that under HA 1996 s 40(5) there is no requirement to serve an initial notice in relation to a resolution for voluntary winding up where the landlord must obtain the consent of the Relevant Authority before passing the special resolution pursuant to HA 1996 schedule 1 para 12(4) (for an industrial and provident society) and para 13(6) (for a company) .

Failure to serve the notices

Any step purportedly taken without the requisite initial notice having been given under section 40 is ineffective (section 40(6) HA 1996). The failure to give the further notice under section 41 does not affect the validity of any step taken however the 28 day moratorium applied by section 42 below does not begin to run until the requisite further notice has been given – section 41(5) HA 1996.

Proceedings or enforcement action to which s 40 and 41 do not apply

There is no definition of 'enforcement of security over land'. Logically, the requirements of service of notice do not apply to the appointment of a Law of Property Act receiver or an administrative receiver (which can still be appointed after 15 September 2003 in relation to a registered social landlord – see IA 1986 s 72G). This is because a receiver acts as agent for the mortgagor. Likewise, where a director, administrator or liquidator of a company proposes to make a voluntary arrangement with the company's creditors no notices need to be served; however the arrangement will not take effect unless the Relevant Authority has given its consent (HA 1996 schedule 1 para 13(5)).

8.4

42 Moratorium on disposal of land, &c

(1) Where any of the steps mentioned in section 41 is taken in relation to a registered social landlord, there is a moratorium on the disposal of land held by the landlord.

(2) During the moratorium the consent of the Relevant Authority under this section is required (except as mentioned below) for any disposal of land held by the landlord, whether by the landlord itself or any person having a power of disposal in relation to the land.

Consent under this section may be given in advance and may be given subject to conditions.

(3) Consent is not required under this section for any such disposal as is mentioned in section 10(1), (2) or (3) (lettings and other disposals not requiring consent under section 9).

(4) A disposal made without the consent required by this section is void.

(5) Nothing in this section prevents a liquidator from disclaiming any land held by the landlord as onerous property.

(6) The provisions of this section apply in relation to any existing or future interest of the landlord in rent or other receipts arising from land as they apply to an interest in land.

Notes

S 42

This provision applies a moratorium where any of the following steps are taken:
(a)   There is enforcement of security against an industrial and provident society, company or charity;
(b)   An administration order is made in respect of a company or an administration is appointed under IA 1986 Sch B1 para 14, para 22;;
(c)   A compulsory winding up order is made against an Industrial and Provident Society or company;
(d)   An Industrial and Provident Society or company enters into voluntary winding up.

The moratorium begins when the step in question is taken and ends at the end of the period of 28 days beginning with the day on which the further notice is given to the Relevant Authority under s 41 above(see s 43(1) HA 1996).

S 42(2)

During the moratorium the consent of the Relevant Authority is required for any disposal of land held by the landlord. The disposal applies not only to a disposal by the landlord but also to any person having a power of disposal in relation to the land (see s 42(2)) ie a liquidator, administrative receiver, receiver or administrator. The moratorium extends not only to land but also to any existing or future interest of the landlord in rent or other receipts arising from the land – HA 1996 s 42(6). Consent may be given in advance and/or may be given subject to conditions. It is theoretically possible that consent could be obtained after the service of the first notice and before the taking of any of the steps mentioned in s 41 HA 1996.

There are certain exceptions to the requirement for consent. These are set out in s 42(3) HA 1996.

S 42(5)

Nothing in section 42 prevents a liquidator from disclaiming any land held by the landlord as onerous property pursuant to sections 178–182 IA 1986.

8.5

43 Period of moratorium

(1) The moratorium in consequence of the taking of any step as mentioned in section 41—
  (a)   begins when the step is taken, and
  (b)   ends at the end of the period of 28 days beginning with the day on which notice of its having been taken was given to the Relevant Authority under that section,
subject to the following provisions.

(2) The taking of any further step as mentioned in section 41 at a time when a moratorium is already in force does not start a further moratorium or affect the duration of the existing one.

(3) A moratorium may be extended from time to time with the consent of all the landlord's secured creditors.

Notice of any such extension shall be given by the Relevant Authority to—
  (a)   the landlord, and
  (b)   any liquidator, administrative receiver, receiver or administrator appointed in respect of the landlord or any land held by it.

(4) If during a moratorium the Relevant Authority considers that the proper management of the landlord's land can be secured without making proposals under section 44 (proposals as to ownership and management of landlord's land), the Relevant Authority may direct that the moratorium shall cease to have effect.

Before making any such direction the Relevant Authority shall consult the person who took the step which brought about the moratorium.

(5) When a moratorium comes to an end, or ceases to have effect under subsection (4), the [Relevant Authority] shall give notice of that fact to the landlord and the landlord's secured creditors.

(6) When a moratorium comes to an end (but not when it ceases to have effect under subsection (4)), the following provisions of this section apply.

The Relevant Authority's notice shall, in such a case, inform the landlord and the landlord's secured creditors of the effect of those provisions.

(7) If any further step as mentioned in section 41 is taken within the period of three years after the end of the original period of the moratorium, the moratorium may be renewed with the consent of all the landlord's secured creditors (which may be given before or after the step is taken).

Notice of any such renewal shall be given by the Relevant Authority to the persons to whom notice of an extension is required to be given under subsection (3).

(8) If a moratorium ends without any proposals being agreed, then, for a period of three years the taking of any further step as mentioned in section 41 does not start a further moratorium except with the consent of the landlord's secured creditors as mentioned in subsection (7) above.

Notes

S 43(2)

If a second 'triggering step' for the purpose of s 41 occurs within the moratorium period, there is no fresh moratorium or extension to the existing moratorium (s 43(2) HA 1996).

S 43(3)

A moratorium may be extended with the consent of all of the landlord's secured creditors. 'Secured creditors' means a creditor who holds a mortgage or charge (including a floating charge) over land held by the landlord or any existing or future interest of the landlord in rents or other receipts from land – see HA 1996 s 39(2). Notice of an extension must be given to the landlord and to any liquidator, administrative receiver, receiver or administrator appointed in respect of the landlord or any land held by it.

The ending of the moratorium

The moratorium will end either:
(a)   On the Relevant Authority directing that the moratorium shall cease to have effect before it expires by effluxion of time – see s 43(4). It may only do this if it considers that the proper management of the land can be achieved without proposals under HA 1996 s 44;
(b)   The expiry of the 28 day period;
(c)   The expiry of any extended period (as agreed by all of the secured creditors).

Notice of the ending or cessation of the moratorium must be served by the Relevant Authority on the landlord and the secured creditors (HA 1996 s 43(6)). If a further triggering step is taken within three years of the end of the original moratorium (but not its cessation by the Relevant Authority under s 43(4)) then the moratorium can be renewed with the consent of all of the landlord's secured creditors – HA 1996 s 43(7). If this consent is not given there will not be a further moratorium (s 43(8)). Note that these provisions do not remove the requirements to serve initial and further notices under s 40 and 41 within the 3–year period.

8.6

44 Proposals as to ownership and management of landlord's land

(1) During the moratorium (see sections 42 and 43) the Relevant Authority may make proposals as to the future ownership and management of the land held by the registered social landlord, designed to secure the continued proper management of the landlord's land by a registered social landlord.

(2) In drawing up its proposals the Relevant Authority—
   (a)   shall consult the landlord and, so far as is practicable, its tenants, and
   (b)   shall have regard to the interests of all the landlord's creditors, both secured and unsecured.

(3) The Relevant Authority shall also consult—
   (a)   where the landlord is an industrial and provident society, the appropriate registrar, and
   (b)   where the landlord is a registered charity, the Charity Commissioners.

(4) No proposals shall be made under which—
   (a)   a preferential debt of the landlord is to be paid otherwise than in priority to debts which are not preferential debts, or
   (b)   a preferential creditor is to be paid a smaller proportion of his preferential debt than another preferential creditor, except with the concurrence of the creditor concerned.

In this subsection references to preferential debts and preferential creditors have the same meaning as in the Insolvency Act 1986.

(5) So far as practicable no proposals shall be made which have the effect that unsecured creditors of the landlord are in a worse position than they would otherwise be.

(6) Where the landlord is a charity the proposals shall not require the landlord to act outside the terms of its trusts, and any disposal of housing accommodation occupied under a tenancy or licence from the landlord must be to another charity whose objects appear to the Relevant Authority to be, as nearly as practicable, akin to those of the landlord.

(7) The Relevant Authority shall serve a copy of its proposals on—
   (a)   the landlord and its officers,
   (b)   the secured creditors of the landlord, and
   (c)   any liquidator, administrator, administrative receiver or receiver appointed in respect of the landlord or its land;
and it shall make such arrangements as it considers appropriate to see that the members, tenants and unsecured creditors of the landlord are informed of the proposals.

8.7

45 Effect of agreed proposals

(1) The following provisions apply if proposals made by the Relevant Authority under section 44 are agreed, with or without modifications, by all the secured creditors of the registered social landlord.

(2) Once agreed the proposals are binding on the Relevant Authority, the landlord, all the landlord's creditors (whether secured or unsecured) and any liquidator, administrator, administrative receiver or receiver appointed in respect of the landlord or its land.

(3) It is the duty of—
   (a)   the members of the committee where the landlord is an industrial and provident society,

> (b)   the directors where the landlord is a company registered under the Companies Act 1985 (including a company which is a registered charity), and
>
> (c)   the trustees where the landlord is a charitable trust,
>
> to co-operate in the implementation of the proposals.
>
> This does not mean that they have to do anything contrary to any fiduciary or other duty owed by them.
>
> (4) The Relevant Authority shall serve a copy of the agreed proposals on—
>
> (a)   the landlord and its officers,
>
> (b)   the secured creditors of the landlord, and
>
> (c)   any liquidator, administrator, administrative receiver or receiver appointed in respect of the landlord or its land, and
>
> (d)   where the landlord is an industrial and provident society or registered charity, the Financial Services Authority]or the Charity Commissioners, as the case may be;
>
> and it shall make such arrangements as it considers appropriate to see that the members, tenants and unsecured creditors of the landlord are informed of the proposals.
>
> (5) The proposals may subsequently be amended with the consent of the Relevant Authority and all the landlord's secured creditors.
>
> Section 44(2) to (7) and subsections (2) to (4) above apply in relation to the amended proposals as in relation to the original proposals.

Notes

SS 44, 45

The purpose of the moratorium is to ensure so far as possible that the land of the registered social landlord continues to be facilitated for such use. In practice, this means the transfer of the land to another registered social landlord. Section 45 gives the Relevant Authority the power during the moratorium to make proposals as to the future ownership and management of the land held by the registered social landlord in order to fulfil this aim.

The effect of the proposals on creditors

Any proposals made by the Relevant Authority must take into account the interests of all of the landlord's creditors, both secured and unsecured (s 44(2)). No proposals shall be made under which a preferential debt is subrogated to a non-preferential debt or preferential creditors are not dealt with pari passu (unless a preferential creditor agrees to receive a smaller proportion of his debt than another preferential creditor) – HA 1996 s 44(4). So far as practicable, no proposals shall be made which have the effect that the unsecured creditors of the landlord are in a worse position that they otherwise would be (s 44(5). However, it is only the secured creditors who have the power to agree to the proposals, and for them to be binding all of the secured creditors must agree – HA 1996 s 45(1). Once agreed the proposals are binding on all of the creditors, both secured and unsecured (HA 1996 s 45(2)). They are also binding on any liquidator, administrative receiver, receiver or administrator – HA 1996 s 45(2).

Amendment of the agreed proposals

The agreed proposals can only be amended with the consent of the Relevant Authority and all the landlord's secured creditors – HA 1996 s 45(5).

8.8

46 Appointment of manager to implement agreed proposals

(1) Where proposals agreed as mentioned in section 45 so provide, the Relevant Authority may by order ... appoint a manager to implement the proposals or such of them as are specified in the order.

(2) If the landlord is a registered charity, the Relevant Authority shall give notice to the Charity Commissioners of the appointment.

(3) Where proposals make provision for the appointment of a manager, they shall also provide for the payment of his reasonable remuneration and expenses.

(4) The Relevant Authority may give the manager directions in relation to the carrying out of his functions.

(5) The manager may apply to the High Court for directions in relation to any particular matter arising in connection with the carrying out of his functions.

A direction of the court supersedes any direction of the [Relevant Authority] in respect of the same matter.

(6) If a vacancy occurs by death, resignation or otherwise in the office of manager, the Relevant Authority may by further order ... fill the vacancy.

[(7) An order under this section—
  (a) if made by the Housing Corporation, shall be made under its seal, and
  (b) if made by the Secretary of State, shall be made in writing.

Notes

S 46

The Relevant Authority has the power to appoint a manager to implement the agreed proposals. If so appointed the manager has the standing to apply to the High Court for directions (HA 1996 s 46(5)) and any direction of the Court will supersede any direction of the Relevant Authority in respect of the same matter (HA 1996 s 46(5)).

8.9

47 Powers of the manager

(1) An order under section 46(1) shall confer on the manager power generally to do all such things as are necessary for carrying out his functions.

(2) The order may include the following specific powers—
  1 Power to take possession of the land held by the landlord and for that purpose to take any legal proceedings which seem to him expedient.
  2 Power to sell or otherwise dispose of the land by public auction or private contract.
  3 Power to raise or borrow money and for that purpose to grant security over the land.

4   Power to appoint a solicitor or accountant or other professionally qualified person to assist him in the performance of his functions.

5   Power to bring or defend legal proceedings relating to the land in the name and on behalf of the landlord.

6   Power to refer to arbitration any question affecting the land.

7   Power to effect and maintain insurance in respect of the land.

8   Power where the landlord is a body corporate to use the seal of the body corporate for purposes relating to the land.

9   Power to do all acts and to execute in the name and on behalf of the landlord any deed, receipt or other document relating to the land.

10   Power to appoint an agent to do anything which he is unable to do for himself or which can more conveniently be done by an agent, and power to employ and dismiss any employees.

11   Power to do all such things (including the carrying out of works) as may be necessary in connection with the management or transfer of the land.

12   Power to make any payment which is necessary or incidental to the performance of his functions.

13   Power to carry on the business of the landlord so far as relating to the management or transfer of the land.

14   Power to grant or accept a surrender of a lease or tenancy of any of the land, and to take a lease or tenancy of any property required or convenient for the landlord's housing activities.

15   Power to make any arrangement or compromise on behalf of the landlord in relation to the management or transfer of the land.

16   Power to do all other things incidental to the exercise of any of the above powers.

(3) In carrying out his functions the manager acts as the landlord's agent and he is not personally liable on a contract which he enters into as manager.

(4) A person dealing with the manager in good faith and for value is not concerned to inquire whether the manager is acting within his powers.

(5) The manager shall, so far as practicable, consult the landlord's tenants about any exercise of his powers which is likely to affect them and inform them about any such exercise of his powers.

Notes

S 47

A manager has the general power to all such things necessary for the carrying out of his functions (HA 1996 s 47(1)). In addition, s 47(2) sets out the powers that may be included in an order appointing a manager. Note that the manager is the agent of the landlord when carrying out his functions and is not personally liable on a contract that he enters into as manager (HA 1996 s 47(3)).

8.10

48 Powers of the manager: transfer of engagements

(1) An order under section 46(1) may, where the landlord is an industrial and provident society, give the manager power to make and execute on behalf of the society an instrument transferring the engagements of the society.

(2) Any such instrument has the same effect as a transfer of engagements under section 51 or 52 of the Industrial and Provident Societies Act 1965 (transfer of engagements by special resolution to another society or a company).

In particular, its effect is subject to section 54 of that Act (saving for rights of creditors).

(3) A copy of the instrument, signed by the manager, shall be sent to the Financial Services Authority and registered by it; and until that copy is so registered the instrument shall not take effect.

(4) It is the duty of the manager to send a copy for registration within 14 days from the day on which the instrument is executed; but this does not invalidate registration after that time.

8.11

49 Assistance by the Relevant Authority

(1) The Relevant Authority may give such assistance as it thinks fit—
  (a) to the landlord, for the purpose of preserving the position pending the making of and agreement to proposals;
  (b) to the landlord or a manager appointed under section 46, for the purpose of carrying out any agreed proposals.

(2) The Relevant Authority may, in particular—
  (a) lend staff;
  (b) pay or secure payment of the manager's reasonable remuneration and expenses;
  (c) give such financial assistance as appears to the [Relevant Authority] to be appropriate.

(3) The giving by the Housing Corporation of the following forms of assistance requires]the consent of the Secretary of State—
  (a) making grants or loans;
  (b) agreeing to indemnify the manager in respect of liabilities incurred or loss or damage sustained by him in connection with his functions;
  (c) paying or guaranteeing the repayment of the principal of, the payment of interest on and the discharge of any other financial obligation in connection with any sum borrowed (before or after the making of the order) and secured on any land disposed of.

Notes

S 49

This provision sets out the nature of the assistance that the Relevant Authority can give:

(a)   To the landlord to preserve the position pending the making of and agreement of proposals; and

(b)   To the landlord or a manager appointed under s 46, for the purposes of carrying out any agreed proposals.

8.12

50 Application to court to secure compliance with agreed proposals

(1) The landlord or any creditor of the landlord may apply to the High Court on the ground that an action of the manager appointed under section 46 is not in accordance with the agreed proposals.

On such an application the court may confirm, reverse or modify any act or decision of the manager, give him directions or make such other order as it thinks fit.

(2) The Relevant Authority or any other person bound by agreed proposals may apply to the High Court on the ground that any action, or proposed action, by another person bound by the proposals is not in accordance with those proposals.

On such an application the court may—

(a)   declare any such action to be ineffective, and

(b)   grant such relief by way of injunction, damages or otherwise as appears to the court appropriate.

Notes

S 50(1)

This provision gives a power to the landlord or any creditor (secured or unsecured) to apply to the High Court to challenge an action taken by a manager on the basis that it is not in accordance with the agreed proposals. The court's powers on such an application are wide – it can confirm, reverse or modify any act or decision of the manager, give him directions or make such order as it thinks fit.

S 50(2)

The class of potential applicants is wider in respect of s 50(2). The application may be made by the Relevant Authority or any person bound by agreed proposals. These persons are set out in HA 1996 s 45(2) and are (in addition to the Relevant Authority) the landlord, all the landlord's creditors and any liquidator, administrator, administrative receiver or receiver appointed in respect of the landlord or its land. The circumstances in which an application can be made are also wider, because s 50(2) applies to proposed actions as well as to executed actions. However, the powers of the court are not quite as wide as they are in relation to an application under s 50(1).

Insolvency Act 2000

2000 CHAPTER 39

An Act to amend the law about insolvency; to amend the Company Directors Disqualification Act 1986; and for connected purposes.

[30th November 2000]

BE IT ENACTED by the Queen's most Excellent Majesty, by and with the advice and consent of the Lords Spiritual and Temporal, and Commons, in this present Parliament assembled, and by the authority of the same, as follows:—

9.1–9.14

14 Model law on cross-border insolvency

(1) The Secretary of State may by regulations make any provision which he considers necessary or expedient for the purpose of giving effect, with or without modifications, to the model law on cross-border insolvency.

(2) In particular, the regulations may—
  (a)   apply any provision of insolvency law in relation to foreign proceedings (whether begun before or after the regulations come into force),
  (b)   modify the application of insolvency law (whether in relation to foreign proceedings or otherwise),
  (c)   amend any provision of section 426 of the Insolvency Act 1986 (co-operation between courts),
and may apply or, as the case may be, modify the application of insolvency law in relation to the Crown.

(3) The regulations may make different provision for different purposes and may make—
  (a)   any supplementary, incidental or consequential provision, or
  (b)   any transitory, transitional or saving provision,
which the Secretary of State considers necessary or expedient.

(4) In this section—
  'foreign proceedings' has the same meaning as in the model law on cross-border insolvency,
  'insolvency law' has the same meaning as in section 426(10)(a) and (b) of the Insolvency Act 1986,
  'the model law on cross-border insolvency' means the model law contained in Annex I of the report of the 30th session of UNCITRAL.

(5) Regulations under this section are to be made by statutory instrument and may only be made if a draft has been laid before and approved by resolution of each House of Parliament.

(6) Making regulations under this section requires the agreement—
    (a)   if they extend to England and Wales, of the Lord Chancellor,
    (b)   if they extend to Scotland, of the Scottish Ministers.

Notes

The United Nations Commission on International Trade Law ('UNICITRAL') Model Law was brought into force under the Cross-Border Insolvency Regulations 2006 (SI 2006/1030) with effect from 6 April 2006 in a modified form. The Model Law generally applies to both corporate and individual debtors in circumstances where a foreign representative requests assistance from the court in respect of foreign insolvency proceedings ; (b) there are concurrent insolvency proceedings in England and another country; (c) foreign creditors wish to become involved in insolvency proceedings in England. See the UNICITRAL Model Law and the Cross-Border Insolvency Regulations which appear in unannotated form in this work.

Landlord and Tenant (Covenants) Act 1995

Excluded assignments

10.1

11 Assignments in breach of covenant or by operation of law

(1) This section provides for the operation of sections 5 to 10 in relation to assignments in breach of a covenant of a tenancy or assignments by operation of law ("excluded assignments").

(2) In the case of an excluded assignment subsection (2) or (3) of section 5—
- (a) shall not have the effect mentioned in that subsection in relation to the tenant as from that assignment, but
- (b) shall have that effect as from the next assignment (if any) of the premises assigned by him which is not an excluded assignment.

(3) In the case of an excluded assignment subsection (2) or (3) of section 6 or 7—
- (a) shall not enable the landlord or former landlord to apply for such a release as is mentioned in that subsection as from that assignment, but
- (b) shall apply on the next assignment (if any) of the reversion assigned by the landlord which is not an excluded assignment so as to enable the landlord or former landlord to apply for any such release as from that subsequent assignment.

(4) Where subsection (2) or (3) of section 6 or 7 does so apply—
- (a) any reference in that section to the assignment (except where it relates to the time as from which the release takes effect) is a reference to the excluded assignment; but
- (b) in that excepted case and in section 8 as it applies in relation to any application under that section made by virtue of subsection (3) above, any reference to the assignment or proposed assignment is a reference to any such subsequent assignment as is mentioned in that subsection.

(5) In the case of an excluded assignment section 9—
- (a) shall not enable the tenant or landlord and his assignee to apply for an agreed apportionment to become binding in accordance with section 10 as from that assignment, but
- (b) shall apply on the next assignment (if any) of the premises or reversion assigned by the tenant or landlord which is not an excluded assignment so as to enable him and his assignee to apply for such an apportionment to become binding in accordance with section 10 as from that subsequent assignment.

(6) Where section 9 does so apply—

(a)   any reference in that section to the assignment or the assignee under it is a reference to the excluded assignment and the assignee under that assignment; but

(b)   in section 10 as it applies in relation to any application under section 9 made by virtue of subsection (5) above, any reference to the assignment or proposed assignment is a reference to any such subsequent assignment as is mentioned in that subsection.

(7) If any such subsequent assignment as is mentioned in subsection (2), (3) or (5) above comprises only part of the premises assigned by the tenant or (as the case may be) only part of the premises the reversion in which was assigned by the landlord on the excluded assignment—

(a)   the relevant provision or provisions of section 5, 6, 7 or 9 shall only have the effect mentioned in that subsection to the extent that the covenants or covenant in question fall or falls to be complied with in relation to that part of those premises; and

(b)   that subsection may accordingly apply on different occasions in relation to different parts of those premises.

Notes

S 11

This provision modifies the application of s 5 to 10 of the Act in respect of "excluded assignments", so as to prevent those sections applying if an assignment is an excluded assignment. "Excluded assignments" are assignments made in breach of covenant or assignments by operation of law. This definition therefore includes the vesting of a landlord or a tenant's interest in a trustee in bankruptcy.

The effect of section 11 when a tenant is adjudged bankrupt

On the vesting of the tenant's interest in his trustee in bankruptcy the following sections of the Act do not have effect:

(a)   **Section 5** – as such, the tenant is not released from the tenant covenants of the tenancy and he continues to have the benefit of the landlord's covenants. Section 5 will only apply to the next non-excluded assignment of the tenant's interest. In practice, unless a trustee in bankruptcy can quickly assign the tenant's interest under the lease he is likely to disclaim the lease.

(b)   **Sections 9, 10** These sections ordinarily apply when there is an assignment of part of the demised premises or part of the reversion and the assignor and assignee agree between themselves as to the apportionment of a non-attributable tenant or landlord covenant. The Act sets out a mechanism whereby the assignor and assignee can apply to make the apportionment binding on the landlord or tenant (as the case may be). These provisions are excluded in the case of an excluded assignment e g one of two or more joint tenants (or landlords) is adjudged bankrupt and his interest vests in his trustee in bankruptcy. Sections 9 and 10 will only apply to the next assignment by the tenant or landlord that is not an excluded assignment.

The effect of section 11 when a landlord is adjudged bankrupt

On the vesting of the landlord's interest in his trustee in bankruptcy the following sections of the Act do not have effect:

(a)   **Sections 6, 7** As such, the landlord (or a former landlord who is still bound by a landlord covenant of the tenancy) may not apply for a release of his liability. Sections 6 and 7 will only apply to the next non-excluded assignment of the landlord's interest.

(b) **Sections 9, 10** See the notes to "the effect of section 11 when a tenant is adjudged bankrupt" above.

Forfeiture and disclaimer

10.2

21 Forfeiture or disclaimer limited to part only of demised premises

(1) Where—
- (a) as a result of one or more assignments a person is the tenant of part only of the premises demised by a tenancy, and
- (b) under a proviso or stipulation in the tenancy there is a right of re-entry or forfeiture for a breach of a tenant covenant of the tenancy, and
- (c) the right is (apart from this subsection) exercisable in relation to that part and other land demised by the tenancy,

the right shall nevertheless, in connection with a breach of any such covenant by that person, be taken to be a right exercisable only in relation to that part.

(2) Where—
- (a) a company which is being wound up, or a trustee in bankruptcy, is as a result of one or more assignments the tenant of part only of the premises demised by a tenancy, and
- (b) the liquidator of the company exercises his power under section 178 of the Insolvency Act 1986, or the trustee in bankruptcy exercises his power under section 315 of that Act, to disclaim property demised by the tenancy,

the power is exercisable only in relation to the part of the premises referred to in paragraph (a).

Notes

S 21

The effect of this section is that a disclaimer served by a liquidator or trustee in bankruptcy will only apply to that part of the demised premises of which the insolvent person is the tenant. This section only has any practical application in circumstances where there have been assignment(s) of part or parts of premises that were originally let to one tenant. This section only applies to new tenancies under the Act ie a tenancy entered into after 1st January 1996 otherwise than in pursuance of an agreement entered into before that date or a court order made before that date (see sections 1(1) and (3) of the Act and SI 1995/2963).

Law of Property Act 1925

SS 101 – 110

101 Powers incident to estate or interest of mortgage

(1) A mortgagee, where the mortgage is made by deed, shall, by virtue of this Act, have the following powers, to the like extent as if they had been in terms conferred by the mortgage deed, but not further (namely):–

   (i) A power, when the mortgage money has become due, to sell, or to concur with any other person in selling, the mortgaged property, or any part thereof, either subject to prior charges or not, and either together or in lots, by public auction or by private contract, subject to such conditions respecting title, or evidence of title, or other matter, as the mortgagee thinks fit, with power to vary any contract for sale, and to buy in at an auction, or to rescind any contract for sale, and to re-sell, without being answerable for any loss occasioned thereby; and

   (ii) A power, at any time after the date of the mortgage deed, to insure and keep insured against loss or damage by fire any building, or any effects or property of an insurable nature, whether affixed to the freehold or not, being or forming part of the property which or an estate or interest wherein is mortgaged, and the premiums paid for any such insurance shall be a charge on the mortgaged property or estate or interest, in addition to the mortgage money, and with the same priority, and with interest at the same rate, as the mortgage money; and

   (iii) A power, when the mortgage money has become due, to appoint a receiver of the income of the mortgaged property, or any part thereof; or, if the mortgaged property consists of an interest in income, or of a rentcharge or an annual or other periodical sum, a receiver of that property or any part thereof; and

   (iv) A power, while the mortgagee is in possession, to cut and sell timber and other trees ripe for cutting, and not planted or left standing for shelter or ornament, or to contract for any such cutting and sale, to be completed within any time not exceeding twelve months from the making of the contract.

(1A) Subsection (1)(i) is subject to s 21 of the Commonhold and Leasehold Reform Act 2002 (no disposition of part-units)

(2) Where the mortgage deed is executed after the thirty-first day of December, nineteen hundred and eleven, the power of sale aforesaid includes the following powers as incident thereto (namely):—

   (i) A power to impose or reserve or make binding, as far as the law permits, by covenant, condition, or otherwise, on the unsold part of the mortgaged property or any part thereof, or on the purchaser and any property sold, any restriction or reservation with respect to building on or other user of land, or with respect to mines and minerals, or for the purpose of the more beneficial working thereof, or with respect to any other thing:

(ii) A power to sell the mortgaged property, or any part thereof, or all or any mines and minerals apart from the surface:—

    (a) With or without a grant or reservation of rights of way, rights of water, easements, rights, and privileges for or connected with building or other purposes in relation to the property remaining in mortgage or any part thereof, or to any property sold: and

    (b) With or without an exception or reservation of all or any of the mines and minerals in or under the mortgaged property, and with or without a grant or reservation of powers of working, wayleaves, or rights of way, rights of water and drainage and other powers, easements, rights, and privileges for or connected with mining purposes in relation to the property remaining unsold or any part thereof, or to any property sold: and

    (c) With or without covenants by the purchaser to expend money on the land sold.

(3) The provisions of this Act relating to the foregoing powers, comprised either in this section, or in any other section regulating the exercise of those powers, may be varied or extended by the mortgage deed, and, as so varied or extended, shall, as far as may be, operate in the like manner and with all the like incidents, effects, and consequences, as if such variations or extensions were contained in this Act.

(4) This section applies only if and as far as a contrary intention is not expressed in the mortgage deed, and has effect subject to the terms of the mortgage deed and to the provisions therein contained.

(5) Save as otherwise provided, this section applies where the mortgage deed is executed after the thirty-first day of December, eighteen hundred and eighty-one.

(6) The power of sale conferred by this section includes such power of selling the estate in fee simple or any leasehold reversion as is conferred by the provisions of this Act relating to the realisation of mortgages.

Notes

S 101

Insofar as they are not excluded by the mortgage deed the combined effect of the provisions of sections 101(1) and 103 LPA 1925 is to abrogate the general legal principle that where a legal mortgage has been created, whether by demise or legal charge, and no provision is made for retention of possession by the mortgagor, the mortgagee is entitled to immediate possession or receipt of the rents and profits at any time after the execution of the mortgage, for the purposes of protecting or enforcing his security. This is so whether or not there has been any default on the mortgagor's part and whether or not the mortgagor has a cross claim against the mortgagee (*TSB Bank plc v Platts (No 2)* [1998] 2 BCLC 1).

The statutory powers contained in s 101 LPA 1925 arise (in the absence of contrary terms in the deed – see s 101(4)) when:

- the mortgage is made by deed; and
- the mortgage money is due–this is either if the legal date for redemption (if any) has passed or any instalment of the mortgage debt under an instalment mortgage has fallen due (*Payne v Cardiff RDC* [1932] 1 KB 241).

However, s 103 LPA 1925 states that the powers shall not be exercisable except in the circumstances set out in that section (to which see the notes to s 103 LPA 1925 below). It is therefore necessary to read sections 101 and 103 side by side.

S 101(1) 'where the mortgage is made by deed'

It is necessary for the mortgage to be created by deeds for the powers set out in s 101 to arise. The powers do not apply to mortgages (eg debentures) that are made under hand but not under deed. The statutory powers apply to all legal and equitable mortgages that are created by deed. In the event that a debenture is not made by deed, a mortgagee can not achieve a sale without an order of the court and he must persuade the court to exercise its discretionary power of sale pursuant to s 91 of the Law of Property Act 1925.

The s 101 powers apply to land charges registrable under Class A (other than a land improvement charge registered after 31 December 1969) and Class B, because such land charges take effect as if they were created by deed by way of legal mortgage – see s 4(1) of the Land Charges Act 1972.

Section 101 applies to mortgage deed executed on or after 31 December 1881 (see s 101(5)), save that the powers incidental to the statutory power for sale which are contained in s 101(2) only apply to mortgage deeds created after 31 December 1911.

S 101(1)(i) – the power of sale

In order to exercise a power of sale a mortgagee is entitled to take possession without a court order – see *Ropaigealach v Barclays Bank plc* [2000] 1 QB 263 (but the property must be unoccupied if it comprises of or includes a dwelling, otherwise the mortgagee will fall foul of s 6 of the Criminal Law Act 1977 and s 126 of the Consumer Credit Act 1974). The mortgagee has no duty at any time to exercise his powers as mortgagee to sell or take any other action; he may remain passive *Silven Properties Ltd v Royal Bank of Scotland plc* [2003] EWCA Civ 1409, [2003] BCC 1002.

S 101(1)(ii) – power to insure the mortgaged property

This provision gives a mortgagee a limited power to insure all or part of the mortgaged property. The power is subject to the restrictions set out in s 108(2) LPA 1925. The premiums paid for any such insurance are a charge on the mortgaged property, with the same priority and with interest at the same rate as the mortgage money. Although the premiums are a charge, they can not be recovered from the mortgagee as a debt, in the absence of a covenant to pay them.

S 101(1)(iii) – the appointment of a receiver over the income of the mortgaged property

Who may be appointed a receiver?

There is no requirement that the person appointed as a receiver be a licensed insolvency practitioner, provided that he is of full age, not a body corporate and is not an undischarged bankrupt.

The mechanics of appointing a receiver

A receiver is appointed under hand (section 109(1) LPA 1925) and the appointment takes effect when the instrument of appointment is handed to the receiver in such circumstances that the fact of the appointment is communicated to him and he accepts the appointment (*Cripps (Pharmaceuticals) Ltd v Wickenden* [1973] 1 WLR 944).

How soon can a receiver be appointed upon a default by the mortgagor?

Once a creditor is entitled to demand repayment of all money secured to him as mortgagee there is no need for him to specify the precise amount of the debt in making a demand for the moneys due and a debtor who is required to pay money on demand is allowed only such time as is necessary to implement the mechanics of payment needed to discharge the debt before being in default. In light of modern methods of communication and transfer of money which are available the time can be as little as one hour, after which a mortgagee can validly appoint a receiver –see *Bank of Baroda v Panessar* [1987] 2 WLR 208, *Sheppard and Looper Ltd v TSB Bank (No 2)* [1996] 2 BCC 965.

Powers that may be delegated to the receiver by the mortgagee

The instrument of appointment of a receiver may include:

(a)   A delegation by the mortgagee to the receiver of the powers of leasing and accepting surrenders of leases or any specified lease exercisable by the mortgagee (sections 99(19), 100(13) LPA 1925);

(b)   A direction to apply the balance of any money remaining after providing for the payments referred to in s 109(8)(i) to (iv) LPA 1925 (which are effectively the first calls on any money received and to which see the notes to s 108 below) in or towards discharge of the principal money owing to the mortgagee (s 109(8)(v) LPA 1925).

Powers, remuneration and duties of a receiver

These are set out in s 109; see the notes to this section in relation thereto.

The right of the mortgagee to rely on his powers of sale or to appoint a receiver in the event of the insolvency of the mortgagor

(i) Bankruptcy of the mortgagor – sale of the property

After presentation of a bankruptcy petition the court has the discretion to stay any action, execution or legal process against the property of person of the debtor (s 285(1) IA 1986). This discretion is potentially wide enough to catch court proceedings by a mortgagee for an order for sale, however a stay is in practice very unlikely to be ordered because this would create an anomaly with the situation post-bankruptcy.

After the bankruptcy of a mortgagor, or the appointment of an interim receiver, a mortgagee may still enforce his security (s 285(3) & (4) and 286(6) IA 1986). After the sale of the mortgaged property, the mortgagee can prove as an unsecured creditor for the shortfall (if any). However note the provision of s 110(1) LPA 1925, which states that where the mortgagee seeks to solely rely on the bankruptcy of the mortgagor (and this includes a winding up of the mortgagor –see s 205(1)(i) LPA 1925) as his ground for selling the property or appointing a receiver, he may not do so without the leave of the court (this is so even if he would not otherwise need leave).

Where a mortgagee seeks an order for the sale of mortgaged property of the bankrupt, see also IR 6.197 – 6.199, which deal with, amongst other matters, the power of the court to order the taking of accounts and enquiries on such an application.

(ii) Bankruptcy of the mortgagor – appointment of a receiver

After the bankruptcy of the mortgagor or the appointment of an interim receiver, the mortgagee can enforce his right under the mortgage deed to appoint a receiver – see s 285(4) and 286(6) IA 1986. However, on the bankruptcy of a mortgagor a receiver appointed (whether before or after the bankruptcy order is made) cannot logically act as the agent of the mortgagor. The appointment of the receiver will be valid and he will be entitled to the rents and profits, however usually he will be deemed to be the agent of the mortgagee (with the consequence that the mortgagee will be treated as having entered into possession).

(iii) IVA – sale of the property

The effect of an interim order is that no proceedings or execution or other legal process may be commenced or continued except with the leave of the court – s 252 IA 1986. This would cover an application by a mortgagee to court for an order for sale. By analogy with *McMullen & Sons v Cerrone* [1994] BCC 25, where it was held that s 252 IA 1986 does not prevent a landlord from exercising his right to distrain, the section is arguably not wide enough to cover situations where a mortgagee does not require a court order in order to sell the property. A creditors' meeting called for the purposes of approving IVA proposals shall not approve any proposal or modification which affects the right of a secured creditor of the debtor to enforce his security, except with the concurrence of the creditor concerned – s 258(4) IA 1986. As such, once the proposals are approved a secured creditor can enforce his rights, including his power of sale.

(iv) IVA – appointment of a receiver

There is no reference in ss 252, 254 or 258 IA 1986 to a secured creditor requiring leave to enforce his security or being prohibited from enforcing his security (and the appointment of a receiver is a method of enforcement).

(v) Liquidation of the mortgagor – sale of the property

Upon the compulsory liquidation of a mortgagor, between the presentation of a petition and the making of a winding up order the company or any creditor of contributory may apply to the court for a stay of any proceedings (section 126(1) IA 1986). After a winding up order is made or a provisional liquidator has been appointed no claim or proceeding shall be proceeded with or commenced against the company except with the leave of the court and subject to such terms as the court thinks fit (section 130(2) IA 1986). The courts are very reluctant to interfere with the right of a mortgagor by refusing an order for sale and the usual rule is that leave will be granted.

(vi) Liquidation of the mortgagor – appointment of a receiver

Prior to a winding up order being made, a receiver is the agent of the mortgagor (section 109 LPA 1925) and it is submitted that the appointment of a receiver is not an 'action or proceeding' for the purposes of s 126 IA 1986. As such, the court does not have the discretion to prevent the appointment of a receiver.

After a winding up order is made, the appointment of a receiver will necessitate him going into possession as agent of the mortgagor (he will no longer be able to act as the agent of the mortgagor – see *Re Northern Garage Ltd* [1946] Ch 188 and *Gosling v Gaskell* [1897] AC 575). Leave will therefore be required, however in practice it will invariably be granted – see *Re Henry Pound, Son & Hutchins* (1889) 42 Ch D 402.

(vii) Administration – sale of the property

Between the application for an administration order and the order itself, or between the filing of a notice of intention to appoint an administrator and the date the appointment takes effect or five days have elapsed without an appointment being made; and at any time the company is in administration a mortgagee is restricted in enforcing a security except with the leave of the court or permission is given by the administrator (Sch B1 paras 42–44). The guidelines that the court applied on an application for leave under the former administration regime are set out in *Re Atlantic Computer Systems plc* [1992] Ch 505.

(viii) Administration – appointment of a receiver

See (vii) above. The court has refused to grant leave to a secured creditor to enforce its security where it would have appointed a receiver, which would inevitably have resulted in the costs of the receivership being added to the security – see *Royal Trust v Buchler* [1989] BCLC 130. Any LPA receiver appointed prior to the administration shall vacate his office if required to do so by an administrator – Sch B1 para 41(2).

(ix) CVA – sale of the property

Where after 1 January 2003 the directors of the company seek and obtain a moratorium in accordance with IA 1986 Sch A1, no steps may be taken to enforce any security over the company's property except with the leave of the court – Sch A1 para 12(1)(g) IA 1986.

A creditors' meeting summoned to approve any CVA proposals or modifications shall not approve any proposal or modification which effects the right of a secured creditor to enforce his security, except with the concurrence of the creditor concerned.

(x) CVA – appointment of a receiver

See (ix) above.

S 101(2) – Powers incidental to the power of sale

This section sets out powers that are incidental to the power of sale contained in s 101(1)(i). These powers apply if the mortgage deed was executed after 31 December 1911.

S 101(3) – Variation or extension of the statutory powers

The powers set out in s 101(1) may be varied or extended by the mortgage deed, however insofar as the deed does this, the varied or extended powers are still subject to the provisions of the LPA 1925 (and as such are only exercisable in accordance with s 103 LPA 1925).

S 101(4) – Statutory powers only apply so far as a contrary intention is not expressed in the mortgage deed

It is open to a mortgagee to exclude or vary the provisions of the Act. In practice, sections 101 and 103 LPA 1925 are sometimes entirely excluded from a mortgage deed. Often they are not entirely excluded but instead the mortgagee's powers to sell and to appoint a receiver are frequently varied. In particular, s 103 LPA 1925 is often excluded or varied so that the power to sell or appoint a receiver can be exercised after a shorter period than that stated in s 103 LPA 1925.

11.2

103 Regulation of exercise of power of sale

A mortgagee shall not exercise the power of sale conferred by this Act unless and until—

(i) Notice requiring payment of the mortgage money has been served on the mortgagor or one of two or more mortgagors, and default has been made in payment of the mortgage money, or of part thereof, for three months after such service; or

(ii) Some interest under the mortgage is in arrear and unpaid for two months after becoming due; or

(iii) There has been a breach of some provision contained in the mortgage deed or in this Act, or in an enactment replaced by this Act, and on the part of the mortgagor, or of some person concurring in making the mortgage, to be observed or performed, other than and besides a covenant for payment of the mortgage money or interest thereon.

Notes

S 103

This section sets out the circumstances in which the statutory power for sale in s 101 LPA 1925 can be exercised once it has arisen. For a recent discussion of the principles which apply to the exercise of the power of sale by a mortgagee see *Silven Properties Ltd v Royal Bank of Scotland plc* [2003] BCC 1002.

The ground usually relied upon is that found in s 103(ii). If the mortgagee intends to rely on the ground set out in s 103(i) notice must be served on the mortgagor. In practice the restrictions set out in s 103 are often modified or excluded pursuant to the power to do so in sections 101(3) and/or 101(4) LPA 1925. The mortgagee's power of sale survives any disclaimer of the mortgaged property by the mortgagor's liquidator or trustee in bankruptcy – *Hindcastle Ltd v Barbara Attenborough Associates* [1997] AC 70.

11.3

104 Conveyance on sale

(1) A mortgagee exercising the power of sale conferred by this Act shall have power, by deed, to convey the property sold, for such estate and interest therein as he is by this Act authorised to sell or convey or may be the subject of the mortgage, freed from all estates, interests, and rights to which the mortgage has priority, but subject to all estates, interests, and rights which have priority to the mortgage.

(2) Where a conveyance is made in exercise of the power of sale conferred by this Act, or any enactment replaced by this Act, the title of the purchaser shall not be impeachable on the ground—

(a)   that no case had arisen to authorise the sale; or

(b)   that due notice was not given; or

(c)   where the mortgage is made after the commencement of this Act, that leave of the court, when so required, was not obtained; or

(d)   whether the mortgage was made before or after such commencement, that the power was otherwise improperly or irregularly exercised;

and a purchaser is not, either before or on conveyance, concerned to see or inquire whether a case has arisen to authorise the sale, or due notice has been given, or the power is otherwise properly and regularly exercised; but any person damnified by an unauthorised, or improper, or irregular exercise of the power shall have his remedy in damages against the person exercising the power.

(3) A conveyance on sale by a mortgagee, made after the commencement of this Act, shall be deemed to have been made in exercise of the power of sale conferred by this Act unless a contrary intention appears.

11.4

105 Application of proceeds of sale

The money which is received by the mortgagee, arising from the sale, after discharge of prior incumbrances to which the sale is not made subject, if any, or after payment into court under this Act of a sum to meet any prior incumbrance, shall be held by him in trust to be applied by him, first, in payment of all costs, charges, and expenses properly incurred by him as incident to the sale or any attempted sale, or otherwise; and secondly, in discharge of the mortgage money, interest, and costs, and other money, if any, due under the mortgage; and the residue of the money so received shall be paid to the person entitled to the mortgaged property, or authorised to give receipts for the proceeds of the sale thereof.

Notes

S 105

See however IR 1986 r 6.199 which sets out the application of proceeds of sale where there is a sale by a mortgagee of land belonging to a bankrupt. The court's power to direct a sale of mortgage land pursuant to IR 1986 r 6.197 is in addition to any statutory powers of sale that a mortgagee may have.

11.5

106 Provisions as to exercise of power of sale

(1) The power of sale conferred by this Act may be exercised by any person for the time being entitled to receive and give a discharge for the mortgage money.

(2) The power of sale conferred by this Act does not affect the right of foreclosure.

(3) The mortgagee shall not be answerable for any involuntary loss happening in or about the exercise or execution of the power of sale conferred by this Act, or of any trust connected therewith, or, where the mortgage is executed after the thirty-first day of December, nineteen hundred and eleven, of any power or provision contained in the mortgage deed.

(4) At any time after the power of sale conferred by this Act has become exercisable, the person entitled to exercise the power may demand and recover from any person, other than a person having in the mortgaged property an estate, interest, or right in priority to the mortgage, all the deeds and documents relating to the property, or to the title thereto, which a purchaser under the power of sale would be entitled to demand and recover from him.

11.6

107 Mortgagee's receipts, discharges, etc

(1) The receipt in writing of a mortgagee shall be a sufficient discharge for any money arising under the power of sale conferred by this Act, or for any money or securities comprised in his mortgage, or arising thereunder; and a person paying or transferring the same to the mortgagee shall not be concerned to inquire whether any money remains due under the mortgage.

(2) Money received by a mortgagee under his mortgage or from the proceeds of securities comprised in his mortgage shall be applied in like manner as in this Act directed respecting money received by him arising from a sale under the power of sale conferred by this Act, but with this variation, that the costs, charges, and expenses payable shall include the costs, charges, and expenses properly incurred of recovering and receiving the money or securities, and of conversion of securities into money, instead of those incident to sale.

11.7

108 Amount and application of insurance money

(1) The amount of an insurance effected by a mortgagee against loss or damage by fire under the power in that behalf conferred by this Act shall not exceed the amount specified in the mortgage deed, or, if no amount is therein specified two third parts of the amount that would be required, in case of total destruction, to restore the property insured.

(2) An insurance shall not, under the power conferred by this Act, be effected by a mortgagee in any of the following cases (namely):—

(i) Where there is a declaration in the mortgage deed that no insurance is required:

(ii) Where an insurance is kept up by or on behalf of the mortgagor in accordance with the mortgage deed:

(iii) Where the mortgage deed contains no stipulation respecting insurance, and an insurance is kept up by or on behalf of the mortgagor with the consent of the mortgagee to the amount to which the mortgagee is by this Act authorised to insure.

(3) All money received on an insurance of mortgaged property against loss or damage by fire or otherwise effected under this Act, or any enactment replaced by this Act, or on an insurance for the maintenance of which the mortgagor is liable under the mortgage deed, shall, if the mortgagee so requires, be applied by the mortgagor in making good the loss or damage in respect of which the money is received.

(4) Without prejudice to any obligation to the contrary imposed by law, or by special contract, a mortgagee may require that all money received on an insurance of mortgaged property against loss or damage by fire or otherwise effected under this Act, or any enactment replaced by this Act, or on an insurance for the maintenance of which the mortgagor is liable under the mortgage deed, be applied in or towards the discharge of the mortgage money.

11.8

109 Appointment, powers, remuneration and duties of receiver

(1) A mortgagee entitled to appoint a receiver under the power in that behalf conferred by this Act shall not appoint a receiver until he has become entitled to exercise the power of sale conferred by this Act, but may then, by writing under his hand, appoint such person as he thinks fit to be receiver.

(2) A receiver appointed under the powers conferred by this Act, or any enactment replaced by this Act, shall be deemed to be the agent of the mortgagor; and the mortgagor shall be solely responsible for the receiver's acts or defaults unless the mortgage deed otherwise provides.

(3) The receiver shall have power to demand and recover all the income of which he is appointed receiver, by action, distress, or otherwise, in the name either of the mortgagor or of the mortgagee, to the full extent of the estate or interest which the mortgagor could dispose of, and to give effectual receipts accordingly for the same, and to exercise any powers which may have been delegated to him by the mortgagee pursuant to this Act.

(4) A person paying money to the receiver shall not be concerned to inquire whether any case has happened to authorise the receiver to act.

(5) The receiver may be removed, and a new receiver may be appointed, from time to time by the mortgagee by writing under his hand.

(6) The receiver shall be entitled to retain out of any money received by him, for his remuneration, and in satisfaction of all costs, charges, and expenses incurred by him as receiver, a commission at such rate, not exceeding five%um on the gross amount of all money received, as is specified in his appointment, and if no rate is so specified, then at the rate

of five% um on that gross amount, or at such other rate as the court thinks fit to allow, on application made by him for that purpose.

(7) The receiver shall, if so directed in writing by the mortgagee, insure to the extent, if any, to which the mortgagee might have insured and keep insured against loss or damage by fire, out of the money received by him, any building, effects, or property comprised in the mortgage, whether affixed to the freehold or not, being of an insurable nature.

(8) Subject to the provisions of this Act as to the application of insurance money, the receiver shall apply all money received by him as follows, namely:—

(i) In discharge of all rents, taxes, rates, and outgoings whatever affecting the mortgaged property; and

(ii) In keeping down all annual sums or other payments, and the interest on all principal sums, having priority to the mortgage in right whereof he is receiver; and

(iii) In payment of his commission, and of the premiums on fire, life, or other insurances, if any, properly payable under the mortgage deed or under this Act, and the cost of executing necessary or proper repairs directed in writing by the mortgagee; and

(iv) In payment of the interest accruing due in respect of any principal money due under the mortgage; and

(v) In or towards discharge of the principal money if so directed in writing by the mortgagee;

and shall pay the residue, if any, of the money received by him to the person who, but for the possession of the receiver, would have been entitled to receive the income of which he is appointed receiver, or who is otherwise entitled to the mortgaged property.

Notes

S 109(1)

The power to appoint a receiver does not arise until a mortgagee is entitled to exercise his power of sale pursuant to s 103 LPA 1925. See also the notes under s 101(1)(iii) on the appointment of a receiver.

S 109(2) – receiver deemed to be the agent of the mortgagor

There is no statutory requirement that the deemed agency ends on the insolvency of the mortgagor (as compared with an administrative receiver, whose deemed agency on behalf of a company was automatically terminated on the company going in to liquidation – see s 44(1)(a) IA 1986). It has however been held that the agency of an LPA receiver ceases upon the winding up of the mortgagor (whether compulsory or voluntary) – *Gosling v Gaskell* [1897] AC 575 and *Thornes v Todd* [1926] 2 KB 511. Logically, the agency also ceases on a bankruptcy, where the bankrupt's interest in the mortgaged property vests in first the Official Receiver and then his trustee in bankruptcy.

Whilst an LPA receiver is ordinarily an agent for the mortgagor, in certain cases the acceptance by the receiver of rent from an unauthorised tenant of the mortgagor can create a new tenancy between the mortgagee (usually a bank) and the tenant – see *Mann v Nijar & another* CA 18.12.98 (Lawtell). The determination of a receiver's deemed agency does not terminate his appointment and he will be entitled to the rents and profits, however usually he will be deemed to be the agent of the mortgagee (with the consequence that the mortgagee will be treated as having entered into possession).

S 109(3) – the powers of a receiver

The powers of an LPA receiver, unless modified or extended in the mortgage deed, are very restrictive. For instance, unless he is given the express power to do so in the mortgage deed an LPA receiver does not have the power to carry on a business operated on the mortgaged property by the mortgagor, to borrow money on the mortgaged property or to sell all or any part of the mortgaged property (see *Medforth v Blake* [2000] Ch 86).

Receiver's power to carry on a business

Subject to his primary duty to try to bring about a situation in which interest on the secured debt can be paid and the debt itself repaid, a receiver owes a duty to manage the property with due diligence. This does not place an obligation on a receiver to continue to carry on a business on the mortgaged premises previously carried on by the mortgagor but, if the receiver does carry on the business, he is required to take reasonable steps in order to try to do so profitably – see *Medforth v Blake* [2000] Ch 86. A claim against a receiver for breach of his duty to manage the property with due diligence is not an action on a specialty and the usual 6 year limitation period applies – *Raja v Lloyds TSB Bank Ltd* [2001] EWCA Civ 210, 82 P & CR 191.

Receiver's power of sale

Where a mortgage deed creates an express power of sale in favour of a receiver, the mortgagor will have to convey the property unless the receiver is given power of attorney to execute deeds in the name of the mortgagor. In the absence of such a power of attorney a trustee in bankruptcy or liquidator would have to join in any sale by a receiver on the mortgagor being declared bankrupt or going into liquidation.

A sale by a receiver pursuant to a mortgage deed is not a disposition for the purposes of s 127 IA 1986 (the relevant disposition in such a case would be the mortgage and not the sale under the mortgage – see *Re French's Wine Bar Ltd* (1987) 3 BCC 173). A receiver like a mortgagee is not under a duty to progress applications for planning permission or complete the grant of leases which would allegedly improve the value of the security; he is entitled to sell property in the condition in which it stood at the date of appointment without investing money or time in increasing its likely sale value: *Silven Properties Ltd v Royal Bank of Scotland plc* [2003] EWCA Civ 1409, [2003] BCC 1002.

S 109(5) – Removal of a receiver

A mortgagee may remove a receiver under a written instrument. Although a receiver is deemed to be the agent of the mortgagor, a mortgagor may not dismiss him – *Gomba Holdings UK Ltd v Minories Finance Ltd* [1988] 1 WLR 1231 at 1233. Agency principles are of limited use in analysing the relationship of the receiver and the mortgagor as the agency is primarily a device to protect the mortgagee: *Silven Properties Ltd v Royal Bank of Scotland plc* [2003] EWCA Civ 1409, [2003] BCC 1002.

S 109(6) – Receiver's remuneration

The document appointing the receiver should state his remuneration (which should be no more than 5% of the gross amount of all money received). If his remuneration is not so fixed, he is entitled by way of default to 5% on that gross amount or alternatively he may apply to the court to fix such rate as it thinks fit, however this is only necessary if the receiver wishes to receive a higher rate; see *Marshall v Cottingham* [1982] Ch 82.

S 109(8) – application of money received by a receiver

This section sets out the order of priority that applies to the application of money (other than insurance money) received by a receiver. Technically, the receiver has a discretion about whether or not to apply this statutory order and pay any particular creditor.

S 109(8)(i) – rents, taxes, rates and outgoings affecting the mortgaged property

Taxes include the payment to the Commissioners of VAT on rent collected *Sargent v Commissioners of Customs & Excise* [1995] 1 WLR 821. Note however that the commissioners are not entitled to treat the receiver as a taxable person so as to make him personally liable for the VAT (although query whether this would be the case post liquidation or bankruptcy, when the receiver would cease to act as the agent of the mortgagor). A receiver of empty property is not under an obligation to exercise his discretion and pay unpaid non-domestic property unoccupied property rates (which do not form part of the expenses of the receivership either) *Re Sobam BV and Satelscopp BV; Brown v Corporation of London* [1996] 1 WLR 1070.

11.9

110 Effect of bankruptcy of the mortgagor on the power to sell or appoint a receiver

(1) Where the statutory or express power for a mortgagee either to sell or to appoint a receiver is made exercisable by reason of the mortgagor ... being adjudged a bankrupt, such power shall not be exercised only on account of the ... adjudication, without the leave of the court.

(2) This section applies only where the mortgage deed is executed after the commencement of this Act.

Notes

This section applies if the only ground upon which a mortgagee seeks to exercise his power of sale or appoint a receiver is the bankruptcy of the mortgagor. 'Bankruptcy' includes a winding up of the mortgagee –see s 205(1)(i) LPA 1925.

Limited Liability Partnerships Act 2000

2000 CHAPTER 12

An Act to make provision for limited liability partnerships.

[20th July 2000]

BE IT ENACTED by the Queen's most Excellent Majesty, by and with the advice and consent of the Lords Spiritual and Temporal, and Commons, in this present Parliament assembled, and by the authority of the same, as follows:—

Introductory

12.1–12.9

1 Limited liability partnerships

(1) There shall be a new form of legal entity to be known as a limited liability partnership.

(2) A limited liability partnership is a body corporate (with legal personality separate from that of its members) which is formed by being incorporated under this Act; and—

    (a) in the following provisions of this Act (except in the phrase 'oversea limited liability partnership'), and

    (b) in any other enactment (except where provision is made to the contrary or the context otherwise requires),

references to a limited liability partnership are to such a body corporate.

(3) A limited liability partnership has unlimited capacity.

(4) The members of a limited liability partnership have such liability to contribute to its assets in the event of its being wound up as is provided for by virtue of this Act.

(5) Accordingly, except as far as otherwise provided by this Act or any other enactment, the law relating to partnerships does not apply to a limited liability partnership.

(6) The Schedule (which makes provision about the names and registered offices of limited liability partnerships) has effect.

7 Ex-members

(1) This section applies where a member of a limited liability partnership has either ceased to be a member or—

(a)   has died,

(b)   has become bankrupt ,or had his estate sequestrated or has been wound up,

(c)   has granted a trust deed for the benefit of his creditors, or

(d)   has assigned the whole or any part of his share in the limited liability partnership (absolutely or by way of charge or security).

(2) In such an event the former member or—

(a)   his personal representative,

(b)   his trustee in bankruptcy or permanent or interim trustee (within the meaning of the Bankruptcy (Scotland) Act 1985) or liquidator,

(c)   his trustee under the trust deed for the benefit of his creditors, or

(d)   his assignee,

may not interfere in the management or administration of any business or affairs of the limited liability partnership.

(3) But subsection (2) does not affect any right to receive an amount from the limited liability partnership in that event.

Regulations

12.10

14 Insolvency and winding up

(1) Regulations shall make provision about the insolvency and winding up of limited liability partnerships by applying or incorporating, with such modifications as appear appropriate, Parts I to IV, VI and VII of the Insolvency Act 1986.

(2) Regulations may make other provision about the insolvency and winding up of limited liability partnerships, and provision about the insolvency and winding up of oversea limited liability partnerships, by—

(a)   applying or incorporating, with such modifications as appear appropriate, any law relating to the insolvency or winding up of companies or other corporations which would not otherwise have effect in relation to them, or

(b)   providing for any law relating to the insolvency or winding up of companies or other corporations which would otherwise have effect in relation to them not to apply to them or to apply to them with such modifications as appear appropriate.

(3) In this Act 'oversea limited liability partnership' means a body incorporated or otherwise established outside Great Britain and having such connection with Great Britain, and such other features, as regulations may prescribe.

Notes

S 14

The relevant regulations are the Limited Liability Partnerships Regulations 2001 (SI 2001/1090). These apply certain parts of IA 1986 with appropriate modifications. These Regulations have recently been amended by the Limited Liability Partnerships (Amendment) Regulations 2005 (SI 2005/1989).

12.11

15 Application of company law etc

Regulations may make provision about limited liability partnerships and oversea limited liability partnerships (not being provision about insolvency or winding up) by—

(a) applying or incorporating, with such modifications as appear appropriate, any law relating to companies or other corporations which would not otherwise have effect in relation to them,

(b) providing for any law relating to companies or other corporations which would otherwise have effect in relation to them not to apply to them or to apply to them with such modifications as appear appropriate, or

(c) applying or incorporating, with such modifications as appear appropriate, any law relating to partnerships.

17 General

(1) In this Act 'regulations' means regulations made by the Secretary of State by statutory instrument.

(2) Regulations under this Act may in particular—

(a) make provisions for dealing with non-compliance with any of the regulations (including the creation of criminal offences),

(b) impose fees (which shall be paid into the Consolidated Fund), and

(c) provide for the exercise of functions by persons prescribed by the regulations.

(3) Regulations under this Act may—

(a) contain any appropriate consequential, incidental, supplementary or transitional provisions or savings, and

(b) make different provision for different purposes.

(4) No regulations to which this subsection applies shall be made unless a draft of the statutory instrument containing the regulations (whether or not together with other provisions) has been laid before, and approved by a resolution of, each House of Parliament.

(5) Subsection (4) applies to—

(a) regulations under section 14(2) not consisting entirely of the application or incorporation (with or without modifications) of provisions contained in or made under the Insolvency Act 1986,

(b) regulations under section 15 not consisting entirely of the application or incorporation (with or without modifications) of provisions contained in or made under Part I, Chapter VIII of Part V, Part VII, Parts XI to XIII, Parts XVI to XVIII, Part XX or Parts XXIV to XXVI of the Companies Act 1985,

(c) regulations under section 14 or 15 making provision about oversea limited liability partnerships, and

(d) regulations under section 16.

(6) A statutory instrument containing regulations under this Act shall (unless a draft of it has been approved by a resolution of each House of Parliament) be subject to annulment in pursuance of a resolution of either House of Parliament.

Matrimonial Causes Act 1973

13.1

39 Settlement, etc, made in compliance with a property adjustment order may be avoided on bankruptcy of settlor

The fact that a settlement or transfer of property had to be made in order to comply with a property adjustment order shall not prevent that settlement or transfer from being a transaction in respect of which an order may be made under section 339 or 340 of the Insolvency Act 1986 (transfers at an undervalue and preferences).

Notes

S 39

This provision makes it clear that the mere fact that there has been a court order does not prevent a transfer or settlement from being challenged by a trustee in bankruptcy on the grounds that it was at an undervalue or amounted to a preference. This is so even though the debtor himself could not have impugned the settlement or transfer (for instance because it was an order made by consent). Difficult questions arise in a transaction at an undervalue claim on the assessment of the consideration provided by one spouse to another when trying to ascertain whether it is "significantly less" than the consideration provided by the other party. Often one spouse is taking an interest in the former matrimonial property and a property adjustment order may be made which may be difficult to unscramble absent proof of lack of good faith (*Harman v Glencross* [1986] Fam 81 – a decision under the Bankruptcy Act 1914). It was held in *Re Abbott (A Bankrupt), ex p Trustee of Property of the Bankrupt v Abbott* [1982] 3 WLR 86 that a wife who relinquishes a claim under s 24 Matrimonial Causes Act 1973 in return for the right to a part of her husband's share of the proceeds for sale of the matrimonial home was a purchaser of that right for valuable consideration.

Where a bankrupt agrees to an order for financial relief (particularly by consent) shortly before the presentation of a bankruptcy petition that order may constitute a preference however. To prove a preference it must be shown that the spouse receiving the benefit of the order (usually the wife) is a "creditor" (IA 1986 s 340(3)); a wife with a claim for maintenance is a creditor of her bankrupt husband adopting the wide definition of "creditor" which includes contingent and unascertained creditors (IA 1986 s 383, s 382(1), (3)). A consent order made s 23(1)(b) MCA 1973 makes the beneficiary of the order a secured creditor *Platt v Platt* (1976) 6 Fam Law 107 and this might be used to argue that a previously unsecured spouse has been preferred by the creation of a security. Section 39 only applies to orders made by the court prior to the presentation of a bankruptcy petition. In cases where such an order is made after the presentation of a petition but before the making of a bankruptcy order the order will be void as a disposition of the bankrupt's property within IA 1986 s 284(1) unless ratified by the court: *In Re Flint* [1993] Ch 319. In circumstances where there is an order that one party do forthwith transfer his interest in a property to another party and in default of compliance the requisite documentation may be signed by a District Judge, the proposed transferee obtains an immediate proprietary interest in the property: *Mountney v Treharne* [2002] EWCA Civ 1174,

[2002] BPIR 556. This is so notwithstanding the fact that there has not been a formal transfer of the property from the proposed transferor to the proposed transferee. In cases where there is such an order and the proposed transferor is subsequently adjudged bankrupt the only course open to a trustee in bankruptcy is to apply for the order to be set aside on the grounds that it was at an undervalue or amounted to a preference.

The "relevant time" for the purposes of IA 1986 s 339, 340 will be calculated by reference to the date that the order is perfected or the date on which the decree is made absolute, whichever is the later (a property adjustment order under section 24 of the Matrimonial Causes Act 1973 can be made before or after the decree is made absolute but does not take effect until the decree has been made absolute – see s 24(1), (3) of the Matrimonial Causes Act 1973).

————

Proceeds of Crime Act 2002

2002 CHAPTER 29

14.1

An Act to establish the Assets Recovery Agency and make provision about the appointment of its Director and his functions (including Revenue functions), to provide for confiscation orders in relation to persons who benefit from criminal conduct and for restraint orders to prohibit dealing with property, to allow the recovery of property which is or represents property obtained through unlawful conduct or which is intended to be used in unlawful conduct, to make provision about money laundering, to make provision about investigations relating to benefit from criminal conduct or to property which is or represents property obtained through unlawful conduct or to money laundering, to make provision to give effect to overseas requests and orders made where property is found or believed to be obtained through criminal conduct, and for connected purposes.

[24th July 2002]

Be it enacted by the Queen's most Excellent Majesty, by and with the advice and consent of the Lords Spiritual and Temporal, and Commons, in this present Parliament assembled, and by the authority of the same, as follows:—

Introductory notes

The Proceeds of Crime Act 2002 (PoCA) widened the jurisdiction to confiscate benefits obtained through crime. Before the coming into force of PoCA the jurisdiction was limited to the proceeds of drug trafficking (Drug Trafficking Act 1994) and other specified offences (Part VI of the Criminal Justice Act 1988). That legislation continues to apply in relation to offences committed before 24 March 2003.

PoCA now applies to all offences committed on or after 24 March 2003 and enables the court to act where property is suspected of representing the proceeds either of a 'criminal lifestyle' or of particular criminal conduct. An order may even be made, where statutory assumptions about 'criminal lifestyle' apply, where the property is found, on the balance of probabilities, to be the proceeds of an offence with which the defendant was not even charged.

In deciding what order to make under PoCA the court must determine first the amount of the benefit from the offender's lifestyle or conduct and secondly the 'available amount' that might be realised from the offender's realisable property (referred to in PoCA as 'free property'). In considering what the offender's realisable property comprises, the court may include assets which the offender has disposed of by way of gifts and disposals at an undervalue made in certain circumstances. Gifts or disposals at an undervalue caught by PoCA are called 'tainted gifts'. The 'available amount' is the aggregate of the offender's 'free property' and 'tainted gifts.' The detailed provisions of PoCA relating to the making and enforcement of confiscation orders and as to what constitutes 'free property' and 'tainted gifts' are outside the scope of this work.

The phrase 'confiscation order' is something of a misnomer because the effect of the order is not to confiscate or attach specific property. Rather the criminal court has power, in addition to any other sentence, to require the offender to pay a sum of money. The order may enforced as a fine (but serving a term of imprisonment in default does not satisfy the obligation to pay); or the Director of the Assets Recovery Agency may be appointed as the enforcement authority in which case he will have additional powers to enforce the order by a number of other means provided for in PoCA. The significance of this in the context of insolvency is that the order does not itself give the Asset Recovery Agency or the Crown any proprietary right and therefore does not, without more, take any assets out of the offender's estate.

PoCA specifically provides for restraint orders to be made to preserve assets available to satisfy confiscation orders and for enforcement by means of the appointment of a receiver, both to get in and manage property that is the subject of a restraint order (a receiver appointed at this stage is called a 'management receiver'); and, once a confiscation order is made, to get in and realise any available property (in which case the receiver is called an 'enforcement receiver'). A restraint order may be made at any time after an investigation has been started if there is reason to believe that the alleged offender has benefited from his criminal conduct. It is therefore possible for a restraint order to be made before any criminal proceedings (other than in relation to the anticipated confiscation) are commenced. In addition the fact that criminal proceedings do not result in a confiscation order is not necessarily the end of the matter, because PoCA enables fresh confiscation proceedings to be brought within 6 years where fresh evidence becomes available or within 2 years if no order was originally made because the offender absconded and the prosecution applies to the court to proceed in his absence. There are also provisions allowing the court to re-open the issues of the amount of benefit and 'available amount' if there is reason to believe that this will result in an increase. A restraint order may be made if the confiscation issue is reopened for any of these reasons.

The previous legislation contained powers to enforce confiscation orders by way of charging order (which took the charged asset out of the insolvent estate), but those powers are not repeated in PoCA. Instead PoCA gives the management or enforcement receiver extremely wide powers in relation to available realisable property (although the extent to which those powers may be exercised is curtailed where property is already the subject of a charging order made under the previous confiscation legislation).

There are specific provisions to deal with the position where property is either the subject matter of a restraint order or in the hands of a receiver and the offender is subsequently made bankrupt or where any available property is held by a company which is subsequently wound up or goes into receivership pursuant to a floating charge. Given the restrictions on the appointment of administrative receivers under the Enterprise Act 2002 (and the widening of the use of administration as a means of corporate rescue and the replacement pursuant to that Act, of IA 1986 Part II with the new Sch B1) it is surprising that the Enterprise Act 2002 did not contain any amendments to PoCA to extend the provisions of s 430 PoCA to administrators appointed by debenture holders under the new insolvency regime.

In broad terms the scheme of PoCA, so far as insolvency is concerned, is that the confiscation order or restraint order or appointment of a receiver in anticipation of a confiscation order will take precedence where it predates the insolvency. Conversely, the confiscation proceedings will not affect an existing bankruptcy or winding up or receivership. s 417 PoCA provides that property in respect of which a receiver has been appointed under PoCA or which is subject to a restraint order will not form part of the bankrupt's estate, and there are restrictions in s 419 PoCA on proceedings under IA 1986 s 339 and 423. Sections 426ff. PoCA apply the same general rules to the winding up of companies holding realisable property available to satisfy a confiscation order.

A significant development from the previous legislation is that whereas the Criminal Justice Act 1988 and Drug Trafficking Act 1994 only dealt with company winding up, under PoCA assets secured under a floating charge are not available to a receiver appointed under a debenture (s 430). However under the Enterprise Act 2002 the ability of a floating charge holder to appoint a receiver is severely restricted, and debenture-holders have power to appoint administrators under the new IA 1986 Sch B1 para 14. PoCA says almost nothing at all about administrations and it is not clear how far the permission of the administrator or the Companies Court is necessary before a restraint order may be made or a management or enforcement receiver can be appointed in respect of the assets of a company in administration under the new administration provisions of IA 1986.

Protection of insolvency practitioners

PoCA contains provisions protecting insolvency practitioners who deal with property that is the subject of a restraint orders provided that they believe and have reasonable grounds for believing that they are entitled to do so (see s 432 below). In addition to the powers of the criminal courts, PoCA introduces a new and draconian power to bring civil proceedings for a 'recovery order' even where no criminal proceedings are brought. The effect of a civil recovery order is to vest the property to which the order relates in the 'Trustee for Civil Recovery'. The interrelationship between civil recovery proceedings and insolvency is governed by s 311 PoCA. Where an individual is bankrupt or the subject of an IVA or a company is being wound up or is the subject of a CVA then the civil proceedings may not be commenced or continued in respect of recoverable property which is part of the insolvent estate without the permission of the court seised of the insolvency proceedings. There are detailed provisions as to what constitutes 'recoverable property' which are outside the scope of this work.

Insolvency

14.2

311 Insolvency

(1) Proceedings for a recovery order may not be taken or continued in respect of property to which subsection (3) applies unless the appropriate court gives leave and the proceedings are taken or (as the case may be) continued in accordance with any terms imposed by that court.

(2) An application for an order for the further detention of any cash to which subsection (3) applies may not be made under section 295 unless the appropriate court gives leave.

(3) This subsection applies to recoverable property, or property associated with it, if—

(a) it is an asset of a company being wound up in pursuance of a resolution for voluntary winding up,

(b) it is an asset of a company and a voluntary arrangement under Part 1 of the 1986 Act, or Part 2 of the 1989 Order, has effect in relation to the company,

(c) an order under section 2 of the 1985 Act, section 286 of the 1986 Act or Article 259 of the 1989 Order (appointment of interim trustee or interim receiver) has effect in relation to the property,

(d) it is an asset comprised in the estate of an individual who has been adjudged bankrupt or, in relation to Scotland, of a person whose estate has been sequestrated,

(e) it is an asset of an individual and a voluntary arrangement under Part 8 of the 1986 Act, or Part 8 of the 1989 Order, has effect in relation to him, or

(f)   in relation to Scotland, it is property comprised in the estate of a person who has granted a trust deed within the meaning of the 1985 Act.

(4) An application under this section, or under any provision of the 1986 Act or the 1989 Order, for leave to take proceedings for a recovery order may be made without notice to any person.

(5) Subsection (4) does not affect any requirement for notice of an application to be given to any person acting as an insolvency practitioner or to the official receiver (whether or not acting as an insolvency practitioner).

(6) References to the provisions of the 1986 Act in sections 420 and 421 of that Act, or to the provisions of the 1989 Order in Articles 364 or 365 of that Order, (insolvent partnerships and estates of deceased persons) include subsections (1) to (3) above.

(7) In this section—
(a)   the 1985 Act means the Bankruptcy (Scotland) Act 1985 (c 66),
(b)   the 1986 Act means the Insolvency Act 1986 (c 45),
(c)   the 1989 Order means the Insolvency (Northern Ireland) Order 1989 (SI 1989/2405 (NI 19)),
and in subsection (8) 'the applicable enactment' means whichever enactment mentioned in paragraphs (a) to (c) is relevant to the resolution, arrangement, order or trust deed mentioned in subsection (3).

(8) In this section—
(a)   an asset means any property within the meaning of the applicable enactment or, where the 1985 Act is the applicable enactment, any property comprised in an estate to which the 1985 Act applies,
(b)   the appropriate court means the court which, in relation to the resolution, arrangement, order or trust deed mentioned in subsection (3), is the court for the purposes of the applicable enactment or, in relation to Northern Ireland, the High Court,
(c)   acting as an insolvency practitioner has the same meaning as in section 433,
(d)   other expressions used in this section and in the applicable enactment have the same meaning as in that enactment.

Notes

S 311

This provision applies in all parts of the United Kingdom and deals solely with the position in relation to civil recovery proceedings. The provisions in relation to insolvency and criminal confiscation proceedings are found in Part 9 of PoCA.

Civil recovery proceedings (including proceedings for an interim receiver) may only be brought or continued against property to which s 311(3) applies with the permission of the appropriate court. The 'appropriate court' is the court in which the insolvency proceedings are pending or to which any application relating to the insolvency would be made under the appropriate insolvency legislation. The section applies to the types of insolvency proceedings listed in s 311(3) namely:
(i)   company voluntary winding up
(ii)   company voluntary arrangement

(iii)   interim receivership under *IA 1986 s 286*
(iv)   bankruptcy
(v)   individual voluntary arrangement.

The list clearly does not include compulsory winding up administration or receivership other than an interim receivership. However the list is extended by s 311(6) to cover the estates of deceased persons and insolvent partnerships. In an administration permission would be required under IA 1986 Sch B1 para 43. In *Q3 Media Limited (Ch D (Rimer J)* 22/5/2006, Lawtel) the court refused to make an administration order on the basis that the company was subject to an interim receiving order (see s 246 PoCA) and it was likely that all the company's property was 'recoverable property' and not available for the creditors.

Whereas PoCA creates a situation where existing orders in relation to criminal confiscation will trump a subsequent insolvency and vice versa, that does not appear to be the case with civil proceedings. Proceedings for a recovery order may only be brought or continued with leave and the court will have to consider how the making of such an order will affect the bankruptcy. If the recovery proceedings are allowed to be brought or continued and the Assets Recovery Agency succeeds in establishing the grounds for the order then s 266 provides that the court must make an order. A recovery order is an order vesting the recoverable property in the Trustee for Civil Recovery.

S 311(1)

The '1985 Act,' '1986 Act' and '1989 Order' are defined in s 311(7).

S 311(4), (5)

Whilst s 311(4) provides that the application for permission may be made without notice, this is qualified by s 311(5) which provides that notice must be given to any person acting as an insolvency practitioner or to the official receiver, whether or not he is acting as an insolvency practitioner.

Acting as an insolvency practitioner has the same meaning as in s 433 PoCA which incorporates IA 1986 s 388. The notice must be given not only to the trustee in bankruptcy or liquidator or interim receiver or supervisor of a voluntary arrangement as the case may be, but also to any administrative receiver or any other person acting as an insolvency practitioner whose powers in relation to any recoverable property might be affected by the recovery proceedings.

Part 9
Insolvency etc

Bankruptcy in England and Wales

14.3

417 Modifications of the 1986 Act

(1) This section applies if a person is adjudged bankrupt in England and Wales.

(2) The following property is excluded from his estate for the purposes of Part 9 of the 1986 Act—

(a)   property for the time being subject to a restraint order which was made under section 41, 120 or 190 before the order adjudging him bankrupt;

(b)   any property in respect of which an order under section 50 or 52 is in force;

(c) any property in respect of which an order under section 128(3) is in force;

(d) any property in respect of which an order under section 198 or 200 is in force.

(3) Subsection (2)(a) applies to heritable property in Scotland only if the restraint order is recorded in the General Register of Sasines or registered in the Land Register of Scotland before the order adjudging the person bankrupt.

(4) If in the case of a debtor an interim receiver stands at any time appointed under section 286 of the 1986 Act and any property of the debtor is then subject to a restraint order made under section 41, 120 or 190 the powers conferred on the receiver by virtue of that Act do not apply to property then subject to the restraint order.

Notes

S 417

This provision applies only to bankruptcies and not to individual voluntary arrangements. The general effect of this section is to take assets against which enforcement action has been taken in connection with confiscation proceedings under PoCA out of the bankrupt's estate. What this provision does is to remove from the estate any property that is subject to a restraint order or the appointment of an enforcement receiver made before the bankruptcy order (even if made after the presentation of the petition). The restraint order therefore operates as a form of attachment or security and not merely as an injunction and in that respect it is more powerful than a freezing order in ordinary civil proceedings.

S 417(2), (3)

These subsections apply to the bankruptcy of any person holding realisable property that is the subject matter of a restraint order or the appointment of an enforcement receiver. PoCA envisages that a restraint order will be made at an early stage, that a management receiver will (or may) be appointed to get or protect the assets subject to that order, and that once a confiscation order is made an enforcement receiver will be appointed to enforce it.

S 417(4)

Equally where an interim receiver has been appointed under IA 1986 s 286 his powers will not apply to any property caught by the restraint order.

14.4

418 Restriction of powers

(1) If a person is adjudged bankrupt in England and Wales the powers referred to in subsection (2) must not be exercised in relation to the property referred to in subsection (3).

(2) These are the powers—

(a) the powers conferred on a court by sections 41 to 67 and the powers of a receiver appointed under section 48, 50 or 52;

(b) the powers conferred on a court by sections 120 to 136 and Schedule 3 and the powers of an administrator appointed under section 125 or 128(3);

>   (c)   the powers conferred on a court by sections 190 to 215 and the powers of a receiver appointed under section 196, 198 or 200.
>
> (3) This is the property—
>   (a)   property which is for the time being comprised in the bankrupt's estate for the purposes of Part 9 of the 1986 Act;
>   (b)   property in respect of which his trustee in bankruptcy may (without leave of the court) serve a notice under section 307, 308 or 308A of the 1986 Act (after-acquired property, tools, tenancies etc);
>   (c)   property which is to be applied for the benefit of creditors of the bankrupt by virtue of a condition imposed under section 280(2)(c) of the 1986 Act;
>   (d)   in a case where a confiscation order has been made under section 6 or 156 of this Act, any sums remaining in the hands of a receiver appointed under section 50, 52, 198 or 200 of this Act after the amount required to be paid under the confiscation order has been fully paid;
>   (e)   in a case where a confiscation order has been made under section 92 of this Act, any sums remaining in the hands of an administrator appointed under section 128 of this Act after the amount required to be paid under the confiscation order has been fully paid.
>
> (4) But nothing in the 1986 Act must be taken to restrict (or enable the restriction of) the powers referred to in subsection (2).
>
> (5) In a case where a petition in bankruptcy was presented or a receiving order or adjudication in bankruptcy was made before 29 December 1986 (when the 1986 Act came into force) this section has effect with these modifications—
>   (a)   for the reference in subsection (3)(a) to the bankrupt's estate for the purposes of Part 9 of that Act substitute a reference to the property of the bankrupt for the purposes of the 1914 Act;
>   (b)   omit subsection (3)(b);
>   (c)   for the reference in subsection (3)(c) to section 280(2)(c) of the 1986 Act substitute a reference to section 26(2) of the 1914 Act;
>   (d)   for the reference in subsection (4) to the 1986 Act substitute a reference to the 1914 Act.

Notes

S 418

This provision is the converse of s 417 and provides that where a bankruptcy order has already been made then no restraint order may be made and no receiver may be appointed in respect of any property that would otherwise vest in or be available to the trustee in bankruptcy or to the creditors as a condition of the bankrupt's discharge.

S 418(4)

Once it is established that an asset is available to satisfy any confiscation order that has been or may be made, then nothing in IA 1986 is to be taken as affecting the court's or the receiver's powers under PoCA. This subsection makes it clear that the only restriction on the exercise of the court's or a receivers' powers are those contained in PoCA. The powers of the court to make a restraint order to appoint a receiver and the court's power to make a what is in effect a third party debt order under s 67 PoCA are all discretionary and the subsection ensures that nothing in IA 1986 is to affect the exercise of that discretion. Thus, for example, the fact that the Assets Recovery Agency or the Crown will receive a preference is not to affect the exercise of that discretion.

S 418(5)

The principles contained in the previous subsections are extended to pre IA 1986 bankruptcies.

14.5

419 Tainted gifts

(1) This section applies if a person who is adjudged bankrupt in England and Wales has made a tainted gift (whether directly or indirectly).

(2) No order may be made under section 339, 340 or 423 of the 1986 Act (avoidance of certain transactions) in respect of the making of the gift at any time when—

   (a)   any property of the recipient of the tainted gift is subject to a restraint order under section 41, 120 or 190, or

   (b)   there is in force in respect of such property an order under section 50, 52, 128(3), 198 or 200.

(3) Any order made under section 339, 340 or 423 of the 1986 Act after an order mentioned in subsection (2)(a) or (b) is discharged must take into account any realisation under Part 2, 3 or 4 of this Act of property held by the recipient of the tainted gift.

(4) A person makes a tainted gift for the purposes of this section if he makes a tainted gift within the meaning of Part 2, 3 or 4.

(5) In a case where a petition in bankruptcy was presented or a receiving order or adjudication in bankruptcy was made before 29 December 1986 (when the 1986 Act came into force) this section has effect with the substitution for a reference to section 339, 340 or 423 of the 1986 Act of a reference to section 27, 42 or 44 of the 1914 Act.

Notes

S 419

Because PoCA allows the court to treat 'tainted gifts' made by the offender as realisable property in the hands of the recipient, this section restricts the ability of the trustee in bankruptcy to obtain orders under IA 1986 s 339, 340, 423 and ensures that where a person has made a gift that is caught by PoCA the subject matter of the tainted gift is available to satisfy a confiscation order.

S 419(2)

This prevents the court from making an order in respect of a gift or preference under IA 1986 s 339, 340, 423 at any time when either a restraint order is in force in relation to the property in the hands of the recipient or where an enforcement receiver has been appointed in relation to that property.

S 419(3)

Where an order under IA 1986 s 339, 340, 423 is made after the conclusion of the criminal proceedings, then the order must take into account any realisations under the confiscation proceedings of property held by the recipient. This is to avoid the injustice to the recipient of having to disgorge the value of the gift twice, first in relation to the confiscation and then on the avoidance of the gift in proceedings brought by the trustee in bankruptcy.

Winding up in England and Wales and Scotland

14.6

426 Winding up under the 1986 Act

(1) In this section 'company' means any company which may be wound up under the 1986 Act.

(2) If an order for the winding up of a company is made or it passes a resolution for its voluntary winding up, the functions of the liquidator (or any provisional liquidator) are not exercisable in relation to the following property—

    (a)   property for the time being subject to a restraint order which was made under section 41, 120 or 190 before the relevant time;

    (b)   any property in respect of which an order under section 50 or 52 is in force;

    (c)   any property in respect of which an order under section 128(3) is in force;

    (d)   any property in respect of which an order under section 198 or 200 is in force.

(3) Subsection (2)(a) applies to heritable property in Scotland only if the restraint order is recorded in the General Register of Sasines or registered in the Land Register of Scotland before the relevant time.

(4) If an order for the winding up of a company is made or it passes a resolution for its voluntary winding up the powers referred to in subsection (5) must not be exercised in the way mentioned in subsection (6) in relation to any property—

    (a)   which is held by the company, and

    (b)   in relation to which the functions of the liquidator are exercisable.

(5) These are the powers—

    (a)   the powers conferred on a court by sections 41 to 67 and the powers of a receiver appointed under section 48, 50 or 52;

    (b)   the powers conferred on a court by sections 120 to 136 and Schedule 3 and the powers of an administrator appointed under section 125 or 128(3);

    (c)   the powers conferred on a court by sections 190 to 215 and the powers of a receiver appointed under section 196, 198 or 200.

(6) The powers must not be exercised—

    (a)   so as to inhibit the liquidator from exercising his functions for the purpose of distributing property to the company's creditors;

(b)   so as to prevent the payment out of any property of expenses (including the remuneration of the liquidator or any provisional liquidator) properly incurred in the winding up in respect of the property.

(7) But nothing in the 1986 Act must be taken to restrict (or enable the restriction of) the exercise of the powers referred to in subsection (5).

(8) For the purposes of the application of Parts 4 and 5 of the 1986 Act (winding up) to a company which the Court of Session has jurisdiction to wind up, a person is not a creditor in so far as any sum due to him by the company is due in respect of a confiscation order made under section 6, 92 or 156.

(9) The relevant time is—

(a)   if no order for the winding up of the company has been made, the time of the passing of the resolution for voluntary winding up;

(b)   if such an order has been made, but before the presentation of the petition for the winding up of the company by the court such a resolution has been passed by the company, the time of the passing of the resolution;

(c)   if such an order has been made, but paragraph (b) does not apply, the time of the making of the order.

(10) In a case where a winding up of a company commenced or is treated as having commenced before 29 December 1986, this section has effect with the following modifications—

(a)   in subsections (1) and (7) for 'the 1986 Act' substitute 'the Companies Act 1985';

(b)   in subsection (8) for 'Parts 4 and 5 of the 1986 Act' substitute 'Parts 20 and 21 of the Companies Act 1985'.

Notes

S 426

This provision and s 427 apply principles similar to those that take effect in relation to bankruptcy to company winding up. The general rule is that the confiscation will take priority over the winding up unless the winding up has already occurred. This is judged according to whether a restraint order is in place at the 'relevant time', which is defined in s 426(9). The section applies only to winding up and has no application to voluntary arrangements, administrations or receiverships (including administrative receiverships), although in the case of receiverships s 430 will govern the position relating to floating charge assets.

S 426(1)

The section applies to all companies that may be wound up under IA 1986 and so extends to Scotland and also to unregistered companies (including foreign companies) subject to the winding up jurisdiction under Part V of IA 1986 as well as to limited liability partnerships in England and Wales and Scotland (see s 431).

S 426(2), (3)

These subsections carry into the effect the principle that an existing order under PoCA will take precedence over a subsequent winding up. They achieve this object by providing that a liquidator's or provisional liquidator's powers are not exercisable in respect of any property that is the subject of a restraint order, or in respect of which an enforcement receiver has been appointed.

S 426(4)–(6)

These provisions give precedence to an existing winding up. The court's and receiver's powers under PoCA must not be exercised so as to inhibit the liquidator from exercising his functions for the purpose of distributing property to the company's creditors or to prevent the payment of any expenses (including the liquidator's or provisional liquidator's remuneration) properly incurred in the winding up (but only to the extent that such expenses were incurred in relation to the property in question).

S 426(7)

As with bankruptcy once it is established that an asset is available to satisfy any confiscation order that has been or may be made, then nothing in IA 1986 is to be taken as affecting the court's or the receiver's powers under PoCA. This subsection makes it clear that the only restriction on the exercise of the court's or a receiver's powers are those contained in PoCA. The powers of the court to make a restraint order, to appoint a receiver and the court's power to make what is in effect a third party debt order under s 67 PoCA are all discretionary and the subsection ensures that nothing in IA 1986 is to affect the exercise of that discretion. Thus, for example, the fact that the Assets Recovery Agency or the Crown will receive a preference is not to affect the exercise of that discretion.

S 426(8)

A person owed money in respect of a confiscation order is not a creditor for the purposes of IA 1986.

S 426(9)

The relevant time is the earlier of any winding up resolution or order affecting the company. It is the date of the order that is important, not the date of presentation of the petition on which an order is made.

14.7

427 Tainted gifts

(1) In this section 'company' means any company which may be wound up under the 1986 Act.

(2) This section applies if—
  (a) an order for the winding up of a company is made or it passes a resolution for its voluntary winding up, and
  (b) it has made a tainted gift (whether directly or indirectly)

(3) No order may be made under section 238, 239 or 423 of the 1986 Act (avoidance of certain transactions) and no decree may be granted under section 242 or 243 of that Act (gratuitous alienations and unfair preferences), or otherwise, in respect of the making of the gift at any time when—
  (a) any property of the recipient of the tainted gift is subject to a restraint order under section 41, 120 or 190, or
  (b) there is in force in respect of such property an order under section 50, 52, 128(3), 198 or 200.

(4) Any order made under section 238, 239 or 423 of the 1986 Act or decree granted under section 242 or 243 of that Act, or otherwise, after an order mentioned in subsection (3)(a) or (b) is discharged must take into account any realisation under Part 2, 3 or 4 of this Act of property held by the recipient of the tainted gift.

(5) A person makes a tainted gift for the purposes of this section if he makes a tainted gift within the meaning of Part 2, 3 or 4.

(6) In a case where the winding up of a company commenced or is treated as having commenced before 29 December 1986 this section has effect with the substitution—

(a) for references to section 239 of the 1986 Act of references to section 615 of the Companies Act 1985 (c 6);

(b) for references to section 242 of the 1986 Act of references to section 615A of the Companies Act 1985;

(c) for references to section 243 of the 1986 Act of references to section 615B of the Companies Act 1985.

Notes

S 427

Because PoCA allows the court to treat 'tainted gifts' made by the offender as realisable property in the hands of the recipient, this section restricts the ability of the liquidator to obtain an order under IA 1986 s 238, 239, 423 and ensures that where a gift has been made and is caught by the Act the subject matter of the tainted gift is available to satisfy a confiscation order.

S 427(1)

The section applies to all companies that may be wound up under IA 1986 and also to unregistered companies (including foreign companies) subject to the winding up jurisdiction under Part V IA 1986 as well as limited liability partnerships in England and Wales and Scotland (see s 431).

S 427(2), (3)

These provisions prevent the court from making an order in respect of the gift or preference under IA 1986 s 238, 239, 423 at any time when either a restraint order is in force in relation to the property in the hands of the recipient or where an enforcement receiver has been appointed in relation to that property.

S 427(4)

Where an order under IA 1986 s 238, 239, 423 is made after the conclusion of the criminal proceedings, then the order must take into account any realisations under the confiscation proceedings of property held by the recipient. This is to avoid the injustice of the recipient having to disgorge the value of the gift twice, first in relation to the confiscation and then on the avoidance of the gift in proceedings brought by the liquidator.

Floating charges

14.8

430 Floating charges

(1) In this section 'company' means a company which may be wound up under

    (a)   the 1986 Act, or

    (b)   the 1989 Order.

(2) If a company holds property which is subject to a floating charge, and a receiver has been appointed by or on the application of the holder of the charge, the functions of the receiver are not exercisable in relation to the following property—

    (a)   property for the time being subject to a restraint order which was made under section 41, 120 or 190 before the appointment of the receiver;

    (b)   any property in respect of which an order under section 50 or 52 is in force;

    (c)   any property in respect of which an order under section 128(3) is in force;

    (d)   any property in respect of which an order under section 198 or 200 is in force.

(3) Subsection (2)(a) applies to heritable property in Scotland only if the restraint order is recorded in the General Register of Sasines or registered in the Land Register of Scotland before the appointment of the receiver.

(4) If a company holds property which is subject to a floating charge, and a receiver has been appointed by or on the application of the holder of the charge, the powers referred to in subsection (5) must not be exercised in the way mentioned in subsection (6) in relation to any property—

    (a)   which is held by the company, and

    (b)   in relation to which the functions of the receiver are exercisable.

(5) These are the powers—

    (a)   the powers conferred on a court by sections 41 to 67 and the powers of a receiver appointed under section 48, 50 or 52;

    (b)   the powers conferred on a court by sections 120 to 136 and Schedule 3 and the powers of an administrator appointed under section 125 or 128(3);

    (c)   the powers conferred on a court by sections 190 to 215 and the powers of a receiver appointed under section 196, 198 or 200.

(6) The powers must not be exercised—

    (a)   so as to inhibit the receiver from exercising his functions for the purpose of distributing property to the company's creditors;

    (b)   so as to prevent the payment out of any property of expenses (including the remuneration of the receiver) properly incurred in the exercise of his functions in respect of the property.

(7) But nothing in the 1986 Act or the 1989 Order must be taken to restrict (or enable the restriction of) the exercise of the powers referred to in subsection (5).

(8) In this section 'floating charge' includes a floating charge within the meaning of section 462 of the Companies Act 1985 (c 6).

Notes

S 430

This provision extends the general principle that confiscation takes precedence over a subsequent insolvency to receiverships of assets caught by floating charges. This will include (but is not limited to) most administrative receiverships where the receiver is appointed under a debenture containing both fixed and floating charges. As with the other sections relating to company insolvency 'company' is widely defined and will include unregistered companies liable to be wound up under IA 1986 as well as limited liability partnerships in England and Wales and Scotland (see s 431).

The Enterprise Act 2002 severely restricted the ability of the holder of a floating charge to appoint an administrative receiver, but enables the holder of a qualifying floating charge to appoint an administrator out of court (see IA 1986, Sch B1 para 14). However, the Enterprise Act 2002 did not amend PoCA with the result that s 430 says nothing about floating charge assets (or any assets) in an administration. Indeed PoCA says almost nothing at all about administrations and it is not clear how far the permission of the administrator or the Companies Court is necessary before a restraint order may be made or a management or enforcement receiver can be appointed in respect of the assets of a company in administration under the new administration provisions of IA 1986. A prior fixed charge will have priority over a confiscation order unless the grant of the charge was itself a 'tainted gift.'

S 430(2), (3)

Where a restraint order has been made or an enforcement receiver has been appointed in respect of any property which is subject to a floating charge, and a receiver is appointed his functions are not exercisable in respect of that property.

S 430(4)–(6)

If a receiver has already been appointed in respect of floating charge assets then the receivership has precedence and the powers of the court or of a receiver appointed under PoCA must not be exercised so as to inhibit the receiver under the charge from exercising his functions for the purpose of distributing property to the company's creditors or to prevent the payment of any expenses (including his remuneration) properly incurred in the receivership (but only to the extent that such expenses were incurred in relation to the property in question).

S 430(7)

As with winding up, once it is established that an asset is available to satisfy any confiscation order that has been or may be made, then nothing in IA 1986 is to be taken as affecting the court's or the receiver's powers under PoCA. This subsection makes it clear that the only restriction on the exercise of the court's or a receiver's powers are those contained in PoCA. The powers of the court to make a restraint order, to appoint a receiver and the court's power to make what is in effect a third party debt order under s 67 PoCA are all discretionary and the subsection ensures that nothing in IA 1986 is to affect the exercise of that discretion.

Limited liability partnerships

14.9

431 Limited liability partnerships

(1) In sections 426, 427 and 430 'company' includes a limited liability partnership which may be wound up under the 1986 Act.

(2) A reference in those sections to a company passing a resolution for its voluntary winding up is to be construed in relation to a limited liability partnership as a reference to the partnership making a determination for its voluntary winding up.

Insolvency practitioners

14.10

432 Insolvency practitioners

(1) Subsections (2) and (3) apply if a person acting as an insolvency practitioner seizes or disposes of any property in relation to which his functions are not exercisable because—

    (a)   it is for the time being subject to a restraint order made under section 41, 120 or 190, or

    (b)   it is for the time being subject to an interim receiving order made under section 246 or an interim administration order made under section 256,

and at the time of the seizure or disposal he believes on reasonable grounds that he is entitled (whether in pursuance of an order of a court or otherwise) to seize or dispose of the property.

(2) He is not liable to any person in respect of any loss or damage resulting from the seizure or disposal, except so far as the loss or damage is caused by his negligence.

(3) He has a lien on the property or the proceeds of its sale—

    (a)   for such of his expenses as were incurred in connection with the liquidation, bankruptcy, sequestration or other proceedings in relation to which he purported to make the seizure or disposal, and

    (b)   for so much of his remuneration as may reasonably be assigned to his acting in connection with those proceedings.

(4) Subsection (2) does not prejudice the generality of any provision of the 1985 Act, the 1986 Act, the 1989 Order or any other Act or Order which confers protection from liability on him.

(5) Subsection (7) applies if—

    (a)   property is subject to a restraint order made under section 41, 120 or 190,

    (b)   a person acting as an insolvency practitioner incurs expenses in respect of property subject to the restraint order, and

    (c)   he does not know (and has no reasonable grounds to believe) that the property is subject to the restraint order.

(6) Subsection (7) also applies if—

    (a)   property is subject to a restraint order made under section 41, 120 or 190,

    (b)   a person acting as an insolvency practitioner incurs expenses which are not ones in respect of property subject to the restraint order, and

    (c)   the expenses are ones which (but for the effect of the restraint order) might have been met by taking possession of and realising property subject to it.

(7) Whether or not he has seized or disposed of any property, he is entitled to payment of the expenses under—

    (a)   section 54(2), 55(3), 56(2) or 57(3) if the restraint order was made under section 41;

> (b) section 130(3) or 131(3) if the restraint order was made under section 120;
>
> (c) section 202(2), 203(3), 204(2) or 205(3) if the restraint order was made under section 190.
>
> (8) Subsection (10) applies if—
>
> (a) property is subject to an interim receiving order made under section 246 or an interim administration order made under section 256,
>
> (b) a person acting as an insolvency practitioner incurs expenses in respect of property subject to the order, and
>
> (c) he does not know (and has no reasonable grounds to believe) that the property is subject to the order.
>
> (9) Subsection (10) also applies if—
>
> (a) property is subject to an interim receiving order made under section 246 or an interim administration order made under section 256,
>
> (b) a person acting as an insolvency practitioner incurs expenses which are not ones in respect of property subject to the order, and
>
> (c) the expenses are ones which (but for the effect of the order) might have been met by taking possession of and realising property subject to it.
>
> (10) Whether or not he has seized or disposed of any property, he is entitled to payment of the expenses under section 280.

Notes

S 432

This provision provides important protection for office holders who inadvertently deal with assets caught by orders made under PoCA. Any person acting as an insolvency practitioner who seizes or disposes of property that is subject to a restraint order or an interim receiving order will not be liable for any loss or damage resulting from such seizure or disposal provided that at the time of the seizure or disposal he both believed, and had reasonable grounds for believing, that he was entitled to do so. In such circumstances he will also have a lien for his expenses and remuneration in connection with the bankruptcy or liquidation or other proceedings.

When read with s 433 PoCA it is clear that this section is not restricted to persons acting as insolvency practitioners in bankruptcy or winding up. The protection is extended to any person acting as an insolvency practitioner within the meaning of IA 1986 s 388 and so extends to provisional liquidators, administrators, administrative receivers, supervisors of voluntary arrangements, interim receivers, trustees of deeds of arrangements and the holders of all the offices referred to in IA 1986 s 388.

S 432(10)

It is provided under s 280 PoCA that in civil recovery proceedings the proceeds of any property vested in the Trustee for Civil Recovery under a recovery order are to be applied first in payment of any sums payable under s 272 PoCA (payments to holders of 'associated property' and to 'excepted joint owners') and then in payment under s 232 PoCA. In general terms 'associated property' is any interest in the recoverable property or any other interest in the property in which the recoverable property subsists and includes the tenancy of a tenant in common whose interest is not subject to confiscation; and an 'excepted joint owner' is a joint owner whose interest is not liable to be confiscated (ss 245 and 270(4) PoCA).

14.11

433 Meaning of insolvency practitioner

(1) This section applies for the purposes of section 432.

(2) A person acts as an insolvency practitioner if he so acts within the meaning given by section 388 of the 1986 Act or Article 3 of the 1989 Order; but this is subject to subsections (3) to (5).

(3) The expression 'person acting as an insolvency practitioner' includes the official receiver acting as receiver or manager of the property concerned.

(4) In applying section 388 of the 1986 Act under subsection (2) above—
   (a) the reference in section 388(2)(a) to a permanent or interim trustee in sequestration must be taken to include a reference to a trustee in sequestration;
   (b) section 388(5) (which includes provision that nothing in the section applies to anything done by the official receiver or the Accountant in Bankruptcy) must be ignored.

(5) In applying Article 3 of the 1989 Order under subsection (2) above, paragraph (5) (which includes provision that nothing in the Article applies to anything done by the official receiver) must be ignored.

Interpretation

14.12

434 Interpretation

(1) The following paragraphs apply to references to Acts or Orders—
   (a) the 1913 Act is the Bankruptcy (Scotland) Act 1913 (c 20);
   (b) the 1914 Act is the Bankruptcy Act 1914 (c 59);
   (c) the 1985 Act is the Bankruptcy (Scotland) Act 1985 (c 66);
   (d) the 1986 Act is the Insolvency Act 1986 (c 45);
   (e) the 1989 Order is the Insolvency (Northern Ireland) Order 1989 (SI 1989/2405 (NI 19)).

(2) An award of sequestration is made on the date of sequestration within the meaning of section 12(4) of the 1985 Act.

(3) This section applies for the purposes of this Part.

Third Parties (Rights Against Insurers) Act 1930

1930 CHAPTER 25

Introductory notes

Before this Act came into force, a claimant had no special rights with respect to a defendant's liability insurance. Consequently, if the defendant was insolvent, the claimant had to prove in the defendant's bankruptcy or winding up in the normal way, and would of course frequently get nothing, even if the defendant had full insurance cover for the liability in question. This was perceived as unjust, particularly in the case of motor insurance, and so this Act was passed to transfer the insured's rights under the insurance policy to the claimant.

The Act comes into operation upon the insolvency of the assured which is widely defined (s 1(1)). Therefore until the insolvency occurs a third party will not generally be entitled to an injunction to prevent a settlement of the assured's claim; this is notwithstanding that it is clear that the result of a settlement is that the assured will be insolvent when the third party establishes its claim *Normid Housing Association v Ralphs* [1989] 1 Lloyd's Rep 265. The Act does not apply to companies wound up voluntarily merely for the purposes of reconstruction or amalgamation (s 1(6)).

There are two features of the Act which limit its value to third parties: (1) the third party merely steps into the shoes of the insured. Consequently the insurer can raise any defence against the third party which would have been available against the insured; (2) since the rights transferred by the Act are subject to the terms of the policy, the third party will normally have to establish the insured's liability before he can claim against the insurer. Generally this will mean obtaining a judgment.

An Act to confer on third parties rights against insurers of third-party risks in the event of the insured becoming insolvent, and in certain other events

[10th July 1930]

15.1

1 Rights of third parties against insurers on bankruptcy, etc, of the insured

(1) Where under any contract of insurance a person (hereinafter referred to as the insured) is insured against liabilities to third parties which he may incur, then—

    (a)   in the event of the insured becoming bankrupt or making a composition or arrangement with his creditors; or

    (b)   in the case of the insured being a company, in the event of a winding-up order being made, or a resolution for a voluntary winding-up being passed, with respect to the company, or of the company entering administration or of a receiver or manager of the company's business or undertaking being duly appointed, or of possession being taken, by or on behalf of the holders of any

debentures secured by a floating charge, of any property comprised in or subject to the charge or of a voluntary arrangement
proposed for the purposes of Part I of the Insolvency Act 1986
being approved under that Part;

if, either before or after that event, any such liability as aforesaid is
incurred by the insured, his rights against the insurer under the contract
in respect of the liability shall, notwithstanding anything in any Act or
rule of law to the contrary, be transferred to and vest in the third party to
whom the liability was so incurred.

(2) Where the estate of any person falls to be administered in accordance
with an order under section 421 of the Insolvency Act 1986, then, if any
debt provable in bankruptcy (in Scotland, any claim accepted in the
sequestration) is owing by the deceased in respect of a liability against
which he was insured under a contract of insurance as being a liability to
a third party, the deceased debtor's rights against the insurer under the
contract in respect of that liability shall, notwithstanding anything in any
such order, be transferred to and vest in the person to whom the debt is
owing.

(3) In so far as any contract of insurance made after the commencement
of this Act in respect of any liability of the insured to third parties
purports, whether directly or indirectly, to avoid the contract or to alter
the rights of the parties thereunder upon the happening to the insured of
any of the events specified in paragraph (a) or paragraph (b) of subsection (1) of this section or upon the estate of any person falling to be
administered in accordance with an order under section 421 of the
Insolvency Act 1986, the contract shall be of no effect.

(4) Upon a transfer under subsection (1) or subsection (2) of this section,
the insurer shall, subject to the provisions of section three of this Act, be
under the same liability to the third party as he would have been under to
the insured, but—

    (a)   if the liability of the insurer to the insured exceeds the liability of
the insured to the third party, nothing in this Act shall affect the
rights of the insured against the insurer in respect of the excess;
and

    (b)   if the liability of the insurer to the insured is less than the liability
of the insured to the third party, nothing in this Act shall affect
the rights of the third party against the insured in respect of the
balance.

(5) For the purposes of this Act, the expression "liabilities to third
parties", in relation to a person insured under any contract of insurance,
shall not include any liability of that person in the capacity of insurer
under some other contract of insurance.

(6) This Act shall not apply—

    (a)   where a company is wound up voluntarily merely for the pur-
poses of reconstruction or of amalgamation with another company; or

> (b)   to any case to which subsections (1) and (2) of section seven of the Workmen's Compensation Act 1925 applies.

Notes

S 1(1)

'under any contract of insurance'

The Act applies to mutual insurance (*Re Allobrogia SS Corpn* [1978] 3 All ER 423) but not to reinsurance.

Foreign insurers and insolvencies

It is not clear when the Act applies, if there is a foreign aspect to the case. *Dicey & Morris on The Conflict of Laws (13th ed), para 35–042*, expresses one view–that the question of third party rights is governed by the same law as that which governs the underlying contract of insurance. On that basis the Act would apply to any insurance policy governed by English law, even if the insurer was based abroad. However by virtue of s 1(1), the Act only has effect in the event of the insured's bankruptcy or winding up (or other specified insolvency proceedings), which probably means English proceedings of this description.

Before the EC Regulation on Insolvency Proceedings 2000 came into force, English winding up proceedings could be brought in respect of a foreign corporation if there was sufficient connection with the jurisdiction, and in particular assets in England. A claim against an insurer could constitute such an asset *Re Compania Merabello San Nicholas SA* [1973] Ch 75 (and see notes to IA 1986 s 220 dealing with unregistered companies). However the EC Regulation will only allow insolvency proceedings to be brought in England against a debtor the centre of whose main interests are in another EU Member State if that debtor has an establishment in England (see the notes to EC Regulation on Insolvency Proceedings 2000).

'liabilites to third parties'

This includes contractual liabilities *First National Tricity Firehouse Ltd v OT Computers Ltd* [2004] EWCA Civ 654, [2004] 3 WLR 886.

'either before or after that event'

The liability to the third party may be incurred before or after the relevant event of insolvency.

'any such liability ... is incurred by the insured'

The rights of the insured against the insurer are transferred at the date of insolvency *First National Tricity Finance Ltd v OT Computers Ltd* [2004] 3 WLR 886. However, these rights will not generally give rise to legal liability on the part of the insurer until the liability of the insured has been established: *Post Office v Norwich Union Fire Ins Sy Ltd* [1967] 2 QB 363, *Bradley v Eagle Star Ins Co Ltd* [1989] AC 957. Unless there is some less stringent requirement in the policy, this will require court proceedings, an arbitration award, or a settlement agreement. In most cases therefore the third party will have to commence proceedings and obtain a judgment. If the insured is already subject to insolvency proceedings, the court's permission will have to be obtained (IA 1986 s 130(2) (liquidation), s 285 (bankruptcy), Sch B1 para 43(6) (administration)). This is likely to be readily granted (*see Post Office v Norwich Union pp 377,378 (above)*).

"rights against the insurer"

The Act does not transfer an assured's claim to the third party but the *"rights against the insurer under the contract in respect of the liability"*. The relevant limitation period will be 6 years unless the rights transferred to the third party are in the nature of a "speciality" in which case the period will be 12 years (The Limitation Act 1980, s 5, s 8). The difficulty may be in ascertaining when the limitation period begins to run. The assured's right of action against the insurer arises when the assured's liability to the third party is determined by agreement, judgment or arbitration award *Bradley v Eagle Star* [1989] AC 957; if at that time the assured is not insolvent (within the Act) the rights transferred to the third party on a subsequent insolvency are arguably subject to a limitation period that has begun to run. In that case the third party will have to issue within 6 years of the accrual of the assured's right of action against the insurer otherwise the claim will be statute barred *Lefevre v White* [1990] 1 Lloyd's Rep 569, 578. Although it may be possible to argue that the limitation period only begins to run on the date of the accrual of the third party's cause of action against the insurer (that is, the insolvency of the assured under the Act, *The Felice* [1990] 2 Lloyd's Rep 21n), this interpretation does some damage to the words of the Act.

Voluntary arrangements

The Act takes effect if the insured enters into a CVA or IVA, as well as other forms of insolvency: s 1(1). Care has to be taken to ensure that the terms of voluntary arrangements do not prejudice creditors who may have a claim under the Act. In *Sea Voyager Maritime Inc & ors v Bielecki* [1999] 1 All ER 628 a creditor had a professional negligence claim against an individual who entered an IVA. The court held that the creditor was unfairly prejudiced by the IVA since it included an implied term that creditors could not commence proceedings, and this would prevent the claimant establishing the insured's liability, which he had to do in order to claim against the insurer (see above).

Prior to *First National Tricity Finance Ltd v OT Computers Ltd* [2004] EWCA Civ 654, [2004] 3 WLR 886 it was thought that the third party had no rights against the insurers until the insured's liability had been established and prior to that point such rights were assets in the voluntary arrangement and could be compromised. Consequently the court directed a supervisor of a voluntary arrangement to accept an offer of settlement by insurers in *Jackson v Greenfield & ors* [1998] BPIR 699. That case would probably be decided differently today.

Dissolved companies

If the insured company has actually been dissolved, it will not be possible to obtain a judgment against it and thereby establish its liability. In these circumstances the third party will have to make an application under CA 1985 s 651 to restore the company to the register. Such an application must be made within two years from dissolution, except in personal injury cases or claims under the Fatal Accidents Act 1976.

Where a company has been struck off the register by the Registrar of Companies as a defunct company under CA 1985 s 652 the company may be restored to the register under CA 1985 s 653 and such an application must be made within 20 years of the date of publication in the Gazette of the notice stating that the company will be struck off the register. The court will make an order for restoration to allow a claim to be made by a third party under the Act usually subject to a condition that the restoration to the register is solely for the purpose of such proceedings.

Defences available to the insurer under the policy

The third party merely steps into the insured's shoes, and acquires no greater rights against the insurer: *The Padre Island* [1984] 2 Lloyd's Rep 408. The insurer can raise any defence against the third party which would have been available against the insured. In particular the insurer can rely on the following:

(1) Misrepresentation, non-disclosure or breach of warranty;
(2) Failure to observe notice requirements;
(3) An arbitration clause in the policy;
(4) The principle that there can be no recovery for a loss intentionally caused by the criminal or tortious act of the insured: *Charlton v Fisher* [2001] EWCA Civ 112, [2001] 3 WLR 1435.
(5) A stipulation that the insured must pay the claim first before he has any right of reimbursement from the insurer (the "pay to be paid" provision: *The Fanti* [1989] 1 Lloyd's Rep 239.

In the case of motor insurance some of these difficulties have been removed by the Road Traffic Act 1988, s 151, which gives third parties improved rights against insurers.

Effect of transfer of rights to the third party

The third party is entitled to bring proceedings directly against the insurer in his own name: *Greenlees v Port of Manchester* [1933] SC 383. If the insurance does not cover all the insured's liability to the third party (if, for example there is a policy limit or excess), the third party can prove in the liquidation or bankruptcy for the balance: s 1(4)(b).

S 1(3)

"Pay to be paid" clauses

The Act seeks to ban provisions under which the liability of the insurer to the third party is precluded on the insolvency of the assured. However "pay to be paid" or "pay first" clauses do not fall foul of s 1(3). See *The Fanti*, discussed above. Similarly s 1(3) does not prevent claims handling rights being transferred to an insurer in the event of insolvency: *Centre Reinsurance International Co v Freakley* [2005] EWCA Civ 115, [2005] All ER (D) 172 (Feb).

S 1(4)

In Sea Voyager Maritime v Bielecki [1999] 1 All ER 628 the court rejected the argument that this subsection prevented the third party from recovering from the insurer any more than its entitlement under a voluntary arrangement. However, the court also held that the terms of the arrangement in that case should be construed as precluding the third party from obtaining a judgment against the debtor for more than the agreed proposals provided. This of course, would normally have the effect of limiting the insurer's liability to the same extent. Thus it is important to consider the terms of the specific voluntary arrangement in question when dealing with the question of recovery from insurer.

15.2

2 Duty to give necessary information to third parties

(1) In the event of any person becoming bankrupt or making a composition or arrangement with his creditors, or in the event of the estate of any person falling to be administered in accordance with an order under section 421 of the Insolvency Act 1986, or in the event of a winding-up order being made, or a resolution for a voluntary winding-up being passed, with respect to any company or of the company entering administration or of a receiver or manager of the company's business or undertaking being duly appointed or of possession being taken by or on behalf of the holders of any debentures secured by a floating charge of any property comprised in or subject to the charge it shall be the duty of the bankrupt, debtor, personal representative of the deceased debtor or company, and, as the case may be, of the trustee in bankruptcy, trustee, liquidator, administrator, receiver, or manager, or person in possession of the property to give at the request of any person claiming that the bankrupt, debtor, deceased debtor, or company is under a liability to him such information as may reasonably be required by him for the purpose of ascertaining whether any rights have been transferred to and vested in him by this Act and for the purpose of enforcing such rights, if any, and any contract of insurance, in so far as it purports, whether directly or indirectly, to avoid the contract or to alter the rights of the parties

thereunder upon the giving of any such information in the events aforesaid or otherwise to prohibit or prevent the giving thereof in the said events shall be of no effect.

(1A) The reference in subsection (1) of this section to a trustee includes a reference to the supervisor of a voluntary arrangement proposed for the purposes of, and approved under, Part I or Part VIII of the Insolvency Act 1986.

(2) If the information given to any person in pursuance of subsection (1) of this section discloses reasonable ground for supposing that there have or may have been transferred to him under this Act rights against any particular insurer, that insurer shall be subject to the same duty as is imposed by the said subsection on the persons therein mentioned.

The duty to give information imposed by this section shall include a duty to allow all contracts of insurance, receipts for premiums, and other relevant documents in the possession or power of the person on whom the duty is so imposed to be inspected and copies thereof to be taken.

Notes

S 2

Duty to provide information and documents

If the third party knows the identity of the insurer then an application can be made for joinder of the insurer to seek a declaration that the insurer is liable to indemnify the assured in respect of the third party's claim *Brice v Wackerbath* [1974] 2 Lloyd's Rep 274, 276. However, a third party will not usually know the identity of the assured's insurance company. In these circumstances assistance may be obtained from s 2 which obliges officeholders to give a third party information although it is now clear that the third party will normally be entitled to this information before the establishment of the insured's liability: *First National Tricity Finance Ltd v OT Computers Ltd* [2004] 3 WLR 886.

15.3

3 Settlement between insurers and insured persons

Where the insured has become bankrupt or where in the case of the insured being a company, a winding-up order or an administration order has been made or a resolution for a voluntary winding-up has been passed, with respect to the company, no agreement made between the insurer and the insured after liability has been incurred to a third party and after the commencement of the bankruptcy or winding-up or the day of the making of the administration order, as the case may be, nor any waiver, assignment, or other disposition made by, or payment made to the insured after the commencement or day aforesaid shall be effective to defeat or affect the rights transferred to the third party under this Act, but

> those rights shall be the same as if no such agreement, waiver, assignment, disposition or payment had been made.

Notes

S 3

Pre liquidation/administration

The above provision does not apply to agreements made before the commencement of the winding up or administration though such agreements which benefit the insurer may in appropriate circumstances be challenged as a transaction at an undervalue or preference (see IA 1986 s 238, 239, 339, 340).

15.4

3A Application to limited liability partnerships

(1) This Act applies to limited liability partnerships as it applies to companies.

(2) In its application to limited liability partnerships, references to a resolution for a voluntary winding-up being passed are references to a determination for a voluntary winding-up being made.

15.5

4 Application to Scotland

. . . .

15.6

5 Short title

This Act may be cited as the Third Parties (Rights Against Insurers) Act 1930.

Part Three

Administration of Insolvent Estates of Deceased Persons Order 1986

(SI 1986/1999)

Notes

This Order was made under the powers in IA 1986 s 421. An estate of a deceased person is insolvent if, when all its assets are realised, the estate's debts and other liabilities cannot be met (IA 1986 s 421(4)). In such a case, beneficiaries under any will or on an intestacy receive nothing and the only issue is what order the creditors should be paid in.

There are three ways of administering an insolvent estate, namely:

(a) by the deceased's personal representative out of court. In practice, this is the method that is usually adopted;

(b) by the deceased's personal representative under directions of the court pursuant to an administration order (CPR Part 64);

(c) in bankruptcy, pursuant to an insolvency administration order made by the bankruptcy court. The Administration of Insolvent Estates of Deceased Persons Order 1986 applies and modifies, where necessary, the relevant parts of the IA 1986. In practice this method is not often used, however it does have some advantages, for instance any trustee of the estate has the power to make an application to set aside a transaction entered into by the deceased at an undervalue or to set aside a preference.

On a practical level, note that the Supreme Court Act 1981 s 113(1) empowers the court to grant probate or letters of administration in respect of any part of a deceased's estate, for example it allows a grant limited for purposes (such as a testator's literary works) or for a limited time (such as until a beneficiary attains majority). However, no such power applies where the estate is known to be insolvent and so the grant cannot be severed. The only exception is that it is allowable to have a separate grant with regard to a trust estate in which the deceased had no beneficial interest (s 113(2) SCA 1981).

16.1–16.3

1 This Order may be cited as the Administration of Insolvent Estates of Deceased Persons Order 1986 and shall come into force on 29th December 1986.

2 In this Order—
'the Act' means the Insolvency Act 1986;
'insolvency administration order' means an order for the administration in bankruptcy of the insolvent estate of a deceased debtor (being an individual at the date of his death);
'insolvency administration petition' means a petition for an insolvency administration order; and
'the Rules' means the Insolvency Rules 1986.

3 (1) The provisions of the Act specified in Parts II and III of Schedule 1 to this Order shall apply to the administration in bankruptcy of the

insolvent estates of deceased persons dying before presentation of a bankruptcy petition with the modifications specified in those Parts and with any further such modifications as may be necessary to render them applicable to the estate of a deceased person and in particular with the modifications specified in Part I of that Schedule, and the provisions of the Rules, the Insolvency Regulations 1986 and any order made under section 415 of the Act (fees and deposits) shall apply accordingly.

(2) In the case of any conflict between any provision of the Rules and any provision of this Order, the latter provision shall prevail.

Notes

Art 3(1)

If the estate is being administered in bankruptcy under an insolvency administration order all of the provisions of s 264 to 437 IA 1986 apply except for the following:

Sections 265, 268, 270, 274–275, 279–281, 282(2) & (3), 286(2), 290, 350(3), 352–358, 360–362, 364, 387(2)–(4), 411, 414, 416–417, 421–422, 427, 429 and paragraphs 13, IV & V of Schedule 11 to the Insolvency Act 1986. In addition, section 292(2) IA 1986 does not apply – see art 4(3) and the notes below.

Whilst all the other provisions of s 264 to 427 IA 1986 apply, some apply with modifications. All of the applicable provisions are listed, together with any modifications, in Parts II and III of Schedule 1 to this Order. Those sections that are modified by the order are set out below, together with the location of the relevant modification.

It is important to note that the modifications listed in sch1 Parts II and III must be read in the light of the general modifications to the IA 1986 listed in sch1 Part 1; those general modifications substitute references for the standard terminology as stated in Part I that one finds in the bankruptcy legislation. The court will adopt a purposive approach to making sense of the modified provisions *Re Vos* [2006] BPIR 348; that case concerned the modifications to IA 1986 s 284 in the context of the Order and the court construed the modified s 284 to apply to dispositions by a personal representative from the date of death of the deceased person to the date of the vesting of the estate in the trustee.

Section which is modified	Where to find the modification in the Order (SI 1986 No 1999)
264	Sch 1 Pt II paragraph 1
266	Sch 1 Pt II paragraph 2
267	Sch 1 Pt II paragraph 3
269	Sch 1 Pt II paragraph 4
271	Sch 1 Pt II paragraph 5
272	Sch 1 Pt II paragraph 6
273	Sch 1 Pt II paragraph 7
278	Sch 1 Pt II paragraph 10
283–285	Sch 1 Pt II paragraph 12
288	Sch 1 Pt II paragraph 15
289	Sch 1 Pt II paragraph 16
297(4)	Sch 1 Pt II paragraph 18

Section which is modified	Where to find the modification in the Order (SI 1986 No 1999)
305	Sch 1 Pt II paragraph 20
307	Sch 1 Pt II paragraph 22
328 & 329	Sch 1 Pt II paragraph 24
330	Sch 1 Pt II paragraph 25
341	Sch 1 Pt II paragraph 27
359	Sch 1 Pt II paragraph 29
382	Sch 1 Pt II paragraph 31
385	Sch 1 Pt II paragraph 33
387(6)(a) & (b)	Sch 1 Pt II paragraph 35

The relevant parts of the Order and the IA 1986 should be referred to where necessary. The following points are however of note:

(1) The power to apply for a transaction to be set aside as a preference by the deceased (s 340 IA 1986) as modified by this Order), a transaction at an undervalue (s 339 IA 1986 as modified by this Order) or an extortionate credit bargain entered into by the deceased with a creditor (s 343 IA 1986 as modified by this Order) is only available when the estate in administered in bankruptcy under an insolvency administration order;

(2) The persons who may present a petition for an insolvency administration order are:

    (a) the deceased's personal representative (section 272 IA 1986 as modified). In such a case, prescribed Form 6 (contained in Schedule 3 to the Order) must be used for the petition;

    (b) a creditor whose debt would have been sufficient to support a bankruptcy petition (ie £750 or more) against the deceased if he were still alive (section 264(1)(a) IA 1986 as modified). In such a case, prescribed Form 1 (contained in Schedule 3 to the Order) must be used for the petition;

    (c) a supervisor of, or any person bound by, an IVA entered into by the deceased (section 264(1)(c) IA 1986 as modified). In such a case, prescribed Form 2 (contained in Schedule 3 to the Order) must be used for the petition;

    (d) the Official Petitioner where a criminal bankruptcy order has been made against the deceased (section 264(1)(d) IA 1986 as modified). In such a case, prescribed Form 3 (contained in Schedule 3 to the Order) must be used for the petition.

Individual Voluntary Arrangements

Where the debtor dies after an interim order is made (and whether or not the arrangement is approved by the deceased person's creditors) IA 1986 s 256–263 apply with the following modifications:

Section which is modified	Where to find the modification in the Order (SI 1986 No 1999)
256	Sch 1 Pt III paragraph 1
257	Sch 1 Pt III paragraph 2
260–262	Sch 1 Pt III paragraph 13
263	Sch 1 Pt III paragraph 4

If the debtor dies after an interim order is made but before the meeting of creditors is held, the nominee of the debtor shall give notice to the court of the debtor's death and upon receiving such a notice the court must discharge the interim order – section 256 IA 1986 as modified by

Part III. Where a debtor dies after the proposal has been accepted sections 260 to 262 IA 1986 (effect of approval, effect where debtor is an undischarged bankrupt and challenge of meeting's decision) cease to apply on the death of the debtor.

Art 3(2)

This article deals with the priority as between two statutory instruments. It states that the Order will prevail over IR 1986 in the case of a conflict. It does not affect the proposition that where subordinate legislation modifies provisions in primary legislation, it should be construed restrictively: *In re Palmer deceased* [1994] Ch 316. Insofar as there is any conflict between the IA 1986 and the Order, the IA 1986 will prevail.

___

16.4

4(1) Where the estate of a deceased person is insolvent and is being administered otherwise than in bankruptcy, subject to paragraphs (2) and (3) below, the same provisions as may be in force for the time being under the law of bankruptcy with respect to the assets of individuals adjudged bankrupt shall apply to the administration of the estate with respect to the respective rights of secured and unsecured creditors, to debts and liabilities provable, to the valuation of future and contingent liabilities and to the priorities of debts and other payments.

(2) The reasonable funeral, testamentary and administration expenses have priority over the preferential debts listed in Schedule 6 to the Act.

(3) Section 292(2) of the Act shall not apply.

___

Notes

Art 4(1)

Where the insolvent estate is being administered by the deceased's personal representatives out of court or under the directions of the court (pursuant to an administration order) the only bankruptcy rules that apply are those 'with respect to the respective rights of secured and unsecured creditors, to debts and liabilities provable, to the valuation of future and contingent liabilities and to the priorities of debts and other payments'. The effect of this article is that the same rules will apply in relation to these matters irrespective of which of the three methods of administration is used.

'The respective rights of secured and unsecured creditors'

A secured creditor of the deceased person has the following choices available:
(1)   The secured creditor can rely on its security and not prove in the deceased's insolvency at all – See s 285(4) IA 1986. This is the best route to adopt if the security is sufficient to pay off the debt in full;
(2)   The secured creditor can realise its security and just prove in the deceased's insolvency for the balance of the debt (s 322(1) IA 1986). This is the obvious route to adopt where the security is insufficient;
(3)   The secured creditor can set a value on its security and then prove for the balance in the deceased's insolvency (IR 1986 r 6.96, 6.98, 6.115 to 6.118). By doing this the secured creditor avoids selling his security but there are risks involved. If the valuation is too low, the personal representatives or trustee in bankruptcy will have the right to redeem the security at the value set, whilst if the value set is too high the secured creditor will prove for too small a balance;

(4)   The secured creditor can surrender its security and prove in the deceased's insolvency for the whole of the debt (IR 1986 r 6.109(2)). Insofar as this course is adopted (and it is not to be recommended if the security has any value at all) the secured creditor is in the same position and entitled to the same priority as an unsecured creditor.

'Debts and liabilities provable'

All of the deceased's debts and liabilities, present or future, certain or contingent, are provable against an insolvent estate. If the value is uncertain, it must be estimated (IA 1986 s 322(3)).

Where there have been mutual credits, mutual debts or other mutual dealings between the deceased and any creditor of the deceased proving or claiming to prove for a debt an account shall be taken of what is due from each party to the other in respect of the mutual dealings and the sums due from one party shall be set off against the sums due form the other party – IA 1986 s 323.

'Priority of debts and other payments'

The order of priority is as follows:
(1)   Reasonable funeral, testamentary and administration expenses;
(2)   Specially preferred debts;
(3)   Preferential debts (as set out in Schedule 6 to the IA 1986);
(4)   Ordinary debts ie all other debts except deferred debts;
(5)   Interest;
(6)   Deferred debts eg a loan from the deceased's spouse.

A personal representative will be personally liable if he fails to observe the priority order and pays an inferior debt before all superior debts of which he has notice have been paid. If he had no notice of the superior debt at the time, he will not be liable – see *Harman v Harman* (1686) 3 Mod Rep 115, 2 Show 492.

Likewise, if a personal representative pays a debt in full when there are insufficient funds to pay in full all the creditors of the class in question, he will be personally liable to the other creditors in that class. If the personal representative paid the debt in full in good faith at a time when he had no reason to believe that the estate was insolvent he will not be liable to the creditors who lose out – see Administration of Estates Act 1971 s 10(2).

Art 4(2)

This article makes it clear that whichever method of administration is used in respect of the insolvent estate, the reasonable funeral, testamentary and administration expenses always have priority over all other liabilities. In the event of a deficiency at this point, funeral expenses probably have priority over testamentary and administration expenses – see *R v Wade* (1818) 5 Price 621; *Re Walter, Slocock v Official Receiver* [1929] 1 Ch 647.

Testamentary and administration expenses are all the expenses incidental to the proper performance of their duties by the personal representatives. They include the legal costs of obtaining the grant of representation and administering the estate and the costs and expenses incurred in maintaining and disposing of the deceased's assets.

Art 4(3)

This article removes the requirement that the trustee (and therefore personal representative) of a bankrupt estate has to be a qualified insolvency practitioner and allows the possibility of a non–IP being appointed as the personal representative. Where the personal representative is an insolvency practitioner the relevant parts of Part XIII of the IA 1986 apply.

16.5

5(1) If a debtor by or against whom a bankruptcy petition has been presented dies, the proceedings in the matter shall, unless the court otherwise orders, be continued as if he were alive, with the modifications specified in Schedule 2 to this Order.

(2) The reasonable funeral and testamentary expenses have priority over the preferential debts listed in Schedule 6 to the Act.

(3) If a debtor dies after presentation of a bankruptcy petition but before service, the court may order service to be effected on his personal representative or such other person as it thinks fit.

Notes

Art 5(1)

The death of a debtor will not thwart a bankruptcy petition that has already been presented *Berti v Steele Raymond* [2002] BPIR 683; the court may order the appointment of a person to represent the deceased's estate (CPR Part 19.8 and IR 1986 r 7.51). Proceedings will continue, and the only modifications to the IA 1986 are to s 288(1) and (2), (which in their modified form deal with the submission of a statement of affairs by the personal representative or such other person as the court may direct within 56 days of a request for the same from the official receiver); and s 330(4)(b) (dealing with the trustee in bankruptcy's obligation to declare a final dividend, if any, without regard to the right of any personal representative of a debtor dying after the presentation of a bankruptcy petition in respect of reasonable funeral and testamentary expenses of which notice has not already been given to the trustee).

Art 5(2)

This must be subject to the application of s 330(4)(b) as modified, to which see the notes to article 5(1) above.

SCHEDULE I
Provisions of the Act applying with relevant modifications to the Administration in bankruptcy of insolvent estates of deceased persons dying before presentation of a bankruptcy petition
Article 3

Part I

General modifications of Provisions of the Act

16.6
Except in so far as the context otherwise requires, for any such reference as is specified in column 1 of the Table set out below there shall be substituted the reference specified in column 2.

Reference in provision of the Act specified in Part II of this Schedule (1)	Substituted references (2)
the bankrupt; the debtor	the deceased debtor or his personal representative (or if there is no personal representative such person as the court may order) as the case may require.
the bankrupt's estate	the deceased debtor's estate.
the commencement of the bankruptcy	the date of the insolvency administration order.
a bankruptcy order	an insolvency administration order.
an individual being adjudged bankrupt	an insolvency administration order being made.
a debtor's petition	a petition by the personal representative of a deceased debtor for an insolvency administration order.

Part II

Provisions of the Act not included in Part III of this Schedule

16.7

The following provisions of the Act shall apply:—

1 Section 264 with the following modifications:—
   (a) the words 'against an individual' shall be omitted;
   (b) at the end of paragraph 1(a) there shall be added the words 'in Form 1 set out in Schedule 3 to the Administration of Insolvent Estates of Deceased Persons Order 1986';
   (c) paragraph 1(b) shall be omitted;
   (ca) at the end of paragraph 1(ba) there shall be added the words 'in Form 1, with such variations as the case requires (if any), set out in Schedule 3 to the Administration of Insolvent Estates of Deceased Persons Order 1986'
   (cb) at the end of paragraph 1(bb) there shall be added the words 'in Form 1, with such variations as the case requires (if any), set out in Schedule 3 to the Administration of Insolvent Estates of Deceased Persons Order 1986'
   (d) in paragraph 1(c) after the words 'Part VIII' there shall be added the words 'in Form 2 set out in the said Schedule 3';
   (e) at the end of paragraph 1(d) there shall be added the words 'in Form 3 set out in the said Schedule 3 in any case where a creditor could present such a petition under paragraph (a) above'; and

(f)   at the end of subsection (2) there shall be added the words 'in Form 4 set out in the said Schedule 3'.

2 Section 266 with the following modifications:—
    (a)   for subsection (1) there shall be substituted the following:—

'(1) An insolvency administration petition shall,
    (a)   if a liquidator (within the meaning of Article 2(b) of the EC Regulation) has been appointed in proceedings by virtue of Article 3(1) of the EC Regulation in relation to the deceased debtor, be served on him;
    (b)   unless the court otherwise directs, be served on the personal representative; and
    (c)   be served on such other persons as the court may direct.'; and
(b) in subsection (3) for the words 'bankruptcy petition' there shall be substituted the words 'petition to the court for an insolvency administration order with or without costs'.

3 Section 267 with the following modifications to subsection (2):—
    (a)   before the words 'at the time' there shall be inserted the words 'had the debtor been alive'; and
    (b)   for paragraphs (a) to (d) there shall be substituted the following:—
    '(a)   the amount of the debt, or the aggregate amount of the debts, owed by the debtor would have been equal to or exceeded the bankruptcy level, or
    (b)   the debt, or each of the debts, owed by the debtor would have been for a liquidated sum payable to the petitioning creditor, or one or more of the petitioning creditors, either immediately or at some certain future time, and would have been unsecured.'.

4 Section 269 with the modification that in subsection (2) for the words 'sections 267 to 270' there shall be substituted the words 'section 267 and this section'.

5 Section 271 as if for that section there were substituted the following:—

'271 (1) The court may make an insolvency administration order on a petition for such an order under section 264(1) if it is satisfied—
    (a)   that the debt, or one of the debts, in respect of which the petition was presented is a debt which,
        (i)   having been payable at the date of the petition or having since become payable, has neither been paid nor secured or compounded for; or
        (ii)   has no reasonable prospect of being able to be paid when it falls due; and
    (b)   that there is a reasonable probability that the estate will be insolvent.

(2) A petition for an insolvency administration order shall not be presented to the court after proceedings have been commenced in any court of justice for the administration of the deceased debtor's estate.

(3) Where proceedings have been commenced in any such court for the administration of the deceased debtor's estate, that court may, if satisfied

that the estate is insolvent, transfer the proceedings to the court exercising jurisdiction for the purposes of the Parts in the second Group of Parts.

(4) Where proceedings have been transferred to the court exercising jurisdiction for the purposes of the Parts in the second Group of Parts, that court may make an insolvency administration order in Form 5 set out in Schedule 3 to the Administration of Insolvent Estates of Deceased Persons Order 1986 as if a petition for such an order had been presented under section 264.

(5) Nothing in sections 264, 266, 267, 269 or 271 or 273 shall invalidate any payment made or any act or thing done in good faith by the personal representative before the date of the insolvency administration order.'

6 Section 272(1) with the following modifications:—
  (a)   after the word 'petition' there shall be inserted the words 'in Form 6 set out in Schedule 3 to the Administration of Insolvent Estates of Deceased Persons Order 1986'; and
  (b)   for the words 'debtor is unable to pay his debts' there shall be substituted the words 'estate of a deceased debtor is insolvent'.

7 Section 273 as if for that section there were substituted the following:—

'**273** The court shall make an insolvency administration order in Form 4 set out in Schedule 3 to the Administration of Insolvent Estates of Deceased Persons Order 1986 on the hearing of a petition presented under section 272 if it is satisfied that the deceased debtor's estate is insolvent.'

8 Section 276(2).

9 Section 277.

10 Section 278 except paragraph (b) as if for paragraph (a) there were substituted the following:—
  '(a)   commences with the day on which the insolvency administration order is made;'.

11 Section 282(1) and (4).

12 Sections 283 to 285 with the modification that they shall have effect as if the petition had been presented and the insolvency administration order had been made on the date of death of the deceased debtor, and with the following modifications to section 283:—
  (a)   in subsection (2)(b), for the words 'bankrupt and his family' there shall be substituted the words 'family of the deceased debtor'; and
  (b)   after subsection (4) there shall be added the following subsection:—

'(4A) References in any of this Group of Parts to property, in relation to a deceased debtor, include the capacity to exercise and take proceedings for exercising all such powers over or in respect of property as might have been exercised by his personal representative for the benefit of the estate on the date of the insolvency administration order and as are specified in subsection (4) above.'

13 Section 286(1) and (3) to (8).

14 Section 287.

15 Section 288 with the modification that for subsections (1) and (2) there shall be substituted the following:—

'(1) Where an insolvency administration order has been made, the personal representative, or if there is no personal representative such person as the court may on the application of the official receiver direct, shall submit to the official receiver a statement of the deceased debtor's affairs containing particulars of the assets and liabilities of the estate as at the date of the insolvency administration order together with other particulars of the affairs of the deceased debtor in Form 7 set out in Schedule 3 to the Administration of Insolvent Estates of Deceased Persons Order 1986 or as the official receiver may require.

(2) The statement shall be submitted before the end of the period of fifty–six days beginning with the date of a request by the official receiver for the statement or such longer period as he or the court may allow.'

16 Section 289 as if for that section there were substituted the following:—

'**289** The official receiver is not under any duty to investigate the conduct and affairs of the deceased debtor unless he thinks fit but may make such report (if any) to the court as he thinks fit.'

17 Section 291.

18 Sections 292 to 302, except section 297(4), with the modification that, where a meeting of creditors is summoned for the purposes of any provision in those sections, the rules regarding the trustee in bankruptcy and the creditors' committee shall apply accordingly.

19 Sections 303 and 304.

20 Section 305 with the modification that after subsection (4) there shall be added the following subsection:—

'(5) In the exercise of his functions under this section where an insolvency administration order has been made, the trustee shall have regard to any claim by the personal representative to payment of reasonable funeral, testamentary and administration expenses incurred by him in respect of the deceased debtor's estate or, if there is no such personal representative, to any claim by any other person to payment of any such expenses incurred by him in respect of the estate provided that the trustee has sufficient funds in hand for the purpose, and such claims shall have priority over the preferential debts listed in Schedule 6 to this Act.'

21 Section 306.

22 Section 307 with the modification that in subsection (1) for the words 'commencement of the bankruptcy' there shall be substituted the words 'date of death of the deceased debtor'.

23 Sections 308 to 327.

24 Sections 328 and 329 with the modification that for the words 'commencement of the bankruptcy', wherever they occur, there shall be substituted the words 'date of death of the deceased debtor'.

25 Section 330 with the following modifications

    (a)   in subsection (5) for the words 'the bankrupt is entitled to the surplus' there shall be substituted the words 'the surplus shall be paid to the personal representative unless the court otherwise orders', and

    (b)   after subsection (5) there shall be added:–

(6) Subsection (5) is subject to Article 35 of the EC Regulation (surplus in secondary proceedings to be transferred to main proceedings)

26 Sections 331 to 340.

27 Section 341 with the modification that in subsection (1)(a) for the words 'day of the presentation of the bankruptcy petition' onwards there shall be substituted the words 'date of death of the deceased debtor'.

28 Sections 342 to 349, 350(1), (2), (4) to (6) and 351 except paragraphs (a) and (b).

29 Section 359 with the following modifications:—

    (a)   subsection (1), and the reference to that subsection in subsection (3), shall be omitted; and

    (b)   in subsection (2), for the words 'petition or in the initial period' there shall be substituted the words 'the date of death of the deceased debtor'.

30 Sections 363 and 365 to 381.

31 Section 382 with the modification that in the definition of 'bankruptcy debt' for the words 'commencement of the bankruptcy', wherever they occur, there shall be substituted the words 'date of death of the deceased debtor'.

32 Sections 383 and 384.

33 Section 385 with the modification that at the end of the definition of 'the court' there shall be added the words 'and subject thereto 'the court' means the court within the jurisdiction of which the debtor resided or carried on business for the greater part of the six months immediately prior to his death'.

34 Section 386.

35 Section 387(1), (5) and (6) with the modification that in subsection (6)(a) and (b) for the reference to the making of the bankruptcy order there shall be substituted a reference to the date of death of the deceased debtor.

36 Sections 388 to 410, 412, 413, 415, 418 to 420, 423 to 426, 428, 430 to 436 and 437 so far as it relates to Parts II, except paragraph 13, IV and V of Schedule 11 to the Act.

Part III

Provisions of Part VIII of the Act relating to individual voluntary Arrangements

16.8

The following provisions of the Act shall apply where court has made an interim order under section 252 of the Act in respect of an individual who subsequently dies:—

1 Section 256 with the modification that where the individual dies before he has submitted the document and statement referred to in subsection (2), after subsection (1) there shall be added the following subsections:—

'(1A) The nominee shall after the death of the individual comes to his knowledge give notice to the court that the individual has died.

(1B) After receiving such a notice the court shall discharge the order mentioned in subsection (1) above.'.

2 Section 257 with the modification that where the individual dies before a creditors' meeting has been held then no such meeting shall be held and, if the individual was at the date of his death an undischarged bankrupt, the personal representative shall give notice of the death to the trustee of his estate and the official receiver.

3 Sections 258 and 259.

4 Sections 260 to 262 with the modification that they shall cease to apply on or after the death of the individual.

5 Section 263 with the modification that where the individual dies after a voluntary arrangement has been approved, then—

(a) in subsection (3), for the words 'debtor, any of his' there shall be substituted the words 'personal representative of the deceased debtor, any of the deceased debtor's'; and

(b) the supervisor shall give notice to the court that the individual has died.

SCHEDULE 2
Death of debtor after presentation of a bankruptcy petition
Article 5

16.9

Modifications

1 For subsections (1) and (2) of section 288 of the Act there shall be substituted the following:—

'(1) Where a bankruptcy order has been made otherwise than on a debtor's petition and the debtor has subsequently died without submitting a statement of his affairs to the official receiver, the personal representative or such other person as the court, on the application of the official receiver, may direct shall submit to the official receiver a statement of the deceased debtor's affairs containing particulars of the assets and liabilities of the estate as at the date of the order together with other particulars of the affairs of the deceased debtor in Form 7 set out in Schedule 3 to the Administration of Insolvent Estates of Deceased Persons Order 1986 or as the official receiver may require, and the Rules shall apply to such a statement as they apply to an ordinary statement of affairs of a debtor.

(2) The statement shall be submitted before the end of the period of fifty–six days beginning with the date of a request by the official receiver for the statement or such longer period as he or the court may allow.'

2 At the end of section 330(4)(b) of the Act there shall be added the words 'and of the personal representative of a debtor dying after the presentation of a bankruptcy petition in respect of reasonable funeral and testamentary expenses of which notice has not already been given to the trustee'.

SCHEDULE 3
Forms relating to Administration in Bankruptcy of Insolvent Estates of Deceased Debtors
Schedule 1, Part II, paras 1, 5–7, 15, Schedule 2, para 1

16.9A

Form 1

The Administration of Insolvent Estates of Deceased Persons Order 1986: Creditor's Petition for Insolvency Administration Order

(TITLE)

I/We (insert full name(s) and address(es) of petitioner(s)) petition the court that an order be made for the administration of the insolvent estate in bankruptcy of the late (insert full name, and former occupation of deceased debtor) ....

[also known as (insert in full any other name(s) by which the deceased debtor was known)]

[and lately residing at (insert any address(es) at which the deceased debtor has resided at or after the time the petition debt was incurred)]

[and lately carrying on business as (insert trading name (adding 'with another or others' if this was so), business address(es) and nature of business(es) carried on by the deceased debtor at or after the time the petition debt was incurred)]

who died on (insert date of death)

and say as follows:—

1   The deceased debtor for the greater part of six months immediately preceding the date of death (delete as applicable) [resided at] [carried on business at] .... within the district of this court (or as the case may be following the terms of Rule 6.9)

2   The estate of the deceased debtor is justly and truly indebted to me/us in the aggregate sum of £ (please give the amount of debt(s), what they relate to and when they were incurred. Please show separately the amount or rate of any interest or other charge not previously notified to the deceased debtor and the reason why you are claiming it.)

3   The above–mentioned debt is for a liquidated sum payable (state date payable or 'immediately' if this is so) and the estate of the deceased debtor is according to my/our information and belief insufficient to pay his debts.

4   I/We do not, nor does any person on my/our behalf, hold any security on the deceased debtor's estate, or any part thereof, for the payment of the above–mentioned sum.

OR

I/We hold security for the payment of (delete as appropriate) [part of] the above–mentioned sum. I/We will give up such security for the benefit of all the creditors in the event of an insolvency administration order being made.

OR

I/We hold security for the payment of part of the above–mentioned sum and I/We estimate the value of such security to be £. This petition is not made in respect of the secured part of my/our debt.

5   The will of the deceased debtor was on (insert date will proved) proved by (insert full names and addresses of parties proving will)

OR

The letters of administration of his estate were on (insert date letters of administration granted) granted to (insert full names and addresses of parties letters of administration granted to)

Endorsement

This petition having been presented to the court on .... it is ordered that the petition shall be heard as follows:—

Date ....

Time .... hours

Place .... and you (insert full names and addresses of parties given notice) are to take notice that if you intend to oppose the petition you must not later than 7 days before the day fixed for the hearing:

(i)   file in court a notice specifying the grounds on which you object to the making of an insolvency administration order

(ii)   send a copy of the notice to the petitioner or his solicitor.

The solicitor to the petitioning creditor is:—(only to be completed where the petitioning creditor is represented by a solicitor

Name ....

Address ....

Telephone Number ....

Reference ....

16.10

Form 2

The Administration of Insolvent Estates of Deceased Persons Order 1986: Petition for Insolvency Administration Order by Supervisor of Voluntary Arrangement or Person Bound by it

(TITLE)

I/We (insert full name(s) and address(es) of petitioner(s)) petition the court that an order be made for the administration of the insolvent estate in bankruptcy of the late (insert full name, and former occupation of deceased debtor)

[also known as (insert in full any other name(s) by which the deceased debtor was known)]

[and lately residing at (insert any address(es) at which the deceased debtor has resided at or after the time the petition debt was incurred)]

[and lately carrying on business as (insert trading name (adding 'with another or others' if this was so), business address(es) and nature of business(es) carried on by the deceased debtor at or after the time the petition debt was incurred)]

and say as follows:—

1   The deceased debtor for the greater part of six months immediately preceding the date of death ((f) Delete as applicable) [resided at] [carried on business at] .... within the district of this court (or as the case may be following the terms of Rule 6.9)

2   On (insert date the deceased entered into voluntary arrangement) a voluntary arrangement proposed by the deceased debtor was approved by his creditors and I am (delete as applicable) a person who is for the time being bound by the said voluntary arrangement and (insert name of supervisor) is the supervisor/(insert name of supervisor) the supervisor of the said voluntary arrangement.

3   The deceased debtor died on (insert date of death)

4   The will of the deceased debtor was on (insert date will proved) proved by (insert full names and addresses of parties proving will)

OR

The letters of administration of his estate were on (insert date letters of administration granted) granted to (insert full names and addresses of parties letters of administration granted to)

5   The estate of the deceased debtor is according to my/our information and belief insufficient to pay his debts.

Endorsement

This petition having been presented to the court on .... it is ordered that the petition shall be heard as follows:—

Date .. ..

Time .... hours

Place .... and you (insert full names and addresses of parties given notice) are to take notice that if you intend to oppose the petition you must not later than 7 days before the day fixed for the hearing:

   (i)   file in court a notice specifying the grounds on which you object to the making of an insolvency administration order

   (ii)   send a copy of the notice to the petitioner or his solicitor.

The solicitor to the petitioning creditor is:—(only to be completed where the petitioning creditor is represented by a solicitor)

Name ....

Address ....

Telephone Number ....

Reference ....

16.11

Form 3

The Administration of Insolvent Estates of Deceased Persons Order 1986: Criminal Bankruptcy Petition for an Insolvency Administration Order

(TITLE)

I, (delete as appropriate) the Official Petitioner of .... or I/We (insert full name(s) and address(es) of petitioner(s) if other than the Official Petitioner)

petition the court that an order be made for the administration of the insolvent estate in bankruptcy of the late (insert full name, and former occupation of deceased debtor)

[also known as (insert in full any other name(s) by which the deceased debtor was known)]

[and lately residing at (insert any address(es) at which the deceased debtor has resided at or after the time the petition debt was incurred)]

[and lately carrying on business as (insert trading name (adding 'with another or others' if this was so), business address(es) and nature of business(es) carried on by the deceased debtor at or after the time the petition debt was incurred)

who died on (insert date of death)

and say as follows:—

1   A criminal bankruptcy order was made against the said (insert full name, and former occupation of deceased debtor) at the (insert name of the court at which the criminal bankruptcy order was made) court on (insert date) and an office copy of the order is annexed to this petition.

2   The said order remains in force.

OR

The said order was amended by the Court of Appeal on (insert date) and an office copy of the order of the Court of Appeal is annexed to this petition and the order as amended by the Court of Appeal remains in force.

3   According to the said criminal bankruptcy order the late (insert full name, and former occupation of deceased debtor) is indebted to (insert names and addresses of the persons specified in the order as having suffered loss or damage) in the aggregate sum of (state the amount of loss or damage suffered as specified in the order)

4   The will of the deceased debtor was on (insert date will proved) proved by (insert full names and addresses of parties proving will)

OR

The letters of administration of his estate were on (insert date letters of administration granted) granted to (insert full names and addresses of parties letters of administration granted to)

5   The estate of the deceased debtor is according to my/our information and belief insufficient to pay his debts.

Endorsement

This petition having been presented to the court on .... it is ordered that the petition shall be heard as follows:—

Date. ....

Time .... hours

Place .... and you (insert full names and addresses of parties given notice) are to take notice that if you intend to oppose the petition you must not later than 7 days before the day fixed for the hearing:

(i)   file in court a notice specifying the grounds on which you object to the making of an insolvency administration order

(ii)   send a copy of the notice to the petitioner or his solicitor.

The solicitor to the petitioning creditor is:— (only to be completed where the petitioning creditor is represented by a solicitor)

Name ....

Address ....

Telephone Number ....

Reference ....

16.12

Form 4

The Administration of Insolvent Estates of Deceased Persons Order 1986: Insolvency Administration Order

(TITLE)

Upon the petition of (insert full name of petitioner) ....

dated (insert date of petition) ....

and numbered (insert court number of petition) ....

and upon hearing ....

and upon reading the evidence ....

It is ordered that the estate of (insert full name of deceased debtor) ....

formerly of (insert residential address of deceased debtor at date of death) ....

who died insolvent, be administered in bankruptcy and that the costs of this application be (terms of any order as to payment of costs of application)

16.13

Form 5

The Administration of Insolvent Estates of Deceased Persons Order 1986: Insolvency Administration Order on Transfer of Proceedings

(TITLE)

Proceedings for the administration of the estate of the late (insert full name of deceased debtor) having been commenced in (insert name of court in which proceedings commenced) court on (insert date) ....

And whereas the Court did on (insert date) transfer such proceedings to this Court ....

It is ordered that the estate of (insert full name of deceased debtor) who died insolvent, be administered in bankruptcy ....

16.14

Form 6

The Administration of Insolvent Estates of Deceased Persons Order 1986: Petition by Personal Representative for Insolvency Administration Order

(TITLE)

I/We (insert full name(s) and address(es) of petitioner(s)) .... petition the court that an order be made for the administration of the insolvent estate in bankruptcy .. .. .of the late (insert full name, and former occupation of deceased debtor) .... (also known as (insert in full any other name(s) by which the deceased debtor was known)) ....(and lately residing at (insert any address(es) at which the deceased debtor has resided at or after the time in which the outstanding liabilities were incurred)) .... (and lately carrying on business as (insert trading name (adding 'with another or others' if this was so), business address(es) and nature of business(es) carried on by deceased debtor who died on (insert date of death) ....

and say as follows:—

1   (delete as appropriate) I am/We are the personal representative(s) of the deceased debtor and his will was on (insert date will proved) proved by (insert full names and addresses of parties proving will) ....

OR

that the letters of administration of his estate were on (insert date letters of administration granted) .... granted to (insert full names and addresses of parties letters of administration granted to) ....

2   The deceased debtor for the greater part of six months immediately preceding the date of death (delete as appropriate) (resided at) (carried on business at) .... within the district of this court ((m) Or as the case may be following the terms of Rule 6.9) ....

3   The estate of the deceased debtor is according to my/our information and belief insufficient to pay his debts.

16.15

Form 7

The Administration of Insolvent Estates of Deceased Persons Order 1986: Statement of Affairs (Deceased Insolvent)

(NOTE:

These details will be the same as those shown at the top of the petition)

IN THE ....

IN BANKRUPTCY NO ....

OF 19 ....

RE ....

THE 'GUIDANCE NOTES' BOOKLET TELLS YOU HOW TO COMPLETE THIS FORM EASILY AND CORRECTLY

Show the financial position of the deceased debtor by completing all the pages of this form which will then be the Statement of Affairs.

Affidavit

THIS AFFIDAVIT MUST BE SWORN BEFORE A SOLICITOR OR COMMISSIONER OF OATHS OR AN OFFICER OF THE COURT DULY AUTHORISED TO ADMINISTER OATHS WHEN YOU HAVE COMPLETED THE REST OF THIS FORM

I (insert your full name and occupation) .... of (insert your full address). ....

Make oath and say that the several pages marked .... are to the best of my knowledge and belief a full, true and complete statement of the affairs of the deceased debtor as at ... ... the date of the insolvency administration/ bankruptcy order.

Sworn at ....

Date .... Signature(s) ....

Before me ....

A Solicitor or Commissioner of Oaths or Duly authorised officer

Before swearing the affidavit, the Solicitor, Commissioner or duly authorised officer is particularly requested to make sure that the full name, address and description of the deponent are stated, and to initial any crossings–out or other alterations in the printed form. A defect in the affidavit in any of the above respects will mean that it will be refused by the court, and will need to be re–sworn.

16.16

A

IS ANYONE CLAIMING SOMETHING OF THE DECEASED DEBTOR'S TO CLEAR OR REDUCE THEIR CLAIM?

If 'YES' give details below: ....

Tick Box Yes .... No ....

Name of creditor	Address (with postcode)	Amount owed to creditor £	What property is claimed and what is it worth?
1			
2			
3			
4			
Signature			
Date			

16.17

B

	Tick Box
1 Has the deceased debtor any creditors under hire–purchase or conditional sale agreements?	Tick Box
If 'YES' name the creditors and give a description of the goods subject to each agreement and the amount owed	YES/NO
2. Has the deceased debtor any liability under leasing agreements?	YES/NO
If 'YES' name the creditors and give details of the property leased	
3. Are any other creditors claiming title to goods that they supplied to the deceased debtor?	YES/NO
If 'YES' name the creditor and give details of the goods claimed	
Signature	
Dated	

16.18

C

LIST THE REST OF THE CREDITORS HERE

1	2	3	4	5
No	Name of creditor or claimant	Address (with postcode)	Creditor's claim at date of death	Creditor's claim at date of insolvency administration bankruptcy order
Signature Date				

16.19

D

1   Did the deceased have any personal bank accounts, including joint accounts? Tick Box Yes/No

If 'YES' state where they and how much is in them now ....

2   Did the deceased have any business bank accounts, including joint accounts? Yes .... .No ....

If 'YES' state the name of the accounts, where they are and how much is in them now. ....

3   Did the deceased have any building society accounts, or an interest in one? Yes .... .No ....

If 'YES' state where they are and how much is in them now. ....

Signature .... Date ....

16.20

D1

4   Are there any other savings? Yes .... No ....

If 'YES' state the amounts and where they are ....

5   Did the deceased debtor have any interest in any life policies? Yes .... No. ....

If 'YES' state with whom they were effected, the policy numbers, and any value to the estate ....

6.   Did the deceased debtor have an interest, of value, in any other policies or agreements? Yes .... No ....

If 'YES' state with whom they were effected, the policy or agreement numbers and the value to the estate ....

Signature .... Dated ....

16.21

E

(This table sets out any debts due to the estate. Due to its complexity, it has proved impossible to obtain a satisfactory reproduction on the database. It has therefore been omitted. Please see the original.)

16.22

F

Property

NOW SHOW ANYTHING OF THE DECEASED DEBTOR'S WHICH MAY BE OF VALUE AND IS NOT SHOWN ON ANOTHER PAGE:	£
a) Cash deposited with solicitor at	
b) Cash in hand	
c) Stock in trade at	
d) Machinery at	
e) Trade fixtures, fittings, utensils etc at	
f) Farming stock at	
g) Growing crops and tenant rights at	
h) Household furniture and effects at	
i) Stocks and shares in	
j) Any interests under wills etc	
k) Motor vehicles (give details)	
l) Bills of exchange, promissory notes etc available as assets	

m) Other property viz .... Signature .... Date	

16.23

G

1   Is there any claim against the estate for funeral, testamentary and administration expenses? YES/NO

If 'YES' give details below ... ...

2   Did the deceased debtor have any assets when he died which are not now
shown in this statement of affairs? YES/NO

If 'YES' list them below and state what has happened to them ... ...

Signature .... Dated ....

16.24

H

Statement of the dealings and administration of the estate since the date of death

Receipts £	Payments £
Signature Date	

Enterprise Act 2002 (Commencement No 4 and Transitional Provisions and Savings) Order 2003

(2003 No 2093)

Made: 8th August 2003

The Secretary of State, in exercise of the powers conferred upon her by sections 276(2) and 279 of the Enterprise Act 2002 hereby makes the following Order:—

17.1

1 Citation and interpretation

(1) This Order may be cited as the Enterprise Act 2002 (Commencement No 4 and Transitional Provisions and Savings) Order 2003.

(2) In this Order, except where otherwise stated, references to sections and Schedules are references to sections of, and Schedules to, the Enterprise Act 2002.

(3) In this Order references to sequestration are references to sequestration within the meaning of the Bankruptcy (Scotland) Act 1985.

(4) Except in relation to sequestration, expressions used in this Order which are used in the Insolvency Act 1986 shall have the same meaning as in that Act.

(5) In articles 4, 5 and 6 references to provisions of, and procedures under, the Insolvency Act 1986 include references to those provisions and procedures as they are applied by or under the provisions of any enactment.

17.2

2 Appointed days

(1) Subject as set out in this Order, the day appointed for the coming into force of the provisions in Schedule 1 to this Order is 15th September 2003 (hereafter referred to as "the first commencement date").

(2) Subject as set out in this Order, the day appointed for the coming into force of the provisions in Schedule 2 to this Order is 1st April 2004 (hereafter referred to as "the second commencement date").

17.3

3 Administration—transitional provisions

(1) In this article "the former administration provisions" means the law relating to administration under Part II of the Insolvency Act 1986 and

section 62(2)(a) of the Criminal Justice Act 1988 without the amendments and repeals made by the provisions of the Enterprise Act 2002 mentioned in paragraph (2).

(2) In a case where a petition for an administration order has been presented before the first commencement date—

(a) section 248 and Schedules 16 and 17; and

(b) section 278(2) and Schedule 26 as respects the repeals relating to sections 212, 230(1), 231, 232, 240(1) and 245(3) of the Insolvency Act 1986, the entries in Schedule 10 to the Insolvency Act 1986 in respect of sections 12(2), 15(8), 18(5), 21(3), 22(6), 23(3), 24(7) and 27(6) of that Act and section 62(2)(a) of the Criminal Justice Act 1988,

shall have no effect.

(3) The former administration provisions shall continue to apply insofar as is necessary to give effect to—

(a) the Insolvent Partnerships Order 1994;

(b) regulation 5 of the Limited Liability Partnerships Regulations 2001; and

(c) the Financial Services and Markets Act 2000 (Administration Orders relating to Insurers) Order 2002.

17.4

4 Abolition of Crown preference—transitional provisions

(1) This article applies to a case where before the first commencement date—

(a) a petition for an administration order pursuant to Part II of the Insolvency Act 1986 is presented;

(b) a voluntary arrangement under Part I of the Insolvency Act 1986 has effect;

(c) a receiver is appointed under the terms of a charge (which when created was a floating charge) in relation to the property of a company subject to the charge;

(d) a petition for a winding-up order is presented;

(e) a resolution for the winding up of the company is passed;

(f) a petition for a bankruptcy order (or, in Scotland, for sequestration) is presented; or

(g) a voluntary arrangement pursuant to Part VIII of the Insolvency Act 1986 has effect.

[(1A) This article also applies to a case where—

(a) an administration order under Part II of the Insolvency Act 1986 is made on a petition presented prior to the first commencement date;

(b) that order is discharged; and

(c) immediately on the discharge of that order—

(i) a winding-up order is made in respect of the company in question; or

(ii) a resolution for the winding up of the company is passed,

on or after the first commencement date.

(1B) This article also applies to a case where—

   (a)   a winding-up order is made on a petition presented prior to the first commencement date; and

   (b)   the company in question enters administration by virtue of an order made under paragraphs 37 or 38 of Schedule B1 to the Insolvency Act 1986.

(1C) This article also applies to a case where—

   (a)   a resolution for the winding up of a company is passed before the first commencement date; and

   (b)   the company enters administration by virtue of an order made under paragraph 38 of Schedule B1 to the Insolvency Act 1986.

(1D) This article also applies to a case where—

   (a)   a receiver is appointed before the first commencement date in respect of a company;

   (b)   the receiver vacates office; and

   (c)   the company in respect of which the receiver is appointed enters administration within the meaning of paragraph 1(2)(b) of Schedule B1 to the Insolvency Act 1986 during the period that the receiver is in office or immediately after the end of that period.]

(2) This article also applies to a case where proposals for a voluntary arrangement under Part I of the Insolvency Act 1986 are made (whether before or after the first commencement date) by—

   (a)   a liquidator in a winding up where the winding-up petition is presented or, as the case may be, the resolution for winding up is passed, before the first commencement date; or

   (b)   an administrator appointed in relation to an administration under Part II of the Insolvency Act 1986 where the administration order is made on a petition which is presented before the first commencement date.

(3) This article also applies to a case in which a proposal for a voluntary arrangement under Part VIII of the Insolvency Act 1986 is made (whether before or after the first commencement date) by a person who was adjudged bankrupt on a petition which was presented before the first commencement date.

(4) In a case to which this article applies—

   (a)   the provisions of section 251; and

   (b)   the provisions of section 278(2) and Schedule 26 as respects the repeals relating to paragraphs 1 to 3 and 8 to 8C in Schedule 3 to the Bankruptcy (Scotland) Act 1985, paragraphs 1 to 7 of Schedule 6 to the Insolvency Act 1986, the table in paragraph 32 of Schedule 29 to the Income and Corporation Taxes Act 1988, paragraphs 21A and 22 of Schedule 2 to the Finance Act 1991, paragraph 73 of Schedule 2 to the Social Security (Consequential Provisions) Act 1992, sections 36(1) to (3) of the Finance Act 1993, paragraphs 13(1) and 13(2) of Schedule 6 and paragraph 7(2) of Schedule 7 to the Finance Act 1994, paragraph 8 of Schedule 14 to the Value Added Tax Act 1994, section 17 of the Finance Act 1995, paragraphs 12(1) and 12(2) of Schedule 5 to the Finance Act 1996, sections 166(7)(a), 183(3)(a) and 189(4) of the Employment Rights Act 1996, paragraph 6 of Schedule 2 to the Finance Act 1997, paragraphs 2 and 3 of Schedule 7 to the Finance Act 2000 and paragraphs 17(1) and (2) and 18 of Schedule 5 to the Finance Act 2001,

shall not have effect.

17.5

5 Liquidator's powers

The insertion of paragraph 3A into Schedule 4 of the Insolvency Act 1986 by section 253 (Liquidator's powers) shall have no effect in relation to any proceedings of a kind mentioned in paragraph 3A which were commenced prior to the first commencement date.

17.6

6 Powers of trustee in bankruptcy

The insertion of paragraph 2A into Schedule 5 of the Insolvency Act 1986 by section 262 (Powers of Trustee) shall have no effect in relation to any proceedings of a kind mentioned in paragraph 2A which were commenced prior to the first commencement date.

17.7

7 Bankruptcy restrictions orders

Where a court is considering whether or not a bankruptcy restrictions order should be made pursuant to the provisions of section 281A and Schedule 4A to the Insolvency Act 1986, it shall not take into account any conduct of the bankrupt before the second commencement date.

17.8

8 Transitional provisions—old summary cases

(1) This article applies to a bankruptcy (other than one where the bankrupt has received his discharge) where a certificate of summary administration under section 275 of the Insolvency Act 1986 is in force on the second commencement date.

(2) In a case to which this article applies sections 275, 292(1), 293(1), 294(1), 297, 298(3), 300(5), 300(6) and 300(7) of the Insolvency Act 1986 shall continue to have effect.

(3) Where on or after the second commencement date the court revokes a certificate of summary administration under section 275(3) of the Insolvency Act 1986 as it has effect by virtue of paragraph (2), the relevant period for the purposes of paragraph 4(1)(b) of Schedule 19 shall be the period specified in section 279(1)(b) of the Insolvency Act 1986 as it had effect immediately prior to the second commencement date.

SCHEDULE I

Article 2(1)

17.9

The provisions referred to in Article 2(1) are—

section 248 (replacement of Part II of the Insolvency Act 1986), and Schedules 16 and 17 (except paragraphs 14 and 59 of Schedule 17)

section 249 (special administration regimes)

section 250 (prohibition of appointment of administrative receivers) (to the extent it is not already in force) and Schedule 18

section 251 (abolition of Crown preference)

section 252 (unsecured creditors)

section 253 (liquidator's powers)

section 254 (application of insolvency law to foreign company)

section 255 (application of law about company arrangement or administration to non-company)

section 262 (powers of trustee in bankruptcy)

section 278(2) and Schedule 26 (but only insofar as is necessary to give effect to the repeals relating to paragraphs 1 to 3 and 8 to 8C of Schedule 3 to the Bankruptcy (Scotland) Act 1985, section 212, 230(1), 231, 232, 240(1), 245(3) and Schedule 10 to the Insolvency Act 1986 (except those relating to the entries relating to sections 31, 361 and 362), paragraph 32 of Schedule 29 to the Income and Corporation Taxes Act 1988, section 62(2)(a) of the Criminal Justice Act 1988, paragraphs 21A and 22 of Schedule 2 to the Finance Act 1991, paragraph 73 of Schedule 2 to the Social Security (Consequential Provisions) Act 1992, sections 36(1) to (3) of the Finance Act 1993, paragraphs 13(1) and 13(2) of Schedule 6 and paragraph 7(2) of Schedule 7 to the Finance Act 1994, paragraph 8 of Schedule 14 to the Value Added Tax Act 1994, section 17 of the Finance Act 1995, paragraphs 12(1) and 12(2) of Schedule 5 to the Finance Act 1996, sections 166(7)(a), 183(3)(a) and 189(4) of the Employment Rights Act 1996, paragraph 6 of Schedule 2 to the Finance Act 1997, paragraphs 2 and 3 of Schedule 7 to the Finance Act 2000 and paragraphs 17(1) and (2) and 18 of Schedule 5 to the Finance Act 2001).

SCHEDULE 2

Article 2(2)

17.10

The provisions referred to in Article 2(2) are—

section 256 (duration of bankruptcy) and Schedule 19 (except paragraph 8 of Schedule 19)

section 257 (post discharge restrictions) and Schedules 20 and 21

section 258 (investigation by official receiver)

section 259 (income payments order)

section 260 (income payments agreement)

section 261 (bankrupt's home)

section 263 (repeal of certain bankruptcy offences)

section 264 (individual voluntary arrangements) and Schedule 22

section 265 (disqualification from office: justice of the peace)

section 266 (disqualification from office: Parliament)

section 267 (disqualification from office: local government)

section 268 (disqualification from office: general)

section 269 (minor and consequential amendments) and Schedule 23
section 270 (fees) [section 270(3)]
section 271 (Insolvency Services Account: interest)
section 272 (Insolvency Services Account)
section 278(2) and Schedule 26 (but only insofar as is necessary to give effect to the repeals relating to sections 81(1) and 82(2) of the Local Government Act 1972, paragraph 22 of Schedule 8 to the Insolvency Act 1985, sections 275, 282(5), 292(1)(a), 293(1), 294(1), 297, 298(3), 300, 310(1), 361, 362, 405, 427 of the Insolvency Act 1986, the entries relating to sections 31, 361 and 362 in Schedule 10 to the Insolvency Act 1986 and section 65 of the Justices of the Peace Act 1997).

EXPLANATORY NOTE
(This note is not part of the Order)

This Order brings into force with minor exceptions the provisions of the Enterprise Act 2002 relating to insolvency.

The following provisions are brought into force on 15th September 2003 ("the first commencement date"):
section 248 (replacement of Part II of the Insolvency Act 1986), and Schedules 16 and 17 (except paragraphs 14 and 59 of Schedule 17)
section 249 (special administration regimes)
section 250 (prohibition of appointment of administrative receivers) (to the extent it is not already in force) and Schedule 18
section 251 (abolition of crown preference)
section 252 (unsecured creditors)
section 253 (liquidator's powers)
section 254 (application of insolvency law to foreign company)
section 255 (application of law about company arrangement or administration to non-company)
section 262 (powers of trustee in bankruptcy)
section 278(2) and Schedule 26 (but only insofar as is necessary to give effect to the repeals relating to paragraphs 1 to 3 and 8 to 8C of Schedule 3 to the Bankruptcy (Scotland) Act 1985, sections 212, 230(1), 231, 232, 240(1), 245(3) and Schedule 10 to the Insolvency Act 1986 (except those relating to the entries relating to sections 31, 361 and 362), paragraph 32 of Schedule 29 to the Income and Corporation Taxes Act 1988, section 62(2)(a) of the Criminal Justice Act 1988, paragraphs 21A and 22 of Schedule 2 to the Finance Act 1991, paragraph 73 of Schedule 2 to the Social Security (Consequential Provisions) Act 1992, sections 36(1) to (3) of the Finance Act 1993, paragraphs 13(1) and 13(2) of Schedule 6 and paragraph 7(2) of Schedule 7 to the Finance Act 1994, paragraph 8 of Schedule 14 to the Value Added Tax Act 1994, section 17 of the Finance Act 1995, paragraphs 12(1) and 12(2) of Schedule 5 to the Finance Act 1996, sections 166(7)(a), 183(3)(a) and 189(4) of the Employment Rights Act 1996, paragraph 6 of Schedule 2 to the Finance Act 1997, paragraphs 2 and 3 of Schedule 7 to the Finance Act 2000 and paragraphs 17(1) and (2) and 18 of Schedule 5 to the Finance Act 2001).

The following provisions are brought into force on 1st April 2004 ("the second commencement date"):

section 256 (duration of bankruptcy) and Schedule 19 (except paragraph 8 of Schedule 19)

section 257 (post discharge restrictions) and Schedules 20 and 21

section 258 (investigation by official receiver)

section 259 (income payments order)

section 260 (income payments agreement)

section 261 (bankrupt's home)

section 263 (repeal of certain bankruptcy offences)

section 264 (individual voluntary arrangements) and Schedule 22

section 265 (disqualification from office: justice of the peace)

section 266 (disqualification from office: Parliament)

section 267 (disqualification from office: local government)

section 268 (disqualification from office: general)

section 269 (minor and consequential amendments) and Schedule 23

section 270 (fees)

section 271 (Insolvency Services Account: interest)

section 272 (Insolvency Services Account)

section 278(2) and Schedule 26 (but only insofar as is necessary to give effect to the repeals relating to sections 81(1) and 82(2) of the Local Government Act 1972, paragraph 22 of Schedule 8 to the Insolvency Act 1985, sections 275, 282(5), 292(1)(a), 293(1), 294(1), 297, 298(3), 300, 310(1), 361, 362, 405, 427 of the Insolvency Act 1986, the entries relating to sections 31, 361 and 362 in Schedule 10 to the Insolvency Act 1986 and section 65 of the Justices of the Peace Act 1997).

The main features of the provisions brought into force by this Order on [... ... ...] are the replacement of the provisions relating to the procedure of administration under Part II of the Insolvency Act 1986, the prohibition (subject to certain exceptions) on the appointment of administrative receivers, the abolition of Crown preference and the creation out of assets subject to a floating charge of a fund for the benefit of unsecured creditors. The remaining provisions of the Enterprise Act 2002 relating to individual insolvency in England and Wales and miscellaneous matters are brought into force from the 1 April 2004. These include the reduction in the period of bankruptcy for those bankrupts who co-operate with the Official Receiver from 3 years to a maximum of one year, the introduction of a procedure under which the court may make an order imposing restrictions on bankrupts who have been guilty of misconduct and provisions which provide for the official receiver to act in certain types of individual voluntary arrangement.

The Order contains a number of transitional and saving provisions. These are as follows.

Article 3 of the Order contains transitional provisions in relation to cases where petitions for administration orders were presented prior to the first commencement date. The old law will continue to apply in those cases. It also saves the operation of the old law for the purposes of giving effect to the Insolvent Partnerships Order 1994, regulation 5 of the Limited Liability Partnerships Regulations 2001; and the Financial Services and Markets Act 2000 (Administration Orders relating to Insurers) Order 2002. Article 4 of the Order contains transitional provisions in relation to the abolition of preferential status for Crown debts. Broadly speaking preferential status will continue to apply in those cases which were started before the first commencement date. The provisions of article 4 (and articles 5 and 6) apply in cases where the provisions of the Insolvency Act 1986 are applied to other situations, for example in relation to insolvent partnerships (*See article 1(5)*).

Articles 5 and 6 make transitional provisions in relation to certain types of proceedings taken by liquidators and trustees in bankruptcy. Section 253 of the Enterprise Act 2002 amends Schedule 4 to the Insolvency Act 1986 so that proceedings under sections 213, 214, 238, 239, 242, 243 or 423 can only be brought with sanction (usually from the creditors' committee). Similarly section 262 of the Enterprise Act 2002 amends Schedule 5 to the Insolvency Act 1986 to provide that a trustee in bankruptcy can only bring proceedings under sections 339, 340 or 423 with sanction (usually from the creditors' committee). Articles 5 and 6 provide that these amendments to the 1986 Act are not to affect any proceedings that are already on foot under the provisions of the Insolvency Act 1986 mentioned above.

Article 7 provides that where a court is considering whether to make a bankruptcy restrictions order it cannot take into account any conduct of the bankrupt which occurred prior to the second commencement date.

Article 8 contains transitional provisions in relation to existing bankruptcies in England and Wales where a certificate of summary administration was in force.

A regulatory impact assessment identifying the costs of the insolvency provisions of the Enterprise Act 2002 to business and the exchequer was published at the time the Act received Royal Assent in November 2002. It is available from www.dti.gov.uk/enterpriseact/rias.htm.

Insolvency Act 1986 (Prescribed Part) Order 2003

(2003 No 2097)

Made: 8th August 2003

Laid before Parliament: 13th August 2003

Coming into force: 15th September 2003

The Secretary of State, in exercise of the power conferred on her by section 176A of the Insolvency Act 1986, hereby makes the following Order:

Notes

Pursuant to IA 1986 s 176A(2) a liquidator or administrator or receiver—

(a)   shall make a 'prescribed part' of the company's net property available for the satisfaction of unsecured debts, and

(b)   shall not distribute that part to the proprietor of a floating charge except in so far as it exceeds the amount required for the satisfaction of unsecured debts.

However IA 1986 s 176(A)(2) shall not apply to a company if—

(a)   the company's net property is less than the 'prescribed minimum', and

(b)   the liquidator, administrator or receiver thinks that the cost of making a distribution to unsecured creditors would be disproportionate to the benefits.

The Insolvency Act 1986 (Prescribed Part) Order 2003 sets the "prescribed minimum" value of the company's net property for the purposes of the above provisions at £10,000; details of how the "prescribed part" of the company's net property available for the satisfaction of unsecured debts is to be calculated; and puts an upper limit on the value of the "prescribed part" of the company's net property at £600,000. See further the notes to IA 1986 s 176A.

18.1

1 Citation, Commencement and Interpretation

(1) This Order may be cited as the Insolvency Act 1986 (Prescribed Part) Order 2003 and shall come into force on 15th September 2003.

(2) In this order "the 1986 Act" means the Insolvency Act 1986.

18.2

2 Minimum value of the company's net property

For the purposes of section 176A(3)(a) of the 1986 Act the minimum value of the company's net property is £10,000.

18.3

3 Calculation of prescribed part

(1) The prescribed part of the company's net property to be made available for the satisfaction of unsecured debts of the company pursuant to section 176A of the 1986 Act shall be calculated as follows—

(a) where the company's net property does not exceed £10,000 in value, 50% of that property;

(b) subject to paragraph (2), where the company's net property exceeds £10,000 in value the sum of—

    (i) 50% of the first £10,000 in value; and

    (ii) 20% of that part of the company's net property which exceeds £10,000 in value.

(2) The value of the prescribed part of the company's net property to be made available for the satisfaction of unsecured debts of the company pursuant to section 176A shall not exceed £600,000.

Nigel Griffiths,

Parliamentary Under-Secretary of State for Small Business and Enterprise

Department of Trade and Industry

8th August 2003

EXPLANATORY NOTE

(This note is not part of the Order)

This Order sets out the method of calculation of the prescribed part referred to in section 176A of the Insolvency Act 1986 (c 45), which was inserted into that Act by section 251 of the Enterprise Act 2002 (c 40). The prescribed part is a part of the insolvency estate of a company which, but for section 176A, would have been available to the holders of debentures secured by floating charges. From the coming into force of section 176A and this Order, the amount of money reflecting the prescribed part as calculated by virtue of this Order will need to be set aside to satisfy the claims of unsecured creditors under the section.

Insolvency Regulations 1994

(1994 No 2507)

Made: 26th September 1994

The Secretary of State, in exercise of the powers conferred on him by Rule 12.1 of the Insolvency Rules 1986 and sections 411 and 412 of, and paragraphs 27 of Schedule 8 and 30 of Schedule 9 to, the Insolvency Act 1986 and of all other powers enabling him in that behalf, hereby makes the following Regulations:—

Part I
General

19.1

1 Citation and commencement

These Regulations may be cited as the Insolvency Regulations 1994 and shall come into force on 24th October 1994.

2 Revocations

Subject to regulation 37 below, the Regulations listed in Schedule 1 to these Regulations are hereby revoked.

3 Interpretation and application

(1) In these Regulations, except where the context otherwise requires—
["bank" means—
    (a)   a person who has permission under Part 4 of the Financial Services and Markets Act 2000 to accept deposits, or
    (b)   an EEA firm of the kind mentioned in paragraph 5(b) of Schedule 3 to that Act, which has permission under paragraph 15 of that Schedule (as a result of qualifying for authorisation under paragraph 12(1) of that Schedule) to accept deposits;]
"bankrupt" means the bankrupt or his estate;
"company" means the company which is being wound up;
"creditors' committee" means any committee established under section 301;
["electronic transfer" means transmission by any electronic means;]
"liquidation committee" means, in the case of a winding up by the court, any committee established under section 141 and, in the case of a creditors' voluntary winding up, any committee established under section 101;
"liquidator" includes, in the case of a company being wound up by the court, the official receiver when so acting;
"local bank" means any bank in, or in the neighbourhood of, the insolvency district, or the district in respect of which the court has winding-up jurisdiction, in which the proceedings are taken, or in the locality in which any business of the company or, as the case may be, the bankrupt is carried on;

"local bank account" means, in the case of a winding up by the court, a current account opened with a local bank under regulation 6(2) below and, in the case of a bankruptcy, a current account opened with a local bank under regulation 21(1) below;

"payment instrument" means a cheque or payable order;

"the Rules" means the Insolvency Rules 1986; and

"trustee", subject to regulation 19(2) below, means trustee of a bankrupt's estate including the official receiver when so acting;

and other expressions used in these Regulations and defined by the Rules have the meanings which they bear in the Rules.

(2) A Rule referred to in these Regulations by number means the Rule so numbered in the Rules.

(3) Any application to be made to the Secretary of State or to the Department or anything required to be sent to the Secretary of State or to the Department under these Regulations shall be addressed to the Department of Trade and Industry, The Insolvency Service, PO Box 3690, Birmingham B2 4UY.

(4) Where a regulation makes provision for the use of a form obtainable from the Department, the Department may provide different forms for different cases arising under that regulation.

(5) Subject to regulation 37 below, these Regulations [(except for regulations 3A and 36A)] apply—

    (a)   to winding-up proceedings commenced on or after 29th December 1986; and

    (b)   to bankruptcy proceedings where the bankruptcy petition is or was presented on or after that day.

[(6) Regulation 3A applies in any case where a company entered into administration on or after 15th September 2003 other than a case where the company entered into administration by virtue of a petition presented before that date.

(7) Regulation 36A applies in any case where an insolvency practitioner is appointed on or after 1st April 2005.]

[Part 1A
Administration]

19.2

[3A Disposal of company's records and provision of information to the Secretary of State]

[(1) The person who was the last administrator of a company which has been dissolved may, at any time after the expiration of a period of one year from the date of dissolution, destroy or otherwise dispose of the books, papers and other records of the company.

(2) An administrator or former administrator shall within 14 days of a request by the Secretary of State give the Secretary of State particulars of any money in his hands or under his control representing unclaimed or

undistributed assets of the company or dividends or other sums due to any person as a member or former member of the company.]

Part 2
Winding up

19.3

4 Introductory

This Part of these Regulations relates to—
    (a)   voluntary winding up and
    (b)   winding up by the court
of companies which the courts in England and Wales have jurisdiction to wind up.

Payments Into and Out of the Insolvency Services Account

19.4

5 Payments into the Insolvency Services Account

(1) In the case of a winding up by the court, subject to regulation 6 below, the liquidator shall pay all money received by him in the course of carrying out his functions as such without any deduction into the Insolvency Services Account kept by the Secretary of State with the Bank of England to the credit of the company once every 14 days or forthwith if £5,000 or more has been received.

[(2) In the case of a voluntary winding up, the liquidator may make payments into the Insolvency Services Account to the credit of the company.]

[(3) Every payment of money into the Insolvency Services Account under this regulation shall be—
    (a)   made through the Bank Giro system; or
    (b)   sent direct to the Bank of England, Threadneedle Street, London EC2R 8AH by cheque drawn in favour of the "Insolvency Services Account" and crossed "A/c payee only" "Bank of England": or
    (c)   made by electronic transfer,
and the liquidator shall on request be given by the Department a receipt for the money so paid.]

(4) Every payment of money [made under sub-paragraph (a) or (b) of paragraph (3) above] shall be accompanied by a form obtainable from the Department for that purpose or by a form that is substantially similar. [Every payment of money made under sub-paragraph (c) of paragraph (3) above shall specify the name of the liquidator making the payment and the name of the company to whose credit such payment is made.]

(5) Where in a voluntary winding up a liquidator pays any unclaimed dividend into the Insolvency Services Account, he shall at the same time give notice to the Secretary of State, on a form obtainable from the

Department or on one that is substantially similar, of the name and address of the person to whom the dividend is payable and the amount of the dividend.

19.5

6 Local bank account and handling of funds not belonging to the company

(1) This regulation does not apply in the case of a voluntary winding up.

(2) Where the liquidator intends to exercise his power to carry on the business of the company, he may apply to the Secretary of State for authorisation to open a local bank account, and the Secretary of State may authorise him to make his payments into and out of a specified bank, subject to a limit, instead of into and out of the Insolvency Services Account if satisfied that an administrative advantage will be derived from having such an account.

(3) Money received by the liquidator relating to the purpose for which the account was opened may be paid into the local bank account to the credit of the company to which the account relates.

(4) Where the liquidator opens a local bank account pursuant to an authorisation granted under paragraph (2) above, he shall open and maintain the account in the name of the company.

(5) Where money which is not an asset of the company is provided to the liquidator for a specific purpose, it shall be clearly identifiable in a separate account.

(6) The liquidator shall keep proper records, including documentary evidence of all money paid into and out of every local bank account opened and maintained under this regulation.

(7) The liquidator shall pay without deduction any surplus over any limit imposed by an authorisation granted under paragraph (2) above into the Insolvency Services Account in accordance with regulation 5 above as that regulation applies in the case of a winding up by the court.

(8) As soon as the liquidator ceases to carry on the business of the company or vacates office or an authorisation given in pursuance of an application under paragraph (2) above is withdrawn, he shall close the account and pay any balance into the Insolvency Services Account in accordance with regulation 5 above as that regulation applies in the case of a winding up by the court.

19.6

7 Payment of disbursements etc out of the Insolvency Services Account

[(A1) Paragraphs (1) to (3) of this regulation are subject to paragraph (3A).]

(1) In the case of a winding up by the court, on application to the Department, the liquidator shall be repaid all necessary disbursements made by him, and expenses properly incurred by him, in the course of his administration to the date of his vacation of office out of any money standing to the credit of the company in the Insolvency Services Account.

(2) In the case of a winding up by the court, the liquidator shall on application to the Department obtain payment instruments to the order of the payee for sums which become payable on account of the company for delivery by the liquidator to the persons to whom the payments are to be made.

(3) In the case of a voluntary winding up, where the liquidator requires to make payments out of any money standing to the credit of the company in the Insolvency Services Account in respect of the expenses of the winding up, he shall apply to the Secretary of State who may either authorise payment to the liquidator of the sum required by him, or may direct payment instruments to be issued to the liquidator for delivery by him to the persons to whom the payments are to be made.

[(3A) In respect of an application made by the liquidator under paragraphs (1) to (3) above, the Secretary of State, if requested to do so by the liquidator, may, at his discretion,
- (a)   make the payment which is the subject of the application to the liquidator by electronic transfer; or
- (b)   as an alternative to the issue of payment instruments, make payment by electronic transfer to the persons to whom the liquidator would otherwise deliver payment instruments.]

(4) Any application under this regulation shall be made by the liquidator on a form obtainable from the Department for the purpose or on a form that is substantially similar.

(5) In the case of a winding up by the court, on the liquidator vacating office, he shall be repaid by any succeeding liquidator out of any funds available for the purpose any necessary disbursements made by him and any expenses properly incurred by him but not repaid before he vacates office.

Dividends to Creditors and Returns of Capital to Contributories of a Company

19.7

8 Payment

[(A1) Paragraphs (1) to (3) of this regulation are subject to paragraph (3A).]

(1) In the case of a winding up by the court, the liquidator shall pay every dividend by payment instruments which shall be prepared by the Department on the application of the liquidator and transmitted to him for distribution amongst the creditors.

(2) In the case of a winding up by the court, the liquidator shall pay every return of capital to contributories by payment instruments which shall be prepared by the Department on application.

(3) In the case of a voluntary winding up, where the liquidator requires to make payments out of any money standing to the credit of the company in the Insolvency Services Account by way of distribution, he shall apply in writing to the Secretary of State who may either authorise payment to the liquidator of the sum required by him, or may direct payment

instruments to be issued to the liquidator for delivery by him to the persons to whom the payments are to be made.

[(3A) In respect of an application made by the liquidator under paragraphs (1) to (3) above, the Secretary of State, if requested to do so by the liquidator, may, at his discretion,

(a)   as an alternative to the issue of payment instruments, make payment by electronic transfer to the persons to whom the liquidator would otherwise deliver payment instruments; or

(b)   make the payment which is the subject of the application to the liquidator by electronic transfer.]

(4) Any application under this regulation for a payment instrument [or payment by electronic transfer] shall be made by the liquidator on a form obtainable from the Department for the purpose or on a form which is substantially similar.

(5) In the case of a winding up by the court, the liquidator shall enter the total amount of every dividend and of every return to contributories that he desires to pay under this regulation in the records to be kept under regulation 10 below in one sum.

(6) On the liquidator vacating office, he shall send to the Department any valid unclaimed or undelivered payment instruments for dividends or returns to contributories after endorsing them with the word "cancelled".

Investment or Otherwise Handling of Funds in Winding up of Companies and Payment of Interest

19.8

9

(1) When the cash balance standing to the credit of the company in the account in respect of that company kept by the Secretary of State is in excess of the amount which, in the opinion of the liquidator, is required for the immediate purposes of the winding up and should be invested, he may request the Secretary of State to invest the amount not so required in Government securities, to be placed to the credit of that account for the company's benefit.

(2) When any of the money so invested is, in the opinion of the liquidator, required for the immediate purposes of the winding up, he may request the Secretary of State to raise such sum as may be required by the sale of such of those securities as may be necessary.

(3) In cases where investments have been made at the request of the liquidator in pursuance of paragraph (1) above and additional sums to the amounts so invested, including money received under paragraph (7) below, are paid into the Insolvency Services Account to the credit of the company, a request shall be made to the Secretary of State by the liquidator if it is desired that these additional sums should be invested.

(4) Any request relating to the investment in, or sale of, as the case may be, Treasury Bills made under paragraphs (1), (2) or (3) above shall be made on a form obtainable from the Department or on one that is substantially similar and any request relating to the purchase or sale, as

the case may be, of any other type of Government security made under the provisions of those paragraphs shall be made in writing.

(5) Any request made under paragraphs (1), (2) or (3) above shall be sufficient authority to the Secretary of State for the investment or sale as the case may be.

[(6) Subject to paragraphs (6A) and (6B), at any time after 1st April 2004 whenever there are any monies standing to the credit of the company in the Insolvency Services Account the company shall be entitled to interest on those monies at the rate of 4.25% per annum.

(6A) Interest shall cease to accrue pursuant to paragraph (6) from the date of receipt by the Secretary of State of a notice in writing from the liquidator that in the opinion of the liquidator it is necessary or expedient in order to facilitate the conclusion of the winding up that interest should cease to accrue but interest shall start to accrue again pursuant to paragraph (6) where the liquidator gives a further notice in writing to the Secretary of State requesting that interest should start to accrue again.

(6B) The Secretary of State may by notice published in the London Gazette vary the rate of interest prescribed by paragraph (6) and such variation shall have effect from the day after the date of publication of the notice in the London Gazette or such later date as may be specified in the notice.]

(7) All money received in respect of investments and interest earned under this regulation shall be paid into the Insolvency Services Account to the credit of the company.

(8) In addition to the application of paragraphs (1) to (7) above, in a voluntary winding up:
  (a) any money invested or deposited at interest by the liquidator shall be deemed to be money under his control, and when such money forms part of the balance of funds in his hands or under his control relating to the company required to be paid into the Insolvency Services Account under regulation 5 above, the liquidator shall realise the investment or withdraw the deposit and shall pay the proceeds into that Account: Provided that where the money is invested in Government securities, such securities may, with the permission of the Secretary of State, be transferred to the control of the Secretary of State instead of being forthwith realised and the proceeds paid into the Insolvency Services Account; and
  (b) where any of the money represented by securities transferred to the control of the Secretary of State pursuant to sub-paragraph (a) above is, in the opinion of the liquidator, required for the immediate purposes of the winding up he may request the Secretary of State to raise such sums as may be required by the sale of such of those securities as may be necessary and such request shall be sufficient authority to the Secretary of State for the sale and the Secretary of State shall pay the proceeds of the realisation into the Insolvency Services Account in accordance with paragraph (7) above and deal with them in the same way as other money paid into that Account may be dealt with.

Records to be Maintained by Liquidators and the Provision of Information

19.9

10 Financial records

(1) This regulation does not apply in the case of a members' voluntary winding up.

(2) The liquidator shall prepare and keep—
    (a) separate financial records in respect of each company; and
    (b) such other financial records as are required to explain the receipts and payments entered in the records described in sub-paragraph (a) above or regulation 12(2) below, including an explanation of the source of any receipts and the destination of any payments;

and shall, subject to regulation 12(2) below as to trading accounts, from day to day enter in those records all the receipts and payments (including, in the case of a voluntary winding up, those relating to the Insolvency Services Account) made by him.

(3) In the case of a winding up by the court, the liquidator shall obtain and keep bank statements relating to any local bank account in the name of the company.

(4) The liquidator shall submit financial records to the liquidation committee when required for inspection.

(5) In the case of a winding up by the court, if the liquidation committee is not satisfied with the contents of the financial records submitted under paragraph (4) above it may so inform the Secretary of State, giving the reasons for its dissatisfaction, and the Secretary of State may take such action as he thinks fit.

19.10

11 Provision of information by liquidator

(1) In the case of a winding up by the court, the liquidator shall, within 14 days of the receipt of a request for a statement of his receipts and payments as liquidator from any creditor, contributory or director of the company, supply free of charge to the person making the request, a statement of his receipts and payments as liquidator during the period of one year ending on the most recent anniversary of his becoming liquidator which preceded the request.

(2) In the case of a voluntary winding up, the liquidator shall, on request from any creditor, contributory or director of the company for a copy of a statement for any period, including future periods, sent to the registrar of companies under section 192, send such copy free of charge to the person making the request and the copy of the statement shall be sent within 14 days of the liquidator sending the statement to the registrar or the receipt of the request whichever is the later.

19.11

12 Liquidator carrying on business

(1) This regulation does not apply in the case of a members' voluntary winding up.

(2) Where the liquidator carries on any business of the company, he shall—
  (a) keep a separate and distinct account of the trading, including, where appropriate, in the case of a winding up by the court, particulars of all local bank account transactions; and
  (b) incorporate in the financial records required to be kept under regulation 10 above the total weekly amounts of the receipts and payments made by him in relation to the account kept under sub-paragraph (a) above.

19.12

13 Retention and delivery of records

(1) All records kept by the liquidator under regulations 10 and 12(2) and any such records received by him from a predecessor in that office shall be retained by him for a period of 6 years following—
  (a) his vacation of office, or
  (b) in the case of the official receiver, his release as liquidator under section 174,
unless he delivers them to another liquidator who succeeds him in office.

(2) Where the liquidator is succeeded in office by another liquidator, the records referred to in paragraph (1) above shall be delivered to that successor forthwith, unless, in the case of a winding up by the court, the winding up is for practical purposes complete and the successor is the official receiver, in which case the records are only to be delivered to the official receiver if the latter so requests.

19.13

14 Provision of accounts by liquidator and audit of accounts

(1) The liquidator shall, if required by the Secretary of State at any time, send to the Secretary of State an account in relation to the company of the liquidator's receipts and payments covering such period as the Secretary of State may direct and such account shall, if so required by the Secretary of State, be certified by the liquidator.

(2) Where the liquidator in a winding up by the court vacates office prior to the holding of the final general meeting of creditors under section 146, he shall within 14 days of vacating office send to the Secretary of State an account of his receipts and payments as liquidator for any period not covered by an account previously so sent by him or if no such account has been sent, an account of his receipts and payments in respect of the whole period of his office.

(3) In the case of a winding up by the court, where:
  (a) a final general meeting of creditors has been held pursuant to section 146, or
  (b) a final general meeting is deemed to have been held by virtue of Rule 4.125(5),
the liquidator shall send to the Secretary of State, in case (a), within 14 days of the holding of the final general meeting of creditors and, in case (b), within 14 days of his report to the court pursuant to Rule 4.125(5), an account of his receipts and payments as liquidator which are not covered

by any previous account so sent by him, or if no such account has been sent an account of his receipts and payments in respect of the whole period of his office.

(4) In the case of a winding up by the court, where a statement of affairs has been submitted under the Act, any account sent under this regulation shall be accompanied by a summary of that statement of affairs and shall show the amount of any assets realised and explain the reasons for any non-realisation of any assets not realised.

(5) In the case of a winding up by the court, where a statement of affairs has not been submitted under the Act, any account sent under this regulation shall be accompanied by a summary of all known assets and their estimated values and shall show the amounts actually realised and explain the reasons for any non-realisation of any assets not realised.

(6) Any account sent to the Secretary of State shall, if he so requires, be audited, but whether or not the Secretary of State requires the account to be audited, the liquidator shall send to the Secretary of State on demand any documents (including vouchers and bank statements) and any information relating to the account.

19.14

15 Production and inspection of records

(1) The liquidator shall produce on demand to the Secretary of State, and allow him to inspect, any accounts, books and other records kept by him (including any passed to him by a predecessor in office), and this duty to produce and allow inspection shall extend—

    (a) to producing and allowing inspection at the premises of the liquidator; and

    (b) to producing and allowing inspection of any financial records of the kind described in regulation 10(2)(b) above prepared by the liquidator (or any predecessor in office of his) before 24th October 1994 and kept by the liquidator;

and any such demand may—

    (i) require the liquidator to produce any such accounts, books or other records to the Secretary of State, and allow him to inspect them—

        (A) at the same time as any account is sent to the Secretary of State under regulation 14 above; or

        (B) at any time after such account is sent to the Secretary of State;

    whether or not the Secretary of State requires the account to be audited; or

    (ii) where it is made for the purpose of ascertaining whether the provisions of these Regulations relating to the handling of money received by the liquidator in the course of carrying out his functions have been or are likely to be complied with, be made at any time, whether or not an account has been sent or should have been sent to the Secretary of State under regulation 14 above and whether or not the Secretary of State has required any account to be audited.

(2) The liquidator shall allow the Secretary of State on demand to remove and take copies of any accounts, books and other records kept by the liquidator (including any passed to him by a predecessor in office), whether or not they are kept at the premises of the liquidator.

19.15

16 Disposal of company's books, papers and other records

(1) The liquidator in a winding up by the court, on the authorisation of the official receiver, during his tenure of office or on vacating office, or the official receiver while acting as liquidator, may at any time sell, destroy or otherwise dispose of the books, papers and other records of the company.

(2) In the case of a voluntary winding up, the person who was the last liquidator of a company which has been dissolved may, at any time after the expiration of a period of one year from the date of dissolution, destroy or otherwise dispose of the books, papers and other records of the company.

19.16

17 Voluntary liquidator to provide information to Secretary of State

(1) In the case of a voluntary winding up, a liquidator or former liquidator, whether the winding up has been concluded under Rule 4.223 or not, shall, within 14 days of a request by the Secretary of State, give the Secretary of State particulars of any money in his hands or under his control representing unclaimed or undistributed assets of the company or dividends or other sums due to any person as a member or former member of the company and such other particulars as the Secretary of State may require for the purpose of ascertaining or getting in any money payable into the Insolvency Services Account.

(2) The particulars referred to in paragraph (1) above shall, if the Secretary of State so requires, be certified by the liquidator, or former liquidator, as the case may be.

19.17

18 Payment of unclaimed or undistributed assets, dividends or other money on dissolution of company

In the case of a company which has been dissolved, notwithstanding anything in these Regulations, any money in the hands of any or any former liquidator at the date of dissolution of the company or his earlier vacation of office, representing unclaimed or undistributed assets of the company or dividends or held by the company in trust in respect of dividends or other sums due to any person as a member or former member of the company, shall forthwith be paid by him into the Insolvency Services Account.

Part 3
Bankruptcy

19.18

19 Introductory

(1) This Part of these Regulations relates to bankruptcy and extends to England and Wales only.

(2) In addition to the application of the provisions of this Part to the official receiver when acting as trustee, the provisions of this Part (other than regulations 30 and 31) shall also apply to him when acting as receiver or manager under section 287 and the term "trustee" shall be construed accordingly.

Payments Into and Out of the Insolvency Services Account

19.19

20 Payments into the Insolvency Services Account

(1) Subject to regulation 21 below, the trustee shall pay all money received by him in the course of carrying out his functions as such without any deduction into the Insolvency Services Account kept by the Secretary of State with the Bank of England to the credit of the bankrupt once every 14 days or forthwith if £5,000 or more has been received.

[(2) Every payment of money into the Insolvency Services Account under this regulation shall be—
   (a)   made through the Bank Giro system; or
   (b)   sent direct to the Bank of England, Threadneedle Street, London EC2R 8AH by cheque drawn in favour of the "Insolvency Services Account" and crossed "A/c payee only" "Bank of England"; or
   (c)   made by electronic transfer,
and the trustee shall on request be given by the Department a receipt for the money so paid.]

(3) Every payment of money [made under sub-paragraph (a) or (b) of paragraph (2) above] shall be accompanied by a form obtainable from the Department for that purpose or by a form that is substantially similar. [Every payment of money made under sub-paragraph (c) of paragraph (2) above shall specify the name of the trustee making the payment and the name of the bankrupt to whose credit such payment is made.]

19.20

21 Local bank account and handling of funds not forming part of the bankrupt's estate

(1) Where the trustee intends to exercise his power to carry on the business of the bankrupt, he may apply to the Secretary of State for authorisation to open a local bank account, and the Secretary of State may authorise him to make his payments into and out of a specified bank, subject to a limit, instead of into and out of the Insolvency Services Account if satisfied that an administrative advantage will be derived from having such an account.

(2) Money received by the trustee relating to the purpose for which the account was opened may be paid into the local bank account to the credit of the bankrupt to whom the account relates.

(3) Where the trustee opens a local bank account pursuant to an authorisation granted under paragraph (1) above he shall open and maintain the account in the name of the bankrupt.

(4) Where money which does not form part of the bankrupt's estate is provided to the trustee for a specific purpose it shall be clearly identifiable in a separate account.

(5) The trustee shall keep proper records, including documentary evidence of all money paid into and out of every local bank account opened and maintained under this regulation.

(6) The trustee shall pay without deduction any surplus over any limit imposed by an authorisation granted under paragraph (1) above into the Insolvency Services Account in accordance with regulation 20(1) above.

(7) As soon as the trustee ceases to carry on the business of the bankrupt or vacates office or an authorisation given in pursuance of an application under paragraph (1) above is withdrawn, he shall close the account and pay any balance into the Insolvency Services Account in accordance with regulation 20(1) above.

19.21

22 Payment of disbursements etc out of the Insolvency Services Account

[(A1) Paragraphs (1) and (2) of this regulation are subject to paragraph (2A).]

(1) On application to the Department, the trustee shall be repaid all necessary disbursements made by him, and expenses properly incurred by him, in the course of his administration to the date of his vacation of office out of any money standing to the credit of the bankrupt in the Insolvency Services Account.

(2) The trustee shall on application to the Department obtain payment instruments to the order of the payee for sums which become payable on account of the bankrupt for delivery by the trustee to the persons to whom the payments are to be made.

[(2A) In respect of an application made by the trustee under paragraph (1) or (2) above, the Secretary of State, if requested to do so by the trustee, may, at his discretion,
   (a) make the payment which is the subject of the application to the trustee by electronic transfer; or
   (b) as an alternative to the issue of payment instruments, make payment by electronic transfer to the persons to whom the trustee would otherwise deliver payment instruments.]

(3) Any application under this regulation shall be made on a form obtainable from the Department or on one that is substantially similar.

(4) On the trustee vacating office, he shall be repaid by any succeeding trustee out of any funds available for the purpose any necessary disbursements made by him and any expenses properly incurred by him but not repaid before he vacates office.

Dividends to Creditors

19.22

23 Payment

(1) [Subject to paragraph (1A),] the trustee shall pay every dividend by payment instruments which shall be prepared by the Department on the application of the trustee and transmitted to him for distribution amongst the creditors.

[(1A) In respect of an application made by the trustee under paragraph (1) above, the Secretary of State, if requested to do so by the trustee, may, at his discretion, as an alternative to the issue of payment instruments, make payment by electronic transfer to the persons to whom the trustee would otherwise deliver payment instruments.]

(2) Any application under this regulation for a payment instrument [or payment by electronic transfer] shall be made by the trustee on a form obtainable from the Department for the purpose or on a form which is substantially similar.

(3) The trustee shall enter the total amount of every dividend that he desires to pay under this regulation in the records to be kept under regulation 24 below in one sum.

(4) On the trustee vacating office, he shall send to the Department any valid unclaimed or undelivered payment instruments for dividends after endorsing them with the word "cancelled".

19.23

[23A Investment or otherwise handling of funds in bankruptcy and payment of interest]

[(1) When the cash balance standing to the credit of the bankrupt in the account in respect of that bankrupt kept by the Secretary of State is in excess of the amount which, in the opinion of the trustee, is required for the immediate purposes of the bankruptcy and should be invested, he may request the Secretary of State to invest the amount not so required in Government securities, to be placed to the credit of that account for the benefit of the bankrupt.

(2) When any of the money so invested is, in the opinion of the trustee, required for the immediate purposes of the bankruptcy, he may request the Secretary of State to raise such sum as may be required by the sale of such of those securities as may be necessary.

(3) In cases where investments have been made at the request of the trustee in pursuance of paragraph (1) above and additional sums to the amounts so invested, including money received under paragraph (7) below, are paid into the Insolvency Services Account to the credit of the bankrupt, a request shall be made to the Secretary of State by the trustee if it is desired that these additional funds should be invested.

(4) Any request relating to the investment in, or sale of, as the case may be, Treasury Bills under paragraphs (1), (2) or (3) above shall be made on a form obtainable from the Department or on one that is substantially similar and any request relating to the purchase or sale, as the case may be, of any other type of Government security made under the provisions of those paragraphs shall be made in writing.

(5) Any request made under paragraphs (1), (2) or (3) above shall be sufficient authority to the Secretary of State for the investment or sale as the case may be.

[(6) Subject to paragraphs (6A) and (6B), at any time after 1st April 2004 whenever there are any monies standing to the credit of the estate of the bankrupt in the Insolvency Services Account the estate shall be entitled to interest on those monies at the rate of 4.25% per annum.

(6A) Interest shall cease to accrue pursuant to paragraph (6) from the date of receipt by the Secretary of State of a notice in writing from the trustee that in the opinion of the trustee it is necessary or expedient in order to facilitate the conclusion of the bankruptcy that interest should cease to accrue but interest shall start to accrue again pursuant to paragraph (6) where the trustee gives a further notice in writing to the Secretary of State requesting that interest should start to accrue again.

(6B) The Secretary of State may by notice published in the London Gazette vary the rate of interest prescribed by paragraph (6) and such variation shall have effect from the day after the date of publication of the notice in the London Gazette or such later date as may be specified in the notice.]

(7) All money received in respect of investments and interest earned under this regulation shall be paid into the Insolvency Services Account to the credit of the bankrupt.]

Records to be Maintained by Trustees and the Provision of Information

19.24

24 Financial records

(1) The trustee shall prepare and keep—
  (a) separate financial records in respect of each bankrupt; and
  (b) such other financial records as are required to explain the receipts and payments entered in the records described in sub-paragraph (a) above or regulation 26 below, including an explanation of the source of any receipts and the destination of any payments;
and shall, subject to regulation 26 below as to trading accounts, from day to day enter in those records all the receipts and payments made by him.

(2) The trustee shall obtain and keep bank statements relating to any local bank account in the name of the bankrupt.

(3) The trustee shall submit financial records to the creditors' committee when required for inspection.

(4) If the creditors' committee is not satisfied with the contents of the financial records submitted under paragraph (3) above it may so inform

the Secretary of State, giving the reasons for its dissatisfaction and the Secretary of State may take such action as he thinks fit.

25 Provision of information by trustee

The trustee shall, within 14 days of the receipt of a request from any creditor or the bankrupt for a statement of his receipts and payments as trustee, supply free of charge to the person making the request, a statement of his receipts and payments as trustee during the period of one year ending on the most recent anniversary of his becoming trustee which preceded the request.

26 Trustee carrying on business

Subject to paragraph (2) below, where the trustee carries on any business of the bankrupt, he shall—

    (a)   keep a separate and distinct account of the trading, including, where appropriate, particulars of all local bank account transactions; and

    (b)   incorporate in the financial records required to be kept under regulation 24 above the total weekly amounts of the receipts and payments made by him in relation to the account kept under paragraph (a) above.

27 Retention and delivery of records

(1) All records kept by the trustee under regulations 24 and 26 and any such records received by him from a predecessor in that office shall be retained by him for a period of 6 years following—

    (a)   his vacation of office, or

    (b)   in the case of the official receiver, his release as trustee under section 299,

unless he delivers them to another trustee who succeeds him in office.

(2) Where the trustee is succeeded in office by another trustee, the records referred to in paragraph (1) above shall be delivered to that successor forthwith, unless the bankruptcy is for practical purposes complete and the successor is the official receiver, in which case the records are only to be delivered to the official receiver if the latter so requests.

28 Provision of accounts by trustee and audit of accounts

(1) The trustee shall, if required by the Secretary of State at any time, send to the Secretary of State an account of his receipts and payments as trustee of the bankrupt covering such period as the Secretary of State may direct and such account shall, if so required by the Secretary of State, be certified by the trustee.

(2) Where the trustee vacates office prior to the holding of the final general meeting of creditors under section 331, he shall within 14 days of vacating office send to the Secretary of State an account of his receipts and payments as trustee for any period not covered by an account previously so sent by him, or if no such account has been sent, an account of his receipts and payments in respect of the whole period of his office.

(3) Where:

(a) a final general meeting of creditors has been held pursuant to section 331, or

(b) a final general meeting is deemed to have been held by virtue of Rule 6.137(5),

the trustee shall send to the Secretary of State, in case (a), within 14 days of the holding of the final general meeting of creditors and, in case (b), within 14 days of his report to the court pursuant to Rule 6.137(5), an account of his receipts and payments as trustee which are not covered by any previous account so sent by him, or if no such account has been sent, an account of his receipts and payments in respect of the whole period of his office.

(4) Where a statement of affairs has been submitted under the Act, any account sent under this regulation shall be accompanied by a summary of that statement of affairs and shall show the amount of any assets realised and explain the reasons for any non-realisation of any assets not realised.

(5) Where a statement of affairs has not been submitted under the Act, any account sent under this regulation shall be accompanied by a summary of all known assets and their estimated values and shall show the amounts actually realised and explain the reasons for any non-realisation of any assets not realised.

(6) Any account sent to the Secretary of State shall, if he so requires, be audited, but whether or not the Secretary of State requires the account to be audited, the trustee shall send to the Secretary of State on demand any documents (including vouchers and bank statements) and any information relating to the account.

29 Production and inspection of records

(1) The trustee shall produce on demand to the Secretary of State, and allow him to inspect, any accounts, books and other records kept by him (including any passed to him by a predecessor in office), and this duty to produce and allow inspection shall extend—

(a) to producing and allowing inspection at the premises of the trustee; and

(b) to producing and allowing inspection of any financial records of the kind described in regulation 24(1)(b) above prepared by the trustee before 24th October 1994 and kept by him;

and any such demand may—

(i) require the trustee to produce any such accounts, books or other records to the Secretary of State, and allow him to inspect them—

(A) at the same time as any account is sent to the Secretary of State under regulation 28 above; or

(B) at any time after such account is sent to the Secretary of State;

whether or not the Secretary of State requires the account to be audited; or

(ii) where it is made for the purpose of ascertaining whether the provisions of these Regulations relating to the handling of money received by the trustee in the course of carrying out his functions have been or are likely to be complied with, be made at any time, whether or not an account has been sent or should have been sent to the Secretary of State under regulation 28 above and whether or not the Secretary of State has required any account to be audited.

(2) The trustee shall allow the Secretary of State on demand to remove and take copies of any accounts, books and other records kept by the trustee (including any passed to him by a predecessor in office), whether or not they are kept at the premises of the trustee.

30 Disposal of bankrupt's books, papers and other records

The trustee, on the authorisation of the official receiver, during his tenure of office or on vacating office, or the official receiver while acting as trustee, may at any time sell, destroy or otherwise dispose of the books, papers and other records of the bankrupt.

31 Payment of unclaimed or undistributed assets, dividends or other money

Notwithstanding anything in these Regulations, any money—
    (a)   in the hands of the trustee at the date of his vacation of office, or
    (b)   which comes into the hands of any former trustee at any time after his vacation of office,
representing, in either case, unclaimed or undistributed assets of the bankrupt or dividends, shall forthwith be paid by him into the Insolvency Services Account.

Part 4
Claiming Money Paid into the Insolvency Services Account

19.25

32

(1) Any person claiming to be entitled to any money paid into the Insolvency Services Account may apply to the Secretary of State for payment and shall provide such evidence of his claim as the Secretary of State may require.

(2) Any person dissatisfied with the decision of the Secretary of State in respect of his claim made under this regulation may appeal to the court.

Part 5
Remuneration of Official Receiver

19.26

33 ...

...

19.27

34 ...

...

19.28

[35 Official receiver's general remuneration while acting as interim receiver, provisional liquidator, liquidator or trustee]

[(1) The official receiver shall be entitled to remuneration calculated in accordance with the applicable hourly rates set out in paragraph (2) for services provided by him (or any of his officers) in relation to—

(a) a distribution made by him when acting as liquidator or trustee to creditors (including preferential or secured creditors or both such classes of creditor);

(b) the realisation of assets on behalf of the holder of a fixed or floating charge or both types of those charges;

(c) the supervision of a special manager;

(d) the performance by him of any functions where he acts as provisional liquidator; or

(e) the performance by him of any functions where he acts as an interim receiver.

(2) The applicable hourly rates referred to in paragraph (1) are—

(a) in relation to the official receiver of the London insolvency district, those set out in Table 2 in Schedule 2; and

(b) in relation to any other official receiver, those set out in Table 3 in Schedule 2.]

36 ...

...

[Part 5A
Information about Time Spent on a Case to be Provided by Insolvency Practitioner to Creditors etc]

19.29

[36A

[(1) Subject as set out in this regulation, in respect of any case in which he acts, an insolvency practitioner shall on request in writing made by any person mentioned in paragraph (2), supply free of charge to that person a statement of the kind described in paragraph (3).

(2) The persons referred to in paragraph (1) are—

(a) any creditor in the case;

(b) where the case relates to a company, any director or contributory of that company; and

(c) where the case relates to an individual, that individual.

(3) The statement referred to in paragraph (1) shall comprise in relation to the period beginning with the date of the insolvency practitioner's appointment and ending with the relevant date the following details—

(a) the total number of hours spent on the case by the insolvency practitioner and any staff assigned to the case during that period;

(b) for each grade of individual so engaged, the average hourly rate at which any work carried out by individuals in that grade is charged; and

(c)   the number of hours spent by each grade of staff during that period.

(4) In relation to paragraph (3) the "relevant date" means the date next before the date of the making of the request on which the insolvency practitioner has completed any period in office which is a multiple of six months or, where the insolvency practitioner has vacated office, the date that he vacated office.

(5) Where an insolvency practitioner has vacated office, an obligation to provide information under this regulation shall only arise in relation to a request that is made within 2 years of the date he vacates office.

(6) Any statement required to be provided to any person under this regulation shall be supplied within 28 days of the date of the receipt of the request by the insolvency practitioner.

(7) In this regulation the expression "insolvency practitioner" shall be construed in accordance with section 388 of the Insolvency Act 1986.]

Part 6
Transitional and Saving Provisions

19.30

37

The Regulations shall have effect subject to the transitional and saving provisions set out in Schedule 3 to these Regulations.

SCHEDULE 1
Regulation 2

19.31

...

SCHEDULE 2
Regulations 33 to 36
TABLE 1

19.32

< ... >

[Table 2 – London rates

Grade according to the Insolvency Service grading structure/Status of Official	Total hourly rate £
D2/Official Receiver	65
C2/Deputy or Assistant Official Receiver	55

Grade according to the Insolvency Service grading structure/Status of Official	Total hourly rate £
C1/Senior Examiner	50
B3/Examiner	40
B2/Administrator	40
B1/Examiner	35
B1/Administrator	40
A2/Administrator	35
A1/Administrator	30

Table 3 – Provincial rates

Grade according to the Insolvency Service grading structure/Status of Official	Total hourly rate £
D2/Official Receiver	60
C2/Deputy or Assistant Official Receiver	50
C1/Senior Examiner	45
B3/Examiner	40
B2/Administrator	37
B1/Examiner	33
B1/Administrator	36
A2/Administrator	31
A1/Administrator	27

SCHEDULE 3

Regulation 37

19.33

Interpretation

1

In this Schedule the expression "the former Regulations" means the Insolvency Regulations 1986 as amended by the Insolvency (Amendment) Regulations 1987, the Insolvency (Amendment) Regulations 1988 and the Insolvency (Amendment) Regulations 1991.

Requests pursuant to regulation 13(1) of the former Regulations

2

Any request made pursuant to regulation 13(1) of the former Regulations which has not been complied with prior to 24th October 1994 shall be treated, in the case of a company that is being wound up by the court, as a request made pursuant to regulation 11(1) of these Regulations and, in the case of a bankruptcy, as a request made pursuant to regulation 25 of these Regulations and in each case the request shall be treated as if it had been made on 24th October 1994.

Things done under the provisions of the former Regulations

3

So far as anything done under, or for the purposes of, any provision of the former Regulations could have been done under, or for the purposes of, the corresponding provision of these Regulations, it is not invalidated by the revocation of that provision but has effect as if done under, or for the purposes of, the corresponding provision.

Time periods

4

Where any period of time specified in a provision of the former Regulations is current immediately before 24th October 1994, these Regulations have effect as if the corresponding provision of these Regulations had been in force when the period began to run; and (without prejudice to the foregoing) any period of time so specified and current is deemed for the purposes of these Regulations—

(a) to run from the date or event from which it was running immediately before 24th October 1994, and

(b) to expire whenever it would have expired if these Regulations had not been made;

and any rights, obligations, requirements, powers or duties dependent on the beginning, duration or end of such period as above-mentioned shall be under these Regulations as they were or would have been under the former Regulations.

References to other provisions

5

Where in any provision of these Regulations there is reference to another provision of these Regulations, and the first-mentioned provision operates, or is capable of operating, in relation to things done or omitted, or events occurring or not occurring, in the past (including in particular past acts of compliance with the former Regulations), the reference to that other provision is to be read as including a reference to the corresponding provision of the former Regulations.

Provisions of Schedule to be without prejudice to the operation of sections 16 and 17 of the Interpretation Act 1978

6

The provisions of this Schedule are to be without prejudice to the operation of sections 16 and 17 of the Interpretation Act 1978 (saving from, and effect of, repeals) as they are applied by section 23 of that Act.

Meaning of "corresponding provision"

7

(1) A provision in the former Regulations, except regulation 13(1) of those Regulations, is to be regarded as the corresponding provision of a

provision in these Regulations notwithstanding any modifications made to the provision as it appears in these Regulations.

(2) Without prejudice to the generality of the term "corresponding provision" the following table shall, subject to sub-paragraph (3) below, have effect in the interpretation of that expression with a provision of these Regulations listed in the left hand column being regarded as the corresponding provision of a provision of the former Regulations listed opposite it in the right hand column and that latter provision being regarded as the corresponding provision of the first-mentioned provision:

19.34

Table

Provision in these Regulations	Provision in the former Regulations
5(1), 5(3), 5(4)	4
5(2), 5(3), 5(4)	24
6	6
7(1), 7(2), 7(4), 7(5)	5
7(3), 7(4)	25
8(1), 8(2), 8(4), 8(5), 8(6)	15
8(3), 8(4)	25
9	18 & 34
10	9, 27
11(2)	31
12	10, 28
13	10A, 28A
15	12A, 30A
16(1)	14
16(2)	32
17	35
18	16, 33
20	4
21	6
22	5
23	15
24	9
26	10
27	10A
29	12A
30	14
31	16A
32	17, 33
33 Table 1 in Schedule 2	19
35 Tables 2 and 3 in Schedule 2	20

Provision in these Regulations	Provision in the former Regulations
36 Table 1 in Schedule 2	22

19.35

(3) Where a provision of the former Regulations is expressed in the Table in sub-paragraph (2) above to be the corresponding provision of a provision in these Regulations and the provision in the former Regulations was capable of applying to other proceedings in addition to those to which the provision in these Regulations is capable of applying, the provision in the former Regulations shall be construed as the corresponding provision of the provision in these Regulations only to the extent that they are both capable of applying to the same type of proceedings.

The Land Registration Rules 2003

(SI 2003 No 1417)

Notes

The Land Registration Rules 2003, which replace the Land Registration Rules 1925 in their entirety, came into force on 13 October 2003 (being the day on which the Land Registration Act 2002 section 1 came into force) – see SI 2003/1725 articles 2(1).

A bankrupt proprietor is capable, in the absence of any mention of the bankruptcy on the register, of passing a legal title to a purchaser in good faith for money or money's worth who at the time of the disposition had no notice of the bankruptcy petition or adjudication – see section 85(6) LRA 2002. A person to whom a registrable disposition is made is not required to make any searches under the Land Charges Act 1972 (section 86(7) LRA 2002). Section 86 LRA 2002 and rules 165–171 LRR 2003 include two methods that can be utilised to prevent such a disposition occurring.

The first (set out in section 86(2) to (4) LRA 2002 and rules 165–167 LRR 2003) creates a system for the registration by the Land Registrar of a bankruptcy notice (on presentation of the bankruptcy petition) followed by a bankruptcy restriction (on the making of a bankruptcy order). The second (set out in rule 168) allows for the trustee in bankruptcy to be registered as the proprietor of the property. This rule also applies where a trustee is appointed pursuant to an insolvency administration order. These remedies are not exclusive of one another, although if a bankruptcy notice or bankruptcy restriction has been registered, it will be cancelled once the trustee in bankruptcy has been registered as proprietor.

These methods do not however apply where one of two or more joint proprietors is made bankrupt.

Bankruptcy notices and restrictions replace creditors' notices and bankruptcy prohibitions which were registered by the Land Registrar under the LRR 1925. Such notices and/or prohibitions registered before the coming into force of LRA 2002 will remain on the register. Creditors' notices and bankruptcy prohibitions could not be entered against land where one of two or more joint proprietors had a petition presented against him or was adjudged bankrupt and this remains the case for bankruptcy notices and restrictions. This is because bankruptcy notices and restrictions can only be registered in relation to estates which appears to be affected (see section 86(2) and (4) LRA 2002) and the legal estate is not vested in the bankrupt (or the person against whom a petition is presented) but rather in that person together with another or others jointly. In addition, the legal estate does not form part of the bankrupt's estate (section 283(3) IA 1986). See also the Land Registry Practice Guide 34 on 'Personal Insolvency' and in particular paragraph 3.2. This useful guide can be found by accessing the Land Registry web site at www.landregistry.gov.uk.

Where a bankruptcy order is made against one of two or more joint registered proprietors the official receiver or the trustee in bankruptcy of the bankrupt can:

(a) apply to register a Form J restriction (see LRR 2003 rule 93(j)) which reads as follows;

'No disposition of [the registered estate or registered charge dated [date]] is to be registered without a certificate signed by the applicant for registration or his conveyancer that written notice of the disposition was given to [name of trustee in bankruptcy] (the trustee in bankruptcy of [name of bankrupt person]) at [address for service].'

(b) Apply for a Form A restriction if there is not already one registered (because prior to the bankruptcy order being made there was an equitable joint tenancy) (see LRR 2003 rule 93(a)).

The trustee in bankruptcy cannot be registered as proprietor because whilst the effect of a bankruptcy order is to sever an equitable joint tenancy (*Re Turner* [1974] 1 WLR 1556 and *Re Gorman* [1990] 1 WLR 616) a bankrupt can not be divested of his legal estate because a joint tenancy can not be severed – section 36 of the Law of Property Act 1925.

20.1

165 Bankruptcy notice

(1) The bankruptcy notice in relation to a registered estate must be entered in the proprietorship register and the bankruptcy notice in relation to a registered charge must be entered in the charges register in the following form—

'BANKRUPTCY NOTICE entered under section 86(2) of the Land Registration Act 2002 in respect of a pending action, as the title of the [proprietor of the registered estate] *or* [the proprietor of the charge dated ..... referred to above] appears to be affected by a petition in bankruptcy against [*name of debtor*], presented in the [*name*] Court (Court Reference Number ....) (Land Charges Reference Number PA . ...).'

(2) The registrar must give notice of the entry of a bankruptcy notice to the proprietor of the registered estate or registered charge to which it relates.

(3) In this rule, 'bankruptcy notice' means the notice which the registrar must enter in the register under section 86(2) of the Act.

Notes

R 165

It is the Chief Land Registrar who is required to register a bankruptcy notice. The trigger for the Chief Land Registrar to do so will be the application by the court at which the petition is filed for the registration of the same in the register of pending actions (see IR 6.13 & 6.43 and sections 5(1)(b) and (3)(b) Land Charges Act 1972). Whilst the registration of a bankruptcy petition under the Land Charges Act 1972 will have no effect upon the debtor's registered land, the Chief Land Registrar is responsible for the Land Charges Department and HM Land Registry. When he receives an application to register a petition as a land charge, he is also under a duty to register a bankruptcy notice against any registered title that appears to be affected. He does this by carrying out a search against the index of proprietors' names and the index of proprietors of registered charges that he keeps pursuant to Land Registration Rules 2003 rule 11.

Problems may arise where the details of the proprietor's name, address and description on the register do not tally with the particulars given in the petition. In such a case, the Chief Land Registrar has a discretion not to register a bankruptcy notice – see LRR 2003 rule 167(2).

20.2

166 Bankruptcy restriction

(1) The bankruptcy restriction in relation to a registered estate must be entered in the proprietorship register and the bankruptcy restriction in relation to a registered charge must be entered in the charges register in the following form—

'BANKRUPTCY RESTRICTION entered under section 86(4) of the Land Registration Act 2002, as the title of [the proprietor of the registered estate] *or* [the proprietor of the charge dated .... referred to above] appears to be affected by a bankruptcy order made by the [*name*] Court (Court Reference Number ....) against [*name of debtor*] (Land Charges Reference Number WO ....).

[No disposition of the registered estate] *or* [No disposition of the charge] is to be registered until the trustee in bankruptcy of the property of the bankrupt is registered as proprietor of the [registered estate] *or* [charge].'

(2) The registrar must give notice of the entry of a bankruptcy restriction to the proprietor of the registered estate or registered charge to which it relates.

(3) In this rule, 'bankruptcy restriction' means the restriction which the registrar must enter in the register under section 86(4) of the Act.

Notes

R 166

As with a bankruptcy notice, the responsibility for registering a bankruptcy restriction rests with the Chief Land Registrar. He must do so as soon as practicable after the registration of a bankruptcy order under the Land Charges Act 1972.

A bankruptcy restriction prevents any disposition or dealing with the registered title or a registered charge, eg the creation of a lease or a sub-charge. The restriction will not prevent the registration of a transmission to the trustee in bankruptcy – see section 86(3)(b) Land Registration Act 2002. Under section 61(4) LRA 1925 it was expressly stated that the entry of a bankruptcy inhibition was without prejudice to dealings with or in right of interests or charges having priority over the estate or charge of the bankrupt proprietor. There is no such equivalent provision in section 86(4) LRA 2002 relating to bankruptcy restrictions, however a restriction does not confer priority under LRA 2002 and therefore the registration of a bankruptcy restriction will not prevent a previously registered chargee from dealing with his charge or relying on his statutory powers (to which see sections 101–110 Law of Property Act 1925 and the notes thereto) or relying on any express powers contained in his charge. The restriction will however apply to a disposition by a receiver appointed by a prior chargee, because the receiver is the agent of the (bankrupt) chargor.

'no disposition'

The wording of the bankruptcy notice prevents any 'dispositions' of the registered estate or charge and differs from the wording in the bankruptcy prohibition which prevented any 'dealing or transmission'. The exclusion of the word 'transmission' in the bankruptcy notice suggests that it will not prevent the registration of a personal representative of a bankrupt proprietor.

20.3

167 Action of the registrar in relation to bankruptcy entries

(1) Where the registrar is satisfied that—
  (a) the bankruptcy order has been annulled, or
  (b) the bankruptcy petition has been dismissed or withdrawn with the court's permission, or

> (c)   the bankruptcy proceedings do not affect or have ceased to affect
> the registered estate or registered charge in relation to which a
> bankruptcy notice or bankruptcy restriction has been entered on
> the register,
> he must as soon as practicable cancel any bankruptcy notice or bank-
> ruptcy restriction which relates to that bankruptcy order, to that bank-
> ruptcy petition or to those proceedings from the register.
>
> (2) Where it appears to the registrar that there is doubt as to whether the
> debtor or bankrupt is the same person as the proprietor of the registered
> estate or registered charge in relation to which a bankruptcy notice or
> bankruptcy restriction has been entered, he must as soon as practicable
> take such action as he considers necessary to resolve the doubt.
>
> (3) In this rule—
> 'bankruptcy notice' means the notice which the registrar must enter in
> the register under section 86(2) of the Act, and
> 'bankruptcy restriction' means the restriction which the registrar must
> enter in the register under section 86(4) of the Act.

Notes

R 167(1)(a) – 'bankruptcy order has been annulled'

In such a case if the bankrupt was the sole registered proprietor a bankruptcy notice will have been registered and (depending on how soon the bankruptcy order is annulled after it was made) a bankruptcy restriction may also have been entered (at which point the bankruptcy notice ceases to have effect – see section 68(3)(a) LRA 2003). An application to cancel a bankruptcy notice or restriction must be made on Land Registry Form AP1 and be accompanied by an office copy of the order in question. The order must expressly authorise the cancellation of the pending land action and/or the bankruptcy order in the register of writs and orders affecting land at the Land Charges Department under the reference numbers set out in the bankruptcy notice and/or bankruptcy restriction.

R 167(1)(b) – 'the bankruptcy petition has been dismissed or withdrawn with the court's permission'

The application to cancel the bankruptcy notice must be on Land Registry Form AP1 and be accompanied by an office copy of the order in question. The order must expressly authorise the cancellation of the pending land action at the Land Charges Department under the reference number set out in the bankruptcy notice.

R 167(1)(c) – 'the bankruptcy proceedings do not affect or have ceased to affect the registered estate or registered charge in relation to which a bankruptcy notice or bankruptcy restriction has been entered on the register.'

This rule does not apply to a discharge from bankruptcy, which of itself does not re-vest property in the debtor. Nor does it apply where a bankrupt has obtained an order under section 1(6) Land Charges Act 1972 ordering that the registration of a bankruptcy petition and/or order be vacated. Such an order does not re-vest property in the bankrupt.

The rule could however apply in a number of circumstances, including the following:

(i)   Where the registered proprietor was never the subject matter of a bankruptcy petition and/or order, for instance because the registered proprietor has a very similar name to a debtor against whom a petition has been presented. In this respect see the notes to rule 167(2) below and the consequence of failing to reply to enquiries sent by the Land

Registry. If an entry is made against a person's title and that person is not the bankrupt, and the entry is a recent one, the Land Registry will usually remove it upon the person signing and returning a disclaimer supplied by the Land Registry. In some cases (for example in respect of an entry made a few years ago) the Land Registry may require a statutory declaration to similar effect. The Land Registry will not accept on its own a clear Land Charges search showing that the registration of the bankruptcy petition and/or order under the Land Charges Act 1972 is no longer subsisting; further evidence will also be required before the bankruptcy notice and/or restriction is removed;

(ii) Where the trustee in bankruptcy obtains a charging order under section 313 IA 1986 over the bankrupt's property. Such an order must provide that the property will cease to be comprised in the bankrupt's estate and will vest the interest in the bankrupt subject to the charging order and any prior charges (see section 313(3) IA 1986). The trustee in bankruptcy shall, forthwith after the making of such an order, send notice of it and its effect to the Chief Land Registrar (see IR 1986 rule 6.237(8)), who will cancel the bankruptcy notice and/or bankruptcy restriction. Note that in such a case a bankruptcy notice and/or restriction will only have been registered if the bankrupt was the sole registered proprietor. The effect of a section 313 order is to create an equitable charge which the trustee in bankruptcy can protect by applying for a notice to be entered on the Charges Register by lodging form AN1 (if an agreed notice is being applied for) or UN1 (if a unilateral notice is being applied for) and a certified copy of the charging order. Where the legal title is vested jointly in the debtor and another or others an order under section 313 IA 1986 will take effect as an equitable charge and can be protected by the registration of a Form K restriction (see LRR 2003 rule 93(k));

(iii) Where the property has ceased to form part of the bankrupt's estate by virtue of the application of section 283A(2) IA 1986 or the transitional provisions in section 261(8) Enterprise Act 2002.

R 167(2)

This rule gives the Chief Land Registrar a discretion as to whether or not to register a bankruptcy notice or restriction. Where the details of the proprietor's name, address and description on the register kept by the Land Registry under section 11 LRA 2002 do not tally with the particulars given in the petition or bankruptcy order, the Land Registry will make an enquiry of the registered proprietor under LRR 2003 rule 167(2) as to whether he or she is the person referred to in the bankruptcy proceedings. If the registered proprietor signs and returns the statement on the form provided to the effect that he or she is not the person referred to, the Land Registry usually takes not further action. If the first enquiry from the Land Registry is not replied to a second will be sent. If this is not replied to the Land Registry will usually register a bankruptcy notice or restriction.

20.4

168 Registration of trustee in bankruptcy

(1) Where—

(a) a proprietor has had a bankruptcy order made against him, or

(b) an insolvency administration order has been made in respect of a deceased proprietor,
and the bankrupt's or deceased's registered estate or registered charge has vested in the trustee in bankruptcy, the trustee may apply for the alteration of the register by registering himself in place of the bankrupt or deceased proprietor.

(2) The application must be supported by, as appropriate—

(a) the bankruptcy order relating to the bankrupt or the insolvency administration order relating to the deceased's estate, and

(b)   a certificate signed by the trustee that the registered estate or registered charge is comprised in the bankrupt's estate or deceased's estate, and

(c)   where the official receiver is the trustee, a certificate by him to that effect, and, where the trustee is another person, the evidence referred to in paragraph (3).

(3) The evidence referred to at paragraph (2)(c) is—

(a)   his certificate of appointment as trustee by the meeting of the bankrupt's or deceased debtor's creditors or

(b)   his certificate of appointment as trustee by the Secretary of State, or

(c)   the order of the court appointing him trustee.

(4) In this rule, 'insolvency administration order' has the same meaning as in section 385(1) of the Insolvency Act 1986.

Notes

R 168

Where the sole proprietor of property or a charge is adjudged bankrupt the property or charge will form part of the bankrupt's estate (see section 283 IA 1986) and when the trustee in bankruptcy is appointed it will automatically vest in the trustee (see section 306 IA 1986). The trustee has an option to apply to be registered as proprietor under LRA 2003 rule 168(1). This also applied to a trustee in bankruptcy appointed under an insolvency administration order. There is no requirement for a trustee in bankruptcy to apply to be registered as proprietor before he sells the property or charge in question. An application by a trustee in bankruptcy under LRR 2003 rule 168(1) must be made on Land Registry Form AP1 and accompanied by the evidence set out in rule 168(2). Registration will be completed in the name of the Official Receiver or other trustee and LRR 2003 rule 170 sets out the form that the description of the trustee in the register will take.

Change of trustee in bankruptcy

Where a trustee in bankruptcy who has been registered as a proprietor vacates his office rule 169 stipulates what evidence must be provided in support of an application to register the replacement trustee in bankruptcy as proprietor (if the replacement trustee chooses to make such an application).

20.5

169 Trustee in bankruptcy vacating office

(1) This rule applies where—

(a)   a trustee in bankruptcy, who has been registered as proprietor, vacates his office, and

(b)   the official receiver or some other person has been appointed the trustee of the relevant bankrupt's estate, and

(c)   he official receiver or that person applies to be registered as proprietor in place of the former trustee.

(2) The application referred to in paragraph (1)(c) must be supported by the evidence required by rule 168(2)(c).

20.6

170 Description of trustee in register

Where the official receiver or another trustee in bankruptcy is registered as proprietor, the words 'Official Receiver and trustee in bankruptcy of [name]' or 'Trustee in bankruptcy of [name]' must be added to the register, as appropriate.

20.7

171 Proceedings under the EC Regulation on insolvency proceedings

(1) A relevant person may apply for a note of a judgement opening insolvency proceedings to be entered in the register.

(2) An application under paragraph (1) must be accompanied by such evidence as the registrar may reasonably require.

(3) Following an application under paragraph (1) if the registrar is satisfied that the judgement opening insolvency proceedings has been made he may enter a note of the judgement in the register.

(4) In this rule—

'judgement opening insolvency proceedings' means a judgement opening proceedings within the meaning of article 3(1) of the Regulation,
'Regulation' means Council Regulation (EC) No 1346/2000,
'relevant person' means any person or body authorised under the provisions of article 22 of the Regulation to request or require an entry to be made in the register in respect of the judgement opening insolvency proceedings the subject of the application.

Notes

R 171(1)

The EC Regulation on Insolvency Proceedings 2000 applies both to individual debtors and to legal persons.

R 171(2)

In most cases the appropriate evidence in support of an application will be an official copy of the judgment together with a certified translation of it.

Limited Liability Partnerships Regulations 2001

(2001 No 1090)

Made: 19th March 2001

Coming into force: 6th April 2001

Notes

These Regulations apply certain parts of the legislation affecting companies to limited liability partnerships ('LLPs'). In this edition of this work, the individual parts of the regulations are not annotated. Particular attention should be paid to the fact that the schedules to the Regulations work in different ways – some apply the sections appearing in them and others exclude the mentioned sections. It should also be noted that certain parts of the Regulations are not reproduced in this work; a complete version of the Regulations can be found at www.opsi.go-v.uk. The Regulations were most recently amended by the Limited Liability Partnerships (Amendment) Regulations 2005 (SI 2005/1989). However, the reader is referred to the 'Explanatory Note' (below) which accompanied the Regulations as they set out their broad structure.

EXPLANATORY NOTE
(This note is not part of the Regulations)

21.1

The Limited Liability Partnerships Act 2000 provided for the creation of Limited Liability Partnerships (LLPs) and for the making of regulations concerning them. These Regulations regulate LLPs by applying to them, with appropriate modifications, the appropriate provisions of the existing law which relate to companies and partnerships.

The Regulations are structured in seven parts accompanied by six schedules. They apply to LLPs, with appropriate modifications to reflect the structure of LLPs, a large number of the provisions contained within the Companies Acts 1985 and 1989, the Insolvency Act 1986 and the Company Directors Disqualification Act 1986.

The Regulations amend the relevant primary legislation by way of general modifications which, provide that references to a company include references to a limited liability partnership, and references to a director or officer include a reference to a member of an LLP. Throughout the Schedules to the Regulations there are references to designated members. This category of member is responsible for a number of administrative and filing duties of the LLP but is also representative of the LLP and its membership in circumstances such as the appointment, removal and remuneration of auditors.

Part I of the Regulations contains the citation, commencement and interpretation provisions to be applied to the Regulations, and gives the date on which they come into force.

Part II of, and Schedule 1 to, the Regulations apply the provisions of Part VII of the Companies Act 1985 (accounts and audit) and its attendant Schedules to LLPs with appropriate modifications. Schedule 1 lists only those sections contained in Part VII of the Companies Act 1985, (including the Schedules related to those sections), which have been modified in their application to LLPs or not applied to LLPs. Therefore, if Schedule 1 does not refer to a particular section, which is contained in Part VII of the Companies Act 1985, or paragraph of a relevant Schedule, then that section or paragraph will apply to LLPs, subject only to the general amendments set out in regulation 3. The accounts and audit provisions, as applied by Part II of, and Schedule 1 to, the Regulations, impose accounting requirements on LLPs which are similar to those for companies. They require that LLPs file annual accounts with the registrar of companies, and place audit requirements on LLPs similar to those imposed on companies. They also define the form and content of the accounts, and allow derogations for small and medium sized LLPs.

Part III of and Schedule 2 to the Regulations apply to LLPs the remainder of the provisions of the Companies Act 1985 together with Part II of the Companies Act 1989 with appropriate modifications. Schedule 2 lists all those sections which apply to LLPs. If Schedule 2 does not refer to a particular section of the Companies Act 1985 then that section will not apply to LLPs. Part III of and Schedule 2 to the Regulations regulate an LLP by applying provisions, many of which are the same as or similar to those imposed on companies, but which reflect the different nature and structure of LLPs. They include provision for:

the execution of documents including bills of exchange and promissory notes and the execution of deeds abroad;

the registration of debenture holders including, a right for the holders of debentures issued by an LLP to inspect the register, the liability of trustees of debentures and perpetual debentures;

the officers and registered office including a requirement to register changes in the registered office of an LLP with the registrar of companies;

company identification—the name of an LLP is to appear outside its place of business and on correspondence, in addition an LLP may have a common seal;

annual return—this part of the regulations provides that it is the duty of an LLP to deliver an annual return to the registrar of companies and sets out requirements as to the content of the annual return;

auditors—an LLP is, in general, required to appoint auditors, provision is made for the appointment of auditors by the Secretary of State where an LLP is in default, the auditors have various rights including the right to have access to an LLP's books, accounts and information as necessary, the right to attend meetings of the LLP, and certain rights in the event of being removed or not being re-appointed, provision is also made for the resignation of auditors and the making of a statement by a person ceasing to hold office as auditor;

registration of charges—sections 395 to 408, 410 to 423 of the Companies Act 1985, will apply to LLPs, with modifications, until section 92 of the Companies Act 1989 is commenced or some other amendment is made;

arrangements and reconstructions—an LLP will have the power to compromise with its creditors and members, the sections set out detailed provisions concerning the circulation of information on any compromise together with provisions for facilitating an LLP's reconstruction or amalgamation;

investigation of LLPs and their affairs—an investigation of an LLP may be made following its own application of that of its members, the sections set out detailed provisions concerning investigations, the production of documents and evidence, contempt of court, inspectors' reports and the use of inspectors' reports as evidence;

fraudulent trading is punished in the case of an LLP in the same was as a company;

unfair prejudice—Schedule 2 applies the Companies Act 1985 so that, in general, there is a remedy for the members of an LLP should they suffer unfair prejudice, the members of a limited liability partnership may, however, by unanimous agreement exclude the right contained in section 459 (1) for such period as may be agreed;

matters arising subsequent to winding up—the provisions deal with various matters including the power of the court to declare the dissolution of a company void, the striking out by the registrar of companies of a defunct company and crown disclaimer of property vesting as bona vacantia;

registrar of companies—Schedule 2 sets out the registrar's functions and offices in relation to LLPs;

miscellaneous and supplementary provisions—the provisions deal with various matters including the form of company registers etc, the use of computers for company records, the service of documents, the powers of a court to grant relief in certain cases, and the punishment of offences.

Part III of the Regulations also applies the provisions of the Company Directors Disqualification Act 1986 to limited liability partnerships with appropriate modifications. These provide that members of an LLP will be subject to the same penalties that currently apply to company directors under the CDDA 1986 and may be disqualified from being the member of an LLP or a director of a company under those provisions.

Part IV of, and Schedule 3 to, the Regulations apply to LLPs the First and Third Groups of Parts of the Insolvency Act 1986, with appropriate modifications. Schedule 3 lists only those sections contained in the First or Third Group of Parts which have been modified or omitted in their application to LLPs. If there is no reference in Schedule 3 to a particular section contained in the First or Third Group of Parts of the Insolvency Act 1986 then that section will apply to LLPs subject to the general modifications contained in Regulation 5. The insolvency provisions as applied to LLPs include provisions for voluntary arrangements, administration orders, receivership, winding-up and liquidations. The most notable modifications of the provisions which apply to companies are, an additional section, section 214A and the re-worded section 74.

The new Section 214A provides that withdrawals made by members during the two years prior to the commencement of winding-up will be subject to claw back if it is proved that at the time of the withdrawal the member knew or had reasonable grounds for believing that the LLP was, or would be made, insolvent. The modified section 74 provides that in the event that an LLP is wound up, both past and present members of the LLP are liable to contribute to the assets of the LLP to the extent that they have agreed to do so with the other members, in the limited liability partnership agreement.

Part V of the Regulations apply the provisions contained in Parts XV and XXIV of the Financial Services and Markets Act 2000 to LLPs. These Parts provide for insolvency arrangements of LLPs which are authorised under FSMA 2000. In addition, these Parts give the Authority powers to ask the courts to wind up, or initiate other insolvency procedures against, authorised and certain other persons. It also enables the Authority to be heard by the court when such proceedings are commenced by third parties.

Part VI of the Regulations provides for default provisions governing the rights and duties of members, which modify those contained in section 24 of the Partnership Act 1890. They will apply when there is no existing limited liability partnership agreement, or where the agreement does not wholly deal with a particular issue.

Schedule 4 to the Regulations lists those provisions contained in the First and Third Group of Parts of the Insolvency Act 1986 which are not applied to Scotland. The provisions wholly or partly concern matters which are set out in Section C 2 of the Fifth Schedule of the Scotland Act 1998 as being exceptions to the reservation.

Part VII of, and Schedule 5 to, the Regulations apply a number of general and consequential amendments to other Acts of Parliament.

Part VII of, and Schedule 6 to, the Regulations apply to LLPs certain pieces of subordinate legislation made under the Companies Act 1985, the Insolvency Act 1986 and other primary legislation.

Whereas a draft of these Regulations has been approved by a resolution of each House of Parliament pursuant to section 17(4) of the Limited Liability Partnerships Act 2000;

Now, therefore, the Secretary of State, in exercise of the powers conferred on him by sections 14, 15, 16 and 17 of the Limited Liability Partnerships Act 2000 and all other powers enabling him in that behalf hereby makes the following Regulations:

Part I
Citation, Commencement and Interpretation

21.2

1 Citation and commencement

These Regulations may be cited as the Limited Liability Partnerships Regulations 2001 and shall come into force on 6th April 2001.

2 Interpretation

In these Regulations—
    'the 1985 Act' means the Companies Act 1985;
    'the 1986 Act' means the Insolvency Act 1986;
    'the 2000 Act' means the Financial Services and Markets Act 2000;
    'devolved', in relation to the provisions of the 1986 Act, means the provisions of the 1986 Act which are listed in Schedule 4 and, in their application to Scotland, concern wholly or partly, matters which are set out in Section C 2 of Schedule 5 to the Scotland Act 1998 as being exceptions to the reservations made in that Act in the field of insolvency;
    'limited liability partnership agreement', in relation to a limited liability partnership, means any agreement express or implied between the members of the limited liability partnership or between the limited liability partnership and the members of the limited liability partnership which determines the mutual rights and duties of the members, and their rights and duties in relation to the limited liability partnership;
    'the principal Act' means the Limited Liability Partnerships Act 2000; and
    'shadow member', in relation to limited liability partnerships, means a person in accordance with whose directions or instructions the members of the limited liability partnership are accustomed to act (but so that a person is not deemed a shadow member by reason only that the members of the limited partnership act on advice given by him in a professional capacity).

Part II
Accounts and Audit

21.3

3 Application of the accounts and audit provisions of the 1985 Act to limited liability partnerships

(1) Subject to paragraph (2), the provisions of Part VII of the 1985 Act (Accounts and Audit) shall apply to limited liability partnerships.

(2) The enactments referred to in paragraph (1) shall apply to limited liability partnerships, except where the context otherwise requires, with the following modifications—
    (a)   references to a company shall include references to a limited liability partnership;

(b) references to a director or to an officer of a company shall include references to a member of a limited liability partnership;

(c) references to other provisions of the 1985 Act and to provisions of the Insolvency Act 1986 shall include references to those provisions as they apply to limited liability partnerships in accordance with Parts III and IV of these Regulations;

(d) the modifications set out in Schedule 1 to these Regulations; and

(e) such further modifications as the context requires for the purpose of giving effect to those provisions as applied by this Part of these Regulations.

Part III
Companies Act 1985 and Company Directors Disqualification Act 1986

21.4

4 Application of the remainder of the provisions of the 1985 Act and of the provisions of the Company Directors Disqualification Act 1986 to limited liability partnerships

(1) The provisions of the 1985 Act specified in the first column of Part I of Schedule 2 to these Regulations shall apply to limited liability partnerships, except where the context otherwise requires, with the following modifications—

(a) references to a company shall include references to a limited liability partnership;

(b) references to the Companies Acts shall include references to the principal Act and regulations made thereunder;

(c) references to the Insolvency Act 1986 shall include references to that Act as it applies to limited liability partnerships by virtue of Part IV of these Regulations;

(d) references in a provision of the 1985 Act to other provisions of that Act shall include references to those other provisions as they apply to limited liability partnerships by virtue of these Regulations;

(e) references to the memorandum of association of a company shall include references to the incorporation document of a limited liability partnership;

(f) references to a shadow director shall include references to a shadow member;

(g) references to a director of a company or to an officer of a company shall include references to a member of a limited liability partnership;

(h) the modifications, if any, specified in the second column of Part I of Schedule 2 opposite the provision specified in the first column; and

(i) such further modifications as the context requires for the purpose of giving effect to that legislation as applied by these Regulations.

(2) The provisions of the Company Director Disqualification Act 1986 shall apply to limited liability partnerships, except where the context otherwise requires, with the following modifications—

(a) references to a company shall include references to a limited liability partnership;

(b) references to the Companies Acts shall include references to the principal Act and regulations made thereunder and references to the companies legislation shall include references to the principal Act, regulations made thereunder and to any enactment applied by regulations to limited liability partnerships;

(d) references to the Insolvency Act 1986 shall include references to that Act as it applies to limited liability partnerships by virtue of Part IV of these Regulations;

(e) references to the memorandum of association of a company shall include references to the incorporation document of a limited liability partnership;

(f) references to a shadow director shall include references to a shadow member;

(g) references to a director of a company or to an officer of a company shall include references to a member of a limited liability partnership;

(h) the modifications, if any, specified in the second column of Part II of Schedule 2 opposite the provision specified in the first column; and

(i) such further modifications as the context requires for the purpose of giving effect to that legislation as applied by these Regulations.

Part IV
Winding Up and Insolvency

21.5

5 Application of the 1986 Act to limited liability partnerships

(1) Subject to paragraphs (2) and (3), the following provisions of the 1986 Act, shall apply to limited liability partnerships—

(a) Parts I, II, III, IV, VI and VII of the First Group of Parts (company insolvency; companies winding up),

(b) the Third Group of Parts (miscellaneous matters bearing on both company and individual insolvency; general interpretation; final provisions).

(2) The provisions of the 1986 Act referred to in paragraph (1) shall apply to limited liability partnerships, except where the context otherwise requires, with the following modifications—

(a) references to a company shall include references to a limited liability partnership;

(b) references to a director or to an officer of a company shall include references to a member of a limited liability partnership;

(c) references to a shadow director shall include references to a shadow member;

(d) references to the 1985 Act, the Company Directors Disqualification Act 1986, the Companies Act 1989 or to any provisions of those Acts or to any provisions of the 1986 Act shall include references to those Acts or provisions as they apply to limited liability partnerships by virtue of the principal Act;

(e) references to the memorandum of association of a company and to the articles of association of a company shall include references to the limited liability partnership agreement of a limited liability partnership;

(f) the modifications set out in Schedule 3 to these Regulations; and

(g) such further modifications as the context requires for the purpose of giving effect to that legislation as applied by these Regulations.

(3) In the application of this regulation to Scotland, the provisions of the 1986 Act referred to in paragraph (1) shall not include the provisions listed in Schedule 4 to the extent specified in that Schedule.

Part V
Financial Services and Markets

21.6

6 Application of provisions contained in Parts XV and XXIV of the 2000 Act to limited liability partnerships

(1) Subject to paragraph (2), sections 215(3),(4) and (6), 356, 359(1) to (4), 361 to 365, 367, 370 and 371 of the 2000 Act shall apply to limited liability partnerships.

(2) The provisions of the 2000 Act referred to in paragraph (1) shall apply to limited liability partnerships, except where the context otherwise requires, with the following modifications—

(a) references to a company shall include references to a limited liability partnership;

(b) references to body shall include references to a limited liability partnership; and

(c) references to the 1985 Act, the 1986 Act or to any of the provisions of those Acts shall include references to those Acts or provisions as they apply to limited liability partnerships by virtue of the principal Act.

Part VI
Default Provision

21.7

7 Default provision for limited liability partnerships

The mutual rights and duties of the members and the mutual rights and duties of the limited liability partnership and the members shall be determined, subject to the provisions of the general law and to the terms of any limited liability partnership agreement, by the following rules:

(1) All the members of a limited liability partnership are entitled to share equally in the capital and profits of the limited liability partnership.

(2) The limited liability partnership must indemnify each member in respect of payments made and personal liabilities incurred by him—

(a) in the ordinary and proper conduct of the business of the limited liability partnership; or

(b) in or about anything necessarily done for the preservation of the business or property of the limited liability partnership.

(3) Every member may take part in the management of the limited liability partnership.

(4) No member shall be entitled to remuneration for acting in the business or management of the limited liability partnership.

(5) No person may be introduced as a member or voluntarily assign an interest in a limited liability partnership without the consent of all existing members.

(6) Any difference arising as to ordinary matters connected with the business of the limited liability partnership may be decided by a majority of the members, but no change may be made in the nature of the business of the limited liability partnership without the consent of all the members.

(7) The books and records of the limited liability partnership are to be made available for inspection at the registered office of the limited liability partnership or at such other place as the members think fit and every member of the limited liability partnership may when he thinks fit have access to and inspect and copy any of them.

(8) Each member shall render true accounts and full information of all things affecting the limited liability partnership to any member or his legal representatives.

(9) If a member, without the consent of the limited liability partnership, carries on any business of the same nature as and competing with the limited liability partnership, he must account for and pay over to the limited liability partnership all profits made by him in that business.

(10) Every member must account to the limited liability partnership for any benefit derived by him without the consent of the limited liability partnership from any transaction concerning the limited liability partnership, or from any use by him of the property of the limited liability partnership, name or business connection.

8 Expulsion

No majority of the members can expel any member unless a power to do so has been conferred by express agreement between the members.

Part VII
Miscellaneous

21.8

9 General and consequential amendments

(1) Subject to paragraph (2), the enactments mentioned in Schedule 5 shall have effect subject to the amendments specified in that Schedule.

(2) In the application of this regulation to Scotland—

(a) paragraph 15 of Schedule 5 which amends section 110 of the 1986 Act shall not extend to Scotland; and

(b) paragraph 22 of Schedule 5 which applies to limited liability partnerships the culpable officer provisions in existing primary legislation shall not extend to Scotland insofar as it relates to matters which have not been reserved by Schedule 5 to the Scotland Act 1998.

10 Application of subordinate legislation

(1) The subordinate legislation specified in Schedule 6 shall apply as from time to time in force to limited liability partnerships and—

(a) in the case of the subordinate legislation listed in Part I of that Schedule with such modifications as the context requires for the purpose of giving effect to the provisions of the Companies Act 1985 which are applied by these Regulations;

(b) in the case of the subordinate legislation listed in Part II of that Schedule with such modifications as the context requires for the purpose of giving effect to the provisions of the Insolvency Act 1986 which are applied by these Regulations; and

(c) in the case of the subordinate legislation listed in Part III of that Schedule with such modifications as the context requires for the purpose of giving effect to the provisions of the Business Names Act 1985 and the Company Directors Disqualification Act 1986 which are applied by these Regulations.

(2) In the case of any conflict between any provision of the subordinate legislation applied by paragraph (1) and any provision of these Regulations, the latter shall prevail.

Kim Howells,

Parliamentary Under-Secretary of State,

for Consumers and Corporate Affairs,

Department of Trade and Industry

19th March 2001

SCHEDULE I
Modifications to Provisions of Part VII of the 1985 Act Applied by these Regulations

Regulation 3

21.9

(*Omitted*)

SCHEDULE 2
Regulation 4

Part I
Modifications to Provisions of the 1985 Act Applied to Limited Liability Partnerships

21.10

Provisions	Modifications
	Insert a new subsection (5):
	' (5) Part II of the Companies Act 1989 shall apply in respect of auditors of limited liability partnerships as if the limited liability partnerships were companies formed and registered under this Act, and references in Part II to an officer of a company shall include reference to a member of a limited liability partnership.'
	In the title to the section for the existing wording substitute 'Appointment of auditors'.
	Omit subsection (1).
	For subsection (2) substitute:
	' (2) The designated members of a limited liability partnership shall appoint the auditors for the first financial year in respect of which auditors are appointed before the end of that financial year and thereafter before the expiration of not more than two months following the approval of the accounts for the preceding financial year in accordance with section 233.'.
	For subsection (3) substitute:
	' (3) The auditor of a limited liability partnership shall hold office until not later than the expiration of two months following the approval in accordance with section 233 of the accounts for the financial year in respect of which the auditor was appointed.'
	For subsection (4) substitute:
	' (4) If the designated members fail to exercise their powers under subsection (2), the powers may be exercised by the members of the limited liability partnership in a meeting convened for the purpose'.
	In subsection (1), omit the words 're-appointed or deemed to be re-appointed'.
	In subsection (2), for the word 'officer' substitute the words 'designated member'.
	In subsection (1), for 'directors, or the company in general meeting,' substitute 'designated members'.

	Omit subsection (3). Omit subsection (4). For subsection (3) substitute: ' (3) The designated members may appoint auditors and the auditors so appointed shall hold office until the expiration of two months following the approval in accordance with section 233 of the accounts for the financial year in respect of which the auditor was appointed.'

Registration of charges

The following references are to sections of the 1985 Act which were replaced by section 92 of the Companies Act 1989. They will apply to limited liability partnerships until the said section 92 is commenced.

395 (certain charges void if not registered)	
396 (charges which have to be registered)	In subsection (1) delete paragraphs (b) and (g).
397 (formalities of registration (debentures))	In subsection (1), paragraph (b) for the word 'resolutions' substitute 'determinations of the limited liability partnership'.
398 (verification of charge on property outside United Kingdom)	
399 (company's duty to register charges it creates)	
400 (charges existing on property acquired)	
401 (register of charges to be kept by registrar of companies)	
402 (endorsement of certificate on debentures)	
403 (entries of satisfaction and release)	In subsection (1A), after 'of the company' insert 'or designated member, administrator or administrative receiver of the limited liability partnership'.
404 (rectification of register of charges)	In subsection (1), omit the words 'or shareholders'.
405 (registration of enforcement of security)	
406 (companies to keep copies of instruments creating charges)	
407 (company's register of charges)	In subsection (1), for 'limited company' substitute 'company (including limited liability partnership)'.
408 (right to inspect instruments which create charges etc)	In subsection (1) delete 'in general meeting'.
410 (charges void unless registered)	In subsection (4) delete paragraph (b) and sub-paragraph (ii) of paragraph (c). In subsection (5) for 'an incorporated company' substitute 'a limited liability partnership'.

411 (charges on property outside the United Kingdom)	
412 (negotiable instrument to secure book debts)	
413 (charges associated with debentures)	In subsection (2)(b), for the word 'resolutions' substitute 'determinations of the limited liability partnership'.
414 (charge by way of ex facie absolute disposition, etc)	
415 (company's duty to register charges created by it)	
416 (duty to register charges existing on property acquired)	
417 (register of charges to be kept by registrar of companies)	
418 (certificate of registration to be issued)	
419 (entries of satisfaction and relief)	In subsection (1A), after the words 'of the company' insert 'or a designated member, liquidator, receiver or administrative receiver of the limited liability partnership'.
420 (rectification of the register)	Omit the words 'or shareholders'.
421 (copies of instruments creating charges to be kept by the company)	
422 (company's register of charges)	
423 (right to inspect copies of instruments, and the company's register)	In subsection (1) delete 'in general meeting'.
Arrangements and Reconstructions	
425 (power of company to compromise with creditors and members)	
subsection (3)	Omit the words 'and a copy of every such order shall be annexed to every copy of the company's memorandum issued after the order has been made or, in the case of a company not having a memorandum, of every copy so issued of the instrument constituting the company or defining its constitution.' For the semi-colon after the word 'registration' substitute a full stop.
subsection (6)	Omit subsection (6).
426 (information as to compromise to be circulated)	
subsection (2)	Omit the words 'as directors or'.
427 (provisions for facilitating company reconstruction or amalgamation)	
subsection (3)	In paragraph (b) for the words 'policies or other like interests' substitute 'policies, other like interests or, in the case of a limited liability partnership, property or interests in the limited liability partnership'.

subsection (6)	For the words "company' includes only a company as defined in section 735(1)' substitute "company' includes only a company as defined in section 735(1) or a limited liability partnership'.
Fraudulent Trading	
458 (punishment for fraudulent trading)	
Protection of company's members against unfair prejudice	
459 (order on application of company member)	At the beginning of subsection (1), insert the words 'Subject to subsection (1A),'. After subsection (1) insert as subsection (1A): ' The members of a limited liability partnership may by unanimous agreement exclude the right contained in subsection 459(1) for such period as shall be agreed. The agreement referred to in this subsection shall be recorded in writing.' Omit subsections (2) and (3).
460 (order on application of Secretary of State)	... Omit subsection (2).
461 (provisions as to orders and petitions under this Part)	In subsection (2)(d) for the words 'the shares of any members of the company by other members or by the company itself and, in the case of a purchase by the company itself, the reduction of the company's capital accordingly' substitute the words 'the shares of any members in the limited liability partnership by other members or by the limited liability partnership itself.'. In subsection (3) for the words 'memorandum or articles' substitute the words 'limited liability partnership agreement'. For the existing words of subsection (4) substitute the words 'Any alteration in the limited liability partnership agreement made by virtue of an order under this Part is of the same effect as if duly agreed by the members of the limited liability partnership and the provisions of this Act apply to the limited liability partnership agreement as so altered accordingly.'. Omit subsection (5).
Matters arising subsequent to winding up	
651 (power of court to declare dissolution of company void)	

652 (registrar may strike defunct company off the register)	In subsection (6) paragraph (a) omit the word 'director'.
652A (registrar may strike private company off the register on application)	In this section the references to 'a private company' shall include a reference to 'a limited liability partnership'.
subsection (1)	In subsection (1) the following shall be substituted for the existing wording
	'On application by two or more designated members of a limited liability partnership, the registrar of companies may strike the limited liability partnership's name off the register'.
	Omit subsection 2(a) and in subsection 2(b) after the word 'be' insert the word 'made'.
	In subsection (6), omit the word 'director'.
652B (duties in connection with making an application under section 652A)	In paragraph (a) of subsection (5) for 'no meetings are' substitute 'no meeting is'.
	In paragraph (b) of subsection (5) for 'meetings summoned under that section fail' substitute 'the meeting summoned under that section fails'.
	In paragraph (c) of subsection (5) for 'meetings' substitute 'a meeting'.
	In paragraph (d) of subsection (5) for 'at previous meetings' substitute 'at a previous meeting'.
652C (directors' duties following application under section 652A)	In subsection (2), for the words 'is a director of the company' substitute 'is a designated member of the limited liability partnership'.
	In subsection (2) omit paragraph (d).
	In subsection (5) for the words 'is a director of the company' substitute 'is a designated member of the limited liability partnership'.
	In subsection (6), omit paragraph (d).
652D (sections 652B and 652C: supplementary provisions)	
652E (sections 652B and 652C: enforcement)	
652F (other offences connected with section 652A)	
653 (objection to striking off by person aggrieved)	
654 (property of dissolved company to be bona vacantia)	
655 (effect on section 654 of company's revival after dissolution)	

656 (crown disclaimer of property vesting as bona vacantia) 657 (effect of crown disclaimer under section 656) 658 (liability for rent charge on company's land after dissolution)	
735A (relationship of this Act to the Insolvency Act)	In subsection (1), delete all the references to provisions of the 1985 Act other than the references to sections 425(6)(a), 460(2) and 728

Part II
Modifications to the Company Directors Disqualification Act 1986

21.11

Part II of Schedule I	After paragraph 8 insert—
	'8A The extent of the member's and shadow members' responsibility for events leading to a member or shadow member, whether himself or some other member or shadow member, being declared by the court to be liable to make a contribution to the assets of the limited liability partnership under section 214A of the Insolvency Act 1986.'

SCHEDULE 3
Modifications to the 1986 Act

Regulation 5

21.12

Provisions	Modifications
Section 1 (those who may propose an arrangement)	
subsection (1)	For 'The directors of a company' substitute 'A limited liability partnership' and delete 'to the company and'.
subsection (3)	At the end add 'but where a proposal is so made it must also be made to the limited liability partnership'.
[Section 1A (moratorium)	

subsection (1)	For 'the directors of an eligible company intend' substitute 'an eligible limited liability partnership intends'. For 'they' substitute 'it'.]
The following modifications to sections 2 to 7 apply where a proposal under section 1 has been made by the limited liability partnership.	
Section 2 (procedure where the nominee is not the liquidator or administrator)	
[subsection (1)	For 'the directors do' substitute 'the limited liability partnership does'.]
subsection (2)	In paragraph [(aa)] for 'meetings of the company and of it creditors' substitute 'a meeting of the creditors of the limited liability partnership'; In paragraph (b) for the first 'meetings' substitute 'a meeting' and for the second 'meetings' substitute 'meeting'.
subsection (3)	For 'the person intending to make the proposal' substitute 'the designated members of the limited liability partnership'.
subsection (4)	[In paragraph (a)] for 'the person intending to make the proposal' substitute 'the designated members of the limited liability partnership '. [In paragraph (b) for 'that person' substitute 'those designated members'.]
Section 3 (summoning of meetings)	
subsection (1)	For 'such meetings as are mentioned in section 2(2)' substitute 'a meeting of creditors' and for 'those meetings' substitute 'that meeting'.
subsection (2)	Delete subsection (2).
Section 4 (decisions of meetings)	
subsection (1)	For 'meetings' substitute 'meeting'.
subsection (5)	For 'each of the meetings' substitute 'the meeting'.
new subsection (5A)	Insert a new subsection (5A) as follows—

	'(5A) If modifications to the proposal are proposed at the meeting the chairman of the meeting shall, before the conclusion of the meeting, ascertain from the limited liability partnership whether or not it accepts the proposed modifications; and if at that conclusion the limited liability partnership has failed to respond to a proposed modification it shall be presumed not to have agreed to it.'
subsection (6)	For 'either' substitute 'the'; after 'the result of the meeting', in the first place where it occurs, insert '(including, where modifications to the proposal were proposed at the meeting, the response to those proposed modifications made by the limited liability partnership)'; and at the end add 'and to the limited liability partnership'.
[Section 4A (approval of arrangement)	
subsection (2)	Omit '—(a)'.
	For 'both meetings' substitute 'the meeting'.
	Omit the words from ', or' to 'that section'.
subsection (3)	Omit.
subsection (4)	Omit.
subsection (5)	Omit.
subsection (6)	Omit.]
Section 5 (effect of approval)	
...	...
subsection (4)	For 'each of the reports' substitute 'the report'.
Section 6 (challenge of decisions)	
subsection (1)	For ... 'either of the meetings' substitute 'the meeting'.

subsection (2)	For 'either of the meetings' substitute 'the meeting' and after paragraph [(aa)] add a new paragraph [(ab) as follows— '(ab)] any member of the limited liability partnership; and'. Omit the word 'and' at the end of paragraph (b) and omit paragraph (c).
subsection (3)	For 'each of the reports' substitute 'the report'.
subsection (4)	For subsection (4) substitute the following— '(4) Where on such an application the court is satisfied as to either of the grounds mentioned in subsection (1), it may do one or both of the following, namely— (a) revoke or suspend [any decision approving the voluntary arrangement which has effect under section 4A]; (b) give a direction to any person for the summoning of a further meeting to consider any revised proposal the limited liability partnership may make or, in a case falling within subsection (1)(b), a further meeting to consider the original proposal.'.
subsection (5)	For ... 'meetings' substitute 'a meeting' ... and for 'person who made the original proposal' substitute 'limited liability partnership'.
[Section 6A (false representations, etc)	
subsection (1)	Omit 'members or'.]
Section 7 (implementation of proposal)	
...	...
[subsection (2)	In paragraph (a) omit 'one or both of' and for 'meetings' substitute 'meeting'.]

The following modifications to sections 2 and 3 apply where a proposal under section 1 has been made, [the limited liability partnership is in administration], by the administrator or, where the limited liability partnership is being wound up, by the liquidator.

Section 2 (procedure where the nominee is not the liquidator or administrator)	
subsection (2)	In paragraph (a) for 'meetings of the company' substitute 'meetings of the members of the limited liability partnership'.
Section 3 (summoning of meetings)	
subsection (2)	For 'meetings of the company' substitute 'a meeting of the members of the limited liability partnership'.
...	...
...	...
< ... >	...
...	...
...	...
...	...
Section 73 (alternative modes of winding up)	
subsection (1)	Delete ', within the meaning given to that expression by section 735 of the Companies Act,'.
Section 74 (liability as contributories of present and past members)	
For section 74 there shall be substituted the following—	

	'74. When a limited liability partnership is wound up every present and past member of the limited liability partnership who has agreed with the other members or with the limited liability partnership that he will, in circumstances which have arisen, be liable to contribute to the assets of the limited liability partnership in the event that the limited liability partnership goes into liquidation is liable, to the extent that he has so agreed, to contribute to its assets to any amount sufficient for payment of its debts and liabilities, and the expenses of the winding up, and for the adjustment of the rights of the contributories among themselves. However, a past member shall only be liable if the obligation arising from such agreement survived his ceasing to be a member of the limited liability partnership.'
Section 75 to 78	Delete sections 75 to 78.
Section 79 (meaning of 'contributory')	
subsection (1)	In subsection (1) for 'every person' substitute '(a) every present member of the limited liability partnership and (b) every past member of the limited liability partnership'.
subsection (2)	After 'section 214 (wrongful trading)' insert 'or 214A (adjustment of withdrawals)'.
subsection (3)	Delete subsection (3).
Section 83 (companies registered under Companies Act, Part XXII, Chapter II)	Delete section 83.
Section 84 (circumstances in which company may be wound up voluntarily)	

subsection (1)	For subsection (1) substitute the following— '(1) A limited liability partnership may be wound up voluntarily when it determines that it is to be wound up voluntarily.'
subsection (2)	Omit subsection (2).
[subsection (2A)	For 'company passes a resolution for voluntary winding up' substitute 'limited liability partnership determines that it is to be wound up voluntarily' and for 'resolution' where it appears for the second time substitute 'determination'.
subsection (2B)	For 'resolution for voluntary winding up may be passed only' substitute 'determination to wind up voluntarily may only be made' and in sub-paragraph (b), for 'passing of the resolution' substitute 'making of the determination'.]
subsection (3)	For subsection (3) substitute the following— '(3) Within 15 days after a limited liability partnership has determined that it be wound up there shall be forwarded to the registrar of companies either a printed copy or else a copy in some other form approved by the registrar of the determination.'
subsection [(5)]	After subsection [(4)] insert a new subsection [(5)]— '[(5)] If a limited liability partnership fails to comply with this regulation the limited liability partnership and every designated member of it who is in default is liable on summary conviction to a fine not exceeding level 3 on the standard scale.'
Section 85 (notice of resolution to wind up)	

subsection (1)	For subsection (1) substitute the following— '(1) When a limited liability partnership has determined that it shall be wound up voluntarily, it shall within 14 days after the making of the determination give notice of the determination by advertisement in the Gazette.'
Section 86 (commencement of winding up)	
	Substitute the following new section— '86 A voluntary winding up is deemed to commence at the time when the limited liability partnership determines that it be wound up voluntarily.'.
Section 87 (effect on business and status of company)	
subsection (2)	In subsection (2), for 'articles' substitute 'limited liability partnership agreement'.
Section 88 (avoidance of share transfers, etc after winding-up resolution)	
	For 'shares' substitute 'the interest of any member in the property of the limited liability partnership'.
Section 89 (statutory declaration of solvency)	
	For 'director(s)' wherever it appears in section 89 substitute 'designated member(s)';
subsection (2)	For paragraph (a) substitute the following— '(a) it is made within the 5 weeks immediately preceding the date when the limited liability partnership determined that it be wound up voluntarily or on that date but before the making of the determination, and'.
subsection (3)	For 'the resolution for winding up is passed' substitute 'the limited liability partnership determined that it be wound up voluntarily'.

subsection (5)	For 'in pursuance of a resolution passed' substitute 'voluntarily'.
Section 90 (distinction between 'members' and 'creditors' voluntary winding up)	
	For 'directors" substitute 'designated members".
Section 91 (appointment of liquidator)	
subsection (1)	Delete 'in general meeting'.
subsection (2)	For the existing wording substitute '(2) On the appointment of a liquidator the powers of the members of the limited liability partnership shall cease except to the extent that a meeting of the members of the limited liability partnership summoned for the purpose or the liquidator sanctions their continuance.' After subsection (2) insert— '(3) Subsections (3) and (4) of section 92 shall apply for the purposes of this section as they apply for the purposes of that section.'
Section 92 (power to fill vacancy in office of liquidator)	
subsection (1)	For 'the company in general meeting' substitute 'a meeting of the members of the limited liability partnership summoned for the purpose'.
subsection (2)	For 'a general meeting' substitute 'a meeting of the members of the limited liability partnership'.
subsection (3)	In subsection (3), for 'articles' substitute 'limited liability partnership agreement'.

new subsection (4)	Add a new subsection (4) as follows— '(4) The quorum required for a meeting of the members of the limited liability partnership shall be any quorum required by the limited liability partnership agreement for meetings of the members of the limited liability partnership and if no requirement for a quorum has been agreed upon the quorum shall be 2 members.'
Section 93 (general company meeting at each year's end)	
subsection (1)	For 'a general meeting of the company' substitute 'a meeting of the members of the limited liability partnership'.
new subsection (4)	Add a new subsection (4) as follows— '(4) subsections (3) and (4) of section 92 shall apply for the purposes of this section as they apply for the purposes of that section.'
Section 94 (final meeting prior to dissolution)	
subsection (1)	For 'a general meeting of the company' substitute 'a meeting of the members of the limited liability partnership'.
new subsection (5A)	Add a new subsection (5A) as follows— '(5A) Subsections (3) and (4) of section 92 shall apply for the purposes of this section as they apply for the purposes of that section.'
subsection (6)	For 'a general meeting of the company' substitute 'a meeting of the members of the limited liability partnership'.
Section 95 (effect of company's insolvency)	
subsection (1)	For 'directors'' substitute 'designated members''.

subsection (7)	For subsection (7) substitute the following— '(7) In this section 'the relevant period' means the period of 6 months immediately preceding the date on which the limited liability partnership determined that it be wound up voluntarily.'
Section 96 (conversion to creditors' voluntary winding up)	
paragraph (a)	For 'directors" substitute 'designated members".
paragraph (b)	Substitute a new paragraph (b) as follows— '(b) the creditors' meeting was the meeting mentioned in section 98 in the next Chapter;'.
Section 98 (meeting of creditors)	
subsection (1)	For paragraph (a) substitute the following— '(a) cause a meeting of its creditors to be summoned for a day not later than the 14th day after the day on which the limited liability partnership determines that it be wound up voluntarily;'.
subsection (5)	For 'were sent the notices summoning the company meeting at which it was resolved that the company be wound up voluntarily' substitute 'the limited liability partnership determined that it be wound up voluntarily'.
Section 99 (directors to lay statement of affairs before creditors)	
subsection (1)	For 'the directors of the company' substitute 'the designated members' and for 'the director so appointed' substitute 'the designated member so appointed'.
subsection (2)	For 'directors' substitute 'designated members'.
subsection (3)	For 'directors' substitute 'designated members' and for 'director' substitute 'designated member'.

Section 100 (appointment of liquidator)	
subsection (1)	For 'The creditors and the company at their respective meetings mentioned in section 98' substitute 'The creditors at their meeting mentioned in section 98 and the limited liability partnership'.
subsection (3)	Delete 'director,'.
Section 101 (appointment of liquidation committee)	
subsection (2)	For subsection (2) substitute the following— '(2) If such a committee is appointed, the limited liability partnership may, when it determines that it be wound up voluntarily or at any time thereafter, appoint such number of persons as they think fit to act as members of the committee, not exceeding 5.'
Section 105 (meetings of company and creditors at each year's end)	
subsection (1)	For 'a general meeting of the company' substitute 'a meeting of the members of the limited liability partnership'.
new subsection (5)	Add a new subsection (5) as follows— '(5) Subsections (3) and (4) of section 92 shall apply for the purposes of this section as they apply for the purposes of that section.'
Section 106 (final meeting prior to dissolution)	
subsection (1)	For 'a general meeting of the company' substitute 'a meeting of the members of the limited liability partnership',
new subsection (5A)	After subsection (5) insert a new subsection (5A) as follows— '5A) Subsections (3) and (4) of section 92 shall apply for the purposes of this section as they apply for the purposes of that section.'

subsection (6)	For 'a general meeting of the company' substitute 'a meeting of the members of the limited liability partnership'.
Section 110 (acceptance of shares, etc, as consideration for sale of company property)	For the existing section substitute the following: '(1) This section applies, in the case of a limited liability partnership proposed to be, or being, wound up voluntarily, where the whole or part of the limited liability partnership's business or property is proposed to be transferred or sold to another company whether or not it is a company within the meaning of the Companies Act ('the transferee company') or to a limited liability partnership ('the transferee limited liability partnership') (2) With the requisite sanction, the liquidator of the limited liability partnership being, or proposed to be, wound up ('the transferor limited liability partnership') may receive, in compensation or part compensation for the transfer or sale, shares, policies or other like interests in the transferee company or the transferee limited liability partnership for distribution among the members of the transferor limited liability partnership. 3) The sanction required under subsection (2) is— (a) in the case of a members' voluntary winding up, that of a determination of the limited liability partnership at a meeting of the members of the limited liability partnership conferring either a general authority on the liquidator or an authority in respect of any particular arrangement, (subsections (3) and (4) of section 92 to apply for this purpose as they apply for the purposes of that section), and

	b) in the case of a creditor's voluntary winding up, that of either court or the liquidation committee.
	4) Alternatively to subsection (2), the liquidator may (with the sanction) enter into any other arrangement whereby the members of the transferor limited liability partnership may, in lieu of receiving cash, shares, policies or other like interests (or in addition thereto), participate in the profits, or receive any other benefit from the transferee company or the transferee limited liability partnership.
	(5) A sale or arrangement in pursuance of this section is binding on members of the transferor limited liability partnership.
	(6) A determination by the limited liability partnership is not invalid for the purposes of this section by reason that it is made before or concurrently with a determination by the limited liability partnership that it be wound up voluntarily or for appointing liquidators; but, if an order is made within a year for winding up the limited liability partnership by the court, the determination by the limited liability partnership is not valid unless sanctioned by the court.'
Section 111 (dissent from arrangement under section 110)	

subsections (1)–(3)	For subsections (1)–(3) substitute the following— '(1) This section applies in the case of a voluntary winding up where, for the purposes of section 110(2) or (4), a determination of the limited liability partnership has provided the sanction requisite for the liquidator under that section. (2) If a member of the transferor limited liability partnership who did not vote in favour of providing the sanction required for the liquidator under section 110 expresses his dissent from it in writing addressed to the liquidator and left at the registered office of the limited liability partnership within 7 days after the date on which that sanction was given, he may require the liquidator either to abstain from carrying the arrangement so sanctioned into effect or to purchase his interest at a price to be determined by agreement or arbitration under this section. (3) If the liquidator elects to purchase the member's interest, the purchase money must be paid before the limited liability partnership is dissolved and be raised by the liquidator in such manner as may be determined by the limited liability partnership.'
subsection (4)	Omit subsection (4).
Section 117 (high court and county court jurisdiction)	
subsection (2)	Delete 'Where the amount of a company's share capital paid up or credited as paid up does not exceed £120,000, then (subject to this section)'.
subsection (3)	Delete subsection (3).
Section 120 (court of session and sheriff court jurisdiction)	
subsection (3)	Delete 'Where the amount of a company's share capital paid up or credited as paid up does not exceed £120,000,'.

subsection (5)	Delete subsection (5).
Section 122 (circumstances in which company may be wound up by the court)	
subsection (1)	For subsection (1) substitute the following— '(1) A limited liability partnership may be wound up by the court if— (a) the limited liability partnership has determined that the limited liability partnership be wound up by the court, (b) the limited liability partnership does not commence its business within a year from its incorporation or suspends its business for a whole year, (c) the number of members is reduced below two, (d) the limited liability partnership is unable to pay its debts, ... [(da) at the time at which a moratorium for the limited liability partnership under section 1A comes to an end, no voluntary arrangement approved under Part I has effect in relation to the limited liability partnership,] (e) the court is of the opinion that it is just and equitable that the limited liability partnership should be wound up.'
Section 124 (application for winding up)	
subsections (2), (3)and (4)(a)	Delete these subsections.
[subsection (3A)	For '122(1)(fa)' substitute '122(1)(da)'.]
Section 124A (petition for winding-up on grounds of public interest)	
subsection (1)	[Omit paragraphs (b) and (bb).]
Section 126 (power to stay or restrain proceedings against company)	
subsection (2)	Delete subsection (2).
Section 127 (avoidance of property dispositions, etc)	

[subsection (1)]	For 'any transfer of shares' substitute 'any transfer by a member of the limited liability partnership of his interest in the property of the limited liability partnership'.
Section 129 (commencement of winding up by the court)	
subsection (1)	For 'a resolution has been passed by the company' substitute 'a determination has been made' and for 'at the time of the passing of the resolution' substitute 'at the time of that determination'.
Section 130 (consequences of winding-up order)	
subsection (3)	Delete subsection (3).
Section 148 (settlement of list of contributories and application of assets)	
subsection (1)	Delete ', with power to rectify the register of members in all cases where rectification is required in pursuance of the Companies Act or this Act,'.
Section 149 (debts due from contributory to company)	
subsection (1)	Delete 'the Companies Act or'.
subsection (2)	Delete subsection (2).
subsection (3)	Delete ', whether limited or unlimited,'.
Section 160 (delegation of powers to liquidator (England and Wales))	
subsection (1)	In subsection (1)(b) delete 'and the rectifying of the register of members'.
subsection (2)	For subsection (2) substitute the following— '(2) But the liquidator shall not make any call without the special leave of the court or the sanction of the liquidation committee.'
Section 165 (voluntary winding up)	

subsection (2)	In paragraph (a) for 'an extraordinary resolution of the company' substitute 'a determination by a meeting of the members of the limited liability partnership'.
subsection (4)	For paragraph (c) substitute the following— '(c) summon meetings of the members of the limited liability partnership for the purpose of obtaining their sanction or for any other purpose he may think fit.'
new subsection (4A)	Insert a new subsection (4A) as follows— '(4A) Subsections (3) and (4) of section 92 shall apply for the purposes of this section as they apply for the purposes of that section.'
Section 166 (creditors' voluntary winding up)	
subsection (5)	In paragraph (b) for 'directors' substitute 'designated members'.
Section 171 (removal, etc (voluntary winding up))	
subsection (2)	For paragraph (a) substitute the following— '(a) in the case of a members' voluntary winding up, by a meeting of the members of the limited liability partnership summoned specially for that purpose, or'.
subsection (6)	In paragraph (a) for 'final meeting of the company' substitute 'final meeting of the members of the limited liability partnership' and in paragraph (b) for 'final meetings of the company' substitute 'final meetings of the members of the limited liability partnership'.
new subsection (7)	Insert a new subsection (7) as follows— '(7) Subsections (3) and (4) of section 92 are to apply for the purposes of this section as they apply for the purposes of that section.'
Section 173 (release (voluntary winding up))	

subsection (2)	In paragraph (a) for 'a general meeting of the company' substitute 'a meeting of the members of the limited liability partnership'.
Section 183 (effect of execution or attachment (England and Wales))	
subsection (2)	Delete paragraph (a).
Section 184 (duties of sheriff (England and Wales))	
subsection (1)	For 'a resolution for voluntary winding up has been passed' substitute 'the limited liability partnership has determined that it be wound up voluntarily'.
subsection (4)	Delete 'or of a meeting having been called at which there is to be proposed a resolution for voluntary winding up,' and 'or a resolution is passed (as the case may be)'.
Section 187 (power to make over assets to employees)	
	Delete section 187.
Section 194 (resolutions passed at adjourned meetings)	
	After 'contributories' insert 'or of the members of a limited liability partnership'.
Section 195 (meetings to ascertain wishes of creditors or contributories)	
subsection (3)	Delete 'the Companies Act or'.
Section 206 (fraud, etc in anticipation of winding up)	
subsection (1)	For 'passes a resolution for voluntary winding up' substitute 'makes a determination that it be wound up voluntarily'.
Section 207 (transactions in fraud of creditors)	
subsection (1)	For 'passes a resolution for voluntary winding up' substitute 'makes a determination that it be wound up voluntarily'.

Section 210 (material omissions from statement relating to company's affairs)	
subsection (2)	For 'passed a resolution for voluntary winding up' substitute 'made a determination that it be wound up voluntarily'.
Section 214 (wrongful trading)	
subsection (2)	Delete from 'but the court shall not' to the end of the subsection.
After section 214	Insert the following new section 214A
	'214A Adjustment of withdrawals
	(1) This section has effect in relation to a person who is or has been a member of a limited liability partnership where, in the course of the winding up of that limited liability partnership, it appears that subsection (2) of this section applies in relation to that person.
	(2) This subsection applies in relation to a person if—
	(a) within the period of two years ending with the commencement of the winding up, he was a member of the limited liability partnership who withdrew property of the limited liability partnership, whether in the form of a share of profits, salary, repayment of or payment of interest on a loan to the limited liability partnership or any other withdrawal of property, and
	(b) it is proved by the liquidator to the satisfaction of the court that at the time of the withdrawal he knew or had reasonable ground for believing that the limited liability partnership—
	(i) was at the time of the withdrawal unable to pay its debts within the meaning of section 123, or

(ii) would become so unable to pay its debts after the assets of the limited liability partnership had been depleted by that withdrawal taken together with all other withdrawals (if any) made by any members contemporaneously with that withdrawal or in contemplation when that withdrawal was made.

(3) Where this section has effect in relation to any person the court, on the application of the liquidator, may declare that that person is to be liable to make such contribution (if any) to the limited liability partnership's assets as the court thinks proper.

(4) The court shall not make a declaration in relation to any person the amount of which exceeds the aggregate of the amounts or values of all the withdrawals referred to in subsection (2) made by that person within the period of two years referred to in that subsection.

(5) The court shall not make a declaration under this section with respect to any person unless that person knew or ought to have concluded that after each withdrawal referred to in subsection (2) there was no reasonable prospect that the limited liability partnership would avoid going into insolvent liquidation.

(6) For the purposes of subsection (5) the facts which a member ought to know or ascertain and the conclusions which he ought to reach are those which would be known, ascertained, or reached by a reasonably diligent person having both:

(a) the general knowledge, skill and experience that may reasonably be expected of a person carrying out the same functions as are carried out by that member in relation to the limited liability partnership, and

	(b) the general knowledge, skill and experience that that member has.
	(7) For the purposes of this section a limited liability partnership goes into insolvent liquidation if it goes into liquidation at a time when its assets are insufficient for the payment of its debts and other liabilities and the expenses of the winding up.
	(8) In this section 'member' includes a shadow member.
	(9) This section is without prejudice to section 214.'
Section 215 (proceedings under ss 213, 214)	
subsection (1)	Omit the word 'or' between the words '213' and '214' and insert after '214' 'or 214A'.
subsection (2)	For 'either section' substitute 'any of those sections'.
subsection (4)	For 'either section' substitute 'any of those sections'.
subsection (5)	For 'Sections 213 and 214' substitute 'Sections 213, 214 or 214A'.
Section 218 (prosecution of delinquent officers and members of company)	
subsection (1)	For 'officer, or any member, of the company' substitute 'member of the limited liability partnership'.
subsections (3), (4) and (6)	For 'officer of the company, or any member of it,' substitute 'officer or member of the limited liability partnership'.
< ... >	...
Section 247 ('insolvency' and 'go into liquidation')	
subsection (2)	For 'passes a resolution for voluntary winding up' substitute 'makes a determination that it be wound up voluntarily' and for 'passing such a resolution' substitute 'making such a determination'.
[subsection (3)	For 'resolution for voluntary winding up' substitute 'determination to wind up voluntarily'.]

Section 249 ('connected with a company')	For the existing words substitute 'For the purposes of any provision in this Group of Parts, a person is connected with a company (including a limited liability partnership) if— (a) he is a director or shadow director of a company or an associate of such a director or shadow director (including a member or a shadow member of a limited liability partnership or an associate of such a member or shadow member); or (b) he is an associate of the company or of the limited liability partnership.'
Section 250 ('member' of a company)	Delete section 250.
Section 251 (expressions used generally)	Delete the word 'and' appearing after the definition of 'the rules' and insert the word 'and' after the definition of 'shadow director'. After the definition of 'shadow director' insert the following— ''shadow member', in relation to a limited liability partnership, means a person in accordance with whose directions or instructions the members of the limited liability partnership are accustomed to act (but so that a person is not deemed a shadow member by reason only that the members of the limited liability partnership act on advice given by him in a professional capacity);'.
Section 386 (categories of preferential debts)	
subsection (1)	In subsection (1), omit the words 'or an individual'.
subsection (2)	In subsection (2), omit the words 'or the individual'.
Section 387 ('the relevant date')	

subsection (3)	[In paragraph (ab) for 'passed a resolution for voluntary winding up' substitute 'made a determination that it be wound up voluntarily'.] In paragraph (c) for 'passing of the resolution for the winding up of the company' substitute 'making of the determination by the limited liability partnership that it be wound up voluntarily'.
subsection (5)	Omit subsection (5).
subsection (6)	Omit subsection (6).
Section 388 (meaning of 'act as insolvency practitioner')	
subsection (2)	Omit subsection (2).
subsection (3)	Omit subsection (3).
subsection (4)	Delete "company' means a company within the meaning given by section 735(1) of the Companies Act or a company which may be wound up under Part V of this Act (unregistered companies);' and delete "interim trustee' and 'permanent trustee' mean the same as the Bankruptcy (Scotland) Act 1985'.
Section 389 (acting without qualification an offence)	
subsection (1)	Omit the words 'or an individual'.
[Section 389A (authorisation of nominees and supervisors)	
subsection (1)	Omit 'or Part VIII'.]
Section 402 (official petitioner)	Delete section 402.
Section 412 (individual insolvency rules (England and Wales))	Delete section 412.
Section 415 (Fees orders (individual insolvency proceedings in England and Wales))	Delete section 415.
Section 416 (monetary limits (companies winding up))	

subsection (1)	In subsection (1), omit the words 'section 117(2) (amount of company's share capital determining whether county court has jurisdiction to wind it up);' and the words 'section 120(3) (the equivalent as respects sheriff court jurisdiction in Scotland);'.
subsection (3)	In subsection (3), omit the words '117(2), 120(3) or'.
Section 418 (monetary limits (bankruptcy))	Delete section 418.
Section 420 (insolvent partnerships)	Delete section 420.
Section 421 (insolvent estates of deceased persons)	Delete section 421.
Section 422 (recognised banks, etc)	Delete section 422.
[Section 426A (disqualification from Parliament (England and Wales))	Omit.
Section 426B (devolution)	Omit.
Section 426C (irrelevance of privilege)	Omit.]
Section 427 (parliamentary disqualification)	Delete section 427.
Section 429 (disabilities on revocation or administration order against an individual)	Delete section 429.
Section 432 (offences by bodies corporate)	
subsection (2)	Delete 'secretary or'.
Section 435 (meaning of 'associate')	

new subsection (3A)	Insert a new subsection (3A) as follows— '(3A) A member of a limited liability partnership is an associate of that limited liability partnership and of every other member of that limited liability partnership and of the husband or wife [or civil partner] or relative of every other member of that limited liability partnership.'.
subsection (11)	For subsection (11) there shall be substituted '(11) In this section 'company' includes any body corporate (whether incorporated in Great Britain or elsewhere); and references to directors and other officers of a company and to voting power at any general meeting of a company have effect with any necessary modifications.'
Section 436 (expressions used generally)	The following expressions and definitions shall be added to the section— 'designated member' has the same meaning as it has in the Limited Liability Partnerships Act 2000; 'limited liability partnership' means a limited liability partnership formed and registered under the Limited Liability Partnerships Act 2000; 'limited liability partnership agreement', in relation to a limited liability partnership, means any agreement, express or implied, made between the members of the limited liability partnership or between the limited liability partnership and the members of the limited liability partnership which determines the mutual rights and duties of the members, and their rights and duties in relation to the limited liability partnership.
Section 437 (transitional provisions, and savings)	Delete section 437.

Section 440 (extent (Scotland)) subsection (2)	In subsection (2), omit paragraph (b).
Section 441 (extent (Northern Ireland))	Delete section 441.
Section 442 (extent (other territories))	Delete section 442.
[Schedule A1 Paragraph 6 sub-paragraph (1)	For 'directors of a company wish' substitute 'limited liability partnership wishes'.
	For 'they' substitute 'the designated members of the limited liability partnership'.
sub-paragraph (2)	For 'directors' substitute 'the designated members of the limited liability partnership'.
	In sub-paragraph (c), for 'meetings of the company and' substitute 'a meeting of'.
Paragraph 7 sub-paragraph (1)	For 'directors of a company' substitute 'designated members of the limited liability partnership'.
	In sub-paragraph (e)(iii), for 'meetings of the company and' substitute 'a meeting of'.
Paragraph 8 sub-paragraph (2)	For 'meetings' substitute 'meeting'.
	For 'are' substitute 'is'.
	Omit the words in parenthesis.
sub-paragraph (3)	For 'either of those meetings' substitute 'the meeting'.
	For 'those meetings were' substitute 'that meeting was'.
	Omit the words in parenthesis.
sub-paragraph (4)	For 'either' substitute 'the'.
sub-paragraph (6)(c)	For 'one or both of the meetings' substitute 'the meeting'.
Paragraph 9	

sub-paragraph (1)	For 'directors' substitute 'designated members of the limited liability partnership'.
sub-paragraph (2)	For 'directors' substitute 'designated members of the limited liability partnership'.
Paragraph 12	
sub-paragraph (1)(b)	Omit.
sub-paragraph (1)(c)	For 'resolution may be passed' substitute 'determination that it may be wound up may be made'.
sub-paragraph (2)	For 'transfer of shares' substitute 'any transfer by a member of the limited liability partnership of his interest in the property of the limited liability partnership'.
Paragraph 20	
sub-paragraph (8)	For 'directors' substitute 'designated members of the limited liability partnership'.
sub-paragraph (9)	For 'directors' substitute 'designated members of the limited liability partnership'.
Paragraph 24	
sub-paragraph (2)	For 'directors' substitute 'designated members of the limited liability partnership'.
Paragraph 25	
sub-paragraph (2)(c)	For 'directors' substitute 'designated members of the limited liability partnership'.
Paragraph 26	
sub-paragraph (1)	Omit ', director'.
Paragraph 29	
sub-paragraph (1)	For 'meetings of the company and its creditors' substitute 'a meeting of the creditors of the limited liability partnership'.
Paragraph 30	
sub-paragraph (1)	For 'meetings' substitute 'meeting'.
new sub-paragraph (2A)	Insert new sub-paragraph (2A) as follows—

	'(2A) If modifications to the proposal are proposed at the meeting the chairman of the meeting shall, before the conclusion of the meeting, ascertain from the limited liability partnership whether or not it accepts the proposed modifications; and if at that conclusion the limited liability partnership has failed to respond to a proposed modification it shall be presumed not to have agreed to it.'.
sub-paragraph (3)	For 'either' substitute 'the'.
	After 'the result of the meeting' in the first place where it occurs insert ' (including, where modifications to the proposal were proposed at the meeting, the response to those proposed modifications made by the limited liability partnership)'.
	At the end add 'and to the limited liability partnership'.
Paragraph 31	
sub-paragraph (1)	For 'meetings' substitute 'meeting'.
sub-paragraph (7)	For 'directors of the company' substitute 'designated members of the limited liability partnership'.
	For 'meetings (or either of them)' substitute 'meeting'.
	For 'directors' substitute 'limited liability partnership'.
	For 'those meetings' substitute 'that meeting'.
Paragraph 32	
sub-paragraph (2)	For sub-paragraphs (a) and (b) substitute 'with the day on which the meeting summoned under paragraph 29 is first held.'.
Paragraph 36	
sub-paragraph (2)	For sub-paragraph (2) substitute—
	'(2) The decision has effect if, in accordance with the rules, it has been taken by the creditors' meeting summoned under paragraph 29.'.
sub-paragraph (3)	Omit.
sub-paragraph (4)	Omit.
sub-paragraph (5)	Omit.

Paragraph 37	
sub-paragraph (5)	For 'each of the reports of the meetings' substitute 'the report of the meeting'.
Paragraph 38	
sub-paragraph (1)(a)	For 'one or both of the meetings' substitute 'the meeting'.
sub-paragraph (1)(b)	For 'either of those meetings' substitute 'the meeting'.
sub-paragraph (2)(a)	For 'either of the meetings' substitute 'the meeting'.
	After sub-paragraph (2)(a) insert new (aa) as follows—
	'(aa) any member of the limited liability partnership;'.
sub-paragraph (2)(b)	Omit 'creditors''.
sub-paragraph (3)(a)	For 'each of the reports' substitute 'the report'.
sub-paragraph (3)(b)	Omit 'creditors''.
sub-paragraph (4)(a)(ii)	Omit 'in question'.
sub-paragraph (4)(b)(i)	For 'further meetings' substitute 'a further meeting' and for 'directors' substitute 'limited liability partnership'.
sub-paragraph (4)(b)(ii)	Omit 'company or (as the case may be) creditors''.
sub-paragraph (5)	For 'directors do' substitute 'limited liability partnerships does'.
Paragraph 39	
sub-paragraph (1)	For 'one or both of the meetings' substitute 'the meeting'.
Schedule B1	
Paragraph 2	
sub-paragraph (c)	For 'company or its directors' substitute 'limited liability partnership'.
Paragraph 8	
sub-paragraph (1)(a)	For 'resolution for voluntary winding up' substitute 'determination to wind up voluntarily'.
Paragraph 9	Omit.
Paragraph 12	
sub-paragraph (1)(b)	Omit.
Paragraph 22	For sub-paragraph (1) substitute—

	'(1) A limited liability partnership may appoint an administrator.'.
	Omit sub-paragraph (2).
Paragraph 23	
sub-paragraph (1)(b)	Omit 'or its directors'.
Paragraph 42	
sub-paragraph (2)	For 'resolution may be passed for the winding up of' substitute 'determination to wind up voluntarily may be made by'.
Paragraph 61	For paragraph 61 substitute—'
	'61 The administrator has power to prevent any person from taking part in the management of the business of the limited liability partnership and to appoint any person to be a manager of that business.'.
Paragraph 62	At the end add the following—
	'Subsections (3) and (4) of section 92 shall apply for the purposes of this paragraph as they apply for the purposes of that section.'.
Paragraph 83	
sub-paragraph (6)(b)	For 'resolution for voluntary winding up' substitute 'determination to wind up voluntarily'.
sub-paragraph (8)(b)	For 'passing of the resolution for voluntary winding up' substitute 'determination to wind up voluntarily'.
sub-paragraph (8)(e)	For 'passing of the resolution for voluntary winding up' substitute 'determination to wind up voluntarily'.
Paragraph 87	
sub-paragraph (2)(b)	Insert at the end 'or'.
sub-paragraph (2)(c)	Omit ', or'.
sub-paragraph (2)(d)	Omit the words from '(d)' to 'company'.
Paragraph 89	
sub-paragraph (2)(b)	Insert at the end 'or'.
sub-paragraph (2)(c)	Omit ', or'.
sub-paragraph (2)(d)	Omit the words from '(d)' to 'company'.
Paragraph 91	

sub-paragraph (1)(c)	Omit.
Paragraph 94	Omit.
Paragraph 95	For 'to 94' substitute 'and 93'.
Paragraph 97	
sub-paragraph (1)(a)	Omit 'or directors'.
Paragraph 103	
sub-paragraph (5)	Omit.
Paragraph 105	Omit.]
Schedule 1	
Paragraph 19	For paragraph 19 substitute the following— '19. Power to enforce any rights the limited liability partnership has against the members under the terms of the limited liability partnership agreement.'
Schedule 10	
[Section 6A(1)	In the entry relating to section 6A omit 'members' or'.]
Section 85(2)	In the entry relating to section 85(2) for 'resolution for voluntary winding up' substitute 'making of determination for voluntary winding up'.
Section 89(4)	In the entry relating to section 89(4) for 'Director' substitute 'Designated member'.
Section 93(3)	In the entry relating to section 93(3) for 'general meeting of the company' substitute 'meeting of members of the limited liability partnership'.
Section 99(3)	In the entries relating to section 99(3) for 'director' and 'directors' where they appear substitute 'designated member' or 'designated members' as appropriate.
Section 105(3)	In the entry relating to section 105(3) for 'company general meeting' substitute 'meeting of the members of the limited liability partnership'.
Section 106(6)	In the entry relating to section 106(6) for 'final meeting of the company' substitute 'final meeting of the members of the limited liability partnership'.

Sections 353(1)to 362	Delete the entries relating to sections 353(1) to 362 inclusive.
Section 429(5)	Delete the entry relating to section 429(5).
[Schedule A1, paragraph 9(2)	For 'Directors' substitute 'Designated Members'.
Schedule A1, paragraph 20(9)	For 'Directors' substitute 'Designated Members'.
Schedule B1, paragraph 27(4)	Omit 'or directors'.
Schedule B1, paragraph 29(7)	Omit 'or directors'.
Schedule B1, paragraph 32	Omit 'or directors'.]

SCHEDULE 4

21.13

(*Omitted*)

SCHEDULE 5
General and Consequential Amendments in Other Legislation

21.14

(*Omitted*)

SCHEDULE 6
Application of Subordinate Legislation
Regulation 10

Part I
Regulations Made under the 1985 Act

21.15

(*Omitted*)

Part II
Regulations Made under the 1986 Act

21.16

1

Insolvency Practitioners Regulations 1990

2

The Insolvency Practitioners (Recognised Professional Bodies) Order 1986

3

The Insolvency Rules 1986 and the Insolvency (Scotland) Rules 1986 (except in so far as they relate to the exceptions to the reserved matters specified in section C 2 of Part II of Schedule 5 to the Scotland Act 1998)

4

The Insolvency Fees Order 1986

5

The Co-operation of Insolvency Courts (Designation of Relevant Countries and Territories) Order 1986

6

The Co-operation of Insolvency Courts (Designation of Relevant Countries and Territories) Order 1996

7

The Co-operation of Insolvency Courts (Designation of Relevant Country) Order 1998

8

Insolvency Proceedings (Monetary Limits) Order 1986

9

Insolvency Practitioners Tribunal (Conduct of Investigations) Rules 1986

10

Insolvency Regulations 1994

11

Insolvency (Amendment) Regulations 2000

Part III
Regulations Made under other Legislation

21.17

1

Company and Business Names Regulations 1981

2

The Companies (Disqualification Orders) Regulations 1986

3

The Insolvent Companies (Disqualification of Unfit Directors) Proceedings Rules 1987

4

The Contracting Out (Functions of the Official Receiver) Order 1995

5

The Uncertificated Securities Regulations 1995

6

The Insolvent Companies (Reports on Conduct of Directors) Rules 1996

7

The Insolvent Companies (Reports on Conduct of Directors) (Scotland) Rules 1996

United Nations Commission on International Trade Law (UNCITRAL) model law on cross-border insolvency regulations

---

Notes

The United Nations Commission on International Trade Law ('UNICITRAL') Model Law in a modified form was brought into force under the Cross-Border Insolvency Regulations 2006 (SI 2006/1030) with effect from 6 April 2006. IA 2000 s 14 enabled regulations to be made by the Secretary of State for the purpose of giving effect, with or without modifications, to the Model Law. The Model Law generally applies to both corporate and individual debtors in circumstances where; (a) a foreign representative requests assistance from the court in respect of foreign insolvency proceedings; (b) there are concurrent insolvency proceedings in England and another country; (c) foreign creditors wish to become involved in insolvency proceedings in England. See below and the Cross-Border Insolvency Regulations which also appear in unannotated form in this work.

Part One

PREAMBLE

The purpose of this Law is to provide effective mechanisms for dealing with cases of cross-border insolvency so as to promote the objectives of:

(a) Cooperation between the courts and other competent authorities of this State and foreign States involved in cases of cross-border insolvency;

(b) Greater legal certainty for trade and investment;

(c) Fair and efficient administration of cross-border insolvencies that protects the interests of all creditors and other interested persons, including the debtor;

(d) Protection and maximization of the value of the debtor's assets; and

(e) Facilitation of the rescue of financially troubled businesses, thereby protecting investment and preserving employment.

Chapter I
General provisions

22.1

1 Scope of application

1. This Law applies where:

(a) Assistance is sought in this State by a foreign court or a foreign representative in connection with a foreign proceeding; or

(b) Assistance is sought in a foreign State in connection with a proceeding under *[identify laws of the enacting State relating to insolvency]*; or

(c) A foreign proceeding and a proceeding under *[identify laws of the enacting State relating to insolvency]* in respect of the same debtor are taking place concurrently; or

(d) Creditors or other interested persons in a foreign State have an interest in requesting the commencement of, or participating in, a proceeding under *[identify laws of the enacting State relating to insolvency]*.

2. This Law does not apply to a proceeding concerning *[designate any types of entities, such as banks or insurance companies, that are subject to a special insolvency regime in this State and that this State wishes to exclude from this Law]*.

22.2

2 Definitions

For the purposes of this Law:

(a) "Foreign proceeding" means a collective judicial or administrative proceeding in a foreign State, including an interim proceeding, pursuant to a law relating to insolvency in which proceeding the assets and affairs of the debtor are subject to control or supervision by a foreign court, for the purpose of reorganization or liquidation;

(b) "Foreign main proceeding" means a foreign proceeding taking place in the State where the debtor has the centre of its main interests;

(c) "Foreign non-main proceeding" means a foreign proceeding, other than a foreign main proceeding, taking place in a State where the debtor has an establishment within the meaning of subparagraph (f) of this article;

(d) "Foreign representative" means a person or body, including one appointed on an interim basis, authorized in a foreign proceeding to administer the reorganization or the liquidation of the debtor's assets or affairs or to act as a representative of the foreign proceeding;

(e) "Foreign court" means a judicial or other authority competent to control or supervise a foreign proceeding;

(f) "Establishment" means any place of operations where the debtor carries out a non-transitory economic activity with human means and goods or services.

22.3

3 International obligations of this State

To the extent that this Law conflicts with an obligation of this State arising out of any treaty or other form of agreement to which it is a party with one or more other States, the requirements of the treaty or agreement prevail.

22.4

4 Competent court or authority

The functions referred to in this Law relating to recognition of foreign proceedings and cooperation with foreign courts shall be performed by *[specify the court, courts, authority or authorities competent to perform those functions in the enacting State].*

Notes

A State where certain functions relating to insolvency proceedings have been conferred upon government-appointed officials or bodies might wish to include in article 4 or elsewhere in chapter I the following provision:

"Nothing in this Law affects the provisions in force in this State governing the authority of *[insert the title of the government-appointed person or body]*.".

22.5

5 Authorization of [insert the title of the person or body administering reorganization or liquidation under the law of the enacting State] to act in a foreign State

A *[insert the title of the person or body administering a reorganization or liquidation under the law of the enacting State]* is authorized to act in a foreign State on behalf of a proceeding under *[identify laws of the enacting State relating to insolvency]*, as permitted by the applicable foreign law.

22.6

6 Public policy exception

Nothing in this Law prevents the court from refusing to take an action governed by this Law if the action would be manifestly contrary to the public policy of this State.

22.7

7 Additional assistance under other laws

Nothing in this Law limits the power of a court or a *[insert the title of the person or body administering a reorganization or liquidation under the law of the enacting State]* to provide additional assistance to a foreign representative under other laws of this State.

22.8

8 Interpretation

In the interpretation of this Law, regard is to be had to its international origin and to the need to promote uniformity in its application and the observance of good faith.

Chapter II
Access of foreign representatives and creditors to courts in this state

22.9

9 Right of direct access

A foreign representative is entitled to apply directly to a court in this State.

22.10

10 Limited jurisdiction

The sole fact that an application pursuant to this Law is made to a court in this State by a foreign representative does not subject the foreign representative or the foreign assets and affairs of the debtor to the jurisdiction of the courts of this State for any purpose other than the application.

22.11

11 Application by a foreign representative to commence a proceeding under *[identify laws of the enacting State relating to insolvency]*

A foreign representative is entitled to apply to commence a proceeding under *[identify laws of the enacting State relating to insolvency]* if the conditions for commencing such a proceeding are otherwise met.

22.12

12 Participation of a foreign representative in a proceeding under *[identify laws of the enacting State relating to insolvency]*

Upon recognition of a foreign proceeding, the foreign representative is entitled to participate in a proceeding regarding the debtor under *[identify laws of the enacting State relating to insolvency]*.

22.13

13 Access of foreign creditors to a proceeding under [identify laws of the enacting State relating to insolvency]

1. Subject to paragraph 2 of this article, foreign creditors have the same rights regarding the commencement of, and participation in, a proceeding under *[identify laws of the enacting State relating to insolvency]* as creditors in this State.

2. Paragraph 1 of this article does not affect the ranking of claims in a proceeding under *[identify laws of the enacting State relating to insolvency]*, except that the claims of foreign creditors shall not be ranked lower than *[identify the class of general non-preference claims, while providing that a foreign claim is to be ranked lower than the general non-preference claims if an*

> *equivalent local claim (e g claim for a penalty or deferred-payment claim) has a rank lower than the general non-preference claims].*

Notes

The enacting State may wish to consider the following alternative wording to replace paragraph 2 of article 13(2):

22.14

"2. Paragraph 1 of this article does not affect the ranking of claims in a proceeding under *[identify laws of the enacting State relating to insolvency]* or the exclusion of foreign tax and social security claims from such a proceeding. Nevertheless, the claims of foreign creditors other than those concerning tax and social security obligations shall not be ranked lower than *[identify the class of general non-preference claims, while providing that a foreign claim is to be ranked lower than the general non-preference claims if an equivalent local claim (e g claim for a penalty or deferred-payment claim) has a rank lower than the general non-preference claims].*".

22.15

14 Notification to foreign creditors of a proceeding under [identify laws of the enacting State relating to insolvency]

1. Whenever under *[identify laws of the enacting State relating to insolvency]* notification is to be given to creditors in this State, such notification shall also be given to the known creditors that do not have addresses in this State. The court may order that appropriate steps be taken with a view to notifying any creditor whose address is not yet known.

2. Such notification shall be made to the foreign creditors individually, unless the court considers that, under the circumstances, some other form of notification would be more appropriate. No letters rogatory or other, similar formality is required.

3. When a notification of commencement of a proceeding is to be given to foreign creditors, the notification shall:
   (a) Indicate a reasonable time period for filing claims and specify the place for their filing;
   (b) Indicate whether secured creditors need to file their secured claims; and
   (c) Contain any other information required to be included in such a notification to creditors pursuant to the law of this State and the orders of the court.

Chapter III
Recognition of a foreign proceeding and relief

22.16

15 Application for recognition of a foreign proceeding

1. A foreign representative may apply to the court for recognition of the foreign proceeding in which the foreign representative has been appointed.

2. An application for recognition shall be accompanied by:
  (a) A certified copy of the decision commencing the foreign proceeding and appointing the foreign representative; or
  (b) A certificate from the foreign court affirming the existence of the foreign proceeding and of the appointment of the foreign representative; or
  (c) In the absence of evidence referred to in subparagraphs (a) and (b), any other evidence acceptable to the court of the existence of the foreign proceeding and of the appointment of the foreign representative.

3. An application for recognition shall also be accompanied by a statement identifying all foreign proceedings in respect of the debtor that are known to the foreign representative.

4. The court may require a translation of documents supplied in support of the application for recognition into an official language of this State.

22.17

16 Presumptions concerning recognition

1. If the decision or certificate referred to in paragraph 2 of article 15 indicates that the foreign proceeding is a proceeding within the meaning of subparagraph (a) of article 2 and that the foreign representative is a person or body within the meaning of subparagraph (d) of article 2, the court is entitled to so presume.

2. The court is entitled to presume that documents submitted in support of the application for recognition are authentic, whether or not they have been legalized.

3. In the absence of proof to the contrary, the debtor's registered office, or habitual residence in the case of an individual, is presumed to be the centre of the debtor's main interests.

22.18

17 Decision to recognize a foreign proceeding

1. Subject to article 6, a foreign proceeding shall be recognized if:
  (a) The foreign proceeding is a proceeding within the meaning of subparagraph (a) of article 2;
  (b) The foreign representative applying for recognition is a person or body within the meaning of subparagraph (d) of article 2;
  (c) The application meets the requirements of paragraph 2 of article 15; and
  (d) The application has been submitted to the court referred to in article 4.

2. The foreign proceeding shall be recognized:
  (a) As a foreign main proceeding if it is taking place in the State where the debtor has the centre of its main interests; or
  (b) As a foreign non-main proceeding if the debtor has an establishment within the meaning of subparagraph (f) of article 2 in the foreign State.

3. An application for recognition of a foreign proceeding shall be decided upon at the earliest possible time.

4. The provisions of articles 15, 16, 17 and 18 do not prevent modification or termination of recognition if it is shown that the grounds for granting it were fully or partially lacking or have ceased to exist.

22.19

18 Subsequent information

From the time of filing the application for recognition of the foreign proceeding, the foreign representative shall inform the court promptly of:

    (a)   Any substantial change in the status of the recognized foreign proceeding or the status of the foreign representative's appointment; and

    (b)   Any other foreign proceeding regarding the same debtor that becomes known to the foreign representative.

22.20

19 Relief that may be granted upon application for recognition of a foreign proceeding

1. From the time of filing an application for recognition until the application is decided upon, the court may, at the request of the foreign representative, where relief is urgently needed to protect the assets of the debtor or the interests of the creditors, grant relief of a provisional nature, including:

    (a)   Staying execution against the debtor's assets;

    (b)   Entrusting the administration or realization of all or part of the debtor's assets located in this State to the foreign representative or another person designated by the court, in order to protect and preserve the value of assets that, by their nature or because of other circumstances, are perishable, susceptible to devaluation or otherwise in jeopardy;

    (c)   Any relief mentioned in paragraph 1(c), (d) and (g) of article 21.

2. *[Insert provisions (or refer to provisions in force in the enacting State) relating to notice.]*

3. Unless extended under paragraph 1(f) of article 21, the relief granted under this article terminates when the application for recognition is decided upon.

4. The court may refuse to grant relief under this article if such relief would interfere with the administration of a foreign main proceeding.

22.21

20 Effects of recognition of a foreign main proceeding

1. Upon recognition of a foreign proceeding that is a foreign main proceeding,

    (a)   Commencement or continuation of individual actions or individual proceedings concerning the debtor's assets, rights, obligations or liabilities is stayed;

    (b)   Execution against the debtor's assets is stayed; and

    (c)   The right to transfer, encumber or otherwise dispose of any assets of the debtor is suspended.

2. The scope, and the modification or termination, of the stay and suspension referred to in paragraph 1 of this article are subject to *[refer to any provisions of law of the enacting State relating to insolvency that apply to exceptions, limitations, modifications or termination in respect of the stay and suspension referred to in paragraph 1 of this article]*.

3. Paragraph 1(a) of this article does not affect the right to commence individual actions or proceedings to the extent necessary to preserve a claim against the debtor.

4. Paragraph 1 of this article does not affect the right to request the commencement of a proceeding under *[identify laws of the enacting State relating to insolvency]* or the right to file claims in such a proceeding.

22.22

21 Relief that may be granted upon recognition of a foreign proceeding

1. Upon recognition of a foreign proceeding, whether main or non-main, where necessary to protect the assets of the debtor or the interests of the creditors, the court may, at the request of the foreign representative, grant any appropriate relief, including:

   (a) Staying the commencement or continuation of individual actions or individual proceedings concerning the debtor's assets, rights, obligations or liabilities, to the extent they have not been stayed under paragraph 1(a) of article 20;

   (b) Staying execution against the debtor's assets to the extent it has not been stayed under paragraph 1(b) of article 20;

   (c) Suspending the right to transfer, encumber or otherwise dispose of any assets of the debtor to the extent this right has not been suspended under paragraph 1(c) of article 20;

   (d) Providing for the examination of witnesses, the taking of evidence or the delivery of information concerning the debtor's assets, affairs, rights, obligations or liabilities;

   (e) Entrusting the administration or realization of all or part of the debtor's assets located in this State to the foreign representative or another person designated by the court;

   (f) Extending relief granted under paragraph 1 of article 19;

   (g) Granting any additional relief that may be available to *[insert the title of a person or body administering a reorganization or liquidation under the law of the enacting State]* under the laws of this State.

2. Upon recognition of a foreign proceeding, whether main or non-main, the court may, at the request of the foreign representative, entrust the distribution of all or part of the debtor's assets located in this State to the foreign representative or another person designated by the court, provided that the court is satisfied that the interests of creditors in this State are adequately protected.

3. In granting relief under this article to a representative of a foreign non-main proceeding, the court must be satisfied that the relief relates to assets that, under the law of this State, should be administered in the foreign non-main proceeding or concerns information required in that proceeding.

22.23

22 Protection of creditors and other interested persons

1. In granting or denying relief under article 19 or 21, or in modifying or terminating relief under paragraph 3 of this article, the court must be satisfied that the interests of the creditors and other interested persons, including the debtor, are adequately protected.

2. The court may subject relief granted under article 19 or 21 to conditions it considers appropriate.

3. The court may, at the request of the foreign representative or a person affected by relief granted under article 19 or 21, or at its own motion, modify or terminate such relief.

22.24

23 Actions to avoid acts detrimental to creditors

1. Upon recognition of a foreign proceeding, the foreign representative has standing to initiate *[refer to the types of actions to avoid or otherwise render ineffective acts detrimental to creditors that are available in this State to a person or body administering a reorganization or liquidation]*.

2. When the foreign proceeding is a foreign non-main proceeding, the court must be satisfied that the action relates to assets that, under the law of this State, should be administered in the foreign non-main proceeding.

22.25

24 Intervention by a foreign representative in proceedings in this State

Upon recognition of a foreign proceeding, the foreign representative may, provided the requirements of the law of this State are met, intervene in any proceedings in which the debtor is a party.

Chapter IV
Cooperation with foreign courts and foreign representatives

22.26

25 Cooperation and direct communication between a court of this State and foreign courts or foreign representatives

1. In matters referred to in article 1, the court shall cooperate to the maximum extent possible with foreign courts or foreign representatives, either directly or through a *[insert the title of a person or body administering a reorganization or liquidation under the law of the enacting State]*.

2. The court is entitled to communicate directly with, or to request information or assistance directly from, foreign courts or foreign representatives.

22.27

26 Cooperation and direct communication between the [insert the title of a person or body administering a reorganization or liquidation under the law of the enacting State] and foreign courts or foreign representatives

1. In matters referred to in article 1, a *[insert the title of a person or body administering a reorganization or liquidation under the law of the enacting State]* shall, in the exercise of its functions and subject to the supervision of the court, cooperate to the maximum extent possible with foreign courts or foreign representatives.

2. The *[insert the title of a person or body administering a reorganization or liquidation under the law of the enacting State]* is entitled, in the exercise of its functions and subject to the supervision of the court, to communicate directly with foreign courts or foreign representatives.

22.28

27 Forms of cooperation

Cooperation referred to in articles 25 and 26 may be implemented by any appropriate means, including:
- (a) Appointment of a person or body to act at the direction of the court;
- (b) Communication of information by any means considered appropriate by the court;
- (c) Coordination of the administration and supervision of the debtor's assets and affairs;
- (d) Approval or implementation by courts of agreements concerning the coordination of proceedings;
- (e) Coordination of concurrent proceedings regarding the same debtor;
- (f) *[The enacting State may wish to list additional forms or examples of cooperation].*

Chapter V
Concurrent proceedings

22.29

28 Commencement of a proceeding under *[identify laws of the enacting State relating to insolvency]* after recognition of a foreign main proceeding

After recognition of a foreign main proceeding, a proceeding under *[identify laws of the enacting State relating to insolvency]* may be commenced only if the debtor has assets in this State; the effects of that proceeding shall be restricted to the assets of the debtor that are located in this State and, to the extent necessary to implement cooperation and coordination under articles 25, 26 and 27, to other assets of the debtor that, under the law of this State, should be administered in that proceeding.

22.30

29 Coordination of a proceeding under *[identify laws of the enacting State relating to insolvency]* and a foreign proceeding

Where a foreign proceeding and a proceeding under *[identify laws of the enacting State relating to insolvency]* are taking place concurrently regarding the same debtor, the court shall seek cooperation and coordination under articles 25, 26 and 27, and the following shall apply:

(a) When the proceeding in this State is taking place at the time the application for recognition of the foreign proceeding is filed,
    (i) Any relief granted under article 19 or 21 must be consistent with the proceeding in this State; and
    (ii) If the foreign proceeding is recognized in this State as a foreign main proceeding, article 20 does not apply;

(b) When the proceeding in this State commences after recognition, or after the filing of the application for recognition, of the foreign proceeding,
    (i) Any relief in effect under article 19 or 21 shall be reviewed by the court and shall be modified or terminated if inconsistent with the proceeding in this State; and
    (ii) If the foreign proceeding is a foreign main proceeding, the stay and suspension referred to in paragraph 1 of article 20 shall be modified or terminated pursuant to paragraph 2 of article 20 if inconsistent with the proceeding in this State;

(c) In granting, extending or modifying relief granted to a representative of a foreign non-main proceeding, the court must be satisfied that the relief relates to assets that, under the law of this State, should be administered in the foreign non-main proceeding or concerns information required in that proceeding.

22.31

30 Coordination of more than one foreign proceeding

In matters referred to in article 1, in respect of more than one foreign proceeding regarding the same debtor, the court shall seek cooperation and coordination under articles 25, 26 and 27, and the following shall apply:

(a) Any relief granted under article 19 or 21 to a representative of a foreign non-main proceeding after recognition of a foreign main proceeding must be consistent with the foreign main proceeding;

(b) If a foreign main proceeding is recognized after recognition, or after the filing of an application for recognition, of a foreign non-main proceeding, any relief in effect under article 19 or 21 shall be reviewed by the court and shall be modified or terminated if inconsistent with the foreign main proceeding;

(c) If, after recognition of a foreign non-main proceeding, another foreign non-main proceeding is recognized, the court shall grant, modify or terminate relief for the purpose of facilitating coordination of the proceedings.

22.32

31 Presumption of insolvency based on recognition of a foreign main proceeding

In the absence of evidence to the contrary, recognition of a foreign main proceeding is, for the purpose of commencing a proceeding under *[identify laws of the enacting State relating to insolvency]*, proof that the debtor is insolvent.

22.33

32 Rule of payment in concurrent proceedings

Without prejudice to secured claims or rights in rem, a creditor who has received part payment in respect of its claim in a proceeding pursuant to a law relating to insolvency in a foreign State may not receive a payment for the same claim in a proceeding under *[identify laws of the enacting State relating to insolvency]* regarding the same debtor, so long as the payment to the other creditors of the same class is proportionately less than the payment the creditor has already received.

Cross-Border Insolvency Regulations 2006

(2006 No 1030)

Made: 3rd April 2006

Coming into force: 4th April 2006

Notes

The United Nations Commission on International Trade Law ('UNICITRAL') Model Law in a modified form was brought into force under these Regulations with effect from 6 April 2006. IA 2000 s 14 enabled regulations to be made by the Secretary of State for the purpose of giving effect, with or without modifications, to the Model Law. The Model Law generally applies to both corporate and individual debtors in circumstances where a foreign representative requests assistance from the court in respect of foreign insolvency proceedings; (b) there are concurrent insolvency proceedings in England and another country; (c) foreign creditors wish to become involved in insolvency proceedings in England. See below and the UNICITRAL Model Law which appear in unannotated form in this work.

These Regulations are made in exercise of the powers conferred by section 14 of the Insolvency Act 2000.

In accordance with section 14(6) of that Act, the Lord Chancellor and the Scottish Ministers have agreed to the making of these Regulations.

A draft of these Regulations has been laid before Parliament in accordance with section 14(5) of that Act and approved by a resolution of each House of Parliament.

Accordingly, the Secretary of State makes the following Regulations:

23.1

1 Citation, commencement and interpretation

(1) These Regulations may be cited as the Cross-Border Insolvency Regulations 2006 and shall come into force on the day after the day on which they are made.

(2) In these Regulations 'the UNCITRAL Model Law' means the Model Law on cross-border insolvency as adopted by the United Nations Commission on International Trade Law on 30th May 1997.

23.2

2 UNCITRAL Model Law to have force of law

(1) The UNCITRAL Model Law shall have the force of law in Great Britain in the form set out in Schedule 1 to these Regulations (which contains the UNCITRAL Model Law with certain modifications to adapt it for application in Great Britain).

(2) Without prejudice to any practice of the courts as to the matters which may be considered apart from this paragraph, the following documents may be considered in ascertaining the meaning or effect of any provision of the UNCITRAL Model Law as set out in Schedule 1 to these Regulations—

    (a)   the UNCITRAL Model Law;

    (b)   any documents of the United Nations Commission on International Trade Law and its working group relating to the preparation of the UNCITRAL Model Law; and

    (c)   the Guide to Enactment of the UNCITRAL Model Law (UNCITRAL document A/CN 9/442) prepared at the request of the United Nations Commission on International Trade Law made in May 1997.

23.3

3 Modification of British insolvency law

(1) British insolvency law (as defined in article 2 of the UNCITRAL Model Law as set out in Schedule 1 to these Regulations) and Part 3 of the Insolvency Act 1986 shall apply with such modifications as the context requires for the purpose of giving effect to the provisions of these Regulations.

(2) In the case of any conflict between any provision of British insolvency law or of Part 3 of the Insolvency Act 1986 and the provisions of these Regulations, the latter shall prevail.

23.4

4 Procedural matters in England and Wales

Schedule 2 to these Regulations (which makes provision about procedural matters in England and Wales in connection with the application of the UNCITRAL Model Law as set out in Schedule 1 to these Regulations) shall have effect.

23.5

5 Procedural matters in Scotland

Schedule 3 to these Regulations (which makes provision about procedural matters in Scotland in connection with the application of the UNCITRAL Model Law as set out in Schedule 1 to these Regulations) shall have effect.

23.6

6 Notices delivered to the registrar of companies

Schedule 4 to these Regulations (which makes provision about notices delivered to the registrar of companies under these Regulations) shall have effect.

23.7

7 Co-operation between courts exercising jurisdiction in relation to cross-border insolvency

(1) An order made by a court in either part of Great Britain in the exercise of jurisdiction in relation to the subject matter of these Regulations shall be enforced in the other part of Great Britain as if it were made by a court exercising the corresponding jurisdiction in that other part.

(2) However, nothing in paragraph (1) requires a court in either part of Great Britain to enforce, in relation to property situated in that part, any order made by a court in the other part of Great Britain.

(3) The courts having jurisdiction in relation to the subject matter of these Regulations in either part of Great Britain shall assist the courts having the corresponding jurisdiction in the other part of Great Britain.

23.8

8 Disapplication of section 388 of the Insolvency Act 1986

Nothing in section 388 of the Insolvency Act 1986 applies to anything done by a foreign representative—

   (a)   under or by virtue of these Regulations;

   (b)   in relation to relief granted or cooperation or coordination provided under these Regulations.

Gerry Sutcliffe

Parliamentary Under Secretary of State for Employment Relations and Consumer Affairs,

Department of Trade and Industry

3rd April 2006

I agree to the making of these Regulations

29th March 2006

Falconer of Thoroton, C

The Scottish Ministers agree to the making of these Regulations

Allan Wilson

A member of the Scottish Executive

30th March 2006

SCHEDULE 1
UNCITRAL Model Law on Cross-Border Insolvency
Regulation 2(1)

Chapter I
General Provisions

Article 1 Scope of Application

23.9

1

This Law applies where—

(a) assistance is sought in Great Britain by a foreign court or a foreign representative in connection with a foreign proceeding; or

(b) assistance is sought in a foreign State in connection with a proceeding under British insolvency law; or

(c) a foreign proceeding and a proceeding under British insolvency law in respect of the same debtor are taking place concurrently; or

(d) creditors or other interested persons in a foreign State have an interest in requesting the commencement of, or participating in, a proceeding under British insolvency law.

23.10

2

This Law does not apply to a proceeding concerning—

(a) a company holding an appointment under Chapter 1 of Part 2 of the Water Industry Act 1991 (water and sewage undertakers) or a qualifying licensed water supplier within the meaning of section 23(6) of that Act (meaning and effect of special administration order);

(b) Scottish Water established under section 20 of the Water Industry (Scotland) Act 2002 (Scottish Water);

(c) a protected railway company within the meaning of section 59 of the Railways Act 1993 (railway administration order) (including that section as it has effect by virtue of section 19 of the Channel Tunnel Rail Link Act 1996 (administration));

(d) a licence company within the meaning of section 26 of the Transport Act 2000 (air traffic services);

(e) a public private partnership company within the meaning of section 210 of the Greater London Authority Act 1999 (public-private partnership agreement);

(f) a protected energy company within the meaning of section 154(5) of the Energy Act 2004 (energy administration orders);

(g) a building society within the meaning of section 119 of the Building Societies Act 1986 (interpretation);

(h) a UK credit institution or an EEA credit institution or any branch of either such institution as those expressions are defined by regulation 2 of the Credit Institutions (Reorganisation and Winding Up) Regulations 2004 (interpretation);

(i) a third country credit institution within the meaning of regulation 36 of the Credit Institutions (Reorganisation and Winding Up) Regulations 2004 (interpretation of this Part);

(j) a person who has permission under or by virtue of Parts 4 or 19 of the Financial Services and Markets Act 2000 to effect or carry out contracts of insurance;

(k) an EEA insurer within the meaning of regulation 2 of the Insurers (Reorganisation and Winding Up) Regulations 2004 (interpretation);

(l) a person (other than one included in paragraph 2(j)) pursuing the activity of reinsurance who has received authorisation for that activity from a competent authority within an EEA State; or

(m)   any of the Concessionaires within the meaning of section 1 of the Channel Tunnel Act 1987.

23.11

3

In paragraph 2 of this article—
- (a)   in sub-paragraph (j) the reference to 'contracts of insurance' must be construed in accordance with—
  - (i)   section 22 of the Financial Services and Markets Act 2000 (classes of regulated activity and categories of investment);
  - (ii)   any relevant order under that section; and
  - (iii)   Schedule 2 to that Act (regulated activities);
- (b)   in sub-paragraph (1) 'EEA State' means a State, other than the United Kingdom, which is a contracting party to the agreement on the European Economic Area signed at Oporto on 2 May 1992.

23.12

4

The court shall not grant any relief, or modify any relief already granted, or provide any co-operation or coordination, under or by virtue of any of the provisions of this Law if and to the extent that such relief or modified relief or cooperation or coordination would—
- (a)   be prohibited under or by virtue of—
  - (i)   Part 7 of the Companies Act 1989;
  - (ii)   Part 3 of the Financial Markets and Insolvency (Settlement Finality) Regulations 1999; or
  - (iii)   Part 3 of the Financial Collateral Arrangements (No 2) Regulations 2003;

  in the case of a proceeding under British insolvency law; or
- (b)   interfere with or be inconsistent with any rights of a collateral taker under Part 4 of the Financial Collateral Arrangements (No 2) Regulations 2003 which could be exercised in the case of such a proceeding.

23.13

5

Where a foreign proceeding regarding a debtor who is an insured in accordance with the provisions of the Third Parties (Rights against Insurers) Act 1930 is recognised under this Law, any stay and suspension referred to in article 20(1) and any relief granted by the court under article 19 or 21 shall not apply to or affect—
- (a)   any transfer of rights of the debtor under that Act; or
- (b)   any claim, action, cause or proceeding by a third party against an insurer under or in respect of rights of the debtor transferred under that Act.

23.14

6

Any suspension under this Law of the right to transfer, encumber or otherwise dispose of any of the debtor's assets—

(a) is subject to section 26 of the Land Registration Act 2002 where owner's powers are exercised in relation to a registered estate or registered charge;

(b) is subject to section 52 of the Land Registration Act 2002, where the powers referred to in that section are exercised by the proprietor of a registered charge; and

(c) in any other case, shall not bind a purchaser of a legal estate in good faith for money or money's worth unless the purchaser has express notice of the suspension.

23.15

7

In paragraph 6—

(a) 'owner's powers' means the powers described in section 23 of the Land Registration Act 2002 and 'registered charge' and 'registered estate' have the same meaning as in section 132(1) of that Act; and

(b) 'legal estate' and 'purchaser' have the same meaning as in section 17 of the Land Charges Act 1972.

Article 2 Definitions

23.16

For the purposes of this Law—

(a) 'British insolvency law' means—

(i) in relation to England and Wales, provision extending to England and Wales and made by or under the Insolvency Act 1986 (with the exception of Part 3 of that Act) or by or under that Act as extended or applied by or under any other enactment (excluding these Regulations); and

(ii) in relation to Scotland, provision extending to Scotland and made by or under the Insolvency Act 1986 (with the exception of Part 3 of that Act), the Bankruptcy (Scotland) Act 1985 or by or under those Acts as extended or applied by or under any other enactment (excluding these Regulations);

(b) 'British insolvency officeholder' means—

(i) the official receiver within the meaning of section 399 of the Insolvency Act 1986 when acting as liquidator, provisional liquidator, trustee, interim receiver or nominee or supervisor of a voluntary arrangement;

(ii) a person acting as an insolvency practitioner within the meaning of section 388 of that Act but shall not include a person acting as an administrative receiver; and

(iii) the Accountant in Bankruptcy within the meaning of section 1 of the Bankruptcy (Scotland) Act 1985 when acting as interim or permanent trustee;

(c) 'the court' except as otherwise provided in articles 14(4) and 23(6)(b), means in relation to any matter the court which in accordance with the provisions of article 4 of this Law has jurisdiction in relation to that matter;

(d) 'the EC Insolvency Regulation' means Council Regulation (EC) No 1346/2000 of 29 May 2000 on Insolvency Proceedings;

(e) 'establishment' means any place of operations where the debtor carries out a non-transitory economic activity with human means and assets or services;

(f) 'foreign court' means a judicial or other authority competent to control or supervise a foreign proceeding;

(g) 'foreign main proceeding' means a foreign proceeding taking place in the State where the debtor has the centre of its main interests;

(h) 'foreign non-main proceeding' means a foreign proceeding, other than a foreign main proceeding, taking place in a State where the debtor has an establishment within the meaning of sub-paragraph (e) of this article;

(i) 'foreign proceeding' means a collective judicial or administrative proceeding in a foreign State, including an interim proceeding, pursuant to a law relating to insolvency in which proceeding the assets and affairs of the debtor are subject to control or supervision by a foreign court, for the purpose of reorganisation or liquidation;

(j) 'foreign representative' means a person or body, including one appointed on an interim basis, authorised in a foreign proceeding to administer the reorganisation or the liquidation of the debtor's assets or affairs or to act as a representative of the foreign proceeding;

(k) 'hire-purchase agreement' includes a conditional sale agreement, a chattel leasing agreement and a retention of title agreement;

(l) 'section 426 request' means a request for assistance in accordance with section 426 of the Insolvency Act 1986 made to a court in any part of the United Kingdom;

(m) 'secured creditor' in relation to a debtor, means a creditor of the debtor who holds in respect of his debt a security over property of the debtor;

(n) 'security' means—
  (i) in relation to England and Wales, any mortgage, charge, lien or other security; and
  (ii) in relation to Scotland, any security (whether heritable or moveable), any floating charge and any right of lien or preference and any right of retention (other than a right of compensation or set off);

(o) in the application of Articles 20 and 23 to Scotland, 'an individual' means any debtor within the meaning of the Bankruptcy (Scotland) Act 1985;

(p) in the application of this Law to Scotland, references howsoever expressed to—
  (i) 'filing' an application or claim are to be construed as references to lodging an application or submitting a claim respectively;
  (ii) 'relief' and 'standing' are to be construed as references to 'remedy' and 'title and interest' respectively; and

> (iii) a 'stay' are to be construed as references to restraint, except in relation to continuation of actions or proceedings when they shall be construed as a reference to sist; and

(q) references to the law of Great Britain include a reference to the law of either part of Great Britain (including its rules of private international law).

Article 3 International Obligations of Great Britain Under the EC Insolvency Regulation

To the extent that this Law conflicts with an obligation of the United Kingdom under the EC Insolvency Regulation, the requirements of the EC Insolvency Regulation prevail.

Article 4 Competent Court

23.17

1

The functions referred to in this Law relating to recognition of foreign proceedings and cooperation with foreign courts shall be performed by the High Court and assigned to the Chancery Division, as regards England and Wales and the Court of Session as regards Scotland.

23.18

2

Subject to paragraph 1 of this article, the court in either part of Great Britain shall have jurisdiction in relation to the functions referred to in that paragraph if—

(a) the debtor has—
  (i) a place of business; or
  (ii) in the case of an individual, a place of residence; or
  (iii) assets,
  situated in that part of Great Britain; or

(b) the court in that part of Great Britain considers for any other reason that it is the appropriate forum to consider the question or provide the assistance requested.

23.19

3

In considering whether it is the appropriate forum to hear an application for recognition of a foreign proceeding in relation to a debtor, the court shall take into account the location of any court in which a proceeding under British insolvency law is taking place in relation to the debtor and the likely location of any future proceedings under British insolvency law in relation to the debtor.

Article 5 Authorisation of British Insolvency Officeholders to Act in a Foreign State

23.20

A British insolvency officeholder is authorised to act in a foreign State on behalf of a proceeding under British insolvency law, as permitted by the applicable foreign law.

Article 6 Public Policy Exception

23.21

Nothing in this Law prevents the court from refusing to take an action governed by this Law if the action would be manifestly contrary to the public policy of Great Britain or any part of it.

Article 7 Additional Assistance under other Laws

23.22

Nothing in this Law limits the power of a court or a British insolvency officeholder to provide additional assistance to a foreign representative under other laws of Great Britain.

Article 8 Interpretation

23.23

In the interpretation of this Law, regard is to be had to its international origin and to the need to promote uniformity in its application and the observance of good faith.

Chapter II
Access of Foreign Representatives and Creditors to Courts in Great Britain

Article 9 Right of Direct Access

23.24

A foreign representative is entitled to apply directly to a court in Great Britain.

Article 10 Limited Jurisdiction

23.25

The sole fact that an application pursuant to this Law is made to a court in Great Britain by a foreign representative does not subject the foreign representative or the foreign assets and affairs of the debtor to the jurisdiction of the courts of Great Britain or any part of it for any purpose other than the application.

Article 11 Application by a Foreign Representative to Commence a Proceeding under British Insolvency Law

23.26

A foreign representative appointed in a foreign main proceeding or foreign non-main proceeding is entitled to apply to commence a proceeding under British insolvency law if the conditions for commencing such a proceeding are otherwise met.

Article 12 Participation of a Foreign Representative in a Proceeding under British Insolvency Law

23.27

Upon recognition of a foreign proceeding, the foreign representative is entitled to participate in a proceeding regarding the debtor under British insolvency law.

Article 13 Access of Foreign Creditors to a Proceeding under British Insolvency Law

23.28

1

Subject to paragraph 2 of this article, foreign creditors have the same rights regarding the commencement of, and participation in, a proceeding under British insolvency law as creditors in Great Britain.

23.29

2

Paragraph 1 of this article does not affect the ranking of claims in a proceeding under British insolvency law, except that the claim of a foreign creditor shall not be given a lower priority than that of general unsecured claims solely because the holder of such a claim is a foreign creditor.

23.30

3

A claim may not be challenged solely on the grounds that it is a claim by a foreign tax or social security authority but such a claim may be challenged—

    (a)   on the ground that it is in whole or in part a penalty, or

    (b)   on any other ground that a claim might be rejected in a proceeding under British insolvency law.

Article 14 Notification to Foreign Creditors of a Proceeding under British Insolvency Law

23.31

1

Whenever under British insolvency law notification is to be given to creditors in Great Britain, such notification shall also be given to the known creditors that do not have addresses in Great Britain. The court may order that appropriate steps be taken with a view to notifying any creditor whose address is not yet known.

23.32

2

Such notification shall be made to the foreign creditors individually, unless—

(a) the court considers that under the circumstances some other form of notification would be more appropriate; or

(b) the notification to creditors in Great Britain is to be by advertisement only, in which case the notification to the known foreign creditors may be by advertisement in such foreign newspapers as the British insolvency officeholder considers most appropriate for ensuring that the content of the notification comes to the notice of the known foreign creditors.

23.33

3

When notification of a right to file a claim is to be given to foreign creditors, the notification shall—

(a) indicate a reasonable time period for filing claims and specify the place for their filing;

(b) indicate whether secured creditors need to file their secured claims; and

(c) contain any other information required to be included in such a notification to creditors pursuant to the law of Great Britain and the orders of the court.

23.34

4

In this article 'the court' means the court which has jurisdiction in relation to the particular proceeding under British insolvency law under which notification is to be given to creditors.

Chapter III
Recognition of a Foreign Proceeding and Relief

Article 15 Application for Recognition of a Foreign Proceeding

23.35

1

A foreign representative may apply to the court for recognition of the foreign proceeding in which the foreign representative has been appointed.

23.36

2

An application for recognition shall be accompanied by—

(a) a certified copy of the decision commencing the foreign proceeding and appointing the foreign representative; or

(b) a certificate from the foreign court affirming the existence of the foreign proceeding and of the appointment of the foreign representative; or

(c)   in the absence of evidence referred to in sub-paragraphs (a) and (b), any other evidence acceptable to the court of the existence of the foreign proceeding and of the appointment of the foreign representative.

23.37

3

An application for recognition shall also be accompanied by a statement identifying all foreign proceedings, proceedings under British insolvency law and section 426 requests in respect of the debtor that are known to the foreign representative.

23.38

4

The foreign representative shall provide the court with a translation into English of documents supplied in support of the application for recognition.

Article 16 Presumptions Concerning Recognition

23.39

1

If the decision or certificate referred to in paragraph 2 of article 15 indicates that the foreign proceeding is a proceeding within the meaning of sub-paragraph (i) of article 2 and that the foreign representative is a person or body within the meaning of sub-paragraph (j) of article 2, the court is entitled to so presume.

23.40

2

The court is entitled to presume that documents submitted in support of the application for recognition are authentic, whether or not they have been legalised.

23.41

3

In the absence of proof to the contrary, the debtor's registered office, or habitual residence in the case of an individual, is presumed to be the centre of the debtor's main interests.

Article 17 Decision to Recognise a Foreign Proceeding

23.42

1

Subject to article 6, a foreign proceeding shall be recognised if—
    (a)   it is a foreign proceeding within the meaning of sub-paragraph (i) of article 2;

(b)   the foreign representative applying for recognition is a person or body within the meaning of sub-paragraph (j) of article 2;

(c)   the application meets the requirements of paragraphs 2 and 3 of article 15; and

(d)   the application has been submitted to the court referred to in article 4.

23.43

2

The foreign proceeding shall be recognised—

(a)   as a foreign main proceeding if it is taking place in the State where the debtor has the centre of its main interests; or

(b)   as a foreign non-main proceeding if the debtor has an establishment within the meaning of sub-paragraph (e) of article 2 in the foreign State.

23.44

3

An application for recognition of a foreign proceeding shall be decided upon at the earliest possible time.

23.45

4

The provisions of articles 15 to 16, this article and article 18 do not prevent modification or termination of recognition if it is shown that the grounds for granting it were fully or partially lacking or have fully or partially ceased to exist and in such a case, the court may, on the application of the foreign representative or a person affected by recognition, or of its own motion, modify or terminate recognition, either altogether or for a limited time, on such terms and conditions as the court thinks fit.

Article 18 Subsequent Information

23.46

From the time of filing the application for recognition of the foreign proceeding, the foreign representative shall inform the court promptly of—

(a)   any substantial change in the status of the recognised foreign proceeding or the status of the foreign representative's appointment; and

(b)   any other foreign proceeding, proceeding under British insolvency law or section 426 request regarding the same debtor that becomes known to the foreign representative.

Article 19 Relief that may be granted upon Application for Recognition of a Foreign Proceeding

23.47

1

From the time of filing an application for recognition until the application is decided upon, the court may, at the request of the foreign representative, where relief is urgently needed to protect the assets of the debtor or the interests of the creditors, grant relief of a provisional nature, including—

    (a)   staying execution against the debtor's assets;

    (b)   entrusting the administration or realisation of all or part of the debtor's assets located in Great Britain to the foreign representative or another person designated by the court, in order to protect and preserve the value of assets that, by their nature or because of other circumstances, are perishable, susceptible to devaluation or otherwise in jeopardy; and

    (c)   any relief mentioned in paragraph 1 (c), (d) or (g) of article 21.

23.48

2

Unless extended under paragraph 1(f) of article 21, the relief granted under this article terminates when the application for recognition is decided upon.

23.49

3

The court may refuse to grant relief under this article if such relief would interfere with the administration of a foreign main proceeding.

Article 20 Effects of Recognition of a Foreign Main Proceeding

23.50

1

Upon recognition of a foreign proceeding that is a foreign main proceeding, subject to paragraph 2 of this article—

    (a)   commencement or continuation of individual actions or individual proceedings concerning the debtor's assets, rights, obligations or liabilities is stayed;

    (b)   execution against the debtor's assets is stayed; and

    (c)   the right to transfer, encumber or otherwise dispose of any assets of the debtor is suspended.

23.51

2

The stay and suspension referred to in paragraph 1 of this article shall be—

    (a)   the same in scope and effect as if the debtor, in the case of an individual, had been adjudged bankrupt under the Insolvency Act 1986 or had his estate sequestrated under the Bankruptcy (Scotland) Act 1985, or, in the case of a debtor other than an individual, had been made the subject of a winding-up order under the Insolvency Act 1986; and

    (b)   subject to the same powers of the court and the same prohibitions, limitations, exceptions and conditions as would apply under the law of Great Britain in such a case, and the provisions of paragraph 1 of this article shall be interpreted accordingly.

23.52

3

Without prejudice to paragraph 2 of this article, the stay and suspension referred to in paragraph 1 of this article, in particular, does not affect any right—
- (a) to take any steps to enforce security over the debtor's property;
- (b) to take any steps to repossess goods in the debtor's possession under a hire-purchase agreement;
- (c) exercisable under or by virtue of or in connection with the provisions referred to in article 1(4); or
- (d) of a creditor to set off its claim against a claim of the debtor,

being a right which would have been exercisable if the debtor, in the case of an individual, had been adjudged bankrupt under the Insolvency Act 1986 or had his estate sequestrated under the Bankruptcy (Scotland) Act 1985, or, in the case of a debtor other than an individual, had been made the subject of a winding-up order under the Insolvency Act 1986.

23.53

4

Paragraph 1(a) of this article does not affect the right to—
- (a) commence individual actions or proceedings to the extent necessary to preserve a claim against the debtor; or
- (b) commence or continue any criminal proceedings or any action or proceedings by a person or body having regulatory, supervisory or investigative functions of a public nature, being an action or proceedings brought in the exercise of those functions.

23.54

5

Paragraph 1 of this article does not affect the right to request or otherwise initiate the commencement of a proceeding under British insolvency law or the right to file claims in such a proceeding.

23.55

6

In addition to and without prejudice to any powers of the court under or by virtue of paragraph 2 of this article, the court may, on the application of the foreign representative or a person affected by the stay and suspension referred to in paragraph 1 of this article, or of its own motion, modify or terminate such stay and suspension or any part of it, either altogether or for a limited time, on such terms and conditions as the court thinks fit.

Article 21 Relief that may be Granted upon Recognition of a Foreign Proceeding

23.56

1

Upon recognition of a foreign proceeding, whether main or non-main, where necessary to protect the assets of the debtor or the interests of the creditors, the court may, at the request of the foreign representative, grant any appropriate relief, including—

(a) staying the commencement or continuation of individual actions or individual proceedings concerning the debtor's assets, rights, obligations or liabilities, to the extent they have not been stayed under paragraph 1(a) of article 20;

(b) staying execution against the debtor's assets to the extent it has not been stayed under paragraph 1(b) of article 20;

(c) suspending the right to transfer, encumber or otherwise dispose of any assets of the debtor to the extent this right has not been suspended under paragraph 1(c) of article 20;

(d) providing for the examination of witnesses, the taking of evidence or the delivery of information concerning the debtor's assets, affairs, rights, obligations or liabilities;

(e) entrusting the administration or realisation of all or part of the debtor's assets located in Great Britain to the foreign representative or another person designated by the court;

(f) extending relief granted under paragraph 1 of article 19; and

(g) granting any additional relief that may be available to a British insolvency officeholder under the law of Great Britain, including any relief provided under paragraph 43 of Schedule B1 to the Insolvency Act 1986.

23.57

2

Upon recognition of a foreign proceeding, whether main or non-main, the court may, at the request of the foreign representative, entrust the distribution of all or part of the debtor's assets located in Great Britain to the foreign representative or another person designated by the court, provided that the court is satisfied that the interests of creditors in Great Britain are adequately protected.

23.58

3

In granting relief under this article to a representative of a foreign non-main proceeding, the court must be satisfied that the relief relates to assets that, under the law of Great Britain, should be administered in the foreign non-main proceeding or concerns information required in that proceeding.

23.59

4

No stay under paragraph 1(a) of this article shall affect the right to commence or continue any criminal proceedings or any action or proceedings by a person or body having regulatory, supervisory or investigative functions of a public nature, being an action or proceedings brought in the exercise of those functions.

Article 22 Protection of Creditors and other Interested Persons

23.60

1

In granting or denying relief under article 19 or 21, or in modifying or terminating relief under paragraph 3 of this article or paragraph 6 of article 20, the court must be satisfied that the interests of the creditors (including any secured creditors or parties to hire-purchase agreements) and other interested persons, including if appropriate the debtor, are adequately protected.

23.61

2

The court may subject relief granted under article 19 or 21 to conditions it considers appropriate, including the provision by the foreign representative of security or caution for the proper performance of his functions.

23.62

3

The court may, at the request of the foreign representative or a person affected by relief granted under article 19 or 21, or of its own motion, modify or terminate such relief.

Article 23 Actions to Avoid Acts Detrimental to Creditors

23.63

1

Subject to paragraphs 6 and 9 of this article, upon recognition of a foreign proceeding, the foreign representative has standing to make an application to the court for an order under or in connection with sections 238, 239, 242, 243, 244, 245, 339, 340, 342A, 343, and 423 of the Insolvency Act 1986 and sections 34, 35, 36, 36A and 61 of the Bankruptcy (Scotland) Act 1985.

23.64

2

Where the foreign representative makes such an application ('an article 23 application'), the sections referred to in paragraph 1 of this article and sections 240, 241, 341, 342, 342B to 342F, 424 and 425 of the Insolvency Act 1986 and sections 36B and 36C of the Bankruptcy (Scotland) Act 1985 shall apply—

    (a)   whether or not the debtor, in the case of an individual, has been adjudged bankrupt or had his estate sequestrated, or, in the case of a debtor other than an individual, is being wound up or is in administration, under British insolvency law; and

    (b)   with the modifications set out in paragraph 3 of this article.

23.65

3

The modifications referred to in paragraph 2 of this article are as follows—

    (a)   for the purposes of sections 241(2A)(a) and 342(2A)(a) of the Insolvency Act 1986, a person has notice of the relevant proceedings if he has notice of the opening of the relevant foreign proceeding;

    (b)   for the purposes of sections 240(1) and 245(3) of that Act, the onset of insolvency shall be the date of the opening of the relevant foreign proceeding;

    (c)   the periods referred to in sections 244(2), 341(1)(a) to (c) and 343(2) of that Act shall be periods ending with the date of the opening of the relevant foreign proceeding;

    (d)   for the purposes of sections 242(3)(a), (3)(b) and 243(1) of that Act, the date on which the winding up of the company commences or it enters administration shall be the date of the opening of the relevant foreign proceeding; and

    (e)   for the purposes of sections 34(3)(a), (3)(b), 35(1)(c), 36(1)(a) and (1)(b) and 61(2) of the Bankruptcy (Scotland) Act 1985, the date of sequestration or granting of the trust deed shall be the date of the opening of the relevant foreign proceeding.

23.66

4

For the purposes of paragraph 3 of this article, the date of the opening of the foreign proceeding shall be determined in accordance with the law of the State in which the foreign proceeding is taking place, including any rule of law by virtue of which the foreign proceeding is deemed to have opened at an earlier time.

23.67

5

When the foreign proceeding is a foreign non-main proceeding, the court must be satisfied that the article 23 application relates to assets that, under the law of Great Britain, should be administered in the foreign non-main proceeding.

23.68

6

At any time when a proceeding under British insolvency law is taking place regarding the debtor—

(a) the foreign representative shall not make an article 23 application except with the permission of—
 (i) in the case of a proceeding under British insolvency law taking place in England and Wales, the High Court; or
 (ii) in the case of a proceeding under British insolvency law taking place in Scotland, the Court of Session; and
(b) references to 'the court' in paragraphs 1, 5 and 7 of this article are references to the court in which that proceeding is taking place.

23.69

7

On making an order on an article 23 application, the court may give such directions regarding the distribution of any proceeds of the claim by the foreign representative, as it thinks fit to ensure that the interests of creditors in Great Britain are adequately protected.

23.70

8

Nothing in this article affects the right of a British insolvency office-holder to make an application under or in connection with any of the provisions referred to in paragraph 1 of this article.

23.71

9

Nothing in paragraph 1 of this article shall apply in respect of any preference given, floating charge created, alienation, assignment or relevant contributions (within the meaning of section 342A(5) of the Insolvency Act 1986) made or other transaction entered into before the date on which this Law comes into force.

Article 24 Intervention by a Foreign Representative in Proceedings in Great Britain

23.72

Upon recognition of a foreign proceeding, the foreign representative may, provided the requirements of the law of Great Britain are met, intervene in any proceedings in which the debtor is a party.

Chapter IV
Cooperation with Foreign Courts and Foreign Representatives

Article 25 Cooperation and Direct Communication between a Court of Great Britain and Foreign Courts or Foreign Representatives

23.73

1

In matters referred to in paragraph 1 of article 1, the court may cooperate to the maximum extent possible with foreign courts or foreign representatives, either directly or through a British insolvency officeholder.

23.74

2

The court is entitled to communicate directly with, or to request information or assistance directly from, foreign courts or foreign representatives.

Article 26 Cooperation and Direct Communication between the British Insolvency Officeholder and Foreign Courts or Foreign Representatives

23.75

1

In matters referred to in paragraph 1 of article 1, a British insolvency officeholder shall to the extent consistent with his other duties under the law of Great Britain, in the exercise of his functions and subject to the supervision of the court, cooperate to the maximum extent possible with foreign courts or foreign representatives.

23.76

2

The British insolvency officeholder is entitled, in the exercise of his functions and subject to the supervision of the court, to communicate directly with foreign courts or foreign representatives.

Article 27 Forms of Cooperation

23.77

Cooperation referred to in articles 25 and 26 may be implemented by any appropriate means, including—
  (a)   appointment of a person to act at the direction of the court;
  (b)   communication of information by any means considered appropriate by the court;
  (c)   coordination of the administration and supervision of the debtor's assets and affairs;
  (d)   approval or implementation by courts of agreements concerning the coordination of proceedings;
  (e)   coordination of concurrent proceedings regarding the same debtor.

Chapter V
Concurrent Proceedings

Article 28 Commencement of a Proceeding Under British Insolvency Law after Recognition of a Foreign Main Proceeding

23.78

After recognition of a foreign main proceeding, the effects of a proceeding under British insolvency law in relation to the same debtor shall, insofar as the assets of that debtor are concerned, be restricted to assets that are located in Great Britain and, to the extent necessary to implement cooperation and coordination under articles 25, 26 and 27, to other assets of the debtor that, under the law of Great Britain, should be administered in that proceeding.

Article 29 Coordination of a Proceeding under British Insolvency Law and a Foreign Proceeding

23.79

Where a foreign proceeding and a proceeding under British insolvency law are taking place concurrently regarding the same debtor, the court may seek cooperation and coordination under articles 25, 26 and 27, and the following shall apply—

(a) when the proceeding in Great Britain is taking place at the time the application for recognition of the foreign proceeding is filed—

(i) any relief granted under article 19 or 21 must be consistent with the proceeding in Great Britain; and

(ii) if the foreign proceeding is recognised in Great Britain as a foreign main proceeding, article 20 does not apply;

(b) when the proceeding in Great Britain commences after the filing of the application for recognition of the foreign proceeding—

(i) any relief in effect under article 19 or 21 shall be reviewed by the court and shall be modified or terminated if inconsistent with the proceeding in Great Britain;

(ii) if the foreign proceeding is a foreign main proceeding, the stay and suspension referred to in paragraph 1 of article 20 shall be modified or terminated pursuant to paragraph 6 of article 20, if inconsistent with the proceeding in Great Britain; and

(iii) any proceedings brought by the foreign representative by virtue of paragraph 1 of article 23 before the proceeding in Great Britain commenced shall be reviewed by the court and the court may give such directions as it thinks fit regarding the continuance of those proceedings; and

(c) in granting, extending or modifying relief granted to a representative of a foreign non-main proceeding, the court must be satisfied that the relief relates to assets that, under the law of Great Britain, should be administered in the foreign non-main proceeding or concerns information required in that proceeding.

Article 30 Coordination of more than one Foreign Proceeding

23.80

In matters referred to in paragraph 1 of article 1, in respect of more than one foreign proceeding regarding the same debtor, the court may seek cooperation and coordination under articles 25, 26 and 27, and the following shall apply—

(a) any relief granted under article 19 or 21 to a representative of a foreign non-main proceeding after recognition of a foreign main proceeding must be consistent with the foreign main proceeding;

(b) if a foreign main proceeding is recognised after the filing of an application for recognition of a foreign non-main proceeding, any relief in effect under article 19 or 21 shall be reviewed by the court and shall be modified or terminated if inconsistent with the foreign main proceeding; and

(c) if, after recognition of a foreign non-main proceeding, another foreign non-main proceeding is recognised, the court shall grant, modify or terminate relief for the purpose of facilitating coordination of the proceedings.

Article 31 Presumption of Insolvency Based on Recognition of a Foreign Main Proceeding

23.81

In the absence of evidence to the contrary, recognition of a foreign main proceeding is, for the purpose of commencing a proceeding under British insolvency law, proof that the debtor is unable to pay its debts or, in relation to Scotland, is apparently insolvent within the meaning given to those expressions under British insolvency law.

Article 32 Rule of Payment in Concurrent Proceedings

23.82

Without prejudice to secured claims or rights in rem, a creditor who has received part payment in respect of its claim in a proceeding pursuant to a law relating to insolvency in a foreign State may not receive a payment for the same claim in a proceeding under British insolvency law regarding the same debtor, so long as the payment to the other creditors of the same class is proportionately less than the payment the creditor has already received.

SCHEDULE 2
Procedural Matters in England and Wales
Regulation 4

Part 1
Introductory Provisions

23.83

1 Interpretation

(1) In this Schedule—

'the 1986 Act' means the Insolvency Act 1986;

'article 21 relief application' means an application to the court by a foreign representative under article 21(1) or (2) of the Model Law for relief;

'business day' means any day other than a Saturday, a Sunday, Christmas Day, Good Friday or a day which is a bank holiday in England and Wales under or by virtue of the Banking and Financial Dealings Act 1971;

'CPR' means the Civil Procedure Rules 1998 and 'CPR' followed by a Part or rule by number means the Part or rule with that number in those Rules;

'enforcement officer' means an individual who is authorised to act as an enforcement officer under the Courts Act 2003;

'file in court' and 'file with the court' means deliver to the court for filing;

'the Gazette' means the London Gazette;

'interim relief application' means an application to the court by a foreign representative under article 19 of the Model Law for interim relief;

'main proceedings' means proceedings opened in accordance with Article 3(1) of the EC Insolvency Regulation and falling within the definition of insolvency proceedings in Article 2(a) of the EC Insolvency Regulation;

'member State liquidator' means a person falling within the definition of liquidator in Article 2(b) of the EC Insolvency Regulation appointed in proceedings to which it applies in a member State other than the United Kingdom;

'the Model Law' means the UNCITRAL Model Law as set out in Schedule 1 to these Regulations;

'modification or termination order' means an order by the court pursuant to its powers under the Model Law modifying or terminating recognition of a foreign proceeding, the stay and suspension referred to in article 20(1) or any part of it or any relief granted under article 19 or 21 of the Model Law;

'originating application' means an application to the court which is not an application in pending proceedings before the court;

'ordinary application' means any application to the court other than an originating application;

'practice direction' means a direction as to the practice and procedure of any court within the scope of the CPR;

'recognition application' means an application to the court by a foreign representative in accordance with article 15 of the Model Law for an order recognising the foreign proceeding in which he has been appointed;

'recognition order' means an order by the court recognising a proceeding the subject of a recognition application as a foreign main proceeding or foreign non-main proceeding, as appropriate;

'relevant company' means a company within the meaning of section 735(1) of the Companies Act 1985 or an unregistered company within the meaning of Part 5 of the 1986 Act which is subject to a requirement imposed by virtue of section 690A, 691(1) or 718 of the Companies Act 1985;

'review application' means an application to the court for a modification or termination order;

'the Rules' means the Insolvency Rules 1986 and 'Rule' followed by a number means the rule with that number in those Rules;

'secondary proceedings' means proceedings opened in accordance with Articles 3(2) and 3(3) of the EC Insolvency Regulation and falling within the definition of winding up proceedings in Article 2(c) of the EC Insolvency Regulation;

'territorial proceedings' means proceedings opened in accordance with Articles 3(2) and 3(4) of the EC Insolvency Regulation and falling within the definition of insolvency proceedings in Article 2(a) of the EC Insolvency Regulation.

(2) Expressions defined in the Model Law have the same meaning when used in this Schedule.

(3) In proceedings under these Regulations, 'Registrar' means—

(a)   a Registrar in Bankruptcy of the High Court; and

(b)   where the proceedings are in a district registry, the district judge.

(4) References to the 'venue' for any proceedings or attendance before the court, are to the time, date and place for the proceedings or attendance.

(5) References in this Schedule to ex parte hearings shall be construed as references to hearings without notice being served on any other party, and references to applications made ex parte as references to applications made without notice being served on any other party; and other references which include the expression 'ex parte' shall be similarly construed.

(6) References in this Schedule to a debtor who is of interest to the Financial Services Authority are references to a debtor who—

(a)   is, or has been, an authorised person within the meaning of section 31 of the Financial Services and Markets Act 2000 (authorised persons);

(b)   is, or has been, an appointed representative within the meaning of section 39 (exemption of appointed representatives) of that Act; or

(c)   is carrying on, or has carried on, a regulated activity in contravention of the general prohibition.

(7) In sub-paragraph (6) 'the general prohibition' has the meaning given by section 19 of the Financial Services and Markets Act 2000 and the reference to a 'regulated activity' must be construed in accordance with—

(a)   section 22 of that Act (classes of regulated activity and categories of investment);

(b)   any relevant order under that section; and

(c)   Schedule 2 to that Act (regulated activities).

(8) References in this Schedule to a numbered form are to the form that bears that number in Schedule 5.

Part 2
Applications to Court for Recognition of Foreign Proceedings

23.84

2 Affidavit in support of recognition application

A recognition application shall be in Form ML1 and shall be supported by an affidavit sworn by the foreign representative complying with paragraph 4.

23.85

3 Form and content of application

The application shall state the following matters—

(a) the name of the applicant and his address for service within England and Wales;

(b) the name of the debtor in respect of which the foreign proceeding is taking place;

(c) the name or names in which the debtor carries on business in the country where the foreign proceeding is taking place and in this country, if other than the name given under sub-paragraph (b);

(d) the principal or last known place of business of the debtor in Great Britain (if any) and, in the case of an individual, his usual or last known place of residence in Great Britain (if any);

(e) any registered number allocated to the debtor under the Companies Act 1985;

(f) brief particulars of the foreign proceeding in respect of which recognition is applied for, including the country in which it is taking place and the nature of the proceeding;

(g) that the foreign proceeding is a proceeding within the meaning of article 2(i) of the Model Law;

(h) that the applicant is a foreign representative within the meaning of article 2(j) of the Model Law;

(i) the address of the debtor's centre of main interests and, if different, the address of its registered office or habitual residence, as appropriate; and

(j) if the debtor does not have its centre of main interests in the country where the foreign proceeding is taking place, whether the debtor has an establishment within the meaning of article 2(e) of the Model Law in that country, and if so, its address.

23.86

4 Contents of affidavit in support

(1) There shall be attached to the application an affidavit in support which shall contain or have exhibited to it—

(a) the evidence and statement required under article 15(2) and (3) respectively of the Model Law;

(b) any other evidence which in the opinion of the applicant will assist the court in deciding whether the proceeding the subject of the application is a foreign proceeding within the meaning of article 2(i) of the Model Law and whether the applicant is a foreign representative within the meaning of article 2(j) of the Model Law;

(c) evidence that the debtor has its centre of main interests or an establishment, as the case may be, within the country where the foreign proceeding is taking place; and

(d) any other matters which in the opinion of the applicant will assist the court in deciding whether to make a recognition order.

(2) The affidavit shall state whether, in the opinion of the applicant, the EC Insolvency Regulation applies to any of the proceedings identified in

accordance with article 15(3) of the Model Law and, if so, whether those proceedings are main proceedings, secondary proceedings or territorial proceedings.

(3) The affidavit shall also have exhibited to it the translations required under article 15(4) of the Model Law and a translation in English of any other document exhibited to the affidavit which is in a language other than English.

(4) All translations referred to in sub-paragraph (3) must be certified by the translator as a correct translation.

23.87

5 The hearing and powers of court

(1) On hearing a recognition application the court may in addition to its powers under the Model Law to make a recognition order—
  (a) dismiss the application;
  (b) adjourn the hearing conditionally or unconditionally;
  (c) make any other order which the court thinks appropriate.

(2) If the court makes a recognition order, it shall be in Form ML2.

23.88

6 Notification of subsequent information

(1) The foreign representative shall set out any subsequent information required to be given to the court under article 18 of the Model Law in a statement which he shall attach to Form ML3 and file with the court.

(2) The statement shall include—
  (a) details of the information required to be given under article 18 of the Model Law; and
  (b) in the case of any proceedings required to be notified to the court under that article, a statement as to whether, in the opinion of the foreign representative, any of those proceedings are main proceedings, secondary proceedings or territorial proceedings under the EC Insolvency Regulation.

(3) The foreign representative shall send a copy of the Form ML3 and attached statement filed with the court to the following—
  (a) the debtor; and
  (b) those persons referred to in paragraph 26(3).

Part 3
Applications for Relief Under the Model Law

23.89

7 Application for interim relief—affidavit in support

(1) An interim relief application must be supported by an affidavit sworn by the foreign representative stating—
  (a) the grounds on which it is proposed that the interim relief applied for should be granted;

(b)   details of any proceeding under British insolvency law taking place in relation to the debtor;

(c)   whether, to the foreign representative's knowledge, an administrative receiver or receiver or manager of the debtor's property is acting in relation to the debtor;

(d)   an estimate of the value of the assets of the debtor in England and Wales in respect of which relief is applied for;

(e)   whether, to the best of the knowledge and belief of the foreign representative, the interests of the debtor's creditors (including any secured creditors or parties to hire-purchase agreements) and any other interested parties, including if appropriate the debtor, will be adequately protected;

(f)   whether, to the best of the foreign representative's knowledge and belief, the grant of any of the relief applied for would interfere with the administration of a foreign main proceeding; and

(g)   all other matters that in the opinion of the foreign representative will assist the court in deciding whether or not it is appropriate to grant the relief applied for.

23.90

8 Service of interim relief application not required

Unless the court otherwise directs, it shall not be necessary to serve the interim relief application on, or give notice of it to, any person.

23.91

9 The hearing and powers of court

On hearing an interim relief application the court may in addition to its powers under the Model Law to make an order granting interim relief under article 19 of the Model Law—

(a)   dismiss the application;

(b)   adjourn the hearing conditionally or unconditionally;

(c)   make any other order which the court thinks appropriate.

23.92

10 Application for relief under article 21 of the Model Law—affidavit in support

An article 21 relief application must be supported by an affidavit sworn by the foreign representative stating—

(a)   the grounds on which it is proposed that the relief applied for should be granted;

(b)   an estimate of the value of the assets of the debtor in England and Wales in respect of which relief is applied for;

(c)   in the case of an application by a foreign representative who is or believes that he is a representative of a foreign non-main proceeding, the reasons why the applicant believes that the relief relates to assets that, under the law of Great Britain, should be administered in the foreign non-main proceeding or concerns information required in that proceeding;

(d) whether, to the best of the knowledge and belief of the foreign representative, the interests of the debtor's creditors (including any secured creditors or parties to hire-purchase agreements) and any other interested parties, including if appropriate the debtor, will be adequately protected; and

(e) all other matters that in the opinion of the foreign representative will assist the court in deciding whether or not it is appropriate to grant the relief applied for.

23.93

11 The hearing and powers of court

On hearing an article 21 relief application the court may in addition to its powers under the Model Law to make an order granting relief under article 21 of the Model Law—

(a) dismiss the application;

(b) adjourn the hearing conditionally or unconditionally;

(c) make any other order which the court thinks appropriate.

Part 4
Replacement of Foreign Representative

23.94

12 Application for confirmation of status of replacement foreign representative

(1) This paragraph applies where following the making of a recognition order the foreign representative dies or for any other reason ceases to be the foreign representative in the foreign proceeding in relation to the debtor.

(2) In this paragraph 'the former foreign representative' shall mean the foreign representative referred to in sub-paragraph (1).

(3) If a person has succeeded the former foreign representative or is otherwise holding office as foreign representative in the foreign proceeding in relation to the debtor, that person may apply to the court for an order confirming his status as replacement foreign representative for the purpose of proceedings under these Regulations.

23.95

13 Contents of application and affidavit in support

(1) An application under paragraph 12(3) shall in addition to the matters required to be stated by paragraph 19(2) state the following matters—

(a) the name of the replacement foreign representative and his address for service within England and Wales;

(b) details of the circumstances in which the former foreign representative ceased to be foreign representative in the foreign proceeding in relation to the debtor (including the date on which he ceased to be the foreign representative);

   (c)   details of his own appointment as replacement foreign repre-
       sentative in the foreign proceeding (including the date of that
       appointment).

(2) The application shall be accompanied by an affidavit in support sworn
by the applicant which shall contain or have attached to it—
   (a)   a certificate from the foreign court affirming—
       (i)   the cessation of the appointment of the former foreign
           representative as foreign representative; and
      (ii)   the appointment of the applicant as the foreign representa-
           tive in the foreign proceeding; or
   (b)   in the absence of such a certificate, any other evidence acceptable
       to the court of the matters referred to in paragraph (a); and
   (c)   a translation in English of any document exhibited to the
       affidavit which is in a language other than English.

(3) All translations referred to in paragraph (c) must be certified by the
translator as a correct translation.

23.96

14 The hearing and powers of court

(1) On hearing an application under paragraph 12(3) the court may—
   (a)   make an order confirming the status of the replacement foreign
       representative as foreign representative for the purpose of pro-
       ceedings under these Regulations;
   (b)   dismiss the application;
   (c)   adjourn the hearing conditionally or unconditionally;
   (d)   make an interim order;
   (e)   make any other order which the court thinks appropriate, includ-
       ing in particular an order making such provision as the court
       thinks fit with respect to matters arising in connection with the
       replacement of the foreign representative.

(2) If the court dismisses the application, it may also if it thinks fit make
an order terminating recognition of the foreign proceeding and—
   (a)   such an order may include such provision as the court thinks fit
       with respect to matters arising in connection with the termina-
       tion; and
   (b)   paragraph 15 shall not apply to such an order.

Part 5
Reviews of Court Orders

23.97

15 Reviews of court orders—where court makes order of its own motion

(1) The court shall not of its own motion make a modification or
termination order unless the foreign representative and the debtor have
either—
   (a)   had an opportunity of being heard on the question; or
   (b)   consented in writing to such an order.

(2) Where the foreign representative or the debtor desires to be heard on the question of such an order, the court shall give all relevant parties notice of a venue at which the question will be considered and may give directions as to the issues on which it requires evidence.

(3) For the purposes of sub-paragraph (2), all relevant parties means the foreign representative, the debtor and any other person who appears to the court to have an interest justifying his being given notice of the hearing.

(4) If the court makes a modification or termination order, the order may include such provision as the court thinks fit with respect to matters arising in connection with the modification or termination.

23.98

16 Review application—affidavit in support

A review application must be supported by an affidavit sworn by the applicant stating—

    (a)   the grounds on which it is proposed that the relief applied for should be granted;

    (b)   whether, to the best of the knowledge and belief of the applicant, the interests of the debtor's creditors (including any secured creditors or parties to hire-purchase agreements) and any other interested parties, including if appropriate the debtor, will be adequately protected; and

    (c)   all other matters that in the opinion of the applicant will assist the court in deciding whether or not it is appropriate to grant the relief applied for.

23.99

17 Hearing of review application and powers of the court

On hearing a review application, the court may in addition to its powers under the Model Law to make a modification or termination order—

    (a)   dismiss the application;

    (b)   adjourn the hearing conditionally or unconditionally;

    (c)   make an interim order;

    (c)   make any other order which the court thinks appropriate, including an order making such provision as the court thinks fit with respect to matters arising in connection with the modification or termination.

Part 6
Court Procedure and Practice with Regard to Principal Applications and Orders

23.100

18 Preliminary and interpretation

(1) This Part applies to—

    (a)   any of the following applications made to the court under these Regulations—

      (i)   a recognition application;
      (ii) an article 21 relief application;
      (iii) an application under paragraph 12(3) for an order confirming the status of a replacement foreign representative;
      (iv) a review application; and

  (b) any of the following orders made by the court under these Regulations—
      (i)   a recognition order;
      (ii) an order granting interim relief under article 19 of the Model Law;
      (iii) an order granting relief under article 21 of the Model Law;
      (iv) an order confirming the status of a replacement foreign representative; and
      (v) a modification or termination order.

23.101

19 Form and contents of application

(1) Subject to sub-paragraph (4) every application to which this Part applies shall be an ordinary application and shall be in Form ML5.

(2) Each application shall be in writing and shall state—
  (a) the names of the parties;
  (b) the nature of the relief or order applied for or the directions sought from the court;
  (c) the names and addresses of the persons (if any) on whom it is intended to serve the application;
  (d) the names and addresses of all those persons on whom these Regulations require the application to be served (so far as known to the applicant); and
  (e) the applicant's address for service.

(3) The application must be signed by the applicant if he is acting in person, or, when he is not so acting, by or on behalf of his solicitor.

(4) This paragraph does not apply to a recognition application.

23.102

20 Filing of application

(1) The application (and all supporting documents) shall be filed with the court, with a sufficient number of copies for service and use as provided by paragraph 21(2).

(2) Each of the copies filed shall have applied to it the seal of the court and be issued to the applicant; and on each copy there shall be endorsed the date and time of filing.

(3) The court shall fix a venue for the hearing of the application and this also shall be endorsed on each copy of the application issued under sub-paragraph (2).

23.103

21 Service of the application

(1) In sub-paragraph (2), references to the application are to a sealed copy of the application issued by the court together with any affidavit in support of it and any documents exhibited to the affidavit.

(2) Unless the court otherwise directs, the application shall be served on the following persons, unless they are the applicant—

    (a)   on the foreign representative;

    (b)   on the debtor;

    (c)   if a British insolvency officeholder is acting in relation to the debtor, on him;

    (d)   if any person has been appointed an administrative receiver of the debtor or, to the knowledge of the foreign representative, as a receiver or manager of the property of the debtor in England and Wales, on him;

    (e)   if a member State liquidator has been appointed in main proceedings in relation to the debtor, on him;

    (f)   if to the knowledge of the foreign representative a foreign representative has been appointed in any other foreign proceeding regarding the debtor, on him;

    (g)   if there is pending in England and Wales a petition for the winding up or bankruptcy of the debtor, on the petitioner;

    (h)   on any person who to the knowledge of the foreign representative is or may be entitled to appoint an administrator of the debtor under paragraph 14 of Schedule B1 to the 1986 Act (appointment of administrator by holder of qualifying floating charge); and

    (i)   if the debtor is a debtor who is of interest to the Financial Services Authority, on that Authority.

23.104

22 Manner in which service to be effected

(1) Service of the application in accordance with paragraph 21(2) shall be effected by the applicant, or his solicitor, or by a person instructed by him or his solicitor, not less than 5 business days before the date fixed for the hearing.

(2) Service shall be effected by delivering the documents to a person's proper address or in such other manner as the court may direct.

(3) A person's proper address is any which he has previously notified as his address for service within England and Wales; but if he has not notified any such address or if for any reason service at such address is not practicable, service may be effected as follows—

    (a)   (subject to sub-paragraph (4)) in the case of a company incorporated in England and Wales, by delivery to its registered office;

    (b)   in the case of any other person, by delivery to his usual or last known address or principal place of business in Great Britain.

(4) If delivery to a company's registered office is not practicable, service may be effected by delivery to its last known principal place of business in Great Britain.

(5) Delivery of documents to any place or address may be made by leaving them there or sending them by first class post in accordance with the provisions of paragraphs 70 and 75(1).

23.105

23 Proof of service

(1) Service of the application shall be verified by an affidavit of service in Form ML6, specifying the date on which, and the manner in which, service was effected.

(2) The affidavit of service, with a sealed copy of the application exhibited to it, shall be filed with the court as soon as reasonably practicable after service, and in any event not less than 1 business day before the hearing of the application.

23.106

24 In case of urgency

Where the case is one of urgency, the court may (without prejudice to its general power to extend or abridge time limits)—
- (a) hear the application immediately, either with or without notice to, or the attendance of, other parties; or
- (b) authorise a shorter period of service than that provided for by paragraph 22(1),

and any such application may be heard on terms providing for the filing or service of documents, or the carrying out of other formalities, as the court thinks fit.

23.107

25 The hearing

(1) At the hearing of the application, the applicant and any of the following persons (not being the applicant) may appear or be represented—
- (a) the foreign representative;
- (b) the debtor and, in the case of any debtor other than an individual, any one or more directors or other officers of the debtor, including—
  - (i) where applicable, any person registered under Part 23 of the Companies Act 1985 as authorised to represent the debtor in respect of its business in England and Wales;
  - (ii) in the case of a debtor which is a partnership, any person who is an officer of the partnership within the meaning of article 2 of the Insolvent Partnerships Order 1994;
- (c) if a British insolvency officeholder is acting in relation to the debtor, that person;
- (d) if any person has been appointed an administrative receiver of the debtor or as a receiver or manager of the property of the debtor in England and Wales, that person;
- (e) if a member State liquidator has been appointed in main proceedings in relation to the debtor, that person;
- (f) if a foreign representative has been appointed in any other foreign proceeding regarding the debtor, that person;
- (g) any person who has presented a petition for the winding up or bankruptcy of the debtor in England and Wales;

(h)   any person who is or may be entitled to appoint an administrator of the debtor under paragraph 14 of Schedule B1 to the 1986 Act (appointment of administrator by holder of qualifying floating charge);

(i)   if the debtor is a debtor who is of interest to the Financial Services Authority, that Authority; and

(j)   with the permission of the court, any other person who appears to have an interest justifying his appearance.

23.108

26 Notification and advertisement of order

(1) If the court makes any of the orders referred to in paragraph 18(1)(b), it shall as soon as reasonably practicable send two sealed copies of the order to the foreign representative.

(2) The foreign representative shall send a sealed copy of the order as soon as reasonably practicable to the debtor.

(3) The foreign representative shall, as soon as reasonably practicable after the date of the order give notice of the making of the order—

(a)   if a British insolvency officeholder is acting in relation to the debtor, to him;

(b)   if any person has been appointed an administrative receiver of the debtor or, to the knowledge of the foreign representative, as a receiver or manager of the property of the debtor, to him;

(c)   if a member State liquidator has been appointed in main proceedings in relation to the debtor, to him;

(d)   if to his knowledge a foreign representative has been appointed in any other foreign proceeding regarding the debtor, that person;

(e)   if there is pending in England and Wales a petition for the winding up or bankruptcy of the debtor, to the petitioner;

(f)   to any person who to his knowledge is or may be entitled to appoint an administrator of the debtor under paragraph 14 of Schedule B1 to the 1986 Act (appointment of administrator by holder of qualifying floating charge);

(g)   if the debtor is a debtor who is of interest to the Financial Services Authority, to that Authority;

(h)   to such other persons as the court may direct.

(4) In the case of an order recognising a foreign proceeding in relation to the debtor as a foreign main proceeding, or an order under article 19 or 21 of the Model Law staying execution, distress or other legal process against the debtor's assets, the foreign representative shall also, as soon as reasonably practicable after the date of the order give notice of the making of the order—

(a)   to any enforcement officer or other officer who to his knowledge is charged with an execution or other legal process against the debtor or its property; and

(b)   to any person who to his knowledge is distraining against the debtor or its property.

(5) In the application of sub-paragraphs (3) and (4) the references to property shall be taken as references to property situated within England and Wales.

(6) Where the debtor is a relevant company, the foreign representative shall send notice of the making of the order to the registrar of companies before the end of the period of 5 business days beginning with the date of the order. The notice to the registrar of companies shall be in Form ML7.

(7) The foreign representative shall advertise the making of the following orders once in the Gazette and once in such newspaper as he thinks most appropriate for ensuring that the making of the order comes to the notice of the debtor's creditors—
  (a) a recognition order;
  (b) an order confirming the status of a replacement foreign representative; and
  (c) a modification or termination order which modifies or terminates recognition of a foreign proceeding,
and the advertisement shall be in Form ML8.

23.109

27 Adjournment of hearing; directions

(1) This paragraph applies in any case where the court exercises its power to adjourn the hearing of the application.

(2) The court may at any time give such directions as it thinks fit as to—
  (a) service or notice of the application on or to any person, whether in connection with the venue of a resumed hearing or for any other purpose;
  (b) the procedure on the application;
  (c) the manner in which any evidence is to be adduced at a resumed hearing and in particular as to—
      (i)   the taking of evidence wholly or in part by affidavit or orally;
      (ii) the cross-examination on the hearing in court or in chambers, of any deponents to affidavits;
  (d) the matters to be dealt with in evidence.

Part 7
Applications to the Chief Land Registrar

23.110

28 Applications to Chief Land Registrar following court orders

(1) Where the court makes any order in proceedings under these Regulations which is capable of giving rise to an application or applications under the Land Registration Act 2002, the foreign representative shall, as soon as reasonably practicable after the making of the order or at the appropriate time, make the appropriate application or applications to the Chief Land Registrar.

(2) In sub-paragraph (1) an appropriate application is—
  (a) in any case where—

> (i) a recognition order in respect of a foreign main proceeding or an order suspending the right to transfer, encumber or otherwise dispose of any assets of the debtor is made, and
>
> (ii) the debtor is the registered proprietor of a registered estate or registered charge and holds it for his sole benefit,
>
> an application under section 43 of the Land Registration Act 2002 for a restriction of the kind referred to in sub-paragraph (3) to be entered in the relevant registered title; and
>
> (b) in any other case, an application under the Land Registration Act 2002 for such an entry in the register as shall be necessary to reflect the effect of the court order under these Regulations.
>
> (3) The restriction referred to in sub-paragraph (2)(a) is a restriction to the effect that no disposition of the registered estate or registered charge (as appropriate) by the registered proprietor of that estate or charge is to be completed by registration within the meaning of section 27 of the Land Registration Act 2002 except under a further order of the court.

Part 8
Misfeasance

23.111

29 Misfeasance by foreign representative

(1) The court may examine the conduct of a person who—

    (a) is or purports to be the foreign representative in relation to a debtor; or

    (b) has been or has purported to be the foreign representative in relation to a debtor.

(2) An examination under this paragraph may be held only on the application of—

    (a) a British insolvency officeholder acting in relation to the debtor;

    (b) a creditor of the debtor; or

    (c) with the permission of the court, any other person who appears to have an interest justifying an application.

(3) An application under sub-paragraph (2) must allege that the foreign representative—

    (a) has misapplied or retained money or other property of the debtor;

    (b) has become accountable for money or other property of the debtor;

    (c) has breached a fiduciary or other duty in relation to the debtor; or

    (d) has been guilty of misfeasance.

(4) On an examination under this paragraph into a person's conduct the court may order him—

    (a) to repay, restore or account for money or property;

    (b) to pay interest;

    (c) to contribute a sum to the debtor's property by way of compensation for breach of duty or misfeasance.

(4) In sub-paragraph (3) 'foreign representative' includes a person who purports or has purported to be a foreign representative in relation to a debtor.

Part 9
General Provision as to Court Procedure and Practice

23.112

30 Principal court rules and practice to apply with modifications

(1) The CPR and the practice and procedure of the High Court (including any practice direction) shall apply to proceedings under these Regulations in the High Court with such modifications as may be necessary for the purpose of giving effect to the provisions of these Regulations and in the case of any conflict between any provision of the CPR and the provisions of these Regulations, the latter shall prevail.

(2) All proceedings under these Regulations shall be allocated to the multi-track for which CPR Part 29 (the multi-track) makes provision, and accordingly those provisions of the CPR which provide for allocation questionnaires and track allocation shall not apply.

23.113

31 Applications other than the principal applications – preliminary

Paragraphs 32 to 37 of this Part apply to any application made to the court under these Regulations, except any of the applications referred to in paragraph 18(1)(a).

23.114

32 Form and contents of application

(1) Every application shall be in the form appropriate to the application concerned. Forms ML4 and ML5 shall be used for an originating application and an ordinary application respectively under these Regulations.

(2) Each application shall be in writing and shall state—
  (a) the names of the parties;
  (b) the nature of the relief or order applied for or the directions sought from the court;
  (c) the names and addresses of the persons (if any) on whom it is intended to serve the application or that no person is intended to be served;
  (d) where these Regulations require that notice of the application is to be given to specified persons, the names and addresses of all those persons (so far as known to the applicant); and
  (e) the applicant's address for service.

(3) An originating application shall set out the grounds on which the applicant claims to be entitled to the relief or order sought.

(4) The application must be signed by the applicant if he is acting in person or, when he is not so acting, by or on behalf of his solicitor.

23.115

33 Filling and service of application

(1) The application shall be filed in court, accompanied by one copy and a number of additional copies equal to the number of persons who are to be served with the application.

(2) Subject as follows in this paragraph and in paragraph 34, or unless the court otherwise orders, upon the presentation of the documents mentioned in sub-paragraph (1), the court shall fix a venue for the application to be heard.

(3) Unless the court otherwise directs, the applicant shall serve a sealed copy of the application, endorsed with the venue of the hearing, on the respondent named in the application (or on each respondent if more than one).

(4) The court may give any of the following directions—

    (a)   that the application be served upon persons other than those specified by the relevant provision of these Regulations;

    (b)   that the giving of notice to any person may be dispensed with;

    (c)   that notice be given in some way other than that specified in sub-paragraph (3).

(5) Subject to sub-paragraph (6), the application must be served at least 10 business days before the date fixed for the hearing.

(6) Where the case is one of urgency, the court may (without prejudice to its general power to extend or abridge time limits)—

    (a)   hear the application immediately, either with or without notice to, or the attendance of, other parties; or

    (b)   authorise a shorter period of service than that provided for by sub-paragraph (5);

and any such application may be heard on terms providing for the filing or service of documents, or the carrying out of other formalities, as the court thinks fit.

23.116

34 Other hearings *ex parte*

(1) Where the relevant provisions of these Regulations do not require service of the application on, or notice of it to be given to, any person, the court may hear the application *ex parte*.

(2) Where the application is properly made *ex parte*, the court may hear it forthwith, without fixing a venue as required by paragraph 33(2).

(3) Alternatively, the court may fix a venue for the application to be heard, in which case paragraph 33 applies (so far as relevant).

23.117

35 Use of affidavit evidence

(1) In any proceedings evidence may be given by affidavit unless the court otherwise directs; but the court may, on the application of any party, order the attendance for cross-examination of the person making the affidavit.

(2) Where, after such an order has been made, the person in question does not attend, his affidavit shall not be used in evidence without the permission of the court.

23.118

36 Filling and service of affidavits

(1) Unless the court otherwise allows—
  (a)   if the applicant intends to rely at the first hearing on affidavit evidence, he shall file the affidavit or affidavits (if more than one) in court and serve a copy or copies on the respondent, not less than 10 business days before the date fixed for the hearing; and
  (b)   where a respondent to an application intends to oppose it and to rely for that purpose on affidavit evidence, he shall file the affidavit or affidavits (if more than one) in court and serve a copy or copies on the applicant, not less than 5 business days before the date fixed for the hearing.

(2) Any affidavit may be sworn by the applicant or by the respondent or by some other person possessing direct knowledge of the subject matter of the application.

23.119

37 Adjournment of hearings; directions

The court may adjourn the hearing of an application on such terms (if any) as it thinks fit and in the case of such an adjournment paragraph 27(2) shall apply.

23.120

38 Transfer of proceedings within the High Court

(1) The High Court may, having regard to the criteria in CPR rule 30.3(2), order proceedings in the Royal Courts of Justice or a district registry, or any part of such proceedings (such as an application made in the proceedings), to be transferred—
  (a)   from the Royal Courts of Justice to a district registry; or
  (b)   from a district registry to the Royal Courts of Justice or to another district registry.

(2) The High Court may order proceedings before a district registry for the detailed assessment of costs to be transferred to another district registry if it is satisfied that the proceedings could be more conveniently or fairly taken in that other district registry.

(3) An application for an order under sub-paragraph (1) or (2) must, if the claim is proceeding in a district registry, be made to that registry.

(4) A transfer of proceedings under this paragraph may be ordered—
  (a)   by the court of its own motion; or
  (b)   on the application of a person appearing to the court to have an interest in the proceedings.

(5) Where the court orders proceedings to be transferred, the court from which they are to be transferred must give notice of the transfer to all the parties.

(6) An order made before the transfer of the proceedings shall not be affected by the order to transfer.

23.121

39 Transfer of proceedings – actions to avoid act detrimental to creditors

(1) If—
- (a) in accordance with article 23(6) of the Model Law, the court grants a foreign representative permission to make an application in accordance with paragraph 1 of that article; and
- (b) the relevant proceedings under British insolvency law taking place regarding the debtor are taking place in the county court,

the court may also order those proceedings to be transferred to the High Court.

(2) Where the court makes an order transferring proceedings under sub-paragraph (1)—
- (a) it shall send sealed copies of the order to the county court from which the proceedings are to be transferred, and to the official receivers attached to that court and the High Court respectively; and
- (b) the county court shall send the file of the proceedings to the High Court.

(3) Following compliance with this paragraph, if the official receiver attached to the court to which the proceedings are transferred is not already, by virtue of directions given by the Secretary of State under section 399(6)(a) of the 1986 Act, the official receiver in relation to those proceedings, he becomes, in relation to those proceedings, the official receiver in place of the official receiver attached to the other court concerned.

23.122

40 Shorthand writers

(1) The judge may in writing nominate one or more persons to be official shorthand writers to the court.

(2) The court may, at any time in the course of proceedings under these Regulations, appoint a shorthand writer to take down the evidence of a person examined in pursuance of a court order under article 19 or 21 of the Model Law.

(3) The remuneration of a shorthand writer appointed in proceedings under these Regulations shall be paid by the party at whose instance the appointment was made or otherwise as the court may direct.

(4) Any question arising as to the rates of remuneration payable under this paragraph shall be determined by the court in its discretion.

23.123

41 Enforcement procedure

In any proceedings under these Regulations, orders of the court may be enforced in the same manner as a judgment to the same effect.

23.124

42 Title of proceedings

(1) Every proceeding under these Regulations shall, with any necessary additions, be intituled 'IN THE MATTER OF ... (naming the debtor to which the proceedings relate) AND IN THE MATTER OF THE CROSS-BORDER INSOLVENCY REGULATIONS 2006'.

(2) Sub-paragraph (1) shall not apply in respect of any form prescribed under these Regulations.

23.125

43 Court records

The court shall keep records of all proceedings under these Regulations, and shall cause to be entered in the records the taking of any step in the proceedings, and such decisions of the court in relation thereto, as the court thinks fit.

23.126

44 Inspection of records

(1) Subject as follows, the court's records of proceedings under these Regulations shall be open to inspection by any person.

(2) If in the case of a person applying to inspect the records the Registrar is not satisfied as to the propriety of the purpose for which inspection is required, he may refuse to allow it. That person may then apply forthwith and *ex parte* to the judge, who may refuse the inspection or allow it on such terms as he thinks fit.

(3) The decision of the judge under sub-paragraph (2) is final.

23.127

45 File of court proceedings

(1) In respect of all proceedings under these Regulations, the court shall open and maintain a file for each case; and (subject to directions of the Registrar) all documents relating to such proceedings shall be placed on the relevant file.

(2) No proceedings under these Regulations shall be filed in the Central Office of the High Court.

23.128

46 Right to inspect the file

(1) In the case of any proceedings under these Regulations, the following have the right, at all reasonable times, to inspect the court's file of the proceedings—
  (a) the Secretary of State;
  (b) the person who is the foreign representative in relation to the proceedings;
  (c) if a foreign representative has been appointed in any other foreign proceeding regarding the debtor to which the proceedings under these Regulations relate, that person;

(d)   if a British insolvency officeholder is acting in relation to the debtor to which the proceedings under these Regulations relate, that person;

(e)   any person stating himself in writing to be a creditor of the debtor to which the proceedings under these Regulations relate;

(f)   if a member State liquidator has been appointed in relation to the debtor to which the proceedings under these Regulations relate, that person; and

(g)   the debtor to which the proceedings under these Regulations relate, or, if that debtor is a company, corporation or partnership, every person who is, or at any time has been—

    (i)   a director or officer of the debtor;

    (ii) a member of the debtor; or

    (iii) where applicable, a person registered under Part 23 of the Companies Act 1985 as authorised to represent the debtor in respect of its business in England and Wales.

(2) The right of inspection conferred as above on any person may be exercised on his behalf by a person properly authorised by him.

(3) Any person may, by leave of the court, inspect the file.

(4) The right of inspection conferred by this paragraph is not exercisable in the case of documents, or parts of documents, as to which the court directs (either generally or specially) that they are not to be made open to inspection without the court's permission.

An application for a direction of the court under this sub-paragraph may be made by the foreign representative or by any party appearing to the court to have an interest.

(5) If, for the purpose of powers conferred by the 1986 Act or the Rules, the Secretary of State or the official receiver wishes to inspect the file of any proceedings under these Regulations, and requests the transmission of the file, the court shall comply with such request (unless the file is for the time being in use for the court's purposes).

(6) Paragraph 44(2) and (3) apply in respect of the court's file of any proceedings under these Regulations as they apply in respect of court records.

(7) Where these Regulations confer a right for any person to inspect documents on the court's file of proceedings, the right includes that of taking copies of those documents on payment of the fee chargeable under any order made under section 92 of the Courts Act 2003.

23.129

47 Copies of court orders

(1) In any proceedings under these Regulations, any person who under paragraph 46 has a right to inspect documents on the court file also has the right to require the foreign representative in relation to those proceedings to furnish him with a copy of any court order in the proceedings.

(2) Sub-paragraph (1) does not apply if a copy of the court order has been served on that person or notice of the making of the order has been given to that person under other provisions of these Regulations.

23.130

48 Filing of Gazette notices and advertisements

(1) In any court in which proceedings under these Regulations are pending, an officer of the court shall file a copy of every issue of the Gazette which contains an advertisement relating to those proceedings.

(2) Where there appears in a newspaper an advertisement relating to proceedings under these Regulations pending in any court, the person inserting the advertisement shall file a copy of it in that court.

The copy of the advertisement shall be accompanied by, or have endorsed on it, such particulars as are necessary to identify the proceedings and the date of the advertisement's appearance.

(3) An officer of any court in which proceedings under these Regulations are pending shall from time to time file a memorandum giving the dates of, and other particulars relating to, any notice published in the Gazette, and any newspaper advertisements, which relate to proceedings so pending.

The officer's memorandum is prima facie evidence that any notice or advertisement mentioned in it was duly inserted in the issue of the newspaper or the Gazette which is specified in the memorandum.

23.131

49 Persons incapable of managing their affairs – introductory

(1) Paragraphs 50 to 52 apply where in proceedings under these Regulations it appears to the court that a person affected by the proceedings is one who is incapable of managing and administering his property and affairs either—
   (a) by reason of mental disorder within the meaning of the Mental Health Act 1983; or
   (b) due to physical affliction or disability.

(2) The person concerned is referred to as 'the incapacitated person'.

23.132

50 Appointment of another person to act

(1) The court may appoint such person as it thinks fit to appear for, represent or act for the incapacitated person.

(2) The appointment may be made either generally or for the purpose of any particular application or proceeding, or for the exercise of particular rights or powers which the incapacitated person might have exercised but for his incapacity.

(3) The court may make the appointment either of its own motion or on application by—
   (a) a person who has been appointed by a court in the United Kingdom or elsewhere to manage the affairs of, or to represent, the incapacitated person; or

    (b)   any relative or friend of the incapacitated person who appears to the court to be a proper person to make the application; or

    (c)   in any case where the incapacitated person is the debtor, the foreign representative.

(4) Application under sub-paragraph (3) may be made *ex parte*; but the court may require such notice of the application as it thinks necessary to be given to the person alleged to be incapacitated, or any other person, and may adjourn the hearing of the application to enable the notice to be given.

23.133

51 Affidavit in support of application

An application under paragraph 50(3) shall be supported by an affidavit of a registered medical practitioner as to the mental or physical condition of the incapacitated person.

23.134

52 Service of notices following appointment

Any notice served on, or sent to, a person appointed under paragraph 50 has the same effect as if it had been served on, or given to, the incapacitated person.

23.135

53 Rights of audience

Rights of audience in proceedings under these Regulations are the same as obtain in proceedings under British insolvency law.

23.136

54 Right of attendance

(1) Subject as follows, in proceedings under these Regulations, any person stating himself in writing, in records kept by the court for that purpose, to be a creditor of the debtor to which the proceedings relate, is entitled at his own cost, to attend in court or in chambers at any stage of the proceedings.

(2) Attendance may be by the person himself, or his solicitor.

(3) A person so entitled may request the court in writing to give him notice of any step in the proceedings; and, subject to his paying the costs involved and keeping the court informed as to his address, the court shall comply with the request.

(4) If the court is satisfied that the exercise by a person of his rights under this paragraph has given rise to costs for the estate of the debtor which would not otherwise have been incurred and ought not, in the circumstances, to fall on that estate, it may direct that the costs be paid by the person concerned, to an amount specified.

The rights of that person under this paragraph shall be in abeyance so long as those costs are not paid.

(5) The court may appoint one or more persons to represent the creditors of the debtor to have the rights conferred by this paragraph, instead of the rights being exercised by any or all of them individually.

If two or more persons are appointed under this paragraph to represent the same interest, they must (if at all) instruct the same solicitor.

23.137

55 Right of attendance for member state liquidator

For the purposes of paragraph 54(1), a member State liquidator appointed in relation to a debtor subject to proceedings under these Regulations shall be deemed to be a creditor.

23.138

56 British insolvency officeholder's solicitor

Where in any proceedings the attendance of the British insolvency officeholder's solicitor is required, whether in court or in chambers, the British insolvency officeholder himself need not attend, unless directed by the court.

23.139

57 Formal defects

No proceedings under these Regulations shall be invalidated by any formal defect or by any irregularity, unless the court before which objection is made considers that substantial injustice has been caused by the defect or irregularity, and that the injustice cannot be remedied by any order of the court.

23.140

58 Restrictions on concurrent proceedings and remedies

Where in proceedings under these Regulations the court makes an order staying any action, execution or other legal process against the property of a debtor, service of the order may be effected by sending a sealed copy of the order to whatever is the address for service of the claimant or other party having the carriage of the proceedings to be stayed.

23.141

59 Affidavit

(1) Where in proceedings under these Regulations, an affidavit is made by any British insolvency officeholder acting in relation to the debtor, he shall state the capacity in which he makes it, the position which he holds and the address at which he works.

(2) Any officer of the court duly authorised in that behalf, may take affidavits and declarations.

(3) Subject to sub-paragraph (4), where these Regulations provide for the use of an affidavit, a witness statement verified by a statement of truth may be used as an alternative.

(4) Sub-paragraph (3) does not apply to paragraphs 4 (affidavit in support of recognition application), 7 (affidavit in support of interim relief application), 10 (affidavit in support of article 21 relief application), 13 (affidavit in support of application regarding status of replacement foreign representative) and 16 (affidavit in support of review application).

23.142

60 Security in court

(1) Where security has to be given to the court (otherwise than in relation to costs), it may be given by guarantee, bond or the payment of money into court.

(2) A person proposing to give a bond as security shall give notice to the party in whose favour the security is required, and to the court, naming those who are to be sureties to the bond.

(3) The court shall forthwith give notice to the parties concerned of a venue for the execution of the bond and the making of any objection to the sureties.

(4) The sureties shall make an affidavit of their sufficiency (unless dispensed with by the party in whose favour the security is required) and shall, if required by the court, attend the court to be cross-examined.

23.143

61 Further information and disclosure

(1) Any party to proceedings under these Regulations may apply to the court for an order—
    (a)   that any other party—
        (i)   clarify any matter which is in dispute in the proceedings; or
        (ii) give additional information in relation to any such matter,
    in accordance with CPR Part 18 (further information); or
    (b)   to obtain disclosure from any other party in accordance with CPR Part 31 (disclosure and inspection of documents).

(2) An application under this paragraph may be made without notice being served on any other party.

23.144

62 Office copies of document

(1) Any person who has under these Regulations the right to inspect the court file of proceedings may require the court to provide him with an office copy of any document from the file.

(2) A person's right under this paragraph may be exercised on his behalf by his solicitor.

(3) An office copy provided by the court under this paragraph shall be in such form as the Registrar thinks appropriate, and shall bear the court's seal.

23.145

63 'The court'

(1) Anything to be done in proceedings under these Regulations by, to or before the court may be done by, to or before a judge of the High Court or a Registrar.

(2) Where these Regulations require or permit the court to perform an act of a formal or administrative character, that act may be performed by a court officer.

Part 10
Costs and Detailed Assessment

23.146

64 Requirement to assess costs by the detailed procedure

In any proceedings before the court, the court may order costs to be decided by detailed assessment.

23.147

65 Costs of officers charged with execution of writs or other process

(1) Where by virtue of article 20 of the Model Law or a court order under article 19 or 21 of the Model Law an enforcement officer, or other officer, charged with execution of the writ or other process—
   (a)   is required to deliver up goods or money; or
   (b)   has deducted costs from the proceeds of an execution or money paid to him,
the foreign representative may require in writing that the amount of the enforcement officer's or other officer's bill of costs be decided by detailed assessment.

(2) Where such a requirement is made, if the enforcement officer or other officer does not commence detailed assessment proceedings within 3 months of the requirement under sub-paragraph (1), or within such further time as the court, on application, may permit, any claim by the enforcement officer or other officer in respect of his costs is forfeited by such failure to commence proceedings.

(3) Where, in the case of a deduction of costs by the enforcement officer or other officer, any amount deducted is disallowed at the conclusion of the detailed assessment proceedings, the enforcement officer or other officer shall forthwith pay a sum equal to that disallowed to the foreign representative for the benefit of the debtor.

23.148

66 Final costs certificate

(1) A final costs certificate of the costs officer is final and conclusive as to all matters which have not been objected to in the manner provided for under the rules of the court.

(2) Where it is proved to the satisfaction of a costs officer that a final costs certificate has been lost or destroyed, he may issue a duplicate.

Part 11
Appeals in Proceedings Under these Regulations

23.149

67 Appeals from court orders

(1) An appeal from a decision of a Registrar of the High Court in proceedings under these Regulations lies to a single judge of the High Court; and an appeal from a decision of that judge on such an appeal lies, with the permission of the Court of Appeal, to the Court of Appeal.

(2) An appeal from a decision of a judge of the High Court in proceedings under these Regulations which is not a decision on an appeal made to him under sub-paragraph (1) lies, with the permission of that judge or the Court of Appeal, to the Court of Appeal.

23.150

68 Procedure on appeals

(1) Subject as follows, CPR Part 52 (appeals to the Court of Appeal) and its practice direction apply to appeals in proceedings under these Regulations.

(2) The provisions of Part 4 of the practice direction on Insolvency Proceedings supporting CPR Part 49 relating to first appeals (as defined in that Part) apply in relation to any appeal to a single judge of the High Court under paragraph 67, with any necessary modifications.

(3) In proceedings under these Regulations, the procedure under CPR Part 52 is by ordinary application and not by appeal notice.

Part 12
General

23.150A

69 Notices

(1) All notices required or authorised by or under these Regulations to be given must be in writing, unless it is otherwise provided, or the court allows the notice to be given in some other way.

(2) Where in proceedings under these Regulations a notice is required to be sent or given by any person, the sending or giving of it may be proved by means of a certificate by that person that he posted the notice, or instructed another person (naming him) to do so.

(3) A certificate under this paragraph may be endorsed on a copy or specimen of the notice to which it relates.

23.151

70 'Give notice' etc

(1) A reference in these Regulations to giving notice, or to delivering, sending or serving any document, means that the notice or document may be sent by post.

(2) Subject to paragraph 75, any form of post may be used.

(3) Personal service of a document is permissible in all cases.

(4) Notice of the venue fixed for an application may be given by service of the sealed copy of the application under paragraph 33(3).

23.152

71 Notice, etc to solicitors

Where in proceedings under these Regulations a notice or other document is required or authorised to be given to a person, it may, if he has indicated that his solicitor is authorised to accept service on his behalf, be given instead to the solicitor.

23.153

72 Notice to joint British insolvency officeholders

Where two or more persons are acting jointly as the British insolvency officeholder in proceedings under British insolvency law, delivery of a document to one of them is to be treated as delivery to them all.

23.154

73 Forms for use in proceedings under these Regulations

(1) The forms contained in Schedule 5 to these Regulations shall be used in, and in connection with, proceedings under these Regulations.

(2) The forms shall be used with such variations, if any, as the circumstances may require.

23.155

74 Time limits

(1) The provisions of CPR Rule 2.8 (time) apply, as regards computation of time, to anything required or authorised to be done by these Regulations.

(2) The provisions of CPR rule 3.1(2)(a) (the court's general powers of management) apply so as to enable the court to extend or shorten the time for compliance with anything required or authorised to be done by these Regulations.

23.156

75 Service by post

(1) For a document to be properly served by post, it must be contained in an envelope addressed to the person on whom service is to be effected, and pre-paid for first class post.

(2) A document to be served by post may be sent to the last known address of the person to be served.

(3) Where first class post is used, the document is treated as served on the second business day after the date of posting, unless the contrary is shown.

(4) The date of posting is presumed, unless the contrary is shown, to be the date shown in the post-mark on the envelope in which the document is contained.

23.157

76 General provisions as to service and notice

Subject to paragraphs 22, 75 and 77, CPR Part 6 (service of documents) applies as regards any matter relating to the service of documents and the giving of notice in proceedings under these Regulations.

23.158

77 Service outside the jurisdiction

(1) Sections III and IV of CPR Part 6 (service out of the jurisdiction and service of process of foreign court) do not apply in proceedings under these Regulations.

(2) Where for the purposes of proceedings under these Regulations any process or order of the court, or other document, is required to be served on a person who is not in England and Wales, the court may order service to be effected within such time, on such person, at such place and in such manner as it thinks fit, and may also require such proof of service as it thinks fit.

(3) An application under this paragraph shall be supported by an affidavit stating—
    (a)   the grounds on which the application is made; and
    (b)   in what place or country the person to be served is, or probably may be found.

23.159

78 False claim of status as creditor

(1) Rule 12.18 (false claim of status as creditor, etc) shall apply with any necessary modifications in any case where a person falsely claims the status of a creditor of a debtor, with the intention of obtaining a sight of documents whether on the court's file or in the hands of the foreign representative or other person, which he has not under these Regulations any right to inspect.

(2) Rule 21.21 and Schedule 5 of the Rules shall apply to an offence under Rule 12.18 as applied by sub-paragraph (1) as they apply to an offence under Rule 12.18.

23.160

79 The Gazette

(1) A copy of the Gazette containing any notice required by these Regulations to be gazetted is evidence of any fact stated in the notice.

(2) In the case of an order of the court notice of which is required by these Regulations to be gazetted, a copy of the Gazette containing the notice may in any proceedings be produced as conclusive evidence that the order was made on the date specified in the notice.

SCHEDULE 3
Procedural Matters in Scotland
Regulation 5

Part I
Interpretation

23.161

1 Interpretation

(1) In this Schedule—
'the 1986 Act' means the Insolvency Act 1986;
'article 21 remedy application' means an application to the court by a foreign representative under article 21(1) or (2) of the Model Law for remedy;
'business day' means any day other than a Saturday, a Sunday, Christmas Day, Good Friday or a day which is a bank holiday in Scotland under or by virtue of the Banking and Financial Dealings Act 1971;
'the Gazette' means the Edinburgh Gazette;
'main proceedings' means proceedings opened in accordance with Article 3(1) of the EC Insolvency Regulation and falling within the definition of insolvency proceedings in Article 2(a) of the EC Insolvency Regulation;
'member State liquidator' means a person falling within the definition of liquidator in Article 2(b) of the EC Insolvency Regulation appointed in proceedings to which it applies in a member State other than the United Kingdom;
'the Model Law' means the UNCITRAL Model Law as set out in Schedule 1 to these Regulations;
'modification or termination order' means an order by the court pursuant to its powers under the Model Law modifying or terminating recognition of a foreign proceeding, the sist, restraint or suspension referred to in article 20(1) or any part of it or any remedy granted under article 19 or 21 of the Model Law;
'recognition application' means an application to the court by a foreign representative in accordance with article 15 of the Model Law for an order recognising the foreign proceeding in which he has been appointed;
'recognition order' means an order by the court recognising a proceeding the subject of a recognition application as a foreign main proceeding or foreign non-main proceeding, as appropriate;
'relevant company' means a company within the meaning of section 735(1) of the Companies Act 1985 or an unregistered company within the meaning of Part 5 of the 1986 Act which is subject to a requirement imposed by virtue of section 690A, 691(1) or 718 of the Companies Act 1985;

'review application' means an application to the court for a modification or termination order.

(2) Expressions defined in the Model Law have the same meaning when used in this Schedule.

(3) References in this Schedule to a debtor who is of interest to the Financial Services Authority are references to a debtor who—

    (a)   is, or has been, an authorised person within the meaning of section 31 of the Financial Services and Markets Act 2000 (authorised persons);

    (b)   is, or has been, an appointed representative within the meaning of section 39 (exemption of appointed representatives) of that Act; or

    (c)   is carrying, or has carried on, a regulated activity in contravention of the general prohibition.

(4) In sub-paragraph (3) 'the general prohibition' has the meaning given by section 19 of the Financial Services and Markets Act 2000 and the reference to a 'regulated activity' must be construed in accordance with—

    (a)   section 22 of that Act (classes of regulated activity and categories of investment);

    (b)   any relevant order under that section; and

    (c)   Schedule 2 to that Act (regulated activities).

(4) References in this Schedule to a numbered form are to the form that bears that number in Schedule 5.

Part 2
The Foreign Representative

23.162

2 Application for confirmation of status of replacement foreign representative

(1) This paragraph applies where following the making of a recognition order the foreign representative dies or for any other reason ceases to be the foreign representative in the foreign proceedings in relation to the debtor.

(2) In this paragraph 'the former foreign representative' means the foreign representative referred to in sub-paragraph (1).

(3) If a person has succeeded the former foreign representative or is otherwise holding office as foreign representative in the foreign proceeding in relation to the debtor, that person may apply to the court for an order confirming his status as replacement foreign representative for the purpose of proceedings under these Regulations.

(4) If the court dismisses an application under sub-paragraph (3) then it may also, if it thinks fit, make an order terminating recognition of the foreign proceeding and—

    (a)   such an order may include such provision as the court thinks fit with respect to matters arising in connection with the termination; and

(b)   paragraph 5 shall not apply to such an order.

23.163

3 Misfeasance by a foreign representative

(1) The court may examine the conduct of a person who—
   (a)   is or purports to be the foreign representative in relation to a debtor, or
   (b)   has been or has purported to be the foreign representative in relation to a debtor.

(2) An examination under this paragraph may be held only on the application of—
   (a)   a British insolvency officeholder acting in relation to the debtor,
   (b)   a creditor of the debtor, or
   (c)   with the permission of the court, any other person who appears to have an interest justifying an application.

(3) An application under sub-paragraph (2) must allege that the foreign representative—
   (a)   has misapplied or retained money or other property of the debtor,
   (b)   has become accountable for money or other property of the debtor,
   (c)   has breached a fiduciary duty or other duty in relation to the debtor, or
   (d)   has been guilty of misfeasance.

(4) On an examination under this paragraph into a person's conduct the court may order him—
   (a)   to repay, restore or account for money or property;
   (b)   to pay interest;
   (c)   to contribute a sum to the debtor's property by way of compensation for breach of duty or misfeasance.

(5) In sub-paragraph (3), 'foreign representative' includes a person who purports or has purported to be a foreign representative in relation to a debtor.

Part 3
Court Procedure and Practice

23.163A

4 Preliminary and interpretation

(1) This Part applies to—
   (a)   any of the following applications made to the court under these Regulations—
      (i)   a recognition application;
      (ii)   an article 21 remedy application;
      (iii)   an application under paragraph 2(3) for an order confirming the status of a replacement foreign representative;
      (iv)   a review application; and

   (b)   any of the following orders made by the court under these Regulations—

      (i)   a recognition order;

      (ii)   an order granting interim remedy under article 19 of the Model Law;

      (iii)   an order granting remedy under article 21 of the Model Law;

      (iv)   an order confirming the status of a replacement foreign representative; or

      (v)   a modification or termination order.

23.164

5 Reviews of court orders—where court makes order of its own motion

(1) The court shall not of its own motion make a modification or termination order unless the foreign representative and the debtor have either—

   (a)   had an opportunity of being heard on the question, or

   (b)   consented in writing to such an order.

(2) If the court makes a modification or termination order, the order may include such provision as the court thinks fit with respect to matters arising in connection with the modification or termination.

23.165

6 The hearing

(1) At the hearing of the application, the applicant and any of the following persons (not being the applicant) may appear or be represented—

   (a)   the foreign representative;

   (b)   the debtor and, in the case of any debtor other than an individual, any one or more directors or other officers of the debtor, including—

      (i)   where applicable, any person registered under Part 23 of the Companies Act 1985 as authorised to represent the debtor in respect of its business in Scotland;

      (ii)   in the case of a debtor which is a partnership, any person who is a member of the partnership;

   (c)   if a British insolvency officeholder is acting in relation to the debtor, that person;

   (d)   if any person has been appointed an administrative receiver of the debtor or as a receiver or manager of the property of the debtor, that person;

   (e)   if a member State liquidator has been appointed in main proceedings in relation to the debtor, that person;

   (f)   if a foreign representative has been appointed in any other foreign proceeding regarding the debtor, that person;

   (g)   any person who has presented a petition for the winding up or sequestration of the debtor in Scotland;

   (h)   any person who is or may be entitled to appoint an administrator of the debtor under paragraph 14 of Schedule B1 to the 1986 Act (appointment of administrator by holder of qualifying floating charge);

(i) if the debtor is a debtor who is of interest to the Financial Services Authority, that Authority; and
(j) with the permission of the court, any other person who appears to have an interest justifying his appearance.

23.166

7 Notification and advertisement of order

(1) This paragraph applies where the court makes any of the orders referred to in paragraph 4(1)(b).

(2) The foreign representative shall send a certified copy of the interlocutor as soon as reasonably practicable to the debtor.

(3) The foreign representative shall, as soon as reasonably practicable after the date of the order, give notice of the making of the order—
    (a) if a British insolvency officeholder is acting in relation to the debtor, to him;
    (b) if any person has been appointed an administrative receiver of the debtor or, to the knowledge of the foreign representative, as a receiver or manager of the property of the debtor, to him;
    (c) if a member State liquidator has been appointed in main proceedings in relation to the debtor, to him;
    (d) if to his knowledge a foreign representative has been appointed in any other foreign proceeding regarding the debtor, that person;
    (e) if there is pending in Scotland a petition for the winding up or sequestration of the debtor, to the petitioner;
    (f) to any person who to his knowledge is or may be entitled to appoint an administrator of the debtor under paragraph 14 of Schedule B1 to the 1986 Act (appointment of administrator by holder of qualifying floating charge);
    (g) if the debtor is a debtor who is of interest to the Financial Services Authority, to that Authority; and
    (h) to such persons as the court may direct.

(4) Where the debtor is a relevant company, the foreign representative shall send notice of the making of the order to the registrar of companies before the end of the period of 5 business days beginning with the date of the order. The notice to the registrar of companies shall be in Form ML7.

(5) The foreign representative shall advertise the making of the following orders once in the Gazette and once in such newspaper as he thinks most appropriate for ensuring that the making of the order comes to the notice of the debtor's creditors—
    (a) a recognition order,
    (b) an order confirming the status of a replacement foreign representative, and
    (c) a modification or termination order which modifies or terminates recognition of a foreign proceeding,
and the advertisement shall be in Form ML8.

23.167

8 Registration of court order

(1) Where the court makes a recognition order in respect of a foreign main proceeding or an order suspending the right to transfer, encumber or otherwise dispose of any assets of the debtor being heritable property, the clerk of the court shall send forthwith a certified copy of the order to the keeper of the register of inhibitions and adjudications for recording in that register.

(2) Recording under sub-paragraph (1) or (3) shall have the effect as from the date of the order of an inhibition and of a citation in an adjudication of the debtor's heritable estate at the instance of the foreign representative.

(3) Where the court makes a modification or termination order, the clerk of the court shall send forthwith a certified copy of the order to the keeper of the register of inhibitions and adjudications for recording in that register.

(4) The effect mentioned in sub-paragraph (2) shall expire—
  (a) on the recording of a modification or termination order under sub-paragraph (3); or
  (b) subject to sub-paragraph (5), if the effect has not expired by virtue of paragraph (a), at the end of the period of 3 years beginning with the date of the order.

(5) The foreign representative may, if recognition of the foreign proceeding has not been modified or terminated by the court pursuant to its powers under the Model Law, before the end of the period of 3 years mentioned in sub-paragraph (4)(b), send a memorandum in a form prescribed by the Court of Session by act of sederunt to the keeper of the register of inhibitions and adjudications for recording in that register, and such recording shall renew the effect mentioned in sub-paragraph (2); and thereafter the said effect shall continue to be preserved only if such memorandum is so recorded before the expiry of every subsequent period of 3 years.

23.168

9 Right to inspect court process

(1) In the case of any proceedings under these Regulations, the following have the right, at all reasonable times, to inspect the court process of the proceedings—
  (a) the Secretary of State;
  (b) the person who is the foreign representative in relation to the proceedings;
  (c) if a foreign representative has been appointed in any other foreign proceeding regarding the debtor, that person;
  (d) if a British insolvency officeholder is acting in relation to the debtor, that person;
  (e) any person stating himself in writing to be a creditor of the debtor to which the proceedings under these Regulations relate;

(f) if a member State liquidator has been appointed in relation to a debtor which is subject to proceedings under these Regulations, that person; and

(g) the debtor to which the proceedings under these Regulations relate, or, if that debtor is a company, corporation or partnership, every person who is, or at any time has been—

(i) a director or officer of the debtor,

(ii) a member of the debtor, or

(iii) where applicable, a person registered under Part 23 of the Companies Act 1985 as authorised to represent the debtor in respect of its business in Scotland.

(2) The right of inspection conferred as above on any person may be exercised on his behalf by a person properly authorised by him.

23.169

10 Copies of court orders

(1) In any proceedings under these Regulations, any person who under paragraph 9 has a right to inspect documents in the court process also has the right to require the foreign representative in relation to those proceedings to furnish him with a copy of any court order in the proceedings.

(2) Sub-paragraph (1) does not apply if a copy of the court order has been served on that person or notice of the making of the order has been given to that person under other provisions of these Regulations.

23.170

11 Transfer of proceedings—actions to avoid acts detrimental to creditors

If, in accordance with article 23(6) of the Model Law, the court grants a foreign representative permission to make an application in accordance with paragraph (1) of that article, it may also order the relevant proceedings under British insolvency law taking place regarding the debtor to be transferred to the Court of Session if those proceedings are taking place in Scotland and are not already in that court.

Part 3
General

23.171

12 Giving of notices, etc

(1) All notices required or authorised by or under these Regulations to be given, sent or delivered must be in writing, unless it is otherwise provided, or the court allows the notice to be sent or given in some other way.

(2) Any reference in these Regulations to giving, sending or delivering a notice or any such document means, without prejudice to any other way and unless it is otherwise provided, that the notice or document may be

sent by post, and that, subject to paragraph 13, any form of post may be used. Personal service of the notice or document is permissible in all cases.

(3) Where under these Regulations a notice or other document is required or authorised to be given, sent or delivered by a person ('the sender') to another ('the recipient'), it may be given, sent or delivered by any person duly authorised by the sender to do so to any person duly authorised by the recipient to receive or accept it.

(4) Where two or more persons are acting jointly as the British insolvency officeholder in proceedings under British insolvency law, the giving, sending or delivering of a notice or document to one of them is to be treated as the giving, sending or delivering of a notice or document to each or all.

23.172

13 Sending by post

(1) For a document to be properly sent by post, it must be contained in an envelope addressed to the person to whom it is to be sent, and pre-paid for either first or second class post.

(2) Any document to be sent by post may be sent to the last known address of the person to whom the document is to be sent.

(3) Where first class post is used, the document is to be deemed to be received on the second business day after the date of posting, unless the contrary is shown.

(4) Where second class post is used, the document is to be deemed to be received on the fourth business day after the date of posting, unless the contrary is shown.

23.173

14 Certificate of giving notice, etc

(1) Where in any proceedings under these Regulations a notice or document is required to be given, sent or delivered by any person, the date of giving, sending or delivery of it may be proved by means of a certificate by that person that he gave, posted or otherwise sent or delivered the notice or document on the date stated in the certificate, or that he instructed another person (naming him) to do so.

(2) A certificate under this paragraph may be endorsed on a copy of the notice to which it relates.

(3) A certificate purporting to be signed by or on behalf of the person mentioned in sub-paragraph (1) shall be deemed, unless the contrary is shown, to be sufficient evidence of the matters stated therein.

23.174

15 Forms for use in proceedings under these Regulations

(1) Forms ML7 and ML8 contained in Schedule 5 to these Regulations shall be used in, and in connection with, proceedings under these Regulations.

(2) The forms shall be used with such variations, if any, as the circumstances may require.

SCHEDULE 4
Notices Delivered to the Registrar of Companies
Regulation 6

23.175

1 Interpretation

(1) In this Schedule—
    'the 1985 Act' means the Companies Act 1985;
    'electronic communication' means the same as in the Electronic Communications Act 2000;
    'Model Law notice' means a notice delivered to the registrar of companies under paragraph 26(6) of Schedule 2 or paragraph 7(4) of Schedule 3.

(2) Expressions defined in the Model Law or Schedule 2 or 3, as appropriate, have the same meaning when used in this Schedule.

(3) References in this Schedule to delivering a notice include sending, forwarding, producing or giving it.

23.176

2 Functions of the registrar of companies

(1) Where a Model Law notice is delivered to the registrar of companies in respect of a relevant company, the registrar shall enter a note in the register relating to that company.

(2) The note referred to in sub-paragraph (1) shall contain the following particulars, in each case as stated in the notice delivered to the registrar—
    (a)   brief details of the court order made;
    (b)   the date of the court order; and
    (c)   the name and address for service of the person who is the foreign representative in relation to the company.

23.177

3 Registrar of companies to whom notices to be delivered

(1) References in Schedules 2 and 3 to the registrar of companies in relation to a relevant company shall be construed in accordance with the following provisions.

(2) The notices which a relevant company is required to deliver to the registrar of companies shall be delivered—
    (a)   to the registrar for England and Wales if the company has a relevant presence in England and Wales, and
    (b)   to the registrar for Scotland if the company has a relevant presence in Scotland,
and if the relevant company has a relevant presence in both parts of Great Britain, the notices shall be delivered to both registrars.

(3) For the purposes of this paragraph a 'relevant presence' means—

(a)   in the case of a company within the meaning of section 735(1) of the 1985 Act, its registered office,

(b)   in the case of an unregistered company within the meaning of Part 5 of the 1986 Act which is subject to a requirement imposed by virtue of section 690A of the 1985 Act, a branch,

(c)   in the case of an unregistered company within the meaning of Part 5 of the 1986 Act which is subject to a requirement imposed by virtue of section 691(1) of the 1985 Act, an established place of business, and

(d)   in the case of an unregistered company within the meaning of Part 5 of the 1986 Act which is subject to a requirement imposed by virtue of section 718 of the 1985 Act, a principal place of business.

23.178

4 Delivery to registrar of notices

(1) Electronic communications may be used for the delivery of any Model Law notice, provided that such delivery is in such form and manner as is directed by the registrar.

(2) Where the Model Law notice is required to be signed, it shall instead be authenticated in such manner as is directed by the registrar.

(3) If a Model Law notice is delivered to the registrar which does not comply with the requirements of these Regulations, he may serve on the person by whom the notice was delivered (or, if there are two or more such persons, on any of them) a notice (a non-compliance notice) indicating the respect in which the Model Law notice does not comply.

(4) Where the registrar serves a non-compliance notice, then, unless a replacement Model Law notice—

(a)   is delivered to him within 14 days after the service of the non-compliance notice, and

(b)   complies with the requirements of these Regulations or is not rejected by him for failure to comply with those requirements,

the original Model Law notice shall be deemed not to have been delivered to him.

23.179

5 Enforcement of foreign representative's duty to give notice to registrar

(1) If a foreign representative, having made default in complying with paragraph 26(6) of Schedule 2 or paragraph 7(4) of Schedule 3 fails to make good the default within 14 days after the service of a notice on the foreign representative requiring him to do so, the court may, on an application made to it by any creditor, member, director or other officer of the debtor or by the registrar of companies, make an order directing the foreign representative to make good the default within such time as may be specified in the order.

(2) The court's order may provide that all costs of and incidental to the application shall be borne by the foreign representative.

23.180

6 Rectification of the register under court order

(1) The registrar shall remove from the register any note, or part of a note—

(a) that relates to or is derived from a court order that the court has declared to be invalid or ineffective, or

(b) that the court declares to be factually inaccurate or derived from something that is factually inaccurate or forged,

and that the court directs should be removed from the register.

(2) The court order must specify what is to be removed from the register and indicate where on the register it is and the registrar shall carry out his duty under sub-paragraph (1) within a reasonable time of receipt by him of the relevant court order.

EXPLANATORY NOTE

(This note is not part of the Regulations)

On 30th May 1997 the United Nations Commission on International Trade Law ('UNCITRAL') adopted the text of a model law on cross-border insolvency, which was approved by a resolution of the United Nations General Assembly on 15th December 1997. These Regulations give effect to the model law in Great Britain.

Regulation 2 of the Regulations provides that the UNCITRAL model law shall have the force of law in Great Britain in the form set out in Schedule 1 to the Regulations (the Model Law) and provides that in interpreting the Model Law the courts can have regard to other documents including the Guide to Enactment of the Model Law published by UNCITRAL (ISBN 92–1–133608–2). The model law and Guide may be accessed at http://www.uncitral.org/uncitral/en/uncitral–texts/insolvency/1997Model.html.

Chapter I of the Model Law contains General Provisions (articles 1 to 8). Article 1 sets out the scope of application of the Model Law, which may apply in a number of cross-border situations, and also lists certain bodies to which the Model Law does not apply. Article 3 of the Model Law clarifies that Council Regulation (EC) No 1346/2000 of 29th May 2000 on Insolvency Proceedings prevails over the Model Law.

Chapter II (articles 9 to 14) relates to the access of foreign representatives and creditors to courts in Great Britain and their rights to participate in an insolvency proceeding in Great Britain.

Chapter III of the Model Law deals with recognition of foreign proceedings and relief. Articles 15 to 17 set out criteria for determining whether a foreign proceeding is to be recognised and, if so whether as a foreign main proceeding or as a foreign non-main proceeding (see articles 16, 17 and definitions in article 2).

Articles 19 to 21 set out the effects of recognition and the relief available to a foreign representative. The relief accorded upon recognition of a foreign main proceeding is listed in article 20(1). Article 21 of the Model Law provides for the court to grant discretionary relief for the benefit of any recognised foreign proceeding, whether main or non-main. Urgently needed relief may be granted by the court on an interim basis pending a decision on recognition (article 19).

Chapter IV of the Model Law provides for the British courts and British insolvency officeholders to cooperate with foreign courts or foreign representatives in the areas covered by the Model Law (articles 25 to 27).

Chapter V of the Model Law (articles 28 to 32) provides for the coordination of a British insolvency proceeding and a foreign proceeding concerning the same debtor and facilitates coordination between two or more foreign proceedings concerning the same debtor.

Schedule 2 to the Regulations sets out procedural matters in relation to proceedings under the Model Law in England and Wales. Parts 2 to 5 of the Schedule contain details of the form and content of specified applications under the Model Law and Part 6 sets out more detailed procedural requirements in respect of those applications. Part 7 of Schedule 2 provides for applications to be made in appropriate cases to the Chief Land Registrar in connection with court orders under the Regulations. Part 8 provides for a summary remedy against foreign representatives guilty of misfeasance. Parts 9 to 12 contain general provision as to court procedure and practice and appeals in connection with proceedings under the Regulations, costs and other general matters.

Schedule 3 of the Regulations sets out miscellaneous procedural matters in relation to proceedings under the Model Law in Scotland.

Schedule 4 makes provision in relation to notices delivered to the registrar of companies under the Regulations.

Schedule 5 contains forms prescribed for use in connection with proceedings under the Regulations.

A full regulatory impact assessment has not been produced for this instrument as it has a negligible impact on the costs of business.

Part Four

Practice Direction: Insolvency proceedings

Part One

General

24.1

1

1.1 In this Practice Direction:
- (1) "The Act" means the Insolvency Act 1986 and includes the Act as applied to limited liability partnerships by the Limited Liability Partnerships Regulations 2001;
- (2) "The Insolvency Rules" means the rules for the time being in force and made under s 411 and s 412 of the Act in relation to insolvency proceedings;
- (3) "CPR" means the Civil Procedure Rules and "CPR" followed by a Part or rule by number means the Part or rule with that number in those Rules;
- (4) "RSC" followed by an Order by number means the Order with that number set out in Schedule 1 to the CPR;
- (5) "Insolvency proceedings" means any proceedings under the Act, the Insolvency Rules, the Administration of Insolvent Estates of Deceased Persons Order 1986 (SI 1986/1999), the Insolvent Partnerships Order 1986 (SI 1986/2124) or the Insolvent Partnerships Order 1994 (SI 1994/2421).
- (6) References to a "company" shall include a limited liability partnership and references to a "contributory" shall include a member of a limited liability partnership.

1.2 This Practice Direction shall come into effect on 26th April 1999 and shall replace all previous Practice Notes and Practice Directions relating to insolvency proceedings.

1.3 Except where the Insolvency Rules otherwise provide, service of documents in insolvency proceedings in the High Court will be the responsibility of the parties and will not be undertaken by the court.

1.4 Where CPR Part 2.4 provides for the court to perform any act, that act may be performed by a Registrar in Bankruptcy for the purpose of insolvency proceedings in the High Court.

1.5 A writ of execution to enforce any order made in insolvency proceedings in the High Court may be issued on the authority of a Registrar.

1.6

(1) This paragraph applies where an insolvency practitioner ("the outgoing office holder") holds office as a liquidator, administrator, trustee or supervisor in more than one case and dies, retires from practice as an insolvency practitioner or is otherwise unable or unwilling to continue in office.

(2) A single application may be made to a Judge of the Chancery Division of the High Court by way of ordinary application in Form 7.2 for the appointment of a substitute office holder or office holders in all cases in which the outgoing office holder holds office, and for the transfer of each such case to the High Court for the purpose only of making such an order.

(3) The application may be made by any of the following:

(i) the outgoing office holder (if he is able and willing to do so);

(ii) any person who holds office jointly with the outgoing office holder;

(iii) any person who is proposed to be appointed as a substitute for the outgoing office holder; or

(iv) any creditor in the cases where the substitution is proposed to be made.

(4) The outgoing office holder (if he is not the applicant) and every person who holds office jointly with the office holder must be made a respondent to the application, but it is not necessary to join any other person as a respondent or to serve the application upon any other person unless the Judge or Registrar in the High Court so directs.

(5) The application should contain schedules setting out the nature of the office held, the identity of the Court currently having jurisdiction over each case and its name and number.

(6) The application must be supported by evidence setting out the circumstances which have given rise to the need to make a substitution and exhibiting the written consent to act of each person who is proposed to be appointed in place of the outgoing office holder.

(7) The Judge will in the first instance consider the application on paper and make such order as he thinks fit. In particular he may do any of the following:

(i) make an order directing the transfer to the High Court of those cases not already within its jurisdiction for the purpose only of the substantive application;

(ii) if he considers that the papers are in order and that the matter is straightforward, make an order on the substantive application;

(iii) give any directions which he considers to be necessary including (if appropriate) directions for the joinder of any additional respondents or requiring the service of the application on any person or requiring additional evidence to be provided;

(iv) if he does not himself make an order on the substantive application when the matter is first before him, give directions for the further consideration of the substantive application by himself or another Judge of the Chancery Division or adjourn the substantive application to the Registrar for him to make such order upon it as is appropriate.

(8) An order of the kind referred to in sub-paragraph (6)(i) shall follow the draft order in Form PDIP 3 set out in the Schedule hereto and an order granting the substantive application shall follow the draft order in Form PDIP 4 set out in the schedule hereto (subject in each case to such modifications as may be necessary or appropriate).

(9) It is the duty of the applicant to ensure that a sealed copy of every order transferring any case to the High Court and of every order which is made on a substantive application is lodged with the court having jurisdiction over each case affected by such order for filing on the court file relating to that case.

(10) It will not be necessary for the file relating to any case which is transferred to the High Court in accordance with this paragraph to be sent to the High Court unless a Judge or Registrar so directs.

Part Two
Companies

24.1A

2 Advertisement of Winding Up Petition

2.1 Insolvency Rule 4.11(2)(b) is mandatory, and designed to ensure that the class remedy of winding up by the court is made available to all creditors, and is not used as a means of putting pressure on the company to pay the petitioner's debt. Failure to comply with the rule, without good reason accepted by the court, may lead to the summary dismissal of the petition on the return date (Insolvency Rule 4.11(5)). If the court, in its discretion, grants an adjournment, this will be on condition that the petition is advertised in due time for the adjourned hearing. No further adjournment for the purpose of advertisement will normally be granted.

2.2 Copies of every advertisement published in connection with a winding up petition must be lodged with the Court as soon as possible after publication and in any event not later than the day specified in Insolvency Rule 4.14 of the Insolvency Rules 1986. This direction applies even if the advertisement is defective in any way (eg is published at a date not in accordance with the Insolvency Rules, or omits or misprints some important words) or if the petitioner decides not to pursue the petition (eg on receiving payment).

3 Certificate of compliance – time for filing

3.1 In the High Court in order to assist practitioners and the Court the time laid down by Insolvency Rule 4.14 of the Insolvency Rules 1986, for filing a certificate of compliance and a copy of the advertisement, is hereby extended to not later than 4.30 pm on the Friday preceding the day on which the petition is to be heard. Applications to file the certificate and the copy advertisement after 4.30 pm on the Friday will only be allowed if some good reason is shown for the delay.

4 Errors in Petitions

4.1 Applications for leave to amend errors in petitions which are discovered subsequent to a winding up order being made should be made to the Court Manager in the High Court and to the District Judge in the county court.

4.2 Where the error is an error in the name of the company, the Court Manager in the High Court and the District Judge in the county court may make any necessary amendments to ensure that the winding up order is drawn with the correct name of the company inserted. If there is any doubt, eg where there might be another company in existence which could be confused with the company to be wound up, the Court Manager will refer the application to the Registrar and the District Judge may refer it to the Judge.

4.3 Where an error is an error in the registered office of the company and any director or member of the company claims that the company was unaware of the petition by reason of it having been served at the wrong registered office it will be open to them to apply to rescind the winding up order in the usual way.

4.4 Where it is discovered that the company had been struck off the Register of Companies prior to the winding up order being made, the matter must be restored to the list before the order is entered to enable an order for the restoration of the name to be made as well as the order to wind up.

5 Distribution of Business

5.1 The following applications shall be made direct to the Judge and, unless otherwise ordered, shall be heard in public:—
   (1)   Applications to commit any person to prison for contempt;
   (2)   Applications for urgent interim relief (eg applications pursuant to s 127 of the Act prior to any winding up order being made);
   (3)   Applications to restrain the presentation or advertisement of a petition to wind up; or
   (4)   Applications for the appointment of a provisional liquidator;
   (5)   Petitions for administration orders or an interim order upon such a Petition;
   (6)   Applications after an administration order has been made pursuant to s 14(3) of the Act (for directions) or s 18(3) of the Act (to vary or discharge the order);
   (7)   Petitions to discharge administration orders and to wind up;
   (8)   Applications pursuant to s 5(3) of the Act (to stay a winding up or discharge an administration order or for directions) where a voluntary arrangement has been approved;
   (9)   Appeals from a decision made by a County Court or by a Registrar of the High Court.

5.2 Subject to paragraph 5.4 below all other applications shall be made to the Registrar or the District Judge in the first instance who may give any necessary directions and may, in the exercise of his discretion, either hear and determine it himself or refer it to the Judge.

5.3 The following matters will also be heard in public:
   (1)   Petitions to wind up;

(2)   Public examinations;

(3)   All matters and applications heard by the Judge, except those referred by the Registrar or the District Judge to be heard in private or so directed by the Judge to be heard.

5.4 In accordance with directions given by the Lord Chancellor the Registrar has authorised certain applications in the High Court to be dealt with by the Court Manager of the Companies Court, pursuant to Insolvency Rule 13.2(2). The applications are:

(1)   To extend or abridge time prescribed by the Insolvency Rules in connection with winding up (Insolvency Rules 4.3 and 12.9);

(2)   For substituted service of winding up petitions (Insolvency Rule 4.8(6));

(3)   To withdraw petitions (Insolvency Rule 4.15);

(4)   For the substitution of a petitioner (Insolvency Rule 4.19);

(5)   By the Official Receiver for limited disclosure of a statement of affairs (Insolvency Rule 4.35);

(6)   By the Official Receiver for relief from duties imposed upon him by the rules (Insolvency Rule 4.47);

(7)   By the Official Receiver for permission to give notice of a meeting by advertisement only (Insolvency Rule 4.59);

(8)   To transfer proceedings from the High Court to a County Court (Insolvency Rule 7.11);

(9)   For permission to amend any originating application.

[NB In District Registries all such applications must be made to the District Judge.]

6 Drawing Up for Orders

6.1 The Court will draw up all orders except orders on the application of the Official Receiver or for which the Treasury Solicitor is responsible under the existing practice.

7 Rescission of a Winding Up Order

7.1 Any application for the rescission of a winding up order shall be made within seven days after the date on which the order was made (Insolvency Rule 7.47(4)). Notice of any such application must be given to the Official Receiver.

7.2 Applications will only be entertained if made (a) by a creditor, or (b) by a contributory, or (c) by the company jointly with a creditor or with a contributory. The application must be supported by written evidence of assets and liabilities.

7.3 In the case of an unsuccessful application the costs of the petitioning creditor, the supporting creditors and of the Official Receiver will normally be ordered to be paid by the creditor or the contributory making or joining in the application. The reason for this is that if the costs of an unsuccessful application are made payable by the company, they fall unfairly on the general body of creditors.

7.4 Cases in which the making of the winding up order has not been opposed may, if the application is made promptly, be dealt with on a statement by the applicant's legal representative of the circumstances; but apart from such cases, the court will normally require any application to be supported by written evidence.

7.5 There is no need to issue a form of application (Form 7.2) as the petition is restored before the Court.

8 Restraint of Presentation of a Winding-up Petition

8.1 An application to restrain presentation of a Winding up petition must be made to the Judge by the issue of an Originating Application (Form 7.1).

Part Three
Personal Insolvency-Bankruptcy

24.1B

9 Distribution of Business

9.1 The following applications shall be made direct to the Judge and unless otherwise ordered shall be heard in public:
  (1) Applications for the committal of any person to prison for contempt;
  (2) Application for injunctions or for the modification or discharge of injunctions;
  (3) Applications for interlocutory relief or directions after the matter has been referred to the Judge.

9.2 All other applications shall be made to the Registrar or the District Judge in the first instance. He shall give any necessary directions and may, if the application is within his jurisdiction to determine, in his discretion either hear and determine it himself or refer it to the Judge.

9.3 The following matters shall be heard in public:
  (1) The public examination of debtors;
  (2) Opposed applications for discharge or for the suspension or lifting of the suspension of discharge;
  (3) Opposed applications for permission to be a director;
  (4) In any case where the petition was presented or the receiving order or order for adjudication was made before the appointed day, those matters and applications specified in Rule 8 of the Bankruptcy Rules 1952;
  (5) All matters and applications heard by the Judge, except matters and applications referred by the Registrar or the District Judge to be heard by the Judge in private or directed by the Judge to be so heard.

9.4 All petitions presented will be listed under the name of the debtor.

9.5 In accordance with Directions given by the Lord Chancellor the Registrar has authorised certain applications in the High Court to be dealt with by the Court Manager of the Bankruptcy Court pursuant to Insolvency Rule 13.2(2). The applications are:
  (1) by petitioning creditors: to extend time for hearing petitions (s 376 of the Act).

(2) by the Official Receiver:
    (a) To transfer proceedings from the High Court to a County Court (Insolvency Rule 7.13);
    (b) to amend the full title of the proceedings (Insolvency Rules 6.35 and 6.47).

[NB In District Registries all such applications must be made to the District Judge]

24.2

10 Service abroad of statutory demand

10.1 A statutory demand is not a document issued by the Court. Leave to serve out of the jurisdiction is not, therefore, required.

10.2 Insolvency Rule 6.3(2) ("Requirements as to service") applies to service of the statutory demand whether outside or within the jurisdiction.

10.3 A creditor wishing to serve a statutory demand outside the jurisdiction in a foreign country with which a civil procedure convention has been made (including the Hague Convention) may and, if the assistance of a British Consul is desired, must adopt the procedure prescribed by rule 6.25. In the case of any doubt whether the country is a "convention country", enquiries should be made of the Queen's Bench Masters' Secretary Department, Room E216, Royal Courts of Justice.

10.4 In all other cases, service of the demand must be effected by private arrangement in accordance with Insolvency Rule 6.3(2) and local foreign law.

10.5 When a statutory demand is to be served out of the jurisdiction, the time limits of 21 days and 18 days respectively referred to in the demand must be amended. For this purpose reference should be made to the table set out in the practice direction supplementing Section III of Part 6.

10.6 A creditor should amend the statutory demand as follows:
    (1) For any reference to 18 days there must be substituted the appropriate number of days set out in the table plus 4 days, and
    (2) for any reference to 21 days must be substituted the appropriate number of days in the table plus 7 days.

Attention is drawn to the fact that in all forms of the statutory demand the figure 18 and the figure 21 occurs in more than one place.

Notes

Para 10(2)

In aooordanoo with IR 1086 r 6.3(2) oorvioo of tho otatutory domand ohould bo poroonal service if practical. If personal service is not practical then the creditor must do all that is reasonably practical to bring the demand to the attention of the debtor.

Para 10(3)

Regard should also be had to CPR Part 6 as regards the effecting of service and time limits.

24.3

11 Substituted service statutory demands:

11.1 The creditor is under an obligation to do all that is reasonable to bring the statutory demand to the debtor's attention and, if practicable, to cause personal service to be effected. Where it is not possible to effect prompt personal service, service may be effected by other means such as first class post or by insertion through a letter box.

11.2 Advertisement can only be used as a means of substituted service where:
  (1) The demand is based on a judgment or order of any Court;
  (2) The debtor has absconded or is keeping out of the way with a view to avoiding service; and,
  (3) There is no real prospect of the sum due being recovered by execution or other process.

As there is no statutory form of advertisement, the Court will accept an advertisement in the following form:

24.4

Statutory demand

(Debt for liquidated sum payable immediately following a judgment or order of the Court)

To (Block letters)

of

TAKE NOTICE that a statutory demand has been issued by:

Name of Creditor:

Address:

The creditor demands payment of £   the amount now due on a judgment or order of the (High Court of Justice   Division) (............ county court) dated the   day of 199   .

The statutory demand is an important document and it is deemed to have been served on you on the date of the first appearance of this advertisement. You must deal with this demand within 21 days of the service upon you or you could be made bankrupt and your property and goods taken away from you. If you are in any doubt as to your position, you should seek advice immediately from a solicitor or your nearest Citizens' Advice Bureau. The statutory demand can be obtained or is available for inspection and collection from:

Name:

Address:

(Solicitor for) the Creditor

Tel. No   Reference:

You have only 21 days from the date of the first appearance of this advertisement before the creditor may present a Bankruptcy Petition. You have only 18 days from that date within which to apply to the Court to set aside the demand.

11.3 In all cases where substituted service is effected, the creditor must have taken all those steps which would justify the Court making an order for substituted service of a petition. The steps to be taken to obtain an order for substituted service of a petition are set out below. Failure to comply with these requirements may result in the Court declining to file the petition: Insolvency Rule 6.11(9).

24.5

Petitions

11.4 In most cases, evidence of the following steps will suffice to justify an order for substituted service:

(1) One personal call at the residence and place of business of the debtor where both are known or at either of such places as is known. Where it is known that the debtor has more than one residential or business address, personal calls should be made at all the addresses.

(2) Should the creditor fail to effect service, a first class prepaid letter should be written to the debtor referring to the call(s), the purpose of the same and the failure to meet with the debtor, adding that a further call will be made for the same purpose on the   day of   19   at   hours at   (place). At least two business days notice should be given of the appointment and copies of the letter sent to all known addresses of the debtor. The appointment letter should also state that:

   (a) in the event of the time and place not being convenient, the debtor is to name some other time and place reasonably convenient for the purpose;

   (b) (Statutory Demands) if the debtor fails to keep the appointment the creditor proposes to serve the debtor by [advertisement] [post] [insertion through a letter box] or as the case may be, and that, in the event of a bankruptcy petition being presented, the Court will be asked to treat such service as service of the demand on the debtor;

   (c) (Petitions) if the debtor fails to keep the appointment, application will be made to the Court for an order for substituted service either by advertisement, or in such other manner as the Court may think fit.

(3) In attending any appointment made by letter, inquiry should be made as to whether the debtor has received all letters left for him. If the debtor is away, inquiry should also be made as to whether or not letters are being forwarded to an address within the jurisdiction (England and Wales) or elsewhere.

(4) If the debtor is represented by a Solicitor, an attempt should be made to arrange an appointment for personal service through such Solicitor. The Insolvency Rules enable a Solicitor to accept service of a statutory demand on behalf of his client but there is no similar provision in respect of service of a bankruptcy petition.

> (5) The written evidence filed pursuant to Insolvency Rule 6.11 should deal with all the above matters including all relevant facts as to the debtor's whereabouts and whether the appointment letter(s) have been returned.
>
> 11.5 Where the Court makes an order for service by first class ordinary post, the order will normally provide that service be deemed to be effected on the seventh day after posting. The same method of calculating service may be applied to calculating the date of service of a statutory demand.

Notes

Paras 11.1–11.3

Paragraph 11 deals with the conditions which must be fulfilled by a petitioning creditor in order to be entitled to effect substituted service of a statutory demand or a petition. Regard should also be had to the notes for IR 1986 r 6.3. Paragraph 11.2 sets out the wording which must be used when advertising a statutory demand.

Paras 11.4–11.5

These provisions deal with substituted service of a petition. In particular they set out the evidence which a court will require in order to permit substituted service. It is to be noted that all the steps under Paragraph 11.4 should be taken if possible and evidence should be produced of the attempts. Paragraph 11.4 is in essence an explanation of the requirements of IR 1986 r 6.11(6) *Anderson v Kas Bank NV* [2004] BPIR 685. The manner in which an application for substituted service is made is found in IR 1986 r 6.14(2).

24.6

12 Setting aside a statutory demand

12.1 The application (Form 6.4) and written evidence in support (Form 6.5) exhibiting a copy of the statutory demand must be filed in Court within 18 days of service of the statutory demand on the debtor. Where service is effected by advertisement in a newspaper the period of 18 days is calculated from the date of the first appearance of the advertisement. Three copies of each document must be lodged with the application to enable the Court to serve notice of the hearing date on the applicant, the creditor and the person named in Part B of the statutory demand.

12.2 Where, to avoid expense, copies of the documents are not lodged with the application in the High Court, any order of the Registrar fixing a venue is conditional upon copies of the documents being lodged on the next business day after the Registrar's order otherwise the application will be deemed to have been dismissed.

12.3 Where the statutory demand is based on a judgment or order, the Court will not at this stage go behind the judgment or order and inquire into the validity of the debt nor, as a general rule, will it adjourn the application to await the result of an application to set aside the judgment or order.

12.4 Where the debtor (a) claims to have a counterclaim, set off or cross demand (whether or not he could have raised it in the action in which the judgment or order was obtained) which equals or exceeds the amount of the debt or debts specified in the statutory demand, or (b) disputes the debt (not being a debt subject to a judgment or order) the Court will normally set aside the statutory demand if, in its opinion, on the evidence there is a genuine triable issue.

12.5 A debtor who wishes to apply to set aside a statutory demand after the expiration of 18 days from the date of service of the statutory demand must apply for an extension of time within which to apply. If the applicant wishes to apply for an injunction to restrain presentation of a petition the application must be made to the Judge. Paragraphs 1 and 2 of Form 6.5 (Affidavit in Support of Application to set Aside Statutory Demand) should be used in support of the application for an extension of time with the following additional paragraphs:

"(3) That to the best of my knowledge and belief the creditor(s) named in the demand has/have not presented a petition against me.

(4) That the reasons for my failure to apply to set aside the demand within 18 days after service are as follows: ..."

If application is made to restrain presentation of a bankruptcy petition the following additional paragraph should be added:

"(5) Unless restrained by injunction the creditor(s) may present a bankruptcy petition against me."

Notes

Para 12

This provision set out formalities regarding applications to set aside a statutory demand and it supplements the provisions of IR 1986 r 6.4, 6.5 to which reference should be made. The formalities dealt with under this paragraph are the form of any application, the evidence in support and the timing the application which must be made within 18 days from the date of service of the demand. If this time limit is not met then the application must request an extension of time.

Para 12.4

This provision deals with the tests the court will apply when considering an application under IR 1986 r 6.5 and these provisions have the force of law (*Society of Lloyd's v Bowman* [2004] EWCA Civ 1886, [2004] BPIR 324). In particular the paragraph sets out that as regards a claim for a set-off, counterclaim or cross demand or a disputed debt the relevant tests are whether there is a genuine triable issue. This is a lesser burden than the test which is applicable under CPR Part 24 (*Kellar v BBR Graphic Engineers (Yorks) Ltd* [2002] BPIR 544); see further the notes to IR 1986 r 6.5.

Para 12.5

An application made outside the 18 day time limit will not prevent the presentation of a petition under IA 1986 s 267: *Chohan v Times Newspapers Ltd* [2001] 1 WLR 184. Therefore if an application is made outside the 18 day time limit the application should also include an application to restrain presentation of a bankruptcy petition. The paragraph deals with the additional requirements in the application in this is required.

24.7

13 Proof of service of a statutory demand

13.1 Insolvency Rule 6.11(3) provides that, if the Statutory Demand has been served personally, the written evidence must be provided by the person who effected that service. Insolvency Rule 6.11(4) provides that, if service of the demand (however effected) has been acknowledged in writing, the evidence of service must be provided by the creditor or by a person acting on his behalf. Insolvency Rule 6.11(5) provides that, if neither paragraphs (3) or (4) apply, the written evidence must be provided by a person having direct knowledge of the means adopted for serving the demand.

13.2 Form 6.11 (Evidence of personal service of the statutory demand): this form should only be used where the demand has been served personally and acknowledged in writing (see Insolvency Rule 6.11(4)). If the demand has not been acknowledged in writing, the written evidence should be provided by the Process Server and Paragraphs 2 and 3 (part of Form 6.11) should be omitted (See Insolvency Rule 6.11(3)).

13.3 Form 6.12 (Evidence of Substituted Service of the Statutory Demand): this form can be used whether or not service of the demand has been acknowledged in writing. Paragraphs 4 and 5 (part) provide for the alternatives. Practitioners are reminded, however, that the appropriate person to provide the written evidence may not be the same in both cases. If the demand has been acknowledged in writing, the appropriate person is the creditor or a person acting on his behalf. If the demand has not been acknowledged, that person must be someone having direct knowledge of the means adopted for serving the demand.

Practitioners may find it more convenient to allow process servers to carry out the necessary investigation whilst reserving to themselves the service of the demand. In these circumstances Paragraph 1 should be deleted and the following paragraph substituted:

"1.   Attempts have been made to serve the demand, full details of which are set out in the accompanying affidavit of ...".

13.4 "Written evidence" means an affidavit or a witness statement.

Notes

Para 13

This provision deals with the evidence which a creditor needs to provide to the court when presenting a bankruptcy petition as regards service of a statutory demand and the relevant forms which should be used appropriate to the manner in which the demand was served. The paragraph should be read in conjunction with IR 1986 r 6.11, 6.12.

14 Extension of Hearing Date of Petition

14.1 Late applications for extension of hearing dates under Insolvency Rule 6.28, and failure to attend on the listed hearing of a petition, will be dealt with as follows:

(1)   If an application is submitted less than two clear working days before the hearing date (for example, later than Monday for

Thursday, or Wednesday for Monday) the costs of the application will not be allowed under Insolvency Rule 6.28(3).

(2) If the petition has not been served and no extension has been granted by the time fixed for the hearing of the petition, and if no one attends for the hearing, the petition will be re-listed for hearing about 21 days later. The Court will notify the petitioning creditor's solicitors (or the petitioning creditor in person), and any known supporting or opposing creditors or their solicitors, of the new date and times. Written evidence should then be filed on behalf of the petitioning creditor explaining fully the reasons for the failure to apply for an extension or to appear at the hearing, and (if appropriate) giving reasons why the petition should not be dismissed.

(3) On the re-listed hearing the Court may dismiss the petition if not satisfied it should be adjourned or a further extension granted.

14.2 All applications for extension should include a statement of the date fixed for the hearing of the petition.

14.3 The petitioning creditor should attend (by solicitors or in person) on or before the hearing date to ascertain whether the application has reached the file and been dealt with. It should not be assumed that an extension will be granted.

15 Bankruptcy Petion

To help in the completion of the form of a creditor's bankruptcy petition, attention is drawn to the following points:

15.1 The petition does not require dating, signing or witnessing.

15.2 In the title it is only necessary to recite the debtor's name eg *Re John William Smith* or *Re J W Smith (Male)*. Any alias or trading name will appear in the body of the petition. This also applies to all other statutory forms other than those which require the "full title".

15.3 Where the petition is based on a statutory demand, only the debt claimed in the demand may be included in the petition.

15.4 In completing Paragraph 2 of the petition, attention is drawn to Insolvency Rule 6.8(1)(a) to (c), particularly where the "aggregate sum" is made up of a number of debts.

15.5 Date of service of the statutory demand (paragraph 4 of the petition):

(1) In the case of personal service, the date of service as set out in the affidavit of service should be recited and whether service is effected *before/after* 1700 hours on Monday to Friday or at any time on a Saturday or a Sunday: see CPR Part 6.7(2) and (3).

(2) In the case of substituted service (otherwise than by advertisement), the date alleged in the affidavit of service should be recited: see "11. Substituted Service" above.

(3) In the strictly limited case of service by advertisement under Insolvency Rule 6.3, the date to be alleged is the date of the advertisement's appearance or, as the case may be, its first appearance: see Insolvency Rules 6.3(3) and 6.11(8).

15.6 There is no need to include in the petition details of the person authorised to present it.

15.7 Certificates at the end of the petition:
(1) The period of search for prior petitions has been reduced to eighteen months.
(2) Where a statutory demand is based wholly or in part on a county court judgment, the following certificate is to be added:

"I/We certify that on the of 19 I/We attended on the county court and was/were informed by an officer of the Court that no money had been paid into Court in the action or matter v Claim No pursuant to the statutory demand."

This certificate will not be required when the demand also requires payment of a separate debt, not based on a county court judgement, the amount of which exceeds the bankruptcy level (at present £750).

15.8 Deposit on petition: the deposit will be taken by the Court and forwarded to the Official Receiver. In the High Court, the petition fee and deposit should be handed to the Supreme Court Accounts Office, Fee Stamping Room, who will record the receipt and will impress two entries on the original petition, one in respect of the Court fee and the other in respect of the deposit. In the county court, the petition fee and deposit should be handed to the duly authorised officer of the Court's staff who will record its receipt.

In all cases cheque(s) for the whole amount should be made payable to 'HM Paymaster General'.

15.9 On the hearing of a petition for a bankruptcy order, in order to satisfy the Court that the debt on which the petition is founded has not been paid or secured or compounded the Court will normally accept as sufficient a certificate signed by the person representing the petitioning creditor in the following form:

"I certify that I have/my firm has made enquiries of the petitioning creditor(s) within the last business day prior to the hearing/adjourned hearing and to the best of my knowledge and belief the debt on which the petition is founded is still due and owing and has not been paid or secured or compounded save as to ......
Signed .... Dated ......"

For convenience in the High Court this certificate will be incorporated in the attendance slip, which will be filed after the hearing. A fresh certificate will be required on each adjourned hearing.

15.10 On the occasion of the adjourned hearing of a petition for a bankruptcy order, in order to satisfy the Court that the petitioner has complied with Insolvency Rule 6.29, the petitioner will be required to file written evidence of the manner in which notice of the making of the order of adjournment and of the venue for the adjourned hearing has been sent to:
(i) the debtor; and
(ii) any creditor who has given notice under Insolvency Rule 6.23 but was not present at the hearing when the order for adjournment was made.

16 Orders without Attendance

16.1 In suitable cases the High Court will normally be prepared to make orders under Part VIII of the Act (Individual Voluntary Arrangements), without the attendance of either party, provided there is no bankruptcy order in existence and (so far as is known) no pending petition. The orders are:

(1) A fourteen day interim order with the application adjourned 14 days for consideration of the nominee's report, where the papers are in order, and the nominee's signed consent to act includes a waiver of notice of the application or a consent by the nominee to the making of an interim order without attendance.

(2) A standard order on consideration of the nominee's report, extending the interim order to a date 7 weeks after the date of the proposed meeting, directing the meeting to be summoned and adjourning to a date about 3 weeks after the meeting. Such an Order may be made without attendance if the nominee's report has been delivered to the Court and complies with Section 256(1) of the Act and Insolvency Rule 5.10(2) and (3) and proposes a date for the meeting not less than 14 days from that on which the nominee's report is filed in Court under Insolvency Rule 5.10 nor more than 28 days from that on which that report is considered by the Court under Insolvency Rule 5.12.

(3) A "concertina" Order, combining orders as under (1) and (2) above. Such an order may be made without attendance if the initial application for an interim order is accompanied by a report of the nominee and the conditions set out in (1) and (2) above are satisfied.

(4) A final order on consideration of the Chairman's report. Such an order may be made without attendance if the Chairman's report has been filed and complies with Insolvency Rule 5.22(1). The order will record the effect of the Chairman's report and may discharge the interim order.

16.2 Provided that the conditions as under 16.1(2) and (4) above are satisfied and that the appropriate report has been lodged with the Court in due time the parties need not attend or be represented on the adjourned hearing for consideration of the Nominee's report or of the Chairman's report (as the case may be) unless they are notified by the Court that attendance is required. Sealed copies of the order made (in all four cases as above) will be posted by the Court to the applicant or his Solicitor and to the Nominee.

16.3 In suitable cases the Court may also make consent orders without attendance by the parties. The written consent of the parties will be required. Examples of such orders are as follows:

(1) On applications to set aside a statutory demand, orders:
    (a) dismissing the application, with or without an order for costs as may be agreed (permission will be given to present a petition on or after the seventh day after the date of the order, unless a different date is agreed);
    (b) setting aside the demand, with or without an order for costs as may be agreed; or

  (c) giving permission to withdraw the application with or without an order for costs as may be agreed.

(2) On petitions: where there is a list of supporting or opposing creditors in Form 6.21, or a statement signed by or on behalf of the petitioning creditor that no notices have been received from supporting or opposing creditors, orders:

  (a) dismissing the petition, with or without an order for costs as may be agreed, or

  (b) if the petition has not been served, giving permission to withdraw the petition (with no order for costs).

(3) On other applications, orders:

  (a) for sale of property, possession of property, disposal of proceeds of sale

  (b) giving interim directions

  (c) dismissing the application, with or without an order for costs as may be agreed

  (d) giving permission to withdraw the application, with or without an order for costs as may be agreed.

If, (as may often be the case with orders under subparagraphs (3)(a) or (b) above) an adjournment is required, whether generally with liberty to restore or to a fixed date, the order by consent may include an order for the adjournment. If adjournment to a date is requested, a time estimate should be given and the Court will fix the first available date and time on or after the date requested.

16.4 The above lists should not be regarded as exhaustive, nor should it be assumed that an order will be made without attendance as requested.

16.5 The procedure outlined above is designed to save time and costs but is not intended to discourage attendance.

16.6 Applications for consent orders without attendance should be lodged at least two clear working days (and preferably longer) before any fixed hearing date.

16.7 Whenever a document is lodged or a letter sent, the correct case number, code (if any) and year (for example 123/SD/99 or 234/99) should be quoted. A note should also be given of the date and time of the next hearing (if any).

16.8 Attention is drawn to Paragraph 4.4(4) of the Practice Direction relating to CPR Part 44.

16A Bankruptcy restriction orders

Making the application

16A.1 An application for a bankruptcy restrictions order is made as an ordinary application in the bankruptcy.

16A.2 The application must be made within one year beginning with the date of the bankruptcy order unless the court gives permission for the application to be made after that period. The one year period does not run while the bankrupt's discharge has been suspended under section 279(3) of the Insolvency Act 1986.

16A.3 An application for a bankruptcy restrictions order may be made by the Secretary of State or the Official Receiver ("the Applicant"). The application must be supported by a report which must include:

(a) a statement of the conduct by reference to which it is alleged that it is appropriate for a bankruptcy restrictions order to be made; and

(b) the evidence relied on in support of the application (r 6.241 Insolvency Rules 1986).

16A.4 The report is treated as if it were an affidavit (r 7.9(2) Insolvency Rules 1986) and is prima facie evidence of any matter contained in it (r 7.9(3)).

16A.5 The application may be supported by evidence from other witnesses which may be given by affidavit or (by reason of r 7.57(5) Insolvency Rules 1986) by witness statement verified by a statement of truth.

16A.6 The court will fix a first hearing which must be not less than 8 weeks from the date when the hearing is fixed (r 6.241(4) Insolvency Rules 1986).

16A.7 Notice of the application and the venue fixed by the court must be served by the Applicant on the bankrupt not more than 14 days after the application is made. Service of notice must be accompanied by a copy of the application together with the evidence in support and a form of acknowledgment of service.

16A.8 The bankrupt must file in court an acknowledgment of service not more than 14 days after service of the application on him, indicating whether or not he contests the application. If he fails to do so he may attend the hearing of the application but may not take part in the hearing unless the court gives permission.

Opposing the application

16A.9 If the bankrupt wishes to oppose the application, he must within 28 days of service on him of the application and the evidence in support (or such longer period as the court may allow) file in court and (within three days thereof) serve on the Applicant any evidence which he wishes the court to take into consideration. Such evidence should normally be in the form of an affidavit or a witness statement verified by a statement of truth.

16A.10 The Applicant must file any evidence in reply within 14 days of receiving the evidence of the bankrupt (or such longer period as the court may allow) and must serve it on the bankrupt as soon as reasonably practicable.

Hearings

16A.11 Any hearing of an application for a bankruptcy restrictions order must be in public (r 6.241(5) Insolvency Rules 1986). The hearing will generally be before the registrar or district judge in the first instance who may:

(1) adjourn the application and give directions;

(2) make a bankruptcy restrictions order; or

(3) adjourn the application to the judge.

Making a bankruptcy restrictions order

16A.12 When the court is considering whether to make a bankruptcy restrictions order, it must not take into account any conduct of the bankrupt prior to 1 April 2004 (art. 7 Enterprise Act (Commencement No 4 and Transitional Provisions and Savings) Order 2003).

16A.13 The court may make a bankruptcy restrictions order in the absence of the bankrupt and whether or not he has filed evidence (r 6.244 Insolvency Rules 1986).

16A.14 When a bankruptcy restrictions order is made the court must send two sealed copies of the order to the Applicant (r 6.244(2) Insolvency Rules 1986), and as soon as reasonably practicable after receipt, the Applicant must send one sealed copy to the bankrupt (r 6.244(3)).

16A.15 A bankruptcy restrictions order comes into force when it is made and must specify the date on which it will cease to have effect, which must be between two and 15 years from the date on which it is made.

Interim bankruptcy restriction orders

16A.16 An application for an interim bankruptcy restrictions order may be made any time between the institution of an application for a bankruptcy restrictions order and the determination of that application (Sch 4A para. 5 Insolvency Act 1986). The application is made as an ordinary application in the bankruptcy.

16A.17 The application must be supported by a report as evidence in support of the application (r 6.246(1) Insolvency Rules 1986) which must include evidence of the bankrupt's conduct which is alleged to constitute the grounds for making an interim bankruptcy restrictions order and evidence of matters relating to the public interest in making the order.

16A.18 Notice of the application must be given to the bankrupt at least two business days before the date fixed for the hearing unless the court directs otherwise (r 6.245).

16A.19 Any hearing of the application must be in public (r 6.245).

16A.20 The court may make an interim bankruptcy restrictions order in the absence of the bankrupt and whether or not he has filed evidence (r 6.247).

16A.21 The bankrupt may apply to the court to set aside an interim bankruptcy restrictions order. The application is made by ordinary application in the bankruptcy and must be supported by an affidavit or witness statement verified by a statement of truth stating the grounds on which the application is made (r 6.248(2)).

16A.22 The bankrupt must send the Secretary of State, not less than 7 days before the hearing, notice of his application, notice of the venue, a copy of his application and a copy of the supporting affidavit. The Secretary of State may attend the hearing and call the attention of the court to any matters which seem to him to be relevant, and may himself give evidence or call witnesses.

16A.23 Where the court sets aside an interim bankruptcy restrictions order, two sealed copies of the order must be sent by the court, as soon as reasonably practicable, to the Secretary of State.

16A.24 As soon as reasonably practicable after receipt of sealed copies of the order, the Secretary of State must send a sealed copy to the bankrupt.

Bankruptcy restrictions undertakings

16A.25 Where a bankrupt has given a bankruptcy restrictions undertaking, the Secretary of State must file a copy in court and send a copy to the bankrupt as soon as reasonably practicable (r 6.250).

16A.26 The bankrupt may apply to annul a bankruptcy restrictions undertaking. The application is made as an ordinary application in the bankruptcy and must be supported by an affidavit or witness statement verified by a statement of truth stating the grounds on which it is made.

16A.27 The bankrupt must give notice of his application and the venue together with a copy of his affidavit in support to the Secretary of State at least 28 days before the date fixed for the hearing.

16A.28 The Secretary of State may attend the hearing and call the attention of the court to any matters which seem to him to be relevant and may himself give evidence or call witnesses.

16A.29 The court must send a sealed copy of any order annulling or varying the bankruptcy restrictions undertaking to the Secretary of State and the bankrupt.

Part Four

24.8

17 Appeals in insolvency proceedings

17.1 This Part shall come into effect on 2nd May 2000 and shall replace and revoke Paragraph 17 of, and be read in conjunction with the Practice Direction – Insolvency Proceedings which came into effect on 26th April 1999 as amended.

17.2
   (1) An appeal from a decision of a county court (whether made by a District Judge or a Circuit Judge) or of a Registrar of the High Court in insolvency proceedings ('a first appeal') lies to a Judge of the High Court pursuant to s 375(2) of the Act and Insolvency Rules 7.47(2) and 7.48(2) (as amended by s 55 of the Access to Justice Act 1999).
   (2) The procedure and practice for a first appeal are governed by Insolvency Rule 7.49 which imports the procedure and practice of the Court of Appeal. The procedure and practice of the Court of Appeal is governed by CPR Part 52 and its Practice Direction, which are subject to the provisions of the Act, the Insolvency Rules and this Practice Direction: see CPR Part 52 rule 1(4).
   (3) A first appeal (as defined above) does not include an appeal from a decision of a Judge of the High Court.

17.3
   (1) Section 55 of the Access to Justice Act 1999 has amended s 375(2) of the Act and Insolvency Rules 7.47(2) and 7.48(2) so

> that an appeal from a decision of a Judge of the High Court made on a first appeal lies, with the permission of the Court of Appeal, to the Court of Appeal.
>
> (2) An appeal from a Judge of the High Court in insolvency proceedings which is not a decision on a first appeal lies, with the permission of the Judge or of the Court of Appeal, to the Court of Appeal (see CPR Part 52 rule 3);
>
> (3) The procedure and practice for appeals from a decision of a Judge of the High Court in insolvency proceedings (whether made on a first appeal or not) are also governed by Insolvency Rule 7.49 which imports the procedure and practice of the Court of Appeal as stated at Paragraph 17.2(2) above.
>
> 17.4 CPR Part 52 and its Practice Direction and Forms apply to appeals from a decision of a Judge of the High Court in insolvency proceedings.
>
> 17.5 An appeal from a decision of a Judge of the High Court in insolvency proceedings requires permission as set out in Paragraph 17.3(1) and (2) above.
>
> 17.6 A first appeal does not require the permission of any court.

Notes

Para 17

This details the procedure to be adopted in relation to both first appeals to a High Court Judge and appeals to the Court of Appeal. It is important to note that no permission to appeal is required for a first appeal from a decision of a county court judge or registrar. However it may be that an appeal in insolvency proceedings against a summary assessment of costs alone will require permission: *Re Michaelides* [2004] BPIR 613. For appeals and reviews of court orders in relation to the winding up of companies see IR 1986 7.47 and Paragraph 7 above.

In relation to individual insolvency appeals each court has the power to review, rescind or vary any order made in the exercise of its jurisdiction; see IA 1986 s 375(1). The court has a wide discretion to rescind any order made in the exercise of the bankruptcy jurisdiction, but the onus is on the applicant to show the existence of exceptional circumstances, or at the very least in the form of some substantial new material or argument that justifies the court in changing its mind: *Papanicola v Humphreys* [2005] EWHC 335 (Ch), [2005] 2 All ER 418. *In Re a Debtor No 8 of 1997* it was held that the discretion to review under IA 1986 s 375(1) was a jurisdiction to be exercised on rare occasions when necessary to prevent a miscarriage of justice.

Such a review under s 375(1) differs from an appeal under IA1986 s 375(2) which lies to a higher court and is a true appeal and not a rehearing *in re Gilmartin* [1989] 1 WLR 513. The distinction is notable in relation to the admission of new evidence—see *in Re a Debtor (No 32–5d–1991)* [1993] 1 WLR 314 where it was held that on an application for a review under s 375 the court could as a matter of discretion admit fresh evidence notwithstanding that it was available at the time of the original hearing. Under Paragraph 17.18 below the admission of new evidence on appeal is more difficult to achieve.

Para 17.6

The Court observed in *Re Michaelides* [2003] EWHC 3029 (Ch), [2004] BPIR 613 that an appeal against a summary assessment of costs would require permission despite it being a decision in the course of insolvency proceedings.

17.7 Except as provided in this Part, CPR Part 52 and its Practice Direction and Forms do not apply to first appeals, but Paragraphs 17.8 to 17.23 inclusive of this Part apply only to first appeals.

17.8 Interpretation:

   (a)   the expressions 'appeal court', 'lower court', 'appellant', 'respondent' and 'appeal notice' have the meanings given in CPR Part 52.1(3);

   (b)   'Registrar of Appeals' means in relation to an appeal filed at the Royal Courts of Justice in London a Bankruptcy Registrar, and in relation to an appeal filed in a District Registry in accordance with Paragraph 17.10(2) and (3) below a District Judge of the relevant District Registry.

   (c)   'appeal date' means the date fixed by the appeal court for the hearing of the appeal or the date fixed by the appeal court upon which the period within which the appeal will be heard commences.

17.9 An appellant's notice and a respondent's notice shall be in Form PDIP 1 and PDIP 2 set out in the Schedule hereto.

17.10

   (1)   An appeal from a decision of a Registrar in Bankruptcy shall, or from any decision made in any county court may, be filed at the Royal Courts of Justice in London.

   (2)   An appeal from a decision made in the county court exercising jurisdiction over an area within the Birmingham, Bristol, Cardiff, Leeds, Liverpool, Manchester, Newcastle Upon Tyne or Preston Chancery District Registries may be filed in the Chancery District Registry of the High Court appropriate to the area in which the decision was made.

17.11

   (1)   Where a party seeks an extension of time in which to file an appeal notice it must be requested in the appeal notice and the appeal notice should state the reason for the delay and the steps taken prior to the application being made; the court will fix a date for the hearing of the application and notify the parties of the date and place of hearing;

   (2)   The appellant must file the appellant's notice at the appeal court within –

      (a)   such period as may be directed by the lower court; or

      (b)   where the court makes no such direction, 14 days after the date of the decision of the lower court which the appellant wishes to appeal.

   (3)   Unless the appeal court orders otherwise, an appeal notice must be served by the appellant on each respondent –

      (a)   as soon as practicable; and

      (b)   in any event not later than 7 days, after it is filed.

17.12

   (1)   A respondent may file and serve a respondent's notice.

   (2)   A respondent who wishes to ask the appeal court to uphold the order of the lower court for reasons different from or additional to those given by the lower court must file a respondent's notice.

   (3)   A respondent's notice must be filed within –
        (a)   such period as may be directed by the lower court; or
        (b)   where the court makes no such direction, 14 days after the date on which the respondent is served with the appellant's notice.
   (4)   Unless the appeal court orders otherwise a respondent's notice must be served by the respondent on the appellant and any other respondent –
        (a)   as soon as practicable; and
        (b)   in any event not later than 7 days, after it is filed.

17.13
   (1)   An application to vary the time limit for filing an appeal notice must be made to the appeal court.
   (2)   The parties may not agree to extend any date or time limit set by –
        (a)   this Practice Direction; or
        (b)   an order of the appeal court or the lower court.

17.14 Unless the appeal court or the lower court orders otherwise an appeal shall not operate as a stay of any order or decision of the lower court.

17.15 An appeal notice may not be amended without the permission of the appeal court.

17.16 A Judge of the appeal court may strike out the whole or part of an appeal notice where there is compelling reason for doing so.

17.17
   (1)   In relation to an appeal the appeal court has all the powers of the lower court.
   (2) The appeal court has power to –
        (a)   affirm, set aside or vary any order or judgment made or given by the lower court;
        (b)   refer any claim or issue for determination by the lower court;
        (c)   order a new trial or hearing;
        (d)   make a costs order.
   (3)   The appeal court may exercise its powers in relation to the whole or part of an order of the lower court.

17.18
   (1)   Every appeal shall be limited to a review of the decision of the lower court.
   (2)   Unless it orders otherwise, the appeal court will not receive –
        (a)   oral evidence; or
        (b)   evidence which was not before the lower court.
   (3)   The appeal court will allow an appeal where the decision of the lower court was –
        (a)   wrong; or
        (b)   unjust because of a serious procedural or other irregularity in the proceedings in the lower court.
   (4)   The appeal court may draw any inference of fact which it considers justified on the evidence.

(5) At the hearing of the appeal a party may not rely on a matter not contained in his appeal notice unless the appeal court gives permission.

17.19 The following applications shall be made to a Judge of the appeal court:
(1) for injunctions pending a substantive hearing of the appeal;
(2) for expedition or vacation of the hearing date of an appeal;
(3) for an order striking out the whole or part of an appeal notice pursuant to Paragraph 17.16 above;
(4) for a final order on paper pursuant to Paragraph 17.22(8) below.

17.20
(1) All other interim applications shall be made to the Registrar of Appeals in the first instance who may in his discretion either hear and determine it himself or refer it to the Judge.
(2) An appeal from a decision of a Registrar of Appeals lies to a Judge of the appeal court and does not require the permission of either the Registrar of Appeals or the Judge.

17.21 The procedure for interim applications is by way of ordinary application (see Insolvency Rule 12.7 and Sch 4, Form 7.2).

17.22 The following practice applies to all first appeals to a Judge of the High Court whether filed at the Royal Courts of Justice in London, or filed at one of the other venues referred to in Paragraph 17.10 above:
(1) on filing an appellant's notice in accordance with Para-graph 17.11(2) above, the appellant must file:
   (a) two copies of the appeal notice for the use of the court, one of which must be stamped with the appropriate fee, and a number of additional copies equal to the number of persons who are to be served with it pursuant to Paragraph 17.22(4) below;
   (b) a copy of the order under appeal; and
   (c) an estimate of time for the hearing.
(2) the above documents may be lodged personally or by post and shall be lodged at the address of the appropriate venue listed below:
   (a) if the appeal is to be heard at the Royal Courts of Justice in London the documents must be lodged at Room 110, Thomas More Building, The Royal Courts of Justice, Strand, London WC2A 2LL;
   (b) if the appeal is to be heard in Birmingham, the documents must be lodged at the District Registry of the Chancery Division of the High Court, 33 Bull Street, Birmingham B4 6DS;
   (c) if the appeal is to be heard in Bristol the documents must be lodged at the District Registry of the Chancery Division of the High Court, Third Floor, Greyfriars, Lewins Mead, Bristol, BS1 2NR;
   (d) if the appeal is to be heard in Cardiff the documents must be lodged at the District Registry in the Chancery Division of the High Court, First Floor, 2 Park Street, Cardiff, CF10 1ET;

(e) if the appeal is to be heard in Leeds the documents must be lodged at the District Registry of the Chancery Division of the High Court, The Court House, 1 Oxford Row, Leeds LS1 3BG;

(f) if the appeal is to be heard in Liverpool the documents must be lodged at the District Registry of the Chancery Division of the High Court, Liverpool Combined Court Centre, Derby Square, Liverpool L2 1XA;

(g) if the appeal is to be heard in Manchester the documents must be lodged at the District Registry of the Chancery Division of the High Court, Courts of Justice, Crown Square, Manchester, M60 9DJ;

(h) if the appeal is to be heard at Newcastle Upon Tyne the documents must be lodged at the District Registry of the Chancery Division of the High Court, The Law Courts, Quayside, Newcastle Upon Tyne NE1 3LA;

(i) if the appeal is to be heard in Preston the documents must be lodged at the District Registry of the Chancery Division of the High Court, The Combined Court Centre, Ringway, Preston PR1 2LL.

(3) if the documents are correct and in order the court at which the documents are filed will fix the appeal date and will also fix the place of hearing. That court will send letters to all the parties to the appeal informing them of the appeal date and of the place of hearing and indicating the time estimate given by the appellant. The parties will be invited to notify the court of any alternative or revised time estimates. In the absence of any such notification the estimate of the appellant will be taken as agreed. The court will also send to the appellant a document setting out the court's requirement concerning the form and content of the bundle of documents for the use of the Judge. Not later than 7 days before the appeal date the bundle of documents must be filed by the appellant at the address of the relevant venue as set out in sub-paragraph 17.22(2) above and a copy of it must be served by the appellant on each respondent. The bundle should include an approved transcript of the judgment of the lower court or, where there is no officially recorded judgment, the document(s) referred to in paragraph 5.12 of the Practice Direction to CPR Part 52.

(4) the appeal notice must be served on all parties to the proceedings in the lower court who are directly affected by the appeal. This may include the Official Receiver, liquidator or trustee in bankruptcy.

(5) the appeal notice must be served by the appellant or by the legal representative of the appellant and may be effected by:
(a) any of the methods referred to in CPR Part 6 rule 2; or
(b) with permission of the court, an alternative method pursuant to CPR Part 6 rule 8.

(6) service of an appeal notice shall be proved by a Certificate of Service in accordance with CPR Part 6 rule 10 (CPR Form N215) which must be filed at the relevant venue referred to at Paragraph 17.22(2) above immediately after service.

(7) skeleton arguments, accompanied by a written chronology of events relevant to the appeal, should be filed at the address of the appropriate venue as set out in sub-paragraph 17.22(2) above, at least two clear days before the date fixed for the hearing. Failure to lodge may result in an adverse costs order being made by the Judge on the hearing of the appeal.

(8) where an appeal has been settled or where an appellant does not wish to continue with the appeal, the appeal may be disposed of on paper without a hearing. It may be dismissed by consent but the appeal court will not make an order allowing an appeal unless it is satisfied that the decision of the lower court was wrong. Any consent order signed by each party or letters of consent from each party must be lodged not later than 24 hours before the date fixed for the hearing of the appeal at the address of the appropriate venue as set out in sub-paragraph 17.22(2) above and will be dealt with by the Judge of the appeal court. Attention is drawn to paragraph 4.4(4) of the Practice Direction to CPR Part 44 regarding costs where an order is made by consent without attendance.

17.23 Only the following paragraphs of the Practice Direction to CPR Part 52, with any necessary modifications, shall apply to first appeals: 5.12 and 5.14 to 5.20 inclusive.

17.24

(1) Where, under the procedure relating to appeals in insolvency proceedings prior to the coming into effect of this Part of this Practice Direction, an appeal has been set down in the High Court or permission to appeal to the Court of Appeal has been granted before 2nd May 2000, the procedure and practice set out in this Part of this Practice Direction shall apply to such an appeal after that date.

(2) Where, under the procedure relating to appeals in insolvency proceedings prior to the coming into effect of this Part of this Practice Direction, any person has failed before 2nd May 2000 either:

 (a) in the case of a first appeal, to set down in the High Court an appeal which relates to an order made (county court) or sealed (High Court) after 27th March 2000 and before 2nd May 2000, or

 (b) in the case of an appeal from a decision of a Judge of the High Court, to obtain any requisite permission to appeal to the Court of Appeal which relates to an order sealed in the same period,

the time for filing an appeal notice is extended to 16th May 2000 and application for any such permission should be made in the appeal notice.

17.25 This paragraph applies where a judge of the High Court has made a Bankruptcy order or a winding-up order or dismissed an appeal against such an order and an application is made for a stay of proceedings pending appeal.

(1) the judge will not normally grant a stay of all proceedings but will confine himself to a stay of advertisement of the proceedings.

(2)   where the judge has granted permission to appeal any stay of advertisement will normally be until the hearing of the appeal but on terms that the stay will determine without further order if an appellant's notice is not filed within the period prescribed by the rules.

(3)   where the judge has refused permission to appeal any stay of advertisement will normally be for a period not exceeding 28 days. Application for any further stay of advertisement should be made to the Court of Appeal.

Notes

Para 17.17, 17.18

These provisions confirm that a first appeal is a true appeal limited to a review of the decision of the lower court and will not be a re-hearing; *In re Gilmartin* [1989] 1 WLR 513. An appeal will only be allowed if the decision of the lower court was wrong or unjust because of some serious procedural or other irregularity.

The court will not receive evidence on the appeal which was not before the lower court nor oral evidence unless it gives permission. Where there is a trial or hearing on the merits the principles in *Ladd v Marshall* [1954] 1 WLR 1489 are relevant and the case is persuasive authority on the question of admission of new evidence on appeal: *Hamilton v Al Fayed* (2001) Times, 25 January. However the court is not fettered by *Ladd v Marshall* for the purposes of admitting fresh evidence on an appeal of an application to set aside a statutory demand as the application itself was not a trial or hearing on the merits: *Salvidge v Hussein* [1999] BPIR 410, *Heavy Duty Parts Ltd v Anelay* [2004] EWHC 960 (Ch), [2004] BPIR 729. In every case consideration needs to be given to the nature of the application being appealed.

Forms

The relevant forms to be used in conjunction with the Practice Direction: Insolvency Proceedings (PDIP1–PDIP4) can be downloaded from www.lcd.gov.uk.

Chancery Division: Practice note on the hearing of Insolvency proceedings

25.1

1 The following statement was issued by the Vice-Chancellor.

2 This Practice Note supersedes all previous Practice Statements of the Bankruptcy Registrars dealing with jurisdiction and work distribution and the Guidelines issued by the Insolvency Court Users' Committee in November 1988.

3 As a general rule all petitions, claims and applications (except for those listed in paragraph 4 below) should be listed for initial hearing before a registrar or district judge in accordance with rule 7.6(2) Insolvency Rules 1986.

4 The following applications should always be listed before a judge:

Proceedings relating to insolvent companies
- applications for committal for contempt
- applications for an administration order
- applications for an injunction
- applications for the appointment of a provisional liquidator
- interim applications and applications for directions or case management after any proceedings have been referred or adjourned to the judge (except where liberty to apply to the registrar or district judge has been given);

Proceedings relating to insolvent individuals
- applications for committal for contempt
- applications for an injunction
- interim applications and applications for directions or case management after any proceedings have been referred or adjourned to the judge (except where liberty to apply to the registrar or district judge has been given).

5 When deciding whether to hear proceedings themselves or refer or adjourn them to the judge, the registrar or district judge should have regard to the following factors:
- the complexity of the proceedings
- whether the proceedings raise new or controversial points of law
- the likely date and length of the hearing
- public interest in the proceedings

> - the availability in the court which is likely to hear the proceedings of relevant specialist expertise.
>
> 6 Litigants and their advisors are reminded that paragraph 17 of the Practice Direction on Insolvency Proceedings applies to appeals and that an appeal from a registrar, district judge or county court judge lies, in the first instance and without permission, to a single judge of the High Court.

Vice Chancellor

23 May 2005

Notes

Though this Practice Note is not expressed as amending the rules relating to distribution of business in para 5 Practice Direction: Insolvency Proceedings, Civil Procedure, Vol. 2, Section 3E it appears that it was intended that a registrar or district judge should have a wider jurisdiction and the rules relating to work distribution are now contained in this Practice Note. However in practice an application for a validation order under s 127 is usually made before the Judge rather than a registrar or district judge.

Practice Statement – the fixing and approval of the remuneration of appointees (2004)

Notes

This Practice Statement came into force in relation to most applications to fix remuneration issued after 1 October 2004. It was compiled shortly after the decision in *Re Cabletel Installations Limited* [2005] BPIR 28 in which Mr.Registrar Baister (as he then was) heard an application from administrators under IR 1986 r 2.47 for the fixing of their remuneration by the court. The administration was an "old style" administration and a director who was also a creditor of the company challenged the amount of remuneration which the administrators sought to obtain. The case itself was unusual in that the court heard witness evidence over a number of days and at the IA 1986 s 23 creditors' meeting to approve the proposals of the administrators the creditors resolved not to approve the administrators' fees; it should also be noted that he administration was a non trading administration. After a detailed analysis of the breakdown of the fees involved the court substantially reduced the fees claimed by the administrators relying on *Mirror Group Newspapers plc v Maxwell (No 2)* [1998] 1 BCLC 638 and *Re Independent Insurance Co Ltd (No 2)* [2003] EWHC 51 (Ch), [2003] 1 BCLC 640.

The approach of the court in *Re Cabletel Installations Limited* to the fixing of remuneration was not unique and it adopted the principles of transparency and value for money established in *Mirror Group Newspapers plc v Maxwell (No 2)* [1998] 1 BCLC 638 and *Re Independent Insurance Co Ltd (No 2)* [2003] EWHC 51 (Ch), [2003] 1 BCLC 640. Prior to the more interventionist role adopted by the court in those cases there were few reported decisions on the fixing of remuneration. The Practice Statement has promoted a number of guiding principles which must be considered by interested parties and the court in the fixing of remuneration.

Part One

General

26.1

1 Definitions and interpretation

1.1

In this Practice Statement:

(1) "appointee" means:
    (i) A provisional liquidator appointed under Section 135 of the Insolvency Act;
    (ii) A special manager appointed under Section 177 or Section 370 of the Insolvency Act;

    (iii) A liquidator appointed by the members of a company or partnership or by the creditors of a company or partnership or by the Secretary of State pursuant to Section 137 of the Insolvency Act, or by the court pursuant to Section 140 of the Insolvency Act;

    (iv) An administrator of a company appointed to manage the property, business and affairs of that company under the Insolvency Act or other enactment and to which the provisions of the Insolvency Act are applicable;

    (v) A trustee in bankruptcy (other than the Official Receiver) appointed under the Insolvency Act;

    (vi) A nominee or supervisor of a voluntary arrangement under Part I or Part VIII of the Insolvency Act;

    (vii) A licensed insolvency practitioner appointed by the court pursuant to Section 273 of the Insolvency Act;

    (viii) An interim receiver appointed by the court pursuant to Section 286 of the Insolvency Act;

(2) "Appointment" means the appointment as an appointee;

(3) "Assessor" means a person appointed in accordance with Rule 35.15 of the CPR;

(4) "CPR" means the Civil Procedure Rules 1998 (as amended);

(5) "The court" means the court exercising jurisdiction in respect of the appointment in accordance with the Insolvency Act and the Insolvency Rules or other relevant enactment and / or applicable rules;

(6) "The guiding principles" means the statements of principle contained in paragraph 3.4;

(7) "Insolvency Act" means the Insolvency Act 1986 (as amended);

(8) "Insolvency Rules" means the Insolvency Rules 1986 (as amended);

(9) "The objective" means the objective stated in paragraph 3.2.

Notes

Para 1.1(1)

The Practice Statement does not apply to the fixing of the remuneration of administrative receivers or receivers. The fixing of their remuneration is initially at least a matter of contract between the receiver and appointor in the case of out of court appointed receivers. However a disgruntled creditor could seek to challenge the remuneration of a receiver on the basis of an application for directions (IA 1986 s 35, 36, *Munns v Perkins* [2002] BPIR 120) seeking a detailed assessment pursuant to the CPR if appropriate.

26.2

1.2 References to paragraphs are references to paragraphs of this Practice Statement.

26.3

2 Applicability

2.1 This Practice Statement shall, save to the extent and as may otherwise be ordered by the court, apply to all appointees in respect of:

(1) any application to the court by an appointee for the fixing and approval of his remuneration where his remuneration has not otherwise already been fixed and approved;

(2) any application to the court by an appointee for the fixing and approval of his remuneration in circumstances where he considers that the amount of his remuneration as fixed and approved by resolution of the members of the partnership or company or the creditors' committee or the liquidation committee or by resolution of the general body of creditors (as appropriate) is insufficient;

(3) any application by a person who may be permitted to apply under the Insolvency Act, the Insolvency Rules, or otherwise including by reference to the jurisdiction of the court to supervise the conduct of one of its officers and the inherent jurisdiction of the Supreme Court and is dissatisfied with the remuneration of an appointee that has otherwise been fixed and approved on the basis that such remuneration is excessive.

2.2 This Practice Statement shall come into effect on 1 October 2004 and shall apply to all applications for the fixing and approval of the remuneration of an appointee issued after that date.

3 The objective and the guiding principles

3.1 This Practice Statement is supplemental to the Insolvency Act, the Insolvency Rules and such other enactments or rules as have been or may be introduced and which are relevant to the fixing and approval of the remuneration of an appointee.

3.2 The objective of this Practice Statement is to ensure that the remuneration of an appointee which is fixed and approved by the court is fair, reasonable and commensurate with the nature and extent of the work properly undertaken by the appointee in any given case and is fixed and approved by reference to a process which is consistent and predictable.

3.3 Set out below are the guiding principles by reference to which applications for the fixing and approval of the remuneration of appointees are to be considered both by applicants, in the preparation and presentation of their application, and by the court which is required to determine such applications.

3.4 The guiding principles are as follows:
    (1)   "Justification": It is for the appointee who seeks to be remunerated at a particular level and / or in a particular manner to justify

his claim and in order to do so the appointee should be prepared to provide full particulars of the basis for and the nature of his claim for remuneration.

(2) "The benefit of the doubt": The corollary of guiding principle (1) is that on any application for the fixing and approval of the remuneration of an appointee, if after considering the evidence before it and after having regard to the guiding principles (in particular guiding principle (3)), the matters contained in paragraph 5.2 (in particular paragraph 5.2(10)) and the matters referred to in paragraph 5.3 (as appropriate) there remains any element of doubt as to the appropriateness, fairness or reasonableness of the amount sought to be fixed and approved (whether arising from a lack of particularity as to the basis for and the nature of the appointee's claim to remuneration or otherwise) such element of doubt should be resolved by the court against the appointee.

(3) "Professional integrity": The court should give weight to the fact that the appointee is a member of a regulated profession (where such is the case) and as such is subject to rules and guidance as to professional conduct and (where such is the case) the fact that the appointee is an officer of the court.

(4) "The value of the service rendered": the remuneration of an appointee should reflect and should be fixed and approved so as to reward the value of the service rendered by the appointee, not simply to reimburse the appointee in respect of time expended and cost incurred.

(5) "Fair and reasonable": the amount of the remuneration to be fixed and approved by the court should be fair and reasonable and represent fair and reasonable remuneration for the work properly undertaken or to be undertaken.

(6) "Proportionality":

(i) "Proportionality of information": in considering the nature and extent of the information which should be provided by an appointee in respect of an application for the fixing and approval of his remuneration the court, the appointee and any other parties to the application shall have regard to what is proportionate by reference to the amount of remuneration to be fixed and approved, the nature, complexity and extent of the work to be completed (where the application relates to future remuneration) or that has been completed by the appointee and the value and nature of the assets and liabilities with which the appointee will have to deal or has had to deal;

(ii) "Proportionality of remuneration": the amount of remuneration to be fixed and approved by the court should be proportional to the nature, complexity and extent of the work to be completed (where the application relates to future remuneration) or that has been completed by the appointee and the value and nature of the assets and / or potential assets and the liabilities and / or potential liabilities with which the appointee will have to deal or has had to deal, the nature and degree of the responsibility to which the appointee has been subject in any given case, the nature and extent of the risk (if any) assumed by the appointee and the efficiency (in respect of both time and cost) with which the appointee has completed the work undertaken;

(7) "Professional guidance": In respect of an application for the fixing and approval of the remuneration of an appointee, the appointee may have regard to the relevant and current statements of practice promulgated by any relevant regulatory and professional bodies in relation to the fixing and approval of the remuneration of an appointee. In considering an application for the fixing or approval of the remuneration of an appointee, the court may also have regard to such statements of practice and the extent of compliance with such statements of practice by the appointee.

(8) "Impracticability": where the appointee has not, either upon or shortly after the commencement of his appointment, sought to have the basis upon which his remuneration is to be fixed approved by the members of the partnership or the company, the creditors' committee, the liquidation committee or the general body of creditors (as appropriate) and in circumstances where the appointee considers that it will be impracticable to have his remuneration fixed and / or approved in such a manner, he may, as soon as reasonably practicable after his appointment, apply to the court to have the basis upon which he is to be remunerated fixed and for directions as to the manner in which his remuneration is to be approved (which may include provision for payments to be made on account). In circumstances where such an application may be made, to the extent that such an application is not made but the appointee subsequently makes an application to the court for the fixing and approval of the whole or any part of his remuneration, an explanation as to why no earlier application was made shall be provided to the court.

Notes

Para 3.4(2)

It is therefore important for the appointee to appreciate that the burden of persuading the court to fix the remuneration requested is firmly placed on the appointee.

Para 3.4(7)

The court in *Re Cabletel Installations Limited* [2005] BPIR 28 described the Statement of Insolvency Practice 9 which dealt with remuneration issues as a '... limited effort to deal with the matters thrown up by Ferris J ...' in *Mirror Group Newspapers plc v Maxwell (No 2)* [1998] 1 BCLC 638.

Para 3.4(8)

It is important that the appointee makes an application to court to fix remuneration quickly if the creditors have not fixed the remuneration or the appointee considers that it would be impracticable for them to fix it. If as in *Re Cabletel Installations Limited* itself an administrator refuses to end the administration until the remuneration is fixed the court will potentially regard such conduct as an abuse.

Part Two
The fixing and approval of remuneration

26.4

4 Distribution of business

4.1 All applications for the fixing and approval of the remuneration of an appointee shall in the first instance (unless otherwise ordered by the court, having regard to the particular circumstances of an application) be made, where the court is the High Court to a Registrar or a District Judge in the appropriate District Registry of the High Court or, where the court is a county court, a District Judge in the appropriate county court.

4.2 On the hearing of the application the court shall consider the evidence then available to it and may either summarily determine the application or adjourn it giving such directions as it thinks appropriate. Such directions may include a direction that:

(1) an assessor or a Costs Judge prepare a report to the court in respect of the remuneration which is sought to be fixed and approved; and / or

(2) the application be heard by the Registrar or the District Judge sitting with or without an assessor or a Costs Judge or by a Judge sitting with or without an assessor or a Costs Judge.

4.3 In the usual course an application for the fixing and approval of the remuneration of an appointee should be determined by a Registrar or a District Judge sitting without an assessor or a Costs Judge and without the need for a report from an assessor or a Costs Judge.

4.4 The court may give the directions referred to in paragraphs 4.2(1) and (2) where it considers this to be appropriate having regard to the size and complexity of the case or in the event that the application gives rise to complicated issues of fact or of law. The court ought only to make an order for the involvement of a Costs Judge in circumstances where it considers the involvement of an assessor is (for whatever reason) not appropriate and that the application can only properly be determined by reference to the particular expertise and assistance that can be provided by a Costs Judge.

4.5 A list of suitably qualified persons appointed by the court to act as assessors in respect of applications for the fixing and approval of the remuneration of an appointee is available from the court.

4.6 The reasonable costs of an assessor appointed by the court shall be paid from the assets under the control of the appointee.

Notes

Para 4.2

In *Re Independent Insurance Co Ltd (No 2)* [2003] EWHC 51 (Ch), [2003] 1 BCLC 640 Ferris J sat with an assessor who was an experienced insolvency solicitor.

26.5

5 Relevant criteria and procedure

5.1 When considering an application for the fixing and approval of the remuneration of an appointee the court shall have regard to the objective, the guiding principles and all relevant circumstances including the matters referred to in paragraph 5.2 and where appropriate paragraph 5.3, each of which should be addressed in the evidence placed before the court.

5.2 On any application for the fixing and approval of the remuneration of an appointee, the appointee should:
  (1) Provide a narrative description and explanation of:
    (i) the background to, the relevant circumstances of and the reasons for the appointment;
    (ii) the work undertaken or to be undertaken in respect of the appointment and in respect of which work the remuneration of the appointee is sought to be fixed and approved, which description should be divided, insofar as possible, into individual tasks or categories of task. General descriptions of work, tasks, or categories of task should (insofar as possible) be avoided;
    (iii) the reasons why it is or was considered reasonable and / or necessary and / or beneficial for such work to be conducted, giving details of why particular tasks or categories of task were undertaken and why such tasks or categories of task are to be undertaken or have been undertaken by particular individuals and in a particular manner;
    (iv) the amount of time to be spent or that has been spent in respect of work to be completed or that has been completed and in respect of which the fixing and approval of remuneration is sought and which it is considered is fair, reasonable and proportionate;
    (v) what is likely to be and has been achieved, the benefits that are likely to and have accrued as a consequence of the work that is to be or has been completed, the manner in which the work required in respect of the appointment is progressing and what, in the opinion of the appointee, remains to be achieved.

(2) Provide details sufficient for the court to determine the application by reference to the criteria which is required to be taken into account by reference to the Insolvency Rules and any other applicable enactments or rules relevant to the fixing and approval of the remuneration of an appointee.

(3) Provide a statement of the total number of hours of work undertaken or to be undertaken in respect of which the fixing and approval of remuneration is sought, together with a breakdown of such hours by individual member of staff and individual tasks or categories of tasks to be performed or that have been performed. Details should also be given of:
  (i) the tasks or categories of tasks to be undertaken as a proportion of the total amount of work to be undertaken in respect of which the fixing and approval of remuneration is sought and the tasks

or categories of tasks that have been undertaken as a proportion of the total amount of work that has been undertaken in respect of which the fixing and approval of remuneration is sought; and

(ii) the tasks or categories of task to be completed by individual members of staff or grade of personnel including the appointee as a proportion of the total amount of work to be completed by all members of staff including the appointee in respect of which the fixing and approval of remuneration is sought, or the tasks or categories of task that have been completed by individual members of staff or grade of personnel as a proportion of the total amount of work that has been completed by all members of staff including the appointee in respect of which the fixing and approval of remuneration is sought.

(4) Provide a statement of the total amount to be charged for the work to be undertaken or that has been undertaken in respect of which the fixing and approval of remuneration is sought which should include:

(i) a breakdown of such amounts by individual member of staff and individual task or categories of task performed;

(ii) details of the time expended and the remuneration charged in respect of each individual task or category of task as a proportion (respectively) of the total time expended and the total remuneration charged.

In respect of an application pursuant to which the amount of the appointee's remuneration is to be fixed and approved on the basis of a percentage of the value of the assets realised and / or distributed, the appointee shall provide (for the purposes of comparison) the same details as are required by this paragraph (4), but on the basis of what would have been charged had he been seeking remuneration on the basis of the time properly spent by him and his staff.

(5) Provide details of each individual to be engaged or who has been engaged in work in respect of the appointment and in respect of which the fixing and approval of remuneration is sought, including details of their relevant experience, training, qualifications and the level of their seniority.

(6) Provide an explanation of:

(i) the steps, if any, to be taken or that have been taken by the appointee to avoid duplication of effort and cost in respect of the work to be completed or that has been completed in respect of which the fixing and approval of the remuneration is sought; and

(ii) the steps to be taken or that have been taken to ensure that the work to be completed or that has been completed is to be or was undertaken by individuals of appropriate experience and seniority relative to the nature of the work to be or that has been undertaken.

(7) Provide details of the individual rates charged by the appointee and members of his staff in respect of the work to be completed or that has been completed and in respect of which the remuneration is sought to be fixed and approved. Such details should include:

(i) a general explanation of the policy adopted in relation to the fixing or calculation of such rates;

(ii) in relation to charges in respect of secretarial, administrative and cashiering services (and / or such other charges as might also otherwise be regarded as an overhead cost forming a component part of the rates charged by the appointee and members of his staff), an explanation as to why (where this is the case) such costs are to be or have been charged for separately together with confirmation that where such work is to be or has been charged for separately such work will not or has not also been charged for as part of the rates that are to be or have been charged by the appointee and / or members of his staff;

(iii) a description of the manner in which the appointee and members of his staff record the nature of the work they will undertake or have undertaken in respect of which the fixing and approval of remuneration is sought and the manner in which the amount of time spent in carrying out such work is recorded. This explanation should include, in circumstances where time is charged for on the basis of a unit of time a description of such unit and the practice and policy applied in recording time spent by reference to that unit.

As regards sub-paragraphs (i) to (iii) of this paragraph (7) only subparagraph (iii) shall apply to applications to which paragraph 5.3 applies.

(8) Where the application for the fixing and approval of remuneration is in respect of a period of time during which the charge out rates of the appointee and / or members of his staff engaged in work in respect of the appointment have increased, provide an explanation of the nature, extent and reason for such increase and the date when such increase took effect.

This paragraph (8) does not apply to applications to which paragraph 5.3 applies.

(9) Provide details of any remuneration previously fixed and approved in relation to the appointment (whether by the court or otherwise) including in particular the amounts that were previously sought to be fixed and approved and the amounts that were in fact fixed and approved and the basis upon which such amounts were fixed and approved.

(10) In order that the court may be able to consider the views of those persons

which the appointee considers have an interest in the assets that are under his control, provide details of:

(i) what (if any) consultation has taken place between the appointee and those persons and if no such consultation has taken place an explanation should be given as to the reason why; and

(ii) the number and value of the interests of the persons consulted including details of the proportion (by number and by value) of the interests of such persons by reference to the entirety of those persons having an interest in the assets under the control of the appointee.

(11) Provide such other relevant information as the appointee considers, in the circumstances, ought to be provided to the court.

Notes

Para 5.2(7)

The modern practice is to charge in units of 6 minutes; however some firms of insolvency practitioners have in the past adopted charging units of 15 minutes. It is doubtful whether 15 minute units can be justified.

26.6

5.3 This paragraph applies to applications where the remuneration of the appointee is to be fixed and approved on the basis of a percentage of the value of the assets realised and / or distributed. On such applications in addition to the matters referred to in paragraph 5.2 (as applicable) the appointee shall:

(1) Provide a full description of the basis of and reasons for his remuneration being sought to be fixed and approved by reference to a percentage of the value of the assets realised and / or distributed.

(2) Provide a full explanation of the basis upon which the percentage rates to be applied to the values of the assets realised and / or distributed have been chosen.

(3) Provide a statement that to the best of the appointee's belief the percentage rates which are sought to be applied are similar to the percentage rates that are applied or have been applied in respect of other appointments of a similar nature.

(4) By reference to the matters contained in paragraph 5.2 (as applicable), provide a comparison of the amount to be charged by reference to a percentage of the value of the assets realised and / or distributed and an estimate of the amount that would otherwise have been charged if the remuneration was to be fixed by reference to the time properly given by him and his staff.

(5) Provide a comparison between the amounts to be charged by reference to a percentage of the value of the assets realised and / or distributed using the percentage rates sought to be fixed and approved by the court and the percentage rates provided for by the scale of fees referred to in Schedule 6 to the Insolvency Rules.

5.4 If and insofar as any of the matters referred to in paragraph 5.2 or 5.3 (as appropriate) are not addressed in the evidence placed before the court on the hearing of an application for the fixing and approval of the remuneration of an appointee an explanation for why this is the case should be included in such evidence.

5.5 Notwithstanding that the expenses and disbursements of the appointee and his staff are not required to be approved by the court on any application by the appointee for the fixing and approval of his remuneration, a summary of the amount and nature of such expenses and disbursements incurred during the relevant period should be provided as should an explanation of the steps taken by the appointee to subject such expenses and disbursements to critical scrutiny.

5.6 There should be included in the evidence placed before the court by the appointee in respect of any application for the fixing and approval of the remuneration of an appointee the following documents:

(1) A copy of the most recent receipts and payments account;

(2) Copies of any reports by the appointee to the persons having an interest in the assets under his control relevant to the period for which the remuneration sought to be fixed and approved relates;

(3) Schedules or such other representations of the information referred to in paragraphs 5.2 and 5.3 such as are likely to be of assistance to the court in fixing and approving the remuneration of the appointee.

(4) Evidence of consultation with those persons having an interest in the assets under the control of appointee in relation to the fixing and approval of the remuneration of the appointee.

5.7 On any application for the fixing and approval of remuneration of an appointee the court may make an order permitting payments of remuneration to be made on account subject to final approval whether by the court or otherwise.

5.8 Unless otherwise ordered by the court (or as may otherwise be provided for in any enactment or rules of procedure) the costs of and occasioned by an application for the fixing and / or approval of the remuneration of an appointee shall be paid from the assets under the control of the appointee.

Stephen Baister

Chief Registrar

15 July 2004

Notes

Para 5.6(4)

It is not entirely clear what is meant by " *evidence of consultation*" nor the width of the category of persons included as *"having an interest in the assets"*; it appears that both phrases may require an appointee to go beyond what is required by the relevant rules of disclosure to creditors and other interested parties.

Practice Direction: Directors Disqualification Proceedings

Part One

27.1

1 Application and Interpretation

1.1 In this practice direction—
   (1) "the Act" means the Company Directors Disqualification Act 1986 (as amended);
   (2) "the Disqualification Rules" means the rules for the time being in force made under section 411 of the Insolvency Act 1986 in relation to disqualification proceedings;[1]
   (3) "the Insolvency Rules" means the rules for the time being in force made under sections 411 and 412 of the Insolvency Act 1986 in relation to insolvency proceedings;
   (4) "CPR" means the Civil Procedure Rules 1998 and "CPR" followed by "Part" or "Rule" and a number means the part or Rule with that number in those Rules;
   (5) "disqualification proceedings" has the meaning set out in paragraph 1.3 below;
   (6) "a disqualification application" is an application under the Act for the making of a disqualification order;
   (7) "registrar" means any judge of the High Court or the county court who is a registrar within the meaning of the Insolvency Rules;
   (8) "companies court registrar" means any judge of the High Court sitting in the Royal Courts of Justice in London who is a registrar within the meaning of the Insolvency Rules;
   (9) except where the context otherwise requires references to—
      (a) "company" or "companies" shall include references to "partnership" or "partnerships" and to "limited liability partnership" and "limited liability partnerships"
      (b) "director" shall include references to an "officer" of a partnership and to a "member" of a limited liability partnership
      (c) "shadow director" shall include references to a "shadow member" of a limited liability partnership
   and, in appropriate cases, the forms annexed to this practice direction shall be varied accordingly;

1943

(10) "disqualification order" has the meaning set out in section 1 of the Act and "disqualification undertaking" has the meaning set out in section 1A of the Act;

(11) a "Section 8A application" is an application under section 8A of the Act to reduce the period for which a disqualification undertaking is in force or to provide for it to cease to be in force.

1.2 This practice direction shall come into effect on 26 April 1999 and shall replace all previous practice directions relating to disqualification proceedings.

1.3 This practice direction applies to the following proceedings ("disqualification proceedings")—

(1) disqualification applications made—

(a) under section 2(2)(a) of the Act (after the person's conviction of an indictable offence in connection with the affairs of a company);

(b) under section 3 of the Act (on the ground of persistent breaches of provisions of companies legislation);

(c) under section 4 of the Act (on the ground of fraud etc);

(d) by the Secretary of State or the official receiver under section 7(1) of the Act (on the ground of the person's unfitness to be concerned in the management of a company); or

(e) by the Secretary of State under section 8 of the Act (following a report made by inspectors or in consequence of information or documents obtained);

(2) any application made under section 7(2) or 7(4) of the Act; and

(3) any application made under sections 12(2) or 17 of the Act and any application for permission to act notwithstanding a disqualification order which was made under any statutory predecessor of the Act;

(4) any application for a court order made under CPR Part 23 in the course of any of the proceedings set out in sub-paragraphs (1) to (3) above;

(5) any application under the Act to the extent provided for by subordinate legislation;[2]

(6) any section 8A application.

27.2

2 Multi-track

2.1 All disqualification proceedings are allocated to the multi-track. The CPR relating to allocation questionnaires and track allocation shall not apply.

27.3

3 Rights of Audience

3.1 Official receivers and deputy official receivers have right of audience in any proceedings to which this Practice Direction applies, including cases where a disqualification application is made by the Secretary of State or by the official receiver at his direction, and whether made in the High Court or a county court.[3]

Part Two
Disqualification Applications

27.4

4 Commencement

4.1 A disqualification application must be commenced by a claim form issued—
   (1)   in the High Court out of the office of the companies court registrar or a chancery district registry; and
   (2)   in the county court, out of a county court office.

Sections 2(2)(a), 3(4), 4(2), 6(3) and 8(3) of the Act identify the courts which have jurisdiction to deal with disqualification applications.

4.2 Disqualification applications shall be made by the issue of a claim form in the form annexed hereto and the use of the procedure set out in CPR Part 8,[4] as modified by this practice direction and (where the application is made under sections 7 or 8 of the Act) the Disqualification Rules. CPR rule 8.1(3) (power of the Court to order the application to continue as if the claimant had not used the Part 8 Procedure) shall not apply.

4.3 When the claim form is issued, the claimant will be given a date for the first hearing of the disqualification application. This date is to be not less than eight weeks from the date of issue of the claim form.[6] The first hearing will be before a registrar.

27.5

5 Headings

5.1 Every claim form by which a disqualification application under the Act is begun and all affidavits, notices and other documents in the proceedings must be entitled in the matter of the company or companies in question and in the matter of the Act. In the case of any disqualification application under section 7 of the Act it is not necessary to mention in the heading any company other than that referred to in section 6(1)(a) of the Act.

27.6

6 The Claim Form

6.1 CPR Rule 8.2 does not apply. The claim form must state—
   (1)   that CPR Part 8 (as modified by this practice direction) applies, and (if the application is made under sections 7 or 8 of the Act) that the disqualification application is made in accordance with the Disqualification Rules;[7]
   (2)   that the claimant seeks a disqualification order, and the section of the Act pursuant to which the disqualification application is made;
   (3)   the period for which, in accordance with the Act, the court has power to impose a disqualification period.
The periods are as follows—
      (a)   where the application is under section 2 of the Act, for a period of up to 15 years;

(b)   where the application is under section 3 of the Act, for a period of up to 5 years;

(c)   where the application is under section 4 of the Act, for a period of up to 15 years;

(d)   where the application is under section 5 of the Act, for a period of up to 5 years;

(e)   where the application is under section 7 of the Act, for a period of not less than 2, and up to 15, years;[8]

(f)   where the application is under section 8 of the Act, for a period of up to 15 years;[9]

(4)   in cases where the disqualification application is made under sections 7 or 8 of the Act, that on the first hearing of the application, the court may hear and determine it summarily, without further or other notice to the defendant, and that, if the application is so determined, the court may impose a period of disqualification of up to 5 years but that if at the hearing of the application the court, on the evidence then before it, is minded to impose, in the case of any defendant, disqualification for any period longer than 5 years, it will not make a disqualification order on that occasion but will adjourn the application to be heard (with further evidence, if any) at a later date that will be notified to the defendant;[10]

(5)   that any evidence which the defendant wishes the court to take into consideration must be filed in court in accordance with the time limits set out in paragraph 9 below (which time limits shall be set out in the notes to the Claim Form).[11]

27.7

7 Service of the Claim Form

7.1 Service of claim forms in disqualification proceedings will be the responsibility of the claimant and will not be undertaken by the court.

7.2 The claim form shall be served by the claimant on the defendant. It may be served by sending it by first class post to his last known address; and the date of service shall, unless the contrary is shown, be deemed to be the 7th day following that on which the claim form was posted.[12] CPR r 6.7(1) shall be modified accordingly. Otherwise CPR Part 6 applies.[13]

7.3 Where any claim form or order of the court or other document is required under any disqualification proceedings to be served on any person who is not in England and Wales, the court may order service on him to be effected within such time and in such manner as it thinks fit, may require such proof of service as it thinks fit,[14] and may give such directions as to acknowledgement of service as it thinks fit.

7.4 The claim form served on the defendant shall be accompanied by an acknowledgement of service.

27.8

8 Acknowledgement of Service

8.1 The form of acknowledgement of service is annexed to this practice direction. CPR rules 8.3(2) and 8.3(3)(a) do not apply to disqualification applications.

8.2 The form of acknowledgement of service shall state that the defendant should indicate[15]—

(1) whether he contests the application on the grounds that, in the case of any particular company—

(a) he was not a director or shadow director of that company at a time when conduct of his, or of other persons, in relation to that company is in question; or

(b) his conduct as director or shadow director of that company was not as alleged in support of the application for a disqualification order;

(2) whether, in the case of any conduct of his, he disputes the allegation that such conduct makes him unfit to be concerned in the management of a company; and

(3) whether he, while not resisting the application for a disqualification order, intends to adduce mitigating factors with a view to reducing the period of disqualification.

8.3 The defendant shall—

(1) (subject to paragraph 7.2 above) file an acknowledgement of service in the prescribed form not more than 14 days after service of the claim form; and

(2) serve a copy of the acknowledgement of service on the claimant and any other party.

8.4 Where the defendant has failed to file an acknowledgement of service and the time period for doing so has expired, the defendant may attend the hearing of the application but may not take part in the hearing unless the court gives permission.

27.9

9 Evidence

9.1 Evidence in disqualification applications shall be by affidavit, except where the official receiver is a party, in which case his evidence may be in the form of a written report (with or without affidavits by other persons) which shall be treated as if it had been verified by affidavit by him and shall be prima facie evidence of any matter contained in it.[16]

9.2 In the affidavits or (as the case may be) the official receiver's report in support of the application, there shall be included a statement of the matters by reference to which it is alleged that a disqualification order should be made against the defendant.[17]

9.3 When the claim form is issued—

(1) the affidavit or report in support of the disqualification application must be filed in court;

(2) exhibits must be lodged with the court where they shall be retained until the conclusion of the proceedings; and

(3) copies of the affidavit/report and exhibits shall be served with the claim form on the defendant.[18]

9.4 The defendant shall, within 28 days from the date of service of the claim form[19]—

(1) file in court any affidavit evidence in opposition to the disqualification application that he or she wishes the court to take into consideration; and

(2) lodge the exhibits with the court where they shall be retained until the conclusion of the proceedings; and

(3) at the same time, serve upon the claimant a copy of the affidavits and exhibits.

9.5 In cases where there is more than one defendant, each defendant is required to serve his evidence on the other defendants unless the court otherwise orders.

9.6 The claimant shall, within 14 days from receiving the copy of the defendant's evidence[20]—

(1) file in court any further affidavit or report in reply he wishes the court to take into consideration; and

(2) lodge the exhibits with the court where they shall be retained until the conclusion of the proceedings; and

(3) at the same time serve a copy of the affidavits/reports and exhibits upon the defendant.

9.7 Prior to the first hearing of the disqualification application, the time for serving evidence may be extended by written agreement between the parties. After the first hearing, the extension of time for serving evidence is governed by CPR rules 2.11 and 29.5.

9.8 So far as is possible all evidence should be filed before the first hearing of the disqualification application.

27.10

10 The First Hearing of the Disqualification Application

10.1 The date fixed for the first hearing of the disqualification application shall be not less than 8 weeks from the date of issue of the claim form.[21]

10.2 The hearing shall in the first instance be before the registrar.[22]

10.3 The registrar shall either determine the case on the date fixed or give directions and adjourn it.[23]

10.4 All interim directions should insofar as possible be sought at the first hearing of the disqualification application so that the disqualification application can be determined at the earliest possible date. The parties should take all such steps as they respectively can to avoid successive directions hearings.

10.5 In the case of disqualification applications made under sections 7 or 8 of the Act, the registrar shall adjourn the case for further consideration if—

(1) he forms the provisional opinion that a disqualification order ought to be made, and that a period of disqualification longer than 5 years is appropriate;[24] or

(2) he is of opinion that questions of law or fact arise which are not suitable for summary determination.[25]

10.6 If the registrar adjourns the application for further consideration he shall—

(1) direct whether the application is to be heard by a registrar or by a judge.[26] This direction may at any time be varied by the court

either on application or of its own initiative. If the court varies the direction in the absence of any of the parties, notice will be given to the parties;

(2) consider whether or not to adjourn the application to a judge so that the judge can give further directions;

(3) consider whether or not to make any direction with regard to fixing the trial date or a trial window;

(4) state the reasons for the adjournment.[27]

27.11

11 Case Management

11.1 On the first or any subsequent hearing of the disqualification application, the registrar may also give directions as to the following matters—

(1) the filing in court and the service of further evidence (if any) by the parties;[28]

(2) the time-table for the steps to be taken between the giving of directions and the hearing of the application;

(3) such other matters as the registrar thinks necessary or expedient with a view to an expeditious disposal of the application or the management of it generally;[29]

(4) the time and place of the adjourned hearing;[30] and

(5) the manner in which and the time within which notice of the adjournment and the reasons for it are to be given to the parties.[31]

11.2 Where a case is adjourned other than to a judge, it may be heard by the registrar who originally dealt with the case or by another registrar.[32]

11.3 If the companies court registrar adjourns the application to a judge, all directions having been complied with and the evidence being complete, the application will be referred to the Listing Office and any practice direction relating to listing shall apply accordingly.

11.4 In all disqualification applications, the Court may direct a pre-trial review ("PTR"), a case management conference or pre-trial check lists (listing questionnaires) (in the form annexed to this practice direction) and will fix a trial date or trial period in accordance with the provisions of CPR Part 29: the Multi-Track as modified by any relevant practice direction made thereunder.

11.5 In contested disqualification applications, the registrar may, at a hearing of the claim, direct—

(1) that a PTR be fixed for a date as soon as practicable after the close of evidence;

(2) that each party complete a pre-trial check list and return it to the court not later than two clear working days before the hearing of the PTR.

11.6 At the hearing of the PTR, the registrar may give any further directions as appropriate and, where the application is to be heard in the Royal Courts of Justice in London, unless the trial date has already been fixed, may direct the parties (by Counsel's clerks if applicable), to attend the Registrar at a specified time and place in order solely to fix a trial date. The court will give notice of the date fixed for the trial to the parties.

11.7 In all cases, the parties must inform the court immediately of any material change to the information provided in a pre-trial checklist.

27.12

12 The Trial

12.1 Trial bundles containing copies of—
  (1)   the claim form;
  (2)   the acknowledgement of service;
  (3)   all evidence filed by or on behalf of each of the parties to the proceedings, together with the exhibits thereto;
  (4)   all relevant correspondence; and
  (5)   such other documents as the parties consider necessary;

shall be lodged with the court.

12.2 Skeleton arguments should be prepared by all the parties in all but the simplest cases whether the case is to be heard by a registrar or a judge. They should comply with all relevant guidelines.

12.3 The advocate for the claimant should also in all but the simplest cases provide: (a) a chronology; (b) a dramatis personae; (c) in respect of each defendant, a list of references to the relevant evidence.

12.4 The documents mentioned in paragraph 12.1–12.3 above must be delivered to the court in accordance with any order of the court and/or any relevant practice direction.[33]
  (1)   If the case is to be heard by a judge sitting in the Royal Courts of Justice, London, but the name of the judge is not known, or the judge is a deputy judge, these documents must be delivered to the Clerk of the Lists. If the name of the judge (other than a deputy judge) is known, these documents must be delivered to the judge's clerk;
  (2)   If the case is to be heard by a companies court registrar, these documents must be delivered to Room 409, Thomas More Building, Royal Courts of Justice. Copies must be provided to the other party so far as possible when they are delivered to the court;
  (3)   If the case is to be heard in the Chancery district registries in Birmingham, Bristol, Cardiff, Leeds, Liverpool, Manchester, Newcastle, or Preston, the addresses for delivery are set out in Annex 1;
  (4)   If the case is to be heard in a county court, the documents should be delivered to the relevant county court office.

12.5 Copies of documents delivered to the court must, so far as possible, be provided to each of the other parties to the disqualification application.

12.6 The provisions in paragraphs 12.1 to 12.5 above are subject to any order of the court making different provision.

Part Three
Applications under sections 7(2) and 7(4) of the Act

27.13

13 Summary Procedure

13.1 If the parties decide to invite the court to deal with the disqualification application under the procedure adopted in *Re Carecraft Construction Co Ltd* [1994] 1 WLR 172, they should inform the court immediately and obtain a date for the hearing of the application.

13.2 Whenever the *Carecraft* procedure is adopted, the claimant must—
  (1) except where the court otherwise directs, submit a written statement containing in respect of each defendant any material facts which (for the purposes of the application) are either agreed or not opposed (by either party); and
  (2) specify in writing the period of disqualification which the parties accept that the agreed or unopposed facts justify or the band of years (eg 4 to 6 years) or bracket (ie 2 to 5 years; 6 to 10 years; 11 to 15 years) into which they will submit the case falls.

13.3 Paragraph 12.4 of the above applies to the documents mentioned in paragraph 13.2 above unless the court otherwise directs.

13.4 Unless the Court otherwise orders, a hearing under the *Carecraft* procedure will be held in private.

13.5 If the Court is minded to make a disqualification order having heard the parties' representations, it will usually give judgment and make the disqualification order in public. Unless the Court otherwise orders, the written statement referred to in paragraph 13.2 shall be annexed to the disqualification order.

13.6 If the Court refuses to make the disqualification order under the *Carecraft* procedure, the Court shall give further directions for the hearing of the application.

27.14

14 Making and Setting Aside of Disqualification Order

14.1 The court may make a disqualification order against the defendant, whether or not the latter appears, and whether or not he has completed and returned the acknowledgement of service of the claim form, or filed evidence.[34]

14.2 Any disqualification order made in the absence of the defendant may be set aside or varied by the court on such terms as it thinks just.[35]

27.15

15 Service of Disqualification Orders

15.1 Service of disqualification orders will be the responsibility of the claimant.

27.16

16 Commencement of Disqualification Order

16.1 Unless the court otherwise orders, the period of disqualification imposed by a disqualification order shall begin at the end of the period of 21 days beginning with the date of the order.[36]

Part Three
Applications under sections 7(2) and 7(4) of the Act

27.17

17 Applications for Permission to Make a Disqualification Application After the End of the Period of 2 Years Specified in Section 7(2) of the Act

17.1 Such applications shall be made by Application Notice under CPR Part 23, and the Part 23 Practice Direction shall apply save as modified below.

27.18

18 Applications for Extra Information Made Under Section 7(4) of the Act

18.1 Such applications may be made—
  (1) by Practice Form N.208 under CPR Part 8; or
  (2) by Application Notice in existing disqualification claim proceedings.

27.19

19 Provisions Applicable to Applications Under Sections 7(2) And 7(4) of the Act

19.1 **Headings:**
  (1) Every claim form and notice by which such an application is begun and all witness statements affidavits, notices and other documents in relation thereto must be entitled in the matter of the company or companies in question and in the matter of the Act.

19.2 **Service:**
  (1) Service of application notices seeking orders under section 7(2) or 7(4) of the Act will be the responsibility of the applicant and will not be undertaken by the court.
  (2) Where any application notice or order of the court or other document is required in any application under section 7(2) or section 7(4) of the Act to be served on any person who is not in England and Wales, the court may order service on him to be effected within such time and in such manner as it thinks fit, may require such proof of service as it thinks fit, and may make such directions as to acknowledgement of service as it thinks fit.

Part Four
Applications for permission to Act
27.20

20 Commencing an Application for Permission to Act

20.1 This practice direction governs applications for permission made under—
(1) sections 1(1), 1A(1) and section 17 of the Act;
(2) section 12 of the Act; and
(3) any application for permission made under any disqualification order which was made under any statutory predecessor of the Act.

20.2 Sections 12 and 17 of the Act identify the courts which have jurisdiction to deal with applications for permission to act. Subject to these sections, such applications may be made—
(1) by Practice Form N.208 under CPR Part 8; or
(2) by application notice in an existing disqualification application.

27.21

21 Headings

21.1 Every claim form by which an application for permission to act is begun, and all affidavits, notices and other documents in the application must be entitled in the matter of the company or companies in question and in the matter of the Act.

21.2 Every application notice by which an application for permission to act is made and all affidavits, notices and other documents in the application shall be entitled in the same manner as the heading of the claim form in the existing disqualification application.

27.22

22 Evidence

22.1 Evidence in support of an application for permission to act shall be by affidavit.

27.23

23 Service

23.1 In all cases, the claim form or application notice (as appropriate), together with the evidence in support thereof, must be served on the Secretary of State.

Part Five
Applications
27.24

24 Form of Application

24.1 CPR Part 23 and the Part 23 practice direction (General Rules about Applications for Court Orders) shall apply in relation to applications governed by this practice direction (see paragraph 1.3(4) above) save as modified below.

27.25

25 Headings

25.1 Every notice and all witness statements and affidavits in relation thereto must be entitled in the same manner as the Claim Form in the proceedings in which the application is made.

27.26

26 Service

26.1 Service of application notices in disqualification proceedings will be the responsibility of the parties and will not be undertaken by the court.

26.2 Where any application notice or order of the court or other document is required in any application to be served on any person who is not in England and Wales, the court may order service on him to be effected within such time and in such manner as it thinks fit, and may also require such proof of service as it thinks fit.

Part Six
Disqualification proceedings other than in the Royal Courts of Justice

27.27

27.1 Where a disqualification application or a section 8A application is made by a claim form issued other than in the Royal Courts of Justice this practice direction shall apply with the following modifications.

(1) Upon the issue of the claim form the court shall endorse it with the date and time for the first hearing before a district judge. The powers exercisable by a registrar under this practice direction shall be exercised by a district judge.

(2) If the district judge (either at the first hearing or at any adjourned hearing before him) directs that the disqualification claim or section 8A application is to be heard by a High Court judge or by an authorised circuit judge he will direct that the case be entered forthwith in the list for hearing by that judge and the court will allocate (i) a date for the hearing of the trial by that judge and (ii) unless the district judge directs otherwise a date for the hearing of a PTR by the trial judge.

Part Seven
Disqualification undertakings

27.28

28 Costs

28.1 The general rule is that the court will order the defendant to pay the costs of the Secretary of State (and, in the case of a disqualification application made under section 7(1)(b) of the Act, the costs of the official receiver) if—

(1) a disqualification application under section 7 or section 8 of the Act has been commenced; and

(2) that application is discontinued because the Secretary of State has accepted a disqualification undertaking under section 1A of that Act.

28.2 The general rule will not apply where the court considers that the circumstances are such that it should make another order.

Applications under section 8A of the Act to reduce the period for which a disqualification undertaking is in force or to provide for it to cease to be in force

27.29

29 Headings

29.1 Every claim form by which a section 8A application is begun and all affidavits, notices and other documents in the proceedings must be entitled in the matter of a disqualification undertaking and its date and in the matter of the Act.

27.30

30 Commencement: the Claim Form

30.1 A section 8A application must be commenced by a claim form issued—
   (1) in the High Court out of the office of the companies court registrar or a chancery district registry; and
   (2) in the county court, out of a county court office.

Section 8A(3) identifies the courts which have jurisdiction to deal with section 8A applications.

30.2 A section 8A application shall be made by the issue of a Part 8 claim form in the form annexed hereto and the use of the procedure set out in CPR Part 8, as modified by this practice direction. CPR rule 8.1(3) (power of the Court to order the application to continue as if the claimant had not used the Part 8 procedure) shall not apply.

30.3 When the claim form is issued, the claimant will be given a date for the first hearing of the section 8A application. This date is to be not less than eight weeks from the date of issue of the claim form. The first hearing will be before registrar.

30.4 CPR Rule 8.2 does not apply. The claim form must state—
   (1) that CPR Part 8 (as modified by this practice direction) applies;
   (2) the form of order the claimant seeks.

30.5 The Secretary of State shall be made the defendant to the section 8A application.

30.6 Service of claim forms in disqualification proceedings will be the responsibility of the claimant and will not be undertaken by the court. The claim form shall be served by the claimant on The Treasury Solicitor, Queen Anne's Chambers, 28 Broadway, London, SW1H 9JS. It may be served by sending it by first class post and the date of service shall, unless the contrary is shown, be deemed to be the 7th day following that on which the claim form was posted. CPR r 6.7(1) shall be modified accordingly. Otherwise CPR Part 6 applies.[37]

30.7 Where any order of the court or other document is required to be served on any person who is not in England and Wales, the court may order service on him to be effected within such time and in such manner as it thinks fit and may require such proof of service as it thinks fit.

30.8 The claim form served on the defendant shall be accompanied by an acknowledgement of service in the form annexed hereto.

27.31

31 Acknowledgement of Service

31.1 The defendant shall—
    (1)   (subject to paragraph 7.2 above) file an acknowledgement of service in the relevant practice form not more than 14 days after service of the claim form; and
    (2)   serve a copy of the acknowledgement of service on the claimant and any other party.

31.2 Where the defendant has failed to file an acknowledgement of service and the time period for doing so has expired, the defendant may nevertheless attend the hearing of the application and take part in the hearing as provided for by section 8A(2) of the Act. However, this is without prejudice to the Court's case management powers and its powers to make costs orders.

27.32

32 Evidence

32.1 Evidence in section 8A applications shall be by affidavit.

32.2 When the claim form is issued—
    (1)   the affidavit in support of the section 8A application must be filed in court;
    (2)   exhibits must be lodged with the court where they shall be retained until the conclusion of the proceedings; and
    (3)   copies of the affidavit and exhibits shall be served with the claim form on the defendant.

32.3 The defendant shall, within 28 days from the date of service of the claim form—
    (1)   file in court any affidavit evidence that he wishes the court to take into consideration on the application; and
    (2)   lodge the exhibits with the court where they shall be retained until the conclusion of the proceedings; and
    (3)   at the same time, serve upon the claimant a copy of the affidavits and exhibits.

32.4 The claimant shall, within 14 days from receiving the copy of the defendant's evidence—
    (1)   file in court any further affidavit evidence in reply he wishes the court to take into consideration; and

(2) lodge the exhibits with the court where they shall be retained until the conclusion of the proceedings; and

(3) at the same time serve a copy of the affidavits and exhibits upon the defendant.

32.5 Prior to the first hearing of the section 8A application, the time for serving evidence may be extended by written agreement between the parties. After the first hearing, the extension of time for serving evidence is governed by CPR rules 2.11 and 29.5.

32.6 So far as is possible all evidence should be filed before the first hearing of the section 8A application.

27.33

33 Hearings and Case Management

33.1 The date fixed for the first hearing of the section 8A application shall be not less than 8 weeks from the date of issue of the claim form.

33.2 The hearing shall in the first instance be before the registrar.

33.3 The registrar shall either determine the case on the date fixed or give directions and adjourn it.

33.4 All interim directions should insofar as possible be sought at the first hearing of the section 8A application so that the section 8A application can be determined at the earliest possible date. The parties should take all such steps as they respectively can to avoid successive directions hearings.

33.5 If the registrar adjourns the application for further consideration he shall—

(1) direct whether the application is to be heard by a registrar or by a judge. This direction may at any time be varied by the court either on application or of its own initiative. If the court varies the direction in the absence of any of the parties, notice will be given to the parties;

(2) consider whether or not to adjourn the application to a judge so that the judge can give further directions;

(3) consider whether or not to make any direction with regard to fixing the trial date or a trial window.

33.6 On the first or any subsequent hearing of the section 8A application, the registrar may also give directions as to the following matters—

(1) the filing in court and the service of further evidence (if any) by the parties;

(2) the time-table for the steps to be taken between the giving of directions and the hearing of the section 8A application;

(3) such other matters as the registrar thinks necessary or expedient with a view to an expeditious disposal of the section 8A application or the management of it generally;

(4) the time and place of the adjourned hearing.

33.7 Where a case is adjourned other than to a judge, it may be heard by the registrar who originally dealt with the case or by another registrar.

33.8 If the companies court registrar adjourns the application to a judge, all directions having been complied with and the evidence being complete, the application will be referred to the Listing Office and any practice direction relating to listing shall apply accordingly.

33.9 In all disqualification applications, the Court may direct a pre-trial review ("PTR"), a case management conference or pre-trial check lists (listing questionnaires) (in the form annexed to this practice direction) and will fix a trial date or trial period in accordance with the provisions of CPR Part 29: The Multi-Track, as modified by any relevant practice direction made thereunder.

33.10 The registrar may, at a hearing of the section 8A application, direct—

    (1)   that a PTR be fixed for a date as soon as practicable after the close of evidence;

    (2)   that each party complete a pre-trial check list and return it to the court not later than two clear working days before the hearing of the PTR.

33.11 At the hearing of the PTR, the registrar may give any further directions as appropriate and, where the application is to be heard in the Royal Courts of Justice in London, unless the trial date has already been fixed, may direct the parties (by Counsel's clerks, if applicable) to attend the Registrar at a specified time and place in order solely to fix a trial date. The court will give notice of the date fixed for the trial to the parties.

33.12 In all cases, the parties must inform the court immediately of any material change to the information provided in a pre-trial check list.

27.34

34 The Trial

34.1 Trial bundles containing copies of—

    (1)   the claim form;

    (2)   the acknowledgement of service;

    (3)   all evidence filed by or on behalf of each of the parties to the proceedings, together with the exhibits thereto;

    (4)   all relevant correspondence; and

    (5)   such other documents as the parties consider necessary, shall be lodged with the court.

34.2 Skeleton arguments should be prepared by all the parties in all but the simplest cases whether the case is to be heard by a registrar or a judge. They should comply with all relevant guidelines.

34.3 The advocate for the claimant should also in all but the simplest cases provide: (a) a chronology; (b) a dramatis personae.

34.4 The documents mentioned in paragraph 34.1–34.3 above must be delivered to the court in accordance with any order of the court and/or and relevant practice direction 38.

    (1)   If the case is to be heard by a judge sitting in the Royal Courts of Justice, London, but the name of the judge is not known, or the judge is a deputy judge, these documents must be delivered to

the Clerk of the Lists. If the name of the judge (other than a deputy judge) is known, these documents must be delivered to the judge's clerk;

(2) If the case is to be heard by a companies court registrar, these documents must be delivered to Room 409, Thomas More Building, Royal Courts of Justice. Copies must be provided to the other party so far as possible when they are delivered to the court;

(3) If the case is to be heard in the Chancery district registries in Birmingham, Bristol, Cardiff, Leeds, Liverpool, Manchester, Newcastle, or Preston, the addresses for delivery are set out in Annex 1;

(4) If the case is to be heard in a county court, the documents should be delivered to the relevant county court office.

34.5 Copies of documents delivered to the court must, so far as possible, be provided to each of the other parties to the claim.

34.6 The provisions in paragraphs 34.1 to 34.5 above are subject to any order of the court making different provision.

27.35

Annex I

Birmingham: The Chancery Listing Officer, The District Registry of the Chancery Division of the High Court, 33 Bull Street, Birmingham B4 6DS.

Bristol: The Chancery Listing Officer, The District Registry of the Chancery Division of the High Court, 3rd Floor, Greyfriars, Lewins Mead, Bristol BS1 2NR.

Cardiff: The Chancery Listing Officer, The District Registry of the Chancery Division of the High Court, 1st Floor, 2 Park Street, Cardiff CF10 1ET.

Leeds: The Chancery Listing Officer, The District Registry of the Chancery Division of the High Court, Leeds Combined Court Centre, The Court House, 1 Oxford Row, Leeds LS1 3BG.

Liverpool and Manchester: The Chancery Listing Officer, The District Registry of the Chancery Division of the High Court, Manchester Courts of Justice, Crown Square, Manchester M60 9DJ.

Newcastle: The Chancery Listing Officer, The District Registry of the Chancery Division of the High Court, The Law Courts, Quayside, Newcastle upon Tyne NE1 3LA.

Preston: The Chancery Listing Officer, The District Registry of the Chancery Division of the High Court, The Combined Court Centre, Ringway, Preston PR1 2LL.

Index

I

M

P